The New
ANALYTICAL
GREEK
LEXICON

The New
ANALYTICAL
GREEK
LEXICON

Wesley J. Perschbacher

Editor

HENDRICKSON
PUBLISHERS
PEABODY, MASSACHUSETTS 01961-3473

Copyright © 1990 by Hendrickson Publishers, Inc.
P.O. Box 3473
Peabody, Massachusetts 01961–3473
All rights reserved.
Printed in the United States of America

ISBN 0–943575–33–8

Second printing — February 1992

Library of Congress Cataloging-in-Publication Data

Perschbacher, Wesley J.
   The new analytical Greek lexicon of the New Testament: every
word and inflection of the Greek New Testament arranged alpha-
betically and with grammatical analyses: a complete series of
Greek paradigms, with grammatical remarks and explanations /
Wesley J. Perschbacher.
      p.   cm.
   ISBN 0–943575–33–8
   1. Greek language, Biblical—Glossaries, vocabularies, etc.
2. Greek language, Biblical—Grammar.   3. Bible.   N.T.   Greek—
Study.   I. Title.
PA881.P54   1990
487′.4—dc20   90–23777
                                                          CIP

TABLE OF CONTENTS

PREFACE

The goal of George V. Wigram's *Analytical Greek Lexicon of the New Testament,* originally published by Samuel Bagster & Sons in 1852, was to aid the reader in acquiring a knowledge of the Greek New Testament. The aim of *The New Analytical Greek Lexicon* clearly remains the same. While the original edition ably served thousands of readers for over a century, this newly revised edition provides numerous corrections and improvements that greatly enhance its usefulness.

The introductory tables of paradigms and explanatory grammatical remarks have been edited and revised with a view toward making them more accessible and more useful to the contemporary reader. One improvement was the elimination of forms not found in the Greek New Testament, such as the dual form of nouns, adjectives, pronouns, etc. Since these forms are not encountered in the New Testament and are seldom taught in New Testament Greek courses, it was clearly better not to include them.

In addition to including over 500 Greek forms not found in the original work, *The New Analytical Greek Lexicon* offers a new format featuring eleven distinct elements designed to afford immediate access to a wide range of important data. Please refer to the Table of Features which follows for an illustration and explanation of the elements of the new format.

While every attempt has been made to ensure the accuracy and completeness of the entries, the human factor dictates that perfection is an impossibility. Any corrections and suggestions for improving future editions will be appreciated.[†]

My gratitude and appreciation are extended to Hendrickson Publishers for recognizing the need for this revision. I especially wish to thank David Townsley and Phil Frank for their expertise, support, and enthusiastic encouragement throughout the editing of this work.

Wesley J. Perschbacher

([†]The second printing has afforded the opportunity to correct a number of minor typographical errors found in the first printing—Publisher.)

TABLE OF FEATURES

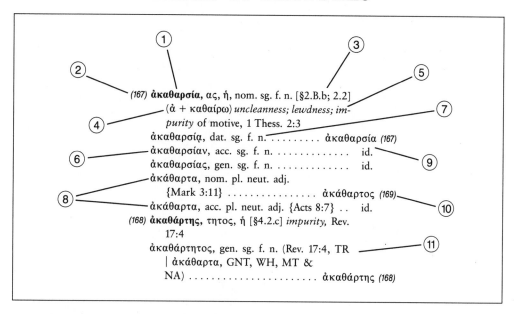

(1) The lexical form is given in bold face type.

(2) Every lexical form (and a few nonlexical forms) is coded with the numbering used in *Strong's Exhaustive Concordance.* This numbering system is used in a wide variety of Greek and Hebrew reference works to make them more accessible to readers with a limited knowledge of the biblical languages. A dagger (†) or a double dagger (‡) appended to the Strong's number indicates that the form listed is a variant spelling or variant form of the Greek word found in Strong's *Greek Dictionary* under that number. The double dagger (‡) also indicates that the form listed is in its proper position in the alphabetical order but is consequently out of position in the Strong's numerical order. The appendix beginning on page 447 gives a complete list of these forms and indicates where in the numerical order they may be found.

(3) When applicable, a cross reference is given in brackets indicating the relevant table(s) and/or section(s) of grammatical remarks in the introductory matter.

(4) If the word is a compound, it is often broken down into its respective components.

(5) An English gloss or a brief definition is given for lexical forms. With few exceptions, no attempt has been made to change or update the definitions found in Wigram's edition.

(6) Nonlexical forms appear in regular type. This is a comprehensive listing of all the forms in the Greek New Testament. When ν is movable, it is given in parentheses.

(7) The complete parsing, including gender, voice, and mood of every word is included.

(8) Words having the same spelling but different parsing forms are given separate entries. A form with more than one gender receives an entry for each gender, e.g., ἀκάθαρτα (nom. pl. neut. adj.) and ἀκάθαρτα (acc. pl. neut. adj.), and each is followed by a N.T. reference given in braces where an example of its usage can be found.

(9) The lexical form corresponding to each parsed form is given. When the lexical form repeats, id. (= idem, the same) is used.

(10) The Strong's number for the corresponding lexical form is given to facilitate locating the form. See (2) above for an explanation of the significance of a dagger (†) or a double dagger (‡) appended to the Strong's number.

(11) Variant readings are listed that occur in TR (Textus Receptus = Beza's or Stephanus' text), MT (Majority Text), WH (Westcott & Hort), GNT (United Bible Societies' *Greek New Testament*, 3rd ed.), and NA (Nestle—Aland, *Novum Testamentum*, 26th ed.)

ABBREVIATIONS

absol. absolutely, without case or
  adjunct
acc. accusative case
act. active voice
adj. adjective
adv. adverb
al. *alibi,* in other texts
al. freq. *alibi frequenter,* in many
  other texts
Ant. Antiquities of Josephus
aor. aorist
Att. Attic dialect
compar. comparative
conj. conjunction
contr. contraction, contracted
dat. dative case
dep. deponent
dimin. diminutive
esp. especially
et and
etc. *et cetera*
e.g. *exempli gratia,* for example
f. feminine gender
freq. with al, *alibi frequenter,* in
  many other texts
fut. future tense
gen. genitive case
genr. generally, in a general sense,
  not affected by
i.e. *id est,* that is
id., idem. the same
imper. imperative mood
imperf. imperfect tense
impers. impersonal
impl. implication
indecl. indeclinable
indic. indicative mood
infin. infinitive
interj. interjection
interrog. interrogative, interrogation
intrans. intransitive

i.q. *idem quod,* the same as
Lat. Latin
lit. literally
LXX Septuagint
m. masculine gender
met. metaphorically
metath. metathesis, the transposition of letters
meton. by metonymy
mid. middle voice
n. noun
neut. neuter gender
N.T. New Testament
nom. nominative case
obsol. obsolete
O.T. Old Testament
opt. optative mood
part. participle
pass. passive voice
perf. perfect tense
pers. person
pl. plural
pluperf. pluperfect
pr. properly, proper
pres. present tense
prep. preposition
pron. pronoun
q.v. *quod vide,* which see
rem. remark(s) in the Tables of
  Paradigms
sc. *scilicet,* that is to say
seq. *sequente,* as seq. gen., *se-*
  quente genitivo, with a genitive
  following
sg. singular
signif. significance
spc. specially, i.e., in a special and
  local meaning
subj. subjunctive mood
subst. substantive
superl. superlative

sync. syncope, contraction
synec. synecdoche
tab. table(s) in the Tables of
  Paradigms
trans. transitively
trop. tropically, i.e., turned aside
  from its strict literal meaning
v(v). verse(s)
v.r. a variant reading to the common text
viz. *videlicet,* that is, namely
voc. vocative case
2× two times
3× three times
§ Section(s) in the Tables of
  Paradigms
ὁ attached to a word shows it to be
  masculine; ἡ, to be feminine; ὁ, ἡ,
  to be common, i.e., masculine or
  feminine; and τό, to be neuter.

AUTHORITIES REFERRED TO

GNT *The Greek New Testament,*
  3rd. edition, United Bible Socie-
  ties, 1975.
MT *The Greek New Testament*
  According to the Majority Text,
  Hodges & Farstad, eds., 1982.
NA *Novum Testamentum,* 26th
  edition, Nestle, Aland, et al., eds.,
  1979.
TR *Textus Receptus,* The Received
  Text
TRb TR, Beza's text, 1598.
TRs TR, Stephanus' text
  (= R. Estienne), 1550.
WH *The New Testament in the*
  Original Greek, Westcott and
  Hort, eds., 1881.

TABLES OF PARADIGMS OF
GREEK DECLENSIONS AND CONJUGATIONS,
WITH EXPLANATORY GRAMMATICAL REMARKS

SECTION 1—THE ARTICLE

TABLE A—THE ARTICLE

	Singular					Plural			
	M.	F.	N.			M.	F.	N.	
N.	ὁ	ἡ	τό	*the*		οἱ	αἱ	τά	*the*
G.	τοῦ	τῆς	τοῦ	*of the*		τῶν	τῶν	τῶν	*of the*
D.	τῷ	τῇ	τῷ	*to the*		τοῖς	ταῖς	τοῖς	*to the*
A.	τόν	τήν	τό	*the*		τούς	τάς	τά	*the*

REMARKS

1. The article has no vocative. ὦ, which sometimes precedes a noun in the vocative, is an interjection.

2. The article takes the consonant τ in every case, except in the nominative singular masculine and feminine ὁ, ἡ, and in the nominative plural masculine and feminine οἱ, αἱ, where the τ is superseded by the rough breathing (ʽ).*

3. In every declension the dative singular ends in ι; but when ι unites, to form a diphthong, with a preceding *long* vowel, as is the case in the dative of the first and second declensions, it is, by a general rule of the language, placed in a subscript position, e.g., ῳ. The same vowel also invariably enters into the ending of the dative plural.

4. The genitive plural, in all genders, ends in ων. This is the case also in every declension, without exception.

---

* There are two breathings or aspirations, smooth and rough. A smooth breathing is not sounded in pronunciation; a rough breathing is like our aspirated *h* (e.g., *heaven*). They are placed on initial vowels and diphthongs, e.g., ἐγώ, *I*, ἡμεῖς, *we*; αὐτός, *himself*, αὐτοῦ, *of himself*. The initial vowel υ always receives the rough breathing; other vowels take smooth or rough, according to circumstances. The letter ρ is the only consonant which receives a breathing. This is invariably when ρ is initial and it is invariably rough (e.g., *rhetoric*).

There are three accents, the acute (´), the grave (`), and the circumflex (˜). Accents are useful not merely as limited guides in pronunciation, but by their position accents also help distinguish between words of the same orthography but very different meaning; e.g., μόνην, *only, alone*, μονήν, *staying, dwelling*; or χειρῶν, *hand*, χείρων, *worse*.

SECTION 2—NOUNS SUBSTANTIVE

TABLE B—FIRST DECLENSION

			Singular			Plural
(a)	N.	ἡ	κεφαλή, *the head*	αἱ		κεφαλαί
	G.	τῆς	κεφαλῆς	τῶν		κεφαλῶν
	D.	τῇ	κεφαλῇ	ταῖς		κεφαλαῖς
	A.	τὴν	κεφαλήν	τὰς		κεφαλάς
	V.		κεφαλή			κεφαλαί
(b)	N.	ἡ	ἡμέρα, *the day*	αἱ		ἡμέραι
	G.	τῆς	ἡμέρας	τῶν		ἡμερῶν
	D.	τῇ	ἡμέρᾳ	ταῖς		ἡμέραις
	A.	τὴν	ἡμέραν	τὰς		ἡμέρας
	V.		ἡμέρα			ἡμέραι
(c)	N.	ὁ	ποιητής, *the poet*	οἱ		ποιηταί
	G.	τοῦ	ποιητοῦ	τῶν		ποιητῶν
	D.	τῷ	ποιητῇ	τοῖς		ποιηταῖς
	A.	τὸν	ποιητήν	τοὺς		ποιητάς
	V.		ποιητά			ποιηταί
(d)	N.	ὁ	νεανίας, *the young man*	οἱ		νεανίαι
	G.	τοῦ	νεανίου	τῶν		νεανιῶν
	D.	τῷ	νεανίᾳ	τοῖς		νεανίαις
	A.	τὸν	νεανίαν	τοὺς		νεανίας
	V.		νεανία			νεανίαι

REMARKS

1. All nominative nouns ending in η keep that vowel in every case of the singular and are declined like κεφαλή.

2. All nominative nouns ending in ρα or α *pure* (i.e., preceded by a vowel), as φιλία, *friendship*, keep α in every case, like ἡμέρα. But in the New Testament the word σπεῖρα, *a band or troop*, has genitive σπείρης; Acts 10:1; 21:31; 17:1. This is according to the Ionic dialect.

3. All other nouns ending in α, if they are not preceded by a vowel or ρ, form the genitive singular in ης, and the dative singular in η. In the accusative singular they resume α; e.g.,

N. V. δόξα, *glory*   D. δόξῃ
G.   δόξης   A. δόξαν

The plural endings are always like those of the feminine article.

4. Nominative nouns in ης and ας form the genitive singular in ου, like the masculine article. In the other cases, those in ης retain η, as in κεφαλή; those in ας keep α, as in ἡμέρα. The Doric ending α (contracted from αο), for ου, is found in Attic Greek, especially in the case of proper names; e.g., Καλλίας, genitive Καλλία; so also Θωμᾶς, *Thomas*, genitive Θωμᾶ, etc.

5. Words such as μνᾶ, genitive μνᾶς (contracted from μνάα, μνάας), *a mina or pound*, are declined like ἡμέρα. Foreign names in ης sometimes form the genitive in η; e.g., Ἰωσῆς, *Joses*, genitive Ἰωσῆ.

6. The vocative singular of nouns in ης and ας is formed by dropping the σ of the nominative. But most nouns in ης form the vocative in α *short*, especially those in της, as ποιητής, vocative ποιητά. Those in πης, compounded of ὄψ, *an eye*, as κυνώπης, *shameless*, vocative κυνῶπα. Compounds of μετρέω, *to measure*, as γεωμέτρης, *a geometer*, vocative γεωμέτρα. Of πωλέω, *to sell*, as βιβλιοπώλης, *a bookseller*, vocative βιβλιοπῶλα. Of τρίβω, *to wear*, hence *to exercise*, as παιδοτρίβης, *a trainer of boys*, vocative παιδοτρίβα.

SECTION 3—NOUNS SUBSTANTIVE

TABLE C—SECOND DECLENSION

		Singular			Plural	
(a)	N.	ὁ	λόγος, *the word*		οἱ	λόγοι
	G.	τοῦ	λόγου		τῶν	λόγων
	D.	τῷ	λόγῳ		τοῖς	λόγοις
	A.	τὸν	λόγον		τοὺς	λόγους
	V.		λόγε			λόγοι
(b)	N.	ἡ	ὁδός, *the road*		αἱ	ὁδοί
	G.	τῆς	ὁδοῦ		τῶν	ὁδῶν
	D.	τῇ	ὁδῷ		ταῖς	ὁδοῖς
	A.	τὴν	ὁδόν		τοὺς	ὁδούς
	V.		ὁδέ			ὁδοί
(c)	N.	τὸ	δῶρον, *the gift*		τὰ	δῶρα
	G.	τοῦ	δώρου		τῶν	δώρων
	D.	τῷ	δώρῳ		τοῖς	δώροις
	A.	τὸ	δῶρον		τοὺς	δώρους
	V.		δῶρον			δῶρα

REMARKS

1. This declension comprises masculine and feminine nouns in ος, which follow the endings of the masculine article and form the vocative in ε; also neuter nouns in ον, which follow the neuter article. The genitive singular is in ου.

2. The neuters nominative, accusative, and vocative are alike in the singular and plural, and in the plural these cases (except in the Attic declension) end in α.

3. Some nouns of this declension, whose endings are preceded by ε, ον, ο, are contracted in all cases; e.g.,

Masculine	*Neuter*
N. νόος, νοῦς, *the mind*	N. ὀστέον, ὀστοῦν, *a bone*
G. νόου, νοῦ, etc.	G. ὀστέου, ὀστοῦ, etc.
Pl. (None)	Pl. ὀστέα, ὀστᾶ, etc.

So πλόος, πλοῦς, *a voyage*, plural πλόοι, πλοῖ; πλόων, πλῶν; πλόοις, πλοῖς; πλόους, πλοῦς.

4. The Attics frequently omit the ν of the accusative singular; e.g., Κῶ, the island *Cos*, for Κῶν; Ἀπολλώ, for Ἀπολλῶν, etc.

5. The first two declensions are termed *parisyllabic*, or *inseparable*, as having in each case the same number of syllables. The third declension is called *imparisyllabic*, or *separable*, because in the genitive and following cases it has one syllable more than it does in the nominative and vocative singular.

SECTION 4—NOUNS SUBSTANTIVE

TABLE D—THIRD DECLENSION

		Singular			Plural	
(a)	N.	ὁ	Ἕλλην, *the Greek*		οἱ	Ἕλληνες
	G.	τοῦ	Ἕλληνος		τῶν	Ἑλλήνων
	D.	τῷ	Ἕλληνι		τοῖς	Ἕλλησι
	A.	τὸν	Ἕλληνα		τοὺς	Ἕλληνας
	V.		Ἕλλην			Ἕλληνες

TABLE D—THIRD DECLENSION (Cont.)

			Singular		Plural
(b)	N.	ἡ	λαμπάς, *the lamp*	αἱ	λαμπάδες
	G.	τῆς	λαμπάδος	τῶν	λαμπάδων
	D.	τῇ	λαμπάδι	ταῖς	λαμπάσι
	A.	τὴν	λαμπάδα	τὰς	λαμπάδας
	V.		λαμπάς		λαμπάδες
(c)	N.	τὸ	σῶμα, *the body*	τὰ	σώματα
	G.	τοῦ	σώματος	τῶν	σωμάτων
	D.	τῷ	σώματι	τοῖς	σώμασι
	A.	τὸ	σῶμα	τὰ	σώματα
	V.		σῶμα		σώματα

REMARKS

1. This declension contains nouns of all genders and includes nine endings: four vowels, α, ι, υ, ω, and five consonants, ν, ρ, σ, ξ, ψ. The vocative is generally like the nominative. Exceptions will be indicated shortly.

2. The genitive singular is always in ος. The consonant which precedes this ending is found in all the following cases, except (generally) the dative plural, rules for the formation of which will presently be given. The nominative in this declension is not the stem of the noun. This is to be found in the genitive by dropping the ending ος, according to the following rules:

(*a*) A mute (consonantal stop) of the first order* (labials: π, β, φ) before the genitive ending indicates a nominative in ψ; e.g., genitive Ἄραβος, nominative Ἄραψ, *an Arabian*; ὠπός, nominative ὤψ, *an eye*.

(*b*) A mute of the second order (gutturals: κ, γ, χ) indicates a nominative in ξ; e.g., genitive ἅρπαγος, nominative ἅρπαξ, *rapacious*; ὄνυχος, nominative ὄνυξ, *a nail, claw*; λάρυγγος, nominative λάρυγξ, *the throat*. But νύξ, *night*, makes νυκτός.

(*c*) A mute of the third order (dentals: τ, δ, θ) indicates a nominative in ς; e.g., genitive ἐλπίδος, nominative ἐλπίς, *hope*; γέλωτος, nominative γέλως, *laughter*. Except neuters in μα, genitive ματος, as σῶμα, σώματος; also ἧπαρ, ἥπατος, *the liver*; ὕδωρ, ὕδατος, *water*; φρέαρ, φρέατος, *a pit*; μέλι, μέλιτος, *honey*; and a few other neuters.

(*d*) ντ indicates ς or ν; e.g., genitive γίγαντος, nominative γίγας, *a giant*; ὀδόντος, nominative ὀδούς, *a tooth*; δράκοντος, nominative δράκων, *a dragon*.

(*e*) ν indicates ς or ν; e.g., μέλανος, nominative μέλας, *black*; φρενός, nominative φρήν, *the mind*.

(*f*) ρ indicates ρ; e.g., θηρός, nominative θήρ, *a wild beast*; πυρός, nominative πῦρ, *fire*.

(*g*) ος pure (preceded by a vowel) indicates ς; e.g., τριήρεος, nominative τριήρης, *a galley*.

3. (*a*) The dative plural always ends in σι. It is formed from the dative singular by inserting σ before ι; e.g., μάρτυρ, *a witness*, dative singular μάρτυρι, dative plural μάρτυρσι (μάρτυσι(ν) Acts 10:41) ῥήτωρ, *an orator*, . . . ῥήτορι, . . . ῥήτορσι(ν); κόραξ, *a raven*, . . . κόρακι, . . . κόραξι(ν) (for κόρακσι[ν]).

(*b*) If a mute of the third order (τ, δ, θ) occurs in the singular it is dropped in the plural; e.g., λαμπάς, λαμπάδι, λαμπάσι(ν); σῶμα, σώματος, σώμασι(ν); οὖς, ὠτός, ὠσί(ν); πούς, ποδός, ποσί(ν).

(*c*) ν is also dropped, whether alone, as Ἕλλην, Ἕλληνι, Ἕλλησι(ν), or joined to a mute of the third order, as λύσας, *having loosed*, λύσαντι, λύσασι(ν).

(*d*) If the dative singular ends in οντι (ντ being

*The following Table of Mutes may be found useful:

	First Order Labials	Second Order Gutturals (Palatals)	Third Order Dentals
Smooth	Π	Κ	Τ
Middle	Β	Γ	Δ
Aspirate	Φ	Χ	Θ

The letters of each column are of the same nature and are, in certain circumstances, interchanged. If two successive consonants occur in the same syllable, *both* must be smooth, as ἑπτά, *seven*; middle, as ἕβδομος, *seventh*, or aspirate, as φθόνος, *envy*. Two successive syllables seldom begin with an aspirate; τρέχω, not θρέχω, *I run*; τριχός, not θριχός, from θρίξ, *hair*.

dropped), the o is changed into ου; e.g., λέων, *a lion*, λέοντι, λέουσι(ν).

(*e*) If the dative singular ends in εντι (ντ being dropped), the ε is changed into ει; e.g., λυθείς, *having been loosed*, λυθέντι, λυθεῖσι(ν).

4. Some nouns in ις and υς (and a few in ους) take two endings in the accusative singular, α and ν; e.g., ἔρις, ἔριδος, *strife*, accusative ἔριδα and ἔριν (ἔριν in the New Testament) plural ἔριδες and ἔρεις; χάρις,

χάριτος, *grace*, accusative χάριτα and χάριν; κλείς, κλειδός, *a key*, accusative κλεῖδα, and κλεῖν. Ὄρνις, ὄρνιθος, *a bird*, makes accusative singular ὄρνιθα and ὄρνιν; accusative plural ὄρνιθας and ὄρνις. With the exception of κλείς, nouns with the ending ν in the accusative (unless the genitive ends in ος *pure*) must have the nominative singular *unaccented* on the last syllable; e.g., ἔρις, χάρις.

SECTION 5 — NOUNS SUBSTANTIVE

TABLE E — CONTRACTED NOUNS

			Singular		Plural				Singular		Plural
(*a*)	N.	ἡ	τριήρης, *the galley*	αἱ	τριήρεις	(*b*)	N.	τὸ	τεῖχος, *the wall*	τὰ	τείχη
	G.	τῆς	τριήρους	τῶν	τριηρῶν		G.	τοῦ	τείχους	τῶν	τειχῶν
	D.	τῇ	τριήρει	ταῖς	τριήρεσι(ν)		D.	τῷ	τείχει	τοῖς	τείχεσι(ν)
	A.	τὴν	τριήρη	τὰς	τριήρεις		A.	τὸ	τεῖχος	τὰ	τείχη
	V.		τρίηρες		τριήρεις		V.		τεῖχος		τείχη
(*c*)	N.	ἡ	πόλις, *the city*	αἱ	πόλεις	(*d*)	N.	ὁ	βασιλεύς, *the king*	οἱ	βασιλεῖς
	G.	τῆς	πόλεως	τῶν	πόλεων		G.	τοῦ	βασιλέως	τῶν	βασιλέων
	D.	τῇ	πόλει	ταῖς	πόλεσι(ν)		D.	τῷ	βασιλεῖ	τοῖς	βασιλεῦσι(ν)
	A.	τὴν	πόλιν	τὰς	πόλεις		A.	τὸν	βασιλέα	τοὺς	βασιλεῖς
	V.		πόλι		πόλεις		V.		βασιλεῦ		βασιλεῖς
(*e*)	N.	ὁ	πέλεκυς, *the hatchet*	οἱ	πελέκεις	(*f*)	N.	τὸ	ἄστυ, *the city*	τὰ	ἄστη
	G.	τοῦ	πελέκεως	τῶν	πελεκέων		G.	τοῦ	ἄστεως	τῶν	ἀστέων
	D.	τῷ	πελέκει	τοῖς	πελέκεσι(ν)		D.	τῷ	ἄστει	τοῖς	ἄστεσι(ν)
	A.	τὸν	πέλεκυν	τοὺς	πελέκεις		A.	τὸ	ἄστυ	τὰ	ἄστη
	V.		πέλεκυ		πελέκεις		V.		ἄστυ		ἄστη
(*g*)	N.	ὁ	ἰχθύς, *the fish*	οἱ	ἰχθύες	(*h*)	N.	ἡ	αἰδώς, *modesty*	αἱ	αἰδοί
	G.	τοῦ	ἰχθύος	τῶν	ἰχθύων		G.	τῆς	αἰδοῦς	τῶν	αἰδῶν
	D.	τῷ	ἰχθύϊ	τοῖς	ἰχθύσι(ν)		D.	τῇ	αἰδοῖ	ταῖς	αἰδοῖς
	A.	τὸν	ἰχθύν	τοὺς	ἰχθύας		A.	τὴν	αἰδώ	τὰς	αἰδούς
	V.		ἰχθύ		ἰχθύες		V.		αἰδοῖ		αἰδοί
(*i*)	N.	ἡ	ἠχώ, *the echo*	αἱ	ἠχοί	(*j*)	N.	τὸ	κέρας, *the horn*	τὰ	κέρατα
	G.	τῆς	ἠχοῦς	τῶν	ἠχῶν		G.	τοῦ	κέρατος	τῶν	κεράτων
	D.	τῇ	ἠχοῖ	ταῖς	ἠχοῖς		D.	τῷ	κέρατι	τοῖς	κέρασι(ν)
	A.	τὴν	ἠχώ	τὰς	ἠχοῦς		A.	τὸ	κέρας	τὰ	κέρατα
	V.		ἠχοῖ		ἠχοί		V.		κέρας		κέρατα

REMARKS

1. The above ten nouns represent all the varieties which can occur. (See Remark 4.) They are all of the third declension. The genitive singular ends in ος *pure*, except nouns in ρας, in which the contraction is formed after dropping the τ of the genitive; e.g., κέρατος, κέραος, κέρως.

2. The contracted nominative and accusative plural are always alike. The ending ης is confined to proper names, and adjectives (such as ἀληθής), τριήρης itself being an adjective, at full length τριήρης ναῦς, *a vessel with three tiers of oars*.

3. The ending ος is limited to neuter nouns. The genitive plural is often uncontracted: e.g., ἄνθεων, *of flowers* (from ἄνθος), not ἀνθῶν.

4. The ending ι is also confined to neuter, and mostly foreign, nouns: e.g., σίνηπι (σίναπι, New Testament), *mustard*, genitive σινήπιος, εος, εως; dative σινήπιι, εϊ; plural σινήπια, σινήπεα; πέπερι, *pepper*; στίμμι, *antimony*, etc. The only true Greek word ending in ι seems to be μέλι, *honey*, declined like σῶμα, σώματος (μέλι, μέλιτος).

5. The ending ευς is found only in masculine nouns; e.g., βασιλεύς, *a king*, βραβεύς, *an umpire*, ἱερεύς, *a priest*, φονεύς, *a murderer*, etc. Nouns in υς, genitive εος, are like βασιλεύς, except that the accusative singular is in υν; e.g., πῆχυς, *a cubit*, genitive εος, εως, accusative πῆχυν.

6. Nouns in υς, genitive υος, are contracted in the plural in ῦς; e.g., nominative ἰχθύες, ἰχθῦς, accusative ἰχθύας, ἰχθῦς.

7. All nouns ending in ως, ω (αἰδώς, ἠχώ) are feminine. The last form in the Table E includes only neuter nouns in ρας and ας *pure*; e.g., τέρας, *a wonder*; γῆρας, *old age*; κρέας, *flesh*, etc.

8. (*a*) The dative plural is never contracted, because its ending σι(ν) begins with a consonant. The genitive plural is sometimes contracted, but only in nouns ending in ης, ος, and ας. Ις and υς always form the accusative singular in ν.

(*b*) Lastly, as we have seen in πόλεις, πόλιας, πόλις, contraction sometimes occurs even in nouns which have a consonant before the ending; e.g., accusative plural ὄρνιθας, ὄρνις, *birds*; κλεῖδας, κλεῖς, from κλείς, κλειδός, *a key*.

SECTION 6—IRREGULARITIES OF DECLENSION

REMARKS

1. Some nouns in ηρ, genitive ερος, in certain cases drop the ε, though the ending be preceded by a consonant: they form the dative plural in ασι(ν).

		Singular			Plural
N.	ὁ	πατήρ, *the father*	οἱ	πατέρες
G.	τοῦ	πατρός		τῶν	πατέρων
D.	τῷ	πατρί		τοῖς	πατράσι(ν)
A.	τὸν	πατέρα		τοὺς	πατέρας
V.		πάτερ			πατέρες

2. So also μήτηρ, *mother*, and θυγάτηρ, *daughter*. Ἡ γαστήρ, *the belly*, dative plural γαστήρασι(ν), rarely γαστράσι(ν). In ὁ ἀνήρ, *the man*, we find the vowel ε rejected in all cases, except the vocative singular, and supplied by δ, for the sake of euphony, or better pronunciation.

		Singular		Plural
N.	ὁ	ἀνήρ, *the man*	οἱ	ἄνδρες
G.	τοῦ	ἀνδρός	τῶν	ἀνδρῶν
D.	τῷ	ἀνδρί	τοῖς	ἀνδράσι(ν)
A.	τὸν	ἄνδρα	τοὺς	ἄνδρας
V.		ἄνερ		ἄνδρες

3. A very small number of nouns belong to the parisyllabic (inseparable) form of declension; e.g., nominative Ἰησοῦς, *Jesus*, genitive and dative Ἰησοῦ, accusative Ἰησοῦν, vocative Ἰησοῦ.

4. Most belong to the imparisyllabic (separable) declension. A few are given here:

(*a*) Nominative Ζεύς, *Jupiter*, genitive Διός, dative Διί, accusative Δία, vocative Ζεῦ.

(*b*) Nominative γυνή, *a woman*, genitive γυναικός, and the rest of the cases as if from nominative γύναιξ, except vocative singular γύναι. Nominative γάλα, *milk*, genitive γάλακτος, dative γάλακτι, accusative γάλα.

(*c*) Nominative ἀστήρ, *a star*, genitive ἀστέρος; the irregularity is in the dative plural ἀστράσι(ν).

(*d*) ἄρς (not used in nominative), *a lamb*, genitive ἀρνός, dative ἀρνί, dative plural ἀνάσι(ν).

(*e*) Nominative κύων, *a dog*, genitive κυνός, dative κυνί, accusative κύνα, vocative κύον. Plural κύνες, κυνῶν, κυσί(ν), κύνας.

(*f*) Nominative ἡ χείρ, *the hand*, genitive χειρός, dative χειρί, accusative χεῖρα. Plural χεῖρες, χειρῶν, χερσί(ν), χεῖρας.

(*g*) ἡ ναῦς, *the ship*, νεώς, νεῖ, ναῦν. Plural νῆες, νεῶν, ναυσί(ν), ναῦς. Attic form (the word occurs only once in the New Testament), τὴν ναῦν, Acts 27:41.

(*h*) βοῦς, *an ox or cow*, genitive βοός, dative βοΐ, accusative βοῦν. Plural βόες, genitive βοῶν, dative βουσί(ν), accusative βόας, βοῦς (βόας in the New Testament). The forms βοῦς, genitive νοός, dative νοΐ, also occur; and πλοῦς, genitive πλοός, Acts 27:9.

5. Defective nouns. Some of these are formed only in the plural; e.g., τὰ Διονύσια, *the festivals of Bacchus*; τὰ ἐγκαίνια, *the feast of dedication*, John 10:22. Others only in the nominative and accusative; e.g., τὸ ὄναρ, *the dream*; others only in the nominative; e.g., τὸ ὄφελος, *the advantage*.

6. Indeclinable nouns have one ending for all cases.

These are:

(*a*) some foreign nouns; e.g., τὸ Πάσχα, *the Pass-over*, genitive τοῦ Πάσχα, dative τῷ Πάσχα, etc., only in the singular.

(*b*) The cardinal numbers, from 5 to 100 inclusive.

(*c*) The names of *letters*; e.g., ἄλφα, βῆτα, etc.

7. A few nouns are of different genders in the sin-gular and plural; e.g., ὁ δεσμός, *the bond*, plural τὰ δεσμά; ὁ λύχνος, *the light*, τὰ λύχνα. But οἱ λύχνοι, in New Testament, Luke 12:35.

8. The word σάββατον, ου, τό, forms, in the New Testament σάββασι(ν), in the dative plural, according to the third declension. Matt. 12:1, 5, et al.

SECTION 7—DECLENSION OF ADJECTIVES

TABLE F—CLASS I—PARISYLLABIC

		Singular				Plural	
	M.	F.	N.		M.	F.	N.
N.	ἀγαθός	ἀγαθή	ἀγαθόν, *good*		ἀγαθοί	ἀγαθαί	ἀγαθά
G.	ἀγαθοῦ	ἀγαθῆς	ἀγαθοῦ		ἀγαθῶν	ἀγαθῶν	ἀγαθῶν
D.	ἀγαθῷ	ἀγαθῇ	ἀγαθῷ		ἀγαθοῖς	ἀγαθαῖς	ἀγαθοῖς
A.	ἀγαθόν	ἀγαθήν	ἀγαθόν		ἀγαθούς	ἀγαθάς	ἀγαθά
V.	ἀγαθέ	ἀγαθή	ἀγαθόν		ἀγαθοί	ἀγαθαί	ἀγαθά

REMARKS

1. The masculine of ἀγαθός is declined like λόγος, the feminine like κεφαλή, and the neuter like δῶρον. But if the feminine is in α *pure*, as ἅγιος, ἁγία, ἅγιον, *holy*; or in ρα, as ἱερός, ἱερά, ἱερόν, *sacred*; α is retained throughout.

2. Many adjectives (especially in Attic Greek, and those *compounded* or *derived*) have only two endings, ος for masculine and feminine, and ον for neuter; e.g., masculine and feminine ἔνδοξος, neuter ἔνδοξον, *illustrious*; ἄφθαρτος, ἄφθαρτον, *incorruptible*; βασίλειος, βασίλειον, *royal*; ἀΐδιος, ἀΐδιον, *eternal*; αἰώνιος, αἰώνιον, *everlasting*. But αἰωνίαν, accusative singular feminine, occurs *twice* in the New Testament, 2 Thess. 2:16; Heb. 9:12.

TABLE G—CLASS II—IMPARISYLLABIC

		Singular			Plural	
		M. & F.	N.		M. & F.	N.
(*a*)	N.	εὐδαίμων	εὔδαιμον, *fortunate*		εὐδαίμονες	εὐδαίμονα
	G.	εὐδαίμονος	εὐδαίμονος		εὐδαιμόνων	εὐδαιμόνων
	D.	εὐδαίμονι	εὐδίμονι		εὐδαίμοσι(ν)	εὐδαίμοσι(ν)
	A.	εὐδαίμονα	εὔδαιμον		εὐδαίμονας	εὐδαίμονα
	V.	εὔδαιμον	εὔδαιμον		εὐδαίμονες	εὐδαίμονα
(*b*)	N.	ἀληθής	ἀληθές, *true*		ἀληθεῖς	ἀληθῆ
	G.	ἀληθοῦς	ἀληθοῦς		ἀληθοῦς	ἀληθῶν
	D.	ἀληθεῖ	ἀληθεῖ		ἀληθεῖ	ἀληθέσι(ν)
	A.	ἀληθῆ	ἀληθές		ἀληθές	ἀληθῆ
	V.	ἀληθές	ἀληθές		ἀληθεῖς	ἀληθῆ

3. σώφρων, *prudent*, ἄφρων, *foolish*; ἐλεήμων, *merciful*; ἄρρην, genitive ενος, *male*, etc., are declined like εὐδαίμων.

4. (*a*) A large number are declined like ἀληθής; e.g., εὐγενής, *nobly born, noble*; πλήρης, *full*; ἀσθενής, *weak*; ἀκριβής, *exact*; εὐσεβής, *pious*; etc.

(*b*) A few are contracted in every case and occur most frequently in the contracted form; so ἁπλόος, ἁπλοῦς, *simple*; διπλόος, διπλοῦς, *double*; τετραπλόος, οῦς, *quadruple*; etc. E.g.,

N.	χρύσεος	χρυσέη	χρυσέον, *of gold*
	χρυσοῦς	χρυσῆ	χρυσοῦν
G.	χρυσέου	χρυσέης	χρυσέου
	χρυσοῦ	χρυσῆς	χρυσοῦ, etc.

(*c*) Nominative ἀργύρεος, ἀργυροῦς, ἀργυρέα, ἀργυρᾶ, ἀργύρεον, ἀργυροῦν, *of silver*. Genitive ἀργυρέου, ἀργυροῦ, ἀργυρέας, ἀργυρᾶς, ἀργυρέου, ἀργυροῦ. The feminine has α, because ρ precedes the ending.

TABLE H—CLASS III

		Singular				Plural		
		M.	F.	N.		M.	F.	N.
(*a*)	N.	μέλας	μέλαινα	μέλαν, *black*		μέλανες	μέλαιναι	μέλανα
	G.	μέλανος	μελαίνης	μέλανος		μελάνων	μελαινῶν	μελάνων
	D.	μέλανι	μελαίνῃ	μέλανι		μέλασι(ν)	μελαίναις	μέλασι(ν)
	A.	μέλαν	μέλαιναν	μέλαν		μέλανας	μελαίνας	μέλανα
	V.	μέλαν	μέλαινα	μέλαν				
(*b*)	N.	πᾶς	πᾶσα	πᾶν		πάντες	πᾶσαι	πάντα
	G.	παντός	πάσης	παντός		πάντων	πασῶν	πάντων
	D.	παντί	πάσῃ	παντί		πᾶσι(ν)	πάσαις	πᾶσι(ν)
	A.	πάντα	πᾶσαν	πᾶν		πάντας	πάσας	πάντα
	V.	πάντες	πᾶσαι	πᾶν				

Other Forms

		M.	F.	N.			M.	F.	N.
(*c*)	N.	τέρην	τέρεινα	τέρεν, *tender*		(*e*) N.	χαρίεις	χαρίεσσα	χαρίεν, *graceful*
	G.	τέρενος	τερείνης	τέρενος		G.	χαρίεντος	χαριέσσης	χαρίεντος
(*d*)	N.	ἑκών	ἑκοῦσα	ἑκόν, *willing*		(*f*) N.	τιμήεις	τιμήεσσα	τιμῆεν, *precious*
	G.	ἑκόντος	ἑκούσης	ἑκόντος		Contract	τιμῆς	τιμῆσσα	τιμῆν
						G.	τιμῆντος	τιμήσσης	τιμῆντος

		Singular				Plural		
		M.	F.	N.		M.	F.	N.
(*g*)	N.	ἡδύς	ἡδεῖα	ἡδύ, *sweet*		ἡδεῖς	ἡδεῖαι	ἡδέα
	G.	ἡδέος	ἡδείας	ἡδέος		ἡδέων	ἡδειῶν	ἡδέων
	D.	ἡδεῖ	ἡδείᾳ	ἡδεῖ		ἡδέσι(ν)	ἡδείαις	ἡδέσι(ν)
	A.	ἡδύν	ἡδεῖαν	ἡδύ		ἡδεῖς	ἡδείας	ἡδέα
	V.	ἡδύ	ἡδεῖα	ἡδύ		ἡδεῖς	ἡδεῖαι	ἡδέα

---

5. It will be seen that this class of adjectives follows the third declension in the masculine and neuter and the first in the feminine. Of those in υς, εια, υ, the masculine is like πέλεκυς, the feminine like ἡμέρα, and the neuter like ἄστυ.

6. Sometimes the ending εος of the genitive singular is contracted into ους; e.g., ἥμισυς, half, genitive ἡμίσεος, contracted ἡμίσους, Mark 6:23.

7. The two adjectives, πολύς, much, and μέγας, great, belong to the third class with respect to the nominative and accusative singular, and to the first class in all the other cases.

		Singular			Plural		
		M.	F.	N.	M.	F.	N.
(a)	N.	πολύς	πολλή	πολύ	πολλοί	πολλαί	πολλά
	G.	πολλοῦ	πολλῆς	πολλοῦ	πολλῶν	πολλῶν	πολλῶν
	D.	πολλῷ	πολλῇ	πολλῷ	πολλοῖς	πολλαῖς	πολλοῖς
	A.	πολύν	πολλήν	πολύ	πολλούς	πολλάς	πολλά
(b)	N.	μέγας	μεγάλη	μέγα	μεγάλοι	μεγάλαι	μεγάλα
	G.	μεγάλου	μεγάλης	μεγάλου	μεγάλων	μεγάλων	μεγάλων
	D.	μεγάλῳ	μεγάλῃ	μεγάλῳ	μεγάλοις	μεγάλαις	μεγάλοις
	A.	μέγαν	μεγάλην	μέγα	μεγάλους	μεγάλας	μεγάλα

8. Of irregular adjectives, πρᾶος, gentle, may be noticed.

		Singular			Plural		
		M.	F.	N.	M.	F.	N.
(a)	N.	πρᾶος or πρᾷος	πραεῖα	πρᾷον	πραεῖς or πρᾷοι	πραεῖαι	πραέα
	G.	πρᾷου	πραείας	πρᾷου	πραέων	πραειῶν	πραέων

The feminine and plural are formed from πραΰς, which is also found, Matt. 21:5.

SECTION 8 — COMPARISON OF ADJECTIVES

REMARKS

1. Comparatives usually end in τερος, τερα, τερον; superlatives in τατος, τατη, τατον; e.g., First Class — σοφός, wise, σοφώτερος, σοφώτατος. ἅριος, holy, ἁγιώτερος, ἁγιάτατος. Second Class — σώφρων, prudent, σωφρονέστερος, σωφρονέστατος. εὐσεβής, pious, εὐσεβέστερος, εὐσεβέστατος. Third Class — μέλας, black, μελάντερος, μελάντατος. εὐρύς, broad, εὐρύτερος, εὐρύτατος. All these are declined like ἀγαθός, except that α appears in all cases of the feminine comparative because the nominative singular ends in ρα.

2. Many comparatives have ιων, sometimes ων, for masculine and feminine endings, their superlatives ιστος, ιστη, ιστον; e.g., First Class — κακός, bad, κακίων, κάκιστος; καλός, beautiful, κυλλίων, κάλλιστος. Third Class — ἡδύς, sweet, ἡδίων, ἥδιστος. πολύς, much, many, πλείων, πλεῖστος. μέγας, great, μείζων, μέγιστος. μειζότερος is found in the New Testament, 3 John 4.

3. All comparatives in ιων and ων are declined as the following:

	Singular		Plural	
	M. & F.	N.	M. & F.	N.
N.	μείζων, greater	μεῖζον	μείζονες	μείζονα, μείζω
G.	μείζονος	μείζονος	μειζόνων	μειζόνων
D.	μείζονι	μείζονι	μείζοσι(ν)	μείζοσι(ν)
A.	μείζονα, μείζω	μεῖζον	μείζονας	μείζονα, μείζω

4. Adjectives in ος form the comparative in οτερος, if the syllable preceding ος has a diphthong or a vowel long by nature or by position (followed by two consonants or a double letter); e.g., κοῦφος, light, κουφότερος, κουφότατος; ἔνδοξος, illustrious, ἐνδοξότερος, ἐνδοξότατος. In ωτερος, if the vowel preceding ος is short; e.g., σοφός, wise, σοφώτερος, σοφώτατος. Some change ος of the simple, uncompared form into εστερος; e.g., σπουδαῖος, diligent, σπουδαιέστερος (σπουδαιότερος in the New Testament, 2 Cor. 8:17, 22).

Contracted adjectives in οος — ους, take εστερος; e.g., ἁπλόος, ἁπλοῦς, ἁπλοέστερος contracted ἁπλούστερος. διπλόος, διπλοῦς, makes διπλότερος in the New Testament, Matt. 23:15.

5. The following show some irregularity; ἐλαχύς, *small*, ἐλάσσων (for ἐλαχίων), ἐλάχιστος, from which a further comparative, ἐλαχιστότερος, is formed. Eph. 3:8. ταχύς, *swift*, θάσσων (for ταχίων), Attic θάττων, τάχιστος. From the root word κρατύς, *strong*, are formed κρείσσων (κρείττων), κράτιστος. From κακός, *bad*, χείρων (also κακίων, and κακώτερος), χείριστος.

From μικρός, *little*, μείων (μικρότερος in the New Testament). Also ἥσσων (ἥττων) ἥκιστος. From πολύς, *much, many*, πλείων, πλεῖστος, etc.

6. Some comparatives and superlatives are formed from prepositions; e.g., πρό, *before*, πρότερος (πρότατος, contracted into), πρῶτος, *first*. ὑπέρ, *above*, ὑπέρτερος, ὑπέρτατος, and ὕπατος, *supreme*. ἐξ, *out of*, ἔσχατος, *extreme, last*.

The above appear to be a sufficient number of instances, though not including *all* the varieties of comparison.

SECTION 9—THE NUMERALS

TABLE I—CARDINAL NUMBERS

		M.	F.	N.	
(a)	N.	εἷς	μία	ἕν, *one*	(b) δύο, *two*, for all genders
	G.	ἑνός	μιᾶς	ἑνός	δύο
	D.	ἑνί	μιᾷ	ἑνί	δυσί(ν)
	A.	ἕνα	μίαν	ἕν	δύο

		M.	F.	N.	
(c)	N.	τρεῖς	τρεῖς	τρία, *three*	(d) τέσσαρες τέσσαρα, *four*
	G.	τριῶν	τριῶν	τριῶν	τεσσάρων
	D.	τρισί(ν)	τρισί(ν)	τρισί(ν)	τέσσαρσι(ν)
	A.	τρεῖς	τρεῖς	τρία	τέσσαρας

Indeclinable (from 5 to 100)

(e)		
πέντε	*five*
ἕξ	*six*
ἑπτα	*seven*
ὀκτώ	*eight*
ἐννέα	*nine*
δέκα	*ten*
ἕνδεκα	*eleven*
δώδεκα	*twelve*
εἴκοσι	*twenty*
τριάκοντα	*thirty*
τεσσαράκοντα	*forty*
πεντήκοντα	*fifty*
ἑξήκοντα	*sixty*
ἑβδομήκοντα	*seventy*
ὀγδοήκοντα	*eighty*
ἐννενήκοντα	*ninety*
ἑκατόν	*a hundred*

	M.	F.	N.	
(f)	διακόσιοι	διακόσιαι	διακόσια	*200*
	τριακόσιοι	τριακόσιαι	τριακόσια	*300*
	χίλιοι	χίλιαι	χίλια	*1000*
	μύριοι	μύριαι	μύρια	*10,000*

Ordinals

(g)		
πρῶτος	*first*
δεύτερος	*second*
τρίτος	*third*
τέταρτος	*fourth*
πέμπτος	*fifth*, etc.
εἰκοστός	*twentieth*
τριακοστός	*thirtieth*
ἑκατοστός	*hundredth*
διακοσιοστός	*two hundredth*
χιλιοστός	*thousandth*, etc.

REMARK

All the declinable ordinals are formed according to the first and second declensions; e.g., πρῶτος, η, ον, δεύτερος, α, ον.

SECTION 10 — PRONOMINAL ADJECTIVES

TABLE J

αὐτός, reflexive *self*

		Singular			Plural		
		M.	F.	N.	M.	F.	N.
(a)	N.	αὐτός	αὐτή	αὐτό	αὐτοί	αὐταί	αὐτά
	G.	αὐτοῦ	αὐτῆς	αὐτοῦ	αὐτῶν	αὐτῶν	αὐτῶν
	D.	αὐτῷ	αὐτῇ	αὐτῷ	αὐτοῖς	αὐταῖς	αὐτοῖς
	A.	αὐτόν	αὐτήν	αὐτό	αὐτούς	αὐτάς	αὐτά

Demonstratives, ὅδε, οὗτος, ἐκεῖνος

(b)	N.	ὅδε	ἥδε	τόδε	οἵδε	αἵδε	τάδε
	G.	τοῦδε	τῆσδε	τοῦδε	τῶνδε	τῶνδε	τῶνδε
	D.	τῷδε	τῇδε	τῷδε	τοῖσδε	ταῖσδε	τοῖσδε
	A.	τόνδε	τήνδε	τόδε	τούσδε	τάσδε	τάδε
(c)	N.	οὗτος	αὕτη	τοῦτο	οὗτοι	αὗται	ταῦτα
	G.	τούτου	ταύτης	τούτου	τούτων	τούτων	τούτων
	D.	τούτῳ	ταύτῃ	τούτῳ	τούτοις	ταύταις	τούτοις
	A.	τοῦτον	ταύτην	τοῦτο	τούτους	ταύτας	ταῦτα
(d)	N.	ἐκεῖνος	ἐκείνη	ἐκεῖνο	ἐκεῖνοι	ἐκεῖναι	ἐκεῖνα
	G.	ἐκείνου	ἐκείνης	ἐκείνου	ἐκείνων	ἐκείνων	ἐκείνων
	D.	ἐκείνῳ	ἐκείνῃ	ἐκείνῳ	ἐκείνοις	ἐκείναις	ἐκείνοις
	A.	ἐκεῖνον	ἐκείνην	ἐκεῖνο	ἐκείνους	ἐκείνας	ἐκεῖνα

τίς, interrogative pronoun, *who?*

(e)	N.	τίς	τίς	τί	τίνες	τίνες	τίνα
	G.	τίνος	τίνος	τίνος	τίνων	τίνων	τίνων
	D.	τίνι	τίνι	τίνι	τίσι(ν)	τίσι(ν)	τίσι(ν)
	A.	τίνα	τίνα	τί	τίνας	τίνας	τίνα

τις, indefinite pronoun

(f)	N.	τις	τις	τι	τινες	τινες	τινα
	G.	τινος	τινος	τινος	τινων	τινων	τινων
	D.	τινι	τινι	τινι	τισι(ν)	τισι(ν)	τισι(ν)
	A.	τινα	τινα	τι	τινας	τινας	τινα

The relative pronoun ὅς, *who, which*

(g)	N.	ὅς	ἥ	ὅ	οἵ	αἵ	ἅ
	G.	οὗ	ἧς	οὗ	ὧν	ὧν	ὧν
	D.	ᾧ	ᾗ	ᾧ	οἷς	αἷς	οἷς
	A.	ὅν	ἥν	ὅ	οὕς	ἅς	ἅ

The relative pronoun, combined with τις, *whoever*

(h)	N.	ὅστις	ἥτις	ὅτι	οἵτινες	αἵτινες	ἅτινα
	G.	οὗτινος	ἧστινος	οὗτινος	ὧτίνων	ὧτίνων	ὧτίνων
	D.	ᾧτινι	ἧτινι	ᾧτινι	οἷστισι(ν)	αἷστισι(ν)	οἷστισι(ν)
	A.	ὅντινα	ἥτινα	ὅτι	οὕστινας	ἅστινας	ἅτινα

REMARKS

1. The article ὁ, ἡ, τό may be considered as a demonstrative. Combined with the particle δε, ὅδε, ἥδε, τόδε, its meaning is more precise: *this one, this here.*

2. Αὐτός is declined like ἀγαθός, except that ν is absent in the neuter. It is always marked with the *smooth* breathing. If the article precedes αὐτός, it means *the same*; e.g., ὁ αὐτὸς βασιλεύς, *the same king.*

3. Οὗτος, αὕτη, τοῦτο, *this*, indicates present or near objects. Ἐκεῖνος, *that*, points to absent or distant objects.

4. The difference between τις, indefinite, *some one, any one*, and τίς, interrogative, *who?* will be easily perceived. The interrogative τίς has the acute accent always on the first syllable of each case. It may be noticed that in Attic Greek τοῦ and τῷ are used for τίνος and τίνι, and του and τῳ as enclitics, for τινος and τινι. In the New Testament an example of the latter usage occurs in the variant reading, ὥσπερεὶ τῷ ἐκτρώματι, 1 Cor. 15:8, where the common text has the article.

5. Δεῖνα, or ὁ δεῖνα, *such a one*, is generally indeclinable, but it is sometimes declined thus: nominative δεῖνα, genitive δεῖνος, dative δεῖνι, accusative δεῖνα. Plural—nominative δεῖνες, genitive δείνων.

6. The following adjectives may be included here:

   (*a*) ἄλλος, ἄλλη, ἄλλο, *other.* Declined like αὐτός.

   (*b*) ἕτερος, ἑτέρα, ἕτερον, *other.*

   (*c*) μηδείς (μηδὲ εἷς), μηδεμία, μηδέν, *none, no one.* οὐδείς (οὐδὲ εἷς), οὐδεμία, οὐδέν, *none, no one.* So οὐθείς.

   (*d*) ἕκαστος, τη, τον, *each* of more than two.

   (*e*) Nominative and accusative ἄμφω, *both, two together*; genitive and dative ἀμφοῖν. Ἀμφότερος, ρα, ρον, the same meaning.

   (*f*)

   G. plural ἀλλήλων, *of each other*
   D. plural ἀλλήλοις, ἀλλήλαις, ἀλλήλοις, *to each other*
   A. plural ἀλλήλους, ἀλλήλας, ἀλλήλα, *each other*

7. The following form a class.

	Demonstratives	Interrogatives	Correlatives
(*a*)	τοῖος, *such* τοιοῦτος, *such*	ποῖος, *of what kind?* (Relative, ὁποῖος)	οἷος, *such as*, or, *of what kind* ὅσος, *how great, as great as* In plural *whosoever*
(*b*)	τόσος, *so much* τοσοῦτος, *so much*	πόσος, *how great?* In Plural *how many?*	ἡλίκος, *how great*, referring to
(*c*)	τηλίκος, *so great* τηλικοῦτος, *so great*	πηλίκος, *how great?* or, *of what age?*	*age* or *size*

8. Of these, τοιοῦτος, τοσοῦτος, and τηλικοῦτος are declined like οὗτος; but the Attic Greeks make the neuter τοιοῦτον and τοσοῦτον. In the New Testament we find neuter τοιοῦτον, Matt. 18:5, and Acts 21:25; τοσοῦτον, Heb. 12:1. Τοῖος, τοιόσδε, οἷος, and ποῖος are declined according to Section 7, Remark 1.

SECTION 11—THE PRONOUNS

TABLE K—PERSONAL PRONOUNS

		Singular	Plural			Singular	Plural
(*a*)	N.	ἐγώ, *I*	ἡμεῖς, *we*	(*b*)	N.	σύ, *you*	ὑμεῖς, *you*
	G.	ἐμοῦ, μου	ἡμῶν		G.	σοῦ	ὑμῶν
	D.	ἐμοί, μοι	ἡμῖν		D.	σοί	ὑμῖν
	A.	ἐμέ, με	ἡμᾶς		A.	σέ	ὑμᾶς

Compounds

(*c*) 1st Pers. Sg.   3rd Pers. Sg.

	M.	F.	N.		M.	F.	N.
G.	ἐμαυτοῦ	ἐμαυτῆς	ἐμαυτοῦ, *of myself*	G.	ἑαυτοῦ	ἑαυτῆς	ἑαυτοῦ, *of him/her/itself*
D.	ἐμαυτῷ	ἐμαυτῇ	ἐμαυτῷ	D.	ἑαυτῷ	ἑαυτῇ	ἑαυτῷ
A.	ἐμαυτόν	ἐμαυτήν	ἐμαυτό	A.	ἑαυτόν	ἑαυτήν	ἑαυτό

TABLE K—PERSONAL PRONOUNS (Cont.)

2nd Pers. Sg.			3rd Pers. Plural		
M.	F.	N.	M.	F.	N.
G. σεαυτοῦ	σεαυτῆς	σεαυτοῦ, *of yourself*	G. ἑαυτῶν	ἑαυτῶν	ἑαυτῶν, *of themselves*
D. σεαυτῷ	σεαυτῇ	σεαυτῷ	D. ἑαυτοῖς	ἑαυταῖς	ἑαυτοῖς
A. σεαυτόν	σεαυτήν	σεαυτό	A. ἑαυτούς	ἑαυτάς	ἑαυτά

REMARKS

1. The place of the 3rd personal pronoun is supplied in the oblique cases from αὐτός, αὐτή, αὐτό, Section 10, Table J.

2. The compounds ἐμαυτοῦ and σεαυτοῦ have no plural. *Of ourselves* is expressed by ἡμῶν αὐτῶν; *to ourselves*, by ἡμῖν αὐτοῖς, etc.

3. The possessive pronominal adjectives are as follows: ἐμός, ἐμή, ἐμόν, *mine*; σός, σή, σόν, *thine*; ὅς, ἥ, ἥν, *his*; ἡμέτερος, ρα, ρον, *ours*; ὑμέτερος, ρα, ρον, *yours.*

SECTION 12—THE VERB SUBSTANTIVE

TABLE L

	INDICATIVE	IMPERATIVE	SUBJUNCTIVE	OPTATIVE	INFINITIVE	PARTICIPLE
Present	*I am*, etc.					
Sg.	εἰμί		ὦ	εἴην	εἶναι	M. ὤν, ὄντος
	εἶ	ἴσθι	ᾖς	εἴης		F. οὖσα, οὔσης
	ἐστί(ν)	ἔστω or ἤτω	ᾖ	εἴη		N. ὄν, ὄντος
Pl.	ἐσμέν		ὦμεν	εἴημεν		M. ὄντες, ὄντων
	ἐστέ	ἔστε	ἦτε	εἴητε		F. οὖσαι, οὐσῶν
	εἰσί(ν)	ἔστωσαν	ὦσι(ν)	εἴησαν		N. ὄντα, ὄντων
Imperfect	*I was*, etc.					
Sg.	ἤμην					
	ἦς or ἦσθα					
	ἦν					
Pl.	ἦμεν or ἤμεθα					
	ἦτε					
	ἦσαν					
Future	*I shall be*, etc.					
Sg.	ἔσομαι				ἔσεσθαι	M. ἐσόμενος, ου
	ἔσῃ					F. ἐσομένη, ης
	ἔσται					N. ἐσόμενον, ου
Pl.	ἐσόμεθα					
	ἔσεσθε					
	ἔσονται					

Present Participle, the type of all participles in ων, without exception

		Singular			Plural	
	M.	F.	N.	M.	F.	N.
N.	ὤν	οὖσα	ὄν	ὄντες	οὖσαι	ὄντα
G.	ὄντος	οὔσης	ὄντος	ὄντων	οὐσῶν	ὄντων
D.	ὄντι	οὔσῃ	ὄντι	οὖσι(ν)	οὔσαις	οὖσι(ν)
A.	ὄντα	οὖσαν	ὄν	ὄντας	οὔσας	ὄντα

REMARKS

1. In the present, the 2nd person εἶ is the ordinary form. ἔνι occurs for ἔνεστι.

2. In the imperfect the 2nd person is ordinarily ἦσθα, Matt. 26:69. Another form of the imperfect occurs in the lst person plural ἤμεθα, Matt. 23:30. ἤτω occurs, as 3rd person singular of the imperative.

3. The future, in all its moods, is of the middle form. The 2nd person singular is originally ἔσεσαι. By dropping σ is formed ἔσεαι, and by contracting εα into η and subscribing the ι, ἔσῃ is formed. This remark applies to all 2nd person singular in η of passive and middle verbs, without exception.

4. The verb substantive has neither perfect, pluperfect, nor aorist. The imperfect supplies the place of these tenses.

SECTION 13—REGULAR VERB IN Ω

TABLE M—ACTIVE VOICE

	INDICATIVE	IMPERATIVE	SUBJUNCTIVE	OPTATIVE	INFINITIVE	PARTICIPLES
Present	*I loose,* etc.					
Sg.	λύω		λύω	λύοιμι	λύειν	M. λύων
	λύεις	λύε	λύῃς	λύοις		λύοντος
	λύει	λυέτω	λύῃ	λύοι		F. λύουσα
Pl.	λύομεν		λύωμεν	λύοιμεν		λυούσης
	λύετε	λύετε	λύητε	λύοιτε		N. λύον
	λύουσι(ν)	λυέτωσαν	λύωσι(ν)	λύοιεν		λύοντος
Imperfect						
Sg.	ἔλυον					
	ἔλυες					
	ἔλυε(ν)					
Pl.	ἐλύομεν					
	ἐλύετε					
	ἔλυον					
Future						
Sg.	λύσω				λύσειν	M. λύσων
	λύσεις					λύσοντος
	λύσει					F. λύσουσα
Pl.	λύσομεν					λυσούσης
	λύσετε					N. λῦσον
	λύσουσι(ν)					λύσοντος
Aorist						
Sg.	ἔλυσα		λύσω	λύσαιμι	λῦσαι	M. λύσας
	ἔλυσας	λῦσον	λύσῃς	λύσαις		λύσαντος
	ἔλυσε(ν)	λυσάτω	λύσῃ	λύσαι		F. λύσασα
Pl.	ἐλύσαμεν		λύσωμεν	λύσαιμεν		λυσάσης
	ἐλύσατε	λύσατε	λύσητε	λύσαιτε		N. λῦσον
	ἔλυσαν	λυσάτωσαν	λύσωσι(ν)	λύσαιεν		λύσαντος

TABLE M—ACTIVE VOICE (Cont.)

	INDICATIVE	IMPERATIVE	SUBJUNCTIVE	OPTATIVE	INFINITIVE	PARTICIPLE
Perfect						
Sg.	λέλυκα				λελυκέναι	M. λελυκώς
	λέλυκας	λέλυκε				λελυκότος
	λέλυκε(ν)	λελυκέτω				F. λελυκυῖα
Pl.	λελύκαμεν					λελυκυίας
	λελύκατε	λελύκετε				N. λελυκός
	λελύκασι(ν)	λελυκέτωσαν				λελυκότος
Pluperfect						
Sg.	ἐλελύκειν					
	ἐλελύκεις					
	ἐλελύκει					
Pl.	ἐλελύκειμεν					
	ἐλελύκειτε					
	ἐλελύκεισαν					

REMARKS

1. Syllabic augment, so named because it adds a syllable to the tense, occurs in the imperfect, the first aorist (in the indicative mood), and pluperfect; e.g., ἔλυον, ἔλυσα, ἐλελύκειν. Verbs beginning with ῥ double that ῥ after the augment; e.g., ῥίπτω, *I cast*, ἔρριπτον. The Attic dialect gives η for ε in three verbs; viz., βούλομαι, *I wish*, ἠβουλόμην; δύναμαι, *I am able*, ἠδυνάμην; μέλλω, *I am about, I intend*, ἤμελλον.

2. Temporal augment, so called as lengthening the *time*, or quantity, in pronunciation. It occurs when the verb begins with one of the vowels α, ε, or ο; α being lengthened into η, e.g., ἀνύτω, *I accomplish*, ἤνυτον; ε into η, ἐθέλω, *I wish*, ἤθελον; ο into ω, ὁρίζω, *I limit*, ὤριζον. Or with one of the diphthongs αι, οι, or αυ; αι into η, αἰτέω, *I ask*, ᾔτεον; οι into ῳ, οἰκέω, *I inhabit*, ᾤκεον; αυ into ηυ, αὐξάνω, *I increase*, ηὔξανον.

3. The long vowels η, ω, and the three diphthongs ει, ευ, ου are unchanged, and ι, υ, merely lengthened in quantity; e.g., ἠχέω, *I resound*, ἤχεον; ὤθω, *I push*, ὤθον; ἱκετεύω, *I supplicate*, ἱκέτευον; ὑβρίζω, *I assault*, ὕβριζον, εἰκάζω, *I imagine*, εἴκαζον; εὐθύνω, *I direct*, εὔθυνον; οὐτάζω, *I wound*, οὔταζον. But the Attics often change ευ into ηυ; e.g., εὔχομαι, *I pray*, ηὐχόμην.

4. Several verbs beginning with ε receive the augment by inserting ι; e.g., ἔχω, *I have*, εἶχον; ἐργάζομαι, *I work*, εἰργαζόμην; ἐάω, *I permit*, εἴαον, contract εἴων, etc. So ἔθω, perfect εἴωθα, *I am accustomed*, ω being interposed, and ἐθίζω, *I accustom*, perfect passive εἴθισμαι. The verb ὁράω, *I see*, receives both the syllabic and temporal augments, ε and ω; e.g., ὁράω, ἑώραον, contract ἑώρων; perfect Attic ἑώρακα, for ὤρακα.

5. Reduplication. (*a*) This consists of ε added to the first consonant of the root, as in λέλυκα. All verbs beginning with a consonant have the reduplication in the perfect and retain it in all the moods.

(*b*) Verbs beginning with a vowel or a diphthong receive no reduplication, the first letter of the perfect being the same as that of the imperfect; e.g., ἀνύτω, imperfect ἤνυτον, perfect ἤνυκα. In such cases the temporal augment is retained through all the moods.

6. (*a*) If the first consonant of the present is an aspirate, it is replaced in the reduplication by the corresponding smooth consonant; e.g., φιλέω, *I love*, πεφίληκα; θύω, *I sacrifice*, τέθυκα.

(*b*) Verbs which begin with ῥ, a double letter, or two consonants lack the reduplication; e.g., ῥάπτω, *I sew*, ἔρραφα; ψάλλω, *I play on an instrument*, ἔψαλκα; σπείρω, *I sow*, ἔσπαρκα.

(*c*) As exceptions to this rule may be mentioned, verbs beginning with a mute and a liquid; e.g., γράφω, *I write*, γέγραφα; κλίνω, *I incline*, κέκλικα. Some beginning with πτ; e.g., πέπτωκα, from the old form πτύω, *I fall*.

7. (*a*) The Attics change the reduplications λε and με in the perfect into ει; e.g., λαμβάνω, *I take* (old form λήβω) εἴληφα, for λέληφα; μείρω, *I divide*, εἴμαρμαι, for μέμαρμαι.

(*b*) What is called the Attic reduplication occurs in some verbs beginning with a vowel. It consists in a repetition of the two first letters of the verb before the temporal augment; e.g., ὀρύπτω, *I dig*, perfect ὤρυχα, Attic ὀρώρυχα; ἐλαύνω, *I drive*, perfect ἤλακα, Attic ἐλήλακα.

(*c*) If the third syllable, counting the reduplication, is long, it is shortened; e.g., ἀλείφω, *I anoint*, ἤλειφα, Attic ἀλήλιφα; ἀκούω, *I hear*, ἤκουσα, Attic ἀκήκοα.

(*d*) In the second aorist* this reduplication continues through the moods, but the temporal augment does not go beyond the indicative; e.g., from ἄγω, *I lead*, 2nd aorist ἤγαγον (by transposition for ἄγηγον), but infinitive ἀγαγεῖν.

8. Formation of the tenses of the active voice. Indicative mood.

(*a*) The present is formed from the root and the ending ω, εις, ει. Third person plural ουσι(ν), like the dative plural of the present participle.

(*b*) The imperfect is formed from the present by prefixing the augment and changing ω into ον; λύω, ἔλυον. The 3rd person plural is like the lst person singular in this tense.

(*c*) The future is the root, with the addition of the ending σω, σεις, σει, etc.

(*d*) The aorist is formed from the future by prefixing the augment and changing σω into σα; λύσω, ἔλυσα. The 3rd person plural is formed by adding ν to the 1st person singular; ἔλυσα, ἔλυσαν.

(*e*) The perfect is formed from the future by changing σω into κα and prefixing the reduplication. Modifications of this ending will be hereafter noted.

(*f*) The pluperfect is formed from the perfect by prefixing the augment ε and changing the final α into ειν; λέλυκα, ἐλελύκειν. Sometimes the augment is omitted; e.g., πεπιστεύκεισαν.

9. Imperative. (*a*) The present is formed by changing ω of the present indicative into ε; e.g., λύω, λύε, λυέτω, etc.

(*b*) The imperative aorist is in ον, ατω; e.g., λῦσον, λυσάτω.

(*c*) The perfect is the same in form as the 3rd person singular of the perfect indicative; e.g., λέλυκε. All the 3rd persons singular and plural of the imperative have ω in the ending.

10. Subjunctive. (*a*) The present subjunctive is formed from the present indicative by changing the short vowels into long ones and adding the iota subscript where it occurs; e.g., indicative λύω, λύεις, λύει; subjunctive λύω, λύῃς, λύῃ.

(*b*) The 2nd person plural λύητε has no iota subscript, there being none in the corresponding persons of the indicative.

11. Optative. (*a*) The present, future, and perfect optative are formed by changing the last letter of the same tenses of the indicative into οιμι; e.g., present λύω, optative λύοιμι; future λύσω, optative λύσοιμι; perfect λέλυκα, optative λελύκοιμι.

(*b*) The aorist optative drops the augment, and changes α into αιμι; e.g., ἔλυσα, λύσαιμι.

12. Infinitive. All tenses ending in ω in the indicative form the infinitive in ειν; the aorist forms it in αι, and the perfect in έναι.

13. Participles. Those tenses having the infinitive in ειν form the participle in ων, ουσα, ον. The aorist participle ends in ας, ασα, αν; λύσας, λύσασα, λῦσαν, genitive λύσαντος, λυσάσης, λύσαντος, etc. The perfect participle ends in ως, υια, ος; λελυκώς, λελυκυῖα, λελυκός, genitive λελυκότος, λελυκυίας, λελυκότος, etc. They are all declined like adjectives of the third class.

---

* It will be observed that in the Paradigm given above (λύω), the second aorist does not occur. This tense is regarded by Burnouf as only another form of what is usually called the first aorist, since it appears that if one aorist is used in a given verb, the other does not occur, at least in the same dialect. Buttmann (as quoted by Burnouf) states that no verb in which the second aorist is the same in form with the imperfect, or would differ only in the quantity of the penultimate syllable, can have this aorist, at any rate in the active voice.

Remarks on the second aorist will be found below, Section 24.

SECTION 14—REGULAR VERB IN Ω

TABLE N—PASSIVE VOICE					
	INDICATIVE	IMPERATIVE	SUBJUNCTIVE	OPTATIVE	INFINITIVE	PARTICIPLES
Present Sg.	*I am loosed*, etc.				
	λύομαι		λύωμαι	λυοίμην	λύεσθαι	M. λυόμενος
	λύῃ	λύου	λύῃ	λύοιο		λυομένου
	λύεται	λυέσθω	λύηται	λύοιτο		F. λυομένη
Pl.	λυόμεθα		λυώμεθα	λυοίμεθα		λυομένης
	λύεσθε	λύεσθε	λύησθε	λύοισθε		N. λυόμενον
	λύονται	λυέσθωσαν	λύωνται	λύοιντο		λυομένου

TABLE N — PASSIVE VOICE (Cont.)

	INDICATIVE	IMPERATIVE	SUBJUNCTIVE	OPTATIVE	INFINITIVE	PARTICIPLE	
Imperfect							
Sg.	ἐλυόμην						
	ἐλύου						
	ἐλύετο						
Pl.	ἐλυόμεθα						
	ἐλύεσθε						
	ἐλύοντο						
Future							
Sg.	λυθήσομαι				λυθήσεσθαι	M.	λυθησόμενος
	λυθήσῃ						λυθησομένου
	λυθήσεται					F.	λυθησομένη
Pl.	λυθησόμεθα						λυθησομένης
	λυθήσεσθε					N.	λυθησόμενον
	λυθήσονται						λυθησομένου
Aorist							
Sg.	ἐλύθην		λυθῶ	λυθείην	λυθῆναι	M.	λυθείς
	ἐλύθης	λύθητι	λυθῇς	λυθείης			λυθέντος
	ἐλύθη	λυθήτω	λυθῇ	λυθείη		F.	λυθεῖσα
Pl.	ἐλύθημεν		λυθῶμεν	λυθείημεν			λυθείσης
	ἐλύθητε	λύθητε	λυθῆτε	λυθείητε		N.	λυθέν
	ἐλύθησαν	λυθήτωσαν	λυθῶσι(ν)	λυθείησαν			λυθέντος
Perfect							
Sg.	λέλυμαι		λελυμένος ὦ		λελύσθαι	M.	λελυμένος
	λέλυσαι	λέλυσο	λελυμένος ᾖς				λελυμένου
	λέλυται	λελύσθω	λελυμένος ᾖ			F.	λελυμένη
Pl.	λελύμεθα		λελυμένος ὦμεν				λελυμένης
	λέλυσθε	λέλυσθε	λελυμένοι ἦτε			N.	λελυμένον
	λέλυνται	λελύσθωσαν	λελυμένοι ὦσι				λελυμένου
Pluperfect							
Sg.	ἐλελύμην						
	ἐλέλυσο						
	ἐλέλυτο						
Pl.	ἐλελύμεθα						
	ἐλέλυσθε						
	ἐλέλυντο						
3rd Future							
Sg.	λελύσομαι			λελυσοίμην	λελύσεσθαι	M.	λελυσομένος
	λελύσῃ			λελύσοιο			λελυσομένου
	λελύσεται			λελύσοιτο		F.	λελυσομένη
Pl.	λελυσόμεθα			λελυσοίμεθα			λελυσομένης
	λελύσεσθε			λελύσοισθε		N.	λελυσόμενον
	λελύσονται			λελυσοίμεθον			λελυσομένου

REMARKS

1. (a) The present passive is formed from the present active by changing ω into ομαι; λύω, λύομαι.

(b) The imperfect passive from the imperfect active, by changing ον into ομην; ἔλυον, ἐλυόμην.

(*c*) The future passive by adding the ending θησομαι to the stem of the verb, especially as it appears in the future active and the perfect, and aspirating a preceding consonant; λύω, λυθήσομαι; σκοτίζω, σκοτίσω, σκοτισθήσομαι; ἄγω, ἄξω, ἀχθήσομαι. Some verbs have another form, termed the second future, which exhibits the same change of the stem of the verb as the second aorist active, with the ending ησομαι; δέρω, δαρήσομαι; ἀλλάσσω, ἀλλαγήσομαι.

(*d*) The aorist passives of the first and second form have the ending ην in place of ησομαι in the futures, and prefix the augment; λύω, ἐλύθην; πέμπω, ἐπέμθην; στρέφω, ἐστράφην; κρύπτω, ἐκρύβην.

(*e*) The ending of the perfect passive is μαι; λέλυκα, λέλυμαι; τετέλεκα, τετέλεσμαι; γέγραφα, γέγραμμαι.

(*f*) The pluperfect is formed from the perfect by changing μαι into μην and prefixing the augment; λέλυμαι, ἐλελύμην. The augment is sometimes omitted; e.g., νενομοθέτητο, for ἐνενομοθέτητο.

(*g*) The third future, which mainly belongs to the passive voice, is formed from one of the perfects by substituting the ending σομαι; κέκραγα (κεκράγσομαι) κεκράξομαι; γέγραπται (γεγράπσομαι) γεγράψομαι.

2. (*a*) The imperative passive is formed from the indicative by the following changes:

Present indicative 1st person λύω
   Imperative λύου
   3rd person λυέσθω
Aorist indicative 3rd person ἐλύθη
   Imperative λύθητι
   3rd person λυθήτω
Pluperfect indicative 2nd person ἐλέλυσο
   Imperative λέλυσο
   3rd person λελύσθω

(*b*) The 2nd person in ου of the imperfect is formed from εσο by dropping σ and contracting εο into ου; e.g., ἐλύεσο, ἐλύεο, ἐλύου.

3. (*a*) The present passive subjunctive is formed from the present passive indicative by changing the short vowels into long ones; e.g., λύομαι, λύωμαι. The 2nd person singular is from ησαι, thus: ησαι, ηαι, ῃ.

(*b*) The aorist passive subjunctive from that of the aorist passive indicative by dropping the augment and changing ην into ω; ἐλύθην, λυθῶ.

(*c*) The perfect passive subjunctive, usually, by a combination of the perfect passive participle with the present subjunctive of the verb εἶναι, ὦ, ᾖς, ᾖ.

4. (*a*) The optative passive is formed by changing the ending of the passive indicative ομαι into οιμην; e.g., present indicative λύομαι, optative λυοίμην.

(*b*) The aorist passive drops the augment and changes ην into ειην; ἐλύθην, λυθείην. The plural is frequently contracted; e.g., λυθεῖμεν, λυθεῖτε, λυθεῖεν.

5. (*a*) The passive infinitive of the tenses ending in μαι is formed from the 3rd person of the indicative by changing ται into σθαι; e.g., present λύεται, infinitive λύεσθαι; future λυθήσεται, infinitive λυθήσεσθαι.

(*b*) The aorist passive infinitive drops the augment and changes ην into ηναι; ἐλύθην, λυθῆναι; ἐκρύβην, κρυβῆναι.

6. (*a*) The passive participle of every tense in μαι ends in μενος; e.g., present λύομαι, participle λυόμενος, future λυθήσομαι, participle λυθησόμενος; third future λελύσομαι, participle λελυσόμενος, etc. All these are declined like ἀγαθός, ή, όν.

(*b*) The passive participle of the aorist drops the augment and changes ην into εις; ἐλύθην, λυθείς; ἐστράφην, στραφείς. It is declined like adjectives of the third class.

SECTION 15—REGULAR VERB IN Ω

TABLE O—MIDDLE VOICE					
INDICATIVE	IMPERATIVE	SUBJUNCTIVE	OPTATIVE	INFINITIVE	PARTICIPLE
Future I shall loose, etc.					
Sg. λύσομαι				λύσεσθαι	M. λυσόμενος
λύσῃ					λυσομένου
λύσεται					F. λυσομένη
Pl. λυσόμεθα					λυσομένης
λύσεσθε					N. λυσόμενον
λύσονται					λυσομένου
Aorist					
Sg. ἐλυσάμην		λύσωμαι	λυσαίμην	λύσασθαι	M. λυσάμενος
ἐλύσω	λῦσαι	λύσῃ	λύσαιο		λυσαμένου
ἐλύσατο	λυσάσθω	λύσηται	λύσαιτο		F. λυσαμένη
Pl. ἐλυσάμεθα		λυσώμεθα	λυσαίμεθα		λυσαμένης
ἐλύσασθε	λύσασθε	λύσησθε	λύσαισθε		N. λυσάμενον
ἐλύσαντο	λυσάσθωσαν	λύσωνται	λύσαιντο		λυσαμένου

REMARKS

1. The middle voice has only two tenses peculiar to itself, the future and the aorist. As to the other tenses, the passive form is used to indicate reflexive action: thus the present, λύομαι, may mean *I am loosed* (passive), or, *I loose myself* (middle).

2. The tense ending in α, e.g., κέκραγα, πέφευγα, commonly called the perfect middle, but which is, in fact, only a second form of the perfect active, will be noticed hereafter.

3. (*a*) The future middle is formed from the future active by changing ω into ομαι; λύσω, λύσομαι.

(*b*) The aorist middle from the aorist active, by adding μην; ἔλυσα, ἐλυσάμην. The 2nd person, ἐλύσω, from ἐλύσασο, by dropping σ and contracting αο into ω.

SECTION 16—CONTRACTED VERB IN Ε'Ω

TABLE P—ACTIVE VOICE						
	INDICATIVE	IMPERATIVE	SUBJUNCTIVE	OPTATIVE	INFINITIVE	PARTICIPLE
Present	*I love*, etc.					
Sg.	φιλῶ		φιλῶ	φιλοῖμι	φιλεῖν	M. φιλῶν
	φιλεῖς	φίλει	φιλῇς	φιλοῖς		φιλοῦντος
	φιλεῖ	φιλείτω	φιλῇ	φιλοῖ		F. φιλοῦσα
Pl.	φιλοῦμεν		φιλῶμεν	φιλοῖμεν		φιλούσης
	φιλεῖτε	φιλεῖτε	φιλῆτε	φιλοῖτε		N. φιλοῦν
	φιλοῦσι(ν)	φιλείτωσαν	φιλῶσι(ν)	φιλοῖεν		φιλοῦντος
Imperfect						
Sg.	ἐφίλουν					
	ἐφίλεις					
	ἐφίλει					
Pl.	ἐφιλοῦμεν					
	ἐφιλεῖτε					
	ἐφίλουν					
Future	φιλήσω				φιλήσειν	φιλήσων, σοντος
Aorist	ἐφίλησα	φίλησον	φιλήσω	φιλήσαιμι	φιλῆσαι	φιλήσας, σαντος
Perfect	πεφίληκα	πεφίληκε			πεφιληκέναι	πεφιληκώς, κότος
Pluperfect	ἐπεφιλήκειν					

REMARKS

1. Rules of contraction; ε disappears before long vowels and diphthongs, εε is contracted into ει, εο into ου.

2. The contraction takes place only in the present and imperfect, because in these tenses alone the ending begins with a vowel.

3. In the future and perfect these verbs change often (not invariably) ε and α into η, and o into ω, i.e., the short vowels of the root into their corresponding long ones; e.g., present φιλέω, future φιλήσω, perfect πεφίληκα. τιμάω, τιμήσω, τετίμηκα, δηλόω, δηλώσω, δεδήλωκα.

4. Since the uncontracted tenses are conjugated like λύω, only the first persons are given.

5. As regards the reduplication in the perfect, we find πεφίληκα, not φεφίληκα, because two successive syllables cannot begin with the same aspirate.

6. In place of the optative φιλοῖμι, the Attics wrote φιλοίην, φιλοίης, φιλοίη; but the 3rd person plural is always φιλοῖεν (not φιλοίησαν). The 1st and 2nd person plural φιλοίημεν, φιλοίητε, are scarcely used, on account of their length.

SECTION 17—CONTRACTED VERB IN ΕΏ

TABLE Q—PASSIVE VOICE

	INDICATIVE	IMPERATIVE	SUBJUNCTIVE	OPTATIVE	INFINITIVE	PARTICIPLES
Present	*I am loved*, etc.					
Sg.	φιλοῦμαι		φιλῶμαι	φιλοίμην	φιλεῖσθαι	M. φιλούμενος
	φιλῇ	φιλοῦ	φιλῇ	φιλοῖο		φιλουμένου
	φιλεῖται	φιλείσθω	φιλῆται	φιλοῖτο		F. φιλουμένη
Pl.	φιλούμεθα		φιλώμεθα	φιλοίμεθα		φιλουμένης
	φιλεῖσθε	φιλεῖσθε	φιλῆσθε	φιλοῖσθε		N. φιλούμενον
	φιλοῦνται	φιλείσθωσαν	φιλῶνται	φιλοῖντο		φιλουμένου
Imperfect						
Sg.	ἐφιλούμην					
	ἐφιλοῦ					
	ἐφιλεῖτο					
Pl.	ἐφιλούμεθα					
	ἐφιλεῖσθε					
	ἐφιλοῦντο					
Future	φιληθήσομαι				φιληθήσεσθαι	φιληθησόμενος, ου
Aorist	ἐφιλήθην	φιλήθητι	φιληθῶ	φιληθείην	φιληθῆναι	φιληθείς, θέντος
Perfect	πεφίλημαι	πεφίλησο	πεφιλημένος ὦ		πεφιλῆσθαι	πεφιλημένος, ου
Pluperfect	ἐπεφιλήμην					

MIDDLE VOICE

	INDICATIVE	IMPERATIVE	SUBJUNCTIVE	OPTATIVE	INFINITIVE	PARTICIPLES
Future	φιλήσομαι				φιλήσεσθαι	φιλησόμενος, ου
Aorist	ἐφιλησάμην	φίλησαι	φιλήσωμαι	φιλησαίμην	φιλήσασθαι	φιλησάμενος, ου

REMARKS

1. The contraction takes place, as in the active voice, only in the present and imperfect; and, if φιλε be considered as the stem, the endings are the same as in λύομαι.

2. Another form of the perfect, subjunctive, and optative, πεφιλῶμαι and πεφιλήμην, will be hereafter noted.

SECTION 18—CONTRACTED VERB IN ΑΏ

TABLE R—ACTIVE VOICE

	INDICATIVE	IMPERATIVE	SUBJUNCTIVE	OPTATIVE	INFINITIVE	PARTICIPLES
Present	*I honor*, etc.					
Sg.	τιμῶ		τιμῶ	τιμῷμι	τιμάειν	M. τιμῶν
	τιμᾷς	τίμα	τιμᾷς	τιμῷς		τιμῶντος
	τιμᾷ	τιμάτω	τιμᾷ	τιμῷ		F. τιμῶσα
Pl.	τιμῶμεν		τιμῶμεν	τιμῷμεν		τιμώσης
	τιμᾶτε	τιμᾶτε	τιμᾶτε	τιμῷτε		N. τιμῶν
	τιμῶσι(ν)	τιμάτωσαν	τιμῶσι(ν)	τιμῷεν		τιμῶντος

TABLE R—ACTIVE VOICE (Cont.)

	INDICATIVE	IMPERATIVE	SUBJUNCTIVE	OPTATIVE	INFINITIVE	PARTICIPLE
Imperfect						
Sg.	ἐτίμων					
	ἐτίμας					
	ἐτίμα					
Pl.	ἐτιμῶμεν					
	ἐτιμᾶτε					
	ἐτίμων					
Future	τιμήσω				τιμήσειν	τιμήσων, σοντος
Aorist	ἐτίμησα	τίμησον	τιμήσω	τιμήσαιμι	τιμῆσαι	τιμήσας, σαντος
Perfect	τετίμηκα	τετίμηκε	τετιμήκω		τετιμηκέναι	τετιμηκώς, κότος
Pluperfect	ἐτετιμήκειν					

REMARKS

1. Rules of contraction; 1st, αο, αω, αον into ω; 2nd, αοι into ῳ (ι subscript); 3rd, αε, αη, into α; 4th, αει, αη, into ᾳ (ι subscript).

2. For the optative, instead of τιμῴμι, the Attics wrote also τιμῴην, τιμῴης, τιμῴη, τιμῴημεν, τιμῴητε, τιμῷεν.

SECTION 19—CONTRACTED VERB IN A'Ω

TABLE S—PASSIVE VOICE

	INDICATIVE	IMPERATIVE	SUBJUNCTIVE	OPTATIVE	INFINITIVE	PARTICIPLES
Present	*I am honored*, etc.					
Sg.	τιμῶμαι		τιμῶμαι	τιμῴμην	τιμᾶσθαι	M. τιμώμενος
	τιμᾷ	τιμῶ	τιμᾷ	τιμῷο		τιμωμένου
	τιμᾶται	τιμάσθω	τιμᾶται	τιμῷτο		F. τιμωμένη
Pl.	τιμώμεθα		τιμώμεθα	τιμῴμεθα		τιμωμένης
	τιμᾶσθε	τιμᾶσθε	τιμᾶσθε	τιμῷσθε		N. τιμώμενον
	τιμῶνται	τιμάσθωσαν	τιμῶνται	τιμῷντο		τιμωμένου
Imperfect						
Sg.	ἐτιμώμην					
	ἐτιμῶ					
	ἐτιμᾶτο					
Pl.	ἐτιμώμεθα					
	ἐτιμᾶσθε					
	ἐτιμῶντο					
Future	τιμηθήσομαι				τιμηθήσεσθαι	τιμηθησόμενος, ου
Aorist	ἐτιμήθην	τιμήθητι	τιμηθῶ	τιμηθείην	τιμηθῆναι	τιμηθείς, θέντος
Perfect	τετίμημαι	τετίμησο	τετιμημένος ὦ		τετιμῆσθαι	τετιμημένος, ου
Pluperfect	ἐτετιμήμην					

TABLE S (Cont.)

MIDDLE VOICE

	INDICATIVE	IMPERATIVE	SUBJUNCTIVE	OPTATIVE	INFINITIVE	PARTICIPLE
Future	τιμήσομαι				τιμήσεσθαι	τιμησόμενος, ου
Aorist	ἐτιμησάμην	τίμησαι	τιμήσωμαι	τιμησαίμην	τιμήσασθαι	τιμησάμενος, ου

REMARKS

1. The 3rd person singular of the imperfect would originally be ἐτιμάεσο; by dropping σ and contracting εο into ου, we have ἐτιμάου, then ἐτιμῶ.

2. The present subjunctive, after contraction, is the same as that of the indicative (as also in the active voice); because αε and αη are alike contracted in α.

SECTION 20 — CONTRACTED VERB IN O΄Ω

TABLE T — ACTIVE VOICE

	INDICATIVE	IMPERATIVE	SUBJUNCTIVE	OPTATIVE	INFINITIVE	PARTICIPLES
Present	*I show*, etc.					
Sg.	δηλῶ		δηλῶ	δηλοῖμι	δηλοῦν	M. δηλῶν
	δηλοῖς	δήλου,	δηλοῖς	δηλοῖς		δηλοῦντος
	δηλοῖ	δηλούτω	δηλοῖ	δηλοῖ		F. δηλοῦσα
Pl.	δηλοῦμεν		δηλῶμεν	δηλοῖμεν		δηλούσης
	δηλοῦτε	δηλοῦτε	δηλῶτε	δηλοῖτε		N. δηλοῦν
	δηλοῦσι(ν)	δηλούτωσαν	δηλῶσι(ν)	δηλοῖεν		δηλοῦντος
Imperfect						
Sg.	ἐδήλουν					
	ἐδήλους					
	ἐδήλου					
Pl.	ἐδηλοῦμεν					
	ἐδηλοῦτε					
	ἐδήλουν					
Future	δηλώσω				δηλώσειν	δηλώσων, σοντος
Aorist	ἐδήλωσα	δήλωσον	δηλώσω	δηλώσαιμι	δηλῶσαι	δηλώσας, σαντος
Perfect	δεδήλωκα	δεδήλωκε			δεδηλωκέναι	δεδηλωκώς, κότος
Pluperfect	ἐδεδηλώκειν					

REMARKS

1. Rules of contraction: 1st, οε, οο, οου, into ου; 2nd, οη, οω, into ω; 3rd, οη, οει, οοι, into οι. In the infinitive, όειν is contracted into οῦν.

2. Instead of the form δηλοῖμι for the optative, the Attics also wrote δηλοίην, δηλοίης, δηλοίη, etc.

SECTION 21 — CONTRACTED VERB IN Ο΄Ω

TABLE U — PASSIVE VOICE

	INDICATIVE	IMPERATIVE	SUBJUNCTIVE	OPTATIVE	INFINITIVE	PARTICIPLES
Present	*I am shown, etc.*					
Sg.	δηλοῦμαι		δηλῶμαι	δηλοίμην	δηλοῦσθαι	M. δηλούμενος
	δηλοῖ	δηλοῦ	δηλοῖ	δηλοῖο		δηλουμένου
	δηλοῦται	δηλούσθω	δηλῶται	δηλοῖτο		F. δηλουμένη
Pl.	δηλούμεθα		δηλώμεθα	δηλοίμεθα		δηλουμένης
	δηλοῦσθε	δηλοῦσθε	δηλῶσθε	δηλοῖσθε		N. δηλούμενον
	δηλοῦνται	δηλούσθωσαν	δηλῶνται	δηλοῖντο		δηλουμένου
Imperfect						
Sg.	ἐδηλούμην					
	ἐδηλοῦ					
	ἐδηλοῦτο					
Pl.	ἐδηλούμεθα					
	ἐδηλοῦσθε					
	ἐδηλοῦντο					
Future	δηλωθήσομαι				δηλωθήσεσθαι	δηλωθησόμενος, ου
Aorist	ἐδηλώθην	δηλώθητι	δηλωθῶ	δηλωθείην	δηλωθῆναι	δηλωθείς, θέντος
Perfect	δεδήλωμαι	δεδήλωσο	δεδηλωμένος ὦ		δεδηλῶσθαι	δεδηλωμένος, ου
Pluperfect	ἐδεδηλώμην					

MIDDLE VOICE

	INDICATIVE	IMPERATIVE	SUBJUNCTIVE	OPTATIVE	INFINITIVE	PARTICIPLES
Future	δηλώσομαι				δηλώσεσθαι	δηλωσόμενος, ου
Aorist	ἐδηλωσάμην	δήλωσαι	δηλώσωμαι	δηλωσαίμην	δηλώσασθαι	δηλωσάμενος, ου

SECTION 22 — REMARKS ON VERBS IN Ω PURE, I.E., PRECEDED BY A VOWEL

1. Many verbs in έω make the future in έσω (not ήσω); e.g., τελέω, *I finish*, τελέσω; ἀρκέω, ἀρκέσω. Some have both forms; e.g., αἰνέω, *I praise*, αἰνέσω, and αἰνήσω; φορέω, *I bear*, φορέσω, and φορήσω.

2. Of verbs in άω, many keep α in the future. Those which have ε or ι before άω; e.g., ἐάω, *I permit*, ἐάσω; θεάομαι, *I behold*, θεάσομαι, perfect τεθέαμαι, aorist ἐθεάθην. Those in ράω; e.g., ὁράω, *I see*, ὁράσω (not used). Those in λάω; e.g., γελάω, *I laugh*, γελάσω; κλάω, *I break*, κλάσω. Also κρεμάω, *I hang up*, κρεμάσω; σπάω, *I draw*, σπάσω. But χράω, *I lend*, has χρήσω; τλάω, *I bear*, τλήσω.

3. Of verbs in όω a very few keep ο in the future; e.g., ἀρόω, *I plough*, ἀρόσω. All others have ω, as δηλώσω.

4. Future and aorist passive. Many verbs have σ before θήσομαι in the future and before θην in the aorist; e.g.,

χρίω, *I anoint*, χρίσω, χρισθήσομαι, ἐχρίσθην; τελέω, *I finish*, τελέσω, τελεσθήσομαι, ἐτελέσθην; κλείω, *I shut*, κλείσω, κλεισθήσομαι, ἐκλείσθην; ἀκούω, *I hear*, ἀκούσω, ἀκουσθήσομαι, ἠκούσθην. Indeed, almost all verbs which have a short vowel or a diphthong before the ending receive σ; καλέω, *I call*, καλέσω, makes κέκληκα, κέκλημαι, ἐκλήθην, as if from κλέω, κλήσω. But κέκληκα is for κεκάλεκα, by contraction.

5. Perfect passive. Generally, verbs which have σ in the future and aorist passive have it also in the perfect; e.g., τετέλεσμαι, κέχρισμαι, κέκλεισμαι, ἤκουσμαι. But some have σ in the aorist and not in the perfect; e.g., μνάομαι, *I remember*, ἐμνήσθην, but μέμνημαι; παύω, *I cause to cease*, ἐπαύσθην, but πέπαυμαι.

6. The perfect passive of verbs which have σ before μαι is conjugated as follows:

	INDICATIVE	PLUPERFECT	IMPERATIVE	SUBJUNCTIVE	INFINITIVE	PARTICIPLE
Perfect						
Sg.	ἤκουσμαι	ἠκούσμην		ἠκουσμένος ὦ	ἠκοῦσθαι	M. ἠκουσμένος
	ἤκουσαι	ἤκουσο	ἤκουσο	ἠκουσμένος ᾖς		F. ἠκουσμένη
	ἤκουσται	ἤκουστο	ἠκούσθω	ἠκουσμένος ᾖ		N. ἠκουσμένον
Pl.	ἠκούσμεθα	ἠκούσμεθα		ἠκουσμένοι ὦμεν		
	ἤκουσθε	ἤκουσθε	ἤκουσθε	ἠκουσμένοι ἦτε		
	ἠκουσμένοι εἰσί(ν)	ἠκουσμένοι ἦσαν	ἠκούσθωσαν	ἠκουσμένοι ὦσι(ν)		

7. According to the analogy of λέλυται, λέλυνται, the 3rd person plural of ἤκουσμαι should be ἤκουσνται. The harshness of three consecutive consonants is avoided by combining the 3rd person plural indicative of εἶναι, *to be*, with the perfect participle ἠκουσμένοι εἰσί(ν). The same remark applies to the pluperfect, where the 3rd person plural imperfect of εἰμί is used; ἠκουσμένοι ἦσαν.

SECTION 23—REMARKS ON VERBS WHICH HAVE A CONSONANT OR CONSONANTS BEFORE Ω

1. Future and aorist active. (*a*) All verbs which have in the stem form a mute of the first order, Β, Π, Φ, form the future in ψω; e.g., τρίβω, *I bruise*, τρίψω; γράφω, *I write*, γράψω.

(*b*) Those which have a mute of the second order, Γ, Κ, Χ, form it in ξω; e.g., λέγω, *I say*, λέξω; βρέχω, *I wet*, βρέξω. So in the middle form, δέχομαι, future δέξομαι, etc.

(*c*) Those which have a mute of the third order, Δ, Τ, Θ, form it in σω; e.g., ᾄδω, *I sing*, ᾄσω; ἀνύτω, *I finish*, ἀνύσω; πλήθω, *I fill*, πλήσω.

2. If the stem has τ before π, as in τύπτω, the τ is lost in the future; e.g., τύψω. The aorists are in ψα, ξα, and σα; e.g., ἔτυψα, ἔλεξα, ἤνυσα.

3. Future and aorist passive. (*a*) Verbs which have in the stem a mute of the first order form the future passive in φθήσομαι; e.g., τύπτω, τυφθήσομαι.

(*b*) Those with a mute of the second order form it in χθήσομαι; e.g., λέγω, λεχθήσομαι.

(*c*) Those with a mute of the third order, in σθήσομαι; e.g., ἀνύτω, ἀνυσθήσομαι.

4. Since the aorist passive is formed from the future by changing θήσομαι into θην, the aorist will be, for the first order, φθην, ἐτύφθην; for the second, χθην, ἐλέχθην; for the third, σθην, ἠνύσθην.

5. Future and aorist middle. For the future, the ω of the future active is changed into ομαι; e.g., τύψω, τύψομαι; λέξω, λέξομαι; ἀνύσω, ἀνύσομαι. For the aorist μην is added to the aorist active; e.g., ἔτυψα, ἐτυψάμην; ἔλεξα, ἐλεξάμην; ἤνυσα, ἠνυσάμην.

6. Perfect and pluperfect active. Verbs which have the future in ψω, form the perfect in φα; e.g., τύψω, τέτυφα. Those with the future in ξω, form the perfect in χα, with χ; e.g., πράξω, πέπραχα. Those with the future in σω, form the perfect in κα, with κ; e.g., πείσω, πέπεικα. The pluperfect is regularly formed by changing α into ειν, and prefixing the augment; e.g., τέτυφα, ἐτετύφειν, etc.

7. Perfect and pluperfect passive. Verbs which have the perfect active in φα, form the perfect passive in μμαι, with double μ; e.g., τέτυφα, τέτυμμαι (by assimilation for τέτυπμαι). Those which have the perfect active in χ, with χ, form the perfect passive in γμαι; e.g., πέπραχα, πέπραγμαι. Those with the perfect active in κα, with κ, form the perfect passive in σμαι; e.g., πέπεικα, πέπεισμαι. The pluperfect is formed by changing μαι into μην, and prefixing the augment; ἐτετύμμην, ἐλελέγμην.

8. Example of perfect passive in μμαι, from τύπτω, *I strike* —

	INDICATIVE	PLUPERFECT	IMPERATIVE	SUBJUNCTIVE	INFINITIVE	PARTICIPLE
Perfect						
Sg.	τέτυμμαι	ἐτετύμμην		τετυμμένος ὦ	τετύφθαι	M. τετυμμένος
	τέτυψαι	ἐτέτυψο	τέτυψο	τετυμμένος ᾖς		F. τετυμμένη
	τέτυπται	ἐτέτυπτο	τετύφθω	τετυμμένος ᾖ		N. τετυμμένον
Pl.	τετύμμεθα	ἐτετύμμεθα		τετυμμένοι ὦμεν		
	τέτυφθε	ἐτέτυφθε	τέτυφθε	τετυμμένοι ἦτε		
	τετυμμένοι εἰσί(ν)	τετυμμένοι ἦσαν	τετύφθωσαν	τετυμμένοι ὦσι(ν)		

9. Perfect passive in γμαι, from λέγω, *I say*.

	INDICATIVE	PLUPERFECT	IMPERATIVE	SUBJUNCTIVE	INFINITIVE	PARTICIPLE
Perfect						
Sg.	λέλεγμαι	ἐλελέγμην		λελεγμένος ὦ	λελέχθαι	M. λελεγμένος
	λέλεξαι	ἐλέλεξο	λέλεξο	λελεγμένος ᾖς		F. λελεγμένη
	λέλεκται	ἐλέλεκτο	λελέχθω	λελεγμένος ᾖ		N. λελεγμένον
Pl.	λελέγμεθα	ἐλελέγμεθα		λελεγμένοι ὦμεν		
	λέλεχθε	ἐλέλεχθε	λέλεχθε	λελεγμένοι ἦτε		
	λελεγμένοι εἰσί(ν)	λελεγμένοι ἦσαν	λελέχθωσαν	λελεγμένοι ὦσι(ν)		

Ἐλέγχω, *I convict*, forms the perfect ἐλήλεγμαι. But the γ of the stem reappears in the 2nd and 3rd persons, ἐλήλεγξαι, ἐλήλεγκται; in the future, ἐλεγχθήσομαι, and in the aorist, ἠλέγχθην.

10. The conjugation of all perfect passives in σμαι accords with the example already given; Section 22, Remark 6.

SECTION 24—REMARKS ON THE SECOND AORIST AND SECOND FUTURE

1. Very few verbs have both the 1st and 2nd aorist active. Both forms of the aorist have the same significance.

2. The active and middle voices each have only one form of the future: the passive has two, without difference of meaning, though very few verbs exhibit both. The third future, already noticed, has a distinct meaning.

3. The stem portion of the second form of the future in the passive voice is the same as that of the second aorist active: the ending is ησομαι; e.g., ἔτυπον, τυπήσομαι, ήσῃ, ήσεται. Infinitive τυπήσεσθαι. Participle τυπησόμενος.

4. The future middle is in many verbs used simply as the future of the active voice; e.g., ἀκούω, future ἀκούσομαι.

5. The second aorist active has the ending and augment of the imperfect. It is generally characterized by certain changes, in respect of the present, either in the final consonant of the root, or its vowel portion, or both. The penultimate syllable of this tense is mostly short in quantity. This form of the aorist has been supposed to be derived from an older and simpler form of the present. It is conjugated like the imperfect, but has all the moods; e.g., Indicative ἔτυπον, ες, ε. Imperative τύπε, τυπέτω. Subjunctive τύπω, ῃς, ῃ. Optative τύποιμι, οις, οι, Infinitive τυπεῖν. Participle τυπών, όντος

6. The second aorist passive is formed from the active by changing ον into ην and prefixing the augment; e.g., Indicative ἐτύπην, ης, η. Imperative τύπηθι, ήτω. Subjunctive τυπῶ, ῇς, ῇ. Optative τυπείην, είης, είη. Infinitive τυπῆναι. Participle τυπείς, έντος. Very few verbs have both the active and passive second aorist.

7. The second aorist middle is formed from that of the active by changing ον into όμην; e.g., Indicative ἐτυπόμην, ου, ετο. Imperative τυποῦ, έσθω. Subjunctive τύπωμαι, ῃ, ηται. Optative τυποίμην, οιο, οιτο. Infinitive τυπέσθαι. Participle τυπόμενος.

8. Changes in the second aorist. (*a*) Several verbs change π of the present into β; e.g., κρύπτω, *I hide*, 2nd aorist passive ἐκρύβην; βλάπτω, *I hurt*, ἐβλάβην, as if from underived verbs in βω.

(*b*) Others change π into φ; e.g., ῥίπτω, *I cast*, ἐρρίφην; βάπτω, *I dip*, ἐβάφην, as if from underived verbs in φω. So θάπτω, *I bury*, makes aorist passive ἐτάφην.

(*c*) ψύχω, *I cool*, changes χ into γ; e.g., ψύχω, future ψύξω, 2nd aorist passive ἐψύγην, 2nd future ψυγήσομαι.

9. If the ending of the present is preceded by η, it is changed in the 2nd aorist into α short; e.g., λήβω (root form of λαμβάνω, *I take*), ἔλαβον; λήθω, primitive of λανθάνω, *I am hidden*, ἔλαθον. But, πλήσσω, *I strike*, makes ἐπλήγην. If the ending of the present is preceded by the diphthongs ει, ευ, they are shortened by dropping the ι; e.g., λείπω, *I leave*, ἔλιπον; φεύγω, *I flee*, ἔφυγον.

10. Verbs of two syllables, with ε before the ending, preceded (or followed) by ρ or λ, change the ε into α in the 2nd aorist; e.g., τρέπω, *I turn*, ἔτραπον; τρέφω, *I nourish*, ἐτράφην.

11. Contracted verbs have no 2nd aorist or 2nd future. So, generally, other verbs in ω pure. But a few have the 2nd aorist passive; e.g., καίω, *I burn*, ἐκάην; φύω, *I produce*, ἐφύην.

SECTION 25—REMARKS ON THE SECOND OR MIDDLE PERFECT

1. This form is properly a second perfect active and is formed by adding α to the stem (τυπ), and prefixing the reduplication; e.g., τέτυπα. Indicative perfect τέτυπα, ας, ε. Pluperfect ἐτετύπειν, εις, ει. Imperative τέτυπε, τετυπέτω. Subjunctive τετύπω, ῃς, ῃ. Optative τετύποιμι, οις, οι. Infinitive τετυπέναι. Participle τετυπώς, υῖα, ός; τετυπότος, υίας, ότος.

2. Very few verbs in ω pure have the 2nd perfect; contracted verbs never, because they all easily form the 1st perfect in κα.

3. In some verbs the 2nd perfect is alone used; e.g., φεύγω, I flee, πέφευγα.

4. In some verbs with both perfects, the 1st has an active, the 2nd a neuter or intransitive sense; e.g., πείθω, I persuade, 1st perfect πέπεικα, I have persuaded; 2nd perfect πέποιθα, I trust. So ἀνέῳχα τὴν θύραν, I have opened the door; ἀνέῳγεν ἡ θύρα, the door is open; ἐγήγερκα, I have aroused; ἐγρήγορα, I am awake; ὀλώλεκα, I have lost; ὄλωλα, I am ruined, etc.

5. Verbs which have αι in the present change it into η in the 2nd perfect; e.g., φαίνω, I show, πέφηνα. Those of two syllables which have ε in the present change it into ο; e.g., κτείνω, ἔκτονα. Lastly, ει of the present is changed into οι; e.g., λείπω, λέλοιπα; ἀμείβω, I change, ἤμοιβα; πείθω, πέποιθα.

SECTION 26—REMARKS ON VERBS IN ΖΩ AND ΣΣΩ

1. Most of these verbs come from root words in ω pure and therefore form the future in σω and the perfect in κα. They take σ in the future, aorist, and perfect passive; e.g., ὁρίζω, I limit, ὁρίσω, ὥρισα, ὥρικα, ὥρισμαι, 1st aorist ὡρίσθην. The penultimate syllable of their futures in ασω and ισω is always short.

2. Several of them appear to come from stems in γω and form the future in ξω and the perfect in χα; e.g., στίζω, I puncture, στίξω, ἔστιγμαι; κράζω, I cry, κράξω, 2nd perfect κέκραγα. A few form the future both in σω and ξω; e.g., ἁρπάζω, I carry off, ἁρπάσω and ἁρπάξω.

3. The verbs in σσω seem also to come from root words in γω, and form the future in ξω, and the perfect in χα; e.g., πράσσω, I do, πράξω, πέπραχα, πέπραγμαι; τάσσω, I appoint, future τάξω, makes 2nd aorist passive ἐτάγην; σφάττω, I slay, σφάξω, ἐσφάγην; ἁρπάζω, I carry off, 2nd aorist passive ἡρπάγην; ἀλλάττω, I change, ἀλλάξω, 2nd aorist passive ἡλλάγην. A very few come from stems in ω pure and form the future in σω; e.g., πλάσσω, I form, πλάσω, πέπλασμαι.

4. The verbs ending in ζω form the most numerous class in the language next to those in ω pure. The Attic Greeks change the ending σσω into ττω; e.g., πράττω, for πράσσω, ἀλάττω, for ἀλάσσω, etc.

SECTION 27—REMARKS ON VERBS IN ΛΩ, ΜΩ, ΝΩ, ΡΩ

1. Active voice. Future and first aorist. (a) These verbs do not take σ in the future ('Αποτίνω, I repay, makes future ἀποτίσω, but is, in fact, a compound of τίω), which they form in ῶ, and conjugate like the contracted form of φιλέω; e.g., κρίνω, I judge, κρινῶ; νέμω, I distribute, νεμῶ; ἀμύνω, I defend, ἀμυνῶ.

(b) If the present has two consonants, one is dropped in order to shorten the syllable which precedes the ending; e.g., ψάλλω, I play on an instrument, ψαλῶ; κάμνω, I labor, καμῶ; στέλλω, I send, στελῶ; ἀγγέλλω, I announce, ἀγγελῶ.

(c) If the diphthongs αι or ει precede the ending, they are shortened by dropping the ι; e.g., φαίνω, I show, φανῶ; σημαίνω, I signify, σημανῶ; σπείρω, I sow, σπερῶ.

(d) But in the first aorist the ι occurs, even if absent in the present; e.g., νέμω, future νεμῶ, aorist ἔνειμα; ἀγγέλλω, ἀγγελῶ, ἤγγειλα; σπείρω, σπερῶ, ἔσπειρα; στέλλω, στελῶ, ἔστειλα.

(e) The α of the future is changed into η in the aorist, especially in Attic Greek; e.g., ψάλλω, ψαλῶ, ἔψηλα; φαίνω, φανῶ, ἔφηνα; σημαίνω, σημανῶ, ἐσήμηνα. The α, however, is often retained and is long in quantity. It especially occurs when preceded by ρ; e.g., μαραίνω, I wither, μαρανῶ, ἐμάρανα.

(f) The vowel, then, which precedes the ending, is short in the future and long in the 1st aorist.

2. Perfect. (a) This tense in these verbs is formed from the future by changing ῶ into κα; e.g., ψάλλω, ψαλῶ, ἔψαλκα; ἀγγέλλω, ἀγγελῶ, ἤγγελκα. The consonant ν becomes γ before κ; e.g., φαίνω, φανῶ, πέφαγκα; πλατύνω, perfect active πεπλάτυγκα, perfect passive

πεπλάτυμα, 1st aorist passive ἐπλατύνθην.

(*b*) Dissyllables (words with only two syllables) in λω and ρω which have ε in the future, change it into α in the perfect; e.g., στέλλω, στελῶ, ἔσταλκα; σπείρω, σπερῶ, ἔσπαρκα; φθείρω, φθερῶ, ἔφθαρκα.

(*c*) Dissyllables in ίνω and ύνω drop the ν in the perfect tense, which they form as if they came from ίω and ύω; e.g., κρίνω, κρινῶ, κέκρικα; πλύνω, *I wash*, πλυνῶ, πέπλυκα: κλίνω sometimes resumes the ν in the 1st aorist passive ἐκλίνθην, for ἐκλίθην. Those in είνω form the perfect as if they came from άω; e.g., τείνω, *I stretch*, τενῶ, τέτακα, as if from the present τάω.

(*d*) Several verbs in μω and μνω form the perfect in ηκα, as if the future were in ήσω, e.g., νέμω, νεμῶ, νενέμηκα; κάμνω, καμῶ, καμοῦμαι, κέκμηκα (for κεκάμηκα), 2nd aorist ἔκαμον; τέμνω, τέτμηκα (for τετάμηκα); μένω, μενῶ, μεμένηκα; etc. So βάλλω, βαλῶ, βέβληκα (for βεβάληκα), 2nd aorist ἔβαλον.

3. Passive voice. First future, first aorist, and perfect. These tenses are directly derived from the perfect active by changing κα into μαι, θήσομαι, and θην; e.g., perfect active βέβληκα, βέβλημαι, βληθήσομαι, ἐβλήθην; etc.:

μιαίνω, future μιανῶ, makes perfect passive μεμίασμαι 1st aorist passive ἐμιάνθην.

4. Second aorist, active and passive, and second future passive. (*a*) Dissyllables change their vowel into α to form the 2nd aorist; e.g., σπείρω, σπερῶ, 2nd aorist passive ἐσπάρην; φθείρω, φθερῶ, 2nd aorist passive ἐφθάρην. But, ἀγγέλλω, 2nd aorist passive ἠγγέλην.

(*b*) The 2nd aorist is formed in general as in other classes of verbs; e.g., κάμνω; φαίνω, 2nd aorist passive ἐφάνην; χαίρω, 2nd aorist passive ἐχάρην.

(*c*) So in the case of the 2nd future passive; e.g., φαίνω, 2nd future passive φανήσομαι.

5. Second or middle perfect. All dissyllable verbs (of those in λω, μω, νω, ρω) which have ε in the future, takes ο in the 2nd perfect (Section 25, Remark 5); e.g., σπείρω, σπερῶ, ἔσπορα. All those which have αι in the present and α in the future take η in the 2nd perfect; e.g., φαίνω, future φανῶ, 2nd perfect πέφηνα; θάλλω, *I flourish*, τέθηλα.

6. It should be observed that the future middle of these verbs ends in ουμαι; e.g., αἰσχύνομαι, *I am ashamed*, αἰσχυνοῦμαι.

SECTION 28—VERBS IN MI

REMARKS

1. These are formed from roots in έω, άω, όω, ύω, from which they differ as to conjugation in three tenses, the present, imperfect, and second aorist. The remaining tenses are regularly formed.

2. The root forms θέω, *I place*, στάω, *I set up*, δόω, *I give*, and δεικνύω, *I show*, may be taken as examples. To form a verb in μι from θέω, (1) the ω is changed into μι. (2) ε, the short vowel, becomes η; θημι. (3) ι with the reduplication is prefixed; τίθημι.

3. From στάω, (1) α is changed into η; στημι. (2) ι

with the rough breathing is prefixed; ἵστημι. So when the root begins with πτ, ι aspirated is prefixed instead of the reduplication; e.g., πτάω, ἵπταμαι.

4. From δόω, ο being changed into ω, we have δωμι, and, with the reduplication, δίδωμι.

5. From δεικνύω, and all those which end in ύω, the change of the last letter ω into μι is sufficient; δεικνύω, δείκνυμι. In the Tables, the middle voice is given before the passive to show more clearly the relation of the 2nd aorist middle with the 2nd aorist active.

TABLE V—τίθημι, ACTIVE VOICE

	INDICATIVE	IMPERATIVE	SUBJUNCTIVE	OPTATIVE	INFINITIVE	PARTICIPLES
Present	*I place*, etc.					
Sg.	τίθημι		τιθῶ	τιθείην	τιθέναι	M. τιθείς
	τίθης	τίθει	τιθῇς	τιθείης		τιθέντος
	τίθησι(ν)	τιθέτω	τιθῇ	τιθείη		F. τιθεῖσα
Pl.	τίθεμεν		τιθῶμεν	τιθείημεν		τιθείσης
	τίθετε	τίθετε	τιθῆτε	τιθείητε		N. τιθέν
	τιθεῖσι(ν)	τιθέτωσαν	τιθῶσι(ν)	τιθείησαν		τιθέντος
Imperfect						
Sg.	ἐτίθην					
	ἐτίθης					
	ἐτίθη					
Pl.	ἐτίθεμεν					
	ἐτίθετε					
	ἐτίθεσαν					

TABLE V—τίθημι, ACTIVE VOICE (Cont.)

	INDICATIVE	IMPERATIVE	SUBJUNCTIVE	OPTATIVE	INFINITIVE	PARTICIPLE
2nd Aorist						
Sg.	ἔθην		θῶ	θείην	θεῖναι	M. θείς
	ἔθης	θές	θῇς	θείης		θέντος
	ἔθη	θέτω	θῇ	θείη		F. θεῖσα
Pl.	ἔθεμεν		θῶμεν	θείημεν		θείσης
	ἔθετε	θέτε	θῆτε	θείητε		N. θέν
	ἔθεσαν	θέτωσαν	θῶσι(ν)	θείησαν		θέντος
Future	θήσω				θήσειν	M. θήσων, σοντος
1st Aorist	ἔθηκα					
Perfect	τέθεικα	τέθεικε			τεθεικέναι	M. τεθεικώς, κότος
Pluperfect	ἐτεθείκειν					

TABLE W—τίθημι, MIDDLE VOICE

	INDICATIVE	IMPERATIVE	SUBJUNCTIVE	OPTATIVE	INFINITIVE	PARTICIPLES
Present						
Sg.	τίθεμαι		τιθῶμαι	τιθείμην	τίθεσθαι	M. τιθέμενος
	τίθεσαι	τίθεσο	τιθῇ	τιθεῖο		τιθεμένου
	τίθεται	τιθέσθω	τιθῆται	τιθεῖτο		F. τιθεμένη
Pl.	τιθέμεθα		τιθώμεθα	τιθείμεθα		τιθεμένης
	τίθεσθε	τίθεσθε	τιθῆσθε	τιθεῖσθε		N. τιθέμενον
	τίθενται	τιθέσθωσαν	τιθῶνται	τιθεῖντο		τιθεμένου
Imperfect						
Sg.	ἐτιθέμην					
	ἐτίθεσο					
	ἐτίθετο					
Pl.	ἐτιθέμεθα					
	ἐτίθεσθε					
	ἐτίθεντο					
2nd Aorist						
Sg.	ἐθέμην		θῶμαι	θείμην	θέσθαι	M. θέμενος
	ἔθεσο	θέσο	θῇ	θεῖο		θεμένου
	ἔθετο	θέσθω	θῆται	θεῖτο		F. θεμένη
Pl.	ἐθέμεθα		θώμεθα	θείμεθα		θεμένης
	ἔθεσθε	θέσθε	θῆσθε	θεῖσθε		N. θέμενον
	ἔθεντο	θέσθωσαν	θῶνται	θεῖντο		θεμένου
Future	θήσομαι				θήσεσθαι	M. θησόμενος, ου
1st Aorist	ἐθηκάμην					M. θηκάμενος, ου

6. Present and imperfect active. For τιθεῖσι(ν), the Attics wrote τεθεᾶσι(ν). The imperfect ἐτίθην, ης, η, is conjugated like the aorist passive ἐλύθην; but, ἐτίθεμεν, etc., not ἐτίθημεν.

7. The second aorist is formed from the imperfect by dropping the duplication τι; e.g., imperfect ἐτίθην, 2nd aorist ἔθην. It takes the long vowel in the singular, the short in the plural, ἔθην, ης, η; plural ἔθεμεν, etc. The imperative θές is an abbreviation for θέτι.

8. Middle voice. (a) The present middle (or passive) is formed by changing μι into μαι and resuming the short vowel of the root; e.g., τίθημι, τίθεμαι. It is con-

jugated like the perfect passive of λύω, the 2nd and 3rd person singular being in the full, not the contracted form. But ἔθου occurs for ἔθεσο.

(b) The subjunctive is formed from the subjunctive active by adding μαι; e.g., τιθῶ, τιθῶμαι.

(c) The optative is regularly formed from the indicative by changing μαι into ίμην; e.g., τίθεμαι, τιθείμην.

(d) The second aorist is formed, like that of the active voice, from the imperfect by dropping τι; e.g., ἐ-τιθέμην, ἐθέμην. In the imperative the contracted from θοῦ for θέσο is found in παράθου; 2 Tim. 2:2.

9. (a) The future is formed from the root θέω; e.g., future active θήσω; middle θήσομαι.

(b) The first aorist ends, not in σα, but in κα; ἔθηκα, κας, κε, etc. It is scarcely used, either in the active or middle except in certain persons of the indicative.

(c) There are two other aorists in κα; e.g., ἔδωκα from δίδωμι, and ἦκα from ἵημι.

(d) The perfect has the diphthong ει, as if from θείω; e.g., τέθεικα, pluperfect ἐτεθείκειν.

10. Passive voice. The following are the tenses in use: the present and imperfect are like those of the middle.

	INDICATIVE	IMPERATIVE	SUBJUNCTIVE	OPTATIVE	INFINITIVE	PARTICIPLES
1st Future	τεθήσομαι				τεθήσεσθαι	τεθησόμενος
1st Aorist	ἐτέθην	τέθητι	τεθῶ	τεθείην	τεθῆναι	τεθείς
Perfect	τέθειμαι	τέθεισο	τεθειμένος ὦ		τεθεῖσθαι	τεθειμένος
Pluperfect	ἐτεθείμην					

SECTION 29—VERBS IN MI

TABLE X—ἵστημι, ACTIVE VOICE

	INDICATIVE	IMPERATIVE	SUBJUNCTIVE	OPTATIVE	INFINITIVE	PARTICIPLES
Present	*I set*, etc.					
Sg.	ἵστημι		ἱστῶ	ἱσταίην	ἱστάναι	M. ἱστάς
	ἵστης	ἵσταθι	ἱστῇς	ἱσταίης		ἱστάντος
	ἵστησι(ν)	ἱστάτω	ἱστῇ	ἱσταίη		F. ἱστᾶσα
Pl.	ἵσταμεν		ἱστῶμεν	ἱσταίημεν		ἱστάσης
	ἵστατε	ἵστατε	ἱστῆτε	ἱστείητε		N. ἱστάν
	ἱστᾶσι(ν)	ἱστάτωσαν	ἱστῶσι(ν)	ἱσταίησαν		ἱστάντος
Imperfect						
Sg.	ἵστην					
	ἵστης					
	ἵστη					
Pl.	ἵσταμεν					
	ἵστατε					
	ἵστασαν					
2nd Aorist						
Sg.	ἔστην ·		στῶ	σταίην	στῆναι	M. στάς
	ἔστης	στῆθι	στῇς	σταίης		στάντος
	ἔστη	στήτω	στῇ	σταίη		F. στᾶσα
Pl.	ἔστημεν		στῶμεν	σταίημεν		στάσης
	ἔστητε	στῆτε	στῆτε	σταίητε		N. στάν
	ἔστησαν	στήτωσαν	στῶσι(ν)	σταίησαν		στάντος
Future	στήσω				στήσειν	στήσων, σοντος
1st Aorist	ἔστησα	στῆσον	στήσω	στήσαιμι	στῆσαι	στήσας, σαντος
Perfect	ἔστηκα	ἔστηκε			ἑστηκέναι	ἑστηκώς, κότος
Pluperfect	ἑστήκειν					

TABLE Y—ἵστημι, MIDDLE VOICE

	INDICATIVE	IMPERATIVE	SUBJUNCTIVE	OPTATIVE	INFINITIVE	PARTICIPLES
Present						
Sg.	ἵσταμαι		ἱστῶμαι	ἱσταίμην	ἵστασθαι	M. ἱστάμενος
	ἵστασαι	ἵστασο	ἱστῇ	ἱσταῖο		ἱσταμένου
	ἵσταται	ἱστάσθω	ἱστῆται	ἱσταῖτο		F. ἱσταμένη
Pl.	ἱστάμεθα		ἱστώμεθα	ἱσταίμεθα		ἱσταμένης
	ἵστασθε	ἵστασθε	ἱστῆσθε	ἱσταῖσθε		N. ἱστάμενον
	ἵστανται	ἱστάσθωσαν	ἱστῶνται	ἱσταῖντο		ἱσταμένου
Imperfect						
Sg.	ἱστάμην					
	ἵστασο					
	ἵστατο					
Pl.	ἱστάμεθα					
	ἵστασθε					
	ἵσταντο					
2nd Aorist						
Sg.	ἐστάμην		στῶμαι	σταίμην	στάσθαι	M. στάμενος
	ἔστασο	στάσο	στῇ	σταῖο		σταμένου
	ἔστατο	στάσθω	στῆται	σταῖτο		F. σταμένη
Pl.	ἐστάμεθα		στώμεθα	σταίμεθα		σταμένης
	ἔστασθε	στάσθε	στῆσθε	σταῖσθε		N. στάμενον
	ἔσταντο	στάσθωσαν	στῶνται	σταῖντο		σταμένου
Future	στήσομαι				στήσεσθαι	στησόμενος, ου
1st Aorist	ἐστησάμην	στῆσαι	στήσωμαι	στησαίμην	στήσασθαι	στησάμενος, ου

REMARKS

1. The 2nd aorist is formed by dropping ι of the present and prefixing the augment, ἔστην. This tense keeps the long vowel η in the plural, as is the case with all verbs in μι which come from roots in ἀω.

2. The imperative takes θι in the 2nd person, because the root does not have an aspirated consonant, as is the case in τίθετι. It takes the short vowel in the present, ἵσταθι; the long in the 2nd aorist, στῆθι: ἀνάστα occurs for ἀνάστηθι.

3. The subjunctive present and 2nd aorist takes η, as in those of τίθημι; e.g., ἱστῶ, ῇς, ῇ; στῶ, στῇς, στῇ: so in the middle; ἱστῶμαι, ῇ, ῆται. But also sometimes α; ἱστῶ, ᾷς, ᾷ, ἱστῶμαι, ᾷ, ᾶται; but these are formed from ἱστάω, not ἵστημι.

4. The perfect ἔστηκα is regularly formed from the future στήσω. Its augment ε has the rough breathing. This perfect has the sense of the Latin *stare, to stand*, and signifies *I am placed*, or, *I stand*, in a present sense. So the pluperfect ἑστήκειν (also εἱστήκειν), *I was standing, I stood*.

5. The present ἵστημι, imperfect ἵστην, future στήσω, 1st aorist ἔστησα, participle ἱστάς, all have an active or transitive force; the perfect ἔστηκα, pluperfect ἑστήκειν, 2nd aorist ἔστην, 2nd aorist participle στάς, a neuter or intransitive sense.

6. Passive voice. The present and imperfect are like those of the middle.

	INDICATIVE	IMPERATIVE	SUBJUNCTIVE	OPTATIVE	INFINITIVE	PARTICIPLES
1st Future	σταθήσομαι				σταθήσεσθαι	σταθησόμενος
1st Aorist	ἐστάθην	στάθητι	σταθῶ	σταθείην	σταθῆναι	σταθείς
Perfect	ἔσταμαι	ἔστασο	ἐσταμένος ὦ		ἑστάσθαι	ἐσταμένος
Pluperfect	ἐστάμην					

SECTION 30—VERBS IN MI

TABLE Z—δίδωμι, ACTIVE VOICE

	INDICATIVE	IMPERATIVE	SUBJUNCTIVE	OPTATIVE	INFINITIVE	PARTICIPLES
Present	*I give*, etc.					
Sg.	δίδωμι		διδῶ	διδοίην	διδόναι	M. διδούς
	δίδως	δίδοθι	διδῷς	διδοίης		διδόντος
	δίδωσι(ν)	διδότω	διδῷ	διδοίη		F. διδοῦσα
Pl.	δίδομεν		διδῶμεν	διδοίημεν		διδούσης
	δίδοτε	δίδοτε	διδῶτε	διδοίητε		N. διδόν
	διδοῦσι(ν)	διδότωσαν	διδῶσι(ν)	διδοίησαν		διδόντος
Imperfect						
Sg.	ἐδίδων					
	ἐδίδως					
	ἐδίδω					
Pl.	ἐδίδομεν					
	ἐδίδοτε					
	ἐδίδοσαν					
2nd Aorist						
Sg.	ἔδων		δῶ	δοίην	δοῦναι	M. δούς
	ἔδως	δός	δῷς	δοίης		δόντος
	ἔδω	δότω	δῷ	δοίη		F. δοῦσα
Pl.	ἔδομεν		δῶμεν	δοίημεν		δούσης
	ἔδοτε	δότε	δῶτε	δοίητε		N. δόν
	ἔδοσαν	δότωσαν	δῶσι(ν)	δοίησαν		δόντος
Future	δώσω				δώσειν	δώσων, σοντος
1st Aorist	ἔδωκα					
Perfect	δέδωκα	δέδωκε			δεδωκέναι	δεδωκώς, κότος
Pluperfect	ἐδεδώκειν					

TABLE AA—δίδωμι, MIDDLE VOICE

	INDICATIVE	IMPERATIVE	SUBJUNCTIVE	OPTATIVE	INFINITIVE	PARTICIPLES
Present						
Sg.	δίδομαι		διδῶμαι	διδοίμην	δίδοσθαι	M. διδόμενος
	δίδοσαι	δίδοσο	διδῷ	διδοῖο		διδομένου
	δίδοται	διδόσθω	διδῶται	διδοῖτο		F. διδομένη
Pl.	διδόμεθα		διδώμεθα	διδοίμεθα		διδομένης
	δίδοσθε	δίδοσθε	διδῶσθε	διδοῖσθε		N. διδόμενον
	δίδονται	διδόσθωσαν	διδῶνται	διδοῖντο		διδομένου
Imperfect						
Sg.	ἐδιδόμην					
	ἐδίδοσο					
	ἐδίδοτο					
Pl.	ἐδιδόμεθα					
	ἐδίδοσθε					
	ἐδίδοντο					

TABLE AA—δίδωμι, MIDDLE VOICE (Cont.)

	INDICATIVE	IMPERATIVE	SUBJUNCTIVE	OPTATIVE	INFINITIVE	PARTICIPLE
2nd Aorist						
Sg.	ἐδόμην		δῶμαι	δοίμην	δόσθαι	M. δόμενος
	ἔδοσο	δόσο	δῷ	δοῖο		δομένου
	ἔδοτο	δόσθω	δῶται	δοῖτο		F. δομένη
Pl.	ἐδόμεθα		δώμεθα	δοίμεθα		δομένης
	ἔδοσθε	δόσθε	δῶσθε	δοῖσθε		N. δόμενον
	ἔδοντο	δόσθωσαν	δῶνται	δοῖντο		δομένου
Future	δώσομαι				δώσεσθαι	δωσόμενος, ου
1st Aorist	ἐδωκάμην					

REMARKS

1. δίδωμι takes (like τίθημι) σ in the 2nd aorist imperative; δός for δόθι, like θές for θέτι. It has a diphthong in the infinitive of the same tense, δοῦναι; and in the two participles, διδούς and δούς, like τιθείς and θείς.

2. The present and 2nd aorist subjunctive, active and middle, retain ω in all the persons: ι is iota subscript in those persons in which verbs in όω have the diphthong οι; e.g., δηλῶ, οἷς, οἷ; διδῶ, ῷς, ῷ.

3. For διδοῦσι, 3rd person plural present, the Attic Greeks write διδόασι, like τιθέασι.

4. Passive voice. The present and imperfect are like those of the middle.

	INDICATIVE	IMPERATIVE	SUBJUNCTIVE	OPTATIVE	INFINITIVE	PARTICIPLES
1st Future	δοθήσομαι				δοθήσεσθαι	δοθησόμενος
1st Aorist	ἐδόθην	δόθητι	δοθῶ	δοθείην	δοθῆναι	δοθείς
Perfect	δίδομαι	δέδοσο	δεδομένος ὦ		δεδόσθαι	δεδομένος
Pluperfect	ἐδεδόμην					

5. For δῶ, δῷς, δῷ, the forms δώω, δώῃς, δώῃ also occur in the Ionic dialect.

SECTION 31—VERBS IN MI

TABLE BB—δείκνυμι, ACTIVE VOICE

	INDICATIVE	IMPERATIVE	INFINITIVE	PARTICIPLES
Present	*I show*, etc.			
Sg.	δείκνυμι		δεικνύναι	M. δεικνύς
	δείκνυς	δείκνυθι		δεικνύντος
	δείκνυσι(ν)	δεικνύτω		F. δεικνῦσα
Pl.	δείκνυμεν			δεικνύσης
	δείκνυτε	δείκνυτε		N. δεικνύν
	δεικνύασι(ν)	δεικνύτωσαν		δεικνύντος
Imperfect				
Sg.	ἐδείκνυν			
	ἐδείκνυς			
	ἐδείκνυ			
Pl.	ἐδείκνυμεν			
	ἐδείκνυτε			
	ἐδείκνυσαν			

TABLE BB—δείκνυμι (Cont.)

PASSIVE AND MIDDLE VOICES

		INDICATIVE	IMPERATIVE	INFINITIVE	PARTICIPLES	
Present						
	Sg.	δείκνυμαι		δείκνυσθαι	M.	δεικνύμενος
		δείκνυσαι	δείκνυσο			δεικνυμένου
		δείκνυται	δεικνύσθω		F.	δεικνυμένη
	Pl.	δεικνύμεθα				δεικνυμένης
		δείκνυσθε	δείκνυσθε		N.	δεικνυμένον
		δείκνυνται	δεικνύσθων			δεικνυμένου
Imperfect						
	Sg.	ἐδεικνύμην				
		ἐδείκνυσο				
		ἐδείκνυτο				
	Pl.	ἐδεικνύμεθα				
		ἐδείκνυσθε				
		ἐδείκνυντο				

REMARKS

1. (*a*) The subjunctive and optative are formed from the verb in ύω; e.g., δεικνύω, ῃς, ῃ; δεικνύοιμι, οις, οι.

(*b*) The future, 1st aorist, perfect, and pluperfect come regularly from the root δείκω; e.g., δείξω, δέδειχα, δέδειγμαι, ἐδείχθην, etc.

(*c*) Verbs in υμι of more than two syllables are without the 2nd aorist. But those of two syllables are generally only used in the 2nd aorist; e.g., ἔφυν, from φύω, *I produce*; ἔδυν, from δύνω, δύω, *I enter*.

(*d*) Several others are limited in their use to the 2nd aorist; e.g., τλάω, τλῆμι, *I bear*, ἔτλην; γνόω, γνῶμι, *I know*, ἔγνων; βάω, βῆμι, *I walk*, ἔβην. These keep the long vowel in the plural: ἔβημεν, ἔγνωμεν. They take θε in the imperative; βῆθι, γνώθι. But κατάβα

occurs for κατάθηθι, and ἀνάβα for ἀνάβηθι.

2. The imperfect of verbs in μι, especially in the singular, is often conjugated like contracted verbs; e.g., ἐτίθεον, ουν; ἵσταον, ων; ἐδίδοον, ουν. So in the imperative, τίθεε, τίθει; ἵστα ε, ἵστη (for ἵστα); δίδοε, δίδου. In those in υμι, θι is sometimes dropped; δείκνυ for δείκνυθι.

3. In Attic Greek, the present and 2nd aorist middle optative are sometimes formed in οίμην, οιο, οιτο; e.g., τίθοιτο, as if from τίθομαι. The optative present and 2nd aorist are sometimes contracted in the plural number; e.g., τιθεῖμεν, τιθεῖτε, τιθεῖεν; ἰσταῖμεν, ἰσταῖτε, ἰσταῖεν; διδοῖμεν, διδοῖτε, διδοῖεν; so θεῖμεν, θεῖτε, θεῖεν, etc.

SECTION 32—VERBS IN MI

TABLE CC—ἵημι, ACTIVE VOICE

		INDICATIVE	IMPERATIVE	SUBJUNCTIVE	OPTATIVE	INFINITIVE	PARTICIPLES	
Present		*I send, etc.*						
	Sg.	ἵημι		ἰῶ	ἰείην	ἰέναι	M.	ἰείς
		ἵης	ἵεθι	ἰῇς	ἰείης			ἰέντος
		ἵησι(ν)	ἰέτω	ἰῇ	ἰείη		F.	ἰεῖσα
	Pl.	ἵεμεν		ἰῶμεν	ἰείημεν			ἰείσης
		ἵετε	ἵετε	ἰῆτε	ἰείητε		N.	ἰέν
		ἰεῖσι(ν)	ἰέτωσαν	ἰῶσι(ν)	ἰείησαν			ἰέντος

TABLE CC—ἵημι, ACTIVE VOICE (Cont.)

	INDICATIVE	IMPERATIVE	SUBJUNCTIVE	OPTATIVE	INFINITIVE	PARTICIPLE
Imperfect						
Sg.	ἵην					
	ἵης					
	ἵη					
Pl.	ἵεμεν					
	ἵετε					
	ἵεσαν					
2nd Aorist						
Sg.	ἦν		ὧ	εἵην	εἶναι	M. εἵς
	ἧς	ἕς	ᾖς	εἵης		ἕντος
	ἦ	ἕτω	ᾖ	εἵη		F. εἷσα
Pl.	ἕμεν		ὧμεν	εἵημεν		εἵσης
	ἕτε	ἕτε	ἦτε	εἵητε		N. ἕν
	ἕσαν	ἕτωσαν	ὧσι(ν)	εἵησαν		ἕντος
Future	ἥσω				ἥσειν	ἥσων, ἥσοντος
	ἥσεις					
	ἥσει					
Aorist	ἧκα					
	ἧκας					
	ἧκε(ν)					
Perfect	εἷκα				εἱκέναι	εἱκώς, εἱκότος
	εἷκας					
	εἷκε					
Pluperfect	εἵκειν					
	εἵκεις					
	εἵκει					

MIDDLE VOICE

	INDICATIVE	IMPERATIVE	SUBJUNCTIVE	OPTATIVE	INFINITIVE	PARTICIPLE
Present	ἵεμαι		ἱῶμαι	ἱείμην	ἵεσθαι	ἱέμενος, ου
	ἵεσαι	ἵεσο	ἱῇ	ἱεῖο		
	ἵεται	ἱέσθω	ἱῆται	ἱεῖτο		
Imperfect	ἱέμην					
	ἵεσο					
	ἵετο					
2nd Aorist	ἕμην		ὧμαι	εἵμην	ἕσθαι	ἕμενος, ου
	ἕσο	ἕσο	ᾖ	εἷο		
	ἕτο	ἕσθω	ἦται	εἷτο		
Future	ἥσομαι				ἥσεσθαι	ἡσόμενος, ου
	ἥσῃ					
	ἥσεται					
1st Aorist	ἡκάμην					

TABLE CC—ἵημι (Cont.)

PASSIVE VOICE

	INDICATIVE	IMPERATIVE	SUBJUNCTIVE	OPTATIVE	INFINITIVE	PARTICIPLE
1st Future	ἐθήσομαι				ἐθήσεσθαι	ἐθησόμενος, ου
1st Aorist	ἔθην or εἵθην	ἔθητι ἐθήτω	ἐθῶ ἐθῇς ἐθῇ	ἐθείην	ἐθῆναι	ἐθείς, ἐθέντος
Perfect	εἷμαι εἷσαι εἷται	εἷσο εἷσθω	εἱμένος ὦ		εἷσθαι	εἱμένος, ου
Pluperfect	εἵμην εἷσο εἷτο					

REMARKS

1. The simple form of this verb is rarely encountered. The compound ἀνίημι occurs frequently in the New Testament, as does ἀφίημι.

2. The following are the principal forms of ἀφίημι, which present some irregularity: ἀφεῖς, 2nd perfect singular present (as if from ἀφέω); ἤφιον, ες, ε, imperfect (as if from ἀφίω); ἀφέωνται, for ἀφεῖνται, 3rd person plural perfect passive.

SECTION 33—VERBS IN MI

TABLE DD—φημι, ἵσημι, κεῖμαι

	INDICATIVE	IMPERATIVE	SUBJUNCTIVE	OPTATIVE	INFINITIVE	PARTICIPLES
Present	*I say*, etc.					
Sg.	φημί		φῶ	φαίην	φάναι	M. φάς
	φής	φαθί	φῇς	φαίης		F. φᾶσα
	φησί(ν)	φάτω	φῇ	φαίη		N. φάν
Pl.	φαμέν					
	φατέ					
	φασί(ν)					
Imperfect						
Sg.	ἔφην					
	ἔφης					
	ἔφη					
Pl.	ἔφαμεν					
	ἔφατε					
	ἔφασαν					
Future	φήσω					

TABLE DD—φημι, ἴσημι, κεῖμαι (Cont.)

	INDICATIVE	IMPERATIVE	SUBJUNCTIVE	OPTATIVE	INFINITIVE	PARTICIPLE
Aorist	ἔφησα		φήσω	φήσαιμι	φῆσαι	φήσας
Present	*I know*, etc.				ἰσάναι	M. ἴσας
Sg.	ἴσημι					F. ἴσασα
	ἴσης	ἴσθι				N. ἴσαν
	ἴσησι(ν)	ἴστω				
Pl.	ἴσμεν					
	ἴστε	ἴστε				
	ἴσατε	ἴστωσαν				
Imperfect						
Sg.	ἴσην					
	ἴσης					
	ἴση					
Pl.	ἴσαμεν					
	ἴσατε					
	ἴσασαν					
Present	*I lie* (on the ground), etc.				κεῖσθαι	M. κείμενος
Sg.	κεῖμαι					F. κειμένη
	κεῖσαι	κεῖσο				N. κείμενον
	κεῖται	κείσθω, etc.				
Pl.	κείμεθα					
	κεῖσθε					
	κεῖνται					
Imperfect						
Sg.	ἐκείμην					
	ἔκεισο					
	ἔκειτο					
Pl.	ἐκείμεθα					
	ἔκεισθε					
	ἔκειντο					

REMARKS

1. Of φημί, the 1st person singular (φημί), 3rd person singular (φησί[v]), 3rd person plural (φασί[v]), of the present indicative, and the 3rd person singular of the imperfect (ἔφη), are the only forms which occur in the New Testament.

2. The verb ἴσημι is seldom used (ἴσασι and ἴστε are found in the New Testament); it is perhaps connected with the obsolete εἴδω, future εἴσω, the forms of which will be hereafter noticed.

3. Ἐπίσταμαι, *I know*, of doubtful derivation, is conjugated like the middle voice of ἴστημι.

4. Of εἴμι, *I go* (primitive ἴω), a few tenses may be mentioned. Present singular εἴμι, εἴς or εἴ; plural ἴμεν, ἴτε, ἴασι. Past tense, singular ἤειν, ἤεις, ἤει; plural ἤειμεν, ἤειτε, ἤεισαν and ἤεσαν. Infinitive ἰέναι. Participle ἰών, ἰοῦσα, ἰόν, ἰόντος, ἰούσης, ἰόντος, etc. The following (compounded) forms occur in the New Testament: ἀπήεσαν, εἰσίασιν, εἰσήει, εἰσιέναι. ἐξήεσαν, ἐξιέναι, ἐξιόντων. ἐπιούσῃ, present participle dative singular feminine of ἐπιέναι. συνιόντος, genitive singular participle present of σύνειμι, Luke 8:4.

SECTION 34—REMARKS ON THE AUGMENT OF COMPOUNDED VERBS

1. Verbs compounded with a preposition. (*a*) If the preposition changes the meaning of the verb, the augment and reduplication are placed after the preposition; e.g., προστάττω, I *enjoin*, προσέταττον; εἰσάγω, I *introduce*, εἰσῆγον.

(*b*) If the preposition ends with a vowel, this is elided; e.g., διασπείρω, I *disperse*, διέσπειρον. But περί retains its ι; e.g., περιάγειν, περιέθηκε: and πρό (generally) its ο; e.g., προάγειν. The ο of πρό is often combined with the initial ε of a verb; e.g., προὔβην for προέβην; προὔβαλον for προέβαλον.

(*c*) If ἐν and σύν have lost or changed their ν because of the consonant following them, this ν reappears before the augment; e.g., ἐμβλέπω, I *look upon*, ἐνέβλεπον; συλλέγω, I *collect*, συνέλεγον; συζητῶ, συνεζήτουν, etc.

(*d*) Some verbs take the augment both before and after the preposition; e.g., ἀνορθόω, I *correct*, ἠνώρθουν; ἀνέχομαι, I *sustain*, ἠνειχόμην.

2. If the preposition does not change the meaning of the verb, the augment usually comes before it; e.g., (ἵζω) καθίζω, I *sit down*, ἐκάθιζον (εὕδω) καθεύδω, I *sleep*, ἐκάθευδον. But some take the augment after: e.g., προφητεύω, προεφήτευον; παρανομέω, παρηνόμησα.

3. Verbs compounded, but not with a preposition.

(*a*) Those compounded with the privative particle α take the temporal augment η; e.g., ἀδικέω, I *act unjustly*, ἠδίκουν, etc.

(*b*) Those compounded with εὖ, if the verb begins with a vowel capable of augment, take η after εὖ; e.g., εὐεργετέω, I *benefit*, εὐηργέτουν.

(*c*) If the verb begins with a consonant or a long vowel, εὖ remains invariable, or else is changed into ηὖ, according to the Attic dialect; e.g., εὐδοκέω, ηὐδόκησα (also εὐδόκησα); εὐλογέω, ηὐλόγουν, ηὐλόγησα (also εὐλόγησα).

SECTION 35—REMARKS ON TENSES MORE OR LESS IRREGULAR

1. Verbs in έω uncontracted. Dissyllables in έω are not usually contracted in the 1st person singular or the 1st and 3rd person plural of the present; e.g., πλέω, I *sail*, πλέομεν, πλέουσι(ν); imperfect ἔπλεον. Nor are they contracted in the subjunctive and optative. The contracted form πνεῖ, however, occurs, John 3:8.

2. In some verbs in άω, αε is contracted into η, instead of into α; e.g., ζάω, I *live*, ζῇς, ζῇ, infinitive ζῆν; πεινάω, I *am hungry*, πεινῇς, ῇ, infinitive πεινῆν. So διψάω, I *thirst*; and χράομαι, I *use*, χρῇ, χρῆται, infinitive χρῆσθαι.

3. Futures in εύσω and αύσω, from verbs in έω and άω. A very few, as ῥέω, I *flow*, πλέω, I *sail*, πνέω, I *blow*, form the future in εύσω; e.g., ῥεύσω, πλεύσω (πλεύσομαι), πνεύσω. Two in αίω, κλαίω, I *weep*, and καίω, I *burn*, form it in αύσω; e.g., κλαύσω, καύσω. So perfect passive κέκαυμαι, aorist passive ἐκαύθην.

4. Aspirated futures. Four verbs, ἔχω, τρέχω, τύφω, and τρέφω, take as the first letter of the future the aspirate which is in the second syllable of the present; e.g., ἕξω, θρέξομαι, θύψω, θρέψω.

5. Some verbs, though their ending is not preceded by a vowel, form the future in ήσω; e.g., θέλω, θελήσω; μέλλω, μελλήσω; αὐξάνω (αὔξω), αὐξήσω; βούλομαι, βουλήσομαι (aorist ἐβουλήθην). So μάχομαι, μαχέσομαι.

6. Three futures, though uncontracted, omit σ; e.g., πίομαι, I *shall drink*, from πίνω; ἔδομαι, φάγομαι, I *shall eat*, which serve as futures to ἐσθίω.

7. In the verb πίπτω, I *fall* (root πέτω), σ occurs in the 2nd aorist, ἔπεσον.

Besides ἔθηκα, ἦκα, and ἔδωκα, already cited, one or two others may be mentioned as lacking σ in the 1st aorist; e.g., ἤνεγκα (root ἐνέγκω), used as 1st aorist of φέρω; εἶπα, and 2nd aorist εἶπον (root ἔπω), which verb keeps the ι throughout the moods.

8. Perfect actives without κ. One of two may be here given; e.g., τεθνηκέναι, *to have died*, by contraction, τεθνάναι, participle τεθνεώς for τεθνηκώς. From ἵστημι, ἕστηκα, plural ἑστήκαμεν, contract ἕσταμεν, ἕστατε, ἑστᾶσι; pluperfect plural ἕσταμεν, ἕστατε, ἕστασαν; imperative ἕσταθι, ἑστάτω, etc.; subjunctive ἑστῶ; optative ἑσταίην; infinitive ἑστάναι; participle ἑστώς, ἑστῶσα, ἑστός, genitive ἑστῶτος, ἑστώσης, ἑστῶτος, etc.

9. Perfect passive. τρέφω, στρέφω, and τρέπω take α in this tense; τέθραμμαι, ἔστραμμαι, τέτραμμαι. In the 1st aorist passive ε reappears; e.g., ἐθρέφθην, ἐστρέφθην.

10. Verbal adjectives in τέος may be noted here. They are used to signify *necessity*; e.g., λυτέος, *that ought to be, or must be, loosed*, and are formed from the participle of the 1st aorist passive by changing the ending θείς into τέος. One instance, at least, occurs in the New Testament, βλητέος from βληθείς, of βάλλω, I *cast*.

11. In Attic Greek, the ending of the 2nd person singular passive or middle is usually ει, instead of η: always in these three verbs; βούλομαι, *I will*, βούλει; οἴομαι, *I think*, οἴει; ὄψομαι, *I shall see*, ὄψει. Futures in ουμαι are also inflected by ει; e.g., ἀπολοῦμαι, *I shall perish*, ἀπολεῖ, ἀπολεῖται. So also, after the contraction of the active future (very frequent in verbs in ζω); e.g., from κομίζω, future κομίσω, Attic κομιῶ, future middle κομιοῦμαι, κομιεῖ, κομιεῖται.

12. Occasionally such aorist forms as ἐξῆλθα, ἔπεσα, ἀνεῦρα, etc. are found where the 2nd aorist would be more usual.

13. The ending ασι(ν) of the perfect active is sometimes shortened into αν; e.g., πέπτωκαν for πεπτώκασι(ν), from πίπτω (variant reading). So γέγοναν for γεγόνασι(ν), etc. On the other hand (chiefly in the Alexandrian dialect), the ending ον is lengthened into οσαν; e.g., ἤλθοσαν for ἦλθον (variant reading). So ἐδολιοῦσαν for ἐδολίουν, imperfect of δολιόω.

SECTION 36 — REMARKS ON DEFECTIVE AND IRREGULAR VERBS

(A notice of those which occur in the New Testament may be found useful, though *not all* the forms given appear in the sacred text.)

1. Those which borrow some tenses from verbs of similar meaning, but different root:

αἱρέω, *I take*, future αἱρήσω, perfect ᾕρηκα, perfect passive ᾕρημαι, aorist ᾑρέθην, future passive αἱρεθήσομαι; (from ἕλω) 2nd aorist εἷλον, 2nd aorist middle εἱλόμην.

εἰπεῖν, *to speak*, has only 2nd aorist and some persons of 1st aorist εἶπα. Its other tenses are 1st (from λέγω); 2nd (from εἴρω), future ἐρῶ; 3rd (from ῥέω), perfect εἴρηκα, perfect passive εἴρημαι, aorist ἐρρέθην, or ἐρρήθην.

ἔρχομαι, *I come*, imperfect ἠρχόμην (from ἐλεύθω) future ἐλεύσομαι, 2nd aorist ἤλυθον, ἦλθον, 2nd perfect ἐλήλυθα, pluperfect ἐληλύθειν.

ἐσθίω, *I eat*, perfect ἐδήδοκα, perfect passive ἐδήδομαι and ἐδήδεσμαι (from φάγω) 2nd aorist ἔφαγον, future φάγομαι.

τρώγω, *I eat*, forms 2nd aorist ἔτραγον.

ὁράω, *I see*, imperfect ἑώρων, perfect ἑώρακα, perfect passive ἑώραμαι, aorist passive infinitive ὁρασθῆναι; (from εἴδω), 2nd aorist εἶδον, ἰδέ, ἴδω, ἴδοιμι, ἰδεῖν; middle εἰδόμην, etc. (from ὄπτω, ὄτομαι), future ὄψομαι, aorist ὤφθην, perfect ὦμαι.

τρέχω, *I run*, future θρέξομαι, aorist ἔθρεξα, etc. (from δρέμω, δράμα), future δραμοῦμαι, 2nd aorist ἔδραμον, perfect δεδράμηκα, 2nd perfect δέδρομα.

ῥέω, *I flow*, 2nd aorist ἐρρύην, hence παραρρυῶμεν, Heb. 2:1, from παραρρέω.

χέω, *I pour*, future χεύσω and χέω, 1st aorist ἔχευσα, ἔχευα and ἔχεα, infinitive χέαι.

φέρω, *I bear*, *carry*, imperfect ἔφερον (from οἴω), future οἴσω, future passive οἰσθήσομαι; (from ἐνέγκω) aorist ἤνεγκα and ἤνεγκον, perfect ἐνήνοχα, perfect passive ἐνήνεγμαι, aorist ἠνέχθην, future ἐνεχθήσομαι.

2. Endings νω, άνω.

αἰσθάνομαι, *I perceive*, 2nd aorist ᾐσθόμην, future αἰσθήσομαι, perfect ᾔσθημαι.

ἁμαρτάνω, *I err*, *sin*, 2nd aorist ἥμαρτον, infinitive ἁμαρτεῖν, future ἁμαρτήσω.

βλαστάνω, *I bud* (root βλάστω), 2nd aorist ἔβλαστον, infinitive βλαστεῖν, future βλαστήσω.

δάκνω, *I bite* (root δήκω), 2nd aorist ἔδακον, future δήξομαι, perfect passive δέδηγμαι.

θιγγάνω (θίγω), *I touch*, 2nd aorist ἔθιγον, future θίξω and θίξομαι.

ἱκάνω, ἱκνέομαι, *I come* (root ἴκω), 2nd aorist ἱκόμην, perfect ἶγμαι, with ἀπό, ἀφῖγμαι.

λαγχάνω, *I set by lot* (root λήχω), 2nd aorist ἔλαχον, future λήξομαι, perfect εἴληχα, 2nd perfect λέλογχα.

λαμβάνω, *I take* (root λήβω), 2nd aorist ἔλαβον, future λή(μ)ψομαι, perfect εἴληφα, perfect passive εἴλημμαι.

λανθάνω, *I am hidden* (root λήθω), future λήσω, 2nd aorist ἔλαθον, 2nd perfect λέληθα. λανθάνομαι, *I forget*, 2nd aorist ἐλαθόμην, perfect λέλησμαι.

μανθάνω, *I learn* (root μήθω or μάθω), 2nd aorist ἔμαθον, infinitive μαθεῖν, future μαθήσω, perfect μεμάθηκα.

ἐλαύνω, *I drive*, future ἐλάσω, 1st aorist ἤλασα, perfect ἐλήλακα, etc.

πυνθάνομαι, *I inquire* (root πεύθομαι), 2nd aorist ἐπυθόμην, future πεύσομαι, perfect πέπυσμαι.

τυγχάνω, *I obtain* (root τεύχω), future τεύξομαι, perfect τετύχηκα, 2nd aorist ἔτυχον.

3. Ending σκω, from ω pure.

ἀρέσκω, *I please* (root ἀρέω), future ἀρέσκω, 1st aorist ἤρεσα, 1st aorist passive ἠρέσθην.

βιβρώσκω, *I eat* (root βρόω), future βρώσω, βρώσομαι, perfect βέβρωκα, 2nd aorist ἔβρων.

μεθύσκω, *I inebriate* (μεθύω), future μεθύσω, etc.

γηράσκω, *I grow old* (root γηράω), future γηράσομαι, aorist infinitive γηράναι or γηρᾶναι, participle γήρας, γήραντος.

γινώσκω, *I know* (root γνόω), future γνώσομαι, perfect ἔγνωκα, perfect passive ἔγνωσμαι, 2nd aorist active ἔγνων, γνῶθι, γνῶ, γνοίην, γνῶναι, participle γνούς, γνόντος; hence ἀναγινώσκω, *I read*, 1st aorist ἀνέγνωσα.

μιμνήσκω, *I call to mind* (root γνάω), perfect μέμνημαι,

1

I remember, aorist ἐμνήσθην.

πιπράσκω, *I sell* (root περάω), future περάσω, perfect πέπρακα (for πεπέρακα), perfect passive πέπραμαι, aorist ἐπράθην, 3rd future πεπράσομαι.

ἀναλίσκω, *I consume* (root ἀλόω, ἄλωμι), future ἀναλώσω, perfect ἀνήλωκα, 1st aorist passive ἀνηλώθην, etc.

4. Endings σκω and σχω, from ω impure (not preceded by a vowel).

εὑρίσκω, *I find* (root εὕρω), 2nd aorist εὗρον, infinitive εὑρεῖν, future εὑρήσω, perfect εὕρηκα, perfect passive εὕρημαι, aorist εὑρέθην; also εὕρησα and εὑράμην, 1st aorist active and middle

θνήσκω, *I die* (root θάνω), 2nd aorist ἔθανον, future θανοῦμαι, perfect τέθνηκα.

πάσχω, *I suffer* (root πάθω), 2nd aorist ἔπαθον (root πένθω), future πείσομαι, 2nd perfect πέπονθα.

ἔχω, *I have*, imperfect εἶχον, future ἕξω (root σχώ), 2nd aorist ἔσχον, σχές, σχῶ, σχοίην, σχεῖν, from which a new future σχήσω, and perfect ἔσχηκα. From σχῶ also comes ἴσχω, *I hold*, and the compound ὑπισχνέομαι, *I promise*, 2nd aorist ὑπεσχόμην, future ὑποσχήσομαι, perfect ὑπέσχημαι.

5. Ending υμι. ἀμφιέννυμι, *I clothe* (root ἀμφιέω), future ἀμφιέσω, ἀμφιῶ, perfect passive ἠμφίεσμαι.

ζώννυμι, *I gird*, future ζώσω, 1st aorist middle ἐζωσάμην, perfect passive ἔζωσμαι.

κατάγνυμι, *I break in pieces*, future κατεάξω, 1st aorist κατέαξα, 2nd aorist passive κατεάγην.

κεράννυμι, *I mingle* (root κεράω), future κεράσω, perfect passive κεκέρασμαι, aorist ἐκεράσθην, by syncope κέκραμαι, ἐκράθην.

κορέννυμι, *I satiate*, future κορέσω, perfect passive κεκόρεσμαι, aorist ἐκορέσθην.

κρεμάννυμι, *I suspend* (root κρεμάω), future κρεμάσω, κρεμῶ, 1st aorist passive ἐκρεμάσθην. Also κρέμαμαι, future κρεμήσομαι.

μίγνυμι, *I mix* (root μίσγω, μίγω), future μίξω, perfect passive μέμιγμαι.

ὄλλυμι, *I destroy* (root ὄλω), future ὀλέσω, έω, ῶ, 1st aorist ὤλεσα, perfect ὀλώλεκα, future middle ὀλοῦμαι, 2nd aorist middle ὠλόμην, 2nd perfect ὄλωλα, participle ὀλωλώς, ὀλωλυῖα, ὀλωλός.

ὄμνυμι, *I swear* (root ὀμόω), 1st aorist ὤμοσα, perfect ὀμώμοκα, perfect passive ὀμώμοσμαι (root ὄμω), future ὀμοῦμαι, ὀμεῖ, ὀμεῖται, infinitive ὀμεῖσθαι.

πετάννυμι, *I expand*, future πετάσω, 1st aorist ἐπέτασα, etc.

πήγνυμι, *I fix* (root πήγω), future πήξω, 1st aorist ἔπηξα, perfect passive πέπηγμαι, aorist ἐπήχθην, 2nd aorist passive ἐπάγην, 2nd perfect πέπηγα; the two last in a neuter sense.

ῥήγνυμι, ῥήσσω, *I break* (root ῥήγω), future ῥήξω, 1st aorist ἔρρηξα, 2nd aorist passive ἐρράγην, 2nd perfect ἔρρωγα, in a neuter sense.

ῥώννυμι, *I strengthen* (root ῥόω), future ῥώσω, perfect passive ἔρρωμαι, aorist ἐρρώσθην, imperative perfect passive ἔρρωσο, *farewell*.

σβέννυμι, *I extinguish* (root σβέω), future σβέσω, perfect passive ἔσβεσμαι, 1st aorist passive ἐσβέσθην; (root σβέω, σβῆμι) 2nd aorist ἔσβην, perfect ἔσβηκα.

στρώννυμι, *I spread out*, future στρώσω, 1st aorist ἔστρωσα, perfect passive ἔστρωμαι.

SECTION 37—REMARKS ON IRREGULAR VERBS CONTINUED—VARIOUS ENDINGS

1. ἅλλομαι, *I leap*, future ἁλοῦμαι, 1st aorist ἡλάμην.

(ἀνά, κατά) βαίνω (root βάω, βῆμι), future βήσομαι, perfect βέβηκα, 2nd aorist ἔβην; βήσω and ἔβησα in active sense.

ἀνοίγω, *I open*, imperfect ἀνέῳγον, 1st aorist ἀνέῳξα and ἤνοιξα, perfect ἀνέῳχα, perfect passive ἀνέῳγμαι, ἠνέῳγμαι, 1st aorist passive ἀνεῴχθην, ἠνεῴχθην, ἠνοίχθην, 2nd aorist passive ἠνοίγην, 2nd future ἀνοιγήσομαι, 2nd perfect ἀνέῳγα, in neuter sense.

γίνομαι, *I become* (root γένω), 2nd aorist ἐγενόμην, 2nd perfect γέγονα, future γενήσομαι, perfect passive γεγένημαι, aorist passive ἐγενήθην.

δύναμαι, *I am able*, imperfect ἐδυνάμην and ἠδυνάμην, future δυνήσομαι, aorist ἐδυνήθην and ἠδυνήθην, perfect δεδύνημαι.

δέω, *I bind*, future δήσω, 1st aorist ἔδησα, perfect δέδεκα, perfect passive δέδεμαι, aorist ἐδέθην.

δέω, *I want*, future δεήσω; impersonal δεῖ, *it is necessary*, future δεήσει, etc.; passive δέομαι, *I pray*, also

I want, future δεήσομαι, aorist ἐδεήθην.

ἐγείρω, *I arouse*, future ἐγερῶ, perfect Attic ἐγήγερκα; middle ἐγείρομαι, *I awake*, 1st aorist ἠγειράμην, perfect passive ἐγήγερμαι, future ἐγερθήσομαι, aorist ἠγέρθην, 2nd aorist middle ἠγρόμην (for ἠγερόμην), 2nd perfect ἐγρήγορα, whence a new present, γρηγορέω, *I watch*.

εἴδω, *I see* (not used in the present), 2nd aorist εἶδον, infinitive ἰδεῖν; 2nd perfect οἶδα, *I know*; pluperfect ᾔδειν, *I knew*. The forms are as follows: perfect indicative singular οἶδα, οἶσθα, οἶδας, οἶδε, plural (from ἴσημι) ἴσμεν, ἴστε, ἴσασι; imperative ἴσθι, ἴστω, etc.; pluperfect ᾔδειν, ᾔδεις, ᾔδει, plural ᾔδειμεν, ᾔδειτε, ᾔδεισαν; subjunctive εἰδῶ; optative εἰδείην; infinitive εἰδέναι; participle εἰδώς, εἰδυῖα, εἰδός; future εἴσομαι, εἴσῃ, εἴσεται, etc.; also εἰδήσω, as if from εἰδέω, ῶ.

εἴκω, 2nd perfect ἔοικα, *I resemble*; participle ἐοικώς.

κτείνω, *I kill* (in New Testament ἀποκτείνω, and, in

variant readings, ἐπικτένω and ἀποκτέννω), future κτενῶ, 1st aorist ἔκτεινα, 1st aorist passive ἐκτάνθην, infinitive ἀποκτανθῆναι.

μαρτύρομαι, *I witness*, future μαρτυροῦμαι, 1st aorist ἐμαρτυράμην.

οἴομαι, *I think*, imperfect ᾠόμην (also οἶμαι, ᾤμην), future οἰήσομαι, aorist ᾠήθην, infinitive οἰηθῆναι.

ὀνίνημι, *I help* (root ὀνάω), future middle ὀνήσομαι, aorist ὠνησάμην, optative ὀναίμην.

πίνω, *I drink*, future πίομαι, πίεσαι, also πιοῦμαι, 2nd aorist ἔπιον (root πόω), perfect πέπωκα, perfect passive πέπομαι, 1st aorist ἐπόθην (κατεπόθην).

πίπτω, *I fall* (root πέτω), future πεσοῦμαι, 1st aorist ἔπεσα, 2nd aorist ἔπεσον (root πτόω), perfect πέπτωκα.

σπένδω, *I pour out*, future σπείσω, perfect ἔσπεικα, perfect passive ἔσπεισμαι, aorist ἐσπείσθην.

σῴζω, *I save*, perfect passive σέσωμαι and σέσωσμαι, aorist ἐσώθην.

aorist ἐσώθην.

τίκτω, *I bring forth* (root τέκω), future τέξομαι, 2nd aorist ἔτεκον, 1st aorist passive ἐτέχθην, 2nd perfect τέτοκα.

φθάνω, *I anticipate*, future φθάσω, 1st aorist ἔφθασα, perfect ἔφθακα (root φθάω, φθῆμι), 2nd aorist ἔφθην, future φθήσομαι.

2. A few verbs in έω and άω form some tenses as if the verb terminated in ω impure.

γαμέω, *I marry* (root γάμω), 1st aorist ἔγημα and ἐγάμησα, perfect γεγάμηκα, regular.

δαμάω, *I tame* (root δάμνω), 2nd aorist ἔδαμον, 2nd aorist passive ἐδάμην, perfect δέδμηκα (for δεδάμηκα).

δοκέω, *I appear* (root δόκω), future δόξω, 1st aorist ἔδοξα, perfect passive δέδογμαι. Impersonally, δοκεῖ, *it seems good*, ἔδοξε, etc.

μυκάομαι, *I roar* (root μύκω), 2nd aorist ἔμυκον, 2nd perfect μέμυκα.

SECTION 38—REMARKS ON SOME PERFECT TENSES EMPLOYED AS PRESENTS

1. In a considerable number of verbs the perfect is used in a strictly present sense. The explanation of this usage is simply derived from the complete idea conveyed by the perfect tense, as in the following examples.

2. ἔθω, *I accustom myself*, εἴωθα, *I have accustomed myself*; hence, *I am accustomed*.

εἴδω, *I see*, οἶδα, *I know*.

ἔοικα, *I resemble*.

θνήσκω, *I die*, τέθνηκα, *I have suffered death*; hence, *I am dead*.

ἵστημι, *I place*, ἕστηκα (ἐμαυτόν), *I have placed myself*; hence, *I stand*.

κτάομαι, *I acquire*, κέκτημαι, *I have acquired and retain*; hence, *I possess*.

μνάομαι, *I call to mind*, μέμνημαι, *I have called to mind and retain*; hence, *I remember*.

So also in the perfect passive; e.g., οἱ κεκλημένοι, *those who are in receipt of a call or invitation*; hence, *the invited ones, the guests*.

SECTION 39—THE USE OF THE TENSES

The use of the *present* and *future* tenses is sufficiently explained by their names. But the present is sometimes used as a lively expression of a past action; as, ἄγουσιν αὐτὸν πρὸς τοὺς Φαρισαίους, John 9:13; and also of a certain futurity: as, μετὰ τρεῖς ἡμέρας ἐγείρομαι, Matt. 27:63. The indicative of the future occasionally has the force of the imperative mood: as, ἔσεσθε οὖν ὑμεῖς τέλειοι, Matt. 5:48. The *imperfect* expresses a prolonged or recurrent action in past time. The *aorist* is strictly the expression of a momentary or transient single action, being thus distinguished from the imperfect; and in the indicative mood it ordinarily signifies

past time. It is, however, used of a prolonged action, if there is no positive need to make a direct expression of that circumstance. It is thus of constant use in the narrative of past transactions. The *perfect* conveys the double notion of an action terminated in past time, and of its effect existing in the present: as, γυνὴ δέδεται, 1 Cor. 7:39. The *pluperfect* expresses the effect as past, as well as the action. In the case of certain verbs, the latter part of the entire idea conveyed by these two tenses is so prominent that they virtually become a present and imperfect respectively: as, οἶδα, *I know*, ᾔδειν, *I knew*.

SECTION 40—THE USE OF THE INFINITIVE MOOD

A verb in the infinitive mood, either alone or in combination with other words, mostly expresses either the subject of another verb: as, μακάριόν ἐστι διδόναι, Acts

20:35; or the object of relation of the action or condition expressed by a verb, participle, or adjective: as, ἐπιποθῶ ἰδεῖν ὑμᾶς, Rom. 1:11; δυνατὸς κωλῦσαι, Acts

11:17; οὐκ ἔστιν ἐμὸν δοῦναι, Matt. 20:23. The most usual grammatical situation of a verb in the infinitive is in immediate dependence on another verb. A verb in the infinitive with the neuter article (τό) prefixed becomes, by the inflection of the article, admissible into the various grammatical positions of the substantive: as, γνώμη τοῦ ὑποστρέφειν, Acts 20:3; διὰ παντὸς τοῦ

ζῆν, Heb. 2:15; ἐν τῷ ἱερατεύειν αὐτόν, Luke 1:8. The infinitive is always a legitimate construction, though not the only one, after the particles πρίν and ὥστε: as, πρὶν γενέσθαι, John 14:29; ὥστε μὴ ἰσχύειν τινά, Matt. 8:28. A participle takes the place of an infinitive in dependence upon certain verbs: as, ἐπαύσατο λαλῶν, Luke 5:4; ὁρῶ σε ὄντα, Acts 8:23.

SECTION 41—THE USE OF THE SUBJUNCTIVE MOOD

In the principal verb of a sentence, the subjunctive mood is an expression of deliberative interrogation: as, δῶμεν, ἢ μὴ δῶμεν; Mark 12:15, *Should we pay, or should we not pay?* καὶ τί εἴπω; John 12:27, *And what should I say?* This is termed its deliberative use. In the first person plural, it has also the suggestive force which is usually classed as an imperative: as, ἄγωμεν εἰς τὰς ἐχομένας κωμοπόλεις, Mark 1:38; *Let us go into the next towns.* This usage, if not actually identical with it, is nearly related to the preceding. The aorist of this mood is used as an imperative with the particle μή: as, μὴ σαλπίσῃς, Matt. 6:2. The construction of the subjunctive with the combined particles οὐ μή is a form

of absolute negation: as, οὐ μὴ νίψῃς, John 13:8. The future indicative is also used in the same construction. In dependent clauses, the subjunctive is the ordinary mood after ἐάν, ἄν used hypothetically, and relative words when ἄν is subjoined to them: as, ὅταν (ὅτε ἄν), ὃς ἄν, etc., as also πρίν and ἕως with ἄν subjoined. It is also the ordinary construction with the particles ἵνα, ὡς, ὅπως when expressing purpose: as, ἵνα πληρωθῇ, Matt. 2:15. The same is the case when purpose is implied, though not expressed directly: as, τὸ κατάλυμα, ὅπου—φάγω, Mark 14:14. The future indicative is also constructed with ὡς and ὅπως, and in the New Testament sometimes also with ἵνα.

SECTION 42—THE USE OF THE OPTATIVE MOOD

In the principal verb, the optative mood is a simple form of wishing: as, τὸ ἀργύριον—εἴη εἰς ἀπώλειαν, Acts 8:20. In the combination with the particle ἄν, it is an expression of a conditional futurity: as, πῶς ἂν δυναίμην; Acts 8:31, *How should I be able?* In dependent clauses, it is sometimes employed in oblique narration, that is, when the sentiments of a person are made

a matter of narration, instead of being expressed in direct personal terms: as, ἐπυνθάνετο, τί εἴη ταῦτα, Luke 15:26. The optative following the particle εἰ is one of the forms of a hypothetical clause, but of rare occurrence in the New Testament; as is also its use after particles expressing purpose.

SECTION 43—THE AGREEMENT OF THE VERB

In Greek, as in language in general, the verb is ordinarily put in the same number and person as its subject, or nominative case. This is its agreement, or concord. There is, however, this special exception; that, when a word in the plural, expressing the subject, is also in the neuter gender, the verb is usually in the singular: as, πάντα δι' αὐτοῦ ἐγένετο, John 1:3. A subject in the singular, when the idea conveyed by the word is that of plurality, may have its verb in the plural: as, ὄχλος ἔστρωσαν, Matt. 21:8. This is termed a rational, as distinguished from a formal, agreement. When a verb is

in the plural, as having several joint subjects, and these are of different persons, its agreement will be with the first person in preference to the second, and with the second in preference to the third. Since the verb, by its inflection alone always implies its pronominal subject in the first and second persons, these are, accordingly, not necessary to be expressed for the purpose of mere clarity: when, therefore, they are expressed, it is a mark of point or emphasis on the subject of the verb, of some kind or degree. And the same is the case to a certain extent with the third person.

SECTION 44—THE AGREEMENT OF THE ADJECTIVE, PARTICIPLE, AND PRONOUN

The adjective, the participle, and the pronoun agree with the substantive to which they have relation, in

gender, number, and case. Rational agreements are also admissible, as in the case of the verb. An adjective, participle, or pronoun in the masculine gender without any substantive expressed has relation to persons; but in the neuter, to things: as, μακάριοι οἱ πενθοῦντες, Matt. 5:4; πάντα ταῦτα ἐφυλαξάμην, Matt. 19:20. The relative pronoun, being either the subject of the verb in its own clause or the object of the governing force of some word in that clause, agrees with its antecedent in gender and number only: if it is in the nominative case, it is also reckoned of the same person with the antecedent.

SECTION 45—THE USE OF THE NOMINATIVE CASE

A nominative case with the article prefixed is sometimes used for the vocative: as, τὸ πνεῦμα τὸ ἄλαλον, Mark 9:25. A substantive or adjective which is attached to a neuter or passive verb, as a necessary supplement to the sense, is put in the same case with the subject of the verb; which, except in case of an infinitive, will be the nominative: as, ἐγώ εἰμι ἡ ὁδός, John 14:6; ὁ λόγος σὰρξ ἐγένετο, John 1:14; αὐτοὶ υἱοὶ θεοῦ κληθήσονται, Matt. 5:9; πεπεισμένος ἐστὶν Ἰωάννην προφήτην εἶναι, Luke 20:6. If, instead of a verb, a participle is used, the case of the participle is continued in the supplemental word: as, Φοίβην οὖσαν διάκονουν, Rom. 16:1; ἡμῖν Ῥωμαίοις οὖσι(ν), Acts 16:21. Of the same principle is the rule of apposition, namely, that two terms for the same thing, in the same grammatical clause, are put in the same case: as, παραγίνεται Ἰωάννης ὁ βαπτιστής, Matt. 3:1; ἐν ἡμέραις Ἡρῴδου τοῦ βασιλέως, Matt. 2:1; παραβάτην ἐμαυτὸν συνιστάνω, Gal. 2:18; ὑμᾶς—ἔθετο ἐπισκόπους, Acts 20:28.

SECTION 46—THE USE OF THE ACCUSATIVE CASE

The accusative is the governing case of by far the greater number of transitive verbs and may therefore by regarded as the ordinary case of the direct object of a verb. The subject of a verb in the infinitive mood is ordinarily in the accusative case: as, πάντας ἀνθρώπους θέλει σωθῆναι, 1 Tim. 2:4. But, if the subject of the verb in the infinitive is the same as that of the principal verb on which it depends, it is in the nominative: as, δέομαι τὸ μὴ παρὼν θαρρῆσαι, 2 Cor. 10:2; φάσκοντες εἶναι σοφοί, Rom. 1:22. An object of relation, or in limitation, as distinguished from one which is direct, is also in the accusative; and in this way the case is found after adjectives, passive verbs, and a previous governing accusative: as, σκηνοποιοὶ τὴν τέχνην, Acts 18:3; δαρήσεται πολλάς, Luke 12:47; δεδεμένος τοὺς πόδας, John 11:44; γάλα ὑμᾶς ἐπότισα, 1 Cor. 3:2. When the relative would, by its own governing case, be in the accusative, it sometimes exchanges this case for the genitive or dative of its antecedent: as, ἐπὶ πᾶσιν οἷς ἤκουσαν, Luke 2:20; ἐκ τοῦ ὕδατος οὗ ἐγὼ δώσω, John 4:14. This is termed attraction. The accusative is employed in designations of space and time: as, ἀπέχουσαν σταδίους ἑξήκοντα, Luke 24:13; ὡσεὶ ὥραν ἐννάτην, Acts 10:3.

SECTION 47—THE USE OF THE GENITIVE CASE

The most simple and ordinary use of the genitive is to place a substantive in immediate construction with another substantive. This construction is an expression of some simple and obvious relation between the things signified by the two substantives; and thus the substantive in the genitive comes variously to signify a possessor, origin, cause, matter, object, etc. In the New Testament, the genitive in construction has also the force of a qualifying adjective: as, τὸν οἰκονόμον τῆς ἀδικίας, Luke 16:8. This is a Hebraism.

An absolute participial clause, so termed, is one which has its subject distinct from the principal subject of the sentence of which it forms a part. Such clauses are distinguished by having their subject in the genitive case, hence termed the genitive absolute: as, τοῦ δαιμονίου ἐξελθόντος, ἐλάλησεν ὁ κωφός, Luke 11:14.

The genitive is used in designations of price: as, ἐπράθη τριακοσίων δηναρίων, John 12:5. Akin to this is when the genitive is required by the adjective ἄξιος. It is also found in designations of time, John 3:2. The genitive is constructed with words, that is, verbs and adjectives, implying—

(1) exclusive distinction: as, for instance, διαφέρειν, 1 Cor. 15:41, and all comparatives: hence

(2) superiority, especially power and rule, Rom. 14:9; 1 Tim. 2:12.

(3) inclusive distinction: as, for instance, distributives and superlatives, Luke 16:5; 1 Cor. 15:9.

(4) deprivation, Luke 16:4; abstinence, Acts 20:29; and cessation, 1 Pet. 4:1.

(5) fulness and its opposites: emptiness, deficiency, need, Luke 5:12; John 2:7; 1 Tim. 1:6; James 1:5.

(6) desire, objective pursuit, Matt. 5:28.

(7) bodily perception, except sight, Matt. 2:9.

(8) mental perception, as, for instance, memory, knowledge, Luke 18:32. But words of this class, as well as the preceding one, are also constructed with the accusative, Luke 9:45.

Certain verbs in the middle voice govern the genitive, as, ἅπτομαι, ἔχομαι, γεύομαι, ὀρέγομαι, ἐπιλανθάνομαι, Matt. 8:15; Heb. 6:9; Mark 9:1; 1 Tim. 3:1; Heb. 6:10. Also certain verbs compounded of

κατά, and conveying by their compositon the idea of untoward action: as, κατηγορῶ, καταμαρτυρῶ, καταδυναστεύω, κατακυριεύω, καταφρονῶ, Matt. 12:10; Mark 14:60; James 2:6; Acts 19:16; Matt. 6:24. A criminal charge or sentence is expressed in the genitive, Matt. 26:66. The object of a partial action is in the genitive, Mark 2:21; Acts 27:36; Mark 9:27. The construction of the genitive after verbs substantive is the same, in effect, with its immediate dependence upon a substantive, Matt. 19:15; 1 Cor. 6:19; Heb. 12:11.

SECTION 48—THE USE OF THE DATIVE CASE

As a general principle, that to which anything is represented as accruing, is expressed in the dative case. It is thus constructed with words implying—

(1) address, Matt. 3:7; Luke 1:19; Acts 26:29.

(2) bestowal, Matt. 4:9; Acts 3:14.

(3) approach, Luke 7:12.

(4) gain or loss, advantage or disadvantage, Matt. 5:44; Luke 4:22; Matt. 23:31; Heb. 8:8; Matt. 3:16; Rom. 14:6, 7.

(5) credence, reliance, Matt. 21:25; 2 Cor. 10:7.

(6) submission, subservience, Acts 5:36; Luke 2:51; Acts 13:36.

To these must be added words signifying adaptation,

likeness, equality, 2 Cor. 2:6; Heb. 6:7; Eph. 5:3; James 1:6; Luke 7:32; Matt. 20:12. The dative is an expression of instrumentality, Matt. 8:16; Mark 5:3; as also causation, method, agency, and other kindred notions, Rom. 11:20; Acts 15:1; Phil. 2:7; 1 Cor. 14:20. The dative is used in designations of time, Luke 12:20; Acts 13:20. Certain verbs in the middle voice are followed by the dative; as, χρῶμαι, διαλέγομαι, κρίνομαι, Acts 27:17; Heb. 12:5; Matt. 5:40. The dative is frequently found in dependence upon a preposition involved in a compound verb, Mark 3:10; Acts 13:43; 2 Pet. 1:9; Matt. 26:53.

SECTION 49—PREPOSITIONS, ADVERBS, AND CONJUNCTIONS

The various governing cases required by the several prepositions are given at length in the Lexicon. Some prepositions are occasionally used as adverbs without a case, 2 Cor. 11:23; and are also prefixed to adverbs, Matt. 4:17; Acts 28:23. Certain adverbs may have a governing case, ordinarily the genitive, Matt. 10:29; John

6:23; Matt. 13:34. The Greek language exhibits a peculiar usage in the repetition of a negative, Matt. 22:16; John 15:5; Mark 1:44. Words directly united by a simple conjunction are ordinarily in the same grammatical construction.

LEXICON

A

(1) **A, α,** *Alpha,* the first letter of the Greek alphabet, and used for the *first,* in the titles of 1 Cor., 1 Thess., 1 Tim., 1 Pet., and 1 John (Rev. 1:8, 11; 21:6; 22:13, MT & TR | ἄλφα, GNT, WH & NA)

ἅ, nom. pl. neut. relative pron. [§10.J.g] {Col. 2:17} . . . . ὅς *(3739)*

ἅ, acc. pl. neut. relative pron. [§10.J.g] {Col. 2:18} . . . . id.

(2) **Ἀαρών,** ὁ, *Aaron,* pr. name, indecl.

(3) **Ἀβαδδών,** ὁ, *Abaddon,* pr. name, indecl. (Rev. 9:11, GNT, WH, NA & TR | Ἀββαδών, MT)

ἀβαρῆ, acc. sg. m. adj. . . . . ἀβαρής *(4)*

(4) **ἀβαρής,** ές [§7.G.b] (ἀ + βάρος) *not burdensome, not chargeable,* 2 Cor. 11:9

(5) **Ἀββᾶ,** indecl. Aramaic or Syriac אַבָּא, *father* (Mark 14:36; Rom. 8:15; Gal. 4:6, TR | Ἀββά, WH & MT | Αββα, GNT | αββα, NA)

(‡3) **Ἀββαδών,** ὁ, *Abbadon,* pr. name, indecl. (Rev. 9:11, MT | ἀβαδδών, GNT, WH, NA & TR)

(†6) **Ἄβελ,** ὁ, *Abel,* pr. name, indecl. (Matt. 23:35; Luke 11:51; Heb. 11:4; 12:24, GNT, MT, WH & NA | Ἅβελ, TR)

(7) **Ἀβιά,** ὁ, *Abia,* pr. name, indecl.

(†8) **Ἀβιαθάρ,** ὁ, *Abiathar,* pr. name, indecl. (Mark 2:26, GNT, WH & NA | Ἀβιάθαρ, MT & TR)

(9) **Ἀβιληνή,** ῆς, ἡ [§2.B.a] *Abilene,* a district of the Syrian Decapolis; from *Abila,* the chief town

Ἀβιληνῆς, gen. sg. fem. n. (Luke 3:1, GNT, TR, MT & NA | Ἀβελληνῆς, WH) . . Ἀβιληνή *(9)*

(10) **Ἀβιούδ,** ὁ, *Abihud,* pr. name, indecl.

(11) **Ἀβραάμ,** ὁ, *Abraham,* pr. name, indecl.

ἄβυσσον, acc. sg. fem. n. [§3.C.b] . . . . ἄβυσσος *(12)*

(12) **ἄβυσσος,** ου, ἡ, *bottomless; place of the dead, hell*

ἀβύσσου, gen. sg. f. n. . . . . ἄβυσσος *(12)*

(13) **Ἄγαβος,** ου, ὁ, nom. sg. m. n., *Agabus,* pr.

name (Acts 11:28; 21:10, WH & TR | Ἄγαβος, GNT, MT & NA)

ἀγαγεῖν, 2 aor. act. infin. [§13.7.d] . . . . . ἄγω *(71)*

ἀγάγετε, 2 pers. pl. 2 aor. act. imper. . . . . id.

ἀγάγῃ, 3 pers. sg. 2 aor. act. subj. . . . . . . id.

ἀγαγόντα, acc. sg. m. 2 aor. act. part. . . . id.

ἀγαγόντες, nom. pl. m. 2 aor. act. part. . . id.

ἀγάγωσιν, 3 pers. pl. 2 aor. act. subj. (Mark 13:11, MT & TR | ἄγωσιν, GNT, WH & NA) . . . . id.

ἀγαθά nom. pl. neut. adj. [§7.F.a] {Rom. 3:8} . . . . ἀγαθός *(18)*

ἀγαθά, acc. pl. neut. adj. {Rom. 10:15} . . . id.

ἀγαθάς, acc. pl. f. adj. . . . . id.

ἀγαθέ, voc. sg. m. adj. . . . . id.

ἀγαθή, nom. sg. f. adj. . . . . id.

ἀγαθῇ, dat. sg. f. adj. . . . . id.

ἀγαθήν, acc. sg. f. adj. . . . . id.

ἀγαθῆς, gen. sg. f. adj. . . . . id.

ἀγαθοεργεῖν, pres. act. infin. . . . . . . ἀγαθοεργέω *(14)*

(14) **ἀγαθοεργέω,** ῶ, fut. ἀγαθουργήσω [§16.P] (ἀγαθός + ἔργον) *to do good, confer benefits,* 1 Tim. 6:18

ἀγαθοῖς, dat. pl. m. adj. {1 Pet. 2:18} . . . ἀγαθός *(18)*

ἀγαθοῖς, dat. pl. neut. adj. {Eph. 2:10} . . id.

ἀγαθόν, acc. sg. m. adj. {Mark 10:18} . . . id.

ἀγαθόν, nom. sg. neut. adj. {Matt. 7:17} . id.

ἀγαθόν, acc. sg. neut. adj. {Matt. 19:16} . id.

ἀγαθοποιεῖτε, 2 pers. pl. pres. act. imper. . . . . ἀγαθοποιέω *(15)*

(15) **ἀγαθοποιέω,** ῶ, fut. ἀγαθοποιήσω [§16.P] (ἀγαθός + ποιέω) *to do good, benefit, do well*

ἀγαθοποιῆσαι, aor. act. infin. . . . . . ἀγαθοποιέω *(15)*

ἀγαθοποιῆτε, 2 pers. pl. pres. act. subj. . . id.

(16) **ἀγαθοποιΐα,** ας, ἡ [§2.B.b; 2.2] *well-doing, probity,* 1 Pet. 4:19

ἀγαθοποιΐᾳ, dat. sg. f. n. . . . . ἀγαθοποιΐα *(16)*

(17) **ἀγαθοποιός,** όν, *doing good* or *right;* subst., *a well-doer*

ἀγαθοποιοῦντας, acc. pl. m. pres. act. part. . . . . ἀγαθοποιέω *(15)*

ἀγαθοποιοῦντες, nom. pl. m. pres. act. part. id.

ἀγαθοποιοῦσαι, nom. pl. f. pres. act. part. id.

ἀγαθοποιῶν, nom. sg. m. pres. act. part.
{3 John 11} . . . . ἀγαθοποιέω *(15)*
ἀγαθοποιῶν, gen. pl. m. adj.
{1 Pet. 2:14} . . . . ἀγαθοποιός *(17)*
(18) **ἀγαθός,** ή, όν, nom. sg. m. adj., *good, profitable, generous, beneficent, upright, virtuous* [§7.F.a]
ἀγαθοῦ, gen. sg. m. adj. {Matt. 12:35} . . ἀγαθός *(18)*
ἀγαθοῦ, gen. sg. neut. adj. {Matt. 19:17} . id.
ἀγαθουργῶν, nom. sg. m. pres. act. part. (Acts 14:17, GNT, WH & NA | ἀγαθοποιῶν, MT & TR) . . . . ἀγαθοεργέω *(14)*
ἀγαθούς, acc. pl. m. adj. . . . . ἀγαθός *(18)*
ἀγαθῷ, dat. sg. m. adj. {2 Thess. 2:17} . . id.
ἀγαθῷ, dat. sg. neut. adj. {1 Tim. 5:10} . . id.
ἀγαθῶν, gen. pl. m. adj. {James 3:17} . . . id.
ἀγαθῶν, gen. pl. neut. adj. {1 Tim. 2:10} . id.
(19) **ἀγαθωσύνη,** ης, ή, nom. sg. f. n. [§2.B.a]
goodness, virtue, beneficence
ἀγαθωσύνῃ, dat. sg. f. n. . . . . ἀγαθωσύνη *(19)*
ἀγαθωσύνης, gen. sg. f. n. . . . . id.
ἀγαλλιαθῆναι, aor. pass. dep. infin. (John 5:35, GNT, WH, MT & NA | ἀγαλλιασθῆναι, TR) . . . . ἀγαλλιάω *(21)*
ἀγαλλιάσει, dat. sg. f. n. . . . . ἀγαλλίασις *(20)*
ἀγαλλιάσεως, gen. sg. f. n. . . . . id.
ἀγαλλιᾶσθε, 2 pers. pl. pres. mid./pass. dep. indic. [§19.S] {1 Pet. 1:6} . . . . ἀγαλλιάω *(21)*
ἀγαλλιᾶσθε, 2 pers. pl. pres. mid./pass. dep. imper. {Matt. 5:12} . . . . id.
ἀγαλλιασθῆναι, aor. pass. dep. infin. (John 5:35, TR | ἀγαλλιαθῆναι, GNT, WH, MT & NA) . . . . id.
(20) **ἀγαλλίασις,** εως, ή, nom. sg. f. n. [§5.E.c] *exultation, extreme joy*
ἀγαλλιᾶτε, 2 pers. pl. pres. act. imper. (1 Pet. 1:8, WH | ἀγαλλιᾶσθε, GNT, MT, TR & NA) . . . . ἀγαλλιάω *(21)*
(21) **ἀγαλλιάω,** ῶ, fut. ἀγαλλιάσω [§22.2] *to celebrate, praise;* also equivalent to ἀγαλλιάομαι, ῶμαι, *to exult, rejoice exceedingly; to desire ardently,* John 8:56
ἀγαλλιώμεθα, 1 pers. pl. pres. mid./pass. dep. subj. (Rev. 19:7, MT & TR | ἀγαλλιῶμεν, GNT, WH & NA) . . . . ἀγαλλιάω *(21)*
ἀγαλλιῶμεν, 1 pers. pl. pres. act. subj. (Rev. 19:7, GNT, WH & NA | ἀγαλλιώμεθα, MT & TR) . . . . id.
ἀγαλλιώμενοι, nom. pl. m. pres. mid./pass. dep. part. [§19.S] . . . . id.
ἀγάμοις, dat. pl. m. n. . . . . ἄγαμος *(22)*
(22) **ἄγαμος,** ου, ὁ, nom. sg. m. n. [§3.C.a] (ἀ + γάμος) *unmarried* {1 Cor. 7:32}
(22) **ἄγαμος,** ου, ή, nom. sg. f. n. [§3.C.b] (ἀ + γάμος) *unmarried* {1 Cor. 7:11, 34}

ἀγανακτεῖν, pres. act. infin. . . . . ἀγανακτέω *(23)*
(23) **ἀγανακτέω,** ῶ, fut. ἀγανακτήσω [§16.P] *to be pained; to be angry, vexed, indignant; to manifest indignation*
ἀγανάκτησιν, acc. sg. f. n. . . . . . . ἀγανάκτησις *(24)*
(24) **ἀγανάκτησις,** εως, ή [§5.E.c] *indignation,* 2 Cor. 7:11
ἀγανακτοῦντες, nom. pl. m. pres. act. part. . . . . ἀγανακτέω *(23)*
ἀγανακτῶν, nom. sg. m. pres. act. part. . . id.
ἀγαπᾷ, 3 pers. sg. pres. act. indic. [§18.R] {John 10:17} . . . . ἀγαπάω *(25)*
ἀγαπᾷ, 3 pers. sg. pres. act. subj. {John 14:23} . . . . id.
ἀγάπαις, dat. pl. f. n. . . . . ἀγάπη *(26)*
ἀγαπᾶν, pres. act. infin. (GNT, MT & NA | ἀγαπᾷν, WH & TR) . . . . ἀγαπάω *(25)*
ἀγαπᾷς, 2 pers. sg. pres. act. indic. . . . . . . id.
ἀγαπᾶτε, 2 pers. pl. pres. act. indic. {Luke 6:32} . . . . id.
ἀγαπᾶτε, 2 pers. pl. pres. act. subj. {John 13:34} . . . . id.
ἀγαπᾶτε, 2 pers. pl. pres. act. imper. {Luke 6:27} . . . . id.
ἀγαπάτω, 3 pers. sg. pres. act. imper. . . . . id.
(25) **ἀγαπάω,** ῶ, fut. ἀγαπήσω, perf. ἠγάπηκα [§18.R] *to love, value, esteem, feel or manifest generous concern for, be faithful towards; to delight in, to set store upon,* Rev. 12:11
(26) **ἀγάπη,** ης, ή, nom. sg. f. n. [§2.B.a] *love, generosity, kindly concern, devotedness;* pl. *love-feasts,* Jude 12
ἀγάπῃ, dat. sg. f. n. . . . . ἀγάπη *(26)*
ἀγαπηθήσεται, 3 pers. sg. fut. pass. indic. [§19.S] . . . . ἀγαπάω *(25)*
ἀγάπην, acc. sg. f. n. . . . . ἀγάπη *(26)*
ἀγάπης, gen. sg. f. n. . . . . id.
ἀγαπήσαντι, dat. sg. m. aor. act. part. (Rev. 1:5, TR | ἀγαπῶντι, GNT, WH, MT & NA) . . . . ἀγαπάω *(25)*
ἀγαπήσαντος, gen. sg. m. aor. act. part. . . id.
ἀγαπήσας, nom. sg. m. aor. act. part. . . . id.
ἀγαπήσατε, 2 pers. pl. aor. act. imper. . . . id.
ἀγαπήσει, 3 pers. sg. fut. act. indic. [§16.3] id.
ἀγαπήσεις, 2 pers. sg. fut. act. indic. . . . . id.
ἀγαπήσητε, 2 pers. pl. aor. act. subj. . . . . id.
ἀγαπήσω, 1 pers. sg. fut. act. indic. . . . . . id.
ἀγαπητά, nom. pl. neut. adj.
{Eph. 5:1} . . . . ἀγαπητός *(27)*
ἀγαπητά, acc. pl. neut. adj. {1 Cor. 4:14} . id.
ἀγαπητέ, voc. sg. m. adj. . . . . id.
ἀγαπητῇ, dat. sg. f. adj. (Philemon 2, MT & TR | ἀδελφῇ, GNT, WH & NA) . . . . id.
ἀγαπητήν, acc. sg. f. adj. . . . . id.

ἀγαπητοί, nom. pl. m. adj.
{Rom. 11:28} . . . .'. . . . . ἀγαπητός *(27)*

ἀγαπητοί, voc. pl. m. adj. {Rom. 12:19} . .   id.

ἀγαπητοῖς, dat. pl. m. adj. . . . . id.

ἀγαπητόν, acc. sg. m. adj. {Philemon 16} .   id.

ἀγαπητόν, nom. sg. neut. adj. {1 Cor. 4:17}   id.

(27) **ἀγαπητός**, ή, όν, nom. sg. m. adj. [§7.F.a] *be-*
loved, dear; worthy of love

ἀγαπητοῦ, gen. sg. m. adj. . . . . ἀγαπητός *(27)*

ἀγαπητῷ, dat. sg. m. adj. {Philemon 1} . .   id.

ἀγαπητῷ, dat. sg. neut. adj. {2 Tim. 1:2} .   id.

ἀγαπῶ, 1 pers. sg. pres. act. indic. contracted
form of . . . . ἀγαπάω *(25)*

ἀγαπῶμαι, 1 pers. sg. pres. pass. indic. . . .   id.

ἀγαπῶμεν, 1 pers. pl. pres. act. indic.
{1 John 3:14} . . . .   id.

ἀγαπῶμεν, 1 pers. pl. pres. act. subj.
{1 John 3:11} . . . .   id.

ἀγαπῶν, nom. sg. m. pres. act. part. . . . . .   id.

ἀγαπῶντας, acc. pl. m. pres. act. part. . . .   id.

ἀγαπῶντι, dat. sg. m. pres. act. part. (Rev. 1:5,
GNT, WH, MT & NA | ἀγαπήσαντι,
TR) . . . .   id.

ἀγαπώντων, gen. pl. m. pres. act. part. . .   id.

ἀγαπῶσι(ν), 3 pers. pl. pres. act. indic.
{Luke 6:32}. . . . .   id.

ἀγαπῶσιν, dat. pl. m. pres. act. part.
{1 Cor. 2:9} . . . .   id.

(†28) **Ἀγάρ**, ἡ, pr. name, indecl., *Agar* (Gal.
4:24, 25, GNT, MT & NA | Ἄγαρ, TR
| Ἅγαρ, WH)

ἀγγαρεύουσι(ν), 3 pers. pl. pres. act.
indic. . . . . ἀγγαρεύω *(29)*

ἀγγαρεύσει, 3 pers. sg. fut. act. indic. . . . .   id.

(29) **ἀγγαρεύω**, fut. ἀγγαρεύσω [§13.M] (ἄγγα-
ρος, a Persian courier, or messenger, who
had authority to press into his service men,
horses, etc.) *to press,* or *compel* another
to go somewhere, or carry some burden

ἀγγεῖα, acc. pl. neut. n. (Matt. 13:48, MT &
TR | ἄγγη, GNT, WH & NA) . . . . . ἀγγεῖον *(30)*

ἀγγείοις, dat. pl. neut. n. . . . .   id.

(30) **ἀγγεῖον**, ου, τό [§3.C.c] *a vessel, utensil,* Matt.
25:4

(31) **ἀγγελία**, ας, ἡ, nom. sg. f. n. [§2.B.b; 2.2] *a*
message, doctrine, or *precept,* delivered in
the name of any one

ἀγγέλλουσα, nom. sg. f. pres. act. part. (John
20:18, GNT, WH, NA | ἀπαγγέλλουσα,
MT & TR) . . . . ἀγγέλλω *(‡32)*

(‡32) **ἀγγέλλω**, *to tell, to announce*

ἄγγελοι, nom. pl. m. n. . . . . ἄγγελος *(32)*

ἀγγέλοις, dat. pl. m. n. . . . .   id.

ἄγγελον, acc. sg. m. n. . . . .   id.

(32) **ἄγγελος**, ου, ὁ, nom. sg. m. n. [§3.C.a,b] *one*

sent, a messenger, angel

ἀγγέλου, gen. sg. m. n. . . . . ἄγγελος *(32)*

ἀγγέλους, acc. pl. m. n. . . . .   id.

ἀγγέλῳ, dat. sg. m. n. . . . .   id.

ἀγγέλων, gen. pl. m. n. . . . .   id.

ἄγγη, acc. pl. neut. n. (Matt. 13:48, GNT,
WH & NA | ἀγγεῖα, MT & TR) . . . ἄγγος *(‡30)*

(‡30) **ἄγγος**, ους, τό, *vessel, container,* Matt. 13:48

(33) **ἄγε**, a particle of exhortation, *come, come now*
{James 4:13; 5:1}

ἄγε, 2 pers. sg. pres. act. imper. {2 Tim. 4:11}   ἄγω *(71)*

ἄγει, 3 pers. sg. pres. act. indic. . . . .   id.

ἄγειν, pres. act. infin. . . . .   id.

(34) **ἀγέλη**, ης, ἡ, nom. sg. f. n. [§2.B.a] *a drove,*
flock, herd

ἀγέλην, acc. sg. f. n. . . . . ἀγέλη *(34)*

(35) **ἀγενεαλόγητος**, ον, nom. sg. m. adj. [§7.2]
(ἀ + γενεαλογέω) *not included in a pedi-*
gree; independent of pedigree

ἀγενῆ, acc. pl. neut. adj. . . . . ἀγενής *(36)*

(36) **ἀγενής**, ές [§7.G.b] (ἀ + γένος) *ignoble, base*

ἄγεσθαι, pres. pass. infin. . . . .   ἄγω *(71)*

ἄγεσθε, 2 pers. pl. pres. pass. indic. . . . . .   id.

ἁγία, nom. sg. f. adj. {1 Cor. 7:34} . . . . . ἅγιος *(40)*

ἅγια, nom. pl. neut. adj. {1 Cor. 7:14} . . .   id.

ἅγια, acc. pl. neut. adj. {Heb. 9:25} . . . . .   id.

ἁγίᾳ, dat. sg. f. adj. . . . .   id.

ἁγιάζει, 3 pers. sg. pres. act. indic. . . . . . ἁγιάζω *(37)*

ἁγιάζεται, 3 pers. sg. pres. pass. indic. . . .   id.

ἁγιαζόμενοι, nom. pl. m. pres. pass. part.   id.

ἁγιαζομένους, acc. pl. m. pres. pass. part.   id.

ἁγιάζον, nom. sg. neut. pres. act. part. . . .   id.

(37) **ἁγιάζω**, 1 pers. sg. pres. act. indic., fut.
ἁγιάσω, perf. pass. ἡγίασμαι [§26.1] *to*
separate, consecrate; cleanse, purify, sanc-
tify; regard or *reverence as holy*

ἁγιάζων, nom. sg. m. pres. act. part. . . . ἁγιάζω *(37)*

ἅγιαι, nom. pl. f. adj. . . . . ἅγιος *(40)*

ἁγίαις, dat. pl. f. adj. . . . .   id.

ἁγίαν, acc. sg. f. adj. . . . .   id.

ἁγίας, gen. sg. f. adj. . . . .   id.

ἁγιάσαι, 3 pers. sg. aor. act. opt. . . . . . . ἁγιάζω *(37)*

ἁγιάσας, nom. sg. m. aor. act. part. (Matt.
23:17, GNT, WH & NA | ἁγιάζων, MT
& TR) . . . .   id.

ἁγιάσατε, 2 pers. pl. aor. act. imper. . . . .   id.

ἁγιάσῃ, 3 pers. sg. aor. act. subj. . . . .   id.

ἁγιασθήτω, 3 pers. sg. aor. pass. imper. . .   id.

ἁγιασμόν, acc. sg. m. n. . . . . ἁγιασμός *(38)*

(38) **ἁγιασμός**, οῦ, ὁ, nom. sg. m. n. [§3.C.a] *sanc-*
tification, moral purity, sanctity

ἁγιασμῷ, dat. sg. m. n. . . . . ἁγιασμός *(38)*

ἁγίασον, 2 pers. sg. aor. act. imper. . . . . ἁγιάζω *(37)*

ἅγιε, voc. sg. m. adj. . . . . ἅγιος *(40)*

ἅγιοι, nom. pl. m. adj. {Rev. 18:20} . . . . .   id.

ἅγιοι, voc. pl. m. adj. {Heb. 3:1} . . . . . . ἅγιος *(40)*

ἁγίοις, dat. pl. m. adj. . . . . id.

ἅγιον, acc. sg. m. adj. {Acts 3:14} . . . . . . id.

(39) ἅγιον, nom. sg. neut. adj. {Acts 10:44} . . . id.

ἅγιον, acc. sg. neut. adj. {Acts 10:47} . . . . id.

(40) **ἅγιος**, α, ον, nom. sg. m. adj. [§7.1] *separate from common condition and use; dedicated,* Luke 2:23; *hallowed;* used of things, τὰ ἅγια, *the sanctuary;* and of persons, *saints,* e.g., members of the first Christian communities; *pure, righteous,* ceremonially or morally; *holy*

(41) **ἁγιότης**, ητος, ἡ [§4.2.c] *holiness, sanctity,* Heb. 12:10

ἁγιότητι, dat. sg. f. n. (2 Cor. 1:12, WH | ἁπλότητι, GNT, MT, TR & NA) . . . ἁγιότης *(41)*

ἁγιότητος, gen. sg. f. n. . . . . id.

ἁγίου, gen. sg. m. adj. {Acts 6:13} . . . . . ἅγιος *(40)*

ἁγίου, gen. sg. neut. adj. {Acts 6:5} . . . . id.

ἁγίους, acc. pl. m. adj. . . . . id.

ἁγίῳ, dat. sg. m. adj. {Matt. 24:15} . . . . id.

ἁγίῳ, dat. sg. neut. adj. {Mark 12:36} . . . id.

ἁγίων, gen. pl. m. adj. {Rev. 5:8} . . . . . . id.

ἁγίων, gen. pl. neut. adj. {Heb. 8:2} . . . . id.

(42) **ἁγιωσύνη**, ης, ἡ [§2.B.a] *sanctification, sanctity, holiness*

ἁγιωσύνῃ, dat. sg. f. n. . . . . ἁγιωσύνη *(42)*

ἁγιωσύνην, acc. sg. f. n. . . . . id.

ἁγιωσύνης, gen. sg. f. n. . . . . id.

ἁγιωτάτῃ, dat. sg. f. superl. adj. [§8.4] . . . ἅγιος *(40)*

ἀγκάλας, acc. pl. f. n. . . . . ἀγκάλη *(43)*

(43) **ἀγκάλη**, ης, ἡ [§2.B.a] *the arm,* Luke 2:28

(44) **ἄγκιστρον**, ου, τό [§3.C.c] *a hook, fish-hook,* Matt. 17:27

ἄγκιστρον, acc. sg. neut. n. . . . . ἄγκιστρον *(44)*

(45) **ἄγκυρα**, ας, ἡ [§2.B.b] *an anchor,* Acts 27:29, 30, 40

ἄγκυραν, acc. sg. f. n. . . . . ἄγκυρα *(45)*

ἀγκύρας, acc. pl. f. n. . . . . id.

ἀγνά, nom. pl. neut. adj. . . . . ἁγνός *(53)*

ἀγνάς, acc. pl. f. adj. . . . . id.

(46) **ἄγναφος**, ον [§7.2] (ἀ + γνάπτω, *to dress*) *unmilled, unshrunken; new,* Matt. 9:16; Mark 2:21

ἀγνάφου, gen. sg. neut. adj. . . . . ἄγναφος *(46)*

(47) **ἁγνεία**, ας, ἡ [§2.B.b; 2.2] *purity, chastity,* 1 Tim. 4:12; 5:2

ἁγνείᾳ, dat. sg. f. n. (1 Tim. 4:12; 5:2, GNT, MT, TR & NA | ἁγνίᾳ, WH) . . . . . ἁγνεία *(47)*

ἁγνή, nom. sg. f. adj. . . . . ἁγνός *(53)*

ἁγνήν, acc. sg. f. adj. . . . . id.

ἁγνίζει, 3 pers. sg. pres. act. indic. . . . . ἁγνίζω *(48)*

(48) **ἁγνίζω**, fut. ἁγνίσω [§26.1] *to purify; to purify morally, reform.* ἁγνίζομαι, perf. ἥγνισμαι, aor. ἡγνίσθην, *to live like one under*

a vow of abstinence, as the Nazirites

ἁγνίσατε, 2 pers. pl. aor. act. imper. . . . . ἁγνίζω *(48)*

ἁγνισθείς, nom. sg. m. aor. pass. part. . . . id.

ἁγνίσθητι, 2 pers. sg. aor. pass. imper. . . . id.

(49) **ἁγνισμός**, οῦ, ὁ [§3.C.a] *purification, abstinence,* Acts 21:26

ἁγνισμοῦ, gen. sg. m. n. . . . . ἁγνισμός *(49)*

ἁγνίσωσιν, 3 pers. pl. aor. act. subj. . . . . ἁγνίζω *(48)*

ἀγνοεῖ, 3 pers. sg. pres. act. indic. . . . . . ἀγνοέω *(50)*

ἀγνοεῖν, pres. act. infin. . . . . id.

ἀγνοεῖται, 3 pers. sg. pres. pass. indic. (1 Cor. 14:38, GNT, WH & NA | ἀνοείτω, MT & TR) . . . . id.

ἀγνοεῖτε, 2 pers. pl. pres. act. indic. . . . . . id.

ἀγνοείτω, 3 pers. sg. pres. act. imper. (1 Cor. 14:38, MT & TR | ἀγνοεῖται, GNT, WH & NA) . . . . id.

(50) **ἀγνοέω**, ῶ, fut. ἀγνοήσω [§16.P] *to be ignorant; not to understand; sin through ignorance*

(51) **ἀγνόημα**, ατος, τό [§4.D.c] *error, sin of ignorance,* Heb. 9:7

ἀγνοημάτων, gen. pl. neut. n. . . . . ἀγνόημα *(51)*

ἀγνοήσαντες, nom. pl. m. aor. act. part. . . . . ἀγνοέω *(50)*

(52) **ἄγνοια**, ας, ἡ [§2.B.b; 2.2] *ignorance*

ἀγνοίᾳ, dat. sg. f. n. . . . . ἄγνοια *(52)*

ἄγνοιαν, acc. sg. f. n. . . . . id.

ἀγνοίας, gen. sg. f. n. . . . . id.

ἀγνόν, acc. sg. m. adj. . . . . ἁγνός *(53)*

(53) **ἁγνός**, ή, όν, nom. sg. m. adj. [§7.F.a] *pure, chaste, modest, innocent, blameless*

ἀγνοοῦμεν, 1 pers. pl. pres. act. indic. . . ἀγνοέω *(50)*

ἀγνοούμενοι, nom. pl. m. pres. pass. part. id.

ἀγνοούμενος, nom. sg. m. pres. pass. part. id.

ἀγνοοῦντες, nom. pl. m. pres. act. part. . . id.

ἀγνοοῦσι(ν), 3 pers. pl. pres. act. indic. {2 Pet. 2:12} . . . . id.

ἀγνοοῦσι(ν), dat. pl. m. pres. act. part. {Heb. 5:2} . . . . id.

(54) **ἁγνότης**, τητος, ἡ [§4.2.c] *purity, life of purity,* 2 Cor. 6:6

ἁγνότητι, dat. sg. f. n. . . . . ἁγνότης *(54)*

ἁγνότητος, gen. sg. f. n. (2 Cor. 11:3, GNT, WH & NA | MT & TR omit) . . . . . . id.

ἁγνούς, acc. pl. m. adj. . . . . ἁγνός *(53)*

ἁγνῶν, nom. sg. m. pres. act. part. . . . ἀγνοέω *(50)*

(55) **ἁγνῶς**, adv., *purely, with sincerity,* Phil. 1:17

(56) **ἀγνωσία**, ας, ἡ [§2.B.b; 2.2] (ἀ + γνῶσις) *ignorance,* 1 Cor. 15:34; 1 Pet. 2:15

ἀγνωσίαν, acc. sg. f. n. . . . . ἀγνωσία *(56)*

(57) **ἄγνωστος**, ον [§7.2] (ἀ + γνωστός) *unknown,* Acts 17:23

ἀγνώστῳ, dat. sg. m. adj. . . . . ἄγνωστος *(57)*

ἀγόμενα, acc. pl. neut. pres. pass. part. . . . ἄγω *(71)*

ἀγομένους, acc. pl. m. pres. pass. part. (Luke 21:12, MT & TR | ἀπαγομένους, GNT, WH & NA) . . . . ἄγω *(71)*

ἀγομένων, gen. pl. m. pres. pass. part. (Matt. 14:6, MT & TR | γενομένοις, GNT, WH & NA) . . . . id.

ἄγονται, 3 pers. pl. pres. pass. indic. . . . . id.

ἄγοντες, nom. pl. m. pres. act. part. . . . . . id.

(58) **ἀγορά**, ᾶς, ἡ [§2.B.b; 2.2] (ἀγείρω, to gather together) *a place of public concourse, forum, market-place; things said in the market, provision*

ἀγορᾷ, dat. sg. f. n. . . . . ἀγορά *(58)*

ἀγοράζει, 3 pers. sg. pres. act. indic. . . ἀγοράζω *(59)*

ἀγοράζοντας, acc. pl. m. pres. act. part. . id.

ἀγοράζοντες, nom. pl. m. pres. act. part. . id.

(59) **ἀγοράζω**, fut. ἀγοράσω [§26.1] perf. pass. ἠγόρασμαι, aor. pass. ἠγοράσθην, *to buy; redeem, acquire* by a ransom or price paid

ἀγοραῖοι, nom. pl. m. adj. (with ἡμέραν understood) . . . . ἀγοραῖος *(60)*

(60) **ἀγοραῖος**, ον [§7.2] *one who visits the forum; a lounger, one who idles away his time in public places, a low fellow,* Acts 17:5; *pertaining to the forum, judicial;* ἀγόραιοι, *court days,* Acts 19:38

ἀγοραῖς, dat. pl. f. n. . . . . ἀγορά *(58)*

ἀγοραίων, gen. pl. m. adj. . . . . ἀγοραῖος *(60)*

ἀγοράν, acc. sg. f. n. . . . . ἀγορά *(58)*

ἀγορᾶς, gen. sg. f. n. . . . . id.

ἀγοράσαι, aor. act. infin. . . . . ἀγοράζω *(59)*

ἀγοράσαντα, acc. sg. m. aor. act. part. . . . id.

ἀγοράσας, nom. sg. m. aor. act. part. . . . id.

ἀγοράσατε, 2 pers. pl. aor. act. imper. . . . id.

ἀγοράσει, 3 pers. sg. aor. act. imper. (Luke 22:36, GNT, WH, TR & NA | ἀγοράσει, MT) . . . . id.

ἀγορασάτω, 3 pers. sg. fut. act. indic. (Luke 22:36, MT | ἀγορασάτω, GNT, WH, TR & NA) . . . . id.

ἀγοράσομεν, 1 pers. pl. fut. act. indic. (John 6:5, MT & TR | ἀγοράσωμεν, GNT, WH & NA) . . . . id.

ἀγόρασον, 2 pers. sg. aor. act. imper. . . . . id.

ἀγοράσωμεν, 1 pers. pl. aor. act. subj. . . . id.

ἀγοράσωσι(ν), 3 pers. pl. aor. act. subj. . . id.

ἄγουσι(ν), 3 pers. pl. pres. act. indic. . . . . ἄγω *(71)*

(61) **ἄγρα**, ας, ἡ [§2.B.b; 2.2] *a catching, thing taken, draught* of fishes, Luke 5:4, 9

ἄγρᾳ, dat. sg. f. n. . . . . ἄγρα *(61)*

ἀγράμματοι, nom. pl. m. adj. . . . . ἀγράμματος *(62)*

(62) **ἀγράμματος**, ον [§7.2] (ἀ + γράμμα) *illiterate, unlearned* Acts 4:13

ἄγραν, acc. sg. f. n. . . . . ἄγρα *(61)*

(63) **ἀγραυλέω**, ῶ, fut. ἀγραυλήσω [§16.P] (ἀγρός

+ αὐλή) *to remain in the open air,* especially *by night,* Luke 2:8

ἀγραυλοῦντες, nom. pl. m. pres. act. part. . . . . ἀγραυλέω *(63)*

ἀγρεύσωσι(ν), 3 pers. pl. aor. act. subj. . . ἀγρεύω *(64)*

(64) **ἀγρεύω**, fut. ἀγρεύσω [§13.M] *to take in hunting, catch,* Mark 12:13

ἄγρια, nom. pl. neut. adj. . . . . ἄγριος *(66)*

(65) **ἀγριέλαιος**, ου, ἡ, nom. sg. f. n. [§3.C.b] (ἄγριος + ἐλαία) *a wild olive-tree, oleaster,* Rom. 11:17, 24

ἀγριελαίου, gen. sg. f. n. . . . . ἀγριέλαιος *(65)*

ἄγριον, nom. sg. neut. adj. {Matt. 3:4} . ἄγριος *(66)*

ἄγριον, acc. sg. neut. adj. {Mark 1:6} . . . . id.

(66) **ἄγριος**, ία, ιον [§7.1] *belonging to the field, wild; fierce, raging*

Ἀγρίππα, gen. sg. m. n. {Acts 25:23} Ἀγρίππας *(67)*

Ἀγρίππα, voc. sg. m. n. {Acts 25:24} . . . . id.

(67) **Ἀγρίππας**, α, ὁ, nom. sg. m. n. [§2.4] *Agrippa,* pr. name

ἀγρόν, acc. sg. m. n. . . . . ἀγρός *(68)*

(68) **ἀγρός**, οῦ, ὁ, nom. sg. m. n. [§3.C.a] *a field,* especially *a cultivated field;* pl. *the country; lands, farms, villages*

ἀγροῦ, gen. sg. m. n. . . . . ἀγρός *(68)*

ἀγρούς, acc. pl. m. n. . . . . id.

ἀγρυπνεῖτε, 2 pers. pl. pres. act. imper. . . . . ἀγρυπνέω *(69)*

(69) **ἀγρυπνέω**, ῶ, fut. ἀγρυπνήσω [§16.P] *to be awake, watch; to be watchful, vigilant*

(70) **ἀγρυπνία**, ας, ἡ [§2.B.b; 2.2] *want of sleep, watching,* 2 Cor. 6:5; 11:27

ἀγρυπνίαις, dat. pl. f. n. . . . . ἀγρυπνία *(70)*

ἀγρυπνοῦντες, nom. pl. m. pres. act. part. . . . . ἀγρυπνέω *(69)*

ἀγρυπνοῦσιν, 3 pers. pl. pres. act. indic. . . id.

ἀγρῷ, dat. sg. m. n. . . . . ἀγρός *(68)*

ἀγρῶν, gen. pl. m. n. (Mark 11:8, GNT, WH & NA | δένδρων, MT & TR) . . . . id.

(71) **ἄγω**, 1 pers. sg. pres. act. indic., fut. ἄξω [§23.1.b] perf. ἦχα and ἀγήοχα [§23.6] 2 aor. ἤγαγον [§13.7.d] fut. pass. ἀχθήσομαι [§23.3.b] aor. pass. ἤχθην [§23.4] perf. pass. ἦγμαι [§23.7] *to lead, bring; lead away, drive off,* as a booty of cattle; *conduct, accompany; lead out, produce; conduct with force, drag, hurry away; guide, incite, entice; convey one's self, go, go away; pass or spend* as *time; celebrate*

(72) **ἀγωγή**, ῆς, ἡ [§2.B.a] *guidance, mode of instruction, discipline, course of life,* 2 Tim. 3:10

ἀγωγῇ, dat. sg. f. n. . . . . ἀγωγή *(72)*

ἄγωμεν, 1 pers. pl. pres. act. subj. . . . . . . ἄγω *(71)*

(73) **ἀγών**, ῶνος, ὁ [§4.2.e] *place of contest, race-*

course, stadium; a contest, strife, conten-
tion; peril, toil
ἀγῶνα, acc. sg. m. n. . . . . ἀγών *(73)*
ἀγῶνι, dat. sg. m. n. . . . . id.
(74) **ἀγωνία, ας, ἡ** [§2.B.b; 2.2] *contest, violent*
struggle; agony, anguish, Luke 22:44
ἀγωνίᾳ, dat. sg. f. n. . . . . ἀγωνία *(74)*
ἀγωνίζεσθε, 2 pers. pl. pres. mid./pass. dep.
imper. . . . . ἀγωνίζομαι *(75)*
(75) **ἀγωνίζομαι,** fut. ἀγωνίσομαι, perf. ἠγώνισμαι
[§26.1] *to be a combatant in the public*
games; to contend, fight, strive earnestly
ἀγωνιζόμεθα, 1 pers. pl. pres. mid./pass. dep.
indic. (1 Tim. 4:10, GNT, WH & NA |
ὀνειδιζόμεθα, MT & TR) . . . . id.
ἀγωνιζόμενος, nom. sg. m. pres. mid./pass.
dep. part. . . . . id.
ἀγωνίζου, 2 pers. sg. pres. mid./pass. dep.
imper. . . . . id.
ἄγωσιν, 3 pers. pl. pres. act. subj. (Mark
13:11, GNT, WH & NA | ἀγάγωσιν, MT
& TR) . . . . ἄγω *(71)*
(76) **Ἀδάμ, ὁ,** *Adam,* pr. name, indecl.
ἀδάπανον, acc. sg. neut. adj. . . . . ἀδάπανος *(77)*
(77) **ἀδάπανος, ον** [§7.2] (ἀ + δαπάνη) *without*
expense, gratuitous, 1 Cor. 9:18
(78) **Ἀδδί, ὁ,** *Addi,* pr. name, indecl. (Luke 3:28,
GNT, MT, TR & NA | ᾽Αδδεί, WH)
ἀδελφαί, nom. pl. f. n. . . . . ἀδελφή *(79)*
ἀδελφάς, acc. pl. f. n. . . . . id.
ἀδελφέ, voc. sg. m. n. . . . . ἀδελφός *(80)*
(79) **ἀδελφή, ῆς, ἡ,** nom. sg. f. n. [§2.B.a] *a sis-*
ter; near kinswoman, or female relative, a
female member of the Christian com-
munity
ἀδελφῇ, dat. sg. f. n. (Philemon 2, GNT, WH
& NA | ἀγαπητῇ, MT & TR) . . . . . ἀδελφή *(79)*
ἀδελφήν, acc. sg. f. n. . . . . id.
ἀδελφῆς, gen. sg. f. n. . . . . id.
ἀδελφοί, nom. pl. m. n. {Acts 28:15} . ἀδελφός *(80)*
ἀδελφοί, voc. pl. m. n. {Acts 28:17} . . . . . id.
ἀδελφοῖς, dat. pl. m. n. . . . . id.
ἀδελφόν, acc. sg. m. n. . . . . id.
(80) **ἀδελφός, οῦ, ὁ,** nom. sg. m. n. [§3.C.a] (ἀ +
δελφύς, *the womb) a brother, near kins-*
man or relative; one of the same nation or
nature; one of equal rank and dignity; an
associate, a member of the Christian com-
munity
(81) **ἀδελφότης, τητος, ἡ** [§4.2.c] *brotherhood, the*
body of the Christian brotherhood, 1 Pet.
2:17; 5:9
ἀδελφότητα, acc. sg. f. n. . . . . ἀδελφότης *(81)*
ἀδελφότητι, dat. sg. f. n. . . . . id.
ἀδελφοῦ, gen. sg. m. n. . . . . ἀδελφός *(80)*

ἀδελφούς, acc. pl. m. n. . . . . ἀδελφός *(80)*
ἀδελφῷ, dat. sg. m. n. . . . . id.
ἀδελφῶν, gen. pl. m. n. . . . . id.
ᾄδη, voc. sg. m. n. (1 Cor. 15:55, TR | Ἅιδη,
MT | θάνατε, GNT, WH & NA) . . . . ᾄδης *(86)*
ᾄδη, dat. sg. m. n. (Luke 16:23, GNT, WH,
TR & NA | Ἅιδη, MT) . . . . id.
ἄδηλα, nom. pl. neut. adj. . . . . ἄδηλος *(82)*
ἄδηλον, acc. sg. f. adj. . . . . id.
(82) **ἄδηλος, ον** [§7.2] (ἀ + δῆλος) *not apparent*
or obvious; uncertain, not distinct, Luke
11:44; 1 Cor. 14:8
(83) **ἀδηλότης, τητος, ἡ** [§4.2.c] *uncertainty, in-*
constancy, 1 Tim. 6:17
ἀδηλότητι, dat. sg. f. n. . . . . ἀδηλότης *(83)*
(84) **ἀδήλως,** adv., *not manifestly, uncertainly,*
dubiously, 1 Cor. 9:26
ἀδημονεῖν, pres. act. infin. . . . . ἀδημονέω *(85)*
(85) **ἀδημονέω, ῶ,** fut. ἀδημονήσω [§16.P] *to be*
depressed or dejected, full of anguish or
sorrow
ἀδημονῶν, nom. sg. m. pres. act.
part. . . . . ἀδημονέω *(85)*
ᾄδην, acc. sg. m. n. (Acts 2:27, 31, GNT, WH
& NA | Ἅιδου, MT | ᾄδου, TR) . . . . ᾄδης *(86)*
(86) **ᾄδης, ου, ὁ,** nom. sg. m. n. [§2.B.c] *the in-*
visible abode or mansion of the dead; the
place of punishment, hell; the lowest place
or condition, Matt. 11:23; Luke 10:15
(87) **ἀδιάκριτος, ον,** nom. sg. f. adj. [§7.2] (ἀ +
διακρίνω) *undistinguishing, impartial,*
James 3:17
ἀδιάλειπτον, acc. sg. f. adj. . . . . . . ἀδιάλειπτος *(88)*
(88) **ἀδιάλειπτος, ον,** nom. sg. f. adj. [§7.2] (ἀ +
διαλείπω) *unceasing, constant, settled,*
Rom. 9:2; 2 Tim. 1:3
(89) **ἀδιαλείπτως,** adv., *unceasingly, by an unvary-*
ing practice
(90) **ἀδιαφθορία, ας, ἡ** [§2.B.b; 2.2] (ἀ +
διαφθορά) *incorruptness, genuineness,*
pureness
ἀδιαφθορίαν, acc. sg. f. n. (Tit. 2:7, MT &
TR | ἀφθορίαν, GNT, WH &
NA) . . . . ἀδιαφθορία *(90)*
ἀδικεῖσθε, 2 pers. pl. pres. pass. indic. . . ἀδικέω *(91)*
ἀδικεῖτε, 2 pers. pl. pres. act. indic. . . . . . id.
(91) **ἀδικέω, ῶ,** fut. ἀδικήσω, perf. ἀδίκηκα
[§16.P] *to act unjustly; wrong; injure; vi-*
olate a law
ἀδικηθέντος, gen. sg. m. aor. pass. part. ἀδικέω *(91)*
ἀδικηθῇ, 3 pers. sg. aor. pass. subj. . . . . . id.
(92) **ἀδίκημα, ατος, τό,** nom. sg. neut. n. [§4.D.c]
an act of injustice, crime {Acts 18:14}
ἀδίκημα, acc. sg. neut. n. {Acts 24:20} ἀδίκημα *(92)*
ἀδικήματα, acc. pl. neut. n. . . . . id.

ἀδικῆσαι, aor. act. infin. . . . . ἀδικέω (91)
ἀδικήσαντος, gen. sg. m. aor. act. part. . . . id.
ἀδικησάτω, 3 pers. sg. aor. act. imper. . . . . id.
ἀδικήσει, 3 pers. sg. fut. act. indic. (Luke
    10:19, WH & TRb | ἀδικήσῃ, GNT, MT,
    NA & TRs) . . . . id.
ἀδικήσῃ, 3 pers. sg. aor. act. subj. (Luke
    10:19, GNT, MT, NA & TRs | ἀδικήσει,
    WH & TRb) . . . . id.
ἀδικήσῃς, 2 pers. sg. aor. act. subj. . . . . . id.
ἀδικήσητε, 2 pers. pl. aor. act. subj. . . . . . id.
ἀδικήσουσιν, 3 pers. pl. fut. act. indic. (Rev.
    9:4, GNT, WH & NA | ἀδικήσωσι(ν),
    MT & TR) . . . . id.
ἀδικήσωσι(ν), 3 pers. pl. aor. act. subj. (Rev.
    9:4, MT & TR | ἀδικήσουσιν, GNT, WH
    & NA) . . . . id.
(93) **ἀδικία,** ας, ἡ, nom. sg. f. n. [§2.B.b; 2.2] *in-*
    justice, wrong; iniquity, falsehood, deceit-
    fulness
ἀδικίᾳ, dat. sg. f. n. . . . . ἀδικία (93)
ἀδικίαις, dat. pl. f. n. . . . . id.
ἀδικίαν, acc. sg. f. n. . . . . id.
ἀδικίας, gen. sg. f. n. . . . . id.
ἄδικοι, nom. pl. m. adj. . . . . ἄδικος (94)
(94) **ἄδικος,** ον, nom. sg. m. adj. [§7.2] (ἀ + δίκη)
    unjust, unrighteous, iniquitous, vicious; de-
    ceitful, fallacious
ἀδικούμενοι, nom. pl. m. pres. pass. part.
    (2 Pet. 2:13, GNT, WH & NA | κομι-
    ούμενοι, MT & TR) . . . . ἀδικέω (91)
ἀδικούμενον, acc. sg. m. pres. pass. part. . id.
ἀδίκους, acc. pl. m. adj. . . . . ἄδικος (94)
ἀδικοῦσι(ν), 3 pers. pl. pres. act. indic. . . ἀδικέω (91)
ἀδίκῳ, dat. sg. m. adj. . . . . ἄδικος (94)
ἀδικῶ, 1 pers. sg. pres. act. indic. . . . . . . ἀδικέω (91)
ἀδίκων, gen. pl. m. adj. {Acts 24:15} . . . ἄδικος (94)
ἀδικῶν, nom. sg. m. pres. act. part.
    {Acts 7:27} . . . . ἀδικέω (91)
(95) **ἀδίκως,** adv., *unjustly, undeservedly,* 1 Pet.
    2:19
(‡689) **Ἀδμίν,** ὁ, *Admin,* pr. name indecl. (Luke 3:33,
    GNT & NA | Ἀράμ, MT & TR |
    Ἀδμείν, WH)
ἀδόκιμοι, nom. pl. m. adj. . . . . ἀδόκιμος (96)
ἀδόκιμον, acc. sg. m. adj. . . . . id.
(96) **ἀδόκιμος,** ον, nom. sg. m. adj. [§7.2] (ἀ +
    δόκιμος) *unable to stand test, rejected, re-*
    fuse, worthless
ἄδολον, acc. sg. neut. adj. . . . . ἄδολος (97)
(97) **ἄδολος,** ον [§7.2] (ἀ + δόλος) *without de-*
    ceit, sincere, 1 Pet. 2:2
ᾄδοντες, nom. pl. m. pres. act. part. . . . . . ᾄδω (103)
ᾅδου, gen. sg. m. n. . . . . ᾅδης (86)
ᾄδουσι(ν), 3 pers. pl. pres. act. indic. . . . . ᾄδω (103)

(98) **Ἀδραμυττηνός,** ή, όν [§7.F.a] *of Adramyttium,*
    a Greek city on the coast of Aeolia, in Asia
    Minor
Ἀδραμυττηνῷ, dat. sg. neut. adj. (Acts 27:2,
    GNT, MT, TR & NA | Ἀδραμυντηνῷ,
    WH) . . . . Ἀδραμυττηνός (98)
Ἀδρίᾳ, dat. sg. m. n. (Acts 27:27, GNT, MT,
    TR & NA | Ἀδρίᾳ, WH) . . . . Ἀδρίας (99)
(99) **Ἀδρίας,** ου, ὁ [§2.B.d] *the Adriatic sea*
(100) **ἁδρότης,** τητος, ἡ [§4.2.c] (ἁδρός, *mature,*
    full) abundance, 2 Cor. 8:20
ἁδρότητι, dat. sg. f. n. . . . . ἁδρότης (100)
ἀδύνατα, nom. pl. neut. adj. . . . . ἀδύνατος (102)
(101) **ἀδυνατέω,** ῶ, fut. ἀδυνατήσω [§16.P] *not to*
    be able; to be impossible
ἀδυνατήσει, 3 pers. sg. fut. act.
    indic. . . . . ἀδυνατέω (101)
ἀδύνατον, nom. sg. neut. adj. . . . . . . ἀδύνατος (102)
(102) **ἀδύνατος,** ον, nom. sg. m. adj. [§7.2] (ἀ +
    δύναμαι) *impotent, weak; impossible*
ἀδυνάτων, gen. pl. m. adj. . . . . ἀδύνατος (102)
(103) **ᾄδω** (contr. from ἀείδω) fut. ᾄσω, and
    ᾄσομαι [§23.1.c] *to sing*
(104) **ἀεί,** adv., *always, for ever, aye*
ἀέρα, acc. sg. m. n. . . . . ἀήρ (109)
ἀέρος, gen. sg. m. n. [§4.2.f] . . . . id.
ἀετοί, nom. pl. m. n. . . . . ἀετός (105)
(105) **ἀετός,** οῦ, ὁ [§3.C.a] *an eagle*
ἀετοῦ, gen. sg. m. n. . . . . ἀετός (105)
ἀετῷ, dat. sg. m. n. . . . . id.
ἄζυμα, nom. pl. neut. adj. . . . . ἄζυμος (106)
ἄζυμοι, nom. pl. m. adj. . . . . ἄζυμος (106)
ἀζύμοις, dat. pl. neut. adj. . . . . id.
(106) **ἄζυμος,** ον [§7.2] (ἀ + ζύμη) *unleavened;* τὰ
    ἄζυμα, *the feast of unleavened bread;* met.
    pure from foreign matter, unadulterated,
    genuine; τὸ ἄζυμον, *genuineness,* 1 Cor.
    5:7, 8
ἀζύμων, gen. pl. neut. adj. . . . . ἄζυμος (106)
(107) **Ἀζώρ,** ὁ, *Azor,* pr. name indecl.
Ἄζωτον, acc. sg. f. n. . . . . Ἄζωτος (108)
(108) **Ἄζωτος,** ου, ἡ [§3.C.b] *Azotus, Ashdod,* a
    seaport in Palestine, Acts 8:40
(109) **ἀήρ,** ἀέρος, ὁ, nom. sg. m. n. [§4.2.f] *air, at-*
    mosphere
ἀθά, Aramaic with μαράν (1 Cor. 16:22,
    WH & TR | Μαρανα θα, GNT, MT &
    NA) . . . . μαρὰν ἀθά (3134)
(110) **ἀθανασία,** ας, ἡ [§2.B.b; 2.2] (ἀ + θάνατος)
    immortality, 1 Cor. 15:53, 54; 1 Tim. 6:16
ἀθανασίαν, acc. sg. f. n. . . . . ἀθανασία (110)
ἀθεμίτοις, dat. pl. f. adj. . . . . ἀθέμιτος (111)
ἀθέμιτον, nom. sg. neut. adj. . . . . id.
(111) **ἀθέμιτος,** ον [§7.2] (ἀ + θεμιτός, *lawful)*
    unlawful, criminal, wicked, Acts 10:28;

1 Pet. 4:3

ἄθεοι, nom. pl. m. adj. . . . . ἄθεος *(112)*

(112) **ἄθεος, ον** [§7.2] (ἀ + θεός) *an atheist; godless, estranged from the knowledge and worship of the true God,* Eph. 2:12

(113) **ἄθεσμος, ον** [§7.2] (ἀ + θεσμός, *law*) *lawless, unrestrained, licentious,* 2 Pet. 2:7; 3:17

ἀθέσμων, gen. pl. m. adj. . . . . ἄθεσμος *(113)*

ἀθετεῖ, 3 pers. sg. pres. act. indic. . . . . . ἀθετέω *(114)*

ἀθετεῖτε, 2 pers. pl. pres. act. indic. . . . . . id.

(114) **ἀθετέω, ῶ,** fut. ἀθετήσω [§16.P] (ἀ + τίθημι) pr. *to displace, set aside; to abrogate, annul, violate, swerve from; reject, condemn*

ἀθετῆσαι, aor. act. infin. . . . . ἀθετέω *(114)*

ἀθετήσας, nom. sg. m. aor. act. part. . . . . id.

ἀθέτησιν, acc. sg. f. n. . . . . ἀθέτησις *(115)*

(115) **ἀθέτησις, εως, ἡ,** nom. sg. f. n. [§5.E] *abrogation, annulling,* Heb. 7:18; 9:26

ἀθετήσω, 1 pers. sg. fut. act. indic. . . . . ἀθετέω *(114)*

ἀθετοῦσι(ν), 3 pers. pl. pres. act. indic. . . . id.

ἀθετῶ, 1 pers. sg. pres. act. indic. contr. . . id.

ἀθετῶν, nom. sg. m. pres. act. part. . . . . . id.

(116) **Ἀθῆναι, ῶν, αἱ** [§2.B.a] *Athens,* one of the most important cities of Greece, called from Ἀθήνη, *Minerva,* to whom it was dedicated

Ἀθηναῖοι, nom. pl. m. adj.
{Acts 17:21} . . . . Ἀθηναῖος *(117)*

Ἀθηναῖοι, voc. pl. m. adj. {Acts 17:22} . . . id.

(117) **Ἀθηναῖος, αία, αῖον** [§7.1] *Athenian, inhabiting or belonging to Athens*

Ἀθήναις, dat. pl. f. n. . . . . Ἀθῆναι *(116)*

Ἀθηνῶν, gen. pl. f. n. . . . . id.

(118) **ἀθλέω, ῶ,** fut. ἀθλήσω, perf. ἤθληκα [§16.P] (ἆεθλος, *strife, contest*) *to strive, contend, be a champion in the public games,* 2 Tim. 2:5(2×)

ἀθλῇ, 3 pers. sg. pres. act. subj. . . . . ἀθλέω *(118)*

ἀθλήσῃ, 3 pers. sg. aor. act. subj. . . . . id.

ἄθλησιν, acc. sg. f. n. . . . . ἄθλησις *(119)*

(119) **ἄθλησις, εως, ἡ** [§5.E.c] *contest, combat, struggle, conflict,* Heb. 10:32

(‡4867) **ἀθροίζω,** fut. ἀθροίσω, perf. ἤθροικα [§26.1] (ἀθρόος, *collected, crowded*) *to collect in a body*

(120) **ἀθυμέω, ῶ,** fut. ἀθυμήσω [§16.P] (ἀ + θυμός) *to despond, be disheartened,* Col. 3:21

ἀθυμῶσιν, 3 pers. pl. pres. act. subj. . . ἀθυμέω *(120)*

ἀθῷον, acc. sg. neut. adj. (Matt. 27:4, GNT & NA | ἀθῶον, MT & TR | δίκαιον, WH) . . . . ἀθῷος *(†121)*

(†121) **ἀθῷος, ον,** nom. sg. m. adj. [§7.2] (ἀ + θωή, *a penalty*) *unpunished;* metaph. *innocent* (Matt. 27:24, GNT, WH & NA | ἀθῶος,

MT & TR)

αἱ, nom. pl. f. article {Mark 15:41b} . . . . . ὁ *(3588)*

αἵ, nom. pl. f. relative pronoun [§10.J.g] {Mark 15:41a} . . . . ὅς *(3739)*

αἵ τε, nom. pl. f. article before enclitic {Rom. 1:26} . . . . ὁ *(3588)*

αἰγείοις, dat. pl. neut. adj. (Heb. 11:37, GNT, MT, TR & NA | αἰγίοις, WH) . . . . αἴγειος *(122)*

(122) **αἴγειος, εία, ειον** [§7.1] (αἴξ, γός, *a goat*) *belonging to a goat,* Heb. 11:37

αἰγιαλόν, acc. sg. m. n. . . . . αἰγιαλός *(123)*

(123) **αἰγιαλός, οῦ, ὁ** [§3.C.a] *seashore*

Αἰγύπτιοι, nom. pl. m. adj. . . . . Αἰγύπτιος *(124)*

Αἰγύπτιον, acc. sg. m. adj. . . . . id.

(124) **Αἰγύπτιος, α, ον,** nom. sg. m. adj. *Egyptian*

Αἰγυπτίων, gen. pl. m. adj. . . . . Αἰγύπτιος *(124)*

Αἴγυπτον, acc. sg. f. n. . . . . Αἴγυπτος *(125)*

(125) **Αἴγυπτος, ου, ἡ,** nom. sg. f. n. [§3.C.b] *Egypt*

Αἰγύπτου, gen. sg. f. n. . . . . Αἴγυπτος *(125)*

Αἰγύπτῳ, dat. sg. f. n. . . . . id.

Ἅιδῃ, voc. sg. m. n. (1 Cor. 15:55, MT | ᾅδη, TR | θάνατε, GNT, WH & NA) . . . Ἅιδης *(‡86)*

Ἅιδῃ, dat. sg. m. n. (Luke 16:23, MT | ᾅδη, GNT, WH, TR & NA) . . . . id.

(‡86) **Ἅιδης, nom. sg. m. n.** [§2.B.c] *the invisible abode or mansion of the dead; the place of punishment, hell; the lowest place or condition* (Rev. 6:8; 20:13, 14, MT | ᾅδης, GNT, WH, TR & NA)

ἀϊδίοις, dat. pl. m. adj. . . . . ἀΐδιος *(126)*

(126) **ἀΐδιος, ον,** nom. sg. m. adj. [§7.2] (ἀεί) *always existing, eternal,* Rom. 1:20; Jude 6

Ἅιδου, acc. sg. m. n. (Matt. 11:23; 16:18; Luke 10:15; Rev. 1:18, MT | ᾅδου, GNT, WH, TR & NA) . . . . Ἅιδης *(‡86)*

αἰδοῦς, gen. sg. f. n. . . . . αἰδώς *(127)*

(127) **αἰδώς, οῦς, ἡ** [§5.E.h] *modesty, reverence,* 1 Tim. 2:9; Heb. 12:28

Αἰθιόπων, gen. pl. m. n. . . . . Αἰθίοψ *(128)*

(128) **Αἰθίοψ, οπος, ὁ,** nom. sg. m. n. [§4.2.a] *an Ethiopian*

(129) **αἷμα, ατος, τό,** nom. sg. neut. n. [§4.D.c] *blood; of the color of blood; bloodshed; blood-guiltiness; natural descent* {John 6:55}

αἷμα, acc. sg. neut. n. {John 6:54} . . . . . . αἷμα *(129)*

αἵματα, nom. pl. neut. n. (Rev. 18:24, MT | αἷμα, GNT, WH, TR & NA) . . . . . . id.

(130) **αἱματεκχυσία, ας, ἡ** [§2.B.b; 2.2] (αἷμα + ἔκχυσις, from ἐκχέω) *an effusion or shedding of blood,* Heb. 9:22

αἱματεκχυσίας, gen. sg. f. n. . . . αἱματεκχυσία *(130)*

αἵματι, dat. sg. neut. n. . . . . αἷμα *(129)*

αἵματος, gen. sg. neut. n. . . . . id.

αἱμάτων, gen. pl. neut. n. . . . . id.

(131) **αἱμορροέω**, ῶ, fut. αἱμορροήσω [§16.P] (αἷμα
+ ῥόος, from ῥέω) *to have a flux of blood,*
Matt. 9:20

αἱμορροοῦσα, nom. sg. f. pres. act.
part. . . . . αἱμορροέω *(131)*

Αἰνέα, voc. sg. m. n. . . . . Αἰνέας *(132)*

Αἰνέαν, acc. sg. m. n. . . . . id.

(132) **Αἰνέας**, ου, ὁ [§2.B.d] *Aeneas*, pr. name

αἰνεῖν, pres. act. infin. . . . . αἰνέω *(134)*

αἰνεῖτε, 2 pers. pl. pres. act. imper. . . . . . . id.

αἰνέσεως, gen. sg. f. n. . . . . αἴνεσις *(133)*

(133) **αἴνεσις**, εως, ἡ [§5.E.c] *praise*, Heb. 13:15

(134) **αἰνέω**, ῶ, fut. αἰνέσω [§22.1] *to praise, celebrate*

(135) **αἴνιγμα**, ατος, τό (αἰνίσσω, *to intimate obscurely*) *an enigma, any thing obscurely expressed or intimated,* 1 Cor. 13:12

αἰνίγματι, dat. sg. neut. n. . . . . αἴνιγμα *(135)*

αἶνον, acc. sg. m. . . . . αἶνος *(136)*

(136) **αἶνος**, ου, ὁ [§3.C.a] *praise*, Matt. 21:16; Luke
18:43

αἰνοῦντα, acc. sg. m. pres. act. part. . . . . αἰνέω *(134)*

αἰνοῦντες, nom. pl. m. pres. act. part. . . . id.

αἰνούντων, gen. pl. m. pres. act. part. . . . id.

αἰνῶν, nom. sg. m. pres. act. part. {Acts 3:8} id.

(137) **Αἰνών**, ἡ, *Enon*, pr. name, indecl. {John 3:23}

αἶρε, 2 pers. sg. pres. act. imper. . . . . αἴρω *(142)*

αἴρει, 3 pers. sg. pres. act. indic. . . . . id.

αἴρεις, 2 pers. sg. pres. act. indic. . . . . id.

(138) **αἱρέομαι**, 1 pers. sg. pres. mid. indic. . . αἱρέω *(‡138)*

αἱρέσεις, nom. pl. f. n. {Gal. 5:20} . . . αἵρεσις *(139)*

αἱρέσεις, acc. pl. f. n. {2 Pet. 2:1} . . . . id.

αἱρέσεως, gen. sg. f. n. . . . . id.

αἵρεσιν, acc. sg. f. n. . . . . id.

(139) **αἵρεσις**, εως, ἡ, nom. sg. f. n. [§5.E.c] strictly,
a choice or option; hence, *a sect, faction;*
by impl. *discord, contention*

αἴρεται, 3 pers. sg. pres. pass. indic. . . . . . αἴρω *(142)*

αἴρετε, 2 pers. pl. pres. act. imper. . . . . . . id.

(140) **αἱρετίζω**, fut. αἱρετίσω [§26.1] aor. ἡρέτισα
[§13.2] *to choose, choose with delight or
love,* Matt. 12:18

αἱρετικόν, acc. sg. m. adj. . . . . αἱρετικός *(141)*

(141) **αἱρετικός**, ή, όν [§3.C.a] subst. adj., *one who
creates or fosters factions,* Tit. 3:10

(‡138) **αἱρέω**, ῶ, fut. αἱρήσω, perf. ᾕρηκα, perf.
pass. ᾕρημαι, mid. αἱρέομαι, οῦμαι, 2 aor.
εἱλόμην [§36.1] *to take;* mid. *to choose*

αἱρήσομαι, 1 pers. sg. fut. mid. indic. . . αἱρέω *(‡138)*

αἱρόμενον, acc. sg. m. pres. pass. part. . . αἴρω *(142)*

αἴροντος, gen. sg. m. pres. act. part. . . . . . id.

(142) **αἴρω**, fut. ἀρῶ [§27.1.c] aor., ἦρα, *to take up,
lift, raise; bear, carry; take away, remove;
destroy, kill*

αἴρων, nom. sg. m. pres. act. part. . . . . . . αἴρω *(142)*

αἴρωσιν, 3 pers. pl. pres. act. subj. . . . . . . αἴρω *(142)*

αἷς, dat. pl. f. relative pron. [§10.J.g] . . . . ὅς *(3739)*

(143) **αἰσθάνομαι**, fut. αἰσθήσομαι, 2 aor., ᾐσθόμην
[§36.2] *to perceive, understand,* Luke 9:45

αἰσθήσει, dat. sg. f. n. . . . . αἴσθησις *(144)*

(144) **αἴσθησις**, εως, ἡ [§5.E.c] *perception, understanding,* Phil. 1:9

αἰσθητήρια, acc. pl. neut. n. . . . . . αἰσθητήριον *(145)*

(145) **αἰσθητήριον**, ου, τό [§3.C.c] *an organ of perception; internal sense,* Heb. 5:14

αἴσθωνται, 3 pers. pl. 2 aor. mid. dep.
subj. . . . . αἰσθάνομαι *(143)*

αἰσχροκερδεῖς, acc. pl. m. adj. . αἰσχροκερδής *(146)*

αἰσχροκερδῆ, acc. sg. m. adj. . . . . id.

(146) **αἰσχροκερδής**, ές [§7.G.b] (αἰσχρός +
κέρδος) *eager for dishonorable gain, sor-
did,* 1 Tim. 3:3, 8; Tit. 1:7

(147) **αἰσχροκερδῶς**, adv., *for the sake of base gain,
sordidly,* 1 Pet. 5:2

(148) **αἰσχρολογία**, ας, ἡ [§2.B.b; 2.2] (αἰσχρός +
λόγος) *vile or obscene language, foul talk,*
Col. 3:8

αἰσχρολογίαν, acc. sg. f. n. . . . . . . αἰσχρολογία *(148)*

(149) **αἰσχρόν**, nom. sg. neut. adj. . . . . αἰσχρός *(150)*

(150) **αἰσχρός**, ά, όν [§7.1] strictly, *deformed,* opposed to καλός; metaph. *indecorous, in-
decent, dishonorable, vile*

(151) **αἰσχρότης**, τητος, ἡ, nom. sg. f. n. [§4.2.c]
indecorum, indecency, Eph. 5:4

αἰσχροῦ, gen. sg. neut. . . . . αἰσχρός *(150)*

αἰσχύνας, acc. pl. f. n. . . . . αἰσχύνη *(152)*

αἰσχυνέσθω, 3 pers. sg. pres. pass.
imper. αἰσχύνομαι *(153)*

(152) **αἰσχύνη**, ης, ἡ, nom. sg. f. n. [§2.B.a] *shame,
disgrace; cause of shame, dishonorable
conduct*

αἰσχύνῃ, dat. sg. f. n. . . . . αἰσχύνη *(152)*

αἰσχύνης, gen. sg. f. n. . . . . id.

αἰσχυνθήσομαι, 1 pers. sg. fut. pass. indic.
[§27.3] . . . . αἰσχύνομαι *(153)*

αἰσχυνθῶμεν, 1 pers. pl. aor. pass. subj. . . id.

(153) **αἰσχύνομαι**, 1 pers. sg. pres. mid./pass. indic.,
fut. αἰσχυνοῦμαι and αἰσχυνθήσομαι
[§27.6] *to be ashamed, confounded*

αἰτεῖν, pres. act. infin. . . . . αἰτέω *(154)*

αἰτεῖς, 2 pers. sg. pres. act. indic. . . . . id.

αἰτεῖσθαι, pres. mid. infin. [§17.Q] . . . . . . id.

αἰτεῖσθε, 2 pers. pl. pres. mid. indic. . . . . . id.

αἰτεῖτε, 2 pers. pl. pres. act. indic.
{James 4:3} . . . . id.

αἰτεῖτε, 2 pers. pl. pres. act. imper.
{Matt. 7:7} . . . . id.

αἰτείτω, 3 pers. sg. pres. act. imper. . . . . . id.

(154) **αἰτέω**, ῶ, fut. αἰτήσω, aor. ᾔτησα [§16.P] *to
ask, request; demand; desire,* Acts 7:46

(155) **αἴτημα**, ατος, τό, nom. sg. neut. n. [§4.D.c]
    a thing asked or sought for; petition, re-
    quest, Luke 23:24; 1 John 5:15
αἰτήματα, nom. pl. neut. n. {Phil. 4:6} . αἴτημα (155)
αἰτήματα, acc. pl. neut. n. {1 John 5:15} . id.
αἰτῆσαι, aor. act. infin. . . . . αἰτέω (154)
αἰτήσας, nom. sg. m. aor. act. part. . . . . . . id.
αἰτήσασθε, 2 pers. pl. aor. mid. imper. (John
    15:7, GNT, WH & NA | αἰτήσεσθε, MT
    & TR) . . . . id.
αἰτήσει, 3 pers. sg. fut. act. indic. . . . . id.
αἰτήσεσθε, 2 pers. pl. fut. mid. indic. . . . . . id.
αἰτήσῃ, 3 pers. sg. aor. act. subj. (Matt.
    7:9, 10; Luke 11:12, MT & TR | αἰτήσει,
    GNT, WH & NA) . . . . id.
αἰτήσῃ, 2 pers. sg. aor. mid. subj.
    {John 11:22} . . . . id.
αἰτήσῃς, 2 pers. sg. aor. act. subj. . . . . id.
αἰτήσηται, 3 pers. sg. aor. mid. subj. . . . . id.
αἰτήσητε, 2 pers. pl. aor. act. subj. . . . . . . id.
αἰτήσομαι, 2 pers. sg. fut. mid. indic. (Mark
    6:24, MT & TR | αἰτήσωμαι, GNT, WH
    & NA) . . . . id.
αἴτησον, 2 pers. sg. aor. act. imper. . . . . . id.
αἰτήσουσιν, 3 pers. pl. fut. act. indic. . . . . id.
αἰτήσωμαι, 1 pers. sg. aor. mid. subj. (Mark
    6:24, GNT, WH & NA | αἰτήσομαι, MT
    & TR) . . . . id.
αἰτήσωμεν, 1 pers. pl. aor. act. subj. . . . . . id.
αἰτήσωνται, 3 pers. pl. aor. mid. subj. . . . id.
(156) **αἰτία**, ας, ἡ, nom. sg. f. n. [§2.B.b; 2.2] *cause,*
    motive, incitement; accusation, crime, case
(157) **αἰτίαμα**, ατος, τό [§4.D.c] *charge, accusation*
αἰτιάματα, acc. pl. neut. n. (Acts 25:7, TR |
    αἰτιώματα, GNT, WH, MT & NA) αἰτίαμα (157)
αἰτίαν, acc. sg. f. n. . . . . αἰτία (156)
αἰτίας, gen. sg. f. n. {Mark 15:26} . . . . . . id.
αἰτίας, acc. pl. f. n. {Acts 15:27} . . . . id.
αἴτινες, nom. pl. f. rel. pron. [§10.J.h] . . ὅστις (3748)
(158) **αἴτιον**, acc. sg. neut. adj. . . . . αἴτιος (159)
(159) **αἴτιος**, α, ον, nom. sg. m. adj. [§7.2]
    causative; αἴτιος, *an author or causer,*
    Heb. 5:9; τὸ αἴτιον, equivalent to αἰτία
αἰτίου, gen. sg. neut. adj. . . . . αἴτιος (159)
(‡157) **αἰτίωμα**, ατος, τό [§4.D.c] *charge, accusation*
αἰτιώματα, acc. pl. neut. n. (Acts 25:7, GNT,
    WH, MT & NA | αἰτιάματα, TR) αἰτίωμα (‡157)
αἰτοῦμαι, 1 pers. sg. pres. mid. indic. . . . αἰτέω (154)
αἰτούμεθα, 1 pers. pl. pres. mid. indic. . . . id.
αἰτούμενοι, nom. pl. m. pres. mid. part. . . id.
αἰτοῦντι, dat. sg. m. pres. act. part. . . . . . id.
αἰτοῦσα, nom. sg. f. pres. act. part. . . . . . id.
αἰτοῦσι(ν), 3 pers. pl. pres. act. indic.
    {1 Cor. 1:22} . . . . id.
αἰτοῦσιν, dat. pl. m. pres. act. part.

{Matt. 7:11} . . . . αἰτέω (154)
αἰτώμεθα, 1 pers. pl. pres. mid. subj. . . . . id.
αἰτῶμεν, 1 pers. pl. pres. act. subj. . . . . . . id.
αἰτῶν, 1 pers. sg. m. pres. act. part. . . . . . id.
(160) **αἰφνίδιος**, ον, nom. sg. m. adj. [§7.2] *unfore-*
    seen, unexpected, sudden, Luke 21:34
    {1 Thess. 5:3}
αἰφνίδιος, nom. sg. f. adj. {Luke 21:34} αἰφνίδιος (160)
αἰχμαλωσίαν, acc. sg. f. n. . . . . αἰχμαλωσία (161)
(161) **αἰχμαλωσία**, ας, ἡ [§2.B.b; 2.2] *captivity, state*
    of captivity; captive multitude, Eph. 4:8;
    Rev. 13:10(2×)
αἰχμαλωτεύοντες, nom. pl. m. pres. act. part.
    (2 Tim. 3:6, MT & TR | αἰχμαλωτί-
    ζοντες, GNT, WH & NA) . . . αἰχμαλωτεύω (162)
(162) **αἰχμαλωτεύω**, fut. αἰχμαλωτεύσω [§13.M] *to*
    lead captive; met. *to captivate,* Eph. 4:8;
    2 Tim. 3:6
αἰχμαλωτίζοντα, acc. sg. m. pres. act.
    part. . . . . αἰχμαλωτίζω (163)
αἰχμαλωτίζοντες, nom. pl. m. pres. act. part. id.
(163) **αἰχμαλωτίζω**, fut. αἰχμαλωτίσω [§26.1] *to*
    lead captive; by impl. *to subject,* Luke
    21:24; Rom. 7:23; 2 Cor. 10:5
αἰχμαλωτισθήσονται, 3 pers. pl. fut. pass.
    indic. . . . . αἰχμαλωτίζω (163)
αἰμαλώτοις, dat. pl. m. n. . . . . . . αἰχμάλωτος (†164)
(†164) **αἰχμάλωτος**, ου, ὁ [§3.C.a] (αἰχμή, *a spear,* and
    ἁλίσκομαι, *to capture*) *a captive,* Luke 4:18
(165) **αἰών**, ῶνος, ὁ [§4.2.e] pr. *a period of time of*
    significant character; life; an era; an age:
    hence, *a state of things marking an age or*
    era; the present order of nature; the nat-
    ural condition of man, the world; ὁ αἰών,
    illimitable duration, eternity; as also, οἱ
    αἰῶνες, ὁ αἰὼν τῶν αἰώνων, οἱ αἰῶνες
    τῶν αἰώνων; by an Aramaism οἱ αἰῶνες,
    the material universe, Heb. 1:2
αἰῶνα, acc. sg. m. n. . . . . id.
αἰῶνας, acc. pl. m. n. . . . . id.
αἰῶνι, dat. sg. m. n. . . . . id.
αἰώνια, nom. pl. neut. adj. . . . . αἰώνιος (166)
αἰωνίαν, acc. sg. f. adj. [§7.2] . . . . id.
αἰωνίοις, dat. pl. m. adj. . . . . id.
αἰώνιον, acc. sg. m. adj. {2 Thess. 1:9} . . id.
αἰώνιον, acc. sg. f. adj. {2 Cor. 5:1} . . . . id.
αἰώνιον, nom. sg. neut. adj. {1 Tim. 6:16} id.
αἰώνιον, acc. sg. neut. adj. {2 Cor. 4:17} . id.
(166) **αἰώνιος**, ον [§7.2] *indeterminate as to dura-*
    tion, eternal, everlasting
αἰώνιος, nom. sg. f. adj. . . . . αἰώνιος (166)
αἰωνίου, gen. sg. m. adj. {Rom. 16:26} . . . id.
αἰωνίου, gen. sg. f. adj. {Heb. 9:15} . . . . . id.
αἰωνίου, gen. sg. neut. adj. {Heb. 9:14} . . id.
αἰωνίους, acc. pl. f. adj. . . . . id.

αἰωνίων, gen. pl. m. adj. . . . . αἰώνιος *(166)*

αἰῶνος, gen. sg. m. n. . . , ... αἰών *(165)*

αἰώνων, gen. pl. m. n. . . . . id.

αἰῶσι(ν), dat. pl. m. n. . . . . id.

(167) **ἀκαθαρσία,** ας, ἡ, nom. sg. f. n. [§2.B.b; 2.2] (ἀ + καθαίρω) *uncleanness; lewdness; impurity* of motive, 1 Thess. 2:3

ἀκαθαρσίᾳ, dat. sg. f. n. . . . . ἀκαθαρσία *(167)*

ἀκαθαρσίαν, acc. sg. f. n. . . . . id.

ἀκαθαρσίας, gen. sg. f. n. . . . . id.

ἀκάθαρτα, nom. pl. neut. adj. {Mark 3:11} . . . . ἀκάθαρτος *(169)*

ἀκάθαρτα, acc. pl. neut. adj. {Acts 8:7} . . id.

(168) **ἀκαθάρτης,** τητος, ἡ [§4.2.c] *impurity,* Rev. 17:4

ἀκαθάρτητος, gen. sg. f. n. (Rev. 17:4, TR | ἀκάθαρτα, GNT, WH, MT & NA) . . . . ἀκαθάρτης *(168)*

ἀκαθάρτοις, dat. pl. neut. adj. . . . . ἀκάθαρτος *(169)*

ἀκάθαρτον, acc. sg. m. adj. {Acts 10:28} . id.

ἀκάθαρτον, nom. sg. neut. adj. {Mark 1:26} id.

ἀκάθαρτον, acc. sg. neut. adj. {Mark 3:30} id.

(169) **ἀκάθαρτος,** ον, nom. sg. m. adj. [§7.2] *impure, unclean; lewd; foul*

ἀκαθάρτου, gen. sg. neut. adj. . . . . ἀκάθαρτος *(169)*

ἀκαθάρτῳ, dat. sg. neut. adj. . . . . id.

ἀκαθάρτων, gen. pl. neut. adj. . . . . id.

(170) **ἀκαιρέομαι,** οῦμαι, fut. ἀκαιρήσομαι [§17.Q] (ἀ + καιρός) *to be without opportunity or occasion,* Phil. 4:10

(171) **ἀκαίρως,** adv., *unseasonably,* 2 Tim. 4:2

(172) **ἄκακος,** ον, nom. sg. m. adj. [§7.2] (ἀ + κακός) *free from evil, innocent, blameless; artless, simple,* Rom. 16:18; Heb. 7:26

ἀκάκων, gen. pl. m. adj. . . . . ἄκακος *(172)*

(173) **ἄκανθα,** ης, ἡ [§2.3] *a thorn, thornbush,* Matt. 7:16

ἄκανθαι, nom. pl. f. n. . . . . ἄκανθα *(173)*

ἀκάνθας, acc. pl. f. n. . . . . id.

ἀκάνθινον, acc. sg. m. adj. . . . . ἀκάνθινος *(174)*

(174) **ἀκάνθινος,** η, ον [§7.2] *thorny, made of thorns,* Mark 15:17; John 19:5

ἀκανθῶν, gen. pl. f. n. . . . . ἄκανθα *(173)*

ἄκαρπα, nom. pl. neut. adj. . . . . ἄκαρπος *(175)*

ἄκαρποι, nom. pl. m. adj. . . . . id.

ἀκάρποις, dat. pl. neut. adj. . . . . id.

(175) **ἄκαρπος,** ον, nom. sg. m. adj. [§7.2] (ἀ + καρπός) *without fruit, unfruitful, barren;* by impl. *noxious*

ἀκάρπους, acc. pl. m. adj. . . . . ἄκαρπος *(175)*

ἀκατάγνωστον, acc. sg. m. adj. ἀκατάγνωστος *(176)*

(176) **ἀκατάγνωστος,** ον [§7.2] (ἀ + καταγινώσκω) pr. *not worthy of condemnation* by a judge; hence, *irreprehensible,* Tit. 2:8

ἀκατακάλυπτον, acc. sg. f.

adj. . . . . ἀκατακάλυπτος *(177)*

(177) **ἀκατακάλυπτος,** ον [§7.2] (ἀ + κατακαλύπτω) *uncovered, unveiled,* 1 Cor. 11:5, 13

ἀκατακαλύπτῳ, dat. sg. f. adj. ἀκατακάλυπτος *(177)*

ἀκατάκριτον, acc. sg. m. adj. . . . ἀκατάκριτος *(178)*

(178) **ἀκατάκριτος,** ον [§7.2] (ἀ + κατακρίνω) *uncondemned* in a public trial, Acts 16:37; 22:25

ἀκατακρίτους, acc. pl. m. adj. . . ἀκατάκριτος *(178)*

(179) **ἀκατάλυτος,** ον [§7.2] (ἀ + καταλύω) *incapable of dissolution, indissoluble;* hence, *enduring, everlasting,* Heb. 7:16

ἀκαταλύτου, gen. sg. f. adj. . . . . . ἀκατάλυτος *(179)*

(†180) **ἀκατάπαστος,** ον [§7.2] (ἀ + κατάπαστος, *filled, satiated,* from πατέομαι, *to taste*) *unsatisfied, insatiable*

ἀκαταπάστους, acc. pl. m. adj. (2 Pet. 2:14, WH | ἀκαταπαύστους, GNT, MT, TR & NA) . . . . ἀκατάπαστος *(†180)*

(180) **ἀκατάπαυστος,** ον [§7.2] (ἀ + καταπαύω) *which cannot be restrained* from a thing, *unceasing*

ἀκαταπαύστους, acc. pl. m. adj. (2 Pet. 2:14, GNT, MT, TR & NA | ἀκαταπάστους, WH) . . . . ἀκατάπαυστος *(180)*

(181) **ἀκαταστασία,** ας, ἡ, nom. sg. f. n. [§2.B.b; 2.2] (ἀ + καθίσταμαι, *to be in a fixed and tranquil state*) pr. *instability;* hence, *an unsettled state; disorder, commotion, tumult, sedition,* Luke 21:9; 1 Cor. 14:33; 2 Cor. 6:5; 12:20; James 3:16

ἀκαταστασίαι, nom. pl. f. n. . . . ἀκαταστασία *(181)*

ἀκαταστασίαις, dat. pl. f. n. . . . . id.

ἀκαταστασίας, gen. sg. f. n. {1 Cor. 14:33} id.

ἀκαταστασίας, acc. pl. f. n. {Luke 21:9} . id.

ἀκατάστατον, nom. sg. neut. adj. (James 3:8, GNT, WH & NA | ἀκατάσχετον, MT & TR) . . . . ἀκατάστατος *(182)*

(182) **ἀκατάστατος,** ον, nom. sg. m. adj. [§7.2] (ἀ + καθίσταμαι) *unstable, inconstant; unquiet, turbulent,* James 1:8

ἀκατάσχετον, nom. sg. neut. adj. (James 3:8, MT & TR | ἀκατάστατον, GNT, WH & NA) . . . . ἀκατάσχετος *(183)*

(183) **ἀκατάσχετος,** ον [§7.2] (ἀ + κατέχω) *not coercible, irrestrainable, untamable, unruly,* James 3:8

(†184) **Ἀκελδαμάχ,** τό, *Akeldama,* pr. name, indecl. (Acts 1:19, GNT, WH & NA | Ἀκέλδαμα, MT | Ἀκελδαμά, TR)

ἀκέραιοι, nom. pl. m. adj. . . . . ἀκέραιος *(185)*

(185) **ἀκέραιος,** ον [§7.2] (ἀ + κεράννυμι, *to mix*) pr. *unmixed:* hence, *without mixture of vice or deceit, sincere, artless, blameless,*

Matt. 10:16; Rom. 16:19; Phil. 2:15

ἀκεραίους, acc. pl. m. adj. . . . . ἀκέραιος *(185)*

ἀκήκοα, 1 pers. sg. 2 perf. act. indic. Att.
[§13.7.b,c] (Acts 9:13, MT & TR |
ἤκουσα, GNT, WH & NA) . . . . . . ἀκούω *(191)*

ἀκηκόαμεν, 1 pers. pl. 2 perf. act. indic. Att. id.

ἀκηκόασι(ν), 3 pers. pl. 2 perf. act. indic.
Att. . . . . id.

ἀκηκόατε, 2 pers. pl. 2 perf. act. indic. Att. id.

ἀκηκοότας, acc. pl. m. 2 perf. act. part. Att. id.

ἀκλινῆ, acc. sg. f. adj. . . . . ἀκλινής *(186)*

(186) **ἀκλινής,** ές [§7.G.b] (ἀ + κλίνω) *not declin-
ing, unwavering, steady,* Heb. 10:23

(187) **ἀκμάζω,** fut. ἀκμάσω [§26.1] *to flourish,
ripen, be in one's prime,* Rev. 14:18

(†188) **ἀκμή,** ῆς, ἡ [§2.B.a] (ἀκή, idem) pr. *the point
of a weapon; point of time:* ἀκμήν, for
κατἀκμήν, adv., *yet, still, even now,* Matt.
15:16

(188) **ἀκμήν,** acc. sg. f. n. . . . . ἀκμή *(†188)*

ἀκοαί, nom. pl. f. n. . . . . ἀκοή *(189)*

ἀκοαῖς, dat. pl. f. n. . . . . id.

ἀκοάς, acc. pl. f. n. . . . . id.

(189) **ἀκοή,** ῆς, ἡ, nom. sg. f. n. [§2.B.a] *hearing;
the act or sense of hearing,* 1 Cor. 12:17;
2 Pet. 2:8, et al.; *the instrument of hearing, the ear,* Mark 7:35, et al.; *a thing
heard;* announcement, *instruction, doctrine,* John 12:38; Rom. 10:16; *report,*
Matt. 4:24, et al.

ἀκοῇ, dat. sg. f. n. . . . . ἀκοή *(189)*

ἀκοήν, acc. sg. f. n. . . . . id.

ἀκοῆς, gen. sg. f. n. . . . . id.

ἀκολουθεῖ, 3 pers. sg. pres. act. indic.
{Luke 9:49} . . . . ἀκολουθέω *(190)*

ἀκολούθει, 2 pers. sg. pres. act. imper.
{Luke 9:59} . . . . id.

ἀκολουθεῖν, pres. act. infin. (Mark 8:34,
GNT, MT & NA | ἐλθεῖν, WH & TR |
John 13:37, WH | ἀκολουθῆσαι, GNT,
MT, TR & NA) . . . . id.

ἀκολουθείτω, 3 pers. sg. pres. act. imper. . id.

(190) **ἀκολουθέω,** ῶ, fut. ἀκολουθήσω, perf.
ἠκολούθηκα [§16.P] *to follow; follow* as
a disciple; *imitate*

ἀκολουθῆσαι, aor. act. infin. . . . . . ἀκολουθέω *(190)*

ἀκολουθήσαντες, nom. pl. m. aor. act. part. id.

ἀκολουθησάντων, gen. pl. m. aor. act. part. id.

ἀκολουθήσατε, 2 pers. pl. aor. act. imper. id.

ἀκολουθήσει, 3 pers. sg. fut. act. indic. (Mark
16:17, WH | παρακολουθήσει, GNT, MT,
TR & NA) . . . . id.

ἀκολουθήσεις, 2 pers. sg. fut. act. indic. . id.

ἀκολουθήσουσιν, 3 pers. pl. fut. act. indic.
(John 10:5, GNT, WH & NA | ἀκολου-

θήσωσιν, MT & TR) . . . . ἀκολουθέω *(190)*

ἀκολουθήσω, 1 pers. sg. fut. act. indic. . . id.

ἀκολουθήσωσιν, 3 pers. pl. aor. act. subj.
(John 10:5, MT & TR | ἀκολουθήσουσιν,
GNT, WH & NA) . . . . id.

ἀκολουθοῦντα, acc. sg. m. pres. act. part. id.

ἀκολουθοῦντας, acc. pl. m. pres. act. part. id.

ἀκολουθοῦντες, nom. pl. m. pres. act. part. id.

ἀκολουθοῦντι, dat. sg. m. pres. act. part. . id.

ἀκολουθούσης, gen. sg. f. pres. act. part. . id.

ἀκολουθοῦσι(ν), 3 pers. pl. pres. act. indic.
{Mark 6:1} . . . . id.

ἀκολουθοῦσιν, dat. pl. m. pres. act. part.
{Matt. 8:10} . . . . id.

ἀκολουθῶν, nom. sg. m. pres. act. part. . . id.

ἄκουε, 2 pers. sg. pres. act. imper. . . . . . ἀκούω *(191)*

ἀκούει, 3 pers. sg. pres. act. indic. . . . . . . id.

ἀκούειν, pres. act. infin. . . . . id.

ἀκούεις, 2 pers. sg. pres. act. indic. . . . . . id.

ἀκούεται, 3 pers. sg. pres. pass. indic. [§14.N] id.

ἀκούετε, 2 pers. pl. pres. act. indic.
{Matt. 13:17} . . . . id.

ἀκούετε, 2 pers. pl. pres. act. imper.
{Matt. 15:10} . . . . id.

ἀκουέτω, 3 pers. sg. pres. act. imper. . . . . id.

ἀκούομεν, 1 pers. pl. pres. act. indic. . . . . id.

ἀκούοντα, acc. sg. m. pres. act. part.
{Luke 2:46} . . . . id.

ἀκούοντα, nom. pl. neut. pres. act. part.
{Acts 13:48} . . . . id.

ἀκούοντας, acc. pl. m. pres. act. part. . . . id.

ἀκούοντες, nom. pl. m. pres. act. part. . . . id.

ἀκούοντι, dat. sg. m. pres. act. part. . . . . . id.

ἀκούοντος, gen. sg. m. pres. act. part. . . . id.

ἀκουόντων, gen. pl. m. pres. act. part. . . . id.

ἀκούουσι(ν), 3 pers. pl. pres. act. indic.
{Mark 4:20} . . . . id.

ἀκούουσι(ν), dat. pl. m. pres. act. part.
{Luke 6:27} . . . . id.

ἀκοῦσαι, aor. act. infin. . . . . id.

ἀκούσαντες, nom. pl. m. aor. act. part. . . id.

ἀκουσάντων, gen. pl. m. aor. act. part. . . . id.

ἀκούσας, nom. sg. m. aor. act. part. . . . . . id.

ἀκούσασα, nom. sg. f. aor. act. part. . . . . . id.

ἀκούσασιν, dat. pl. m. aor. act. part. . . . . . id.

ἀκούσατε, 2 pers. pl. aor. act. imper. . . . . id.

ἀκουσάτω, 3 pers. sg. aor. act. imper. . . . . id.

ἀκουσάτωσαν, 3 pers. pl. aor. act. imper. . id.

ἀκούσει, 3 pers. sg. fut. act. indic. . . . . . . id.

ἀκούσεσθε, 2 pers. pl. fut. mid. dep. indic. id.

ἀκούσετε, 2 pers. pl. fut. act. indic. . . . . . id.

ἀκούσῃ, 2 pers. sg. fut. mid. dep. indic.
{Acts 25:22} . . . . id.

ἀκούσῃ, 3 pers. sg. aor. act. subj. {Acts 3:23} id.

ἀκούσητε, 2 pers. pl. aor. act. subj. . . . . . id.

ἀκουσθεῖσι(ν), dat. pl. neut. aor. pass.
part. . . . . ἀκούω *(191)*
ἀκουσθῇ, 3 pers. sg. aor. pass. subj. . . . . . id.
ἀκουσθήσεται, 3 pers. sg. fut. pass. indic.
[§22.4] . . . . id.
ἀκουσόμεθα, 1 pers. pl. fut. mid. dep. indic.   id.
ἀκούσονται, 3 pers. pl. fut. mid. dep. indic.   id.
ἀκούσουσι(ν), 3 pers. pl. fut. act. indic. . .   id.
ἀκούσω, 1 pers. sg. aor. act. subj. (Phil. 1:27,
MT & TR | ἀκούω, GNT, WH & NA)   id.
ἀκούσωσι(ν), 3 pers. pl. aor. act. subj. . . .   id.
(191) **ἀκούω**, 1 pers. sg. pres. act. indic., fut.
ἀκούσομαι, and, later, ἀκούσω [§13.M]
perf. ἀκήκοα [§13.7.b,c] perf. pass. ἤκουσμαι [§22.6] aor. pass. ἠκούσθην, *to hear;*
to hearken, listen to, Mark 4:3; Luke 19:48;
to heed, obey, Matt. 18:15; Acts 4:19, et
al.; *to understand,* 1 Cor. 14:2; *to take in*
or admit to mental acceptance, Mark 4:33;
John 8:43, 47 {John 5:30}
ἀκούω, 1 pers. sg. pres. act. subj.
{Phil. 1:27} . . . . ἀκούω *(191)*
ἀκούων, nom. sg. m. pres. act. part. . . . . .   id.
ἀκούωσι(ν), 3 pers. pl. pres. act. subj. . . .   id.
(192) **ἀκρασία**, ας, ἡ [§2.B.b; 2.2] *intemperance, in-*
continence, Matt. 23:25; *unruly appetite,*
lustfulness, 1 Cor. 7:5
ἀκρασίαν, acc. sg. f. n. . . . . ἀκρασία *(192)*
ἀκρασίας, gen. sg. f. n. (Matt. 23:25, GNT,
NA, TR & WH | ἀδικίας, MT) . . . . .   id.
ἀκρατεῖς, nom. pl. m. adj. . . . . ἀκρατής *(193)*
(193) **ἀκρατής**, ές [§7.G.b] (ἀ + κράτος) *not mas-*
ter of one's self, intemperate, 2 Tim. 3:3
(194) **ἄκρατος**, ον [§7.2] (ἀ + κεράννυμι) *unmixed,*
unmingled wine, Rev. 14:10
ἀκράτου, gen. sg. m. adj. . . . . ἄκρατος *(194)*
(195) **ἀκρίβεια**, ας, ἡ [§2.B.b; 2.2] *accuracy, exact-*
ness; preciseness, or *rigor, severe discipline,*
Acts 22:3
ἀκρίβειαν, acc. sg. f. n. . . . . ἀκρίβεια *(195)*
ἀκριβεστάτην, acc. sg. f. superl. adj.
[§8.1] . . . . ἀκριβής *(‡196)*
(197) ἀκριβέστερον, compar. adv. . . . . . ἀκριβῶς *(199)*
(‡196) **ἀκριβής**, ές [§7.4.a] *accurate, exact,* Acts
18:26; 23:15, 20; 24:22; *precise, severe, rig-*
orous, Acts 26:5
(198) **ἀκριβόω**, ῶ, fut. ἀκριβώσω, perf. ἠκρίβωκα
[§20.T] *to inquire accurately,* or *assidu-*
ously, Matt. 2:7, 16: compare verse 8
(199) **ἀκριβῶς**, adv., *accurately, diligently,* Matt.
2:8; Luke 1:3; Acts 18:25; *circumspectly,*
strictly, Eph. 5:15; *precisely, distinctly,*
1 Thess. 5:2
ἀκρίδας, acc. pl. f. n. . . . . ἀκρίς *(200)*
ἀκρίδες, nom. pl. f. n. . . . .   id.

ἀκρίδων, gen. pl. f. n. . . . . ἀκρίς *(200)*
(200) **ἀκρίς**, ίδος, ἡ [§4.2.c] *a locust,* Matt. 3:4;
Mark 1:6; Rev. 9:3, 7
ἀκροαταί, nom. pl. m. n. . . . . ἀκροατής *(202)*
(201) **ἀκροατήριον**, ου, τό [§3.C.c] (ἀκροάομαι, *to*
hear) *a place of audience,* Acts 25:23
ἀκροατήριον, acc. sg. neut. n. . . . ἀκροατήριον *(201)*
(202) **ἀκροατής**, οῦ, ὁ, nom. sg. m. n. [§2.B.c] *a*
hearer, Rom. 2:13; James 1:22, 23, 25
(203) **ἀκροβυστία**, ας, ἡ, nom. sg. f. n. [§2.B.b; 2.2]
(ἄκρον + βύω, *to cover*) *the prepuce, fore-*
skin; uncircumcision, the state of being un-
circumcised, Rom. 4:10, et al.; the abstract
being put for the concrete, *uncircumcised*
men, i.e., *Gentiles,* Rom. 4:9, et al.
ἀκροβυστίᾳ, dat. sg. f. n. . . . . ἀκροβυστία *(203)*
ἀκροβυστίαν, acc. sg. f. n. . . . .   id.
ἀκροβυστίας, gen. sg. f. n. . . . .   id.
ἀκρογωνιαῖον, acc. sg. m. adj. . . ἀκρογωνιαῖος *(204)*
(204) **ἀκρογωνιαῖος**, α, ον [§7.1] (ἄκρος + γωνία)
corner-foundation stone, Eph. 2:20; 1 Pet.
2:6
ἀκρογωνιαίου, gen. sg. m. adj. . ἀκρογωνιαῖος *(204)*
(205) **ἀκροθίνιον**, ου, τό [§3.C.c] (ἄκρος + θίν, *a*
heap) *the first-fruits* of the produce of the
ground, which were taken from the top of
the heap and offered to the gods; *the best*
and choicest of the spoils of war, usually
collected in a heap, Heb. 7:4
ἀκροθινίων, gen. pl. neut. n. . . . . . ἀκροθίνιον *(205)*
(206) **ἄκρον**, ου, τό [§3.C.c] *the top, tip, end, ex-*
tremity, Mark. 13:27; Luke 16:24; Heb.
11:21
ἄκρον, acc. sg. neut. n. . . . . ἄκρον *(206)*
ἄκρου, gen. sg. neut. n. . . . .   id.
ἄκρων, gen. pl. neut. n. . . . .   id.
Ἀκύλαν, acc. sg. m. n. . . . . Ἀκύλας *(207)*
(207) **Ἀκύλας**, α, ὁ, nom. sg. m. n. [§2.4] *Aquila,*
pr. name
ἀκυροῖ, 3 pers. sg. pres. act. indic. . . . ἀκυρόω *(208)*
ἀκυροῦντες, nom. pl. m. pres. act. part. . .   id.
(208) **ἀκυρόω**, ῶ, fut. ἀκυρώσω [§20.T] (ἀ +
κυρόω) *to deprive of authority, annul, ab-*
rogate, Matt. 15:6; Mark 7:13; Gal. 3:17
(209) **ἀκωλύτως**, adv. (ἀ + κωλύω) *without hin-*
drance, freely, Acts 28:31
(210) **ἄκων**, ουσα, ον, nom. sg. m. adj. (for ἀέκων,
from ἀ + ἑκών, *willing*) *unwilling*
[§7.H.d] 1 Cor. 9:17
(‡217) **ἅλα**, ατος, τό, *salt* (Mark 9:50, GNT, WH
& NA | ἅλας, MT & TR)
ἅλα, acc. sg. neut. n. . . . . ἅλα *(‡217)*
(211) **ἀλάβαστρον**, ου, τό [§3.C.c] *alabaster; a vase*
to hold perfumed ointment, properly made
of alabaster, but also of other materials,

Matt. 26:7; Mark 14:3; Luke 7:37

ἀλάβαστρον, acc. sg. neut. n. . . . . ἀλάβαστρον *(211)*

ἀλαζόνας, acc. pl. m. n. . . . . ἀλαζών *(213)*

(212) **ἀλαζονεία**, ας, ἡ, nom. sg. f. n. [§2.B.b; 2.2]
ostentation; presumptuous speech, James
4:16; *haughtiness* (1 John 2:16, GNT, MT,
TR & NA | ἀλαζονία, WH)

ἀλαζονείαις, dat. pl. f. n. (James 4:16, GNT,
MT, TR & NA | ἀλαζονίας,
WH) . . . . ἀλαζονεία *(212)*

ἀλαζόνες, nom. pl. m. n. . . . . ἀλαζών *(213)*

(213) **ἀλαζών**, όνος, ὁ [§7.G.a] *ostentatious, vain-
glorious, arrogant, boasting,* Rom. 1:30;
2 Tim. 3:2

ἀλαλάζον, nom. sg. neut. pres. act.
part. . . . . ἀλαλάζω *(214)*

ἀλαλάζοντας, acc. pl. m. pres. act. part. . id.

(214) **ἀλαλάζω**, fut. ἀλαλάξω and ἀλαλάξομαι
[§26.2] pr. *to raise the war-cry,* ἀλαλά:
hence, *to utter* other *loud sounds; to wail,*
Mark. 5:38; *to tinkle, ring,* 1 Cor. 13:1

ἀλαλήτοις, dat. pl. m. adj. . . . . ἀλάλητος *(215)*

(215) **ἀλάλητος**, ον [§7.2] (ἀ + λαλέω) *unutterable,*
or, *unexpressed,* Rom. 8:26

ἄλαλον, nom. sg. neut. adj.
{Mark 9:17} . . . . ἄλαλος *(216)*

ἄλαλον, acc. sg. neut. adj. {Mark 9:25} . . id.

(216) **ἄλαλος**, ον [§7.2] (ἀ + λαλέω) *unable to
speak, dumb,* Mark 7:37

ἀλάλους, acc. pl. m. adj. . . . . ἄλαλος *(216)*

(217) **ἅλας**, ατος, τό, nom. sg. neut. n. [§4.2.c] *salt,*
Mark 9:50, et al.; met. Matt. 5:13; met.
the salt of wisdom and prudence, Col. 4:6
{Mark 9:50a,b}

ἅλας, acc. sg. neut. n. (Mark 9:50c, MT &
TR | ἅλα, GNT, WH & NA) . . . . . . ἅλας *(217)*

ἅλατι, dat. sg. neut. n. . . . . id.

(218) **ἀλείφω**, fut. ἀλείψω [§23.1.a] *to anoint* with
oil or ointment

ἄλειψαι, 2 pers. sg. aor. mid. imper. . . . ἀλείφω *(218)*

ἀλείψαντες, nom. pl. m. aor. act. part. . . . id.

ἀλείψασα, nom. sg. f. aor. act. part. . . . . . id.

ἀλείψωσιν, 3 pers. pl. aor. act. subj. . . . . id.

ἀλέκτορα, acc. sg. m. n. . . . . ἀλέκτωρ *(220)*

(219) **ἀλεκτοροφωνία**, ας, ἡ [§2.B.b; 2.2] (ἀλέκτωρ
+ φωνή) *the cock-crowing, the third watch
of the night,* intermediate to mid-night and
daybreak, and termed *cock-crow,* Mark
13:35

ἀλεκτοροφωνίας, gen. sg. f. n. ἀλεκτοροφωνία *(219)*

(220) **ἀλέκτωρ**, ορος, ὁ, nom. sg. m. n. [§4.2.f] *a
cock,* Matt. 26:34; Mark 14:30; Luke
22:34; John 13:38

(221) **Ἀλεξανδρεύς**, έως, ὁ, nom. sg. m. n. [§5.E.d]
a native of Alexandria, an Alexandrine

Ἀλεξανδρέων, gen. pl. m. n. . . . . Ἀλεξανδρεύς *(221)*

Ἀλεξανδρῖνον, acc. sg. neut. adj. (Acts 27:6,
GNT, MT, TR & NA | Ἀλεξανδρινόν,
WH) . . . . Ἀλεξανδρῖνος *(222)*

(222) **Ἀλεξανδρῖνος**, η, ον [§7.F.a] *Alexandrian*

Ἀλεξανδρίνῳ, dat. sg. neut. adj. (Acts 28:11,
GNT, MT, TR & NA | Ἀλεξανδρινῷ,
WH) . . . . Ἀλεξανδρῖνος *(222)*

Ἀλέξανδρον, acc. sg. m. n. . . . . . Ἀλέξανδρος *(223)*

(223) **Ἀλέξανδρος**, ου, ὁ, nom. sg. m. n. [§3.C.a]
Alexander, pr. name   I. *The High Priest's
kinsman,* Acts 4:6   II. *A Jew of Ephesus,*
Acts 19:33   III. *The coppersmith,* 1 Tim.
1:20; 2 Tim. 4:14   IV. *Son of Simon of
Cyrene,* Mark 15:21

Ἀλεξάνδρου, gen. sg. m. n. . . . . . Ἀλέξανδρος *(223)*

(224) **ἄλευρον**, ου, τό [§3.C.c] (ἀλέω, *to grind*)
meal, flour, Matt. 13:33; Luke 13:21

ἀλεύρου, gen. sg. neut. n. . . . . ἄλευρον *(224)*

(225) **ἀλήθεια**, ας, ἡ, nom. sg. f. n. [§2.B.b; 2.2]
truth, verity, Mark 5:33; *love of truth, ve-
racity, sincerity,* 1 Cor. 5:8, et al.; *divine
truth* revealed to man, John 1:17, et al.;
practice in accordance with Gospel *truth,*
John 3:21; 2 John 4, et al.

ἀληθείᾳ, dat. sg. f. n. . . . . ἀλήθεια *(225)*

ἀλήθειαν, acc. sg. f. n. . . . . id.

ἀληθείας, gen. sg. f. n. . . . . id.

ἀληθεῖς, nom. pl. m. adj. . . . . ἀληθής *(227)*

ἀληθές, nom. sg. neut. adj. {Acts 12:9} . . . id.

ἀληθές, acc. sg. neut. adj. {John 4:18} . . . id.

ἀληθεύοντες, nom. pl. m. pres. act.
part. . . . . ἀληθεύω *(226)*

(226) **ἀληθεύω**, fut. ἀληθεύσω [§13.M] *to speak or
maintain the truth; to act truly or sincerely,*
Gal. 4:16; Eph. 4:15

ἀληθεύων, nom. sg. m. pres. act. part. ἀληθεύω *(226)*

ἀληθῆ, acc. sg. f. adj. {1 Pet. 5:12} . . . . ἀληθής *(227)*

ἀληθῆ, nom. pl. neut. adj. {John 10:41} . . id.

ἀληθῆ, acc. pl. neut. adj. {John 19:35} . . . id.

(227) **ἀληθής**, ές, nom. sg. m. adj. [§7.G.b] *true,*
John 4:18, et al.; *worthy of credit,* John
5:31; *truthful,* John 7:18, et al. {John 3:33}

ἀληθής, nom. sg. f. adj. {John 5:31} . . ἀληθής *(227)*

ἀληθιναί, nom. pl. f. adj. . . . . ἀληθινός *(228)*

ἀληθινή, nom. sg. f. adj. . . . . id.

ἀληθινῆς, gen. sg. f. adj. . . . . id.

ἀληθινοί, nom. pl. m. adj. . . . . id.

ἀληθινόν, acc. sg. m. adj. {John 6:32} . . . id.

ἀληθινόν, nom. sg. neut. adj. {John 1:9} . id.

ἀληθινόν, acc. sg. neut. adj. {Luke 16:11} . id.

(228) **ἀληθινός**, ή, όν, nom. sg. m. adj. [§7.F.a] *ster-
ling,* Luke 16:11; *real,* John 6:32; 1 Thess.
1:9, et al.; *unfeigned, trustworthy, true,*
John 19:35, et al.

ἀληθινῷ, dat. sg. m. adj. . . . . ἀληθινός (228)
ἀληθινῶν, gen. pl. neut. adj. . . . . id.
ἀληθοῦς, gen. sg. f. adj. . . . . ἀληθής (227)
ἀληθουσαι, nom. pl. f. pres. act. part. . . ἀλήθω (229)
(229) **ἀλήθω,** fut. ἀλήσω [§23.1.c] (ἀλέω, idem) *to grind,* Matt. 24:41; Luke 17:35
(230) **ἀληθῶς,** adv., *truly, really,* Matt. 14:33, et al.; *certainly, of a truth,* John 17:8; Acts 12:11: *truly, veraciously,* John 4:42, et al.
ἀλί, dat. sg. m. n. (Mark 9:49, MT & TR | GNT, WH & NA omit) . . . . ἅλς (251)
ἁλιεῖς, nom. pl. m. n. (Matt. 4:18, GNT, MT, TR & NA | ἁλεεῖς, WH) . . . . ἁλιεύς (231)
ἁλιεῖς, acc. pl. m. n. (Matt. 4:19, GNT, MT, TR & NA | ἁλεεῖς, WH) . . . . id.
ἁλιεύειν, pres. act. infin. . . . . ἁλιεύω (232)
(231) **ἁλιεύς,** έως, ὁ [§5.E.d] *a fisherman,* Matt. 4:18, 19; Mark 1:16, 17; Luke 5:2
(232) **ἁλιεύω,** fut. ἁλιεύσω [§13.M] *to fish,* John 21:3
(233) **ἁλίζω,** fut. ἁλίσω [§26.1] *to salt, season with salt, preserve by salting,* Matt. 5:13; Mark 9:49
(†234) **ἀλίσγημα,** ατος, τό [§4.D.c] (ἀλισγέω, *to pollute,* in the LXX) *pollution, defilement,* Acts 15:20
ἀλισγημάτων, gen. pl. neut. n. . . . . ἀλίσγημα (†234)
ἀλισθήσεται, 3 pers. sg. fut. pass. ind. . . ἁλίζω (233)
ἀλλ᾽, aspirated form of . . . . ἀλλά (235)
(235) **ἀλλά,** conj. *but; however; but still more;* ἀλλάγε, *at all events;* ἀλλή, *unless, except.* Ἀλλά also serves to introduce a sentence with keenness and emphasis, Rom. 6:5; 7:7; Phil. 3:8; John 16:2
ἄλλα, nom. pl. neut. adj. {Matt. 13:5} . . ἄλλος (243)
ἄλλα, acc. pl. neut. adj. {Matt. 25:16} . . . id.
ἀλλαγησόμεθα, 1 pers. pl. 2 fut. pass. indic. . . . . ἀλλάσσω (236)
ἀλλαγήσονται, 3 pers. pl. 2 fut. pass. indic. id.
ἄλλαι, nom. pl. f. adj. . . . . ἄλλος (243)
ἀλλάξαι, aor. act. infin. . . . . ἀλλάσσω (236)
ἀλλάξει, 3 pers. sg. fut. act. indic. . . . . . . id.
ἄλλας, acc. pl. f. adj. . . . . ἄλλος (243)
(236) **ἀλλάσσω,** fut. ἀλλάξω, aor. pass. ἠλλάχθην, 2 aor. pass. ἠλλάγην, fut. ἀλλαγήσομαι [§26.3] *to change, alter, transform,* Acts 6:14 Rom. 1:23; 1 Cor. 15:51, 52; Gal. 4:20; Heb. 1:12
(237) **ἀλλαχόθεν,** adv. (ἄλλος + θεν, denoting *from a place) from another place or elsewhere,* John 10:1
ἀλλαχοῦ, adv., *elsewhere* (Mark 1:38, GNT, WH & NA | MT & TR omit)
ἄλλη, nom. sg. f. adj. . . . . ἄλλος (243)
(238) **ἀλληγορέω,** ῶ [§16.P] (ἄλλος + ἀγορεύω, *to

speak) to say what is either designed or fitted to convey a meaning other than the literal one, to allegorize;* ἀλληγορούμενος, *adapted to another meaning, otherwise significant,* Gal. 4:24
ἀλληγορούμενα, nom. pl. neut. pres. pass. part. . . . . ἀλληγορέω (238)
ἀλλήλοις, dat. pl. m. reciprocal pron. {Gal. 5:13} . . . . ἀλλήλων (240)
ἀλλήλοις, dat. pl. neut. reciprocal pron. {Gal. 5:17} . . . . id.
(239) **Ἀλληλούϊα,** Hebrew הַלְלוּ־יָהּ, *praise ye Jehovah* (Rev. 19:1, 3, 4, 6, MT & TR | Ἀλληλουϊά, GNT & NA | Ἁλληλουιά, WH)
ἀλλήλους, acc. pl. m. reciprocal pron. ἀλλήλων (240)
(240) **ἀλλήλων,** gen. pl. m. reciprocal pron. [§10.6.f] *one another, each other* {Rom. 2:15}
ἀλλήλων, gen. pl. neut. reciprocal pron. {1 Cor. 12:25} . . . . ἀλλήλων (240)
ἄλλην, acc. sg. f. adj. . . . . ἄλλος (243)
ἄλλης, gen. sg. f. adj. . . . . id.
ἄλλο, nom. sg. neut. adj. {Rev. 12:3} . . . . id.
ἄλλο, acc. sg. neut. adj. {Rev. 13:11} . . . . id.
(241) **ἀλλογενής,** ές, nom. sg. m. adj. [§7.G.b] (ἄλλος + γένος) *of another race or nation,* i.e., not a Jew; *a stranger, foreigner,* Luke 17:18
ἄλλοι, nom. pl. m. adj. . . . . ἄλλος (243)
ἄλλοις, dat. pl. m. adj. . . . . id.
(242) **ἄλλομαι,** fut. ἁλοῦμαι, aor., ἡλάμην [§37.1] *to leap, jump, leap up,* Acts 3:8; 14:10; *to spring,* as water, John 4:14
ἀλλόμενος, nom. sg. m. pres. mid./pass. dep. part. . . . . ἄλλομαι (242)
ἀλλομένου, gen. sg. neut. pres. mid./pass. dep. part. . . . . id.
ἄλλον, acc. sg. m. adj. . . . . ἄλλος (243)
(243) **ἄλλος,** η, ο, nom. sg. m. adj. [§10.6.a] *another, some other;* ὁ ἄλλος, *the other;* οἱ ἄλλοι, *the others, the rest*
ἀλλοτρία, dat. sg. f. adj. . . . . ἀλλότριος (245)
ἀλλοτρίαις, dat. pl. f. adj. . . . . id.
ἀλλοτρίαν, acc. sg. f. adj. . . . . id.
(244) **ἀλλοτριεπίσκοπος,** ου, ὁ, nom. sg. m. n. [§3.C.a,b] (ἀλλότριος + ἐπίσκοπος) pr. *one who meddles with the affairs of others, a busybody in other men's matters; factious* (1 Pet. 4:15, GNT, WH & NA | ἀλλοτριοεπίσκοπος, MT & TR)
ἀλλοτριοεπίσκοπος, nom. sg. m. n. (1 Pet. 4:15, MT & TR | ἀλλοτριεπίσκοπος, GNT, WH & NA) . . . . . ἀλλοτριεπίσκοπος (244)
ἀλλοτρίοις, dat. pl. m. adj. . . . . ἀλλότριος (245)
ἀλλότριον, acc. sg. m. adj. . . . . id.

(245) **ἀλλότριος**, α, ον [§7.1] *belonging to another,*
Luke 16:12, et al.; *foreign,* Acts 7:6; Heb.
11:9; *a foreigner, alien,* Matt. 17:25
ἀλλοτρίῳ, dat. sg. m. adj.
{John 10:5} . . . . ἀλλότριος *(245)*
ἀλλοτρίῳ, dat. sg. neut. adj. {Luke 16:12}   id.
ἀλλοτρίων, gen. pl. m. adj. . . . . id.
ἄλλου, gen. sg. m. adj. . . . . ἄλλος *(243)*
ἄλλους, acc. pl. m. adj. . . . . id.

(246) **ἀλλόφυλος**, ον [§7.2] (ἄλλος + φυλή) *of another race or nation,* i.e., not a Jew, *a foreigner,* Acts 10:28
ἀλλοφύλῳ, dat. sg. m. adj. . . . . . . ἀλλόφυλος *(246)*
ἄλλῳ, dat. sg. m. adj. . . . . ἄλλος *(243)*
ἄλλων, gen. pl. m. adj. . . . . id.

(247) **ἄλλως**, adv., *otherwise,* 1 Tim. 5:25

(248) **ἀλοάω**, ῶ, fut. ἀλοήσω [§18.R] and ἀλοάσω
[§22.2] *to thresh; to tread, or thresh out,*
1 Cor. 9:9, 10; 1 Tim. 5:18
ἄλογα, nom. pl. neut. adj. . . . . ἄλογος *(249)*
ἄλογον, nom. sg. neut. adj. . . . . id.

(249) **ἄλογος**, ον [§7.2] (ἀ + λόγος) *without speech
or reason, irrational, brute,* 2 Pet. 2:12;
Jude 10; *unreasonable, absurd,* Acts 25:27

(250) **ἀλόη**, ης, ἡ [§2.B.a] also termed ξυλαλόη,
ἀγάλλοχον, *aloe, lign-aloe,* a tree which
grows in India and Cochin-China, the
wood of which is soft and bitter, though
highly aromatic. It is used by the Orien-
tals as a perfume; and employed for the
purposes of embalming, John 19:39
ἀλόης, gen. sg. f. n. . . . . ἀλόη *(250)*
ἀλοῶν, nom. sg. m. pres. act. part. . . . . ἀλοάω *(248)*
ἀλοῶντα, acc. sg. m. pres. act. part. . . . . . id.

(251) **ἅλς**, ἁλός, ὁ [§4.1; 4.2] *salt,* Mark 9:49
ἁλυκόν, acc. sg. neut. adj. . . . . ἁλυκός *(252)*

(252) **ἁλυκός**, ή, όν [§7.F.a] *brackish, bitter, salt,*
James 3:12

(†253) **ἄλυπος**, ον [§7.2] (ἀ + λύπη) *free from grief
or sorrow,* Phil 2:28

(253) **ἀλυπότερος**, nom. sg. m. compar. adj.
[§8.4] . . . . ἄλυπος *(†253)*
ἀλύσει, dat. sg. f. n. . . . . ἄλυσις *(254)*
ἀλύσεις, nom. pl. f. n. {Acts 12:7} . . . . . . id.
ἀλύσεις, acc. pl. f. n. {Mark 5:4} . . . . id.
ἀλύσεσι(ν), dat. pl. f. n. . . . . id.
ἄλυσιν, acc. sg. f. n. . . . . id.

(254) **ἅλυσις**, εως, ἡ [§5.E.c] *a chain,* Mark 5:3, 4
ἀλυσιτελές, nom. sg. neut. adj. . . . ἀλυσιτελής *(255)*

(255) **ἀλυσιτελής**, ές [§7.G.b] (ἀ + λυσιτελής, i.e.
λύων τὰ τέλη) pr. *bringing in no revenue
or profit;* hence, *unprofitable, useless; det-
rimental; ruinous, disastrous,* Heb. 13:17

(‡1) **Ἄλφα**, τό, indecl. first letter of Greek alphabet, *Alpha* (Rev. 1:8; 21:6; 22:13, GNT,

WH, MT & NA | A, TR)

(256) **Ἁλφαῖος**, ου, ὁ, *Alphaeus,* pr. name   I.
Father of James the less   II. *Father of Levi,*
(or Matthew) Mark 2:14
Ἁλφαίου, gen. sg. m. n. . . . . Ἁλφαῖος *(256)*

(257) **ἅλων**, ωνος, ἡ [§4.D.a] (a later form of ἅλως,
ω, ἡ) *a threshing-floor, a place where corn
is trodden out;* meton. *the corn which is
trodden out,* Matt. 3:12; Luke 3:17
ἅλωνα, acc. sg. f. n. . . . . ἅλων *(257)*
ἀλώπεκες, nom. pl. f. n. . . . . ἀλώπηξ *(258)*
ἀλώπεκι, dat. sg. f. n. . . . . id.

(258) **ἀλώπηξ**, εκος, ἡ [§4.2.b] *a fox,* Matt. 8:20;
Luke 9:58; met. *a fox-like, crafty man,*
Luke 13:32
ἅλωσιν, acc. sg. f. n. . . . . ἅλωσις *(259)*

(259) **ἅλωσις**, εως, ἡ [§5.E.c] (ἁλίσκομαι, *to take*)
a taking, catching, capture, 2 Pet. 2:12

(260) **ἅμα**, adv., *with, together with; at the same time*
ἀμαθεῖς, nom. pl. m. adj. . . . . ἀμαθής *(261)*

(261) **ἀμαθής**, ές [§7.G.b] (ἀ + μανθάνω) *unlearned, uninstructed, rude,* 2 Pet. 3:16
ἀμαράντινον, acc. sg. m. adj. . . . ἀμαράντινος *(262)*

(262) **ἀμαράντινος**, η, ον [§7.2] (ἀ + μαραίνομαι)
unfading; hence, *enduring* 1 Pet. 5:4
ἀμάραντος, acc. sg. f. adj. . . . . ἀμάραντος *(263)*

(263) **ἀμάραντος**, ον, *unfading;* hence, *enduring*
1 Pet. 1:4
ἁμάρτανε, 2 pers. sg. pres. act.
imper. ἁμαρτάνω *(264)*
ἁμαρτάνει, 3 pers. sg. pres. act. indic. . . . id.
ἁμαρτάνειν, pres. act. infin. . . . . id.
ἁμαρτάνετε, 2 pers. pl. pres. act. indic.
{1 Cor. 8:12} . . . . id.
ἁμαρτάνετε, 2 pers. pl. pres. act. imper.
{1 Cor. 15:34} . . . . id.
ἁμαρτάνοντα, acc. sg. m. pres. act. part. .
ἁμαρτάνοντας, acc. pl. m. pres. act. part.
ἁμαρτάνοντες, nom. pl. m. pres. act. part.
ἁμαρτανόντων, gen. pl. m. pres. act. part.
ἁμαρτάνουσι(ν), dat. pl. m. pres. act. part. id.

(264) **ἁμαρτάνω**, fut. ἁμαρτήσομαι and, later,
ἁμαρτήσω, aor. ἡμάρτησα, 2 aor. ἥμαρ-
τον [§36.2] pr. *to miss a mark; to be in error,* 1 Cor. 15:34; Tit. 3:11; *to sin,* John
5:14, et al.; *to be guilty of wrong,* Matt.
18:15, et al.
ἁμαρτάνων, nom. sg. m. pres. act.
part. . . . . ἁμαρτάνω *(264)*
ἁμάρτῃ, 3 pers. sg. 2 aor. act. subj. . . . . . id.

(265) **ἁμάρτημα**, ατος, τό, nom. sg. neut. n. [§4.D.c]
an error; sin, offence, Mark 3:28; 4:12;
Rom. 3:25; 1 Cor. 6:18
ἁμαρτήματα, nom. pl. neut. n. . . . . ἁμάρτημα *(265)*
ἁμαρτήματος, gen. sg. neut. n. (Mark 3:29,

GNT, WH & NA | κρίσεως, MT &
TR) . . . . ἁμάρτημα (265)
ἁμαρτημάτων, gen. pl. neut. n. . . . . id.
ἁμαρτήσαντας, acc. pl. m. aor. act.
     part. . . . . ἁμαρτάνω (264)
ἁμαρτήσαντος, gen. sg. m. aor. act. part.   id.
ἁμαρτησάντων, gen. pl. m. aor. act. part.   id.
ἁμαρτήσασιν, dat. pl. m. aor. act. part. . .   id.
ἁμαρτήσει, 3 pers. sg. fut. act. indic. . . . .   id.
ἁμαρτήσῃ, 3 pers. sg. aor. act. subj. . . . . .   id.
ἁμαρτήσομεν, 1 pers. pl. fut. act. indic. (Rom.
     6:15, MT & TR | ἁμαρτήσωμεν, GNT,
     WH & NA) . . . . id.
ἁμαρτήσωμεν, 1 pers. pl. aor. act. subj. (Rom.
     6:15, GNT, WH & NA | ἁμαρτήσομεν,
     MT & TR) . . . . id.
ἁμάρτητε, 2 pers. pl. 2 aor. act. subj. . . . .   id.
(266) ἁμαρτία, ας, ἡ, nom. sg. f. n. [§2.B.b; 2.2] er-
     ror; offence, sin, Matt. 1:21, et al.; a prin-
     ciple or cause of sin, Rom. 7:7; proneness
     to sin, sinful propensity, Rom. 7:17, 20;
     guilt or imputation of sin, John 9:41; Heb.
     9:26, et al.; a guilty subject, sin-offering,
     expiatory victim, 2 Cor. 5:21
ἁμαρτίᾳ, dat. sg. f. n. . . . . ἁμαρτία (266)
ἁμαρτίαι, nom. pl. f. n. . . . . id.
ἁμαρτίαις, dat. pl. f. n. . . . . id.
ἁμαρτίαν, acc. sg. f. n. . . . . id.
ἁμαρτίας, gen. sg. f. n. {Heb. 9:28b} . . . . id.
ἁμαρτίας, acc. pl. f. n. {Heb. 9:28a} . . . . id.
ἁμαρτιῶν, gen. pl. f. n. . . . . id.
ἁμάρτυρον, acc. sg. m. adj. . . . . . . ἁμάρτυρος (267)
(267) ἁμάρτυρος, ον [§7.2] (ἀ + μάρτυς) without
     testimony or witness, without evidence,
     Acts 14:17
ἁμαρτωλοί, nom. pl. m. adj.
     {Luke 6:32} . . . . ἁμαρτωλός (268)
ἁμαρτωλοί, voc. pl. m. adj. {James 4:8} .   id.
ἁμαρτωλοῖς, dat. pl. m. adj. . . . . id.
ἁμαρτωλόν, acc. sg. m. adj. . . . . id.
(268) ἁμαρτωλός, όν, nom. sg. m. adj. [§7.2] one
     who deviates from the path of virtue, a sin-
     ner, Mark 2:17, et al.; depraved, Mark
     8:38; sinful, detestable, Rom. 7:13
     {Luke 5:8}
ἁμαρτωλός, nom. sg. f. adj.
     {Luke 7:37, 39} . . . . ἁμαρτωλός (268)
ἁμαρτωλούς, acc. pl. m. adj. . . . . id.
ἁμαρτωλῷ, dat. sg. m. adj. {Luke 15:7} . . id.
ἁμαρτωλῷ, dat. sg. f. adj. {Mark 8:38} . . id.
ἁμαρτωλῶν, gen. pl. m. adj. . . . . id.
ἄμαχον, acc. sg. m. adj. . . . . ἄμαχος (269)
(269) ἄμαχος, ον [§7.2] (ἀ + μάχομαι) not disposed
     to fight; not quarrelsome or contentious,
     1 Tim. 3:3; Tit. 3:2

ἀμάχους, acc. pl. m. adj. . . . . ἄμαχος (269)
(270) ἀμάω, ῶ, fut. ἀμήσω [§18.R] to collect; to
     reap, mow or cut down, James 5:4
(†271) ἀμέθυσος, ου, ἡ, nom. sg. f. n. an amethyst
     (Rev. 21:20, MT | ἀμέθυστος, GNT, WH,
     TR & NA)
(271) ἀμέθυστος, ου, ἡ, nom. sg. f. n. [§3.C.b] (ἀ
     + μεθύω) an amethyst, a gem of a deep
     purple or violet color, so called from its
     supposed efficacy in keeping off drunken-
     ness (Rev. 21:20, GNT, WH, TR & NA
     | ἀμέθυσος, MT)
ἀμέλει, 2 pers. sg. pres. act. imper. . . . . ἀμελέω (272)
(272) ἀμελέω, ῶ, fut. ἀμελήσω, perf. ἠμέληκα
     [§16.P] (ἀμελής, ἀ + μέλει) not to care for,
     to neglect, disregard, Matt. 22:5; 1 Tim.
     4:14; Heb. 2:3; 8:9; 2 Pet. 1:12
ἀμελήσαντες, nom. pl. m. aor. act.
     part. . . . . ἀμελέω (272)
ἀμελήσω, 1 pers. sg. fut. act. indic. (2 Pet.
     1:12, MT & TR | μελλήσω, GNT, WH
     & NA) . . . . id.
ἄμεμπτοι, nom. pl. m. adj. . . . . ἄμεμπτος (273)
(273) ἄμεμπτος, ον, nom. sg. m. adj. [§7.2] (ἀ +
     μεμπτος, from μέμφομαι) blameless, ir-
     reprehensible, without defect, Luke 1:6;
     Phil. 2:15; 1 Thess. 3:13; Heb. 8:7
     {Phil. 3:6}
ἄμεμπτος, nom. sg. f. adj.
     {Heb. 8:7} . . . . ἄμεμπτος (273)
ἀμέμπτους, acc. pl. f. adj. . . . . id.
(274) ἀμέμπτως, adv., blamelessly, unblamably, un-
     exceptionably, 1 Thess. 2:10; 5:23
(275) ἀμέριμνος, ον [§7.2] (ἀ + μέριμνα) free from
     care or solicitude, Matt. 28:14; 1 Cor. 7:32
ἀμερίμνους, acc. pl. m. adj. . . . . ἀμέριμνος (275)
ἀμετάθετον, acc. sg. m. adj. . . . . . ἀμετάθετος (276)
(276) ἀμετάθετος, ον [§7.2] (ἀ + μετατίθημι) un-
     changeable, Heb. 6:17, 18
ἀμεταθέτων, gen. pl. neut. adj. . . . ἀμετάθετος (276)
ἀμετακίνητοι, nom. pl. m. adj. . ἀμετακίνητος (277)
(277) ἀμετακίνητος, ον [§7.2] (ἀ + μετακινέω) im-
     movable, firm, 1 Cor. 15:58
ἀμεταμέλητα, nom. pl. neut.
     adj. . . . . ἀμεταμέλητος (278)
ἀμεταμέλητον, acc. sg. f. adj. . . . . id.
(278) ἀμεταμέλητος, ον [§7.2] (ἀ + μεταμέλομαι)
     not to be repented of; by impl. irrevoca-
     ble, enduring, Rom. 11:29; 2 Cor. 7:10
ἀμετανόητον, acc. sg. f. adj. . . . . . ἀμετανόητος (279)
(279) ἀμετανόητος, ον [§7.2] (ἀ + μετανοέω) im-
     penitent, obdurate, Rom. 2:5
ἄμετρα, acc. pl. neut. adj. . . . . ἄμετρος (280)
(280) ἄμετρος, ον [§7.2] (ἀ + μέτρον) without or
     beyond measure, regardless of measure,

2 Cor. 10:13, 15

(281) **ἀμήν**, used as a particle both of affirmation and assent (Hebrew אָמֵן, *firm, faithful, true*) *in truth, verily, most certainly; so be it*; ὁ ἀμήν, *the faithful and true one*, Rev. 3:14

ἀμησάντων, gen. pl. m. aor. act. part. .. ἀμάω (270)

(282) **ἀμήτωρ**, ορος, ὁ, ἡ, nom. sg. m. adj. [§7.G.a] (ἀ + μήτηρ) pr. *without mother; independent of maternal descent*, Heb. 7:3

ἀμίαντον, acc. sg. f. adj. . . . . ἀμίαντος (283)

(283) **ἀμίαντος**, ον, nom. sg. m. adj. [§7.2] (ἀ + μιαίνω) pr. *unstained, unsoiled*; met. *undefiled, chaste*, Heb. 13:4; *pure, sincere*, James 1:27; *inviolate, unimpaired*, 1 Pet. 1:4 {Heb. 7:26}

ἀμίαντος, nom. sg. f. adj.
   {Heb. 13:4} . . . . ἀμίαντος (283)

(284) **Ἀμιναδάβ**, ὁ, *Aminadab*, pr. name, indecl.

ἄμμον, acc. sg. f. n. . . . . ἄμμος (285)

(285) **ἄμμος**, ου, ἡ, nom. sg. f. n. [§3.C.b] *sand*, Matt. 7:26; et al.

(286) **ἀμνός**, οῦ, ὁ, nom. sg. m. n. [§3.C.a] *a lamb*, John 1:29, 36; Acts 8:32; 1 Pet. 1:19

ἀμνοῦ, gen. sg. m. n. . . . . ἀμνός (286)

ἀμοιβάς, acc. pl. f. n. . . . . ἀμοιβή (287)

(287) **ἀμοιβή**, ῆς, ἡ [§2.B.a] (ἀμείβω, ἀμείβομαι, *to requite*) *requital*; of kind offices, *recompense*, 1 Tim. 5:4

ἄμπελον, acc. sg. f. n. . . . . ἄμπελος (288)

(288) **ἄμπελος**, ου, ἡ, nom. sg. f. n. [§3.C.b] *a vine, grape-vine*

ἀμπέλου, gen. sg. f. n. . . . . ἄμπελος (288)

ἀμπελουργόν, acc. sg. m. adj. . . . ἀμπελουργός (289)

(289) **ἀμπελουργός**, οῦ, ὁ, ἡ [§3.C.a] (ἄμπελος + ἔργον) *a vine-dresser*, Luke 13:7

ἀμπέλῳ, dat. sg. f. n. . . . . ἄμπελος (288)

(290) **ἀμπελών**, ῶνος, ὁ [§4.D.a] *a vineyard*

ἀμπελῶνα, acc. sg. m. n. . . . . ἀμπελών (290)

ἀμπελῶνι, dat. sg. m. n. . . . . id.

ἀμπελῶνος, gen. sg. m. n. . . . . id.

Ἀμπλίαν, acc. sg. m. n. (Rom. 16:8, MT & TR | Ἀμπλιᾶτον, GNT, WH & NA) . . . . Ἀμπλίας (291)

(291) **Ἀμπλίας**, ου, ὁ, *Amplias*, pr. name, [§2.B.d]

Ἀμπλιᾶτον, acc. sg. m. n. (Rom. 16:8, GNT, WH & NA | Ἀμπλίαν, MT & TR) . . . . Ἀμπλιᾶτος (†291)

(†291) **Ἀμπλιᾶτος**, ου, ὁ, *Ampliatus*, pr. name

(†292) **ἀμύνω**, fut. ἀμυνῶ [§27.1.a] aor., ἤμυνα, *to ward off; to help, assist*; mid. ἀμύνομαι, *to repel from oneself, resist, make a defence; to assume the office of protector and avenger*, Acts 7:24

ἀμφί, prep. *about, round about* (only occurs

in composition in the N.T.)

ἀμφιάζει, 3 pers. sg. pres. act. indic. (Luke 12:28, WH | ἀμφιέζει, GNT & NA | ἀμφιέννυσι(ν), MT & TR) . . . . . ἀμφιάζω (‡294)

(‡294) **ἀμφιάζω**, same signif. as ἀμφιέννυμι

ἀμφιβάλλοντας, acc. pl. m. pres. act. part. (Mark 1:16, GNT, WH & NA | βάλλοντας, MT & TR) . . . . ἀμφιβάλλω (‡906)

(‡906) **ἀμφιβάλλω**, fut. ἀμφιβαλῶ [§27.1.b] (ἀμφί + βάλλω) *to throw around; to cast* a net

(293) **ἀμφίβληστρον**, ου, τό [§3.C.c] pr. *what is thrown around*, e.g., a garment; *a large kind of fish-net, drag*, Matt. 4:18; Mark 1:16

ἀμφίβληστρον, acc. sg. neut. n. ἀμφίβληστρον (293)

ἀμφιέζει, 3 pers. sg. pres. act. indic. (Luke 12:28, GNT & NA | ἀμφιάζει, WH | ἀμφιέννυσι(ν), MT & TR) . . . . ἀμφιέζω (†294)

(†294) **ἀμφιέζω**, same signif. as ἀμφιέννυμι

(294) **ἀμφιέννυμι**, fut. ἀμφιέσω, perf. pass. ἠμφίεσμαι [§36.5] (ἀμφί + ἕννυμι, *to put on*) *to clothe, invest*, Matt. 6:30; 11:8; Luke 7:25; 12:28

ἀμφιέννυσι(ν), 3 pers. sg. pres. act. indic. [§31.BB] . . . . ἀμφιέννυμι (294)

Ἀμφίπολιν, acc. sg. f. n. . . . . Ἀμφίπολις (295)

(295) **Ἀμφίπολις**, εως, ἡ [§5.E.c] *Amphipolis*, a city of Thrace, on the river Strymon, Acts 17:1

(296) **ἄμφοδον**, ου, τό [§3.C.c] (equivalent to ἄμφοδος, ου, ἡ, from ἀμφί + ὁδός) pr. *a road leading round a town or village; the street of a village*, Mark 11:4

ἀμφόδου, gen. sg. neut. n. . . . . ἄμφοδον (296)

ἀμφότερα, acc. pl. neut. adj. . . . . . ἀμφότερος (297)

ἀμφότεροι, nom. pl. m. adj. . . . . id.

ἀμφοτέροις, dat. pl. m. adj. . . . . id.

(297) **ἀμφότερος**, α, ον [§10.6.e] (ἄμφω, *both*) *both*. Only plural in the N.T.

ἀμφοτέρους, acc. pl. m. adj. . . . . . ἀμφότερος (297)

ἀμφοτέρων, gen. pl. m. adj. (Acts 19:16, GNT, WH & NA | αὐτῶν, MT & TR) . . . . id.

ἄμωμα, nom. pl. neut. adj. (Phil. 2:15, GNT, WH & NA | ἀμώμητα, MT & TR) . . . . ἄμωμος (299)

ἀμώμητα, nom. pl. neut. adj. (Phil. 2:15, MT & TR | ἄμωμα, GNT, WH & NA) . . . . ἀμώμητος (298)

ἀμώμητοι, nom. pl. m. adj. . . . . id.

(298) **ἀμώμητος**, ον [§7.2] (ἀ + μῶμος) *blameless, irreprehensible*, Phil. 2:15; 2 Pet. 3:14

ἄμωμοι, nom. pl. m. adj. . . . . ἄμωμος (299)

ἄμωμον, acc. sg. m. adj. {Heb. 9:14} . . . . id.

(299') **ἄμωμον**, ου, τό [§3.C.c] *amomum*, an odoriferous shrub, from which a precious ointment was prepared {Rev. 18:13} ἄμωμον, acc. sg. neut. n. . . . . ἄμωμον *(299)*

(299) **ἄμωμος,** ον [§7.2] (ἀ + μῶμος) *blameless*
ἄμωμος, nom. sg. f. adj. . . . . ἄμωμος *(299)*
ἀμώμου, gen. sg. m. adj. . . . . id.
ἀμώμους, acc. pl. m. adj. . . . . id.

(300) **Ἀμών,** ὁ, *Amon,* pr. name, indecl. (Matt. 1:10,
MT & TR | Ἀμώς, GNT, WH & NA)

(301) **Ἀμώς,** ὁ, *Amos,* pr. name, indecl.

(302) **ἄν,** a particle. For the various constructions
of this particle, and their significance, consult a grammar. At the beginning of a
clause, it is another form of ἐάν, *if,* John
20:23

(303) **ἀνά,** prep. used in the N.T. only in certain
forms. ἀνὰ μέρος, *in turn;* ἀνὰ μέσον,
through the midst, between; ἀνὰ
δηνάριον, *at the rate of a denarius;* with
numerals, ἀνὰ ἑκατόν, *in parties of a hundred.* In composition, *step by step, up,
back, again*
ἀνάβα, 2 pers. sg. 2 aor. act. imper. by apocope for ἀνάβηθι [§31.1.d] . . . . . . ἀναβαίνω *(305)*

(304) **ἀναβαθμός,** οῦ, ὁ [§3.C.a] *the act of ascend-
ing; means of ascent, steps, stairs,* Acts
21:35, 40
ἀναβαθμούς, acc. pl. m. n. . . . . ἀναβαθμός *(304)*
ἀναβαθμῶν, gen. pl. m. n. . . . . id.
ἀναβαίνει, 3 pers. sg. pres. act.
indic. . . . . ἀναβαίνω *(305)*
ἀναβαίνειν, pres. act. infin. . . . . id.
ἀναβαίνομεν, 1 pers. pl. pres. act. indic. . . id.
ἀναβαῖνον, nom. sg. neut. pres. act. part.
{Rev. 11:7} . . . . id.
ἀναβαῖνον, acc. sg. neut. pres. act. part.
{Rev. 13:1} . . . . id.
ἀναβαίνοντα, acc. sg. m. pres. act. part. . . id.
ἀναβαίνοντας, acc. pl. m. pres. act. part. . id.
ἀναβαίνοντες, nom. pl. m. pres. act. part. . id.
ἀναβαινόντων, gen. pl. ˙m. pres. act. part. . id.
ἀναβαίνουσιν, 3 pers. pl. pres. act. indic. . id.

(305) **ἀναβαίνω,** 1 pers. sg. pres. act. indic., fut.
ἀναβήσομαι, perf. ἀναβέβηκα, 2 aor.
ἀνέβην [§37.1] (ἀνά + βαίνω) *to go up,
ascend,* Matt. 5:1, et al.; *to climb,* Luke
19:4; *to go on board,* Mark 6:51; *to rise,
mount upwards,* as smoke, Rev. 8:4; *to
grow or spring up,* as plants, Matt. 13:7;
to spring up, arise, as thoughts, Luke 24:38
ἀναβαίνων, nom. sg. m. pres. act.
part. . . . . ἀναβαίνω *(305)*

(†306) **ἀναβάλλω,** fut. ἀναβαλῶ [§27.1.a,b] perf.
ἀναβέβληκα [§27.2.d] (ἀνά + βάλλω) *to
throw back;* mid. *to put off, defer, adjourn,*
Acts 24:22
ἀναβάντα, acc. sg. m. 2 aor. act.

part. . . . . ἀναβαίνω *(305)*
ἀναβάντες, nom. pl. m. 2 aor. act. part. . id.
ἀναβάντων, gen. pl. m. 2 aor. act. part. . . id.
ἀναβάς, nom. sg. m. 2 aor. act. part. . . . . id.
ἀνάβατε, 2 pers. pl. 2 aor. act. imper. (Rev.
11:12, GNT, WH & NA | ἀνάβητε, MT
& TR) . . . . id.
ἀναβέβηκα, 1 pers. sg. perf. act. indic. . . . id.
ἀναβέβηκεν, 3 pers. sg. perf. act. indic. . . id.
ἀναβήσεται, 3 pers. sg. fut. mid. dep. indic. id.
ἀνάβητε, 2 pers. pl. 2 aor. act. imper. . . . . id.

(307) **ἀναβιβάζω,** fut. ἀναβιβάσω, aor. ἀνεβίβασα
[§26.1] (ἀνά + βιβάζω) *to cause to come
up or ascend, draw or bring up,* Matt.
13:48
ἀναβιβάσαντες, nom. pl. m. aor. act.
part. . . . . ἀναβιβάζω *(307)*
ἀναβλέπουσι(ν), 3 pers. pl. pres. act.
indic. . . . . ἀναβλέπω *(308)*

(308) **ἀναβλέπω,** fut. ἀναβλέψω [§23.1.a] (ἀνά +
βλέπω) *to look upwards,* Matt. 14:19, et
al.; *to see again, recover sight,* Matt. 11:5,
et al.
ἀναβλέψαι, aor. act. infin. (Mark 8:25, MT
& TR | διέβλεψεν, GNT, WH &
NA) . . . . ἀναβλέπω *(308)*
ἀναβλέψαντος, gen. sg. m. aor. act. part. . id.
ἀναβλέψας, nom. sg. m. aor. act. part. . . . id.
ἀναβλέψασαι, nom. pl. f. aor. act. part. . . id.
ἀναβλέψῃ, 3 pers. sg. aor. act. subj. . . . . . id.
ἀναβλέψῃς, 2 pers. sg. aor. act. subj. . . . . id.
ἀνάβλεψιν, acc. sg. f. n. . . . . ἀνάβλεψις *(309)*

(309) **ἀνάβλεψις,** εως, ἡ [§5.E.c] *recovery of sight,*
Luke 4:18
ἀνάβλεψον, 2 pers. sg. aor. act.
imper. . . . . ἀναβλέπω *(308)*
ἀναβλέψω, 1 pers. sg. aor. act. subj. . . . . . id.

(310) **ἀναβοάω,** ῶ [§18.R] fut. ἀναβοήσομαι, aor.,
ἀνεβόησα (ἀνά + βοάω) *to cry out or
aloud, exclaim,* Matt. 27:46; Mark 15:8;
Luke 9:38
ἀναβοήσας, nom. sg. m. aor. act. part. (Mark
15:8, MT & TR | ἀναβάς, GNT, WH &
NA) . . . . ἀναβοάω *(310)*

(311) **ἀναβολή,** ῆς, ἡ [§2.B.a] *delay,* Acts 25:17
ἀναβολήν, acc. sg. f. n. . . . . ἀναβολή *(311)*
ἀναγαγεῖν, 2 aor. act. infin. [§13.7.d] . . . ἀνάγω *(321)*

(‡508) **ἀνάγαιον,** ου, τό, *an upper room*
ἀνάγαιον, acc. sg. neut. n. (Mark 14:15; Luke
22:12, GNT, WH & NA | ἀνώγεον, MT
& TR) . . . . ἀνάγαιον *(‡508)*
ἀναγαγών, nom. sg. m. 2 aor. act. part. ἀνάγω *(321)*
ἀναγγεῖλαι, aor. act. infin. [§27.1.d] ἀναγγέλλω *(312)*
ἀνάγγειλον, 2 pers. sg. aor. act. imper. (Mark
5:19, MT & TR | ἀπάγγειλον, GNT, WH

& NA) . . . . ἀναγγέλλω *(312)*

ἀναγγελεῖ, 3 pers. sg. fut. act. indic. . . . . . id.

ἀναγγέλλομεν, 1 pers. pl. pres. act. indic.   id.

ἀναγγέλλοντες, nom. pl. m. pres. act. part.   id.

(312) **ἀναγγέλλω**, fut. ἀναγγελῶ, aor. ἀνήγγειλα [§27.1.b,d] 2 aor., pass. ἀνηγγέλην [§27.4.a] (ἀνά + ἀγγέλλω) *to bring back word, announce, report*, Mark 5:14, et al.; *to declare, set forth, teach* John 4:25, et al.

ἀναγγέλλων, nom. sg. m. pres. act. part. . . . . ἀναγγέλλω *(312)*

ἀναγγελῶ, 1 pers. sg. fut. act. indic. (John 16:25, MT & TR | ἀπαγγελῶ, GNT, WH & NA) . . . . id.

(313) **ἀναγεννάω**, ῶ, fut. ἀναγεννήσω [§18.R] perf. pass. ἀναγεγέννημαι (ἀνά + γεννάω) *to beget or bring forth again; to regenerate*, 1 Pet. 1:3, 23

ἀναγεγεννημένοι, nom. pl. m. pres. pass. part. ἀναγεννάω *(313)*

ἀναγεννήσας, nom. sg. m. aor. act. part. .   id.

ἀνάγεσθαι, pres. pass. infin. . . . . ἀνάγω *(321)*

ἀναγινώσκεις, 2 pers. sg. pres. act. indic. ἀναγινώσκω *(314)*

ἀναγινώσκεται, 3 pers. sg. pres. pass. indic. (2 Cor. 3:15, MT & TR | ἀναγινώσκηται, GNT, WH & NA) . . . . id.

ἀναγινώσκετε, 2 pers. pl. pres. act. indic.   id.

ἀναγινώσκηται, 3 pers. sg. pres. pass. subj. (2 Cor. 3:15, GNT, WH & NA | ἀναγινώσκεται, MT & TR) . . . . id.

ἀναγινωσκομένας, acc. pl. f. pres. pass. part.   id.

ἀναγινωσκομένη, nom. sg. f. pres. pass. part.   id.

ἀναγινωσκόμενος, nom. sg. m. pres. pass. part. . . . . id.

ἀναγινώσκοντες, nom. pl. m. pres. act. part.   id.

ἀναγινώσκοντος, gen. sg. m. pres. act. part.   id.

(314) **ἀναγινώσκω** [§36.3] fut. ἀναγνώσομαι, 2 aor., ἀνέγνων, aor. pass. ἀνεγνώσθην (ἀνά + γινώσκω) *to gather exact knowledge of, recognize, discern;* especially, *to read*

ἀναγινώσκων, nom. sg. m. pres. act. part. ἀναγινώσκω *(314)*

ἀναγκάζεις, 2 pers. sg. pres. act. indic. ἀναγκάζω *(315)*

ἀναγκάζουσιν, 3 pers. pl. pres. act. indic.   id.

(315) **ἀναγκάζω**, fut. ἀναγκάσω [§26.1] *to force, compel*, Acts 28:19, et al.; *to constrain, urge*, Luke 14:23, et al.

ἀναγκαῖα, nom. pl. neut. adj. . . . . . ἀναγκαῖος *(316)*

ἀναγκαίας, acc. pl. f. adj. . . . . id.

ἀναγκαῖον, nom. sg. neut. adj. {Acts 13:41}   id.

ἀναγκαῖον, acc. sg. neut. adj. {2 Cor. 9:5}   id.

(316) **ἀναγκαῖος**, α, ον [§7.1] *necessary, indispensable*, 1 Cor. 12:22; *necessary, needful,*

right, proper, Acts 13:46; 2 Cor. 9:5; Phil. 1:24; 2:25; Heb. 8:3; *near, intimate, closely connected,* as friends, Acts 10:24

ἀναγκαιότερον, nom. sg. neut. compar. adj. [§8.4] . . . . ἀναγκαῖος *(316)*

ἀναγκαίους, acc. pl. m. adj. . . . . id.

ἀνάγκαις, dat. pl. f. n. . . . . ἀνάγκη *(†318)*

ἀνάγκασον, 2 pers. sg. aor. act. imper. . . . . ἀναγκάζω *(315)*

(317) **ἀναγκαστῶς**, adv., *by constraint or compulsion, unwillingly,* opposite to ἑκουσίως, 1 Pet. 5:2

(†318) **ἀνάγκη**, ης, ἡ, nom. sg. f. n. [§2.B.a] (ἄγχω, *to compress*) *necessity,* Matt. 18:7, et al.; *constraint, compulsion,* 2 Cor. 9:7, et al.; *obligation of duty,* moral or spiritual *necessity,* Rom. 13:5, et al.; *distress, trial, affliction,* Luke 21:23; 1 Cor. 7:26; 2 Cor. 6:4; 12:10; 1 Thess. 3:7

ἀνάγκῃ, dat. sg. f. n. . . . . ἀνάγκη *(†318)*

ἀνάγκην, acc. sg. f. n. . . . . id.

ἀνάγκης, gen. sg. f. n. . . . . id.

ἀναγνόντες, nom. pl. m. 2 aor. act. part. ἀναγινώσκω *(314)*

ἀναγνούς, nom. sg. m. 2 aor. act. part. . .   id.

ἀναγνῶναι, 2 aor. act. infin. [§36.3] . . . . . id.

(†319) **ἀναγνωρίζω**, fut. ἀναγνωρίσω, aor. pass. ἀνεγνωρίσθην [§26.1] (ἀνά + γνωρίζω) *to recognize;* pass. *to be made known, or to cause one's self to be recognized,* Acts 7:13

ἀναγνώσει, dat. sg. f. n. . . . . ἀνάγνωσις *(320)*

ἀναγνωσθῇ, 3 pers. sg. aor. pass. subj. ἀναγινώσκω *(314)*

ἀναγνωσθῆναι, aor. pass. infin. . . . . id.

ἀνάγνωσιν, acc. sg. f. n. . . . . ἀνάγνωσις *(320)*

(320) **ἀνάγνωσις**, εως, ἡ [§5.E.c] *reading,* Acts 13:15; 2 Cor. 3:14; 1 Tim. 4:13

ἀναγνῶτε, 2 pers. pl. 2 aor. act. subj. . . . . ἀναγινώσκω *(314)*

ἀναγομένοις, dat. pl. m. pres. pass. part. . . . . ἀνάγω *(321)*

(321) **ἀνάγω**, fut. ἀνάξω [§23.1.b] 2 aor. ἀνήγαγον [§13.7.d] aor. pass. ἀνήχθην (ἀνά + ἄγω) *to conduct; to lead or convey* up from a lower place to a higher, Luke 4:5, et al.; *to offer up,* as a sacrifice, Acts 7:41; *to lead out, produce,* Acts 12:4; mid. ἀνάγομαι, aor. ἀνήχθην, as a nautical term, *to set sail, put to sea,* Luke 8:22, et al.

(322) **ἀναδείκνυμι**, or ἀναδεικνύω, fut. ἀναδείξω [§31.BB] (ἀνά + δείκνυμι) pr. *to show anything by raising it aloft,* as a torch; *to display, manifest, show plainly or openly,* Acts 1:24; *to mark out, constitute, appoint* by some outward sign, Luke 10:1

ἀναδείξεως, gen. sg. f. n. . . . . ἀνάδειξις *(323)*

(323) **ἀνάδειξις**, εως, ἡ [§5.E.c] *a showing forth, manifestation; public entrance upon the duty or office to which one is consecrated,* Luke 1:80

ἀνάδειξον, 2 pers. sg. aor. act. imper. . . . . ἀναδείκνυμι *(322)*

ἀναδεξάμενος, nom. sg. m. aor. mid. dep. part. . . . . ἀναδέχομαι *(324)*

(324) **ἀναδέχομαι**, fut. ἀναδέξομαι [§23.1.b] (ἀνά + δέχομαι) *to receive,* as opposed to shunning or refusing; *to receive* with hospitality, Acts 28:7; *to embrace* a proffer or promise, Heb. 11:17

(325) **ἀναδίδωμι**, fut. ἀναδώσω, 2 aor. ἀνέδων [§30.Z] (ἀνά + δίδωμι) *to give forth, up, or back; to deliver, present,* Acts 23:33

ἀναδόντες, nom. pl. m. 2 aor. act. part. . . . . ἀναδίδωμι *(325)*

(326) **ἀναζάω**, ῶ, fut. ἀναζήσω [§18.R] (ἀνά + ζάω) *to live again, recover life,* Rom. 14:9; Rev. 20:5; *to revive, recover activity,* Rom. 7:9; met. *to live a new and reformed life,* Luke 15:24, 32

(327) **ἀναζητέω**, ῶ, fut. ἀναζητήσω [§16.P] (ἀνά + ζητέω) *to track; to seek diligently, inquire after, search for,* Luke 2:44; Acts 11:25

ἀναζητῆσαι, aor. act. infin. . . . . ἀναζητέω *(327)*
ἀναζητοῦντες, nom. pl. m. pres. act. part. (Luke 2:45, GNT, WH & NA | ζητοῦντες, MT & TR) . . . . id.

(328) **ἀναζώννυμι**, fut. ἀναζώσω [§31.BB] (ἀνά + ζώννυμι) *to gird* with a belt or girdle; mid. ἀναζώννυμαι, aor. ἀνεζωσάμην, *to gird one's self,* 1 Pet. 1:13

ἀναζωπυρεῖν, pres. act. infin. . . . . ἀναζωπυρέω *(329)*

(329) **ἀναζωπυρέω**, ῶ, fut. ἀναζωπυρήσω [§16.P] (ἀνά + ζωπυρέω, *to receive a fire,* from ζωός + πῦρ) pr. *to kindle up a dormant fire;* met. *to revive, excite; to stir up, quicken* one's powers, 2 Tim. 1:6

ἀναζωσάμενοι, nom. pl. m. aor. mid. part. . . . . ἀναζώννυμι *(328)*

(330) **ἀναθάλλω**, fut. ἀναθαλῶ [§27.1.b] 2 aor. ἀνέθαλον (ἀνά + θάλλω, *to thrive, flourish*) pr. *to recover verdure, flourish again;* met. *to receive, to recover activity,* Phil. 4:10

(331) **ἀνάθεμα**, ατος, τό, nom. sg. neut. n. [§4.D.c] (a later equivalent to ἀνάθημα) *a devoted thing,* but ordinarily in a bad sense, *a person* or *thing accursed,* Rom. 9:3; 1 Cor. 12:3; 16:22; Gal. 1:8, 9; *a curse, execration, anathema,* Acts 23:14

ἀναθέματι, dat. sg. neut. n. . . . . ἀνάθεμα *(331)*
ἀναθεματίζειν, pres. act. infin. . . . ἀναθεματίζω *(332)*

(332) **ἀναθεματίζω**, fut. ἀναθεματίσω [§26.1] *to declare* any one *to be* ἀνάθεμα; *to curse, bind by a curse,* Mark 14:71; Acts 23:12, 14, 21

(333) **ἀναθεωρέω**, ῶ, fut. ἀναθεωρήσω [§16.P] (ἀνά + θεωρέω) *to view, behold attentively, contemplate,* Acts 17:23; Heb. 13:7

ἀναθεωροῦντες, nom. pl. m. pres. act. part. . . . . ἀναθεωρέω *(333)*
ἀναθεωρῶν, nom. sg. m. pres. act. part. . . id.

(334) **ἀνάθημα**, ατος, τό [§4.D.c] *a gift* or *offering consecrated to God,* Luke 21:5

ἀναθήμασι(ν), dat. pl. neut. n. (Luke 21:5, GNT & NA) . . . . ἀνάθημα *(334)*

(335) **ἀναίδεια**, ας, ἡ [§2.B.b; 2.2] (ἀ + αἰδώς) pr. *impudence;* hence, *importunate solicitation, pertinacious importunity,* without regard to time, place, or person, Luke 11:8

ἀναίδειαν, acc. sg. f. n. (Luke 11:8, GNT, MT, TR & NA | ἀναιδίαν, WH) . . . . . ἀναίδεια *(335)*
ἀναιρεθῆναι, aor. pass. infin. [§36.1] . . ἀναιρέω *(337)*
ἀναιρεῖ, 3 pers. sg. pres. act. indic. . . . . . . id.
ἀναιρεῖν, pres. act. infin. . . . . id.
ἀναιρεῖσθαι, pres. pass. infin. [§17.Q] . . . id.
ἀναιρέσει, dat. sg. f. n. . . . . ἀναίρεσις *(336)*

(336) **ἀναίρεσις**, εως, ἡ [§5.E.c] *a taking up* or *away; a putting to death, murder,* Acts 8:1; 22:20

(337) **ἀναιρέω**, ῶ, fut. ἀναιρήσω, 2 aor., ἀνεῖλον, aor. pass. ἀνῃρέθην [§36.1] (ἀνά + αἱρέω) pr. *to take up, lift,* as from the ground; *to take off, put to death, kill, murder,* Matt. 2:16, et al.; *to take away, abolish, abrogate,* Heb. 10:9; mid. *to take up* infants in order to bring them up, Acts 7:21

ἀναιρουμένων, gen. pl. m. pres. pass. part. . . . . ἀναιρέω *(337)*
ἀναιρούντων, gen. pl. m. pres. act. part. . id.
ἀναίτιοι, nom. pl. m. adj. . . . . ἀναίτιος *(338)*

(338) **ἀναίτιος**, ον [§7.2] (ἀ + αἰτία) *guiltless, innocent,* Matt. 12:5, 7

ἀναιτίους, acc. pl. m. adj. . . . . ἀναίτιος *(338)*

(339) **ἀνακαθίζω**, fut. ἀνακαθίσω [§26.1] (ἀνά + καθίζω) *to set up;* intrans. *to sit up,* Luke 7:15; Acts 9:40

ἀνακαινίζειν, pres. act. infin. . . . . . ἀνακαινίζω *(340)*

(340) **ἀνακαινίζω**, fut. ἀνακαινίσω [§26.1] (ἀνά + καινίζω) *to renovate, renew,* Heb. 6:6

ἀνακαινούμενον, acc. sg. m. pres. pass. part. . . . . ἀνακαινόω *(341)*
ἀνακαινοῦται, 3 pers. sg. pres. pass. indic. [§21.U] . . . . id.

(341) **ἀνακαινόω**, ῶ, fut. ἀνακαινώσω [§20.T] (ἀνά + καινός) *to invigorate, renew,* 2 Cor.

4:16; Col. 3:10

ἀνακαινώσει, dat. sg. f. n. ...... ἀνακαίνωσις *(342)*

ἀνακαινώσεως, gen. sg. f. n. .... id.

(342) **ἀνακαίνωσις,** εως, ἡ [§5.E.c] *renovation, renewal,* Rom. 12:2; Tit. 3:5

ἀνακαλυπτόμενον, nom. sg. neut. pres. pass. part. .... ἀνακαλύπτω *(343)*

(343) **ἀνακαλύπτω,** fut. ἀνακαλύψω [§23.1.a] (ἀνά + καλύπτω) *to unveil, uncover;* pass. *to be unveiled,* 2 Cor. 3:18; met. *to be disclosed* in true character and condition, 2 Cor. 3:14

(344) **ἀνακάμπτω,** fut. ἀνακάψω [§23.1.a] (ἀνά + κάμπτω) pr. *to reflect, bend back;* hence, *to bend back* one's course, *return,* Matt. 2:12; Luke 10:6; Acts 18:21; Heb. 11:15

ἀνακάμψαι, aor. act. infin. ...... ἀνακάμπτω *(344)*

ἀνακάμψει, 3 pers. sg. fut. act. indic. .... id.

ἀνακάμψω, 1 pers. sg. fut. act. indic. .... id.

(†345) **ἀνάκειμαι,** fut. ἀνακείσομαι [§33.DD] (ἀνά + κεῖμαι) *to be laid up,* as offerings; later, *to lie, be in a recumbent posture, recline* at table, Matt. 9:10, et al.

ἀνακειμένοις, dat. pl. m. pres. mid./pass. dep. part. .... ἀνάκειμαι *(†345)*

ἀνακείμενον, nom. sg. neut. pres. mid./pass. dep. part. (Mark 5:40, MT & TR | GNT, WH & NA omit) .... id.

ἀνακείμενος, nom. sg. m. pres. mid./pass. dep. part. .... id.

ἀνακειμένου, gen. sg. m. pres. mid./pass. dep. part. .... id.

ἀνακειμένους, acc. pl. m. pres. mid./pass. dep. part. .... id.

ἀνακειμένων, gen. pl. m. pres. mid./pass. dep. part. .... id.

ἀνακεῖται, 3 pers. sg. pres. mid./pass. dep. indic. (Luke 7:37, MT & TR | κατάκειται, GNT, WH & NA) ...... id.

ἀνακεκαλυμμένῳ, dat. sg. neut. perf. pass. part. .... ἀνακαλύπτω *(343)*

ἀνακεκύλισται, 3 pers. sg. perf. pass. indic. (Mark 16:4, WH | ἀποκεκύλισται, GNT, MT, TR & NA) .... ἀνακυλίω *(‡617)*

ἀνακεφαλαιοῦται, 3 pers. sg. pres. pass. indic. .... ἀνακεφαλαιόω *(†346)*

(†346) **ἀνακεφαλαιόω,** ῶ, fut. ἀνακεφαλαιώσω [§20.T] (ἀνά + κεφάλαιον) *to bring together several things under one, reduce under one head; to comprise,* Rom. 13:9; Eph. 1:10

ἀνακεφαλαιώσασθαι, aor. mid. dep. infin. .... ἀνακεφαλαιόω *(†346)*

ἀνακλιθῆναι, aor. pass. infin. ...... ἀνακλίνω *(347)*

ἀνακλιθήσονται, 3 pers. pl. fut. pass. indic. .... id.

ἀνακλῖναι, aor. act. infin. (Mark 6:39, GNT, MT, TR & NA | ἀνακλιθῆναι, WH) .... ἀνακλίνω *(347)*

ἀνακλινεῖ, 3 pers. sg. fut. act. indic. ..... id.

(347) **ἀνακλίνω,** fut. ἀνακλινῶ [§27.1.a] (ἀνά + κλίνω) *to lay down,* Luke 2:7; *to cause to recline* at table, etc. Mark 6:39; Luke 9:15; 12:37; mid. ἀνακλίνομαι, aor. (pass. form) ἀνεκλίθην, fut. (pass. form) ἀνακλιθήσομαι, *to recline at table,* Matt. 8:11, et al.

(348) **ἀνακόπτω,** fut. ἀνακόψω [§23.1.a] (ἀνά + κόπτω) pr. *to beat back;* hence, *to check, impede, hinder, restrain,* Gal. 5:7

(349) **ἀνακράζω,** fut. ἀνακράξομαι [§26.1] aor., ἀνέκραξα, in N.T. (ἀνά + κράζω) *to cry aloud, exclaim, shout,* Mark 1:23; 6:49; Luke 4:33; 8:28; 23:18

ἀνακράξας, nom. sg. m. aor. act. part. .... ἀνακράζω *(349)*

ἀνακριθῶ, 1 pers. sg. aor. pass. subj. ἀνακρίνω *(350)*

ἀνακρίναντες, nom. pl. m. aor. act. part. . id.

ἀνακρίνας, nom. sg. m. aor. act. part. ... id.

ἀνακρίνει, 3 pers. sg. pres. act. indic. ... id.

ἀνακρίνεται, 3 pers. sg. pres. pass. indic. . id.

ἀνακρινόμεθα, 1 pers. pl. pres. pass. indic. id.

ἀνακρίνοντες, nom. pl. m. pres. act. part. id.

ἀνακρίνουσιν, dat. pl. m. pres. act. part. . id.

(350) **ἀνακρίνω,** 1 pers. sg. pres. act. indic., fut. ἀνακρινῶ [§27.1.a] aor. ἀνέκρινα, aor. pass. ἀνεκρίθην (ἀνά + κρίνω) *to sift; to examine closely,* Acts 17:11; *to scrutinize, scan,* 1 Cor. 2:14, 15; 9:3; *to try judicially,* Luke 23:14, et al.; *to judge, give judgment upon,* 1 Cor. 4:3, 4; *to put questions, be inquisitive,* 1 Cor. 10:25, 27

ἀνακρίνων, nom. sg. m. pres. act. part. .... ἀνακρίνω *(350)*

ἀνακρίσεως, gen. sg. f. n. .... ἀνάκρισις *(351)*

(351) **ἀνάκρισις,** εως, ἡ [§5.E.c] *investigation, judicial examination, hearing of a cause,* Acts 25:26

(‡617) **ἀνακυλίω,** *to roll back,* Mark 16:4

(352) **ἀνακύπτω,** fut. ἀνακύψω [§23.1.a] (ἀνά + κύπτω) pr. *to raise up one's self, look up,* Luke 13:11; John 8:7, 10; met. *to look up cheerily, to be cheered,* Luke 21:28

ἀνακύψαι, aor. act. infin. ...... ἀνακύπτω *(352)*

ἀνακύψας, nom. sg. m. aor. act. part. ... id.

ἀνακύψατε, 2 pers. pl. aor. act. imper. ... id.

ἀναλάβετε, 2 pers. pl. 2 aor. act. imper. .... ἀναλαμβάνω *(353)*

ἀναλαβόντες, nom. pl. m. 2 aor. act. part. id.

ἀναλαβών, nom. sg. m. 2 aor. act. part. .. id.

ἀναλαμβάνειν, pres. act. infin. .... id.

(353) **ἀναλαμβάνω,** fut. ἀναλήψομαι (ἀναλήμ-
ψομαι) 2 aor. ἀνέλαβον, aor. pass. ἀνε-
λήφθην (ἀνελήμφθην) [§36.2] *to take up,
receive up,* Mark 16:19, et al.; *to take up,
carry,* Acts 7:43; *to take on board,* Acts
20:13, 14; *to take* in company, Acts 23:31;
2 Tim. 4:11

ἀναλημφθείς, nom. sg. m. aor. pass. part.
(Acts 1:11, GNT, WH & NA | ἀναλη-
φθείς, MT & TR) . . . . ἀναλαμβάνω *(353)*

ἀναλήμψεως, gen. sg. f. n. (Luke 9:51, GNT,
WH & NA | ἀναλήψεως, MT &
TR) . . . . ἀνάλημψις *(†354)*

(†354) **ἀνάλημψις,** εως, ἡ [§5.E.c] *a taking up, receiving up,* Luke 9:51

ἀναληθείς, nom. sg. m. aor. pass. part. (Acts
1:11, MT & TR | ἀναλημφθείς, GNT,
WH & NA) . . . . ἀναλαμβάνω *(353)*

ἀναλήψεως, gen. sg. f. n. (Luke 9:51, MT &
TR | ἀναλήμψεως, GNT, WH &
NA) . . . . ἀνάληψις *(354)*

(354) **ἀνάληψις,** εως, ἡ [§5.E.c] *a taking up, receiving up,* Luke 9:51

(355) **ἀναλίσκω,** fut. ἀναλώσω, aor. ἀνήλωσα and
ἀνάλωσα, aor. pass. ἀνηλώθην and
ἀναλώθην [§36.3] (ἀνά + ἁλίσκω) *to use
up; to consume, destroy,* Luke 9:54; Gal.
5:15; 2 Thess. 2:8

(356) **ἀναλογία,** ας, ἡ [§2.B.b; 2.2] (ἀνά + λόγος)
analogy, ratio, proportion, Rom. 12:6

ἀναλογίαν, acc. sg. f. n. . . . . ἀναλογία *(356)*

(357) **ἀναλογίζομαι,** fut. ἀναλογίσομαι [§26.1] (ἀνά
+ λογίζομαι) *to consider attentively,* Heb.
12:3

ἀναλογίσασθε, 2 pers. pl. aor. mid. dep.
imper. . . . . ἀναλογίζομαι *(357)*

ἄναλον, nom. sg. neut. adj. . . . . ἄναλος *(358)*

(358) **ἄναλος,** ον [§7.2] (ἀ + ἅλς) *without saltness,
without the taste and pungency of salt, insipid,* Mark 9:50

ἀναλῦσαι, aor. act. infin. . . . . ἀναλύω *(360)*

ἀναλύσει, 3 pers. sg. fut. act. indic. (Luke
12:36, MT & TR | ἀναλύσῃ, GNT, WH
& NA) . . . . id.

ἀναλύσεως, gen. sg. f. n. . . . . ἀνάλυσις *(359)*

ἀναλύσῃ, 3 pers. sg. aor. act. subj. (Luke
12:36, GNT, WH & NA | ἀναλύσει, MT
& TR) . . . . ἀναλύω *(360)*

(359) **ἀνάλυσις,** εως, ἡ [§5.E.c] pr. *dissolution;* met.
departure, death, 2 Tim. 4:6

(360) **ἀναλύω,** fut. ἀναλύσω [§13.M] (ἀνά + λύω)
pr. *to loose, dissolve;* intrans. *to loose* in
order to departure; *to depart,* Luke 12:36;
to depart from life, Phil. 1:23

ἀναλωθῆτε, 2 pers. pl. aor. pass.

subj. . . . . ἀναλίσκω *(355)*

ἀναλῶσαι, aor. act. infin. . . . . id.

ἀναλώσει, 3 pers. sg. fut. act. indic. (2 Thess.
2:8, MT & TR | ἀνελεῖ, GNT, WH &
NA) . . . . id.

(361) **ἀναμάρτητος,** ον, nom. sg. m. adj. [§7.2] (ἀ
+ ἁμαρτάνω) *without sin, guiltless,* John
8:7

ἀναμένειν, pres. act. infin. . . . . ἀναμένω *(362)*

(362) **ἀναμένω,** fut. ἀναμενῶ [§27.1.a] (ἀνά +
μένω) *to await, wait for, expect,* 1 Thess.
1:10

(‡303) **ἀναμέσον,** compound form of ἀνὰ μέσον
(Rev. 7:17, TRs | ἀνα μέσον, GNT, MT,
TRb, WH & NA)

ἀναμιμνήσκεσθε, 2 pers. pl. pres. mid. imper.
(Heb. 10:32, GNT, MT & NA | ἀνα-
μιμνήσκεσθε, WH & TR) . . ἀναμιμνήσκω *(†363)*

ἀναμιμνησκομένου, gen. sg. m. pres. mid.
part. (2 Cor. 7:15, GNT, MT & NA |
ἀναμιμνησκομένου, WH & TR) . . . . . id.

(†363) **ἀναμιμνήσκω,** 1 pers. sg. pres. act. indic., fut.
ἀναμνήσω (ἀνά + μιμνήσκω) *to remind,
cause to remember,* 1 Cor. 4:17; *to exhort,*
2 Tim. 1:6; mid. ἀναμιμνήσκομαι, aor.
(pass. form) ἀνεμνήσθην, *to call to mind,
recollect, remember,* Mark 14:72; 2 Cor.
7:15; Heb. 10:32 (2 Tim. 1:6, GNT, MT
& NA | ἀναμιμνήσκω, WH & TR)

ἀναμνήσει, 3 pers. sg. fut. act.
indic. . . . . ἀναμιμνήσκω *(†363)*

ἀναμνησθείς, nom. sg. m. aor. pass. dep.
part. . . . . id.

ἀνάμνησιν, acc. sg. f. n. . . . . ἀνάμνησις *(364)*

(364) **ἀνάμνησις,** εως, ἡ, nom. sg. f. n. [§5.E.c] *remembrance; a commemoration, memorial,*
Luke 22:19; 1 Cor. 11:24, 25; Heb. 10:3

ἀνανεοῦσθαι, pres. pass. infin. [§21.U] ἀνανεόω *(365)*

(365) **ἀνανεόω,** ῶ, fut. ἀνανεώσω [§20.T] *to renew;*
pass. *to be renewed, be renovated,* by inward reformation, Eph. 4:23

(366) **ἀνανήφω,** fut. ἀνανήψω [§23.1.a] (ἀνά +
νήφω) *to become sober;* met. *to recover so-
briety* of mind, 2 Tim. 2:26

ἀνανήψωσιν, 3 pers. pl. aor. act.
subj. . . . . ἀνανήφω *(366)*

Ἀνανία, voc. sg. m. n. (Acts 5:3; 9:10, GNT,
WH, MT & NA | Ἀνανία, TR) . . Ἀνανίας *(367)*

Ἀνανίαν, acc. sg. m. n. (Acts 9:12, GNT, WH,
MT & NA | Ἀνανίαν, TR) . . . . id.

(367) **Ἀνανίας,** ου, ὁ, nom. sg. m. n. [§2.B.d] *Ana-
nias,* pr. name   I. *A Christian of Jerusalem,* Acts 5:1, etc.   II. *A Christian of
Damascus,* Acts 9:12, etc.   III. *High
Priest,* Acts 23:2; 24:1 (GNT, WH, MT &

NA | Ἀνανίας, TR)

(368) **ἀναντίρρητος**, ον [§7.2] (ἀ + ἀντερῶ) *not to be contradicted, indisputable,* Acts 19:36
ἀναντιρρήτων, gen. pl. m. adj. (Acts 19:36, GNT, MT, TR & NA | ἀναντιρήτων, WH) . . . . ἀναντίρρητος (368)

(369) **ἀναντιρρήτως**, adv., pr. *without contradiction* or *gainsaying; without hesitation, promptly* (Acts 10:29, GNT, MT, TR & NA | ἀναντιρήτως WH)
ἀνάξιοι, nom. pl. m. adj. . . . . ἀνάξιος (370)

(370) **ἀνάξιος**, ον [§7.2] (ἀ + ἄξιος) *inadequate, unworthy,* 1 Cor. 6:2

(371) **ἀναξίως**, adv., *unworthily, in an improper manner,* 1 Cor. 11:27, 29
ἀναπαήσονται, 3 pers. pl. 2 fut. pass. indic. (Rev. 14:13, GNT, WH & NA | ἀναπαύσωνται, MT & TR) . . . . ἀναπαύω (373)
ἀναπαύεσθε, 2 pers. pl. pres. mid. indic. or imper. . . . . id.
ἀναπαύεται, 3 pers. sg. pres. mid. indic. . . id.
ἀναπαύου, 2 pers. sg. pres. mid. imper. . . . id.
ἀναπαύσασθε, 2 pers. pl. aor. mid. imper. (Mark 6:31, GNT, WH & NA | ἀναπαύεσθε, MT & TR) . . . . id.
ἀνάπαυσιν, acc. sg. f. n. . . . . ἀνάπαυσις (372)

(372) **ἀνάπαυσις**, εως, ἡ [§5.E.c] *rest, intermission,* Matt. 11:29; Rev. 4:8; 14:11; *meton. place of rest, fixed habitation,* Matt. 12:43; Luke 11:24
ἀνάπαυσον, 2 pers. sg. aor. act. imper. ἀναπαύω (373)
ἀναπαύσονται, 3 pers. pl. fut. mid. indic. (Rev. 6:11, GNT, WH & NA | ἀναπαύσωνται, MT & TR) . . . . id.
ἀναπαύσω, 1 pers. sg. fut. act. indic. . . . . id.
ἀναπαύσωνται, 3 pers. pl. aor. mid. subj. (Rev. 6:11; 14:13, MT & TR | Rev. 6:11, ἀναπαύσονται, GNT, WH & NA | Rev. 14:13, ἀναπαήσονται, GNT, WH & NA) id.

(373) **ἀναπαύω**, fut. ἀναπαύσω [§13.M] (ἀνά + παύω) *to cause to rest, to soothe, refresh,* Matt. 11:28, et al.; mid. *to take rest, repose, refreshment,* Matt. 26:45; et al.; *to have a fixed place of rest, abide, dwell,* 1 Pet. 4:14
ἀναπείθει, 3 pers. sg. pres. act. indic. ἀναπείθω (374)

(374) **ἀναπείθω**, fut. ἀναπείσω [§23.1.c] (ἀνά + πείθω) *to persuade* to a different opinion, *to seduce,* Acts 18:13

(‡376) **ἀνάπειρος**, ον, *maimed, deprived of some member of the body,* or *at least of its use*
ἀναπείρους, acc. pl. m. adj. (Luke 14:13, 21, GNT, WH & NA | ἀναπήρους, MT & TR) . . . . ἀνάπειρος (‡376)

(375) **ἀναπέμπω**, fut. ἀναπέμψω [§23.1.a] (ἀνά + πέμπω) *to send back,* Philemon 12; *to send up, remit* to a tribunal, Luke 23:7, 11, 15
ἀναπέμψω, 1 pers. sg. aor. act. subj. (Acts 25:21, GNT, WH & NA | πέμψω, MT & TR) . . . . ἀναπέμπω (375)
ἀναπέπαυται, 3 pers. sg. perf. pass. indic. . . . . ἀναπαύω (373)
ἀνάπεσαι, 2 pers. sg. aor. mid. imper. (Luke 17:7, TR | ἀνάπεσε, GNT, WH, MT & NA) . . . . ἀναπίπτω (377)
ἀνάπεσε, 2 pers. sg. 2 aor. act. imper. (Luke 14:10; 17:7, GNT, WH & NA | ἀνάπεσον, Luke 14:10, TR | ἀνάπεσαι, Luke 17:7, TR) . . . . id.
ἀναπεσεῖν, 2 aor. act. infin. [§37.1] . . . . . . id.
ἀνάπεσον, 2 pers. sg. aor. act. imper. (Luke 14:10, TR | ἀνάπεσε, GNT, WH, MT & NA) . . . . id.
ἀναπεσών, nom. sg. m. 2 aor. act. part. . . id.

(‡450) **ἀναπηδάω**, ῶ, fut. ἀναπηδήσω [§18.R] (ἀνά + πηδάω) *to leap up*
ἀναπηδήσας, nom. sg. m. aor. act. part. (Mark 10:50, GNT, WH & NA | ἀναστάς, MT & TR) . . . . ἀναπηδάω (‡450)

(376) **ἀνάπηρος**, ον [§7.2] (ἀνά + πηρός, *maimed*) *maimed, deprived of some member of the body,* or *at least of its use,* Luke 14:13, 21
ἀναπήρους, acc. pl. m. adj. (Luke 14:13, 21, MT & TR | ἀναπείρους, GNT, WH & NA) . . . . ἀνάπηρος (376)

(377) **ἀναπίπτω**, fut. ἀναπεσοῦμαι, 2 aor., ἀνέπεσον [§37.1] (ἀνά + πίπτω) *to fall* or *recline backwards; to recline* at table, etc., Luke 11:37, et al.; *to throw one's self back,* John 21:20
ἀναπληροῦται, 3 pers. sg. pres. pass. indic. [§21.U] . . . . ἀναπληρόω (378)

(378) **ἀναπληρόω**, ῶ, fut. ἀναπληρώσω [§20.T] (ἀνά + πληρόω) *to fill up, complete,* 1 Thess. 2:6; *to fulfil, confirm,* as a prophecy by the event, Matt. 13:14; *to fill the place of any one,* 1 Cor. 14:16; *to supply, make good,* 1 Cor. 16:17; Phil. 2:30; *to observe fully, keep* the law, Gal. 6:2
ἀναπληρῶν, nom. sg. m. pres. act. part. . . . . ἀναπληρόω (378)
ἀναπληρῶσαι, aor. act. infin. . . . . id.
ἀναπληρώσατε, 2 pers. pl. aor. act. imper. (Gal. 6:2, WH, MT & TR | ἀναπληρώσετε, GNT & NA) . . . . id.
ἀναπληρώσετε, 2 pers. pl. fut. act. indic. (Gal. 6:2, GNT & NA | ἀναπληρώσατε, WH, MT & TR) . . . . id.
ἀναπληρώσῃ, 3 pers. sg. aor. act. subj. . . . id.

(379) **ἀναπολόγητος,** ον, nom. sg. m. adj. [§7.2] (ἀ + ἀπολογέομαι) *inexcusable,* Rom. 1:20; 2:1

ἀναπολογήτους, acc. pl. m. adj. ἀναπολόγητος *(379)*

ἀνάπτει, 3 pers. sg. pres. act. indic. ... ἀνάπτω *(381)*

ἀναπτύξας, nom. sg. m. aor. act. part. (Luke 4:17, GNT, MT, TR & NA | ἀνοίξας, WH) .... ἀναπτύσσω *(380)*

(380) **ἀναπτύσσω,** fut. ἀναπτύξω [§26.3] (ἀνά + πτύσσω) *to roll back, unroll, unfold,* Luke 4:17

(381) **ἀνάπτω,** fut. ἀνάψω [§23.1.a] (ἀνά + ἅπτω) *to light, kindle, set on fire,* Luke 12:49; Acts 28:2; James 3:5

(382) **ἀναρίθμητος,** ον [§7.2] (ἀ + ἀριθμός) *innumerable,* Heb. 11:12

ἀναρίθμητος, nom. sg. f. adj. ... ἀναρίθμητος *(382)*

ἀνασείει, 3 pers. sg. pres. act. indic. .. ἀνασείω *(383)*

(383) **ἀνασείω,** fut. ἀνασείσω [§13.M] (ἀνά + σείω) pr. *to shake up;* met. *to stir up, instigate,* Mark. 15:11; Luke 23:5

ἀνασκευάζοντες, nom. pl. m. pres. act. part. .... ἀνασκευάζω *(384)*

(384) **ἀνασκευάζω,** fut. ἀνασκευάσω [§26.1] (ἀνά + σκευάζω, from σκεῦος) pr. *to collect one's effects* or *baggage* (σκεύη) in order to remove; *to lay waste by carrying off* or *destroying* every thing; met. *to unsettle, pervert, subvert,* Acts 15:24

ἀνασπάσει, 3 pers. sg. fut. act. indic. ἀνασπάω *(385)*

(385) **ἀνασπάω,** ῶ, fut. ἀνασπάσω [§22.2] (ἀνά + σπάω) *to draw up, to draw out,* Luke 14:5; Acts 11:10

ἀνάστα, 2 pers. sg. 2 aor. act. imper. by apocope for ἀνάστηθι [§29.2] .... ἀνίστημι *(450)*

ἀναστάν, nom. sg. neut. 2 aor. act. part. . id.

ἀναστάντες, nom. pl. m. 2 aor. act. part. id.

ἀναστάς, nom. sg. m. 2 aor. act. part. ... id.

ἀναστᾶσα, nom. sg. f. 2 aor. act. part. ... id.

ἀναστάσει, dat. sg. f. n. .... ἀνάστασις *(386)*

ἀναστάσεως, gen. sg. f. n. .... id.

ἀνάστασιν, acc. sg. f. n. .... id.

(386) **ἀνάστασις,** εως, ἡ, nom. sg. f. n. [§5.E.c] *a raising* or *rising up; resurrection* Matt. 22:23, et al.; meton. *the author of resurrection,* John 11:25; met. *an uprising* into a state of higher advancement and blessedness, Luke 2:34

ἀναστατοῦντες, nom. pl. m. pres. act. part. .... ἀναστατόω *(387)*

(387) **ἀναστατόω,** ῶ, fut. ἀναστατώσω [§20.T] i.e. ἀνάστατον ποιεῖν, *to lay waste, destroy; to disturb, throw into commotion,* Acts 17:6; *to excite to sedition and tumult,* Acts 21:38; *to disturb* the mind of any one by

doubts, etc.; *to subvert, unsettle,* Gal. 5:12

ἀναστατώσαντες, nom. pl. m. aor. act. part. .... ἀναστατόω *(387)*

ἀναστατώσας, nom. sg. m. aor. act. part. id.

ἀνασταυροῦντας, acc. pl. m. pres. act. part. .... ἀνασταυρόω *(388)*

(388) **ἀνασταυρόω,** ῶ, fut. ἀνασταυρώσω [§20.T] (ἀνά + σταυρόω) pr. *to crucify;* met. *to crucify* by indignity, Heb. 6:6

(389) **ἀναστενάζω,** fut. ἀναστενάξω [§26.2] (ἀνά + στενάζω) *to sigh, groan deeply,* Mark 8:12

ἀναστενάξας, nom. sg. m. aor. act. part. .... ἀναστενάζω *(389)*

ἀναστῇ, 3 pers. sg. 2 aor. act. subj. .. ἀνίστημι *(450)*

ἀνάστηθι, 2 pers. sg. 2 aor. act. imper. ... id.

ἀναστῆναι, 2 aor. act. infin. .... id.

ἀναστήσας, nom. sg. m. aor. act. part. ... id.

ἀναστήσει, 3 pers. sg. fut. act. indic. .... id.

ἀναστήσειν, fut. act. infin. (Acts 2:30, MT & TR | GNT, WH & NA omit) ..... id.

ἀναστήσεται, 3 pers. sg. fut. mid. indic. [§29.Y] .... id.

ἀναστήσονται, 3 pers. pl. fut. mid. indic. . id.

ἀναστήσω, 1 pers. sg. fut. act. indic. {John 6:40} .... id.

ἀναστήσω, 1 pers. sg. aor. act. subj. {John 6:39} .... id.

ἀναστράφητε, 2 pers. pl. 2 aor. pass. imper. [§24.10] .... ἀναστρέφω *(390)*

ἀναστρέφεσθαι, pres. pass. infin. .... id.

ἀναστρεφομένους, acc. pl. m. pres. pass. part. .... id.

ἀναστρεφομένων, gen. pl. m. pres. pass. part. .... id.

(390) **ἀναστρέφω,** fut. ἀναστρέψω [§23.1.a] (ἀνά + στρέφω) *to overturn, throw down,* John 2:15; *to turn back, return,* Acts 5:22; 15:16; mid. ἀναστρέφομαι, 2 aor. (pass. form) ἀνεστράφην, *to abide, spend time,* Matt. 17:22; *to live, to conduct one's self,* 2 Cor. 1:12; Eph. 2:3; 1 Tim. 3:15; Heb. 13:18; 1 Pet. 1:17; 2 Pet. 2:18; *to gaze,* Heb. 10:33

ἀναστρέψαντες, nom. pl. m. aor. act. part. .... ἀναστρέφω *(390)*

ἀναστρέψω, 1 pers. sg. fut. act. indic. ... id.

ἀναστροφαῖς, dat. pl. f. n. ...... ἀναστροφή *(391)*

(391) **ἀναστροφή,** ῆς, ἡ [§2.B.a] *conversation, mode of life, conduct, deportment,* Gal. 1:13, et al.

ἀναστροφῇ, dat. sg. f. n. .... ἀναστροφή *(391)*

ἀναστροφήν, acc. sg. f. n. .... id.

ἀναστροφῆς, gen. sg. f. n. .... id.

ἀναστῶσι(ν), 3 pers. pl. 2 aor. act. subj. .... ἀνίστημι *(450)*

ἀνατάξασθαι, aor. mid. dep.
infin. . . . . ἀνατάσσομαι *(392)*
(392) **ἀνατάσσομαι,** fut. ἀνατάξομαι [§23.7] (ἀνά
+ τάσσω) pr. *to arrange;* hence, *to com-
pose,* Luke 1:1
ἀνατεθραμμένος, nom. sg. m. perf. pass. part.
[§35.9] . . . . ἀνατρέφω *(397)*
ἀνατείλαντος, gen. sg. m. aor. act.
part. ἀνατέλλω *(393)*
ἀνατείλῃ, 3 pers. sg. aor. act. subj. . . . . . . id.
ἀνατέλλει, 3 pers. sg. pres. act. indic. . . . . id.
ἀνατέλλουσαν, acc. sg. f. pres. act. part. . id.
(393) **ἀνατέλλω,** fut. ἀνατελῶ, aor. ἀνέτειλα
[§27.1.b,d] (ἀνά + τέλλω, *to make to rise*)
to cause to rise, Matt. 5:45; intrans. *to rise,*
as the sun, stars, etc., Matt. 4:16, et al.;
to spring by birth, Heb. 7:14
ἀνατέταλκεν, 3 pers. sg. perf. act.
indic. . . . . ἀνατέλλω *(393)*
(†394) **ἀνατίθημι,** mid. ἀνατίθεμαι [§28.V; 28.W] 2
aor. ἀνεθέμην (ἀνά + τίθημι) *to submit*
to a person's *consideration, statement,* or
report of matters, Acts 25:14; Gal. 2:2
(395) **ἀνατολή,** ῆς, ἡ, nom. sg. f. n. [§2.B.a] pr. *a
rising* of the sun, etc.; *the place of rising,
the east,* as also pl. ἀνατολαί, Matt. 2:1, 2,
et al.; met. *the dawn* or *day-spring,* Luke
1:78
ἀνατολῇ, dat. sg. f. n. . . . . ἀνατολή *(395)*
ἀνατολῆς, gen. sg. f. n. . . . . id.
ἀναταλῶν, gen. pl. f. n. . . . . id.
ἀνατρέπουσι(ν), 3 pers. pl. pres. act.
indic. . . . . ἀνατρέπω *(396)*
(396) **ἀνατρέπω,** fut. ἀνατρέψω [§23.1.a] (ἀνά +
τρέπω) pr. *to overturn, overthrow;* met. *to
subvert, corrupt,* 2 Tim. 2:18; Tit. 1:11
(397) **ἀνατρέφω,** fut. ἀναθρέψω [§35.4] perf. pass.
ἀνατέθραμμαι [§35.9] 2 aor. pass.
ἀνετράφην [§24.10] (ἀνά + τρέφω) *to
nurse,* as an infant, Acts 7:20; *to bring up,
educate,* Acts 7:21; 22:3
ἀναφαίνεσθαι, pres. pass. infin. . . . . ἀναφαίνω *(398)*
(398) **ἀναφαίνω,** fut. ἀναφανῶ [§27.4.b] (ἀνά +
φαίνω) *to bring to light, display;* mid. and
pass. *to appear,* Luke 19:11; a nautical
term, *to come in sight of,* Acts 21:3
ἀναφάναντες, nom. pl. m. 2 aor. act. part.
(Acts 21:3, GNT, WH, TR & NA |
ἀναφανέντες, MT) . . . . ἀναφαίνω *(398)*
ἀναφανέντες, nom. pl. m. 2 aor. act. part.
(Acts 21:3, MT | ἀναφάναντες, GNT,
WH, TR & NA) . . . . id.
ἀναφέρει, 3 pers. sg. pres. act. indic. . ἀναφέρω *(399)*
ἀναφέρειν, pres. act. infin. . . . . id.
(399) **ἀναφέρω,** fut. ἀνοίσω, aor. ἀνήνεγκα, 2 aor.

ἀνήνεγκον [§36.1] (ἀνά + φέρω) *to bear*
or *carry upwards, lead up,* Matt. 17:1, et
al.; *to offer* sacrifices, Heb. 7:27, et al.; *to
bear aloft* or *sustain* a burden, as sins,
1 Pet. 2:24; Heb. 9:28
ἀναφέρωμεν, 1 pers. pl. pres. act.
subj. ἀναφέρω *(399)*
(400) **ἀναφωνέω,** ῶ, fut. ἀναφωνήσω [§16.P] (ἀνά
+ φωνέω) *to exclaim, cry out,* Luke 1:42
ἀναχθέντες, nom. pl. m. aor. pass. part. ἀνάγω *(321)*
ἀναχθῆναι, aor. pass. infin. . . . . id.
ἀνάχυσιν, acc. sg. f. n. . . . . ἀνάχυσις *(401)*
(401) **ἀνάχυσις,** εως, ἡ [§5.E.c] (ἀναχέω, *to pour
out*) *a pouring out;* met. *excess,* 1 Pet. 4:4
ἀναχωρεῖτε, 2 pers. pl. pres. act.
imper. . . . . ἀναχωρέω *(402)*
(402) **ἀναχωρέω,** ῶ, fut. ἀναχωρήσω [§16.P] (ἀνά
+ χωρέω) *to go backward; to depart, go
away,* Matt. 2:12, et al.; *to withdraw, retire,* Matt. 9:24; Acts 23:19; 26:31
ἀναχωρήσαντες, nom. pl. m. aor. act.
part. ἀναχωρέω *(402)*
ἀναχωρησάντων, gen. pl. m. aor. act. part. id.
ἀναχωρήσας, nom. sg. m. aor. act. part. . id.
ἀνάψαντες, nom. pl. m. aor. act. part. (Acts
28:2, MT & TR | ἅψαντες, GNT, WH
& NA) . . . . ἀνάπτω *(381)*
ἀναψύξεως, gen. sg. f. n. . . . . ἀνάψυξις *(403)*
(403) **ἀνάψυξις,** εως, ἡ [§5.E.c] pr. *a refreshing cool-
ness* after heat; met. *refreshing, recreation,
rest,* Acts 3:19
(404) **ἀναψύχω,** fut. ἀναψύξω [§23.1.b] (ἀνά +
ψύχω) *to recreate by fresh air; to refresh,
cheer,* 2 Tim. 1:16
ἄνδρα, acc. sg. m. n. [§6.2] . . . . ἀνήρ *(435)*
ἀνδραποδισταῖς, dat. pl. m. n. ἀνδραποδιστής *(405)*
(405) **ἀνδραποδιστής,** οῦ, ὁ [§2.B.c] (ἀνδράποδον,
a slave) *a man-stealer, kidnapper,* 1 Tim.
1:10
ἄνδρας, acc. pl. m. n. . . . . ἀνήρ *(435)*
ἀνδράσι(ν), dat. pl. m. n. . . . . id.
Ἀνδρέᾳ, dat. sg. m. n. . . . . Ἀνδρέας *(406)*
Ἀνδρέαν, acc. sg. m. n. . . . . id.
(406) **Ἀνδρέας,** ου, ὁ, nom. sg. m. n. [§2.B.d] *An-
drew,* pr. name
Ἀνδρέου, gen. sg. m. n. . . . . Ἀνδρέας *(406)*
ἄνδρες, nom. pl. m. n. {Acts 1:10} . . . . . ἀνήρ *(435)*
ἄνδρες, voc. pl. m. n. {Acts 1:11} . . . . id.
ἀνδρί, dat. sg. m. n. . . . . id.
ἀνδρίζεσθε, 2 pers. pl. pres. mid./pass. dep.
imper. ἀνδρίζω *(†407)*
(†407) **ἀνδρίζω,** fut. ἀνδρίσω [§26.1] *to render brave*
or *manly;* mid. *to show* or *behave one's self
like a man,* 1 Cor. 16:13
Ἀνδρόνικον, acc. sg. m. n. . . . . . . Ἀνδρόνικος *(408)*

(408) **Ἀνδρόνικος**, ου, ὁ [§3.C.a] *Andronicus*, pr.
name, Rom. 16:7
ἀνδρός, gen. sg. m. n. . . . . ἀνήρ (435)
ἀνδροφόνοις, dat. pl. m. n. . . . . . ἀνδροφόνος (409)
(409) **ἀνδροφόνος**, ου, ὁ [§3.C.a] (ἀνήρ + φόνος)
a homicide, man-slayer, murderer, 1 Tim.
1:9
ἀνδρῶν, gen. pl. m. n. . . . . ἀνήρ (435)
ἀνεβαίνομεν, 1 pers. pl. imperf. act.
  indic. . . . . ἀναβαίνω (305)
ἀνέβαινον, 3 pers. pl. imperf. act. indic. . . id.
ἀνεβάλετο, 3 pers. sg. 2 aor. mid.
  indic. ἀναβάλλω (†306)
ἀνέβη, 3 pers. sg. 2 aor. act. indic. . . ἀναβαίνω (305)
ἀνέβημεν, 1 pers. pl. 2 aor. act. indic. (Acts
  21:6, GNT & NA | ἐπέβημεν, MT & TR
  | ἐνέβημεν, WH) . . . . id.
ἀνέβην, 1 pers. sg. 2 aor. act. indic. [§37.1] id.
ἀνέβησαν, 3 pers. pl. 2 aor. act. indic. . . . id.
ἀνέβλεψα, 1 pers. sg. aor. act. indic. ἀναβλέπω (308)
ἀνέβλεψαν, 3 pers. pl. aor. act. indic. . . . . id.
ἀνέβλεψε(ν), 3 pers. sg. aor. act. indic. . . . id.
ἀνεβόησε(ν), 3 pers. sg. aor. act.
  indic. . . . . ἀναβοάω (310)
ἀνεγίνωσκε(ν), 3 pers. sg. imperf. act.
  indic. ἀναγινώσκω (314)
ἀνέγκλητοι, nom. pl. m. adj. . . . . ἀνέγκλητος (410)
ἀνέγκλητον, acc. sg. m. adj. . . . . id.
(410) **ἀνέγκλητος**, ον, nom. sg. m. adj. [§7.2] (ἀ
  + ἐγκαλέω) *not arraigned; unblamable, irreproachable,* 1 Cor. 1:8; Col. 1:22; 1 Tim.
  3:10; Tit. 1:6, 7
ἀνεγκλήτους, acc. pl. m. adj. . . . . ἀνέγκλητος (410)
ἀνεγνωρίσθη, 3 pers. sg. aor. pass.
  indic. . . . . ἀναγνωρίζω (†319)
ἀνέγνωσαν, 3 pers. pl. 2 aor. act. indic.
  [§31.1.d] . . . . ἀναγινώσκω (314)
ἀνέγνωτε, 2 pers. pl. 2 aor. act. indic. [§36.3] id.
ἀνέδειξεν, 3 pers. sg. aor. act.
  indic. ἀναδείκνυμι (322)
ἀνέζησαν, 3 pers. pl. aor. act. indic. (Rev.
  20:5, TR | ἔζησαν, GNT, WH, MT &
  NA) . . . . ἀναζάω (326)
ἀνέζησε(ν), 3 pers. sg. aor. act. indic. . . . id.
ἀνεζήτουν, 3 pers. pl. imperf. act.
  indic. . . . . ἀναζητέω (327)
ἀνεθάλετε, 2 pers. pl. 2 aor. act. indic.
  [§27.3.b] . . . . ἀναθάλλω (330)
ἀνεθεματίσαμεν, 1 pers. pl. aor. act.
  indic. . . . . ἀναθεματίζω (332)
ἀνεθεμάτισαν, 3 pers. pl. aor. act. indic. . id.
ἀνεθέμην, 1 pers. sg. 2 aor. mid.
  indic. . . . . ἀνατίθημι (†394)
ἀνέθετο, 3 pers. sg. 2 aor. mid. indic. [§28.W] id.
ἀνέθη, 3 pers. sg. aor. pass.

  indic. [§32.CC] . . . . ἀνίημι (447)
ἀνεθρέψατο, 3 pers. sg. aor. mid. indic.
  [§35.4] . . . . ἀνατρέφω (397)
ἀνεῖλαν, 3 pers. pl. aor. act. indic. [§35.12]
  (Acts 10:39, GNT, WH & NA | ἀνεῖλον,
  MT & TR) . . . . ἀναιρέω (337)
ἀνείλατε, 2 pers. pl. 2 aor. act. indic. (Acts
  2:23, GNT, WH & NA | ἀνείλετε, MT
  & TR) . . . . id.
ἀνείλατο, 3 pers. sg. 2 aor. mid. indic. (Acts
  7:21, GNT, WH & NA | ἀνείλετο, MT
  & TR) . . . . id.
ἀνεῖλε(ν), 3 pers. sg. 2 aor. act. indic. [§36.1] id.
ἀνεῖλες, 2 pers. sg. 2 aor. act. indic. . . . . . id.
ἀνείλετε, 2 pers. pl. 2 aor. act. indic. (Acts
  2:23, MT & TR | ἀνείλατε, GNT, WH
  & NA) . . . . id.
ἀνείλετο, 3 pers. sg. 2 aor. mid. indic. (Acts
  7:21, MT & TR | ἀνείλατο, GNT, WH
  & NA) . . . . id.
ἀνεῖλον, 3 pers. pl. 2 aor. act. indic. (Acts
  10:39, MT & TR | ἀνεῖλαν, GNT, WH
  & NA) . . . . id.
ἀνείχεσθε, 2 pers. pl. imperf. mid./pass. dep.
  indic. . . . . ἀνέχομαι (430)
ἀνεκάθισε(ν), 3 pers. sg. aor. act.
  indic. . . . . ἀνακαθίζω (339)
(411) **ἀνεκδιήγητος**, ον [§7.2] (ἀ + ἐκδιηγέομαι)
  *which cannot be related, inexpressible, un-
  utterable,* 2 Cor. 9:15
ἀνεκδιηγήτῳ, dat. sg. f. adj. . . . . ἀνεκδιήγητος (411)
ἀνέκειτο, 3 pers. sg. imperf. mid./pass. dep.
  indic. . . . . ἀνάκειμαι (†345)
(412) **ἀνεκλάλητος**, ον [§7.2] (ἀ + ἐκλαλέω) *un-
  speakable, ineffable,* 1 Pet. 1:8
ἀνεκλαλήτῳ, dat. sg. f. adj. . . . . ἀνεκλάλητος (412)
ἀνέκλειπτον, acc. sg. m. adj. . . . . ἀνέκλειπτος (413)
(413) **ἀνέκλειπτος**, ον [§7.2] (ἀ + ἐκλείπω) *unfailing, exhaustless,* Luke 12:33
ἀνεκλίθη, 3 pers. sg. aor. pass. indic. (Luke
  7:36, MT & TR | κατεκλίθη, GNT, WH
  & NA) . . . . ἀνακλίνω (347)
ἀνέκλιναν, 3 per. pl. aor. act. indic. (Luke
  9:15, MT & TR | κατέκλιναν, GNT,
  WH. & NA) . . . . id.
ἀνέκλινεν, 3 pers. sg. aor. act. indic. . . . . id.
ἀνέκοψε(ν), 3 pers. sg. aor. act. indic. (Gal.
  5:7, TR | ἐνέκοψεν, GNT, WH, MT &
  NA) . . . . ἀνακόπτω (348)
ἀνέκραγον, 3 pers. pl. 2 aor. act. indic. (Luke
  23:18, GNT, WH & NA | ἀνέκραξαν,
  MT & TR) . . . . ἀνακράζω (349)
ἀνέκραξαν, 3 pers. pl. aor. act. indic. . . . . id.
ἀνέκραξε(ν), 3 pers. sg. aor. act. indic. . . . id.
(†414) **ἀνεκτός**, όν [§7.2] *tolerable, supportable,*

Matt. 10:15; 11:22, 24; Mark 6:11; Luke
10:12, 14
ἀνεκτότερον, nom. sg. sg. compar.
adj. . . . . ἀνεκτός (†414)
ἀνέκυψεν, 3 pers. sg. aor. act. indic. (John 8:7,
GNT & NA | ἀναβλέψας, MT | ἀνα-
ύψας, TR | WH omits) . . . . ἀνακύπτω (352)
ἀνελάβετε, 2 pers. pl. 2 aor. act.
indic. . . . . ἀναλαμβάνω (353)
ἀνελεήμονας, acc. pl. m. adj. . . . . . ἀνελεήμων (415)
(415) ἀνελεήμων, ον [§7.G.a; 7.3] (ἀ + ἐλεήμων)
unmerciful, uncompassionate, cruel, Rom.
1:31
ἀνελεῖ, 3 pers. sg. fut. act. indic. (2 Thess. 2:8,
GNT, WH & NA | ἀναλώσει, MT &
TR) . . . . ἀναιρέω (337)
ἀνελεῖν, 2 aor. act. infin. . . . . id.
(‡448) ἀνέλεος, ον [§7.2] (ἀ + ἔλεος) pitiless (James
2:13, GNT, WH, MT & NA | ἀνίλεως,
TR)
ἀνέλεος, nom. sg. f. adj. . . . . ἀνέλεος (‡448)
ἀνελήμφθη, 3 pers. sg. aor. pass. indic. (Acts
1:2; 10:16, GNT, WH & NA | ἀνελήφθη,
MT & TR) . . . . ἀναλαμβάνω (353)
ἀνελήφθη, 3 pers. sg. aor. pass. indic. (Acts
1:2; 10:16, MT & TR | ἀνελήμφθη, GNT,
WH & NA) . . . . id.
ἀνέλωσι(ν), 3 pers. pl. aor. act. subj.
§36.1] . . . . ἀναιρέω (337)
ἀνεμιζομένῳ, dat. sg. m. pres. pass.
part. . . . . ἀνεμίζω (416)
(416) ἀνεμίζω, fut. ἀνεμίσω [§26.1] to agitate with
the wind; pass. to be agitated or driven by
the wind, James 1:6
ἀνεμνήσθη, 3 pers. sg. aor. pass.
indic. . . . . ἀναμιμνήσκω (†363)
ἄνεμοι, nom. pl. m. n. . . . . ἄνεμος (417)
ἀνέμοις, dat. pl. m. n. . . . . id.
ἄνεμον, acc. sg. m. n. . . . . id.
(417) ἄνεμος, ου, ὁ, nom. sg. m. n. [§3.C.a] the
wind; met. a wind of shifting doctrine,
Eph. 4:14
ἀνέμου, gen. sg. m. n. . . . . ἄνεμος (417)
ἀνέμους, acc. pl. m. n. . . . . id.
ἀνέμῳ, dat. sg. m. n. . . . . id.
ἀνέμων, gen. pl. m. n. . . . . id.
ἀνένδεκτον, nom. sg. neut. adj. . . . ἀνένδεκτος (418)
(418) ἀνένδεκτος, ον [§7.2] (ἀ + ἐνδέχεται, it is
possible) impossible, what cannot be, Luke
17:1
ἀνενέγκαι, aor. act. infin. [§36.1] . . . . ἀναφέρω (399)
ἀνενέγκας, nom. sg. m. aor. act. part. . . . id.
ἀνενεγκεῖν, 2 aor. act. infin. . . . . id.
ἀνέντες, nom. pl. m. 2 aor. act. part. . . . ἀνίημι (447)
ἀνεξεραύνητα, nom. pl. neut. adj. (Rom.

11:33, GNT, WH & NA | ἀνεξερεύνητα,
MT & TR) . . . . ἀνεξεραύνητος (†419)
(†419) ἀνεξεραύνητος, ον, unfathomable, incapable
of human explanation
ἀνεξερεύνητα, nom. pl. neut. adj. (Rom.
11:33, MT & TR | ἀνεξεραύνητα, GNT,
WH & NA) . . . . ἀνεξερεύνητος (419)
(419) ἀνεξερεύνητος, ον [§7.2] (ἀ + ἐξερευνάω)
unsearchable, inscrutable, Rom. 11:33
ἀνεξίκακον, acc. sg. m. adj. . . . . . ἀνεξίκακος (420)
(420) ἀνεξίκακος, ον [§7.2] (ἀνέχομαι + κακός)
enduring or patient under evils and injuries, 2 Tim. 2:24
ἀνεξιχνίαστοι, nom. pl. f. adj. . . . ἀνεξιχνίαστος (421)
(421) ἀνεξιχνίαστος, ον [§7.2] (ἀ + ἐξιχνιάζω) to
track out, ἴχνος, a track which cannot be
explored, inscrutable, incomprehensible,
Rom. 11:33; Eph. 3:8
ἀνεξιχνίαστον, acc. sg. m. adj. . . ἀνεξιχνίαστος (421)
ἀνέξομαι, 1 pers. sg. fut. mid. dep. indic.
[§23.1.b] . . . . ἀνέχομαι (430)
ἀνέξονται, 3 pers. pl. fut. mid. dep. indic. . id.
ἀνεπαίσχυντον, acc. sg. m. adj. ἀνεπαίσχυντος (422)
(422) ἀνεπαίσχυντος, ον [§7.2] (ἀ + ἐπαισχύνομαι)
without cause of shame, irreproachable,
2 Tim. 2:15
ἀνέπαυσαν, 3 pers. pl. aor. act. indic. ἀναπαύω (373)
ἀνέπεμψα, 1 pers. sg. aor. act. indic. ἀναπέμπω (375)
ἀνέπεμψεν, 3 pers. sg. aor. act. indic. . . . . id.
ἀνέπεσαν, 3 pers. pl. aor. act. indic. (Mark
6:40; John 6:10, GNT, WH & NA |
ἀνέπεσον, MT & TR) . . . . ἀναπίπτω (377)
ἀνέπεσε(ν), 3 pers. sg. 2 aor. act. indic. . . id.
ἀνέπεσον, 3 pers. pl. 2 aor. act. indic. (Mark
6:40; John 6:10, MT & TR | ἀνέπεσαν,
GNT, WH & NA) . . . . id.
ἀνεπίλημπτοι, nom. pl. m. adj. (1 Tim. 5:7,
GNT, WH & NA | ἀνεπίληπτοι, MT &
TR) . . . . ἀνεπίλημπτος (†423)
ἀνεπίλημπτον, acc. sg. m. adj. {1 Tim. 3:2} id.
ἀνεπίλημπτον, acc. sg. f. adj. {1 Tim. 6:14} id.
(†423) ἀνεπίλημπτος, ον [§7.2] (ἀ + ἐπιλαμβάνω)
pr. not to be laid hold of; met. irreprehensible, unblamable, 1 Tim. 3:2; 5:7; 6:14
ἀνεπίληπτοι, nom. pl. m. adj. (1 Tim. 5:7,
MT & TR | ἀνεπίλημπτοι, GNT, WH &
NA) . . . . ἀνεπίληπτος (423)
ἀνεπίληπτον, acc. sg. m. adj. {1 Tim. 3:2} id.
ἀνεπίληπτον, acc. sg. f. adj. {1 Tim. 6:14} id.
(423) ἀνεπίληπτος, ον [§7.2] (ἀ + ἐπιλαμβάνω) pr.
not to be laid hold of; met. irreprehensible,
unblamable, 1 Tim. 3:2; 5:7; 6:14
ἀνεπλήρωσαν, 3 pers. pl. aor. act.
indic. . . . . ἀναπληρόω (378)
ἄνερ, voc. sg. m. n. . . . . ἀνήρ (435)

(424) **ἀνέρχομαι,** fut. ἀνελεύσομαι, 2 aor. ἀνῆλθον [§36.1] (ἀνά + ἔρχομαι) *to ascend, go up,* John 6:3; Gal. 1:17, 18

ἀνέσεισαν, 3 pers. pl. aor. act. indic. . ἀνασείω *(383)*

ἄνεσιν, acc. sg. f. n. . . . . ἄνεσις *(425)*

(425) **ἄνεσις,** εως, ἡ, nom. sg. f. n. [§5.E.c] pr. *the relaxing* of a state of constraint; *relaxation* of rigor of confinement, Acts 24:23; met. *ease, rest, peace, tranquility,* 2 Cor. 2:13; 7:5; 8:13; 2 Thess. 1:7

ἀνεσπάσθη, 3 pers. sg. aor. pass. indic. . . . . ἀνασπάω *(385)*

ἀνέστη, 3 pers. sg. 2 aor. act. indic. [§29.X] . . . . ἀνίστημι *(450)*

ἀνέστησαν, 3 pers. pl. aor. act. indic. . . . . id.

ἀνέστησε(ν), 3 pers. sg. aor. act. indic. . . . id.

ἀνεστράφημεν, 1 pers. pl. 2 aor. pass. indic. [§24.10] . . . . ἀναστρέφω *(390)*

ἀνέστρεψε(ν), 3 pers. sg. aor. act. indic. (John 2:15, MT & TR | ἀνέτρεψεν, GNT, WH & NA) . . . . id.

ἀνεσχόμην, 1 pers. sg. 2 aor. mid. indic. (Acts 18:14, GNT, WH & NA | ἠνεσχόμην, MT & TR) . . . . ἀνέχομαι *(430)*

ἀνετάζειν, pres. act. infin. . . . . ἀνετάζω *(426)*

ἀνετάζεσθαι, pres. pass. infin. . . . . id.

(426) **ἀνετάζω,** fut. ἀνετάσω [§26.1] *to examine thoroughly; to examine* by torture, Acts 22:24, 29

ἀνέτειλε(ν), 3 pers. sg. aor. act. indic. [§27.1.d] . . . . ἀνατέλλω *(393)*

ἀνετράφη, 3 pers. sg. 2 aor. pass. indic. [§24.10] . . . . ἀνατρέφω *(397)*

ἀνέτρεψεν, 3 pers. sg. aor. act. indic. (John 2:15, GNT, WH & NA | ἀνέστρεψε(ν), MT & TR) . . . . ἀνατρέπω *(396)*

(427) **ἄνευ,** prep. governing the gen., *without,* Matt. 10:29; 1 Pet. 3:1; 4:9

(428) **ἀνεύθετος,** ον [§7.2] (ἀ + εὔθετος) *not commodious, inconvenient,* Acts 27:12

ἀνευθέτου, gen. sg. m. adj. . . . . ἀνεύθετος *(428)*

ἀνεῦραν, 3 pers. pl. 2 aor. act. indic. [§35.12] (Luke 2:16, GNT, WH & NA | ἀνεῦρον, MT & TR) . . . . ἀνευρίσκω *(429)*

(429) **ἀνευρίσκω,** fut. ἀνευρήσω [§36.4] (ἀνά + εὑρίσκω) *to find by diligent search,* Luke 2:16; Acts 21:4

ἀνεῦρον, 3 pers. pl. 2 aor. act. indic. (Luke 2:16, MT & TR | ἀνεῦραν, GNT, WH & NA) . . . . ἀνευρίσκω *(429)*

ἀνευρόντες, nom. pl. m. 2 aor. act. part. . id.

ἀνεφέρετο, 3 pers. sg. imperf. pass. indic. . . . . ἀναφέρω *(399)*

ἀνεφώνησε(ν), 3 pers. sg. aor. act. indic. . . . . ἀναφωνέω *(400)*

ἀνέχεσθε, 2 pers. pl. pres. mid./pass. dep. indic. {2 Thess. 1:4} . . . . ἀνέχομαι *(430)*

ἀνέχεσθε, 2 pers. pl. pres. mid./pass. dep. imper. {Heb. 13:22} . . . . ; id.

(430) **ἀνέχομαι,** fut. ἀνέξομαι, imperf. ἀνειχόμην, ἠνειχόμην, 2 aor. ἠνεσχόμην [§34.1.d] (ἀνά + ἔχω) *to endure patiently,* 1 Cor. 4:12; 2 Cor. 11:20; 2 Thess. 1:4; *to bear with,* Matt. 17:17, et al.; *to suffer, admit, permit,* Acts 18:14; 2 Cor. 11:4; 2 Tim. 4:3; Heb. 13:22

ἀνεχόμεθα, 1 pers. pl. pres. mid./pass. dep. indic. ἀνέχομαι *(430)*

ἀνεχόμενοι, nom. pl. m. pres. mid./pass. dep. part. . . . . id.

ἀνεχώρησαν, 3 pers. pl. aor. act. indic. . . . . ἀναχωρέω *(402)*

ἀνεχώρησε(ν), 3 pers. sg. aor. act. indic. . id.

(†431) **ἀνεψιός,** οῦ, ὁ, nom. sg. m. n. [§3.C.a] *a nephew, cousin,* Col. 4:10

ἀνέψυξε(ν), 3 pers. sg. aor. act. indic. . . . . ἀναψύχω *(404)*

ἀνέῳγε(ν), 3 pers. sg. 2 perf. act. indic. [§25.4] . . . . ἀνοίγω *(455)*

ἀνεῳγμένας, acc. pl. f. perf. pass. part. [§37.1] . . . . id.

ἀνεῳγμένη, nom. sg. f. perf. pass. part. (Rev. 4:1, MT | ἠνεῳγμένη, GNT, WH, TR & NA) . . . . id.

ἀνεῳγμένην, acc. sg. f. perf. pass. part. (Rev. 3:8, MT & TR | ἠνεῳγμένην, GNT, WH & NA) . . . . id.

ἀνεῳγμένης, gen. sg. f. perf. pass. part. {2 Cor. 2:12} . . . . id.

ἀνεῳγμένον, acc. sg. m. perf. pass. part. {Acts 10:11} . . . . id.

ἀνεῳγμένον, acc. sg. neut. perf. pass. part. (Rev. 10:2, MT & TR | ἠνεῳγμένον, GNT, WH & NA | ἀνεῳγμένον, Rev. 10:8, MT | ἠνεῳγμένον GNT, TR, WH & NA) . . . . id.

ἀνεῳγμένος, nom. sg. m. perf. pass. part. id.

ἀνεῳγμένους, acc. pl. m. perf. pass. part. (Acts 7:56, MT & TR | διηνοιγμένους, GNT, WH & NA) . . . . id.

ἀνεῳγμένων, gen. pl. m. perf. pass. part. . id.

ἀνεῳγότα, acc. sg. m. 2 perf. pass. part. [§37.1] . . . . id.

ἀνέῳξε(ν), 3 pers. sg. aor. act. indic. . . . . id.

ἀνεῴχθη, 3 pers. sg. aor. pass. indic. [§37.1] id.

ἀνεῳχθῆναι, aor. pass. infin. . . . . id.

ἀνεῴχθησαν, 3 pers. pl. aor. pass. indic. . id.

ἀνήγαγον, 3 pers. pl. 2 aor. act. indic. Att. [§13.7.b,d] . . . . ἀνάγω *(321)*

ἀνήγγειλαν, 3 pers. pl. aor. act. indic.

[§27.1.d] . . . . ἀναγγέλλω *(312)*
ἀνήγγειλε(ν), 3 pers. sg. aor. act. indic. (John
  5:15, GNT, MT, TR & NA | εἶπεν, WH) id.
ἀνηγγέλη, 3 pers. sg. 2 aor. pass. indic.
  [§27.4.b] . . . . id.
ἀνήγγελλον, 3 pers. pl. imperf. act. indic.
  (Acts 14:27, GNT, WH & NA |
  ἀνήγγειλαν, MT & TR) . . . . id.
(432) **ἄνηθον,** ου, τό [§3.C.c] *anethum, dill,* an aromatic plant, Matt. 23:23
ἄνηθον, acc. sg. neut. n. . . . . ἄνηθον *(432)*
ἀνῆκεν, 3 pers. sg. imperf. act. indic. . . ἀνήκω *(433)*
ἀνῆκον, acc. sg. neut. pres. act. part. . . . . id.
ἀνήκοντα, nom. pl. neut. pres. act. part. (Eph.
  5:4, MT & TR | ἀνῆκεν, GNT, WH &
  NA) . . . . id.
(433) **ἀνήκω** (ἀνά + ἥκω) *to come up to, to per-*
  tain to; ἀνήκει, impers. *it is fit, proper, be-*
  coming, Col. 3:18; Eph. 5:4; Philemon 8
ἀνῆλθε(ν), 3 pers. sg. 2 aor. act.
  indic. . . . . ἀνέρχομαι *(424)*
ἀνῆλθον, 1 pers. sg. 2 aor. act. indic. . . . . id.
ἀνήμεροι, nom. pl. m. adj. . . . . ἀνήμερος *(434)*
(434) **ἀνήμερος,** ον [§7.2] (ἀ + ἥμερος, *gentle,*
  mild) ungentle, fierce, ferocious, 2 Tim. 3:3
ἀνήνεγκεν, 3 pers. sg. aor. act. indic. ἀναφέρω *(399)*
(435) **ἀνήρ,** ἀνδρός, ὁ, nom. sg. m. n. [§6.2] *a male*
  person of full age and stature, as opposed
  to a child or female, 1 Cor. 13:11, et al.;
  a husband, Matt. 1:16, et al.; *a man, hu-*
  man being, individual, Luke 11:31, et al.;
  used also pleonastically with other nouns
  and adjectives Luke 5:8; Acts 1:16, et al.
ἀνῃρέθη, 3 pers. sg. aor. pass. indic.
  [§36.1] . . . . ἀναιρέω *(337)*
ἀνήφθη, 3 pers. sg. aor. pass. indic.
  [§23.4] . . . . ἀνάπτω *(381)*
ἀνήχθη, 3 pers. sg. aor. pass. indic. . . . . ἀνάγω *(321)*
ἀνήχθημεν, 1 pers. pl. aor. pass. indic. . . . id.
ἀνήχθησαν, 3 pers. pl. aor. pass. indic. . . . id.
(‡473) **ἀνθ᾽,** for ἀντί; ἀνθ᾽ ὧν, *on which account,*
  wherefore; because
ἀνθέξεται, 3 pers. sg. fut. mid. dep. indic.
  [§35.4] . . . . ἀντέχομαι *(472)*
ἀνθέστηκε(ν), 3 pers. sg. perf. act. indic.
  (2 Tim. 4:15, MT & TR | ἀντέστη, GNT,
  WH & NA) . . . . ἀνθίστημι *(436)*
ἀνθεστηκότες, nom. pl. m. perf. act. part. id.
ἀνθίστανται, 3 pers. pl. pres. mid. indic.
  [§29.Y] . . . . id.
ἀνθίστατο, 3 pers. sg. imperf. mid. indic. . . id.
(436) **ἀνθίστημι,** fut. ἀντιστήσω (ἀντί + ἵστημι) *to*
  set in opposition; intrans. 2 aor. ἀντέστην,
  perf. ἀνθέστηκα [§29.X] and mid., *to op-*
  pose, resist, stand out against

(437) **ἀνθομολογέομαι,** οῦμαι [§17.Q] (ἀντί +
  ὁμολογέω) pr. *to come to an agreement;*
  hence, *to confess openly what is due; to*
  confess, give thanks, render praise, Luke
  2:38
(438) **ἄνθος,** ους, τό, nom. sg. neut. n. [§5.E.b] *a*
  flower, James 1:10, 11; 1 Pet. 1:24(2×)
ἄνθρακας, acc. pl. m. n. . . . . ἄνθραξ *(440)*
(439) **ἀνθρακιά,** ᾶς, ἡ [§2.B.b; 2.2] *a mass* or *heap*
  of live coals, John 18:18; 21:9
ἀνθρακιάν, acc. sg. f. n. . . . . ἀνθρακιά *(439)*
(440) **ἄνθραξ,** ακος, ὁ [§4.2.b] *a coal, burning coal,*
  Rom. 12:20
ἀνθρωπάρεσκοι, nom. pl. m.
  adj. . . . . ἀνθρωπάρεσκος *(441)*
(441) **ἀνθρωπάρεσκος,** ον [§7.2] (ἄνθρωπος +
  ἀρέσκω) *desirous of pleasing men,* Eph.
  6:6; Col. 3:22
ἄνθρωπε, voc. sg. m. n. . . . . ἄνθρωπος *(444)*
ἀνθρωπίνη, dat. sg. f. adj. . . . . ἀνθρώπινος *(442)*
ἀνθρωπίνης, gen. sg. f. adj. . . . . id.
ἀνθρώπινον, acc. sg. neut. adj. . . . . id.
(442) **ἀνθρώπινος,** η, ον, nom. sg. m. adj. [§7.F.a]
  human, belonging to man, 1 Cor. 2:4, 13;
  4:3; 10:13; James 3:7; 1 Pet. 2:13; *suited*
  to man, Rom. 6:19
ἀνθρωπίνων, gen. pl. m. adj. (Acts 17:25,
  GNT, WH & NA | ἀνθρώπων, MT &
  TR) . . . . ἀνθρώπινος *(442)*
ἄνθρωποι, nom. pl. m. n. . . . . ἄνθρωπος *(444)*
ἀνθρώποις, dat. pl. m. n. . . . . id.
(443) **ἀνθρωποκτόνος,** ον, nom. sg. m. adj. [§3.C.a]
  (ἄνθρωπος + κτείνω) *a homicide, mur-*
  derer, John 8:44; 1 John 3:15
ἄνθρωπον, acc. sg. m. n. . . . . ἄνθρωπος *(444)*
(444) **ἄνθρωπος,** ου, ὁ, nom. sg. m. n. [§3.C.a] *a*
  human being, John 16:21; Phil. 2:7, et al.;
  an individual, Rom. 3:28, et al. freq.; used
  also pleonastically with other words, Matt.
  11:19; et al.; met. *the* spiritual frame of the
  inner *man,* Rom. 7:22; Eph. 3:16; 1 Pet.
  3:4
ἀνθρώπου, gen. sg. m. n. . . . . ἄνθρωπος *(444)*
ἀνθρώπους, acc. pl. m. n. . . . . id.
ἀνθρώπῳ, dat. sg. m. n. . . . . id.
ἀνθρώπων, gen. pl. m. n. . . . . id.
ἀνθυπατεύοντος, gen. sg. m. pres. act. part.
  (Acts 18:12, MT & TR | ἀνθυπάτου
  ὄντος, GNT, WH & NA) . . . . ἀνθυπατεύω *(445)*
(445) **ἀνθυπατεύω,** fut. ἀνθυπατεύσω [§13.M] *to be*
  proconsul, Acts 18:12
ἀνθύπατοι, nom. pl. m. n. . . . . ἀνθύπατος *(446)*
ἀνθύπατον, acc. sg. m. n. . . . . id.
(446) **ἀνθύπατος,** ου, ὁ, nom. sg. m. n. [§3.C.a]
  (ἀντί + ὕπατος, *a consul) a proconsul,*

Acts 13:7, 8, 12; 19:38

ἀνθυπάτου, gen. sg. m. n. (Acts 18:12, with ὄντος, GNT, WH & NA | ἀνθυπατεύοντος, MT & TR) . . . . ἀνθύπατος *(446)*

ἀνθυπάτῳ, dat. sg. m. n. . . . . id.

ἀνθωμολογεῖτο, 3 pers. sg. imperf. mid./pass. dep. indic. [§34.1.a,b] . . . . ἀνθομολογέομαι *(437)*

ἀνιέντες, nom. pl m. pres. act. part. . . . . ἀνίημι *(447)*

(447) **ἀνίημι**, fut. ἀνήσω, 2 aor. ἀνῆν, subj. ἀνῶ, aor. pass. ἀνέθην [§32.CC] (ἀνά + ἵημι) *to loose, slacken,* Acts 27:40; *to unbind, unfasten,* Acts 16:26; *to omit, dispense with,* Eph. 6:9; *to leave* or *neglect,* Heb. 13:5

(448) **ἀνίλεως**, ον, nom. sg. f. adj. [§7.G.b] (ἀ + ἵλεως) *uncompassionate, unmerciful, stern* (James 2:13, TR | ἀνέλεος, GNT, WH, MT & NA)

ἀνίπτοις, dat. pl. m. adj. . . . . ἄνιπτος *(449)*

(449) **ἄνιπτος**, ον [§7.2] (ἀ + νίπτω) *unwashed,* Matt. 15:20; Mark 7:2, 5

ἀνιστάμενος, nom. sg. m. pres. mid. part. . . . . ἀνίστημι *(450)*

ἀνίστασθαι, pres. mid. infin. [§29.Y] . . . . id.

ἀνίσταται, 3 pers. sg. pres. mid. indic. . . . id.

(450) **ἀνίστημι**, fut. ἀναστήσω, aor. ἀνέστησα [§29.X] trans. *to cause to stand up* or *rise,* Acts 9:41; *to raise up,* as the dead, John 6:39, et al.; *to raise up* into existence, Matt. 22:24, et al.; intrans. 2 aor. ἀνέστην, imper. ἀνάστηθι, ἀνάστα, and mid., *to rise up,* Matt. 9:9, et al.; *to rise up* into existence, Acts 7:18; 20:30

(451) **Ἄννα**, ης, ἡ nom. sg. f. n. [§2.3] *Anna,* pr. name (Luke 2:36, GNT, WH, MT & NA | Ἅννα, TR)

Ἄννα, gen. sg. m. n. (Luke 3:2, GNT, WH, MT & NA | Ἅννα, TR) . . . . Ἄννας *(452)*

Ἄνναν, acc. sg. m. n. (John 18:13, GNT, WH, MT & NA | Ἅννα, TR) . . . . id.

(452) **Ἄννας**, α, ὁ, nom. sg. m. n. [§2.4] *Annas,* pr. name (GNT, WH, MT & NA | Ἅννας, TR)

ἀνόητοι, nom. pl. m. adj. {Gal. 3:3} . ἀνόητος *(453)*

ἀνόητοι, voc. pl. m. adj. {Gal. 3:1} . . . . . id.

ἀνόητοις, dat. pl. m. adj. . . . . id.

(453) **ἀνόητος**, ον [§7.2] (ἀ + νοέω) *inconsiderate, unintelligent, unwise;* Luke 24:25; Rom. 1:14; Gal. 3:1, 3; Tit. 3:3; *brutish,* 1 Tim. 6:9

ἀνοήτους, acc. pl. f. adj. . . . . ἀνόητος *(453)*

(454) **ἄνοια**, ας, ἡ, nom. sg. f. n. [§2.B.b; 2.2] (ἀ + νοῦς) *want of understanding; folly, rashness, madness,* Luke 6:11; 2 Tim. 3:9

ἀνοίας, gen. sg. f. n. . . . . ἄνοια *(454)*

ἀνοίγει, 3 pers. sg. pres. act. indic. . . . . ἀνοίγω *(455)*

ἀνοίγειν, pres. act. infin. . . . . id.

ἀνοιγήσεται, 3 pers. sg. 2 fut. pass. indic. . id.

(455) **ἀνοίγω**, fut. ἀνοίξω, aor. ἀνέῳξα, ἤνοιξα, perf. ἀνέῳχα [§37.1] (ἀνά + οἴγω) trans. *to open,* Matt. 2:11, et al.; intrans. 2 perf. ἀνέῳγα, perf. pass. ἀνέῳγμαι, ἠνέῳγμαι, aor. pass. ἀνεῴχθην, ἠνεῴχθην, ἠνοίχθην, *to be opened, to be open,* Matt. 3:16; John 1:52, et al.

ἀνοίγων, nom. sg. m. pres. act. part. . . ἀνοίγω *(455)*

ἀνοιγῶσιν, 3 pers. pl. 2 aor. pass. subj. (Matt. 20:33, GNT, WH & NA | ἀνοιχθῶσιν, MT & TR) . . . . id.

(456) **ἀνοικοδομέω**, ῶ, fut. ἀνοικοδομήσω [§16.P] (ἀνά + οἰκοδομέω) *to rebuild,* Acts 15:16 (2×)

ἀνοικοδομήσω, 1 pers. sg. fut. act. indic. . . . . ἀνοικοδομέω *(456)*

ἀνοῖξαι, aor. act. infin. . . . . ἀνοίγω *(455)*

ἀνοίξαντες, nom. pl. m. aor. act. part. . . . id.

ἀνοίξας, nom. sg. m. aor. act. part. . . . . . id.

ἀνοίξει, 3 pers. sg. fut. act. indic. (Rev. 3:7, MT | ἀνοίγει, GNT, WH, TR & NA) id.

ἀνοίξει, dat. sg. f. n. {Eph. 6:19} . . . . ἄνοιξις *(457)*

ἀνοίξῃ, 3 pers. sg. aor. act. subj. . . . . . ἀνοίγω *(455)*

(457) **ἄνοιξις**, εως, ἡ [§5.E.c] *an opening, act of opening,* Eph. 6:19

ἄνοιξον, 2 pers. sg. aor. act. imper. . . . . ἀνοίγω *(455)*

ἀνοίξω, 1 pers. sg. fut. act. indic. . . . . id.

ἀνοίξωσιν, 3 pers. pl. aor. act. subj. . . . . . id.

ἀνοιχθῶσιν, 3 pers. pl. aor. pass. subj. [§37.1] (Matt. 20:33, MT & TR | GNT, WH & NA) . . . . id.

(458) **ἀνομία**, ας, ἡ, nom. sg. f. n. [§2.B.b; 2.2] *lawlessness; violation of law,* 1 John 3:4; *iniquity, sin,* Matt. 7:23, et al.

ἀνομίᾳ, dat. sg. f. n. . . . . ἀνομία *(458)*

ἀνομίαι, nom. pl. f. n. . . . . id.

ἀνομίαν, acc. sg. f. n. . . . . id.

ἀνομίας, gen. sg. f. n. . . . . id.

ἀνομιῶν, gen. pl. f. n. . . . . id.

ἀνόμοις, dat. pl. m. adj. {1 Tim. 1:9} . . ἄνομος *(459)*

ἀνόμοις, dat. pl. neut. adj. {2 Pet. 2:8} . . id.

(459) **ἄνομος**, ον, nom. sg. m. adj. [§7.2] (ἀ + νόμος) *lawless, without law, not subject to law,* 1 Cor. 9:21; *lawless, violating law, wicked, impious,* Acts 2:23, et al.; *a transgressor,* Mark 15:28; Luke 22:37

ἀνόμους, acc. pl. m. adj. . . . . ἄνομος *(459)*

ἀνόμων, gen. pl. m. adj. . . . . id.

(460) **ἀνόμως**, adv., *without* the intervention of *law,* Rom. 2:12 (2×)

(461) **ἀνορθόω**, ῶ, fut. ἀνορθώσω [§20.T] (ἀνά + ὀρθόω) *to restore to straightness* or *erect-*

ness, Luke 13:13; *to re-invigorate,* Heb. 12:12; *to re-erect,* Acts 15:16

ἀνορθώσατε, 2 pers. pl. aor. act.

imper. . . . . ἀνορθόω *(461)*

ἀνορθώσω, 1 pers. sg. fut. act. indic. . . . . id.

ἀνόσιοι, nom. pl. m. adj. . . . . ἀνόσιος *(462)*

ἀνοσίοις, dat. pl. m. adj. . . . . id.

(462) **ἀνόσιος,** ον [§7.2] (ἀ + ὅσιος, *pious*) *impious, unholy,* 1 Tim. 1:9; 2 Tim. 3:2

(463) **ἀνοχή,** ῆς, ἡ [§2.B.a] (ἀνέχομαι) *forbearance, patience,* Rom. 2:4; 3:26

ἀνοχῇ, dat. sg. f. n. . . . . ἀνοχή *(463)*

ἀνοχῆς, gen. sg. f. n. . . . . id.

ἀνταγωνιζόμενοι, nom. pl. m. pres. mid./pass. dep. part. . . . . . . ἀνταγωνίζομαι *(464)*

(464) **ἀνταγωνίζομαι,** fut. ἀνταγωνίσομαι [§26.1] (ἀντί + ἀγωνίζομαι) *to contend, strive against,* Heb. 12:4

(465) **ἀντάλλαγμα,** ατος, τό [§4.D.c] (ἀνταλλάσσω, *to exchange*) *a price paid in exchange* for a thing; *compensation, equivalent ransom,* Matt. 16:26; Mark 8:37

ἀντάλλαγμα, acc. sg. neut. n. . . . ἀντάλλαγμα *(465)*

(466) **ἀνταναπληρόω,** ῶ, fut. ἀνταναπληρώσω [§20.T] (ἀντί + ἀναπληρόω) *to fill up, complete, supply,* Col. 1:24

ἀνταναπληρῶ, 1 pers. sg. pres. act. indic. . . . . ἀνταναπληρόω *(466)*

(467) **ἀνταποδίδωμι,** fut. ἀνταποδώσω, 2 aor. ἀνταπέδων [§30.Z] aor. pass. ἀνταπεδόθην [§30.4] (ἀντί + ἀποδίδωμι) *to repay, requite, recompense,* Luke 14:14(2×); Rom. 11:35; 12:19; 1 Thess. 3:9; 2 Thess. 1:6; Heb. 10:30

ἀνταποδοθήσεται, 3 pers. sg. fut. pass. indic. . . . . ἀνταποδίδωμι *(467)*

(468) **ἀνταπόδομα,** ατος, τό, nom. sg. neut. n. [§4.D.c] *requital, recompense, retribution* {Luke 14:12}

ἀνταπόδομα, acc. sg. neut. n. {Rom. 11:9} . . . . ἀνταπόδομα *(468)*

ἀνταπόδοσιν, acc. sg. f. n. . . . . . ἀνταπόδοσις *(469)*

(469) **ἀνταπόδοσις,** εως, ἡ [§5.E.c] *recompense, reward,* Col. 3:24

ἀνταποδοῦναι, 2 aor. act. infin. . ἀνταποδίδωμι *(467)*

ἀνταποδώσω, 1 pers. sg. fut. act. indic. . . id.

ἀνταποκριθῆναι, aor. pass. dep. infin. . . . . ἀνταποκρίνομαι *(470)*

(470) **ἀνταποκρίνομαι,** aor. (pass. form) ἀνταπεκρίθην [§27.3] (ἀντί + ἀποκρίνομαι) *to answer, speak in answer,* Luke 14:6; *to reply against, contradict, dispute,* Rom. 9:20

ἀνταποκρινόμενος, nom. sg. m. pres. mid./pass. dep. part. . . . . . ἀνταποκρίνομαι *(470)*

(†471) **ἀντειπεῖν,** 2 aor. act. infin. [§36.1] . . ἀντιλέγω *(†483)*

ἀντελάβετο, 3 pers. sg. 2 aor. mid. dep. indic. . . . . ἀντιλαμβάνω *(†482)*

ἀντέλεγον, 3 pers. pl. imperf. act. indic. . . . . ἀντιλέγω *(†483)*

ἀντελοιδόρει, 3 pers. sg. imperf. act. indic. [§34.1.a,b] . . . . ἀντιλοιδορέω *(486)*

ἀντέστη, 3 pers. sg. 2 aor. act. indic. (2 Tim. 4:15, GNT, WH & NA | ἀνθέστηκε(ν), MT & TR) . . . . ἀνθίστημι *(436)*

ἀντέστην, 1 pers. sg. 2 aor. act. indic. [§29.X] id.

ἀντέστησαν, 3 pers. pl. 2 aor. act. indic. . id.

ἀντέχεσθε, 2 pers. pl. pres. mid./pass. dep. imper. . . . . ἀντέχομαι *(472)*

(472) **ἀντέχομαι,** fut. ἀνθέξομαι [§35.4] (ἀντί + ἔχω) *to hold firmly, cling* or *adhere to; to be devoted to* any one, Luke 16:13; Tit. 1:9; *to exercise a zealous care for* any one, 1 Thess. 5:14

ἀντεχόμενον, acc. sg. m. pres. mid./pass. dep. part. . . . . ἀντέχομαι *(472)*

(473) **ἀντί,** prep. *over against;* hence, *in correspondence to, answering to,* John 1:16; *in place of,* Matt. 2:22, et al.; *in retribution* or *return for,* Matt. 5:38, et al.; *in consideration of,* Heb. 12:2, 16; *on account of,* Matt. 17:27; ἀνθ᾽ ὧν, *because,* Luke 1:20, et al.

ἀντιβάλλετε, 2 pers. pl. pres. act. indic. ἀντιβάλλω *(474)*

(474) **ἀντιβάλλω** (ἀντί + βάλλω) pr. *to throw* or *toss from one to another;* met. *to agitate, to converse* or *discourse about,* Luke 24:17

ἀντιδιατιθεμένους, acc. pl. m. pres. mid. part. . . . . ἀντιδιατίθημι *(475)*

(475) **ἀντιδιατίθημι** (ἀντί + διατίθημι) *to set opposite;* mid. *to be of an opposite opinion, to be adverse;* part. ἀντιδιατιθέμενος, *opponent,* 2 Tim. 2:25

(476) **ἀντίδικος,** ου, nom. sg. m. n. [§3.C.a] (ἀντί + δίκη) *an opponent in a lawsuit,* Matt. 5:25(2×); Luke 12:58; 18:3; *an adversary,* 1 Pet. 5:8

ἀντιδίκου, gen. sg. m. n. . . . . ἀντίδικος *(476)*

ἀντιδίκῳ, dat. sg. m. n. . . . . id.

ἀντιθέσεις, acc. pl. f. n. . . . . ἀντίθεσις *(477)*

(477) **ἀντίθεσις,** εως, ἡ [§5.E.c] (ἀντί + τίθημι) pr. *opposition;* hence, *a question proposed for dispute, disputation,* 1 Tim. 6:20

(478) **ἀντικαθίστημι,** fut. ἀνικαταστήσω [§29.X] (ἀντί + καθίστημι) trans. *to set in opposition;* intrans. 2 aor. ἀντικατέστην, *to withstand, resist,* Heb. 12:4

ἀντικαλέσωσι(ν), 3 pers. pl. aor. act. subj. . . . . ἀντικαλέω *(479)*

(479) **ἀντικαλέω,** ῶ (ἀντί + καλέω) *to invite in re-*

turn, Luke 14:12

ἀντικατέστητε, 2 pers. pl. 2 aor. act. indic. . . . . ἀντικαθίστημι *(478)*

(480) **ἀντίκειμαι,** fut. ἀντικείσομαι [§33.DD] (ἀντί + κεῖμαι) pr. *to occupy an opposite position;* met. *to oppose, be adverse to,* Gal. 5:17; 1 Tim. 1:10; part. ἀντικείμενος, *opponent, hostile,* Luke 13:17, et al.

ἀντικείμενοι, nom. pl. m. pres. mid./pass. dep. part. . . . . ἀντίκειμαι *(480)*

ἀντικείμενος, nom. sg. m. pres. mid./pass. dep. part. . . . . id.

ἀντικειμένῳ, dat. sg. m. pres. mid./pass. dep. part. . . . . id.

ἀντικειμένων, gen. pl. m. pres. mid./pass. dep. part. . . . . id.

ἀντίκειται, 3 pers. sg. pres. mid./pass. dep. indic. . . . . id.

(481) **ἀντικρύ,** adv., *opposite to, over against* (Acts 20:15, MT & TR | ἀντικρυς, GNT, WH & NA)

(†481) **ἀντικρυς,** adv., *opposite to, over against* (Acts 20:15, GNT, WH & NA | ἀντικρύ, MT & TR)

ἀντιλαμβάνεσθαι, pres. mid./pass. dep. infin. . . . . ἀντιλαμβάνω *(†482)*

ἀντιλαμβανόμενοι, nom. pl. m. pres. mid./pass. dep. part. . . . . id.

(†482) **ἀντιλαμβάνω,** fut. ἀντιλή(μ)ψομαι [§36.2] (ἀντιλαμβάνω, *to take in turn*) *to aid, assist, help,* Luke 1:54; Acts 20:35; *to be a recipient,* 1 Tim. 6:2

ἀντιλέγει, 3 pers. sg. pres. act. indic. ἀντιλέγω *(†483)*

ἀντιλέγεται, 3 pers. sg. pres. pass. indic. . id.

ἀντιλεγόμενον, acc. sg. neut. pres. pass. part. id.

ἀντιλέγοντα, acc. sg. m. pres. act. part. . . id.

ἀντιλέγοντας, acc. pl. m. pres. act. part. . id.

ἀντιλέγοντες, nom. pl. m. pres. act. part. (Luke 20:27, GNT, MT, TR & NA | λέγοντες, WH) . . . . id.

ἀντιλεγόντων, gen. pl. m. pres. act. part. . id.

(†483) **ἀντιλέγω,** fut. ἀντιλέξω [§23.1.b] 2 aor. ~~ἀντεῖπον~~ (ἀντί + λέγω) *to speak against, contradict; to gainsay, deny,* Luke 20:27; *to oppose,* John 19:12; Acts 13:45; 28:19; Rom. 10:21; Tit. 1:9; 2:9; pass. *to be spoken against, decried,* Luke 2:34; Acts 28:22

ἀντιλήψεις, acc. pl. f. n. (1 Cor. 12:28, MT & TR | ἀντιλήμψεις, GNT, WH & NA) . . . . ἀντίληψις *(484)*

(484) **ἀντίληψις,** εως, ἡ [§5.E.c] *aid, assistance;* meton. *one who aids* or *assists, a help,* 1 Cor. 12:28

ἀντιλήμψεις, acc. pl. f. n. (1 Cor. 12:28, GNT,

WH & NA | ἀντιλήψεις, MT & TR) . . . . ἀντιλήμψις *(†484)*

(†484) **ἀντιλήμψις,** εως, ἡ, *help, helpful deeds*

(485) **ἀντιλογία,** ας, ἡ [§2.B.b; 2.2] *contradiction, question,* Heb. 6:16; 7:7; *opposition, rebellion,* Jude 11; *contumely,* Heb. 12:3

ἀντιλογίᾳ, dat. sg. f. n. . . . . ἀντιλογία *(485)*

ἀντιλογίαν, acc. sg. f. n. . . . . id.

ἀντιλογίας, gen. sg. f. n. . . . . id.

(486) **ἀντιλοιδορέω,** ῶ, fut. ἀντιλοιδορήσω [§16.P] (ἀντί + λοιδορέω) *to reproach* or *revile again* or *in return,* 1 Pet. 2:23

(487) **ἀντίλυτρον,** ου, τό [§3.C.c] (ἀντί + λύτρον) *a ransom,* 1 Tim. 2:6

ἀντίλυτρον, acc. sg. neut. n. . . . . . . ἀντίλυτρον *(487)*

(488) **ἀντιμετρέω,** ῶ, fut. ἀντιμετρήσω [§16.P] (ἀντί + μετρέω) *to measure in return,* Luke 6:38; Matt. 7:2

ἀντιμετρηθήσεται, 3 pers. sg. fut. pass. indic. [§17.Q] . . . . ἀντιμετρέω *(488)*

(489) **ἀντιμισθία,** ας, ἡ [§2.B.b; 2.2] (ἀντί + μισθός) *a retribution, recompense,* Rom. 1:27; 2 Cor. 6:13

ἀντιμισθίαν, acc. sg. f. n. . . . . ἀντιμισθία *(489)*

Ἀντιοχέα, acc. sg. m. n. . . . . Ἀντιοχεύς *(491)*

(490) **Ἀντιόχεια,** ας, ἡ [§2.B.b; 2.2] *Antioch,* pr. name I. *Antioch,* the metropolis of Syria, where the disciples first received the name of Christians II. *Antioch,* a city of Pisidia, Acts 13:14; 14:19; 2 Tim. 3:11

Ἀντιοχείᾳ, dat. sg. f. n. . . . . Ἀντιόχεια *(490)*

Ἀντιόχειαν, acc. sg. f. n. . . . . id.

Ἀντιοχείας, gen. sg. f. n. . . . . id.

(491) **Ἀντιοχεύς,** έως, ὁ [§5.E.d] *an inhabitant of Antioch,* Acts 6:5

(492) **ἀντιπαρέρχομαι,** fut. ἀντιπαρελεύσομαι, 2 aor. ἀντιπαρῆλθον [§36.1] (ἀντί + παρέρχομαι) *to pass over against, to pass along* without noticing, Luke 10:31, 32

ἀντιπαρῆλθεν, 3 pers. sg. 2 aor. act. indic. . . . . ἀντιπαρέρχομαι *(492)*

(493) **Ἀντίπας,** α, ὁ, nom. sg. m. n. [§2.4] *Antipas,* pr. name

Ἀντιπατρίδα, acc. sg. f. n. . . . . Ἀντιπατρίς *(494)*

(494) **Ἀντιπατρίς,** ίδος, ἡ [§4.2.c] *Antipatris,* a city of Palestine, Acts 23:31

(†495) **ἀντιπέρα,** adv., *opposite* (Luke 8:26, GNT, WH & NA | ἀντιπέραν, MT & TR)

(495) **ἀντιπέραν,** adv., *over against, on the opposite side* (Luke 8:26, MT & TR | ἀντιπέρα, GNT, WH & NA)

ἀντιπίπτετε, 2 pers. pl. pres. act. indic. . . . . ἀντιπίπτω *(496)*

(496) **ἀντιπίπτω,** fut. ἀντιπεσοῦμαι [§37.1] (ἀντί + πίπτω) pr. *to fall upon, rush upon* any one;

hence, *to resist by force, oppose, strive against,* Acts 7:51

ἀντιστῆναι, 2 aor. act. infin. [§29.X] ἀνθίστημι *(436)*

ἀντίστητε, 2 pers. pl. 2 aor. act. imper. . .   id.

ἀντιστρατευόμενον, acc. sg. m. pres. mid./pass. dep. part. . . . . . ἀντιστρατεύομαι *(497)*

(497) **ἀντιστρατεύομαι** [§15.O] (ἀντί + στρατεύω) *to war against; to contravene, oppose,* Rom. 7:23

ἀντιτάσσεται, 3 pers. sg. pres. mid. indic. ἀντιτάσσω *(†498)*

ἀντιτασσόμενος, nom. sg. m. pres. mid. part.   id.

ἀντιτασσομένων, gen. pl. m. pres. mid. part.   id.

(†498) **ἀντιτάσσω**, fut. ἀντιτάξω [§26.3] (ἀντί + τάσσω) *to post in adverse array,* as an army; mid. *to set oneself in opposition, resist,* Acts 18:6; Rom. 13:2; James 5:6; *to be averse,* James 4:6; 1 Pet. 5:5

ἀντίτυπα, acc. pl. neut. adj. . . . . . . ἀντίτυπος *(†499)*

(499) ἀντίτυπον, nom. sg. neut. adj. . . . . . . id.

(†499) **ἀντίτυπος**, ον [§7.2] (ἀντί + τύπος) *of correspondent stamp* or *form; corresponding, in correspondent fashion,* 1 Pet. 3:21; τὸ ἀντίτυπον, *a copy, representation,* Heb. 9:24

ἀντίχριστοι, nom. pl. m. n. . . . . . . ἀντίχριστος *(500)*

(500) **ἀντίχριστος**, ου, ὁ, nom. sg. m. n. [§3.C.a] (ἀντί + Χριστός) *antichrist, an opposer of Christ,* 1 John 2:18, 22; 4:3; 2 John 7

ἀντιχρίστου, gen. sg. m. n. . . . . . . ἀντίχριστος *(500)*

ἀντλεῖν, pres. act. infin. . . . . ἀντλέω *(501)*

(501) **ἀντλέω**, ῶ, fut. ἀντλήσω [§16.P] (ἄντλος, *a sink*) *to draw,* e.g., wine, water, etc.; John 2:8, 9; 4:7, 15

(502) **ἄντλημα**, ατος, τό [§4.D.c] pr. *that which is drawn; a bucket, vessel for drawing water,* John 4:11

ἄντλημα, acc. sg. neut. n. . . . . ἄντλημα *(502)*

ἀντλῆσαι, aor. act. infin. . . . . ἀντλέω *(501)*

ἀντλήσατε, 2 pers. pl. aor. act. imper. . . . id.

ἀντοφθαλμεῖν, pres. act. infin. . . ἀντοφθαλμέω *(503)*

(503) **ἀντοφθαλμέω**, ῶ, fut. ἀντοφθαλμήσω [§16.P] (ἀντί + ὀφθαλμός) pr. *to look in the face,* i.e., rectis oculis; met. a nautical term, *to bear up against* the wind, Acts 27:15

ἄνυδροι, nom. pl. f. adj. . . . . ἄνυδρος *(504)*

(504) **ἄνυδρος**, ον [§7.2] (ἀ + ὕδωρ) *without water, dry,* 2 Pet. 2:17; Jude 12; τόποι ἄνυδροι, *dry places,* and therefore, in the East, *barren, desert,* Matt. 12:43; Luke 11:24

ἀνύδρων, gen. pl. m. adj. . . . . ἄνυδρος *(504)*

ἀνυπόκριτον, acc. sg. f. adj. . . . . ἀνυπόκριτος *(505)*

(505) **ἀνυπόκριτος**, ον, nom. sg. f. adj. [§7.2] (ἀ + ὑποκρίνομαι) *unfeigned, real, sincere,* Rom. 12:9, et al.

ἀνυποκρίτου, gen. sg. f. adj. . . . . ἀνυπόκριτος *(505)*

ἀνυποκρίτῳ, dat. sg. f. adj. . . . . id.

ἀνυπότακτα, acc. pl. neut. adj. . . ἀνυπότακτος *(506)*

ἀνυπότακτοι, nom. pl. m. adj. . . . . id.

ἀνυποτάκτοις, dat. pl. m. adj. . . . . id.

ἀνυπότακτον, acc. sg. neut. adj. . . . . id.

(506) **ἀνυπότακτος**, ον [§7.2] (ἀ + ὑποτάσσω) *not subjected, not made subordinate,* Heb. 2:8; *insubordinate, refractory, disorderly, contumacious, lawless,* 1 Tim. 1:9; Tit. 1:6, 10

(507) **ἄνω**, adv., *above,* Acts 2:19; *up, upwards,* John 11:41; ὁ, ἡ, τό, ἄνω, *that which is above,* John 8:23, et al.; ἕως ἄνω, *to the top* {John 2:7}

ἀνῶ, 1 pers. sg. 2 aor. act. subj. {Heb. 13:5} . . . . ἀνίημι *(447)*

(508) **ἀνώγεον**, or ἀνώγαιον, or ἀνώγεων, or ἀνάγειον, ου, τό [§3.C.e] (ἄνω + γῆ) *an upper room* or *chamber*

ἀνώγεον, acc. sg. neut. n. (Mark 14:15; Luke 22:12, MT & TR | ἀνάγαιον, GNT, WH & NA) . . . . ἀνώγεον *(508)*

(509) **ἄνωθεν**, adv., of place, *from above, from a higher place,* John 3:31; et al.; of time, *from the first* or *beginning,* Acts 26:5; *from the source,* Luke 1:3; *again, anew,* John 3:3, 7; Gal. 4:9; with a preposition, *the top* or *upper part,* Matt. 27:51

ἀνωρθώθη, 3 pers. sg. aor. pass. indic. [§34.1.d] . . . . ἀνορθόω *(461)*

ἀνωτερικά, acc. pl. neut. adj. . . . . . ἀνωτερικός *(510)*

(510) **ἀνωτερικός**, ή, όν [§7.F.a] *upper, higher, inland,* Acts 19:1

ἀνώτερον, acc. sg. neut. adj. . . . . ἀνώτερος *(511)*

(511) **ἀνώτερος**, α, ον [§7.1] (compar. of ἄνω) *higher, superior; to a higher place,* Luke 14:10; *above, before,* Heb. 10:8

ἀνωφελεῖς, nom. pl. f. adj. . . . . ἀνωφελής *(†512)*

ἀνωφελές, acc. sg. neut. adj. . . . . id.

(†512) **ἀνωφελής**, ές [§7.G.b] (ἀ + ὠφελέω) *useless, unprofitable,* Tit. 3:9; Heb. 7:18

ἄξει, 3 pers. sg. fut. act. indic. . . . . ἄγω *(71)*

ἀξία, nom. sg. f. adj. {Matt. 10:13} . . . . . ἄξιος *(514)*

ἄξια, nom. pl. neut. adj. {Rom. 8:18} . . . . id.

ἄξια, acc. pl. neut. adj. {Luke 12:48} . . . . id.

(513) **ἀξίνη**, ης, ἡ, nom. sg. f. n. [§2.B.a] *an axe,* Matt. 3:10; Luke 3:9

ἄξιοι, nom. pl. m. adj. . . . . ἄξιος *(514)*

ἄξιον, acc. sg. m. adj. {Matt. 3:8} . . . . . . id.

ἄξιον, nom. sg. neut. adj. {Luke 23:15} . . id.

ἄξιον, acc. sg. neut. adj. {Acts 23:29} . . . id.

(514) **ἄξιος**, ία, ιον, nom. sg. m. adj. [§7.1] pr. *of equal value; worthy, estimable,* Matt. 10:11, 13, et al.; *worthy of, deserving,* either good or evil, Matt. 10:10, et al.; *correspondent to,* Matt. 3:8; Luke 3:8; Acts

26:20; *comparable, countervailing,* Rom.
8:18; *suitable, due,* Luke 23:41

ἀξιοῦμεν, 1 pers. pl. pres. act. indic. . . . . ἀξιόω *(515)*

ἀξίους, acc. pl. m. adj. . . . . ἄξιος *(514)*

ἀξιούσθωσαν, 3 pers. pl. pers. pass.
imper. . . . . ἀξιόω *(515)*

(515) **ἀξιόω,** ῶ, fut. ἀξιώσω [§20.T] perf. pass.
ἠξίωμαι, *to judge* or *esteem worthy* or *deserving; to deem fitting, to require,* Acts
15:38; 28:22

ἀξιωθήσεται, 3 pers. sg. fut. pass. indic. . ἀξιόω *(515)*

(516) **ἀξίως,** adv., *worthily,* Col. 1:10, et al.; *suit-
ably, in a manner becoming,* Rom. 16:2,
et al.

ἀξιώσῃ, 3 pers. sg. aor. act. subj. . . . . . . ἀξιόω *(515)*

ἄξων, nom. sg. m. fut. act. part. . . . . ἄγω *(71)*

ἀόρατα, nom. pl. neut. adj. . . . . ἀόρατος *(517)*

ἀόρατον, acc. sg. m. adj. . . . . id.

(517) **ἀόρατος,** ον [§7.2] (ἀ + ὁράω) *invisible,* Rom.
1:20; Col. 1:15, 16; 1 Tim. 1:17; Heb. 11:27

ἀοράτου, gen. sg. m. adj. . . . . ἀόρατος *(517)*

ἀοράτῳ, dat. sg. m. adj. . . . . id.

ἀπ᾽ , by apostrophe for the prep. . . . . . . ἀπό *(575)*

ἀπάγαγε, 2 pers. sg. 2 aor. act. imper.
[§13.7.b,d] (Acts 23:17, GNT, MT, TR &
NA | ἄπαγε, WH) . . . . ἀπάγω *(520)*

ἀπαγάγετε, 2 pers. pl. 2 aor. act. imper. (Mark
14:44, MT & TR | ἀπάγετε, GNT, WH
& NA) . . . . id.

ἀπαγαγών, nom. sg. m. 2 aor. act. part. (Luke
13:15, GNT, MT, TR & NA | ἀπάγων,
WH) . . . . id.

ἀπαγγεῖλαι, aor. act. infin. [§27.1.d] ἀπαγγέλλω *(518)*

ἀπαγγείλατε, 2 pers. pl. aor. act. imper. . . id.

ἀπάγγειλον, 2 pers. sg. aor. act. imper. (Mark
5:19, GNT, WH & NA | ἀνάγγειλον, MT
& TR) . . . . id.

ἀπαγγελεῖ, 3 pers. sg. fut. act. indic. . . id.

ἀπαγγέλλει, 3 pers. sg. pres. act. indic. (Acts
17:30, WH | παραγγέλλει, GNT, MT, TR
& NA) . . . . id.

ἀπαγγέλλομεν, 1 pers. pl. pres. act. indic. id.

ἀπαγγέλλοντας, acc. pl. m. pres. act. part. id.

ἀπαγγέλλοντες, nom. pl. m. pres. act. part. id.

ἀπαγγέλλουσα, nom. sg. f. pres. act. part.
(John 20:18, MT & TR | ἀγγέλλουσα,
GNT, WH & NA) . . . . id.

ἀπαγγέλλουσιν, 3 pers. pl. pres. act. indic. id.

(518) **ἀπαγγέλλω,** fut. ἀπαγγελῶ [§27.1.b] aor.
ἀπήγγειλα [§27.1.b] 2 aor. pass.
ἀπηγγέλην [§27.4.a] (ἀπό + ἀγγέλλω) *to
enounce that with which a person is
charged,* or *which is called for by circumstances; to carry back word,* Matt. 2:8, et
al.; *to report,* Matt. 8:33, et al.; *to declare*

plainly, Heb. 2:12; *to announce* formally,
1 John 1:2, 3

ἀπαγγέλλων, nom. sg. m. pres. act.
part. . . . . ἀπαγγέλλω *(518)*

ἀπαγγελῶ, 1 pers. sg. fut. act. indic. . . . . . id.

ἄπαγε, 2 pers. sg. pres. act. imper. (Acts 23:17,
WH | ἀπάγαγε, GNT, MT, TR &
NA) . . . . ἀπάγω *(520)*

ἀπάγετε, 2 pers. pl. pres. act. imper. (Mark
14:44, GNT, WH & NA | ἀπαγάγετε,
MT & TR) . . . . id.

ἀπαγόμενοι, nom. pl. m. pres. pass. part. . id.

ἀπαγομένους, acc. pl. m. pres. pass. part.
(Luke 21:12, GNT, WH & NA | ἀγομέ-
νους, MT & TR) . . . . id.

ἀπάγουσα, nom. sg. f. pres. act. part. . . . id.

(†519) **ἀπάγχω,** fut. ἀπάγξω [§23.1.b] (ἀπό + ἄγχω,
to compress) *to strangle;* mid. *to choke* or
strangle one's self, hang one's self, Matt.
27:5

(520) **ἀπάγω,** fut. ἀπάξω [§23.1.b] 2 aor. ἀπήγαγον
[§13.7.b,d] aor. pass. ἀπήχθην (ἀπό +
ἄγω) *to lead away,* Matt. 26:57, et al.; *to
conduct,* Matt. 7:13, 14; pass. *to be led off
to execution,* Acts 12:19; met. *to be led
astray, seduced,* 1 Cor. 12:2

ἀπάγων, nom. sg. m. pres. act. part. (Luke
13:15, WH | ἀπαγαγών, GNT, MT, TR
& NA) . . . . ἀπάγω *(520)*

(521) **ἀπαίδευτος,** ον [§7.2] (ἀ + παιδεύω) *uninstructed, ignorant; silly, unprofitable*

ἀπαιδεύτους, acc. pl. f. adj. . . . . . . ἀπαίδευτος *(521)*

(522) **ἀπαίρω,** fut. ἀπαρῶ [§27.1.c] aor. pass.
ἀπήρθην [§27.3] subj. ἀπαρθῶ (ἀπό +
αἴρω) *to take away;* pass. *to be taken
away; to be withdrawn,* Matt. 9:15; Mark
2:20; Luke 5:35

ἀπαίτει, 2 pers. sg. pres. act. imper. . . ἀπαιτέω *(523)*

(523) **ἀπαιτέω,** ῶ, fut. ἀπαιτήσω [§16.P] (ἀπό +
αἰτέω) *to demand, require,* Luke 12:20; *to
demand back,* Luke 6:30

ἀπαιτοῦσιν, 3 pers. pl. pres. act. indic. (Luke
12:20, GNT, MT, TR & NA | αἰτοῦσιν,
WH) . . . . ἀπαιτέω *(523)*

(524) **ἀπαλγέω,** ῶ, fut. ἀπαλγήσω, perf. ἀπήλγηκα
[§16.P] (ἀπό + ἀλγέω, *to be in pain,
grieve*) pr. *to desist from grief;* hence, *to
become insensible* or *callous,* Eph. 4:19

ἀπαλλάξη, 3 pers. sg. aor. act.
subj. . . . . ἀπαλλάσσω(525)

ἀπαλλάσσεσθαι, pres. pass. infin. . . . . id.

(525) **ἀπαλλάσσω,** fut. ἀπαλλάξω, aor. pass.
ἀπηλλάχθην [§26.3; 26.4] perf. pass.
ἀπήλλαγμαι [§26.3] 2 aor. pass.
ἀπηλλάγην [§26.3] (ἀπό + ἀλλάσσω) *to*

set free, deliver, set at liberty, Heb. 2:15;
to rid judicially, Luke 12:58; mid. *to depart, remove,* Acts 19:12

(526) **ἀπαλλοτριόω, ῶ,** fut. ἀπαλλοτριώσω [§20.T]
perf. pass. ἀπηλλοτρίωμαι [§21.U] (ἀπό +
ἀλλοτριόω, *to alienate*) pass. *to be alien-
ated from, be a stranger to;* perf. part.
ἀπηλλοτριωμένος, *alien,* Eph. 2:12; 4:18;
Col. 1:21

(527) **ἀπαλός, ή, όν,** nom. sg. m. adj. [§7.F.a] *soft,
tender,* Matt. 24:32; Mark 13:28

ἅπαν, nom. sg. neut. adj. [§7.H.b] . . . . . . ἅπας (537)
ἅπαντα, acc. sg. m. adj. {Luke 3:21} . . . . id.
ἅπαντα, nom. pl. neut. adj. {Acts 4:32} . . id.
ἅπαντα, acc. pl. neut. adj. {Acts 2:44} . . . id.
ἅπαντας, acc. pl. m. adj. . . . . id.

(528) **ἀπαντάω, ῶ,** fut. ἀπαντήσω [§18.R] (ἀπό +
ἀντάω, *to meet*) *to meet,* Matt. 28:9, et
al.; *to encounter,* Luke 14:31

ἅπαντες, nom. pl. m. adj. . . . . ἅπας (537)
ἀπαντῆσαι, aor. act. infin. (Luke 14:31; Acts
16:16, MT & TR | ὑπαντῆσαι, GNT, WH
& NA) . . . . ἀπαντάω (528)
ἀπαντήσει, 3 pers. sg. fut. act. indic. . . . . id.
ἀπάντησιν, acc. sg. f. n. . . . . ἀπάντησις (529)

(529) **ἀπάντησις, εως, ή** [§5.E.c] *a meeting, encounter;* εἰς ἀπάντησιν, *to meet,* Matt.
25:1, 6; Acts 28:15; 1 Thess. 4:17

ἀπάντων, gen. pl. neut. adj. . . . . ἅπας (537)

(530) **ἅπαξ,** adv., *once,* 2 Cor. 11:25, et al.; *once for
all,* Heb. 6:4; 9:26, 28; 10:2; 1 Pet.
3:18, 20; Jude 3; εἰδὼς ἅπαξ, *knowing
once for ever, unfailingly, constantly,* Jude 5

ἀπαράβατον, acc. sg. f. adj. . . . . . ἀπαράβατος (531)

(531) **ἀπαράβατος, ον** [§7.2] (ἀ + παραβαίνω) *not
transient; not to be superseded, unchangeable,* Heb. 7:24

(532) **ἀπαρασκεύαστος, ον** [§7.2] (ἀ + παρασκευάζω) *unprepared,* 2 Cor. 9:4

ἀπαρασκευάστους, acc. pl. m.
adj. . . . . ἀπαρασκεύαστος (532)
ἀπαρθῇ, 3 pers. sg. aor. pass. subj. . . . ἀπαίρω (522)

(533) **ἀπαρνέομαι, οῦμαι,** fut. ἀπαρνήσομαι, 2 fut.
pass. ἀπαρνηθήσομαι [§17.Q] (ἀπό +
ἀρνέομαι) *to deny, disown,* Matt. 26:34,
et al.; *to renounce, disregard,* Matt. 16:24,
et al.

ἀπαρνηθήσεται, 3 pers. sg. fut. pass.
indic. . . . . ἀπαρνέομαι (533)
ἀπαρνησάσθω, 3 pers. sg. aor. mid. dep.
imper. . . . . id.
ἀπαρνήσῃ, 2 pers. sg. fut. mid. dep. indic.
{Luke 22:61} . . . . id.
ἀπαρνήσῃ, 2 pers. sg. aor. mid. dep. subj.
{Luke 22:34} . . . . id.

ἀπαρνήσομαι, 1 pers. sg. fut. mid. dep.
indic. . . . . ἀπαρνέομαι (533)
ἀπαρνήσωμαι, 1 pers. sg. aor. mid. dep. subj.
(Mark 14:31, MT | ἀπαρνήσομαι, GNT,
WH, TR & NA) . . . . id.

(534) **ἀπάρτι,** or ἀπ᾽ ἄρτι, *forthwith, at once,* John
13:19; 14:7; *henceforward,* Matt. 26:29;
Rev. 14:13; *hereafter,* Matt. 26:64; John
1:52 (Rev. 14:13, TRs | ἀπ᾽ ἄρτι, GNT,
WH, MT, TRb & NA)

ἀπαρτισμόν, acc. sg. m. n. . . . . . . ἀπαρτισμός (535)

(535) **ἀπαρτισμός, οῦ, ὁ** [§3.C.a] (ἀπαρτίζω, *to perfect,* from ἀπό + ἄρτιος) *completion, perfection,* Luke 14:28

(536) **ἀπαρχή, ῆς, ή,** nom. sg. f. n. [§2.B.a] (ἀπό
+ ἀρχή) pr. *the first act of a sacrifice;*
hence, *the firstfruits, first portion, firstling,*
Rom. 8:23, et al.

ἀπαρχήν, acc. sg. f. n. . . . . ἀπαρχή (536)

(537) **ἅπας, ασα, αν,** nom. sg. m. adj. [§7.H.b] (a
strengthened form of πᾶς) *all, the whole*

ἅπασαν, acc. sg. f. adj. . . . . ἅπας (537)
ἅπασι(ν), dat. pl. m. adj. (Luke 3:16, MT &
TR | πᾶσιν, GNT, WH & NA) . . . . . . id.

(‡782) **ἀπασπάζομαι,** fut. ἀπασπάσομαι, *to salute,
greet,* Acts 21:6

ἀπάταις, dat. pl. f. n. . . . . ἀπάτη (539)
ἀπατάτω, 3 pers. sg. pres. act. imper. . ἀπατάω (538)

(538) **ἀπατάω, ῶ,** fut. ἀπατήσω [§18.R] aor. pass.
ἠπατήθην, *to deceive, seduce into error,*
Eph. 5:6; 1 Tim. 2:14; James 1:26

(539) **ἀπάτη, ης, ή,** nom. sg. f. n. [§2.B.a] *deceit,
deception, delusion*

ἀπάτῃ, dat. sg. f. n. . . . . ἀπάτη (539)
ἀπατηθεῖσα, nom. sg. f. aor. pass. part. [§19.S]
(1 Tim. 2:14, MT & TR | ἐξαπατηθεῖσα,
GNT, WH & NA) . . . . ἀπατάω (538)
ἀπάτης, gen. sg. f. n. . . . . ἀπάτη (539)
ἀπατῶν, nom. sg. m. pres. act. part. . . ἀπατάω (538)

(540) **ἀπάτωρ, ορος, ὁ, ή,** nom. sg. m. adj. [§4.2.f]
(ἀ + πατήρ) pr. *without a father, father-
less;* hence, *independent of paternal descent,* Heb. 7:3

(541) **ἀπαύγασμα, ατος, τό,** nom. sg. neut. n.
[§4.D.c] (ἀπό + αὐγάζω) *an effulgence,*
Heb. 1:3

ἀπαχθῆναι, aor. pass. infin. [§23.4] . . . . ἀπάγω (520)
ἀπέβησαν, 3 pers. pl. 2 aor. act. indic.
[§37.1] . . . . ἀποβαίνω (576)
ἀπέβλεπε(ν), 3 pers. sg. imperf. act.
indic. . . . . ἀποβλέπω (578)
ἀπέδειξεν, 3 pers. sg. aor. act. indic.
[§31.1.b] . . . . ἀποδείκνυμι (584)
ἀπεδέξαντο, 3 pers. pl. aor. mid. dep. indic.
(Acts 21:17, GNT, WH & NA | ἐδέξαντο,

MT & TR) . . . . ἀποδέχομαι *(588)*
ἀπεδέξατο, 3 pers. sg. aor. mid. dep.
    indic. . . . . id.
ἀπέδετο, 3 pers. sg. 2 aor. mid. indic. (Heb.
    12:16, GNT, WH & NA | ἀπέδοτο, MT
    & TR) . . . . ἀποδίδωμι *(591)*
ἀπεδέχετο, 3 pers. sg. imperf. mid./pass. dep.
    indic. . . . . ἀποδέχομαι *(588)*
ἀπεδέχθησαν, 3 pers. pl. aor. pass. indic.
    [§23.4] (Acts 15:4, MT & TR |
    παρεδέχθησαν, GNT, WH & NA) . . . id.
ἀπεδήμησεν, 3 pers. sg. aor. act.
    indic. . . . . ἀποδημέω *(589)*
ἀπεδίδουν, 3 pers. pl. imperf. act. indic.
    [§31.2] . . . . ἀποδίδωμι *(591)*
ἀπεδοκίμασαν, 3 pers. pl. aor. act.
    indic. ἀποδοκιμάζω *(593)*
ἀπεδοκιμάσθη, 3 pers. sg. aor. pass. indic.   id.
ἀπέδοντο, 3 pers. pl. 2 aor. mid. indic.
    [§30.AA] . . . . ἀποδίδωμι *(591)*
ἀπέδοσθε, 2 pers. pl. 2 aor. mid. indic. . . id.
ἀπέδοτο, 3 pers. sg. 2 aor. mid. indic. (Heb.
    12:16, MT & TR | ἀπέδετο, GNT, WH
    & NA) . . . . id.
ἀπέδωκεν, 3 pers. sg. aor. act. indic. [§30.Z]   id.
ἀπέθανε(ν), 3 pers. sg. 2 aor. act. indic.
    [§36.4] . . . . ἀποθνήσκω *(†599)*
ἀπεθάνετε, 2 pers. pl. 2 aor. act. indic. . . . id.
ἀπεθάνομεν, 1 pers. pl. 2 aor. act. indic. . id.
ἀπέθανον, 1 pers. sg. 2 aor. act. indic.
    {Rom. 7:10} . . . . id.
ἀπέθανον, 3 pers. pl. 2 aor. act. indic.
    {Rom. 5:15} . . . . id.
ἀπέθεντο, 3 pers. pl. 2 aor. mid. indic.
    [§28.W] . . . . ἀποτίθημι *(659)*
ἀπέθετο, 3 pers. sg. 2 aor. mid. indic. (Matt.
    14:3, GNT, WH & NA | ἔθετο, MT &
    TR) . . . . id.
ἀπέθνησκεν, 3 pers. sg. imperf. act. indic.
    (Luke 8:42, GNT & NA | ἀπέθνησκεν,
    WH, MT & TR) . . . . ἀποθνήσκω *(†599)*
(†542) **ἀπεῖδον**, subj. ἀπίδω, see ἀφοράω *(872)*
(543) **ἀπείθεια**, ας, ἡ [§2.B.b; 2.2] *an uncompliant
    disposition; obstinacy, contumacy, disobe-
    dience, unbelief,* Rom. 11:30, 32; Eph. 2:2;
    5:6; Heb. 4:6, 11; Col. 3:6
ἀπειθείᾳ, dat. sg. f. n. (Rom. 11:30, GNT,
    MT, TR & NA | ἀπειθίᾳ, WH) . . ἀπείθεια *(543)*
ἀπείθειαν, acc. sg. f. n. (Rom. 11:32, GNT,
    MT, TR & NA | ἀπειθίαν, WH) . . . . . id.
ἀπειθείας, gen. sg. f. n. (Eph. 2:2; 5:6, GNT,
    MT, TR & NA | ἀπειθίας, WH) . . . . id.
ἀπειθεῖς, nom. pl. m. adj.
    {2 Tim. 3:2} . . . . ἀπειθής *(545)*
ἀπειθεῖς, acc. pl. m. adj. {Luke 1:17} . . . . id.

(544) **ἀπειθέω**, ῶ, fut. ἀπειθήσω [§16.P] *to be un-
    compliant; to refuse belief, disbelieve,* John
    3:36, et al.; *to refuse belief and obedience,
    be contumacious,* Rom. 10:21; 1 Pet. 3:20
    et al.; *to refuse conformity,* Rom. 2:8
(545) **ἀπειθής**, ές, nom. sg. m. adj. [§7.G.b] (ἀ +
    πείθω) *who will not be persuaded, uncom-
    pliant; disobedient,* Acts 26:19; Rom. 1:30;
    2 Tim. 3:2; *untoward, contumacious,* Luke
    1:17; Tit. 1:16; 3:3
ἀπειθήσαντες, nom. pl. m. aor. act. part. (Acts
    14:2, GNT, WH & NA | ἀπειθοῦντες,
    MT & TR) . . . . ἀπειθέω *(544)*
ἀπειθήσασι(ν), dat. pl. m. aor. act. part. .   id.
ἀπειθοῦντα, acc. sg. m. pres. act. part. . . . id.
ἀπειθοῦντες, nom. pl. m. pres. act. part. .   id.
ἀπειθούντων, gen. pl. m. pres. act. part. . . id.
ἀπειθοῦσι(ν), 3 pers. pl. pres. act. indic.
    {1 Pet. 3:1} . . . . id.
ἀπειθοῦσι(ν), dat. pl. m. pres. act. part.
    {Rom. 2:8} . . . . id.
ἀπειθῶν, nom. sg. m. pres. act. part. . . . . id.
ἀπειλάς, acc. pl. f. n. . . . . ἀπειλή *(547)*
(546) **ἀπειλέω**, ῶ, and, later, also ἀπειλοῦμαι, fut.
    ἀπειλήσω, aor. ἠπείλησα [§16.P] *to threat-
    en, menace, rebuke* Acts 4:17; 1 Pet. 2:23
(547) **ἀπειλή**, ῆς, ἡ [§2.B.a] *threat, commination,*
    Acts 4:17, 29; 9:1; *harshness of language,*
    Eph. 6:9
ἀπειλῇ, dat. sg. f. n. (Acts 4:17, MT & TR
    | GNT, WH & NA omit) . . . . ἀπειλή *(547)*
ἀπειλήν, acc. sg. f. n. . . . . id.
ἀπειλῆς, gen. sg. f. n. . . . . id.
ἀπειλησώμεθα, 1 pers. pl. aor. mid.
    subj. . . . . ἀπειλέω *(546)*
(548) **ἄπειμι**, 1 pers. sg. pres. indic., fut. ἀπέσομαι
    (ἀπό + εἰμί) *to be absent*
(549) **ἄπειμι**, imperf. ἀπῄειν [§33.4] (ἀπό + εἶμι,
    to go) *to go away, depart,* Acts 17:10
ἀπειπάμεθα, 1 pers. pl. 2 aor. mid. indic.
    [§13.4] . . . . ἀπεῖπον *(†550)*
(†550) **ἀπεῖπον**, 2 aor. act. indic., *to tell out; to re-
    fuse, forbid;* aor. mid. ἀπειπάμην, *to re-
    nounce, disclaim,* 2 Cor. 4:2
(551) **ἀπείραστος**, ον, nom. sg. m. adj. [§7.2] (ἀ +
    πειράζω) *not having tried, inexperienced,*
    or, *untried,* or, *incapable of being tried,*
    James 1:13
(552) **ἄπειρος**, ον, nom. sg. m. adj. [§7.2] (ἀ +
    πεῖρα) *inexperienced, unskillful, ignorant,*
    Heb. 5:13
ἀπεῖχεν, 3 pers. sg. imperf. act. indic. (Matt.
    14:24 with σταδίους πολλοὺς ἀπὸ τῆ γῆς,
    GNT, WH & NA | μέσον τῆς θαλάσσης
    ἦν, MT & TR) . . . . ἀπέχω *(568)*

ἀπεκαλύφθη, 3 pers. sg. aor. pass.
  indic. . . . . ἀποκαλύπτω (601)
ἀπεκάλυψας, 2 pers. sg. aor. act. indic. . . id.
ἀπεκάλυψε(ν), 3 pers. sg. aor. act. indic. . id.
ἀπεκατεστάθη, 3 pers. sg. aor. pass. indic.
  (Matt. 12:13; Mark 3:5; Luke 6:10, GNT,
  WH & NA | ἀποκατεστάθη, MT &
  TR) . . . . ἀποκαθίστημι (600)
ἀπεκατέστη, 3 pers. sg. aor. act. indic. (Mark
  8:25, GNT, WH & NA | ἀποκατεστάθη,
  MT & TR) . . . . id.
ἀπεκδέχεται, 3 pers. sg. pres. mid./pass. dep.
  indic. . . . . ἀποδέχομαι (588)
(553) ἀπεκδέχομαι, fut. ἀπεκδέξομαι [§23.1.b]
  (ἀπό + ἐκδέχομαι) to expect, wait or look
  for, Rom. 8:19, 23, 25; 1 Cor. 1:7; Gal.
  5:5; Phil. 3:20; Heb. 9:28
ἀπεκδεχόμεθα, 1 pers. pl. pres. mid./pass.
  dep. indic. . . . . ἀπεκδέχομαι (553)
ἀπεκδεχόμενοι, nom. pl. m. pres. mid./pass.
  dep. part. . . . . id.
ἀπεκδεχομένοις, dat. pl. m. pres. mid./pass.
  dep. part. . . . . id.
ἀπεκδεχομένους, acc. pl. m. pres. mid./pass.
  dep. part. . . . . id.
(554) ἀπεκδύομαι, fut. ἀπεκδύσομαι [§15.O] (ἀπό
  + ἐκδύω) to put off, renounce, Col. 3:9;
  to despoil a rival, Col. 2:15
ἀπεκδυσάμενοι, nom. pl. m. aor. mid. dep.
  part. . . . . ἀπεκδύομαι (554)
ἀπεκδυσάμενος, nom. sg. m. aor. mid. dep.
  par. . . . . id.
ἀπεκδύσει, dat. sg. f. n. . . . . ἀπέκδυσις (555)
(555) ἀπέκδυσις, εως, ἡ [§5.E.c] a putting or strip-
  ping off, renunciation, Col. 2:11
ἀπεκεφάλισα, 1 pers. sg. aor. act.
  indic. . . . . ἀποκεφαλίζω (607)
ἀπεκεφάλισε(ν), 3 pers. sg. aor. act. indic. id.
ἀπέκοψαν, 3 pers. pl. aor. act.
  indic. . . . . ἀποκόπτω (609)
ἀπέκοψε(ν), 3 pers. sg. aor. act. indic.
  [§23.1.a; 23.2] . . . . id.
ἀπεκρίθη, 3 pers. sg. aor. mid. dep.
  indic. . . . . ἀποκρίνομαι (611)
ἀπεκρίθην, 1 pers. sg. aor. mid. dep. indic.
  [§27.3] . . . . id.
ἀπεκρίθης, 2 pers. sg. aor. mid. dep. indic. id.
ἀπεκρίθησαν, 3 pers. pl. aor. mid. dep. indic. id.
ἀπεκρίνατο, 3 pers. sg. aor. mid. dep. indic. id.
ἀπέκρυψας, 2 pers. sg. aor. act.
  indic. . . . . ἀποκρύπτω (613)
ἀπέκρυψε(ν), 3 pers. sg. aor. act. indic. (Matt.
  25:18, MT & TR | ἔκρυψεν, GNT, WH
  & NA) . . . . id.
ἀπεκτάνθη, 3 pers. sg. aor. pass. indic.

[§37.1] . . . . ἀποκτείνω (615)
ἀπεκτάνθησαν, 3 pers. pl. aor. pass. indic. id.
ἀπέκτειναν, 3 pers. pl. aor. act. indic.
  [§27.1.d] . . . . id.
ἀπεκτείνατε, 2 pers. pl. aor. act. indic. . . . id.
ἀπέκτεινεν, 3 pers. sg. aor. act. indic. . . . . id.
ἀπεκύησεν, 3 pers. sg. aor. act. indic. ἀποκυέω (616)
ἀπεκύλισε(ν), 3 pers. sg. aor. act.
  indic. ἀποκυλίω (617)
ἀπέλαβεν, 3 pers. sg. 2 aor. act.
  indic. . . . . ἀπολαμβάνω (618)
ἀπέλαβες, 2 pers. sg. 2 aor. act. indic. . . . id.
(556) ἀπελαύνω, fut. ἀπελάσω, aor. ἀπήλασα
  [§36.2] (ἀπό + ἐλαύνω) to drive away,
  Acts 18:16
ἀπελεγμόν, acc. sg. m. n. . . . . ἀπελεγμός (557)
(557) ἀπελεγμός, οῦ, ὁ [§3.C.a] (ἀπελέγχω, to refute, from ἀπό + ἐλέγχω) pr. refutation;
  by impl. disesteem, contempt, Acts 19:27
ἀπέλειπον, 1 pers. sg. imperf. act. indic.
  (2 Tim. 4:13, 20; Tit. 1:5, WH |
  ἀπέλιπον, 2 Tim. 4:13, 20, GNT, MT, TR
  & NA | κατέλιπον, Tit. 1:5, MT &
  TR) . . . . ἀπολείπω (620)
ἀπέλειχον, 3 pers. pl. imperf. act. indic. (Luke
  16:21, MT & TR | ἐπέλειχον, GNT, WH
  & NA) . . . . ἀπολείχω (621)
(558) ἀπελεύθερος, ου, ὁ, ἡ, nom. sg. m. n. [§3.C.a]
  (ἀπό + ἐλεύθερος) a freed-man, 1 Cor.
  7:22
ἀπελεύσομαι, 1 pers. sg. fut. mid. dep.
  indic. . . . . ἀπέρχομαι (565)
ἀπελευσόμεθα, 1 pers. pl. fut. mid. dep.
  indic. . . . . id.
ἀπελεύσονται, 3 pers. pl. fut. mid. dep. indic. id.
ἀπεληλύθεισαν, 3 pers. pl. pluperf. act. indic. id.
ἀπελήλυθε(ν), 3 pers. sg. 2 perf. act. indic. id.
ἀπελθεῖν, 2 aor. act. infin. . . . . id.
ἀπέλθῃ, 3 pers. sg. 2 aor. act. subj. (Matt.
  5:30, GNT, WH & NA | βληθῇ, MT &
  TR) . . . . id.
ἀπέλθητε, 2 pers. pl. 2 aor. act. subj. . . . . id.
ἀπελθόντες, nom. pl. m. 2 aor. act. part. . id.
ἀπελθόντι, dat. sg. m. 2 aor. act. part. . . . id.
ἀπελθόντων, gen. pl. m. 2 aor. act. part. . id.
ἀπελθοῦσα, nom. sg. f. 2 aor. act. part. . . id.
ἀπελθοῦσαι, nom. pl. f. 2 aor. act. part. . . id.
ἀπέλθω, 1 pers. sg. 2 aor. act. subj. . . . . . id.
ἀπελθών, nom. sg. m. 2 aor. act. part. . . . id.
ἀπέλθωσιν, 3 pers. pl. 2 aor. act. subj. . . . id.
ἀπέλιπον, 1 pers. sg. 2 aor. act. indic. [§24.9]
  (2 Tim. 4:13, 20, GNT, MT, TR & NA
  | ἀπέλειπον, WH) . . . . ἀπολείπω (620)
Ἀπελλῆν, acc. sg. m. n. . . . . Ἀπελλῆς (559)
(559) Ἀπελλῆς, οῦ, ὁ [§2.B.c] Apelles, proper name,

Rom. 16:10

ἀπελογεῖτο, 3 pers. sg. imperf. mid./pass. dep.
indic. . . . . ἀπολογέομαι *(626)*

ἀπελούσασθε, 2 pers. pl. aor. mid. indic.
[§15.O] . . . . ἀπολούω *(628)*

ἀπελπίζοντες, nom. pl. m. pres. act.
part. ἀπελπίζω *(560)*

(560) **ἀπελπίζω,** fut. ἀπελπίσω [§26.1] (ἀπό +
ἐλπίζω) *to lay aside hope, despond, de-*
spair; also, *to hope for* something *in return,*
Luke 6:35

ἀπέλυεν, 3 pers. sg. imperf. act. indic. . ἀπολύω *(630)*

ἀπελύθησαν, 3 pers. pl. aor. pass. indic.
[§14.N] . . . . id.

ἀπελύοντο, 3 pers. pl. imperf. mid. indic. . id.

ἀπέλυσαν, 3 pers. pl. aor. act. indic. [§13.M] id.

ἀπέλυσε(ν), 3 pers. sg. aor. act. indic. . . . . id.

(561) **ἀπέναντι,** adv. (ἀπό + ἔναντι) *opposite to,*
over against, Matt. 21:2; 27:61; *contrary*
to, in opposition to, against, Acts 17:7;
before, in the presence of, Matt. 27:24;
Acts 3:16

ἀπενεγκεῖν, 2 aor. act. infin. [§36.1] . ἀποφέρω *(667)*

ἀπενεχθῆναι, aor. pass. infin. . . . . id.

ἀπενίψατο, 3 pers. sg. aor. mid. indic.
[§23.5] . . . . ἀπονίπτω *(633)*

ἀπεξεδέχετο, 3 pers. sg. imperf. mid./pass.
dep. indic. (1 Pet. 3:20, GNT, WH, MT &
NA | ἅπαξ ἐξεδέχετο, TR) . . ἀπεκδέχομαι *(553)*

ἀπέπεσαν, 3 pers. pl. 2 aor. act. indic. (Acts
9:18, GNT, WH & NA | ἀπέπεσον, MT
& TR) . . . . ἀποπίπτω *(634)*

ἀπέπεσον, 3 pers. pl. 2 aor. act. indic. [§37.1]
(Acts 9:18, MT & TR | ἀπέπεσαν, GNT,
WH & NA) . . . . id.

ἀπεπλανήθησαν, 3 pers. pl. aor. pass. indic.
[§19.5] . . . . ἀποπλανάω *(635)*

ἀπέπλευσαν, 3 pers. pl. aor. act.
indic. ἀποπλέω *(636)*

ἀπέπλυναν, 3 pers. pl. aor. act. indic. (Luke
5:2, MT & TR | ἔπλυνον, GNT, WH &
NA) . . . . ἀποπλύνω *(637)*

ἀπεπνίγη, 3 pers. sg. 2 aor. pass. indic.
[§24.6] . . . . ἀποπνίγω *(638)*

ἀπέπνιξαν, 3 pers. pl. aor. act. indic. . . . . id.

ἀπεράντοις, dat. pl. f. adj. . . . . ἀπέραντος *(562)*

(562) **ἀπέραντος,** ον [§7.2] (ἀ + πέρας) *unlimited,*
interminable, endless, 1 Tim. 1:4

(563) **ἀπερισπάστως,** adv. (ἀ + περισπάω) *with-*
out distraction, without care or *solicitude,*
1 Cor. 7:35

ἀπερίτμητοι, voc. pl. m. adj. . . . . ἀπερίτμητος *(564)*

(564) **ἀπερίτμητος,** ον [§7.2] (ἀ + περιτέμνω)
pr. *uncircumcised;* met. *uncircumcised*
in respect of untowardness and obduracy

Acts 7:51

ἀπέρχεσθαι, pres. mid./pass. dep. infin. (Acts
23:32, GNT, WH & NA | πορεύεσθαι,
MT & TR) . . . . ἀπέρχομαι *(565)*

ἀπέρχῃ, 2 pers. sg. pres. mid./pass. dep. subj. id.

(565) **ἀπέρχομαι,** fut. ἀπελεύσομαι, 2 aor. ἀπῆλθον
[§36.1] pass. ἀπελήλυθα (ἀπό + ἔρχομαι)
to go away, depart, Matt. 8:18, et al.; *to*
go forth, pervade, as a rumor, Matt. 4:24;
to arrive at a destination, Luke 23:33; *to*
pass away, disappear, Rev. 21:4;
ἀπέρχομαι ὀπίσω, *to follow,* Mark 1:20,
et al.

ἀπερχομένων, gen. pl. f. pres. mid./pass. dep.
part. ἀπέρχομαι *(565)*

ἀπέσπασε(ν), 3 pers. sg. aor. act.
indic. ἀποσπάω *(645)*

ἀπεσπάσθη, 3 pers. sg. aor. pass. indic. . . id.

ἀπεστάλη, 3 pers. sg. 2 aor. pass. indic.
[§27.4.b] . . . . ἀποστέλλω *(649)*

ἀπεστάλην, 1 pers. sg. 2 aor. pass. indic. . id.

ἀπέσταλκα, 1 pers. sg. perf. act. indic.
[§27.2.b] . . . . id.

ἀπεστάλκαμεν, 1 pers. pl. perf. act. indic. id.

ἀπεστάλκαν, 3 pers. pl. perf. act. indic. (Acts
16:36, GNT, WH & NA | ἀπεστάλκασιν,
MT & TR) . . . . id.

ἀπεστάλκασιν, 3 pers. pl. perf. act. indic.
(Acts 16:36, MT & TR | ἀπεστάλκαν,
GNT, WH & NA) . . . . id.

ἀπεστάλκατε, 2 pers. pl. perf. act. indic. . id.

ἀπέσταλκε(ν), 3 pers. sg. perf. act. indic. . id.

ἀπέσταλμαι, 1 pers. sg. perf. pass. indic.
(Luke 4:43, MT & TR | ἀπεστάλην,
GNT, WH & NA) . . . . id.

ἀπεσταλμένα, nom. pl. neut. perf. pass. part.
(Rev. 5:6, TR | ἀπεσταλμένοι, GNT, WH
& NA | ἀποστελλόμενα, MT) . . . . . . id.

ἀπεσταλμένοι, nom. pl. m. perf. pass. part. id.

ἀπεσταλμένος, nom. sg. m. perf. pass. part. id.

ἀπεσταλμένους, acc. pl. m. perf. pass. part. id.

ἀπεστέγασαν, 3 pers. pl. aor. act.
indic. ἀποστεγάζω *(648)*

ἀπέστειλα, 1 pers. sg. aor. act. indic.
[§27.1.d] . . . . ἀποστέλλω *(649)*

ἀπεστείλαμεν, 1 pers. pl. aor. act. indic. (Acts
21:25, WH | ἐπεστείλαμεν, GNT, MT,
TR & NA) . . . . id.

ἀπέστειλαν, 3 pers. pl. aor. act. indic. . . . id.

ἀπέστειλας, 2 pers. sg. aor. act. indic. . . . id.

ἀπέστειλε(ν), 3 pers. sg. aor. act. indic. . . id.

ἀπεστερημένος, nom. sg. m. perf. pass. part.
(James 5:4, GNT, MT, TR & NA |
ἀφυστερημένος, WH) . . . . ἀποστερέω *(650)*

ἀπεστερημένων, gen. pl. m. perf. pass. part. id.

ἀπέστη, 3 pers. sg. 2 aor. act. indic. . ἀφίστημι *(868)*
ἀπέστησαν, 3 pers. pl. 2 aor. act. indic. . . . id.
ἀπέστησε(ν), 3 pers. sg. aor. act. indic. . . . id.
ἀπεστράφησαν, 3 pers. pl. 2 aor. pass. indic.
    [§24.10] . . . . ἀποστρέφω *(654)*
ἀπέστρεψε(ν), 3 pers. sg. aor. act. indic.
    [§23.2] (Matt. 27:3, MT & TR |
    ἔστρεψεν, GNT, WH & NA) . . . . . . id.
ἀπετάξατο, 3 pers. sg. aor. mid. dep. indic.
    [§26.3] (Acts 18:21, MT & TR |
    ἀποταξάμενος, GNT, WH &
    NA) . . . . ἀποτάσσομαι *(657)*
ἀπεφθέγξατο, 3 pers. sg. aor. mid. dep. indic.
    [§23.1.b] . . . . ἀποφθέγγομαι *(669)*
(566) ἀπέχει, 3 pers. sg. pres. act. indic. . . . . . ἀπέχω *(568)*
ἀπέχεσθαι, pres. mid. infin. . . . . id.
ἀπέχεσθε, 2 pers. pl. pres. mid. imper. . . . id.
ἀπέχετε, 2 pers. pl. pres. act. indic. . . . . . id.
ἀπέχῃς, 2 pers. sg. pres. act. subj. . . . . . . id.
ἀπέχοντος, gen. sg. m. pres. act. part. . . . id.
ἀπέχουσαν, acc. sg. f. pres. act. part. . . . . id.
ἀπέχουσι(ν), 3 pers. pl. pres. act. indic. . . id.
(568) **ἀπέχω**, 1 pers. sg. pres. act. indic., fut. ἀφέξω
    [§35.4] (ἀπό + ἔχω) trans. *to have in full
    what is due or is sought,* Matt. 6:2, 5, 16;
    Luke 6:24; Phil. 4:18; *to have altogether,*
    Philemon 15; hence, impers. ἀπέχει, *it is
    enough,* Mark 14:41; intrans. *to be distant,*
    Luke 7:6, et al.; *to be estranged,* Matt.
    15:8; Mark 7:6; mid. *to abstain from,* Acts
    15:20, et al.
ἀπεχωρίσθη, 3 pers. sg. aor. pass.
    indic. . . . . ἀποχωρίζω *(673)*
ἀπήγαγεν, 3 pers. sg. 2 aor. act. indic.
    [§13.7.d] (Acts 24:7, TR | GNT, WH, MT
    & NA omit) . . . . ἀπάγω *(520)*
ἀπήγαγον, 3 pers. pl. 2 aor. act. indic. . . . id.
ἀπήγγειλαν, 3 pers. pl. aor. act. indic.
    [§27.1.d] . . . . ἀπαγγέλλω *(518)*
ἀπήγγειλε(ν), 3 pers. sg. aor. act. indic. . . id.
ἀπηγγέλη, 3 pers. sg. 2 aor. pass. indic.
    [§27.4.a] . . . . id.
ἀπήγγελλον, 1 pers. sg. imperf. act. indic.
    (Acts 26:20, GNT, WH, TRb & NA |
    ἀπαγγέλλων, MT & TRs) . . . . id.
ἀπήγξατο, 3 pers. sg. aor. mid. indic.
    [§23.1.b] . . . . ἀπάγχω *(†519)*
ἀπήεσαν, 3 pers. pl. imperf. indic.
    [§33.4] . . . . ἄπειμι *(549)*
ἀπήλασεν, 3 pers. sg. aor. act. indic.
    [§36.2] . . . . ἀπελαύνω *(556)*
ἀπηλγηκότες, nom. pl. m. perf. act.
    part. . . . . ἀπαλγέω *(524)*
ἀπῆλθα, 1 pers. sg. 2 aor. act. indic. [§35.12]
    (Rev. 10:9, GNT, WH & NA | ἀπῆλθον,

    MT & TR) . . . . ἀπέρχομαι *(565)*
ἀπῆλθαν, 3 pers. pl. 2 aor. act. indic. . . . . id.
ἀπῆλθε(ν), 3 pers. sg. 2 aor. act. indic. [§36.1] id.
ἀπῆλθον, 1 pers. sg. 2 aor. act. indic.
    {Gal. 1:17} . . . . id.
ἀπῆλθον, 3 pers. pl. 2 aor. act. indic.
    {John 6:22} . . . . id.
ἀπηλλάχθαι, perf. pass. infin.
    [§26.3] . . . . ἀπαλλάσσω *(525)*
ἀπηλλοτριωμένοι, nom. pl. m. perf. pass.
    part. . . . . ἀπαλλοτριόω *(526)*
ἀπηλλοτριωμένους, acc. pl. m. perf. pass.
    part. . . . . id.
ἀπήνεγκαν, 3 pers. pl. aor. act. indic.
    [§36.1] . . . . ἀποφέρω *(667)*
ἀπήνεγκε(ν), 3 pers. sg. aor. act. indic. . . . id.
ἀπήντησαν, 3 pers. pl. aor. act. indic. ἀπαντάω *(528)*
ἀπήντησεν, 3 pers. sg. aor. act. indic. (Matt.
    28:9; Mark 5:2, MT & TR | ὑπήντησεν,
    GNT, WH & NA) . . . . id.
ἀπησπασάμεθα, 1 pers. pl. aor. mid. dep.
    indic. (Acts 21:6, GNT, WH & NA |
    ἀσπασάμενοι, MT & TR) . . ἀπασπάζομαι *(‡782)*
ἀπίδω, 1 pers. sg. 2 aor. act. subj. [§36.1] (Phil.
    2:23, MT & TR | ἀφίδω, GNT, WH &
    NA) . . . . ἀφοράω *(872)*
(569) **ἀπιστέω**, ῶ, fut. ἀπιστήσω [§16.P] *to refuse
    belief, be incredulous, disbelieve,* Mark
    16:11, 16; Luke 24:11, 41; Acts 28:24; *to
    prove false, violate one's faith, be unfaith-
    ful,* 2 Tim. 2:13; Rom. 3:3
ἀπιστήσας, nom. sg. m. aor. act. part. ἀπιστέω *(569)*
(570) **ἀπιστία**, ας, ἡ, nom. sg. f. n. [§2.B.b; 2.2] *un-
    belief, want of trust and confidence; a state
    of unbelief,* 1 Tim. 1:13; *violation of faith,
    faithlessness,* Rom. 3:3; Heb. 3:12, 19
ἀπιστίᾳ, dat. sg. f. n. . . . . ἀπιστία *(570)*
ἀπιστίαν, acc. sg. f. n. . . . . id.
ἀπιστίας, gen. sg. f. n. . . . . id.
ἄπιστοι, nom. pl. m. adj. . . . . ἄπιστος *(571)*
ἀπίστοις, dat. pl. m. adj. . . . . id.
ἄπιστον, acc. sg. m. adj. {1 Cor. 7:13} . . . id.
ἄπιστον, acc. sg. f. adj. {1 Cor. 7:12} . . . id.
ἄπιστον, nom. sg. neut. adj. {Acts 26:8} . id.
(571) **ἄπιστος**, ον, nom. sg. m. adj. [§7.2] (ἀ +
    πιστός) *unbelieving, without confidence* in
    any one, Matt. 17:17, et al.; *violating one's
    faith, unfaithful, false, treacherous,* Luke
    12:46; *an unbeliever, infidel, pagan,* 1 Cor.
    6:6, et al.; pass. *incredible,* Acts 26:8
    {1 Cor. 7:14a}
ἄπιστος, nom. sg. f. adj.
    {1 Cor. 7:14b} . . . . ἄπιστος *(571)*
ἄπιστος, voc. sg. f. adj. {Matt. 17:17} . . . id.
ἀπίστου, gen. sg. m. adj. . . . . id.

ἀπιστοῦμεν, 1 pers. pl. pres. act.
indic. . . . . ἀπιστέω (569)
ἀπιστούντων, gen. pl. m. pres. act. part. .   id.
ἀπιστοῦσιν, dat. pl. m. pres. act. part. (1 Pet.
2:7, GNT, WH & NA | ἀπειθοῦσι(ν),
MT & TR) . . . .   id.
ἀπίστων, gen. pl. m. adj. . . . . ἄπιστος (571)
(572) ἁπλότης, ητος, ἡ [§4.2.c] *simplicity, sincer-*
ity, purity or *probity of mind,* Rom. 12:8;
2 Cor. 1:12; 11:3; Eph. 6:5; Col. 3:22; *lib-*
erality, as arising from simplicity and frankness of character, 2 Cor. 8:2; 9:11, 13
ἁπλότητα, acc. sg. f. n. . . . . ἁπλότης (572)
ἁπλότητι, dat. sg. f. n. . . . . id.
ἁπλότητος, gen. sg. f. n. . . . . id.
(573) ἁπλοῦς, ῆ, οῦν, nom. sg. m. adj. [§7.4.c] pr.
single; hence, *simple, uncompounded;*
sound, perfect, Matt. 6:22; Luke 11:34
(574) ἁπλῶς, adv., *in simplicity; sincerely, really,* or,
liberally, bountifully, James 1:5
(575) ἀπό, prep., pr. *forth, from, away from;* hence,
it variously signifies *departure; distance of*
time or *place; avoidance; riddance; deri-*
vation from a quarter, source, or *material;*
origination from agency or *instrumentality*
(576) ἀποβαίνω, fut. ἀποβήσομαι, 2 aor. ἀπέβην
[§37.1] (ἀπό + βαίνω) *to step off; to dis-*
embark from a ship, Luke 5:2; John 21:9;
to become, result, happen, Luke 21:13;
Phil. 1:19
ἀποβάλητε, 2 pers. pl. 2 aor. act.
subj. . . . . ἀποβάλλω (577)
(577) ἀποβάλλω, fut. ἀποβαλῶ, 2 aor. ἀπέβαλον
[§27.2.d] (ἀπό + βάλλω) *to cast* or *throw*
off, cast aside, Mark 10:50
ἀποβάλλειν, pres. act. infin. (Rev. 3:2, MT
| ἀποθανεῖν, GNT, WH, TR &
NA) . . . . ἀποβάλλω (577)
ἀποβαλών, nom. sg. m. 2 aor. act. part. . .   id.
ἀποβάντες, nom. pl. m. 2 aor. act.
part. . . . . ἀποβαίνω (576)
ἀποβήσεται, 3 pers. sg. fut. mid. dep. indic.   id.
(578) ἀποβλέπω, fut. ἀποβλέψω [§23.1.a] (ἀπό +
βλέπω) pr. *to look off from all other ob-*
jects and at a single one; hence, *to turn a*
steady gaze, to look with fixed and earn-
est attention, Heb. 11:26
ἀπόβλητον, nom. sg. neut. adj. . . . . ἀπόβλητος (579)
(579) ἀπόβλητος, ον [§7.2] pr. *to be cast away;* met.
to be contemned, regarded as vile, 1 Tim.
4:4
(580) ἀποβολή, ῆς, ἡ, nom. sg. f. n. [§2.B.a] *a cast-*
ing off; rejection, reprobation, Rom. 11:15;
loss, deprivation, of life, etc., Acts 27:22
ἀπογεγραμμένων, gen. pl. m. perf. pass.

part. . . . . ἀπογράφω (583)
ἀπογενόμενοι, nom. pl. m. 2 aor. mid. dep.
part. . . . . ἀπογίνομαι (†581)
(†581) ἀπογίνομαι, 2 aor. indic. ἀπεγενόμην [§37.1]
(ἀπό + γίνομαι) *to be away from, uncon-*
nected with; to die; met. *to die to a thing*
by renouncing it, 1 Pet. 2:24
ἀπογράφεσθαι, pres. mid./pass. infin.
{Luke 2:3} . . . . ἀπογράφω (583)
ἀπογράφεσθαι, pres. pass. infin. {Luke 2:1}   id.
(582) ἀπογραφή, ῆς, ἡ, nom. sg. f. n. [§2.B.a] *a reg-*
ister, inventory; registration, enrollment,
Luke 2:2; Acts 5:37
ἀπογραφῆς, gen. sg. f. n. . . . . ἀπογραφή (582)
(583) ἀπογράφω, fut. ἀπογράψω [§23.1.a] (ἀπό +
γράφω) pr. *to copy;* hence, *to register, en-*
rol, Luke 2:1; Heb. 12:23; mid. *to procure*
the registration of one's name, to give in
one's name for registration, Luke 2:3, 5
ἀπογράψασθαι, aor. mid. infin. . . . . ἀπογράφω (583)
ἀποδεδειγμένον, acc. sg. m. perf. pass. part.
[§31.1.b] . . . . ἀποδείκνυμι (584)
ἀποδεδοκιμασμένον, acc. sg. m. perf. pass.
part. . . . . ἀποδοκιμάζω (593)
(584) ἀποδείκνυμι, fut. ἀποδείξω [§31.BB] *to point*
out, display; to prove, evince, demonstrate,
Acts 25:7; *to designate, proclaim, hold*
forth, 2 Thess. 2:4; *to constitute, appoint,*
Acts 2:22; 1 Cor. 4:9; 2 Thess. 2:4
ἀποδεικνύντα, acc. sg. m. pres. act.
part. . . . . ἀποδείκνυμι (584)
ἀποδεῖξαι, aor. act. infin. . . . . id.
ἀποδείξει, dat. sg. f. n. . . . . ἀπόδειξις (585)
(585) ἀπόδειξις, εως, ἡ [§5.E.c] *manifestation,*
demonstration, indubitable proof, 1 Cor.
2:4
(†586) ἀποδεκατεύω, 1 pers. sg. pres. act. indic., *to*
tithe, give one tenth (Luke 18:12, WH |
ἀποδεκατῶ, GNT, MT, TR & NA)
ἀποδεκατοῦν, pres. act. infin. . . . ἀποδεκατόω (586)
ἀποδεκατοῦτε, 2 pers. pl. pres. act. indic.   id.
ἀποδεκατῶ, 1 pers. sg. pres. act. indic. (Luke
18:12, GNT, MT, TR & NA |
ἀποδεκατεύω, WH) . . . . id.
(586) ἀποδεκατόω, ῶ, fut. ἀποδεκατώσω [§20.T]
(ἀπό + δεκατόω) *to pay* or *give tithes of,*
Matt. 23:23; Luke 11:42; 18:12; *to tithe,*
levy tithes upon, Heb. 7:5
ἀπόδεκτον, nom. sg. neut. adj. . . . . ἀπόδεκτος (587)
(587) ἀπόδεκτος, ον [§7.2] *acceptable,* 1 Tim. 2:3;
5:4
ἀποδεξάμενοι, nom. pl. m. aor. mid. dep.
part. . . . . ἀποδέχομαι (588)
ἀποδεξάμενος, nom. sg. m. aor. mid. dep.
part. (Luke 9:11, GNT, WH & NA |

δεξάμενος, MT & TR) . . . . . ἀποδέχομαι (588)

ἀποδέξασθαι, aor. mid. dep. infin. . . . . . . id.

(588) **ἀποδέχομαι,** fut. ἀποδέξομαι [§23.1.b] (ἀπό + δέχομαι) *to receive* kindly or heartily, *welcome,* Luke 8:40; Acts 15:4; 18:27; 28:30; *to receive* with hearty assent, *embrace,* Acts 2:41; *to accept* with satisfaction, Acts 24:3

ἀποδεχόμεθα, 1 pers. pl. pres. mid./pass. dep. indic. . . . . ἀποδέχομαι (588)

(589) **ἀποδημέω,** ῶ, fut. ἀποδημήσω [§16.P] *to be absent from one's home* or *country; to go on travel,* Matt. 21:33; 25:14, 15; Mark 12:1; Luke 15:13; 20:9

(590) **ἀπόδημος,** ον, nom. sg. m. adj. [§7.2] (ἀπό + δῆμος) *absent* in foreign countries, Mark 13:34

ἀποδημῶν, nom. sg. m. pres. act. part. . . . . ἀποδημέω (589)

ἀποδιδόναι, pres. act. infin. . . . . ἀποδίδωμι (591)

ἀποδιδόντες, nom. pl. m. pres. act. part. . id.

ἀποδιδότω, 3 pers. sg. pres. act. imper. . id.

ἀποδιδοῦν, acc. sg. neut. pres. act. part. (Rev. 22:2, GNT, WH, TR & NA | ἀποδιδοῦς, MT) . . . . id.

ἀποδιδοῦς, nom. sg. m. pres. act. part. (Rev. 22:2, MT | ἀποδιδοῦν, GNT, WH, TR & NA) . . . . id.

(591) **ἀποδίδωμι,** 1 pers. sg. pres. act. indic., fut. ἀποδώσω, aor. ἀπέδωκα, 2 aor. ἀπέδων, aor. pass. ἀπεδόθην [§30.Z] (ἀπό + δίδωμι) *to give in answer to a claim* or *expectation; to render* a due, Matt. 12:36; 16:27; 21:41; 22:21, et al.; *to recompense,* Matt. 6:4, 6, 18; *to discharge* an obligation, Matt. 5:33; *to pay* a debt, Matt. 5:26, et al.; *to render back, requite,* Rom. 12:17, et al.; *to give back, restore,* Luke 4:20; 9:42; *to refund,* Luke 10:35; 19:8, mid., *to sell,* Acts 5:8; 7:9; Heb. 12:16; pass., *to be sold,* Matt. 18:25; *to be given up* at a request, Matt. 27:58

ἀποδίδωσι(ν), 3 pers. sg. pres. act. indic. . . . . ἀποδίδωμι (591)

ἀποδιορίζοντες, nom. pl. m. pres. act. part. . . . . ἀποδιορίζω (592)

(592) **ἀποδιορίζω,** fut. ἀποδιορίσω [§26.1] (ἀπό + διορίζω, *to set bounds*) pr. *to separate by intervening boundaries; to separate*

ἀποδοθῆναι, aor. pass. infin. [§30.4] ἀποδίδωμι (591)

(593) **ἀποδοκιμάζω,** fut. ἀποδοκιμάσω [§26.1] (ἀπό + δοκιμάζω) *to reject upon trial; to reject,* Matt. 21:42; Mark 12:10; Luke 20:17; 1 Pet. 2:4, 7; pass., *to be disallowed* a claim, Luke 9:22; 17:25; Heb. 12:17

ἀποδοκιμασθῆναι, aor. pass. infin. . . . . ἀποδοκιμάζω (593)

ἀπόδος, 2 pers. sg. 2 aor. act. imper. [§30.1] . . . . ἀποδίδωμι (591)

ἀπόδοτε, 2 pers. pl. 2 aor. act. imper. . . . . id.

ἀποδοῦναι, 2 aor. act. infin. . . . . id.

ἀποδούς, nom. sg. m. 2 aor. act. part. . . . id.

(594) **ἀποδοχή,** ῆς, ἡ [§2.B.a] pr. *reception, welcome;* met. *reception* of hearty assent, 1 Tim. 1:15; 4:9

ἀποδοχῆς, gen. sg. f. n. . . . . ἀποδοχή (594)

ἀποδῷ, 3 pers. sg. 2 aor. act. subj. . ἀποδίδωμι (591)

ἀποδῴη, 3 pers. sg. 2 aor. act. opt. [§30.5] (2 Tim. 4:14, MT & TR | ἀποδώσει, GNT, WH & NA) . . . . id.

ἀποδῷς, 2 pers. sg. 2 aor. act. subj. . . . . . id.

ἀποδώσει, 3 pers. sg. fut. act. indic. . . . . . id.

ἀποδώσεις, 2 pers. sg. fut. act. indic. . . . . id.

ἀποδώσοντες, nom. pl. m. fut. act. part. . id.

ἀποδώσουσι(ν), 3 pers. pl. fut. act. indic. . id.

ἀποδώσω, 1 pers. sg. fut. act. indic. . . . . . id.

ἀποθανεῖν, 2 aor. act. infin. [§36.4] . . . . ἀποθνήσκω (†599)

ἀποθανεῖσθε, 2 pers. pl. fut. mid. dep. indic. id.

ἀποθανεῖται, 3 pers. sg. fut. mid. dep. indic. id.

ἀποθάνῃ, 3 pers. sg. 2 aor. act. subj. . . . . id.

ἀποθανόντα, nom. pl. neut. 2 aor. act. part. id.

ἀποθανόντες, nom. pl. m. 2 aor. act. part. id.

ἀποθανόντι, dat. sg. m. 2 aor. act. part. . . id.

ἀποθανόντος, gen. sg. m. 2 aor. act. part. . id.

ἀποθανοῦνται, 3 pers. pl. fut. mid. dep. indic. (Matt. 26:52, MT | ἀπολοῦνται, GNT, WH, TR & NA) . . . . id.

ἀποθάνωμεν, 1 pers. pl. 2 aor. act. subj. . . id.

ἀποθανών, nom. sg. m. 2 aor. act. part. . . id.

ἀποθέμενοι, nom. pl. m. 2 aor. mid. part. [§28.W] . . . . ἀποτίθημι (659)

ἀποθέσθαι, 2 aor. mid. infin. . . . . id.

ἀπόθεσθε, 2 pers. pl. 2 aor. mid. imper. . . id.

(595) **ἀπόθεσις,** εως, ἡ, nom. sg. f. n. [§5.E.c] *a putting off* or *away, laying aside,* 1 Pet. 3:21; 2 Pet. 1:14

ἀποθήκας, acc. pl. f. n. . . . . ἀποθήκη (596)

(596) **ἀποθήκη,** ης, ἡ, nom. sg. f. n. [§2.B.a] *a place where anything is laid up for preservation, repository, granary, storehouse, barn,* Matt. 3:12; 6:26; 13:30; Luke 3:17; 12:18, 24

ἀποθήκην, acc. sg. f. n. . . . . ἀποθήκη (596)

ἀποθησαυρίζοντας, acc. pl. m. pres. act. part. . . . . ἀποθησαυρίζω (597)

(597) **ἀποθησαυρίζω,** fut. ἀποθησαυρίσω [§26.1] (ἀπό + θησαυρίζω) pr. *to lay up in store, hoard;* met. *to treasure up, secure,* 1 Tim. 6:19

ἀποθλίβουσι(ν), 3 pers. pl. pres. act.
    indic. . . . . ἀποθλίβω *(598)*
(598) **ἀποθλίβω,** fut. ἀποθλίψω [§23.1.a] (ἀπό +
    θλίβω) pr. *to press out; to press close, press*
    upon, crowd, Luke 8:45
ἀποθνήσκει, 3 pers. sg. pres. act. indic. (GNT,
    MT & NA | ἀποκνήσκει, WH &
    TR) . . . . ἀποθνήσκω *(†599)*
ἀποθνήσκειν, pres. act. infin. (GNT, MT &
    NA | ἀποθνήσκειν, WH & TR) . . . . . id.
ἀποθνήσκομεν, 1 pers. pl. pres. act. indic.
    (GNT, MT & NA | ἀποθνήσκομεν, WH
    & TR) . . . . id.
ἀποθνήσκοντες, nom. pl. m. pres. act. part.
    (GNT, MT & NA | ἀποθνήσκοντες, WH
    & TR) . . . . id.
ἀποθνήσκουσιν, 3 pers. pl. pres. act. indic.
    (1 Cor. 15:22, GNT, MT & NA |
    ἀποθνήσκουσιν, WH & TR) . . . . id.
(†599) **ἀποθνήσκω,** 1 pers. sg. pres. act. indic., fut.
    ἀποθανοῦμαι, 2 aor. ἀπέθανον [§36.4]
    (ἀπό + θνήσκω) *to die,* Matt. 8:32, et al.;
    to become putrescent, rot, as seeds, John
    12:24; 1 Cor. 15:36; *to wither, become dry,*
    as a tree, Jude 12; met. *to die* the death of
    final condemnation and misery, John 6:50;
    8:21, 24; *to die* to a thing by renunciation
    or utter separation, Rom. 6:2; Gal. 2:19;
    Col. 3:3 (1 Cor. 15:31, GNT, MT & NA
    | ἀποθνήσκω, WH & TR)
ἀποθνήσκωμεν, 1 pers. pl. pres. act. subj.
    (GNT, MT & TR | ἀποθνήσκωμεν, WH
    & TR) . . . . ἀποθνήσκω *(†599)*
ἀποθνήσκων, nom. sg. m. pres. act. part.
    (GNT, MT & NA | ἀποθνήσκων, WH &
    TR) . . . . id.
ἀποθώμεθα, 1 pers. pl. 2 aor. mid.
    subj. . . . . ἀποτίθημι *(659)*
ἀποκαθιστᾷ, 3 pers. sg. pres. act. indic. (Mark
    9:12, MT & TR | ἀποκαθιστάνει, GNT,
    WH & NA) . . . . ἀποκαθίστημι *(600)*
ἀποκαθιστάνει, 3 pers. sg. pres. act. indic.
    (Mark 9:12, GNT, WH & NA | ἀποκαθ-
    ιστᾷ, MT & TR) . . . . id.
ἀποκαθιστάνεις, 2 pers. sg. pres. act.
    indic. . . . . ἀποκαθίστημι *(600)*
(600) **ἀποκαθίστημι** (or ἀποκαθιστάνω) fut.
    ἀποκαταστήσω, aor. pass. ἀπεκατεστά-
    θην [§29.X; 29.6] (ἀπό + καθίστημι) *to*
    restore a thing to its former place or state,
    Matt. 12:13; 17:11; Mark 3:5; 8:25, et al.
ἀποκαλύπτεσθαι, pres. pass.
    infin. . . . . ἀποκαλύπτω *(601)*
ἀποκαλύπτεται, 3 pers. sg. pres. pass. indic. id.
(601) **ἀποκαλύπτω,** fut. ἀποκαλύψω (ἀπό + κα-

λύπτω) pr. *uncover; to reveal,* Matt. 11:25;
    et al.; pass. *to be disclosed,* Luke 2:35;
    Eph. 3:5; *to be plainly signified, distinctly*
    declared, Rom. 1:17, 18; *to be set forth, an-*
    nounced, Gal. 3:23; *to be discovered* in
    true character, 1 Cor. 3:13; *to be manif-*
    ested, appear, John 12:38; Rom. 8:18;
    2 Thess. 2:3, 6, 8; 1 Pet. 1:5; 5:1
ἀποκαλυφθῇ, 3 pers. sg. aor. pass. subj.
    [§23.4] . . . . ἀποκαλύπτω *(601)*
ἀποκαλυφθῆναι, aor. pass. infin. . . . . id.
ἀποκαλυφθήσεται, 3 pers. sg. fut. pass. indic. id.
ἀποκαλυφθῶσιν, 3 pers. pl. aor. pass. subj. id.
ἀποκαλύψαι, aor. act. infin. . . . . id.
ἀποκαλύψει, 3 pers. sg. fut. act. indic.
    {Phil. 3:15} . . . . id.
ἀποκαλύψει, dat. sg. f. n.
    {1 Cor. 14:6} . . . . ἀποκάλυψις *(602)*
ἀποκαλύψεις, acc. pl. f. n. . . . . id.
ἀποκαλυψέων, gen. pl. f. n. . . . . id.
ἀποκαλύψεως, gen. sg. f. n. . . . . id.
ἀποκάλυψιν, acc. sg. f. n. . . . . id.
(602) **ἀποκάλυψις,** εως, ἡ, nom. sg. f. n. [§5.E.c]
    a disclosure, revelation, Rom. 2:5, et al.;
    manifestation, appearance, Rom. 8:19;
    1 Cor. 1:7; 2 Thess. 1:7; 1 Pet. 1:7, 13; 4:13;
    met. spiritual *enlightenment,* Luke 2:32
(603) **ἀποκαραδοκία,** ας, ἡ, nom. sg. f. n. [§2.B.b;
    2.2] (ἀπό + καραδοκέω, *to watch with*
    the head stretched out, to keep an eager
    look-out; from κάρα, *the head,* and
    δοκεύω, *to watch*) *earnest expectation,*
    eager hope, Rom. 8:19; Phil. 1:20
ἀποκαραδοκίαν, acc. sg. f. n. . ἀποκαραδοκία *(603)*
ἀποκαταλλάξαι, aor. act.
    infin. . . . . ἀποκαταλλάσσω *(604)*
ἀποκαταλλάξῃ, 3 pers. sg. aor. act. subj. . id.
(604) **ἀποκαταλλάσσω,** fut. ἀποκαταλλάξω
    [§26.3] (ἀπό + καταλλάσσω) *to transfer*
    from a certain state to another which is
    quite different; hence, *to reconcile, restore*
    to favor, Eph. 2:16; Col. 1:20, 22
ἀποκατασταθῶ, 2 pers. sg. aor. pass. subj.
    [§29.6] . . . . ἀποκαθίστημι *(600)*
ἀποκαταστάσεως, gen. sg.
    f. n. . . . . ἀποκατάστασις *(605)*
(605) **ἀποκατάστασις,** εως, ἡ [§5.E.c] pr. *a restitu-*
    tion or restoration of a thing to its former
    state; hence, *the renovation* of a new and
    better era, Acts 3:21
ἀποκαταστήσει, 3 pers. sg. fut. act.
    indic. . . . . ἀποκαθίστημι *(600)*
ἀποκατεστάθη, 3 pers. sg. aor. pass. indic.
    (Matt. 12:13; Mark 3:5; 8:25; Luke 6:10,
    MT & TR | ἀπεκατέστη, Mark 8:25,

GNT, WH & NA | ἀπεκατεστάθη, Matt. 12:13; Mark 3:5; Luke 6:10, GNT, WH & NA) . . . . ἀποκαθίστημι *(600)*

ἀποκατήλλαξεν, 3 pers. sg. aor. act. indic. (Col. 1:22, GNT, WH, TRb & NA | Col. 1:21, MT & TRs) . . . . ἀποκαταλλάσσω *(604)*

(606) **ἀπόκειμαι**, fut. ἀποκείσομαι [§33.DD] (ἀπό + κεῖμαι) *to be laid up, preserved,* Luke 19:20; *to be in store, be reserved, await* any one, Col. 1:5; 2 Tim. 4:8; Heb. 9:27

ἀποκειμένην, acc. sg. f. pres. mid./pass. dep. part. . . . . ἀπόκειμαι *(606)*

ἀπόκειται, 3 pers. sg. pres. mid./pass. dep. indic. . . . . id.

ἀποκεκρυμμένην, acc. sg. f. perf. pass. part. [§23.7] . . . . ἀποκρύπτω *(613)*

ἀποκεκρυμμένον, acc. sg. neut. perf. pass. part. . . . . id.

ἀποκεκρυμμένου, gen. sg. neut. perf. pass. part. . . . . id.

ἀποκεκυλισμένον, acc. sg. m. perf. pass. part. . . . . ἀποκυλίω *(617)*

ἀποκεκύλισται, 3 pers. sg. perf. pass. indic. (Mark 16:4, GNT, MT, TR & NA | ἀνακεκύλισται, WH) . . . . id.

(607) **ἀποκεφαλίζω**, fut. ἀποκεφαλίσω [§26.1] (ἀπό + κεφαλή) *to behead,* Matt. 14:10; Mark 6:16, 27; Luke 9:9

ἀποκλείσῃ, 3 pers. sg. aor. act. subj. ἀποκλείω *(608)*

(608) **ἀποκλείω**, fut. ἀποκλείσω [§13.M] (ἀπό + κλείω) *to close, shut up,* Luke 13:25

(609) **ἀποκόπτω**, fut. ἀποκόψω [§23.1.a] (ἀπό + κόπτω) *to cut off,* Mark 9:43, 45; John 18:10, 26; Acts 27:32; Gal. 5:12

ἀπόκοψον, 2 pers. sg. aor. act. imper. . . . . ἀποκόπτω *(609)*

ἀποκόψονται, 3 pers. pl. fut. mid. indic. . id.

ἀποκριθείς, nom. sg. m. aor. pass. dep. part. . . . . ἀποκρίνομαι *(611)*

ἀποκριθεῖσα, nom. sg. f. aor. pass. dep. part. id.

ἀποκριθέν, nom. sg. neut. aor. pass. dep. part. . . . . id.

ἀποκριθέντες, nom. pl. m. aor. pass. dep. part. . . . . id.

ἀποκριθῇ, 3 pers. sg. aor. pass. dep. subj. (Mark 9:6, GNT, WH & NA | λαλήσῃ, MT & TR) . . . . id.

ἀποκριθῆναι, aor. pass. dep. infin. . . . . . . id.

ἀποκριθήσεται, 3 pers. sg. fut. pass. dep. indic. . . . . id.

ἀποκριθήσονται, 3 pers. pl. fut. pass. dep. indic. . . . . id.

ἀποκρίθητε, 2 pers. pl. aor. pass. dep. imper. {Mark 11:29} . . . . id.

ἀποκριθῆτε, 2 pers. pl. aor. pass. dep. subj.

{Luke 22:68} . . . . ἀποκρίνομαι *(611)*

ἀποκριθῶσι(ν), 3 pers. pl. aor. pass. dep. subj. . . . . id.

(610) **ἀπόκριμα**, ατος, τό [§4.D.c] *a judicial sentence,* 2 Cor. 1:9

ἀπόκριμα, acc. sg. neut. n. . . . . ἀπόκριμα *(610)*

ἀποκρίνεσθαι, pres. mid./pass. dep. infin. . . . . ἀποκρίνομαι *(611)*

ἀποκρίνεται, 3 pers. sg. pres. mid./pass. dep. indic. . . . . id.

ἀποκρίνῃ, 2 pers. sg. pres. mid./pass. dep. indic. . . . . id.

(611) **ἀποκρίνομαι** [§27.3] aor. ἀπεκρινάμην and, later, also (pass. form) ἀπεκρίθην, fut. (pass. form) ἀποκριθήσομαι (ἀποκρίνω, *to separate,* from ἀπό + κρίνω) *to answer,* Matt. 3:15, et al.; in N.T. *to respond* to certain present circumstances, *to avow,* Matt. 11:25, et al.

ἀποκρίσει, dat. sg. f. n. . . . . ἀπόκρισις *(612)*

ἀποκρίσεσιν, dat. pl. f. n. . . . . id.

ἀπόκρισιν, acc. sg. f. n. . . . . id.

(612) **ἀπόκρισις**, εως, ἡ [§5.E.c] *an answer, reply,* Luke 2:47; 20:26; John 1:22; 19:9

(613) **ἀποκρύπτω**, fut. ἀποκρύψω [§23.1.a] (ἀπό + κρύπτω) *to hide away; to conceal, withhold from sight* or *knowledge,* Matt. 11:25; 25:18, et al.

ἀπόκρυφοι, nom. pl. m. adj. . . . . . . ἀπόκρυφος *(614)*

ἀπόκρυφον, nom. sg. neut. adj. . . . . id.

(614) **ἀπόκρυφος**, ον [§7.2] *hidden away; concealed,* Mark 4:22; Luke 8:17; *stored up,* Col. 2:3

ἀποκτανθείς, nom. sg. m. aor. pass. part. . . . . ἀποκτείνω *(615)*

ἀποκτανθῆναι, aor. pass. infin. [§37.1] . . . id.

ἀποκτανθῶσι(ν), 3 pers. pl. aor. pass. subj. id.

ἀποκτεῖναι, aor. act. infin. . . . . id.

ἀποκτεινάντων, gen. pl. m. aor. act. part. . id.

ἀποκτείνας, nom. sg. m. aor. act. part. . . id.

ἀποκτείνει, 3 pers. sg. pres. act. indic. (2 Cor. 3:6, WH & TR | ἀποκτέννει, GNT & NA | ἀποκτένει, MT) . . . . id.

ἀποκτείνεσθαι, pres. pass. infin. (Rev. 6:11, TR | ἀποκτέννεσθαι, GNT, WH & NA | ἀποκτένεσθαι, MT) . . . . id.

ἀποκτείνοντες, nom. pl. m. pres. act. part. (Mark 12:5, TR | ἀποκτέννοντες, GNT & NA | ἀποκτεννύντες, WH | ἀποκτένοντες, MT) . . . . id.

ἀποκτεινόντων, gen. pl. m. pres. act. part. (Luke 12:4, GNT, WH, TR & NA | ἀποκτενόντων, MT) . . . . id.

ἀποκτείνουσα, nom. sg. f. pres. act. part. (Matt. 23:37; Luke 13:34, GNT, WH, NA

& TR | ἀποκτένουσα, MT) .... ἀποκτείνω *(615)*

(615) **ἀποκτείνω,** fut. ἀποκτενῶ, aor. pass. ἀπεκτάνθην [§37.1] (ἀπό + κτείνω) *to kill,* Matt. 14:5; *to destroy, annihilate,* Matt. 10:28; *to destroy* a hostile principle, Eph. 2:16; met. *to kill* by spiritual condemnation, Rom. 7:11; 2 Cor. 3:6

ἀποκτείνωμεν, 1 pers. pl. pres. act. subj. .... ἀποκτείνω *(615)*

ἀποκτείνωσι(ν), 3 pers. pl. pres. act. subj.   id.

ἀποκτένει, 3 pers. sg. pres. act. indic. (2 Cor. 3:6, MT | ἀποκτέννει, GNT & NA | ἀποκτείνει, WH & TR) .... ἀποκτείνω *(615)*

ἀποκτενεῖ, 3 pers. sg. fut. act. indic. {John 8:22} .... id.

ἀποκτενεῖτε, 2 pers. pl. fut. act. indic. ... id.

ἀποκτένεσθαι, pres. pass. infin. (Rev. 6:11, MT | ἀποκτείνεσθαι, TR | ἀποκτέννεσθαι, GNT, WH & NA) .... id.

ἀποκτέννει, 3 pers. sg. pres. act. indic. (2 Cor. 3:6, GNT, WH & NA | ἀποκτείνει, TR | ἀποκτένει, MT) .... ἀποκτέννω *(†615)*

ἀποκτέννεσθαι, pres. pass. infin. (Rev. 6:11, GNT, WH & NA | ἀποκτείνεσθαι, TR | ἀποκτένεσθαι, MT) .... id.

ἀποκτέννοντες, nom. pl. m. pres. act. part. (Mark 12:5, GNT & NA | ἀποκτεννύντες, WH | ἀποκτένοντες, MT | ἀποκτείνοντες, TR) .... id.

ἀποκτεννόντων, gen. pl. m. pres. act. part. (Matt. 10:28, GNT & NA | ἀποκτεινόντων, WH) .... id.

ἀποκτένοντες, nom. pl. m. pres. act. part. (Mark 12:5, MT | ἀποκτέννοντες, GNT & NA | ἀπεκτείνοντες, TR | ἀπεκτεννύντες, WH) .... ἀποκτένω *(†615)*

ἀποκτενόντων, gen. pl. m. pres. act. part. (Matt. 10:28; Luke 12:4, MT | ἀποκτεινόντων, Luke 12:4, GNT, WH, TR & NA | ἀποκτεννόντων, Matt. 10:28, GNT & NA | ἀποκτεινόντων, Matt. 10:28, WH & TR) .... id.

ἀποκτένουσα, nom. sg. f. pres. act. part. (Matt. 23:37; Luke 13:34, MT | ἀποκτείνουσα, GNT, WH, TR & NA)   id.

(†615) **ἀποκτέννω,** *to kill, to destroy* a hostile principle

ἀποκτενοῦσι(ν), 3 pers. pl. fut. act. indic. .... ἀποκτένω *(†615)*

ἀποκτενῶ, 1 pers. sg. fut. act. indic. ..... id.

(†615) **ἀποκτένω,** *to kill, to destroy* a hostile principle

ἀποκύει, 3 pers. sg. pres. act. indic. .. ἀποκυέω *(616)*

(616) **ἀποκυέω, ῶ,** fut. ἀποκυήσω [§16.P] (ἀπό + κυέω) pr. *to bring forth,* as women; met. *to generate, produce,* James 1:15; *to gen-*

---

erate by spiritual birth, James 1:18

ἀποκυλίσει, 3 pers. sg. fut. act. indic. .... ἀποκυλίω *(617)*

(617) **ἀποκυλίω,** fut. ἀποκυλίσω [§13.M] (ἀπό + κυλίω) *to roll away,* Matt. 28:2; Mark 16:3, 4; Luke 24:2

ἀπολαβεῖν, 2 aor. act. infin. (Luke 6:34, MT & TR | λαβεῖν, GNT, WH & NA) .... ἀπολαμβάνω *(618)*

ἀπολάβῃ, 3 pers. sg. 2 aor. act. subj. .... id.

ἀπολάβητε, 2 pers. pl. 2 aor. act. subj. (2 John 8, GNT, WH & NA | ἀπολάβωμεν, MT & TR) .... id.

ἀπολαβόμενος, nom. sg. m. 2 aor. mid. part.   id.

ἀπολάβωμεν, 1 pers. pl. 2 aor. act. subj. . id.

ἀπολάβωσι(ν), 3 pers. pl. 2 aor. act. subj.   id.

ἀπολαμβάνειν, pres. act. infin. (3 John 8, MT & TR | ὑπολαμβάνειν, GNT, WH & NA) .... id.

ἀπολαμβάνομεν, 1 pers. pl. pres. act. indic.   id.

ἀπολαμβάνοντες, nom. pl. m. pres. act. part.   id.

(618) **ἀπολαμβάνω,** fut. ἀπολή(μ)ψομαι, 2 aor. ἀπέλαβον (ἀπό + λαμβάνω) *to receive* what is due, sought, or needed, Luke 23:41; Rom. 1:27; Gal. 4:5; Col. 3:24; 2 John 8; *to receive in full,* Luke 16:25; *to receive back, recover,* Luke 6:34; 15:27; 18:30; *to receive* in hospitality, welcome, 3 John 8; mid. *to take aside, lead away,* Mark 7:33

ἀπόλαυσιν, acc. sg. f. n. .... ἀπόλαυσις *(619)*

(619) **ἀπόλαυσις, εως, ἡ** [§5.E.c] (ἀπολαύω, *to obtain a portion* of a thing, *enjoy*) *beneficial participation,* 1 Tim. 6:17; *enjoyment, pleasure,* Heb. 11:25

ἀπολείπεται, 3 pers. sg. pres. pass. indic. .... ἀπολείπω *(620)*

(620) **ἀπολείπω,** fut. ἀπολείψω [§23.1.a] (ἀπό + λείπω) *to leave, leave behind;* pass. *to be left, remain,* 2 Tim. 4:13, 20; Heb. 4:6, 9; 10:26; *to relinquish, forsake, desert,* Jude 6

ἀπολεῖσθε, 2 pers. pl. fut. mid. indic. ἀπόλλυμι *(622)*

ἀπολεῖται, 3 pers. sg. 2 fut. mid. indic. .. id.

(621) **ἀπολείχω,** fut. ἀπολείξω [§23.1.b] (ἀπό + λείχω, *to lick*) pr. *to lick off; to cleanse by licking, lick clean,* Luke 16:21

ἀπολελυμένην, acc. sg. f. perf. pass. part. [§14.N] .... ἀπολύω *(630)*

ἀπολελυμένον, acc. sg. m. perf. pass. part. id.

ἀπολέλυσαι, 2 pers. sg. perf. pass. indic. . id.

ἀπολελύσθαι, perf. pass. infin. .... id.

ἀπολέσαι, aor. act. infin. .... id.

ἀπολέσας, nom. sg. m. aor. act. part. .... id.

ἀπολέσει, 3 pers. sg. fut. act. indic. . ἀπόλλυμι *(622)*

ἀπολέσῃ, 3 pers. sg. aor. act. subj. ...... id.

ἀπολέσητε, 2 pers. pl. aor. act. subj. (2 John

8, GNT, WH & NA | ἀπολέσωμεν, MT
& TR) . . . . ἀπόλλυμι *(622)*
ἀπολέσθαι, 2 aor. mid. infin. . . . . id.
ἀπολέσουσιν, 3 pers. pl. fut. act. indic. (Mark
11:18, TR | ἀπολέσωσι(ν), GNT, WH,
MT & NA) . . . . id.
ἀπολέσω, 1 pers. sg. aor. act. subj. . . . . . . id.
ἀπολέσωμεν, 1 pers. pl. aor. act. subj. (2 John
8, MT & TR | ἀπολέσητε, GNT, WH &
NA) . . . . id.
ἀπολέσωσι(ν), 3 pers. pl. aor. act. subj. . . . id.
ἀπολήμψεσθε, 2 pers. pl. fut. mid. dep. indic.
(Col. 3:24, GNT, WH & NA |
ἀπολήψεσθε, TR | λήψεσθε,
MT) . . . . ἀπολαμβάνω *(618)*
ἀπόληται, 3 pers. sg. 2 aor. mid.
subj. . . . . ἀπόλλυμι *(622)*
ἀπολήψεσθε, 2 pers. pl. fut. mid. dep. indic.
(Col. 3:24, MT & TR | ἀπολήμψεσθε,
GNT, WH & NA | λήψεσθε,
MT) . . . . ἀπολαμβάνω *(618)*
ἀπολιπόντας, acc. pl. m. 2 aor. act. part.
[§24.9] . . . . ἀπολείπω *(620)*
ἀπόλλυε, 2 pers. sg. pres. act. imper. ἀπόλλυμι *(622)*
ἀπολλύει, 3 pers. sg. pres. act. indic. (John
12:25, GNT, WH & NA | ἀπολέσει, MT
& TR) . . . . id.
ἀπόλλυμαι, 1 pers. sg. pres. mid. indic. . . . id.
ἀπολλύμεθα, 1 pers. pl. pres. mid. indic. . . id.
ἀπολλυμένην, acc. sg. f. pres. mid. part. . id.
ἀπολλύμενοι, nom. pl. m. pres. mid./pass.
part. . . . . id.
ἀπολλυμένοις, dat. pl. m. pres. mid./pass.
part. . . . . id.
ἀπολλυμένου, gen. sg. neut. pres. mid. part. id.
(622) **ἀπόλλυμι**, fut. ἀπολέσω and ἀπολῶ, aor.
ἀπώλεσα, perf. ἀπολώλεκα (ἀπό +
ὄλλυμι) *to destroy utterly; to kill,* Matt.
2:13; et al.; *to bring to nought, make void,*
1 Cor. 1:19; *to lose, be deprived of,* Matt.
10:42, et al.; mid. ἀπόλλυμαι,
ἀπολοῦμαι, 2 aor. ἀπωλόμην, 2 perf.
ἀπόλωλα, *to be destroyed, perish,* Matt.
9:17, et al.; *to be put to death, to die,* Matt.
26:52, et al.; *to be lost, to stray,* Matt.
10:6, et al.
ἀπόλλυνται, 3 pers. pl. pres. pass. indic.
(Matt. 9:17, GNT, WH & NA | ἀπο-
λοῦνται, MT & TR) . . . . ἀπόλλυμι *(622)*
ἀπόλλυται, 3 pers. sg. pres. pass. indic. (Mark
2:22; 1 Cor. 8:11, GNT, WH & NA |
ἀπολοῦνται, Mark 2:22, MT & TR |
ἀπολεῖται, 1 Cor. 8:11, MT & TR) . . . id.
(623) **Ἀπολλύων**, οντος, ἡ, nom. sg. m. n. [§7.H.d]
Apollyon, Destroyer, i.q. Ἀβαδδών,

Rev. 9:11
Ἀπολλῶ, gen. sg. m. n. (1 Cor. 16:12, GNT
& NA | Ἀπολλώ, WH, MT &
TR) . . . . Ἀπολλῶς *(†625)*
Ἀπολλῶ, acc. sg. m. n. [§3.4] (Acts 19:1, GNT
& NA | Ἀπολλώ, WH, MT & TR) . . id.
Ἀπολλῶν, acc. sg. m. n. (1 Cor. 4:6; Tit. 3:13,
GNT & NA | Ἀπολλών, WH & MT |
Ἀπολλώ, TR) . . . . id.
(624) **Ἀπολλωνία**, ας, ἡ [§2.B.b; 2.2] *Apollonia,* a
city of Macedonia, Acts 17:1
Ἀπολλωνίαν, acc. sg. f. n. . . . . Ἀπολλωνία *(624)*
(†625) **Ἀπολλῶς**, ῶ, ὁ, nom. sg. m. n. [§3.C.d] *Apol-
los,* pr. name
ἀπολογεῖσθαι, pres. mid./pass. dep.
infin. . . . . ἀπολογέομαι *(626)*
(626) **ἀπολογέομαι**, οῦμαι, fut. ἀπολογήσομαι, aor.
ἀπελογησάμην and, pass. form.
ἀπελογήθην [§17.Q] (ἀπό + λόγος) *to defend one's self against a charge, to make
a defence,* Luke 12:11; 21:14, et al.
ἀπολογηθῆναι, aor. pass. dep.
infin. . . . . ἀπολογέομαι *(626)*
ἀπολογήσησθε, 2 pers. pl. aor. mid. dep.
subj. . . . . id.
(627) **ἀπολογία**, ας, ἡ, nom. sg. f. n. [§2.B.b; 2.2]
a verbal defence, Acts 22:1; 25:16, et al.
ἀπολογίᾳ, dat. sg. f. n. . . . . ἀπολογία *(627)*
ἀπολογίαν, acc. sg. f. n. . . . . id.
ἀπολογίας, gen. sg. f. n. . . . . id.
ἀπολογοῦμαι, 1 pers. sg. pres. mid./pass. dep.
indic. . . . . ἀπολογέομαι *(626)*
ἀπολογούμεθα, 1 pers. pl. pres. mid./pass.
dep. indic. . . . . id.
ἀπολογουμένου, gen. sg. m. pres. mid./pass.
dep. part. . . . . id.
ἀπολογουμένων, gen. pl. m. pres. mid./pass.
dep. part. . . . . id.
ἀπολομένου, gen. sg. m. 2 aor. mid.
part. . . . . ἀπόλλυμι *(622)*
ἀπολοῦνται, 3 pers. pl. fut. mid. indic.
[§36.5] . . . . id.
ἀπόλουσαι, 2 pers. sg. aor. mid.
imper. . . . . ἀπολούω *(628)*
(628) **ἀπολούω**, fut. ἀπολούσω [§13.M] (ἀπό +
λούω) *to cleanse by bathing;* mid. *to
cleanse one's self; to procure one's self to
be cleansed;* met., of sin, Acts 22:16; 1 Cor.
6:11
ἀπολύει, 3 pers. sg. pres. act. indic. (Mark
6:45, GNT, WH & NA | ἀπολύσῃ, MT
& TR) . . . . ἀπολύω *(630)*
ἀπολύειν, pres. act. infin. . . . . id.
ἀπολύεις, 2 pers. sg. pres. act. indic. . . . . id.
ἀπολύετε, 2 pers. pl. pres. act. imper. . . . . id.

ἀπολυθέντες, nom. pl. m. aor. pass.
part. . . . . ἀπολύω (630)
ἀπολυθήσεσθε, 2 pers. pl. fut. pass. indic.   id.
ἀπολυθῆτε, 2 pers. pl. aor. pass. subj. . . .   id.
ἀπολῦσαι, aor. act. infin. . . . .   id.
ἀπολύσας, nom. sg. m. aor. act. part. . . .   id.
ἀπολύσασα, nom. sg. f. aor. act. part. (Mark
10:12, GNT, WH & NA | ἀπολύσῃ, MT
& TR) . . . .   id.
ἀπολύσῃ, 3 pers. sg. aor. act. subj. . . . . .   id.
ἀπολύσῃς, 2 pers. sg. aor. act. subj. . . . .   id.
ἀπολύσητε, 2 pers. pl. aor. act. subj. (Luke
22:68, MT & TR | GNT, WH & NA
omit) . . . .   id.
ἀπόλυσον, 2 pers. sg. aor. act. imper. . . . .   id.
ἀπολύσω, 1 pers. sg. fut. act. indic.
{Luke 23:16} . . . .   id.
ἀπολύσω, 1 pers. sg. aor. act. subj.
{Mark 8:3} . . . .   id.
ἀπολυτρώσεως, gen. sg. f. n. . . . ἀπολύτρωσις (629)
ἀπολύτρωσιν, acc. sg. f. n. . . . .   id.
(629) **ἀπολύτρωσις**, εως, ἡ, nom. sg. f. n. [§5.E.c]
(ἀπολυτρόω, to dismiss for a ransom paid,
from ἀπό + λυτρόω) redemption, a deliverance procured by the payment of a ransom; meton. the author of redemption,
1 Cor. 1:30; deliverance, simply, the idea
of a ransom being excluded, Luke 21:28;
Heb. 11:35
(630) **ἀπολύω**, fut. ἀπολύσω [§13.M] (ἀπό + λύω)
pr. to loose; to release from a tie or burden,
Matt. 18:27; to divorce, Matt. 1:19, et al.;
to remit, forgive, Luke 6:37; to liberate, discharge, Matt. 27:15, et al.; to dismiss,
Matt. 15:23; Acts 19:40; to allow to depart, to send away, Matt. 14:15, et al.; to
permit, or, signal departure from life, Luke
2:29; mid. to depart, Acts 28:25; pass. to
be rid, Luke 13:12
ἀπολύων, nom. sg. m. pres. act. part. . ἀπολύω (630)
ἀπολῶ, 1 pers. sg. fut. act. indic. . . . ἀπόλλυμι (622)
ἀπολωλός, acc. sg. neut. 2 perf. act. part.   id.
ἀπολωλότα, acc. sg. neut. 2 perf. act. part.   id.
ἀπολωλώς, nom. sg. m. 2 perf. act. part.   id.
ἀπόλωνται, 3 pers. pl. 2 aor. mid. subj. . .   id.
ἀπομασσόμεθα, 1 pers. pl. pres. mid.
indic. ἀπομάσσω (†631)
(†631) **ἀπομάσσω**, fut. ἀπομάξω [§26.3] (ἀπό +
μάσσω, to wipe) to wipe off; mid. to wipe
off one's self, Luke 10:11
ἀπονέμοντες, nom. pl. m. pres. act.
part. . . . . ἀπονέμω (632)
(632) **ἀπονέμω**, fut. ἀπονεμῶ [§27.1.a] (ἀπό +
νέμω, to allot) to portion off; to assign,
bestow, 1 Pet. 3:7

(633) **ἀπονίπτω**, fut. ἀπονίψω [§23.1.a] (ἀπό +
νίπτω) to cleanse a part of the body by
washing; mid., of one's self, Matt. 27:24
ἀπόντες, nom. pl. m. pres. part. . . . . . . ἄπειμι (548)
(634) **ἀποπίπτω**, fut. ἀποπεσοῦμαι, 2 aor.
ἀπέπεσον [§37.1] (ἀπό + πίπτω) to fall
off or from, Acts 9:18
ἀποπλανᾶν, pres. act. infin. (Mark 13:22,
GNT, MT & NA | ἀποπλανᾷν, WH &
TR) . . . . ἀποπλανάω (635)
(635) **ἀποπλανάω**, ῶ, fut. ἀποπλανήσω [§18.R]
(ἀπό + πλανάω) to cause to wander; met.
to deceive, pervert, seduce, Mark 13:22;
pass. to wander; met. to swerve from,
apostatize, 1 Tim. 6:10
ἀποπλεῖν, pres. act. infin. . . . . ἀποπλέω (636)
ἀποπλεύσαντες, nom. pl. m. aor. act. part.   id.
(636) **ἀποπλέω**, ῶ, fut. ἀποπλεύσομαι, aor.
ἀπέπλευσα [§35.3] (ἀπό + πλέω) to depart by ship, sail away, Acts 13:4; 14:26;
20:15; 27:1
(637) **ἀποπλύνω**, fut. ἀποπλυνῶ [§27.1.a] (ἀπό +
πλύνω) to wash, rinse, Luke 5:2
(638) **ἀποπνίγω**, fut. ἀποπνίξω [§23.1.b] 2 aor.
pass. ἀπεπνίγην (ἀπό + πνίγω) to choke,
suffocate, Matt. 13:7; Luke 8:33; to drown,
Luke 8:7
ἀπορεῖσθαι, pres. mid. infin. (Luke 24:4,
GNT, WH & NA | διαπορεῖσθαι, MT &
TR) . . . . ἀπορέω (639)
(639) **ἀπορέω**, ῶ, fut. ἀπορήσω [§16.P] and
ἀπορέομαι, οῦμαι [§17.Q] (ἀ + πόρος, a
way) pr. to be without means; met. to hesitate, be at a stand, be in doubt and perplexity, John 13:22; Acts 25:20; 2 Cor. 4:8;
Gal. 4:20
(640) **ἀπορία**, ας, ἡ [§2.B.b; 2.2] doubt, uncertainty,
perplexity, Luke 21:25
ἀπορίᾳ, dat. sg. f. n. . . . . ἀπορία (640)
ἀπορίψαντας, acc. pl. m. aor. act. part. (Acts
27:43, GNT, WH & NA | ἀπορρίψαν-
τας, MT & TR) . . . . ἀπο(ρ)ρίπτω (†641)
ἀποροῦμαι, 1 pers. sg. pres. mid. indic. ἀπορέω (639)
ἀπορούμενοι, nom. pl. m. pres. mid. part.   id.
ἀπορούμενος, nom. sg. m. pres. mid. part.   id.
(†641) **ἀπο(ρ)ρίπτω**, fut. ἀπορίψω [§23.1.a] (ἀπό +
ῥίπτω) to throw off
ἀπορρίψαντας, acc. pl. m. aor. act. part. (Acts
27:43, MT & TR | ἀπορίψαντας, GNT,
WH & NA) . . . . ἀπο(ρ)ρίπτω (†641)
(642) **ἀπορφανίζω**, fut. ἀπορφανίσω [§26.1] (ἀπό +
ὀρφανός) to deprive, bereave, 1 Thess. 2:17
ἀπορφανισθέντες, nom. pl. m. aor. pass.
part. ἀπορφανίζω (642)
(†643) **ἀποσκευάζομαι**, fut. ἀποσκευάσομαι [§26.1]

(ἀποσκευάζω, *to pack up articles*, σκεύη, *for removal*) *to prepare for a journey, take one's departure*, Acts 21:15
ἀποσκευασάμενοι, nom. pl. m. aor. mid. dep. part. (Acts 21:15, TR | ἐπισκευασάμενοι, GNT, WH, MT & NA) .. ἀποσκευάζομαι (†643)

(644) **ἀποσκίασμα**, ατος, τό, nom. sg. neut. n. [§4.D.c] (ἀπό + σκιάζω, *to throw a shadow*, from σκιά) *a shadow cast;* met. *a shade, the slightest trace*, James 1:17
ἀποσπᾶν, pres. act. infin. (Acts 20:30, GNT, MT & NA | ἀποσπᾶν, WH & TR) . . . . ἀποσπάω (645)
ἀποσπασθέντες, acc. pl. m. aor. pass. part. . . . . id.

(645) **ἀποσπάω**, ῶ, fut. ἀποσπάσω [§22.2] (ἀπό + σπάω) *to draw away from; to draw out* or *forth*, Matt. 26:51; *to draw away, seduce*, Acts 20:30; mid. aor., pass. form, ἀπεσπάσθην, *to separate one's self, to part*, Luke 22:41; Acts 21:1
ἀποσταλέντι, dat. sg. neut. 2 aor. pass. part. . . . . ἀποστέλλω (649)
ἀποσταλῶσι(ν), 3 pers. pl. 2 aor. pass. subj. [§27.4.a,b] . . . . id.
ἀποστάντα, acc. sg. m. 2 aor. act. part. . . . . ἀφίστημι (868)
ἀποστάς, nom. sg. m. 2 aor. act. part. . . . id.

(646) **ἀποστασία**, ας, ἡ, nom. sg. f. n. [§2.B.b; 2.2] *a falling away, a defection, apostasy*, Acts 21:21; 2 Thess 2:3
ἀποστασίαν, acc. sg. f. n. . . . . ἀποστασία (646)

(647) **ἀποστάσιον**, ου, τό [§3.C.c] *defection, desertion*, as of a freedman from a patron; in N.T. *the act of putting away a wife, repudiation, divorce*, Matt. 19:7; Mark 10:4; meton. *a bill of repudiation, deed of divorce*, Matt. 5:31
ἀποστάσιον, acc. sg. neut. n. . . . . ἀποστάσιον (647)
ἀποστασίου, gen. sg. neut. n. . . . . id.

(648) **ἀποστεγάζω**, fut. ἀποστεγάσω [§26.1] (ἀπό + στέγη) *to remove* or *break through a covering* or *roof* of a place, Mark 2:4
ἀποστεῖλαι, aor. act. infin. . . . . ἀποστέλλω (649)
ἀποστείλαντα, acc. sg. m. aor. act. part. . id.
ἀποστείλαντας, acc. pl. m. aor. act. part. (Acts 15:33, GNT, WH & NA | ἀποστόλους, MT & TR) . . . . id.
ἀποστείλαντες, nom. pl. m. aor. act. part. id.
ἀποστείλας, nom. sg. m. aor. act. part. . . id.
ἀποστείλῃ, 3 pers. sg. aor. act. subj. . . . id.
ἀπόστειλον, 2 pers. sg. aor. act. imper. . . id.
ἀποστείλω, 1 pers. sg. aor. act. subj. (Acts 7:34, GNT, WH & NA | ἀποστελῶ, MT & TR) . . . . id.
ἀποστελεῖ, 3 pers. sg. fut. act. indic. . . . . id.

ἀποστέλλει, 3 pers. sg. pres. act. indic. . . . . ἀποστέλλω (649)
ἀποστέλλειν, pres. act. infin. . . . . id.
ἀποστέλλῃ, 3 pers. sg. pres. act. subj. . . . id.
ἀποστελλόμενα, nom. pl. neut. pres. pass. part. . . . . id.
ἀποστέλλουσιν, 3 pers. pl. pres. act. indic. id.

(649) **ἀποστέλλω**, 1 pers. sg. pres. act. indic., fut. ἀποστελῶ [§27.1.b] aor. ἀπέστειλα [§27.1.d] perf. ἀπέσταλκα [§27.2.b] perf. pass. ἀπέσταλμαι [§27.3] 2 aor. pass. ἀπεστάλην [§27.4.b] (ἀπό + στέλλω) *to send forth* a messenger, agent, message, or command, Matt. 2:16; 10:5, et al.; *to put forth into action*, Mark 4:29; *to liberate, rid*, Luke 4:19; *to dismiss, send away*, Mark 12:3, et al.
ἀποστελῶ, 1 pers. sg. fut. act. indic. . . . . ἀποστέλλω (649)
ἀποστερεῖσθε, 2 pers. pl. pres. pass. indic. . . . . ἀποστερέω (650)
ἀποστερεῖτε, 2 pers. pl. pres. act. indic. {1 Cor. 6:8} . . . . id.
ἀποστερεῖτε, 2 pers. pl. pres. act. imper. {1 Cor. 7:5} . . . . id.

(650) **ἀποστερέω**, ῶ, fut. ἀποστερήσω [§16.P] perf. pass. ἀπεστέρημαι [§17.Q] (ἀπό + στερέω, *to deprive*) *to deprive, detach; to debar*, 1 Cor. 7:5; *to deprive* in a bad sense, *defraud*, Mark 10:19; 1 Cor. 6:7; mid. *to suffer one's self to be deprived* or *defrauded*, 1 Cor. 6:8; pass. *to be destitute* or *devoid of*, 1 Tim. 6:5; *to be unjustly withheld*, James 5:4
ἀποστερήσῃς, 2 pers. sg. aor. act. subj. . . . . ἀποστερέω (650)
ἀποστῇ, 3 pers. sg. 2 aor. act. subj. [§29.3] . . . . ἀφίστημι (868)
ἀποστῆναι, 2 aor. act. infin. . . . . id.
ἀποστήσονται, 3 pers. pl. fut. mid. dep. indic. . . . . id.
ἀπόστητε, 2 pers. pl. 2 aor. act. imper. . . . id.
ἀποστήτω, 3 pers. sg. 2 aor. act. imper. . . id.

(651) **ἀποστολή**, ῆς, ἡ [§2.B.a] *a sending, expedition; office* or *duty of one sent as a messenger* or *agent; office of an apostle, apostleship*, Acts 1:25; Rom. 1:5; 1 Cor. 9:2; Gal. 2:8
ἀποστολήν, acc. sg. f. n. . . . . ἀποστολή (651)
ἀποστολῆς, gen. sg. f. n. . . . . id.
ἀπόστολοι, nom. pl. m. n. . . . . ἀπόστολος (652)
ἀποστόλοις, dat. pl. m. n. . . . . id.
ἀπόστολον, acc. sg. m. n. . . . . id.

(652) **ἀπόστολος**, ου, ὁ, nom. sg. m. n. [§3.C.a] *one sent as a messenger* or *agent, the bearer of*

a commission, messenger, John 13:16, et al.; *an apostle,* Matt. 10:2, et al.

ἀποστόλου, gen. sg. m. n. . . . . ἀπόστολος *(652)*

ἀποστόλους, acc. pl. m. n. . . . . id.

ἀποστόλων, gen. pl. m. n. . . . . id.

ἀποστοματίζειν, pres. act. infin. ἀποστοματίζω *(653)*

(653) **ἀποστοματίζω,** fut. ἀποστοματίσω [§26.1] (ἀπό + στόμα) pr. *to speak* or *repeat off-hand;* also, *to require* or *lead* others *to speak without premeditation,* as by questions calculated to elicit unpremeditated answers, *to endeavor to entrap into unguarded language,* Luke 11:53

ἀποστραφῇς, 2 pers. sg. 2 aor. pass. subj. (with mid. sense) . . . . ἀποστρέφω *(654)*

ἀποστρέφειν, pres. act. infin. . . . . id.

ἀποστρεφόμενοι, nom. pl. m. pres. mid. part. . . . . id.

ἀποστρεφομένων, gen. pl. m. pres. mid. part.   id.

ἀποστρέφοντα, acc. pl. m. pres. act. part.   id.

(654) **ἀποστρέφω,** fut. ἀποστρέψω [§23.1.a] (ἀπό + στρέφω) *to turn away; to remove,* Acts 3:26; Rom. 11:26; 2 Tim. 4:4; *to turn a people from their allegiance to their sovereign, pervert, incite to revolt,* Luke 23:14; *to replace, restore,* Matt. 26:52; 27:3; mid. 2 aor., pass. form. ἀπεστράφην [§24.10] *to turn away from* any one, *to slight, reject, repulse,* Matt. 5:42; Tit. 1:14; Heb. 12:25; *to desert,* 2 Tim. 1:15

ἀποστρέψει, 3 pers. sg. fut. act. indic. ἀποστρέφω *(654)*

ἀπόστρεψον, 2 pers. sg. aor. act. imper. . . id.

ἀποστρέψουσιν, 3 pers. pl. fut. act. indic.   id.

(655) **ἀποστυγέω,** ῶ, fut. ἀποστυγήσω [§16.P] (ἀπό + στυγέω, *to hate*) *to shrink from with abhorrence, detest,* Rom. 12:9

ἀποστυγοῦντες, nom. pl. m. pres. act. part. . . . . ἀποστυγέω *(655)*

ἀποσυνάγωγοι, nom. pl. m. adj. . . . . ἀποσυνάγωγος *(656)*

(656) **ἀποσυνάγωγος,** ον, nom. sg. m. adj. [§7.2] (ἀπό + συναγωγή) *expelled* or *excluded from the synagogue, excommunicated, cut off from the rights and privileges of a Jew, excluded from society,* John 9:22; 12:42; 16:2

ἀποσυναγώγους, acc. pl. m. adj. . . . . ἀποσυνάγωγος *(656)*

ἀποταξάμενος, nom. sg. m. aor. mid. part. . . . . ἀποτάσσομαι *(657)*

ἀποτάξασθαι, aor. mid. infin. . . . . id.

ἀποτάσσεται, 3 pers. sg. pres. mid. indic.   id.

(657) **ἀποτάσσομαι,** fut. ἀποτάξομαι [§26.3] (ἀποτάσσω, *to set apart,* from ἀπό +

τάσσω) *to take leave of, bid farewell to,* Luke 9:61; Acts 18:18, 21; 2 Cor. 2:13; *to dismiss, send away,* Mark 6:46; *to renounce, forsake,* Luke 14:33

ἀποτελεσθεῖσα, nom. sg. f. aor. pass. part. . . . . ἀποτελέω *(658)*

(658) **ἀποτελέω,** ῶ, fut. ἀποτελέσω [§22.1] aor. pass. ἀπετελέσθην [§22.4] (ἀπό + τελέω) *to complete;* pass. *to be perfected, to arrive at full stature* or *measure,* James 1:15

ἀποτελῶ, 1 pers. sg. pres. act. indic. (Luke 13:32, GNT, WH & NA | ἐπιτελῶ, MT & TR) . . . . ἀποτελέω *(658)*

(659) **ἀποτίθημι,** fut. ἀποθήσω [§28.V] mid. ἀποτίθεμαι, 2 aor. ἀπεθέμην [§28.W] *to lay off, lay down* or *aside,* as garments, Acts 7:58; met. *to lay aside, put off, renounce,* Rom. 13:12; Eph. 4:22, 25; Col. 3:8, et al.

ἀποτινάξας, nom. sg. m. aor. act. part. ἀποτινάσσω *(660)*

ἀποτινάξατε, 2 pers. pl. aor. act. imper. (Luke 9:5, MT & TR | ἀποτινάσσετε, GNT, WH & NA) . . . . id.

ἀποτινάσσετε, 2 pers. pl. pres. act. imper. (Luke 9:5, GNT, WH & NA | ἀποτινάξατε, MT & TR) . . . . id.

(660) **ἀποτινάσσω,** fut. ἀποτινάξω [§26.3] (ἀπό + τινάσσω, *to shake*) *to shake off,* Luke 9:5; Acts 28:5

(661) **ἀποτίνω,** fut. ἀποτίσω [§27.1 note] (ἀπό + τίνω) *to pay off* what is claimed or due; *to repay, refund, make good,* Philemon 19

ἀποτίσω, 1 pers. sg. fut. act. indic. . . . ἀποτίνω *(661)*

ἀποτολμᾷ, 3 pers. sg. pres. act. indic. ἀποτολμάω *(662)*

(662) **ἀποτολμάω,** ῶ, fut. ἀποτολμήσω [§18.R] (ἀπό + τολμάω) *to dare* or *risk outright; to speak outright, without reserve* or *restraint,* Rom. 10:20

(663) **ἀποτομία,** ας, ἡ, nom. sg. f. n. [§2.B.b; 2.2] (ἀπότομος, *cut off sheer,* from ἀποτέμνω, *to cut off,* from ἀπό + τέμνω) pr. *abruptness;* met. *summary severity, rigor,* Rom. 11:22(2×)

ἀποτομίαν, acc. sg. f. n. . . . . ἀποτομία *(663)*

(664) **ἀποτόμως,** adv., *sharply, severely,* 2 Cor. 13:10; Tit. 1:13

ἀποτρέπου, 2 pers. sg. pres. mid. imper. ἀποτρέπω *(665)*

(665) **ἀποτρέπω,** fut. ἀποτρέψω [§23.1.a] (ἀπό + τρέπω) *to turn* any one *away* from a thing; mid. *to turn one's self away* from any one; *to avoid, shun,* 2 Tim. 3:5

(666) **ἀπουσία,** ας, ἡ [§2.B.b; 2.2] *absence,* Phil. 2:12

ἀπουσίᾳ, dat. sg. f. n. . . . . ἀπουσία (666)

ἀποφέρεσθαι, pres. pass. infin. (Acts 19:12, GNT, WH & NA | ἐπιφέρεσθαι, MT & TR) . . . . ἀποφέρω (667)

(667) **ἀποφέρω**, fut. ἀποίσω, aor. ἀπήνεγκα, 2 aor. ἀπήνεγκον, aor. pass. ἀπηνέχθην [§36.1] (ἀπό + φέρω) *to bear* or *carry away, conduct away,* Mark 15:1; Luke 16:22; 1 Cor. 16:3; Rev. 17:3; 21:10

ἀποφεύγοντας, acc. pl. m. pres. act. part. (2 Pet. 2:18, GNT, WH & NA | ἀποφυγόντας, MT & TR) . . . . . ἀποφεύγω (668)

(668) **ἀποφεύγω**, fut. ἀποφεύξομαι [§23.1.b] 2 aor. ἀπέφυγον [§24.9] (ἀπό + φεύγω) *to flee from, escape;* met. *to be rid, be freed from,* 2 Pet. 1:4; 2:18, 20

ἀποφθέγγεσθαι, pres. mid./pass. dep. infin. . . . . ἀποφθέγγομαι (669)

(669) **ἀποφθέγγομαι**, 1 pers. sg. pres. mid./pass. dep. indic., fut. ἀποφθέγξομαι [§23.1.b] (ἀπό + φθέγγομαι) *to speak out, declare,* particularly solemn, weighty, or pithy sayings, Acts 2:4, 14; 26:25

(670) **ἀποφορτίζομαι**, fut. ἀποφορτίσομαι [§26.1] (ἀπό + φόρτος) *to unlade,* Acts 21:3

ἀποφορτιζόμενον, nom. sg. neut. pres. mid./pass. dep. part. . . . . ἀποφορτίζομαι (670)

ἀποφυγόντας, acc. pl. m. 2 aor. act. part. (2 Pet. 2:18, MT & TR | ἀποφεύγοντας, GNT, WH & NA) . . . . ἀποφεύγω (668)

ἀποφυγόντες, nom. pl. m. 2 aor. act. part.   id.

ἀποχρήσει, dat. sg. f. n. . . . . ἀπόχρησις (671)

(671) **ἀπόχρησις**, εως, ἡ [§5.E.c] (ἀποχράομαι, *to use up, consume by use*) *a using up,* or, *a discharge of an intended use,* Col. 2:22

ἀποχωρεῖ, 3 pers. sg. pres. act. indic. . . . . ἀποχωρέω (672)

ἀποχωρεῖτε, 2 pers. pl. pres. act. imper. . .   id.

(672) **ἀποχωρέω**, ῶ, fut. ἀποχωρήσω [§16.P] (ἀπό + χωρέω) *to go from* or *away, depart,* Matt. 7:23; Luke 9:39; Acts 13:13

ἀποχωρήσας, nom. sg. m. aor. act. part. . . . . ἀποχωρέω (672)

(673) **ἀποχωρίζω**, fut. ἀποχωρίσω, aor. pass. ἀπεχωρίσθην [§26.1] (ἀπό + χωρίζω) *to separate;* pass. *to be swept aside,* Rev. 6:14; mid. *to part,* Acts 15:39

ἀποχωρισθῆναι, aor. pass. infin. . . . ἀποχωρίζω (673)

ἀποψυχόντων, gen. pl. m. pres. act. part. . . . . ἀποψύχω (674)

(674) **ἀποψύχω**, fut. ἀποψύξω [§23.1.b] (ἀπό + ψύχω) pr. *to breathe out, faint away, die;* met. *to faint at heart, be dismayed,* Luke 21:26

(675) **Ἄππιος φόρος**, ου, ὁ, *the forum* or *market-*

place, of Appius; a village on the Appian road, near Rome, Acts 28:15

Ἀππίου φόρου, gen. sg. m. n. . . . Ἄππιος φόρος (675)

ἀπρόσιτον, acc. sg. neut. adj. . . . . . ἀπρόσιτος (676)

(676) **ἀπρόσιτος**, ον [§7.2] (ἀ + προσιτός, *accessible,* from πρόσειμι, *to approach*) *unapproached, unapproachable,* 1 Tim. 6:16

ἀπρόσκοποι, nom. pl. m. adj. . . . ἀπρόσκοπος (677)

ἀπρόσκοπον, acc. sg. f. adj. . . . .   id.

(677) **ἀπρόσκοπος**, ον (ἀ + προσκοπή) *not stumbling* or *jarring;* met. *not stumbling* or *jarring* against moral rule, *unblamable, clear,* Acts 24:16; Phil. 1:10; *free from offensiveness,* 1 Cor. 10:32

(678) **ἀπροσωπολήμπτως**, adv. (ἀ + προσωπολήπτέω) *without respect of persons, impartially* (1 Pet. 1:17, GNT, WH & NA | ἀπροσωπολήπτως, MT & TR)

(679) **ἄπταιστος**, ον (ἀ + πταίω) *free from stumbling;* met. *free from* moral *stumbling* or *offence; irreprehensible,* Jude 24

ἀπταίστους, acc. pl. m. adj. . . . . ἄπταιστος (679)

ἅπτει, 3 pers. sg. pres. act. indic. . . . . ἅπτω (681)

ἅπτεσθαι, pres. mid. infin. . . . .   id.

ἅπτεσθε, 2 pers. pl. pres. mid. imper. . . . .   id.

ἅπτεται, 3 pers. sg. pres. mid. indic. . . . . .   id.

ἅπτηται, 3 pers. sg. pres. mid. subj. . . . . .   id.

ἅπτου, 2 pers. sg. pres. mid. imper. . . . . .   id.

(681) **ἅπτω**, fut. ἅπψω [§23.1.a] pr. *to bring in contact, fit, fasten; to light, kindle,* Mark 4:21; Luke 8:16, et al.; mid. ἅπτομαι, fut. ἅψομαι, aor. ἡψάμην, *to touch,* Matt. 8:3, et al.; *to meddle, venture to partake,* Col. 2:21; *to have intercourse with, to know carnally,* 1 Cor. 7:1; by impl. *to harm,* 1 John 5:18

(682) **Ἀπφία**, ας, ἡ, *Apphia,* pr. name, Philemon 2

Ἀπφίᾳ, dat. sg. f. n. . . . . Ἀπφία (682)

ἀπωθεῖσθε, 2 pers. pl. pres. mid./pass. dep. indic. . . . . ἀπωθέω (†683)

(†683) **ἀπωθέω**, ῶ, fut. ἀπωθήσω and ἀπωθώσω, and mid. ἀπωθέομαι, οῦμαι, aor. ἀπωσάμην (ἀπό + ὠθέω, *to thrust*) *to thrust away, repel from one's self, repulse,* Acts 7:27; *to refuse, reject, cast off,* Acts 7:39; 13:46; Rom. 11:1, 2; 1 Tim. 1:19

(684) **ἀπώλεια**, ας, ἡ nom. sg. f. n. [§2.B.b; 2.2] *consumption, destruction; waste, profusion,* Matt. 26:8; Mark 14:4; *destruction, state of being destroyed,* Acts 25:6; eternal *ruin, perdition,* Matt. 7:13; Acts 8:20, et al.

ἀπωλείαις, dat. pl. f. n. (2 Pet. 2:2, TR | ἀσελγείαις, GNT, WH, NA, MT & NA) . . . . ἀπώλεια (684) ἀπώλειαν, acc. sg. f. n. . . . . ἀπώλεια *(684)*

ἀπωλείας, gen. sg. f. n. . . . . id.

ἀπώλεσα, 1 pers. sg. aor. act. indic. . ἀπόλλυμι *(622)*

ἀπώλεσε(ν), 3 pers. sg. aor. act. indic. . . . id.

ἀπώλετο, 3 pers. sg. 2 aor. mid. indic. . . . id.

ἀπώλλυντο, 3 pers. pl. imperf. mid. indic.
(1 Cor. 10:9, GNT, WH & NA |
ἀπώλοντο, MT & TR) . . . . id.

ἀπώλοντο, 3 pers. pl. 2 aor. mid. indic. . . id.

ἀπών, nom. sg. m. pres. part. . . . . ἄπειμι *(548)*

ἀπωσάμενοι, nom. pl. m. aor. mid. dep.
part. . . . . ἀπωθέω *(†683)*

ἀπώσαντο, 3 pers. pl. aor. mid. dep. indic. id.

ἀπώσατο, 3 pers. sg. aor. mid. dep. indic. id.

(685) **ἀρά,** ᾶς, ἡ [§2.B.b; 2.2] pr. *a prayer;* more
commonly *a prayer for evil; curse, cursing,
imprecation,* Rom. 3:14

(686) **ἄρα,** a particle which denotes, first, transition
from one thing to another by natural se-
quence; secondly, logical inference; in
which case the premises are either expressed, Matt. 12:28, or to be variously
supplied. *Therefore, then, consequently;
should it so result,* Acts 17:27 {Gal. 2:21}

(687) **ἆρα,** stronger form of the preceding, used
mainly in interrogations, Luke 18:8; Acts
8:30; {Gal. 2:17}

Ἄραβες, nom. pl. m. n. . . . . Ἄραψ *(690)*

(688) **Ἀραβία,** ας, ἡ [§2.B.b; 2.2] *Arabia*

Ἀραβίᾳ, dat. sg. f. n. . . . . ·. . . Ἀραβία *(688)*

Ἀραβίαν, acc. sg. f. n. . . . . id.

ἄραγε, the particle ἄρα combined with γε
(WH & TR | ἄρα γε, GNT, MT & NA) ἄρα *(686)*

ἆραι, aor. act. infin. . . . . αἴρω *(142)*

(689) **Ἀράμ,** ὁ, *Aram,* pr. name, indecl.

ἄραντες, nom. pl. m. aor. act. part. . . . . αἴρω *(142)*

ἄρας, nom. sg. m. aor. act. part. {1 Cor. 6:15} id.

ἀρᾶς, gen. sg. f. n. {Rom. 3:14} . . . . ἀρά *(685)*

ἄρατε, 2 pers. pl. aor. act. imper. . . . . . . αἴρω *(142)*

ἀράτω, 3 pers. sg. aor. act. imper. . . . . . . id.

(‡729) **ἄραφος,** ον, nom. sg. m. adj. [§7.2] (ἀ +
ῥάπτω, *to sew) not sewed, without seam,*
John 19:23

(690) **Ἄραψ,** αβος, ὁ [§4.2.a] *an Arabian,* Acts 2:11

ἀργαί, nom. pl. f. adj. . . . . ἀργός *(692)*

ἀργεῖ, 3 pers. sg. pres. act. indic. . . . . . . ἀργέω *(691)*

(691) **ἀργέω,** ῶ, fut. ἀργήσω [§16.P] pr. *to be unemployed; to be inoperative, to linger,* 2 Pet.
2:3

ἀργή, nom. sg. f. adj. (James 2:20, GNT, WH
& NA | νεκρά, MT & TR) . . . . ἀργός *(692)*

ἀργοί, nom. pl. m. adj. . . . . id.

ἀργόν, nom. sg. neut. adj. . . . . id.

(692) **ἀργός,** ή, όν [§7.F.a] (ἀ + ἔργον) contr. from
ἀεργός, pr. *inactive, unemployed,* Matt.

20:3, 6; *idle, averse from labor* 1 Tim.
5:13; Tit. 1:12; met. 2 Pet. 1:8; *unprofitable, hollow,* or by impl., *injurious,* Matt.
12:36

ἀργούς, acc. pl. m. adj. . . . . ἀργός *(692)*

ἀργυρᾶ, nom. pl. neut. adj.
{2 Tim. 2:20} . . . . ἀργυροῦς *(‡693)*

ἀργυρᾶ, acc. pl. neut. adj. {Rev. 9:20} . . . id.

(693) **ἀργύρεος,** έα, εον, contr. οῦς, ᾶ, οῦν [§7.4.c]
made of silver, Acts 19:24; 2 Tim. 2:20;
Rev. 9:20

ἀργύρια, acc. pl. neut. n. . . . . ἀργύριον *(694)*

(694) **ἀργύριον,** ου, τό, nom. sg. neut. n. [§3.C.c]
silver; meton. *money;* spc. *a piece of silver money, a shekel* {Acts 8:20}

ἀργύριον, acc. sg. neut. n. {Luke 9:3} ἀργύριον *(694)*

ἀργυρίου, gen. sg. neut. n. . . . . id.

ἀργυρίῳ, dat. sg. neut. n. . . . . id.

(695) **ἀργυροκόπος,** ου, ὁ, nom. sg. m. n. [§3.C.a]
(ἄργυρος + κόπτω) *a forger of silver, sil-
versmith,* Acts 19:24

ἄργυρον, acc. sg. m. n. . . . . ἄργυρος *(696)*

(696) **ἄργυρος,** ου, ὁ, nom. sg. m. n. [§3.C.a] *silver;*
meton. *anything made of silver; money,*
James 5:3

ἀργύρου, gen. sg. m. n. . . . . ἄργυρος *(696)*

(‡693) **ἀργυροῦς,** ᾶ, οῦν [§7.4.c] *made of silver,* Acts
19:24; 2 Tim. 2:20; Rev. 9:20

ἀργυροῦς, acc. pl. m. adj. . . . . ἀργυροῦς *(‡693)*

ἀργύρῳ, dat. sg. m. n. . . . . ἄργυρος *(696)*

ἀρεῖ, 3 pers. sg. fut. act. indic. αἴρω (John
16:22, WH | αἴρει, GNT, MT, TR &
NA) . . . . αἴρω *(142)*

Ἄρειον πάγον, acc. sg. m. n. . . Ἄρειος πάγος *(697)*

(697) **Ἄρειος πάγος,** ου, ὁ, *the Areopagus* or *Hill
of Mars,* in Athens, Acts 17:22

Ἀρείου πάγου, gen. sg. m. n. ·. . Ἄρειος πάγος *(697)*

(698) **Ἀρεοπαγίτης,** ου, ὁ, nom. sg. m. n. [§2.B.c]
a judge of the court of Areopagus, Acts
17:34

ἀρέσαι, aor. act. infin. . . . . ἀρέσκω *(700)*

ἀρεσάσης, gen. sg. f. aor. act. part. (Mark
6:22, MT & TR | ἤρεσεν, GNT, WH &
NA) . . . . id.

ἀρέσει, 3 pers. sg. fut. act. indic. [§36.3]
(1 Cor. 7:32, 33, 34, MT & TR | ἀρέσῃ,
GNT, WH & NA) . . . . id.

ἀρέσῃ, 3 pers. sg. aor. act. subj. . . . . id.

(†699) **ἀρεσκεία,** ας, ἡ [§2.B.b; 2.2] *a pleasing, desire of pleasing* Col. 1:10

ἀρεσκείαν, acc. sg. n. (Col. 1:10, GNT, MT,
TR & NA | ἀρεσκίαν, WH) . . . ἀρεσκεία *(†699)*

ἀρέσκειν, pres. act. infin. . . . . ἀρέσκω *(700)*

ἀρεσκέτω, 3 pers. sg. pres. act. imper. . . . id.

ἀρέσκοντες, nom. pl. m. pres. act. part. . . id.

ἀρεσκόντων, gen. pl. m. pres. act.
part. . . . . ἀρέσκω *(700)*

(700) **ἀρέσκω,** 1 pers. sg. pres. act. indic., fut.
ἀρέσω, imperf. ἤρεσκον, aor. ἤρεσα, *to*
please, Matt. 14:6, et al.; *to be pleasing,*
acceptable, Acts 6:5; *to consult the plea-*
sure of any one, Rom. 15:1, 2, 3; 1 Cor.
10:33; *to seek favor with,* Gal. 1:10;
1 Thess. 2:4

ἀρεστά, acc. pl. neut. adj. . . . . ἀρεστός *(701)*
ἀρεστόν, nom. sg. neut. adj. . . . . id.

(701) **ἀρεστός,** ή, όν [§7.F.a] *pleasing, acceptable,*
John 3:22; 8:29; Acts 12:3; *deemed proper,*
Acts 6:2

Ἀρέτα, gen. sg. m. n. . . . . Ἀρέτας *(702)*

(702) **Ἀρέτας,** α, ὁ [§2.4] *Aretas,* pr. name, 2 Cor.
11:32

ἀρετάς, acc. pl. f. n. . . . . ἀρετή *(703)*

(703) **ἀρετή,** ῆς, ἡ, nom. sg. f. n. [§2.B.a] *goodness,*
good quality of any kind; *a gracious act*
of God, 1 Pet. 2:9; 2 Pet. 1:3; *virtue,*
uprightness, Phil. 4:8; 2 Pet. 1:5

ἀρετῇ, dat. sg. f. n. . . . . ἀρετή *(703)*
ἀρετήν, acc. sg. f. n. . . . . id.
ἀρετῆς, gen. sg. f. n. (2 Pet. 1:3, MT, WH &
TR | ἀρετῇ, GNT & NA) . . . . id.
ἄρῃ, 3 pers. sg. aor. act. subj. . . . . αἴρω *(142)*

(704) **ἀρήν,** ἀρνός, ὁ, nom. not in use, pl. ἄρνας,
a sheep, lamb, Luke 10:3

ἄρῃς, 2 pers. sg. aor. act. subj. . . . . αἴρω *(142)*
ἀρθῇ, 3 pers. sg. aor. pass. subj. (1 Cor. 5:2,
GNT, WH & NA | ἐξαρθῇ, MT & TR) id.
ἀρθήσεται, 3 pers. sg. fut. pass. indic. [§27.3] id.
ἄρθητι, 2 pers. sg. aor. pass. imper. . . . . . id.
ἀρθήτω, 3 pers. sg. aor. pass. imper. . . . . . id.
ἀρθῶσιν, 3 pers. pl. aor. pass. subj. . . . . . id.

(705) **ἀριθμέω,** ῶ, fut. ἀριθμήσω [§16.P] aor.
ἠρίθμησα, perf. pass. ἠρίθμημαι, *to*
number, Matt. 10:30; Luke 12:7; Rev. 7:9

ἀριθμῆσαι, aor. act. infin. . . . . ἀριθμέω *(705)*
ἀριθμόν, acc. sg. m. n. . . . . ἀριθμός *(706)*

(706) **ἀριθμός,** οῦ, ὁ, nom. sg. m. n. [§3.C.a] *a*
number, Luke 22:3; John 6:10; Acts 4:4;
Rev. 20:8; 13:18

ἀριθμοῦ, gen. sg. m. n. . . . . ἀριθμός *(706)*
ἀριθμῷ, dat. sg. m. n. . . . . id.

(707) **Ἀριμαθαία,** ας, ἡ [§2.B.b; 2.2] *Arimathea,* a
town of Palestine

Ἀριμαθαίας, gen. sg. f. n. . . . . Ἀριμαθαία *(707)*
Ἀρίσταρχον, acc. sg. m. n. . . . . Ἀρίσταρχος *(708)*

(708) **Ἀρίσταρχος,** ου, ὁ, nom. sg. m. n. [§3.C.a]
Aristarchus, pr. name, Acts 19:29

Ἀριστάρχου, gen. sg. m. n. . . . . Ἀρίσταρχος *(708)*

(709) **ἀριστάω,** ῶ, fut. ἀριστήσω [§18.R] aor.
ἠρίστησα, *to take the first meal, breakfast,*

John 21:12, 15; also, *to take a mid-day*
meal, Luke 11:37

ἀριστερά, nom. sg. f. adj. . . . . ἀριστερός *(710)*

(710) **ἀριστερός,** ά, όν [§7.1] *the left;* ἀριστερά, sc.
χείρ, *the left hand,* Matt. 6:3; so ἐξ
ἀριστερῶν, sc. μερῶν, Luke 23:33; 2 Cor.
6:7

ἀριστερῶν, gen. pl. m. adj. . . . . ἀριστερός *(710)*
ἀριστήσατε, 2 pers. pl. aor. act.
imper. . . . . ἀριστάω *(709)*
ἀριστήσῃ, 3 pers. sg. aor. act. subj. . . . . . id.

(711) **Ἀριστόβουλος,** ου, ὁ [§3.C.a] *Aristobulus,* pr.
name, Rom. 16:10

Ἀριστοβούλου, gen. sg. m. n. . . . Ἀριστόβουλος *(711)*

(712) **ἄριστον,** ου, τό [§3.C.c] pr. *the first meal,*
breakfast; afterwards extended to signify
also *a slight mid-day meal, luncheon,* Matt.
22:4

ἄριστον, nom. sg. neut. n. . . . . ἄριστον *(712)*
ἀρίστου, gen. sg. neut. n. . . . . id.
ἀρκεῖ, 3 pers. sg. pres. act. indic. . . . . . . ἀρκέω *(714)*
ἀρκεῖσθε, 2 pers. pl. pres. pass. imper. . . . id.
ἀρκέσῃ, 3 pers. sg. aor. act. subj. . . . . . . id.
ἀρκεσθησόμεθα, 1 pers. pl. fut. pass. indic.
[§22.4] . . . . id.
ἀρκετόν, nom. sg. neut. adj. . . . . ἀρκετός *(713)*

(713) **ἀρκετός,** ή, όν nom. sg. m. adj. [§7.F.a] *suf-*
ficient, enough, Matt. 6:34; 10:25; 1 Pet.
4:3

(714) **ἀρκέω,** ῶ, fut. ἀρκέσω [§22.1] aor. ἤρκεσα,
pr. *to ward off;* thence; *to be of service,*
avail; to suffice, be enough, Matt. 25:9, et
al.; pass. *to be contented, satisfied,* Luke
3:14; 1 Tim. 6:8; Heb. 13:5; 3 John 10

(†715) **ἄρκος,** ου, ὁ, ἡ, *a bear*
ἄρκου, gen. sg. f. n. (Rev. 13:2, GNT, WH,
MT & NA | ἄρκτου, TR) . . . . ἄρκος *(†715)*
ἀρκούμενοι, nom. pl. m. pres. pass.
part. . . . . ἀρκέω *(714)*
ἀρκούμενος, nom. sg. m. pres. pass. part. id.
ἀρκοῦσιν, 3 pers. pl. pres. act. indic. . . . . id.

(715) **ἄρκτος,** ου, ὁ, ἡ [§3.C.a,b] *a bear,* Rev. 13:2
ἄρκτου, gen. sg. f. n. (Rev. 13:2, TR | ἄρκου,
GNT, WH, MT & NA) . . . . ἄρκτος *(715)*

(716) **ἅρμα,** ατος, τό [§4.D.c] *a chariot, vehicle,* Acts
8:28, 29, 38

ἅρμα, acc. sg. neut. n. . . . . ἅρμα *(716)*

(717) **Ἁρμαγεδδών,** οῦ, τό, nom. sg. neut. n. *Ar-*
mageddon (Rev. 16:16, GNT & NA |
Ἁρμαγεδδῶν, TR | Μαγεδών, MT | Ἅρ
Μαγεδών, WH)

ἅρματι, dat. sg. neut. n. . . . . ἅρμα *(716)*
ἅρματος, gen. sg. neut. n. . . . . id.
ἁρμάτων, gen. pl. neut. n. . . . . id.

(718) **ἁρμόζω,** fut. ἁρμόσω [§26.1] *to fit together;*

mid. ἁρμόζομαι, aor. ἡρμοσάμην, *to join,*
unite in marriage, *espouse, betroth,* 2 Cor.
11:2

(719) **ἁρμός,** οῦ, ὁ [§3.C.a] *a joint* or *articulation*
of the bones, Heb. 4:12

ἁρμῶν, gen. pl. m. n. . . . . ἁρμός *(719)*

ἄρνας, acc. pl. m. n. [§6.4.d] . . . . ἀρήν *(704)*

ἀρνεῖσθαι, pres. mid./pass. dep. infin. (Acts
4:16, GNT, WH & NA | ἀρνήσασθαι,
MT & TR) . . . . ἀρνέομαι *(720)*

(720) **ἀρνέομαι,** οῦμαι, fut. ἀρνήσομαι [§17.Q] perf.
(pass. form) ἤρνημαι, aor. ἠρνησάμην, *to*
deny, disclaim, disown, Matt. 10:33; et al.;
to renounce, Tit. 2:12, et al.; *to decline, re-*
fuse, Heb. 11:24; absol. *to deny, contra-*
dict, Luke 8:45, et al.

ἀρνησάμενοι, nom. pl. m. aor. mid. dep.
part. . . . . ἀρνέομαι *(720)*

ἀρνησάμενος, nom. sg. m. aor. mid. dep.
part. . . . . id.

ἀρνήσασθαι, aor. mid. dep. infin. . . . . id.

ἀρνησάσθω, 3 pers. sg. aor. mid. dep. imper.
(Luke 9:23, GNT, WH & NA |
ἀπαρνησάσθω, MT & TR) . . . . id.

ἀρνήσεται, 3 pers. sg. fut. mid. dep. indic. id.

ἀρνήσῃ, 2 pers. sg. aor. mid. dep. subj. (John
13:38, GNT, WH & NA | ἀπαρνήσῃ, MT
& TR) . . . . id.

ἀρνήσηται, 3 pers. sg. aor. mid. dep. subj. id.

ἀρνήσομαι, 1 pers. sg. fut. mid. dep. indic. id.

ἀρνησόμεθα, 1 pers. pl. fut. mid. dep. indic.
(2 Tim. 2:12, GNT, WH & NA |
ἀρνούμεθα, MT & TR) . . . . id.

(‡2496) **Ἀρνί,** m. indecl. n. *Arni,* proper name (Luke
3:33, GNT & NA | Ἀρνεί, WH | Ἰωράμ,
MT | TR omits)

ἀρνία, acc. pl. neut. n. . . . . ἀρνίον *(721)*

(721) **ἀρνίον,** ου, τό, nom. sg. neut. n. [§3.C.c] *a*
young lamb, lambkin, lamb, John 21:15;
Rev. 5:6, 8

ἀρνίου, gen. sg. neut. n. . . . . ἀρνίον *(721)*

ἀρνίῳ, dat. sg. neut. n. . . . . id.

ἀρνούμεθα, 1 pers. pl. pres. mid./pass. dep.
indic. (2 Tim. 2:12, MT & TR |
ἀρνησόμεθα, GNT, WH & NA) . ἀρνέομαι *(720)*

ἀρνούμενοι, nom. pl. m. pres. mid./pass. dep.
part. . . . . id.

ἀρνούμενος, nom. sg. m. pres. mid./pass. dep.
part. . . . . id.

ἀρνουμένων, gen. pl. m. pres. mid./pass. dep.
part. . . . . id.

ἀρνοῦνται, 3 pers. pl. pres. mid./pass. dep.
indic. . . . . id.

ἀρξάμενοι, nom. pl. m. aor. mid. part. . . . ἄρχω *(757)*

ἀρξάμενον, nom. sg. neut. aor. mid. part.

(Luke 24:47, MT & TR | ἀρξάμενοι,
GNT, WH & NA) . . . . ἄρχω *(757)*

ἀρξάμενον, acc. sg. neut. aor. mid. part. (Acts
10:37, MT & TR | ἀρξάμενος, GNT,
WH & NA) . . . . id.

ἀρξάμενος, nom. sg. m. aor. mid. part. . . id.

ἀρξαμένου, gen. sg. m. aor. mid. part. . . . id.

ἄρξασθαι, aor. mid. infin. . . . . id.

ἄρξεσθε, 2 pers. pl. fut. mid. indic. . . . . . id.

ἄρξῃ, 2 pers. sg. aor. mid. subj. . . . . id.

ἄρξησθε, 2 pers. pl. aor. mid. subj. . . . . . id.

ἄρξηται, 3 pers. sg. aor. mid. subj. . . . . . id.

ἄρξονται, 3 pers. pl. fut. mid. indic. . . . . id.

ἄρξωνται, 3 pers. pl. aor. mid. subj. . . . . id.

ἆρον, 2 pers. sg. aor. act. imper. . . . . αἴρω *(142)*

ἀροτριᾶν, pres. act. infin. (1 Cor. 9:10, GNT,
MT & NA | ἀροτριᾷν, WH &
TR) . . . . ἀροτριάω *(†722)*

(†722) **ἀροτριάω,** ῶ, fut. ἀροτριάσω [§22.2.a] *to*
plough, Luke 17:7; 1 Cor. 9:10

ἀροτριῶν, nom. sg. m. pres. act.
part. . . . . ἀροτριάω *(†722)*

ἀροτριῶντα, acc. sg. m. pres. act. part. . . id.

(723) **ἄροτρον,** ου, τό [§3.C.c] (ἀρόω, *to plough*)
a plough, Luke 9:62

ἄροτρον, acc. sg. neut. n. . . . . ἄροτρον *(723)*

ἀροῦσι(ν), 3 pers. pl. fut. act. indic. . . . . αἴρω *(142)*

ἁρπαγέντα, acc. sg. m. 2 aor. pass.
part. . . . . ἁρπάζω *(726)*

ἅρπαγες, nom. pl. m. adj. [§4.2.b] . . . . ἅρπαξ *(727)*

(724) **ἁρπαγή,** ῆς, ἡ [§2.B.a] *plunder, pillage, rapine;*
the act of plundering, Heb. 10:34; *prey,*
spoil, or, *rapacity,* Matt. 23:25; Luke 11:39

ἁρπαγήν, acc. sg. f. n. . . . . ἁρπαγή *(724)*

ἁρπαγῆς, gen. sg. f. n. . . . . id.

ἁρπαγησόμεθα, 1 pers. pl. 2 fut. pass. indic.
[§24.3] . . . . ἁρπάζω *(726)*

ἁρπαγμόν, acc. sg. m. n. . . . . ἁρπαγμός *(725)*

(725) **ἁρπαγμός,** οῦ, ὁ [§3.C.a] *rapine, robbery,*
eager seizure; in N.T., *a thing retained with*
an eager grasp, or *eagerly claimed and con-*
spicuously exercised, Phil. 2:6

ἁρπάζει, 3 pers. sg. pres. act. indic. . . . ἁρπάζω *(726)*

ἁρπάζειν, pres. act. infin. . . . . id.

ἁρπάζοντες, nom. pl. m. pres. act. part. . . id.

ἁρπάζουσιν, 3 pers. pl. pres. act. indic. . . id.

(726) **ἁρπάζω,** fut. ἁρπάσω and ἁρπάξω [§26.2]
aor. ἥρπασα, aor. pass. ἡρπάσθην, 2 aor.
pass. ἡρπάγην [§24.6] *to seize,* as a wild
beast, John 10:12; *take away by force,*
snatch away, Matt. 13:19; John 10:28, 29;
Acts 23:10; Jude 23; met. *to seize on with*
avidity, eagerly, appropriate, Matt. 11:12;
to convey away suddenly, transport hastily,
John 6:15, et al.

(727) ἅρπαξ, αγος, ὁ, ἡ, τό, nom. sg. m. adj. [§4.2.b] pr. *ravenous, ravening,* as a wild beast, Matt. 7:15; met. *rapacious, given to extortion and robbery, an extortioner,* Luke 18:11; 1 Cor. 5:10, 11; 6:10

ἅρπαξιν, dat. pl. m. adj. . . . . ἅρπαξ (727)

ἁρπάσαι, aor. act. infin. . . . . ἁρπάζω (726)

ἁρπάσει, 3 pers. sg. fut. act. indic. . . . . . . id.

(728) ἀρραβών, ῶνος, ὁ, nom. sg. m. n. [§4.2.e] (Hebrew עֵרָבוֹן) *a pledge, earnest,* 2 Cor. 1:22; 5:5; Eph. 1:14

ἀρραβῶνα, acc. sg. m. n. . . . . ἀρραβών (728)

(729) ἄρραφος, ον, nom. sg. m. adj. [§7.2] (ἀ + ῥάπτω, *to sew) not sewed, without seam* John 19:23

ἄρρενα, acc. sg. neut. n. (Rev. 12:5, 13, MT & TR | ἄρσεν, Rev. 12:5, GNT, WH & NA | ἄρσενα, Rev. 12:13, GNT, WH & NA) . ἄρρην (730)

ἄρρενες, nom. pl. neut. n. (Rom. 1:27, MT & TR | ἄρσενες, GNT, WH & NA) . id.

(730) ἄρρην, ἄρρεν, ενος, ὁ, τό [§7.2] *male, of the male sex,* Rom. 1:27; Rev. 12:5, 13

ἄρρητα, acc. pl. neut. adj. . . . . ἄρρητος (731)

(731) ἄρρητος, ον [§7.2] (ἀ + ῥητός) pr. *not spoken; what ought not to be spoken, secret; which cannot be spoken* or *uttered, ineffable,* 2 Cor. 12:4

ἄρρωστοι, nom. pl. m. adj. . . . . ἄρρωστος (732)

ἀρρώστοις, dat. pl. m. adj. . . . . id.

(732) ἄρρωστος, ον [§7.2] (ἀ + ῥώννυμι) *infirm, sick, an invalid,* Matt. 14:14; Mark 6:5, 13; 16:18; 1 Cor. 11:30

ἀρρώστους, acc. pl. m. adj. . . . . ἄρρωστος (732)

ἄρσεν, nom. sg. neut. n. {Gal. 3:28} . . ἄρσην (‡730)

ἄρσεν, acc. sg. neut. n. {Matt. 19:4} . . . . id.

ἄρσενα, acc. sg. m. n. (Rev. 12:13, GNT, WH & NA | ἄρρενα, MT & TR) . . . . id.

ἄρσενες, nom. pl. m. n. . . . . id.

ἀρσενοκοῖται, nom. pl. m. n. . . ἀρσενοκοίτης (733)

ἀρσενοκοίταις, dat. pl. m. n. . . . . id.

(733) ἀρσενοκοίτης, ου, ὁ [§2.B.c] (ἄρσην + κοίτη) *one who lies with a male, a sodomite,* 1 Cor. 6:9; 1 Tim. 1:10

ἄρσεσι(ν), dat. pl. m. n. . . . . ἄρσην (‡730)

(‡730) ἄρσην, ἄρσεν, ενος, ὁ, τό [§7.3] *male, of the male sex,* Matt. 19:4; Mark 10:6; Luke 2:23; Rom. 1:27; Gal. 3:28

Ἀρτεμᾶν, acc. sg. m. n. . . . . Ἀρτεμᾶς (734)

(734) Ἀρτεμᾶς, ᾶ, ὁ [§2.4] *Artemas,* pr. name, Tit. 3:12

Ἀρτέμιδος, gen. sg. f. n. . . . . Ἄρτεμις (735)

(735) Ἄρτεμις, ιδος, ἡ, nom. sg. f. n. [§4.2.c] *Artemis* or *Diana,* Acts 19:24, 27, 28, 34

ἀρτέμονα, acc. sg. m. n. [§4.2.e] (Acts 27:40, MT & TR | ἀρτέμωνα, GNT, WH &

NA) . . . . ἀρτέμων (736)

(736) ἀρτέμων, ωνος, ὁ (ἀρτάω, *to suspend) a topsail, artemon, supparum;* or, according to others, *the dolon* of Pliny and Pollux, a small sail near the prow of the ship, which was hoisted when the wind was too strong to use larger sails, Acts 27:40

ἀρτέμωνα, acc. sg. m. n. (Acts 27:40, GNT, WH & NA | ἀρτέμονα, MT & TR) . . . . ἀρτέμων (736)

(737) ἄρτι, adv., of time, pr. *at the present moment, close upon it either before or after; now, at the present juncture,* Matt. 3:15; *forthwith, presently; just now, recently,* 1 Thess. 3:6; ἕως ἄρτι, *until now, hitherto,* Matt. 11:12; John 2:10, et al.; ἀπ᾽ ἄρτι, or ἀπάρτι, *from this time, henceforth,* Matt. 23:39; et al.

ἀρτιγέννητα, nom. pl. neut. adj. . ἀρτιγέννητος (738)

(738) ἀρτιγέννητος, ον [§7.2] (ἄρτι + γεννάω) *just born, new-born,* 1 Pet. 2:2

(739) ἄρτιος, α, ον, nom. sg. m. adj. [§7.2] (ἄρω, *to fit, adapt) entirely suited; complete* in accomplishment, *ready,* 2 Tim. 3:17

ἄρτοι, nom. pl. m. n. . . . . ἄρτος (740)

ἄρτοις, dat. pl. m. n. . . . . id.

ἄρτον, acc. sg. m. n. . . . . id.

(740) ἄρτος, ου, ὁ, nom. sg. m. n. [§3.C.a] *bread; a loaf* or *thin cake of bread,* Matt. 26:26; et al.; *food,* Matt. 15:2; Mark 3:20, et al.; *bread, maintenance, living, necessaries of life,* Matt. 6:11; Luke 11:3; 2 Thess. 3:8

ἄρτου, gen. sg. m. n. . . . . ἄρτος (740)

ἄρτους, acc. pl. m. n. . . . . id.

ἀρτυθήσεται, 3 pers. sg. fut. pass. indic. ἀρτύω (741)

ἀρτύσετε, 2 pers. pl. fut. act. indic. . . . . id.

(741) ἀρτύω (or ἀρτύνω) fut. ἀρτύσω [§13.M] fut. pass. ἀρτυθήσομαι, perf. pass. ἤρτυμαι (ἄρω, *to fit) pr. to fit, prepare; to season, make savoury,* Mark 9:50; Luke 14:34; Col. 4:6

ἄρτῳ, dat. sg. m. n. . . . . ἄρτος (740)

ἄρτων, gen. pl. m. n. . . . . id.

(742) Ἀρφαξάδ, ὁ, *Arphaxad,* pr. name, indecl., Luke 3:36

(743) ἀρχάγγελος, ου, ὁ, nom. sg. m. n. [§3.C.a] (ἀρχή + ἄγγελος) *an archangel, chief angel,* 1 Thess. 4:16; Jude 9

ἀρχαγγέλου, gen. sg. m. n. . . . . . . ἀρχάγγελος (743)

ἀρχαί, nom. pl. f. n. . . . . ἀρχή (746)

ἀρχαῖα, nom. pl. neut. adj. . . . . ἀρχαῖος (744)

ἀρχαίοις, dat. pl. m. adj. . . . . id.

ἀρχαῖον, acc. sg. m. adj. (Rev. 20:2, MT & TR | ἀρχαῖος, GNT, WH & NA) . . . . id.

(744) ἀρχαῖος, αία, αῖον, nom. sg. m. adj. [§7.1] *old,*

ancient, of former age, Matt. 5:21, 27, 33, et al.; of long standing, old, veteran, Acts 21:16; ἀφήμερῶν ἀρχαίων, from early days, from an early period, of the Gospel, Acts 15:7

ἀρχαίου, gen. sg. m. adj. . . . . ἀρχαῖος (744)

ἀρχαῖς, dat. pl. m. n. . . . . ἀρχή (746)

ἀρχαίῳ, dat. sg. m. adj. . . . . ἀρχαῖος (744)

ἀρχαίων, gen. pl. m. adj. {Luke 9:19} . . . id.

ἀρχαίων, gen. pl. f. adj. {Acts 15:7} . . . . . id.

ἀρχάς, acc. pl. f. n. . . . . ἀρχή (746)

ἄρχειν, pres. act. infin. . . . . ἄρχω (757)

(745) Ἀρχέλαος, ου, ὁ, nom. sg. m. n. [§3.C.a] Archelaus, pr. name, Matt. 2:22

(746) ἀρχή, ῆς, ἡ, nom. sg. f. n. [§2.B.a] a beginning, Matt. 24:8, et al.; an extremity, corner, or, an attached cord, Acts 10:11; 11:5; first place, headship; high estate, eminence, Jude 6; authority, Luke 20:20, et al.; an authority, magistrate, Luke 12:11; a principality, prince, of spiritual existence, Eph. 3:10; 6:12, et al.; ἀπ᾽ ἀρχῆς, ἐξ ἀρχῆς, from the first, originally, Matt. 19:4, 8; Luke 1:2; John 6:64; 2 Thess. 2:13; 1 John 1:1; 2:7, et al.; ἐν ἀρχῇ, κατ᾽ ἀρχάς, in the beginning of things, John 1:1, 2; Heb. 1:10; ἐν ἀρχῇ, at the first, Acts 11:15; τὴν ἀρχήν, used adverbially, wholly, altogether, John 8:25

ἀρχῇ, dat. sg. f. n. . . . . ἀρχή (746)

ἀρχηγόν, acc. sg. m. n. . . . . ἀρχηγός (747)

(747) ἀρχηγός, οῦ, ὁ [§3.C.a] (ἀρχή + ἄγω) a chief, leader, prince, Acts 5:31; a prime author, Acts 3:15; Heb. 2:10; 12:2

ἀρχήν, acc. sg. f. n. . . . . ἀρχή (746)

ἀρχῆς, gen. sg. f. n. . . . . id.

(748) ἀρχιερατικός, όν [§7.2] pontifical, belonging to or connected with the high-priest or his office, Acts 4:6

ἀρχιερατικοῦ, gen. sg. neut. adj. ἀρχιερατικός (748)

ἀρχιερέα, acc. sg. m. n. . . . . ἀρχιερεύς (749)

ἀρχιερεῖ, dat. sg. m. n. . . . . id.

ἀρχιερεῖς, nom. pl. m. n. {Matt. 21:15} . . id.

ἀρχιερεῖς, acc. pl. m. n. {Matt. 2:4} . . . . . id.

(749) ἀρχιερεύς, έως, ὁ, nom. sg. m. n. [§5.E.d] (ἀρχή + ἱερεύς) a high-priest, chief-priest

ἀρχιερεῦσι(ν), acc. pl. m. n. . . . . . . ἀρχιερεύς (749)

ἀρχιερέων, gen. pl. m. n. . . . . id.

ἀρχιερέως, gen. sg. m. n. . . . . id.

ἀρχιποίμενος, gen. sg. m. n.

[§4.2.e] . . . . ἀρχιποίμην (750)

(750) ἀρχιποίμην, ενος, ὁ (ἀρχή + ποιμήν) chief shepherd, 1 Pet. 5:4

(751) Ἄρχιππος, ου, ὁ, Archippus, pr. name

Ἀρχίππῳ, dat. sg. m. n. . . . . Ἄρχιππος (751)

ἀρχισυνάγωγοι, nom. pl. m. n. ἀρχισυνάγωγος (752)

ἀρχισυνάγωγον, acc. sg. m. n. . . . . id.

(752) ἀρχισυνάγωγος, ου, ὁ, nom. sg. m. n. [§3.C.a] (ἀρχή + συναγωγή) a president or moderating elder of a synagogue, Mark 5:22, 35, 36, 38; Luke 8:49, et al.

ἀρχισυναγώγου, gen. sg. m. n. ἀρχισυνάγωγος (752)

ἀρχισυναγώγῳ, dat. sg. m. n. . . . . id.

ἀρχισυναγώγων, gen. pl. m. n. . . . . id.

(753) ἀρχιτέκτων, ονος, ὁ, nom. sg. m. n. [§4.2.e] (ἀρχή + τέκτων) architect, head or master-builder, 1 Cor. 3:10

(754) ἀρχιτελώνης, ου, ὁ, nom. sg. m. n. [§2.B.d] (ἀρχή + τελώνης) a chief publican, chief collector of the customs or taxes, Luke 19:2

(755) ἀρχιτρίκλινος, ου, ὁ, nom. sg. m. n. [§3.C.a] (ἀρχή + τρίκλινος, triclinium, a diningroom in which three couches were placed round the table, etc.) director of a feast, John 2:8, 9

ἀρχιτρικλίνῳ, dat. sg. m. n. . . . ἀρχιτρίκλινος (755)

ἀρχόμεθα, 1 pers. pl. pres. mid. indic. . . ἄρχω (757)

ἀρχόμενος, nom. sg. m. pres. mid. part. . . id.

ἀρχομένων, gen. pl. m. pres. mid. part. . . id.

ἄρχοντα, acc. sg. m. n. . . . . ἄρχων (758)

ἄρχοντας, acc. pl. m. n. . . . . id.

ἄρχοντες, nom. pl. m. n. {Acts 3:17} . . . . id.

ἄρχοντες, voc. pl. m. n. {Acts 4:8} . . . . . . id.

ἄρχοντι, dat. sg. m. n. . . . . id.

ἄρχοντος, gen. sg. m. n. . . . . id.

ἀρχόντων, gen. pl. m. n. . . . . id.

ἄρχουσιν, dat. pl. m. n. . . . . id.

(757) ἄρχω, fut. ἄρξω [§23.1.b] pr. to be first; to govern, Mark 10:42; Rom. 15:12; mid. to begin, Matt. 4:17; et al.; to take commencement, Luke 24:27; 1 Pet. 4:17

(758) ἄρχων, οντος, ὁ, nom. sg. m. n. [§4.2.d] one invested with power and dignity, chief, ruler, prince, magistrate, Matt. 9:23; 20:25, et al.

ἀρῶ, 1 pers. sg. fut. act. indic. [§27.1.c] . . αἴρω (142)

(759) ἄρωμα, ατος, τό [§4.D.c] an aromatic substance, spice, etc. Mark 16:1; Luke 23:56; 24:1 John 19:40

ἀρώματα, acc. pl. neut. n. . . . . ἄρωμα (759)

ἀρωμάτων, gen. pl. neut. n. . . . . id.

ἅς, acc. pl. f. relative pron. [§10.J.g] . . . . . ὅς (3739)

(760) Ἀσά, ὁ, Asa, pr. name indecl. (Matt. 1:7, 8, MT & TR | Ἀσάφ, GNT, WH & NA)

ἀσάλευτον, acc. sg. f. adj. . . . . ἀσάλευτος (761)

(761) ἀσάλευτος, ον, nom. sg. f. adj. [§7.2] (ἀ + σαλεύω) unshaken, immovable, Acts 27:41; met. firm, stable, enduring, Heb. 12:28

(‡760) Ἀσάφ, ὁ, Asaph, pr. name indecl. (Matt.

1:7, 8, GNT, WH & NA | Ἀσά, MT & TR)

ἄσβεστον, acc. sg. neut. adj. . . . . ἄσβεστος *(762)*

(762) **ἄσβεστος,** ον [§7.2] (ἀ + σβέννυμι) *unquenched; inextinguishable, unquenchable,* Matt. 3:12; Mark 9:43, 45; Luke 3:17

ἀσβέστῳ, dat. sg. neut. adj. . . . . ἄσβεστος *(762)*

(763) **ἀσέβεια,** ας, ἡ [§2.B.b; 2.2] *impiety, ungodliness; dishonesty, wickedness,* Rom. 1:18; 11:26; 2 Tim. 2:16; Tit. 2:12; Jude 15, 18

ἀσέβειαν, acc. sg. f. n. . . . . ἀσέβεια *(763)*

ἀσεβείας, gen. sg. f. n. {2 Tim. 2:16} . . . . id.

ἀσεβείας, acc. pl. f. n. {Rom. 11:26} . . . . id.

ἀσεβεῖν, pres. act. infin. (2 Pet. 2:6, MT & TRs | ἀσεβέσιν, GNT, WH & NA) ἀσεβέω *(764)*

ἀσεβεῖς, nom. pl. m. adj. . . . . ἀσεβής *(765)*

ἀσεβειῶν, gen. pl. f. n. . . . . ἀσέβεια *(763)*

ἀσεβέσι(ν), dat. pl. m. adj. . . . . ἀσεβής *(765)*

(764) **ἀσεβέω,** ῶ, fut. ἀσεβήσω [§16.P] perf. ἠσέβηκα, aor. ἠσέβησα, *to be impious, to act impiously* or *wickedly, live an impious life,* 2 Pet. 2:6; Jude 15

ἀσεβῆ, acc. sg. m. adj. . . . . ἀσεβής *(765)*

(765) **ἀσεβής,** ές, nom. sg. m. adj. [§7.G.b] (ἀ + σέβομαι) *impious, ungodly; wicked, sinful,* Rom. 4:5; 5:6, et al.

ἀσεβῶν, gen. pl. m. adj. . . . . ἀσεβής *(765)*

(766) **ἀσέλγεια,** ας, ἡ, nom. sg. f. n. [§2.B.b; 2.2] (ἀσελγής, *outrageous*) *intemperance; licentiousness, lasciviousness,* Rom. 13:13, et al.; *insolence, outrageous behavior,* Mark 7:22

ἀσελγείᾳ, dat. sg. f. n. . . . . ἀσέλγεια *(766)*

ἀσελγείαις, dat. pl. f. n. . . . . id.

ἀσέλγειαν, acc. sg. f. n. . . . . id.

(767) **ἄσημος,** ον [§7.2] (ἀ + σῆμα) pr. *not marked;* met. *not noted, not remarkable, unknown to fame, ignoble, mean, inconsiderable,* Acts 21:39

ἀσήμου, gen. sg. f. adj. . . . . ἄσημος *(767)*

(768) **Ἀσήρ,** ὁ, *Aser,* pr. name, indecl.

ἀσθενεῖ, 3 pers. sg. pres. act. indic. . . . ἀσθενέω *(770)*

(769) **ἀσθένεια,** ας, ἡ, nom. sg. f. n. [§2.B.b; 2.2] *want of strength, weakness, feebleness,* 1 Cor. 15:43; bodily *infirmity, state of ill health, sickness,* Matt. 8:17; Luke 5:15, et al.; met. *infirmity, frailty, imperfection,* intellectual and moral, Rom. 6:19; 1 Cor. 2:3; Heb. 5:2; 7:28; *suffering, affliction, distress, calamity,* Rom. 8:26, et al.

ἀσθενείᾳ, dat. sg. f. n. . . . . ἀσθένεια *(769)*

ἀσθενείαις, dat. pl. f. n. . . . . id.

ἀσθένειαν, acc. sg. f. n. . . . . id.

ἀσθενείας, gen. sg. f. n. {Luke 13:12} . . . . id.

ἀσθενείας, acc. pl. f. n. {Luke 13:11} . . . . id.

ἀσθενεῖς, nom. pl. m. adj. {1 Cor. 4:10} . . . . ἀσθενής *(772)*

ἀσθενεῖς, acc. pl. m. adj. {1 Cor. 9:22} . . . id.

ἀσθενειῶν, gen. pl. f. n. . . . . ἀσθένεια *(769)*

ἀσθενές, nom. sg. neut. adj. {1 Cor. 1:25} . . . . ἀσθενής *(772)*

ἀσθενές, acc. sg. neut. adj. {Heb. 7:18} . . id.

ἀσθενέσιν, dat. pl. m. adj. . . . . id.

ἀσθενέστερα, nom. pl. neut. compar. adj. [§8.1] . . . . id.

ἀσθενεστέρῳ, dat. sg. neut. compar. adj. . id.

(770) **ἀσθενέω,** ῶ, fut. ἀσθενήσω [§16.P] aor. ἠσθένησα, *to be weak, infirm, deficient in strength; to be inefficient,* Rom. 8:3; 2 Cor. 13:3; *to be sick,* Matt. 25:36, et al.; met. *to be weak* in faith, *to doubt, hesitate, be unsettled, timid,* Rom. 14:1; 1 Cor. 8:9, 11, 12; 2 Cor. 11:29; *to be deficient in authority, dignity,* or *power, be contemptible,* 2 Cor. 11:21; 13:3, 9; *to be afflicted, distressed, needy,* Acts 20:35; 2 Cor. 12:10; 13:4, 9

ἀσθενῆ, acc. sg. m. adj. {Matt. 25:44} ἀσθενής *(772)*

ἀσθενῆ, acc. pl. neut. adj. {1 Cor. 1:27} . . id.

(771) **ἀσθένημα,** ατος, τό [§4.D.c] pr. *weakness, infirmity,* met. *doubt, scruple, hesitation,* Rom. 15:1

ἀσθενήματα, acc. pl. neut. n. . . . . . . ἀσθένημα *(771)*

(772) **ἀσθενής,** ές, nom. sg. m. adj. [§7.4.a] (ἀ + σθένος, *strength*) *without strength, weak, infirm,* Matt. 26:41; Mark 14:38; 1 Pet. 3:7; *helpless,* Rom. 5:6; *imperfect, inefficient,* Gal. 4:9; *feeble, without energy,* 2 Cor. 10:10; *infirm* in body, *sick, sickly,* Matt. 25:39, 43, 44, et al.; *weak,* mentally or spiritually, *dubious, hesitating,* 1 Cor. 8:7, 10; 9:22; 1 Thess. 5:14; *afflicted, distressed, oppressed with calamities,* 1 Cor. 4:10 {Matt. 25:43}

ἀσθενής, nom. sg. f. adj. {Matt. 26:41} . . . . ἀσθενής *(772)*

ἀσθενήσας, nom. sg. m. aor. act. part. ἀσθενέω *(770)*

ἀσθενήσασαν, acc. sg. f. aor. act. part. . . . id.

ἀσθενοῦμεν, 1 pers. pl. pres. act. indic. . . id.

ἀσθενοῦντα, acc. sg. m. pres. act. part. . . id.

ἀσθενοῦντας, acc. pl. m. pres. act. part. . . id.

ἀσθενούντων, gen. pl. m. pres. act. part. . id.

ἀσθενοῦς, gen. sg. m. adj. . . . . ἀσθενής *(772)*

ἀσθενοῦσαν, acc. sg. f. pres. act. part. ἀσθενέω *(770)*

ἀσθενοῦσιν, dat. pl. m. pres. act. part. (1 Cor. 8:9, MT & TR | ἀσθενέσιν, GNT, WH & NA) . . . . id.

ἀσθενῶ, 1 pers. sg. pres. act. indic. {2 Cor. 11:29} . . . . id.

ἀσθενῶ, 1 pers. sg. pres. act. subj.

{2 Cor. 12:10} . . . . ἀσθενέω (770)

ἀσθενῶμεν, 1 pers. pl. pres. act. subj. . . . . id.

ἀσθενῶν, nom. sg. m. pres. act. part.
{Rom. 14:2} . . . . id.

ἀσθενῶν, gen. pl. m. adj. {Rom. 5:6} . ἀσθενής (772)

(773) Ἀσία, ας, ἡ, nom. sg. f. n. [§2.B.b; 2.2] (unless
it be the f. adj. γῆ being understood) Asia,
the Roman province, Acts 19:27

Ἀσίᾳ, dat. sg. f. n. . . . . Ἀσία (773)

Ἀσίαν, acc. sg. f. n. . . . . id.

Ἀσιανοί, nom. pl. m. n. . . . . Ἀσιανός (774)

(774) Ἀσιανός, οῦ, ὁ [§3.C.a] belonging to the Roman province of Asia, Acts 20:4

(775) Ἀσιάρχης, ου, ὁ [§2.B.c] (Ἀσία + ἀρχή) an
Asiarch, an officer in the province of Asia,
as in other eastern provinces of the Roman empire, selected, with others, from the
more opulent citizens, to preside over the
things pertaining to religious worship, and
to exhibit annual public games at their own
expense in honor of the gods, in the manner of the aediles at Rome, Acts 19:31

Ἀσιαρχῶν, gen. pl. m. n. . . . . Ἀσιάρχης (775)

Ἀσίας, gen. sg. f. n. . . . . Ἀσία (773)

(776) ἀσιτία, ας, ἡ [§2.B.b; 2.2] abstinence from
food, fasting, Acts 27:21

ἀσιτίας, gen. sg. f. n. . . . . ἀσιτία (776)

ἄσιτοι, nom. pl. m. adj. . . . . ἄσιτος (777)

(777) ἄσιτος, ον [§7.2] (ἀ + σῖτος) abstaining from
food, fasting, Acts 27:33

(778) ἀσκέω, ῶ, fut. ἀσκήσω [§16.P] pr. to work
materials; absol. to train or exert one's self,
make endeavor, Acts 24:16

ἀσκοί, nom. pl. m. n. . . . . ἀσκός (779)

(779) ἀσκός, οῦ, ὁ [§3.C.a] a leathern bag or bottle, bottle of skin, Matt. 9:17; Mark 2:22;
Luke 5:37, 38

ἀσκούς, acc. pl. m. n. . . . . ἀσκός (779)

ἀσκῶ, 1 pers. sg. pres. act. indic. contr. ἀσκέω (778)

(780) ἀσμένως, adv., gladly, joyfully, Acts 2:41;
21:17

ἄσοφοι, nom. pl. m. adj. . . . . ἄσοφος (781)

(781) ἄσοφος, ον [§7.2] (ἀ + σοφός) unwise; destitute of Christian wisdom, Eph. 5:15

ἀσπάζεσθαι, pres. mid./pass. dep.
infin. . . . . ἀσπάζομαι (782)

ἀσπάζεται, 3 pers. sg. pres. mid./pass. dep.
indic. . . . . id.

(782) ἀσπάζομαι, 1 pers. sg. pres. mid./pass. dep.
indic., fut. ἀσπάσομαι [§26.1] aor.
ἠσπασάμην, perf. ἤσπασμαι, to salute,
greet, welcome, express good wishes, pay
respects, Matt. 10:12; Mark 9:15; et al.
freq.; to bid farewell, Acts 20:1; 21:6; to
treat with affection, Matt. 5:47; met. to

embrace mentally, welcome to the heart of
understanding, Heb. 11:13

ἀσπάζονται, 3 pers. pl. pres. mid./pass. dep.
indic. . . . . ἀσπάζομαι (782)

ἀσπάζου, 2 pers. sg. pres. mid./pass. dep.
imper. . . . . id.

ἄσπασαι, 2 pers. sg. aor. mid. dep. imper. id.

ἀσπασάμενοι, nom. pl. m. aor. mid. dep.
part. . . . . id.

ἀσπασάμενος, nom. sg. m. aor. mid. dep.
part. . . . . id.

ἀσπάσασθε, 2 pers. pl. aor. mid. dep. imper. id.

ἀσπάσησθε, 2 pers. pl. aor. mid. dep. subj. id.

ἀσπασμόν, acc. sg. m. n. . . . . ἀσπασμός (783)

(783) ἀσπασμός, οῦ, ὁ, nom. sg. m. n. [§3.C.a] sal-
utation, greeting, Matt. 23:7; Mark 12:38,
et al.

ἀσπασμοῦ, gen. sg. m. n. . . . . ἀσπασμός (783)

ἀσπασμούς, acc. pl. m. n. . . . . id.

ἀσπασόμενοι, nom. pl. m. fut. mid. dep. part.
(Acts 25:13, TR | ἀσπασάμενοι, GNT,
WH, MT & NA) . . . . id.

ἀσπίδων, gen. pl. f. n. [§4.2.c] . . . . ἀσπίς (785)

ἄσπιλοι, nom. pl. m. adj. . . . . ἄσπιλος (784)

ἄσπιλον, acc. sg. m. adj. {James 1:27} . . . id.

ἄσπιλον, acc. sg. f. adj. {1 Tim. 6:14} . . . id.

(784) ἄσπιλος, ον [§7.2] (ἀ + σπίλος) spotless, un-
blemished, pure, 1 Tim. 6:14; James 1:27;
1 Pet. 1:19; 2 Pet. 3:14

ἀσπίλου, gen. sg. m. adj. . . . . ἄσπιλος (784)

(785) ἀσπίς, ίδος, ἡ, an asp, a species of serpent of
the most deadly venom, Rom. 3:13

ἄσπονδοι, nom. pl. m. adj. . . . . ἄσπονδος (786)

(786) ἄσπονδος, ον [§7.2] (ἀ + σπονδή, a libation
usually conjoined with the making of a
treaty) pr. unwilling to make a treaty;
hence, implacable, irreconcilable, Rom.
1:31; 2 Tim. 3:3

ἀσπόνδους, acc. pl. m. adj. (Rom. 1:31, MT
& TR | GNT, WH & NA omit) . ἄσπονδος (786)

(787) ἀσσάριον, ου, τό [§3.C.c] dimin. of the Latin
as, a Roman brass coin of the value of one-
tenth of a denarius, or δραχμή, used to
convey the idea of a trifle or very small
sum, like the term a mil (equals one-tenth
of a cent) Matt. 10:29; Luke 12:6

ἀσσαρίου, gen. sg. neut. n. . . . . ἀσσάριον (787)

ἀσσαρίων, gen. pl. neut. n. . . . . id.

(‡4565) Ἀσσάρων, ωνος, ὁ, Saron, a level tract of Palestine, between Caesarea and Joppa

Ἀσσάρωνα, acc. pl. m. n. (Acts 9:35, MT |
Σαρῶνα, GNT, WH & NA | Σάρωνα,
TRb | Σαρωνᾶν, TRs) . . . . Ἀσσάρων (‡4565)

(788) ἆσσον, adv., nearer; very nigh, close; used as
the compar. of ἄγχι {Acts 27:13}

Ἆσσον, acc. sg. f. n. {Acts 20:13, 14} . Ἆσσος *(789)*

(789) Ἆσσος, ου, ἡ [§3.C.b] *Assos, a maritime city of Mysia, in Asia Minor, Acts 20:13, 14*

(790) ἀστατέω, ῶ, fut. ἀστατήσω [§16.P] (ἄστατος, *unfixed, unstable,* from ἀ + ἵστημι) *to be unsettled, to be a wanderer, be homeless,* 1 Cor. 4:11

ἀστατοῦμεν, 1 pers. pl. pres. act. indic. . . . . ἀστατέω *(790)*

ἀστεῖον, acc. sg. neut. adj. . . . . ἀστεῖος *(791)*

(791) ἀστεῖος, α, ον, nom. sg. m. adj. [§7.1] (ἄστυ, *a city*) pr. *belonging to a city; well bred, polite, polished;* hence, *elegant, fair, comely, beautiful,* Acts 7:20; Heb. 11:23

ἀστέρα, acc. sg. m. n. . . . . ἀστήρ *(792)*
ἀστέρας, acc. pl. m. n. . . . . id.
ἀστέρες, nom. pl. m. n. . . . . id.
ἀστέρος, gen. sg. m. n. [§4.2.f] . . . . id.
ἀστέρων, gen. pl. m. n. . . . . id.

(792) ἀστήρ, έρος, ὁ, nom. sg. m. n. [§6.4.c] *a star, luminous body like a star, luminary,* Matt. 2:2, 7, 9, 10; Rev. 1:16, et al.

ἀστήρικτοι, nom. pl. m. adj. . . . . . ἀστήρικτος *(793)*

(793) ἀστήρικτος, ον [§7.2] (ἀ + στηρίζω) *not made firm; unsettled, unstable, unsteady,* 2 Pet. 2:14; 3:16

ἀστηρίκτους, acc. pl. f. adj. . . . . . . ἀστήρικτος *(793)*
ἄστοργοι, nom. pl. m. adj. . . . . ἄστοργος *(794)*

(794) ἄστοργος, ον [§7.2] (ἀ + στοργή, *natural or instinctive affection*) *devoid of natural or instinctive affection, without affection to kindred,* Rom. 1:31; 2 Tim. 3:3

ἀστόργους, acc. pl. m. adj. . . . . ἄστοργος *(794)*

(795) ἀστοχέω, ῶ, fut. ἀστοχήσω [§16.P] aor. ἠστόχησα (ἀ + στόχος, *a mark*) pr. *to miss the mark;* met. *to err, deviate, swerve from,* 1 Tim. 1:6; 6:21; 2 Tim. 2:18

ἀστοχήσαντες, nom. pl. m. aor. act. part. . . . . ἀστοχέω *(795)*

ἄστρα, nom. pl. neut. n. . . . . ἄστρον *(798)*
ἀστραπαί, nom. pl. f. n. . . . . ἀστραπή *(796)*

(796) ἀστραπή, ῆς, ἡ, nom. sg. f. n. [§2.B.a] *lightning,* Matt. 24:27; *brightness, lustre,* Luke 11:36

ἀστραπῇ, dat. sg. f. n. . . . . ἀστραπή *(796)*
ἀστραπήν, acc. sg. f. n. . . . . id.
ἀστράπτουσα, nom. sg. f. pres. act. part. . . . . ἀστράπτω *(797)*
ἀστραπτούσαις, dat. pl. f. pres. act. part. (Luke 24:4, MT & TR | ἀστραπτούσῃ, GNT, WH & NA) . . . . id.
ἀστραπτούσῃ, 3 pers. sg. aor. act. subj. (Luke 24:4, GNT, WH & NA | ἀστραπτούσαις, MT & TR) . . . . id.

(797) ἀστράπτω, fut. ἀστράψω [§23.1.a] *to lighten,*

flash as lightning, Luke 17:24; *to be bright, shining,* Luke 24:4

ἄστροις, dat. pl. neut. n. . . . . ἄστρον *(798)*

(798) ἄστρον, ου, τό [§3.C.c] *a constellation; a star,* Luke 21:25; Acts 7:43; 27:20; Heb. 11:12

ἄστρον, acc. sg. neut. n. . . . . ἄστρον *(798)*
ἄστρων, gen. pl. neut. n. . . . . id.

Ἀσύγκριτον, acc. sg. m. n. (Rom 16:14, GNT, MT, TR & NA | Ἀσύνκριτον, WH) . . . . Ἀσύγκριτος *(799)*

(799) Ἀσύγκριτος, ου, ὁ, *Asyncritus,* pr. name, Rom. 16:14

ἀσύμφωνοι, nom. pl. m. adj. . . . . . ἀσύμφωνος *(800)*

(800) ἀσύμφωνος, ον [§7.2] (ἀ + σύμφωνος) *discordant in sound;* met. *discordant, at difference,* Acts 28:25

ἀσύνετοι, nom. pl. m. adj. . . . . ἀσύνετος *(801)*

(801) ἀσύνετος, ον [§7.2] (ἀ + συνετός from συνίημι) *unintelligent, dull,* Matt. 15:16; Mark 7:18; *reckless, perverse,* Rom. 1:21, 31; *unenlightened, heathenish,* Rom. 10:19

ἀσύνετος, nom. sg. f. adj. . . . . ἀσύνετος *(801)*
ἀσυνέτους, acc. pl. m. adj. . . . . id.
ἀσυνέτῳ, dat. sg. neut. adj. . . . . id.

(802) ἀσύνθετος, ον [§7.2] (ἀ + συντίθεμαι, *to make a covenant*) *regardless of covenants, perfidious,* Rom. 1:31

ἀσυνθέτους, acc. pl. m. adj. . . . . . . ἀσύνθετος *(802)*

(803) ἀσφάλεια, ας, ἡ, nom. sg. f. n. [§2.B.b; 2.2] pr. *state of security from falling, firmness; safety, security,* 1 Thess. 5:3; *certainty, truth,* Luke 1:4; *means of security,* Acts 5:23

ἀσφαλείᾳ, dat. sg. f. n. . . . . ἀσφάλεια *(803)*
ἀσφάλειαν, acc. sg. f. n. . . . . id.
ἀσφαλές, nom. sg. neut. adj. {Phil. 3:1} . . . . ἀσφαλής *(804)*
ἀσφαλές, acc. sg. neut. adj. {Acts 21:34} . id.
ἀσφαλῆ, acc. sg. f. adj. . . . . id.

(804) ἀσφαλής, ές [§7.G.b] (ἀ + σφάλλομαι, *to stumble, fall*) pr. *firm, secure from falling; firm, sure, steady, immovable,* Heb. 6:19; met. *certain, sure,* Acts 21:34; 22:30; 25:26; *safe, making secure,* Phil. 3:1

(805) ἀσφαλίζω, fut. ἀσφαλίσω [§26.1] *to make fast, safe,* or *secure,* Matt. 27:64, 65, 66; Acts 16:24

ἀσφαλίσασθε, 2 pers. pl. aor. mid. dep. imper. ἀσφαλίζω *(805)*
ἀσφαλισθῆναι, aor. pass. infin. . . . . id.

(806) ἀσφαλῶς, adv., *securely, safely; without fail, safely,* Mark 14:44; Acts 16:23; *certainly, assuredly,* Acts 2:36

ἀσχήμονα, nom. pl. neut. adj. . . . . . . ἀσχήμων *(809)*

ἀσχημονεῖ, 3 pers. sg. pres. act.
indic. ἀσχημονέω *(807)*
ἀσχημονεῖν, pres. act. infin. . . . . id.

(807) **ἀσχημονέω**, ῶ, fut. ἀσχημονήσω [§16.P] *to behave in an unbecoming manner or indecorously*, 1 Cor. 13:5; *to behave in a manner open to censure*, 1 Cor. 7:36

(808) **ἀσχημοσύνη**, ης, ἡ [§2.B.a] pr. *external indecorum; nakedness, shame, pudenda*, Rev. 16:15; *indecency, infamous lust* or *lewdness*, Rom. 1:27
ἀσχημοσύνην, acc. sg. f. n. . . . . . ἀσχημοσύνη *(808)*

(809) **ἀσχήμων**, ον [§7.G.a] (ἀ + σχῆμα) *indecorous, uncomely, indecent*, 1 Cor. 12:23

(810) **ἀσωτία**, ας, ἡ, nom. sg. f. n. [§2.B.b; 2.2] (pr. *the disposition and life of one who is* ἄσωτος, *abandoned, recklessly debauched*) *profligacy, dissoluteness, debauchery*, Eph. 5:18; Tit. 1:6; 1 Pet. 4:4
ἀσωτίας, gen. sg. f. n. . . . . ἀσωτία *(810)*

(811) **ἀσώτως**, adv., *dissolutely, profligately*, Luke 15:13

(812) **ἀτακτέω**, ῶ, fut. ἀτακτήσω [§16.P] pr. *to infringe* military *order*; met. *to be irregular, behave disorderly*, 2 Thess. 3:7

(813) **ἄτακτος**, ον [§7.2] (ἀ + τάσσω) pr. used of soldiers, *disorderly*; met. *irregular* in conduct, *disorderly*, 1 Thess. 5:14
ἀτάκτους, acc. pl. m. adj. . . . . ἄτακτος *(813)*

(814) **ἀτάκτως**, adv., *disorderly*, 2 Thess. 3:6, 11

(815) **ἄτεκνος**, ον, nom. sg. m. adj. [§7.2] (ἀ + τέκνον) *childless*, Luke 20:28, 29, 30
ἀτενίζετε, 2 pers. pl. pres. act. indic. . . ἀτενίζω *(816)*
ἀτενίζοντες, nom. pl. m. pres. act. part. . . id.

(816) **ἀτενίζω**, fut. ἀτενίσω, aor. ἠτένισα [§26.1] (ἀτενής, *intent*) *to fix one's eyes upon, look steadily, gaze intently*, Luke 4:20, et al.
ἀτενίσαι, aor. act. infin. . . . . ἀτενίζω *(816)*
ἀτενίσαντες, nom. pl. m. aor. act. part. . . id.
ἀτενίσας, nom. sg. m. aor. act. part. . . . . id.
ἀτενίσασα, nom. sg. f. aor. act. part. . . . . id.

(817) **ἀτέρ**, prep. with gen. *without*, Luke 22:6, 35
ἀτιμάζεις, 2 pers. sg. pres. act. indic. . ἀτιμάζω *(818)*
ἀτιμάζεσθαι, pres. mid./pass. infin. . . . . . id.
ἀτιμάζετε, 2 pers. pl. pres. act. indic. . . . . id.

(818) **ἀτιμάζω**, fut. ἀτιμάσω [§26.1] aor. ἠτίμασα, aor. pass. ἠτιμάσθην, *to dishonor, slight*, John 8:49; Rom. 2:23; James 2:6; *to treat with contumely* or *indignity*, Luke 20:11; Acts 5:41; *to abuse, debase*, Rom. 1:24
ἀτιμάσαντες, nom. pl. m. aor. act.
part. . . . . ἀτιμάζω *(818)*
ἀτιμασθῆναι, aor. pass. infin. . . . . id.

(‡821) **ἀτιμάω**, ῶ, fut. ἀτιμήσω [§18.R] *to dishonor*

(819) **ἀτιμία**, ας, ἡ, nom. sg. f. n. [§2.B.b; 2.2] *dis-*

honor, infamy, Rom. 1:26; *indecorum*, 1 Cor. 11:14; *meanness, vileness*, 1 Cor. 15:43; 2 Cor. 6:8; *a mean use*, Rom. 9:21; 2 Tim. 2:20; κατὰ ἀτιμίαν, *slightingly, disparagingly*, 2 Cor. 11:21
ἀτιμίᾳ, dat. sg. f. n. . . . . ἀτιμία *(819)*
ἀτιμίαν, acc. sg. f. n. . . . . id.
ἀτιμίας, gen. sg. f. n. . . . . id.
ἄτιμοι, nom. pl. m. adj. . . . . ἄτιμος *(820)*

(820) **ἄτιμος**, ον, nom. sg. m. adj. [§7.2] (ἀ + τιμή) *unhonored, without honor*, Matt. 13:57; Mark 6:4; *ignoble*, 1 Cor. 4:10; 12:23
ἀτιμότερα, acc. pl. neut. compar. adj. . . ἄτιμος *(820)*

(821) **ἀτιμόω**, ῶ [§20.T] perf. pass. ἠτίμωμαι, *to dishonor; to outrage*, Mark 12:4
ἄτινα, nom. pl. neut. relative pron.
[§10.J.h] . . . . ὅστις *(3748)*
ἀτμίδα, acc. sg. f. n. . . . . ἀτμίς *(822)*

(822) **ἀτμίς**, ίδος, ἡ, nom. sg. f. n. [§4.2.d] *an exhalation, vapor, smoke* Acts 2:19; James 4:14

(823) **ἄτομος**, ον [§7.2] (ἀ + τέμνω) *indivisible*, and by impl. *exceedingly minute*; ἐν ἀτόμῳ, sc. χρόνῳ, *in an indivisible point of time, in an instant* or *moment*, 1 Cor. 15:52
ἀτόμῳ, dat. sg. neut. adj. . . . . ἄτομος *(823)*
ἄτοπον, nom. sg. neut. adj. (Acts 25:5, GNT, WH & NA | τούτῳ, MT & TR) . . ἄτοπος *(824)*
ἄτοπον, acc. sg. neut. adj. {Acts 28:6} . . . id.

(824) **ἄτοπος**, ον [§7.2] (ἀ + τόπος) pr. *out of place; inopportune, unsuitable, absurd; new, unusual, strange*; in N.T. *improper, amiss, wicked*, Luke 23:41; 2 Thess. 3:2; *noxious, harmful*, Acts 28:6
ἀτόπων, gen. pl. m. adj. . . . . ἄτοπος *(824)*

(825) **Ἀττάλεια**, ας, ἡ [§2.B.b; 2.2] *Attalia*, a city of Pamphylia, Acts 14:25
Ἀττάλειαν, acc. sg. f. n. (Acts 14:25, GNT, MT, TR & NA | Ἀτταλίαν, WH) . . . . Ἀττάλεια *(825)*

(826) **αὐγάζω**, fut. αὐγάσω [§26.1] *to see distinctly, discern*, or, intrans., *to shine, give light*, 2 Cor. 4:4
αὐγάσαι, aor. act. infin. . . . . αὐγάζω *(826)*

(827) **αὐγή**, ῆς, ἡ [§2.B.a] *radiance; daybreak*, Acts 20:11
αὐγῆς, gen. sg. f. n. . . . . αὐγή *(827)*

(828) **Αὔγουστος**, ου, ὁ, Καῖσαρ, *Caesar Augustus*, Luke 2:1
Αὐγούστου, gen. sg. m. n. . . . . Αὔγουστος *(828)*
αὐθάδεις, nom. pl. m. adj. . . . . αὐθάδης *(829)*
αὐθάδη, acc. sg. m. adj. . . . . id.

(829) **αὐθάδης**, ες [§7.G.b] (αὐτός + ἥδομαι) *one who pleases himself, willful, obstinate; arrogant, imperious*, Tit. 1:7; 2 Pet. 2:10

αὐθαίρετοι, nom. pl. m. adj. . . . . . . αὐθαίρετος (830)

(830) αὐθαίρετος, ον, nom. sg. m. adj. [§7.2] (αὐτός + αἱρέομαι) pr. *one who chooses his own course of action; acting spontaneously, of one's own accord,* 2 Cor. 8:3, 17

αὐθεντεῖν, pres. act. infin. . . . . αὐθεντέω (831)

(831) αὐθεντέω, ῶ, fut. αὐθεντήσω [§16.P] (*to be* αὐθέντες, *one acting by his own authority or power,* contr. from αὐτοέντης, *one who executes with his own hand*) *to have authority over, domineer,* 1 Tim. 2:12

(832) αὐλέω, ῶ, fut. αὐλήσω [§16.P] aor. ηὔλησα, *to play on a pipe* or *flute, pipe,* Matt. 11:17; Luke 7:32; 1 Cor. 14:7

(833) αὐλή, ῆς, ἡ [§2.B.a] pr. *an unroofed enclosure; court-yard; sheepfold,* John 10:1, 16; *an exterior court,* i.q. προαύλιον, an enclosed place between the door and the street, Rev. 11:2; *an interior court, quadrangle,* the open court in the middle of Oriental houses, which are commonly built in the form of a square enclosing this court, Matt. 26:58, 69, et al.; by synec. *a house, mansion, palace,* Matt. 26:3; Luke 11:21

αὐλῇ, dat. sg. f. n. . . . . αὐλή (833)

αὐλήν, acc. sg. f. n. . . . . id.

αὐλῆς, gen. sg. f. n. . . . . id.

αὐλητάς, acc. pl. m. n. . . . . αὐλητής (834)

(834) αὐλητής, οῦ, ὁ [§2.B.c] *a player on a pipe* or *flute,* Matt. 9:23; Rev. 18:22

αὐλητῶν, gen. pl. m. n. . . . . αὐλητής (834)

(835) αὐλίζομαι, fut. αὐλίσομαι [§26.1] aor. (pass. form) ηὐλίσθην, pr. *to pass the time in a court-yard; to lodge, bivouac;* hence, *to pass the night* in any place, *to lodge at night, pass* or *remain through the night,* Matt. 21:17; Luke 21:37

(836) αὐλός, οῦ, ὁ, nom. sg. m. n. [§3.C.a] *a pipe* or *flute,* 1 Cor. 14:7

αὐλούμενον, nom. sg. neut. pres. pass. part. . . . . αὐλέω (832)

αὐξάνει, 3 pers. sg. pres. act. indic. . . . αὐξάνω (837)

αὐξάνειν, pres. act. infin. . . . . id.

αὐξάνετε, 2 pers. pl. pres. act. imper. . . . . id.

αὐξανόμενα, acc. pl. neut. pres. pass. part. (Mark 4:8, GNT, WH & NA | αὐξάνοντα, MT & TR) . . . . id.

αὐξανομένης, gen. sg. f. pres. pass. part. . id.

αὐξανόμενοι, nom. pl. m. pres. pass. part. id.

αὐξανόμενον, nom. sg. neut. pres. pass. part. (Col. 1:6, GNT, WH, MT & NA | TR omits) . . . . id.

αὐξάνοντα, acc. sg. m. pres. act. part. (Mark 4:8, TR | αὐξανόμενα, GNT, WH & NA) . . . . id.

αὐξάνουσιν, 3 pers. pl. pres. act. indic. (Matt. 6:28, GNT, WH & NA | αὐξάνει, MT & TR) . . . . αὐξάνω (837)

(837) αὐξάνω, or αὔξω, fut. αὐξήσω [§35.5] aor. ηὔξησα, aor. pass. ηὐξήθην, trans. *to cause to grow* or *increase;* pass. *to be increased, enlarged,* Matt. 13:32; 1 Cor. 3:6, 7, et al.; intrans. *to increase, grow,* Matt. 6:28; Mark 4:8, et al.

αὐξάνων, nom. sg. m. pres. act. part. . αὐξάνω (837)

αὔξει, 3 pers. sg. pres. act. indic. . . . . id.

αὐξηθῇ, 3 pers. sg. aor. pass. subj. . . . . . . id.

αὐξηθῆτε, 2 pers. pl. aor. pass. subj. . . . . id.

αὐξήσαι, 3 pers. sg. aor. act. opt. (2 Cor. 9:10, MT & TR | αὐξήσει, GNT, WH & NA) id.

αὐξήσει, 3 pers. sg. fut. act. indic. . . . . . . id.

αὔξησιν, acc. sg. f. n. . . . . αὔξησις (838)

(838) αὔξησις, εως, ἡ [§5.E.c] *increase, growth,* Eph. 4:16; Col. 2:19

αὐξήσωμεν, 1 pers. pl. aor. act. subj. . . . αὐξάνω (837)

(839) αὔριον, adv., *to-morrow,* Matt. 6:30, et al.; ἡ αὔριον, sc. ἡμέρα, *the morrow, the next day,* Matt. 6:34, et al.

(840) αὐστηρός, ά, όν, nom. sg. m. adj. [§7.1] pr. *harsh, sour in flavor;* met. *harsh, rigid, ungenerous,* Luke 19:21, 22

αὐτά, nom. pl. neut. personal pron. {John 5:36b} . . . . αὐτός (846)

αὐτά, acc. pl. neut. personal pron. {John 5:36a} . . . . id.

αὗται, nom. pl. f. demons. pron. . . . . . . οὗτος (3778)

αὐταῖς, dat. pl. f. personal pron. . . . . . . αὐτός (846)

(841) αὐτάρκεια, ας, ἡ [§2.B.b; 2.2] *a competence of the necessaries of life,* 2 Cor. 9:8; *a frame of mind viewing one's lot as sufficient, contentedness,* 1 Tim. 6:6

αὐτάρκειαν, acc. sg. f. n. . . . . . . αὐτάρκεια (841)

αὐταρκείας, gen. sg. f. n. . . . . id.

(842) αὐτάρκης, ες, nom. sg. m. adj. [§7.G.b] (αὐτός + ἀρκέω) pr. *sufficient* or *adequate in one's self; contented with one's lot,* Phil. 4:11

αὐτάς, acc. pl. f. personal pron. . . . . αὐτός (846)

αὐτή, nom. sg. f. personal pron. {Luke 2:37} id.

αὕτη, nom. sg. f. demons. pron. {Luke 2:36} . . . . οὗτος (3778)

αὗτη, contraction of ἑαυτῆς (Luke 2:37, 38; 7:12, TR | αὐτή, GNT, WH, MT & NA) . . . . ἑαυτοῦ (1438)

αὐτῇ, dat. sg. f. personal pron. . . . . αὐτός (846)

αὐτήν, acc. sg. f. personal pron. . . . . id.

αὐτῆς, gen. sg. f. personal pron. . . . . id.

αὐτό, nom. sg. neut. personal pron. {1 Cor. 12:11} . . . . id.

αὐτό, acc. sg. neut. personal pron.

{1 Cor. 12:8} . . . . αὐτός *(846)*

αὐτοί, nom. pl. m. personal pron. . . . . . . id.

αὐτοῖς, dat. pl. m. personal pron.
{John 10:25} . . . . id.

αὐτοῖς, dat. pl. neut. personal pron.
{John 10:28} . . . . id.

(843) **αὐτοκατάκριτος**, ον, nom. sg. m. adj. [§7.2]
(αὐτός + κατακρίνω) *self-condemned*,
Tit. 3:11

αὐτομάτη, nom. sg. f. adj. . . . . αὐτόματος *(844)*

(844) **αὐτόματος**, η, ον [§7.F.a] (αὐτός + μέμαα,
to be excited) self-excited, acting spontane-
ously, spontaneous, of his own accord,
Mark 4:28; Acts 12:10

αὐτόν, acc. sg. m. personal pron. . . . . . . αὐτός *(846)*

αὐτόπται, nom. pl. m. adj. . . . . αὐτόπτης *(845)*

(845) **αὐτόπτης**, ου, ὁ [§2.B.c] (αὐτό + ὄψομαι) *an*
eye-witness, Luke 1:2

(846) **αὐτός**, ή, ό, nom. sg. m. personal pron.
[§10.J.b; 10.2] a reflexive pron. *self, very;*
alone, Mark 6:31; 2 Cor. 12:13; *of one's*
self, of one's own motion, John 16:27; used
also in the oblique cases independently as
a personal pron. of the third person; ὁ
αὐτός, *the same; unchangeable,* Heb. 1:12;
κατὰ τὸ αὐτό, *at the same time, together,*
Acts 14:1; ἐπὶ τὸ αὐτό, *in one and the same*
place, Matt. 22:34; *at the same time, to-*
gether, Acts 3:1 (For a full account of the
uses of αὐτός, consult a grammar.)

αὐτοῦ, gen. sg. m. personal pron.
{Luke 9:26} . . . . αὐτός *(846)*

αὐτοῦ, gen. sg. neut. personal pron.
{John 3:8} . . . . id.

(847) **αὐτοῦ**, adv., of place, pr. *in the very place;*
here, there, in this or *that place,* Matt.
26:36; Acts 15:34; 18:19; 21:4 {Luke 9:27}

(848) **αὐτοῦ**, ῆς, οὖ, reciprocal pronoun contr. from
ἑαυτοῦ, ῆς, οὖ, *himself, herself, itself*
(Mark 12:6; John 9:21, TR | GNT, WH,
MT & NA omit in Mark 12:6 and have
ἑαυτοῦ in John 9:21)

αὐτούς, acc. pl. m. personal pron. . . . . . αὐτός *(846)*

αὐτοφώρῳ, dat. sg. m. adj. (John 8:4, GNT,
MT & NA | ἐπαυτοφώρῳ, TR | WH
omits) . . . . αὐτόφωρος *(‡1888)*

(‡1888) **αὐτόφωρος**, ον (αὐτός + φώρ, *a thief*) pr.
caught in the act of theft

(849) **αὐτόχειρ**, ρος, ὁ [§4.2.f] (αὐτός + χείρ) *act-*
ing or *doing anything with one's own*
hands, Acts 27:19

αὐτόχειρες, nom. pl. m. adj. . . . . . . αὐτόχειρ *(849)*

αὐτῷ, dat. sg. m. personal pron.
{John 11:39} . . . . αὐτός *(846)*

αὐτῷ, dat. sg. neut. personal pron.

{John 11:38} . . . . αὐτός *(846)*

αὐτῷ, dat. sg. m. contracted form of ἑαυτῷ
(Phil. 3:21, WH | αὐτῷ, GNT, MT, TR
& NA) . . . . αὐτοῦ *(848)*

αὐτῶν, gen. pl. m. personal pron.
{Rev. 9:17} . . . . αὐτός *(846)*

αὐτῶν, gen. pl. f. personal pron. {Rev. 9:11} id.

αὐτῶν, gen. pl. neut. personal pron.
{Rev. 9:16} . . . . id.

αὐτῶν, contracted form of ἑαυτοῦ (2 Cor. 3:5,
WH | ἑαυτῶν, GNT, MT, TR &
NA) . . . . αὐτοῦ *(848)*

αὐχεῖ, 3 pers. sg. pres. act. indic. (James 3:5,
with μεγάλα, GNT, WH & NA |
μεγαλαυχεῖ, MT & TR) . . . . αὐχέω *(‡3166)*

(‡3166) **αὐχέω**, ῶ, *to boast*

(850) **αὐχμηρός**, ά, όν [§7.1] (αὐχμέω, *to be dry,*
squalid, filthy) squalid, filthy; by impl.
dark, obscure, murky, 2 Pet. 1:19

αὐχμηρῷ, dat. sg. m. adj. . . . . αὐχμηρός *(850)*

ἀφ᾽, prep. by apostrophe for ἀπό . . . . . . ἀπό *(575)*

ἀφαιρεθήσεται, 3 pers. sg. fut. pass.
indic. . . . . ἀφαιρέω *(851)*

ἀφαιρεῖν, pres. act. infin. . . . . id.

ἀφαιρεῖται, 3 pers. sg. pres. mid. indic.
[§17.Q] . . . . id.

(851) **ἀφαιρέω**, ῶ, fut. ἀφαιρήσω and ἀφελῶ, 2 aor.
ἀφεῖλον [§36.1] aor. pass. ἀφαιρεθήσομαι
(ἀπό + αἱρέω) *to take away, remove,* Luke
1:25; 10:42; et al.; *to take off, cut off, re-*
move by cutting off, Matt. 26:51; Mark
14:47; Luke 22:50

ἀφαιρῇ, 3 pers. sg. pres. act. subj. (Rev.
22:19a, TR | ἀφέλῃ, GNT, WH, MT &
NA) . . . . ἀφαιρέω *(851)*

ἀφαιρήσει, 3 pers. sg. fut. act. indic. (Rev.
22:19b, TR | ἀφελεῖ, GNT, WH & NA
| ἀφέλοι, MT) . . . . id.

(852) **ἀφανής**, ές [§7.G.b] (ἀ + φαίνω) *out of sight;*
not manifest, hidden, concealed, Heb. 4:13

ἀφανής, nom. sg. f. adj. . . . . ἀφανής *(852)*

ἀφανίζει, 3 pers. sg. pres. act. indic. . . ἀφανίζω *(853)*

ἀφανιζομένη, nom. sg. f. pres. pass. part. . id.

ἀφανίζουσι(ν), 3 pers. pl. pres. act. indic. . id.

(853) **ἀφανίζω**, fut. ἀφανίσω [§26.1] *to remove out*
of sight, cause to disappear; pass. *to dis-*
appear, vanish, James 4:14; by impl. *to de-*
stroy, consume, so that nothing shall be left
visible, Matt. 6:19, 20; met. *to spoil, de-*
form, disfigure, Matt. 6:16

ἀφανίσθητε, 2 pers. pl. aor. pass.
imper. . . . . ἀφανίζω *(853)*

(854) **ἀφανισμός**, οῦ, ὁ [§3.C.a] *a disappearing, van-*
ishing away; met. *destruction, abolition,*
abrogation, Heb. 8:13

ἀφανισμοῦ, gen. sg. m. . . . . ἀφανισμός *(854)*

(855) **ἄφαντος**, ον, nom. sg. m. adj. [§7.2] (ἀ + φαίνω) *not appearing, not seen, invisible;* hence, ἄφαντος γενέσθαι, *to disappear, vanish,* Luke 24:31

(856) **ἀφεδρών**, ῶνος, ὁ [§4.2.e] (ἀπό + ἕδρα, *a seat*) *a privy,* Matt. 15:17; Mark 7:19

ἀφεδρῶνα, acc. sg. m. n. . . . . ἀφεδρών *(856)*

ἀφεθῇ, 3 pers. sg. aor. pass. subj.
[§32.CC] . . . . ἀφίημι *(863)*

ἀφέθησαν, 3 pers. pl. aor. pass. indic. . . . . id.

ἀφεθήσεται, 3 pers. sg. fut. pass. indic. . . id.

(857) **ἀφειδία**, ας, ἡ [§2.B.b; 2.2] (ἀ + φείδομαι) pr. *the disposition of one who is* ἀφειδής, *unsparing;* hence, in N.T. *unsparingness* in the way of rigorous treatment, *nonindulgence,* Col. 2:23

ἀφειδίᾳ, dat. sg. f. n. . . . . ἀφειδία *(857)*

ἀφεῖλεν, 3 pers. sg. 2 aor. act. indic.
[§36.1] . . . . ἀφαιρέω *(851)*

ἀφεῖναι, aor. pass. infin. (Luke 5:21, GNT, WH & NA | ἀφιέναι, MT & TR) . . ἀφίημι *(863)*

ἀφεῖς, 2 pers. sg. pres. act. indic. of ἀφέω, ῶ, an irregular form of ἀφίημι [§32.2] (Rev. 2:20, GNT, WH, MT & NA | ἐᾷς, TR)   id.

ἀφείς, nom. sg. m. 2 aor. act. part.
{Matt. 13:36} . . . . id.

ἀφελεῖ, 3 pers. sg. 2 fut. act. indic. (Rev. 22:19, GNT, WH & NA | ἀφαιρήσει, TR | ἀφέλοι, MT) . . . . ἀφαιρέω *(851)*

ἀφελεῖν, 2 aor. act. infin. . . . . id.

ἀφέλῃ, 3 pers. sg. 2 aor. act. subj. (Rev. 22:19, GNT, WH, MT & NA | ἀφαιρῇ, TR)   id.

ἀφέλοι, 3 pers. sg. 2 aor. act. opt. (Rev. 22:19, MT | ἀφελεῖ, GNT, WH & NA | ἀφαιρήσει, TR) . . . . id.

(858) **ἀφελότης**, τητος, ἡ [§4.2.c] (ἀφελής, *not rough, plain,* met. *simple, sincere,* from ἀ + φελλεύς, *a rough, stony region*) *sincerity, simplicity,* Acts 2:46

ἀφελότητι, dat. sg. f. n. . . . . ἀφελότης *(858)*

ἀφέλωμαι, 1 pers. sg. 2 aor. mid.
subj. . . . . ἀφαιρέω *(851)*

ἀφέντες, nom. pl. m. 2 aor. act. part. . . . ἀφίημι *(863)*

ἄφες, 2 pers. sg. 2 aor. act. imper. [§32.CC]   id.

ἀφέσει, dat. sg. f. n. . . . . ἄφεσις *(859)*

ἄφεσιν, acc. sg. f. n. . . . . id.

(859) **ἄφεσις**, εως, ἡ, nom. sg. f. n. [§5.E.c] *dismission, deliverance* from captivity, Luke 4:18(2×); *remission, forgiveness, pardon,* Matt. 26:28, et al.

ἄφετε, 2 pers. pl. 2 aor. act. imper. . . . . ἀφίημι *(863)*

ἀφέωνται, 3 pers. pl. perf. pass. indic. [§32.2]   id.

ἀφῇ, 3 pers. sg. 2 aor. act. subj. . . . . id.

(860) **ἀφή**, ῆς, ἡ [§2.B.a] (ἅπτω, *to fasten*) *a fasten-*

ing; a ligature, by which the different members are connected, *commissure, joint,* Eph. 4:16; Col. 2:19

ἀφῆκα, 1 pers. sg. aor. act. indic.
[§28.9.c] . . . . ἀφίημι *(863)*

ἀφήκαμεν, 1 pers. sg. aor. act. indic. . . . . id.

ἀφῆκαν, 3 pers. pl. aor. act. indic. . . . . . . id.

ἀφῆκας, 2 pers. sg. aor. act. indic. (Rev. 2:4, MT & TR | ἀφῆκες, GNT, WH & NA)   id.

ἀφήκατε, 2 pers. pl. aor. act. indic. . . . . . id.

ἀφῆκε(ν), 3 pers. sg. aor. act. indic. . . . . . id.

ἀφῆκες, 2 pers. sg. aor. act. indic. (Rev. 2:4, GNT, WH & NA | ἀφῆκας, MT & TR)   id.

ἀφῆς, gen. sg. f. n. . . . . ἀφή *(860)*

ἀφήσει, 3 pers. sg. fut. act. indic. . . . . . . ἀφίημι *(863)*

ἀφήσεις, 2 pers. sg. fut. act. indic. . . . . . . id.

ἀφήσουσι(ν), 3 pers. pl. fut. act. indic. . . . id.

ἀφήσω, 1 pers. sg. fut. act. indic. . . . . id.

ἀφῆτε, 2 pers. pl. 2 aor. act. subj. . . . . id.

(861) **ἀφθαρσία**, ας, ἡ [§2.B.b; 2.2] *incorruptibility,* 1 Cor. 15:42, 53, 54; *immortality,* Rom. 2:7; 2 Tim. 1:10; *soundness, purity;* ἐν ἀφθαρσίᾳ, *purely, sincerely* or *constantly, unfailingly,* Eph. 6:24

ἀφθαρσίᾳ, dat. sg. f. n. . . . . ἀφθαρσία *(861)*

ἀφθαρσίαν, acc. sg. f. n. . . . . id.

ἄφθαρτοι, nom. pl. m. adj. . . . . ἄφθαρτος *(862)*

ἄφθαρτον, acc. sg. m. adj. {1 Cor. 9:25} .   id.

ἄφθαρτον, acc. sg. f. adj. {1 Pet. 1:4} . . . . id.

(862) **ἄφθαρτος**, ον, [§7.2] (ἀ + φθείρω) *incorruptible, immortal, imperishable, undying, enduring,* Rom. 1:23; 1 Cor. 9:25; 15:52, et al.

ἀφθάρτου, gen. sg. m. adj.
{Rom. 1:23} . . . . ἄφθαρτος *(862)*

ἀφθάρτου, gen. sg. f. adj. {1 Pet. 1:23} . . . id.

ἀφθάρτῳ, dat. sg. m. adj. {1 Tim. 1:17} . . id.

ἀφθάρτῳ, dat. sg. neut. adj. {1 Pet. 3:4} . . id.

(‡90) **ἀφθορία**, ας, ἡ [§2.B.b; 2.2] Tit. 2:7, pr. *incapability of decay;* met. *incorruptness, integrity, genuineness, purity*

ἀφθορίαν, acc. sg. f. n. (Tit. 2:7, GNT, WH & NA | ἀδιαφθορίαν, MT & TR) ἀφθορία *(‡90)*

ἀφίδω, 1 pers. sg. 2 aor. act. subj. (Phil. 2:23, GNT, WH & NA | ἀπίδω, MT & TR) . . . . ἀφοράω *(872)*

ἀφίεμεν, 1 pers. pl. pres. act. indic. (Matt. 6:12; Luke 11:4, MT & TR | ἀφήκαμεν, Matt. 6:12 GNT, WH & NA | ἀφίομεν, Luke 11:4, GNT, WH & NA) . . . . . ἀφίημι *(863)*

ἀφιέναι, pres. act. infin. . . . . id.

ἀφίενται, 3 pers. pl. pres. pass. indic. . . . . id.

ἀφίεται, 3 pers. sg. pres. pass. indic. . . . . . id.

ἀφίετε, 2 pers. pl. pres. act. indic.
{Mark 7:12} . . . . id.

ἀφίετε, 2 pers. pl. pres. act. imper.
{Mark 11:25} . . . . ἀφίημι *(863)*
ἀφιέτω, 3 pers. sg. pres. act. imper. . . . . . id.

(863) **ἀφίημι**, 1 pers. sg. pres. act. indic. [§32.CC]
fut. ἀφήσω, aor. ἀφῆκα, aor. pass.
ἀφείθην and ἀφέθην, fut. pass.
ἀφεθήσομαι, imperf. 3 pers. sg. ἤφιε(ν),
Mark 1:34; 11:16; perf. pass. 3 pers. pl.
ἀφέωνται, pres. 2 pers. sg. ἀφεῖς, v.r., Rev.
2:20 (ἀπό + ἵημι) *to send away, dismiss,*
suffer to depart; to emit, send forth; τὴν
φωνήν, *the voice, to cry out, utter an ex-*
clamation, Mark 15:37; τὸ πνεῦμα, *the*
spirit, to expire, Matt. 27:50; *to omit, pass*
over or *by; to let alone, care not for,* Matt.
15:14; 23:23; Heb. 6:1; *to permit, suffer,*
let, forbid not; to give up, yield, resign,
Matt. 5:40; *to remit, forgive, pardon; to*
relax, suffer to become less intense, Rev.
2:4; *to leave, depart from; to desert, for-*
sake; to leave remaining or *alone; to leave*
behind, sc. at one's death, Mark 12:19, 20,
21, 22; John 14:27
ἀφίησι(ν), 3 pers. sg. pres. act. indic. . . . ἀφίημι *(863)*
ἀφίκετο, 3 pers. sg. 2 aor. mid. dep.
indic. ἀφικνέομαι *(864)*

(864) **ἀφικνέομαι**, οῦμαι, fut. ἀφίξομαι, 2 aor.
ἀφικόμην [§36.2] (ἀπό + ἱκνέομαι, *to*
come, arrive) *to come, arrive at; to reach*
as a report, Rom. 16:19
ἀφιλάγαθοι, nom. pl. m. adj. . . . . ἀφιλάγαθος *(865)*

(865) **ἀφιλάγαθος**, ον [§7.2] (ἀ, φίλος + ἀγαθός)
not a lover of, inimical to, good and good
men, 2 Tim. 3:3
ἀφιλάργυρον, acc. sg. m. adj. . . . ἀφιλάργυρος *(866)*

(866) **ἀφιλάργυρος**, ον, nom. sg. m. adj. [§7.2] (ἀ,
φίλος + ἄργυρος) *not fond of money, not*
covetous, liberal, generous, 1 Tim. 3:3;
Heb. 13:5
ἄφιξιν, acc. sg. f. n. . . . . ἄφιξις *(867)*

(867) **ἄφιξις**, εως, ἡ [§5.E.c] *arrival; departure,* Acts
20:29
ἀφίομεν, 1 per. pl. pres. act. indic. (Luke 11:4,
GNT, WH & NA | ἀφίεμεν, MT &
TR) . . . . ἀφίημι *(863)*
ἀφίουσιν, 3 pers. pl. pres. act. indic. (Rev. 11:9,
GNT, WH & NA | ἀφήσουσι(ν), MT &
TR) . . . . id.
ἀφίστανται, 3 pers. pl. pres. mid./pass. dep.
indic. [§29.Y] . . . . ἀφίστημι *(868)*
ἀφίστασο, 2 pers. sg. pres. mid./pass. dep.
imper. (1 Tim. 6:5, MT & TR | GNT, WH
& NA omit) . . . . id.
ἀφίστατο, 3 pers. sg. imperf. mid./pass. dep.
indic. . . . . id.

(868) **ἀφίστημι** [§29.X] fut. ἀποστήσω, aor.
ἀπέστησα (ἀπό + ἵστημι) trans. *to put*
away, separate; to draw off or *away, with-*
draw, induce to revolt, Acts 5:37; intrans.,
perf. ἀφέστηκα, 2 aor. ἀπέστην, and
mid., *to depart, go away from,* Luke 2:37,
et al.; met. *to desist* or *refrain from, let*
alone, Acts 5:38; 22:29; 2 Cor. 12:8; *to*
make defection, fall away, apostatize, Luke
8:13; 1 Tim. 4:1; Heb. 3:12; *to withdraw*
from, have no intercourse with, 1 Tim. 6:5;
to abstain from, 2 Tim. 2:19

(869) **ἄφνω**, adv., *suddenly, unexpectedly,* Acts 2:2;
16:26; 28:6

(870) **ἀφόβως**, adv. (ἄφοβος, *fearless,* from ἀ +
φόβος) *fearlessly, boldly, intrepidly,* Phil.
1:14; *securely, peacefully, tranquilly,* Luke
1:74; 1 Cor. 16:10; *impudently, shame-*
lessly, Jude 12

(871) **ἀφομοιόω**, ἀφομοιώσω, fut. ώσω [§20.T]
(ἀπό + ὁμοιόω) *to assimilate, cause to re-*
semble, Heb. 7:3

(872) **ἀφοράω**, ῶ, fut. ἀπόψομαι, 2 aor. ἀπεῖδον
[§36.1] (ἀπό + ὁράω) *to view with undi-*
vided attention by looking away from every
other object; *to regard fixedly and ear-*
nestly, Heb. 12:2; *to see distinctly,* Phil 2:23
ἀφοριεῖ, 3 pers. sg. fut. act. indic. (Matt.
25:32, MT & TR | ἀφορίσει, GNT, WH
& NA) . . . . ἀφορίζω *(873)*
ἀφορίζει, 3 pers. sg. pres. act. indic. . . . . id.

(873) **ἀφορίζω**, fut. ἀφορίσω and ἀφοριῶ, perf.
pass. ἀφώρισμαι [§26.1] (ἀπό + ὁρίζω) *to*
limit off; to separate, sever from the rest,
Matt. 13:49, et al.; *to separate* from society, *cut off from all intercourse, excom-*
municate, Luke 6:22; *to set apart, select,*
Acts 13:2; Rom. 1:1; Gal. 1:15
ἀφοριοῦσι(ν), 3 pers. pl. fut. act. indic. Att.
[§35.11] . . . . ἀφορίζω *(873)*
ἀφορίσας, nom. sg. m. aor. act. part. . . . . id.
ἀφορίσατε, 2 pers. pl. aor. act. imper. . . . id.
ἀφορίσει, 3 pers. sg. fut. act. indic. (Matt.
25:32, GNT, WH & NA | ἀφοριεῖ, MT
& TR) . . . . id.
ἀφορίσθητε, 2 pers. pl. aor. pass. imper. . . id.
ἀφορίσωσιν, 3 pers. pl. aor. act. subj. . . . . id.

(874) **ἀφορμή**, ῆς, ἡ [§2.B.a] (ἀπό + ὁρμή) pr. *a*
starting point; means to accomplish an object; *occasion, opportunity,* Rom. 7:8, 11,
et al.
ἀφορμήν, acc. sg. f. n. . . . . ἀφορμή *(874)*
ἀφορῶντες, nom. pl. m. pres. act.
part. . . . . ἀφοράω *(872)*
ἀφρίζει, 3 pers. sg. pres. act. indic. . . . . ἀφρίζω *(875)*

(875) **ἀφρίζω,** fut. ἀφρίσω [§26.1] *to froth, foam,*
  Mark 9:18, 20
  ἀφρίζων, nom. sg. m. pres. act. part. .. ἀφρίζω (875)
  ἄφρον, voc. sg. m. adj. (Luke 12:20, MT &
    TRb | ἄφρων, GNT, WH, TRs &
    NA) . . . . ἄφρων (878)
  ἄφρονα, acc. sg. m. adj. . . . . id.
  ἄφρονες, nom. pl. m. adj. {Eph. 5:17} . . . id.
  ἄφρονες, voc. pl. m. adj. {Luke 11:40} . . . id.
  ἀφρόνων, gen. pl. m. adj. . . . . id.
(876) **ἀφρός,** οῦ, ὁ [§3.C.a] *froth, foam,* Luke 9:39
(877) **ἀφροσύνη,** ης, ἡ, nom. sg. f. n. [§2.B.a] *in-*
  considerateness, folly; boastful *folly,* 2 Cor.
  11:1, 17, 21; in N.T. *foolishness, levity,*
  wickedness, impiety, Mark 7:22
  ἀφροσύνῃ, dat. sg. f. n. . . . . ἀφροσύνη (877)
  ἀφροσύνης, gen. sg. f. n. . . . . id.
  ἀφροῦ, gen. sg. m. n. . . . . ἀφρός (876)
(878) **ἄφρων,** ον, nom. sg. m. adj. [§7.G.a; 7.3] (ἀ
  + φρήν) *unwise, inconsiderate, simple,*
  foolish, Luke 11:40; 12:20; 1 Cor. 15:36;
  ignorant, religiously *unenlightened,* Rom.
  2:20; Eph. 5:17; 1 Pet. 2:15; boastfully
  foolish, vain, 2 Cor. 11:16, 19; {2 Cor.
  12:6, 11}
  ἄφρων, voc. sg. m. adj. (1 Cor. 15:36, GNT,
    WH & NA | ἄφρον, MT & TR) . . . ἄφρων (878)
(879) **ἀφυπνόω,** ῶ, fut. ἀφυπνώσω [§20.T] (ἀπό +
  ὕπνος) *to awake from sleep;* in N.T. *to go*
  off into sleep, fall asleep, Luke 8:23
  ἀφύπνωσε(ν), 3 pers. sg. aor. act.
    indic. . . . . ἀφυπνόω (879)
(‡650) **ἀφυστερέω,** ῶ, *to withhold*
  ἀφυστερημένος, nom. sg. m. perf. pass. part.
    (James 5:4, WH | ἀπεστερημένος, GNT,
    MT, TR & NA) . . . . ἀφυστερέω (‡650)
  ἀφῶμεν, 1 pers. pl. 2 aor. act. subj. . . . ἀφίημι (863)
  ἀφωμοιωμένος, nom. sg. m. perf. pass.
    part. . . . . ἀφομοιόω (871)
  ἀφῶν, gen. pl. f. n. . . . . ἀφή (860)
  ἄφωνα, acc. pl. neut. adj. . . . . ἄφωνος (880)
  ἄφωνον, nom. sg. neut. adj. . . . . id.
(880) **ἄφωνος,** ον, nom. sg. m. adj. [§7.2] (ἀ +
  φωνή) *dumb, destitute of the power of*
  speech, 1 Cor. 12:2; 2 Pet. 2:16; *silent,*
  mute, uttering no voice, Acts 8:32; *inartic-*
  ulate, consisting of inarticulate sounds, un-
  meaning, 1 Cor. 14:10
  ἀφώριζεν, 3 pers. sg. imperf. act.
    indic. . . . . ἀφορίζω (873)
  ἀφώρισε(ν), 3 pers. sg. aor. act. indic. . . . id.
  ἀφωρισμένος, nom. sg. m. perf. pass. part. . id.
(†881) **Ἀχάζ,** ὁ, *Achaz,* pr. name, indecl. (Matt.
  1:9a, 9b, GNT, MT & NA | Ἄχαζ, TR
  | Ἄχας, WH)

(882) **Ἀχαΐα,** ας, ἡ, nom. sg. m. n. [§2.B.b; 2.2]
  Achaia, the Roman province, comprehend-
  ing all Greece to the south of Thessaly
  (GNT, MT, TR & NA | Ἀχαία, WH)
  Ἀχαΐα, dat. sg. f. n. (GNT, MT, TR & NA
    | Ἀχαία, WH) . . . . Ἀχαΐα (882)
  Ἀχαΐαν, acc. sg. f. n. (GNT, MT, TR & NA
    | Ἀχαία, WH) . . . . id.
  Ἀχαΐας, gen. sg. f. n. (GNT, MT, TR & NA
    | Ἀχαία, WH) . . . . id.
(883) **Ἀχαϊκός,** οῦ, ὁ, *Achaicus,* pr. name, 1 Cor.
  16:17
  Ἀχαϊκοῦ, gen. sg. m. n. . . . . Ἀχαϊκός (883)
  ἀχάριστοι, nom. pl. m. adj. . . . . ἀχάριστος (884)
(884) **ἀχάριστος,** ον [§7.2] (ἀ + χάρις) *unthank-*
  ful, ungrateful, Luke 6:35; 2 Tim. 3:2
  ἀχαρίστους, acc. pl. m. adj. . . . . . . ἀχάριστος (884)
(‡881) **Ἄχας,** ὁ, indecl. n. *Achaz* (Matt. 1:9a, 9b,
  WH | Ἄχαζ, TR | Ἀχάζ, GNT, MT &
  NA)
(885) **Ἀχείμ,** ὁ, *Achim,* pr. name, indecl. (Matt. 1:14,
  MT, WH & TR | Ἀχίμ, GNT & NA)
  ἀχειροποίητον, acc. sg. m. adj. {Mark
    14:58} . . . . ἀχειροποίητος (886)
  ἀχειροποίητον, acc. sg. f. adj. {2 Cor. 5:1}   id.
(886) **ἀχειροποίητος,** ον [§7.2] (ἀ + χειροποίητος)
  not made with hands, Mark 14:58; 2 Cor.
  5:1; Col. 2:11
  ἀχειροποιήτῳ, dat. sg. f. adj. . . ἀχειροποίητος (886)
  ἀχθῆναι, aor. pass. infin. [§23.4] . . . . ἄγω (71)
  ἀχθήσεσθε, 2 pers. pl. fut. pass. indic. . . . id.
(‡885) **Ἀχίμ,** ὁ, *Achim,* pr. name, indecl. (Matt. 1:14,
  GNT & N | Ἀχείμ, MT, WH & TR)
(887) **ἀχλύς,** ύος, ἡ, nom. sg. f. n. [§5.E.g] *a mist;*
  darkening, dimness, of the sight, Acts 13:11
  ἀχρεῖοι, nom. pl. m. adj. . . . . ἀχρεῖος (888)
  ἀχρεῖον, acc. sg. m. adj. . . . . id.
(888) **ἀχρεῖος,** ον [§7.2] (ἀ + χρεία) *useless, unpro-*
  fitable, worthless, Matt. 25:30; *unmeritor-*
  ious, Luke 17:10
(889) **ἀχρειόω,** ῶ, fut. ἀχρειώσω [§20.T] aor. pass.
  ἠχρειώθην, *to render useless;* met. pass. *to*
  become corrupt, depraved, Rom. 3:12
  ἄχρηστον, acc. sg. m. adj. . . . . ἄχρηστος (890)
(890) **ἄχρηστος,** ον [§7.2] (ἀ + χρηστός) *unuseful,*
  useless, unprofitable, and by impl. *detri-*
  mental, causing loss, Philemon 11
(891) **ἄχρι,** or ἄχρις, originally an adv., of place;
  used as a prep., with respect to place, *as*
  far as; to time, *until, during;* as a conj. *until*
(892) **ἄχυρον,** ου, τό [§3.C.c] *chaff, straw broken*
  up by treading out the grain, Matt. 3:12;
  Luke 3:17
  ἄχυρον, acc. sg. neut. n. . . . . ἄχυρον (892)
  ἀψάμενος, nom. sg. m. aor. mid. part. . . . ἅπτω (681)

ἄψαντες, nom. pl. m. aor. act. part. (Acts 28:2, GNT, WH & NA | ἀνάψαντες, MT & TR) . . . . ἄπτω *(681)*

ἀψάντων, gen. pl. m. aor. act. part. (Luke 22:55, MT & TR | περιαψάντων, GNT, WH & NA) . . . . id.

ἄψας, nom. sg. m. aor. act. part. . . . . id.

(893) **ἀψευδής**, ές, nom. sg. m. adj. [§7.G.b] (ἀ + ψευδής) *free from falsehood; incapable of falsehood,* Tit. 1:2

ἄψῃ, 2 pers. sg. aor. mid. subj. . . . . ἄπτω *(681)*

ἄψηται, 3 pers. sg. aor. mid. subj. . . . . . . id.

ἄψινθον, acc. sg. f. n. . . . . ἄψινθος *(894)*

(894) **ἄψινθος**, ου, ἡ, nom. sg. f. n. [§3.C.b] *wormwood,* Rev. 8:11; where, as a proper name, it is masculine, Rev. 8:11

ἄψυχα, nom. pl. neut. adj. . . . . ἄψυχος *(895)*

(895) **ἄψυχος**, ον [§7.2] (ἀ + ψυχή) *void of life* or *sense, inanimate,* 1 Cor. 14:7

ἄψωμαι, 1 pers. sg. aor. mid. subj. . . . . . . ἄπτω *(681)*

ἄψωνται, 3 pers. pl. aor. mid. subj. . . . . . id.

B

Β′, *beta,* second letter of Greek alphabet; used as *second* in titles of N.T. writings.

(896) **Βάαλ**, ὁ, *Baal,* pr. name, indecl. (Hebrew בַּעַל) Rom. 11:4

(897) **Βαβυλών**, ῶνος, ἡ, nom. sg. f. n. [§4.2.e] *Babylon,* 1 Pet. 5:13

Βαβυλῶνι, dat. sg. f. n. . . . . Βαβυλών *(897)*

Βαβυλῶνος, gen. sg. f. n. . . . . id.

βαθέα, acc. pl. neut. adj. (Rev. 2:24, GNT, WH, MT & NA | βάθη, TR) . . . . . βαθύς *(901)*

βαθεῖ, dat. sg. m. adj. . . . . id.

βαθέος, gen. sg. m. adj. of βάθος (Luke 24:1, TR | βαθέως, GNT, WH, MT & NA) id.

βαθέως, gen. sg. m. adj. (Luke 24:1, GNT, WH, MT & NA | βαθέος, TR) . . . . . id.

βάθη, acc. pl. neut. n. . . . . βάθος *(899)*

βαθμόν, acc. sg. m. n. . . . . βαθμός *(898)*

(898) **βαθμός**, οῦ, ὁ [§3.C.a] (βαίνω, *to walk, go*) pr. *a step, stair;* met. *grade* of dignity, *degree, rank, standing,* 1 Tim. 3:13

(899) **βάθος**, ους, τό, nom. sg. neut. n. [§5.E.b] *depth;* τὸ βάθος, *deep water,* Luke 5:4; Matt. 13:5, et al.; met. *fulness, abundance, immensity,* Rom. 11:33; *an extreme degree,* 2 Cor. 8:2; pl. *profundities, deep-laid plans,* 1 Cor. 2:10; Rev. 2:24 {Rom. 11:33}

βάθος, acc. sg. neut. n. {Luke 5:4} . . . . . βάθος *(899)*

βάθους, gen. sg. neut. n. . . . . id.

βαθύ, nom. sg. neut. adj. . . . . βαθύς *(901)*

(900) **βαθύνω**, fut. βαθυνῶ [§27.1.a] *to deepen, excavate,* Luke 6:48

(901) **βαθύς**, εῖα, ύ [§7.H.g] *deep,* John 4:11; met. *deep, profound,* Acts 20:9; ὄρθρου βαθέος, lit. *at deep morning twilight, at the earliest dawn,* Luke 24:1

βαῖα, acc. pl. neut. n. . . . . βαῖον *(902)*

(902) **βάϊον**, or βαῖον, ου, τό, *a palm branch,* John 12:13

(903) **Βαλαάμ**, ὁ, *Balaam,* pr. name, indecl.

(904) **Βαλάκ**, ὁ, *Balak,* pr. name, indecl., Rev. 2:14

βαλάντια, acc. pl. neut. n. (Luke 12:33, MT & TR | βαλλάντια, GNT, WH & NA) . . . . βαλάντιον *(905)*

(905) **βαλάντιον**, ου, τό [§3.C.c] *a bag, purse,* Luke 10:4; 12:33; 22:35, 36

βαλάντιον, acc. sg. neut. n. (Luke 10:4; 22:36, MT & TR | βαλλάντιον, GNT, WH & NA) . . . . βαλάντιον *(905)*

βαλαντίου, gen. sg. neut. n. (Luke 22:35, MT & TR | βαλλαντίου, GNT, WH & NA) id.

βάλε, 2 pers. sg. 2 aor. act. imper. . . . . . βάλλω *(906)*

βαλεῖ, 3 pers. sg. fut. act. indic. (Luke 12:58, GNT, WH & NA | βάλῃ, TR | βάλλῃ, MT) . . . . id.

βαλεῖν, 2 aor. act. infin. . . . . id.

βάλετε, 2 pers. pl. 2 aor. act. imper. . . . . . id.

βαλέτω, 3 pers. sg. 2 aor. act. imper. . . . . id.

βάλῃ, 3 pers. sg. 2 aor. act. subj. . . . . id.

βάλητε, 2 pers. pl. 2 aor. act. subj. . . . . . . id.

βαλλάντια, acc. pl. neut. n. (Luke 12:33, GNT, WH & NA | βαλάντια, MT & TR) . . . . βαλλάντιον *(†905)*

(†905) **βαλλάντιον**, ου, τό, *a bag, purse*

βαλλάντιον, acc. sg. neut. n. (Luke 10:4; 22:36, GNT, WH & NA | βαλάντιον, MT & TR) . . . . βαλλάντιον *(†905)*

βαλλαντίου, gen. sg. neut. n. (Luke 22:35, GNT, WH & NA | βαλαντίου, MT & TR) . . . . id.

βάλλει, 3 pers. sg. pres. act. indic. . . . . . βάλλω *(906)*

βάλλειν, pres. act. infin. (Rev. 2:10, GNT, WH & NA | βάλειν, MT & TR) . . . . id.

βάλλεται, 3 pers. sg. pres. pass. indic. . . . id.

βάλλῃ, 3 pers. sg. pres. act. subj. (Luke 12:58; John 5:7, TR | Luke 12:58, βαλεῖ, GNT, WH & NA | Luke 12:58, βάλῃ, MT | John 5:7, βάλῃ, GNT, WH, MT & NA) id.

βάλλομεν, 1 pers. pl. pres. act. indic. . . . . id.

βαλλόμενα, nom. pl. neut. pres. pass. part. id.

βαλλόμενον, acc. sg. m. pres. pass. part. . id.

βάλλοντας, acc. pl. m. pres. act. part. (Mark 1:16, MT & TR | ἀμφιβάλλοντας, GNT, WH & NA) . . . . id.

βάλλοντες, nom. pl. m. pres. act. part. . . . id.

βαλλόντων, gen. pl. m. pres. act. part. . βάλλω *(906)*
βάλλουσαν, acc. sg. f. pres. act. part. . . . .   id.
βάλλουσι(ν), 3 pers. pl. pres. act. indic. . .   id.
(906) **βάλλω,** 1 pers. sg. pres. act. indic., fut. βαλῶ
     [§27.1.b] 2 aor. ἔβαλον [§27.2.d] perf.
     βέβληκα, perf. pass. βέβλημαι, aor. pass.
     ἐβλήθην, fut. pass. βληθήσομαι [§27.3] *to*
     throw, cast; to lay, Rev. 2:22; Matt. 8:6, 14,
     et al.; *to put, place,* James 3:3; *to place,*
     deposit, Matt. 27:6; Mark 12:41-44; Luke
     21:1-4; John 12:6; *to pour,* John 13:5; *to*
     thrust, John 18:11; 20:27; Mark 7:33; Rev.
     14:19; *to send forth,* Matt. 10:34; *to as-*
     sault, strike, Mark 14:65; met. *to suggest,*
     John 13:2; intrans. *to rush, beat,* as the
     wind, Acts 27:14
βαλόντων, gen. pl. m. 2 aor. act. part. (Mark
     12:43, TR | βαλλόντων, GNT, WH, MT
     & NA) . . . . βάλλω *(906)*
βαλοῦσα, nom. sg. f. 2 aor. act. part. . . . .   id.
βαλοῦσιν, 3 pers. pl. fut. act. indic. . . . . .   id.
βαλῶ, 1 pers. sg. fut. act. indic. (Rev. 2:24,
     TR | βάλλω, GNT, WH, MT & NA) .   id.
βάλω, 1 pers. sg. 2 aor. act. subj.
     {John 20:25} . . . .   id.
βαλῶσιν, 3 pers. pl. 2 aor. act. subj. . . . .   id.
βαπτίζει, 3 pers. sg. pres. act. indic. . . βαπτίζω *(907)*
βαπτίζειν, pres. act. infin. . . . .   id.
βαπτίζεις, 2 pers. sg. pres. act. indic. . . .   id.
βαπτίζομαι, 1 pers. sg. pres. pass. indic. . .   id.
βαπτιζόμενοι, nom. pl. m. pres. pass. part.   id.
βαπτίζονται, 3 pers. pl. pres. pass. indic. .   id.
βαπτίζοντες, nom. pl. m. pres. act. part. .   id.
βαπτίζοντος, gen. sg. m. pres. act. part.
     (Mark 6:24, GNT, WH & NA |
     βαπτιστοῦ, MT & TR) . . . .   id.
(907) **βαπτίζω,** 1 pers. sg. pres. act. indic., fut.
     βαπτίσω [§26.1] aor. ἐβάπτισα, perf. pass.
     βεβάπτισμαι, aor. pass. ἐβαπτίσθην, pr.
     to dip, immerse; to cleanse or *purify by*
     washing; to administer the rite of baptism,
     to baptize; met. with various reference to
     the ideas associated with Christian baptism
     as an act of dedication, e.g. marked desig-
     nation, devotion, trial, etc.; mid. *to pro-*
     cure baptism for one's self, to undergo
     baptism, Acts 22:16
βαπτίζων, nom. sg. m. pres. act. part. . βαπτίζω *(907)*
βάπτισαι, 2 pers. sg. aor. mid. imper. . . . .   id.
βαπτίσει, 3 pers. sg. fut. act. indic. . . . . . .   id.
βαπτισθείς, nom. sg. m. aor. pass. part. . .   id.
βαπτισθέντες, nom. pl. m. aor. pass. part.   id.
βαπτισθέντος, gen. sg. m. aor. pass. part.   id.
βαπτισθῆναι, aor. pass. infin. . . . .   id.
βαπτισθήσεσθε, 2 pers. pl. fut. pass. indic.   id.

βαπτισθήτω, 3 pers. sg. aor. pass.
     imper. . . . . βαπτίζω *(907)*
(908) **βάπτισμα,** ατος, τό, nom. sg. neut. n. [§4.D.c]
     pr. *immersion; baptism, ordinance of bap-*
     tism, Matt. 3:7; Rom. 6:4, et al.; met. *bap-*
     tism in the trial of suffering, Matt.
     20:22, 23; Mark 10:38, 39 {Mark 11:30}
βάπτισμα, acc. sg. neut. n.
     {Mark 10:38–39} . . . . βάπτισμα *(908)*
βαπτίσματι, dat. sg. neut. n. (Col. 2:12, MT,
     WH & TR | βαπτισμῷ, GNT & NA)   id.
βαπτίσματος, gen. sg. neut. n. . . . .   id.
βαπτισμοῖς, dat. pl. m. n. . . . . βαπτισμός *(909)*
(909) **βαπτισμός,** οῦ, ὁ [§3.C.a] pr. *an act of dip-*
     ping or *immersion: a baptism,* Heb. 6:2;
     an ablution, Mark 7:4, 8; Heb. 9:10
βαπτισμούς, acc. pl. m. n. . . . . βαπτισμός *(909)*
βαπτισμῷ, dat. sg. m. n. (Col. 2:12, GNT &
     NA | βαπτίσματι, MT, WH & TR) . .   id.
βαπτισμῶν, gen. pl. m. n. . . . .   id.
βαπτιστήν, acc. sg. m. n. . . . . βαπτιστής *(910)*
(910) **βαπτιστής,** οῦ, ὁ, nom. sg. m. n. [§2.B.c] *one*
     who baptizes, a baptist, Matt. 3:1;
     11:11, 12, et al.
βαπτιστοῦ, gen. sg. m. n. . . . . βαπτιστής *(910)*
βαπτίσωνται, 3 pers. pl. aor. mid.
     subj. . . . . βαπτίζω *(907)*
(911) **βάπτω,** fut. βάψω [§23.1.a] aor. ἔβαψα, perf.
     pass. βέβαμμαι [§23.7] *to dip,* John 13:26;
     Luke 16:24; *to dye,* Rev. 19:13
(‡920) **βάρ,** ὁ, indecl. (Aramaic or Syriac בַּר) *a son*
     (Matt. 16:17, with 'Ιωνᾶ, TR | Βαριωνᾶ,
     GNT, WH, MT & NA)
Βαραββᾶν, acc. sg. m. n. . . . . Βαραββᾶς *(912)*
(912) **Βαραββᾶς,** ᾶ, ὁ, nom. sg. m. n. [§2.4] *Barab-*
     bas, pr. name
(913) **Βαράκ,** ὁ, *Barak,* pr. name, indecl., Heb. 11:32
(914) **Βαραχίας,** ου, ὁ [§2.B.d] *Barachias,* pr. name,
     Matt. 23:35
Βαραχίου, gen. sg. m. n. . . . . Βαραχίας *(914)*
βάρβαροι, nom. pl. m. adj. . . . . βάρβαρος *(915)*
βαρβάροις, dat. pl. m. adj. . . . .   id.
(915) **βάρβαρος,** ον, nom. sg. m. adj. [§7.2] pr. *one*
     to whom a pure Greek dialect is not na-
     tive; one who is not a proper Greek, a bar-
     barian, Rom. 1:14; Col. 3:11; Acts 28:2, 4;
     a foreigner speaking a strange language,
     1 Cor. 14:11
βαρέα, acc. pl. neut. adj. . . . . βαρύς *(926)*
βάρει, dat. sg. neut. n. . . . . βάρος *(922)*
βαρεῖαι, nom. pl. f. adj. . . . . βαρύς *(926)*
βαρεῖς, nom. pl. m. adj. . . . .   id.
βαρείσθω, 3 pers. sg. pres. pass. imper. . βαρέω *(916)*
(916) **βαρέω,** ῶ, fut. βαρήσω [§16.P] perf. pass.
     βεβάρημαι, *to be heavy upon, weigh*

down, burden, oppress, as sleep, Matt.
26:43; Mark 14:40; Luke 9:32; surfeiting,
v.r. Luke 21:34; calamities, 2 Cor. 1:8; 5:4;
or, trouble, care, expense, etc. 1 Tim. 5:16

(917) **βαρέως**, adv., heavily; met. with difficulty,
dully, stupidly, Matt. 13:15; Acts 28:27

βάρη, acc. pl. neut. n. . . . . βάρος (922)

βαρηθῶσιν, 3 pers. pl. aor. pass. subj. (Luke
21:34, GNT, WH, MT & NA | βαρυν-
θῶσιν, TR) . . . . βαρέω (916)

Βαρθολομαῖον, acc. sg. m. n. . . Βαρθολομαῖος (918)

(918) **Βαρθολομαῖος**, ου, ὁ, nom. sg. m. n. [§3.C.a]
Bartholomew, pr. name

Βαριησοῦ, gen. sg. m. n. (Acts 13:6, GNT &
NA | Βαριησοῦς, WH & TR | Βαρ-
ιησοῦν, MT) . . . . Βαριησοῦς (919)

Βαριησοῦν, acc. sg. m. n. (Acts 13:6, MT |
Βαριησοῦς, WH & TR | Βαριησοῦ, GNT
& NA) . . . . id.

(919) **Βαριησοῦς**, οῦ, ὁ, nom. sg. m. n. [§6.3] Bar-
jesus, pr. name (Acts 13:6, WH & TR |
Βαριησοῦν, MT | Βαριησοῦ, GNT &
NA)

(†920) **Βὰρ Ἰωνᾶ**, or **Βαριωνᾶς**, ᾶ, ὁ, Bar-jona, pr.
name (Matt. 16:17, TR | Βαριωνᾶ, GNT,
WH, MT & NA)

(†920) **Βαριωνᾶ**, Bar-jona, pr. name (Matt. 16:17,
GNT, WH, MT & NA | Βὰρ Ἰωνᾶ, TR)

Βαρναβᾶ, gen. sg. m. n. (GNT, MT & NA
| Βαρνάβα, WH) . . . . Βαρναβᾶς (921)

Βαρναβᾷ, dat. sg. m. n. (GNT, MT & NA
| Βαρνάβᾳ, WH) . . . . id.

Βαρναβᾶν, acc. sg. m. n. (GNT, MT & NA
| Βαρνάβαν, WH) . . . . id.

(921) **Βαρναβᾶς**, ᾶ, ὁ, nom. sg. m. n. [§2.2] Barnabas, pr. name

(922) **βάρος**, ους, τό [§5.E.b] weight, heaviness; a
burden, anything grievous and hard to be
borne, Matt. 20:12; Acts 15:28; Rev. 2:24;
burden, charge or weight, influence, dignity, honor, 1 Thess. 2:6; with another
noun in government, fulness, abundance,
excellence, 2 Cor. 4:17

βάρος, acc. sg. neut. n. . . . . βάρος (922)

βαρούμενοι, nom. pl. m. pres. pass.
part. . . . . βαρέω (916)

Βαρσαβᾶν, acc. sg. m. n. (Acts 1:23, MT &
TR | Βαρσαββᾶν, GNT, WH &
NA) . . . . Βαρσαβᾶς (923)

(923) **Βαρσαβᾶς**, or Βαρσαββᾶς, ᾶ, ὁ [§2.4] Barsabas, pr. name   I. Joseph, surnamed Justus, Acts 1:23   II. Judas, Acts 15:22

Βαρσαββᾶν, acc. sg. m. n. (Acts 1:23, GNT,
WH & NA | Βαρσαβᾶν, MT &
TR) . . . . Βαρσαββᾶς (923)

(†924) **Βαρτίμαιος**, ου, ὁ, nom. sg. m. n. Bartimaeus,
pr. name, Mark 10:46

βαρυνθῶσιν, 3 pers. pl. aor. pass. subj. (Luke
21:34, TR | βαρηθῶσιν, GNT, WH, MT
& NA) . . . . βαρύνω (925)

(925) **βαρύνω**, fut. βαρυνῶ [§27.1.a] aor. pass.
ἐβαρύνθην, Luke 21:34; to be heavy upon,
weigh down, burden, oppress; surfeiting

(926) **βαρύς**, εῖα, ύ [§7.H.g] heavy; met. burdensome, oppressive or difficult of observance,
as precepts, Matt. 23:4; 1 John 5:3;
weighty, important, momentous, Matt.
23:23; Acts 25:7; grievous, oppressive, af-
flictive, violent, rapacious, Acts 20:29; au-
thoritative, strict, stern, severe, 2 Cor. 10:10

βαρύτερα, acc. pl. neut. compar. adj.
[§8.1] . . . . βαρύς (926)

βαρυτίμου, gen. sg. neut. adj. . . . . . . βαρύτιμος (927)

(927) **βαρύτιμος**, ον [§7.2] (βαρύς + τιμή) of great
price, precious, Matt. 26:7

βασανιζομένη, nom. sg. f. pres. pass.
part. . . . . βασανίζω (928)

βασανιζόμενον, nom. sg. neut. pres. pass.
part. . . . . id.

βασανιζόμενος, nom. sg. m. pres. pass. part.   id.

βασανιζομένους, acc. pl. m. pres. pass. part.   id.

(928) **βασανίζω**, fut. βασανίσω [§26.1] aor. pass.
ἐβασανίσθην, pr. to apply the lapis Lydius
or touchstone; met. to examine, scrutinize,
try, either by words or torture; in N.T. to
afflict, torment; pass. to be afflicted, tormented, pained, by diseases, Matt. 8:6,
29, 35 et al.; to be tossed, agitated, as by
the waves, Matt. 14:24

βασανίσαι, aor. act. infin. . . . . βασανίζω (928)

βασανίσῃς, 2 pers. sg. aor. act. subj. . . . . id.

βασανισθήσεται, 3 pers. sg. fut. pass. indic.   id.

βασανισθήσονται, 3 pers. pl. fut. pass. indic.   id.

βασανισθῶσι(ν), 3 pers. pl. aor. pass. subj.
(Rev. 9:5, MT & TR | βασανισθήσονται,
GNT, WH & NA) . . . . id.

βασανισμόν, acc. sg. m. n. . . . . . . βασανισμός (929)

(929) **βασανισμός**, οῦ, ὁ, nom. sg. m. n. [§3.C.a]
pr. examination by the lapis Lydius or by
torture; torment, torture, Rev. 9:5; 14:11;
18:7, 10, 15

βασανισμοῦ, gen. sg. m. n. . . . . . . βασανισμός (929)

βασανισταῖς, dat. pl. m. n. . . . . . . βασανιστής (930)

(930) **βασανιστής**, οῦ, ὁ [§2.B.c] pr. an inquisitor,
tormentor; in N.T. a keeper of a prison,
gaoler, Matt. 18:34

βασάνοις, dat. pl. f. n. . . . . βάσανος (931)

(931) **βάσανος**, ου, ἡ [§3.C.b] pr. lapis Lydius, a species of stone from Lydia, which being ap-
plied to metals was thought to indicate any

alloy which might be mixed with them, and therefore used in the trial of metals; hence, *examination* of a person, especially by torture; in N.T. *torture, torment, severe pain,* Matt. 4:24; Luke 16:23, 28

βασάνου, gen. sg. f. n. . . . . βάσανος *(931)*

βάσεις, nom. pl. f. n. . . . . βάσις *(939)*

βασιλέα, acc. sg. m. n. . . . . βασιλεύς *(935)*

βασιλεῖ, dat. sg. m. n. . . . . id.

(932) **βασιλεία,** ας, ἡ, nom. sg. f. n. [§2.B.b; 2.2] *a kingdom, realm,* the region or country governed by a king; *kingly power, authority, dominion, reign; royal dignity, the title and honor of king;* ἡ βασιλεία, Matt. 9:35, ἡ βασιλεία τοῦ θεοῦ — τοῦ Χριστοῦ — τοῦ οὐρανοῦ — τῶν οὐρανῶν, *the reign* or *kingdom of the Messiah,* both in a false and true conception of it; used also with various limitation, of its administration and coming history, as in the parables; its distinctive nature, Rom. 14:17; its requirements, privileges, rewards, consummation

βασιλείᾳ, dat. sg. f. n. . . . . βασιλεία *(932)*

βασιλεῖαι, nom. pl. f. n. (Rev. 11:15, TR | βασιλεία, GNT, WH, MT & NA) . . . . id.

βασιλείαν, acc. sg. f. n. . . . . id.

βασιλείας, gen. sg. f. n. {Matt. 4:23} . . . . id.

βασιλείας, acc. pl. f. n. {Matt. 4:8} . . . . . id.

βασιλείοις, dat. pl. m. adj. . . . . βασίλειος *(934)*

(933) **βασίλειον,** nom. sg. neut. adj. . . . . id.

(934) **βασίλειος,** ον [§7.2] *royal, regal;* met. *possessed of high prerogatives and distinction,* 1 Pet. 2:9; τὰ βαείλεια, sc. δώματα, *regal mansions, palaces,* Luke 7:25

βασιλεῖς, nom. pl. m. n. {Rev. 17:12} βασιλεύς *(935)*

βασιλεῖς, acc. pl. m. n. {Rev. 16:14} . . . . . id.

βασιλείων, gen. pl. m. n. (Matt. 11:8, MT | βασιλέων, GNT, WH, TR & NA) . . . . βασίλειος *(934)*

βασιλεῦ, voc. sg. m. n. . . . . βασιλεύς *(935)*

βασιλεύει, 3 pers. sg. pres. act. indic. βασιλεύω *(936)*

βασιλεύειν, pres. act. infin. . . . . id.

βασιλευέτω, 3 pers. sg. pres. act. imper. . . . id.

βασιλευόντων, gen. pl. m. pres. act. part. . id.

βασιλεύουσιν, 3 pers. pl. pres. act. indic. (Rev. 5:10, WH | βασιλεύσουσιν, GNT, MT & NA | βασιλεύσομεν, TR) . . . . id.

(935) **βασιλεύς,** έως, ὁ, nom. sg. m. n. [§5.E.d] *a king, monarch, one possessing regal authority*

βασιλεῦσαι, aor. act. infin. [§13.12] . . βασιλεύω *(936)*

βασιλεύσει, 3 pers. sg. fut. act. indic. . . . . id.

βασιλεύσῃ, 3 pers. sg. aor. act. subj. . . . . . id.

βασιλεῦσι(ν), dat. pl. m. n. . . . . βασιλεύς *(935)*

βασιλεύσομεν, 1 pers. pl. fut. act. indic. (Rev.

5:10, TR | βασιελύσουσιν, GNT, MT & NA | βασιλεύουσιν, WH) . . . . βασιλεύω *(936)*

βασιλεύσουσι(ν), 3 pers. pl. fut. act. indic. id.

(936) **βασιλεύω,** fut. βασιλεύσω [§13.M] *to possess regal authority, be a king, reign; to rule, govern,* Matt. 2:22; met. *to be in force, predominate, prevail,* Rom. 5:14, 17, 21; met. *to be in kingly case, fare royally,* 1 Cor. 4:8

βασιλέων, gen. pl. m. n. . . . . βασιλεύς *(935)*

βασιλέως, gen. sg. m. n. . . . . id.

βασιλικήν, acc. sg. f. adj. . . . . βασιλικός *(937)*

βασιλικῆς, gen. sg. f. adj. . . . . id.

βασιλικόν, acc. sg. m. adj. . . . . id.

(937) **βασιλικός,** ή, όν, nom. sg. m. adj. [§7.F.a] *royal, regal,* Acts 12:20, 21; βασιλικός, used as a subst. *a person attached to the king, courtier;* met. *royal, of the highest excellence,* James 2:8

(938) **βασίλισσα,** ης, ἡ, nom. sg. f. n. [§2.B.a] (a later form of βασιλίς) *a queen,* Matt. 12:42; Luke 11:31; Acts 8:27; Rev. 18:7

βασιλίσσης, gen. sg. f. n. . . . . βασίλισσα *(938)*

(939) **βάσις,** εως, ἡ [§5.E.c] (βαίνω) pr. *a step; the foot,* Acts 3:7

(940) **βασκαίνω,** fut. βασκανῶ, aor. ἐβάσκηνα and ἐβάσκανα [§27.1.c,e] pr. *to slander;* thence, *to bewitch* by spells, or by any other means; *to delude,* Gal. 3:1

βαστάζει, 3 pers. sg. pres. act. indic. . βαστάζω *(941)*

βαστάζειν, pres. act. infin. . . . . id.

βαστάζεις, 2 pers. sg. pres. act. indic. . . . . id.

βαστάζεσθαι, pres. pass. infin. . . . . id.

βαστάζετε, 2 pers. pl. pres. act. imper. . . . . id.

βαστάζοντες, nom. pl. m. pres. act. part. . id.

βαστάζοντος, gen. sg. neut. pres. act. part. id.

(941) **βαστάζω,** 1 pers. sg. pres. act. indic., fut. βαστάσω, aor. ἐβάστασα [§26.1] pr. *to lift, raise, bear aloft; to bear, carry* in the hands or about the person; *carry* as a message, Acts 9:15; *to take away, remove,* Matt. 8:17; John 20:15; *to take up,* John 10:31; Luke 14:27; *to bear* as a burden, *endure, suffer; to sustain,* Rom. 11:18; *to bear with, tolerate; to sustain* mentally, *comprehend,* John 16:12

βαστάζων, nom. sg. m. pres. act. part. . . . . βαστάζω *(941)*

βαστάσαι, aor. act. infin. . . . . id.

βαστάσασα, nom. sg. f. aor. act. part. . . . id.

βαστάσασι(ν), dat. pl. m. aor. act. part. . . id.

βαστάσει, 3 pers. sg. fut. act. indic. . . . . . id.

(942) **βάτος,** ου, ὁ, ἡ [§3.C.a,b] *a bush, bramble,* Mark 12:26, et al.

(943) **βάτος,** ου, ὁ (Hebrew בַּת) *a bath,* a measure for liquids, which is stated by Josephus

(*Ant.* 8.57) to contain seventy-two sextarii, or about thirteen and one half gallons.
Others estimate it to be nine gallons; and
others, seven and one half gallons, Luke
16:6

βάτου, gen. sg. m. n. . . . . βάτος *(942)*

βάτους, acc. pl. m. n. (Hebrew בַּת) . . . . βάτος *(943)*

βάτραχοι, nom. pl. m. n. . . . . βάτραχος *(944)*

βατράχοις, dat. pl. m. n. (Rev. 16:13, TR |
βατράχοι, GNT, WH, MT & NA) . . . id.

(944) **βάτραχος,** ου, ὁ [§3.C.a] *a frog,* Rev. 16:13

βατταλογήσητε, 2 pers. pl. aor. act. subj.
(Matt. 6:7, GNT, WH & NA | βαττο-
λογήσητε, MT & TR) . . . . . . βαττολογέω *(945)*

(945) **βαττολογέω,** ῶ, fut. βαττολογήσω [§16.P]
(βάττος, *a stammerer*) pr. *to stammer;*
hence, *to babble; to use vain repetitions,*
Matt. 6:7

βάτῳ, dat. sg. m. n. . . . . βάτος *(942)*

βάψας, nom. sg. m. aor. act. part. . . . . . βάπτω *(911)*

βάψῃ, 3 pers. sg. aor. act. subj. . . . . id.

βάψω, 1 pers. sg. fut. act. indic. (John 13:26,
GNT, WH & NA | ἐμβάψας, MT &
TR) . . . . id.

(946) **βδέλυγμα,** ατος, τό, nom. sg. neut. n. [§4.D.c]
an abomination, an abominable thing,
Matt. 24:15; Mark 13:14, et al.; *idolatry
with all its pollutions,* Rev. 17:4, 5; 21:7
{Luke 16:15}

βδέλυγμα, acc. sg. neut. n.
{Matt. 24:15} . . . . βδέλυγμα *(946)*

βδελυγμάτων, gen. pl. neut. n. . . . . id.

βδελυκτοί, nom. pl. m. adj. . . . . . . βδελυκτός *(947)*

(947) **βδελυκτός,** ή, όν [§7.F.a] *abominable, detestable,* Tit. 1:16

(†948) **βδελύσσομαι,** fut. βδελύξομαι, perf.
ἐβδέλυγμαι [§26.3] *to abominate, loathe,
detest, abhor,* Rom. 2:22; pass. *to be
abominable, detestable,* Rev. 21:8

βδελυσσόμενος, nom. sg. m. pres. mid./pass.
dep. part. . . . . βδελύσσομαι *(†948)*

βεβαία, nom. sg. f. adj. . . . . βέβαιος *(949)*

βεβαίαν, acc. sg. f. adj. . . . . id.

(949) **βέβαιος,** αία, ον, nom. sg. m. adj. [§7.1]
(βέβαα, perf. of βαίνω) *firm, stable, steadfast,* Heb. 3:6, 14; 6:19; *sure, certain, established,* Rom. 4:16, et al.

βεβαιότερον, acc. sg. m. compar. adj.
[§8.4] . . . . βέβαιος *(949)*

βεβαιούμενοι, nom. pl. m. pres. pass.
part. . . . . βεβαιόω *(950)*

βεβαιοῦντος, gen. sg. m. pres. act. part. . . id.

βεβαιοῦσθαι, pres. pass. infin. [§21.U] . . . . id.

(950) **βεβαιόω,** ῶ, fut. βεβαιώσω, aor. ἐβεβαίωσα
[§20.T] *to confirm, establish; to render*

constant and unwavering, 1 Cor. 1:8, et al.;
to strengthen or *establish* by arguments or
proofs, *ratify,* Mark 16:20; *to verify,* as
promises, Rom. 15:8

βεβαιῶν, nom. sg. m. pres. act. part. . βεβαιόω *(950)*

βεβαιῶσαι, aor. act. infin. . . . . id.

βεβαιώσει, 3 pers. sg. fut. act. indic.
{1 Cor. 1:8} . . . . id.

βεβαιώσει, dat. sg. f. n. {Phil. 1:7} . . βεβαίωσις *(951)*

βεβαίωσιν, acc. sg. f. n. . . . . id.

(951) **βεβαίωσις,** εως, ἡ [§5.E.c] *confirmation, firm
establishment,* Phil. 1:7; Heb. 6:16

βεβαμμένον, acc. sg. neut. perf. pass.
part. . . . . βάπτω *(911)*

βεβαπτισμένοι, nom. pl. m. perf. pass. part. id.

βεβαρημένοι, nom. pl. m. perf. pass.
part. . . . . βαρέω *(916)*

βεβήλοις, dat. pl. m. adj. . . . . βέβηλος *(952)*

(952) **βέβηλος,** ον, nom. sg. m. adj. [§7.2] (βαίνω,
to tread, and βηλός, *a threshold*) pr. *what
is open and accessible to all;* hence, *profane, not religious, not connected with religion; unholy; a despiser, scorner,* 1 Tim.
1:9; 4:7, et al.

βεβήλους, acc. pl. m. adj.
{1 Tim. 4:7} . . . . βέβηλος *(952)*

βεβήλους, acc. pl. f. adj. {1 Tim. 6:20} . . id.

βεβηλοῦσι(ν), 3 pers. pl. pres. act.
indic. . . . . βεβηλόω *(953)*

(953) **βεβηλόω,** ῶ, fut. βεβηλώσω, aor. ἐβεβήλωσα
[§20.T] *to profane, pollute, violate,* Matt.
12:5; Acts 24:6

βεβηλῶσαι, aor. act. infin. . . . . βεβηλόω *(953)*

βέβληκε(ν), 3 pers. sg. perf. act. indic.
[§27.2.d] (Mark 12:43, MT & TR |
ἔβαλεν, GNT, WH & NA) . . . . βάλλω *(906)*

βεβληκότος, gen. sg. m. perf. act. part. . . id.

βεβλημένην, acc. sg. f. perf. pass. part. . . id.

βεβλημένον, acc. sg. m. perf. pass. part. . . id.

βεβλημένος, nom. sg. m. perf. pass. part. . . id.

βέβληται, 3 pers. sg. perf. pass. indic. . . . . id.

βεβρωκόσιν, dat. pl. m. perf. act. part.
[§36.3] . . . . βιβρώσκω *(977)*

(†954) **Βεελζεβούβ,** ὁ, *Beelzeboub,* pr. name, indecl.
(Matt. 10:25, TRb | Βεεζεβούλ, WH |
Βεελζεβούλ, GNT, TRs & NA)

(954) **Βεελζεβούλ,** ὁ, *Beelzeboul,* pr. name, indecl.
(Matt. 10:25, GNT, TRs & NA |
Βεελζεβούβ, TRb | Βεεζεβούλ, WH)

βέλη, acc. pl. neut. n. . . . . βέλος *(956)*

(†955) **Βελίαρ,** ὁ, *Belial,* pr. name, indecl. (2 Cor.
6:15, GNT, MT & NA | Βελίαρ, WH &
TRs | Βελίαλ, TRb)

(‡4476) **βελόνη,** ης, ἡ [§2.B.a] v.r. pr. *the point of a
spear; a needle,* Luke 18:25

βελόνης, gen. sg. f. n. (Luke 18:25, GNT, WH & NA | ῥαφίδος, MT & TR) . . . βελόνη (‡4476)

(956) **βέλος**, ους, τό [§5.E.c] *a missile weapon, dart, arrow,* Eph. 6:16

βέλτιον, acc. sg. neut. n. used adverbially . . . . βελτίων (†957)

(†957) **βελτίων**, ον, compar. adj. of ἀγαθός [§8.3] *better;* βέλτιον, as an adv., *very well, too well to need informing,* 2 Tim. 1:18

(958) **Βενιαμίν**, ὁ, *Benjamin,* pr. name, indecl. (GNT, MT, TR & NA | Βενιαμείν, WH | Rom. 11:1, Βενιαμίν, TRb)

(959) **Βερνίκη**, ης, ἡ, nom. sg. f. n. [§2.B.a] *Bernice,* pr. name, Acts 25:23

Βερνίκης, gen. sg. f. n. . . . . Βερνίκη (959)

(960) **Βέροια**, ας, ἡ [§2.B.b; 2.2] *Berea,* a town of Macedonia

Βεροίᾳ, dat. sg. f. n. . . . . Βέροια (960)

(961) **Βεροιαῖος**, α, ον, nom. sg. m. adj. [§7.1] *belonging to Berea,* Acts 20:4

Βέροιαν, acc. sg. f. n. . . . . Βέροια (960)

(‡1007) **Βεώρ**, ὁ, indecl. pr. name, *Beor* (2 Pet. 2:15, WH | Βοσόρ, GNT, MT, TR & NA)

(962) **Βηθαβαρά**, ᾶς, ἡ [§2.B.b; 2.2] *Bethabara,* a town of Palestine, John 1:28

Βηθαβαρᾷ, dat. sg. f. n. (John 1:28, TR | Βηθανίᾳ, GNT, WH, MT & NA) . . . . Βηθαβαρά (962)

(963) **Βηθανία**, ας, ἡ, nom. sg. f. n. [§2.B.b; 2.2] *Bethany* I. A village near Jerusalem, at the Mount of Olives, Matt. 21:17; Mark 11:1, et al. II. A village beyond the Jordan, John 1:28

Βηθανίᾳ, dat. sg. f. n. . . . . Βηθανία (963)
Βηθανίαν, acc. sg. f. n. . . . . id.
Βηθανίας, gen. sg. f. n. . . . . id.

(964) **Βηθεσδά**, ἡ, *Bethesda,* indecl., a pool in Jerusalem (John 5:2, MT & TR | Βηθζαθά, GNT, WH & NA)

(†964) **Βηθζαθα**, ἡ, *Bethzatha,* indecl. (John 5:2, GNT, WH & NA | Βηθεσδά, MT & TR)

(†965) **Βηθλέεμ**, ἡ, *Bethlehem,* indecl., a town in Palestine (GNT & NA | Βηθλεέμ, MT, WH & TR)

(966) **Βηθσαϊδά**, ἡ, *Bethsaida,* indecl. I. A city of Galilee, Matt. 11:21; Mark 6:45, et al. II. A city of Lower Gaulanitis, near the Lake of Gennesareth, Luke 9:10

Βηθσαϊδάν, acc. sg. f. n. . . . . Βηθσαϊδά (966)

(†967) **Βηθσφαγή**, ἡ, *Bethphage,* indecl. (Matt. 21:1; Mark 11:1, MT | Βηθφαγή, GNT, WH, TR & NA)

(967) **Βηθφαγή**, ἡ, *Bethphage,* indecl., a part of the Mount of Olives

(968) **βῆμα**, ατος, τό [§4.D.c] (βαίνω) *a step, foot-*

step, foot-breadth, space to set the foot on, Acts 7:5; *an elevated place ascended by steps, tribunal, throne,* Matt. 27:19; Acts 12:21, et al.

βῆμα, acc. sg. neut. n. . . . . βῆμα (968)
βήματι, dat. sg. neut. n. . . . . id.
βήματος, gen. sg. neut. n. . . . . id.

(969) **βήρυλλος**, ου, ὁ, ἡ, nom. sg. m. n. [§3.C.a,b] *a beryl,* a precious stone of a sea-green color, found chiefly in India

(970) **βία**, ας, ἡ [§2.B.b; 2.2] *force, impetus, violence,* Acts 5:26; 21:35, et al.

βιάζεται, 3 pers. sg. pres. mid. indic. {Luke 16:16} . . . . βιάζω (971)
βιάζεται, 3 pers. sg. pres. pass. indic. {Matt. 11:12} . . . . id.

(971) **βιάζω**, fut. βιάσω [§26.1] and mid. βιάζομαι, *to urge, constrain, overpower by force; to press earnestly forward, to rush,* Luke 16:16; pass. *to be an object of an impetuous movement,* Matt. 11:12

βιαίας, gen. sg. f. adj. . . . . βίαιος (972)

(972) **βίαιος**, α, ον [§7.1] *violent, vehement,* Acts 2:2

βίαν, acc. sg. f. n. . . . . βία (970)
βίας, gen. sg. f. n. . . . . id.
βιασταί, nom. pl. m. n. . . . . βιαστής (973)

(973) **βιαστής**, οῦ, ὁ [§2.B.c] *one who uses violence, or is impetuous; one who is forceful* in eager pursuit, Matt. 11:12

(974) **βιβλαρίδιον**, ου, τό [§3.C.c] (dimin. of βιβλάριον, *a roll*) *a small volume* or *scroll, a little book,* Rev. 10:2, 8, 9, 10

βιβλαρίδιον, acc. sg. neut. n. . . . . . βιβλαρίδιον (974)
βιβλία, nom. pl. neut. n. {Rev. 20:12} . βιβλίον (975)
βιβλία, acc. pl. neut. n. {John 21:25} . . . . id.
βιβλίοις, dat. pl. neut. n. . . . . id.

(975) **βιβλίον**, ου, τό, nom. sg. neut. n. [§3.C.c] (pr. dimin. of βίβλος) *a written volume* or *roll, book,* Luke 4:17, 20, et al.; *a scroll, bill, billet,* Matt. 19:7; Mark 10:4 {Rev. 6:14}

βιβλίον, acc. sg. neut. n. {Rev. 5:1} . . . βιβλίον (975)
βιβλίου, gen. sg. neut. n. . . . . id.
βιβλίῳ, dat. sg. neut. n. . . . . id.

(976) **βίβλος**, ου, ἡ, nom. sg. f. n. [§3.C.b] pr. *the inner bark* or *rind of the papyrus,* which was anciently used instead of paper; hence, *a written volume* or *roll, book, catalogue, account,* Matt. 1:1; Mark 12:26, et al.

βίβλου, gen. sg. f. n. . . . . βίβλος (976)
βίβλους, acc. pl. f. n. . . . . id.
βίβλῳ, dat. sg. f. n. . . . . id.

(977) **βιβρώσκω**, fut. βιβρώσομαι, perf. βέβρωκα [§36.3] *to eat,* John 6:13

(978) **Βιθυνία**, ας, ἡ [§2.B.b; 2.2] *Bithynia,* a province of Asia Minor

Βιθυνίαν, acc. sg. f. n. . . . . Βιθυνία *(978)*
Βιθυνίας, gen. sg. f. n. . . . . id.
βίον, acc. sg. m. n. . . . . βίος *(979)*
(979) **βίος**, ου, ὁ [§3.C.a] *life; means of living; suste-nance, maintenance, substance, goods,* Mark 12:44, et al.
βίου, gen. sg. m. n. . . . . βίος *(979)*
(980) **βιόω**, ῶ, fut. βιώσω, aor. ἐβίωσα [§20.T] *to live,* 1 Pet. 4:2
βιῶσαι, aor. act. infin. . . . . βιόω *(980)*
βίωσιν, acc. sg. f. n. . . . . βίωσις *(981)*
(981) **βίωσις**, εως, ἡ [§5.E.c] *manner of life,* Acts 26:4
βιωτικά, acc. pl. neut. adj. . . . . βιωτικός *(982)*
βιωτικαῖς, dat. pl. f. adj. . . . . id.
(982) **βιωτικός**, ή, όν [§7.F.a] *pertaining to this life* or *the things of this life,* Luke 21:34; 1 Cor. 6:3, 4
βλαβεράς, acc. pl. f. adj. . . . . βλαβερός *(983)*
(983) **βλαβερός**, ά, όν [§7.1] *hurtful,* 1 Tim. 6:9
(984) **βλάπτω**, fut. βλάψω, aor. ἔβλαψα [§23.1.a; 23.2] pr. *to weaken, hinder, disable; to hurt, harm, injure,* Mark 16:18; Luke 4:35
βλαστᾷ, 3 pers. sg. pres. act. subj. (as if from βλαστάω | Mark 4:27, GNT, WH & NA | βλαστάνη, MT & TR) . . . . . . βλαστάνω *(985)*
βλαστάνη, 3 pers. sg. pres. act. subj. (Mark 4:27, MT & TR | βλαστᾷ, GNT, WH & NA) . . . . id.
(985) **βλαστάνω**, fut. βλαστήσω, aor. ἐβλάστησα, 2 aor. ἔβλαστον [§36.2] intrans. *to germinate, bud, sprout, spring up,* Matt. 13:26; Mark 4:27; Heb. 9:4; trans. and causat. *to cause to shoot, to produce, yield,* James 5:18
βλαστήσασα, nom. sg. f. aor. act. part. . . . . βλαστάνω *(985)*
Βλάστον, acc. sg. m. n. . . . . Βλάστος *(986)*
(986) **Βλάστος**, ου, ὁ [§3.C.a] *Blastus,* pr. name, Acts 12:20
βλάσφημα, acc. pl. neut. adj. . . . . . βλάσφημος *(989)*
βλασφημεῖ, 3 pers. sg. pres. act. indic. . . . . βλασφημέω *(987)*
βλασφημεῖν, pres. act. infin. . . . . id.
βλασφημεῖς, 2 pers. sg. pres. act. indic. . . id.
βλασφημείσθω, 3 pers. sg. pres. pass. imper. id.
βλασφημεῖται, 3 pers. sg. pres. pass. indic. [§17.Q] . . . . id.
(987) **βλασφημέω**, ῶ, fut. βλασφημήσω [§16.P] perf. βεβλασφήμηκα, aor. ἐβλασφήμησα, *to calumniate, revile, treat with calumny and contumely,* Matt. 27:39, et al.; *to speak of God* or *divine things in terms of impious irreverence, to blaspheme,* Matt. 9:3; 26:65, et al.

βλασφημηθήσεται, 3 pers. sg. fut. pass. indic. βλασφημέω *(987)*
βλασφημῆσαι, aor. act. infin. . . . . id.
βλασφημήσαντι, dat. sg. m. aor. act. part. id.
βλασφημήση, 3 pers. sg. aor. act. subj. . . . id.
βλασφημήσωσιν, 3 pers. pl. aor. act. subj. id.
βλασφημῆται, 3 pers. sg. pres. pass. subj. id.
(988) **βλασφημία**, ας, ἡ, nom. sg. f. n. [§2.B.b; 2.2] *calumny, railing, reproach,* Matt. 15:19; Mark 7:22, et al.; *blasphemy,* Matt. 12:31; 26:65, et al.
βλασφημίαι, nom. pl. f. n. . . . . βλασφημία *(988)*
βλασφημίαν, acc. sg. f. n. . . . . id.
βλασφημίας, gen. sg. f. n. {Rev. 13:1} . . . . id.
βλασφημίας, acc. pl. f. n. {Rev. 13:5} . . . . id.
βλάσφημοι, nom. pl. m. adj. . . . . . βλάσφημος *(989)*
βλάσφημον, acc. sg. m. adj. {1 Tim. 1:13} id.
βλάσφημον, acc. sg. f. adj. {2 Pet. 2:11} . . id.
(989) **βλάσφημος**, ον [§7.2] *calumnious, railing, re-proachful,* 2 Tim. 3:2; 2 Pet. 2:11; *blas-phemous,* Acts 6:11, 13; 1 Tim. 1:13
βλασφημοῦμαι, 1 pers. sg. pres. pass. indic. . . . . βλασφημέω *(987)*
βλασφημούμεθα, 1 pers. pl. pres. pass. indic. id.
βλασφημούμενοι, nom. pl. m. pres. pass. part. (1 Cor. 4:13, MT & TR | δυσφημούμενοι, GNT, WH & NA) . . . . id.
βλασφημοῦντας, acc. pl. m. pres. act. part. id.
βλασφημοῦντες, nom. pl. m. pres. act. part. id.
βλασφημούντων, gen. pl. m. pres. act. part. id.
βλασφημοῦσι(ν), 3 pers. pl. pres. act. indic. id.
βλάψαν, nom. sg. neut. aor. act. part. . βλάπτω *(984)*
βλάψει, 3 pers. sg. fut. act. indic. (Mark 16:18, TR | βλάψη, GNT, WH, MT & NA) . id.
βλάψη, 3 pers. sg. aor. act. subj. (Mark 16:18, GNT, WH, MT & NA | βλάψει, TR) . id.
(990) **βλέμμα**, ατος, τό [§4.D.c] *a look; the act of seeing, sight,* 2 Pet. 2:8
βλέμματι, dat. sg. neut. n. . . . . βλέμμα *(990)*
βλέπε, 2 pers. sg. pres. act. imper. . . . . . βλέπω *(991)*
βλέπει, 3 pers. sg. pres. act. indic. . . . . id.
βλέπειν, pres. act. infin. . . . . id.
βλέπεις, 2 pers. sg. pres. act. indic. . . . . . . id.
βλέπετε, 2 pers. pl. pres. act. indic. {Matt. 24:2} . . . . id.
βλέπετε, 2 pers. pl. pres. act. imper. {Matt. 24:4} . . . . id.
βλεπέτω, 3 pers. sg. pres. act. imper. . . . . id.
βλέπη, 3 pers. sg. pres. act. subj. . . . . id.
βλέπης, 2 pers. sg. pres. act. subj. . . . . . . id.
βλέπομεν, 1 pers. pl. pres. act. indic. . . . . id.
βλεπόμενα, nom. pl. neut. pres. pass. part. {2 Cor. 4:18c,d} . . . . id.
βλεπόμενα, acc. pl. neut. pres. pass. part. {2 Cor. 4:18a,b} . . . . id.

βλεπομένη, nom. sg. f. pres. pass. part. . βλέπω (991)
βλεπόμενον, acc. sg. neut. pres. pass. part.
   (Heb. 11:3, GNT, WH & NA | βλεπό-
   μενα, MT & TR) . . . . id.
βλεπομένων, gen. pl. neut. pres. pass. part. id.
βλέποντα, acc. sg. m. pres. act. part. . . . . id.
βλέποντας, acc. pl. m. pres. act. part. . . . id.
βλέποντες, nom. pl. m. pres. act. part. . . . id.
βλεπόντων, gen. pl. m. pres. act. part. . . . id.
βλέπουσι(ν), 3 pers. pl. pres. act. indic. . . id.
(991) **βλέπω**, 1 pers. sg. pres. act. indic., fut. βλέψω,
   aor. ἔβλεψα [§23.1.a; 23.2] *to have the fa-*
   culty of sight, to see, Matt. 12:22, et al.;
   to exercise sight, to see, Matt. 6:4, et al.;
   to look towards or at, Matt. 22:16, et al.;
   to face, Acts 27:12; *to take heed,* Matt.
   24:4, et al.; in N.T., βλέπειν ἀπό, *to be-*
   ware of, shun, Mark 8:15; trans., *to cast*
   a look on, Matt. 5:28; *to see, behold,*
   Matt. 13:17, et al.; *to observe,* Matt. 7:3,
   et al.; *to have an eye to, see to,* Mark 13:9;
   Col. 4:17; 2 John 8; *to discern* mentally,
   perceive, Rom. 7:23; 2 Cor. 7:8; James
   2:22; *to guard against,* Phil. 3:2; pass., *to*
   be an object of sight, be visible, Rom. 8:24,
   et al.
βλέπων, nom. sg. m. pres. act. part. . . . . βλέπω (991)
βλέπωσι(ν), 3 pers. pl. pres. act. subj. . . . id.
βλέψετε, 2 pers. pl. fut. act. indic. . . . . . . id.
βλέψον, 2 pers. sg. aor. act. imper. . . . . . . id.
βλέψουσιν, 3 pers. pl. fut. act. indic. (Rev.
   11:9, TR | βλέπουσιν, GNT, WH, MT &
   NA) . . . . id.
βληθείς, nom. sg. m. aor. pass. part. (Luke
   23:19, GNT, WH & NA | βεβλημένος,
   MT & TR) . . . . βάλλω (906)
βληθείσῃ, dat. sg. f. aor. pass. part. . . . . . id.
βληθέν, nom. sg. neut. aor. pass. part. (Matt.
   5:13, GNT, WH & NA | βληθῆναι, MT
   & TR) . . . . id.
βληθῇ, 3 pers. sg. aor. pass. subj. . . . . id.
βληθῆναι, aor. pass. infin. . . . . id.
βληθήσεται, 3 pers. sg. fut. pass. indic.
   [§27.3] . . . . id.
βληθήσῃ, 2 pers. sg. fut. pass. indic. . . . . id.
βλήθητι, 2 pers. sg. aor. pass. imper. . . . . . id.
βλητέον, nom. sg. neut. adj. . . . . βλητέος (992)
(992) **βλητέος**, α, ον, verbal adj. [§35.10] *requiring*
   to be cast or *put,* Mark 2:22; Luke 5:38
βοαί, nom. pl. f. n. . . . . βοή (995)
(993) **Βοανηργές**, *Boanerges,* pr. name, indecl.
   (Mark 3:17, GNT, WH & NA |
   Βοανεργές, MT & TR)
βόας, acc. pl. m. n. [§6.4.h] . . . . βοῦς (1016)
(994) **βοάω**, ῶ, fut. βοήσω, aor. ἐβόησα [§18.R] *to*

cry out; to exclaim, proclaim, Matt. 3:3;
   15:34; Acts 8:7, et al.; πρός τινα, *to in-*
   voke, implore the aid of any one, Luke 18:7
(‡1003) **Βοές**, ὁ, *Boaz,* pr. name, indecl. (Matt. 1:5;
   Luke 3:32, WH | Βόες, GNT & NA |
   Βοόζ, TR | Βόοζ, MT)
(995) **βοή**, ῆς, ἡ [§2.B.b; 2.2] *a cry, outcry, excla-*
   mation, James 5:4
βοήθει, 2 pers. sg. pres. act. imper. . . . . βοηθέω (997)
(996) **βοήθεια**, ας, ἡ [§2.B.b; 2.2] *help, succor,* Heb.
   4:16; meton. pl. *helps, contrivances for re-*
   lief and safety, Acts 27:17
βοηθείαις, dat. pl. f. n. . . . . βοήθεια (996)
βοήθειαν, acc. sg. f. n. . . . . id.
βοηθεῖτε, 2 pers. pl. pres. act. imper. . . βοηθέω (997)
(997) **βοηθέω**, ῶ, fut. βοηθήσω, aor. ἐβοήθησα
   [§16.P] (βοή + θέω, *to run*) *to run to the*
   aid of those who cry for help; to advance
   to the assistance of any one, help, aid, suc-
   cor, Matt. 15:25; Mark 9:22, 24, et al.
βοηθῆσαι, aor. act. infin. . . . . βοηθέω (997)
βοήθησον, 2 pers. sg. aor. act. imper. . . . . id.
(998) **βοηθός**, οῦ, ὁ, nom. sg. m. n. [§3.C.a] *a*
   helper, Heb. 13:6
βόησον, 2 pers. sg. aor. act. imper. . . . . . βοάω (994)
βόθυνον, acc. sg. m. n. . . . . βόθυνος (999)
(999) **βόθυνος**, ου, ὁ [§3.C.a] *a pit, well* or *cistern,*
   Matt. 12:11; 15:14; Luke 6:39
(1000) **βολή**, ῆς, ἡ [§2.B.a] *a cast, a throw; the dis-*
   tance to which a thing can be thrown, Luke
   22:41
βολήν, acc. sg. f. n. . . . . βολή (1000)
βολίδι, dat. sg. f. n. βολίς (Heb. 12:20, TR
   | GNT, WH, MT & NA omit) . . . . . βολίς (1002)
(1001) **βολίζω**, fut. βολίσω, aor ἐβόλισα [§26.1] *to*
   heave the lead, sound, Acts 27:28
(1002) **βολίς**, ίδος, ἡ [§4.2.c] *a missile weapon, dart,*
   javelin, Heb. 12:20; also, *a plummet, lead*
   for sounding
βολίσαντες, nom. pl. m. aor. act. part. βολίζω (1001)
(†1003) **Βοόζ**, ὁ, *Booz,* pr. name, indecl. (Matt. 1:5;
   Luke 3:32, TR | Βόοζ, MT | Βόες, Matt.
   1:5, GNT, WH & NA | Βόος, Luke 3:32
   GNT & NA | Βόος, WH)
(1003) **Βοός**, ὁ, *Boaz,* pr. name, indecl. (Luke 3:32,
   WH | Βόος, GNT & NA | Βοόζ, TR |
   Βόοζ, MT)
(1004) **βόρβορος**, ου, ὁ [§3.C.a] *mud, mire, dung,*
   filth, 2 Pet. 2:22
βορβόρου, gen. sg. m. n. . . . . βόρβορος (1004)
βορρᾶ, gen. sg. m. n. . . . . βορρᾶς (1005)
(1005) **βορρᾶς**, ᾶ, ὁ [§2.4] i.q. βορέας, pr. *the north*
   or *N.N.E. wind;* meton. *the north,* Luke
   13:29; Rev. 21:13
βόσκε, 2 pers. sg. pres. act. imper. . . . . βόσκω (1006)

βόσκειν, pres. act. infin. . . . . βόσκω *(1006)*

βοσκομένη, nom. sg. f. pres. pass. part. . . id.

βοσκομένων, gen. pl. m. pres. pass. part.
(Luke 8:32, MT & TR | βοσκομένη,
GNT, WH & NA) . . . . id.

βόσκοντες, nom. pl. m. pres. act. part. . . id.

(1006) **βόσκω,** fut. βοσκήσω [§35.5] aor. ἐβόσκησα,
to feed, pasture, tend while grazing;
βόσκομαι, *to feed, be feeding,* Matt.
8:30, 33; Luke 8:32, 34, et al.

(1007) **Βοσόρ,** ὁ, *Bosor,* pr. name, indecl. (2 Pet. 2:15,
GNT, MT, TR & NA | Βεώρ, WH)

(1008) **βοτάνη,** ης, ἡ [§2.B.a] *herb, herbage, produce
of the earth,* Heb. 6:7

βοτάνην, acc. sg. f. n. . . . . βοτάνη *(1008)*

βότρυας, acc. pl. m. n. . . . . βότρυς *(1009)*

(1009) **βότρυς,** υος, ὁ [§5.E.g] *a bunch* or *cluster of
grapes,* Rev. 14:18

βουλάς, acc. pl. f. n. . . . . βουλή *(1012)*

βούλει, 2 pers. sg. pres. mid./pass. dep. indic.
Att. [§35.11] . . . . βούλομαι *(1014)*

βούλεσθε, 2 pers. pl. pres. mid./pass. dep.
indic. . . . . id.

βούλεται, 3 pers. sg. pres. mid./pass. dep.
indic. . . . . id.

βουλεύεται, 3 pers. sg. pres. mid./pass. dep.
indic. (Luke 14:31, MT & TR | βουλεύ-
σεται, GNT, WH & NA) . . . . βουλεύομαι *(‡1011)*

(‡1011) **βουλεύομαι,** 1 pers. sg. pres. mid./pass. dep.
indic., *to resolve, decide*

βουλευόμενος, nom. sg. m. pres. mid./pass.
dep. part. (2 Cor. 1:17, MT & TR |
βουλόμενος, GNT, WH &
NA) . . . . βουλεύομαι *(‡1011)*

βουλεύσεται, 3 pers. sg. fut. mid. dep. indic.
(Luke 14:31, GNT, WH & NA |
βουλεύεται, MT & TR) . . . . id.

(1010) **βουλευτής,** οῦ, ὁ, nom. sg. m. n. [§2.B.c] *a
counsellor, senator; member of the San-
hedrin,* Mark 15:43; Luke 23:50

(1011) **βουλεύω,** fut. βουλεύσω [§13.M] *to give counsel, to deliberate;* mid. βουλεύομαι, *to deliberate,* Luke 14:31; John 12:10; Acts 5:33;
to purpose, determine, Acts 15:37; 27:39;
2 Cor. 1:17

(1012) **βουλή,** ῆς, ἡ, nom. sg. f. n. [§2.B.a] *counsel,
purpose, design, determination, decree,*
Luke 7:30; 23:51; et al. freq.; by impl. *secret thoughts, cogitations* of the mind,
1 Cor. 4:5

βουλῇ, dat. sg. f. n. . . . . βουλή *(1012)*

βουληθείς, nom. sg. m. aor. pass. dep.
part. . . . . βούλομαι *(1014)*

βουλήθῃ, 3 pers. sg. aor. pass. dep. subj. . id.

(1013) **βούλημα,** ατος, τό [§4.D.c] *purpose, will, de-*

termination, Acts 27:43; Rom. 9:19

βούλημα, acc. sg. neut. (1 Pet. 4:3, GNT, WH
& NA | θέλημα, MT & TR) . . . . βούλημα *(1013)*

βουλήματι, dat. sg. neut. n. . . . . id.

βουλήματος, gen. sg. neut. n. . . . . id.

βουλήν, acc. sg. f. n. . . . . βουλή *(1012)*

βουλῆς, gen. sg. f. n. . . . . id.

βούληται, 3 pers. sg. pres. mid./pass. dep.
subj. . . . . βούλομαι *(1014)*

βούλοιτο, 3 pers. sg. pres. mid./pass. dep.
opt. . . . . id.

(1014) **βούλομαι,** 1 pers. sg. pres. mid./pass. dep.
indic., fut. βουλήσομαι [§35.5] imperf.
ἐβουλόμην and Att. ἠβουλόμην, aor.
(pass. form) ἐβουλήθην and ἠβουλήθην,
perf. (pass. form) βεβούλημαι, *to be willing, disposed,* Mark 15:15; Acts 25:20;
28:18, et al.; *to intend,* Matt. 1:19; Acts
5:28; 12:4; 2 Cor. 1:15; *to desire,* 1 Tim.
6:9; *to choose, be pleased,* John 18:39; Acts
18:15; James 3:4; *to will, decree, appoint,*
Luke 22:42; James 1:18; 1 Cor. 12:11;
1 Tim. 2:8; 5:14, et al.; ἐβουλόμην, *I could
wish,* Acts 25:22

βουλόμεθα, 1 pers. pl. pres. mid./pass. dep.
indic. . . . . βούλομαι *(1014)*

βουλόμενοι, nom. pl. m. pres. mid./pass. dep.
part. . . . . id.

βουλόμενος, nom. sg. m. pres. mid./pass. dep.
part. . . . . id.

βουλομένου, gen. sg. m. pres. mid./pass. dep.
part. . . . . id.

βουλομένους, acc. pl. m. pres. mid./pass. dep.
part. . . . . id.

βοῦν, acc. sg. m. n. . . . . βοῦς *(1016)*

βουνοῖς, dat. pl. m. n. . . . . βουνός *(1015)*

(1015) **βουνός,** οῦ, ὁ, nom. sg. m. n. [§3.C.a] *a hill,
hillock, rising ground,* Luke 3:5; 23:30

(1016) **βοῦς,** βοός, ὁ, ἡ, nom. sg. m. n. [§6.4.h] *an
ox, a bull* or *cow,* an animal of the ox kind,
Luke 13:15, et al.

βοῶν, gen. pl. m. n. . . . . βοῦς *(1016)*

βοῶντα, nom. pl. neut. pres. act. part. . . βοάω *(994)*

βοῶντες, nom. pl. m. pres. act. part. . . . . id.

βοῶντος, gen. sg. m. pres. act. part. . . . . . id.

βοώντων, gen. pl. m. pres. act. part. . . . . id.

(1017) **βραβεῖον,** ου, τό [§3.C.c] (βραβεύς, *a judge*
or *arbiter in the public games*) *a prize* bestowed on victors in the public games, such
as a crown, wreath, chaplet, garland, etc.,
1 Cor. 9:24; Phil. 3:14

βραβεῖον, acc. sg. neut. n. . . . . βραβεῖον *(1017)*

βραβευέτω, 3 pers. sg. pres. act.
imper. . . . . βραβεύω *(1018)*

(1018) **βραβεύω,** fut. βραβεύσω [§13.M] pr. *to be a*

director or arbiter in the public games; in
N.T. to preside, direct, rule, govern, be pre-
dominant, Col. 3:15

βραδεῖς, nom. pl. m. adj. . . . . βραδύς *(1021)*

βραδύνει, 3 pers. sg. pres. act. indic. . βραδύνω *(1019)*

(1019) **βραδύνω**, fut. βραδυνῶ [§27.1.a] to be slow,
to delay, 1 Tim. 3:15; 2 Pet. 3:9

βραδύνω, 1 pers. sg. pres. act. subj. . βραδύνω *(1019)*

(1020) **βραδυπλοέω**, ῶ, fut. βραδυπλοήσω [§16.P]
(βραδύς + πλέω) to sail slowly, Acts 27:7

βραδυπλοοῦντες, nom. pl. m. pres. act.
part. . . . . βραδυπλοέω *(1020)*

(1021) **βραδύς**, εῖα, ύ, nom. sg. m. adj. [§7.H.g] slow,
not hasty, James 1:19; slow of understand-
ing, heavy, stupid, Luke 24:25

(1022) **βραδύτης**, τητος, ἡ [§4.2.c] slowness, tardi-
ness, delay, 2 Pet. 3:9

βραδύτητα, acc. sg. f. n. (2 Pet. 3:9, GNT,
MT & NA | βραδθτῆτα, WH &
TR) . . . . βραδύτης *(1022)*

βραχέων, gen. pl. neut. adj. . . . . βραχύς *(1024)*

βραχίονι, dat. sg. m. n. . . . . βραχίων *(1023)*

βραχίονος, gen. sg. m. n. . . . . id.

(1023) **βραχίων**, ονος, ὁ, nom. sg. m. n. [§4.2.e] the
arm; the arm as a symbol of power, Luke
1:51; John 12:38; Acts 13:17

βραχύ, acc. sg. neut. adj. . . . . βραχύς *(1024)*

(1024) **βραχύς**, εῖα, ύ [§7.H.g] short, brief; few, small,
Luke 22:58; John 6:7, et al.

βρέξαι, aor. act. infin. . . . . βρέχω *(1026)*

βρέφη, nom. pl. neut. n. {1 Pet. 2:2} . . βρέφος *(1025)*

βρέφη, acc. pl. neut. n. {Luke 18:15} . . . . . id.

(1025) **βρέφος**, ους, τό, nom. sg. neut. n. [§5.E.b]
a child; whether unborn, an embryo, fetus,
Luke 1:41, 44; or just born, an infant, Luke
2:12, 16; Acts 7:19; or partly grown, Luke
18:15; 2 Tim. 3:15; met. a babe in simplicity of faith, 1 Pet. 2:2 {Luke 1:41}

βρέφος, acc. sg. neut. n. {Luke 2:12} . βρέφος *(1025)*

βρέφους, gen. sg. neut. n. . . . . id.

βρέχει, 3 pers. sg. pres. act. indic. . . . . βρέχω *(1026)*

βρέχειν, pres. act. infin. . . . . id.

βρέχῃ, 3 pers. sg. pres. act. subj. . . . . id.

(1026) **βρέχω**, fut. βρέξω, aor. ἔβρεξα [§23.1.b; 23.2]
to wet, moisten, Luke 7:38; to rain, cause
or send rain, Matt. 5:45; Luke 17:29, et al.

βρονταί, nom. pl. f. n. . . . . βροντή *(1027)*

(1027) **βροντή**, ῆς, ἡ [§2.B.a] thunder, Mark 3:17;
John 12:29, et al.

βροντήν, acc. sg. f. n. . . . . βροντή *(1027)*

βροντῆς, gen. sg. f. n. . . . . id.

βροντῶν, gen. pl. f. n. . . . . id.

(1028) **βροχή**, ῆς, ἡ, nom. sg. f. n. [§2.B.a] rain,
Matt. 7:25, 27

βρόχον, acc. sg. m. n. . . . . βρόχος *(1029)*

(1029) **βρόχος**, ου, ὁ [§3.C.a] a cord, noose, 1 Cor.
7:35

(1030) **βρυγμός**, οῦ, ὁ, nom. sg. m. n. [§3.C.a] gnash-
ing of teeth together

βρύει, 3 pers. sg. pres. act. indic. . . . . βρύω *(1032)*

(1031) **βρύχω**, fut. βρύξω [§23.1.b] to grate or gnash
the teeth, Acts 7:54

(1032) **βρύω**, pr. to be full, to swell with anything;
to emit, send forth, James 3:11

(1033) **βρῶμα**, ατος, τό, nom. sg. neut. n. [§4.D.c]
food, Matt. 14:15; Mark 7:19, et al.; solid
food, 1 Cor. 3:2 {1 Cor. 8:8}

βρῶμα, acc. sg. neut. n. {1 Cor. 10:3} . βρῶμα *(1033)*

βρώμασι(ν), dat. pl. neut. n. . . . . id.

βρώματα, nom. pl. neut. n. {1 Cor. 6:13} . . id.

βρώματα, acc. pl. neut. n. {Luke 9:13} . . . id.

βρώματι, dat. sg. neut. n. . . . . id.

βρώματος, gen. sg. neut. n. . . . . id.

βρωμάτων, gen. pl. neut. n. . . . . id.

βρώσει, dat. sg. f. n. . . . . βρῶσις *(1035)*

βρώσεως, gen. sg. f. n. . . . . id.

βρώσιμον, acc. sg. neut. adj. . . . . . βρώσιμος *(1034)*

(1034) **βρώσιμος**, ον [§7.2] eatable, that may be
eaten, Luke 24:41

βρῶσιν, acc. sg. f. n. . . . . βρῶσις *(1035)*

(1035) **βρῶσις**, εως, ἡ, nom. sg. f. n. [§5.E.c] eating,
the act of eating, Rom. 14:17; 1 Cor. 8:4,
et al.; meat, food, John 6:27; Heb. 12:16;
a canker or rust, aerugo, Matt. 6:19, 20

βυθίζεσθαι, pres. pass. infin. . . . . βυθίζω *(1036)*

βυθίζουσι(ν), 3 pers. pl. pres. act. indic. . . id.

(1036) **βυθίζω**, fut. βυθίσω, aor. ἐβύθισα [§26.1] to
immerse, submerge, cause to sink, Luke
5:7; to plunge deep, drown, 1 Tim. 6:9

(1037) **βυθός**, οῦ, ὁ [§3.C.a] the bottom, lowest part;
the deep, sea, 2 Cor. 11:25

βυθῷ, dat. sg. m. n. . . . . βυθός *(1037)*

βυρσεῖ, dat. sg. m. n. . . . . βυρσεύς *(1038)*

(1038) **βυρσεύς**, έως, ὁ [§5.E.d] (βύρσα, a hide) a
tanner, leather-dresser, Acts 9:43; 10:6, 32

βυρσέως, gen. sg. m. n. . . . . βυρσεύς *(1038)*

βύσσινον, nom. sg. neut. adj.
{Rev. 19:8b} . . . . βύσσινος *(1039)*

βύσσινον, acc. sg. neut. adj. {Rev. 19:8a} . id.

(1039) **βύσσινος**, η, ον [§7.F.a] made of byssus or fine
cotton, Rev. 18:16

βυσσίνου, gen. sg. neut. adj. (Rev. 18:12,
GNT, WH, MT & NA | βύσσου,
TR) . . . . βύσσινος *(1039)*

βύσσον, acc. sg. f. n. . . . . βύσσος *(1040)*

(1040) **βύσσος**, ου, ἡ [§3.C.b] byssus, a species of fine
cotton highly prized by the ancients, Luke
16:19, v.r.; Rev. 18:12

βύσσου, gen. sg. f. n. (Rev. 18:12, TR | βυσ-
σίνου, GNT, WH, MT & NA) . . . βύσσος *(1040)*

βωμόν, acc. sg. m. n. . . . . βωμός *(1041)*

(1041) **βωμός**, οῦ, ὁ [§3.C.a] pr. *a slightly-elevated spot, base, pedestal;* hence, *an altar,* Acts 17:23

Γ

Γ, γ, gamma, third letter of the Greek alphabet; *third* in titles of N.T. writings.

(†1042) **Γαββαθα,** *Gabbatha,* pr. name, indecl. (John 19:13, GNT & NA | Γαββαθά, WH | Γαββαθᾶ, MT & TR)

(1043) **Γαβριήλ,** ὁ, *Gabriel,* pr. name, indecl.

(1044) **γάγγραινα,** ης, ἡ, nom. sg. f. n. [§2.3] (γράω, γραίνω, *to eat, gnaw) gangrene, mortification,* 2 Tim. 2:17

(1045) **Γάδ,** ὁ, *Gad,* pr. name, indecl., Rev. 7:5

(1046) **Γαδαρηνός,** ή, όν [§7.F] *an inhabitant of Gadara,* the chief city of Perea

Γαδαρηνῶν, gen. pl. m. adj. . . . . . Γαδαρηνός *(1046)*

(1047) **γάζα,** ης, ἡ, *a treasure, treasury,* Acts 8:27

(1048) **Γάζα,** ης, ἡ [§2.3] *Gaza,* a strong city of Palestine, Acts 8:26

Γάζαν, acc. sg. f. n. . . . . Γάζα *(1048)*

γάζης, gen. sg. f. n. . . . . γάζα *(1047)*

(1049) **γαζοφυλάκιον,** ου, τό [§3.C.c] (γάζα + φυλακή) *a treasury; the sacred treasury,* Mark 12:41, 43; Luke 21:1; John 8:20

γαζοφυλάκιον, acc. sg. neut. n. γαζοφυλάκιον *(1049)*

γαζοφυλακίου, gen. sg. neut. n. . . . . id.

γαζοφυλακίῳ, dat. sg. neut. n. . . . . id.

Γάϊον, acc. sg. m. n. (Acts 19:29; 1 Cor. 1:14, GNT, MT, TR & NA | Γαῖον, WH) Γάϊος *(1050)*

(1050) **Γάϊος,** ου, ὁ, nom. sg. m. n. [§3.C.a] *Gaius,* pr. name   I. Of Macedonia, Acts 19:29   II. Of Corinth, 1 Cor. 1:14   III. Of Derbe, Acts 20:4   IV. A Christian to whom John addressed his third Epistle, 3 John 1 (Acts 20:4; Rom. 16:23, GNT, MT, TR & NA | Γαῖος, WH)

Γαΐῳ, dat. sg. m. n. (3 John 1, GNT, MT, TR & NA | Γαίῳ, WH) . . . . Γάϊος *(1050)*

(1051) **γάλα,** γάλακτος, τό [§6.4.b] *milk,* 1 Cor. 9:7; met. spiritual *milk,* consisting in the elements of Christian instruction, 1 Cor. 3:2; Heb. 5:12, 13; spiritual *nutriment,* 1 Pet. 2:2

γάλα, acc. sg. neut. n. . . . . γάλα *(1051)*

γάλακτος, gen. sg. neut. n. . . . . id.

Γαλάται, voc. pl. m. n. . . . . Γαλάτης *(1052)*

Γαλάτας, acc. sg. m. n. (Gal. 6:18, TRs | GNT, WH, MT, TRb & NA omit) . . . id.

(1052) **Γαλάτης,** ου, ὁ, *a Galatian, inhabitant of*

Galatia, Gal. 3:1

(1053) **Γαλατία,** ας, ἡ [§2.B.b; 2.2] *Galatia or Gallo-Graecia,* a province of Asia Minor

Γαλατίαν, acc. sg. f. n. . . . . Γαλατία *(1053)*

Γαλατίας, gen. sg. f. n. . . . . id.

Γαλατικήν, acc. sg. f. adj. . . . . . . Γαλατικός *(1054)*

(1054) **Γαλατικός,** ή, όν [§7.F.a] *Galatian*

(1055) **γαλήνη,** ης, ἡ, nom. sg. f. n. [§2.B.a] *tranquillity of the sea, a calm,* Matt. 8:26; Mark 4:39; Luke 8:24

(1056) **Γαλιλαία,** ας, ἡ, nom. sg. f. n. [§2.B.b; 2.2] *Galilee,* a district of Palestine north of Samaria, Matt. 4:15

Γαλιλαίᾳ, dat. sg. f. n. . . . . Γαλιλαία *(1056)*

Γαλιλαίαν, acc. sg. f. n. . . . . id.

Γαλιλαίας, gen. sg. f. n. . . . . id.

Γαλιλαῖοι, nom. pl. m. n. {Acts 2:7} . . . . Γαλιλαῖος *(1057)*

Γαλιλαῖοι, voc. pl. m. n. {Acts 1:11} . . . . . id.

(1057) **Γαλιλαῖος,** ου, ὁ, nom. sg. m. n. [§3.C.a] *a native of Galilee*

Γαλιλαίου, gen. sg. m. n. . . . . Γαλιλαῖος *(1057)*

Γαλιλαίους, acc. pl. m. n. . . . . id.

Γαλιλαίων, gen. pl. m. n. . . . . id.

(1058) **Γαλλίων,** ωνος, ὁ, nom. sg. m. n. [§4.2.e] *Gallio,* pr. name, Acts 18:14

Γαλλίωνι, dat. sg. m. n. . . . . Γαλλίων *(1058)*

Γαλλίωνος, gen. sg. m. n. . . . . id.

(1059) **Γαμαλιήλ,** ὁ, *Gamaliel,* pr. name, indecl.

γαμεῖν, pres. act. infin. . . . . γαμέω *(1060)*

γαμείτωσαν, 3 pers. pl. pres. act. imper. . . id.

(1060) **γαμέω,** ῶ, fut. γαμήσω, perf. γεγάμηκα, aor. ἔγημα and ἐγάμησα, aor. pass. ἐγαμήθην [§37.2] *to marry,* Matt. 5:32, et al.; absol. *to marry, enter the marriage state,* Matt. 19:10, et al.; mid. *to marry, be married,* Mark 10:12; 1 Cor. 7:39

γαμηθῇ, 3 pers. sg. aor. pass. subj. (Mark 10:12, MT & TR | γαμήσῃ, GNT, WH & NA) . . . . γαμέω *(1060)*

γαμηθῆναι, aor. pass. infin. . . . . id.

γαμῆσαι, aor. act. infin. . . . . id.

γαμήσας, nom. sg. m. aor. act. part. . . . . . id.

γαμήσασα, nom. sg. f. aor. act. part. . . . . . id.

γαμησάτωσαν, 3 pers. pl. aor. act. imper. . . id.

γαμήσῃ, 3 pers. sg. aor. act. subj. . . . . id.

γαμήσῃς, 2 pers. sg. aor. act. subj. (1 Cor. 7:28, GNT, WH & NA | γήμῃς, MT & TR) . . . . id.

γαμίζονται, 3 pers. pl. pres. pass. indic. (Matt. 22:30; Mark 12:25; Luke 20:35, GNT, WH & NA | ἐκγαμίζονται, Matt. 22:30; Luke 20:35, MT & TR | γαμίσκονται, Mark 12:25, MT & TR) . . . . γαμίζω *(†1061)*

γαμίζοντες, nom. pl. m. pres. act. part. (Matt.

24:38, GNT, WH & NA | ἐκγαμίζοντες,
MT & TR) . . . . γαμίζω (†1061)

(†1061) **γαμίζω**, fut. γαμίσω [§26.1] *to give in marriage, permit to marry*, v.r. 1 Cor. 7:38

γαμίζων, nom. sg. m. pres. act. part. (1 Cor.
7:38, GNT, WH & NA | ἐκγαμίζων, MT
& TR) . . . . γαμίσκω (1061)

(†1061) **γαμίσκομαι**, pass. *to be given in marriage*,
Mark 12:25

γαμίσκονται, 3 pers. pl. pres. pass.
indic. . . . . γαμίσκω (1061)

(1061) **γαμίσκω**, fut. γαμίσω, *to give in marriage*, v.r.
Matt. 24:38

γάμον, acc. sg. m. n. . . . . γάμος (1062)

(1062) **γάμος**, ου, ὁ, nom. sg. m. n. [§3.C.a] *a wedding; nuptial festivities, a marriage festival*, Matt. 22:2; 25:10; John 2:1, 2; Rev.
19:7, 9; any *feast* or *banquet*, Luke 12:36;
14:8; *the marriage state*, Heb. 13:4

γάμου, gen. sg. m. n. . . . . γάμος (1062)
γαμοῦντες, nom. pl. m. pres. act. part. . γαμέω (1060)
γάμους, acc. pl. m. n. . . . . γάμος (1062)
γαμοῦσι(ν), 3 pers. pl. pres. act. indic. . γαμέω (1060)
γάμων, gen. pl. m. n. {Luke 12:36} . . . . γάμος (1062)
γαμῶν, nom. sg. m. pres. act. part.
{Luke 16:18} . . . . γαμέω (1060)

(1063) **γάρ**, a causal particle or conjunction, *for*; it
is, however, frequently used with an ellipsis of the clause to which it has reference,
and its force must then be variously expressed: Matt. 15:27; 27:23, et al.: it is also
sometimes epexegetic, or introductory of
an intimated detail of circumstances, *now,
then, to wit*, Matt. 1:18

γαστέρες, nom. pl. f. n. . . . . γαστήρ (1064)

(1064) **γαστήρ**, τρός, ἡ [§6.2] *the belly, stomach; the
womb*, Luke 1:31; ἐν γαστρὶ ἔχειν, *to be
with child*, Matt. 1:18, 23; 24:19, et al.;
γαστέρες, *paunches, gluttons*, Tit. 1:12

γαστρί, dat. sg. f. n. . . . . γαστήρ (1064)

(†1065) **γε**, an enclitic particle imparting emphasis; indicating that a particular regard is to be had
to the term to which it is attached. Its force
is to be conveyed, when this is possible, by
various expressions; *at least, indeed, even*

γεγαμηκόσι(ν), dat. pl. m. perf. act.
part. . . . . γαμέω (1060)

γεγενήμεθα, 1 pers. pl. perf. pass. indic. (John
8:41, MT & TR | γεγεννήμεθα, GNT &
NA | ἐγεννήθημεν, WH) . . . . . γίνομαι (1096)

γεγενημένα, nom. pl. neut. perf. pass. part.
(2 Pet. 2:12, MT & TR | γεγεννημένα,
GNT, WH & NA) . . . . id.

γεγενημένον, acc. sg. neut. perf. pass. part.   id.

γεγενῆσθαι, perf. pass. infin. . . . . id.

γεγένησθε, 2 pers. pl. perf. pass. indic.
(1 Thess. 2:8, MT & TR | ἐγενήθητε,
GNT, WH & NA) . . . . id.

γεγέννηκα, 1 pers. sg. perf. act. indic. . γεννάω (1080)

γεγέννημαι, 1 pers. sg. perf. pass. indic. . . id.

γεγεννήμεθα, 1 pers. pl. perf. pass. indic.
(John 8:41, GNT & NA | γεγενήμεθα,
MT & TR | ἐγεννήθημεν, WH) . . . . . id.

γεγεννημένα, nom. pl. neut. perf. pass. part.
(2 Pet. 2:12, GNT, WH & NA |
γεγενημένα, MT & TR) . . . . id.

γεγεννημένον, acc. sg. m. perf. pass. part.
{1 John 5:1} . . . . id.

γεγεννημένον, nom. sg. neut. perf. pass. part.
{1 John 5:4} . . . . id.

γεγεννημένος, nom. sg. m. perf. pass. part.   id.

γεγεννημένου, gen. sg. m. perf. pass. part.   id.

γεγέννηται, 3 pers. sg. perf. pass. indic. . . id.

γέγονα, 1 pers. sg. 2 perf. act. indic. . . γίνομαι (1096)

γεγόναμεν, 1 pers. pl. 2 perf. act. indic. . . id.

γέγοναν, 3 pers. pl. 2 perf. act. indic. contr.
[§35.13] . . . . id.

γέγονας, 2 pers. sg. 2 perf. act. indic. . . id.

γεγόνασι(ν), 3 pers. pl. 2 perf. act. indic. . id.

γεγόνατε, 2 pers. pl. 2 perf. act. indic. . . . id.

γεγόνει, 3 pers. sg. pluperf. act. indic. (Acts
4:22, GNT, WH & NA | ἐγεγόνει, MT
& TR) . . . . id.

γέγονε(ν), 3 pers. pl. 2 perf. act. indic. . . . id.

γεγονέναι, 2 perf. act. infin. . . . . id.

γεγονός, nom. sg. neut. 2 perf. act. part.
{Mark 5:14} . . . . id.

γεγονός, acc. sg. neut. 2 perf. act. part.
{Luke 2:15} . . . . id.

γεγονότας, acc. pl. m. 2 perf. act. part. . . id.

γεγονότες, nom. pl. m. 2 perf. act. part. . id.

γεγονότι, dat. sg. neut. 2 perf. act. part. . id.

γεγονυῖα, nom. sg. f. 2 perf. act. part. . . id.

γεγονώς, nom. sg. m. 2 perf. act. part. . . . id.

γεγραμμένα, nom. pl. neut. perf. pass. part.
[§13.6.c] {John 12:16} . . . . γράφω (1125)

γεγραμμένα, acc. pl. neut. perf. pass. part.
{Rev. 1:3} . . . . id.

γεγραμμένας, acc. pl. f. perf. pass. part. . id.

γεγραμμένη, nom. sg. f. perf. pass. part. (Luke
23:38, MT & TR | GNT, WH & NA
omit) . . . . id.

γεγραμμένην, acc. sg. f. perf. pass. part. . id.

γεγραμμένοι, nom. pl. m. perf. pass. part. . id.

γεγραμμένοις, dat. pl. neut. perf. pass. part. . id.

γεγραμμένον, nom. sg. neut. perf. pass. part.
{John 2:17} . . . . id.

γεγραμμένον, acc. sg. neut. perf. pass. part.
{Rev. 2:17} . . . . id.

γεγραμμένος, nom. sg. m. perf. pass. part.   id.

γεγραμμένων, gen. pl. m. perf. pass. part.
{Rev. 22:19} . . . . γράφω *(1125)*

γεγραμμένων, gen. pl. neut. perf. pass. part.
{Rev. 20:12} . . . . id.

γέγραπται, 3 pers. sg. perf. pass. indic.
[§23.8] . . . . id.

γέγραφα, 1 pers. sg. perf. act. indic. [§13.6.c]   id.

γεγυμνασμένα, acc. pl. neut. perf. pass.
part. . . . . γυμνάζω *(1128)*

γεγυμνασμένην, acc. sg. f. perf. pass. part.   id.

γεγυμνασμένοις, dat. pl. m. perf. pass. part.   id.

(1066) **Γεδεών**, ὁ, *Gideon*, pr. name, indecl., Heb.
11:32

(1067) **γέεννα**, ης, ἡ [§2.3] (Hebrew גֵּיא הִנֹּם) *Gehenna*, pr. *the valley of Hinnom*, south of
Jerusalem, once celebrated for the horrid
worship of Moloch, and afterwards polluted with every species of filth, as well as
the carcasses of animals, and dead bodies
of malefactors; to consume which, in order to avert the pestilence which such a
mass of corruption would occasion, constant fires were kept burning; hence, *hell,
the fires of Tartarus, the place of punishment in Hades*, Matt. 5:22, 29, 30; 10:28;
18:9, et al.

γέενναν, acc. sg. f. n. . . . . γέεννα *(1067)*

γεέννῃ, dat. sg. f. n. . . . . id.

γεέννης, gen. sg. f. n. . . . . id.

(†1068) **Γεθσημανί**, *Gethsamane*, pr. name, indecl.
(Matt. 26:36; Mark 14:32, GNT & NA
| Γεθσημανῆ, MT & TR | Γεθσημανεί,
WH)

γείτονας, acc. pl. m. n. {Luke 14:12} . . γείτων *(1069)*

γείτονας, acc. pl. f. n. {Luke 15:9} . . . . . . id.

γείτονες, nom. pl. m. n. . . . . id.

(1069) **γείτων**, ονος, ὁ, ἡ [§4.2.e] *a neighbor*, Luke
14:12; 15:6, 9; John 9:8

γελάσετε, 2 pers. pl. fut. act. indic. . . . . γελάω *(1070)*

(1070) **γελάω**, ῶ, fut. γελάσομαι, and, later, γελάσω
[§22.2.c] aor. ἐγέλασα, *to laugh, smile*; by
impl. *to be merry, happy, to rejoice*, Luke
6:21, 25

γελῶντες, nom. pl. m. pres. act. part. . . γελάω *(1070)*

(1071) **γέλως**, ωτος, ὁ, nom. sg. m. n. [§4.2.c]
laughter; by impl. *mirth, joy, rejoicing*,
James 4:9

γέμει, 3 pers. sg. pres. act. indic. . . . . γέμω *(1073)*

γεμίζεσθαι, pres. pass. infin. . . . . γεμίζω *(1072)*

(1072) **γεμίζω**, fut. γεμίσω [§26.1] aor. ἐγέμισα, aor.
pass. ἐγεμίσθην, *to fill*, Matt. 4:37; 15:36,
et al.

γεμίσαι, aor. act. infin. (Luke 15:16, with τὴν
κοιλίαν αὐτοῦ, MT & TR | χορτασθῆ-
ναι, GNT, WH & NA) . . . . γεμίζω *(1072)*

γεμίσας, nom. sg. m. aor. act. part. . . . γεμίζω *(1072)*

γεμίσατε, 2 pers. pl. aor. act. imper. . . . . . id.

γεμισθῇ, 3 pers. sg. aor. pass. subj. . . . . . . id.

γέμον, acc. sg. neut. pres. act. part. . . . . . γέμω *(1073)*

γέμοντα, nom. pl. neut. pres. act. part.
{Rev. 4:6} . . . . id.

γέμοντα, acc. pl. neut. pres. act. part. (Rev.
17:3, GNT, WH & NA | γέμον, MT &
TR) . . . . id.

γεμόντων, gen. pl. f. pres. act. part. (Rev. 21:9,
GNT, WH & NA | γεμούσας, MT &
TR) . . . . id.

γεμούσας, acc. pl. f. pres. act. part. . . . . . id.

γέμουσιν, 3 pers. pl. pres. act. indic. . . . . . id.

(1073) **γέμω**, fut. γεμῶ [§27.1.a] *to be full*, Matt.
23:27; Luke 11:39, et al.

(1074) **γενεά**, ᾶς, ἡ, nom. sg. f. n. [§2.B.b; 2.2] pr.
birth; hence, *progeny; a generation* of mankind, Matt. 11:16; 23:36, et al.; *a generation*, a step in a genealogy, Matt. 1:17; *a
generation*, an interval of time, *an age*; in
N.T. *course of life*, in respect of its events,
interests, or character, Luke 16:8; Acts
13:36 {Mark 8:12}

γενεά, voc. sg. f. n. {Mark 9:19} . . . . . . γενεά *(1074)*

γενεᾷ, dat. sg. f. n. . . . . id.

γενεαί, nom. pl. f. n. . . . . id.

γενεαῖς, dat. pl. f. n. . . . . id.

(1075) **γενεαλογέω**, ῶ, fut. γενεαλογήσω [§16.P]
(γενεά + λέγω) *to reckon one's descent,
derive one's origin*, Heb. 7:6

(1076) **γενεαλογία**, ας, ἡ [§2.B.b; 2.2] *genealogy, catalogue of ancestors, history of descent*,
1 Tim. 1:4 Tit. 3:9

γενεαλογίαις, dat. pl. f. n. . . . . γενεαλογία *(1076)*

γενεαλογίας, acc. pl. f. n. . . . . id.

γενεαλογούμενος, nom. sg. m. pres. pass.
part. . . . . γενεαλογέω *(1075)*

γενεάν, acc. sg. f. n. . . . . γενεά *(1074)*

γενεᾶς, gen. sg. f. n. {Luke 7:31} . . . . id.

γενεάς, acc. pl. f. n. {Luke 1:50} . . . . id.

γένει, dat. sg. neut. n. . . . . γένος *(1085)*

γενέσει, dat. sg. f. n. (Luke 1:14, GNT, WH
& NA | γεννήσει, MT & TR) . . . . γένεσις *(1078)*

γενέσεως, gen. sg. f. n. . . . . id.

γενέσθαι, 2 aor. mid. dep. infin. . . . . . γίνομαι *(1096)*

γένεσθε, 2 pers. pl. 2 aor. mid. dep. imper.
(1 Pet. 1:16, TR | ἔσεσθε, GNT, WH &
NA | γίνεσθε, MT) . . . . id.

γενέσθω, 3 pers. sg. 2 aor. mid. dep. imper.   id.

(1077) **γενέσια**, ων, τά [§3.C.c] pr. *a day observed in
memory of the dead*; in N.T. equivalent to
γενέθλια, *celebration of one's birthday,
birthday-festival*, Matt. 14:6; Mark 6:21

γενεσίοις, dat. pl. neut. n. . . . . γενέσια *(1077)*

(1078) **γένεσις**, εως, ἡ, nom. sg. f. n. [§5.E.c] *birth, nativity,* Matt. 1:18; Luke 1:14; James 1:23; *successive generation, descent, lineage,* Matt. 1:1; meton. *life,* James 3:6 (Matt. 1:18, GNT, WH & NA | γέννησις, MT & TR)

γενεσίων, gen. pl. neut. n. (Matt. 14:6, MT & TR | γενεσίοις, GNT, WH & NA) . . . . γενέσια *(1077)*

(1079) **γενετή**, ῆς, ἡ [§2.B.a] *birth,* John 9:1

γενετῆς, gen. sg. f. n. . . . . γενετή *(1079)*

γενεῶν, gen. pl. f. n. . . . . γενεά *(1074)*

γένη, nom. pl. neut. n. {1 Cor. 12:10} . . . γένος *(1085)*

γένη, acc. pl. neut. n. {1 Cor. 12:28} . . . . . id.

γενηθέντας, acc. pl. m. aor. pass. dep. part. . . . . γίνομαι *(1096)*

γενηθέντες, nom. pl. m. aor. pass. dep. part.   id.

γενηθέντων, gen. pl. neut. aor. pass. dep. part. . . . . id.

γενηθῆναι, aor. pass. dep. infin. . . . . id.

γενήθητε, 2 pers. pl. aor. pass. dep. imper.   id.

γενηθήτω, 3 pers. sg. aor. pass. dep. imper.   id.

γενηθῶμεν, 1 pers. pl. aor. pass. dep. subj.   id.

(‡1081) **γένημα**, ατος, τό [§4.D.c] v.r. Luke 22:18; 2 Cor. 9:10, *natural produce, fruit, increase*

γενήματα, acc. pl. neut. n. . . . . γένημα *(‡1081)*

γενήματος, gen. sg. neut. n. (Matt. 26:29; Mark 14:25; Luke 22:18, GNT, WH & NA | γεννήματος, TR | MT has γεννήματος in Matt. 26:29 and γενήματος in Mark 14:25; Luke 22:18)   id.

γενήσεσθε, 2 pers. pl. fut. mid. dep. indic. . . . . γίνομαι *(1096)*

γενήσεται, 3 pers. sg. fut. mid. dep. indic.   id.

γένησθε, 2 pers. pl. 2 aor. mid. dep. subj.   id.

γενησόμενον, acc. sg. neut. fut. mid. dep. part. . . . . id.

γενήσονται, 3 pers. pl. fut. mid. dep. indic. (John 10:16, GNT, WH & NA | γενήσεται, MT & TR) . . . . id.

γένηται, 3 pers. sg. 2 aor. mid. dep. subj. .   id.

γεννᾶται, 3 pers. sg. pres. pass. indic. [§19.S] . . . . γεννάω *(1080)*

(1080) **γεννάω**, ῶ, fut. γεννήσω [§18.R] perf. γεγέννηκα, aor. ἐγέννησα, perf. pass. γεγέννημαι, aor. pass. ἐγεννήθην, used of men, *to beget, generate,* Matt. 1:2-16, et al.; of women, *to bring forth, bear, give birth to,* Luke 1:13, 57, et al.; pass. *to be born, produced,* Matt. 2:1, 4, et al.; met. *to produce, excite, give occasion to, effect,* 2 Tim. 2:23; from the Hebrew, *to constitute as son, to constitute as king,* or *as the representative* or *vicegerent of God,* Acts 13:33; Heb. 1:5; 5:5; by impl. *to be a par-*

ent to any one; pass. *to be a son* or *child to* any one, John 1:13; 1 Cor. 4:15, et al.

γεννηθείς, nom. sg. m. aor. pass. part. γεννάω *(1080)*

γεννηθέν, nom. sg. neut. aor. pass. part. . .   id.

γεννηθέντος, gen. sg. m. aor. pass. part. . .   id.

γεννηθέντων, gen. pl. m. aor. pass. part. .   id.

γεννηθῇ, 3 pers. sg. aor. pass. subj. . . . . . .   id.

γεννηθῆναι, aor. pass. infin. . . . .   id.

(1081) **γέννημα**, ατος, τό [§4.D.c] *what is born* or *produced, offspring, progeny, brood,* Matt. 3:7; 12:34, et al.; *fruit, produce,* Matt. 26:29; Mark 14:25, et al.; *fruit, increase,* Luke 12:18; 2 Cor. 9:10

γεννήματα, acc. pl. neut. n. (2 Cor. 9:10, TR | γενήματα, GNT, WH, MT & NA) . . . . γέννημα *(1081)*

γεννήματα, voc. pl. neut. n. {Luke 3:7} . .   id.

γεννήματος, gen. sg. neut. n. (Matt. 26:29; Mark 14:25; Luke 22:18, MT & TR | γενήματος, GNT, WH & NA) . . . . . .   id.

γεννήσαντα, acc. sg. m. aor. act. part. γεννάω *(1080)*

(1082) **Γεννησαρέτ**, ἡ, *Gennesaret,* a lake of Palestine, called also the *Sea of Tiberias* (GNT, WH, MT, TR & NA | Mark 6:53, Γενησαρέτ, TR)

γεννήσει, 3 pers. sg. fut. act. indic. {Luke 1:13} . . . . γεννάω *(1080)*

γεννήσει, dat. sg. f. n. (Luke 1:14, MT & TR | γενέσει, GNT, WH & NA) . . . . γέννησις *(1083)*

γεννήσῃ, 3 pers. sg. aor. act. subj. . . . . γεννάω *(1080)*

(1083) **γέννησις**, εως, ἡ, nom. sg. f. n. [§5.E.c] *birth, nativity* (Matt. 1:18, MT & TR | γένεσις, GNT, WH & NA)

γεννητοῖς, dat. pl. m. adj. . . . . γεννητός *(1084)*

(1084) **γεννητός**, ἡ, όν [§7.F.a] *born* or *produced of,* Matt. 11:11; Luke 7:28

γεννώμενον, nom. sg. neut. pres. pass. part. . . . . γεννάω *(1080)*

γεννῶσα, nom. sg. f. pres. act. part. . . . . .   id.

γεννῶσι(ν), 3 pers. pl. pres. act. indic. . . .   id.

γένοιτο, 3 pers. sg. 2 aor. mid. dep. opt. . . . . γίνομαι *(1096)*

γενόμενα, acc. pl. neut. 2 aor. mid. dep. part.   id.

γενόμεναι, nom. pl. f. 2 aor. mid. dep. part.   id.

γενομένην, acc. sg. f. 2 aor. mid. dep. part.   id.

γενομένης, gen. sg. f. 2 aor. mid. dep. part.   id.

γενόμενοι, nom. pl. m. 2 aor. mid. dep. part.   id.

γενομένοις, dat. pl. m. 2 aor. mid. dep. part. {Mark 16:10} . . . . id.

γενομένοις, dat. pl. neut. 2 aor. mid. dep. part. {Matt. 14:6} . . . . id.

γενόμενον, acc. sg. m. 2 aor. mid. dep. part. {Luke 18:24} . . . . id.

γενόμενον, acc. sg. neut. 2 aor. mid. dep. part. {Luke 23:47} . . . . id.

γενόμενος, nom. sg. m. 2 aor. mid. dep.
part. . . . . γίνομαι *(1096)*
γενομένου, gen. sg. m. 2 aor. mid. dep. part.
{Acts 25:15} . . . . id.
γενομένου, gen. sg. neut. 2 aor. mid. dep. part.
{Acts 28:9} . . . . id.
γενομένων, gen. pl. m. 2 aor. mid. dep. part.
{Acts 21:17} . . . . id.
γενομένων, gen. pl. f. 2 aor. mid. dep. part.
{Luke 24:5} . . . . id.
γενομένων, gen. pl. neut. 2 aor. mid. dep.
part. (Heb. 9:11, GNT, WH & NA |
μελλόντων, MT & TR) . . . . id.
(1085) **γένος**, ους, τό, nom. sg. neut. n. [§5.E.b] *offspring, progeny*, Acts 17:28, 29; *family,
kindred, lineage*, Acts 7:13, et al.; *race, nation, people*, Mark 7:26; Acts 4:36, et al.;
kind, sort, species, Matt. 13:47, et al.
{Acts 7:13}
γένος, acc. sg. neut. n. {Acts 7:19} . . . . . γένος *(1085)*
γένους, gen. sg. neut. n. . . . . id.
γένωμαι, 1 pers. sg. 2 aor. mid. dep.
subj. . . . . γίνομαι *(1096)*
γενώμεθα, 1 pers. pl. 2 aor. mid. dep. subj. id.
γένωνται, 3 pers. pl. 2 aor. mid. dep. subj. id.
(‡1046) **Γερασηνός**, ή, όν, *Gerasene*, belonging to the
city of Gerasa
Γερασηνῶν, gen. pl. m. n. (Mark 5:1; Luke
8:26, 37, GNT, WH & NA | Γαδαρηνῶν,
MT & TR) . . . . Γερασηνός *(‡1046)*
(1086) **Γεργεσηνός**, ή, όν [§3.C.a] *a Gergesene, an
inhabitant of Gergasa*, a city in Peraea
Γεργεσηνῶν, gen. pl. m. n. (Matt. 8:28, MT
& TR | Γαδαρηνῶν, GNT, WH &
NA) . . . . Γεργεσηνός *(1086)*
(1087) **γερουσία**, ας, ἡ [§2.B.b; 2.2] *a senate, assembly of elders; the elders* of Israel collectively, Acts 5:21
γερουσίαν, acc. sg. f. n. . . . . γερουσία *(1087)*
(1088) **γέρων**, οντος, ὁ, nom. sg. m. n. [§4.2.d] *an
old man*, John 3:4
(1089) **γεύομαι**, fut. γεύσομαι, aor. ἐγευσάμην
[§15.O] (mid. of γεύω, *to cause to taste*) *to
taste*, Matt. 27:34; John 2:9; absol. *to take
food*, Acts 10:10, et al.; met. *to have perception of, experience*, Heb. 6:4, 5; 1 Pet.
2:3; θανάτου γεύεσθαι, *to experience
death, to die*, Matt. 16:28, et al.
γευσάμενος, nom. sg. m. aor. mid. dep.
part. . . . . γεύομαι *(1089)*
γευσαμένους, acc. pl. m. aor. mid. dep. part. id.
γεύσασθαι, aor. mid. dep. part. infin. . . . . id.
γεύσεται, 3 pers. sg. fut. mid. dep. indic. . id.
γεύση, 2 pers. sg. aor. mid. dep. subj. . . . . id.
γεύσηται, 3 pers. sg. aor. mid. dep. subj. . id.

γεύσονται, 3 pers. pl. fut. mid. dep. indic.
(Luke 9:27, TR | γεύσωνται, GNT, WH,
MT & NA) . . . . γεύομαι *(1089)*
γεύσωνται, 3 pers. pl. aor. mid. dep. subj. id.
γεωργεῖται, 3 pers. sg. pres. pass.
indic. . . . . γεωργέω *(1090)*
(1090) **γεωργέω**, ῶ, fut. γεωργήσω [§16.P] *to culti-
vate, till the earth*, Heb. 6:7
(1091) **γεώργιον**, ου, τό, nom. sg. neut. n. [§3.C.c]
cultivated field or *ground, a farm*, 1 Cor.
3:9
γεωργοί, nom. pl. m. n. . . . . γεωργός *(1092)*
γεωργοῖς, dat. pl. m. n. . . . . id.
γεωργόν, acc. sg. m. n. . . . . id.
(1092) **γεωργός**, οῦ, ὁ, nom. sg. m. n. [§3.C.a] (γῆ
+ ἔργον) *a husbandman, one who tills the
earth*, 2 Tim. 2:6; James 5:7; in N.T. spc.
a vine-dresser, keeper of a vineyard, i.q.
ἀμπελουργός, Matt. 21:33, 34, et al.
γεωργούς, acc. pl. m. n. . . . . γεωργός *(1092)*
γεωργῶν, gen. pl. m. n. . . . . id.
(1093) **γῆ**, γῆς, ἡ, nom. sg. f. n. [§2.B.a] (contr. from
γέα) *earth, soil*, Matt. 13:5; Mark 4:8, et
al.; *the ground, surface of the earth*, Matt.
10:29; Luke 6:49, et al.; *the land*, as opposed to the sea or a lake, Luke 5:11; John
21:8, 9, 11; *the earth, world*, Matt.
5:18, 35, et al.; by synec. *the inhabitants
of the earth*, Matt. 5:13; 6:10; 10:34; *a
land, region, tract, country, territory*, Matt.
2:20; 14:34; by way of eminence, *the chosen land*, Matt. 5:5; 24:30; 27:45; Eph.
6:3; *the inhabitants of a region* or *country*, Matt. 10:15; 11:24, et al. {Matt. 5:18}
γῆ, voc. sg. f. n. {Matt. 2:6} . . . . γῆ *(1093)*
γῇ, dat. sg. f. n. id.
γήμας, nom. sg. m. aor. act. part. (Matt.
22:25, GNT, WH & NA | γαμήσας, MT
& TR) . . . . γαμέω *(1060)*
γήμῃ, 3 pers. sg. aor. act. subj. . . . . id.
γήμῃς, 2 pers. sg. aor. act. subj. (1 Cor. 7:28,
MT & TR | γαμήσῃς, GNT, WH & NA) id.
γῆν, acc. sg. f. n. . . . . γῆ *(1093)*
γήρᾳ, dat. sg. neut. n. (Luke 1:36, TR | γήρει,
GNT, WH, MT & NA) . . . . γῆρας *(1094)*
(1094) **γῆρας**, ους or ως, τό [§5.E.j] dat. γήραϊ,
γήρᾳ, also γήρει, *old age*, Luke 1:36
γηράσῃς, 2 pers. sg. aor. act. subj. . . γηράσκω *(1095)*
γηράσκον, nom. sg. neut. pres. act.
part. . . . . γηράσκω *(1095)*
(1095) **γηράσκω**, or γηράω, ῶ, fut. γηράσομαι, aor.
ἐγήρασα and ἐγήρανα, *to be or become
old*, John 21:18; Heb. 8:13
γήρει, dat. sg. neut. n. (Luke 1:36, GNT, WH,
MT & NA | γήρᾳ, TR) . . . . γῆρας *(1094)*

γῆς, gen. sg. f. n. . . . . γῆ *(1093)*

γίνεσθαι, pres. mid./pass. dep. infin. . . γίνομαι *(1096)*

γίνεσθε, 2 pers. pl. pres. mid./pass. dep. imper. . . . . id.

γινέσθω, 3 pers. sg. pres. mid./pass. dep. imper. . . . . id.

γίνεται, 3 pers. pres. mid./pass. dep. indic. id.

(1096) **γίνομαι** [§37.1] (a later form of γίγνομαι) fut. γενήσομαι, perf. γέγονα and γεγένημαι, aor. ἐγενήθην, 2 aor. ἐγενόμην, *to come into existence; to be created, exist by creation,* John 1:3, 10; Heb. 11:3; James 3:9; *to be born, produced, grow,* Matt. 21:19; John 8:58; et al.; *to arise, come on, occur,* as the phenomena of nature, etc.; Matt. 8:24, 26; 9:16, et al.; *to come, approach,* as morning or evening, Matt. 8:16; 14:15, 23; *to be appointed, constituted, established,* Mark 2:27; Gal. 3:17, et al.; *to take place, come to pass, happen, occur,* Matt. 1:22; 24:6, 20, 21, 34, et al. freq.; *to be done, performed, effected,* Matt. 21:42, et al.; *to be fulfilled, satisfied,* Matt. 6:10; 26:42, et al.; *to come into a particular state* or *condition; to become, assume the character and appearance* of anything, Matt. 5:45; 12:45, et al. *to become* or *be made* anything, *be changed* or *converted,* Matt. 4:3; 21:42; Mark 1:17, et al.; *to be, esse,* Matt. 11:26; 19:8; γίνεσθαι ὑπό τινα, *to be subject to,* Gal. 4:4; γίνεσθαι ἐν ἑαυτῷ, *to come to one's self, to recover from a trance* or *surprise,* Acts 12:11; μὴ γένοιτο, *let it not be, far be it from, God forbid,* Luke 20:16; Rom. 3:4, 31, et al.; *to be kept, celebrated, solemnized,* as festivals, Matt. 26:2, et al.; *to be finished, completed,* Heb. 4:3

γινόμενα, acc. pl. neut. pres. mid./pass. dep. part. . . . . γίνομαι *(1096)*

γινόμεναι, nom. pl. f. pres. mid./pass. dep. part. (Mark 6:2, GNT, WH & NA | γίνονται, MT & TR) . . . . id.

γινομένας, acc. pl. f. pres. mid./pass. dep. part. (Acts 8:13, GNT, WH, TRs & NA | γινόμενα, MT & TRb) . . . . id.

γινομένη, nom. sg. f. pres. mid./pass. dep. part. . . . . id.

γινομένῃ, dat. sg. f. pres. mid./pass. dep. part. id.

γινομένης, gen. sg. f. pres. mid./pass. dep. part. (Acts 23:10, GNT, WH & NA | γενομένης, MT & TR) . . . . id.

γινόμενοι, nom. pl. m. pres. mid./pass. dep. part. . . . . id.

γινομένοις, dat. pl. neut. pres. mid./pass. dep.

part. . . . . γίνομαι *(1096)*

γινόμενον, acc. sg. m. pres. mid./pass. dep. part. {John 6:19} . . . . id.

γινόμενον, nom. sg. neut. pres. mid./pass. dep. part. {Acts 12:9} . . . . id.

γινόμενον, acc. sg. neut. pres. mid./pass. dep. part. {Acts 28:6} . . . . id.

γινομένου, gen. sg. neut. pres. mid./pass. dep. part. (John 13:2, GNT, WH & NA | γενομένου, MT & TR) . . . . id.

γινομένων, gen. pl. neut. pres. mid./pass. dep. part. . . . . id.

γίνονται, 3 pers. pl. pres. mid./pass. dep. indic. (Mark 6:2, MT & TR | γινόμεναι, GNT, WH & NA) . . . . id.

γίνου, 2 pers. sg. pres. mid./pass. dep. imper. id.

γινώμεθα, 1 pers. pl. pres. mid./pass. dep. subj. . . . . id.

γίνωνται, 3 pers. pl. pres. mid./pass. dep. subj. . . . . id.

γίνωσκε, 2 pers. sg. pres. act. imper. . γινώσκω *(1097)*

γινώσκει, 3 pers. sg. pres. act. indic. . . . . . id.

γινώσκειν, pres. act. infin. . . . . id.

γινώσκεις, 2 pers. sg. pres. act. indic. . . . . id.

γινώσκεται, 3 pers. sg. pres. pass. indic. . . id.

γινώσκετε, 2 pers. pl. pres. act. indic. {Matt. 24:32} . . . . id.

γινώσκετε, 2 pers. pl. pres. act. imper. {Luke 10:11} . . . . id.

γινωσκέτω, 3 pers. sg. pres. act. imper. . . id.

γινώσκῃ, 3 pers. sg. pres. act. subj. . . . . . . id.

γινώσκητε, 2 pers. pl. pres. act. subj. (John 10:38, GNT, WH & NA | πιστεύσητε, MT & TR) . . . . id.

γινώσκομαι, 1 pers. sg. pres. pass. indic. (John 10:14, MT & TR | γινώσκουσι, GNT, WH & NA) . . . . id.

γινώσκομεν, 1 pers. pl. pres. act. indic. . . id.

γινωσκομένη, nom. sg. f. pres. pass. part. id.

γινώσκοντες, nom. pl. m. pres. act. part. . id.

γινώσκουσι, 3 pers. pl. pres. act. indic. (John 10:14b, GNT, WH & NA | γινώσκομαι, MT & TR) . . . . id.

γινώσκουσι(ν), dat. pl. m. pres. act. part. {Rom. 7:1} . . . . id.

(1097) **γινώσκω**, 1 pers. sg. pres. act. indic., [§36.3] (a later form of γιγνώσκω) fut. γνώσομαι, perf. ἔγνωκα, 2 aor. ἔγνων, perf. pass. ἔγνωσμαι, aor. pass. ἐγνώσθην, *to know,* whether the action be inceptive or complete and settled; *to perceive,* Matt. 22:18; Mark 5:29; 8:17; 12:12; Luke 8:46; *to mark, discern,* Matt. 25:24; Luke 19:44; *to ascertain by examination,* Mark 6:38; John 7:51; Acts 23:28; *to understand,*

Mark 4:13; Luke 18:34; John 12:16; 13:7;
Acts 8:30; 1 Cor. 14:7, 9; *to acknowledge,*
Matt. 7:23; 2 Cor. 3:2; *to resolve, conclude,* Luke 16:4; John 7:26; 17:8; *to be assured,* Luke 21:20; John 6:69; 8:52; 2 Pet.
1:20; *to be skilled, to be master of* a thing,
Matt. 16:3; Acts 21:37; *to know* carnally,
Matt. 1:25; Luke 1:34; from the Hebrew,
to view with favor, 1 Cor. 8:3; Gal. 4:9

γινώσκωμεν, 1 pers. pl. pres. act.
subj. . . . . γινώσκω (1097)
γινώσκων, nom. sg. m. pres. act. part. . . . id.
γινώσκωσι(ν), 3 pers. pl. pres. act. subj. . . id.

(1098) **γλεῦκος**, ους, τό [§7.E.b] pr. *the unfermented
juice of grapes, must;* hence, *sweet new
wine,* Acts 2:13

γλεύκους, gen. sg. neut. n. . . . . γλεῦκος (1098)
γλυκύ, nom. sg. neut. adj.
{Rev. 10:9, 10} . . . . γλυκύς (1099)
γλυκύ, acc. sg. neut. adj. {James 3:11–12} id.

(1099) **γλυκύς**, εῖα, ύ [§7.H.g] *sweet,* James 3:11, 12;
Rev. 10:9, 10

(1100) **γλῶσσα**, ης, ἡ, nom. sg. f. n. [§2.3] *the
tongue,* Mark 7:33, 35, et al.; meton.
speech, talk, 1 John 3:18; *a tongue, language,* Acts 2:11; 1 Cor. 13:1, et al.; meton. *a language not proper to a speaker,
a gift* or *faculty of such language,* Mark
16:17; 1 Cor. 14:13, 14, 26, et al.; from Hebrew, *a nation,* as defined by its language,
Rev. 5:9, et al.; met. *a tongue-shaped
flame,* Acts 2:3

γλῶσσαι, nom. pl. f. n. . . . . γλῶσσα (1100)
γλώσσαις, dat. pl. f. n. . . . . id.
γλῶσσαν, acc. sg. f. n. . . . . id.
γλώσσας, acc. pl. f. n. . . . . id.
γλώσση, dat. sg. f. n. . . . . id.
γλώσσης, gen. sg. f. n. . . . . id.

(1101) **γλωσσόκομον**, ου τό [§3.C.c] (γλῶσσα +
κομέω, *to keep, preserve*) pr. *a box for
keeping the tongues, mouth-pieces,* or *reeds
of musical instruments;* hence, genr. *any
box* or *receptacle;* in N.T. *a purse, money-
bag,* John 12:6; 13:29

γλωσσόκομον, acc. sg. neut. n. . γλωσσόκομον (1101)
γλωσσῶν, gen. pl. f. n. . . . . γλῶσσα (1100)

(1102) **γναφεύς**, έως, ὁ, nom. sg. m. n. [§5.E.d]
(γνάφος, *a teasel* or *thistle*) *a fuller,* part
of whose business it was to raise a nap by
means of teasels, etc., Mark 9:3

γνήσιε, voc. sg. m. adj. . . . . γνήσιος (1103)
γνήσιον, acc. sg. neut. adj. . . . . id.

(1103) **γνήσιος**, α, ον [§7.1] *lawful, legitimate,* as
children; *genuine,* in faith, etc.; 1 Tim. 1:2;
Tit. 1:4; *true, sincere,* 2 Cor. 8:8; Phil. 4:3

γνησίῳ, dat. sg. neut. adj. . . . . γνήσιος (1103)

(1104) **γνησίως**, adv., *genuinely, sincerely,* Phil. 2:20
γνοῖ, 3 pers. sg. 2 aor. act. subj. [§30.5] (Mark
5:43; 9:30; Luke 19:15, GNT, WH & NA
| γνῷ, MT & TR) . . . . γινώσκω (1097)
γνόντα, acc. sg. m. 2 aor. act. part. . . . . . id.
γνόντες, nom. pl. m. 2 aor. act. part. . . . . id.
γνούς, nom. sg. m. 2 aor. act. part. [§36.3] id.

(1105) **γνόφος**, ου, ὁ [§3.C.a] *a thick cloud, darkness,* Heb. 12:18

γνόφῳ, dat. sg. m. n. . . . . γνόφος (1105)
γνῶ, 1 pers. sg. 2 aor. act. subj. . . . . γινώσκω (1097)
γνῷ, 3 pers. sg. 2 aor. act. subj. . . . . id.
γνῶθι, 2 pers. sg. 2 aor. act. imper. . . . . . . id.

(1106) **γνώμη**, ης, ἡ, nom. sg. f. n. [§2.B.a] *the
mind,* as the means of knowing and judg-
ing; *assent,* Philemon 14; *purpose, resolution,* Acts 20:3; *opinion, judgment,*
1 Cor. 1:10; 7:40; *suggestion, suggested
advice,* as distinguished from positive injunction, 1 Cor. 7:25; 2 Cor. 8:10 (Acts
20:3, MT & TR | γνώμης, GNT, WH
& NA)

γνώμη, dat. sg. f. n. . . . . γνώμη (1106)
γνώμην, acc. sg. f. n. . . . . id.
γνώμης, gen. sg. f. n. . . . . id.
γνῶναι, 2 aor. act. infin. . . . . γινώσκω (1097)
γνωριζέσθω, 3 pers. sg. pres. pass.
imper. . . . . γνωρίζω (1107)
γνωρίζομεν, 1 pers. pl. pres. act. indic. . . . id.

(1107) **γνωρίζω**, 1 pers. sg. pres. act. indic., fut.
γνωρίσω [§26.1] Att. γνωριῶ [§35.11] aor.
ἐγνώρισα, aor. pass. ἐγνωρίσθην, *to make
known, reveal, declare,* John 15:15; 17:26,
et al.; *to know,* Phil. 1:22

γνωριοῦσι(ν), 3 pers. pl. fut. act. indic. Att.
[§35.11] (Col. 4:9, MT & TR |
γνωρίσουσι(ν), GNT, WH & NA) γνωρίζω (1107)
γνωρίσαι, aor. act. infin. . . . . id.
γνωρίσας, nom. sg. m. aor. act. part. . . . . id.
γνωρίσει, 3 pers. sg. fut. act. indic. . . . . . . id.
γνωρίση, 3 pers. sg. aor. act. subj. . . . . id.
γνωρισθέντος, gen. sg. neut. aor. pass. part. id.
γνωρισθῆ, 3 pers. sg. aor. pass. subj. . . . . id.
γνωρίσουσι(ν), 3 pers. pl. fut. act. indic. (Col.
4:9, GNT, WH & NA | γνωριοῦσι(ν),
MT & TR) . . . . id.
γνωρίσω, 1 pers. sg. fut. act. indic. . . . . . . id.
γνῷς, 2 pers. sg. 2 aor. act. subj. . . . . γινώσκω (1097)
γνώσει, dat. sg. f. n. . . . . γνῶσις (1108)
γνώσεσθε, 2 pers. pl. fut. mid. dep.
indic. . . . . γινώσκω (1097)
γνώσεται, 3 pers. sg. fut. mid. dep. indic. . id.
γνώσεως, gen. sg. f. n. . . . . γνῶσις (1108)
γνώση, 2 pers. sg. fut. mid. dep.

indic. . . . . γινώσκω *(1097)*

γνωσθέντες, nom. pl. m. aor. pass. part. . . id.

γνώσθῃ, 3 pers. sg. aor. pass. subj. (Luke 8:17, GNT, WH & NA | γνωσθήσεται, MT & TR) . . . . id.

γνωσθήσεται, 3 pers. sg. fut. pass. indic. . id.

γνωσθήτω, 3 pers. sg. aor. pass. imper. . . . id.

γνῶσιν, 3 pers. pl. 2 aor. act. subj. {Rev. 3:9} id.

γνῶσιν, acc. sg. f. n. {Luke 1:77} . . . . γνῶσις *(1108)*

(1108) **γνῶσις**, εως, ἡ, nom. sg. f. n. [§5.E.c] *knowledge,* Luke 1:77; *knowledge* of an especial kind and relatively high character, Luke 11:52; Rom. 2:20; 1 Tim. 6:20; more particularly in respect of Christian enlightenment, Rom. 15:14; 1 Cor. 8:10; 12:8; 2 Cor. 11:6, et al.

γνώσομαι, 1 pers. sg. fut. mid. dep. indic. . . . . γινώσκω *(1097)*

γνωσόμεθα, 1 pers. pl. fut. mid. dep. indic. (1 John 3:19, GNT, WH & NA | γινώσκομεν, MT & TR) . . . . id.

γνώσονται, 3 pers. pl. fut. mid. dep. indic. id.

γνωστά, nom. pl. neut. adj. . . . . γνωστός *(1110)*

γνώστην, acc. sg. m. n. . . . . γνώστης *(1109)*

(1109) **γνώστης**, ου, ὁ [§2.B.c] *one acquainted with* a thing, *knowing, skilful,* Acts 26:3

γνωστοί, nom. pl. m. adj. . . . . γνωστός *(1110)*

γνωστοῖς, dat. pl. m. adj. . . . . id.

γνωστόν, nom. sg. neut. adj. . . . . id.

(1110) **γνωστός**, ή, όν, nom. sg. m. adj. [§7.F.a] *known,* John 18:15, 16, et al.; *certain, incontrovertible,* Acts 4:16; τὸ γνωστόν, *that which is known or is cognizable, the unquestionable attributes,* Rom. 1:19; subst. *an acquaintance,* Luke 2:44; 23:49

γνῶτε, 2 pers. pl. 2 aor. act. imper. {Luke 21:20} . . . . γινώσκω *(1097)*

γνῶτε, 2 pers. pl. 2 aor. act. subj. {John 10:38} . . . . id.

γνώτω, 3 pers. sg. 2 aor. act. imper. . . . . id.

γογγύζετε, 2 pers. pl. pres. act. imper. . . γογγύζω *(1111)*

γογγύζοντος, gen. sg. m. pres. act. part. . . id.

γογγύζουσι(ν), 3 pers. pl. pres. act. indic. . id.

(1111) **γογγύζω**, fut. γογγύσω, aor. ἐγόγγυσα [§26.1] *to speak privately and in a low voice, mutter,* John 7:32; *to utter secret and sullen discontent, express indignant complaint, murmur, grumble,* Matt. 20:11; Luke 5:30; John 6:41, 43, 61

(1112) **γογγυσμός**, οῦ, ὁ, nom. sg. m. n. [§3.C.a] *a muttering, murmuring, low and suppressed discourse,* John 7:12; *the expression of secret and sullen discontent, murmuring, complaint,* Acts 6:1; Phil. 2:14; 1 Pet. 4:9

γογγυσμοῦ, gen. sg. m. n. (1 Pet. 4:9, GNT,

WH & NA | γογγυσμῶν, MT & TR) . . . . γογγυσμός *(1112)*

γογγυσμῶν, gen. pl. m. n. . . . . id.

γογγυσταί, nom. pl. m. n. . . . . γογγυστής *(1113)*

(1113) **γογγυστής**, οῦ, ὁ [§2.B.c] *a murmurer,* Jude 16

(1114) **γόης**, ητος, ὁ [§4.2.c] *a juggler, diviner;* hence, by impl. *an impostor, cheat,* 2 Tim. 3:13

γόητες, nom. pl. m. n. . . . . γόης *(1114)*

(1115) **Γολγοθᾶ**, ἡ, nom. sg. f. pr. name, *Golgotha,* John 19:17

Γολγοθᾶν, acc. sg. f. n. (Mark 15:22, GNT | Γαλγοθάν, WH & NA | Γολγοθᾶ, MT & TR) . . . . Γολγοθᾶ *(1115)*

γόμον, acc. sg. m. n. . . . . γόμος *(1117)*

(1116) **Γόμορρα**, ας, ἡ, nom. sg. f. n., and Γόμορρα, ων, τά, *Gomorrha,* pr. name

Γομόρρας, gen. sg. f. n. . . . . Γόμορρα *(1116)*

Γομόρροις, dat. pl. neut. n. (Mark 6:11, MT & TR | GNT, WH & NA omit) . . . . . id.

Γομόρρων, gen. pl. neut. n. . . . . id.

(1117) **γόμος**, ου, ὁ [§3.C.a] *the lading* of a ship, Acts 21:3; by impl. *merchandise,* Rev. 18:11, 12

γόνασιν, dat. pl. neut. n. . . . . γόνυ *(1119)*

γόνατα, acc. pl. neut. n. . . . . id.

γονεῖς, nom. pl. m. n. {John 9:20} . . . . γονεύς *(1118)*

γονεῖς, acc. pl. m. n. {John 9:18} . . . . . . id.

(1118) **γονεύς**, έως, ὁ [§5.E.d] *a father;* pl. *parents,* Matt. 10:21; Luke 2:27, 41; 2 Cor. 12:14

γονεῦσι(ν), dat. pl. m. n. . . . . γονεύς *(1118)*

γονέων, gen. pl. m. n. . . . . id.

(1119) **γόνυ**, γόνατος, τό, nom. sg. neut. n. *the knee,* Luke 22:41; Heb. 12:12, et al {Rom. 14:11}

γόνυ, acc. sg. neut. n. {Rom. 11:4} . . . . . . γόνυ *(1119)*

(1120) **γονυπετέω**, ῶ, fut. γονυπετήσω, aor. ἐγονυπέτησα [§16.P] (γόνυ + πίπτω) *to fall upon one's knees, to kneel before,* Matt. 17:14; 27:29; Mark 1:40; 10:17

γονυπετήσαντες, nom. pl. m. aor. act. part. . . . . γονυπετέω *(1120)*

γονυπετήσας, nom. sg. m. aor. act. part. . id.

γονυπετῶν, nom. sg. m. pres. act. part. . . id.

(1121) **γράμμα**, ατος, τό, nom. sg. neut. n. [§4.D.c] pr. *that which is written or drawn; a letter, character of the alphabet,* Luke 23:38; *a writing, book,* John 5:47; *an acknowledgment of debt, an account, a bill, note,* Luke 16:6, 7; *an epistle, letter,* Acts 28:21; Gal. 6:11; ἱερὰ γράμματα, *Holy writ, the sacred books of the Old Testament, the Jewish Scriptures,* 2 Tim. 3:15; spc. *the letter* of the law of Moses, *the bare literal sense,* Rom. 2:27, 29; 2 Cor. 3:6, 7; pl. *letters, learning,* John 7:15; Acts 26:24 {2 Cor. 3:6}

γράμμα, acc. sg. neut. n. (Luke 16:6, MT &

TR | γράμματα, GNT, WH &
NA) . . . . γράμμα *(1121)*
γράμμασιν, dat. pl. neut. n. . . . . id.
γράμματα, nom. pl. neut. n. {Acts 26:24}   id.
γράμματα, acc. pl. neut. n. {Acts 25:21} .   id.
γραμματεῖς, nom. pl. m. n.
    {Matt. 23:2} . . . . γραμματεύς *(1122)*
γραμματεῖς, acc. pl. m. n. {Matt. 23:34} .   id.
γραμματεῖς, voc. pl. m. n. {Matt. 23:13} .   id.
(1122) **γραμματεύς**, έως, ὁ, nom. sg. m. n. [§5.E.d]
    a scribe; a clerk, town-clerk, registrar, re-
    corder, Acts 19:35; *one skilled in the Jew-*
    ish law, a teacher or interpreter of the law,
    Matt. 2:4; 5:20, et al. freq.; genr. *a reli-*
    gious teacher, Matt. 13:52; by synec. *any*
    one distinguished for learning or wisdom,
    1 Cor. 1:20
γραμματεῦσι(ν), dat. pl. m. n. . . . γραμματεύς *(1122)*
γραμματέων, gen. pl. m. n. . . . . id.
γράμματι, dat. sg. neut. n. . . . . γράμμα *(1121)*
γράμματος, gen. sg. neut. n. . . . . id.
γραπτόν, acc. sg. neut. adj. . . . . γραπτός *(1123)*
(1123) **γραπτός**, ή, όν [§7.F.a] *written,* Rom. 2:15
γραφαί, nom. pl. f. n. . . . . γραφή *(1124)*
γραφαῖς, dat. pl. f. n. . . . . id.
γραφάς, acc. pl. f. n. . . . . id.
γράφε, 2 pers. sg. pres. act. imper. . . . . γράφω *(1125)*
γράφει, 3 pers. sg. pres. act. indic. . . . . . id.
γράφειν, pres. act. infin. . . . . id.
γράφεσθαι, pres. pass. infin. . . . . id.
(1124) **γραφή**, ῆς, ἡ, nom. sg. f. n. [§2.B.a] *a writ-*
    ing; in N.T. *the Holy Scriptures, the Jew-*
    ish Scriptures, or *Books of the Old*
    Testament, Matt. 21:42; John 5:39, et al.;
    by synec. *doctrines, declarations, oracles,*
    or *promises* contained in the sacred books,
    Matt. 22:29; Mark 12:24; et al.; spc. *a*
    prophecy, Matt. 26:54; Mark 14:49; Luke
    4:21; 24:27, 32; with the addition of
    προφητική, Rom. 16:26; of τῶν
    προφητῶν, Matt. 26:56
γραφῇ, dat. sg. f. n. . . . . γραφή *(1124)*
γραφήν, acc. sg. f. n. . . . . id.
γραφῆς, gen. sg. f. n. . . . . id.
γράφηται, 3 pers. sg. pres. pass. subj. . . . γράφω *(1125)*
γράφομεν, 1 pers. pl. pres. act. indic. . . . . id.
γροφόμενα, acc. pl. neut. pres. pass. part.   id.
(1125) **γράφω**, 1 pers. sg. pres. act. indic., fut.
    γράψω, aor. ἔγραψα [§23.1.a; 23.2] perf.
    γέγραφα [§23.6] *to engrave, write,* accord-
    ing to the ancient method of writing on
    plates of metal, waxes tables, etc., John
    8:6, 8; *to write* on parchment, paper, etc.,
    generally, Matt. 27:37, et al.; *to write* let-
    ters to another, Acts 23:25; 2 Cor. 2:9;

13:10, et al.; *to describe in writing,* John
1:46; Rom. 10:5; *to inscribe* in a catalogue,
etc., Luke 10:20; Rev. 13:8; 17:8, et al.; *to*
write a law, *command,* or *enact in writing,*
Mark 10:5; 12:19; Luke 2:23, et al.
γράφων, nom. sg. m. pres. act. part. (2 John
    5, GNT, WH, MT, TRb & NA | γράφω,
    TRs) . . . . γράφω *(1125)*
γραφῶν, gen. pl. f. n. {Rom. 15:4} . . . . γραφή *(1124)*
γράψαι, aor. act. infin. . . . . γράφω *(1125)*
γράψαντες, nom. pl. m. aor. act. part. . . . id.
γράψας, nom. sg. m. aor. act. part. . . . . . id.
γράψῃς, 2 pers. sg. aor. act. subj. . . . . . . id.
γράψον, 2 pers. sg. aor. act. imper. . . . . . id.
γράψω, 1 pers. sg. fut. act. indic. {Rev. 3:12}   id.
γράψω, 1 pers. sg. aor. act. subj. (Acts 25:26,
    GNT, WH & NA | γράψαι, MT & TR)   id.
γραώδεις, acc. pl. m. adj. . . . . γραώδης *(1126)*
(1126) **γραώδης**, ες [§7.G.b] (γραῦς, *an old woman*)
    old-womanish; by impl. *silly, absurd,*
    1 Tim. 4:7
γρηγορεῖτε, 2 pers. pl. pres. act.
    imper. γρηγορέω *(1127)*
(1127) **γρηγορέω**, ῶ, fut. γρηγορήσω [§16.P] aor.
    ἐγρηγόρησα (a later form from pref.
    ἐγρήγορα) *to be awake, to watch,* Matt.
    26:38, 40, 41; Mark 14:34, 37, 38; *to be*
    alive, 1 Thess. 5:10; met. *to be watchful,*
    attentive, vigilant, circumspect, Matt.
    25:13; Mark 13:35, et al.
γρηγορῇ, 3 pers. sg. pres. act. subj. . γρηγορέω *(1127)*
γρηγορῆσαι, aor. act. infin. . . . . id.
γρηγορήσατε, 2 pers. pl. aor. act. imper. .   id.
γρηγορήσῃς, 2 pers. sg. aor. act. subj. . . .   id.
γρηγοροῦντας, acc. pl. m. pres. act. part. .   id.
γρηγοροῦντες, nom. pl. m. pres. act. part.   id.
γρηγορῶμεν, 1 pers. pl. pres. act. subj. . . . id.
γρηγορῶν, nom. sg. m. pres. act. part. . . .   id.
γυμνά, nom. pl. neut. adj. . . . . γυμνός *(1131)*
γύμναζε, 2 pers. sg. pres. act. imper. . γυμνάζω *(1128)*
(1128) **γυμνάζω**, fut. γαμνάσω [§26.1] perf. pass.
    γεγύμνασμαι, pr. *to train in gymnastic dis-*
    cipline; hence, *to exercise* in anything, *train*
    to use, discipline, 1 Tim. 4:7; Heb. 5:14;
    12:11; 2 Pet. 2:14
(1129) **γυμνασία**, ας, ἡ, nom. sg. f. n. [§2.B.b; 2.2]
    pr. *gymnastic exercise;* hence, *bodily dis-*
    cipline of any kind, 1 Tim. 4:8
γυμνήν, acc. sg. f. adj. . . . . γυμνός *(1131)*
γυμνητεύομεν, 1 pers. pl. pres. act. indic.
    (1 Cor. 4:11, MT & TR | γυμνιτεύομεν,
    GNT, WH & NA) . . . . γυμνητεύω *(1130)*
(1130) **γυμνητεύω**, fut. γυμνητεύσω [§13.M] *to be*
    naked; by synec. *to be poorly clad* or *des-*
    titute of proper and sufficient clothing,

1 Cor. 4:11

γυμνιτεύομεν, 1 pers. pl. pres. act. indic.
(1 Cor. 4:11, GNT, WH & NA | γυμνη-
τεύομεν, MT & TR) . . . . γυμνιτεύω *(1130)*

(1130) **γυμνιτεύω**, fut. γυμνιτεύσω [§13.M] *to be
poorly clad*

γυμνοί, nom. pl. m. adj. . . . . γυμνός *(1131)*

γυμνόν, acc. sg. m. adj. . . . . id.

(1131) **γυμνός**, ή, όν, nom. sg. m. adj. [§7.F.a] *naked,
without clothing,* Mark 14:51, 52; *with-
out the upper garment, and clad only with
an inner garment or tunic,* John 21:7;
*poorly or meanly clad, destitute of proper
and sufficient clothing,* Matt. 25:36, 38,
43, 44; Acts 19:16; James 2:15; met. *un-
clothed with a body,* 2 Cor. 5:3; *not covered, uncovered, open, manifest,* Heb. 4:13;
bare, mere, 1 Cor. 15:37; *naked of* spiritual *clothing,* Rev. 3:17; 16:15; 17:16

(1132) **γυμνότης**, τητος, ή, nom. sg. f. n. [§4.2.c]
*nakedness; want of proper and sufficient
clothing,* Rom. 8:35; 2 Cor. 11:27; spiritual *nakedness, being destitute of* spiritual
clothing, Rev. 3:18

γυμνότητι, dat. sg. f. n. . . . . γυμνότης *(1132)*

γυμνότητος, gen. sg. f. n. . . . . id.

γυμνοῦ, gen. sg. neut. adj. . . . . γυμνός *(1131)*

γυμνούς, acc. pl. m. adj. . . . . id.

γύναι, voc. sg. f. n. [§6.4.b] . . . . γυνή *(1135)*

γυναῖκα, acc. sg. f. n. . . . . id.

γυναικάρια, acc. pl. neut. n. . . . . . γυναικάριον *(1133)*

(1133) **γυναικάριον**, ου, τό [§3.C.c] (dimin. of γυνή)
*a little woman, muliercula; a trifling, weak,
silly woman,* 2 Tim. 3:6

γυναῖκας, acc. pl. f. n. . . . . γυνή *(1135)*

(1134) **γυναικεῖος**, εία, αῖον [§7.1] *pertaining to
women, female,* 1 Pet. 3:7

γυναικείῳ, dat. sg. neut. adj. . . . . . γυναικεῖος *(1134)*

γυναῖκες, nom. pl. f. n. . . . . γυνή *(1135)*

γυναικί, dat. sg. f. n. . . . . id.

γυναικός, gen. sg. f. n. . . . . id.

γυναικῶν, gen. pl. f. n. . . . . id.

γυναιξί(ν), dat. pl. f. n. . . . . id.

(1135) **γυνή**, γυναικός, ή, nom. sg. f. n. [§6.4.b] *a
woman,* Matt. 5:28, et al.; *a married
woman, wife,* Matt. 5:31, 32; 14:3, et al.;
in the voc. ὦ γύναι, *O woman!* an ordinary mode of addressing females under
every circumstance; met. used of the
Church, as united to Christ, Rev. 19:7; 21:9

(1136) **Γώγ**, ὁ, *Gog,* pr. name of a nation, indecl.,
Rev. 20:8

(1137) **γωνία**, ας, ή [§2.B.b; 2.2] *an exterior angle,
projecting corner,* Matt. 6:5; 21:42, et al.;
an interior angle; by impl. *a dark corner,*

obscure place, Acts 26:26; *corner, extremity,* or *quarter* of the earth, Rev. 7:1; 20:8

γωνίᾳ, dat. sg. f. n. . . . . γωνία *(1137)*

γωνίαις, dat. pl. f. n. . . . . id.

γωνίας, gen. sg. f. n. {Matt. 21:42} . . . . id.

γωνίας, acc. pl. f. n. {Rev. 7:1} . . . . id.

Δ

δ' for δέ before ἄν . . . . δέ *(1161)*

(1138) **Δαβίδ**, ὁ, *David,* pr. name, indecl. (MT & TR
| Δαυίδ, GNT & NA | Δαυείδ, WH)

δαίμονες, nom. pl. m. n. . . . . δαίμων *(1142)*

δαιμόνια, nom. pl. neut. n.
{Luke 8:30} . . . . δαιμόνιον *(1140)*

δαιμόνια, acc. pl. neut. n. {Luke 8:27} . . . id.

δαιμονίζεται, 3 pers. sg. pres. mid./pass. dep.
indic. δαιμονίζομαι *(1139)*

(1139) **δαιμονίζομαι**, fut. δαιμονίσομαι [§26.1] aor.
pass. ἐδαιμονίσθην [§26.1] in N.T. *to be
possessed, afflicted, vexed, by a demon* or
evil spirit, i.q. δαιμόνιον ἔχειν, Matt. 4:24;
8:16, 28, 33, et al.

δαιμονιζόμενοι, nom. pl. m. pres. mid./pass.
dep. part. . . . . δαιμονίζομαι *(1139)*

δαιμονιζόμενον, acc. sg. m. pres. mid./pass.
dep. part. . . . . id.

δαιμονιζόμενος, nom. sg. m. pres. mid./pass.
dep. part. . . . . id.

δαιμονιζομένου, gen. sg. m. pres. mid./pass.
dep. part. . . . . id.

δαιμονιζομένους, acc. pl. m. pres. mid./pass.
dep. part. . . . . id.

δαιμονιζομένῳ, dat. sg. m. pres. mid./pass.
dep. part. . . . . id.

δαιμονιζομένων, gen. pl. m. pres. mid./pass.
dep. part. . . . . id.

δαιμονίοις, dat. pl. neut. n. . . . . δαιμόνιον *(1140)*

(1140) **δαιμόνιον**, ου, τό, nom. sg. neut. n. [§3.C.c]
a heathen god, deity, Acts 17:18; 1 Cor.
10:20, 21; Rev. 9:20; in N.T., *a demon, evil
spirit,* Matt. 7:22; 9:33, 34; 10:8; 12:24,
et al. {John 10:21}

δαιμόνιον, acc. sg. neut. n.
{John 10:20} . . . . δαιμόνιον *(1140)*

δαιμονίου, gen. sg. neut. n. . . . . id.

δαιμονισθείς, nom. sg. m. aor. pass. dep.
part. . . . . δαιμονίζομαι *(1139)*

(1141) **δαιμονιώδης**, ες, nom. sg. f. adj. [§7.G.b] *pertaining to* or *proceeding from demons;
demoniacal, devilish,* James 3:15

δαιμονίων, gen. pl. neut. n. . . . . δαιμόνιον *(1140)*

δαίμονος, gen. sg. m. n. (Luke 8:29, MT &

TR | δαιμονίου, GNT, WH & NA) δαίμων *(1142)*
δαιμόνων, gen. pl. m. n. (Rev. 16:14, TR |
δαιμονίων, GNT, WH, MT & NA | Rev.
18:2, MT & TR | δαιμονίων, GNT, WH
& NA) . . . . id.

(1142) **δαίμων**, ονος, ὁ [§4.2.e] *a god, a superior
power;* in N.T. *a malignant demon, evil angel,* Matt. 8:31; Mark 5:12; Luke 8:29; Rev.
16:14; 18:2
δάκνετε, 2 pers. pl. pres. act. indic. . . . δάκνω *(1143)*

(1143) **δάκνω**, fut. δήξομαι, 2 aor. ἔδακον, perf.
δέδηχα [§36.2] *to bite, sting;* met. *to mo-
lest, vex, injure,* Gal. 5:15

(1144) **δάκρυ**, υος, τό [§4.1] *a tear*

(1144) **δάκρυον**, ου, τό [§3.C.c] *a tear*
δάκρυον, acc. sg. neut. n. . . . . δάκρυον *(1144)*
δάκρυσι(ν), dat. pl. neut. n. . . . . δάκρυ *(1144)*

(1145) **δακρύω**, fut. δακρύσω [§13.M] aor.
ἐδάκρυσα [§13.M] *to shed tears, weep,*
John 11:35
δακρύων, gen. pl. neut. n. . . . . δάκρυον *(1144)*
δακτύλιον, acc. sg. m. n. . . . . δακτύλιος *(1146)*

(1146) **δακτύλιος**, ου, ὁ [§3.C.a] *a ring for the finger,*
Luke 15:22
δάκτυλον, acc. sg. m. n. . . . . δάκτυλος *(1147)*

(1147) **δάκτυλος**, ου, ὁ [§3.C.a] *a finger,* Matt. 23:4;
Mark 7:33; et al.; from Hebrew, *power,*
Luke 11:20
δακτύλου, gen. sg. m. n. . . . . δάκτυλος *(1147)*
δακτύλους, acc. pl. m. n. . . . . id.
δακτύλῳ, dat. sg. m. n. . . . . id.
δακτύλων, gen. pl. m. n. . . . . id.

(1148) **Δαλμανουθά**, ἡ, *Dalmanutha,* indecl., a small
town on the shore of the Sea of Tiberias,
Mark 8:10

(1149) **Δαλματία**, ας, ἡ [§2.B.b; 2.2] *Dalmatia,*
2 Tim. 4:10
Δαλματίαν, acc. sg. f. n. . . . . Δαλματία *(1149)*
δαμάζεται, 3 pers. sg. pres. pass.
indic. δαμάζω *(1150)*

(1150) **δαμάζω**, fut. δαμάσω [§26.1] aor. ἐδάμασα,
perf. pass. δεδάμασμαι (δαμάω, the same)
to subdue, tame, Mark 5:4; James 3:7; met.
to restrain within proper limits, James 3:8
δαμάλεως, gen. sg. f. n. . . . . δάμαλις *(1151)*

(1151) **δάμαλις**, εως, ἡ [§5.E.c] *a heifer,* Heb. 9:13

(1152) **Δάμαρις**, ιδος, ἡ, nom. sg. f. n. [§4.2.c]
Damaris, pr. name, Acts 17:34
δαμάσαι, aor. act. infin. . . . . δαμάζω *(1150)*

(1153) **Δαμασκηνός**, ή, όν [§7.F] *A Damascene, a
native of Damascus,* 2 Cor. 11:32
Δαμασκηνῶν, gen. pl. m. adj. . . Δαμασκηνός *(1153)*
Δαμασκόν, acc. sg. f. n. . . . . Δαμασκός *(1154)*

(1154) **Δαμασκός**, οῦ, ἡ [§3.C.b] *Damascus,* the capital city of Syria

Δαμασκῷ, dat. sg. f. n. . . . . Δαμασκός *(1154)*
δανείζετε, 2 pers. pl. pres. act. imper. (Luke
6:35, MT & TR | δανίζετε, GNT, WH
& NA) . . . . δανείζω *(1155)*
δανείζητε, 2 pers. pl. pres. act. subj. (Luke
6:34, MT & TR | δανίσητε, GNT, WH
& NA) . . . . id.
δανείζουσιν, 3 pers. pl. pres. act. indic. (Luke
6:34, MT & TR | δανίζουσιν, GNT, WH
& NA) . . . . id.

(1155) **δανείζω**, fut. δανείσω [§26.1] aor. ἐδάνεισα,
to lend money, Luke 6:34, 35; mid. *to borrow money,* Matt. 5:42

(1156) **δάνειον**, ου, τό [§3.C.c] (δάνος, *a gift, loan*)
a loan, debt, Matt. 18:27
δάνειον, acc. sg. neut. n. (Matt. 18:27, GNT,
MT, TR & NA | δάνιον, WH) . . . δάνειον *(1156)*
δανείσασθαι, aor. mid. infin. (Matt. 5:42, MT
& TR | δανίσασθαι, GNT, WH &
NA) . . . . δανείζω *(1155)*
δανειστῇ, dat. sg. m. n. (Luke 7:41, MT &
TR | δανιστῇ, GNT, WH &
NA) . . . . δανειστής *(1157)*

(1157) **δανειστής**, οῦ, ὁ [§2.B.c] *a lender, creditor,*
Luke 7:41
δανίζετε, 2 pers. pl. pres. act. imper. (Luke
6:35, GNT, WH & NA | δανείζετε, MT
& TR) . . . . δανίζω *(‡1155)*
δανίζουσιν, 3 pers. pl. pres. act. indic. (Luke
6:34, GNT, WH & NA | δανείζουσιν,
MT & TR) . . . . id.

(‡1155) **δανίζω**, *to lend money*

(1158) **Δανιήλ**, ὁ, *Daniel,* pr. name, indecl.
δανίσασθαι, aor. mid. infin. (Matt. 5:42,
GNT, WH & NA | δανείσασθαι, MT &
TR) . . . . δανίζω *(‡1155)*
δανίσητε, 2 pers. pl. aor. act. subj. (Luke 6:34,
GNT, WH & NA | δανείζητε, MT &
TR) . . . . id.
δανιστῇ, dat. sg. m. n. . . . . δανιστής *(‡1157)*

(‡1157) **δανιστής**, οῦ, ὁ, *a money-lender, creditor*

(1159) **δαπανάω**, ῶ, fut. δαπανήσω [§18.R] aor.
ἐδαπάνησα, *to expend, be at expense,*
Mark 5:26; Acts 21:24; 2 Cor. 12:15; *to
spend, waste, consume by extravagance,*
Luke 15:14 James 4:3

(1160) **δαπάνη**, ης, ἡ [§2.B.a] *expense, cost,* Luke
14:28
δαπάνην, acc. sg. f. n. . . . . δαπάνη *(1160)*
δαπανήσαντος, gen. sg. m. aor. act.
part. δαπανάω *(1159)*
δαπανήσασα, nom. sg. f. aor. act. part. . . id.
δαπανήσητε, 2 pers. pl. aor. act. subj. . . . id.
δαπάνησον, 2 pers. sg. aor. act. imper. . . . id.
δαπανήσω, 1 pers. sg. fut. act. indic. . . . . id.

δαρήσεσθε, 2 pers. pl. 2 fut. pass. indic. . δέρω *(1194)*
δαρήσεται, 3 pers. sg. 2 fut. pass. indic. . . .   id.

(‡1138) **Δαυίδ**, ὁ, *David,* pr. name, indecl. (GNT &
NA | Δαβίδ, MT & TR | Δαυείδ, WH)

(1161) **δέ**, a conjunctive particle, marking the superaddition of a clause, whether in opposition
or in continuation, to what has preceded,
and it may be variously rendered *but, on
the other hand, and, also, now,* etc.; καὶ
δέ, when there is a special superaddition
in continuation, *too, yea,* etc. It sometimes
is found at the commencement of the apodosis of a sentence, Acts 11:17. It serves also
to mark the resumption of an interrupted
discourse, 2 Cor. 2:10; Gal. 2:6
δεδάμασται, 3 pers. sg. perf. pass.
indic. . . . . δαμάζω *(1150)*
δεδεκάτωκε(ν), 3 pers. sg. perf. act.
indic. . . . . δεκατόω *(1183)*
δεδεκάτωται, 3 pers. sg. perf. pass. indic.   id.
δέδεκται, 3 pers. sg. perf. mid./pass. dep.
indic. [§23.7] . . . . δέχομαι *(1209)*
δεδεκώς, nom. sg. m. perf. act. part.
[§37.1] . . . . δέω *(1210)*
δέδεμαι, 1 pers. sg. perf. pass. indic. . . . .   id.
δεδεμένα, nom. pl. neut. perf. pass. part. .   id.
δεδεμένην, acc. sg. f. perf. pass. part. . . . .   id.
δεδεμένον, acc. sg. m. perf. pass. part.
{John 18:24} . . . .   id.
δεδεμένον, nom. sg. neut. perf. pass. part.
{Matt. 16:19} . . . .   id.
δεδεμένος, nom. sg. m. perf. pass. part. . .   id.
δεδεμένους, acc. pl. m. perf. pass. part. . .   id.
δέδεσαι, 2 pers. sg. perf. pass. indic. . . . .   id.
δεδέσθαι, perf. pass. infin. . . . .   id.
δέδεται, 3 pers. sg. perf. pass. indic. . . . . .   id.
δεδικαίωμαι, 1 pers. sg. perf. pass. indic.
[§21.U] . . . . δικαιόω *(1344)*
δεδικαιωμένος, nom. sg. m. perf. pass. part.   id.
δεδικαίωται, 3 pers. sg. perf. pass. indic. .   id.
δεδιωγμένοι, nom. pl. m. perf. pass.
part. διώκω *(1377)*
δεδοκιμάσμεθα, 1 pers. pl. perf. pass.
indic. . . . . δοκιμάζω *(1381)*
δεδομένην, acc. sg. f. perf. pass. part.
[§30.4] . . . . δίδωμι *(1325)*
δεδομένον, nom. sg. neut. perf. pass. part.   id.
δεδόξασμαι, 1 pers. sg. perf. pass.
indic. . . . . δοξάζω *(1392)*
δεδοξασμένη, dat. sg. f. perf. pass. part. .   id.
δεδοξασμένον, nom. sg. neut. perf. pass.
part. . . . .   id.
δεδόξασται, 3 pers. sg. perf. pass. indic. .   id.
δέδοται, 3 pers. sg. perf. pass. indic.
[§30.4] . . . . δίδωμι *(1325)*

δεδουλεύκαμεν, 1 pers. pl. perf. act.
indic. . . . . δουλεύω *(1398)*
δεδουλωμένας, acc. pl. f. perf. pass.
part. δουλόω *(1402)*
δεδουλωμένοι, nom. pl. m. perf. pass. part.   id.
δεδούλωται, 3 pers. sg. perf. pass. indic. .   id.
δέδωκα, 1 pers. sg. perf. act. indic.
[§30.Z] . . . . δίδωμι *(1325)*
δέδωκας, 2 pers. sg. perf. act. indic. . . . . .   id.
δεδώκει, 3 pers. sg. pluperf. act. indic. Att.
for ἐδεδώκει . . . .   id.
δεδώκεισαν, 3 pers. pl. pluperf. act. indic. Att.
for ἐδεδώκεισαν . . . .   id.
δέδωκε(ν), 3 pers. sg. perf. act. indic. . . . .   id.
δεδωκότι, dat. sg. m. perf. act. part. (Rev. 13:4,
MT | ἔδωκεν, GNT, WH, TR & NA)   id.
δεδωρημένης, gen. sg. f. perf. pass.
part. δωρέομαι *(1433)*
δεδώρηται, 3 pers. sg. perf. pass. indic. . .   id.
δέῃ, 3 pers. sg. pres. subj. . . . . δεῖ *(1163)*
δεηθέντων, gen. pl. m. aor. pass. dep.
part. . . . . δέομαι *(1189)*
δεήθητε, 2 pers. pl. aor. pass. dep. imper. .   id.
δεήθητι, 2 pers. sg. aor. pass. dep. imper. .   id.
δεήσει, dat. sg. f. n. . . . . δέησις *(1162)*
δεήσεις, acc. pl. f. n. . . . .   id.
δεήσεσι(ν), dat. pl. f. n. . . . .   id.
δεήσεως, gen. sg. f. n. . . . .   id.
δέησιν, acc. sg. f. n. . . . .   id.
(1162) **δέησις**, εως, ἡ, nom. sg. f. n. [§5.E.c] *want,
entreaty; prayer, supplication,* Luke 1:13;
2:37; 5:33, et al.
δεθῆναι, aor. pass. infin. . . . . δέω *(1210)*
(1163) **δεῖ**, 3 pers. sg. pres. indic. impers., fut. δεήσει,
aor. ἐδέησε(ν), imperf. ἔδει, subj. δέῃ, in-
fin. δεῖν, part. δέον, *it is binding, it is necessary, it behooves, it is proper; it is
inevitable,* Acts 21:22
(1164) **δεῖγμα**, ατος, τό [§4.D.c] pr. *that which is
shown, a specimen, sample;* met. *an ex-
ample* by way of warning, Jude 7
δεῖγμα, acc. sg. neut. n. . . . . δεῖγμα *(1164)*
(1165) **δειγματίζω**, fut. δειγματίσω, aor. ἐδειγμάτισα
[§26.1] *to make a public show or specta-
cle of* Col. 2:15
δειγματίσαι, aor. act. infin. (Matt. 1:19, GNT,
WH & NA | παραδειγματίσαι, MT &
TR) . . . . δειγματίζω *(1165)*
δεικνύειν, pres. act. infin. . . . . δείκνυμι *(†1166)*
δεικνύεις, 2 pers. sg. pres. act. indic. . . . .   id.
(†1166) **δείκνυμι**, 1 pers. sg. pres. act. indic., fut.
δείξω, aor. ἔδειξα, aor. pass. ἐδείχθην
[§31.BB] *to show, point out, present to the
sight,* Matt. 4:8; 8:4, et al.; *to exhibit,
permit to see, cause to be seen,* John 2:18;

10:32; 1 Tim. 6:15; *to demonstrate, prove,*
James 2:18; 3:13; met. *to teach, make
known, declare, announce,* Matt. 16:21;
John 5:20; Acts 10:28, et al.

δεικνύντος, gen. sg. m. pres. act. part. (Rev.
22:8, MT | δεικνύοντος, GNT, WH, TR
& NA) . . . . δείκνυμι (†1166)

δεικνύοντος, gen. sg. m. pres. act. part. (Rev.
22:8, GNT, WH, TR & NA | δεικνύντος,
MT) . . . . id.

δείκνυσιν, 3 pers. sg. pres. act. indic. . . . . id.

(1167) **δειλία**, ας, ἡ [§2.B.b; 2.2] *timidity,* 2 Tim. 1:7

δειλίας, gen. sg. f. n. . . . . δειλία (1167)

δειλιάτω, 3 pers. sg. pres. act. imper. . δειλιάω (1168)

(1168) **δειλιάω**, ῶ, fut. δειλιάσω [§22.2] *to be timid,
be in fear,* John 14:27

δειλοί, nom. pl. m. adj. . . . . δειλός (1169)

δειλοῖς, dat. pl. m. adj. . . . . id.

(1169) **δειλός**, ή, όν [§7.F.a] *timid, fearful, pusillan-
imous, cowardly,* Matt. 8:26; Mark 4:40;
Rev. 21:8

δεῖν, pres. infin. δεῖ (1163)

(1170) **δεῖνα**, ὁ, ἡ, τό [§10.5] *such a one, a certain
one,* Matt. 26:18

δεῖνα, acc. sg. m. adj. . . . . δεῖνα (1170)

(1171) **δεινῶς**, adv. (δεινός, *terrible, vehement*)
dreadfully, grievously, greatly, vehemently,
Matt. 8:6; Luke 11:53

δεῖξαι, aor. act. infin. . . . . δείκνυμι (†1166)

δείξατε, 2 pers. pl. aor. act. imper. (Luke
20:24, GNT, WH & NA | ἐπιδείξατε,
MT & TR) . . . . id.

δειξάτω, 3 pers. sg. aor. act. imper. . . . . . id.

δείξει, 3 pers. sg. fut. act. indic. . . . . id.

δεῖξον, 2 pers. sg. aor. act. imper. . . . . id.

δείξω, 1 pers. sg. fut. act. indic. {Rev. 4:1} id.

δείξω, 1 pers. sg. aor. act. subj. {Acts 7:3} id.

(1172) **δειπνέω**, ῶ, fut. δειπνήσω and δειπνήσομαι,
aor. ἐδείπνησα [§16.P] *to sup,* Luke 17:8;
22:20; 1 Cor. 11:25; Rev. 3:20

δειπνῆσαι, aor. act. infin. . . . . δειπνέω (1172)

δειπνήσω, 1 pers. sg. fut. act. indic.
{Rev. 3:20} . . . . id.

δειπνήσω, 1 pers. sg. aor. act. subj.
{Luke 17:8} . . . . id.

δείπνοις, dat. pl. neut. n. . . . . δεῖπνον (1173)

(1173) **δεῖπνον**, ου, τό [§3.C.c] pr. *a meal; supper,
the principal meal taken in the evening,*
Luke 14:12; John 13:2, 4, et al.; meton.
food, 1 Cor. 11:21; *a feast, banquet,* Matt.
23:6; Mark 6:21; 12:39, et al.

δεῖπνον, acc. sg. neut. n. . . . . δεῖπνον (1173)

δείπνου, gen. sg. neut. n. . . . . id.

δείπνῳ, dat. sg. neut. n. . . . . id.

δείραντες, nom. pl. m. aor. act. part.

[§27.1.d] . . . . δέρω (1194)

δεισιδαιμονεστέρους, acc. pl. m. compar. adj.
[§8.1] . . . . δεισιδαίμων (‡1174)

(1175) **δεισιδαιμονία**, ας, ἡ [§2.B.b; 2.2] *fear of the
gods;* in a bad sense, *superstition; a form
of religious belief,* Acts 25:19

δεισιδαιμονίας, gen. sg. f. n. . . . δεισιδαιμονία (1175)

(‡1174) **δεισιδαίμων**, ον [§7.G.a] (δείδω, *to fear,* and
δαίμων) *reverencing the gods and divine
things, religious;* in a bad sense, *supersti-
tious;* in N.T. *careful and precise in the discharge of religious services,* Acts 17:22

δειχθέντα, acc. sg. m. aor. pass. part.
[§31.1.b] . . . . δείκνυμι (†1166)

(1176) **δέκα**, οἱ, αἱ, τά, indecl. numeral, *ten,* Matt.
20:24; 25:1, et al.; ἡμερῶν δέκα, *ten days,
a few days, a short time,* Rev. 2:10

(1177) **δεκαδύο**, οἱ, αἱ, τά, indecl. numeral (δέκα +
δύο) i.q. δώδεκα, *twelve* (Acts 19:7; 24:11;
MT & TR: Rev. 21:16, MT | δώδεκα,
GNT, WH & NA | Rev. 21:16, δώδεκα, TR)

δεκαόκτω, indecl. numeral (δέκα + ὀκτώ)
eighteen (Luke 13:4, 11, GNT & NA |
δέκα ὀκτώ, WH | δέκα καὶ ὀκτώ, MT
& TR)

(1178) **δεκαπέντε**, οἱ, αἱ, τά, indecl. numeral (δέκα
+ πέντε) *fifteen,* John 11:18; Acts 27:28;
Gal. 1:18

Δεκαπόλει, dat. sg. f. n. . . . . Δεκάπολις (1179)

Δεκαπόλεως, gen. sg. f. n. . . . . id.

(1179) **Δεκάπολις**, εως, ἡ [§5.E.c] *Decapolis,* a district of Palestine beyond Jordan, Mark 5:20

δεκάτας, acc. pl. f. n. . . . . δεκάτη (1181)

(1180) **δεκατέσσαρες**, οἱ, αἱ, τά, nom. pl. f. numeral
(δέκα + τέσσαρες) *fourteen,* Matt. 1:17;
2 Cor. 12:2; Gal. 2:1

δεκατεσσάρων, gen. pl. neut.
numeral . . . . δεκατέσσαρες (1180)

(1181) **δεκάτη**, ης, ἡ, nom. sg. f. n. *a tithe,* the tenth
part of anything

δεκάτη, nom. sg. fem. adj. . . . . δέκατος (1182)

δεκάτην, acc. sg. f. n. . . . . δεκάτη (1181)

δέκατον, nom. sg. neut. adj. . . . . δέκατος (1182)

(1182) **δέκατος**, η, ον, nom. sg. m. adj. [§7.F.a] *tenth,*
John 1:40; Rev. 11:13; 21:20; δεκάτη, sc.
μερίς, *a tenth part, tithe,* Heb. 7:2, 4, 8, 9

(1183) **δεκατόω**, ῶ, fut. δεκατώσω [§20.T] perf.
δεδεκάτωκα, *to cause to pay tithes;* pass.
to be tithed, pay tithes, Heb. 7:6, 9

δεκτήν, acc. sg. f. adj. . . . . δεκτός (1184)

δεκτόν, acc. sg. m. adj. . . . . id.

(1184) **δεκτός**, ή, όν, nom. sg. m. adj. [§7.F.a] *ac-
cepted, acceptable, agreeable, approved,*
Luke 4:24; Acts 10:35; Phil. 4:18; by impl.
when used of a certain time, *marked by* di-

vine *acceptance, propitious,* Luke 4:19;
2 Cor. 6:2

δεκτῷ, dat. sg. m. adj. . . . . δεκτός *(1184)*

δελεαζόμενος, nom. sg. m. pres. pass.
part. . . . . δελεάζω *(1185)*

δελεάζοντες, nom. pl. m. pres. act. part. . ·id.

δελεάζουσιν, 3 pers. pl. pres. act. indic. . . id.

(1185) **δελεάζω,** fut. δελεάσω [§26.1] (δέλεαρ, *a
bait*) pr. *to entrap, take or catch* with a bait;
met. *allure, entice, delude,* James 1:14;
2 Pet. 2:14, 18

δένδρα, nom. pl. neut. n. {Jude 12} . . δένδρον *(1186)*

δένδρα, acc. pl. neut. n. {Rev. 7:3} . . . . . id.

(1186) **δένδρον,** ου, τό, nom. sg. neut. n. [§3.C.c] *a
tree,* Matt. 3:10; 7:17; 13:32 {Matt.
12:33c}

δένδρον, acc. sg. neut. n.
{Matt. 12:33a,b} . . . . δένδρον *(1186)*

δένδρων, gen. pl. neut. n. . . . . id.

δέξαι, 2 pers. sg. aor. mid. dep.
imper. . . . . δέχομαι *(1209)*

δεξαμένη, nom. sg. f. aor. mid. dep. part. . id.

δεξάμενοι, nom. pl. m. aor. mid. dep. part. . id.

δεξάμενος, nom. sg. m. aor. mid. dep. part. . id.

δέξασθαι, aor. mid. dep. infin. . . . . id.

δέξασθε, 2 pers. pl. aor. mid. dep. imper. . id.

δέξηται, 3 pers. sg. aor. mid. dep. subj. . . id.

δεξιά, nom. sg. f. adj. {Luke 6:6} . . . . . δεξιός *(1188)*

δεξιά, acc. pl. neut. adj. {John 21:6} . . . . id.

δεξιᾷ, dat. sg. f. adj. . . . . id.

δεξιάν, acc. sg. f. adj. . . . . id.

δεξιᾶς, gen. sg. f. adj. {Acts 3:7} . . . . . . id.

δεξιάς, acc. pl. f. adj. {Gal. 2:9} . . . . id.

δεξιοῖς, dat. pl. neut. adj. . . . . id.

(1187) **δεξιολάβος,** ου, ὁ [§3.C.a] (δεξιός +
λαμβάνω) *one posted on the right hand;
a flank guard; a light armed spearman,*
Acts 23:23

δεξιολάβους, acc. pl. m. n. . . . . . . δεξιολάβος *(1187)*

δεξιόν, acc. sg. m. adj. {Rev. 10:2} . . . . δεξιός *(1188)*

δεξιόν, acc. sg. neut. adj. {John 18:10} . . . id.

(1188) **δεξιός,** ά, όν, nom. sg. m. adj. [§7.1] *right,*
as opposed to left, Matt. 5:29, 30; Luke
6:6, et al.; ἡ δεξιά, sc. χείρ, *the right hand,*
Matt. 6:3; 27:29, et al.; τὰ δεξιά, sc. μέρη,
*the parts towards the right hand, the right
hand side;* καθίζειν, or, καθῆσθαι, or,
ἑστάναι, ἐκ δεξιῶν (μερῶν) τινος, *to sit
or stand at the right hand of any one,* as
a mark of the highest honor and dignity
which he can bestow, Matt. 20:21; 26:64,
et al.; εἶναι ἐκ δεξιῶν (μερῶν) τινος, *to
be at one's right hand,* as a helper, Acts
2:25; δεξιὰς (χεῖρας) διδόναι, *to give the
right hand* to any one, as a pledge of sin-

cerity in one's promises, Gal. 2:9

δεξιῶν, gen. pl. m. adj. . . . . δεξιός *(1188)*

δέξωνται, 3 pers. pl. aor. mid. dep.
subj. . . . . δέχομαι *(1209)*

(1189) **δέομαι,** 1 pers. sg. pres. mid./pass. dep. indic.,
fut. δεήσομαι, aor. (pass. form) ἐδεήθην,
to be in want, to need; to ask, request,
Matt. 9:38; Luke 5:12; 8:28, 38, et al.; in
N.T. absol. *to pray, offer prayer, beseech,
supplicate,* Luke 21:36; 22:32; Acts 4:31;
8:22, 24, et al.

δεόμεθα, 1 pers. pl. pres. mid./pass. dep.
indic. . . . . δέομαι *(1189)*

δεόμενοι, nom. pl. m. pres. mid./pass. dep.
part. . . . . id.

δεόμενος, nom. sg. m. pres. mid./pass. dep.
part. . . . . id.

(‡1163) **δέον,** nom. sg. neut. pres. part. [§37.1] (part.
of δεῖ) *necessary,* 1 Pet. 1:6; *proper, right,*
Acts 19:36; 1 Tim. 5:13

δέοντα, acc. pl. neut. pres. part. . . . . δέον *(‡1163)*

(‡127) **δέος,** δέους, τό (δείδω, *to fear*) *fear*

δέους, gen. sg. neut. n. (Heb. 12:28, GNT,
WH & NA | αἰδοῦς, MT & TR) . . . . δέος *(‡127)*

(1190) **Δερβαῖος,** α, ον, nom. sg. m. adj. *an inhabitant of Derbe,* Acts 20:4

(1191) **Δέρβη,** ης, ἡ [§2.B.a] *Derbe,* a city of Lycaonia

Δέρβην, acc. sg. f. n. . . . . Δέρβη *(1191)*

δέρει, 3 pers. sg. pres. act. indic. . . . . . . δέρω *(1194)*

δέρεις, 2 pers. sg. pres. act. indic. . . . . . . id.

(1192) **δέρμα,** ατος, τό [§4.D.c] *the skin* of an animal, Heb. 11:37

δέρμασιν, dat. pl. neut. n. . . . . δέρμα *(1192)*

δερματίνην, acc. sg. f. adj. . . . . δερμάτινος *(1193)*

(1193) **δερμάτινος,** η, ον [§7.F.a] *made of skin, leathern,* Matt. 3:4; Mark 1:6

δέροντες, nom. pl. m. pres. act. part. . . . δέρω *(1194)*

(1194) **δέρω,** fut. δερῶ [§27.1.a] aor. ἔδειρα [§27.1.d]
2 fut. pass. δαρήσομαι [§27.4.c] *to skin,
flay;* hence, *to beat, scourge,* Matt. 21:35;
Mark 12:3, 5; 13:9, et al.

δέρων, nom. sg. m. pres. act. part. . . . . . δέρω *(1194)*

δεσμά, nom. pl. neut. n. {Acts 16:26} . δεσμός *(1199)*

δεσμά, acc. pl. neut. n. {Luke 8:29} . . . . . id.

δεσμάς, acc. pl. f. n. . . . . δεσμή *(1197)*

δεσμεύουσι(ν), 3 pers. pl. pres. act.
indic. . . . . δεσμεύω *(1195)*

(1195) **δεσμεύω,** fut. δεσμεύσω [§13.M] *to bind, bind
up,* as a bundle, Matt. 23:4; *to bind, confine,* Acts 22:4

δεσμεύων, nom. sg. m. pres. act.
part. . . . . δεσμεύω *(1195)*

(1196) **δεσμέω,** ῶ, fut. δεσμήσω [§16.P] *to bind, confine,* i.q. δεσμεύω, Luke 8:29

(1197) **δεσμή,** ης, ἡ [§2.B.a] *a bundle,* as of tares,

Matt. 13:20

δέσμιοι, nom. pl. m. n. . . . . δέσμιος *(1198)*

δεσμίοις, dat. pl. m. n. (Heb. 10:34, GNT, WH & NA | δεσμοῖς, MT & TR) . . .   id.

δέσμιον, acc. sg. m. n. . . . .   id.

(1198) **δέσμιος**, ου, ὁ, nom. sg. m. n. [§3.C.a] *one bound, a prisoner*, Matt. 27:15, 16; Mark 15:6, et al.

δεσμίους, acc. pl. m. n. . . . . δέσμιος *(1198)*

δεσμίων, gen. pl. m. n. . . . .   id.

δεσμοῖς, dat. pl. m. n. . . . . δεσμός *(1199)*

(1199) **δεσμός**, οῦ, ὁ, nom. sg. m. n. [§6.7] pl. τὰ δεσμά, and οἱ δεσμοί [§6.7] *a bond, anything by which one is bound, a cord, chain, fetters*, etc.; and by meton. *imprisonment*, Luke 8:29; Acts 16:26; 20:23, et al.; *a string or ligament*, as of the tongue, Mark 7:35; met. *an impediment, infirmity*, Luke 13:16

δεσμοῦ, gen. sg. m. n. . . . . δεσμός *(1199)*

δεσμούς, acc. pl. m. n. . . . .   id.

δεσμοφύλακι, dat. sg. m. n. . . . . δεσμοφύλαξ *(1200)*

(1200) **δεσμοφύλαξ**, ακος, ὁ, nom. sg. m. n. [§4.2.b] (δεσμός + φυλάσσω) *a keeper of a prison, jailer*, Acts 16:23, 27, 36

δεσμῶν, gen. pl. m. n. . . . . δεσμός *(1199)*

δεσμώτας, acc. pl. m. n. . . . . δεσμώτης *(1202)*

(1201) **δεσμωτήριον**, ου, τό [§3.C.c] (δεσμόω, *to bind*) *a prison*, Matt. 11:2; Acts 5:21, 23; 16:26

δεσμωτήριον, acc. sg. neut. n. . . δεσμωτήριον *(1201)*

δεσμωτηρίου, gen. sg. neut. n. . . . .   id.

δεσμωτηρίῳ, dat. sg. neut. n. . . . .   id.

(1202) **δεσμώτης**, ου, ὁ [§2.B.c] (δεσμόω) *a prisoner*, i.q. δέσμιος, Acts 27:1, 42

δέσποτα, voc. sg. m. n. [§2.6] . . . . . δεσπότης *(1203)*

δεσπόταις, dat. pl. m. n. . . . .   id.

δεσπότας, acc. pl. m. n. . . . .   id.

δεσπότῃ, dat. sg. m. n. . . . .   id.

δεσπότην, acc. sg. m. n. . . . .   id.

(1203) **δεσπότης**, ου, ὁ, nom. sg. m. n. [§2.B.c] *a lord, master*, especially of slaves, 1 Tim. 6:1, 2; 2 Tim. 2:21; Tit. 2:9; 1 Pet. 2:18; by impl. as denoting the possession of supreme authority, *Lord, sovereign*, used of God, Luke 2:29; Acts 4:24; Rev. 6:10; and of Christ, 2 Pet. 2:1; Jude 4

(1204) **δεῦρο**, adv., *hither, here;* used also as a sort of imperative, *come, Come hither!* Matt. 19:21; Mark 10:21, et al.; used of time, ἄχρι τοῦ δεῦρο, sc. χρόνου, *to the present time*, Rom. 1:13

(1205) **δεῦτε**, i.e., δεῦρ' ἴτε, an exclamation in the plural, of which the singular form is δεῦρο, *come*, Matt. 4:19; 11:28, et al.; as a par-

ticle of exhortation, incitement, etc., and followed by an imperative, *come now*, etc., Matt. 21:38; 28:6, et al.

δευτέρα, nom. sg. f. adj. . . . . δεύτερος *(1208)*

δευτέρᾳ, dat. sg. f. adj. . . . .   id.

δευτεραῖοι, nom. pl. m. adj. . . . . . δευτεραῖος *(1206)*

(1206) **δευτεραῖος**, αία, αῖον [§7.1] *on the second day* of a certain state or process, and used as an epithet of the subject or agent, Acts 28:13

δευτέραν, acc. sg. f. adj. . . . . δεύτερος *(1208)*

δευτέρας, gen. sg. f. adj. . . . .   id.

δεύτερον, nom. sg. neut. adj. {Rev. 4:7} . .   id.

δεύτερον, acc. sg. neut. adj. {Rev. 19:3} . .   id.

δεύτερον, acc. sg. neut. adj. as adv. {John 3:4} . . . .   id.

(1207) **δευτερόπρωτος**, ον [§7.2] (δεύτερος + πρῶτος) *second-first*, an epithet of uncertain meaning, but probably appropriated of unleavened bread, Luke 6:1

δευτεροπρώτῳ, dat. sg. neut. adj. (Luke 6:1, MT & TR | διαπορεύεσθαι, GNT, WH & NA) . . . . δευτερόπρωτος *(1207)*

(1208) **δεύτερος**, α, ον, nom. sg. m. adj. [§7.1] *second*, Matt. 22:26, et al.; τὸ δεύτερον, *again, the second time, another time*, Jude 5; so ἐκ δευτέρου, Matt. 26:42, et al.; and ἐν τῷ δευτέρῳ, Acts 7:13

δευτέρου, gen. sg. m. adj. {Rev. 2:11} . . . . δεύτερος *(1208)*

δευτέρου, gen. sg. neut. adj. {Rev. 6:3} . .   id.

δευτέρῳ, dat. sg. m. adj. {Acts 13:33} . . .   id.

δευτέρῳ, dat. sg. neut. adj. {Acts 7:13} . .   id.

δέχεται, 3 pers. sg. pres. mid./pass. dep. indic. . . . . δέχομαι *(1209)*

δέχηται, 3 pers. sg. pres. mid./pass. dep. subj. (Mark 9:37, GNT, WH & NA | δέξηται, MT & TR) . . . .   id.

(1209) **δέχομαι**, fut. δέξομαι, perf. (pass. form) δέδεγμαι [§23.1.b; 23.7] aor. ἐδεξάμην, *to take* into one's hands, etc., Luke 2:28; 16:6, 7, et al.; *to receive*, Acts 22:5; 28:21; Phil. 4:18; *to receive into and retain, contain*, Acts 3:21; met. *to receive* by the hearing, *learn, acquire a knowledge of*, 2 Cor. 11:4; James 1:21; *to receive, admit, grant access to, receive kindly, welcome*, Matt. 10:40, 41; 18:5, et al.; *to receive* in hospitality, *entertain*, Luke 9:53; Heb. 11:31; *to bear with, bear patiently*, 2 Cor. 11:16; met. *to receive, approve, assent to*, Matt. 11:14; Luke 8:13; Acts 8:14; 11:1, et al.; *to admit*, and by impl. *to embrace, follow*, 1 Cor. 2:14; 2 Cor. 8:17, et al.

δεχόμενος, nom. sg. m. pres. mid./pass. dep.

part. . . . . δέχομαι *(1209)*

δέχονται, 3 pers. pl. pres. mid./pass. dep.
indic. . . . . id.

δέχωνται, 3 pers. pl. pres. mid./pass. dep.
subj. . . . . id.

(1210) **δέω,** fut. δήσω, perf. δέδεκα, aor. ἔδησα,
perf. pass. δέδεμαι, aor. pass. ἐδέθην
[§37.1] *to bind, tie,* Matt. 13:30; 21:2, et
al.; *to bind, confine,* Matt. 27:2; 14:3, et
al.; *to impede, hinder,* 2 Tim. 2:9; *to bind
with infirmity,* Luke 13:16; *to bind by a legal or moral tie, as marriage,* Rom. 7:2;
1 Cor. 7:27, 39; by impl. *to impel, compel,* Acts 20:22; in N.T. *to pronounce or
declare to be binding or obligatory, or, to
declare to be prohibited and unlawful,*
Matt. 16:19; 18:18

(1211) **δή,** a particle serving to add an intensity of
expression to a term or clause. Its simplest
and most ordinary uses are when it gives
impressiveness to an affirmation, *indeed,
really, doubtless,* Matt. 13:23; 2 Cor. 12:1;
or earnestness to a call, injunction, or entreaty, Luke 2:15; Acts 13:2; 15:36

δηλοῖ, 3 pers. sg. pres. act. indic. . . . . . δηλόω *(1213)*
δῆλον, acc. sg. m. adj. {Matt. 26:73} . . δῆλος *(1212)*
δῆλον, nom. sg. neut. adj. {Gal. 3:11} . . . id.

(1212) **δῆλος,** η, ον, pr. *clearly visible; plain, manifest, evident,* Matt. 26:73; 1 Cor. 15:27;
Gal. 3:11; 1 Tim. 6:7

δηλοῦντος, gen. sg. neut. pres. act.
part. . . . . δηλόω *(1213)*

(1213) **δηλόω,** ῶ, fut. δηλώσω [§20.T] aor.
ἐδήλωσα, *to render manifest or evident;
to make known, to tell, relate, declare,*
1 Cor. 1:11; Col. 1:8; *to show, point out,
bring to light,* 1 Cor. 3:13; *to intimate, signify,* Heb. 9:8; 12:27; 1 Pet. 1:11

δηλώσας, nom. sg. m. aor. act. part. . . δηλόω *(1213)*
δηλώσει, 3 pers. sg. fut. act. indic. . . . . . . id.

(1214) **Δημᾶς,** ᾶ, ὁ, nom. sg. m. n. [§2.4] *Demas,*
pr. name

(1215) **δημηγορέω,** ῶ, fut. δαμηγορήσω [§16.P]
(δῆμος + ἀγορεύω) *to address a public assembly, to deliver an harangue or public
oration,* Acts 12:21

(1216) **Δημήτριος,** ου, ὁ, nom. sg. m. n. [§3.C.a]
Demetrius, pr. name   I. *The Ephesian sil-
versmith,* Acts 19:24, 38   II. *A certain
Christian,* 3 John 12

Δημητρίῳ, dat. sg. m. n. . . . . Δημήτριος *(1216)*

(1217) **δημιουργός,** οῦ, ὁ, nom. sg. m. n. [§3.C.a]
(δῆμος + ἔργον) pr. *one who labors for
the public,* or, *exercises some public calling; an architect,* especially, the Divine

Architect of the universe, Heb. 11:10

δῆμον, acc. sg. m. n. . . . . δῆμος *(1218)*

(1218) **δῆμος,** ου, ὁ, nom. sg. m. n. [§3.C.a] *the people,* Acts 12:22; 17:5; 19:30, 33

δημοσίᾳ, dat. sg. f. adj. {Acts 5:18} . δημόσιος *(1219)*
δημοσίᾳ, dat. sg. f. adj. as adv. {Acts 16:37}   id.

(1219) **δημόσιος,** α, ον [§7.1] *public, belonging to the
public,* Acts 5:18; δημοσίᾳ, *publicly,* Acts
16:37; 18:28; 20:20

δήμῳ, dat. sg. m. n. . . . . δῆμος *(1218)*
δηνάρια, acc. pl. neut. n. . . . . δηνάριον *(1220)*

(1220) **δηνάριον,** ου, τό [§3.C.c] Latin *denarius,* a Roman silver coin; the name originally meant
ten asses

δηνάριον, acc. sg. neut. n. . . . . δηνάριον *(1220)*
δηναρίου, gen. sg. neut. n. . . . . id.
δηναρίων, gen. pl. neut. n. . . . . id.

(1221) **δήποτε,** an intensive combination of the particle δή with ποτε as an intensive (John 5:4,
MT & TR | GNT, WH & NA omit)

(1222) **δήπου,** adv., *now in some way, surely* (Heb.
2:16, GNT, MT, TR & NA | δή που,
WH)

δῆσαι, aor. act. infin. . . . . δέω *(1210)*
δήσαντες, nom. pl. m. aor. act. part. . . . . id.
δήσας, nom. sg. m. aor. act. part. . . . . id.
δήσατε, 2 pers. pl. aor. act. imper. . . . . . . id.
δήσῃ, 3 pers. sg. aor. act. subj. . . . . id.
δήσῃς, 2 pers. sg. aor. act. subj. . . . . id.
δήσητε, 2 pers. pl. aor. act. subj. . . . . id.
δήσουσιν, 3 pers. pl. fut. act. indic. . . . . . id.
δι᾽, by apostrophe for διά . . . . διά *(1223)*

(1223) **διά,** prep. with a genitive, *through,* used of
place or medium, Matt. 7:13; Luke 6:1;
2 Cor. 11:33, et al.; *through,* of time, *during, in the course of,* Heb. 2:15; Acts 5:19,
et al.; *through,* of immediate agency, causation, instrumentality, *by means of, by,*
John 1:3; Acts 3:18, et al.; of means or
manner, *through, by, with,* Luke 8:4;
2 Cor. 5:7; 8:8, et al.; of state or condition, *in a state of,* Rom. 4:11, et al.; with
an accusative, used of causation which is
not direct and immediate in the production
of a result, *on account of, because of, for
the sake of, with a view to,* Mark 2:27;
John 1:31, et al.; rarely, *through, while subject to* a state of untoward circumstances,
Gal. 4:13

Δία, acc. sg. m. n. [§6.4.a] . . . . Ζεύς *(2203)*

(1224) **διαβαίνω,** fut. διαβήσομαι, 2 aor. διέβην
[§37.1] (διά + βαίνω) *to pass through* or
over, Luke 16:26; Acts 16:9; Heb. 11:29

(1225) **διαβάλλω,** fut. διαβαλῶ [§27.1.b] (διά +
βάλλω) *to throw* or *convey through* or

over; to thrust through; to defame, inform against, Luke 16:1

διαβάς, nom. sg. m. 2 aor. act. part.   διαβαίνω *(1224)*

(1226) **διαβεβαιόομαι,** οῦμαι [§21.U] (διά + βεβαιόω) *to assert strongly, asseverate,* 1 Tim. 1:7; Tit. 3:8

διαβεβαιοῦνται, 3 pers. pl. pres. mid./pass. dep. indic. . . . . διαβεβαιόομαι *(1226)*

διαβεβαιοῦσθαι, pres. mid./pass. dep. infin.   id.

διαβῆναι, 2 aor. act. infin. . . . . διαβαίνω *(1224)*

(1227) **διαβλέπω,** fut. διαβλέψω [§23.1.a] (διά + βλέπω) *to look through; to view steadily; to see clearly* or *steadily,* Matt. 7:5; Luke 6:42

διαβλέψεις, 2 pers. sg. fut. act. indic. . . . . διαβλέπω *(1227)*

διάβολοι, nom. pl. m. adj. . . . . διάβολος *(1228)*

βιάβολον, acc. sg. m. adj. . . . . id.

(1228) **διάβολος,** ον, nom. sg. m. adj. [§7.2] *a calumniator, slanderer,* 1 Tim. 3:11; 2 Tim. 3:3; Tit. 2:3; *a treacherous informer, traitor,* John 6:70; ὁ διάβολος, *the devil*

διαβόλου, gen. sg. m. adj. . . . . διάβολος *(1228)*

διαβόλους, acc. pl. f. adj. . . . . id.

διαβόλῳ, dat. sg. m. adj. . . . . id.

διαγγελῇ, 3 pers. sg. 2 aor. pass. subj. . . . . διαγγέλλω *(1229)*

διάγγελλε, 2 pers. sg. pres. act. imper. . . . id.

(1229) **διαγγέλλω,** aor. διήγγειλα [§27.1.b,d] 2 aor. pass. διηγγέλην [§27.4.a] (διά + ἀγγέλλω) *to publish abroad,* Luke 9:60; Rom. 9:17; *to certify* to the public, Acts 21:26; *to tell, announce, give notice of, divulge, publish abroad,* Acts 21:26; *to declare, promulgate, teach,* Luke 9:60; from the Hebrew, *to celebrate, praise,* Rom. 9:17

διαγγέλλων, nom. sg. m. pres. act. part. . . . . διαγγέλλω *(1229)*

διαγενομένου, gen. sg. m. 2 aor. mid. dep. part. {Acts 27:9} . . . . διαγίνομαι *(1230)*

διαγενομένου, gen. sg. neut. 2 aor. mid. dep. part. {Mark 16:1} . . . . id.

διαγενομένων, gen. pl. f. 2 aor. mid. dep. part. . . . . id.

(1230) **διαγίνομαι,** fut. διαγενήσομαι, 2 aor. διεγενόμην [§37.1] (διά + γίνομαι) *to continue through; to intervene, elapse,* Mark 16:1; Acts 25:13; 27:9

διαγινώσκειν, pres. act. infin. . . . . διαγινώσκω *(1231)*

(1231) **διαγινώσκω,** fut. διαγνώσομαι [§36.3] (διά + γινώσκω) pr. *to distinguish; to resolve determinately; to examine, inquire into,* judicially, Acts 23:15; 24:22

(1232) **διαγνωρίζω,** fut. διαγνωρίσω [§26.1] (διά +

γνωρίζω) *to tell abroad, publish,* Luke 2:17

διάγνωσιν, acc. sg. f. n. . . . . διάγνωσις *(1233)*

(1233) **διάγνωσις,** εως, ἡ [§5.E.c] pr. *an act of distinguishing* or *discernment; a determination; examination* judicially, *hearing, trial,* Acts 25:21

διαγνώσομαι, 1 pers. sg. fut. mid. dep. indic. . . . . διαγινώσκω *(1231)*

(1234) **διαγογγύζω,** fut. διαγογγύσω [§26.1] (διά + γογγύζω) *to murmur, mutter,* Luke 15:2; 19:7

διάγοντες, nom. pl. m. pres. act. part. . διάγω *(1236)*

(1235) **διαγρηγορέω,** ῶ, fut. διαγρηγορήσω [§16.P] (διά + γρηγορέω) *to remain awake; to wake thoroughly,* Luke 9:32

διαγρηγορήσαντες, nom. pl. m. aor. act. part. διαγρηγορέω *(1235)*

(1236) **διάγω,** fut. διάξω [§23.1.b] (διά + ἄγω) *to conduct* or *carry through* or *over; to pass* or *spend* time, *live,* 1 Tim. 2:2; Tit. 3:3

διάγωμεν, 1 pers. pl. pres. act. subj. . . . διάγω *(1236)*

διαδεξάμενοι, nom. pl. m. aor. mid. dep. part. διαδέχομαι *(1237)*

(1237) **διαδέχομαι,** fut. διαδέξομαι [§23.1.b] (διά + δέχομαι) *to receive by transmission; to receive by succession,* Acts 7:45

(1238) **διάδημα,** ατος, τό [§4.D.c] (διαδέω, διά + δέω) pr. *a band* or *fillet; a diadem,* the badge of a sovereign, Rev. 12:3; 13:1; 19:12

διαδήματα, nom. pl. neut. n. {Rev. 19:12} . . . . διάδημα *(1238)*

διαδήματα, acc. pl. neut. n. {Rev. 13:1} . . id.

(1239) **διαδίδωμι,** fut. διαδώσω, aor. διέδωκα [§30.Z] (διά + δίδωμι) *to deliver from hand to hand; to distribute, divide,* Luke 11:22; 18:22; John 6:11 Acts 4:35

διαδίδωσιν, 3 pers. sg. pres. act. indic. . . . . διαδίδωμι *(1239)*

διαδιδώσουσιν, 3 pers. pl. pres. act. indic. (Rev. 17:13, TR | διδόασιν, GNT, WH, MT & NA) . . . . id.

διάδος, 2 pers. sg. 2 aor. act. imper. [§30.1]   id.

διάδοχον, acc. sg. m. n. . . . . διάδοχος *(1240)*

(1240) **διάδοχος,** ου, ὁ [§3.C.a] *a successor,* Acts 24:27

(1241) **διαζώννυμι,** or διαζωννύω, fut. διαζώσω [§31.BB] perf. pass. διέζωσμαι (διά + ζώννυμι) *to gird firmly round,* John 13:4, 5; mid. *to gird round one's self,* John 21:7

διαθέμενος, nom. sg. m. 2 aor. mid. part. [§28.W] . . . . διατίθημι (†1303)

διαθεμένου, gen. sg. m. 2 aor. mid. part. . id.

διαθῆκαι, nom. pl. f. n. . . . . διαθήκη *(1242)*

(1242) **διαθήκη,** ης, ἡ, nom. sg. f. n. [§2.B.a] *a tes-*

tamentary disposition, will; a covenant,
Heb. 9:16, 17: Gal. 3:15; in N.T., *a covenant* of God with men, Gal. 3:17; 4:24;
Heb. 9:4; Matt. 26:28, et al.; *the writings
of the old covenant,* 2 Cor. 3:14

διαθήκῃ, dat. sg. f. n. . . . . διαθήκη *(1242)*

διαθήκην, acc. sg. f. n. . . . . id.

διαθήκης, gen. sg. f. n. . . . . id.

διαθηκῶν, gen. pl. f. n. . . . . id.

διαθήσομαι, 1 pers. sg. fut. mid. dep.
indic. . . . . διατίθημι *(†1303)*

διαιρέσεις, nom. pl. f. n. . . . . διαίρεσις *(1243)*

(1243) **διαίρεσις**, εως, ἡ [§5.E.c] *a distinction, difference, diversity,* 1 Cor. 12:4, 5, 6

(1244) **διαιρέω**, ῶ, fut. διαιρήσω, 2 aor. διεῖλον
[§36.1] (διά + αἱρέω) *to divide, to divide
out, distribute,* Luke 15:12; 1 Cor. 12:11

διαιροῦν, nom. sg. neut. pres. act.
part. . . . . διαιρέω *(1244)*

(‡1245) **διακαθαίρω**, *to cleanse thoroughly*

διακαθᾶραι, aor. act. infin. (Luke 3:17, GNT,
WH & NA | καὶ διακαθαριεῖ, MT &
TR) . . . . διακαθαίρω *(‡1245)*

διακαθαριεῖ, 3 pers. sg. fut. act. indic. Att.
[§35.1] . . . . διακαθαρίζω *(1245)*

(1245) **διακαθαρίζω**, fut. διακαθαριῶ (διά +
καθαρίζω) *to cleanse thoroughly,* Matt.
3:12; Luke 3:17

(1246) **διακατελέγχομαι**, fut. διακατελέγξομαι
[§23.1.b] (διά, κατά, + ἐλέγχομαι) *to
maintain discussion strenuously and thoroughly,* Acts 18:28

διακατηλέγχετο, 3 pers. sg. imperf.
mid./pass. dep. indic. . . . . διακατελέγχομαι *(1246)*

διακονεῖ, 3 pers. sg. pres. act. indic.
{1 Pet. 4:11} . . . . διακονέω *(1247)*

διακόνει, 2 pers. sg. pres. act. imper.
{Luke 17:8} . . . . id.

διακονεῖν, pres. act. infin. . . . . id.

διακονείτωσαν, 3 pers. pl. pres. act. imper. id.

(1247) **διακονέω**, ῶ, fut. διακονήσω [§16.P] imperf.
ἐδιακόνουν, aor. ἐδιακόνησα, perf.
δεδιακόνηκα, but later, διηκόνουν,
διηκόνησα, δεδιηκόνηκα, *to wait, attend
upon, serve,* Matt. 8:15; Mark 1:31; Luke
4:39, et al.; *to be an attendant or assistant,*
Acts 19:22; *to minister to, relieve, assist,* or
*supply with the necessaries of life, provide
the means of living,* Matt. 4:11; 27:55;
Mark 1:13; 15:41; Luke 8:3, et al.; *to fill
the office of* διάκονος, *deacon, perform
the duties of deacon,* 1 Tim. 3:10, 13; 1 Pet.
4:11; *to convey in charge, administer,*
2 Cor. 3:3; 8:19, 20; 1 Pet. 1:12; 4:10; pass.
to receive service, Matt. 20:28; Mark 10:45

διακονῇ, 3 pers. sg. pres. act. subj. . . διακονέω *(1247)*

διακονηθεῖσα, nom. sg. f. aor. pass. part. . id.

διακονηθῆναι, aor. pass. infin. [§17.Q] . . . id.

διακονῆσαι, aor. act. infin. . . . . id.

διακονήσαντες, nom. pl. m. aor. act. part. id.

διακονήσει, 3 pers. sg. fut. act. indic. . . . .id.

(1248) **διακονία**, ας, ἡ, nom. sg. f. n. [§2.B.b; 2.2]
*serving, service, waiting, attendance, the
act of rendering friendly offices,* Luke
10:40; 2 Tim. 4:11; Heb. 1:14; *relief, aid,*
Acts 6:2; 11:29; 2 Cor. 8:4; 9:1, 12, 13; *a
commission,* Acts 12:25; Rom. 15:31; *a
commission or ministry* in the service of
the Gospel, Acts 1:17, 25; 20:24; Rom.
11:13; 2 Cor. 4:1; 5:18; 1 Tim. 1:12; *service*
in the Gospel, Acts 6:4; 21:19; 1 Cor. 16:15;
2 Cor. 6:3; 11:8; Eph. 4:12; Rev. 2:19; *a
function, ministry,* or *office* in the Church,
Rom. 12:7; 1 Cor. 12:5; Col. 4:17; 2 Tim.
4:5; *a ministering* in the conveyance of a
revelation from God, 2 Cor. 3:7, 8, 9

διακονίᾳ, dat. sg. f. n. . . . . διακονία *(1248)*

διακονίαν, acc. sg. f. n. . . . . id.

διακονίας, gen. sg. f. n. . . . . id.

διακονιῶν, gen. pl. f. n. . . . . id.

διάκονοι, nom. pl. m. n. . . . . διάκονος *(1249)*

διακόνοις, dat. pl. m. n. . . . . id.

διάκονον, acc. sg. m. n. {Rom. 15:8} . . . . id.

διάκονον, acc. sg. f. n. {Rom. 16:1} . . . . . id.

(1249) **διάκονος**, ου, ὁ, ἡ, nom. sg. m. n. [§3.C.a,b]
one who renders service to another; *an attendant, servant,* Matt. 20:26; 22:13; John
2:5, 9, et al.; *one who executes a commission, a deputy,* Rom. 13:4; Χριστοῦ,
Θεοῦ, ἐν κυρίῳ, etc. *a commissioned minister or preacher* of the Gospel, 1 Cor. 3:5;
2 Cor. 6:4, et al.; *a minister* charged with
an announcement or sentence, 2 Cor. 3:6;
Gal. 2:17; Col. 1:23; *a minister* charged
with a significant characteristic, Rom. 15:8;
a servitor, devoted follower, John 12:26; *a
deacon or deaconess,* whose official duty
was to superintend the alms of the Church,
with other kindred services, Rom. 16:1;
Phil. 1:1; 1 Tim. 3:8, 12

διακόνου, gen. sg. f. n. (Rom. 16:27, TR |
GNT, WH, MT & NA omit) . . . διάκονος *(1249)*

διακονουμένη, dat. sg. f. pres. pass.
part. . . . . διακονέω *(1247)*

διακονοῦντες, nom. pl. m. pres. act. part. id.

διακονούντων, gen. pl. m. pres. act. part. id.

διακόνους, acc. pl. m. n. . . . . διάκονος *(1249)*

διακονοῦσαι, nom. pl. f. pres. act.
part. . . . . διακονέω *(1247)*

διακονῶν, nom. sg. m. pres. act. part. . . . id.

διακόσιαι, nom. pl. f. numeral . . . . . διακόσιοι *(1250)*

διακοσίας, acc. pl. f. numeral . . . . id.

(1250) **διακόσιοι,** αι, α [§9.I.e] *two hundred,* Mark 6:37; John 6:7, et al.

διακοσίους, acc. pl. m. numeral . . . διακόσιοι *(1250)*

διακοσίων, gen. pl. m. numeral {John 21:8}   id.

διακοσίων, gen. pl. neut. numeral {John 6:7}   id.

διακούσομαι, 1 pers. sg. fut. mid. dep.
indic. . . . . διακούω *(†1251)*

(†1251) **διακούω,** fut. διακούσομαι (διά + ἀκούω) *to hear* a thing *through; to hear* judicially, Acts 23:35

διακριθῇ, 3 pers. sg. aor. pass. subj. . . διακρίνω *(1252)*

διακριθῆτε, 2 pers. pl. aor. pass. subj. . . . id.

διακρῖναι, aor. act. infin. . . . . id.

διακρίναντα, acc. sg. m. aor. act. part. (Acts 11:12, GNT, WH & NA | διακρινόμενον, MT & TR) . . . . id.

διακρίνει, 3 pers. sg. pres. act. indic. . . . . id.

διακρίνειν, pres. act. infin. . . . . id.

διακρινέτωσαν, 3 pers. pl. pres. act. imper.   id.

διακρινόμενοι, nom. pl. m. pres. mid. part. (Jude 22, MT & TR | διακρινομένους, GNT, WH & NA) . . . . id.

διακρινόμενον, acc. sg. m. pres. mid. part. (Acts 11:12, MT & TR | διακρίναντα, GNT, WH & NA) . . . . id.

διακρινόμενος, nom. sg. m. pres. mid. part.   id.

διακρινομένους, acc. pl. m. pres. mid. part. (Jude 22, GNT, WH & NA | διακρινό-μενοι, MT & TR) . . . . id.

(1252) **διακρίνω,** fut. διακρινῶ [§27.1.a] (διά + κρίνω) *to separate, sever; to make a distinction or difference,* Acts 15:9; 1 Cor. 11:29; *to make to differ, distinguish, prefer, confer a superiority,* 1 Cor. 4:7; *to examine, scrutinize, estimate,* 1 Cor. 11:31; 14:29; *to discern, discriminate,* Matt. 16:3; *to judge, to decide a cause,* 1 Cor. 6:5; mid. διακρίνομαι, aor. (pass. form) διεκρίθην, *to dispute, contend,* Acts 11:2; Jude 9; *to make a distinction* mentally James 2:4; Jude 22: in N.T. *to hesitate, be in doubt, doubt,* Matt. 21:21; Mark 11:23, et al.

διακρίνων, nom. sg. m. pres. act. part. . . . . διακρίνω *(1252)*

διακρίσεις, nom. pl. f. n. {1 Cor. 12:10} . . . . διάκρισις *(1253)*

διακρίσεις, acc. pl. f. n. {Rom. 14:1} . . . . id.

διάκρισιν, acc. sg. f. n. . . . . id.

(1253) **διάκρισις,** εως, ἡ [§5.E.c] *a separation; a distinction,* or, *doubt,* Rom. 14:1; *a discerning, the act of discerning or distinguishing,* Heb. 5:14; *the faculty of distinguishing and estimating,* 1 Cor. 12:10

(1254) **διακωλύω,** fut. διακωλύσω [§13.M] (διά + κωλύω) *to hinder, restrain, prohibit,* Matt. 3:14

(1255) **διαλαλέω,** ῶ, fut. διαλαλήσω [§16.P] (διά + λαλέω) *to talk with;* by impl. *to consult, deliberate,* Luke 6:11; *to divulge, publish, spread by rumor,* Luke 1:65

διαλέγεται, 3 pers. sg. pres. mid./pass. dep.
indic. . . . . διαλέγομαι *(1256)*

(1256) **διαλέγομαι,** fut. διαλέξομαι, aor. (pass. form) διελέχθην [§23.4] (διά + λέγω) *to discourse, argue, reason,* Acts 17:2, 17; 24:12, et al.; *to address, speak to,* Heb. 12:5; *to contend, dispute,* Mark 9:34; Jude 9

διαλεγόμενον, acc. sg. m. pres. mid./pass. dep. part. . . . . διαλέγομαι *(1256)*

διαλεγόμενος, nom. sg. m. pres. mid./pass. dep. part. . . . . id.

διαλεγομένου, gen. sg. m. pres. mid./pass. dep. part. . . . . id.

(1257) **διαλείπω,** fut. διαλείψω [§23.1.a] 2 aor. διέλιπον [§24.9] (διά + λείπω) *to leave an interval; to intermit, cease,* Luke 7:45

(1258) **διάλεκτος,** ου, ἡ [§3.C.b] *speech; manner of speaking; peculiar language* of a nation, *dialect, vernacular idiom,* Acts 1:19; 2:6, 8; 21:40; 22:2; 26:14

διαλέκτῳ, dat. sg. f. n. . . . . διάλεκτος *(1258)*

διαλλάγηθι, 2 pers. sg. 2 aor. pass. imper. . . . . διαλλάσσω *(1259)*

(1259) **διαλλάσσω** (διά + ἀλλάσσω) *to change, exchange;* pass. διαλλάσσομαι, 2 aor. διηλλάγην [§26.3] *to be reconciled* to another, Matt. 5:24

διαλογίζεσθαι, pres. mid./pass. dep.
infin. . . . . διαλογίζομαι *(1260)*

διαλογίζεσθε, 2 pers. pl. pres. mid./pass. dep.
indic. . . . . id.

(1260) **διαλογίζομαι,** fut. διαλογίσομαι [§26.1] (διά + λογίζομαι) pr. *to make a settlement of accounts; to reason, deliberate, ponder, consider,* Matt. 16:7, 8; Mark 2:6, 8; John 11:50, et al.; *to dispute, contend,* Mark 9:33

διαλογιζόμενοι, nom. pl. m. pres. mid./pass. dep. part. . . . . διαλογίζομαι *(1260)*

διαλογιζομένων, gen. pl. m. pres. mid./pass. dep. part. . . . . id.

διαλογίζονται, 3 pers. pl. pres. mid./pass. dep.
indic. . . . . id.

διαλογισμοί, nom. pl. m. n. . . . . . . διαλογισμός *(1261)*

διαλογισμοῖς, dat. pl. m. n. . . . . id.

διαλογισμόν, acc. sg. m. n. . . . . id.

(1261) **διαλογισμός,** οῦ, ὁ, nom. sg. m. n. [§3.C.a] *reasoning, retiocination, thought, cogita-*

tion, purpose, Matt. 15:19; Mark 7:21, et
al.; *discourse, dispute, disputation, conten-*
tion, Luke 9:46, et al.; *doubt, hesitation,*
scruple, Luke 24:38
διαλογισμοῦ, gen. sg. m. n. (1 Tim. 2:8, GNT,
MT, TR & NA | διαλογισμῶν,
WH) . . . . διαλογισμός *(1261)*
διαλογισμούς, acc. pl. m. n. . . . . id.
διαλογισμῶν, gen. pl. m. n. . . . . id.
(1262) **διαλύω,** fut. διαλύσω [§13.M] (διά + λύω) *to*
dissolve, dissipate, disperse, Acts 5:36
διαμαρτυράμενοι, nom. pl. m. aor. mid. dep.
part. . . . . διαμαρτύρομαι *(1263)*
διαμαρτυράμενος, nom. sg. m. aor. mid. dep.
part. (Acts 28:23, MT & TR | διαμαρτυ-
ρόμενος, GNT, WH & NA) . . . . id.
διαμαρτύρασθαι, aor. mid. dep. infin. . . . id.
διαμαρτύρεται, 3 pers. sg. pres. mid./pass.
dep. indic. . . . . id.
διαμαρτύρηται, 3 pers. sg. pres. mid./pass.
dep. subj. . . . . id.
(1263) **διαμαρτύρομαι,** 1 pers. sg. pres. mid./pass.
dep. indic., fut. διαμαρτυροῦμαι, aor.
διεμαρτυράμην [§37.1] (διά +
μαρτύρομαι) *to make solemn affirmation,*
protest; to make a solemn and earnest
charge, Luke 16:28; Acts 2:40, et al.; *to de-*
clare solemnly and earnestly, Acts 8:25;
18:5, et al.
διαμαρτυρόμενος, nom. sg. m. pres.
mid./pass. dep. part. . . . . . . διαμαρτύρομαι *(1263)*
(1264) **διαμάχομαι,** fut. διαμάχέσομαι, contr.
διαμαχοῦμαι (διά + μάχομαι) *to fight*
out, to fight resolutely; met. *to contend*
vehemently, insist, Acts 23:9
διαμείνῃ, 3 pers. sg. aor. act. subj. . . . διαμένω *(1265)*
διαμεμενηκότες, nom. pl. m. perf. act. part.
[§27.2.d] . . . . id.
διαμεμερισμένοι, nom. pl. m. perf. pass.
part. . . . . διαμερίζω *(1266)*
διαμένει, 3 pers. sg. pres. act. indic. . . διαμένω *(1265)*
διαμένεις, 2 pers. sg. pres. act. indic. . . . . id.
(1265) **διαμένω,** fut. διαμενῶ, aor. διέμεινα
[§27.1.a,d] perf. διαμεμένηκα (διά +
μένω) *to continue throughout; to continue,*
be permanent or unchanged, Luke 1:22;
Gal. 2:5; Heb. 1:11; 2 Pet. 3:4; *to continue,*
remain constant, Luke 22:28
διαμεριζόμεναι, nom. pl. f. pres. mid./pass.
part. . . . . διαμερίζω *(1266)*
διαμεριζόμενοι, nom. pl. m. pres. mid. part. id.
διαμερίζονται, 3 pers. pl. pres. mid. indic.
(Mark 15:24, GNT, WH, MT & NA |
διεμέριζον, TR) . . . . id.
(1266) **διαμερίζω,** fut. διαμερίσω [§26.1] (διά +

μερίζω) *to divide into parts and distribute,*
Matt. 27:35; Mark 15:24; Acts 2:3, et al.;
pass. in N.T. *to be in a state of dissension,*
Luke 11:17, 18; 12:52, 53
διαμερίσατε, 2 pers. pl. aor. act.
imper. διαμερίζω *(1266)*
διαμερισθεῖσα, nom. sg. f. aor. pass. part. id.
διαμερισθήσεται, 3 pers. sg. fut. pass. indic.
(Luke 12:53, MT & TR | διαμερισθή-
σονται, GNT, WH & NA) . . . . id.
διαμερισθήσονται, 3 pers. pl. fut. pass. indic.
(Luke 12:53, GNT, WH & NA | διαμερι-
σθήσεται, MT & TR) . . . . id.
διαμερισμόν, acc. sg. m. n. . . . . . διαμερισμός *(1267)*
(1267) **διαμερισμός,** οῦ, ὁ [§3.C.a] *division;* met. in
N.T. *disunion, dissension,* Luke 12:51
διανεμηθῇ, 3 pers. sg. aor. pass. subj. διανέμω *(1268)*
(1268) **διανέμω,** fut. διανεμῶ [§27.1.a] aor. pass.
διενεμήθην (διά + νέμω) *to distribute; to*
divulge, spread abroad, Acts 4:17
(1269) **διανεύω,** fut. διανεύσω [§13.M] (διά + νεύω)
to signify by a nod, beckon, make signs,
Luke 1:22
διανεύων, nom. sg. m. pres. act. part. διανεύω *(1269)*
(1270) **διανόημα,** ατος, τό [§4.D.c] (διανοέομαι, *to*
turn over in the mind, think, from διά +
νοές) *thought,* Luke 11:17
διανοήματα, acc. pl. neut. n. . . . . . . διανόημα *(1270)*
(1271) **διάνοια,** ας, ἡ [§2.B.b; 2.2] (διά + νοέω) pr.
thought, intention; the mind, intellect,
understanding, Matt. 22:37; Mark 12:30;
Luke 10:27; et al.; *an operation of the*
understanding, thought, imagination, Luke
1:51; *insight, comprehension,* 1 John 5:20;
mode of thinking and feeling, disposition
of mind and heart, the affections, Eph. 2:3;
Col. 1:21
διανοίᾳ, dat. sg. f. n. . . . . διάνοια *(1271)*
διάνοιαν, acc. sg. f. n. . . . . id.
διανοίας, gen. sg. f. n. . . . . id.
διανοῖγον, nom. sg. neut. pres. act.
part. . . . . διανοίγω *(1272)*
(1272) **διανοίγω,** fut. διανοίξω [§37.1] (διά +
ἀνοίγω) *to open,* Mark 7:34, 35; Luke
2:23; 24:31; met. *to open* the sense of a
thing, *explain, expound,* Luke 24:32; Acts
17:3; διανοίγειν τὸν νοῦν, τὴν καρδίαν,
to open the mind, the heart, so as to understand and receive, Luke 24:45; Acts 16:14
διανοίγων, nom. sg. m. pres. act.
part. . . . . διανοίγω *(1272)*
διανοίχθητι, 2 pers. sg. aor. pass. imper. . . id.
διανοιῶν, gen. pl. f. n. . . . . διάνοια *(1271)*
(1273) **διανυκτερεύω,** fut. διανυκτερεύσω [§13.M]
(διά + νύξ) *to pass the night, spend the*

whole night, Luke 6:12

διανυκτερεύων, nom. sg. m. pres. act.

part. . . . . διανυκτερεύω *(1273)*

διανύσαντες, nom. pl. m. aor. act.

part. . . . . διανύω *(1274)*

(1274) **διανύω,** fut. διανύσω [§13.M] (διά + ἀνύω,
to accomplish) *to complete, finish,* Acts
21:7

(1275) **διαπαντός,** same signif. as διὰ παντός,
through all time; throughout; always,
Mark 5:5, et al.; *continually* by stated rout-
ine, Luke 24:53; Heb. 9:6 (TRs | διὰ
παντός, GNT, WH, MT, TRb & NA)

διαπαρατριβαί, nom. pl. f. n. (1 Tim. 6:5,
GNT, WH, MT & NA | παραδιατριβαί,
TR) . . . . διαπαρατριβή *(‡3859)*

(‡3859) **διαπαρατριβή,** ῆς, ἡ [§2.B.a] (διά +
παρατριβή, *collision, altercation,* from
παρατρίβω, *to rub against,* παρά +
τρίβω) *pertinacious disputation*

διαπεράσαντες, nom. pl. m. aor. act.

part. . . . . διαπεράω *(1276)*

διαπεράσαντος, gen. sg. m. aor. act. part. id.

(1276) **διαπεράω,** ῶ, fut. διαπεράσω [§22.2] (διά +
περάω) *to pass through or over,* Matt. 9:1;
14:34; Mark 5:21, et al.

διαπερῶν, acc. sg. neut. pres. act.

part. . . . . διαπεράω *(1276)*

διαπερῶσιν, 3 pers. pl. pres. act. subj. [§18.R] id.

διαπλεύσαντες, nom. pl. m. aor. act.

part. . . . . διαπλέω *(1277)*

(1277) **διαπλέω,** fut. διαπλεύσομαι [§35.3] aor.
διέπλευσα (διά + πλέω) *to sail through
or over,* Acts 27:5

(†1278) **διαπονέομαι,** οῦμαι [§17.Q] fut.
διαπονήσομαι, aor. διεπονήθην (διαπο-
νέω, *to elaborate,* from διά + πονέω) pr.
*to be thoroughly exercised with labor; to
be wearied; to be vexed,* Acts 4:2; 16:18

διαπονηθείς, nom. sg. m. aor. mid. dep.

part. . . . . διαπονέομαι *(†1278)*

διαπονούμενοι, nom. pl. m. pres. mid./pass.

dep. part. . . . . id.

διαπορεῖσθαι, pres. pass. infin. (Luke 24:4,
MT & TR | ἀπορεῖσθαι, GNT, WH &
NA) . . . . διαπορέω *(1280)*

διαπορεύεσθαι, pres. mid./pass. dep. infin.
(Luke 6:1, GNT, WH & NA | δευτε-
ροπρώτῳ, MT & TR) . . . . . διαπορεύομαι *(1279)*

(1279) **διαπορεύομαι,** fut. διαπορεύσομαι [§14.N]
(διά + πορεύομαι) *to go or pass through,*
Luke 6:1; 13:22; Acts 16:4; *to pass by,* Luke
18:36, same signif. as παρέρχομαι, Luke
18:37

διαπορευόμενος, nom. sg. m. pres. mid./pass.

dep. part. . . . . διαπορεύομαι *(1279)*

διαπορευομένου, gen. sg. m. pres. mid./pass.

dep. part. . . . . id.

(1280) **διαπορέω,** ῶ, fut. διαπορήσω [§16.P] (διά +
ἀπορέω) *to be utterly at a loss; to be in
doubt and perplexity,* Luke 9:7; 24:4; et al.

(1281) **διαπραγματεύομαι,** fut. διαπραγματεύσομαι
[§15.O] (διά + πραγματεύομαι) *to de-
spatch a matter thoroughly; to make profit
in business, gain in trade,* Luke 19:15

(1282) **διαπρίω,** fut. διαπρίσω [§13.M] (διά + πρίω)
*to divide with a saw, saw asunder; to grate
the teeth in a rage;* pass. met. *to be cut* to
the heart, *to be enraged,* Acts 5:33; 7:54

διαρήξας, nom. sg. m. aor. act. part. (Mark
14:63, WH | διαρρήξας, GNT, MT, TR
& NA) . . . . δια(ρ)ρήσσω *(†1284)*

διαρήσσων, nom. sg. m. pres. act. part. (Luke
8:29, WH | διαρρήσσων, GNT, MT, TR
& NA) . . . . id.

(1283) **διαρπάζω,** fut. διαρπάσω [§26.2] (διά +
ἁρπάζω) *to plunder, spoil, pillage,* Matt.
12:29(2×); Mark 3:27(2×)

διαρπάσαι, aor. act. infin. . . . . διαρπάζω *(1283)*

διαρπάσει, 3 pers. sg. fut. act. indic. (Matt.
12:29; Mark 3:27, GNT, WH, TR & NA
| διαρπάσῃ, MT) . . . . id.

διαρπάσῃ, 3 pers. sg. aor. act. subj. (Matt.
12:29; Mark 3:27, MT | διαρπάσει, GNT,
WH, TR & NA) . . . . id.

(†1284) **διαρρήγνυμι,** and δια(ρ)ρήσσω, fut.
δια(ρ)ρήξω [§36.5] (διά + ῥήγνυμι) *to
break asunder, rend, tear, burst,* Matt.
26:65, et al.

διαρρήξαντες, nom. pl. m. aor. act.

part. . . . . διαρρήγνυμι *(†1284)*

διαρρήξας, nom. sg. m. aor. act. part. (Mark
14:63, GNT, MT, TR & NA | διαρήξας,
WH) . . . . id.

(†1284) **δια(ρ)ρήσσω,** and διαρρήγνυμι fut.
δια(ρ)ρήξω [§36.5] (διά + ῥήγνυμι) *to
break asunder, rend, tear, burst,* Matt.
26:65, et al.

διαρρήσσων, nom. sg. m. pres. act. part.
(Luke 8:29, GNT, MT, TR & NA |
διαρήσσων, WH) . . . . δια(ρ)ρήσσω *(†1284)*

(1285) **διασαφέω,** ῶ, fut. διασαφήσω [§16.P] aor.
διεσάφησα (διά + σαφής, *manifest*) *to
make known, declare, tell plainly, or fully,*
Matt. 18:31

διασάφησον, 2 pers. sg. aor. act. imper. (Matt.
13:36, GNT, WH & NA | φράσον, MT
& TR) . . . . διασαφέω *(1285)*

διασείσητε, 2 pers. pl. aor. act. subj. . διασείω *(1286)*

(1286) **διασείω,** fut. διασείσω [§13.M] (διά + σείω)

pr. *to shake thoroughly or violently; to harass, intimidate, extort from,* Luke 3:14

(1287) διασκορπίζω, fut. διασκορπίσω [§26.1] (διά + σκορπίζω) *to disperse, scatter,* Matt. 26:31; Mark 14:27, et al.; *to dissipate, waste,* Luke 15:13; 16:1; *to winnow,* or, *to strew,* Matt. 25:24, 26

διασκορπίζων, nom. sg. m. pres. act.
part. . . . . διασκορπίζω *(1287)*

διασκορπισθήσεται, 3 pers. sg. fut. pass. indic. (Matt. 26:31; Mark 14:27, MT & TR | διασκορπισθήσονται, GNT, WH & NA) . . . . id.

διασκορπισθήσονται, 3 pers. pl. fut. pass. indic. (Matt. 26:31; Mark 14:27, GNT, WH & NA | διασκορπισθήσεται, MT & TR) . . . . id.

διασπαρέντες, nom. pl. m. 2 aor. pass. part. [§27.4.b] . . . . διασπείρω *(1289)*

διασπασθῇ, 3 pers. sg. aor. pass. subj. . . . . διασπάω *(1288)*

(1288) διασπάω, ῶ, fut. διασπάσομαι [§22.2] perf. pass. διέσπασμαι, aor. pass. διεσπάσθην (διά + σπάω) *to pull or tear asunder or in pieces, burst,* Mark 5:4; Acts 23:10

(1289) διασπείρω, fut. διασπερῶ [§27.1.c] 2 aor. pass. διεσπάρην [§27.4.a] (διά + σπείρω) *to scatter abroad or in every direction,* as seen; *to disperse,* Acts 8:1, 4; 11:19

(1290) διασπορά, ᾶς, ἡ [§2.B.b; 2.2] pr. *a scattering,* as of seed; *dispersion;* in N.T. meton. *the dispersed portion* of the Jews, specially termed *the dispersion,* John 7:35; James 1:1; 1 Pet. 1:1

διασπορᾷ, dat. sg. f. n. . . . . διασπορά *(1290)*
διασποράν, acc. sg. f. n. . . . . id.
διασπορᾶς, gen. sg. f. n. . . . . id.
διαστάσης, gen. sg. f. 2 aor. act. part. [§29.X] . . . . διΐστημι *(1339)*

διαστελλόμενον, acc. sg. neut. pres. pass. part. . . . . διαστέλλω *(†1291)*

(†1291) διαστέλλω (διά + στέλλω) *to separate, distinguish;* mid. διαστέλλομαι, aor. διεστειλάμην [§27.1.d] *to determine, issue a decision; to state or explain distinctly and accurately;* hence, *to admonish, direct, charge, command,* Acts 15:24; Heb. 12:20; when followed by a negative clause, *to interdict, prohibit,* Matt. 16:20; Mark 5:43, et al.

(1292) διάστημα, ατος, τό, nom. sg. neut. n. [§4.D.c] *interval, space, distance,* Acts 5:7

διαστήσαντες, nom. pl. m. aor. act. part. . . . . διΐστημι *(1339)*

(1293) διαστολή, ῆς, ἡ, nom. sg. f. n. [§2.B.a] *dis-* tinction, difference, Rom. 3:22; 10:12; 1 Cor. 14:7

διαστολήν, acc. sg. f. n. . . . . διαστολή *(1293)*

διαστρέφοντα, acc. sg. m. pres. act. part. . . . . διαστρέφω *(1294)*

(1294) διαστρέφω, fut. διαστρέψω [§23.1.a] perf. pass. διέστραμμαι [§23.7.8] (διά + στρέφω) *to distort, turn away;* met. *to pervert, corrupt,* Matt. 17:17; Luke 9:41, et al.; *to turn out of the way, cause to make defection,* Luke 23:2; Acts 13:8; διεστραμμένος, *perverse, corrupt, erroneous*

διαστρέφων, nom. sg. m. pres. act. part. . . . . διαστρέφω *(1294)*
διαστρέψαι, aor. act. infin. . . . . id.

(†1295) διασῴζω, fut. διασώσω, aor. pass. διεσώθην [§26.1] (διά + σῴζω) *to bring safely through; to convey in safety,* Acts 23:24; pass. *to reach a place or state of safety,* Acts 27:44; 28:1, 4; 1 Pet. 3:20; *to heal, to restore to health,* Matt. 14:36; Luke 7:3

διασωθέντα, acc. sg. m. aor. pass. part. . . . . διασῴζω *(†1295)*
διασωθέντες, nom. pl. m. aor. pass. part. . id.
διασωθῆναι, aor. pass. infin. . . . . id.
διασῶσαι, aor. act. infin. . . . . id.
διασώσῃ, 3 pers. sg. aor. act. subj. . . . . id.
διασώσωσι(ν), 3 pers. pl. aor. act. subj. . . id.

διαταγάς, acc. pl. f. n. . . . . διαταγή *(1296)*
διαταγείς, nom. sg. m. 2 aor. pass. part. [§26.3] . . . . διατάσσω *(1299)*

(1296) διαταγή, ῆς, ἡ [§2.B.a] *an injunction, institute, ordinance,* Rom. 13:2; Acts 7:53

διαταγῇ, dat. sg. f. n. . . . . διαταγή *(1296)*

(1297) διάταγμα, ατος, τό [§4.D.c] *a mandate, commandment, ordinance,* Heb. 11:23

διάταγμα, acc. sg. neut. n. . . . . διάταγμα *(1297)*
διαταξάμενος, nom. sg. m. aor. mid. part. . . . . διατάσσω *(1299)*
διατάξομαι, 1 pers. sg. fut. mid. dep. indic. id.

(1298) διαταράσσω, fut. διαταράξω [§26.3] (διά + ταράσσω) *to throw into a state of perturbation, to move or trouble greatly,* Luke 1:29

διατάσσομαι, 1 pers. sg. pres. mid. indic. . . . . διατάσσω *(1299)*

(1299) διατάσσω, fut. διατάξω [§26.3] and mid. διατάσσομαι (διά + τάσσω) pr. *to arrange, make a precise arrangement; to prescribe,* 1 Cor. 11:34; 16:1; Tit. 1:5; *to direct,* Luke 8:55; Acts 20:13; *to charge,* Matt. 11:1; *to command,* Acts 18:2, et al.; *to ordain,* Gal. 3:19

διατάσσων, nom. sg. m. pres. act. part. . . . . διατάσσω *(1299)*

διαταχθέντα, acc. pl. neut. aor. pass.
part. . . . . διατάσσω *(1299)*
διατελεῖτε, 2 pers. pl. pres. act.
indic. . . . . διατελέω *(1300)*

(1300) **διατελέω**, ῶ, fut. διατελέσω [§22.1] (διά + τελέω) *to complete, finish;* intrans. *to continue, persevere,* in a certain state or course of action, Acts 27:33

διατεταγμένον, acc. sg. neut. perf. pass.
part. . . . . διατάσσω *(1299)*
διατεταγμένος, nom. sg. m. perf. pass. part.   id.
διατεταχέναι, perf. act. infin. (Acts 18:2,
GNT, WH, TR & NA | τεταχέναι, MT)   id.
διατηροῦντες, nom. pl. m. pres. act.
part. . . . . διατηρέω *(1301)*

(1301) **διατηρέω**, ῶ, fut. διατηρήσω [§16.P] (διά + τηρέω) *to watch carefully, guard with vigilance; to treasure up,* Luke 2:51; ἑαυτὸν ἐκ, *to keep one's self from, to abstain wholly from,* Acts 15:29

(1302) **διατί**, i.e., διὰ τί, interrog. *For what? Why? Wherefore?* Matt. 9:14; 13:10; Luke 19:23, 31 (TR | διὰ τί, GNT, WH, MT & NA)

διατίθεμαι, 1 pers. sg. pres. mid. indic.
[§28.W] . . . . διατίθημι *(†1303)*

(†1303) **διατίθημι** [§28.V] (διά + τίθημι) *to arrange;* mid. διατίθεμαι, fut. διαθήσομαι, 2 aor. διεθέμην, *to arrange according to one's own mind; to make a disposition, to make a will; to settle the terms of a covenant, to ratify,* Acts 3:25; Heb. 8:10; 10:16; *to assign,* Luke 22:29

διατρίβοντες, nom. pl. m. pres. act.
part. . . . . διατρίβω *(1304)*

(1304) **διατρίβω**, fut. διατρίψω [§23.1.a] (διά + τρίβω) pr. *to rub, wear away by friction;* met. *to pass or spend* time, *to remain, stay, tarry, continue,* John 3:22; 11:54; Acts 12:19; 14:3, 28, et al.

διατρίψας, nom. sg. m. aor. act.
part. . . . . διατρίβω *(1304)*
διατροφάς, acc. pl. f. n. . . . . διατροφή *(1305)*

(1305) **διατροφή**, ῆς, ἡ [§2.B.a] (διατρέφω, *to nourish*) *food, sustenance,* 1 Tim. 6:8

(1306) **διαυγάζω**, fut. διαυγάσω [§26.1] (διά + αὐγάζω) *to shine through, shine out, dawn,* 2 Pet. 1:19

διαυγάσῃ, 3 pers. sg. aor. act. subj. . διαυγάζω *(1306)*

(†1307) **διαυγής**, ές, nom. sg. m. adj. [§7.G.b] (διά + αὐγή) *translucent, transparent, pellucid* (Rev. 21:21, GNT, MT, WH & NA | διαφανής, TR)

(1307) **διαφανής**, ές, nom. sg. m. adj. [§7.G.b] (διαφαίνω, *to show through*) *transparent, pellucid* (Rev. 21:21, TR | διαυγής, GNT,

MT, WH & NA)

διαφέρει, 3 pers. sg. pres. act. indic. . διαφέρω *(1308)*
διαφέρετε, 2 pers. pl. pres. act. indic. . . . .   id.
διαφερομένων, gen. pl. m. pres. pass. part.   id.
διαφέροντα, acc. pl. neut. pres. act. part. .   id.

(1308) **διαφέρω**, fut. διοίσω, aor. διήνεγκα, 2 aor. διήνεγκον [§36.1] (διά + φέρω) *to convey through, across,* Mark 11:16; *to carry different ways or into different parts, separate;* pass. *to be borne, driven, or tossed hither and thither,* Acts 27:27; *to be promulgated, proclaimed, published,* Acts 13:49; intrans. met. *to differ,* 1 Cor. 15:41; *to excel, be better or of greater value, be superior,* Matt. 6:26; 10:31; et al.; impers. διαφέρει, *it makes a difference, it is of consequence;* with οὐδέν, *it makes no difference, it is nothing,* Gal. 2:6

(1309) **διαφεύγω**, fut. διαφεύξομαι, 2 aor. διέφυγον [§24.5] (διά + φεύγω) *to flee through, escape by flight,* Acts 27:42

διαφημίζειν, pres. act. infin. . . . . . . διαφημίζω *(1310)*

(1310) **διαφημίζω**, fut. διαφημίσω [§26.1] διεφήμισα (διά + φημή) *to report, proclaim, publish, spread abroad,* Matt. 9:31; 28:15; Mark 1:45

διαφθεῖραι, aor. act. infin. . . . . διαφθείρω *(1311)*
διαφθείρει, 3 pers. sg. pres. act. indic. . . . .   id.
διαφθείρεται, 3 pers. sg. pres. pass. indic. .   id.
διαφθείροντας, acc. pl. m. pres. act. part.   id.

(1311) **διαφθείρω**, fut. διαφθερῶ, aor. διέφθειρα, perf. διέφθαρκα [§27.1.c,d; 27.2.b] 2 aor. pass. διεφθάρην, perf. pass. διέφθαρμαι [§27.3; 27.4.a] (διά + φθείρω) *to corrupt or destroy utterly; to waste, bring to decay,* Luke 12:33; 2 Cor. 4:16; *to destroy,* Rev. 8:9; 11:18, met. *to corrupt, pervert utterly,* 1 Tim. 6:5

(1312) **διαφθορά**, ᾶς, ἡ [§2.B.b; 2.2] *corruption, dissolution,* Acts 2:27, 31; 13:34, 35, 36, 37

διαφθοράν, acc. sg. f. n. . . . . διαφθορά *(1312)*
διάφορα, acc. pl. neut. adj. . . . . διάφορος *(1313)*
διαφόροις, dat. pl. m. adj. . . . .   id.

(1313) **διάφορος**, ον [§7.2] *different, diverse, of different kinds,* Rom. 12:6; Heb. 9:10; *excellent, superior,* Heb. 1:4; 8:6

διαφορωτέρας, gen. sg. f. compar. adj. [§8.1; 8.4] . . . . διάφορος *(1313)*
διαφορώτερον, acc. sg. neut. compar. adj.   id.
διαφύγῃ, 3 pers. sg. 2 aor. act. subj. (Acts 27:42, GNT, WH, MT & NA | διαφύγοι, TR) . . . . διαφεύγω *(1309)*
διαφύγοι, 3 pers. sg. 2 aor. act. opt. [§24.9] (Acts 27:42, TR | διαφύγῃ, GNT, WH, MT & NA) . . . .   id.

διαφυλάξαι, aor. act. infin. . . . . . διαφυλάσσω (1314)

(1314) **διαφυλάσσω**, fut. διαφυλάξω [§26.3] (διά + φυλάσσω) *to keep or guard carefully or with vigilance; to guard, protect*

(†1315) **διαχειρίζω**, and διαχειρίζομαι [§26.1] (διά + χείρ) pr. *to have in the hands, to manage;* mid. later, *to kill,* Acts 5:30; 26:21

διαχειρίσασθαι, aor. mid. infin. . . . διαχειρίζω (†1315)

διαχλευάζοντες, nom. pl. m. pres. act. part. (Acts 2:13, GNT, WH & NA | χλευάζοντες, MT & TR) . . . . διαχλευάζω (‡5512)

(‡5512) **διαχλευάζω**, fut. διαχλευάσω [§26.1] (διά + χλευάζω) *to jeer outright, deride,* Acts 2:13

διαχωρίζεσθαι, pres. mid./pass. dep. infin. . . . . διαχωρίζομαι (1316)

(1316) **διαχωρίζομαι**, fut. διαχωρίσομαι (mid. of διαχωρίζω, *to separate,* from διά + χωρίζω) *to depart, go away*

διδακτικόν, acc. sg. m. adj. . . . . . . διδακτικός (1317)

(1317) **διδακτικός**, ή, όν [§7.F.a] *apt or qualified to teach,* 1 Tim. 3:2; 2 Tim. 2:24

διδακτοί, nom. pl. m. adj. . . . . διδακτός (1318)

διδακτοῖς, dat. sg. m. adj. . . . . id.

(1318) **διδακτός**, ή, όν [§7.F.a] pr. *taught, teachable,* of things; in N.T. *taught,* of persons, John 6:45; 1 Cor. 2:13

διδάξαι, aor. act. infin. . . . . διδάσκω (1321)

διδάξει, 3 pers. sg. fut. act. indic. . . . . id.

διδάξῃ, 3 pers. sg. aor. act. subj. . . . . id.

δίδαξον, 2 pers. sg. aor. act. imper. . . . . . . id.

διδάξωσιν, 3 pers. pl. aor. act. subj. . . . . . . id.

διδάσκαλε, voc. sg. m. n. . . . . διδάσκαλος (1320)

(1319) **διδασκαλία**, ας, ή, nom. sg. f. n. [§2.B.b; 2.2] *the act or occupation of teaching,* Rom. 12:7; 1 Tim. 4:13, et al.; *information, instruction,* Rom. 15:4; 2 Tim. 3:16; *matter taught, precept, doctrine,* Matt. 15:9; 1 Tim. 1:10, et al.

διδασκαλία, dat. sg. f. n. . . . . . . διδασκαλία (1319)

διδασκαλίαις, dat. pl. f. n. . . . . id.

διδασκαλίαν, acc. sg. f. n. . . . . id.

διδασκαλίας, gen. sg. f. n. {1 Tim. 4:6} . . id.

διδασκαλίας, acc. pl. f. n. {Matt. 15:9} . . id.

διδάσκαλοι, nom. pl. m. n. . . . . . διδάσκαλος (1320)

διδάσκαλον, acc. sg. m. n. . . . . id.

(1320) **διδάσκαλος**, ου, ὁ, nom. sg. m. n. [§3.C.a] *a teacher, master,* Rom. 2:20, et al.; in N.T. as an equivalent to ῥαββί, John 1:39, et al.

διδασκάλους, acc. pl. m. n. . . . . . διδάσκαλος (1320)

διδασκάλων, gen. pl. m. n. . . . . id.

δίδασκε, 2 pers. sg. pres. act. imper. . διδάσκω (1321)

διδάσκει, 3 pers. sg. pres. act. indic. . . . . . id.

διδάσκειν, pres. act. infin. . . . . id.

διδάσκεις, 2 pers. sg. pres. act. indic. . . . . id.

διδάσκῃ, 3 pers. sg. pres. act. subj. . . . . . . id.

διδάσκοντες, nom. pl. m. pres. act. part. . . . . διδάσκω (1321)

διδάσκοντι, dat. sg. m. pres. act. part. . . . id.

διδάσκοντος, gen. sg. m. pres. act. part. . . id.

(1321) **διδάσκω**, 1 pers. sg. pres. act. indic., fut. διδάξω, perf. δεδίδαχα [§23.1.a,b; 23.6] aor. ἐδίδαξα, aor. pass. ἐδιδάχθην [§23.2; 23.4] *to teach,* Matt. 4:23; 22:16, et al.; *to teach or speak in a public assembly,* 1 Tim. 2:12; *to direct, admonish,* Matt. 28:15; Rom. 2:21, et al.

διδάσκων, nom. sg. m. pres. act. part. . . . . διδάσκω (1321)

διδαχαῖς, dat. pl. f. n. . . . . διδαχή (1322)

(1322) **διδαχή**, ῆς, ἡ, nom. sg. f. n. [§2.B.a] *instruction, the giving of instruction, teaching,* Mark 4:2; 12:38, et al.; *instruction, what is taught, doctrine,* Matt. 16:12; John 7:16, 17, et al.; meton. *mode of teaching and kind of doctrine taught,* Matt. 7:28; Mark 1:27

διδαχῇ, dat. sg. f. n. . . . . διδαχή (1322)

διδαχήν, acc. sg. f. n. . . . . id.

διδαχῆς, gen. sg. f. n. . . . . id.

διδόασιν, 3 pers. pl. pres. act. indic. for διδοῦσι [§30.3] (Rev. 17:13, GNT, WH, MT & NA | διαδιδώσουσιν, TR) . . δίδωμι (1325)

διδόμενον, nom. sg. neut. pres. pass. part. id.

διδόναι, pres. act. infin. . . . . id.

διδόντα, acc. sg. m. pres. act. part. (1 Thess. 4:8, GNT, WH & NA | δόντα, MT & TR) . . . . id.

διδόντα, nom. pl. neut. pres. act. part. {1 Cor. 14:7} . . . . id.

διδόντες, nom. pl. m. pres. act. part. . . . . id.

διδόντι, dat. sg. m. pres. act. part. . . . . . . id.

διδόντος, gen. sg. m. pres. act. part. . . . . . id.

δίδοται, 3 pers. sg. pres. pass. indic. . . . . . id.

δίδοτε, 2 pers. pl. pres. act. imper. . . . . . . id.

δίδου, 2 pers. sg. pres. act. imper. [§31.2] . id.

διδούς, nom. sg. m. pres. act. part. . . . . . . id.

δίδραχμα, acc. pl. neut. n. . . . . δίδραχμον (1323)

(1323) **δίδραχμον**, ου, τό [§3.C.c] (δίς + δραχμή) *a didrachmon or double drachm,* a silver coin equal to the drachm of Alexandria, to two Attic drachms, to two Roman denarii, and to the half-shekel of the Jews, Matt. 17:24(2×)

(1324) **Δίδυμος**, ου, ὁ, nom. sg. m. n. [§3.C.a] *a twin; Didymus,* the Greek equivalent to the name Thomas, John 11:16; 20:24; 21:2

διδῶ, 1 pers. sg. pres. act. subj. (Rev. 3:9, GNT, WH & NA | δίδωμι, MT & TR) . . . . δίδωμι (1325)

(1325) **δίδωμι**, 1 pers. sg. pres. act. indic., fut. δώσω,

perf. δέδωκα, aor. ἔδωκα, 2 aor. ἔδων,
perf. pass. δέδομαι, aor. pass. ἐδόθην, *to
give, bestow, present,* Matt. 4:9; 6:11; John
3:16; 17:2, et al. freq.; *to give, cast, throw,*
Matt. 7:6; *to supply, suggest,* Matt. 10:19;
Mark 13:11; *to distribute* alms, Matt.
19:21; Luke 11:41, et al.; *to pay* tribute,
etc., Matt. 22:17; Mark 12:14; Luke 20:22;
to be the author or source of a thing, Luke
12:51; Rom. 11:8, et al.; *to grant, permit,
allow,* Acts 2:27; 13:35; Matt. 13:11; 19:11,
et al.; *to deliver to, entrust, commit to the
charge* of anyone, Matt. 25:15; Mark 12:9,
et al.; *to give or deliver up,* Luke 22:19;
John 6:51, et al.; *to reveal, teach,* Acts 7:38;
to appoint, constitute, Eph. 1:22; 4:11; *to
consecrate, devote, offer in sacrifice,* 2 Cor.
8:5; Gal. 1:4; Rev. 8:3, et al.; *to present,
expose* one's self in a place, Acts 19:31; *to
recompense,* Rev. 2:23; *to attribute, ascribe,*
John 9:24; Rev. 11:13; from the Hebrew,
to place, put, fix, inscribe, Heb. 8:10;
10:16, et al.; *to infix, impress,* 2 Cor. 12:7;
Rev. 13:16; *to inflict,* John 18:22; 19:3;
2 Thess. 1:8; *to give in charge, assign,* John
5:36; 17:4; Rev. 9:5; *to exhibit, put forth,*
Matt. 24:24; Acts 2:19; *to yield, bear* fruit,
Matt. 13:8; διδόναι ἐργασίαν, *to endeavor, strive,* Luke 12:58; διδόναι ἀπόκρισιν,
to answer, reply, John 1:22; διδόναι τόπον,
to give place, yield, Luke 14:9; Rom. 12:19
δίδωσι(ν), 3 pers. sg. pres. act. indic.
  [§30.Z] . . . . δίδωμι *(1325)*
διέβησαν, 3 pers. pl. 2 aor. act. indic.
  [§37.1] . . . . διαβαίνω *(1224)*
διέβλεψεν, 3 pers. sg. aor. act. indic. (Mark
  8:25, GNT, WH & NA | ἐποίησεν αὐτὸν
  ἀναβλέψαι, MT & TR) . . . . διαβλέπω *(1227)*
διεβλήθη, 3 pers. sg. aor. pass.
  indic. διαβάλλω *(1225)*
διεγείρειν, pres. act. infin. . . . . διεγείρω *(1326)*
διεγείρετο, 3 pers. sg. pres. pass. indic. (John
  6:18, GNT, WH & NA | διηγείρετο, MT
  & TR) . . . . id.
διεγείρουσιν, 3 pers. pl. pres. act. indic. (Mark
  4:38, MT & TR | ἐγείρουσιν, GNT, WH
  & NA) . . . . id.
(1326) **διεγείρω**, 1 pers. sg. pres. act. indic., fut. διεγερῶ,
  aor. pass. διηγέρθην [§37.1] (διά + ἐγείρω) *to
  arouse or awake thoroughly,* Matt. 1:24; Mark
  4:38, 39; Luke 8:24; pass. *to be raised, excited,
  agitated,* as a sea, John 6:18; met. *to stir up,
  arouse, animate,* 2 Pet. 1:13; 3:1
διεγερθείς, nom. sg. m. aor. pass.
  part. διεγείρω *(1326)*

διεγνώρισαν, 3 pers. pl. aor. act. indic. (Luke
  2:17, MT & TR | ἐγνώρισαν, GNT, WH
  & NA) . . . . διαγνωρίζω *(1232)*
διεγόγγυζον, 3 pers. pl. imperf. act.
  indic. διαγογγύζω *(1234)*
διεδίδετο, 3 pers. sg. imperf. pass. indic. (Acts
  4:35, GNT, WH & NA | διεδίδοτο, MT
  & TR) . . . . διαδίδωμι *(1239)*
διεδίδοτο, 3 pers. sg. imperf. pass. indic.
  [§30.4] (Acts 4:35, MT & TR | διεδίδετο,
  GNT, WH & NA) . . . . id.
διέδωκε(ν), 3 pers. sg. aor. act. indic. . . . . id.
διεζώσατο, 3 pers. sg. aor. mid. indic.
  [§31.BB] . . . . διαζώννυμι *(1241)*
διέζωσεν, 3 pers. sg. aor. act. indic. . . . . . id.
διεζωσμένος, nom. sg. m. perf. pass. part. . id.
διέθετο, 3 pers. sg. 2 aor. mid. indic.
  [§30.AA] . . . . διατίθημι (†1303)
διεῖλεν, 3 pers. sg. 2 aor. act. indic.
  [§36.1] . . . . διαιρέω *(1244)*
διεκρίθη, 3 pers. sg. aor. pass. indic.
  [§27.3] . . . . διακρίνω *(1252)*
διεκρίθητε, 2 pers. pl. aor. pass. indic. . . . id.
διέκρινε(ν), 3 pers. sg. aor. act. indic. . . . . id.
διεκρίνομεν, 1 pers. pl. imperf. act. indic. . id.
διεκρίνοντο, 3 pers. pl. imperf. mid. indic. . id.
διεκώλυεν, 3 pers. sg. imperf. act.
  indic. διακωλύω *(1254)*
διελαλεῖτο, 3 pers. sg. imperf. pass. indic.
  [§17.Q] . . . . διαλαλέω *(1255)*
διελάλουν, 3 pers. pl. imperf. act. indic. . . id.
διελέγετο, 3 pers. sg. imperf. mid./pass. dep.
  indic. διαλέγομαι *(1256)*
διελέξατο, 3 pers. sg. aor. mid. dep. indic.
  (Acts 17:2; 18:19, GNT, WH & NA | Acts
  17:2, MT, διελέξατο; TR, διελέγετο | Acts
  18:19, διελέχθη, MT & TR) . . . . id.
διελεύσεται, 3 pers. sg. fut. mid. dep.
  indic. διέρχομαι *(1330)*
διελέχθη, 3 pers. sg. aor. pass. dep. indic.
  [§23.4] (Acts 18:19, MT & TR |
  διελέξατο, GNT, WH & NA) . διαλέγομαι *(1256)*
διελέχθησαν, 3 pers. pl. aor. pass. dep. indic. id.
διεληλυθότα, acc. sg. m. 2 perf. act.
  part. διέρχομαι *(1330)*
διελθεῖν, 2 aor. act. infin. . . . . id.
διελθόντα, acc. sg. m. 2 aor. act. part. . . . id.
διελθόντες, nom. pl. m. 2 aor. act. part. . id.
διέλθω, 1 pers. sg. 2 aor. act. subj. . . . . . id.
διέλθωμεν, 1 pers. pl. 2 aor. act. subj. . . . id.
διελθών, nom. sg. m. 2 aor. act. part. . . . . id.
διέλιπε(ν), 3 pers. sg. 2 aor. act. indic.
  [§24.9] . . . . διαλείπω *(1257)*
διελογίζεσθε, 2 pers. pl. imperf. mid./pass.
  dep. indic. . . . . διαλογίζομαι *(1260)*

διελογίζετο, 3 pers. sg. imperf. mid./pass. dep.
indic. . . . . διαλογίζομαι *(1260)*
διελογίζοντο, 3 pers. pl. imperf. mid./pass.
dep. indic. . . . . id.
διελύθησαν, 3 pers. pl. aor. pass. indic.
[§14.N] . . . . διαλύω *(1262)*
διεμαρτυράμεθα, 1 pers. pl. aor. mid. dep.
indic. . . . . διαμαρτύρομαι *(1263)*
διεμαρτύρατο, 3 pers. sg. aor. mid. dep. indic.
[§37.1] . . . . id.
διεμαρτύρετο, 3 pers. sg. imperf. mid./pass.
dep. indic. (Acts 2:40, MT & TR |
διεμαρτύρατο, GNT, WH & NA) . . . . id.
διεμαρτύρω, 2 pers. sg. aor. mid. dep. indic.   id.
διεμάχοντο, 3 pers. pl. imperf. mid./pass. dep.
indic. . . . . διαμάχομαι *(1264)*
διέμενε(ν), 3 pers. sg. imperf. act.
indic. . . . . διαμένω *(1265)*
διεμέριζον, 3 pers. pl. imperf. act.
indic. . . . . διαμερίζω *(1266)*
διεμερίσαντο, 3 pers. pl. aor. mid. indic. .   id.
διεμερίσθη, 3 pers. sg. aor. pass. indic. . . .   id.
διενέγκῃ, 3 pers. sg. 2 aor. act. subj.
[§36.1] . . . . διαφέρω *(1308)*
(‡1760) **διενθυμέομαι,** οῦμαι (διά + ἐνθυμέομαι) *to
revolve thoroughly in the mind, consider
carefully*
διενθυμουμένου, gen. sg. m. pres. mid./pass.
dep. part. (Acts 10:19, GNT, WH, MT &
NA | ἐνθυμουμένου, TR) . . . διενθυμέομαι *(‡1760)*
διεξελθοῦσα, nom. sg. f. 2 aor. act. part. (Acts
28:3, MT | ἐξελθοῦσα, GNT, WH, TR
& NA) . . . . διεξέρχομαι *(‡1831)*
(‡1831) **διεξέρχομαι,** fut. διεξελεύσομαι (διά +
ἐξέρχομαι) *to come out through* anything,
find one's way out
(1327) **διέξοδος,** ου, ἡ [§3.C.b] (διά + ἔξοδος) *a passage throughout; a line of road, a thor-
oughfare,* Matt. 22:9
διεξόδους, acc. pl. f. n. . . . . διέξοδος *(1327)*
διεπέρασε(ν), 3 pers. sg. aor. act.
indic. . . . . διαπεράω *(1276)*
διεπορεύετο, 3 pers. sg. imperf. mid./pass.
dep. indic. . . . . διαπορεύομαι *(1279)*
διεπορεύοντο, 3 pers. pl. imperf. mid./pass.
dep. indic. . . . . id.
διεπραγματεύσαντο, 3 pers. pl. aor. mid. dep.
indic. (Luke 19:15, GNT, WH & NA |
διεπραγματεύσατο, MT &
TR) . . . . διαπραγματεύομαι *(1281)*
διεπραγματεύσατο, 3 pers. sg. aor. mid. dep.
indic. (Luke 19:15, MT & TR | διεπρα-
γματεύσαντο, GNT, WH & NA) . . . . id.
διεπρίοντο, 3 pers. pl. imperf. pass.
indic. . . . . διαπρίω *(1282)*

διέρηξεν, 3 pers. sg. aor. act. indic. (Matt.
26:65, WH | διέρρηξε(ν), GNT, MT, TR
& NA) . . . . δια(ρ)ρήσσω *(†1284)*
διερήσσετο, 3 pers. sg. imperf. pass. indic.
(Luke 5:6, WH | διερρήσσετο, GNT &
NA | διερρήγνυτο, MT & TR) . . . . . id.
διερμηνεύει, 3 pers. sg. pres. act. indic. (1 Cor.
14:5, MT | διερμηνεύῃ, GNT, WH, TR
& NA) . . . . διερμηνεύω *(1329)*
διερμηνευέτω, 3 pers. sg. pres. act. imper.   id.
διερμηνεύῃ, 3 pers. sg. pres. act. subj. . . .   id.
διερμηνευομένη, nom. sg. f. pres. pass. part.   id.
διερμηνεύουσι(ν), 3 pers. pl. pres. act. indic.   id.
διερμήνευσεν, 3 pers. sg. aor. act. indic. (Luke
24:27, GNT, WH & NA | διηρμήνευεν,
MT & TR) . . . . id.
(1328) **διερμηνευτής,** οῦ, ὁ, nom. sg. m. n. [§2.B.c]
an interpreter, 1 Cor. 14:28
(1329) **διερμηνεύω,** fut. διερμηνεύσω [§13.M] a late
compound used as an equivalent to the
simple ἑρμηνεύω, *to explain, interpret,
translate,* Luke 24:27; Acts 9:36; 1 Cor.
14:5, 13, 27; *to be able to interpret,* 1 Cor.
12:30
διερρήγνυτο, 3 pers. sg. imperf. pass. indic.
(Luke 5:6, MT & TR | διερρήσσετο,
GNT & NA | διερήσσετο,
WH) . . . . διαρρήγνυμι *(†1284)*
διέρρηξε(ν), 3 pers. sg. aor. act. indic. (Matt.
26:65, GNT, MT, TR & NA | διέρηξεν,
WH) . . . . id.
διερρήσσετο, 3 pers. sg. imperf. pass. indic.
(Acts 5:6, GNT & NA | διερήσσετο, WH
| διερρήγνυτο, MT & TR) . δια(ρ)ρήσσω *(†1284)*
διέρχεσθαι, pres. mid./pass. dep.
infin. . . . . διέρχομαι *(1330)*
διέρχεται, 3 pers. sg. pres. mid./pass. dep.
indic. . . . . id.
(1330) **διέρχομαι,** 1 pers. sg. pres. mid./pass. dep.
indic., fut. διελεύσεται, 2 aor. διῆλθον
[§36.1] (διά + ἔρχομαι) *to pass through,*
Mark 10:25 Luke 4:30, et al.; *to pass over,
cross,* Mark 4:35; Luke 8:22; *to pass
along,* Luke 19:4; *to proceed,* Luke 2:15;
Acts 9:38, et al.; *to travel through* or *over*
a country, *wander about,* Matt. 12:43;
Luke 9:6, et al.; *to transfix, pierce,* Luke
2:35; *to spread abroad, be prevalent,* as a
rumor, Luke 5:15; met. *to extend to,* Rom.
5:12
διερχόμενον, acc. sg. m. pres. mid./pass. dep.
part. . . . . διέρχομαι *(1330)*
διερχόμενος, nom. sg. m. pres. mid./pass.
dep. part. . . . . id.
διέρχωμαι, 1 pers. sg. pres. mid./pass. dep.

subj. (John 4:15, GNT, WH & NA | ἔρχο-
μαι, MT | ἔρχωμαι, TR) . . . . . . διέρχομαι *(1330)*

(1331) **διερωτάω**, ῶ, fut. διερωτήσω [§18.R] (διά +
ἐρωτάω) *to sift by questioning,* of persons;
in N.T., of things, *to ascertain by inquiry,*
Acts 10:17

διερωτήσαντες, nom. pl. m. aor. act.
part. . . . . διερωτάω *(1331)*

διεσάφησαν, 3 pers. pl. aor. act.
indic. διασαφέω *(1285)*

διεσκόρπισα, 1 pers. sg. aor. act.
indic. διασκορπίζω *(1287)*

διεσκόρπισας, 2 pers. sg. aor. act. indic. . id.

διεσκόρπισε(ν), 3 pers. sg. aor. act. indic.   id.

διεσκορπίσθησαν, 3 pers. pl. aor. pass. indic.   id.

διεσκορπισμένα, acc. pl. neut. perf. pass.
part. . . . . id.

διεσπάρησαν, 3 pers. pl. aor. pass. indic.
[§27.4.a,b] . . . . διασπείρω *(1289)*

διεσπᾶσθαι, perf. pass. infin. . . . . . . διασπάω *(1288)*

διεστειλάμεθα, 1 pers. pl. aor. mid.
indic. διαστέλλω *(†1291)*

διεστείλατο, 3 pers. sg. aor. mid. indic.
[§27.1.d] . . . . id.

διεστέλλετο, 3 pers. sg. imperf. mid. indic.   id.

διέστη, 3 pers. sg. 2 aor. act. indic. . . διΐστημι *(1339)*

διεστραμμένα, acc. pl. neut. perf. pass. part.
[§35.9] . . . . διαστρέφω *(1294)*

διεστραμμένη, voc. sg. f. perf. pass. part. . id.

διεστραμμένης, gen. sg. f. perf. pass. part.   id.

διεσώθησαν, 3 pers. pl. aor. pass. indic.
[§37.1] . . . . διασῴζω *(†1295)*

διέταξα, 1 pers. sg. aor. act. indic. . διατάσσω *(1299)*

διεταξάμην, 1 pers. sg. aor. mid. indic. . . id.

διετάξατο, 3 pers. sg. aor. mid. indic. . . . . id.

διέταξε(ν), 3 pers. sg. aor. act. indic. . . . . id.

διεταράχθη, 3 pers. sg. aor. pass.
indic. διαταράσσω *(1298)*

διετήρει, 3 pers. sg. imperf. act.
indic. . . . . διατηρέω *(1301)*

(1332) **διετής**, ές [§7.G.b] (δίς + ἔτος) *of two years;
of the age of two years,* Matt. 2:16

(1333) **διετία**, ας, ἡ [§2.B.b; 2.2] *the space of two
years,* Acts 24:27; 28:30

διετίαν, acc. sg. f. n. . . . . διετία *(1333)*

διετίας, gen. sg. f. n. . . . . id.

διετοῦς, gen. sg. m. adj. . . . . διετής *(1332)*

διέτριβε(ν), 3 pers. sg. imperf. act.
indic. . . . . διατρίβω *(1304)*

διέτριβον, 3 pers. pl. imperf. act. indic. . . id.

διετρίψαμεν, 1 pers. pl. aor. act. indic. . . . id.

διέτριψαν, 3 pers. pl. aor. act. indic. . . . . . id.

διεφέρετο, 3 pers. sg. imperf. pass.
indic. . . . . διαφέρω *(1308)*

διεφήμισαν, 3 pers. pl. aor. act.

indic. διαφημίζω *(1310)*

διεφημίσθη, 3 pers. sg. aor. pass. indic. . . id.

διεφθάρη, 3 pers. sg. 2 aor. pass. indic. (Rev.
8:9, MT & TR | διεφθάρησαν, GNT,
WH & NA) . . . . διαφθείρω *(1311)*

διεφθάρησαν, 3 pers. pl. 2 aor. pass. indic.
(Rev. 8:9, GNT, WH & NA | διεφθάρη,
MT & TR) . . . . id.

διεφθαρμένων, gen. pl. m. perf. pass. part.   id.

διέφθειρε, 3 pers. sg. imperf. act. indic. (Rev.
19:2, MT | ἔφθειρε(ν), GNT, WH, TR &
NA) . . . . id.

διεχειρίσασθε, 2 pers. pl. aor. mid.
indic. διαχειρίζω *(†1315)*

διήγειραν, 3 pers. pl. aor. act. indic. . διεγείρω *(1326)*

διηγείρετο, 3 pers. sg. imperf. pass. indic.
(John 6:18, MT & TR | διεγείρετο, GNT,
WH & NA) . . . . id.

(1334) **διηγέομαι**, οῦμαι, fut. διηγήσομαι [§17.Q]
(διά + ἡγέομαι) pr. *to lead throughout;
to declare thoroughly, detail, recount, relate, tell,* Mark 5:16; 9:9; Luke 8:39; Acts
8:33; Heb. 11:32, et al.

διηγήσαντο, 3 pers. pl. aor. mid. dep.
indic. διηγέομαι *(1334)*

διηγήσατο, 3 pers. sg. aor. mid. dep. indic.   id.

διηγήσεται, 3 pers. sg. fut. mid. dep. indic.   id.

διήγησιν, acc. sg. f. n. . . . . διήγησις *(†1335)*

(†1335) **διήγησις**, εως, ἡ [§5.E.c] *a narration, relation,
history,* Luke 1:1

διηγήσωνται, 3 pers. pl. aor. mid. dep.
subj. . . . . διηγέομαι *(1334)*

διηγοῦ, 2 pers. sg. pres. mid./pass. dep. imper.   id.

διηγούμενον, acc. sg. m. pres. mid./pass. dep.
part. . . . . id.

διηκόνει, 3 pers. sg. imperf. act.
indic. . . . . διακονέω *(1247)*

διηκονήσαμεν, 1 pers. pl. aor. act. indic. . . id.

διηκόνησε(ν), 3 pers. sg. aor. act. indic. . . id.

διηκόνουν, 3 pers. pl. imperf. act. indic. . . id.

διῆλθεν, 3 pers. sg. 2 aor. act. indic.
[§36.1] . . . . διέρχομαι *(1330)*

διῆλθον, 1 pers. sg. 2 aor. act. indic.
{Acts 20:25} . . . . id.

διῆλθον, 3 pers. sg. 2 aor. act. indic.
{Acts 8:4} . . . . id.

διηνεκές, acc. sg. neut. adj. . . . . διηνεκής *(†1336)*

(†1336) **διηνεκής**, ές [§7.G.b] (διά + ἠνεκής, *extended, prolonged*) *continuous, uninter-
rupted;* εἰς τὸ διηνεκές, *perpetually,* Heb.
7:3; 10:1, 12, 14

διήνοιγεν, 3 pers. sg. imperf. act. indic.
[§37.1] . . . . διανοίγω *(1272)*

διηνοιγμένους, acc. pl. m. perf. pass. part.
(Acts 7:56, GNT, WH & NA | ἀνεῳ-

γμένους, MT & TR) . . . . διανοίγω *(1272)*
διήνοιξε(ν), 3 pers. sg. aor. act. indic. . . . . id.
διηνοίχθησαν, 3 pers. pl. aor. pass. indic. . id.
διηπόρει, 3 pers. sg. imperf. act.
    indic. . . . . διαπορέω *(1280)*
διηπόρουν, 3 pers. pl. imperf. act. indic. . . id.
διηποροῦντο, 3 pers. pl. imperf. mid. indic.
    (Acts 2:12, WH | διηπόρουν, GNT, MT,
    NA & TR) . . . . id.
διηρμήνευεν, 3 pers. sg. imperf. act. indic.
    (Luke 24:27, MT & TR | διερμήνευσεν,
    GNT, WH & NA) . . . . διερμηνεύω *(1329)*
διήρχετο, 3 pers. sg. imperf. mid./pass. dep.
    indic. . . . . διέρχομαι *(1330)*
διήρχοντο, 3 pers. pl. imperf. mid./pass. dep.
    indic. . . . . id.
διθάλασσον, acc. sg. m. adj. . . . . διθάλασσος *(1337)*
(1337) **διθάλασσος**, ον [§7.2] (δίς, + θάλασσα)
    washed on both sides by the sea; τόπος
    διθάλασσος, *a shoal or sand-bank formed
    by the confluence of opposite currents,* Acts
    27:41
(1338) **διϊκνέομαι**, οῦμαι, fut. διϊκνίξομαι [§36.2]
    (διά + ἱκνέομαι) *to go or pass through;
    to penetrate,* Heb. 4:12
διϊκνούμενος, nom. sg. m. pres. mid./pass.
    dep. part. (Heb. 4:12, GNT, MT, TR &
    NA | διικνούμενος, WH) . . . . . διϊκνέομαι *(1338)*
(1339) **διΐστημι**, fut. διαστήσω [§29.X] (διά +
    ἵστημι) *to set at an interval, apart; to sta-
    tion at an interval* from a former position,
    Acts 27:28; intrans. 2 aor. διέστην, *to
    stand apart; to depart, be parted,* Luke
    24:51; of time, *to intervene, be interposed,*
    Luke 22:59
διϊσχυρίζετο, 3 pers. sg. imperf. mid./pass.
    dep. indic. (Luke 22:59; Acts 12:15, GNT,
    MT, TR & NA | διισχυρίζετο,
    WH) . . . . διϊσχυρίζομαι *(1340)*
(1340) **διϊσχυρίζομαι**, fut. διϊσχυρίσομαι (διά +
    ἰσχυρίζομαι, from ἰσχυρός) *to feel or ex-
    press reliance; to affirm confidently, as-
    everate,* Luke 22:59; Acts 12:15
δικαία, nom. sg. f. adj. {John 5:30} . . δίκαιος *(1342)*
δίκαια, nom. pl. neut. adj. {1 John 3:12} . id.
δίκαιαι, nom. pl. f. adj. . . . . id.
δικαίαν, acc. sg. f. adj. . . . . id.
δικαίας, gen. sg. f. adj. . . . . id.
δίκαιε, voc. sg. m. adj. . . . . id.
δίκαιοι, nom. pl. m. adj. {Rom. 5:19} . . . id.
δικαιοῖ, 3 pers. sg. pres. act. indic.
    {Gal. 3:8} . . . . δικαιόω *(1344)*
δικαίοις, dat. pl. m. adj. . . . . δίκαιος *(1342)*
(1341) **δικαιοκρισία**, ας, ἡ [§2.B.b; 2.2] (δίκαιος +
    κρίσις) *just or righteous judgment,* Rom. 2:5

δικαιοκρισίας, gen. sg. f. n. . . . . δικαιοκρισία *(1341)*
δίκαιον, acc. sg. m. adj. {2 Pet. 2:7} . . δίκαιος *(1342)*
δίκαιον, nom. sg. neut. adj. {Eph. 6:1} . . id.
δίκαιον, acc. sg. neut. adj. {2 Pet. 1:13} . . id.
(1342) **δίκαιος**, αία, αιον, nom. sg. m. adj. [§7.1]
    used of things, *just, equitable, fair,* Matt.
    20:4; Luke 12:57; John 5:30; Col. 4:1, et
    al.; of persons, *just, righteous,* absolutely,
    John 17:25; Rom. 3:10, 26; 2 Tim. 4:8;
    1 Pet. 3:18; 1 John 1:9; 2:1, 29; Rev. 16:5;
    righteous by account and acceptance, Rom.
    2:13; 5:19, et al.; in ordinary usage, *just,
    upright, innocent, pious,* Matt. 5:45; 9:13,
    et al. freq.; ὁ δίκαιος, *the Just One,* one
    of the distinctive titles of the Messiah, Acts
    3:14; 7:52; 22:14
(1343) **δικαιοσύνη**, ης, ἡ, nom. sg. f. n. [§2.B.a] *fair
    and equitable dealing, justice,* Acts 17:31;
    Heb. 11:33; Rom. 9:28; *rectitude, virtue,*
    Luke 1:75; Eph. 5:9; in N.T. *generosity,
    alms,* 2 Cor. 9:10, v.r.; Matt. 6:1; *piety,
    godliness,* Rom. 6:13, et al.; *investiture
    with the attribute of righteousness, accep-
    tance as righteous, justification,* Rom. 4:11;
    10:4, et al. freq.; *a provision or mean for
    justification,* Rom. 1:17; 2 Cor. 3:9, et al.;
    an instance of justification, 2 Cor. 5:21
δικαιοσύνῃ, dat. sg. f. n. . . . . δικαιοσύνη *(1343)*
δικαιοσύνην, acc. sg. f. n. . . . . id.
δικαιοσύνης, gen. sg. f. n. . . . . id.
δικαίου, gen. sg. m. adj. . . . . δίκαιος *(1342)*
δικαιούμενοι, nom. pl. m. pres. pass.
    part. . . . . δικαιόω *(1344)*
δικαιοῦν, pres. act. infin. (Luke 10:29, MT &
    TR | δικαιῶσαι, GNT, WH & NA) . . id.
δικαιοῦντα, acc. sg. m. pres. act. part. . . . id.
δικαιοῦντες, nom. pl. m. pres. act. part. . id.
δικαίους, acc. pl. m. adj. . . . . δίκαιος *(1342)*
δικαιοῦσθαι, pres. pass. infin. [§21.U] δικαιόω *(1344)*
δικαιοῦσθε, 2 pers. pl. pres. pass. indic. . . id.
δικαιοῦται, 3 pers. sg. pres. pass. indic. . . id.
(1344) **δικαιόω**, ῶ, fut. δικαιώσομαι and δικαιώσω,
    aor. ἐδικαίωσα, perf. pass. δεδικαίωμαι,
    aor. pass. ἐδικαιώθην [§20.T; 21.U] pr. *to
    make or render right or just;* mid. *to act
    with justice,* Rev. 22:11; *to avouch to be
    good and true, to vindicate,* Matt. 11:19;
    Luke 7:29, et al.; *to set forth as good and
    just,* Luke 10:29; 16:15; in N.T. *to hold as
    guiltless, to accept as righteous, to justify,*
    Rom. 3:26, 30; 4:5; 8:30, 33, et al.; pass.
    to be held acquitted, to be cleared, Acts
    13:39; Rom. 3:24; 6:7; *to be approved, to
    stand approved, to stand accepted,* Rom.
    2:13; 3:20, 28, et al.

δικαίῳ, dat. sg. m. adj. . . . . δίκαιος *(1342)*
δικαιωθέντες, nom. pl. m. aor. pass.
    part. . . . . δικαιόω *(1344)*
δικαιωθῆναι, aor. pass. infin. . . . . id.
δικαιωθῇς, 2 pers. sg. aor. pass. subj. . . . . id.
δικαιωθήσεται, 3 pers. sg. fut. pass. indic. id.
δικαιωθήσῃ, 2 pers. sg. fut. pass. indic. . . id.
δικαιωθήσονται, 3 pers. pl. fut. pass. indic. id.
δικαιωθήτω, 3 pers. sg. aor. pass. imper. (Rev.
    22:11, TR | δικαιοσύνην ποιησάτω,
    GNT, WH, MT & NA) . . . . id.
δικαιωθῶμεν, 1 pers. pl. aor. pass. subj. . . id.
(1345) **δικαίωμα**, ατος, τό, nom. sg. neut. n. [§4.D.c]
    pr. *a rightful act, act of justice, equity; a*
    sentence, of condemnation, Rev. 15:4; in
    N.T., of acquittal, *justification,* Rom. 5:16;
    a decree, law, ordinance, Luke 1:6; Rom.
    1:32; 2:26; 8:4; Heb. 9:1, 10; *a meritori-*
    ous act, an instance of perfect righteous-
    ness, Rom. 5:18; *state of righteousness,*
    Rev. 19:8 {Rom. 8:4}
δικαίωμα, acc. sg. neut. n.
    {Rom. 1:32} . . . . δικαίωμα *(1345)*
δικαιώμασι(ν), dat. pl. neut. n. . . . . id.
δικαιώματα, nom. pl. neut. n. {Heb. 9:10} id.
δικαιώματα, acc. pl. neut. n. {Heb. 9:1} . id.
δικαιώματος, gen. sg. neut. n. . . . . id.
δικαίων, gen. pl. m. adj. {Luke 1:17} . δίκαιος *(1342)*
δικαιῶν, nom. sg. m. pres. act. part.
    {Rom. 8:33} . . . . δικαιόω *(1344)*
(1346) **δικαίως**, adv., *justly, with strict justice,* 1 Pet.
    2:23; *deservedly,* Luke 23:41; *as it is right,*
    fit or proper, 1 Cor. 15:34; *uprightly, hon-*
    estly, piously, religiously, 1 Thess. 2:10;
    Tit. 2:12
δικαιῶσαι, aor. act. infin. (Luke 10:29, GNT,
    WH & NA | δικαιοῦν, MT &
    TR) . . . . δικαιόω *(1344)*
δικαιώσει, 3 pers. sg. fut. act. indic. . . . . . id.
δικαίωσιν, acc. sg. f. n. . . . . δικαίωσις *(1347)*
(1347) **δικαίωσις**, εως, ἡ [§5.E.c] pr. *a making right*
    or just; a declaration of right or justice; a
    judicial sentence; in N.T., *acquittal, accep-*
    tance, justification, Rom. 4:25; 5:18
δικαστήν, acc. sg. f. n. . . . . δικαστής *(1348)*
(1348) **δικαστής**, οῦ, ὁ [§2.B.c] (δικάζω, *to judge*)
    a judge, Luke 12:14; Acts 7:27, 35
(1349) **δίκη**, ης, ἡ, nom. sg. f. n. [§2.B.a] *right, jus-*
    tice; in N.T. *judicial punishment, venge-*
    ance, 2 Thess. 1:9; Jude 7; *sentence of*
    punishment, judgment, Acts 25:15; *person-*
    ified, *the goddess of justice or vengeance,*
    Nemesis, Paena, Acts 28:4
δίκην, acc. sg. f. n. . . . . δίκη *(1349)*
δίκτυα, nom. pl. neut. n. (Luke 5:6, GNT,

WH & NA | δίκτυον, MT & TR) δίκτυον *(1350)*
δίκτυα, acc. pl. neut. n. {Luke 5:5} . . . . id.
(1350) **δίκτυον**, ου, τό, nom. sg. neut. n. [§3.C.c] *a*
    net, fishing-net, Matt. 4:20, 21, et al.
    {John 21:11b}
δίκτυον, acc. sg. neut. n.
    {John 21:11a} . . . . δίκτυον *(1350)*
(1351) **δίλογος**, ον [§7.2] (δίς + λόγος) pr. *saying*
    the same thing twice; in N.T. *double-*
    tongued, speaking one thing and meaning
    another, deceitful in words, 1 Tim. 3:8
διλόγους, acc. pl. m. adj. . . . . δίλογος *(1351)*
(1352) **διό** (i.e., δι’ ὅ) *on which account, wherefore,*
    therefore, Matt. 27:8; 1 Cor. 12:3, et al.
διοδεύσαντες, nom. pl. m. aor. act.
    part. . . . . διοδεύω *(1353)*
(1353) **διοδεύω**, fut. διοδεύσω [§13.M] (διά +
    ὁδεύω) *to travel through* a place, *traverse,*
    Luke 8:1; Acts 17:1
(1354) **Διονύσιος**, ου, ὁ, nom. sg. m. n. *Dionysius,*
    pr. name, Acts 17:34
(1355) **διόπερ**, conj. strengthened from διό, *on this*
    very account, for this very reason, where-
    fore, 1 Cor. 8:13; 10:14; 14:13
(1356) **διοπετής**, ές [§7.G.b] (Ζεύς, Διός, + πίπτω)
    which fell from Jupiter, or heaven; τοῦ
    Διοπετοῦς, sc. ἀγάλματος, Acts 19:35
διοπετοῦς, gen. sg. m. adj. . . . . Διοπετής *(1356)*
(‡2735) **διόρθωμα**, ατος, τό [§4.D.c] (διορθόω, *to cor-*
    rect, from διά + ὀρθόω, *to make straight,*
    from ὀρθός) *correction, emendation, refor-*
    mation, Acts 24:3
διορθωμάτων, gen. pl. neut. n. (Acts 24:2,
    GNT, WH & NA | κατορθωμάτων, Acts
    24:2, MT & TRb | κατορθωμάτων, Acts
    24:3, TRs) . . . . διόρθωμα *(‡2735)*
διορθώσεως, gen. sg. f. n. . . . . διόρθωσις *(1357)*
(1357) **διόρθωσις**, εως, ἡ [§5.E.c] (διορθόω, *to cor-*
    rect) *a complete rectification, reformation,*
    Heb. 9:10
διορυγῆναι, 2 aor. pass. infin. [§26.3] (Matt.
    24:43; Luke 12:39, MT & TR | διορυ-
    χθῆναι, GNT, WH & NA) . . . . . διορύσσω *(1358)*
διορύσσουσι(ν), 3 pers. pl. pres. act. indic. id.
(1358) **διορύσσω**, fut. διορύξω (δία + ὀρύσσω) *to*
    dig or break through, Matt. 6:19, 20,
    24:43; Luke 12:39
διορυχθῆναι, aor. pass. infin. (Matt. 24:43;
    Luke 12:39, GNT, WH & NA | διορυ-
    γῆναι, MT & TR) . . . . διορύσσω *(1358)*
Διός, gen. sg. m. n. [§6.4.a] . . . . Ζεύς *(2203)*
(1359) **Διόσκουροι**, or Διόσκοροι, ων, οἱ [§3.C.a]
    (Ζεύς, Διός, + κοῦρος, *a youth*) *the Di-*
    oscuri, Castor and Pollux, sons of Jupiter
    by Leda, and patrons of sailors, Acts 28:11

Διοσκούροις, dat. pl. m. n. ..... Διόσκουροι *(1359)*

(1360) **διότι,** conj. (διά, ὅτι) *on the account that, because,* Luke 2:7; 21:28; *in as much as,* Luke 1:13; Acts 18:10, et al.

(1361) **Διοτρέφης,** ους, ὁ, nom. sg. m. n. [§5.E.a] *Diotrephes,* pr. name (3 John 9, GNT, MT, WH & NA | Διοτρεφής, TR)

διπλᾶ, acc. pl. neut. adj. .... διπλόος *(†1362)*

διπλῆς, gen. sg. f. adj. .... id.

(†1362) **διπλόος,** οῦς, ῆ, οῦν [§7.4.b] *double,* Matt. 23:15; 1 Tim. 5:17; Rev. 18:6

διπλότερον, acc. sg. m. compar. adj. [§8.4] .... διπλόος *(†1362)*

διπλοῦν, acc. sg. neut. adj. .... id.

(1363) **διπλόω,** ῶ, fut. διπλώσω, aor. ἐδίπλωσα [§20.T] *to double; to render back double,* Rev. 18:6

διπλώσατε, 2 pers. pl. aor. act. imper. . διπλόω *(1363)*

(1364) **δίς,** adv., *twice,* Mark 14:30, 72, et al.; in the sense of *entirely, utterly,* Jude 12; ἅπαξ καὶ δίς, *once and again, repeatedly,* Phil. 4:16

δισμυριάδες, nom. pl. f. numeral (Rev. 9:16, GNT & NA | δίς μυριάδες, WH | δύο μυριάδες, TR | μυριάδες, MT) δισμυριάς *(‡3461)*

(‡3461) **δισμυριάς,** άδος, ἡ, *twice ten thousand, two myriads*

(1365) **διστάζω,** fut. διστάσω [§26.1] aor. ἐδίστασα, *to doubt, waver, hesitate,* Matt. 14:31; 28:17

δίστομον, acc. sg. f. adj. .... δίστομος *(1366)*

(1366) **δίστομος,** ον [§7.2] (δίς + στόμα) pr. *having two mouths; two-edged,* Heb. 4:12; Rev. 1:16; 2:12

δίστομος, nom. sg. f. adj. .... δίστομος *(1366)*

(1367) **δισχίλιοι,** αι, α, nom. pl. m. numeral (δίς + χίλιοι) *two thousand,* Mark 5:13

διϋλίζοντες, nom. pl. m. pres. act. part. (Matt. 23:24, GNT, MT, TR & NA | διυλίζοντες, WH) .... διϋλίζω *(†1368)*

(†1368) **διϋλίζω,** fut. διϋλίσω [§26.1] (διά + ὑλίζω, *to strain, filter*) *to strain, filter thoroughly; to strain out or off,* Matt. 23:24

διχάσαι, aor. act. infin. .... διχάζω *(1369)*

(1369) **διχάζω,** fut. διχάσω [§26.1] (δίχα, *apart*) *to cut asunder, disunite;* met. *to cause to disagree, set at variance,* Matt. 10:35

(1370) **διχοστασία,** ας, ἡ [§2.B.b; 2.2] (δίχα + στάσις) *a standing apart; a division, dissension,* Rom. 16:17; 1 Cor. 3:3; Gal. 5:20

διχοστασίαι, nom. pl. f. n. ...... διχοστασία *(1370)*

διχοστασίας, acc. pl. f. n. .... id.

(1371) **διχοτομέω,** ῶ, fut. διχοτομήσω [§16.P] (δίχα + τέμνω) pr. *to cut into two parts, cut asunder;* in N.T. *to inflict a punishment of extreme severity,* Matt. 24:51; Luke 12:46

διχοτομήσει, 3 pers. sg. fut. act.

indic. .... διχοτομέω *(1371)*

διψᾷ, 3 pers. sg. pres. act. subj. .... διψάω *(1372)*

(1372) **διψάω,** ῶ, fut. διψήσω [§18.R] aor. ἐδίψησα (δίψα, *thirst*) *to thirst, be thirsty,* Matt. 25:35, 37, 42, 44, et al.; met. *to thirst after* in spirit, *to desire or long for ardently,* Matt. 5:6; John 4:14; 6:35, et al.

δίψει, dat. sg. neut. n. .... δίψος *(1373)*

διψήσει, 3 pers. sg. fut. act. indic. ... διψάω *(1372)*

διψήσῃ, 3 pers. sg. aor. act. subj. (John 4:14; 6:35, MT & TR | διψήσει, GNT, WH & NA) .... id.

διψήσουσιν, 3 pers. pl. fut. act. indic. ... id.

(1373) **δίψος,** ους, τό [§5.E.b] *thirst,* 2 Cor. 11:27

δίψυχοι, nom. pl. m. adj. .... δίψυχος *(1374)*

(1374) **δίψυχος,** ον, nom. sg. m. adj. [§7.2] (δίς + ψυχή) *double-minded, inconstant, fickle,* James 1:8

διψῶ, 1 pers. sg. pres. act. indic. contr. {John 19:28} .... διψάω *(1372)*

διψῶ, 1 pers. sg. pres. act. subj. {John 4:15} id.

διψῶμεν, 1 pers. pl. pres. act. subj. ..... id.

διψῶν, nom. sg. m. pres. act. part. ...... id.

διψῶντα, acc. sg. m. pres. act. part. ..... id.

διψῶντες, nom. pl. m. pres. act. part. .... id.

διψῶντι, dat. sg. m. pres. act. part. ..... id.

διωγμοῖς, dat. pl. m. n. .... διωγμός *(1375)*

διωγμόν, acc. sg. m. n. .... id.

(1375) **διωγμός,** οῦ, ὁ, nom. sg. m. n. [§3.C.a] pr. *chase, pursuit; persecution,* Matt. 13:21; Mark 4:17; 10:30, et al.

διωγμοῦ, gen. sg. m. n. .... διωγμός *(1375)*

διωγμούς, acc. pl. m. n. .... id.

διωγμῶν, gen. pl. m. n. .... id.

διώδευε(ν), 3 pers. sg. imperf. act.

indic. .... διοδεύω *(1353)*

δίωκε, 2 pers. sg. pres. act. imper. .... διώκω *(1377)*

διώκεις, 2 pers. sg. pres. act. indic. ..... id.

διώκετε, 2 pers. pl. pres. act. imper. ..... id.

διώκομαι, 1 pers. sg. pres. pass. indic. ... id.

διωκόμενοι, nom. pl. m. pres. pass. part. . id.

διώκοντα, nom. pl. neut. pres. act. part. . id.

διώκοντας, acc. pl. m. pres. act. part. ... id.

διώκοντες, nom. pl. m. pres. act. part. ... id.

διωκόντων, gen. pl. m. pres. act. part. ... id.

διώκτην, acc. sg. m. n. .... διώκτης *(1376)*

(1376) **διώκτης,** ου, ὁ [§2.B.c] *a persecutor,* 1 Tim. 1:13

(1377) **διώκω,** 1 pers. sg. pres. act. indic., fut. διώξω, aor. ἐδίωξα [§23.1.b; 23.2] perf. pass. δεδίωγμαι, aor. pass. ἐδιώχθην [§23.7; 23.4] *to put in rapid motion; to pursue; to follow, pursue the direction of,* Luke 17:23; *to follow eagerly, endeavor earnestly to acquire,* Rom. 9:30, 31; 12:13, et al.; *to press*

forwards, Phil 3:12, 14; *to pursue* with malignity, *persecute,* Matt. 5:10, 11, 12, 44, et al.

διώκωμεν, 1 pers. pl. pres. act. subj. . . διώκω *(1377)*
διώκων, nom. sg. m. pres. act. part. . . . . . id.
διώκωνται, 3 pers. pl. pres. pass. subj. . . . id.
διώκωσιν, 3 pers. pl. pres. act. subj. . . . . . id.
διωξάτω, 3 pers. sg. aor. act. imper. . . . . . id.
διώξετε, 2 pers. pl. fut. act. indic. . . . . id.
διώξητε, 2 pers. pl. aor. act. subj. . . . . id.
διώξουσι(ν), 3 pers. pl. fut. act. indic. . . . id.
διώξωσι(ν), 3 pers. pl. aor. act. subj. . . . . id.
διωχθήσονται, 3 pers. pl. fut. pass. indic. . id.
(1378) **δόγμα,** ατος, τό, nom. sg. neut. n. [§4.D.c]
a decree, statute, ordinance, Luke 2:1; Acts
16:4; 17:7; Eph. 2:15; Col. 2:14
δόγμασι(ν), dat. pl. neut. n. . . . . δόγμα *(1378)*
δόγματα, acc. pl. neut. n. . . . . id.
δογματίζεσθε, 2 pers. pl. pres. pass.
indic. δογματίζω *(1379)*
(1379) **δογματίζω,** fut. δογματίσω [§26.1] *to decree,
prescribe an ordinance;* mid. *to suffer laws
to be imposed on one's self, to submit to,
bind one's self by, ordinances,* Col. 2:20
δογμάτων, gen. pl. neut. n. . . . . δόγμα *(1378)*
δοθείη, 3 pers. sg. aor. pass. opt. [§30.4] (Eph.
6:19, TR | δοθῇ, GNT, WH, MT &
NA) . . . . δίδωμι *(1325)*
δοθεῖσα, nom. sg. f. aor. pass. part. . . . . . id.
δοθεῖσαν, acc. sg. f. aor. pass. part. . . . . . id.
δοθείσῃ, dat. sg. f. aor. pass. part. . . . . . . id.
δοθείσης, gen. sg. f. aor. pass. part. . . . . . id.
δοθέντος, gen. sg. neut. aor. pass. part. . . id.
δοθῇ, 3 pers. sg. aor. pass. subj. . . . . id.
δοθῆναι, aor. pass. infin. [§30.4] . . . . id.
δοθήσεται, 3 pers. sg. fut. pass. indic. . . . id.
δοῖ, 3 pers. sg. 2 aor. act. subj. (for δῷ,)
[§30.5] (Mark 8:37, GNT, WH & NA |
δώσει, MT & TR) . . . . id.
δοκεῖ, 3 pers. sg. pres. act. indic.
[§37.2] . . . . δοκέω *(1380)*
δοκεῖν, pres. act. infin. . . . . id.
δοκεῖς, 2 pers. sg. pres. act. indic. . . . . . . id.
δοκεῖτε, 2 pers. pl. pres. act. indic.
{John 5:39} . . . . id.
δοκεῖτε, 2 pers. pl. pres. act. imper.
{John 5:45} . . . . id.
(1380) **δοκέω,** ῶ, fut. δόξω, aor. ἔδοξα [§37.2] *to
think, imagine, suppose, presume,* Matt.
3:9; 6:7, et al.; *to seem, appear,* Luke
10:36; Acts 17:18, et al.; impers. δοκεῖ, *it
seems; it seems good, best, or right, it pleases,* Luke 1:3; Acts 15:22, 25, et al.
δοκῇ, 3 pers. sg. pres. act. subj. . . . . . . δοκέω *(1380)*
δοκιμάζει, 3 pers. sg. pres. act.

indic. δοκιμάζω *(1381)*
δοκιμάζειν, pres. act. infin. . . . . id.
δοκιμάζεις, 2 pers. sg. pres. act. indic. . . . id.
δοκιμαζέσθωσαν, 3 pers. pl. pres. pass.
imper. . . . . id.
δοκιμάζετε, 2 pers. pl. pres. act. indic. (Luke
12:56, MT & TR | δοκιμάζειν, GNT,
WH & NA) . . . . id.
δοκιμάζετε, 2 pers. pl. pres. act. imper.
{1 John 4:1} . . . . id.
δοκιμαζέτω, 3 pers. sg. pres. act. imper. . . id.
δοκιμαζομένου, gen. sg. neut. pres. pass.
part. . . . . id.
δοκιμάζοντες, nom. pl. m. pres. act. part. . id.
δοκιμάζοντι, dat. sg. m. pres. act. part. . . id.
(1381) **δοκιμάζω,** fut. δοκιμάσω [§26.1] aor.
ἐδοκίμασα, perf. pass. δεδοκίμασμαι, *to
prove* by trial; *to test, assay* metals, 1 Pet.
1:7; *to prove, try, examine, scrutinize,* Luke
14:19; Rom. 12:2, et al.; *to put to the proof,
tempt,* Heb. 3:9; *to approve* after trial,
judge worthy, choose, Rom. 14:22; 1 Cor.
16:3; 2 Cor. 8:22; et al.; *to decide upon*
after examination, *judge of, distinguish,
discern,* Luke 12:56; Rom. 2:18; Phil. 1:10
δοκιμάζων, nom. sg. m. pres. act.
part. . . . . δοκιμάζω *(1381)*
δοκιμάσαι, aor. act. infin. . . . . id.
δοκιμάσει, 3 pers. sg. fut. act. indic. . . . . . id.
δοκιμάσητε, 2 pers. pl. aor. act. subj. . . . . id.
(†1381) **δοκιμασία,** ας, ἡ [§2.B.b; 2.2] *proof, probation,* Heb. 3:9
δοκιμασίᾳ, dat. sg. f. n. (Heb. 3:9, GNT, WH
& NA | ἐδοκίμασαν, MT &
TR) . . . . δοκιμασία *(†1381)*
(1382) **δοκιμή,** ῆς, ἡ, nom. sg. f. n. [§2.B.a] *trial,
proof* by trial, 2 Cor. 8:2; *the state or disposition of that which has been tried and
approved, approved character or temper,*
Rom. 5:4; 2 Cor. 2:9, et al.; *proof, document, evidence,* 2 Cor. 13:3
δοκιμῇ, dat. sg. f. n. . . . . δοκιμή *(1382)*
δοκιμήν, acc. sg. f. n. . . . . id.
δοκιμῆς, gen. sg. f. n. . . . . id.
(1383) **δοκίμιον,** ου, τό, nom. sg. neut. n. [§3.C.c]
*that by means of which anything is tried,
proof, criterion, test; trial, the act of trying or putting to proof,* James 1:3; *approved character,* 1 Pet. 1:7
δόκιμοι, nom. pl. m. adj. . . . . δόκιμος *(1384)*
δόκιμον, acc. sg. m. adj. . . . . id.
(1384) **δόκιμος,** ον, nom. sg. m. adj. [§7.2] *proved,
tried; approved* after examination and trial,
Rom. 16:10; James 1:12, et al.; by impl. *acceptable,* Rom. 14:18

δοκόν, acc. sg. f. n. . . . . δοκός *(1385)*

(1385) **δοκός,** οῦ, ἡ, nom. sg. f. n. [§3.C.b] *a beam or spar* of timber, Matt. 7:3, 4, 5; Luke 6:41, 42

δοκοῦμεν, 1 pers. pl. pres. act. indic. . . δοκέω *(1380)*

δοκοῦν, acc. sg. neut. pres. act. part. . . . . id.

δοκοῦντα, nom. pl. neut. pres. act. part. . id.

δοκοῦντες, nom. pl. m. pres. act. part. . . . id.

δοκούντων, gen. pl. m. pres. act. part. . . . id.

δοκοῦσα, nom. sg. f. pres. act. part. . . . . . id.

δοκοῦσι(ν), 3 pers. pl. pres. act. indic. {Matt. 6:7} . . . . id.

δοκοῦσι(ν), dat. pl. m. pres. act. part. {Gal. 2:2} . . . . id.

δοκῶ, 1 pers. sg. pres. act. indic. contr. . . id.

δοκῶν, nom. sg. m. pres. act. part. . . . . . . id.

δόλιοι, nom. pl. m. adj. . . . . δόλιος *(1386)*

(1386) **δόλιος,** ία, ιον [§7.1] and ος, ον [§7.2] *fraudulent, deceitful,* 2 Cor. 11:13

(1387) **δολιόω,** ῶ, fut. δολιώσω [§20.T] *to deceive, use fraud or deceit,* Rom. 3:13

δόλον, acc. sg. m. n. . . . . δόλος *(1388)*

(1388) **δόλος,** ου, ὁ, nom. sg. m. n. [§3.C.a] pr. *a bait or contrivance for entrapping; fraud, deceit, insidious artifice, guile,* Matt. 26:4; Mark 7:22; 14:1, et al.

δόλου, gen. sg. m. n. . . . . δόλος *(1388)*

δολοῦντες, nom. pl. m. pres. act. part. . δολόω *(1389)*

(1389) **δολόω,** ῶ, fut. δολώσω [§20.T] pr. *to entrap, beguile; to adulterate, corrupt, falsify,* 2 Cor. 4:2

δόλῳ, dat. sg. m. n. . . . . δόλος *(1388)*

(1390) **δόμα,** ατος, τό [§4.D.c] *a gift, present,* Matt. 7:11, et al.

δόμα, acc. sg. neut. n. . . . . δόμα *(1390)*

δόματα, acc. pl. neut. n. . . . . id.

δόντα, acc. sg. m. 2 aor. act. part. [§30.Z] . . . . δίδωμι *(1325)*

δόντι, dat. sg. m. 2 aor. act. part. (2 Cor. 8:16, GNT & NA | διδόντι, WH, MT & TR) id.

δόντος, gen. sg. m. 2 aor. act. part. . . . . . id.

(1391) **δόξα,** ης, ἡ, nom. sg. f. n. [§2.3] pr. *a seeming; appearance; a notion, imagination, opinion; the opinion which obtains respecting one; reputation, credit, honor, glory;* in N.T. *honorable consideration,* Luke 14:10; *praise, glorification, honor,* John 5:41, 44; Rom. 4:20; 15:7, et al.; *dignity, majesty,* Rom. 1:23; 2 Cor. 3:7, et al.; *a glorious manifestation, glorious working,* John 11:40; 2 Pet. 1:3; et al.; pl. *dignitaries,* 2 Pet. 2:10; Jude 8: *glorification* in a future state of bliss, 2 Cor. 4:17; 2 Tim. 2:10, et al.; *pride, ornament,* 1 Cor. 11:15; 1 Thess. 2:20; *splendid array, pomp, mag-*

nificence, Matt. 6:29; 19:28, et al.; *radiance, dazzling lustre,* Luke 2:9; Acts 22:11, et al.

δοξάζειν, pres. act. infin. . . . . δοξάζω *(1392)*

δοξάζεται, 3 pers. sg. pres. pass. indic. . . . id.

δοξαζέτω, 3 pers. sg. pres. act. imper. . . . id.

δοξάζηται, 3 pers. sg. pres. pass. subj. . . . id.

δοξάζητε, 2 pers. pl. pres. act. subj. . . . . . id.

δοξαζόμενος, nom. sg. m. pres. pass. part. id.

δοξάζοντες, nom. pl. m. pres. act. part. . . id.

(1392) **δοξάζω,** 1 pers. sg. pres. act. indic., fut. δοξάσω [§26.1] aor. ἐδόξασα, perf. pass. δεδόξασμαι, aor. pass. ἐδοξάσθην, according to the various significations of δόξα, *to think, suppose, judge; to extol, magnify,* Matt. 6:2; Luke 4:15, et al.; in N.T. *to adore, worship,* Rom. 1:21, et al.; *to invest with dignity or majesty,* 2 Cor. 3:10; Heb. 5:5, et al.; *to signalize with a manifestation of dignity, excellence, or majesty,* John 12:28; 13:32, et al.; *to glorify* by admission to a state of bliss, *to beatify,* Rom. 8:30, et al.

δοξάζων, nom. sg. m. pres. act. part. . . . . id.

δόξαν, acc. sg. f. n. . . . . δόξα *(1391)*

δόξαντες, nom. pl. m. aor. act. part. . . δοκέω *(1380)*

δόξας, acc. pl. f. n. . . . . δόξα *(1391)*

δοξάσαι, aor. act. infin. . . . . δοξάζω *(1392)*

δοξάσατε, 2 pers. pl. aor. act. imper. . . . . id.

δοξάσει, 3 pers. sg. fut. act. indic. . . . . . . id.

δοξάσῃ, 3 pers. sg. aor. act. subj. . . . . id.

δοξασθῇ, 3 pers. sg. aor. pass. subj. . . . . . id.

δοξασθῶσιν, 3 pers. pl. aor. pass. subj. . . id.

δόξασον, 2 pers. sg. aor. act. imper. . . . . . id.

δοξάσω, 1 pers. sg. fut. act. indic. {John 12:28} . . . . id.

δοξάσω, 1 pers. sg. aor. act. subj. {John 8:54} . . . . id.

δοξάσωσι(ν), 3 pers. pl. aor. act. subj. . . . id.

δόξῃ, 3 pers. sg. aor. act. subj. {John 16:2} . . . . δοκέω *(1380)*

δόξῃ, dat. sg. f. n. {John 17:5} . . . . δόξα *(1391)*

δόξης, gen. sg. f. n. . . . . id.

δόξητε, 2 pers. pl. aor. act. subj. . . . . . δοκέω *(1380)*

δόξω, 2 pers. sg. aor. act. subj. . . . . id.

(1393) **Δορκάς,** άδος, ἡ, nom. sg. f. n. [§4.2.c] *Dorcas,* pr. name, signifying *a gazelle or antelope,* Acts 9:36, 39

δός, 2 pers. sg. 2 aor. act. imper. [§30.1] . . . . δίδωμι *(1325)*

δόσεως, gen. sg. f. n. . . . . δόσις *(1394)*

(1394) **δόσις,** εως, ἡ, nom. sg. f. n. [§5.E.c] pr. *giving, outlay;* Phil. 4:15; *a donation, gift,* James 1:17

δότε, 2 pers. pl. 2 aor. act. imper. . . . . δίδωμι *(1325)* δότην, acc. sg. m. n. . . . . δότης *(1395)*

(1395) **δότης**, ου, ὁ [§2.B.c] *a giver,* 2 Cor. 9:7

δότω, 3 pers. sg. 2 aor. act. imper. . . . . δίδωμι *(1325)*

δοῦλα, acc. pl. neut. adj. . . . . δοῦλος *(†1401)*

(1396) **δουλαγωγέω**, ῶ, fut. δουλαγωγήσω [§16.P]
(δοῦλος + ἄγω) pr. *to bring into slavery;
to treat as a slave; to discipline into subjection,* 1 Cor. 9:27

δουλαγωγῶ, 1 pers. sg. pres. act. ind.
contr. . . . . δουλαγωγέω *(1396)*

δούλας, acc. pl. f. n. . . . . δούλη *(1399)*

δοῦλε, voc. sg. m. n. . . . . δοῦλος *(†1401)*

(1397) **δουλεία**, ας, ἡ [§2.B.b; 2.2] *slavery, bondage,
servile condition;* in N.T. met. with refer-
ence to degradation and unhappiness,
thraldom spiritual or moral, Rom. 8:15, 21;
Gal. 4:24; 5:1; Heb. 2:15

δουλείαν, acc. sg. f. n. . . . . δουλεία *(1397)*

δουλείας, gen. sg. f. n. . . . . id.

δουλεύει, 3 pers. sg. pres. act. indic. . δουλεύω *(1398)*

δουλεύειν, pres. act. infin. . . . . id.

δουλεύετε, 2 pers. pl. pres. act. indic. or imper.
{Col. 3:24} . . . . id.

δουλεύετε, 2 pers. pl. pres. act. imper.
{Gal. 5:13} . . . . id.

δουλευέτωσαν, 3 pers. pl. pres. act. imper. id.

δουλεύοντες, nom. pl. m. pres. act. part. . id.

δουλεύουσιν, 3 pers. pl. pres. act. indic. . . id.

δουλεῦσαι, aor. act. infin. (Gal. 4:9, WH |
δουλεύειν, GNT, MT, TR & NA) . . . . id.

δουλεύσει, 3 pers. sg. fut. act. indic. . . . . . id.

δουλεύσουσιν, 3 pers. pl. fut. act. indic. (Acts
7:7, GNT, WH & NA | δουλεύσωσι(ν),
MT & TR) . . . . id.

δουλεύσωσι(ν), 3 pers. pl. aor. act. subj. (Acts
7:7, MT & TR | δουλεύσουσιν, GNT,
WH & NA) . . . . id.

(1398) **δουλεύω**, 1 pers. sg. pres. act. indic., fut.
δουλεύσω [§13.M] perf. δεδούλευκα, aor.
ἐδούλευσα, *to be a slave or servant; to be
in slavery or subjection,* John 8:33; Acts
7:7; Rom. 9:12; *to discharge the duties of
a slave or servant,* Eph. 6:7; 1 Tim. 6:2;
*to serve, be occupied in the service of, be
devoted, subservient,* Matt. 6:24; Luke
15:29; Acts 20:19; Rom. 14:18; 16:18 et al.;
met. *to be enthralled, involved in a slav-
ish service,* spiritually or morally, Gal.
4:9, 25; Tit. 3:3

δουλεύων, nom. sg. m. pres. act.
part. . . . . δουλεύω *(1398)*

(1399) **δούλη**, ης, ἡ, nom. sg. f. n., *female slave,
bondmaid*

δούλης, gen. sg. f. n. . . . . δούλη *(1399)*

δοῦλοι, nom. pl. m. n. . . . . δοῦλος *(†1401)*

δούλοις, dat. pl. m. n. . . . . δοῦλος *(†1401)*

(1400) δοῦλον, acc. sg. m. n. . . . . id.

(†1401) **δοῦλος**, η, ον, *as a slave, servile, subject*

(1401) **δοῦλος**, ου, ὁ, nom. sg. m. n. *enslaved, enthralled, subservient,* Rom. 6:19; as a subst.
δοῦλος, *a male slave, or servant,* of various degrees, Matt. 8:9, et al. freq.; *a servitor, person of mean condition,* Phil. 2:7;
fem. δούλη, *a female slave; a handmaiden,*
Luke 1:38, 48; Acts 2:18; δοῦλος, used figuratively, in a bad sense, *one involved in*
moral or spiritual *thraldom,* John 8:34;
Rom. 6:17, 20; 1 Cor. 7:23; 2 Pet. 2:19; in
a good sense, *a* devoted *servant or minister,* Acts 16:17; Rom. 1:1, et al.; *one
pledged or bound to serve,* 1 Cor. 7:22;
2 Cor. 4:5

δούλου, gen. sg. m. n. . . . . id.

δούλους, acc. pl. m. n. . . . . id.

(1402) **δουλόω**, ῶ, fut. δουλώσω [§20.T] aor.
ἐδούλωσα, perf. pass. δεδούλωμαι, aor.
pass. ἐδουλώθην, *to reduce to servitude,
enslave, oppress by retaining in servitude,*
Acts 7:6; 2 Pet. 2:19; met. *to render subservient,* 1 Cor. 9:19; pass. *to be under restraint,* 1 Cor. 7:15; *to be in bondage,*
spiritually or morally, Gal. 4:3; Tit. 2:3;
to become devoted to the service of, Rom.
6:18, 22

δούλῳ, dat. sg. m. n. . . . . δοῦλος *(†1401)*

δουλωθέντες, nom. pl. m. aor. pass.
part. . . . . δουλόω *(1402)*

δούλων, gen. pl. m. n. . . . . δοῦλος *(†1401)*

δουλώσουσιν, 3 pers. pl. fut. act.
indic. . . . . δουλόω *(1402)*

δοῦναι, 2 aor. act. infin. [§30.Z] . . . . . δίδωμι *(1325)*

δούς, nom. sg. m. 2 aor. act. part. . . . . . . id.

(1403) **δοχή**, ῆς, ἡ [§2.B.a] pr. *reception* of guests;
in N.T. *a banquet, feast,* Luke 5:29;
14:13

δοχήν, acc. sg. f. n. . . . . δοχή *(1403)*

δράκοντα, acc. sg. m. n. . . . . δράκων *(1404)*

δράκοντι, dat. sg. m. n. (Rev. 13:4, GNT,
WH, MT & NA | δράκοντα, TR) . . . id.

δράκοντος, gen. sg. m. n. . . . . id.

(1404) **δράκων**, οντος, ὁ, nom. sg. m. n. [§4.2.d] *a
dragon or large serpent;* met. *the devil or
Satan,* Rev. 12:3, 4, 7, 9, 13, 16, 17; 13:2,
4, 11; 16:13; 20:2

δραμών, nom. sg. m. 2 aor. act. part.
[§36.1] . . . . τρέχω *(5143)*

(1405) **δράσσομαι** [§26.3] (δράξ, *the fist*) pr. *to grasp
with the hand, clutch; to lay hold of, seize,
take, catch,* 1 Cor. 3:19

δρασσόμενος, nom. sg. m. pres. mid./pass.

dep. part. . . . . δράσσομαι *(1405)*

δραχμάς, acc. pl. f. n. . . . . δραχμή *(1406)*

(1406) **δραχμή**, ῆς, ἡ [§2.B.a] *a drachm,* an Attic silver coin of nearly the same value as the Roman *denarius,* Luke 15:8, 9

δραχμήν, acc. sg. f. n. . . . . δραχμή *(1406)*

(1407) **δρέπανον**, ου, τό [§3.C.c] (δρέπω, *to crop, cut off) an instrument with a curved blade,* as *a sickle,* Mark 4:29; Rev. 14:14, 15, 16, 17, 18, 19

δρέπανον, acc. sg. neut. n. . . . . δρέπανον *(1407)*

δρόμον, acc. sg. m. n. . . . . δρόμος *(1408)*

(1408) **δρόμος**, ου, ὁ [§3.C.a] (δέδρομα) *a course, race, race-course;* met. *course* of life or ministry, *career,* Acts 13:25; 20:24; 2 Tim. 4:7

(1409) **Δρούσιλλα**, ης, ἡ [§2.3] *Drusilla,* pr. name, Acts 24:24

Δρουσίλλῃ, dat. sg. f. n. . . . . Δρούσιλλα *(1409)*

δυναίμην, 1 pers. sg. pres. mid./pass. dep. opt. . . . . δύναμαι *(1410)*

δύναιντο, 3 pers. pl. pres. mid./pass. dep. opt.   id.

(1410) **δύναμαι**, 1 pers. sg. pres. mid./pass. dep. indic., fut. δυνήσομαι, imperf. ἐδυνάμην and ἠδυνάμην, aor. ἐδυνησάμην and (pass. form) ἐδυνάσθην, ἐδυνήθην, ἠδυνήθην [§37.1] *to be able,* either intrinsically and absolutely, which is the ordinary signification; or, for specific reasons, Matt. 9:15; Luke 16:2

δυνάμεθα, 1 pers. pl. pres. mid./pass. dep. indic. . . . . δύναμαι *(1410)*

δυνάμει, dat. sg. f. n. . . . . δύναμις *(1411)*

δυνάμεις, nom. pl. f. n. {Matt. 13:54} . . . id.

δυνάμεις, acc. pl. f. n. {Matt. 13:58} . . . . id.

δυνάμενα, acc. pl. neut. pres. mid./pass. dep. part. . . . . δύναμαι *(1410)*

δυνάμεναι, nom. pl. f. pres. mid./pass. dep. part. . . . . id.

δυναμένη, nom. sg. f. pres. mid./pass. dep. part. . . . . id.

δυνάμενοι, nom. pl. m. pres. mid./pass. dep. part. . . . . id.

δυνάμενον, acc. sg. m. pres. mid./pass. dep. part. . . . . id.

δυνάμενος, nom. sg. m. pres. mid./pass. dep. part. . . . . id.

δυναμένου, gen. sg. m. pres. mid./pass. dep. part. {Acts 24:11} . . . . id.

δυναμένου, gen. sg. neut. pres. mid./pass. dep. part. {Acts 27:15} . . . . id.

δυναμένους, acc. pl. m. pres. mid./pass. dep. part. . . . . id.

δυναμένῳ, dat. sg. m. pres. mid./pass. dep. part. . . . . id.

δυναμένων, gen. pl. m. pres. mid./pass. dep. part. . . . . δύναμαι *(1410)*

δυνάμεσι(ν), dat. pl. f. n. . . . . δύναμις *(1411)*

δυνάμεων, gen. pl. f. n. . . . . id.

δυνάμεως, gen. sg. f. n. . . . . id.

δύναμιν, acc. sg. f. n. . . . . id.

(1411) **δύναμις**, εως, ἡ, nom. sg. f. n. [§5.E.c] *power; strength, ability,* Matt. 25:15; Heb. 11:11; *efficacy,* 1 Cor. 4:19, 20; Phil. 3:10; 1 Thess. 1:5; 2 Tim. 3:5; *energy,* Col. 1:29; 2 Tim. 1:7; *meaning, purport* of language, 1 Cor. 14:11; *authority,* Luke 4:36; 9:1; *might, power, majesty,* Matt. 22:29; 24:30; Acts 3:12; Rom. 9:17; 2 Thess. 1:7; 2 Pet. 1:16; in N.T. *a manifestation or instance of power, mighty means,* Acts 8:10; Rom. 1:16; 1 Cor. 1:18, 24; ἡ δύναμις, *omnipotence,* Matt. 26:64; Luke 22:69; Matt. 14:62; pl. *authorities,* Rom. 8:38; Eph. 1:21; 1 Pet. 3:22; *miraculous power,* Mark 5:30; Luke 1:35; 5:17; 6:19; 8:46; 24:49; 1 Cor. 2:4; *a miracle,* Matt. 11:20, 21, et al. freq.; *a worker of miracles,* 1 Cor. 12:28, 29; from the Hebrew αἱ δυνάμεις τῶν οὐρανῶν, *the heavenly luminaries,* Matt. 24:29; Mark 13:25; Luke 21:26; αἱ δυνάμεις, *the* spiritual *powers,* Matt. 14:2; Mark 6:14

δυναμούμενοι, nom. pl. m. pres. pass. part. . . . . δυναμόω *(1412)*

(1412) **δυναμόω**, ῶ, fut. δυναμώσω [§20.T] *to strengthen, confirm,* Col. 1:11

δύνανται, 3 pers. pl. pres. mid./pass. dep. indic. . . . . δύναμαι *(1410)*

δύνασαι, 2 pers. sg. pres. mid./pass. dep. indic. . . . . id.

δύνασθαι, pres. mid./pass. dep. infin. . . . . id.

δύνασθε, 2 pers. pl. pres. mid./pass. dep. indic. . . . . id.

δυνάστας, acc. pl. m. n. . . . . δυνάστης *(1413)*

(1413) **δυνάστης**, ου, ὁ, nom. sg. m. n. [§2.B.c] *a potentate, sovereign, prince,* Luke 1:52; 1 Tim. 6:15; *a person of rank and authority, a grandee,* Acts 8:27

δυνατά, nom. pl. neut. adj. . . . . δυνατός *(1415)*

δύναται, 3 pers. sg. pres. mid./pass. dep. indic. . . . . δύναμαι *(1410)*

δυνατεῖ, 3 pers. sg. pres. act. indic. . . δυνατέω *(1414)*

(1414) **δυνατέω**, ῶ, fut. δυνατήσω [§16.P] *to be powerful, mighty, to show one's self powerful,* 2 Cor. 13:3, v.r. Rom. 14:4

δυνατοί, nom. pl. m. adj. . . . . δυνατός *(1415)*

δυνατόν, nom. sg. neut. adj. {Rom. 12:18} id.

δυνατόν, acc. sg. neut. adj. {Rom. 9:22} . id.

(1415) **δυνατός**, ή, όν, nom. sg. m. adj. [§7.F.a] *able,*

having power, powerful, mighty; δυνατὸς
εἶναι, *to be able,* i.q. δύνασθαι, Luke 14:31;
Acts 11:17, et al.; ὁ δυνατός, *the Mighty
One, God,* Luke 1:49; τὸ δυνατόν, *power,*
i.q. δύναμις, Rom. 9:22; *valid, powerful,
efficacious,* 2 Cor. 10:4; *distinguished for
rank, authority, or influence,* Acts 25:5;
1 Cor. 1:26; *distinguished for skill or excellence,* Luke 24:19; Acts 7:22; Rom. 15:1;
δυνατόν and δυνατά, *possible, capable of
being done,* Matt. 19:26; 24:24; et al.

δύνη, 2 pers. sg. pres. mid. dep. indic. contr.
for δύνασαι . . . . δύναμαι *(1410)*

δυναθῆτε, 2 pers. pl. aor. pass. dep. subj.
[§37.1] . . . . id.

δυνήσεσθε, 2 pers. pl. fut. mid. dep. indic. id.

δυνήσεται, 3 pers. sg. fut. mid. dep. indic. id.

δυνήσῃ, 2 pers. sg. fut. mid. dep. indic. . . id.

δυνησόμεθα, 1 pers. pl. fut. mid. dep. indic. id.

δυνήσονται, 3 pers. pl. fut. mid. dep. indic. id.

δύνηται, 3 pers. sg. pres. mid./pass. dep. subj. id.

δύνοντος, gen. sg. m. pres. act. part. . . . . δύνω *(1416)*

(1416) **δύνω,** 2 aor. ἔδυν [§31.1.c] *to sink, go down,
set* as the sun, Mark 1:32; Luke 4:40

δύνωνται, 3 pers. pl. pres. mid./pass. dep.
subj. δύναμαι *(1410)*

(1417) **δύο** [§9.I.b] both indecl. and also with dat.
δυσί(ν), *two,* Matt. 6:24; 21:28, 31, et al.
freq.; οἱ δύο, *both,* John 20:4; δύο ἢ τρεῖς,
two or three, some, a few, Matt. 18:20;
from the Hebrew, δύο δύο, *two and two,*
Mark 6:7, i.q. ἀνὰ δύο, Luke 10:1, and
κατὰ δύο, 1 Cor. 14:27

(1418) **δυσ-,** an inseparable particle, conveying the notion of untowardness, as *hard, ill, unlucky,
dangerous,* like the English *un-, mis-;* opp.
to εὖ

δυσβάστακτα, acc. pl. neut.
adj. . . . . δυσβάστακτος *(1419)*

(1419) **δυσβάστακτος,** ον [§7.2] (δυς + βαστάζω)
*difficult or grievous to be borne, oppres-
sive,* Matt. 23:4; Luke 11:46

(1420) **δυσεντερία,** ας, ἡ [§2.B.b; 2.2] (δυς + ἔντε-
ρον, *an intestine*) *a dysentery,* Acts 28:8
δυσεντερίᾳ, dat. sg. f. n. (Acts 28:8, MT &
TR | δυσεντερίῳ, GNT, WH &
NA) . . . . δυσεντερία *(1420)*

(†1420) **δυσεντέριον,** ου, τό, *dysentery*
δυσεντερίῳ, dat. sg. f. n. (Acts 28:8, GNT,
WH & NA | δυσεντερίᾳ, MT &
TR) . . . . δυσεντέριον *(†1420)*

(1421) **δυσερμήνευτος,** ον, nom. sg. m. adj. [§7.2]
(δυς + ἑρμηνεύω) *difficult to be explained,
hard to be understood,* Heb. 5:11

δυσί(ν), dat. pl. m. numeral {Luke 12:52} . δύο *(1417)*

δυσί(ν), dat. pl. f. numeral {Matt. 22:40} . δύο *(1417)*

δύσκολον, nom. sg. neut. adj. . . . . . δύσκολος *(1422)*

(1422) **δύσκολος,** ον [§7.2] (δυς + κόλον, *food*) pr.
*peevish about food; hard to please, dis-
agreeable;* in N.T., *difficult,* Mark 10:24

(1423) **δυσκόλως,** adv., *with difficulty, hardly,* Matt.
19:23; Mark 10:23, et al.

(1424) **δυσμή,** ῆς, ἡ [§2.B.a] *a sinking or setting;* pl.
δυσμαί, *the setting of the sun;* hence, *the
west,* Matt. 8:11; 24:27, et al.

δυσμῶν, gen. pl. f. n. . . . . δυσμή *(1424)*

δυσνόητα, nom. pl. neut. adj. . . . . δυσνόητος *(1425)*

(1425) **δυσνόητος,** ον [§7.2] (δυς + νοητός, from
νοέω) *hard to be understood,* 2 Pet. 3:16

(‡987) **δυσφημέω,** ῶ, fut. δυσφημήσω [§16.P] pr. *to
use ill words; to reproach, revile,* 1 Cor.
4:13

(1426) **δυσφημία,** ας, ἡ [§2.B.b; 2.2] (δυς + φήμη)
*ill words; words of ill omen; reproach, con-
tumely,* 2 Cor. 6:8

δυσφημίας, gen. sg. f. n. . . . . δυσφημία *(1426)*

δυσφημούμενοι, nom. pl. m. pres. pass. part.
(1 Cor. 4:13, GNT, WH & NA |
βλασφημούμενοι, MT & TR) . . δυσφημέω *(‡987)*

δῷ, 3 pers. sg. 2 aor. act. subj. . . . . δίδωμι *(1325)*

(1427) **δώδεκα,** οἱ, αἱ, τά, indecl. numeral (δύο +
δέκα) *twelve,* Matt. 9:20; 10:1, et al.; οἱ
δώδεκα, *the twelve* apostles, Matt.
26:14, 20, et al.

(1428) **δωδέκατος,** η, ον, nom. sg. m. adj. [§7.F.a]
the twelfth, Rev. 21:20

(1429) **δωδεκάφυλον,** ου, τό, nom. sg. neut. n.
[§3.C.c] (δώδεκα + φυλή) *twelve tribes,*
Acts 26:7

δώῃ, 3 pers. sg. 2 aor. act. subj. (Eph. 1:17;
2 Tim. 2:25, GNT & NA | δῴη, WH |
Eph. 1:17, δῴη, MT & TR | 2 Tim. 2:25,
δῷ, MT & TR) . . . . δίδωμι *(1325)*

δῴη, 3 pers. sg. 2 aor. act. opt. [§30.5] . . id.

(1430) **δῶμα,** ατος, τό [§4.D.e] pr. *a house;* synec.
a roof, Matt. 10:27; 24:17, et al.

δῶμα, acc. sg. neut. n. . . . . δῶμα *(1430)*

δώματος, gen. sg. neut. n. . . . . id.

δωμάτων, gen. pl. neut. n. . . . . id.

δῶμεν, 1 pers. pl. 2 aor. act. subj.
[§30.Z] . . . . δίδωμι *(1325)*

δῶρα, nom. pl. neut. n. {Heb. 9:9} . . . δῶρον *(1435)*

δῶρα, acc. pl. neut. n. {Heb. 5:1} . . . . id.

(1431) **δωρεά,** ᾶς, ἡ, nom. sg. f. n. [§2.B.b; 2.2] *a
gift, free gift, benefit,* John 4:10; Acts 2:38,
et al.

δωρεᾷ, dat. sg. f. n. . . . . δωρεά *(1431)*

δωρεάν, acc. sg. f. n. {John 4:10} . . . . id.

(1432) **δωρεάν,** adverbial acc. of δωρεά, *gratis, gra-
tuitously, freely,* Matt. 10:8; Rom. 3:24, et

al.; in N.T. *undeservedly, without cause,* John 15:25; *in vain,* Gal. 2:21 {John 15:25}

δωρεᾶς, gen. sg. f. n. . . . . δωρεά *(1431)*

(1433) **δωρέομαι,** οῦμαι, fut. δωρήσομαι [§17.Q] perf. δεδώρημαι, *to give freely, grant,* Mark 15:45; 2 Pet. 1:3, 4

(1434) **δώρημα,** ατος, τό, nom. sg. neut. n. [§4.D.c] *a gift, free gift,* Rom. 5:16; James 1:17

δώροις, dat. pl. neut. n. . . . . δῶρον *(1435)*

(1435) **δῶρον,** ου, τό, nom. sg. neut. n. [§3.C.c] *a gift, present,* Matt. 2:11; Eph. 2:8; Rev. 11:10; *an offering, sacrifice,* Matt. 5:23, 24; 8:4, et al.; δῶρον, sc. ἐστι(ν), *it is consecrated to God,* Matt. 15:5; Mark 7:11; *contribution* to the temple, Luke 21:1, 4 {Matt. 23:19a}

δῶρον, acc. sg. neut. n. {Matt. 23:19b} δῶρον *(1435)*

δώρῳ, dat. sg. neut. n. . . . . id.

δῷς, 2 pers. sg. 2 aor. act. subj. [§30.Z] . . . . δίδωμι *(1325)*

δώσει, 3 pers. sg. fut. act. indic. . . . . id.

δώσεις, 2 pers. sg. fut. act. indic. . . . . id.

δώσῃ, 3 pers. sg. aor. act. subj. (as if from ἔδωκα for the usual aor. ἔδωκα) . . . . . id.

δῶσι(ν), 3 pers. pl. 2 aor. act. subj. . . . . . id.

δώσομεν, 1 pers. pl. fut. act. indic. (Mark 6:37, GNT, WH & NA | δῶμεν, MT & TR) . . . . id.

δώσουσι(ν), 3 pers. pl. fut. act. indic. . . . . id.

δώσω, 1 pers. sg. fut. act. indic. . . . . id.

δώσωμεν, 1 pers. pl. aor. act. subj. (Rev. 19:7, GNT & NA | δώσομεν, WH | δῶμεν, MT & TR) . . . . id.

δώσωσιν, 3 pers. pl. aor. act. subj. (Rev. 13:16, MT | δῶσι(ν), GNT, WH, TR & NA) id.

δῶτε, 2 pers. pl. 2 aor. act. subj. . . . . id.

Ε

(1436) **ἔα,** interjection, *Ha!* an expression of surprise or displeasure, Matt 1:24; Luke 4:34

(1437) **ἐάν,** conj., *if.* The particulars of the use of ἐάν must be learned from the grammars. Ἐὰν μή, *except, unless;* also equivalent to ἀλλά, Gal. 2:16. Ἐάν, in N.T. as in the later Greek, is substituted for ἄν after relative words, Matt. 5:19, et al. freq.

(†1437) **ἐάνπερ,** a strengthening of ἐάν, by the enclitic particle περ, *if it be that, if at all events,* Heb. 3:6, 14; 6:3

ἐᾷς, 2 pers. sg. pres. act. indic. (Rev. 2:20, TR | ἀφεῖς, GNT, WH, MT & NA) . . . . . ἐάω *(1439)*

ἐάσαντες, nom. pl. m. aor. act. part. . . . . id.

ἐάσατε, 2 pers. pl. aor. act. imper. (Acts 5:38, MT & TR | ἄφετε, GNT, WH & NA) . . . . ἐάω *(1439)*

ἐάσει, 3 pers. sg. fut. act. indic. . . . . id.

ἐᾶτε, 2 pers. pl. pres. act. imper. . . . . id.

ἑαυτά, acc. pl. neut. 3 pers. reflexive pron. . . . . ἑαυτοῦ *(1438)*

ἑαυταῖς, dat. pl. f. 3 pers. reflexive pron. . . id.

ἑαυτάς, acc. pl. f. 3 pers. reflexive pron. . . id.

ἑαυτῇ, dat. sg. f. 3 pers. reflexive pron. . . . id.

ἑαυτήν, acc. sg. f. 3 pers. reflexive pron. . . id.

ἑαυτῆς, gen. sg. f. 3 pers. reflexive pron. . . id.

ἑαυτό, acc. sg. neut. 3 pers. reflexive pron. (Rev. 4:8, with ἓν καθ᾽, TR | καθ᾽ ἓν αὐτῶν, GNT, WH & NA | ἓν καθ᾽ ἕν, MT) . . . . id.

ἑαυτοῖς, dat. pl. m. 3 pers. reflexive pron. id.

ἑαυτόν, acc. sg. m. 3 pers. reflexive pron. . id.

(1438) **ἑαυτοῦ,** ῆς, οῦ, gen. sg. m. 3 pers. reflexive pron., pl. ἑαυτῶν [§11.K.d] *himself, herself, itself,* Matt. 8:22; 12:26; 9:21, et al.; also used for the first and second persons, Rom. 8:23; Matt. 23:31; also equivalent to ἀλλήλων, Mark 10:26; John 12:19; ἀφ᾽ ἑαυτοῦ, ἀφ᾽ ἑαυτῶν, *of himself, themselves, voluntarily, spontaneously,* Luke 12:57; 21:30, et al.; *of one's own will merely,* John 5:19; δι᾽ ἑαυτοῦ, *of itself, in its own nature,* Rom. 14:14; ἐξ ἑαυτῶν, *of one's own self merely,* 2 Cor. 3:5; καθ᾽ ἑαυτόν, *by one's self, alone,* Acts 28:16; James 2:17; παρ᾽ ἑαυτῷ, *with one's self, at home,* 1 Cor. 16:2; πρὸς ἑαυτόν, *to one's self, to one's home,* Luke 24:12; John 20:10; or, *with one's self,* Luke 18:11

ἑαυτούς, acc. pl. m. 3 pers. reflexive pron. . . . . ἑαυτοῦ *(1438)*

ἑαυτῷ, dat. sg. m. 3 pers. reflexive pron. . . id.

ἑαυτῶν, gen. pl. m. 3 pers. reflexive pron. . id.

(1439) **ἐάω,** ῶ, fut. ἐάσω [§22.2] imperf. εἴων, aor. εἴασα [§13.4] *to let, allow, permit, suffer to be done,* Matt. 24:43; Luke 4:41, et al.; *to let be, let alone, desist from,* Luke 22:51; Acts 5:38; *to commit* a ship to the sea, *let her drive,* Acts 27:40

ἐβάθυνε(ν), 3 pers. sg. aor. act. indic. . . βαθύνω *(900)*

ἔβαλαν, 3 pers. pl. 2 aor. act. indic. (Acts 16:37, GNT, WH & NA | ἔβαλον, MT & TR) . . . . βάλλω *(906)*

ἔβαλε(ν), 3 pers. sg. 2 aor. act. indic. [§27.4.b] . . . . id.

ἔβαλλον, 3 pers. pl. imperf. act. indic. . . . id.

ἔβαλον, 3 pers. pl. 2 aor. act. indic. . . . . . id.

ἐβάπτιζεν, 3 pers. sg. imperf. act. indic. . . . . βαπτίζω *(907)*

ἐβαπτίζοντο, 3 pers. pl. imperf. pass.
    indic. . . . . βαπτίζω (907)
ἐβάπτισα, 1 pers. sg. aor. act. indic. . . . . . id.
ἐβαπτίσαντο, 3 pers. pl. aor. mid. indic.
    (1 Cor. 10:2, MT, WH & TR | ἐβαπτί-
    σθησαν, GNT & NA) . . . . id.
ἐβάπτισε(ν), 3 pers. sg. aor. act. indic. . . . id.
ἐβαπτίσθη, 3 pers. sg. aor. pass. indic. [§26.1] id.
ἐβαπτίσθημεν, 1 pers. pl. aor. pass. indic.   id.
ἐβαπτίσθησαν, 3 pers. pl. aor. pass. indic.   id.
ἐβαπτίσθητε, 2 pers. pl. aor. pass. indic. . .   id.
ἐβαρήθημεν, 1 pers. pl. aor. pass. indic. . βαρέω (916)
ἐβασάνιζεν, 3 pers. sg. imperf. act.
    indic. . . . . βασανίζω (928)
ἐβασάνισαν, 3 pers. pl. aor. act. indic. . . . id.
ἐβασίλευσαν, 3 pers. pl. aor. act.
    indic. . . . . βασιλεύω (936)
ἐβασίλευσας, 2 pers. sg. aor. act. indic. . .   id.
ἐβασιλεύσατε, 2 pers. pl. aor. act. indic. . .   id.
ἐβασίλευσε(ν), 3 pers. sg. aor. act. indic. .   id.
ἐβάσκανε(ν), 3 pers. sg. aor. act.
    indic. . . . . βασκαίνω (940)
ἐβάσταζεν, 3 pers. sg. imperf. act.
    indic. . . . . βαστάζω (941)
ἐβαστάζετο, 3 pers. sg. imperf. pass. indic.   id.
ἐβάστασαν, 3 pers. pl. aor. act. indic. . . . .   id.
ἐβάστασας, 2 pers. sg. aor. act. indic. . . .   id.
ἐβάστασεν, 3 pers. sg. aor. act. indic. . . .   id.
ἐβδελυγμένοις, dat. pl. m. perf. pass. part.
    [§26.3] . . . . βδελύσσομαι (†948)
ἐβδόμη, dat. sg. f. adj. . . . . ἕβδομος (1442)
(1440) ἑβδομήκοντα, οἱ, αἱ, τά, indecl. numeral, sev-
    enty, Acts 7:14, et al.; οἱ ἑβδομήκοντα, the
    seventy disciples, Luke 10:1, 17
(†1440) ἑβδομηκονταέξ, indecl. numeral, seventy-six
    (Acts 27:37, TR | ἑβδομήκοντα ἕξ, GNT,
    WH, MT & NA)
(1441) ἑβδομηκοντάκις, adv., seventy times, Matt.
    18:22
ἑβδόμην, acc. sg. f. adj. . . . . ἕβδομος (1442)
ἑβδόμης, gen. sg. f. adj. . . . . id.
(1442) ἕβδομος, η, ον, nom. sg. m. adj. [§7.F.a] sev-
    enth, John 4:52; Heb. 4:4, et al.
ἑβδόμου, gen. sg. m. adj. . . . . ἕβδομος (1442)
ἐβεβαιώθη, 3 pers. sg. aor. pass. indic. βεβαιόω (950)
ἐβέβλητο, 3 pers. sg. pluperf. pass. indic.
    [§13.8.f] . . . . βάλλω (906)
(1443) Ἔβερ, ὁ, Heber, pr. name, indecl. (Luke 3:35,
    GNT, WH, MT, TRs & NA | Ἐβέρ,
    TRb)
ἐβλάστησε(ν), 3 pers. sg. aor. act. indic.
    [§36.2] . . . . βλαστάνω (985)
ἐβλασφήμει, 3 pers. sg. imperf. act.
    indic. . . . . βλασφημέω (987)
ἐβλασφήμησαν, 3 pers. pl. aor. act. indic.   id.

ἐβλασφήμησε(ν), 3 pers. sg. aor. act.
    indic. . . . . βλασφημέω (987)
ἐβλασφήμουν, 3 pers. pl. imperf. act. indic.   id.
ἔβλεπε(ν), 3 pers. sg. imperf. act. indic. . βλέπω (991)
ἔβλεπον, 3 pers. pl. imperf. act. indic. . . .   id.
ἔβλεψα, 1 pers. sg. aor. act. indic. . . . . . .   id.
ἐβλήθη, 3 pers. sg. aor. pass. indic.
    [§27.3] . . . . βάλλω (906)
ἐβλήθησαν, 3 pers. pl. aor. pass. indic. . . .   id.
ἐβοήθησα, 1 pers. sg. aor. act. indic. . . βοηθέω (997)
ἐβοήθησεν, 3 pers. sg. aor. act. indic. . . . .   id.
ἐβόησε(ν), 3 pers. sg. aor. act. indic. . . . . βοάω (994)
ἐβούλετο, 3 pers. sg. imperf. mid./pass. dep.
    indic. (Acts 15:37, GNT, WH & NA |
    ἐβουλεύσατο, MT & TR) . . . . . . βούλομαι (1014)
ἐβουλεύοντο, 3 pers. pl. imperf. mid./pass.
    dep. indic. . . . . βουλεύω (1011)
ἐβουλεύσαντο, 3 pers. pl. aor. mid. dep.
    indic. . . . . id.
ἐβουλεύσατο, 3 pers. sg. aor. mid. dep. indic.
    (Acts 15:37, MT & TR | ἐβούλετο, GNT,
    WH & NA) . . . . id.
ἐβουλήθη, 3 pers. sg. aor. pass. dep.
    indic. . . . . βούλομαι (1014)
ἐβουλήθην, 1 pers. sg. aor. pass. dep. indic.
    (2 John 12, GNT, WH, MT & NA |
    ἠβουλήθην, TR) . . . . id.
ἐβουλόμην, 1 pers. sg. imperf. mid./pass. dep.
    indic. . . . . id.
ἐβούλοντο, 3 pers. pl. imperf. mid./pass. dep.
    indic. . . . . id.
ἐβόων, 3 pers. pl. imperf. act. indic. (Acts
    21:34, MT & TR | ἐπεφώνουν, GNT,
    WH & NA) . . . . βοάω (994)
Ἑβραΐδι, dat. sg. f. n. [§4.2.c] . . . . . . Ἑβραΐς (1446)
Ἑβραϊκοῖς, dat. pl. neut. adj. (Luke 23:38,
    MT & TR | GNT, WH & NA
    omit) . . . . Ἑβραϊκός (1444)
(1444) Ἑβραϊκός, ή, όν [§7.F.a] Hebrew, Luke 23:38
Ἑβραῖοι, nom. pl. m. adj. . . . . Ἑβραῖος (1445)
(1445) Ἑβραῖος, αία, αῖον, nom. sg. m. adj. [§7.1]
    or ου, ὁ, a Hebrew, one descended from
    Abraham the Hebrew, 2 Cor. 11:22; Phil.
    3:5; in N.T., a Jew of Palestine, opp. to
    Ἑλληνιστής, Acts 6:1
Ἑβραίους, acc. pl. m. adj. . . . . Ἑβραῖος (1445)
(1446) Ἑβραΐς, ΐδος, ἡ [§4.2.c] sc. διάλεκτος, the
    Hebrew dialect, i.e., the Hebrew-Aramaic
    dialect of Palestine, Acts 21:40, et al.
(1447) Ἑβραϊστί, adv., in Hebrew, John 5:2; 19:13,
    et al.
Ἑβραίων, gen. pl. m. adj. . . . . Ἑβραῖος (1445)
ἔβρεξε(ν), 3 pers. sg. aor. act. indic. . . . βρέχω (1026)
ἔβρυχον, 3 pers. pl. imperf. act. indic. . βρύχω (1031)
ἐγάμησεν, 3 pers. sg. aor. act. indic. . . . γαμέω (1060)

ἐγαμίζοντο, 3 pers. pl. imperf. pass. indic.
(Luke 17:27, GNT, WH & NA | ἐξεγα-
μίζοντο, MT & TR) . . . . γαμίζω (†1061)

ἐγάμουν, 3 pers. pl. imperf. act. indic. . γαμέω (1060)

ἐγγεγραμμένη, nom. sg. f. perf. pass. part.
[§23.7] . . . . ἐγγράφω (1449)

ἐγγέγραπται, 3 pers. sg. perf. pass. indic.
(Luke 10:20, GNT & NA | ἐγράφη, MT
& TR | ἐνγέγραπται, WH) . . . . id.

ἐγγιεῖ, 3 pers. sg. fut. act. indic. Att. [§35.11]
(James 4:8, GNT, MT, TR & NA |
ἐγγίσει, WH) . . . . ἐγγίζω (1448)

ἐγγίζει, 3 pers. sg. pres. act. indic. . . . . id.
ἐγγίζειν, pres. act. infin. . . . . id.
ἐγγίζομεν, 1 pers. pl. pres. act. indic. . . . . id.
ἐγγίζοντες, nom. pl. m. pres. act. part. . . . id.
ἐγγίζοντι, dat. sg. m. pres. act. part. . . . . . id.
ἐγγίζοντος, gen. sg. m. pres. act. part. . . . id.
ἐγγιζόντων, gen. pl. m. pres. act. part. . . . id.
ἐγγίζουσαν, acc. sg. f. pres. act. part. . . . . id.
ἐγγίζουσιν, 3 pers. pl. pres. act. indic. . . . . id.

(1448) ἐγγίζω, fut. ἐγγίσω, Att. ἐγγιῶ, perf. ἤγγικα,
aor. ἤγγισα [§26.1] pr. to cause to approach; in N.T. intrans. to approach, draw
near, Matt. 21:1; Luke 18:35, et al.; met.
to be at hand, impend, Matt. 3:2; 4:17, et
al.; μέχρι θανάτου ἐγγίζειν, to be at the
point of death, Phil. 2:30; from Hebrew to
draw near to God, to offer Him reverence
and worship, Matt. 15:8; Heb. 7:19; James
4:8; used of God, to draw near to men, assist them, bestow favors on them, James
4:8

ἐγγίσαι, aor. act. infin. . . . . ἐγγίζω (1448)
ἐγγίσαντος, gen. sg. m. aor. act. part. . . . . id.
ἐγγίσας, nom. sg. m. aor. act. part. . . . . . id.
ἐγγίσατε, 2 pers. pl. aor. act. imper. . . . . . id.
ἐγγίσει, 3 pers. sg. fut. act. indic. (James 4:8,
WH | ἐγγιεῖ, GNT, MT, TR & NA) . . id.

(1449) ἐγγράφω, fut. ἐγγράψω [§23.1.a] perf. pass.
ἐγγέγραμμαι [§23.7] (ἐν + γράφω) to engrave, inscribe; met. ἐγγεγραμμένος, imprinted, 2 Cor. 3:2, 3

(1450) ἔγγυος, ον, nom. sg. m. adj. [§7.2] (from
ἐγγύη, a pledge) a surety, sponsor, Heb.
7:22

(1451) ἐγγύς, adv., near, as to place, Luke 19:11, et
al.; close at hand, Rom. 10:8; near, in respect of ready interposition, Phil. 4:5; near,
as to time, Matt. 24:32, 33, et al.; near to
God, as being in covenant with him, Eph.
2:13; οἱ ἐγγύς, the people near to God, the
Jews, Eph. 2:17

(1452) ἐγγύτερον, adv. (pr. neut. of ἐγγύτερος, compar. of ἐγγύς) nearer, Rom. 13:11

ἐγεγόνει, 3 pers. sg. pluperf. act. indic.
[§13.8.f] . . . . γίνομαι (1096)

ἔγειραι, 2 pers. sg. aor. mid. imper. (MT &
TR | ἔγειρε, GNT, WH & NA) . . . . ἐγείρω (1453)

ἐγεῖραι, aor. act. infin. {Matt. 3:9} . . . . . id.
ἐγείραντα, acc. sg. m. aor. act. part. . . . . . id.
ἐγείραντος, gen. sg. m. aor. act. part. . . . . id.
ἐγείρας, nom. sg. m. aor. act. part. . . . . . . id.

ἔγειρε, 2 pers. sg. pres. act. imper. (GNT, WH
& NA | ἔγειραι, MT & TR) . . . . id.

ἐγείρει, 3 pers. sg. pres. act. indic. . . . . . . id.
ἐγείρειν, pres. act. infin. . . . . id.
ἐγείρεσθε, 2 pers. pl. pres. mid./pass. imper. id.
ἐγείρεται, 3 pers. sg. pres. pass. indic. . . . id.
ἐγείρετε, 2 pers. pl. pres. act. imper. . . . . . id.
ἐγείρηται, 3 pers. sg. pres. pass. subj. . . . . id.
ἐγείρομαι, 1 pers. sg. pres. pass. indic. . . . id.
ἐγείρονται, 3 pers. pl. pres. pass. indic. . . id.
ἐγείροντι, dat. sg. m. pres. act. part. . . . . . id.

ἐγείρου, 2 pers. sg. pres. mid./pass. imper.
(Luke 8:54, MT & TR | ἔγειρε, GNT,
WH & NA) . . . . id.

ἐγείρουσιν, 3 pers. pl. pres. act. indic. (Mark
4:38, GNT, WH & NA | διεγείρουσιν,
MT & TR) . . . . id.

(1453) ἐγείρω [§37.1] fut. ἐγερῶ, perf. ἐγήγερκα, aor.
ἤγειρα, perf. pass. ἐγήγερμαι, aor. pass.
ἠγέρθην, to excite, arouse, awaken, Matt.
8:25, et al.; mid. to awake, Matt. 2:13,
20, 21, et al.; met. mid. to rouse one's self
to a better course of conduct, Rom. 13:11;
Eph. 5:14; to raise from the dead, John
12:1, et al.; and mid. to rise from the dead,
Matt. 27:52; John 5:21, et al.; met. to raise
as it were from the dead, 2 Cor. 4:14; to
raise up, cause to rise up from a recumbent posture, Acts 3:7; and mid. to rise up,
Matt. 17:7, et al.; to restore to health,
James 5:15; met. et seq. ἐπί, to excite to
war; mid. to rise up against, Matt. 24:7,
et al.; to raise up again, rebuild, John
2:19, 20; to raise up from a lower place,
to draw up or out of a ditch, Matt. 12:11;
from Hebrew, to raise up, to cause to arise
or exist, Acts 13:22, 23; mid. to arise, exist,
appear, Matt. 3:9; 11:11, et al.

ἐγέμισαν, 3 pers. pl. aor. act. indic. . . . γεμίζω (1072)
ἐγέμισεν, 3 pers. sg. aor. act. indic. . . . . . . id.
ἐγεμίσθη, 3 pers. sg. aor. pass. indic. . . . . . id.

ἐγένεσθε, 2 pers. pl. 2 aor. mid. dep.
indic. . . . . γίνομαι (1096)

ἐγένετο, 3 pers. sg. 2 aor. mid. dep. indic.
[§37.1] . . . . id.

ἐγενήθη, 3 pers. sg. aor. pass. dep. indic. . . id.
ἐγενήθημεν, 1 pers. pl. aor. pass. dep. indic. id.

ἐγενήθην, 1 pers. sg. aor. pass. dep. indic.
(Eph. 3:7, GNT, WH & NA | ἐγενόμην,
MT & TR) . . . . γίνομαι *(1096)*
ἐγενήθησαν, 3 pers. pl. aor. pass. dep. indic. id.
ἐγενήθητε, 2 pers. pl. aor. pass. dep. indic. id.
ἐγεννήθη, 3 pers. sg. aor. pass. indic. . . γεννάω *(1080)*
ἐγεννήθημεν, 1 pers. pl. aor. pass. indic. . . id.
ἐγεννήθης, 2 pers. sg. aor. pass. indic. . . . id.
ἐγεννήθησαν, 3 pers. pl. aor. pass. indic. . id.
ἐγέννησα, 1 pers. sg. aor. act. indic. . . . . id.
ἐγέννησαν, 3 pers. pl. aor. act. indic. . . . id.
ἐγέννησε(ν), 3 pers. sg. aor. act. indic. . . . id.
ἐγενόμην, 1 pers. sg. 2 aor. mid. dep.
indic. . . . . γίνομαι *(1096)*
ἐγένοντο, 3 pers. pl. 2 aor. mid. dep. indic. id.
ἐγένου, 2 pers. sg. 2 aor. mid. dep. indic. id.
ἐγερεῖ, 3 pers. sg. fut. act. indic. [§37.1] ἐγείρω *(1453)*
ἐγερεῖς, 2 pers. sg. fut. act. indic. . . . . . . id.
ἐγερθείς, nom. sg. m. aor. pass. part. . . . . id.
ἐγερθέντι, dat. sg. m. aor. pass. part. . . . . id.
ἐγερθῇ, 3 pers. sg. aor. pass. subj. . . . . id.
ἐγερθῆναι, aor. pass. infin. . . . . id.
ἐγερθήσεται, 3 pers. sg. fut. pass. indic. . . id.
ἐγερθήσονται, 3 pers. pl. fut. pass. indic. . id.
ἐγέρθητε, 2 pers. pl. aor. pass. imper. . . . . id.
ἐγέρθητι, 2 pers. sg. aor. pass. imper. . . . . id.
ἔγερσιν, acc. sg. f. n. . . . . ἔγερσις *(1454)*
(1454) **ἔγερσις**, εως, ἡ [§5.E.c] pr. *the act of waking
or rising up; resurrection, resuscitation,*
Matt. 27:53

ἐγερῶ, 1 pers. sg. fut. act. indic. . . . . . . ἐγείρω *(1453)*
ἐγεύσασθε, 2 pers. pl. aor. mid. dep.
indic. . . . . γεύομαι *(1089)*
ἐγεύσατο, 3 pers. sg. aor. mid. dep. indic.
[§15.O] . . . . id.
ἐγηγερμένον, acc. sg. m. perf. pass.
part. . . . . ἐγείρω *(1453)*
ἐγήγερται, 3 pers. sg. perf. pass. indic. . . . id.
ἔγημα, 1 pers. sg. aor. act. indic.
[§37.2] . . . . γαμέω *(1060)*
ἐγίνετο, 3 pers. sg. imperf. mid./pass. dep.
indic. . . . . γίνομαι *(1096)*
ἐγίνωσκε(ν), 3 pers. sg. imperf. act.
indic. . . . . γινώσκω *(1097)*
ἐγίνωσκον, 3 pers. pl. imperf. act. indic. . id.
(1455) **ἐγκάθετος**, ον [§7.2] (ἐν + καθίημι) *sub-
orned,* Luke 20:20
ἐγκαθέτους, acc. pl. m. adj. (Luke 20:20,
GNT, MT, TR & NA | ἐνκαθέτους,
WH) . . . . ἐγκάθετος *(1455)*
(1456) **ἐγκαίνια**, ίων, τά, nom. pl. neut. n. [§6.5] (ἐν
+ καινός) *initiation, consecration;* in N.T.
the feast of dedication, an annual festival
of eight days in the month Kisleu, John
10:22

(1457) **ἐγκαινίζω**, fut. ἐγκαινίσω [§26.1] aor.
ἐνεκαίνισα, perf. pass. ἐγκεκαίνισμαι, *to
handsel, initiate, consecrate, dedicate, renovate; to institute,* Heb. 9:18; 10:20
ἐγκακεῖν, pres. act. infin. (Luke 18:1; Eph.
3:13, GNT & NA | ἐνκακεῖν, WH |
ἐκκακεῖν, MT & TR) . . . . ἐγκακέω *(‡1573)*
(‡1573) **ἐγκακέω**, ῶ, fut. ἐγκακήσω, probably the
same signif. as ἐκκακέω, *to despond, be
faint-hearted, be remiss*
ἐγκακήσητε, 2 pers. pl. aor. act. subj.
(2 Thess. 3:13, GNT & NA | ἐνκακή-
σητε, WH | ἐκκακήσητε, MT &
TR) . . . . ἐγκακέω *(‡1573)*
ἐγακοῦμεν, 1 pers. pl. pres. act. indic. (2 Cor.
4:1, 16, GNT, WH & NA | ἐκκακοῦμεν,
MT & TR) . . . . id.
ἐγκακῶμεν, 1 pers. pl. pres. act. subj. (Gal.
6:9, GNT & NA | ἐνκακῶμεν, WH |
ἐκκακῶμεν, MT & TR) . . . . id.
ἐγκαλεῖσθαι, pres. pass. infin. . . . . . . ἐγκαλέω *(1458)*
ἐγκαλείτωσαν, 3 pers. pl. pres. act. imper. id.
ἐγκαλέσει, 3 pers. sg. fut. act. indic. . . . . . id.
(1458) **ἐγκαλέω**, ῶ, fut. ἐγκαλέσω [§22.1] (ἐν +
καλέω) *to bring a charge against, accuse;
to institute judicial proceedings,* Acts
19:38, 40; 23:28, 29; 26:2, 7; Rom. 8:33
ἐγκαλοῦμαι, 1 pers. sg. pres. pass. indic.
[§17.Q] . . . . ἐγκαλέω *(1458)*
ἐγκαλούμενον, acc. sg. m. pres. pass. part. id.
ἐγκαταλειπόμενοι, nom. pl. m. pres. pass.
part. ἐγκαταλείπω *(1459)*
ἐγκαταλείποντες, nom. pl. m. pres. act. part. id.
(1459) **ἐγκαταλείπω**, fut. ἐγκαταλείψω [§23.1.a] 2
aor. ἐγκατέλιπον [§24.9] (ἐν +
καταλείπω) *to leave* in a place or situation,
Acts 2:27; *to leave behind; to forsake,
abandon,* Matt. 27:46, et al.; *to leave,* as
a remnant from destruction, Rom. 9:29
ἐγκαταλείπω, 1 pers. sg. pres. act. subj. (Heb.
13:5, MT | ἐγκαταλίπω, GNT, WH, TR
& NA) . . . . ἐγκαταλείπω *(1459)*
ἐγκαταλείψεις, 2 pers. sg. fut. act. indic. . id.
ἐγκαταλίπω, 1 pers. sg. 2 aor. act. subj. (Heb.
13:5, GNT, WH, TR & NA | ἐγκατα-
λείπω, MT) . . . . id.
ἐγκατέλειπεν, 3 pers. sg. imperf. act. indic.
(2 Tim. 4:10, WH | ἐγκατέλιπεν, GNT,
MT, TR & NA) . . . . id.
ἐγκατέλειπον, 3 pers. pl. imperf. act. indic.
(2 Tim. 4:16, WH | ἐγκατέλιπον, GNT,
MT, TR & NA) . . . . id.
ἐγκατελείφθη, 3 pers. sg. aor. pass. indic.
(Acts 2:31, GNT, WH & NA | κατε-
λείφθη, MT & TR) . . . . id.

ἐγκατέλιπεν, 3 pers. sg. 2 aor. act.
  indic. . . . . ἐγκαταλείπω *(1459)*
ἐγκατέλιπες, 2 pers. sg. 2 aor. act. indic. .   id.
ἐγκατέλιπον, 3 pers. pl. 2 aor. act. indic.
  (2 Tim. 4:16, GNT, MT, TR & NA |
  ἐγκατέλειπον, WH) . . . .   id.
(1460) ἐγκατοικέω, ῶ, fut. ἐγκατοικήσω [§16.P] (ἐν
  + κατοικέω) *to dwell in, or among,* 2 Pet.
  2:8
ἐγκατοικῶν, nom. sg. m. pres. act. part.
  (2 Pet. 2:8, GNT, MT, TR & NA |
  ἐνκατοικῶν, WH) . . . . ἐγκατοικέω *(1460)*
(‡2744) ἐγκαυχάομαι, ῶμαι, fut. ἐκαυχήσομαι (ἐν +
  καυχάομαι) *to boast in, or of,* 2 Thess. 1:4
ἐγκαυχᾶσθαι, pres. mid./pass. dep. infin.
  (2 Thess. 1:4, GNT & NA | ἐνκαυχᾶ-
  σθαι, WH | καυχᾶσθαι, MT &
  TR) . . . . ἐγκαυχάομαι *(‡2744)*
ἐγκεκαίνισται, 3 pers. sg. perf. pass. indic.
  (Heb. 9:18, GNT, MT, TR & NA |
  ἐνκεκαίνισται, WH) . . . . ἐγκαινίζω *(1457)*
(1461) ἐγκεντρίζω, fut. ἐγκεντρίσω [§26.1] (ἐν +
  κεντρίζω, *to prick*) *to ingraft;* met. Rom.
  11:17, 19, 23, 24
ἐγκεντρίσαι, aor. act. infin. (Rom. 11:23,
  GNT, MT, TR & NA | ἐνκεντρίσαι,
  WH) . . . . ἐγκεντρίζω *(1461)*
ἐγκεντρισθήσονται, 3 pers. pl. fut. pass. indic.
  (Rom. 11:23, GNT, MT, TR & NA |
  ἐνκεντρισθήσονται, WH) . . . .   id.
ἐγκεντρισθῶ, 1 pers. sg. aor. pass. subj. (Rom.
  11:19, GNT, MT, TR & NA | ἐνκεν-
  τρισθῶ, WH) . . . .   id.
(1462) ἔγκλημα, ατος, τό [§4.D.c] *an accusation,*
  charge, crimination, Acts 23:29; 25:16
ἔγκλημα, acc. sg. neut. n. . . . . ἔγκλημα *(1462)*
ἐγκλήματος, gen. sg. neut. n. . . . .   id.
(1463) ἐγκομβόομαι, οῦμαι, fut. ἐγκομβώσομαι
  [§21.U] (κόμβος, *a string, band;* from
  which ἐγκόμβωμα, *a garment which is*
  fastened by tying) pr. *to put on a garment*
  which is to be tied; in N.T. *to put on, clothe*
  one's self with; met. 1 Pet. 5:5
ἐγκομβώσασθε, 2 pers. pl. aor. mid. dep.
  imper. . . . . ἐγκομβόομαι *(1463)*
(1464) ἐγκοπή, ῆς, ἡ [§2.B.a] pr. *an incision,* e.g. a
  trench, etc., cut in the way of an enemy;
  an impediment, hindrance, 1 Cor. 9:12
ἐγκοπήν, acc. sg. f. n. (1 Cor. 9:12, GNT, MT,
  TR & NA | ἐνκοπήν, WH) . . . . . . ἐγκοπή *(1464)*
ἐγκόπτεσθαι, pres. pass. infin. (1 Pet. 3:7,
  GNT, WH, MT & NA | ἐκκόπτεσθαι,
  TR) . . . . ἐγκόπτω *(1465)*
(1465) ἐγκόπτω, fut. ἐγκόψω [§23.1.a] (ἐν + κόπτω)
  pr. *to cut or strike in;* hence, *to impede,*

interrupt, hinder, Rom. 15:22; 1 Thess.
  2:18; 1 Pet. 3:7; Gal. 5:7
ἐγκόπτω, 1 pers. sg. pres. act. subj. . ἐγκόπτω *(1465)*
(1466) ἐγκράτεια, ας, ἡ, nom. sg. f. n. [§2.B.b; 2.2]
  self-control, continence, temperance, Acts
  24:25, et al.
ἐγκρατείᾳ, dat. sg. f. n. . . . . ἐγκράτεια *(1466)*
ἐγκράτειαν, acc. sg. f. n. . . . .   id.
ἐγκρατείας, gen. sg. f. n. . . . .   id.
ἐγκρατεύεται, 3 pers. sg. pres. mid./pass. dep.
  indic. . . . . ἐγκρατεύομαι *(1467)*
(1467) ἐγκρατεύομαι, fut. ἐγκρατεύσομαι [§14.N] *to*
  possess the power of self-control or con-
  tinence, 1 Cor. 7:9; *to practise abstinence,*
  1 Cor. 9:25
ἐγκρατεύονται, 3 pers. pl. pres. mid./pass.
  dep. indic. . . . . ἐγκρατεύομαι *(1467)*
ἐγκρατῆ, acc. sg. m. adj. . . . . ἐγκρατής *(1468)*
(1468) ἐγκρατής, ές [§7.G.b] (κράτος) *strong, stout;*
  possessed of mastery; master of self, Tit.
  1:8
ἐγκρῖναι, aor. act. infin. (2 Cor. 10:12, GNT,
  MT, TR & NA | ἐνκρῖναι, WH) . ἐγκρίνω *(1469)*
(1469) ἐγκρίνω, fut. ἐγκρινῶ [§27.1.a] (ἐν + κρίνω)
  to judge or reckon among, consider as be-
  longing to, adjudge to the number of, class
  with, place in the same rank, 2 Cor. 10:12
(1470) ἐγκρύπτω, fut. ἐγκρύψω [§23.1.a] (ἐν +
  κρύπτω) *to conceal in* anything; *to mix,*
  intermix, Matt. 13:33; Luke 13:21
(1471) ἔγκυος, ου, ἡ [§3.C.b] (ἐν + κύω) *with child,*
  pregnant, Luke 2:5
ἐγκύῳ, dat. sg. f. n. (Luke 2:5, GNT, MT, TR
  & NA | ἐνκύῳ, WH) . . . . ἔγκυος *(1471)*
ἔγνω, 3 pers. sg. 2 aor. act. indic.
  [§36.3] . . . . γινώσκω *(1097)*
ἔγνωκα, 1 pers. sg. perf. act. indic. . . . . . .   id.
ἐγνώκαμεν, 1 pers. pl. perf. act. indic. . . .   id.
ἔγνωκαν, 3 pers. pl. perf. act. indic. . . .   id.
ἔγνωκας, 2 pers. sg. perf. act. indic. . . .   id.
ἐγνώκατε, 2 pers. pl. perf. act. indic. . . .   id.
ἐγνώκειτε, 2 pers. pl. pluperf. act. indic. .   id.
ἔγνωκε(ν), 3 pers. sg. perf. act. indic. . . .   id.
ἐγνωκέναι, perf. act. infin. (1 Cor. 8:2, GNT,
  WH & NA | εἰδέναι, MT & TR) . . . .   id.
ἐγνωκότες, nom. pl. m. perf. act. part. . . .   id.
ἔγνων, 1 pers. sg. 2 aor. act. indic. . . . . .   id.
ἐγνώρισα, 1 pers. sg. aor. act. indic. . . γνωρίζω *(1107)*
ἐγνωρίσαμεν, 1 pers. pl. aor. act. indic. . . .   id.
ἐγνώρισαν, 3 pers. pl. aor. act. indic. (Luke
  2:17, GNT, WH & NA | διεγνώρισαν,
  MT & TR) . . . .   id.
ἐγνώρισας, 2 pers. sg. aor. act. indic. . . .   id.
ἐγνώρισε(ν), 3 pers. sg. aor. act. indic. . . .   id.
ἐγνωρίσθη, 3 pers. sg. aor. pass. indic. . . .   id.

ἔγνως, 2 pers. sg. 2 aor. act. indic. .. γινώσκω (1097)
ἔγνωσαν, 3 pers. pl. 2 aor. act. indic. .... id.
ἐγνώσθη, 3 pers. sg. aor. pass. indic. [§36.3]   id.
ἔγνωσται, 3 pers. sg. perf. pass. indic. ...   id.
ἐγόγγυζον, 3 pers. pl. imperf. act.
    indic. .... γογγύζω (1111)
ἐγόγγυσαν, 3 pers. pl. aor. act. indic. ...   id.
ἔγραφεν, 3 pers. sg. imperf. act. indic. . γράφω (1125)
ἐγράφη, 3 pers. sg. 2 aor. pass. indic. [§24.6]   id.
ἔγραψα, 1 pers. sg. aor. act. indic. ......   id.
ἔγραψαν, 3 pers. pl. aor. act. indic. ......   id.
ἐγράψατε, 2 pers. pl. aor. act. indic. .....   id.
ἔγραψε(ν), 3 pers. sg. aor. act. indic. ....   id.
ἐγρηγόρησεν, 3 pers. sg. aor. act.
    indic. .... γρηγορέω (1127)
ἐγχρῖσαι, aor. act. infin. (Rev. 3:18, GNT, WH
    & NA | ἐγχρίσῃ, MT | ἔγχρισον,
    TR) .... ἐγχρίω (1472)
ἐγχρίσῃ, 3 pers. sg. aor. act. subj. (Rev. 3:18,
    MT | ἐγχρῖσαι, GNT, WH & NA | ἔγχρι-
    σον, TR) ....   id.
ἔγχρισον, 2 pers. sg. aor. act. imper. (Rev.
    3:18, TR | ἐγχρῖσαι, GNT, WH & NA |
    ἐγχρίσῃ, MT) ....   id.
(1472) ἐγχρίω, fut. ἐγχρίσω [§13.M] (ἐν + χρίω) to
    rub in, anoint, Rev. 3:18
(1473) ἐγώ, 1 pers. sg. personal pron., gen. ἐμοῦ and
    μου [§11.K.a] I
ἐδάκρυσεν, 3 pers. sg. aor. act. indic. . δακρύω (1145)
(1474) ἐδαφίζω, fut. ἐδαφίσω, Att. ἐδαφιῶ [§26.1]
    pr. to form a level and firm surface; to level
    with the ground, overthrow, raze, destroy,
    Luke 19:44
ἐδαφιοῦσι(ν), 3 pers. pl. fut. act. indic. Att.
    [§35.11] .... ἐδαφίζω (1474)
(1475) ἔδαφος, ους, τό [§5.E.b] pr. a bottom, base;
    hence, the ground, Acts 22:7
ἔδαφος, acc. sg. neut. n. .... ἔδαφος (1475)
ἐδέετο, 3 pers. sg. imperf. mid./pass. dep.
    indic. (Luke 8:38, MT & TR | ἐδεῖτο,
    GNT, WH & NA) .... δέομαι (1189)
ἐδεήθη, 3 pers. sg. aor. pass. indic. [§37.1]   id.
ἐδεήθην, 1 pers. sg. aor. pass. indic. .....   id.
ἔδει, 3 pers. sg. imperf. indic. of δεῖ, impers.
    [§37.1] .... δεῖ (1163)
ἐδειγμάτισεν, 3 pers. sg. aor. act.
    indic. .... δειγματίζω (1165)
ἔδειξα, 1 pers. sg. aor. act. indic. .. δείκνυμι (†1166)
ἔδειξε(ν), 3 pers. sg. aor. act. indic. [§31.BB]   id.
ἔδειραν, 3 pers. pl. aor. act. indic.
    [§27.1.d] .... δέρω (1194)
ἐδεῖτο, 3 pers. sg. imperf. mid./pass. dep.
    indic. (Luke 8:38, GNT, WH & NA |
    ἐδέετο, MT & TR) .... δέομαι (1189)
ἐδεξάμεθα, 1 pers. pl. aor. mid. dep.

indic. .... δέχομαι (1209)
ἐδέξαντο, 3 pers. pl. aor. mid. dep. indic. .   id.
ἐδέξασθε, 2 pers. pl. aor. mid. dep. indic. .   id.
ἐδέξατο, 3 pers. sg. aor. mid. dep. indic. .   id.
ἐδεσμεῖτο, 3 pers. sg. imperf. pass. indic.
    [§17.Q] (Luke 8:29, MT & TR | ἐδε-
    σμεύετο, GNT, WH & NA) ..... δεσμέω (1196)
ἐδεσμεύετο, 3 pers. sg. imperf. pass. indic.
    (Luke 8:29, GNT, WH & NA | ἐδεσμεῖτο,
    MT & TR) .... δεσμεύω (1195)
ἐδήλου, 3 pers. sg. imperf. act. indic. .. δηλόω (1213)
ἐδηλώθη, 3 pers. sg. aor. pass. indic. [§21.U]   id.
ἐδήλωσε(ν), 3 pers. sg. aor. act. indic. ...   id.
ἐδημηγόρει, 3 pers. sg. imperf. act.
    indic. .... δημηγορέω (1215)
ἔδησαν, 3 pers. pl. aor. act. indic. .... δέω (1210)
ἔδησεν, 3 pers. sg. aor. act. indic. ....   id.
ἐδίδαξα, 1 pers. sg. aor. act. indic. .. διδάσκω (1321)
ἐδίδαξαν, 3 pers. pl. aor. act. indic. .....   id.
ἐδίδαξας, 2 pers. sg. aor. act. indic. .....   id.
ἐδίδαξε(ν), 3 pers. sg. aor. act. indic. ....   id.
ἐδίδασκε(ν), 3 pers. sg. imperf. act. indic.   id.
ἐδίδασκον, 3 pers. pl. imperf. act. indic. .   id.
ἐδιδάχθην, 1 pers. sg. aor. pass. indic. ..   id.
ἐδιδάχθησαν, 3 pers. pl. aor. pass. indic.
    [§23.4] ....   id.
ἐδιδάχθητε, 2 pers. pl. aor. pass. indic. ...   id.
ἐδίδοσαν, 3 pers. pl. imperf. act. indic. (John
    19:3, GNT, WH & NA | ἐδίδουν, MT &
    TR) .... δίδωμι (1325)
ἐδίδου, 3 pers. sg. imperf. act. indic. ....   id.
ἐδίδουν, 3 pers. pl. imperf. act. indic. [§31.1]   id.
ἐδικαιώθη, 3 pers. sg. aor. pass. indic. δικαιόω (1344)
ἐδικαιώθητε, 2 pers. pl. aor. pass. indic. ...   id.
ἐδικαίωσαν, 3 pers. pl. aor. act. indic. ...   id.
ἐδικαίωσε(ν), 3 pers. sg. aor. act. indic. ..   id.
ἐδίστασαν, 3 pers. pl. aor. act. indic. . διστάζω (1365)
ἐδίστασας, 2 pers. sg. aor. act. indic. ....   id.
ἐδίψησα, 1 pers. sg. aor. act. indic. .... διψάω (1372)
ἐδίωκε(ν), 3 pers. sg. imperf. act. indic. διώκω (1377)
ἐδίωκον, 1 pers. sg. imperf. act. indic.
    {Acts 26:11} ....   id.
ἐδίωκον, 3 pers. pl. imperf. act. indic.
    {John 5:16} ....   id.
ἐδίωξα, 1 pers. sg. aor. act. indic. ......   id.
ἐδίωξαν, 3 pers. pl. aor. act. indic. ......   id.
ἐδίωξε(ν), 3 pers. sg. aor. act. indic. ....   id.
ἐδόθη, 3 pers. sg. aor. pass. indic.
    [§30.4] .... δίδωμι (1325)
ἐδόθησαν, 3 pers. pl. aor. pass. indic. ...   id.
ἐδόκει, 3 pers. sg. imperf. act. indic. .. δοκέω (1380)
ἐδοκιμάσαμεν, 1 pers. pl. aor. act.
    indic. .... δοκιμάζω (1381)
ἐδοκίμασαν, 3 pers. pl. aor. act. indic. ...   id.
ἐδόκουν, 3 pers. pl. imperf. act. indic. . δοκέω (1380)

ἐδολιοῦσαν, 3 pers. pl. imperf. act. indic.
[§35.13] . . . . δολιόω *(1387)*
ἔδοξα, 1 pers. sg. aor. act. indic.
[§37.2] . . . . δοκέω *(1380)*
ἐδόξαζε(ν), 3 pers. sg. imperf. act.
indic. . . . . δοξάζω *(1392)*
ἐδόξαζον, 3 pers. pl. imperf. act. indic. . . id.
ἔδοξαν, 3 pers. pl. aor. act. indic. . . . . . δοκέω *(1380)*
ἐδόξασα, 1 pers. sg. aor. act. indic. . . δοξάζω *(1392)*
ἐδόξασαν, 3 pers. pl. aor. act. indic. . . . . . id.
ἐδόξασε(ν), 3 pers. sg. aor. act. indic. . . . . id.
ἐδοξάσθη, 3 pers. sg. aor. pass. indic. . . . . id.
ἔδοξε(ν), 3 pers. sg. aor. act. indic. . . . . δοκέω *(1380)*
ἐδουλεύσατε, 2 pers. pl. aor. act.
indic. . . . . δουλεύω *(1398)*
ἐδούλευσεν, 3 pers. sg. aor. act. indic. . . . id.
ἐδουλώθητε, 2 pers. pl. aor. pass.
indic. . . . . δουλόω *(1402)*
ἐδούλωσα, 1 pers. sg. aor. act. indic. . . . . id.
ἑδραῖοι, nom. pl. m. adj. . . . . ἑδραῖος *(1476)*
(1476) **ἑδραῖος**, αία, αῖον, nom. sg. m. adj. [§7.1]
(ἕδρα, *a seat*) *sedentary*; met. *settled,*
steady, firm, steadfast, constant, 1 Cor.
7:37; 15:58; Col. 1:23
(1477) **ἑδραίωμα**, ατος, τό, nom. sg. neut. n. [§4.D.c]
(ἑδραιόω, *to settle,* from preceding) *a ba-*
sis, foundation, 1 Tim. 3:15
ἔδραμε(ν), 3 pers. sg. 2 aor. act. indic.
[§36.1] . . . . τρέχω *(5143)*
ἔδραμον, 1 pers. sg. 2 aor. act. indic.
{Phil. 2:16} . . . . id.
ἔδραμον, 3 pers. pl. 2 aor. act. indic.
{Matt. 28:8} . . . . id.
ἔδυ, 3 pers. sg. 2 aor. act. indic. [§31.1.c] (Mark
1:32, GNT, MT, TR & NA | ἔδυσεν,
WH) . . . . δύνω *(1416)*
ἐδυναμώθησαν, 3 pers. pl. aor. pass. indic.
(Heb. 11:34, GNT, WH & NA |
ἐνεδυναμώθησαν, MT & TR) . . . δυναμόω *(1412)*
ἐδύναντο, 3 pers. pl. imperf. mid./pass. dep.
indic. (Mark 4:33, MT | ἠδύνατο, GNT,
WH, TR & NA) . . . . δύναμαι *(1410)*
ἐδύνασθε, 2 pers. pl. imperf. mid./pass. dep.
indic. (1 Cor. 3:2, GNT, WH, MT & NA
| ἠδύνασθε, TR) . . . . id.
ἐδύνατο, 3 pers. sg. imperf. mid./pass. dep.
indic. . . . . id.
ἔδυσεν, 3 pers. sg. aor. act. indic. (Mark 1:32,
WH | ἔδυ, GNT, MT, TR & NA) . . . δύνω *(1416)*
ἔδωκα, 1 pers. sg. aor. act. indic.
[§29.9.c] . . . . δίδωμι *(1325)*
ἐδώκαμεν, 1 pers. pl. aor. act. indic. . . . . id.
ἔδωκαν, 3 pers. pl. aor. act. indic. . . . . . . id.
ἔδωκας, 2 pers. sg. aor. act. indic. . . . . . . id.
ἐδώκατε, 2 pers. pl. aor. act. indic. . . . . . . id.

ἔδωκε(ν), 3 pers. sg. aor. act. indic. . . . δίδωμι *(1325)*
ἐδωρήσατο, 3 pers. sg. aor. mid. dep.
indic. . . . . δωρέομαι *(1433)*
Ἐζεκίαν, acc. sg. m. n. (Matt. 1:9, TR |
Ἐζεκίαν, GNT, MT, WH & NA) Ἐζεκίας *(1478)*
(1478) **Ἐζεκίας**, ου, ὁ, nom. sg. m. n. [§2.B.d] *Eze-*
kias, pr. name (Matt. 1:10, TR | Ἐζεκίας,
GNT, MT, WH & NA)
ἐζημιώθην, 1 pers. sg. aor. pass. indic. . ζημιόω *(2210)*
ἔζησα, 1 pers. sg. aor. act. indic. . . . . ζάω *(2198)*
ἔζησαν, 3 pers. pl. aor. act. indic. . . . . . . id.
ἔζησε(ν), 3 pers. sg. aor. act. indic. . . . . . . id.
ἐζῆτε, 2 pers. pl. imperf. act. indic. [§35.2] id.
ἐζήτει, 3 pers. sg. imperf. act. indic. . . . ζητέω *(2212)*
ἐζητεῖτε, 2 pers. pl. imperf. act. indic. . . . . id.
ἐζητεῖτο, 3 pers. sg. imperf. pass. indic. . . id.
ἐζητήσαμεν, 1 pers. pl. aor. act. indic. . . . id.
ἐζήτησαν, 3 pers. pl. aor. act. indic. . . . . . id.
ἐζήτησε(ν), 3 pers. sg. aor. act. indic. . . . . id.
ἐζητοῦμεν, 1 pers. pl. imperf. act. indic. (Luke
2:48, GNT, MT, TR & NA | ζητοῦμεν,
WH) . . . . id.
ἐζήτουν, 3 pers. pl. imperf. act. indic. . . . . id.
ἐζυμώθη, 3 pers. sg. aor. pass. indic. . . ζυμόω *(2220)*
ἐζωγρημένοι, nom. pl. m. perf. pass.
part. . . . . ζωγρέω *(2221)*
ἔζων, 1 pers. sg. imperf. act. indic. . . . . . ζάω *(2198)*
ἐζώννυες, 2 pers. sg. imperf. act.
indic. . . . . ζωννύω *(2224)*
ἐθαμβήθησαν, 3 pers. pl. aor. pass.
indic. . . . . θαμβέω *(2284)*
ἐθαμβοῦντο, 3 pers. pl. imperf. pass. indic. . id.
ἐθανατώθητε, 2 pers. pl. aor. pass.
indic. . . . . θανατόω *(2289)*
ἐθαύμαζε(ν), 3 pers. sg. imperf. act.
indic. . . . . θαυμάζω *(2296)*
ἐθαύμαζον, 3 pers. pl. imperf. act. indic. . . id.
ἐθαύμασα, 1 pers. sg. aor. act. indic. . . . . id.
ἐθαύμασαν, 3 pers. pl. aor. act. indic. . . . . id.
ἐθαύμασας, 2 pers. sg. aor. act. indic. . . . . id.
ἐθαύμασε(ν), 3 pers. sg. aor. act. indic. . . . id.
ἐθαυμάσθη, 3 pers. sg. aor. pass. indic. (Rev.
13:3, GNT, WH, MT & NA | ἐθαύμασεν,
TR) . . . . id.
ἔθαψαν, 3 pers. pl. aor. act. indic. . . . . θάπτω *(2290)*
ἐθεάθη, 3 pers. sg. aor. pass. indic. . . θεάομαι *(2300)*
ἐθεασάμεθα, 1 pers. pl. aor. mid. dep. indic. id.
ἐθεάσαντο, 3 pers. pl. aor. mid. dep. indic. id.
ἐθεάσασθε, 2 pers. pl. aor. mid. dep. indic. id.
ἐθεάσατο, 3 pers. sg. aor. mid. dep. indic. id.
ἔθει, dat. sg. neut. n. . . . . ἔθος *(1485)*
(†1479) **ἐθελοθρησκεία**, ας, ἡ [§2.B.b; 2.2] (ἐθέλω +
θρησκεία) *self-devised worship, supererog-*
atory worship, will-worship, Col. 2:23
ἐθελοθρησκείᾳ, dat. sg. f. n. (Col. 2:23, MT

& TR | ἐθελοθρησκίᾳ, GNT, WH &
NA) . . . . ἐθελοθρησκεία (†1479)

(1479) **ἐθελοθρησκία**, ας, ἡ, *self-made religion*, Col.
2:23

ἐθελοθρησκίᾳ, dat. sg. f. n. (Col. 2:23, GNT,
WH & NA | ἐθελοθρησκεία, MT &
TR) . . . . ἐθελοθρησκία (1479)

(‡2309) **ἐθέλω**, see θέλω (2309)

ἐθεμελίωσας, 2 pers. sg. aor. act.
indic. θεμελιόω (2311)

ἔθεντο, 3 pers. pl. 2 aor. mid. indic.
[§28.W] . . . . τίθημι (5087)

ἐθεράπευεν, 3 pers. sg. imperf. act. indic.
(Luke 4:40, GNT, WH & NA | ἐθερά-
πευσεν, MT & TR) . . . . θεραπεύω (2323)

ἐθεραπεύθη, 3 pers. sg. aor. pass. indic. . . id.

ἐθεραπεύθησαν, 3 pers. pl. aor. pass. indic. id.

ἐθεράπευον, 3 pers. pl. imperf. act. indic. . id.

ἐθεραπεύοντο, 3 pers. pl. imperf. pass. indic. id.

ἐθεράπευσε(ν), 3 pers. sg. aor. act. indic. . id.

ἐθερίσθη, 3 pers. sg. aor. pass. indic. . . θερίζω (2325)

ἐθερμαίνοντο, 3 pers. pl. imperf. mid./pass.
dep. indic. . . . . θερμαίνω (2328)

ἔθεσθε, 2 pers. pl. 2 aor. mid. indic. . . . τίθημι (5087)

ἔθεσι(ν), dat. pl. neut. n. . . . . ἔθος (1485)

ἔθετο, 3 pers. sg. 2 aor. mid. indic.
[§28.8.d] . . . . τίθημι (5087)

ἐθεώρει, 3 pers. sg. imperf. act. indic. . θεωρέω (2334)

ἐθεώρησαν, 3 pers. pl. aor. act. indic. . . . id.

ἐθεώρουν, 1 pers. pl. imperf. act. indic.
{Luke 10:18} . . . . id.

ἐθεώρουν, 3 pers. pl. imperf. act. indic.
{John 6:2} . . . . id.

ἔθη, acc. pl. neut. n. . . . . ἔθος (1485)

ἔθηκα, 1 pers. sg. aor. act. indic.
[§28.9.b] . . . . τίθημι (5087)

ἔθηκαν, 3 pers. pl. aor. act. indic. . . . . id.

ἔθηκας, 2 pers. sg. aor. act. indic. . . . . id.

ἔθηκε(ν), 3 pers. sg. aor. act. indic. . . . . . . id.

ἐθήλασαν, 3 pers. pl. aor. act. indic. (Luke
23:29, MT & TR | ἔθρεψαν, GNT, WH
& NA) . . . . θηλάζω (2337)

ἐθήλασας, 2 pers. sg. aor. act. indic. . . . . . id.

ἐθηριομάχησα, 1 pers. sg. aor. act.
indic. . . . . θηριομαχέω (2341)

ἐθησαυρίσατε, 2 pers. pl. aor. act.
indic. . . . . θησαυρίζω (2343)

(1480) **ἐθίζω**, fut. ἐθίσω, perf. pass. εἴθισμαι [§13.4]
to accustom; pass. *to be customary,* Luke
2:27

(1481) **ἐθνάρχης**, ου, ὁ, nom. sg. m. n. [§2.B.c]
(ἔθνος + ἄρχω) *a governor, chief, or head
of any tribe or nation, prefect,* 2 Cor. 11:32

ἔθνει, dat. sg. neut. n. . . . . ἔθνος (1484)

ἔθνεσι(ν), dat. pl. neut. n. . . . . id.

ἔθνη, nom. pl. neut. n. {Acts 13:48} . . . . ἔθνος (1484)

ἔθνη, acc. pl. neut. n. {Acts 13:46} . . . . . . id.

ἔθνη, voc. pl. neut. n. {Rom. 15:10, 11} . . . id.

ἐθνικοί, nom. pl. m. adj. . . . . ἐθνικός (1482)

(1482) **ἐθνικός**, ή, όν, nom. sg. m. adj. [§7.F.a] *na-
tional;* in N.T. *Gentile, heathen, not Israelites,* Matt. 6:7; 18:17

ἐθνικῶν, gen. pl. m. adj. (3 John 7, GNT, WH
& NA | ἐθνῶν, MT & TR) . . . . . ἐθνικός (1482)

(1483) **ἐθνικῶς**, adv., *after the manner of the Gentiles, heathenishly,* Gal. 2:14

(1484) **ἔθνος**, ους, τό, nom. sg. neut. n. [§5.E.b] *a
multitude, company,* Acts 17:26; 1 Pet. 2:9;
Rev. 21:24; *a nation, people,* Matt. 20:25;
21:43; et al.; pl. ἔθνη, from the Hebrew,
nations or people as distinguished from the
Jews, *the heathen, Gentiles,* Matt. 4:15;
10:5; Luke 2:32, et al. {Matt. 24:7a}

ἔθνος, acc. sg. neut. n. {Matt. 24:7b} . . ἔθνος (1484)

ἔθνους, gen. sg. neut. n. . . . . id.

ἐθνῶν, gen. pl. neut. n. . . . . id.

ἐθορύβουν, 3 pers. pl. imperf. act.
indic. θορυβέω (2350)

(1485) **ἔθος**, ους, τό, nom. sg. neut. n. [§5.E.b] *a custom, usage,* Luke 2:42; 22:39, et al.; *an institute, rite,* Luke 1:9; Acts 6:14; 15:1, et al.
{John 19:40}

ἔθος, acc. sg. neut. n. {Luke 1:9} . . . . ἔθος (1485)

ἔθου, 2 pers. sg. 2 aor. mid. indic.
[§28.8.a] . . . . τίθημι (5087)

ἐθρέψαμεν, 1 pers. pl. aor. act. indic. . . τρέφω (5142)

ἔθρεψαν, 3 pers. pl. aor. act. indic. (Luke
23:29, GNT, WH & NA | ἐθήλασαν, MT
& TR) . . . . id.

ἐθρέψατε, 2 pers. pl. aor. act. indic. . . . . . id.

ἐθρηνήσαμεν, 1 pers. pl. aor. act.
indic. θρηνέω (2354)

ἐθρήνουν, 3 pers. pl. imperf. act. indic. . . . id.

ἐθύθη, 3 pers. sg. aor. pass. indic. (1 Cor 5:7,
TRb | ἐτύθη, GNT, WH, MT, TRs &
NA) . . . . θύω (2380)

ἐθυμώθη, 3 pers. sg. aor. pass. indic. . . θυμόω (2373)

ἔθυον, 3 pers. pl. imperf. act. indic. . . . . . θύω (2380)

ἔθυσας, 2 pers. sg. aor. act. indic. . . . . id.

ἔθυσεν, 3 pers. sg. aor. act. indic. . . . . id.

ἐθῶν, gen. pl. neut. n. . . . . ἔθος (1485)

(1487) **εἰ**, conj., *if,* Matt. 4:3, 6; 12:7; Acts 27:39, et
al. freq.; *since,* Acts 4:9, et al.; *whether,*
Mark 9:23; Acts 17:11, et al.; *that,* in certain expressions, Acts 26:8, 23; Heb. 7:15;
by a suppression of the apodosis of a sentence, εἰ serves to express a wish; *O if! O
that!* Luke 19:42; 22:42; also a strong negation, Mark 8:12; Heb. 3:11; 4:3; εἰ καί,
if even, though, although, Luke 18:4, et al.;

εἰ μή, *unless, except,* Matt. 11:27, et al.;
also equivalent to ἀλλά, *but,* Matt. 12:4;
Mark 13:32; Luke 4:26, 27; εἰ μήτι, *unless perhaps, unless it be,* Luke 9:13, et al.;
εἴ τις, εἴ τι, pr. *if any one; whosoever,
whatsoever,* Matt. 18:28, et al. The syn-
tax of this particle must be learned from
the grammars. As an interrogative particle, *whether,* Acts 17:11, et al.; in N.T. as
a mere note of interrogation, Luke 22:49,
et al. {John 1:25}

(‡1536) εἴ, before enclitic, εἴ τις {2 John 10}

(1488) εἴ, 2 pers. sg. pres. indic. [§12.1]
{John 1:25} . . . . εἰμί (1510)

εἴα, 3 pers. sg. imperf. act. indic. [§13.4] . ἐάω (1439)

εἴασαν, 3 pers. pl. aor. act. indic. . . . . id.

εἴασε(ν), 3 pers. sg. aor. act. indic. . . . . . . id.

(1489) εἴγε, see γε (1065) (Eph. 3:2; 4:21; Col. 1:23,
TR | εἴ γε, GNT, WH, MT & NA)

εἴδαμεν, 1 pers. pl. 2 aor. act. indic. (Matt.
25:37, 38, WH and Acts 4:20, GNT, WH
& NA | εἴδομεν, Matt. 25:37, 38, GNT,
MT, TR & NA and Acts 4:20, MT &
TR) . . . . εἶδον (‡3708)

εἴδαν, 3 pers. pl. for εἶδον [§35.12] (Matt.
13:17; Luke 10:24; John 1:39; Acts 9:35;
12:16, GNT, WH & NA | εἶδον, MT &
TR) . . . . id.

(‡2397) εἰδέα, ας, ἡ, nom. sg. f. n., *appearance, face*
(Matt. 28:3, GNT, WH & NA | ἰδέα, MT
& TR)

εἴδει, dat. sg. neut. n. . . . . εἶδος (1491)

(1490) εἰ δὲ μή(γε), particles, *if not, otherwise*

εἶδε(ν), 3 pers. sg. 2 aor. act. indic.
[§36.1] . . . . εἶδον (‡3708)

εἰδέναι, perf. act. infin. [§37.1] . . . . οἶδα (‡1492)

εἶδες, 2 pers. sg. 2 aor. act. indic. . . . . . εἶδον (‡3708)

εἴδετε, 2 pers. pl. 2 aor. act. indic. . . . . . . id.

εἰδῆς, 2 pers. sg. perf. act. subj. [§37.1] . οἶδα (‡1492)

εἰδήσουσι(ν), 3 pers. pl. fut. act. indic. . . . id.

εἰδῆτε, 2 pers. pl. perf. act. subj. . . . . id.

εἴδομεν, 1 pers. pl. 2 aor. act. indic. . . . εἶδον (‡3708)

(‡3708) εἶδον, 1 pers. sg. 2 aor. act. indic. (used as the
2 aor. of ὁράω) imper. ἰδέ and ἔδε, opt.
ἴδοιμι, subj. ἴδω, infin. ἰδεῖν, part. ἰδών
[§36.1] of perception by sight, *see, percieve*
{John 18:26}

εἶδον, 3 pers. pl. 2 aor. act. indic. {John
19:33} . . . . εἶδον (‡3708)

(1491) εἶδος, ους, τό, nom. sg. neut. n. [§5.E.b]
(εἴδω, a form not in use, *to see*) *form, external appearance,* Luke 3:22; 9:29; John
5:37; *kind, species,* 1 Thess. 5:22; *sight,
perception,* 2 Cor. 5:7 {Luke 9:29}

εἴδος, acc. sg. neut. n. {John 5:37} . . . . . εἶδος (1491)

εἰδόσι(ν), dat. pl. m. perf. act. part.
[§37.1] . . . . οἶδα (‡1492)

εἰδότα, nom. pl. neut. perf. act. part. . . . . id.

εἰδότας, acc. pl. m. perf. act. part. . . . . . . id.

εἰδότες, nom. pl. m. perf. act. part. . . . . . id.

εἰδότι, dat. sg. m. perf. act. part. . . . . id.

εἴδους, gen. sg. neut. n. . . . . εἶδος (1491)

εἰδυῖα, nom. sg. f. perf. act. part. . . . . . . οἶδα (‡1492)

(1492) εἰδῶ, 1 pers. sg. perf. act. subj. . . . . id.

εἴδωλα, acc. pl. neut. n. . . . . εἴδωλον (1497)

(1493) εἰδωλεῖον, ου, τό [§3.C.c] *a heathen temple,*
1 Cor. 8:10

εἰδωλείῳ, dat. sg. neut. n. (1 Cor. 8:10, GNT,
MT, TR & NA | εἰδωλίῳ, WH) . εἰδωλεῖον (1493)

εἰδωλόθυτα, acc. pl. neut. adj. . . εἰδωλόθυτος (†1494)

εἰδωλόθυτον, nom. sg. neut. adj. {1 Cor.
10:19} . . . . id.

(1494) εἰδωλόθυτον, acc. sg. neut. adj. {1 Cor. 8:7} id.

(†1494) εἰδωλόθυτος, ον [§7.2] (εἴδωλον + θύω) pr.
sacrificed to an idol; meton. *the remains
of victims sacrificed to idols,* reserved for
eating, Acts 15:29; 21:25, et al.

εἰδωλοθύτων, gen. pl. neut. adj. εἰδωλόθυτος (†1494)

εἰδωλολάτραι, nom. pl. m. n. . . εἰδωλολάτρης (1496)

εἰδωλολάτραις, dat. pl. m. n. . . . . id.

(†1495) εἰδωλολατρεία, ας, ἡ, nom. sg. f. n. [§2.B.b;
2.2] (εἴδωλον + λατρεία) *idolatry, worship of idols,* 1 Cor. 10:14; Gal. 5:20, et
al. (Gal. 5:20; Col. 3:5, MT & TR |
εἰδωλολατρία, GNT, WH & NA)

εἰδωλολατρείαις, dat. pl. f. n. (1 Pet. 4:3, MT
& TR | εἰδωλολατρίαις, GNT, WH &
NA) . . . . εἰδωλολατρία (‡1495)

εἰδωλολατρείας, gen. sg. f. n. (1 Cor. 10:14,
MT & TR | εἰδωλολατρίας, GNT, WH
& NA) . . . . id.

(1496) εἰδωλολάτρης, ου, ὁ, nom. sg. m. n. [§2.B.c]
(εἴδωλον + λάτρις, *a servant, worshipper*) *an idolater, worshipper of idols,* 1 Cor.
5:10, 11; 6:9; 10:7, et al.

(‡1495) εἰδωλολατρία, ας, ἡ, nom. sg. f. n. *idolatry,
worship of idols* (Gal. 5:20; Col. 3:5,
GNT, WH & NA | εἰδωλολατρεία, MT
& TR)

εἰδωλολατρίαις, dat. pl. f. n. (1 Pet. 4:3, GNT,
WH & NA | εἰδωλολατρείαις, MT &
TR) . . . . εἰδωλολατρεία (†1495)

εἰδωλολατρίας, gen. sg. f. n. (1 Cor. 10:14,
GNT, WH & NA | εἰδωλολατρείας, MT
& TR) . . . . id.

(1497) εἴδωλον, ου, τό, nom. sg. neut. n. [§3.C.c] pr.
a form, shape, figure; image or statue;
hence, *an idol, image of a god,* Acts 7:41,
et al.; meton. *a heathen god,* 1 Cor. 8:4, 7,
et al.; for εἰδωλόθυτον, *the flesh of victims*

sacrificed to idols, Acts 15:20

εἰδώλου, gen. sg. neut. n. . . . . εἴδωλον *(1497)*

εἰδώλῳ, dat. sg. neut. n. . . . . id.

εἰδώλων, gen. pl. neut. n. . . . . id.

εἴδωμεν, 1 pers. pl. perf. act. subj. . . . . . οἶδα *(‡1492)*

εἰδώς, nom. sg. m. perf. act. part. . . . . id.

εἴη, 3 pers. sg. pres. opt. . . . . εἰμί *(1510)*

(†1498) εἴης, 2 pers. sg. pres. opt. (Rev. 3:15, TR | ἧς, GNT, WH, MT & NA) . . . . id.

εἰθισμένον, acc. sg. neut. perf. pass. part. [§13.4] . . . . ἐθίζω *(1480)*

(1499) **εἰ καί,** *even if, even though, although*

(‡1752) **εἴκενεν,** equivalent to ἕνεκα, *on account of,* 2 Cor. 7:12 (3×)

(1500) **εἰκῆ,** adv., *without plan or system; without cause, lightly, rashly,* Matt. 5:22; Col. 2:18; *to no purpose, in vain,* Rom. 13:4; 1 Cor. 15:2; Gal. 3:4; 4:11

εἰκόνα, acc. sg. f. n. . . . . εἰκών *(1504)*

εἰκόνι, dat. sg. f. n. . . . . id.

εἰκόνος, gen. sg. f. n. . . . . id.

(1501) **εἴκοσι(ν),** οἱ, αἱ, τά, nom. pl. m. numeral, *twenty,* Luke 14:31, et al.

εἰκοσιπέντε, indecl. numeral, *twenty-five* (John 6:19, TR | εἴκοσι πέντε, GNT, WH, MT & NA)

εἰκοσιτέσσαρες, numeral (εἴκοσι + τέσσαρες) *twenty-four* (Rev. 5:8, 14, TR | εἴκοσι τέσσαρες, GNT, WH, MT & NA)

εἰκοσιτρεῖς, numeral, *twenty-three* (1 Cor. 10:8, TR | εἴκοσι τρεῖς, GNT, WH, MT & NA)

(1502) **εἴκω,** fut. εἴξω, *to yield, give place, submit,* Gal. 2:5

(1504) **εἰκών,** όνος, ἡ, nom. sg. f. n. [§4.D.a] (εἴκω, an obsolete form, *to be like*) *a material image, likeness, effigy,* Matt. 22:20; Mark 12:16, et al.; *a similitude, representation, exact image,* 1 Cor. 11:7, et al.; *resemblance,* Rom. 8:29, et al.

εἵλατο, 3 pers. sg. aor. mid. indic. [§35.12] (2 Thess. 2:13, GNT, WH & NA | εἵλετο, MT & TR) . . . . αἱρέω *(‡138)*

εἵλετο, 3 pers. sg. 2 aor. mid. indic. [§36.1] (2 Thess. 2:13, MT & TR | εἵλατο, GNT, WH & NA) . . . . id.

εἴληφα, 1 pers. sg. perf. act. indic. [§13.7.a] . . . . λαμβάνω *(2983)*

εἴληφας, 2 pers. sg. perf. act. indic. (Rev. 3:3; 11:17, GNT, MT, TR & NA | εἴληφες, WH) . . . . id.

εἴληφε(ν), 3 pers. sg. perf. act. indic. . . . . id.

εἰληφώς, nom. sg. m. perf. act. part. . . . . id.

(1505) **εἰλικρίνεια,** ας, ἡ [§2.B.b; 2.2] *clearness, pur-*

ity; met. *sincerity, integrity, ingenuousness,* 1 Cor. 5:8, et al.

εἰλικρινείᾳ, dat. sg. f. n. (2 Cor 1:12, GNT, MT, TR & NA | εἰλικρινίᾳ, WH) . . . . εἰλικρίνεια *(1505)*

εἰλικρινείας, gen. sg. f. n. (1 Cor. 5:8; 2 Cor. 2:17; GNT, MT, TR & NA | εἰλικρινίας, WH) . . . . id.

εἰλικρινεῖς, nom. pl. m. adj. . . . . . . εἰλικρινής *(1506)*

εἰλικρινῆ, acc. sg. f. adj. . . . . id.

(1506) **εἰλικρινής,** ές [§7.G.b] (εἵλη, *sunshine,* and κρίνω) pr. *that which being viewed in the sunshine is found clear and pure;* met. *spotless, sincere, ingenuous,* Phil. 1:10; 2 Pet. 3:1

εἰλισσόμενον, nom. sg. neut. pres. pass. part. (Rev. 6:14, TR | ἑλισσόμενον, GNT, WH & NA | ἑλισσόμενος, MT) . . . . . εἰλίσσω *(1507)*

(1507) **εἰλίσσω,** fut. εἰλίξω [§26.2] (properly Ionic for ἑλίσσω | εἰλέω, *to roll*) *to roll up,* Rev. 6:14

εἷλκον, 3 pers. pl. imperf. act. indic. [§13.4] . . . . ἕλκω *(†1670)*

εἵλκυσαν, 3 pers. pl. aor. act. indic. . . . ἑλκύω *(†1670)*

εἵλκυσε(ν), 3 pers. sg. aor. act. indic. . . . . id.

εἱλκωμένος, nom. sg. m. perf. pass. part. (Luke 16:20, GNT, WH & NA | ἡλκωμένος, MT & TR) . . . . ἑλκόω *(1669)*

(1508) **εἰ μή,** conditional and negative particles, *except, if not*

(1509) **εἰ μήτι,** *unless indeed, unless perhaps*

(1510) **εἰμί,** 1 pers. sg. pres. indic., [§12.L] imperf. ἦν and ἤμην, fut. ἔσομαι, imper. ἔσθι, ἔστω and ἤτω, subj. ὦ, infin. εἶναι, part. ὤν, a verb of existence, *to be, to exist,* John 1:1; 17:5; Matt. 6:30; Luke 4:25, et al. freq.; ἐστί(ν), *it is possible, proper,* Heb. 9:5; a simple copula to the subject and predicate, and therefore in itself affecting the force of the sentence only by its tense, mood, etc., John 1:1; 15:1, et al. freq.; it also forms a frequent circumlocution with the participles of the present and perfect of other verbs, Matt. 19:22; Mark 2:6, et al.

(1511) **εἶναι,** pres. infin. . . . . εἰμί *(1510)*

εἴξαμεν, 1 pers. pl. aor. act. indic. . . . . . . εἴκω *(1502)*

εἶπα, 1 pers. sg. aor. act. indic. [§35.7] . εἶπον *(‡3004)*

εἶπαν, 3 pers. pl. 2 aor. act. indic. (Matt. 2:5, et al., GNT, WH & NA | εἶπον, MT & TR) . . . . id.

εἶπας, 2 pers. sg. 2 aor. act. indic. {Matt. 26:25} . . . . id.

εἶπας, nom. sg. m. 2 aor. act. part. (Acts 22:24; 24:22; 27:35, GNT, WH & NA | εἰπών, MT & TR) . . . . id.

εἴπατε, 2 pers. pl. 2 aor. act. indic.

{Luke 12:3} . . . . εἶπον *(‡3004)*
εἴπατε, 2 pers. pl. 2 aor. act. imper.
    {Luke 13:32} . . . . id.
εἰπάτω, 3 pers. sg. 2 aor. act. imper. . . . . . id.
εἰπάτωσαν, 3 pers. pl. 2 aor. act. imper. . . . id.
εἰπέ, 2 pers. sg. 2 aor. act. imper. . . . . id.
εἰπεῖν, 2 aor. act. infin. . . . . id.
εἶπε(ν), 3 pers. sg. 2 aor. act. indic. . . . . . id.
(1512) **εἴπερ**, a strengthening of εἰ by the enclitic par-
    ticle περ, *if indeed, if it be so that,* Rom.
    8:9; 1 Cor. 15:15; *since indeed, since,*
    2 Thess. 1:6; 1 Pet. 2:3; *although indeed,*
    1 Cor. 8:5
εἶπες, 2 pers. sg. 2 aor. act. indic. (Mark
    12:32, GNT, WH & NA | εἶπας, MT &
    TR) . . . . εἶπον *(‡3004)*
εἴπῃ, 3 pers. sg. 2 aor. act. subj. . . . . id.
εἴπῃς, 2 pers. sg. 2 aor. act. subj. . . . . id.
εἴπητε, 2 pers. pl. 2 aor. act. subj. . . . . . . id.
(‡3004) **εἶπον**, 1 pers. sg. 2 aor. act. indic. (used as the
    2 aor. of λέγω) *to say, speak* {Luke 24:24;
    John 6:36}
εἶπον, 3 pers. pl. 2 aor. act. indic.
    {John 6:34} . . . . εἶπον *(‡3004)*
εἰπόν, 2 pers. sg. 2 aor. act. imper. (Mark 13:4;
    Luke 20:2; Acts 28:26, GNT, WH & NA
    | εἰπέ, MT & TR) . . . . id.
εἰπόντα, acc. sg. m. 2 aor. act. part. . . . . . id.
εἰπόντες, nom. pl. m. 2 aor. act. part. . . . id.
εἰπόντι, dat. sg. m. 2 aor. act. part. (Matt.
    12:48, MT & TR | λέγοντι, GNT, WH
    & NA) . . . . id.
εἰπόντος, gen. sg. m. 2 aor. act. part. . . . . id.
εἰποῦσα, nom. sg. f. 2 aor. act. part. . . . id.
εἴπω, 1 pers. sg. 2 aor. act. subj. . . . . id.
εἴπωμεν, 1 pers. pl. 2 aor. act. subj. . . . . . id.
εἰπών, nom. sg. m. 2 aor. act. part. . . . . . id.
(1513) **εἴπως** (εἰ + πώς) *if by any means, if possibly*
    (Acts 27:12, et al. TR | εἴ πως, GNT, WH,
    MT & NA)
εἴπωσι(ν), 3 pers. pl. 2 aor. act. subj. . . . εἶπον *(‡3004)*
εἰργάζετο, 3 pers. sg. imperf. mid./pass. dep.
    indic. (Acts 18:3, MT & TR | ἠργάζετο,
    GNT & NA | ἠργάζοντο, WH) ἐργάζομαι *(2038)*
εἰργασάμεθα, 1 pers. pl. aor. mid. dep. indic.
    (2 John 8, GNT, MT, TR & NA |
    ἠργασάμεθα, WH) . . . . id.
εἰργάσαντο, 3 pers. pl. aor. mid. dep. indic.
    (Heb. 11:33, GNT, MT, TR & NA |
    ἠργάσαντο, WH) . . . . id.
εἰργάσατο, 3 pers. sg. aor. mid. dep. indic.
    (Matt. 25:16; 26:10; Mark 14:6, MT &
    TR | ἠργάσατο, GNT, WH & NA) . . id.
εἰργασμένα, nom. pl. neut. perf. pass. part. id.
εἴρηκα, 1 pers. sg. perf. act. indic. Att.

[§36.1] . . . . ῥέω *(4483)*
εἴρηκαν, 3 pers. pl. perf. act. indic. Att.
    [§35.13] . . . . id.
εἴρηκας, 2 pers. sg. perf. act. indic. Att. . . id.
εἰρήκασι(ν), 3 pers. pl. perf. act. indic. Att. id.
εἰρήκατε, 2 pers. pl. perf. act. indic. Att. . id.
εἰρήκει, 3 pers. sg. pluperf. act. indic. Att. id.
εἴρηκε(ν), 3 pers. sg. perf. act. indic. Att. . id.
εἰρηκέναι, perf. act. infin. (Heb. 10:15, GNT,
    WH & NA | προειρηκέναι, MT & TR) id.
εἰρηκότος, gen. sg. neut. perf. act. part. Att. id.
εἰρημένον, nom. sg. neut. perf. pass. part. Att.
    {Acts 2:16} . . . . id.
εἰρημένον, acc. sg. neut. perf. pass. part. Att.
    {Acts 13:40} . . . . id.
εἰρηνεύετε, 2 pers. pl. pres. act.
    imper. . . . . εἰρηνεύω *(1514)*
εἰρηνεύοντες, nom. pl. m. pres. act. part. . id.
(1514) **εἰρηνεύω**, fut. εἰρηνεύσω [§13.M] *to be at
    peace; to cultivate peace, concord, or har-
    mony,* Matt. 9:50; Rom. 12:18, et al.
(1515) **εἰρήνη**, ης, ἡ, nom. sg. f. n. [§2.B.a] *peace,*
    Luke 14:32; Acts 12:20, et al.; *tranquillity,*
    Luke 11:21; John 16:33; 1 Thess. 5:3; *con-
    cord, unity, love of peace,* Matt. 10:34;
    Luke 12:51, et al.; meton. *the author of
    peace or concord,* Eph. 2:14; from the He-
    brew *felicity, every kind of blessing and
    good,* Luke 1:79; 2:14, 29, et al.; meton.
    *a salutation expressive of good wishes, a
    benediction, blessing,* Matt. 10:13, et al.
εἰρήνη, dat. sg. f. n. . . . . εἰρήνη *(1515)*
εἰρήνην, acc. sg. f. n. . . . . id.
εἰρήνης, gen. sg. f. n. . . . . id.
εἰρηνική, nom. sg. f. adj. . . . . εἰρηνικός *(1516)*
εἰρηνικόν, acc. sg. f. adj. . . . . id.
(1516) **εἰρηνικός**, ή, όν [§7.F.a] *pertaining to peace;
    peaceable, disposed to peace and concord,*
    James 3:17; from the Hebrew, *profitable,
    blissful,* Heb. 12:11
(1517) **εἰρηνοποιέω**, ῶ, fut. εἰρηνοποιήσω [§16.P]
    (εἰρήνη + ποιέω) *to make peace, restore
    concord,* Col. 1:20
εἰρηνοποιήσας, nom. sg. m. aor. act.
    part. εἰρηνοποιέω *(1517)*
εἰρηνοποιοί, nom. pl. m. adj. . . . . εἰρηνοποιός *(1518)*
(1518) **εἰρηνοποιός**, ον, *a peace-maker, one who cul-
    tivates peace and concord,* Matt. 5:9
εἴρηται, 3 pers. sg. perf. pass. indic.
    [§36.1] . . . . ῥέω *(4483)*
εἴρω, an almost obsolete pres., fut. ἐρῶ [§36.1]
    to say, speak, etc., joined in usage with the
    forms λέγω, εἶπον, and εἴρηκα
(1519) **εἰς**, prep., *into,* Matt. 2:11, et al.; *to, as far as,
    to the extent of,* Matt. 2:23; 4:24, et al.;

until, John 13:1, et al.; *against,* Matt. 18:15; Luke 12:10; *before, in the presence of,* Acts 22:30, et al.; *in order to, for, with a view to,* Mark 1:38, et al.; *for the use or service of,* John 6:9; Luke 9:13; 1 Cor. 16:1; *with reference to,* 2 Cor. 10:13, 16; *in accordance with,* Matt. 12:41; Luke 11:32; 2 Tim. 2:26; also equivalent to ἐν, John 1:18, et al.; *by,* in forms of swearing, Matt. 5:35, et al.; from the Hebrew, εἶναι, γίνεσθαι εἰς, *to become, result in, amount to,* Matt. 19:5; 1 Cor. 4:3, et al.; εἰς τί, *why, wherefore,* Matt. 26:8 {Matt. 8:18}

(1520) **εἷς,** μία, ἕν, nom. sg. m. numeral, gen. ἑνός, μιᾶς, ἑνός [§9.I.a] *one,* Matt. 10:29, et al. freq.; *only,* Mark 12:6; *one* virtually by union, Matt. 19:5, 6; John 10:30; *one and the same,* Luke 12:52; Rom. 3:30, et al.; *one* in respect of office and standing, 1 Cor. 3:8; equivalent to τις, *a certain one,* Matt. 8:19; 16:14, et al.; *a, an,* Matt. 21:19; James 4:13, et al.; εἷς ἕκαστος, *each one, every one,* Luke 4:40; Acts 2:3, et al.; εἷς τὸν ἕνα, *one another,* 1 Thess. 5:11; εἷς — καὶ εἷς, *the one — and the other,* Matt. 20:21, et al.; εἷς καθ᾽ εἷς and ὁδὲ καθ᾽ εἷς, *one by one, one after another, in succession,* Mark 14:19; John 8:9, et al.; from the Hebrew as an ordinal, *first,* Matt. 28:1, et al. {Matt. 8:19}

εἰσάγαγε, 2 pers. sg. 2 aor. act. imper. [§13.7.d] . . . . εἰσάγω *(1521)*

εἰσαγαγεῖν, 2 aor. act. infin. . . . . id.

εἰσαγάγῃ, 3 pers. sg. 2 aor. act. subj. . . . . id.

εἰσάγεσθαι, pres. pass. infin. . . . . id.

(1521) **εἰσάγω,** fut. εἰσάξω [§23.1.b] (εἰς + ἄγω) *to lead or bring in, introduce, conduct or usher in or to* a place or person, Luke 2:27; 14:21; 22:54, et al.

εἰσακουσθείς, nom. sg. m. aor. pass. part. . . . . εἰσακούω *(1522)*

εἰσακουσθήσονται, 3 pers. pl. fut. pass. indic. . . . . id.

εἰσακούσονται, 3 pers. pl. fut. mid. dep. indic. . . . . id.

(1522) **εἰσακούω,** fut. εἰσκούσομαι (εἰς + ἀκούω) *to hear or hearken to, to heed,* 1 Cor. 14:21; *to listen to* the prayers of any one, *accept one's petition,* Matt. 6:7; Luke 1:13; Acts 10:31; Heb. 5:7

εἰσδέξομαι, 1 pers. sg. fut. mid. dep. indic. . . . . εἰσδέχομαι *(1523)*

(1523) **εἰσδέχομαι,** fut. εἰσδέξομαι [§23.1.b] (εἰς + δέχομαι) *to admit; to receive into favor, receive kindly, accept with favor,* 2 Cor. 6:17

εἰσδραμοῦσα, nom. sg. f. 2 aor. act. part. [§36.1] . . . . εἰστρέχω *(1532)*

(1524) **εἴσειμι** [§33.4] (εἰς + εἶμι, *to go*) imperf. εἰσῄειν, *to go in, enter,* Acts 3:3; 21:18, 26; Heb. 9:6

εἰσελεύσεσθαι, fut. mid. dep. infin. [§36.1] . . . . εἰσέρχομαι *(1525)*

εἰσελεύσεται, 3 pers. sg. fut. mid. dep. indic.   id.

εἰσελεύσομαι, 1 pers. sg. fut. mid. dep. indic.   id.

εἰσελεύσονται, 3 pers. pl. fut. mid. dep. indic.   id.

εἰσελήλυθαν, 3 pers. pl. 2 perf. act. indic. [§35.13] (James 5:4, WH | GNT, MT, TR & NA) . . . . id.

εἰσεληλύθασιν, 3 pers. pl. 2 perf. act. indic. (James 5:4, GNT, MT, TR & NA | εἰσελήλυθαν, WH) . . . . id.

εἰσεληλύθατε, 2 pers. pl. 2 perf. act. indic.   id.

εἰσέλθατε, 2 pers. pl. aor. act. imper. [§35.12] (Matt. 7:13, GNT, WH & NA | εἰσέλθετε, MT & TR) . . . . id.

εἰσελθάτω, 3 pers. sg. aor. act. imper. [§35.12] (Mark 13:15, GNT, WH & NA | εἰσ- ελθέτω, MT & TR) . . . . id.

εἴσελθε, 2 pers. sg. 2 aor. act. imper. . . . . id.

εἰσελθεῖν, 2 aor. act. infin. . . . . id.

εἰσέλθετε, 2 pers. pl. 2 aor. act. imper. (Matt. 7:13, MT & TR | εἰσέλθατε, GNT, WH & NA) . . . . id.

εἰσελθέτω, 3 pers. sg. 2 aor. act. imper. (Mark 13:15, MT & TR | εἰσελθάτω, GNT, WH & NA) . . . . id.

εἰσέλθῃ, 3 pers. sg. 2 aor. act. subj. . . . . . id.

εἰσέλθῃς, 2 pers. sg. 2 aor. act. subj. . . . . id.

εἰσέλθητε, 2 pers. pl. 2 aor. act. subj. . . . . id.

εἰσελθόντα, acc. sg. m. 2 aor. act. part. {Acts 9:2} . . . . id.

εἰσελθόντα, nom. pl. neut. 2 aor. act. part. {Luke 11:26} . . . . id.

εἰσελθόντες, nom. pl. m. 2 aor. act. part. . id.

εἰσελθόντι, dat. sg. m. 2 aor. act. part. . . id.

εἰσελθόντος, gen. sg. m. 2 aor. act. part. . id.

εἰσελθόντων, gen. pl. m. 2 aor. act. part. . id.

εἰσελθοῦσα, nom. sg. f. 2 aor. act. part. . . id.

εἰσελθοῦσαι, nom. pl. f. 2 aor. act. part. . . id.

εἰσελθούσης, gen. sg. f. 2 aor. act. part. . . id.

εἰσέλθωμεν, 1 pers. pl. 2 aor. act. subj. . . id.

εἰσελθών, nom. sg. m. 2 aor. act. part. . . . id.

εἰσέλθωσι(ν), 3 pers. pl. 2 aor. act. subj. . id.

εἰσενεγκεῖν, 2 aor. act. infin. . . . . εἰσφέρω *(1533)*

εἰσενέγκῃς, 2 pers. sg. aor. act. subj. [§36.1] id.

εἰσενέγκωσιν, 3 pers. pl. 2 aor. act. subj. . id.

εἰσεπήδησαν, 3 pers. pl. aor. act. indic. (Acts 14:14, MT & TR | ἐξεπήδησαν, GNT, WH & NA) . . . . εἰσπηδάω *(1530)*

εἰσεπήδησε(ν), 3 pers. sg. aor. act. indic. . id.

εἰσεπορεύετο, 3 pers. sg. imperf. mid./pass.
dep. indic. . . . . εἰσπορεύομαι *(1531)*
εἰσέρχεσθε, 2 pers. pl. pres. mid./pass. dep.
indic. . . . . εἰσέρχομαι *(1525)*
εἰσερχέσθωσαν, 3 pers. pl. pres. mid./pass.
dep. imper. id.
εἰσέρχεται, 3 pers. sg. pres. mid./pass. dep.
indic. . . . . id.
εἰσέρχησθε, 2 pers. pl. pres. mid./pass. dep.
subj. . . . . id.
(1525) **εἰσέρχομαι** [§36.1] fut. εἰσελεύσομαι, 2 aor.
εἰσῆλθον (εἰς + ἔρχομαι) *to go or come
in, enter,* Matt. 7:13; 8:5, 8, et al.; spc. *to
enter* by force, *break in,* Mark 3:27; Acts
20:29; met. with εἰς κόσμον, *to begin to
exist, come into existence,* Rom. 5:12;
2 John 7; or, *to make one's appearance on
earth,* Heb. 10:5; *to enter into or take possession of,* Luke 22:3; John 13:27; *to enter into, enjoy, partake of,* Matt. 19:23, 24,
et al.; *to enter into* any one's labor, *be* his
successor, John 4:38; *to fall into, be placed
in* certain circumstances, Matt. 26:41, et
al.; *to be put into,* Matt. 15:11; Acts 11:8;
to present one's self before, Acts 19:30; met.
to arise, spring up, Luke 9:46; from the Hebrew, εἰσέρχεσθαι καὶ ἐξέρχεσθαι, *to go
in and out, to live, discharge the ordinary
functions of life,* Acts 1:21
εἰσερχόμεθα, 1 pers. pl. pres. mid./pass. dep.
indic. . . . . εἰσέρχομαι *(1525)*
εἰσερχομένην, acc. sg. f. pres. mid./pass. dep.
part. . . . . id.
εἰσερχόμενοι, nom. pl. m. pres. mid./pass.
dep. part. . . . . id.
εἰσερχόμενον, nom. sg. neut. pres. mid./pass.
dep. part. . . . . id.
εἰσερχόμενος, nom. sg. m. pres. mid./pass.
dep. part. . . . . id.
εἰσερχομένου, gen. sg. m. pres. mid./pass.
dep. part. . . . . id.
εἰσερχομένους, acc. pl. m. pres. mid./pass.
dep. part. . . . . id.
εἰσήγαγε(ν), 3 pers. sg. 2 aor. act. indic.
[§34.1.a] . . . . εἰσάγω *(1521)*
εἰσήγαγον, 3 pers. pl. 2 aor. act. indic.
[§13.7.b,d] . . . . id.
εἰσῄει, 3 pers. sg. pluperf. act. indic.
[§33.4] . . . . εἴσειμι *(1524)*
εἰσηκούσθη, 3 pers. sg. aor. pass. indic.
[§22.4] . . . . εἰσακούω *(1522)*
εἰσήλθαμεν, 1 pers. pl. aor. act. indic. (Acts
28:16, WH | εἰσήλθομεν, GNT, MT, TR
& NA) . . . . εἰσέρχομαι *(1525)*
εἰσήλθατε, 2 pers. pl. aor. act. indic. [§35.12]

(Luke 11:52, GNT, WH & NA | εἰσήλ-
θετε, MT & TR) . . . . εἰσέρχομαι *(1525)*
εἰσῆλθε(ν), 3 pers. sg. 2 aor. act. indic. . . . id.
εἰσῆλθες, 2 pers. sg. 2 aor. act. indic. . . . id.
εἰσήλθετε, 2 pers. pl. 2 aor. act. indic. (Luke
11:52, MT & TR | εἰσήλθατε, GNT, WH
& NA) . . . . id.
εἰσήλθομεν, 1 pers. pl. 2 aor. act. indic. . . id.
εἰσῆλθον, 1 pers. sg. 2 aor. act. indic.
{Luke 7:44} . . . . id.
εἰσῆλθον, 3 pers. pl. 2 aor. act. indic.
{Luke 8:33} . . . . id.
εἰσηνέγκαμεν, 1 pers. pl. aor. act. indic.
[§36.1] . . . . εἰσφέρω *(1533)*
εἰσίασιν, 3 pers. pl. pres. indic. for εἰσεῖσιν
[§33.4] . . . . εἴσειμι *(1524)*
εἰσιέναι, pres. infin. . . . . id.
(1526) εἰσί(ν), 3 pers. pl. pres. indic. [§12.L] . . . . εἰμί *(1510)*
(1527) **εἷς καθ' εἷς,** numeral *one* joined by preposition κατά, *one by one, one after another,
in succession*
εἰσκαλεσάμενος, nom. sg. m. aor. mid. dep.
indic. εἰσκαλέω *(1528)*
(1528) **εἰσκαλέω,** ῶ, fut. εἰσκαλέσω, and mid.
εἰσκαλέομαι, οῦμαι [§17.Q] (εἰς + καλέω)
to call in; to invite in
εἴσοδον, acc. sg. f. n. . . . . εἴσοδος *(1529)*
(1529) **εἴσοδος,** ου, ἡ, nom. sg. f. n. [§3.C.b] (εἰς +
ὁδός) *a place of entrance; the act of en-
trance,* Heb. 10:19; *admission, reception,*
1 Thess. 1:9; 2 Pet. 1:11; *a coming, approach, access,* 1 Thess. 2:1; *entrance* upon
office, *commencement* of ministry, Acts
13:24
εἰσόδου, gen. sg. f. n. . . . . εἴσοδος *(1529)*
(1530) **εἰσπηδάω,** ῶ, fut. εἰσπηδήσω [§18.R] (εἰς +
πηδάω, *to leap*) *to leap or spring in, rush
in eagerly,* Acts 14:14; 16:29
εἰσπορεύεται, 3 pers. sg. pres. mid./pass. dep.
indic. . . . . εἰσπορεύομαι *(1531)*
(1531) **εἰσπορεύομαι,** fut. εἰσπορεύσομαι [§14.N]
(εἰς + πορεύομαι) *to go or come in, enter,*
Mark 1:21; 5:40, et al.; *to come to, visit,*
Acts 28:30; *to be put in,* Matt. 15:17; Mark
7:15, 18, 19; *to intervene,* Mark 4:19; from
the Hebrew, εἰσπορεύεσθαι καὶ ἐκπορεύεσθαι, equivalent to εἰσέρχεσθαι καὶ
ἐξέρξεσθαι, above, Acts 9:28
εἰσπορευόμεναι, nom. pl. f. pres. mid./pass.
dep. part. . . . . εἰσπορεύομαι *(1531)*
εἰσπορευόμενοι, nom. pl. m. pres. mid./pass.
dep. part. . . . . id.
εἰσπορευόμενον, nom. sg. neut. pres.
mid./pass. dep. part. . . . . id.
εἰσπορευόμενος, nom. sg. m. pres. mid. or

mid./pass. dep. part. . . . . εἰσπορεύομαι *(1531)*
εἰσπορευομένους, acc. pl. m. pres. mid. or
    mid./pass. dep. part. . . . . id.
εἰσπορευομένων, gen. pl. m. pres. mid./pass.
    dep. part. . . . . id.
εἰσπορεύονται, 3 pers. pl. pres. mid./pass.
    dep. indic. . . . . id.
εἱστήκει, 3 pers. sg. pluperf. act. indic. [§29.4]
    (GNT, MT, TR & NA | ἱστήκει,
    WH) . . . . ἵστημι *(2476)*
εἱστήκεισαν, 3 pers. pl. pluperf. act. indic.
    (GNT, MT, TR & NA | ἱστήκεισαν,
    WH) . . . . id.
(1532) **εἰστρέχω**, 2 aor. εἰσέδραμον [§36.1] (εἰς +
    τρέχω) *to run in,* Acts 12:14
εἰσφέρεις, 2 pers. sg. pres. act. indic. . εἰσφέρω *(1533)*
εἰσφέρεται, 3 pers. sg. pres. pass. indic. . . id.
(1533) **εἰσφέρω**, fut. εἰσοίσω, aor. εἰσήνεγκα, 2 aor.
    εἰσήνεγκον [§36.1] (εἰς + φέρω) *to bring
    in, to, or into,* Luke 5:18, 19; 1 Tim. 6:7;
    Heb. 13:11; *to bring to* the ears of any one,
    to announce, Acts 17:20; *to lead into,* Matt.
    6:13; Luke 11:4
εἰσφέρωσιν, 3 pers. pl. pres. act. subj. (Luke
    12:11, GNT, WH & NA | προσφέρωσιν,
    MT & TR) . . . . εἰσφέρω *(1533)*
(1534) **εἶτα**, adv., *then, afterwards, thereupon,* Mark
    4:17, 28; Luke 8:12, et al.; *in the next
    place,* 1 Cor. 12:28; *besides,* Heb. 12:9
(1535) **εἴτε**, conj., *whether*
(‡1534) **εἶτεν**, adv. *then, afterwards, thereupon* (Mark
    4:28, WH | εἶτα, GNT, MT, TR & NA)
(1536) **εἴ τις**, particle with indef. pron., *everyone who*
    or *whoever, everything that* or *whatever*
εἶχαν, 3 pers. pl. imperf. act. indic. (Rev.
    9:8, 9, WH | εἶχον, GNT, MT, TR &
    NA) . . . . ἔχω *(2192)*
εἶχε(ν), 3 pers. sg. imperf. act. indic. [§13.4] id.
εἶχες, 2 pers. sg. imperf. act. indic. . . . . . . id.
εἴχετε, 2 pers. pl. imperf. act. indic. . . . . . id.
εἴχομεν, 1 pers. pl. imperf. act. indic. . . . . id.
εἶχον, 1 pers. sg. imperf. act. indic.
    {Luke 19:20} . . . . id.
εἶχον, 3 pers. pl. imperf. act. indic.
    {Luke 4:40} . . . . id.
εἴχοσαν, 3 pers. pl. imperf. act. indic. for
    εἶχον [§35.13] (John 15:22, 24, GNT, WH
    & NA | εἶχον, MT & TR) . . . . id.
(‡1486) **εἴωθα**, 2 perf. from an old pres. ἔθω, with a
    present signification, [§38.2] pluperf.
    εἰώθειν, part. εἰωθώς, *to be accustomed,
    to be usual,* Matt. 27:15, et al.
εἰώθει, 3 pers. sg. pluperf. act. indic. . . εἴωθα *(‡1486)*
εἰωθός, acc. sg. neut. 2 perf. act. part. . . . id.
εἴων, 3 pers. pl. imperf. act. indic. [§13.4] ἐάω *(1439)*

(1537) **ἐκ**, prep. before a consonant; ἐξ, before a
    vowel; *from, out of,* a place, Matt. 2:15;
    3:17; *of, from, out of,* denoting origin or
    source, Matt. 1:3; 21:19; *of, from* some ma-
    terial, Matt. 3:9; Rom. 9:21; *of, from,
    among,* partitively, Matt. 6:27; 21:31;
    Mark 9:17; *from,* denoting cause, Rev.
    8:11; 17:6; means or instrument, Matt.
    12:33, 37; *by, through,* denoting the author
    or efficient cause, Matt. 1:18; John 10:32;
    of, denoting the distinguishing mark of a
    class, Rom. 2:8; Gal. 3:7, et al.; *of time,
    after,* 2 Cor. 4:6; Rev. 17:11; *from, after,
    since,* Matt. 19:12; Luke 8:27; *for, with,* de-
    noting a rate of payment, price, Matt. 20:2;
    27:7; *at,* denoting position, Matt.
    20:21, 23; after passive verbs, *by, of, from,*
    marking the agent, Matt. 15:5; Mark 7:11;
    forming with certain words a periphrasis
    for an adverb, Matt. 26:42, 44; Mark 6:51;
    Luke 23:8; put after words of freeing, Rom.
    7:24; 2 Cor. 1:10; used partitively after
    verbs of eating, drinking, etc., John 6:26;
    1 Cor. 9:7
ἐκαθάρισε(ν), 3 pers. sg. aor. act.
    indic. . . . . καθαρίζω *(2511)*
ἐκαθαρίσθη, 3 pers. sg. aor. pass. indic.
    [§26.1] (Matt. 8:3, GNT, MT, TR & NA
    | ἐκαθερίσθη, WH) . . . . id.
ἐκαθαρίσθησαν, 3 pers. pl. aor. pass. indic. id.
ἐκαθέζετο, 3 pers. sg. imperf. mid./pass. dep.
    indic. [§34.2] . . . . καθέζομαι *(2516)*
ἐκαθεζόμην, 1 pers. sg. imperf. mid./pass.
    dep. indic. . . . . id.
ἐκάθευδε(ν), 3 pers. sg. imperf. act. indic.
    [§34.2] . . . . καθεύδω *(2518)*
ἐκάθευδον, 3 pers. pl. imperf. act. indic. . id.
ἐκάθητο, 3 pers. sg. imperf. mid./pass. dep.
    indic. . . . . κάθημαι *(2521)*
ἐκάθισα, 1 pers. sg. aor. act. indic.
    [§34.2] . . . . καθίζω *(2523)*
ἐκάθισαν, 3 pers. pl. aor. act. indic. . . . . . id.
ἐκάθισε(ν), 3 pers. sg. aor. act. indic. . . . id.
ἐκάκωσαν, 3 pers. pl. aor. act. indic. . κακόω *(2559)*
ἐκάκωσε(ν), 3 pers. sg. aor. act. indic. . . . id.
ἐκάλεσα, 1 pers. sg. aor. act. indic. . . . καλέω *(2564)*
ἐκάλεσαν, 3 pers. pl. aor. act. indic. (Matt.
    10:25, TR | ἐπεκάλεσαν, GNT, WH, MT
    & NA) . . . . id.
ἐκάλεσε(ν), 3 pers. sg. aor. act. indic. . . . . id.
ἐκάλουν, 3 pers. pl. imperf. act. indic. . . . id.
ἐκάμμυσαν, 3 pers. pl. aor. act. indic. καμμύω *(2576)*
ἔκαμψαν, 3 pers. pl. aor. act. indic. . . κάμπτω *(2578)*
ἐκαρτέρησε(ν), 3 pers. sg. aor. act.
    indic. . . . . καρτερέω *(2594)*

ἑκάστη, nom. sg. f. adj. . . . . ἕκαστος (1538)
ἑκάστην, acc. sg. f. adj. . . . . id.
ἕκαστοι, nom. pl. m. adj. (Phil. 2:4, GNT,
   WH & NA | ἕκαστος, MT & TR) . . . id.
ἑκάστοις, dat. pl. m. adj. (Rev. 6:11, TR |
   ἑκάστῳ, GNT, WH & NA | MT omits) id.
ἕκαστον, acc. sg. m. adj. {Luke 16:5} . . . . id.
ἕκαστον, nom. sg. neut. adj. {Luke 6:44} id.
ἕκαστον, acc. sg. neut. adj. {1 Cor. 12:18} id.
(1538) ἕκαστος, η, ον, nom. sg. m. adj. [§10.6.d] *each
   one, every one separately,* Matt. 16:27;
   Luke 13:15, et al.
(1539) ἑκάστοτε, adv., *always,* 2 Pet. 1:15
ἑκάστου, gen. sg. m. adj.
   {1 Cor. 3:13} . . . . ἕκαστος (1538)
ἑκάστου, gen. sg. neut. adj. {Eph. 4:16} . id.
ἑκάστῳ, dat. sg. m. adj. {1 Cor. 12:11} . . . id.
ἑκάστῳ, dat. sg. neut. adj. {1 Cor. 15:38} . id.
(1540) ἑκατόν, οἱ, αἱ, τά, indecl. numeral, *one hundred,* Matt. 13:8; Mark 4:8, et al.
(†1541) ἑκατονταετής, ές, nom. sg. m. adj. [§5.E.a]
   (ἑκατόν + ἔτος) *a hundred years old*
   (Rom. 4:19, GNT, WH & NA | ἑκατον-
   ταέτης, MT & TR)
ἑκατονταπλασίονα, acc. sg. m. adj.
   {Luke 8:8} . . . . ἑκατονταπλασίων (1542)
ἑκατονταπλασίονα, acc. pl. neut. adj.
   {Matt. 19:29} . . . . id.
(1542) ἑκατονταπλασίων, ον [§8.3] *a hundredfold,
   centuple,* Matt. 19:29, et al.
ἑκατοντάρχας, acc. pl. m. n. (Acts 21:32,
   GNT, WH & NA | ἑκατοντάρχους, MT
   & TR) . . . . ἑκατοντάρχης (1543)
ἑκατοντάρχῃ, dat. sg. m. n. . . . . id.
(1543) ἑκατοντάρχης, ου, ὁ, nom. sg. m. n. [§2.B.c]
   commander of a hundred men, a centurion
ἑκατόνταρχον, acc. sg. m. n. . . ἑκατόνταρχος (1543)
(1543) ἑκατόνταρχος, ου, ὁ, nom. sg. m. n. [§3.C.a]
   (ἑκατόν + ἄρχος) *commander of a hundred men, a centurion,* Matt. 8:5, 8, 13;
   Luke 7:2, 6, et al.
ἑκατοντάρχου, gen. sg. m. n. . . ἑκατόνταρχος (1543)
ἑκατοντάρχους, acc. pl. m. n. (Acts 21:32,
   MT & TR | ἑκατοντάρχας, GNT, WH
   & NA) . . . . id.
ἑκατοντάρχῳ, dat. sg. m. n. (Matt. 8:13, TR
   | ἑκατοντάρχῃ, GNT, WH, MT & NA) id.
ἑκατοντάρχων, gen. pl. m. n. . . . . id.
ἐκαυμαστίσθη, 3 pers. sg. aor. pass. indic.
   [§26.1] . . . . καυματίζω (2739)
ἐκαυματίσθησαν, 3 pers. pl. aor. pass. indic.
(‡1545) ἐκβαίνω, fut. ἐκβήσομαι, 2 aor. ἐξέβην
   [§37.1] (ἐκ + βαίνω) *to go forth, go out of*
ἔκβαλε, 2 pers. sg. 2 aor. act. imper. ἐκβάλλω (1544)
ἐκβαλεῖν, 2 aor. act. infin. . . . . id.

ἐκβάλετε, 2 pers. pl. 2 aor. act.
   imper. . . . . ἐκβάλλω (1544)
ἐκβάλῃ, 3 pers. sg. 2 aor. act. subj. . . . . . id.
ἐκβάλλει, 3 pers. sg. pres. act. indic. . . . . id.
ἐκβάλλειν, pres. act. infin. . . . . id.
ἐκβάλλεις, 2 pers. sg. pres. act. indic. . . . id.
ἐκβάλλεται, 3 pers. sg. pres. pass. indic. . id.
ἐκβάλλετε, 2 pers. pl. pres. act. imper. . . id.
ἐκβάλλῃ, 3 pers. sg. pres. act. subj. (Mark
   7:26; Luke 10:2, TR | ἐκβάλῃ, GNT, WH,
   MT & NA) . . . . id.
ἐκβαλλόμενοι, nom. pl. m. pres. mid. part. id.
ἐκβαλλομένους, acc. pl. m. pres. pass. part. id.
ἐκβάλλοντα, acc. sg. m. pres. act. part. . . id.
ἐκβάλλουσι(ν), 3 pers. pl. pres. act. indic. id.
(1544) ἐκβάλλω, 1 pers. sg. pres. act. indic., fut.
   ἐκβαλῶ [§27.1.b] 2 aor. ἐξέβαλον [§27.2.d]
   (ἐκ + βάλλω) *to cast out, eject by force,*
   Matt. 15:17; Acts 27:38; *to expel, force away,*
   Luke 4:29; Acts 7:58; *to refuse,* John 6:37;
   to extract, Matt. 7:4; *to reject with contempt,
   despise, contemn,* Luke 6:22; in N.T. *to send
   forth, send out,* Matt. 9:38; Luke 10:2; *to
   send away, dismiss,* Matt. 9:25; Mark 1:12;
   met. *to spread abroad,* Matt. 12:20; *to bring
   out, produce,* Matt. 12:35; 13:52, et al.
ἐκβάλλων, nom. sg. m. pres. act.
   part. . . . . ἐκβάλλω (1544)
ἐκβάλλωσι(ν), 3 pers. pl. pres. act. subj.
   (Luke 9:40, TR | ἐκβάλωσιν, GNT, WH,
   MT & NA) . . . . id.
ἐκβαλόντες, nom. pl. m. 2 aor. act. part. . id.
ἐκβαλοῦσα, nom. sg. f. 2 aor. act. part. . . id.
ἐκβαλοῦσι(ν), 3 pers. pl. fut. act. indic. . . id.
ἐκβάλω, 1 pers. sg. 2 aor. act. subj. . . . . . id.
ἐκβαλών, nom. sg. m. 2 aor. act. part. . . . id.
ἐκβάλωσι(ν), 3 pers. pl. 2 aor. act. subj. . . id.
ἔκβασιν, acc. sg. f. n. . . . . ἔκβασις (1545)
(1545) ἔκβασις, εως, ἡ [§5.E.c] (ἐκβαίνω) *way out,
   egress;* hence, *result, issue,* Heb. 13:7;
   means of clearance or successful endurance,
   1 Cor. 10:13
ἐκβεβλήκει, 3 pers. sg. pluperf. act. indic.
   [§13.8.f] . . . . ἐκβάλλω (1544)
ἐκβληθέντος, gen. sg. neut. aor. pass. part. id.
ἐκβληθήσεται, 3 pers. sg. fut. pass. indic.
   [§27.3] . . . . id.
ἐκβληθήσονται, 3 pers. pl. fut. pass. indic. id.
(1546) ἐκβολή, ῆς, ἡ [§2.B.a] *a casting out;* especially,
   a throwing overboard of a cargo, Acts
   27:18
ἐκβολήν, acc. sg. f. n. . . . . ἐκβολή (1546)
ἐκγαμίζονται, 3 pers. pl. pres. pass. indic.
   (Matt. 22:30: Luke 20:35, MT & TR |
   γαμίζονται, GNT, WH & NA) . . ἐκγαμίζω (1547)

ἐκγαμίζοντες, nom. pl. m. pres. act. part.
(Matt. 24:38, MT & TR | γαμίζοντες,
GNT, WH & NA) . . . . ἐκγαμίζω *(1547)*
(1547) ἐκγαμίζω, fut. ἐκγαμίσω [§26.1] (ἐκ +
γαμίζω) *to give in marriage,* Matt. 22:30;
24:38; Luke 17:27; 1 Cor. 7:38
ἐκγαμίζων, nom. sg. m. pres. act. part. (1 Cor.
7:38a, 38b, MT & TR | γαμίζων, GNT,
WH & NA) . . . . ἐκγαμίζω *(1547)*
ἐκγαμίσκονται, 3 pers. pl. pres. pass. indic.
(Luke 20:34, MT & TR | γαμίσκονται,
GNT, WH & NA) . . . . ἐκγαμίσκω *(1548)*
(1548) ἐκγαμίσκω (ἐκ + γαμίσκω) i.q. ἐκγαμίζω,
Luke 20:34, 35
ἔκγονα, acc. pl. neut. adj. . . . . ἔκγονος *(†1549)*
(†1549) ἔκγονος, ον [§7.2] (ἐκγίνομαι, *to be born*)
born of, descended from; ἔκγονα, *descendants, grandchildren,* 1 Tim. 5:4
(1550) ἐκδαπανάω, ῶ, fut. ἐκδαπανήσω [§18.R] (ἐκ
+ δαπανάω) *to expend, consume, ex-
haust,* 2 Cor. 12:15
ἐκδαπανηθήσομαι, 1 pers. sg. fut. pass.
indic. . . . . ἐκδαπανάω *(1550)*
ἐκδέχεσθε, 2 pers. pl. pres. mid./pass. dep.
imper. . . . . ἐκδέχομαι *(1551)*
ἐκδέχεται, 3 pers. sg. pres. mid./pass. dep.
indic. . . . . id.
(1551) ἐκδέχομαι, 1 pers. sg. pres. mid./pass. dep.
indic., fut. ἐκδέξομαι [§23.1.b] (ἐκ +
δέχομαι) pr. *to receive from* another; *to expect, look for,* Acts 17:16, et al.; *to wait
for, to wait,* 1 Cor. 11:33; 1 Pet. 3:20, et al.
ἐκδεχόμενος, nom. sg. m. pres. mid./pass.
dep. part. . . . . ἐκδέχομαι *(1551)*
ἐκδεχομένου, gen. sg. m. pres. mid./pass. dep.
part. . . . . id.
ἐκδεχομένων, gen. pl. m. pres. mid./pass.
dep. part. (John 5:3, MT & TR | GNT,
WH & NA omit) . . . . id.
(1552) ἔκδηλος, ον, nom. sg. m. adj. [§7.2] (ἐκ +
δῆλος) *clearly manifest, evident,* 2 Tim.
3:9
(1553) ἐκδημέω, ῶ, fut. ἐκδημήσω [§16.P] (ἐκ +
δῆμος) pr. *to be absent from home, go
abroad, travel;* hence, *to be absent from*
any place or person, 2 Cor. 5:6, 8, 9
ἐκδημῆσαι, aor. act. infin. . . . . ἐκδημέω *(1553)*
ἐκδημοῦμεν, 1 pers. pl. pres. act. indic. . . id.
ἐκδημοῦντες, nom. pl. m. pres. act. part. . id.
(1554) ἐκδίδωμι, fut. ἐκδώσω [§30.Z] 2 aor. mid.
ἐξεδόμην (ἐκ + δίδωμι) *to give out, to
give up; to put out* at interest; in N.T. *to
let out* to tenants, Matt. 21:33, 41, et al.
(1555) ἐκδιηγέομαι, οῦμαι, fut. ἐκδιηγήσομαι
[§17.Q] (ἐκ + διηγέομαι) *to narrate fully,*

detail, Acts 13:14; 15:3
ἐκδιηγῆται, 3 pers. sg. pres. mid./pass. dep.
subj. . . . . ἐκδιηγέομαι *(1555)*
ἐκδιηγούμενοι, nom. pl. m. pres. mid./pass.
dep. part. . . . . id.
ἐκδικεῖς, 2 pers. sg. pres. act. indic. . ἐκδικέω *(1556)*
(1556) ἐκδικέω, ῶ, fut. ἐκδικήσω [§16.P] pr. *to execute right and justice; to punish,* 2 Cor.
10:6; in N.T. *to right, avenge* a person,
Luke 18:3, 5, et al.
ἐκδικῆσαι, aor. act. infin. . . . . ἐκδικέω *(1556)*
ἐκδικήδεως, gen. sg. f. n. . . . . ἐκδίκησις *(1557)*
ἐκδίκησιν, acc. sg. f. n. . . . . id.
(1557) ἐκδίκησις, εως, ἡ, nom. sg. f. n. [§5.E.c] *satisfaction; vengeance, punishment, retrib-
utive justice,* Luke 21:22; Rom. 12:19, et
al.; ἐκδίκησιν ποιεῖν, *to vindicate, avenge,*
Luke 18:7, 8, et al.; διδόναι ἐκδίκησιν, *to
inflict vengeance,* 2 Thess. 1:8
ἐκδίκησον, 2 pers. sg. aor. act. imper. ἐκδικέω *(1556)*
ἐκδικήσω, 1 pers. sg. fut. act. indic. . . . . . id.
(1558) ἔκδικος, ον, nom. sg. m. adj. [§7.2] (ἐκ +
δίκη) *maintaining right; an avenger, one
who inflicts punishment,* Rom. 13:4;
1 Thess. 4:6
ἐκδικοῦντες, nom. pl. m. pres. act.
part. . . . . ἐκδικέω *(1556)*
(1559) ἐκδιώκω, fut. ἐκδιώξω [§23.1.b] (ἐκ +
διώκω) pr. *to chase away, drive out;* in
N.T. *to persecute, vex, harass,* Luke 11:49;
1 Thess. 2:15
ἐκδιωξάντων, gen. pl. m. aor. act.
part. . . . . ἐκδιώκω *(1559)*
ἐκδιώξουσιν, 3 pers. pl. fut. act. indic. (Luke
11:49, MT & TR | διώξουσιν, GNT, WH
& NA) . . . . id.
ἐκδόσεται, 3 pers. sg. fut. mid. dep. indic.
[§30.AA] (Matt. 21:41, TR | ἐκδώσεται,
GNT, WH, MT & NA) . . . . ἐκδίδωμι *(1554)*
ἔκδοτον, acc. sg. m. adj. . . . . ἔκδοτος *(1560)*
(1560) ἔκδοτος, ον [§7.2] *delivered up,* Acts 2:23
(1561) ἐκδοχή, ῆς, ἡ, nom. sg. f. n. [§2.B.a] in N.T.
a looking for, expectation, Heb. 10:27
ἐκδυσαμένοι, nom. pl. m. aor. mid. part.
(2 Cor. 5:3, GNT, MT, TR & NA |
ἐνδυσάμενοι, WH) . . . . ἐκδύω *(1562)*
ἐκδύσαντες, nom. pl. m. aor. act. part. . . id.
ἐκδύσασθαι, aor. mid. infin. . . . . id.
(1562) ἐκδύω, or δύνω, fut. ἐκδύσω [§13.M] (ἐκ +
δύνω) pr. *to go out from; to take off, strip,
unclothe,* Matt. 27:28, 31, et al.; mid. *to
lay aside, to put off,* 2 Cor. 5:4
ἐκδώσεται, 3 pers. sg. fut. mid. dep. indic.
(Matt. 21:41, GNT, WH, MT & NA |
ἐκδόσεται, TR) . . . . ἐκδίδωμι *(1554)*

(1563) **ἐκεῖ**, adv., *there, in that place,* Matt. 2:13, 15, et al.; *thither,* Matt. 2:22; 17:20, et al.

(1564) **ἐκεῖθεν**, adv., *from there, thence,* Matt. 4:21; 5:26, et al.

ἐκεῖνα, nom. pl. neut. demonstrative pron. (Mark 7:15, MT & TR | GNT, WH & NA omit) . . . . ἐκεῖνος (1565)

ἐκεῖνα, acc. pl. neut. demonstrative pron. {Acts 20:2} . . . . id.

ἐκεῖναι, nom. pl. f. demonstrative pron. . . id.

ἐκείναις, dat. pl. f. demonstrative pron. . . id.

ἐκείνας, acc. pl. f. demonstrative pron. . . . id.

ἐκείνη, nom. sg. f. demonstrative pron. . . . id.

ἐκείνη, dat. sg. f. demonstrative pron. . . . . id.

ἐκείνην, acc. sg. f. demonstrative pron. . . . id.

ἐκείνης, gen. sg. f. demonstrative pron. . . . id.

ἐκεῖνο, nom. sg. neut. demonstrative pron. {Mark 7:20} . . . . id.

ἐκεῖνο, acc. sg. neut. demonstrative pron. {Matt. 24:43} . . . . id.

ἐκεῖνοι, nom. pl. m. demonstrative pron. . id.

ἐκείνοις, dat. pl. m. demonstrative pron. . id.

ἐκεῖνον, acc. sg. m. demonstrative pron. . . id.

(1565) **ἐκεῖνος**, η, ο, nom. sg. m. demonstrative pron. [§10.J; 10.3] used with reference to a thing previously mentioned or implied, or already familiar; *that, this, he,* etc., Matt. 17:27; 10:14; 2 Tim. 4:8, et al.; in contrast with οὗτος, referring to the former of two things previously mentioned, Luke 18:14, et al.

ἐκείνου, gen. sg. m. demonstrative pron. {John 18:13} . . . . ἐκεῖνος (1565)

ἐκείνου, gen. sg. neut. demonstrative pron. {John 19:31} . . . . id.

ἐκείνους, acc. pl. m. demonstrative pron. . id.

ἐκείνῳ, dat. sg. m. demonstrative pron. . . id.

ἐκείνων, gen. pl. m. demonstrative pron. {Matt. 25:19} . . . . id.

ἐκείνων, gen. pl. f. demonstrative pron. {Matt. 24:29} . . . . id.

ἐκείνων, gen. pl. neut. demonstrative pron. {Matt. 15:22} . . . . id.

(1566) **ἐκεῖσε**, adv., *thither, there,* Acts 21:3; 22:5

ἔκειτο, 3 pers. sg. imperf. mid./pass. dep. indic. κεῖμαι (2749)

ἐκέκραξα, 1 pers. sg. aor. act. indic. (Acts 24:21, GNT, WH & NA | ἔκραξα, MT & TR) . . . . κράζω (2896)

ἐκέλευον, 3 pers. pl. imperf. act. indic. κελεύω (2753)

ἐκέλευσα, 1 pers. sg. aor. act. indic. . . . . . id.

ἐκέλευσε(ν), 3 pers. sg. aor. act. indic. . . . id.

ἐκένωσε(ν), 3 pers. sg. aor. act. indic. . κενόω (2758)

ἐκέρασε(ν), 3 pers. sg. aor. act. indic. [§36.5] . . . . κεράννυμι (2767)

ἐκέρδησα, 1 pers. sg. aor. act. indic. κερδαίνω (2770)

ἐκέρδησας, 2 pers. sg. aor. act. indic. . . . . id.

ἐκέρδησε(ν), 3 pers. sg. aor. act. indic. . . . id.

ἐκεφαλαίωσαν, 3 pers. pl. aor. act. indic. . . . . κεφαλαιόω (2775)

(1567) **ἐκζητέω**, ῶ, fut. ἐκζητήσω [§16.P] (ἐκ + ζητέω) *to seek out, investigate diligently, scrutinize,* 1 Pet. 1:10; *to ask for, beseech earnestly,* Heb. 12:17; *to seek diligently or earnestly after,* Acts 15:17; Rom. 3:11; Heb. 11:6; from the Hebrew, *to require, exact, demand,* Luke 11:50, 51

ἐκζητηθῇ, 3 pers. sg. aor. pass. subj. . ἐκζητέω (1567)

ἐκζητηθήσεται, 3 pers. sg. fut. pass. indic. id.

ἐκζητήσας, nom. sg. m. aor. act. part. . . . id.

ἐκζητήσεις, acc. pl. f. n. (1 Tim. 1:4, GNT, WH & NA | ζητήσεις, MT & TR) . . . . ἐκζήτησις (‡2214)

(‡2214) **ἐκζήτησις**, εως, ἡ, *useless speculation*

ἐκζητήσωσιν, 3 pers. pl. aor. act. subj. . . . . ἐκζητέω (1567)

ἐκζητοῦσιν, dat. pl. m. pres. act. part. . . . id.

ἐκζητῶν, nom. sg. m. pres. act. part. . . . . id.

ἐκηρύξαμεν, 1 pers. pl. aor. act. indic. . . . . κηρύσσω (2784)

ἐκήρυξαν, 3 pers. pl. aor. act. indic. . . . . . id.

ἐκήρυξεν, 3 pers. sg. aor. act. indic. . . . . . id.

ἐκήρυσσε(ν), 3 pers. sg. imperf. act. indic. id.

ἐκήρυσσον, 3 pers. pl. imperf. act. indic. . id.

ἐκηρύχθη, 3 pers. sg. aor. pass. indic. [§26.3] id.

ἐκθαμβεῖσθαι, pres. pass. infin. . . . . ἐκθαμβέω (1568)

ἐκθαμβεῖσθε, 2 pers. pl. pres. pass. imper. id.

(1568) **ἐκθαμβέω**, ῶ [§17.Q] *to be amazed, astonished, awe-struck,* Mark 9:15; 14:33; 16:5, 6

ἔκθαμβοι, nom. pl. m. adj. . . . . ἔκθαμβος (1569)

(1569) **ἔκθαμβος**, ον [§7.2] (ἐκ + θάμβος) *amazed, awe-struck,* Acts 3:11

(‡2296) **ἐκθαυμάζω**, *to wonder at, wonder greatly*

ἔκθετα, acc. pl. neut. adj. . . . . ἔκθετος (1570)

(1570) **ἔκθετος**, ον [§7.2] *exposed, cast out, abandoned,* Acts 7:19

ἐκινδύνευον, 3 pers. pl. imperf. act. indic. κινδυνεύω (2793)

ἐκινήθη, 3 pers. sg. aor. pass. indic. . . . κινέω (2795)

ἐκινήθησαν, 3 pers. pl. aor. pass. indic. . . id.

(1571) **ἐκκαθαίρω**, fut. ἐκκαθαρῶ, aor. ἐξεκάθηρα, and, later, ἐξεκάθαρα [§27.1.c,e] (ἐκ + καθαίρω) *to cleanse thoroughly, purify,* 2 Tim. 2:21; *to purge out, eliminate,* 1 Cor. 5:7

ἐκκαθάρατε, 2 pers. pl. aor. act. imper. ἐκκαθαίρω (1571)

ἐκκαθάρῃ, 3 pers. sg. aor. act. subj. . . . . . id.

(1572) **ἐκκαίω**, aor. pass. ἐξεκαύθην [§35.3]

(ἐκκαίω, *to kindle up,* ἐκ + καίω) *to blaze out, to be inflamed,* Rom. 1:27

ἐκκακεῖν, pres. act. infin. (Luke 18:1; Eph. 3:13, MT & TR | ἐγκακεῖν, GNT & NA | ἐνκακεῖν, WH) . . . . ἐκκακέω (1573)

(1573) **ἐκκακέω,** ῶ, fut. ἐκκακήσω [§16.P] (ἐκ + κακός) *to lose spirits, to be faint-hearted, despond,* Eph. 3:13; *to faint, to flag, be remiss, indolent, slothful,* Luke 18:1; Gal. 6:9; 2 Cor. 4:1, 16; 2 Thess. 3:13

ἐκκακήσητε, 2 pers. pl. aor. act. subj. (2 Thess. 3:13, MT & TR | ἐγκακήσητε, GNT & NA | ἐνκακήσητε, WH) ἐκκακέω (1573)

ἐκκακοῦμεν, 1 pers. pl. pres. act. indic. (2 Cor. 4:1, MT & TR | ἐγκακοῦμεν, GNT, WH & NA) . . . . id.

ἐκκακῶμεν, 1 pers. pl. pres. act. subj. (Gal. 6:9, MT & TR | ἐγκακῶμεν, GNT & NA | ἐνκακῶμεν, WH) . . . . id.

(1574) **ἐκκεντέω,** ῶ, fut. ἐκκεντήσω [§16.P] (ἐκ + κεντέω) *to stab, pierce deeply, transfix,* John 19:37

ἐκκεχυμένον, nom. sg. neut. perf. pass. part. (Luke 11:50, GNT, WH & NA | ἐκχυνόμενον, MT & TR) . . . . ἐκχέω (1632)

ἐκκέχυται, 3 pers. sg. perf. pass. indic. . . . id.

(1575) **ἐκκλάω,** fut. ἐκκλάσω [§22.2] aor. pass. ἐξεκλάσθην (ἐκ + κλάω) *to break off,* Rom. 11:17, 19, 20

ἐκκλεῖσαι, aor. act. infin. . . . . ἐκκλείω (1576)

(1576) **ἐκκλείω,** fut. ἐκκλείσω [§22.4] (ἐκ + κλείω) *to shut out, exclude; to shut off, separate, insulate;* Gal. 4:17; *to leave no place for, eliminate,* Rom. 3:27

(1577) **ἐκκλησία,** ας, ἡ, nom. sg. f. n. [§2.B.b; 2.2] (ἐκκαλέω, *to summon forth*) *a popular assembly,* Acts 19:32, 39, 40; in N.T. *the congregation* of the children of Israel, Acts 7:38; transferred to the Christian body, of which the congregation of Israel was a figure, *the Church,* 1 Cor. 12:28; Col. 1:18, et al.; a local portion of the Church, *a local church,* Rom. 16:1, et al.; *a Christian congregation,* 1 Cor. 14:4, et al.

ἐκκλησίᾳ, dat. sg. f. n. . . . . ἐκκλησία (1577)

ἐκκλησίαι, nom. pl. f. n. . . . . id.

ἐκκλησίαις, dat. pl. f. n. . . . . id.

ἐκκλησίαν, acc. sg. f. n. . . . . id.

ἐκκλησίας, gen. sg. f. n. {Acts 15:4} . . . . . id.

ἐκκλησίας, acc. pl. f. n. {Acts 15:41} . . . . id.

ἐκκλησιῶν, gen. pl. f. n. . . . . id.

ἐκκλίνατε, 2 pers. pl. aor. act. imper. (Rom. 16:17, MT & TR | ἐκκλίνετε, GNT, WH & NA) . . . . ἐκκλίνω (1578)

ἐκκλινάτω, 3 pers. sg. aor. act. imper. . . . id.

ἐκκλίνετε, 2 pers. pl. pres. act. imper. (Rom. 16:17, GNT, WH & NA | ἐκκλίνατε, MT & TR) . . . . ἐκκλίνω (1578)

(1578) **ἐκκλίνω,** fut. ἐκκλινῶ [§27.1.a] (ἐκ + κλίνω) *to deflect, deviate,* Rom. 3:12; *to decline or turn away from, avoid,* Rom. 16:17; 1 Pet. 3:11

(1579) **ἐκκολυμβάω,** ῶ, fut. ἐκκολυμβήσω [§18.R] (ἐκ + κολυμβάω) *to swim out* to land, Acts 27:42

ἐκκολυμβήσας, nom. sg. m. aor. act. part. . . . . ἐκκολυμβάω (1579)

(1580) **ἐκκομίζω,** fut. ἐκκομίσω [§26.1] (ἐκ + κομίζω) *to carry out, bring out;* especially, *to carry out* a corpse for burial, Luke 7:12

ἐκκοπήσῃ, 2 pers. sg. 2 fut. pass. indic. [§24.6] . . . . ἐκκόπτω (1581)

ἐκκόπτεσθαι, pres. pass. infin. (1 Pet. 3:7, TR | ἐγκόπτεσθαι, GNT, WH, MT & NA) id.

ἐκκόπτεται, 3 pers. sg. pres. pass. indic. . id.

(1581) **ἐκκόπτω,** fut. ἐκκόψω [§23.1.a] (ἐκ + κόπτω) *to cut out; to cut off,* Matt. 3:10; 5:30, et al.; met. *to cut off* occasion, *remove, prevent,* 2 Cor. 11:12; *to render ineffectual,* 1 Pet. 3:7

ἐκκόψεις, 2 pers. sg. fut. act. indic. . ἐκκόπτω (1581)

ἔκκοψον, 2 pers. sg. aor. act. imper. . . . . . id.

ἐκκόψω, 1 pers. sg. aor. act. subj. . . . . . . id.

(†1582) **ἐκκρέμαννυμι** *to hang upon* a speaker, *fondly listen to, be earnestly attentive,* Luke 19:48

ἔκλαιε(ν), 3 pers. sg. imperf. act. indic. κλαίω (2799)

ἔκλαιον, 1 pers. sg. imperf. act. indic. {Rev. 5:4} . . . . id.

ἔκλαιον, 3 pers. pl. imperf. act. indic. {Luke 8:52} . . . . id.

(1583) **ἐκλαλέω,** ῶ, fut. ἐκλαλήσω [§16.P] (ἐκ + λαλέω) *to speak out; to tell, utter, divulge,* Acts 23:22

ἐκλαλῆσαι, aor. act. infin. . . . . ἐκλαλέω (1583)

(1584) **ἐκλάμπω,** fut. ἐκλάμψω [§23.1.a] (ἐκ + λάμπω) *to shine out or forth, be resplendent,* Matt. 13:43

ἐκλάμψουσιν, 3 pers. pl. fut. act. indic. . . . . ἐκλάμπω (1584)

(†1585) **ἐκλανθάνω** [§36.2] (ἐκ + λανθάνω) *to make to forget quite;* mid. ἐκλανθάνομαι, perf. (pass. form) ἐκλέλησμαι, *to forget entirely,* Heb. 12:5

ἔκλασα, 1 pers. sg. aor. act. indic. . . . . . κλάω (2806)

ἔκλασε(ν), 3 pers. sg. aor. act. indic. . . . . id.

ἐκλαύσατε, 2 pers. pl. aor. act. indic. [§35.3] . . . . κλαίω (2799)

ἔκλαυσε(ν), 3 pers. sg. aor. act. indic. . . . id.

(†1586) **ἐκλέγω,** fut. ἐκλέξω [§23.1.b] *to pick out;* in N.T. mid. ἐκλέγομαι, aor. ἐξελεξάμην, *to* *choose, select,* Luke 6:13; 10:42, et al.; in N.T. *to choose out* as the recipients of special favor and privilege, Acts 13:17; 1 Cor. 1:27, et al.

ἐκλείπῃ, 3 pers. sg. pres. act. subj. (Luke 22:32, TR | ἐκλίπῃ, GNT, WH, MT & NA) . . . . ἐκλείπω *(1587)*

ἐκλείπητε, 2 pers. pl. pres. act. subj. (Luke 16:9, MT | ἐκλίπῃ, GNT, WH & NA | ἐκλίπητε, TR) . . . . id.

ἐκλειπόντος, gen. sg. m. pres. act. part. (Luke 23:45, WH | ἐκλιπόντος, GNT & NA | ἐσκοτίσθη, MT & TR) . . . . id.

(1587) **ἐκλείπω,** fut. ἐκλείψω [§23.1.a] (ἐκ + λείπω) intrans. *to fail,* Luke 22:32; *to come to an end,* Heb. 1:12; *to be defunct,* Luke 16:9

ἔκλεισε(ν), 3 pers. sg. aor. act. indic. . . κλείω *(2808)*

ἐκλείσθη, 3 pers. sg. aor. pass. indic. [§22.4]   id.

ἐκλείσθησαν, 3 pers. pl. aor. pass. indic. .   id.

ἐκλείψουσι(ν), 3 pers. pl. fut. act. indic. . . . . ἐκλείπω *(1587)*

ἐκλεκτῇ, dat. sg. f. adj. . . . . ἐκλεκτός *(1588)*

ἐκλεκτῆς, gen. sg. f. adj. . . . . id.

ἐκλεκτοί, nom. pl. m. adj. . . . . id.

ἐκλεκτοῖς, dat. pl. m. adj. . . . . id.

ἐκλεκτόν, acc. sg. m. adj. {1 Pet. 2:4, 6} .   id.

ἐκλεκτόν, nom. sg. neut. adj. {1 Pet. 2:9}   id.

(1588) **ἐκλεκτός,** ή, όν, nom. sg. m. adj. [§7.F.a] *chosen out, selected;* in N.T. *chosen* as a recipient of special privilege, *elect,* Col. 3:12, et al.; *specially beloved,* Luke 23:35; *possessed of prime excellence, exalted,* 1 Tim. 5:21; *choice, precious,* 1 Pet. 2:4, 6

ἐκλεκτούς, acc. pl. m. adj. . . . . ἐκλεκτός *(1588)*

ἐκλεκτῶν, gen. pl. m. adj. . . . . id.

ἐκλελεγμένος, nom. sg. m. perf. pass. part. (Luke 9:35, GNT, WH & NA | ἀγαπητός, MT & TR) . . . . ἐκλέγω *(†1586)*

ἐκλέλησθε, 2 pers. pl. perf. pass. indic. [§36.2] . . . . ἐκλανθάνω *(†1585)*

ἐκλελυμένοι, nom. pl. m. perf. pass. part. (Matt. 9:36, TR | ἐσκυλμένοι, GNT, WH, MT & NA) . . . . ἐκλύω *(1590)*

ἐκλεξαμένοις, dat. pl. m. aor. mid. part. (Acts 15:25, GNT, WH & NA | ἐκλεξαμένους, MT & TR) . . . . ἐκλέγω *(†1586)*

ἐκλεξάμενος, nom. sg. m. aor. mid. part. .   id.

ἐκλεξαμένους, acc. pl. m. aor. mid. part. .   id.

ἔκλεψαν, 3 pers. pl. aor. act. indic. . . . κλέπτω *(2813)*

ἐκλήθη, 3 pers. sg. aor. pass. indic. [§22.4] . . . . καλέω *(2564)*

ἐκλήθης, 2 pers. sg. aor. pass. indic. . . . . . id.

ἐκλήθητε, 2 pers. pl. aor. pass. indic. . . . . id.

ἐκληρώθημεν, 1 pers. pl. aor. pass. indic. . . . . κληρόω *(2820)*

ἔκλιναν, 3 pers. pl. aor. act. indic. . . . . κλίνω *(2827)*

ἐκλίπῃ, 3 pers. sg. 2 aor. act. subj. (Luke 16:9; 22:32, GNT, WH & NA | ἐκλίπῃ, Luke 22:32, MT; ἐκλείπητε, Luke 16:9, MT | ἐκλίπητε, Luke 16:9, TR; ἐκλείπῃ, Luke 22:32, TR) . . . . ἐκλείπω *(1587)*

ἐκλίπητε, 2 pers. pl. 2 aor. act. subj. [§24.9] (Luke 16:9, TR | ἐκλίπῃ, GNT, WH & NA | ἐκλείπητε, MT) . . . . id.

ἐκλιπόντος, gen. sg. m. 2 aor. act. part. (Luke 23:45, GNT & NA | ἐκλειπόντος, WH | ἐσκοτίσθη, MT & TR) . . . . id.

(1589) **ἐκλογή,** ῆς, ἡ, nom. sg. f. n. [§2.b.a] *the act of choosing out, election;* in N.T. *election to privilege by divine grace,* Rom. 11:5, et al.; ἡ ἐκλογή, *the aggregate of those who are chosen, the elect,* Rom. 11:7; ἐκλογῆς, equivalent to ἐκλεκτόν, by Hebraism, Acts 9:15

ἐκλογήν, acc. sg. f. n. . . . . ἐκλογή *(1589)*

ἐκλογῆς, gen. sg. f. n. . . . . id.

ἐκλυθήσονται, 3 pers. pl. fut. pass. indic. . . . . ἐκλύω *(1590)*

ἐκλυθῶσιν, 3 pers. pl. aor. pass. subj. . . . . id.

ἐκλυόμενοι, nom. pl. m. pres. pass. part. . . . . id.

ἐκλύου, 2 pers. sg. pres. pass. imper. . . . . id.

(1590) **ἐκλύω** [§14.N] (*to loosen, debilitate,* ἐκ + λύω) *to be weary, exhausted, faint,* Matt. 9:36; 15:32; Mark 8:3; Gal. 6:9; *to faint, despond,* Heb. 12:3, 5

ἐκμάξασα, nom. sg. f. aor. act. part. ἐκμάσσω *(1591)*

ἐκμάσσειν, pres. act. infin. . . . . id.

(1591) **ἐκμάσσω,** fut. ἐκμάξω [§26.3] (ἐκ + μάσσω) *to wipe off; to wipe dry,* Luke 7:38, 44; John 11:2; 12:3; 13:5

(†1592) **ἐκμυκτηρίζω,** fut. ἐκμυκτηρίσω [§26.1] (ἐκ + μυκτηρίζω, from μυκτήρ, *the nose*) *to mock, deride, scoff at,* Luke 16:14; 23:35

(1593) **ἐκνεύω,** fut. ἐκνεύσομαι [§35.3] aor. ἐξένευσα, pr. *to swim out, to escape by swimming;* hence, generally, *to escape, get clear of* a place, John 5:13; though ἐκνεύσας, in this place, may be referred to ἐκνεύω, *to deviate, withdraw*

(1594) **ἐκνήφω,** fut. ἐκνήψω [§23.1.a] (ἐκ + νήφω) pr. *to awake sober after intoxication;* met. *to shake off mental bewilderment, to wake up* from delusion and folly, 1 Cor. 15:34

ἐκνήψατε, 2 pers. pl. aor. act. imper. . ἐκνήφω *(1594)*

ἐκοιμήθη, 3 pers. sg. aor. pass. indic. . κοιμάω *(2837)*

ἐκοιμήθησαν, 3 pers. pl. aor. pass. indic. .   id.

ἐκοινώνησαν, 3 pers. pl. aor. act. indic. . . . . κοινωνέω *(2841)*

ἐκοινώνησεν, 3 pers. sg. aor. act. indic. . . id.

ἐκολάφισαν, 3 pers. pl. aor. act.
indic. . . . . κολαφίζω *(2852)*
ἐκολλήθη, 3 pers. sg. aor. pass. indic. κολλάω *(2853)*
ἐκολλήθησαν, 3 pers. pl. aor. pass. indic. (Rev.
18:5, GNT, WH, MT, TRb & NA |
ἠκολούθησαν, TRs) . . . . id.
ἐκολοβώθησαν, 3 pers. pl. aor. pass.
indic. . . . . κολοβόω *(2856)*
ἐκολόβωσε(ν), 3 pers. sg. aor. act. indic. . id.
ἐκομισάμην, 1 pers. sg. aor. mid.
indic. . . . . κομίζω *(2865)*
ἐκομίσαντο, 3 pers. pl. aor. mid. indic. . . id.
ἐκομίσατο, 3 pers. sg. aor. mid. indic. . . . id.
ἐκόπασεν, 3 pers. sg. aor. act. indic. . κοπάζω *(2869)*
ἐκοπίασα, 1 pers. sg. aor. act. indic. . . κοπιάω *(2872)*
ἐκοπίασας, 2 pers. sg. aor. act. indic. (Rev.
2:3, MT | κεκοπίακες, GNT, WH & NA
| κεκοπίακες καὶ οὐ κέκμηκας, TR) . id.
ἐκοπίασεν, 3 pers. sg. aor. act. indic. . . . . id.
ἔκοπτον, 3 pers. pl. imperf. act. indic. . κόπτω *(2875)*
ἐκόπτοντο, 3 pers. pl. imperf. mid. indic. . id.
ἐκόσμησαν, 3 pers. pl. aor. act. indic. κοσμέω *(2885)*
ἐκόσμουν, 3 pers. pl. imperf. act. indic. . . id.
ἑκοῦσα, nom. sg. f. adj. . . . . ἑκών *(1635)*
(1595) ἑκούσιον, acc. sg. neut. adj. . . . . . ἑκούσιος *(†1595)*
(†1595) ἑκούσιος, α, ον, *voluntary, spontaneous,* Philemon 14
(1596) ἑκουσίως, adv., *voluntarily, spontaneously,*
Heb. 10:26; 1 Pet. 5:2
ἐκούφιζον, 3 pers. pl. imperf. act.
indic. κουφίζω *(2893)*
ἐκόψασθε, 2 pers. pl. aor. mid. indic. . κόπτω *(2875)*
(1597) ἔκπαλαι, adv. (ἐκ + πάλαι) *of old, long since,*
2 Pet. 2:3; 3:5
(1598) ἐκπειράζω, fut. ἐκπειράσω [§26.1] (ἐκ +
πειράζω) *to tempt, put to the proof,* Matt.
4:7; Luke 4:12; 1 Cor. 10:9; *to try, sound,*
Luke 10:25
ἐκπειράζωμεν, 1 pers. pl. pres. act.
subj. ἐκπειράζω *(1598)*
ἐκπειράζων, nom. sg. m. pres. act. part. . . id.
ἐκπειράσεις, 2 pers. sg. fut. act. indic. . . . id.
(1599) ἐκπέμπω, fut. ἐκπέμψω [§23.1.a] (ἐκ +
πέμπω) *to send out, or away,* Acts 13:4;
17:10
ἐκπεμφθέντες, nom. pl. m. aor. pass.
part. ἐκπέμπω *(1599)*
ἐκπεπλήρωκε(ν), 3 pers. sg. perf. act.
indic. ἐκπληρόω *(1603)*
ἐκπέπτωκας, 2 pers. sg. perf. act. indic.
[§37.1] ἐκπίπτω (Rev. 2:5, TR | πέπτω-
κας, GNT, MT & NA | πέπτωκες,
WH) . . . . ἐκπίπτω *(1601)*
ἐκπέπτωκεν, 3 pers. sg. perf. act. indic. . . id.
(‡4057) ἐκπερισσοῦ, adv., *exceedingly, vehemently*

(1 Thess. 3:10; 5:13, with ὑπέρ TRs | ὑπέρ
ἐκ περισσοῦ, TRb | ὑπερεκπερισσοῦ,
GNT, WH & NA)
(‡4057) ἐκπερισσῶς, adv. (strengthened from
περισσῶς) *exceedingly, vehemently* (Mark
14:31, GNT, WH & NA | ἐκ περισσοῦ,
MT & TR)
ἐκπεσεῖν, 2 aor. act. infin. [§37.1] . . . ἐκπίπτω *(1601)*
ἐκπέσητε, 2 pers. pl. 2 aor. act. subj. . . . . id.
ἐκπέσωμεν, 1 pers. pl. 2 aor. act. subj. (Acts
27:29, GNT, WH, MT, TRb & NA |
ἐκπέσωσιν, TRs) . . . . id.
ἐκπέσωσι(ν), 3 pers. pl. 2 aor. act. subj. . . id.
(1600) ἐκπετάννυμι, fut. ἐκπετάσω [§36.5] (ἐκ +
πετάννυμι) *to stretch forth, expand, extend,* Rom. 10:21
ἐκπεφευγέναι, 2 perf. act. infin.
[§25.3] . . . . ἐκφεύγω *(1628)*
(‡1530) ἐκπηδάω, ῶ, fut. ἐκπηδήσω [§18.R] (ἐκ +
πηδάω, *to leap, spring*) *to leap forth, rush
out,* Acts 14:14
ἐκπίπτει, 3 pers. sg. pres. act. indic. (1 Cor.
13:8, MT & TR | πίπτει, GNT, WH &
NA) . . . . ἐκπίπτω *(1601)*
ἐκπίπτοντες, nom. pl. m. pres. act. part.
(Mark 13:25, MT & TR | πίπτοντες,
GNT, WH & NA) . . . . id.
(1601) ἐκπίπτω, fut. ἐκπεσοῦμαι, perf. ἐκπέπτωκα,
aor. ἐξέπεσα, 2 aor. ἐξέπεσον [§37.1] *to
fall off or from,* Mark 13:25; Acts 12:7;
27:32, et al.; met. *to fall from, forfeit, lose,*
Gal. 5:4; 2 Pet. 3:17; Rev. 2:5; *to be cast
ashore,* Acts 27:17, 26, 29; *to fall to the
ground, be fruitless, ineffectual,* Rom. 9:6;
to cease, come to an end, 1 Cor. 13: 8
ἐκπλεῦσαι, aor. act. infin. [§35.3] . . . . ἐκπλέω *(1602)*
(1602) ἐκπλέω, fut. ἐκπλεύσομαι, aor. ἐξέπλευσα
(ἐκ + πλέω) *to sail out of or from* a place,
Acts 15:39; 18:18; 20:6
(1603) ἐκπληρόω, ῶ, fut. ἐκπληρώσω [§20.T] (ἐκ
+ πληρόω) *to fill out, complete, fill up;*
met. *to fulfil, perform, accomplish,* Acts
13:32
ἐκπλήρωσιν, acc. sg. f. n. . . . . . . ἐκπλήρωσις *(1604)*
(1604) ἐκπλήρωσις, εως, ἡ [§5.E.c] pr. *a filling up,
completion;* hence, *a fulfilling, accomplishment,* Acts 21:26
ἐκπλήσσεσθαι, pres. pass. infin. (Matt. 13:54,
GNT, WH & NA | ἐκπλήττεσθαι, MT
& TR) . . . . ἐκπλήσσω *(1605)*
ἐκπλησσόμενος, nom. sg. m. pres. pass. part.
(Acts 13:12, GNT, MT, TR & NA |
ἐκπληττόμενος, WH) . . . . id.
(1605) ἐκπλήσσω, or ἐκπλήττω, fut. ἐκπλήξω
[§26.3] 2 aor. pass. ἐξεπλάγην [§24.9] (ἐκ

+ πλήσσω) pr. *to strike out of;* hence, *to strike out of* one's wits, *to astound, amaze;* pass. Matt. 7:28; 13:54, et al.

ἐκπλήττεσθαι, pres. pass. infin. (Matt. 13:54, MT & TR | ἐκπλήσσεσθαι, GNT, WH & NA) . . . . ἐκπλήσσω *(1605)*

ἐκπληττόμενος, nom. sg. m. pres. pass. part. (Acts 13:12, WH | ἐκπλησσόμενος, GNT, MT, TR & NA) . . . . id.

(1606) **ἐκπνέω,** fut. ἐκπνεύσω, and ἐκπνεύσομαι [§35.3] (ἐκ + πνέω) *to breathe out; to expire, die,* Mark 15:37, 39; Luke 23:46

ἐκπορεύεσθαι, pres. mid./pass. dep. infin. . . . . ἐκπορεύομαι *(1607)*

ἐκπορευέσθω, 3 pers. sg. pres. mid./pass. dep. imper. . . . . id.

ἐκπορεύεται, 3 pers. sg. pres. mid./pass. dep. indic. . . . . id.

(1607) **ἐκπορεύομαι,** fut. ἐκπορεύσομαι [§14.N] (ἐκ + πορεύομαι) *to go from* or *out of* a place, *depart from,* Mark 11:19; 13:1, et al.; *to be voided,* Mark 7:19; *to be cast out,* Matt. 17:21; *to proceed from, be spoken,* Matt. 4:4; 15:11, et al.; *to burst forth,* Rev. 4:5; *to be spread abroad,* Luke 4:37; *to flow out,* Rev. 22:1; from the Hebrew, ἐκπορεύομαι καὶ εἰσπορεύομαι. See εἰσέρχομαι *(1525),* Acts 9:28

ἐκπορευόμενα, nom. pl. neut. pres. mid./pass. dep. part. . . . . ἐκπορεύομαι *(1607)*

ἐκπορευομένη, nom. sg. f. pres. mid./pass. dep. part. id.

ἐκπορευομένῃ, dat. sg. f. pres. mid./pass. dep. part. (Rev. 19:21, TR | ἐξελθούσῃ, GNT, WH, MT & NA) . . . . id.

ἐκπορευόμενοι, nom. pl. m. pres. mid./pass. dep. part. . . . . id.

ἐκπορευομένοις, dat. pl. m. pres. mid. or mid./pass. dep. part. . . . . id.

ἐκπορευόμενον, acc. sg. m. pres. mid./pass. dep. part. {Rev. 22:1} . . . . id.

ἐκπορευόμενον, nom. sg. neut. pres. mid./pass. dep. part. {Matt. 15:11} . . . . id.

ἐκπορευόμενος, nom. sg. m. pres. mid./pass. dep. part. . . . . id.

ἐκπορευομένου, gen. sg. m. pres. mid./pass. dep. part. {Mark 10:17} . . . . id.

ἐκπορευομένου, gen. sg. neut. pres. mid./pass. dep. part. {Rev. 9:18} . . . . id.

ἐκπορευομένῳ, dat. sg. neut. pres. mid. or mid./pass. dep. part. . . . . id.

ἐκπορευομένων, gen. pl. m. pres. mid./pass. dep. part. . . . . id.

ἐκπορεύονται, 3 pers. pl. pres. mid./pass. dep. indic. . . . . id.

ἐκπορεύσονται, 3 pers. pl. fut. mid. dep. indic. . . . . ἐκπορεύομαι *(1607)*

ἐκπορνεύσασαι, nom. pl. f. aor. act. part. . . . . ἐκπορνεύω *(1608)*

(1608) **ἐκπορνεύω,** fut. ἐκπορνεύσω [§13.M] (ἐκ + πορνεύω) *to be given to fornication,* Jude 7

(1609) **ἐκπτύω,** fut. ἐκπτύσω and ἐκπτύσομαι [§13.M] (ἐκ + πτύω) *to spit out;* met. *to reject,* Gal. 4:14

ἔκραζε(ν), 3 pers. sg. imperf. act. indic. . . . . κράζω *(2896)*

ἔκραζον, 3 pers. pl. imperf. act. indic. . . . id.

ἔκραξα, 1 pers. sg. aor. act. indic. (Acts 24:21, MT & TR | ἐκέκραξα, GNT, WH & NA) . . . . id.

ἔκραξαν, 3 pers. pl. aor. act. indic. . . . . . . id.

ἔκραξε(ν), 3 pers. sg. aor. act. indic. . . . . . id.

ἐκραταιοῦτο, 3 pers. sg. imperf. pass. indic. . . . . κραταιόω *(2901)*

ἐκρατήσαμεν, 1 pers. pl. aor. act. indic. . . . . κρατέω *(2902)*

ἐκράτησαν, 3 pers. pl. aor. act. indic. . . . . id.

ἐκρατήσατε, 2 pers. pl. aor. act. indic. . . . id.

ἐκράτησε(ν), 3 pers. sg. aor. act. indic. . . . id.

ἐκρατοῦντο, 3 pers. pl. imperf. pass. indic. . . id.

ἐκραύγαζον, 3 pers. pl. imperf. act. indic. (John 12:13, GNT, WH & NA | ἔκραζον, MT & TR) . . . . κραυγάζω *(2905)*

ἐκραύγασαν, 3 pers. pl. aor. act. indic. . . . id.

ἐκραύγασε(ν), 3 pers. sg. aor. act. indic. . . id.

(1610) **ἐκριζόω, ῶ,** fut. ἐκριζώσω [§20.T] (ἐκ + ῥιζόω, ῥίζα) *to root up, eradicate,* Matt. 13:29; 15:13; Luke 17:6; Jude 12

ἐκριζωθέντα, nom. pl. neut. aor. pass. part. . . . . ἐκριζόω *(1610)*

ἐκριζωθήσεται, 3 pers. sg. fut. pass. indic. id.

ἐκριζώθητι, 2 pers. sg. aor. pass. imper. . . id.

ἐκριζώσητε, 2 pers. pl. aor. act. subj. . . . . id.

ἐκρίθη, 3 pers. sg. aor. pass. indic. [§27.3] . . . . κρίνω *(2919)*

ἐκρίθησαν, 3 pers. pl. aor. pass. indic. . . . id.

ἔκρινα, 1 pers. sg. aor. act. indic. . . . . id.

ἔκρινας, 2 pers. sg. aor. act. indic. . . . . . . id.

ἔκρινε(ν), 3 pers. sg. aor. act. indic. . . . . . id.

ἐκρινόμεθα, 1 pers. pl. imperf. pass. indic. id.

ἐκρύβη, 3 pers. sg. 2 aor. pass. indic. [§24.8.a] . . . . κρύπτω *(2928)*

ἔκρυψα, 1 pers. sg. aor. act. indic. . . . . . . id.

ἔκρυψαν, 3 pers. pl. aor. act. indic. . . . . . . id.

ἔκρυψας, 2 pers. sg. aor. act. indic. (Matt. 11:25, GNT, WH & NA | ἀπέκρυψας, MT & TR) . . . . id.

ἔκρυψε(ν), 3 pers. sg. aor. act. indic. . . . . id.

ἐκστάσει, dat sg. f. n. . . . . ἔκστασις *(1611)*

ἐκστάσεως, gen. sg. f. n. . . . . id.

(1611) **ἔκστασις**, εως, ἡ, nom. sg. f. n. [§5.E.c] pr. *a displacement;* hence, *a displacement of the mind from its ordinary state and self-possession; amazement, astonishment,* Mark 5:42; *excess of fear; fear, terror,* Mark 16:8; Luke 5:26; Acts 3:10; in N.T. *an ecstasy, a trance,* Acts 10:10; 11:5; 22:17

(1612) **ἐκστρέφω**, fut. ἐκστρέψω, perf. pass. ἐξέστραμμαι [§35.9] (ἐκ + στρέφω) pr. *to turn out of, to turn inside out;* hence, *to change entirely;* in N.T. pass. *to be perverted,* Tit. 3:11

ἐκσῶσαι, aor. act. infin. (Acts 27:39, WH | ἐξῶσαι, GNT, MT, TR & NA) .. ἐκσῴζω *(‡1856)*

(‡1856) **ἐκσῴζω**, *to save from,* either to keep or to rescue from danger

ἐκταράσσουσιν, 3 pers. pl. pres. act. indic. ἐκταράσσω *(1613)*

(1613) **ἐκταράσσω**, fut. ἐκταράξω [§26.3] (ἐκ + ταράσσω) *to disturb, disquiet, throw into confusion,* Acts 16:20

ἐκτεθέντα, acc. sg. m. aor. pass. part. (Acts 7:21, MT & TR | ἐκτεθέντος, GNT, WH & NA) . . . . ἐκτίθημι *(1620)*

ἐκτεθέντος, gen. sg. m. aor. pass. part. (Acts 7:21, GNT, WH & NA | ἐκτεθέντα, MT & TR) . . . . id.

ἐκτείνας, nom. sg. f. aor. act. part. . . . ἐκτείνω *(1614)*

ἐκτείνειν, pres. act. infin. . . . . id.

ἔκτεινον, 2 pers. sg. aor. act. imper. . . . . . id.

(1614) **ἐκτείνω**, fut. ἐκτενῶ [§27.1.c] (ἐκ + τείνω) *to stretch out,* Matt. 8:3; 12:13, et al.; *to lay* hands on any one, Luke 22:53; *to exert* power and energy, Acts 4:30; *to cast out, let down* an anchor, Acts 27:30

ἐκτελέσαι, aor. act. infin. . . . . ἐκτελέω *(1615)*

(1615) **ἐκτελέω**, ῶ, fut. ἐκτελέσω [§22.1] (ἐκ + τελέω) *to bring quite to an end, to finish, complete,* Luke 14:29, 30

(1616) **ἐκτένεια**, ας, ἡ [§2.B.b; 2.2] pr. *extension;* in N.T. *intenseness, intentness;* ἐν ἐκτενείᾳ, *intently, assiduously,* Acts 26:7

ἐκτενείᾳ, dat. sg. f. n. . . . . ἐκτένεια *(1616)*

ἐκτενεῖς, 2 pers. sg. fut. act. indic. . . . ἐκτείνω *(1614)*

(1617) **ἐκτενέστερον**, adv., *very earnestly,* Luke 22:44; pr. neut. compar. of ἐκτενής

ἐκτενῆ, acc. sg. f. adj. . . . . ἐκτενής *(1618)*

(1618) **ἐκτενής**, ές, nom. sg. f. adj. [§7.G.b] pr. *extended;* met. *intense, earnest, fervent,* Acts 12:5; 1 Pet. 4:8 (Acts 12:5, MT & TR | GNT, WH & NA)

(1619) **ἐκτενῶς**, adv., *intensely, fervently, earnestly,* 1 Pet. 1:22

ἔκτη, nom. sg. f. adj. . . . . ἕκτος *(1623)*

ἔκτην, acc. sg. f. adj. . . . . id.

ἕκτης, gen. sg. f. adj. . . . . ἕκτος *(1623)*

ἐκτησάμην, 1 pers. sg. aor. mid. dep. indic. . . . . κτάομαι *(2932)*

ἐκτήσατο, 3 pers. sg. aor. mid. dep. indic. id.

(1620) **ἐκτίθημι**, fut. ἐκθήσω [§28.V] (ἐκ + τίθημι) pr. *to place outside, put forth; to expose* an infant, Acts 7:21; met. *to set forth, declare, explain,* Acts 11:4; 18:26; 28:23

ἐκτιναξάμενοι, nom. pl. m. aor. mid. part. . . . . ἐκτινάσσω *(1621)*

ἐκτιναξάμενος, nom. sg. m. aor. mid. part. id.

ἐκτινάξατε, 2 pers. pl. aor. act. imper. . . . id.

(1621) **ἐκτινάσσω**, fut. ἐκτινάξω [§26.3] (ἐκ + τινάσσω, *to shake*) *to shake out, shake off,* Matt. 10:14; Mark 6:11, et al.

ἔκτισας, 2 pers. sg. aor. act. indic. . . . . κτίζω *(2936)*

ἔκτισε(ν), 3 pers. sg. aor. act. indic. . . . . . id.

ἐκτίσθη, 3 pers. sg. aor. pass. indic. . . . . . id.

ἐκτίσθησαν, 3 pers. pl. aor. pass. indic. . . id.

ἔκτισται, 3 pers. sg. perf. pass. indic. . . . . id.

(1622) **ἐκτός**, adv. (ἐκ) *without, on the outside;* τὸ ἐκτός, *the exterior, outside,* Matt. 23:26; met. *besides,* Acts 26:22; 1 Cor. 15:27; ἐκτὸς εἰ μή, *unless, except,* 1 Cor. 14:5, et al. {Acts 26:22}

(1623) **ἕκτος**, η, ον, nom. sg. m. adj. [§7.F.a] *sixth,* Matt. 20:5; 27:45, et al. {Rev. 9:13}

ἐκτραπῇ, 3 pers. sg. 2 aor. pass. subj. [§24.10] . . . . ἐκτρέπω *(1624)*

ἐκτραπήσονται, 3 pers. pl. 2 fut. pass. indic. id.

ἐκτρεπόμενος, nom. sg. m. pres. mid. part. id.

(1624) **ἐκτρέπω**, fut. ἐκτρέψω [§23.1.a] (ἐκ + τρέπω) *to turn out or aside,* Heb. 12:13; 2 aor. mid. (pass. form) ἐξετράπην, *to turn aside or away, swerve,* 1 Tim. 1:6; 5:15; 2 Tim. 4:4; *to turn from, avoid,* 1 Tim. 6:20

ἐκτρέφει, 3 pers. sg. pres. act. indic. . ἐκτρέφω *(1625)*

ἐκτρέφετε, 2 pers. pl. pres. act. imper. . . . id.

(1625) **ἐκτρέφω**, fut. ἐκθρέψω [§35.4] (ἐκ + τρέφω) *to nourish, promote health and strength,* Eph. 5:29; *to bring up, educate,* Eph. 6:4

ἐκτρέφωσιν, 3 pers. pl. pres. act. subj. (Rev. 12:6, MT | τρέφωσιν, GNT, WH, TR & NA) . . . . ἐκτρέφω *(1625)*

(1626) **ἔκτρωμα**, ατος, τό [§4.D.c] (ἐκτιτρώσκω, *to cause abortion*) *an abortion, fetus prematurely born; a puny birth,* 1 Cor. 15:8

ἐκτρώματι, dat. sg. neut. n. . . . . ἔκτρωμα *(1626)*

ἕκτῳ, dat. sg. m. adj. . . . . ἕκτος *(1623)*

ἐκύκλευσαν, 3 pers. pl. aor. act. indic. (Rev. 20:9, GNT, WH, MT & NA | ἐκύκλωσαν, TR) . . . . κυκλεύω *(‡2944)*

ἐκύκλωσαν, 3 pers. pl. aor. act. indic. κυκλόω *(2944)*

ἐκυλίετο, 3 pers. sg. imperf. mid./pass.

indic. κυλίω *(†2947)*

ἐκφέρειν, pres. act. infin. . . . . ἐκφέρω *(1627)*

ἐκφέρουσα, nom. sg. f. pres. act. part. . . . id.

(1627) **ἐκφέρω,** fut. ἐξοίσω, aor. ἐξήνεγκα, 2 aor.
ἐξήνεγκον [§36.1] (ἐκ + φέρω) *to bring
forth, carry out,* Luke 15:22; Acts 5:15;
1 Tim. 6:7; *to carry out* for burial, Acts
5:6, 9, 10; *to produce, yield,* Heb. 6:8

(1628) **ἐκφεύγω,** fut. ἐκφεύξομαι, 2 aor. ἐξέφυγον
[§25.3] 2 perf. ἐκπέφευγα [§24.9] (ἐκ +
φεύγω) intrans. *to flee out, to make an
escape,* Acts 16:27; 19:16; trans. *to escape,
avoid,* Luke 21:36; Rom. 2:3, et al.

ἐκφεύξῃ, 2 pers. sg. fut. mid. dep.
indic. ἐκφεύγω *(1628)*

ἐκφευξόμεθα, 1 pers. pl. fut. mid. dep. indic. id.

ἐκφοβεῖν, pres. act. infin. . . . . ἐκφοβέω *(1629)*

(1629) **ἐκφοβέω,** ῶ, fut. ἐκφοβήσω [§16.P] (ἐκ +
φοβέω) *to terrify,* 2 Cor. 10:9

ἔκφοβοι, nom. pl. m. adj. . . . . ἔκφοβος *(1630)*

(1630) **ἔκφοβος,** ον, nom. sg. m. adj. [§7.2] (ἐκ +
φόβος) *affrighted,* Mark 9:6; Heb. 12:21

ἐκφυγεῖν, 2 aor. act. infin. . . . . ἐκφεύγω *(1628)*

ἐκφύγωσιν, 3 pers. pl. 2 aor. act. subj. . . . id.

ἐκφύῃ, 3 pers. sg. pres. act. subj. . . . . . . ἐκφύω *(1631)*

(1631) **ἐκφύω,** fut. ἐκφύσω [§13.M] (ἐκ + φύω) *to
generate; to put forth, shoot,* Matt. 24:32;
Mark 13:28

ἐκχέαι, aor. act. infin. [§36.1] . . . . ἐκχέω *(1632)*

ἐκχέατε, 2 pers. pl. aor. act. imper. (Rev. 16:1,
MT & TR | ἐκχέετε, GNT, WH & NA) id.

ἐκχέετε, 2 pers. pl. pres. act. imper. (Rev. 16:1,
GNT, WH & NA | ἐκχέατε, MT & TR) id.

ἐκχεῖται, 3 pers. sg. pres. pass. indic. . . . . id.

(1632) **ἐκχέω,** fut. ἐκχεῶ, aor. ἐξέχεα, perf.
ἐκκέχυκα, perf. pass. ἐκκέχυμαι, aor.
pass. ἐξεχύθην [§36.1] *to pour out,* Rev.
16:1, 2, 3, et al.; *to shed* blood, Matt.
26:28; Mark 14:24, et al.; pass. *to gush
out,* Acts 1:18; *to spill, scatter,* Matt. 9:17;
John 2:15; met. *to give largely, bestow liberally,* Acts 2:17, 18, 33; 10:45, et al.; pass.
to rush headlong into anything, *be abandoned to,* Jude 11

ἐκχεῶ, 1 pers. sg. fut. act. indic. . . . . . . ἐκχέω *(1632)*

ἐκχυθήσεται, 3 pers. sg. fut. pass.
indic. ἐκχύν(ν)ω *(†1632)*

ἐκχυννόμενον, nom. sg. neut. pres. pass. part.
(Matt. 23:35; 26:28; Mark 14:24; Luke
11:50; 22:20, GNT, WH & NA | ἐκ-
χυνόμενον, MT & TR) . . . . id.

(†1632) **ἐκχύν(ν)ω,** a later form equivalent to ἐκχέω,
Matt. 23:35, et al.

ἐκχυνόμενον, nom. sg. neut. pres. pass. part.
(Matt. 23:35; 26:28; Mark 14:24; Luke

11:50; 22:20, MT & TR | ἐκχυννόμενον,
GNT, WH & NA) . . . . ἐκχύν(ν)ω *(†1632)*

ἐκχωρείτωσαν, 3 pers. pl. pres. act.
imper. ἐκχωρέω *(1633)*

(1633) **ἐκχωρέω,** ῶ, fut. ἐκχωρήσω [§16.P] (ἐκ +
χωρέω) *to go out, depart from, flee,* Luke
21:21

(1634) **ἐκψύχω,** fut. ἐκψύξω [§23.1.b] *to expire, give
up the ghost,* Acts 5:5, 10; 12:23

ἐκωλύθην, 1 pers. sg. aor. pass. indic. . κωλύω *(2967)*

ἐκωλύομεν, 1 pers. pl. imperf. act. indic.
(Mark 9:38; Luke 9:49, GNT, WH & NA
| ἐκωλύσαμεν, MT & TR) . . . . id.

ἐκωλύσαμεν, 1 pers. pl. aor. act. indic. (Mark
9:38; Luke 9:49, MT & TR | ἐκωλύομεν,
GNT, WH & NA) . . . . id.

ἐκωλύσατε, 2 pers. pl. aor. act. indic. . . . . id.

ἐκώλυσε(ν), 3 pers. sg. aor. act. indic. . . . id.

(1635) **ἑκών,** οῦσα, όν, nom. sg. m. adj. [§7.H.d]
willing, voluntary, Rom. 8:20; 1 Cor. 9:17

ἔλαβε(ν), 3 pers. sg. 2 aor. act. indic.
[§24.9] . . . . λαμβάνω *(2983)*

ἔλαβες, 2 pers. sg. 2 aor. act. indic. . . . . . id.

ἐλάβετε, 2 pers. pl. 2 aor. act. indic. . . . . . id.

ἐλάβομεν, 1 pers. pl. 2 aor. act. indic. . . . . id.

ἔλαβον, 1 pers. sg. 2 aor. act. indic.
{John 10:18} . . . . id.

ἔλαβον, 3 pers. pl. 2 aor. act. indic.
{John 12:13} . . . . id.

ἔλαθε(ν), 3 pers. sg. 2 aor. act. indic.
[§24.9] . . . . λανθάνω *(2990)*

ἔλαθον, 3 pers. pl. 2 aor. act. indic. . . . . . id.

(1636) **ἐλαία,** ας, ἡ [§2.B.b; 2.2] *an olive tree,* Matt.
21:1; 24:3, et al.; *an olive, fruit of the olive
tree,* James 3:12

ἐλαίᾳ, dat. sg. f. n. . . . . ἐλαία *(1636)*

ἐλαῖαι, nom. pl. f. n. . . . . id.

ἐλαίας, gen. sg. f. n. {Rom. 11:17} . . . . . . id.

ἐλαίας, acc. pl. f. n. {James 3:12} . . . . . . id.

(1637) **ἔλαιον,** ου, τό [§3.C.c] *olive oil, oil,* Matt.
25:3, 4, 8; Mark 6:13, et al.

ἔλαιον, acc. sg. neut. n. . . . . ἔλαιον *(1637)*

ἐλαίου, gen. sg. neut. n. . . . . id.

ἐλαίῳ, dat. sg. neut. n. . . . . id.

ἐλαιῶν, gen. pl. f. n. . . . . ἐλαία *(1636)*

(1638) **ἐλαιών,** ῶνος, ὁ [§4.2.e] *an olive garden;* in
N.T. the mount *Olivet,* Acts 1:12

ἐλαιῶνος, gen. sg. m. n. . . . . ἐλαιών *(1638)*

ἐλάκησε(ν), 3 pers. sg. aor. act. indic. λάσκω *(†2997)*

ἐλάλει, 3 pers. sg. imperf. act. indic. . . λαλέω *(2980)*

ἐλαλήθη, 3 pers. sg. aor. pass. indic. . . . . id.

ἐλάλησα, 1 pers. sg. aor. act. indic. . . . . . id.

ἐλαλήσαμεν, 1 pers. pl. aor. act. indic. . . . id.

ἐλάλησαν, 3 pers. pl. aor. act. indic. . . . . . id.

ἐλαλήσατε, 2 pers. pl. aor. act. indic. . . . . id.

ἐλάλησε(ν), 3 pers. sg. aor. act.
  indic. . . . . λαλέω *(2980)*
ἐλαλοῦμεν, 1 pers. pl. imperf. act. indic. . id.
ἐλάλουν, 1 pers. sg. imperf. act. indic.
  {1 Cor. 13:11} . . . . id.
ἐλάλουν, 3 pers. pl. imperf. act. indic.
  {Luke 2:15} . . . . id.
ἐλάμβανον, 3 pers. pl. imperf. act.
  indic. . . . . λαμβάνω *(2983)*
Ἐλαμῖται, nom. pl. m. n. (Acts 2:9, GNT,
  MT, TR & NA | Ἐλαμεῖται,
  WH) . . . . Ἐλαμίτης *(1639)*
(1639) **Ἐλαμίτης**, ου, ὁ [§2.B.c] *an Elamite; an in-*
  habitant of Elam, a province of Persia, Acts
  2:9
ἔλαμψε(ν), 3 pers. sg. aor. act. indic. . . λάμπω *(2989)*
ἐλάσσονι, dat. sg. m. adj. . . . . ἐλάσσων *(1640)*
ἐλάσσω, acc. sg. m. adj. contr. . . . . id.
(1640) **ἐλάσσων**, or **ἐλάττων**, ον [§8.5] (compar. of
  the old word ἐλαχύς) *less; less* in age,
  younger, Rom. 9:12; *less* in dignity, *infer-*
  ior, Heb. 7:7; *less* in quality, *inferior,*
  worse, John 2:10
ἐλατόμησεν, 3 pers. sg. aor. act.
  indic. λατομέω *(2998)*
ἐλάτρευσαν, 3 pers. pl. aor. act.
  indic. . . . . λατρεύω *(3000)*
ἔλαττον, nom. sg. neut. adj.
  {Heb. 7:7} . . . . ἐλάττων *(1640)*
ἔλαττον, acc. sg. neut. adj. {1 Tim. 5:9} . . id.
(1641) **ἐλαττονέω**, ῶ, fut. ἐλαττονήσω, aor.
  ἠλαττόνησα [§16.P] trans. *to make less;* intrans. *to be less, inferior; to have too lit-*
  tle, want, lack, 2 Cor. 8:15
ἐλαττοῦσθαι, pres. pass. infin. [§21.U] ἐλαττόω *(1642)*
(1642) **ἐλαττόω**, ῶ, fut. ἐλαττώσω, perf. pass.
  ἠλάττωμαι [§20.T; 21.U] *to make less or*
  inferior, Heb. 2:7; pass. *to be made less or*
  inferior, Heb. 2:9; *to decline* in importance,
  John 3:30
ἐλαύνειν, pres. act. infin. . . . . ἐλαύνω *(1643)*
ἐλαυνόμενα, nom. pl. neut. pres. pass. part. id.
ἐλαυνόμεναι, nom. pl. f. pres. pass. part. . id.
(1643) **ἐλαύνω**, fut. ἐλάσω, perf. ἐλήλακα [§36.2]
  to drive, urge forward, spur on, Luke 8:29;
  James 3:4; 2 Pet. 2:17; *to impel* a vessel by
  oars, *to row,* Mark 6:48; John 6:19
(1644) **ἐλαφρία**, ας, ἡ [§2.B.b; 2.2] *lightness* in
  weight; hence, *lightness of mind, levity,*
  2 Cor. 1:17
ἐλαφρίᾳ, dat. sg. f. n. . . . . ἐλαφρία *(1644)*
ἐλαφρόν, nom. sg. neut. adj. . . . . ἐλαφρός *(1645)*
(1645) **ἐλαφρός**, ά, όν [§7.1] *light, not heavy,* Matt.
  11:30; 2 Cor. 4:17
ἔλαχε(ν), 3 pers. sg. 2 aor. act. indic.

  [§36.2] . . . . λαγχάνω *(2975)*
ἐλαχίστη, nom. sg. f. adj. . . . . ἐλάχιστος *(1646)*
ἐλάχιστον, acc. sg. neut. adj. . . . . id.
(1646) **ἐλάχιστος**, η, ον, nom. sg. m. adj. [§8.5]
  (superl. of μικρός, from ἐλαχύς) *smallest,*
  least, Matt. 2:6; 5:19, et al.
(1647) **ἐλαχιστότερος**, α, ον [§8.5] (compar. of preceding) *far less, far inferior,* Eph. 3:8
ἐλαχιστοτέρῳ, dat. sg. m. compar.
  adj. . . . . ἐλαχιστότερος *(1647)*
ἐλαχίστου, gen. sg. neut. adj. . . . . . ἐλάχιστος *(1646)*
ἐλαχίστῳ, dat. sg. neut. adj. . . . . id.
ἐλαχίστων, gen. pl. m. adj. {Matt. 25:40} id.
ἐλαχίστων, gen. pl. f. adj. {Matt. 5:19} . . id.
ἐλαχίστων, gen. pl. neut. adj. {1 Cor. 6:2} id.
(1648) **Ἐλεάζαρ**, ὁ, *Eleazar,* pr. name, indecl.
ἐλεᾶτε, 2 pers. pl. pres. act. imper. (Jude 22,
  23, GNT, WH & NA | Jude 22, ἐλεεῖτε,
  MT & TR | Jude 23, MT & TR
  omit) . . . . ἐλεάω *(‡1653)*
(‡1653) **ἐλεάω**, ῶ, fut. ἐλεήσω, same signif. as ἐλεέω,
  ῶ, Rom. 9:16, 18; Jude 23
ἔλεγε(ν), 3 pers. sg. imperf. act. indic. . . λέγω *(3004)*
ἐλέγετε, 2 pers. pl. imperf. act. indic. . . . id.
ἐλεγμόν, acc. sg. m. n. (2 Tim. 3:16, GNT,
  WH & NA | ἔλεγχον, MT &
  TR) . . . . ἐλεγμός *(‡1650)*
(‡1650) **ἐλεγμός**, οῦ, ὁ [§3.C.a] v.r. 2 Tim. 3:16, a later
  equivalent to ἔλεγχος
ἐλέγξαι, aor. act. infin. (Jude 15, GNT, WH,
  MT & NA | ἐξελέγξαι, TR) . . . . . . ἐλέγχω *(1651)*
ἐλέγξει, 3 pers. sg. fut. act. indic. . . . . . . id.
ἔλεγξιν, acc. sg. f. n. . . . . ἔλεγξις *(1649)*
(1649) **ἔλεγξις**, εως, ἡ [§5.E.c] (a later form for
  ἔλεγχος) *reproof, confutation,* 2 Pet. 2:16
ἔλεγξον, 2 pers. sg. aor. act. imper. . . . ἐλέγχω *(1651)*
ἔλεγον, 1 pers. sg. imperf. act. indic.
  {Acts 25:20} . . . . λέγω *(3004)*
ἔλεγον, 3 pers. pl. imperf. act. indic.
  {Acts 21:4} . . . . id.
ἔλεγχε, 2 pers. sg. pres. act. imper. . . . ἐλέγχω *(1651)*
ἐλέγχει, 3 pers. sg. pres. act. indic. . . . . . id.
ἐλέγχειν, pres. act. infin. . . . . id.
ἐλέγχεται, 3 pers. sg. pres. pass. indic. . . . id.
ἐλέγχετε, 2 pers. pl. pres. act. imper. . . . . id.
ἐλεγχθῇ, 3 pers. sg. aor. pass. subj. [§23.9] id.
ἐλεγχόμενα, nom. pl. neut. pres. pass. part. id.
ἐλεγχόμενοι, nom. pl. m. pres. pass. part. id.
ἐλεγχόμενος, nom. sg. m. pres. pass. part. id.
ἔλεγχον, acc. sg. m. n. (2 Tim. 3:16, MT &
  TR | ἐλεγμόν, GNT, WH & NA) . ἔλεγχος *(1650)*
(1650) **ἔλεγχος**, ου, ὁ, nom. sg. m. n. [§3.C.a] pr. *a*
  trial in order to proof, a proof; meton. *a*
  certain persuasion, Heb. 11:1; *reproof,*
  refutation, 2 Tim. 3:16

(1651) **ἐλέγχω**, 1 pers. sg. pres. act. indic., fut.
ἐλέγξω, aor. ἤλεγξα, aor. pass. ἠλέγχθην
[§23.9] *to put to proof, to test; to convict*,
John 8:46; James 2:9; *to refute, confute*,
1 Cor. 14:24; Tit. 1:9; *to detect, lay bare,
expose*, John 3:20; Eph. 5:11, 13; *to reprove, rebuke*, Matt. 18:15; Luke 3:19;
1 Tim. 5:20, et al.; *to discipline, chastise*,
Heb. 12:5; Rev. 3:19; pass. *to experience
conviction*, John 8:9; 1 Cor. 14:24
ἐλεεῖ, 3 pers. sg. pres. act. indic.
{Rom. 9:18} . . . . ἐλεέω (1653)
ἐλέει, dat. sg. neut. n. {Rom. 11:31} . . . . ἔλεος (1656)
(1652) **ἐλεεινός**, ή, όν, nom. sg. m. adj. [§7.F.a] *piti-
able, wretched, miserable*, 1 Cor. 15:19
(Rev. 3:17, GNT, MT, TR & NA |
ἐλεινός, WH)
ἐλεεινότεροι, nom. pl. m. compar. adj.
[§8.4] . . . . ἐλεεινός (1652)
ἐλεεῖτε, 2 pers. pl. pres. act. imper. (Jude 22,
MT & TR | ἐλεᾶτε, GNT, WH &
NA) . . . . ἐλεέω (1653)
(1653) **ἐλεέω**, ῶ, fut. ἐλεήσω, aor. ἠλέησα [§16.P]
perf. pass. ἠλέημαι, aor. pass. ἠλεήθην
[§17.Q] *to pity, commiserate, have compassion on*; pass. *to receive pity, experience
compassion*, Matt. 5:7; 9:27; 15:22, et al.;
*to be gracious to any one, show gracious
favor and saving mercy towards*; pass. *to
be an object of gracious favor and saving
mercy*, Rom. 9:15, 16, 18; 11:30, 31, 32, et
al.; spc. *to obtain pardon and forgiveness*,
1 Tim. 1:13, 16
ἐλεηθέντες, nom. pl. m. aor. pass. part. ἐλεέω (1653)
ἐλεηθήσονται, 3 pers. pl. fut. pass. indic. .   id.
ἐλεηθῶσι(ν), 3 pers. pl. aor. pass. subj. . . .   id.
ἐλεήμονες, nom. pl. m. adj. . . . . ἐλεήμων (1655)
ἐλεημοσύναι, nom. pl. f. n. . . . . . ἐλεημοσύνη (1654)
ἐλεημοσύνας, acc. pl. f. n. . . . .   id.
(1654) **ἐλεημοσύνη**, ης, ἡ, nom. sg. f. n. [§2.B.a] *pity,
compassion*; in N.T. *alms, almsgiving*,
Matt. 6:2, 3, 4; Luke 11:41, et al.
ἐλεημοσύνην, acc. sg. f. n. . . . . . . ἐλεημοσύνη (1654)
ἐλεημοσυνῶν, gen. pl. f. n. . . . .   id.
(1655) **ἐλεήμων**, ον, nom. sg. m. adj. [§7.G.a; 7.3]
merciful, pitiful, ccompassionate, Matt.
5:7; Heb. 2:17
ἐλεῆσαι, aor. act. infin. . . . . ἐλεέω (1653)
ἐλεήσῃ, 3 pers. sg. aor. act. subj. . . . .   id.
ἐλέησον, 2 pers. sg. aor. act. imper. . . . . .   id.
ἐλεήσω, 1 pers. sg. fut. act. indic. . . . . . .   id.
ἔλεον, acc. sg. m. n. (Matt. 9:13, et al. MT
& TR | ἔλεος, GNT, WH & NA) . . ἔλεος (1656)
(1656) **ἔλεος**, ου, τό nom. sg. neut. n. and in N.T. ους,
τό [§5.E.b] *pity, mercy, compassion*, Matt.

9:13; 12:7; Luke 1:50, 78, et al.; meton.
benefit which results from compassion,
kindness, mercies, blessings, Luke 1:54,
58, 72; 10:37; Rom. 9:23, et al.
{James 2:13b}
ἔλεος, acc. sg. neut. n. {James 2:13a} . . ἔλεος (1656)
ἐλεοῦντος, gen. sg. m. pres. act. part. (Rom.
9:16, MT & TR | ἐλεῶντος, GNT, WH
& NA) . . . . ἐλεέω (1653)
ἐλέους, gen. sg. neut. n. . . . . ἔλεος (1656)
ἐλευθέρα, nom. sg. f. adj. . . . . ἐλεύθερος (1658)
ἐλευθέρας, gen. sg. f. adj. . . . .   id.
(1657) **ἐλευθερία**, ας, ἡ, nom. sg. f. n. [§2.B.b; 2.2]
liberty, freedom, 1 Cor. 10:29; Gal. 2:4,
et al.
ἐλευθερίᾳ, dat. sg. f. n. . . . . ἐλευθερία (1657)
ἐλευθερίαν, acc. sg. f. n. . . . .   id.
ἐλευθερίας, gen. sg. f. n. . . . .   id.
ἐλεύθεροι, nom. pl. m. adj. . . . . ἐλεύθερος (1658)
(1658) **ἐλεύθερος**, α, ον, nom. sg. m. adj. [§7.1] *free,
in a state of freedom* as opposed to slav-
ery, 1 Cor. 12:13; Gal. 3:28, et al.; *free, ex-
empt*, Matt. 17:26; 1 Cor. 7:39, et al.;
unrestricted, unfettered, 1 Cor. 9:1; *free
from the dominion of sin*, etc., John 8:36;
Rom. 6:20; *free in the possession of Gospel privileges*, 1 Pet. 2:16
ἐλευθέρους, acc. pl. m. adj. . . . . ἐλεύθερος (1658)
(1659) **ἐλευθερόω**, ῶ, fut. ἐλευθερώσω [§20.T] *to
free, set free*, John 8:32, 36; Rom. 6:18, 22,
et al.
ἐλευθερωθέντες, nom. pl. m. aor. pass. part.
[§21.U] . . . . ἐλευθερόω (1659)
ἐλευθερωθήσεται, 3 pers. sg. fut. pass. indic.   id.
ἐλευθέρων, gen. pl. m. adj. . . . . ἐλεύθερος (1658)
ἐλευθερώσει, 3 pers. sg. fut. act.
indic. . . . . ἐλευθερόω (1659)
ἐλευθερώσῃ, 3 pers. sg. aor. act. subj. . . .   id.
ἐλεύκαναν, 3 pers. pl. aor. act. indic.
[§27.1.e] . . . . λευκαίνω (3021)
ἐλεύσεται, 3 pers. sg. fut. mid. dep. indic.
[§36.1] . . . . ἔρχομαι (2064)
ἐλεύσεως, gen. sg. f. n. . . . . ἔλευσις (1660)
(1660) **ἔλευσις**, εως, ἡ [§5.E.c] (obsol. ἐλεύθω) *a
coming, advent*, Acts 7:52
ἐλεύσομαι, 1 pers. sg. fut. mid. dep. indic.
[§36.1] . . . . ἔρχομαι (2064)
ἐλευσόμεθα, 1 pers. pl. fut. mid. dep. indic.   id.
ἐλεύσονται, 3 pers. pl. fut. mid. dep. indic.   id.
ἐλεφάντινον, acc. sg. neut. adj. . . . ἐλεφάντινος (1661)
(1661) **ἐλεφάντινος**, η, ον [§7.F.a] (ἐλέφας, *ivory*)
ivory, made of ivory, Rev. 18:12
ἐλεῶ, 1 pers. sg. pres. act. subj. . . . . ἐλεέω (1653)
ἐλεῶν, nom. sg. m. pres. act. part. . . . . . .   id.
ἐλεῶντος, gen. sg. m. pres. act. part. (Rom.

9:16, GNT, WH & NA | ἐλεοῦντος, MT
& TR) . . . . ἐλεάω (‡1653)
ἐληλακότες, nom. pl. m. perf. act. part. Att.
for ἠλακότες [§13.7.b] . . . . ἐλαύνω (1643)
ἐλήλυθα, 1 pers. sg. 2 perf. act. indic.
[§36.1] . . . . ἔρχομαι (2064)
ἐλήλυθας, 2 pers. sg. 2 perf. act. indic. . . . id.
ἐλήλύθει, 3 pers. sg. pluperf. act. indic. . . id.
ἐληλύθεισαν, 3 pers. pl. pluperf. act. indic. id.
ἐλήλυθε(ν), 3 pers. sg. 2 perf. act. indic. . . id.
ἐληλυθότα, acc. sg. m. 2 perf. act. part. . . id.
ἐληλυθότες, nom. pl. m. 2 perf. act. part. . id.
ἐληλυθυῖαν, acc. sg. f. 2 perf. act. part. . . id.
ἐλθάτω, 3 pers. sg. aor. act. imper. [§35.12]
(Matt. 10:13, GNT, WH & NA | ἐλθέτω,
MT & TR | Matt. 6:10, WH | ἐλθέτω,
GNT, MT, TR & NA) . . . . id.
ἐλθέ, 2 pers. sg. 2 aor. act. imper. . . . . . . id.
ἐλθεῖν, 2 aor. act. infin. . . . . id.
ἐλθέτω, 3 pers. sg. 2 aor. act. imper. . . . . id.
ἔλθη, 3 pers. sg. 2 aor. act. subj. . . . . id.
ἔλθης, 2 pers. sg. 2 aor. act. subj. . . . . . . id.
ἔλθητε, 2 pers. pl. 2 aor. act. subj. (Mark
14:38, GNT, WH & NA | εἰσέλθητε, MT
& TR) . . . . id.
ἐλθόν, nom. sg. neut. 2 aor. act. part. . . . . id.
ἐλθόντα, acc. sg. m. 2 aor. act. part. (Matt.
17:25, GNT, WH & NA | ὅτε εἰσῆλθεν,
MT & TR) . . . . id.
ἐλθόντα, nom. pl. neut. 2 aor. act. part.
{Matt. 13:4} . . . . id.
ἐλθόντας, acc. pl. m. 2 aor. act. part. . . . . id.
ἐλθόντες, nom. pl. m. 2 aor. act. part. . . . id.
ἐλθόντι, dat. sg. m. 2 aor. act. part. . . . . . id.
ἐλθόντος, gen. sg. m. 2 aor. act. part. . . . . id.
ἐλθόντων, gen. pl. m. 2 aor. act. part. . . . . id.
ἐλθοῦσα, nom. sg. f. 2 aor. act. part. . . . . id.
ἐλθοῦσαι, nom. pl. f. 2 aor. act. part. . . . . id.
ἐλθούσης, gen. sg. f. 2 aor. act. part. . . . . id.
ἔλθω, 1 pers. sg. 2 aor. act. subj. . . . . id.
ἐλθών, nom. sg. m. 2 aor. act. part. . . . . . id.
ἔλθωσι(ν), 3 pers. pl. 2 aor. act. subj. . . . . id.
(1662) Ἐλιακείμ, ὁ, Eliakim, pr. name, indecl. (Matt.
1:13; Luke 3:30, MT, WH & TR |
Ἐλιακίμ, GNT & NA)
(†1662) Ἐλιακίμ, ὁ, Eliakim, pr. name, indecl. (Matt.
1:13; Luke 3:30, GNT & NA | Ἐλιακείμ,
WH, MT & TR)
(‡3395) ἔλιγμα, ατος, τό, a roll
ἔλιγμα, acc. sg. neut. n. (John 19:39, WH |
μίγμα, GNT, MT, TR & NA) . . . . ἔλιγμα (‡3395)
(1663) Ἐλιέζερ, ὁ, Eliezer, pr. name, indecl., Luke
3:29
ἐλιθάσθην, 1 pers. sg. aor. pass. indic.
[§26.1] . . . . λιθάζω (3034)

ἐλιθάσθησαν, 3 pers. pl. aor. pass.
indic. . . . . λιθάζω (3034)
ἐλιθοβόλησαν, 3 pers. pl. aor. pass.
indic. . . . . λιθοβολέω (3036)
ἐλιθοβόλουν, 3 pers. pl. imperf. act. indic. id.
ἑλίξεις, 2 pers. sg. fut. act. indic. . . . . . ἑλίσσω (1667)
(1664) Ἐλιούδ, ὁ, Eliud, pr. name, indecl.
(1665) Ἐλισάβετ, ἡ, Elisabeth, pr. name, indecl.
(GNT, MT, TR & NA | Ἐλεισάβετ, WH)
(†1666) Ἐλισαῖος, ου, ὁ, Elisha, pr. name
Ἐλισαίου, gen. sg. m. n. (Luke 4:27, GNT,
WH & NA | Ἐλισσαίου, MT &
TR) . . . . Ἐλισαῖος (†1666)
(1666) Ἐλισσαῖος, ου, ὁ [§3.C.a] Elisaeus, pr. name;
in O.T. Elisha
Ἐλισσαίου, gen. sg. m. n. (Luke 4:27, MT
& TR | Ἐλισαίου, GNT, WH &
NA) . . . . Ἐλισσαῖος (1666)
ἑλισσόμενον, acc. sg. neut. pres. pass. part.
(Rev. 6:14, GNT, WH & NA | ἑλισσό-
μενος, MT | εἱλισσόμενον, TR) . . . ἑλίσσω (1667)
ἑλισσόμενος, nom. sg. m. pres. pass. part.
(Rev. 6:14, MT | ἑλισσόμενον, GNT, WH
& NA | εἱλισσόμενον, TR) . . . . id.
(1667) ἑλίσσω, fut. ἑλίξω [§26.3] to roll, fold up, as
garments, Heb. 1:12
ἕλκη, acc. pl. neut. n. . . . . ἕλκος (1668)
(1668) ἕλκος, ους, τό, nom. sg. neut. n. [§5.E.b] pr.
a wound; hence, an ulcer, sore, Luke 16:21;
Rev. 16:2, 11
ἕλκουσιν, 3 pers. pl. pres. act. indic. . . . ἕλκω (†1670)
(1669) ἑλκόω, ῶ, fut. ἑκώσω [§20.T] to ulcerate, ex-
ulcerate; pass. to be afflicted with ulcers,
Luke 16:20
ἑλκύσαι, aor. act. infin. (John 21:6, GNT,
WH, MT, TRb & NA | ἑλκῦσαι,
TRs) . . . . ἕλκύω (†1670)
ἑλκύσῃ, 3 pers. sg. aor. act. subj. . . . . . . id.
ἑλκύσω, 1 pers. sg. fut. act. indic. . . . . . . id.
(†1670) ἕλκω, and ἑλκύω, imperf. εἷλκον, fut.
ἑλκύσω, aor. εἵλκυσα [§13.4] to draw,
drag, John 21:6, 11; Acts 16:19; 21:30;
James 2:6; to draw a sword, unsheath,
John 18:10; met. to draw mentally and
morally, John 6:44; 12:32
ἑλκῶν, gen. pl. neut. n. . . . . ἕλκος (1668)
Ἑλλάδα, acc. sg. f. n. . . . . Ἑλλάς (1671)
(1671) Ἑλλάς, άδος, ἡ [§4.D.b] Hellas, Greece;
in N.T. the southern portion of Greece
as distinguished from Macedonia, Acts
20:2
(1672) Ἕλλην, ηνος, ὁ, nom. sg. m. n. [§4.D.a] a
Greek, Acts 18:17; Rom. 1:14; one not a
Jew, a Gentile, Acts 14:1; 16:1, 3, et al.
Ἕλληνας, acc. pl. m. n. . . . . Ἕλλην (1672)

Ἕλληνες, nom. pl. m. n. . . . . Ἕλλην *(1672)*

Ἕλληνι, dat. sg. m. n. . . . . Ἕλλην *(1672)*

Ἑλληνίδων, gen. pl. f. n. . . . . Ἑλληνίς *(1674)*

Ἑλληνικῇ, dat. sg. f. adj. . . . . Ἑλληνικός *(1673)*

Ἑλληνικοῖς, dat. pl. neut. adj. (Luke 23:38,
    MT & TR | GNT, WH & NA omit) .   id.

(1673) **Ἑλληνικός**, ή, όν [§4.2.c] *Greek, Grecian,*
    Luke 23:38; Rev. 9:11

(1674) **Ἑλληνίς**, ίδος, ή, nom. sg. f. n. [§4.2.c] *a fe-*
    male Greek, Mark 7:26; Acts 17:12

Ἑλληνιστάς, acc. pl. m. n. . . . . . Ἑλληνιστής *(1675)*

(1675) **Ἑλληνιστής**, οῦ, ὁ [§2.B.c] (ἑλληνίζω, *to im-*
    itate the Greeks) pr. *one who uses the lan-*
    guage and follows the customs of the
    Greeks; in N.T. *a Jew by blood, but a na-*
    tive of a Greek-speaking country, Helle-
    nist, Acts 6:1; 9:29

(1676) **Ἑλληνιστί**, adv., *in the Greek language,* John
    19:20; Acts 21:37

Ἑλληνιστῶν, gen. pl. m. n. . . . . . Ἑλληνιστής *(1675)*

Ἕλληνος, gen. sg. m. n. . . . . Ἕλλην *(1672)*

Ἑλλήνων, gen. pl. m. n. . . . . id.

Ἕλλησι(ν), dat. pl. m. n. . . . . id.

ἐλλόγα, 2 pers. sg. pres. act. imper. (Philemon
    18, GNT, WH & NA | ἐλλόγει, MT &
    TR) . . . . ἐλλογάω *(†1677)*

ἐλλογᾶται, 3 pers. sg. pres. pass. indic. (Rom.
    5:13, WH | ἐλλογεῖται, GNT, MT, TR &
    NA) . . . . id.

(†1677) **ἐλλογάω**, ῶ, fut. ἐλλογήσω, same signif. as
    ἐλλογέω

ἐλλόγει, 2 pers. sg. pres. act. imper. (Philemon
    18, MT & TR | ἐλλόγα, GNT, WH &
    NA) . . . . ἐλλογέω *(1677)*

ἐλλογεῖται, 3 pers. sg. pres. pass. indic. (Rom.
    5:13, GNT, MT, TR & NA | ἐλλογᾶται,
    WH) . . . . id.

(1677) **ἐλλογέω**, ῶ, fut. ἐλλογήσω [§16.P] (ἐν +
    λόγος) *to enter in an account, to put to*
    one's account, Philemon 18; in N.T. *to im-*
    pute, Rom. 5:13

(†1678) **Ἐλμαδάμ**, ὁ, *Elmadam,* pr. name, indecl.
    (Luke 3:28, GNT, WH & NA | Ἐλμω-
    δάμ, MT & TR)

(1678) **Ἐλμωδάμ**, ὁ, *Elmodam,* pr. name, indecl.
    (Luke 3:28, MT & TR | Ἐλμαδάμ, GNT,
    WH & NA)

ἐλογιζόμην, 1 pers. sg. imperf. mid./pass. dep.
    indic. . . . . λογίζομαι *(3049)*

ἐλογίζοντο, 3 pers. pl. imperf. mid./pass. dep.
    indic. (Mark 11:31, MT & TR | διελο-
    γίζοντο, GNT, WH & NA) . . . . id.

ἐλογίσθη, 3 pers. sg. aor. pass. indic. . . . . id.

ἐλογίσθημεν, 1 pers. pl. aor. pass. indic. . . id.

ἐλοιδόρησαν, 3 pers. pl. aor. act.

indic. . . . . λοιδορέω *(3058)*

ἑλόμενος, nom. sg. m. 2 aor. mid. part. αἱρέω *(‡138)*

ἔλουσεν, 3 pers. sg. aor. act. indic. . . . . λούω *(3068)*

ἐλπίδα, acc. sg. f. n. . . . . ἐλπίς *(1680)*

ἐλπίδι, dat. sg. f. n. . . . . id.

ἐλπίδος, gen. sg. f. n. . . . . id.

ἐλπίζει, 3 pers. sg. pres. act. indic. . . . ἐλπίζω *(1679)*

ἐλπίζετε, 2 pers. pl. pres. act. indic. (Luke
    6:34, GNT, WH, MT, TRs & NA |
    ἐλπίζητε, TRb) . . . . id.

ἐλπίζητε, 2 pers. pl. pres. act. subj. (Luke
    6:34, TRb | ἐλπίζετε, GNT, WH, MT,
    TRs & NA) . . . . id.

ἐλπίζομεν, 1 pers. pl. pres. act. indic. . . . id.

ἐλπιζομένων, gen. pl. neut. pres. pass. part. id.

ἐλπίζουσαι, nom. pl. f. pres. act. part. . . . id.

(1679) **ἐλπίζω**, 1 pers. sg. pres. act. indic., fut.
    ἐλπίσω, Att. ἐλπιῶ [§26.1; 35.11] perf.
    ἤλπικα, aor. ἤλπισα, *to hope, expect,* Luke
    23:8; 24:21, et al.; *to repose hope and con-*
    fidence in, trust, confide, Matt. 12:21; John
    5:45, et al.

ἐλπίζων, nom. sg. m. pres. act. part. . . ἐλπίζω *(1679)*

ἐλπιοῦσι(ν), 3 pers. pl. act. indic. Att. [§35.11] id.

(1680) **ἐλπίς**, ίδος, ή, nom. sg. f. n. [§4.2.c] pr. *ex-*
    pectation; hope, Acts 24:15; Rom. 5:4, et
    al.; meton. *the object of hope, thing hoped*
    for, Rom. 8:24; Gal. 5:5, et al.; *the author*
    or source of hope, Col. 1:27; 1 Tim. 1:1,
    et al.; *trust, confidence,* 1 Pet. 1:21; ἐπ'
    ἐλπίδι, *in security, with a guarantee,* Acts
    2:26; Rom. 8:20

ἐλπίσατε, 2 pers. pl. aor. act. imper. . . . ἐλπίζω *(1679)*

ἔλυε(ν), 3 pers. sg. imperf. act. indic. . . . . λύω *(3089)*

ἐλύετο, 3 pers. sg. imperf. pass. indic. . . . id.

ἐλύθη, 3 pers. sg. aor. pass. indic. [§14.1.d] id.

ἐλύθησαν, 3 pers. pl. aor. pass. indic. . . . id.

ἐλυμαίνετο, 3 pers. sg. imperf. mid./pass. dep.
    indic. . . . . λυμαίνομαι *(3075)*

(1681) **Ἐλύμας**, α, ὁ, nom. sg. m. n. [§2.4] *Elymas,*
    pr. name, Acts 13:8

ἐλυπήθη, 3 pers. sg. aor. pass. indic.
    [§17.Q] . . . . λυπέω *(3076)*

ἐλυπήθησαν, 3 pers. pl. aor. pass. indic. . . id.

ἐλυπήθητε, 2 pers. pl. aor. pass. indic. . . . id.

ἐλύπησα, 1 pers. sg. aor. act. indic. . . . . . . id.

ἐλύπησεν, 3 pers. sg. aor. act. indic. . . . . . id.

ἔλυσεν, 3 pers. sg. aor. act. indic. . . . . λύω *(3089)*

ἐλυτρώθητε, 2 pers. pl. aor. pass.
    indic. . . . . λυτρόω *(3084)*

(†1682) **Ἐλωΐ** (Aramaic אֱלָהִי) *my God* (Mark 15:34,
    MT & TR | Ἐλωΐ, WH | ελωι, GNT &
    NA)

ἐμά, nom. pl. neut. 1 pers. possessive pron.
    {John 10:14b} . . . . ἐμός *(1699)*

ἐμά, acc. pl. neut. 1 pers. possessive pron.
{John 10:14a} . . . . ἐμός *(1699)*

ἔμαθεν, 3 pers. sg. 2 aor. act. indic.
[§24.5] . . . . μανθάνω *(3129)*

ἔμαθες, 2 pers. sg. 2 aor. act. indic. . . . . id.

ἐμάθετε, 2 pers. pl. 2 aor. act. indic. . . . . id.

ἐμαθητεύθη, 3 pers. sg. aor. pass. indic. (Matt.
27:57, GNT, WH & NA | ἐμαθήτευσε(ν),
MT & TR) . . . . μαθητεύω *(3100)*

ἐμαθήτευσε(ν), 3 pers. sg. aor. act. indic.
(Matt. 27:57, MT & TR | ἐμαθητεύθη,
GNT, WH & NA) . . . . id.

ἔμαθον, 1 pers. sg. 2 aor. act. indic. . . μανθάνω *(3129)*

ἐμαρτύρει, 3 pers. sg. imperf. act.
indic. . . . . μαρτυρέω *(3140)*

ἐμαρτυρεῖτο, 3 pers. sg. imperf. pass. indic.   id.

ἐμαρτυρήθη, 3 pers. sg. aor. pass. indic. . .   id.

ἐμαρτυρήθησαν, 3 pers. pl. aor. pass. indic.   id.

ἐμαρτυρήσαμεν, 1 pers. pl. aor. act. indic. .   id.

ἐμαρτύρησαν, 3 pers. pl. aor. act. indic. . .   id.

ἐμαρτύρησε(ν), 3 pers. sg. aor. act. indic. .   id.

ἐμαρτύρουν, 3 pers. pl. imperf. act. indic.   id.

ἐμάς, acc. pl. f. 1 pers. possessive pron. . ἐμός *(1699)*

ἐμασσῶντο, 3 pers. pl. imperf. mid./pass. dep.
indic. (Rev. 16:10, TR | ἐμασῶντο, GNT,
WH, MT & NA) . . . . μασ(σ)άομαι *(3145)*

ἐμαστίγωσε(ν), 3 pers. sg. aor. act.
indic. μαστιγόω *(3146)*

ἐμασῶντο, 3 pers. pl. imperf. mid./pass. dep.
indic. (Rev. 16:10, GNT, WH, MT & N
| ἐμασσῶντο, TR) . . . . μασ(σ)άομαι *(3145)*

ἐματαιώθησαν, 3 pers. pl. aor. pass.
indic. . . . . ματαιόω *(3154)*

ἐμαυτόν, acc. sg. m. reflexive pron. . . . ἐμαυτοῦ *(1683)*

(1683) ἐμαυτοῦ, ῆς, οῦ, gen. sg. m. reflexive pron.
[§11.K.d] (ἐμοῦ + αὐτοῦ) *myself,* Luke 7:7;
John 5:31, et al.

ἐμαυτῷ, dat. sg. m. reflexive pron. . . . ἐμαυτοῦ *(1683)*

ἐμάχοντο, 3 pers. pl. imperf. mid./pass. dep.
indic. . . . . μάχομαι *(3164)*

ἐμβαίνοντος, gen. sg. m. pres. act. part.
(Mark 5:18, GNT, WH & NA | ἐμβάν-
τος, MT & TR) . . . . ἐμβαίνω *(1684)*

(1684) ἐμβαίνω, fut. ἐμβήσομαι, 2 aor. ἐνέβην
[§37.1] (ἐν + βαίνω) *to step in; to go on
board* a ship, *embark,* Matt. 8:23; 9:1;
13:2, et al.

ἐμβαλεῖν, 2 aor. act. infin. . . . . ἐμβάλλω *(1685)*

(1685) ἐμβάλλω, fut. ἐμβαλῶ, 2 aor. ἐνέβαλον
[§27.1.b; 27.2.d] (ἐν + βάλλω) *to cast into,*
Luke 12:5

ἐμβάντα, acc. sg. m. 2 aor. act. part. . ἐμβαίνω *(1684)*

ἐμβάντες, nom. pl. m. 2 aor. act. part. . . . id.

ἐμβάντι, dat. sg. m. 2 aor. act. part. . . . . . id.

ἐμβάντος, gen. sg. m. 2 aor. act. part. (Mark

5:18, MT & TR | ἐμβαίνοντος, GNT,
WH & NA) . . . . ἐμβαίνω *(1684)*

ἐμβάντων, gen. pl. m. 2 aor. act. part. (Matt.
14:32, MT & TR | ἀναβάντων, GNT,
WH & NA) . . . . id.

ἐμβαπτόμενος, nom. sg. m. pres. mid.
part. . . . . ἐμβάπτω *(1686)*

(1686) ἐμβάπτω, fut. ἐμβάψω [§23.1.a] (ἐν + βάπτω)
to dip in, Matt. 26:23; John 13:26; mid.
ἐμβάπτομαι, *to dip* for food in a dish,
Mark 14:20

ἐμβάς, nom. sg. m. 2 aor. act. part. . . ἐμβαίνω *(1684)*

(1687) ἐμβατεύω, fut. ἐμβατεύσω [§13.M] (ἐν +
βαίνω) pr. *to step into or upon;* met. *to
search into, investigate; to pry into intru-
sively,* Col. 2:18

ἐμβατεύων, nom. sg. m. pres. act.
part. . . . . ἐμβατεύω *(1687)*

ἐμβάψας, nom. sg. m. aor. act. part. ἐμβάπτω *(1686)*

ἐμβῆναι, 2 aor. act. infin. [§37.1] . . . . ἐμβαίνω *(1684)*

(1688) ἐμβιβάζω, fut. ἐμβιβάσω [§26.1] (ἐν +
βιβάζω) *to cause to step into or upon; to
set in or upon;* especially, *to put on board,*
Acts 27:6

ἐμβλέποντες, nom. pl. m. pres. act. part. (Acts
1:11, GNT, MT, TR & NA | βλέποντες,
WH) . . . . ἐμβλέπω *(1689)*

(1689) ἐμβλέπω, fut. ἐμβλέψω [§23.1.a] (ἐν +
βλέπω) *to look attentively, gaze earnestly,*
at an object, followed by εἰς, Matt. 6:26;
Acts 1:11; *to direct a glance, to look search-
ingly or significantly,* at a person, followed
by the dat., Mark 10:21; 14:67; Luke 22:61,
et al.; absol. *to see clearly,* Mark 8:25; Acts
22:11

ἐμβλέψας, nom. sg. m. aor. act. part. ἐμβλέπω *(1689)*

ἐμβλέψασα, nom. sg. f. aor. act. part. . . . id.

ἐμβλέψατε, 2 pers. pl. aor. act. imper. . . . id.

(1690) ἐμβριμάομαι, ῶμαι, fut. ἐμβριμήσομαι [§19.S]
(ἐν + βριμάομαι, *to snort) to be greatly
fretted or agitated,* John 11:33; *to charge
or forbid sternly or vehemently,* Matt.
9:30; Mark 1:43; *to express indignation,
to censure,* Mark 14:5

ἐμβριμησάμενος, nom. sg. m. aor. mid. dep.
part. . . . . ἐμβριμάομαι *(1690)*

ἐμβριμώμενος, nom. sg. m. pres. mid./pass.
dep. part. . . . . id.

(1691) ἐμέ, acc. sg. 1 pers. personal pron. [§11.K.a] ἐγώ *(1473)*

ἐμεγάλυνε(ν), 3 pers. sg. imperf. act.
indic. . . . . μεγαλύνω *(3170)*

ἐμεγαλύνετο, 3 pers. sg. imperf. pass. indic.   id.

ἐμεθύσθησαν, 3 pers. pl. aor. pass. indic.
[§22.4] . . . . μεθύω *(3184)*

ἐμείναμεν, 1 pers. pl. aor. act. indic.

[§27.1.d] . . . . μένω *(3306)*
ἔμειναν, 3 pers. pl. aor. act. indic. . . . . id.
ἔμεινε(ν), 3 pers. sg. aor. act. indic. . . . . . id.
ἔμελεν, 3 pers. sg. imperf. act. indic. . . . μέλει *(‡3199)*
ἐμελέτησαν, 3 pers. pl. aor. act.
    indic. . . . . μελετάω *(3191)*
ἔμελλε(ν), 3 pers. sg. imperf. act. indic. μέλλω *(3195)*
ἔμελλες 2 pers. sg. imperf. act. indic. (Rev.
    3:2, MT | μέλλει, GNT, WH, TR & NA)   id.
ἔμελλον, 1 pers. sg. imperf. act. indic. (Rev.
    10:4, MT & TR | ἤμελλον, GNT, WH
    & NA) . . . . id.
ἔμελλον, 3 pers. pl. imperf. act. indic.
    {John 7:39} . . . . id.
ἐμέμψαντο, 3 pers. pl. aor. mid. dep. indic.
    [§23.5] (Mark 7:2, MT & TR | GNT,
    WH & NA omit) . . . . μέμφομαι *(3201)*
ἔμενε(ν), 3 pers. sg. imperf. act. indic. . . μένω *(3306)*
ἔμενον, 3 pers. pl. imperf. act. indic. . . . . id.
ἐμέρισε(ν), 3 pers. sg. aor. act. indic. . . μερίζω *(3307)*
ἐμερίσθη, 3 pers. sg. aor. pass. indic. . . . . id.
ἐμέσαι, aor. act. infin. . . . . ἐμέω *(1692)*
ἐμεσίτευσεν, 3 pers. sg. aor. act.
    indic. μεσιτεύω *(3315)*
ἐμέτρησε(ν), 3 pers. sg. aor. act.
    indic. . . . . μετρέω *(3354)*
(1692) **ἐμέω,** ῶ, fut. ἐμέσω [§22.1] *to vomit,* Rev. 3:16
ἐμή, nom. sg. f. 1 pers. possessive pron. . ἐμός *(1699)*
ἐμῇ, dat. sg. f. 1 pers. possessive pron. . . . id.
ἐμήν, acc. sg. f. 1 pers. possessive pron. . . id.
ἐμήνυσεν, 3 pers. sg. aor. act. indic. . . . μηνύω *(3377)*
ἐμῆς, gen. sg. f. 1 pers. possessive pron. . ἐμός *(1699)*
ἔμιξε(ν), 3 pers. sg. aor. act. indic.
    [§36.5] . . . . μίγνυμι *(3396)*
ἐμίσησα, 1 pers. sg. aor. act. indic. . . . . μισέω *(3404)*
ἐμίσησαν, 3 pers. pl. aor. act. indic. . . . . . id.
ἐμίσησας, 2 pers. sg. aor. act. indic. . . . . . id.
ἐμίσησεν, 3 pers. sg. aor. act. indic. . . . . . id.
ἐμισθώσατο, 3 pers. sg. aor. mid.
    indic. . . . . μισθόω *(3409)*
ἐμίσουν, 3 pers. pl. imperf. act. indic. . . μισέω *(3404)*
(1693) **ἐμμαίνομαι,** fut. ἐμμανοῦμαι [§24.4] (ἐν +
    μαίνομαι) *to be mad against, be furious*
    towards, Acts 26:11
ἐμμαινόμενος, nom. sg. m. pres. mid./pass.
    dep. part. . . . . ἐμμαίνομαι *(1693)*
(1694) **Ἐμμανουήλ,** ὁ, *Emmanuel,* pr. name, indecl.,
    Matt. 1:23
(1695) **Ἐμμαούς,** ἡ, *Emmaus,* pr. name, indecl., of
    a village near Jerusalem, Luke 24:13
ἐμμένει, 3 pers. sg. pres. act. indic. . . . ἐμμένω *(1696)*
ἐμμένειν, pres. act. infin. . . . . id.
(1696) **ἐμμένω,** fut. ἐμμενῶ [§27.1.a] (ἐν + μένω) pr.
    to remain in a place; met. *to abide by, to*
    continue firm in, persevere in, Acts 14:22;

Gal. 3:10; Heb. 8:9
(1697) **Ἐμμόρ,** ὁ, *Emmor,* pr. name, indecl. (Acts
    7:16, MT & TRs | Ἐμόρ, TRb | Ἐμμώρ,
    GNT, WH & NA)
(†1697) **Ἐμμώρ,** ὁ, *Emmor,* pr. name, indecl. (Acts
    7:16, GNT, WH & NA | Ἐμμόρ, MT &
    TRs | Ἐμόρ, TRb)
ἐμνημόνευον, 3 pers. pl. imperf. act.
    indic. μνημονεύω *(3421)*
ἐμνημόνευσε(ν), 3 pers. sg. aor. act. indic.   id.
ἐμνήσθη, 3 pers. sg. aor. pass. indic.
    [§36.3] . . . . μιμνήσκω *(†3403)*
ἐμνήσθημεν, 1 pers. pl. aor. pass. indic. . . id.
ἐμνήσθην, 1 pers. sg. aor. pass. indic. . . . id.
ἐμνήσθησαν, 3 pers. pl. aor. pass. indic. . . id.
ἐμνηστευμένη, dat. sg. f. perf. pass. part.
    (Luke 2:5, GNT, WH & NA | μεμνη-
    στευμένη, MT & TR) . . . . μνηστεύω *(3423)*
ἐμνηστευμένην, acc. sg. f. perf. pass. part.
    (Luke 1:27, GNT, WH & NA | μεμνη-
    στευμένην, MT & TR) . . . . id.
(1698) ἐμοί, dat. sg. 1 pers. personal pron.
    {John 18:35} . . . . ἐγώ *(1473)*
(1698) ἐμοί, nom. pl. m. 1 pers. possessive pron.
    {John 18:36} . . . . ἐμός *(1699)*
ἐμοῖς, dat. pl. neut. 1 pers. possessive pron.   id.
ἐμοίχευσεν, 3 pers. sg. aor. act. indic. μοιχεύω *(3431)*
ἐμόλυναν, 3 pers. pl. aor. act. indic. . . μολύνω *(3435)*
ἐμολύνθησαν, 3 pers. pl. aor. pass. indic. . . id.
ἐμόν, acc. sg. m. 1 pers. possessive pron.
    {John 8:43} . . . . ἐμός *(1699)*
ἐμόν, nom. sg. neut. 1 pers. possessive pron.
    {John 4:34} . . . . id.
ἐμόν, acc. sg. neut. 1 pers. possessive pron.
    {John 6:38} . . . . id.
(1699) **ἐμός,** ή, όν, nom. sg. m. 1 pers. possessive
    pron. [§11.3] *my, mine,* John 7:16; 8:37,
    et al.
ἐμοσχοποίησαν, 3 pers. pl. aor. act.
    indic. . . . . μοσχοποιέω *(3447)*
(1700) ἐμοῦ, gen. sg. 1 pers. personal pron.
    {John 16:32} . . . . ἐγώ *(1473)*
(1700) ἐμοῦ, gen. sg. neut. 1 pers. possessive pron.
    {John 16:14} . . . . ἐμός *(1699)*
ἐμούς, acc. pl. m. 1 pers. possessive pron.   id.
(†1701) **ἐμπαιγμονή,** ῆς, ἡ [§2.B.a] *mocking, scoffing,*
    derision, 2 Pet. 3:3.
ἐμπαιγμονῇ, dat. sg. f. n. (2 Pet. 3:3, GNT,
    WH & NA | MT & TR
    omit) . . . . ἐμπαιγμονή *(†1701)*
(1701) **ἐμπαιγμός,** οῦ, ὁ [§3.C.a] *mocking, scoffing,*
    scorn, Heb. 11:36
ἐμπαιγμῶν, gen. pl. m. n. . . . . ἐμπαιγμός *(1701)*
ἐμπαίζειν, pres. act. infin. . . . . ἐμπαίζω *(1702)*
ἐμπαίζοντες, nom. pl. m. pres. act. part. .   id.

(1702) **ἐμπαίζω**, fut. ἐμπαίξω [§26.2] (ἐν + παίζω) to *play upon, deride, mock, treat with scorn and contumely*, Matt. 20:19; 27:29, et al.; by impl. *to delude, deceive*, Matt. 2:16

ἐμπαῖκται, nom. pl. m. n. . . . . ἐμπαίκτης (1703)

(1703) **ἐμπαίκτης**, ου, ὁ [§2.B.c] *a mocker, derider, scoffer*, 2 Pet. 3:3; Jude 18

ἐμπαῖξαι, aor. act. infin. . . . . ἐμπαίζω (1702)
ἐμπαίξας, nom. sg. m. aor. act. part. . . . . id.
ἐμπαίξουσιν, 3 pers. pl. fut. act. indic. . . . id.
ἐμπαιχθήσεται, 3 pers. sg. fut. pass. indic. id.
ἐμπεπλησμένοι, nom. pl. m. perf. pass.
    part. . . . . ἐμπί(μ)πλημι (†1705)

(1704) **ἐμπεριπατέω**, ῶ, fut. ἐμπεριπατήσω [§16.P] (ἐν + περιπατέω) pr. *to walk about in a place*; met. in M.T. *to live among, be conversant with*

ἐμπεριπατήσω, 1 pers. sg. fut. act. indic.
    (2 Cor. 6:16, GNT, MT, TR & NA |
    ἐνπεριπατήσω, WH) . . . . . . ἐμπεριπατέω (1704)
ἐμπεσεῖν, 2 aor. act. infin. [§37.1] . . . ἐμπίπτω (1706)
ἐμπεσεῖται, 3 pers. sg. fut. mid. dep. indic.
    (Luke 14:5, MT & TR | πεσεῖται, GNT,
    WH & NA) . . . . id.
ἐμπέσῃ, 3 pers. sg. 2 aor. act. subj. . . . . . id.
ἐμπεσόντος, gen. sg. m. 2 aor. act. part. . id.
ἐμπεσοῦνται, 3 pers. pl. fut. mid. dep. indic.
    (Luke 6:39, GNT, WH & NA | πεσοῦν-
    ται, MT & TR) . . . . id.

(†1705) **ἐμπί(μ)πλημι**, and ἐμπιπλάω, ῶ, fut. ἐμπλήσω, aor. pass. ἐνεπλήσθην (ἐν + πίμπλημι) *to fill*, Acts 14:17; pass. *to be satisfied, satiated, full*, Luke 1:53; 6:25; John 6:12; met. *to have the full enjoyment of*, Rom. 15:24

(‡1714) **ἐμπί(μ)πρημι**, *to set on fire, burn down*
ἐμπιπλῶν, nom. sg. m. pres. act.
    part. . . . . ἐμπιπλάω (†1705)
ἐμπίπτουσιν, 3 pers. pl. pres. act.
    indic. . . . . ἐμπίπτω (1706)

(1706) **ἐμπίπτω**, fut. ἐμπεσοῦμαι, 2 aor. ἐνέπεσον [§37.1] (ἐν + πίπτω) *to fall into*, Matt. 12:11; Luke 14:5; *to encounter*, Luke 10:36; *to be involved in*, 1 Tim. 3:6, 7; 6:9; εἰς χεῖρας, *to fall under the chastisement of*, Heb. 10:31

ἐμπλακέντες, nom. pl. m. 2 aor. pass. part.
    [§24.10] . . . . ἐμπλέκω (1707)
ἐμπλέκεται, 3 pers. sg. pres. pass. indic. . . id.

(1707) **ἐμπλέκω**, fut. ἐμπλέξω [§23.1.b] (ἐν + πλέκω) pr. *to intertwine*; met. *to implicate, entangle, involve*; pass. *to be implicated, involved, or to entangle one's self in*, 2 Tim. 2:4; 2 Pet. 2:20

ἐμπλησθῶ, 1 pers. sg. aor. pass.
    subj. . . . . ἐμπί(μ)πλημι (†1705)

(1708) **ἐμπλοκή**, ῆς, ἡ [§2.B.a] *braiding or plaiting* of hair, 1 Pet. 3:3

ἐμπλοκῆς, gen. sg. f. n. . . . . ἐμπλοκή (1708)

(1709) **ἐμπνέω**, fut. ἐμπνεύσω [§35.3] (ἐν + πνέω) *to breathe into or upon; to respire, breathe*; met. *to breathe of, be animated with the spirit of*, Acts 9:1

ἐμπνέων, nom. sg. m. pres. act. part. (Acts 9:1,
    GNT, MT, TR & NA | ἐνπνέων,
    WH) . . . . ἐμπνέω (1709)

(1710) **ἐμπορεύομαι**, fut. ἐμπορεύσομαι [§15.O] (ἐν + πορεύομαι) *to travel; to travel for business' sake; to trade, traffic*, James 4:13; by impl., trans., *to make a gain of, deceive for one's own advantage*, 2 Pet. 2:3

ἐμπορευσόμεθα, 1 pers. pl. fut. mid. dep.
    indic. (James 4:13, GNT, WH, TRb & NA
    | ἐμπορευσώμεθα, MT &
    TRs) . . . . ἐμπορεύομαι (1710)
ἐμπορεύσονται, 3 pers. pl. fut. mid. dep.
    indic. . . . . id.
ἐμπορευσώμεθα, 1 pers. pl. aor. mid. dep.
    subj. (James 4:13, MT & TRs | ἐμπο-
    ρευσόμεθα, GNT, WH, TRb & NA) . id.

(1711) **ἐμπορία**, ας, ἡ [§2.B.b; 2.2] *traffic, trade*, Matt. 22:5

ἐμπορίαν, acc. sg. f. n. . . . . ἐμπορία (1711)

(1712) **ἐμπόριον**, ου, τό [§3.C.c] *a mart, marketplace, emporium*; met. *traffic*, John 2:16

ἐμπορίου, gen. sg. neut. n. . . . . ἐμπόριον (1712)
ἔμποροι, nom. pl. m. n. . . . . ἔμπορος (1713)

(1713) **ἔμπορος**, ου, ὁ [§3.C.a] (ἐν + πόρος) pr. *a passenger by sea; a traveller; one who travels about for traffic, a merchant*, Matt. 13:45; Rev. 18:3, 11, 15, 23

ἐμπόρῳ, dat. sg. m. n. . . . . ἔμπορος (1713)

(1714) **ἐμπρήθω**, fut. ἐμπρήσω [§23.1.c] *to set on fire, to burn*, Matt. 22:7

(1715) **ἔμπροσθεν**, adv., used also as a prep., *before, in front of*, Luke 19:4; Phil. 3:13; *before, in the presence of, in the face of*, Matt. 5:24; 23:14; *before, previous to*, John 1:15, 27, 30; from the Hebrew, *in the sight or estimation of*, Matt. 11:26; 18:14, et al.

ἐμπτύειν, pres. act. infin. . . . . ἐμπτύω (1716)
ἐμπτύσαντες, nom. pl. m. aor. act. part. . id.
ἐμπτυσθήσεται, 3 pers. sg. fut. pass. indic. id.
ἐμπτύσσουσιν, 3 pers. pl. fut. act. indic. . id.

(1716) **ἐμπτύω**, fut. ἐμπτύσω [§13.M] (ἐν + πτύω) *to spit upon*, Matt. 26:67; 27:30, et al.

ἐμφανῆ, acc. sg. m. adj. . . . . ἐμφανής (1717)

(1717) **ἐμφανής**, ές, nom. sg. m. adj. [§7.G.b] (ἐν + φαίνω) *apparent, conspicuous, obvious to*

the sight, Acts 10:40; met. *manifest,
known, comprehended*, Rom. 10:20
ἐμφανίζειν, pres. act. infin. . . . . ἐμφανίζω *(1718)*
ἐμφανίζουσιν, 3 pers. pl. pres. act. indic. .   id.
(1718) **ἐμφανίζω,** fut. ἐμφανίσω, aor. ἐνεφάνισα
[§26.1] *to cause to appear clearly; to communicate, report,* Acts 23:15, 22; *to bring
charges against,* Acts 24:1; 25:2, 15; *to
manifest, intimate plainly,* Heb. 11:14; *to
reveal, make known,* John 14:21, 22; pass.
to appear, be visible, Matt. 27:53; *to
present one's self,* Heb. 9:24
ἐμφανίσατε, 2 pers. pl. aor. act.
imper. . . . . ἐμφανίζω *(1718)*
ἐμφανισθῆναι, aor. pass. infin. . . . . id.
ἐμφανίσω, 1 pers. sg. fut. act. indic. . . . . . id.
ἔμφοβοι, nom. pl. m. adj. . . . . ἔμφοβος *(1719)*
(1719) **ἔμφοβος,** ον, nom. sg. m. adj. [§7.2] (ἐν +
φόβος) *terrible;* in N.T. *terrified, affrighted,*
Luke 24:5, 37; Acts 10:4; 22:9, et al.
ἐμφόβων, gen. pl. m. adj. . . . . ἔμφοβος *(1719)*
(1720) **ἐμφυσάω,** ῶ, fut. ἐμφυσήσω [§18.R] (ἐν +
φυσάω, *to breathe*) *to blow or breathe into,
inflate;* in N.T. *to breathe upon,* John 20:22
ἔμφυτον, acc. sg. m. adj. . . . . ἔμφυτος *(1721)*
(1721) **ἔμφυτος,** ον [§7.2] (ἐν + φύω) *implanted, in-
grafted, infixed,* James 1:21
ἐμῷ, dat. sg. m. 1 pers. possessive pron.
{John 8:31} . . . . ἐμός *(1699)*
ἐμῷ, dat. sg. neut. 1 pers. possessive pron.
{Rom. 3:7} . . . . id.
ἐμῶν, gen. pl. neut. 1 pers. possessive pron.   id.
ἐμώρανεν, 3 pers. sg. aor. act. indic. . μωραίνω *(3471)*
ἐμωράνθησαν, 3 pers. pl. aor. pass. indic.   id.
(1722) **ἐν,** prep. pr. referring to place, *in,* Matt. 8:6;
Mark 12:26; Rev. 6:6, et al. freq.; *upon,*
Luke 8:32, et al.; *among,* Matt. 11:11, et
al.; *before, in the presence of,* Mark 8:38,
et al.; *in the sight, estimation of,* 1 Cor.
14:11, et al.; *before,* judicially, 1 Cor. 6:2;
in, of state, occupation, habit, Matt. 21:22;
Luke 7:25; Rom. 4:10, et al.; *in the case
of,* Matt. 17:12, et al.; *in respect of,* Luke
1:7; 1 Cor. 1:7, et al.; *on occasion of, on
the ground of,* Matt. 6:7; Luke 1:21, et al.;
used of the thing by which an oath is made,
Matt. 5:34, et al.; of the instrument,
means, efficient cause, Rom. 12:21; Acts
4:12, et al.; *equipped with, furnished with,*
1 Cor. 4:21; Heb. 9:25, et al.; *arrayed with,
accompanied by,* Luke 14:31; Jude 14, et
al.; of time, *during, in the course of,* Matt.
2:1, et al.; in N.T. of demoniacal possession, *possessed by,* Mark 5:2, et al.
ἕν with accent followed by enclitic . . . . ἐν *(1722)*

ἕν, nom. sg. neut. numeral {Matt. 5:30} . .   εἷς *(1520)*
ἕν, acc. sg. neut. numeral {Matt. 5:41} . . .   id.
ἕνα, acc. sg. m. numeral . . . .   id.
(1723) **ἐναγκαλίζομαι,** fut. ἐναγκαλίσομαι [§26.1] (ἐν
+ ἀγκάλη) *to take into or embrace in one's
arms,* Mark 9:36; 10:16
ἐναγκαλισάμενος, nom. sg. m. aor. mid. dep.
part. . . . . ἐναγκαλίζομαι *(1723)*
(1724) **ἐνάλιος,** ία, ιον, or ον [§7.1; 7.2] (ἐν + ἅλς)
marine, living in the sea, James 3:7
ἐναλίων, gen. pl. neut. adj. . . . . ἐνάλιος *(1724)*
(1725) **ἔναντι,** adv. (ἐν + ἀντί) *over against, in the
presence of,* Luke 1:8
ἐναντία, acc. pl. neut. adj. . . . . ἐναντίος *(1727)*
ἐναντίας, gen. sg. f. adj. . . . . id.
ἐναντίον, acc. sg. neut. adj. {Acts 28:17} .   id.
(1726) **ἐναντίον,** adv. (pr. neut. of ἐναντίος) *before,
in the presence of,* Mark 2:12; Luke 20:26;
Acts 8:32; from the Hebrew, *in the sight
or estimation of,* Acts 7:10; with τοῦ θεοῦ,
an intensive expression, Luke 24:19
(1727) **ἐναντίος,** ία, ίον, nom. sg. m. adj. [§7.1] *opposite to, over against,* Mark 15:39; *con-
trary,* as the wind, Matt. 14:24; Acts 26:9;
28:17; ὁ ἐξ ἐναντίας, *an adverse party, enemy,* Tit. 2:8; *adverse, hostile, counter,*
1 Thess. 2:15
ἐναντίους, acc. pl. m. adj. . . . . ἐναντίος *(1727)*
ἐναντίων, gen. pl. m. adj. . . . . id.
ἐναρξάμενοι, nom. pl. m. aor. mid. dep.
part. ἐνάρχομαι *(1728)*
ἐναρξάμενος, nom. sg. m. aor. mid. dep.
part. . . . . id.
(1728) **ἐνάρχομαι,** fut. ἐνάρξομαι [§23.1.b] (ἐν +
ἄρχομαι) *to begin, commence,* Gal. 3:3;
Phil. 1:6
ἐνάτῃ, dat. sg. f. adj. (Mark 15:34, GNT,
WH, MT & NA | ἐννάτῃ, TR) . . . ἔνατος *(‡1766)*
ἐνάτην, acc. sg. f. adj. (Matt. 20:5; 27:46; Acts
3:1; 10:3, 30, GNT, WH, MT & NA |
ἐννάτην, TR) . . . . id.
ἐνάτης, gen. sg. f. adj. (Matt. 27:45; Mark
15:33; Luke 23:44, GNT, WH, MT & NA
| ἐννάτης, TR) . . . . id.
(‡1766) **ἔνατος,** η, ον, nom. sg. m. adj., *the ninth,* for
ἔννατος (Rev. 21:20, GNT, WH, MT, TRs
& NA | ἔννατος, TRb)
ἐναυάγησα, 1 pers. sg. aor. act.
indic. . . . . ναυαγέω *(3489)*
ἐναυάγησαν, 3 pers. pl. aor. act. indic. . . . id.
ἐνγέγραπται, 3 pers. sg. perf. pass. indic.
(Luke 10:20, WH | ἐγγέγραπται, GNT &
NA | ἐγράφη, MT & TR) . . . . . ἐνγράφω *(‡1125)*
(‡1125) **ἐνγράφω,** *to inscribe, write in; enter in a register, enroll*

ἐνδεδυμένοι, nom. pl. m. perf. mid.
part. . . . . ἐνδύω *(1746)*
ἐνδεδυμένον, acc. sg. m. perf. mid. part. .   id.
ἐνδεδυμένος, nom. sg. m. perf. mid. part.   id.
(1729) **ἐνδεής**, ές, nom. sg. m. adj. [§7.G.b] *indigent,
poor, needy,* Acts 4:34
(1730) **ἔνδειγμα**, ατος, τό, nom. sg. neut. n. [§4.D.c]
a token, evidence, proof, 2 Thess. 1:5
(1731) **ἐνδείκνυμι**, fut. ἐνδείξομαι [§31.BB] (mid. of
ἐνδείκνυμι, *to point out) to manifest, display,* Rom. 9:17, 22; Heb. 6:10, et al.; *to
give outward proof of,* Rom. 2:15; *to display* a certain bearing towards a person;
hence, *to perpetrate openly,* 2 Tim. 4:14
ἐνδεικνύμενοι, nom. pl. m. pres. mid. part.
(2 Cor. 8:24, GNT & NA | ἐνδείξασθε,
WH, MT & TR) . . . . ἐνδείκνυμι *(1731)*
ἐνδεικνυμένους, acc. pl. m. pres. mid. part.   id.
ἐνδείκνυνται, 3 pers. pl. pres. mid. indic. .   id.
ἐνδείκνυσθαι, pres. mid. infin. . . . .   id.
ἐνδείξασθαι, aor. mid. infin. . . . .   id.
ἐνδείξασθε, 2 pers. pl. aor. mid. imper. (2 Cor.
8:24, WH, MT & TR | ἐνδεικνύμενοι,
GNT & NA) . . . .   id.
ἐνδείξηται, 3 pers. sg. aor. mid. subj. . . . .   id.
ἔνδειξιν, acc. sg. f. n. . . . . ἔνδειξις *(1732)*
(1732) **ἔνδειξις**, εως, ἡ, nom. sg. f. n. [§5.E.c] *a
pointing out;* met. *manifestation, public
declaration,* Rom. 3:25, 26; *a token, sign,
proof,* i.q. ἔνδειγμα, 2 Cor. 8:24; Phil. 1:28
ἐνδείξωμαι, 1 pers. sg. aor. mid.
subj. . . . . ἐνδείκνυμι *(1731)*
(1733) **ἕνδεκα**, οἱ, αἱ, τά (εἷς, ἕν, + δέκα) *eleven,*
indecl. numeral, Matt. 28:16; Mark 16:14,
et al.
ἐνδεκάτην, acc. sg. f. adj. . . . . ἑνδέκατος *(1734)*
(1734) **ἑνδέκατος**, η, ον, nom. sg. m. adj. [§7.F.a]
eleventh, Matt. 20:6, 9; Rev. 21:20
(1735) ἐνδέχεται, 3 pers. sg. pres. mid./pass. dep.
indic. impersonal . . . . ἐνδέχομαι *(†1735)*
(†1735) **ἐνδέχομαι**, *to admit, approve; to be possible,*
impersonal, *it is possible,* Luke 13:33
(1736) **ἐνδημέω**, ῶ, fut. ἐνδημήσω [§16.P] (ἐν +
δῆμος) *to dwell in* a place, *be at home,*
2 Cor. 5:6, 8, 9
ἐνδημῆσαι, aor. act. infin. . . . . ἐνδημέω *(1736)*
ἐνδημοῦντες, nom. pl. m. pres. act. part. .   id.
ἐνδιδύσκουσιν, 3 pers. pl. pres. act. indic.
(Mark 15:17, GNT, WH & NA | ἐνδύ-
ουσιν, MT & TR) . . . . ἐνδιδύσκω *(1737)*
(1737) **ἐνδιδύσκω**, a later form, equivalent to ἐνδύω,
Luke 8:27; 16:19; and v.r. Mark 15:17
ἔνδικον, acc. sg. f. adj. {Heb. 2:2} . . . ἔνδικος *(1738)*
ἔνδικον, nom. sg. neut. adj. {Rom. 3:8} . .   id.
(1738) **ἔνδικος**, ον [§7.2] (ἐν + δίκη) *fair, just,* Rom.

3:8; Heb. 2:2
(1739) **ἐνδόμησις**, εως, ἡ, nom. sg. f. n. [§5.E.c]
(ἐνδομέω) pr. *a thing built in;* in N.T. *a
building, structure* (Rev. 21:18, MT & TR
| ἐνδώμησις, GNT, WH & NA)
(1740) **ἐνδοξάζω**, fut. ἐνδοξάσω [§26.1] (ἐν +
δοξάζω) *to invest with glory;* pass. *to be
glorified, to be made a subject of glorification,* 2 Thess. 1:10, 12
ἐνδοξασθῇ, 3 pers. sg. aor. pass.
subj. . . . . ἐνδοξάζω *(1740)*
ἐνδοξασθῆναι, aor. pass. infin. . . . .   id.
ἔνδοξοι, nom. pl. m. adj. . . . . ἔνδοξος *(1741)*
ἐνδόξοις, dat. pl. neut. adj. . . . .   id.
ἔνδοξον, acc. sg. f. adj. . . . .   id.
(1741) **ἔνδοξος**, ον [§7.2] (ἐν + δόξα) *honored,*
1 Cor. 4:10; *notable, memorable,* Luke
13:17; *splendid, gorgeous,* Luke 7:25; *in
unsullied array,* Eph. 5:27
ἐνδόξῳ, dat. sg. m. adj. . . . . ἔνδοξος *(1741)*
(1742) **ἔνδυμα**, ατος, τό, nom. sg. neut. n. [§4.D.c]
clothing, a garment, Matt. 6:25, 28;
22:11, 12, et al.; in particular, *an outer garment, cloak, mantle,* Matt. 3:4 {Matt.
28:3}
ἔνδυμα, acc. sg. neut. n. {Matt. 22:11} ἔνδυμα *(1742)*
ἐνδύμασι(ν), dat. pl. neut. n. . . . .   id.
ἐνδύματος, gen. sg. neut. n. . . . .   id.
ἐνδυναμοῦ, 2 pers. sg. pres. pass. imper.
[§21.U] . . . . ἐνδυναμόω *(1743)*
ἐνδυναμοῦντι, dat. sg. m. pres. act. part. .   id.
ἐνδυναμοῦσθε, 2 pers. pl. pres. pass. imper.   id.
(1743) **ἐνδυναμόω**, ῶ, fut. ἐνδυναμώσω [§20.T] (ἐν
+ δύναμις) *to empower, invigorate,* Phil.
4:13; 1 Tim. 1:12; 2 Tim. 4:17; mid. *to
summon up vigor, put forth energy,* Eph.
6:10; 2 Tim. 2:1; pass. *to acquire strength,
be invigorated, be strong,* Acts 9:22; Rom.
4:20; Heb. 11:34
ἐνδυναμώσαντι, dat. sg. m. aor. act.
part. . . . . ἐνδυναμόω *(1743)*
ἐνδύνοντες, nom. pl. m. pres. act.
part. . . . . ἐνδύνω *(1744)*
(1744) **ἐνδύνω**, *sink into, enter, creep in*
ἐνδύουσιν, 3 pers. pl. pres. act. indic. (Mark
15:17, MT & TR | ἐνδιδύσκουσιν, GNT,
WH & NA) . . . . ἐνδύω *(1746)*
ἐνδυσάμενοι, nom. pl. m. aor. mid. part. .   id.
ἐνδυσάμενος, nom. sg. m. aor. mid. part.   id.
ἐνδύσασθαι, aor. mid. infin. . . . .   id.
ἐνδύσασθε, 2 pers. pl. aor. mid. imper.   id.
ἐνδύσατε, 2 pers. pl. aor. act. imper. . . . .   id.
ἐνδύσεως, gen. sg. f. n. . . . . ἔνδυσις *(1745)*
ἐνδύσησθε, 2 pers. pl. aor. mid. subj. . . ἐνδύω *(1746)*
ἐνδύσηται, 3 pers. sg. aor. mid. subj. . . . .   id.

(1745) **ἔνδυσις**, εως, ἡ [§5.E.c] *a putting on, or wearing* of clothes, 1 Pet. 3:3

ἐνδυσώμεθα, 1 pers. pl. aor. mid. subj. . ἐνδύω *(1746)*

(1746) **ἐνδύω**, fut. ἐνδύσω [§13.M] (ἐν + δύω) *to enter*, 2 Tim. 3:6; *to put on, clothe, invest, array*, Matt. 27:31; Mark 15:17, 20; mid. *clothe one's self, be clothed or invested*, Matt. 22:11, 27, 31, et al.; trop. *to be invested* with spiritual gifts, graces, or character, Luke 24:49; Rom. 13:14, et al.

(‡1739) **ἐνδώμησις**, εως, ἡ, nom. sg. f. n. (Rev. 21:18, GNT, WH & NA | ἐνδόμησις, MT & TR)

ἐνέβη, 3 pers. sg. 2 aor. act. indic. [§37.1] . . . . ἐμβαίνω *(1684)*

ἐνέβημεν, 1 pers. pl. 2 aor. act. indic. (Acts 21:6, WH | ἀνέβημεν, GNT & NA | ἐπέβημεν, MT & TR) . . . . id.

ἐνέβησαν, 3 pers. pl. 2 aor. act. indic. . . . id.

ἐνεβίβασεν, 3 pers. sg. aor. act. indic. . . . . ἐμβιβάζω *(1688)*

ἐνέβλεπεν, 3 pers. sg. imperf. act. indic. (Mark 8:25, GNT, WH & NA | ἀνέβλεψε, MT | ἐνέβλεψέ(ν), TR) . . ἐμβλέπω *(1689)*

ἐνέβλεπον, 3 pers. pl. imperf. act. indic. [§34.1] . . . . id.

ἐνέβλεψε(ν), 3 pers. sg. aor. act. indic. . . . id.

ἐνεβριμήθη, 3 pers. sg. aor. pass. dep. indic. (Matt. 9:30, GNT, WH & NA | ἐνεβριμήσατο, MT & TR) . . . . . . ἐμβριμάομαι *(1690)*

ἐνεβριμήσατο, 3 pers. sg. aor. mid. dep. indic. id.

ἐνεβριμῶντο, 3 pers. pl. imperf. mid./pass. dep. indic. . . . . id.

ἐνέγκαι, 2 aor. act. infin. (Mark 6:27, GNT, WH & NA | ἐνεχθῆναι, MT & TR) φέρω *(5342)*

ἐνέγκαντες, nom. pl. m. aor. act. part. [§36.1] (Luke 15:23, MT & TR | φέρετε, GNT, WH & NA) . . . . id.

ἐνέγκας, nom. sg. m. aor. act. part. . . . . . id.

ἐνέγκατε, 2 pers. pl. aor. act. imper. . . . . . id.

ἐνεγκεῖν, 2 aor. act. infin. (Matt. 7:18, WH | ποιεῖν, GNT, MT, TR & NA) . . . . . . id.

ἐνεδείξασθε, 2 pers. pl. aor. mid. indic. . . . . ἐνδείκνυμι *(1731)*

ἐνεδείξατο, 3 pers. sg. aor. mid. indic. . . . id.

ἐνεδιδύσκετο, 3 pers. sg. imperf. mid. indic. . . . . ἐνδιδύσκω *(1737)*

(1747) **ἐνέδρα**, ας, ἡ [§2.B.b; 2.2] (ἐν + ἕδρα) pr. *a sitting in or on a spot; an ambush, ambuscade*, or *lying in wait*, Acts 23:16; 25:3

ἐνέδραν, acc. sg. f. n. . . . . ἐνέδρα *(1747)*

ἐνεδρεύοντες, nom. pl. m. pres. act. part. . . . . ἐνεδρεύω *(1748)*

ἐνεδρεύουσι(ν), 3 pers. pl. pres. act. indic. id.

(1748) **ἐνεδρεύω**, fut. ἐνεδρεύσω [§13.M] *to lie in*

wait or ambush for, Acts 23:21; *to endeavor to entrap*, Luke 11:54

(1749) **ἔνεδρον**, ου, τό [§3.C.c] i.q. ἐνέδρα, Acts 23:16

ἔνεδρον, acc. sg. neut. n. (Acts 23:16, MT & TRs | ἐνέδραν, GNT, WH, TRb & NA) . . . . ἔνεδρον *(1749)*

ἐνεδυναμοῦτο, 3 pers. sg. imperf. pass. indic. . . . . ἐνδυναμόω *(1743)*

ἐνεδυναμώθη, 3 pers. sg. aor. pass. indic. . id.

ἐνεδυναμώθησαν, 3 pers. pl. aor. pass. indic. (Heb. 11:34, MT & TR | ἐδυναμώθησαν, GNT, WH & NA) . . . . id.

ἐνεδυνάμωσε(ν), 3 pers. sg. aor. act. indic. id.

ἐνέδυσαν, 3 pers. pl. aor. act. indic. . . . ἐνδύω *(1746)*

ἐνεδύσασθε, 2 pers. pl. aor. mid. indic. . . id.

ἐνεδύσατο, 3 pers. sg. aor. mid. indic. (Luke 8:27, GNT, WH & NA | ἐνεδιδύσκετο, MT & TR) . . . . id.

(1750) **ἐνειλέω**, ῶ, fut. ἐνειλήσω [§16.P] (ἐν + εἰλέω) *to inwrap, envelope*, Mark 15:46

ἐνείλησε(ν), 3 pers. sg. aor. act. indic. ἐνειλέω *(1750)*

(1751) **ἔνειμι** [§12.L] (ἐν + εἰμί) *to be in or within*; τὰ ἐνόντα, *those things which are within*, Luke 11:41

ἐνεῖχεν, 3 pers. sg. imperf. act. indic. . . ἐνέχω *(1758)*

(1752) **ἕνεκα**, or ἕνεκεν, or εἵνεκεν, adv., *on account of, for the sake of, by reason of*, Matt. 5:10, 11; 10:18, 39, et al.

ἐνεκαίνισεν, 3 pers. sg. aor. act. indic. . . . . ἐγκαινίζω *(1457)*

ἐνεκάλουν, 3 pers. pl. imperf. act. indic. . . . . ἐγκαλέω *(1458)*

(†1752) **ἕνεκεν**, adv., *on account of, for the sake of, by reason of*

ἐνεκεντρίσθης, 2 pers. sg. aor. pass. indic. . . . . ἐγκεντρίζω *(1461)*

ἐνεκοπτόμην, 1 pers. sg. imperf. pass. indic. . . . . ἐγκόπτω *(1465)*

ἐνέκοψεν, 3 pers. sg. aor. act. indic. . . . . . id.

ἐνέκρυψεν, 3 pers. sg. aor. act. indic. . . . . id.

ἐνέμειναν, 3 pers. pl. aor. act. indic. [§34.1.c] . . . . ἐμμένω *(1696)*

ἐνέμεινεν, 3 pers. sg. aor. act. indic. (Acts 28:30, GNT, WH & NA | ἔμεινε(ν), MT & TR) . . . . id.

ἐνένευον, 3 pers. pl. imperf. act. indic. . ἐννεύω *(1770)*

(‡1768) **ἐνενήκοντα**, indecl. numeral, *ninety* (Matt. 18:12, 13; Luke 15:4, 7, GNT, WH, MT & NA | ἐννενηκονταεννέα, TR)

ἐνεοί, nom. pl. m. n. (Acts 9:7, GNT, WH, MT & NA | ἐννεοί, TR) . . . . ἐνεός *(‡1769)*

(‡1769) **ἐνεός**, ά, όν, *dumb, speechless*

ἐνέπαιζον, 3 pers. pl. imperf. act. indic. . . . . ἐμπαίζω *(1702)* ἐνέπαιξαν, 3 pers. pl. aor. act. indic. . ἐμπαίζω (1702)

ἐνεπαίχθη, 3 pers. sg. aor. pass. indic. . . . id.

ἐνέπλησεν, 3 pers. sg. aor. act.

indic. . . . . ἐμπί(μ)πλημι (†1705)

ἐνεπλήσθησαν, 3 pers. pl. aor. pass. indic.   id.

ἐνέπρησε(ν), 3 pers. sg. aor. act.

indic. . . . . ἐμπί(μ)πρημι (‡1714)

ἐνέπτυον, 3 pers. pl. imperf. act. indic. ἐμπτύω (1716)

ἐνέπτυσαν, 3 pers. pl. aor. act. indic. . . . . id.

ἐνεργεῖ, 3 pers. sg. pres. act. indic. . . . ἐνεργέω (1754)

(1753) **ἐνέργεια**, ας, ἡ [§2.B.b; 2.2] *energy, efficacy, power,* Phil. 3:21; Col. 2:12; *active energy, operation,* Eph. 4:16; Col. 1:29, et al.

ἐνέργειαν, acc. sg. f. n. . . . . ἐνέργεια (1753)

ἐνεργείας, gen. sg. f. n. . . . . id.

ἐνεργεῖν, pres. act. infin. . . . . ἐνεργέω (1754)

ἐνεργεῖται, 3 pers. sg. pres. mid. indic.

[§17.Q] . . . . id.

(1754) **ἐνεργέω**, ῶ, fut. ἐνεργήσω, aor. ἐνήργησα [§16.P] *to effect,* 1 Cor. 12:6, 11; Gal. 3:5; Eph. 1:11; Phil. 2:13; *to put into operation,* Eph. 1:20; absol. *to be active,* Matt. 14:2; Mark 6:14; Eph. 2:2; in N.T. *to communicate energy and efficiency,* Gal. 2:8; pass. or mid. *to come into activity, be actively developed; to be active, be in operation,* towards a result, 2 Cor. 4:12; 2 Thess. 2:7; *to be an active power or principle,* Rom. 7:5; 1 Thess. 2:12; part. ἐνεργούμενος, *instinct with activity; in action, operative,* 2 Cor. 1:6; Gal. 5:6; Eph. 3:20; Col. 1:29; *earnest,* James 5:16

(1755) **ἐνέργημα**, ατος, τό [§4.D.c] *an effect, thing effected,* 1 Cor. 12:6; *operation, working,* 1 Cor. 12:10

ἐνεργήματα, nom. pl. neut. n. . . . . . ἐνέργημα (1755)

ἐνεργημάτων, gen. pl. neut. n. . . . . id.

(1756) **ἐνεργής**, ές, nom. sg. m. adj. [§7.G.b] (ἐν + ἔργον) *active,* Philemon 6; *efficient, energetic,* Heb. 4:12; *adapted to accomplish* a thing, *effectual,* 1 Cor. 16:9 {Heb. 4:12}

ἐνεργής, nom. sg. f. adj. {1 Cor. 16:9} ἐνεργής (1756)

ἐνεργήσας, nom. sg. m. aor. act. part. ἐνεργέω (1754)

ἐνεργουμένη, nom. sg. f. pres. mid. part. . id.

ἐνεργουμένην, acc. sg. f. pres. mid. part. . id.

ἐνεργουμένης, gen. sg. f. pres. mid. part. . id.

ἐνεργοῦντος, gen. sg. m. pres. act. part. {Eph. 1:11} . . . . id.

ἐνεργοῦντος, gen. sg. neut. pres. act. part. {Eph. 2:2} . . . . id.

ἐνεργοῦσιν, 3 pers. pl. pres. act. indic. . . id.

ἐνεργῶν, nom. sg. m. pres. act. part. . . . id.

ἐνέστηκεν, 3 pers. sg. perf. act. indic. [§29.X] . . . . ἐνίστημι (1764)

ἐνεστηκότα, acc. sg. m. perf. act. part. . . . id.

ἐνεστῶσαν, acc. sg. f. perf. act. part. [§35.8] . . . . ἐνίστημι (1764)

ἐνεστῶτα, nom. pl. neut. perf. act. part. . . id.

ἐνεστῶτος, gen. sg. m. perf. act. part. . . . id.

ἐνετειλάμην, 1 pers. sg. aor. mid. dep. indic. . . . . ἐντέλλομαι (1781)

ἐνετείλατο, 3 pers. sg. aor. mid. dep. indic. [§27.1.d] . . . . id.

ἐνετρεπόμεθα, 1 pers. pl. imperf. mid. indic. . . . . ἐντρέπω (1788)

ἐνετύλιξεν, 3 pers. sg. aor. act. indic. . . . . ἐντυλίσσω (1794)

ἐνέτυχεν, 3 pers. sg. 2 aor. act. indic. (Acts 25:24, WH | ἐνέτυχον, GNT, MT, TR & NA) . . . . ἐντυγχάνω (1793)

ἐνέτυχον, 3 pers. pl. 2 aor. act. indic. (Acts 25:24, GNT, MT, TR & NA | ἐνέτυχεν, WH) . . . . id.

(1757) **ἐνευλογέω**, ῶ, fut. ἐνευλογήσω [§16.P] (ἐν + εὐλογέω) *to bless in respect of, or by means of,* Acts 3:25; Gal. 3:8

ἐνευλογηθήσονται, 3 pers. pl. fut. pass. indic. . . . . ἐνευλογέω (1757)

ἐνεφάνισαν, 3 pers. pl. aor. act. indic. . . . . ἐμφανίζω (1718)

ἐνεφάνισας, 2 pers. sg. aor. act. indic. . . . id.

ἐνεφανίσθησαν, 3 pers. pl. aor. pass. indic.   id.

ἐνεφύσησε(ν), 3 pers. sg. aor. act. indic. . . . . ἐμφυσάω (1720)

ἐνέχειν, pres. act. infin. . . . . ἐνέχω (1758)

ἐνέχεσθε, 2 pers. pl. pres. pass. imper. . . . id.

ἐνεχθεῖσαν, acc. sg. f. aor. pass. part. [§36.1] . . . . φέρω (5342)

ἐνεχθείσης, gen. sg. f. aor. pass. part. . . . . id.

ἐνεχθῆναι, aor. pass. infin. (Mark 6:27, MT & TR | ἐνέγκαι, GNT, WH & NA) . . id.

(1758) **ἐνέχω**, fut. ἐνέξω, imperf. ἐνεῖχον [§13.4] (ἐν + ἔχω) *to hold within; to fix upon;* in N.T. intrans. (sc. χόλον) *to entertain a grudge against,* Mark 6:19; *to be exasperated against,* Luke 11:53; pass. *to be entangled, held fast in,* Gal. 5:1

ἐνηργεῖτο, 3 pers. sg. imperf. mid. indic. . . . . ἐνεργέω (1754)

ἐνήργηκεν, 3 pers. sg. perf. act. indic. (Eph. 1:20, WH | ἐνήργησεν, GNT, MT, TR & NA) . . . . id.

ἐνήργησε(ν), 3 pers. sg. aor. act. indic. . . . id.

(1759) **ἐνθάδε**, adv. (ἔνθα, here, + δε, an enclitic particle) pr. *hither, to this place,* John 4:15, 16, et al.; also, *here, in this place,* Luke 24:41, et al.

(†1759) **ἔνθεν**, adv., *hence, from this place,* v.r. Luke 16:26

ἐνθυμεῖσθε, 2 pers. pl. pres. mid./pass. dep.

indic. . . . . ἐνθυμέομαι *(1760)*

(1760) **ἐνθυμέομαι**, οὖμαι, fut. ἐνθυμήσομαι, aor.
(pass. form) ἐνεθυμήθην [§17.Q] (ἐν +
θυμός) *to ponder in one's mind, think of,
meditate on,* Matt. 1:20; 9:4; Acts 10:19

ἐνθυμηθέντος, gen. sg. m. aor. pass. dep.
part. . . . . ἐνθυμέομαι *(1760)*

ἐνθυμήσεις, acc. pl. f. n. . . . . ἐνθύμησις *(1761)*

ἐνθυμήσεων, gen. pl. f. n. . . . . id.

ἐνθυμήσεως, gen. sg. f. n. . . . . id.

(1761) **ἐνθύμησις**, εως, ἡ [§5.E.c] *the act of thought,
cogitation, reflection,* Matt. 9:4; 12:25;
Heb. 4:12; *the result of thought, invention,
device,* Acts 17:29

ἐνθυμουμένου, gen. sg. m. pres. mid./pass.
dep. part. (Acts 10:19, TR | διενθυμου-
μένου, GNT, WH, MT & NA) ἐνθυμέομαι *(1760)*

ἑνί, dat. sg. m. numeral {Col. 4:6} . . . . . . εἷς *(1520)*

ἑνί, dat. sg. neut. numeral {Rom. 5:18} . . . id.

(1762) **ἔνι**, for ἔνεστι [§12.1] *there is in, there is contained, there exists,* Gal. 3:28(3×); Col.
3:11; James 1:17

ἐνιαυτόν, acc. sg. m. n. . . . . ἐνιαυτός *(1763)*

(1763) **ἐνιαυτός**, οῦ, ὁ [§3.C.a] (ἔνος) *a year,* more
particularly as being a cycle of seasons, and
in respect of its revolution, John 11:49, 51;
18:13, et al.; in N.T. *an era,* Luke 4:19

ἐνιαυτοῦ, gen. sg. m. n. . . . . ἐνιαυτός *(1763)*

ἐνιαυτούς, acc. pl. m. n. . . . . id.

ἐνίκησα, 1 pers. sg. aor. act. indic. . . . . νικάω *(3528)*

ἐνίκησαν, 3 pers. pl. aor. act. indic. . . . . . id.

ἐνίκησεν, 3 pers. sg. aor. act. indic. . . . . . id.

(1764) **ἐνίστημι**, fut. ἐνεστήσω [§29.X] (ἐν + ἵστημι)
to place in or upon; intrans., perf.
ἐνέστηκα, part. ἐνεστηκώς, and ἐνεστώς,
fut. mid. ἐνστήσομαι, *to stand close upon;
to be at hand, impend, to be present,* Rom.
8:38; 2 Thess. 2:2, et al.

ἐνισχύθη, 3 pers. sg. aor. pass. indic. (Acts
9:19, WH | ἐνίσχυσεν, GNT, MT, TR &
NA) . . . . ἐνισχύω *(1765)*

ἐνίσχυσεν, 3 pers. sg. aor. act. indic. (Acts
9:19, GNT, MT, TR & NA | ἐνισχύθη,
WH) . . . . id.

(1765) **ἐνισχύω**, fut. ἐνισχύσω [§13.M] (ἐν + ἰσχύω)
to strengthen, impart strength and vigor,
Luke 22:43; intrans. *to gain, acquire, or
recover strength and vigor, be strengthened,*
Acts 9:19

ἐνισχύων, nom. sg. m. pres. act. part. ἐνισχύω *(1765)*

ἔνιψα, 1 pers. sg. aor. act. indic. . . . . . . νίπτω *(3538)*

ἐνιψάμην, 1 pers. sg. aor. mid. indic. . . . . id.

ἐνίψατο, 3 pers. sg. aor. mid. indic. . . . . . id.

ἔνιψε(ν), 3 pers. sg. aor. act. indic. . . . . . . id.

ἐνκακεῖν, pres. act. infin. (Luke 18:1; Eph.

3:13, WH | ἐγκακεῖν, GNT & NA |
ἐκκακεῖν, MT & TR) . . . . ἐνκακέω *(‡1573)*

(‡1573) **ἐνκακέω**, ῶ, *to lose heart*

ἐνκακήσητε, 2 pers. pl. aor. act. subj.
(2 Thess. 3:13, WH | ἐγκακήσητε, GNT
& NA | ἐκκακήσητε, MT &
TR) . . . . ἐνκακέω *(‡1573)*

ἐνκακῶμεν, 1 pers. pl. pres. act. subj. (Gal.
6:9, WH | ἐγκακῶμεν, GNT & NA |
ἐκκακῶμεν, MT & TR) . . . . . ἐνκακέω *(‡1573)*

(‡2620) **ἐνκαυχάομαι**, ῶμαι, *to take pride in, glory in*

ἐνκαυχᾶσθαι, pres. mid./pass. dep. infin.
(2 Thess. 1:4, WH | ἐγκαυχᾶσθαι, GNT
& NA | καυχᾶσθαι, MT &
TR) . . . . ἐνκαυχάομαι *(‡2620)*

ἐννάτῃ, dat. sg. f. adj. (Mark 15:34, TR |
ἐνάτῃ, GNT, WH, MT & NA) . . . ἔννατος *(1766)*

ἐννάτην, acc. sg. f. adj. (Matt. 20:5; 27:46;
Acts 3:1; 10:3, 30, TR | ἐνάτην, GNT,
WH, MT & NA) . . . . id.

ἐννάτης, gen. sg. f. adj. (Matt. 27:45; Mark
15:33; Luke 23:44, TR | ἐνάτης, GNT,
WH, MT & NA) . . . . id.

(1766) **ἔννατος**, η, ον, nom. sg. m. adj. [§7.F.a] *ninth,*
Matt. 20:5; Rev. 21:20, et al.

(1767) **ἐννέα**, οἱ, αἱ, τά, indecl. numeral, *nine,* Luke
17:17

(†1768) **ἐννενήκοντα**, οἱ, αἱ, τά, indecl. numeral,
ninety

(1768) **ἐννενήκονταεννέα**, οἱ, αἱ, τά, indecl. numeral,
ninety-nine (Matt. 18:12, 13; Luke 15:4, 7,
TR | ἐνενήκοντα ἐννέα, GNT, WH, MT
& NA)

ἐννεοί, nom. pl. m. adj. (Acts 9:7, TR | ἐνεοί,
GNT, WH, MT & NA) . . . . ἐννεός *(1769)*

(1769) **ἐννεός**, ον [§7.2] *stupid; dumb; struck dumb
with amazement, bewildered, stupefied,*
Acts 9:7

(1770) **ἐννεύω**, fut. ἐννεύσω [§13.M] (ἐν + νεύω) *to
nod at, signify by a nod; to make signs; to
intimate by signs,* Luke 1:62

(1771) **ἔννοια**, ας, ἡ [§2.B.b; 2.2] (ἐν + νοέω, νοῦς)
notion, idea; thought, purpose, intention,
Heb. 4:12; 1 Pet. 4:1

ἔννοιαν, acc. sg. f. n. . . . . ἔννοια *(1771)*

ἐννοιῶν, gen. pl. f. n. . . . . id.

(1772) **ἔννομος**, ον, nom. sg. m. adj. [§7.2] (ἐν +
νόμος) *within law; lawful, legal,* Acts
19:39; in N.T. *subject or under a law, obedient to a law,* 1 Cor. 9:21

ἐννόμῳ, dat. sg. f. adj. . . . . ἔννομος *(1772)*

(†1773) **ἔννυχα**, adv., *by night* (Mark 1:35, GNT, WH
& NA | ἔννυχον, MT & TR)

(1773) **ἔννυχον**, adv., *by night* (Mark 1:35, MT &
TR | ἔννυχα, GNT, WH & NA)

(†1773) **ἔννυχος**, ον [§7.2] (ἐν + νύξ) *nocturnal*

(1774) **ἐνοικέω**, ῶ, fut. ἐνοικήσω [§16.P] (ἐν + οἰκέω) *to dwell in, inhabit;* in N.T. met. *to be indwelling* spiritually, Rom. 8:11; Col. 3:16; 2 Tim. 1:14; *to be infixed* mentally, 2 Tim. 1:5; of the Deity, *to indwell,* by special presence, 2 Cor. 6:16

ἐνοικείτω, 3 pers. sg. pres. act. imper. ἐνοικέω *(1774)*

ἐνοικήσω, 1 pers. sg. fut. act. indic. . . . . . id.

ἐνοικοῦν, acc. sg. neut. pres. act. part. (Rom. 8:11, MT & TRs | ἐνοικοῦντος, GNT, WH, TRb & NA) . . . . id.

ἐνοικοῦντος, gen. sg. neut. pres. act. part. id.

ἐνοικοῦσα, nom. sg. f. pres. act. part. (Rom. 7:17, WH | οἰκοῦσα, GNT, MT, TR & NA) . . . . id.

ἐνόμιζεν, 3 pers. sg. imperf. act. indic. νομίζω *(3543)*

ἐνομίζετο, 3 pers. sg. imperf. pass. indic. . id.

ἐνομίζομεν, 1 pers. pl. imperf. act. indic. (Acts 16:13, GNT, WH & NA | ἐνομίζετο, MT & TR) . . . . id.

ἐνόμιζον, 3 pers. pl. imperf. act. indic. . . . id.

ἐνόμισαν, 3 pers. pl. aor. act. indic. . . . . . id.

ἐνόμισας, 2 pers. sg. aor. act. indic. . . . . . id.

ἐνόντα, acc. pl. neut. pres. part. . . . . ἔνειμι *(1751)*

(‡3726) **ἐνορκίζω**, 1 pers. sg. pres. act. indic., fut. ἐνορκίσω (ἐν + ὁρκίζω) *to adjure* (1 Thess. 5:27, GNT, WH & NA | ὁρκίζω, MT & TR)

ἑνός, gen. sg. m. numeral {Rom. 5:17} . . . εἷς *(1520)*

ἑνός, gen. sg. neut. numeral {Rom. 5:18} . id.

ἐνοσφίσατο, 3 pers. sg. aor. mid. indic. . . . . νοσφίζω *(†3557)*

(1775) **ἑνότης**, ητος, ἡ [§4.2.c] *oneness, unity,* Eph. 4:3, 13

ἑνότητα, acc. sg. f. n. . . . . ἑνότης *(1775)*

(1776) **ἐνοχλέω**, ῶ, fut. ἐνοχλήσω [§16.P] (ἐν + ὀχλέω) *to trouble, annoy; to be a trouble,* Heb. 12:15

ἐνοχλῇ, 3 pers. sg. pres. act. subj. . . . ἐνοχλέω *(1776)*

ἐνοχλούμενοι, nom. pl. m. pres. pass. part. (Luke 6:18, GNT, WH & NA | ὀχλούμενοι, MT & TR) . . . . id.

ἔνοχοι, nom. pl. m. adj. . . . . ἔνοχος *(1777)*

ἔνοχον, acc. sg. m. adj. . . . . id.

(1777) **ἔνοχος**, ον, nom. sg. m. adj. [§7.2] *held in or by; subjected to,* Heb. 2:15; *subject to, liable to,* Matt. 5:21, 22; 26:66; Mark 3:29; 14:64; *an offender against,* 1 Cor. 11:27; James 2:10

ἐνστήσονται, 3 pers. pl. fut. mid. dep. indic. [§29.Y] . . . . ἐνίστημι *(1764)*

(1778) **ἔνταλμα**, ατος, τό [§4.D.c] equivalent to ἐντολή, *a precept, commandment, ordinance,* Matt. 15:9; Mark 7:7; Col. 2:22

ἐντάλματα, acc. pl. neut. n. . . . . ἔνταλμα *(1778)*

ἐνταφιάζειν, pres. act. infin. . . . . . . ἐνταφιάζω *(1779)*

(1779) **ἐνταφιάζω**, fut. ἐνταφιάσω [§26.1] (ἐντάφιος, θάπτω) *to prepare* a body *for burial,* Matt. 26:12; absol. *to make the ordinary preparations for burial,* John 19:40

ἐνταφιάσαι, aor. act. infin. . . . . ἐνταφιάζω *(1779)*

ἐνταφιασμόν, acc. sg. m. n. . . . . ἐνταφιασμός *(1780)*

(1780) **ἐνταφιασμός**, οῦ, ὁ [§3.C.a] *preparation* of a corpse *for burial,* Mark 14:8; John 12:7

ἐνταφιασμοῦ, gen. sg. m. n. . . . . ἐνταφιασμός *(1780)*

ἐντειλάμενος, nom. sg. m. aor. mid./pass. dep. part. . . . . ἐντέλλομαι *(1781)*

ἐντελεῖται, 3 pers. sg. fut. mid./pass. dep. indic. [§35.11] . . . . id.

(1781) **ἐντέλλομαι**, 1 pers. sg. pres. mid./pass. dep. indic., fut. ἐντελοῦμαι, aor. ἐνετειλάμην [§27.1.d] perf. ἐντέταλμαι [§27.2.b] *to enjoin, charge, command,* Matt. 4:6; 15:4; 17:9, et al.; *to direct,* Matt. 19:7; Mark 10:3

ἐντέταλται, 3 pers. sg. perf. pass. indic. ἐντέλλομαι *(1781)*

ἐντετυλιγμένον, acc. sg. neut. perf. pass. part. ἐντυλίσσω *(1794)*

ἐντετυπωμένη, nom. sg. f. perf. pass. part. . . . . ἐντυπόω *(1795)*

(1782) **ἐντεῦθεν**, adv., *hence, from this place,* Matt. 17:20; Luke 4:9, et al.; ἐντεῦθεν καὶ ἐντεῦθεν, *hence and hence, on each side,* Rev. 22:2; *hence, from this cause,* James 4:1

ἐντεύξεις, acc. pl. f. n. . . . . ἔντευξις *(1783)*

ἐντεύξεως, gen. sg. f. n. . . . . id.

(1783) **ἔντευξις**, εως, ἡ [§5.E.c] pr. *a meeting with;* hence, *converse, address; prayer, supplication, intercession,* 1 Tim. 2:1; 4:5

ἔντιμον, acc. sg. m. adj. . . . . ἔντιμος *(1784)*

(1784) **ἔντιμος**, ον, nom. sg. m. adj. [§7.2] (ἐν + τιμή) *honored, estimable, dear,* Luke 7:2; 14:8; Phil. 2:29; *highly-valued, precious, costly,* 1 Pet. 2:4, 6

ἐντιμότερος, nom. sg. m. compar. adj. [§8.4] . . . . ἔντιμος *(1784)*

ἐντιμους, acc. pl. m. adj. . . . . id.

ἐντολαί, nom. pl. f. n. . . . . ἐντολή *(1785)*

ἐντολαῖς, dat. pl. f. n. . . . . id.

ἐντολάς, acc. pl. f. n. . . . . id.

(1785) **ἐντολή**, ῆς, ἡ, nom. sg. f. n. [§2.B.a] *an injunction; a precept, commandment,* Matt. 5:19; 15:3, 6, et al.; *an order, direction,* Acts 17:15; *an edict,* John 11:57; *a direction,* Mark 10:5; *a commission,* John 10:18, *a charge* of matters to be proclaimed or received, John 12:49, 50; 1 Tim. 6:14;

2 Pet. 2:21, et al.

ἐντολήν, acc. sg. f. n. . . . . ἐντολή *(1785)*

ἐντολῆς, gen. sg. f. n. . . . . id.

ἐντολῶν, gen. pl. f. n. . . . . id.

ἐντόπιοι, nom. pl. m. adj. . . . . ἐντόπιος *(1786)*

(1786) **ἐντόπιος**, ον [§7.2] (ἐν + τόπος) i.q. ἔντο-
πος, *in or of a place; an inhabitant, citizen*, Acts 21:12

(1787) **ἐντός**, adv., *inside, within*, Luke 17:21; τὸ
ἐντός, *the interior, inside*, Matt. 23:26

ἐντραπῇ, 3 pers. sg. 2 aor. pass. subj.
[§24.10] . . . . ἐντρέπω *(1788)*

ἐντραπήσονται, 3 pers. pl. 2 fut. pass. indic. id.

ἐντρέπομαι, 1 pers. sg. pres. pass. indic. . . id.

ἐντρεπόμενος, nom. sg. m. pres. pass. part. id.

(1788) **ἐντρέπω**, fut. ἐντρέψω [§23.1.a] (ἐν + τρέπω)
pr. *to turn* one *back upon himself;* hence,
to put to shame, make ashamed; pass.
ἐντρέπομαι, fut. (pass. form) ἐντραπή-
σομαι, 2 aor. (pass. form) ἐνετράπην
[§24.10] *to revere, reverence, regard*, Matt.
21:37; Mark 12:6, et al.; absol. *to feel
shame, be put to shame*, 2 Thess. 3:14;
Tit. 2:8

ἐντρέπων, nom. sg. m. pres. act. part. ἐντρέπω *(1788)*

ἐντρεφόμενος, nom. sg. m. pres. pass.
part. . . . . ἐντρέφω *(1789)*

(1789) **ἐντρέφω**, fut. ἐνθρέψω [§35.4] (ἐν + τρέφω)
to nourish in, bring up or educate in; pass.
to be imbued, 1 Tim. 4:6

(1790) **ἔντρομος**, ον, nom. sg. m. adj. [§7.2] (ἐν +
τρόμος) *trembling, terrified*, Acts 7:32;
16:29; Heb. 12:21

(1791) **ἐντροπή**, ῆς, ἡ [§2.B.a] *reverence;* in N.T.
shame, 1 Cor. 6:5; 15:34

ἐντροπήν, acc. sg. f. n. . . . . ἐντροπή *(1791)*

(1792) **ἐντρυφάω**, ῶ, fut. ἐντρυφήσω [§18.R] (ἐν +
τρυφάω) *to live luxuriously, riot, revel*,
2 Pet. 2:13

ἐντρυφῶντες, nom. pl. m. pres. act.
part. ἐντρυφάω *(1792)*

ἐντυγχάνει, 3 pers. sg. pres. act.
indic. ἐντυγχάνω *(1793)*

ἐντυγχάνειν, pres. act. infin. . . . . id.

(1793) **ἐντυγχάνω**, fut. ἐντεύξομαι, 2 aor. ἐνέτυχον
[§36.2] (ἐν + τυγχάνω) *to fill in with,
meet; to have converse with, address; to address or apply to any one*, Acts 25:24; ὑπέρ
τινος, *to intercede for any one, plead the
cause of*, Rom. 8:27, 34; Heb. 7:25; κατά
τινος, *to address a representation or suit
against any one, to accuse, complain of*,
Rom. 11:2

(1794) **ἐντυλίσσω**, fut. ἐντυλίξω, perf. pass.
ἐντετύλιγμαι [§26.3] (ἐν + τυλίσσω) *to*

wrap up in, inwrap, envelope, Matt. 27:59;
Luke 23:53; *to wrap up, roll or fold together*, John 20:7

(1795) **ἐντυπόω**, ῶ, fut. ἐντυπώσω [§20.T] (ἐν +
τυπόω, from τύπος, *an impress*) *to impress
a figure, instamp, engrave*, 2 Cor. 3:7

(1796) **ἐνυβρίζω**, fut. ἐνυβρίσω [§26.1] (ἐν + ὕβρις)
to insult, outrage, contemn, Heb. 10:29

ἐνυβρίσας, nom. sg. m. aor. act.
part. ἐνυβρίζω *(1796)*

ἔνυξε(ν), 3 pers. sg. aor. act. indic. . . . . νύσσω *(3572)*

ἐνύπνια, acc. pl. neut. n. (Acts 2:17, MT &
TR | ἐνυπνίοις, GNT, WH &
NA) . . . . ἐνύπνιον *(1798)*

ἐνυπνιαζόμενοι, nom. pl. m. pres. mid./pass.
dep. part. . . . . ἐνυπνιάζω *(†1797)*

(†1797) **ἐνυπνιάζω**, fut. ἐνυπνιάσω [§26.1] and
ἐνυπνιάζομαι, fut. (pass. form) ἐνυπνι-
ασθήσομαι, *to dream*, in N.T. *to dream
under supernatural impression*, Acts 2:17;
to dream delusion, Jude 8

ἐνυπνιασθήσονται, 3 pers. pl. fut. pass.
indic. ἐνυπνιάζω *(†1797)*

ἐνυπνίοις, dat. pl. neut. n. (Acts 2:17, GNT,
WH & NA | ἐνύπνια, MT &
TR) . . . . ἐνύπνιον *(1798)*

(1798) **ἐνύπνιον**, ου, τό [§3.C.c] (pr. neut. of
ἐνύπνιος, *presented during sleep*, from ἐν
+ ὕπνος) *a dream;* in N.T. *a supernatural
suggestion or impression received during
sleep, a sleep-vision*, Acts 2:17

ἐνύσταξαν, 3 pers. pl. aor. act. indic. νυστάζω *(3573)*

ἐνῴκησε(ν), 3 pers. sg. aor. act. indic.
[§13.2] . . . . ἐνοικέω *(1774)*

(1799) **ἐνώπιον**, adv. (pr. neut. of ἐνώπιος, *in sight
or front*) *before, in the presence of*, Luke
5:25; 8:47; *in front of*, Rev. 4:5, 6; *immediately preceding* as a forerunner, Luke
1:17; Rev. 16:19; from the Hebrew, *in the
presence of*, metaphysically, *i.e.* in the
sphere of sensation or thought, Luke 12:9;
15:10; Acts 10:31; *in the eyes of, in the judgment of*, Luke 16:15; 24:11; Acts 4:19, et al.

(1800) **Ἐνώς**, ὁ, *Enos*, pr. name, indecl., Luke 3:38

(1801) **ἐνωτίζομαι**, fut. ἐνωτίσομαι, aor. ἐνωτισάμην
[§26.1] (ἐν + οὖς) *to give ear, listen,
hearken to*, Acts 2:14

ἐνωτίσασθε, 2 pers. pl. aor. mid. dep.
imper. ἐνωτίζομαι *(1801)*

(1802) **Ἐνώχ**, ὁ, *Enoch*, pr. name, indecl. (Luke 3:37;
Heb. 11:5; Jude 14, GNT, MT, TR & NA
| Ἐνώχ, WH)

ἐξ, prep. ἐκ before a vowel {Matt. 18:12} . ἐκ *(1537)*

(1803) **ἕξ**, οἱ, αἱ, τά, indecl. numeral, *six*, Matt. 17:1;
Mark 9:2, et al. {Matt. 17:1}

ἐξαγαγεῖν, 2 aor. act. infin. [§13.7.b,d] . ἐξάγω *(1806)*

ἐξαγαγέτωσαν, 3 pers. pl. 2 aor. act. imper.   id.

ἐξαγαγόντες, nom. pl. m. 2 aor. act. part.   id.

ἐξαγαγών, nom. sg. m. 2 aor. act. part. . .   id.

ἐξαγγείλητε, 2 pers. pl. aor. act. subj.
[§27.1.d] . . . . ἐξαγγέλλω *(1804)*

(1804) **ἐξαγγέλλω,** fut. ἐξαγγελῶ [§27.1.b] (ἐξ + ἀγγέλλω) *to tell forth, divulge, publish; to declare abroad, celebrate,* 1 Pet. 2:9

ἐξάγει, 3 pers. sg. pres. act. indic. . . . . . ἐξάγω *(1806)*

ἐξαγοραζόμενοι, nom. pl. m. pres. mid.
part. . . . . ἐξαγοράζω *(1805)*

(1805) **ἐξαγοράζω,** fut. ἐξαγοράσω [§26.1] (ἐξ + ἀγοράζω) *to buy out* of the hands of a person; *to redeem, set free,* Gal. 3:13; mid. *to redeem, buy off, to secure for one's self or one's own use; to rescue* from loss or misapplication, Eph. 5:16; Col. 4:5

ἐξαγοράσῃ, 3 pers. sg. aor. act.
subj. . . . . ἐξαγοράζω *(1805)*

ἐξάγουσιν, 3 pers. pl. pres. act. indic. . . ἐξάγω *(1806)*

(1806) **ἐξάγω,** fut. ἐξάξω [§23.1.b] 2 aor. ἐξήγαγον [§13.7.b,d] (ἐξ + ἄγω) *to bring or lead forth, conduct out of,* Mark 8:23; 15:20; Luke 24:50, et al.

(1807) **ἐξαιρέω, ῶ,** fut. ἐξαιρήσω, 2 aor. ἐξεῖλον [§36.1] (ἐξ + αἱρέω) *to take out of; to pluck out, tear out,* Matt. 5:29; 18:9; mid. *to take out of, select, choose,* Acts 26:17; *to rescue, deliver,* Acts 7:10, 34; 12:11; 23:27; Gal. 1:4

ἐξαιρούμενος, nom. sg. m. pres. mid.
part. . . . . ἐξαιρέω *(1807)*

(1808) **ἐξαίρω,** fut. ἐξαρῶ [§27.1.c] (ἐξ + αἴρω) pr. *to lift up out of;* in N.T. *to remove, eject,* 1 Cor. 5:2, 13

(†1809) **ἐξαιτέω, ῶ,** fut. ἐξαιτήσω [§16.P] (ἐξ + αἰτέω) *to ask for from; to demand;* mid. *to demand for one's self,* Luke 22:31; also, *to obtain by asking*

(1810) **ἐξαίφνης,** adv. (ἐξ + αἴφνης) *suddenly, unexpectedly,* Mark 13:36, et al. (Mark 13:36; Luke 2:13; 9:39; Acts 9:3; 22:6, GNT, MT, TR & NA | ἐξέφνης, WH)

(1811) **ἐξακολουθέω, ῶ,** fut. ἐξακολουθήσω [§16.P] (ἐξ + ἀκολουθέω) *to follow out; to imitate,* 2 Pet. 2:2, 15; *to observe as a guide,* 2 Pet. 1:16

ἐξακολουθήσαντες, nom. pl. m. aor. act.
part. ἐξακολουθέω *(1811)*

ἐξακολουθήσουσιν, 3 pers. pl. fut. act. indic.   id.

(1812) **ἐξακόσιοι, αι, α,** nom. pl. m. numeral (ἐξ + ἑκατόν) *six hundred,* Rev. 13:18; 14:20 (Rev. 13:18, GNT, WH & NA | χξϛ΄, MT & TR)

ἐξακοσίων, gen. pl. m. numeral . . . . ἑξακόσιοι *(1812)*

ἐξαλειφθῆναι, aor. pass. infin. . . . . . . ἐξαλείφω *(1813)*

(1813) **ἐξαλείφω,** fut. ἐξαλείψω [§23.1.a] (ἐξ + ἀλείφω) pr. *to anoint or smear over;* hence *to wipe off or away,* Rev. 7:17; 21:4; *to blot out, obliterate, expunge,* Col. 2:14; Rev. 3:5; met. *to wipe out* guilt, Acts 3:19

ἐξαλείψας, nom. sg. m. aor. act.
part. . . . . ἐξαλείφω *(1813)*

ἐξαλείψει, 3 pers. sg. fut. act. indic. . . . . . id.

ἐξαλείψω, 1 pers. sg. fut. act. indic. . . . . . id.

(1814) **ἐξάλλομαι,** fut. ἐξαλοῦμαι [§37.1] (ἐξ + ἄλλομαι) *to leap or spring up or forth,* Acts 3:8

ἐξαλλόμενος, nom. sg. m. pres. mid./pass.
dep. part. . . . . ἐξάλλομαι *(1814)*

ἐξανάστασιν, acc. sg. f. n. . . . . . ἐξανάστασις *(1815)*

(1815) **ἐξανάστασις, εως, ἡ** [§5.E.c] (ἐξ + ἀνάστασις) *a raising up; a dislodgment; a rising up; a resurrection from* the dead, Phil. 3:11

ἐξαναστήσῃ, 3 pers. sg. aor. act.
subj. . . . . ἐξανίστημι *(1817)*

(1816) **ἐξανατέλλω,** fut. ἐξανατελῶ [§27.1.b] (ἐξ + ἀνατέλλω) *to raise up, make to spring up;* intrans. *to rise up, sprout, spring up or forth,* Matt. 13:5; Mark 4:5

ἐξανέστησαν, 3 pers. pl. 2 aor. act.
indic. . . . . ἐξανίστημι *(1817)*

ἐξανέτειλε(ν), 3 pers. sg. aor. act. indic.
[§27.1.d] . . . . ἐξανατέλλω *(1816)*

(1817) **ἐξανίστημι,** fut. ἐξαναστήσω [§29.X] (ἐξ + ἀνίστημι) *to cause to rise up, raise up;* from the Hebrew, *to raise up* into existence, Mark 12:19; Luke 20:28; intrans. 2 aor. ἀνέστην, *to rise up from, stand forth,* Acts 15:5

(1818) **ἐξαπατάω, ῶ,** fut. ἐξαπατήσω [§18.R] (ἐξ + ἀπατάω) pr. *to deceive thoroughly; to deceive, delude, beguile,* Rom. 7:11; 16:8; 1 Cor. 3:18, et al.

ἐξαπατάτω, 3 pers. sg. pres. act.
imper. . . . . ἐξαπατάω *(1818)*

ἐξαπατηθεῖσα, nom. sg. f. aor. act. part.
(1 Tim. 2:14, GNT, WH & NA | ἀπατηθεῖσα, MT & TR) . . . . id.

ἐξαπατήσῃ, 3 pers. sg. aor. act. subj. . . . . id.

ἐξαπατῶσι(ν), 3 pers. pl. pres. act. indic. . id.

ἐξαπεστάλη, 3 pers. sg. 2 aor. pass. indic.
(Acts 13:26, GNT, WH & NA | ἀπεστάλη, MT & TR) . . . . ἐξαποστέλλω *(1821)*

ἐξαπέστειλαν, 3 pers. pl. aor. act. indic. . . id.

ἐξαπέστειλε(ν), 3 pers. sg. aor. act. indic.
[§27.1.d] . . . . id.

(1819) **ἐξάπινα,** adv., a later form for ἐξαπίνης, *sud-*

denly, immediately, unexpectedly, Mark 9:8

(†1820) ἐξαπορέω, ῶ, and ἐξαπορέομαι, οῦμαι, fut. ἐξαπορήσομαι (ἐξ + ἀπορέω) *to be in the utmost perplexity or despair,* 2 Cor. 1:8; 4:8

ἐξαπορηθῆναι, aor. pass. infin. ... ἐξαπορέω (†1820)

ἐξαπορούμενοι, nom. pl. m. pres. mid./pass. dep. part. . . . . id.

(1821) ἐξαποστέλλω, 1 pers. sg. pres. act. indic.
ἐξαποστέλλω [§27.1.b] (ἐξ + ἀποστέλλω) *to send out or forth; to send away, dismiss,* Luke 1:53, et al.; *to despatch* on a service or agency, Acts 7:12, et al.; *to send forth* as a pervading influence, Gal. 4:6 (Luke 24:49, WH | ἀποστέλλω, GNT, MT, TR & NA)

ἐξαποστελῶ, 1 pers. sg. fut. act. indic. . . . . ἐξαποστέλλω (1821)

ἐξάρατε, 2 pers. pl. aor. act. imper. (1 Cor. 5:13, GNT, WH & NA | ἐξαρεῖτε, MT & TR) . . . . ἐξαίρω (1808)

ἐξαρεῖτε, 2 pers. pl. fut. act. indic. (1 Cor. 5:13, MT & TR | ἐξάρατε, GNT, WH & NA) . . . . id.

ἐξαρθῇ, 3 pers. sg. aor. pass. subj. [§27.3] (1 Cor. 5:2, MT & TR | ἀρθῇ, GNT, WH & NA) . . . . id.

(1822) ἐξαρτίζω, fut. ἐξαρτίσω, perf. pass. ἐξήρτισμαι [§26.1] (ἐξ + ἄρτιος) *to equip or furnish completely,* 2 Tim. 3:17; *to complete* time, Acts 21:5

ἐξαρτίσαι, aor. act. infin. . . . . ἐξαρτίζω (1822)

(1823) ἐξαστράπτω, fut. ἐξαστράψω [§23.1.a] (ἐξ + ἀστράπτω) pr. *to flash forth;* hence, *to glisten,* Luke 9:29

ἐξαστράπτων, nom. sg. m. pres. act. part. . . . . ἐξαστράπτω (1823)

(1824) ἐξαυτῆς, adv. (ἐξ αὐτῆς, sc. τῆς ὥρας) lit. *at the very time; presently, instantly, immediately,* Mark 6:25; Acts 10:33; 11:11, et al.

ἐξέβαλε(ν), 3 pers. sg. 2 aor. act. indic. [§27.2.d] . . . . ἐκβάλλω (1544)

ἐξέβαλλον, 3 pers. pl. imperf. act. indic. . . id.

ἐξεβάλομεν, 1 pers. pl. 2 aor. act. indic. . . id.

ἐξέβαλον, 3 pers. pl. 2 aor. act. indic. . . . id.

ἐξέβησαν, 3 pers. pl. 2 aor. act. indic. (Heb. 11:15, GNT, WH & NA | ἐξῆλθον, MT & TR) . . . . ἐκβαίνω (‡1545)

ἐξεβλήθη, 3 pers. sg. aor. pass. indic. [§27.3] . . . . ἐκβάλλω (1544)

ἐξεγαμίζοντο, 3 pers. pl. imperf. pass. indic. (Luke 17:27, MT & TR | ἐγαμίζοντο, GNT, WH & NA) . . . . ἐκγαμίζω (1547)

ἐξεγερεῖ, 3 pers. sg. fut. act. indic. . . ἐξεγείρω (1825)

(1825) ἐξεγείρω, fut. ἐξεγερῶ [§27.1.c] (ἐξ + ἐγείρω) *to excite, arouse* from sleep; *to raise up* from the dead, 1 Cor. 6:14; *to raise up* into existence, or into a certain condition, Rom. 9:17

ἐξέδετο, 3 pers. sg. 2 aor. mid. indic. (Matt. 21:33; Mark 12:1; Luke 20:9, GNT, WH & NA | ἐξέδοτο, MT & TR) . . . ἐκδίδωμι (1554)

ἐξεδέχετο, 3 pers. sg. imperf. mid./pass. dep. indic. . . . . ἐκδέχομαι (1551)

ἐξεδίκησε(ν), 3 pers. sg. aor. act. indic. . . . . ἐκδικέω (1556)

ἐξέδοτο, 3 pers. sg. 2 aor. mid. indic. [§30.AA] (Matt. 21:33; Mark 12:1; Luke 20:9, MT & TR | ἐξέδετο, GNT, WH & NA) . . . . ἐκδίδωμι (1554)

ἐξέδυσαν, 3 pers. pl. aor. act. indic. ... ἐκδύω (1562)

ἐξεζήτησαν, 3 pers. pl. aor. act. indic. ἐκζητέω (1567)

ἐξεθαμβήθη, 3 pers. sg. aor. pass. indic. (Mark 9:15, TR | ἐξεθαμβήθησαν, GNT, WH, MT & NA) . . . . ἐκθαμβέω (1568)

ἐξεθαμβήθησαν, 3 pers. pl. aor. pass. indic.   id.

ἐξεθαύμαζον, 3 pers. pl. imperf. act. indic. (Mark 12:17, GNT, WH & NA | ἐθαύμασαν, MT & TR) . . . . ἐκθαυμάζω (‡2296)

ἐξέθεντο, 3 pers. pl. 2 aor. mid. indic. [§28.W] . . . . ἐκτίθημι (1620)

ἕξει, 3 pers. sg. fut. act. indic. [§35.4] ... ἔχω (2192)

ἐξειλάμην, 1 pers. sg. 2 aor. mid. indic. (Acts 23:27, GNT, WH & NA | ἐξειλόμην, MT & TR) . . . . ἐξαιρέω (1807)

ἐξείλατο, 3 pers. sg. aor. mid. indic. (Acts 7:10; 12:11, GNT, WH & NA | ἐξείλετο, MT & TR) . . . . id.

ἐξείλετο, 3 pers. sg. 2 aor. mid. indic. [§36.1] (Acts 7:10; 12:11, MT & TR | ἐξείλατο, GNT, WH & NA) . . . . id.

ἐξειλόμην, 1 pers. sg. 2 aor. mid. indic. (Acts 23:27, MT & TR | ἐξειλάμην, GNT, WH & NA) . . . . id.

(1826) ἔξειμι (ἐξ + εἶμι) [§33.4] imperf. ἐξῄειν, infin. ἐξιέναι, part. ἐξιών, *to go out or forth,* Acts 13:42; *to depart,* Acts 17:15; 20:7; ἐπὶ τὴν γῆν, *to get to land,* from the water, Acts 27:43

ἕξεις, 2 pers. sg. fut. act. indic. . . . . ἔχω (2192)

ἐξεκαύθησαν, 3 pers. pl. aor. pass. indic. [§35.3] . . . . ἐκκαίω (1572)

ἐξεκέντησαν, 3 pers. pl. aor. act. indic. . . . . ἐκκεντέω (1574)

ἐξεκλάσθησαν, 3 pers. pl. aor. pass. indic. [§22.4] . . . . ἐκκλάω (1575)

ἐξεκλείσθη, 3 pers. sg. aor. pass. indic. . . . . ἐκκλείω (1576)

ἐξέκλιναν, 3 pers. pl. aor. act. indic. . . ἐκκλίνω (1578)

ἐξεκομίζετο, 3 pers. sg. imperf. pass.

indic. ἐκκομίζω *(1580)*
ἐξεκόπης, 2 pers. sg. 2 aor. pass. indic.
[§24.6] . . . . ἐκκόπτω *(1581)*
ἐξεκρέματο, 3 pers. sg. imperf. mid.
indic. . . . . ἐκκρέμαννυμι *(†1582)*
ἔξελε, 2 pers. sg. 2 aor. act. imper. . . . ἐξαιρέω *(1807)*
ἐξελέγξαι, aor. act. infin. (Jude 15, TR |
ἐλέγξαι, GNT, WH, MT & NA) ἐξελέγχω *(1827)*
ἐξελέγοντο, 3 pers. pl. imperf. mid.
indic. . . . . ἐκλέγω *(†1586)*
(1827) **ἐξελέγχω** [§23.1.b] (ἐξ + ἐλέγχω) *to search
thoroughly, to test; to convict, condemn,*
Jude 15
ἐξελεξάμην, 1 pers. sg. aor. mid.
indic. . . . . ἐκλέγω *(†1586)*
ἐξελέξαντο, 3 pers. pl. aor. mid. indic. . . . id.
ἐξελέξασθε, 2 pers. pl. aor. mid. indic. . . . id.
ἐξελέξατο, 3 pers. sg. aor. mid. indic. . . . . id.
ἐξελέξω, 2 pers. sg. aor. mid. indic. . . . . . id.
ἐξελέσθαι, 2 aor. mid. infin. [§36.1] . . ἐξαιρέω *(1807)*
ἐξελεύσεται, 3 pers. sg. fut. mid. dep. indic.
[§36.1] . . . . ἐξέρχομαι *(1831)*
ἐξελεύσονται, 3 pers. pl. fut. mid. dep. indic. id.
ἐξελήλυθα, 1 pers. sg. perf. act. indic. (Mark
1:38, MT & TR | ἐξῆλθον, GNT, WH &
NA) . . . . id.
ἐξεληλύθασιν, 3 pers. pl. perf. act. indic. . id.
ἐξεληλύθατε, 2 pers. pl. perf. act. indic. (Luke
7:26, MT & TR | ἐξήλθατε, GNT, WH
& NA) . . . . id.
ἐξεληλύθει, 3 pers. sg. pluperf. act. indic. . id.
ἐξελήλυθε(ν), 3 pers. sg. perf. act. indic. . . id.
ἐξεληλυθός, acc. sg. neut. perf. act. part. . id.
ἐξεληλυθότας, acc. pl. m. perf. act. part. . id.
ἐξεληλυθυῖαν, acc. sg. f. perf. act. part. (Luke
8:46, GNT, WH & NA | ἐξελθοῦσαν,
MT & TR) . . . . id.
ἐξέληται, 3 pers. sg. 2 aor. mid. subj. ἐξαιρέω *(1807)*
ἐξέλθατε, 2 pers. pl. aor. act. imper. [§35.12]
(2 Cor. 6:17; Rev. 18:4, GNT, WH & NA
| ἐξέλθετε, TR | 2 Cor. 6:17, ἐξέλθετε;
Rev. 18:4, ἔξελθε, MT) . . . . ἐξέρχομαι *(1831)*
ἔξελθε, 2 pers. sg. 2 aor. act. imper. . . . . . id.
ἐξελθεῖν, 2 aor. act. infin. . . . . id.
ἐξέλθετε, 2 pers. pl. 2 aor. act. imper. (2 Cor.
6:17, MT & TR; Rev. 18:4, TR |
ἐξέλθατε, GNT, WH & NA) . . . . id.
ἐξέλθῃ, 3 pers. sg. 2 aor. act. subj. . . . . . . id.
ἐξέλθῃς, 2 pers. sg. 2 aor. act. subj. . . . . . id.
ἐξέλθητε, 2 pers. pl. 2 aor. act. subj. . . . . id.
ἐξελθόντα, acc. sg. m. 2 aor. act. part.
{Matt. 26:71} . . . . id.
ἐξελθόντα, nom. pl. neut. 2 aor. act. part.
{Mark 5:13} . . . . id.
ἐξελθόντες, nom. pl. m. 2 aor. act. part. . id.

ἐξελθόντι, dat. sg. m. 2 aor. act.
part. . . . . ἐξέρχομαι *(1831)*
ἐξελθόντος, gen. sg. m. 2 aor. act. part.
{Luke 11:53} . . . . id.
ἐξελθόντος, gen. sg. neut. 2 aor. act. part.
{Luke 11:14} . . . . id.
ἐξελθόντων, gen. pl. m. 2 aor. act. part. . . id.
ἐξελθοῦσα, nom. sg. f. 2 aor. act. part. . . id.
ἐξελθοῦσαι, nom. pl. f. 2 aor. act. part. . . id.
ἐξελθοῦσαν, acc. sg. f. 2 aor. act. part. . . . id.
ἐξελθούσῃ, dat. sg. f. 2 aor. act. part. (Rev.
19:21, GNT, WH, MT & NA | ἐκπο-
ρευομένῃ, TR) . . . . id.
ἐξελθών, nom. sg. m. 2 aor. act. part. . . . id.
ἐξελκόμενος, nom. sg. m. pres. pass.
part. . . . . ἐξέλκω *(1828)*
(1828) **ἐξέλκω**, fut. ἐξελξω [§23.1.b] (ἐξ + ἕλκω) *to
draw or drag out;* met. *to withdraw, allure,
hurry away,* James 1:14
ἐξέμαξε(ν), 3 pers. sg. aor. act.
indic. . . . . ἐκμάσσω *(1591)*
ἐξέμασσε(ν), 3 pers. sg. imperf. act. indic. id.
ἐξεμυκτήριζον, 3 pers. pl. imperf. act.
indic. . . . . ἐκμυκτηρίζω *(†1592)*
ἐξενέγκαντες, nom. pl. m. aor. act. part.
[§36.1] . . . . ἐκφέρω *(1627)*
ἐξενέγκατε, 2 pers. pl. aor. act. imper. . . . id.
ἐξενεγκεῖν, 2 aor. act. infin. . . . . id.
ἐξένευσεν, 3 pers. sg. aor. act. indic. . . ἐκνεύω *(1593)*
ἐξένισε(ν), 3 pers. sg. aor. act. indic. . . ξενίζω *(3579)*
ἐξενοδόχησεν, 3 pers. sg. aor. act.
indic. . . . . ξενοδοχέω *(3580)*
ἐξέπεμψαν, 3 pers. pl. aor. act. indic. ἐκπέμπω *(1599)*
ἐξέπεσαν, 3 pers. pl. aor. act. indic. [§37.1]
(Acts 12:7, GNT, WH & NA | ἐξέπεσον,
MT & TR) . . . . ἐκπίπτω *(1601)*
ἐξεπέσατε, 2 pers. pl. aor. act. indic. . . . . id.
ἐξέπεσε(ν), 3 pers. sg. 2 aor. act. indic. . . id.
ἐξέπεσον, 3 pers. pl. 2 aor. act. indic. (Acts
12:7, MT & TR | ἐξέπεσαν, GNT, WH
& NA) . . . . id.
ἐξεπέτασα, 1 pers. sg. aor. act.
indic. . . . . ἐκπετάννυμι *(1600)*
ἐξεπήδησαν, 3 pers. pl. aor. act. indic. (Acts
14:14, GNT, WH & NA | εἰσεπήδησαν,
MT & TR) . . . . ἐκπηδάω *(‡1530)*
ἐξεπλάγησαν, 3 pers. pl. 2 aor. pass. indic.
[§24.9] . . . . ἐκπλήσσω *(1605)*
ἐξέπλει, 3 pers. sg. imperf. act. indic. . ἐκπλέω *(1602)*
ἐξεπλεύσαμεν, 1 pers. pl. aor. act. indic.
[§35.3] . . . . ἐκπλέω *(1602)*
ἐξεπλήσσετο, 3 pers. sg. imperf. pass.
indic. | ἐκπλήσσω *(1605)*
ἐξεπλήσσοντο, 3 pers. pl. imperf. pass. indic. id.
ἐξέπνευσε(ν), 3 pers. sg. aor. act. indic.

[§35.3] . . . . ἐκπνέω (1606)

ἐξεπορεύετο, 3 pers. sg. imperf. mid./pass.
dep. indic. . . . . ἐκπορεύομαι (1607)

ἐξεπορεύοντο, 3 pers. pl. imperf. mid./pass.
dep. indic. (Mark 11:19, GNT, WH & NA
| ἐξεπορεύετο, MT & TR) . . . . id.

ἐξεπτύσατε, 2 pers. pl. aor. act. indic. ἐκπτύω (1609)

(1829) ἐξέραμα, ατος, τό [§4.D.c] (ἐξεράω, to vomit)
vomit, 2 Pet. 2:22

ἐξέραμα, acc. sg. neut. n. . . . . ἐξέραμα (1829)

(†1830) ἐξεραυνάω, ῶ, to search out, to examine
closely, 1 Pet. 1:10

(1830) ἐξερευνάω, ῶ, fut. ἐξερευνήσω [§18.K] (ἐξ +
ἐρευνάω) to search out, to examine closely,
1 Pet. 1:10

ἐξέρχεσθαι, pres. mid./pass. dep. infin. (Acts
19:12, MT & TR | ἐκπορεύεσθαι, GNT,
WH & NA) . . . . ἐξέρχομαι (1831)

ἐξέρχεσθε, 2 pers. pl. pres. mid./pass. dep.
imper. . . . . id.

ἐξέρχεται, 3 pers. sg. pres. mid./pass. dep.
indic. . . . . id.

(1831) ἐξέρχομαι [§36.1] fut. ἐξελεύσομαι, 2 aor.
ἐξῆλθον, perf. ἐξελήλυθα (ἐξ + ἔρχομαι)
to go or come out of; to come out, Matt.
5:26; 8:34, et al.; to proceed, emanate, take
rise from, Matt. 2:6; 15:18; 1 Cor. 14:36,
et al.; to come abroad, 1 John 4:1, et al.;
to go forth, go away, depart, Matt. 9:31;
Luke 5:8, et al.; to escape, John 10:39; to
pass away, come to an end, Acts 16:19

ἐξερχόμενοι, nom. pl. m. pres. mid./pass. dep.
part. . . . . ἐξέρχομαι (1831)

ἐξερχόμενος, nom. sg. m. pres. mid./pass.
dep. part. . . . . id.

ἐξερχομένων, gen. pl. m. pres. mid./pass. dep.
part. . . . . id.

ἐξέρχονται, 3 pers. pl. pres. mid./pass. dep.
indic. . . . . id.

ἐξερχώμεθα, 1 pers. pl. pres. mid./pass. dep.
subj. . . . . id.

ἐξεστακέναι, perf. act. infin. . . . . ἐξίστημι (1839)

ἐξέστη, 3 pers. sg. 2 aor. act. indic. [§29.X] id.

ἐξέστημεν, 1 pers. pl. 2 aor. act. indic. . . . id.

ἐξέστησαν, 3 pers. pl. 2 aor. act. indic. . . id.

(1832) ἔξεστι(ν), 3 pers. sg. pres. indic. impersonal,
part. ἐξόν, it is possible; it is permitted,
it is lawful, Matt. 12:2, 4, et al.

ἐξέστραπται, 3 pers. sg. perf. pass. indic.
[§35.9] . . . . ἐκστρέφω (1612)

(1833) ἐξετάζω, fut. ἐξετάσω [§26.1] (ἐξ + ἐτάζω,
to inquire, examine) to search out; to inquire by interrogation, examine strictly,
Matt. 2:8; 10:11; to interrogate, John 21:12

ἐξετάσαι, aor. act. infin. . . . . ἐξετάζω (1833)

ἐξετάσατε, 2 pers. pl. aor. act. imper. ἐξετάζω (1833)

ἕξετε, 2 pers. pl. fut. act. indic. [§35.4] . . ἔχω (2192)

ἐξετείνατε, 2 pers. pl. aor. act. indic. . ἐκτείνω (1614)

ἐξέτεινε(ν), 3 pers. sg. aor. act. indic.
[§27.1.d] . . . . id.

ἐξετίθετο, 3 pers. sg. imperf. mid.
indic. . . . . ἐκτίθημι (1620)

ἐξετράπησαν, 3 pers. pl. 2 aor. pass. indic.
[§24.10] . . . . ἐκτρέπω (1624)

ἐξέφυγον, 1 pers. sg. 2 aor. act. indic.
{2 Cor. 11:33} . . . . ἐκφεύγω (1628)

ἐξέφυγον, 3 pers. pl. 2 aor. act. indic. (Heb.
12:25, GNT, WH & NA | ἔφυγον, MT
& TR) . . . . id.

ἐξέχεαν, 3 pers. pl. aor. act. indic.
[§36.1] . . . . ἐκχέω (1632)

ἐξέχεε(ν), 3 pers. sg. aor. act. indic. . . . . id.

ἐξεχεῖτο, 3 pers. sg. imperf. pass. indic. (Acts
22:20, MT & TR | ἐξεχύννετο, GNT,
WH & NA) . . . . id.

ἐξεχύθη, 3 pers. sg. aor. pass. indic. . . . . id.

ἐξεχύθησαν, 3 pers. pl. aor. pass. indic. . . id.

ἐξεχύννετο, 3 pers. sg. imperf. pass. indic.
(Acts 22:20, GNT, WH & NA | ἐξεχεῖτο,
MT & TR) . . . . ἐκχύν(ν)ω (†1632)

ἐξέψυξε(ν), 3 pers. sg. aor. act. indic.
[§23.3] . . . . ἐκψύχω (1634)

ἐξήγαγε(ν), 3 pers. sg. 2 aor. act. indic.
[§13.7.b,d] . . . . ἐξάγω (1806)

ἐξήγειρα, 1 pers. sg. aor. act. indic.
[§27.1.d] . . . . ἐξεγείρω (1825)

ἐξηγεῖτο, 3 pers. sg. imperf. mid./pass. dep.
indic. . . . . ἐξηγέομαι (1834)

(1834) ἐξηγέομαι, οῦμαι, fut. ἐξηγήσομαι [§17.Q] (ἐξ
+ ἡγέομαι) to be a leader; to detail, to set
forth in language; to tell, narrate, recount,
Luke 24:35; Acts 10:8, et al.; to make
known, reveal, John 1:18

ἐξηγησάμενος, nom. sg. m. aor. mid. dep.
part. . . . . ἐξηγέομαι (1834)

ἐξηγήσατο, 3 pers. sg. aor. mid. dep. indic. id.

ἐξηγόρασεν, 3 pers. sg. aor. act.
indic. ἐξαγοράζω (1805)

ἐξηγουμένων, gen. pl. m. pres. mid./pass. dep.
part. . . . . ἐξηγέομαι (1834)

ἐξηγοῦντο, 3 pers. pl. imperf. mid./pass. dep.
indic. . . . . id.

ἐξῄεσαν, 3 pers. pl. imperf. indic.
[§33.4] . . . . ἔξειμι (1826)

(1835) ἑξήκοντα, οἱ, αἱ, τά, indecl. numeral, sixty,
Matt. 13:8, 23, et al.

ἐξῆλθαν, 3 pers. pl. 2 aor. act. indic. (Acts
16:40; 1 John 2:19; GNT, WH & NA |
ἐξῆλθον, MT & TR) . . . . ἐξέρχομαι (1831)

ἐξήλθατε, 2 pers. pl. aor. act. indic. (Matt.

11:7, 8, 9; 26:55; Mark 14:48; Luke 7:24, 25, 26; 22:52, GNT, WH & NA | ἐξ-ήλθετε, MT & TR) . . . . ἐξέρχομαι *(1831)*

ἐξῆλθε(ν), 3 pers. sg. 2 aor. act. indic. [§36.1]   id.

ἐξῆλθες, 2 pers. sg. 2 aor. act. indic. . . . . . id.

ἐξήλθετε, 2 pers. pl. 2 aor. act. indic. (Matt. 11:7, 8, 9; 26:55; Mark 14:48; Luke 7:24, 25, 26; 22:52, MT & TR | ἐξήλθατε, GNT, WH & NA) . . . . id.

ἐξήλθομεν, 1 pers. pl. 2 aor. act. indic. . . . id.

ἐξῆλθον, 1 pers. sg. 2 aor. act. indic. {John 8:42} . . . . id.

ἐξῆλθον, 3 pers. pl. 2 aor. act. indic. {John 4:30} . . . . id.

ἐξήνεγκεν, 3 pers. sg. aor. act. indic. (Mark 8:23, GNT, WH & NA | ἐξήγαγεν, MT & TR) . . . . ἐκφέρω *(1627)*

ἐξηπάτησε(ν), 3 pers. sg. aor. act. indic. . . . . ἐξαπατάω *(1818)*

ἐξηραμμένην, ἀcc. sg. f. perf. pass. part. [§27.2.a; 27.3] . . . . ξηραίνω *(3583)*

ἐξήρανε(ν), 3 pers. sg. aor. act. indic. [§27.1.e] . . . . id.

ἐξηράνθη, 3 pers. sg. aor. pass. indic. . . . . id.

ἐξήρανται, 3 pers. sg. perf. pass. indic. . . . id.

ἐξηραύνησαν, 3 pers. pl. aor. act. indic. (1 Pet. 1:10, GNT, WH & NA | ἐξηρεύνησαν, MT & TR) . . . . ἐξεραυνάω *(†1830)*

ἐξηρεύνησαν, 3 pers. pl. aor. act. indic. (1 Pet. 1:10, MT & TR | ἐξηραύνησαν, GNT, WH & NA) . . . . ἐξερευνάω *(1830)*

ἐξηρτισμένος, nom. sg. m. perf. pass. part. . . . . ἐξαρτίζω *(1822)*

ἐξήρχετο, 3 pers. sg. imperf. mid./pass. dep. indic. ἐξέρχομαι *(1831)*

ἐξήρχοντο, 3 pers. pl. imperf. mid./pass. dep. indic. . . . . id.

(1836) ἐξῆς, adv., *successively, in order;* in N.T. with the article ὁ, ἡ, τό, ἐξῆς, *next,* Luke 7:11; 9:37, et al.

ἐξητήσατο, 3 pers. sg. aor. mid. indic. [§13.2] . . . . ἐξαιτέω *(†1809)*

(†1837) ἐξηχέω, ῶ, fut. ἐξηχήσω [§16.P] perf. pass. ἐξήχημαι (ἐξ + ἠχέω) *to make to sound forth or abroad;* pass. *to sound forth, to come abroad,* 1 Thess. 1:8

ἐξήχηται, 3 pers. sg. perf. pass. indic. ἐξηχέω *(†1837)*

ἐξιέναι, pres. infin. [§33.4] . . . . ἔξειμι *(1826)*

ἔξιν, acc. sg. f. n. . . . . ἕξις *(1838)*

ἐξιόντων, gen. pl. m. 2 aor. part. [§33.4] . . . . ἔξειμι *(1826)*

(1838) ἕξις, εως, ἡ [§5.E.c] *a condition of body or mind,* strictly, as resulting from practice; *habit,* Heb. 5:14

ἐξίσταντο, 3 pers. pl. imperf. mid. indic.

[§29.Y] . . . . ἐξίστημι *(1839)*

ἐξιστάνων, nom. sg. m. pres. act. part. (Acts 8:9, GNT, WH & NA | ἐξιστῶν, MT & TR) . . . . id.

ἐξίστασθαι, pres. mid. infin. . . . . id.

ἐξίστατο, 3 pers. sg. imperf. mid. indic. . . id.

(1839) ἐξίστημι, or ἐξιστάνω, fut. ἐκστήσω, aor. ἐξέστησα, later perf. ἐξέστακα [§29.X] (ἐξ + ἵστημι) trans. pr. *to put out of its place; to astonish, amaze,* Luke 24:22; Acts 8:9, 11; intrans. 2 aor. ἐξέστην, and mid. ἐξίσταμαι, *to be astonished,* Matt. 12:23, et al.; *to be beside one's self,* Mark 3:21; 2 Cor. 5:13

ἐξιστῶν, nom. sg. m. pres. act. part. (Acts 8:9, MT & TR | ἐξιστάνων, GNT, WH & NA) . . . . ἐξίστημι *(1839)*

ἐξισχύσητε, 2 pers. pl. aor. act. subj. . ἐξισχύω *(1840)*

(1840) ἐξισχύω, fut. ἐξισχύσω [§13.M] (ἐξ + ἰσχύω) *to be fully able,* Eph. 3:18

ἔξοδον, acc. sg. f. n. . . . . ἔξοδος *(1841)*

(1841) ἔξοδος, ου, ἡ [§3.C.b] (ἐξ + ὁδός) *a way out, a going out; a going out, departure,* Heb. 11:22; met. *a departure* from life, *decease, death,* Luke 9:31; 2 Pet. 1:15

ἐξόδου, gen. sg. f. n. . . . . ἔξοδος *(1841)*

ἐξοίσουσι(ν), 3 pers. pl. fut. act. indic. [§36.1] . . . . ἐκφέρω *(1627)*

ἐξολεθρευθήσεται, 3 pers. sg. fut. pass. indic. (Acts 3:23, GNT, WH & NA | ἐξολο-θρευθήσεται, MT & TR) . . . . ἐξολεθρεύω *(†1842)*

(†1842) ἐξολεθρεύω, *to destroy utterly, root out*

ἐξολοθρευθήσεται, 3 pers. sg. fut. pass. indic. (Acts 3:23, MT & TR | ἐξολεθρευθή-σεται, GNT, WH & NA) . . . . ἐξολοθρεύω *(1842)*

(1842) ἐξολοθρεύω, fut. ἐξολοθρεύσω [§13.M] (ἐξ + ὀλοθρεύω) *to destroy utterly, exterminate*

ἐξομολογεῖσθε, 2 pers. pl. pres. mid. imper. ἐξομολογέω *(1843)*

(1843) ἐξομολογέω, ῶ, fut. ἐξολομογήσω [§16.P] (ἐξ + ὁμολογέω) *to agree, bind one's self, promise,* Luke 22:6; mid. *to confess,* Matt. 3:6; *to profess openly,* Phil. 2:11; Rev. 3:5; *to make open avowal* of benefits; *to praise, celebrate,* Matt. 11:25; Luke 10:21, et al.

ἐξομολογήσεται, 3 pers. sg. fut. mἐξομολογέω indic. . . . . id.

ἐξομολογήσηται, 3 pers. sg. aor. mid. subj. (Phil. 2:11, GNT, WH, TR & NA | ἐξομολογήσεται, MT) . . . . id.

ἐξομολογήσομαι, 1 pers. sg. fut. mid. indic. id.

ἐξομολογοῦμαι, 1 pers. sg. pres. mid. indic. [§17.Q] . . . . id.

ἐξομολογούμενοι, nom. pl. m. pres. mid.

part. . . . . ἐξομολογέω *(1843)*

ἐξόν, nom. sg. neut. pres. part.
(impers.) . . . . ἔξεστι(ν) *(1832)*

(1844) **ἐξορκίζω**, 1 pers. sg. pres. act. indic., fut.
ἐξορκίσω [§26.1] (ἐξ + ὁρκίζω) *to put an
oath* to a person, *to adjure*, Matt. 26:63

(1845) **ἐξορκιστής**, οῦ, ὁ [§2.B.c] pr. *one who puts
an oath;* in N.T. *an exorcist, one who by
various kinds of incantations*, etc., *pretended to expel demons*, Acts 19:13

ἐξορκιστῶν, gen. pl. m. n. . . . . . . ἐξορκιστής *(1845)*

ἐξορύξαντες, nom. pl. m. aor. act.
part. ἐξορύσσω *(1846)*

(1846) **ἐξορύσσω**, fut. ἐξορύξω [§26.3] (ἐξ +
ὀρύσσω) *to dig out or through, force up*,
Mark 2:4; *to pluck out* the eyes, Gal. 4:15

(†1847) **ἐξουδενέω**, ῶ, fut. ἐξουδενήσω, same signif.
as ἐξουδενόω

ἐξουδενηθῇ, 3 pers. sg. aor. pass. subj. (Mark
9:12, GNT, WH & NA | ἐξουδενωθῇ,
MT & TR) . . . . ἐξουδενέω *(†1847)*

(1847) **ἐξουδενόω**, ῶ, fut. ἐξουδενώσω [§20.T]
equivalent to ἐξουθενέω

ἐξουδενωθῇ, 3 pers. sg. aor. pass. subj. (Mark
9:12, MT & TR | ἐξουδενηθῇ, GNT, WH
& NA) . . . . ἐξουδενόω *(1847)*

ἐξουθενεῖς, 2 pers. sg. pres. act.
indic. . . . . ἐξουθενέω *(1848)*

ἐξουθενεῖτε, 2 pers. pl. pres. act. imper. . .   id.

ἐξουθενείτω, 3 pers. sg. pres. act. imper. . .   id.

(1848) **ἐξουθενέω**, ῶ, fut. ἐξουθενήσω [§16.P] (ἐξ +
οὐθέν, a later form of οὐδέν) *to make light
of, set at naught, despise, contemn, treat
with contempt and scorn*, Luke 18:9, et al.;
to neglect, disregard, 1 Thess. 5:20;
ἐξουθενημένος, *paltry, contemptible*,
2 Cor. 10:10; *of small account*, 1 Cor. 1:28;
6:4; by impl. *to reject with contempt*, Acts
4:11

ἐξουθενηθείς, nom. sg. m. aor. pass.
part. . . . . ἐξουθενέω *(1848)*

ἐξουθενημένα, acc. pl. neut. perf. pass. part.   id.

ἐξουθενημένος, nom. sg. m. perf. pass. part.   id.

ἐξουθενημένους, acc. pl. m. perf. pass. part.   id.

ἐξουθενήσας, nom. sg. m. aor. act. part. .   id.

ἐξουθενήσατε, 2 pers. pl. aor. act. indic. . .   id.

ἐξουθενήσῃ, 3 pers. sg. aor. act. subj. . . . .   id.

ἐξουθενοῦντας, acc. pl. m. pres. act. part.   id.

(1849) **ἐξουσία**, ας, ἡ, nom. sg. f. n. [§2.B.b; 2.2]
power, ability, faculty, Matt. 9:8; 10:1, et
al.; *efficiency, energy*, Luke 4:32, et al.; *liberty, licence*, John 10:18; Acts 5:4; *authority, rule, dominion, jurisdiction*, Matt. 8:9;
28:18; meton. pl. *authorities, potentates,
powers*, Luke 12:11; 1 Cor. 15:24; Eph.

1:21; *right, authority, full power*, Matt. 9:6;
21:23; *privilege, prerogative*, John 1:12; perhaps, *a veil*, 1 Cor. 11:10

ἐξουσίᾳ, dat. sg. f. n. . . . . ἐξουσία *(1849)*

ἐξουσιάζει, 3 pers. sg. pres. act.
indic. . . . . ἐξουσιάζω *(1850)*

ἐξουσιάζοντες, nom. pl. m. pres. act. part.   id.

(1850) **ἐξουσιάζω**, fut. ἐξουσιάσω [§26.1] *to have or
exercise power or authority over* any one,
Luke 22:25; *to possess independent control over*, 1 Cor. 7:4 (2×); pass. *to be subject to, under the power or influence of*,
1 Cor. 6:12

ἐξουσίαι, nom. pl. f. n. . . . . ἐξουσία *(1849)*

ἐξουσίαις, dat. pl. f. n. . . . .   id.

ἐξουσίαν, acc. sg. f. n. . . . .   id.

ἐξουσίας, gen. sg. f. n. {Col. 2:10} . . . . . .   id.

ἐξουσίας, acc. pl. f. n. {Col. 2:15} . . . . . .   id.

ἐξουσιασθήσομαι, 1 pers. sg. fut. pass.
indic. . . . . ἐξουσιάζω *(1850)*

ἔξουσιν, 3 pers. pl. fut. act. indic. [§35.4] ἔχω *(2192)*

ἐξουσιῶν, gen. pl. f. n. . . . . ἐξουσία *(1849)*

(1851) **ἐξοχή**, ῆς, ἡ [§2.B.a] (ἐξέχω, *to be prominent*)
pr. *prominency, anything prominent;* in
N.T. *eminence, distinction*, Acts 25:23

ἐξοχήν, acc. sg. f. n. . . . . ἐξοχή *(1851)*

(1852) **ἐξυπνίζω**, fut. ἐξυπνίσω [§26.1] *to awake,
arouse* from sleep, John 11:11

ἐξυπνίσω, 1 pers. sg. aor. act. subj. . ἐξυπνίζω *(1852)*

(1853) **ἔξυπνος**, ον, nom. sg. m. adj. [§7.2] (ἐξ +
ὕπνος) *awake, aroused from sleep*, Acts
16:27

ἐξυρημένη, dat. sg. f. perf. pass. part.
[§19.S] . . . . ξυράω *(3587)*

(1854) **ἔξω**, adv. (ἐξ) *without, out of doors;* Matt.
12:46, 47; ὁ, ἡ, τὸ ἔξω, *outer, external,
foreign*, Acts 26:11; 2 Cor. 4:16; met. *not
belonging to one's community*, Mark 4:11;
1 Cor. 5:12, 13; *out, away*, from a place or
person, Matt. 5:13; 13:48; as a prep., *out
of*, Mark 5:10, et al.

(1855) **ἔξωθεν**, adv., *outwardly, externally*, Matt.
23:27, 28; Mark 7:15; ὁ, ἡ, τὸ ἔξωθεν,
outer, external, Matt. 23:25; Luke 11:39;
τὸ ἔξωθεν, *the exterior*, Luke 11:40. οἱ
ἔξωθεν, *those who are without* the Christian community, 1 Tim. 3:7, et al.

(1856) **ἐξωθέω**, ῶ, fut. ἐξωθήσω, and ἐξώσω, aor.
ἐξέωσα, in N.T. ἔξωσα (ἐξ + ὠθέω) *to expel, drive out*, Acts 7:45; *to propel, urge
forward*, Acts 27:39

ἐξωμολόγησε(ν), 3 pers. sg. aor. act. indic.
[§13.2] . . . . ἐξομολογέω *(1843)*

ἐξῶσαι, aor. act. infin. (Acts 27:39, GNT, MT,
TR & NA | ἐκσῶσαι, WH) . . . . . . ἐξωθέω *(1856)*

ἐξῶσεν, 3 pers. sg. aor. act. indic. . . . . ἐξωθέω *(1856)*

ἐξώτερον, acc. sg. neut. adj. . . . . ἐξώτερος *(1857)*

(1857) **ἐξώτερος,** α, ον [§7.1] (compar. of ἔξω) *outer, exterior, external,* Matt. 8:12; 22:13; 25:30

(‡1503) **ἔοικα,** perf. with pres. signif. [§38.2] from obsolete εἴκω, *to be like,* James 1:6, 23

ἔοικε(ν), 3 pers. sg. 2 perf. act. indic. [§37.1] . . . . ἔοικα *(‡1503)*

ἑόρακα, 1 pers. sg. perf. act. indic. (1 Cor. 9:1, GNT, WH & NA | ἑώρακα, MT & TR) . . . . ὁράω *(3708)*

ἑόρακαν, 3 pers. pl. perf. act. indic. (Col. 2:1, GNT, WH & NA | ἑωράκασι(ν), MT & TR) . . . . id.

ἑόρακεν, 3 pers. sg. perf. act. indic. (Col. 2:18, GNT, WH & NA | ἑώρακεν, MT & TR)　id.

(1858) **ἑορτάζω,** fut. ἑορτάσω [§26.1] *to keep a feast, celebrate a festival,* 1 Cor. 5:8

ἑορτάζωμεν, 1 pers. pl. pres. act. subj. . . . . ἑορτάζω *(1858)*

(1859) **ἑορτή,** ῆς, ἡ, nom. sg. f. n. [§2.B.a] *a solemn feast, public festival,* Luke 2:41; 22:1; John 13:1; spc. used of *the passover,* Matt. 26:5; 27:15, et al.

ἑορτῇ, dat. sg. f. n. . . . . ἑορτή *(1859)*

ἑορτήν, acc. sg. f. n. . . . . id.

ἑορτῆς, gen. sg. f. n. . . . . id.

ἐπ᾽, by apostrophe for ἐπί . . . . ἐπί *(1909)*

ἐπαγαγεῖν, 2 aor. act. infin. [§13.7.d] . . ἐπάγω *(1863)*

ἐπαγγειλάμενον, acc. sg. m. aor. mid. dep. part. . . . . ἐπαγγέλλομαι *(†1861)*

ἐπαγγειλάμενος, nom. sg. m. aor. mid. dep. part. . . . . id.

(1860) **ἐπαγγελία,** ας, ἡ, nom. sg. f. n. [§2.B.b; 2.2] *annunciation,* 2 Tim. 1:1; *a promise, act of promising,* Acts 13:23, 32; 23:21; meton. *the thing promised, promised favor and blessing,* Luke 24:49; Acts 1:4, et al.

ἐπαγγελίᾳ, dat. sg. f. n. . . . . ἐπαγγελία *(1860)*

ἐπαγγελίαι, nom. pl. f. n. . . . . id.

ἐπαγγελίαις, dat. pl. f. n. . . . . id.

ἐπαγγελίαν, acc. sg. f. n. . . . . id.

ἐπαγγελίας, gen. sg. f. n. {Heb. 6:15} . . . id.

ἐπαγγελίας, acc. pl. f. n. {Heb. 6:12} . . . . id.

ἐπαγγελιῶν, gen. pl. f. n. . . . . id.

ἐπαγγελλομέναις, dat. pl. f. pres. mid./pass. dep. part. . . . . ἐπαγγέλλομαι *(†1861)*

ἐπαγγελλόμενοι, nom. pl. m. pres. mid./pass. dep. part. . . . . id.

(†1861) **ἐπαγγέλλομαι,** *to declare, to promise, undertake,* Mark 14:11; Rom. 4:21, et al.; *to profess,* 1 Tim. 2:10

(1862) **ἐπάγγελμα,** ατος, τό [§4.D.c] *a promise,* 2 Pet. 3:13; meton. *promised favor or*

blessing, 2 Pet. 1:4

ἐπάγγελμα, acc. sg. neut. n. . . . . . . ἐπάγγελμα *(1862)*

ἐπαγγέλματα, nom. pl. neut. n. . . . . id.

ἐπάγοντες, nom. pl. m. pres. act. part. . ἐπάγω *(1863)*

(1863) **ἐπάγω,** fut. ἐπάξω [§23.1.b] 2 aor. ἐπήγαγον [§13.7.b,d] (ἐπί + ἄγω) *to bring upon, cause to come upon,* 2 Pet. 2:1, 5; met. *to cause to be imputed or attributed to, to bring* guilt *upon,* Acts 5:28

ἐπαγωνίζεσθαι, pres. mid./pass. dep. infin. . . . . ἐπαγωνίζομαι *(1864)*

(1864) **ἐπαγωνίζομαι,** fut. ἐπαγωνίσομαι [§26.1] (ἐπί + ἀγωνίζομαι) *to contend strenuously in defence of,* Jude 3

ἔπαθε(ν), 3 pers. sg. 2 aor. act. indic. [§36.4] . . . . πάσχω *(3958)*

ἐπάθετε, 2 pers. pl. 2 aor. act. indic. . . . . id.

ἔπαθον, 1 pers. sg. 2 aor. act. indic. . . . . id.

ἐπαθροιζομένων, gen. pl. m. pres. pass. part. . . . . ἐπαθροίζω *(1865)*

(1865) **ἐπαθροίζω,** fut. ἐπαθροίσω [§26.1] (ἐπί + ἀθροίζω) *to gather together, to collect close upon, or beside;* mid. *to crowd upon,* Luke 11:29

ἐπαιδεύθη, 3 pers. sg. aor. pass. indic.　παιδεύω *(3811)*

ἐπαίδευον, 3 pers. pl. imperf. act. indic. . . id.

ἐπαινέσατε, 2 pers. pl. aor. act. imper. (Rom. 15:11, MT & TR | ἐπαινεσάτωσαν, GNT, WH & NA) . . . . ἐπαινέω *(1867)*

ἐπαινεσάτωσαν, 3 pers. pl. aor. act. imper. (Rom. 15:11, GNT, WH & NA | ἐπαινέσατε, MT & TR) . . . . id.

ἐπαινέσω, 1 pers. sg. aor. act. subj. . . . . . id.

Ἐπαίνετον, acc. sg. m. n. . . . . Ἐπαίνετος *(1866)*

(1866) **Ἐπαίνετος,** ου, ὁ [§3.C.a] *Epaenetus,* pr. name, Rom. 16:5

(1867) **ἐπαινέω,** ῶ, fut. ἐπαινέσω and ἐπαινέσομαι [§22.1] aor. ἐπήνεσα (ἐπί + αἰνέω) *to praise, commend, applaud,* Luke 16:8; Rom. 15:11; 1 Cor. 11:2, 17, 22(2×)

ἔπαινον, acc. sg. m. n. . . . . ἔπαινος *(1868)*

(1868) **ἔπαινος,** ου, ὁ, nom. sg. m. n. [§3.C.a] (ἐπί + αἶνος) *praise, applause, honor paid,* Rom. 2:29; 2 Cor. 8:18, et al.; meton. *ground or reason of praise or commendation,* Phil. 4:8; *approval,* Rom. 13:3; 1 Pet. 2:14; 1 Cor. 4:5

ἐπαινῶ, 1 pers. sg. pres. act. indic. . . . ἐπαινέω *(1867)*

ἐπαίρεται, 3 pers. sg. pres. mid. indic. . ἐπαίρω *(1869)*

ἐπαιρόμενον, acc. sg. neut. pres. mid. part.　id.

ἐπαίροντας, acc. pl. m. pres. act. part. . . . id.

(1869) **ἐπαίρω,** fut. ἐπαρῶ, aor. ἐπῆρα [§27.1.c,ε] aor. pass. ἐπήρθην, *to lift up, raise, elevate; to hoist,* Acts 27:40; τὴν φωνήν, *to lift up the voice, to speak in a loud voice,* Luke 11:27;

τὰς χεῖρας, *to lift up the hands* in prayer, Luke 24:50; 1 Tim. 2:8; τοὺς ὀφθαλμούς, *to lift up the eyes, to look,* Matt. 17:8; τὴν κεφαλήν, *to lift up the head, to be encouraged, animated,* Luke 21:28; τὴν πτέρναν, *to lift up the heel, to attack, assault;* or, *to seek one's overthrow or destruction,* John 13:18; pass. *to be borne upwards,* Acts 1:9; met. mid. *to exalt one's self, assume consequence, be elated,* 2 Cor. 10:5, et al.

ἔπαισε(ν), 3 pers. sg. aor. act. indic. .... παίω *(3817)*

ἐπαισχύνεσθε, 2 pers. pl. pres. mid./pass. dep. indic. .... ἐπαισχύνομαι *(1870)*

ἐπαισχύνεται, 3 pers. sg. pres. mid./pass. dep. indic. .... id.

ἐπαισχύνθη, 3 pers. sg. aor. pass. dep. indic. (2 Tim. 1:16, GNT, WH, MT & NA | ἐπῃσχύνθη, TR) .... id.

ἐπαισχυνθῇ, 3 pers. sg. aor. pass. dep. subj. id.

ἐπαισχυνθῇς, 2 pers. sg. aor. pass. dep. subj. id.

ἐπαισχυνθήσεται, 3 pers. sg. fut. pass. dep. indic. .... id.

(1870) **ἐπαισχύνομαι,** 1 pers. sg. pres. mid./pass. dep. indic., aor. ἐπῃσχύνθην [§13.2] fut. ἐπαισχυνθήσομαι (ἐπί + αἰσχύνομαι) *to be ashamed of,* Mark 8:38; Luke 9:26, et al.

ἐπαιτεῖν, pres. act. infin. .... ἐπαιτέω *(1871)*

(1871) **ἐπαιτέω,** ῶ, fut. ἐπαιτήσω [§16.P] (ἐπί + αἰτέω) *to prefer a suit or request in respect of certain circumstances; to ask alms, beg,* Luke 16:3

ἐπαιτῶν, nom. sg. m. pres. act. part. (Luke 18:35, GNT, WH & NA | προσαιτῶν, MT & TR) .... ἐπαιτέω *(1871)*

(1872) **ἐπακολουθέω,** ῶ, fut. ἐπακολουθήσω [§16.P] (ἐπί + ἀκολουθέω) *to follow upon; to accompany, be attendant,* Mark 16:20; *to appear in the sequel,* 1 Tim. 5:24; met. *to follow* one's steps, *to imitate,* 1 Pet. 2:21; *to follow* a work, *pursue, prosecute, be studious of, devoted to,* 1 Tim. 5:10

ἐπακολουθήσητε, 2 pers. pl. aor. act. subj. .... ἐπακολουθέω *(1872)*

ἐπακολουθούντων, gen. pl. neut. pres. act. part. .... id.

ἐπακολουθοῦσιν, 3 pers. pl. pres. act. indic. id.

(1873) **ἐπακούω,** fut. ἐπακούσομαι (ἐπί + ἀκούω) *to listen or hearken to; to hear with favor,* 2 Cor. 6:2

(1874) **ἐπακροάομαι,** ῶμαι [§19.S] (ἐπί + ἀκροάομαι, *to hear) to hear, hearken, listen to,* Acts 16:25

(1875) **ἐπάν,** conj. (ἐπεί + ἄν) *whenever, as soon as,*

Matt. 2:8; Luke 11:22, 34

ἐπανάγαγε, 2 pers. sg. 2 aor. act. imper. .... ἐπανάγω *(1877)*

ἐπαναγαγεῖν, 2 aor. act. infin. [§13.7.d] .. id.

ἐπαναγαγών, nom. sg. m. 2 aor. act. part. (Matt. 21:18, WH | ἐπανάγων, GNT, MT, TR & NA) .... id.

(1876) **ἐπάναγκες,** adv. (ἐπί + ἀνάγκη) *of necessity, necessarily;* τὰ ἐπάναγκες, *necessary things,* Acts 15:28

(1877) **ἐπανάγω,** fut. ἐπανάξω [§23.1.b] 2 aor. ἐπανήγαγον (ἐπί + ἀνάγω) *to bring up or back;* intrans. *to return,* Matt. 21:18; a nautical term, *to put off from shore,* Luke 5:3, 4

ἐπανάγων, nom. sg. m. pres. act. part. (Matt. 21:18, GNT, MT, TR & NA | ἐπαναγαγών, WH) .... ἐπανάγω *(1877)*

(†1878) **ἐπαναμιμνήσκω,** fut. ἐπαναμνήσω [§36.3] (ἐπί + ἀναμιμνήσκω) *to remind, put in remembrance*

ἐπαναμιμνήσκων, nom. sg. m. pres. act. part. (Rom. 15:15, GNT, MT & NA | ἐπαναμιμνήσκων, WH & TR) . ἐπαναμιμνήσκω *(†1878)*

ἐπαναπαήσεται, 3 pers. sg. fut. mid. dep. indic. (Luke 10:6, GNT, WH & NA | ἐπαναπαύσεται, MT & TR) .... id.

ἐπαναπαύῃ, 2 pers. sg. pres. mid./pass. dep. indic. .... ἐπαναπαύομαι *(1879)*

(1879) **ἐπαναπαύομαι,** fut. ἐπαναπαύσομαι [§13.M] (ἐπί + ἀναπαύομαι) pr. *to make to rest upon;* mid. *to rest upon; to abide with,* Luke 10:6; *to rely on, confide in, abide by confidingly,* Rom. 2:17

ἐπαναπαύσεται, 3 pers. sg. fut. mid. dep. indic. (Luke 10:6, MT & TR | ἐπαναπαήσεται, GNT, WH & NA) .... ἐπαναπαύομαι *(1879)*

ἐπαναστήσονται, 3 pers. pl. fut. mid. dep. indic. [§29.Y] .... ἐπανίστημι *(†1881)*

ἐπανελθεῖν, 2 aor. act. infin. .... ἐπανέρχομαι *(1880)*

ἐπανέρχεσθαι, pres. mid./pass. dep. infin. id.

(1880) **ἐπανέρχομαι,** 2 aor. ἐπανῆλθον [§36.1] (ἐπί + ἀνέρχομαι) *to come back, return,* Luke 10:35; 19:15

(†1881) **ἐπανίστημι** [§29.X] (ἐπί + ἀνίστημι) *to raise up against;* mid. *to rise up against,* Matt. 10:21; Mark 13:12

ἐπανόρθωσιν, acc. sg. f. n. ..... ἐπανόρθωσις *(1882)*

(1882) **ἐπανόρθωσις,** εως, ἡ [§5.E.c] (ἐπανορθόω, *to set upright again; to set to rights;* ἐπί + ἀνορθόω) *correction, reformation,* 2 Tim. 3:16

(1883) **ἐπάνω,** adv. (ἐπί + ἄνω) *above, over, upon,* of place, Matt. 2:9; 5:14; *over,* of author-

ity, Luke 19:17, 19; *above, more than,*
Mark 14:5, et al.

ἐπάξας, nom. sg. m. aor. act. part. . . . . ἐπάγω *(1863)*

ἐπᾶραι, aor. act. infin. [§27.1.f] . . . . . ἐπαίρω *(1869)*

ἐπάραντες, nom. pl. m. aor. act. part. . . . id.

ἐπάρας, nom. sg. m. aor. act. part. . . . . . id.

ἐπάρασα, nom. sg. f. aor. act. part. . . . . id.

ἐπάρατε, 2 pers. pl. aor. act. imper. . . . . id.

ἐπάρατοι, nom. pl. m. adj. (John 7:49, GNT,
WH & NA | ἐπικατάρατοι, MT &
TR) . . . . ἐπάρατος *(‡1944)*

(‡1944) **ἐπάρατος**, ον [§7.2] *accursed*

ἐπαρκείτω, 3 pers. sg. pres. act.
imper. ἐπαρκέω *(1884)*

ἐπαρκέσῃ, 3 pers. sg. aor. act. subj. . . . . . id.

(1884) **ἐπαρκέω**, ῶ, fut. ἐπαρκέσω [§22.1] (ἐπί +
ἀρκέω) pr. *to ward off; to assist, relieve,
succor;* 1 Tim. 5:10, 16 (2×)

ἐπαρρησιάζετο, 3 pers. sg. imperf. mid./pass.
dep. indic. . . . . παρρησιάζομαι *(3955)*

ἐπαρρησιασάμεθα, 1 pers. pl. aor. mid. dep.
indic. . . . . id.

ἐπαρρησιάσατο, 3 pers. sg. aor. mid. dep.
indic. . . . . id.

(†1885) **ἐπαρχεία**, ας, ἡ, *province*
ἐπαρχείᾳ, dat. sg. f. n. (Acts 25:1, GNT, WH
& NA | ἐπαρχίᾳ, MT & TR) . . ἐπαρχεία *(†1885)*

ἐπαρχείας, gen. sg. f. n. (Acts 23:34, GNT,
WH & NA | ἐπαρχίας, MT & TR) . . id.

(1885) **ἐπαρχία**, ας, ἡ [§2.B.b; 2.2] (ἔπαρχος, *a prefect,* etc.) *a prefecture, province,* Acts 23:34;
25:1

ἐπαρχίᾳ, dat. sg. f. n. (Acts 25:1, MT & TR
| ἐπαρχείᾳ, GNT, WH & NA) . . . ἐπαρχία *(1885)*

ἐπαρχίας, gen. sg. f. n. (Acts 23:34, MT &
TR | ἐπαρχείας, GNT, WH & NA) . . id.

ἐπάταξεν, 3 pers. sg. aor. act. indic. πατάσσω *(3960)*

ἐπατήθη, 3 pers. sg. aor. pass. indic. . . πατέω *(3961)*

(1886) **ἔπαυλις**, εως, ἡ, nom. sg. f. n. [§5.E.c] (ἐπί
+ αὐλίζομαι) pr. *a place to pass the night
in; a cottage;* in N.T. *a dwelling, habitation,* Acts 1:20

ἐπαύοντο, 3 pers. pl. imperf. mid. indic. παύω *(3973)*

(1887) **ἐπαύριον**, adv. (ἐπί + αὔριον) *tomorrow;* ἡ
ἐπαύριον, sc. ἡμέρα, *the next or follow-
ing day,* Matt. 27:62; Mark 11:12, et al.

ἐπαυσάμην, 1 pers. sg. aor. mid. indic. . παύω *(3973)*

ἐπαύσαντο, 3 pers. pl. aor. mid. indic. . . . id.

ἐπαύσατο, 3 pers. sg. aor. mid. indic. . . . id.

(1888) **ἐπαυτοφώρῳ**, adv. (ἐπί + αὐτόφωρος, from
αὐτός + φώρ, *a thief*) pr. *in the very theft;*
in N.T. *in the very act* (John 8:4, TR |
αὐτοφώρῳ, GNT, WH & NA)

Ἐπαφρᾶ, gen. sg. m. n. [§2.4] . . . . Ἐπαφρᾶς *(1889)*

(1889) **Ἐπαφρᾶς**, ᾶ, ὁ, nom. sg. m. n. *Epaphras,*

pr. name

ἐπαφρίζοντα, nom. pl. neut. pres. act.
part. . . . . ἐπαφρίζω *(1890)*

(1890) **ἐπαφρίζω**, fut. ἐπαφρίσω [§26.1] (ἐπί +
ἀφρίζω) *to foam out; to pour out like
foam, vomit forth,* Jude 13

Ἐπαφρόδιτον, acc. sg. m. n. . . . Ἐπαφρόδιτος *(1891)*

(1891) **Ἐπαφρόδιτος**, ου, ὁ [§3.C.a] *Epaphroditus,*
pr. name

Ἐπαφροδίτου, gen. sg. m. n. . . Ἐπαφρόδιτος *(1891)*

ἐπαχύνθη, 3 pers. sg. aor. pass. indic. παχύνω *(3975)*

ἐπέβαλεν, 3 pers. sg. 2 aor. act.
indic. . . . . ἐπιβάλλω *(1911)*

ἐπέβαλλεν, 3 pers. sg. imperf. act. indic. . id.

ἐπέβαλον, 3 pers. pl. 2 aor. act. indic. (Mark
11:7, MT & TR | ἐπιβάλλουσιν, GNT,
WH & NA) . . . . id.

ἐπέβημεν, 1 pers. pl. 2 aor. act. indic. [§37.1]
(Acts 21:6, MT & TR | ἀνέβημεν, GNT
& NA | ἐνέβημεν, WH) . . . . ἐπιβαίνω *(1910)*

ἐπέβην, 1 pers. sg. 2 aor. act. indic. . . . . . id.

ἐπεβίβασαν, 3 pers. pl. aor. act.
indic. . . . . ἐπιβιβάζω *(1913)*

ἐπίβλεψεν, 3 pers. sg. aor. act. indic. ἐπιβλέπω *(1914)*

ἐπεγέγραπτο, 3 pers. sg. pluperf. pass. indic.
[§23.8] . . . . ἐπιγράφω *(1924)*

(1892) **ἐπεγείρω**, fut. ἐπιγερῶ [§27.1.c] (ἐπί +
ἐγείρω) *to raise or stir up against, excite
or instigate against,* Acts 13:50; 14:2

ἐπεγίνωσκον, 3 pers. pl. imperf. act.
indic. . . . . ἐπιγινώσκω *(1921)*

ἐπεγνωκέναι, perf. act. infin. . . . . id.

ἐπεγνωκόσι(ν), dat. pl. m. perf. act. part. id.

ἐπέγνωμεν, 1 pers. pl. 2 aor. act. indic. (Acts
28:1, GNT, WH & NA | ἐπέγνωσαν, MT
& TR) . . . . id.

ἐπέγνωσαν, 3 pers. pl. 2 aor. act. indic. . . id.

ἐπεγνώσθην, 1 pers. sg. aor. pass. indic. . . id.

ἐπέγνωτε, 2 pers. pl. 2 aor. act. indic. . . . id.

ἐπέδειξεν, 3 pers. sg. aor. act. indic. (Luke
24:40, MT & TR | ἔδειξεν, GNT, WH
& NA) . . . . ἐπιδείκνυμι *(1925)*

ἐπεδίδου, 3 pers. sg. imperf. act. indic.
[§31.2] . . . . ἐπιδίδωμι *(1929)*

ἐπεδόθη, 3 pers. sg. aor. pass. indic. [§30.4] id.

ἐπέδωκαν, 3 pers. pl. aor. act. indic. . . . . id.

ἐπεζήτησεν, 3 pers. sg. aor. act.
indic. . . . . ἐπιζητέω *(1934)*

ἐπεζήτουν, 3 pers. pl. imperf. act. indic. (Luke
4:42, GNT, WH, MT & NA | ἐζήτουν,
TR) . . . . id.

ἐπέθεντο, 3 pers. pl. 2 aor. mid. indic.
[§28.W] . . . . ἐπιτίθημι *(2007)*

ἐπέθηκαν, 3 pers. pl. aor. act. indic. [§28.U] id.

ἐπέθηκε(ν), 3 pers. sg. aor. act. indic. . . . . id.

ἐπεθύμει, 3 pers. sg. imperf. act.
    indic. . . . . ἐπιθυμέω *(1937)*
ἐπεθύμησα, 1 pers. sg. aor. act. indic. . . . . id.
ἐπεθύμησαν, 3 pers. pl. aor. act. indic. . . . id.
(1893) **ἐπεί,** conj., *when, after, as soon as,* Luke 7:1;
    since, because, in as much as, Matt. 18:32;
    27:6; *for, for then, for else, since in that*
    case, Rom. 3:6; 11:6, et al.
ἐπεῖδεν, 3 pers. sg. 2 aor. act. indic. . . ἐπεῖδον *(1896)*
(1894) **ἐπειδή,** conj. (ἐπεί + δή) *since, because, in as*
    much as, Matt. 21:46; Luke 11:6; Acts
    13:46, et al.
(1895) **ἐπειδήπερ,** conj. (ἐπειδή + περ) *since now,*
    since indeed, considering that, Luke 1:1
(1896) **ἐπεῖδον,** 2 aor. of ἐφοράω [§36.1] imper.
    ἔπιδε, *to look upon, regard;* in N.T. *to look*
    upon with favor, Luke 1:25; *to mark* with
    disfavor, Acts 4:29
ἔπειθεν, 3 pers. sg. imperf. act. indic. . . πείθω *(3982)*
ἐπείθετο, 3 pers. sg. imperf. pass. indic. . . id.
ἔπειθον, 3 pers. pl. imperf. act. indic. . . . . id.
ἐπείθοντο, 3 pers. pl. imperf. pass. indic. . id.
(‡1966) **ἔπειμι** [§33.4] (ἐπί + εἶμι) part. ἐπιών, *to*
    come upon; to come after; to succeed im-
    mediately, Acts 7:26; 16:11; 20:15; 21:18;
    23:11
ἐπείνασα, 1 pers. sg. aor. act. indic. . . πεινάω *(3983)*
ἐπείνασαν, 3 pers. pl. aor. act. indic. . . . . id.
ἐπείνασε(ν), 3 pers. sg. aor. act. indic. . . . id.
(1897) **ἐπείπερ,** conj. (ἐπεί + περ) *since indeed, see-*
    ing that (Rom. 3:30, MT & TR | εἴπερ,
    GNT, WH & NA)
ἐπείραζεν, 3 pers. sg. imperf. act. indic. (Acts
    9:26, GNT, WH & NA | ἐπειρᾶτο, MT
    & TR) . . . . πειράζω *(3985)*
ἐπείραζον, 3 pers. pl. imperf. act. indic. . . id.
ἐπείρασαν, 3 pers. pl. aor. act. indic. . . . . id.
ἐπείρασας, 2 pers. sg. aor. act. indic. (Rev. 2:2,
    GNT, WH, MT & NA | ἐπειράσω, TR) id.
ἐπείρασε(ν), 3 pers. sg. imperf. act. indic. . id.
ἐπειράσθησαν, 3 pers. pl. aor. pass. indic.
    (Heb. 11:37, MT & TR | GNT, WH &
    NA omit) . . . . id.
ἐπειράσω, 2 pers. sg. aor. mid. indic. (Rev.
    2:2, TR | ἐπείρασας, GNT, WH, MT &
    NA) . . . . id.
ἐπειρᾶτο, 3 pers. sg. imperf. mid./pass. dep.
    indic. (Acts 9:26, MT & TR | ἐπείραζεν,
    GNT, WH & NA) . . . . πειράομαι *(‡3987)*
ἐπειρῶντο, 3 pers. pl. imperf. mid./pass. dep.
    indic. . . . . id.
(1898) **ἐπεισαγωγή,** ῆς, ἡ, nom. sg. f. n. [§2.B.a] (ἐπί
    + εἰσάγω) *a superinduction, a further in-*
    troduction, whether by way of addition or
    substitution

ἔπεισαν, 3 pers. pl. aor. act. indic. . . . . . πείθω *(3982)*
ἐπεισελεύσεται, 3 pers. sg. fut. mid. dep.
    indic. (Luke 21:35, GNT, WH & NA |
    ἐπελεύσεται, MT & TR) . . ἐπεισέρχομαι *(‡1904)*
(‡1904) **ἐπεισέρχομαι,** fut. ἐπεισελεύσομαι [§36.1] (ἐπί
    + εἰσέρχομαι) *to come in upon, invade,*
    surprise
ἐπείσθησαν, 3 pers. pl. aor. pass. indic.
    [§23.4] . . . . πείθω *(3982)*
(1899) **ἔπειτα,** adv. (ἐπί + εἶτα) *thereupon, then, af-*
    ter that, in the next place, afterwards,
    Mark 7:5; Luke 16:7, et al.
ἐπεῖχεν, 3 pers. sg. imperf. act. indic.
    [§13.4] . . . . ἐπέχω *(1907)*
ἐπεκάθισαν, 3 pers. pl. aor. act. indic. (Matt.
    21:7, MT & TR | ἐπεκάθισεν, GNT, WH
    & NA) . . . . ἐπικαθίζω *(1940)*
ἐπεκάθισεν, 3 pers. sg. aor. act. indic. (Matt.
    21:7, GNT, WH & NA | ἐπεκάθισαν,
    MT & TR) . . . . id.
ἐπεκάλεσαν, 3 pers. pl. aor. act. indic. (Matt.
    10:25, GNT, WH, MT & NA | ἐκά-
    λεσαν, TR) . . . . ἐπικαλέω *(†1941)*
ἐπεκαλύφθησαν, 3 pers. pl. aor. pass.
    indic. ἐπικαλύπτω *(1943)*
ἐπέκειλαν, 3 pers. pl. aor. act. indic. (Acts
    27:41, GNT, WH & NA | ἐπώκειλαν,
    MT & TR) . . . . ἐπικέλλω *(‡2027)*
(1900) **ἐπέκεινα,** adv. (i.e., ἐπ' ἐκεῖνα) *on yonder side,*
    beyond, Acts 7:43
ἐπέκειντο, 3 pers. pl. imperf. mid./pass. dep.
    indic. . . . . ἐπίκειμαι *(1945)*
ἐπέκειτο, 3 pers. sg. imperf. mid./pass. dep.
    indic. . . . . id.
ἐπεκέκλητο, 3 pers. sg. pluperf. mid. dep.
    indic. . . . . ἐπικαλέω *(†1941)*
ἐπεκλήθη, 3 pers. sg. aor. pass. indic. [§22.4] id.
ἐπέκρινε(ν), 3 pers. sg. aor. act.
    indic. . . . . ἐπικρίνω *(1948)*
(1901) **ἐπεκτείνομαι** [§27.1.c] (ἐπί + ἐκτείνομαι) pr.
    to stretch out farther; in N.T. mid. *to reach*
    out towards, strain for, Phil. 3:13
ἐπεκτεινόμενος, nom. sg. m. pres. mid. or
    mid./pass. dep. part. . . . . ἐπεκτείνομαι *(1901)*
ἐπελάβετο, 3 pers. sg. 2 aor. mid. dep. indic.
    [§36.2] . . . . ἐπιλαμβάνω *(†1949)*
ἐπελάθετο, 3 pers. sg. 2 aor. mid. dep. indic.
    [§36.2] . . . . ἐπιλανθάνομαι *(1950)*
ἐπελάθοντο, 3 pers. pl. 2 aor. mid. dep. indic. id.
ἐπέλειχον, 3 pers. pl. imperf. act. indic. (Luke
    16:21, GNT, WH & NA | ἀπέλειχον, MT
    & TR) . . . . ἐπιλείχω *(‡621)*
ἐπελεύσεται, 3 pers. sg. fut. mid. dep.
    indic. . . . . ἐπέρχομαι *(1904)*
ἐπέλθῃ, 3 pers. sg. 2 aor. act. subj. . . . . . . id.

ἐπελθόντος, gen. sg. neut. 2 aor. act.
part. . . . . ἐπέρχομαι *(1904)*
ἐπελθών, nom. sg. m. 2 aor. act. part. . . . id.
ἐπέλυε(ν), 3 pers. sg. imperf. act.
indic. . . . . ἐπιλύω *(1956)*
ἐπέμεινα, 1 pers. sg. aor. act. indic.
[§27.1.d] . . . . ἐπιμένω *(1961)*
ἐπεμείναμεν, 1 pers. pl. aor. act. indic. . . . id.
ἐπεμελήθη, 3 pers. sg. aor. pass. dep.
indic. . . . . ἐπιμελέομαι *(1959)*
ἐπέμενε(ν), 3 pers. sg. imperf. act.
indic. . . . . ἐπιμένω *(1961)*
ἐπέμενον, 3 pers. pl. imperf. act. indic. . . . id.
ἐπέμφθη, 3 pers. sg. aor. pass. indic.
[§23.4] . . . . πέμπω *(3992)*
ἔπεμψα, 1 pers. sg. aor. act. indic. . . . . . . id.
ἐπέμψαμεν, 1 pers. pl. aor. act. indic. . . . . id.
ἐπέμψατε, 2 pers. pl. aor. act. indic. . . . . . id.
ἔπεμψε(ν), 3 pers. sg. aor. act. indic. . . . . . id.
ἐπενδύσασθαι, aor. mid. infin. . . . . . ἐπενδύω *(‡1902)*
ἐπενδύτην, acc. sg. f. n. . . . . ἐπενδύτης *(1903)*
(1903) **ἐπενδύτης**, ου, ὁ [§2.B.c] *the outer or upper tunic,* worn between the inner tunic and the external garments
(‡1902) **ἐπενδύω**, fut. ἐπενδύσω [§13.M] (ἐπί + ἐνδύω) *to put on over or in addition to;* mid. *to put on one's self in addition; to be further invested,* 2 Cor. 5:2, 4
ἐπενεγκεῖν, 2 aor. act. infin. [§36.1] . . ἐπιφέρω *(2018)*
ἐπένευσεν, 3 pers. sg. aor. act. indic. . ἐπινεύω *(1962)*
ἐπενθήσατε, 2 pers. pl. aor. act. indic. πενθέω *(3996)*
ἐπέπεσαν, 3 pers. pl. aor. act. indic. (Rom. 15:3, GNT, WH & NA | ἐπέπεσον, MT & TR) . . . . ἐπιπίπτω *(1968)*
ἐπέπεσε(ν), 3 pers. sg. 2 aor. act. indic. [§37.1] . . . . id.
ἐπέπεσον, 3 pers. pl. 2 aor. act. indic. (Rom. 15:3, MT & TR | ἐπέπεσαν, GNT, WH & NA) . . . . id.
ἐπεποίθει, 3 pers. sg. 2 pluperf. act. indic. [§25.5] . . . . πείθω *(3982)*
ἐπερίσσευον, 3 pers. pl. imperf. act. indic. . . . . περισσεύω *(4052)*
ἐπερίσσευσαν, 3 pers. pl. aor. act. indic. (John 6:13, GNT, WH & NA | ἐπερίσσευσε(ν), MT & TR) . . . . id.
ἐπερίσσευσε(ν), 3 pers. sg. aor. act. indic. id.
(1904) **ἐπέρχομαι**, fut. ἐπελεύσομαι [§36.1] 2 aor. ἐπῆλθον (ἐπί + ἔρχομαι) *to come to,* Acts 14:19; *to come upon,* Luke 1:35; 21:26; Acts 1:8; James 5:1; *to come upon* unexpectedly, *overtake,* Luke 21:35; *to be coming on, to succeed,* Eph. 2:7; *to occur, happen to,* Acts 8:24; 13:40; *to come against, attack,* Luke 11:22

ἐπερχομέναις, dat. pl. f. pres. mid./pass. dep.
part. . . . . ἐπέρχομαι *(1904)*
ἐπερχομένοις, dat. pl. m. pres. mid./pass. dep.
part. . . . . id.
ἐπερχομένων, gen. pl. m. pres. mid./pass.
dep. part. . . . . id.
ἐπερωτᾶν, pres. act. infin. (Luke 20:40, GNT, MT & NA | ἐπερωτᾶν, WH & TR) . . . . ἐπερωτάω *(1905)*
ἐπερωτᾷς, 2 pers. sg. pres. act. indic. (John 18:21, MT & TR | ἐρωτᾷς, GNT, WH & NA) . . . . id.
ἐπερωτάτωσαν, 3 pers. pl. pres. act. imper. id.
(1905) **ἐπερωτάω**, ῶ, fut. ἐπερωτήσω [§18.R] (ἐπί + ἐρωτάω) *to interrogate, question, ask,* Matt. 12:10; 17:10, et al.; in N.T. *to request, require,* Matt. 16:1; from the Hebrew, ἐπερωτᾶν τὸν θεόν, *to seek after, desire an acquaintance with God,* Rom. 10:20
ἐπερωτηθείς, nom. sg. m. aor. pass.
part. . . . . ἐπερωτάω *(1905)*
(1906) **ἐπερώτημα**, ατος, τό, nom. sg. neut. n. [§4.D.c] pr. *an interrogation, question;* in N.T. *profession, pledge,* 1 Pet. 3:21
ἐπερωτῆσαι, aor. act. infin. . . . . . ἐπερωτάω *(1905)*
ἐπερωτήσας, nom. sg. m. aor. act. part. . . id.
ἐπερωτήσατε, 2 pers. pl. aor. act. imper. (John 9:23, GNT, WH & NA | ἐρωτήσατε, MT & TR) . . . . id.
ἐπερώτησον, 2 pers. sg. aor. act. imper. (John 18:21, MT & TR | ἐρώτησον, GNT, WH & NA) . . . . id.
ἐπερωτήσω, 1 pers. sg. fut. act. indic. . . . id.
ἐπερωτῶ, 1 pers. sg. pres. act. indic. (Luke 6:9, GNT, WH & NA | ἐπερωτήσω, MT & TR) . . . . id.
ἐπερωτῶντα, acc. sg. m. pres. act. part. . . id.
ἐπερωτῶντες, nom. pl. m. aor. act. part. (John 8:7, MT | ἐρωτῶντες, GNT, WH, TR & NA) . . . . id.
ἐπερωτῶσιν, 3 pers. pl. pres. act. indic. {Mark 7:5} . . . . id.
ἐπερωτῶσι(ν), dat. pl. m. pres. act. part. {Rom. 10:20} . . . . id.
ἔπεσα, 1 pers. sg. 2 aor. act. indic. [§35.12] . . . . πίπτω *(4098)*
ἔπεσαν, 3 pers. pl. 2 aor. act. indic. (GNT, NA & sometimes TR) . . . . id.
ἔπεσε(ν), 3 pers. sg. 2 aor. act. indic. [§35.7] id.
ἐπεσκέψασθε, 2 pers. pl. aor. mid. dep.
indic. ἐπισκέπτομαι *(1980)*
ἐπεσκέψατο, 3 pers. sg. aor. mid. dep. indic. id.
ἐπεσκίαζεν, 3 pers. sg. imperf. act. indic. (Luke 9:34, GNT, WH & NA | ἐπεσκί-

ασεν, MT & TR) . . . . ἐπισκιάζω *(1982)*

ἐπεσκίασεν, 3 pers. sg. aor. act. indic. . . . id.

ἔπεσον, 1 pers. sg. 2 aor. act. indic. [§37.1]
(Acts 22:7; Rev. 19:10, TR | ἔπεσα, GNT,
WH & NA) . . . . πίπτω *(4098)*

ἔπεσον, 3 pers. pl. 2 aor. act. indic. (Matt.
17:6; John 18:6; 1 Cor. 10:8; Rev. 5:8; 7:11;
16:19, MT & TR | ἔπεσαν, GNT, WH &
NA) . . . . id.

ἐπέσπειρεν, 3 pers. sg. imperf. act. indic.
(Matt. 13:25, GNT, WH & NA | ἔσπει-
ρε(ν), MT & TR) . . . . ἐπισπείρω *(‡4687)*

ἐπέστειλα, 1 pers. sg. aor. act. indic.
[§27.1.d] . . . . ἐπιστέλλω *(1989)*

ἐπεστείλαμεν, 1 pers. pl. aor. act. indic. (Acts
21:25, GNT, MT, TR & NA | ἀπεστεί-
λαμεν, WH) . . . . id.

ἐπέστη, 3 pers. sg. 2 aor. act. indic.
[§29.X] . . . . ἐφίστημι *(2186)*

ἐπεστήριξαν, 3 pers. pl. aor. act.
indic. ἐπιστηρίζω *(1991)*

ἐπέστησαν, 3 pers. pl. 2 aor. act.
indic. . . . . ἐφίστημι *(2186)*

ἐπεστράφητε, 2 pers. pl. 2 aor. pass. indic.
[§24.10] . . . . ἐπιστρέφω *(1994)*

ἐπέστρεψα, 1 pers. sg. aor. act. indic. . . . . id.

ἐπέστρεψαν, 3 pers. pl. aor. act. indic. . . . id.

ἐπεστρέψατε, 2 pers. pl. aor. act. indic. . . . id.

ἐπέστρεψε(ν), 3 pers. sg. aor. act. indic. . . id.

ἐπέσχε(ν), 3 pers. sg. 2 aor. act. indic.
[§36.4] . . . . ἐπέχω *(1907)*

ἐπέταξας, 2 pers. sg. aor. act. indic. ἐπιτάσσω *(2004)*

ἐπέταξε(ν), 3 pers. sg. aor. act. indic. . . . id.

ἐπετίθεσαν, 3 pers. pl. imperf. act. indic. (Acts
8:17, GNT, WH & NA | ἐπετίθουν, MT
& TR) . . . . ἐπιτίθημι *(2007)*

ἐπετίθουν, 3 pers. pl. imperf. act. indic. [§31.2]
(Acts 8:17, MT & TR | ἐπετίθεσαν, GNT,
WH & NA) . . . . id.

ἐπετίμα, 3 pers. sg. imperf. act.
indic. . . . . ἐπιτιμάω *(2008)*

ἐπετίμησαν, 3 pers. pl. aor. act. indic. . . . id.

ἐπετίμησε(ν), 3 pers. sg. aor. act. indic. . . id.

ἐπετίμων, 3 pers. pl. imperf. act. indic.
[§18.R] . . . . id.

ἐπετράπη, 3 pers. sg. aor. pass. indic.
[§24.10] . . . . ἐπιτρέπω *(2010)*

ἐπέτρεψε(ν), 3 pers. sg. aor. act. indic. . . . id.

ἐπέτυχε(ν), 3 pers. sg. 2 aor. act. indic.
[§36.2] . . . . ἐπιτυγχάνω *(2013)*

ἐπέτυχον, 2 pers. pl. 2 aor. act. indic. . . . id.

ἐπεφάνη, 3 pers. sg. 2 aor. pass. indic.
[§27.4.b] . . . . ἐπιφαίνω *(2014)*

ἐπέφερον, 2 pers. pl. imperf. act. indic. (Acts
25:18, MT & TR | ἔφερον, GNT, WH &

NA) . . . . ἐπιφέρω *(2018)*

ἐπεφώνει, 3 pers. sg. imperf. act.
indic. . . . . ἐπιφωνέω *(2019)*

ἐπεφώνουν, 3 pers. pl. imperf. act. indic. . . id.

ἐπέφωσκε(ν), 3 pers. sg. imperf. act.
indic. . . . . ἐπιφώσκω *(2020)*

ἔπεχε, 2 pers. sg. pres. act. imper. . . . . . ἐπέχω *(1907)*

ἐπεχείρησαν, 3 pers. pl. aor. act.
indic. . . . . ἐπιχειρέω *(2021)*

ἐπεχείρουν, 3 pers. pl. imperf. act. indic. . . id.

ἐπέχοντες, nom. pl. m. pres. act. part. . ἐπέχω *(1907)*

ἐπέχρισε(ν), 3 pers. sg. aor. act.
indic. . . . . ἐπιχρίω *(2025)*

(1907) **ἐπέχω**, fut. ἐφέξω, imperf. ἐπεῖχον, 2 aor.
ἐπέσχον [§36.4] (ἐπί + ἔχω) trans. *to hold
out, present, exhibit, display,* Phil. 2:16; intrans. *to observe, take heed to, attend to,*
Luke 14:7; Acts 3:5; 1 Tim. 4:16; *to stay,
delay,* Acts 19:22

ἐπέχων, nom. sg. m. pres. act. part. . . . ἐπέχω *(1907)*

ἐπηγγείλαντο, 3 pers. pl. aor. mid./pass. dep.
indic. [§27.1.d] . . . . ἐπαγγέλλομαι *(†1861)*

ἐπηγγείλατο, 3 pers. sg. aor. mid. dep. indic. id.

ἐπήγγελται, 3 pers. sg. perf. mid./pass. dep.
indic. [§27.3] . . . . id.

ἐπήγειραν, 3 pers. pl. aor. act. indic. ἐπεγείρω *(1892)*

ἐπηκολούθησε(ν), 3 pers. sg. aor. act.
indic. . . . . ἐπακολουθέω *(1872)*

ἐπήκουσα, 1 pers. sg. aor. act. indic. ἐπακούω *(1873)*

ἐπηκροῶντο, 3 pers. pl. imperf. mid./pass.
dep. indic. . . . . ἐπακροάομαι *(1874)*

ἐπῆλθαν, 3 pers. pl. aor. act. indic. [§35.12]
(Acts 14:19, GNT, WH & NA | ἐπῆλθον,
MT & TR) . . . . ἐπέρχομαι *(1904)*

ἐπῆλθον, 3 pers. pl. 2 aor. act. indic. (Acts
14:19, MT & TR | ἐπῆλθαν, GNT, WH
& NA) . . . . id.

ἐπήνεσεν, 3 pers. sg. aor. act. indic.
[§13.2] . . . . ἐπαινέω *(1867)*

ἔπηξεν, 3 pers. sg. aor. act. indic.
[§36.5] . . . . πήγνυμι *(4078)*

ἐπῆραν, 3 pers. pl. aor. act. indic. . . . . ἐπαίρω *(1869)*

ἐπηρεάζοντες, nom. pl. m. pres. act.
part. . . . . ἐπηρεάζω *(1908)*

ἐπηρεαζόντων, gen. pl. m. pres. act. part. id.

(1908) **ἐπηρεάζω**, fut. ἐπηρεάσω [§26.1] *to harass,
insult,* Matt. 5:44; Luke 6:28; *to traduce,
calumniate,* 1 Pet. 3:16

ἐπῆρε(ν), 3 pers. sg. aor. act. indic. . . . ἐπαίρω *(1869)*

ἐπήρθη, 3 pers. sg. aor. pass. indic. [§27.3] id.

ἐπήρκεσεν, 3 pers. sg. aor. act. indic. ἐπαρκέω *(1884)*

ἐπηρώτα, 3 pers. sg. imperf. act.
indic. . . . . ἐπερωτάω *(1905)*

ἐπηρώτησαν, 3 pers. pl. aor. act. indic. . . id.

ἐπηρώτησε(ν), 3 pers. sg. aor. act. indic. . id.

ἐπηρώτων, 3 pers. pl. imperf. act.
indic. . . . . ἐπερωτάω *(1905)*

ἐπῃσχύνθη, 3 pers. sg. aor. pass. indic. [§13.2]
(2 Tim. 1:16, TR | ἐπαισχύνθη, GNT,
WH, MT & NA) . . . . ἐπαισχύνομαι *(1870)*

(1909) **ἐπί**, pres. with the gen., *upon, on,* Matt. 4:6;
9:2; 27:19, et al.; *in,* of locality, Mark 8:4,
et al.; *near upon, by, at,* Matt. 21:19; John
21:1, et al.; *upon, over,* of authority, Matt.
2:22; Acts 8:27, et al.; *in the presence of,*
especially in a judicial sense, 2 Cor. 7:14;
Acts 25:9, et al.; *in the case of, in respect
of,* John 6:2; Gal. 3:16; *in the time of, at
the time of,* Acts 11:28; Rom. 1:10, et al.;
ἐπ' ἀληθείας, *really, bona fide,* Mark
12:32, et al.; with the dat., *upon, on,* Matt.
14:8; Mark 2:21; Luke 12:44, et al.; *close
upon, by,* Matt. 24:33; John 4:6, et al.; *in
the neighborhood or society of,* Acts 28:14;
over, of authority, Matt. 24:47, et al.; *to,*
of addition, *besides,* Matt. 25:20; Eph.
6:16; Col. 3:14, et al.; supervening *upon,
after,* 2 Cor. 1:4; 7:4; *immediately upon,*
John 4:27; *upon,* of the object of an act,
towards, to, Mark 5:33; Luke 18:7; Acts
5:35, et al.; *against,* of hostile posture or
disposition, Luke 12:52, et al.; *in dependence upon,* Matt. 4:4; Luke 5:5; Acts 14:3,
et al.; *upon the ground of,* Matt. 19:9;
Luke 1:59; Phil. 1:3; Heb. 7:11; 8:6; 9:17,
et al.; *with a view to,* Gal. 5:13; 1 Thess.
4:7, et al.; with the acc., *upon,* with the
idea of previous or present motion, Matt.
4:5; 14:19, 26, et al.; *towards,* of place, *to,*
Matt. 3:13; 22:34, et al.; *towards,* of the
object of an action, Luke 6:35; 9:38, et al.;
against, of hostile movement, Matt. 10:21,
et al.; *over,* of authority, Luke 1:33, et al.;
to the extent of, both of place and time,
Rev. 21:16; Rom. 7:1, et al.; *near, by,* Matt.
9:9, et al.; *about, at,* of time, Acts 3:1, et
al.; *in order to, with a view to, for the purpose of,* Matt. 3:7; Luke 7:44, et al.

ἐπίασον, 3 pers. pl. aor. act. indic. . . . . πιάζω *(4084)*
ἐπιάσατε, 2 pers. pl. aor. act. indic. . . . . . id.
ἐπίασεν, 3 pers. sg. aor. act. indic. . . . . . id.
ἐπιάσθη, 3 pers. sg. aor. pass. indic. [§26.1] id.
ἐπιβαίνειν, pres. act. infin. (Acts 21:4, GNT,
WH & NA | ἀναβαίνειν, MT &
TR) . . . . ἐπιβαίνω *(1910)*

(1910) **ἐπιβαίνω**, fut. ἐπιβήσομαι, perf. ἐπιβέβηκα,
2 aor. ἐπέβην [§37.1] (ἐπί + βαίνω) pr. *to
step upon; to mount,* Matt. 21:5; *to go on
board,* Acts 21:2; 27:2, *to enter,* Acts 20:18;
to enter upon, Acts 25:1

ἐπιβαλεῖν, 2 aor. act. infin. . . . . ἐπιβάλλω *(1911)*
ἐπιβάλλει, 3 pers. sg. pres. act. indic. . . . . id.
ἐπιβάλλον, acc. sg. neut. pres. act. part. . . id.
ἐπιβάλλουσιν, 3 pers. pl. pres. act. indic.
(Mark 11:7, GNT, WH & NA | ἐπέ-
βαλον, MT & TR) . . . . id.

(1911) **ἐπιβάλλω**, fut. ἐπιβαλῶ, 2 aor. ἐπέβαλον
[§27.1.b; 27.2.d] (ἐπί + βάλλω) *to cast or
throw upon,* Mark 11:7; 1 Cor. 7:35; *to lay
on, apply to,* Luke 9:62; *to put on, sew on,*
Matt. 9:16; Luke 5:36; τὰς χεῖρας, *to lay
hands on, offer violence to, seize,* Matt.
26:50, et al.; also, *to lay hand to, undertake, commence,* Acts 12:1; intrans. *to rush,
dash, beat into,* Mark 4:37; *to ponder, reflect on,* Mark 14:72; *to fall to one's share,
pertain to,* Luke 15:12

ἐπιβαλοῦσιν, 3 pers. pl. fut. act.
indic. . . . . ἐπιβάλλω *(1911)*
ἐπιβάλω, 1 pers. sg. 2 aor. act. subj. . . . . . id.
ἐπιβαλών, nom. sg. m. 2 aor. act. part. . . id.
ἐπιβάντες, nom. sg. m. 2 aor. act.
part. . . . . ἐπιβαίνω *(1910)*

(1912) **ἐπιβαρέω**, ῶ, fut. ἐπιβαρήσω [§16.P] (ἐπί +
βαρέω) *to burden;* met. *to be burdensome,
chargeable to,* 1 Thess. 2:9; 2 Thess. 3:8;
to bear hard upon, overcharge, overcensure,
2 Cor. 2:5

ἐπιβαρῆσαι, aor. act. infin. . . . . ἐπιβαρέω *(1912)*
ἐπιβαρῶ, 1 pers. sg. pres. act. subj. . . . . . . id.
ἐπιβάς, nom. sg. m. 2 aor. act. part. . ἐπιβαίνω *(1910)*
ἐπιβεβηκώς, nom. sg. m. perf. act. part. . id.

(1913) **ἐπιβιβάζω**, fut. ἐπιβιβάσω [§26.1] (ἐπί +
βιβάζω) *to cause to ascend or mount, to
set upon,* Luke 10:34; 19:35; Acts 23:24

ἐπιβιβάσαντες, nom. pl. m. aor. act.
part. . . . . ἐπιβιβάζω *(1913)*
ἐπιβιβάσας, nom. sg. m. aor. act. part. . . . id.

(1914) **ἐπιβλέπω**, fut. ἐπιβλέψω [§23.1.a] (ἐπί +
βλέπω) *to look upon; to regard* with partiality, James 2:3; *to regard* with kindness and
favor, *to compassionate,* Luke 1:48; 9:38

ἐπιβλέψαι, aor. act. infin. (Luke 9:38, GNT,
WH, MT & NA | ἐπίβλεψον,
TR) . . . . ἐπιβλέπω *(1914)*
ἐπιβλέψητε, 2 pers. pl. aor. act. subj. . . . . id.
ἐπίβλεψον, 2 pers. sg. aor. act. imper. (Luke
9:38, TR | ἐπιβλέψαι, GNT, WH, MT &
NA) . . . . id.

(1915) **ἐπίβλημα**, ατος, τό [§4.D.c] *that which is put
over or upon;* in N.T. *a patch,* Matt. 9:16;
Mark 2:21; Luke 5:36(2×)

ἐπίβλημα, acc. sg. neut. n. . . . . ἐπίβλημα *(1915)*

(1916) **ἐπιβοάω**, ῶ, fut. ἐπιβοήσω [§18.R] (ἐπί +
βοάω) *to cry out to or against, to vo-*

ciferate, Acts 25:24

ἐπιβουλαῖς, dat. pl. f. n. . . . . ἐπιβουλή *(1917)*

(1917) **ἐπιβουλή,** ῆς, ἡ, nom. sg. f. n. [§2.B.a] (ἐπί + βουλή) *a purpose or design against* any one; *conspiracy, plot,* Acts 9:24; 20:3, 19; 23:30

ἐπιβουλῆς, gen. sg. f. n. . . . . ἐπιβουλή *(1917)*

ἐπιβοῶντες, nom. pl. m. pres. act. part. (Acts 25:24, MT & TR | βοῶντες, GNT, WH & NA) . . . . ἐπιβοάω *(1916)*

ἐπιγαμβρεύσει, 3 pers. sg. fut. act. indic. . . . . ἐπιγαμβρεύω *(1918)*

(1918) **ἐπιγαμβρεύω,** fut. ἐπιγαμβρεύσω [§13.M] (ἐπί + γαμβρεύω, *to marry*) *to marry* a wife *by the law of affinity,* Matt. 22:24

ἐπιγεγραμμένα, acc. pl. neut. perf. pass. part. . . . . ἐπιγράφω *(1924)*

ἐπιγεγραμμένη, nom. sg. f. perf. pass. part.   id.

ἐπίγεια, nom. pl. neut. adj. {1 Cor. 15:40} . . . . ἐπίγειος *(1919)*

ἐπίγεια, acc. pl. neut. adj. {Phil. 3:19} . . .   id.

(1919) **ἐπίγειος,** ον [§7.2] (ἐπί + γῆ) pr. *on the earth,* Phil. 2:10; *earthly, terrestrial,* John 3:12; 1 Cor. 15:40; 2 Cor. 5:1; Phil. 3:19; *earthly, low, grovelling,* James 3:15

ἐπίγειος, nom. sg. f. adj. . . . . ἐπίγειος *(1919)*

ἐπιγείων, gen. pl. neut. adj. . . . .   id.

ἐπιγενομένου, gen. sg. m. 2 aor. mid. dep. part. . . . . ἐπιγίνομαι *(1920)*

(1920) **ἐπιγίνομαι** [§37.1] (ἐπί + γίνομαι) *to come on, spring up,* as the wind, Acts 28:13

ἐπιγινώσκει, 3 pers. sg. pres. act. indic. . . . . ἐπιγινώσκω *(1921)*

ἐπιγινώσκεις, 2 pers. sg. pres. act. indic. .   id.

ἐπιγινώσκετε, 2 pers. pl. pres. act. indic. {2 Cor. 1:13} . . . .   id.

ἐπιγινώσκετε, 2 pers. pl. pres. act. imper. {1 Cor. 16:18} . . . .   id.

ἐπιγινωσκέτω, 3 pers. sg. pres. act. imper.   id.

ἐπιγινωσκόμενοι, nom. pl. m. pres. pass. part. . . . .   id.

(1921) **ἐπιγινώσκω,** fut. ἐπιγνώσομαι, aor. pass. ἐπεγνώσθην [§36.3] (ἐπί + γινώσκω) pr. *to make* a thing *a subject of observation;* hence, *to arrive at knowledge from preliminaries; to attain to a knowledge of,* Matt. 11:27, et al.; *to ascertain,* Luke 7:37; 23:7, et al.; *to perceive,* Mark 2:8; 5:30, et al.; *to discern, detect,* Matt. 7:16, 20, et al.; *to recognize,* Mark 6:33; Luke 24:16, 31; Acts 3:10, et al.; *to acknowledge, admit,* 1 Cor. 14:37; 1 Tim. 4:3, et al.; pass. *to have one's character discerned and acknowledged,* 2 Cor. 6:9; from the Hebrew, *to regard with favor and kindness,* 1 Cor. 16:18

ἐπιγνόντες, nom. pl. m. 2 aor. act. part. . . . . ἐπιγινώσκω *(1921)*

ἐπιγνόντων, gen. pl. m. 2 aor. act. part. (Acts 19:34, TR | ἐπιγνόντες, GNT, WH, MT & NA) . . . .   id.

ἐπιγνούς, nom. sg. m. 2 aor. act. part. . . .   id.

ἐπιγνοῦσα, nom. sg. f. 2 aor. act. part. . . .   id.

ἐπιγνοῦσιν, dat. pl. m. 2 aor. act. part. . . .   id.

ἐπιγνῷ, 3 pers. sg. 2 aor. act. subj. . . . . . .   id.

ἐπιγνῶναι, 2 aor. act. infin. . . . .   id.

ἐπιγνῷς, 2 pers. sg. 2 aor. act. subj. . . . . .   id.

ἐπιγνώσει, dat. sg. f. n. . . . . ἐπίγνωσις *(1922)*

ἐπιγνώσεσθε, 2 pers. pl. fut. mid. dep. indic. . . . . ἐπιγινώσκω *(1921)*

ἐπιγνώσεως, gen. sg. f. n. . . . . ἐπίγνωσις *(1922)*

ἐπίγνωσιν, acc. sg. f. n. . . . .   id.

(1922) **ἐπίγνωσις,** εως, ἡ, nom. sg. f. n. [§5.E.c] *the coming at the knowledge* of a thing, *ascertainment,* Rom. 3:20; *a distance perception or impression, acknowledgment,* Col. 2:2, et al.

ἐπιγνώσομαι, 1 pers. sg. fut. mid. dep. indic. . . . . ἐπιγινώσκω *(1921)*

(1923) **ἐπιγραφή,** ῆς, ἡ, nom. sg. f. n. [§2.B.a] *an inscription; a legend* of a coin, Matt. 22:20; Mark 12:16; Luke 20:24; *a label* of a criminal's name and offence, Mark 15:26; Luke 23:38

ἐπιγραφήν, acc. sg. f. n. . . . . ἐπιγραφή *(1923)*

(1924) **ἐπιγράφω,** fut. ἐπιγράψω [§23.1.a] (ἐπί + γράφω) *to imprint a mark on; to inscribe, engrave, write on,* Mark 15:26; Acts 17:23; Rev. 21:12; met. *to imprint, impress deeply on,* Heb. 8:10; 10:16

ἐπιγράψω, 1 pers. sg. fut. act. indic. ἐπιγράφω *(1924)*

ἔπιδε, 2 pers. sg. 2 aor. act. imper. . . . ἐπεῖδον *(1896)*

ἐπιδεικνύμεναι, nom. pl. f. pres. mid. part. . . . . ἐπιδείκνυμι *(1925)*

(1925) **ἐπιδείκνυμι,** or ἐπιδεικνύω, and mid. ἐπιδείνυμαι, fut. ἐπιδείξω [§31.BB] (ἐπί + δείκνυμι) *to exhibit,* Matt. 16:1: Acts 9:39; *to show,* Matt. 22:19; Luke 17:14; 20:24; 24:40; *to point out,* Matt. 24:1; *to demonstrate, prove,* Acts 18:28; Heb. 6:17

ἐπιδεικνύς, nom. sg. m. pres. act. part. . . . . ἐπιδείκνυμι *(1925)*

ἐπιδεῖξαι, aor. act. infin. . . . .   id.

ἐπιδείξατε, 2 pers. pl. aor. act. imper. . . . .   id.

ἐπιδέχεται, 3 pers. sg. pres. mid./pass. dep. indic. . . . . ἐπιδέχομαι *(1926)*

(1926) **ἐπιδέχομαι,** fut. ἐπιδέξομαι [§23.1.b] (ἐπί + δέχομαι) *to admit; to receive kindly, welcome, entertain,* 3 John 10: met. *to admit, approve, assent to,* 3 John 9

(1927) **ἐπιδημέω,** ῶ, fut. ἐπιδημήσω [§16.P] (ἐπί +

δῆμος) *to dwell among a people; to be at home among one's own people;* and in N.T. *to sojourn as a stranger among another people,* Acts 2:10; 17:21

ἐπιδημοῦντες, nom. pl. m. pres. act. part. . . . . ἐπιδημέω *(1927)*

ἐπιδιατάσσεται, 3 pers. sg. pres. mid./pass. dep. indic. . . . . ἐπιδιατάσσομαι *(1928)*

(1928) **ἐπιδιατάσσομαι,** fut. ἐπιτιατάξομαι [§26.3] (ἐπί + διατάσσω) *to enjoin* anything *additional, superadd an injunction,* etc. {Gal. 3:15}

(1929) **ἐπιδίδωμι,** fut. ἐπιδώσω [§30.Z] (ἐπί + δίδωμι) *to give in addition;* also, *to give to, deliver to, give into one's hands,* Matt. 7:9, 10; Luke 4:17; 24:30, 42, et al.; intrans. probably a nautical term, *to commit a ship to the wind, let her drive,* Acts 27:15

(1930) **ἐπιδιορθόω,** ῶ, fut. ἐπιδιορθώσω [§20.T] (ἐπί + διορθόω) *to set further to rights, to carry on an amendment,* Tit. 1:5

ἐπιδιορθώσῃ, 2 pers. sg. aor. mid. subj. ἐπιδιορθόω *(1930)*

ἐπιδόντες, nom. pl. m. 2 aor. act. part. . . . . ἐπιδίδωμι *(1929)*

ἐπιδυέτω, 3 pers. sg. pres. act. imper. . . . ἐπιδύω *(1931)*

(1931) **ἐπιδύω,** fut. ἐπιδύσω (ἐπί + δύω) *of the sun, to set upon, to set during,* Eph. 4:26

ἐπιδώσει, 3 pers. sg. fut. act. indic. . ἐπιδίδωμι *(1929)*

ἐπιδώσω, 1 pers. sg. fut. act. indic. (John 13:26, MT & TR | δώσω, GNT, WH & NA) . . . . id.

ἔπιε(ν), 3 pers. sg. 2 aor. act. indic. [§37.1] . . . . πίνω *(4095)*

(1932) **ἐπιείκεια,** ας, ἡ [§2.B.b; 2.2] *reasonableness, equity;* in N.T. *gentleness, mildness,* 2 Cor. 10:1; *lenity, clemency,* Acts 24:4

ἐπιεικείᾳ, dat. sg. f. n. (Acts 24:4, GNT, MT, TR & NA | ἐπιεικία, WH) . . . . . ἐπιείκεια *(1932)*

ἐπιεικείας, gen. sg. f. n. (2 Cor. 10:1, GNT, MT, TR & NA | ἐπιεικίας, WH) . . . . id.

ἐπιεικεῖς, acc. pl. m. adj. . . . . ἐπιεικής *(1933)*

ἐπιεικές, nom. sg. neut. adj. . . . . id.

ἐπιεικέσιν, dat. pl. m. adj. . . . . id.

ἐπιεικῆ, acc. sg. m. adj. . . . . id.

(1933) **ἐπιεικής,** ές [§7.G.b] (ἐπί + εἰκός) pr. *suitable; fair, reasonable; gentle, mild, patient,* 1 Tim. 3:3; Tit. 3:2; James 3:17; 1 Pet. 2:18; τὸ ἐπιεικές, *mildness, gentleness, probity,* Phil. 4:5

ἐπιεικής, nom. sg. f. adj. . . . . ἐπιεικής *(1933)*

ἐπιζητεῖ, 3 pers. sg. pres. act. indic. . ἐπιζητέω *(1934)*

ἐπιζητεῖτε, 2 pers. pl. pres. act. indic. . . . . id.

(1934) **ἐπιζητέω,** ῶ, fut. ἐπιζητήσω [§16.P] (ἐπί +

ζητέω) *to seek for, make search for,* Acts 12:19; *to require, demand,* Matt. 12:39; 16:4; Acts 19:39; *to desire, endeavor to obtain,* Rom. 11:7; Heb. 11:14, et al.; *to seek with care and anxiety,* Matt. 6:32

ἐπιζητήσας, nom. sg. m. aor. act. part. . . . . ἐπιζητέω *(1934)*

ἐπιζητοῦμεν, 1 pers. pl. pres. act. indic. . . id.

ἐπιζητοῦσι(ν), 3 pers. pl. pres. act. indic. . id.

ἐπιζητῶ, 1 pers. sg. pres. act. indic. . . . . . id.

(1935) **ἐπιθανάτιος,** ον [§7.2] (ἐπί + θάνατος) *condemned to death, under sentence of death,* 1 Cor. 4:9

ἐπιθανατίους, acc. pl. m. adj. . . . . ἐπιθανάτιος *(1935)*

ἐπιθεῖναι, 2 aor. act. infin. [§28.U] . . ἐπιτίθημι *(2007)*

ἐπιθείς, nom. sg. m. 2 aor. act. part. . . . . . id.

ἐπιθέντα, acc. sg. m. 2 aor. act. part. . . . . id.

ἐπιθέντες, nom. pl. m. 2 aor. act. part. . . . id.

ἐπιθέντος, gen. sg. m. 2 aor. act. part. . . . id.

ἐπίθες, 2 pers. sg. 2 aor. act. imper. . . . . . id.

ἐπιθέσεως, gen. sg. f. n. . . . . ἐπίθεσις *(1936)*

(1936) **ἐπίθεσις,** εως, ἡ [§5.E.c] *the act of placing upon, imposition* of hands, Acts 8:18, et al.

ἐπιθῇ, 3 pers. sg. 2 aor. act. subj. . . . ἐπιτίθημι *(2007)*

ἐπιθῇς, 2 pers. sg. 2 aor. act. subj. . . . . . . id.

ἐπιθῆσαι, aor. act. infin. (Rev. 22:18, MT | ἐπιθήσει, GNT, WH, TR & NA) . . . . id.

ἐπιθήσει, 3 pers. sg. fut. act. indic. (Rev. 22:18, GNT, WH, TR & NA | ἐπιθῆσαι, MT) id.

ἐπιθήσεται, 3 pers. sg. fut. mid. indic. [§28.W] . . . . id.

ἐπιθήσουσι(ν), 3 pers. pl. fut. act. indic. . . id.

ἐπιθυμεῖ, 3 pers. sg. pres. act. indic. . ἐπιθυμέω *(1937)*

ἐπιθυμεῖτε, 2 pers. pl. pres. act. indic. . . . . id.

(1937) **ἐπιθυμέω,** ῶ, fut. ἐπιθυμήσω [§16.P] (ἐπί + θυμός) *to set the heart upon; to desire, long for, have earnest desire,* Matt. 13:17; Luke 15:16, et al.; *to lust after,* Matt. 5:28, et al.; spc. *to covet,* Rom. 13:9, et al.

ἐπιθυμῆσαι, aor. act. infin. . . . . ἐπιθυμέω *(1937)*

ἐπιθυμήσεις, 2 pers. sg. fut. act. indic. . . . id.

ἐπιθυμήσετε, 2 pers. pl. fut. act. indic. . . . id.

ἐπιθυμήσουσιν, 3 pers. pl. fut. act. indic. . id.

ἐπιθυμητάς, acc. pl. m. n. . . . . ἐπιθυμητής *(1938)*

(1938) **ἐπιθυμητής,** οῦ, ὁ [§2.B.c] *one who has an ardent desire for* anything, 1 Cor. 10:6

(1939) **ἐπιθυμία,** ας, ἡ, nom. sg. f. n. [§2.B.b; 2.2] *earnest desire,* Luke 22:15, et al.; *irregular or violent desire, cupidity,* Mark 4:19, et al.; spc. impure *desire, lust,* Rom. 1:24, et al.; met. *the object of desire, what enkindles desire,* 1 John 2:16, 17

ἐπιθυμίᾳ, dat. sg. f. n. . . . . ἐπιθυμία *(1939)*

ἐπιθυμίαι, nom. pl. f. n. . . . . id.

ἐπιθυμίαις, dat. pl. f. n. . . . . id.

ἐπιθυμίαν, acc. sg. f. n. . . . . ἐπιθυμία *(1939)*
ἐπιθυμίας, gen. sg. f. n. {Rev. 18:14} . . . . id.
ἐπιθυμίας, acc. pl. f. n. {John 8:44} . . . . id.
ἐπιθυμιῶν, gen. pl. f. n. . . . . id.
ἐπιθυμοῦμεν, 1 pers. pl. pres. act.
    indic. ἐπιθυμέω *(1937)*
ἐπιθυμοῦσιν, 3 pers. pl. pres. act. indic. . . id.
ἐπιθυμῶν, nom. sg. m. pres. act. part. . . . id.
ἐπιθῶ, 1 pers. sg. 2 aor. act. subj.
    [§28.U] . . . . ἐπιτίθημι *(2007)*
(1940) ἐπικαθίζω, fut. ἐπικαθίσω [§26.1] (ἐπί +
    καθίζω) *to cause to sit upon, seat upon,*
    Matt. 21:7; or according to the v.r.,
    ἐπεκάθισεν, intrans. *to sit upon*
ἐπικαλεῖσθαι, pres. pass. infin. . . . . ἐπικαλέω *(†1941)*
ἐπικαλεῖσθε, 2 pers. pl. pres. mid. indic. . id.
ἐπικαλεῖται, 3 pers. sg. pres. pass. indic. . id.
ἐπικαλεσάμενος, nom. sg. m. aor. mid. part. id.
ἐπικαλεσαμένου, gen. sg. m. aor. mid. part. id.
ἐπικαλέσασθαι, aor. mid. infin. . . . . id.
ἐπικαλέσηται, 3 pers. sg. aor. mid. subj. . id.
ἐπικαλέσονται, 3 pers. pl. fut. mid. indic.
    (Rom. 10:14, MT & TR | ἐπικαλέσωνται,
    GNT, WH & NA) . . . . id.
ἐπικαλέσωνται, 3 pers. pl. aor. mid. indic.
    (Rom. 10:14, GNT, WH & NA |
    ἐπικαλέσονται, MT & TR) . . . . id.
(†1941) ἐπικαλέω, ῶ, fut. ἐπικαλέσω, perf. pass.
    ἐπικέκληται, aor. pass. ἐπεκλήθην [§22.1;
    22.4] (ἐπί + καλέω) *to call on; to attach*
    or connect a name, Acts 15:17; James 2:7;
    to attach an additional name, to surname,
    Matt. 10:3, et al.; pass. *to receive an ap-*
    pellation or surname, Heb. 11:16; mid. *to*
    call upon, invoke, 2 Cor. 1:23, et al.; *to ap-*
    peal to, Acts 25:11, 12, 21
ἐπικαλοῦμαι, 1 pers. sg. pres. mid.
    indic. ἐπικαλέω *(†1941)*
ἐπικαλουμένοις, dat. pl. m. pres. mid. part. id.
ἐπικαλούμενον, acc. sg. m. pres. mid. part.
    {Acts 7:59} . . . . id.
ἐπικαλούμενον, acc. sg. m. pres. pass. part.
    {Acts 11:13} . . . . id.
ἐπικαλούμενος, nom. sg. m. pres. pass. part. id.
ἐπικαλουμένου, gen. sg. m. pres. pass. part. id.
ἐπικαλουμένους, acc. pl. m. pres. mid. part. id.
ἐπικαλουμένων, gen. pl. m. pres. mid. part. id.
(†1942) ἐπικάλυμμα, ατος, τό [§4.D.c] *a covering, veil;*
    met. *a cloak,* 1 Pet. 2:16
ἐπικάλυμμα, acc. sg. neut. n. . . . ἐπικάλυμμα *(†1942)*
(1943) ἐπικαλύπτω, fut. ἐπικαλύψω [§23.1.a] (ἐπί +
    καλύπτω) *to cover over;* met. *to cover or*
    veil by a pardon, Rom. 4:7
ἐπικατάρατοι, nom. pl. m. adj. (John 7:49,
    MT & TR | ἐπάρατοι, GNT, WH &

NA) . . . . ἐπικατάρατος *(1944)*
(1944) ἐπικατάρατος, ον, nom. sg. m. adj. [§7.2] (ἐπί
    + κατάρατος) *cursed, accursed; subject to*
    the curse of condemnation, Gal. 3:10; *in-*
    famous, Gal. 3:13; *outcast, vile,* John 7:49
(1945) ἐπίκειμαι, fut. ἐπικείσομαι [§33.DD] (ἐπί +
    κεῖμαι) *to lie upon, be placed upon,* John
    11:38; 21:9; *to press, urge upon,* Luke 5:1;
    Acts 27:20; *be urgent, importunate upon,*
    Luke 23:23; *to be imposed upon, be im-*
    posed by law, Heb. 9:10; by necessity,
    1 Cor. 9:16
ἐπικείμενα, nom. pl. neut. pres. mid./pass.
    dep. part. . . . . ἐπίκειμαι *(1945)*
ἐπικείμενον, acc. sg. neut. pres. mid./pass.
    dep. part. . . . . id.
ἐπικειμένου, gen. sg. m. pres. mid./pass. dep.
    part. . . . . id.
ἐπικεῖσθαι, pres. mid./pass. dep. infin. . . . id.
ἐπίκειται, 3 pers. sg. pres. mid./pass. dep.
    indic. . . . . id.
ἐπικέκλησαι, 2 pers. sg. perf. mid.
    indic. . . . . ἐπικαλέω *(†1941)*
ἐπικέκληται, 3 pers. sg. perf. pass. indic. . id.
(‡2027) ἐπικέλλω, equivalent to ἐποκέλλω, *to push*
    a ship *to shore,* Acts 27:41
ἐπικληθείς, nom. sg. m. aor. pass.
    part. ἐπικαλέω *(†1941)*
ἐπικληθέν, acc. sg. neut. aor. pass. part. . . id.
ἐπικληθέντα, acc. sg. m. aor. pass. part. . . id.
(1946) Ἐπικούρειος, ου, ὁ, *an Epicurean, follower*
    of the philosophy of Epicurus, Acts 17:18
Ἐπικουρείων, gen. pl. m. n. (Acts 17:18,
    GNT, MT, TR & NA | Ἐπικουρίων,
    WH) . . . . Ἐπικούρειος *(1946)*
(1947) ἐπικουρία, ας, ἡ [§2.B.b; 2.2] (ἐπίκουρος, *a*
    helper) help, assistance, Acts 26:22
ἐπικουρίας, gen. sg. f. n. . . . . ἐπικουρία *(1947)*
ἐπικράνθη, 3 pers. sg. aor. pass. indic.
    [§27.3] . . . . πικραίνω *(4087)*
ἐπικράνθησαν, 3 pers. pl. aor. pass. indic. id.
(1948) ἐπικρίνω, fut. ἐπικρινῶ [§27.1.a] (ἐπί +
    κρίνω) *to decide; to decree,* Luke 23:24
ἐπιλαβέσθαι, 2 aor. mid. dep.
    infin. . . . . ἐπιλαμβάνω *(†1949)*
ἐπιλαβόμενοι, nom. pl. m. 2 aor. mid. dep.
    part. . . . . id.
ἐπιλαβόμενος, nom. sg. m. 2 aor. mid. dep.
    part. . . . . id.
ἐπιλαβομένου, gen. sg. m. 2 aor. mid. dep.
    part. . . . . id.
ἐπιλαβοῦ, 2 pers. sg. 2 aor. mid. dep. imper. id.
ἐπιλάβωνται, 3 pers. pl. 2 aor. mid. dep. subj. id.
ἐπιλαθέσθαι, 2 aor. mid. dep. infin.
    [§36.2] . . . . ἐπιλανθάνομαι *(1950)*

ἐπιλαμβάνεται, 3 pers. sg. pres. mid./pass.
dep. indic. . . . . ἐπιλαμβάνω *(†1949)*

(†1949) **ἐπιλαμβάνω,** fut. ἐπιλήμψομαι [§36.2] and
mid. ἐπιλαμβάνομαι (ἐπί + λαμβάνω) *to
take hold of,* Matt. 14:31; Mark 8:23; *to
lay hold of, seize,* Luke 23:26; Acts 16:19,
et al.; met. *to seize on* as a ground of accusation, Luke 20:20, 26; *to grasp, obtain
as if by seizure,* 1 Tim. 6:12, 19; *to assume
a portion of, to assume the nature of,* or,
to attach or ally one's self to, Heb. 2:16
ἐπιλανθάνεσθε, 2 pers. pl. pres. mid./pass.
dep. imper. . . . . ἐπιλανθάνομαι *(1950)*

(1950) **ἐπιλανθάνομαι,** fut. ἐπιλήσομαι, 2 aor.
ἐπελαθόμην [§36.2] (ἐπί + λανθάνω) *to
forget,* Matt. 16:5, et al.; *to be forgetful,
neglectful of, to disregard,* Phil. 3:13; Heb.
6:10, et al.; perf. pass. part. ἐπιλελησ-
μένος, in N.T. in a passive sense, *for-
gotten,* Luke 12:6
ἐπιλανθανόμενος, nom. sg. m. pres.
mid./pass. dep. part. . . . . . . ἐπιλανθάνομαι *(1950)*
ἐπιλεγομένη, nom. sg. f. pres. pass.
part. . . . . ἐπιλέγω *(†1951)*

(†1951) **ἐπιλέγω,** fut. ἐπιλέξω [§23.1.b] (ἐπί + λέγω)
to call, denominate, John 5:2; mid. *to select for one's self, choose,* Acts 15:40

(1952) **ἐπιλείπω,** fut. ἐπιλείψω [§23.1.a] (ἐπί +
λείπω) *to be insufficient, to run short, to
fail,* Heb. 11:32

(‡621) **ἐπιλείχω,** fut. ἐπιλείξω (ἐπί + λείχω) *to lick,*
Luke 16:21
ἐπιλείψει, 3 pers. sg. fut. act. indic. . . ἐπιλείπω *(1952)*
ἐπιλελησμένον, nom. sg. neut. perf. pass.
part. . . . . ἐπιλανθάνομαι *(1950)*
ἐπιλεξάμενος, nom. sg. m. aor. mid.
part. . . . . ἐπιλέγω *(†1951)*

(1953) **ἐπιλησμονή,** ῆς, ἡ [§2.B.a] *forgetfulness, oblivion,* James 1:25
ἐπιλησμονῆς, gen. sg. f. n. . . . . . . ἐπιλησμονή *(1953)*
ἐπίλοιπον, acc. sg. m. adj. . . . . ἐπίλοιπος *(1954)*

(1954) **ἐπίλοιπος,** ον [§7.2] *remaining, still left,* 1 Pet.
4:2
ἐπιλυθήσεται, 3 pers. sg. fut. pass.
indic. . . . . ἐπιλύω *(1956)*
ἐπιλύσεως, gen. sg. f. n. . . . . ἐπίλυσις *(1955)*

(1955) **ἐπίλυσις,** εως, ἡ [§5.E.c] *a loosing, liberation;*
met. *interpretation of* what is enigmatical
and obscure, 2 Pet. 1:20

(1956) **ἐπιλύω,** fut. ἐπιλύσω [§13.M] (ἐπί + λύω) *to
loose* what has previously been fastened or
entangled, as a knot; met. *to solve, to explain,* what is enigmatical, as a parable,
Mark 4:34; *to settle, put an end to* a matter of debate, Acts 19:39

(1957) **ἐπιμαρτυρέω,** ῶ, fut. ἐπιμαρτυρήω [§16.P]
(ἐπί + μαρτυρέω) *to bear testimony to; to
testify solemnly,* 1 Pet. 5:12
ἐπιμαρτυρῶν, nom. sg. m. pres. act.
part. ἐπιμαρτυρέω *(1957)*
ἐπιμεῖναι, aor. act. infin. [§27.1.d] . . . . ἐπιμένω *(1961)*
ἐπιμείνης, 2 pers. sg. aor. act. subj. (Rom.
11:22, MT & TR | ἐπιμένης, GNT, WH
& NA) . . . . id.
ἐπιμείνωσι(ν), 3 pers. pl. aor. act. subj. (Rom.
11:23, MT & TR | ἐπιμένωσι(ν), GNT,
WH & NA) . . . . id.

(1958) **ἐπιμέλεια,** ας, ἡ [§2.B.b; 2.2] (ἐπιμελής, *careful*) *care, attention,* Acts 27:3
ἐπιμελείας, gen. sg. f. n. . . . . ἐπιμέλεια *(1958)*

(1959) **ἐπιμελέομαι,** οῦμαι, fut. (pass. form) ἐπι-
μεληθήσομαι, and, later, ἐπιμελήσομαι,
aor. (pass. form) ἐπεμελήθην [§17.Q] (ἐπί
+ μέλομαι) *to take care of,* Luke 10:34;
1 Tim. 3:5
ἐπιμελήθητι, 2 pers. sg. aor. pass.
imper. . . . . ἐπιμέλομαι *(†1959)*
ἐπιμελήσεται, 3 pers. sg. fut. mid. dep. indic.   id.

(†1959) **ἐπιμέλομαι** (ἐπί + μέλομαι) *to take care of,*
Luke 10:34; 1 Tim. 3:5

(1960) **ἐπιμελῶς,** adv. (ἐπιμελής, *careful*) *carefully,
diligently,* Luke 15:8
ἐπίμενε, 2 pers. sg. pres. act. imper. . . ἐπιμένω *(1961)*
ἐπιμένειν, pres. act. infin. . . . . id.
ἐπιμένετε, 2 pers. pl. pres. act. indic. . . . . id.
ἐπιμένῃς, 2 pers. sg. pres. act. subj. (Rom.
11:22, GNT, WH & NA | ἐπιμείνης, MT
& TR) . . . . id.
ἐπιμένομεν, 1 pers. pl. pres. act. indic. (Rom.
6:1, MT | ἐπιμένωμεν, GNT, WH & NA
| ἐπιμενοῦμεν, TR) . . . . id.
ἐπιμενόντων, gen. pl. m. pres. act. part. . . id.
ἐπιμενοῦμεν, 1 pers. pl. fut. act. indic. (Rom.
6:1, TR | ἐπιμένωμεν, GNT, WH & NA
| ἐπιμένομεν, MT) . . . . id.

(1961) **ἐπιμένω,** 1 pers. sg. pres. act. indic., fut.
ἐπιμενῶ [§27.1.a] (ἐπί + μένω) *to stay
longer, prolong a stay, remain on,* Acts
10:48; 15:34, et al.; *to continue, persevere,*
John 8:7; Acts 12:16; *to adhere to, continue
to embrace,* Acts 13:43; Rom. 11:22; *to persist in,* Rom. 6:1, et al. (1 Cor. 16:8, WH
| ἐπιμενῶ, GNT, MT, TR & NA)
ἐπιμενῶ, 1 pers. sg. fut. act. indic. (1 Cor. 16:8,
GNT, MT, TR & NA | ἐπιμένω,
WH) . . . . ἐπιμένω *(1961)*
ἐπιμένωμεν, 1 pers. pl. pres. act. subj. (Rom.
6:1, GNT, WH & NA | ἐπιμένομεν, MT
| ἐπιμενοῦμεν, TR) . . . . id.
ἐπιμένωσι(ν), 3 pers. pl. pres. act. subj. (Rom.

11:23, GNT, WH & NA | ἐπιμείνωσι(ν),
MT & TR) . . . . ἐπιμένω *(1961)*

(1962) **ἐπινεύω**, fut. ἐπινεύσω [§13.M] (ἐπί + νεύω)
to nod to; met. *to assent to, consent*, Acts
18:20

(1963) **ἐπίνοια**, ας, ἡ, nom. sg. f. n. [§2.B.b; 2.2] (ἐπί
+ νοῦς) *cogitation, purpose, device*, Acts
8:22

ἔπινον, 3 pers. pl. imperf. act. indic. . . . . πίνω *(4095)*
ἐπίομεν, 1 pers. pl. 2 aor. act. indic.
[§37.1] . . . . id.
ἔπιον, 3 pers. pl. 2 aor. act. indic. . . . . . . id.

(1964) **ἐπιορκέω**, ῶ, fut. ἐπιορκήσω [§16.P] *to for-
swear one's self, to fail of observing one's
oath*, Matt. 5:33

ἐπιορκήσεις, 2 pers. sg. fut. act.
indic. . . . . ἐπιορκέω *(1964)*
ἐπιόρκοις, dat. pl. m. adj. . . . . ἐπίορκος *(1965)*

(1965) **ἐπίορκος**, ον [§7.2] (ἐπί + ὅρκος) *one who
violates his oath, perjured*, 1 Tim. 1:10

(†1966) ἐπιούσῃ, dat. sg. f. pres. part. [§33.4] . ἔπειμι *(‡1966)*
ἐπιούσιον, acc. sg. m. adj. . . . . . . ἐπιούσιος *(1967)*

(1967) **ἐπιούσιος**, ον [§7.2] *supplied with the coming day* (ἡ ἐπιοῦσα) *daily or sufficient*,
Matt. 6:11; Luke 11:3

ἐπιπεπτωκός, nom. sg. neut. perf. act.
part. . . . . ἐπιπίπτω *(1968)*
ἐπιπεσόντες, nom. pl. m. 2 aor. act. part. id.
ἐπιπεσών, nom. sg. m. 2 aor. act. part. (John
13:25, MT & TR | ἀναπεσών, GNT, WH
& NA) . . . . id.
ἐπιπίπτειν, pres. act. infin. . . . . id.

(1968) **ἐπιπίπτω**, fut. ἐπιπεσοῦμαι, 2 aor. ἐπέπεσον
[§37.1] (ἐπί + πίπτω) *to fall upon; to
throw one's self upon*, Luke 15:20; John
13:25; Acts 20:10, 37; *to press, urge upon*,
Mark 3:10; *to light upon*, Rom. 15:3; *to
come over*, Acts 13:11; *to come upon, fall
upon* mentally or spiritually, Luke 1:12;
Acts 8:16; 10:10, 44; 11:15; 19:17

ἐπιπλήξῃς, 2 pers. sg. aor. act.
subj. . . . . ἐπιπλήσσω *(1969)*

(1969) **ἐπιπλήσσω** (or ἐπιπλήττω) fut. ἐπιπλήξω
[§26.3] (ἐπί + πλήσσω) pr. *to inflict blows
upon*; met. *to chide, reprove*, 1 Tim. 5:1

(1970) **ἐπιπνίγω**, fut. ἐπιπνίξω [§23.1.b] (ἐπί +
πνίγω) pr. *to suffocate*; met. *to choke, obstruct the growth of*, Luke 8:7

ἐπιποθεῖ, 3 pers. sg. pres. act. indic. . ἐπιποθέω *(1971)*

(1971) **ἐπιποθέω**, ῶ, fut. ἐπιποθήσω [§19.P] (ἐπί +
ποθέω) *to desire besides*; also, *to desire earnestly, long for*, 2 Cor. 5:2; *to have a strong
bent*, James 4:5; by impl. *to love, have affection for*, 2 Cor. 9:14, et al.

ἐπιποθήσατε, 2 pers. pl. aor. act.

imper. . . . . ἐπιποθέω *(1971)*
ἐπιπόθησιν, acc. sg. f. n. . . . . ἐπιπόθησις *(1972)*

(1972) **ἐπιπόθησις**, εως, ἡ [§5.E.c] *earnest desire,
strong affection*, 2 Cor. 7:7, 11

ἐπιπόθητοι, nom. pl. m. adj. . . . . . ἐπιπόθητος *(1973)*

(1973) **ἐπιπόθητος**, ον [§7.2] *earnestly desired,
longed for*, Phil. 4:1

(1974) **ἐπιποθία**, ας, ἡ [§2.B.b; 2.2] *earnest desire*,
Rom. 15:23

ἐπιποθίαν, acc. sg. f. n. (Rom. 15:23, GNT,
MT, TR & NA | ἐπιπόθειαν,
WH) . . . . ἐπιποθία *(1974)*
ἐπιποθοῦντες, nom. pl. m. pres. act.
part. . . . . ἐπιποθέω *(1971)*
ἐπιποθούντων, gen. pl. m. pres. act. part. . id.
ἐπιποθῶ, 1 pers. sg. pres. act. indic. . . . . . id.
ἐπιποθῶν, nom. sg. m. pres. act. part. . . . id.

(1975) **ἐπιπορεύομαι**, fut. ἐπιπορεύσομαι [§14.N]
(ἐπί + πορεύομαι) *to travel to; to come
to*, Luke 8:4

ἐπιπορευομένων, gen. pl. m. pres. mid./pass.
dep. part. . . . . ἐπιπορεύομαι *(1975)*
ἐπίπρασκον, 3 pers. pl. imperf. act.
indic. . . . . πιπράσκω *(4097)*
ἔπιπτεν, 3 pers. sg. imperf. act. indic. (Mark
14:35, GNT, WH & NA | ἔπεσεν, MT &
TR) . . . . πίπτω *(4098)*
ἐπιράπτει, 3 pers. sg. pres. act. indic. (Mark
2:21, GNT, WH & NA | ἐπιρράπτει, MT
& TR) . . . . ἐπιράπτω *(1976)*

(1976) **ἐπιράπτω**, *to sew on*, Mark 2:21

(1977) **ἐπιρίπτω**, *to throw upon, cast upon*

ἐπιρίψαντες, nom. pl. m. aor. act. part. (Luke
19:35; 1 Pet. 5:7, GNT, WH & NA |
ἐπιρρίψαντες, MT & TR) . . . . . . ἐπιρίπτω *(1977)*
ἐπιρράπτει, 3 pers. sg. pres. act. indic. (Mark
2:21, MT & TR | ἐπιράπτει, GNT, WH
& NA) . . . . ἐπιρράπτω *(‡1976)*

(‡1976) **ἐπιρράπτω**, fut. ἐπιρράψω [§23.1.a] (ἐπί +
ράπτω) *to sew upon*

(†1977) **ἐπιρρίπτω**, fut. ἐπιρρίψω (ἐπί + ρίπτω) *to
throw or cast upon*, Luke 19:35; met. *to
devolve upon, commit to*, in confidence,
1 Pet. 5:7

ἐπιρρίψαντες, nom. pl. m. aor. act. part.
(Luke 19:35; 1 Pet. 5:7, MT & TR |
ἐπιρίψαντες, GNT, WH & NA) ἐπιρρίπτω *(†1977)*
ἐπίσημοι, nom. pl. m. adj. . . . . ἐπίσημος *(1978)*
ἐπίσημον, acc. sg. m. adj. . . . . id.

(1978) **ἐπίσημος**, ον [§7.2] (ἐπί + σῆμα) pr. *bearing a distinctive mark or device; noted, eminent*, Rom. 16:7; *notorious*, Matt. 27:16

ἐπισιτισμόν, acc. sg. m. n. . . . . . . ἐπισιτισμός *(1979)*

(1979) **ἐπισιτισμός**, οῦ, ὁ [§3.C.a] (ἐπισιτίζομαι, *to
provision*, from ἐπί + σιτίζω, *to feed*, from

σῖτος) *supply of food, provisions,* Luke 9:12

ἐπισκέπτεσθαι, pres. mid./pass. dep. infin. . . . . ἐπισκέπτομαι *(1980)*

ἐπισκέπτῃ, 2 pers. sg. pres. mid./pass. dep. indic. . . . . id.

(1980) **ἐπισκέπτομαι,** fut. ἐπισκέψομαι [§23.1.a] (ἐπί + σκέπτομαι) *to look at observantly, to inspect; to look out, select,* Acts 6:3; *to go see, visit,* Acts 7:23; 15:36; *to visit* for the purpose of comfort and relief, Matt. 25:36, 43; James 1:27; from the Hebrew, of God, *to visit,* with gracious interposition, Luke 1:68, 78, et al.

(‡643) **ἐπισκευάζομαι,** fut. ἐπισκευάσομαι [§26.1] (ἐπισκευάζω, *to put in readiness*) *to prepare for a journey,* v.r. Acts 21:15

ἐπισκευασάμενοι, nom. pl. m. aor. mid. dep. part. (Acts 21:15, GNT, WH, MT & NA | ἀποσκευασάμενοι, TR) . . ἐπισκευάζομαι *(‡643)*

ἐπισκέψασθαι, aor. mid. dep. infin. . . . . ἐπισκέπτομαι *(1980)*

ἐπισκέψασθε, 2 pers. pl. aor. mid. dep. imper. id.

ἐπισκέψεται, 3 pers. sg. fut. mid. dep. indic. (Luke 1:78, GNT, WH & NA | ἐπεσκέψατο, MT & TR) . . . . id.

ἐπισκεψώμεθα, 1 pers. pl. aor. mid. dep. subj. . . . . id.

(1981) **ἐπισκηνόω, ῶ,** fut. ἐπισκηνώσω [§20.T] (ἐπί + σκηνή, *a tent*) *to quarter in or at;* met. *to abide upon,* 2 Cor. 12:9

ἐπισκηνώσῃ, 3 pers. sg. aor. act. subj. ἐπισκηνόω *(1981)*

ἐπισκιάζουσα, nom. sg. f. pres. act. part. ἐπισκιάζω *(1982)*

(1982) **ἐπισκιάζω,** fut. ἐπισκιάσω [§26.1] (ἐπί + σκιάζω, *to shade,* from σκιά) *to overshadow,* Matt. 17:5, et al.; met. *to overshadow, to shed influence upon,* Luke 1:35

ἐπισκιάσει, 3 pers. sg. fut. act. indic. . . . . ἐπισκιάζω *(1982)*

ἐπισκιάσῃ, 3 pers. sg. aor. act. subj. . . . . . id.

(1983) **ἐπισκοπέω, ῶ,** fut. ἐπισκοπήσω [§16.P] (ἐπί + σκοπέω) *to look at, inspect;* met. *to be circumspect, heedful,* Heb. 12:15; *to oversee, to exercise the office of* ἐπίσκοπος, 1 Pet. 5:2

(1984) **ἐπισκοπή, ῆς, ἡ** [§2.B.a] *inspection, oversight, visitation;* of God, *visitation, interposition,* whether in mercy or judgment, Luke 19:44; 1 Pet. 2:12; *the office of an ecclesiastical overseer,* 1 Tim. 3:1; from the Hebrew, *charge, function,* Acts 1:20

ἐπισκοπήν, acc. sg. f. n. . . . . ἐπισκοπή *(1984)*

ἐπισκοπῆς, gen. sg. f. n. . . . . id.

ἐπισκόποις, dat. pl. m. n. . . . . . . ἐπίσκοπος *(1985)*

ἐπίσκοπον, acc. sg. m. n. . . . . id.

(1985) **ἐπίσκοπος, ου, ὁ** [§3.C.a] (ἐπί + σκοπός) pr. *an inspector, overseer; a watcher, guardian,* 1 Pet. 2:25; in N.T. *an ecclesiastical overseer,* Acts 20:28; Phil. 1:1; 1 Tim. 3:2; Tit. 1:7

ἐπισκοποῦντες, nom. pl. m. pres. act. part. ἐπισκοπέω *(1983)*

ἐπισκόπους, acc. pl. m. n. . . . . . . ἐπίσκοπος *(1985)*

(1986) **ἐπισπάομαι,** fut. ἐπισπάσομαι [§18.R] (ἐπί + σπάω) *to draw upon or after;* in N.T. mid. *to obliterate circumcision* by artificial extension of the foreskin, 1 Cor. 7:18

ἐπισπάσθω, 3 pers. sg. pres. mid./pass. dep. imper. . . . . ἐπισπάομαι *(1986)*

(‡4687) **ἐπισπείρω,** fut. ἐπισπερῶ (ἐπί + σπείρω) *to sow in or among,* Matt. 13:25

(1987) **ἐπίσταμαι,** 1 pers. sg. pres. mid./pass. dep. indic., [§33.3] *to be versed in, to be master of,* 1 Tim. 6:4; *to be acquainted with,* Acts 18:25; 19:15; Jude 10: *to know,* Acts 10:28, et al.; *to remember, comprehend,* Mark 14:68

ἐπιστάμενος, nom. sg. m. pres. mid./pass. dep. part. . . . . ἐπίσταμαι *(1987)*

ἐπίστανται, 3 pers. pl. pres. mid./pass. dep. indic. . . . . id.

ἐπιστάντες, nom. pl. m. 2 aor. act. part. . . . . ἐφίστημι *(2186)*

ἐπιστάς, nom. sg. m. 2 aor. act. part. [§29.X] id.

ἐπιστᾶσα, nom. sg. f. 2 aor. act. part. . . . id.

ἐπίστασθε, 2 pers. pl. pres. mid./pass. dep. indic. . . . . ἐπίσταμαι *(1987)*

ἐπίστασιν, acc. sg. f. n. (Acts 24:12, GNT, WH & NA | ἐπισύστασιν, MT & TR) . . . . ἐπίστασις *(‡1999)*

(‡1999) **ἐπίστασις,** nom. sg. f. n. ἐπίστασις, εως, ἡ [§5.E.c] pr. *care of, attention to* (2 Cor. 11:28, GNT, WH & NA | ἐπισύστασις, MT & TR)

ἐπιστάτα, voc. sg. m. n. [§2.6] . . . . ἐπιστάτης *(1988)*

ἐπίσταται, 3 pers. sg. pres. mid./pass. dep. indic. ἐπίσταμαι *(1987)*

(1988) **ἐπιστάτης, ου, ὁ** [§2.B.c] pr. *one who stands by; one who is set over;* in N.T., in voc., equivalent to διδάσκαλε, or ῥαββί, *master, doctor,* Luke 5:5; 8:24, 45, et al.

ἐπιστεῖλαι, aor. act. infin. [§27.1.d] ἐπιστέλλω *(1989)*

(1989) **ἐπιστέλλω,** fut. ἐπιστελῶ [§27.1.b] (ἐπί + στέλλω) *to send word to, to send injunctions,* Acts 15:20; 21:25; *to write to, write* a letter, Heb. 13:22

ἐπίστευεν, 3 pers. sg. imperf. act. indic. . . . . πιστεύω *(4100)*

ἐπιστεύετε, 2 pers. pl. imperf. act.
 indic. . . . . πιστεύω *(4100)*
ἐπιστεύθη, 3 pers. sg. aor. pass. indic. . . . . id.
ἐπιστεύθην, 1 pers. sg. aor. pass. indic. . . . id.
ἐπιστεύθησαν, 3 pers. pl. aor. pass. indic. . . id.
ἐπίστευον, 3 pers. pl. imperf. act. indic. . . id.
ἐπίστευσα, 1 pers. sg. aor. act. indic. . . . . id.
ἐπιστεύσαμεν, 1 pers. pl. aor. act. indic. . . id.
ἐπίστευσαν, 3 pers. pl. aor. act. indic. . . . id.
ἐπίστευσας, 2 pers. sg. aor. act. indic. . . . id.
ἐπιστεύσατε, 2 pers. pl. aor. act. indic. . . . id.
ἐπίστευσε(ν), 3 pers. sg. aor. act. indic. . . id.
ἐπιστῇ, 3 pers. sg. 2 aor. act. subj.
 [§29.3] . . . . ἐφίστημι *(2186)*
ἐπίστηθι, 2 pers. sg. 2 aor. act. imper. . . . . id.
(1990) **ἐπιστήμων**, ον, nom. sg. m. adj. [§7.G.a]
 knowing, discreet, James 3:13
ἐπιστηρίζοντες, nom. pl. m. pres. act.
 part. . . . . ἐπιστηρίζω *(1991)*
(1991) **ἐπιστηρίζω**, fut. ἐπιστηρίξω [§26.2] (ἐπί +
 στηρίζω) pr. *to cause to rest or lean on,
 to settle upon;* met. *to conform, strengthen,
 establish,* Acts 14:22; 15:32, 41; 18:23
ἐπιστηρίζων, nom. sg. m. pres. act.
 part. . . . . ἐπιστηρίζω *(1991)*
ἐπιστολαί, nom. pl. f. n. . . . . ἐπιστολή *(1992)*
ἐπιστολαῖς, dat. pl. f. n. . . . . id.
ἐπιστολάς, acc. pl. f. n. . . . . id.
(1992) **ἐπιστολή**, ῆς, ἡ, nom. sg. f. n. [§2.B.a] *word
 sent; an order, command; an epistle, let-
 ter,* Acts 9:2; 15:30, et al.
ἐπιστολῇ, dat. sg. f. n. . . . . ἐπιστολή *(1992)*
ἐπιστολήν, acc. sg. f. n. . . . . id.
ἐπιστολῆς, gen. sg. f. n. . . . . id.
ἐπιστολῶν, gen. pl. f. n. . . . . id.
ἐπιστομίζειν, pres. act. infin. . . . . . ἐπιστομίζω *(1993)*
(1993) **ἐπιστομίζω**, fut. ἐπιστομίσω [§26.1] (ἐπί +
 στόμα) *to apply a curb or muzzle;* met. *to
 put to silence,* Tit. 1:11
ἐπιστραφείς, nom. sg. m. 2 aor. pass. part.
 [§24.10] . . . . ἐπιστρέφω *(1994)*
ἐπιστραφήτω, 3 pers. sg. 2 aor. pass. imper. id.
ἐπιστραφῶσι(ν), 3 pers. pl. 2 aor. pass. subj.
 (John 12:40, MT & TR | στραφῶσιν,
 GNT, WH & NA) . . . . id.
ἐπιστρέφειν, pres. act. infin. . . . . id.
ἐπιστρέφετε, 2 pers. pl. pres. act. indic. . . id.
ἐπιστρέφουσιν, dat. pl. m. pres. act. part. . . id.
(1994) **ἐπιστρέφω**, fut. ἐπιστρέψω, 2 aor. pass.
 ἐπεστράφην [§24.10] (ἐπί + στρέφω)
 trans. *to turn towards; to turn round; to
 bring back, convert,* Luke 1:16, 17; James
 5:19, 20; intrans. and mid. *to turn one's
 self upon or towards,* Acts 9:40; Rev. 1:12;
 to turn about, Matt. 9:22, et al.; *to turn*

 back, return, Matt. 12:44, et al.; met. *to
 be converted,* Acts 28:27, et al.
ἐπιστρέψαι, aor. act. infin. . . . . ἐπιστρέφω *(1994)*
ἐπιστρέψαντες, nom. pl. m. aor. act. part. id.
ἐπιστρέψας, nom. sg. m. aor. act. part. . . id.
ἐπιστρέψατε, 2 pers. pl. aor. act. imper. . . id.
ἐπιστρεψάτω, 3 pers. sg. aor. act. imper. . id.
ἐπιστρέψει, 3 pers. sg. fut. act. indic. . . . . id.
ἐπιστρέψῃ, 3 pers. sg. aor. act. subj. . . . . . id.
ἐπιστρέψω, 1 pers. sg. fut. act. indic. . . . . id.
ἐπιστρέψωσι(ν), 3 pers. pl. aor. act. subj. . id.
(1995) **ἐπιστροφή**, ῆς, ἡ [§2.B.a] *a turning towards,
 a turning about;* in N.T. met. *conversion,*
 Acts 15:3
ἐπιστροφήν, acc. sg. f. n. . . . . ἐπιστροφή *(1995)*
ἐπιστώθης, 2 pers. sg. aor. pass. indic.
 [§21.U] . . . . πιστόω *(4104)*
ἐπισυναγαγεῖν, 2 aor. act. infin.
 [§13.7.d] . . . . ἐπισυνάγω *(1996)*
ἐπισυνάγει, 3 pers. sg. pres. act. indic. . . . id.
(1996) **ἐπισυνάγω**, fut. ἐπισυνάξω [§23.1.b] (ἐπί +
 συνάγω) *to gather to* a place; *to gather together, assemble, convene,* Matt. 23:37;
 24:31, et al.
(1997) **ἐπισυναγωγή**, ῆς, ἡ [§2.B.a] *the act of being
 gathered together or assembled,* 2 Thess.
 2:1; *an assembling together,* Heb. 10:25
ἐπισυναγωγήν, acc. sg. f. n. . . . . ἐπισυναγωγή *(1997)*
ἐπισυναγωγῆς, gen. sg. f. n. . . . . id.
ἐπισυνάξαι, aor. act. infin. . . . . ἐπισυνάγω *(1996)*
ἐπισυνάξει, 3 pers. sg. fut. act. indic. . . . . id.
ἐπισυνάξουσι(ν), 3 pers. pl. fut. act. indic. id.
ἐπισυναχθεισῶν, gen. pl. f. aor. pass. part. id.
ἐπισυναχθήσονται, 3 pers. pl. fut. pass. indic.
 (Luke 17:37, GNT, WH & NA | συνα-
 χθήσονται, MT & TR) . . . . id.
ἐπισυνηγμένη, nom. sg. f. perf. pass. part. id.
ἐπισυντρέχει, 3 pers. sg. pres. act.
 indic. . . . . ἐπισυντρέχω *(1998)*
(1998) **ἐπισυντρέχω** (ἐπί + συντρέχω) *to run together* to a place, Mark 9:25
ἐπισύστασιν, acc. sg. f. n. (Acts 24:12, MT
 & TR | ἐπίστασιν, GNT, WH &
 NA) . . . . ἐπισύστασις *(1999)*
(1999) **ἐπισύστασις**, εως, ἡ, nom. sg. f. n. [§5.E.c]
 (ἐπισυνίσταμαι) *a gathering, concourse,
 tumult,* Acts 24:12; *a crowding* of calls
 upon the attention and thoughts (2 Cor.
 11:28, MT & TR | ἐπίστασις, GNT, WH
 & NA)
(2000) **ἐπισφαλής**, ές [§7.G.b] (ἐπί + σφάλλω, *to
 supplant) on the verge of falling, unsteady;*
 met. *insecure, hazardous, dangerous,* Acts
 27:9
ἐπισφαλοῦς, gen. sg. m. adj. . . . . . ἐπισφαλής *(2000)*

ἐπίσχυον, 3 pers. pl. imperf. act.
indic. . . . . ἐπισχύω *(2001)*

(2001) ἐπισχύω, fut. ἐπισχύσω [§13.M] (ἐπί + ἰσχύω) *to strengthen;* intrans. *to gather strength;* met. *to be urgent, to press on* a point, Luke 23:5

ἐπισωρεύσουσι(ν), 3 pers. pl. fut. act.
indic. . . . . ἐπισωρεύω *(2002)*

(2002) ἐπισωρεύω, fut. ἐπισωρεύσω (ἐπί + σωρεύω, from σωρός, *a heap*) *to heap up, accumulate largely;* met. *to procure in abundance,* 2 Tim. 4:3

(2003) ἐπιταγή, ῆς, ἡ [§2.B.a] (a later form for ἐπίταξις or ἐπίταγμα) *injunction,* 1 Cor. 7:6, 25; 2 Cor. 8:8; *a decree,* Rom. 16:26; 1 Tim. 1:1; Tit. 1:3; *authoritativeness, strictness,* Tit. 2:15

ἐπιταγήν, acc. sg. f. n. . . . . ἐπιταγή *(2003)*
ἐπιταγῆς, gen. sg. f. n. . . . . id.
ἐπιτάξῃ, 3 pers. sg. aor. act. subj. . . ἐπιτάσσω *(2004)*
ἐπιτάσσει, 3 pers. sg. pres. act. indic. . . . . id.
ἐπιτάσσειν, pres. act. infin. . . . . id.

(2004) ἐπιτάσσω, 1 pers. sg. pres. act. indic., fut. ἐπιτάξω [§26.3] (ἐπί + τάσσω) *to set over or upon; to enjoin, charge,* Mark 1:27; 6:39; Luke 4:36, et al.

ἐπιτεθῇ, 3 pers. sg. aor. pass. subj. [§28.10] (Mark 4:21, MT & TR | τεθῇ, GNT, WH & NA) . . . . ἐπιτίθημι *(2007)*
ἐπιτελεῖν, pres. act. infin. . . . . ἐπιτελέω *(2005)*
ἐπιτελεῖσθαι, pres. pass. infin. . . . . id.
ἐπιτελεῖσθε, 2 pers. pl. pres. mid./pass. indic. id.
ἐπιτελέσαι, aor. act. infin. . . . . id.
ἐπιτελέσας, nom. sg. f. aor. act. part. . . . . id.
ἐπιτελέσατε, 2 pers. pl. aor. act. imper. . . id.
ἐπιτελέσει, 3 pers. sg. fut. act. indic. [§22.1] id.
ἐπιτελέσῃ, 3 pers. sg. aor. act. subj. . . . . . id.

(2005) ἐπιτελέω, ῶ, fut. ἐπιτελέσω [§22.1] (ἐπί + τελέω) *to bring to an end; to finish, complete, perfect,* Rom. 15:28; 2 Cor. 8:6, 11; *to perform,* Luke 13:32; *to carry into practice, to realize,* 2 Cor. 7:1; *to discharge,* Heb. 9:6; *to execute,* Heb. 8:5; *to carry out to completion,* Phil. 1:6; mid. *to end, make an end,* Gal. 3:3; pass. *to be fully undergone, endured,* 1 Pet. 5:9

ἐπιτελοῦντες, nom. pl. m. pres. act.
part. . . . . ἐπιτελέω *(2005)*
ἐπιτελῶ, 1 pers. sg. pres. act. indic. (Luke 13:32, MT & TR | ἀποτελῶ, GNT, WH & NA) . . . . id.
ἐπιτέτραπται, 3 pers. sg. perf. pass. indic. [§35.9] (1 Cor. 14:34, MT & TR | ἐπιτρέπεται, GNT, WH & NA) . . . . ἐπιτρέπω *(2010)*
ἐπιτήδεια, acc. pl. neut. adj. . . . . . . ἐπιτήδειος *(2006)*

(2006) ἐπιτήδειος, εία, ειον [§7.1] (ἐπιτηδές, *fit*) *fit, suitable, necessary,* James 2:16

ἐπιτιθέασιν, 3 pers. pl. pres. act. indic. Att. for ἐπιτιθεῖσι [§28.6] . . . . ἐπιτίθημι *(2007)*
ἐπιτίθει, 2 pers. sg. pres. act. imper. [§31.2] id.
ἐπιτιθείς, nom. sg. m. pres. act. part. (Luke 4:40, GNT, WH & NA | ἐπιθείς, MT & TR) . . . . id.
ἐπιτίθεσθαι, pres. mid. infin. . . . . id.
ἐπιτιθῇ, 3 pers. sg. pres. act. subj. (Rev. 22:18, MT & TR | ἐπιθῇ, GNT, WH & NA) id.

(2007) ἐπιτίθημι, fut. ἐπιθήσω [§28.V] (ἐπί + τίθημι) *to put, place, or lay upon,* Matt. 9:18; Luke 4:40, et al.; *to impose* a name, Mark 3:16, 17; *to inflict,* Acts 16:23; Luke 10:30; Rev. 22:18; mid. *to impose with authority,* Acts 15:28; *to lade,* Acts 28:10; *to set or fall upon, assail, assault, attack,* Acts 18:10

ἐπιτίθησιν, 3 pers. sg. pres. act.
indic. . . . . ἐπιτίθημι *(2007)*
ἐπιτιμᾶν, pres. act. infin. (Matt. 16:22; Mark 8:32, GNT, MT & NA | ἐπιτιμᾶν, WH & TR) . . . . ἐπιτιμάω *(2008)*

(2008) ἐπιτιμάω, ῶ, fut. ἐπιτιμήσω [§18.R] (ἐπί + τιμάω) pr. *to set a value upon; to assess a penalty; to allege as a crimination;* hence, *to reprove, chide, censure, rebuke, reprimand,* Matt. 19:13; Luke 23:40, et al.; in N.T. *to admonish strongly, enjoin strictly,* Matt. 12:16; Luke 17:3

ἐπιτιμήσαι, 3 pers. sg. aor. act. opt. . ἐπιτιμάω *(2008)*
ἐπιτιμήσας, nom. sg. m. aor. act. part. . . . id.
ἐπιτίμησον, 2 pers. sg. aor. act. imper. . . . id.

(2009) ἐπιτιμία, ας, ἡ, nom. sg. f. n. [§2.B.b; 2.2] used in N.T. in the sense of ἐπιτίμημα or ἐπιτίμησις, *a punishment, penalty,* 2 Cor. 2:6

ἐπιτιμῶν, nom. sg. m. pres. act. part. ἐπιτιμάω *(2008)*
ἐπιτρέπεται, 3 pers. sg. pres. pass.
indic. . . . . ἐπιτρέπω *(2010)*
ἐπιτρέπῃ, 3 pers. sg. pres. act. subj. . . . . . id.

(2010) ἐπιτρέπω, 1 pers. sg. pres. act. indic., fut. ἐπιτρέψω [§23.1.a] 2 aor. pass. ἐπετράπην [§24.10] perf. ἐπιτέτραμμαι [§35.9] (ἐπί + τρέπω) *to give over, to leave to the entire trust or management* of any one; hence, *to permit, allow, suffer,* Matt. 8:21; Mark 5:13, et al.

ἐπιτρέψαντος, gen. sg. m. aor. act.
part. . . . . ἐπιτρέπω *(2010)*
ἐπιτρέψῃ, 3 pers. sg. aor. act. subj. . . . . . . id.
ἐπίτρεψον, 2 pers. sg. aor. act. imper. . . . . id.

(2011) ἐπιτροπή, ῆς, ἡ [§2.B.a] *a trust; a commission,* Acts 26:12

ἐπιτροπῆς, gen. sg. f. n. . . . . ἐπιτροπή *(2011)*

(2012) **ἐπίτροπος**, ου, ὁ [§3.C.a] *one to whose charge or control a thing is left; a steward, bailiff, agent, manager,* Matt. 20:8; *steward or overseer* of the revenue, *treasurer,* Luke 8:3; *a guardian* of children, Gal. 4:2

ἐπιτρόπου, gen. sg. m. n. . . . . ἐπίτροπος *(2012)*

ἐπιτρόπους, acc. pl. m. n. . . . . id.

ἐπιτρόπῳ, dat. sg. m. n. . . . . id.

(2013) **ἐπιτυγχάνω**, 2 aor. ἐπέτυχον [§36.2] (ἐπί + τυγχάνω) *to light upon, find; to hit, reach; to acquire, obtain, attain,* Rom. 11:7; Heb. 6:15; 11:33; James 4:2

ἐπιτυχεῖν, 2 aor. act. infin. . . . . . . ἐπιτυγχάνω *(2013)*

ἐπιφαινόντων, gen. pl. neut. pres. act.

part. ἐπιφαίνω *(2014)*

(2014) **ἐπιφαίνω**, fut. ἐπιφανῶ, aor. ἐπέφηνα, later and in N.T. ἐπέφανα [§27.1.c,e] 2 aor. pass. ἐπεφάνην [§27.4.b] (ἐπί + φαίνω) *to make to appear, to display;* pass. *to be manifested, revealed,* Tit. 2:11; 3:4; intrans. *to give light, shine,* Luke 1:79; Acts 27:20

ἐπιφᾶναι, aor. act. infin. [§27.1.f] . . . ἐπιφαίνω *(2014)*

(2015) **ἐπιφάνεια**, ας, ἡ [§2.B.b; 2.2] *appearance, manifestation,* 1 Tim. 6:14; 2 Tim. 1:10, et al.; *glorious display,* 2 Thess. 2:8

ἐπιφανείᾳ, dat. sg. f. n. . . . . ἐπιφάνεια *(2015)*

ἐπιφάνειαν, acc. sg. f. n. . . . . id.

ἐπιφανείας, gen. sg. f. n. . . . . id.

ἐπιφανῆ, acc. sg. f. adj. . . . . ἐπιφανής *(2016)*

(2016) **ἐπιφανής**, ές [§7.G.b] pr. *in full and clear view; splendid, glorious, illustrious,* Acts 2:20

ἐπιφαύσει, 3 pers. sg. fut. act.

indic. . . . . ἐπιφαύσκω *(†2017)*

(†2017) **ἐπιφαύσκω**, in N.T. fut. ἐπιφαύσω (φῶς) *to shine upon, give light to, enlighten,* Eph. 5:14

ἐπιφέρειν, pres. act. infin. (Phil. 1:16, MT & TR | Phil. 1:17, ἐγείρειν, GNT, WH & NA) . . . . ἐπιφέρω *(2018)*

ἐπιφέρεσθαι, pres. pass. infin. (Acts 19:12, MT & TR | ἀποφέρεσθαι, GNT, WH & NA) id.

(2018) **ἐπιφέρω**, fut. ἐποίσω, 2 aor. ἐπήνεγκον [§36.1] (ἐπί + φέρω) *to bring upon or against,* Acts 25:18; Jude 9: *to inflict,* Rom. 3:5; *to bring to, apply to,* Acts 19:12; *to bring in addition, add, superadd,* Phil. 1:16

ἐπιφέρων, nom. sg. m. pres. act. part. ἐπιφέρω *(2018)*

(2019) **ἐπιφωνέω**, ῶ, fut. ἐπιφωνήσω [§16.P] (ἐπί + φωνέω) *to cry aloud, raise a shout* at a speaker, whether applaudingly, Acts 12:22, or the contrary, *to clamor at,* Luke 23:21; Acts 22:24

ἐπιφωσκούσῃ, dat. sg. f. pres. act.

part. ἐπιφώσκω *(2020)*

(2020) **ἐπιφώσκω**, a varied form of ἐπιφαύσκω, *to*

dawn, Matt. 28:1; hence, used of the reckoned commencement of the day, *to be near commencing, to dawn on,* Luke 23:54

(2021) **ἐπιχειρέω**, ῶ, fut. ἐπιχειρήσω [§16.P] (ἐπί + χείρ) *to put hand to* a thing; *to undertake, attempt,* Luke 1:1; Acts 9:29; 19:13

(2022) **ἐπιχέω**, fut. ἐπιχεύσω [§36.1] (ἐπί + χέω) *to pour upon,* Luke 10:34

ἐπιχέων, nom. sg. m. pres. act. part. . . ἐπιχέω *(2022)*

(2023) **ἐπιχορηγέω**, ῶ, fut. ἐπιχορηγήσω [§16.P] (ἐπί + χορηγέω) *to supply further; to superadd,* 2 Pet. 1:5; *to supply, furnish, give,* 2 Cor. 9:10; Gal. 3:5; 2 Pet. 1:11; pass. *to gather vigor,* Col. 2:19

ἐπιχορηγηθήσεται, 3 pers. sg. fut. pass.

indic. . . . . ἐπιχορηγέω *(2023)*

ἐπιχορηγήσατε, 2 pers. pl. aor. act. imper. id.

(2024) **ἐπιχορηγία**, ας, ἡ [§2.B.b; 2.2] *supply, aid,* Eph. 4:16; Phil. 1:19

ἐπιχορηγίας, gen. sg. f. n. . . . . ἐπιχορηγία *(2024)*

ἐπιχορηγούμενον, nom. sg. neut. pres. pass.

part. ἐπιχορηγέω *(2023)*

ἐπιχορηγῶν, nom. sg. m. pres. act. part. . id.

(2025) **ἐπιχρίω**, fut. ἐπιχρίσω [§22.4] (ἐπί + χρίω) *to smear upon, to anoint,* John 9:6, 11

ἐπλανήθησαν, 3 pers. pl. aor. pass.

indic. . . . . πλανάω *(4105)*

ἐπλάνησε(ν), 3 pers. sg. aor. act. indic. . . id.

ἐπλάσθη, 3 pers. sg. aor. pass. indic. . πλάσσω *(4111)*

ἐπλέομεν, 1 pers. pl. imperf. act. indic.

[§35.1] . . . . πλέω *(4126)*

ἐπλεόνασε(ν), 3 pers. sg. aor. act.

indic. πλεονάζω *(4121)*

ἐπλεονέκτησα, 1 pers. sg. aor. act.

indic. . . . . πλεονεκτέω *(4122)*

ἐπλεονεκτήσαμεν, 1 pers. pl. aor. act. indic. id.

ἐπλεονέκτησεν, 3 pers. sg. aor. act. indic. id.

ἐπλήγη, 3 pers. sg. 2 aor. pass. indic.

[§24.9] . . . . πλήσσω *(4141)*

ἐπληθύνετο, 3 pers. sg. imperf. pass.

indic. πληθύνω *(4129)*

ἐπληθύνθη, 3 pers. sg. aor. pass. indic. . . . id.

ἐπληθύνοντο, 3 pers. pl. imperf. pass. indic. (Acts 9:31, MT & TR | ἐπληθύνετο, GNT, WH & NA) . . . . id.

ἐπλήρου, 3 pers. sg. imperf. act. indic. πληρόω *(4137)*

ἐπληροῦντο, 3 pers. pl. imperf. pass. indic. id.

ἐπληροῦτο, 3 pers. sg. imperf. pass. indic. id.

ἐπληρώθη, 3 pers. sg. aor. pass. indic. . . . id.

ἐπλήρωσαν, 3 pers. pl. aor. act. indic. . . id.

ἐπλήρωσε(ν), 3 pers. sg. aor. act. indic. . . id.

ἔπλησαν, 3 pers. pl. aor. act. indic. . πίμπλημι *(‡4130)*

ἐπλήσθη, 3 pers. sg. aor. pass. indic. [§23.4] id.

ἐπλήσθησαν, 3 pers. pl. aor. pass. indic. . id.

ἐπλούτησαν, 3 pers. pl. aor. act.

indic. . . . . πλουτέω *(4147)*
ἐπλουτήσατε, 2 pers. pl. aor. act. indic. . . . id.
ἐπλουτίσθητε, 2 pers. pl. aor. pass. indic.
[§26.1] . . . . πλουτίζω *(4148)*
ἔπλυναν, 3 pers. pl. aor. act. indic. . . . . πλύνω *(4150)*
ἔπλυνον, 3 pers. pl. imperf. act. indic. (Luke
5:2, GNT, WH & NA | ἀπέπλυναν, MT
& TR) . . . . id.
ἔπνευσαν, 3 pers. pl. aor. act. indic.
[§35.3] . . . . πνέω *(4154)*
ἔπνιγε(ν), 3 pers. sg. imperf. act. indic. . πνίγω *(4155)*
ἐπνίγοντο, 3 pers. pl. imperf. pass. indic. . id.
ἔπνιξαν, 3 pers. pl. aor. act. indic. (Matt. 13:7,
GNT & NA | ἐπέπνιξαν, WH, MT &
TR) . . . . id.
ἐποίει, 3 pers. sg. imperf. act. indic. . . . . ποιέω *(4160)*
ἐποιεῖτε, 2 pers. pl. imperf. act. indic. . . . . id.
ἐποίησα, 1 pers. sg. aor. act. indic. . . . . . . id.
ἐποιήσαμεν, 1 pers. pl. aor. act. indic. . . . id.
ἐποιησάμην, 1 pers. sg. aor. mid. indic. . . id.
ἐποίησαν, 3 pers. pl. aor. act. indic. . . . . . id.
ἐποιήσαντο, 3 pers. pl. aor. mid. indic. (Acts
8:2, MT & TR | ἐποίησαν, GNT, WH &
NA) . . . . id.
ἐποίησας, 2 pers. sg. aor. act. indic. . . . . . id.
ἐποιήσατε, 2 pers. pl. aor. act. indic. . . . . . id.
ἐποίησε(ν), 3 pers. sg. aor. act. indic. . . . . id.
ἐποικοδομεῖ, 3 pers. sg. pres. act.
indic. . . . . ἐποικοδομέω *(2026)*
(2026) **ἐποικοδομέω**, ῶ, fut. ἐποιδοκομήσω [§16.P]
(ἐπί + οἰκοδομέω) met. *to build upon,*
1 Cor. 3:10, 12, 14; pass. met. *to be built*
upon as parts of a spiritual structure, Eph.
2:20; *to build up, carry up a building;* met.
to build up in spiritual advancement, Acts
20:32, et al.
ἐποικοδομηθέντες, nom. pl. m. aor. pass.
part. . . . . ἐποικοδομέω *(2026)*
ἐποικοδομῆσαι, aor. act. infin. (Acts 20:32,
MT & TR | οἰκοδομῆσαι, GNT, WH &
NA) . . . . id.
ἐποικοδόμησεν, 3 pers. sg. aor. act. indic.
(1 Cor. 3:14, GNT, WH, MT & NA |
ἐπῳκοδόμησε(ν), TR) . . . . id.
ἐποικοδομούμενοι, nom. pl. m. pres. pass.
part. . . . . id.
ἐποικοδομοῦντες, nom. pl. m. pres. act. part. id.
ἐποίουν, 3 pers. pl. imperf. act. indic. . . ποιέω *(4160)*
ἐποιοῦντο, 3 pers. pl. imperf. mid. indic. . id.
(2027) **ἐποκέλλω**, aor. ἐπώκειλα [§27.1.d] (ἐπί +
ὀκέλλω, idem) *to run* a ship *aground,* Acts
27:41
ἐπολέμησαν, 3 pers. pl. aor. act. indic. (Rev.
12:7, TR | ἐπολέμησε(ν), GNT, WH, MT
& NA) . . . . πολεμέω *(4170)*

ἐπολέμησε(ν), 3 pers. sg. aor. act. indic. (Rev.
12:7, GNT, WH, MT & NA | ἐπολέ-
μησαν, TR) . . . . πολεμέω *(4170)*
ἐπονομάζῃ, 2 pers. sg. pres. pass.
indic. . . . . ἐπονομάζω *(2028)*
(2028) **ἐπονομάζω**, fut. ἐπονομάσω [§26.1] (ἐπί +
ὀνομάζω) *to attach a name to;* pass. *to be*
named, to be styled, Rom. 2:17
ἐπόπται, nom. pl. m. n. . . . . ἐπόπτης *(2030)*
ἐποπτεύοντες, nom. pl. m. pres. act. part.
(1 Pet. 2:12, GNT, WH & NA | ἐποπτεύ-
σαντες, MT & TR) . . . . ἐποπτεύω *(2029)*
ἐποπτεύσαντες, nom. pl. m. aor. act. part. id.
(2029) **ἐποπτεύω**, fut. ἐποπτεύσω [§13.M] *to look*
upon, observe, watch; to witness, be an
eye-witness of, 1 Pet. 2:12; 3:2
(2030) **ἐπόπτης**, ου, ὁ [§2.B.c] (ἐπί + ὄψομαι) *a*
looker-on, eye-witness, 2 Pet. 1:16
ἐπορεύετο, 3 pers. sg. imperf. mid./pass. dep.
indic. πορεύομαι *(4198)*
ἐπορεύθη, 3 pers. sg. aor. pass. dep. indic. id.
ἐπορεύθησαν, 3 pers. pl. aor. pass. dep. indic. id.
ἐπορευόμεθα, 1 pers. pl. imperf. mid./pass.
dep. indic. . . . . id.
ἐπορευόμην, 1 pers. sg. imperf. mid./pass.
dep. indic. . . . . id.
ἐπορεύοντο, 3 pers. pl. imperf. mid./pass. dep.
indic. . . . . id.
ἐπόρθει, 3 pers. sg. imperf. act. indic. . πορθέω *(4199)*
ἐπόρθουν, 1 pers. sg. imperf. act. indic. . . id.
ἐπόρνευσαν, 3 pers. pl. aor. act.
indic. . . . . πορνεύω *(4203)*
(2031) **ἔπος**, ους, τό [§5.E.b] (εἶπον) *a word, that*
which is expressed by words; ὡς ἔπος
εἰπεῖν, *so to say, if the expression may be*
allowed. Heb. 7:9
ἔπος, acc. sg. neut. n. . . . . ἔπος *(2031)*
ἐπότιζεν, 3 pers. sg. imperf. act. indic. ποτίζω *(4222)*
ἐπότισα, 1 pers. sg. aor. act. indic. . . . . . . id.
ἐποτίσαμεν, 1 pers. pl. aor. act. indic. . . . id.
ἐποτίσατε, 2 pers. pl. aor. act. indic. . . . . . id.
ἐπότισεν, 3 pers. sg. aor. act. indic. . . . . . id.
ἐποτίσθημεν, 1 pers. pl. aor. pass. indic
[§26.1] . . . . id.
ἐπουράνια, nom. pl. neut. adj.
{1 Cor. 15:40} . . . . ἐπουράνιος *(2032)*
ἐπουράνια, acc. pl. neut. adj. {John 3:12} id.
ἐπουράνιοι, nom. pl. m. adj. . . . . id.
ἐπουρανίοις, dat. pl. neut. adj. . . . . id.
ἐπουράνιον, acc. sg. f. adj. . . . . id.
(2032) **ἐπουράνιος**, ον, nom. sg. m. adj. [§7.2] (ἐπί
+ οὐρανός) *heavenly,* in respect of local-
ity, Eph. 1:20; Phil. 2:10, et al.; τὰ
ἐπουράνια, *the upper regions* of the air,
Eph. 6:12; *heavenly,* in respect of essence

and character, *unearthly,* 1 Cor. 15:48, 49,
et al.; met. *divine, spiritual,* John 3:12,
et al.

ἐπουρανίου, gen. sg. m. adj.
　{1 Cor. 15:49} . . . . ἐπουράνιος *(2032)*

ἐπουρανίου, gen. sg. f. adj. {Heb. 3:1} . . . id.

ἐπουρανίῳ, dat. sg. f. adj. . . . . id.

ἐπουρανίων, gen. pl. m. adj. {Phil. 2:10} . id.

ἐπουρανίων, gen. pl. neut. adj. {1 Cor. 15:40} id.

ἐπράθη, 3 pers. sg. aor. pass. indic.
　[§36.3] . . . . πιπράσκω *(4097)*

ἔπραξα, 1 pers. sg. aor. act. indic. . . . πράσσω *(4238)*

ἐπράξαμεν, 1 pers. pl. aor. act. indic. . . . . id.

ἔπραξαν, 3 pers. pl. aor. act. indic. . . . . . id.

ἐπράξατε, 2 pers. pl. aor. act. indic. . . . . . id.

ἔπραξε(ν), 3 pers. sg. aor. act. indic. [§26.8] id.

ἔπρεπε(ν), 3 pers. sg. imperf. act.
　indic. . . . . πρέπει *(†4241)*

ἐπρίσθησαν, 3 pers. pl. aor. pass. indic.
　[§22.4] . . . . πρίζω *(4249)*

ἐπροφήτευον, 3 pers. pl. imperf. act. indic.
　(Acts 19:6, GNT, WH & NA |
　προεφήτευον, MT & TR) . . . . προφητεύω *(4395)*

ἐπροφητεύσαμεν, 1 pers. pl. aor. act. indic.
　(Matt. 7:22, GNT, WH & NA | προ-
　εφητεύσαμεν, MT & TR) . . . . id.

ἐπροφήτευσαν, 3 pers. pl. aor. act. indic.
　(Matt. 11:13, GNT, WH & NA | προ-
　εφήτευσαν, MT & TR) . . . . id.

ἐπροφήτευσεν, 3 pers. sg. aor. act. indic.
　(Matt. 15:7; Mark 7:6; Luke 1:67; John
　11:51, GNT, WH & NA | προεφήτευ-
　σε(ν) MT & TR) . . . . id.

(2033) ἑπτά, οἱ, αἱ, τά, *seven,* indecl. numeral, Matt.
　15:34, 37, et al.; by Jewish usage for a
　round number, Matt. 12:45; Luke 11:26

ἔπταισαν, 3 pers. pl. aor. act. indic. . . . πταίω *(4417)*

(2034) ἑπτάκις, adv., *seven times,* Matt. 18:21, 22;
　Luke 17:4(2×)

(2035) ἑπτακισχίλιοι, αι, α (ἑπτάκις + χίλιοι) *seven
　thousand,* Rom. 11:4

ἑπτακισχιλίους, acc. pl. m. adj. ἑπτακισχίλιοι *(2035)*

ἔπτυσε(ν), 3 pers. sg. aor. act. indic. . . . . πτύω *(4429)*

ἐπτώχευσε(ν), 3 pers. sg. aor. act.
　indic. . . . . πτωχεύω *(4433)*

ἐπύθετο, 3 pers. sg. 2 aor. mid. dep. indic.
　[§36.2] . . . . πυνθάνομαι *(4441)*

ἐπύθοντο, 3 pers. pl. 2 aor. mid. dep. indic.
　(Acts 10:18, WH | ἐπυνθάνοντο, GNT,
　MT, TR & NA) . . . . id.

ἐπυνθάνετο, 3 pers. sg. imperf. mid./pass. dep.
　indic. . . . . id.

ἐπυνθάνοντο, 3 pers. pl. imperf. mid./pass.
　dep. indic. . . . . id.

(2036) ἔπω, see εἶπον *(‡3004)*

ἐπώκειλαν, 3 pers. pl. aor. act. indic. (Acts
　27:41, MT & TR | ἐπέκειλαν, GNT, WH
　& NA) . . . . ἐποκέλλω *(2027)*

ἐπῳκοδόμησεν, 3 pers. sg. aor. act. indic.
　[§13.2] (1 Cor. 3:14, TR | ἐποικοδόμησεν,
　GNT, WH, MT & NA) . . . . ἐποικοδομέω *(2026)*

ἐπώλησε(ν), 3 pers. sg. aor. act. indic. . πωλέω *(4453)*

ἐπώλουν, 3 pers. pl. imperf. act. indic. . . . id.

ἐπωρώθη, 3 pers. sg. aor. pass. indic. . πωρόω *(4456)*

ἐπωρώθησαν, 3 pers. pl. aor. pass. indic. . id.

ἐπώρωσεν, 3 pers. sg. aor. act. indic. (John
　12:40, GNT, WH & NA | πεπώρωκεν,
　MT & TR) . . . . id.

ἐραβδίσθην, 3 pers. sg. aor. pass. indic.
　(2 Cor. 11:25, GNT, WH, MT & NA |
　ἐρραβδίσθην, TR) . . . . ῥαβδίζω *(4463)*

ἐράντισεν, 3 pers. sg. aor. act. indic. (Heb.
　9:19, 21, GNT, WH & NA | ἐρράντι-
　σε(ν), MT & TR) . . . . ῥαντίζω *(4472)*

ἐράπισαν, 3 pers. pl. aor. act. indic. (Matt.
　26:67, GNT, WH & NA | ἐρράπισαν,
　MT & TR) . . . . ῥαπίζω *(4474)*

Ἔραστον, acc. sg. m. n. . . . . Ἔραστος *(2037)*

(2037) Ἔραστος, ου, ὁ, nom. sg. m. n. [§3.C.a] *Er-
　astus,* pr. name, Acts 19:22

ἐραυνᾷ, 3 pers. sg. pres. act. indic. (1 Cor.
　2:10, GNT, WH & NA | ἐρευνᾷ, MT &
　TR) . . . . ἐραυνάω *(‡2045)*

ἐραυνᾶτε, 2 pers. pl. pres. act. indic. or imper.
　(John 5:39, GNT, WH & NA | ἐρευνᾶτε,
　MT & TR) . . . . id.

(‡2045) ἐραυνάω, *to search,* examine

ἐραύνησον, 2 pers. sg. aor. act. imper. (John
　7:52, GNT, WH & NA | ἐρεύνησον, MT
　& TR) . . . . ἐραυνάω *(‡2045)*

ἐραυνῶν, nom. sg. m. pres. act. part. (Rom.
　8:27; Rev. 2:23, GNT, WH & NA |
　ἐρευνῶν, MT & TR) . . . . id.

ἐραυνῶντες, nom. pl. m. pres. act. part. (1 Pet.
　1:11, GNT, WH & NA | ἐρευνῶντες, MT
　& TR) . . . . id.

ἔργα, nom. pl. neut. n. {John 7:7} . . . . . ἔργον *(2041)*

ἔργα, acc. pl. neut. n. {John 7:3} . . . . id.

ἐργάζεσθαι, pres. mid./pass. dep.
　infin. . . . . ἐργάζομαι *(2038)*

ἐργάζεσθε, 2 pers. pl. pres. mid./pass. dep.
　indic. {James 2:9} . . . . id.

ἐργάζεσθε, 2 pers. pl. pres. mid./pass. dep.
　imper. {John 6:27} . . . . id.

ἐργάζεται, 3 pers. sg. pres. mid./pass. dep.
　indic. . . . . id.

ἐργάζῃ, 2 pers. sg. pres. mid./pass. dep. indic. id.

(2038) ἐργάζομαι, 1 pers. sg. pres. mid./pass. dep.
　indic., fut. ἐργάσομαι, aor. εἰργασάμην,
　perf. εἴργασμαι [§13.4] intrans. *to work,*

labor, Matt. 21:28; Luke 13:14; *to trade, traffic, do business*, Matt. 25:16; Rev. 18:17; *to act, exert one's power, be active*, John 5:17; trans. *to do, perform, commit*, Matt. 26:10; John 6:28; *to be engaged in, occupied upon*, 1 Cor. 9:13; Rev. 18:17; *to acquire, gain by one's labor*, John 6:27, et al.

ἐργαζόμενοι, nom. pl. m. pres. mid./pass. dep. part. . . . . ἐργάζομαι *(2038)*

ἐργαζόμενος, nom. sg. m. pres. mid./pass. dep. part. . . . . id.

ἐργαζομένους, acc. pl. m. pres. mid./pass. dep. part. . . . . id.

ἐργαζομένῳ, dat. sg. m. pres. mid./pass. dep. part. . . . . id.

ἐργάζονται, 3 pers. pl. pres. mid./pass. dep. part. . . . . id.

ἐργάζου, 2 pers. sg. pres. mid./pass. dep. imper. . . . . id.

ἐργαζώμεθα, 1 pers. pl. pres. mid./pass. dep. subj. . . . . id.

ἐργάσῃ, 2 pers. sg. aor. mid. dep. subj. . . . id.

(2039) ἐργασία, ας, ἡ [§2.B.b; 2.2] *work, labor;* in N.T. ἐργασίαν διδόναι, *operam dare, to endeavor, strive*, Luke 12:58; *performance, practice*, Eph. 4:19; *a trade, business, craft*, Acts 19:25, *gain* acquired by labor or trade, *profit*, Acts 16:16, 19; 19:24, 25

ἐργασίαν, acc. sg. f. n. . . . . ἐργασία *(2039)*

ἐργασίας, gen. sg. f. n. . . . . id.

ἐργάται, nom. pl. m. n. . . . . ἐργάτης *(2040)*

ἐργάτας, acc. pl. m. n. . . . . id.

ἐργάτην, acc. sg. m. n. . . . . id.

(2040) ἐργάτης, ου, ὁ, nom. sg. m. n. [§2.B.c] *a workman, laborer*, Matt. 9:37, 38; 20:1, 2, 8; met. *a spiritual* workman *or* laborer, 2 Cor. 11:13, et al.; *an artisan, artificer*, Acts 19:25; *a worker, practicer*, Luke 13:27

ἐργατῶν, gen. pl. m. n. . . . . ἐργάτης *(2040)*

ἔργοις, dat. pl. neut. n. . . . . ἔργον *(2041)*

(2041) ἔργον, ου, τό, nom. sg. neut. n. [§3.C.c] *anything done or to be done; a deed, work, action*, John 3:21; Eph. 2:10; 2 Cor. 9:8, et al. freq.; *duty enjoined, office, charge, business*, Mark 13:34; John 4:34, et al. freq.; *a process, course of action*, James 1:4; *a work, product of an action or process*, Acts 7:41; Heb. 1:10, et al.; *substance in effect*, Rom. 2:15 {John 6:29}

ἔργον, acc. sg. neut. n. {John 7:21} . . . . ἔργον *(2041)*

ἔργου, gen. sg. neut. n. . . . . id.

ἔργῳ, dat. sg. neut. n. . . . . id.

ἔργων, gen. pl. neut. n. . . . . id.

ἐρεθίζετε, 2 pers. pl. pres. act. imper. . ἐρεθίζω *(2042)*

(2042) ἐρεθίζω, fut. ἐρεθίσω, aor. ἠρέθισα [§26.1] (ἐρέθω, idem. from ἔρις) *to provoke, to irritate, exasperate*, Col. 3:21; *to incite, stimulate*, 2 Cor. 9:2

ἐρεῖ, 3 pers. sg. fut. act. indic. . . . . εἶπον *(‡3004)*

(2043) ἐρείδω, fut. ἐρείσω, aor. ἤρεισα [§23.1.c] *to make to lean upon; to fix firmly;* intrans. *to become firmly fixed, stick fast*, Acts 27:41

ἔρεις, nom. pl. f. n. (2 Cor. 12:20, MT & TR | ἔρις, GNT, WH & NA) . . . . . . ἔρις *(2054)*

ἔρεις, acc. pl. f. n. [§4.4] {Tit. 3:9} . . . . . id.

ἐρεῖς, 2 pers. sg. fut. act. indic. {Matt. 7:4} . . . . εἶπον *(‡3004)*

ἐρείσασα, nom. sg. f. aor. act. part. . . . ἐρείδω *(2043)*

ἐρεῖτε, 2 pers. pl. fut. act. indic. . . . . . εἶπον *(‡3004)*

(2044) ἐρεύγομαι, fut. ἐρεύξομαι [§23.1.b] *to vomit, disgorge;* met. *to utter, declare openly*, Matt. 13:35

ἐρευνᾷ, 3 pers. sg. pres. act. indic. (1 Cor. 2:10, MT & TR | ἐραυνᾷ, GNT, WH & NA) . . . . ἐρευνάω *(2045)*

ἐρευνᾶτε, 2 pers. pl. pres. act. indic. or imper. (John 5:39, MT & TR | ἐραυνᾶτε, GNT, WH & NA) . . . . id.

(2045) ἐρευνάω, ῶ, fut. ἐρευνήσω [§18.R] *to search, trace, investigate, explore*, John 5:39; 7:52, et al.

ἐρεύνησον, 2 pers. sg. aor. act. imper. (John 7:52, MT & TR | ἐραύνησον, GNT, WH & NA) . . . . ἐρευνάω *(2045)*

ἐρευνῶν, nom. sg. m. pres. act. part. (Rom. 8:27; Rev. 2:23, MT & TR | ἐραυνῶν, GNT, WH & NA) . . . . id.

ἐρευνῶντες, nom. pl. m. pres. act. part. (1 Pet. 1:11, MT & TR | ἐραυνῶντες, GNT, WH & NA) . . . . id.

ἐρεύξομαι, 1 pers. sg. fut. mid. dep. indic. . . . . ἐρεύγομαι *(2044)*

(2046) ἐρέω, see εἶπον *(‡3004)*

(2047) ἐρημία, ας, ἡ [§2.B.b; 2.2] *a solitude, uninhabited region, waste, desert*, Matt. 15:33, et al.

ἐρημίᾳ, dat. sg. f. n. . . . . ἐρημία *(2047)*

ἐρημίαις, dat. pl. f. n. . . . . id.

ἐρημίας, gen. sg. f. n. . . . . id.

ἐρήμοις, dat. pl. m. adj. {Mark 1:45} . ἔρημος *(2048)*

ἐρήμοις, dat. pl. f. adj. {Luke 5:16} . . . . . id.

ἔρημον, acc. sg. m. adj. {Mark 1:35} . . . . id.

ἔρημον, acc. sg. f. adj. {Mark 1:12} . . . . . id.

(2048) ἔρημος, ον, nom. sg. m. adj. [§7.2; 7.F.a] *lone, desert, waste, uninhabited*, Matt. 14:13, 15; Mark 6:31, 32, 35; *lone abandoned* to ruin, Matt. 23:38; Luke 13:35; met. *lone, unmarried*, Gal. 4:27; as a subst. *a desert,*

uninhabited region, waste, Matt. 3:1; 24:26; Acts 7:36, et al.{Mark 6:35}

ἔρημος, nom. sg. f. adj. {Acts 1:20} .. ἔρημος *(2048)*

ἐρήμου, gen. sg. f. adj. . . . . id.

ἐρήμους, acc. pl. f. adj. . . . . id.

ἐρημοῦται, 3 pers. sg. pres. pass. indic. . . . . ἐρημόω *(2049)*

(2049) **ἐρημόω**, ῶ, fut. ἐρημώσω, perf. pass. ἠρήμωμαι, aor. pass. ἠρημώθην [§20.Τ; 21.U] *to lay waste, make desolate, bring to ruin,* Matt. 12:25; Luke 11:17; Rev. 17:16; 18:17, 19

ἐρήμῳ, dat. sg. m. adj. {Luke 9:12} .. ἔρημος *(2048)*

ἐρήμῳ, dat. sg. f. adj. {Luke 4:1} . . . . . . id.

ἐρημώσεως, gen. sg. f. n. . . . . ἐρήμωσις *(2050)*

(2050) **ἐρήμωσις**, εως, ἡ, nom. sg. f. n. [§5.E.c] *desolation, devastation,* Matt. 24:15; Mark 13:14, et al.

ἔριδες, nom. pl. f. n. . . . . ἔρις *(2054)*

ἔριδι, dat. sg. f. n. . . . . id.

ἔριδος, gen. sg. f. n. . . . . id.

(2051) **ἐρίζω**, fut. ἐρίσω [§26.1] *to quarrel; to wrangle; to use the harsh tone of a wrangler or brawler, to grate,* Matt. 12:19

(2052) **ἐριθεία**, ας, ἡ, nom. sg. f. n. [§2.B.b; 2.2] (ἐριθεύομαι, *to serve for hire, to serve a party,* from ἔριθος, *a hired laborer) the service of a party, party spirit; feud, faction,* 2 Cor. 12:20; *contentious disposition,* James 3:14, et al.; by impl. *untowardness, disobedience,* Rom. 2:8 (James 3:16, GNT, MT, TR & NA | ἐριθία, WH)

ἐριθεῖαι, nom. pl. f. n. (2 Cor. 12:20; Gal. 5:20, GNT, MT, TR & NA | ἐριθίαι, WH) . . . . ἐριθεία *(2052)*

ἐριθείαν, acc. sg. f. n. (Phil. 2:3; James 3:14, GNT, MT, TR & NA | ἐριθίαν, WH) . id.

ἐριθείας, gen. sg. f. n. (Rom. 2:8; Phil. 1:17, GNT, MT, TR & NA | ἐριθίας, WH) . id.

ἐριμμένοι, nom. pl. m. perf. pass. part. (Matt. 9:36, WH | ἐρριμμένοι, GNT, WH, MT, TR & NA) . . . . ῥίπτω *(4496)*

ἔριν, acc. sg. f. n. [§4.4] . . . . ἔρις *(2054)*

(2053) **ἔριον**, ου, τό, nom. sg. neut. n. [§3.C.c] (ἔρος, εἶρος, idem) *wool,* Heb. 9:19; Rev. 1:14

ἐρίου, gen. sg. neut. n. . . . . ἔριον *(2053)*

(2054) **ἔρις**, ιδος, ἡ, nom. sg. f. n. [§4.2.c] *altercation, strife,* Rom. 13:13; *contentious disposition,* Rom. 1:29; Phil. 1:15, et al.

ἐρίσει, 3 pers. sg. fut. act. indic. . . . . . . ἐρίζω *(2051)*

ἐρίφια, acc. pl. neut. n. . . . . ἐρίφιον *(2055)*

(2055) **ἐρίφιον**, ου, τό [§3.C.a] *a goat, kid,* Matt. 25:33

ἔριφον, acc. sg. m. n. . . . . ἔριφος *(2056)*

(2056) **ἔριφος**, ου, ὁ [§3.C.a,b] *a goat, kid,* Matt.

25:32; Luke 15:29

ἐρίφων, gen. pl. m. n. . . . . ἔριφος *(2056)*

ἔριψαν, 3 pers. pl. aor. act. indic. (Acts 27:19, WH | ἔρριψαν, GNT & NA | ἐρρίψαμεν, MT & TR) . . . . ῥίπτω *(4496)*

Ἑρμᾶν, acc. sg. m. n. . . . . Ἑρμᾶς *(2057)*

(2057) **Ἑρμᾶς**, ᾶ, ὁ [§2.4] *Hermas,* pr. name, Rom. 16:14

Ἑρμῆν, acc. sg. m. n. . . . . Ἑρμῆς *(2060)*

(2058) **ἑρμηνεία**, ας, ἡ, nom. sg. f. n. [§2.B.b; 2.2] *interpretation, explanation,* 1 Cor. 14:26; meton. *the power or faculty of interpreting,* 1 Cor. 12:10

ἑρμηνείαν, acc. sg. f. n. . . . . ἑρμηνεία *(2058)*

ἑρμηνεύεται, 3 pers. sg. pres. pass. indic. . . . . ἑρμηνεύω *(2059)*

ἑρμηνευόμενον, nom. sg. neut. pres. pass. part. (John 1:38, MT & TRb, 1:39, TRs | μεθερμηνευόμενον, GNT, WH & NA) id.

ἑρμηνευόμενος, nom. sg. m. pres. pass. part. id.

(2059) **ἑρμηνεύω**, fut. ἑρμηνεύσω [§13.M] (ἑρμηνεύς, *an interpreter) to explain, interpret, translate,* John 1:39, 43; 9:7; Heb. 7:2

(2060) **Ἑρμῆς**, οῦ, ὁ [§2.B.c] *Hermes* or *Mercury,* son of Jupiter and Maia, the messenger and interpreter of the gods, and the patron of eloquence, learning, etc., Acts 14:12

(2061) **Ἑρμογένης**, ους, ὁ, nom. sg. m. n. [§5.E.a] *Hermogenes,* pr. name, 2 Tim. 1:15

ἐροῦμεν, 1 pers. pl. fut. act. indic. . . . . εἶπον (‡3004)

ἐροῦσι(ν), 3 pers. pl. fut. act. indic. . . . . . id.

ἑρπετά, nom. pl. neut. n. {Acts 10:12} ἑρπετόν *(2062)*

ἑρπετά, acc. pl. neut. n. {Acts 11:6} . . . . . id.

(2062) **ἑρπετόν**, οῦ, τό [§3.C.c] (ἕρπω, *to creep) a creeping animal, a reptile,* Acts 10:12, et al.

ἑρπετῶν, gen. pl. neut. n. . . . . ἑρπετόν *(2062)*

ἐρραβδίσθην, 1 pers. sg. aor. pass. indic. (2 Cor. 11:25, TR | ἐραβδίσθην, GNT, WH, MT & NA) . . . . ῥαβδίζω *(4463)*

ἐρράντισε(ν), 3 pers. sg. aor. act. indic. (Heb. 9:19, 21, MT & TR | ἐράντισεν, GNT, WH & NA) . . . . ῥαντίζω *(4472)*

ἐρραντισμένοι, nom. pl. m. perf. pass. part. (Heb. 10:22, MT & TR | ῥεραντισμένοι, GNT, WH & NA) . . . . id.

ἐρράπισαν, 3 pers. pl. aor. act. indic. (Matt. 26:67, MT & TR | ἐράπισαν, GNT, WH & NA) . . . . ῥαπίζω *(4474)*

ἐρρέθη, 3 pers. sg. aor. pass. indic. . . . . . . ῥέω *(4482)*

ἐρρέθησαν, 3 pers. pl. aor. pass. indic. (Gal. 3:16, GNT, WH, MT & NA | ἐρρήθησαν, TR) . . . . id.

ἐρρήθη, 3 pers. sg. aor. pass. indic. (Rom. 9:12, 26, TRs | ἐρρέθη, GNT, WH, MT, TRb & NA) . . . . id.

ἐρρήθησαν, 3 pers. pl. aor. pass. indic. (Gal. 3:16, TR | ἐρρέθησαν, GNT, WH, MT & NA) . . . . ῥέω *(4482)*

ἔρρηξεν, 3 pers. sg. aor. act. indic. [§36.5] . . . . ῥήγνυμι *(4486)*

ἐρριζωμένοι, nom. pl. m. perf. pass. part. . . . . ῥιζόω *(4492)*

ἐρριμμένοι, nom. pl. m. perf. pass. part. (Matt. 9:36, GNT, MT, TR & NA | ἐριμμένοι, WH) . . . . ῥίπτω *(4496)*

ἔρριπται, 3 pers. sg. perf. pass. indic. [§13.6.b] . . . . id.

ἐρρίψαμεν, 1 pers. pl. aor. act. indic. (Acts 27:19, MT & TR | ἔρριψαν, GNT & NA | ἔριψαν, WH) . . . . id.

ἔρριψαν, 3 pers. pl. aor. act. indic. (Matt. 15:30; Acts 27:19, GNT, MT, TR & NA | ἔριψαν, WH) . . . . id.

ἐρρύσατο, 3 pers. sg. aor. mid./pass. dep. indic. (2 Cor. 1:10; Col. 1:13; 2 Tim. 3:11; 2 Pet. 2:7, GNT, MT, TR & NA | ἐρύσατο, WH) . . . . ῥύομαι *(4506)*

ἐρρύσθην, 1 pers. sg. aor. pass. indic. (2 Tim. 4:17, GNT, MT, TR & NA | ἐρύσθην, WH) . . . .

ἔρρωσθε, 2 pers. pl. perf. pass. imper. ῥώννυμι *(4517)*

ἔρρωσο, 2 pers. sg. perf. pass. imper. (Acts 23:30, MT & TR | GNT, WH & NA omit) . . . . id.

ἐρυθρᾷ, dat sg. f. adj. . . . . ἐρυθρός *(2063)*

ἐρυθράν, acc. sg. f. adj. . . . . id.

(2063) **ἐρυθρός**, ά, όν [§7.1] *red,* Acts 7:36; Heb. 11:29

ἐρύσθην, 3 pers. sg. aor. pass. indic. (2 Tim. 4:17, WH | ἐρρύσθην, GNT, MT, TR & NA) . . . . ῥύομαι *(4506)*

ἔρχεσθαι, pres. mid./pass. dep. infin. . ἔρχομαι *(2064)*

ἔρχεσθε, 2 pers. pl. pres. mid./pass. dep. imper. . . . . id.

ἐρχέσθω, 3 pers. sg. pres. mid./pass. dep. imper. . . . . id.

ἔρχεται, 3 pers. sg. pres. mid./pass. dep. indic. . . . . id.

ἔρχῃ, 2 pers. sg. pres. mid./pass. dep. indic. id.

ἔρχηται, 3 pers. sg. pres. mid./pass. dep. subj. id.

(2064) **ἔρχομαι**, 1 pers. sg. pres. mid./pass. dep. indic., fut. ἐλεύσομαι, 2 aor. ἄλυθον, by synec. ἦλθον, perf. ἐλήλυθα [§36.1] *to come, to go, to pass.* By the combination of this verb with other terms, a variety of meaning results, which, however, is due, not to a change of meaning in the verb, but to the adjuncts. Ὁ ἐρχόμενος, *He who is coming, the expected Messiah,* Matt. 11:3, et al.

ἐρχόμεθα, 1 pers. pl. pres. mid./pass. dep. indic. . . . . ἔρχομαι *(2064)*

ἐρχόμενα, acc. pl. neut. pres. mid./pass. dep. part. . . . . id.

ἐρχομένη, nom. sg. f. pres. mid./pass. dep. part. . . . . id.

ἐρχομένην, acc. sg. f. pres. mid./pass. dep. part. (Acts 18:21, MT & TR | GNT, WH & NA omit) . . . . id.

ἐρχομένης, gen. sg. f. pres. mid./pass. dep. part. . . . . id.

ἐρχόμενοι, nom. pl. m. pres. mid./pass. dep. part. . . . . id.

ἐρχόμενον, acc. sg. m. pres. mid./pass. dep. part. {Matt. 16:28} . . . . id.

ἐρχόμενον, acc. sg. neut. pres. mid./pass. dep. part. {Matt. 3:16} . . . . id.

ἐρχόμενος, nom. sg. m. pres. mid./pass. dep. part. . . . . id.

ἐρχομένου, gen. sg. m. pres. mid./pass. dep. part. . . . . id.

ἐρχομένους, acc. pl. m. pres. mid./pass. dep. part. . . . . id.

ἐρχομένῳ, dat. sg. m. pres. mid./pass. dep. part. {Luke 18:30} . . . . id.

ἐρχομένῳ, dat. sg. neut. pres. mid./pass. dep. part. {Acts 13:44} . . . . id.

ἐρχομένων, gen. pl. m. pres. mid./pass. dep. part. . . . . id.

ἔρχονται, 3 pers. pl. pres. mid./pass. dep. indic. . . . . id.

ἔρχου, 2 pers. sg. pres. mid./pass. dep. imper. id.

ἔρχωμαι, 1 pers. sg. pres. mid./pass. dep. subj. (John 4:15, TR | διέρχωμαι, GNT, WH & NA | ἔρχομαι, MT) . . . . id.

ἐρῶ, 1 pers. sg. fut. act. indic. . . . . εἶπον *(‡3004)*

ἐρωτᾷ, 3 pers. sg. pres. act. indic. {John 16:5} . . . . ἐρωτάω *(2065)*

ἐρωτᾷ, 3 pers. sg. pres. act. subj. {John 16:30} . . . . id.

ἐρωτᾶν, pres. act. infin. (John 16:19, GNT, MT & NA | ἐρωτᾷν, WH & TR) . . . . id.

ἐρωτᾷς, 2 pers. sg. pres. act. indic. . . . . id.

(2065) **ἐρωτάω**, ῶ, fut. ἐρωτήσω [§18.R] *to ask, interrogate, inquire of,* Matt. 21:24; Luke 20:3; in N.T. *to ask, request, beg, beseech,* Matt. 15:23; Luke 4:38; John 14:16, et al.

ἐρωτῆσαι, aor. act. infin. . . . . ἐρωτάω *(2065)*

ἐρωτήσατε, 2 pers. pl. aor. act. imper. . . . id.

ἐρωτήσετε, 2 pers. pl. fut. act. indic. . . . . id.

ἐρωτήσῃ, 3 pers. sg. aor. act. subj. . . . . . . id.

ἐρώτησον, 2 pers. sg. aor. act. imper. (John 18:21, GNT, WH & NA | ἐπερώτησαν, MT & TR) . . . . id.

ἐρωτήσω, 1 pers. sg. fut. act. indic.

{Luke 20:3} . . . . ἐρωτάω *(2065)*

ἐρωτήσω, 1 pers. sg. aor. act. subj.

    {Luke 22:68} . . . . id.

ἐρωτήσωσιν, 3 pers. pl. aor. act. subj. . . . id.

ἐρωτῶ, 1 pers. sg. pres. act. indic. . . . . id.

ἐρωτῶμεν, 1 pers. pl. pres. act. indic. . . . . id.

ἐρωτῶν, nom. sg. m. pres. act. part. . . . . . id.

ἐρωτῶντες, nom. pl. m. pres. act. part. . . id.

ἐρωτώντων, gen. pl. m. pres. act. part. . . . id.

ἐσαλεύθη, 3 pers. sg. aor. pass. indic.

    [§14.N] . . . . σαλεύω *(4531)*

ἐσάλευσε(ν), 3 pers. sg. aor. act. indic. . . . id.

ἐσάλπισε(ν), 3 pers. sg. aor. act.

    indic. σαλπίζω *(4537)*

ἔσβεσαν, 3 pers. pl. aor. act. indic.

    [§36.5] . . . . σβέννυμι *(4570)*

ἐσεβάσθησαν, 3 pers. pl. aor. mid. dep. indic.

    [§26.1] . . . . σεβάζομαι *(4573)*

ἐσείσθη, 3 pers. sg. aor. pass. indic. . . . . σείω *(4579)*

ἐσείσθησαν, 3 pers. pl. aor. pass. indic.

    [§22.4] . . . . id.

ἔσεσθαι, fut. infin. . . . . εἰμί *(1510)*

ἔσεσθε, 2 pers. pl. fut. indic. . . . . id.

ἔσῃ, 2 pers. sg. fut. indic. . . . . id.

ἐσήμαινεν, 3 pers. sg. imperf. act. indic. (Acts
    11:28, WH | ἐσήμανεν(ν), GNT, MT, TR
    & NA) . . . . σημαίνω *(4591)*

ἐσήμανε(ν), 3 pers. sg. aor. act. indic.

    [§27.1.e] . . . . id.

(2066) ἐσθής, ῆτος, ἡ [§4.2.c] (ἕννυμι, *to clothe*) a
    robe, vestment, raiment, Luke 23:11; Acts
    1:10, et al.

ἐσθήσεσι(ν), dat. pl. f. n. . . . . ἔσθησις *(2067)*

(2067) ἔσθησις, εως, ἡ [§5.E.c] *a garment, robe, rai-
    ment,* Luke 24:4

ἐσθῆτα, acc. sg. f. n. . . . . ἐσθής *(2066)*

ἔσθητε, 2 pers. pl. pres. act. subj. (Luke 22:30,
    GNT, WH & NA | ἐσθίητε, MT &
    TR) . . . . ἔσθω *(†2068)*

ἐσθῆτι, dat. sg. f. n. . . . . ἐσθής *(2066)*

ἐσθίει, 3 pers. sg. pres. act. indic. . . . . . . ἐσθίω *(2068)*

ἐσθίειν, pres. act. infin. . . . . id.

ἐσθίετε, 2 pers. pl. pres. act. indic.
    {1 Cor. 10:31} . . . . id.

ἐσθίετε, 2 pers. pl. pres. act. imper.
    {1 Cor. 10:28} . . . . id.

ἐσθιέτω, 3 pers. sg. pres. act. imper. . . . . . id.

ἐσθίῃ, 3 pers. sg. pres. act. subj. . . . . id.

ἐσθίητε, 2 pers. pl. pres. act. subj. . . . . id.

ἐσθίοντα, acc. sg. m. pres. act. part. . . . . . id.

ἐσθίοντας, acc. pl. m. pres. act. part. (Mark
    7:2, MT & TR | ἐσθίουσιν, GNT, WH
    & NA) . . . . id.

ἐσθίοντες, nom. pl. m. pres. act. part. . . . id.

ἐσθίοντι, dat. sg. m. pres. act. part. . . . . . id.

ἐσθιόντων, gen. pl. m. pres. act. part. . . ἐσθίω *(2068)*

ἐσθίουσι(ν), 3 pers. pl. pres. act. indic. . . . id.

(2068) ἐσθίω, fut. φάγομαι, 2 aor. ἔφαγον [§36.1] *to
    eat,* Matt. 12:1; 15:27; ἐσθίειν καὶ πίνειν,
    to eat and drink, to eat and drink in the
    usual manner, follow the common mode
    of living,* Matt. 11:18; also with the associ-
    ated notion of supposed security, Luke
    17:27; *to feast, banquet,* Matt. 24:49; met.
    to *devour, consume,* Heb. 10:27; James
    5:3; from the Hebrew, ἄρτον ἐσθίειν, *to
    eat bread, to take food, take the usual
    meals,* Matt. 15:2, et al.

ἐσθίων, nom. sg. m. pres. act. part. . . . . ἐσθίω *(2068)*

ἐσθίωσιν, 3 pers. pl. pres. act. subj. . . . . . id.

ἔσθοντες, nom. pl. m. pres. act. part. (Luke
    10:7, WH | ἐσθίοντες, GNT, MT, TR &
    NA) . . . . ἔσθω *(†2068)*

(†2068) ἔσθω, equivalent to ἐσθίω

ἔσθων, nom. sg. m. pres. act. part. (Luke 7:33,
    WH | ἐσθίων, GNT, MT, TR &
    NA) . . . . ἔσθω *(†2068)*

ἐσίγησαν, 3 pers. pl. aor. act. indic. . . . σιγάω *(4601)*

ἐσίγησε(ν), 3 pers. sg. aor. act. indic. . . . . id.

ἐσιώπα, 3 pers. sg. imperf. act. indic. σιωπάω *(4623)*

ἐσιώπων, 3 pers. pl. imperf. act. indic. . . . id.

ἐσκανδαλίζοντο, 3 pers. pl. imperf. pass.
    indic. . . . . σκανδαλίζω *(4624)*

ἐσκανδαλίσθησαν, 3 pers. pl. aor. pass.
    indic. . . . . id.

ἔσκαψε(ν), 3 pers. sg. aor. act. indic. σκάπτω *(4626)*

ἐσκήνωσεν, 3 pers. sg. aor. act. indic. σκηνόω *(4637)*

ἐσκίρτησε(ν), 3 pers. sg. aor. act.
    indic. . . . . σκιρτάω *(4640)*

ἐσκληρύνοντο, 3 pers. pl. imperf. pass.
    indic. σκληρύνω *(4645)*

ἐσκόρπισεν, 3 pers. sg. aor. act.
    indic. . . . . σκορπίζω *(4650)*

ἐσκοτίσθη, 3 pers. sg. aor. pass.
    indic. . . . . σκοτίζω *(4654)*

ἐσκοτισμένοι, nom. pl. m. perf. pass. part.
    (Eph. 4:18, MT & TR | ἐσκοτωμένοι,
    GNT, WH & NA) . . . . id.

ἐσκοτώθη, 3 pers. sg. aor. pass. indic. (Rev.
    9:2, GNT, WH & NA | ἐσκοτίσθη, MT
    & TR) . . . . σκοτόω *(4656)*

ἐσκοτωμένη, nom. sg. f. perf. pass. part. . id.

ἐσκοτωμένοι, nom. pl. m. perf. pass. part.
    (Eph. 4:18, GNT, WH & NA | ἐσκο-
    τισμένοι, MT & TR) . . . . id.

ἐσκυλμένοι, nom. pl. m. perf. pass. part.
    (Matt. 9:36, GNT, WH, MT & NA |
    ἐκλελυμένοι, TR) . . . . σκύλλω *(4660)*

(2069) Ἐσλί, ὁ, *Esli,* pr. name, indecl. (Luke 3:25,
    GNT & NA | Ἐσλεί, WH | Ἐσλί,

MT & TR)

(2070) **ἐσμέν**, 1 pers. pl. pres. indic. . . . . εἰμί *(1510)*

ἐσμυρνισμένον, acc. sg. m. perf. pass.
part. . . . . σμυρνίζω *(4669)*

(2071) **ἔσομαι**, 1 pers. sg. fut. indic. . . . . εἰμί *(1510)*

ἐσόμεθα, 1 pers. pl. fut. indic. . . . . id.

ἐσόμενον, acc. sg. neut. fut. part. . . . . . . id.

ἐσόμενος, nom. sg. m. fut. part. (Rev. 16:5,
TR | ὅσιος, GNT, WH, MT & NA) . . id.

ἔσονται, 3 pers. pl. fut. indic. . . . . id.

(2072) **ἔσοπτρον**, ου, τό [§3.C.c] (ὄψομαι) *mirror,*
speculum, James 1:23; 1 Cor. 13:12

ἐσόπτρου, gen. sg. neut. n. . . . . ἔσοπτρον *(2072)*

ἐσόπτρῳ, dat. sg. neut. n. . . . . id.

ἐσπάραξεν, 3 pers. sg. aor. act. indic. [§26.3]
(Mark 9:20, MT & TR | συνεσπάραξεν,
GNT, WH & NA) . . . . σπαράσσω *(4682)*

ἐσπαργανωμένον, acc. sg. neut. perf. pass.
part. . . . . σπαργανόω *(4683)*

ἐσπαργάνωσεν, 3 pers. sg. aor. act. indic. id.

ἐσπαρμένον, acc. sg. m. perf. pass. part.
{Mark 4:15} . . . . σπείρω *(4687)*

ἐσπαρμένον, acc. sg. neut. perf. pass. part.
{Matt. 13:19} . . . . id.

ἐσπαταλήσατε, 2 pers. pl. aor. act.
indic. . . . . σπαταλάω *(4684)*

ἔσπειρα, 1 pers. sg. aor. act. indic. . . . σπείρω *(4687)*

ἐσπείραμεν, 1 pers. pl. aor. act. indic. . . . id.

ἔσπειρας, 2 pers. sg. aor. act. indic. . . . . . id.

ἔσπειρε(ν), 3 pers. sg. aor. act. indic. . . . . id.

(2073) **ἑσπέρα**, ας, ἡ, nom. sg. f. n. [§2.B.b; 2.2]
(fem. of ἕσπερος) *evening,* Luke 24:29;
Acts 4:3; 28:23

ἑσπέραν, acc. sg. f. n. . . . . ἑσπέρα *(2073)*

ἑσπέρας, gen. sg. f. n. . . . . id.

ἔσπευδε(ν), 3 pers. sg. imperf. act.
indic. . . . . σπεύδω *(4692)*

ἐσπιλωμένον, acc. sg. m. perf. pass. part.
[§21.U] . . . . σπιλόω *(4695)*

ἐσπλαγχνίσθη, 3 pers. sg. aor. pass. dep.
indic. . . . . σπλαγχνίζομαι *(4697)*

ἐσπούδασα, 1 pers. sg. aor. act.
indic. . . . . σπουδάζω *(4704)*

ἐσπουδάσαμεν, 1 pers. pl. aor. act. indic. . id.

(2074) **Ἐσρώμ**, ὁ, *Esrom,* pr. name, indecl.

(‡2274) **ἐσσόομαι**, οῦμαι, aor. ἡσσώθην [§21.U] *to be*
inferior to; to fare worse, to be in a less fa-
vored condition, 2 Cor. 12:13

ἐστάθη, 3 pers. sg. aor. pass. indic.
[§29.6] . . . . ἵστημι *(2476)*

ἐστάθην, 1 pers. sg. aor. pass. indic. (Rev.
12:18, TR; Rev. 13:1, MT | Rev. 12:18,
GNT, WH & NA) . . . . id.

ἐστάθησαν, 3 pers. pl. aor. pass. indic. (Luke
24:17, GNT, WH & NA | ἔστε, MT &

TR) . . . . ἵστημι *(2476)*

ἔσται, 3 pers. sg. fut. indic. [§12.L] . . . . . εἰμί *(1510)*

ἑστάναι, perf. act. infin. [§35.8] . . . . . ἵστημι *(2476)*

ἐσταυρώθη, 3 pers. sg. aor. pass.
indic. . . . . σταυρόω *(4717)*

ἐσταυρωμένον, acc. sg. m. perf. pass. part. id.

ἐσταυρωμένος, nom. sg. m. perf. pass. part. id.

ἐσταύρωσαν, 3 pers. pl. aor. act. indic. . . id.

ἐσταυρώσατε, 2 pers. pl. aor. act. indic. . . id.

ἐσταύρωται, 3 pers. sg. perf. pass. indic. . id.

(2075) **ἔστε**, 2 pers. pl. pres. indic. [§12.L] . . . . . εἰμί *(1510)*

ἐστέναξε(ν), 3 pers. sg. aor. act.
indic. . . . . στενάζω *(4727)*

ἐστερεοῦντο, 3 pers. pl. imperf. pass. indic.
[§21.U] . . . . στερεόω *(4732)*

ἐστερεώθησαν, 3 pers. pl. aor. pass. indic. id.

ἐστερέωσε(ν), 3 pers. sg. aor. act. indic. . . id.

ἐστεφανωμένον, acc. sg. m. perf. pass.
part. στεφανόω *(4737)*

ἐστεφάνωσας, 2 pers. sg. aor. act. indic. . id.

ἔστη, 3 pers. sg. 2 aor. act. indic.
[§29.1.5] . . . . ἵστημι *(2476)*

ἕστηκα, 1 pers. sg. perf. act. indic. [§38.2] id.

ἑστήκαμεν, 1 pers. pl. perf. act. indic.
[§29.4.5] . . . . id.

ἕστηκας, 2 pers. sg. perf. act. indic. . . . . . id.

ἑστήκασι(ν), 3 pers. pl. perf. act. indic. . . id.

ἑστήκατε, 2 pers. pl. perf. act. indic. . . . . id.

ἕστηκεν, 3 pers. sg. imperf. act. indic. (John
8:44, GNT, WH, MT & NA | ἔστηκεν,
TR) . . . . id.

ἕστηκε(ν), 3 pers. sg. perf. act. indic.
{John 1:26} . . . . id.

ἑστήκεισαν, 3 pers. pl. pluperf. act. indic.
Att. for εἱστήκεισαν [§29.4.5] (Rev. 7:11,
TR | εἱστήκεισαν, GNT, MT & NA |
ἱστήκεισαν, WH) . . . . id.

ἑστηκός, nom. sg. neut. perf. act. part. . . id.

ἑστηκότα, acc. sg. m. perf. act. part. (Mark
13:14, GNT, WH & NA | ἑστώς, MT &
TRb | ἑστός, TRs) . . . . id.

ἑστηκότες, nom. pl. m. perf. act. part. . . . id.

ἑστηκότων, gen. pl. m. perf. act. part. . . . id.

ἑστηκώς, nom. sg. m. perf. act. part. . . . . id.

ἐστηριγμένους, acc. pl. m. perf. pass.
part. . . . . στηρίζω *(4741)*

ἐστήρικται, 3 pers. sg. perf. pass. indic.
[§26.2] . . . . id.

ἐστήριξε(ν), 3 pers. sg. aor. act. indic. (Luke
9:51, MT & TR | ἐστήρισεν, GNT, WH
& NA) . . . . id.

ἐστήρισεν, 3 pers. sg. aor. act. indic. (Luke
9:51, GNT, WH & NA | ἐστήριξεν, MT
& TR) . . . . id.

ἔστησαν, 3 pers. pl. 2 aor. act. indic.

[§29.5] . . . . ἵστημι *(2476)*
ἕστησεν, 3 pers. sg. aor. act. indic. . . . . . . id.
(2076) ἐστί(ν), 3 pers. sg. pres. indic. . . . . εἰμί *(1510)*
ἐστός, acc. sg. neut. 2 perf. act. part. . . ἵστημι *(2476)*
ἐστράφη, 3 pers. sg. 2 aor. pass. indic.
[§24.10] . . . . στρέφω *(4762)*
ἐστράφησαν, 3 pers. pl. 2 aor. pass. indic. id.
ἔστρεψε(ν), 3 pers. sg. aor. act. indic. . . . . id.
ἐστρηνίασε(ν), 3 pers. sg. aor. act. indic. . id.
ἐστρωμένον, acc. sg. neut. perf. pass. part.
[§36.5] . . . . στρώννυμι *(4766)*
ἐστρώννυον, 3 pers. pl. imperf. act. indic. id.
ἔστρωσαν, 3 pers. pl. aor. act. indic. . . . . id.
(2077) ἔστω, 3 pers. sg. pres. imper. [§12.L] . . . . εἰμί *(1510)*
ἐστώς, nom. sg. m. perf. act. part.
[§35.8] . . . . ἵστημι *(2476)*
ἐστῶσα, nom. sg. f. perf. act. part. (John 8:9,
TR | οὖσα, GNT, WH, MT & NA) . . id.
ἐστῶσαι, nom. pl. f. perf. act. part. (Rev. 11:4,
TR | ἐστῶτες, GNT, WH, MT & NA) id.
ἔστωσαν, 3 pers. pl. pres. imper. [§12.L] . . εἰμί *(1510)*
ἐστῶτα, acc. sg. m. perf. act. part.
{John 20:14} . . . . ἵστημι *(2476)*
ἐστῶτα, acc. pl. neut. perf. act. part.
{Luke 5:2} . . . . id.
ἐστῶτας, acc. pl. m. perf. act. part. . . . . id.
ἐστῶτες, nom. pl. m. perf. act. part. . . . . id.
ἐστῶτος, gen. sg. m. perf. act. part. . . . . id.
ἐστώτων, gen. pl. m. perf. act. part. . . . . id.
ἐσυκοφάντησα, 1 pers. sg. aor. act.
indic. . . . . συκοφαντέω *(4811)*
ἐσύλησα, 1 pers. sg. aor. act. indic.
[§18.R] . . . . συλάω *(4813)*
ἔσυρον, 3 pers. pl. imperf. act. indic. . . . σύρω *(4951)*
ἐσφάγης, 2 pers. sg. 2 aor. pass. indic.
[§26.3] . . . . σφάζω *(4969)*
ἐσφαγμένην, acc. sg. f. perf. pass. part. . . id.
ἐσφαγμένον, nom. sg. neut. perf. pass. part. id.
ἐσφαγμένου, gen. sg. neut. perf. pass. part. id.
ἐσφαγμένων, gen. pl. m. perf. pass. part. . id.
ἔσφαξε(ν), 3 pers. sg. aor. act. indic. . . . . id.
ἐσφράγισεν, 3 pers. sg. aor. act.
indic. σφραγίζω *(4972)*
ἐσφραγίσθητε, 2 pers. pl. aor. pass. indic. . id.
ἐσφραγισμέναι, nom. pl. f. perf. pass. part.
(Rev. 7:5, 8, MT | ἐσφραγισμένοι, GNT,
WH, TR & NA) . . . . id.
ἐσφραγισμένοι, nom. pl. m. perf. pass. part. id.
ἐσφραγισμένων, gen. pl. m. perf. pass. part.
[§26.1] . . . . id.
ἔσχατα, nom. pl. neut. adj.
{Matt. 12:45} . . . . ἔσχατος *(2078)*
ἔσχατα, acc. pl. neut. adj. {Rev. 2:19} . . . id.
ἐσχάταις, dat. pl. f. adj. . . . . id.
ἐσχάτας, acc. pl. f. adj. . . . . id.

ἐσχάτη, nom. sg. f. adj. . . . . ἔσχατος *(2078)*
ἐσχάτῃ, dat. sg. f. adj. . . . . id.
ἔσχατοι, nom. pl. m. adj. . . . . id.
ἔσχατον, acc. sg. m. adj. {Matt. 5:26} . . . id.
ἔσχατον, acc. sg. neut. adj. {Mark 12:22} id.
(2078) **ἔσχατος**, η, ον, nom. sg. m. adj. [§8.6] *far-
thest; last, latest,* Matt. 12:45; Mark 12:6;
lowest, Matt. 19:30; 20:16, et al.; *in the
lowest plight,* 1 Cor. 4:9
ἐσχάτου, gen. sg. m. adj. {Jude 18} . . ἔσχατος *(2078)*
ἐσχάτου, gen. sg. neut. adj. {Heb. 1:2} . . . id.
ἐσχάτους, acc. pl. m. adj. . . . . id.
ἐσχάτῳ, dat. sg. m. adj. . . . . id.
ἐσχάτων, gen. pl. m. adj. {Matt. 20:8} . . id.
ἐσχάτων, gen. pl. f. adj. {Rev. 21:9} . . . . . id.
(2079) **ἐσχάτως**, adv., *extremely;* ἐσχάτως ἔχειν, *to
be in the last extremity,* Mark 5:23
ἔσχε(ν), 3 pers. sg. 2 aor. act. indic.
[§36.4] . . . . ἔχω *(2192)*
ἔσχες, 2 pers. sg. 2 aor. act. indic. . . . . . . id.
ἔσχηκα, 1 pers. sg. perf. act. indic. . . . . . . id.
ἐσχήκαμεν, 1 pers. pl. perf. act. indic. . . . id.
ἔσχηκεν, 3 pers. sg. perf. act. indic. . . . . . id.
ἐσχηκότα, acc. sg. m. perf. act. part. . . . . id.
ἐσχίσθη, 3 pers. sg. aor. pass. indic.
[§26.1] . . . . σχίζω *(4977)*
ἐσχίσθησαν, 3 pers. pl. aor. pass. indic. . . id.
ἔσχομεν, 1 pers. pl. 2 aor. act. indic. . . . ἔχω *(2192)*
ἔσχον, 1 pers. sg. 2 aor. act. indic. {Jude 3} id.
ἔσχον, 3 pers. pl. 2 aor. act. indic.
{Matt. 22:28} . . . . id.
(2080) **ἔσω**, adv., for the more usual form εἴσω, *in,
within, in the interior of,* Matt. 26:58; John
20:26, et al.; ὁ, ἡ, τὸ ἔσω, *inner, interior,
internal;* met. *within* the pale of community, 1 Cor. 5:12; ὁ ἔσω ἄνθρωπος, *the inner man, the mind, soul,* Rom. 7:22
ἐσῴζοντο, 3 pers. pl. imperf. pass. indic.
(Mark 6:56, GNT & NA | ἐσώζοντο,
WH, MT & TR) . . . . σῴζω *(†4982)*
(2081) **ἔσωθεν**, adv., *from within, from the interior,*
Mark 7:21, 23; *within, in the internal
parts,* Matt. 7:15, et al.; ὁ, ἡ, τὸ ἔσωθεν,
interior, internal, Luke 11:39, 40; ὁ ἔσωθεν
ἄνθρωπος, *the mind, soul,* 2 Cor. 4:16
ἐσώθη, 3 pers. sg. aor. pass. indic.
[§37.1] . . . . σῴζω *(†4982)*
ἐσώθημεν, 1 pers. pl. aor. pass. indic. . . . . id.
ἔσωσε(ν), 3 pers. sg. aor. act. indic. . . . . . id.
ἐσωτέραν, acc. sg. f. adj. . . . . ἐσώτερος *(2082)*
ἐσώτερον, acc. sg. neut. adj. . . . . id.
(2082) **ἐσώτερος**, α, ον [§7.1] *inner, interior,* Acts
16:24; Heb. 6:19
ἑταῖρε, voc. sg. m. n. . . . . ἑταῖρος *(2083)*
ἑταίροις, dat. pl. m. n. (Matt. 11:16, TR |

ἑτέροις, GNT, WH, MT & NA) .. ἑταῖρος *(2083)*

(2083) **ἑταῖρος, ου, ὁ** [§3.C.a] *a companion, associate, fellow-comrade, friend,* Matt. 11:16; 20:13; 22:12; 26:50

ἔταξαν, 3 pers. pl. aor. act. indic. ..... τάσσω *(5021)*

ἐτάξατο, 3 pers. sg. aor. mid. indic. ..... id.

ἐταπείνωσεν, 3 pers. sg. aor. act. indic. .... ταπεινόω *(5013)*

ἐτάραξαν, 3 pers. pl. aor. act. indic. ταράσσω *(5015)*

ἐτάραξεν, 3 pers. sg. aor. act. indic. ..... id.

ἐτάρασσε(ν), 3 pers. sg. imperf. act. indic. (John 5:4, MT & TR | GNT, WH & NA omit) .... id.

ἐταράχθη, 3 pers. sg. aor. pass. indic. .... id.

ἐταράχθησαν, 3 pers. pl. aor. pass. indic. . id.

ἐτάφη, 3 pers. sg. 2 aor. pass. indic. [§24.8.b] .... θάπτω *(2290)*

ἐτέθη, 3 pers. sg. aor. pass. indic. [§28.10] .... τίθημι *(5087)*

ἐτέθην, 1 pers. sg. aor. pass. indic. ...... id.

ἐτέθησαν, 3 pers. pl. aor. pass. indic. .... id.

ἐτεθνήκει, 3 pers. sg. pluperf. act. indic. [§36.4] (John 11:21, MT & TR | ἀπέθανεν, GNT, WH & NA) .... θνήσκω *(2348)*

ἔτει, dat. sg. neut. n. .... ἔτος *(2094)*

ἔτεκε(ν), 3 pers. sg. 2 aor. act. indic. [§37.1] .... τίκτω *(5088)*

ἐτεκνοτρόφησεν, 3 pers. sg. aor. act. indic. .... τεκνοτροφέω *(5044)*

ἐτελειώθη, 3 pers. sg. aor. pass. indic. [§21.U] .... τελειόω *(5048)*

ἐτελείωσα, 1 pers. sg. aor. act. indic. [§20.T] (John 17:4, MT & TR | τελειώσας, GNT, WH & NA) .... id.

ἐτελείωσεν, 3 pers. sg. aor. act. indic. .... id.

ἐτέλεσαν, 3 pers. pl. aor. act. indic. ... τελέω *(5055)*

ἐτέλεσεν, 3 pers. sg. aor. act. indic. ..... id.

ἐτελέσθη, 3 pers. sg. aor. pass. indic. [§22.4] id.

ἐτελεύτησε(ν), 3 pers. sg. aor. act. indic. .... τελευτάω *(5053)*

ἑτέρα, nom. sg. f. adj. {John 19:37} ... ἕτερος *(2087)*

ἕτερα, acc. pl. neut. adj. {Matt. 12:45} ... id.

ἑτέρᾳ, dat. sg. f. adj. .... id.

ἕτεραι, nom. pl. f. adj. .... id.

ἑτέραις, dat. pl. f. adj. .... id.

ἑτέραν, acc. sg. f. adj. .... id.

ἑτέρας, gen. sg. f. adj. .... id.

ἑτερογλώσσοις, dat. pl. m. adj. ἑτερόγλωσσος *(2084)*

(2084) **ἑτερόγλωσσος, ον** [§7.2] (ἕτερος + γλῶσσα) *one who speaks another or foreign language,* 1 Cor. 14:21

ἑτεροδιδασκαλεῖ, 3 pers. sg. pres. act. indic. .... ἑτεροδιδασκαλέω *(2085)*

ἑτεροδιδασκαλεῖν, pres. act. infin. ...... id.

(2085) **ἑτεροδιδασκαλέω, ῶ,** fut. ἑτεροδιδασκα-

λήσω [§16.P] (ἕτερος + διδασκαλία) *to teach other or different doctrine,* and spc. *what is foreign to the Christian religion,* 1 Tim. 1:3; 6:3

(2086) **ἑτεροζυγέω, ῶ** (ἕτερος + ζυγέω) *to be unequally yoked or matched,* 2 Cor. 6:14

ἑτεροζυγοῦντες, nom. pl. m. pres. act. part. .... ἑτεροζυγέω *(2086)*

ἕτεροι, nom. pl. m. adj. .... ἕτερος *(2087)*

ἑτέροις, dat. pl. m. adj. {Acts 2:40} ..... id.

ἑτέροις, dat. pl. neut. adj. {Matt. 11:16} .. id.

ἕτερον, acc. sg. m. adj. {Acts 12:17} ..... id.

ἕτερον, nom. sg. neut. adj. {Acts 4:12} ... id.

ἕτερον, acc. sg. neut. adj. {2 Cor. 11:4} .. id.

(2087) **ἕτερος, α, ον,** nom. sg. m. adj. [§10.6.b] *other,* Matt. 12:45, et al.; *another, some other,* Matt. 8:21, et al.; *besides,* Luke 23:32; ὁ ἕτερος, *the other* of two, Matt. 6:24; τῇ ἑτέρᾳ, *on the next day,* Acts 20:15; 27:3; ὁ ἕτερος, *one's neighbor,* Rom. 13:8, et al.; *different,* Luke 9:29, et al.; *foreign, strange,* Acts 2:4; 1 Cor. 14:21; *illicit,* Jude 7

ἑτέρου, gen. sg. m. adj. .... ἕτερος *(2087)*

ἑτέρους, acc. pl. m. adj. .... id.

ἑτέρῳ, dat. sg. m. adj. {Luke 14:31} ..... id.

ἑτέρῳ, dat. sg. neut. adj. {Luke 5:7} ..... id.

ἑτέρων, gen. pl. m. adj. {2 Cor. 8:8} ... id.

ἑτέρων, gen. pl. neut. adj. (Acts 19:39, MT & TR | περαιτέω, GNT, WH & NA) . id.

(2088) **ἑτέρως,** adv., *otherwise, differently,* Phil. 3:15

ἔτεσι(ν), dat. pl. neut. n. .... ἔτος *(2094)*

ἐτέχθη, 3 pers. sg. aor. pass. indic. [§37.1] .... τίκτω *(5088)*

ἔτη, nom. pl. neut. n. {Heb. 1:12} ...... ἔτος *(2094)*

ἔτη, acc. pl. neut. n. {John 5:5} .... id.

ἐτηρεῖτο, 3 pers. sg. imperf. pass. indic. [§17.Q] .... τηρέω *(5083)*

ἐτήρησα, 1 pers. sg. aor. act. indic. ...... id.

ἐτήρησαν, 3 pers. pl. aor. act. indic. ..... id.

ἐτήρησας, 2 pers. sg. aor. act. indic. ..... id.

ἐτήρουν, 1 pers. sg. imperf. act. indic. {John 17:12} .... id.

ἐτήρουν, 3 pers. pl. imperf. act. indic. {Matt. 27:36} .... id.

(2089) **ἔτι,** adv., *yet, still,* Matt. 12:46; *still, further, longer,* Luke 16:2; *further, besides, in addition,* Matt. 18:16; *with a compar. yet, still,* Phil. 1:9

ἐτίθει, 3 pers. sg. imperf. act. indic. [§31.2] .... τίθημι *(5087)*

ἐτίθεσαν, 3 pers. pl. imperf. act. indic. (Mark 6:56, GNT, WH & NA | ἐτίθουν, MT & TR) .... id.

ἐτίθουν, 3 pers. pl. imperf. act. indic. .... id.

ἔτιλλον, 3 pers. pl. imperf. act. indic. ... τίλλω *(5089)*

ἐτίμησαν, 3 pers. pl. aor. act. indic. . . . . τιμάω *(5091)*
ἐτιμήσαντο, 3 pers. pl. aor. mid. indic. . . . id.
ἕτοιμα, nom. pl. neut. adj.
{Luke 14:17} . . . . ἕτοιμος *(2092)*
ἕτοιμα, acc. pl. neut. adj. {2 Cor. 10:16} . . id.
ἑτοίμαζε, 2 pers. sg. pres. act. imper. ἑτοιμάζω *(2090)*
(2090) **ἑτοιμάζω,** fut. ἑτοιμάσω [§26.1] *to make ready, prepare,* Matt. 22:4; 26:17, et al.
ἑτοιμάσαι, aor. act. infin. . . . . ἑτοιμάζω *(2090)*
ἑτοιμάσας, nom. sg. m. aor. act. part. . . . id.
ἑτοιμάσατε, 2 pers. pl. aor. act. imper. . . . id.
ἑτοιμασθῇ, 3 pers. sg. aor. pass. subj. . . . . id.
(2091) **ἑτοιμασία,** ας, ἡ [§2.B.b; 2.2] *preparation; preparedness, readiness, alacrity,* Eph. 6:15
ἑτοιμασίᾳ, dat. sg. f. n. . . . . ἑτοιμασία *(2091)*
ἑτοιμάσομεν, 1 pers. pl. fut. act. indic. (Matt. 26:17; Mark 14:12; Luke 22:9, MT | GNT, WH, TR & NA) . . . . ἑτοιμάζω *(2090)*
ἑτοίμασον, 2 pers. sg. aor. act. imper. . . . . id.
ἑτοιμάσω, 1 pers. sg. aor. act. subj. . . . . . id.
ἑτοιμάσωμεν, 1 pers. pl. aor. act. subj. (Matt. 26:17; Mark 14:12; Luke 22:9, GNT, WH, NA & TR | ἑτοιμάσομεν, MT) . . . . . . id.
ἑτοίμην, acc. sg. f. adj. . . . . ἕτοιμος *(2092)*
ἕτοιμοι, nom. pl. m. adj. {Matt. 24:44} . . id.
ἕτοιμοι, nom. pl. f. adj. {Matt. 25:10} . . . id.
ἕτοιμον, acc. sg. neut. adj. . . . . id.
(2092) **ἕτοιμος,** η, ον, nom. sg. m. adj., *ready, prepared,* Matt. 22:4, 8; Mark 14:15, et al.
ἑτοίμους, acc. pl. m. adj. . . . . ἕτοιμος *(2092)*
ἑτοίμῳ, dat. sg. m. adj. . . . . id.
(2093) **ἑτοίμως,** adv., *in readiness, preparedly,* Acts 21:13, et al.
ἐτόλμα, 3 pers. sg. imperf. act. indic.
[§18.R] . . . . τολμάω *(5111)*
ἐτόλμησε(ν), 3 pers. sg. aor. act. indic. . . . id.
ἐτόλμων, 3 pers. pl. imperf. act. indic. . . . id.
(2094) **ἔτος,** ους, τό [§5.E.b] *a year,* Luke 2:41; 3:23, et al.
ἔτος, acc. sg. neut. n. . . . . ἔτος *(2094)*
ἐτρέχετε, 2 pers. pl. imperf. act. indic. . τρέχω *(5143)*
ἔτρεχον, 3 pers. pl. imperf. act. indic. . . . . id.
ἐτροποφόρησεν, 3 pers. sg. aor. act.
indic. τροποφορέω *(5159)*
ἐτρύγησε(ν), 3 pers. sg. aor. act. indic. τρυγάω *(5166)*
ἐτρυφήσατε, 2 pers. pl. aor. act. indic. τρυφάω *(5171)*
ἐτύθη, 3 pers. sg. aor. pass. indic. [§14.N]
(1 Cor. 5:7, GNT, WH, MT, TRs & NA
| ἐθύθη, TRb) . . . . θύω *(2380)*
ἐτυμπανίσθησαν, 3 pers. pl. aor. pass.
indic. . . . . τυμπανίζω *(5178)*
ἔτυπτεν, 3 pers. sg. imperf. act. indic. . . τύπτω *(5180)*
ἔτυπτον, 3 pers. pl. imperf. act. indic. . . . . id.
ἐτύφλωσε(ν), 3 pers. sg. aor. act.
indic. . . . . τυφλόω *(5186)*

ἐτῶν, gen. pl. neut. n. . . . . ἔτος *(2094)*
(2095) **εὖ,** adv., *well, good, happily, rightly,* Mark 14:7; Acts 15:29; *Well! Well done!* Matt. 25:21, 23, et al.
(†2096) **Εὖα,** ας, ἡ, nom. sg. f. n., *Eva, Eve,* pr. name (1 Tim. 2:13, GNT, WH, MT & NA | Εὕα, TR)
εὐαγγελίζεσθαι, pres. mid. infin. . . εὐαγγελίζω *(2097)*
εὐαγγελίζεται, 3 pers. sg. pres. mid. indic.
{Gal. 1:9, 23} . . . . id.
εὐαγγελίζεται, 3 pers. sg. pres. pass. indic.
{Luke 16:16} . . . . id.
εὐαγγελίζηται, 3 pers. sg. pres. mid. subj.
(Gal. 1:8, GNT, TR & NA | εὐαγγελίζεται, MT | εὐαγγελίσηται, WH) . . . . id.
εὐαγγελίζομαι, 2 pers. sg. pres. mid. indic. id.
εὐαγγελιζόμεθα, 1 pers. pl. pres. mid. indic. id.
εὐαγγελιζόμενοι, nom. pl. m. pres. mid. part. id.
εὐαγγελιζόμενος, nom. sg. m. pres. mid.
part. . . . . id.
εὐαγγελιζομένου, gen. sg. m. pres. mid. part. id.
εὐαγγελιζομένῳ, dat. sg. m. pres. mid. part. id.
εὐαγγελιζομένων, gen. pl. m. pres. mid. part. id.
εὐαγγελίζονται, 3 pers. pl. pres. pass. indic. id.
(2097) **εὐαγγελίζω,** fut. εὐαγγελίσω [§26.1] *to address with good tidings,* Rev. 10:7; 14:6; but elsewhere mid. εὐαγγελίζομαι, *to proclaim as good tidings, to announce good tidings of,* Luke 1:19, et al.; *to address with good tidings,* Acts 13:32; 14:15; *to address with Gospel teaching, evangelize,* Acts 16:10; Gal. 1:9; absol. *to announce the good tidings* of the Gospel, Luke 4:18; 9:6, et al.; pass. *to be announced as good tidings,* Luke 16:16; *to be addressed with good tidings,* Matt. 11:5; Luke 7:22; Heb. 4:2
εὐαγγελίζωμαι, 1 pers. sg. pres. mid.
subj. . . . . εὐαγγελίζω *(2097)*
(2098) **εὐαγγέλιον,** ου, τό, nom. sg. neut. n. [§3.C.e] (εὖ + ἄγγελος) *glad tidings, good or joyful news,* Matt. 4:23; 9:35; *the Gospel; doctrines of the Gospel,* Matt. 26:13; Mark 8:35; meton. *the preaching of, or instruction in, the Gospel,* 1 Cor. 4:15; 9:14, et al. {1 Thess. 1:5}
εὐαγγέλιον, acc. sg. neut. n.
{1 Thess. 2:2} . . . . εὐαγγέλιον *(2098)*
εὐαγγελίου, gen. sg. neut. n. . . . . id.
εὐαγγελίσαι, aor. act. infin. . . . . . εὐαγγελίζω *(2097)*
εὐαγγελισάμενοι, nom. pl. m. aor. mid. part. id.
εὐαγγελισαμένου, gen. sg. m. aor. mid. part. id.
εὐαγγελισαμένων, gen. pl. m. aor. mid. part. id.
εὐαγγελίσασθαι, aor. mid. infin. . . . . id.
εὐαγγελίσηται, 3 pers. sg. aor. mid. subj. (Gal. 1:8, WH | εὐαγγελίζηται, GNT, TR &

NA | εὐαγγελίζεται, MT) . . . . εὐαγγελίζω *(2097)*
εὐαγγελισθέν, nom. sg. neut. aor. pass. part.
{1 Pet. 1:25} . . . . id.
εὐαγγελισθέν, acc. sg. neut. aor. pass. part.
{Gal. 1:11} . . . . id.
εὐαγγελισθέντες, nom. pl. m. aor. pass. part. id.
εὐαγγελιστάς, acc. pl. m. n. . . . εὐαγγελιστής *(2099)*
(2099) **εὐαγγελιστής**, οῦ, ὁ [§2.B.c] pr. *one who an-nounces glad tidings; an evangelist, preacher of the Gospel, teacher of the Christian religion,* Acts 21:8; Eph. 4:11; 2 Tim. 4:5
εὐαγγελιστοῦ, gen. sg. m. n. . . . εὐαγγελιστής *(2099)*
εὐαγγελίσωμαι, 1 pers. pl. aor. mid.
subj. . . . . εὐαγγελίζω *(2097)*
εὐαγγελίῳ, dat. sg. neut. n. . . . . . . εὐαγγέλιον *(2098)*
Εὔαν, acc. sg. f. n. (2 Cor. 11:3, GNT, WH, MT & NA | Εὔαν, TR) . . . . Εὔα *(†2096)*
εὐαρεστεῖται, 3 pers. sg. pres. pass. indic.
[§17.Q] . . . . εὐαρεστέω *(2100)*
(2100) **εὐαρεστέω**, ῶ, fut. εὐαρεστήσω, perf. εὐηρέστηκα [§16.P] *to please well,* Heb. 11:5, 6; pass. *to take pleasure in, be well pleased with,* Heb. 13:6
εὐαρεστηκέναι, perf. act. infin. (Heb. 11:5, GNT, WH & NA | εὐηρεστηκέναι, MT & TR) . . . . εὐαρεστέω *(2100)*
εὐαρεστῆσαι, aor. act. infin. . . . . id.
εὐάρεστοι, nom. pl. m. adj. . . . . . . εὐάρεστος *(2101)*
εὐάρεστον, acc. sg. f. adj. {Rom. 12:1} . . . id.
εὐάρεστον, nom. sg. neut. adj. {Rom. 12:2} id.
εὐάρεστον, acc. sg. neut. adj. {Heb. 13:21} id.
(2101) **εὐάρεστος**, ον, nom. sg. m. adj. [§7.2] (εὐ + ἀρεστός, from ἀρέσκω) *well-pleasing, ac-ceptable, grateful,* Rom. 12:1, 2, et al.
εὐαρέστους, acc. pl. m. adj. . . . . . εὐάρεστος *(2101)*
(2102) **εὐαρέστως**, adv., *acceptably,* Heb. 12:28
(2103) **Εὔβουλος**, ου, ὁ, nom. sg. m. n. [§3.C.a] *Eu-bulus,* pr. name, 2 Tim. 4:21
(‡2095) **εὖγε**, adv., *Well done!* (Luke 19:17, GNT, WH & NA | Εὖ, MT & TR)
εὐγενεῖς, nom. pl. m. adj. . . . . εὐγενής *(†2104)*
εὐγενέστεροι, nom. pl. m. compar. adj. [§8.1] id.
(†2104) **εὐγενής**, ές, nom. sg. m. adj. [§7.4.a] (εὐ + γένος) *well-born, of high rank, honorable,* Luke 19:12; 1 Cor. 1:26; *generous, ingen-uous, candid,* Acts 17:11
(2105) **εὐδία**, ας, ἡ, nom. sg. f. n. [§2.B.b; 2.2] (εὐ + Ζεύς, Διός, *Jupiter,* lord of the air and heavens) *serenity of the heavens, a cloud-less sky, fair or fine weather,* Matt. 16:2
εὐδοκεῖ, 3 pers. sg. pres. act. indic. . . εὐδοκέω *(2106)*
(2106) **εὐδοκέω**, ῶ, fut. εὐδοκήσω [§16.P] (εὐ + δοκέω) *to think well, approve, acquiesce, take delight or pleasure,* Matt. 3:17; 17:5;

Mark 1:11; Luke 3:22; 12:32; et al.
εὐδόκησα, 1 pers. sg. aor. act. indic.
[§34.3.c] . . . . εὐδοκέω *(2106)*
εὐδοκήσαμεν, 1 pers. pl. aor. act. indic.
(1 Thess. 3:1, GNT, MT, TR & NA | ηὐδοκήσαμεν, WH) . . . . id.
εὐδόκησαν, 3 pers. pl. aor. act. indic. (Rom. 15:26, 27, GNT, MT, TR & NA | ηὐδόκησαν, WH) . . . . id.
εὐδοκήσαντες, nom. pl. m. aor. act. part. id.
εὐδόκησας, 2 pers. sg. aor. act. indic. . . . . id.
εὐδόκησε(ν), 3 pers. sg. aor. act. indic. . . . id.
(2107) **εὐδοκία**, ας, ἡ, nom. sg. f. n. [§2.B.b; 2.2] *ap-probation; good will, favor,* Luke 2:14; *good pleasure, purpose, intention,* Matt. 11:26; Luke 10:21; Eph. 1:5, 9; Phil. 2:13; by impl. *desire,* Rom. 10:1
εὐδοκίαν, acc. sg. f. n. . . . . εὐδοκία *(2107)*
εὐδοκίας, gen. sg. f. n. . . . . id.
εὐδοκοῦμεν, 1 pers. pl. pres. act. indic.
{2 Cor. 5:8} . . . . εὐδοκέω *(2106)*
εὐδοκοῦμεν, 1 pers. pl. imperf. act. indic.
{1 Thess. 2:8} . . . . id.
εὐδοκῶ, 1 pers. sg. pres. act. indic. . . . . . . id.
(2108) **εὐεργεσία**, ας, ἡ [§2.B.b; 2.2] *well-doing, a good deed, benefit conferred,* Acts 4:9; *duty, good offices,* 1 Tim. 6:2
εὐεργεσίᾳ, dat. sg. f. n. . . . . εὐεργεσία *(2108)*
εὐεργεσίας, gen. sg. f. n. . . . . id.
εὐεργέται, nom. pl. m. n. . . . . εὐεργέτης *(2110)*
(2109) **εὐεργετέω**, ῶ, fut. εὐεργετήσω [§16.P] *to do good, exercise beneficence,* Acts 10:38
(2110) **εὐεργέτης**, ου, ὁ [§2.B.c] (εὐ + ἔργον) *a well-doer; a benefactor,* Luke 22:25
εὐεργετῶν, nom. sg. m. pres. act.
part. . . . . εὐεργετέω *(2109)*
εὐηγγελίζετο, 3 pers. sg. imperf. mid.
indic. εὐαγγελίζω *(2097)*
εὐηγγελίζοντο, 3 pers. pl. imperf. mid. indic.
(Acts 8:25, GNT, WH & NA | εὐηγγε-λίσαντο, MT & TR) . . . . id.
εὐηγγελισάμεθα, 1 pers. pl. aor. mid. indic. id.
εὐηγγελισάμην, 1 pers. sg. aor. mid. indic. id.
εὐηγγελίσαντο, 3 pers. pl. aor. mid. indic.
(Acts 8:25, MT & TR | εὐηγγελίζοντο, GNT, WH & NA) . . . . id.
εὐηγγελίσατο, 3 pers. sg. aor. mid. indic. . id.
εὐηγγέλισε(ν), 3 pers. sg. aor. act. indic. . . id.
εὐηγγελίσθη, 3 pers. sg. aor. pass. indic. . . id.
εὐηγγελισμένοι, nom. pl. m. perf. pass. part. id.
εὐηρεστηκέναι, perf. act. infin. [§34.3.b]
(Heb. 11:5, MT & TR | εὐαρεστηκέναι, GNT, WH & NA) . . . . εὐαρεστέω *(2100)*
εὐθεῖα, nom. sg. f. adj. . . . . εὐθύς *(2117)*
εὐθεῖαν, acc. sg. f. adj. . . . . id.

εὐθείας, acc. pl. f. adj. . . . . εὐθύς (2117)

εὔθετον, acc. sg. f. adj. {Heb. 6:7} . . . . εὔθετος (2111)

εὔθετον, nom. sg. neut. adj. {Luke 14:35} .   id.

(2111) εὔθετος, ον, nom. sg. m. adj. [§7.2] (εὐ + τίθημι) pr. *well arranged, rightly disposed; fit, proper, adapted,* Luke 9:62; 14:35; *useful,* Heb. 6:7

(2112) εὐθέως, adv., *immediately, forthwith, instantly, at once,* Matt. 8:3; 13:5, et al.

(2113) εὐθυδρομέω, ῶ, fut. εὐθυδρομήσω [§16.P] (εὐθύς + δρόμος) *to run on a straight course; to sail on a direct course,* Acts 16:11; 21:1

εὐθυδρομήσαμεν, 1 pers. pl. aor. act. indic. εὐθυδρομέω (2113)

εὐθυδρομήσαντες, nom. pl. m. aor. act. part.   id.

εὐθυμεῖ, 3 pers. sg. pres. act. indic. . . . εὐθυμέω (2114)

εὐθυμεῖν, pres. act. infin. . . . .   id.

εὐθυμεῖτε, 2 pers. pl. pres. act. imper. . . . .   id.

(2114) εὐθυμέω, ῶ, fut. εὐθυμήσω [§16.P] *to be cheerful, be in good spirits, take courage,* Acts 27:22, 25; James 5:13

εὔθυμοι, nom. pl. m. adj. . . . . εὔθυμος (2115)

(2115) εὔθυμος, ον [§7.2] (εὐ + θυμός) *to good cheer or courage, cheerful,* Acts 27:36

(†2115) εὐθυμότερον, adv. [§8.4] (pr. neut. compar. of the preceding) *more cheerfully* (Acts 24:10, MT & TR | GNT, WH & NA)

(†2115) εὐθύμως, adv., *cheerfully* (Acts 24:10, GNT, WH & NA | εὐθυμότερον, MT & TR)

εὐθύνατε, 2 pers. pl. aor. act. imper. [§13.3] . . . . εὐθύνω (2116)

εὐθύνοντος, gen. sg. m. pres. act. part. . . .   id.

(2116) εὐθύνω, fut. εὐθυνῶ, aor. εὔθυνα [§27.1.a,f] *to guide straight; to direct, guide, steer* a ship, James 3:4; *to make straight,* John 1:23

(2117) εὐθύς, εῖα, ύ [§7.H.g] *straight,* Matt. 3:3; Mark 1:3; met. *right, upright, true,* Acts 8:21, et al.

(†2117) εὐθύς, adv., *straight forwards; directly, immediately, instantly, forthwith,* Matt. 3:16; 13:20, 21, et al.

(2118) εὐθύτης, τητος, ἡ [§4.2.c] *rectitude, righteousness, equity,* Heb. 1:8

εὐθύτητος, gen. sg. f. n. . . . . εὐθύτης (2118)

(2119) εὐκαιρέω, ῶ, fut. εὐκαιρήσω [§16.P] aor. ηὐκαίρησα, *to have convenient time or opportunity, have leisure,* Mark 6:31; 1 Cor. 16:12; *to be at leisure* for a thing, *to be disposed to attend, to give time,* Acts 17:21

εὐκαιρήσῃ, 3 pers. sg. aor. act. subj. εὐκαιρέω (2119)

(2120) εὐκαιρία, ας, ἡ [§2.B.b; 2.2] *convenient opportunity, favorable occasion,* Matt. 26:16; Luke 22:6

εὐκαιρίαν, acc. sg. f. n. . . . . εὐκαιρία (2120)

εὔκαιρον, acc. sg. f. adj. . . . . εὔκαιρος (2121)

(2121) εὔκαιρος, ον [§7.2] (εὐ + καιρός) *timely, opportune, seasonable, convenient,* Mark 6:21; Heb. 4:16

εὐκαίρου, gen. sg. f. adj. . . . . εὔκαιρος (2121)

εὐκαίρουν, 3 pers. pl. imperf. act. indic. . . . . εὐκαιρέω (2119)

(2122) εὐκαίρως, adv., *opportunely, seasonable, conveniently,* Mark 14:11; 2 Tim. 4:2

εὐκοπώτερον, nom. sg. neut. compar. adj. . . . . εὐκοπώτερος (2123)

(2123) εὐκοπώτερος, α, ον, compar. of εὔκοπος, *easy* (from εὐ + κόπος) [§8.4] *easier, more feasible,* Matt. 9:5; 19:24; Mark 2:9, et al.

(2124) εὐλάβεια, ας, ἡ [§2.B.b; 2.2] *the disposition of one who is* εὐλαβής, *caution, circumspection;* in N.T. *reverence* to God, *piety,* Heb. 5:7; 12:28

εὐλαβείας, gen. sg. f. n. . . . . εὐλάβεια (2124)

εὐλαβεῖς, nom. pl. m. adj. . . . . εὐλαβής (2126)

(2125) εὐλαβέομαι, οῦμαι, fut. εὐλαβήσομαι, aor. (pass. form) ηὐλαβήθην [§17.Q] *to be cautious or circumspect; to fear, be afraid or apprehensive,* Acts 23:10; in N.T. absol. *to reverence* God, *to be influenced by pious awe,* Heb. 11:7

εὐλαβηθείς, nom. sg. m. aor. pass. part. . . . . εὐλαβέομαι (2125)

(2126) εὐλαβής, ές, nom. sg. m. adj. [§7.G.b] (εὐ + λαμβάνω) pr. *taking hold of well,* i.e., *warily;* hence, *cautious, circumspect; full of reverence* towards God, *devout, pious, religious,* Luke 2:25; Acts 2:5; 8:2

εὐλόγει, 3 pers. sg. imperf. act. indic. (Mark 10:16, MT | κατευλόγει, GNT, WH & NA | ηὐλόγει, TR) . . . . εὐλογέω (2127)

εὐλογεῖν, pres. act. infin. . . . .   id.

εὐλογεῖται, 3 pers. sg. pres. pass. indic. [§17.Q] . . . .   id.

εὐλογεῖτε, 2 pers. pl. pres. act. imper. . . . .   id.

(2127) εὐλογέω, ῶ, fut. εὐλογήσω, perf. εὐλόγηκα [§16.P] (εὐ + λόγος) pr. *to speak well of,* in N.T. *to bless, ascribe praise and glorification,* Luke 1:64, et al.; *to bless, invoke a blessing upon,* Matt. 5:44, et al.; *to bless, confer a favor or blessing upon,* Eph. 1:3; Heb. 6:14; pass. *to be blessed, to be an object of favor or blessing,* Luke 1:28, et al.

εὐλογηθήσονται, 3 pers. pl. fut. pass. indic. (Acts 3:25, WH | ἐνευλογηθήσονται, GNT, MT, TR & NA) . . . . εὐλογέω (2127)

εὐλόγηκε(ν), 3 pers. sg. perf. act. indic. . .   id.

εὐλογημένη, nom. sg. f. perf. pass. part. .   id.

εὐλογημένοι, nom. pl. m. perf. pass. part.   id.

εὐλογημένος, nom. sg. m. perf. pass. part.   id.

εὐλογῆς, 2 pers. sg. pres. act. subj. (1 Cor.
14:16, GNT, WH & NA | εὐλογήσῃς,
MT & TR) . . . . εὐλογέω (2127)
εὐλογήσας, nom. sg. m. aor. act. part. . . . id.
εὐλόγησε(ν), 3 pers. sg. aor. act. indic. . . . id.
εὐλογήσῃς, 2 pers. sg. aor. act. subj. (1 Cor.
14:16, MT & TR | εὐλογῆς, GNT, WH
& NA) . . . . id.
εὐλογήσω, 1 pers. sg. fut. act. indic. . . . . . id.
(2128) εὐλογητός, ον, nom. sg. m. adj. [§7.2] worthy
of praise or blessing, blessed, Mark 14:61;
Luke 1:68, et al.
εὐλογητοῦ, gen. sg. m. adj. . . . . . . εὐλογητός (2128)
(2129) εὐλογία, ας, ἡ, nom. sg. f. n. [§2.B.b; 2.2] pr.
good speaking; fair speech, flattery, Rom.
16:18; in N.T. blessing, praise, celebration,
1 Cor. 10:16; Rev. 5:12, 13; invocation of
good, benediction, James 3:10; a divine
blessing or boon, Rom. 15:29, et al.; a gift,
benevolence, 2 Cor. 9:5; a frank gift, as opposed to πλεονεξία, 2 Cor. 9:5; ἐπ'
εὐλογίαις, liberally, 2 Cor. 9:6
εὐλογίᾳ, dat. sg. f. n. . . . . εὐλογία (2129)
εὐλογίαις, dat. pl. f. n. . . . . id.
εὐλογίαν, acc. sg. f. n. . . . . id.
εὐλογίας, gen. sg. f. n. . . . . id.
εὐλογοῦμεν, 1 pers. pl. pres. act.
indic. . . . . εὐλογέω (2127)
εὐλογοῦντα, acc. sg. m. pres. act. part. . . . id.
εὐλογοῦνται, 3 pers. pl. pres. pass. indic. . . id.
εὐλογοῦντες, nom. pl. m. pres. act. part. . . id.
εὐλογῶν, nom. sg. m. pres. act. part. . . . . id.
(2130) εὐμετάδοτος, ον [§7.2] (εὖ + μεταδίδωμι)
really in imparting, liberal, bountiful,
1 Tim. 6:18
εὐμεταδότους, acc. pl. m. adj. . . εὐμετάδοτος (2130)
(2131) Εὐνίκη, ης, ἡ [§2.B.a] Eunice, pr. name,
2 Tim. 1:5
Εὐνίκῃ, dat. sg. f. n. (2 Tim. 1:5, GNT, WH,
MT, TRb & NA | Εὐνείκῃ, TRs) . . Εὐνίκη (2131)
(2132) εὐνοέω, ῶ, fut. εὐνοήσω [§16.P] (εὔνοος, εὖ
+ νόος, νοῦς) to have kind thoughts, be
well affected or kindly disposed towards,
Matt. 5:25
(2133) εὔνοια, ας, ἡ [§2.B.b; 2.2] (εὔνοος) good will,
kindliness; heartiness, Eph. 6:7; conjugal
duty, 1 Cor. 7:3
εὔνοιαν, acc. sg. f. n. (1 Cor. 7:3, MT & TR
| GNT, WH & NA omit) . . . . εὔνοια (2133)
εὐνοίας, gen. sg. f. n. . . . . id.
(2134) εὐνουχίζω, fut. εὐνουχίσω [§26.1] aor.
εὐνούχισα, to emasculate, make a eunuch;
to impose chaste abstinence on, to bind to
a practical emasculation, Matt. 19:12
εὐνούχισαν, 3 pers. pl. aor. act.

indic. . . . . εὐνουχίζω (2134)
εὐνουχίσθησαν, 3 pers. pl. aor. act. indic. . . id.
εὐνοῦχοι, nom. pl. m. n. . . . . εὐνοῦχος (2135)
(2135) εὐνοῦχος, ου, ὁ, nom. sg. m. n. [§3.C.a]
(εὐνή, a bed, + ἔχω) pr. one who has
charge of the bedchamber; hence, a eunuch, one emasculated, Matt. 19:12; as eu-
nuches in the East often rose to places of
power and trust, hence, a minister of a
court, Acts 8:27, 34
εὐνοῶν, nom. sg. m. pres. act. part. . . . εὐνοέω (2132)
εὐξαίμην, 1 pers. sg. aor. mid. dep. opt.
[§23.1.b] . . . . εὔχομαι (2172)
(2136) Εὐοδία, ας, ἡ [§2.B.b; 2.2] Euodia, pr. name,
Phil. 4:2
Εὐοδίαν, acc. sg. f. n. (Phil. 4:2, GNT, WH,
MT, TRb & NA | Εὐωδίαν, TRs) . Εὐοδία (2136)
εὐοδοῦσθαι, pres. pass. infin. . . . . εὐοδόω (2137)
εὐοδοῦται, 3 pers. sg. pres. pass. indic. . . id.
(2137) εὐοδόω, ῶ, fut. εὐοδώσω [§20.T] (εὖ + ὁδός)
to give a prosperous journey; cause to pros-
per or be successful; pass. to have a prosperous journey, to succeed in a journey,
Rom. 1:10; met. to be furthered, to pros-
per, temporally or spiritually, 1 Cor. 16:2;
3 John 2 (2×)
εὐοδωθήσομαι, 1 pers. sg. fut. pass.
indic. εὐοδόω (2137)
εὐοδῶται, 3 pers. sg. pres. pass. subj. . . . . id.
εὐπάπεδρον, acc. sg. neut. adj. (1 Cor. 7:35,
GNT, WH & NA | εὐπρόσεδρον, MT &
TR) . . . . εὐπάρεδρος (‡2145)
(‡2145) εὐπάρεδρος, ον [§7.2] (εὖ + πάρεδρος, one
who sits by, an assistant, assessor, from
παρά + ἕδρα, a seat) constantly attending; assiduous, devoted to; τὸ εὐπάρεδρον,
assiduity, devotedness, v.r. 1 Cor. 7:35
(2138) εὐπειθής, ές, nom. sg. m. adj. [§7.G.b] (εὖ +
πείθω) easily persuaded, pliant, James 3:17
εὐπερίστατον, acc. sg. f. adj. . . . εὐπερίστατος (2139)
(2139) εὐπερίστατος, ον [§7.2] (εὖ + περιΐσταμαι)
easily or constantly environing or besetting,
Heb. 12:1
(2140) εὐποιΐα, ας, ἡ [§2.B.b; 2.2] (εὖ + ποιέω) doing good, beneficence, Heb. 13:16
εὐποιΐας, gen. sg. f. n. (Heb. 13:16, GNT, MT,
TR & NA | εὐποιΐας, WH) . . . . . . εὐποιΐα (2140)
(2141) εὐπορέω [§17.Q] (εὐπορέω, to supply, from
εὔπορος, easy, abounding, in easy circumstances) to be in prosperous circumstances,
enjoy plenty, Acts 11:29
εὐπορεῖτο, 3 pers. sg. imperf. mid. indic. (Acts
11:29, GNT, WH, MT & NA |
ηὐπορεῖτο, TR) . . . . εὐπορέω (2141)
(2142) εὐπορία, ας, ἡ, nom. sg. f. n. [§2.B.b; 2.2]

(εὔπορος) *wealth, abundance,* Acts 19:25

(2143) **εὐπρέπεια,** ας, ἡ, nom. sg. f. n. (εὐπρεπής, *well-looking,* from εὖ + πρέπει) *grace, beauty,* James 1:11

(2144) **εὐπρόσδεκτος,** ον, nom. sg. m. adj. [§7.2] (εὖ + προσδέχομαι) *acceptable, grateful, pleasing,* Rom. 15:16, 31; 2 Cor. 8:12; 1 Pet. 2:5; in N.T. *gracious* {2 Cor. 6:2}
εὐπρόσδεκτος, nom. sg. f. adj.
{2 Cor. 8:12} . . . . εὐπρόσδεκτος (2144)
εὐπροσδέκτους, acc. pl. f. adj. . . . . id.
εὐπρόσεδρον, acc. sg. neut. adj. (1 Cor. 7:35, MT & TR | εὐπάρεδρον, GNT, WH & NA) . . . . εὐπρόσεδρος (2145)

(2145) **εὐπρόσεδρος,** ον [§7.2] (εὖ + πρόσεδρος, *an assessor) constantly attending, assiduous, devoted to,* 1 Cor. 7:35; equivalent to εὐπάρεδρος

(2146) **εὐπροσωπέω,** ῶ, fut. εὐπροσωπήσω [§16.P] (εὐπρόσωπος, *of a fair countenance,* from εὖ + πρόσωπον) *to carry or make a fair appearance, to be specious*
εὐπροσωπῆσαι, aor. act. infin. . . . εὐπροσωπέω (2146)

(‡2148) **εὐρακύλων,** ωνος, ὁ, nom. sg. m. n., *the north-east wind,* from the Latin words Eurus and Aquilo (Acts 27:14, GNT, WH & NA | Εὐροκλύδων, MT & TR)
εὔραμεν, 1 pers. pl. 2 aor. act. indic. (Luke 23:2, GNT, WH & NA | εὔρομεν, MT & TR) . . . . εὑρίσκω (2147)
εὐράμενος, nom. sg. m. 2 aor. mid. part. [§36.4] . . . . id.
εὑρεθείς, nom. sg. m. aor. pass. part. . . . . id.
εὑρέθη, 3 pers. sg. aor. pass. indic. . . . . . . id.
εὑρεθῇ, 3 pers. sg. aor. pass. subj. . . . . id.
εὑρέθημεν, 1 pers. pl. aor. pass. indic. . . . id.
εὑρέθην, 1 pers. sg. aor. pass. indic. . . . . . id.
εὑρεθῆναι, aor. pass. infin. . . . . id.
εὑρέθησαν, 3 pers. pl. aor. pass. indic. . . . id.
εὑρεθήσεται, 3 pers. sg. fut. pass. indic. (2 Pet. 3:10, GNT, WH & NA | κατακαήσεται, MT & TR) . . . . id.
εὑρεθησόμεθα, 1 pers. pl. fut. pass. indic.   id.
εὑρεθῆτε, 2 pers. pl. aor. pass. subj. . . . . . id.
εὑρεθῶ, 1 pers. sg. aor. pass. subj. . . . . . . id.
εὑρεθῶσι(ν), 3 pers. pl. aor. pass. subj. . . . id.
εὑρεῖν, 2 aor. act. infin. . . . . id.
εὗρε(ν), 3 pers. sg. 2 aor. act. indic. . . . . . id.
εὗρες, 2 pers. sg. 2 aor. act. indic. . . . . . . id.
εὕρῃ, 3 pers. sg. 2 aor. act. subj. . . . . id.
εὕρηκα, 1 pers. sg. perf. act. indic. [§36.4] id.
εὑρήκαμεν, 1 pers. pl. perf. act. indic. . . . id.
εὑρηκέναι, perf. act. infin. (Rom. 4:1, GNT, MT, TR & NA | WH omits) . . . . id.
εὕρῃς, 2 pers. sg. 2 aor. act. subj. (Rev. 18:14,

MT | εὑρήσουσιν, GNT, WH & NA | εὑρήσῃς, TR) . . . . εὑρίσκω (2147)
εὑρήσει, 3 pers. sg. fut. act. indic. . . . . . . id.
εὑρήσεις, 2 pers. sg. fut. act. indic. . . . . . . id.
εὑρήσετε, 2 pers. pl. fut. act. indic. . . . . . . id.
εὑρήσῃς, 2 pers. sg. aor. act. subj. (Rev. 18:14, TR | εὑρήσουσιν, GNT, WH & NA | εὕρῃς, MT) . . . . id.
εὑρήσομεν, 1 pers. pl. fut. act. indic. . . . . id.
εὑρήσουσιν, 3 pers. pl. fut. act. indic. . . . . id.
εὕρητε, 2 pers. pl. 2 aor. act. subj. . . . . . . id.
εὑρίσκει, 3 pers. sg. pres. act. indic. . . . . . id.
εὑρίσκετο, 3 pers. sg. imperf. pass. indic. (Heb. 11:5, MT & TR | ηὑρίκετο, GNT, WH & NA) . . . . id.
εὑρισκόμεθα, 1 pers. pl. pres. pass. indic. . id.
εὑρίσκομεν, 1 pers. pl. pres. act. indic. . . . id.
εὕρισκον, 3 pers. pl. imperf. act. indic. {Luke 19:48} . . . . id.
εὕρισκον, nom. sg. neut. pres. act. part. {Luke 11:24} . . . . id.
εὑρίσκοντες, nom. pl. m. pres. act. part. . id.

(2147) **εὑρίσκω,** 1 pers. sg. pres. act. indic., [§36.4] fut. εὑρήσω, perf. εὕρηκα, 2 aor. εὗρον, aor. pass. εὑρέθην, later aor. εὕρησα, and aor. mid. εὑράμην, Heb. 9:12; *to find, to meet with, light upon;* Matt. 18:28; 20:6; *to find out, to detect, discover,* Luke 23:2, 4, 14; *to acquire, obtain, win, gain,* Luke 1:30; 9:12; *to find mentally, to comprehend, recognize,* Acts 17:27; Rom. 7:21; *to find* by experience, *observe, gather,* Rom. 7:18; *to devise* as feasible, Luke 5:19; 19:48
εὕροιεν, 3 pers. pl. 2 aor. apt. . . . . . . εὑρίσκω (2147)

(2148) **Εὐροκλύδων,** ωνος, ὁ, nom. sg. m. n. [§4.D.a] (εὖρος, *the east wind,* κλύδων, *a wave) Euroclydon,* the name of a tempestuous wind (Acts 27:14, MT & TR | εὐρακύλων, GNT, WH & NA)
εὕρομεν, 1 pers. pl. 2 aor. act. indic. . εὑρίσκω (2147)
εὗρον, 1 pers. sg. 2 aor. act. indic. {Luke 7:9}   id.
εὗρον, 3 pers. pl. 2 aor. act. indic. {Luke 7:10} . . . . id.
εὑρόντες, nom. pl. m. 2 aor. act. part. . . . id.
εὑροῦσα, nom. sg. f. 2 aor. act. part. . . . id.
εὑροῦσαι, nom. pl. f. 2 aor. act. part. . . . id.

(2149) **εὐρύχωρος,** ον [§7.2] (εὐρύς, *broad,* + χώρα) *spacious; broad, wide,* Matt. 7:13
εὐρύχωρος, nom. sg. f. n. . . . . εὐρύχωρος (2149)
εὕρω, 1 pers. sg. 2 aor. act. subj. . . . . εὑρίσκω (2147)
εὕρωμεν, 1 pers. pl. 2 aor. act. subj. . . . . . id.
εὑρών, nom. sg. m. 2 aor. act. part. . . . . . id.
εὕρωσι(ν), 3 pers. pl. 2 aor. act. indic. . . . id.

(2150) **εὐσέβεια,** ας, ἡ, nom. sg. f. n. [§2.B.b; 2.2] *reverential feeling; piety, devotion, godli-*

ness, Acts 3:12; 1 Tim. 2:2; 4:7, 8, et al.;
religion, the Christian religion, 1 Tim. 3:16

εὐσεβείᾳ, dat. sg. f. n. . . . . εὐσέβεια *(2150)*
εὐσεβείαις, dat. pl. f. n. . . . . id.
εὐσέβειαν, acc. sg. f. n. . . . . id.
εὐσεβείας, gen. sg. f. n. . . . . id.
εὐσεβεῖν, pres. act. infin. . . . . εὐσεβέω *(2151)*
εὐσεβεῖς, acc. pl. m. adj. . . . . εὐσεβής *(2152)*
εὐσεβεῖτε, 2 pers. pl. pres. act. indic. . εὐσεβέω *(2151)*

(2151) **εὐσεβέω**, ῶ, fut. εὐσεβήσω [§16.P] *to exer-*
cise piety; towards a deity, *to worship,* Acts
17:23; towards relatives, *to be dutiful to-*
wards, 1 Tim. 5:4

εὐσεβῆ, acc. sg. m. adj. . . . . εὐσεβής *(2152)*

(2152) **εὐσεβής**, ές, nom. sg. m. adj. [§7.G.b] (εὐ +
σέβομαι) *reverent; pious, devout, religious,*
Acts 10:2, 7; 22:12; 2 Pet. 2:9

(2153) **εὐσεβῶς**, adv., *piously, religiously,* 2 Tim.
3:12; Tit. 2:12

εὔσημον, acc. sg. m. adj. . . . . εὔσημος *(2154)*

(2154) **εὔσημος**, ον [§7.2] (εὐ + σῆμα) pr. *well*
marked, strongly marked; met. *significant,*
intelligible, perspicuous, 1 Cor. 14:9

εὔσπλαγχνοι, nom. pl. m. adj. . . εὔσπλαγχνος *(2155)*

(2155) **εὔσπλαγχνος**, ον [§7.2] (εὐ + σπλάγχνον) in
N.T. *tender-hearted, compassionate,* Eph.
4:32; 1 Pet. 3:8

εὔσχημον, acc. sg. neut. adj. . . . . . . εὐσχήμων *(2158)*
εὐσχήμονα, nom. pl. neut. adj. . . . . id.
εὐσχήμονας, acc. pl. m. adj. . . . . id.
εὐσχημόνων, gen. pl. m. adj. . . . . id.

(2156) **εὐσχημόνως**, adv., *in a becoming manner,*
with propriety, decently, gracefully, Rom.
13:13; 1 Cor. 14:40; 1 Thess. 4:12

(2157) **εὐσχημοσύνη**, ης, ἡ [§2.B.a] *comeliness, grace-*
fulness; artificial *comeliness, ornamental*
array, embellishment, 1 Cor. 12:23

εὐσχημοσύνην, acc. sg. f. n. . . . . εὐσχημοσύνη *(2157)*

(2158) **εὐσχήμων**, ον, nom. sg. m. adj. [§7.G.a] (εὐ
+ σχῆμα) *of good appearance, pleasing to*
look upon, comely, 1 Cor. 12:24; met. *be-*
coming, decent, τὸ εὔσχημον, *decorum,*
propriety, 1 Cor. 7:35; *honorable, reput-*
able, of high standing and influence, Mark
15:43; Acts 13:50; 17:12

(2159) **εὐτόνως**, adv. (εὔτονος, *on the stretch,* from
εὐ + τείνω) *intensely, vehemently, stren-*
uously, Luke 23:10; Acts 18:28

(2160) **εὐτραπελία**, ας, ἡ, nom. sg. f. n. [§2.B.b; 2.2]
(εὐτράπελος, *ready, witty,* from εὐ +
τρέπω) *facetiousness, pleasantry;* hence,
buffoonery, ribaldry, Eph. 5:4

(2161) **Εὔτυχος**, ου, ὁ, nom. sg. m. n. [§3.C.a] *Eu-*
tychus, pr. name, Acts 20:9

εὔφημα, nom. pl. neut. adj. . . . . εὔφημος *(2163)*

(2162) **εὐφημία**, ας, ἡ [§2.B.b; 2.2] pr. *use of words*
of good omen; hence, *favorable expression,*
praise, commendation, 2 Cor. 6:8

εὐφημίας, gen. sg. f. n. . . . . εὐφημία *(2162)*

(2163) **εὔφημος**, ον [§7.2] (εὐ + φήμη) pr. *of good*
omen, auspicious; hence, *of good report,*
commendable, laudable, reputable, Phil.
4:8

(2164) **εὐφορέω**, ῶ, fut. εὐφορήσω [§16.P] (εὔφορος,
εὐ + φέρω) *to bear or bring forth well or*
plentifully, yield abundantly, Luke 12:16

εὐφόρησεν, 3 pers. sg. aor. act. indic. εὐφορέω *(2164)*
εὐφραίνεσθαι, pres. pass. infin. . . . . εὐφραίνω *(2165)*
εὐφραίνεσθε, 2 pers. pl. pres. pass. imper. id.
εὐφραινόμενος, nom. sg. m. pres. pass. part. id.
εὐφραίνονται, 3 pers. pl. pres. pass. indic.
(Rev. 11:10, GNT, WH & NA | εὐφραν-
θήσονται, MT & TR) . . . . id.
εὐφραίνοντο, 3 pers. pl. imperf. pass. indic. id.
εὐφραίνου, 2 pers. sg. pres. pass. imper. . . id.

(2165) **εὐφραίνω**, fut. εὐφρανῶ, aor. εὔφρηνα +
εὔφρανα [§27.1.c,e] (εὔφρων, εὐ + φρήν)
to gladden, 2 Cor. 2:2; pass. *to be glad,*
exult, rejoice, Luke 12:19; Acts 2:26; mid.
to feast in token of joy, keep a day of re-
joicing, Luke 15:23, 24, 29, 32, et al.

εὐφραίνων, nom. sg. m. pres. act.
part. . . . . εὐφραίνω *(2165)*
εὐφράνθη, 3 pers. sg. aor. pass. indic. (Acts
2:26, MT & TR | ηὐφράνθη, GNT, WH
& NA) . . . . id.
εὐφρανθῆναι, aor. pass. infin. . . . . id.
εὐφρανθήσονται, 3 pers. pl. fut. pass. indic.
(Rev. 11:10, MT & TR | εὐφραίνονται,
GNT, WH & NA) . . . . id.
εὐφράνθητε, 2 pers. pl. aor. pass. imper. . . id.
εὐφράνθητι, 2 pers. sg. aor. pass. imper. . . id.
εὐφρανθῶ, 1 pers. sg. aor. pass. subj. . . . . id.
εὐφρανθῶμεν, 1 pers. pl. aor. pass. subj. . id.
Εὐφράτῃ, dat. sg. m. n. . . . . Εὐφράτης *(2166)*
Εὐφράτην, acc. sg. m. n. . . . . id.

(2166) **Εὐφράτης**, ου, ὁ [§2.B.c] the river *Euphrates*

(2167) **εὐφροσύνη**, ης, ἡ [§2.B.a] (εὔφρων) *joy, glad-*
ness, rejoicing, Acts 2:28; 14:17

εὐφροσύνης, gen. sg. f. n. . . . . εὐφροσύνη *(2167)*
εὐχαριστεῖ, 3 pers. sg. pres. act.
indic. . . . . εὐχαριστέω *(2168)*
εὐχαριστεῖν, pres. act. infin. . . . . id.
εὐχαριστεῖς, 2 pers. sg. pres. act. indic. . . id.
εὐχαριστεῖτε, 2 pers. pl. pres. act. imper. . id.

(2168) **εὐχαριστέω**, ῶ, fut. εὐχαριστήσω [§16.P] aor.
εὐχαρίστησα, *to thank,* Luke 17:16, et al.;
absol. *to give thanks,* Matt. 15:36; 26:27,
et al.; pass. *to be made a matter of thank-*
fulness, 2 Cor. 1:11

εὐχαριστηθῇ, 3 pers. sg. aor. pass.

   subj. εὐχαριστέω *(2168)*

εὐχαρίστησαν, 3 pers. pl. aor. act. indic.

   (Rom. 1:21, MT & TR | ηὐχαρίστησαν,

   GNT, WH & NA) . . . . id.

εὐχαριστήσαντος, gen. sg. m. aor. act. part.   id.

εὐχαριστήσας, nom. sg. m. aor. act. part.   id.

εὐχαρίστησε(ν), 3 pers. sg. aor. act. indic.   id.

(2169) **εὐχαριστία**, ας, ἡ, nom. sg. f. n. [§2.B.b; 2.2]

   gratitude, thankfulness, Acts 24:3; *thanks,*

   the act of giving thanks, thanksgiving,

   1 Cor. 14:16, et al.; *conversation marked*

   by the gentle cheerfulness of a grateful

   heart, as contrasted with the unseemly

   mirth of εὐτραπελία, Eph. 5:4

εὐχαριστίᾳ, dat. sg. f. n. . . . . εὐχαριστία *(2169)*

εὐχαριστίαν, acc. sg. f. n. . . . . id.

εὐχαριστίας, gen. sg. f. n. {1 Tim. 4:3} . . id.

εὐχαριστίας, acc. pl. f. n. {1 Tim. 2:1} . . . id.

εὐχαριστιῶν, gen. pl. f. n. . . . . id.

εὐχάριστοι, nom. pl. m. adj. . . . . . εὐχάριστος *(2170)*

(2170) **εὐχάριστος**, ον [§7.2] (εὖ + χάρις) *grateful,*

   pleasing; grateful, mindful of benefits,

   thankful, Col. 3:15

εὐχαριστοῦμεν, 1 pers. pl. pres. act.

   indic. . . . . εὐχαριστέω *(2168)*

εὐχαριστοῦντες, nom. pl. m. pres. act. part.   id.

εὐχαριστῶ, 1 pers. sg. pres. act. indic. . . .   id.

εὐχαριστῶν, nom. sg. m. pres. act. part. . .   id.

εὔχεσθε, 2 pers. pl. pres. mid./pass. dep.

   imper. (James 5:16, GNT, MT, TR & NA

   | προσεύχεσθε, WH) . . . . εὔχομαι *(2172)*

(2171) **εὐχή**, ῆς, ἡ, nom. sg. f. n. [§2.B.a] *a wish,*

   prayer, James 5:15; *a vow,* Acts 21:23

εὐχήν, acc. sg. f. n. . . . . εὐχή *(2171)*

(2172) **εὔχομαι**, 1 pers. sg. pres. mid./pass. dep.

   indic., fut. εὔξομαι, aor. εὐξάμην [§23.1.c]

   to pray, offer prayer, Acts 26:29; 2 Cor.

   13:7, 9; James 5:16; *to wish, desire,* Acts

   27:29; Rom. 9:3; 3 John 2

εὐχόμεθα, 1 pers. pl. pres. mid./pass. dep.

   indic. εὔχομαι *(2172)*

εὔχρηστον, acc. sg. m. adj.

   {Philemon 11} . . . . εὔχρηστος *(2173)*

εὔχρηστον, nom. sg. neut. adj. {2 Tim. 2:21}   id.

(2173) **εὔχρηστος**, ον, nom. sg. m. adj. [§7.2] (εὖ +

   χρηστός) *highly useful, very profitable,*

   2 Tim. 2:21; 4:11; Philemon 11

(2174) **εὐψυχέω**, ῶ, fut. εὐψυχήσω [§16.P] (εὔψυχος,

   of good courage, εὖ + ψυχή) *to be ani-*

   mated, encouraged, in good spirits, Phil.

   2:19

εὐψυχῶ, 1 pers. sg. pres. act. subj. . . εὐψυχέω *(2174)*

(2175) **εὐωδία**, ας, ἡ, nom. sg. f. n. [§2.B.b; 2.2]

   (εὐώδης, εὖ + ὄδωδα, perf. from. ὄζω)

a sweet smell, grateful odor, fragrance,

   2 Cor. 2:15; Eph. 5:2; Phil. 4:18

(‡2136) **Εὐωδία**, ας, ἡ, *Euodia,* pr. name

   Εὐωδίαν, acc. sg. f. n. (Phil. 4:2, TR |

   Εὐοδίαν, GNT, WH, MT & NA) Εὐωδία *(‡2136)*

εὐωδίας, gen. sg. f. n. . . . . εὐωδία *(2175)*

εὐώνυμον, acc. sg. m. adj.

   {Rev. 10:2} . . . . εὐώνυμος *(2176)*

εὐώνυμον, acc. sg. f. adj. {Acts 21:3} . . . . id.

(2176) **εὐώνυμος**, ον [§7.2] (εὖ + ὄνομα) *of good*

   name or omen; used also as an euphem-

   ism by the Greeks instead of ἀριστερός,

   which was a word of bad import, as all

   omens on the left denoted misfortune; *the*

   left, Matt. 20:21, 23; 25:33, 41, et al.

εὐωνύμων, gen. pl. m. adj. . . . . εὐώνυμος *(2176)*

ἐφ᾿, for ἐπί, before an aspirated vowel . . . ἐπί *(1909)*

ἔφαγε(ν), 3 pers. sg. 2 aor. act. indic.

   [§36.1] . . . . ἐσθίω *(2068)*

ἐφάγετε, 2 pers. pl. 2 aor. act. indic. . . . . . id.

ἐφάγομεν, 1 pers. pl. 2 aor. act. indic. . . . id.

ἔφαγον, 1 pers. sg. 2 aor. act. indic.

   {Rev. 10:10} . . . . id.

ἔφαγον, 3 pers. pl. 2 aor. act. indic.

   {John 6:23} . . . . id.

(2177) **ἐφάλλομαι**, fut. ἐφαλοῦμαι [§24.4] (ἐπί +

   ἄλλομαι) *to leap or spring upon, assault,*

   Acts 19:16

ἐφαλλόμενος, nom. sg. m. pres. mid./pass.

   dep. part. (Acts 19:16, MT & TR | ἐφαλό-

   μενος, GNT, WH & NA) . . . . . ἐφάλλομαι *(2177)*

ἐφαλόμενος, nom. sg. m. aor. mid. dep. part.

   (Acts 19:16, GNT, WH & NA | ἐφαλ-

   λόμενος, MT & TR) . . . . id.

ἐφανερώθη, 3 pers. sg. aor. pass.

   indic. φανερόω *(5319)*

ἐφανερώθησαν, 3 pers. pl. aor. pass. indic.   id.

ἐφανέρωσα, 1 pers. sg. aor. act. indic. . . . id.

ἐφανέρωσε(ν), 3 pers. sg. aor. act. indic. .   id.

ἐφάνη, 3 pers. sg. 2 aor. pass. indic.

   [§27.4.b] . . . . φαίνω *(5316)*

ἐφάνησαν, 3 pers. pl. 2 aor. pass. indic. . . id.

(2178) **ἐφάπαξ**, adv. (ἐπί + ἅπαξ) *once for all,* Rom.

   6:10; *at once,* 1 Cor. 15:6

ἔφασκεν, 3 pers. sg. imperf. act. indic. φάσκω *(5335)*

ἐφείσατο, 3 pers. sg. aor. mid. dep. indic.

   [§23.5] . . . . φείδομαι *(5339)*

ἔφερεν, 3 pers. sg. imperf. act. indic. . . . φέρω *(5342)*

ἐφερόμεθα, 1 pers. pl. imperf. pass. indic. id.

ἔφερον, 3 pers. pl. imperf. act. indic. . . . . id.

ἐφέροντο, 3 pers. pl. imperf. pass. indic. . id.

Ἐφεσίνης, gen. sg. f. n. (Rev. 2:1, TR |

   Ἐφέσῳ, GNT, WH, MT & NA) Ἐφεσῖνος *(2179)*

(2179) **Ἐφεσῖνος**, η, ον [§27.F.a] *Ephesian,* Rev. 2:1

Ἐφέσιοι, nom. pl. m. adj. . . . . Ἐφέσιος *(2180)*

Ἐφέσιον, acc. sg. m. adj. .... Ἐφέσιος *(2180)*
(2180) **Ἐφέσιος,** α, ον [§7.1] *Ephesian,* belonging to
Ephesus, Acts 19:28, 34, 35; 21:29
Ἐφεσίους, acc. pl. m. adj. (Eph. 6:24, TRs
| GNT, WH, MT, TRb & NA
omit) .... Ἐφέσιος *(2180)*
Ἐφεσίων, gen. pl. m. adj. .... id.
Ἔφεσον, acc. sg. f. n. .... Ἔφεσος *(2181)*
(2181) **Ἔφεσος,** ου, ἡ [§3.C.b] *Ephesus,* a celebrated
city of Asia Minor
Ἐφέσου, gen. sg. f. n. .... Ἔφεσος *(2181)*
ἐφέστηκε(ν), 3 pers. sg. perf. act. indic.
[§29.X] .... ἐφίστημι *(2186)*
ἐφεστώς, nom. sg. m. perf. act. part. [§35.8] id.
ἐφεστῶτα, acc. sg. m. perf. act. part. .... id.
Ἐφέσῳ, dat. sg. f. n. .... Ἔφεσος *(2181)*
ἐφευρετάς, acc. pl. m. n. .... ἐφευρετής *(2182)*
(2182) **ἐφευρετής,** οῦ, ὁ [§2.B.c] (ἐφευρίσκω, *to come
upon, find, discover,* from ἐπί + εὑρίσκω)
an inventor, deviser, Rom. 1:30
ἔφη, 3 pers. sg. imperf. indic. [§33.1] .... φημί *(5346)*
(2183) **ἐφημερία,** ας, ἡ [§2.B.b; 2.2] pr. *daily course;
the daily service* of the temple; *a course* of
priests to which the daily service for a week
was allotted in rotation, Luke 1:5, 8
ἐφημερίας, gen. sg. f. n. .... ἐφημερία *(2183)*
(2184) **ἐφήμερος,** ον [§7.2] (ἐπί + ἡμέρα) *lasting for
a day; daily; sufficient for a day, necessary
for every day,* James 2:15
ἐφημέρου, gen. sg. f. adj. .... ἐφήμερος *(2184)*
ἔφθακε, 3 pers. sg. perf. act. indic. (1 Thess.
2:16, MT | ἔφθασε(ν), GNT, WH, TR &
NA) .... φθάνω *(5348)*
ἐφθάσαμεν, 1 pers. pl. aor. act. indic. .... id.
ἔφθασε(ν), 3 pers. sg. aor. act. indic. (1 Thess.
2:16, GNT, WH, TR & NA | ἔφθακε,
MT) .... id.
ἐφθείραμεν, 1 pers. pl. aor. act. indic. . φθείρω *(5351)*
ἔφθειρε(ν), 3 pers. sg. imperf. act. indic. (Rev.
19:2, GNT, WH, TR & NA | διέφθειρε,
MT) .... id.
ἐφικέσθαι, 2 aor. mid. dep. infin. . ἐφικνέομαι *(2185)*
(2185) **ἐφικνέομαι,** οῦμαι, fut. ἐφίξομαι, 2 aor.
ἐφικόμην [§36.2] (ἐπί + ἱκνέομαι, *to
come)* to come or reach to, to reach a certain point or end; to reach, arrive at, 2 Cor.
10:13, 14
ἐφικνούμενοι, nom. pl. m. pres. mid./pass.
dep. part. .... ἐφικνέομαι *(2185)*
ἐφίλει, 3 pers. sg. imperf. act. indic. ... φιλέω *(5368)*
ἐφιμώθη, 3 pers. sg. aor. pass. indic. .. φιμόω *(5392)*
ἐφίμωσε(ν), 3 pers. sg. aor. act. indic. .... id.
ἐφίσταται, 3 pers. sg. pres. mid. indic.
[§29.Y] .... ἐφίστημι *(2186)*
(2186) **ἐφίστημι,** fut. ἐπιστήσω [§29.X] (ἐπί +

ἵστημι) trans. *to place upon, over, close by;*
intrans., perf. ἐφέστηκα, part. ἐφεστώς,
2 aor., ἐπέστην, mid. ἐφίσταμαι, *to stand
by or near,* Luke 2:38; 4:39; *to come suddenly upon,* Luke 2:9; 24:4; *to come upon,
assault,* Acts 6:12; 17:5; *to come near, approach,* Luke 10:40; *to impend, be instant,
to be at hand,* 1 Thess. 5:3; *to be present,*
Acts 28:2; *to be pressing, urgent, earnest,*
2 Tim. 4:2
ἐφοβεῖτο, 3 pers. sg. imperf. mid./pass. dep.
indic. .... φοβέω *(5399)*
ἐφοβήθη, 3 pers. sg. aor. pass. dep. indic. . id.
ἐφοβήθησαν, 3 pers. pl. aor. pass. dep. indic. id.
ἐφοβούμην, 1 pers. sg. imperf. mid./pass. dep.
indic. .... id.
ἐφοβοῦντο, 3 pers. pl. imperf. mid./pass. dep.
indic. .... id.
ἐφονεύσατε, 2 pers. pl. aor. act. indic. φονεύω *(5407)*
ἐφορέσαμεν, 1 pers. pl. aor. act. indic. . φορέω *(5409)*
(†2187) **Ἐφραίμ,** ὁ, *Ephraim,* pr. name, indecl. (John
11:54, GNT, WH, MT & NA | Ἐφραῖμ,
TR)
ἔφραξαν, 3 pers. pl. aor. act. indic. .. φράσσω *(5420)*
ἐφρονεῖτε, 2 pers. pl. imperf. act.
indic. .... φρονέω *(5426)*
ἐφρόνουν, 1 pers. sg. imperf. act. indic. .. id.
ἐφρούρει, 3 pers. sg. imperf. act.
indic. .... φρουρέω *(5432)*
ἐφρουρούμεθα, 1 pers. pl. imperf. pass. indic. id.
ἐφρύαξαν, 3 pers. pl. aor. act. indic. φρυάσσω *(5433)*
ἔφυγε(ν), 3 pers. sg. 2 aor. act. indic.
[§24.9] .... φεύγω *(5343)*
ἔφυγον, 3 pers. pl. 2 aor. act. indic. ..... id.
ἐφύλαξα, 1 pers. sg. aor. act. indic. . φυλάσσω *(5442)*
ἐφυλαξάμην, 1 pers. sg. aor. mid. indic. .. id.
ἐφυλάξατε, 2 pers. pl. aor. act. indic. .... id.
ἐφύλαξε(ν), 3 pers. sg. aor. act. indic. .... id.
ἐφυσιώθησαν, 3 pers. pl. aor. pass. indic.
[§21.U] .... φυσιόω *(5448)*
ἐφύτευον, 3 pers. pl. imperf. act. indic. φυτεύω *(5452)*
ἐφύτευσα, 1 pers. sg. aor. act. indic. ..... id.
ἐφύτευσεν, 3 pers. sg. aor. act. indic. ..... id.
(2188) **ἐφφαθά,** indecl. (Aramaic אֶתְפְּתַח) *be thou
opened,* Mark 7:34
ἐφώνει, 3 pers. sg. imperf. act. indic. .. φωνέω *(5455)*
ἐφώνησαν, 3 pers. pl. aor. act. indic. .... id.
ἐφώνησε(ν), 3 pers. sg. aor. act. indic. ... id.
ἐφώτισεν, 3 pers. sg. aor. act. indic. .. φωτίζω *(5461)*
ἐφωτίσθη, 3 pers. sg. aor. pass. indic. .... id.
ἔχαιρεν, 3 pers. sg. imperf. act. indic. . χαίρω *(5463)*
ἔχαιρον, 3 pers. pl. imperf. act. indic. .... id.
ἐχαλάσθην, 1 pers. sg. aor. pass. indic.
[§22.4] .... χαλάω *(5465)*
ἐχάρη, 3 pers. sg. 2 aor. pass. dep. indic.

[§27.4.b] . . . . χαίρω *(5463)*
ἐχάρημεν, 1 pers. pl. 2 aor. pass. dep. indic.   id.
ἐχάρην, 1 pers. sg. 2 aor. pass. dep. indic.   id.
ἐχάρησαν, 3 pers. pl. 2 aor. pass. dep. indic.   id.
ἐχάρητε, 2 pers. pl. 2 aor. pass. dep. indic.   id.
ἐχαρίσατο, 3 pers. sg. aor. mid. dep.
    indic. χαρίζομαι *(5483)*
ἐχαρίσθη, 3 pers. sg. aor. pass. indic. . . . . id.
ἐχαρίτωσεν, 3 pers. sg. aor. act.
    indic. . . . . χαριτόω *(5487)*
ἔχε, 2 pers. sg. pres. act. imper. . . . . ἔχω *(2192)*
ἔχει, 3 pers. sg. pres. act. indic. . . . . id.
ἔχειν, pres. act. infin. . . . . id.
ἔχεις, 2 pers. sg. pres. act. indic. . . . . id.
ἔχετε, 2 pers. pl. pres. act. indic.
    {Mark 11:25} . . . . id.
ἔχετε, 2 pers. pl. pres. act. imper.
    {Mark 11:22} . . . . id.
ἐχέτω, 3 pers. sg. pres. act. imper. . . . . . . id.
ἔχῃ, 3 pers. sg. pres. act. subj. . . . . id.
ἔχητε, 2 pers. pl. pres. act. subj. . . . . id.
(‡5504) **ἐχθές,** adv., *yesterday* (John 4:52; Acts 7:28;
    Heb. 13:8, GNT, WH & NA | χθές, MT
    & TR)
(2189) **ἔχθρα, ας, ἡ,** nom. sg. f. n. [§2.B.b; 2.2] *en-*
    mity, discord, feud, Luke 23:12; Gal. 5:20;
    alienation, Eph. 2:14, 16; *a principle or*
    state of enmity, Rom. 8:7
ἔχθρᾳ, dat. sg. f. n. . . . . ἔχθρα *(2189)*
ἔχθραι, nom. pl. f. n. . . . . id.
ἔχθραν, acc. sg. f. n. . . . . id.
ἐχθρέ, voc. sg. m. adj. . . . . ἐχθρός *(2190)*
ἐχθροί, nom. pl. m. adj. . . . . id.
ἐχθρόν, acc. sg. m. adj. . . . . id.
(2190) **ἐχθρός, ά, όν,** nom. sg. m. adj. [§7.1] *hated,*
    under disfavor, Rom. 11:28; *inimical, hos-*
    tile, Matt. 13:28; Col. 1:21; as a subst., *an*
    enemy, adversary, Matt. 5:43, 44; 10:36,
    et al.
ἐχθροῦ, gen. sg. m. adj. . . . . ἐχθρός *(2190)*
ἐχθρούς, acc. pl. m. adj. . . . . id.
ἐχθρῶν, gen. pl. adj. m. . . . . id.
(2191) **ἔχιδνα, ης, ἡ,** nom. sg. f. n. [§2.B; 2.3] (ἔχις)
    a viper, poisonous serpent, Acts 28:3; used
    also fig. of persons, Matt. 3:7
ἐχιδνῶν, gen. pl. f. n. . . . . ἔχιδνα *(2191)*
ἐχλεύαζον, 3 pers. pl. imperf. act.
    indic. . . . . χλευάζω *(5512)*
ἔχοι, 3 pers. sg. pres. act. opt. . . . . ἔχω *(2192)*
ἔχοιεν, 3 pers. pl. pres. act. opt. . . . . id.
ἔχομεν, 1 pers. pl. pres. act. indic. . . . . . . id.
ἐχόμενα, acc. pl. neut. pres. pass. part. . . . id.
ἐχομένας, acc. pl. f. pres. pass. part. . . . . id.
ἐχομένῃ, dat. sg. f. pres. pass. part. . . . . . id.
ἔχον, nom. sg. neut. pres. act. part.

{Acts 1:12} . . . . ἔχω *(2192)*
ἔχον, acc. sg. neut. pres. act. part.
    {Acts 24:25} . . . . id.
ἔχοντα, acc. sg. m. pres. act. part.
    {Mark 9:17} . . . . id.
ἔχοντα, nom. pl. neut. pres. act. part.
    {Mark 6:34} . . . . id.
ἔχοντας, acc. pl. m. pres. act. part. . . . . . . id.
ἔχοντες, nom. pl. m. pres. act. part. . . . . . id.
ἔχοντι, dat. sg. m. pres. act. part. . . . . id.
ἔχοντος, gen. sg. m. pres. act. part.
    {Rev. 16:9} . . . . id.
ἔχοντος, gen. sg. neut. pres. act. part.
    {Rev. 17:7} . . . . id.
ἐχόντων, gen. pl. m. pres. act. part. . . . . . id.
ἐχορτάσθησαν, 3 pers. pl. aor. pass. indic.
    [§26.1] . . . . χορτάζω *(5526)*
ἐχορτάσθητε, 2 pers. pl. aor. pass. indic. . . id.
ἔχουσα, nom. sg. f. pres. act. part. . . . . . . ἔχω *(2192)*
ἔχουσαι, nom. pl. f. pres. act. part. . . . . . . id.
ἐχούσαις, dat. pl. f. pres. act. part. . . . . . . id.
ἔχουσαν, acc. sg. f. pres. act. part. . . . . . . id.
ἐχούσῃ, dat. sg. f. pres. act. part. . . . . id.
ἐχούσης, gen. sg. f. pres. act. part. . . . . . . id.
ἔχουσι(ν), 3 pers. pl. pres. act. indic. . . . . id.
ἐχρηματίσθη, 3 pers. sg. aor. pass.
    indic. . . . . χρηματίζω *(5537)*
ἐχρησάμεθα, 1 pers. pl. aor. mid. dep. indic.
    [§19.S] . . . . χράομαι *(5530)*
ἐχρησάμην, 1 pers. sg. aor. mid. dep. indic. id.
ἔχρισας, 2 pers. sg. aor. act. indic. . . . . . χρίω *(5548)*
ἔχρισε(ν), 3 pers. sg. aor. act. indic. . . . . . id.
ἐχρῶντο, 3 pers. pl. imperf. mid./pass. dep.
    indic. . . . . χράομαι *(5530)*
(2192) **ἔχω,** 1 pers. sg. pres. act. indic., [§36.4] fut.
    ἕξω, imperf. εἶχον, 2 aor. ἔσχον, perf.
    ἔσχηκα, *to hold,* Rev. 1:16, et al.; *to seize,*
    possess a person, Mark 16:8; *to have, pos-*
    sess, Matt. 7:29, et al. freq.; *to have, have*
    ready, be furnished with, Matt. 5:23; John
    5:36; 6:68, et al.; *to have* as a matter of
    crimination, Matt. 5:23; Mark 11:25, et
    al.; *to have* at command, Matt. 27:65; *to*
    have the power, *be able,* Matt. 18:25; Luke
    14:14; Acts 4:14, et al.; *to have* in marriage,
    Matt. 14:4, et al.; *to have, be affected by,*
    subjected to, Matt. 3:14; 12:10; Mark 3:10;
    John 12:48; 15:22, 24; 16:21, 22; Acts
    23:29; 1 Tim. 5:12; Heb. 7:28; 1 John 1:8;
    4:18; χάραν ἔχειν, *to feel gratitude, be*
    thankful, 1 Tim. 1:12; 2 Tim. 1:3; Phile-
    mon 7; *to hold, esteem, regard,* Matt. 14:5;
    Luke 14:18, 19, et al.; *to have or hold* as
    an object of knowledge, faith, or practice,
    John 5:38, 42; 14:21; 1 John 5:12; 2 John

9; *to hold on* in entire possession, *to retain*, Rom. 15:4; 2 Tim. 1:13; Heb. 12:28; intrans. with adverbs or adverbial expressions, *to be, to fare*, Matt. 9:12; Mark 2:17; 5:23; Luke 5:31; John 4:52; Acts 7:1; 12:15; 15:36; 21:13; 2 Cor. 10:6; 12:14; 1 Tim. 5:25; 1 Pet. 4:5; τὸ νῦν ἔχον, *for the present;* in N.T. ἔχειν ἐν γαστρί, *to be pregnant*, Matt. 1:18, et al.; as also ἔχειν κοίτην, Rom. 9:10; ἔχειν δαιμόνιον, *to be possessed*, Matt. 11:18, et al.; of time, *to have continued, to have lived*, John 5:5, 6; 8:57; of space, *to embrace, be distant*, Acts 1:12; mid. pr. *to hold by, cling to;* hence, *to border upon, be next*, Mark 1:38; Luke 13:33; Acts 20:15; 21:26; *to tend immediately to*, Heb. 6:9 {1 Cor. 12:21}

ἔχω, 1 pers. sg. pres. act. subj.
{1 Cor. 13:1–3} . . . . ἔχω *(2192)*

ἔχωμεν, 1 pers. pl. pres. act. subj. . . . . . . id.

ἔχων, nom. sg. m. pres. act. part. . . . . . . id.

ἐχωρίσθη, 3 pers. sg. aor. pass. indic. . χωρίζω *(5563)*

ἔχωσι(ν), 3 pers. pl. pres. act. subj. . . . . . .ἔχω *(2192)*

ἐψευδομαρτύρουν, 3 pers. pl. imperf. act.
indic. . . . . ψευδομαρτυρέω *(5576)*

ἐψεύσω, 2 pers. sg. aor. mid. dep. indic.
[§23.5] . . . . ψεύδω *(‡5574)*

ἐψηλάφησαν, 3 pers. pl. aor. act.
indic. . . . . ψηλαφάω *(5584)*

ἑώρακα, 1 pers. sg. perf. act. indic. Att. for
ὥρακα [§13.4] . . . . ὁράω *(3708)*

ἑωράκαμεν, 1 pers. pl. perf. act. indic. Att.   id.

ἑώρακαν, 3 pers. pl. perf. act. indic. [§35.13]
(Luke 9:36, GNT, WH & NA | ἑωρά-
κασιν, MT & TR) . . . . id.

ἑώρακας, 2 pers. sg. perf. act. indic. Att.
[§13.4] . . . . id.

ἑωράκασι(ν), 3 pers. pl. perf. act. indic. Att.   id.

ἑωράκατε, 2 pers. pl. perf. act. indic. Att.   id.

ἑωράκει, 3 pers. sg. pluperf. act. indic. Att.   id.

ἑώρακε(ν), 3 pers. sg. perf. act. indic. Att.   id.

ἑωρακέναι, perf. act. infin. Att. . . . . id.

ἑωρακότες, nom. pl. m. perf. act. part. Att.   id.

ἑωρακώς, nom. sg. m. perf. act. part. Att.   id.

ἑώρων, 3 pers. pl. imperf. act. indic. Att.
[§36.1] (John 6:2, MT & TR | ἐθεώρουν,
GNT, WH & NA) . . . . id.

(2193) ἕως, conj. of time, *while, as long as*, John 9:4; *until*, Matt. 2:9; Luke 15:4; as also in N.T. ἕως οὗ, ἕως ὅτου, Matt. 5:18, 26; ἕως ἄρτι, *until now*, Matt. 11:12; ἕως πότε, *until when, how long*, Matt. 17:17; ἕως σήμερον, *until this day, to this time*, 2 Cor. 3:15; as a prep. of time, *until*, Matt. 24:21; of place, *unto, even to*, Matt. 11:23; Luke

2:15; ἕως ἄνω, *to the brim*, John 2:7; ἕως εἰς, *even to, as far as*, Luke 24:50; ἕως κάτω, *to the bottom;* ἕως ὧδε, *to this place*, Luke 23:5; of state, *unto, even to*, Matt. 26:38; of number, *even, so much as*, Rom. 3:12, et al. freq.

Z

(2194) **Ζαβουλών**, ὁ, *Zabulon*, pr. name, indecl.

Ζακχαῖε, voc. sg. m. n. . . . . Ζακχαῖος *(2195)*

(2195) **Ζακχαῖος**, ου, ὁ, nom. sg. m. n. [§3.C.a]
Zacchaeus, pr. name,

(2196) **Ζάρα**, ὁ, *Zara*, pr. name, indecl. (Matt. 1:3, GNT & NA | Ζαρά, WH, MT & TR)

Ζαχαρία, voc. sg. m. n. . . . . Ζαχαρίας *(2197)*

Ζαχαρίαν, acc. sg. m. n. . . . . id.

(2197) **Ζαχαρίας**, ου, ὁ, nom. sg. m. n. [§2.B.d]
Zacharias, pr. name   I. *Son of Barachias*, Matt. 23:35; Luke 11:51   II. *Father of John the Baptist*, Luke 1:5, et al.

Ζαχαρίου, gen. sg. m. n. . . . . Ζαχαρίας *(2197)*

(2198) **ζάω**, ζῶ, ζῇς, ζῇ [§35.2] fut. ζήσω and ζήσομαι, aor. ἔζησα, perf. ἔζηκα, *to live, to be possessed of vitality, to exercise the functions of life*, Matt. 27:63; Acts 17:28, et al.; τὸ ζῆν, *life*, Heb. 2:15; *to have means of subsistence*, 1 Cor. 9:14; *to live, to pass existence* in a specific manner, Luke 2:36; 15:13, et al.; *to be instinct with life and vigor;* hence, ζῶν, *living*, an epithet of God, in a sense peculiar to Himself; ἐλπὶς ζῶσα, *a living hope* in respect of vigor and constancy, 1 Pet. 1:3; ὕδωρ ζῶν, *living water* in respect of a full and unfailing flow, John 4:10, 11; *to be alive* with cheered and hopeful feelings, 1 Thess. 3:8; *to be alive* in a state of salvation from spiritual death, 1 John 4:9, et al.

Ζεβεδαῖον, acc. sg. m. n. . . . . Ζεβεδαῖος *(2199)*

(2199) **Ζεβεδαῖος**, ου, ὁ [§3.C.a] *Zebedee*, pr. name

Ζεβεδαίου, gen. sg. m. n. . . . . Ζεβεδαῖος *(2199)*

ζέοντες, nom. pl. m. pres. act. part.
[§35.1] . . . . ζέω *(2204)*

(2200) **ζεστός**, ή, όν, nom. sg. m. adj. [§7.F.a] pr. *boiled; boiling, boiling hot;* met. *glowing with zeal, fervent*, Rev. 3:15, 16

ζεύγη, acc. pl. neut. n. . . . . ζεῦγος *(2201)*

(2201) **ζεῦγος**, ους, τό, nom. sg. neut. n. [§5.E.b] *a yoke* of animals; *a pair, couple*, Luke 2:24; 14:19

(2202) **ζευκτηρία**, ας, ἡ [§2.B.b; 2.2] (pr. fem. of ζευκτήριος, from ζεύγνυμι, *to yoke, join*)

a fastening, band, Acts 27:40

ζευκτηρίας, acc. pl. f. n. . . . . ζευκτηρία *(2202)*

(2203) **Ζεύς, Διός, ὁ** [§6.4.a] the supreme God of the Greeks answering to the *Jupiter* of the Romans, Acts 14:12, 13

(2204) **ζέω,** fut. ζέσω [§22.2] *to boil, to be hot,* in N.T. met. *to be fervent, ardent, zealous,* Acts 18:25; Rom. 12:11

ζέων, nom. sg. m. pres. act. part. [§35.1] . ζέω *(2204)*

ζῇ, 3 pers. sg. pres. act. indic. [§35.2] . . . . ζάω *(2198)*

ζήλευε, 2 pers. sg. pres. act. imper. (Rev. 3:19, GNT, WH, MT & NA | ζήλωσον, TR) . . . . ζηλεύω *(‡2206)*

(‡2206) **ζηλεύω,** fut. ζηλεύσω, *to be zealous, earnest,* i.q.

ζῆλοι, nom. pl. m. n. (2 Cor. 12:20; Gal. 5:20, MT & TR | ζῆλος, GNT, WH & NA) . . . . ζῆλος *(2205)*

ζηλοῖ, 3 pers. sg. pres. act. indic. {1 Cor. 13:4} . . . . ζηλόω *(2206)*

ζῆλον, acc. sg. m. n. . . . . ζῆλος *(2205)*

(2205) **ζῆλος, ου, ὁ,** nom. sg. m. n. and ους, τό [§3.C.a] in a good sense, *generous rivalry; noble aspiration;* in N.T. *zeal, ardor in behalf of, ardent affection,* John 2:17; Rom. 10:2; in a bad sense, *jealousy, envy, malice,* Acts 13:45; Rom. 13:13; *indignation, wrath,* Acts 5:17, et al. {2 Cor. 12:20}

ζῆλος, nom. sg. neut. n. {2 Cor. 9:2} . . ζῆλος *(2205)*

ζῆλος, acc. sg. neut. n. {Phil. 3:6} . . . . . . id.

ζήλου, gen. sg. m. n. . . . . id.

ζηλοῦσθαι, pres. pass. infin. [§21.U] . . . ζηλόω *(2206)*

ζηλοῦσιν, 3 pers. pl. pres. act. indic. . . . . . id.

ζηλοῦτε, 2 pers. pl. pres. act. indic. {James 4:2} . . . . id.

ζηλοῦτε, 2 pers. pl. pres. act. subj. {Gal. 4:17} . . . . id.

ζηλοῦτε, 2 pers. pl. pres. act. imper. {1 Cor. 14:1} . . . . id.

(2206) **ζηλόω, ῶ,** fut. ζηλώσω [§20.T] *to have strong affection towards, be ardently devoted to,* 2 Cor. 11:2; *to make a show of affection and devotion towards,* Gal. 4:17; *to desire earnestly, aspire eagerly after,* 1 Cor. 12:31; 14:1, 39; absol. *to be fervent, to be zealous,* Rev. 3:19; *to be jealous, envious, spiteful,* Acts 7:9; 17:5; 1 Cor. 13:4; James 4:2; pass. *to be an object of warm regard and devotion,* Gal. 4:18

ζηλῶ, 1 pers. sg. pres. act. indic. . . . . . . ζηλόω *(2206)*

ζήλῳ, dat. sg. m. n. . . . . ζῆλος *(2205)*

ζηλώσαντες, nom. pl. m. aor. act. part. ζηλόω *(2206)*

ζήλωσον, 2 pers. sg. aor. act. imper. (Rev. 3:19, TR | ζήλευε, GNT, WH, MT & NA) . . . . id.

ζηλωταί, nom. pl. m. n. . . . . ζηλωτής *(2207)*

ζηλωτήν, acc. sg. m. n. . . . . id.

(2207) **ζηλωτής, οῦ, ὁ,** nom. sg. m. n. [§2.B.c] pr. *a generous rival, an imitator;* in N.T. *an aspirant,* 1 Cor. 14:12; Tit. 2:14; *a devoted adherent, a zealot,* Acts 21:20; 22:3; Gal. 1:14

(2209) **ζημία, ας, ἡ** [§2.B.b; 2.2] *damage, loss, detriment,* Acts 27:10, 21; Phil. 3:7, 8

ζημίαν, acc. sg. f. n. . . . . ζημία *(2209)*

ζημίας, gen. sg. f. n. . . . . id.

(2210) **ζημιόω, ῶ,** fut. ζημιώσω [§20.T] *to visit with loss or harm;* pass. *to suffer loss or detriment,* 1 Cor. 3:15; 2 Cor. 7:9; *to lose, to forfeit,* Matt. 16:26; Mark 8:36; Phil. 3:8

ζημιωθείς, nom. sg. m. aor. pass. part. ζημιόω *(2210)*

ζημιωθῇ, 3 pers. sg. aor. pass. subj. . . . . . id.

ζημιωθῆναι, aor. pass. indic. (Mark 8:36, GNT, WH & NA | ζημιωθῇ, MT & TR) . id.

ζημιωθήσεται, 3 pers. sg. fut. pass. indic. . id.

ζημιωθῆτε, 2 pers. pl. aor. pass. subj. . . . . id.

ζῆν, pres. act. infin. [§35.2] (GNT, MT & NA | ζῇν, WH & TR) . . . . ζάω *(2198)*

Ζηνᾶν, acc. sg. m. n. . . . . Ζηνᾶς *(2211)*

(2211) **Ζηνᾶς, ᾶ, ὁ** [§2.4] *Zenas,* pr. name, Tit. 3:13

ζῇς, 2 pers. sg. pres. act. indic. . . . . ζάω *(2198)*

ζήσασα, nom. sg. f. aor. act. part. . . . . . . id.

ζήσει, 3 pers. sg. fut. act. indic. (John 6:51, 57, 58, GNT, WH & NA | ζήσεται, MT & TR) . . . . id.

ζήσεσθε, 2 pers. pl. fut. mid. dep. indic. . . id.

ζήσεται, 3 pers. sg. fut. mid. dep. indic. . . id.

ζήσετε, 2 pers. pl. fut. act. indic. (John 14:19, GNT, WH & NA | ζήσεσθε, MT & TR) . id.

ζήσῃ, 2 pers. sg. fut. act. indic. {Luke 10:28} id.

ζήσῃ, 2 pers. sg. aor. act. subj. (Mark 5:23, GNT, WH & NA | ζήσεται, MT & TR) . id.

ζησόμεθα, 1 pers. pl. fut. mid. dep. indic. (2 Cor. 13:4, MT & TR | ζήσομεν, GNT, WH & NA) . . . . id.

ζήσομεν, 1 pers. pl. fut. act. indic. . . . . . . id.

ζήσονται, 3 pers. pl. fut. mid. dep. indic. (John 5:25, MT & TR | ζήσουσιν, GNT, WH & NA) . . . . id.

ζήσουσιν, 3 pers. pl. fut. act. indic. (John 5:25, GNT, WH & NA | ζήσονται, MT & TR) . . . . id.

ζήσω, 1 pers. sg. aor. act. subj. . . . . id.

ζήσωμεν, 1 pers. pl. aor. act. subj. . . . . . . id.

ζῆτε, 2 pers. pl. pres. act. indic. . . . . id.

ζητεῖ, 3 pers. sg. pres. act. indic. {1 Cor. 13:5} . . . . ζητέω *(2212)*

ζήτει, 2 pers. sg. pres. act. imper. {1 Cor. 7:27} . . . . id.

ζητεῖν, pres. act. infin. . . . . id.

ζητεῖς, 2 pers. sg. pres. act. indic. . . . . . ζητέω *(2212)*

ζητεῖται, 3 pers. sg. pres. pass. indic. . . . . id.

ζητεῖτε, 2 pers. pl. pres. act. indic.
{Matt. 28:5} . . . . id.

ζητεῖτε, 2 pers. pl. pres. act. imper.
{Matt. 6:33} . . . . id.

ζητείτω, 3 pers. sg. pres. act. imper. . . . . . id.

(2212) **ζητέω**, ῶ, fut. ζητήσω [§16.P] *to seek, look for,* Matt. 18:12; Luke 2:48, 49; *to search after,* Matt. 13:45; *to be on the watch for,* Matt. 26:16; *to pursue, endeavor to obtain,* Rom. 2:7; 1 Pet. 3:11, et al.; *to desire, wish, want,* Matt. 12:47; *to seek, strive for,* Matt. 6:33; *to endeavor,* Matt. 21:46; *to require, demand, ask for,* Mark 8:11; Luke 11:16; 12:48; *to inquire or ask questions, question,* John 16:19; *to deliberate,* Mark 11:18; Luke 12:29; in N.T. from Hebrew, ζητεῖν τὴν ψυχήν, *to seek the life* of any one, *to seek to kill,* Matt. 2:20

ζητηθήσεται, 3 pers. sg. fut. pass. indic.
[§17.Q] . . . . ζητέω *(2212)*

(2213) **ζήτημα**, ατος, τό, nom. sg. neut. n. [§4.D.c] *a question; a subject of debate or controversy,* Acts 15:2; 18:15; 23:29, et al. (Acts 18:15, MT & TR | ζητήματα, GNT, WH & NA)

ζητήματα, nom. pl. neut. n. (Acts 18:15, GNT, WH & NA | ζήτημα, MT & TR) . ζήτημα *(2213)*

ζητήματα, acc. pl. neut. n. {Acts 25:19} . . id.

ζητήματος, gen. sg. neut. n. . . . . id.

ζητημάτων, gen. pl. neut. n. . . . . id.

ζητῆσαι, aor. act. infin. . . . . ζητέω *(2212)*

ζητησάτω, 3 pers. sg. aor. act. imper. . . . . id.

ζητήσεις, acc. pl. f. n. . . . . ζήτησις *(2214)*

ζητήσετε, 2 pers. pl. fut. act. indic. . . . . ζητέω *(2212)*

ζητήσεως, gen. sg. f. n. (Acts 15:2, 7, GNT, WH & NA; Acts 15:2, MT | Acts 15:2, 7, συζητήσεως, TR; Acts 15:7, MT) . ζήτησις *(2214)*

ζητήσῃ, 3 pers. sg. aor. act. subj. . . . . . . ζητέω *(2212)*

ζήτησιν, acc. sg. f. n. . . . . ζήτησις *(2214)*

(2214) **ζήτησις**, εως, ἡ, nom. sg. f. n. [§5.E.c] *a seeking; an inquiry, a question; a dispute, debate, discussion,* John 3:25; 1 Tim. 1:4; *a subject of dispute or controversy,* Acts 25:20, et al.

ζήτησον, 2 pers. sg. aor. act. imper. . . . . ζητέω *(2212)*

ζητήσουσιν, 3 pers. pl. fut. act. indic. . . . . id.

ζητοῦμεν, 1 pers. pl. pres. act. indic. (Luke 2:48, WH | ἐζητοῦμεν, GNT, MT, TR & NA) . . . . id.

ζητοῦν, nom. sg. neut. pres. act. part. . . . . id.

ζητοῦντες, nom. pl. m. pres. act. part. . . . id.

ζητοῦντι, dat. sg. m. pres. act. part. . . . . . id.

ζητούντων, gen. pl. m. pres. act. part. . . . id.

ζητοῦσι(ν), 3 pers. pl. pres. act. indic.
{Rom. 11:3} . . . . ζητέω *(2212)*

ζητοῦσιν, dat. pl. m. pres. act. part.
{Rom. 10:20} . . . . id.

ζητῶ, 1 pers. sg. pres. act. indic. . . . . id.

ζητῶν, nom. sg. m. pres. act. part. . . . . . . id.

ζιζάνια, nom. pl. neut. n.
{Matt. 13:26} . . . . ζιζάνιον *(2215)*

ζιζάνια, acc. pl. neut. n. {Matt. 13:25} . . . id.

(2215) **ζιζάνιον**, ου, τό [§3.C.c] *zizanium, darnel, spurious wheat,* a plant found in Palestine, which resembles wheat both in its stalk and grain, but is worthless and deleterious, Matt. 13:26, 27, 29, 30, 36, 38, 40

ζιζανίων, gen. pl. neut. n. . . . . ζιζάνιον *(2215)*

(2216) **Ζοροβαβέλ**, ὁ, *Zorobabel,* pr. name, indecl. (Matt. 1:12, 13; Luke 3:27, GNT, MT & NA | Ζοροβάβελ, WH & TR)

ζόφον, acc. sg. m. n. . . . . ζόφος *(2217)*

(2217) **ζόφος**, ου, ὁ, nom. sg. m. n. [§3.C.a] *gloom, thick darkness,* 2 Pet. 2:4, 17; Jude 6, 13

ζόφου, gen. sg. m. n. . . . . ζόφος *(2217)*

ζόφῳ, dat. sg. m. n. (Heb. 12:18, GNT, WH & NA | σκότῳ, MT & TR) . . . . id.

ζυγόν, acc. sg. m. n. . . . . ζυγός *(2218)*

(2218) **ζυγός**, οῦ, ὁ, nom. sg. m. n. [§3.C.a] a collateral form of ζυγόν (ζεύγνυμι) pr. *a cross bar or band; a yoke;* met. *a yoke* of servile condition, 1 Tim. 6:1; *a yoke* of service or obligation, Matt. 11:29, 30; Acts 15:10; Gal. 5:1; *the beam* of a balance; *a balance,* Rev. 6:5

ζυγῷ, dat. sg. m. n. . . . . ζυγός *(2218)*

(2219) **ζύμη**, ης, ἡ, nom. sg. f. n. [§2.B.a] *leaven,* Matt. 16:12; 13:33; met. *leaven* of the mind and conduct, by a system of doctrine or morals, used in a bad sense, Matt. 16:6, 11; 1 Cor. 5:6, et al.

ζύμῃ, dat. sg. f. n. . . . . ζύμη *(2219)*

ζύμην, acc. sg. f. n. . . . . id.

ζύμης, gen. sg. f. n. . . . . id.

ζυμοῖ, 3 pers. sg. pres. act. indic. . . . . . ζυμόω *(2220)*

(2220) **ζυμόω**, ῶ, fut. ζυμώσω [§20.T] *to leaven, cause to ferment,* Matt. 13:33; Luke 13:21; 1 Cor. 5:6; Gal. 5:9

ζῶ, 1 pers. sg. pres. act. indic. . . . . ζάω *(2198)*

ζῷα, nom. pl. neut. n. (GNT, WH, MT & NA | ζῶα, TR) . . . . ζῷον *(†2226)*

(2221) **ζωγρέω**, ῶ, fut. ζωγρήσω, perf. ἐζώγρηκα [§16.P] (ζωός, *alive,* + ἀγρεύω) pr. *to take alive, take prisoner in war* instead of killing; *to take captive, enthral,* 2 Tim. 2:26; also, *to catch* animals, as fish; in which sense it is used figuratively, Luke 5:10

ζωγρῶν, nom. sg. m. pres. act. part. . . ζωγρέω *(2221)*

(2222) **ζωή**, ῆς, ἡ, nom. sg. f. n. [§2.B.a] *life, living existence*, Luke 16:25; Acts 17:25; in N.T. spiritual *life* of deliverance from the proper penalty of sin, which is expressed by θάνατος, John 6:51; Rom. 5:18; 6:4, et al.; the final *life* of the redeemed, Matt. 25:46, et al.; *life, source* of spiritual *life*, John 5:39; 11:25; Col. 3:4
ζωῇ, dat. sg. f. n. . . . . ζωή (2222)
ζωήν, acc. sg. f. n. . . . . id.
ζωῆς, gen. sg. f. n. . . . . id.
ζῶμεν, 1 pers. pl. pres. act. indic. {Rom. 14:8a} . . . . ζάω (2198)
ζῶμεν, 1 pers. pl. pres. act. subj. {Rom. 14:8b,c} . . . . id.
ζῶν, nom. sg. m. pres. act. part. {John 6:51} id.
ζῶν, acc. sg. neut. pres. act. part. {John 4:10} id.
ζώνας, acc. pl. f. n. . . . . ζώνη (2223)
(2223) **ζώνη**, ης, ἡ, nom. sg. f. n. [§2.B.a] *a zone, belt, girdle*, Matt. 3:4; 10:9, et al.
ζώνην, acc. sg. f. n. . . . . ζώνη (2223)
(2224) **ζώννυμι**, and in N.T. ζωννύω, fut. ζώσω [§31.BB] *to gird, gird on, put on one's girdle*, John 21:18(2×)
ζῶντα, acc. sg. m. pres. act. part. {Acts 1:3} . . . . ζάω (2198)
ζῶντα, acc. pl. neut. pres. act. part. {Acts 7:38} . . . . id.
ζῶντας, acc. pl. m. pres. act. part. . . . . . . id.
ζῶντες, nom. pl. m. pres. act. part. . . . . . . id.
ζῶντι, dat. sg. m. pres. act. part. . . . . . . id.
ζῶντος, gen. sg. m. pres. act. part. {Matt. 16:16} . . . . id.
ζῶντος, gen. sg. neut. pres. act. part. {John 7:38} . . . . id.
ζώντων, gen. pl. m. pres. act. part. . . . . . . id.
ζωογονεῖσθαι, pres. pass. infin. [§17.Q] (Acts 7:19, GNT, MT & NA | ζωογονεῖσθαι, WH & TR) . . . . ζωογονέω (†2225)
(†2225) **ζωογονέω**, ῶ, fut. ζωογονήσω [§16.P] (ζωός + γόνος) pr. *to bring forth living creatures;* in N.T. *to preserve alive, save*, Luke 17:33; Acts 7:19
ζωογονήσει, 3 pers. sg. fut. act. indic. (Luke 17:33, GNT, MT & NA | ζωογονήσει, WH & TR) . . . . ζωογονέω (†2225)
ζωογονοῦντος, gen. sg. m. pres. act. part. (1 Tim. 6:13, GNT & NA | ζωογονοῦντος, WH | ζωοποιοῦντος, MT & TR) id.
(†2226) **ζῶον**, ου, τό, nom. sg. neut. n. [§3.C.c] *a living creature, animal*, Heb. 13:11; 2 Pet. 2:12, et al. (GNT, MT & NA | ζῶον, WH & TR)
ζωοποιεῖ, 3 pers. sg. pres. act. indic. (John 5:21(2×); 2 Cor. 3:6, GNT, MT & NA

| ζωοποιεῖ, WH & TR; John 5:21(2×), MT) . . . . ζωοποιέω (†2227)
ζωοποιεῖται, 3 pers. sg. pres. pass. indic. (1 Cor. 15:36, GNT, MT & NA | ζωοποιεῖται, WH & TR) . . . . id.
(†2227) **ζωοποιέω**, ῶ, fut. ζωοποιήσω [§16.P] (ζωός + ποιέω) pr. *to engender living creatures; to quicken, make alive, vivify*, Rom. 4:17; 8:11; 1 Cor. 15:36; in N.T. met. *to quicken* with the life of salvation, John 6:63; 2 Cor. 3:6, et al.
ζωοποιηθείς, nom. sg. m. aor. pass. part. (1 Pet. 3:18, GNT & NA | ζωοποιηθείς, WH, MT & TR) . . . . ζωοποιέω (†2227)
ζωοποιηθήσονται, 3 pers. pl. fut. pass. indic. (1 Cor. 15:22, GNT, MT & NA | ζωοποιηθήσονται, WH & TR) . . . . . . id.
ζωοποιῆσαι, aor. act. infin. (Gal. 3:21, GNT, MT & NA | ζωοποιῆσαι, WH & TR) id.
ζωοποιήσει, 3 pers. sg. fut. act. indic. (Rom. 8:11, GNT & NA | ζωοποιήσει, WH, MT & TR) . . . . id.
ζωοποιοῦν, nom. sg. neut. pres. act. part. (John 6:63, GNT & NA | ζωοποιοῦν, WH, MT & TR) . . . . id.
ζωοποιοῦν, acc. sg. neut. pres. act. part. (1 Cor. 15:45, GNT, MT & NA | ζωοποιοῦν, WH & TR) . . . . id.
ζωοποιοῦντος, gen. sg. m. pres. act. part. (Rom. 4:17, GNT & NA | ζωοποιοῦντος, WH, MT & TR) . . . . id.
ζώου, gen. sg. neut. n. (Rev. 6:3, 5, 7, GNT, WH, MT & NA | ζώου, TR) . . . . . . ζῶον (†2226)
ζῶσα, nom. sg. f. pres. act. part. . . . . ζάω (2198)
ζῶσαι, 2 pers. sg. aor. mid. imper. (Acts 12:8, GNT, WH & NA | περίζωσαι, MT & TR) . . . . ζώννυμι (2224)
ζῶσαν, acc. sg. f. pres. act. part. . . . . . . ζάω (2198)
ζώσας, acc. pl. f. pres. act. part. (Rev. 7:17, TR | ζωῆς, GNT, WH, MT & NA) . . id.
ζώσει, 3 pers. sg. fut. act. indic. . . . . . ζώννυμι (2224)
ζῶσιν, 3 pers. pl. pres. act. indic. {Luke 20:38} . . . . ζάω (2198)
ζῶσιν, 3 pers. pl. pres. act. subj. {2 Cor. 5:15} . . . . id.
ζώων, gen. pl. neut. n. (GNT, WH, MT & NA | ζώων, TR) . . . . ζῶον (†2226)

H

ἡ, nom. sg. f. article [§1.A] {1 Cor. 7:15} . ὁ (3588)
ἥ, nom. sg. f. relative pron. [§10.J.g] {Luke 2:37} . . . . ὅς (3739)

(2228) **ἤ,** disjunctive particle, *either, or,* Matt. 6:24, et al.; after comparatives, and ἄλλος, ἕτερος, expressed or implied, *than,* Matt. 10:15; 18:8; Acts 17:21; 24:21; intensive after ἀλλά and πρίν, Luke 12:51; Matt. 1:18; it also serves to point an interrogation, Rom. 3:29, et al. {1 Cor. 7:15a}

(2229) **ἦ,** a particle occurring in the N.T. only in the combination ἦ μήν, introductory to the terms of an oath (Heb. 6:14, MT & TR | Εἰ μήν, GNT, WH & NA)

ᾖ, 3 pers. sg. pres. subj. [§12.L] {1 Tim. 4:15} . . . . εἰμί *(1510)*

ᾗ, dat. sg. f. relative pron. [§10.J.g] {1 Tim. 4:6} . . . . ὅς *(3739)*

ἠβουλήθην, 1 pers. sg. aor. pass. dep. indic. [§13.1] (2 John 12, TR | ἐβουλήθην, GNT, WH, MT & NA) . . . . βούλομαι *(1014)*

ἤγαγε(ν), 3 pers. sg. 2 aor. act. indic. [§13.7.d] . . . . ἄγω *(71)*

ἠγάγετε, 2 pers. pl. 2 aor. act. indic. . . . . . id.

ἤγαγον, 3 pers. pl. 2 aor. act. indic. . . . . . id.

ἠγαλλιάσατο, 3 pers. sg. aor. mid. dep. indic. . . . . ἀγαλλιάω *(21)*

ἠγαλλίασε(ν), 3 pers. sg. aor. act. indic. . . id.

ἠγαλλιᾶτο, 3 pers. sg. imperf. mid./pass. dep. indic. (Acts 16:34, MT | ἠγαλλιάσατο, GNT, WH, TR & NA) . . . . id.

ἠγανάκτησαν, 3 pers. pl. aor. act. indic. . . . . ἀγανακτέω *(23)*

ἠγανάκτησε(ν), 3 pers. sg. aor. act. indic. id.

ἠγάπα, 3 pers. sg. imperf. act. indic. . . ἀγαπάω *(25)*

ἠγαπᾶτε, 2 pers. pl. imperf. act. indic. . . . id.

ἠγαπήκαμεν, 1 pers. pl. perf. act. indic. (1 John 4:10, GNT, WH & NA | ἠγαπήσαμεν, MT & TR) . . . . id.

ἠγαπηκόσι(ν), dat. pl. m. perf. act. part. [§16.3] . . . . id.

ἠγαπημένην, acc. sg. f. perf. pass. part. . . id.

ἠγαπημένοι, nom. pl. m. perf. pass. part. . id.

ἠγαπημένοις, dat. pl. m. perf. pass. part. (Jude 1, GNT, WH & NA | ἡγιασμένοις, MT & TR) . . . . id.

ἠγαπημένῳ, dat. sg. m. perf. pass. part. . . id.

ἠγάπησα, 1 pers. sg. aor. act. indic. . . . . . id.

ἠγαπήσαμεν, 1 pers. pl. aor. act. indic. (1 John 4:10, MT & TR | ἠγαπήκαμεν, GNT, WH & NA) . . . . id.

ἠγάπησαν, 3 pers. pl. aor. act. indic. . . . . id.

ἠγάπησας, 2 pers. sg. aor. act. indic. . . . . id.

ἠγάπησε(ν), 3 pers. sg. aor. act. indic. . . . id.

ἠγγάρευσαν, 3 pers. pl. aor. act. indic. . . . . ἀγγαρεύω *(29)*

ἤγγιζε(ν), 3 pers. sg. imperf. act. indic. . ἐγγίζω *(1448)*

ἤγγικε(ν), 3 pers. sg. perf. act. indic. . . . . id.

ἤγγισαν, 3 pers. pl. aor. act. indic. . . . . ἐγγίζω *(1448)*

ἤγγισε(ν), 3 pers. sg. aor. act. indic. . . . . . id.

ἤγειραν, 3 pers. pl. aor. act. indic. . . . . ἐγείρω *(1453)*

ἤγειρε(ν), 3 pers. sg. aor. act. indic. [§27.1.d] id.

ἡγεῖσθαι, pres. mid./pass. dep. infin. [§17.Q] . . . . ἡγέομαι *(2233)*

ἡγεῖσθε, 2 pers. pl. pres. mid./pass. dep. imper. . . . . id.

ἡγείσθωσαν, 3 pers. pl. pres. mid./pass. dep. imper. . . . . id.

ἡγεμόνα, acc. sg. m. n. . . . . ἡγεμών *(2232)*

ἡγεμόνας, acc. pl. m. n. . . . . id.

ἡγεμονεύοντος, gen. sg. m. pres. act. part. . . . . ἡγεμονεύω *(2230)*

(2230) **ἡγεμονεύω,** fut. ἡγεμονεύσω [§13.M] *to be a guide, leader, chief;* in N.T. *to hold the office of a Roman provincial governor,* Luke 2:2; 3:1

ἡγεμόνι, dat. sg. m. n. . . . . ἡγεμών *(2232)*

(2231) **ἡγεμονία,** ας, ἡ [§2.B.b; 2.2] *leadership, sovereignty;* in N.T. *a reign,* Luke 3:1

ἡγεμονίας, gen. sg. f. n. . . . . ἡγεμονία *(2231)*

ἡγεμόνος, gen. sg. m. n. . . . . ἡγεμών *(2232)*

ἡγεμόνων, gen. pl. m. n. . . . . id.

ἡγεμόσιν, dat. pl. m. n. . . . . id.

(2232) **ἡγεμών,** όνος, ὁ, nom. sg. m. n. [§4.2.e] *a guide; a leader; a chieftain, prince,* Matt. 2:6; *a Roman provincial governor,* under whatever title, Matt. 27:2, et al.

ἤγεν, 3 pers. sg. 2 aor. act. indic. (Acts 5:26, GNT, WH & NA | ἤγαγεν, MT & TR) ἄγω *(71)*

(2233) **ἡγέομαι,** οῦμαι, fut. ἡγήσομαι [§17.Q] *to lead the way; to take the lead,* Acts 14:12; *to be chief, to preside, govern, rule,* Matt. 2:6; Acts 7:10; ἡγούμενος, *a chief officer* in the church, Heb. 13:7, 17, 24; also, with perf. ἥγημαι, *to think, consider, count, esteem, regard,* Acts 26:2; 2 Cor. 9:5, et al.

ἠγέρθη, 3 pers. sg. aor. pass. indic. [§37.1] . . . . ἐγείρω *(1453)*

ἠγέρθησαν, 3 pers. pl. aor. pass. indic. . . . id.

ἤγεσθε, 2 pers. pl. imperf. pass. indic. . . ἄγω *(71)*

ἤγετο, 3 pers. sg. imperf. pass. indic. . . . . id.

ἥγημαι, 1 pers. sg. perf. mid./pass. dep. indic. . . . . ἡγέομαι *(2233)*

ἡγησάμενος, nom. sg. m. aor. mid. dep. part. id.

ἡγησάμην, 1 pers. sg. aor. mid. dep. indic. id.

ἡγήσασθε, 2 pers. pl. aor. mid. dep. indic. id.

ἡγήσατο, 3 pers. sg. aor. mid. dep. indic. . id.

ἡγίασε(ν), 3 pers. sg. aor. act. indic. . . . . ἁγιάζω *(37)*

ἡγιάσθη, 3 pers. sg. aor. pass. indic. . . . . . id.

ἡγιάσθητε, 2 pers. pl. aor. pass. indic. . . . id.

ἡγιασμένη, nom. sg. f. perf. pass. part. . . . id.

ἡγιασμένοι, nom. pl. m. perf. pass. part. . . id.

ἡγιασμένοις, dat. pl. m. perf. pass. part. . . id.

ἡγιασμένον, nom. sg. neut. perf. pass.
part. . . . . ἀγιάζω *(37)*
ἡγίασται, 3 pers. sg. perf. pass. indic. . . . . id.
ἡγνικότες, nom. pl. m. perf. act. part. . . ἀγνίζω *(48)*
ἡγνισμένον, acc. sg. m. perf. pass. part. . . id.
ἡγνόουν, 3 pers. pl. imperf. act. indic. . . . ἀγνοέω *(50)*
ἤγοντο, 3 pers. pl. imperf. pass. indic. . . . ἄγω *(71)*
ἠγόραζον, 3 pers. pl. imperf. act.
indic. . . . . ἀγοράζω *(59)*
ἠγόρασα, 1 pers. sg. aor. act. indic. . . . . . id.
ἠγόρασαν, 3 pers. pl. aor. act. indic. . . . . . id.
ἠγόρασας, 2 pers. sg. aor. act. indic. . . . . id.
ἠγόρασεν, 3 pers. sg. aor. act. indic. . . . . . id.
ἠγοράσθησαν, 3 pers. pl. aor. pass. indic. id.
ἠγοράσθητε, 2 pers. pl. aor. pass. indic. . . id.
ἠγορασμένοι, nom. pl. m. perf. pass. part. id.
ἡγοῦμαι, 1 pers. sg. pres. mid./pass. dep.
indic. . . . . ἡγέομαι *(2233)*
ἡγούμενοι, nom. pl. m. pres. mid./pass. dep.
part. . . . . id.
ἡγουμένοις, dat. pl. m. pres. mid./pass. dep.
part. . . . . id.
ἡγούμενον, acc. sg. m. pres. mid./pass. dep.
part. . . . . id.
ἡγούμενος, nom. sg. m. pres. mid./pass. dep.
part. . . . . id.
ἡγουμένους, acc. pl. m. pres. mid./pass. dep.
part. . . . . id.
ἡγουμένων, gen. pl. m. pres. mid./pass. dep.
part. . . . . id.
ἡγοῦνται, 3 pers. pl. pres. mid./pass. dep.
indic. [§17.Q] . . . . id.
ἠγωνίζοντο, 3 pers. pl. imperf. mid./pass. dep.
indic. ἀγωνίζομαι *(75)*
ἠγώνισμαι, 1 pers. sg. perf. mid./pass. dep.
indic. [§26.1] . . . . id.
ᾔδει, 3 pers. sg. pluperf. act. indic.
[§37.1] . . . . οἶδα *(‡1492)*
ᾔδειν, 1 pers. sg. pluperf. act. indic. . . . . . id.
ᾔδεις, 2 pers. sg. pluperf. act. indic. . . . . . id.
ᾔδεισαν, 3 pers. pl. pluperf. act. indic. . . . id.
ᾔδειτε, 2 pers. pl. pluperf. act. indic. . . . . id.
(2234) ἡδέως, adv. (ἡδύς, sweet) *with pleasure,*
gladly, willingly, Mark 6:20; 12:37; 2 Cor.
11:19
(2235) ἤδη, adv., *before now, now, already,* Matt.
3:10; 5:28, et al.; ἤδη ποτέ, *at length,*
Rom. 1:10; Phil. 4:10
ἠδίκηκα, 1 pers. sg. perf. act. indic. (Acts
25:10, WH | ἠδίκησα, GNT, MT, TR &
NA) . . . . ἀδικέω *(91)*
ἠδίκησα, 1 pers. sg. aor. act. indic. [§34.3.a]
(Acts 25:10, GNT, MT, TR & NA |
ἠδίκηκα, WH) . . . . id.
ἠδικήσαμεν, 1 pers. pl. aor. act. indic. . . . id.

ἠδικήσατε, 2 pers. pl. aor. act. indic. . . . ἀδικέω *(91)*
ἠδίκησε(ν), 3 pers. sg. aor. act. indic. . . . . id.
(2236) ἥδιστα, adv. (pr. neut. pl. superl. of ἡδύς) *with*
the greatest pleasure, most gladly, 2 Cor.
12:9, 15
ἡδοναῖς, dat. pl. f. n. . . . . ἡδονή *(2237)*
(2237) ἡδονή, ῆς, ἡ [§2.B.a] (ἡδος) *pleasure, grati-*
fication; esp. sensual pleasure, Luke 8:14;
Tit. 3:3; James 4:3; 2 Pet. 2:13; *a passion,*
James 4:1
ἡδονήν, acc. sg. f. n. . . . . ἡδονή *(2237)*
ἡδονῶν, gen. pl. f. n. . . . . id.
ἠδύναντο, 3 pers. pl. imperf. mid./pass. dep.
indic. Att. for ἐδύναντο [§37.1] . . . δύναμαι *(1410)*
ἠδύνασθε, 2 pers. pl. imperf. mid./pass. dep.
indic. Att. [§13.1] (1 Cor. 3:2, TR | ἐδύ-
νασθε, GNT, WH, MT & NA) . . . . . . id.
ἠδυνάσθη, 3 pers. sg. aor. pass. dep. indic.
(Mark 7:24, WH | ἠδυνήθη, GNT, MT,
TR & NA) . . . . id.
ἠδύνατο, 3 pers. sg. imperf. mid./pass. dep.
indic. Att. id.
ἠδυνήθη, 3 pers. sg. aor. pass. dep. indic. Att.
(Mark 7:24, GNT, MT, TR & NA |
ἠδυνάσθη, WH) . . . . id.
ἠδυνήθημεν, 1 pers. pl. aor. pass. dep. indic.
Att. . . . . id.
ἠδυνήθην, 1 pers. sg. aor. pass. dep. indic.
Att. . . . . id.
ἠδυνήθησαν, 3 pers. pl. aor. pass. dep. indic.
Att. . . . . id.
ἠδυνήθητε, 2 pers. pl. aor. pass. dep. indic.
Att. . . . . id.
(2238) ἡδύοσμον, ου, τό [§3.C.c] (ἡδύς + ὀσμή) *gar-*
den mint, Matt. 23:23; Luke 11:42
ἡδύοσμον, acc. sg. neut. n. . . . . ἡδύοσμον *(2238)*
ἤθελε(ν), 3 pers. sg. imperf. act. indic. . θέλω *(‡2309)*
ἤθελες, 2 pers. sg. imperf. act. indic. . . . . id.
ἠθέλησα, 1 pers. sg. aor. act. indic. . . . . . . id.
ἠθελήσαμεν, 1 pers. pl. aor. act. indic. . . . id.
ἠθέλησαν, 3 pers. pl. aor. act. indic. . . . . . id.
ἠθέλησας, 2 pers. sg. aor. act. indic. . . . . . id.
ἠθελήσατε, 2 pers. pl. aor. act. indic. . . . . id.
ἠθέλησε(ν), 3 pers. sg. aor. act. indic. . . . . id.
ἤθελον, 1 pers. sg. imperf. act. indic. {Gal. 4:20} id.
ἤθελον, 3 pers. pl. imperf. act. indic.
{John 6:11} . . . . id.
ἠθέτησαν, 3 pers. pl. aor. act. indic. . . . ἀθετέω *(114)*
ἤθη, acc. pl. neut. n. . . . . ἦθος *(2239)*
(2239) ἦθος, ους, τό [§5.E.b] pr. *a place of custo-*
mary resort, a haunt; hence, *a settled habit*
of mind and manners, 1 Cor. 15:33
ἠθροισμένους, acc. pl. m. perf. pass. part.
(Luke 24:33, GNT, WH & NA | συνη-
θροισμένους, MT & TR) . . . . . . ἀθροίζω *(‡4867)*

ἠθῶν, gen. pl. neut. n. (Acts 26:3, MT | ἐθῶν, GNT, WH, TR & NA) . . . . ἦθος *(2239)*
ἠκαιρεῖσθε, 2 pers. pl. imperf. mid./pass. dep. indic. . . . . ἀκαιρέομαι *(170)*
ἥκασι(ν), 3 pers. pl. perf. act. indic. (Mark 8:3, GNT, TR & NA | εἰσίν, WH | ἥκουσι, MT) . . . . ἥκω *(2240)*
ἥκει, 3 pers. sg. pres. act. indic. . . . . id.
ἤκμασαν, 3 pers. pl. aor. act. indic. (Rev. 14:18, GNT, WH, TR & NA | ἤκμασεν, MT) . . . . ἀκμάζω *(187)*
ἤκμασεν, 3 pers. sg. aor. act. indic. (Rev. 14:18, MT | ἤκμασαν, GNT, WH, TR & NA) . . . . id.
ἠκολούθει, 3 pers. sg. imperf. act. indic. . . . . ἀκολουθέω *(190)*
ἠκολουθήκαμεν, 1 pers. pl. perf. act. indic. (Mark 10:28, GNT, WH, NA | ἠκολουθήσαμεν, MT & TR) . . . . id.
ἠκολουθήσαμεν, 1 pers. pl. aor. act. indic. id.
ἠκολούθησαν, 3 pers. pl. aor. act. indic. . . id.
ἠκολούθησε(ν), 3 pers. sg. aor. act. indic. id.
ἠκολούθουν, 3 pers. pl. imperf. act. indic. id.
ἧκον, 3 pers. pl. imperf. act. indic. (Acts 28:23, MT & TR | ἦλθον, GNT & NA | ἦλθαν, WH) . . . . ἥκω *(2240)*
ἤκουε(ν), 3 pers. sg. imperf. act. indic. . . ἀκούω *(191)*
ἤκουον, 3 pers. pl. imperf. act. indic. . . . . id.
ἤκουσα, 1 pers. sg. aor. act. indic. . . . . . . id.
ἠκούσαμεν, 1 pers. pl. aor. act. indic. . . . . id.
ἤκουσαν, 3 pers. pl. aor. act. indic. . . . . . id.
ἤκουσας, 2 pers. sg. aor. act. indic. . . . . . id.
ἠκούσατε, 2 pers. pl. aor. act. indic. . . . . . id.
ἤκουσε(ν), 3 pers. sg. aor. act. indic. . . . . id.
ἠκούσθη, 3 pers. sg. aor. pass. indic. [§22.4] id.
ἤκουσι, 3 pers. pl. pres. act. indic. (Mark 8:3, MT | ἥκασι(ν), GNT, WH, TR & NA) id.
ἠκρίβωσε(ν), 3 pers. sg. aor. act. indic. . . . . ἀκριβόω *(198)*
ἠκυρώσατε, 2 pers. pl. aor. act. indic. . ἀκυρόω *(208)*
(2240) ἥκω, 1 pers. sg. pres. act. indic., fut. ἥξω, imperf. ἧκον, later perf. ἧκα,*to become, have arrived,* Luke 15:27, et al.
ἥλατο, 3 pers. sg. aor. mid. dep. indic. (Acts 14:10, GNT, WH & NA | ἥλλετο, MT & TR) . . . . ἅλλομαι *(242)*
ἠλαττόνησε(ν), 3 pers. sg. aor. act. indic. . . . . ἐλαττονέω *(1641)*
ἠλαττωμένον, acc. sg. m. perf. pass. part. . . . . ἐλαττόω *(1642)*
ἠλάττωσας, 2 pers. sg. aor. act. indic. . . . id.
ἠλαύνετο, 3 pers. sg. imperf. pass. indic. . . . . ἐλαύνω *(1643)*
ἠλεήθημεν, 1 pers. pl. aor. pass. indic. . . ἐλεέω *(1653)*
ἠλεήθην, 1 pers. sg. aor. pass. indic. . . . . id.

ἠλεήθητε, 2 pers. pl. aor. pass. indic. . . . . id.
ἠλεημένοι, nom. pl. m. perf. pass. part. ἐλεέω *(1653)*
ἠλεημένος, nom. sg. m. perf. pass. part. . id.
ἠλέησα, 1 pers. sg. aor. act. indic. . . . . id.
ἠλέησε(ν), 3 pers. sg. aor. act. indic. . . . . . id.
ἤλειφε(ν), 3 pers. sg. imperf. act. indic. . ἀλείφω *(218)*
ἤλειφον, 3 pers. pl. imperf. act. indic. . . . . id.
ἤλειψας, 2 pers. sg. aor. act. indic. [§23.2] id.
ἤλειψε(ν), 3 pers. sg. aor. act. indic. . . . . . id.
ἠλευθέρωσε(ν), 3 pers. sg. aor. act. indic. . . . . ἐλευθερόω *(1659)*
ἤλθαμεν, 1 pers. pl. 2 aor. act. indic. (Acts 28:14, GNT, WH & NA | ἤλθομεν, MT & TR) . . . . ἔρχομαι *(2064)*
ἦλθαν, 3 pers. pl. 2 aor. act. indic. (Luke 2:16; John 1:39; 4:27; Acts 12:10; 28:15, GNT, WH & NA | ἦλθον, Luke 2:16; John 1:39; 4:27; Acts 12:10, MT & TR | ἐξῆλθον, Acts 28:15, MT & TR) . . . . id.
ἤλθατε, 2 pers. pl. 2 aor. act. indic. (Matt. 25:36, GNT, WH & NA | ἤλθετε, MT & TR) . . . . id.
ἦλθε(ν), 3 pers. sg. 2 aor. act. indic. [§36.1] id.
ἦλθες, 2 pers. sg. 2 aor. act. indic. . . . . . . id.
ἤλθετε, 2 pers. pl. 2 aor. act. indic. (Matt. 25:36, MT & TR | ἤλθατε, GNT, WH & NA) . . . . id.
ἤλθομεν, 1 pers. pl. 2 aor. act. indic. . . . . id.
ἦλθον, 1 pers. sg. 2 aor. act. indic. {John 12:27} . . . . id.
ἦλθον, 3 pers. pl. 2 aor. act. indic. {John 12:9} . . . . id.
(2241) Ηλι, indecl. (Hebrew אֵלִי) *My God!* (Matt. 27:46, GNT & NA | Ἐλωΐ, WH | Ἠλί, MT & TR)
(†2242) Ἠλί, ὁ, *Eli,* pr. name, indecl. (Luke 3:23, GNT, MT, TRs & NA | Ἡλί, TRb)
Ἠλίᾳ, dat. sg. m. n. (GNT, MT, TRb & NA | Ἠλίᾳ, TRs | Ἠλείᾳ, WH) . . . . . Ἠλίας *(†2243)*
Ἠλίαν, acc. sg. m. n. (GNT, MT, TRb & NA | Ἠλίαν, TRs | Ἠλείαν, WH) . . . . . . id.
(†2243) Ἠλίας, ου, ὁ, nom. sg. m. n. [§2.B.d] *Elias,* pr. name (GNT, MT, TRb & NA | Ἠλίας, TRs | Ἠλείας, WH)
ἡλίκην, acc. sg. f. adj. . . . . ἡλίκος *(2245)*
(2244) ἡλικία, ας, ἡ [§2.B.b; 2.2] (ἧλιξ) *a particular period of life; the period fitted for a particular function, prime,* Heb. 11:11; *full age, years of discretion,* John 9:21, 23; perhaps, *the whole duration of life,* Matt. 6:27; Luke 12:25; otherwise, *stature,* Luke 19:3; Eph. 4:13
ἡλικίᾳ, dat. sg. f. n. . . . . ἡλικία *(2244)*
ἡλικίαν, acc. sg. f. n. . . . . id.
ἡλικίας, gen. sg. f. n. . . . . id.
ἡλίκον, acc. sg. m. adj. {Col. 2:1} . . . . ἡλίκος *(2245)*

ἡλίκον, nom. sg. neut. adj. (James 3:5, GNT,
    WH & NA | ὀλίγον, MT & TR) . . ἡλίκος *(2245)*

(2245) **ἡλίκος,** η, ον [§10.7.c] *as great as; how great,*
    Col. 2:1; James 3:5

ἥλιον, acc. sg. m. n. . . . . ἥλιος *(2246)*

(2246) **ἥλιος,** ου, ὁ, nom. sg. m. n. [§3.C.a] *the sun,*
    Matt. 13:43; 17:2; Mark 1:32, et al.; me-
    ton. *light of the sun, light,* Acts 13:11

Ἠλίου, gen. sg. m. n. (Luke 1:17; 4:25, GNT,
    MT, TRb & NA | Ἡλίου, TRs | Ἠλεία,
    WH) . . . . Ἠλίας *(†2243)*

ἡλίου, gen. sg. m. n. {Luke 4:40} . . . . . ἥλιος *(2246)*

ἡλίῳ, dat. sg. m. n. . . . . id.

ἡλκωμένος, nom. sg. m. perf. pass. part.
    [§21.U] (Luke 16:20, MT & TR | εἱλ-
    κωμένος, GNT, WH & NA) . . . . . . ἑλκόω *(1669)*

ἤλλαξαν, 3 pers. pl. aor. act. indic. . . ἀλλάσσω *(236)*

ἥλλετο, 3 pers. sg. imperf. mid./pass. dep.
    indic. (Acts 14:10, MT & TR | ἥλατο,
    GNT, WH & NA) . . . . ἅλλομαι *(242)*

(2247) **ἧλος,** ου, ὁ [§3.C.a] *a nail,* John 20:25(2×)

ἤλπιζε(ν), 3 pers. sg. imperf. act. indic. ἐλπίζω *(1679)*

ἠλπίζομεν, 1 pers. pl. imperf. act. indic. . . id.

ἠλπίκαμεν, 1 pers. pl. perf. act. indic.
    [§13.5.b] . . . . id.

ἠλπίκατε, 2 pers. pl. perf. act. indic. . . . . id.

ἤλπικεν, 3 pers. sg. perf. act. indic. . . . . . id.

ἠλπικέναι, perf. act. infin. . . . . id.

ἠλπικότες, nom. pl. m. perf. act. part. . . . id.

ἠλπίσαμεν, 1 pers. pl. aor. act. indic. . . . id.

ἥλων, gen. pl. m. n. . . . . ἧλος *(2247)*

ἥμαρτε(ν), 3 pers. sg. 2 aor. act. indic.
    [§36.2] . . . . ἁμαρτάνω *(264)*

ἥμαρτες, 2 pers. sg. 2 aor. act. indic. . . . . id.

ἡμαρτήκαμεν, 1 pers. pl. perf. act. indic. . . id.

ἥμαρτον, 1 pers. sg. 2 aor. act. indic.
    {Matt. 27:4} . . . . id.

ἥμαρτον, 3 pers. pl. 2 aor. act. indic.
    {Rom. 2:12} . . . . id.

(2248) **ἡμᾶς,** acc. pl. 1 pers. personal pron. . . . . . ἐγώ *(1473)*

ἥμεθα, 1 pers. pl. imperf. indic. [§12.2] (Matt.
    23:30(2×); Acts 27:37; Gal. 4:3; Eph. 2:3,
    GNT, WH & NA | ἦμεν, MT & TR) εἰμί *(1510)*

(2249) **ἡμεῖς,** nom. pl. 1 pers. personal pron.
    [§11.K.a] . . . . ἐγώ *(1473)*

ἠμέλησα, 1 pers. sg. aor. act. indic. . . . ἀμελέω *(272)*

ἤμελλε(ν), 3 pers. sg. imperf. act. indic. Att.
    [§13.1] . . . . μέλλω *(3195)*

ἤμελλον, 1 pers. sg. imperf. act. indic. (Rev.
    10:4, GNT, WH & NA | ἔμελλον, MT
    & TR) . . . . id.

ἦμεν, 1 pers. pl. imperf. indic. [§12.L] . . . . εἰμί *(1510)*

(2250) **ἡμέρα,** ας, ἡ, nom. sg. f. n. [§2.B.b; 2.2] *day,*
    a day, the interval from sunrise to sunset,
    opp. to νύξ, Matt. 4:2; 12:40; Luke 2:44;

the interval of twenty-four hours, compre-
hending day and night, Matt. 6:34; 15:32;
from the Hebrew, ἡμέρα καὶ ἡμέρα, *day*
by day, every day, 2 Cor. 4:16; ἡμέραν ἐξ
ἡμέρας, *from day to day, continually,*
2 Pet. 2:8; καθ' ἡμέραν, *every day, daily,*
Acts 17:17; Heb. 3:13; *a point or period of*
time, Luke 19:42; Acts 15:7; Eph. 6:13, et
al.; *a judgment, trial,* 1 Cor. 4:3

ἡμέρᾳ, dat. sg. f. n. . . . . ἡμέρα *(2250)*

ἡμέραι, nom. pl. f. n. . . . . id.

ἡμέραις, dat. pl. f. n. . . . . id.

ἡμέραν, acc. sg. f. n. . . . . id.

ἡμέρας, gen. sg. f. n. {Matt. 27:64} . . . . . id.

ἡμέρας, acc. pl. f. n. {Matt. 27:63} . . . . . id.

ἡμερῶν, gen. pl. f. n. . . . . id.

ἡμετέρα, nom. sg. f. 1 pers. possessive
    pron. . . . . ἡμέτερος *(2251)*

ἡμετέραις, dat. pl. f. 1 pers. possessive pron. id.

ἡμετέραν, acc. sg. f. 1 pers. possessive pron. id.

ἡμετέρας, gen. sg. f. 1 pers. possessive pron. id.

ἡμέτεροι, nom. pl. m. 1 pers. possessive pron. id.

ἡμετέροις, dat. pl. m. 1 pers. possessive pron. id.

ἡμέτερον, acc. sg. m. 1 pers. possessive pron.
    (Acts 24:6, TR | GNT, WH, MT & NA
    omit) . . . . id.

ἡμέτερον, acc. sg. neut. 1 pers. possessive
    pron. (Luke 16:12, WH | ὑμέτερον, GNT,
    MT, TR & NA) . . . . id.

(2251) **ἡμέτερος,** α, ον, 1 pers. possessive pron.
    [§11.3] *our,* Acts 2:11; 24:6, et al.

ἡμετέρων, gen. pl. f. 1 pers. possessive
    pron. . . . . ἡμέτερος *(2251)*

ἦ μήν, particle (Heb. 6:14, MT & TR | Εἰ
    μήν, GNT, WH & NA) . . . . ἦ *(2229)*

(2252) **ἤμην,** 1 pers. sg. imperf. indic. [§12.2] . . . εἰμί *(1510)*

ἡμιθανῆ, acc. sg. m. adj. . . . . ἡμιθανής *(2253)*

(2253) **ἡμιθανής,** ές [§7.G.b] (ἡμι(συς) + θνήσκω)
    half dead, Luke 10:30

(2254) **ἡμῖν,** dat. pl. 1 pers. personal pron. . . . . . ἐγώ *(1473)*

ἡμίση, acc. pl. neut. adj. (Luke 19:8, MT &
    TR | ἡμίσια, GNT, WH & NA) . . ἥμισυς *(†2255)*

ἡμίσια, acc. pl. neut. adj. (Luke 19:8, GNT,
    WH & NA | ἡμίση, MT & TR) . . . . . id.

ἡμίσους, gen. sg. neut. adj. [§7.6] . . . . id.

(2255) **ἥμισυ,** acc. sg. neut. adj. . . . . id.

(†2255) **ἥμισυς,** σεια, συ [§7.H.g] *half,* Mark 6:23;
    Luke 19:8; Rev. 11:11; 12:14

(2256) **ἡμιώριον,** ου, τό [§3.C.c] (ἡμι-+ ὥρα) *half an*
    hour, Rev. 8:1

ἡμιώριον, acc. sg. neut. n. (Rev. 8:1, GNT,
    MT, TR & NA | ἡμίωρον, WH) ἡμιώριον *(2256)*

ἡμύνατο, 3 pers. sg. aor. mid. dep. indic.
    [§13.2] . . . . ἀμύνω *(†292)*

ἠμφιεσμένον, acc. sg. m. perf. pass. part.

[§36.5] .... ἀμφιέννυμι *(294)*

(2257) ἡμῶν, gen. pl. 1 pers. personal pron. ..... ἐγώ *(1473)*

(2258) ἤν, 3 pers. sg. imperf. indic. [§12.2]

{1 John 3:12} .... εἰμί *(1510)*

ἤν, acc. sg. f. relative pron. [§10.J.g]

{1 John 3:11} .... ὅς *(3739)*

ἠνάγκαζον, 1 pers. sg. imperf. act.

indic. .... ἀναγκάζω *(315)*

ἠναγκάσατε, 2 pers. pl. aor. act. indic. ... id.

ἠνάγκασε(ν), 3 pers. sg. aor. act. indic. .. id.

ἠναγκάσθη, 3 pers. sg. aor. pass. indic.

[§26.1] .... id.

ἠναγκάσθην, 1 pers. sg. aor. pass. indic. . id.

ἤνεγκα, 1 pers. sg. aor. act. indic.

[§35.7] .... φέρω *(5342)*

ἤνεγκαν, 3 pers. pl. aor. act. indic. ...... id.

ἤνεγκε(ν), 3 pers. sg. aor. act. indic. ..... id.

ἠνείχεσθε, 2 pers. pl. imperf. mid./pass. dep.

indic. [§34.1.d] (2 Cor. 11:4, TR |

ἀνέχεσθε, GNT, WH & NA | ἠνείχεσθε,

MT) .... ἀνέχομαι *(430)*

ἠνεσχόμην, 1 pers. sg. 2 aor. mid. dep. indic.

(Acts 18:14, MT & TR | ἀνεσχόμην,

GNT, WH & NA) .... id.

ἠνέχθη, 3 pers. sg. aor. pass. indic.

[§36.1] .... φέρω *(5342)*

ἠνεῳγμένη, nom. sg. f. perf. pass. part. ἀνοίγω *(455)*

ἠνεῳγμένην, acc. sg. f. perf. pass. part. (Rev.

3:8, GNT, WH & NA | ἀνεῳγμένην, MT

& TR) .... id.

ἠνεῳγμένον, acc. sg. m. perf. pass. part. (Rev.

19:11, GNT, WH & NA | ἀνεῳγμένον,

MT & TR) .... id.

ἠνεῳγμένον, acc. sg. neut. perf. pass. part.

(Rev. 10:2, 8, GNT, WH & NA |

ἀνεῳγμένον, MT & TR) .... id.

ἠνέῳξεν, 3 pers. sg. aor. act. indic. (John

9:17, 32, GNT, WH & NA | ἤνοιξε(ν),

MT & TR) .... id.

ἠνεῴχθη, 3 pers. sg. aor. pass. indic. (Rev.

20:12, MT & TR | ἠνοίχθη, GNT, WH

& NA) .... id.

ἠνεῴχθησαν, 3 pers. pl. aor. pass. indic. ... id.

(2259) ἡνίκα, adv., *when,* 2 Cor. 3:15, 16

ἠνοίγη, 3 pers. sg. 2 aor. pass. indic.

[§37.1] .... ἀνοίγω *(455)*

ἠνοίγησαν, 3 pers. pl. 2 aor. pass. indic.

(Mark 7:35, GNT, WH & NA | διηνοί-

χθησαν, MT & TR) .... id.

ἤνοιξαν, 3 pers. pl. aor. act. indic. (Rev. 20:12,

MT | ἠνοίχθησαν, GNT, WH & NA |

ἠνεῴχθησαν, TR) .... id.

ἤνοιξε(ν), 3 pers. sg. aor. act. indic. ..... id.

ἠνοίχθη, 3 pers. sg. aor. pass. indic. [§23.4]

ἠνοίχθησαν, 3 pers. pl. aor. pass. indic. (Rev.

20:12, GNT, WH & NA | ἤνοιξαν, MT

| ἠνεῴχθησαν, TR) .... ἀνοίγω *(455)*

ἠντληκότες, nom. pl. m. perf. act.

part. .... ἀντλέω *(501)*

ἥξει, 3 pers. sg. fut. act. indic. .... ἥκω *(2240)*

ἥξῃ, 3 pers. sg. aor. act. subj. (Luke 13:35, MT

& TR | ἥξει, GNT & NA | WH omits)   id.

ἠξίου, 3 pers. sg. imperf. act. indic. ..... ἀξιόω *(515)*

ἠξίωσα, 1 pers. sg. aor. act. indic. .... id.

ἠξίωται, 3 pers. sg. perf. pass. indic. [§21.U]   id.

ἥξουσι(ν), 3 pers. pl. fut. act. indic. ..... ἥκω *(2240)*

ἥξω, 1 pers. sg. fut. act. indic. {Rev. 3:3a,b}   id.

ἥξω, 1 pers. sg. aor. act. subj. {Rev. 2:25}   id.

ἥξωσι(ν), 3 pers. pl. aor. act. subj. (Rev. 3:9,

MT & TR | ἥξουσιν, GNT, WH & NA)   id.

ἠπατήθη, 3 pers. sg. aor. pass. indic. ... ἀπατάω *(538)*

ἠπείθησαν, 3 pers. pl. aor. act. indic. . ἀπειθέω *(544)*

ἠπειθήσατε, 2 pers. pl. aor. act. indic. ...   id.

ἠπείθουν, 3 pers. pl. imperf. act. indic. [§16.P]   id.

ἠπείλει, 3 pers. sg. imperf. act. indic. . ἀπειλέω *(546)*

(2260) ἤπερ (ἤ + περ) an emphatic form of ἤ, *than,*

John 12:43

ἤπιοι, nom. pl. m. adj. (1 Thess. 2:7, MT &

TR | νήπιοι, GNT, WH & NA) .... ἤπιος *(2261)*

ἤπιον, acc. sg. m. adj. .... id.

(2261) ἤπιος, α, ον [§7.1] *mild, gentle, kind*

ἠπίστησαν, 3 pers. pl. aor. act. indic. . ἀπιστέω *(569)*

ἠπίστουν, 3 pers. pl. imperf. act. indic. ...   id.

ἠπόρει, 3 pers. sg. imperf. act. indic. (Mark

6:20, GNT, WH & NA | ἐποίει, MT &

TR) .... ἀπορέω *(639)*

ἥπτοντο, 3 pers. pl. imperf. mid./pass. dep.

indic. (Mark 6:56, MT & TR | ἥψαντο,

GNT, WH & NA) .... ἅπτω *(681)*

(2262) Ἤρ, ὁ, *Er,* pr. name, indecl., Luke 3:28

ἦραν, 3 pers. pl. aor. act. indic. .... αἴρω *(142)*

ἤρατε, 2 pers. pl. aor. act. indic. .... id.

ἠργάζετο, 3 pers. sg. imperf. mid./pass. dep.

indić. (Acts 18:3, GNT & NA | εἰργάζετο,

MT & TR | ἠργάζοντο, WH) . ἐργάζομαι *(2038)*

ἠργάζοντο, 3 pers. pl. imperf. mid./pass. dep.

indic. (Acts 18:3, WH | ἠργάζετο, GNT

& NA | εἰργάζετο, MT & TR) ......   id.

ἠργασάμεθα, 1 pers. pl. aor. mid. dep. indic.

(2 John 8, WH | εἰργασάμεθα, GNT, MT,

TR & NA) .... id.

ἠργάσαντο, 3 pers. pl. aor. mid. dep. indic.

(Heb. 11:33, WH | εἰργάσαντο, GNT,

MT, TR & NA) .... id.

ἠργάσατο, 3 pers. sg. aor. mid. dep. indic.

(Matt. 25:16; 26:10; Mark 14:6, GNT,

WH & NA | εἰργάσατο, MT & TR) .   id.

ἠρέθισε(ν), 3 pers. sg. aor. act. indic. . ἐρεθίζω *(2042)*

ἤρεμον, acc. sg. m. adj. .... ἥρεμος *(2263)*

(2263) ἥρεμος, ον [§7.2] equivalent to the ordinary

form ἠρεμαῖος, *tranquil, quiet,* 1 Tim. 2:2

ἦρε(ν), 3 pers. sg. aor. act. indic. . . . . αἴρω *(142)*

ἤρεσε(ν), 3 pers. sg. aor. act. indic.
　[§36.3] . . . . ἀρέσκω *(700)*

ἤρεσκον, 1 pers. sg. imperf. act. indic. . . . id.

ἡρέτισα, 1 pers. sg. aor. act. indic.
　[§13.2] . . . . αἱρετίζω *(140)*

ἠρημώθη, 3 pers. sg. aor. pass. indic.
　[§21.U] . . . . ἐρημόω *(2049)*

ἠρημωμένην, acc. sg. f. perf. pass. part. . . id.

ἤρθη, 3 pers. sg. aor. pass. indic. [§27.3] . αἴρω *(142)*

ἠριθμημέναι, nom. pl. f. perf. pass.
　part. . . . . ἀριθμέω *(705)*

ἠρίθμηνται, 3 pers. pl. perf. pass. indic.
　[§17.Q] . . . . id.

ἠρίστησαν, 3 pers. pl. aor. act. indic. . ἀριστάω *(709)*

ἦρκεν, 3 pers. sg. perf. act. indic.
　[§27.2.a] . . . . αἴρω *(142)*

ἠρμένον, acc. sg. m. perf. pass. part. . . . . id.

ἡρμοσάμην, 1 pers. sg. aor. mid. indic. ἁρμόζω *(718)*

ἠρνεῖτο, 3 pers. sg. imperf. mid./pass. dep.
　indic. . . . . ἀρνέομαι *(720)*

ἠρνημένοι, nom. pl. m. perf. mid./pass. dep.
　part. . . . . id.

ἠρνήσαντο, 3 pers. pl. aor. mid. dep. indic. id.

ἠρνήσασθε, 2 pers. pl. aor. mid. dep. indic. id.

ἠρνήσατο, 3 pers. sg. aor. mid. dep. indic. id.

ἠρνήσω, 2 pers. sg. aor. mid. dep. indic. . . id.

ἤρνηται, 3 pers. sg. perf. mid. dep. indic. . id.

ἤρξαντο, 3 pers. pl. aor. mid. dep. indic.
　[§23.5] . . . . ἄρχω *(757)*

ἤρξατο, 3 pers. sg. aor. mid. dep. indic. . . id.

Ἡροδίωνα, acc. sg. m. n. (Rom. 16:11, TR
　| Ἡρῳδίωνα, GNT, WH, MT &
　NA) . . . . Ἡρῳδίων *(†2267)*

ἡρπάγη, 3 pers. sg. 2 aor. pass. indic.
　[§26.3] . . . . ἁρπάζω *(726)*

ἥρπασε(ν), 3 pers. sg. aor. act. indic. . . . . id.

ἡρπάσθη, 3 pers. sg. aor. pass. indic. [§26.1] id.

ἠρτυμένος, nom. sg. m. perf. pass. part. ἀρτύω *(741)*

ἤρχετο, 3 pers. sg. imperf. mid./pass. dep.
　indic. . . . . ἔρχομαι *(2064)*

ἤρχοντο, 3 pers. pl. imperf. mid./pass. dep.
　indic. . . . . id.

ἤρχου, 2 pers. sg. imperf. mid./pass. dep.
　indic. . . . . id.

Ἡρῴδῃ, dat. sg. m. n. (GNT, WH, MT &
　NA | Ἡρώδῃ, TR) . . . . Ἡρῴδης *(†2264)*

Ἡρῴδην, acc. sg. m. n. (GNT, WH, MT &
　NA | Ἡρώδην, TR) . . . . id.

(†2264) **Ἡρῴδης**, ου, ὁ, nom. sg. m. n. [§2.B.c]
　Herod, pr. name　I. *Herod the Great,*
　Matt. 2:1, et al.　　II. *Herod Antipas,*
　tetrarch of Galilee and Peraea, Matt. 14:1,
　et al.　　III. *Herod Agrippa,* Acts 12:1, et

al. (GNT, WH, MT & NA | Ἡρώδης,
　TR)

Ἡρῳδιάδα, acc. sg. f. n. (GNT, WH, MT &
　NA | Ἡρωδιάδα, TR) . . . . Ἡρῳδιάς *(†2266)*

Ἡρῳδιάδος, gen. sg. f. n. (GNT, WH, MT
　& NA | Ἡρωδιάδος, TR) . . . . id.

(†2265) **Ἡρῳδιανοί**, ων, οἱ, *Herodians,* partisans of
　Ἡρῴδης, *Herod Antipas,* Matt. 22:16;
　Mark 3:6; 12:13

Ἡρῳδιανῶν, gen. pl. m. n. (GNT, WH, MT
　& NA | Ἡρωδιανῶν, TR) . . Ἡρῳδιανοί *(†2265)*

(†2266) **Ἡρῳδιάς**, αδος, ἡ, nom. sg. f. n. [§4.D.b]
　Herodias, pr. name

(†2267) **Ἡρῳδίων**, ωνος, ὁ [§4.2.e] *Herodian,* pr.
　name, Rom. 16:11

Ἡρῳδίωνα, acc. sg. m. n. (Rom. 16:11, GNT,
　WH, MT & NA | Ἡροδίωνα,
　TR) . . . . Ἡρῳδίων *(†2267)*

Ἡρῴδου, gen. sg. m. n. Ἡρῴδης (GNT,
　WH, MT & NA | Ἡρώδου,
　TR) . . . . Ἡρῴδης *(†2264)*

ἠρώτα, 3 pers. sg. imperf. act. indic.
　[§18.R] . . . . ἐρωτάω *(2065)*

ἠρώτησαν, 3 pers. pl. aor. act. indic. . . . . id.

ἠρώτησε(ν), 3 pers. sg. aor. act. indic. . . . id.

ἠρώτουν, 3 pers. pl. imperf. act. indic. (Matt.
　15:23, GNT, WH & NA | ἠρώτων, MT
　& TR) . . . . id.

ἠρώτων, 3 pers. pl. imperf. act. indic. . . . . id.

ἦς, 2 pers. sg. imperf. indic. [§12.L]
　{John 11:21} . . . . εἰμί *(1510)*

ἧς, gen. sg. f. relative pron. [§10.J.g]
　{John 11:2} . . . . ὅς *(3739)*

ᾖς, 2 pers. sg. pres. subj. . . . . εἰμί *(1510)*

Ἡσαΐᾳ, dat. sg. m. n. (Mark 1:2, GNT & NA
　| Ἡσαΐᾳ, WH | ἐν τοῖς προφήταις, MT
　& TR) . . . . Ἡσαΐας *(2268)*

Ἡσαΐαν, acc. sg. m. n. (Acts 8:28, 30, GNT,
　MT, TR & NA | Ἡσαΐαν, WH) . . . . . id.

(2268) **Ἡσαΐας**, ου, ὁ, nom. sg. m. n. [§2.B.d] *Isaiah,*
　pr. name (GNT, MT, TR & NA |
　Ἡσαΐας, WH | Ἡσαΐας, TRs)

Ἡσαΐου, gen. sg. m. n. (GNT, MT, TR &
　NA | Ἡσαΐου, TR | Ἡσαΐου,
　WH) . . . . Ἡσαΐας *(2268)*

ἦσαν, 3 pers. pl. imperf. indic. [§12.L] . . . εἰμί *(1510)*

(2269) **Ἡσαῦ**, ὁ, *Esau,* pr. name, indecl.

ἠσέβησαν, 3 pers. pl. aor. act. indic. . . ἀσεβέω *(764)*

ἦσθα, 2 pers. sg. imperf. indic. for ἦς
　[§23.2] . . . . εἰμί *(1510)*

ἠσθένει, 3 pers. sg. imperf. act. indic.
　[§16.P] . . . . ἀσθενέω *(770)*

ἠσθενήκαμεν, 1 pers. pl. perf. act. indic.
　(2 Cor. 11:21, GNT, WH & NA | ἠσθε-
　νήσαμεν, MT & TR) . . . . id.

ἠσθένησα, 1 pers. sg. aor. act. indic. . ἀσθενέω *(770)*
ἠσθενήσαμεν, 1 pers. pl. aor. act. indic.
(2 Cor. 11:21, MT & TR | ἠσθενήκαμεν,
GNT, WH & NA) .... id.
ἠσθένησε(ν), 3 pers. sg. aor. act. indic. ... id.
ἤσθιον, 3 pers. pl. imperf. act. indic. ... ἐσθίω *(2068)*
ἠσπάζοντο, 3 pers. pl. imperf. mid./pass. dep.
indic. .... ἀσπάζομαι *(782)*
ἠσπάσατο, 3 pers. sg. aor. mid. dep. indic. id.
ἧσσον, acc. sg. neut. compar. adj. (1 Cor.
11:17; 2 Cor. 12:15, GNT, WH & NA |
ἧττον, MT & TR) .... ἧσσων *(‡2276)*
ἡσσώθητε, 2 pers. pl. aor. pass. indic. (2 Cor.
12:13, GNT, WH & NA | ἡττήθητε, MT
& TR) .... ἑσσόομαι *(‡2274)*
(‡2276) **ἧσσων**, ον, compar. adj. *lesser, inferior,*
weaker
ἠστόχησαν, 3 pers. pl. aor. act. indic.
[§16.P] .... ἀστοχέω *(795)*
ἡσυχάζειν, pres. act. infin. .... ἡσυχάζω *(2270)*
(2270) **ἡσυχάζω**, fut. ἡσυχάσω [§26.1] (ἥσυχος,
quiet) to be still, at rest; to live peaceably,
be quiet, 1 Thess. 4:11; *to rest* from labor,
Luke 23:56; *to be silent or quiet, acquiesce,*
to desist from discussion, Luke 14:4; Acts
11:18; 21:14
ἡσυχάσαμεν, 1 pers. pl. aor. act.
indic. .... ἡσυχάζω *(2270)*
ἡσύχασαν, 3 pers. pl. aor. act. indic. ... id.
(2271) **ἡσυχία**, ας, ἡ [§2.B.b; 2.2] *rest, quiet, tran-*
quillity; a quiet, tranquil life, 2 Thess. 3:12;
silence, silent attention, Acts 22:2; 1 Tim.
2:11, 12
ἡσυχίᾳ, dat. sg. f. n. .... ἡσυχία *(2271)*
ἡσυχίαν, acc. sg. f. n. .... id.
ἡσυχίας, gen. sg. f. n. .... id.
ἡσύχιον, acc. sg. m. adj. .... ἡσύχιος *(2272)*
(2272) **ἡσύχιος**, ον [§7.2] equivalent to ἥσυχος,
quiet, tranquil, peaceful, 1 Tim. 2:2; 1 Pet.
3:4
ἡσυχίου, gen. sg. neut. adj. .... ἡσύχιος *(2272)*
ἠσφαλίσαντο, 3 pers. pl. aor. mid. dep. indic. id.
ἠσφαλίσατο, 3 pers. sg. aor. mid. dep.
indic. .... ἀσφαλίζω *(805)*
ἠτακτήσαμεν, 1 pers. pl. aor. act.
indic. .... ἀτακτέω *(812)*
ἦτε, 2 pers. pl. imperf. indic. [§2.L]
{John 11:21} .... εἰμί *(1510)*
ἦτε, 2 pers. pl. pres. subj. {Rom. 2:25} .. id.
ᾐτήκαμεν, 1 pers. pl. perf. act. indic.
[§13.2] .... αἰτέω *(154)*
ᾐτήσαντο, 3 pers. pl. aor. mid. indic. .... id.
ᾔτησας, 2 pers. sg. aor. act. indic. .... id.
ᾐτήσασθε, 2 pers. pl. aor. mid. indic. .... id.
ᾐτήσατε, 2 pers. pl. aor. act. indic. ...... id.

ᾐτήσατο, 3 pers. sg. aor. mid. indic. .... αἰτέω *(154)*
ἠτίμασαν, 3 pers. pl. aor. act. indic. (Mark
12:4, GNT, WH & NA | ἀπέστειλαν
ἠτιμωμένον, MT & TR) .... ἀτιμάζω *(818)*
ἠτιμάσατε, 2 pers. pl. aor. act. indic. .... id.
ἠτιμωμένον, acc. sg. m. perf. pass. part.
(Mark 12:4, with ἀπέστειλαν, MT & TR
| ἠτίμασαν, GNT, WH & NA) .... ἀτιμόω *(821)*
ἥτις, nom. sg. f. relative pron. [§10.J.h] .. ὅστις *(3748)*
(2273) **ἤτοι**, conj. (ἤ + τοι) in N.T. only in the usage, ἤτοι — ἤ, *whether,* with an elevated
tone
ἡτοίμακα, 1 pers. sg. perf. act. indic. (Matt.
22:4, GNT, WH & NA | ἡτοίμασα, MT
& TR) .... ἑτοιμάζω *(2090)*
ἡτοίμασα, 1 pers. sg. aor. act. indic. (Matt.
22:4, MT & TR | ἡτοίμακα, GNT, WH
& NA) .... id.
ἡτοίμασαν, 3 pers. pl. aor. act. indic. .... id.
ἡτοίμασας, 2 pers. sg. aor. act. indic. .... id.
ἡτοίμασε(ν), 3 pers. sg. aor. act. indic. ... id.
ἡτοιμασμένην, acc. sg. f. perf. pass. part. . id.
ἡτοιμασμένοι, nom. pl. m. perf. pass. part. id.
ἡτοιμασμένοις, dat. pl. m. perf. pass. part. id.
ἡτοιμασμένον, acc. sg. m. perf. pass. part.
{Rev. 12:6} .... id.
ἡτοιμασμένον, nom. sg. neut. perf. pass. part.
{2 Tim. 2:21} .... id.
ἡτοιμασμένον, acc. sg. neut. perf. pass. part.
{Matt. 25:41} .... id.
ἡτοίμασται, 3 pers. sg. perf. pass. indic. .. id.
ἡτοῦντο, 3 pers. pl. imperf. mid. indic.
[§13.2] .... αἰτέω *(154)*
(†2274) **ἡττάομαι**, ῶμαι, fut. ἡττηθήσομαι and
ἡττήσομαι [§19.S] perf. ἥττημαι, *to be less,*
inferior to; to fare worse, to be in a less fa-
vored condition, 2 Cor. 12:13; by impl. *to*
be overcome, vanquished, 2 Pet. 2:19, 20
ἡττήθητε, 2 pers. pl. aor. pass. indic. (2 Cor.
12:13, MT & TR | ἡσσώθητε, GNT, WH
& NA) .... ἡττάομαι *(†2274)*
(2275) **ἥττημα**, ατος, τό nom. sg. neut. n. [§4.D.c]
an inferiority, to a particular standard; *de-*
fault, failure, shortcoming, Rom. 11:12;
1 Cor. 6:7
ἥττηται, 3 pers. sg. perf. mid./pass. dep.
indic. .... ἡττάομαι *(†2274)*
ἧττον, acc. sg. neut. adj. (1 Cor. 11:17; 2 Cor.
12:15, MT & TR | ἧσσον, GNT, WH &
NA) .... ἥττων *(†2276)*
(†2276) **ἥττων**, Att. for ἥσσων, ον [§8.5] *less*
ἡττῶνται, 3 pers. pl. pres. mid./pass. dep.
indic. .... ἡττάομαι *(†2274)*
(2277) **ἤτω**, 3 pers. sg. pres. imper. [§12.2] ...... εἰμί *(1510)*
ηὐδόκησα, 1 pers. sg. aor. act. indic. [§34.3.c]

(Luke 3:22, TR | εὐδόκησα, GNT, WH,
MT & NA) . . . . εὐδοκέω *(2106)*

ηὐδοκήσαμεν, 1 pers. pl. aor. act. indic.
(1 Thess. 3:1, WH | εὐδοκήσαμεν, GNT,
MT, TR & NA) . . . . id.

ηὐδόκησαν, 3 pers. pl. aor. act. indic. (Rom.
15:27, WH | εὐδόκησαν, GNT, MT, TR
& NA) . . . . id.

ηὐδόκησεν, 3 pers. sg. aor. act. indic. (Gal.
1:15; 1 Cor. 10:5, WH | εὐδόκησεν, GNT,
MT, TR & NA) . . . . id.

ηὐδοκοῦμεν, 1 pers. pl. imperf. act. indic.
(1 Thess. 2:8, WH | εὐδοκοῦμεν, GNT,
MT, TR & NA) . . . . id.

ηὐκαίρουν, 3 pers. pl. imperf. act. indic.
[§34.3.c] . . . . εὐκαιρέω *(2119)*

ηὐλήσαμεν, 1 pers. pl. aor. act. indic. . . αὐλέω *(832)*

ηὐλίζετο, 3 pers. sg. imperf. mid./pass. dep.
indic. . . . . αὐλίζομαι *(835)*

ηὐλίσθη, 3 pers. sg. aor. pass. dep. indic. . id.

ηὐλόγει, 3 pers. sg. imperf. act. indic. [§34.3.c]
(Mark 10:16, TR | κατευλόγει, GNT, WH
& NA | εὐλόγει, MT) . . . . εὐλογέω *(2127)*

ηὔξανε(ν), 3 pers. sg. imperf. act. indic.
[§13.2] . . . . αὐξάνω *(837)*

ηὔξησε(ν), 3 pers. sg. aor. act. indic. . . . . . id.

ηὐπορεῖτο, 3 pers. sg. imperf. mid./pass. dep.
indic. (Acts 11:29, TR | εὐπορεῖτο, GNT,
WH, MT & NA) . . . . εὐπορέω *(2141)*

ηὑρίσκετο, 3 pers. sg. imperf. pass. indic.
(Heb. 11:5, GNT, WH & NA | εὑρίσκετο,
MT & TR) . . . . εὑρίσκω *(2147)*

ηὕρισκον, 3 pers. pl. imperf. act. indic. (Mark
14:55; Acts 7:11, GNT, WH & NA |
εὕρισκον, MT & TR) . . . . id.

ηὐφράνθη, 3 pers. sg. aor. pass. indic. (Acts
2:26, GNT, WH & NA | εὐφράνθη, MT
& TR) . . . . εὐφραίνω *(2165)*

ηὐχαρίστησαν, 3 pers. pl. aor. act. indic.
(Rom. 1:21, GNT, WH & NA | εὐχα-
ρίστησαν, MT & TR) . . . . . . εὐχαριστέω *(2168)*

ηὐχόμην, 1 pers. sg. imperf. mid./pass. dep.
indic. . . . . εὔχομαι *(2172)*

ηὔχοντο, 3 pers. pl. imperf. mid./pass. dep.
indic. . . . . id.

ἤφιε(ν), 3 pers. sg. imperf. act. indic.
[§32.2] . . . . ἀφίημι *(863)*

(2278) **ἠχέω**, ῶ, fut. ἠχήσω [§16.P] (ἠχή) *to sound,*
ring, 1 Cor. 13:1 *to roar,* as the sea, Luke
21:25

ἤχθη, 3 pers. sg. aor. pass. indic. [§23.4] . ἄγω *(71)*

ἠχμαλώτευσεν, 3 pers. sg. aor. act. indic.
[§13.2] . . . . αἰχμαλωτεύω *(162)*

(2279) **ἦχος**, ου, ὁ, nom. sg. m. n. [§3.C.a] equivalent to ἠχή, *sound, noise,* Acts 2:2; Heb.

12:19; met. *report, fame, rumor,* Luke 4:37

(†2279) **ἦχος**, ους, τό, *roar, sound, noise,* Luke 21:25

ἤχους, gen. sg. neut. n. (Luke 21:25, GNT,
WH & NA | ἠχούσης, MT & TR) . ἦχος *(†2279)*

ἠχούσης, gen. sg. f. pres. act. part. (Luke
21:25, MT & TR | ἤχους, GNT, WH &
NA) . . . . ἠχέω *(2278)*

ἠχρειώθησαν, 3 pers. pl. aor. pass. indic.
[§21.U] . . . . ἀχρειόω *(889)*

ἤχῳ, dat. sg. m. n. . . . . ἦχος *(2279)*

ἠχῶν, nom. sg. m. pres. act. part. . . . . . ἠχέω *(2278)*

ἥψαντο, 3 pers. pl. aor. mid. dep. indic. . ἅπτω *(681)*

ἥψατο, 3 pers. sg. aor. mid. dep. indic.
[§23.5] . . . . id.

Θ

θά, Aramaic with μαράνα (1 Cor. 16:22, GNT,
MT & NA | ἀθά, WH & TR) . μαρὰν ἀθά *(3134)*

Θαδδαῖον, acc. sg. m. n. . . . . Θαδδαῖος *(2280)*

(2280) **Θαδδαῖος**, ου, ὁ, nom. sg. m. n. [§3.C.a]
Thaddaeus, pr. name

(2281) **θάλασσα**, ης, ἡ, nom. sg. f. n. [§2.3] *the sea,*
Matt. 23:15; Mark 9:42; *a sea,* Acts 7:36;
an inland sea, lake, Matt. 8:24, et al.

θάλασσαν, acc. sg. f. n. . . . . θάλασσα *(2281)*

θαλάσσῃ, dat. sg. f. n. . . . . id.

θαλάσσης, gen. sg. f. n. . . . . id.

θάλπει, 3 pers. sg. pres. act. indic. . . . . θάλπω *(2282)*

θάλπῃ, 3 pers. sg. pres. act. subj. . . . . id.

(2282) **θάλπω**, fut. θάλψω [§23.1.a] *to impart*
warmth; met. *to cherish, nurse, foster,* Eph.
5:29; 1 Thess. 2:7

(2283) **Θαμάρ**, ἡ, *Thamar,* pr. name, indecl. (Matt.
1:3, GNT, MT, TRs & NA | θάμαρ, WH
& TRb)

(2284) **θαμβέω**, ῶ, fut. θαμβήσω [§16.P] aor.
ἐθάμβησα, *to be astonished, amazed,* Acts
9:6; later, pass. *to be astonished, amazed,*
awestruck, Mark 1:27; 10:24, 32

(2285) **θάμβος**, ους, τό, nom. sg. neut. n. [§5.E.b]
astonishment, amazement, awe, Luke 4:36,
et al.

θάμβους, gen. sg. neut. n. . . . . θάμβος *(2285)*

θαμβῶν, nom. sg. m. pres. act. part. (Acts 9:6,
TR | GNT, WH, MT & NA omit) θαμβέω *(2284)*

θανάσιμον, acc. sg. neut. adj. . . . . θανάσιμος *(2286)*

(2286) **θανάσιμος**, ον [§7.2] *deadly, mortal, fatal,*
Mark 16:18

θάνατε, voc. sg. m. n. . . . . θάνατος *(2288)*

θανατηφόρου, gen. sg. m. adj. . . θανατηφόρος *(2287)*

(2287) **θανατηφόρος**, ον [§7.2] (θάνατος + φέρω)
mortiferous, bringing or causing death,

deadly, fatal, James 3:8

θανάτοις, dat. pl. m. n. . . . . θάνατος *(2288)*

θάνατον, acc. sg. m. n. . . . . id.

(2288) **θάνατος,** ου, ὁ, nom. sg. m. n. [§3.C.a] *death, the extinction of life,* whether naturally, Luke 2:26; Mark 9:1; or violently, Matt. 10:21; 15:4; *imminent danger of death,* 2 Cor. 4:11, 12; 11:23; in N.T. spiritual *death,* as opposed to ζωή in its spiritual sense, in respect of a forfeiture of salvation, John 8:51; Rom. 6:16, et al.

θανάτου, gen. sg. m. n. . . . . θάνατος *(2288)*

θανατούμεθα, 1 pers. pl. pres. pass. indic. [§32.U] . . . . θανατόω *(2289)*

θανατούμενοι, nom. pl. m. pres. pass. part.   id.

θανατοῦτε, 2 pers. pl. pres. act. indic. . . . id.

(2289) **θανατόω,** ῶ, fut. θανατώσω, ἐθανάτωσα [§20.T] *to put to death, deliver to death,* Matt. 10:21; 26:59; Mark 13:12; pass. *to be exposed to imminent danger of death,* Rom. 8:36; in N.T. met. *to mortify, subdue,* Rom. 8:13; pass. *to be dead to, to be rid, parted from,* as if by the intervention of death, Rom. 7:4

θανάτῳ, dat. sg. m. n. . . . . θάνατος *(2288)*

θανατωθείς, nom. sg. m. perf. pass. part. . . . . θανατόω *(2289)*

θανατῶσαι, aor. act. infin. . . . . id.

θανατώσουσιν, 3 pers. pl. fut. act. indic. . id.

θανατώσωσι(ν), 3 pers. pl. aor. act. subj. . id.

(2290) **θάπτω,** fut. θάψω [§23.1.a] perf. τέταφα, aor. ἔθαψα, 2 aor. pass. ἐτάφην [§24.8.b] *to bury, inter,* Matt. 8:21, 22; 14:12, et al.

(2291) **Θάρα,** ὁ, *Thara,* pr. name, indecl. (Luke 3:34, GNT, TR & NA | θαρά, WH | θάρρα, MT)

(2292) **θαρρέω,** ῶ, *to be confident, courageous*

θαρρῆσαι, aor. act. infin. . . . . θαρρέω *(2292)*

θαρροῦμεν, 1 pers. pl. pres. act. indic. . . . id.

θαρροῦντας, acc. pl. m. pres. act. part. . . id.

θαρροῦντες, nom. pl. m. pres. act. part. . . id.

θαρρῶ, 1 pers. sg. pres. act. indic. contr. . id.

θάρσει, 2 pers. sg. pres. act. imper. . . . θαρσέω *(2293)*

θαρσεῖτε, 2 pers. pl. pres. act. imper. . . . . id.

(2293) **θαρσέω,** ῶ, and new Attic, θαρρέω, ῶ, fut. θαρρήσω [§16.P] imper. θάρσει, *to be of good courage, be of good cheer,* Matt. 9:2, et al.; *to be confident, hopeful,* 2 Cor. 7:16, et al.; *to be bold, maintain a bold bearing,* 2 Cor. 10:1, 2

(2294) **θάρσος,** ους, τό [§5.E.b] *courage, confidence,* Acts 28:15

θάρσος, acc. sg. neut. n. . . . . θάρσος *(2294)*

(2295) **θαῦμα,** ατος, τό, nom. sg. neut. n. [§4.D.c] *a wonder; wonder, admiration, astonish-*

ment (2 Cor. 11:14, GNT, WH & NA | θαυμαστόν, MT & TR)

θαῦμα, acc. sg. neut. n. {Rev. 17:6} . . . θαῦμα *(2295)*

θαυμάζειν, pres. act. infin. . . . . θαυμάζω *(2296)*

θαυμάζετε, 2 pers. pl. pres. act. indic. {John 7:21} . . . . id.

θαυμάζετε, 2 pers. pl. pres. act. imper. {John 5:28} . . . . id.

θαυμάζητε, 2 pers. pl. pres. act. subj. . . . . id.

θαυμάζοντες, nom. pl. m. pres. act. part. . . id.

θαυμαζόντων, gen. pl. m. pres. act. part. . . id.

(2296) **θαυμάζω,** 1 pers. sg. pres. act. indic., fut. θαυμάσω, and θαυμάσομαι, perf. τεθαύμακα, aor. ἐθαύμασα [§26.1] *to admire, regard with admiration, wonder at,* Luke 7:9; Acts 7:31; *to reverence, adore,* 2 Thess. 1:10; absol. *to wonder, be filled with wonder, admiration,* or *astonishment,* Matt. 8:10; Luke 4:22, et al.

θαυμάζων, nom. sg. m. pres. act. part. . . . . θαυμάζω *(2296)*

θαυμάσαι, aor. act. infin. . . . . id.

θαυμάσαντες, nom. pl. m. aor. act. part. . . id.

θαυμάσατε, 2 pers. pl. aor. act. imper. . . . id.

θαυμάσῃς, 2 pers. sg. aor. act. subj. . . . . . id.

θαυμασθῆναι, aor. pass. infin. . . . . id.

θαυμασθήσονται, 3 pers. pl. fut. pass. indic. (Rev. 17:8, GNT, WH & NA | θαυμάσονται, MT & TR) . . . . id.

θαυμάσια, acc. pl. neut. adj. . . . . . θαυμάσιος *(2297)*

(2297) **θαυμάσιος,** α, ον [§7.1] *wonderful, admirable, marvellous;* τὸ θαυμάσιον, *a wonder, wonderful work,* Matt. 21:15

θαυμάσονται, 3 pers. pl. fut. mid. dep. indic. (Rev. 17:8, MT & TR | θαυμασθήσονται, GNT, WH & NA) . . . . θαυμάζω *(2296)*

θαυμαστά, nom. pl. neut. adj. . . . . θαυμαστός *(2298)*

θαυμαστή, nom. sg. f. adj. . . . . id.

θαυμαστόν, nom. sg. neut. adj. {John 9:30} id.

θαυμαστόν, acc. sg. neut. adj. {Rev. 15:1} . id.

(2298) **θαυμαστός,** ή, όν [§7.F.a] *wondrous, glorious,* 1 Pet. 2:9; Rev. 15:1; *marvellous, strange, uncommon,* Matt. 21:42; Mark 12:11

θάψαι, aor. act. infin. . . . . θάπτω *(2290)*

θαψάντων, gen. pl. m. aor. act. part. . . . . id.

(2299) **θεά,** ᾶς, ἡ [§2.B.b; 2.2] *a goddess,* Acts 19:27, 35, 37

θεαθῆναι, aor. pass. infin. [§22.2] . . . θεάομαι *(2300)*

θεάν, acc. sg. f. n. θεά (Acts 19:37, TR | θεόν, GNT, WH, MT & NA) . . . . θεά *(2299)*

(2300) **θεάομαι,** ῶμαι, fut. θεάσομαι, perf. (pass. form) τεθέαμαι, aor. pass. ἐθεάθην [§19.S] *to gaze upon,* Matt. 6:1; 23:5; Luke 7:24; *to see, discern with the eyes,* Mark

16:11, 14; Luke 5:27; John 1:14, 32, 38, et al.; *to see, visit,* Rom. 15:24

θεᾶς, gen. sg. f. n. . . . . θεά *(2299)*

θεασάμενοι, nom. pl. m. aor. mid. dep. part. . . . . θεάομαι *(2300)*

θεασαμένοις, dat. pl. m. aor. mid. dep. part.   id.

θεασάμενος, nom. sg. m. aor. mid. dep. part.   id.

θεάσασθαι, aor. mid. dep. infin. . . . .   id.

θεάσασθε, 2 pers. pl. aor. mid. dep. imper.   id.

(†2301) **θεατρίζομαι**, fut. θεατρίσομαι, *to be exposed as in a theater, to be made a gazing-stock, object of scorn,* Heb. 10:33

θεατριζόμενοι, nom. pl. m. pres. pass. part. . . . . θεατρίζομαι *(†2301)*

(2302) **θέατρον**, ου, τό, nom. sg. neut. n. [§3.C.c] *a theater, a place where public games and spectacles are exhibited,* Acts 19:29, 31; meton. *a show, gazing-stock* {1 Cor. 4:9}

θέατρον, acc. sg. neut. n. {Acts 19:29} . . . . θέατρον *(2302)*

θεέ, voc. sg. m. n. [§3.1] . . . . θεός *(2316)*

θείας, gen. sg. f. adj. . . . . θεῖος *(2304)*

θεῖναι, 2 aor. act. infin. [§28.V] . . . . . . τίθημι *(5087)*

θεῖον, acc. sg. neut. adj. {Acts 17:29} . . . θεῖος *(2304)*

(2303) **θεῖον**, ου, τό, nom. sg. neut. n. [§3.C.c] *brimstone, sulphur,* Luke 17:29; Rev. 9:18, et al. {Rev. 9:17}

θεῖον, acc. sg. neut. n. {Luke 17:29} . . . . θεῖον *(2303)*

(2304) **θεῖος**, α, ον [§7.1] *divine, pertaining to God,* 2 Pet. 1:3, 4; τὸ θεῖον, *the divine nature, divinity,* Acts 17:29

(2305) **θειότης**, ητος, ἡ, nom. sg. f. n. [§4.2.c] *divinity, deity, godhead, divine majesty,* Rom. 1:20

θείου, gen. sg. neut. n. . . . . θεῖον *(2303)*

θείς, nom. sg. m. 2 aor. act. part. [§28.U] . . . . τίθημι *(5087)*

θείῳ, dat. sg. neut. n. . . . . θεῖον *(2303)*

θειώδεις, acc. pl. m. adj. . . . . θειώδης *(2306)*

(2306) **θειώδης**, ες [§7.G.b] *of brimstone, sulphurous,* Rev. 9:17

θέλει, 3 pers. sg. pres. act. indic. . . . . θέλω *(2309)*

θέλειν, pres. act. infin. . . . .   id.

θέλεις, 2 pers. sg. pres. act. indic. . . . .   id.

θέλετε, 2 pers. pl. pres. act. indic. . . . . . .   id.

θέλῃ, 3 pers. sg. pres. act. subj. . . . .   id.

(2307) **θέλημα**, ατος, τό, nom. sg. neut. n. [§4.D.c] *will, bent, inclination,* 1 Cor. 16:12; Eph. 2:3; 1 Pet. 4:3; *resolve,* 1 Cor. 7:37; *will, purpose, design,* 2 Tim. 2:26; 2 Pet. 1:21; *will, sovereign pleasure, behest,* Matt. 18:14; Luke 12:47; Acts 13:22, et al. freq.; ἐν τῷ θελήματι θεοῦ, *Deo permittente, if God please or permit,* Rom. 1:10 {John 6:39}

θέλημα, acc. sg. neut. n. {John 6:38} . θέλημα *(2307)*

θελήματα, acc. pl. neut. n. . . . .   id.

θελήματι, dat. sg. neut. n. . . . .   id.

θελήματος, gen. sg. neut. n. . . . .   id.

θέλῃς, 2 pers. sg. pres. act. subj. . . . . θέλω *(2309)*

θελήσαντας, acc. pl. m. aor. act. part. . . .   id.

θελήσῃ, 3 pers. sg. aor. act. subj. . . . . . .   id.

θέλησιν, acc. sg. f. n. . . . . θέλησις *(2308)*

(2308) **θέλησις**, εως, ἡ [§5.E.c] *will, pleasure,* Heb. 2:4

θελήσω, 1 pers. sg. aor. act. subj. . . . . . . θέλω *(2309)*

θελήσωσι(ν), 3 pers. pl. aor. act. subj. . . .   id.

θέλητε, 2 pers. pl. pres. act. subj. . . . . . .   id.

θέλοι, 3 pers. sg. pres. act. opt. . . . .   id.

θέλομεν, 1 pers. pl. pres. act. indic. . . . . .   id.

θέλοντα, acc. sg. m. pres. act. part. . . . . .   id.

θέλοντας, acc. pl. m. pres. act. part. . . . . .   id.

θέλοντες, nom. pl. m. pres. act. part. . . . .   id.

θέλοντι, dat. sg. m. pres. act. part. . . . . .   id.

θέλοντος, gen. sg. m. pres. act. part. . . . .   id.

θελόντων, gen. pl. m. pres. act. part. . . . .   id.

θέλουσι(ν), 3 pers. pl. pres. act. indic. . . .   id.

(2309) **θέλω**, 1 pers. sg. pres. act. indic., and ἐθέλω, the former being the present tense form used in N.T., fut. θελήσω and ἐθελήσω, imperf. ἤθελον, aor. ἠθέλησα [§35.5] *to exercise the will,* properly by an unimpassioned operation; *to be willing,* Matt. 17:4, et al.; *to be inclined, disposed,* Rom. 13:3, et al.; *to choose,* Luke 1:62; *to intend, design,* Luke 14:28, et al.; *to will,* John 5:21; 21:22, et al.; ἤθελον, *I could wish,* Gal. 4:20 {John 17:24}

θέλω, 1 pers. sg. pres. act. subj. {John 21:22–23} . . . . θέλω *(2309)*

θέλων, nom. sg. m. pres. act. part. . . . . . .   id.

θέλωσι(ν), 3 pers. pl. pres. act. subj. . . . . .   id.

θεμέλια, acc. pl. neut. n. . . . . θεμέλιον *(†2310)*

θεμέλιοι, nom. pl. m. n. . . . . θεμέλιος *(2310)*

θεμέλιον, acc. sg. m. n. . . . .   id.

(†2310) **θεμέλιον**, ου, τό, and θεμέλιος, ου, ὁ (pr. an adj. from θέμα, τίθημι) *a foundation,* Luke 6:48, 49; Heb. 11:10; met. *a foundation laid in elementary instruction,* Heb. 6:1; *a foundation of a superstructure of faith, doctrine, or hope,* 1 Cor. 3:10, 11, 12; Eph. 2:20; 1 Tim. 6:19; *a foundation laid in a commencement of preaching the Gospel,* Rom. 15:20

(2310) **θεμέλιος**, ου, ὁ, nom. sg. m. n., see θεμέλιον above

θεμελίου, gen. sg. m. n. . . . . θεμέλιος *(2310)*

θεμελίους, acc. pl. m. n. . . . .   id.

θεμελίῳ, dat. sg. m. n. . . . .   id.

(2311) **θεμελιόω**, ῶ, fut. θεμελιώσω, perf.

τεθεμελίωκα, aor. ἐθεμελίωσα [§20.T] *to found, lay the foundation of,* Matt. 7:25; Luke 6:48; Heb. 1:10; met. *to ground, establish, render firm and unwavering,* Eph. 3:17; Col. 1:23; 1 Pet. 5:10

θεμελιῶσαι, 3 pers. sg. aor. act. opt. (1 Pet. 5:10, TR | θεμελιώσει, GNT, MT & NA | WH omits) . . . . θεμελιόω *(2311)*

θεμελιώσει, 3 pers. sg. fut. act. indic. (1 Pet. 5:10, GNT, MT & NA | θεμελιῶσαι, TR | WH omits) . . . . id.

θέμενος, nom. sg. m. 2 aor. mid. part. [§28.W] . . . . τίθημι *(5087)*

θέντες, nom. pl. m. 2 aor. act. part. [§28.U]   id.

θέντος, gen. sg. m. 2 aor. act. part. . . . . . id.

θεοδίδακτοι, nom. pl. m. adj. . . . θεοδίδακτος *(2312)*

(2312) **θεοδίδακτος**, ον [§7.2] (θεός + διδακτός) *taught of God, divinely instructed,* 1 Thess. 4:9

θεοί, nom. pl. m. n. . . . . θεός *(2316)*

θεοῖς, dat. pl. m. n. . . . . id.

(2313) **θεομαχέω**, ῶ, fut. θεομαχήσω [§16.P] (θεός + μάχομαι) *to fight or contend against God, to seek to counteract the divine will,* Acts 23:9

θεομάχοι, nom. pl. m. adj. . . . . θεομάχος *(2314)*

(2314) **θεομάχος**, ον [§7.2] *fighting against God, in conflict with God,* Acts 5:39

θεομαχῶμεν, 1 pers. pl. pres. act. subj. (Acts 23:9, MT & TR | GNT, WH & NA omit) . . . . θεομαχέω *(2313)*

θεόν, acc. sg. m. n. {Acts 20:21} . . . . . . θεός *(2316)*

θεόν, acc. sg. f. n., *a goddess* (Acts 19:37, GNT, WH, MT & NA | θεάν, TR) . . θεός *(2316)*

(2315) **θεόπνευστος**, ον, nom. sg. f. adj. [§7.2] (θεός + πνέω) *divinely inspired,* 2 Tim. 3:16

(2316) **θεός**, οῦ, ὁ, nom. sg. m. n. and ἡ [§3.1] *a deity,* Acts 7:43; 1 Cor. 8:5; *an idol,* Acts 7:40; *God, the true God,* Matt. 3:9, et al. freq.; *God, possessed of true godhead,* John 1:1; Rom. 9:5; from the Hebrew, applied to potentates, John 10:34, 35; τῷ θεῷ, an intensive term, from the Hebrew, *exceedingly,* Acts 7:20, and, perhaps, 2 Cor. 10:4

(2317) **θεοσέβεια**, ας, ἡ [§2.B.b; 2.2] *worshipping of God, reverence towards God, piety*

θεοσέβειαν, acc. sg. f. n. . . . . θεοσέβεια *(2317)*

(2318) **θεοσεβής**, ές, nom. sg. m. adj. [§7.G.b] (θεός + σέβομαι) *reverencing God, pious, godly, devout, a sincere worshipper of God*

θεοστυγεῖς, acc. pl. m. adj. . . . . θεοστυγής *(2319)*

(2319) **θεοστυγής**, ές [§7.G.b] (θεός + στυγέω, *to hate*) *God-hated;* in N.T. *a hater and despiser of God,* Rom. 1:30

(2320) **θεότης**, ητος, ἡ [§4.2.c] *divinity, deity, godhead,* Col. 2:9

θεότητος, gen. sg. f. n. . . . . θεότης *(2320)*

θεοῦ, gen. sg. m. n. . . . . θεός *(2316)*

θεούς, acc. pl. m. n. . . . . id.

Θεόφιλε, voc. sg. m. n. . . . . Θεόφιλος *(2321)*

(2321) **Θεόφιλος**, ου, ὁ [§3.C.a] *Theophilus,* pr. name

(2322) **θεραπεία**, ας, ἡ [§2.B.b; 2.2] *service, attendance; healing, cure,* Luke 9:11; Rev. 22:2; meton. *those who render service, servants, domestics, family household,* Matt. 24:45; Luke 12:42

θεραπείαν, acc. sg. f. n. . . . . θεραπεία *(2322)*

θεραπείας, gen. sg. f. n. . . . . id.

θεραπεύει, 3 pers. sg. pres. act. indic. (Luke 6:7, GNT, WH & NA | θεραπεύσει, MT & TR) . . . . θεραπεύω *(2323)*

θεραπεύειν, pres. act. infin. . . . . id.

θεραπεύεσθαι, pres. pass. infin. [§14.N] . . id.

θεραπεύεσθε, 2 pers. pl. pres. pass. imper.   id.

θεραπεύεται, 3 pers. sg. pres. pass. indic. . id.

θεραπεύετε, 2 pers. pl. pres. act. imper. . . id.

θαραπευθῆναι, aor. pass. infin. . . . . id.

θεραπεύοντες, nom. pl. m. pres. act. part. id.

θεραπεῦσαι, aor. act. infin. . . . . id.

θεραπεύσει, 3 pers. sg. fut. act. indic. . . . . id.

θεράπευσον, 2 pers. sg. aor. act. imper. . . id.

θεραπεύσω, 1 pers. sg. fut. act. indic. . . . . id.

(2323) **θεραπεύω**, fut. θεραπεύσω, aor. ἐθεράπευσα [§13.M] *to serve, minister to, render service and attendance; to render* divine *service, worship,* Acts 17:25; *to heal, cure,* Matt. 4:23, 24; 8:16, et al.; pass. *to receive service,* Acts 17:25

θεραπεύων, nom. sg. m. pres. act. part. . . . . θεραπεύω *(2323)*

(2324) **θεράπων**, οντος, ὁ, nom. sg. m. n. [§4.2.d] *an attendant, a servant; a minister,* Heb. 3:5

θερίζειν, pres. act. infin. . . . . θερίζω *(2325)*

θερίζεις, 2 pers. sg. pres. act. indic. . . . . . . id.

θερίζουσιν, 3 pers. pl. pres. act. indic. . . . id.

(2325) **θερίζω**, 1 pers. sg. pres. act. indic., fut. θερίσω [§26.1] aor. ἐθέρισα, *to gather in harvest, reap,* Matt. 6:26; 25:24, 26; met. *to reap* the reward of labor, 1 Cor. 9:11; 2 Cor. 9:6; *to reap* the harvest of vengeance, Rev. 14:15, 16

θερίζων, nom. sg. m. pres. act. part. . . . θερίζω *(2325)*

θερίσαι, aor. act. infin. . . . . id.

θερισάντων, gen. pl. m. aor. act. part. . . . id.

θερίσει, 3 pers. sg. fut. act. indic. . . . . id.

θερισμόν, acc. sg. m. n. . . . . θερισμός *(2326)*

(2326) **θερισμός**, οῦ, ὁ, nom. sg. m. n. [§3.C.a] *a harvest, the act of gathering in the harvest,*

reaping, John 4:35, et al.; met. *the harvest* of the Gospel, Matt. 9:37, 38; Luke 10:2; *a crop;* met. *the crop* of vengeance, Rev. 14:15

θερισμοῦ, gen. sg. m. n. . . . . θερισμός *(2326)*

θερίσομεν, 1 pers. pl. fut. act. indic. . . θερίζω *(2325)*

θέρισον, 2 pers. sg. aor. act. imper. . . . . . . id.

θερισταί, nom. pl. m. n. . . . . θεριστής *(2327)*

θερισταῖς, dat. pl. m. n. . . . . id.

(2327) **θεριστής**, οῦ, ὁ [§2.B.c] *one who gathers in the harvest, a reaper,* Matt. 13:30, 39

θερμαίνεσθε, 2 pers. pl. pres. mid./pass. imper. θερμαίνω *(2328)*

θερμαινόμενον, acc. sg. m. pres. mid. part.   id.

θερμαινόμενος, nom. sg. m. pres. mid. part.   id.

(2328) **θερμαίνω**, fut. θερμανῶ [§27.1.c] *to warm;* mid. *to warm one's self,* Mark 14:54, 67; John 18:18, 25; James 2:16

(2329) **θέρμη**, ης, ἡ [§2.B.a] (θερμός, θέρω) *heat, warmth,* Acts 28:3

θέρμης, gen. sg. f. n. . . . . θέρμη *(2329)*

(2330) **θέρος**, ους, τό, nom. sg. neut. n. [§5.E.b] *the warm season of the year, summer,* Matt. 24:32; Mark 13:38; Luke 21:30

θέσθε, 2 pers. pl. 2 aor. mid. imper. . . . τίθημι *(5087)*

Θεσσαλονικεῖς, acc. pl. m. n. (1 Thess. 5:28, TRs | GNT, WH, MT, TRb & NA omit) . . . . Θεσσαλονικεύς *(2331)*

(2331) **Θεσσαλονικεύς**, έως, ὁ [§5.E.d] *Thessalonian, of Thessalonica*

Θεσσαλονικέων, gen. pl. m. n. Θεσσαλονικεύς *(2331)*

Θεσσαλονικέως, gen. sg. m. n. . . . . id.

(2332) **Θεσσαλονίκη**, ης, ἡ [§2.B.a] *Thessalonica, a* city of Macedonia

Θεσσαλονίκῃ, dat. sg. f. n. . . . . Θεσσαλονίκη *(2332)*

Θεσσαλονίκην, acc. sg. f. n. . . . . id.

Θεσσαλονίκης, gen. sg. f. n. . . . . id.

θέτε, 2 pers. pl. 2 aor. act. imper. (Luke 21:14, GNT, WH & NA | θέσθε, MT & TR) . . . . τίθημι *(5087)*

(2333) **Θευδᾶς**, ᾶ, ὁ, nom. sg. m. n. [§2.4] *Theudas,* pr. name, Acts 5:36

θεῷ, dat. sg. m. n. . . . . θεός *(2316)*

θεωρεῖ, 3 pers. sg. pres. act. indic. . . . θεωρέω *(2334)*

θεωρεῖν, pres. act. infin. . . . . id.

θεωρεῖς, 2 pers. sg. pres. act. indic. . . . . . . id.

θεωρεῖτε, 2 pers. pl. pres. act. indic. {John 14:19} . . . . id.

θεωρεῖτε, 2 pers. pl. pres. act. imper. {Heb. 7:4} . . . . id.

(2334) **θεωρέω**, ῶ, fut. θεωρήσω [§16.P] *to be a spectator, to gaze on, contemplate; to behold, view* with interest and attention, Matt. 27:55; 28:1, et al.; *to contemplate* mentally, *consider,* Heb. 7:4; in N.T. *to see, per-*

ceive, Mark 3:11, et al.; *to come to a knowledge of,* John 6:40; from the Hebrew, *to experience, undergo,* John 8:51, et al.

θεωρῇ, 3 pers. sg. pres. act. subj. . . . . θεωρέω *(2334)*

θεωρῆσαι, aor. act. infin. . . . . id.

θεωρήσαντες, nom. pl. m. aor. act. part. (Luke 23:48, GNT, WH & NA | θεωροῦντες, MT & TR) . . . . id.

θεωρήσῃ, 3 pers. sg. aor. act. subj. . . . . . . id.

θεωρήσουσιν, 3 pers. pl. fut. act. indic. (John 7:3, GNT, WH & NA | θεωρήσωσι(ν), MT & TR) . . . . id.

θεωρήσωσι(ν), 3 pers. pl. aor. act. subj. (John 7:3, MT & TR | θεωρήσουσιν, GNT, WH & NA) . . . . id.

θεωρῆτε, 2 pers. pl. pres. act. subj. . . . . . . id.

(2335) **θεωρία**, ας, ἡ [§2.B.b; 2.2] *a beholding; a sight, spectacle,* Luke 23:48

θεωρίαν, acc. sg. f. n. . . . . θεωρία *(2335)*

θεωροῦντας, acc. pl. m. pres. act. part. . . . . θεωρέω *(2334)*

θεωροῦντες, nom. pl. m. pres. act. part. . . . id.

θεωροῦντι, dat. sg. m. pres. act. part. (Acts 17:16, MT & TR | θεωροῦντος, GNT, WH & NA) . . . . id.

θεωροῦντος, gen. sg. m. pres. act. part. (Acts 17:16, GNT, WH & NA | θεωροῦντι, MT & TR) . . . . id.

θεωρούντων, gen. pl. m. pres. act. part. . . . id.

θεωροῦσαι, nom. pl. f. pres. act. part. . . . id.

θεωροῦσι(ν), 3 pers. pl. pres. act. indic. . . id.

θεωρῶ, 1 pers. sg. pres. act. indic. . . . . . . id.

θεωρῶν, nom. sg. m. pres. act. part. . . . . . id.

θεωρῶσι(ν), 3 pers. pl. pres. act. subj. . . . id.

θῇ, 3 pers. sg. 2 aor. act. subj. [§28.V] . τίθημι *(5087)*

(2336) **θήκη**, ης, ἡ [§2.B.a] *a repository, receptacle; a case, sheath, scabbard,* John 18:11

θήκην, acc. sg. f. n. . . . . θήκη *(2336)*

θηλαζόντων, gen. pl. m. pres. act. part. . . . . θηλάζω *(2337)*

θηλαζούσαις, dat. pl. f. pres. act. part. . . . id.

(2337) **θηλάζω**, fut. θηλάσω, aor. ἐθήλασα [§26.1] (θηλή, *a nipple*) *to suckle, give suck,* Matt. 24:19; Mark 13:17; Luke 21:23; 23:29; *to suck,* Matt. 21:16; Luke 11:27

θήλειαι, nom. pl. f. adj. . . . . θῆλυς *(2338)*

θηλείας, gen. sg. f. adj. . . . . id.

θῆλυ, nom. sg. neut. adj. {Gal. 3:28} . . . . id.

θῆλυ, acc. sg. neut. adj. {Matt. 19:4} . . . . id.

(2338) **θῆλυς**, θήλεια, θῆλυ [§7.H.g] *female;* τὸ θῆλυ, sc. γένος, *a female,* Matt. 19:4; Mark 10:6; Gal. 3:28; ἡ θήλεια, *woman,* Rom. 1:26, 27

(2339) **θήρα**, ας, ἡ [§2.B.b] (θήρ, *a wild beast*) *hunting, the chase;* met. *means of capture, a*

cause of destruction, Rom. 11:9

θήραν, acc. sg. f. n. . . . . θήρα *(2339)*

θηρεῦσαι, aor. act. infin. . . . . θηρεύω *(2340)*

(2340) **θηρεύω,** fut. θηρεύσω [§13.M] *to hunt, catch;* met. *to seize on, lay hold of,* Luke 11:54

θηρία, nom. pl. neut. n. {Tit. 1:12} . . . θηρίον *(2342)*

θηρία, acc. pl. neut. n. {Acts 11:6} . . . . . id.

(2341) **θηριομαχέω,** ῶ, fut. θηριομαχήσω, aor. ἐθηριομάχησα [§16.P] (θηρίον + μάχομαι) *to fight with wild beasts;* met. *to be exposed to furious hostility,* 1 Cor. 15:32

(2342) **θηρίον,** ου, τό, nom. sg. neut. n. [§3.C.c] (equivalent to θήρ, but pr. a dimin. from it) *a beast, wild animal,* Mark 1:13; Acts 10:12, et al.; met. *a brute, brutish man,* Tit. 1:12 {Rev. 20:10}

θηρίον, acc. sg. neut. n. {Rev. 20:4} . . . θηρίον *(2342)*

θηρίου, gen. sg. neut. n. . . . . id.

θηρίῳ, dat. sg. neut. n. . . . . id.

θηρίων, gen. pl. neut. n. . . . . id.

θησαυρίζειν, pres. act. infin. . . . . . θησαυρίζω *(2343)*

θησαυρίζεις, 2 pers. sg. pres. act. indic. . . id.

θησαυρίζετε, 2 pers. pl. pres. act. imper. . . id.

(2343) **θησαυρίζω,** fut. θησαυρίσω, aor. ἐθησαύρισα [§26.1] *to collect and lay up stores or wealth, treasure up,* Matt. 6:19, 20; *to heap up, accumulate,* Rom. 2:5; 1 Cor. 16:2; *to reserve, keep in store,* 2 Pet. 3:7

θησαυρίζων, nom. sg. m. pres. act. part. . . . . θησαυρίζω *(2343)*

θησαυροί, nom. pl. m. n. . . . . θησαυρός *(2344)*

θησαυρόν, acc. sg. m. n. . . . . id.

(2344) **θησαυρός,** οῦ, ὁ, nom. sg. m. n. [§3.C.a] *a treasury, a store, treasure, precious deposit,* Matt. 6:19, 20, 21, et al.; *a receptacle in which precious articles are kept, a casket,* Matt. 2:11; *a storehouse,* Matt. 12:35

θησαυροῦ, gen. sg. m. n. . . . . θησαυρός *(2344)*

θησαυρούς, acc. pl. m. n. . . . . id.

θησαυρῷ, dat. sg. m. n. . . . . id.

θησαυρῶν, gen. pl. m. n. . . . . id.

θήσει, 3 pers. sg. fut. act. indic. [§28.9.a] . . . . τίθημι *(5087)*

θήσεις, 2 pers. sg. fut. act. indic. . . . . . . id.

θήσω, 1 pers. sg. fut. act. indic. {Matt. 12:18} id.

θήσω, 1 pers. sg. aor. act. subj. {1 Cor. 9:18} id.

(2345) **θιγγάνω,** fut. θίξομαι, 2 aor. ἔθιγον [§36.2] *to touch,* Col. 2:21; Heb. 12:20; *to harm,* Heb. 11:28

θίγῃ, 3 pers. sg. 2 aor. act. subj. . . . . . θιγγάνω *(2345)*

θίγῃς, 2 pers. sg. 2 aor. act. subj. . . . . id.

θλίβεσθαι, pres. pass. infin. . . . . θλίβω *(2346)*

θλιβόμεθα, 1 pers. pl. pres. pass. indic. . . . id.

θλιβόμενοι, nom. pl. m. pres. pass. part. . . id.

θλιβομένοις, dat. pl. m. pres. pass. part. . . id.

θλίβουσιν, dat. pl. m. pres. act. part. . . . θλίβω *(2346)*

(2346) **θλίβω,** fut. θλίψω, perf. pass. τέθλιμμαι [§23.1.a; 23.7] *to squeeze, press; to press upon, encumber, throng, crowd,* Mark 3:9; met. *to distress, afflict,* 2 Cor. 1:6; 4:8, et al.; pass. *to be compressed, narrow,* Matt. 7:14

θλίβωσιν, 3 pers. pl. pres. act. subj. . . . θλίβω *(2346)*

θλίψει, dat. sg. f. n. . . . . θλῖψις (†2347)

θλίψεις, nom. pl. f. n. . . . . id.

θλίψεσι(ν), dat. pl. f. n. . . . . id.

θλίψεων, gen. pl. f. n. . . . . id.

θλίψεως, gen. sg. f. n. . . . . id.

θλῖψιν, acc. sg. f. n. (GNT, MT & NA | θλίψιν, WH & TR) . . . . id.

(†2347) **θλῖψις,** εως, ἡ, nom. sg. f. n. [§5.E.c] pr. *pressure, compression;* met. *affliction, distress of mind,* 2 Cor. 2:4; *distressing circumstances, trial, affliction,* Matt. 24:9, et al. (GNT, MT & NA | θλίψις, WH & TR)

(2348) **θνῄσκω** [§36.4] fut. θανοῦμαι, perf. τέθνηκα, 2 aor. ἔθανον, *to die;* in N.T., only in the perf. and pluperf., τέθνηκα, ἐτεθνήκειν, infin. τεθνάναι, part. τεθνηκώς, *to be dead,* Matt. 2:20; Mark 15:44, et al.

θνητά, acc. pl. neut. adj. . . . . θνητός *(2349)*

θνητῇ, dat. sg. f. adj. . . . . id.

θνητόν, nom. sg. neut. adj. {1 Cor. 15:54} id.

θνητόν, acc. sg. neut. adj. {1 Cor. 15:53} . id.

(2349) **θνητός,** ή, όν [§7.F.a] *mortal, subject to death,* Rom. 6:12; 8:11; 2 Cor. 4:11; τὸ θνητόν, *mortality,* 1 Cor. 15:53, 54; 2 Cor. 5:4

θνητῷ, dat. sg. neut. adj. . . . . θνητός *(2349)*

θορυβάζῃ, 2 pers. sg. pres. pass. indic. (Luke 10:41, GNT, WH & NA | τυρβάζῃ, MT & TR) . . . . θορυβάζομαι (‡5182)

(‡5182) **θορυβάζομαι,** *to be troubled, disturbed*

θορυβεῖσθε, 2 pers. pl. pres. pass. indic. {Mark 5:39} . . . . θορυβέω *(2350)*

θορυβεῖσθε, 2 pers. pl. pres. pass. imper. {Acts 20:10} . . . . id.

(2350) **θορυβέω,** ῶ, fut. θορυβήσω [§16.P] intrans. *to make a din, uproar;* trans. *to disturb, throw into commotion,* Acts 17:5; in N.T. mid. *to manifest agitation of mind, to raise a lament,* Matt. 9:23; Mark 5:39; Acts 20:10

θόρυβον, acc. sg. m. n. . . . . θόρυβος *(2351)*

(2351) **θόρυβος,** ου, ὁ, nom. sg. m. n. [§3.C.a] *an uproar, din; an outward expression of mental agitation, outcry,* Mark 5:38; *a tumult, commotion,* Matt. 26:5, et al.

θορύβου, gen. sg. m. n. . . . . θόρυβος *(2351)*

θορυβούμενον, acc. sg. m. pres. pass. part. . . . . θορυβέω *(2350)*

(2352) **θραύω**, fut. θραύσω, *to break, shiver;* met., perf. pass. part. τεθραυσμένος, *shattered, crushed* by cruel oppression, Luke 4:18

(2353) **θρέμμα**, ατος, τό [§4.D.c] *that which is reared;* pl. *cattle,* John 4:12
θρέμματα, nom. pl. neut. n. . . . . θρέμμα (2353)

(2354) **θρηνέω**, ῶ, fut. θρηνήσω, aor. ἐθρήνησα [§16.P] *to lament, bewail,* Matt. 11:17; Luke 7:32; John 16:20
θρηνήσετε, 2 pers. pl. fut. act. indic. . θρηνέω (2354)

(2355) **θρῆνος**, ου, ὁ, nom. sg. m. n. [§3.C.a] (θρέομαι, *to shriek) wailing, lamentation* (Matt. 2:18, MT & TR | GNT, WH & NA omit)

(2356) **θρησκεία**, ας, ἡ, nom. sg. f. n. [§2.B.b; 2.2] *religious worship,* Col. 2:18; *religion, a religious system,* Acts 26:5; *religion, piety,* James 1:26, 27
θρησκείᾳ, dat. sg. f. n. . . . . θρησκεία (2356)
θρησκείας, gen. sg. f. n. . . . . id.

(2357) **θρῆσκος**, ον, nom. sg. m. adj., *occupied with religious observances;* in N.T. *religious, devout, pious*
θριαμβεύοντι, dat. sg. m. pres. act. part. θριαμβεύω (2358)
θριαμβεύσας, nom. sg. m. aor. act. part. . id.

(2358) **θριαμβεύω**, fut. θριαμβεύσω [§13.M] (θρίαμβος, *a hymn in honor of Bacchus; a triumph)* pr. *to celebrate a triumph;* trans. *to lead in triumph, celebrate a triumph over,* Col. 2:15; in N.T. *to cause to triumph,* or, *to render conspicuous,* 2 Cor. 2:14

(2359) **θρίξ**, τριχός, ἡ, nom. sg. f. n. [§4.2.b] *a hair;* pl. αἱ τρίχες, dat. θριξί(ν), *the hair* of the head, Matt. 5:36; 10:30, et al.; of an animal, Matt. 3:4; Mark 1:6
θριξί(ν), dat. pl. f. n. . . . . θρίξ (2359)
θροεῖσθαι, pres. pass. infin. . . . . θροέω (2360)
θροεῖσθε, 2 pers. pl. pres. pass. imper. . . . id.

(2360) **θροέω**, ῶ, fut. θροήσω [§16.P] (θρόος, *an uproar,* from θρέομαι, *to make a clamor) to cry aloud;* in N.T. pass., *to be disturbed, disquieted, alarmed, terrified,* Matt. 24:6; Mark 13:7; 2 Thess. 2:2
θρόμβοι, nom. pl. m. n. . . . . θρόμβος (2361)

(2361) **θρόμβος**, ου, ὁ [§3.C.a] *a lump;* espec. *a clot* of blood, Luke 22:44
θρόνοι, nom. pl. m. n. . . . . θρόνος (2362)
θρόνον, acc. sg. m. n. . . . . id.

(2362) **θρόνος**, ου, ὁ, nom. sg. m. n. (θράω, *to set) a seat, a throne,* Matt. 5:34; 19:28; Luke 1:52; meton. *power, dominion,* Luke 1:32; Heb. 1:8; *a potentate,* Col. 1:16, et al.
θρόνου, gen. sg. m. n. . . . . θρόνος (2362)
θρόνους, acc. pl. m. n. . . . . id.

θρόνῳ, dat. sg. m. n. . . . . θρόνος (2362)
θρόνων, gen. pl. m. n. . . . . id.

(2363) **Θυάτειρα**, ων, τά, nom. pl. neut. n. [§3.C.c] *Thyatira,* a city of Lydia, Rev. 1:11
Θυατείροις, dat. pl. neut. n. . . . . Θυάτειρα (2363)
Θυατείρων, gen. pl. neut. n. . . . . id.
θύγατερ, voc. sg. f. n. [§6.1.2] . . . . . θυγάτηρ (2364)
θυγατέρα, acc. sg. f. n. . . . . id.
θυγατέρας, acc. pl. f. n. . . . . id.
θυγατέρες, nom. pl. f. n. {Acts 2:17} . . . . id.
θυγατέρες, voc. pl. f. n. {Luke 23:28} . . . id.
θυγατέρων, gen. pl. f. n. . . . . id.

(2364) **θυγάτηρ**, nom. sg. f. n., τέρος, τρός, dat. τέρι, τρί, acc. τέρα, voc. θύγατερ, ἡ [§6.2] *a daughter,* Matt. 9:18; 10:35, 37; in the vocative, an expression of affection and kindness, Matt. 9:22; from the Hebrew, *one of the female posterity* of any one, Luke 1:5; met. *a city,* Matt. 21:5; John 12:15; pl. *female inhabitants,* Luke 23:28 {Mark 5:35}
θυγάτηρ, voc. sg. f. n. {Mark 5:34} . θυγάτηρ (2364)
θυγατρί, dat. sg. f. n. . . . . id.

(2365) **θυγάτριον**, ου, τό, nom. sg. neut. n. [§3.C.c] *a little daughter, female child,* Mark 5:23; 7:25
θυγατρός, gen. sg. f. n. . . . . θυγάτηρ (2364)
θύει, 3 pers. sg. pres. act. indic. (1 Cor. 10:20, MT & TR | θύουσιν, GNT, WH & NA) . . . . θύω (2380)
θύειν, pres. act. infin. . . . . id.

(2366) **θύελλα**, ης, ἡ [§2.3] (θύω, *to rush) a tempest, whirlwind, hurricane,* Heb. 12:18
θυέλλῃ, dat. sg. f. n. . . . . θύελλα (2366)
θύεσθαι, pres. pass. infin. . . . . θύω (2380)
θύϊνον, acc. sg. neut. adj. (Rev. 18:12, GNT, MT, TR & NA | θύινον, WH) . . . . θύϊνος (2367)

(2367) **θύϊνος**, η, ον [§7.F.a] *thyme,* of θυΐα, *thya,* an aromatic evergreen tree, arbor vitae, resembling the cedar, and found in Libya, Rev. 18:12

(2368) **θυμίαμα**, ατος, τό [§4.D.c] *incense, any odoriferous substance burnt in religious worship,* Rev. 5:8; 8:3, 4; 18:13; or, *the act of burning incense,* Luke 1:10, 11
θυμιάματα, nom. pl. neut. n. {Rev. 8:3} . . . . θυμίαμα (2368)
θυμιάματα, acc. pl. neut. n. {Rev. 18:13} . id.
θυμιάματος, gen. sg. neut. n. . . . . id.
θυμιαμάτων, gen. pl. neut. n. . . . . id.
θυμιᾶσαι, aor. act. infin. . . . . θυμιάω (2370)

(2369) **θυμιατήριον**, ου, τό [§3.C.c] *a censer* for burning incense, Heb. 9:4
θυμιατήριον, acc. sg. neut. n. . . . . θυμιατήριον (2369)

(2370) **θυμιάω**, ῶ, fut. θυμιάσω [§18.R] *to burn in-*

cense, Luke 1:9

θυμοί, nom. pl. m. n. . . . . θυμός *(2372)*

(2371) **θυμομαχέω,** ῶ, fut. θυμομαχήσω [§16.P] (θυμός + μάχομαι) *to wage war fiercely; to be warmly hostile to, be enraged against,* Acts 12:20

θυμομαχῶν, nom. sg. m. pres. act. part. . . . . θυμομαχέω *(2371)*

θυμόν, acc. sg. m. n. . . . . θυμός *(2372)*

(2372) **θυμός,** οῦ, ὁ, nom. sg. m. n. [§3.C.a] (θύω, *to rush*) pr. *the soul, mind;* hence, *a strong passion or emotion of the mind; anger, wrath,* Luke 4:28; Acts 19:28, et al.; pl. *swellings of anger,* 2 Cor. 12:20; Gal. 5:20

θυμοῦ, gen. sg. m. n. . . . . θυμός *(2372)*

(2373) **θυμόω,** ῶ, fut. θυμώσω [§20.T] *to provoke to anger;* pass. *to be angered, enraged,* Matt. 2:16

θύουσιν, 3 pers. pl. pres. act. indic. (1 Cor. 10:20(2×), GNT, WH & NA | θύει, MT & TR) . . . . θύω *(2380)*

(2374) **θύρα,** ας, ἡ, nom. sg. f. n. [§2.B.b] *a door, gate,* Matt. 6:6; Mark 1:33; *an entrance,* Matt. 27:60, et al.; in N.T. met. *an opening, occasion, opportunity,* Acts 14:27; 1 Cor. 16:9, et al.; meton. *a medium or means of entrance,* John 10:7, 9

θύρᾳ, dat. sg. f. n. . . . . θύρα *(2374)*

θύραι, nom. pl. f. n. . . . . id.

θύραις, dat. pl. f. n. . . . . id.

θύραν, acc. sg. f. n. . . . . id.

θύρας, gen. sg. f. n. {Acts 12:6} . . . . id.

θύρας, acc. pl. f. n. {Acts 16:27} . . . . id.

θυρεόν, acc. sg. m. n. . . . . θυρεός *(2375)*

(2375) **θυρεός,** οῦ, ὁ [§3.C.a] *a stone or other material employed to close a doorway;* later, *a large oblong shield,* Eph. 6:16

θυρίδος, gen. sg. f. n. . . . . θυρίς *(2376)*

(2376) **θυρίς,** ίδος, ἡ [§4.2.c] *a small opening; a window,* Acts 20:9; 2 Cor. 11:33

θυρῶν, gen. pl. f. n. . . . . θύρα *(2374)*

(2377) **θυρωρός,** οῦ, ὁ, ἡ, nom. sg. m. n. [§3.C.a,b] (θύρα + οὖρος, *a keeper) a door-keeper, porter,* Mark 13:34; John 10:3; 18:16, 17 {John 10:3}

θυρωρός, nom. sg. f. n. {John 18:17} θυρωρός *(2377)*

θυρωρῷ, dat. sg. m. n. {Mark 13:34} . . . . id.

θυρωρῷ, dat. sg. f. n. {John 18:16} . . . . . . id.

θύσατε, 2 pers. pl. aor. act. imper. . . . . . . θύω *(2380)*

θύσῃ, 3 pers. sg. aor. act. subj. . . . . id.

(2378) **θυσία,** ας, ἡ, nom. sg. f. n. [§2.B.b; 2.2] *sacrifice, the act of sacrificing,* Heb. 9:26; *the thing sacrificed, a victim,* Matt. 9:13; 12:7; *the flesh of victims* eaten by the sacrificers, 1 Cor. 10:18; in N.T. *an offering or ser-*

vice to God, Phil. 4:18, et al.

θυσίᾳ, dat. sg. f. n. . . . . θυσία *(2378)*

θυσίαι, nom. pl. f. n. . . . . id.

θυσίαις, dat. pl. f. n. . . . . id.

θυσίαν, acc. sg. f. n. . . . . id.

θυσίας, gen. sg. f. n. {Heb. 9:26} . . . . id.

θυσίας, acc. pl. f. n. {Heb. 10:8} . . . . id.

θυσιαστήρια, acc. pl. neut. n. . . θυσιαστήριον *(2379)*

(2379) **θυσιαστήριον,** ου, τό, nom. sg. neut. n. [§3.C.c] *an altar,* Matt. 5:23, 24; Luke 1:11, et al.; spc. *the altar of burnt-offering,* Matt. 23:35; Luke 11:51; meton. *a class of sacrifices,* Heb. 13:10 {Matt. 23:19}

θυσιαστήριον, acc. sg. neut. n. {Matt. 5:23} . . . . θυσιαστήριον *(2379)*

θυσιαστηρίου, gen. sg. neut. n. . . . . id.

θυσιαστηρίῳ, dat. sg. neut. n. . . . . id.

θυσιῶν, gen. pl. f. n. . . . . θυσία *(2378)*

θῦσον, 2 pers. sg. aor. act. imper. . . . . . . θύω *(2380)*

(2380) **θύω,** fut. θύσω, perf. τέθυκα, aor. ἔθυσα, perf. pass. τέθυμαι, aor. pass. ἐτύθην, *to offer; to kill in sacrifice, sacrifice, immolate,* Acts 14:13, 18, et al.; in N.T. *to slaughter* for food, Matt. 22:4, et al.

θῶ, 1 pers. sg. 2 aor. act. subj. [§28.V] . τίθημι *(5087)*

Θωμᾶ, voc. sg. m. n. (John 20:29, TR | GNT, WH, MT & NA omit) . . . . Θωμᾶς *(2381)*

Θωμᾷ, dat. sg. m. n. . . . . id.

Θωμᾶν, acc. sg. m. n. . . . . id.

(2381) **Θωμᾶς,** ᾶ, ὁ, nom. sg. m. n. [§2.4] *Thomas,* pr. name

θῶμεν, 1 pers. pl. 2 aor. act. subj. (Mark 4:30, GNT, WH & NA | παραβάλωμεν, MT & TR) . . . . τίθημι *(5087)*

θώρακα, acc. sg. m. n. . . . . θώραξ *(2382)*

θώρακας, acc. pl. m. n. . . . . id.

(2382) **θώραξ,** ακος, ὁ [§4.2.b] *a breast-plate, armor for the body,* consisting of two parts, one covering the breast and the other the back, Rev. 9:9, 17; Eph. 6:14; 1 Thess. 5:8

I

(2383) **Ἰάειρος,** ου, ὁ, nom. sg. m. n. [§3.C.a] *Jairus,* pr. name (Mark 5:22; Luke 8:41, MT, WH & TR | Ἰάϊρος, GNT & NA)

ἰαθείς, nom. sg. m. aor. pass. part. . . . . ἰάομαι *(2390)*

ἰαθέντος, gen. sg. m. aor. pass. part. (Acts 3:11, MT & TR | GNT, WH & NA omit) . . . . id.

ἰάθη, 3 pers. sg. aor. pass. indic. . . . . id.

ἰαθῇ, 3 pers. sg. aor. pass. subj. . . . . id.

ἰαθῆναι, aor. pass. infin. . . . . id.

ἰαθήσεται, 3 pers. sg. fut. pass. indic. . ἰάομαι *(2390)*
ἰάθητε, 2 pers. pl. aor. pass. indic.
{1 Pet. 2:24} . . . . id.
ἰαθῆτε, 2 pers. pl. aor. pass. subj.
{James 5:16} . . . . id.
ἰαθήτω, 3 pers. sg. aor. pass. imper. (Luke 7:7,
GNT, WH & NA | ἰαθήσεται, MT &
TR) . . . . id.

(†2383) Ἰάϊρος, ου, ὁ, nom. sg. m. n. *Jairus,* pr. name
(Mark 5:22; Luke 8:41, GNT & NA |
Ἰάειρος, WH, MT & TR)

(2384) Ἰακώβ, ὁ, *Jacob,* pr. name, indecl. I. *Son
of Isaac,* Matt. 1:2, et al. II. *Father of
Joseph, Mary's husband,* Matt. 1:15, 16
Ἰάκωβον, acc. sg. m. n. . . . . Ἰάκωβος *(2385)*

(2385) Ἰάκωβος, ου, ὁ, nom. sg. m. n. [§3.C.a]
James, pr. name I. *Son of Zebedee,* Matt.
4:21, et al. II. *Son of Alphaeus and
Mary, brother of Jude,* Matt. 10:3, et al.
III. *James the less, brother of Jesus,* Gal.
1:19
Ἰακώβου, gen. sg. m. n. . . . . Ἰάκωβος *(2385)*
Ἰακώβῳ, dat. sg. m. n. . . . . id.

(2386) ἴαμα, ατος, τό [§4.D.c] *healing, cure,* 1 Cor.
12:9, 28, 30
ἰαμάτων, gen. pl. neut. n. . . . . ἴαμα *(2386)*

(2387) Ἰαμβρῆς, οῦ, ὁ, nom. sg. m. n. [§2.B.c] *Jam-
bres,* pr. name, 2 Tim. 3:8

(2388) Ἰαννά, ὁ, *Janna,* pr. name, indecl. (Luke 3:24,
MT & TR | Ἰανναί, GNT, WH & NA)

(†2388) Ἰανναί, ὁ, *Jannai,* pr. name, indecl. (Luke
3:24, GNT, WH & NA | Ἰαννά, MT &
TR)

(†2389) Ἰάννης, ου, ὁ, nom. sg. m. n., *Jannes,* pr.
name (2 Tim. 3:8, GNT, MT & NA |
Ἰαννῆς, WH & TR)

(2390) ἰάομαι, ῶμαι [§19.S] fut. ἰάσομαι, aor.
ἰασάμην, perf. pass. ἴαμαι, aor. pass.
ἰάθην, *to heal cure,* Matt. 8:8; Luke 9:2;
met. *to heal,* spiritually, *restore from a state
of sin and condemnation,* Matt. 13:15;
Heb. 12:13, et al.

(†2391) Ἰάρετ, ὁ, *Jared,* pr. name, indecl. (Luke 3:37,
GNT, WH & NA | Ἰαρέδ, MT & TR)
ἰάσασθαι, aor. mid. dep. infin. (Luke 4:18,
MT & TR | GNT, WH & NA
omit) . . . . ἰάομαι *(2390)*
ἰάσατο, 3 pers. sg. aor. mid. dep. indic. . . id.
ἰάσεις, acc. pl. f. n. . . . . ἴασις *(2392)*
ἰάσεως, gen. sg. f. n. . . . . id.
ἰάσηται, 3 pers. sg. aor. mid. dep. subj. ἰάομαι *(2390)*
ἰᾶσθαι, pres. mid./pass. dep. infin. . . . . . . id.
ἴασιν, acc. sg. f. n. . . . . ἴασις *(2392)*

(2392) ἴασις, εως, ἡ [§5.E.c] *healing, cure,* Luke
13:32; Acts 4:22, 30

ἰάσομαι, 1 pers. sg. fut. mid. dep. indic. (Matt.
13:15; Acts 28:27, GNT, WH, MT & NA
and John 12:40, GNT, WH & NA |
ἰάσωμαι, TR and John 12:40, MT &
TR) . . . . ἰάομαι *(2390)*
Ἰάσονα, acc. sg. m. n. . . . . Ἰάσων *(2394)*
Ἰάσονος, gen. sg. m. n. . . . . id.
ἰάσπιδι, dat. sg. f. n. . . . . ἴασπις *(2393)*

(2393) ἴασπις, ιδος, ἡ, nom. sg. f. n. [§4.2.c] *jasper,*
a precious stone of various colors, as pur-
ple, cerulian, green, etc. Rev. 4:3; 21:11,
18, 19
ἰάσωμαι, 1 pers. sg. aor. mid. dep. subj. (Matt.
13:15; Acts 28:27, TR and John 12:40, MT
& TR | ἰάσομαι, GNT, WH &
NA) . . . . ἰάομαι *(2390)*

(2394) Ἰάσων, ονος, ὁ, nom. sg. m. n. [§4.2.e] *Ja-
son,* pr. name
ἰᾶται, 3 pers. sg. pres. mid./pass. dep. indic.
{Acts 9:34} . . . . ἰάομαι *(2390)*
ἴαται, 3 pers. sg. perf. pass. indic.
{Mark 5:29} . . . . id.
ἰᾶτο, 3 pers. sg. imperf. mid./pass. dep. indic. id.
ἰατρέ, voc. sg. m. n. . . . . ἰατρός *(2395)*
ἰατροῖς, dat. pl. m. n. (Luke 8:43, GNT, MT
& NA | ἰατρούς, TR | WH omits) . . . id.

(2395) ἰατρός, οῦ, ὁ, nom. sg. m. n. [§3.C.a] *a
physician,* Matt. 9:12; Mark 2:17; 5:26,
et al.
ἰατροῦ, gen. sg. m. n. . . . . ἰατρός *(2395)*
ἰατρούς, acc. pl. m. n. (Luke 8:43, TR |
ἰατροῖς, GNT, MT & NA | WH omits) id.
ἰατρῶν, gen. pl. m. n. . . . . id.

(‡1427) ιβ′, numeral, *twelve* (Rev. 7:5(3×), 6(3×),
7(3×), 8(3×), TR | δώδεκα, GNT, WH,
MT & NA)

(2396) ἴδε, or ἰδέ, imper. of εἶδον [§36.1] used as an
interj. *Lo! Behold!* John 16:29; 19:4, 5, et
al. {John 11:36}
ἴδε, 2 pers. sg. aor. act. imper.
{John 11:34} . . . . εἶδον *(‡3708)*

(2397) ἰδέα, ας, ἡ, nom. sg. f. n. [§2.B.b; 2.2] *form;
look, aspect* (Matt. 28:3, MT & TR |
εἰδέα, GNT, WH & NA)
ἰδεῖν, 2 aor. act. infin. [§36.1] . . . . εἶδον *(‡3708)*
ἴδετε, 2 pers. pl. 2 aor. act. imper. . . . . . . id.
ἴδῃ, 3 pers. sg. 2 aor. act. subj. . . . . id.
ἴδῃς, 2 pers. sg. 2 aor. act. subj. . . . . id.
ἴδητε, 2 pers. pl. 2 aor. act. subj. . . . . id.
ἴδια, nom. pl. neut. adj. {John 10:12} . . . ἴδιος *(2398)*
ἴδια, acc. pl. neut. adj. {John 10:3–4} . . . . id.
ἰδίᾳ, dat. sg. f. adj. . . . . id.
ἰδίαις, dat. pl. f. adj. . . . . id.
ἰδίαν, acc. sg. f. adj. . . . . id.
ἰδίας, gen. sg. f. adj. {2 Pet. 2:16} . . . . . . id.

ἰδίας, acc. pl. f. adj. {2 Pet. 3:3} ...... ἴδιος (2398)
ἴδιοι, nom. pl. m. adj. .... id.
ἰδίοις, dat. pl. m. adj. {Eph. 5:22} ..... id.
ἰδίοις, dat. pl. neut. adj. {1 Cor. 9:7} .... id.
ἴδιον, acc. sg. m. adj. {1 Cor. 7:2} .... id.
ἴδιον, acc. sg. neut. adj. {1 Cor. 7:7} ..... id.
(2398) ἴδιος, ία, ιον, nom. sg. m. adj. [§7.1] one's
   own, Mark 15:20; John 7:18, et al.; due,
   proper, specially assigned, Gal. 6:9; 1 Tim.
   2:6; 6:15; Tit. 1:3; also used in N.T. as a
   simple possessive, Eph. 5:22, et al.; τὰ
   ἴδια, one's home, household, people, John
   1:11; 16:32; 19:27; οἱ ἴδιοι, members of
   one's own household, friends, John 1:11;
   Acts 24:23, et al.; ἰδίᾳ, adverbially, sever-
   ally, respectively, 1 Cor. 12:11; κατ' ἰδίαν,
   adv., privately, aside, by one's self, alone,
   Matt. 14:13, 23, et al.
ἰδίου, gen. sg. m. adj. {Rom. 8:32} ..... ἴδιος (2398)
ἰδίου, gen. sg. neut. adj. {1 Cor. 7:4} .... id.
ἰδίους, acc. pl. m. adj. .... id.
ἰδίῳ, dat. sg. m. adj. {Rom. 14:4–5} ..... id.
ἰδίῳ, dat. sg. neut. adj. {1 Cor. 15:23} .... id.
ἰδίων, gen. pl. m. adj. {1 Tim. 3:12} ..... id.
ἰδίων, gen. pl. f. adj. {Heb. 7:27} .... id.
ἰδίων, gen. pl. neut. adj. {Heb. 4:10} .... id.
ἰδιῶται, nom. pl. m. n. .... ἰδιώτης (2399)
(2399) ἰδιώτης, ου, ὁ, nom. sg. m. n. [§2.B.c] pr. one
   in private life, one devoid of special learning or gifts, a plain person, Acts 4:13;
   2 Cor. 11:6; ungifted, 1 Cor. 14:16, 23, 24
ἰδιώτου, gen. sg. m. n. .... ἰδιώτης (2399)
ἰδόντες, nom. pl. m. 2 aor. act. part. .. εἶδον (‡3708)
(2400) ἰδού, varied in accent from ἰδοῦ, imper. of
   εἰδόμην, a particle serving to call attention,
   Lo! Matt. 1:23; Luke 1:38; Acts 8:36, et al.
   freq.
(2401) Ἰδουμαία, ας, ἡ [§2.B.b; 2.2] Idumaea, a
   country south of Judea
Ἰδουμαίας, gen. sg. f. n. .... Ἰδουμαία (2401)
ἰδοῦσα, nom. sg. f. 2 aor. act. part. .... εἶδον (‡3708)
(2402) ἰδρώς, ῶτος, ὁ, nom. sg. m. n. [§4.2.c] (ἴδος,
   sweat) sweat, Luke 22:44
ἴδω, 1 pers. sg. 2 aor. act. subj. ...... εἶδον (‡3708)
ἴδωμεν, 1 pers. pl. 2 aor. act. subj. ...... id.
ἰδών, nom. sg. m. 2 aor. act. part. ...... id.
ἴδωσι(ν), 3 pers. pl. 2 aor. act. subj. ..... id.
(†2403) Ἰεζάβελ, ἡ, Jezebel, pr. name, indecl. (Rev.
   2:20, GNT, WH, MT & NA | Ἰεζαβήλ,
   TR)
ἱερά, acc. pl. neut. adj. .... ἱερός (2413)
Ἱεραπόλει, dat. sg. f. n. (Col. 4:13, GNT,
   MT, TR & NA | Ἱερᾷ Πόλει,
   WH) .... Ἱεράπολις (2404)
(2404) Ἱεράπολις, εως, ἡ [§5.E.c] Hierapolis, a

city of Phrygia
(2405) ἱερατεία, ας, ἡ [§2.B.b; 2.2] priesthood, sacerdotal office, Luke 1:9
ἱερατείαν, acc. sg. f. n. (Heb. 7:5, GNT, MT,
   TR & NA | ἱερατίαν, WH) .... ἱερατεία (2405)
ἱερατείας, gen. sg. f. n. (Luke 1:9, GNT, MT,
   TR & NA | ἱερατίας, WH) .... id.
ἱερατεύειν, pres. act. infin. .... ἱερατεύω (2407)
(2406) ἱεράτευμα, ατος, τό, nom. sg. neut. n. [§4.D.c]
   a priesthood; meton. a body of priests
   {1 Pet. 2:9}
ἱεράτευμα, acc. sg. neut. n.
   {1 Pet. 2:5} .... ἱεράτευμα (2406)
(2407) ἱερατεύω, fut. ἱερατεύσω, to officiate as a
   priest, perform sacred rites, Luke 1:8
ἱερέα, acc. sg. m. n. .... ἱερεύς (2409)
ἱερεῖ, dat. sg. m. n. .... id.
ἱερεῖς, nom. pl. m. n. {Acts 4:1} .... id.
ἱερεῖς, acc. pl. m. n. {Luke 6:4} .... id.
Ἱερεμίαν, acc. sg. m. n. (Matt. 16:14, GNT,
   MT, TRb & NA | Ἰερεμίαν, TRs &
   WH) .... Ἱερεμίας (2408)
(2408) Ἱερεμίας, ου, ὁ [§2.B.d] Jeremiah, pr. name
Ἱερεμίου, gen. sg. m. n. (Matt. 2:17; 27:9,
   GNT, MT, TRb & NA | Ἰερεμίου, TRs
   & WH) .... Ἱερεμίας (2408)
(2409) ἱερεύς, έως, ὁ, nom. sg. m. n. [§5.E.d] a
   priest, one who performs sacrificial rites,
   Matt. 8:4; Luke 1:5; John 1:19, et al.
ἱερεῦσι(ν), dat. pl. m. n. .... ἱερεύς (2409)
ἱερέων, gen. pl. m. n. .... id.
(2410) Ἱεριχώ, ἡ, indecl., Jericho, a city of Palestine
   (GNT, MT, TRb & NA | Ἱεριχώ, TRs
   | Ἱερειχώ, WH)
ἱερόθυτον, nom. sg. neut. adj. (1 Cor. 10:28,
   GNT, WH & NA | εἰδωλόθυτον, MT &
   TR) .... ἱερόθυτος (‡1494)
(‡1494) ἱερόθυτος, ον [§7.2] (ἱερός + θύω) offered in
   sacrifice
(2411) ἱερόν, οῦ, τό [§3.C.c] a temple, Matt. 4:5;
   Luke 4:9; Acts 19:27, et al.
ἱερόν, acc. sg. neut. n. .... ἱερόν (2411)
ἱεροπρεπεῖς, acc. pl. f. adj. ...... ἱεροπρεπής (2412)
(2412) ἱεροπρεπής, ές [§7.G.b] (ἱερός + πρέπει) be-
   seeming what is sacred; becoming holy persons, Tit. 2:3
(2413) ἱερός, ά, όν [§7.1] hallowed; holy, divine,
   2 Tim. 3:15; τὰ ἱερά, sacred rites, 1 Cor.
   9:13 (2×)
(2414) Ἱεροσόλυμα, ης, ἡ, nom. sg. f. n., and ων,
   τά, Jerusalem, the Greek forms of
   Ἱερουσαλήμ (Matt. 2:3, GNT, MT, TR
   & NA | Ἱεροσόλυμα, WH)
Ἱεροσόλυμα, acc. sg. f. n. (Matt. 2:1, GNT,
   MT, TR & NA | Ἱεροσόλυμα,

WH) . . . . Ἱεροσόλυμα *(2414)*

Ἱεροσολυμῖται, nom. pl. m. n. (Mark 1:5, GNT, MT, TR & NA | Ἱεροσολυμεῖται, WH) . . . . Ἱεροσολυμίτης *(2415)*

(2415) **Ἱεροσολυμίτης,** ου, ὁ [§2.B.c] *a native of Jerusalem,* Mark 1:5; John 7:25

Ἱεροσολυμιτῶν, gen. pl. m. n. (John 7:25, GNT, MT, TR & NA | Ἱεροσολυμειτῶν, WH) . . . . Ἱεροσολυμίτης *(2415)*

Ἱεροσολύμοις, dat. pl. neut. n. (GNT, MT, TR & NA | Ἱεροσολύμοις, WH) . . . . Ἱεροσόλυμα *(2414)*

Ἱεροσολύμων, gen. pl. neut. n. (GNT, MT, TR & NA | Ἱεροσολύμων, WH) . . . . id.

ἱεροσυλεῖς, 2 pers. sg. pres. act. indic. . . . . ἱεροσυλέω *(2416)*

(2416) **ἱεροσυλέω,** ῶ, fut. ἱεροσυλήσω [§16.P] *to despoil temples, commit sacrilege,* Rom. 2:22

(2417) **ἱερόσυλος,** ον [§7.2] (ἱερός + συλάω) *one who despoils temples, commits sacrilege,* Acts 19:37

ἱεροσύλους, acc. pl. m. adj. . . . . ἱερόσυλος *(2417)*

ἱεροῦ, gen. sg. neut. n. . . . . ἱερόν *(2411)*

ἱερουργοῦντα, acc. sg. m. pres. act. part. . . . . ἱερουργέω *(2418)*

(2418) **ἱερουργέω,** ῶ, fut. ἱερουργήσω [§16.P] (ἱερός + ἔργον) *to officiate as priest, perform sacred rites;* in N.T. *to minister* in a divine commission

(†2419) **Ἱερουσαλήμ,** ἡ, *Jerusalem,* pr. name, indecl. (GNT, WH, MT & NA | Ἱερουσαλήμ, TR)

ἱερῷ, dat. sg. neut. n. . . . . ἱερόν *(2411)*

(2420) **ἱερωσύνη,** ης, ἡ [§2.B.a] *a priesthood, sacerdotal office,* Heb. 7:11, 12, 14

ἱερωσύνην, acc. sg. f. n. . . . . ἱερωσύνη *(2420)*

ἱερωσύνης, gen. sg. f. n. . . . . id.

(2421) **Ἱεσσαί,** ὁ, *Jesse,* pr. name, indecl.

(2422) **Ἱεφθάε,** ὁ, *Jephthae,* pr. name, indecl., Heb. 11:32

Ἰεχονίαν, acc. sg. m. n. . . . . Ἰεχονίας *(2423)*

(2423) **Ἰεχονίας,** ου, ὁ, nom. sg. m. n. [§2.B.d] *Jechonias,* pr. name, Matt. 1:11, 12

Ἰησοῦ, gen. sg. m. n. {Rev. 22:21} . . . Ἰησοῦς *(2424)*

Ἰησοῦ, dat. sg. m. n. {Rev. 1:9} . . . . id.

Ἰησοῦ, voc. sg. m. n. {Rev. 22:20} . . . . . . id.

Ἰησοῦν, acc. sg. m. n. . . . . id.

(2424) **Ἰησοῦς,** οῦ, ὁ, nom. sg. m. n. [§6.3] (Hebrew יְהוֹשׁוּעַ contr. יֵשׁוּעַ) *a Savior, Jesus,* Matt. 1:21, 25; 2:1, et al. freq.; *Joshua,* Acts 7:45; Heb. 4:8; *Jesus,* a Jewish Christian, Col. 4:11

ἱκανά, acc. pl. neut. adj. . . . . ἱκανός *(2425)*

ἱκαναί, nom. pl. f. adj. . . . . id.

ἱκαναῖς, dat. pl. f. adj. . . . . id.

ἱκανάς, acc. pl. f. adj. . . . . ἱκανός *(2425)*

ἱκανοί, nom. pl. m. adj. . . . . id.

ἱκανοῖς, dat. pl. m. adj. . . . . id.

ἱκανόν, acc. sg. m. adj. {Acts 14:3} . . . . . . id.

ἱκανόν, nom. sg. neut. adj. {Luke 22:38} . id.

ἱκανόν, acc. sg. neut. adj. {Acts 17:9} . . . . id.

(2425) **ἱκανός,** ή, όν, nom. sg. m. adj. [§7.F.a] (ἵκω, or, ἱκάνω, *to arrive at, reach to*) *befitting; sufficient, enough,* Luke 22:38; ἱκανὸν ποιεῖν τινί, *to satisfy, gratify,* Mark 15:15; τὸ ἱκανὸν λαμβάνειν, *to take security or bail* of any one, Acts 17:9; or persons, *adequate, competent, qualified,* 2 Cor. 2:16; *fit, worthy,* Matt. 3:11; 8:8; of number or quantity, *considerable, large, great, much,* and pl. *many,* Matt. 28:12; Mark 10:46, et al.

(2426) **ἱκανότης,** ητος, ἡ, nom. sg. f. n. [§4.2.c] *sufficiency, ability, fitness, qualification,* 2 Cor. 3:5

ἱκανοῦ, gen. sg. m. adj. {Mark 19:46} . ἱκανός *(2425)*

ἱκανοῦ, gen. sg. neut. adj. (Luke 23:8, MT & TR | ἱκανῶν, GNT, WH & NA) . . id.

ἱκανούς, acc. pl. m. adj. . . . . id.

(2427) **ἱκανόω,** ῶ, fut. ἱκανώσω [§20.T] aor. ἱκάνωσα, *to make sufficient or competent, qualify,* 2 Cor. 3:6; Col. 1:12

ἱκανῷ, dat. sg. m. adj. . . . . ἱκανός *(2425)*

ἱκανῶν, gen. pl. m. adj. . . . . id.

ἱκανώσαντι, dat. sg. m. aor. act. part. ἱκανόω *(2427)*

ἱκάνωσεν, 3 pers. sg. aor. act. indic. [§13.3] id.

(2428) **ἱκετηρία,** ας, ἡ [§2.B.b; 2.2] (f. of ἱκετήριος, sc. ῥάβδος, from ἱκέτης, *suppliant*) pr. *an olive branch* borne by suppliants in their hands; *supplication,* Heb. 5:7

ἱκετηρίας, acc. pl. f. n. . . . . ἱκετηρία *(2428)*

ἱκμάδα, acc. sg. f. n. . . . . ἱκμάς *(†2429)*

(†2429) **ἱκμάς,** άδος, ἡ [§4.2.c] *moisture,* Luke 8:6

(2430) **Ἰκόνιον,** ου, τό [§3.C.c] *Iconium,* a city of Lycaonia, in Asia Minor

Ἰκόνιον, acc. sg. neut. n. . . . . Ἰκόνιον *(2430)*

Ἰκονίου, gen. sg. neut. n. . . . . id.

Ἰκονίῳ, dat. sg. neut. n. . . . . id.

ἱλαρόν, acc. sg. m. adj. . . . . ἱλαρός *(2431)*

(2431) **ἱλαρός,** ά, όν [§7.1] *cheerful, not grudging,* 2 Cor. 9:7

(2432) **ἱλαρότης,** ητος, ἡ [§4.2.c] *cheerfulness,* Rom. 12:8

ἱλαρότητι, dat. sg. f. n. . . . . id.

ἱλάσθητι, 2 pers. sg. aor. pass. imper. . . . . ἱλάσκομαι *(2433)*

ἱλάσκεσθαι, pres. pass. infin. . . . . id.

(2433) **ἱλάσκομαι,** fut. ἱλάσομαι, aor. pass. ἱλάσθην, *to appease, render propitious;* in N.T. *to expiate, make an atonement or expiation*

for, Heb. 2:17; ἱλάσθητι, *be gracious, show mercy, pardon*, Luke 18:13

ἱλασμόν, acc. sg. m. n. . . . . ἱλασμός (2434)

(2434) **ἱλασμός**, οῦ, ὁ, nom. sg. m. n. [§3.C.a] *propitiation, expiation; one who makes expiation*, 1 John 2:2; 4:10

(2435) **ἱλαστήριον**, ου, τό [§3.C.c] *the cover of the ark of the covenant, the mercy-seat*, Heb. 9:5

ἱλαστήριον, acc. sg. neut. n. . . . . . ἱλαστήριον (2435)

(†2435) **ἱλαστήριος**, α, ον [§7.1] *propitiatory; invested with propitiatory power*, Rom. 3:25; in N.T. and LXX, τὸ ἱλαστήριον, *the cover of the ark of the covenant, the mercy-seat*, Heb. 9:5

(2436) **ἵλεως**, ων, nom. sg. m. adj. (Att. for ἵλαος) *propitious, favorable, merciful, clement*, Heb. 8:12; from the Hebrew, ἵλεως σοι (ὁ θεός) *God have mercy on thee, God forbid, far be it from thee*, Matt. 16:22

(2437) **Ἰλλυρικόν**, οῦ, τό, *Illyricum*, a country between the Adriatic and the Danube

Ἰλλυρικοῦ, gen. sg. neut. n. . . . . . Ἰλλυρικόν (2437)

ἱμάντα, acc. sg. m. n. . . . . ἱμάς (2438)

(2438) **ἱμάς**, άντος, ὁ [§4.d] *a strap or thong of leather*, Acts 22:25; *a shoe-latchet*, Mark 1:7; Luke 3:16; John 1:27

ἱμᾶσιν, dat. pl. m. n. . . . . ἱμάς (2438)

ἱμάτια, nom. pl. neut. n. {Mark 9:3} . ἱμάτιον (2440)

ἱμάτια, acc. pl. neut. n. {Mark 11:7–8} . . id.

(2439) **ἱματίζω**, fut. ἱματίσω, perf. pass. ἱμάτισμαι [§26.1] *to clothe;* pass. *to be clothed*, Mark 5:15; Luke 8:35

ἱματίοις, dat. pl. neut. n. . . . . ἱμάτιον (2440)

(2440) **ἱμάτιον**, ου, τό, nom. sg. neut. n. [§3.C.c] (ἕννυμι, *to clothe*, εἶμα) *a garment; the upper garment, mantle*, Matt. 5:40; 9:16, 20, 21; pl. *the mantle and tunic together*, Matt. 26:65; pl. genr. *garments, raiment*, Matt. 11:8; 24:18, et al. {Heb. 1:11}

ἱμάτιον, acc. sg. neut. n. {Heb. 1:12} . ἱμάτιον (2440)

ἱματίου, gen. sg. neut. n. . . . . id.

ἱματισμένον, acc. sg. m. perf. pass. part. . . . . ἱματίζω (2439)

ἱματισμόν, acc. sg. m. n. . . . . ἱματισμός (2441)

(2441) **ἱματισμός**, οῦ, ὁ, nom. sg. m. n. [§3.C.a] *a garment; raiment, apparel, clothing*, Luke 7:25; 9:29, et al.

ἱματισμοῦ, gen. sg. m. n. . . . . ἱματισμός (2441)

ἱματισμῷ, dat. sg. m. n. . . . . id.

ἱματίῳ, dat. sg. neut. n. . . . . ἱμάτιον (2440)

ἱματίων, gen. pl. neut. n. . . . . id.

ἱμειρόμενοι, nom. pl. m. pres. mid. part. (1 Thess. 2:8, TR | ὁμειρόμενοι, GNT, WH, MT & NA) . . . . ἱμείρω (†2442)

(†2442) **ἱμείρω**, and ἱμείρομαι (ἵμερος, *desire*) *to desire earnestly;* by impl. *to have a strong affection for, love fervently*, 1 Thess. 2:8

(2443) **ἵνα**, conj., *that, in order that*, Matt. 19:13; Mark 1:38; John 1:22; 3:15; 17:1; ἵνα μή, *that not, lest*, Matt. 7:1; in N.T. equivalent to ὥστε, *so that, so as that*, John 9:2, et al.; also, marking a simple circumstance, *the circumstance that*, Matt. 10:25; John 4:34; 6:29 1 John 4:17; 5:3, et al.

(‡3363) **ἵνα μή**, *in order that not, lest*

(2444) **ἱνατί**, adv. (ἵνα + τί) *Why is it that? Wherefore? Why?* Matt. 9:4; 27:46, et al.

(2445) **Ἰόππη**, ης, ἡ [§2.B.a] *Joppa*, a city of Palestine

Ἰόππῃ, dat. sg. f. n. . . . . Ἰόππη (2445)

Ἰόππην, acc. sg. f. n. . . . . id.

Ἰόππης, gen. sg. f. n. . . . . id.

Ἰορδάνῃ, dat. sg. m. n. . . . . Ἰορδάνης (2446)

Ἰορδάνην, acc. sg. m. n. . . . . id.

(2446) **Ἰορδάνης**, ου, ὁ [§2.b.c] *the river Jordan*

Ἰορδάνου, gen. sg. m. n. . . . . Ἰορδάνης (2446)

(2447) **ἰός**, οῦ, ὁ, nom. sg. m. n. [§3.C.a] *a missile weapon, arrow, dart; venom, poison*, Rom. 3:13; James 3:8; *rust*, James 5:3

ἰοῦ, gen. sg. m. n. . . . . ἰός (2447)

(†2448) **Ἰούδα**, gen. sg. m. n. [§2.4] {Luke 1:39} . . . . Ἰούδας (2455)

Ἰούδα, voc. sg. m. n. {Luke 22:48} . . Ἰούδας (2455)

Ἰούδᾳ, dat. sg. m. n. . . . . id.

(2449) **Ἰουδαία**, ας, ἡ, nom. sg. f. n. [§2.B.b; 2.2] *Judea*, Matt. 2:1, 5, 22; 3:1, et al.; meton. *the inhabitants of Judea* {Matt. 3:5}

Ἰουδαία, nom. sg. f. adj. {Mark 1:5} . . . . Ἰουδαῖος (2453)

Ἰουδαίᾳ, dat. sg. f. adj. {Acts 24:24} . . . . id.

Ἰουδαίᾳ, dat. sg. f. n. {Acts 11:29} . . Ἰουδαία (2449)

Ἰουδαίαν, acc. sg. f. n. {John 4:3} . . . . . . id.

Ἰουδαίαν, acc. sg. f. adj. {John 3:22} . . . . Ἰουδαῖος (2453)

Ἰουδαίας, gen. sg. f. adj. {Acts 16:1} . . . . id.

Ἰουδαίας, gen. sg. f. n. {Acts 15:1} . . Ἰουδαία (2449)

Ἰουδαΐζειν, pres. act. infin. . . . . Ἰουδαΐζω (2450)

(2450) **Ἰουδαΐζω**, fut. Ἰουδαΐσω, *to judaize, live like a Jew, follow the manners and customs of the Jews*, Gal. 2:14

Ἰουδαϊκοῖς, dat. pl. m. adj. . . . . . . Ἰουδαϊκός (2451)

(2451) **Ἰουδαϊκός**, ή, όν [§7.F.a] *Jewish, current among the Jews*, Tit. 1:14

(2452) **Ἰδουδαϊκῶς**, adv., *Jewishly, in the manner of Jews*, Gal. 2:14

Ἰουδαῖοι, nom. pl. m. adj. {Acts 2:11} . . . . Ἰουδαῖος (2453)

Ἰουδαῖοι, voc. pl. m. adj. {Acts 2:14} . . . . id.

Ἰουδαίοις, dat. pl. m. adj. . . . . id.

Ἰουδαῖον, acc. sg. m. adj. . . . . id.

(2453) **Ἰουδαῖος**, α, ον, nom. sg. m. adj. [§7.1] (Hebrew יְהוּדִי) *Jewish*, Mark 1:5; John 3:22; Acts 16:1; 24:24; pr. *one sprung from the tribe of Judah, or a subject of the kingdom of Judah*; in N.T. *a descendant of Jacob, a Jew*, Matt. 28:15; Mark 7:3; Acts 19:34; Rom. 2:28, 29, et al.

Ἰουδαίου, gen. sg. m. adj. . . . . Ἰουδαῖος *(2453)*

Ἰουδαίους, acc. pl. m. adj. . . . . id.

(2454) **Ἰουδαϊσμός**, οῦ, ὁ [§3.C.a] *Judaism, the character and condition of a Jew; practice of the Jewish religion*, Gal. 1:13, 14

Ἰουδαϊσμῷ, dat. sg. m. n. . . . . . Ἰουδαϊσμός *(2454)*

Ἰουδαίῳ, dat. sg. m. adj. . . . . Ἰουδαῖος *(2453)*

Ἰουδαίων, gen. pl. m. adj. . . . . id.

Ἰούδαν, acc. sg. m. n. . . . . Ἰούδας *(2455)*

(2455) **Ἰούδας**, α, ὁ, nom. sg. m. n. [§2.4] *Judas, Jude*, pr. name   I. *Judah, son of Jacob; the tribe of Judah*, Matt. 1:2; Luke 1:39, et al.   II. *Juda, son of Joseph, of the ancestry of Jesus*, Luke 3:30   III. *Juda, son of Joanna, of the ancestry of Jesus*, Luke 3:26   IV. *Judas, brother of James, Jude*, Luke 6:16, et al.; Jude 1   V. *Judas Iscariot, son of Simon*, Matt. 10:4; John 6:71, et al.   VI. *Judas, brother of Jesus*, Matt. 13:55; Mark 6:3   VII. *Judas of Galilee*, Acts 5:37   VIII. *Judas, surnamed Barsabas*, Acts 15:22, et al.   IX. *Judas of Damascus*, Acts 9:11

(2456) **Ἰουλία**, ας, ἡ [§2.B.b; 2.2] *Julia*, pr. name, Rom. 16:15

Ἰουλίαν, acc. sg. f. n. . . . . Ἰουλία *(2456)*

(2457) **Ἰούλιος**, ου, ὁ, nom. sg. m. n. [§3.C.a] *Julius*, pr. name

Ἰουλίῳ, dat. sg. m. n. . . . . Ἰούλιος *(2457)*

Ἰουνιᾶν, acc. sg. f. n. (Rom. 16:7, GNT & NA | Ἰουνίαν, WH, MT & TR) . Ἰουνία *(†2458)*

(†2458) **Ἰουνία**, ας, ἡ [§2.4] *Junia*, pr. name

(2459) **Ἰοῦστος**, ου, ὁ, nom. sg. m. n. [§3.C.a] *Justus*, pr. name   I. *Joseph Barsabas*, Acts 1:23   II. *Justus of Corinth*, Acts 18:7   III. *Jesus, called Justus*, Col. 4:11

Ἰούστου, gen. sg. m. n. . . . . Ἰοῦστος *(2459)*

ἱππεῖς, acc. pl. m. n. . . . . ἱππεύς *(2460)*

(2460) **ἱππεύς**, έως, ὁ [§5.E.d] *a horseman*; pl. ἱππεῖς, *horsemen, cavalry*, Acts 23:23, 32

(†2461) **ἱππικός**, ή, όν [§7.F.a] *equestrian*; τὸ ἱππικόν, *cavalry, horse*, Rev. 9:16

ἱππικοῦ, gen. sg. neut. adj. . . . . ἱππικός *(†2461)*

ἵπποις, dat. pl. m. n. . . . . ἵππος *(2462)*

(2462) **ἵππος**, ου, ὁ, nom. sg. m. n. [§3.C.a] *a horse*, James 3:3; Rev. 6:2, 4, 5, 8, et al.

ἵππου, gen. sg. m. n. . . . . ἵππος *(2462)*

ἵππους, acc. pl. m. n. . . . . id.

ἵππων, gen. pl. m. n. . . . . ἵππος *(2462)*

(2463) **ἶρις**, ἴριδος, ἡ, nom. sg. f. n. [§4.2.c] *a rainbow, iris*, Rev. 4:3; 10:1

ἴσα, nom. pl. neut. adj. {Rev. 21:16} . . . . ἴσος *(2470)*

ἴσα, acc. pl. neut. adj. {Luke 6:34} . . . . . id.

(2464) **Ἰσαάκ**, ὁ, *Isaac*, pr. name, indecl.

ἰσάγγελοι, nom. pl. m. adj. . . . . ἰσάγγελος *(2465)*

(2465) **ἰσάγγελος**, ον [§7.2] (ἴσος + ἄγγελος) *equal or similar to angels*

ἴσαι, nom. pl. f. adj. . . . . ἴσος *(2470)*

ἴσασι(ν), 3 pers. pl. perf. act. indic. [§33.2; 37.1] (usually in N.T. οἴδασι) . . . . . . οἶδα *(‡1492)*

(2466) **Ἰσαχάρ**, ὁ, *Issachar*, pr. name, indecl. (Rev. 7:7, MT & TR | Ἰσσαχάρ, GNT, WH & NA)

ἴση, nom. sg. f. adj. . . . . ἴσος *(2470)*

ἴσην, acc. sg. f. adj. . . . . id.

(2468) **ἴσθι**, 2 pers. sg. pres. imper. [§12.L] . . . . . εἰμί *(1510)*

(†2469) **Ἰσκαριώθ**, ὁ, *Iscariot*, indecl. surname of Judas (Mark 3:19; 14:10; Luke 6:16, GNT, WH & NA | Ἰσκαριώτην, MT & TR)

Ἰσκαριώτῃ, dat. sg. m. n. (John 13:26, MT & TR | Ἰσκαριώτου, GNT, WH & NA) . . . . Ἰσκαριώτης *(2469)*

Ἰσκαριώτην, acc. sg. m. n. . . . . id.

(2469) **Ἰσκαριώτης**, ου, ὁ, nom. sg. m. n. [§2.B.c] *Iscariot (man of Carioth)* pr. name

Ἰσκαριώτου, gen. sg. m. n. . . . . Ἰσκαριώτης *(2469)*

ἴσον, acc. sg. m. adj. . . . . ἴσος *(2470)*

(2470) **ἴσος**, η, ον [§7.F.a] *equal, like*, Matt. 20:12; Luke 6:34, et al.; neut. pl. ἴσα, adverbially, *on an equality*, Phil. 2:6; met. *correspondent, consistent*, Mark 14:56, 59

(2471) **ἰσότης**, ητος, ἡ, nom. sg. f. n. [§4.2.c] *equality, equal proportion*, 2 Cor. 8:13, 14; *fairness, equity, what is equitable*, Col. 4:1

ἰσότητα, acc. sg. f. n. . . . . ἰσότης *(2471)*

ἰσότητος, gen. sg. f. n. . . . . ἰσότης *(2471)*

ἰσότιμον, acc. sg. f. adj. . . . . ἰσότιμος *(2472)*

(2472) **ἰσότιμος**, ον [§7.2] (ἴσος + τιμή) *of equal price, equally precious or valuable*, 2 Pet. 1:1

ἴσους, acc. pl. m. adj. . . . . ἴσος *(2470)*

ἰσόψυχον, acc. sg. m. adj. . . . . ἰσόψυχος *(2473)*

(2473) **ἰσόψυχος**, ον [§7.2] (ἴσος + ψυχή) *likeminded, of the same mind and spirit*, Phil. 2:20

(2474) **Ἰσραήλ**, ὁ, *Israel*, pr. name, indecl.

Ἰσραηλῖται, nom. pl. m. n. {Rom. 9:4} (GNT, MT, TR & NA | Ἰσραηλεῖται, WH) . . . . Ἰσραηλίτης *(2475)*

Ἰσραηλῖται, voc. pl. m. n. (GNT, MT, TR & NA | Ἰσραηλεῖται, WH) {Acts 2:22} id.

(2475) **Ἰσραηλίτης**, ου, ὁ, nom. sg. m. n. (GNT, MT, TR & NA | Ἰσραηλείτης, WH) [§2.B.c]

an Israelite, a descendant of Ἰσραήλ, Israel or Jacob, John 1:48; Acts 2:22, et al.

(‡2466) Ἰσσαχάρ, ὁ, Issachar, pr. name, indecl. (Rev. 7:7, GNT, WH & NA | Ἰσαχάρ, MT & TR)

ἱστάνομεν, 1 pers. pl. pres. act. indic. (Rom. 3:31, GNT, WH & NA | ἱστῶμεν, MT & TR) . . . . ἱστάνω (†2476)

(†2476) ἱστάνω, same signif. as ἵστημι

ἴστε, 2 pers. pl. perf. act. imper. for ἴσατε [§37.1] . . . . οἶδα (‡1492)

ἱστήκεισαν, 3 pers. pl. pluperf. act. indic. (Rev. 7:11, WH | εἱστήκεισαν, GNT, MT & NA | ἑστήκεσαν, TR) . . . . ἵστημι (2476)

(2476) ἵστημι, and, in N.T., ἱστάω [§29.X] fut. στήσω, aor. ἔστησα, trans. to make to stand, set, place, Matt. 4:5, et al.; to set forth, appoint, Acts 1:23; to fix, appoint, Acts 17:31; to establish, confirm, Rom. 10:3; Heb. 10:9; to set down, impute, Acts 7:60; to weigh out, pay, Matt. 26:15; intrans. perf. ἕστηκα, infin. ἑστάναι, part. ἑστώς, pluperf. εἱστήκειν, 2 aor. ἔστην, pass. ἵσταμαι, fut. σταθήσομαι, aor. ἐστάθην, to stand, Matt. 12:46, et al.; to stand fast, be firm, be permanent, endure, Matt. 12:25; Eph. 6:13, et al.; to be confirmed, proved, Matt. 18:16; 2 Cor. 13:1; to stop, Luke 7:14; 8:44; Acts 8:38, et al.

ἵστησιν, 3 pers. sg. pres. act. indic. (Matt. 4:5, MT & TR | ἔστησεν, GNT, WH & NA) . . . . ἵστημι (2476)

(2477) ἱστορέω, ῶ, fut. ἱστορήσω [§16.P] (ἵστωρ, knowing) to ascertain by inquiry and examination; to inquire of; in N.T. to visit in order to become acquainted with, Gal. 1:18

ἱστορῆσαι, aor. act. infin. . . . . ἱστορέω (2477)

ἱστῶμεν, 1 pers. pl. pres. act. indic. (Rom. 3:31, MT & TR | ἱστάνομεν, GNT, WH & NA) . . . . ἱστάω (2476)

ἰσχύει, 3 pers. sg. pres. act. indic. . . . . . ἰσχύω (2480)

ἰσχύειν, pres. act. infin. . . . . id.

ἴσχυε(ν), 3 pers. sg. imperf. act. indic. . . . id.

ἰσχύϊ, dat. sg. f. n. . . . . ἰσχύς (2479)

ἰσχύν, acc. sg. f. n. . . . . id.

ἴσχυον, 3 pers. pl. imperf. act. indic. . . . ἰσχύω (2480)

ἰσχύοντες, nom. pl. m. pres. act. part. . . . id.

ἰσχύοντος, gen. sg. m. pres. act. part. . . . . id.

ἰσχύος, gen. sg. f. n. . . . . ἰσχύς (2479)

ἰσχυρά, nom. sg. f. adj. {Rev. 18:10} . ἰσχυρός (2478)

ἰσχυρά, acc. pl. neut. adj. {1 Cor. 1:27} . . id.

ἰσχυρᾷ, dat. sg. f. adj. (Rev. 18:2, GNT, WH, MT & NA | ἰσχύϊ, TR) . . . . id.

ἰσχυραί, nom. pl. f. adj. . . . . id.

ἰσχυράν, acc. sg. f. adj. . . . . ἰσχυρός (2478)

ἰσχυρᾶς, gen. sg. f. adj. . . . . id.

ἰσχυροί, nom. pl. f. adj. . . . . id.

ἰσχυρόν, acc. sg. m. adj. . . . . id.

(2478) ἰσχυρός, ά, όν, nom. sg. m. adj. [§7.1] strong, mighty, robust, Matt. 12:29; Luke 11:21; powerful, mighty, 1 Cor. 1:27; 4:10; 1 John 2:14; strong, fortified, Rev. 18:10; vehement, Matt. 14:30; energetic, 2 Cor. 10:10; sure, firm, Heb. 6:18, et al.

ἰσχυρότεροι, nom. pl. m. compar. adj. [§8.4] . . . . ἰσχυρός (2478)

ἰσχυρότερον, nom. sg. neut. compar. adj. . id.

ἰσχυρότερος, nom. sg. m. compar. adj. . . . id.

ἰσχυροῦ, gen. sg. m. adj. . . . . id.

ἰσχυρῶν, gen. pl. m. adj. {Rev. 19:18} . . . . id.

ἰσχυρῶν, gen. pl. f. adj. {Rev. 19:6} . . . . . id.

(2479) ἰσχύς, ύος, ἡ, nom. sg. f. n. [§5.E.g] strength, might, power, Rev. 18:2; Eph. 1:19; faculty, ability, 1 Pet. 4:11; Mark 12:30, 33; Luke 10:27

ἰσχύσαμεν, 1 pers. pl. aor. act. indic. . . ἰσχύω (2480)

ἴσχυσαν, 3 pers. pl. aor. act. indic. . . . . . . id.

ἴσχυσας, 2 pers. sg. aor. act. indic. . . . . . . id.

ἰσχύσατε, 2 pers. pl. aor. act. indic. . . . . . id.

ἴσχυσε(ν), 3 per. sg. aor. act. indic. . . . . . id.

ἰσχύσουσιν, 3 pers. pl. fut. act. indic. . . . . id.

(2480) ἰσχύω, 1 pers. sg. pres. act. indic., fut. ἰσχύσω [§13.M] aor. ἴσχυσα, to be strong, be well, be in good health, Matt. 9:12; to have power, be able, Matt. 8:28; 26:40; to have power or efficiency, avail, be valid, Gal. 5:6; Heb. 9:17; to be of service, be serviceable, Matt. 5:13; meton. to prevail, Acts 19:16; Rev. 12:8, et al.

(2481) ἴσως, adv., equally; perhaps, it may be that, Luke 20:13

(2482) Ἰταλία, ας, ἡ [§2.B.b; 2.2] Italy

Ἰταλίαν, acc. sg. f. n. . . . . Ἰταλία (2482)

Ἰταλίας, gen. sg. f. n. . . . . id.

Ἰταλικῆς, gen. sg. f. adj. . . . . Ἰταλικός (2483)

(2483) Ἰταλικός, ή, όν [§7.F.a] Italian, Acts 10:1

(†2484) Ἰτουραία, α, ον [§2.B.b; 2.2] Ituraea, a district of Palestine beyond Jordan, Luke 3:1

Ἰτουραίας, gen. sg. f. adj. . . . . Ἰτουραία (†2484)

ἰχθύας, acc. pl. m. n. . . . . ἰχθύς (2486)

ἰχθύδια, acc. pl. neut. n. . . . . ἰχθύδιον (2485)

(2485) ἰχθύδιον, ου, τό [§3.C.c] dimin. of ἰχθύς, a small fish, Matt. 15:34; Mark 8:7

ἰχθύες, nom. pl. m. n. . . . . ἰχθύς (2486)

ἰχθύν, acc. sg. m. n. . . . . id.

ἰχθύος, gen. sg. m. n. . . . . id.

(2486) ἰχθύς, ύος, ὁ [§5.E.g] a fish, Matt. 15:36; 17:27; Luke 5:6, et al.

ἰχθύων, gen. pl. m. n. . . . . ἰχθύς (2486) ἴχνεσι(ν), dat. pl. neut. n. . . . . ἴχνος *(2487)*

(2487) **ἴχνος**, ους, τό [§5.E.b] (ἴκω) *a footstep, track; in N.T. pl. footsteps, line of conduct,* Rom. 4:12; 2 Cor. 12:18; 1 Pet. 2:21

(†2488) **Ἰωαθάμ**, ὁ, *Joatham,* pr. name, indecl. (Matt. 1:9, 9, GNT, WH, MT & NA | Ἰωάθαμ, TR)

(‡2490) **Ἰωανάν**, ὁ, *Joanan,* pr. name, indecl. (Luke 3:27, GNT, WH, MT & NA | Ἰωαννᾶ, TR)

(2489) **Ἰωάννα**, ἡ, nom. sg. f. n., *Joanna,* pr. name Ἰωαννᾶ, gen. sg. f. n. (Luke 3:27, TR | Ἰωανάν, GNT, WH, MT & NA) Ἰωαννᾶς *(2490)*

(2490) **Ἰωαννᾶς**, ᾶ, ὁ [§2.4] *Joanna, Joannas,* pr. name

Ἰωάννῃ, dat. sg. m. n. (GNT, MT, TR & NA | Ἰωάνῃ, WH) . . . . Ἰωάννης *(2491)*

Ἰωάννην, acc. sg. m. n. (GNT, MT, TR & NA | Ἰωάνην, WH) . . . . id.

(2491) **Ἰωάννης**, ου, ὁ, nom. sg. m. n. [§2.B.c] *Joannes, John,* pr. name I. *John the Baptist,* Matt. 3:1, et al. II. *John, son of Zebedee, the apostle,* Matt. 4:21, et al. III. *John, surnamed Mark,* Acts 12:12, et al. IV. *John, the high-priest,* Acts 4:6 (GNT, MT, TR & NA | Ἰωάνης, WH)

Ἰωάννου, gen. sg. m. n. (GNT, MT, TR & NA | Ἰωάνου, WH) . . . . Ἰωάννης *(2491)*

(2492) **Ἰώβ**, ὁ, *Job,* pr. name, indecl.

(‡5601) **Ἰωβήδ**, ὁ, *Jobed,* pr. name, indecl. (Matt. 1:5; Luke 3:32, GNT & NA | Ὠβήδ, MT & TR | Ἰωβήλ, WH)

(‡2448) **Ἰωδά**, ὁ, *Joda,* pr. name, indecl. (Luke 3:26, GNT, WH & NA | Ἰούδα, MT & TR)

(2493) **Ἰωήλ**, ὁ, *Joel,* pr. name, indecl.

ἰώμενος, nom. sg. m. pres. mid./pass. dep. part. . . . . ἰάομαι *(2390)*

Ἰωνᾶ, gen. sg. m. n. . . . . Ἰωνᾶς *(2495)*

(†2494) **Ἰωνάμ**, ὁ, *Jonam,* pr. name, indecl. (Luke 3:30, GNT, WH & NA | Ἰωνάν, MT & TR)

(2494) **Ἰωνάν**, ὁ, *Jonan,* pr. name, indecl. (Luke 3:30, MT & TR | Ἰωνάμ, GNT, WH & NA)

(2495) **Ἰωνᾶς**, ᾶ, ὁ, nom. sg. m. n. [§2.4] *Jonas,* pr. name I. *Jonah, the prophet,* Matt. 12:39, et al. II. *Jonas, father of Simon Peter,* John 1:43, et al.

(2496) **Ἰωράμ**, ὁ, *Joram,* pr. name, indecl.

(†2497) **Ἰωρίμ**, ὁ, *Jorim,* pr. name, indecl. (Luke 3:29, GNT & NA | Ἰωρείμ, WH, MT & TR)

(2498) **Ἰωσαφάτ**, ὁ, *Josaphat,* pr. name, indecl.

(†2499) **Ἰωσῆ**, gen. sg. m. n. (Matt. 27:56; Mark 6:3; 15:40, 47; MT & TR and Luke 3:29, TR | Ἰωσήφ Matt. 27:56, GNT, WH & NA | Ἰωσῆτος Mark 6:3; 15:40, 47, GNT,

WH & NA | Ἰωσή Luke 3:29, MT | Ἰησοῦ, Luke 3:29, GNT, WH & NA) . . . . Ἰωσῆς *(2500)*

(2500) **Ἰωσῆς**, ῆ, or ῆτος, ὁ [§2.5] *Joses,* pr. name I. *Joses, son of Eliezer,* Luke 3:29 II. *Joses, son of Mary, brother of Jesus,* Matt. 13:55 III. *Joses, surnamed Barnabas,* Acts 4:36 (Matt. 13:55; Acts 4:36, MT & TR | Ἰωσήφ, GNT, WH & NA)

Ἰωσῆτος, gen. sg. m. n. (Mark 6:3; 15:40, 47, GNT, WH & NA | Ἰωσῆ, MT & TR) . . . . Ἰωσῆς *(2500)*

(2501) **Ἰωσήφ**, ὁ, *Joseph,* pr. name, indecl. I. *Joseph, son of Jacob,* John 4:5, et al. II. *Joseph, son of Jonan,* Luke 3:30 III. *Joseph, son of Judas,* Luke 3:26 IV. *Joseph, son of Mattathias,* Luke 3:24 V. *Joseph, the husband of Mary,* Matt. 1:16, et al. VI. *Joseph of Arimathea,* Matt. 27:57, et al. VII. *Joseph Barsabas,* Acts 1:23 VIII. *Joseph Barnabas,* Acts 4:36

(†2501) **Ἰωσήχ**, ὁ, *Josech,* pr. name, indecl. (Luke 3:26, GNT, WH & NA | Ἰωσήφ, MT & TR)

Ἰωσίαν, acc. sg. m. n. (Matt. 1:10, GNT, MT, TR & NA | Ἰωσείαν, WH) . . . . . Ἰωσίας *(2502)*

(2502) **Ἰωσίας**, ου, ὁ, nom. sg. m. n. (Matt. 1:11, GNT, MT, TR & NA | Ἰωσείας, WH) [§2.B.d] *Josias,* pr. name

(2503) **ἰῶτα**, τό, indecl., *iota;* in N.T. used like the Hebrew, יוֹד, the smallest letter in the Hebrew alphabet, as an expression for *the least or minutest part; a jot*

Κ

(2504) **κἀγώ**, contracted from καὶ ἐγώ, dat. κἀμοί, acc. κἀμέ, καί retaining, however, its independent force, John 6:57; 10:15, et al.

καθ', by apostrophe for κατά . . . . κατά *(2596)*

(2505) **καθά**, adv. (καθ' ἅ) lit. *according to what; as, according as*

καθαίρει, 3 pers. sg. pres. act. indic. . καθαίρω *(2508)*

καθαιρεῖσθαι, pres. pass. infin. [§17.Q] . . . . καθαιρέω *(2507)*

καθαίρεσιν, acc. sg. f. n. . . . . καθαίρεσις *(2506)*

(2506) **καθαίρεσις**, εως, ἡ [§5.E.c] pr. *a taking down; a pulling down, overthrow, demolition,* 2 Cor. 10:4; met. *a razing* as respects spiritual state, a counter process to religious advancement by apostolic instrumentality, 2 Cor. 10:8; 13:10

(2507) **καθαιρέω**, ῶ, fut. καθαιρήσω, and καθελῶ,

2 aor. καθεῖλον [§36.1] (κατά + αἱρέω)
to take down, Matt. 15:36, 46; Luke
23:53; Acts 13:29; *to pull down, demol-*
ish, Luke 12:18; *to throw or cast down, de-*
grade, Luke 1:52; *to destroy, put an end to*,
Acts 19:27; *to overthrow, conquer*, Acts
13:19; *to pull down, subvert*, 2 Cor. 10:5
καθαιροῦντες, nom. pl. m. pres. act.
    part. . . . . καθαιρέω *(2507)*

(2508) **καθαίρω**, fut. καθαρῶ, perf. pass. κεκά-
θαρμαι [§27.1.c; 27.3] *to cleanse* from filth;
to clear by pruning, *prune*, John 15:2; met.
to cleanse from sin, *make expiation*, Heb.
10:2

(2509) **καθάπερ**, adv. (καθ᾽ ἅ περ) *even as, just as*,
Rom. 4:6, et al.

(2510) **καθάπτω**, fut. καθάψω [§23.1] (κατά +
ἅπτω) trans. *to fasten or fit to;* in N.T.
equivalent to καθάπτομαι, *to fix one's self*
upon, fasten upon; Acts 28:3
καθαρά, nom. sg. f. adj.
    {James 1:27} . . . . καθαρός *(2513)*
καθαρά, nom. pl. neut. adj. {Luke 11:41} .   id.
καθαρᾷ, dat. sg. f. adj. . . . . id.
καθαρᾶς, gen. sg. f. adj. . . . . id.
καθαριεῖ, 3 pers. sg. fut. act. indic. Att. for
    καθαρίσει [§35.1] . . . . καθαρίζω *(2511)*
καθαρίζει, 3 pers. sg. pres. act. indic. . . . . id.
καθαρίζεσθαι, pres. pass. infin. . . . . id.
καθαρίζεται, 3 pers. sg. pres. pass. indic. .   id.
καθαρίζετε, 2 pers. pl. pres. act. indic.
    {Matt. 23:25} . . . . id.
καθαρίζετε, 2 pers. pl. pres. act. imper.
    {Matt. 10:8} . . . . id.
καθαρίζον, nom. sg. neut. pres. act. part.
    (Mark 7:19, MT & TR | καθαρίζων,
    GNT, WH & NA) . . . . id.
καθαρίζονται, 3 pers. pl. pres. pass. indic.   id.

(2511) **καθαρίζω**, fut. καθαρίσω and καθαριῶ, aor.
ἐκαθάρισα [§26.1] a later equivalent to
καθαίρω, *to cleanse, render pure*, Matt.
23:25; Luke 11:39; *to cleanse* from leprosy,
Matt. 8:2, 3; 10:8; met. *to cleanse* from sin,
purify by an expiatory offering, make ex-
piation for, Heb. 9:22, 23; 1 John 1:7; *to*
cleanse from sin, *free from the influence*
of error and sin, Acts 15:9; 2 Cor. 7:1; *to*
pronounce ceremonially *clean*, Acts 10:15;
11:9, et al.
καθαρίζων, nom. sg. m. pres. act. part. (Mark
    7:19, GNT, WH & NA | καθαρίζον, MT
    & TR) . . . . καθαρίζω *(2511)*
καθαρίσαι, aor. act. infin. . . . . id.
καθαρίσας, nom. sg. m. aor. act. part. . . . . id.
καθαρίσατε, 2 pers. pl. aor. act. imper. . . . id.

καθαρίσῃ, 3 pers. sg. aor. act. subj. . . καθαρίζω *(2511)*
καθαρίσθητι, 2 pers. sg. aor. pass. imper. . . id.
καθαρισμόν, acc. sg. m. n. . . . . . καθαρισμός *(2512)*

(2512) **καθαρισμός**, οῦ, ὁ [§3.C.a] ceremonial *cleans-*
ing, purification, Luke 2:22; John 2:6;
mode of purification, John 2:6; 3:35;
cleansing of lepers, Mark 1:44; met. *ex-*
piation, Heb. 1:3; 2 Pet. 1:9, et al.
καθαρισμοῦ, gen. sg. m. n. . . . . . καθαρισμός *(2512)*
καθάρισον, 2 pers. sg. aor. act.
    imper. . . . . καθαρίζω *(2511)*
καθαρίσωμεν, 1 pers. pl. aor. act. subj. . . id.
καθαροί, nom. pl. m. adj. . . . . καθαρός *(2513)*
καθαροῖς, dat. pl. m. adj. . . . . id.
καθαρόν, acc. sg. m. adj. (Rev. 22:1, TR |
    GNT, WH, MT & NA omit) . . . . id.
καθαρόν, nom. sg. neut. adj. {Matt. 23:26}   id.
καθαρόν, acc. sg. neut. adj. {Rev. 15:6} . . id.

(2513) **καθαρός**, ά, όν, nom. sg. m. adj. [§7.1] *clean*
pure, unsoiled, Matt. 23:26; 27:59; met.
clean from guilt, *guiltless, innocent*, Acts
18:6; 20:26; *sincere, unfeigned, upright*,
virtuous, void of evil, Matt. 5:8; John
15:3; *clean* ceremonially, Luke 11:41

(2514) **καθαρότης**, ητος, ἡ [§4.2.c] *cleanness;* ceremonial *purity*, Heb. 9:13
καθαρότητα, acc. sg. f. n. . . . . καθαρότης *(2514)*
καθαρῷ, dat. sg. m. adj. {Rev. 21:18} καθαρός *(2513)*
καθαρῷ, dat. sg. neut. adj. {Heb. 10:22} . id.

(2515) **καθέδρα**, ας, ἡ [§2.B.b] (κατά + ἕδρα) *a seat*,
Matt. 21:12; 23:2; Mark 11:15
καθέδρας, gen. sg. f. n. {Matt. 23:2} καθέδρα *(2515)*
καθέδρας, acc. pl. f. n. {Matt. 21:12} . . id.

(2516) **καθέζομαι**, fut. καθεζοῦμαι, *to seat one's self,*
sit down, Matt. 26:55; Luke 2:46, et al.
καθεζόμενοι, nom. pl. m. pres. mid./pass.
    dep. part. . . . . καθέζομαι *(2516)*
καθεζόμενον, acc. sg. m. pres. mid./pass. dep.
    part. . . . . id.
καθεζόμενος, nom. sg. m. pres. mid./pass.
    dep. part. (Acts 20:9, GNT, WH & NA
    | καθήμενος, MT & TR) . . . . id.
καθεζομένους, acc. pl. m. pres. mid./pass.
    dep. part. id.
καθεῖλε(ν), 3 pers. sg. 2 aor. act. indic.
    [§36.1] . . . . καθαιρέω *(2507)*
καθελεῖν, 2 aor. act. infin. . . . . id.
καθελόντες, nom. pl. m. 2 aor. act. part. . id.
καθελῶ, 1 pers. sg. fut. act. indic. . . . . . id.
καθελών, nom. sg. m. 2 aor. act. part. . . . id.

(2517) **καθεξῆς**, adv. (κατά + ἑξῆς) *in a continual*
order or series, successively, consecutively,
Luke 1:3; Acts 11:4; 18:23; ὁ, ἡ, καθεξῆς,
succeeding, subsequent, Luke 8:1; Acts
3:24

καθεύδει, 3 pers. sg. pres. act. indic. . καθεύδω *(2518)*

καθεύδειν, pres. act. infin. . . . . id.

καθεύδεις, 2 pers. sg. pres. act. indic. . . . . id.

καθεύδετε, 2 pers. pl. pres. act. indic. or
imper. {Luke 22:46} . . . . id.

καθεύδετε, 2 pers. pl. pres. act. imper.
{Matt. 26:45} . . . . id.

καθεύδῃ, 3 pers. sg. pres. act. subj. . . . . . . id.

καθεύδοντας, acc. pl. m. pres. act. part. . . id.

καθεύδοντες, nom. pl. m. pres. act. part. . id.

καθεύδουσι(ν), 3 pers. pl. pres. act. indic. id.

(2518) **καθεύδω,** fut. καθευδήσω (κατά + εὕδω, *to
sleep*) *to sleep, be fast asleep,* Matt. 8:24;
9:24, et al.; met. *to sleep* in spiritual sloth,
Eph. 5:14; 1 Thess. 5:6; *to sleep* the sleep
of death, 1 Thess. 5:10

καθεύδωμεν, 1 pers. pl. pres. act.
subj. . . . . καθεύδω *(2518)*

καθεύδων, nom. sg. m. pres. act. part. . . . id.

κάθῃ, 2 pers. sg. pres. mid./pass. dep. indic.
Att. for κάθησαι, ... κάθημαι *(2521)*

καθηγηταί, nom. pl. m. n. . . . . καθηγητής *(2519)*

(2519) **καθηγητής,** οῦ, ὁ, nom. sg. m. n. [§2.B.c]
(καθηγέομαι, *to lead, conduct,* from κατά
+ ἡγέομαι) pr. *a guide, leader;* in N.T. *a
teacher, instructor,* Matt. 23:8, 10

καθῆκαν, 3 pers. pl. aor. act. indic. . . καθίημι *(2524)*

καθῆκεν, 3 pers. sg. (impers.) imperf. act.
indic. (Acts 22:22, GNT, WH, MT & NA
| καθῆκον, TR) . . . . καθήκω *(2520)*

καθῆκον, nom. sg. neut. (impers.) pres. act.
part. (Acts 22:22, TR | καθῆκεν, GNT,
WH, MT & NA) . . . . id.

καθήκοντα, acc. pl. neut. pres. act. part. . id.

(2520) **καθήκω** (κατά + ἥκω) *to reach, extend to;*
καθήκει, impers. *it is fitting, meet,* Acts
22:22; τὸ καθῆκον, *what is fit, right, duty;*
τὰ μὴ καθήκοντα, by litotes for *what is
abominable or detestable,* Rom. 1:28

(2521) **κάθημαι,** 1 pers. sg. pres. mid./pass. dep.
indic., 2 pers. κάθησαι and κάθῃ, imper.
κάθησο and κάθου (κατά + ἧμαι, *to sit*)
to sit, be sitting, Matt. 9:9; Luke 10:13; *to
be seated,* 1 Cor. 14:30; *to dwell,* Matt.
4:16; Luke 1:79; 21:35, et al.

καθήμεναι, nom. pl. f. pres. mid./pass. dep.
part. . . . . κάθημαι *(2521)*

καθημένην, acc. sg. f. pres. mid./pass. dep.
part. . . . . id.

καθημένης, gen. sg. f. pres. mid./pass. dep.
part. . . . . id.

καθήμενοι, nom. pl. m. pres. mid./pass. dep.
part. . . . . id.

καθημένοις, dat. pl. m. pres. mid./pass. dep.
part. {Matt. 4:16} . . . . id.

καθημένοις, dat. pl. neut. pres. mid./pass.
dep. part. {Matt. 11:16} . . . . κάθημαι *(2521)*

καθήμενον, acc. sg. m. pres. mid./pass. dep.
part. . . . . id.

καθήμενος, nom. sg. m. pres. mid./pass. dep.
part. . . . . id.

καθημένου, gen. sg. m. pres. mid./pass. dep.
part. . . . . id.

καθημένους, acc. pl. m. pres. mid./pass. dep.
part. . . . . id.

καθημένῳ, dat. sg. m. pres. mid./pass. dep.
part. . . . . id.

καθημένων, gen. pl. m. pres. mid./pass. dep.
part. . . . . id.

καθημερινῇ, dat. sg. f. adj. . . . . . καθημερινός *(2522)*

(2522) **καθημερινός,** ή, όν [§7.F.a] (καθ᾽ ἡμέραν, *daily*) *daily, day by day,* Acts 6:1

κάθηνται, 3 pers. pl. pres. mid./pass. dep.
indic. (Rev. 11:16, MT | καθήμενοι, GNT,
WH, TR & NA) . . . . κάθημαι *(2521)*

καθήσεσθε, 2 pers. pl. fut. mid. dep. indic.
(Matt. 19:28; Luke 22:30, GNT & NA |
καθίσεσθε, MT | καθίσεσθε, Matt. 19:28;
καθίσησθε, Luke 22:30, TR | καθῆσθε,
Matt. 19:28; κάθησθε, Luke 22:30, WH) id.

καθῆσθαι, pres. mid./pass. dep. infin. . . . . id.

κάθησθε, 2 pers. pl. pres. mid./pass. dep.
indic. (Luke 22:30, WH | καθήσεσθε,
GNT & NA | καθίσεσθε, MT | καθ-
ίσησθε, TR) . . . . id.

κάθηται, 3 pers. sg. pres. mid./pass. dep.
indic. . . . . id.

καθῆψε(ν), 3 pers. sg. aor. act. indic.
[§23.2] . . . . καθάπτω *(2510)*

καθιεμένην, acc. sg. f. pres. pass.
part. . . . . καθίημι *(2524)*

καθιέμενον, acc. sg. neut. pres. pass. part. id.

καθίζετε, 2 pers. pl. pres. act. indic. .or
imper. . . . . καθίζω *(2523)*

(2523) **καθίζω,** fut. καθίσω, perf. κακάθικα, aor.
ἐκάθισα [§26.1] trans. *to cause to sit, place;*
καθίζομαι, *to be seated, sit,* Matt. 19:28;
Luke 22:30; *to cause to sit* as judges, *place,
appoint,* 1 Cor. 6:4; intrans. *to sit, sit
down,* Matt. 13:48; 26:36; *to remain, stay,
continue,* Luke 24:49

(2524) **καθίημι,** fut. καθήσω, aor. καθῆκα [§32.CC]
(κατά + ἵημι) *to let down, lower,* Luke
5:19; Acts 9:25; 10:11; 11:5

καθίσαι, aor. act. infin. . . . . καθίζω *(2523)*

καθίσαντες, nom. pl. m. aor. act. part. . . id.

καθίσαντος, gen. sg. m. aor. act. part. . . . id.

καθίσας, nom. sg. m. aor. act. part. . . . . . id.

καθίσατε, 2 pers. pl. aor. act. imper. . . . . . id.

καθίσει, 3 pers. sg. fut. act. indic. . . . . id.

καθίσεσθε, 2 pers. pl. fut. mid. dep. indic.
(Matt. 19:28; Luke 22:30, MT | Matt.
19:28 καθίσεσθε; καθίσησθε, Luke 22:30,
TR | καθήσεσθε, GNT & NA | καθ-
ήσεσθε, Matt. 19:28; κάθησθε, Luke
22:30, WH) . . . . καθίζω (2523)
καθίσῃ, 3 pers. sg. aor. act. subj. . . . . id.
καθίσησθε, 2 pers. pl. aor. mid. dep. subj.
(Luke 22:30, TR | καθήσεσθε, GNT &
NA | καθίσεσθε, MT | κάθησθε, WH) id.
καθιστάνοντες, nom. pl. m. pres. act. part.
(Acts 17:15, GNT, WH & NA | καθ-
ιστῶντες, MT & TR) . . . . καθίστημι (2525)
καθίσταται, 3 pers. sg. pres. pass. indic. . . id.
(2525) **καθίστημι**, and in N.T. καθιστάω, ῶ, fut.
καταστήσω, aor. κατέστησα, aor. pass.
κατεστάθην [§29.X.Y] (κατά + ἵστημι)
to place, set, James 3:6; *to set, constitute,
appoint,* Matt. 24:45, 47; Luke 12:14; *to
set down* in a place, *conduct,* Acts 17:15;
to make, render, or cause to be, 2 Pet. 1:8;
pass. *to be rendered,* Rom. 5:19
καθίστησιν, 3 pers. sg. pres. act.
indic. . . . . καθίστημι (2525)
καθιστῶντες, nom. pl. m. pres. act. part.
[§31.2] (Acts 17:15, MT & TR | καθ-
ιστάνοντες, GNT, WH & NA) . καθιστάω (2525)
καθίσωμεν, 1 pers. pl. aor. act. subj. . . καθίζω (2523)
καθίσωσιν, 3 pers. pl. aor. act. subj. . . . . . id.
(2526) **καθό** (καθ' ὅ) *as,* Rom. 8:26; *according as,
in proportion as,* 2 Cor. 8:12; 1 Pet. 4:13
καθολική, nom. sg. f. adj. (James 5:20; 1 Pet.
5:14; 1 John 5:21; 3 John 15; Jude 25, TRs
| GNT, WH, MT, TRb & NA
omit) . . . . καθολικός (2526')
(2526') **καθολικός,** ή, όν, *general, universal*
(2527) **καθόλου** (καθ' ὅλου), adv. *on the whole, in
general, altogether;* and with a negative,
not at all, Acts 4:18
(2528) **καθοπλίζω,** fut. καθοπλίσω [§26.1] (κατά +
ὁπλίζω) *to arm completely,* Luke 11:21
καθορᾶται, 3 pers. sg. pres. pass. indic.
[§19.S] . . . . καθοράω (2529)
(2529) **καθοράω,** ῶ (κατά + ὁράω) pr. *to look down
upon,* in N.T. *to mark, perceive, discern,*
Rom. 1:20
(2530) **καθότι** (καθ' ὅτι) *according as, in proportion
as,* Acts 2:45; 4:35; *inasmuch as,* Luke 1:7;
19:9; Acts 2:24
κάθου, 2 pers. sg. pres. mid./pass. dep.
imper. . . . . κάθημαι (2521)
καθωπλισμένος, nom. sg. m. perf. pass.
part. . . . . καθοπλίζω (2528)
(2531) **καθώς** (κατά + ὡς) *as, in the manner that,*
Matt. 21:6; 26:24; *how, in what manner,*

Acts 15:14; *according as,* Mark 4:33; *inasmuch as,* John 17:2; of time, *when,* Acts
7:17
(‡2509) **καθώσπερ,** adv., *just as, exactly as* (Heb. 5:4,
GNT, MT, WH & NA | καθάπερ, TR)
(2532) **καί,** conj., *and,* Matt. 2:2, 3, 11; 4:22; καὶ . . .
καί, *both . . . and;* as a cumulative parti-
cle, *also, too,* Matt. 5:39; John 8:19; 1 Cor.
11:6, et al.; emphatic, *even, also,* Matt.
10:30; 1 Cor. 2:10, et al.; in N.T. adversa-
tive, *but,* Matt. 11:19, et al.; also introductory of the apodosis of a sentence, James
2:4; Gal. 3:28
Καϊάφα, gen. sg. m. n. (GNT, MT, TR & NA
| Καιάφα, WH) . . . . Καϊάφας (2533)
Καϊάφαν, acc. sg. m. n. (GNT, MT, TR &
NA | Καιάφαν, WH) . . . . id.
(2533) **Καϊάφας,** α, ὁ, nom. sg. m. n. (GNT, MT, TR
& NA | Καιάφας, WH) [§2.4] *Caiaphas,*
pr. name
(2534) **καίγε** (καί + γε) *at least, were it only,* Luke
19:42; *and even, yea too,* Acts 2:18
καίεται, 3 pers. sg. pres. pass. indic. . . . . καίω (2545)
(2535) **Κάϊν,** ὁ, *Cain,* pr. name, indecl. (GNT, MT,
TR & NA | Καίν, WH)
καινά, nom. pl. neut. adj.
{2 Cor. 5:17} . . . . καινός (2537)
καινά, acc. pl. neut. adj. {Rev. 21:5} . . . . . id.
καιναῖς, dat. pl. f. adj. . . . . id.
(†2536) **Καϊνάμ,** ὁ, *Cainan,* pr. name, indecl. (Luke
3:36, 37, GNT & NA | Καινάμ, WH |
Καϊνάν, MT & TR)
(2536) **Καϊνάν,** ὁ, *Cainan,* pr. name, indecl. I. *Cainan, son of Enos,* II. *Cainan, son of Ar-
phaxad* (Luke 3:36, 37, MT & TR |
Καινάμ, WH | Καϊνάμ, GNT & NA)
καινή, nom. sg. f. adj. . . . . καινός (2537)
καινήν, acc. sg. f. adj. . . . . id.
καινῆς, gen. sg. f. adj. . . . . id.
καινόν, acc. sg. m. adj. {Rev. 21:1} . . . . id.
καινόν, nom. sg. neut. adj. {John 19:41} . id.
καινόν, acc. sg. neut. adj. {Rev. 2:17} . . . . id.
(2537) **καινός,** ή, όν [§7.F.a] *new, recently made,*
Matt. 9:17; Mark 2:22; *new* in species,
character, or mode, Matt. 26:28, 29; Mark
14:24, 25; Luke 22:20; John 13:34; 2 Cor.
5:17; Gal. 6:15; Eph. 2:15; 4:24; 1 John
2:7; Rev. 3:12, et al.; *novel, strange,* Mark
1:27; Acts 17:19; *new* to the possessor,
Mark 16:17; *unheard of, unusual,* Mark
1:27; Acts 17:19; met. *renovated, better, of
higher excellence,* 2 Cor. 5:17; Rev. 5:9,
et al.
καινότερον, acc. sg. neut. adj. . . . καινότερος (†2537)
(†2537) **καινότερος,** α, ον [§8.4] compar. of preced-

ing, *newer, more recent;* but used for the positive, *new, novel,* Acts 17:21

(2538) **καινότης**, ητος, ἡ [§4.2.c] *newness,* Rom. 6:4; 7:6

καινότητι, dat. sg. f. n. . . . . καινότης (2538)
καινοῦ, gen. sg. neut. adj. . . . . καινός (2537)
καινούς, acc. pl. m. adj. . . . . id.
καινῷ, dat. sg. neut. adj. . . . . id.
καιόμεναι, nom. pl. f. pres. pass. part. . . καίω (2545)
καιομένη, nom. sg. f. pres. pass. part. . . . id.
καιομένῃ, dat. sg. f. pres. pass. part. . . . . id.
καιομένην, acc. sg. f. pres. pass. part. (Rev. 19:20, MT & TR | καιομένης, GNT, WH & NA) . . . . id.
καιομένης, gen. sg. f. pres. pass. part. (Rev. 19:20, GNT, WH & NA | καιομένην, MT & TR) . . . . id.
καιομένοι, nom. pl. f. pres. pass. part. . . . id.
καιόμενον, nom. sg. neut. pres. pass. part. id.
καιόμενος, nom. sg. m. pres. pass. part. . id.
καίουσι(ν), 3 pers. pl. pres. act. indic. . . . id.

(2539) **καίπερ** (καί + περ) *though, although;* Phil. 3:4; Rev. 17:8, et al.

καιροί, nom. pl. m. n. . . . . καιρός (2540)
καιροῖς, dat. pl. m. n. . . . . id.
καιρόν, acc. sg. m. n. . . . . id.

(2540) **καιρός**, οῦ, ὁ, nom. sg. m. n. [§3.C.a] pr. *fitness, proportion, suitableness; a fitting situation, suitable place,* 1 Pet. 4:17; *a limited period of time marked by a suitableness of circumstances, a fitting season,* 1 Cor. 4:5; 1 Tim. 2:6; 6:15; Tit. 1:3; *opportunity,* Acts 24:25; Gal. 6:10; Heb. 11:15; *a limited period of time marked by characteristic circumstances, a signal juncture, a marked season,* Matt. 16:3; Luke 12:56; 21:8; 1 Pet. 1:11, et al.; *a destined time,* Matt. 8:29; 26:18; Mark 1:15; Luke 21:24; 1 Thess. 5:1, et al.; *a season* in ordinary succession, equivalent to ὥρα, Matt. 13:30; Acts 14:17, et al.; in N.T. *a limited time, a short season,* Luke 4:13, et al.; simply, *a point of time,* Matt. 11:25; Luke 13:1, et al.

καιροῦ, gen. sg. m. n. . . . . καιρός (2540)
καιρούς, acc. pl. m. n. . . . . id.
καιρῷ, dat. sg. m. n. . . . . id.
καιρῶν, gen. pl. m. n. . . . . id.

(2541) **Καῖσαρ**, αρος, ὁ [§4.2.f] *Caesar,* pr. name
Καίσαρα, acc. sg. m. n. . . . . Καῖσαρ (2541)

(2542) **Καισάρεια**, ας, ἡ [§2.B.b; 2.2] *Caesarea* I. *Caesarea Philippi,* Matt. 16:13; Mark 8:27 II. *Caesarea Augusta,* Acts 8:40, et al.
Καισαρείᾳ, dat. sg. f. n. (Acts 10:1, GNT, MT, TR & NA | Καισαρίᾳ, WH) . . Καισάρεια (2542)

Καισάρειαν, acc. sg. f. n. (Acts 8:40; 9:30; 10:24; 12:19; 18:22; 21:8; 23:33; 25:4, 6, 13 | Καισάριαν, WH) . . . . . Καισάρεια (2542)
Καισαρείας, gen. sg. f. n. (Matt. 16:13; Mark 8:27; Acts 11:11; 21:16; 23:23; 25:1 | Καισαρίας, WH) . . . . id.
Καίσαρι, dat. sg. m. n. . . . . Καῖσαρ (2541)
Καίσαρος, gen. sg. m. n. . . . . id.

(2543) **καίτοι** (καί + enclitic τοι) *and yet, though, although,* Heb. 4:3

(2544) **καίτοιγε** (καίτοι + γε) *although indeed,* John 4:2; Acts 14:17; 17:27

(2545) **καίω**, fut. καύσω, aor. pass. ἐκαύθην [§35.3] *to cause to burn, kindle, light,* Matt. 5:15; pass. *to be kindled, burn, flame,* Luke 12:35; met. *to be kindled* into emotion, Luke 24:32; *to consume with fire,* John 15:6; 1 Cor. 13:3

κακά, nom. pl. neut. adj. {Tit. 1:12} . . κακός (2556)
κακά, acc. pl. neut. adj. {2 Tim. 4:14} . . . id.
κακαί, nom. pl. f. adj. . . . . id.

(2546) **κἀκεῖ** (by crasis for καὶ ἐκεῖ) *and there,* Matt. 5:23; 10:11; *there also,* Mark 1:38; *thither also,* Acts 17:13, et al.

(2547) **κἀκεῖθεν** (by crasis for καὶ ἐκεῖθεν) *and thence,* Mark 10:1; Acts 7:4; 14:26; 20:15; 21:1; 27:4, 12; 28:15; *and then, afterwards,* Acts 13:21

κἀκεῖνα, nom. pl. neut. pron. adj. {Matt. 15:18} . . . . κἀκεῖνος (2548)
κἀκεῖνα, acc. pl. neut. pron. adj. {Matt. 23:23} . . . . id.
κἀκεῖνοι, nom. pl. m. pron. adj. . . . . . . id.
κἀκείνοις, dat. pl. m. pron. adj. (Matt. 20:4, TR | καὶ ἐκείνοις, GNT, WH, MT & NA) . . . . id.
κἀκεῖνον, acc. sg. m. pron. adj. . . . . id.

(2548) **κἀκεῖνος**, η, ο, nom. sg. m. pron. adj. (by crasis for καὶ ἐκεῖνος) *and he, she, it; and this, and that,* Matt. 15:18; 23:23; *he, she, it also; this also, that also,* Matt. 20:4
κἀκείνους, acc. pl. m. pron. adj. . . . κἀκεῖνος (2548)
κακήν, acc. sg. f. adj. . . . . κακός (2556)

(2549) **κακία**, ας, ἡ, nom. sg. f. n. [§2.B.b; 2.2] *malice, malignity,* Rom. 1:29; Eph. 4:31; *wickedness, depravity,* Acts 8:22; 1 Cor. 5:8; in N.T. *evil, trouble, calamity,* Matt. 6:34
κακίᾳ, dat. sg. f. n. . . . . κακία (2549)
κακίαν, acc. sg. f. n. . . . . id.
κακίας, gen. sg. f. n. . . . . id.

(2550) **κακοήθεια**, ας, ἡ [§2.B.b; 2.2] (κακός + ἦθος) *disposition for mischief, malignity,* Rom. 1:29
κακοηθείας, gen. sg. f. n. . . . . . . κακοήθεια (2550)
κακοί, nom. pl. m. adj. . . . . κακός (2556)

(2551) **κακολογέω**, ῶ, fut. κακολογήσω [§16.P]
(κακός + λέγω) *to speak evil of, revile,*
abuse, assail with reproaches, Mark 9:39;
Acts 19:9; *to address with offensive lan-*
guage, to treat with disrespect, contemn,
Matt. 15:4; Mark 7:10
κακολογῆσαι, aor. act. infin. .... κακολογέω (2551)
κακολογοῦντες, nom. pl. m. pres. act. part.   id.
κακολογῶν, nom. sg. m. pres. act. part. .   id.
κακόν, nom. sg. neut. adj. {James 3:8}   κακός (2556)
κακόν, acc. sg. neut. adj. {3 John 11} ....   id.
κακοπαθεῖ, 3 pers. sg. pres. act.
     indic. .... κακοπαθέω (2553)
(2552) **κακοπάθεια**, ας, ἡ [§2.B.b; 2.2] *a state of suf-*
fering, affliction, trouble, in N.T. *endur-*
ance in affliction, James 5:10
κακοπαθείας, gen. sg. f. n. (James 5:10, GNT,
     MT, TR, NA | κακοπαθίας,
     WH) .... κακοπάθεια (2552)
(2553) **κακοπαθέω**, ῶ, fut. κακοπαθήσω [§16.P]
(κακός + πάσχω) *to suffer evil or afflic-*
tions, 2 Tim. 2:9; *to be vexed, troubled,*
dejected, James 5:13; in N.T. *to show en-*
durance in trials and afflictions, 2 Tim. 2:3
κακοπάθησον, 2 pers. sg. aor. act.
     imper. .... κακοπαθέω (2553)
κακοπαθίας, gen. sg. f. n. κακοπαθεία, ας,
     ἡ, *trouble, distress, affliction* (James 5:10,
     WH | κακοπαθείας, GNT, MT, TR &
     NA) .... κακοπάθεια (2552)
κακοπαθῶ, 1 pers. sg. pres. act.
     indic. .... κακοπαθέω (2553)
(2554) **κακοποιέω**, ῶ, fut. κακοποιήσω [§16.P]
(κακός + ποιέω) *to cause evil, injure, do*
harm, Mark 3:4; Luke 6:9; *to do evil, com-*
mit sin, 1 Pet. 3:17
κακοποιῆσαι, aor. act. infin. ..... κακοποιέω (2554)
(2555) **κακοποιός**, όν, nom. sg. m. adj. [§7.2] *an evil-*
doer, 1 Pet. 2:12, et al.; *a malefactor, crim-*
inal, John 18:30
κακοποιοῦντας, acc. pl. m. pres. act.
     part. .... κακοποιέω (2554)
κακοποιῶν, nom. sg. m. pres. act. part.
     {3 John 11} .... id.
κακοποιῶν, gen. pl. m. adj.
     {1 Pet. 2:12, 14} .... κακοποιός (2555)
(2556) **κακός**, ή, όν, nom. sg. m. adj. [§7.F.a] *bad,*
of a bad quality or disposition, worthless,
corrupt, depraved, Matt. 21:41; 24:48;
Mark 7:21; *wicked, criminal, morally bad;*
τὸ κακόν, *evil, wickedness, crime,* Matt.
27:23; Acts 23:9; *malediction,* 1 Pet. 3:10;
mischievous, harmful, baneful; τὸ κακόν,
evil, mischief, harm, injury, Tit. 1:12; *af-*
flictive; τὸ κακόν, *evil, misery, affliction,*

suffering, Luke 16:25
κακοῦ, gen. sg. neut. adj. .... κακός (2556)
κακοῦργοι, nom. pl. m. adj. ..... κακοῦργος (2557)
(2557) **κακοῦργος**, ον, nom. sg. m. adj. [§7.2]
(κακός + ἔργον) *an evil-doer, malefactor,*
criminal, Luke 23:32, 33, 39; 2 Tim. 2:9
κακούργους, acc. pl. m. adj. ..... κακοῦργος (2557)
κακούργων, gen. pl. m. adj. .... id.
κακούς, acc. pl. m. adj. .... κακός (2556)
(2558) **κακουχέω**, ῶ, fut. κακουχήσω [§16.P]
(κακός + ἔχω) *to maltreat, afflict, harass;*
pass. *to be afflicted, be oppressed with*
evils, Heb. 11:37; 13:3
κακουχούμενοι, nom. pl. m. pres. pass.
     part. .... κακουχέω (2558)
κακουχουμένων, gen. pl. m. pres. pass. part.   id.
(2559) **κακόω**, ῶ, fut. κακώσω, aor. ἐκάκωσα
[§20.T] *to maltreat, cause evil to, oppress,*
Acts 7:6, 19; 12:1; 18:10; 1 Pet. 3:13; in N.T.
to render ill-disposed, to embitter, Acts 14:2
κακῷ, dat. sg. neut. adj. .... κακός (2556)
κακῶν, gen. pl. m. adj. {Rom. 13:3} .... id.
κακῶν, gen. pl. neut. adj. {Rom. 2:30} .. id.
(2560) **κακῶς**, adv., *ill, badly;* physically *ill, sick,*
Matt. 4:24; 8:16, et al.; *grievously, vehe-*
mently, Matt. 15:22; *wretchedly, miserably,*
Matt. 21:41; *wickedly, reproachfully,* Acts
23:5; *wrongly, criminally,* John 18:23;
amiss, James 4:3
κακῶσαι, aor. act. infin. .... κακόω (2559)
κάκωσιν, acc. sg. f. n. .... κάκωσις (2561)
(2561) **κάκωσις**, εως, ἡ [§5.E.c] *ill-treatment, afflic-*
tion, misery, Acts 7:34
κακώσουσιν, 3 pers. pl. fut. act. indic. κακόω (2559)
κακώσων, nom. sg. m. fut. act. part. .... id.
καλά, nom. pl. neut. adj. {Tit. 3:8} ... καλός (2570)
καλά, acc. pl. neut. adj. {Matt. 5:16} .... id.
(2562) **καλάμη**, ης, ἡ [§2.B.a] *the stalk* of grain,
straw, stubble, 1 Cor. 3:12
καλάμην, acc. sg. f. n. .... καλάμη (2562)
κάλαμον, acc. sg. m. n. .... κάλαμος (2563)
(2563) **κάλαμος**, ου, ὁ, nom. sg. m. n. [§3.C.a] *a*
reed, cane, Matt. 11:7; 12:20; Luke 7:24;
a reed in its various appliances, as, a wand,
a staff, Matt. 27:29, 30, 48; Mark 15:19,
36; *a measuring-rod,* Rev. 11:1; *a writer's*
reed, 3 John 13
καλάμου, gen. sg. m. n. .... κάλαμος (2563)
καλάμῳ, dat. sg. m. n. .... id.
καλεῖ, 3 pers. sg. pres. act. indic. {Luke
     20:44} .... καλέω (2564)
κάλει, 2 pers. sg. pres. act. imper. {Luke 14:13}   id.
καλεῖν, pres. act. infin. .... id.
καλεῖσθαι, pres. pass. infin. [§17.Q] .... id.
καλεῖται, 3 pers. sg. pres. pass. indic. .... id.

καλεῖτε, 2 pers. pl. pres. act.
   indic. . . . . καλέω *(2564)*
καλέσαι, aor. act. infin. . . . . id.
καλέσαντα, acc. sg. m. aor. act. part. . . . . id.
καλέσαντες, nom. pl. m. aor. act. part. . . id.
καλέσαντος, gen. sg. m. aor. act. part. . . . id.
καλέσας, nom. sg. m. aor. act. part. . . . . . id.
καλέσατε, 2 pers. pl. aor. act. imper. . . . . id.
καλέσεις, 2 pers. sg. fut. act. indic. [§22.2] id.
καλέσητε, 2 pers. pl. aor. act. subj. . . . . . id.
κάλεσον, 2 pers. sg. aor. act. imper. . . . . . id.
καλέσουσι(ν), 3 pers. pl. fut. act. indic. . . id.
καλέσω, 1 pers. sg. fut. act. indic. . . . . . . id.
(2564) **καλέω**, ῶ, fut. καλέσω, perf. κέκληκα, aor.
   ἐκάλεσα, perf. pass. κέκλημαι, aor. pass.
   ἐκλήθην [§22.1.4] *to call, call to,* John
   10:3; *to call* into one's presence, *send for*
   a person, Matt. 2:7; *to summon,* Matt.
   2:15; 25:14, et al.; *to invite,* Matt. 22:9,
   et al.; *to call* to the performance of a certain thing, Matt. 9:13; Heb. 11:8, et al.;
   to call to a participation in the privileges
   of the Gospel, Rom. 8:30; 9:24; 1 Cor. 1:9;
   7:18, et al.; *to call* to an office or dignity,
   Heb. 5:4; *to name, style,* Matt. 1:21, et al.;
   pass. *to be styled, regarded,* Matt. 5:9, 19,
   et al.
καλῇ, dat. sg. f. adj. . . . . καλός *(2570)*
καλήν, acc. sg. f. adj. . . . . id.
καλῆς, gen. sg. f. adj. . . . . id.
καλλιέλαιον, acc. sg. f. n. . . . . . . καλλιέλαιος *(2565)*
(2565) **καλλιέλαιος**, ου, ἡ [§3.C.b] (κάλλος + ἔλαιον)
   pr. adj. *productive of good oil;* as subst.
   a cultivated olive tree, Rom. 11:24
(2566) **κάλλιον**, compar. adv. of καλῶς, *full well,*
   Acts 25:10
(†2566) **καλλίων**, ον [§8.2] *better,* Acts 25:10
(2567) **καλοδιδάσκαλος**, ον [§7.2] (καλός +
   διδάσκαλος) *teaching what is good; a*
   teacher of good, Tit. 2:3
καλοδιδασκάλους, acc. pl. f.
   adj. . . . . καλοδιδάσκαλος *(2567)*
καλοί, nom. pl. f. adj. . . . . καλός *(2570)*
(2568) **Καλοὶ Λιμένες**, *Fair Havens,* a harbor of Crete
καλοῖς, dat. pl. m. adj. {Luke 21:5} . . . καλός *(2570)*
καλοῖς, dat. pl. neut. adj. {1 Tim. 5:10} . . id.
καλόν, acc. sg. m. adj. {Matt. 12:33b} . . . id.
καλόν, nom. sg. neut. adj. {Matt. 13:38} . id.
καλόν, acc. sg. neut. adj. {Matt. 12:33a} . id.
(2569) **καλοποιέω**, ῶ, fut. καλοποιήσω [§16.P]
   (καλός + ποιέω) *to do well, do good,*
   2 Thess. 3:13
καλοποιοῦντες, nom. pl. m. pres. act.
   part. . . . . καλοποιέω *(2569)*
(2570) **καλός**, ή, όν, nom. sg. m. adj. [§7.F.a] pr.

beautiful; good, of good quality or dispo-
sition; fertile, rich, Matt. 13:8, 23; *useful,*
profitable, Luke 14:34; καλόν ἐστι(ν), *it*
is profitable, it is well, Matt. 18:8, 9; *ex-*
cellent, choice, select, goodly, Matt.
7:17, 19; καλόν ἐστι(ν), *it is pleasant, de-*
lightful, Matt. 17:4; *just, full* measure, Luke
6:38; *honorable, distinguished,* James 2:7;
good, possessing moral excellence, worthy,
upright, virtuous, John 10:11, 14; 1 Tim.
4:6; τὸ καλόν, and τὸ καλὸν ἔργον, *what*
is good and right, a good deed, rectitude,
virtue, Matt. 5:16; Rom. 7:18, 21; *right,*
duty, propriety, Matt. 15:26; *benefit, fa-*
vor, John 10:32, 33, et al.
καλοῦ, gen. sg. neut. adj. . . . . καλός *(2570)*
καλουμένη, gen. sg. f. pres. pass. part. καλέω *(2564)*
καλουμένῃ, dat. sg. f. pres. pass. part. . . . id.
καλουμένην, acc. sg. f. pres. pass. part. . . id.
καλουμένης, gen. sg. f. pres. pass. part. . . id.
καλούμενον, acc. sg. m. pres. pass. part.
   {Acts 27:8} . . . . id.
καλούμενον, acc. sg. neut. pres. pass. part.
   {Acts 27:16} . . . . id.
καλούμενος, nom. sg. m. pres. pass. part. id.
καλουμένου, gen. sg. m. pres. pass. part.
   {Acts 7:58} . . . . id.
καλουμένου, gen. sg. neut. pres. pass. part.
   {Acts 1:12} . . . . id.
καλοῦνται, 3 pers. pl. pres. pass. indic. . . id.
καλοῦντες, nom. pl. m. pres. act. part. (Mark
   3:31, GNT, WH & NA | φωνοῦντες, MT
   & TR) . . . . id.
καλοῦντος, gen. sg. m. pres. act. part. . . . id.
καλούς, acc. pl. m. adj. . . . . καλός *(2570)*
καλοῦσα, nom. sg. f. pres. act. part. . . καλέω *(2564)*
(†2571) **κάλυμμα**, ατος, τό, nom. sg. neut. n. [§4.D.c]
   a covering; a veil, 2 Cor. 3:13; met. *a veil,*
   a blind to spiritual vision, 2 Cor. 3:15, 16
   {2 Cor. 3:14}
κάλυμμα, acc. sg. neut. n.
   {2 Cor. 3:13} . . . . κάλυμμα *(†2571)*
καλύπτει, 3 pers. sg. pres. act. indic. καλύπτω *(2572)*
καλύπτεσθαι, pres. pass. infin. . . . . id.
(2572) **καλύπτω**, fut. καλύψω [§23.1] aor. ἐκάλυψα,
   perf. pass. κεκάλυμμαι, *to cover,* Matt.
   8:24; Luke 8:16; 23:30; *to hide, conceal,*
   Matt. 10:26; 2 Cor. 4:3; met. *to cover,*
   throw a veil of oblivion *over,* James 5:20;
   1 Pet. 4:8
καλύψατε, 2 pers. pl. aor. act. imper. καλύπτω *(2572)*
καλύψει, 3 pers. sg. fut. act. indic. . . . . . . id.
καλῷ, dat. sg. neut. adj. . . . . καλός *(2570)*
καλῶν, gen. pl. neut. adj. {Heb. 10:24} . . id.
καλῶν, nom. sg. m. pres. act. part.

{1 Thess. 5:24} . . . . καλέω *(2564)*

(2573) **καλῶς,** adv., *well, rightly, suitable, with propriety, becomingly,* 1 Cor. 7:37; 14:17; Gal. 4:17; 5:7, et al.; *truly, justly, correctly,* Mark 12:32; Luke 20:39; John 4:17, et al.; *appositely,* Matt. 15:7; Mark 7:6; *becomingly, honorably,* James 2:3; *well, effectually,* Mark 7:9, 37, et al.; καλῶς εἰπεῖν, *to speak well, praise, applaud,* Luke 6:26; καλῶς ἔχειν, *to be convalescent,* Mark 16:18; καλῶς ποιεῖν, *to do good, confer benefits,* Matt. 5:44; 12:12; *to do well, act virtuously,* Phil. 4:14, et al.

κἀμέ, by crasis for καὶ ἐμέ . . . . κἀγώ *(2504)*

καμήλον, acc. sg. m. n. . . . . κάμηλος *(2574)*

(2574) **κάμηλος,** ου, ὁ, ἡ, *a camel* (Hebrew גָּמָל) Matt. 3:4; 23:24, et al.

καμήλου, gen. sg. m. n. . . . . κάμηλος *(2574)*

κάμητε, 2 pers. pl. 2 aor. act. subj. [§27.2.d] . . . . κάμνω *(2577)*

καμίνου, acc. sg. f. n. . . . . κάμινος *(2575)*

(2575) **κάμινος,** ου, ἡ, [§3.C.b] *a furnace, oven, kiln,* Matt. 13:42, 50; Rev. 1:15; 9:2

καμίνου, gen. sg. f. n. . . . . κάμινος *(2575)*

καμίνῳ, dat. sg. f. n. . . . . id.

(2576) **καμμύω,** fut. καμμύσω, aor. ἐκάμμυσα [§13.M] (contr. for καταμύω, from κατά + μύω) *to shut, close* the eyes, Matt. 13:15; Acts 28:27

κάμνοντα, acc. sg. m. pres. act. part. . κάμνω *(2577)*

(2577) **κάμνω,** fut. καμοῦμαι, perf. κέκμηκα, 2 aor. ἔκαμον [§27.2.d] pr. *to tire with exertion, labor to weariness; to be wearied, tired out, exhausted,* Heb. 12:3; Rev. 2:3; *to labor under disease, be sick,* James 5:15

κἀμοί, by crasis for καὶ ἐμοί . . . . κἀγώ *(2504)*

(2578) **κάμπτω,** 1 pers. sg. pres. act. indic., fut. κάμψω [§23.2] aor. ἔκαμψα, trans. *to bend, inflect* the knee, Rom. 11:4; Eph. 3:14; intrans. *to bend, bow,* Rom. 14:11; Phil. 2:10

κάμψει, 3 pers. sg. fut. act. indic. . . . κάμπτω *(2578)*

κάμψῃ, 3 pers. sg. aor. act. subj. . . . . id.

(2579) **κἄν** (by crasis for καὶ ἐάν) *and if,* Mark 16:18; *also if,* Matt. 21:21; *even if, if even, although,* John 10:38; *if so much as,* Heb. 12:20; also in N.T. simply equivalent to καί, as a particle of emphasis, by a pleonasm of ἄν, *at least, at all events,* Mark 6:56; Acts 5:15; 2 Cor. 11:16

(†2580) **Κανά,** ἡ, indecl. *Cana,* a town of Galilee (GNT, WH, MT & NA | Κανᾷ, TR)

Κανααῖον, acc. sg. m. n. (Mark 3:18, GNT, WH & NA | Κανανίτην, MT & TR) . . . . Κανααῖος *(†2581)*

(†2581) **Κανααῖος,** ου, ὁ, nom. sg. m. n. [§3.C.a] *a*

Canaanite (Matt. 10:4, GNT, WH & NA | Κανανίτης, MT & TR)

Κανανίτην, acc. sg. m. n. (Mark 3:18, MT & TR | Κανααῖον, GNT, WH & NA) . . . . Κανανίτης *(2581)*

(2581) **Κανανίτης,** ου, ὁ, nom. sg. m. n. [§2.B.c] (Aramaic קַנְאָן, from the Hebrew קָנָא, *to be zealous,* i.q. ζηλωτής, *zealot,* Luke 6:15; Acts 1:13) *Canaanite,* Matt. 10:4; Mark 3:18 (Matt. 10:4, MT & TR | Κανααῖος, GNT, WH & NA)

(2582) **Κανδάκη,** ης, ἡ [§2.B.a] *Candace,* pr. name, Acts 8:27

Κανδάκης, gen. sg. f. n. . . . . Κανδάκη *(2582)*

κανόνα, acc. sg. m. n. . . . . κανών *(2583)*

κανόνι, acc. sg. m. n. . . . . id.

κανόνος, gen. sg. m. n. . . . . id.

(2583) **κανών,** όνος, ὁ [§4.2.c] (κάννα or κάνη, *a cane) a measure, rule;* in N.T. *prescribed range* of action or duty, 2 Cor. 10:13, 15, 16; met. *rule* of conduct or doctrine, Gal. 6:16; Phil. 3:16

(2584) **Καπερναούμ,** ἡ, indecl. *Capernaum,* a city of Galilee (MT & TR | Καφαρναούμ, GNT, WH & NA)

καπηλεύοντες, nom. pl. m. pres. act. part. . . . . καπηλεύω *(2585)*

(2585) **καπηλεύω,** fut. καπηλεύσω [§13.M] pr. *to be* κάπηλος, *a retailer, to huckster; to peddle with; to deal paltrily with,* or, *to corrupt, adulterate,* 2 Cor. 2:17

καπνόν, acc. sg. m. n. . . . . καπνός *(2586)*

(2586) **καπνός,** οῦ, ὁ, nom. sg. m. n. [§3.C.a] *smoke,* Act 2:19; Rev. 8:4, et al.

καπνοῦ, gen. sg. m. n. . . . . καπνός *(2586)*

(2587) **Καππαδοκία,** ας, ἡ [§2.B.b; 2.2] *Cappadocia,* a district of Asia Minor

Καππαδοκίαν, acc. sg. f. n. . . . . Καππαδοκία *(2587)*

Καππαδοκίας, gen. sg. f. n. . . . . id.

(2588) **καρδία,** ας, ἡ, nom. sg. f. n. [§2.B.b; 2.2] (κέαρ, idem) *the heart; the heart,* regarded as the seat of feeling, impulse, affection, desire, Matt. 6:21; 22:37; Phil. 1:7; et al.; *the heart,* as the seat of intellect, Matt. 13:15; Rom. 1:21; et al.; *the heart,* as the inner and mental frame, Matt. 5:8; Luke 16:15; 1 Pet. 3:4, et al.; *the conscience,* 1 John 3:20, 21; *the heart, the inner part, middle, center,* Matt. 12:40, et al.

καρδία, dat. sg. f. n. . . . . καρδία *(2588)*

καρδίαι, nom. pl. f. n. . . . . id.

καρδίαις, dat. pl. f. n. . . . . id.

καρδίαν, acc. sg. f. n. . . . . id.

καρδίας, gen. sg. f. n. {Eph. 6:5} . . . . . . id.

καρδίας, acc. pl. f. n. {Eph. 6:22} . . . . . . id.

καρδιογνῶστα, voc. sg. m. n.

[§2.6] .... καρδιογνώστης *(2589)*

(2589) **καρδιογνώστης**, ου, ὁ, nom. sg. m. n. [§2.B.c]
(καρδία + γινώσκω) *heart-knower,*
searcher of hearts, Acts 1:24; 15:8

καρδιῶν, gen. pl. f. n. .... καρδία *(2588)*

καρπόν, acc. sg. m. n. .... καρπός *(2590)*

(2590) **καρπός**, οῦ, ὁ, nom. sg. m. n. [§3.C.a] *fruit,*
Matt. 3:10; 21:19, 34; from the Hebrew,
καρπὸς κοιλίας, *fruit of the womb, off-*
spring, Luke 1:42; καρπὸς ὀσφύος, *fruit*
of the loins, offspring, posterity, Acts 2:30;
καρπὸς χειλέων, *fruit of the lips, praise,*
Heb. 13:15; met. *conduct, actions,* Matt.
3:8; 7:16; Rom. 6:22; *benefit, profit, emol-*
ument, Rom. 1:13; 6:21; *reward,* Phil. 4:17,
et al.

(2591) **Κάρπος**, ου, ὁ, *Carpus,* pr. name

καρποῦ, gen. sg. m. n. .... καρπός *(2590)*

καρπούς, acc. pl. m. n. .... id.

καρποφορεῖ, 3 pers. sg. pres. act.
indic. .... καρποφορέω *(2592)*

(2592) **καρποφορέω**, ῶ, fut. καρποφορήσω, aor.
ἐκαρποφόρησα [§16.P] (καρπός +
φορέω, from φέρω) *to bear fruit, yield,*
Mark 4:28; met. *to bring forth the fruit* of
action or conduct, Matt. 13:23; Rom.7:5;
mid. *to expand by fruitfulness, to develop*
itself by success, Col. 1:6

καρποφορῆσαι, aor. act. infin. .. καρποφορέω *(2592)*

καρποφορήσωμεν, 1 pers. pl. aor. act. subj. id.

καρποφορούμενον, nom. sg. neut. pres. mid.
part. .... id.

καρποφοροῦντες, nom. pl. m. pres. act. part. id.

(2593) **καρποφόρος**, ον [§7.2] *fruitful, adapted to*
bring forth fruit, Acts 14:17

καρποφόρους, acc. pl. m. adj. ... καρποφόρος *(2593)*

καρποφοροῦσιν, 3 pers. pl. pres. act.
indic. .... καρποφορέω *(2592)*

Κάρπῳ, dat. sg. m. n. .... Κάρπος *(2591)*

καρπῶν, gen. pl. m. n. .... καρπός *(2590)*

(2594) **καρτερέω**, ῶ, fut. καρτερήσω, aor.
ἐκαρτέρησα [§16.P] (καρτερός, by metath. from κράτος) *to be stout; to endure*
patiently, bear up with fortitude, Heb.
11:27

(2595) **κάρφος**, ους, τό [§5.E.b] (κάρφω, *to shrivel*)
any small dry thing, as *chaff, stubble,*
splinter, mote, etc.; Matt. 7:3, 4, 5; Luke
6:41, 42

κάρφος, acc. sg. neut. n. .... κάρφος *(2595)*

κατ ᾽ by apostrophe for κατά .... κατά *(2596)*

(2596) **κατά**, prep., with a genitive, *down from,* Matt.
8:32; *down upon, upon,* Mark 14:3; Acts
27:14; *down into;* κατὰ βάθους, *profound,*

deepest, 2 Cor. 8:2; *down over, through-*
out a space, Luke 4:14; 23:5; *concerning,*
in cases of pointed allegation, 1 Cor. 15:15;
against, Matt. 12:30, et al.; *by,* in oaths,
Matt. 26:63, et al.; with an acc. of place,
in the quarter of, about, near, at, Luke
10:32; Acts 2:10; *throughout,* Luke 8:39;
in, Rom. 16:5; *among,* Acts 21:21; *in the*
presence of, Luke 2:31; *in the direction of,*
towards, Acts 8:26; Phil. 3:14; *of time,*
within the range of; during, in the course
of, at, about, Acts 12:1; 27:27; *distribu-*
tively, κατ ᾽ οἶκον, *by houses, from house*
to house, Acts 2:46; κατὰ δύο, *two and*
two, 1 Cor. 14:27; καθ᾽ ἡμέραν, *daily,*
Matt. 26:55, et al.; trop., *according to, con-*
formable to, in proportion to, Matt. 9:29;
25:15; *after the fashion or likeness of,* Heb.
5:6; *in virtue of,* Matt. 19:3; *as respects,*
Rom. 1:3; Acts 25:14; Heb. 9:9

κατάβα, 2 pers. sg. 2 aor. act. imper. [§31.1.d]
Att. for κατάβηθι (Mark 15:30, MT &
TR | καταβάς, GNT, WH &
NA) .... καταβαίνω *(2597)*

καταβαίνει, 3 pers. sg. pres. act. indic. ... id.

καταβαίνειν, pres. act. infin. (Rev. 13:13,
GNT, WH, TR & NA | καταβαίνῃ, MT) id.

καταβαινέτω, 3 pers. sg. pres. act. imper.
(Matt. 24:17, MT & TR | καταβάτω,
GNT, WH & NA) .... id.

καταβαίνῃ, 3 pers. sg. pres. act. subj. (Rev.
13:13, MT | καταβαίνειν, GNT, WH, TR
& NA) .... id.

καταβαῖνον, nom. sg. neut. pres. act. part.
{James 1:17} .... id.

καταβαῖνον, acc. sg. neut. pres. act. part.
{John 1:32–33} .... id.

καταβαίνοντα, acc. sg. m. pres. act. part. id.

καταβαίνοντας, acc. pl. m. pres. act. part. id.

καταβαίνοντες, nom. pl. m. pres. act. part.
(Luke 22:44, MT & TR | καταβαίνοντος,
GNT, WH & NA) .... id.

καταβαίνοντος, gen. sg. m. pres. act. part.
{John 4:51} .... id.

καταβαίνοντος, gen. sg. neut. pres. act. part.
(Luke 22:44, GNT, WH & NA |
καταβαίνοντες, MT & TR) .... id.

καταβαινόντων, gen. pl. m. pres. act. part. id.

καταβαίνουσα, nom. sg. f. pres. act. part.
(Rev. 3:12, GNT, WH, TR & NA |
καταβαίνει, MT) .... id.

καταβαίνουσαν, acc. sg. f. pres. act. part. id.

(2597) **καταβαίνω** [§37.1] fut. καταβήσομαι, 2 aor.
κατέβην, imper. κατάβηθι, and κατάβα,
perf. καταβέβηκα (κατά + βαίνω) *to*

come or *go down, descend,* Matt. 8:1; 17:9; *to lead down,* Acts 8:26; *to come down, fall,* Matt. 7:25, 27, et al.; *to be let down,* Acts 10:11; 11:5

καταβαίνων, nom. sg. m. pres. act. part. . . . . καταβαίνω *(2597)*

καταβαλλόμενοι, nom. pl. m. pres. mid. part. {Heb. 6:1} . . . . καταβάλλω *(2598)*

καταβαλλόμενοι, nom. pl. m. pres. pass. part. {2 Cor. 4:9} . . . . id.

(2598) **καταβάλλω,** fut. καταβαλῶ [§27.1.b] (κατά + βάλλω) *to cast down,* Rev. 12:10; *to prostrate,* 2 Cor. 4:9; mid. *to lay down, lay a foundation,* Heb. 6:1

καταβάν, acc. sg. neut. 2 aor. act. part. . . . . καταβαίνω *(2597)*

καταβάντες, nom. pl. m. 2 aor. act. part.   id.

καταβάντι, dat. sg. m. 2 aor. act. part. (Matt. 8:1, MT & TR | καταβάντος, GNT, WH & NA) . . . . id.

καταβάντος, gen. sg. m. 2 aor. act. part. (Matt. 8:1, GNT, WH & NA | καταβάντι, MT & TR) . . . . id.

(2599) **καταβαρέω,** ῶ, fut. καταβήσω [§16.P] (κατά + βαρέω) pr. *to weigh down,* met. *to burden, be burdensome to,* 2 Cor. 12:16

καταβαρυνόμενοι, nom. pl. m. pres. pass. part. (Mark 14:40, GNT, WH & NA | βεβαρημένοι, MT & TR) . . . καταβαρύνω *(‡916)*

(‡916) **καταβαρύνω,** *to weigh down, depress*

καταβάς, nom. sg. m. 2 aor. act. part. . . . . καταβαίνω *(2597)*

καταβάσει, dat. sg. f. n. . . . . κατάβασις *(2600)*

(2600) **κατάβασις,** εως, ἡ [§5.E.c] *the act of descending; a way down, descent,* Luke 19:37

καταβάτω, 3 pers. sg. 2 aor. act. imper. . . . . καταβαίνω *(2597)*

καταβέβηκα, 1 pers. sg. perf. act. indic. . .   id.

καταβεβηκότες, nom. pl. m. perf. act. part.   id.

καταβῇ, 3 pers. sg. 2 aor. act. subj. . . . . .   id.

κατάβηθι, 2 pers. sg. 2 aor. act. imper. . . .   id.

καταβῆναι, 2 aor. act. infin. . . . .   id.

καταβήσεται, 3 pers. sg. fut. mid. dep. indic. [§37.1] . . . .   id.

καταβήσῃ, 2 pers. sg. fut. mid. dep. indic. (Matt. 11:23; Luke 10:15, GNT, WH & NA | καταβιβασθήσῃ, MT & TR) . . .   id.

(2601) **καταβιβάζω,** fut. καταβιβάσω [§26.1] (κατά + βιβάζω) *to cause to descend, bring or thrust down,* Matt. 11:23; Luke 10:15

καταβιβασθήσῃ, 2 pers. sg. fut. pass. indic. (Matt. 11:23; Luke 10:15, MT & TR | καταβήσῃ, GNT, WH & NA)   καταβιβάζω *(2601)*

(2602) **καταβολή,** ῆς, ἡ [§2.B.a] pr. *a casting down; laying the foundation, foundation; begin-*

ning, commencement, Matt. 13:35; 25:34, et al.; *conception* in the womb, Heb. 11:11

καταβολήν, acc. sg. f. n. . . . . καταβολή *(2602)*

καταβολῆς, gen. sg. f. n. . . . . id.

καταβραβευέτω, 3 pers. sg. pres. act. imper. . . . . καταβραβεύω *(2603)*

(2603) **καταβραβεύω,** fut. καταβραβεύσω [§13.M] (κατά + βραβεύω) pr. *to give an unfavorable decision as respects a prize, to disappoint of the palm;* hence, *to make a victim of practices, to overreach,* Col. 2:18

καταγαγεῖν, 2 aor. act. infin. [§13.7.d] . κατάγω *(2609)*

καταγάγῃ, 3 pers. sg. 2 aor. act. subj. . . . id.

καταγάγῃς, 2 pers. sg. 2 aor. act. subj. . . id.

καταγαγόντες, nom. pl. m. 2 aor. act. part. id.

καταγαγών, nom. sg. m. 2 aor. act. part. . id.

(2604) **καταγγελεύς,** έως, ὁ, nom. sg. m. n. [§5.E.d] *one who announces* anything, *a proclaimer, publisher,* Acts 17:18; equivalent το κατάγγελος

καταγγέλλειν, pres. act. infin. . . . καταγγέλλω *(2605)*

καταγγέλλεται, 3 pers. sg. pres. pass. indic. id.

καταγγέλλετε, 2 pers. pl. pres. act. indic. . id.

καταγγέλλομεν, 1 pers. pl. pres. act. indic. id.

καταγγέλλουσιν, 3 pers. pl. pres. act. indic. {Acts 16:17} . . . . id.

καταγγέλλουσιν, dat. pl. m. pres. act. part. {1 Cor. 9:14} . . . . id.

(2605) **καταγγέλλω,** 1 pers. sg. pres. act. indic., fut. καταγελῶ [§27.1.b] 2 aor. pass. κατηγγέλην [§27.4.a] (κατά + ἀγγέλλω) *to announce, proclaim,* Acts 13:38; in N.T. *to laud, celebrate,* Rom. 1:8

καταγγέλλων, nom. sg. m. pres. act. part. . . . . καταγγέλλω *(2605)*

(2606) **καταγελάω,** ῶ, fut. καταγελάσω, καταγελάσομαι [§22.2] (κατά + γελάω) *to deride, jeer,* Matt. 9:24; Mark 5:40; Luke 8:53

καταγινώσκῃ, 3 pers. sg. pres. act. subj. . . . . καταγινώσκω *(2607)*

(2607) **καταγινώσκω,** fut. καταγνώσομαι [§36.3] (κατά + γινώσκω) *to determine against, condemn, blame, reprehend,* Gal. 2:11; 1 John 3:20, 21

(2608) **κατάγνυμι,** or καταγνύω, fut. κατάξω, and κατεάξω, aor. κατέαξα, 2 aor. pass. κατεάγην [§36.5] (κατά + ἄγνυμι, *to break*) *to break in pieces, crush, break in two,* Matt. 12:20; John 19:31, 32, 33

(‡1125) **καταγράφω,** *to trace, draw in outline*

(2609) **κατάγω,** fut. κατάξω [§23.1.b] 2 aor. κατήγαγον [§13.7.d] (κατά + ἄγω) *to lead, bring,* or *conduct down,* Acts 9:30; 22:30; 23:15, 20, 28; *to bring* a ship *to*

land; pass. κατάγομαι, aor. κατήχθην, *to come to land, land, touch,* Luke 5:11, et al.

(2610) **καταγωνίζομαι**, fut. καταγωνίσομαι, aor. κατηγωνισάμην [§26.1] (κατά + ἀγωνίζομαι) *to subdue, vanquish, conquer,* Heb. 11:33

(2611) **καταδέω**, fut. καταδήσω [§35.1] (κατά + δέω) *to bind down; to bandage* a wound, Luke 10:34

κατάδηλον, nom. sg. neut. adj. . . . κατάδηλος (2612)

(2612) **κατάδηλος**, ον [§7.2] (κατά + δῆλος) *quite manifest or evident,* Heb. 7:15

καταδικάζετε, 2 pers. pl. pres. act. imper. . . . . καταδικάζω (2613)

(2613) **καταδικάζω**, fut. καταδικάσω [§26.1] (κατά + δικάζω) *to give judgment against, condemn,* Matt. 12:7, 37; Luke 6:37; James 5:6

καταδικασθήσῃ, 2 pers. sg. fut. pass. indic. . . . . καταδικάζω (2613)

καταδικασθῆτε, 2 pers. pl. aor. pass. subj.   id.

(‡1349) **καταδίκη**, ης, ἡ [§2.B.a] (κατά + δίκη) *condemnation, sentence of condemnation,* Acts 25:15

καταδίκην, acc. sg. f. n. (Acts 25:15, GNT, WH & NA | δίκην, MT & TR) . . . . καταδίκη (‡1349)

(2614) **καταδιώκω**, fut. καταδιώξω [§23.1.b] (κατά + διώκω) *to follow hard upon; to track, follow perseveringly,* Mark 1:36

καταδουλοῖ, 3 pers. sg. pres. act. indic. . . . . καταδουλόω (2615)

(2615) **καταδουλόω**, ῶ, fut. καταδουλώσω [§20.T] (κατά + δουλόω) *to reduce to absolute servitude, make a slave of,* 2 Cor. 11:20; Gal. 2:4

καταδουλώσουσιν, 3 pers. pl. fut. act. indic. (Gal. 2:4, GNT, WH & NA | καταδουλώσωνται, MT & TR) . . . . . καταδουλόω (2615)

καταδουλώσωνται, 3 pers. pl. aor. mid. subj. (Gal. 2:4, MT & TR | καταδουλώσουσιν, GNT, WH & NA) . . . . id.

καταδυναστευομένους, acc. pl. m. pres. pass. part. . . . . καταδυναστεύω (2616)

καταδυναστεύουσιν, 3 pers. pl. pres. act. indic. . . . . id.

(2616) **καταδυναστεύω**, fut. καταδυναστεύσω [§13.M] (κατά + δυναστεύω, *to rule, reign*) *to tyrannize over, oppress,* Acts 10:38; James 2:6

(‡2652) **κατάθεμα**, ατος, τό, nom. sg. neut. n. [§4.D.c] *an execration, curse;* by meton. *what is worthy of execration* (Rev. 22:3, GNT, WH, MT & NA | κατανάθεμα, TR)

καταθεματίζειν, pres. act. infin. (Matt. 26:74,

GNT, WH, MT & NA | καταναθεματίζειν, TR) . . . . καταθεματίζω (‡2653)

(‡2653) **καταθεματίζω**, fut. καταθεματίσω [§26.1] *to curse,* Matt. 26:74

καταθέσθαι, 2 aor. mid. infin. [§28.W] . . . . κατατίθημι (2698)

καταισχύνει, 3 pers. sg. pres. act. indic. . . . . καταισχύνω (2617)

καταισχύνετε, 2 pers. pl. pres. act. indic. . . id.

καταισχύνῃ, 3 pers. sg. pres. act. subj. . . . id.

καταισχυνθῇ, 3 pers. sg. aor. pass. subj. . . id.

καταισχυνθήσεται, 3 pers. sg. fut. pass. indic. . . . . id.

καταισχυνθῶμεν, 1 pers. pl. aor. pass. subj. id.

καταισχυνθῶσιν, 3 pers. pl. aor. pass. subj. id.

(2617) **καταισχύνω**, fut. κατισχυνῶ [§27.1.a] (κατά + αἰσχύνω) *to shame, put to shame, put to the blush,* 1 Cor. 1:27; pass. *to be ashamed, be put to the blush,* Luke 13:17; *to dishonor, disgrace,* 1 Cor. 11:4, 5; from the Hebrew, *to frustrate, disappoint,* Rom. 5:5; 9:33

κατακαήσεται, 3 pers. sg. 2 fut. pass. indic. . . . . κατακαίω (2618)

κατακαίεται, 3 pers. sg. pres. pass. indic. . . id.

(2618) **κατακαίω**, fut. κατακαύσω [§35.3] 2 aor. pass. κατεκάην (κατά + καίω) *to burn up, consume with fire,* Matt. 3:12; 13:30, 40, et al.

κατακαλύπτεσθαι, pres. pass. infin. . . . . κατακαλύπτω (2619)

κατακαλυπτέσθω, 3 pers. sg. pres. pass. imper. . . . . id.

κατακαλύπτεται, 3 pers. sg. pres. pass. indic.   id.

(2619) **κατακαλύπτω**, mid. κατακαλύπτομαι (κατά + καλύπτω) *to veil;* mid. *to veil one's self, to be veiled or covered,* 1 Cor. 11:6, 7

κατακαυθήσεται, 3 pers. sg. fut. pass. indic. . . . . κατακαίω (2618)

κατακαῦσαι, aor. act. infin. . . . . id.

κατακαύσει, 3 pers. sg. fut. act. indic. . . . id.

κατακαύσουσιν, 3 pers. pl. fut. act. indic.   id.

(2620) **κατακαυχάομαι**, ῶμαι, fut. κατακαυχήσομαι [§19.S] (κατά + καταχάομαι) *to vaunt one's self against, to glory over, to assume superiority over,* Rom. 11:18; James 2:13; 3:14

κατακαυχᾶσαι, 2 pers. sg. pres. mid./pass. dep. indic. . . . . κατακαυχάομαι (2620)

κατακαυχᾶσθε, 2 pers. pl. pres. mid./pass. dep. imper. . . . . id.

κατακαυχᾶται, 3 pers. sg. pres. mid./pass. dep. indic. . . . . id.

κατακαυχῶ, 2 pers. sg. pres. mid./pass. dep. imper. . . . . id.

(2621) **κατάκειμαι,** fut. κατάκείσομαι [§33.DD]
(κατά + κεῖμαι) *to lie, be in a recumbent
position, be laid down,* Mark 1:30; 2:4; *to
recline* at table, Mark 2:15; 14:3, et al.
κατακείμενοι, nom. pl. m. pres. mid./pass.
dep. part. . . . . κατάκειμαι (2621)
κατακείμενον, acc. sg. m. pres. mid./pass.
dep. part. . . . . id.
κατακειμένου, gen. sg. m. pres. mid./pass.
dep. part. . . . . id.
κατακεῖσθαι, pres. mid./pass. dep. infin. . id.
κατάκειται, 3 pers. sg. pres. mid./pass. dep.
indic. (Luke 7:37, GNT, WH & NA |
ἀνάκειται, MT & TR) . . . . id.
κατακέκριται, 3 pers. sg. perf. pass.
indic. . . . . κατακρίνω (2632)

(2622) **κατακλάω,** ῶ, fut. κατακλάσω [§22.2] aor.
κατέκλασα (κατά + κλάω) *to break,
break in pieces,* Mark 6:41; Luke 9:16

(2623) **κατακλείω,** fut. κατακλείσω [§22.4] (κατά
+ κλείω) *to close, shut fast; to shut up,
confine,* Luke 3:20; Acts 26:10

(2624) **κατακληροδοτέω,** ῶ, fut. κατακληροδοτήσω
[§16.P] (κατά, κλῆρος, + δίδωμι) *to divide out by lot, distribute by lot,* Acts 13:19

(†2624) **κατακληρονομέω,** ῶ, fut. κατακληρονο-
μήσω [§16.P] (κατά, κλῆρος, + νέμω, *to
distribute*) same as preceding, for which it
is a v.r.
κατακλιθῆναι, aor. pass. infin.
[§27.3] . . . . κατακλίνω (2625)
κατακλιθῇς, 2 pers. sg. aor. pass. subj. . . id.
κατακλίνατε, 2 pers. pl. aor. act. imper. . . id.

(2625) **κατακλίνω,** fut. κατακλινῶ [§27.1.a] aor.
κατέκλινα, aor. pass. κατεκλίθην (κατά
+ κλίνω) *to cause to lie down, cause to
recline* at table, Luke 9:14; mid. *to lie
down, recline,* Luke 14:8; 24:30

(2626) **κατακλύζω,** fut. κατακλύσω [§26.1] aor. pass.
κατεκλύσθην (κατά + κλύζω, *to lave,
wash*) *to inundate, deluge,* 2 Pet. 3:6
κατακλυσθείς, nom. sg. m. aor. pass.
part. . . . . κατακλύζω (2626)
κατακλυσμόν, acc. sg. m. n. . . κατακλυσμός (2627)

(2627) **κατακλυσμός,** οῦ, ὁ, nom. sg. m. n. [§3.C.a]
an inundation, deluge, Matt. 24:38, 39, et
al.
κατακλυσμοῦ, gen. sg. m. n. . . κατακλυσμός (2627)

(2628) **κατακολουθέω,** ῶ, fut. κατακολουθήσω
[§16.P] (κατά + ἀκολουθέω) *to follow
closely or earnestly,* Luke 23:55; Acts 16:17
κατακολουθήσασα, nom. sg. f. aor. act. part.
(Acts 16:17, MT & TR | κατακολου-
θοῦσα, GNT, WH & NA) . κατακολουθέω (2628)
κατακολουθήσασαι, nom. pl. f. aor. act.

part. . . . . κατακολουθέω (2628)
κατακολουθοῦσα, nom. sg. f. aor. act. part.
(Acts 16:17, GNT, WH & NA | κατα-
λουθήσασα, MT & TR) . . . . id.

(2629) **κατακόπτω,** fut. κατακόψω [§23.1.a] (κατά
+ κόπτω) *to cut or dash in pieces; to
mangle, wound,* Mark 5:5
κατακόπτων, nom. sg. m. pres. act.
part. κατακόπτω (2629)

(2630) **κατακρημνίζω,** fut. κατακρημνίσω [§26.1]
(κατά + κρημνός, *a precipice*) *to cast
down headlong, precipitate,* Luke 4:29
κατακρημνίσαι, aor. act. infin. κατακρημνίζω (2630)
κατακριθήσεται, 3 pers. sg. fut. pass.
indic. κατακρίνω (2632)
κατακριθῆτε, 2 pers. pl. aor. pass. subj.
(James 5:9, TR | κριθῆτε, GNT, WH, MT
& NA) . . . . id.
κατακριθῶμεν, 1 pers. pl. aor. pass. subj. id.

(2631) **κατάκριμα,** ατος, τό, nom. sg. neut. n.
[§4.D.c] *condemnation, condemnatory sentence,* Rom. 5:16, 18 {Rom. 8:1}
κατάκριμα, acc. sg. neut. n.
{Rom. 5:16} . . . . κατάκριμα (2631)
κατακρινεῖ, 3 pers. sg. fut. act.
indic. κατακρίνω (2632)
κατακρίνεις, 2 pers. sg. pres. act. indic. . . id.
κατακρινοῦσιν, 3 pers. pl. fut. act. indic. . id.

(2632) **κατακρίνω,** 1 pers. sg. pres. act. indic., fut.
κατακρινῶ [§27.1.a] aor. κατέκρινα, perf.
pass. κατακέκριμαι, aor. pass. κατεκρί-
θην (κατά + κρίνω) *to give judgment
against, condemn,* Matt. 27:3; John
8:10, 11, et al.; *to condemn, to place in a
guilty light* by contrast, Matt. 12:41, 42;
Luke 11:31, 32; Heb. 11:7
κατακρίνων, nom. sg. m. pres. act. part.
(Rom. 8:34, MT & TR | κατακρινῶν,
GNT, WH & NA) . . . . κατακρίνω (2632)
κατακρινῶν, nom. sg. m. fut. act. part. (Rom.
8:34, GNT, WH & NA | κατακρίνων,
MT & TR) . . . . id.
κατακρίσεως, gen. sg. f. n. . . . . κατάκρισις (2633)
κατάκρισιν, acc. sg. f. n. . . . . id.

(2633) **κατάκρισις,** εως, ἡ [§5.E.c] *condemnation,*
2 Cor. 3:9; *censure,* 2 Cor. 7:3

(‡2955) **κατακύπτω,** *to bend down*
κατακυριεύοντες, nom. pl. m. pres. act.
part. . . . . κατακυριεύω (2634)
κατακυριεύουσιν, 3 pers. pl. pres. act. indic. id.
κατακυριεύσαν, nom. sg. neut. aor. act. part.
(Acts 19:16, MT | κατακυριεύσας, GNT,
WH, TR & NA) . . . . id.
κατακυριεύσας, nom. sg. m. aor. act. part.
(Acts 19:16, GNT, WH, TR & NA |

κατακυριεύσαν, ΜΤ) . . . . . . κατακυριεύω *(2634)*

(2634) **κατακυριεύω,** fut. κατακυριεύσω [§13.Μ] (κατά + κυριεύω) *to get into one's power; in N.T. to bring under, master, overcome,* Acts 19:16; *to domineer over,* Matt. 20:25, *et al.*

κατακύψας, nom. sg. m. aor. act. part. (John 8:8, GNT, WH & NA | κύψας, ΜΤ & TR) . . . . κατακύπτω *(‡2955)*

καταλαβέσθαι, 2 aor. mid. infin. [§36.2] . . . . καταλαμβάνω *(2638)*

καταλάβῃ, 3 pers. sg. 2 aor. act. subj. . . . id.

καταλάβητε, 2 pers. pl. 2 aor. act. subj. . . . id.

καταλαβόμενοι, nom. pl. m. 2 aor. mid. part. . . . . id.

καταλαβόμενος, nom. sg. m. 2 aor. mid. part. (Acts 25:25, ΜΤ & TR | κατελαβόμην, GNT, WH & NA) . . . . id.

καταλάβω, 1 pers. sg. 2 aor. act. subj. . . . id.

καταλαλεῖ, 3 pers. sg. pres. act. indic. καταλαλέω *(2635)*

καταλαλεῖσθε, 2 pers. pl. pres. pass. indic. (1 Pet. 3:16, GNT, WH & NA | καταλαλῶσιν, ΜΤ & TR) . . . . id.

καταλαλεῖτε, 2 pers. pl. pres. act. imper. . id.

(2635) **καταλαλέω,** ῶ, fut. καταλαλήσω [§16.Ρ] (κατά + λαλέω) *to blab out; to speak against, calumniate,* James 4:11; 1 Pet. 2:12; 3:16

(†2636) **καταλαλιά,** ᾶς, ἡ [§2.Β.b; 2.2] *evil-speaking, detraction, backbiting, calumny,* 2 Cor. 12:20; 1 Pet. 2:1

καταλαλιαί, nom. pl. f. n. . . . . . . καταλαλιά *(†2636)*

καταλαλιάς, acc. pl. f. n. . . . . id.

(2637) **κατάλαλος,** ον [§7.2] *slanderous; a detractor, calumniator,* Rom. 1:30

καταλάλους, acc. pl. m. adj. . . . . κατάλαλος *(2637)*

καταλαλοῦσιν, 3 pers. pl. pres. act. indic. καταλαλέω *(2635)*

καταλαλῶν, nom. sg. m. pres. act. part. . id.

καταλαλῶσιν, 3 pers. pl. pres. act. subj. (1 Pet. 3:16, ΜΤ & TR | καταλαλεῖσθε, GNT, WH & NA) . . . . id.

καταλαμβάνομαι, 1 pers. sg. pres. mid. indic. . . . . καταλαμβάνω *(2638)*

(2638) **καταλαμβάνω,** fut. καταλή(μ)ψομαι, 2 aor. κατέλαβον [§36.2] (κατά + λαμβάνω) *to lay hold of, grasp; to obtain, attain,* Rom. 9:30; 1 Cor. 9:24; *to seize, to take possession of,* Mark 9:18; *to come suddenly upon; overtake, surprise,* John 12:35; *to detect in the act, seize,* John 8:3, 4; met. *to comprehend, apprehend,* John 1:5; mid. *to understand, perceive,* Acts 4:13; 10:34, *et al.*

καταλεγέσθω, 3 pers. sg. pres. pass. imper. . . . . καταλέγω *(2639)*

(2639) **καταλέγω,** fut. καταλέξω [§23.1.b] (κατά + λέγω) *to select; to reckon in a number, enter in a list or catalog, enroll,* 1 Tim. 5:9

(2640) **κατάλειμμα,** ατος, τό, nom. sg. neut. n, [§4.d.c] *a remnant, a small residue* (Rom. 9:27, ΜΤ & TR | ὑπόλειμμα, GNT, WH & NA)

καταλείπει, 3 pers. sg. pres. act. indic. καταλείπω *(2641)*

καταλειπομένης, gen. sg. f. pres. pass. part. id.

καταλείποντες, nom. pl. m. pres. act. part. id.

(2641) **καταλείπω,** fut. καταλείψω, 2 aor. κατέλιπον [§24.9] (κατά + λείπω) *to leave behind; to leave behind at death,* Mark 12:19; *to relinquish, let remain,* Mark 14:52; *to quit, depart from, forsake,* Matt. 4:13; 16:4; *to neglect,* Acts 6:2; *to leave alone, or without assistance,* Luke 10:40; *to reserve,* Rom. 11:4

καταλειφθῆναι, aor. pass. infin. [§23.4] . . . . καταλείπω *(2641)*

καταλείψαντας, acc. pl. m. aor. act. part. id.

καταλείψει, 3 pers. sg. fut. act. indic. . . . . id.

καταλελειμμένος, nom. sg. m. perf. pass. part. . . . . id.

(2642) **καταλιθάζω,** fut. καταλιθάσω [§26.1] (κατά + λιθάζω) *to stone, kill by stoning,* Luke 20:6

καταλιθάσει, 3 pers. sg. fut. act. indic. καταλιθάζω *(2642)*

καταλίπῃ, 3 pers. sg. 2 aor. act. subj. . . . . καταλείπω *(2641)*

καταλιπόντες, nom. pl. m. 2 aor. act. part. id.

καταλιπών, nom. sg. m. 2 aor. act. part. . id.

καταλλαγέντες, nom. pl. m. 2 aor. pass. part. . . . . καταλλάσσω *(2644)*

(2643) **καταλλαγή,** ῆς, ἡ, nom. sg. f. n. [§2.Β.a] pr. *an exchange; reconciliation, restoration to favor,* Rom. 5:11; 11:15; 2 Cor. 5:18, 19

καταλλαγήν, acc. sg. f. n. . . . . καταλλαγή *(2643)*

καταλλαγῆς, gen. sg. f. n. . . . . id.

καταλλάγητε, 2 pers. pl. 2 aor. pass. imper. . . . . καταλλάσσω *(2644)*

καταλλαγήτω, 3 pers. sg. 2 aor. pass. imper. id.

καταλλάξαντος, gen. sg. m. aor. act. part. id.

(2644) **καταλλάσσω,** fut. καταλλάξω [§26.3] 2 aor. pass. κατηλλάγην (κατά + ἀλλάσσω) *to change, exchange; to reconcile;* pass. *to be reconciled,* Rom. 5:10; 1 Cor. 7:11; 2 Cor. 5:18, 19, 20

καταλλάσσων, nom. sg. m. pres. act. part. . . . . καταλλάσσω *(2644)*

κατάλοιποι, nom. pl. m. adj. . . . . κατάλοιπος *(2645)*

(2645) **κατάλοιπος,** ον [§7.2] *remaining;* οἱ κατάλοιποι, *the rest,* Acts 15:17
κατάλυε, 2 pers. sg. pres. act. imper. καταλύω *(2647)*
καταλυθῇ, 3 pers. sg. aor. pass. subj. .... id.
καταλυθήσεται, 3 pers. sg. fut. pass. indic.
[§14.N] .... id.

(2646) **κατάλυμα,** ατος, τό, nom. sg. neut. n. [§4.D.c]
a lodging, inn, khan, Luke 2:7; *a guest-*
chamber, Mark 14:14; Luke 22:11
καταλύματι, dat. sg. neut. n. ..... κατάλυμα *(2646)*
καταλῦσαι, aor. act. infin. .... καταλύω *(2647)*
καταλύσει, 3 pers. sg. fut. act. indic. .... id.
καταλύσω, 1 pers. sg. fut. act. indic. .... id.
καταλύσωσι(ν), 3 pers. pl. aor. act. subj. . id.

(2647) **καταλύω,** fut. καταλύσω, aor. pass.
κατελύθην [§13.M; 14.N] (κατά + λύω)
to dissolve; to destroy, demolish, overthrow,
throw down, Matt. 24:2; 26:61; met. *to*
nullify, abrogate, Matt. 5:17; Acts 5:38, 39,
et al.; absol. *to unloose* harness, etc., *to*
halt, to stop for the night, lodge, Luke 9:12
καταλύων, nom. sg. m. pres. act.
part. .... καταλύω *(2647)*
καταμάθετε, 2 pers. pl. 2 aor. act.
imper. .... καταμανθάνω *(2648)*

(2648) **καταμανθάνω,** fut. καταμανθήσομαι, 2 aor.
κατέμαθον [§36.2] (κατά + μανθάνω) *to*
learn or observe thoroughly; to consider
accurately and diligently, contemplate,
mark, Matt. 6:28

(2649) **καταμαρτυρέω,** ῶ, fut. καταμαρτυρήσω
[§26.P] (κατά + μαρτυρέω) *to witness or*
testify against, Matt. 26:62; 27:13, et al.
καταμαρτυροῦσιν, 3 pers. pl. pres. act.
indic. .... καταμαρτυρέω *(2649)*
καταμένοντες, nom. pl. m. pres. act.
part. .... καταμένω *(2650)*

(2650) **καταμένω,** fut. καταμενῶ [§27.1.a] (κατά +
μένω) *to remain; to abide, dwell*
καταμενῶ, 1 pers. sg. fut. act. indic. (1 Cor.
16:6, WH | παραμενῶ, GNT, MT, TR &
NA) .... καταμένω *(2650)*

(2651) **καταμόνας,** adv. (κατά + μόνος) *alone,*
apart, in private (Mark 4:10; Luke 9:18,
TR | κατὰ μόνας, GNT, WH, MT &
NA)

(2652) **κατανάθεμα,** ατος, τό, nom. sg. neut. n.
[§4.D.c] (κατά + ἀνάθεμα) *a curse, exe-*
cration; meton. *one accursed, execrable*
(Rev. 22:3, TR | κατάθεμα, GNT, WH,
MT & NA)
καταναθεματίζειν, pres. act. infin. (Matt.
26:74, TR | καταθεματίζειν, GNT, WH,
MT & NA) .... καταναθεματίζω *(2653)*

(2653) **καταναθεματίζω,** fut. καταναθεματίσω

[§26.1] *to curse,* Matt. 26:74
καταναλίσκον, nom. sg. neut. pres. act.
part. .... καταναλίσκω *(2654)*

(2654) **καταναλίσκω,** fut. καταναλώσω [§36.4]
(κατά + ἀναλίσκω) *to consume,* as fire

(2655) **καταναρκάω,** ῶ, fut. καταναρκήσω [§18.R]
(κατά + ναρκάω, *to grow torpid)* in N.T.
to be torpid to the disadvantage of any one,
to be a dead weight upon; by impl. *to be*
troublesome, burdensome to, in respect of
maintenance, 2 Cor. 11:9; 12:13, 14
καταναρκήσω, 1 pers. sg. fut. act.
indic. .... καταναρκάω *(2655)*

(2656) **κατανεύω,** fut. κατανεύσομαι (κατά + νεύω)
pr. *to nod, signify assent by a nod;* genr.
to make signs, beckon, Luke 5:7
κατανοεῖς, 2 pers. sg. pres. act.
indic. .... κατανοέω *(2657)*

(2657) **κατανοέω,** ῶ, fut. κατανοήσω [§16.P] (κατά
+ νοέω) *to perceive, understand, appre-*
hend, Luke 20:23; *to observe, mark, con-*
template, Luke 12:24, 27; *to discern,*
descry, Matt. 7:3; *to have regard to, make*
account of, Rom. 4:19
κατανοῆσαι, aor. act. infin. ...... κατανοέω *(2657)*
κατανοήσας, nom. sg. m. aor. act. part. . id.
κατανοήσατε, 2 pers. pl. aor. act. imper. . id.
κατανοοῦντι, dat. sg. m. pres. act. part. ... id.
κατανοῶμεν, 1 pers. pl. pres. act. subj. ... id.

(2658) **καταντάω,** ῶ, fut. καταντήσω [§18.K] (κατά.
+ ἀντάω) *to come to, arrive at,* Acts 16:1;
20:15; of an epoch, *to come upon,* 1 Cor.
10:11; met. *to reach, attain to,* Acts 26:7,
et al.
καταντῆσαι, aor. act. infin. ...... καταντάω *(2658)*
καταντήσαντες, nom. pl. m. aor. act. part. id.
καταντήσω, 1 pers. sg. aor. act. subj. .... id.
καταντήσωμεν, 1 pers. pl. aor. act. subj. . id.
κατανύξεως, gen. sg. f. n. .... κατάνυξις *(2659)*

(2659) **κατάνυξις,** εως, ἡ [§5.E.c] in N.T. *deep sleep,*
stupor, dullness, Rom. 11:8

(2660) **κατανύσσω,** fut. κατανύξω, 2 aor. pass.
κατενύγην [§26.3] (κατά + νύσσω) *to*
pierce through; to pierce with compunction
and pain of heart, Acts 2:37

(2661) **καταξιόω,** ῶ, fut. καταξιώσω [§20.T] (κατά
+ ἀξιόω) *to account worthy of,* Luke
20:35; 21:36; Acts 5:41; 2 Thess. 1:5
καταξιωθέντες, nom. pl. m. aor. pass. part.
[§21.U] .... καταξιόω *(2661)*
καταξιωθῆναι, aor. pass. infin. .... id.
καταξιωθῆτε, 2 pers. pl. aor. pass. subj. (Luke
21:36, MT & TR | κατισχύσητε, GNT,
WH & NA) .... id.
καταπατεῖν, pres. act. infin. ..... καταπατέω *(2662)*

καταπατεῖσθαι, pres. pass. infin. . καταπατέω *(2662)*

(2662) **καταπατέω, ῶ,** fut. καταπατήσω [§16.P] (κατά + πατέω) *to trample upon, tread down or under feet,* Matt. 5:13; 7:6; Luke 8:5; 12:1; met. *to trample on* by indignity, *spurn,* Heb. 10:29

καταπατήσας, nom. sg. m. aor. act. part. . . . . καταπατέω *(2662)*

καταπατήσουσιν, 3 pers. pl. fut. act. indic. (Matt. 7:6, GNT, WH & NA | καταπατήσωσιν, MT & TR) . . . . id.

καταπατήσωσιν, 3 pers. pl. aor. act. subj. (Matt. 7:6, MT & TR | καταπατήσουσιν, GNT, WH & NA) . . . . id.

καταπαύσεως, gen. sg. f. n. . . . . κατάπαυσις *(2663)*

κατάπαυσιν, acc. sg. f. n. . . . . id.

(2663) **κατάπαυσις, εως, ἡ** [§5.E.c] pr. *the act of giving rest; a state of settled or final rest,* Heb. 3:11, 18; 4:3, 11, et al.; *a place of rest, place of abode, dwelling, habitation,* Acts 7:49

(2664) **καταπαύω,** fut. καταπαύσω [§13.M] (κατά + παύω) *to cause to cease, restrain,* Acts 14:18; *to cause to rest, give final rest to, to settle finally,* Heb. 4:8; intrans. *to rest, desist from,* Heb. 4:4, 10

καταπεσόντων, gen. pl. m. 2 aor. act. part. καταπίπτω *(2667)*

(2665) **καταπέτασμα, ατος, τό,** nom. sg. neut. n. [§4.D.c] (καταπετάννυμι, *to expand) a veil, curtain,* Matt. 27:51; Mark 15:38; Heb. 6:19; 10:20 {Luke 23:45}

καταπέτασμα, acc. sg. neut. n. {Heb. 9:3} . . . . καταπέτασμα *(2665)*

καταπετάσματος, gen. sg. neut. n. . . . . . . id.

καταπιεῖν, 2 aor. act. infin. (1 Pet. 5:8, GNT, WH & NA | καταπίῃ, MT & TR) . . καταπίνω *(2666)*

καταπίῃ, 3 pers. sg. 2 aor. act. subj. (1 Pet. 5:8, MT & TR | καταπιεῖν, GNT, WH & NA) . . . . id.

καταπίνοντες, nom. pl. m. pres. act. part. . . id.

(2666) **καταπίνω,** fut. καταπίομαι, 2 aor. κατέπιον, aor. pass. κατεπόθην [§37.1] (κατά + πίνω) *to drink, swallow, gulp down,* Matt. 23:24; *to swallow up, absorb,* Rev. 12:16; 2 Cor. 5:4; *to engulf, submerge, overwhelm,* Heb. 11:29; *to swallow greedily, devour,* 1 Pet. 5:8; *to destroy, annihilate,* 1 Cor. 15:54; 2 Cor. 2:7

καταπίπτειν, pres. act. infin. . . . . . καταπίπτω *(2667)*

(2667) **καταπίπτω,** fut. καταπεσοῦμαι, 2 aor. κατέπεσον, perf. καταπέπτωκα [§37.1] (κατά + πίπτω) *to fall down, fall prostrate,* Acts 26:14; 28:6

(2668) **καταπλέω,** fut. καταπλεύσομαι, aor. κατέπλευσα [§35.1.3] (κατά + πλέω) *to*

sail towards land, to come to land, Luke 8:26

καταποθῇ, 3 pers. sg. aor. pass. subj. καταπίνω *(2666)*

(2669) **καταπονέω, ῶ,** fut. καταπονήσω [§16.P] (κατά + πονέω) *to exhaust by labor or suffering; to weary out,* 2 Pet. 2:7; *to overpower, oppress,* Acts 7:24

καταπονούμενον, acc. sg. m. pres. pass. part. καταπονέω *(2669)*

καταπονουμένῳ, dat. sg. m. pres. pass. part. id.

καταποντίζεσθαι, pres. pass. infin. . . . . καταποντίζω *(2670)*

(2670) **καταποντίζω,** fut. καταποντίσω [§26.1] (κατά + ποντίζω, *to sink,* from πόντος) *to sink in the sea;* pass. *to sink,* Matt. 14:30; *to be plunged, submerged,* Matt. 18:6

καταποντισθῇ, 3 pers. sg. aor. pass. subj. . . . . καταποντίζω *(2670)*

(2671) **κατάρα, ας, ἡ,** nom. sg. f. n. [§2.B.b] (κατά + ἀρά) *a cursing, execration, imprecation,* James 3:10; from the Hebrew, *condemnation, doom,* Gal. 3:10, 13; 2 Pet. 2:14; meton., *a doomed one, one on whom condemnation falls,* Gal. 3:13

κατάραν, acc. sg. f. n. . . . . κατάρα *(2671)*

(2672) **καταράομαι, ῶμαι,** fut. καταράσομαι, aor. κατηρασάμην [§19.S] in N.T. perf. pass. part. κατηραμένος, *to curse, to wish evil to, imprecate evil upon,* Matt. 5:44; Mark 11:21, et al.; in N.T. pass. *to be doomed,* Matt. 25:41

κατάρας, gen. sg. f. n. . . . . κατάρα *(2671)*

καταρᾶσθε, 2 pers. pl. pres. mid./pass. dep. imper. . . . . : . . . καταράομαι *(2672)*

καγαργεῖ, 3 pers. sg. pres. act. indic. . . . . καταργέω *(2673)*

καταργεῖται, 3 pers. sg. pres. pass. indic. . id.

(2673) **καταργέω, ῶ** [§16.P] fut. καταργήσω, perf. κατήργηκα, aor. κατήργησα, perf. pass. κατήργημαι, aor. pass. κατηργήθην (κατά + ἀργός) *to render useless or unproductive, occupy unprofitably,* Luke 13:7; *to render powerless,* Rom. 6:6; *to make empty and unmeaning,* Rom. 4:14; *to render null, to abrogate, cancel,* Rom. 3:3, 31; Eph. 2:15, et al.; *to bring to an end,* 1 Cor. 2:6; 13:8; 15:24, 26; 2 Cor. 3:7, et al.; *to destroy, annihilate,* 2 Thess. 2:8; Heb. 2:14; *to free from, dissever from,* Rom. 7:2, 6; Gal. 5:4

καταργηθῇ, 3 pers. sg. aor. pass. subj. καταργέω *(2673)*

καταργηθήσεται, 3 pers. sg. fut. pass. indic. id.

καταργηθήσονται, 3 pers. pl. fut. pass.
indic. . . . . καταργέω (2673)
καταργῆσαι, aor. act. infin. . . . . id.
καταργήσαντος, gen. sg. m. aor. act. part. id.
καταργήσας, nom. sg. m. aor. act. part. . id.
καταργήσει, 3 pers. sg. fut. act. indic. . . . id.
καταργήσῃ, 3 pers. sg. aor. act. subj. . . . . id.
καταργοῦμεν, 1 pers. pl. pres. act. indic. . id.
καταργουμένην, acc. sg. f. pres. pass. part. id.
καταργούμενον, nom. sg. neut. pres. pass.
part. . . . . id.
καταργουμένου, gen. sg. neut. pres. pass.
part. . . . . id.
καταργουμένων, gen. pl. m. pres. pass. part. id.
(2674) **καταριθμέω**, ῶ, fut. καταριθμήσω [§16.P]
(κατά + ἀριθμέω) to enumerate, number
with, count with, Acts 1:17
καταρτίζεσθε, 2 pers. pl. pres. pass.
imper. καταρτίζω (2675)
καταρτίζετε, 2 pers. pl. pres. act. imper. . . id.
καταρτίζοντας, acc. pl. m. pres. act. part. id.
(2675) **καταρτίζω**, fut. καταρτίσω, aor. κατήρτισα
[§26.1] (κατά + ἀρτίζω) to adjust thoroughly; to knit together, unite completely,
1 Cor. 1:10; to frame, Heb. 11:3; to prepare, provide, Matt. 21:16; Heb. 10:5; to
qualify fully, to complete in character, Luke
6:40; Heb. 13:21; 1 Pet. 5:10; perf. pass.
κατηρτισμένος, fit, ripe, Rom. 9:22; to repair, refit, Matt. 4:21; Mark 1:19; to supply, make good, 1 Thess. 3:10; to restore
to a forfeited condition, to reinstate, Gal.
6:1
καταρτίσαι, 3 pers. sg. aor. act. opt.
{Heb. 13:21} . . . . καταρτίζω (2675)
καταρτίσαι, aor. act. infin. {1 Thess. 3:10} id.
καταρτίσει, 3 pers. sg. fut. act. indic. (1 Pet.
5:10, GNT, WH & NA | καταρτίσαι, MT
& TR) . . . . id.
κατάρτισιν, acc. sg. f. n. . . . . κατάρτισις (2676)
(2676) **κατάρτισις**, εως, ἡ [§5.E.c] pr. a complete adjustment; completeness of character, perfection, 2 Cor. 13:9
καταρτισμόν, acc. sg. m. n. . . . . καταρτισμός (2677)
(2677) **καταρτισμός**, οῦ, ὁ [§3.C.a] a perfectly ad-
justed adaptation; complete qualification
for a specific purpose, Eph. 4:12
καταρώμεθα, 1 pers. pl. pres. mid./pass. dep.
indic. καταράομαι (2672)
καταρωμένους, acc. pl. m. pres. mid./pass.
dep. part. id.
κατασείσας, nom. sg. m. aor. act.
part. . . . . κατασείω (2678)
(2678) **κατασείω**, fut. κατασείσω [§13.M] (κατά +
σείω) to shake down or violently; τὴν

χεῖρα, or τῇ χειρί, to wave the hand,
beckon; to sign silence by waving the hand,
Acts 12:17, et al.
(2679) **κατασκάπτω**, fut. κατασκάψω [§23.1.a]
(κατά + σκάπτω) pr. to dig down under,
undermine; by impl. to overthrow, demolish, raze, Rom. 11:3; τὰ κατεσκαμμένα,
ruins, Acts 15:16
κατασκευάζεται, 3 pers. sg. pres. pass.
indic. . . . . κατασκευάζω (2680)
κατασκευαζομένης, gen. sg. f. pres. pass.
part. . . . . id.
(2680) **κατασκευάζω**, fut. κατασκευάσω [§26.1]
(κατά + σκευάζω, from σκεῦος) to prepare, put in readiness, Matt. 11:10; Mark
1:2; Luke 1:17; 7:27; to construct, form,
build, Heb. 3:3, 4; 9:2, 6; 11:7; 1 Pet. 3:20
κατασκευάσας, nom. sg. m. aor. act.
part. . . . . κατασκευάζω (2680)
κατασκευάσει, 3 pers. sg. fut. act. indic. . id.
κατασκηνοῦν, pres. act. infin. (Matt. 13:32;
Mark 4:32. GNT, MT, TR & NA |
κατασκηνοῖν, WH) . . . . κατασκηνόω (2681)
(2681) **κατασκηνόω**, ῶ, fut. κατασκηνώσω [§20.T]
(κατά + σκηνόω, from σκηνή) to pitch
one's tent; in N.T. to rest in a place, settle,
abide, Acts 2:26; to haunt, roost, Matt.
13:32; Mark 4:32; Luke 13:19
κατασκηνώσει, 3 pers. sg. fut. act.
indic. . . . . κατασκηνόω (2681)
κατασκηνώσεις, acc. pl. f. n. . κατασκήνωσις (2682)
(2682) **κατασκήνωσις**, εως, ἡ [§5.E.c] pr. the pitching a tent; a tent; in N.T. a dwelling-place;
a haunt, roost, Matt. 8:20; Luke 9:58
κατασκιάζοντα, nom. pl. neut. pres. act.
part. κατασκιάζω (2683)
(2683) **κατασκιάζω**, fut. κατασκιάσω [§26.1] (κατά
+ σκιάζω, idem) to overshadow, Heb. 9:5
(2684) **κατασκοπέω**, ῶ, fut. κατασκέψομαι, in N.T.
aor. infin. κατασκοπῆσαι (κατά +
σκοπέω) to view closely and accurately; to
spy out, Gal. 2:4
κατασκοπῆσαι, aor. act. infin. . κατασκοπέω (2684)
(2685) **κατάσκοπος**, ου, ὁ [§3.C.a] a scout, spy, Heb.
11:31
κατασκόπους, acc. pl. m. n. . . . κατάσκοπος (2685)
(2686) **κατασοφίζομαι**, fut. κατασοφίσομαι [§26.1]
(κατά + σοφίζω) to exercise cleverness to
the detriment of any one, to outwit; to
make a victim of subtlety, to practise on
by insidious dealing, Acts 7:19
κατασοφισάμενος, nom. sg. m. aor. mid. dep.
part. . . . . κατασοφίζομαι (2686)
κατασταθήσονται, 3 pers. pl. fut. pass. indic.
[§29.6] . . . . καθίστημι (2525)

καταστείλας, nom. sg. m. aor. act.
part. . . . . καταστέλλω *(2687)*

(2687) **καταστέλλω**, fut. καταστελῶ, aor. κατέ-
στειλα [§27.1.b,d] perf. pass. κατέσταλμαι
[§27.3] (κατά + στέλλω) *to arrange, dispose in regular order; to appease, quiet,
pacify,* Acts 19:35, 36

(2688) **κατάστημα**, ατος, τό [§4.D.c] *determinate
state, condition; personal appearance,
mien, deportment,* Tit. 2:3
καταστήματι, dat. sg. neut. n. . . . κατάστημα *(2688)*
καταστήσει, 3 pers. sg. fut. act.
indic. . . . . καθίστημι *(2525)*
καταστήσῃς, 2 pers. sg. aor. act. subj. . . . id.
καταστήσομεν, 1 pers. pl. fut. act. indic. (Acts
6:3, GNT, WH, TR & NA | καταστή-
σωμεν, MT) . . . . id.
καταστήσω, 1 pers. sg. fut. act. indic. . . . id.
καταστήσωμεν, 1 pers. pl. aor. act. subj. (Acts
6:3, MT | καταστήσομεν, GNT, WH, TR
& NA) . . . . id.

(2689) **καταστολή**, ῆς, ἡ [§2.B.a] pr. *an arranging in
order; adjustment of dress;* in N.T. *apparel,
dress,* 1 Tim. 2:9
καταστολῇ, dat. sg. f. n. . . . . καταστολή *(2689)*

(2690) **καταστρέφω**, fut. καταστρέψω [§23.1.a]
(κατά + στρέφω) *to invert; to overturn,
overthrow, throw down,* Matt. 21:12; Mark
11:15

(2691) **καταστρηνιάω**, fut. καταστρηνιάσω (κατά +
στρηνιάω, *to be headstrong, wanton,* from
στρηνής or στρηνός, *hard, harsh*) *to be
headstrong or wanton towards*
καταστρηνιάσωσι(ν), 3 pers. pl. aor. act.
subj. . . . . καταστρηνιάω *(2691)*

(2692) **καταστροφή**, ῆς, ἡ [§2.B.a] *an overthrow, destruction,* 2 Pet. 2:6; met. *overthrow* of
right principle or faith, *utter detriment, perversion,* 2 Tim. 2:14
καταστροφῇ, dat. sg. f. n. . . . . . καταστροφή *(2692)*

(2693) **καταστρώννυμι**, fut. καταστρώσω, aor. pass.
κατεστρώθην [§36.5] (κατά +
στρώννυμι) *to strew down, lay flat;* pass.
to be strewn, laid prostrate in death, 1 Cor.
10:5
κατασύρῃ, 3 pers. sg. aor. act.
subj. κατασύρω *(2694)*

(2694) **κατασύρω** (κατά + σύρω) *to drag down, to
drag away,* Luke 12:58
κατασφάξατε, 2 pers. pl. aor. act.
imper. . . . . κατασφάζω (†*2695*)

(†*2695*) **κατασφάζω**, or κατασφάττω, fut. κατα-
σφάξω [§26.3] (κατά + σφάζω, or σφάττω)
to slaughter, slay, Luke 19:27

(2696) **κατασφραγίζω**, fut. κατασφραγίσω, perf.

pass. κατεσφράγισμαι [§26.1] (κατά +
σφραγίζω) *to seal up,* Rev. 5:1
κατασχέσει, dat. sg. f. n. . . . . . . κατάσχεσις *(2697)*
κατάσχεσιν, acc. sg. f. n. . . . . id.

(2697) **κατάσχεσις**, εως, ἡ [§5.E.c] *a possession,
thing possessed,* Acts 7:5, 45
κατάσχωμεν, 1 pers. pl. 2 aor. act. subj.
[§36.4] . . . . κατέχω *(2722)*

(2698) **κατατίθημι**, fut. κατατιθήσω, aor. κατέθηκα
[§28.V] (κατά + τίθημι) *to lay down, deposit,* Mark 15:46; mid. *to deposit or lay
up for one's self;* χάριν, or χάριτας, *to lay
up a store of favor for one's self, earn a title to favor* at the hands of a person, *to
curry favor with,* Acts 24:27; 25:9

(2699) **κατατομή**, ῆς, ἡ [§2.B.a] (κατατέμνω, *to cut
up,* from κατά + τέμνω) *concision, muti-
lation,* Phil. 3:2
κατατομήν, acc. sg. f. n. . . . . κατατομή *(2699)*
κατατοξευθήσεται, 3 pers. sg. fut. pass. indic.
(Heb. 12:20, TR | GNT, WH, MT & NA
omit) . . . . κατατοξεύω *(2700)*

(2700) **κατατοξεύω**, fut. κατατοξεύσω [§13.M]
(κατά + τοξεύω, *to shoot with a bow*) *to
shoot down* with arrows; *to transfix* with
an arrow or dart, Heb. 12:20

(2701) **κατατρέχω**, fut. καταδραμοῦμαι, 2 aor.
κατέδραμον [§36.1] (κατά + τρέχω) *to
run down,* Acts 21:32
κατάφαγε, 2 pers. sg. 2 aor. act.
imper. κατεσθίω *(2719)*
καταφάγεται, 3 pers. sg. fut. mid. dep. indic.
(John 2:17, GNT, WH, MT & NA |
κατέφαγε(ν), TR) . . . . id.
καταφάγῃ, 3 pers. sg. 2 aor. act. subj. . . . id.
καταφαγών, nom. sg. m. 2 aor. act. part. . id.

(2702) **καταφέρω**, fut. κατοίσω, aor. pass.
κατηνέχθην [§36.1] (κατά + φέρω) *to
bear down; to overpower,* as sleep, Acts
20:9; καταφέρειν ψῆφον, *to give a vote or
verdict,* Acts 26:10
καταφερόμενος, nom. sg. m. pres. pass.
part. . . . . καταφέρω *(2702)*
καταφέροντες, nom. pl. m. pres. act. part.
(Acts 25:7, GNT, WH & NA | φέροντες,
MT & TR) . . . . id.

(2703) **καταφεύγω**, fut. καταφεύξομαι, 2 aor.
κατέφυγον [§24.9] (κατά + φεύγω) *to flee
to* for refuge, Acts 14:6; Heb. 6:18
καταφθαρήσονται, 3 pers. pl. 2 fut. pass.
indic. (2 Pet. 2:12, MT & TR | φθαρή-
σονται, GNT, WH & NA) . . . καταφθείρω *(2704)*

(2704) **καταφθείρω**, fut. καταφθερῶ [§27.1.c] fut.
pass. καταφθαρήσομαι [§27.4.b,c] (κατά
+ φθείρω) *to destroy, cause to perish,*

2 Pet. 2:12; *to corrupt, deprave,* 2 Tim. 3:8

(2705) **καταφιλέω**, ῶ, fut. καταφιλήσω [§16.P]
(κατά + φιλέω) *to kiss affectionately or*
with a semblance of affection, to kiss with
earnest gesture, Matt. 26:49; Luke 7:38;
Acts 20:37, et al.

καταφιλοῦσα, nom. sg. f. pres. act.
part. καταφιλέω (2705)

καταφρονεῖς, 2 pers. sg. pres. act.
indic. . . . . καταφρονέω (2706)

καταφρονεῖτε, 2 pers. pl. pres. act. indic. . id.

καταφρονείτω, 3 pers. sg. pres. act. imper. id.

καταφρονείτωσαν, 3 pers. pl. pres. act.
imper. . . . . id.

(2706) **καταφρονέω**, ῶ, fut. καταφρονήσω [§16.P]
(κατά + φρονέω) pr. *to think in dispar-*
agement of; to contemn, scorn, despise,
Matt. 18:10; Rom. 2:4; *to slight,* Matt.
6:24; Luke 16:13; 1 Cor. 11:22; 1 Tim.
4:12; 6:2; 2 Pet. 2:10; *to disregard,* Heb.
12:2

καταφρονήσας, nom. sg. m. aor. act.
part. . . . . καταφρονέω (2706)

καταφρονήσει, 3 pers. sg. fut. act. indic. . id.

καταφρονήσητε, 2 pers. pl. aor. act. subj. id.

καταφρονηταί, nom. pl. m. n. καταφρονητής (†2707)

(†2707) **καταφρονητής**, οῦ, ὁ [§2.B.c] *a contemner, de-*
spiser, scorner, Acts 13:41

καταφρονοῦντας, acc. pl. m. pres. act.
part. . . . . καταφρονέω (2706)

καταφυγόντες, nom. pl. m. 2 aor. act.
part. . . . . καταφεύγω (2703)

(2708) **καταχέω**, fut. καταχεύσω [§35.1.3] (κατά +
χέω) *to pour down upon,* Matt. 26:7;
Mark 14:3

καταχθέντες, nom. pl. m. aor. pass.
part. . . . . κατάγω (2609)

(2709) **καταχθόνιος**, ον [§7.2] (κατά + χθών, *the*
earth) under the earth, subterranean, infer-
nal, Phil. 2:10

καταχθονίων, gen. pl. m. adj. . . καταχθόνιος (2709)

(2710) **καταχράομαι**, ῶμαι, fut. καταχρήσομαι
[§19.S] (κατά + χράομαι) *to use down-*
right; to use up, consume; to make an un-
restrained use of, use eagerly, 1 Cor. 7:31;
to use to the full, stretch to the utmost,
1 Cor. 9:18

καταχρήσασθαι, aor. mid. dep.
infin. . . . . καταχράομαι (2710)

καταχρώμενοι, nom. pl. m. pres. mid./pass.
dep. part. . . . . id.

καταψύξῃ, 3 pers. sg. aor. act.
subj. . . . . καταψύχω (2711)

(2711) **καταψύχω**, fut. καταψύξω [§23.1.b] (κατά +
ψύχω) *to cool, refresh,* Luke 16:24

κατεαγῶσιν, 3 pers. pl. 2 aor. pass. subj.
[§36.5] . . . . κατάγνυμι (2608)

κατέαξαν, 3 pers. pl. aor. act. indic. . . . . . id.

κατεάξει, 3 pers. sg. aor. act. indic. . . . . . id.

κατέβαινεν, 3 pers. sg. imperf. act.
indic. . . . . καταβαίνω (2597)

κατεβάρησα, 1 pers. sg. aor. act.
indic. . . . . καταβαρέω (2599)

κατέβη, 3 pers. sg. 2 aor. act. indic.
[§31.1.d] . . . . καταβαίνω (2597)

κατέβην, 1 pers. sg. 2 aor. act. indic. [§37.1] id.

κατέβησαν, 3 pers. pl. 2 aor. act. indic. . . id.

κατεβλήθη, 3 pers. sg. aor. pass. indic. [§27.3]
(Rev. 12:10, TR | ἐβλήθη, GNT, WH, MT
& NA) . . . . καταβάλλω (2598)

κατεγέλων, 3 pers. pl. imperf. act.
indic. . . . . καταγελάω (2606)

κατεγνωσμένος, nom. sg. m. perf. pass. part.
[§36.3] . . . . καταγινώσκω (2607)

κατέγραφεν, 3 pers. sg. imperf. act. indic.
(John 8:6, GNT, WH & NA | ἔγραφεν,
MT & TR) . . . . καταγράφω (‡1125)

κατέδησε(ν), 3 pers. sg. aor. act.
indic. . . . . καταδέω (2611)

κατεδικάσατε, 2 pers. pl. aor. act.
indic. . . . . καταδικάζω (2613)

κατεδίωξαν, 3 pers. pl. aor. act. indic. (Mark
1:36, MT & TR | κατεδίωξεν, GNT, WH
& NA) . . . . καταδιώκω (2614)

κατεδίωξεν, 3 pers. sg. aor. act. indic. (Mark
1:36, GNT, WH & NA | κατεδίωξαν,
MT & TR) . . . . id.

κατέδραμεν, 3 pers. sg. 2 aor. act. indic.
[§36.1] . . . . κατατρέχω (2701)

κατέθηκεν, 3 pers. sg. aor. act. indic. (Mark
15:46, MT & TR | ἔθηκεν, GNT, WH &
NA) . . . . κατατίθημι (2698)

κατείδωλον, acc. sg. f. adj. . . . . . . κατείδωλος (2712)

(2712) **κατείδωλος**, ον [§7.2] (κατά + εἴδωλον) *rife*
with idols, sunk in idolatry, grossly idol-
atrous, Acts 17:16

κατειλημμένην, acc. sg. f. perf. pass.
part. . . . . καταλαμβάνω (2638)

κατείληπται, 3 pers. sg. perf. pass. indic.
(John 8:4, GNT, WH & NA | MT omits
| κατειλήφθη, TR) . . . . id.

κατειληφέναι, perf. act. infin. . . . . id.

κατειλήφθη, 3 pers. sg. aor. pass. indic. (John
8:4, TR | κατείληπται, GNT, WH & NA
| MT omits) . . . . id.

κατειργάσατο, 3 pers. sg. aor. mid. dep. indic.
[§13.4] . . . . κατεργάζομαι (2716)

κατειργάσθαι, perf. mid./pass. dep. infin.
(1 Pet. 4:3, GNT, WH & NA | κατερ-
γάσασθαι, MT & TR) . . . . id.

κατειργάσθη, 3 pers. sg. aor. pass.

  indic. . . . . κατεργάζομαι *(2716)*

κατείχετο, 3 pers. sg. imperf. pass. indic.

  (John 5:4, MT & TR | GNT, WH & NA

  omit) . . . . κατέχω *(2722)*

κατειχόμεθα, 1 pers. pl. imperf. pass. indic. id.

κατεῖχον, 3 pers. pl. imperf. act. indic.

  [§13.4] . . . . id.

κατεκάη, 3 pers. sg. 2 aor. pass. indic.

  [§24.11] . . . . κατακαίω *(2618)*

κατέκαιον, 3 pers. pl. imperf. act. indic. . id.

κατέκειτο, 3 pers. sg. imperf. mid./pass. dep.

  indic. . . . . κατάκειμαι *(2621)*

κατέκλασε(ν), 3 pers. sg. aor. act. indic.

  [§22.2] . . . . κατακλάω *(2622)*

κατέκλεισα, 1 pers. sg. aor. act.

  indic. . . . . κατακλείω *(2623)*

κατέκλεισε(ν), 3 pers. sg. aor. act. indic. . id.

κατεκληροδότησεν, 3 pers. sg. aor. act. indic.

  (Acts 13:19, TR | κατεκληρονόμησεν,

  GNT, WH, MT & NA) . κατακληροδοτέω *(2624)*

κατεκληρονόμησεν, 3 pers. sg. aor. act.

  indic. (Acts 13:19, GNT, WH, MT &

  NA | κατεκληροδότησεν,

  TR) . . . . κατακληρονομέω *(†2624)*

κατεκλίθη, 3 pers. sg. aor. pass. indic. (Luke

  7:36, GNT, WH & NA | ἀνεκλίθη, MT

  & TR) . . . . κατακλίνω *(2625)*

κατέκλιναν, 3 pers. pl. aor. act. indic. (Luke

  9:15, GNT, WH & NA | ἀνέκλιναν, MT

  & TR) . . . . id.

κατεκρίθη, 3 pers. sg. aor. pass. indic.

  [§27.3] . . . . κατακρίνω *(2632)*

κατέκριναν, 3 pers. pl. aor. act. indic. . . . id.

κατέκρινε(ν), 3 pers. sg. aor. act. indic. . . id.

κατέλαβε(ν), 3 pers. sg. 2 aor. act.

  indic. . . . . καταλαμβάνω *(2638)*

κατελαβόμην, 1 pers. sg. 2 aor. mid. indic.

  (Acts 25:25, GNT, WH & NA | κατα-

  λαβόμενος, MT & TR) . . . . id.

κατέλειπε(ν), 3 pers. sg. imperf. act. indic.

  (Luke 10:40, WH & MT | κατέλιπε(ν),

  GNT, TR & NA) . . . . καταλείπω *(2641)*

κατελείφθη, 3 pers. sg. aor. pass. indic.

  [§23.4] . . . . id.

κατελήμφθην, 1 pers. sg. aor. pass. indic.

  [§36.2] (Phil. 3:12, GNT, MT, WH & NA

  | κατελήφθην, TR) . . . . καταλαμβάνω *(2638)*

κατελήφθην, 1 pers. sg. aor. pass. indic. (Phil.

  3:12, TR | κατελήμφθην, GNT, MT, WH

  & NA) . . . . id.

κατελθεῖν, 2 aor. act. infin.

  [§36.1] . . . . κατέρχομαι *(2718)*

κατελθόντες, nom. pl. m. 2 aor. act. part. id.

κατελθόντων, gen. pl. m. 2 aor. act. part. id.

κατελθών, nom. sg. m. 2 aor. act.

  part. . . . . κατέρχομαι *(2718)*

κατέλιπε(ν), 3 pers. sg. 2 aor. act. indic.

  [§24.9] . . . . καταλείπω *(2641)*

κατέλιπον, 1 pers. sg. 2 aor. act. indic.

  {Rom. 11:4} . . . . id.

κατέλιπον, 3 pers. pl. 2 aor. act. indic.

  {Luke 20:31} . . . . id.

κατέλυσα, 1 pers. sg. aor. act. indic. καταλύω *(2647)*

(2713) **κατέναντι,** adv. (κατά + ἔναντι) *over against,*

  opposite to, Mark 11:2; 12:41; 13:3; ὁ, ἡ,

  τό, κατέναντι, *opposite,* Luke 19:30;

  before, in the presence of, in the sight of,

  Rom. 4:17

κατενάρκησα, 1 pers. sg. aor. act.

  indic. . . . . καταναρκάω *(2655)*

κατένευσαν, 3 pers. pl. aor. act.

  indic. . . . . κατανεύω *(2656)*

κατενεχθείς, nom. sg. m. aor. pass. part.

  [§36.1] . . . . καταφέρω *(2702)*

κατενόησε(ν), 3 pers. sg. aor. act.

  indic. . . . . κατανοέω *(2657)*

κατενόουν, 1 pers. sg. imperf. act. indic.

  {Acts 11:6} . . . . id.

κατενόουν, 3 pers. pl. imperf. act. indic.

  {Acts 27:39} . . . . id.

κατενύγησαν, 3 pers. pl. 2 aor. pass. indic.

  [§26.3] . . . . κατανύσσω *(2660)*

(2714) **κατενώπιον,** adv., or prep. (κατά + ἐνώπιον)

  in the presence of, in the sight of, 2 Cor.

  2:17; 12:19; Eph. 1:4

κατεξουσιάζουσιν, 3 pers. pl. pres. act.

  indic. . . . . κατεξουσιάζω *(2715)*

(2715) **κατεξουσιάζω,** fut. κατεξουσιάσω [§26.1]

  (κατά + ἐξουσιάζω) *to exercise lordship*

  over, domineer over, Matt. 20:25; Mark

  10:42

κατεπατήθη, 3 pers. sg. aor. pass. indic.

  [§17.Q] . . . . καταπατέω *(2662)*

κατέπαυσαν, 3 pers. pl. aor. act.

  indic. . . . . καταπαύω *(2664)*

κατέπαυσεν, 3 pers. sg. aor. act. indic. . . . id.

κατέπεσε(ν), 3 pers. sg. 2 aor. act. indic.

  (Luke 8:6, GNT, WH & NA | ἔπεσεν,

  MT & TR) . . . . καταπίπτω *(2667)*

κατεπέστησαν, 3 pers. pl. 2 aor. act.

  indic. . . . . κατεφίστημι *(2721)*

κατέπιε(ν), 3 pers. sg. 2 aor. act. indic.

  [§37.1] . . . . καταπίνω *(2666)*

κατέπλευσαν, 3 pers. pl. aor. act. indic.

  [§35.3] . . . . καταπλέω *(2668)*

κατεπόθη, 3 pers. sg. aor. pass. indic.

  [§37.1] . . . . καταπίνω *(2666)*

κατεπόθησαν, 3 pers. pl. aor. pass. indic. . id.

κατεργάζεσθαι, pres. mid./pass. dep.

infin. . . . . κατεργάζομαι *(2716)*
κατεργάζεσθε, 2 pers. pl. pres. mid./pass. dep.
imper. . . . . id.
κατεργάζεται, 3 pers. sg. pres. mid./pass. dep.
indic. . . . . id.
(2716) **κατεργάζομαι**, 1 pers. sg. pres. mid./pass. dep.
indic., fut. κατεργάσομαι (κατά + ἐργάζομαι) *to work out; to effect, produce, bring out as a result,* Rom. 4:15; 5:3; 7:13; 2 Cor. 4:17; 7:10; Phil. 2:12; 1 Pet. 4:3; James 1:3; *to work, practise, realize in practice,* Rom. 1:27; 2:9, et al.; *to work or mould into fitness,* 2 Cor. 5:5; *to despatch, subdue,* Eph. 6:13
κατεργαζομένη, nom. sg. f. pres. mid./pass.
dep. part. . . . . κατεργάζομαι *(2716)*
κατεργαζόμενοι, nom. pl. m. pres. mid./pass.
dep. part. . . . . id.
κατεργαζομένου, gen. sg. m. pres. mid./pass.
dep. part. . . . . id.
κατεργασάμενοι, nom. pl. m. aor. mid. dep.
part. . . . . id.
κατεργασάμενον, acc. sg. m. aor. mid. dep.
part. . . . . id.
κατεργασάμενος, nom. sg. m. aor. mid. dep.
part. . . . . id.
κατεργάσασθαι, aor. mid. dep. infin. (1 Pet.
4:3, MT & TR | κατειργάσθαι, GNT,
WH & NA) . . . . id.
(2718) **κατέρχομαι**, fut. κατελεύσομαι, 2 aor.
κατῆλθον [§36.1] (κατά + ἔρχομαι) *to come or go down,* Luke 4:31; 9:37; Acts 8:5; 9:32, et al.; *to land at, touch at,* Acts 18:22; 27:5
κατερχομένη, nom. sg. f. pres. mid./pass. dep.
part. . . . . κατέρχομαι *(2718)*
κατέσεισε(ν), 3 pers. sg. aor. act.
indic. κατασείω *(2678)*
κατεσθίει, 3 pers. sg. pres. act.
indic. κατεσθίω *(2719)*
κατεσθίετε, 2 pers. pl. pres. act. indic. . . . id.
κατεσθίοντες, nom. pl. m. pres. act. part.
(Mark 12:40, GNT, MT, TR & NA |
κατέσθοντες, WH) . . . . id.
κατεσθίουσι(ν), 3 pers. pl. pres. act. indic. id.
(2719) **κατεσθίω**, fut. καθέδομαι, and καταφάγομαι, 2 aor. κατέφαγον [§36.1] (κατά + ἐσθίω) *to eat up, devour,* Matt. 13:4, et al.; *to consume,* Rev. 11:5, *to expend, squander,* Luke 15:30; met. *to make a prey of, plunder,* Matt. 23:13; Mark 12:40; Luke 20:47; 2 Cor. 11:20; *to vex, injure,* Gal. 5:15
κατεσκαμμένα, acc. pl. neut. perf. pass. part.
(Acts 15:16, GNT, MT, TR & NA |

κατεστραμμένα, WH) . . . . . κατασκάπτω *(2679)*
κατέσκαψαν, 3 pers. pl. aor. act. indic. . . id.
κατεσκεύασε(ν), 3 pers. sg. aor. act.
indic. . . . . κατασκευάζω *(2680)*
κατεσκευάσθη, 3 pers. sg. aor. pass. indic. id.
κατεσκευασμένον, acc. sg. m. perf. pass.
part. . . . . id.
κατεσκευσμένων, gen. pl. m. perf. pass.
part. . . . . id.
κατεσκήνωσεν, 3 pers. sg. aor. act.
indic. . . . . κατασκηνόω *(2681)*
κατεστάθησαν, 3 pers. pl. aor. pass. indic.
[§29.6] . . . . καθίστημι *(2525)*
κατεσταλμένους, acc. pl. m. perf. pass. part.
[§27.3] . . . . καταστέλλω *(2687)*
κατέστησας, 2 pers. sg. aor. act. indic.
[§29.X] (Heb. 2:7, WH & TR | GNT, MT
& NA omit) . . . . καθίστημι *(2525)*
κατέστησε(ν), 3 pers. sg. aor. act. indic. . id.
κατεστραμμένα, acc. pl. neut. perf. pass.
part. (Acts 15:16, WH | κατεσκαμμένα,
GNT, MT, TR & NA) . . . . . καταστρέφω *(2690)*
κατέστρεψε(ν), 3 pers. sg. aor. act. indic. . id.
κατεστρώθησαν, 3 pers. pl. aor. pass.
indic. . . . . καταστρώννυμι *(2693)*
κατεσφραγισμένον, acc. sg. neut. perf. pass.
part. . . . . κατασφραγίζω *(2696)*
κατευθύναι, 3 pers. sg. aor. act. opt.
κατευθύνω {1 Thess. 3:11} . . . . κατευθύνω *(2720)*
κατευθῦναι, aor. act. infin. {Luke 1:79} . . id.
(2720) **κατευθύνω**, fut. κατευθυνῶ, aor. κατεύθυνα
[§27.1.a,f] (κατά + εὐθύνω, from εὐθύς, straight) *to make straight; to direct, guide aright,* Luke 1:79; 1 Thess. 3:11; 2 Thess. 3:5
(‡2127) **κατευλογέω**, ῶ, fut. κατευλογήσω (κατά + εὐλογέω) *to bless,* Mark 10:16
κατευλόγει, 3 pers. sg. imperf. act. indic.
(Mark 10:16, GNT, WH & NA | εὐλόγει,
MT | ηὐλόγει, TR) . . . . κατευλογέω *(‡2127)*
κατέφαγε(ν), 3 pers. sg. 2 aor. act.
indic. κατεσθίω *(2719)*
κατέφαγον, 1 pers. sg. 2 aor. act. indic. . . id.
κατεφθαρμένοι, nom. pl. m. perf. pass. part.
[§27.3] . . . . καταφθείρω *(2704)*
κατεφίλει, 3 pers. sg. imperf. act.
indic. καταφιλέω *(2705)*
κατεφίλησεν, 3 pers. sg. aor. act. indic. . . id.
κατεφίλουν, 3 pers. pl. imperf. act. indic. . id.
(2721) **κατεφίστημι**, intrans. 2 aor. κατεπέστην
[§29.X] (κατά + ἐφίστημι) *to come upon suddenly, rush upon, assault,* Acts 18:12
κατέφυγον, 3 pers. pl. 2 aor. act. indic.
[§24.9] . . . . καταφεύγω *(2703)*
κατέχεεν, 3 pers. sg. aor. act. indic.

[§36.1] . . . . κατάχεω (2708)

κατέχειν, pres. act. infin. . . . . κατέχω (2722)

κατέχετε, 2 pers. pl. pres. act. indic.
{1 Cor. 15:2} . . . . id.

κατέχετε, 2 pers. pl. pres. act. imper.
{1 Cor. 11:2} . . . . id.

κατέχον, acc. sg. neut. pres. act. part. . . . id.

κατέχοντες, nom. pl. m. pres. act. part. . . id.

κατεχόντων, gen. pl. m. pres. act. part. . . id.

κατέχουσι(ν), 3 pers. pl. pres. act. indic. . id.

(2722) **κατέχω**, fut. καθέξω, and κατασχήσω, imperf. κατεῖχον, 2 aor. κατέσχον [§36.4]
(κατά + ἔχω) *to hold down; to detain, retain,* Luke 4:42; Philemon 13; *to hinder,
restrain,* 2 Thess. 2:6, 7; *to hold down-
right, hold in a firm grasp, to have in full
and secure possession,* 1 Cor. 7:30; 2 Cor.
6:10; *to come into full possession of, seize
upon,* Matt. 21:38; *to keep, retain,* 1 Thess.
5:21; *to occupy,* Luke 14:9; met. *to hold
fast* mentally, *retain,* Luke 8:15; 1 Cor.
11:2; 15:2; *to maintain,* Heb. 3:6, 14;
10:23; intrans. a nautical term, *to land,
touch,* Acts 27:40; pass. *to be in the grasp
of, to be bound by,* Rom. 7:6; *to be afflicted with,* John 5:4

κατέχωμεν, 1 pers. pl. pres. act. subj. κατέχω (2722)

κατέχων, nom. sg. m. pres. act. part. . . . . id.

κατήγαγον, 1 pers. sg. 2 aor. act. indic.
[§13.7.d] {Acts 23:28} . . . . κατάγω (2609)

κατήγαγον, 3 pers. pl. 2 aor. act. indic.
{Acts 9:30} . . . . id.

κατηγγείλαμεν, 1 pers. pl. aor. act.
indic. καταγγέλλω (2605)

κατήγγειλαν, 3 pers. pl. aor. act. indic. (Acts
3:24, GNT, WH, MT & NA | προκατ-
ήγγειλαν, TR) . . . . id.

κατηγγέλη, 3 pers. sg. 2 aor. pass. indic.
[§27.4.a] . . . . id.

κατήγγελλον, 3 pers. pl. imperf. act. indic. id.

κατηγορεῖν, pres. act. infin. . . . . . κατηγορέω (2723)

κατηγορεῖσθαι, pres. pass. infin. [§17.Q] . id.

κατηγορεῖται, 3 pers. sg. pres. pass. indic. id.

κατηγορεῖτε, 2 pers. pl. pres. act. indic. . . id.

κατηγορείτωσαν, 3 pers. pl. pres. act. imper. id.

(2723) **κατηγορέω**, ῶ, fut. κατηγορήσω [§16.P]
(κατά + ἀγορεύω, *to harangue) to speak
against, accuse,* Matt. 12:10; 27:12; John
5:45, et al.

κατηγορῆσαι, aor. act. infin. (Acts 28:19, MT
& TR | κατηγορεῖν, GNT, WH &
NA) . . . . κατηγορέω (2723)

κατηγορήσω, 1 pers. sg. fut. act. indic. . . id.

κατηγορήσωσιν, 3 pers. pl. aor. act. subj. id.

(2724) **κατηγορία**, ας, ἡ [§2.B.b; 2.2] *an accusation,*

crimination, Luke 6:7, et al.

κατηγορίᾳ, dat. sg. f. n. . . . . κατηγορία (2724)

κατηγορίαν, acc. sg. f. n. . . . . id.

κατήγοροι, nom. pl. m. n. . . . . . κατήγορος (†2725)

κατηγόροις, dat. pl. m. n. . . . . id.

(†2725) **κατήγορος**, ου, ὁ, nom. sg. m. n. [§3.C.a] *an
accuser,* John 8:10; Acts 23:30, 35; 24:8,
et al. (Rev. 12:10, MT & TR | κατήγωρ,
GNT, WH & NA)

κατηγοροῦμεν, 1 pers. pl. pres. act.
indic. κατηγορέω (2723)

κατηγορούμενος, nom. sg. m. pres. pass.
part. . . . . id.

κατηγόρουν, 3 pers. pl. imperf. act. indic. id.

κατηγοροῦντες, nom. pl. m. pres. act. part. id.

κατηγορούντων, gen. pl. m. pres. act. part. id.

κατηγόρους, acc. pl. m. n. . . . . . κατήγορος (†2725)

κατηγοροῦσι(ν), 3 pers. pl. pres. act.
indic. κατηγορέω (2723)

κατηγορῶν, nom. sg. m. pres. act. part. . . id.

κατηγωνίσαντο, 3 pers. pl. aor. mid. dep.
indic. . . . . καταγωνίζομαι (2610)

(2725) **κατήγωρ**, ορος, ὁ, nom. sg. m. n. [§4.2.f] *an
accuser,* Rev. 12:10, a barbarous form for
κατήγορος (Rev. 12:10, GNT, WH & NA
| κατήγορος, MT & TR)

κατῆλθε(ν), 3 pers. sg. 2 aor. act.
indic. κατέρχομαι (2718)

κατήλθομεν, 1 pers. pl. 2 aor. act. indic. (Acts
21:3; 27:5, GNT, MT, TR & NA | κατ-
ήλθαμεν, WH) . . . . id.

κατῆλθον, 3 pers. pl. 2 aor. act. indic. . . . id.

κατηλλάγημεν, 1 pers. pl. 2 aor. pass. indic.
[§26.3] . . . . καταλλάσσω (2644)

κατήνεγκα, 1 pers. sg. aor. act. indic.
[§36.1] . . . . καταφέρω (2702)

κατήντηκεν, 3 pers. sg. perf. act. indic. (1 Cor.
10:11, GNT, WH & NA | κατήντησεν,
MT & TR) . . . . κατανταάω (2658)

κατηντήσαμεν, 1 pers. pl. aor. act. indic. . id.

κατήντησαν, 3 pers. pl. aor. act. indic. . . . id.

κατήντησε(ν), 3 pers. sg. aor. act. indic. . . id.

κατηξιώθησαν, 3 pers. pl. aor. pass. indic.
[§21.U] . . . . καταξιόω (2661)

κατηραμένοι, nom. pl. m. perf. pass.
part. . . . . καταράομαι (2672)

κατηράσω, 2 pers. sg. aor. mid. dep. indic.
[§15.3.b] . . . . id.

κατηργήθημεν, 1 pers. pl. aor. pass.
indic. . . . . καταργέω (2673)

κατηργήθητε, 2 pers. pl. aor. pass. indic. . id.

κατήργηκα, 1 pers. sg. perf. act. indic. . . . id.

κατήργηται, 3 pers. sg. perf. pass. indic. . . id.

κατηριθμημένος, nom. sg. m. perf. pass.
part. . . . . καταριθμέω (2674)

κατηρτίσθαι, perf. pass. infin. .... καταρτίζω *(2675)*
κατηρτισμένα, acc. pl. neut. perf. pass. part.   id.
κατηρτισμένοι, nom. pl. m. perf. pass. part.   id.
κατηρτισμένος, nom. sg. m. perf. pass. part.   id.
κατηρτίσω, 2 pers. sg. aor. mid. indic.
  [§15.3.b] .... id.
κατησχύνθην, 1 pers. sg. aor. pass. indic.
  [§13.2] .... καταισχύνω *(2617)*
κατησχύνοντο, 3 pers. pl. imperf. pass. indic.   id.
(2726) **κατήφεια**, ας, ή [§2.B.b; 2.2] (κατηφής, *having a downcast look*, κατά + φάος) *dejection, sorrow*, James 4:9
κατήφειαν, acc. sg. f. n. .... κατήφεια *(2726)*
(2727) **κατηχέω**, ῶ, fut. κατηχήσω [§16.P] (κατά + ἠχέω) pr. *to sound in the ears, make the ears ring; to instruct orally, to instruct, inform*, 1 Cor. 14:19; pass. *to be taught, be instructed*, Luke 1:4; Rom. 2:18; Gal. 6:6; *to be made acquainted*, Acts 18:25; *to receive information, hear report*, Acts 21:21, 24
κατηχήθης, 2 pers. sg. aor. pass.
  indic. .... κατηχέω *(2727)*
κατηχήθησαν, 3 pers. pl. aor. pass. indic.   id.
κατηχημένος, nom. sg. m. perf. pass. part.   id.
κατήχηνται, 3 pers. pl. perf. pass. indic. .   id.
κατηχήσω, 1 pers. sg. aor. act. subj. .....   id.
κατήχθημεν, 1 pers. sg. 2 aor. pass. indic.
  [§23.4] .... κατάγω *(2609)*
κατηχούμενος, nom. sg. m. pres. pass.
  part. .... κατηχέω *(2727)*
κατηχοῦντι, dat. sg. m. pres. act. part. ...   id.
(2728) **κατιόω**, ῶ, fut. κατιώσω [§20.T] perf. pass. κατίωμαι (κατά + ἰός) *to cover with rust*; pass. *to rust, become rusty or tarnished*
κατίσχυον, 3 pers. pl. imperf. act.
  indic. .... κατισχύω *(2729)*
κατισχύσητε, 2 pers. pl. pres. act. subj. (Luke 21:36, GNT, WH & NA | καταξιωθῆτε, MT & TR) .... id.
κατισχύσουσιν, 3 pers. pl. fut. act. indic. .   id.
(2729) **κατισχύω**, fut. κατισχύσω [§13.M] (κατά + ἰσχύω) *to overpower*, Matt. 16:18; absol. *to predominate, get the upper hand*, Luke 23:23
κατίωται, 3 pers. sg. perf. pass. indic.
  [§21.U] .... κατιόω *(2728)*
κατοικεῖ, 3 pers. sg. pres. act. indic. κατοικέω *(2730)*
κατοικεῖν, pres. act. infin. .... id.
κατοικεῖς, 2 pers. sg. pres. act. indic. ....   id.
κατοικεῖτε, 2 pers. pl. pres. act. indic. ....   id.
(2730) **κατοικέω**, ῶ, fut. κατοικήσω [§16.P] (κατά + οἰκέω) trans. *to inhabit*, Acts 1:19, et al.; absol. *to have an abode, dwell*, Luke 13:4; Acts 11:29, et al.; *to take up or find an*

abode, Acts 7:2, et al.; *to indwell*, Eph. 3:17; James 4:5, et al.
κατοικῆσαι, aor. act. infin. .... κατοικέω *(2730)*
κατοικήσαντι, dat. sg. m. aor. act. part.
  (Matt. 23:21, MT | κατοικοῦντι, GNT, WH, TR & NA) .... id.
κατοικήσας, nom. sg. m. aor. act. part. ...   id.
κατοίκησιν, acc. sg. f. n. .... κατοίκησις *(2731)*
(2731) **κατοίκησις**, εως, ή [§5.E.c] *an abode, dwelling, habitation*, Mark 5:3
(2732) **κατοικητήριον**, ου, τό, nom. sg. neut. n. [§3.C.c] *the same as the preceding*, Eph. 2:22; {Rev. 18:2}
κατοικητήριον, acc. sg. neut. n.
  {Eph. 2:22} .... κατοικητήριον *(2732)*
(2733) **κατοικία**, ας, ή [§2.B.b; 2.2] *habitation*, i.q. κατοίκησις, Acts 17:26
κατοικίας, gen. sg. f. n. .... κατοικία *(2733)*
(‡2730) **κατοικίζω**, *to cause to dwell*
κατοικοῦντας, acc. pl. m. pres. act.
  part. .... κατοικέω *(2730)*
κατοικοῦντες, nom. pl. m. pres. act. part.   id.
κατοικοῦντι, dat. sg. m. pres. act. part. (Matt. 23:21, GNT, WH, TR & NA | κατοικήσαντι, MT) .... id.
κατοικούντων, gen. pl. m. pres. act. part.   id.
κατοικοῦσιν, dat. pl. m. pres. act. part. ...   id.
κατοικῶν, nom. sg. m. pres. act. part. ...   id.
κατοπτριζόμενοι, nom. pl. m. pres. mid.
  part. .... κατοπτρίζω *(†2734)*
(†2734) **κατοπτρίζω**, fut. κατοπτρίσω [§26.1] (κάτοπτρον, *a mirror*) *to show in a mirror; to present a clear and correct image of a thing*, mid. *to have presented in a mirror, to have a clear image presented*, or, *to reflect*, 2 Cor. 3:18
(2735) **κατόρθωμα**, ατος, τό [§4.D.c] (κατορθόω, *to set upright, accomplish happily*, from κατά + ὀρθόω, *to make straight*) *anything happily and successfully accomplished; a beneficial and worthy deed*, Acts 24:2
κατορθωμάτων, gen. pl. neut. n. (Acts 24:2, MT & TR | διορθωμάτων, GNT, WH & NA) .... κατόρθωμα *(2735)*
(2736) **κάτω**, adv., and prep. (κατά) *down, downwards*, Matt. 4:6; Luke 4:9; *beneath, below, under*, Matt. 27:51; Mark 14:66, et al.; ὁ, ἡ, τό, κάτω, *what is below, earthly*, John 8:23
κατῴκησεν, 3 pers. sg. aor. act. indic.
  [§13.2] .... κατοικέω *(2730)*
κατῴκισεν, 3 pers. sg. aor. act. indic. (James 4:5, GNT, WH & NA | κατῴκησεν, MT & TR) .... κατοικίζω *(‡2730)*
κατώτερα, acc. pl. neut. compar.

adj. . . . . κατώτερος *(2737)*

(2737) **κατώτερος**, α, ον [§7.1] (compar. adj. from κάτω) *lower*, Eph. 4:9

(‡2736) **κατωτέρω**, adv. (compar. of κάτω) *lower, farther down;* of time, *under*, Matt. 2:16

(‡2802) **Καῦδα**, indecl. prop. name of an island, *Clauda* (Acts 27:16, GNT, WH & NA | Κλαύδην, MT & TR)

καυθήσωμαι, 1 pers. sg. fut. pass. subj. (an unusual form | 1 Cor. 13:3, MT & TR | καυχήσωμαι, GNT, WH & NA) . . . . καίω *(2545)*

(2738) **καῦμα**, ατος, τό, nom. sg. neut. n. [§4.D.c] *heat, scorching or burning heat* {Rev. 7:16}

καῦμα, acc. sg. neut. n. {Rev. 16:9} . . . καῦμα *(2738)*

(2739) **καυματίζω**, fut. καυματίσω [§26.1] *to scorch, burn*, Matt. 13:6; Mark 4:6; Rev. 16:8, 9

καυματίσαι, aor. act. infin. . . . . . . καυματίζω *(2739)*

καῦσιν, acc. sg. f. n. . . . . καῦσις *(2740)*

(2740) **καῦσις**, εως, ἡ [§5.E.c] *burning, being burned*, Heb. 6:8

(†2741) **καυσόομαι**, οῦμαι [§21.U] *to be on fire, burn intensely*, 2 Pet. 3:10, 12

καυσούμενα, nom. pl. neut. pres. pass. part. καυσόομαι *(†2741)*

(‡2743) **καυστηριάζω**, same signif. as καυτηριάζω

(2742) **καύσων**, ωνος, ὁ, nom. sg. m. n. [§4.2.e] *fervent scorching heat; the scorching* of the sun, Matt. 20:12; *hot weather, a hot time,* Luke 12:55; *the scorching wind of the East, Eurus,* James 1:11

καύσωνα, acc. sg. m. n. . . . . καύσων *(2742)*

καύσωνι, dat. sg. m. n. . . . . id.

(2743) **καυτηριάζω**, fut. καυτηριάσω [§26.1] perf. pass. κεκαυτηρίασμαι (καυτήριον, *an instrument for branding*, from καίω) *to cauterize, brand;* pass. met. *to be branded* with marks of guilt, or, *to be seared* into insensibility, 1 Tim. 4:2

(2744) **καυχάομαι**, ῶμαι, fut. καυχήσομαι, aor. ἐκαυχησάμην, perf. κεκαύχημαι [§19.S] *to glory, boast*, Rom. 2:17, 23; ὑπέρ τινος, *to boast of* a person or thing, *to undertake a laudatory testimony to*, 2 Cor. 12:5; *to rejoice, exult,* Rom. 5:2, 3, 11, et al.

καυχᾶσαι, 2 pers. sg. pres. mid./pass. dep. indic. for καυχᾷ, a later form combining the inflexions of a contract verb and a verb in μι, ... καυχάομαι *(2744)*

καυχᾶσθαι, pres. mid./pass. dep. infin. . . . id.

καυχᾶσθε, 2 pers. pl. pres. mid./pass. dep. indic. id.

καυχάσθω, 3 pers. sg. pres. mid./pass. dep. imper. id.

(2745) **καύχημα**, ατος, τό, nom. sg. neut. n. [§4.D.c]

a glorying, boasting, 1 Cor. 5:6; *a ground or matter of glorying or boasting,* Rom. 4:2; *joy, exultation,* Phil. 1:26; *laudatory testimony,* 1 Cor. 9:15, 16; 2 Cor. 9:3, et al. {1 Cor. 5:6}

καύχημα, acc. sg. neut. n. {1 Cor. 9:15} . . . . καύχημα *(2745)*

καυχήματος, gen. sg. neut. n. . . . . id.

καυχήσασθαι, aor. mid. dep. infin. καυχάομαι *(2744)*

καυχήσεως, gen. sg. f. n. . . . . καύχησις *(2746)*

καυχήσηται, 3 pers. sg. aor. mid. dep. subj. καυχάομαι *(2744)*

καύχησιν, acc. sg. f. n. . . . . καύχησις *(2746)*

(2746) **καύχησις**, εως, ἡ, nom. sg. f. n. [§5.E.c] a later equivalent to καύχημαι, Rom. 3:27; 2 Cor. 7:4, 14; 11:10, et al.

καυχήσομαι, 1 pers. sg. fut. mid. dep. indic. καυχάομαι *(2744)*

καυχησόμεθα, 1 pers. pl. fut. mid. dep. indic. id.

καυχήσωμαι, 1 pers. sg. aor. mid. dep. subj. id.

καυχήσωνται, 3 pers. pl. aor. mid. dep. subj. id.

καυχῶμαι, 1 pers. sg. pres. mid./pass. dep. indic. id.

καυχώμεθα, 1 pers. pl. pres. mid./pass. dep. indic. id.

καυχώμενοι, nom. pl. m. pres. mid./pass. dep. part. id.

καυχώμενος, nom. sg. m. pres. mid./pass. dep. part. id.

καυχωμένους, acc. pl. m. pres. mid./pass. dep. part. id.

καυχῶνται, 3 pers. pl. pres. mid./pass. dep. indic. id.

(‡2584) **Καφαρναούμ**, ἡ, indecl. pr. name, *Capernaum* (GNT, WH & NA | Καπερναούμ, MT & TR)

(†2747) **Κεγρεαί**, ῶν, αἱ, *Cenchreae*, the port of Corinth on the Saronic Gulf

Κεγχρεαῖς, dat. pl. f. n. (Rom. 16:21, TRs | GNT, WH, MT, TRb & NA omit | Acts 18:18, GNT, MT, TR & NA | Κενχρειαῖς, WH) . . . . Κεγρεαί *(†2747)*

(†2748) **κέδρος**, ου, ἡ [§3.C.b] *a cedar*, John 18:1, where κέρδων is a false reading for the proper name Κεδρών, John 18:1

κέδρων, gen. pl. f. n. (John 18:1, MT, WH & TR | Κεδρών, GNT & NA) . . . κέδρος *(†2748)*

(2748) **Κεδρών**, ὁ, indecl. pr. name, *Cedron*, a mountain torrent near Jerusalem (John 18:1, GNT & NA | Κέδρων, MT, WH & TR)

(2749) **κεῖμαι**, 1 pers. sg. pres. mid./pass. dep. indic., fut. κείσομαι [§33.DD] *to lie, to be laid; to recline, to be lying, to have been laid down*, Matt. 28:6; Luke 2:12, et al.; *to have been laid, placed, set*, Matt. 3:10;

Luke 3:9; John 2:6, et al.; *to be situated,*
as a city, Matt. 5:14; Rev. 21:16; *to be in
store,* Luke 12:19; met. *to be constituted,
established* as a law, 1 Tim. 1:9; in N.T. of
persons, *to be specially set, solemnly appointed, destined,* Luke 2:34; Phil. 1:17;
1 Thess. 3:3; *to lie* under an influence, *to
be involved in,* 1 John 5:19

κείμεθα, 1 pers. pl. pres. mid./pass. dep.
     indic. . . . . κεῖμαι *(2749)*
κείμενα, acc. pl. neut. pres. mid./pass. dep.
     part. . . . . id.
κείμεναι, nom. pl. f. pres. mid./pass. dep.
     part. . . . . id.
κειμένη, nom. sg. f. pres. mid./pass. dep.
     part. . . . . id.
κειμένην, acc. sg. f. pres. mid./pass. dep. part.   id.
κείμενον, acc. sg. m. pres. mid./pass. dep.
     part. {1 Cor. 3:11} . . . . id.
κείμενον, acc. sg. neut. pres. mid./pass. dep.
     part. {John 20:7} . . . . id.
κείμενος, nom. sg. m. pres. mid./pass. dep.
     part. . . . . id.
κειράμενος, nom. sg. m. aor. mid. part.
     [§27.1.d] . . . . κείρω *(2751)*
κείραντος, gen. sg. m. aor. act. part. (Acts
     8:32, GNT, WH, MT & NA | κείροντος,
     TR) . . . . id.
κείρασθαι, aor. mid. infin. . . . . id.
κειράσθω, 3 pers. sg. aor. mid. imper. . . . id.
(2750) **κειρία,** ας, ἡ [§2.B.b; 2.2] *a bandage, swath,
roller,* in N.T. pl. *graveclothes,* John 11:44
κειρίαις, dat. pl. f. n. . . . . κειρία *(2750)*
κείροντος, gen. sg. m. pres. act. part. (Acts
     8:32, TR | κείραντος, GNT, WH, MT &
     NA) . . . . κείρω *(2751)*
(2751) **κείρω,** fut. κερῶ [§27.1.c] aor. mid.
     ἐκειράμην, *to cut off* the hair, *shear, shave,*
     Acts 8:32; 18:18; 1 Cor. 11:6(2×)
κεῖται, 3 pers. sg. pres. mid./pass. dep.
     indic. . . . . κεῖμαι *(2749)*
κεκαθαρισμένους, acc. pl. m. perf. pass. part.
     (Heb. 10:2, GNT, WH & NA | κεκαθ-
     αρμένους, MT & TR) . . . . καθαρίζω *(2511)*
κεκαθαρμένους, acc. pl. m. perf. pass. part.
     [§27.3] (Heb. 10:2, MT & TR | κεκαθ-
     αρισμένους, GNT, WH & NA) . . καθαίρω *(2508)*
κεκάθικε(ν), 3 pers. sg. perf. act.
     indic. . . . . καθίζω *(2523)*
κακαλυμμένον, nom. sg. neut. perf. pass.
     part. . . . . καλύπτω *(2572)*
κεκαυμένῳ, dat. sg. neut. perf. pass.
     part. . . . . καίω *(2545)*
κεκαυστηριασμένων, gen. pl. m. perf. pass.
     part. (1 Tim. 4:2, GNT, WH & NA |

κεκαυτηριασμένων, MT &
     TR) . . . . καυστηριάζω *(‡2743)*
κεκαυτηριασμένων, gen. pl. m. perf. pass.
     part. (1 Tim. 4:2, MT & TR | κεκαυ-
     στηριασμένων, GNT, WH &
     NA) . . . . καυτηριάζω *(2743)*
κεκαύχημαι, 1 pers. sg. perf. mid./pass. dep.
     indic. καυχάομαι *(2744)*
κεκένωται, 3 pers. sg. perf. pass. indic.
     [§21.U] . . . . κενόω *(2758)*
κεκερασμένου, gen. sg. m. perf. pass. part.
     [§36.5] . . . . κεράννυμι *(2767)*
κεκλεισμένον, acc. sg. neut. perf. pass.
     part. . . . . κλείω *(2808)*
κεκλεισμένων, gen. pl. m. perf. pass. part.   id.
κέκλεισται, 3 pers. sg. perf. pass. indic.
     [§22.5.6] . . . . id.
κέκληκεν, 3 pers. sg. perf. act. indic.
     [§22.4] . . . . καλέω *(2564)*
κεκληκότι, dat. sg. m. perf. act. part. . . . id.
κεκληκώς, nom. sg. m. perf. act. part. . . . id.
κεκλημένοι, nom. pl. m. perf. pass. part. . id.
κεκλημένοις, dat. pl. m. perf. pass. part. . id.
κεκλημένος, nom. sg. m. perf. pass. part. . id.
κεκλημένους, acc. pl. m. perf. pass. part. . id.
κεκλημένων, gen. pl. m. perf. pass. part. . id.
κεκληρονόμηκεν, 3 pers. sg. perf. act.
     indic. . . . . κληρονομέω *(2816)*
κέκληται, 3 pers. sg. perf. pass. indic. . καλέω *(2564)*
κέκλικεν, 3 pers. sg. perf. act. indic.
     [§13.6.c] . . . . κλίνω *(2827)*
κέκμηκας, 2 pers. sg. perf. act. indic.
     [§27.2.d] (Rev. 2:3, TR | GNT, WH, MT
     & NA omit) . . . . κάμνω *(2577)*
κεκοιμημένων, gen. pl. m. perf. pass.
     part. . . . . κοιμάω *(2837)*
κεκοίμηται, 3 pers. sg. perf. pass. indic. . . id.
κεκοίνωκε(ν), 3 pers. sg. perf. act.
     indic. . . . . κοινόω *(2840)*
κεκοινωμένους, acc. pl. m. perf. pass. part.
     [§21.U] . . . . id.
κεκοινώνηκε(ν), 3 pers. sg. perf. act.
     indic. . . . . κοινωνέω *(2841)*
κεκονιαμένε, voc. sg. m. perf. pass.
     part. . . . . κονιάω *(2867)*
κεκονιαμένοις, dat. pl. m. perf. pass. part.   id.
κεκοπίακα, 1 pers. sg. perf. act. indic.
     [§22.2] . . . . κοπιάω *(2872)*
κεκοπίακας, 2 pers. sg. perf. act. indic. (Rev.
     2:3, TR | κεκοπίακες, GNT, WH & NA
     | ἐκοπίασας, MT) . . . . id.
κεκοπιάκασι(ν), 3 pers. pl. perf. act. indic.   id.
κεκοπιάκατε, 2 pers. pl. perf. act. indic. .   id.
κεκοπίακες, nom. pl. m. perf. act. part. (Rev.
     2:3, GNT, WH & NA | κεκοπίακας,

TR | ἐκοπίασας, ΜΤ) . . . . κοπιάω *(2872)*
κεκοπιακώς, nom. sg. m. perf. act. part. .   id.
κεκορεσμένοι, nom. pl. m. perf. pass. part.
   [§36.5] . . . . κορέννυμι *(2880)*
κεκοσμημένην, acc. sg. f. perf. pass.
   part. . . . . κοσμέω *(2885)*
κεκοσμημένοι, nom. pl. m. perf. pass. part.   id.
κεκοσμημένον, acc. sg. m. perf. pass. part.   id.
κεκόσμηται, 3 pers. sg. perf. pass. indic. .   id.
κέκραγε(ν), 3 pers. sg. 2 perf. act. indic.
   [§26.2] . . . . κράζω *(2896)*
κεκράξονται, 3 pers. pl. 2 fut. mid. dep. indic.
   [§14.1.g] (Luke 19:40, ΜΤ & TR |
   κράξουσιν, GNT, WH & NA) . . . . . . id.
κεκρατηκέναι, perf. act. infin. . . . . . . κρατέω *(2902)*
κεκράτηνται, 3 pers. pl. perf. pass. indic.   id.
κέκρικα, 1 pers. sg. perf. act. indic.
   [§13.6.c] . . . . κρίνω *(2919)*
κεκρίκατε, 2 pers. pl. perf. act. indic. . . . id.
κεκρίκει, 3 pers. sg. pluperf. act. indic. (Acts
   20:16, GNT, WH & NA | ἔκρινε(ν), ΜΤ
   & TR) . . . . id.
κέκρικεν, 3 pers. sg. perf. act. indic. . . . . id.
κεκριμένα, acc. pl. neut. perf. pass. part. . id.
κέκριται, 3 pers. sg. perf. pass. indic. . . . id.
κεκρυμμένα, acc. pl. neut. perf. pass. part.
   [§23.7] . . . . κρύπτω *(2928)*
κεκρυμμένον, nom. sg. neut. perf. pass. part.   id.
κεκρυμμένος, nom. sg. m. perf. pass. part.   id.
κεκρυμμένου, gen. sg. m. perf. pass. part. . id.
κεκρυμμένῳ, dat. sg. m. perf. pass. part. . id.
κέκρυπται, 3 pers. sg. perf. pass. indic. . . id.
κεκυρωμένην, acc. sg. f. perf. pass. part.
   [§21.U] . . . . κυρόω *(2964)*
κελεύεις, 2 pers. sg. pres. act. indic. . . . κελεύω *(2753)*
κελεύσαντες, nom. pl. m. aor. act. part. . id.
κελεύσαντος, gen. sg. m. aor. act. part. . . id.
κελεύσας, nom. sg. m. aor. act. part. . . . . id.
(†2752) **κέλευσμα,** ατος, τό [§4.D.c] *a word of command; a mutual cheer;* hence, in N.T. *a
   loud shout, an arousing outcry,* 1 Thess.
   4:16
κελεύσματι, dat. sg. neut. n. . . . . . κέλευσμα *(†2752)*
κέλευσον, 2 pers. sg. aor. act. imper. . κελεύω *(2753)*
(2753) **κελεύω,** fut. κελεύσω, aor. ἐκέλευσα [§13.M]
   (κέλω, κέλομαι, idem) *to order, com-
   mand, direct, bid,* Matt. 8:18; 14:19, 28,
   et al.
κενά, acc. pl. neut. adj. . . . . κενός *(2756)*
κενέ, voc. sg. m. adj. . . . . id.
κενή, nom. sg. f. adj. . . . . id.
κενῆς, gen. sg. f. adj. . . . . id.
(2754) **κενοδοξία,** ας, ἡ [§2.B.b; 2.2] *empty conceit,
   vainglory,* Phil. 2:3
κενοδοξίαν, acc. sg. f. n. . . . . κενοδοξία *(2754)*

κενόδοξοι, nom. pl. m. adj. . . . . . . κενόδοξος *(2755)*
(2755) **κενόδοξος,** ον [§7.2] (κενός + δόξα) *vain-
   glorious, desirous of vainglory,* Gal. 5:26
κενοῖς, dat. pl. m. adj. . . . . κενός *(2756)*
κενόν, acc. sg. m. adj. {Mark 12:3} . . . . id.
κενόν, nom. sg. neut. adj. {1 Cor. 15:14} . id.
κενόν, acc. sg. neut. adj. {Phil. 2:16} . . . . id.
(2756) **κενός,** ή, όν, nom. sg. m. adj. [§7.F.a] *empty;
   having nothing, empty-handed,* Mark 12:3;
   met. *vain, fruitless, void of effect,* Acts
   4:25; 1 Cor. 15:10; εἰς κενόν, *in vain, to
   no purpose,* 2 Cor. 6:1, et al.; *hollow, fallacious, false,* Eph. 5:6; Col. 2:8; *inconsiderate, foolish,* James 2:20
κενούς, acc. pl. m. adj. . . . . κενός *(2756)*
(2757) **κενοφωνία,** ας, ἡ [§2.B.b; 2.2] (κενός +
   φωνή) *vain, empty babbling, vain disputation, fruitless discussion,* 1 Tim. 6:20;
   2 Tim. 2:16
κενοφωνίας, acc. pl. f. n. . . . . κενοφωνία *(2757)*
(2758) **κενόω,** ῶ, fut. κενώσω, aor. ἐκένωσα [§20.T]
   to empty, evacuate; ἑαυτόν, *to divest one’s
   self of one’s prerogatives, abase one’s self,*
   Phil. 2:7; *to deprive* a thing *of its proper
   functions,* Rom. 4:14; 1 Cor. 1:17; *to show
   to be without foundation, falsify,* 1 Cor.
   9:15; 2 Cor. 9:3
κέντρα, acc. pl. neut. n. . . . . κέντρον *(2759)*
(2759) **κέντρον,** ου, τό, nom. sg. neut. n. [§3.C.c]
   (κεντέω, *to prick*) *a sharp point; a sting,*
   Rev. 9:10; *a prick, stimulus, goad,* Acts 9:5;
   26:14; met. of death, *destructive power,
   deadly venom,* 1 Cor. 15:55, 56
(2760) **κεντυρίων,** ωνος, ὁ, nom. sg. m. n. [§4.2.e]
   (Lat. centurio, from centum, *a hundred*) in
   its original signification, *a commander of
   a hundred* foot-soldiers, *a centurion,* Mark
   15:39, 44, 45
κεντυρίωνα, acc. sg. m. n. . . . . κεντυρίων *(2760)*
κεντυρίωνος, gen. sg. m. n. . . . . id.
κενωθῇ, 3 pers. sg. aor. pass. subj. . . . . κενόω *(2758)*
(2761) **κενῶς,** adv., *in vain, to no purpose, unmeaning,* James 4:5
κενώσει, 3 pers. sg. fut. act. indic. (1 Cor.
   9:15, GNT, WH & NA | κενώσῃ, ΜΤ &
   TR) . . . . κενόω *(2758)*
κενώσῃ, 3 pers. sg. aor. act. subj. (1 Cor. 9:15,
   ΜΤ & TR | κενώσει, GNT, WH & NA)   id.
(2762) **κεραία,** ας, ἡ, nom. sg. f. n. [§2.B.b; 2.2] pr.
   a horn-like projection, a point, extremity;
   in N.T. *an apex,* or *fine point;* as of letters, used for *the minutest part, a tittle,*
   Matt. 5:18; Luke 16:17
κεραίαν, acc. sg. f. n. . . . . κεραία *(2762)*
(2763) **κεραμεύς,** έως, ὁ, nom. sg. m. n. [§5.E.d] *a*

potter, Matt. 27:7, 10; Rom. 9:21

κεραμέως, gen. sg. m. n. . . . . κεραμεύς *(2763)*

κεραμικά, nom. pl. neut. adj. . . . . κεραμικός *(2764)*

(2764) **κεραμικός,** ή, όν [§7.F.a] *made by a potter, earthen,* Rev. 2:27

(2765) **κεράμιον,** ου, τό [§3.C.a] (dimin. of κέραμος) *an earthenware vessel, a pitcher, jar,* Mark 14:13; Luke 22:10

κεράμιον, acc. sg. neut. n. . . . . κεράμιον *(2765)*

(2766) **κέραμος,** ου, ὁ [§3.C.a] *potter's clay; earthenware; a tile, tiling,* Luke 5:19

κεράμων, gen. pl. m. n. . . . . κέραμος *(2766)*

(2767) **κεράννυμι,** or κεραννύω (κεράω) fut. κεράσω, aor. ἐκέρασα, perf. pass. κέκραμαι, later κεκέρασμαι [§36.5] *to mix, mingle,* drink; *to prepare* for drinking, Rev. 14:10; 18:6 (2×)

(2768) **κέρας,** ατος, τό [§5.E.j] *a horn,* Rev. 5:6; 12:3, et al.; *a horn-like projection* at the corners of an altar, Rev. 9:13; from the Hebrew, *a horn* as a symbol of power, Luke 1:69

κέρας, acc. sg. neut. n. . . . . κέρας *(2768)*

κεράσατε, 2 pers. pl. aor. act. imper. κεράννυμι *(2767)*

κέρατα, nom. pl. neut. n. {Rev. 17:12} . κέρας *(2768)*

κέρατα, acc. pl. neut. n. {Rev. 17:3} . . . . . id.

(2769) **κεράτιον,** όυ, τό [§3.C.c] (dimin. of κέρας) pr. *a little horn;* in N.T. *a pod, the pod of the carob tree,* or *Ceratonia siliqua* of Linnaeus, a common tree in the East and the south of Europe, growing to a considerable size, and producing long slender pods, with a pulp of a sweetish taste, and several brown shining seeds like beans, sometimes eaten by the poorer people in Syria and Palestine, and commonly used for fattening swine, Luke 15:16

κερατίων, gen. pl. neut. n. . . . . κεράτιον *(2769)*

κεράτων, gen. pl. neut. n. . . . . κέρας *(2768)*

(2770) **κερδαίνω,** fut. κερδανῶ, κερδήσω and κέρδομαι [§27.1.c] aor. ἐκέρδησα, *to gain* as a matter of profit, Matt. 25:17, et al.; *to win, acquire possession of,* Matt. 16:26; *to profit in the avoidance of, to avoid,* Acts 27:21; in N.T. Χριστόν, *to win* Christ, *to become possessed of* the privileges of the Gospel, Phil. 3:8; *to win over* from estrangement, Matt. 18:15; *to win over* to embrace the Gospel, 1 Cor. 9:19, 20, 21, 22; 1 Pet. 3:1; absol. *to make gain,* James 4:13

κερδάνω, 1 pers. sg. aor. act. subj. (1 Cor. 9:21, GNT, WH & NA | κερδήσω, MT & TR) . . . . κερδαίνω *(2770)*

κέρδη, nom. pl. neut. n. . . . . κέρδος *(2771)*

κερδηθήσονται, 3 pers. pl. fut. pass. indic. (1 Pet. 3:1, GNT, WH, MT & NA | κερδηθήσωνται, TR) . . . . κερδαίνω *(2770)*

κερδηθήσωνται, 3 pers. pl. aor. pass. subj. (an unusual form | 1 Pet. 3:1, TR | κερδηθήσονται, GNT, WH, MT & NA) . . . id.

κερδῆσαι, aor. act. infin. . . . . id.

κερδήσας, nom. sg. m. aor. act. part. . . . . id.

κερδήσῃ, 3 pers. sg. aor. act. subj. . . . . . id.

κερδήσομεν, 1 pers. pl. fut. act. indic. (James 4:13, GNT, WH & NA | κερδήσωμεν, MT & TR) . . . . id.

κερδήσω, 1 pers. sg. aor. act. subj. . . . . . id.

κερδήσωμεν, 1 pers. pl. aor. act. subj. (James 4:13, MT & TR | κερδήσομεν, GNT, WH & NA) . . . . id.

(2771) **κέρδος,** ους, τό, nom. sg. neut. n. [§5.E.b] *gain, profit,* Phil. 1:21; 3:7; Tit. 1:11

κέρδους, gen. sg. neut. n. . . . . κέρδος *(2771)*

(2772) **κέρμα,** ατος, τό, nom. sg. neut. n. [§4.D.c] *something clipped small; small change, small pieces of money, coin* (John 2:15, GNT, MT, TR & NA | κέρματα, WH)

κέρματα, acc. pl. neut. n. (John 2:15, WH | κέρμα, GNT, MT, TR & NA) . . . . κέρμα *(2772)*

κερματιστάς, acc. pl. m. n. . . . . κερματιστής *(2773)*

(2773) **κερματιστής,** οῦ, ὁ [§2.B.c] *a money changer,* John 2:14

κεφαλαί, nom. pl. f. n. . . . . κεφαλή *(2776)*

(2774) **κεφάλαιον,** ου, τό, nom. sg. neut. n. [§3.C.c] *a sum total; a sum of money, capital,* Acts 22:28; *the crowning or ultimate point* to preliminary matters, Heb. 8:1

κεφαλαίου, gen. sg. neut. n. . . . . . . κεφάλαιον *(2774)*

(2775) **κεφαλαιόω,** ῶ, fut. καφαλαιώσω [§20.T] *to sum up;* but in N.T. equiv. to κεφαλίζω, *to wound on the head,* Mark 12:4

κεφαλάς, acc. pl. f. n. . . . . κεφαλή *(2776)*

(2776) **κεφαλή,** ῆς, ἡ, nom. sg. f. n. [§2.B.a] *the head,* Matt. 5:36; 6:17, et al.; *the head, top;* κεφαλὴ γωνίας, *the head of the corner, the chief corner-stone,* Matt. 21:42; Luke 20:17; met. *the head, superior, chief, principal, one to whom others are subordinate,* 1 Cor. 11:3; Eph. 1:22, et al.

κεφαλῇ, dat. sg. f. n. . . . . κεφαλή *(2776)*

κεφαλήν, acc. sg. f. n. . . . . id.

κεφαλῆς, gen. sg. f. n. . . . . id.

κεφαλίδι, dat. sg. f. n. . . . . κεφαλίς *(2777)*

(2777) **κεφαλίς,** ίδος, ἡ [§4.2.c] (dimin. of κεφαλή) in N.T. *a roll, volume, division* of a book, Heb. 10:7

κεφαλῶν, gen. pl. f. n. . . . . κεφαλή *(2776)*

κεχάρισμαι, 1 pers. sg. perf. mid./pass. dep.

indic. . . . . χαρίζομαι *(5483)*

κεχάρισται, 3 pers. sg. perf. mid./pass. dep.

indic. . . . . id.

κεχαριτωμένη, nom. sg. f. perf. pass. part.

[§21.U] . . . . χαριτόω *(5487)*

κέχρημαι, 1 pers. sg. perf. mid./pass. dep.

indic. (1 Cor. 9:15, GNT, WH & NA |
ἐχρησάμην, MT & TR) . . . . χράομαι *(5530)*

κεχρηματισμένον, nom. sg. neut. perf. pass.

part. . . . . χρηματίζω *(5537)*

κεχρημάτισται, 3 pers. sg. perf. pass. indic.   id.

κεχρυσωμένη, nom. sg. f. perf. pass.

part. χρυσόω *(5558)*

κεχωρισμένος, nom. sg. m. perf. pass.

part. χωρίζω *(5563)*

(‡5392) **κημόω**, ῶ, fut. κημώσω (κημός, *a curb,
bridle, muzzle*) *to muzzle*

κημώσεις, 2 pers. sg. fut. act. indic. (1 Cor.
9:9, GNT & NA | φιμώσεις, WH, MT
& TR) . . . . κημόω *(‡5392)*

κῆνσον, acc. sg. m. n. . . . . κῆνσος *(2778)*

(2778) **κῆνσος**, ου, ὁ [§3.C.a] (Lat. census) *a census,
assessment, enumeration of the people and
a valuation of their property;* in N.T. *tribute, tax,* Matt. 17:25; *poll-tax,* Matt.
22:17, 19; Mark 12:14

κήνσου, gen. sg. m. n. . . . . κῆνσος *(2778)*

κῆπον, acc. sg. m. n. . . . . κῆπος *(2779)*

(2779) **κῆπος**, ου, ὁ, nom. sg. m. n. [§3.C.a] *a
garden, any place planted with trees and
herbs,* Luke 13:19; John 18:1, 26; 19:41

(2780) **κηπουρός**, οῦ, ὁ, nom. sg. m. n. (κῆπος +
οὖρος, *a watcher*) *a garden-keeper, gar-
dener,* John 20:15

κήπῳ, dat. sg. m. n. . . . . κῆπος *(2779)*

(2781) **κηρίον**, ου, τό [§3.C.c] (κηρός, *beeswax*) *a
honeycomb; a comb filled with honey,*
Luke 24:42

κηρίου, gen. sg. neut. n. (Luke 24:42, MT &
TR | GNT, WH & NA omit) . . . . . κηρίον *(2781)*

(2782) **κήρυγμα**, ατος, τό, nom. sg. neut. n. [§4.D.c]
*proclamation, proclaiming, public annun-
ciation,* Matt. 12:41; *public inculcation,
preaching,* 1 Cor. 2:4; 15:14; meton. *what
is publicly inculcated, doctrine,* Rom.
16:25, et al. {1 Cor. 2:4}

κήρυγμα, acc. sg. neut. n.
{Matt. 12:41} . . . . κήρυγμα *(2782)*

κηρύγματι, dat. sg. neut. n. . . . . id.

κηρύγματος, gen. sg. neut. n. . . . . id.

κήρυκα, acc. sg. m. n. (κῆρυξ) . . . . . . κῆρυξ *(2783)*

(2783) **κῆρυξ**, (κῆρυξ) υκος, ὁ, nom. sg. m. n.
[§4.2.b] *a herald, public messenger;* in N.T.
a proclaimer, publisher, preacher, 1 Tim.
2:7; 2 Tim. 1:11; 2 Pet. 2:5

κηρύξαι, aor. act. infin. . . . . κηρύσσω *(2784)*

κηρύξας, nom. sg. m. aor. act. part. . . . . . id.

κηρύξατε, 2 pers. pl. aor. act. imper. . . . . id.

κήρυξον, 2 pers. sg. aor. act. imper. . . . . . id.

κηρύξουσιν, 3 pers. pl. fut. act. indic. (Rom.
10:15, MT & TR | κηρύξωσιν, GNT, WH
& NA) . . . . id.

κηρύξω, 1 pers. sg. aor. act. subj. . . . . . . id.

κηρύξωσιν, 3 pers. pl. aor. act. subj. (Rom.
10:15, GNT, WH & NA | κηρύξουσιν,
MT & TR) . . . . id.

κηρύσσει, 3 pers. sg. pres. act. indic. . . . . id.

κηρύσσειν, pres. act. infin. . . . . id.

κηρύσσεται, 3 pers. sg. pres. pass. indic. . id.

κηρύσσετε, 2 pers. pl. pres. act. imper. . . . id.

κηρύσσομεν, 1 pers. pl. pres. act. indic. . . id.

κηρύσσοντα, acc. sg. m. pres. act. part. . . id.

κηρύσσοντας, acc. pl. m. pres. act. part. . . id.

κηρύσσοντος, gen. sg. m. pres. act. part. . id.

κηρύσσουσιν, 3 pers. pl. pres. act. indic. . id.

(2784) **κηρύσσω**, 1 pers. sg. pres. act. indic., fut.
κηρύξω, aor. ἐκήρυξα [§26.3] *to pub-
lish, proclaim,* as a herald, 1 Cor. 9:27;
to announce openly and publicly, Mark
1:4; Luke 4:18; *to noise abroad,* Mark
1:45; 7:36; *to announce* as a matter of
doctrine, *inculcate, preach,* Matt. 24:14;
Mark 1:38; 13:10; Acts 15:21; Rom. 2:21,
et al.

κηρύσσων, nom. sg. m. pres. act.
part. κηρύσσω *(2784)*

κηρυχθείς, nom. sg. m. aor. pass. part. . . . id.

κηρυχθέντος, gen. sg. neut. aor. pass. part.   id.

κηρυχθῇ, 3 pers. sg. aor. pass. subj. . . . . . id.

κηρυχθῆναι, aor. pass. infin. . . . . id.

κηρυχθήσεται, 3 pers. sg. fut. pass. indic.   id.

(2785) **κῆτος**, ους, τό [§5.E.b] *a large fish, sea mon-
ster, whale,* Matt. 12:40

κήτους, gen. sg. neut. n. . . . . κῆτος *(2785)*

Κηφᾶ, gen. sg. m. n. . . . . Κηφᾶς *(2786)*

Κηφᾷ, dat. sg. m. n. . . . . id.

Κηφᾶν, acc. sg. m. n. (Gal. 1:18, GNT, WH
& NA | Πέτρον, MT & TR) . . . . id.

(2786) **Κηφᾶς**, ᾶ, ὁ, nom. sg. m. n. [§2.4] (Aramaic
כֵּיפָא) *Cephas, Rock,* rendered into Greek
by Πέτρος, John 1:43; 1 Cor. 1:12, et al.

κιβωτόν, acc. sg. f. n. . . . . κιβωτός *(2787)*

(2787) **κιβωτός**, οῦ, ἡ, nom. sg. f. n. [§3.C.b] *a chest,
coffer; the ark* of the covenant, Heb. 9:4;
the ark of Noah, Matt. 24:38; Luke 17:27,
et al.

κιβωτοῦ, gen. sg. f. n. . . . . κιβωτός *(2787)*

(2788) **κιθάρα**, ας, ἡ, nom. sg. f. n. [§2.B.b] *a lyre,*
1 Cor. 14:7; Rev. 5:8; 14:2; 15:2

κιθάραις, dat. pl. f. n. . . . . κιθάρα *(2788)*

κιθάραν, acc. sg. f. n. (Rev. 5:8, GNT, WH & NA | κιθάρας, MT & TR) .... κιθάρα *(2788)*
κιθάρας, acc. pl. f. n. .... id.
(2789) **κιθαρίζω,** fut. κιθαρίσω [§26.1] *to play on a lyre, to harp,* 1 Cor. 14:7; Rev. 14:2
κιθαριζόμενον, nom. sg. neut. pres. pass. part. .... κιθαρίζω *(2789)*
κιθαριζόντων, gen. pl. m. pres. act. part. . id.
(2790) **κιθαρῳδός,** οῦ, ὁ [§3.C.a] (κιθάρα + ἀείδω) *one who plays on the lyre and accompanies it with his voice, a harper,* Rev. 14:2; 18:22
κιθαρῳδῶν, gen. pl. m. n. ...... κιθαρῳδός *(2790)*
(2791) **Κιλικία,** ας, ἡ [§2.B.b; 2.2] *Cilicia,* a province of Asia Minor
Κιλικίαν, acc. sg. f. n. .... Κιλικία *(2791)*
Κιλικίας, gen. sg. f. n. .... id.
(2792) **κινάμωμον,** ου, τό [§3.C.c] *cinnamon,* the aromatic bark of the *laurus cinnamomum,* which grows in Arabia, Syria, etc.
κινάμωμον, acc. sg. neut. n. (Rev. 18:13, MT & TR | κιννάμωμον, GNT, WH & NA) .... κινάμωμον *(2792)*
κινδυνεύει, 3 pers. sg. pres. act. indic. .... κινδυνεύω *(2793)*
κινδυνεύομεν, 1 pers. pl. pres. act. indic. . id.
(2793) **κινδυνεύω,** fut. κινδυνεύσω [§13.M] *to be in danger or peril,* Luke 8:23; Acts 19:27, 40; 1 Cor. 15:30
κινδύνοις, dat. pl. m. n. .... κίνδυνος *(2794)*
(2794) **κίνδυνος,** ου, ὁ, nom. sg. m. n. [§3.C.a] *danger, peril,* Rom. 8:35; 2 Cor. 11:26
(2795) **κινέω,** ῶ, fut. κινήσω, aor. ἐκίνησα [§16.P] (κίω, *to go*) *to set a-going; to move,* Matt. 23:4; *to excite, agitate,* Acts 21:30; 24:5; *to remove,* Rev. 2:5; 6:14; in N.T. κεφαλήν, *to shake the head* in derision, Matt. 27:39; Mark 15:29; mid. *to move, possess the faculty of motion, exercise the functions of life,* Acts 17:28
κινῆσαι, aor. act. infin. .... κινέω *(2795)*
κίνησιν, acc. sg. f. n. (John 5:3, MT & TR | GNT, WH & NA omit) .... κίνησις *(2796)*
(2796) **κίνησις,** εως, ἡ [§5.E.c] *a moving, motion,* John 5:3
κινήσω, 1 pers. sg. fut. act. indic. ..... κινέω *(2795)*
(‡2792) **κιννάμωμον,** ου, τό, *cinnamon*
κιννάμωμον, acc. sg. neut. n. (Rev. 18:13, GNT, WH & NA | κινάμωμον, MT & TR) .... κιννάμωμον *(‡2792)*
κινούμεθα, 1 pers. pl. pres. pass. indic. . κινέω *(2795)*
κινοῦντα, acc. sg. m. pres. act. part. ..... id.
κινοῦντες, nom. pl. m. pres. act. part. ... id.
(2797) **Κίς,** ὁ (Hebrew קִישׁ) *Cis,* pr. name, indecl. (Acts 13:21, GNT, MT, TR & NA | Κείς, WH)

(‡5531) **κίχρημι,** fut. κιχρήσω, aor. ἔχρησα (another form of χράω) *to lend,* Luke 11:5
κλάδοι, nom. pl. m. n. .... κλάδος *(2798)*
κλάδοις, dat. pl. m. n. .... id.
(2798) **κλάδος,** ου, ὁ, nom. sg. m. n. [§3.C.a] *a bough, branch, shoot,* Matt. 13:32; 21:8, et al.; met. *a branch* of a family stock, Rom. 11:16, 21
κλάδους, acc. pl. m. n. .... κλάδος *(2798)*
κλάδων, gen. pl. m. n. .... id.
κλαῖε, 2 pers. sg. pres. act. imper. ..... κλαίω *(2799)*
κλαίειν, pres. act. infin. .... id.
κλαίεις, 2 pers. sg. pres. act. indic. ...... id.
κλαίετε, 2 pers. pl. pres. act. indic. {Mark 5:39} .... id.
κλαίετε, 2 pers. pl. pres. act. imper. {Luke 8:52} .... id.
κλαίοντας, acc. pl. m. pres. act. part. .... id.
κλαίοντες, nom. pl. m. pres. act. part. ... id.
κλαιόντων, gen. pl. m. pres. act. part. ... id.
κλαίουσα, nom. sg. f. pres. act. part. .... id.
κλαίουσαι, nom. pl. f. pres. act. part. .... id.
κλαίουσαν, acc. sg. f. pres. act. part. .... id.
κλαίουσι(ν), 3 pers. pl. pres. act. indic. {Rev. 18:11} .... id.
κλαίουσι(ν), dat. pl. m. pres. act. part. {Mark 16:10} .... id.
(2799) **κλαίω,** fut. κλαύσομαι, in N.T. κλαύσω [§35.3] aor. ἔκλαυσα, intrans. *to weep, shed tears,* Matt. 26:75; Mark 5:38, 39; Luke 19:41; 23:28, et al.; trans. *to weep for, bewail,* Matt. 2:18
κλαίων, nom. sg. m. pres. act. part. ... κλαίω *(2799)*
κλάσαι, aor. act. infin. [§22.2] .... κλάω *(2806)*
κλάσας, nom. sg. m. aor. act. part. ..... id.
κλάσει, dat. sg. f. n. .... κλάσις *(2800)*
(2800) **κλάσις,** εως, ἡ [§5.E.c] *a breaking, the act of breaking,* Luke 24:35; Acts 2:42
(2801) **κλάσμα,** ατος, τό [§4.D.c] *a piece broken off, fragment,* Matt;. 14:20 15:37; Mark 6:43, et al.
κλάσματα, acc. pl. neut. n. .... κλάσμα *(2801)*
κλασμάτων, gen. pl. neut. n. .... id.
(2802) **Κλαύδη,** ης, ἡ [§2.B.a] *Clauda,* a small island near Crete, Acts 27:16
Κλαύδην, acc. sg. f. n. (Acts 27:16, MT & TR | Καῦδα, GNT, WH & NA) .. Κλαύδη *(2802)*
(2803) **Κλαυδία,** ας, ἡ, nom. sg. f. n. [§2.B.b; 2.2] *Claudia,* pr. name
Κλαύδιον, acc. sg. m. n. .... Κλαύδιος *(2804)*
(2804) **Κλαύδιος,** ου, ὁ, nom. sg. m. n. [§3.C.a] *Claudius,* pr. name I. *The fourth Roman Emperor,* Acts 11:28, et al. II. *Claudius Lysias, a Roman captain,* Acts 23:26
Κλαυδίου, gen. sg. m. n. .... Κλαύδιος *(2804)*

(2805) **κλαυθμός**, οῦ, ὁ, nom. sg. m. n. [§3.C.a]
weeping, Matt. 2:18; 8:12, et al.
κλαύσατε, 2 pers. pl. aor. act. imper. . . κλάω *(2806)*
κλαύσετε, 2 pers. pl. fut. act. indic. . . . . . id.
κλαύσῃ, 3 pers. sg. aor. act. subj. . . . . id.
κλαύσονται, 3 pers. pl. fut. mid. dep. indic.
(Rev. 18:9, TR | κλαύσουσι(ν), GNT,
WH, MT & NA) . . . . id.
κλαύσουσι(ν), 3 pers. pl. fut. act. indic. (Rev.
18:9, GNT, WH, MT & NA | κλαύ-
σονται, TR) . . . . id.

(2806) **κλάω**, fut. κλάσω [§22.2] aor. ἔκλασα, *to
break off*; in N.T. *to break bread*, Matt.
14:19, et al.; with figurative reference to the
violent death of Christ, 1 Cor. 11:24
κλεῖδα, acc. sg. f. n. [§4.4] . . . . κλείς *(2807)*
κλεῖδας, acc. pl. f. n. (Matt. 16:19, GNT, WH
& NA | κλεῖς, MT & TR) . . . . id.
κλείει, 3 pers. sg. pres. act. indic. (Rev. 3:7,
TR | κλείσει, GNT, WH, MT &
NA) . . . . κλείω *(2808)*
κλείετε, 2 pers. pl. pres. act. indic. . . . . . . id.
κλεῖν, acc. sg. f. n. (Rev. 3:7; 20:1, GNT, WH,
MT & NA | κλεῖδα, TR) . . . . κλείς *(2807)*

(2807) **κλείς**, ή, nom. sg. f. n. κλειδός, κλειδί,
κλεῖδα, and κλεῖν [§4.4] κλεῖδες and
κλεῖς, *a key*, used in N.T. as the symbol
of power, authority, etc. Matt. 16:19; Rev.
1:18; 3:7; 9:1; 20:1; met. *the key* of entrance into knowledge, Luke 11:52
{Rev. 9:1}
κλεῖς, acc. pl. f. n. for κλεῖδας [§5.8.b]
{Rev. 1:18} . . . . κλείς *(2807)*
κλεῖσαι, aor. act. infin. . . . . κλείω *(2808)*
κλείσας, nom. sg. m. aor. act. part. . . . . . id.
κλείσει, 3 pers. sg. fut. act. indic. (Rev. 3:7,
GNT, WH, MT & NA | κλείει, TR) . id.
κλείσῃ, 3 pers. sg. aor. act. subj. . . . . . . id.
κλεισθῶσιν, 3 pers. pl. aor. pass. subj. . . . id.

(2808) **κλείω**, fut. κλείσω, aor. ἔκλεισα, perf. pass.
κέκλεισμαι, aor. pass. ἐκλείσθην [§22.4]
to close, shut, Matt. 6:6; 25:10, et al.; *to
shut up* a person, Rev. 20:3; met. of the
heavens, Luke 4:25; Rev. 11:6; κλεῖσαι τὰ
σπλάγχνα, *to shut up one's bowels, to be
hard-hearted, void of compassion*, 1 John
3:17; κλείειν τὴν βασιλεία τῶν οὐρανῶν,
*to endeavor to prevent entrance into the
kingdom of heaven*, Matt. 23:14
κλείων, nom. sg. m. pres. act. part. (Rev. 3:7,
GNT, WH & NA | MT & TR
omit) . . . . κλείω *(2808)*

(2809) **κλέμμα**, ατος, τό [§4.D.c] *theft*, Rev. 9:21
κλεμμάτων, gen. pl. neut. n. . . . . κλέμμα *(2809)*

(2810) **Κλεοπᾶς**, ᾶ, ὁ, nom. sg. m. n. [§2.4] *Cleopas*,

pr. name (Luke 24:18, GNT & NA |
Κλεόπας, WH, MT & TR)

(2811) **κλέος**, ους, τό, nom. sg. neut. n. [§5.E.b] pr.
rumor, report; good report, praise, credit,
1 Pet. 2:20
κλέπται, nom. pl. m. n. . . . . κλέπτης *(2812)*
κλέπτας, acc. pl. m. n. (1 Thess. 5:4, WH |
κλέπτης, GNT, MT, TR & NA) . . . . . id.
κλέπτειν, pres. act. infin. . . . . κλέπτω *(2813)*
κλέπτεις, 2 pers. sg. pres. act. indic. . . . . . id.
κλεπτέτω, 3 pers. sg. pres. act. imper. . . . id.

(2812) **κλέπτης**, ου, ὁ, nom. sg. m. n. [§2.B.c] *a thief*,
Matt. 6:19, 20; 24:43, et al.; trop. *a thief*
by imposture, John 10:8
κλέπτουσι(ν), 3 pers. pl. pres. act.
indic. . . . . κλέπτω *(2813)*

(2813) **κλέπτω**, fut. κλέψω, and κλέψομαι [§23.1.a]
2 perf. κέκλοφα [§25.5] aor. ἔκλεψα, *to
steal*, Matt. 6:19, 20; 19:18, et al.; *to take
away stealthily, remove secretly*, Matt.
27:64; 28:13
κλέπτων, nom. sg. m. pres. act. part. . κλέπτω *(2813)*
κλέψεις, 2 pers. sg. fut. act. indic. . . . . . . id.
κλέψῃ, 3 pers. sg. aor. act. subj. . . . . id.
κλέψῃς, 2 pers. sg. aor. act. subj. . . . . id.
κλέψωσιν, 3 pers. pl. aor. act. subj. . . . . . id.
κληθείς, nom. sg. m. aor. pass. part.
[§22.4] . . . . καλέω *(2564)*
κληθέν, nom. sg. neut. aor. pass. part. . . . id.
κληθέντος, gen. sg. m. aor. pass. part. . . . id.
κληθῆναι, aor. pass. infin. . . . . id.
κληθῇς, 2 pers. sg. aor. pass. subj. . . . . . . id.
κληθήσεται, 3 pers. sg. fut. pass. indic. . . id.
κληθήσῃ, 2 pers. sg. fut. pass. indic. . . . . id.
κληθήσονται, 3 pers. pl. fut. pass. indic. . id.
κληθῆτε, 2 pers. pl. aor. pass. subj. . . . . . id.
κληθῶμεν, 1 pers. pl. aor. pass. subj. . . . . id.

(2814) **κλῆμα**, ατος, τό, nom. sg. neut. n. [§4.D.c]
a branch, shoot, twig, esp. of the vine,
{John 15:4, 6}
κλῆμα, acc. sg. neut. n. {John 15:2} . . . κλῆμα *(2814)*
κλήματα, nom. pl. neut. n. . . . . id.
Κλήμεντος, gen. sg. m. n. . . . . Κλήμης *(2815)*

(2815) **Κλήμης**, εντος, ὁ [§4.2.d] *Clemens, Clement*,
pr. name, Latin, Phil. 4:3
κλῆρον, acc. sg. m. n. . . . . κλῆρος *(2819)*
κληρονομεῖ, 3 pers. sg. pres. act.
indic. . . . . κληρονομέω *(2816)*
κληρονομεῖν, pres. act. infin. . . . . id.

(2816) **κληρονομέω**, ῶ, fut. κληρονομήσω [§16.P]
perf. κεκληρονόμηκα, aor. ἐκληρονό-
μησα, pr. *to acquire by lot; to inherit, obtain by inheritance*; in N.T. *to obtain,
acquire, receive possession of*, Matt. 5:5;
19:29, et al.; absol. *to be heir*, Gal. 4:30

κληρονομῆσαι, aor. act. infin. ... κληρονομέω (2816)

κληρονομήσατε, 2 pers. pl. aor. act. imper.   id.

κληρονομήσει, 3 pers. sg. fut. act. indic. .   id.

κληρονομήσῃ, 3 pers. sg. aor. act. subj. (Gal.
4:30, MT & TR | κληρονομήσει, GNT,
WH & NA) ....   id.

κληρονομήσητε, 2 pers. pl. aor. act. subj.   id.

κληρονομήσουσι(ν), 3 pers. pl. fut. act.
indic. ....   id.

κληρονομήσω, 1 pers. sg. fut. act. indic.
{Luke 10:25} ....   id.

κληρονομήσω, 1 pers. sg. aor. act. subj.
{Mark 10:17} ....   id.

(2817) **κληρονομία**, ας, ἡ, nom. sg. f. n. [§2.B.b; 2.2]
an inheritance, patrimony, Matt. 21:38;
Mark 12:7; *a possession, portion, property,*
Acts 7:5; 20:32, et al.; in N.T. *a share, participation* in privileges, Acts 20:32; Eph.
1:14, et al.

κληρονομίαν, acc. sg. f. n. ...... κληρονομία (2817)

κληρονομίας, gen. sg. f. n. .... id.

κληρονόμοι, nom. pl. m. n. ..... κληρονόμος (2818)

κληρονόμοις, dat. pl. m. n. .... id.

κληρονόμον, acc. sg. m. n. .... id.

(2818) **κληρονόμος**, ου, ὁ, nom. sg. m. n. [§3.C.a]
(κλῆρος + νέμομαι) *an heir,* Matt. 21:38;
Gal. 4:1, et al.; *a possessor,* Rom. 4:13;
Heb. 11:7; James 2:5, et al.

κληρονομούντων, gen. pl. m. pres. act.
part. .... κληρονομέω (2816)

κληρονόμους, acc. pl. m. n. .... κληρονόμος (2818)

(2819) **κλῆρος**, ου, ὁ, nom. sg. m. n. [§3.C.a] *a lot,
die, a thing used in determining chances,*
Matt. 27:35; Mark 15:24, et al.; *assign-
ment, investiture,* Acts 1:17, 25; *allotment,
destination,* Col. 1:12; *a part, portion,
share,* Acts 8:21; 26:18; *a* constituent *portion* of the Church, 1 Pet. 5:3

κλήρου, gen. sg. m. n. .... κλῆρος (2819)

κλήρους, acc. pl. m. n. .... id.

(2820) **κληρόω**, ῶ, fut. κληρώσω [§20.T] *to choose
by lot;* mid. κληροῦμαι, aor. (pass. form)
ἐκληρώθην [§21.U] *to obtain by lot or as-
signment; to obtain a portion, receive a
share,* Eph. 1:11

κλήρων, gen. pl. m. n. .... κλῆρος (2819)

κλήσει, dat. sg. f. n. .... κλῆσις (2821)

κλήσεως, gen. sg. f. n. .... id.

κλῆσιν, acc. sg. f. n. .... id.

(2821) **κλῆσις**, εως, ἡ, nom. sg. f. n. [§5.E.c] *a call,
calling, invitation;* in N.T. *the call or invitation* to the privileges of the Gospel,
Rom. 11:29; Eph. 1:18, et al.; *the favor and
privilege of the invitation,* 2 Thess. 1:11;
2 Pet. 1:10; *the temporal condition in*

which the call found a person, 1 Cor. 1:26;
7:20

κλητοί, nom. pl. m. adj. .... κλητός (2822)

κλητοῖς, dat. pl. m. adj. .... id.

(2822) **κλητός**, ή, όν, nom. sg. m. adj. [§7.F.a] *called,
invited,* in N.T. *called* to privileges or functions, Matt. 20:16; 22:14; Rom. 1:1, 6, 7;
1 Cor. 1:1, 2, et al.

κλίβανον, acc. sg. m. n. .... κλίβανος (2823)

(2823) **κλίβανος**, ου, ὁ (Att. κρίβανος) [§3.C.a] *an
oven,* Matt. 6:30; Luke 12:28

(2824) **κλίμα**, ατος, τό [§4.D.c] pr. *a slope; a portion of the* ideal *slope of the earth's surface; a tract or region of* country, Rom.
15:23; 2 Cor. 11:10; Gal. 1:21

κλίμασι(ν), dat. pl. neut. n. .... κλίμα (2824)

κλίματα, acc. pl. neut. n. .... id.

(†2825) **κλινάριον**, ου, τό [§3.C.c] *a small bed or
couch*

κλιναρίων, gen. pl. neut. n. (Acts 5:15, GNT,
WH & NA | κλινῶν, MT &
TR) .... κλινάριον (†2825)

κλίνας, nom. sg. m. aor. act. part. .... κλίνω (2827)

κλίνειν, pres. act. infin. .... id.

κλίνῃ, 3 pers. sg. pres. act. subj. .... id.

(2825) **κλίνη**, ης, ἡ [§2.B.a] *a couch, bed,* Matt.
9:2, 6; Mark 4:21, et al.

κλίνην, acc. sg. f. n. .... κλίνη (2825)

κλίνης, gen. sg. f. n. .... id.

(2826) **κλινίδιον**, ου, τό [§3.C.c] dimin. of κλίνη, *a
small couch or bed,* Luke 5:19, 24

κλινίδιον, acc. sg. neut. n. .... κλινίδιον (2826)

κλινιδίῳ, dat. sg. neut. n. .... id.

κλινουσῶν, gen. pl. f. pres. act. part. ... κλίνω (2827)

(2827) **κλίνω**, fut. κλινῶ, perf. κέκλικα [§27.1.a;
27.2.c] aor. ἔκλινα, pr. trans. *to cause to
slope or bend; to bow down,* Luke 24:5;
John 19:30; *to lay down* to rest, Matt.
8:20; Luke 9:58; *to put to flight* troops,
Heb. 11:34; intrans. of the day, *to decline,*
Luke 9:12; 24:29

κλινῶν, gen. pl. f. n. .... κλίνη (2825)

(2828) **κλισία**, ας, ἡ [§2.B.b; 2.2] pr. *a place for reclining; a tent, seat, couch;* in N.T. *a company of persons reclining* at a meal, Luke
9:14

κλισίας, acc. pl. f. n. .... κλισία (2828)

κλοπαί, nom. pl. f. n. .... κλοπή (2829)

(2829) **κλοπή**, ῆς, ἡ [§2.B.a] *theft,* Matt. 15:19; Mark
7:22

(2830) **κλύδων**, ωνος, ὁ [§4.2.e] (κλύζω, *to dash,
surge, like the waves) a wave, billow, surge,*
Luke 8:24; James 1:6

κλύδωνι, dat. sg. m. n. .... κλύδων (2830)

(2831) **κλυδωνίζομαι**, fut. κληρονομέω, *to be*

tossed by waves; met. *to fluctuate* in opinion, *be agitated, tossed to and fro,* Eph. 4:14

κλυδωνιζόμενοι, nom. pl. m. pres. mid./pass. dep. part. . . . . κλυδωνίζομαι *(2831)*

κλῶμεν, 1 pers. pl. pres. act. indic. . . . . κλάω *(2806)*

κλώμενον, nom. sg. neut. pres. pass. part. (1 Cor. 11:24, MT & TR | GNT, WH & NA omit) . . . . id.

κλῶντες, nom. pl. m. pres. act. part. . . . id.

Κλωπᾶ, gen. sg. m. n. . . . . Κλωπᾶς *(2832)*

(2832) **Κλωπᾶς,** ᾶ, ὁ [§2.4] contr. for Κλεόπας, *Cleopas,* pr. name, John 19:25

κνηθόμενοι, nom. pl. m. pres. pass. part. . . . . κνήθω *(2833)*

(2833) **κνήθω** (κνάω) fut. κνήσω [§23.1.c] *to scratch; to tickle, cause titillation;* in N.T. mid. met. *to procure pleasurable excitement for, to indulge an itching,* 2 Tim. 4:3

Κνίδον, acc. sg. f. n. . . . . Κνίδος *(2834)*

(2834) **Κνίδος,** ου, ἡ [§3.C.b] *Cnidus,* a city of Caria, in Asia Minor, Acts 27:7

κοδράντην, acc. sg. m. n. . . . . κοδράντης *(2835)*

(2835) **κοδράντης,** ου, ὁ, nom. sg. m. n. [§2.B.c] (Lat. *quadrans*) *a Roman brass coin,* equivalent to the *fourth part* of an *as,* or ἀσσάριον, or τὸ δύο λεπτά, Matt. 5:26; Mark 12:42

(2836) **κοιλία,** ας, ἡ, nom. sg. f. n. [§2.B.b; 2.2] (κοῖλος, *hollow*) *a cavity; the belly,* Matt. 15:17; Mark 7:19; *the stomach,* Matt. 12:40; Luke 15:16; *the womb,* Matt. 19:12; Luke 1:15, et al.; from the Hebrew, *the inner self,* John 7:38

κοιλίᾳ, dat. sg. f. n. . . . . κοιλία *(2836)*

κοιλίαι, nom. pl. f. n. . . . . id.

κοιλίαν, acc. sg. f. n. . . . . id.

κοιλίας, gen. sg. f. n. . . . . id.

(2837) **κοιμάω,** ῶ, fut. κοιμήσω [§18.R] perf. pass. κεκοίμημαι, *to lull to sleep;* pass. *to fall asleep, be asleep,* Matt. 28:13; Luke 22:45; met. *to sleep* in death, Acts 7:60; 13:36, et al.

κοιμηθέντας, acc. pl. m. aor. pass. part. . . . . κοιμάω *(2837)*

κοιμηθέντες, nom. pl. m. aor. pass. part. . id.

κοιμηθῇ, 3 pers. sg. aor. pass. subj. . . . . . id.

κοιμηθησόμεθα, 1 pers. pl. fut. pass. indic. id.

κοιμήσεως, gen. sg. f. n. . . . . κοίμησις *(2838)*

(2838) **κοίμησις,** εως, ἡ [§5.E.c] *sleep;* meton. *rest, repose,* John 11:13

κοιμώμενος, nom. sg. m. pres. pass. part. . . . . κοιμάω *(2837)*

κοιμωμένους, acc. pl. m. pres. pass. part. id.

κοιμωμένων, gen. pl. m. pres. pass. part. . id.

κοιμῶνται, 3 pers. pl. pres. pass. indic. . . id.

κοινά, nom. pl. neut. adj. {Acts 4:32} . κοινός *(2839)*

κοινά, acc. pl. neut. adj. {Acts 2:44} . . . . id.

κοιναῖς, dat. pl. f. adj. . . . . id.

κοινήν, acc. sg. f. adj. . . . . id.

κοινῆς, gen. sg. f. adj. . . . . id.

κοινοῖ, 3 pers. sg. pres. act. indic. . . . . κοινόω *(2840)*

κοινόν, acc. sg. m. adj. {Acts 10:28} . . κοινός *(2839)*

κοινόν, nom. sg. neut. adj. {Rom. 14:14} . id.

κοινόν, acc. sg. neut. adj. {Acts 10:14} . . . id.

(2839) **κοινός,** ή, όν [§7.F.a] *common, belonging equally to several,* Acts 2:44; 4:32; in N.T. *common, profane,* Heb. 10:29; ceremonially *unclean,* Mark 7:2; Acts 10:14, et al.

κοίνου, 2 pers. sg. pres. act. imper. . . . κοινόω *(2840)*

κοινοῦν, nom. sg. neut. pres. act. part. (Rev. 21:27, TR | κοινόν, GNT, WH, MT & NA) . . . . id.

κοινοῦντα, nom. pl. neut. pres. act. part. . id.

(2840) **κοινόω,** ῶ, fut. κοινώσω, perf. κεκοίνωκα, aor. ἐκοίνωσα [§20.T] *to make common,* in N.T. *to profane, desecrate,* Acts 21:28; *to render* ceremonially *unclean, defile, pollute,* Matt. 15:11, 18, 20; *to pronounce unclean* ceremonially, Acts 10:15; 11:9

κοινωνεῖ, 3 pers. sg. pres. act. indic. {2 John 11} . . . . κοινωνέω *(2841)*

κοινωνεῖ, 2 pers. sg. pres. act. imper. {1 Tim. 5:22} . . . . id.

κοινωνεῖτε, 2 pers. pl. pres. act. indic. . . . id.

κοινωνείτω, 3 pers. sg. pres. act. imper. . . id.

(2841) **κοινωνέω,** ῶ, fut. κοινωνήσω, perf. κεκοινώνηκα, aor. ἐκοινώνησα [§16.P] *to have in common, share,* Heb. 2:14; *to be associated in, to become a sharer in,* Rom. 15:27; 1 Pet. 4:13; *to become implicated in, be a party to,* 1 Tim. 5:22; 2 John 11: *to associate one's self with* by sympathy and assistance, *to communicate with* in the way of aid and relief, Rom. 12:13; Gal. 6:6

(2842) **κοινωνία,** ας, ἡ, nom. sg. f. n. [§2.B.b; 2.2] *fellowship, partnership,* Acts 2:42; 2 Cor. 6:14; Gal. 2:9; Phil. 3:10; 1 John 1:3, et al.; *participation, communion,* 1 Cor. 10:16, et al.; *aid, relief,* Heb. 13:16, et al.; *contribution in aid,* Rom. 15:26

κοινωνίᾳ, dat. sg. f. n. . . . . κοινωνία *(2842)*

κοινωνίαν, acc. sg. f. n. . . . . id.

κοινωνίας, gen. sg. f. n. . . . . id.

(2843) **κοινωνικός,** ή, όν [§7.F.a] *social;* in N.T. *ready to communicate* in kind offices, *liberal, beneficent,* 1 Tim. 6:18

κοινωνικούς, acc. pl. m. adj. . . . . κοινωνικός *(2843)*

κοινωνοί, nom. pl. m. adj. . . . . κοινωνός *(2844)*

κοινωνόν, acc. sg. m. adj. . . . . id.

(2844) **κοινωνός,** οῦ, ὁ, ἡ, nom. sg. m. n. [§3.C.a,b]

a fellow, partner, Matt. 23:30; Luke 5:10;
1 Cor. 10:18, 20; 2 Cor. 8:23; Philemon 17:
Heb. 10:33; *a sharer, partaker*, 2 Cor. 1:7;
1 Pet. 5:1; 2 Pet. 1:4
κοινωνοῦντες, nom. pl. m. pres. act.
   part. . . . . κοινωνέω *(2841)*
κοινωνούς, acc. pl. m. adj. . . . . κοινωνός *(2844)*
κοινῶσαι, aor. act. infin. . . . . κοινόω *(2840)*
κοίταις, dat. pl. f. n. . . . . κοίτη *(2845)*
(2845) **κοίτη**, ης, ἡ, nom. sg. f. n. [§2.B.a] *a bed*,
Luke 11:7; *the* conjugal *bed*, Heb. 13:4;
meton. *sexual intercourse, concubitus*;
hence, *lewdness, whoredom, chambering*,
Rom. 13:13; in N.T. *conception*, Rom. 9:10
κοίτην, acc. sg. f. n. . . . . κοίτη *(2845)*
κοιτῶνος, gen. sg. m. n. . . . . κοιτών *(2846)*
(2846) **κοιτών**, ῶνος, ὁ [§4.2.e] *a bed-chamber*, Acts
12:20
κοκκίνην, acc. sg. f. adj. . . . . κόκκινος *(2847)*
κόκκινον, acc. sg. neut. adj. . . . . id.
(2847) **κόκκινος**, η, ον [§7.F.a] (κόκκος, *kermes, the
coccus ilicis* of Linnaeus, a small insect,
found on the leaves of the *quercus cocci-
ferus, or holm oak*, which was used by the
ancients, as the cochineal insect now is, for
dyeing a beautiful crimson or deep scarlet
color, and supposed by them to be the
berry of a plant or tree) *dyed with coccus,
crimson, scarlet*, Matt. 27:28; Heb. 9:19;
Rev. 17:3, 4; 18:12, 16
κοκκίνου, gen. sg. neut. adj. . . . . . . κόκκινος *(2847)*
κοκκίνῳ, dat. sg. neut. adj. (Rev. 17:4, TR
  | κόκκινον, GNT, WH, MT & NA) . . id.
κόκκον, acc. sg. m. n. . . . . κόκκος *(2848)*
(2848) **κόκκος**, ου, ὁ, nom. sg. m. n. [§3.C.a] *a ker-
nel, grain, seed*, Matt. 13:31; 17:20, et al.
κόκκῳ, dat. sg. m. n. . . . . κόκκος *(2848)*
κολαζομένους, acc. pl. m. pres. pass.
   part. . . . . κολάζω *(2849)*
(2849) **κολάζω**, fut. κολάσομαι and κολάσω [§26.1]
pr. *to curtail, to coerce; to chastise, punish*, Acts 4:21; 2 Pet. 2:9
(2850) **κολακεία**, ας, ἡ [§2.B.b; 2.2] (κόλαξ, *a flat-
terer) flattery, adulation, obsequiousness*
κολακείας, gen. sg. f. n. (1 Thess. 2:5, GNT,
MT, TR & NA | κολακίας,
WH) . . . . κολακεία *(2850)*
κόλασιν, acc. sg. f. n. . . . . κόλασις *(2851)*
(2851) **κόλασις**, εως, ἡ [§5.E.c] *chastisement, punishment*, Matt. 25:46; *painful disquietude,
torment*, 1 John 4:18
Κολασσαεῖς, acc. pl. m. n. (Col. 4:18, TRs
  | GNT, WH, MT, TRb & NA
omit) . . . . Κολασσαεύς *(‡2858)*
(‡2858) **Κολασσαεύς**, έως, ὁ, *Colossian*, a Colossian

(‡2857) **Κολασσαί**, ῶν, αἱ [§2.B.a] *Colosse*, a city of
Phrygia
Κολασσαῖς, dat. pl. f. n. (Col. 1:2, MT & TR
  | Κολοσσαῖς, GNT, WH &
NA) . . . . Κολασσαί *(‡2857)*
κολάσωνται, 3 pers. pl. aor. mid.
   subj. . . . . κολάζω *(2849)*
κολαφίζειν, pres. act. infin. . . . . κολαφίζω *(2852)*
κολαφίζῃ, 3 pers. sg. pres. act. subj. . . . . . id.
κολαφιζόμεθα, 1 pers. pl. pres. pass. indic. id.
κολαφιζόμενοι, nom. pl. m. pres. pass. part. id.
(2852) **κολαφίζω**, fut. κολαφίσω [§26.1] (κόλαφος,
*a blow with the fist) to beat with the fist,
buffet*, Matt. 26:67; Mark 14:65; met. *to
maltreat, treat with contumely and ignominy*, 1 Cor. 4:11; *to punish*, 1 Pet. 2:20;
to buffet, fret, afflict, 2 Cor. 12:7
κολλᾶσθαι, pres. pass. infin. [§19.S] . κολλάω *(2853)*
(2853) **κολλάω**, ῶ, fut. κολλήσω [§18.R] *to glue or
weld together;* mid. *to adhere to*, Luke
10:11; met. *to attach one's self to, unite
with, associate with*, Luke 15:15; Acts 5:13,
et al.
κολληθέντα, acc. sg. m. aor. pass.
   part. . . . . κολλάω *(2853)*
κολληθέντες, nom. pl. m. aor. pass. part. id.
κολληθήσεται, 3 pers. sg. fut. pass. indic.
  (Matt. 19:5, GNT, WH & NA | προσ-
  κολληθήσεται, MT & TR) . . . . id.
κολλήθητι, 2 pers. sg. aor. pass. imper. . . . id.
(2854) **κολλούριον**, or κολλύριον, ου, τό [§3.C.c]
(dimin. of κολλύρα, *a cake) collyrium,
eye-salve*
κολλούριον, acc. sg. neut. n. (Rev. 3:18, GNT,
WH, TR & NA | κολλύριον,
MT) . . . . κολλούριον *(2854)*
(2855) **κολλυβιστής**, οῦ, ὁ [§2.B.c] (κόλλυβος, *small
coin) a money-changer*, Matt. 21:12; Mark
11:15; John 2:15
κολλυβιστῶν, gen. pl. m. n. . . . . . κολλυβιστής *(2855)*
(‡2854) **κολλύριον**, or κολλύρα, ου, τό [§3.C.c]
(dimin. of κολλύρα, *a cake) collyrium,
eye-salve*
κολλύριον, acc. sg. neut. n. (Rev. 3:18, MT
  | κολλούριον, GNT, WH, TR &
NA) . . . . κολλύριον *(‡2854)*
κολλώμενοι, nom. pl. m. pres. pass.
   part. . . . . κολλάω *(2853)*
κολλώμενος, nom. sg. m. pres. pass. part. id.
(2856) **κολοβόω**, ῶ, fut. κολοβώσω [§20.T]
(κολοβός, *curtailed, mutilated*, from
κόλος, id.) in N.T. of time, *to cut short,
shorten*, Matt. 24:22; Mark 13:20
κολοβωθήσονται, 3 pers. pl. fut. pass.
   indic. . . . . κολοβόω *(2856)*

(2857) **Κολοσσαί, ῶν, αἱ** [§2.B.a] *Colosse,* a city of
Phrygia
Κολοσσαῖς, dat. pl. f. n. (Col. 1:2, GNT, WH
& NA | Κολασσαῖς, MT &
TR) . . . . Κολοσσαί (2857)
κόλποις, dat. pl. m. n. . . . . κόλπος (2859)
κόλπον, acc. sg. m. n. . . . . id.

(2859) **κόλπος, ου, ὁ** [§3.C.a] *the bosom,* Luke
16:22, 23; John 1:18; 13:23; *the bosom of
a garment,* Luke 6:38; *a bay, creek, inlet,*
Acts 27:39
κόλπῳ, dat. sg. m. n. . . . . κόλπος (2859)
κολυμβᾶν, pres. act. infin. (Acts 27:43, GNT,
MT & NA | κολυμβᾶν, WH &
TR) . . . . κολυμβάω (2860)

(2860) **κολυμβάω, ῶ,** fut. κολυμβήσω [§18.R] *to
dive;* in N.T. *to swim,* Acts 27:43

(2861) **κολυμβήθρα, ας, ἡ,** nom. sg. f. n. [§2.B.b] *a
place where any one may swim; a pond,
pool,* John 5:2, 4, 7; 9:7, 11
κολυμβήθρα, dat. sg. f. n. (John 5:4, MT &
TR | GNT, WH & NA omit) κολυμβήθρα (2861)
κολυμβήθραν, acc. sg. f. n. . . . . id.

(2862) **κολωνία, ας, ἡ,** nom. sg. f. n. [§2.B.b; 2.2]
(Latin, *colonia) a Roman colony,* Acts
16:12
κομᾷ, 3 pers. sg. pres. act. subj. . . . . . κομάω (2863)

(2863) **κομάω, ῶ,** fut. κομήσω [§18.R] *to have long
hair, wear the hair long,* 1 Cor. 11:14, 15

(2864) **κόμη, ης, ἡ,** nom. sg. f. n. [§2.B.a] *the hair;
a head of long hair,* 1 Cor. 11:15
κομιεῖσθε, 2 pers. pl. fut. mid. dep. indic. (Att.
for κομίσεσθε) [§35.11] . . . . κομίζω (2865)
κομιεῖται, 3 pers. sg. fut. mid. dep. indic. (Att.
for κομίσεται | Eph. 6:8; Col. 3:25, MT
& TR | κομίσεται, GNT, WH & NA) id.
κομιζόμενοι, nom. pl. m. pres. mid. part. id.

(2865) **κομίζω,** fut. κομίσω and κομιῶ, mid.
κομιοῦμαι, aor. ἐκόμισα [§26.1] [§35.11]
(κομέω, *to take care of)* pr. *to take into
kindly keeping, to provide for; to convey,
bring,* Luke 7:37; mid. *to bring for one's
self; to receive, obtain,* 2 Cor. 5:10; Eph.
6:8, et al.; *to receive again, recover,* Matt.
25:27; Heb. 11:19
κομιούμενοι, nom. pl. m. fut. mid. dep. part.
(2 Pet. 2:13, MT & TR | ἀδικούμενοι,
GNT, WH & NA) . . . . κομίζω (2865)
κομισάμενοι, nom. pl. m. aor. mid. part.
(Heb. 11:13, WH | λαβόντες, GNT, MT,
TR & NA) . . . . id.
κομίσασα, nom. sg. f. aor. act. part. . . . . id.
κομίσεται, 3 pers. sg. fut. mid. dep. indic.
(Eph. 6:8, GNT, WH & NA | κομιεῖται,
MT & TR) . . . . id.

κομίσησθε, 2 pers. pl. aor. mid. subj. . . κομίζω (2865)
κομίσηται, 3 pers. sg. aor. mid. subj. . . . . id.

(2866) **κομψότερον,** adv. (compar. of κόμψως, *well,
smartly)* in N.T. *in better health,* John 4:52

(2867) **κονιάω, ῶ,** fut. κονιάσω [§18.R] perf. pass.
κεκονίαμαι (κόνις, or κονία, *dust, lime-
dust) to whitewash,* or, *plaster,* Matt.
23:27; Acts 23:3
κονιορτόν, acc. sg. m. n. . . . . κονιορτός (2868)

(2868) **κονιορτός, οῦ, ὁ** [§3.C.a] (κόνις + ὄρνυμι,
to raise) dust excited; dust, Matt. 10:14;
Luke 9:5; 10:11; Acts 13:51; 22:23

(2869) **κοπάζω,** fut. κοπάσω [§26.1] pr. *to grow
weary, suffer exhaustion; to abate, be
stilled,* Matt. 14:32; Mark 4:39; 6:51
κοπετόν, acc. sg. m. n. . . . . κοπετός (2870)

(2870) **κοπετός, οῦ, ὁ** [§3.C.a] pr. *a beating* of the
breast, etc., in token of grief; *a wailing, lamentation,* Acts 8:2

(2871) **κοπή, ῆς, ἡ** [§2.B.a] *a stroke, smiting;* in N.T.
slaughter, Heb. 7:1
κοπῆς, gen. sg. f. n. . . . . κοπή (2871)
κοπιᾷ, 3 pers. sg. pres. act. indic. . . . κοπιάω (2872)
κοπιάσαντες, nom. pl. m. aor. act. part.
[§22.2] . . . . id.
κοπιάτω, 3 pers. sg. pres. act. imper. . . . . id.

(2872) **κοπιάω, ῶ,** fut. κοπιάσω [§22.2] perf.
κεκοπίακα, aor. ἐκοπίασα, *to be wearied
or spent with labor, faint from weariness,*
Matt. 11:28; John 4:6; in N.T. *to labor
hard, to toil,* Luke 5:5; John 4:38, et al.
κοπιῶ, 1 pers. sg. pres. act. indic. . . . . κοπιάω (2872)
κοπιῶμεν, 1 pers. pl. pres. act. indic. . . . id.
κοπιῶντα, acc. sg. m. pres. act. part. . . . id.
κοπιῶντας, acc. pl. m. pres. act. part. . . . id.
κοπιῶντες, nom. pl. m. pres. act. part. . . . id.
κοπιῶντι, dat. sg. m. pres. act. part. . . . . id.
κοπιώσας, acc. pl. f. pres. act. part. . . . . id.
κοπιῶσιν, 3 pers. pl. pres. act. indic. (Matt.
6:28, GNT, WH & NA | κοπιᾷ, MT &
TR) . . . . id.
κόποις, dat. pl. m. n. . . . . κόπος (2873)
κόπον, acc. sg. m. n. . . . . id.

(2873) **κόπος, ου, ὁ,** nom. sg. m. n. [§3.C.a] *trouble,
vexation, uneasiness,* Matt. 26:10; Mark
14:6; *labor, wearisome labor, travail, toil,*
1 Cor. 3:8; 15:58, et al.; meton. *the fruit
or consequence of labor,* John 4:38; 2 Cor.
10:15
κόπου, gen. sg. m. n. . . . . κόπος (2873)
κόπους, acc. pl. m. n. . . . . id.

(2874) **κοπρία, ας, ἡ** [§2.B.b; 2.2] *dung, manure,*
Luke 13:8; 14:35
κόπρια, acc. pl. neut. n. (Luke 13:8, GNT,
WH, MT & NA | κοπρίαν, TR) κοπρίον (†2874)

κοπρίαν, acc. sg. f. n. . . . . κοπρία *(2874)*

(†2874) **κοπρίον**, ου, τό [§3.C.c] *dung, manure*

(2875) **κόπτω**, fut. κόψω [§23.1.a] *to smite, cut; to cut off or down,* Matt. 21:8; Mark 11:8; mid. *to beat one's self* in mourning, *lament, bewail,* Luke 8:52; 23:27, et al.

κόπῳ, dat. sg. m. n. . . . . κόπος *(2873)*

κόπων, gen. pl. m. n. . . . . id.

κόρακας, acc. pl. m. n. . . . . κόραξ *(2876)*

(2876) **κόραξ**, ακος, ὁ [§4.2.b] *a raven, crow,* Luke 12:24

(2877) **κοράσιον**, όυ, τό, nom. sg. neut. n. [§3.C.c] (dimin. of κόρη) *a girl, damsel, maiden,* Matt. 9:24, 25; 14:11, et al.

κορασίῳ, dat. sg. neut. n. . . . . κοράσιον *(2877)*

(2878) **κορβᾶν**, ὁ, indecl. or κορβανᾶς, ᾶ, ὁ [§2.4] (Hebrew קָרְבָּן, Aramaic קוּרְבָּנָא, explained in Greek by δῶρον) *corban, a gift, offering, oblation, anything consecrated to God,* Mark 7:11; meton. *the sacred treasury,* Matt. 27:6 (GNT, MT, TR & NA | κορβάν, WH)

κορβανᾶν, acc. sg. m. n. . . . . κορβανᾶς *(†2878)*

(†2878) **κορβανᾶς**, ᾶ, ὁ, *temple treasury*

(2879) **Κορέ**, ὁ, pr. name, indecl. (Hebrew קֹרַח) *Core, Korah* (Jude 11, WH, MT & TR | Κόρε, GNT & NA)

(2880) **κορέννυμι**, fut. κορέσω, perf. pass. κεκόρεσμαι [§36.5] *to satiate, satisfy,* Acts 27:38; 1 Cor. 4:8

κορεσθέντες, nom. pl. m. aor. pass. part. . . . . κορέννυμι *(2880)*

Κορίνθιοι, voc. pl. m. adj. . . . . Κορίνθιος *(2881)*

(2881) **Κορίνθιος**, ία, ιον [§7.1] *Corinthian; an inhabitant of* Κόρινθος, *Corinth,* Acts 18:8; 2 Cor. 6:11

Κορινθίους, acc. pl. m. adj. (1 Cor. 16:24; 2 Cor. 13:13, TRs | GNT, WH, MT, TRb & NA omit) . . . . Κορίνθιος *(2881)*

Κορινθίων, gen. pl. m. adj. . . . . id.

Κόρινθον, acc. sg. f. n. . . . . Κόρινθος *(2882)*

(2882) **Κόρινθος**, ου, ἡ [§3.C.b] *Corinth,* a celebrated city of Greece

Κορίνθου, gen. sg. f. n. (Rom. 16:27, TRs | GNT, WH, MT, TRb & NA omit) . . . . Κόρινθος *(2882)*

Κορίνθῳ, dat. sg. f. n. . . . . id.

Κορνήλιε, voc. sg. m. n. . . . . Κορνήλιος *(2883)*

(2883) **Κορνήλιος**, ου, ὁ, nom. sg. m. n., *Cornelius,* a Latin pr. name

Κορνηλίου, gen. sg. m. n. . . . . Κορνήλιος *(2883)*

Κορνηλίῳ, dat. sg. m. n. (Acts 10:7, MT & TR | αὐτῷ, GNT, WH & NA) . . . . . . id.

(2884) **κόρος**, ου, ὁ [§3.C.a] (Hebrew כֹּר) *a cor,* the largest Jewish measure for things dry, equal

to the homer, and about fifteen bushels English, according to Josephus, (*Ant.* 15.341)

κόρους, acc. pl. m. n. . . . . κόρος *(2884)*

κοσμεῖν, pres. act. infin. . . . . κοσμέω *(2885)*

κοσμεῖτε, 2 pers. pl. pres. act. indic. . . . . . id.

(2885) **κοσμέω**, ῶ, fut. κοσμήσω, perf. κεκόσμηκα, aor. ἐκόσμησα [§16.P] *to arrange, set in order; to adorn, decorate, embellish,* Matt. 12:44; 23:29; *to prepare, put in readiness, trim,* Matt. 25:7; met. *to honor, dignify,* Tit. 2:10

κοσμικάς, acc. pl. f. adj. . . . . κοσμικός *(2886)*

κοσμικόν, acc. sg. neut. adj. . . . . . . κοσμικός *(2886)*

(2886) **κοσμικός**, ή, όν [§7.F.a] pr. *belonging to the universe,* in N.T. *accommodated to the present state of things, adapted to this world, worldly,* Tit. 2:12; τὸ κοσμικόν, as a subst. *the apparatus* for the service of the tabernacle, Heb. 9:1

κόσμιον, acc. sg. m. adj. . . . . κόσμιος *(2887)*

(2887) **κόσμιος**, ον [§7.2] *decorous, well-ordered,* 1 Tim. 2:9; 3:2

κοσμίῳ, dat. sg. f. adj. . . . . κόσμιος *(2887)*

κοσμοκράτορας, acc. pl. m. n. κοσμοκράτωρ *(2888)*

(2888) **κοσμοκράτωρ**, ορος, ὁ [§4.2.f] (κόσμος + κρατέω) pr. *monarch of the world;* in N.T. *a worldly prince, a power paramount in the world* of the unbelieving and ungodly, Eph. 6:12

κόσμον, acc. sg. m. n. . . . . κόσμος *(2889)*

(2889) **κόσμος**, ου, ὁ, nom. sg. m. n. [§3.C.a] pr. *order, regular disposition; ornament, decoration, embellishment,* 1 Pet. 3:3; *the world, the material universe,* Matt. 13:35, et al.; *the world, the aggregate of sensitive existence,* 1 Cor. 4:9; *the* lower *world, the* earth, Mark 16:15, et al.; *the world, the aggregate of mankind,* Matt. 5:14, et al.; *the world, the public,* John 7:4; in N.T. *the present order of things, the secular world,* John 18:36, et al.; *the human race* external to the Jewish nation, *the* heathen *world,* Rom. 11:12, 15; *the world* external to the Christian body, 1 John 3:1, 13, et al.; *the world or material system* of the Mosaic covenant, Gal. 4:3; Col. 2:8, 20

κόσμου, gen. sg. m. n. . . . . κόσμος *(2889)*

κόσμῳ, dat. sg. m. n. . . . . id.

κοσμῶσιν, 3 pers. pl. pres. act. subj. . κοσμέω *(2885)*

(2890) **Κούαρτος**, ου, ὁ, nom. sg. m. n., *Quartus,* a Latin pr. name, Rom. 16:23

(†2891) **κουμ**, Aramaic imper. *stand up* (Mark 5:41, GNT & NA | κούμ, WH | κοῦμι, MT & TR)

(2891) **κοῦμι** (Aramaic קוּמִי, 2 pers. sg. f. imper. of
קוּם, *to arise*) *cumi, arise* (Mark 5:41, MT
& TR | κουμ, GNT & NA | κούμ, WH)

(2892) **κουστωδία**, ας, ἡ [§2.B.b; 2.2] (Latin. *custo-
dia*) *a watch, guard*, Matt. 27:65, 66; 28:11
κουστωδίαν, acc. sg. f. n. . . . . κουστωδία (2892)
κουστωδίας, gen. sg. f. n. . . . . id.

(2893) **κουφίζω**, fut. κουφίσω [§26.1] (κοῦφος, *light*)
to lighten, make light or less heavy, Acts 27:38
κόφινοι, nom. pl. m. n. . . . . κόφινος (2894)

(2894) **κόφινος**, ου, ὁ [§3.C.a] *a basket*, Matt. 14:20;
16:9; Mark 6:43, et al.
κοφίνους, acc. pl. m. n. . . . . κόφινος (2894)
κοφίνων, gen. pl. m. n. (Mark 6:43, GNT,
WH & NA | κοφίνους, MT & TR) . . id.
κόψαντες, nom. pl. m. aor. act. part. (Mark
11:8, GNT, WH & NA | ἔκοπτον, MT
& TR) . . . . κόπτω (2875)
κόψονται, 3 pers. pl. fut. mid. dep. indic. . . id.
κραβάττοις, dat. pl. m. n. (Mark 6:55, GNT,
WH & NA | κραββάτοις, MT &
TR) . . . . κράβαττος (†2895)
κράβαττον, acc. sg. m. n. (GNT, WH & NA
| κράββατον, MT & TR) . . . . id.

(†2895) **κράβαττος**, ου, ὁ, *mattress, pallet, bed*
κραβάττου, gen. sg. m. n. (Acts 9:33, GNT,
WH & NA | κραββάτῳ, MT &
TR) . . . . κράβαττος (†2895)
κραβάττων, gen. pl. m. n. (Acts 5:15, GNT,
WH & NA | κραββάτων, MT & TR) id.
κραββάτοις, dat. pl. m. n. κράββατος (Mark
6:55, MT & TR | κραβάττοις, GNT,
WH & NA) . . . . κράββατος (2895)
κράββατον, acc. sg. m. n. (MT & TR |
κράβαττον, GNT, WH & NA) . . . . . . id.

(2895) **κράββατος**, ου, ὁ [§3.C.a] (Latin *grabatus*) *a
couch* capable of holding one person,
Mark 2:4, 9, 11, 12, et al.
κραββάτῳ, dat. sg. m. n. (Acts 9:33, MT &
TR | κραβάττου, GNT, WH &
NA) . . . . κράββατος (2895)
κραββάτων, gen. pl. m. n. (Acts 5:15, MT &
TR | κραβάττων, GNT, WH & NA) . id.
κράζει, 3 pers. sg. pres. act. indic. . . . . κράζω (2896)
κράζειν, pres. act. infin. . . . . id.
κράζομεν, 1 pers. pl. pres. act. indic. . . . . id.
κρᾶζον, nom. sg. neut. pres. act. part. (Acts 21:36,
MT & TR | κράζοντες, GNT, WH & NA) id.
κρᾶζον, acc. sg. neut. pres. act. part. (Gal. 4:6,
GNT, WH & NA | κράζον, MT & TR) id.
κράζοντα, nom. pl. neut. pres. act. part. (Luke
4:41, WH, MT & TR | κραυγάζοντα,
GNT & NA) . . . . id.
κράζοντας, acc. pl. m. pres. act. part. . . . id.
κράζοντες, nom. pl. m. pres. act. part. . . . id.

κραζόντων, gen. pl. m. pres. act. part. κράζω (2896)
κράζουσι(ν), 3 pers. pl. pres. act. indic. (Rev.
7:10, GNT, WH, MT & NA | κράζοντες,
TR) . . . . id.

(2896) **κράζω**, fut. κεκράξομαι, aor. ἔκραγον, later
fut. κράξω, aor. ἔκραξα, perf. κέκραγα,
with a pres. signif. [§26.2] *to utter a cry,*
Matt. 14:26, et al.; *to exclaim, vociferate,*
Matt. 9:27; John 1:15, et al.; *to cry* for
vengeance, James 5:4; *to cry* in supplication, Rom. 8:15; Gal. 4:6
κράζων, nom. sg. m. pres. act. part. . . κράζω (2896)

(2897) **κραιπάλη**, ης, ἡ [§2.B.a] *debauch*, Luke 21:34
κραιπάλῃ, dat. sg. f. n. (Luke 21:34, GNT,
MT, TR & NA | κρεπάλῃ,
WH) . . . . κραιπάλη (2897)

(2898) **κρανίον**, ου, τό [§3.C.c] (κάρα, *the head*) *a
skull*, Matt. 27:33; Mark 15:22; Luke
23:33; John 19:17
κρανίον, acc. sg. neut. n. . . . . κρανίον (2898)
κρανίου, gen. sg. neut. n. . . . . id.
κράξαν, nom. sg. neut. aor. act. part. (Mark
1:26, MT & TR | φωνῆσαν, GNT, WH
& NA) . . . . κράζω (2896)
κράξαντες, nom. pl. m. aor. act. part. . . . id.
κράξας, nom. sg. m. aor. act. part. . . . . id.
κράξουσιν, 3 pers. pl. fut. act. indic. (Luke
19:40, GNT, WH & NA | κεκράξονται,
MT & TR) . . . . id.
κράσπεδα, acc. pl. neut. n. . . . . . . κράσπεδον (2899)

(2899) **κράσπεδον**, ου, τό [§3.C.c] *a margin, border,*
in N.T. *a fringe, tuft, tassel*, Matt. 9:20;
14:36; 23:5, et al.
κρασπέδου, gen. sg. neut. n. . . . . . κράσπεδον (2899)
κραταιάν, acc. sg. f. adj. . . . . . . κραταιός (2900)

(2900) **κραταιός**, ά, όν [§7.1] *strong, mighty, powerful*, 1 Pet. 5:6
κραταιοῦσθε, 2 pers. pl. pres. pass. imper.
[§21.U] . . . . κραταιόω (2901)

(2901) **κραταιόω**, ῶ, fut. κραταιώσω [§20.T] *to
strengthen, render strong, corroborate,
confirm*; pass. *to grow strong, acquire
strength*, Luke 1:80; 2:40; Eph. 3:16; *to be
firm, resolute*, 1 Cor. 16:13
κραταιωθῆναι, aor. pass. infin. . . . . κραταιόω (2901)
κράτει, dat. sg. neut. n. {Eph. 6:10} . κράτος (2904)
κράτει, 2 pers. sg. pres. act. imper.
{Rev. 3:11} . . . . κρατέω (2902)
κρατεῖν, pres. act. infin. . . . . id.
κρατεῖς, 2 pers. sg. pres. act. indic. . . . . id.
κρατεῖσθαι, pres. pass. infin. [§17.Q] . . . . id.
κρατεῖτε, 2 pers. pl. pres. act. indic. {Mark 7:8} id.
κρατεῖτε, 2 pers. pl. pres. act. imper.
{2 Thess. 2:15} . . . . id.

(2902) **κρατέω**, ῶ, fut. κρατήσω, perf. κεκράτηκα,

aor. ἐκράτησα [§16.P] pr. *to be strong; to be superior* to any one, *subdue, vanquish*, Acts 2:24; *to get into one's power, lay hold of, seize, apprehend*, Matt. 14:3; 18:28; 21:46; *to gain, compass, attain*, Acts 27:13; in N.T. *to lay hold of, grasp, clasp*, Matt. 9:25; Mark 1:31; 5:41; *to retain, keep under reserve*, Mark 9:10; met. *to hold fast, observe*, Mark 7:3, 8; 2 Thess. 2:15; *to hold to, adhere to*, Acts 3:11; Col. 2:19; *to restrain, hinder, repress*, Luke 24:16; Rev. 7:1; *to retain, not to remit*, sins, John 20:23

κρατῆσαι, aor. act. infin. . . . . κρατέω *(2902)*
κρατήσαντες, nom. pl. m. aor. act. part. . id.
κρατήσας, nom. sg. m. aor. act. part. . . . id.
κρατήσατε, 2 pers. pl. aor. act. imper. . . . id.
κρατήσει, 3 pers. sg. fut. act. indic. . . . . . id.
κρατήσωσι(ν), 3 pers. pl. aor. act. subj. . . id.
κρατῆτε, 2 pers. pl. pres. act. subj. . . . . . . id.
κράτιστε, voc. sg. m. adj. . . . . . . κράτιστος *(2903)*
(2903) **κράτιστος**, η, ον [§8.5] (superl. from κρατύς, *strong*) *strongest;* in N.T. κράτιστε, a term of respect, *most excellent, noble, or illustrious*, Luke 1:3; Acts 23:26; 24:3; 26:25
κρατίστῳ, dat. sg. m. adj. . . . . κράτιστος *(2903)*
(2904) **κράτος**, ους, το, nom. sg. neut. n. [§5.E.b] *strength, power, might, force*, Acts 19:20; Eph. 1:19; meton. *a display of might*, Luke 1:51; *power, sway, dominion*, Heb. 2:14; 1 Pet. 4:11; 5:11, et al. {Rev. 1:6}
κράτος, acc. sg. neut. n. {Luke 1:51} . κράτος *(2904)*
κρατοῦντας, acc. pl. m. pres. act.
part. . . . . κρατέω *(2902)*
κρατοῦντες, nom. pl. m. pres. act. part. . . id.
κρατοῦντος, gen. sg. m. pres. act. part. . . id.
κράτους, gen. sg. neut. n. . . . . κράτος *(2904)*
κρατοῦσιν, 3 pers. pl. pres. act. indic. κρατέω *(2902)*
κρατῶμεν, 1 pers. pl. pres. act. subj. . . . . id.
κρατῶν, nom. sg. m. pres. act. part. . . . . id.
κραυγάζοντα, nom. pl. neut. pres. act. part.
(Luke 4:41, GNT & NA | κράζοντας, WH, MT & TR) . . . . κραυγάζω *(2905)*
κραυγαζόντων, gen. pl. m. pres. act. part. id.
(2905) **κραυγάζω**, fut. κραυγάσω, aor. ἐκραύγασα [§26.1] *to cry out, exclaim, vociferate*, Matt. 12:19; 15:22, et al.
κραυγάσει, 3 pers. sg. fut. act.
indic. . . . . κραυγάζω *(2905)*
(2906) **κραυγή**, ῆς, ἡ, nom. sg. f. n. [§2.B.a] *a cry, outcry, clamor, vociferation*, Matt. 25:6; Acts 23:9; Eph. 4:31; Rev. 14:18; *a cry* of sorrow, *wailing, lamentation*, Rev. 21:4; *a cry* for help, *earnest supplication*, Heb. 5:7
κραυγῇ, dat. sg. f. n. . . . . κραυγή *(2906)*
κραυγῆς, gen. sg. f. n. . . . . id.

κρέα, acc. pl. neut. n. . . . . κρέας *(2907)*
(2907) **κρέας**, ατος, τό, pl. κρέατα, κρέα [§5.E.j] *flesh, meat*, Rom. 14:21; 1 Cor. 8:13
κρεῖσσον, nom. sg. neut. adj.
{Phil. 1:23} . . . . κρείσσων *(†2908)*
κρεῖσσον, acc. sg. neut. adj. {1 Cor. 7:38} id.
κρείσσονα, acc. pl. neut. adj. (Heb. 6:9, GNT, WH, MT & NA | κρείττονα, TR) . . . id.
(†2908) **κρείσσων**, or κρείττων, ον [§8.5] (used as the compar. of ἀγαθός) *better, more useful or profitable, more conducive to good*, 1 Cor. 7:9, 38; *superior, more excellent, of a higher nature, more valuable*, Heb. 1:4; 6:9; 7:7, 19, 22, et al.
κρεῖττον, nom. sg. neut. adj.
{1 Cor. 7:9} . . . . κρείττων *(2909)*
κρεῖττον, acc. sg. neut. adj. {Heb. 11:40} . id.
κρείττονα, acc. sg. f. adj. (Heb. 10:34, κρείττονα, GNT, MT, TR & NA | κρείσσονα, WH) . . . . id.
κρείττονα, acc. pl. neut. adj. (1 Cor. 12:31; Heb. 12:24, MT & TR and Heb. 6:9 TR | μείζονα, 1 Cor. 12:31, GNT, WH & NA | κρείσσονα, Heb. 6:9, GNT, WH, MT & NA | κρεῖττον, Heb. 12:24, GNT, WH & NA) . . . . id.
κρείττονος, gen. sg. m. adj. {Heb. 7:7} . . id.
κρείττονος, gen. sg. f. adj. {Heb. 7:19} . . id.
κρείττοσι(ν), dat. pl. f. adj. . . . . id.
(2909) **κρείττων**, or κρείσσων, nom. sg. m. adj. (used as the compar. of ἀγαθός) *better, more useful or profitable, more conducive to good*, 1 Cor. 7:9, 38; *superior, more excellent, of a higher nature, more valuable*, Heb. 1:4; 6:9; 7:7, 19, 22, et al.
κρεμάμενον, acc. sg. neut. pres. mid.
part. . . . . κρεμάννυμι *(2910)*
κρεμάμενος, nom. sg. m. pres. mid. part. id.
(2910) **κρεμάννυμι**, fut. κρεμάσω, aor. ἐκρέμασα, aor. pass. ἐρεμάσθην [§36.5] *to hang, suspend*, Acts 5:30; 10:39; pass. *to be hung, suspended*, Matt. 18:6; Luke 23:39; mid. κρέμαμαι, *to hang, be suspended*, Acts 28:4; Gal. 3:13, et al.; met. κρέμαμαι ἐν, *to hang upon, to be referable to* as an ultimate principle, Matt. 22:40
κρέμανται, 3 pers. pl. pres. pass. indic. (Matt. 22:40, MT & TR | κρέμαται, GNT, WH & NA) . . . . κρεμάννυμι *(2910)*
κρεμάσαντες, nom. pl. m. aor. act. part. . id.
κρεμασθέντων, gen. pl. m. aor. pass. part. id.
κρεμασθῇ, 3 pers. sg. aor. pass. subj. . . . . id.
κρέμαται, 3 pers. sg. pres. pass. indic. (Matt. 22:40, GNT, WH & NA | κρέμανται, MT & TR) . . . . id.

(2911) **κρημνός**, οῦ, ὁ [§3.C.a] *a hanging steep, precipice, a steep bank,* Matt. 8:32; Mark 5:13; Luke 8:33

κρημνοῦ, gen. sg. m. n. . . . . κρημνός *(2911)*

(2912) **Κρής**, ητός, ὁ [§4.2.c] pl. Κρῆτες, *a Cretan, an inhabitant of* Κρήτη, Acts 2:11; Tit. 1:12

(2913) **Κρήσκης**, εντος, ὁ, nom. sg. m. n. [§4.2.d] *Crescens,* a Latin pr. name, 2 Tim. 4:10

Κρῆτες, nom. pl. m. n. . . . . Κρής *(2912)*

(2914) **Κρήτη**, ης, ἡ [§2.B.a] *Crete,* a large island in the eastern part of the Mediterranean

Κρήτῃ, dat. sg. f. n. . . . . Κρήτη *(2914)*

Κρήτην, acc. sg. f. n. . . . . id.

Κρήτης, gen. sg. f. n. . . . . id.

Κρητῶν, gen. pl. m. n. (Tit. 3:15, TRs | GNT, WH, MT, TRb & NA omit) . . . . Κρής *(2912)*

(2915) **κριθή**, ῆς, ἡ [§2.B.a] *barley,* Rev. 6:6

κριθῆναι, aor. pass. infin. . . . . κρίνω *(2919)*

κριθῆς, gen. sg. f. n. (Rev. 6:6, MT & TR | κριθῶν, GNT, WH & NA) . . . . κριθή *(2915)*

κριθήσεσθε, 2 pers. pl. fut. pass. indic. [§27.3] . . . . κρίνω *(2919)*

κριθήσονται, 3 pers. pl. fut. pass. indic. . . id.

κριθῆτε, 2 pers. pl. aor. pass. subj. . . . . . id.

(2916) **κρίθινος**, η, ον [§7.F.a] *made of barley,* John 6:9, 13

κριθίνους, acc. pl. m. adj. . . . . κρίθινος *(2916)*

κριθίνων, gen. pl. m. adj. . . . . id.

κριθῶν, gen. pl. f. n. (Rev. 6:6, GNT, WH & NA | κριθῆς, MT & TR) . . . . κριθή *(2915)*

κριθῶσι(ν), 3 pers. pl. aor. pass. subj. . . κρίνω *(2919)*

(2917) **κρίμα**, ατος, τό nom. sg. neut. n. [§4.D.c] *judgment; a sentence, award,* Matt. 7:2; *a judicial sentence,* Luke 23:40; 24:20; Rom. 2:2; 5:16, et al.; *an adverse sentence,* Matt. 23:14; Rom. 13:2; 1 Tim. 5:12; James 3:1; *judgment, administration of justice,* John 9:39; Acts 24:25, et al.; *execution of justice,* 1 Pet. 4:17; *a lawsuit;* 1 Cor. 6:7; in N.T. *judicial visitation,* 1 Cor. 11:29; 2 Pet. 2:3; *an administrative decree,* Rom. 11:33 {Rom. 2:2}

κρίμα, acc. sg. neut. n. {Rom. 2:3} . . . . κρίμα *(2917)*

κρίματα, nom. pl. neut. n. {Rom. 11:33} . id.

κρίματα, acc. pl. neut. n. {1 Cor. 6:7} . . . id.

κρίματι, dat. sg. neut. n. . . . . id.

κρίματος, gen. sg. neut. n. . . . . id.

κρίνα, acc. pl. neut. n. . . . . κρίνον *(2918)*

κρῖναι, aor. act. infin. [§27.1.f] (1 Pet. 4:5, GNT, MT, TR & NA | κρίνοντι, WH) . . . . κρίνω *(2919)*

κρίναντας, acc. pl. m. aor. act. part. . . . . id.

κρίναντες, nom. pl. m. aor. act. part. . . . . id.

κρίναντος, gen. sg. m. aor. act. part. . . . . id.

κρίνας, nom. sg. m. aor. act. part. (Rev. 18:8,

GNT, WH, MT & NA | κρίνων, TR) . . . . κρίνω *(2919)*

κρίνατε, 2 pers. pl. aor. act. imper. . . . . . . id.

κρίνει, 3 pers. sg. pres. act. indic. {John 7:51} id.

κρινεῖ, 3 pers. sg. fut. act. indic. {John 12:48} id.

κρίνειν, pres. act. infin. . . . . id.

κρίνεις, 2 pers. sg. pres. act. indic. . . . . . . id.

κρίνεσθαι, pres. pass. infin. . . . . id.

κρίνεται, 3 pers. sg. pres. pass. indic. . . . . id.

κρίνετε, 2 pers. pl. pres. act. indic. {John 8:15} . . . . id.

κρίνετε, 2 pers. pl. pres. act. imper. {John 7:24} . . . . id.

κρινέτω, 3 pers. sg. pres. act. imper. . . . . . id.

κρίνῃ, 3 pers. sg. pres. act. subj. . . . . id.

κρίνομαι, 1 pers. sg. pres. pass. indic. . . . . id.

κρινόμενοι, nom. pl. m. pres. pass. part. . id.

κρινόμενος, nom. sg. m. pres. pass. part. . id.

(2918) **κρίνον**, ου, τό [§3.C.c] *a lily,* Matt. 6:28; Luke 12:27

κρίνοντα, acc. sg. m. pres. act. part. . . . κρίνω *(2919)*

κρίνοντες, nom. pl. m. pres. act. part. . . . id.

κρίνοντι, dat. sg. m. pres. act. part. . . . . . id.

κρινοῦμεν, 1 pers. pl. fut. act. indic. . . . . . id.

κρινοῦσι(ν), 3 pers. pl. fut. act. indic. . . . . id.

(2919) **κρίνω**, 1 pers. sg. pres. act. indic., fut. κρινῶ, aor. ἔκρινα, perf. κέκρικα, perf. pass. κέκριμαι, aor. pass. ἐκρίθην, pr. *to separate; to make a distinction between; to exercise judgment upon; to estimate,* Rom. 14:5; *to judge, to assume censorial power over, to call to account,* Matt. 7:1; Luke 6:37; Rom. 2:1, 3; 14:3, 4, 10, 13; Col. 2:16; James 4:11, 12; *to bring under question,* Rom. 14:22; *to judge judicially, to try* as a judge, John 18:31, et al.; *to bring to trial,* Acts 13:27; *to sentence,* Luke 19:22; John 7:51; *to resolve on, decree,* Acts 16:4; Rev. 16:5; absol. *to decide, determine, resolve,* Acts 3:13; 15:19; 27:1, et al.; *to deem,* Acts 13:46; *to form a judgment, pass judgment,* John 8:15, et al.; pass. *to be brought to trial,* Acts 25:10, 20; Rom. 3:4, et al.; *to be brought to account, to incur arraignment, be arraigned,* 1 Cor. 10:29; mid. *to go to law, litigate,* Matt. 5:40; in N.T. *to judge, to visit judicially,* Acts 7:7; 1 Cor. 11:31, 32; 1 Pet. 4:6; *to judge, to right, to vindicate,* Heb. 10:30; *to administer government over, to govern,* Matt. 19:28; Luke 22:30 {John 5:30}

κρινῶ, 1 pers. sg. fut. act. indic. {Luke 19:22} . . . . κρίνω *(2919)*

κρίνω, 1 pers. sg. aor. act. subj. {John 8:16} id.

κρίνωμεν, 1 pers. pl. pres. act. subj. . . . . . id.

κρίνων, nom. sg. m. pres. act. part. . . . . . id.

κρίσει, dat. sg. f. n. . . . . κρίσις *(2920)*
κρίσεις, nom. pl. f. n. . . . . id.
κρίσεως, gen. sg. f. n. . . . . id.
κρίσιν, acc. sg. f. n. . . . . id.

(2920) **κρίσις**, εως, ἡ, nom. sg. f. n., pr. *distinction; discrimination; judgment, decision, award,* John 5:30; 7:24; 8:16; *a judicial sentence,* John 3:19; James 2:13, et al.; *an adverse sentence,* Matt. 23:33; Mark 3:29, et al.; *judgment, judicial process, trial,* Matt. 10:15; John 5:24; 12:31; 16:8, et al.; *judgment, administration of justice,* John 5:22, 27; in N.T. *a court of justice, tribunal,* Matt. 5:21, 22; *an impeachment,* 2 Pet. 2:11; Jude 9; from the Hebrew, *justice, equity,* Matt. 12:18, 20; 23:23; Luke 11:42

Κρίσπον, acc. sg. m. n. . . . . Κρίσπος *(2921)*

(2921) **Κρίσπος**, ου, ὁ, nom. sg. m. n. [§3.C.a] *Crispus,* a Latin pr. name

κριταί, nom. pl. m. n. . . . . κριτής *(2923)*
κριτάς, acc. pl. m. n. . . . . id.
κριτῇ, dat. sg. m. n. . . . . id.
κριτήν, acc. sg. m. n. . . . . id.
κριτήρια, acc. pl. neut. n. . . . . κριτήριον *(2922)*

(2922) **κριτήριον**, ου, τό [§3.C.c] pr. *a standard or means by which to judge, criterion; a court of justice, tribunal,* James 2:6; *a cause, controversy,* 1 Cor. 6:2, 4

κριτηρίων, gen. pl. neut. n. . . . . κριτήριον *(2922)*

(2923) **κριτής**, οῦ, ὁ, nom. sg. m. n. [§2.B.c] *a judge,* Matt. 5:25, et al.; from the Hebrew, *a magistrate, ruler,* Acts 13:20; 24:10

(2924) **κριτικός**, ή, όν, nom. sg. m. adj. [§7.F.a] *able or quick to discern or judge,* Heb. 4:12

κρούειν, pres. act. infin. . . . . κρούω *(2925)*
κρούετε, 2 pers. pl. pres. act. imper. . . . . . id.
κρούοντι, dat. sg. m. pres. act. part. . . . . . id.
κρούσαντος, gen. sg. m. aor. act. part. . . . id.

(2925) **κρούω**, 1 pers. sg. pres. act. indic., fut. κρούσω [§13.M] *to knock* at a door, Matt. 7:7, 8; Luke 11:9, 10; 13:25, et al.

κρούων, nom. sg. m. pres. act. part. . . . κρούω *(2925)*
κρυβῆναι, 2 aor. pass. infin. [§24.8.a] κρύπτω *(2928)*
κρυπτά, nom. pl. neut. adj.
{1 Cor. 14:25} . . . . κρυπτός *(2927)*
κρυπτά, acc. pl. neut. adj. {1 Cor. 4:5} . . . id.

(2926) **κρύπτη**, ης, ἡ [§2.B.a] *a vault or closet, a cell for storage,* Luke 11:33

κρύπτην, acc. sg. f. n. (Luke 11:33, GNT, WH, MT & NA | κρυπτόν, TR) . κρύπτη *(2926)*
κρυπτόν, nom. sg. neut. adj.
{Luke 12:2} . . . . κρυπτός *(2927)*
κρυπτόν, acc. sg. neut. adj. (Luke 11:33, TR | κρύπτην, GNT, WH, MT & NA) . . . id.

(2927) **κρυπτός**, ή, όν, nom. sg. m. adj. [§7.F.a] *hidden, concealed, secret, clandestine,* Matt. 6:4, 6, 18, et al.; τὰ κρυπτά, *secrets,* Rom. 2:16; 1 Cor. 14:25

(2928) **κρύπτω**, fut. κρύψω, aor. ἔκρυψα [§23.1.a; 23.2] perf. pass. κέκρυμμαι [§23.7.8] 2 aor. pass. ἐκρύβην [§24.8.a] *to hide, conceal,* Matt. 5:14, et al.; in N.T. *to lay up in store,* Col. 3:3; Rev. 2:17; κεκρυμμένος, *concealed, secret,* John 19:38

κρυπτῷ, dat. sg. neut. adj. . . . . κρυπτός *(2927)*
κρυσταλλίζοντι, dat. sg. m. pres. act.
part. . . . . κρυσταλλίζω *(2929)*

(2929) **κρυσταλλίζω**, fut. κρυσταλλίσω [§26.1] *to be clear, brilliant like crystal,* Rev. 21:11

κρύσταλλον, acc. sg. m. n. . . . . . κρύσταλλος *(2930)*

(2930) **κρύσταλλος**, ου, ὁ [§3.C.a] (κρύος, *cold*) pr. *clear ice; crystal,* Rev. 4:6; 22:1

κρυστάλλῳ, dat. sg. m. n. . . . . . κρύσταλλος *(2930)*

(‡2927) **κρυφαῖος**, α, ον [§7.1] *secret, hidden,* Matt. 6:18

κρυφαίῳ, dat. sg. neut. adj. (Matt. 6:18, GNT, WH & NA | κρύπτῳ, MT & TR) . . . . κρυφαῖος *(‡2927)*

(†2931) **κρυφῇ**, adv., *in secret, secretly, not openly,* Eph. 5:12

κρύψατε, 2 pers. pl. aor. act. imper. . . κρύπτω *(2928)*

(2932) **κτάομαι**, ῶμαι, fut. κτήσομαι [§19.S] *to get, procure, provide,* Matt. 10:9; *to make gain, gain,* Luke 18:12; *to purchase,* Acts 8:20; 22:28; *to be the cause or occasion of purchasing,* Acts 1:18; *to preserve, save,* Luke 21:19; *to get under control, to be winning the mastery over,* 1 Thess. 4:4; perf. κέκτημαι, *to possess*

κτᾶσθαι, pres. mid./pass. dep. infin. . κτάομαι *(2932)*

(2933) **κτῆμα**, ατος, τό [§4.D.c] *a possession, property,* and spc. *real estate,* Matt. 19:22; Mark 10:22; Acts 2:45; 5:1

κτῆμα, acc. sg. neut. n. . . . . κτῆμα *(2933)*
κτήματα, acc. pl. neut. n. . . . . id.
κτήνη, acc. pl. neut. n. . . . . κτῆνος *(2934)*

(2934) **κτῆνος**, ους, τό [§5.E.b] pr. *property,* generally used in the plural, τὰ κτήνη; *property in animals; a beast of burden,* Luke 10:34; Acts 23:24; *beasts, cattle,* 1 Cor. 15:39; Rev. 18:13

κτῆνος, acc. sg. neut. n. . . . . κτῆνος *(2934)*
κτηνῶν, gen. pl. neut. n. . . . . id.
κτήσασθε, 2 pers. pl. aor. mid. dep. imper.
(Luke 21:19, GNT, MT, TR & NA | κτήσεσθε, WH) . . . . κτάομαι *(2932)*
κτήσεσθε, 2 pers. pl. fut. mid. dep. indic.
(Luke 21:19, WH | κτήσασθε, GNT, MT, TR & NA) . . . . id.

κτήσησθε, 2 pers. pl. aor. mid. dep.
   subj. . . . . κτάομαι *(2932)*
κτήτορες, nom. pl. m. n. . . . . κτήτωρ *(2935)*
(2935) **κτήτωρ,** ορος, ὁ [§4.2.f] *a possessor, owner,*
   Acts 4:34
(2936) **κτίζω,** fut. κτίσω, aor. ἔκτισα, perf. pass.
   ἔκτισμαι [§26.1] pr. *to reduce from a state*
   of disorder and wildness; in N.T. *to call*
   into being, to create, Mark 13:19, et al.;
   to call into individual existence, to frame,
   Eph. 2:15; *to create* spiritually, *to invest*
   with a spiritual *frame,* Eph. 2:10; 4:24
κτίσαντα, acc. sg. m. aor. act. part. . . . κτίζω *(2936)*
κτίσαντι, dat. sg. m. aor. act. part. . . . . . . id.
κτίσαντος, gen. sg. m. aor. act. part. . . . . id.
κτίσας, nom. sg. m. aor. act. part. (Matt.
   19:4, GNT, WH & NA | ποιήσας, MT
   & TR) . . . . id.
κτίσει, dat. sg. f. n. . . . . κτίσις *(2937)*
κτίσεως, gen. sg. f. n. . . . . id.
κτίση, 3 pers. sg. aor. act. subj. . . . . κτίζω *(2936)*
κτισθέντα, acc. sg. m. aor. pass. part. . . . . id.
κτισθέντες, nom. pl. m. aor. pass. part. . . id.
(2937) **κτίσις,** εως, ἡ, nom. sg. f. n. [§5.E.c] pr. *a*
   framing, founding; in N.T. *creation, the act*
   of creating, Rom. 1:20; *creation, the ma-*
   terial universe, Mark 10:6; 13:19; Heb.
   9:11; 2 Pet. 3:4; *a created thing, a creature,*
   Rom. 1:25; 8:39; Col. 1:15; Heb. 4:13; *the*
   human *creation,* Mark 16:15; Rom. 8:19,
   20, 21, 22; Col. 1:23; *a spiritual creation,*
   2 Cor. 5:17; Gal. 6:15; *an institution, or-*
   dinance, 1 Pet. 2:13
(2938) **κτίσμα,** ατος, τό, nom. sg. neut. n. [§4.D.c]
   pr. *a thing founded;* in N.T. *a created be-*
   ing, creature, 1 Tim. 4:4; James 1:18, et al.
κτισμάτων, gen. pl. neut. n. . . . . κτίσμα *(2938)*
κτίστῃ, dat. sg. m. n. . . . . κτίστης *(†2939)*
(†2939) **κτίστης,** ου, ὁ [§2.B.c] *a founder;* in N.T. *a*
   creator, 1 Pet. 4:19
κτῶμαι, 1 pers. sg. pres. mid./pass. dep. indic.
   contr. . . . . κτάομαι *(2932)*
(2940) **κυβεία,** ας, ἡ [§2.B.b; 2.2] (κυβεύω, *to play*
   at dice; from κύβος, *a cube, die*) pr. *dic-*
   ing; met. *sleight, versatile artifice,* Eph.
   4:14
κυβείᾳ, dat. sg. f. n. (Eph. 4:14, GNT, MT,
   TR & NA | κυβίᾳ, WH) . . . . κυβεία *(2940)*
κυβερνήσεις, acc. pl. f. n. . . . . κυβέρνησις *(2941)*
(2941) **κυβέρνησις,** εως, ἡ [§5.E.c] (κυβερνάω, *to*
   steer, direct) *government, office of a gov-*
   ernor or director; meton. *a director,* 1 Cor.
   12:28
κυβερνήτῃ, dat. sg. m. n. . . . . . . κυβερνήτης *(2942)*
(2942) **κυβερνήτης,** ου, ὁ, nom. sg. m. n. [§2.B.c] *a*

pilot, helmsman, Acts 27:11; Rev. 18:17
(‡2944) **κυκλεύω,** fut. κυκλεύσω, aor. ἐκύκλευσα
   [§13.M] *to encircle, encompass,* Rev. 20:9
(2943) **κυκλόθεν,** adv., *around, round about,* Rev.
   4:3, 4, 8; 5:11
(‡2945) **κύκλος,** ου, ὁ [§3.C.a] *a circle;* in N.T. κύκλῳ,
   adverbially, *round, round about, around,*
   Mark 3:34; 6:6, 36, et al.
κυκλουμένην, acc. sg. f. pres. pass. part.
   [§21.U] . . . . κυκλόω *(2944)*
(2944) **κυκλόω,** ῶ, fut. κυκλώσω, aor. ἐκύκλωσα
   [§20.T] *to encircle, surround, encompass,*
   come around, John 10:24; Acts 14:20; spc.
   to beleaguer, Luke 21:20; Rev. 20:9; *to*
   march round, Heb. 11:30
(2945) κύκλῳ, dat. sg. m. n. . . . . . κύκλος *(‡2945)*
κυκλωθέντα, nom. pl. neut. aor. pass.
   part. . . . . κυκλόω *(2944)*
κυκλωσάντων, gen. pl. m. aor. act. part.   id.
(2946) **κύλισμα,** ατος, τό [§4.D.c] pr. *a rolling thing;*
   in N.T. *a place of rolling or wallowing,*
   wallowing-place, 2 Pet. 2:22
κύλισμα, acc. sg. neut. n. (2 Pet. 2:22, MT
   & TR | κυλισμόν, GNT, WH &
   NA) . . . . κύλισμα *(2946)*
κυλισμόν, acc. sg. m. n. (2 Pet. 2:22, GNT,
   WH & NA | κύλισμα, MT &
   TR) . . . . κυλισμός *(†2946)*
(†2946) **κυλισμός,** οῦ, ὁ, *a rolling, wallowing*
(†2947) **κυλίω,** fut. κυλίσω, aor. ἐκύλισα [§13.M] (a
   later form for κυλίνδω) *to roll;* mid. *to roll*
   one's self, to wallow, Mark 9:20
κυλλόν, acc. sg. m. adj. . . . . κυλλός *(2948)*
(2948) **κυλλός,** ή, όν [§7.F.a] pr. *crooked, bent,*
   maimed, lame, crippled, Matt. 18:8, et al.
κυλλούς, acc. pl. m. adj. . . . . κυλλός *(2948)*
(2949) **κῦμα,** ατος, τό [§4.D.c] *a wave, surge, billow,*
   Matt. 8:24; 14:24, et al.
κύματα, nom. pl. neut. n. . . . . κῦμα *(2949)*
κυμάτων, gen. pl. neut. n. . . . . id.
(2950) **κύμβαλον,** ου, τό, nom. sg. neut. n. [§3.C.c]
   (κύμβος, *a hollow*) *a cymbal,* 1 Cor. 13:1
(2951) **κύμινον,** ου, τό, *cumin, cuminum salivum* of
   Linnaeus, a plant, a native of Egypt and
   Syria, whose seeds are of an aromatic,
   warm, bitterish taste, with a strong but not
   disagreeable smell, and used by the ancients
   as a condiment, Matt. 23:23
κύμινον, acc. sg. neut. n. . . . . κύμινον *(2951)*
κυνάρια, nom. pl. neut. n. . . . . κυνάριον *(2952)*
κυναρίοις, dat. pl. neut. n. . . . . id.
(2952) **κυνάριον,** ου, τό [§3.C.c] (dimin. of κύων) *a*
   little dog; a cur, Matt. 15:26, 27; Mark
   7:27, 28
κύνας, acc. pl. m. n. . . . . κύων *(2965)*

κύνες, nom. pl. m. n. . . . . κύων *(2965)*

Κύπριοι, nom. pl. m. n. . . . . Κύπριος *(2953)*

(2953) **Κύπριος**, ου, ὁ, nom. sg. m. n. [§3.C.a] *a Cypriot, an inhabitant of Cyprus*, Acts 4:36; 11:20; 21:16

Κυπρίῳ, dat. sg. m. n. . . . . Κύπριος *(2953)*

Κύπρον, acc. sg. f. n. . . . . Κύπρος *(2954)*

(2954) **Κύπρος**, ου, ἡ [§3.C.b] *Cyprus*, an island in the eastern part of the Mediterranean, Acts 11:19, et al.

Κύπρου, gen. sg. f. n. . . . . Κύπρος *(2954)*

(2955) **κύπτω**, fut. κύψω, aor. ἔκυψα [§23.1.a; 23.2] *to bend forwards, stoop down*, Mark 1:7; John 8:6, 8

Κυρηναῖοι, nom. pl. m. n. . . . . . . Κυρηναῖος *(2956)*

Κυρηναῖον, acc. sg. m. n. . . . . id.

(2956) **Κυρηναῖος**, ου, ὁ, nom. sg. m. n. [§3.C.a] *a Cyrenian, an inhabitant of Cyrene*, Matt. 27:32, et al.

Κυρηναίου, gen. sg. m. n. (Luke 23:26, MT & TR | Κυρηναῖον, GNT, WH & NA) . . . . Κυρηναῖος *(2956)*

Κυρηναίων, gen. pl. m. n. . . . . id.

(2957) **Κυρήνη**, ης, ἡ [§2.B.a] *Cyrene*, a city founded by a colony of Greeks, in Northern Africa, Acts 2:10

Κυρήνην, acc. sg. f. n. . . . . Κυρήνη *(2957)*

(2958) **Κυρήνιος**, ου, ὁ [§3.C.a] *Cyrenius* (perhaps *Quirinus*) pr. name, Luke 2:2

Κυρηνίου, gen. sg. m. n. . . . . Κυρήνιος *(2958)*

(2959) **κυρία**, ας, ἡ [§2.B.b; 2.2] *a lady*, 1 John 1, 5

κυρία, voc. sg. f. n. . . . . κυρία *(2959)*

κυρίᾳ, dat. sg. f. n. . . . . id.

κυριακῇ, dat. sg. f. adj. . . . . κυριακός *(2960)*

κυριακόν, acc. sg. neut. adj. . . . . id.

(2960) **κυριακός**, ή, όν [§7.F.a] *pertaining to the Lord Jesus Christ, the Lord's*, 1 Cor. 11:20; Rev. 1:10

κύριε, voc. sg. m. n. . . . . κύριος *(2962)*

κυριεύει, 3 pers. sg. pres. act. indic. . . κυριεύω *(2961)*

κυριεύομεν, 1 pers. pl. pres. act. indic. . . . id.

κυριευόντων, gen. pl. m. pres. act. part. . . . id.

κυριεύουσιν, 3 pers. pl. pres. act. indic. . . . id.

κυριεύσει, 3 pers. sg. fut. act. indic. . . . . id.

κυριεύσῃ, 3 pers. sg. aor. act. subj. . . . . . id.

(2961) **κυριεύω**, fut. κυριεύσω [§13.M] Rom. 14:9; aor. ἐκυρίευσα, *to be lord over, to be possessed of, mastery over*, Rom. 6:9, 14; 7:1; 2 Cor. 1:24; *to exercise sway over*, Luke 22:25

κύριοι, nom. pl. m. n. {Acts 16:19} . . . κύριος *(2962)*

κύριοι, voc. pl. m. n. {Acts 16:30} . . . . . . id.

κυρίοις, dat. pl. m. n. . . . . id.

κύριον, acc. sg. m. n. . . . . id.

(2962) **κύριος**, ου, ὁ, nom. sg. m. n. [§3.C.a] *a lord,*

master, Matt. 12:8, et al.; *an owner, possessor*, Matt. 20:8, et al.; *a potentate, sovereign*, Acts 25:26; *a power, deity*, 1 Cor. 8:5; *the Lord, Jehovah*, Matt. 1:22, et al.; *the Lord* Jesus Christ, Matt. 24:42; Mark 16:19; Luke 10:1; John 4:1; 1 Cor. 4:5, et al. freq.; κύριε, a term of respect of various force, *Sir, Lord*, Matt. 13:27; Acts 9:6, et al. freq.

(2963) **κυριότης**, ητος, ἡ [§4.2.c] *lordship; constituted authority*, Eph. 1:21; 2 Pet. 2:10; Jude 8; pl. *authorities, potentates*, Col. 1:16

κυριότητα, acc. sg. f. n. . . . . κυριότης *(2963)*

κυριότητες, nom. pl. f. n. . . . . id.

κυριότητος, gen. sg. f. n. . . . . id.

κυρίου, gen. sg. m. n. . . . . κύριος *(2962)*

κυρίῳ, dat. sg. m. n. . . . . id.

κυρίων, gen. pl. m. n. . . . . id.

(2964) **κυρόω**, ῶ, fut. κυρώσω, perf. κεκύρωκα [§20.T] (κῦρος, *authority, confirmation*) *to confirm, ratify*, Gal. 3:15; *to assure*, 2 Cor. 2:8

κυρῶσαι, aor. act. infin. . . . . κυρόω *(2964)*

κυσί(ν), dat. pl. m. n. . . . . κύων *(2965)*

κύψας, nom. sg. m. aor. act. part. . . . . κύπτω *(2955)*

(2965) **κύων**, κυνός, ὁ, nom. sg. m. n. [§6.4.e] *a dog*, Luke 16:21; 2 Pet. 2:22; met. *a dog, a religious corrupter*, Phil. 3:2; *miscreant*, Rev. 22:15

Κῶ, acc. sg. f. n. (Acts 21:1, GNT, WH & NA | Κῶν, MT & TR) . . . . Κῶς *(2972)*

κῶλα, nom. pl. neut. n. . . . . κῶλον *(2966)*

(2966) **κῶλον**, ου, τό [§3.C.c] *a member or limb of the body*, Heb. 3:17

κωλύει, 3 pers. sg. pres. act. indic. . . . . κωλύω *(2967)*

κωλύειν, pres. act. infin. . . . . id.

κωλύεσθαι, pres. pass. infin. . . . . id.

κωλύετε, 2 pers. pl. pres. act. imper. . . . . . id.

κωλυθέντες, nom. pl. m. aor. pass. part. . . id.

κωλύοντα, acc. sg. m. pres. act. part. . . . . id.

κωλυόντων, gen. pl. m. pres. act. part. . . . id.

κωλῦσαι, aor. act. infin. . . . . id.

κωλύσῃς, 2 pers. sg. aor. act. subj. . . . . . . id.

(2967) **κωλύω**, fut. κωλύσω, aor. ἐκώλυσα [§13.M] aor. pass. ἐκωλύθην, *to hinder, restrain, prevent*, Matt. 19:14; Acts 8:36; Rom. 1:13, et al.

κώμας, acc. pl. f. n. . . . . κώμη *(2968)*

(2968) **κώμη**, ης, ἡ [§2.B.a] *a village, a country town*, Matt. 9:35; 10:11; Luke 8:1, et al.

κώμῃ, dat. sg. f. n. (Mark 8:26, MT & TR | κώμην, GNT, WH & NA) . . . . κώμη *(2968)*

κώμην, acc. sg. f. n. . . . . id.

κώμης, gen. sg. f. n. . . . . id.

κῶμοι, nom. pl. m. n. . . . . κῶμος *(2970)*

κώμοις, dat. pl. m. n. . . . . κῶμος *(2970)*
κωμοπόλεις, acc. pl. f. n. . . . . . . κωμόπολις *(2969)*
(2969) **κωμόπολις**, εως, ἡ [§5.E.c] (κώμη + πόλις)
    a large village, open town, Mark 1:38
(2970) **κῶμος**, ου, ὁ [§3.C.a] pr. *a festive procession,*
    a merry-making; in N.T. *a revel, lascivi-*
    ous feasting, Rom. 13:13; Gal. 5:21; 1 Pet.
    4:3
Κῶν, acc. sg. f. n. (Acts 21:1, MT & TR | Κῶ,
    GNT, WH & NA) . . . . Κῶς *(2972)*
κώνωπα, acc. sg. m. n. . . . . κώνωψ *(2971)*
(2971) **κώνωψ**, ωπος, ὁ [§4.2.a] *a gnat, culex,* which
    is found in wine when becoming sour,
    Matt. 23:24
(2972) **Κῶς**, ῶ, ἡ [§3.C.d] *Cos,* an island in the Ae-
    gean sea, Acts 21:1
(2973) **Κωσάμ**, ὁ, *Cosam,* pr. name, indecl., Luke
    3:28
κωφοί, nom. pl. m. adj. . . . . κωφός *(2974)*
κωφόν, acc. sg. m. adj. {Mark 7:32} . . . . id.
κωφόν, nom. sg. neut. adj. {Mark 9:25} . id.
(2974) **κωφός**, ή, όν, nom. sg. m. adj. [§7.F.a] pr.
    blunt, dull, as a weapon; *dull of hearing,*
    deaf, Matt. 11:5; Mark 7:32, 37; Luke
    7:22; *dumb, mute,* Matt. 9:32, 33, et al.;
    meton. *making dumb, causing dumbness,*
    Luke 11:14
κωφούς, acc. pl. m. adj. . . . . κωφός *(2974)*

Λ

λάβε, 2 pers. sg. 2 aor. act. imper. . . λαμβάνω *(2983)*
λαβεῖν, 2 aor. act. infin. [§36.2] . . . . id.
λάβετε, 2 pers. pl. 2 aor. act. imper. . . . . . id.
λαβέτω, 3 pers. sg. 2 aor. act. imper. (Acts
    1:20; Rev. 22:17, GNT, WH & NA |
    λάβοι, Acts 1:20 MT & TR; Rev. 22:17,
    λαβέτω, MT, λαμβανέτω, TR) . . . . . . id.
λάβῃ, 3 pers. sg. 2 aor. act. subj. . . . . id.
λάβητε, 2 pers. pl. 2 aor. act. subj. . . . . . . id.
λάβοι, 3 pers. sg. 2 aor. act. opt. . . . . id.
λαβόντα, acc. sg. m. 2 aor. act. part. . . . . id.
λαβόντας, acc. pl. m. 2 aor. act. part. . . . id.
λαβόντες, nom. pl. m. 2 aor. act. part. . . . id.
λαβοῦσα, nom. sg. f. 2 aor. act. part. . . . . id.
λαβοῦσαι, nom. pl. f. 2 aor. act. part. . . . . id.
λάβω, 1 pers. sg. 2 aor. act. subj. . . . . . . id.
λάβωμεν, 1 pers. pl. 2 aor. act. subj. . . . . id.
λαβών, nom. sg. m. 2 aor. act. part. . . . . . id.
λάβωσι(ν), 3 pers. pl. 2 aor. act. subj. . . . id.
(2975) **λαγχάνω**, fut. λήξομαι, perf. εἴληχα, 2 perf.
    λέλογχα, 2 aor. ἔλαχον [§36.2] *to have as-*
    signed to one, to obtain, receive, Acts 1:17;

2 Pet. 1:1; *to have fall to one by lot,* Luke
    1:9; absol. *to cast lots,* John 19:24
Λάζαρε, voc. sg. m. n. . . . . Λάζαρος *(2976)*
Λάζαρον, acc. sg. m. n. . . . . id.
(2976) **Λάζαρος**, ου, ὁ, nom. sg. m. n. [§3.C.a]
    Lazarus, pr. name
λαθεῖν, 2 aor. act. infin. . . . . λανθάνω *(2990)*
(†2977) **λάθρα**, adv., *secretly, privately* (Matt. 1:19;
    2:7; John 11:28; Acts 16:37, GNT, WH,
    MT & NA | λάθρα, TR)
λαίλαπος, gen. sg. f. n. . . . . λαῖλαψ *(2978)*
(2978) **λαῖλαψ**, απος, ἡ, nom. sg. f. n. [§4.2.a] *a*
    squall of wind, a hurricane, Mark 4:37, et
    al.
λακτίζειν, pres. act. infin. . . . . λακτίζω *(2979)*
(2979) **λακτίζω**, fut. λακτίσω [§26.1] (λάξ, *with the*
    heel) to kick, Acts 9:5; 26:14
λαλεῖ, 3 pers. sg. pres. act. indic.
    {John 16:18} . . . . λαλέω *(2980)*
λάλει, 2 pers. sg. pres. act. imper. {Acts 18:9} id.
λαλεῖν, pres. act. infin. . . . . id.
λαλεῖς, 2 pers. sg. pres. act. indic. . . . . . . id.
λαλεῖσθαι, pres. pass. infin. [§17.Q] . . . . . id.
λαλεῖται, 3 pers. sg. pres. mid. indic. (Heb.
    11:4, MT & TR | λαλεῖ, GNT, WH &
    NA) . . . . id.
λαλεῖτε, 2 pers. pl. pres. act. imper. . . . . . id.
λαλείτω, 3 pers. sg. pres. act. imper. . . . . . id.
λαλείτωσαν, 3 pers. pl. pres. act. imper. . . id.
(2980) **λαλέω**, ῶ, fut. λαλήσω, perf. λελάληκα, aor.
    ἐλάλησα [§16.P] *to make vocal utterance;*
    to babble, to talk; in N.T. absol. *to exer-*
    cise the faculty of speech, Matt. 9:33, et
    al.; *to speak,* Matt. 10:20, et al.; *to hold*
    converse with, to talk with, Matt. 12:46;
    Mark 6:50; Rev. 1:12, et al.; *to discourse,*
    to make an address, Luke 11:37; Acts
    11:20; 21:39, et al.; *to make announce-*
    ment, to make a declaration, Luke 1:55, et
    al.; *to make mention,* John 12:41; Acts
    2:31; Heb. 4:8; 2 Pet. 3:16; trans. *to speak,*
    address, preach, Matt. 9:18; John 3:11; Tit.
    2:1, et al.; *to give utterance to, to utter,*
    Mark 2:7; John 3:34, et al.; *to declare, an-*
    nounce, reveal, Luke 24:25, et al.; *to dis-*
    close, 2 Cor. 12:4
λαλῇ, 3 pers. sg. pres. act. subj. . . . . . . λαλέω *(2980)*
λαληθείς, nom. sg. m. aor. pass. part. . . . id.
λαληθείσης, gen. sg. f. aor. pass. part. . . . id.
λαληθέντος, gen. sg. neut. aor. pass. part. id.
λαληθέντων, gen. pl. neut. aor. pass. part. id.
λαληθῆναι, aor. pass. infin. . . . . id.
λαληθήσεται, 3 pers. sg. fut. pass. indic. . id.
λαληθησομένων, gen. pl. neut. fut. pass.
    part. . . . . id.

λαλῆσαι, aor. act. infin. . . . . λαλέω *(2980)*
λαλήσαντες, nom. pl. m. aor. act. part. . . id.
λαλήσαντος, gen. sg. m. aor. act. part. (Acts
  23:7, MT & TR | εἰπόντος, GNT & NA
  | λαλοῦντος, WH) . . . . id.
λαλήσας, nom. sg. m. aor. act. part. . . . . id.
λαλήσει, 3 pers. sg. fut. act. indic. . . . . . id.
λαλήσετε, 2 pers. pl. fut. act. indic. (Matt.
  10:19, MT & TR | λαλήσητε, GNT, WH
  & NA) . . . . id.
λαλήσῃ, 3 pers. sg. aor. act. subj. . . . . . . id.
λαλήσητε, 2 pers. pl. aor. act. subj. . . . . . id.
λαλήσομεν, 1 pers. pl. fut. act. indic. . . . . id.
λαλήσουσι(ν), 3 pers. pl. fut. act. indic. . . id.
λαλήσω, 1 pers. sg. fut. act. indic.
  {John 14:30} . . . . id.
λαλήσω, 1 pers. sg. aor. act. subj.
  {John 12:49} . . . . id.
λαλήσωσιν, 3 pers. pl. aor. act. subj. (Matt.
  12:36, MT & TR | λαλήσουσιν, GNT,
  WH & NA) . . . . id.
(2981) **λαλιά**, ᾶς, ἡ, nom. sg. f. n. [§2.B.b; 2.2] *talk;*
  in N.T. *matter of discourse,* John 4:42;
  8:43; *language, dialect,* Matt. 26:73; Mark
  14:70
λαλιάν, acc. sg. f. n. . . . . λαλιά *(2981)*
λαλοῦμεν, 1 pers. pl. pres. act. indic. . . λαλέω *(2980)*
λαλουμένη, nom. sg. f. pres. pass. part. . . id.
λαλουμένοις, dat. pl. neut. pres. pass. part. id.
λαλούμενον, acc. sg. m. pres. pass. part.
  {Mark 5:36} . . . . id.
λαλούμενον, nom. sg. neut. pres. pass. part.
  {1 Cor. 14:9} . . . . id.
λαλοῦν, nom. sg. neut. pres. act. part. . . . id.
λαλοῦντα, acc. sg. m. pres. act. part. . . . . id.
λαλοῦντας, acc. pl. m. pres. act. part. . . . id.
λαλοῦντες, nom. pl. m. pres. act. part. . . . id.
λαλοῦντι, dat. sg. m. pres. act. part. . . . . . id.
λαλοῦντος, gen. sg. m. pres. act. part. . . . id.
λαλούντων, gen. pl. m. pres. act. part. . . . id.
λαλοῦσα, nom. sg. f. pres. act. part. (Rev.
  10:8, MT & TR | λαλοῦσαν, GNT, WH
  & NA) . . . . id.
λαλοῦσαι, nom. pl. f. pres. act. part. . . . . id.
λαλοῦσαν, acc. sg. f. pres. act. part. (Rev.
  10:8, GNT, WH & NA | λαλοῦσα, MT
  & TR) . . . . id.
λαλούσης, gen. sg. f. pres. act. part. . . . . . id.
λαλοῦσι(ν), 3 pers. pl. pres. act. indic. . . . id.
λαλῶ, 1 pers. sg. pres. act. indic.
  {1 Cor. 14:18} . . . . id.
λαλῶ, 1 pers. sg. pres. act. subj. {1 Cor. 13:1} id.
λαλῶν, nom. sg. m. pres. act. part. . . . . . . id.
λαλῶσιν, 3 pers. pl. pres. act. subj. . . . . . . id.
(2982) **λαμά** (or λαμμᾶ, Hebrew לְמָה) *For what?*

Why? Wherefore? Matt. 27:46; Mark
  15:34 (Matt. 27:46, TR | λαμμᾶ, Mark
  15:34, TR | λεμα, GNT & NA | λεμά,
  WH)
λαμβάνει, 3 pers. sg. pres. act. indic. λαμβάνω *(2983)*
λαμβάνειν, pres. act. infin. . . . . id.
λαμβάνεις, 2 pers. sg. pres. act. indic. . . . id.
λαμβάνετε, 2 pers. pl. pres. act. indic.
  {John 5:43} . . . . id.
λαμβάνετε, 2 pers. pl. pres. act. imper.
  {2 John 10} . . . . id.
λαμβανέτω, 3 pers. sg. pres. act. imper. (Rev.
  22:17, TR | λαβέτω, GNT, WH, MT &
  NA) . . . . id.
λαμβάνῃ, 3 pers. sg. pres. act. subj. . . . . . id.
λαμβάνομεν, 1 pers. pl. pres. act. indic. . . id.
λαμβανόμενον, nom. sg. neut. pres. pass.
  part. . . . . id.
λαμβανόμενος, nom. sg. m. pres. pass. part. id.
λαμβάνοντες, nom. pl. m. pres. act. part. . id.
λαμβάνουσι(ν), 3 pers. pl. pres. act. indic. id.
(2983) **λαμβάνω**, 1 pers. sg. pres. act. indic., fut.
  λή(μ)ψομαι, perf. εἴληφα, 2 aor. ἔλαβον,
  aor. pass. ἐλήφθην [§36.2] *to take, take up,*
  take in the hand, Matt. 10:38; 13:31, 33,
  et al.; *to take on one's self, sustain,* Matt.
  8:17; *to take, seize, seize upon,* Matt. 5:40;
  21:34; Luke 5:26; 1 Cor. 10:13, et al.; *to*
  catch, Luke 5:5; 2 Cor. 12:16; *to assume,*
  put on, Phil. 2:7; *to make a rightful or suc-*
  cessful assumption of, John 3:27; *to con-*
  ceive, Acts 28:15; *to take* by way of
  provision, Matt. 16:5; *to get, get together,*
  Matt. 16:9; *to receive* as payment, Matt.
  17:24; Heb. 7:8; *to take* to wife, Mark
  12:19; *to admit, give reception to,* John
  6:21; 2 John 10; met. *to give* mental *recep-*
  tion to, John 3:11, et al.; *to be simply re-*
  cipient of, to receive, Matt. 7:8; John
  7:23, 39; 19:30; Acts 10:43; in N.T. λαμβάνειν πεῖραν, *to make encounter* of a
  matter of difficulty or trial, Heb. 11:29, 36;
  λαμβάνειν ἀρχήν, *to begin,* Heb. 2:3;
  λαμβάνειν συμβούλιον, *to take counsel,*
  consult, Matt. 12:14; λαμβάνειν λήθην, *to*
  forget, 2 Pet. 1:9; λαμβάνειν ὑπόμνησιν,
  to recollect, call to mind, 2 Tim. 1:5;
  λαμβάνειν περιτομήν, *to receive circumci-*
  sion, be circumcised, John 7:23; λαμβάνειν καταλλαγήν, *to be reconciled,* Rom.
  5:11; λαμβάνειν κρίμα, *to receive condem-*
  nation or punishment, be punished, Mark
  12:40; from the Hebrew, πρόσωπον λαμβάνειν, *to accept the person* of any one,
  show partiality towards, Luke 20:21

λαμβάνων, nom. sg. m. pres. act.
part. . . . . λαμβάνω (2983)

(2984) **Λάμεχ**, ὁ, *Lamech,* pr. name, indecl., Luke
3:36

(‡2982) **λαμμᾶ,** (or λαμά, Hebrew לָמָה) *For what?*
Why? Wherefore? (Mark 15:34, TR |
λεμα, GNT & NA | λιμά, MT | λεμά,
WH)

λαμπάδας, acc. pl. f. n. . . . . λαμπάς (2985)
λαμπάδες, nom. pl. f. n. . . . . id.
λαμπάδων, gen. pl. f. n. . . . . id.

(2985) **λαμπάς**, άδος, ἡ, nom. sg. f. n. [§4.D.b] *a*
light, Acts 20:8; *a lamp,* Rev. 4:5; *a port-*
able lamp, lantern, or flambeau, Matt.
25:1, 3, 4, 7, 8; John 18:3

λάμπει, 3 pers. sg. pres. act. indic. . . . . λάμπω (2989)
λαμπρά, nom. pl. neut. adj. . . . . λαμπρός (2986)
λαμπρᾷ, dat. sg. f. adj. . . . . id.
λαμπράν, acc. sg. f. adj. . . . . id.
λαμπρόν, acc. sg. m. adj. {Rev. 22:1} . . . . id.
λαμπρόν, acc. sg. neut. adj. {Rev. 15:6} . . id.

(2986) **λαμπρός**, ά, όν, nom. sg. m. adj. [§7.1] *bright,*
resplendent, Rev. 22:16; *clear, pellucid,*
Rev. 22:1; *white, glistering,* Acts 10:30; Rev.
15:6; *of a bright color, gaudy,* Luke 23:11;
by impl. *splendid, magnificent, sumptuous,*
James 2:2, 3; Rev. 18:14

(2987) **λαμπρότης**, ητος, ἡ [§4.2.c] *brightness, splen-*
dor, Acts 26:13

λαμπρότητα, acc. sg. f. n. . . . . . . λαμπρότης (2987)

(2988) **λαμπρῶς**, adv., *splendidly; magnificently,*
sumptuously, Luke 16:19

(2989) **λάμπω,** fut. λάμψω and λάμψομαι, aor.
ἔλαμψα [§23.1.a; 23.2] *to shine, give light,*
Matt. 5:15, 16; 17:2; Luke 17:24, et al.

λάμψαι, aor. act. infin. (2 Cor. 4:6, MT &
TR | λάμψει, GNT, WH & NA) . . λάμπω (2989)
λαμψάτω, 3 pers. sg. aor. act. imper. . . . . id.
λάμψει, 3 pers. sg. fut. act. indic. (2 Cor. 4:6,
GNT, WH & NA | λάμψαι, MT & TR) id.
λανθάνει, 3 pers. sg. pres. act. indic. λανθάνω (2990)
λανθάνειν, pres. act. infin. . . . . id.
λανθανέτω, 3 pers. sg. pres. act. imper. . . id.

(2990) **λανθάνω,** fut. λήσω, 2 aor. ἔλαθον, perf.
λέληθα [§36.2] (λήθω, obsolete) *to be un-*
noticed; to escape the knowledge or obser-
vation of a person, Acts 26:26; 2 Pet.
3:5, 8; absol. *to be concealed, escape de-*
tection, Mark 7:24; Luke 8:47; with a participle of another verb, *to be unconscious*
of an action while the subject or object of
if, Heb. 13:2

(2991) **λαξευτός**, ή, όν [§7.F.a] (λᾶς, *a stone,* and
ξέω, *to cut, hew) cut in stone, hewn out*
of stone or rock, Luke 23:53

λαξευτῷ, dat. sg. neut. adj. . . . . λαξευτός (2991)

(2993) **Λαοδίκεια**, ας, ἡ [§2.B.b; 2.2] *Laodicea,* a city
of Phrygia in Asia Minor

Λαοδικείᾳ, dat. sg. f. n. (Col. 2:1; 4:13, 15;
Rev. 3:14, GNT, MT, TR & NA |
Λαοδικίᾳ, WH) . . . . Λαοδίκεια (2993)
Λαοδίκειαν, acc. sg. f. n. (Rev. 1:11, GNT,
MT, TR & NA | Λαοδικίαν, WH) . . . id.
Λαοδικείας, gen. sg. f. n. (Col. 4:16, GNT,
MT, TR & NA | Λαοδικίας, WH) . . . id.

(2994) **Λαοδικεύς**, έως, ὁ [§5.E.d] *a Laodicean, an*
inhabitant of Laodicea, Col. 4:16; Rev. 3:14

Λαοδικέων, gen. pl. m. n. . . . . Λαοδικεύς (2994)
λαοί, nom. pl. m. n. . . . . λαός (‡2992)
λαοῖς, dat. pl. m. n. . . . . id.
λαόν, acc. sg. m. n. . . . . id.

(‡2992) **λαός**, οῦ, ὁ, nom. sg. m. n. [§3.C.a] *a body*
of people; a concourse of people, a multi-
tude, Matt. 27:25; Luke 8:47, et al.; *the*
common people, Matt. 26:5, et al.; *a*
people, nation, Matt. 2:4; Luke 2:32; Tit.
2:14, et al.; ὁ λαός, *the people* of Israel,
Luke 2:10

λαοῦ, gen. sg. m. n. . . . . λαός (‡2992)

(2995) **λάρυγξ**, υγγος, ὁ, nom. sg. m. n. [§4.2.b] *the*
throat, gullet

(2996) **Λασαία**, ας, ἡ, nom. sg. f. n., *Lasaea,* a maritime town in Crete (Acts 27:8, GNT, MT,
TR & NA | Λασέα, WH)

(†2996) **Λασέα**, ας, ἡ, nom. sg. f. n., *Lasaea* (Acts
27:8, WH | Λασαία, GNT, MT, TR &
NA)

(†2997) **λάσκω,** fut. λακήσω, aor. ἐλάκησα, pr. *to*
emit a sound, ring; hence, *to break with*
a sharp noise; to burst, Acts 1:18

(2998) **λατομέω**, ῶ, fut. λατομήσω, perf. λετατό-
μηκα, aor. ἐλατόμησα [§16.P] (λᾶς, *a*
stone, and τέμνω) *to hew stones; to cut out*
of stone, hew from stone, Matt. 27:60;
Mark 15:46

(2999) **λατρεία**, ας, ἡ, nom. sg. f. n. [§2.B.b; 2.2] *ser-*
vice, servitude; religious service, worship,
John 16:2; Rom. 9:4; 12:1; Heb. 9:1, 6

λατρείαν, acc. sg. f. n. . . . . λατρεία (2999)
λατρείας, gen. sg. f. n. {Heb. 9:1} . . . . . . id.
λατρείας, acc. pl. f. n. {Heb. 9:6} . . . . . . id.
λατρεύειν, pres. act. infin. . . . . λατρεύω (3000)
λατρεύομεν, 1 pers. pl. pres. act. indic. (Heb.
12:28, MT | λατρεύωμεν, GNT, WH, TR
& NA) . . . . id.
λατρεῦον, nom. sg. neut. pres. act. part. . . id.
λατρεύοντα, acc. sg. m. pres. act. part. . . . id.
λατρεύοντας, acc. pl. m. pres. act. part. . . id.
λατρεύοντες, nom. pl. m. pres. act. part. . . id.
λατρεύουσα, nom. sg. f. pres. act. part. . . id.

λατρεύουσι(ν), 3 pers. pl. pres. act.
indic. . . . . λατρεύω *(3000)*
λατρεύσεις, 2 pers. sg. fut. act. indic. . . . . id.
λατρεύσουσι(ν), 3 pers. pl. fut. act. indic. . . id.
(3000) **λατρεύω,** 1 pers. sg. pres. act. indic., fut.
λατρεύσω, aor. ἐλάτρευσα [§13.M]
(λάτρις, *a servant*) *to be a servant, to serve,*
Acts 27:23; *to render religious service and
homage, worship,* Matt. 4:10; Luke 1:74;
spc. *to offer sacrifices, present offerings,*
Heb. 8:5; 9:9
λατρεύωμεν, 1 pers. pl. pres. act. subj. (Heb.
12:28, GNT, WH, TR & NA | λατρεύ-
ομεν, MT) . . . . λατρεύω *(3000)*
λάχανα, acc. pl. neut. n. . . . . λάχανον *(3001)*
(3001) **λάχανον,** ου, τό [§3.C.c] (λαχαίνω, *to dig*) *a
garden herb, vegetable,* Matt. 13:32; Luke
11:42; Rom. 14:2
λαχάνον, acc. sg. neut. n. . . . . λάχανον *(3001)*
λαχάνων, gen. pl. neut. n. . . . . id.
λαχοῦσι(ν), dat. pl. m. 2 aor. act.
part. . . . . λαγχάνω *(2975)*
λάχωμεν, 1 pers. pl. 2 aor. act. subj. . . . . id.
λαῷ, dat. sg. m. n. . . . . λαός *(‡2992)*
λαῶν, gen. pl. m. n. . . . . id.
(3002) **Λεββαῖος,** ου, ὁ, nom. sg. m. n. [§3.C.a]
Lebbaeus, pr. name (Matt. 10:3, MT &
TR | GNT, WH & NA omit)
λέγε, 2 pers. sg. pres. act. imper. . . . . λέγω *(3004)*
λέγει, 3 pers. sg. pres. act. indic. . . . . id.
λέγειν, pres. act. infin. . . . . id.
λέγεις, 2 pers. sg. pres. act. indic. . . . . id.
λέγεσθαι, pres. pass. infin. . . . . id.
λέγεται, 3 pers. sg. pres. pass. indic. . . . . . id.
λέγετε, 2 pers. pl. pres. act. indic.
{Luke 11:18} . . . . id.
λέγετε, 2 pers. pl. pres. act. imper.
{Luke 11:2} . . . . id.
λεγέτω, 3 pers. sg. pres. act. imper. . . . . . . id.
(3003) **λεγεών,** ῶνος, ὁ, nom. sg. m. n. [§4.2.e] *a* Roman *legion;* in N.T. *legion* used indefinitely
for a great number, Matt. 26:53; Mark
5:9, 15 (Mark 5:9; Luke 8:30, MT & TR
| λεγιών, GNT, WH & NA)
λεγεῶνα, acc. sg. m. n. (Mark 5:15, MT &
TR | λεγιῶνα, GNT, WH & NA) . λεγεών *(3003)*
λεγεῶνας, acc. pl. m. n. (Matt. 26:53, MT
& TR | λεγιῶνας, GNT, WH & NA) . id.
λέγῃ, 3 pers. sg. pres. act. subj. . . . . λέγω *(3004)*
λέγητε, 2 pers. pl. pres. act. subj. . . . . id.
(†3003) **λεγιών,** ῶνος, ἡ, nom. sg. f. n., *legion* (Mark
5:9; Luke 8:30, GNT, WH & NA |
λεγεών, MT & TR)
λεγιῶνα, acc. sg. f. n. (Mark 5:15, GNT, WH
& NA | λεγεῶνα, MT & TR) . . . λεγιών *(†3003)*

λεγιῶνας, acc. pl. f. n. (Matt. 26:53, GNT,
WH & NA | λεγεῶνας, MT &
TR) . . . . λεγιών *(†3003)*
λέγομεν, 1 pers. pl. pres. act. indic. . . . . λέγω *(3004)*
λεγόμενα, acc. pl. neut. pres. pass. part. . . id.
λεγομένη, nom. sg. f. pres. pass. part. . . . id.
λεγομένην, acc. sg. f. pres. pass. part. . . . . id.
λεγομένης, gen. sg. f. pres. pass. part. . . . id.
λεγόμενοι, nom. pl. m. pres. pass. part. . . id.
λεγομένοις, dat. pl. neut. pres. pass. part. id.
λεγόμενον, acc. sg. m. pres. pass. part.
{Matt. 27:16} . . . . id.
λεγόμενον, acc. sg. neut. pres. pass. part.
{Matt. 26:36} . . . . id.
λεγόμενος, nom. sg. m. pres. pass. part. . . id.
λεγομένου, gen. sg. m. pres. pass. part. . . id.
λέγον, nom. sg. neut. pres. act. part. . . . . id.
λέγοντα, acc. sg. m. pres. act. part.
{Luke 23:2} . . . . id.
λέγοντα, nom. pl. neut. pres. act. part.
{Luke 4:41} . . . . id.
λέγοντας, acc. pl. m. pres. act. part. . . . . . id.
λέγοντες, nom. pl. m. pres. act. part. . . . . id.
λέγοντι, dat. sg. m. pres. act. part. (Matt.
12:48, GNT, WH & NA | εἰπόντι, MT
& TR) . . . . id.
λέγοντος, gen. sg. m. pres. act. part.
{Rev. 16:5} . . . . id.
λέγοντος, gen. sg. neut. pres. act. part.
{Rev. 16:7} . . . . id.
λεγόντων, gen. pl. m. pres. act. part. . . . . . id.
λέγουσα, nom. sg. f. pres. act. part. . . . . . id.
λέγουσαι, nom. pl. f. pres. act. part. . . . . . id.
λέγουσαν, acc. sg. f. pres. act. part. . . . . . id.
λεγούσης, gen. sg. f. pres. act. part. . . . . . id.
λέγουσι(ν), 3 pers. pl. pres. act. indic.
{Matt. 11:18} . . . . id.
λέγουσιν, dat. pl. m. pres. act. part.
{Matt. 11:17} . . . . id.
(3004) **λέγω,** 1 pers. sg. pres. act. indic., fut. λέξω
[§23.1.b] *to lay, to arrange, to gather; to say,*
Matt. 1:20, et al. freq.; *to speak, make an
address or speech,* Acts 26:1; *to say* mentally, in thought, Matt. 3:9; Luke 3:8; *to say*
in written language, Mark 15:28; Luke 1:63;
John 19:37, et al.; *to say,* as distinguished
from acting, Matt. 23:3; *to mention, speak
of,* Mark 14:71; Luke 9:31; John 8:27; *to tell,
declare, narrate,* Matt. 21:27; Mark 10:32;
to express, Heb. 5:11; *to put forth, propound,*
Luke 5:36; 13:6; John 16:29; *to mean, to intend to signify,* 1 Cor. 1:12; 10:29; *to say, declare, affirm, maintain,* Matt. 3:9; 5:18;
Mark 12:18; Acts 17:7; 26:22; 1 Cor. 1:10,
et al.; *to enjoin,* Acts 15:24; 21:21; Rom.

2:22; *to term, designate, cull,* Matt. 19:17;
Mark 12:37; Luke 20:37; 23:2 1 Cor. 8:5,
et al.; *to call* by a name, Matt. 2:23, et al.;
pass. *to be further named, to be surnamed,*
Matt. 1:16, et al.; *to be explained, inter-
preted,* John 4:25; 20:16, 24; in N.T. σὺ
λέγεις, *thou sayest,* a form of affirmative
answer to a question, Matt. 27:11; Mark
15:2; John 18:37 {1 Tim. 2:7}

λέγω, 1 pers. sg. pres. act. subj.
{Philemon 19} . . . . λέγω *(3004)*
λέγωμεν, 1 pers. pl. pres. act. subj. (2 Cor.
9:4, MT, WH & TR | λέγω, GNT &
NA) . . . . id.
λέγων, nom. sg. m. pres. act. part. . . . . . . id.
λέγωσι(ν), 3 pers. pl. pres. act. subj. . . . . . id.
λείας, acc. pl. f. adj. . . . . λεῖος *(3006)*
(3005) **λεῖμμα,** ατος, τό, nom. sg. neut. n. [§4.D.c]
pr. *a remnant;* in N.T. *a small residue*
(Rom. 11:5, GNT, MT, TR & NA |
λίμμα, WH)
(3006) **λεῖος,** εία, εῖον [§7.1] *smooth, level, plain,*
Luke 3:5
λείπει, 3 pers. sg. pres. act. indic. . . . . . λείπω *(3007)*
λείπεται, 3 pers. sg. pres. pass. indic. . . . . id.
λείπῃ, 3 pers. sg. pres. act. subj. . . . . id.
λειπόμενοι, nom. pl. m. pres. pass. part. . id.
λείποντα, acc. pl. neut. pres. act. part. . . . id.
(3007) **λείπω,** fut. λείψω [§23.1.a] 2 aor. ἔλιπον
[§24.9] trans. *to leave, forsake;* pass. *to be
left, deserted;* by impl. *to be destitute of,
deficient in,* James 1:4, 5; 2:15; intrans. *to
fail, be wanting, be deficient* Luke 18:22,
et al.
(3008) **λειτουργέω,** ῶ, fut. λειτουργήσω, perf.
λελειτούργηκα [§16.P] pr. *to perform some
public service at one's own expense;* in N.T.
to officiate as a priest, Heb. 10:11; *to minister* in the Christian Church, Acts 13:2; *to
minister to, assist, succor,* Rom. 15:27
λειτουργῆσαι, aor. act. infin. . . . . id.
(3009) **λειτουργία,** ας, ἡ [§2.B.b; 2.2] pr. *a public service discharged by a citizen at his own ex-
pense;* in N.T. *a sacred ministration,* Luke
1:23; Phil. 2:17; Heb. 8:6; 9:21; *a kind office, aid, relief,* 2 Cor. 9:12; Phil. 2:30
λειτουργίᾳ, dat. sg. f. n. . . . . λειτουργία *(3009)*
λειτουργίας, gen. sg. f. n. . . . . id.
λειτουργικά, nom. pl. neut. adj. . λειτουργικός *(3010)*
(3010) **λειτουργικός,** ή, όν [§7.F.a] *ministering; engaged in subordinate service,* Heb. 1:14
λειτουργοί, nom. pl. m. n. . . . . λειτουργός *(3011)*
λειτουργόν, acc. sg. m. n. . . . . id.
(3011) **λειτουργός,** οῦ, ὁ, nom. sg. m. n. [§3.C.a]
(λεῖτος, *public,* + ἔργον) pr. *a person of*

*property who performed a public duty or
service to the state at his own expense;* in
N.T. *a minister or servant,* Rom. 13:6, et
al.; *one who ministers relief,* Phil. 2:25
λειτουργούντων, gen. pl. m. pres. act.
part. λειτουργέω *(3008)*
λειτουργούς, acc. pl. m. n. . . . . λειτουργός *(3011)*
λειτουργῶν, nom. sg. m. pres. act.
part. λειτουργέω *(3008)*
λελάληκα, 1 pers. sg. perf. act. indic. . λαλέω *(2980)*
λελάληκεν, 3 pers. sg. perf. act. indic. . . . id.
λελαλημένοις, dat. pl. neut. perf. pass. part. id.
λελάληται, 3 pers. sg. perf. pass. indic. . . id.
λελατομημένον, nom. sg. neut. perf. pass.
part. . . . . λατομέω *(2998)*
λελουμένοι, nom. pl. m. perf. pass. part.
(Heb. 10:22, MT & TR | λελουσμένοι,
GNT, WH & NA) . . . . λούω *(3068)*
λελουμένος, nom. sg. m. perf. pass. part.
[§14.1.e] . . . . id.
λελουσμένοι, nom. pl. m. perf. pass. part.
(Heb. 10:22, GNT, WH & NA | λελου-
μένοι, MT & TR) . . . . id.
λελυμένα, nom. pl. neut. perf. pass. part. λύω *(3089)*
λελυμένον, nom. sg. neut. perf. pass. part.
[§14.N] . . . . id.
λελύπηκεν, 3 pers. sg. perf. act. indic. . λυπέω *(3076)*
λέλυσαι, 2 pers. sg. perf. pass. indic.
[§14.1.e] . . . . λύω *(3089)*
(‡2982) **λεμα,** Aramaic, *For what? Why? Wherefore?*
(Matt. 27:46; Mark 15:34, GNT & NA
| λεμά, WH | λιμά, MT | λαμα, Matt.
27:46, TR | λαμμᾶ, Mark 15:34, TR)
(3012) **λέντιον,** ου, τό [§3.C.c] (Latin *linteum*) *a
coarse cloth,* with which servants were
girded, *a towel, napkin, apron,* John
13:4, 5
λέντιον, acc. sg. neut. n. . . . . λέντιον *(3012)*
λεντίῳ, dat. sg. neut. n. . . . . id.
λέοντι, dat. sg. m. n. . . . . λέων *(†3023)*
λέοντος, gen. sg. m. n. [§4.2.d] . . . . id.
λεόντων, gen. pl. m. n. . . . . id.
λεπίδες, nom. pl. f. n. . . . . λεπίς *(3013)*
(3013) **λεπίς,** ίδος, ἡ [§4.2.c] (λέπω, *to peel or strip
off) a scale, shell, rind, crust, incrustation,*
Acts 9:18
(3014) **λέπρα,** ας, ἡ, nom. sg. f. n. [§2.B.b] *the leprosy,* Matt. 8:3; Mark 1:42; Luke 5:12, 13
λέπρας, gen. sg. f. n. . . . . λέπρα *(3014)*
λεπροί, nom. pl. m. adj. . . . . λεπρός *(3015)*
(3015) **λεπρός,** ά, όν, nom. sg. m. adj. [§3.C.a] *le-
prous; a leper,* Matt. 8:2; 10:8, et al.
λεπροῦ, gen. sg. m. adj. . . . . λεπρός *(3015)*
λεπρούς, acc. pl. m. adj. . . . . id.
λεπτά, acc. pl. neut. adj. . . . . λεπτός *(†3016)*

(3016) λεπτόν, acc. sg. neut. adj. . . . . λεπτός *(†3016)*

(†3016) λεπτός, ά, όν [§3.C.c] (λεπτός, *thin, fine, small*) *a mite,* the smallest Jewish coin, equal to half a κοδράντης, Mark 12:42, et al.

Λευείν, acc. sg. m. n. (Mark 2:14, WH | Λευίν, GNT, MT & NA | λευῖν, TR) . . . . Λευείς *(†3017)*

(†3017) Λευείς, ὁ, nom. sg. m. n. *Levi* (Heb. 7:9, WH | Λευί, GNT, MT & NA | Λευῖ, TR)

(†3017) Λευί, ὁ, *Levi,* pr. name, indecl. I. *Levi, son of Jacob,* Heb. 7:5, et al. II. *Levi, son of Symeon,* Luke 3:29 III. *Levi, son of Melchi,* Luke 3:24 (GNT, MT & NA | Λευῖ, TR | Λευεί, WH)

Λευί, gen. sg. m. n. (Luke 3:24, 29, GNT, MT & NA | Λευῖ, TR | Λευεί, WH) . . . Λευίς *(†3018)*

Λευίν, acc. sg. m. n. (Mark 2:14; Luke 5:27, GNT, MT & NA | Λευῖν, TR | Λευείν, WH) . . . . id.

(†3018) Λευίς, ὁ, nom. sg. m. n. *Levi, son of Alphaeus, the publican,* Mark 2:14 (Luke 5:29, GNT, MT & NA | Λευῖς, TR | Λευείς, WH)

Λευίτας, acc. pl. m. n. (John 1:19, GNT & NA | Λευῖτας, TR | Λευείτας, WH) . . . . Λευίτης *(†3019)*

(†3019) Λευίτης, ου, ὁ, nom. sg. m. n. [§2.B.c] *a Levite, one of the posterity of Levi,* John 1:19 (Luke 10:32; Acts 4:36, GNT, MT & NA | Λευῖτης, TR | Λευείτης, WH)

Λευιτικῆς, gen. sg. f. adj. (Heb. 7:11, GNT, MT & NA | Λευϊτικός, TR | Λευειτικῆς, WH) . . . . Λευιτικός *(†3020)*

(†3020) Λευιτικός, ή, όν [§7.F.a] *Levitical, pertaining to the Levites,* Heb. 7:11

λευκά, nom. pl. neut. adj. {Matt. 17:2} . . . . λευκός *(3022)*

λευκά, acc. pl. neut. adj. {Rev. 3:18} . . . . id.

λευκαί, nom. pl. f. adj. . . . . id.

(3021) λευκαίνω, fut. λευκανῶ, aor. ἐλεύκανα [§27.1.c‚e] *to brighten, to make white,* Mark 9:3; Rev. 7:14

λευκαῖς, dat. pl. f. adj. (Acts 1:10, GNT, WH & NA | λευκῇ, MT & TR) . . . . . . λευκός *(3022)*

λευκᾶναι, aor. act. infin. . . . . λευκαίνω *(3021)*

λευκάς, acc. pl. f. adj. . . . . λευκός *(3022)*

λευκή, nom. sg. f. adj. . . . . id.

λευκῇ, dat. sg. f. adj. (Acts 1:10, MT & TR | λευκαῖς, GNT, WH & NA) . . . . id.

λευκήν, acc. sg. f. adj. . . . . id.

λευκοῖς, dat. pl. m. adj. {Rev. 19:14} . . . . id.

λευκοῖς, dat. pl. neut. adj. {Rev. 3:4} . . . . id.

λευκόν, acc. sg. m. adj. {Rev. 20:11} . . . . id.

λευκόν, nom. sg. neut. adj. {Rev. 1:14} . . . id.

λευκόν, acc. sg. neut. adj. {Rev. 19:14} . . . id.

(3022) λευκός, ή, όν, nom. sg. m. adj. [§7.F.a] pr. *light, bright; white,* Matt. 5:36; 17:2, et al.; *whitening, growing white,* John 4:35

(†3023) λέων, οντος, ὁ, nom. sg. m. n. [§4.2.d] *a lion,* Heb. 11:33; 1 Pet. 5:8, et al.; met. *a lion, cruel adversary, tyrant,* 2 Tim. 4:17; *a lion, a hero, deliverer,* Rev. 5:5

(3024) λήθη, ης, ἡ [§2.B.a] *forgetfulness, oblivion,* 2 Pet. 1:9

λήθην, acc. sg. f. n. . . . . λήθη *(3024)*

λήμψεσθε, 2 pers. pl. fut. mid. dep. indic. (GNT, WH & NA | λήψεσθε, MT & TR) . . . . λαμβάνω *(2983)*

λήμψεται, 3 pers. sg. fut. mid. dep. indic. (GNT, WH & NA | λήψεται, MT & TR) id.

λήμψεως, gen. sg. f. n. (Phil. 4:15, GNT, WH & NA | λήψεως, MT & TR) . . . . λῆμψις *(‡3028)*

(‡3028) λῆμψις, εως, ἡ, *receiving*

λημψόμεθα, 1 pers. pl. fut. mid. dep. indic. (James 3:1, GNT, WH & NA | ληψόμεθα, MT & TR) . . . . λαμβάνω *(2983)*

λήμψονται, 3 pers. pl. fut. mid. dep. indic. (GNT, WH & NA | λήψονται, MT & TR) . . . . id.

ληνόν, acc. sg. f. n. . . . . ληνός *(3025)*

(3025) ληνός, οῦ, ἡ, nom. sg. f. n. [§3.C.b] pr. *a tub, trough; a wine-press,* into which grapes were cast and trodden, Rev. 14:19, 20; 19:15; *a wine-vat,* i.q. ὑπολήνιον, the lower vat into which the juice of the trodden grapes flowed, Matt. 21:33

ληνοῦ, gen. sg. f. n. . . . . ληνός *(3025)*

(3026) λῆρος, ου, ὁ, nom. sg. m. n. [§3.C.a] *idle talk; an empty tale,* Luke 24:11

λησταί, nom. pl. m. n. . . . . λῃστής *(3027)*

λῃσταῖς, dat. pl. m. n. . . . . id.

λῃστάς, acc. pl. m. n. . . . . id.

λῃστήν, acc. sg. m. n. . . . . id.

(3027) λῃστής, οῦ, ὁ, nom. sg. m. n. [§2.B.c] (λῃίζομαι, λῃίς, *plunder*) *a plunderer, robber, highwayman,* Matt. 21:13; 26:55; Mark 11:17; Luke 10:30; 2 Cor. 11:26, et al.; *a bandit, brigand,* Matt. 27:38, 44; Mark 15:27; John 18:40; trop. *a robber, rapacious impostor,* John 10:1, 8

λῃστῶν, gen. pl. m. n. . . . . λῃστής *(3027)*

λήψεσθε, 2 pers. pl. fut. mid. dep. indic. [§36.2] (MT & TR | λήμψεσθε, GNT, WH & NA) . . . . λαμβάνω *(2983)*

λήψεται, 3 pers. sg. fut. mid. dep. indic. (MT & TR | λήμψεται, GNT, WH & NA) id.

λήψεως, gen. sg. f. n. (Phil. 4:15, MT & TR | λήμψεως, GNT, WH & NA) . . . . . λῆψις *(3028)*

(3028) λῆψις, εως, ἡ [§5.E.c] *taking, receiving,*

receipt, Phil. 4:15

ληψόμεθα, 1 pers. pl. fut. mid. dep. indic. (MT & TR | λημψόμεθα, GNT, WH & NA) . . . . λαμβάνω *(2983)*

λήψονται, 3 pers. pl. fut. mid. dep. indic. (MT & TR | λήμψονται, GNT, WH & NA)   id.

(3029) **λίαν**, adv., *much, greatly, exceedingly*, Matt. 2:16; 4:8; 8:28, et al.

λίβα, acc. sg. m. n. . . . . λίψ *(3047)*

λίβανον, acc. sg. m. n. . . . . λίβανος *(3030)*

(3030) **λίβανος**, ου, ὁ [§3.C.a] *arbor thurifera*, the tree producing frankincense, growing in Arabia and Mount Lebanon; in N.T. *frankincense*, the transparent gum which distils from incisions in the tree, Matt. 2:11; Rev. 18:13

λιβανωτόν, acc. sg. m. adj. . . . . λιβανωτός *(3031)*

(3031) **λιβανωτός**, οῦ, ὁ [§3.C.a] *frankincense;* in N.T. *a censer*, Rev. 8:3, 5

(3032) **Λιβερτῖνος**, ου, ὁ (Latin *libertinus*) *a freedman, one who having been a slave has obtained his freedom, or whose father was a freed-man;* in N.T. the λιβερτῖνοι probably denote Jews who had been carried captive to Rome, and subsequently manumitted

λιβερτίνων, gen. pl. m. n. . . . . Λιβερτῖνος *(3032)*

(3033) **Λιβύη**, ης, ἡ [§2.B.a] *Libya*, a part of Africa, bordering on the West of Egypt, Acts 2:10

Λιβύης, gen. sg. f. n. . . . . Λιβύη *(3033)*

λιθάζειν, pres. act. infin. (John 8:5, GNT, WH, MT & NA | λιθοβολεῖσθαι, TR) . . . . λιθάζω *(3034)*

λιθάζετε, 2 pers. pl. pres. act. indic. . . . . . id.

λιθάζομεν, 1 pers. pl. pres. act. indic. . . . . id.

(3034) **λιθάζω**, fut. λιθάσω [§26.1] *to stone, pelt or kill with stones*, John 10:31, 32, 33, et al.

λιθάσαι, aor. act. infin. . . . . λιθάζω *(3034)*

λιθάσαντες, nom. pl. m. aor. act. part. . . . id.

λιθασθῶσιν, 3 pers. pl. aor. pass. subj. . . . id.

λιθάσωσιν, 3 pers. pl. aor. act. subj. . . . . . id.

λίθινα, acc. pl. neut. adj. . . . . λίθινος *(3035)*

λίθιναι, nom. pl. f. adj. . . . . id.

λιθίναις, dat. pl. f. adj. . . . . id.

(3035) **λίθινος**, η, ον [§7.F.a] *made of stone*, John 2:6, et al.

λιθοβολεῖσθαι, pres. pass. infin. [§17.Q] (John 8:5, TR | λιθάζειν, GNT, WH, MT & NA) . . . . λιθοβολέω *(3036)*

(3036) **λιθοβολέω**, ῶ, λιθοβολήσω, aor. ἐλιθοβόλησα [§16.P] (λίθος + βάλλω) *to stone, pelt with stones*, in order to kill, Matt. 21:35; 23:37, et al.

λιθοβοληθήσεται, 3 pers. sg. fut. pass. indic. . . . . λιθοβολέω *(3036)*

λιθοβολῆσαι, aor. act. infin. . . . . . . λιθοβολέω *(3036)*

λιθοβολήσαντες, nom. pl. m. aor. act. part. (Mark 12:4, MT & TR | GNT, WH & NA omit) . . . . id.

λιθοβολοῦσα, nom. sg. f. pres. act. part. . id.

λίθοι, nom. pl. m. n. . . . . λίθος *(3037)*

λίθοις, dat. pl. m. n. . . . . id.

λίθον, acc. sg. m. n. . . . . id.

(3037) **λίθος**, ου, ὁ, nom. sg. m. n. [§3.C.a] *a stone*, Matt. 3:9; 4:3, 6, et al.; used figuratively, of Christ, Eph. 2:20; 1 Pet. 2:6, et al.; of believers, 1 Pet. 2:5; meton. *a tablet of stone*, 2 Cor. 3:7; *a precious stone*, Rev. 4:3, et al.

λιθόστρωτον, acc. sg. neut. adj. . λιθόστρωτος *(3038)*

(3038) **λιθόστρωτος**, ον (*paved with stone*, λίθος + στρώννυμι) *a tassellated pavement*, John 19:13

λίθου, gen. sg. m. n. . . . . λίθος *(3037)*

λίθους, acc. pl. m. n. . . . . id.

λίθῳ, dat. sg. m. n. . . . . id.

λίθων, gen. pl. m. n. . . . . id.

(3039) **λικμάω**, ῶ, fut. λικμήσω [§18.R] pr. *to winnow grain;* in N.T. *to scatter like chaff*, Matt. 21:44; Luke 20:18

λικμήσει, 3 pers. sg. fut. act. indic. . . λικμάω *(3039)*

(‡2982) **λιμά** (or λιμᾶ) Aramaic, *For what? Why? Wherefore?* (Matt. 27:46; Mark 15:34, MT | λεμα, GNT & NA | λεμά, WH | λαμα, Matt. 27:46, TR | λαμμᾶ, Mark 15:34, TR)

λιμένα, acc. sg. m. n. . . . . λιμήν *(3040)*

λιμένας, acc. pl. m. n. . . . . id.

λιμένος, gen. sg. m. n. . . . . id.

(3040) **λιμήν**, ένος, ὁ [§4.2.e] *a port, haven, harbor*, Acts 27:8, 12

(3041) **λίμνη**, ης, ἡ, nom. sg. f. n. [§2.B.a] *a tract of standing water; a lake*, Luke 5:1, et al. (Rev. 20:14, GNT, WH, MT & NA | TR omits)

λίμνῃ, dat. sg. f. n. . . . . λιμήν *(3040)*

λίμνην, acc. sg. f. n. . . . . id.

λίμνης, gen. sg. f. n. . . . . id.

λιμοί, nom. pl. m. n. . . . . λιμός *(3042)*

λιμόν, acc. sg. m. n. . . . . id.

(3042) **λιμός**, οῦ, ὁ, nom. sg. m. n. [§3.C.a] *famine, scarcity of food, want of grain*, Matt. 24:7; *famine, hunger, famishment*, Luke 15:17; Rom. 8:35, et al.

λιμῷ, dat. sg. m. n. . . . . λιμός *(3042)*

(3043) **λίνον**, ου, τό [§3.C.c] *flax;* by meton. *a flaxen wick*, Matt. 12:20; *linen*, Rev. 15:6

λίνον, acc. sg. neut. n. . . . . λίνον *(3043)*

(†3044) **Λῖνος**, ου, ὁ, nom. sg. m. n. *Linus*, pr. name (2 Tim. 4:21, MT & TR | Λίνος, GNT, WH & NA)

(3044) **Λίνος,** ου, ὁ, nom. sg. m. n., *Linus,* pr. name
(2 Tim. 4:21, GNT, WH & NA | Λῖνος,
MT & TR)

λιπαρά, nom. pl. neut. adj. . . . . λιπαρός *(3045)*

(3045) **λιπαρός,** ά, όν [§7.1] (λίπος, *fat, fatness*) *fat;
dainty, delicate, sumptuous,* Rev. 18:14

(3046) **λίτρα,** ας, ἡ [§2.B.b] *a pound, libra,* equivalent to about twelve ounces avoirdupois,
John 12:3; 19:39

λίτραν, acc. sg. f. n. . . . . λίτρα *(3046)*

λίτρας, acc. pl. f. n. . . . . id.

(3047) **λίψ,** λιβός, ὁ [§4.2.a] pr. *the south-west wind;*
meton. *the south-west quarter of the heav-
ens,* Acts 27:12

(†3048) **λογεία,** ας, ἡ, *collection* of money

λογεῖαι, nom. pl. f. n. (1 Cor. 16:2, GNT &
NA | λογίαι, WH, MT & TR) . . . λογεία *(†3048)*

λογείας, gen. sg. f. n. (1 Cor. 16:1, GNT &
NA | λογίας, WH, MT & TR) . . . . . . id.

(3048) **λογία,** ας, ἡ, *a collection* of money

λόγια, acc. pl. neut. n. . . . . λόγιον *(3051)*

λογίαι, nom. pl. f. n. (1 Cor. 16:2, WH, MT
& TR | λογεῖαι, GNT & NA) . . . . . λογία *(3048)*

λογίας, gen. sg. f. n. (1 Cor. 16:1, WH, MT
& TR | λογείας, GNT & NA) . . . . . . id.

λογίζεσθαι, pres. pass. infin. . . . . . . λογίζομαι *(3049)*

λογίζεσθε, 2 pers. pl. pres. mid./pass. dep.
indic. (John 11:50, GNT, WH & NA |
διαλογίζεσθε, MT & TR) . . . . id.

λογίζεσθε, 2 pers. pl. pres. mid./pass. dep.
imper. {Rom. 6:11} . . . . id.

λογιζέσθω, 3 pers. sg. pres. mid./pass. dep.
imper. . . . . id.

λογίζεται, 3 pers. sg. pres. mid./pass. dep.
indic. . . . . id.

λογίζῃ, 2 pers. sg. pres. mid./pass. dep. indic. id.

(3049) **λογίζομαι,** 1 pers. sg. pres. mid./pass. dep.
indic., fut. λογίσομαι, aor. ἐλογισάμην,
aor. pass. ἐλογίσθην, fut. pass. λογισθή-
σομαι, perf. λελόγισμαι [§26.1] pr. *to
count, calculate; to count, enumerate,*
Mark 15:28; Luke 22:37; *to set down* as
a matter of account, 1 Cor. 13:5; 2 Cor.
3:5; 12:6; *to impute,* Rom. 4:3; 2 Cor.
5:19; 2 Tim. 4:16, et al.; *to account,* Rom.
2:26; 8:36; εἰς οὐδὲν λογισθῆναι, *to be set
at nought, despised,* Acts 19:27; *to regard,
deem, consider,* Rom. 6:11; 14:14; 1 Cor.
4:1; 2 Cor. 10:2; Phil. 3:13; *to infer, conclude, presume,* Rom. 2:3; 3:28; 8:18;
2 Cor. 10:2, 7, 11; Heb. 11:19; 1 Pet. 5:12;
to think upon, ponder, Phil. 4:8; absol. *to
reason,* Mark 11:31; 1 Cor. 13:11

λογιζόμεθα, 1 pers. pl. pres. mid./pass. dep.
indic. . . . . λογίζομαι *(3049)*

λογιζόμενος, nom. sg. m. pres. mid./pass.
dep. part. . . . . λογίζομαι *(3049)*

λογιζομένους, acc. pl. m. pres. mid./pass. dep.
part. . . . . id.

λογιζομένῳ, dat. sg. m. pres. mid./pass. dep.
part. . . . . id.

λογικήν, acc. sg. f. adj. . . . . λογικός *(3050)*

λογικόν, acc. sg. neut. adj. . . . . id.

(3050) **λογικός,** ή, όν [§7.F.a] *pertaining to speech;
pertaining to reason;* in N.T. *rational, spiritual, pertaining to the mind and soul,*
Rom. 12:1; 1 Pet. 2:2

(3051) **λόγιον,** ου, τό [§3.C.c] *an oracle, a divine communication or revelation,* Acts 7:38; Rom.
3:2, et al.

(3052) **λόγιος,** ον, nom. sg. m. adj. [§7.2] *gifted with
learning or eloquence,* Acts 18:24

λογισάμενος, nom. sg. m. aor. mid. dep.
part. . . . . λογίζομαι *(3049)*

λογίσασθαι, aor. mid. dep. infin. . . . . . . id.

λογίσηται, 3 pers. sg. aor. mid. dep. subj. id.

λογισθείη, 3 pers. sg. aor. pass. dep. opt. . id.

λογισθῆναι, aor. pass. infin. . . . . id.

λογισθήσεται, 3 pers. sg. fut. pass. indic. . id.

(3053) **λογισμός,** οῦ, ὁ [§3.C.a] pr. *a computation,
act of computing; a thought, cogitation,*
Rom. 2:15; *a conception, device,* 2 Cor.
10:5

λογισμούς, acc. pl. m. n. . . . . λογισμός *(3053)*

λογισμῶν, gen. pl. m. n. . . . . id.

λογίων, gen. pl. neut. n. . . . . λόγιον *(3051)*

λόγοι, nom. pl. m. n. . . . . λόγος *(3056)*

λόγοις, dat. pl. m. n. . . . . id.

λογομαχεῖν, pres. act. infin. . . . . . λογομαχέω *(3054)*

(3054) **λογομαχέω,** ῶ, fut. λογομαχήσω [§16.P]
(λόγος + μάχομαι) *to contend about
words;* by impl. *to dispute about trivial
things*

(3055) **λογομαχία,** ας, ἡ [§2.B.b; 2.2] *contention or
strife about words;* by impl. *a dispute
about trivial things, unprofitable controversy,* 1 Tim. 6:4

λογομαχίας, acc. pl. f. n. . . . . λογομαχία *(3055)*

λόγον, acc. sg. m. n. . . . . λόγος *(3056)*

(3056) **λόγος,** ου, ὁ, nom. sg. m. n. [§3.C.a] *a word,
a thing uttered,* Matt. 12:32, 37; 1 Cor.
14:19; *speech, language, talk,* Matt. 22:15;
Luke 20:20; 2 Cor. 10:10; James 3:2; *converse,* Luke 24:17; *mere talk, wordy show,*
1 Cor. 4:19, 20; Col. 2:23; 1 John 3:18;
*language, mode of discourse, style of speak-
ing,* Matt. 5:37; 1 Cor. 1:17; 1 Thess. 2:5;
a saying, a speech, Mark 7:29; Eph. 4:29;
an expression, form of words, formula,
Matt. 26:44; Rom. 13:9; Gal. 5:14; *a say-*

ing, a thing propounded in discourse, Matt. 7:24; 19:11; John 4:37; 6:60; 1 Tim. 1:15, et al.; *a message, announcement,* 2 Cor. 5:19; *a prophetic announcement,* John 12:38; *an account, statement,* 1 Pet. 3:15; *a story, report,* Matt. 28:15; John 4:39; 21:23; 2 Thess. 2:2; *a written narrative, a treatise,* Acts 1:1; *a set discourse,* Acts 20:7; *doctrine,* John 8:31, 37; 2 Tim. 2:17; *subject-matter,* Acts 15:6; *reckoning, account,* Matt. 12:36; 18:23; 25:19; Luke 16:2; Acts 19:40; 20:24; Rom. 9:28; Phil. 4:15, 17; Heb. 4:13; *a plea,* Matt. 5:32; Acts 19:38; *a motive,* Acts 10:29; *reason,* Acts 18:14; ὁ λόγος, *the word* of God, especially in the Gospel, Matt. 13:21, 22; Mark 16:20; Luke 1:2; Acts 6:4, et al.; ὁ λόγος, *the* divine WORD, or *Logos,* John 1:1

λόγου, gen. sg. m. n. . . . . λόγος (3056)

λόγους, acc. pl. m. n. . . . . id.

(3057) **λόγχη**, ης, ἡ [§2.B.a] pr. *the head of a javelin; a spear, lance,* John 19:34

λόγχη, dat. sg. f. n. . . . . λόγχη (3057)

λόγχην, acc. sg. f. n. (Matt. 27:49, WH | GNT, MT, TR & NA omit) . . . . id.

λόγῳ, dat. sg. m. n. . . . . λόγος (3056)

λόγων, gen. pl. m. n. . . . . id.

λοιδορεῖς, 2 pers. sg. pres. act. indic. . . . . λοιδορέω (3058)

(3058) **λοιδορέω**, ῶ, fut. λοιδορήσω [§16.P] *to revile, rail at,* John 9:28; Acts 23:4, et al.

(3059) **λοιδορία**, ας, ἡ [§2.B.b; 2.2] *reviling, railing,* 1 Tim. 5:14; 1 Pet. 3:9

λοιδορίαν, acc. sg. f. n. . . . . λοιδορία (3059)

λοιδορίας, gen. sg. f. n. . . . . id.

λοίδοροι, nom. pl. m. adj. . . . . λοίδορος (3060)

(3060) **λοίδορος**, ον, nom. sg. m. adj., *reviling, railing; as a subst. a reviler, railer,* 1 Cor. 5:11; 6:10

λοιδορούμενοι, nom. pl. m. pres. pass. part. [§17.Q] . . . . λοιδορέω (3058)

λοιδορούμενος, nom. sg. m. pres. pass. part. id.

λοιμοί, nom. pl. m. n. . . . . λοιμός (3061)

λοιμόν, acc. sg. m. n. . . . . id.

(3061) **λοιμός**, οῦ, ὁ [§3.C.a] *a pestilence, plague,* Matt. 24:7; Luke 21:11; met. *a pest, pestilent fellow,* Acts 24:5

λοιπά, nom. pl. neut. adj. (Eph. 4:17, MT & TR | GNT, WH & NA omit) . . . . λοιπός (‡3062)

λοιπά, acc. pl. neut. adj. {1 Cor. 11:34} . . id.

λοιπαί, nom. pl. f. adj. . . . . id.

λοιπάς, acc. pl. f. adj. . . . . id.

(3062) λοιποί, nom. pl. m. adj. . . . . id.

λοιποῖς, dat. pl. m. adj. {1 Cor. 7:12} . . . . id.

λοιποῖς, dat. pl. neut. adj. {Rom. 1:13} . . . . λοιπός (‡3062)

(3063) λοιπόν, acc. sg. neut. adj. . . . . id.

(‡3062) **λοιπός**, ή, όν [§7.F.a] *remaining; the rest, remainder,* Matt. 22:6, et al.; as an adv., τοῦ λοιποῦ, *henceforth,* Gal. 6:17; τὸ λοιπόν, or λοιπόν, *henceforwards, thenceforwards,* Matt. 26:45; 2 Tim. 4:8; Acts 27:20, et al.; *as to the rest, besides,* 1 Cor. 1:16; *finally,* Eph. 6:10, et al.; ὃ δὲ λοιπόν, *caeterum, but, now,* 1 Cor. 4:2

(3064) λοιποῦ, gen. sg. neut. adj. . . . . λοιπός (‡3062)

λοιπούς, acc. pl. m. adj. . . . . id.

λοιπῶν, gen. pl. m. adj. {Phil. 4:3} . . . . . . id.

λοιπῶν, gen. pl. f. adj. {Rev. 8:13} . . . . . . id.

λοιπῶν, gen. pl. neut. adj. {Luke 12:26} . . id.

Λουκᾶ, gen. sg. m. n. (2 Cor. 13:13, TRs | GNT, WH, MT, TRb & NA omit) Λουκᾶς (3065)

Λουκᾶν, acc. sg. m. n. (Luke 24:53, TRs | GNT, WH, MT, TRb & NA omit) . . . id.

(3065) **Λουκᾶς**, ᾶ, ὁ, nom. sg. m. n. [§2.4] *Lucas, Luke,* pr. name

(3066) **Λούκιος**, ου, ὁ, nom. sg. m. n. [§3.C.a] *Lucius,* pr. name

λουσαμένη, nom. sg. f. aor. mid. part. [§15.O] . . . . λούω (3068)

λούσαντες, nom. pl. m. aor. act. part. . . . id.

λούσαντι, dat. sg. m. aor. act. part. (Rev. 1:5, MT & TR | λύσαντι, GNT, WH & NA) id.

(3067) **λουτρόν**, οῦ, τό [§3.C.c] *a bath, water for bathing; a bathing, washing, ablution,* Eph. 5:26; Tit. 3:5

λουτροῦ, gen. sg. neut. n. . . . . λουτρόν (3067)

λουτρῷ, dat. sg. neut. n. . . . . id.

(3068) **λούω**, fut. λούσω, aor. ἔλουσα [§13.M] perf. pass. λέλουμαι, pr. *to bathe the body,* as distinguished from washing only the extremities, John 13:10; *to bathe, wash,* Acts 9:37; 16:33; Heb. 10:22, 23; 2 Pet. 2:22; met. *to cleanse* from sin, Rev. 1:5

(3069) **Λύδδα**, ης, ἡ [§2.3] *Lydda,* a town in Palestine

Λύδδα, acc. sg. f. n. (Acts 9:32, 35, GNT, WH & NA | Λύδδαν, MT & TR) . Λύδδα (3069)

Λύδδαν, acc. sg. f. n. (Acts 9:32, 35, MT & TR | Λύδδα, GNT, WH & NA) . . . . . id.

Λύδδας, gen. sg. f. n. (Acts 9:38, GNT, WH & NA | Λύδδης, MT & TR) . . . . id.

Λύδδης, gen. sg. f. n. (Acts 9:38, MT & TR | Λύδδας, GNT, WH & NA) . . . . id.

(3070) **Λυδία**, ας, ἡ, nom. sg. f. n. [§2.B.b; 2.2] *Lydia,* pr. name of a woman, Acts 16:14, 40

Λυδίαν, acc. sg. f. n. . . . . Λυδία (3070)

λύει, 3 pers. sg. pres. act. indic. . . . . λύω (3089)

λύετε, 2 pers. pl. pres. act. indic. . . . . id.

λυθείσης, gen. sg. f. aor. pass. part. [§14.N] id.

λυθῇ, 3 pers. sg. aor. pass. subj. . . . . λύω (3089)

λυθῆναι, aor. pass. infin. . . . . id.

λυθήσεται, 3 pers. sg. fut. pass. indic. [§14.1.c] id.

λυθήσονται, 3 pers. pl. fut. pass. indic. . . . id.

(3071) **Λυκαονία**, ας, ἡ [§2.B.b; 2.2] *Lycaonia,* a province of Asia Minor, Acts 14:6

Λυκαονίας, gen. sg. f. n. . . . . Λυκαονία (3071)

(3072) **Λυκαονιστί**, adv., *in the dialect of Lycaonia,* Acts 14:11

(3073) **Λυκία**, ας, ἡ [§2.B.b; 2.2] *Lycia,* a province of Asia Minor, Acts 27:5

Λυκίας, gen. sg. f. n. . . . . Λυκία (3073)

λύκοι, nom. pl. m. n. . . . . λύκος (3074)

λύκον, acc. sg. m. n. . . . . id.

(3074) **λύκος**, ου, ὁ, nom. sg. m. n. [§3.C.a] *a wolf,* Matt. 10:16; Luke 10:3; John 10:12; met. *a person of wolf-like character,* Matt. 7:15; Acts 20:29

λύκων, gen. pl. m. n. . . . . λύκος (3074)

(3075) **λυμαίνομαι**, fut. λυμανοῦμαι (λύμη, *outrage*) *to outrage, violently maltreat;* in N.T. *to make havoc of,* Acts 8:3

λυομένων, gen. pl. neut. pres. pass. part. . λύω (3089)

λύοντες, nom. pl. m. pres. act. part. . . . . . id.

λυόντων, gen. pl. m. pres. act. part. . . . . . id.

λύουσιν, 3 pers. pl. pres. act. indic. . . . . . . id.

λύπας, acc. pl. f. n. . . . . λύπη (3077)

λυπεῖσθαι, pres. pass. infin. [§17.Q] . . . λυπέω (3076)

λυπεῖται, 3 pers. sg. pres. pass. indic. . . . . id.

λυπεῖτε, 2 pers. pl. pres. act. imper. . . . . . id.

(3076) **λυπέω**, ῶ, fut. λυπήσω, perf. λελύπηκα, aor. ἐλύπησα [§16.P] *to occasion grief or sorrow to, to distress,* 2 Cor. 2:2, 5; 7:8; pass. *to be grieved, pained, distressed, sorrowful,* Matt. 17:23; 19:22, et al.; *to aggrieve, cross, vex,* Eph. 4:30; pass. *to feel pained,* Rom. 14:15

(3077) **λύπη**, ης, ἡ, nom. sg. f. n. [§2.B.a] *pain, distress,* John 16:21; *grief, sorrow,* John 16:6, 20, 22, et al.; meton. *cause of grief, trouble, affliction,* 1 Pet. 2:19

λύπῃ, dat. sg. f. n. . . . . λύπη (3077)

λυπηθείς, nom. sg. m. aor. pass. part. (Matt. 14:9, GNT, WH & NA | ἐλυπήθη, MT & TR) . . . . λυπέω (3076)

λυπηθέντες, nom. pl. m. aor. pass. part. . . id.

λυπηθῆναι, aor. pass. infin. . . . . id.

λυπηθήσεσθε, 2 pers. pl. fut. pass. indic. . . id.

λυπηθῆτε, 2 pers. pl. aor. pass. subj. . . . . . id.

λύπην, acc. sg. f. n. . . . . λύπη (3077)

λύπης, gen. sg. f. n. . . . . id.

λυπῆσθε, 2 pers. pl. pres. pass. subj. . . . λυπέω (3076)

λυπούμενοι, nom. pl. m. pres. pass. part. . id.

λυπούμενος, nom. sg. m. pres. pass. part. . id.

λυπῶ, 1 pers. sg. pres. act. indic. contr. . . id.

λῦσαι, aor. act. infin. [§13.12] . . . . λύω (3089)

(3078) **Λυσανίας**, ου, ὁ [§2.B.d] *Lyssanias,* pr. name, Luke 3:1

Λυσανίου, gen. sg. m. n. . . . . Λυσανίας (3078)

λύσαντες, nom. pl. m. aor. act. part. . . . . λύω (3089)

λύσαντι, dat. sg. m. aor. act. part. (Rev. 1:5, GNT, WH & NA | λούσαντι, MT & TR) . . . . id.

λύσας, nom. sg. m. aor. act. part. . . . . . . id.

λύσατε, 2 pers. pl. aor. act. imper. [§13.13] id.

λύσῃ, 3 pers. sg. aor. act. subj. . . . . id.

λύσῃς, 2 pers. sg. aor. act. subj. . . . . id.

λύσητε, 2 pers. pl. aor. act. subj. . . . . id.

(3079) **Λυσίας**, ου, ὁ, nom. sg. m. n. [§2.B.d] *Lysias,* pr. name

λύσιν, acc. sg. f. n. . . . . λύσις (3080)

(3080) **λύσις**, εως, ἡ [§5.E.c] *a loosing;* in N.T. *a release* from the marriage bond, *a divorce,* 1 Cor. 7:27

(3081) λυσιτελεῖ, 3 pers. sg. pres. act. indic. λυσιτελέω (†3081)

(†3081) **λυσιτελέω**, ῶ, λυσιτελήσω [§16.P] (λύω, *to pay,* + τέλος, *an impost*) pr. *to compensate for incurred expense;* by impl. *to be advantageous to, to profit, advantage;* impers. Luke 17:2

λῦσον, 2 pers. sg. aor. act. imper. . . . . . . λύω (3089)

(3082) **Λύστρα**, ας, ἡ, and Λύστρα, ων, τά [§2.B.b; 3.C.c] *Lystra,* a city of Lycaonia, in Asia Minor

Λύστραν, acc. sg. f. n. . . . . Λύστρα (3082)

Λύστροις, dat. pl. neut. n. . . . . id.

λύσω, 1 pers. sg. aor. act. subj. . . . . λύω (3089)

(3083) **λύτρον**, ου, τό [§3.C.c] pr. *price paid; a ransom,* Matt. 20:28; Mark 10:45

λύτρον, acc. sg. neut. n. . . . . λύτρον (3083)

(3084) **λυτρόω**, ῶ, fut. λυτρώσω [§20.T] *to release for a ransom;* mid. *to ransom, redeem, deliver, liberate,* Luke 24:21; Tit. 2:14; 1 Pet. 1:18

λυτροῦσθαι, pres. mid. infin. [§21.U] . λυτρόω (3084)

λυτρώσηται, 3 pers. sg. aor. mid. subj. . . . id.

λύτρωσιν, acc. sg. f. n. . . . . λύτρωσις (3085)

(3085) **λύτρωσις**, εως, ἡ [§5.E.c] *redemption,* Heb. 9:12; *liberation, deliverance,* Luke 1:68; 2:38

λυτρωτήν, acc. sg. m. n. . . . . λυτρωτής (3086)

(3086) **λυτρωτής**, οῦ, ὁ [§2.B.c] *a redeemer; a deliverer,* Acts 7:35

(3087) **λυχνία**, ας, ἡ, nom. sg. f. n. [§2.B.b; 2.2] *a candlestick, lampstand,* Matt. 5:15, et al.; met. *a candlestick,* as a figure of a Christian church, Rev. 1:12, 13, 20; of a teacher or prophet, Rev. 11:4

λυχνίαι, nom. pl. f. n. . . . . λυχνία (3087)

λυχνίαν, acc. sg. f. n. . . . . λυχνία (3087)
λυχνίας, gen. sg. f. n. {Luke 8:16} . . . . . . id.
λυχνίας, acc. pl. f. n. {Rev. 1:12} . . . . id.
λυχνιῶν, gen. pl. f. n. . . . . id.
λύχνοι, nom. pl. m. n. . . . . λύχνος (3088)
λύχνον, acc. sg. f. n. . . . . id.
(3088) λύχνος, ου, ὁ, nom. sg. m. n. [§6.7] *a light,
lamp, candle,* etc., Matt. 5:15; Mark 4:21,
et al.; met. *a lamp,* as a figure of a distinguished teacher, John 5:35
λύχνου, gen. sg. m. n. . . . . λύχνος (3088)
λύχνῳ, dat. sg. m. n. . . . . id.
(3089) λύω, fut. λύσω, perf. λέλυκα, aor. ἔλυσα
[§13.M] perf. pass. λέλυμαι, aor. pass.
ἐλύθην [§14.N] *to loosen, unbind, unfasten,* Mark 1:7, et al.; *to loose, untie,*
Matt. 21:2; John 11:44; *to disengage,*
1 Cor. 7:27; *to set free, set at liberty, deliver,* Luke 13:16; *to break,* Acts 27:41; Rev.
5:2, 5; *to break up, dismiss,* Acts 13:43; *to
destroy, demolish,* John 2:19; Eph. 2:14;
met. *to infringe,* Matt. 5:19; John 5:18;
7:23; *to make void, nullify,* John 10:35; in
N.T. *to declare free,* of privileges, or, in respect of lawfulness, Matt. 16:19, et al.
Λωΐδι, dat. sg. m. n. (2 Tim. 1:5, GNT, MT,
TR & NA | Λωΐδι, WH) . . . . Λωΐς (3090)
(3090) Λωΐς, ΐδος, ἡ [§4.2.c] *Lois,* pr. name of a
woman, 2 Tim. 1:5
(3091) Λώτ, ὁ, *Lot,* pr. name, indecl.

M

(3092) Μαάθ, ὁ, *Maath,* pr. name, indecl. (Luke 3:26,
WH & TR | Μάαθ, GNT, MT & NA)
(†3093) Μαγαδάν, ὁ, *Magadan,* pr. name, indecl.
(Matt. 15:39, GNT, WH & NA | Μα-
γδαλά, MT & TR)
(3093) Μαγδαλά, ἡ, indecl. *Magdala,* a town of Ju-
dea (Matt. 15:39, MT & TR | Μαγαδάν,
GNT, WH & NA)
(3094) Μαγδαληνή, ῆς, ἡ, nom. sg. f. n. [§2.B.a]
Magdalen, pr. name (*of Magdala*)
Μαγδαληνῇ, dat. sg. f. n. . . . . . Μαγδαληνή (3094)
(‡717) Μαγεδών, ὁ, *Mageddo,* indecl. pr. name (Rev.
16:16, WH & MT | Ἁρμαγεδών, GNT
& NA | Ἁρμαγεδδών, TR)
(3095) μαγεία, ας, ἡ [§2.B.b; 2.2] pr. *the system of
the magians; magic,* Acts 8:11
μαγείαις, dat. pl. f. n. (Acts 8:11, GNT, MT,
TR & NA | μαγίαις, WH) . . . . μαγεία (3095)
(3096) μαγεύω, fut. μαγεύσω [§13.M] *to be a magician; to use magical arts, practise magic,*

sorcery, Acts 8:9
μαγεύων, nom. sg. m. pres. act. part. . μαγεύω (3096)
μάγοι, nom. pl. m. n. . . . . μάγος (3097)
μάγον, acc. sg. m. n. . . . . id.
(3097) μάγος, ου, ὁ, nom. sg. m. n. [§3.C.a] (Persian
mogh, Hebrew מַג, akin to μέγας, *magnus*)
*a magus, sage of the magian religion, ma-
gian,* Matt. 2:1, 7, 16; *a magician, sorcerer,*
Acts 13:6, 8
μάγους, acc. pl. m. n. . . . . μάγος (3097)
(3098) Μαγώγ, ὁ, *Magog,* pr. name, indecl., Rev.
20:8
μάγων, gen. pl. m. n. . . . . μάγος (3097)
(†3099) Μαδιάμ, ὁ, indecl. *Madian,* a district of
Arabia Petraea, Acts 7:29
μαθεῖν, 2 aor. act. infin. [§36.2] . . . . μανθάνω (3129)
μάθετε, 2 pers. pl. 2 aor. act. imper. . . . . . id.
μαθηταί, nom. pl. m. n. . . . . μαθητής (3101)
μαθηταῖς, dat. pl. m. n. . . . . id.
μαθητάς, acc. pl. m. n. . . . . id.
μάθητε, 2 pers. pl. 2 aor. act. subj. . . μανθάνω (3129)
μαθητευθείς, nom. sg. m. aor. pass.
part. . . . . μαθητεύω (3100)
μαθητεύσαντες, nom. pl. m. aor. act. part. id.
μαθητεύσατε, 2 pers. pl. aor. act. imper. . . id.
(3100) μαθητεύω, fut. μαθητεύσω, aor. ἐμαθήτευσα
[§13.M] intrans. *to be a disciple, follow as
a disciple,* Matt. 27:57; in N.T. trans. *to
make a disciple of, to train in discipleship,*
Matt. 28:19; Acts 14:21; pass. *to be trained,
disciplined, instructed,* Matt. 13:52
μαθητῇ, dat. sg. m. n. . . . . μαθητής (3101)
μαθητήν, acc. sg. m. n. . . . . id.
(3101) μαθητής, οῦ, ὁ, nom. sg. m. n. [§2.B.c] *a disciple,* Matt. 10:24, 42, et al.
μαθητοῦ, gen. sg. m. n. . . . . μαθητής (3101)
(3102) μαθήτρια, ας, ἡ, nom. sg. f. n. [§2.B.b; 2.2]
a female disciple; a female Christian, Acts
9:36
μαθητῶν, gen. pl. m. n. . . . . μαθητής (3101)
Μαθθαῖον, acc. sg. m. n. (Matt. 9:9; Mark
3:18; Luke 6:15, GNT, WH & NA |
Ματθαῖον, MT & TR) . . . . . . Μαθθαῖος (‡3156)
(‡3156) Μαθθαῖος, ου, ὁ, nom. sg. m. n. *Matthew,* pr.
name (Matt. 10:3; Acts 1:13, GNT, WH &
NA | Ματθαῖος, MT & TR)
(‡3157) Μαθθάν, ὁ, *Mathan,* pr. name, indecl. (Matt.
1:15a, 15b, WH | Ματθάν, GNT, MT, TR
& NA)
(‡3158) Μαθθάτ, ὁ, *Mathat,* pr. name, indecl. (Luke
3:24, 29, GNT & NA | Luke 3:24,
Μαθθάτ; Ματθάτ, Luke 3:29 WH |
Ματθάτ, MT & TR)
Μαθθίαν, acc. sg. m. n. (Acts 1:23, 26, GNT,
WH & NA | Ματθίαν, MT &

TR) . . . . Μαθθίας *(‡3159)*

(‡3159) **Μαθθίας,** ου, ὁ, *Mathias,* pr. name

(†3103) **Μαθουσαλά,** ὁ, *Mathusala,* pr. name, indecl.
(Luke 3:37, GNT, WH & NA | Μαθου-
σάλα, MT & TR)

μαθών, nom. sg. m. 2 aor. act. part. . μανθάνω *(3129)*

(3104) **Μαϊνάν,** ὁ, *Mainan,* pr. name, indecl. (Luke
3:31, MT & TR | Μεννά, GNT, WH &
NA)

μαίνεσθε, 2 pers. pl. pres. mid./pass. dep.
indic. . . . . μαίνομαι *(3105)*

μαίνεται, 3 pers. sg. pres. mid./pass. dep.
indic. . . . . id.

μαίνῃ, 2 pers. sg. pres. mid./pass. dep. indic. id.

(3105) **μαίνομαι,** 1 pers. sg. pres. mid./pass. dep.
indic., fut. μανήσομαι, and μανοῦμαι,
perf. μέμηνα [§25.5] *to be disordered in
mind, mad,* John 10:20, et al.

μακαρία, nom. sg. f. adj. . . . . μακάριος *(3107)*

καμάριαι, nom. pl. f. adj. . . . . id.

μακαρίαν, acc. sg. f. adj. . . . . id.

μακαρίζομεν, 1 pers. pl. pres. act.
indic. . . . . μακαρίζω *(3106)*

(3106) **μακαρίζω,** fut. μακαρίσω, Att. μακαριῶ
[§26.1] *to pronounce happy, felicitate,* Luke
1:48; James 5:11

μακάριοι, nom. pl. m. adj. . . . . μακάριος *(3107)*

μακάριον, acc. sg. m. adj. {Acts 26:2} . . . id.

μακάριον, nom. sg. neut. adj. {Acts 20:35} id.

(3107) **μακάριος,** ία, ιον, nom. sg. m. adj. [§7.1]
(μάκαρ, idem.) *happy, blessed,* Matt. 5:3,
4, 5, 7; Luke 1:45, et al.

μακαρίου, gen. sg. m. adj. . . . . μακάριος *(3107)*

μακαριοῦσι(ν), 3 pers. pl. fut. act. indic. Att.
[§35.1] . . . . μακαρίζω *(3106)*

μακαρισμόν, acc. sg. m. n. . . . . . μακαρισμός *(3108)*

(3108) **μακαρισμός,** οῦ, ὁ, nom. sg. m. n. [§3.C.a]
*a calling happy, the act of pronouncing
happy, felicitation,* Rom. 4:6, 9; *self-
congratulation,* Gal. 4:15

μακαριωτέρα, nom. sg. f. compar. adj.
[§8.4] . . . . μακάριος *(3107)*

Μακεδόνας, acc. pl. m. n. . . . . Μακεδών *(3110)*

Μακεδόνες, nom. pl. m. n. . . . . id.

(3109) **Μακεδονία,** ας, ἡ, nom. sg. f. n. [§2.B.b; 2.2]
Macedonia

Μακεδονίᾳ, dat. sg. f. n. . . . . Μακεδονία *(3109)*

Μακεδονίαν, acc. sg. f. n. . . . . id.

Μακεδονίας, gen. sg. f. n. . . . . id.

Μακεδόνος, gen. sg. m. n. . . . . Μακεδών *(3110)*

Μακεδόσιν, dat. pl. m. n. . . . . id.

(3110) **Μακεδών,** όνος, ὁ, nom. sg. m. n. [§4.2.e]
a native of Macedonia, Acts 16:9, et al.

(3111) **μάκελλον,** ου, τό [§3.C.c] (Latin *macellum*)
a place where all kinds of provision are ex-

posed to sale, provision mart, shambles,
1 Cor. 10:25

μακέλλῳ, dat. sg. neut. n. . . . . μάκελλον *(3111)*

μακρά, acc. pl. neut. adj. . . . . μακρός *(3117)*

μακράν, acc. sg. f. adj. {Luke 15:13} . . . . id.

(3112) **μακράν,** adv. (acc. sg. f. of μακρός) *far, far
off, at a distance, far distant,* Matt. 8:30;
Mark 12:34, et al.; met. οἱ μακράν, *remote, alien,* Eph. 2:13, 17; so οἱ εἰς
μακράν, Acts 2:39 {Luke 15:10}

(3113) **μακρόθεν,** adv., *far off, at a distance, from
afar, from a distance,* Mark 3:8; 11:13;
preceded by ἀπό, in the same sense, Matt.
26:58

μακροθυμεῖ, 3 pers. sg. pres. act.
indic. . . . . μακροθυμέω *(3114)*

μακροθυμεῖτε, 2 pers. pl. pres. act. imper. id.

(3114) **μακροθυμέω,** ῶ, fut. μακροθυμήσω [§16.P]
(μακρόθυμος, μακρός + θυμός) *to be
slow towards, be long-enduring; to exercise patience, be long-suffering, clement, or
indulgent, to forbear,* Matt. 18:26, 29;
1 Cor. 13:4; 1 Thess. 5:14; 2 Pet. 3:9; *to
have patience, endure patiently, wait with
patient expectation,* Heb. 6:15; James
5:7, 8; *to bear long* with entreaties for deliverance and avengement, Luke 18:7

μακροθυμήσας, nom. sg. m. aor. act.
part. . . . . μακροθυμέω *(3114)*

μακροθυμήσατε, 2 pers. pl. aor. act. imper. id.

μακροθύμησον, 2 pers. sg. aor. act. imper. id.

(3115) **μακροθυμία,** ας, ἡ, nom. sg. f. n. [§2.B.b; 2.2]
patience; patient enduring of evil, fortitude,
Col. 1:11; *slowness of avenging injuries,
long-suffering, forbearance, clemency,*
Rom. 2:4; 9:22; 2 Cor. 6:6; *patient expectation,* Heb. 6:12, et al.

μακροθυμίᾳ, dat. sg. f. n. . . . . μακροθυμία *(3115)*

μακροθυμίαν, acc. sg. f. n. . . . . id.

μακροθυμίας, gen. sg. f. n. . . . . id.

μακροθυμῶν, nom. sg. m. pres. act.
part. . . . . μακροθυμέω *(3114)*

(†3116) **μακροθύμως,** adv., *patiently, with indulgence,*
Acts 26:3

(3117) **μακρός,** ά, όν [§7.1] *long;* of space, *far, distant, remote,* Luke 15:13; 19:12; of time,
of long duration; prolix, Matt. 23:13;
Mark 12:40; Luke 20:47

(3118) **μακροχρόνιος,** ον, nom. sg. m. adj. [§7.2]
(μακρός + χρόνος) *of long duration;
long-lived,* Eph. 6:3

μαλακά, acc. pl. neut. adj. . . . . μαλακός *(3120)*

(3119) **μαλακία,** ας, ἡ [§2.B.b; 2.2] *softness; languor,
indisposition, weakness, infirmity of body,*
Matt. 4:23, et al.

μαλακίαν, acc. sg. f. n. . . . . μαλακία *(3119)*

μαλακοί, nom. pl. m. adj. . . . . μαλακός *(3120)*

μαλακοῖς, dat. pl. neut. adj. . . . . id.

(3120) **μαλακός,** ή, όν [§7.F.a] *soft; soft to the touch, delicate,* Matt. 11:8; Luke 7:25; met. *cinaedus, an instrument of unnatural lust, effeminate,* 1 Cor. 6:9

(3121) **Μαλελεήλ,** ὁ, *Maleleel,* pr. name, indecl., Luke 3:37

(3122) **μάλιστα,** adv. (superlative of μάλα, *very, much*) *most, most of all, chiefly, especially,* Acts 20:38; 25:26, et al.

(3123) **μᾶλλον,** adv. (comparative of μάλα) *more, to a greater extent, in a higher degree,* Matt. 18:13; 27:24; John 5:18; 1 Cor. 14:18, et al.; *rather, in preference,* Matt. 10:6; Eph. 4:28, et al.; used in a periphrasis for the comparative, Acts 20:35, et al.; as an intensive with a comparative term, Matt. 6:26; Mark 7:36; 2 Cor. 7:13; Phil. 1:23; μᾶλλον δέ, *yea rather,* or, *more properly speaking,* Rom. 8:34; Gal. 4:9; Eph. 5:11

(3124) **Μάλχος,** ου, ὁ, nom. sg. m. n. [§3.C.a] *Malchus,* pr. name, John 18:10

(3125) **μάμμη,** and μάμμα, ης, ἡ [§2.B.a; 2.3] *a mother;* later, *a grandmother,* 2 Tim. 1:5

μάμμη, dat. sg. f. n. . . . . μάμμη *(3125)*

μαμμωνᾶ, gen. sg. m. n. (Luke 16:9, TR | μαμωνᾶ, GNT, WH, MT & NA) . . . . μαμμωνᾶς *(3126)*

μαμμωνᾷ, dat. sg. m. n. (Matt. 6:24; Luke 16:11, 13, TR | μαμωνᾷ, GNT, WH, MT & NA) . . . . id.

(3126) **μαμμωνᾶς,** or μαμωνᾶς, ᾶ, ὁ [§2.4] (Aramaic מָמוֹנָא) *wealth, riches,* Luke 16:9, 11; personified, like the Greek Πλοῦτος, *Mammon,* Matt. 6:24; Luke 16:13

μαμωνᾶ, gen. sg. m. n. (Luke 16:9, GNT, WH, MT & NA | μαμμωνᾶ, TR) . . . . μαμμωνᾶς *(3126)*

μαμωνᾷ, dat. sg. m. n. (Matt. 6:24; Luke 16:11, 13, GNT, WH, MT & NA | μαμμωνᾷ, TR) . . . . id.

(3127) **Μαναήν,** ὁ, *Manaen,* pr. name, indecl., Acts 13:1

Μανασσῆ, acc. sg. m. n. . . . . Μανασσῆς *(†3128)*

(†3128) **Μανασσῆ,** indecl. and Μανασσῆς, acc. ῆ, ὁ [§2.5] *Manasses,* pr. name I. *The tribe of Manasseh,* Rev. 7:6 II. *Manasseh, king of Judah,* Matt. 1:10

Μανασσῆ, gen. sg. m. n. {Rev. 7:6} . . . . Μανασσῆ *(†3128)*

Μανασσῆ, acc. sg. m. n. {Matt. 1:10} . . . . id.

(3128) Μανασσῆς, nom. sg. m. n. . . . . id.

μανθάνειν, pres. act. infin. (1 Cor. 14:35, WH | μαθεῖν, GNT, MT, TR & NA) . μανθάνω *(3129)*

μανθανέτω, 3 pers. sg. pres. act. imper. . .   id.

μανθανέτωσαν, 3 pers. pl. pres. act. imper.   id.

μανθάνοντα, acc. pl. neut. pres. act. part.   id.

μανθάνουσι(ν), 3 pers. pl. pres. act. indic.   id.

(3129) **μανθάνω,** fut. μαθήσομαι, 2 aor. ἔμαθον, perf. μεμάθηκα [§36.2] *to learn, be taught,* Matt. 9:13; 11:29; 24:32; *to learn* by practice or experience, *acquire a custom or habit,* Phil. 4:11; 1 Tim. 5:4, 13; *to ascertain, be informed,* Acts 23:27, et al. *to understand, comprehend,* Rev. 14:3

μανθάνωσι(ν), 3 pers. pl. pres. act. subj. . . . . μανθάνω *(3129)*

(3130) **μανία,** ας, ἡ [§2.B.b; 2.2] *madness, insanity,* Acts 26:24

μανίαν, acc. sg. f. n. . . . . μανία *(3130)*

(3131) **μάννα,** τό, indecl. (Hebrew מָן, Ex. 16:15) *manna, the miraculous food of the Israelites while in the desert,* John 6:31, 49, 58, et al.

(3132) **μαντεύομαι,** fut. μαντεύσομαι (μάντις, *a soothsayer diviner*) *to utter oracles, to divine,* Acts 16:16

μαντευομένη, nom. sg. f. pres. mid./pass. dep. part. μαντεύομαι *(3132)*

(3133) **μαραίνω,** fut. μαρανῶ, aor. pass. ἐμαράνθην [§27.1.c; 27.3] *to quench, cause to decay, fade, or wither;* pass. *to wither, waste away,* met. *to fade away, disappear, perish,* James 1:11

(3134) **μαρὰν ἀθά,** indecl. (Aramaic מָרְנָא אֲתָה) i.q. κύριος ἔρχεται, *the Lord cometh, or will come* to judgment (1 Cor. 16:22, WH & TR | μαράνα θά, GNT, MT & NA)

(†3134) **μαράνα,** Aramaic with θά *the Lord cometh, or will come* to judgment (1 Cor. 16:22, GNT, MT & NA | μαράν, WH & TR)

μαρανθήσεται, 3 pers. sg. fut. pass. indic. . . . . μαραίνω *(3133)*

μαργαρῖται, nom. pl. m. n. . . . . . . μαργαρίτης *(3135)*

μαργαρίταις, dat. pl. m. n. . . . . . . id.

μαργαρίτας, acc. pl. m. n. . . . . . . id.

μαργαρίτῃ, dat. sg. m. n. (Rev. 18:16, GNT, WH & NA | μαργαρίταις, MT & TR)   id.

μαργαρίτην, acc. sg. m. n. . . . . id.

(3135) **μαργαρίτης,** ου, ὁ [§2.B.c] (μάργαρον, idem) *a pearl,* Matt. 7:6; 13:45, 46, et al.

μαργαρίτου, gen. sg. m. n. . . . . . . μαργαρίτης *(3135)*

μαργαρίτων, gen. pl. m. n. (Rev. 18:12, GNT, WH & NA | μαργαρίτου, MT & TR)   id.

(3136) **Μάρθα,** ας, ἡ, nom. sg. f. n., *Martha,* pr. name

Μάρθαν, acc. sg. f. n. . . . . Μάρθα *(3136)*

Μάρθας, gen. sg. f. n. . . . . id.

(3137) **Μαρία,** ας, ἡ, nom. sg. f. n. (or Μαριάμ, indecl.) *Mary,* pr. name I. *The mother of Jesus,* Matt. 1:16, et al. II. *Mary, wife of Clopas, mother of James,* Mark 15:40; John 19:25, et al. III. *Mary Magdalene,* Matt. 27:56, et al. IV. *Mary, sister of Martha and Lazarus,* Luke 10:39; John 11:1, et al. V. *Mary, mother of John surnamed Mark,* Acts 12:12 VI. *Mary, a Christian at Rome,* Rom. 16:6

Μαρίᾳ, dat. sg. f. n. . . . . Μαρία *(3137)*

(†3137) **Μαριάμ,** ἡ, the indeclinable form of Μαρία

Μαρίαν, acc. sg. f. n. . . . . Μαρία *(3137)*

Μαρίας, gen. sg. f. n. . . . . id.

Μᾶρκον, acc. sg. m. n. (GNT, MT & NA | Μάρκον, WH & TR) . . . . Μᾶρκος *(3138)*

(3138) **Μᾶρκος,** ου, ὁ, nom. sg. m. n., *Marcus, Mark,* pr. name (GNT, MT & NA | Μάρκος, WH & TR)

Μάρκου, gen. sg. m. n. . . . . Μᾶρκος *(3138)*

(3139) **μάρμαρος,** ου, ὁ [§3.C.a] (μαρμαίρω, *to glisten, shine) a white glistening stone; marble,* Rev. 18:12

μαρμάρου, gen. sg. m. n. . . . . μάρμαρος *(3139)*

μάρτυρα, acc. sg. m. n. . . . . μάρτυς *(3144)*

μάρτυρας, acc. pl. m. n. . . . . id.

μαρτυρεῖ, 3 pers. sg. pres. act. indic. . . . . μαρτυρέω *(3140)*

μαρτυρεῖν, pres. act. infin. . . . . id.

μαρτυρεῖς, 2 pers. sg. pres. act. indic. . . . . id.

μαρτυρεῖται, 3 pers. sg. pres. pass. indic. (Heb. 7:17, GNT, WH & NA | μαρτυρεῖ, MT & TR) . . . . id.

μαρτυρεῖτε, 2 pers. pl. pres. act. indic. . . . id.

μάρτυρες, nom. pl. m. n. . . . . μάρτυς *(3144)*

(3140) **μαρτυρέω,** ῶ, fut. μαρτυρήσω, perf. μεμαρτύρηκα, aor. ἐμαρτύρησα [§16.P] trans. *to testify, depose,* John 3:11, 32; 1 John 1:2; Rev. 1:2; 22:20; absol. *to give evidence,* John 18:23; *to bear testimony, testify,* Luke 4:22; John 1:7, 8, et al.; *to bear testimony* in confirmation, Acts 14:3; *to declare* distinctly and formally, John 4:44; pass. *to be the subject of testimony, to obtain attestation* to character, Acts 6:3; 10:22; 1 Tim. 5:10; Heb. 11:2, 4; mid. equivalent to μαρτύρομαι, *to make a solemn appeal,* Acts 26:22; 1 Thess. 2:12

μαρτυρηθέντες, nom. pl. m. aor. pass. part. [§17.Q] . . . . μαρτυρέω *(3140)*

μαρτυρῆσαι, aor. act. infin. . . . . id.

μαρτυρήσαντος, gen. sg. m. aor. act. part. id.

μαρτυρήσας, nom. sg. m. aor. act. part. . . id.

μαρτυρήσει, 3 pers. sg. fut. act. indic. . . . id.

μαρτυρήσῃ, 3 pers. sg. aor. act. subj. . . . . id.

μαρτύρησον, 2 pers. sg. aor. act. imper. . . . . μαρτυρέω *(3140)*

μαρτυρήσω, 1 pers. sg. aor. act. subj. . . . . id.

(3141) **μαρτυρία,** ας, ἡ, nom. sg. f. n. [§2.B.b; 2.2] judicial *evidence,* Mark 14:55, 56, 59; Luke 22:71; *testimony* in general, Tit. 1:13; 1 John 5:9; *testimony, declaration* in a matter of fact or doctrine, John 1:19; 3:11; Acts 22:18, et al.; *attestation* to character, John 5:34, 36, et al.; *reputation,* 1 Tim. 3:7

μαρτυρίαι, nom. pl. f. n. . . . . μαρτυρία *(3141)*

μαρτυρίαν, acc. sg. f. n. . . . . id.

μαρτυρίας, gen. sg. f. n. . . . . id.

(3142) **μαρτύριον,** ου, τό, nom. sg. neut. n. [§3.C.c] *testimony, evidence,* 2 Cor. 1:12; James 5:3; *testification,* Acts 4:33; in N.T. *testimony,* mode of solemn *declaration or testification,* Matt. 8:4; Luke 9:5, et al.; *testimony, matter of solemn declaration,* 1 Cor. 1:6; 2:1; 1 Tim. 2:6; σκηνὴ τοῦ μαρτυρίου, a title of the Mosaic tabernacle, Acts 7:44; Rev. 15:5 {1 Cor. 1:6}

μαρτύριον, acc. sg. neut. n. {Matt. 10:18} . . . . μαρτύριον *(3142)*

μαρτυρίου, gen. sg. neut. n. . . . . id.

(3143) **μαρτύρομαι,** 1 pers. sg. pres. mid./pass. dep. indic., *to call to witness;* intrans. *to make a solemn affirmation or declaration, asseverate,* Acts 20:26; Gal. 5:3; *to make a solemn appeal,* Eph. 4:17

μαρτυρόμενοι, nom. pl. m. pres. mid./pass. dep. part. (1 Thess. 2:12, GNT, WH, MT & NA | μαρτυρούμενοι, TR) . μαρτύρομαι *(3143)*

μαρτυρόμενος, nom. sg. m. pres. mid./pass. dep. part. (Acts 26:22, GNT, WH, MT & NA | μαρτυρούμενος, TR) . . . μαρτύρομαι *(3143)*

μάρτυρος, gen. sg. m. n. . . . . . . μάρτυς *(3144)*

μαρτυροῦμεν, 1 pers. pl. pres. act. indic. . . . . μαρτυρέω *(3140)*

μαρτυρουμένη, nom. sg. f. pres. pass. part. id.

μαρτυρούμενοι, nom. pl. m. pres. mid. part. (1 Thess. 2:12, TR | μαρτυρόμενοι, GNT, WH, MT & NA) . . . . id.

μαρτυρούμενος, nom. sg. m. pres. pass. part. id.

μαρτυρουμένους, acc. pl. m. pres. pass. part. id.

μαρτυροῦν, nom. sg. neut. pres. act. part. id.

μαρτυροῦντες, nom. pl. m. pres. act. part. id.

μαρτυροῦντι, dat. sg. m. pres. act. part. . . id.

μαρτυροῦντος, gen. sg. m. pres. act. part. id.

μαρτυρούντων, gen. pl. m. pres. act. part. id.

μαρτυροῦσαι, nom. pl. f. pres. act. part. . id.

μαρτυρούσης, gen. sg. f. pres. act. part. . . id.

μαρτυροῦσιν, 3 pers. pl. pres. act. indic. . . id.

μαρτυρῶ, 1 pers. sg. pres. act. indic. {John 7:7} . . . . id.

μαρτυρῶ, 1 pers. sg. pres. act. subj.
{John 8:14} .... μαρτυρέω *(3140)*
μαρτυρῶν, nom. sg. m. pres. act. part.
{Rev. 22:20} .... id.
μαρτύρων, gen. pl. m. n. {Rev. 17:6} .. μάρτυς *(3144)*

(3144) **μάρτυς**, υρος, ὁ, ἡ, nom. sg. m. n., a judicial
witness, deponent, Matt. 18:16; Heb.
10:28, et al.; generally, a witness to a circumstance, Luke 24:48; Acts 10:41, et al.;
in N.T. a witness, a testifier, of a doctrine,
Rev. 1:5; 3:14; 11:3; a martyr, Acts 22:20;
Rev. 2:13

μάρτυσι(ν), dat. pl. m. n. [§4.3.a] .... μάρτυς *(3144)*

(3145) **μασ(σ)άομαι**, ῶμαι, fut. μασ(σ)ήσομαι
[§19.S] to chew, masticate; in N.T. to gnaw,
Rev. 16:10

μάστιγας, acc. pl. f. n. .... μάστιξ *(3148)*
μαστιγοῖ, 3 pers. sg. pres. act. indic. μαστιγόω *(3146)*
μάστιγος, gen. sg. f. n. .... μάστιξ *(3148)*

(3146) **μαστιγόω**, ῶ, fut. μαστιγώσω, aor. ἐμαστί-
γωσα [§20.T] to scourge, Matt. 10:17;
20:19, et al.; met. to chastise, Heb. 12:6

μαστίγων, gen. pl. f. n. .... μάστιξ *(3148)*
μαστιγῶσαι, aor. act. infin. .... μαστιγόω *(3146)*
μαστιγώσαντες, nom. pl. m. aor. act. part. id.
μαστιγώσετε, 2 pers. pl. fut. act. indic. .. id.
μαστιγώσουσιν, 3 pers. pl. fut. act. indic. .. id.
μαστίζειν, pres. act. infin. .... id.

(3147) **μαστίζω**, fut. μαστίξω [§26.2] to scourge, Acts
22:25

(3148) **μάστιξ**, ιγος, ἡ [§4.2.b] a scourge, whip, Acts
22:24; Heb. 11:36; met. a scourge of dis-
ease, Mark 3:10; 5:29, 34; Luke 7:21

μάστιξιν, dat. pl. f. n. .... μάστιξ *(3148)*
μαστοί, nom. pl. m. n. .... μαστός *(3149)*
μαστοῖς, dat. pl. m. n. .... id.

(3149) **μαστός**, οῦ, ὁ [§3.C.a] (a collateral form of
μαζός) the breast, pap, Luke 11:27, et al.

ματαία, nom. sg. f. adj. .... μάταιος *(3152)*
ματαίας, gen. sg. f. adj. .... id.
μάταιοι, nom. pl. m. adj. .... id.

(3150) **ματαιολογία**, ας, ἡ [§2.B.b; 2.2] vain talking,
idle disputation, 1 Tim. 1:6

ματαιολογίαν, acc. sg. f. n. ..... ματαιολογία *(3150)*
ματαιολόγοι, nom. pl. m. adj. ... ματαιολόγος *(3151)*

(3151) **ματαιολόγος**, ον [§7.2] (μάταιος + λέγω) a
vain talker, given to vain talking or trivial
disputation, Tit. 1:10

(3152) **μάταιος**, αία, αιον, nom. sg. m. adj. [§7.1; 7.2]
vain, ineffective, bootless, 1 Cor. 3:20;
groundless, deceptive, fallacious, 1 Cor.
15:17; useless, fruitless, unprofitable, Tit.
3:9; James 1:26; from the Hebrew, erroneous
in principle, corrupt, perverted, 1 Pet. 1:18;
τὰ μάταια, superstition, idolatry, Acts 14:15

(3153) **ματαιότης**, ητος, ἡ [§4.2.c] vanity, folly; from
the Hebrew, religious error, Eph. 4:17;
2 Pet. 2:18; false religion, Rom. 8:20

ματαιότητι, dat. sg. f. n. .... ματαιότης *(3153)*
ματαιότητος, gen. sg. f. n. .... id.

(3154) **ματαιόω**, ῶ, fut. ματαιώσω [§20.T] to make
vain; from the Hebrew, pass. to fall into
religious error, to be perverted, Rom. 1:21

ματαίων, gen. pl. m. adj. .... μάταιος *(3152)*

(3155) **μάτην**, adv., in vain, fruitlessly, without profit,
Matt. 15:9; Mark 7:7

Ματθαῖον, acc. sg. m. n. (Matt. 9:9; Mark
3:18; Luke 6:15, MT & TR | Μαθθαῖον,
GNT, WH & NA) .... Ματθαῖος *(3156)*

(3156) **Ματθαῖος**, ου, ὁ, nom. sg. m. n., Matthew,
pr. name (Matt. 10:3; Acts 1:13, MT & TR
| Μαθθαῖος, GNT, WH & NA)

(3157) **Ματθάν**, ὁ, Matthan, pr. name, indecl. (Matt.
1:15a, b, GNT, MT, TR & NA | Μαθθάν,
WH)

(3158) **Ματθάτ**, ὁ, Matthat, pr. name, indecl. (Luke
3:24, 29, MT & TR | Μαθθάτ, GNT &
NA | Ματθάτ, Luke 3:24; Μαθθάτ, Luke
3:29, WH)

Ματθίαν, acc. sg. m. n. (Acts 1:23, 26, MT
& TR | Μαθθίαν, GNT, WH &
NA) .... Ματθίας *(3159)*

(3159) **Ματθίας**, ου, ὁ [§2.B.d] Matthias, pr. name

(3160) **Ματταθά**, ὁ, Mattatha, pr. name, indecl.

(3161) **Ματταθίας**, ου, ὁ [§2.B.d] Mattathias, pr.
name

Ματταθίου, gen. sg. m. n. ...... Ματταθίας *(3161)*
μάχαι, nom. pl. f. n. .... μάχη *(3163)*

(3162) **μάχαιρα**, ας, ἡ, nom. sg. f. n. [§2.B.b] a large
knife, poniard; a sword, Matt. 26:47, 51,
et al.; the sword of the executioner, Acts
12:2; Rom. 8:35; Heb. 11:37; hence,
φορεῖν μάχαιραν, to bear the sword, to
have the power of life and death, Rom.
13:4; meton. war, Matt. 10:34

μαχαίρᾳ, dat. sg. f. n. (MT & TR | μαχαίρῃ,
GNT, WH & NA) .... μάχαιρα *(3162)*
μάχαιραι, nom. pl. f. n. .... id.
μάχαιραν, acc. sg. f. n. .... id.
μαχαίρας, gen. sg. f. n. (MT & TR |
μαχαίρης, GNT, WH & NA) .... id.
μαχαίρῃ, dat. sg. f. n. (GNT, WH & NA |
μαχαίρᾳ MT & TR) .... id.
μαχαίρης, gen. sg. f. n. (GNT, WH & NA
| μαχαίρας, MT & TR) .... id.
μαχαιρῶν, gen. pl. f. n. .... id.
μάχας, acc. pl. f. n. .... μάχη *(3163)*
μάχεσθαι, pres. mid./pass. dep. infin. μάχομαι *(3164)*
μάχεσθε, 2 pers. pl. pres. mid./pass. dep.
indic. .... id.

(3163) **μάχη**, ης, ἡ [§2.B.a] *a fight, battle, conflict;* in N.T. *contention, dispute, strife, controversy,* 2 Cor. 7:5; 2 Tim. 2:23, et al.

(3164) **μάχομαι**, fut. μαχοῦμαι, or μαχέσομαι [§35.5] *to fight; to quarrel,* Acts 7:26; *to contend, dispute,* John 6:52, et al.

μαχομένοις, dat. pl. m. pres. mid./pass. dep. indic. . . . . μάχομαι *(3164)*

(3165) **μέ**, acc. sg. 1 pers. personal pron. [§11.K.a] ἐγώ *(1473)*

μέγα, nom. sg. neut. adj. {Luke 16:26} . μέγας *(3173)*

μέγα, acc. sg. neut. adj. {Luke 4:16} . . . . . id.

μεγάλα, nom. pl. neut. adj. {Luke 21:11} . id.

μεγάλα, acc. pl. neut. adj. {Luke 1:49} . . . id.

μεγάλαι, nom. pl. f. adj. . . . . id.

μεγάλαις, dat. pl. f. adj. . . . . id.

μεγάλας, acc. pl. f. adj. . . . . id.

μεγαλαυχεῖ, 3 pers. sg. pres. act. indic. (James 3:5, MT & TR | μεγάλα αὐχεῖ, GNT, WH & NA) . . . . μεγαλαυχέω *(3166)*

(3166) **μεγαλαυχέω**, ῶ, fut. μεγαλαυχήσω (μέγας + αὐχέω, *to boast*) *to boast, vaunt; to cause a great stir,* James 3:5

μεγαλεῖα, acc. pl. neut. adj. . . . . μεγαλεῖος *(3167)*

(3167) **μεγαλεῖος**, εία, εῖον [§7.1] *magnificent, splendid;* τὰ μεγαλεῖα, *great things, wonderful works,* Luke 1:49; Acts 2:11

(3168) **μεγαλειότης**, ητος, ἡ [§4.2.c] *majesty, magnificence, glory,* Luke 9:43; Acts 19:27; 2 Pet. 1:16

μεγαλειότητα, acc. sg. f. n. (Acts 19:27, MT & TR | μεγαλειότητος, GNT, WH & NA) . . . . μεγαλειότης *(3168)*

μεγαλειότητι, dat. sg. f. n. . . . . id.

μεγαλειότητος, gen. sg. f. n. . . . . id.

μεγάλη, nom. sg. f. adj. . . . . μέγας *(3173)*

μεγάλῃ, dat. sg. f. adj. . . . . id.

μεγάλην, acc. sg. f. adj. . . . . id.

μεγάλης, gen. sg. f. adj. . . . . id.

μεγάλοι, nom. pl. m. adj. . . . . id.

μεγάλοις, dat. pl. m. adj. (Rev. 11:18, MT & TR | μεγάλους, GNT, WH & NA) . . . id.

(3169) **μεγαλοπρεπής**, ές [§7.G.b] (μέγας + πρέπω) pr. *becoming a great man; magnificent, glorious, most splendid,* 2 Pet. 1:17

μεγαλοπρεποῦς, gen. sg. f. adj. μεγαλοπρεπής *(3169)*

μεγάλου, gen. sg. m. adj. . . . . μέγας *(3173)*

μεγάλους, acc. pl. m. adj. . . . . id.

μεγαλύνει, 3 pers. sg. pres. act. indic. . . . . μεγαλύνω *(3170)*

μεγαλυνθῆναι, aor. pass. infin. . . . . id.

μεγαλυνθήσεται, 3 pers. sg. fut. pass. indic. . . . . id.

μεγαλυνόντων, gen. pl. m. pres. act. part. id.

μεγαλύνουσι(ν), 3 pers. pl. pres. act. indic. id.

(3170) **μεγαλύνω**, fut. μεγαλυνῶ, aor. ἐμεγάλυνα [§27.1.a,f] *to enlarge, amplify,* Matt. 23:5; *to manifest in an extraordinary degree,* Luke 1:58; *to magnify, exalt, extol,* Luke 1:46; Acts 5:13, et al.

μεγάλῳ, dat. sg. m. adj. . . . . μέγας *(3173)*

μεγάλων, gen. pl. m. adj. . . . . id.

(3171) **μεγάλως**, adv., *greatly, very much, vehemently,* Phil. 4:10

(3172) **μεγαλωσύνη**, ης, ἡ, nom. sg. f. n. [§2.B.a] *greatness, majesty,* Heb. 1:3; 8:1; ascribed *majesty,* Jude 25

μεγαλωσύνης, gen. sg. f. n. . . . . . μεγαλωσύνη *(3172)*

μέγαν, acc. sg. m. adj. . . . . μέγας *(3173)*

(3173) **μέγας**, μεγάλη, μέγα, nom. sg. m. adj. [§7.7.b] compar. μείζων, superl. μέγιστος, *great, large in size,* Matt. 27:60; Mark 4:32, et al.; *great, much, numerous,* Mark 5:11; Heb. 11:26; *great, grown up, adult,* Heb. 11:24; *great, vehement, intense,* Matt. 2:10; 28:8; *great, sumptuous,* Luke 5:29; *great, important, weighty, of moment,* 1 Cor. 9:11; 13:13 *great, splendid, magnificent,* Rev. 15:3; *extraordinary, wonderful,* 2 Cor. 11:15; *great, solemn,* John 7:37; 19:31; *great in rank, noble,* Rev. 11:18; 13:16; *great in dignity, distinguished, eminent, illustrious, powerful,* Matt. 5:19; 18:1, 4, et al.; *great, arrogant, boastful,* Rev. 13:5

(3174) **μέγεθος**, ους, τό, nom. sg. neut. n. [§5.E.b] *greatness, vastness,* Eph. 1:19

μέγιστα, nom. pl. neut. superl. adj. [§8.2] . . . . μέγας *(3173)*

(†3175) **μεγιστάν**, ᾶνος, ὁ [§4.2.e] *great men, lords, chiefs, nobles, princes,* Mark 6:21; Rev. 6:15; 18:23

(3175) μεγιστάνες, nom. pl. m. n. . . . . . . μεγιστάν *(†3175)*

μεγιστᾶσιν, dat. pl. m. n. . . . . id.

(3176) **μέγιστος**, η, ον [§7.F.a] *greatest; preeminent,* 2 Pet. 1:4

μεθ', by apostrophe for μετά . . . . μετά *(3326)*

μέθαι, nom. pl. f. n. . . . . μέθη *(3178)*

μέθαις, dat. pl. f. n. . . . . id.

μεθερμηνεύεται, 3 pers. sg. pres. pass. indic. μεθερμηνεύω *(3177)*

μεθερμηνευόμενον, nom. sg. neut. pres. pass. part. . . . . id.

μεθερμηνευόμενος, nom. sg. m. pres. pass. part. (Mark 15:22, WH | μεθερμηνευόμενον, GNT, MT, TR & NA) . . . . id.

(3177) **μεθερμηνεύω**, fut. μεθερμηνεύσω [§13.M] (μετά + ἑρμηνεύω) *to translate, interpret,* Matt. 1:23; Mark 5:41, et al.

(3178) **μέθη**, ης, ἡ [§2.B.a] *strong drink; drunken-*

ness, Luke 21:34; *a debauch in drinking,* Rom. 13:13; Gal. 5:21

μέθη, dat. sg. f. n. . . . . μέθη *(3178)*

μεθιστάναι, pres. act. infin. (1 Cor. 13:2, GNT & NA | μεθιστάνειν, WH, MT & TR) . . . . μεθίστημι *(3179)*

μεθιστάνειν, pres. act. infin. (1 Cor. 13:2, WH, MT & TR | μεθιστάναι, GNT & NA) . . . . μεθιστάνω *(3179)*

(3179) **μεθίστημι,** or μεθιστάνω, fut.μεταστήσω [§29.X] aor. μετέστησα (μετά + ἵστημι) *to cause a change of position; to remove, transport,* 1 Cor. 13:2; *to transfer,* Col. 1:13; met. *to cause to change sides;* by impl. *to pervert, mislead,* Acts 19:26; *to remove* from office, *dismiss, discard,* Luke 16:4; Acts 13:22

(3180) **μεθοδεία,** ας, ἡ [§2.B.b; 2.2] (μεθοδεύω, *to trace, investigate; to handle methodically; to handle cunningly;* from μέθοδος, μετά + ὁδός) *artifice, wile,* Eph. 4:14; 6:11

μεθοδείαν, acc. sg. f. n. (Eph. 4:14, GNT, MT, TR & NA | μεθοδίαν, WH) μεθοδεία *(3180)*

μεθοδείας, acc. pl. f. n. (Eph. 6:11, GNT, MT, TR & NA | μεθοδίας, WH) . . . . id.

μεθόρια, acc. pl. neut. n. (Mark 7:24, MT & TR | ὅρια, GNT, WH & NA) . . μεθόριον *(†3181)*

(†3181) **μεθόριον,** ου, τό [§3.C.c] (neut. from μεθόριος, *interjacent,* μετά + ὅρος) *confine, border,* Mark 7:24

μεθύει, 3 pers. sg. pres. act. indic. . . . . . μεθύω *(3184)*

μεθυόντων, gen. pl. m. pres. act. part. . . . id.

μεθύουσαν, acc. sg. f. pres. act. part. . . . . id.

μεθύουσιν, 3 pers. pl. pres. act. indic. . . . . id.

μεθυσθῶσι(ν), 3 pers. pl. aor. pass. subj. . . . . μεθύσκω *(3182)*

μεθύσκεσθαι, pres. pass. infin. . . . . id.

μεθύσκεσθε, 2 pers. pl. pres. pass. imper. . id.

μεθυσκόμενοι, nom. pl. m. pres. pass. part. id.

(3182) **μεθύσκω,** fut. μεθύσω, aor. pass. ἐμεθύσθην [§36.3] *to inebriate, make drunk;* pass. *to be intoxicated, to be drunk,* Luke 12:45; 1 Thess. 5:7, et al.; *to drink freely,* John 2:10

μέθυσοι, nom. pl. m. n. . . . . μέθυσος *(3183)*

(3183) **μέθυσος,** ου, ὁ, ἡ, nom. sg. m. n. [§3.C.a,b] *drunken; a drunkard,* 1 Cor. 5:11; 6:10

(3184) **μεθύω,** fut. μεθύσω [§13.M] (μέθυ, *strong drink) to be intoxicated, be drunk,* Matt. 24:49, et al.

μεῖζον, nom. sg. neut. compar. adj. {Matt. 23:19} . . . . μέγας *(3173)*

μεῖζον, acc. sg. neut. compar. adj. {James 3:1} . . . . id.

(3185) **μεῖζον,** adv., *to a greater degree* {Matt. 20:31}

μείζονα, acc. sg. m. compar. adj. {Heb. 11:26} . . . . μέγας *(3173)*

μείζονα, acc. sg. f. compar. adj. {John 15:13}   id.

μείζονα, acc. pl. neut. compar. adj. {John 1:50} . . . . id.

μείζονας, acc. pl. f. compar. adj. . . . . id.

μείζονες, nom. pl. m. compar. adj. . . . . . . id.

μείζονος, gen. sg. m. compar. adj. {Heb. 6:13, 16} . . . . id.

μείζονος, gen. sg. f. compar. adj. {Heb. 9:11}   id.

μειζοτέραν, acc. sg. f. adj. . . . . . . μειζότερος *(3186)*

(3186) **μειζότερος,** α, ον [§8.2] *greater,* a comparative form of μείζων, 3 John 4

μείζω, acc. sg. f. compar. adj. {John 5:36} . . . . μέγας *(3173)*

μείζω, acc. pl. neut. compar. adj. {John 1:50}   id.

(3187) μείζων, nom. sg. m. compar. adj. [§8.3] {1 John 4:4} . . . . id.

μείζων, nom. sg. f. compar. adj. {1 John 5:9}   id.

μεῖναι, aor. act. infin. [§27.1.d] . . . . μένω *(3306)*

μείναντες, nom. pl. m. aor. act. part. (Acts 20:15, MT & TR | GNT, WH & NA omit) . . . . id.

μείνατε, 2 pers. pl. aor. act. imper. . . . . . . id.

μείνῃ, 3 pers. sg. aor. act. subj. . . . . id.

μείνητε, 2 pers. pl. aor. act. subj. . . . . id.

μεῖνον, 2 pers. sg. aor. act. imper. . . . . . . id.

μείνωσιν, 3 pers. pl. aor. act. subj. . . . . . . id.

μέλαιναν, acc. sg. f. adj. . . . . μέλας *(3189)*

(3188) **μέλαν,** ανος, τό (neut. from μέλας) *ink,* 2 Cor. 3:3; 2 John 12: 3 John 13

μέλανι, dat. sg. neut. adj. . . . . μέλας *(3189)*

μέλανος, gen. sg. neut. adj. . . . . id.

(3189) **μέλας,** αινα, αν, nom. sg. m. adj. [§7.H.a] *black,* Matt. 5:36; Rev. 6:5, 12

(†3190) **Μελεά,** ὁ [§2.4] *Meleas,* indecl. pr. name (Luke 3:31, GNT, WH & NA | Μελεᾶ, MT & TR)

(‡3199) **μέλει,** 3 pers. sg. pres. act. indic. as impersonal μέλω, fut. μελήσει, imperf. ἔμελε, imper. μελέτω, impersonal verb, *there is a care, it concerns,* Matt. 22:16; Acts 18:17; 1 Cor. 9:9, et al.

μέλεσι(ν), dat. pl. neut. n. . . . . μέλος *(3196)*

μελέτα, 2 pers. sg. pres. act. imper. . . μελετάω *(3191)*

μελετᾶτε, 2 pers. pl. pres. act. imper. (Mark 13:11, MT & TR | GNT, WH & NA omit) . . . . id.

(3191) **μελετάω,** ῶ, fut. μελετήσω [§18.R] aor. ἐμελέτησα, *to care for; to bestow careful thought upon, to give painful attention to, be earnest in,* 1 Tim. 4:15; *to devise,* Acts 4:25; absol. *to study beforehand, premeditate,* Mark 13:11

μελέτω, 3 pers. sg. pres. act. imper. . . . . μέλει *(‡3199)*

μέλη, nom. pl. neut. n. {Rom. 12:4b} .. μέλος *(3196)*
μέλη, acc. pl. neut. n. {Rom. 12:4a} .... id.
(3192) **μέλι,** ιτος, τό, nom. sg. neut. n. [§5.4] *honey,*
     Matt. 3:4; Mark 1:6; Rev. 10:9, 10
     {Matt. 3:4}
μέλι, acc. sg. neut. n. {Mark 1:6} ...... μέλι *(3192)*
(3193) **μελίσσιος,** α, ον [§7.1] (μέλισσα, *a bee,* μέλι)
     of bees, made by bees, Luke 24:42
μελισσίου, gen. sg. neut. adj. (Luke 24:42,
     MT & TR | GNT, WH & NA
     omit) .... μελίσσιος *(3193)*
(3194) **Μελίτη,** ης, ἡ, nom. sg. f. n. [§2.B.a] *Melita,*
     an island in the Mediterranean (Acts 28:1,
     GNT, MT, TR & NA | Μελιτήνη, WH)
(†3194) **Μελιτήνη,** nom. sg. f. n., *Melita,* an island in
     the Mediterranean (Acts 28:1, WH |
     Μελίτη, GNT, MT, TR & NA)
μέλλει, 3 pers. sg. pres. act. indic. ..... μέλλω *(3195)*
μέλλειν, pres. act. infin. .... id.
μέλλεις, 2 pers. sg. pres. act. indic. ...... id.
μέλλετε, 2 pers. pl. pres. act. indic. ...... id.
μέλλη, 3 pers. sg. pres. act. subj. ...... id.
μελλήσετε, 2 pers. pl. fut. act. indic. [§35.5] id.
μελλήσω, 1 pers. sg. fut. act. indic. (2 Pet.
     1:12, GNT, WH & NA | οὐκ ἀμελήσω,
     MT & TR) .... id.
μέλλομεν, 1 pers. pl. pres. act. indic. .... id.
μέλλον, acc. sg. neut. pres. act. part. .... id.
μέλλοντα, acc. sg. m. pres. act. part.
     {Acts 13:34} .... id.
μέλλοντα, nom. pl. neut. pres. act. part.
     {1 Cor. 3:22} .... id.
μέλλοντα, acc. pl. neut. pres. act. part.
     {Mark 10:32} .... id.
μέλλοντας, acc. pl. m. pres. act. part. ... id.
μέλλοντες, nom. pl. m. pres. act. part. ... id.
μέλλοντι, dat. sg. m. pres. act. part. ..... id.
μέλλοντος, gen. sg. m. pres. act. part.
     {Acts 18:14} .... id.
μέλλοντος, gen. sg. neut. pres. act. part.
     {Acts 24:25} .... id.
μελλόντων, gen. pl. m. pres. act. part.
     {Rev. 8:13} .... id.
μελλόντων, gen. pl. neut. pres. act. part.
     {Col. 2:17} .... id.
μέλλουσαν, acc. sg. f. pres. act. part. .... id.
μελλούσης, gen. sg. f. pres. act. part. .... id.
μέλλουσι(ν), 3 pers. pl. pres. act. indic. .. id.
(3195) **μέλλω,** 1 pers. sg. pres. act. indic., fut.
     μελλήσω [§35.5] imperf. ἔμελλον, Att.
     ἤμελλον, *to be about to, be on the point
     of,* Matt. 2:13; John 4:47; it serves to ex-
     press in general a settled futurity, Matt.
     11:14; Luke 9:31; John 11:51, et al.; *to in-
     tend,* Luke 10:1, et al.; participle μέλλων,

μέλλουσα, μέλλον, *future* as distinguished
     from past and present, Matt. 12:32; Luke
     13:9, et al.; *to be always, as it were, about
     to do, to delay, linger,* Acts 22:16
μέλλων, nom. sg. m. pres. act. part. ... μέλλω *(3195)*
(3196) **μέλος,** ους, τό, nom. sg. neut. n. [§5.E.b] *a
     member, limb, any part of the body,* Matt.
     5:29, 30; Rom. 12:4; 1 Cor. 6:15; 12:12,
     et al.
(3197) **Μελχί,** ὁ, *Melchi,* pr. name, indecl. (Luke
     3:24, 28, GNT, MT, TR & NA | Μελχεί,
     WH)
(3198) **Μελχισέδεκ,** ὁ, *Melchisedec,* pr. name, indecl.
     (GNT, MT & NA | Μελχισεδέκ, WH &
     TR)
μελῶν, gen. pl. neut. n. .... μέλος *(3196)*
μεμαθηκώς, nom. sg. m. perf. act. part.
     [§36.2] .... μανθάνω *(3129)*
μεμαρτύρηκα, 1 pers. sg. perf. act.
     indic. .... μαρτυρέω *(3140)*
μεμαρτύρηκας, 2 pers. sg. perf. act. indic. id.
μεμαρτύρηκε(ν), 3 pers. sg. perf. act. indic. id.
μεμαρτύρηται, 3 pers. sg. perf. pass. indic. id.
(3200) **μεμβράνα,** ης, ἡ [§2.3] (Latin *membrana*)
     parchment, vellum, 2 Tim. 4:13
μεμβράνας, acc. pl. f. n. .... μεμβράνα *(3200)*
μεμενήκεισαν, 3 pers. pl. pluperf. act. indic.
     for ἐμεμενήκεισαν [§27.2.d] ...... μένω *(3306)*
μεμέρικεν, 3 pers. sg. perf. act. indic. (1 Cor.
     7:17, WH | ἐμέρισεν, GNT, MT, TR &
     NA) .... μερίζω *(3307)*
μεμέρισται, 3 pers. sg. perf. pass. indic. .. id.
μεμεστωμένοι, nom. pl. m. perf. pass. part.
     [§21.U] .... μεστόω *(3325)*
μεμιαμμένοις, dat. pl. m. perf. pass. part.
     (Tit. 1:15, GNT, WH & NA | μεμιασμέ-
     νοις, MT & TR) .... μιαίνω *(3392)*
μεμίανται, 3 pers. sg. perf. pass. indic. ... id.
μεμιασμένοις, dat. pl. m. perf. pass. part.
     [§27.3] (Tit. 1:15, MT & TR |
     μεμιαμμένοις, GNT, WH & NA) .... id.
μεμίγμενα, nom. pl. neut. perf. pass.
     part. .... μίγνυμι *(3396)*
μεμιγμένην, acc. sg. f. perf. pass. part.
     [§36.5] .... id.
μεμιγμένον, acc. sg. neut. perf. pass. part. id.
μεμισήκασι(ν), 3 pers. pl. perf. act.
     indic. .... μισέω *(3404)*
μεμίσηκεν, 3 pers. sg. perf. act. indic. ... id.
μεμισημένου, gen. sg. neut. perf. pass. part.
     [§17.Q] .... id.
μεμνημένος, nom. sg. m. perf. pass. part.
     [§22.5] .... μιμνήσκω *(†3403)*
μέμνησθε, 2 pers. pl. perf. pass. indic. [§36.3] id.
μεμνηστευμένη, dat. sg. f. perf. pass. part.

(Luke 2:5, MT & TR | ἐμνηστευμένῃ, GNT, WH & NA) . . . . μνηστεύω *(3423)*

μεμνηστευμένην, acc. sg. f. perf. pass. part. (Luke 1:27, MT & TR | ἐμνηστευμένην, GNT, WH & NA) . . . . id.

μεμονωμένη, nom. sg. f. perf. pass. part. [§21.U] . . . . μονόω *(3443)*

μεμύημαι, 1 pers. sg. perf. pass. indic. [§38.2] . . . . μυέω *(3453)*

μέμφεται, 3 pers. sg. pres. mid./pass. dep. indic. μέμφομαι *(3201)*

(3201) **μέμφομαι**, fut. μέμψομαι [§23.1.a] aor. ἐμεμψάμην, *to find fault with, blame, censure; to intimate dissatisfaction with,* Heb. 8:8; absol. *to find fault,* Rom. 9:19

μεμφόμενος, nom. sg. m. pres. mid./pass. dep. part. . . . . μέμφομαι *(3201)*

μεμψίμοιροι, nom. pl. m. adj. . . . μεμψίμοιρος *(3202)*

(3202) **μεμψίμοιρος**, ον [§7.2] (μέμψις, *a finding fault,* from μέμφομαι, + μοῖρα, *a portion, lot) finding fault or being discontented with one's lot, querulous; a discontented, querulous person, a repiner,* Jude 16

(3303) **μέν**, a particle serving to indicate that the term or clause with which it is used stands distinguished from another, usually in the sequel, and then mostly with δέ correspondent, Matt. 3:11; 9:39; Acts 1:1; ὁ μέν — ὁ δέ, *this — that, the one — the other,* Phil. 1:16, 17; *one — another,* οἱ μέν — οἱ δέ, *some — others,* Matt. 22:5; ὃς μέν — ὃς δέ, *one — another,* pl. *some —others,* Matt. 13:8; 21:35; ἄλλος μέν —ἄλλος δέ, *one — another,* 1 Cor. 15:39; ὧδε μέν — ἐκεῖ δέ, *here — there,* Heb. 7:8; τοῦτο μέν — τοῦτο δέ, *partly —partly,* Heb. 10:33, et al. freq.

μένε, 2 pers. sg. pres. act. imper. . . . . . . μένω *(3306)*

μένει, 3 pers. sg. pres. act. indic. {1 Cor. 13:13} . . . . id.

μενεῖ, 3 pers. sg. fut. act. indic. (1 Cor. 3:14, GNT, WH & NA | μένει, MT & TR) id.

μένειν, pres. act. infin. . . . . id.

μένεις, 2 pers. sg. pres. act. indic. . . . . id.

μενεῖτε, 2 pers. pl. fut. act. indic. . . . . . id.

μένετε, 2 pers. pl. pres. act. indic./imper. (1 John 2:27, GNT, WH & NA | μενεῖτε, MT & TR) . . . . id.

μένετε, 2 pers. pl. pres. act. imper. {Mark 6:10} . . . . id.

μενέτω, 3 pers. sg. pres. act. imper. . . . . . id.

μένῃ, 3 pers. sg. pres. act. subj. . . . . id.

μένητε, 2 pers. pl. pres. act. subj. (John 15:4, GNT, WH & NA | μείνητε, MT & TR) id.

(‡3104) **Μεννά**, ὁ, *Menna,* pr. name, indecl. (Luke

3:31, GNT, WH & NA | Μαϊνάν, MT & TR)

μένομεν, 1 pers. pl. pres. act. indic. . . . . μένω *(3306)*

μένον, nom. sg. neut. pres. act. part. {Acts 5:4} . . . . id.

μένον, acc. sg. neut. pres. act. part. {John 1:33} . . . . id.

μένοντα, acc. sg. m. pres. act. part. . . . . . id.

μένοντος, gen. sg. m. pres. act. part. . . . . id.

(†3304) **μενοῦν**, particle (Luke 11:28, GNT, WH, MT & NA | μενοῦνγε, TR)

(3304) **μενοῦνγε** (μέν, οὖν, γε) a combination of particles serving to take up what has just preceded, with either addition or abatement, like the Latin *imo; yea indeed, yea truly, yea rather,* Luke 11:28; Rom. 9:20; 10:18; Phil. 3:8

μένουσαν, acc. sg. f. pres. act. part. . . . . μένω *(3306)*

μένουσιν, 3 pers. pl. pres. act. indic. . . . . . . id.

(3305) **μέντοι**, conj. (μέν + τοι) *truly, certainly, sure,* Jude 8; *nevertheless, however,* John 4:27, et al.

(3306) **μένω**, 1 pers. sg. pres. act. indic., fut. μενῶ, perf. μεμένηκα [§27.1.a; 27.2.d] aor. ἔμεινα [§27.1.d] *to stay,* Matt. 26:38; Acts 27:31; *to continue;* 1 Cor. 7:11; 2 Tim. 2:13; *to dwell, lodge, sojourn,* John 1:39; Acts 9:43, et al.; *to remain,* John 9:41; *to rest, settle,* John 1:32, 33; 3:36; *to last, endure,* Matt. 11:23; John 6:27; 1 Cor. 3:14; *to survive,* 1 Cor. 15:6; *to be existent,* 1 Cor. 13:13; *to continue unchanged,* Rom. 9:11; *to be permanent,* John 15:16; 2 Cor. 3:11; Heb. 10:34; 13:14; 1 Pet. 1:23; *to persevere, be constant, be steadfast,* 1 Tim. 2:15; 2 Tim. 3:14; *to abide, to be in close and settled union,* John 6:56; 14:10; 15:4, et al.; *to indwell,* John 5:38; 1 John 2:14; trans. *to wait for,* Acts 20:5, 23 {John 15:10}

μενῶ, 1 pers. sg. fut. act. indic. [§27.1.a] {Phil. 1:25} . . . . μένω *(3306)*

μένων, nom. sg. m. pres. act. part. . . . . . . id.

μέρει, dat. sg. neut. n. . . . . μέρος *(3313)*

μέρη, acc. pl. neut. n. . . . . id.

μερίδα, acc. sg. f. n. . . . . μερίς *(3310)*

μερίδος, gen. sg. f. n. . . . . id.

(3307) **μερίζω**, fut. μερίσω [§26.1] *to divide; to divide out, distribute,* Mark 6:41; *to assign, bestow,* Rom. 12:3; 1 Cor. 7:17; 2 Cor. 10:13; Heb. 7:2; mid. *to share,* Luke 12:13; pass. *to be subdivided, to admit distinctions,* 1 Cor. 1:13; *to be severed* by discord, *be at variance,* Matt. 12:25, et al.; *to differ,* 1 Cor. 7:34

(3308) **μέριμνα**, ης, ἡ, nom. sg. f. n. [§2.3] (μερίζειν
τὸν νοῦν, *dividing the mind*) *care*, Matt.
13:22; Luke 8:14, et al.; *anxious interest*,
2 Cor. 11:28

μεριμνᾷ, 3 pers. sg. pres. act. indic. μεριμνάω (3309)
μέριμναι, nom. pl. f. n. . . . . μέριμνα (3308)
μερίμναις, dat. pl. f. n. . . . . id.
μέριμναν, acc. sg. f. n. . . . . id.
μεριμνᾷς, 2 pers. sg. pres. act. indic. μεριμνάω (3309)
μεριμνᾶτε, 2 pers. pl. pres. act. indic.
{Matt. 6:28} . . . . id.
μεριμνᾶτε, 2 pers. pl. pres. act. imper.
{Matt. 6:25} . . . . id.

(3309) **μεριμνάω**, ῶ, fut. μεριμνήσω [§18.R] aor.
ἐμερίμνησα, *to be anxious, or solicitous*,
Phil. 4:6; *to expend careful thought*, Matt.
6:27; *to concern one's self*, Matt. 6:25, et
al.; *to have the thoughts occupied with*,
1 Cor. 7:32, 33, 34; *to feel an interest in*,
Phil. 2:20

μεριμνήσει, 3 pers. sg. fut. act.
indic. . . . . μεριμνάω (3309)
μεριμνήσητε, 2 pers. pl. aor. act. subj. . . . id.
μεριμνῶν, nom. sg. m. pres. act. part.
{Luke 12:25} . . . . id.
μεριμνῶν, gen. pl. f. n. {Luke 8:14} . μέριμνα (3308)
μεριμνῶσι(ν), 3 pers. pl. pres. act.
subj. . . . . μεριμνάω (3309)

(3310) **μερίς**, ίδος, ἡ, nom. sg. f. n. [§4.2.c] *a part;
a division* of a country, *district, region,
tract*, Acts 16:12; *a portion*, Luke 10:42; *an*
allotted *portion*, Col. 1:12; *a portion* in
common, *share*, Acts 8:21; 2 Cor. 6:15

μερίσασθαι, aor. mid. infin. . . . . μερίζω (3307)
μερισθεῖσα, nom. sg. f. aor. pass. part. . . . id.
μερισθῇ, 3 pers. sg. aor. pass. subj. [§26.1] id.
μερισμοῖς, dat. pl. m. n. . . . . μερισμός (3311)

(3311) **μερισμός**, οῦ, ὁ [§3.C.a] *a dividing, act of dividing*, Heb. 4:12; *distribution, gifts distributed*, Heb. 2:4

μερισμοῦ, gen. sg. m. n. . . . . μερισμός (3311)
μεριστήν, acc. sg. m. n. . . . . μεριστής (3312)

(3312) **μεριστής**, οῦ, ὁ [§2.B.c] *a divider; an appor-
tioner, arbitrator*, Luke 12:14

(3313) **μέρος**, ους, τό, nom. sg. neut. n. [§5.E.b] *a
part, portion, division*, of a whole, Luke
11:36; 15:12; Acts 5:2; Eph. 4:16, et al.;
a piece, fragment, Luke 24:42; John 19:23;
a party, faction, Acts 23:9; allotted *portion,
lot, destiny*, Matt. 24:51; Luke 12:46; *a
calling, craft*, Acts 19:27; *a* partner's *portion, partnership, fellowship*, John 13:8; pl.
μέρη, a local *quarter, district, region*, Matt.
2:22; 16:13; Acts 19:1; Eph. 4:9, et al.; *side*
of a ship, John 21:6; ἐν μέρει, *in respect,*

on the score, 2 Cor. 3:10; 9:3; Col. 2:16;
1 Pet. 4:16; μέρος τι, *partly, in some part*,
1 Cor. 11:18; ἀνὰ μέρος, *alternately, one
after another*, 1 Cor. 14:27; ἀπὸ μέρους,
partly, in some part or measure, 2 Cor.
1:14; ἐκ μέρους, *individually*, 1 Cor. 12:27;
partly, imperfectly, 1 Cor. 13:9; κατὰ
μέρος, *particularly, in detail*, Heb. 9:5
{Rev. 21:8}

μέρος, acc. sg. neut. n. {Rev. 20:6} . . . . μέρος (3313)
μέρους, gen. sg. neut. n. . . . . id.

(3314) **μεσημβρία**, ας, ἡ [§2.B.b; 2.2] (μέσος +
ἡμέρα) *mid-day, noon*, Acts 22:6; meton.
the south, Acts 8:26

μεσημβρίαν, acc. sg. f. n. . . . . μεσημβρία (3314)
μέσης, gen. sg. f. adj. . . . . μέσος (3319)

(3315) **μεσιτεύω**, fut. μεσιτεύσω [§13.M] aor.
ἐμεσίτευσα, *to perform offices between
two parties; to intervene, interpose*, Heb.
6:17

μεσίτῃ, dat. sg. m. n. . . . . μεσίτης (3316)

(3316) **μεσίτης**, ου, ὁ, nom. sg. m. n. [§2.B.c] *one that
acts between two parties; a mediator, one
who interposes to reconcile two adverse
parties*, 1 Tim. 2:5; *an internuncius, one
who is the medium of communication between two parties, a mid-party*, Gal.
3:19, 20; Heb. 8:6, et al.

μεσίτου, gen. sg. m. n. . . . . μεσίτης (3316)
μέσον, acc. sg. neut. adj. . . . . μέσος (3319)

(3317) **μεσονύκτιον**, ου, τό [§3.C.c] (μέσος + νύξ)
midnight, Luke 11:5, et al.

μεσονύκτιον, acc. sg. neut. n. . . . μεσονύκτιον (3317)
μεσονυκτίου, gen. sg. neut. n. . . . . id.

(3318) **Μεσοποταμία**, ας, ἡ [§2.B.b; 2.2] (μέσος +
ποταμός) *Mesopotamia, the country lying
between the rivers Tigris and Euphrates*

Μεσοποταμίᾳ, dat. sg. f. n. . . . Μεσοποταμία (3318)
Μεσοποταμίαν, acc. sg. f. n. . . . . id.

(3319) **μέσος**, η, ον, nom. sg. m. adj. [§7.F.a] *mid,
middle*, Matt. 25:6; Acts 26:13; τὸ μέσον,
the middle, the midst, Matt. 14:24; ἀνὰ
μέσον, *in the midst*; from the Hebrew, *in,
among*, Matt. 13:25; *between*, 1 Cor. 6:5;
διὰ μέσου, *through the midst of*, Luke
4:30; εἰς τὸ μέσον, *into, or in the midst*,
Mark 3:3; Luke 6:8; ἐκ μέσου, *from the
midst, out of the way*, Col. 2:14; 2 Thess.
2:7; from the Hebrew, *from, from among*,
Matt. 13:49; ἐν τῷ μέσῳ, *in the midst*,
Matt. 10:16; *in the midst, in public, publicly*, Matt. 14:6; ἐν μέσῳ, *in the midst of;
among*, Matt. 18:20; κατὰ μέσον τῆς
νυκτός, *about midnight*, Acts 27:27

(3320) **μεσότοιχον**, ου, τό [§3.C.c] (μέσος + τοῖχος)

a middle wall; a partition wall, a barrier,
Eph. 2:14

μεσότοιχον, acc. sg. neut. n. ..... μεσότοιχον *(3320)*

μέσου, gen. sg. neut. adj. .... μέσος *(3319)*

(3321) **μεσουράνημα**, ατος, τό [§4.D.c] (μέσος +
οὐρανός) *the mid-heaven, mid-air,* Rev.
8:13, et al.

μεσουρανήματι, dat. sg. neut. n. μεσουράνημα *(3321)*

μεσούσης, gen. sg. f. pres. act. part. .. μεσόω *(3322)*

(3322) **μεσόω**, ῶ, fut. μεσώσω [§20.T] *to be in the
middle or midst; to be advanced midway,*
John 7:14

Μεσσίαν, acc. sg. m. n. (John 1:41, GNT,
WH, TR & NA | Μεσίαν, MT) . Μεσσίας *(3323)*

(3323) **Μεσσίας**, ου, ὁ, nom. sg. m. n. [§2.B.d]
(Hebrew מָשִׁיחַ, from מָשַׁח, *to anoint*) *the
Messiah, the Anointed One,* i.q. ὁ Χριστός,
John 1:42 (John 4:25, GNT, WH, TR &
NA | Μεσίας, MT)

μεστή, nom. sg. f. adj. .... μεστός *(3324)*

μεστοί, nom. pl. m. adj. .... id.

μεστόν, acc. sg. m. adj. {John 19:29b} ... id.

μεστόν, nom. sg. neut. adj. {John 19:29a} id.

μεστόν, acc. sg. neut. adj. {John 21:11} .. id.

(3324) **μεστός**, ή, όν [§7.F.a] *full, full of, filled with,*
John 19:29, et al.; *replete,* Rom. 1:29;
15:14, et al.

μεστούς, acc. pl. m. adj. .... μεστός *(3324)*

(3325) **μεστόω**, ῶ, fut. μεστώσω [§20.T] *to fill; pass.
to be filled, be full,* Acts 2:13

μέσῳ, dat. sg. neut. adj. .... μέσος *(3319)*

μετ', by apostrophe for μετά .... μετά *(3326)*

(3326) **μετά**, prep., with a genitive, *with, together
with,* Matt. 16:27; 12:41; 26:55; *with, on
the same side or party with, in aid of,* Matt.
12:30; 20:20; *with, by means of,* Acts
13:17; *with,* of conflict, Rev. 11:7; *with,
among,* Luke 24:5; *with, to, towards,* Luke
1:58, 72; with an accusative, *after,* of place,
behind, Heb. 9:3; of time, *after,* Matt. 17:1;
24:29; followed by an infin. with the neut.
article, *after, after that,* Matt. 26:32; Luke
22:20

μετάβα, 2 pers. sg. 2 aor. act. imper. (Matt.
17:20, GNT, WH & NA | μετάβηθι, MT
& TR) .... μεταβαίνω *(3327)*

μεταβαίνετε, 2 pers. pl. pres. act. imper. ... id.

(3327) **μεταβαίνω**, fut. μεταβήσομαι [§37.1] perf.
μεταβέβηκα, 2 aor. μετέβην (μετά +
βαίνω) *to go or pass from one place to another,* John 5:24; *to pass away, be removed,* Matt. 17:20; *to go away, depart,*
Matt. 8:34, et al.

μεταβαλλόμενοι, nom. pl. m. pres. mid. part.
(Acts 28:6, MT & TR | μεταβαλόμενοι,

GNT, WH & NA) .... μεταβάλλω *(3328)*

(3328) **μεταβάλλω** (μετά + βάλλω) *to change;* mid.
to change one's mind, Acts 28:6

μεταβαλόμενοι, nom. pl. m. aor. mid. part.
(Acts 28:6, GNT, WH & NA | μετα-
βαλλόμενοι, MT & TR) ..... μεταβαίνω *(3327)*

μεταβάς, nom. sg. m. 2 aor. act. part. ... id.

μεταβεβήκαμεν, 1 pers. pl. perf. act. indic. id.

μεταβέβηκεν, 3 pers. sg. perf. act. indic. . id.

μεταβῇ, 3 pers. sg. 2 aor. act. subj. ...... id.

μετάβηθι, 2 pers. sg. 2 aor. act. imper. ... id.

μεταβήσεται, 3 pers. sg. fut. mid. dep. indic. id.

μετάγεται, 3 pers. sg. pres. pass. indic. μετάγω *(3329)*

μετάγομεν, 1 pers. pl. pres. act. indic. ... id.

(3329) **μετάγω**, fut. μεγάξω [§23.1.b] (μετά + ἄγω)
*to lead or move from one place to another;
to change direction, to turn about,* James
3:3, 4

μεταδιδόναι, pres. act. infin. .... μεταδίδωμι *(3330)*

μεταδιδούς, nom. sg. m. pres. act. part. .. id.

(3330) **μεταδίδωμι**, fut. μεταδώσω [§30.Z] (μετά +
δίδωμι) *to give a part, to share,* Luke 3:11;
to impart, bestow, Rom. 1:11; 12:8, et al.

μεταδότω, 3 pers. sg. 2 aor. act.
imper. .... μεταδίδωμι *(3330)*

μεταδοῦναι, 2 aor. act. infin. .... id.

μεταδῶ, 1 pers. sg. 2 aor. act. subj. ..... id.

μεταθέσεως, gen. sg. f. n. .... μετάθεσις *(3331)*

μετάθεσιν, acc. sg. f. n. .... id.

(3331) **μετάθεσις**, εως, ἡ, nom. sg. f. n. [§5.E.c] *a
removal, translation,* Heb. 11:5; *a trans-
mutation, change* by the abolition of one
thing, and the substitution of another

(3332) **μεταίρω**, fut. μεταρῶ, aor. μετῆρα [§27.1.c,e]
(μετά + αἴρω) *to remove, transfer;* in N.T.
intrans. *to go away, depart,* Matt. 13:53;
19:1

μετακάλεσαι, 2 pers. sg. aor. mid.
imper. .... μετακαλέω *(3333)*

μετακαλέσομαι, 1 pers. sg. fut. mid. indic. id.

(3333) **μετακαλέω**, ῶ, fut. μετακαλέσω [§22.1]
(μετά + καλέω) *to call from one place into
another;* mid. *to call or send for, invite to
come to oneself,* Acts 7:14, et al.

(3334) **μετακινέω**, ῶ, fut. μετακινήσω [§16.P] (μετά
+ κινέω) *to move away, remove;* pass.
met. *to stir away from, to swerve,* Col. 1:23

μετακινούμενοι, nom. pl. m. pres. pass.
part. .... μετακινέω *(3334)*

μεταλαβεῖν, 2 aor. act. infin. .. μεταλαμβάνω *(3335)*

μεταλαβών, nom. sg. m. 2 aor. act. part. . id.

μεταλαμβάνει, 3 pers. sg. pres. act. indic. id.

μεταλαμβάνειν, pres. act. infin. .... id.

(3335) **μεταλαμβάνω**, fut. μεταλή(μ)ψομαι [§36.2]
2 aor. μετέλαβον (μετά + λαμβάνω) *to*

partake of, share in, Acts 2:46; 2 Tim. 2:6, et al.; *to get, obtain, find,* Acts 24:25

μετάλημψιν, acc. sg. f. n. (1 Tim. 4:3, GNT, WH & NA | μετάληψιν, MT & TR) . . . . μετάλη(μ)ψις *(†3336)*

(†3336) **μετάλη(μ)ψις**, εως, ἡ [§5.E.c] *a partaking of, a being partaken of,* 1 Tim. 4:3

(3337) **μεταλλάσσω**, or μεταλλάττω, fut. μεταλλάξω [§26.3] (μετά + ἀλλάσσω) *to exchange, change for or into, transmute,* Rom. 1:25, 26

μεταμεληθείς, nom. sg. m. aor. pass. dep. part. . . . . μεταμέλομαι *(†3338)*

μεταμεληθήσεται, 3 pers. sg. fut. pass. dep. indic. . . . . id.

(†3338) **μεταμέλομαι**, 1 pers. sg. pres. mid./pass. dep. indic., fut. (pass. form) μεταμεληθήσομαι, aor. (pass. form) μετεμελήθην [§35.5] (μετά + μέλομαι) *to change one's judgment on past points of conduct; to change one's mind and purpose,* Heb. 7:21; *to repent, regret,* Matt. 21:29, 32; 27:3; 2 Cor. 7:8

(3339) **μεταμορφόω**, ῶ, fut. μεταμορφώσω [§20.T] (μετά + μορφόω) *to change the external form, transfigure;* mid. *to change one's form, be transfigured,* Matt. 17:2; Mark 9:2; *to undergo a* spiritual *transformation,* Rom. 12:2; 2 Cor. 3:18

μεταμορφούμεθα, 1 pers. pl. pres. pass. indic. [§21.U] . . . . μεταμορφόω *(3339)*

μεταμορφοῦσθε, 2 pers. pl. pres. pass. imper.   id.

μετανοεῖν, pres. act. infin. . . . . μετανοέω *(3340)*

μετανοεῖτε, 2 pers. pl. pres. act. imper. . . .   id.

(3340) **μετανοέω**, ῶ, fut. μετανοήσω [§16.P] (μετά + νοέω) *to undergo a change in frame of mind and feeling, to repent,* Luke 17:3, 4, et al.; *to make a change of principle and practice, to reform,* Matt. 3:2, et al.

μετανοῆσαι, aor. act. infin. (Rev. 2:21, GNT, WH, MT & NA | μετενόησεν, TR) . . . . μετανοέω *(3340)*

μετανοησάντων, gen. pl. m. aor. act. part.   id.

μετανοήσατε, 2 pers. pl. aor. act. imper. .   id.

μετανοήση, 3 pers. sg. aor. act. subj. . . . .   id.

μετανοήσης, 2 pers. sg. aor. act. subj. . . .   id.

μετανοήσητε, 2 pers. pl. aor. act. subj. (Luke 13:5, WH | μετανοῆτε, GNT, MT, TR & NA) . . . . id.

μετανοήσον, 2 pers. sg. aor. act. imper. . .   id.

μετανοήσουσιν, 3 pers. pl. fut. act. indic. .   id.

μετανοήσωσι(ν), 3 pers. pl. aor. act. subj.   id.

μετανοῆτε, 2 pers. pl. pres. act. subj. . . . .   id.

(3341) **μετάνοια**, ας, ἡ [§2.B.b; 2.2] *a change of mode of thought and feeling, repentance,* Matt.

3:8; Acts 20:21; 2 Tim. 2:25, et al.; practical *reformation,* Luke 15:7, et al.; *reversal* of the past, Heb. 12:17

μετάνοιαν, acc. sg. f. n. . . . . μετάνοια *(3341)*

μετανοίας, gen. sg. f. n. . . . . id.

μετανοοῦντι, dat. sg. m. pres. act. part. . . . . μετανοέω *(3340)*

μετανοῶ, 1 pers. sg. pres. act. indic. . . . .   id.

μετανόωσι(ν), 3 pers. pl. pres. act. subj. (Mark 6:12, GNT, WH & NA | μετανοήσωσι(ν), MT & TR) . . . .   id.

(3342) **μεταξύ**, adv. (μετά) *between,* Matt. 23:35; Luke 11:51; 16:26; Acts 15:9; ἐν τῷ μεταξύ, sc. χρόνῳ, *in the meantime, meanwhile,* John 4:31; in N.T. ὁ μεταξύ, *following, succeeding,* Acts 13:42

μεταπεμπόμενος, nom. sg. m. pres. mid./pass. dep. part. . . . . μεταπέμπω *(3343)*

(3343) **μεταπέμπω**, fut. μεταπέμψω [§23.1.a] (μετά + πέμπω) *to send after;* mid. *to send after or for* any one, *invite to come to one's self,* Acts 10:5, et al.

μεταπεμφθείς, nom. sg. m. aor. pass. part. μεταπέμπω *(3343)*

μετάπεμψαι, 2 pers. sg. aor. mid. dep. imper.   id.

μεταπεμψάμενος, nom. sg. m. aor. mid. dep. part. (Acts 20:1, GNT, WH & NA | προσκαλεσάμενος, MT & TR) . . . . .   id.

μεταπέμψασθαι, aor. mid. dep. infin. . . . .   id.

μεταπέμψηται, 3 pers. sg. aor. mid. dep. subj.   id.

μετασταθῶ, 1 pers. sg. aor. pass. subj. [§29.6] . . . . μεθίστημι *(3179)*

μεταστήσας, nom. sg. m. aor. act. part. [§29.X] . . . . id.

μεταστραφήσεται, 3 pers. sg. 2 fut. pass. indic. . . . . μεταστρέφω *(3344)*

μεταστραφήτω, 3 pers. sg. 2 aor. pass. imper. (James 4:9, MT & TR | μετατραπήτω, GNT, WH & NA) . . . .   id.

(3344) **μεταστρέφω**, fut. μεταστρέψω [§23.1.a] 2 aor. pass. μετεστράφην [§24.10] (μετά + στρέφω) *to turn about; convert* into something else, *change,* Acts 2:20; James 4:9; by impl. *to pervert,* Gal. 1:7

μεταστρέψαι, aor. act. infin. . . . . μεταστρέφω *(3344)*

μετασχηματίζεται, 3 pers. sg. pres. mid. indic. . . . . μετασχηματίζω *(3345)*

μετασχηματιζόμενοι, nom. pl. m. pres. mid. part. . . . . id.

μετασχηματίζονται, 3 pers. pl. pres. pass. indic. . . . . id.

(3345) **μετασχηματίζω**, fut. μετασχηματίσω [§26.1] aor. μετεσχημάτισα (μετά + σχηματίζω, *to fashion,* σχῆμα) *to remodel, transfigure,* Phil. 3:21; mid. *to transform one's self,*

2 Cor. 11:13, 14, 15; *to make an* imaginary *transference* of circumstances from the parties really concerned in them to others, *to transfer* an imagination, 1 Cor. 4:6

μετασχηματίσει, 3 pers. sg. fut. act.
indic. . . . . μετασχηματίζω *(3345)*

μετατιθεμένης, gen. sg. f. pres. pass.
part. . . . . μετατίθημι *(3346)*

μετατιθέντες, nom. pl. m. pres. act. part. . id.

μετατίθεσθε, 2 pers. pl. pres. mid./pass. indic.   id.

(3346) **μετατίθημι,** fut. μετατιθήσω [§27.V] aor. μετέθηκα, aor. pass. μετετέθην (μετά + τίθημι) *to transport,* Acts 7:16; *to transfer,* Heb. 7:12; *to translate* out of the world, Heb. 11:5; met. *to transfer* to other purposes, *to pervert,* Jude 4; mid. *to transfer one's self, to change over,* Gal. 1:6

μετατραπήτω, 3 pers. sg. 2 aor. pass. imper. (James 4:9, GNT, WH & NA | μεταστραφήτω, MT & TR) . . . . . . μετατρέπω *(‡3344)*

(‡3344) **μετατρέπω,** *to turn around, change, alter*

μετέβη, 3 pers. sg. 2 aor. act. indic. [§37.1] . . . . μεταβαίνω *(3327)*

μετέθηκεν, 3 pers. sg. aor. act.
indic. . . . . μετατίθημι *(3346)*

μετεκαλέσατο, 3 pers. sg. aor. mid. indic. [§22.1] . . . . μετακαλέω *(3333)*

μετελάμβανον, 3 pers. pl. imperf. act.
indic. . . . . μεταλαμβάνω *(3335)*

μετεμελήθητε, 2 pers. pl. aor. pass. dep.
indic. . . . . μεταμέλομαι *(†3338)*

μετεμελόμην, 1 pers. sg. imperf. mid./pass.
dep. indic. . . . . id.

μετεμορφώθη, 3 pers. sg. aor. pass.
indic. . . . . μεταμορφόω *(3339)*

μετεμόησαν, 3 pers. pl. aor. act.
indic. . . . . μετανοέω *(3340)*

μετενόησε(ν), 3 pers. sg. aor. act. indic. (Rev. 2:21, TR | μετανοῆσαι, GNT, WH, MT & NA) . . . . id.

(3347) **μετέπειτα,** adv. (μετά + ἔπειτα) *afterwards,* Heb. 12:17

μετεπέμψασθε, 2 pers. pl. aor. mid. dep.
indic. . . . . μεταπέμπω *(3343)*

μετεπέμψατο, 3 pers. sg. aor. mid. dep. indic.   id.

μετέστησεν, 3 pers. sg. aor. act.
indic. . . . . μεθίστημι *(3179)*

μετέσχε(ν), 3 pers. sg. 2 aor. act.
indic. . . . . μετέχω *(3348)*

μετέσχηκεν, 3 pers. sg. perf. act. indic. . . id.

μετεσχημάτισα, 1 pers. sg. aor. act.
indic. . . . . μετασχηματίζω *(3345)*

μετετέθη, 3 pers. sg. aor. pass. indic.
[§28.10] . . . . μετατίθημι *(3346)*

μετετέθησαν, 3 pers. pl. aor. pass. indic. . id.

μετέχειν, pres. act. infin. . . . . μετέχω *(3348)*

μετέχομεν, 1 pers. pl. pres. act. indic. . . . . id.

μετέχουσιν, 3 pers. pl. pres. act. indic. . . . id.

(3348) **μετέχω,** 1 pers. sg. pres. act. indic., fut. μεθέξω [§35.4] perf. μετέσχηκα, 2 aor. μετέσχον [§36.4] (μετά + ἔχω) *to share in, partake,* 1 Cor. 9:10, 12; 10:17, 21, et al.; *to be a member of,* Heb. 7:13

μετέχων, nom. sg. m. pres. act. part. . μετέχω *(3348)*

μετεωρίζεσθε, 2 pers. pl. pres. pass.
imper. . . . . μετεωρίζω *(3349)*

(3349) **μετεωρίζω,** fut. μετεωρίσω [§26.1] (μετέωρος, *raised from the ground) to raise aloft;* met. *to unsettle in mind;* pass. *to be excited with anxiety, be in anxious suspense,* Luke 12:29

μετήλλαξαν, 3 pers. pl. aor. act.
indic. . . . . μεταλλάσσω *(3337)*

μετῆρεν, 3 pers. sg. aor. act. indic.
[§27.1.e] . . . . μεταίρω *(3332)*

(3350) **μετοικεσία,** ας, ἡ [§2.B.b; 2.2] (μετοικέω, *to change one's abode,* μετά + οἰκέω) *change of abode or country, migration,* Matt. 1:11, 12, 17

μετοικεσίαν, acc. sg. f. n. . . . . μετοικεσία *(3350)*

μετοικεσίας, gen. sg. f. n. . . . . id.

(3351) **μετοικίζω,** fut. μετοικίσω [§26.1] (μετά + οἰκίζω, *to fix in a habitation) to cause to change abode, cause to emigrate,* Acts 7:4

μετοικιῶ, 1 pers. sg. fut. act. indic. Att.
[§35.11] . . . . μετοικίζω *(3351)*

(3352) **μετοχή,** ῆς, ἡ, nom. sg. f. n. [§2.B.a] *a sharing, partaking; communion, fellowship,* 2 Cor. 6:14

μέτοχοι, nom. pl. m. adj. . . . . μέτοχος *(3353)*

μετόχοις, dat. pl. m. adj. . . . . id.

(3353) **μέτοχος,** ον [§7.2] *a partaker,* Heb. 3:1, 14; 12:8; *an associate, partner, fellow,* Luke 5:7; Heb. 1:9

μετόχους, acc. pl. m. adj. . . . . μέτοχος *(3353)*

μετρεῖτε, 2 pers. pl. pres. act. indic. . . μετρέω *(3354)*

(3354) **μετρέω,** ῶ, fut. μετρήσω [§16.P] aor. ἐμέτρησα, *to mete, measure,* Matt. 7:2; Rev. 11:1, 2, et al.; met. *to estimate,* 2 Cor. 10:12

μετρηθήσεται, 3 pers. sg. fut. pass.
indic. . . . . μετρέω *(3354)*

μετρήσῃ, 3 pers. sg. aor. act. subj. . . . . . . id.

μετρήσῃς, 2 pers. sg. aor. act. subj. . . . . . id.

μέτρησον, 2 pers. sg. aor. act. imper. . . . . id.

μετρητάς, acc. pl. m. n. . . . . μετρητής *(3355)*

(3355) **μετρητής,** οῦ, ὁ [§2.B.c] pr. *a measurer;* also, *metretes,* Latin *metreta,* equivalent to the Attic ἀμφορεύς, i.e., three-fourths of the Attic μέδιμνος, or Hebrew בַּת, and therefore

equal to about nine gallons, John 2:6

μετριοπαθεῖν, pres. act. infin. . . . μετριοπαθέω *(3356)*

(3356) **μετριοπαθέω, ῶ,** fut. μετριοπαθήσω [§16.P] (μέτριος + πάθος) *to moderate one's passions; to be gentle, compassionate,* Heb. 5:2

(3357) **μετρίως,** adv., *moderately; slightly;* οὐ μετρίως, *no little, not a little, much, greatly,* Acts 20:12

(3358) **μέτρον,** ου, τό [§3.C.c] *measure,* Matt. 7:2; Mark 4:24; Luke 6:38; Rev. 21:17, et al.; *measure, standard,* Eph. 4:13; *extent, compass,* 2 Cor. 10:13; allotted *measure, specific portion,* Rom. 12:3; Eph. 4:7, 16; ἐκ μέτρον, *by measure, with definite limitation,* John 3:34

μέτρον, acc. sg. neut. n. . . . . μέτρον *(3358)*
μέτρου, gen. sg. neut. n. . . . . id.
μετροῦντες, nom. pl. m. pres. act.
  part. . . . . μετρέω *(3354)*
μέτρῳ, dat. sg. neut. n. . . . . μέτρον *(3358)*
μετῴκισεν, 3 pers. sg. aor. act. indic.
  [§13.2] . . . . μετοικίζω *(3351)*

(3359) **μέτωπον,** ου, τό [§3.C.c] (μετά + ὤψ) *forehead, front,* Rev. 7:3; 9:4, et al.

μέτωπον, acc. sg. neut. n. . . . . μέτωπον *(3359)*
μετώπου, gen. sg. neut. n. . . . . id.
μετώπων, gen. pl. neut. n. . . . . id.

(3360) **μέχρι,** and μέχρις before a vowel, adv. of place, *unto, even to,* Rom. 15:19; of time, *until, till,* Matt. 11:23; 13:30, et al.

(3361) **μή,** a particle of negation, *not,* for the particulars of its usage, especially as distinguished from that of οὐ, consult a grammar; as a conjunction, *lest, that not,* Matt. 5:29, 30; 18:10; 24:6; Mark 13:36; μή, or μήτι, or μήποτε, prefixed to an interrogative clause, is a mark of tone, since it expresses an intimation either of the reality of the matters respecting which the question is asked, Matt. 12:23, et al.; or the contrary, John 4:12, et al.

(†3361) **μήγε,** a strengthened form for μή (μή + γε) Matt. 6:1; 9:17, et al.

(3365) **μηδαμῶς,** adv. (μηδαμός, i.q. μηδείς) *by no means,* Acts 10:14; 11:8

(3366) **μηδέ,** conj. *neither,* and repeated, *neither — nor,* Matt. 6:25; 7:6; 10:9, 10; *not even, not so much as,* Mark 2:2, et al.

(3367) **μηδείς,** nom. sg. m. adj., μηδεμία, μηδέν [§10.6.c] (μηδέ, εἷς) *not one, none, no one,* Matt. 8:4, et al.

μηδεμίαν, acc. sg. f. adj. . . . . μηδείς *(3367)*
μηδέν, nom. sg. neut. adj. {Mark 7:15} . . id.
μηδέν, acc. sg. neut. adj. {Acts 10:20} . . . id.
μηδένα, acc. sg. m. adj. . . . . id.

μηδενί, dat. sg. m. adj. {Rom. 13:8} . . . μηδείς *(3367)*
μηδενί, dat. sg. neut. adj. {1 Cor. 1:7} . . . . id.
μηδενός, gen. sg. neut. adj. . . . . id.

(3368) **μηδέποτε,** adv. (μηδέ + ποτε) *not at any time, never,* 2 Tim. 3:7

(3369) **μηδέπω,** adv. (μηδέ + πω) *not yet, not as yet,* Heb. 11:7

Μῆδοι, nom. pl. m. n. . . . . Μῆδος *(3370)*

(3370) **Μῆδος,** ου, ὁ [§3.C.a] *a Mede, a native of Media* in Asia, Acts 2:9

μηθέν, acc. sg. neut. adj. (Acts 27:33, GNT, WH & NA | μηδέν, MT & TR) . . μηδείς *(3367)*

(3371) **μηκέτι,** adv. (μή + ἔτι) *no more, no longer,* Mark 1:45; 2:2, et al.

(3372) **μῆκος,** ους, τό, nom. sg. neut. n. [§5.E.b] *length,* Eph. 3:18; Rev. 21:16

μηκύνηται, 3 pers. sg. pres. pass. subj. μηκύνω *(3373)*

(3373) **μηκύνω,** fut. μηκυνῶ [§27.1.a] *to lengthen, prolong;* mid. *to grow up,* as plants, Mark 4:27

μηλωταῖς, dat. pl. f. n. . . . . μηλωτή *(3374)*

(3374) **μηλωτή,** ῆς, ἡ [§2.B.a] (μῆλον, *a sheep*) *a sheepskin,* Heb. 11:37

(3375) **μήν,** a particle of affirmation, *verily, certainly, truly* {Heb. 6:14}

(3376) **μήν,** μηνός, ὁ, nom. sg. m. n. [§4.2.e] *a month,* Luke 1:24, 26, 36, 56, et al.; in N.T. *the new moon, the day of the new moon,* Gal. 4:10 {Luke 1:36}

μῆνα, acc. sg. m. n. . . . . μήν *(3376)*
μῆνας, acc. pl. m. n. . . . . id.
μηνί, dat. sg. m. n. . . . . id.
μηνυθείσης, gen. sg. f. aor. pass. part.
  [§14.N] . . . . μηνύω *(3377)*
μηνύσαντα, acc. sg. m. aor. act. part. . . . . id.
μηνύσῃ, 3 pers. sg. aor. act. subj. . . . . id.

(3377) **μηνύω,** fut. μηνύσω [§13.M] perf. μεμήνυκα, aor. ἐμήνυσα, *to disclose* what is secret, John 11:57; Acts 23:30; 1 Cor. 10:28; *to declare, indicate,* Luke 20:37

(3378) **μὴ οὐκ,** see μή *(3361)*

(3379) **μήποτε** (μή + ποτε) same signif. and usage as μή *(3361)* Heb. 9:17; Matt. 4:6; 13:15; also, *whether* (Luke 3:15, GNT, MT, NA & TR | μή ποτε, WH)

(‡4225) **μήπου,** or μή που, conj., *that . . . somewhere, that*

(3380) **μήπω,** adv. (μή + πω) *not yet, not as yet,* Rom. 9:11; Heb. 9:8

(3381) **μήπως,** or μή πως, conj. (μή + πως) *lest in any way or means, that in no way,* Acts 27:29; Rom. 11:21; 1 Cor. 8:9; 9:27, et al.; *whether perhaps,* 1 Thess. 3:5

μηρόν, acc. sg. m. n. . . . . μηρός *(3382)*

(3382) **μηρός,** οῦ, ὁ [§3.C.a] *the thigh,* Rev. 19:16

(3383) **μήτε**, conj. (μή + τε) *neither;* μήτε — μήτε, or μὴ — μήτε, or μηδὲ — μητέ, *neither – nor,* Matt. 5:34, 35, 36; Acts 23:8; 2 Thess. 2:2; in N.T. also equivalent to μηδέ, *not even, not so much as,* Mark 3:20

μητέρα, acc. sg. f. n. . . . . μήτηρ *(3384)*

μητέρας, acc. pl. f. n. . . . . id.

(3384) **μήτηρ**, τέρος, τρός, ἡ, nom. sg. f. n. [§6.2] *a mother,* Matt. 1:18; 12:49, 50, et al. freq.; *a parent* city, Gal. 4:26; Rev. 17:5

(3385) **μήτι** (μή + τι) has the same use as μή in the form εἰ μήτε, Luke 9:13, et al.; also when prefixed to an interrogative clause, Matt. 7:16; John 4:29

(3386) **μήτιγε** (μήτι + γε) strengthened for μήτι, *surely then, much more then* (1 Cor. 6:3, GNT, WH & NA | μήτι γε, MT & TR)

(3387) **μήτις** (μήτι + γε) *not any, no one* (Acts 27:42, TR | μή τις, GNT, WH, MT & NA)

(3388) **μήτρα**, ας, ἡ [§2.B.b] *the womb,* Luke 2:23; Rom. 4:19

μητραλῴαις, dat. pl. m. n. (1 Tim. 1:9, TR | μητρολῴαις, GNT, WH, MT & NA) . . . . μητραλῴας *(3389)*

(3389) **μητραλῴας**, ου, ὁ [§2.4] (μήτηρ + ἀλοιάω, poetic for ἀλοάω, *to smite) a striker of his mother, matricide,* 1 Tim. 1:9

μήτραν, acc. sg. f. n. . . . . μήτρα *(3388)*

μήτρας, gen. sg. f. n. . . . . id.

μητρί, dat. sg. f. n. . . . . μήτηρ *(3384)*

μητρολῴαις, dat. pl. m. n. (1 Tim. 1:9, GNT, WH, MT & NA | μητραλῴαις, TR) . . . . μητρολῴας *(†3389)*

(†3389) **μητρολῴας**, ου, ὁ, *a striker of his mother, matricide,* 1 Tim. 1:9

(3390) **μητρόπολις**, εως, ἡ, nom. sg. f. n., *a metropolis, chief city* (1 Tim. 6:21, TRs | GNT, WH, MT, TRb & NA omit)

μητρός gen. sg. f. n. . . . . μήτηρ *(3384)*

(3391) **μία**, nom. sg. f. numeral [§9.I.a] . . . . εἷς *(1520)*

μιᾷ, dat. sg. f. numeral . . . . id.

μιαίνουσι(ν), 3 pers. pl. pres. act. indic. . . . . μιαίνω *(3392)*

(3392) **μιαίνω**, fut. μιανῶ [§27.1.c] aor. ἐμίηνα and ἐμίανα [§27.1.e] perf. μεμίαγκα, perf. pass. μεμίασμαι, aor. pass. ἐμιάνθην [§27.3] pr. *to tinge, dye, stain; to pollute, defile,* ceremonially, John 18:28; *to corrupt, deprave,* Tit. 1:15; Heb. 12:15; Jude 8

μίαν, acc. sg. f. numeral . . . . εἷς *(1520)*

μιανθῶσι(ν), 3 pers. pl. aor. pass. subj. μιαίνω *(3392)*

μιᾶς, gen. sg. f. numeral . . . . εἷς *(1520)*

(3393) **μίασμα**, ατος, τό [§4.D.c] *pollution, moral defilement,* 2 Pet. 2:20

μιάσματα, acc. pl. neut. n. . . . . μίασμα *(3393)*

(3394) **μιασμός**, οῦ, ὁ [§3.C.a] *pollution, defiling,* 2 Pet. 2:10

μιασμοῦ, gen. sg. m. n. . . . . μιασμός *(3394)*

(3395) **μίγμα**, ατος, τό (or μῖγμα) [§4.D.c] *a mixture,* John 19:39

μίγμα, acc. sg. neut. n. (John 19:39, GNT, MT, TR & NA | ἕλιγμα, WH) . . . . μίγμα *(3395)*

(3396) **μίγνυμι**, fut. μίξω [§36.5] aor. ἔμιξα, perf. pass. μέμιγμαι, *to mix, mingle,* Matt. 27:34; Luke 13:1; Rev. 8:7

μικρά, nom. sg. f. adj. . . . . μικρός *(3398)*

μικράν, acc. sg. f. adj. . . . . id.

μικροί, nom. pl. m. adj. . . . . id.

μικροῖς, dat. pl. m. adj. (Rev. 11:18, MT & TR | μικρούς, GNT, WH & NA) . . . . id.

μικρόν, acc. sg. m. adj. {John 12:35} . . . . id.

μικρόν, nom. sg. neut. adj. {Luke 12:32} . id.

(3397) μικρόν, acc. sg. neut. adj. {John 13:33} . . id.

(3398) **μικρός**, ά, όν, nom. sg. m. adj. [§7.1] *little, small* in size, quantity, etc. Matt. 13:32; *small, little* in age, *young, not adult,* Mark 15:40; *little, short* in time, John 7:33; μικρόν, sc. χρόνον, *a little while, a short time,* John 13:33; μετὰ μικρόν, *after a little while, a little while afterwards,* Matt. 26:73; *little* in number, Luke 12:32; *small, little in dignity, low, humble,* Matt. 10:42; 11:11; μικρόν, as an adv., *little, a little,* Matt. 26:39, et al.

μικρότερον, nom. sg. neut. compar. adj. . . . . μικρός *(3398)*

μικρότερος, nom. sg. m. compar. adj. [§8.5] id.

μικροῦ, gen. sg. m. adj. . . . . id.

μικρούς, acc. pl. m. adj. . . . . id.

μικρῷ, dat. sg. m. adj. . . . . id.

μικρῶν, gen. pl. m. adj. . . . . id.

Μίλητον, acc. sg. f. n. . . . . Μίλητος *(3399)*

(3399) **Μίλητος**, ου, ἡ [§3.C.b] *Miletus,* a celebrated city of Caria

Μιλήτου, gen. sg. f. n. . . . . Μίλητος *(3399)*

Μιλήτῳ, dat. sg. f. n. . . . . id.

(3400) **μίλιον**, όυ, τό [§3.C.c] (Latin *miliarium) a Roman mile,* which contained *mille passuum,* 1000 paces, or 8 stadia, i.e., about 1680 English yards, Matt. 5:41

μίλιον, acc. sg. neut. n. . . . . μίλιον *(3400)*

μιμεῖσθαι, pres. mid./pass. dep. infin. μιμέομαι *(3401)*

μιμεῖσθε, 2 pers. pl. pres. mid./pass. dep. imper. . . . . id.

(3401) **μιμέομαι**, οῦμαι, fut. μιμήσομαι [§17.Q] (μῖμος, *an imitator) to imitate, follow* as an example, *strive to resemble,* 2 Thess. 3:7, 9; Heb. 13:7; 3 John 11

μιμηταί, nom. pl. m. n. . . . . μιμητής *(3402)*

(3402) **μιμητής**, οῦ, ὁ [§2.B.c] *an imitator, follower,*

1 Cor. 4:16; Eph. 5:1, et al.

μιμνῄσκεσθε, 2 pers. pl. pres. mid./pass. dep. imper. (Heb. 13:3, GNT, MT & NA | μιμνῄσκεσθε, WH & TR) .... μιμνῄσκω (†3403)

μιμνῄσκῃ, 2 pers. sg. pres. mid./pass. dep. indic. (Heb. 2:6, GNT, MT & NA | μιμνῄσκῃ, WH & TR) .... id.

(†3403) **μιμνῄσκω,** to remind; mid. μιμνῄσκομαι, aor. (pass. form) ἐμνήσθην, fut. μνήσθήσομαι, perf. μέμνημαι, with pres. signif. [§36.3] to remember, recollect, call to mind, Matt. 26:75; Luke 1:54, 72; 16:25; in N.T., in a passive sense, to be called to mind, be borne in mind, Acts 10:31; Rev. 16:19, et al.

μιμοῦ, 2 pers. sg. pres. mid./pass. dep. imper. .... μιμέομαι (3401)

μισεῖ, 3 pers. sg. pres. act. indic. ...... μισέω (3404)

μισεῖν, pres. act. infin. .... id.

μισεῖς, 2 pers. sg. pres. act. indic. .... id.

(3404) **μισέω,** ῶ, fut. μισήσω [§16.P] perf. μεμίσηκα, aor. ἐμίσησα (μῖσος, hatred) to hate, regard with ill-will, Matt. 5:43, 44; 10:22; to detest, abhor, John 3:20; Rom. 7:15; in N.T. to regard with less affection, love less, esteem less, Matt. 6:24; Luke 14:26

μισῇ, 3 pers. sg. pres. act. subj. .... μισέω (3404)

μισήσει, 3 pers. sg. fut. act. indic. .... id.

μισήσεις, 2 pers. sg. fut. act. indic. .... id.

μισήσουσι(ν), 3 pers. pl. fut. act. indic. .. id.

μισήσωσιν, 3 pers. pl. aor. act. subj. ..... id.

(3405) **μισθαποδοσία,** ας, ἡ [§2.B.b; 2.2] (μισθός, ἀποδίδωμι) pr. the discharge of wages; requital; reward, Heb. 10:35; 11:26; punishment, Heb. 2:2

μισθαποδοσίαν, acc. sg. f. n. .. μισθαποδοσία (3405)

(3406) **μισθαποδότης,** ου, ὁ, nom. sg. m. n. [§2.B.c] (μισθός, ἀποδίδωμι) a bestower of remuneration; recompenser, rewarder, Heb. 11:6

μίσθιοι, nom. pl. m. adj. .... μίσθιος (3407)

(3407) **μίσθιος,** ία, ιον [§7.1] hired; as a subst., a hired servant, hireling, Luke 15:17, 19

μισθίων, gen. pl. m. adj. .... μίσθιος (3407)

μισθόν, acc. sg. m. n. .... μισθός (3408)

(3408) **μισθός,** οῦ, ὁ, nom. sg. m. n. [§3.C.a] hire, wages, Matt. 20:8; James 5:4, et al.; reward, Matt. 5:12, 46; 6:1, 2, 5, 16, et al.; punishment, 2 Pet. 2:13, et al.

μισθοῦ, gen. sg. m. n. .... μισθός (3408)

(3409) **μισθόω,** ῶ, fut. μισθώσω [§20.T] to hire out, let out to hire; mid. to hire, Matt. 20:1, 7

(3410) **μίσθωμα,** ατος, τό [§4.D.c] hire, rent; in N.T. a hired dwelling, Acts 28:30

μισθώματι, dat. sg. neut. n. .... μίσθωμα (3410)

μισθώσασθαι, aor. mid. infin. .... μισθόω (3409)

(3411) **μισθωτός,** οῦ, ὁ, nom. sg. m. n. [§3.C.a] a

hireling, Mark 1:20; John 10:12, 13

μισθωτῶν, gen. pl. m. n. .... μισθωτός (3411)

μισούμενοι, nom. pl. m. pres. pass. part. .... μισέω (3404)

μισοῦντας, acc. pl. m. pres. act. part. (Matt. 5:44, TR | μισοῦσιν, MT | GNT, WH & NA omit) .... id.

μισοῦντες, nom. pl. m. pres. act. part. ... id.

μισούντων, gen. pl. m. pres. act. part. ... id.

μισοῦσιν, dat. pl. m. pres. act. part. ..... id.

μισῶ, 1 pers. sg. pres. act. indic. .... id.

μισῶν, nom. sg. m. pres. act. part. .... id.

(3412) **Μιτυλήνη,** ης, ἡ [§2.B.a] Mitylene, the capital city of Lesbos, in the Aegean sea, Acts 20:14

Μιτυλήνην, acc. sg. f. n. .... Μιτυλήνη (3412)

(3413) **Μιχαήλ,** ὁ, Michael, the archangel, indecl.

(3414) **μνᾶ,** ᾶς, ἡ, nom. sg. f. n. (μνάα) [§2.5] Latin mina; a weight, equivalent to 100 drachmae; also a sum, equivalent to 100 drachmae and the sixtieth part of a talent, Luke 19:13, et al.

μνᾶν, acc. sg. f. n. contr. .... μνᾶ (3414)

(3415) **μνάομαι,** ῶμαι [§36.3] see μιμνῄσκω (3403)

μνᾶς, acc. pl. f. n. contr. μνάα .... μνᾶ (3414)

(3416) **Μνάσων,** ωνος, ὁ [§4.2.e] Mnason, pr. name, Acts 21:16

Μνάσωνι, dat. sg. m. n. .... Μνάσων (3416)

(3417) **μνεία,** ας, ἡ [§2.B.b; 2.2] remembrance, recollection, Phil. 1:3; 1 Thess. 3:6; 2 Tim. 1:3; mention; μνείαν ποιεῖσθαι, to make mention, Rom. 1:9; Eph. 1:16; 1 Thess. 1:2; Philemon 4

μνείᾳ, dat. sg. f. n. .... μνεία (3417)

μνείαν, acc. sg. f. n. .... id.

(3418) **μνῆμα,** ατος, τό, nom. sg. neut. [§4.D.c] pr. a memorial, monument; a tomb, sepulchre, Mark 5:5, et al. {Acts 2:29}

μνῆμα, acc. sg. neut. n. {Luke 24:1} ... μνῆμα (3418)

μνήμασιν, dat. pl. neut. n. .... id.

μνήματα, acc. pl. neut. n. (Rev. 11:9, TR | μνῆμα, GNT, WH, MT & NA) ..... id.

μνήματι, dat. sg. neut. n. .... id.

μνημεῖα, nom. pl. neut. n. {Matt. 27:52} .... μνημεῖον (3419)

μνημεῖα, acc. pl. neut. n. {Matt. 23:29} .. id.

μνημείοις, dat. pl. neut. n. .... id.

(3419) **μνημεῖον,** ου, τό, nom. sg. neut. n. [§3.C.c] the same as μνῆμα, Matt. 8:28; 23:29, et al. {John 19:41–42}

μνημεῖον, acc. sg. neut. n. {John 20:1} .... μνημεῖον (3419)

μνημείου, gen. sg. neut. n. .... id.

μνημείῳ, dat. sg. neut. n. .... id.

μνημείων, gen. pl. neut. n. .... id.

(3420) **μνήμη**, ης, ἡ [§2.B.a] *remembrance, recollection, mention;* μνήμην ποιεῖσθαι, *to make mention*, 2 Pet. 1:15

μνήμην, acc. sg. f. n. . . . . μνήμη (3420)

μνημόνευε, 2 pers. sg. pres. act.
imper. μνημονεύω (3421)

μνημονεύει, 3 pers. sg. pres. act. indic. . . . id.

μνημονεύειν, pres. act. infin. . . . . id.

μνημονεύετε, 2 pers. pl. pres. act. indic.
{Matt. 16:9} . . . . id.

μνημονεύετε, 2 pers. pl. pres. act. imper.
{John 15:20} . . . . id.

μνημονεύητε, 2 pers. pl. pres. act. subj. . . id.

μνημονεύοντες, nom. pl. m. pres. act. part. id.

(3421) **μνημονεύω**, fut. μνημονεύσω [§13.M] aor.
ἐμνημόνευσα, *to remember, recollect, call to mind*, Matt. 16:9; Luke 17:32; Acts 20:31, et al.; *to be mindful of, to fix the thoughts upon*, Heb. 11:15; *to make mention, mention, speak of*, Heb. 11:22

μνημονεύωμεν, 1 pers. pl. pres. act.
subj. . . . . μνημονεύω (3421)

(3422) **μνημόσυνον**, ου, τό [§3.C.c] *a record, memorial*, Acts 10:4; honorable *remembrance*, Matt. 26:13; Mark 14:9

μνημόσυνον, acc. sg. neut. n. . . . μνημόσυνον (3422)

μνησθῆναι, aor. pass. infin. . . . . . . μιμνήσκω (†3403)

μνησθῇς, 2 pers. sg. aor. pass. subj. . . . . . id.

μνησθήσομαι, 1 pers. sg. fut. pass. indic.
(Heb. 10:17, GNT, WH & NA | μνησθῶ,
MT & TR) . . . . id.

μνήσθητε, 2 pers. pl. aor. pass. imper. . . . id.

μνήσθητι, 2 pers. sg. aor. pass. imper. . . . . id.

μνησθῶ, 1 pers. sg. aor. pass. subj. . . . . . . id.

μνηστευθείσης, gen. sg. f. aor. pass.
part. . . . . μνηστεύω (3423)

(3423) **μνηστεύω**, fut. μνηστεύσω [§13.M] aor. pass.
ἐμνηστεύθην, *to ask in marriage; to betroth;* pass. *to be betrothed, affianced*, Matt. 1:18; Luke 1:27; 2:5

μογιλάλον, acc. sg. m. adj. . . . . μογιλάλος (3424)

(3424) **μογιλάλος**, ον [§7.2] (μόγις + λαλέω) *having an impediment in one's speech, speaking with difficulty, a stammerer*, Mark 7:32

(3425) **μόγις**, adv. (μόγος, *labor, toil*) *with difficulty, scarcely, hardly* (Luke 9:39, GNT, MT, TR & NA | μόλις, WH)

μόδιον, acc. sg. m. n. . . . . μόδιος (3426)

(3426) **μόδιος**, ου, ὁ [§3.C.a] (Latin *modius*) *a modius*, a Roman measure for things dry, containing 16 sextarii, and equivalent to about *a peck;* in N.T. *a corn measure*, Matt. 5:15; Mark 4:21; Luke 11:33

(3427) **μοί**, dat. sg. 1 pers. personal pron.
[§11.K.a] . . . . ἐγώ (1473)

μοιχαλίδα, acc. sg. f. n. . . . . μοιχαλίς (3428)

μοιχαλίδες, voc. pl. f. n. (James 4:4, GNT,
WH & NA | μοιχοί, MT & TR) . . . . id.

μοιχαλίδι, dat. sg. f. n. . . . . id.

μοιχαλίδος, gen. sg. f. n. . . . . id.

(3428) **μοιχαλίς**, ίδος, ἡ, nom. sg. f. n. [§4.2.c]
(equivalent to μοιχάς, fem. of μοιχός) *an adulteress*, Rom. 7:3; James 4:4; by meton. *an adulterous mien, lustful significance*, 2 Pet. 2:14; from the Hebrew, spiritually *adulterous, faithless, ungodly*, Matt. 12:39; 16:4; Mark 8:38

(†3429) **μοιχάομαι**, ῶμαι, fut. μοιχήσομαι [§19.S]
(mid. of μοιχάω, *to defile a married woman*) *to commit or be guilty of adultery*, Matt. 5:32, et al.

μοιχᾶσθαι, pres. mid./pass. dep. infin. (Matt.
5:32, MT & TR | μοιχευθῆναι, GNT,
WH, NA) . . . . μοιχάομαι (†3429)

μοιχᾶται, 3 pers. sg. pres. mid./pass. dep.
indic. . . . . id.

(3430) **μοιχεία**, ας, ἡ, nom. sg. f. n. [§2.B.b; 2.2]
adultery, Matt. 15:19; Mark 7:21, et al.
(Gal. 5:19, MT & TR | GNT, WH & NA
omit)

μοιχείᾳ, dat. sg. f. n. . . . . μοιχεία (3430)

μοιχεῖαι, nom. pl. f. n. . . . . id.

μοιχεύει, 3 pers. sg. pres. act. indic. . . μοιχεύω (3431)

μοιχεύειν, pres. act. infin. . . . . id.

μοιχεύεις, 2 pers. sg. pres. act. indic. . . . . id.

μοιχευθῆναι, aor. pass. infin. (Matt. 5:32,
GNT, WH & NA | μοιχᾶσθαι, MT &
TR) . . . . id.

μοιχευομένη, nom. sg. f. pres. pass. part.
(John 8:4, GNT, WH, TR & NA |
μοιχευομένην, MT) . . . . id.

μοιχευομένην, acc. sg. f. pres. mid. part. (John
8:4, MT | μοιχευομένη, GNT, WH, TR
& NA) . . . . id.

μοιχεύοντας, acc. pl. m. pres. act. part. . . id.

μοιχεύσεις, 2 pers. sg. fut. act. indic. . . . . id.

μοιχεύσῃς, 2 pers. sg. aor. act. subj. . . . . . id.

(3431) **μοιχεύω**, fut. μοιχεύσω [§13.M] aor.
ἐμοίχευσα, trans. *to commit adultery with, debauch*, Matt. 5:28; absol. and mid. *to commit adultery*, Matt. 5:27; John 8:4, et al.; *to commit* spiritual *adultery, be guilty of idolatry*, Rev. 2:22

μοιχοί, nom. pl. m. n. {Luke 18:11} . . . μοιχός (3432)

μοιχοί, voc. pl. m. n. (James, 4:4, MT & TR
| μοιχαλίδες, GNT, WH & NA) . . . . . id.

(3432) **μοιχός**, οῦ, ὁ [§3.C.a] *an adulterer*, Luke 18:11; 1 Cor. 6:9; Heb. 13:4; James 4:4

μοιχούς, acc. pl. m. n. . . . . μοιχός (3432)

(3433) **μόλις**, adv. (μόλος, *labor*) *with difficulty,*

scarcely, hardly, Acts 14:18; 27:7, 8, 16; Rom. 5:7; 1 Pet. 4:18

(3434) **Μολόχ**, ὁ, *Moloch,* pr. name, indecl., Acts 7:43

μολύνεται, 3 pers. sg. pres. pass. indic. . . . . μολύνω *(3435)*

(3435) **μολύνω**, fut. μολυνῶ [§27.1.a] aor. ἐμόλυνα, perf. pass. μεμόλυσμαι, aor. ἐμολύνθην [§27.3] pr. *to stain, sully; to defile, contaminate* morally, 1 Cor. 8:7; Rev. 14:4; *to soil,* Rev. 3:4

(3436) **μολυσμός**, οῦ, ὁ [§3.C.a] *pollution,* 2 Cor. 7:1

μολυσμοῦ, gen. sg. m. n. . . . . μολυσμός *(3436)*

(3437) **μομφή**, ῆς, ἡ [§2.B.a] *a complaint, cause or ground of complaint,* Col. 3:13

μομφήν, acc. sg. f. n. . . . . μομφή *(3437)*

μόνα, acc. pl. neut. adj. . . . . μόνος *(3441)*

μοναί, nom. pl. f. adj. . . . . μονή *(3438)*

μόνας, acc. pl. f. adj. (Mark 4:10; Luke 9:18, GNT, WH, MT & NA | καταμόνας, TR) . . . . μόνος *(3441)*

(3438) **μονή**, ῆς, ἡ [§2.B.a] *a stay in any place; an abode, dwelling, mansion,* John 14:2, 23

μονήν, acc. sg. f. n. {John 14:23} . . . . . . μονή *(3438)*

μόνην, acc. sg. f. adj. {Luke 10:40} . . . . μόνος *(3441)*

μονογενῆ, acc. sg. m. adj. . . . . . . μονογενής *(3439)*

(3439) **μονογενής**, ές, nom. sg. m. adj. [§7.G.b] (μόνος + γένος) *only-begotten, only-born,* Luke 7:12; 8:42; 9:38; Heb. 11:17; *only-begotten* in respect of peculiar generation, John 1:14, 18; 3:16, 18; 1 John 4:9 {Luke 7:12}

μονογενής, nom. sg. f. adj. {Luke 8:42} . . . . μονογενής *(3439)*

μονογενοῦς, gen. sg. m. adj. . . . . id.

μόνοι, nom. pl. m. adj. . . . . μόνος *(3441)*

μόνοις, dat. pl. m. adj. . . . . id.

μόνον, acc. sg. m. n. adj. {John 17:3} . . . . id.

μόνον, acc. sg. neut. n. adj. {John 17:20} . id.

(3440) **μόνον**, adv., *only,* Matt. 5:47; 8:8; οὐ μόνον— ἀλλὰ καί, *not only—but also,* Matt. 21:21; John 5:18; μὴ μόνον—ἀλλά, *not only— but,* Phil. 2:12, et al.

(3441) **μόνος**, η, ον, nom. sg. m. adj. [§7.F.a] *without accompaniment, alone,* Matt. 14:23; 18:15; Luke 10:40, et al.; *singly existent, sole, only,* John 17:3, et al.; *lone, solitary,* John 8:29; 16:32; *alone* in respect of restriction, *only,* Matt. 4:4; 12:4, et al.; *alone* in respect of circumstances, *only,* Luke 24:18; *not multiplied by reproduction, lone, barren,* John 12:24

μόνου, gen. sg. m. adj. . . . . μόνος *(3441)*

μόνους, acc. pl. m. adj. . . . . id.

μονόφθαλμον, acc. sg. m. adj. . μονόφθαλμος *(3442)*

(3442) **μονόφθαλμος**, ον [§7.2] (μόνος + ὀφθαλμός) *one-eyed; deprived of an eye,* Matt. 18:9; Mark 9:47

(3443) **μονόω**, ῶ, fut. μονώσω [§20.T] perf. pass. μεμόνωμαι, *to leave alone;* pass. *to be left alone, be lone,* 1 Tim. 5:5

μόνῳ, dat. sg. m. adj. . . . . μόνος *(3441)*

(3444) **μορφή**, ῆς, ἡ [§2.B.a] *form,* Mark 16:12; Phil. 2:6, 7

μορφῇ, dat. sg. f. n. . . . . μορφή *(3444)*

μορφήν, acc. sg. f. n. . . . . id.

(3445) **μορφόω**, ῶ, fut. μορφώσω [§20.T] aor. pass. ἐμορφώθην, *to give shape to, mould, fashion,* Gal. 4:19

μορφωθῇ, 3 pers. sg. aor. pass. subj. [§21.U] . . . . μορφόω *(3445)*

μόρφωσιν, acc. sg. f. n. . . . . μόρφωσις *(3446)*

(3446) **μόρφωσις**, εως, ἡ [§5.E.c] pr. *a shaping, moulding;* in N.T. *external form, appearance,* 2 Tim. 3:5; *a settled form,* prescribed *system,* Rom. 2:20

μόσχον, acc. sg. m. adj. . . . . μόσχος *(3448)*

(3447) **μοσχοποιέω**, ῶ, fut. μοσχοποιήσω [§16.P] aor. ἐμοσχοποίησα (μόσχος + ποιέω) *to form an image of a calf,* Acts 7:41

(3448) **μόσχος**, ου, ὁ [§3.C.a] pr. *a tender branch, shoot; a young animal; a calf, young bullock,* Luke 15:23, 27, 30; Heb. 9:12, 19; Rev. 4:7

μόσχῳ, dat. sg. m. n. . . . . μόσχος *(3448)*

μόσχων, gen. pl. m. n. . . . . id.

(3450) μοῦ, gen. sg. 1 pers. personal pron. [§11.K.a] . . . . ἐγώ *(1473)*

(3451) **μουσικός**, ή, όν (μοῦσα, *a muse, song, music*) pr. *devoted to the arts of the Muses; a musician;* in N.T., perhaps, *a singer,* Rev. 18:22

μουσικῶν, gen. pl. m. adj. . . . . μουσικός *(3451)*

μόχθον, acc. sg. m. n. . . . . μόχθος *(‡3449)*

(‡3449) **μόχθος**, ου, ὁ [§3.C.a] *wearisome labor, toil, travail,* 2 Cor. 11:27; 1 Thess. 2:9; 2 Thess. 3:8

μόχθῳ, dat. sg. m. n. . . . . μόχθος *(‡3449)*

(3452) **μυελός**, οῦ, ὁ [§3.C.a] *marrow,* Heb. 4:12

μυελῶν, gen. pl. m. n. . . . . μυελός *(3452)*

(3453) **μυέω**, ῶ, fut. μυήσω [§16.P] perf. pass. μεμύημαι (μύω, *to shut the mouth*) *to initiate, instruct* in the sacred mysteries; in N.T. pass. *to be disciplined* in a practical lesson, *to learn* a lesson, Phil. 4:12

μύθοις, dat. pl. m. n. . . . . μῦθος *(3454)*

(3454) **μῦθος**, ου, ὁ [§3.C.a] *a word, speech, a tale; a fable, figment,* 1 Tim. 1:4, et al.

μύθους, acc. pl. m. n. . . . . μῦθος *(3454)*

(3455) **μυκάομαι**, ῶμαι [§19.S] *to low, bellow,* as a

bull; also, *to roar,* as a lion, Rev. 10:3

μυκᾶται, 3 pers. sg. pres. mid./pass. dep.
indic. . . . . μυκάομαι *(3455)*

μυκτηρίζεται, 3 pers. sg. pres. pass.
indic. μυκτηρίζω *(3456)*

(3456) **μυκτηρίζω,** fut. μυκτηρίσω [§26.1] (μυκτήρ,
*the nose) to contract the nose in contempt
and derision, toss up the nose; to mock,
deride,* Gal. 6:7

(3457) **μυλικός,** ή, όν, nom. sg. m. adj. [§7.F.a]
(μύλη, *a mill) of a mill, belonging to a mill,*
Luke 17:2

μύλινον, acc. sg. m. adj. (Rev. 18:21, GNT,
WH & NA | μύλον, MT & TR) μύλινος *(†3458)*

(†3458) **μύλινος,** η, ον, *belonging to a mill*

μύλον, acc. sg. m. n. (Rev. 18:21, MT & TR
| μύλινον, GNT, WH & NA) . . . . . μύλος *(3458)*

(3458) **μύλος,** ου, ὁ, nom. sg. m. n. [§3.C.a] *a millstone,* Matt. 18:6, et al.

μύλου, gen. sg. m. n. . . . . μύλος *(3458)*

μύλῳ, dat sg. m. n. (Matt. 24:41, GNT, WH
& NA | μύλωνι, MT & TR) . . . . id.

(3459) **μύλων,** ωνος, ὁ [§4.2.e] *a mill-house,* a place
where the grinding of corn was performed,
Matt. 24:41

μύλωνι, dat. sg. m. n. (Matt. 24:41, MT &
TR | μύλῳ, GNT, WH & NA) . . . . μύλων *(3459)*

(3460) **Μύρα,** ων, τά, *Myra,* a city of Lycia, Acts 27:5

Μύρα, acc. pl. neut. n. (Acts 27:5, GNT, MT,
TR & NA | Μύρρα, WH) . . . . Μύρα *(3460)*

μύρα, acc. pl. neut. n. {Luke 23:56} . . . μύρον *(3464)*

μυριάδας, acc. pl. m. numeral . . . . . . μυριάς *(3461)*

μυριάδες, nom. pl. m. numeral . . . . id.

μυριάδων, gen. pl. m. numeral . . . . id.

(3461) **μυριάς,** άδος, ή [§4.D.b] (μυρίος, *innumerable) a myriad, ten thousand,* Acts 19:19;
indefinitely, *a vast multitude,* Luke 12:1;
Acts 21:20, et al.

μυριάσιν, dat. pl. m. numeral . . . . μυριάς *(3461)*

(3462) **μυρίζω,** fut. μυρίσω [§26.1] *to anoint,* Mark
14:8

(3463) **μυρίοι,** αι, α [§9.I.d] (μυρίος, *innumerable)* indefinitely, *a great number,* 1 Cor. 4:15;
14:19; specifically, μύριοι, *a myriad, ten
thousand,* Matt. 18:24

μυρίους, acc. pl. m. adj. . . . . μυρίοι *(3463)*

μυρίσαι, aor. act. infin. . . . . μυρίζω *(3462)*

μυρίων, gen. pl. m. adj. . . . . μυρίοι *(3463)*

(3464) **μύρον,** ου, τό, nom. sg. neut. n. [§3.C.c] pr.
*aromatic juice which distils from trees;
ointment, unguent,* usually perfumed,
Matt. 26:7, 12; Mark 14:3, 4, et al.
{John 12:5}

μύρον, acc. sg. neut. n. {Rev. 18:13} . . . μύρον *(3464)*

μύρου, gen. sg. neut. n. . . . . id.

Μύρρα, acc. pl. neut. n. (Acts 27:5, WH |
Μύρα, GNT, MT, TR & NA) . . . . . Μύρα *(3460)*

μύρῳ, dat. sg. neut. n. . . . . id.

(3465) **Μυσία,** ας, ή [§2.B.b; 2.2] *Mysia,* a province
of Asia Minor

Μυσίαν, acc. sg. f. n. . . . . Μυσία *(3465)*

μυστήρια, acc. pl. neut. n. . . . . μυστήριον *(3466)*

(3466) **μυστήριον,** ου, τό, nom. sg. neut. n. [§3.C.c]
(μύστης, *an initiated person,* μυέω) *a matter to the knowledge of which initiation is
necessary; a secret* which would remain
such but for revelation, Matt. 3:11; Rom.
11:25; Col. 1:26, et al.; *a concealed power
or principle,* 2 Thess. 2:7; *a hidden meaning* of a symbol, Rev. 1:20; 17:7 {Rev. 10:7}

μυστήριον, acc. sg. neut. n.
{Rev. 17:7} . . . . μυστήριον *(3466)*

μυστηρίου, gen. sg. neut. n. . . . . id.

μυστηρίῳ, dat. sg. neut. n. . . . . id.

μυστηρίων, gen. pl. neut. n. . . . . id.

(3467) **μυωπάζω,** fut. μυωπάσω [§26.1] (μύω, *to
shut, close,* + ὤψ) pr. *to close the eyes,
contract the eyelids, wink; to be near-
sighted, dimsighted, purblind,* 2 Pet. 1:9

μυωπάζων, nom. sg. m. pres. act.
part. . . . . μυωπάζω *(3467)*

μώλωπι, dat. sg. m. n. . . . . μώλωψ *(3468)*

(3468) **μώλωψ,** ωπος, ὁ [§4.2.a] *the mark of a blow;
a stripe, a wound,* 1 Pet. 2:24

(†3469) **μωμέομαι,** οῦμαι or μωμάομαι, ῶμαι, fut.
μωμήσομαι [§17.Q] aor. pass. ἐμωμήθην,
to find fault with, censure, blame, 2 Cor.
8:20; passively, 2 Cor. 6:3

μωμηθῇ, 3 pers. sg. aor. pass. subj. μωμέομαι *(†3469)*

μωμήσηται, 3 pers. sg. aor. mid. dep. subj. id.

μῶμοι, nom. pl. m. n. . . . . μῶμος *(3470)*

(3470) **μῶμος,** ου, ὁ [§3.C.a] *blame, ridicule; a disgrace* to society, *a stain,* 2 Pet. 2:13

μωρά, acc. pl. neut. adj. . . . . μωρός *(3474)*

μωραί, nom. pl. f. adj. . . . . id.

(3471) **μωραίνω,** fut. μωρανῶ [§27.1.c] aor.
ἐμώρανα, *to be foolish, to play the fool;*
in N.T. trans. *to make foolish, convict of
folly,* 1 Cor. 1:20; pass. *to be convicted of
folly, to incur the character of folly,* Rom.
1:22; *to be rendered insipid,* Matt. 5:13;
Luke 14:34

μωρανθῇ, 3 pers. sg. aor. pass. subj. . μωραίνω *(3471)*

μωράς, acc. pl. f. adj. . . . . μωρός *(3474)*

μωρέ, voc. sg. m. adj. . . . . id.

(3472) **μωρία,** ας, ή, nom. sg. f. n. [§2.B.b; 2.2] *foolishness,* 1 Cor. 1:18, 21, 23, et al.

μωρίαν, acc. sg. f. n. . . . . μωρία *(3472)*

μωρίας, gen. sg. f. n. . . . . id.

μωροί, nom. pl. m. adj. {1 Cor. 4:10} . . μωρός *(3474)*

μωροί, voc. pl. m. adj. {Matt. 23:17} .. μωρός *(3474)*

(3473) **μωρολογία,** ας, ἡ, nom. sg. f. n. [§2.B.b; 2.2] (μωρός + λόγος) *foolish talk,* Eph. 5:4

μωρόν, nom. sg. neut. adj. . . . . μωρός *(3474)*

(3474) **μωρός,** ά, όν, nom. sg. m. adj. [§7.1] pr. *dull; foolish,* Matt. 7:26; 23:17, 19; 2 Tim. 2:23, et al.; from the Hebrew, *a fool* in senseless wickedness, Matt. 5:22

μωρῷ, dat. sg. m. adj. . . . . μωρός *(3474)*

Μωσέα, acc. sg. m. n. (Luke 16:29, MT & TR | Μωϋσέα, GNT & NA | Μωυσέα, WH) . . . . Μωσῆς *(3475)*

Μωσεῖ, dat. sg. m. n. (MT & TR | Μωϋσεῖ, GNT & NA | Μωυσεῖ, WH) . . . . id.

Μωσέως, gen. sg. m. n. (MT & TR | Μωϋσέως, GNT & NA | Μωυσέως, WH) . . . . id.

Μωσῇ, dat. sg. m. n. (Acts 7:44, MT & TR | Μωϋσῇ, GNT & NA | μωυσῇ, WH) id.

Μωσῆν, acc. sg. m. n. (MT & TR | Μωϋσῆν, GNT & NA | Μωυσῆν, WH) . . . . . . id.

(3475) **Μωσῆς,** έως, ὁ, nom. sg. m. n., *Moses,* pr. name (MT & TR | Μωϋσῆς, GNT & NA | Μωυσῆς, WH)

Μωϋσέα, acc. sg. m. n. (Luke 16:29, GNT & NA | Μωσέα, MT & TR | Μωυσέα, WH) . . . . Μωϋσῆς *(3475)*

Μωϋσεῖ, dat. sg. m. n. (GNT & NA | Μωσεῖ, MT & TR | Μωυσεῖ, WH) . . . . id.

Μωϋσέως, gen. sg. m. n. (GNT & NA | Μωσέως, MT & TR | Μωυσέως, WH) id.

Μωϋσῇ, dat. sg. m. n. (Acts 7:44, GNT & NA | Μωσῇ, Mt & TR | Μωυσῇ, WH) id.

Μωϋσῆν, acc. sg. m. n. (GNT & NA | Μωσῆν, MT & TR | Μωυσῆν, WH) . id.

(3475) **Μωϋσῆς,** έως, ὁ, nom. sg. m. n., *Moses,* pr. name (GNT & NA | Μωυσῆς, WH | Μωσῆς, MT & TR)

N

(3476) **Ναασσών,** ὁ, *Naasson,* pr. name, indecl.

(3477) **Ναγγαί,** ὁ, *Naggai, Nagge,* pr. name, indecl., Luke 3:25

(†3478) **Ναζαρά,** ἡ, *Nazareth,* indecl. (Matt. 4:13; Luke 4:16, GNT, WH & NA | Ναζαρέτ, MT & TR)

(3478) **Ναζαρέτ,** or Ναζαρέθ, ἡ, *Nazareth,* a city of Galilee, indecl.

Ναζαρηνέ, voc. sg. m. n. . . . . Ναζαρηνός *(3479)*

Ναζαρηνόν, acc. sg. m. n. . . . . id.

(3479) **Ναζαρηνός,** οῦ, ὁ, nom. sg. m. n., *an inhabitant of Nazareth* (Mark 10:47, GNT, WH

& NA | Ναζωραῖος, MT & TR)

Ναζαρηνοῦ, gen. sg. m. n. . . . . . . Ναζαρηνός *(3479)*

Ναζωραῖον, acc. sg. m. n. . . . . . . Ναζωραῖος *(3480)*

(3480) **Ναζωραῖος,** ου, ὁ, nom. sg. m. n. [§3.C.a] *a Nazarite; an inhabitant of Nazareth*

Ναζωραίου, gen. sg. m. n. . . . . . . Ναζωραῖος *(3480)*

Ναζωραίων, gen. pl. m. n. . . . . id.

(†3481) **Ναθάμ,** ὁ, *Nathan,* pr. name, indecl. (Luke 3:31, GNT, WH & NA | Ναθάν, MT & TR)

(3481) **Ναθάν,** ὁ, *Nathan,* pr. name, indecl. (Luke 3:31, MT & TR | Ναθάμ, GNT, WH & NA)

(3482) **Ναθαναήλ,** ὁ, *Nathanael,* pr. name, indecl.

(3483) **ναί,** a particle, used to strengthen an affirmation, *verily,* Rev. 22:20; to make an affirmation, or express an assent, *yea, yes,* Matt. 5:37; Acts 5:8, et al.

(‡3497) **Ναιμάν,** ὁ, *Naaman,* pr. name, indecl. (Luke 4:27, GNT, WH & NA | Νεεμάν, MT & TR)

(3484) **Ναΐν,** ἡ, *Nain,* a town of Palestine, indecl. (Luke 7:11, GNT, MT, TR & NA | Ναίν, WH)

ναοῖς, dat. pl. m. n. . . . . ναός *(3485)*

ναόν, acc. sg. m. n. . . . . id.

(3485) **ναός,** οῦ, ὁ, nom. sg. m. n. [§3.C.a] (ναίω, *to dwell*) pr. *a dwelling; the dwelling* of a deity, *a temple,* Matt. 26:61; Acts 7:48, et al.; used figuratively of individuals, John 2:19; 1 Cor. 3:16, et al.; spc. *the cell of a temple;* hence, *the Holy Place* of the Temple of Jerusalem, Matt. 23:35; Luke 1:9, et al.; *a model of a temple, a shrine,* Acts 19:24

ναοῦ, gen. sg. m. n. . . . . ναός *(3485)*

(3486) **Ναούμ,** ὁ, *Naum,* pr. name, indecl., Luke 3:25

ναούς, acc. pl. m. n. . . . . ναός *(3485)*

(3487) **νάρδος,** ου, ἡ [§3.C.b] (Hebrew נֵרְדְּ) *spikenard, andropogon nardus* of Linn., a species of aromatic plant with grassy leaves and a fibrous root, of which the best and strongest grows in India; in N.T. *oil of spikenard,* an oil extracted from the plant, which was highly prized and used as an ointment either pure or mixed with other substances, Mark 14:3; John 12:3

νάρδου, gen. sg. f. n. . . . . νάρδος *(3487)*

(3488) **Νάρκισσος,** ου, ὁ, *Narcissus,* pr. name, Rom. 16:11

Ναρκίσσου, gen. sg. m. n. . . . . . . Νάρκισσος *(3488)*

(3489) **ναυαγέω,** ῶ, fut. ναυαγήσω, aor. ἐναυάγησα [§16.P] (ναῦς + ἄγνυμι, *to break*) *to make shipwreck, be shipwrecked,* 2 Cor. 11:25; Rev. 18:17

(3490) **ναύκληρος**, ου, ὁ [§3.C.a] (ναῦς + κλῆρος)
the master or owner of a ship, Acts 27:11

ναυκλήρῳ, dat. sg. m. n. . . . . ναύκληρος (3490)

ναῦν, acc. sg. f. n. . . . . ναῦς (3491)

(3491) **ναῦς**, νεώς, ἡ [§6.4.g] (νέω, to swim) a ship,
vessel, Acts 27:41

ναῦται, nom. pl. m. n. . . . . ναύτης (3492)

(3492) **ναύτης**, ου, ὁ [§2.B.c] a shipman, sailor, sea-
man, Acts 27:27, 30; Rev. 18:17

ναυτῶν, gen. pl. m. n. . . . . ναύτης (3492)

(3493) **Ναχώρ**, ὁ, Nachor, pr. name, indecl., Luke
3:34

ναῷ, dat. sg. m. n. . . . . ναός (3485)

Νέαν, acc. sg. f. adj. (Acts 16:11, GNT, WH
& NA | Νεάπολιν, MT & TR) . . . . . νέος (3501)

νεανίαν, acc. sg. m. n. . . . . νεανίας (3494)

(3494) **νεανίας**, ου, ὁ, nom. sg. m. n. [§2.B.d] (νεάν,
idem, from νέος) a young man, youth, Acts
20:9; 23:17, 18, 22; used of one who is in
the prime and vigor of life, Acts 7:58

νεανίου, gen. sg. m. n. . . . . νεανίας (3494)

νεανίσκε, voc. sg. m. n. . . . . νεανίσκος (3495)

νεανίσκοι, nom. pl. m. n. {Acts 2:17} . . . id.

νεανίσκοι, voc. pl. m. n. {1 John 2:13–14} id.

νεανίσκον, acc. sg. m. n. . . . . id.

(3495) **νεανίσκος**, ου, ὁ, nom. sg. m. n. [§3.C.a] a
young man, youth, Mark 14:51; 16:5, et
al.; used of one in the prime of life, Matt.
19:20, 22; νεανίσκοι, soldiers, Mark 14:51

Νεάπολιν, acc. sg. f. n. (Acts 16:11, MT &
TR | Νεάν πόλιν, GNT, WH &
NA) . . . . Νεάπολις (3496)

(3496) **Νεάπολις**, εως, ἡ [§5.E.c] Neapolis, a city of
Thrace on the Strymonic gulf, Acts 16:11

νέας, gen. sg. f. adj. {Heb. 12:24} . . . . . . νέος (3501)

νέας, acc. pl. f. adj. {Tit. 2:4} . . . . id.

(3497) **Νεεμάν**, ὁ, Neeman, Naaman, pr. name, in-
decl. (Luke 4:27, MT & TR | Ναιμάν,
GNT, WH & NA)

νεκρά, nom. sg. f. adj. . . . . νεκρός (3498)

νεκράν, acc. sg. f. adj. . . . . id.

νεκροί, nom. pl. m. adj. . . . . id.

νεκροῖς, dat. pl. m. adj. . . . . id.

νεκρόν, acc. sg. m. adj. {Acts 28:6} . . . . . id.

νεκρόν, nom. sg. neut. adj. {Rom. 8:10} . id.

(3498) **νεκρός**, ά, όν, nom. sg. m. adj. [§7.1] (νέκυς,
a dead body) dead, without life, Matt.
11:5; 22:31; met. νεκρός τινι, dead to a
thing, no longer devoted to, or under the
influence of a thing, Rom. 6:11; dead in respect of fruitlessness, James 2:17, 20, 26;
morally or spiritually dead, Rom. 6:13;
Eph. 5:14; dead in alienation from God,
Eph. 2:1, 5; Col. 2:13; subject to death,
mortal, Rom. 8:10; causing death and mis-

ery, fatal, having a destructive power, Heb.
6:1; 9:14, et al.

νεκροῦ, gen. sg. m. adj. . . . . νεκρός (3498)

νεκρούς, acc. pl. m. adj. . . . . id.

(3499) **νεκρόω**, ῶ, fut. νεκρώσω, aor. ἐνέκρωσα
[§20.T] pr. to put to death, kill; in N.T.
met. to deaden, mortify, Col. 3:5; pass. to
be rendered impotent, effete, Rom. 4:19;
Heb. 11:12

νεκρῶν, gen. pl. m. adj. {Heb. 6:2} . . νεκρός (3498)

νεκρῶν, gen. pl. neut. adj. {Heb. 6:1} . . . id.

νεκρώσατε, 2 pers. pl. aor. act. imper. νεκρόω (3499)

νέκρωσιν, acc. sg. f. n. . . . . νέκρωσις (3500)

(3500) **νέκρωσις**, εως, ἡ [§5.E.c] pr. a putting to
death; dying, abandonment to death,
2 Cor. 4:10; deadness, impotency, Rom.
4:19

νενεκρωμένον, acc. sg. neut. perf. pass. part.
[§21.U] . . . . νεκρόω (3499)

νενεκρωμένου, gen. sg. m. perf. pass. part. . id.

νενίκηκα, 1 pers. sg. perf. act. indic. . . νικάω (3528)

νενικήκατε, 2 pers. pl. perf. act. indic. . . . id.

νενομοθέτηται, 3 pers. sg. perf. pass.
indic. . . . . νομοθετέω (3549)

νενομοθέτητο, 3 pers. sg. pluperf. pass. indic.
for ἐνενομοθέθητο [§14.1.f] (Heb. 7:11,
MT & TR | νενομοθέτηται, GNT, WH
& NA) . . . . id.

(‡3561) **νεομηνία**, ας, ἡ, new moon, first of the month
(Col. 2:16, GNT, WH & NA | νουμηνίας,
MT & TR)

νεομηνίας, gen. sg. f. n. (Col. 2:16, GNT, WH
& NA | νουμηνίας, MT & TR) νεομηνία (‡3561)

νέον, acc. sg. m. adj. {Matt. 9:17} . . . . . . νέος (3501)

νέον, nom. sg. neut. adj. {1 Cor. 5:7} . . . . id.

(3501) **νέος**, α, ον, nom. sg. m. adj. [§7.1] recent,
new, fresh, Matt. 9:17; 1 Cor. 5:7; Col.
3:10; Heb. 12:24; young, youthful, Tit.
2:4, et al.

(3502) **νεοσσός**, οῦ, ὁ [§3.C.a] the young of birds,
a young bird, youngling, chick, Luke 2:24

νεοσσούς, acc. pl. m. n. (Luke 2:24, MT &
TR | νοσσούς, GNT, WH & NA) νεοσσός (3502)

(3503) **νεότης**, ητος, ἡ [§4.2.c] youth, Matt. 19:20;
Acts 26:4, et al.

νεότητος, gen. sg. f. n. . . . . νεότης (3503)

νεόφυτον, acc. sg. m. adj. . . . . νεόφυτος (3504)

(3504) **νεόφυτος**, ον [§7.2] (νέος + φύω) newly or
recently planted; met. a neophyte, one
newly implanted into the Christian Church,
a new convert, 1 Tim. 3:6

(3505) **Νέρων**, ωνος, ὁ, Nero, pr. name
Νέρωνι, dat. sg. m. n. (2 Tim. 4:22, TRs |
GNT, WH, MT, TRb & NA omit) . Νέρων (3505)

νεύει, 3 pers. sg. pres. act. indic. . . . . νεύω (3506) νεύσαντος, gen. sg. m. aor. act. part. . . . νεύω *(3506)*

(3506) **νεύω,** fut. νεύσω, aor. ἔνευσα [§13.M] *to nod;*
     to intimate by a nod or significant gesture,
     John 13:24; Acts 24:10

νεφέλαι, nom. pl. f. n. . . . . νεφέλη *(3507)*

νεφέλαις, dat. pl. f. n. . . . . id.

(3507) **νεφέλη,** ης, ἡ, nom. sg. f. n. [§2.B.a] *a cloud,*
     Matt. 17:5; 24:30; 26:64, et al.

νεφέλη, dat. sg. f. n. . . . . νεφέλη *(3507)*

νεφέλην, acc. sg. f. n. . . . . id.

νεφέλης, gen. sg. f. n. . . . . id.

νεφελῶν, gen. pl. f. n. . . . . id.

(†3508) **Νεφθαλείμ,** ὁ, *Nephthalim,* pr. name, indecl.
     (Matt. 4:13, 15; Rev. 7:6, WH, MT & TR
     | Νεφθαλίμ, GNT & NA)

(3508) **Νεφθαλίμ,** ὁ, *Nephthalim,* pr. name, indecl.
     (Matt. 4:13, 15; Rev. 7:6, GNT & NA |
     Νεφθαλείμ, WH, MT & TR)

(3509) **νέφος,** ους, τό [§5.E.b] *a cloud;* trop. *a cloud,*
     a throng of persons, Heb. 12:1

νέφος, acc. sg. neut. n. . . . . νέφος *(3509)*

(3510) **νεφρός,** οῦ, ὁ [§3.C.a] *a kidney;* pl. νεφροί,
     the kidneys, reins; from the Hebrew *the*
     reins regarded as a seat of desire and af-
     fection, Rev. 2:23

νεφρούς, acc. pl. m. n. . . . . νεφρός *(3510)*

νεωκόρον, acc. sg. f. adj. . . . . νεωκόρος *(3511)*

(3511) **νεωκόρος,** ον [§7.2] (ναός, Att. νεώς, +
     κορέω, *to sweep clean*) pr. *one who sweeps*
     or cleanses a temple; generally, *one who*
     has the charge of a temple, aedituus; in
     N.T. *a devotee* city, as having specially dedi-
     cated a temple to some deity

νεωτέρας, acc. pl. f. compar. adj. . . νεώτερος *(‡3501)*

νεωτερικάς, acc. pl. f. adj. . . . . . . νεωτερικός *(3512)*

(3512) **νεωτερικός,** ή, όν [§7.F.a] *juvenile, natural to*
     youth, youthful, 2 Tim. 2:22

νεώτεροι, nom. pl. m. compar. adj. νεώτερος *(‡3501)*

(‡3501) **νεώτερος,** α, ον, nom. sg. m. compar. adj.
     [§7.1] (compar. of νέος) *younger, more*
     youthful, Luke 15:12, 13, et al.

νεωτέρους, acc. pl. m. compar. adj. νεώτερος *(‡3501)*

(3513) **νή,** a particle used in affirmative oaths, *by,*
     1 Cor. 15:31

νήθει, 3 pers. sg. pres. act. indic. . . . . νήθω *(3514)*

νήθουσιν, 3 pers. pl. pres. act. indic. (Matt.
     6:28, GNT, WH & NA | νήθει, MT &
     TR) . . . . id.

(3514) **νήθω,** fut. νήσω [§23.1.c] (νέω, idem) *to spin,*
     Matt. 6:28; Luke 12:27

νηπιάζετε, 2 pers. pl. pres. act. imper. νηπιάζω *(3515)*

(3515) **νηπιάζω,** fut. νηπιάσω [§26.1] *to be childlike,*
     1 Cor. 14:20

νήπιοι, nom. pl. m. adj. . . . . νήπιος *(3516)*

νηπίοις, dat. pl. m. adj. . . . . id.

(3516) **νήπιος,** ία, ον, nom. sg. m. adj. [§3.C.a] (νή
     + ἔπος) pr. *not speaking,* Latin *infans; an*
     infant, babe, child, Matt. 21:16; 1 Cor.
     13:11; *one below the age of manhood, a*
     minor, Gal. 4:1; met. *a babe* in knowledge,
     unlearned, simple, Matt. 11:25; Rom. 2:20

νηπίου, gen. sg. m. adj. . . . . νήπιος *(3516)*

νηπίων, gen. pl. m. adj. . . . . id.

Νηρέα, acc. sg. m. n. . . . . Νηρεύς *(3517)*

(3517) **Νηρεύς,** έως, ὁ [§5.E.d] *Nereus,* pr. name,
     Rom. 16:15

(3518) **Νηρί,** ὁ, *Neri,* pr. name, indecl. (Luke 3:27,
     GNT, MT, TR & NA | Νηρεί, WH)

(3519) **νησίον,** ου, τό [§3.C.c] *a small island,* Acts
     27:16

νησίον, acc. sg. neut. n. . . . . νησίον *(3519)*

νῆσον, acc. sg. f. n. . . . . νῆσος *(3520)*

(3520) **νῆσος,** ου, ἡ, nom. sg. f. n. [§3.C.b] (νέω, *to*
     swim) *an island,* Acts 13:6; 27:26, et al.

νήσου, gen. sg. f. n. . . . . νῆσος *(3520)*

(3521) **νηστεία,** ας, ἡ [§2.B.b; 2.2] *fasting, want of*
     food, 2 Cor. 6:5; 11:27; *a fast,* religious ab-
     stinence *from food,* Matt. 17:21; Luke
     2:37, et al.; spc. *the annual public fast of*
     the Jews, the great day of atonement, oc-
     curring in the month Tisri, corresponding
     to the new moon of October, Acts 27:9

νηστεία, dat. sg. f. n. (Matt. 17:21, MT & TR
     | GNT, WH & NA omit) . . . . νηστεία *(3521)*

νηστείαις, dat. pl. f. n. . . . . id.

νηστείαν, acc. sg. f. n. . . . . id.

νήστεις, acc. pl. m. adj. . . . . νῆστις *(3523)*

νηστειῶν, gen. pl. f. n. . . . . νηστεία *(3521)*

νηστεύειν, pres. act. infin. . . . . νηστεύω *(3522)*

νηστεύητε, 2 pers. pl. pres. act. subj. . . . . id.

νηστεύομεν, 1 pers. pl. pres. act. indic. . . . id.

νηστεύοντες, nom. pl. m. pres. act. part. . id.

νηστευόντων, gen. pl. m. pres. act. part. . id.

νηστεύουσι(ν), 3 pers. pl. pres. act. indic. . id.

νηστεῦσαι, aor. act. infin. (Luke 5:34, GNT,
     WH & NA | νηστεύειν, MT & TR) . . id.

νηστεύσαντες, nom. pl. m. aor. act. part. . id.

νηστεύσας, nom. sg. m. aor. act. part. . . . id.

νηστεύσουσιν, 3 pers. pl. fut. act. indic. . . id.

(3522) **νηστεύω,** 1 pers. sg. pres. act. indic., fut.
     νηστεύσω, aor. ἐνήστευσα [§13.M] *to fast,*
     Matt. 4:2; 6:16, 17, 18; 9:15, et al.

νηστεύων, nom. sg. m. pres. act.
     part. . . . . νηστεύω *(3522)*

(3523) **νῆστις,** ιος, εως [§5.E.c] and ιδος, ὁ, ἡ
     [§4.2.c] (νή + ἐσθίω) *fasting,* Matt. 15:32;
     Mark 8:3

νήσῳ, dat. sg. f. n. . . . . νῆσος *(3520)*

νηφάλεον, acc. sg. m. adj. (1 Tim. 3:2, MT
     & TR | νηφάλιον, GNT, WH &

NA) . . . . νηφάλεος *(3524)*

(3524) **νηφάλεος**, ον, *sober, temperate, abstinent in respect to wine, etc.; in N.T. met., vigilant, circumspect,* 1 Tim. 3:2, 11; Tit. 2:2

νηφαλέους, acc. pl. m. adj. (1 Tim. 3:11; Tit. 2:2, MT & TR | νηφαλίους, GNT, WH & NA) . . . . νηφάλεος *(3524)*

νηφάλιον, acc. sg. m. n. (1 Tim. 3:2, GNT, WH & NA | νηφάλεον, MT & TR) . . . . νηφάλιος *(†3524)*

(†3524) **νηφάλιος**, ον (and later νηφάλεος) ίου, ό, ή [§7.2] *sober, temperate, abstinent in respect to wine, etc.; in N.T. met., vigilant, circumspect,* 1 Tim. 3:2, 11; Tit. 2:2

νηφαλίους, acc. pl. m. adj. (1 Tim. 3:11; Tit. 2:2, GNT, WH & NA | νηφαλέους, MT & TR) . . . . νηφάλιος *(†3524)*

νῆφε, 2 pers. sg. pres. act. imper. . . . . . . νήφω *(3525)*

νήφοντες, nom. pl. m. pres. act. part. . . . . id.

(3525) **νήφω**, fut. νήψω [§23.1.a] aor. ἔνηψα, *to be sober, not intoxicated; in N.T. met., to be vigilant, circumspect,* 1 Thess. 5:6, 8, et al.

νήφωμεν, 1 pers. pl. pres. act. subj. . . . . νήφω *(3525)*

νήψατε, 2 pers. pl. aor. act. imper. . . . . . . id.

(3526) **Νίγερ**, ό, *Niger,* pr. name, probably not declined, Acts 13:1

νικᾷ, 3 pers. sg. pres. act. indic. . . . . . . νικάω *(3528)*

νίκα, 2 pers. sg. pres. act. imper. . . . . id.

Νικάνορα, acc. sg. m. n. . . . . Νικάνωρ *(3527)*

(3527) **Νικάνωρ**, ορος, ό [§4.2.f] *Nicanor,* pr. name, Acts 6:5

(3528) **νικάω**, ῶ, fut. νικήσω, perf. νενίκησα, aor. ἐνίκησα [§18.R] *to conquer, overcome, vanquish, subdue,* Luke 11:22; John 16:33; absol. *to overcome, prevail,* Rev. 5:5; *to come off superior* in a judicial cause, Rom. 3:4

(3529) **νίκη**, ης, ή, nom. sg. f. n. [§2.B.a] *victory;* meton. *a victorious principle,* 1 John 5:4

νικῆσαι, aor. act. infin. . . . . νικάω *(3528)*

νικήσασα, nom. sg. f. aor. act. part. . . . . . id.

νικήσει, 3 pers. sg. fut. act. indic. . . . . id.

νικήσεις, 2 pers. sg. fut. act. indic. (Rom. 3:4, GNT, WH & NA | νικήσῃς, MT & TR) id.

νικήσῃ, 3 pers. sg. aor. act. subj. . . . . id.

νικήσῃς, 2 pers. sg. aor. act. subj. (Rom. 3:4, MT & TR | νικήσεις, GNT, WH & NA) id.

(3530) **Νικόδημος**, ου, ό, nom. sg. m. n. [§3.C.a] *Nicodemus,* pr. name

(3531) **Νικολαΐτης**, ου, ό [§2.B.c] *a Nicolaitan,* or follower of Nicolaus, an heresiarch of the Apostolic age, Rev. 2:6, 15

Νικολαϊτῶν, gen. pl. m. n. . . . . . . Νικολαΐτης *(3531)*

Νικόλαον, acc. sg. m. n. . . . . Νικόλαος *(3532)*

(3532) **Νικόλαος**, ου, ό [§3.C.a] *Nicolaus,* pr. name, Acts 6:5

Νικοπόλεως, gen. sg. f. n. (Tit. 3:15, TRs | GNT, WH, MT, TRb & NA omit) . . . . Νικόπολις *(3533)*

Νικόπολιν, acc. sg. f. n. . . . . id.

(3533) **Νικόπολις**, εως, ή [§5.E.c] *Nicopolis,* a city of Macedonia

(3534) **νῖκος**, ους, τό, nom. sg. neut. n. [§5.E.b] (a later equivalent to νίκη) *victory,* Matt. 12:20; {1 Cor. 15:55}

νῖκος, acc. sg. neut. n. {1 Cor. 15:54} . . νῖκος *(3534)*

νικῶ, 2 pers. sg. pres. pass. imper. . . . . νικάω *(3528)*

νικῶν, nom. sg. m. pres. act. part. . . . . . . id.

νικῶντας, acc. pl. m. pres. act. part. . . . . . id.

νικῶντι, dat. sg. m. pres. act. part. . . . . . . id.

(†3535) **Νινευή**, ή, *Nineveh,* indecl. (Luke 11:32, MT | Νινευΐ, TR | Νινευΐται, GNT, WH & NA)

(3535) **Νινευΐ**, ή, *Nineveh,* the capital of Assyria, indecl. (Luke 11:32, TR | Νινευή, MT | Νινευΐται, GNT, WH & NA)

Νινευΐται, nom. pl. m. n. (Matt. 12:41; Luke 11:32, GNT, MT, TR & NA | Νινευεΐται, WH) . . . . Νινευΐτης *(†3536)*

Νινευΐταις, dat. pl. m. n. (Luke 11:30, GNT, MT & NA | Νινευΐταις, TR | Νινευεΐταις, WH) . . . . id.

(†3536) **Νινευΐτης**, ου, ό [§2.B.c] *a Ninevite, an inhabitant of Nineveh*

νίπτειν, pres. act. infin. . . . . νίπτω *(3538)*

νίπτεις, 2 pers. sg. pres. act. indic. . . . . . . id.

(3537) **νιπτήρ**, ῆρος, ό [§4.2.f] *a basin* for washing some part of the person, John 13:5

νιπτῆρα, acc. sg. m. n. . . . . νιπτήρ *(3537)*

νίπτονται, 3 pers. pl. pres. mid. indic. . . νίπτω *(3538)*

(3538) **νίπτω**, fut. νίψω [§23.1.a] aor. ἔνιψα (a form of later use for νίζω) *to wash;* spc. *to wash* some part of the person, as distinguished from λούω, Matt. 6:17; John 13:8, et al.

νίψαι, 2 pers. sg. aor. mid. imper. . . . . . νίπτω *(3538)*

νιψάμενος, nom. sg. m. aor. mid. part. . . id.

νίψασθαι, aor. mid. infin. . . . . id.

νίψῃς, 2 pers. sg. aor. act. subj. . . . . id.

νίψω, 1 pers. sg. aor. act. subj. . . . . id.

νίψωνται, 3 pers. pl. aor. mid. subj. . . . . . id.

νόει, 2 pers. sg. pres. act. imper. . . . . . . νοέω *(†3539)*

νοεῖτε, 2 pers. pl. pres. act. indic. . . . . . . id.

νοείτω, 3 pers. sg. pres. act. imper. . . . . . . id.

(†3539) **νοέω**, ῶ, fut. νοήσω, aor. ἐνόησα [§16.P] *to perceive, observe; to mark* attentively, Matt. 24:15; Mark 13:14; 2 Tim. 2:7; *to understand, comprehend,* Matt. 15:17, et al.; *to conceive,* Eph. 3:20

(3540) **νόημα**, ατος, τό [§4.D.c] *the mind, the understanding, intellect,* 2 Cor. 3:14; 4:4; *the heart, soul, affections, feelings, disposition,*

2 Cor. 11:3; *a conception of the mind, thought, purpose, device,* 2 Cor. 2:11; 10:5

νόημα, acc. sg. neut. n. . . . . νόημα *(3540)*

νοήματα, nom. pl. neut. n. {2 Cor. 3:14} . id.

νοήματα, acc. pl. neut. n. {2 Cor. 4:4} . . . id.

νοῆσαι, aor. act. infin. . . . . νοέω *(†3539)*

νοήσωσι(ν), 3 pers. pl. aor. act. subj. . . . . id.

νόθοι, nom. pl. m. adj. . . . . νόθος *(3541)*

(3541) **νόθος,** η, ον, *spurious, bastard,* Heb. 12:8

νοΐ, dat. sg. m. n. [§6.4.h] . . . . νοῦς *(3563)*

(3542) **νομή,** ῆς, ἡ [§2.B.a] (νέμω, *to feed*) *pasture, pasturage,* John 10:9; ἔχειν νομήν, *to eat its way, spread corrosion,* 2 Tim. 2:17

νομήν, acc. sg. f. n. . . . . νομή *(3542)*

νομίζει, 3 pers. sg. pres. act. indic. . . . . νομίζω *(3543)*

νομίζειν, pres. act. infin. . . . . id.

νομίζοντες, nom. pl. m. pres. act. part. (Acts 14:19, GNT, WH & NA | νομίσαντες, MT & TR) . . . . id.

νομιζόντων, gen. pl. m. pres. act. part. . . . id.

(3543) **νομίζω,** 1 pers. sg. pres. act. indic., fut. νομίσω, perf. νενόμικα, aor. ἐνόμισα [§26.1] *to own as settled and established; to deem,* 1 Cor. 7:26; 1 Tim. 6:5; *to suppose, presume,* Matt. 5:17; 20:10; Luke 2:44, et al.; pass. *to be usual, customary,* Acts 16:13

νομίζων, nom. sg. m. pres. act. part. . . νομίζω *(3543)*

νομικάς, acc. pl. f. adj. . . . . νομικός *(3544)*

νομικοί, nom. pl. m. adj. . . . . id.

νομικοῖς, dat. pl. m. adj. . . . . id.

νομικόν, acc. sg. m. adj. . . . . id.

(3544) **νομικός,** ή, όν, nom. sg. m. adj. [§7.F.a] *pertaining to law; relating to the* Mosaic *law,* Tit. 3:9; as a subst., *one skilled in law, a jurist, lawyer,* Tit. 3:13; spc. *an interpreter and teacher of the* Mosaic *law,* Matt. 22:35, et al.

νομικούς, acc. pl. m. adj. . . . . νομικός *(3544)*

νομικῶν, gen. pl. m. adj. . . . . id.

(3545) **νομίμως,** adv., *lawfully, agreeably to law or custom, rightfully,* 1 Tim. 1:8; 2 Tim. 2:5

νομίσαντες, nom. pl. m. aor. act. part. νομίζω *(3543)*

νομίσητε, 2 pers. pl. aor. act. subj. . . . . . . id.

(3546) **νόμισμα,** ατος, τό [§4.D.c] pr. *a thing sanctioned by law or custom; lawful money, coin,* Matt. 22:19

νόμισμα, acc. sg. neut. n. . . . . νόμισμα *(3546)*

νομοδιδάσκαλοι, nom. pl. m. n. . . . . νομοδιδάσκαλος *(3547)*

(3547) **νομοδιδάσκαλος,** ου, ὁ, nom. sg. m. n. [§3.C.a] (νόμος + διδάσκαλος) *a teacher and interpreter of the* Mosaic *law,* Luke 5:17, et al.

(3548) **νομοθεσία,** ας, ἡ, nom. sg. f. n. [§2.B.b; 2.2]

legislation; ἡ νομοθεσία, *the gift of the* Divine *law,* or *the* Mosaic *law* itself, Rom. 9:4

(3549) **νομοθετέω,** ῶ, fut. νομοθετήσω [§16.P] *to impose a law, give laws;* in N.T. pass., *to have a law imposed on one's self, receive a law,* Heb. 7:11; *to be enacted, constituted,* Heb. 8:6

(3550) **νομοθέτης,** ου, ὁ, nom. sg. m. n. [§2.B.c] (νόμος + τίθημι) *a legislator, lawgiver,* James 4:12

νόμον, acc. sg. m. n. . . . . νόμος *(3551)*

(3551) **νόμος,** ου, ὁ, nom. sg. m. n. [§3.C.a] (νέμω, *to dispense, distribute*) *a law,* Rom. 4:15; 1 Tim. 1:9; *the* Mosaic *law,* Matt. 5:17, et al. freq.; *the Old Testament Scripture,* John 10:34; *a legal tie,* Rom. 7:2, 3; *a law, a rule, standard,* Rom. 3:27; *a rule* of life and conduct, Gal. 6:2, James 1:25

νόμου, gen. sg. m. n. . . . . νόμος *(3551)*

νόμους, acc. pl. m. n. . . . . id.

νόμῳ, dat. sg. m. n. . . . . id.

νοός, gen. sg. m. n. [§6.4.h] . . . . νοῦς *(3563)*

νοοῦμεν, 1 pers. pl. pres. act. indic. . . . νοέω *(†3539)*

νοούμενα, nom. pl. neut. pres. pass. part. id.

νοοῦντες, nom. pl. m. pres. act. part. . . . . id.

(3552) **νοσέω,** ῶ, fut. νοσήσω [§16.P] *to be sick;* met. *to have a diseased appetite or craving for* a thing, *have an excessive and vicious fondness for* a thing, *to dote,* 1 Tim. 6:4

(3553) **νόσημα,** ατος, τό [§4.D.c] *disease, sickness,* John 5:4

νοσήματι, dat. sg. neut. n. (John 5:4, MT & TR | GNT, WH & NA omit) . . . . νόσημα *(3553)*

νόσοις, dat. pl. f. n. . . . . νόσος *(3554)*

νόσον, acc. sg. f. n. . . . . id.

(3554) **νόσος,** ου, ἡ [§3.C.b] *a disease, sickness, distemper,* Matt. 4:23, 24; 8:17; 9:35, et al.

νόσους, acc. pl. f. n. . . . . νόσος *(3554)*

(3555) **νοσσιά,** ᾶς, ἡ [§2.B.b; 2.2] (contr. for νεοσσιά, from νεοσσός) *as brood* of young birds, Luke 13:34

νοσσία, acc. pl. neut. n. . . . . νοσσίον *(3556)*

νοσσιάν, acc. sg. f. n. . . . . νοσσιά *(3555)*

(3556) **νοσσίον,** ου, τό [§3.C.c] (contr. for νεοσσίον) *the young of birds, a chick;* pl. *a brood* of young birds, Matt. 23:37

(‡3502) **νοσσός,** οῦ, ὁ [§3.C.a] (contr. for νεοσσός) *a young bird,* Luke 2:24

νοσσούς, acc. pl. m. n. (Luke 2:24, GNT, WH & NA | νεοσσούς, MT & TR) . . νοσσός *(‡3502)*

νοσφιζομένους, acc. pl. m. pres. mid. part. . . . . νοσφίζω *(†3557)*

(†3557) **νοσφίζω,** fut. νοσφίσω [§26.1] (νόσφι, *apart, separate*) *to deprive, rob;* mid. *to appropriate; to make secret reservation,* Acts

5:2, 3; *to purloin,* Tit. 2:10

νοσφίσασθαι, aor. mid. infin. . . . . . . νοσφίζω (†3557)

νόσων, gen. pl. f. n. {Luke 6:18} . . . . νόσος (3554)

νοσῶν, nom. sg. m. pres. act. part. {1 Tim. 6:4} . . . . νοσέω (3552)

νότον, acc. sg. m. n. . . . . νότος (3558)

(3558) **νότος,** ου, ὁ [§3.C.a] *the south wind,* Luke 12:55; Acts 27:13; meton. *the south, the southern quarter of the heavens,* Matt. 12:42; Luke 11:31; 13:29; Rev. 21:13

νότου, gen. sg. m. n. . . . . νότος (3558)

(3559) **νουθεσία,** ας, ἡ [§2.B.b; 2.2] *warning, admonition,* 1 Cor. 10:11; Eph. 6:4; Tit. 3:10

νουθεσίᾳ, dat. sg. f. n. . . . . νουθεσία (3559)

νουθεσίαν, acc. sg. f. n. . . . . id.

νουθετεῖν, pres. act. infin. . . . . νουθετέω (3560)

νουθετεῖτε, 2 pers. pl. pres. act. imper. . . . id.

(3560) **νουθετέω,** ῶ, fut. νουθετήσω [§16.P] (νοῦς + τίθημι) pr. *to put in mind; to admonish, warn,* Acts 20:31; Rom. 15:14, et al.

νουθετοῦντας, acc. pl. m. pres. act. part. . . . . νουθετέω (3560)

νουθετοῦντες, nom. pl. m. pres. act. part.   id.

νουθετῶ, 1 pers. sg. pres. act. indic. (1 Cor. 4:14, MT & TR | νουθετῶν, GNT, WH & NA) . . . . id.

νουθετῶν, nom. sg. m. pres. act. part. . . . id.

(3561) **νουμηνία,** ας, ἡ [§2.B.b; 2.2] (contr. for νεομηνία, νέος + μήν) *the new moon*

νουμηνίας, gen. sg. f. n. (Col. 2:16, MT & TR | νεομηνίας, GNT, WH & NA) . . . . νουμηνία (3561)

νοῦν, acc. sg. m. n. . . . . νοῦς (3563)

(3562) **νουνεχῶς,** adv. (νουνεχής, νοῦς + ἔχω) *understandingly, sensibly, discreetly,* Mark 12:34

(3563) **νοῦς,** nom. sg. m. n., νοῦ, and in N.T. νοός, dat. νοΐ, ὁ (contr. for νόος) [§3.3; 6.4.h] *the mind, intellect,* 1 Cor. 14:15, 19; *understanding, intelligent faculty,* Luke 24:45; *intellect, judgment,* Rom. 7:23, 25; *opinion, sentiment,* Rom. 14:5; 1 Cor. 1:10; *mind, thought, conception,* Rom. 11:34; 1 Cor. 2:16; Phil. 4:7; *settled state of mind,* 2 Thess. 2:2; *frame of mind,* Rom. 1:28; 12:2; Col. 2:18; Eph. 4:23; 1 Tim. 6:5; 2 Tim. 3:8; Tit. 1:15

νύκτα, acc. sg. f. n. . . . . νύξ (3571)

νύκτας, acc. pl. f. n. . . . . id.

νυκτί, dat. sg. f. n. . . . . id.

νυκτός, gen. sg. f. n. . . . . id.

Νύμφαν, acc. sg. m. n. (Col. 4:15, GNT, WH & NA | Νυμφᾶν, MT & TR) . . . Νύμφας (3564)

(3564) **Νύμφας,** or Νυμφᾶς, α, ὁ [§2.4] *Nymphas,* pr. name

(3565) **νύμφη,** ης, ἡ, nom. sg. f. n. [§2.B.a] *a bride,* John 3:29; Rev. 18:23; 21:2, 9; 22:17; opposed to πενθερά, *a daughter-in-law,* Matt. 10:35; Luke 12:53

νύμφην, acc. sg. f. n. . . . . νύμφη (3565)

νύνφης, gen. sg. f. n. . . . . id.

νυμφίον, acc. sg. m. n. . . . . νυμφίος (3566)

(3566) **νυμφίος,** ου, ὁ, nom. sg. m. n. [§3.C.a] *a bridegroom,* Matt. 9:15; 25:1, 5, 6, 10, et al.

νυμφίου, gen. sg. m. n. . . . . νυμφίος (3566)

(3567) **νυμφών,** ῶνος, ὁ, nom. sg. m. n. [§4.2.e] *a bridal-chamber;* in N.T. υἱοὶ τοῦ νυμφῶνος, *sons of the bridal-chamber, the bride-groom's attendant friends, groomsmen,* perhaps the same as the Greek παρανύμφιοι, Matt. 9:15; Mark 2:19; Luke 5:34 (Matt. 22:10, WH | γάμος, GNT, MT, TR & NA)

νυμφῶνος, gen. sg. m. n. . . . . νυμφών (3567)

(3568) **νῦν,** adv., *now, at the present time,* Mark 10:30; Luke 6:21, et al. freq.; *just now,* John 11:8, et al.; *forthwith,* John 12:31; καὶ νῦν, *even now, as matters stand,* John 11:22; *now,* expressive of a marked tone of address, Acts 7:34; 13:11; James 4:13; 5:1; τὸ νῦν, *the present time,* Luke 1:48, et al.; τανῦν, or τὰ νῦν, *now,* Acts 4:29, et al.

(3570) **νυνί,** adv., of time, *now, at this very moment,*

(3571) **νύξ,** νυκτός, ἡ, nom. sg. f. n. [§4.2.b] *night,* Matt. 2:14; 28:13; John 3:2; met. spiritual *night,* moral *darkness,* Rom. 13:12; 1 Thess. 5:5

(3572) **νύσσω,** or νύττω, fut. νύξω, aor. ἔνυξα [§26.3] *to prick, pierce,* John 19:34

νυστάζει, 3 pers. sg. pres. act. indic. (2 Pet. 2:3, GNT, WH, TR & NA | νυστάξει, MT) . . . . νυστάζω (3573)

(3573) **νυστάζω,** fut. νυστάσω and νυστάξω [§26.2] *to nod; to nod in sleep; to sink into a sleep,* Matt. 25:5; *to slumber* in inactivity, 2 Pet. 2:3

νυστάξει, 3 pers. sg. fut. act. indic. (2 Pet. 2:3, MT | νυστάζει, GNT, WH, TR & NA) . . . . νυστάζω (3573)

(3574) **νυχθήμερον,** ου, τό [§3.C.c] (νύξ + ἡμέρα) *a day and night, twenty-four hours,* 2 Cor. 11:25

νυχθήμερον, acc. sg. neut. n. . . . . νυχθήμερον (3574)

(3575) **Νῶε,** ὁ, *Noe, Noah,* pr. name, indecl.

νωθροί, nom. pl. m. adj. . . . . νωθρός (3576)

(3576) **νωθρός,** ά, όν [§7.1] *slow, sluggish, untoward,* Heb. 5:11; 6:12

νῶτον, acc. sg. m. n. . . . . νῶτος (3577)

(3577) **νῶτος,** ου, ὁ [§3.C.a] *the back* of men or animals

Ξ

ξέναις, dat. pl. f. adj. . . . . ξένος *(3581)*

(3578) **ξενία,** ας, ἡ [§2.B.b; 2.2] pr. *state of being a guest;* then, *the reception of a guest or stranger, hospitality;* in N.T. *a lodging,* Acts 28:23; Philemon 22

ξενίαν, acc. sg. f. n. . . . . ξενία *(3578)*
ξενίζεσθε, 2 pers. pl. pres. pass. imper. ξενίζω *(3579)*
ξενίζεται, 3 pers. sg. pres. pass. indic. . . . . id.
ξενίζοντα, acc. pl. neut. pres. act. part. . . id.
ξενίζονται, 3 pers. pl. pres. pass. indic. . . . id.

(3579) **ξενίζω,** fut. ξενίσω, aor. ἐξένισα [§26.1] *to receive as a guest, entertain,* Acts 10:23; 28:7; Heb. 13:2; pass. *to be entertained as a guest, to lodge or reside with,* Acts 10:6, 18, 32; 21:16; *to strike with a feeling of strangeness, to surprise;* pass. or mid. *to be struck with surprise, be staggered, be amazed,* 1 Pet. 4:4, 12; intrans. *to be strange;* ξενίζοντα, *strange matters, novelties,* Acts 17:20

ξενίσαντες, nom. pl. m. aor. act. part. . ξενίζω *(3579)*
ξενισθῶμεν, 1 pers. pl. aor. pass. subj. . . . id.

(3580) **ξενοδοχέω,** ῶ, fut. ξενοδοχήσω [§16.P] (ξενοδόχος, ξένος + δέχομαι) *to receive and entertain strangers, exercise hospitality,* 1 Tim. 5:10

ξένοι, nom. pl. m. adj. . . . . ξένος *(3581)*
ξένοις, dat. pl. m. adj. . . . . id.
ξένον, acc. sg. m. adj. . . . . id.

(3581) **ξένος,** η, ον, nom. sg. m. adj., *strange, foreign; alien,* Eph. 2:12, 19; *strange, unexpected, surprising,* 1 Pet. 4:12; *novel,* Heb. 13:9; subst. *a stranger,* Matt. 25:35, et al.; *a host,* Rom. 16:23

ξένου, gen. sg. neut. adj. . . . . ξένος *(3581)*
ξένους, acc. pl. m. adj. . . . . id.
ξένων, gen. pl. neut. adj. . . . . id.

(3582) **ξέστης,** ου, ὁ [§2.B.c] (Latin *sextus* or *sextarius*) *a sextarius,* a Roman measure, containing about one pint English; in N.T. used for *a small vessel, cup, pot,* Mark 7:4, 8

ξεστῶν, gen. pl. m. n. . . . . ξέστης *(3582)*
ξηρά, nom. sg. f. adj. . . . . ξηρός *(3584)*
ξηραίνεται, 3 pers. sg. pres. pass. indic. . . . . ξηραίνω *(3583)*

(3583) **ξηραίνω,** fut. ξηρανῶ, aor. ἐξήρανα [§27.1.c,ε] perf. pass. ἐξήραμμαι, aor. pass. ἐξηράνθην [§27.3] *to dry up, parch,* James 1:11; pass. *to be parched,* Matt. 13:6, et al.; *to be ripened* as corn, Rev. 14:15; *to be withered, to wither,* Mark 11:20; of parts of the body, *to be withered,* Mark 3:1, 3;

to pine, Mark 9:18

ξηράν, acc. sg. f. n. . . . . ξηρός *(3584)*
ξηρᾶς, gen. sg. f. n. . . . . id.

(3584) **ξηρός,** ά, όν [§7.1] *dry, withered,* Luke 23:31; ἡ ξηρά, sc. γῆ, *the dry land, land,* Matt. 23:15; Heb. 11:29; of parts of the body, *withered,* Matt. 12:10

ξηρῷ, dat. sg. neut. adj. . . . . ξηρός *(3584)*
ξηρῶν, gen. pl. m. adj. . . . . id.
ξύλα, acc. pl. neut. n. . . . . ξύλον *(3586)*
ξύλινα, nom. pl. neut. adj.
{2 Tim. 2:20} . . . . ξύλινος *(3585)*
ξύλινα, acc. pl. neut. adj. {Rev. 9:20} . . . . id.

(3585) **ξύλινος,** η, ον [§7.F.a] *wooden, of wood, made of wood*

(3586) **ξύλον,** ου, τό, nom. sg. neut. n. [§3.C.c] *wood, timber,* 1 Cor. 3:12; Rev. 18:12; *stocks,* Acts 16:24; *a club,* Matt. 26:47, 55; *a post, cross, gibbet,* Acts 5:30; 10:39; 13:29; *a tree,* Luke 23:31; Rev. 2:7 {Rev. 22:2}

ξύλον, acc. sg. neut. n. {Rev. 22:14} . . . ξύλον *(3586)*
ξύλου, gen. sg. neut. n. . . . . id.
ξύλῳ, dat. sg. neut. n. . . . . id.
ξύλων, gen. pl. neut. n. . . . . id.
ξυρᾶσθαι, pres. pass. infin. [§19.S] . . . . ξυράω *(3587)*

(3587) **ξυράω,** ῶ, fut. ξυρήσω, aor. ἐξύρησα [§18.R] perf. pass. ἐξύρημαι (ξυρόν, *a razor*) *to cut off the hair, shear, shave,* Acts 21:24; 1 Cor. 11:5, 6

ξυρήσονται, 3 pers. pl. fut. mid. dep. indic. (Acts 21:24, GNT, WH & NA | ξυρήσωνται, MT & TR) . . . . ξυράω *(3587)*
ξηρήσωνται, 3 pers. pl. aor. mid. dep. subj. (Acts 21:24, MT & TR | ξυρήσονται, GNT, WH & NA) . . . . id.

Ο

(3588) **ὁ,** ἡ, τό, nom. sg. m. article, [§1.A and remarks] the prepositive article, answering, to a considerable extent, to the English definite article; but, for the principle and facts of its usage, consult a grammar; ὁ μὲν —ὁ δέ, *the one — the other,* Phil. 1:16, 17; Heb. 7:5, 6, 20, 21, 23, 24; pl. *some —others,* Matt. 13:23; 22:5, 6; ὁ δέ, *but he,* Matt. 4:4; 12:48; οἱ δέ, *but others,* Matt. 28:17, et al.; used, in a poetic quotation, for a personal pronoun, Acts 17:28

ὅ, nom. sg. neut. relative pron. [§10.J.g] {Matt. 10:26} . . . . ὅς *(3739)*
ὅ, acc. sg. neut. relative pron. [§10.J.g]

{Matt. 10:27} . . . . ὅς (3739)

ὀγδόῃ, dat. sg. f. adj. . . . . ὄγδοος (3590)

(3589) ὀγδοήκοντα, οἱ, αἱ, τά, indecl. numeral, *eighty,* Luke 2:37; 16:7

(†3589) ὀγδοηκοντατέσσαρες, ων, οἱ, αἱ, numeral, *eighty-eight*

ὀγδοηκοντατεσσάρων, gen. pl. neut. numeral (Luke 2:37, TR | ὀγδοήκοντα τεσσάρων, GNT, WH, MT & NA) . . . . ὀγδοηκοντατέσσαρες (†3589)

ὄγδοον, acc. sg. m. adj. . . . . ὄγδοος (3590)

(3590) ὄγδοος, η, ον, nom. sg. m. adj. [§7.F.a] *the eighth,* Luke 1:59; Acts 7:8, et al.

ὄγκον, acc. sg. m. n. . . . . ὄγκος (3591)

(3591) ὄγκος, ου, ὁ [§3.C.a] pr. *bulk, weight; a burden, impediment,* Heb. 12:1

(3592) ὅδε, nom. sg. m. demon. pron. [§10.J.a; 10.1] (ὅδε, ἥδε, τόδε, for ὁ, ἡ, τό + δέ) *this, that, he, she, it,* Luke 10:39; 16:25; Acts 15:23, et al. (Luke 16:25, TR | ὧδε, GNT, WH, MT & NA)

(3593) ὁδεύω, fut. ὁδεύσω [§13.M] *to journey, travel,* Luke 10:33

ὁδεύων, nom. sg. m. pres. act. part. . . . ὁδεύω (3593)

ὁδηγεῖ, 3 pers. sg. pres. act. indic. (Rev. 7:17, MT | ὁδηγήσει, GNT, WH, TR & NA) . . . . ὁδηγέω (3594)

ὁδηγεῖν, pres. act. infin. . . . . id.

(3594) ὁδηγέω, ῶ, fut. ὁδηγήσω [§16.P] *to lead, guide,* Matt. 15:14; Luke 6:39; Rev. 7:17; met. *to instruct, teach,* John 16:13; Acts 8:31

ὁδηγῇ, 3 pers. sg. pres. act. subj. . . . . ὁδηγέω (3594)

ὁδηγήσει, 3 pers. sg. fut. act. indic. . . . . . id.

ὁδηγήσῃ, 3 pers. sg. aor. act. subj. (Acts 8:31, MT & TR | ὁδηγήσει, GNT, WH & NA) . . . . id.

ὁδηγοί, nom. pl. m. n. {Matt. 15:14} . ὁδηγός (3595)

ὁδηγοί, voc. pl. m. n. {Matt. 23:16, 24} . . id.

ὁδηγόν, acc. sg. m. n. . . . . id.

(3595) ὁδηγός, οῦ, ὁ [§3.C.a] (ὁδός + ἡγέομαι) *a guide, leader,* Acts 1:16; met. *an instructor, teacher,* Matt. 15:14; 23:16, 24; Rom. 2:19

ὁδηγοῦ, gen. sg. m. n. . . . . ὁδηγός (3595)

ὁδοί, nom. pl. f. n. . . . . ὁδός (3598)

(3596) ὁδοιπορέω, ῶ, fut. ὁδοιπορήσω (ὁδός + πόρος) *to journey, travel,* Acts 10:9

(3597) ὁδοιπορία, ας, ἡ [§2.B.b; 2.2] *a journey, journeying, travel,* John 4:6; 2 Cor. 11:26

ὁδοιπορίαις, dat. pl. f. n. . . . . ὁδοιπορία (3597)

ὁδοιπορίας, gen. sg. f. n. . . . . id.

ὁδοιπορούντων, gen. pl. m. pres. act. part. ὁδοιπορέω (3596)

ὁδοῖς, dat. pl. f. n. . . . . ὁδός (3598)

ὁδόν, acc. sg. f. n. . . . . id.

ὀδόντα, acc. sg. m. n. . . . . ὀδούς (3599)

ὀδόντας, acc. pl. m. n. . . . . id.

ὀδόντες, nom. pl. m. n. . . . . id.

ὀδόντος, gen. sg. m. n. . . . . id.

ὀδόντων, gen. pl. m. n. . . . . id.

(3598) ὁδός, οῦ, ἡ, nom. sg. f. n. [§3.C.b] *a way, road,* Matt. 2:12; 7:13, 14; 8:28; 22:9, 10; *means of access, approach, entrance,* John 14:6; Heb. 9:8; *direction, quarter, region,* Matt. 4:15; 10:5; *the act of journeying, a journey, way, course,* Matt. 10:10; Mark 2:23; 1 Thess. 3:11, et al.; *a journey,* as regards extent, Acts 1:12; met. *a way,* systematic *course* of pursuit, Luke 1:79; Acts 2:28; 16:17; *a way,* systematic *course* of action or conduct, Matt. 21:32; Rom. 11:33; 1 Cor. 4:17, et al.; *a way, system of doctrine,* Acts 18:26; ἡ ὁδός, *the way* of the Christian faith, Acts 19:9, 23; 24:22

ὁδοῦ, gen. sg. f. n. . . . . ὁδός (3598)

ὁδούς, acc. pl. f. n. . . . . id.

(3599) ὀδούς, ὀδόντος, ὁ [§4.2.d] *a tooth,* Matt. 5:38; 8:12, et al.

ὀδύναις, dat. pl. f. n. . . . . ὀδύνη (3601)

ὀδυνᾶσαι, 2 pers. sg. pres. pass. indic. for ὀδυνᾷ, an impure form combining the terminations of a contract verb and a verb in μι . . . . ὀδυνάω (3600)

(3600) ὀδυνάω, ῶ, fut. ὀδυνήσω [§18.R] *to pain* either bodily or mentally; pass. *to be in an agony, be tormented,* Luke 2:48; 16:24, 25; *to be distressed, grieved,* Acts 20:38

(3601) ὀδύνη, ης, ἡ, nom. sg. f. n. [§2.B.a] *pain* of body of mind; *sorrow, grief,* Rom. 9:2; 1 Tim. 6:10

ὀδυνῶμαι, 1 pers. sg. pres. pass. indic. ὀδυνάω (3600)

ὀδυνώμενοι, nom. pl. m. pres. pass. part. . id.

ὀδυρμόν, acc. sg. m. n. . . . . ὀδυρμός (3602)

(3602) ὀδυρμός, οῦ, ὁ, nom. sg. m. n. [§3.C.a] (ὀδύρομαι, *to lament, bewail*) *bitter lamentation, wailing,* Matt. 2:18; meton. *sorrow, mourning,* 2 Cor. 7:7

ὁδῷ, dat. sg. f. n. . . . . ὁδός (3598)

ὁδῶν, gen. pl. f. n. . . . . id.

ὄζει, 3 pers. sg. pres. act. indic. . . . . ὄζω (3605)

Ὀζίαν, acc. sg. m. n., *Ozias,* pr. name (Matt. 1:8, GNT, MT, TR & NA | Ὀζείαν, WH) . . . . Ὀζίας (3604)

(3604) Ὀζίας, ου, ὁ, nom. sg. m. n. (Matt. 1:9, GNT, MT, TR & NA | Ὀζείας, WH) [§2.B.d]

(3605) ὄζω, fut. ὀζήσω and ὀζέσω [§35.5] *to smell, emit an odor; to have an offensive smell, stink,* John 11:39

(3606) ὅθεν, adv., *whence,* Matt. 12:44; Acts 14:26; *from the place where,* Matt. 25:24, 26;

whence, from which circumstance, 1 John 2:18; *wherefore, whereupon,* Matt. 14:7

(3607) **ὀθόνη,** ης, ἡ [§2.B.a] pr. *fine linen; a linen cloth; a sheet,* Acts 10:11; 11:5

ὀθόνην, acc. sg. f. n. . . . . ὀθόνη (3607)
ὀθόνια, acc. pl. neut. n. . . . . ὀθόνιον (3608)
ὀθονίοις, dat. pl. neut. n. . . . . id.

(3608) **ὀθόνιον,** ου, τό [§3.C.c] *a linen cloth;* in N.T. *a swath, bandage* for a corpse, Luke 24:12, et al.

ὀθονίων, gen. pl. neut. n. . . . . ὀθόνιον (3608)
οἱ, nom. pl. m. article . . . . ὁ (3588)
οἵ, nom. pl. m. relative pron. [§10.J.g] . . . . ὅς (3739)
οἷα, nom. sg. f. relative pron. [§10.7] {Mark 13:19} . . . . οἷος (3634)
οἷα, nom. pl. neut. relative pron. {2 Tim. 3:11} . . . . id.
οἷα, acc. pl. neut. relative pron. {Mark 9:3} id.

(‡1492) **οἶδα,** 1 pers. sg. perf. act. indic. [§37.1] 2 perf. from absol. εἴδω, with the sense of the present, [§38.2] pluperf. ᾔδειν, imper. ἴσθι, subj. εἰδῶ, opt. εἰδείην, infin. εἰδέναι, part. εἰδώς, fut. εἴσομαι and εἰδήσω, *to know,* Matt. 6:8, et al.; *to know how,* Matt. 7:11, et al.; from the Hebrew, *to regard with favor,* 1 Thess. 5:12.

οἴδαμεν, 1 pers. pl. perf. act. indic. . . . . οἶδα (‡1492)
οἶδας, 2 pers. sg. perf. act. indic. . . . . id.
οἴδασι(ν), 3 pers. pl. perf. act. indic. . . . . . id.
οἴδατε, 2 pers. pl. perf. act. indic. . . . . id.
οἶδε(ν), 3 pers. sg. perf. act. indic. . . . . id.
οἰέσθω, 3 pers. sg. pres. mid./pass. dep. imper. . . . . οἴομαι (3633)
οἰκεῖ, 3 pers. sg. pres. act. indic. . . . . . . οἰκέω (3611)
οἰκειακοί, nom. pl. m. adj. (Matt. 10:36, MT | οἰκιακοί, GNT, TR, WH & NA) . . . . οἰκειακός (‡3615)

(‡3615) **οἰκειακός,** ή, όν, *belonging to a house*

οἰκειακούς, acc. pl. m. adj. (Matt. 10:25, MT | οἰκιακούς, GNT, WH, TR & NA) . . . . οἰκειακός (‡3615)
οἰκεῖν, pres. act. infin. . . . . οἰκέω (3611)
οἰκεῖοι, nom. pl. m. adj. . . . . οἰκεῖος (3609)

(3609) **οἰκεῖος,** εία, εῖον [§7.1] *belonging to a house, domestic;* pl. *members of a family, immediate kin,* 1 Tim. 5:8; *members of* a spiritual *family,* Eph. 2:19; *members of a* spiritual *brotherhood,* Gal. 6:10

οἰκείους, acc. pl. m. adj. . . . . οἰκεῖος (3609)
οἰκείων, gen. pl. m. adj. . . . . id.
οἰκέται, nom. pl. m. n. . . . . οἰκέτης (3610)

(†3610) **οἰκετεία,** ας, ἡ [§2.B.b; 2.2] *the members, or arrangements, of a household*

οἰκετείας, gen. sg. f. n. (Matt. 24:45, GNT, WH & NA | θεραπείας, MT &

TR) . . . . οἰκετεία (†3610)
οἰκέτην, acc. sg. m. n. . . . . οἰκέτης (3610)

(3610) **οἰκέτης,** ου, ὁ, nom. sg. m. n. [§2.B.c] pr. *an inmate of a house; a domestic servant, household slave,* Luke 16:13; Acts 10:7; Rom. 14:4; 1 Pet. 2:18

οἰκέτου, gen. sg. m. n. (Philemon 25, TRs | GNT, WH, MT, TRb & NA omit) οἰκέτης (3610)
οἰκετῶν, gen. pl. m. n. . . . . id.

(3611) **οἰκέω,** ῶ, fut. οἰκήσω [§16.P] *to dwell in, inhabit,* 1 Tim. 6:16; intrans. *to dwell, live; to cohabit,* 1 Cor. 7:12, 13; *to be indwelling, indwell,* Rom. 7:17, 18, 20; 8:9, 11; 1 Cor. 3:16

(3612) **οἴκημα,** ατος, τό [§4.D.c] *a dwelling;* used in various conventional senses, and among them, *a prison, cell,* Acts 12:7

οἰκήματι, dat. sg. neut. n. . . . . οἴκημα (3612)

(3613) **οἰκητήριον,** ου, τό [§3.C.c] *a habitation, dwelling, an abode,* Jude 6; trop. *the personal abode* of the soul, 2 Cor. 5:2

οἰκητήριον, acc. sg. neut. n. . . . . . οἰκητήριον (3613)

(3614) **οἰκία,** ας, ἡ, nom. sg. f. n. [§2.B.b; 2.2] *a house, dwelling, an abode,* Matt. 2:11; 7:24, 27, et al.; trop. *the* bodily *abode* of the soul, 2 Cor. 5:1; meton. *a household, family,* Matt. 10:13; 12:25; meton. *goods, property, means,* Matt. 23:13, et al.

οἰκίᾳ, dat. sg. f. n. . . . . οἰκία (3614)
οἰκιακοί, nom. pl. m. n. . . . . οἰκιακός (3615)

(3615) **οἰκιακός,** οῦ, ὁ, nom. sg. m. n. [§3.C.a] *belonging to a house;* pl. *the members of a household or family, kindred,* Matt. 10:25, 36

οἰκιακούς, acc. pl. m. n. (Matt. 10:25, GNT, WH, TR & NA | οἰκειακούς, MT) . . . . οἰκιακός (3615)
οἰκίαν, acc. sg. f. n. . . . . οἰκία (3614)
οἰκίας, gen. sg. f. n. {Mark 13:15} . . . . . . id.
οἰκίας, acc. pl. f. n. {Mark 12:40} . . . . . . id.
οἰκιῶν, gen. pl. f. n. . . . . id.
οἰκοδεσποτεῖν, pres. act. infin. . οἰκοδεσποτέω (3616)

(3616) **οἰκοδεσποτέω,** ῶ, fut. οἰκοδεσποτήσω [§16.P] pr. *to be master of a household; to occupy one's self in the management of a household,* 1 Tim. 5:14

οἰκοδεσπότῃ, dat. sg. m. n. . . . οἰκοδεσπότης (3617)
οἰκοδεσπότην, acc. sg. m. n. . . . . id.

(3617) **οἰκοδεσπότης,** ου, ὁ, nom. sg. m. n. [§2.B.c] (οἶκος + δεσπότης) *the master or head of a house or family,* Matt. 10:25; 13:27, 52, et al.

οἰκοδεσπότου, gen. sg. m. n. . . οἰκοδεσπότης (3617)
οἰκοδομαί, nom. pl. f. n. . . . . οἰκοδομή (3619)
οἰκοδομάς, acc. pl. f. n. . . . . id.

οἰκοδομεῖ, 3 pers. sg. pres. act. indic. . . . . οἰκοδομέω *(3618)*

οἰκοδομεῖν, pres. act. infin. . . . . id.

οἰκοδομεῖσθε, 2 pers. pl. pres. pass. indic. or imper. . . . . id.

οἰκοδομεῖται, 3 pers. sg. pres. pass. indic.   id.

οἰκοδομεῖτε, 2 pers. pl. pres. act. indic. {Matt. 23:29} . . . . id.

οἰκοδομεῖτε, 2 pers. pl. pres. act. imper. {1 Thess. 5:11} . . . . id.

(3618) **οἰκοδομέω, ῶ,** fut. οἰκοδομήσω [§16.P] aor. ᾠκοδόμησα [§13.2] perf. pass. ᾠκοδόμημαι, *to build a house; to build,* Matt. 7:24, et al.; *to repair, embellish, and amplify* a building, Matt. 23:29, et al.; *to construct, establish,* Matt. 16:18; met. *to contribute to advancement* in religious knowledge, *to edify,* 1 Cor. 14:4, 17; *to advance* a person's spiritual condition, *to edify,* 1 Cor. 8:1, et al.; pass. *to make* spiritual *advancement, be edified,* Acts 9:31; *to advance* in presumption, *be emboldened,* 1 Cor. 8:10

(3619) **οἰκοδομή, ῆς, ἡ,** nom. sg. f. n. [§2.B.a] pr. *the act of building; a building, structure,* Matt. 24:1, et al.; in N.T. *a spiritual structure,* as instanced in the Christian body, 1 Cor. 3:9; Eph. 2:21; religious *advancement, edification,* Rom. 14:19; 1 Cor. 14:3, et al.

οἰκοδομήθη, 3 pers. sg. aor. pass. indic. (John 2:20, GNT, WH & NA | ᾠκοδομήθη, MT & TR) . . . . οἰκοδομέω *(3618)*

οἰκοδομηθήσεται, 3 pers. sg. fut. pass. indic.   id.

οἰκοδομήν, acc. sg. f. n. . . . . οἰκοδομή *(3619)*

οἰκοδομῆς, gen. sg. f. n. . . . . id.

οἰκοδομῆσαι, aor. act. infin. . . . . . οἰκοδομέω *(3618)*

οἰκοδομήσαντι, dat. sg. m. aor. act. part. .   id.

οἰκοδόμησεν, 3 pers. sg. aor. act. indic. (Acts 7:47, GNT, WH & NA | ᾠκοδόμησεν, MT & TR) . . . . id.

οἰκοδομήσετε, 2 pers. pl. fut. act. indic. . .   id.

οἰκοδομῆσθαι, perf. pass. infin. (Luke 6:48, GNT, WH & NA | τεθεμελίωτο, MT & TR) . . . . id.

οἰκοδομήσω, 1 pers. sg. fut. act. indic. . . .   id.

(3620) **οἰκοδομία, ας, ἡ** [§2.B.b; 2.2] pr. *a building of a house;* met. spiritual *advancement, edification,* v.r. 1 Tim. 1:4

(†3621) **οἰκοδόμος, ου, ὁ** [§3.C.a] (οἶκος + δέμω, *to construct*) *a builder, architect,* Acts 4:11

οἰκοδομούμεναι, nom. pl. f. pres. pass. part. (Acts 9:31, MT & TR | οἰκοδομουμένη, GNT, WH & NA) . . . . οἰκοδομέω *(3618)*

οἰκοδομουμένη, nom. sg. f. pres. pass. part.

(Acts 9:31, GNT, WH & NA | οἰκοδομούμεναι, MT & TR) . . . . οἰκοδομέω *(3618)*

οἰκοδομοῦντες, nom. pl. m. pres. act. part.   id.

οἰκοδομοῦντι, dat. sg. m. pres. act. part. .   id.

οἰκοδομούντων, gen. pl. m. pres. act. part. (Acts 4:11, MT & TR | οἰκοδομῶν, GNT, WH & NA) . . . . id.

οἰκοδομῶ, 1 pers. sg. pres. act. indic. {Gal. 2:18} . . . . id.

οἰκοδομῶ, 1 pers. sg. pres. act. subj. {Rom. 15:20} . . . . id.

οἰκοδομῶν, nom. sg. m. pres. act. part. {Matt. 27:40} . . . . id.

οἰκοδόμων, gen. pl. m. n. (Acts 4:11, GNT, WH & NA | οἰκοδομούντων, MT & TR) . . . . οἰκοδόμος *(†3621)*

οἴκοις, dat. pl. m. n. . . . . οἶκος *(3624)*

οἶκον, acc. sg. m. n. . . . . id.

οἰκονομεῖν, pres. act. infin. . . . . . . οἰκονομέω *(3621)*

(3621) **οἰκονομέω, ῶ,** fut. οἰκοδομήσω [§16.P] *to manage a household; to manage the affairs of any one, be steward,* Luke 16:2

(3622) **οἰκονομία, ας, ἡ,** nom. sg. f. n. [§2.B.b; 2.2] pr. *the management of a household; a stewardship,* Luke 16:2, 3, 4; in N.T. *an* apostolic *stewardship, a* ministerial *commission* in the publication and furtherance of the Gospel, 1 Cor. 9:17; Eph. 1:10; 3:2; Col. 1:25; or, *an arranged plan, a scheme,* Eph. 1:10; *a due discharge of a commission,* 1 Tim. 1:4 (Eph. 3:9, GNT, WH, MT & NA | κοινωνία, TR)

οἰκονομίαν, acc. sg. f. n. . . . . οἰκονομία *(3622)*

οἰκονομίας, gen. sg. g. n. . . . . id.

οἰκονόμοι, nom. pl. m. n. . . . . οἰκονόμος *(3623)*

οἰκονόμοις, dat. pl. m. n. . . . . id.

οἰκονόμον, acc. sg. m. n. . . . . id.

(3623) **οἰκονόμος, ου, ὁ,** nom. sg. m. n. [§3.C.a] (οἶκος + νέμω, *to administer*) *the manager of a household; a steward,* Luke 12:42; 16:1, 3, 8; 1 Cor. 4:2; *a manager, trustee,* Gal. 4:2; *a public steward, treasurer,* Rom. 16:23; *a spiritual steward, the holder of a commission* in the service of the Gospel, 1 Cor. 4:1; Tit. 1:7; 1 Pet. 4:10

οἰκονόμους, acc. pl. m. n. . . . . οἰκονόμος *(3623)*

(3624) **οἶκος, ου, ὁ,** nom. sg. m. n. [§3.C.a] *a house, dwelling,* Matt. 9:6, 7; Mark 2:1, 11; 3:20, et al.; *place of abode, seat, site,* Matt. 23:38; Luke 13:35; met. *a spiritual house or structure,* 1 Pet. 2:5; meton. *a household, family,* Luke 10:5; 11:17; *a spiritual household,* 1 Tim. 3:15; Heb. 3:6; *family, lineage,* Luke 1:27, 69; 2:4; from the Hebrew, *a people, nation,* Matt. 10:6; 15:24

οἴκου, gen. sg. m. n. . . . . οἶκος *(3624)*

(3625) **οἰκουμένη,** ης, ἡ, nom. sg. f. n. (pr. f. part. pass. of οἰκέω) sc. γῆ, *the habitable earth, world,* Matt. 24:14; Rom. 10:18; Heb. 1:6, et al.; used, however, with various restrictions of meaning, according to the context, Luke 2:1; Acts 17:6, et al.; meton. *the inhabitants of the earth, the whole human race, mankind,* Acts 17:31; 19:27; Rev. 3:10

οἰκουμένῃ, dat. sg. f. n. . . . . οἰκουμένη *(3625)*

οἰκουμένην, acc. sg. f. n. . . . . id.

οἰκουμένης, gen. sg. f. n. . . . . id.

(†3626) **οἰκουργός,** ον (οἶκος + ἔργον) *one who is occupied in domestic affairs,* Tit. 2:5

οἰκουργούς, acc. pl. f. adj. (Tit. 2:5, GNT, WH & NA | οἰκουρούς, MT & TR) . . . . οἰκουργός *(†3626)*

(3626) **οἰκουρός,** ον [§7.2] (οἶκος + οὖρος, *a watcher*) pr. *a keeper or guard of a house; home-keeper, stay-at-home, domestic,* Tit. 2:5

οἰκουρούς, acc. pl. f. adj. (Tit. 2:5, MT & TR | οἰκουργούς, GNT, WH & NA) . . . . οἰκουρός *(3626)*

οἴκους, acc. pl. m. n. . . . . οἶκος *(3624)*

οἰκοῦσα, nom. sg. f. pres. act. part. . . . . οἰκέω *(3611)*

οἰκτειρήσω, 1 pers. sg. fut. act. indic. (Rom. 9:15, WH, MT & TR | οἰκτιρήσω, GNT & NA) . . . . οἰκτείρω *(†3627)*

(†3627) **οἰκτείρω,** later fut. οἰτειρήσω (οἶκτος, *compassion*) *to compassionate, have compassion on, exercise grace or favor towards*

οἰκτείρω, 1 pers. sg. pres. act. subj. (Rom. 9:15, WH, MT & TR | οἰκτίρω, GNT & NA) . . . . οἰκτείρω *(†3627)*

οἰκτιρήσω, 1 pers. sg. fut. act. indic. (Rom. 9:15, GNT & NA | οἰκτειρήσω, WH, MT & TR) . . . . οἰκτίρω *(‡3627)*

οἰκτιρμοί, nom. pl. m. n. . . . . οἰκτιρμός *(3628)*

οἰκτίρμονες, nom. pl. m. adj. . . . . . οἰκτίρμων *(3629)*

(3628) **οἰκτιρμός,** οῦ, ὁ [§3.C.a] *compassion; kindness,* in relieving sorrow and want, Phil. 2:1; Col. 3:12; *favor, grace, mercy,* Rom. 12:1; 2 Cor. 1:3

οἰκτιρμοῦ, gen. sg. m. n. (Col. 3:12, GNT, WH, MT & NA | οἰκτιρμῶν, TR) . . . . οἰκτιρμός *(3628)*

οἰκτιρμῶν, gen. pl. m. n. {Heb. 10:28} . . . id.

(3629) **οἰκτίρμων,** ον, nom. sg. m. adj. [§7.G.a] *compassionate, merciful,* Luke 6:36; {James 5:11}

(‡3627) **οἰκτίρω,** *to have compassion on*

οἰκτίρω, 1 pers. sg. pres. act. subj. (Rom. 9:15, GNT & NA | οἰκτείρω, WH, MT & TR) . . . . οἰκτίρω *(‡3627)*

οἴκῳ, dat. sg. m. n. . . . . οἶκος *(3624)*

οἴκων, gen. pl. m. n. {1 Tim. 3:12} . . . . . id.

οἰκῶν, nom. sg. m. pres. act. part. {1 Tim. 6:16} . . . . οἰκέω *(3611)*

οἶμαι, 1 pers. sg. pres. mid./pass. dep. indic. (by sync.) . . . . οἴομαι *(3633)*

οἶνον, acc. sg. m. n. . . . . οἶνος *(3631)*

(3630) **οἰνοπότης,** ου, ὁ, nom. sg. m. n. [§2.B.c] (οἶνος + πότης, πίνω) *wine-drinking;* in a bad sense, *a wine-bibber, tippler,* Matt. 11:19; Luke 7:34

(3631) **οἶνος,** ου, ὁ, nom. sg. m. n. [§3.C.a] *wine,* Matt. 9:17; Mark 2:22, et al.; meton. *the vine and its clusters,* Rev. 6:6; met. οἶνος, *a potion,* οἶνος τοῦ θυμοῦ, *a furious potion,* Rev. 14:8, 10; 16:19; 17:2; 18:3

οἴνου, gen. sg. m. n. . . . . οἶνος *(3631)*

(3632) **οἰνοφλυγία,** ας, ἡ [§2.B.b; 2.2] (οἰνόφλυξ, οἶνος + φλύω, *to bubble over, overflow) a debauch with wine, drunkenness,* 1 Pet. 4:3

οἰνοφλυγίαις, dat. pl. f. n. . . . . . . οἰνοφλυγία *(3632)*

οἴνῳ, dat. sg. m. n. . . . . οἶνος *(3631)*

(3633) **οἴομαι,** sync. οἶμαι, fut. οἰήσομαι [§37.1] *to think, suppose, imagine, presume,* John 21:25; Phil. 1:16; James 1:7

οἰόμενοι, nom. pl. m. pres. mid./pass. dep. part. . . . . οἴομαι *(3633)*

οἷοι, nom. pl. m. correlative pron. . . . . . . οἷος *(3634)*

οἷον, acc. sg. m. correlative pronoun {Phil. 1:30} . . . . id.

οἷον, nom. sg. neut. correlative pronoun {Rom. 9:6} . . . . id.

(3634) **οἷος,** οἵα, οἷον, nom. sg. m., [§10.7] correlative pronoun to ποῖος and τοῖος, *what, of what kind or sort, as,* Matt. 24:21; Mark 9:3, et al.; οὐχ, οἷον, *not so as, not as implying,* Rom. 9:6

οἵου, gen. sg. neut. correlative pronoun (Luke 9:55, MT & TR | GNT, WH & NA omit) . . . . οἷος *(3634)*

οἵους, acc. pl. neut. correlative pronoun . . id.

οἷς, dat. pl. m. relative pronoun {Eph. 2:3} ὅς *(3739)*

οἷς, dat. pl. neut. relative pronoun {Eph. 2:10} . . . . id.

οἴσει, 3 pers. sg. fut. act. indic. [§36.1] . . φέρω *(5342)*

οἴσουσι(ν), 3 pers. pl. fut. act. indic. . . . . . id.

οἵτινες, nom. pl. m. relative pronoun . . . ὅστις *(3748)*

(3635) **ὀκνέω,** ῶ, fut. ὀκνήσω, aor. ὤκνησα [§16.P] (ὄκνος, *backwardness, slowness) to be slow, loth; to delay, hesitate,* Acts 9:38

ὀκνηρέ, voc. sg. m. adj. . . . . ὀκνηρός *(3636)*

ὀκνηροί, nom. pl. m. adj. . . . . id.

ὀκνηρόν, nom. sg. neut. adj. . . . . id.

(3636) **ὀκνηρός,** ά, όν [§7.1] *slow; slothful, indolent, idle,* Matt. 25:26; Rom. 12:11; *tedious,*

troublesome, Phil. 3:1

ὀκνῆσαι, aor. act. infin. (Acts 9:38, MT &
TR | ὀκνήσῃς, GNT, WH & NA) . ὀκνέω *(3635)*

ὀκνήσῃς, 2 pers. sg. aor. act. sub. (Acts 9:38,
GNT, WH & NA | ὀκνῆσαι, MT & TR)   id.

(3637) **ὀκταήμερος**, ον, nom. sg. m. adj. [§7.2]
(ὄκτω + ἡμέρα) *on the eighth day*, Phil.
3:5

(3638) **ὀκτώ**, οἱ, αἱ, τά, numeral, *eight*, Luke 2:21;
9:28, et al.

ὄλεθρον, acc. sg. m. n. . . . . ὄλεθρος *(3639)*

(3639) **ὄλεθρος**, ου, ὁ, nom. sg. m. n. [§3.C.a]
(ὄλλυμι, *to destroy*) *perdition, destruction*,
1 Cor. 5:5, et al.

ὄλη, nom. sg. f. adj. . . . . ὅλος *(3650)*
ὄλῃ, dat. sg. f. adj. . . . . id.
ὄλην, acc. sg. f. adj. . . . . id.
ὄλης, gen. sg. f. adj. . . . . id.
ὀλίγα, acc. pl. neut. adj. . . . . ὀλίγος *(3641)*
ὀλίγαι, nom. pl. f. adj. . . . . id.
ὀλίγας, acc. pl. f. adj. . . . . id.
ὀλίγην, acc. sg. f. adj. . . . . id.
ὀλίγης, gen. sg. f. adj. . . . . id.
ὀλίγοι, nom. pl. m. adj. . . . . id.
ὀλίγοις, dat. pl. m. adj. . . . . id.
ὀλίγον, acc. sg. m. adj. {Acts 14:28} . . . . . id.
ὀλίγον, nom. sg. neut. adj. {Luke 7:47a} . id.
ὀλίγον, acc. sg. neut. adj. {Luke 7:47b} . . id.

(†3641) **ὀλίγον**, adv. (pr. neut. of ὀλίγος) *a little*, Mark
1:19; 6:31, et al.

ὀλιγόπιστε, voc. sg. m. adj. . . . . . ὀλιγόπιστος *(3640)*

(†3640) **ὀλιγοπιστία**, ας, ἡ, *littleness or imperfectness
of faith*, Matt. 17:20

ὀλιγοπιστίαν, acc. sg. f. n. (Matt. 17:20,
GNT, WH & NA | ἀπιστίαν, MT &
TR) . . . . ὀλιγοπιστία *(†3640)*

ὀλιγόπιστοι, voc. pl. m. adj. . . . . ὀλιγόπιστος *(3640)*

(3640) **ὀλιγόπιστος**, ον [§7.2] (ὀλίγος + πίστις)
*scant of faith, of little faith, one whose faith
is small and weak*, Matt. 6:30; 8:26, et al.

(3641) **ὀλίγος**, η, ον, nom. sg. m. adj. [§7.F.a] *little,
small*, in number, etc.; pl. *few*, Matt. 7:14;
9:37; 20:16; Luke 13:23; δὶ ὀλίγων, sc.
λόγων, *in a few words, briefly*, 1 Pet. 5:12;
little in time, *short, brief*, Acts 14:28; Rev.
12:12; πρὸς ὀλίγον, sc. χρόνον, *for a short
time, for a little while*, James 4:14; *little,
small, light*, etc., in magnitude, amount,
etc., Luke 7:47; Acts 12:18; 15:2; ἐν ὀλίγῳ,
concisely, briefly, Eph. 3:3; *almost*, Acts
26:28, 29

ὀλίγου, gen. sg. m. adj. . . . . ὀλίγος *(3641)*

(3642) **ὀλιγόψυχος**, ον [§7.2] (ὀλίγος + ψυχή) *faint-
hearted, desponding*, 1 Thess. 5:14

ὀλιγοψύχους, acc. pl. m. adj. . . . . ὀλιγόψυχος *(3642)*

ὀλίγῳ, dat. sg. m. adj. {1 Tim. 5:23} . . ὀλίγος *(3641)*
ὀλίγῳ, dat. sg. neut. adj. {Eph. 3:3} . . . . . id.
ὀλίγων, gen. pl. neut. adj. . . . . id.
ὀλιγώρει, 2 pers. sg. pres. act.
imper. . . . . ὀλιγωρέω *(3643)*

(3643) **ὀλιγωρέω**, ῶ, fut. ὀλιγωρήσω [§16.P] (ὀλίγος
+ ὤρα, *care*) *to neglect, regard slightly,
make light of, despise, contemn*, Heb. 12:5

(‡3641) **ὀλίγως**, adv., *little, scarcely* (2 Pet. 2:18, GNT,
WH & NA | ὄντως, MT & TR)

(3644) **ὀλοθρευτής**, οῦ, ὁ [§2.B.c] *a destroyer*, 1 Cor.
10:10

ὀλοθρευτοῦ, gen. sg. m. n. . . . . . . ὀλοθρευτής *(3644)*

(3645) **ὀλοθρεύω**, fut. ὀλοθρεύσω [§13.M] *to destroy,
cause to perish*, Heb. 11:28

ὀλοθρεύων, nom. sg. m. pres. act.
part. . . . . ὀλοθρεύω *(3645)*

(3646) **ὁλοκαύτωμα**, ατος, τό [§4.D.c] (ὁλόκαυτοω,
to offer a whole burnt-offering, ὁλόκαυ-
τος, ὅλος + καίω) *a holocaust, whole
burnt-offering*, Mark 12:33; Heb. 10:6, 8

ὁλοκαυτώματα, acc. pl. neut. n. ὁλοκαύτωμα *(3646)*
ὁλοκαυτωμάτων, gen. pl. neut. n. . . . . . . id.

(3647) **ὁλοκληρία**, ας, ἡ [§2.B.b; 2.2] *perfect soundness*, Acts 3:16

ὁλοκληρίαν, acc. sg. f. n. . . . . ὁλοκληρία *(3647)*
ὁλόκληροι, nom. pl. m. adj. . . . . . ὁλόκληρος *(3648)*
ὁλόκληρον, nom. sg. neut. adj. . . . . id.

(3648) **ὁλόκληρος**, ον [§7.2] (ὅλος + κλῆρος)
*whole, having all its parts, sound, perfect,
complete in every part*; in N.T. *the whole*,
1 Thess. 5:23; morally, *perfect, faultless,
blameless*, James 1:4

ὀλολύζοντες, nom. pl. m. pres. act.
part. . . . . ὀλολύζω *(3649)*

(3649) **ὀλολύζω**, fut. ὀλολύξω, aor. ὠλόλυξα [§26.2]
pr. *to cry aloud in invocation; to howl, utter cries of distress, lament, bewail*, James
5:1

ὅλον, acc. sg. m. adj. {Gal. 5:3} . . . . . . ὅλος *(3650)*
ὅλον, nom. sg. neut. adj. {1 Cor. 12:17} . . id.
ὅλον, acc. sg. neut. adj. {Gal. 5:9} . . . . . . id.

(3650) **ὅλος**, η, ον, nom. sg. m. adj. [§7.F.a] *all,
whole, entire*, Matt. 1:22; 4:23, 24, et al.
freq.

ὁλοτελεῖς, acc. pl. m. adj. . . . . ὁλοτελής *(3651)*

(3651) **ὁλοτελής**, ές [§7.G.b] (ὅλος + τέλος) *complete; all, the whole*, 1 Thess. 5:23

ὅλου, gen. sg. m. adj. {John 19:23} . . . . . ὅλος *(3650)*
ὅλου, gen. sg. neut. adj. {Acts 10:22} . . . . id.
ὅλους, acc. pl. m. adj. . . . . id.

Ὀλυμπᾶν, acc. sg. m. n. . . . . Ὀλυμπᾶς *(3652)*

(3652) **Ὀλυμπᾶς**, ᾶ, ὁ [§2.4] *Olympas*, pr. name,
Rom. 16:15

(3653) **ὄλυνθος**, ου, ὁ [§3.C.a] *an unripe or unsea-*

sonable fig, such as, shaded by the foliage, does not ripen at the usual season, but hangs on the trees during winter, Rev. 6:13

ὀλύνθους, acc. pl. m. n. . . . . ὄλυνθος (3653)

ὅλῳ, dat. sg. m. adj. {Rom. 1:8} . . . . . . ὅλος (3650)

ὅλῳ, dat. sg. neut. adj. {Phil. 1:13} . . . . . id.

(3654) **ὅλως,** adv., *wholly, altogether; actually, really,* 1 Cor. 5:1; 6:7; 15:29; with a negative, *at all,* Matt. 5:34

(3655) **ὄμβρος,** ου, ὁ, nom. sg. m. n. [§3.C.a] (Latin *imber*) *rain, a storm of rain,* Luke 12:54

(‡2442) **ὀμείρομαι,** *to desire earnestly, have a strong affection for,* 1 Thess. 2:8

ὀμειρόμενοι, nom. pl. m. pres. mid./pass. dep. part. (1 Thess. 2:8, GNT, WH, MT & NA | ἱμειρόμενοι, TR) . . . . ὀμείρομαι (‡2442)

ὁμιλεῖν, pres. act. infin. . . . . ὁμιλέω (3656)

(3656) **ὁμιλέω,** ῶ, fut. ὁμιλήσω [§16.P] *to be in company with, associate with; to converse with, talk with,* Luke 24:14, 15; Acts 20:11; 24:26

ὁμιλήσας, nom. sg. m. aor. act. part. . ὁμιλέω (3656)

(3657) **ὁμιλία,** ας, ἡ [§2.B.b; 2.2] *intercourse, communication, converse,* 1 Cor. 15:33

ὁμιλίαι, nom. pl. f. n. . . . . ὁμιλία (3657)

(3658) **ὅμιλος,** ου, ὁ, nom. sg. m. n. [§3.C.a] (ὁμοῦ + ἴλη, *a band*) *a multitude, company, crowd* (Rev. 18:17, TR | GNT, WH, MT & NA omit)

ὁμίχλαι, nom. pl. f. n. (2 Pet. 2:17, GNT, WH & NA | νεφέλαι, MT & TR) . . . . ὁμίχλη (‡3507)

(‡3507) **ὁμίχλη,** ης, ἡ [§2.B.a] *a mist, fog, a cloud*

(3659) **ὄμμα,** ατος, τό [§4.D.c] *the eye,* Matt. 20:34; Mark 8:23

ὄμματα, acc. pl. neut. n. . . . . ὄμμα (3659)

ὀμμάτων, gen. pl. neut. n. (Matt. 20:34, GNT, WH & NA | ὀφθαλμῶν, MT & TR)   id.

ὀμνύει, 3 pers. sg. pres. act. indic. . . . . ὀμνύω (3660)

ὀμνύειν, pres. act. infin. . . . . id.

ὀμνύετε, 2 pers. pl. pres. act. imper. . . . . . id.

ὀμνύναι, aor. act. infin. (Mark 14:71, GNT, WH, MT & NA | ὀμνύειν, TR) . . . . . id.

ὀμνύουσι(ν), 3 pers. pl. pres. act. indic. . . id.

(3660) **ὀμνύω,** or ὄμνυμι, fut. ὀμοῦμαι, perf. ὀμώμοκα, aor. ὤμοσα [§36.5] *to swear,* Matt. 5:34, et al.; *to promise with an oath,* Mark 6:23; Acts 2:30; 7:17, et al.

(3661) **ὁμοθυμαδόν,** adv. (ὁμοῦ + θυμός) *with one mind, with one accord, unanimously.* Acts 1:14; Rom. 15:6; *together, at once, at the same time,* Acts 2:1, 46; 4:24, et al.

ὁμοία, nom. sg. f. adj. {Rev. 4:6} . . . . ὅμοιος (3664)

ὅμοια, nom. pl. neut. adj. {Rev. 9:7} . . . . id.

ὅμοια, acc. pl. neut. adj. {Rev. 13:11} . . . . id.

ὁμοιάζει, 3 pers. sg. pres. act. indic. (Mark 14:70, MT & TR | GNT, WH & NA

omit) . . . . ὁμοιάζω (3662)

(3662) **ὁμοιάζω,** fut. ὁμοιάσω [§26.1] *to be like, resemble,* Mark 14:70

ὅμοιαι, nom. pl. f. adj. . . . . ὅμοιος (3664)

ὁμοίας, acc. pl. f. adj. . . . . id.

ὅμοιοι, nom. pl. m. adj. . . . . id.

ὅμοιον, acc. sg. m. adj. {Rev. 14:14} . . . . id.

ὅμοιον, nom. sg. neut. adj. {Rev. 21:18} . . id.

ὅμοιον, acc. sg. neut. adj. {Acts 17:29} . . . id.

ὁμοιοπαθεῖς, nom. pl. m. adj. . . . ὁμοιοπαθής (3663)

(3663) **ὁμοιοπαθής,** ές, nom. sg. m. adj. [§7.G.b] (ὅμοιος + πάθος) *being affected in the same way* as another, *subject to the same incidents, of like infirmities, subject to the same frailties and evils,* Acts 14:15; James 5:17

(3664) **ὅμοιος,** οία, οιον, nom. sg. m. adj., [§7.1] (ὁμός, *like*) *like, similar, resembling,* Matt. 11:16; 13:31, 33, 44, 45, 47, 52; John 8:55, et al. freq.; *like, of similar drift and force,* Matt. 22:39; Mark 12:31

(3665) **ὁμοιότης,** ητος, ἡ [§4.2.c] *likeness, similitude,* Heb. 4:15; 7:15

ὁμοιότητα, acc. sg. f. n. . . . . ὁμοιότης (3665)

(3666) **ὁμοιόω,** ῶ, fut. ὁμοιώσω, aor. ὡμοίωσα [§20.T] *to make like, cause to be like or resemble, assimilate;* pass. *to be made like, become like, resemble,* Matt. 6:8; 13:24; 18:23; *to liken, compare,* Matt. 7:24, 26; 11:16, et al.

ὁμοιωθέντες, nom. pl. m. aor. pass. part. [§21.U] . . . . ὁμοιόω (3666)

ὁμοιωθῆναι, aor. pass. infin. . . . . id.

ὁμοιωθήσεται, 3 pers. sg. fut. pass. indic. . id.

ὁμοιωθῆτε, 2 pers. pl. aor. pass. subj. . . . . id.

(3667) **ὁμοίωμα,** ατος, τό [§4.D.c] pr. *that which is conformed or assimilated; form, shape, figure,* Rev. 9:7; *likeness, resemblance, similitude,* Rom. 1:23; 5:14; 6:5; 8:3; Phil. 2:7

ὁμοιώματα, nom. pl. neut. n. . . . . . . ὁμοίωμα (3667)

ὁμοιώματι, dat. sg. neut. n. . . . . id.

(3668) **ὁμοίως,** adv., *likewise, in a similar manner,* Matt. 22:26; 27:41; Mark 4:16, et al.

ὁμοίωσιν, acc. sg. f. n. . . . . ὁμοίωσις (3669)

(3669) **ὁμοίωσις,** εως, ἡ [§5.E.c] pr. *assimilation; likeness, resemblance,* James 3:9

ὁμοιώσω, 1 pers. sg. fut. act. indic. . . ὁμοιόω (3666)

ὁμοιώσωμεν, 1 pers. pl. aor. act. subj. . . . . id.

ὁμολογεῖ, 3 pers. sg. pres. act. indic. . . . . ὁμολογέω (3670)

ὁμολογεῖται, 3 pers. sg. pres. pass. indic. . . id.

(3670) **ὁμολογέω,** ῶ, fut. ὁμολογήσω, aor. ὡμολόγησα [§16.P] (ὁμός, *like,* and λόγος) *to speak in accordance, adopt the same terms of language; to engage, prom-*

ise, Matt. 14:7; *to admit, avow frankly*, John 1:20; Acts 24:14; *to confess*, 1 John 1:9; *to profess, confess*, John 9:22; 12:42; Acts 23:8, et al.; *to avouch, declare openly and solemnly*, Matt. 7:23; in N.T. ὁμολογεῖν ἐν, *to accord belief*, Matt. 10:32; Luke 12:8; *to accord approbation*, Luke 12:8; from the Hebrew, *to accord praise*, Heb. 13:15

ὁμολογήσαντες, nom. pl. m. aor. act. part. . . . . ὁμολογέω *(3670)*

ὁμολογήσει, 3 pers. sg. fut. act. indic. . . . id.

ὁμολογήσῃ, 3 pers. sg. aor. act. subj. . . . . id.

ὁμολογήσῃς, 2 pers. sg. aor. act. subj. . . . id.

ὁμολογήσω, 1 pers. sg. fut. act. indic. . . . id.

(3671) **ὁμολογία**, ας, ἡ [§2.B.b; 2.2] *assent, consent; profession*, 2 Cor. 9:13; 1 Tim. 6:12, 13; Heb. 3:1; 4:14; 10:23

ὁμολογίαν, acc. sg. f. n. . . . . ὁμολογία *(3671)*

ὁμολογίας, gen. sg. f. n. . . . . id.

(3672) **ὁμολογουμένως**, adv. (ὁμολογούμενος, pres. pass. part. of ὁμολογέω) *confessedly, avowedly, without controversy*, 1 Tim. 3:16

ὁμολογοῦντες, nom. pl. m. pres. act. part. . . . . ὁμολογέω *(3670)*

ὁμολογούντων, gen. pl. m. pres. act. part. id.

ὁμολογοῦσι(ν), 3 pers. pl. pres. act. indic. id.

ὁμολογῶ, 1 pers. sg. pres. act. indic. . . . . id.

ὁμολογῶμεν, 1 pers. pl. pres. act. subj. . . id.

ὁμολογῶν, nom. sg. m. pres. act. part. . . . id.

ὀμόσαι, aor. act. infin. [§36.5] . . . . . . ὀμνύω *(3660)*

ὀμόσας, nom. sg. m. aor. act. part. . . . . . id.

ὀμόσῃ, 3 pers. sg. aor. act. subj. . . . . id.

ὀμόσῃς, 2 pers. sg. aor. act. subj. . . . . id.

ὁμότεχνον, acc. sg. m. adj. . . . . . . ὁμότεχνος *(3673)*

(3673) **ὁμότεχνος**, ον [§7.2] (ὁμός, *the same*, and τέχνη) *to the same trade or occupation*, Acts 18:3

(3674) **ὁμοῦ**, adv. (ὁμός) *together; in the same place*, John 21:2; *together at the same time*, John 4:36; 20:4

ὁμόφρονες, nom. pl. m. adj. . . . . . . ὁμόφρων *(3675)*

(3675) **ὁμόφρων**, ον [§7.G.a] (ὁμός + φρήν) *of like mind, of the same mind, like-minded*, 1 Pet. 3:8

(3676) **ὅμως**, conj. (ὁμός) *yet, nevertheless*; with μέντοι, *but nevertheless, but for all that*, John 12:42; *even, though it be but*, 1 Cor. 14:7; Gal. 3:15

ὄν, nom. sg. neut. pres. part. {Mark 4:31} εἰμί *(1510)*

ὅν, acc. sg. m. relative pronoun [§10.J.g] {Mark 6:16} . . . . ὅς *(3739)*

ὀναίμην, 1 pers. sg. 2 aor. mid. dep. opt. [§37.1] . . . . ὀνίνημι *(3685)*

(3677) **ὄναρ**, τό, indecl. [§6.5] *a dream*, Matt. 1:20;

2:12, 13, 19, 22; 27:19

(3678) **ὀνάριον**, ου, τό [§3.C.c] (dimin. of ὄνος) *a young ass, an ass's colt*, John 12:14

ὀνάριον, acc. sg. neut. n. . . . . ὀνάριον *(3678)*

ὀνειδίζειν, pres. act. infin. . . . . ὀνειδίζω *(3679)*

ὀνειδίζεσθε, 2 pers. pl. pres. pass. indic. . . id.

ὀνειδιζόμεθα, 1 pers. pl. pres. pass. indic. (1 Tim. 4:10, MT & TR | ἀγωνιζόμεθα, GNT, WH & NA) . . . . id.

ὀνειδίζοντος, gen. sg. m. pres. act. part. . . id.

ὀνειδιζόντων, gen. pl. m. pres. act. part. . id.

(3679) **ὀνειδίζω**, fut. ὀνειδίσω, aor. ὠνείδισα [§26.1] *to censure, inveigh against*, Matt. 11:20; Mark 16:14; *to upbraid*, James 1:5; *to revile, insult with opprobrious language*, Matt. 5:11, et al.

ὀνειδισμοί, nom. pl. m. n. . . . . ὀνειδισμός *(3680)*

ὀνειδισμοῖς, dat. pl. m. n. . . . . id.

ὀνειδισμόν, acc. sg. m. n. . . . . id.

(3680) **ὀνειδισμός**, οῦ, ὁ [§3.C.a] *censure*, 1 Tim. 3:7; *reproach, reviling, contumely*, Rom. 15:3, et al.

ὀνειδίσωσι(ν), 3 pers. pl. aor. act. subj. . . . . ὀνειδίζω *(3679)*

(3681) **ὄνειδος**, ους, τό [§5.E.b] pr. *fame, report, character*; usually, *reproach, disgrace*, Luke 1:25

ὄνειδος, acc. sg. neut. n. . . . . ὄνειδος *(3681)*

Ὀνήσιμον, acc. sg. m. n. . . . . Ὀνήσιμος *(3682)*

(3682) **Ὀνήσιμος**, ου, ὁ [§3.C.a] *Onesimus*, pr. name Ὀνησίμου, gen. sg. m. n. (Col. 4:18, TRs | GNT, WH, MT, TRb & NA omit) . . . . Ὀνήσιμος *(3682)*

Ὀνησίμῳ, dat. sg. m. n. . . . . id.

(3683) **Ὀνησίφορος**, ου, ὁ, *Onesiphorus*, pr. name, 2 Tim. 1:16; 4:19

Ὀνησιφόρου, gen. sg. m. n. . . . . Ὀνησίφορος *(3683)*

(3684) **ὀνικός**, ή, όν, nom. sg. m. adj. [§7.F.a] *pertaining to an ass*; μύλος ὀνικός, *a millstone turned by an ass, a large or an upper millstone*, Matt. 18:6; Luke 17:2

(3685) **ὀνίνημι**, fut. ὀνήσω, *to help, profit, benefit*; mid. ὀνίναμαι, 2 aor. ὠνήμην and ὠνάμην, opt. ὀναίμην, *to receive profit, pleasure*, etc.; with a gen., *to have joy of*, Philemon 20

(3686) **ὄνομα**, ατος, τό, nom. sg. neut. n. [§4.D.c] *a name; the proper name* of a person, etc., Matt. 1:23, 25; 10:2; 27:32, et al.; *a mere name or reputation*, Rev. 3:1; in N.T. *a name* as the representative of a person, Matt. 6:9; Luke 6:22; 11:2; *the name* of the author of a commission, delegated authority, or religious profession, Matt. 7:22; 10:22; 12:21; 18:5, 20; 19:29; 21:9; 28:19;

Acts 3:16; 4:7, 12, et al.; εἰς ὄνομα, ἐν ὀνόματι, *on the score of being* possessor of a certain character, Matt. 10:41, 42; Mark 9:41 {Luke 1:27}

ὄνομα, acc. sg. neut. n. {Luke 1:31} ... ὄνομα *(3686)*

ὀναμάζειν, pres. act. infin. .... ὀνομάζω *(3687)*

ὀνομάζεσθω, 3 pers. sg. pres. pass. imper.   id.

ὀνομάζεται, 3 pers. sg. pres. pass. indic. ..   id.

ὀνομαζόμενος, nom. sg. m. pres. pass. part.   id.

ὀνομαζομένου, gen. sg. neut. pres. pass. part.   id.

(3687) **ὀνομάζω,** fut. ὀνομάσω [§26.1] *to name,* Luke 6:14; *to style, entitle,* Luke 6:13; 1 Cor. 5:11; *to make mention of,* 1 Cor. 5:1; Eph. 5:3; *to make known,* Rom. 15:20; *to pronounce* in exorcism, Acts 19:13; in N.T. *to profess,* 2 Tim. 2:19

ὀνομάζων, nom. sg. m. pres. act. part. .... ὀνομάζω *(3687)*

ὀνόματα, nom. pl. neut. n. {Matt. 10:2} .... ὄνομα *(3686)*

ὀνόματα, acc. pl. neut. n. {Mark 3:17} ..   id.

ὀνόματι, dat. sg. neut. n. ....   id.

ὀνόματος, gen. sg. neut. n. ....   id.

ὀνομάτων, gen. pl. neut. n. ....   id.

ὄνον, acc. sg. m. n. {Luke 13:15} ...... ὄνος *(3688)*

ὄνον, acc. sg. f. n. {Matt. 21:2, 5, 7} ....   id.

(3688) **ὄνος,** ου, ὁ, ἡ, nom. sg. m. n. [§3.C.a,b] *an ass,* male or female, Matt. 21:2, 5, 7, et al. (Luke 14:5, TR | υἱός, GNT, WH, MT & NA)

ὄνου, gen. sg. f. n. .... ὄνος *(3688)*

ὄνπερ, acc. sg. m. relative pronoun with particle (with ἠτοῦντο, Mark 15:6, MT & TR | ὃν παρῃτοῦντο, GNT, WH & NA) .... ὅσπερ *(3746)*

ὄντα, acc. sg. m. pres. part. [§12.L] {John 1:48} .... εἰμί *(1510)*

ὄντα, nom. pl. neut. pres. part. {1 Cor. 12:12}   id.

ὄντα, acc. pl. neut. pres. part. {1 Cor. 1:28}   id.

ὄντας, acc. pl. m. pres. part. ....   id.

ὄντες, nom. pl. m. pres. part. ....   id.

ὄντι, dat. sg. m. pres. part. ....   id.

ὄντος, gen. sg. m. pres. part. {John 5:13}   id.

ὄντος, gen. sg. neut. pres. part. {Acts 7:5}   id.

ὄντων, gen. pl. m. pres. part. {John 21:11}   id.

ὄντων, gen. pl. neut. pres. part. {Acts 19:36}   id.

(3689) **ὄντως,** adv. (ὤν, ὄντος, pres. part. of εἰμί) *really, in truth, truly,* Mark 11:32; Luke 23:47, et al.

ὀξεῖα, nom. sg. f. adj. .... ὀξύς *(3691)*

ὀξεῖαν, acc. sg. f. adj. ....   id.

ὀξεῖς, nom. pl. m. adj. ....   id.

(3690) **ὄξος,** ους, τό [§5.E.b] *vinegar; a wine of sharp flavor, posca,* which was an ordinary beverage, and was often mixed with bitter

herbs, etc., and thus given to the condemned criminals in order to stupefy them, and lessen their sufferings, Matt. 27:34, 48; Mark 15:36; Luke 23:36; John 19:29, 30

ὄξος, acc. sg. neut. n. ....⸱... ὄξος *(3690)*

ὄξους, gen. sg. neut. n. ....   id.

ὀξύ, acc. sg. neut. adj. .... ὀξύς *(3691)*

(3691) **ὀξύς,** εῖα, ύ [§7.H.g] *sharp, keen,* Rev. 1:16; 2:12; 14:14, 17, 18; 19:15; *swift, nimble,* Rom. 3:15

ὀπαῖς, dat. pl. f. n. .... ὀπή *(3692)*

(3692) **ὀπή,** ῆς, ἡ [§2.B.a] *a hole; a hole, vent, opening,* James 3:11; *a hole, cavern,* Heb. 11:38

ὀπῆς, gen. sg. f. n. .... ὀπή *(3692)*

(3693) **ὄπισθεν,** adv., of place, *from behind, behind, after, at the back of,* Matt. 9:20; 15:23, et al.

(3694) **ὀπίσω,** adv., *behind, after, at one's back,* Matt. 4:19; Luke 7:38; Rev. 1:10; τὰ ὀπίσω, *the things which are behind,* Phil. 3:14; ὀπίσω and εἰς τὰ ὀπίσω, *back, backwards,* Matt. 24:18; Mark 13:16; Luke 9:62

ὅπλα, nom. pl. neut. n. {2 Cor. 10:4} .. ὅπλον *(3696)*

ὅπλα, acc. pl. neut. n. {Rom. 6:13} .....   id.

(3695) **ὁπλίζω,** fut. ὁπλίσω [§26.1] *to arm, equip;* mid. *to arm one's self, equip one's self,* 1 Pet. 4:1

ὁπλίσασθε, 2 pers. pl. aor. mid. imper. ὁπλίζω *(3695)*

(3696) **ὅπλον,** ου, τό [§3.C.c] *an implement,* Rom. 6:13; pl. τὰ ὅπλα, *arms, armor, weapons,* whether offensive or defensive, John 18:3; Rom. 13:12; 2 Cor. 6:7; 10:4

ὅπλων, gen. pl. neut. n. .... ὅπλον *(3696)*

ὁποίαν, acc. sg. f. adj. .... ὁποῖος *(3697)*

ὁποῖοι, nom. pl. m. adj. ....   id.

ὁποῖον, nom. sg. neut. adj. ....   id.

(3697) **ὁποῖος,** οία, οῖον, nom. sg. neut. adj., [§10.7.a] *what, of what sort or manner,* 1 Cor. 3:13; Gal. 2:6; 1 Thess. 1:9; James 1:24; after τοιοῦτος, *as,* Acts 26:29

(3698) **ὁπότε,** adv., *when* (Luke 6:3, MT & TR | ὅτε, GNT, WH & NA)

(3699) **ὅπου,** adv., *where, in which place, in what place,* Matt. 6:19, 20, 21; Rev. 2:13; *whither, to what place,* John 8:21; 14:4; ὅπου ἄν, or ἐάν, *wherever, in whatever place,* Matt. 24:28; *whithersoever,* Matt. 8:19; James 3:4; met. *where, in which thing, state,* etc., Col. 3:11; *whereas,* 1 Cor. 3:3; 2 Pet. 2:11

(3700) **ὀπτάνομαι,** *to be seen, appear,* Acts 1:3

ὀπτανόμενος, nom. sg. m. pres. mid./pass. dep. part. .... ὀπτάνομαι *(3700)*

(3701) **ὀπτασία,** ας, ἡ [§2.B.b; 2.2] (ὀπτάζω, equiv.

to ὁράω) *a vision, apparition,* Luke 1:22;
24:23; Acts 26:19; 2 Cor. 12:1

ὀπτασίᾳ, dat. sg. f. n. . . . . ὀπτασία *(3701)*

ὀπτασίαν, acc. sg. f. n. . . . . id.

ὀπτασίας, acc. pl. f. n. . . . . id.

(3702) **ὀπτός,** ή, όν [§7.F.a] (ὀπτάω, *to roast*) *dressed
by fire, roasted, broiled,* etc., Luke 24:42

ὀπτοῦ, gen. sg. m. adj. . . . . ὀπτός *(3702)*

(3703) **ὀπώρα,** ας, ή, nom. sg. f. n. [§2.B.b] *autumn;
the fruit season;* meton. *fruits,* Rev. 18:14

(3704) **ὅπως,** adv., *how, in what way or manner, by
what means,* Matt. 22:15; Luke 24:20;
conj. *that, in order that,* and ὅπως μή, *that
not, lest,* Matt. 6:2, 4, 5, 16, 18; Acts 9:2,
et al. freq.

ὁρᾷ, 3 pers. sg. pres. act. indic. . . . . . . ὁράω *(3708)*

ὅρα, 2 pers. sg. pres. act. imper. . . . . id.

(3705) **ὅραμα,** ατος, τό, nom. sg. neut. n. [§4.D.c]
a thing seen, sight, appearance, Acts 7:31;
a vision, Matt. 17:9; Acts 9:10, 12, et al.
{Acts 16:9}

ὅραμα, acc. sg. neut. n. {Acts 16:10} . . ὅραμα *(3705)*

ὁράματι, dat. sg. neut. n. . . . . id.

ὁράματος, gen. sg. neut. n. . . . . id.

ὁράσει, dat. sg. f. n. . . . . ὅρασις *(3706)*

ὁράσεις, acc. pl. f. n. . . . . id.

(3706) **ὅρασις,** εως, ή, nom. sg. f. n. [§5.E.c] *seeing,
sight; appearance, aspect, a vision,* Acts
2:17; Rev. 9:17 (Rev. 4:3, MT | ὁράσει,
GNT, WH, TR & NA)

ὁρατά, nom. pl. neut. adj. . . . . ὁρατός *(3707)*

ὁρᾶτε, 2 pers. pl. pres. act. indic.
{James 2:24} . . . . ὁράω *(3708)*

ὁρᾶτε, 2 pers. pl. pres. act. imper.
{1 Thess. 5:15} . . . . ὁράω *(3708)*

(3707) **ὁρατός,** ή, όν [§7.F.a] *visible,* Col. 1:16

(3708) **ὁράω,** ῶ, fut. ὄψομαι, rarely aor. ὡψάμην,
imperf. ἑώρων, perf. ἑώρακα, 2 aor.
εἶδον, aor. pass. ὤφθην, fut. ὀφθήσομαι
[§36.1] *to see, behold,* Matt. 2:2, et al.
freq.; *to look,* John 19:37; *to visit,* John
16:22; Heb. 13:23; *to mark, observe,* Acts
8:23; James 2:24; *to be admitted to witness,* Luke 17:22; John 3:36; Col. 2:18;
with Θεόν, *to be admitted into the more
immediate presence of God,* Matt. 5:8;
Heb. 12:14; *to attain to a true knowledge
of God,* 3 John 11; *to see to a thing,* Matt.
27:4; Acts 18:15; ὅρα, *see, take care,* Matt.
8:4; Heb. 8:5, et al.; pass. *to appear,* Luke
1:11; Acts 2:3, et al.; *to reveal one's self,*
Acts 26:16; *to present one's self,* Acts 7:26

(3709) **ὀργή,** ῆς, ή, nom. sg. f. n. [§2.B.a] pr. *mental
bent, impulse; anger, indignation, wrath,*
Eph. 4:31; Col. 3:8; μετ' ὀργῆς,

indignantly, Mark 3:5; *vengeance, punishment,* Matt. 3:7; Luke 3:7; 21:23; Rom.
13:4, 5, et al.

ὀργῇ, dat. sg. f. n. . . . . ὀργή *(3709)*

ὀργήν, acc. sg. f. n. . . . . id.

ὀργῆς, gen. sg. f. n. . . . . id.

ὀργίζεσθε, 2 pers. pl. pres. pass. imper. ὀργίζω *(3710)*

ὀργιζόμενος, nom. sg. m. pres. pass. part. id.

(3710) **ὀργίζω,** fut. ὀργίσω and ὀργιῶ [§35.11] aor.
pass. ὠργίσθην, *to provoke to anger, irritate;* pass. *to be angry, indignant, enraged,* Matt. 5:22; 18:34, et al.

ὀργίλον, acc. sg. m. adj. . . . . ὀργίλος *(3711)*

(3711) **ὀργίλος,** η, ον [§7.F.a] *prone to anger, iras-
cible, passionate,* Tit. 1:7

ὀργισθείς, nom. sg. m. aor. pass. part. . ὀργίζω *(3710)*

(3712) **ὀργυιά,** ᾶς, ή [§2.B.b; 2.2] *the space measured
by the arms outstretched; a fathom,* Acts
27:28 (2×)

ὀργυιάς, acc. pl. f. n. . . . . ὀργυιά *(3712)*

ὀρέγεται, 3 pers. sg. pres. mid. indic. . . ὀρέγω (†3713)

ὀρεγόμενοι, nom. pl. m. pres. mid. part. . id.

ὀρέγονται, 3 pers. pl. pres. mid. part. . . . id.

(†3713) **ὀρέγω,** fut. ὀρέξω [§23.1.b] *to extend, stretch
out;* mid. *to stretch one's self out, to reach
forward to;* met. *to desire earnestly, long
after,* 1 Tim. 3:1; Heb. 11:16; by impl. *to
indulge in, be devoted to,* 1 Tim. 6:10

ὄρει, dat. sg. neut. n. . . . . ὄρος *(3735)*

ὀρεινῇ, dat. sg. f. adj. . . . . ὀρεινός *(3714)*

ὀρεινήν, acc. sg. f. adj. . . . . id.

(3714) **ὀρεινός,** ή, όν [§7.F.a] *mountainous, hilly,*
Luke 1:39, 65

ὀρέξει, dat. sg. f. n. . . . . ὄρεξις *(3715)*

(3715) **ὄρεξις,** εως, ή [§5.E.c] *desire, longing; lust,
concupiscence,* Rom. 1:27

ὄρεσι(ν), dat. pl. neut. n. . . . . ὄρος *(3735)*

ὀρέων, gen. pl. neut. n. . . . . id.

ὄρη, nom. pl. neut. n. {Rev. 16:20} . . . . id.

ὄρη, acc. pl. neut. n. {Matt. 18:12} . . . . . id.

ὀρθάς, acc. pl. f. adj. . . . . ὀρθός *(3717)*

(3716) **ὀρθοποδέω,** ῶ, fut. ὀρθοποδήσω [§16.P]
(ὀρθός + πούς) *to walk in a straight
course; to be straightforward* in moral conduct, Gal. 2:14

ὀρθοποδοῦσι(ν), 3 pers. pl. pres. act.
indic. ὀρθοποδέω *(3716)*

(3717) **ὀρθός,** ή, όν, nom. sg. m. adj. [§7.F.a] (ὄρω,
to raise up) *erect, upright,* Acts 14:10; *plain,
level, straight,* Heb. 12:13

(3718) **ὀρθοτομέω,** ῶ, fut. ὀρθοτομήσω [§16.P]
(ὀρθός + τέμνω) *to cut straight; to direct
aright; to set forth truthfully, without perversion or distortion,* 2 Tim. 2:15

ὀρθοτομοῦντα, acc. sg. m. pres. act.

part. . . . . ὀρθοτομέω *(3718)*

ὄρθριαι, nom. pl. f. adj. (Luke 24:22, MT &
TR | ὀρθριναί, GNT, WH & NA) . ὄρθριος *(3721)*

(3719) **ὀρθρίζω**, fut. ὀρθρίσω [§26.1] *to rise early in
the morning; to come with the dawn,* Luke
21:38

ὀρθριναί, nom. pl. f. adj. (Luke 24:22, GNT,
WH & NA | ὄρθριαι, MT &
TR) . . . . ὀρθρινός *(3720)*

(3720) **ὀρθρινός**, ή, όν, nom. sg. m. adj. [§7.F.a] *of
or belonging to the morning, morning,* a
later form for ὄρθριος (Rev. 22:16, TR |
πρωϊνός, GNT, MT & NA | πρωινός,
WH)

(3721) **ὄρθριος**, α, ον [§7.1] *at daybreak, early,* Luke
24:22

ὄρθρον, acc. sg. m. n. . . . . ὄρθρος *(3722)*

(3722) **ὄρθρος**, ου, ὁ [§3.C.a] *the dawn; the morning,* John 8:2; Acts 5:21; ὄρθος βαθύς, *the
first streak of dawn, the early dawn,* Luke
24:1

ὄρθρου, gen. sg. m. n. . . . . ὄρθρος *(3722)*

(3723) **ὀρθῶς**, adv., *straightly; rightly, correctly,*
Mark 7:35; Luke 7:43, et al.

ὅρια, acc. pl. neut. n. . . . . ὅριον *(3725)*
ὁρίζει, 3 pers. sg. pres. act. indic. . . . . . . ὁρίζω *(3724)*

(3724) **ὁρίζω**, fut. ὁρίσω [§26.1] aor. pass. ὡρίσθην,
perf. ὥρισμαι (ὅρος, *a bound, limit*)
to set bounds to, to bound; to restrict,
Heb. 4:7; *to settle, appoint definitively,*
Acts 17:26; *to fix determinately,* Acts
2:23; *to decree, destine,* Luke 22:22; *to
constitute, appoint,* Acts 10:42; 17:31;
*to characterize with precision, to set forth
distinctively,* Rom. 1:4; absol. *to resolve,*
Acts 11:29

ὁρίοις, dat. pl. neut. n. . . . . ὅριον *(3725)*

(3725) **ὅριον**, ου, τό [§3.C.c] (ὅρος) *a limit, bound,
border of a territory or country;* pl. τὰ
ὅρια, *region, territory, district,* Matt. 2:16;
4:13; 8:34, et al.

ὁρίσας, nom. sg. m. aor. act. part. . . . . . ὁρίζω *(3724)*
ὁρισθέντος, gen. sg. m. aor. pass. part. . . id.
ὁρίων, gen. pl. neut. n. . . . . ὅριον *(3725)*
ὁρκίζομεν, 1 pers. pl. pres. act. indic. (Acts
19:13, MT & TR | ὁρκίζω, GNT, WH &
NA) . . . . ὁρκίζω *(3726)*

(3726) **ὁρκίζω**, 1 pers. sg. pres. act. indic., fut. ὁρκίσω
[§26.1] *to put to an oath; to obtest, adjure,
conjure,* Mark 5:7; Acts 19:13

ὅρκον, acc. sg. m. n. . . . . ὅρκος *(3727)*

(3727) **ὅρκος**, ου, ὁ, nom. sg. m. n. [§3.C.a] *an oath,*
Matt. 14:7, 9; 26:72, et al.; meton. *that
which is solemnly promised, a vow,* Matt.
5:33

ὅρκου, gen. sg. m. n. . . . . ὅρκος *(3727)*
ὅρκους, acc. pl. m. n. . . . . id.
ὅρκῳ, dat. sg. m. n. . . . . id.

(3728) **ὁρκωμοσία**, ας, ἡ [§2.B.b; 2.2] (ὅρκος +
ὄμνυμι) *the act of taking an oath; an oath,*
Heb. 7:20, 21, 28

ὁρκωμοσίας, gen. sg. f. n. . . . . . . ὁρκωμοσία *(3728)*

(3729) **ὁρμάω**, ῶ, fut. ὁρμήσω, aor. ὥρμησα [§18.R]
pr. trans. *to put in motion, incite;* intrans.
to rush, Matt. 8:32; Mark 5:13; Luke 8:33,
et al.

(3730) **ὁρμή**, ῆς, ἡ, nom. sg. f. n. [§2.B.a] (ὅρω,
ὄρνυμι, *to put in motion*) *impetus, impulse; assault, violent attempt,* Acts 14:5;
met. *impulse of mind, purpose, will,* James
3:4

(3731) **ὅρμημα**, ατος, τό [§4.D.c] *violent or impetuous motion; violence,* Rev. 18:21

ὁρμήματι, dat. sg. neut. n. . . . . ὅρμημα *(3731)*
ὄρνεα, nom. pl. neut. n. . . . . ὄρνεον *(3732)*
ὀρνέοις, dat. pl. neut. n. . . . . id.

(3732) **ὄρνεον**, ου, τό [§3.C.c] *a bird, fowl,* Rev. 18:2;
19:17, 21

ὀρνέου, gen. sg. neut. n. . . . . ὄρνεον *(3732)*

(3733) **ὄρνις**, ιθος, ὁ, ἡ, nom. sg. m. n. [§4.4] *a bird,
fowl; the* domestic *hen,* Matt. 23:37; Luke
13:34

(3734) **ὁροθεσία**, ας, ἡ [§2.B.b; 2.2] (ὅρος, *a bound,
limit,* and τίθημι) pr. *the act of fixing boundaries; a bound set, certain bound, fixed
limit,* Acts 17:26

ὁροθεσίας, acc. pl. f. n. . . . . ὁροθεσία *(3734)*

(3735) **ὄρος**, ους, τό, nom. sg. neut. n. [§5.E.b] *a
mountain, hill,* Matt. 5:1, 14; 8:1; 17:20,
et al. {Rev. 6:14}

ὄρος, acc. sg. neut. n. {Rev. 14:1} . . . . . . ὄρος *(3735)*
ὄρους, gen. sg. neut. n. . . . . id.

(3736) **ὀρύσσω**, or ὀρύττω, fut. ὀρύξω, aor. ὥρυξα
[§26.2] *to dig, excavate,* Matt. 21:33;
25:18; Mark 12:1

(3737) **ὀρφανός**, ή, όν, *bereaved* of parents, *orphan,*
James 1:27; *bereaved, desolate,* John 14:18

ὀρφανούς, acc. pl. m. adj. . . . . ὀρφανός *(3737)*

(3738) **ὀρχέομαι**, οῦμαι, fut. ὀρχήσομαι [§17.Q] aor.
ὠρχησάμην, *to dance,* Matt. 11:17, et al.

ὀρχησαμένης, gen. sg. f. aor. mid. dep.
part. . . . . ὀρχέομαι *(3738)*

ὁρῶ, 1 pers. sg. pres. act. indic. . . . . ὁράω *(3708)*
ὁρῶμεν, 1 pers. pl. pres. act. indic. . . . . . id.
ὁρῶν, nom. sg. m. pres. act. part. . . . . . . id.
ὁρῶντες, nom. pl. m. pres. act. part. . . . . id.
ὁρῶσαι, nom. pl. f. pres. act. part. . . . . . . id.

(3739) **ὅς**, ἥ, ὅ, nom. sg. m. relative pronoun, [§10.J.g]
who, which, qui, quae, quod, Matt. 1:16,
23, 25, et al.; in N.T. interrog. ἐφ᾽ ὅ,

wherefore, why, Matt. 26:50; in N.T. ὅς
μὲν — ὃς δέ, for ὁ μὲν — ὁ δέ, Matt.
21:35; 2 Cor. 2:16, et al.

ὅσα, nom. pl. neut. correlative pronoun
{Rom. 15:4} . . . . ὅσος *(3745)*

ὅσα, acc. pl. neut. correlative pronoun
{Rom. 3:19} . . . . id.

ὅσαι, nom. pl. f. correlative pronoun . . . . id.

(3740) **ὁσάκις,** adv., *as often as,* 1 Cor. 11:25, 26;
Rev. 11:6

ὅσας, acc. pl. f. correlative pronoun (Mark
3:28, MT & TR | ὅσα, GNT, WH &
NA) . . . . ὅσος *(3745)*

ὅσια, acc. pl. neut. adj. . . . . ὅσιος *(3741)*

ὅσιον, acc. sg. m. adj. . . . . id.

(3741) **ὅσιος,** ία, ιον, nom. sg. m. adj. [§7.1] pr. *sanctioned by the supreme law of God, and na-
ture; pious, devout,* Tit. 1:8; *pure,* 1 Tim.
2:8; supremely *holy,* Acts 2:27; 13:35; Heb.
7:26; Rev. 15:4; 16:5; τὰ ὅσια, *pledged
bounties, mercies,* Acts 13:34

(3742) **ὁσιότης,** ητος, ἡ [§4.2.c] *piety, sacred observance of all duties towards God, holiness,*
Luke 1:75; Eph. 4:24

ὁσιότητι, dat. sg. f. n. . . . . ὁσιότης *(3742)*

ὁσίους, acc. pl. m. adj. . . . . ὅσιος *(3741)*

(3743) **ὁσίως,** adv., *piously, holily,* 1 Thess. 2:10

(3744) **ὀσμή,** ῆς, ἡ, nom. sg. f. n. [§2.B.a] *smell,
odor; fragrant odor,* John 12:3; Eph. 5:2;
Phil. 4:18; met. 2 Cor. 2:14, 16

ὀσμήν, acc. sg. f. n. . . . . ὀσμή *(3744)*

ὀσμῆς, gen. sg. f. n. . . . . id.

ὅσοι, nom. pl. m. correlative pronoun . . . ὅσος *(3745)*

ὅσον, acc. sg. m. correlative pronoun
{Mark 2:19} . . . . id.

ὅσον, nom. sg. neut. correlative pronoun
{Rev. 21:16} . . . . id.

ὅσον, acc. sg. neut. correlative pronoun
{Mark 7:36} . . . . id.

(3745) **ὅσος,** η, ον [§10.7.b] a correlative pronoun to
τόσος, τοσοῦτος, etc., *as great, as much,*
Mark 7:36; John 6:11; Heb. 1:4; 8:6;
10:25; ἐφ' ὅσον χρόνον, *for how long a
time, while, as long as,* Rom. 7:1; so, ἐφ'
ὅσον, sc. χρόνου, Matt. 9:15; ὅσον
χρόνον, *how long,* Mark 2:19; neut. ὅσον
repeated, ὅσον ὅσον, used to give intensity to other qualifying words, e.g., μικρόν,
the very least, a very very little while, Heb.
10:37; ἐφ' ὅσον, *in as much as,* Matt.
25:40, 45; καθ' ὅσον, *by how much, so
far as,* Heb. 3:3; or, *in as much as, as, so,*
Heb. 7:20; 9:27; pl. ὅσα, *so far as, as
much as,* Rev. 1:2; 18:7; *how great, how
much, how many, what,* Mark 3:8; 5:19,

20; *how many soever, as many as, all who,*
2 Cor. 1:20; Phil. 3:15; 1 Tim. 6:1; ὅσος
ἄν, or ἐάν, *whoever, whatsoever,* Matt.
7:12; 18:18

ὅσους, acc. pl. m. correlative pronoun . . . ὅσος *(3745)*

(3746) **ὅσπερ,** ἥπερ, ὅπερ (ὅς + περ) an emphatic
form of the relative pronoun, Mark 15:6

ὀστέα, acc. pl. neut. n. . . . . ὀστέον *(3747)*

(3747) **ὀστέον,** οὖν, οῦ, τό [§3.3] *a bone,* Matt.
23:27; Luke 24:39, et al.

ὀστέων, gen. pl. neut. n. . . . . ὀστέον *(3747)*

ὀστοῦν, nom. sg. neut. n. contr. . . . . id.

(3748) **ὅστις,** ἥτις, ὅ τι, nom. sg. m. relative pronoun
[§10.J.h] (ὅς + τις) *whoever, whatever;
whosoever, whatsoever,* Matt. 5:39, 41;
13:12; 18:4; its use in place of the simple
relative is also required in various cases,
which may be learned from the grammars;
ἕως ὅτου, sc. χρόνου, *until,* Luke 13:8;
while, Matt. 5:25

ὀστράκινα, nom. pl. neut. adj. . . . . ὀστράκινος *(3749)*

ὀστρακίνοις, dat. pl. neut. adj. . . . . id.

(3749) **ὀστράκινος,** η, ον [§7.F.a] (ὄστρακον, *an
earthen vessel*) *earthen, of earthenware,*
2 Cor. 4:7; 2 Tim. 2:20

(3750) **ὄσφρησις,** εως, ἡ, nom. sg. f. n. [§5.E.c]
(ὀσφραίνομαι, *to smell*) *smell, the sense
of smelling,* 1 Cor. 12:17

ὀσφύας, acc. pl. f. n. . . . . ὀσφύς *(3751)*

ὀσφύες, nom. pl. f. n. . . . . id.

ὀσφύϊ, dat. sg. f. n. . . . . id.

ὀσφύν, acc. sg. f. n. . . . . id.

ὀσφύος, gen. sg. f. n. . . . . id.

(3751) **ὀσφύς,** ύος, ἡ [§5.E.g] pl. αἱ ὀσφύες, *the
loins,* Matt. 3:4; Mark 1:6, et al.

ὅσῳ, dat. sg. neut. correlative pronoun . . ὅσος *(3745)*

ὅσων, gen. pl. m. correlative pronoun . . . . id.

(3752) **ὅταν,** conj. (ὅτε + ἄν) *when, whenever,* Matt.
5:11; 6:2; Mark 3:11; Rev. 4:9, et al. freq.;
in N.T. *in case of, on occasion of,* John 9:5;
1 Cor. 15:27; Heb. 1:6

(3753) **ὅτε,** adv., *when, at the time that, at what time,*
Matt. 7:28; 9:25; Luke 13:35; et al. freq.

ὅ τι, acc. sg. neut. relative pronoun . . . . . ὅστις *(3748)*

(3754) **ὅτι,** conj., *that,* Matt. 2:16, 22, 23; 6:5, 16;
often used pleonastically in reciting
another's words, Matt. 9:18; Luke 19:42;
Acts 5:23; as a causal particle, *for that, for,
because,* Matt. 2:18; 5:3, 4, 5; 13:13; *because, seeing that, since,* Luke 23:40; Acts
1:17

(3755) **ὅτου,** gen. sg. neut. Att. for οὕτινος, relative
pronoun . . . . ὅστις *(3748)*

οὗ, gen. sg. m. relative pronoun
{Matt. 18:7} . . . . ὅς *(3739)*

οὗ, gen. sg. neut. relative pronoun
{Matt. 18:19} . . . . ὅς (3739)

(3756) οὐ before a consonant, οὐκ before a vowel with smooth breathing, and οὐχ before a vowel with rough breathing, adv., of negation, *not, no,* Matt. 5:37; 12:43; 23:37; for the peculiarities of its usage (especially as distinct from μή) consult a grammar

οὔ, negative adv., with an accent when it is last word in a clause, *No!* {Matt. 13:29} . . . οὐ (3756)

(3757) οὗ, adv. (pr. gen. of ὅς) *where, in what place,* Matt. 2:9; 18:20; *whither, to what place,* Luke 10:1; 22:10; 24:28; οὗ ἐάν, *whithersoever,* 1 Cor. 16:6 {Matt. 18:20}

(3758) οὐά, interj. (Latin *vah*) expressive of insult and derision, *Ah! Aha!*

(3759) οὐαί, interj. (Latin *vae*) *Wo! Alas!* Matt. 11:21; 18:7; 23:13, 14, 15, 16, et al.; ἡ οὐαί, subst., *a woe, calamity,* Rev. 9:12; 11:14

οὐδ᾽, for οὐδέ before a consonant . . . . . οὐδέ (3761)

(3760) οὐδαμῶς, adv. (οὐδαμός, *no one, ne unus quidem*) *by no means,* Matt. 2:6

(3761) οὐδέ, adv. (οὐ + δέ) *neither, nor, and not, also not,* Matt. 5:15; 6:15, 20, 26, 28; when single, *not even,* Matt. 6:29; 8:10

(3762) οὐδείς, οὐδεμία, οὐδέν, nom. sg. f. adj. [§10.6.c] (οὐδέ + εἷς) *not one, no one, none, nothing,* Matt. 5:13; 6:24; 19:17; met. οὐδέν, *nothing, of no account, naught,* John 8:54; Acts 21:24

οὐδεμία, nom. sg. f. adj. . . . . οὐδείς (3762)
οὐδεμίαν, acc. sg. f. adj. . . . . id.
οὐδέν, nom. sg. neut. adj. {Mark 7:15} . . id.
οὐδέν, acc. sg. neut. adj. {Mark 7:12} . . . id.
οὐδένα, acc. sg. m. adj. . . . . id.
οὐδενί, dat. sg. m. adj. {Mark 16:8} . . . . . id.
οὐδενί, dat. sg. neut. adj. {Mark 9:29} . . . id.
οὐδενός, gen. sg. m. adj. {Acts 20:24} . . . id.
οὐδενός, gen. sg. neut. adj. {Luke 8:43} . . id.

(3763) οὐδέποτε, adv. (οὐδέ + πότε) *never,* Matt. 7:23; 21:16, 42, et al. freq.

(3764) οὐδέπω, adv. (οὐδέ + πω) *not yet, never yet, never,* Luke 23:53; John 7:39, et al.

(‡3762) οὐθείς, οὐθέν, later forms for οὐδείς, οὐδέν, (3762) 1 Cor. 13:2; 2 Cor. 11:9

οὐθέν, nom. sg. neut. adj. (1 Cor. 13:2, GNT, WH, MT & NA | οὐδέν, TR) . . . . οὐθείς (‡3762)
οὐθέν, acc. sg. neut. adj. {Luke 23:14} . . . id.
οὐθενός, gen. sg. m. adj. (2 Cor. 11:9, GNT, WH & NA | οὐδενός, MT & TR) . . . id.
οὐθενός, gen. sg. neut. adj. (Luke 22:35, GNT, WH, MT & NA | οὐδενός, TR) id.

οὐκ, negative adv. before a vowel with smooth breathing . . . . οὐ (3756)

(3765) οὐκέτι, adv. (οὐκ + ἔτι) *no longer, no more,*

Matt. 22:46, et al.

(3766) οὐκοῦν, adv., *then, therefore;* used interrogatively, John 18:37

(3767) οὖν, conj. expressing either simple sequence or consequence; *then, now then,* Matt. 13:18; John 19:29, et al.; *then, thereupon,* Luke 15:28; John 6:14, et al.; *therefore, consequently,* Matt. 5:48; Mark 10:9, et al.; it also serves to mark the resumption of discourse after an interruption by a parenthesis, 1 Cor. 8:4, et al.

(3768) οὔπω, adv. (οὐ + πω) *not yet,* Matt. 15:17; 16:9; 24:6; John 2:4, et al.

(3769) οὐρά, ᾶς, ἡ, nom. sg. f. n. [§2.B.b] *a tail,* Rev. 9:10, 19; 12:4

οὐραί, nom. pl. f. n. . . . . οὐρά (3769)
οὐραῖς, dat. pl. f. n. . . . . id.
οὐρανέ, voc. sg. m. n. . . . . οὐρανός (3772)

(3770) οὐράνιος, ία, ιον, nom. sg. m. adj., *heavenly, celestial,* Matt. 6:14, 26, 32; 15:13, et al.

οὐρανίου, gen. sg. f. adj. . . . . οὐράνιος (3770)
οὐρανίῳ, dat. sg. f. adj. . . . . id.

(3771) οὐρανόθεν, adv., *from heaven,* Acts 14:17; 26:13

οὐρανοί, nom. pl. m. n. . . . . οὐρανός (3772)
οὐρανοῖς, dat. pl. m. n. . . . . id.
οὐρανόν, acc. sg. m. n. . . . . id.

(3772) οὐρανός, nom. sg. m. n. οὐρανός, οῦ, ὁ [§3.C.a] and pl. οὐρανοί, ῶν, οἱ, *heaven, the heavens, the visible heavens and all their phenomena,* Matt. 5:18; 16:1; 24:29, et al. freq.; *the air, atmosphere,* in which the clouds and tempests gather, the birds fly, etc., Matt. 6:26; 16:2, 3, et al.; *heaven* as the peculiar seat and abode of God, of angels, of glorified spirits, etc., Matt. 5:34, 45, 48; 6:1, 9, 10; 12:50; John 3:13, 31; 6:32, 38, 41, 42, 50, 51, 58; in N.T. *heaven* as a term expressive of the Divine Being, His administration, etc., Matt. 19:14; 21:25; Luke 20:4, 5; John 3:27

οὐρανοῦ, gen. sg. m. n. . . . . οὐρανός (3772)
οὐρανούς, acc. pl. m. n. . . . . id.
οὐρανῷ, dat. sg. m. n. . . . . id.
οὐρανῶν, gen. pl. m. n. . . . . id.
οὐράς, acc. pl. f. n. . . . . οὐρά (3769)
Οὐρβανόν, acc. sg. m. n. . . . . Οὐρβανός (3773)

(3773) Οὐρβανός, οῦ, ὁ [§3.C.a] *Urbanus, Urban,* pr. name, Rom. 16:9

(3774) Οὐρίας, ου, ὁ [§2.B.d] *Urias, Uriah,* pr. name, Matt. 1:6

Οὐρίου, gen. sg. m. n. . . . . Οὐρίας (3774)
οὕς, acc. pl. m. relative pronoun {Mark 2:26} . . . . ὅς (3739)

(3775) οὖς, ὠτός, τό, nom. sg. neut. n. [§4.3.b] *the*

ear, Matt. 10:27; Mark 7:33; Luke 22:50; Acts 7:57, et al. {1 Cor. 2:9}

οὖς, acc. sg. neut. n. {Matt. 10:27} ...... οὖς *(3775)*

οὖσα, nom. sg. f. pres. part. [§12.L] ..... εἰμί *(1510)*

οὖσαι, nom. pl. f. pres. part. .... id.

οὖσαν, acc. sg. f. pres. part. .... id.

οὖσῃ, dat. sg. f. pres. part. .... id.

οὖσης, gen. sg. f. pres. part. .... id.

(3776) **οὐσία**, ας, ἡ [§2.B.b; 2.2] (ὤν, οὖσα, ὄν, part. of εἰμί) *substance, property, goods, fortune,* Luke 15:12, 13

οὐσίαν, acc. sg. f. n. .... οὐσία *(3776)*

οὐσίας, gen. sg. f. n. .... id.

οὖσι(ν), dat. pl. m. pres. part. .... εἰμί *(1510)*

οὖσῶν, gen. pl. f. pres. part. .... id.

(3777) **οὔτε**, conj. (οὐ + τε) *neither, nor,* Luke 20:36; οὔτε — οὔτε, or οὐδὲ — οὔτε, *neither — nor,* Luke 20:35; Gal. 1:12; in N.T. also used singly in the sense of οὐδέ, *not even,* Mark 5:3; Luke 12:26; 1 Cor. 3:2

οὖτοι, nom. pl. m. demonstrative pronoun .... οὖτος *(3778)*

(3778) **οὖτος**, αὖτη, τοῦτο, nom. sg. m. demonstrative pronoun [§10.J.c; 10.3] *this, this* person or thing, Matt. 3:3, 9, 17; 8:9; 10:2; 24:34, et al. freq.; used by way of contempt, *this fellow,* Matt. 13:55; 27:47; αὐτὸ τοῦτο, *this very thing, this same thing,* 2 Cor. 2:3; 7:11; εἰς αὐτὸ τοῦτο, and elliptically, αὐτὸ τοῦτο, *for this same purpose, on this account,* Eph. 6:18, 22; 2 Pet. 1:5; καὶ οὖτος, *and moreover,* Luke 7:12; 16:1; 20:30; καὶ τοῦτο, *and that too,* 1 Cor. 6:6, 8; τοῦτο μὲν — τοῦτο δέ, *partly — partly,* Heb. 10:33

(3779) **οὕτως**, and οὕτω before a consonant, adv., *thus, in this way,* Matt. 1:18; 2:5; 5:16; et al. freq.; ὃς μὲν οὕτως, ὃς δὲ οὕτως, *one so, and another so, one in one way, and another in another,* 1 Cor. 7:7; *so,* Matt. 7:12; 12:40; 24:27, 37, et al. freq.; *thus, under such circumstances,* Acts 20:11; *in such a condition,* viz., one previously mentioned, Acts 27:17; 1 Cor. 7:26, 40; and, perhaps, John 4:6; *in an ordinary way, at ease,* like Latin *sic,* perhaps, John 4:6

οὐχ, negative adv. before a vowel with rough breathing .... οὐ *(3756)*

(3780) **οὐχί**, adv., *not,* John 13:10, 11; when followed by ἀλλά, *nay, not so, by no means,* Luke 1:60; 12:51; used also in negative interrogations, Matt. 5:46, 47; 6:25

ὀφειλάς, acc. pl. f. n. .... ὀφειλή *(3782)*

ὀφείλει, 3 pers. sg. pres. act. indic. ... ὀφείλω *(3784)*

ὀφείλεις, 2 pers. sg. pres. act. indic. ..... id.

ὀφειλέται, nom. pl. m. n. .... ὀφειλέτης *(3781)*

ὀφειλέταις, dat. pl. m. n. .... id.

ὀφείλετε, 2 pers. pl. pres. act. indic. {John 13:14} .... ὀφείλω *(3784)*

ὀφείλετε, 2 pers. pl. pres. act. imper. {Rom. 13:8} .... id.

(3781) **ὀφειλέτης**, ου, ὁ, nom. sg. m. n. [§2.B.c] *a debtor, one who owes,* Matt. 18:24; met. *one who is in any way bound,* or *under obligation* to perform any duty, Rom. 1:14; 8:12; 15:27; Gal. 5:3; in N.T. *one who fails in duty, a delinquent, offender,* Matt. 6:12; *a sinner,* Luke 13:4, cf. v. 2

(3782) **ὀφειλή**, ῆς, ἡ [§2.B.a] *a debt,* Matt. 18:32; met. *a duty, due,* Rom. 13:7; 1 Cor. 7:3

(3783) **ὀφείλημα**, ατος, τό [§4.D.c] *a debt; a due,* Rom. 4:4; in N.T. *a delinquency, offence, fault, sin,* Matt. 6:12, cf. v. 14

ὀφείλημα, acc. sg. neut. n. .... ὀφείλημα *(3783)*

ὀφειλήματα, acc. pl. neut. n. .... id.

ὀφειλήν, acc. sg. f. n. .... ὀφειλή *(3782)*

ὀφείλομεν, 1 pers. pl. pres. act. indic. . ὀφείλω *(3784)*

ὀφειλομένην, acc. sg. f. pres. pass. part. (1 Cor. 7:3, MT & TR | ὀφειλήν, GNT, WH & NA) .... id.

ὀφειλόμενον, acc. sg. neut. pres. pass. part. id.

ὀφείλοντες, nom. pl. m. pres. act. part. .. id.

ὀφείλοντι, dat. sg. m. pres. act. part. .... id.

ὀφείλουσι(ν), 3 pers. pl. pres. act. indic. .. id.

(3784) **ὀφείλω**, fut. ὀφειλήσω [§35.5] 2 aor. ὤφελον, *to owe, be indebted,* Matt. 18:28, 30, 34; *to incur a bond, to be bound to make discharge,* Matt. 23:16, 18; *to be bound or obliged* by what is due or fitting or consequently necessary, Luke 17:10; John 13:14, et al.; *to incur desert, to deserve,* John 19:7; *to be due or fitting,* 1 Cor. 7:3, 36; from the Aramaic, *to be delinquent,* Luke 11:4

ὄφεις, nom. pl. m. n. {Matt. 10:16} ... ὄφις *(3789)*

ὄφεις, acc. pl. m. n. {Mark 16:18} ...... id.

ὄφεις, voc. pl. m. n. {Matt. 23:33} ...... id.

(3785) **ὄφελον** (pr. 2 aor. of ὀφείλω) used in N.T. as an interj., *O that! Would that!* 1 Cor. 4:8; Gal. 5:12, et al.

(3786) **ὄφελος**, ους, τό, nom. sg. neut. n., only in the nom. [§6.5] (ὀφέλω, *to further, augment*) *profit, utility, advantage,* 1 Cor. 15:32, et al.

ὄφεσιν, dat. pl. m. n. (Rev. 9:19, GNT, WH, TR & NA | ὄφεων, MT) .... ὄφις *(3789)*

ὄφεων, gen. pl. m. n. .... id.

ὄφεως, gen. sg. m. n. .... id.

(3787) **ὀφθαλμοδουλεία**, ας, ἡ [§2.B.b; 2.2] (ὀφθαλμός + δουλεία) *eye-service, service*

rendered only while under inspection, Eph.
6:6; Col. 3:22

ὀφθαλμοδουλείαις, dat. pl. f. n. (Col. 3:22,
MT & TR | ὀφθαλμοδουλίᾳ, GNT, WH
& NA) . . . . ὀφθαλμοδουλεία (3787)

ὀφθαλμοδουλείαν, acc. sg. f. n. (Eph. 6:6,
MT & TR | ὀφθαλμοδουλίαν, GNT, WH
& NA) . . . . id.

(†3787) **ὀφθαλμοδουλία**, ας, ἡ, *eye-service*

ὀφθαλμοδουλίᾳ, dat. sg. f. n. (Col. 3:22,
GNT, WH & NA | ὀφθαλμοδουλείαις,
MT & TR) . . . . ὀφθαλμοδουλία (†3787)

ὀφθαλμοδουλίαν, acc. sg. f. n. (Eph. 6:6,
GNT, WH & NA | ὀφθαλμοδουλείαν,
MT & TR) . . . . id.

ὀφθαλμοί, nom. pl. m. n. . . . . ὀφθαλμός (3788)

ὀφθαλμοῖς, dat. pl. m. n. . . . . id.

ὀφθαλμόν, acc. sg. m. n. . . . . id.

(3788) **ὀφθαλμός**, οῦ, ὁ, nom. sg. m. n. [§3.C.a]
(ὄψομαι, ὤφθην) *an eye,* Matt. 5:29, 38;
6:23; 7:3, 4, 5, et al.; ὀφθαλμὸς πονηρός,
an evil eye, an envious eye, envy, Matt.
20:15; Mark 7:22; met. *the* intellectual *eye,*
Matt. 13:15; Mark 8:18; John 12:40; Acts
26:18

ὀφθαλμοῦ, gen. sg. m. n. . . . . ὀφθαλμός (3788)

ὀφθαλμούς, acc. pl. m. n. . . . . id.

ὀφθαλμῷ, dat. sg. m. n. . . . . id.

ὀφθαλμῶν, gen. pl. m. n. . . . . id.

ὀφθείς, nom. sg. m. aor. pass. part.
[§36.1] . . . . ὁράω (3708)

ὀφθέντες, nom. pl. m. aor. pass. part. . . . id.

ὀφθέντος, gen. sg. m. aor. pass. part. . . . . id.

ὀφθήσεται, 3 pers. sg. fut. pass. indic. . . . id.

ὀφθήσομαι, 1 pers. sg. fut. pass. indic. . . . id.

ὄφιν, acc. sg. m. n. . . . . ὄφις (3789)

(3789) **ὄφις**, εως, ὁ, nom. sg. m. n. [§5.E.c] *a serpent,* Matt. 7:10; 10:16; *an* artificial *serpent,* John 3:14; used of *the devil or Satan,*
Rev. 12:9, 14, 15; 20:2; met. *a man of ser-
pentine character,* Matt. 23:33

ὀφρύος, gen. sg. f. n. . . . . ὀφρύς (3790)

(3790) **ὀφρύς**, ύος, ἡ [§5.E.g] *a brow, eye-brow; the
brow* of a mountain, *edge* of a precipice,
Luke 4:29

(3791) **ὀχλέω**, ῶ, fut. ὀχλήσω [§16.P] pr. *to mob; to
vex, trouble,* Luke 6:18; Acts 5:16

ὄχλοι, nom. pl. m. n. . . . . ὄχλος (3793)

ὄχλοις, dat. pl. m. n. . . . . id.

ὄχλον, acc. sg. m. n. . . . . id.

(3792) **ὀχλοποιέω**, ῶ, fut. ὀχλοποιήσω [§16.P]
(ὄχλος + ποιέω) *to collect a mob, create
a tumult,* Acts 17:5

ὀχλοποιήσαντες, nom. pl. m. aor. act.
part. ὀχλοποιέω (3792)

(3793) **ὄχλος**, ου, ὁ, nom. sg. m. n. [§3.C.a] *a crowd,
a confused multitude* of people, Matt. 4:25;
5:1; 7:28; spc. *the common people,* John
7:49; *a multitude, great number,* Luke
5:29; 6:17; Acts 1:15; by impl. *tumult, uproar,* Luke 22:6; Acts 24:18

ὄχλου, gen. sg. m. n. . . . . ὄχλος (3793)

ὀχλούμενοι, nom. pl. m. pres. pass. part.
(Luke 6:18, MT & TR | ἐνοχλούμενοι,
GNT, WH & NA) . . . . ὀχλέω (3791)

ὀχλουμένους, acc. pl. m. pres. pass. part. . id.

ὄχλους, acc. pl. m. n. . . . . ὄχλος (3793)

ὄχλῳ, dat. sg. m. n. . . . . id.

ὄχλων, gen. pl. m. n. . . . . id.

(3794) **ὀχύρωμα**, ατος, τό [§4.D.c] (ὀχυρόω, *to for-
tify,* ὀχυρός, *firm, strong) a stronghold;*
met. *an* opposing *bulwark* of error or vice,
2 Cor. 10:4

ὀχυρωμάτων, gen. pl. neut. n. . . . . . ὀχύρωμα (3794)

ὀψάρια, acc. pl. neut. n. . . . . ὀψάριον (3795)

(3795) **ὀψάριον**, ου, τό [§3.C.c] (dimin. of ὄψον,
*cooked provision as distinguished from
bread; a dainty dish; fish) a little fish,* John
6:9, 11; 21:9, 10, 13

ὀψάριον, acc. sg. neut. n. . . . . ὀψάριον (3795)

ὀψαρίων, gen. pl. neut. n. . . . . id.

(3796) **ὀψέ**, adv., *late;* put for *the first watch, at evening,* Mark 11:19; 13:35; ὀψὲ σαββάτων,
after the close of the Sabbath, Matt. 28:1

ὄψει, 2 pers. sg. fut. mid. dep. indic. Att.
[§35.11] (Matt. 27:4; John 1:50; 11:40, MT
& TR | ὄψῃ, GNT, WH & NA) . . . ὁράω (3708)

ὄψεσθε, 2 pers. pl. fut. mid. dep. indic. . . id.

ὄψεται, 3 pers. sg. fut. mid. dep. indic. . . . id.

ὄψῃ, 2 pers. sg. fut. mid. dep. indic. (Matt.
27:4; John 1:50; 11:50, GNT, WH & NA
| ὄψει, MT & TR) . . . . id.

ὄψησθε, 2 pers. pl. aor. mid. dep. subj. (Luke
13:28, WH, MT & TR | ὄψεσθε, GNT
& N) . . . . id.

ὀψία, nom. sg. f. adj. . . . . ὄψιος (†3798)

ὀψίας, gen. sg. f. adj. . . . . id.

ὄψιμον, acc. sg. m. adj. . . . . ὄψιμος (3797)

(3797) **ὄψιμος**, ον [§7.2] *late; latter,* James 5:7; poetic and later prose for ὄψιος

ὄψιν, acc. sg. f. n. . . . . ὄψις (3799)

(†3798) **ὄψιος**, ία, ιον [§7.1] *late,* Mark 11:11; ἡ ὀψία,
sc. ὥρα, *evening,* two of which were reck-
oned by the Hebrews; one, from the ninth
hour until sunset, Matt. 8:16; 14:15, et al.;
and the other, from sunset until dark,
Matt. 14:23; 16:2, et al.

(3799) **ὄψις**, εως, ἡ, nom. sg. f. n. [§5.E.c] *a sight;
the face, visage, countenance,* John 11:44;
Rev. 1:16; *external appearance,* John 7:24

ὄψομαι, 1 pers. sg. fut. mid. dep. indic.
[§36.1] . . . . ὁράω (3708)
ὀψόμεθα, 1 pers. pl. fut. mid. dep. indic. . id.
ὄψονται, 3 pers. pl. fut. mid. dep. indic. . . id.
ὀψώνια, nom. pl. neut. n. . . . . ὀψώνιον (3800)
ὀψωνίοις, dat. pl. neut. n. . . . . id.
(3800) ὀψώνιον, ου, τό [§3.C.c] (ὄψον, cooked pro-
    visions, etc.) provisions; a stipend or pay
    of soldiers, Luke 3:14; 1 Cor. 9:7; wages
    of any kind, 2 Cor. 11:8; due wages, a
    stated recompense, Rom. 6:23
ὀψώνιον, acc. sg. neut. n. . . . . ὀψώνιον (3800)

Π

παγίδα, acc. sg. f. n. . . . . παγίς (3803)
παγιδεύσωσιν, 3 pers. pl. aor. act.
    subj. . . . . παγιδεύω (3802)
(3802) παγιδεύω, fut. παγιδεύσω [§13.M] to ensnare,
    entrap, entangle, Matt. 22:15
παγίδος, gen. sg. f. n. . . . . παγίς (3803)
(3803) παγίς, ίδος, ἡ, nom. sg. f. n. [§4.2.c] a snare,
    trap, gin, Luke 21:35; met. artifice, strat-
    agem, device, wile, 1 Tim. 3:7; 6:9; 2 Tim.
    2:26; met. a trap of ruin, Rom. 11:9
πάγον, acc. sg. m. n. . . . . πάγος (‡697)
(‡697) πάγος, ου, ὁ [§3.C.a] a hill; Ἄρειος πάγος,
    Areopagus, the hill of Mars, at Athens, Acts
    17:19, 22
πάγου, gen. sg. m. n. . . . . πάγος (‡697)
πάθει, dat. sg. neut. n. . . . . πάθος (3806)
παθεῖν, 2 aor. act. infin. [§36.4] . . . . . πάσχω (3958)
πάθη, acc. pl. neut. n. . . . . πάθος (3806)
πάθῃ, 3 pers. sg. 2 aor. act. subj. . . . . . πάσχω (3958)
(3804) πάθημα, ατος, τό [§4.D.c] what is suffered;
    suffering, affliction, Rom. 8:18; 2 Cor. 1:5,
    6, 7; Phil. 3:10, et al.; emotion, passion,
    Rom. 7:5; Gal. 5:24
πάθημα, acc. sg. neut. n. . . . . πάθημα (3804)
παθήμασι(ν), dat. pl. neut. n. . . . . . id.
παθήματα, nom. pl. neut. n. {2 Cor. 1:5} . id.
παθήματα, acc. pl. neut. n. {1 Pet. 1:11} . . id.
παθημάτων, gen. pl. neut. n. . . . . . id.
(3805) παθητός, ή, όν, nom. sg. m. adj. [§7.F.a] pas-
    sible, capable of suffering, liable to suffer;
    in N.T. destined to suffer, Acts 26:23
παθόντας, acc. pl. m. 2 aor. act. part.
    [§36.4] . . . . πάσχω (3958)
παθόντος, gen. sg. m. 2 aor. act. part. . . . id.
(3806) πάθος, ους, τό [§5.E.b] suffering; an affection,
    passion, Rom. 1:26, et al.
πάθος, acc. sg. neut. n. . . . . πάθος (3806)
παθοῦσα, nom. sg. f. 2 aor. act. part. . πάσχω (3958)

παθών, nom. sg. m. 2 aor. act. part. . . . πάσχω (3958)
παῖδα, acc. sg. m. n. . . . . παῖς (3816)
παιδαγωγόν, acc. sg. m. n. . . . . . παιδαγωγός (3807)
(3807) παιδαγωγός, οῦ, ὁ, nom. sg. m. n. [§3.C.a]
    (παῖς + ἀγωγός, ἄγω) a pedagogue, child-
    tender, a person, usually a slave or freed-
    man, to whom the care of the boys of a
    family was committed, whose duty it was
    to attend them at their play, lead them to
    and from the public school, and exercise
    a constant superintendence over their con-
    duct and safety; in N.T. an ordinary direc-
    tor or minister contrasted with an Apostle,
    as a pedagogue occupies an inferior posi-
    tion to a parent, 1 Cor. 4:15; a term ap-
    plied to the Mosaic law, as dealing with
    men as in a state of mere childhood and
    tutelage, Gal. 3:24, 25
παιδαγωγούς, acc. pl. m. n. . . . . . παιδαγωγός (3807)
παιδαρίοις, dat. pl. neut. n. (Matt. 11:16, TR
    | παιδίοις, GNT, WH, MT &
    NA) . . . . παιδάριον (3808)
(3808) παιδάριον, ου, τό, nom. sg. neut. n. [§3.C.c]
    (dimin. of παῖς) a little boy, child; a boy,
    lad, Matt. 11:16; John 6:9
παῖδας, acc. pl. m. n. . . . . παῖς (3816)
(3809) παιδεία, ας, ἡ, nom. sg. f. n. [§2.B.b; 2.2]
    (παιδεύω) education, training up, nurture
    of children, Eph. 6:4; instruction, disci-
    pline, 2 Tim. 3:16; in N.T. correction, chas-
    tisement, Heb. 12:5, 7, 8, 11
παιδείᾳ, dat. sg. f. n. . . . . παιδεία (3809)
παιδείαν, acc. sg. f. n. . . . . id.
παιδείας, gen. sg. f. n. . . . . id.
παιδεύει, 3 pers. sg. pres. act. indic. . . παιδεύω (3811)
παιδευθῶσι(ν), 3 pers. pl. aor. pass. subj.
    [§14.3.b] . . . . id.
παιδευόμεθα, 1 pers. pl. pres. pass. indic. . id.
παιδευόμενοι, nom. pl. m. pres. pass. part. id.
παιδεύοντα, acc. sg. m. pres. act. part. . . . id.
παιδεύουσα, nom. sg. f. pres. act. part. . . id.
παιδεύσας, nom. sg. m. aor. act. part. . . . id.
παιδευτάς, acc. pl. m. n. . . . . παιδευτής (3810)
παιδευτήν, acc. sg. f. n. . . . . id.
(3810) παιδευτής, οῦ, ὁ [§2.B.c] a preceptor, instruc-
    tor, teacher, pr. of boys; genr. Rom. 2:20;
    in N.T. a chastiser, Heb. 12:9
(3811) παιδεύω, 1 pers. sg. pres. act. indic., fut.
    παιδεύσω [§13.M] aor. ἐπαίδευσα, to ed-
    ucate, instruct children, Acts 7:22; 22:3;
    genr. παιδεύομαι, to be taught, learn,
    1 Tim. 1:20; to admonish, instruct by ad-
    monition, 2 Tim. 2:25; Tit. 2:12; in N.T.
    to chastise, chasten, 1 Cor. 11:32; 2 Cor.
    6:9; Heb. 12:6, 7, 10; Rev. 3:19; of crimi-

nals, *to scourge*, Luke 23:16, 22

παιδία, nom. pl. neut. n.
{Matt. 19:13} . . . . παιδίον *(3813)*

παιδία, acc. pl. neut. n. {Matt. 19:14} . . . . id.

παιδία, voc. pl. neut. n. {1 John 2:18} . . . id.

(3812) **παιδιόθεν**, adv., *from childhood, from a child*,
Mark 9:21

παιδίοις, dat. pl. neut. n. . . . . παιδίον *(3813)*

(3813) **παιδίον**, ου, τό, nom. sg. neut. n. [§3.C.c]
(dimin. of παῖς) *an infant, babe*, Matt. 2:8,
et al.; but usually in N.T. as equiv. to παῖς,
Matt. 14:21; Mark 7:28, et al. freq.; pl.
voc. used by way of endearment, *my dear
children*, 1 John 2:18, et al.; also as a term
of familiar address, *children, my lads*, John
21:5 {Luke 1:66}

παιδίον, acc. sg. neut. n. {Luke 1:59} . παιδίον *(3813)*

παιδίον, voc. sg. neut. n. {Luke 1:76} . . . . id.

παιδίου, gen. sg. neut. n. . . . . id.

παιδίσκας, acc. pl. f. n. . . . . παιδίσκη *(3814)*

(3814) **παιδίσκη**, ης, ἡ, nom. sg. f. n. [§2.B.a] (f. dimin. of παῖς) *a girl, damsel, maiden; a fe-
male slave or servant*, Matt. 26:69; Mark
14:66, 69, et al.

παιδίσκην, acc. sg. f. n. . . . . παιδίσκη *(3814)*

παιδίσκης, gen. sg. f. n. . . . . id.

παιδισκῶν, gen. pl. f. n. . . . . id.

παιδίων, gen. pl. neut. n. . . . . παιδίον *(3813)*

παιδός, gen. sg. m. n. {Luke 1:54} . . . . . . παῖς *(3816)*

παιδός, gen. sg. f. n. {Luke 8:51} . . . . id.

παίδων, gen. pl. m. n. . . . . id.

παίζειν, pres. act. infin. . . . . παίζω *(3815)*

(3815) **παίζω**, fut. παίξομαι [§26.2] *to play in the manner of children; to sport, to practise the festive gestures* of idolatrous worship, 1 Cor. 10:7

(3816) **παῖς**, παιδός, ὁ, ἡ, nom. sg. m. n. [§4.2.c] *a
child* in relation to parents, of either sex,
John 4:51, et al.; *a child* in respect of age,
either male or female, and of all ages from
infancy up to manhood, *a boy, youth, girl,
maiden*, Matt. 2:16; 17:18; Luke 2:43;
8:54; *a servant, slave*, Matt. 8:6, 8, 13, cf.
v. 9; Luke 7:7, cf. v. 3, 10; *an attendant,
minister*, Matt. 14:2; Luke 1:69; Acts 4:25;
also, Luke 1:54; or, perhaps, *a child* in respect of fatherly regard {Luke 7:7}

παῖς, nom. sg. f. n. {Luke 8:54} . . . . παῖς *(3816)*

παίσας, nom. sg. m. aor. act. part. . . . . . παίω *(3817)*

παίσῃ, 3 pers. sg. aor. act. subj. . . . . id.

παισίν, dat. pl. m. n. [§4.3.b] . . . . παῖς *(3816)*

(3817) **παίω**, fut. παίσω, perf. πέπαικα, aor. ἔπαισα
[§13.M] *to strike, smite*, with the fist, Matt.
26:68; Luke 22:64; with a sword, Mark
14:47; John 18:10; *to strike* as a scorpion,
to sting, Rev. 9:5

Πακατιανῆς, gen. sg. f. adj. (1 Tim. 6:21, TRs
| GNT, WH, MT, TRb & NA
omit) . . . . Πακατιανή *(3818)*

(3818) **Πακατιανή**, ῆς, ἡ, *Pacatiana*

(3819) **πάλαι**, adv., *of old, long ago*, Matt. 11:21;
Luke 10:13; Heb. 1:1; Jude 4; οἱ πάλαι, *old,
former*, 2 Pet. 1:9; *some time since, already*,
Mark 15:44

παλαιά, nom. sg. f. adj. {1 John 2:7} παλαιός *(3820)*

παλαιά, acc. pl. neut. adj. {Matt. 13:52} . id.

παλαιᾷ, dat. sg. f. adj. . . . . id.

παλαιάν, acc. sg. f. adj. . . . . id.

παλαιᾶς, gen. sg. f. adj. . . . . id.

παλαιόν, acc. sg. m. adj. {Luke 5:39} . . . . id.

παλαιόν, acc. sg. neut. adj. {Luke 5:36} . . id.

(3820) **παλαιός**, ά, όν, nom. sg. m. adj. [§7.1] *old,
not new or recent*, Matt. 9:16, 17; 13:52;
Luke 5:36, et al.

(3821) **παλαιότης**, ητος, ἡ [§4.2.c] *oldness, antiqua-
tedness, obsoleteness*, Rom. 7:6

παλαιότητι, dat. sg. f. n. . . . . παλαιότης *(3821)*

παλαιοῦ, gen. sg. neut. adj. . . . . παλαιός *(3820)*

παλαιούμενα, acc. sg. neut. pres. pass.
part. . . . . παλαιόω *(3822)*

παλαιούμενοι, acc. pl. neut. pres. pass. part. id.

παλαιούμενον, nom. sg. neut. pres. pass. part.
[§21.U] . . . . id.

παλαιούς, acc. pl. m. adj. . . . . παλαιός *(3820)*

(3822) **παλαιόω**, ῶ, fut. παλαιώσω, perf.
πεπαλαίωκα [§20.T] *to make old; pass. to
grow old, to become worn or effete*, Luke
12:33; Heb. 1:11; met. *to treat as anti-
quated, to abrogate, supersede*, Heb. 8:13

παλαιῶ, dat. sg. neut. adj. . . . . παλαιός *(3820)*

παλαιωθήσονται, 3 pers. pl. fut. pass.
indic. . . . . παλαιόω *(3822)*

(3823) **πάλη**, ης, ἡ, nom. sg. f. n. [§2.B.a] (πάλλω,
*to swing round, sway backward and for-
ward*) *wrestling; struggle, contest*, Eph.
6:12

(3824) **παλιγγενεσία**, ας, ἡ [§2.B.b; 2.2] (πάλιν +
γένεσις) *a new birth; regeneration, renovation*, Matt. 19:28; Tit. 3:5

παλιγγενεσίᾳ, dat. sg. f. n. (Matt. 19:28,
GNT, MT, TR & NA | παλινγενεσία,
WH) . . . . παλιγγενεσία *(3824)*

παλιγγενεσίας, gen. sg. f. n. (Tit. 3:5, GNT,
MT, TR & NA | παλινγενεσίας, WH) id.

(3825) **πάλιν**, adv., pr. *back; again, back again*, John
10:17; Acts 10:16; 11:10, et al.; *again by
repetition*, Matt. 26:43, et al.; *again in continuation*, *further*, Matt. 5:33; 13:44,
45, 47; 18:19; *again, on the other hand*,
1 John 2:8, et al.

(3826) **παμπληθεί**, adv. (πᾶς + πλῆθος) *the whole*

multitude together, all at once, Luke 23:18

παμπόλλου, gen. sg. m. adj. (Mark 8:1, MT & TR | πάλιν πολλοῦ, GNT, WH & NA) . . . . πάμπολυς *(3827)*

(3827) **πάμπολυς**, παμπόλλη, πάμπολυ [§7.7.a] (πᾶς + πολύς) *very many, very great, vast*

(3828) **Παμφυλία**, ας, ἡ [§2.B.b; 2.2] *Pamphylia, a country of Asia Minor*

Παμφυλίαν, acc. sg. f. n. . . . . Παμφυλία *(3828)*

Παμφυλίας, gen. sg. f. n. . . . . id.

πᾶν, nom. sg. neut. adj. {Phil. 2:10} . . . . πᾶς *(3956)*

πᾶν, acc. sg. neut. adj. {Phil. 2:9} . . . . id.

πανδοχεῖ, dat. sg. m. n. . . . . πανδοχεύς *(3830)*

(3829) **πανδοχεῖον**, ου, τό [§3.C.c] *a public inn, place where travelers may lodge,* called in the East by the name of *menzil, khan, caravanserai,* Luke 10:34

πανδοχεῖον, acc. sg. neut. n. . . . . πανδοχεῖον *(3829)*

(3830) **πανδοχεύς**, έως, ὁ [§5.E.d] (a later form for πανδοκεύς, πᾶς + δέχομαι) *the keeper of a public inn or caravanserai, a host,* Luke 10:35

πανηγύρει, dat. sg. f. n. . . . . πανήγυρις *(3831)*

(3831) **πανήγυρις**, εως, ἡ [§5.E.c] (πᾶς + ἄγυρις, *an assembly*) pr. *an assembly of an entire people; a solemn gathering at a festival; a festive convocation,* Heb. 12:23

(†3832) **πανοικεί**, adv. (πᾶς + οἶκος) *with one's whole household or family* (Acts 16:34, GNT, WH & NA | πανοικί, MT & TR)

(3832) **πανοικί**, adv., *with all his house, with his whole family* (Acts 16:34, MT & TR | πανοικεί, GNT, WH & NA)

(3833) **πανοπλία**, ας, ἡ [§2.B.b; 2.2] (πᾶς + ὅπλον) *panoply, complete armor, a complete suit of armor,* both offensive and defensive, as the shield, sword, spear, helmet, breastplate, etc., Luke 11:22; Eph. 6:11, 13

πανοπλίαν, acc. sg. f. n. . . . . πανοπλία *(3833)*

(3834) **πανουργία**, ας, ἡ [§2.B.b; 2.2] *knavery, craft, cunning,* Luke 20:23; 1 Cor. 3:19, et al.

πανουργίᾳ, dat. sg. f. n. . . . . πανουργία *(3834)*

πανουργίαν, acc. sg. f. n. . . . . id.

(3835) **πανοῦργος**, ον, nom. sg. m. n. [§7.2] (πᾶς + ἔργον) pr. *ready to do anything;* hence, *crafty, cunning, artful, wily*

πάντα, acc. sg. m. adj. {Acts 10:43b} . . . . πᾶς *(3956)*

πάντα, nom. pl. neut. adj. {Acts 10:12} . . id.

πάντα, acc. pl. neut. adj. {Acts 10:33b} . . id.

πάντας, acc. pl. m. adj. . . . . id.

(‡3837) **πανταχῇ**, adv., *everywhere* (Acts 21:28, GNT, WH & NA | πανταχοῦ, MT & TR)

(3836) **πανταχόθεν**, adv., *from all parts, from every quarter* (Mark 1:45, MT & TR | πάντοθεν, GNT, WH & NA)

(3837) **πανταχοῦ**, adv., *in all places, everywhere,* Mark 16:20; Luke 9:6, et al.

παντελές, acc. sg. neut. adj. . . . . παντελής *(3838)*

(3838) **παντελής**, ές [§7.G.b] (πᾶς + τέλος) *perfect, complete;* εἰς τὸ παντελές, adverbially, *throughout, through all time, ever,* Heb. 7:25; with a negative, *at all,* Luke 13:11

πάντες, nom. pl. m. adj. . . . . πᾶς *(3956)*

(†3839) **πάντη**, adv., *everywhere; in every way, in every instance,* Acts 24:3

παντί, dat. sg. m. adj. {1 Cor. 1:5b} . . . . . πᾶς *(3956)*

παντί, dat. sg. neut. adj. {1 Cor. 1:5a} . . . . id.

(3840) **πάντοθεν**, adv. (πᾶς + θεν) *from every place, from all parts,* John 18:20; *on all sides, on every side, round about,* Luke 19:43; Heb. 9:4

παντοκράτορος, gen. sg. m. n. . . παντοκράτωρ *(3841)*

(3841) **παντοκράτωρ**, ορος, ὁ, nom. sg. m. n. [§4.2.f] (πᾶς + κράτος) *almighty, omnipotent,* 2 Cor. 6:18; Rev. 1:8; 4:8, et al.

παντός, gen. sg. m. adj. {Matt. 13:19} . . . πᾶς *(3956)*

παντός, gen. sg. neut. adj. {Matt. 13:47} . id.

(3842) **πάντοτε**, adv., *always, at all times, ever,* Matt. 26:11; Mark 14:7; Luke 15:31; 18:1, et al.

πάντων, gen. pl. m. adj. {Luke 21:17} . . . πᾶς *(3956)*

πάντων, gen. pl. neut. adj. {Luke 21:12} . id.

(3843) **πάντως**, adv., *wholly, altogether; at any rate, by all means,* 1 Cor. 9:22; by impl. *surely, assuredly, certainly,* Luke 4:23; Acts 18:21; 21:22; 28:4; 1 Cor. 9:10; οὐ πάντως, *in nowise, not in the least,* Rom. 3:9; 1 Cor. 5:10; 16:12

παρ', by apostrophe for παρά . . . . παρά *(3844)*

(3844) **παρά**, prep., with a genitive, *from,* indicating source or origin, Matt. 2:4, 7; Mark 8:11; Luke 2:1, et al.; οἱ παρ' αὐτοῦ, *his relatives or kinsmen,* Mark 3:21; τὰ παρ' αὐτῆς πάντα, *all her substance, property,* etc., Mark 5:26; with a dative, *with, by, nigh to, in, among,* etc., Matt. 6:1; 19:26; 21:25; 22:25; παρ' ἑαυτῷ, *at home,* 1 Cor. 16:2; *in the sight of, in the judgment or estimation of,* 1 Cor. 3:19; 2 Pet. 2:11; 3:8; with an accusative, motion, *by, near to, along,* Matt. 4:18; motion, *towards, to, at,* Matt. 15:30; Mark 2:13; motion terminating in rest, *at, by, near, by the side of,* Mark 4:1, 4; Luke 5:1; 8:5; *in deviation from, in violation of, inconsistently with,* Acts 18:13; Rom. 1:26; 11:24; *above, more than,* Luke 13:2, 4; Rom. 1:25; after comparatives, Luke 3:13; 1 Cor. 3:11; *except, save,* 2 Cor. 11:24; *beyond, past,* Heb. 11:11; *in respect of, on the score of,* 1 Cor. 12:15, 16

παραβαίνετε, 2 pers. pl. pres. act.

indic. παραβαίνω (3845)
παραβαίνουσι(ν), 3 pers. pl. pres. act. indic.   id.

(3845) **παραβαίνω**, fut. παραβήσομαι, 2 aor.
παρέβην [§37.1] (παρά + βαίνω) pr. *to
step by the side of; to deviate;* met. *to transgress, violate,* Matt. 15:2, 3; 2 John 9; *to
incur forfeiture,* Acts 1:25
παραβαίνων, nom. sg. m. pres. act. part.
(2 John 9, MT & TR | προάγων, GNT,
WH & NA) . . . . παραβαίνω (3845)

(3846) **παραβάλλω**, fut. παραβαλῶ [§27.1.b] (παρά
+ βάλλω) *to cast or throw by the side of;*
met. *to compare,* Mark 4:30; absol., a
nautical term, *to bring-to, land,* Acts 20:15
παραβάλωμεν, 1 pers. pl. 2 aor. act. subj.
(Mark 4:30, MT & TR | θῶμεν, GNT,
WH & NA) . . . . παραβάλλω (3846)
παραβάσει, dat. sg. f. n. . . . . παράβασις (3847)
παραβάσεων, gen. pl. f. n. . . . . id.
παραβάσεως, gen. sg. f. n. . . . . id.

(3847) **παράβασις**, εως, ἡ, nom. sg. f. n. [§5.E.c] *a
stepping by the side, deviation; a transgression, violation of law,* Rom. 2:23; 4:15,
et al.
παραβάται, nom. pl. m. n. . . . . . . παραβάτης (3848)
παραβάτην, acc. sg. m. n. . . . . id.

(3848) **παραβάτης**, ου, ὁ, nom. sg. m. n. [§2.B.c] *a
transgressor, violator of law,* Rom.
2:25, 27; Gal. 2:18; James 2:9, 11

(3849) **παραβιάζομαι**, fut. παραβιάσομαι [§26.1]
(παρά + βιάζω) *to force; to constrain,
press* with urgent entreaties, Luke 24:29;
Acts 16:15
παραβολαῖς, dat. pl. f. n. . . . . παραβολή (3850)
παραβολάς, acc. pl. f. n. . . . . id.

(‡3851) **παραβολεύομαι**, fut. παραβολεύσομαι
(παράβολος, *risking, venturesome*) *to
stake or risk one's self,* Phil. 2:30
παραβολευσάμενος, nom. sg. m. aor. mid.
dep. part. (Phil. 2:30, GNT, WH & NA
| παραβουλευσάμενος, MT &
TR) . . . . παραβολεύομαι (‡3851)

(3850) **παραβολή**, ῆς, ἡ, nom. sg. f. n. [§2.B.a] *a placing one thing by the side of another; a comparing; a parallel case cited in illustration;
a comparison, simile, similitude,* Mark
4:30; Heb. 11:19; *a parable,* a short relation under which something else is figured,
or in which that which is fictitious is employed to represent that which is real, Matt.
13:3, 10, 13, 18, 24, 31, 33, 34, 36, 53;
21:33, 45; 22:1; 24:32, et al.; in N.T. *a
type, pattern, emblem,* Heb. 9:9; *a sentiment, grave and sententious precept,
maxim,* Luke 14:7; *an obscure and enig-*

*matical saying, anything expressed in re-
mote and ambiguous terms,* Matt. 13:35;
Mark 7:17; *a proverb, adage,* Luke 4:23
παραβολῇ, dat. sg. f. n. . . . . παραβολή (3850)
παραβολήν, acc. sg. f. n. . . . . id.
παραβολῆς, gen. sg. f. n. . . . . id.

(3851) **παραβουλεύομαι**, fut. παραβουλεύσομαι
[§15.O] (παρά + βουλεύω) *to be reckless,
regardless,* Phil. 2:30
παραβουλευσάμενος, nom. sg. m. aor. mid.
dep. part. (Phil. 2:30, MT & TR |
παραβολευσάμενος, GNT, WH &
NA) . . . . παραβουλεύομαι (3851)
παραγγείλαντες, nom. pl. m. aor. act. part.
[§27.1.d] . . . . παραγγέλλω (3853)
παραγγείλας, nom. sg. m. aor. act. part. . id.
παραγγείλῃς, 2 pers. sg. aor. act. subj. . . . id.

(3852) **παραγγελία**, ας, ἡ [§2.B.b; 2.2] *a command,
order, charge,* Acts 5:28; *direction, precept,*
1 Thess. 4:2, et al.
παραγγελίᾳ, dat. sg. f. n. . . . . παραγγελία (3852)
παραγγελίαν, acc. sg. f. n. . . . . id.
παραγγελίας, gen. sg. f. n. {1 Tim. 1:5} . . id.
παραγγελίας, acc. pl. f. n. {1 Thess. 4:2} . id.
παράγγελλε, 2 pers. sg. pres. act.
imper. παραγγέλλω (3853)
παραγγέλλει, 3 pers. sg. pres. act. indic.
(Mark 8:6; Acts 17:30, GNT & NA |
Mark 8:6, παραγγέλλει, WH; Acts 17:30,
ἀπαγγέλλει, WH | παρήγγειλε, Mark 8:6,
MT & TR | Acts 17:30, παραγγέλλει,
MT & TR) . . . . id.
παραγγέλλειν, pres. act. infin. . . . . id.
παραγγέλλομεν, 1 pers. pl. pres. act. indic. id.

(3853) **παραγγέλλω**, 1 pers. sg. pres. act. indic., fut.
παραγγελῶ [§27.1.b] (παρά + ἀγγέλλω)
*to announce, notify; to command, direct,
charge,* Matt. 10:5; Mark 6:8; 8:6; Luke
9:21, et al.; *to charge, obtest, entreat solemnly,* 1 Tim. 6:13
παραγγέλλων, nom. sg. m. pres. act.
part. παραγγέλλω (3853)
παράγει, 3 pers. sg. pres. act. indic. . . παράγω (3855)
παραγενόμενοι, nom. pl. m. 2 aor. mid. dep.
part. [§37.1] . . . . παραγίνομαι (3854)
παραγενόμενον, acc. sg. m. 2 aor. mid. dep.
part. . . . . id.
παραγενόμενος, nom. sg. m. 2 aor. mid. dep.
part. . . . . id.
παραγενομένου, gen. sg. m. 2 aor. mid. dep.
part. . . . . id.
παραγενομένους, acc. pl. m. 2 aor. mid. dep.
part. . . . . id.
παραγένωμαι, 1 pers. sg. 2 aor. mid. dep.
subj. . . . . id.

παραγένωνται, 3 pers. pl. 2 aor. mid. dep.
subj. . . . . παραγίνομαι *(3854)*
παράγεται, 3 pers. sg. pres. mid.
indic. . . . . : . . . . παράγω *(3855)*
παραγίνεται, 3 pers. sg. pres. mid./pass. dep.
indic. . . . . παραγίνομαι *(3854)*
(3854) **παραγίνομαι**, fut. παραγενήσομαι, 2 aor.
παρεγενόμην [§37.1] (παρά + γίνομαι) *to
be by the side of; to come, approach, arrive,* Matt. 2:1; 3:13; Mark 14:43; Luke
7:4, et al.; seq. ἐπί, *to come upon* in order to seize, Luke 22:52; *to come forth in
public, make appearance,* Matt. 3:1; Heb.
9:11
παράγοντα, acc. sg. m. pres. act.
part. . . . . παράγω *(3855)*
παράγοντι, dat. sg. m. pres. act. part. . . . . id.
(3855) **παράγω**, fut. παράξω [§23.1.b] (παρά + ἄγω)
to lead beside; intrans. *to pass along or by,*
Matt. 20:30; John 9:1; *to pass on,* Matt.
9:9, 27; intrans. and mid. *to pass away, be
in a state of transition,* 1 Cor. 7:31; 1 John
2:8, 17
παράγων, nom. sg. m. pres. act. part. παράγω *(3855)*
παραδεδομένοι, nom. pl. m. perf. pass.
part. παραδίδωμι *(3860)*
παραδέδοται, 3 pers. sg. perf. pass. indic.
[§30.4] . . . . id.
παραδεδώκεισαν, 3 pers. pl. pluperf. act.
indic. [§13.8.f] . . . . id.
παραδεδωκόσι(ν), dat. pl. m. perf. act. part.
[§30.Z] . . . . id.
παραδειγματιζόντας, acc. pl. m. pres. act.
part. . . . . παραδειγματίζω *(3856)*
(3856) **παραδειγματίζω**, fut. παραδειγματίσω [§26.1]
(παράδειγμα, *an example*) *to make an example of; to expose to ignominy and
shame,* Matt. 1:19; Heb. 6:6
παραδειγματίσαι, aor. act. infin. (Matt. 1:19,
MT & TR | δειγματίσαι, GNT, WH &
NA) . . . . παραδειγματίζω *(3856)*
παράδεισον, acc. sg. m. n. . . . . . . παράδεισος *(3857)*
(3857) **παράδεισος**, ου, ὁ [§3.C.a] (*of Oriental origin;* in the Hebrew פַּרְדֵּס) *a park, a forest
where wild beasts were kept for hunting;
a pleasure-park, a garden of trees of various kinds;* used in the LXX for *the Garden of Eden;* in N.T. the celestial *paradise,*
Luke 23:43; 2 Cor. 12:4; Rev. 2:7
παραδείσου, gen. sg. m. n. (Rev. 2:7, TR |
παραδείσῳ, GNT, WH, MT &
NA) . . . . παράδεισος *(3857)*
παραδείσῳ, dat. sg. m. n. . . . . id.
παραδέξονται, 3 pers. pl. fut. mid./pass. dep.
indic. . . . . παραδέχομαι *(3858)*

παραδέχεσθαι, pres. mid./pass. dep.
infin. . . . . παραδέχομαι *(3858)*
παραδέχεται, 3 pers. sg. pres. mid./pass. dep.
indic. . . . . id.
(3858) **παραδέχομαι**, fut. παραδέξομαι [§23.1.b]
(παρά + δέχομαι) *to accept, receive;* met.
to receive, admit, yield assent to, Mark
4:20; Acts 16:21; 22:18; 1 Tim. 5:19; in
N.T. *to receive or embrace with favor, approve, love,* Heb. 12:6
παραδέχονται, 3 pers. pl. pres. mid./pass.
dep. indic. . . . . παραδέχομαι *(3858)*
παραδέχου, 2 pers. sg. pres. mid./pass. dep.
imper. . . . . id.
παραδιατριβαί, nom. pl. f. n. (1 Tim. 6:5, TR
| διαπαρατριβαί, GNT, WH, MT &
NA) . . . . παραδιατριβή *(3859)*
(3859) **παραδιατριβή**, ῆς, ἡ [§2.B.a] (παρά +
διατριβή, *waste of time, delay*) *useless disputation,* 1 Tim. 6:5
παραδιδόμεθα, 1 pers. pl. pres. pass. indic.
[§30.AA] . . . . παραδίδωμι *(3860)*
παραδιδόναι, pres. act. infin. . . . . id.
παραδιδόντα, acc. sg. m. pres. act. part. . id.
παραδιδόντες, nom. pl. m. pres. act. part. id.
παραδιδόντος, gen. sg. m. pres. act. part. id.
παραδίδοσθαι, pres. pass. infin. . . . . id.
παραδίδοται, 3 pers. sg. pres. pass. indic. id.
παραδιδούς, nom. sg. m. pres. act. part. . id.
παραδιδῷ, 3 pers. sg. pres. act. subj. (1 Cor.
15:24, GNT, WH & NA | παραδῷ, MT
& TR) . . . . id.
(3860) **παραδίδωμι**, fut. παραδώσω [§30.Z] (παρά
+ δίδωμι) *to give over, hand over, deliver
up,* Matt. 4:12; 5:25; 10:4, 17, et al.; *to
commit, intrust,* Matt. 11:27; 25:14, et al.;
to commit, commend, Acts 14:26; 15:40;
to yield up, John 19:30; 1 Cor. 15:24; *to
abandon,* Acts 7:42; Eph. 4:19; *to stake,
hazard,* Acts 15:26; *to deliver* as a matter
of injunction, instruction, etc., Mark 7:13;
Luke 1:2; Acts 6:14, et al.; absol. *to render
a yield, to be matured,* Mark 4:29
παραδίδως, 2 pers. sg. pres. act.
indic. . . . . παραδίδωμι *(3860)*
παραδιδῶσιν, 3 pers. pl. pres. act. subj. (Matt.
10:19, MT & TR | παραδῶσιν, GNT,
WH & NA) . . . . id.
παραδοθείς, nom. sg. m. aor. pass. part.
[§30.4] . . . . id.
παραδοθείσῃ, dat. sg. f. aor. pass. part. . . id.
παραδοθείσης, gen. sg. f. aor. pass. part. . id.
παραδοθῆναι, aor. pass. infin. . . . . id.
παραδοθήσεσθε, 2 pers. pl. fut. pass. indic. id.
παραδοθήσεται, 3 pers. sg. fut. pass. indic. id.

παραδοθῶ, 1 pers. sg. aor. pass.
subj. . . . . παραδίδωμι (3860)
παραδοῖ, 3 pers. sg. 2 aor. act. subj. [§30.5]
(Mark 4:29; 14:10, 11; John 13:2, GNT,
WH & NA | παραδῷ, MT & TR) . . . id.
παραδόντος, gen. sg. m. 2 aor. act. part. . id.
παράδοξα, acc. pl. neut. adj. . . . . . παράδοξος (3861)
(3861) **παράδοξος**, ον [§7.2] (παρὰ δόξαν, *beside expectation*) *unexpected; strange, wonderful, astonishing,* Luke 5:26
παραδόσει, dat. sg. f. n. . . . . παράδοσις (3862)
παραδόσεις, acc. pl. f. n. . . . . id.
παραδόσεων, gen. pl. f. n. . . . . id.
παράδοσιν, acc. sg. f. n. . . . . id.
(3862) **παράδοσις**, εως, ἡ [§5.E.c] *delivery, handing over, transmission;* in N.T. *what is transmitted* in the way of teaching, *precept, doctrine,* 1 Cor. 11:2; 2 Thess. 2:15; 3:6; *tradition, traditionary law,* handed down from age to age, Matt. 15:2, 3, 6, et al.
παραδοῦναι, 2 aor. act. infin.
[§30.1] . . . . παραδίδωμι (3860)
παραδούς, nom. sg. m. 2 aor. act. part. . . id.
παραδῶ, 1 pers. sg. 2 aor. act. subj. . . . . id.
παραδῷ, 3 pers. sg. 2 aor. act. subj. . . . . id.
παραδώσει, 3 pers. sg. fut. act. indic. . . . id.
παραδῶσιν, 3 pers. pl. 2 aor. act. subj. (Matt. 10:19, GNT, WH & NA | παραδιδῶσιν, MT & TR) . . . . id.
παραδώσουσι(ν), 3 pers. pl. fut. act. indic. id.
παραδώσω, 1 pers. sg. fut. act. indic. . . . . id.
παραδώσων, nom. sg. m. fut. act. part. . . id.
παραζηλοῦμεν, 1 pers. pl. pres. act.
indic. . . . . παραζηλόω (3863)
(3863) **παραζηλόω**, ῶ, fut. παραζηλώσω [§20.T] (παρά + ζηλόω) *to provoke to jealousy,* Rom. 10:19; *to excite to emulation,* Rom. 11:11, 14; *to provoke to indignation,* 1 Cor. 10:22
παραζηλῶσαι, aor. act. infin. . . . . παραζηλόω (3863)
παραζηλώσω, 1 pers. sg. fut. act. indic.
{Rom. 10:19} . . . . id.
παραζηλώσω, 1 pers. sg. aor. act. subj.
{Rom. 11:14} . . . . id.
παραθαλασσίαν, acc. sg. f.
adj. . . . . παραθαλάσσιος (3864)
(3864) **παραθαλάσσιος**, ία, ιον [§7.1] (παρά + θάλασσα) *by the sea-side, situated on the sea-coast, maritime,* Matt. 4:13
παραθεῖναι, 2 aor. act. infin.
[§28.V] . . . . παρατίθημι (3908)
(3865) **παραθεωρέω**, ῶ, fut. παραθεωρήσω [§16.P] (παρά + θεωρέω) *to look at things placed side by side,* as in comparison, *to compare in thus looking, to regard less in compari-*

son, overlook, neglect, Acts 6:1
(3866) **παραθήκη**, ης, ἡ [§2.B.a] *a deposit, a thing committed to one's charge, a trust,* 2 Tim. 1:12; 1 Tim. 6:20; 2 Tim. 1:14
παραθήκην, acc. sg. f. n. . . . . παραθήκη (3866)
παραθήσομαι, 1 pers. sg. fut. mid. dep. indic.
[§28.W] (Luke 23:46, MT & TR | παρατίθεμαι, GNT, WH & NA) . . . παρατίθημι (3908)
παραθήσω, 1 pers. sg. fut. act. indic. . . . . id.
παράθου, 2 pers. sg. 2 aor. mid. indic.
[§28.8.d] . . . . id.
παραθῶσιν, 3 pers. pl. 2 aor. act. subj. (Mark 6:41, MT & TR | παρατιθῶσιν, GNT, WH & NA) . . . . id.
(3867) **παραινέω**, ῶ, fut. παραινέσω [§22.1] (παρά + αἰνέω) *to advise, exhort,* Acts 27:9, 22
παραινῶ, 1 pers. sg. pres. act. indic. παραινέω (3867)
παραιτεῖσθαι, pres. mid./pass. dep.
infin. . . . . παραιτέομαι (3868)
(3868) **παραιτέομαι**, οῦμαι, fut. παραιτήσομαι [§17.Q] (παρά + αἰτέω) *to entreat; to beg off, excuse one's self,* Luke 14:18, 19; *to deprecate, entreat against,* Acts 25:11; Heb. 12:19; *to decline receiving, refuse, reject,* 1 Tim. 4:7; 5:11; Tit. 3:10; Heb. 12:25; *to decline, avoid, shun,* 2 Tim. 2:23
παραιτησάμενοι, nom. pl. m. aor. mid. dep.
part. . . . . παραιτέομαι (3868)
παραιτήσησθε, 2 pers. pl. aor. mid. dep. subj. id.
παραιτοῦ, 2 pers. sg. pres. mid./pass. dep.
imper. . . . . id.
παραιτοῦμαι, 1 pers. sg. pres. mid./pass. dep.
indic. . . . . id.
(†3869) **παρακαθέζομαι**, aor. (pass. form) (παρά + καθέζομαι) *to sit down by,* Luke 10:39
παρακαθεσθεῖσα, nom. sg. f. aor. pass. dep.
part. (Luke 10:39, GNT, WH & NA | παρακαθίσασα, MT & TR) . . παρακαθέζομαι (†3869)
(3869) **παρακαθίζω**, fut. παρακαθίσω [§26.1] (παρά + καθίζω) *to set beside;* intrans. *to sit by the side of, sit near,* Luke 10:39
παρακαθίσασα, nom. sg. f. aor. act. part. (Luke 10:39, MT & TR | παρακαθεσθεῖσα, GNT, WH & NA) . . παρακαθίζω (3869)
παρακαλεῖ, 3 pers. sg. pres. act. indic.
{Mark 5:23} . . . . παρακαλέω (3870)
παρακάλει, 2 pers. sg. pres. act. imper.
{1 Tim. 6:2} . . . . id.
παρακαλεῖν, pres. act. infin. . . . . id.
παρακαλεῖσθε, 2 pers. pl. pres. pass. imper. id.
παρακαλεῖται, 3 pers. sg. pres. pass. indic. id.
παρακαλεῖτε, 2 pers. pl. pres. act. imper. . id.
παρακαλέσαι, 3 pers. sg. aor. act. opt.
{1 Thess. 3:2} . . . . id.

παρακαλέσαι, aor. act. infin.
{2 Thess. 2:17} .... παρακαλέω *(3870)*
παρακαλέσας, nom. sg. m. aor. act. part.   id.
παρακαλέση, 3 pers. sg. aor. act. subj. ...   id.
παρακάλεσον, 2 pers. sg. aor. act. imper. .   id.
(3870) **παρακαλέω**, ῶ, fut. παρακαλέσω [§22.1]
(παρά + καλέω) *to call for, invite to come,
send for,* Acts 28:20; *to call upon, exhort,
admonish, persuade,* Luke 3:18; Acts 2:40;
11:23; *to beg, beseech, entreat, implore,*
Matt. 8:5, 31; 18:29; Mark 1:40; *to animate, encourage, comfort, console,* Matt.
2:18; 5:4; 2 Cor. 1:4, 6; pass. *to be
cheered, comforted,* Luke 16:25; Acts
20:12; 2 Cor. 7:13, et al.
παρακαλούμεθα, 1 pers. pl. pres. pass.
indic. .... παρακαλέω *(3870)*
παρακαλοῦμεν, 1 pers. pl. pres. act. indic.   id.
παρακαλοῦντες, nom. pl. m. pres. act. part.   id.
παρακαλοῦντος, gen. sg. m. pres. act. part.   id.
παρακαλοῦσιν, 3 pers. pl. pres. act. indic.   id.
(3871) **παρακαλύπτω**, fut. παρακαλύψω [§23.1.a]
(παρά + καλύπτω) *to cover over, veil;*
met. pass. *to be veiled* from comprehension, Luke 9:45
παρακαλῶ, 1 pers. sg. pres. act.
indic. .... παρακαλέω *(3870)*
παρακαλῶν, nom. sg. m. pres. act. part. .   id.
παρακαλῶνται, 3 pers. pl. pres. pass. subj.   id.
(3872) **παρακαταθήκη**, ης, ἡ [§2.B.a] (παρακατα-
τίθημι, *to lay down by, deposit) a deposit,
a thing committed to one's charge, a trust,*
1 Tim. 6:20; 2 Tim. 1:14
παρακαταθήκην, acc. sg. f. n. (1 Tim. 6:20,
TR | παραθήκην, GNT, WH, MT &
NA) .... παρακαταθήκη *(3872)*
(3873) **παράκειμαι** [§33.DD] (παρά + κεῖμαι) *to lie
near, be adjacent;* met. *to be at hand, be
present,* Rom. 7:18, 21
παράκειται, 3 pers. sg. pres. mid./pass. dep.
indic. .... παράκειμαι *(3873)*
παρακεκαλυμμένον, nom. sg. neut. perf.
pass. part. .... παρακαλύπτω *(3871)*
παρακεκλήμεθα, 1 pers. pl. perf. pass. indic.
[§22.4] .... παρακαλέω *(3870)*
παρακεχειμακότι, dat. sg. m. perf. act.
part. .... παραχειμάζω *(3914)*
παρακληθῆναι, aor. pass. infin. .. παρακαλέω *(3870)*
παρακληθήσονται, 3 pers. pl. fut. pass. indic.   id.
παρακληθῶσιν, 3 pers. pl. aor. pass. subj.   id.
παρακλήσει, dat. sg. f. n. ..... παράκλησις *(3874)*
παρακλήσεως, gen. sg. f. n. .... id.
παράκλησιν, acc. sg. f. n. .... id.
(3874) **παράκλησις**, εως, ἡ, nom. sg. f. n. [§5.E.c]
a calling upon, exhortation, incitement,

persuasion, Rom. 12:8; 1 Cor. 14:3; *hor-
tatory instruction,* Acts 13:15; 15:31; *entreaty, importunity, earnest supplication,*
2 Cor. 8:4; *solace, consolation,* Luke 2:25;
Rom. 15:4, 5; 2 Cor. 1:3, 4, 5, 6, 7; *cheering and supporting influence,* Acts 9:31; *joy,
gladness, rejoicing,* 2 Cor. 7:13; *cheer, joy,
enjoyment,* Luke 6:24
παράκλητον, acc. sg. m. n. ..... παράκλητος *(3875)*
(3875) **παράκλητος**, ου, ὁ, nom. sg. m. n. [§3.C.a]
*one called or sent for to assist another; an
advocate, one who pleads the cause of another,* 1 John 2:1; genr. *one present to
render various beneficial service,* and thus
the Paraclete, whose influence and operation were to compensate for the departure
of Christ himself, John 14:16, 26; 15:26;
16:7
(3876) **παρακοή**, ῆς, ἡ, nom. sg. f. n. [§2.B.a] *an erroneous or imperfect hearing; disobedience,*
Rom. 5:19; *a deviation from obedience,*
2 Cor. 10:6; Heb. 2:2
παρακοήν, acc. sg. f. n. .... παρακοή *(3876)*
παρακοῆς, gen. sg. f. n. .... id.
(3877) **παρακολουθέω**, ῶ, fut. παρακολουθήσω
[§16.P] (παρά + ἀκολουθέω) *to follow or
accompany closely; to accompany, attend,
characterize,* Mark 16:17; *to follow* with
the thoughts, *trace,* Luke 1:3; *to conform
to,* 1 Tim. 4:6; 2 Tim. 3:10
παρακολουθήσει, 3 pers. sg. fut. act. indic.
(Mark 16:17, GNT, MT, TR & NA |
ἀκολουθήσει, WH) ..... παρακολουθέω *(3877)*
παρακούσας, nom. sg. m. aor. act. part.
(Mark 5:36, GNT, WH & NA | ἀούσας,
MT & TR) .... παρακούω *(3878)*
παρακούσῃ, 3 pers. sg. aor. act. subj. .... id.
(3878) **παρακούω**, fut. παρακούσομαι (παρά +
ἀκούω) *to hear amiss, to fail to listen, neglect to obey, disregard,* Matt. 18:17 (2×)
(3879) **παρακύπτω**, παρακύψω [§23.1.a] (παρά +
κύπτω) *to stoop beside; to stoop down* in
order to take a view, Luke 24:12; John
20:5, 11; *to bestow a close and attentive
look, to look intently, to penetrate,* James
1:25; 1 Pet. 1:12
παρακύψαι, aor. act. infin. ...... παρακύπτω *(3879)*
παρακύψας, nom. sg. m. aor. act. part. ... id.
παράλαβε, 2 pers. sg. 2 aor. act.
imper. .... παραλαμβάνω *(3880)*
παραλαβεῖν, 2 aor. act. infin. .... id.
παραλαβόντα, acc. sg. m. 2 aor. act. part.   id.
παραλαβόντες, nom. pl. m. 2 aor. act. part.   id.
παραλαβών, nom. sg. m. 2 aor. act. part.   id.
παραλαμβάνει, 3 pers. sg. pres. act. indic.   id.

παραλαμβάνεται, 3 pers. sg. pres. pass.
indic. . . . . παραλαμβάνω *(3880)*
παραλαμβάνοντες, nom. pl. m. pres. act.
part. . . . . id.
παραλαμβάνουσιν, 3 pers. pl. pres. act. indic.   id.

(3880) **παραλαμβάνω,** fut. παραλή(μ)ψομαι [§36.2]
2 aor. παρέλαβον (παρά + λαμβάνω) pr.
*to take to one's side; to take, receive to one's
self,* Matt. 1:20; John 14:3; *to take* with
one's self, Matt. 2:13, 14, 20, 21; 4:5, 8;
to receive in charge or possession, Col.
4:17; Heb. 12:28; *to receive* as a matter of
instruction, Mark 7:4; 1 Cor. 11:23; 15:3;
to receive, admit, acknowledge, John 1:11;
1 Cor. 15:1; Col. 2:6; pass. *to be carried
off,* Matt. 24:40, 41; Luke 17:34, 35, 36

(3881) **παραλέγομαι** (παρά + λέγω, *to gather*) *to
gather* a course *along; to sail by, coast
along,* Acts 27:8, 13
παραλεγόμενοι, nom. pl. m. pres. mid./pass.
dep. part. . . . . παραλέγομαι *(3881)*
παραλελυμένα, acc. pl. neut. perf. pass.
part. παραλύω *(3886)*
παραλελυμένοι, nom. pl. m. perf. pass. part.   id.
παραλελυμένος, nom. sg. m. perf. pass. part.   id.
παραλελυμένῳ, dat. sg. m. perf. pass. part.   id.
παραλημφθήσεται, 3 pers. sg. fut. pass. indic.
[§36.2] (Luke 17:34, 35, GNT, WH & NA
| παραληφθήσεται, MT &
TR) . . . . παραλαμβάνω *(3880)*
παραλήμψομαι, 1 pers. sg. fut. mid. dep.
indic. (John 14:3, GNT, WH & NA |
παραλήψομαι, MT & TR) . . . . id.
παραληφθήσεται, 3 pers. sg. fut. pass. indic.
(Luke 17:34, 35, MT & TR | παραλημ-
φθήσεται, GNT, WH & NA) . . . . id.
παραλήψομαι, 1 pers. sg. fut. mid. dep. indic.
(John 14:3, MT & TR | παραλήμψομαι,
GNT, WH & NA) . . . . id.

(3882) **παράλιος,** ον [§7.2] (παρά + ἄλς) *adjacent
to the sea, maritime;* ἡ παράλιος, sc.
χώρα, *the sea-coast,* Luke 6:17
παραλίου, gen. sg. f. adj. . . . . παράλιος *(3882)*

(3883) **παραλλαγή,** ῆς, ἡ, nom. sg. f. n. [§2.B.a]
(παραλλάσσω, *to interchange*) *a shifting,
mutation, change,* James 1:17
παραλογίζηται, 3 pers. sg. pres. mid./pass.
dep. subj. . . . . παραλογίζομαι *(3884)*

(3884) **παραλογίζομαι,** fut. παραλογίσομαι [§26.1]
(παρά + λογίζομαι) *to misreckon, make
a false reckoning; to impose upon, deceive,
delude, circumvent,* Col. 2:4; James 1:22
παραλογιζόμενοι, nom. pl. m. pres.
mid./pass. dep. part. . . . . . . παραλογίζομαι *(3884)*
παραλυτικόν, acc. sg. m. adj. . . παραλυτικός *(3885)*

(3885) **παραλυτικός,** ή, όν, nom. sg. m. adj. [§7.F.a]
paralytic, palsied, Matt. 4:24; 8:6; 9:2, 6,
et al.
παραλυτικούς, acc. pl. m. adj. . . παραλυτικός *(3885)*
παραλυτικῷ, dat. sg. m. adj. . . . . id.

(3886) **παραλύω,** fut. παραλύσω [§13.M] (παρά +
λύω) *to unloose from proper fixity or con-
sistency of substance; to enervate or par-
alyze* the body or limbs; pass. *to be
enervated or enfeebled,* Heb. 12:12; pass.
perf. part. παραλελυμένος, *paralytic,* Luke
5:18, 24, et al.
παραμείνας, nom. sg. m. aor. act.
part. . . . . παραμένω *(3887)*
παραμένειν, pres. act. infin. . . . . id.

(3887) **παραμένω,** fut. παραμενῶ, aor. παρέμεινα
[§27.1.a,d] *to stay beside; to continue, stay,
abide,* 1 Cor. 16:6; Heb. 7:23; met. *to remain constant in, persevere in,* James 1:25
παραμενῶ, 1 pers. sg. fut. act.
indic. . . . . παραμένω *(3887)*
παραμυθεῖσθε, 2 pers. pl. pres. mid./pass. dep.
imper. . . . . παραμυθέομαι *(3888)*

(3888) **παραμυθέομαι,** οῦμαι, fut. παραμυθήσομαι
[§17.Q] (παρά + μυθέομαι, *to speak,* from
μῦθος) *to exercise a gentle influence by
words; to soothe, comfort, console,* John
11:19, 31; 1 Thess. 5:14; *to cheer, exhort,*
1 Thess. 2:11
παραμυθήσωνται, 3 pers. pl. aor. mid. dep.
subj. . . . . παραμυθέομαι *(3888)*

(3889) **παραμυθία,** ας, ἡ [§2.B.b; 2.2] *comfort, encouragement,* 1 Cor. 14:3
παραμυθίαν, acc. sg. f. n. . . . . παραμυθία *(3889)*

(3890) **παραμύθιον,** ου, τό, nom. sg. neut. n. [§3.C.c]
gentle cheering, encouragement, Phil. 2:1
παραμυθούμενοι, nom. pl. m. pres. mid./pass.
dep. part. . . . . παραμυθέομαι *(3888)*

(3891) **παρανομέω,** ῶ, fut. παρανομήσω [§16.P]
(παρά + νόμος) *to violate or transgress
the law,* Acts 23:3

(3892) **παρανομία,** ας, ἡ [§2.B.b; 2.2] *violation of the
law, transgression,* 2 Pet. 2:16
παρανομίας, gen. sg. f. n. . . . . παρανομία *(3892)*
παρανομῶν, nom. sg. m. pres. act.
part. . . . . παρανομέω *(3891)*
παραπεσόντας, acc. pl. m. 2 aor. act. part.
[§37.1] . . . . παραπίπτω *(3895)*

(3893) **παραπικραίνω,** fut. παραπικρανῶ, aor.
παρεπίκρανα [§27.1.c,e] (παρά +
πικραίνω) pr. *to incite to bitter feelings;
to provoke;* absol. *to act provokingly, be
refractory,* Heb. 3:16

(3894) **παραπικρασμός,** οῦ, ὁ [§3.C.a] *exacerbation,
exasperation, provocation; contumacy,*

rebellion, Heb. 3:8, 15

παραπικρασμῷ, dat. sg. m. n. παραπικρασμός *(3894)*

(3895) **παραπίπτω,** fut. παραπεσοῦμαι, 2 aor. παρέπεσον [§37.1] (παρά + πίπτω) pr. *to fall by the side of;* met. *to fall off or away from, make defection from,* Heb. 6:6

παραπλεῦσαι, aor. act. infin. . . . . . παραπλέω *(3896)*

(3896) **παραπλέω,** fut. παραπλεύσομαι [§35.1.3] (παρά + πλέω) *to sail by or past* a place, Acts 20:16

(3897) **παραπλήσιον,** adv., *near to, with a near approach to,* Phil. 2:27

(†3897) **παραπλήσιος,** ον [§7.2] (παρά + πλησίος, *near*) pr. *near alongside;* met. *like, similar;* neut. παραπλήσιον, adverbially, *near to, with a near approach to,* Phil. 2:27

(3898) **παραπλησίως,** adv., *like, in the same or like manner,* Heb. 2:14

παραπορεύεσθαι, pres. mid./pass. dep. infin. (Mark 2:23, GNT, MT, TR & NA | διαπορεύεσθαι, WH) . . . . παραπορεύομαι *(3899)*

(3899) **παραπορεύομαι,** fut. παραπορεύσομαι [§14.N] (παρά + πορεύομαι) *to pass by the side of; to pass along,* Matt. 27:39; Mark 11:20; 15:29, et al.

παραπορευόμενοι, nom. pl. m. pres. mid./pass. dep. part. . . . . . παραπορεύομαι *(3899)*

(3900) **παράπτωμα,** ατος, τό nom. sg. neut. n. [§4.D.c] pr. *a stumbling aside, a false step;* in N.T. *a trespass, fault, offence, transgression,* Matt. 6:14, 15; Mark 11:25, 26; Rom. 4:25, et al.; *a fall, defalcation* in faith, Rom. 11:11, 12

παραπτώμασι(ν), dat. pl. neut. n. παράπτωμα *(3900)*
παραπτώματα, acc. pl. neut. n. . . . . id.
παραπτώματι, dat. sg. neut. n. . . . . id.
παραπτώματος, gen. sg. neut. n. . . . . id.
παραπτωμάτων, gen. pl. neut. n. . . . . id.

(†3901) **παραρρέω,** fut. παραρρεύσομαι, 2 aor. παρερρύην [§36.1] (παρά + ῥέω) *to flow beside; to glide aside from; to fall off* from profession, *decline* from steadfastness, *make forfeit* of faith. Heb. 2:1

παραρρυῶμεν, 1 pers. pl. 2 aor. act. subj. (Heb. 2:1, MT & TR | παραρυῶμεν, GNT, WH & NA) . . . . παραρρέω *(†3901)*

παραρυῶμεν, 1 pers. pl. 2 aor. act. subj. (Heb. 2:1, GNT, WH & NA | παραρρυῶμεν, MT & TR) . . . . id.

(†3902) **παράσημον,** ου, τό [§3.C.c] (παρά + σῆμα) *a distinguishing mark; an ensign or device* of a ship, Acts 28:11

παρασήμῳ, dat. sg. neut. n. . . . . παράσημον *(†3902)*
παρασκευαζόντων, gen. pl. m. pres. act.

part. . . . . παρασκευάζω *(3903)*

(3903) **παρασκευάζω,** fut. παρασκευάσω [§26.1] (παρά + σκευάζω, *to equip*) *to prepare, make ready,* 2 Cor. 9:2, 3; mid. *to prepare one's self, put one's self in readiness,* Acts 10:10; 1 Cor. 14:8

παρασκευάσεται, 3 pers. sg. fut. mid. dep. indic. . . . . παρασκευάζω *(3903)*

(3904) **παρασκευή,** ῆς, ἡ, nom. sg. f. n. [§2.B.a] *a getting ready, preparation;* in N.T. *preparation* for a feast, *day of preparation,* Matt. 27:62; Mark 15:42, et al.

παρασκευήν, acc. sg. f. n. . . . . . . παρασκευή *(3904)*
παρασκευῆς, gen. sg. f. n. (Luke 23:54, GNT, WH & NA | παρασκευή, MT & TR) id.
παραστῆναι, 2 aor. act. infin. [§29.X] {Acts 27:24} . . . . παρίστημι *(3936)*
παραστῆναι, aor. act. infin. {Acts 24:13} . id.
παραστήσατε, 2 pers. pl. aor. act. imper. . id.
παραστήσει, 3 pers. sg. fut. act. indic. . . . id.
παραστήσῃ, 3 pers. sg. aor. act. subj. . . . . id.
παραστησόμεθα, 1 pers. pl. fut. mid. dep. indic. [§29.Y] . . . . id.
παραστήσωμεν, 1 pers. pl. aor. act. subj. . . id.
παραστῆτε, 2 pers. pl. 2 aor. act. subj. . . . id.
παρασχών, nom. sg. m. 2 aor. act. part. . . . . παρέχω *(3930)*

(3905) **παρατείνω** (παρά + τείνω) *to extend, stretch out; to prolong, continue,* Acts 20:7

παρατηρεῖσθε, 2 pers. pl. pres. mid. indic. . . . . παρατηρέω *(3906)*

(3906) **παρατηρέω,** ῶ, fut. παρατηρήσω [§16.P] (παρά + τηρέω) *to watch narrowly,* Acts 9:24; *to observe or watch insidiously,* Mark 3:2; Luke 6:7; 14:1; 20:20; *to observe scrupulously,* Gal. 4:10

παρατηρήσαντες, nom. pl. m. aor. act. part. παρατηρέω *(3906)*
παρατηρήσεως, gen. sg. f. n. . . . παρατήρησις *(3907)*

(3907) **παρατήρησις,** εως, ἡ [§5.E.c] *careful watching, intent observation,* Luke 17:20

παρατηρούμενοι, nom. pl. m. pres. mid. part. παρατηρέω *(3906)*
παρατίθεμαι, 1 pers. sg. pres. mid. indic. [§28.W] . . . . παρατίθημι *(3908)*
παρατιθέμενα, acc. pl. neut. pres. pass. part. id.
παρατιθέμεμον, acc. sg. neut. pres. pass. part. id.
παρατιθέμενος, nom. sg. m. pres. mid. part. id.
παρατιθέναι, aor. pass. infin. (Mark 8:7, GNT, WH & NA | παραθεῖναι, MT & TR) . . . . παρατίθημι *(3908)*
παρατιθέσθωσαν, 3 pers. pl. pres. pass. imper. . . . . id.

(3908) **παρατίθημι,** fut. παραθήσω [§28.V] (παρά + τίθημι) *to place by the side of, or near; to*

set before, Mark 6:41; 8:6, 7; Luke 9:16;
met. *to set or lay before, propound,* Matt.
13:24, 31; *to inculcate,* Acts 17:3; *to deposit, commit to the charge of, intrust,*
Luke 12:48; 23:46; *to commend,* Acts
14:23
παρατιθῶσιν, 3 pers. pl. pres. act. subj. (Mark
8:6, GNT, WH & NA | παραθῶσι(ν),
MT & TR) . . . . παρατίθημι *(3908)*
παρατυγχάνοντας, acc. pl. m. pres. act.
part. . . . . παρατυγχάνω *(3909)*
(3909) **παρατυγχάνω,** fut. παρατεύξομαι, 2 aor.
παρέτυχον [§36.2] (παρά + τυγχάνω) *to
happen, to chance upon, chance to meet,*
Acts 17:17
(3910) **παραυτίκα,** adv. (παρά + αὐτίκα) *instantly,
immediately;* ὁ, ἡ, τό, παραυτίκα, *momentary, transient,* 2 Cor. 4:17
παραφέρεσθε, 2 pers. pl. pres. pass. imper.
(Heb. 13:9, GNT, WH, MT & NA |
περιφέρεσθε, TR) . . . . παραφέρω *(3911)*
παραφερόμεναι, nom. pl. f. pres. pass. part.
(Jude 12, GNT, WH, MT & NA | περιφερόμεναι, TR) . . . . id.
(3911) **παραφέρω,** fut. παροίσω, 2 aor. παρήνεγκον
[§36.1] (παρά + φέρω) *to carry past; to
cause to pass away,* Mark 14:36; Luke
22:42; pass. *to be swept along,* Jude 12;
to be led away, misled, seduced, Heb. 13:9
(3912) **παραφρονέω,** ῶ, fut. παραφρονήσω [§16.P]
(παρά + φρονέω) *to be beside one's wits;*
παραφρονῶν, *in foolish style,* 2 Cor. 11:23
(3913) **παραφρονία,** ας, ἡ [§2.B.b; 2.2] *madness,
folly,* 2 Pet. 2:16
παραφρονίαν, acc. sg. f. n. . . . . . παραφρονία *(3913)*
παραφρονῶν, nom. sg. m. pres. act.
part. . . . . παραφρονέω *(3912)*
(3914) **παραχειμάζω** (παρά + χειμάζω) *to winter,
spend the winter,* Acts 27:12; 28:11; 1 Cor.
16:6; Tit. 3:12
παραχειμάσαι, aor. act. infin. . . παραχειμάζω *(3914)*
(3915) **παραχειμασία,** ας, ἡ [§2.B.b; 2.2] *a wintering*
in a place, Acts 27:12
παραχειμασίαν, acc. sg. f. n. . . . παραχειμασία *(3915)*
παραχειμάσω, 1 pers. sg. fut. act.
indic. . . . . παραχειμάζω *(3914)*
(3916) **παραχρῆμα,** adv. (παρά + χρῆμα) *forthwith,
immediately,* Matt. 21:19, 20; Luke 1:64,
et al.
παρδάλει, dat. sg. f. n. . . . . πάρδαλις *(3917)*
(3917) **πάρδαλις,** εως, ἡ [§5.E.c] (equiv. to πάρδος)
a leopard or panther, Rev. 13:2
παρεβάλομεν, 1 pers. pl. 2 aor. act. indic.
[§27.2.d] . . . . παραβάλλω *(3846)*
παρέβη, 3 pers. sg. 2 aor. act. indic.

[§37.1] . . . . παραβαίνω *(3845)*
παρεβιάσαντο, 3 pers. pl. aor. mid. dep.
indic. . . . . παραβιάζομαι *(3849)*
παρεβιάσατο, 3 pers. sg. aor. mid. dep. indic. id.
παρεγένετο, 3 pers. sg. 2 aor. mid. dep. indic.
[§37.1] . . . . παραγίνομαι *(3854)*
παρεγενόμην, 1 pers. sg. 2 aor. mid. dep.
indic. . . . . id.
παρεγένοντο, 3 pers. pl. 2 aor. mid. dep.
indic. . . . . id.
παρεγίνοντο, 3 pers. pl. imperf. mid./pass.
dep. indic. . . . . id.
παρεδέχθησαν, 3 pers. pl. aor. pass. indic.
(Acts 15:4, GNT, WH & NA | ἀπεδέχθησαν, MT & TR) . . . . . . παραδέχομαι *(3858)*
παρεδίδετο, 3 pers. sg. imperf. pass. indic.
(1 Cor. 11:23, GNT, WH & NA | παρεδίδοτο, MT & TR) . . . . παραδίδωμι *(3860)*
παρεδίδοσαν, 3 pers. pl. imperf. act. indic.
(Acts 16:4, GNT, WH & NA | παρεδίδουν, MT & TR) . . . . id.
παρεδίδοτο, 3 pers. sg. imperf. pass. indic.
[§30.AA] (1 Cor. 11:23, MT & TR |
παρεδίδετο, GNT, WH & NA) . . . . . . id.
παρεδίδου, 3 pers. sg. imperf. act. indic.
[§31.2] . . . . id.
παρεδίδουν, 3 pers. pl. imperf. act. indic. . id.
παρεδόθη, 3 pers. sg. aor. pass. indic. [§30.4] id.
παρεδόθην, 1 pers. sg. aor. pass. indic. . . . id.
παρεδόθητε, 2 pers. pl. aor. pass. indic. . . id.
παρέδοσαν, 3 pers. pl. 2 aor. act. indic. . . id.
παρεδρεύοντες, nom. pl. m. pres. act. part.
(1 Cor. 9:13, GNT, WH & NA | προσεδρεύοντες, MT & TR) . . . . . . παρεδρεύω *(‡4332)*
(‡4332) **παρεδρεύω,** fut. παρεδρεύσω [§13.M]
(πάρεδρος, *one who sits by,* παρά +
ἕδρα) *to sit near; to attend, serve,* 1 Cor.
9:13
παρέδωκα, 1 pers. sg. aor. act. indic.
[§28.9.b,c] . . . . παραδίδωμι *(3860)*
παρεδώκαμεν, 1 pers. pl. aor. act. indic. . id.
παρέδωκαν, 3 pers. pl. aor. act. indic. . . . id.
παρέδωκας, 2 pers. sg. aor. act. indic. . . . id.
παρεδώκατε, 2 pers. pl. aor. act. indic. . . id.
παρέδωκε(ν), 3 pers. sg. aor. act. indic. . . id.
παρέθεντο, 3 pers. pl. 2 aor. mid. indic.
[§28.W] . . . . παρατίθημι *(3908)*
παρεθεωροῦντο, 3 pers. pl. imperf. pass.
indic. . . . . παραθεωρέω *(3865)*
παρέθηκαν, 3 pers. pl. aor. act.
indic. . . . . παρατίθημι *(3908)*
παρέθηκε(ν), 3 pers. sg. aor. act. indic. . . id.
πάρει, 2 pers. sg. pres. indic. . . . . πάρειμι *(3918)*
παρειμένας, acc. pl. f. perf. pass.
part. . . . . παρίημι *(3935)*

(3918) **πάρειμι** [§12.L] (παρά + εἰμί) *to be beside; to be present,* Luke 13:1, et al.; *to be come,* Matt. 26:50; John 7:6; 11:28; Col. 1:6, et al.; *to be in possession,* Heb. 13:5; 2 Pet. 1:9, 12; part. παρών, οὖσα, όν, *present,* 1 Cor. 5:3; τὸ παρόν, *the present time, the present,* Heb. 12:11
παρεῖναι, pres. infin. {Acts 24:19} . . . πάρειμι *(3918)*
παρεῖναι, 2 aor. act. infin.
{Luke 11:42} . . . . παρίημι *(3935)*

(3919) **παρεισάγω**, fut. παρεισάξω [§23.1.b] (παρά + εἰσάγω) *to introduce stealthily,* 2 Pet. 2:1

(3920) **παρείσακτος**, ον [§7.2] *clandestinely introduced, brought in stealthily,* Gal. 2:4
παρεισάκτους, acc. pl. m. adj. . . παρείσακτος *(3920)*
παρεισάξουσιν, 3 pers. pl. fut. act. indic. παρεισάγω *(3919)*
παρεισεδύησαν, 3 pers. pl. 2 aor. pass. indic. (Jude 4, WH | παρεισέδυσαν, GNT, MT, TR & NA) . . . . παρεισδύω *(†3921)*

(†3921) **παρεισδύω**, or παρεισδύνω, fut. παρεισδύσω, aor. παρεισέδυσα (παρά + εἰσδύω) *to enter privily, creep in stealthily, steal in*
παρεισέδυσαν, 3 pers. pl. aor. act. indic. (Jude 4, GNT, MT, TR & NA | παρεισεδύησαν, WH) . . . . παρεισδύω *(†3921)*
παρεισενέγκαντες, nom. pl. m. aor. act. part. [§36.1] . . . . παρεισφέρω *(3923)*

(3922) **παρεισέρχομαι**, 2 aor. παρεισῆλθον [§36.1] (παρά + εἰσέρχομαι) *to supervene,* Rom. 5:20; *to steal in,* Gal. 2:4
παρεισῆλθεν, 3 pers. sg. 2 aor. act. indic. . . . . παρεισέρχομαι *(3922)*
παρεισῆλθον, 3 pers. pl. 2 aor. act. indic. . . id.
πάρεισιν, 3 pers. pl. pres. indic. . . . . . πάρειμι *(3918)*
παρειστήκεισαν, 3 pers. pl. pluperf. act. indic. [§29.4] . . . . παρίστημι *(3936)*

(3923) **παρεισφέρω**, fut. παρεισοίσω, aor. παρεισήνεγκα [§36.1] (παρά + εἰσφέρω) *to bring in beside; to bring into play, superinduce, exhibit in addition,* 2 Pet. 1:5
παρεῖχε(ν), 3 pers. sg. imperf. act. indic. [§13.4] . . . . παρέχω *(3930)*
παρείχετο, 3 pers. sg. imperf. mid. indic. . . id.
παρεῖχον, 3 pers. pl. imperf. act. indic. . . . id.
παρεκάλει, 3 pers. sg. imperf. act. indic. παρακαλέω *(3870)*
παρεκάλεσα, 1 pers. sg. aor. act. indic. [§22.1] . . . . id.
παρεκάλεσαν, 3 pers. pl. aor. act. indic. . . id.
παρεκάλεσας, 2 pers. sg. aor. act. indic. . . id.
παρεκάλεσε(ν), 3 pers. sg. aor. act. indic. . . id.
παρεκαλοῦμεν, 1 pers. pl. imperf. act. indic. . . id.

παρεκάλουν, 3 pers. pl. imperf. act. indic. . . . . παρακαλέω *(3870)*
παρεκλήθη, 3 pers. sg. aor. pass. indic. [§22.4] . . . . id.
παρεκλήθημεν, 1 pers. pl. aor. pass. indic. . . id.
παρεκλήθησαν, 3 pers. pl. aor. pass. indic. . . id.

(3924) **παρεκτός**, adv. (παρά + ἐκτός) *without, on the outside; except,* Matt. 5:32; Acts 26:29; τὰ παρεκτός, *other matters,* 2 Cor. 11:28
παρέκυψεν, 3 pers. sg. aor. act. indic. . . . . παρακύπτω *(3879)*
παρέλαβε(ν), 3 pers. sg. 2 aor. act. indic. [§36.2] . . . . παραλαμβάνω *(3880)*
παρέλαβες, 2 pers. sg. 2 aor. act. indic. . . . id.
παρελάβετε, 2 pers. pl. 2 aor. act. indic. . . id.
παρέλαβον, 1 pers. sg. 2 aor. act. indic. {1 Cor. 15:3} . . . . id.
παρέλαβον, 3 pers. pl. 2 aor. act. indic. {John 1:11} . . . . id.
παρελάβοσαν, 3 pers. pl. 2 aor. act. indic. [§35.13] (2 Thess. 3:6, GNT & NA | παρέλαβον, MT | παρέλαβεν, TR | παρελάβετε, WH) . . . . id.
παρελέγοντο, 3 pers. pl. imperf. mid./pass. dep. indic. . . . . παραλέγομαι *(3881)*
παρελεύσεται, 3 pers. sg. fut. mid. dep. indic. [§36.1] . . . . παρέρχομαι *(3928)*
παρελεύσονται, 3 pers. pl. fut. mid. dep. indic. . . . . id.
παρεληλυθέναι, 2 perf. act. infin. . . . . id.
παρεληλυθώς, nom. sg. m. 2 perf. act. part. . . id.
παρελθάτω, 3 pers. sg. 2 aor. act. imper. [§35.12] (Matt. 26:39, GNT, WH & NA | παρελθέτω, MT & TR) . . . . id.
παρελθεῖν, 2 aor. act. indic. . . . . id.
παρελθέτω, 3 pers. sg. 2 aor. act. imper. (Matt. 26:39, MT & TR | παρελθάτω, GNT, WH & NA) . . . . id.
παρέλθη, 3 pers. sg. 2 aor. act. subj. . . . . . id.
παρελθόντες, nom. pl. m. 2 aor. act. part. . . id.
παρελθών, nom. sg. m. 2 aor. act. part. . . id.
παρέλθωσι(ν), 3 pers. pl. 2 aor. act. subj. . . id.
παρεμβαλοῦσιν, 3 pers. pl. fut. act. indic. (Luke 19:43, GNT, WH & NA | περιβαλοῦσιν, MT & TR) . . . . . παρεμβάλλω *(‡4016)*

(‡4016) **παρεμβάλλω,** *to cast up, set up, throw up* a palisade
παρεμβολάς, acc. pl. f. n. . . . . παρεμβολή *(3925)*

(3925) **παρεμβολή**, ῆς, ἡ [§2.B.a] (παρεμβάλλω, *to interpose or insert,* παρά + ἐμβάλλω) *an insertion besides;* later, *a marshalling* of an army; *an array* of battle, *army,* Heb. 11:34; *a camp,* Heb. 13:11, 13; Rev. 20:9; *a standing camp, fortress, citadel, castle,* Acts 21:34, 37; 22:24; 23:10, 16, 32

παρεμβολήν, acc. sg. f. n. . . . . . . παρεμβολή *(3925)*
παρεμβολῆς, gen. sg. f. n. . . . . id.
παρένεγκε, 2 pers. sg. 2 aor. act. imper.
[§36.1] . . . . παραφέρω *(3911)*
παρενεγκεῖν, 2 aor. act. infin. (Luke 22:42,
MT & TR | παρένεγκε, GNT, WH &
NA) . . . . id.
παρενοχλεῖν, pres. act. infin. . . . παρενοχλέω *(3926)*
(3926) **παρενοχλέω, ῶ,** fut. παρενοχλήσω [§16.P]
(παρά + ἐνοχλέω) *to superadd molesta-
tion; to trouble, harass,* Acts 15:19
παρέξει, 3 pers. sg. fut. act. indic. (Luke 7:4,
MT & TR | παρέξῃ, GNT, WH &
NA) . . . . παρέχω *(3930)*
παρέξῃ, 3 pers. sg. 2 fut. mid. dep. indic. or
aor. act. subj. (Luke 7:4, GNT, WH & NA
| παρέξει, MT & TR) . . . . id.
παρεπίδημοι, nom. pl. m. adj. . . παρεπίδημος *(3927)*
παρεπιδήμοις, dat. pl. m. adj. . . . . id.
(3927) **παρεπίδημος,** ον [§7.2] (παρά + ἐπίδημος)
*residing in a country not one's own, a so-
journer, stranger,* Heb. 11:13; 1 Pet. 1:1;
2:11
παρεπιδήμους, acc. pl. m. adj. . . παρεπίδημος *(3927)*
παρεπίκραναν, 3 pers. pl. aor. act. indic.
[§27.1.e] . . . . παραπικραίνω *(3893)*
παρεπορεύοντο, 3 pers. pl. imperf. mid./pass.
dep. indic. (Mark 9:30, GNT, MT, TR &
NA | ἐπορεύοντο, WH) . . παραπορεύομαι *(3899)*
παρέρχεσθε, 2 pers. pl. pres. mid./pass. dep.
indic. . . . . παρέρχομαι *(3928)*
παρέρχεται, 3 pers. sg. pres. mid./pass. dep.
indic. . . . . id.
(3928) **παρέρχομαι,** fut. παρελεύσομαι, 2 aor.
παρῆλθον [§36.1] (παρά + ἔρχομαι) *to
pass beside, pass along, pass by,* Matt.
8:28; Mark 6:48; *to pass, elapse,* as time,
Matt. 14:15; Acts 27:9; *to pass away, be
removed,* Matt. 26:39, 42; Mark 14:35;
met. *to pass away, disappear, vanish, perish,* Matt. 5:18; 24:34, 35; *to become vain,
be rendered void,* Matt. 5:18; Mark 13:31;
trans. *to pass by, disregard, neglect,* Luke
11:42; 15:29; *to come to the side of, come
to,* Luke 12:37; 17:7
πάρεσιν, acc. sg. f. n. . . . . πάρεσις *(3929)*
(3929) **πάρεσις,** εως, ἡ [§5.E.c] *a letting pass; a passing over,* Rom. 3:25
παρεσκευασμένοι, nom. pl. m. perf. pass.
part. [§26.1] . . . . παρασκευάζω *(3903)*
παρεσκεύασται, 3 pers. sg. perf. pass. indic. id.
πάρεσμεν, 1 pers. pl. pres. indic. . . . . πάρειμι *(3918)*
παρέσται, 3 pers. sg. fut. indic. (Rev. 17:8,
GNT, WH, MT & NA | καίπερ ἐστιν,
TR) . . . . id.

πάρεστε, 2 pers. pl. pres. indic. . . . . . . πάρειμι *(3918)*
παρέστη, 3 pers. sg. 2 aor. act. indic.
[§29.X] . . . . παρίστημι *(3936)*
παρέστηκεν, 3 pers. sg. perf. act. indic. . . id.
παρεστηκόσιν, dat. pl. m. perf. act. part.
(Mark 14:69, MT & TR | παρεστῶσιν,
GNT, WH & NA) . . . . id.
παρεστηκότων, gen. pl. m. perf. act. part. id.
παρεστηκώς, nom. sg. m. perf. act. part. . id.
παρέστησαν, 3 pers. pl. aor. act. indic. . . . id.
παρεστήσατε, 2 pers. pl. aor. act. indic. . . id.
παρέστησεν, 3 pers. sg. aor. act. indic. . . . id.
πάρεστι(ν), 3 pers. sg. pres. indic. . . . . πάρειμι *(3918)*
παρεστῶσιν, dat. pl. m. perf. act. part.
[§35.8] . . . . παρίστημι *(3936)*
παρεστῶτα, acc. sg. m. perf. act. part. contr. id.
παρεστῶτες, nom. pl. m. perf. act. part.
contr. . . . . id.
παρέσχον, 3 pers. pl. 2 aor. act. indic.
[§36.4] . . . . παρέχω *(3930)*
παρέτεινε(ν), 3 pers. sg. imperf. act.
indic. . . . . παρατείνω *(3905)*
παρετήρουν, 3 pers. pl. imperf. act.
indic. . . . . παρατηρέω *(3906)*
παρετηροῦντο, 3 pers. pl. imperf. mid. indic.
(Luke 6:7; Acts 9:24, GNT, WH & NA |
παρετήρουν, MT & TR) . . . . id.
πάρεχε, 2 pers. sg. pres. act. imper. . . παρέχω *(3930)*
παρέχειν, pres. act. infin. . . . . id.
παρέχεσθε, 2 pers. pl. pres. mid. imper. . . . id.
παρέχετε, 2 pers. pl. pres. act. indic. . . . . id.
παρεχέτω, 3 pers. sg. pres. act. imper. . . . id.
παρεχόμενος, nom. sg. m. pres. mid. part. id.
παρέχοντι, dat. sg. m. pres. act. part. . . . . id.
παρέχουσι(ν), 3 pers. pl. pres. act. indic. . id.
(3930) **παρέχω,** fut. παρέξω, 2 aor. παρέσχον
[§36.4] (παρά + ἔχω) *to hold beside; to
hold out to, offer, present,* Luke 6:29; *to
confer, render,* Luke 7:4; Acts 22:2; 28:2;
Col. 4:1; *to afford, furnish,* Acts 16:16;
17:31; 19:24; 1 Tim. 6:17; *to exhibit,* Tit.
2:7; *to be the cause of, occasion,* Matt.
26:10; Mark 14:6; Luke 11:7, et al.
παρηγγείλαμεν, 1 pers. pl. aor. act. indic.
[§27.1.d] . . . . παραγγέλλω *(3853)*
παρήγγειλαν, 3 pers. pl. aor. act. indic. . . id.
παρήγγειλεν, 3 pers. sg. aor. act. indic. . . . id.
παρήγγελλεν, 3 pers. sg. imperf. act. indic.
(Luke 8:29, WH | παρήγγειλεν, GNT,
MT, TR & NA) . . . . id.
παρηγγέλλομεν, 1 pers. pl. imperf. act. indic. id.
παρῆγεν, 3 pers. sg. imperf. act. indic. (John
8:59, MT & TR | GNT, WH & NA
omit) . . . . παράγω *(3855)*
(3931) **παρηγορία,** ας, ἡ, nom. sg. f. n. [§2.B.b; 2.2]

(παρηγορέω, *to exhort; to console*) *exhortation; comfort, solace, consolation,* Col. 4:11

παρηκολούθηκας, 2 pers. sg. perf. act. indic. . . . . παρακολουθέω *(3877)*

παρηκολουθηκότι, dat. sg. m. perf. act. part.   id.

παρηκολούθησας, 2 pers. sg. aor. act. indic. (2 Tim. 3:10, GNT, WH & NA | παρηκολούθηκας, MT & TR) . . . . id.

παρῆλθε(ν), 3 pers. sg. 2 aor. act. indic. . . . . παρέρχομαι *(3928)*

παρῆλθον, 1 pers. sg. 2 aor. act. indic. . . . id.

παρήνει, 3 pers. sg. imperf. act. indic. [§13.2] . . . . παραινέω *(3867)*

παρῆσαν, 3 pers. pl. imperf. indic. . . . πάρειμι *(3918)*

παρῃτημένον, acc. sg. m. perf. pass. part. [§13.2] . . . . παραιτέομαι *(3868)*

παρῃτήσαντο, 3 pers. pl. aor. mid. dep. indic.   id.

παρῃτοῦντο, 3 pers. pl. imperf. mid./pass. dep. indic. (Mark 15:6, GNT, WH & NA | ὅνπερ ᾐτοῦντο, MT & TR) . . . . id.

(3932) **παρθενία**, ας, ἡ [§2.B.b; 2.2] *virginity,* Luke 2:36

παρθενίας, gen. sg. f. n. . . . . παρθενία *(3932)*

παρθένοι, nom. pl. f. n. . . . . παρθένος *(3933)*

παρθένοις, dat. pl. f. n. . . . . id.

παρθένον, acc. sg. f. n. . . . . id.

(3933) **παρθένος**, ου, ἡ, nom. sg. f. n. [§3.C.b] *a virgin, maid,* Matt. 1:23; 25:1, 7, 11; Acts 21:9, et al.; in N.T. also masc., *chaste,* Rev. 14:4

παρθένου, gen. sg. f. n. . . . . παρθένος *(3933)*

παρθένων, gen. pl. f. n. . . . . id.

Πάρθοι, nom. pl. m. n. . . . . Πάρθος *(3934)*

(3934) **Πάρθος**, ου, ὁ [§3.C.a] *a Parthian, a native of Parthia in central Asia,* Acts 2:9

(3935) **παρίημι**, fut. παρήσω [§32.CC] (παρά + ἵημι) *to let pass beside, let fall beside; to relax;* perf. pass. part. παρειμένος, *hanging down helplessly, unstrung, feeble,* Heb. 12:12

παριστάνετε, 2 pers. pl. pres. act. indic. {Rom. 6:16} . . . . παρίστημι *(3936)*

παριστάνετε, 2 pers. pl. pres. act. imper. {Rom. 6:13} . . . . id.

(3936) **παρίστημι**, and later also παριστάνω, fut. παραστήσω [§29.X] (παρά + ἵστημι) trans. *to place beside; to have in readiness, provide,* Acts 23:24; *to range beside, to place at the disposal of,* Matt. 26:53; Acts 9:41; *to present* to God, *dedicate, consecrate, devote,* Luke 2:22; Rom. 6:13, 19; *to prove, demonstrate, show,* Acts 1:3; 24:13; *to commend, recommend,* 1 Cor. 8:8; intrans. perf. παρέστηκα, part. παρεστώς,

pluperf. παρειστήκειν, 2 aor. παρέστην, and mid., *to stand by or before,* Acts 27:24; Rom. 14:10; *to stand by, to be present,* Mark 14:47, 69, 70; *to stand in attendance, attend,* Luke 1:19; 19:24; of time, *to be present, have come,* Mark 4:29; *to stand by* in aid, *assist, support,* Rom. 16:2

παρίστησι(ν), 3 pers. sg. pres. act. indic. (1 Cor. 8:8, MT & TR | παραστήσει, GNT, WH & NA) . . . . παρίστημι *(3936)*

Παρμενᾶν, acc. sg. m. n. . . . . Παρμενᾶς *(3937)*

(3937) **Παρμενᾶς**, ᾶ, ὁ [§2.4] *Parmenas,* pr. name, Acts 6:5

(3938) **πάροδος**, ου, ἡ [§3.C.b] (παρά + ὁδός) *a way by; a passing by;* ἐν παρόδῳ, *in passing, by the way,* 1 Cor. 16:7

παρόδῳ, dat. sg. f. n. . . . . πάροδος *(3938)*

παροικεῖς, 2 pers. sg. pres. act. indic. . . . . παροικέω *(3939)*

(3939) **παροικέω**, ῶ, fut. παροικήσω [§16.P] *to dwell beside;* later, *to reside in a place as a stranger, sojourn, be a stranger or sojourner,* Luke 24:18; Heb. 11:9

(3940) **παροικία**, ας, ἡ [§2.B.b; 2.2] *a sojourning, temporary residence in a foreign land,* Acts 13:17; 1 Pet. 1:17

παροικίᾳ, dat. sg. f. n. . . . . παροικία *(3940)*

παροικίας, gen. sg. f. n. . . . . id.

πάροικοι, nom. pl. m. adj. . . . . πάροικος *(3941)*

πάροικον, nom. sg. neut. adj. . . . . id.

(3941) **πάροικος**, ον, nom. sg. m. adj. [§7.2] (παρά + οἶκος) *a neighbor;* later, *a sojourner, temporary resident, stranger,* Acts 7:6, 29; Eph. 2:19; 1 Pet. 2:11

παροίκους, acc. pl. m. adj. . . . . πάροικος *(3941)*

(3942) **παροιμία**, ας, ἡ [§2.B.b; 2.2] (πάροιμος, *by the road, trite,* παρά + οἶμος) *a by-word, proverb, adage,* 2 Pet. 2:22; in N.T. *an obscure saying, enigma,* John 16:25, 29; *a parable, similitude, figurative discourse,* John 10:6

παροιμίαις, dat. pl. f. n. . . . . παροιμία *(3942)*

παροιμίαν, acc. sg. f. n. . . . . id.

παροιμίας, gen. sg. f. n. . . . . id.

πάροινον, acc. sg. m. adj. . . . . πάροινος *(3943)*

(3943) **πάροινος**, ον [§7.2] (παρά + οἶνος) pr. *pertaining to wine; given to wine, prone to intemperance, drunken;* hence, *quarrelsome, insolent, overbearing,* 1 Tim. 3:3; Tit. 1:7

(3944) **παροίχομαι**, fut. παροιχήσομαι, perf. παρῴχημαι [§13.2] (παρά, + οἴχομαι, *to depart*) *to have gone by;* perf. part. παρῳχημένος, *by-gone,* Acts 14:16

παρόμοια, acc. pl. neut. adj. . . . . . παρόμοιος *(3946)*

παρομοιάζετε, 2 pers. pl. pres. act.

indic. . . . . παρομοιάζω *(3945)*

(3945) **παρομοιάζω**, fut. παρομοιάσω [§26.1] *to be like, to resemble,* Matt. 23:27

(3946) **παρόμοιος**, οία, οιον [§7.1] (παρά + ὅμοιος) *nearly resembling, similar, like,* Mark 7:8, 13

παρόν, acc. sg. neut. pres. part. . . . . . . πάρειμι *(3918)*

παρόντες, nom. pl. m. pres. part. . . . . . . id.

παρόντος, gen. sg. neut. pres. part. . . . . id.

παροξύνεται, 3 pers. sg. pres. pass. indic. . . . . παροξύνω *(3947)*

(3947) **παροξύνω**, fut. παροξυνῶ [§27.1.a] (παρά + ὀξύνω, *to sharpen,* from ὀξύς) *to sharpen;* met. *to incite, stir up,* Acts 17:16; *to irritate, provoke,* 1 Cor. 13:5

παροξυσμόν, acc. sg. m. n. . . . . . παροξυσμός *(3948)*

(3948) **παροξυσμός**, οῦ, ὁ, nom. sg. m. n. [§3.C.a] *an inciting, incitement,* Heb. 10:24; *a sharp fit of anger, sharp contention, angry dispute,* Acts 15:39

παροργίζετε, 2 pers. pl. pres. act. imper. . . . . παροργίζω *(3949)*

(3949) **παροργίζω**, fut. παροργίσω [§26.1] (παρά + ὀργίζω) *to provoke to anger, irritate, exasperate,* Rom. 10:19; Eph. 6:4

(3950) **παροργισμός**, οῦ, ὁ [§3.C.a] *provocation to anger; anger excited, indignation, wrath,* Eph. 4:26

παροργισμῷ, dat. sg. m. n. . . . . παροργισμός *(3950)*

παροργιῶ, 1 pers. sg. fut. act. indic. Att. [§35.11] . . . . παροργίζω *(3949)*

(3951) **παροτρύνω**, fut. παροτρυνῶ [§27.1.a] (παρά + ὀτρύνω, *to excite*) *to stir up, incite, instigate,* Acts 13:50

παρούσῃ, dat. sg. f. pres. part. . . . . . . πάρειμι *(3918)*

(3952) **παρουσία**, ας, ἡ, nom. sg. f. n. [§2.B.b; 2.2] *presence,* 2 Cor. 10:10; Phil. 2:12; *a coming, arrival, advent,* Phil. 1:26; Matt. 24:3, 27, 37, 39; 1 Cor. 15:23, et al.

παρουσίᾳ, dat. sg. f. n. . . . . παρουσία *(3952)*

παρουσίαν, acc. sg. f. n. . . . . id.

παρουσίας, gen. sg. f. n. . . . . id.

παροῦσιν, dat. pl. neut. pres. part. . . . πάρειμι *(3918)*

παροψίδος, gen. sg. f. n. . . . . παροψίς *(3953)*

(3953) **παροψίς**, ίδος, ἡ [§4.2.c] (παρά + ὄψον) pr. *a dainty side-dish;* meton. *a plate, platter,* Matt. 23:25, 26

(3954) **παρρησία**, ας, ἡ, nom. sg. f. n. [§2.B.b; 2.2] (ῥῆσις, *a speech*) *freedom in speaking, boldness of speech,* Acts 4:13; παρρησίᾳ, as an adv., *freely, boldly,* John 7:13, 26; so μετὰ παρρησίας, Acts 2:29; 4:29, 31; *license, authority,* Philemon 8; *confidence, assurance,* 2 Cor. 7:4; Eph. 3:12; Heb. 3:6; 10:19; *openness, frankness,* 2 Cor. 3:12;

παρρησίᾳ, and ἐν παρρησίᾳ, adverbially, *openly, plainly, perspicuously, unambiguously,* Mark 8:32; John 10:24; *publicly, before all,* John 7:4

παρρησίᾳ, dat. sg. f. n. . . . . παρρησία *(3954)*

παρρησιάζεσθαι, pres. mid./pass. dep. infin. . . . . παρρησιάζομαι *(3955)*

(3955) **παρρησιάζομαι**, fut. παρρησιάσομαι [§26.1] *to speak plainly, freely, boldly, and confidently,* Acts 13:46; 14:3, et al.

παρρησιαζόμενοι, nom. pl. m. pres. mid./pass. dep. part. . . . . παρρησιάζομαι *(3955)*

παρρησιαζόμενος, nom. sg. m. pres. mid./pass. dep. part. . . . . id.

παρρησίαν, acc. sg. f. n. . . . . παρρησία *(3954)*

παρρησίας, gen. sg. f. n. . . . . id.

παρρησιασάμενοι, nom. pl. m. aor. mid. dep. part. . . . . παρρησιάζομαι *(3955)*

παρρησιάσωμαι, 1 pers. sg. aor. mid. dep. subj. . . . . id.

παρῴκησεν, 3 pers. sg. aor. act. indic. [§13.2] . . . . παροικέω *(3939)*

παρών, nom. sg. m. pres. part. (GNT, TR, WH & NA | παρῶν, WH) . . . . πάρειμι *(3918)*

παρωξύνετο, 3 pers. sg. imperf. pass. indic. . . . . παροξύνω *(3947)*

παρώτρυναν, 3 pers. pl. aor. act. indic. . . . . παροτρύνω *(3951)*

παρῳχημέναις, dat. pl. f. perf. mid./pass. dep. part. [§13.2] . . . . παροίχομαι *(3944)*

(3956) **πᾶς**, πᾶσα, πᾶν, nom. sg. m. adj., gen. παντός, πάσης, παντός [§7.H.b] *all;* in the sg. *all, the whole,* usually when the substantive has the article, Matt. 6:29; 8:32; Acts 19:26, et al.; *every,* only with an anarthrous subst., Matt. 3:10; 4:4, et al.; pl. *all,* Matt. 1:17, et al. freq.; πάντα, *in all respects,* Acts 20:35; 1 Cor. 9:25; 10:33; 11:2; by a Hebraism, a negative with πᾶς is sometimes equivalent to οὐδείς or μηδείς, Matt. 24:22; Luke 1:37; Acts 10:14; Rom. 3:20; 1 Cor. 1:29; Eph. 4:29, et al.

πᾶσα, nom. sg. f. adj. . . . . πᾶς *(3956)*

πᾶσαι, nom. pl. f. adj. . . . . id.

πάσαις, dat. pl. f. adj. . . . . id.

πᾶσαν, acc. sg. f. adj. . . . . id.

πάσας, acc. pl. f. adj. . . . . id.

πάσῃ, dat. sg. f. adj. . . . . id.

πάσης, gen. sg. f. adj. . . . . id.

πᾶσι(ν), dat. pl. m. adj. {Rom. 1:7} . . . . . id.

πᾶσι(ν), dat. pl. neut. adj. {Rom. 1:5} . . . id.

(3957) **πάσχα**, τό, indecl. (Hebrew פֶּסַח, Aramaic פַּסְחָא, from פָּסַח, *to pass over*) *the passover, the paschal lamb,* Matt. 26:17; Mark

14:12; met. used of Christ, the true *paschal lamb*, 1 Cor. 5:7; *the feast of the passover, the day on which the paschal lamb was slain and eaten,* the 14th of Nisan, Matt. 26:18; Mark 14:1; Heb. 11:28; more genr. *the whole paschal festival,* including the seven days of *the feast of unleavened bread,* Matt. 26:2; Luke 2:41; John 2:13, et al.

πάσχει, 3 pers. sg. pres. act. indic. .... πάσχω *(3958)*

πάσχειν, pres. act. infin. .... id.

πάσχετε, 2 pers. pl. pres. act. indic. ..... id.

πασχέτω, 3 pers. sg. pres. act. imper. .... id.

πάσχοιτε, 2 pers. pl. pres. act. opt. ...... id.

πάσχομεν, 1 pers. pl. pres. act. indic. .... id.

πάσχοντες, nom. pl. m. pres. act. part. .. id.

(3958) **πάσχω,** fut. πείσομαι, 2 aor. ἔπαθον, perf. πέπονθα [§36.4] *to be affected by* a thing, whether good or bad, *to suffer, endure* evil, Matt. 16:21; 17:12, 15; 27:19; absol. *to suffer* death, Luke 22:15; 24:26, et al.

πάσχων, nom. sg. m. pres. act. part. .. πάσχω *(3958)*

πασῶν, gen. pl. f. adj. .... πᾶς *(3956)*

πατάξαι, aor. act. infin. .... πατάσσω *(3960)*

πατάξας, nom. sg. m. aor. act. part. .... id.

πατάξῃ, 3 pers. sg. aor. act. subj. (Rev. 19:15, GNT, WH, MT & NA | πατάσσῃ, TR) id.

πατάξομεν, 1 pers. pl. fut. act. indic. .... id.

πατάξω, 1 pers. sg. fut. act. indic. ...... id.

(3959) **Πάταρα,** ων, τά [§3.C.c] *Patara,* a city on the sea-coast of Lycia, in Asia Minor, Acts 21:1

Πάταρα, acc. pl. neut. .... Πάταρα *(3959)*

πατάσσῃ, 3 pers. sg. aor. act. subj. (Rev. 19:15, TR | πατάξῃ, GNT, WH, MT & NA) .... πατάσσω *(3960)*

(3960) **πατάσσω,** fut. πατάξω, aor. ἐπάταξα [§26.3] *to strike, beat upon; to smite, wound,* Matt. 26:51; Luke 22:49, 50; by impl. *to kill, slay,* Matt. 26:31; Mark 14:27; Acts 7:24; *to strike gently,* Acts 12:7; from the Hebrew, *to smite* with disease, plagues, etc., Acts 12:23; Rev. 11:6; 19:15

πατεῖ, 3 pers. sg. pres. act. indic. ..... πατέω *(3961)*

πατεῖν, pres. act. infin. .... id.

πάτερ, voc. sg. m. n. [§6.1] .... πατήρ *(3962)*

πατέρα, acc. sg. m. n. .... id.

πατέρας, acc. pl. m. n. .... id.

πατέρες, nom. pl. m. n. {Acts 7:11} ..... id.

πατέρες, voc. pl. m. n. {Acts 7:2} .... id.

πατέρων, gen. pl. m. n. .... id.

(3961) **πατέω,** ῶ, fut. πατήσω [§16.P] (πάτος, *a path*) intrans. *to tread,* Luke 10:19; trans. *to tread* the winepress, Rev. 14:20; 19:15; *to trample,* Luke 21:24; Rev. 11:2

(3962) **πατήρ,** τέρος, τρός, ὁ, nom. sg. m. n. [§6.1]

a father, Matt. 2:22; 4:21, 22; spc. used of God, as the *Father* of man by creation, preservation, etc. Matt. 5:16, 45, 48; and peculiarly as the *Father* of our Lord Jesus Christ, Matt. 7:21; 2 Cor. 1:3; *the founder of a race, remote progenitor, forefather, ancestor,* Matt. 3:9; 23:30, 32; *an elder, senior, father* in age, 1 John 2:13, 14; *a* spiritual *father,* 1 Cor. 4:15; *father* by origination, John 8:44; Heb. 12:9; used as an appellation of honor, Matt. 23:9; Acts 7:2

πατήσουσι(ν), 3 pers. pl. fut. act. indic. πατέω *(3961)*

(3963) **Πάτμος,** ου, ἡ [§3.C.b] *Patmos,* an island in the Aegean sea, Rev. 1:9

Πάτμῳ, dat. sg. f. n. .... Πάτμος *(3963)*

πατουμένη, nom. sg. m. pres. pass. part. [§17.Q] .... πατέω *(3961)*

πατραλῴαις, dat. pl. m. n. πατραλῴας (1 Tim. 1:9, TR | πατρολῴαις, GNT, WH, MT & NA) .... πατραλῴας *(3964)*

(3964) **πατραλῴας,** or πατραλῴης, ου, ὁ [§2.B.c; 2.4] (πατήρ + ἀλοάω or ἀλοιάω, *to smite*) *a striker of his father; a parricide,* 1 Tim. 1:9

πατράσιν, dat. pl. m. n. .... πατήρ *(3962)*

πατρί, dat. sg. m. n. .... id.

(3965) **πατριά,** ᾶς, ἡ, nom. sg. f. n. [§2.B.b; 2.2] *descent, lineage; a family, tribe, race,* Luke 2:4; Acts 3:25; Eph. 3:15

πατριαί, nom. pl. f. n. .... πατριά *(3965)*

πατριάρχαι, nom. pl. m. n. ..... πατριάρχης *(3966)*

πατριάρχας, acc. pl. m. n. .... id.

(3966) **πατριάρχης,** ου, ὁ, nom. sg. m. n. [§2.B.c; 2.4] (πατριά + ἀρχή) *a patriarch, head or founder of a family,* Acts 2:29; 7:8, 9; Heb. 7:4

πατριάρχου, gen. sg. m. n. ...... πατριάρχης *(3966)*

πατριᾶς, gen. sg. f. n. .... πατριά *(3965)*

πατρίδα, acc. sg. f. n. .... πατρίς *(3968)*

πατρίδι, dat. sg. f. n. .... id.

(3967) **πατρικός,** ή, όν [§7.F.a] *from fathers or ancestors, ancestral, paternal,* Gal. 1:14

πατρικῶν, gen. pl. m. adj. .... πατρικός *(3967)*

(3968) **πατρίς,** ίδος, ἡ [§4.2.c] *one's native place, country, or city,* Matt. 13:54, 57; Mark 6:1, 4; Luke 4:23, 24; John 4:44; *a* heavenly *country,* Heb. 11:14

Πατροβᾶν, acc. sg. m. n. (Rom. 16:14, GNT, MT & NA | πατρόβαν, TR & WH) .... Πατροβᾶς *(†3969)*

(†3969) **Πατροβᾶς,** ᾶ, ὁ [§2.4] *Patrobas,* pr. name

πατρολῴαις, dat. pl. m. n. (1 Tim. 1:9, GNT, WH, MT & NA | πατραλῴαις, TR) .... πατρολῴας *(‡3964)*

(‡3964) **πατρολῴας,** ου, ὁ, *one who kills one's father,*

a patricide

(3970) **πατροπαράδοτος**, ον [§7.2] (πατήρ + παραδοτός, from παραδίδωμι) *handed down or received by tradition from one's fathers or ancestors,* 1 Pet. 1:18

πατροπαραδότου, gen. sg. f.
adj. . . . . πατροπαράδοτος (3970)
πατρός, gen. sg. m. n. . . . . πατήρ (3962)
πατρῴοις, dat. pl. neut. adj. . . . . πατρῷος (3971)

(3971) **πατρῷος**, α, ον [§7.1] *received from one's ancestors, paternal, ancestral,* Acts 22:3; 24:14; 28:17

πατρῴου, gen. sg. m. adj. . . . . πατρῷος (3971)
πατρῴῳ, dat. sg. m. adj. . . . . id.
παύεται, 3 pers. sg. pres. mid. indic. . . . παύω (3973)
Παῦλε, voc. sg. m. n. . . . . Παῦλος (3972)
Παῦλον, acc. sg. m. n. . . . . id.

(3972) **Παῦλος**, ου, ὁ, nom. sg. m. n. [§3.C.a] *Paulus, Paul,* pr. name   I. *Paul, the Apostle,* Acts 13:9, et al. freq.   II. *Sergius Paulus, the deputy or proconsul of Cyprus,* Acts 13:7

Παύλου, gen. sg. m. n. . . . . Παῦλος (3972)
Παύλῳ, dat. sg. m. n. . . . . id.
παύομαι, 1 pers. sg. pres. mid. indic. . . . παύω (3973)
παυόμεθα, 1 pers. pl. pres. mid. indic. . . . id.
παύσασθαι, aor. mid. infin. . . . . id.
παυσάτω, 3 pers. sg. aor. act. imper. . . . . id.
παύσῃ, 2 pers. sg. fut. mid. dep. indic. . . id.
παύσονται, 3 pers. pl. fut. mid. dep. indic. id.

(3973) **παύω**, fut. παύσω [§13.M] *to cause to pause or cease, restrain, prohibit,* 1 Pet. 3:10; mid. perf. (pass. form) πέπαυμαι, *to cease, stop, leave off, desist, refrain,* Luke 5:4; 8:24, et al.

(3974) **Πάφος**, ου, ἡ [§3.C.b] *Paphos,* the chief city in the island of Cyprus

Πάφου, gen. sg. f. n. . . . . Πάφος (3974)

(3975) **παχύνω**, fut. παχυνῶ, aor. pass. ἐπαχύνθην [§27.1.a; 27.3] (παχύς, *fat, gross*) *to fatten, make gross;* met. pass. *to be rendered gross, dull, unfeeling,* Matt. 13:15; Acts 28:27

πέδαις, dat. pl. f. n. . . . . πέδη (3976)
πέδας, acc. pl. f. n. . . . . id.

(3976) **πέδη**, ης, ἡ [§2.B.a] (πέζα, *the foot*) *a fetter,* Mark 5:4; Luke 8:29

(3977) **πεδινός**, ή, όν [§7.F.a] (πεδίον, *a plain,* πέδον, *the ground*) *level, flat,* Luke 6:17

πεδινοῦ, gen. sg. m. adj. . . . . πεδινός (3977)
πεζεύειν, pres. act. infin. . . . . πεζεύω (3978)

(3978) **πεζεύω**, fut. πεζεύσω [§13.M] (πέζα, *the foot*) pr. *to travel on foot; to travel by land,* Acts 20:13

(3979) **πεζῇ**, adv. (pr. dat. f. of πεζός, ή, όν, *pedestrian,* from πέζα) *on foot,* or, *by land,*

Matt. 14:13; Mark 6:33
πειθαρχεῖν, pres. act. infin. . . . . . . πειθαρχέω (3980)

(3980) **πειθαρχέω**, ῶ, fut. πειθαρχήσω [§16.P] (πείθομαι + ἀρχή) *to obey* one *in authority,* Acts 5:29, 32; Tit. 3:1; genr. *to obey, follow,* or *conform to advice,* Acts 27:21

πειθαρχήσαντας, acc. pl. m. aor. act.
part. . . . . πειθαρχέω (3980)
πειθαρχοῦσιν, dat. pl. m. pres. act. part. . id.
πείθεις, 2 pers. sg. pres. act. indic. . . . . πείθω (3982)
πείθεσθαι, pres. pass. infin. . . . . id.
πείθεσθε, 2 pers. pl. pres. mid. imper. . . . . id.
πειθοῖ(ς), dat. pl. m. adj. (1 Cor. 2:4, GNT, MT, TR & NA | πιθοῖς, WH) . . . . . πειθός (3981)
πείθομαι, 1 pers. sg. pres. pass. indic. . . πείθω (3982)
πειθόμεθα, 1 pers. pl. pres. pass. indic. (Heb. 13:18, GNT, WH & NA | πεποίθαμεν, MT & TR) . . . . id.
πείθομεν, 1 pers. pl. pres. act. indic. . . . . . id.
πειθομένοις, dat. pl. m. pres. mid. part. . . id.
πειθομένου, gen. sg. m. pres. pass. part. . . id.

(3981) **πειθός**, ή, όν [§7.F.a] *persuasive,* 1 Cor. 2:4
(†3981) **πειθώ**, οῦς, ἡ [§5.E.h] *Suada, the goddess of persuasion; persuasiveness,* 1 Cor. 2:4

(3982) **πείθω**, 1 pers. sg. pres. act. indic., fut. πείσω, perf. πέπεικα [§23.1.c; 23.6] aor. ἔπεισα, perf. pass. πέπεισμαι, aor. pass. ἐπείσθην [§23.4.7] *to persuade, seek to persuade, endeavor to convince,* Acts 18:4; 19:8, 26; 28:23; *to persuade, influence by persuasion,* Matt. 27:20; Acts 13:43; 26:28; *to incite, instigate,* Acts 14:19; *to appease, render tranquil, to quiet,* 1 John 3:19; *to strive to conciliate, aspire to the favor of,* Gal. 1:10; *to pacify, conciliate, win over,* Matt. 28:14; Acts 12:20; pass. and mid. *to be persuaded of, be confident of,* Luke 20:6; Rom. 8:38; Heb. 6:9; *to suffer one's self to be persuaded, yield to persuasion, to be induced,* Acts 21:14; *to be convinced, to believe, yield belief,* Luke 16:31; Acts 17:4; *to assent, listen to, obey, follow,* Acts 5:36, 37, 40; 2 perf. πέποιθα [§25.5] *to be assured, be confident,* 2 Cor. 2:3; Phil. 1:6; Heb. 13:18; *to confide in, trust, rely on, place hope and confidence in,* Matt. 27:43; Mark 10:24; Rom. 2:19

πείθων, nom. sg. m. pres. act. part. . . . . πείθω (3982)
πεῖν, 2 aor. act. infin. . . . . πίνω (4095)
πεινᾷ, 3 pers. sg. pres. act. indic. {2 Cor. 11:21} . . . . πεινάω (3983)
πεινᾷ, 3 pers. sg. pres. act. subj. {Rom. 12:20} . . . . id.
πεινᾶν, pres. act. infin. (Phil. 4:12, GNT, MT & NA | πεινᾷν, WH & TR) . . . . id.

πεινάσετε, 2 pers. pl. fut. act. indic. . . πεινάω *(3983)*
πεινάσῃ, 3 pers. sg. aor. act. subj. . . . . id.
πεινάσουσιν, 3 pers. pl. fut. act. indic. . . . id.
(3983) **πεινάω**, ῶ, fut. πεινάσω [§22.2] and πεινήσω,
    aor. ἐπείνασα (πεῖνα, *hunger*) *to hunger,*
    be hungry, Matt. 4:2; Mark 11:12; *to be*
    exposed to hunger, be famished, 1 Cor.
    4:11; Phil. 4:12; met. *to hunger after, de-*
    sire earnestly, long for, Matt. 5:6
πεινῶμεν, 1 pers. pl. pres. act. indic. . . πεινάω *(3983)*
πεινῶντα, acc. sg. m. pres. act. part. . . . . . id.
πεινῶντας, acc. pl. m. pres. act. part. . . . . id.
πεινῶντες, nom. pl. m. pres. act. part. . . . id.
(3984) **πεῖρα**, ας, ἡ [§2.B.b] *a trial, attempt, endea-*
    vor; λαμβάνειν πεῖραν, *to attempt,* Heb.
    11:29; also, *to experience,* Heb. 11:36
πειράζει, 3 pers. sg. pres. act. indic. . . πειράζω *(3985)*
πειράζεται, 3 pers. sg. pres. pass. indic. . . id.
πειράζετε, 2 pers. pl. pres. act. indic.
    {Acts 15:10} . . . . id.
πειράζετε, 2 pers. pl. pres. act. imper.
    {2 Cor. 13:5} . . . . id.
πειράζῃ, 3 pers. sg. pres. act. subj. . . . . . . id.
πειράζομαι, 1 pers. sg. pres. pass. indic. . . id.
πειραζομένοις, dat. pl. m. pres. pass. part. id.
πειραζόμενος, nom. sg. m. pres. pass. part. id.
πειράζοντες, nom. pl. m. pres. act. part. . id.
(3985) **πειράζω**, fut. πειράσω [§26.1] aor. ἐπείρασα,
    perf. pass. πεπείρασμαι, aor. pass.
    ἐπειράσθην, *to make proof or trial of, put*
    to the proof, whether with good or mis-
    chievous intent, Matt. 16:1; 22:35, et al.;
    absol. *to attempt, essay,* Acts 16:7; 24:6;
    in N.T. *to tempt,* Matt. 4:1, et al.; *to try,*
    subject to trial, 1 Cor. 10:13, et al.
πειράζων, nom. sg. m. pres. act. part. πειράζω *(3985)*
πεῖραν, acc. sg. f. n. . . . . πεῖρα *(3984)*
(‡3987) **πειράομαι**, ῶμαι, fut. πειράσομαι [§19.S] (i.q.
    Att. πειράω) *to try, attempt, essay, endea-*
    vor, Acts 9:26; 26:21
πειράσαι, aor. act. infin. . . . . πειράζω *(3985)*
πειρασθείς, nom. sg. m. aor. pass. part. . . id.
πειρασθῆναι, aor. pass. infin. . . . . id.
πειρασθῇς, 2 pers. sg. aor. pass. subj. . . . . id.
πειρασθῆτε, 2 pers. pl. aor. pass. subj. . . . id.
πειρασμοῖς, dat. pl. m. n. . . . . πειρασμός *(3986)*
πειρασμόν, acc. sg. m. n. . . . . id.
(3986) **πειρασμός**, οῦ, ὁ, nom. sg. m. n. [§3.C.a] *a*
    putting to the proof, proof, trial, 1 Pet.
    4:12; Heb. 3:8; direct *temptation* to sin,
    Luke 4:13; *trial, temptation,* Matt. 6:13;
    26:41; 1 Cor. 10:13, et al.; *trial, calamity,*
    affliction, Luke 22:28, et al.
πειρασμοῦ, gen. sg. m. n. . . . . πειρασμός *(3986)*
πειρασμῷ, dat. sg. m. n. . . . . id.

πειρασμῶν, gen. pl. m. n. . . . . πειρασμός *(3986)*
πείσαντες, nom. pl. m. aor. act. part. . . πείθω *(3982)*
πείσας, nom. sg. m. aor. act. part. . . . . . . id.
πεισθέντες, nom. pl. m. aor. pass. part. (Heb.
    11:13, TR | GNT, WH, MT & NA omit) id.
πεισθῇς, 2 pers. sg. aor. pass. subj. . . . . . . id.
πεισθήσονται, 3 pers. pl. fut. pass. indic. . id.
(3988) **πεισμονή**, ῆς, ἡ, nom. sg. f. n. [§2.B.a] *a yield-*
    ing to persuasion, assent, Gal. 5:8
πείσομεν, 1 pers. pl. fut. act. indic. . . . . πείθω *(3982)*
πελάγει, dat. sg. neut. n. . . . . πέλαγος *(3989)*
(3989) **πέλαγος**, ους, τό [§5.E.b] *the deep, the open*
    sea, Matt. 18:6; *a sea,* contradistinguished
    from the sea in general, and named from
    an adjacent country, Acts 27:5
πέλαγος, acc. sg. neut. n. . . . . πέλαγος *(3989)*
(3990) **πελεκίζω**, fut. πελεκίσω [§26.1] (πέλεκυς, *an*
    axe) *to strike or cut with an axe; to be-*
    head, Rev. 20:4
πέμπει, 3 pers. sg. pres. act. indic. (2 Thess.
    2:11, GNT, WH & NA | πέμψει, MT &
    TR) . . . . πέμπω *(3992)*
πέμπειν, pres. act. infin. . . . . id.
πεμπομένοις, dat. pl. m. pres. pass. part. . id.
πέμποντα, acc. sg. m. pres. act. part. . . . . id.
πέμπτην, acc. sg. f. adj. . . . . πέμπτος *(3991)*
(3991) **πέμπτος**, η, ον, nom. sg. m. adj. [§7.F.a] *fifth,*
    Rev. 6:9; 9:1; 16:10; 21:20
(3992) **πέμπω**, 1 pers. sg. pres. act. indic., fut.
    πέμψω, aor. ἔπεμψα, aor. pass. ἐπέμφθην
    [§23.1.a; 23.2; 23.4] *to send, to despatch*
    on any message, embassy, business, etc.,
    Matt. 2:8; 11:2; 14:10; *to transmit,* Acts
    11:29; Rev. 1:11; *to dismiss, permit to go,*
    Mark 5:12; *to send in or among,* 2 Thess.
    2:11; *to thrust in, or put forth,* Rev.
    14:15, 18
πεμφθέντες, nom. pl. m. aor. pass.
    part. . . . . πέμπω *(3992)*
πέμψαι, aor. act. infin. . . . . id.
πέμψαντα, acc. sg. m. aor. act. part. . . . . . id.
πέμψαντες, nom. pl. m. aor. act. part. . . . id.
πέμψαντι, dat. sg. m. aor. act. part. . . . . . id.
πέμψαντος, gen. sg. m. aor. act. part. . . . . id.
πέμψας, nom. sg. m. aor. act. part. . . . . . . id.
πέμψασιν, dat. pl. m. aor. act. part. . . . . . id.
πέμψει, 3 pers. sg. fut. act. indic. . . . . id.
πέμψῃς, 2 pers. sg. aor. act. subj. . . . . id.
πέμψον, 2 pers. sg. aor. act. imper. . . . . . . id.
πέμψουσιν, 3 pers. pl. fut. act. indic. (Rev.
    11:10, GNT, WH, TR & NA | δώσουσιν,
    MT) . . . . id.
πέμψω, 1 pers. sg. fut. act. indic.
    {John 15:26} . . . . id.
πέμψω, 1 pers. sg. aor. act. subj.

{John 13:20} . . . . πέμπω *(3992)*

πένησιν, dat. pl. m. n. . . . . πένης *(3993)*

(3993) **πένης**, ητος, ὁ [§4.2.c] (πένομαι, *to labor* for one's bread) pr. *one who labors for his bread; poor, needy,* 2 Cor. 9:9

πενθεῖν, pres. act. infin. . . . . πενθέω *(3996)*

(3994) **πενθερά**, ᾶς, ἡ, nom. sg. f. n. [§2.B.b] *a mother-in-law,* Matt. 8:14; 10:35; Mark 1:30; Luke 4:38; 12:53

πενθεράν, acc. sg. f. n. . . . . πενθερά *(3994)*

πενθερᾶς, gen. sg. f. n. . . . . id.

(3995) **πενθερός**, οῦ, ὁ, nom. sg. m. n. [§3.C.a] *a father-in-law*

(3996) **πενθέω**, ῶ, fut. πενθήσω, aor. ἐπένθησα [§16.P] trans. *to lament over,* 2 Cor. 12:21; absol. *to lament, be sad, mourn,* Matt. 5:4; 9:15; Mark 16:10, et al.; mid. *to bewail one's self, to feel compunction,* 1 Cor. 5:2

πενθήσατε, 2 pers. pl. aor. act. imper. . πενθέω *(3996)*

πενθήσετε, 2 pers. pl. fut. act. indic. . . . . . id.

πενθήσουσιν, 3 pers. pl. fut. act. indic. (Rev. 18:11, MT | πενθοῦσι(ν), GNT, WH, TR & NA) . . . . id.

πενθήσω, 1 pers. sg. fut. act. indic. . . . . . . id.

(3997) **πένθος**, ους, τό, nom. sg. neut. n. [§5.E.b] *mourning, sorrow, sadness, grief,* James 4:9, et al. {Rev. 21:4}

πένθος, acc. sg. neut. n. {Rev. 18:7} . . . πένθος *(3997)*

πενθοῦντες, nom. pl. m. pres. act. part. . . . . πενθέω *(3996)*

πενθοῦσι(ν), 3 pers. pl. pres. act. indic. (Rev. 18:11, GNT, WH, TR & NA | πενθήσουσιν, TR) . . . . id.

πενθοῦσι(ν), dat. pl. m. pres. act. part. {Mark 16:10} . . . . id.

πενιχράν, acc. sg. f. adj. . . . . πενιχρός *(†3998)*

(†3998) **πενιχρός**, ά, όν [§7.1] *poor, needy,* Luke 21:2

(3999) **πεντάκις**, adv., *five times,* 2 Cor. 11:24

(4000) **πεντακισχίλιοι**, αι, α, nom. pl. m. numeral (πέντε + χίλιοι) *five times one thousand, five thousand,* Matt. 14:21; 16:9, et al.

πεντακισχιλίους, acc. pl. m. numeral . . . . πεντακισχίλιοι *(4000)*

πεντακισχιλίων, gen. pl. m. numeral . . . . id.

πεντακόσια, acc. pl. neut. numeral . . . . πεντακόσιοι *(4001)*

(4001) **πεντακόσιοι**, αι, α, numeral, *five hundred,* Luke 7:41; 1 Cor. 15:6

πεντακοσίοις, dat. pl. m., numeral . . . . πεντακόσιοι *(4001)*

(4002) **πέντε**, οἱ, αἱ, τά, indecl. numeral, *five,* Matt. 14:17, 19; 16:9, et al.

(4003) **πεντεκαιδέκατος**, η, ον [§7.F.a] (πέντε, καί, and δέκα) *fifteenth*

πεντεκαιδεκάτῳ, dat. sg. neut.

adj. . . . . πεντεκαιδέκατος *(4003)*

(4004) **πεντήκοντα**, οἱ, αἱ, τά, indecl. numeral, *fifty,* Mark 6:40; Luke 7:41, et al.

(†4004) **πεντηκοντατρεῖς**, οἱ, αἱ, τά, numeral, *fifty-three*

πεντηκοντατριῶν, gen. pl. m. numeral (John 21:11, MT & TR | πεντήκοντα τριῶν, GNT, WH & NA) . . . . . πεντηκοντατρεῖς *(†4004)*

(4005) **πεντηκοστή**, ῆς, ἡ [§2.B.a] (f. of πεντηκοστός, *fiftieth*) Pentecost, or *the Feast of Weeks;* one of the three great Jewish festivals, so called because it was celebrated on the *fiftieth* day, reckoning from the second day of the feast of unleavened bread, i.e., from the 16th day of Nisan, Acts 2:1; 20:16; 1 Cor. 16:8

πεντηκοστῆς, gen. sg. f. n. . . . . . πεντηκοστή *(4005)*

πεπαιδευμένος, nom. sg. m. perf. pass. part. . . . . παιδεύω *(3811)*

πεπαλαίωκε(ν), 3 pers. sg. perf. act. indic. [§13.5.a] . . . . παλαιόω *(3822)*

πέπαυται, 3 pers. sg. perf. pass. indic. [§22.5] . . . . παύω *(3973)*

πεπειραμένον, acc. sg. m. perf. pass. part. (Heb. 4:15, MT & TR | πεπειρασμένον, GNT, WH & NA) . . . . πειράομαι *(‡3987)*

πεπειρασμένον, acc. sg. m. perf. pass. part. (Heb. 4:15, GNT, WH & NA | πεπειραμένον, MT & TR) . . . . πειράζω *(3985)*

πέπεισμαι, 1 pers. sg. perf. pass. indic. . πείθω *(3982)*

πεπείσμεθα, 1 pers. pl. perf. pass. indic. . . id.

πεπεισμένος, nom. sg. m. perf. pass. part. id.

πεπελεκισμένων, gen. pl. m. perf. pass. part. . . . . πελεκίζω *(3990)*

πεπιεσμένον, acc. sg. neut. perf. pass. part. . . . . πιέζω *(4085)*

πεπίστευκα, 1 pers. sg. perf. act. indic. . . . . πιστεύω *(4100)*

πεπιστεύκαμεν, 1 pers. pl. perf. act. indic. id.

πεπίστευκας, 2 pers. sg. perf. act. indic. . . id.

πεπιστεύκατε, 2 pers. pl. perf. act. indic. . . id.

πεπιστεύκεισαν, 3 pers. pl. pluperf. act. indic. [§13.8.f] . . . . id.

πεπίστευκεν, 3 pers. sg. perf. act. indic. . . id.

πεπιστευκόσι(ν), dat. pl. m. perf. act. part. id.

πεπιστευκότας, acc. pl. m. perf. act. part. id.

πεπιστευκότες, nom. pl. m. perf. act. part. id.

πεπιστευκότων, gen. pl. m. perf. act. part. id.

πεπιστευκώς, nom. sg. m. perf. act. part. [§13.13] . . . . id.

πεπίστευμαι, 1 pers. sg. perf. pass. indic. . id.

πεπλανημένοις, dat. pl. m. perf. pass. part. . . . . πλανάω *(4105)*

πεπλάνησθε, 2 pers. pl. perf. pass. indic. [§19.S] . . . . id.

πεπλάτυνται, 3 pers. sg. perf. pass. indic.
[§27.2.a] . . . . πλατύνω *(4115)*
πεπληροφορημένοι, nom. pl. m. perf. pass.
part. (Col. 4:12, GNT, WH & NA |
πεπληρωμένοι, MT & TR) . . πληροφορέω *(4135)*
πεπληροφορημένων, gen. pl. neut. perf. pass.
part. . . . . id.
πεπληρώκατε, 2 pers. pl. perf. act.
indic. . . . . πληρόω *(4137)*
πεπλήρωκε(ν), 3 pers. sg. perf. act. indic. id.
πεπληρωκέναι, perf. act. infin. . . . . id.
πεπλήρωμαι, 1 pers. sg. perf. pass. indic. . id.
πεπληρωμένα, acc. pl. neut. perf. pass. part. id.
πεπληρωμένη, nom. sg. f. perf. pass. part. id.
πεπληρωμένην, acc. sg. f. perf. pass. part. id.
πεπληρωμένοι, nom. pl. m. perf. pass. part. id.
πεπληρωμένους, acc. pl. m. perf. pass. part. id.
πεπλήρωται, 3 pers. sg. perf. pass. indic. . id.
πεπλούτηκα, 1 pers. sg. perf. act.
indic. . . . . πλουτέω *(4147)*
πεποίηκα, 1 pers. sg. perf. act. indic. . . . ποιέω *(4160)*
πεποιήκαμεν, 1 pers. pl. perf. act. indic. . . id.
πεποιήκατε, 2 pers. pl. perf. act. indic. (Mark
11:17, GNT, WH & NA | ἐποιήσατε, MT
& TR) . . . . id.
πεποιήκεισαν, 3 pers. pl. pluperf. act. indic.
[§13.8.f] . . . . id.
πεποίηκε(ν), 3 pers. sg. perf. act. indic. . . id.
πεποιηκέναι, perf. act. infin. . . . . id.
πεποιηκόσι(ν), dat. pl. m. perf. act. part. . id.
πεποιηκότες, nom. pl. m. perf. act. part. . id.
πεποιηκότος, gen. sg. m. perf. act. part. . id.
πεποιηκώς, nom. sg. m. perf. act. part. . . id.
πεποιημένων, gen. pl. m. perf. pass. part. id.
πέποιθα, 1 pers. sg. 2 perf. act. indic.
[§25.4.5] . . . . πείθω *(3982)*
πεποίθαμεν, 1 pers. pl. 2 perf. act. indic. . id.
πέποιθας, 2 pers. sg. 2 perf. act. indic. . . . id.
πέποιθεν, 3 pers. sg. 2 perf. act. indic. . . . id.
πεποιθέναι, 2 perf. act. infin. . . . . id.
πεποιθήσει, dat. sg. f. n. . . . . πεποίθησις *(4006)*
πεποίθησιν, acc. sg. f. n. . . . . id.
(4006) **πεποίθησις**, εως, ἡ [§5.E.c] (πέποιθα, 2 perf.
of πείθω) *trust, confidence, reliance,* 2 Cor.
1:15, et al.
πεποιθότας, acc. pl. m. 2 perf. act.
part. . . . . πείθω *(3982)*
πεποιθότες, nom. pl. m. 2 perf. act. part. id.
πεποιθώς, nom. sg. m. 2 perf. act. part. . . id.
πεπολίτευμαι, 1 pers. sg. perf. pass. indic.
[§14.N] . . . . πολιτεύω *(†4176)*
πεπόνθασιν, 3 pers. pl. 2 perf. act. indic.
[§36.4] . . . . πάσχω *(3958)*
πέπονθεν, 3 pers. sg. 2 perf. act. indic. . . . id.
πεπορευμένους, acc. pl. m. perf. mid./pass.

dep. part. . . . . πορεύομαι *(4198)*
πεπότικε(ν), 3 pers. sg. perf. act.
indic. . . . . ποτίζω *(4222)*
πεπραγμένον, nom. sg. neut. perf. pass.
part. . . . . πράσσω *(4238)*
πέπρακε(ν), 3 pers. sg. perf. act.
indic. . . . . πιπράσκω *(4097)*
πεπραμένος, nom. sg. m. perf. pass. part.
[§36.3] . . . . id.
πέπραχα, 1 pers. sg. perf. act. indic. . πράσσω *(4238)*
πεπραχέναι, perf. act. infin. . . . . id.
πέπτωκαν, 3 pers. pl. perf. act. indic. [§35.13]
(Rev. 18:3, WH | πέπωκαν, GNT & NA
| πεπώκασι, MT | πέπωκε(ν), TR) . πίπτω *(4098)*
πέπτωκας, 2 pers. sg. perf. act. indic. (Rev.
2:5, GNT, MT & NA | ἐκπέπτωκας, TR
| πέπτωκες, WH) . . . . id.
πέπτωκες, 2 pers. sg. perf. act. indic. (Rev.
2:5, WH | ἐκπέπτωκας, TR | πέπτωκας,
GNT, MT & NA) . . . . id.
πεπτωκότα, acc. sg. m. perf. act. part.
[§13.6.c] . . . . id.
πεπτωκυῖαν, acc. sg. f. perf. act. part. [§37.1] id.
πεπυρωμένα, acc. pl. neut. perf. pass.
part. . . . . πυρόω *(4448)*
πεπυρωμένης, gen. sg. f. perf. pass. part. (Rev.
1:15, GNT, WH & NA | πεπυρωμένοι,
MT & TR) . . . . id.
πεπυρωμένοι, nom. pl. m. perf. pass. part.
(Rev. 1:15, MT & TR | πεπυρωμένης,
GNT, WH & NA) . . . . id.
πεπυρωμένον, acc. sg. neut. perf. pass. part. id.
πέπωκαν, 3 pers. pl. perf. act. indic. (Rev.
18:3, GNT & NA | πεπώκασι, MT |
πέπωκεν, TR | πέπτωκαν, WH) . . . . πίνω *(4095)*
πεπώκασι, 3 pers. pl. perf. act. indic. (Rev.
18:3, MT | πέπωκαν, GNT & NA |
πέπωκεν, TR | πέπτωκαν, WH) . . . . . id.
πέπωκε(ν), 3 pers. sg. perf. act. indic. [§37.1]
(Rev. 18:3, TR | πέπωκαν, GNT & NA
| πεπώκασι, MT | πέπτωκαν, WH) . . id.
πεπώρωκεν, 3 pers. sg. perf. act. indic. (John
12:40, MT & TR | ἐπώρωσεν, GNT, WH
& NA) . . . . πωρόω *(4456)*
πεπωρωμένη, nom. sg. f. perf. pass. part. id.
πεπωρωμένην, acc. sg. f. perf. pass. part. . id.
(4007) **περ**, enclitic particle, serving to add force to
the word to which it is subjoined
(†4008) **περαιτέρω**, compar. adv. of πέραν (Acts 19:39,
GNT, WH & NA | περὶ ἑτέρων, MT &
TR)
(4008) **πέραν**, adv., *across, beyond, over, on the other
side,* Matt. 4:15, 25; 19:1; John 6:1, 17; ὁ,
ἡ, τό, πέραν, *farther, on the farther side,*
and τὸ πέραν, *the farther side, the other*

side, Matt. 8:18, 28; 14:22, et al.

(4009) **πέρας**, ατος, τό, nom. sg. neut. n. [§4.2.c] *an extremity, end*, Matt. 12:42; Luke 11:31; Rom. 10:18; *an end, conclusion, termination*, Heb. 6:16

πέρατα, acc. pl. neut. n. . . . . πέρας (4009)

περάτων, gen. pl. neut. n. . . . . id.

Πέργαμον, acc. sg. f. n. . . . . Πέργαμος (4010)

(4010) **Πέργαμος**, ου, ή [§3.C.b] *Pergamus*, a city of Mysia, in Asia Minor

Περγάμῳ, dat. sg. f. n. . . . . Πέργαμος (4010)

(4011) **Πέργη**, ης, ή [§2.B.a] *Perga*, the chief city of Pamphylia, in Asia Minor

Πέργη, dat. sg. f. n. . . . . Πέργη (4011)

Πέργην, acc. sg. f. n. . . . . id.

Πέργης, gen. sg. f. n. . . . . id.

(4012) **περί**, prep., with a genitive, pr. of place, *about, around; about, concerning, respecting*, Matt. 2:8; 11:10; 22:31; John 8:18; Rom. 8:3, et al. freq.; with an accusative, of place, *about, around, round about*, Matt. 3:4; Mark 3:34; Luke 13:8; οἱ περί τινα, *the companions* of a person, Luke 22:49; *a person and his companions*, Acts 13:13; simply *a person*, John 11:19; τὰ περί τινα, *the condition, circumstances* of any one, Phil. 2:23; of time, *about*, Matt. 20:3, 5, 6, 9; *about, concerning, respecting, touching*, Luke 10:40; 1 Tim. 1:19; 6:21; Tit. 2:7, et al.

περιάγειν, pres. act. infin. [§34.1.b] . . περιάγω (4013)

περιάγετε, 2 pers. pl. pres. act. indic. . . . . id.

(4013) **περιάγω**, fut. περιάξω (περί + ἄγω) *to lead around, carry about* in one's company, 1 Cor. 9:5; *to traverse*, Matt. 4:23; 9:35; 23:15; Mark 6:6; absol. *to go up and down*, Acts 13:11

περιάγων, nom. sg. m. pres. act. part. περιάγω (4013)

περιαιρεῖται, 3 pers. sg. pres. pass. indic. . . . . περιαιρέω (4014)

(4014) **περιαιρέω**, ῶ, fut. περιαιρήσω, 2 aor. περιεῖλον [§36.1] (περί + αἱρέω) *to take off, lift off, remove*, 2 Cor. 3:16; *to cast off*, Acts 27:40; met. *to cut off* hope, Acts 27:20; met. *to take away* sin, *remove the guilt* of sin, *make expiation for* sin, Heb. 10:11

(‡681) **περιάπτω**, *to light a fire, kindle*, Luke 22:55

(4015) **περιαστράπτω**, fut. περιαστράψω [§23.1.a] (περί + ἀστράπτω) *to lighten around, shine like lightning around*, Acts 9:3; 22:6

περιαστράψαι, aor. act. infin. . περιαστράπτω (4015)

περιαψάντων, gen. pl. m. aor. act. part. (Luke 22:55, GNT, WH & NA | ἁψάντων, MT & TR) . . . . περιάπτω (‡681)

περιβαλεῖται, 3 pers. sg. fut. mid. indic. [§24.4] . . . . περιβάλλω (4016)

περιβάλῃ, 2 pers. sg. 2 aor. mid. subj. . . . id.

περιβάληται, 3 pers. sg. 2 aor. mid. subj. . . id.

(4016) **περιβάλλω**, fut. περιβαλῶ, 2 aor. περιέβαλον, perf. pass. περιβέβλημαι [§27.1.b; 27.3] (περί + βάλλω) *to cast around; to clothe*, Matt. 25:36, 38, 43; mid. *to clothe one's self, to be clothed*, Matt. 6:29, 31; Luke 23:11; John 19:2; Acts 12:8; Rev. 4:4, et al.; *to cast around* a city, *to draw* a line of circumvallation, Luke 19:43

περιβαλοῦ, 2 pers. sg. 2 aor. mid. imper. . . . . περιβάλλω (4016)

περιβαλοῦσιν, 3 pers. pl. fut. act. indic. (Luke 19:43, MT & TR | παρεμβαλοῦσιν, GNT, WH & NA) . . . . id.

περιβαλώμεθα, 1 pers. pl. 2 aor. mid. subj. id.

περιβαλών, nom. sg. m. 2 aor. act. part. . id.

περιβαβλημένη, nom. sg. f. perf. pass. part. id.

περιβεβλημένοι, nom. pl. m. perf. pass. part. id.

περιβεβλημένον, acc. sg. m. perf. pass. part. id.

περιβεβλημένος, nom. sg. m. perf. pass. part. id.

περιβεβλημένους, acc. pl. m. perf. pass. part. id.

(†4017) **περιβλέπομαι**, fut. περιβλέψομαι [§23.1.a] (i.q. περιβλέπω, from περί + βλέπω) trans. *to look around upon*, Mark 3:5, 34; 11:11; Luke 6:10; absol. *to look around*, Mark 5:32; 9:8; 10:23

περιβλεψάμενοι, nom. pl. m. aor. mid. part. . . . . περιβλέπομαι (†4017)

περιβλεψάμενος, nom. sg. m. aor. mid. part. id.

(4018) **περιβόλαιον**, ου, τό, nom. sg. neut. n. [§3.C.c] *that which is thrown around* any one, *clothing, covering, vesture; a cloak, mantle*, Heb. 1:12; *a covering*, 1 Cor. 11:15

περιβολαίου, gen. sg. neut. n. . . . περιβόλαιον (4018)

(4019) **περιδέω**, fut. περιδήσω, perf. pass. περιδέδεμαι [§37.1] (περί + δέω) *to bind round about*; pass. *to be bound around, be bound up*, John 11:44

περιδραμόντες, nom. pl. m. 2 aor. act. part. [§36.1] (Mark 6:55, MT & TR | περιέδραμον, GNT, WH & NA) . . . περιτρέχω (4063)

περιεβάλετε, 2 pers. pl. 2 aor. act. indic. [§34.1.b] . . . . περιβάλλω (4016)

περιεβάλετο, 3 pers. sg. 2 aor. mid. indic. id.

περιεβάλομεν, 1 pers. pl. 2 aor. act. indic. id.

περιέβαλον, 3 pers. pl. 2 aor. act. indic. . . id.

περιεβλέπετο, 3 pers. sg. imperf. mid. indic. . . . . περιβλέπομαι (†4017)

περιεδέδετο, 3 pers. sg. pluperf. pass. indic. . . . . περιδέω (4019)

περιέδραμον, 3 pers. pl. aor. act. indic. (Mark 6:55, GNT, WH & NA | περιδραμόντες,

MT & TR) . . . . περιτρέχω *(4063)*

περιεζωσμέναι, nom. pl. f. perf. pass. part.
[§26.5] . . . . περιζώννυμι *(4024)*

περιεζωσμένοι, nom. pl. m. perf. pass. part. id.

περιεζωσμένον, acc. sg. m. perf. pass. part. id.

περιέθηκαν, 3 pers. pl. aor. act.
indic. . . . . περιτίθημι *(4060)*

περιέθηκε(ν), 3 pers. sg. aor. act. indic. . . id.

περιέκρυβεν, 3 pers. sg. imperf. act. indic.
[§24.8.a] . . . . περικρύπτω *(4032)*

περιέλαμψεν, 3 pers. sg. aor. act.
indic. περιλάμπω *(4034)*

περιελεῖν, 2 aor. act. infin. [§36.1] . περιαιρέω *(4014)*

περιελθόντες, nom. pl. m. 2 aor. act. part.
(Acts 28:13, MT & TR | περιελόντες,
GNT, WH & NA) . . . . περιέρχομαι *(4022)*

περιελόντες, nom. pl. m. 2 aor. act.
part. . . . . περιαιρέω *(4014)*

περιεπάτει, 3 pers. sg. imperf. act.
indic. περιπατέω *(4043)*

περιεπάτεις, 2 pers. sg. imperf. act. indic. id.

περιεπατήσαμεν, 1 pers. pl. aor. act. indic. id.

περιεπατήσατε, 2 pers. pl. aor. act. indic. id.

περιεπάτησε(ν), 3 pers. sg. aor. act. indic. id.

περιεπάτουν, 3 pers. pl. imperf. act. indic. id.

περιέπειραν, 3 pers. pl. aor. act.
indic. . . . . περιπείρω *(4044)*

περιεπεπατήκει, 3 pers. sg. pluperf. act. indic.
(Acts 14:8, MT & TR | περιεπάτησεν,
GNT, WH, NA) . . . . περιπατέω *(4043)*

περιέπεσεν, 3 pers. sg. 2 aor. act. indic.
[§37.1] . . . . περιπίπτω *(4045)*

περιεποιήσατο, 3 pers. sg. aor. mid.
indic. περιποιέω *(†4046)*

περίεργα, acc. pl. neut. adj. . . . . περίεργος *(4021)*

περιεργαζομένους, acc. pl. m. pres. mid./pass.
dep. part. . . . . περιεργάζομαι *(4020)*

(4020) **περιεργάζομαι,** fut. περιεργάσομαι (περί, intensive + ἐργάζομαι) *to do a thing with excessive or superfluous care; to be a busy-body,* 2 Thess. 3:11

περίεργοι, nom. pl. m. adj. . . . . περίεργος *(4021)*

(4021) **περίεργος,** ον [§7.2] (περί + ἔργον) *over careful; officious, a busy-body,* 1 Tim. 5:13; in N.T. περίεργα, *magic arts, sorcery,* Acts 19:19

(4022) **περιέρχομαι,** 2 aor. περιῆλθον [§36.1] (περί + ἔρχομαι) *to go about, wander about, rove,* Acts 19:13; Heb. 11:37; *to go about, visit* from house to house, 1 Tim. 5:13; *to take a circuitous course,* Acts 28:13

περιερχόμεναι, nom. pl. f. pres. mid./pass.
dep. part. . . . . περιέρχομαι *(4022)*

περιερχομένων, gen. pl. m. pres. mid./pass.
dep. part. . . . . id.

περιεσπᾶτο, 3 pers. sg. imperf. pass. indic.
[§19.S] . . . . περισπάω *(4049)*

περιέστησαν, 3 pers. pl. 2 aor. act.
indic. . . . . περιΐστημι *(4026)*

περιεστῶτα, acc. sg. m. perf. act. part. contr.
[§35.8] . . . . id.

περιέσχεν, 3 pers. sg. 2 aor. act.
indic. . . . . περιέχω *(4023)*

περιέτεμεν, 3 pers. sg. 2 aor. act.
indic. περιτέμνω *(4059)*

περιετμήθητε, 2 pers. pl. aor. pass. indic.
[§27.3] . . . . id.

περιέχει, 3 pers. sg. pres. act. indic. . . περιέχω *(4023)*

περιέχουσαν, acc. sg. f. pres. act. part. (Acts 23:25, MT & TR | ἔχουσαν, GNT, WH & NA) . . . . id.

(4023) **περιέχω,** fut. περιέξω, 2 aor. περιέσχον [§36.4] (περί + ἔχω) *to encompass, enclose; to embrace, contain,* as a writing, Acts 23:25; met. *to encompass, seize on* the mind, Luke 5:9; περιέχει, impers. *it is contained, it is among the contents* of a writing, 1 Pet. 2:6

(4024) **περιζώννυμι,** and περιζωννύω, fut. περιζώσω, perf. pass. περιέζωσμαι [§36.5] (περί + ζώννυμι) *to bind around with a girdle, gird;* in N.T. mid. *to gird one's self* in preparation for bodily motion and exertion, Luke 12:37; 17:8, et al.; *to wear a girdle,* Rev. 1:13; 15:6

περίζωσαι, 2 pers. sg. aor. mid. imper. (Acts 12:8, MT & TR | ζῶσαι, GNT, WH & NA) . . . . περιζώννυμι *(4024)*

περιζωσάμενοι, nom. pl. m. aor. mid. part. id.

περιζωσάμενος, nom. sg. m. aor. mid. part. id.

περιζώσεται, 3 pers. sg. fut. mid. indic. . . id.

περιῆγε(ν), 3 pers. sg. imperf. act.
indic. . . . . περιάγω *(4013)*

περιῆλθον, 3 pers. pl. 2 aor. act.
indic. . . . . περιέρχομαι *(4022)*

περιῃρεῖτο, 3 pers. sg. imperf. pass. indic.
[§13.2] . . . . περιαιρέω *(4014)*

περιήστραψεν, 3 pers. sg. aor. act.
indic. . . . . περιαστράπτω *(4015)*

περιθείς, nom. sg. m. 2 aor. act.
part. . . . . περιτίθημι *(4060)*

περιθέντες, nom. pl. m. 2 aor. act. part. . . id.

περιθέσεως, gen. sg. f. n. . . . . περίθεσις *(4025)*

(4025) **περίθεσις,** εως, ἡ [§5.E.c] *a putting on, wearing* of dress, etc., 1 Pet. 3:3

περιΐστασο, 2 pers. sg. pres. mid. imper. [§29.Y] (2 Tim. 2:16; Tit. 3:9, GNT, MT, TR & NA | περίϊστασο, WH) . περιΐστημι *(4026)*

(4026) **περιΐστημι,** fut. περιστήσω [§29.X] (περί + ἵστημι) *to place around;* intrans. 2 aor.

περιέστην, perf. part. περιεστώς, *to stand around,* John 11:42; Acts 25:7; mid. *to keep aloof from, avoid, shun,* 2 Tim. 2:16; Tit. 3:9

(4027) **περικάθαρμα,** ατος, τό [§4.D.c] (περικαθαίρω, *to cleanse, purify,* from περί + καθαίρω) pr. *offscouring, filth;* met. *refuse, outcast,* 1 Cor. 4:13

περικαθάρματα, nom. pl. neut. n. περικάθαρμα *(4027)*
περικαλύπτειν, pres. act. infin. . περικαλύπτω *(4028)*

(4028) **περικαλύπτω,** fut. περικαλύψω [§23.1.a] (περί + καλύπτω) *to cover round about, cover over; to cover* the face, Mark 14:65; *to blindfold,* Luke 22:64; pass. *to be overlaid,* Heb. 9:4

περικαλύψαντες, nom. pl. m. aor. act. part. . . . . περικαλύπτω *(4028)*

(4029) **περίκειμαι,** 1 pers. sg. pres. mid./pass. dep. indic., fut. περικείσομαι [§33.DD] (περί + κεῖμαι) *to lie around, be circumjacent; to environ,* Heb. 12:1; *to be hung around,* Mark 9:42; Luke 17:2; *to have around one's self, to wear,* Acts 28:20; *to be beset,* Heb. 5:2

περικείμενον, acc. sg. neut. pres. mid./pass. dep. part. . . . . περίκειμαι *(4029)*
περίκειται, 3 pers. sg. pres. mid./pass. dep. indic. . . . . id.
περικεκαλυμμένην, acc. sg. f. perf. pass. part. . . . . περικαλύπτω *(4028)*

(4030) **περικεφαλαία,** ας, ἡ (fem. of περικεφάλαιος, περί + κεφαλή) *a helmet,* Eph. 6:17; 1 Thess. 5:8

περικεφαλαίαν, acc. sg. f. n. . . περικεφαλαία *(4030)*
περικρατεῖς, nom. pl. m. adj. . . . . περικρατής *(4031)*

(4031) **περικρατής,** ές [§7.G.b] (περί + κρατέω) *overpowering;* περικρατὴς γενέσθαι, *to become master of, to secure,* Acts 27:16

(4032) **περικρύπτω,** fut. περικρύψω [§23.1.a] 2 aor. περιέκρυβον (περί + κρύπτω) *to conceal by envelopment; to conceal* in retirement, Luke 1:24

περικυκλώσουσι(ν), 3 pers. pl. fut. act. indic. . . . . περικυκλόω *(4033)*

(4033) **περικυκλόω,** ῶ, fut. περικυκλώσω [§20.T] (περί + κυκλόω) *to encircle, surround,* Luke 19:43

(4034) **περιλάμπω,** fut. περιλάμψω [§23.1.a] (περί + λάμπω) *to shine around,* Luke 2:9; Acts 26:13

περιλάμψαν, acc. sg. neut. aor. act. part. . . . . περιλάμπω *(4034)*
περιλειπόμενοι, nom. pl. m. pres. pass. dep. part. . . . . περιλείπω *(4035)*

(4035) **περιλείπω,** fut. περιλείψω [§23.1.a] (περί + λείπω) *to leave remaining;* pass. *to remain, survive,* 1 Thess. 4:15, 17

περίλυπον, acc. sg. m. adj. (Luke 18:24, GNT, MT, TR & NA | WH omits) . . . περίλυπος *(4036)*

(4036) **περίλυπος,** ον, nom. sg. m. adj. [§7.2] (περί + λύπη) *greatly grieved, exceedingly sorrowful,* Matt. 26:38; Mark 14:34, et al. {Mark 6:26}

περίλυπος, nom. sg. f. adj. {Mark 14:34} . . . . περίλυπος *(4036)*
περιμένειν, pres. act. infin. . . . περιμένω *(4037)*

(4037) **περιμένω,** fut. περιμενῶ [§27.1.a] (περί + μένω) *to await, wait for,* Acts 1:4

(4038) **πέριξ,** adv., *round about;* ὁ, ἡ, τό, πέριξ, *circumjacent, neighboring,* Acts 5:16

(4039) **περιοικέω,** ῶ, fut. περιοικήσω [§16.P] *to dwell around, or in the vicinity; to be a neighbor,* Luke 1:65

περίοικοι, nom. pl. m. adj. . . . . . . περίοικος *(4040)*

(4040) **περίοικος,** ον [§7.2] (περί + οἶκος) *one who dwells in the vicinity, a neighbor,* Luke 1:58

περιοικοῦντας, acc. pl. m. pres. act. part. . . . . περιοικέω *(4039)*
περιούσιον, acc. sg. m. adj. . . . . περιούσιος *(4041)*

(4041) **περιούσιος,** ον [§7.2] (περιουσία, *abundance, wealth,* from περίειμι, *to superabound*) *superabundant; peculiar, special,* Tit. 2:14

(4042) **περιοχή,** ῆς, ἡ, nom. sg. f. n. [§2.B.a] *a compass, circumference, contents; a section, a portion* of Scripture, Acts 8:32

περιπατεῖ, 3 pers. sg. pres. act. indic. {1 John 2:11} . . . . περιπατέω *(4043)*
περιπάτει, 2 pers. sg. pres. act. imper. {John 5:8} . . . . id.
περιπατεῖν, pres. act. infin. . . . . id.
περιπατεῖς, 2 pers. sg. pres. act. indic. . . . id.
περιπατεῖτε, 2 pers. pl. pres. act. indic. {Eph. 5:15} . . . . id.
περιπατεῖτε, 2 pers. pl. pres. act. imper. {Eph. 5:8} . . . . id.
περιπατείτω, 3 pers. sg. pres. act. imper. . id.

(4043) **περιπατέω,** ῶ, fut. περιπατήσω [§16.P] (περί + πατέω) *to walk, walk about,* Matt. 9:5; 11:5; 14:25, 26, 29, et al.; *to rove, roam,* 1 Pet. 5:8; with μετά, *to accompany, follow, have intercourse with,* John 6:66; Rev. 3:4; *to walk, frequent* a locality, John 7:1; 11:54; from the Hebrew, *to maintain a* certain *walk* of life and conduct, Rom. 6:4; 8:4, et al.

περιπατῇ, 3 pers. sg. pres. act. subj. . . . . περιπατέω *(4043)*
περιπατῆσαι, aor. act. infin. . . . . id.
περιπατήσαντες, nom. pl. m. aor. act. part.

(Heb. 13:9, MT & TR | περιπατοῦντες,
GNT, WH & NA) . . . . περιπατέω *(4043)*
περιπατήσει, 3 pers. sg. fut. act. indic. (John
8:12, TR | περιπατήσῃ, GNT, WH, MT
& NA) . . . . id.
περιπατήσῃ, 3 pers. sg. aor. act. subj. (John
8:12, GNT, MT, WH & NA | περιπα-
τήσει, TR) . . . . id.
περιπατήσουσι(ν), 3 pers. pl. fut. act. indic. id.
περιπατήσωμεν, 1 pers. pl. aor. act. subj. . id.
περιπατῆτε, 2 pers. pl. pres. act. subj. . . . id.
περιπατοῦμεν, 1 pers. pl. pres. act. indic. . id.
περιπατοῦντα, acc. sg. m. pres. act. part. . id.
περιπατοῦντας, acc. pl. m. pres. act. part. id.
περιπατοῦντες, nom. pl. m. pres. act. part. id.
περιπατοῦντι, dat. sg. m. pres. act. part. . id.
περιπατοῦντος, gen. sg. m. pres. act. part. id.
περιπατοῦσι(ν), 3 pers. pl. pres. act. indic
{Mark 7:5} . . . . id.
περιπατοῦσι(ν), dat. pl. m. pres. act. part.
{Mark 16:12} . . . . id.
περιτατῶμεν, 1 pers. pl. pres. act. subj. . . id.
περιπατῶν, nom. sg. m. pres. act. part. . . id.
(4044) **περιπείρω**, fut. περιπερῶ, aor. περιέπειρα
[§27.1.d] (περί + πείρω) *to put on a spit,
transfix;* met. *to pierce, wound deeply,*
1 Tim. 6:10
περιπεπατήκει, 3 pers. sg. pluperf. act. indic.
(Acts 14:8, MT & TR | περιεπάτησεν,
GNT, WH & NA) . . . . περιπατέω *(4043)*
περιπέσητε, 2 pers. pl. 2 aor. act.
subj. περιπίπτω *(4045)*
περιπεσόντες, nom. pl. m. 2 aor. act. part. id.
(4045) **περιπίπτω**, fut. περιπεσοῦμαι, 2 aor.
περιέπεσον [§37.1] (περί + πίπτω) *to fall
around or upon, to fall in with,* Luke 10:30;
to fall into, light upon, Acts 27:41; *to be
involved in,* James 1:2
(†4046) **περιποιέω**, ῶ, fut. περιποιήσω [§16.P] (περί
+ ποιέω) *to cause to remain over and
above, to reserve, save;* mid. *to acquire,
gain, earn,* 1 Tim. 3:13; *to purchase,* Acts
20:28
περιποιήσασθαι, aor. mid. infin. (Luke 17:33,
GNT, WH & NA | σῶσαι, MT &
TR) . . . . περιποιέω *(†4046)*
περιποιήσεως, gen. sg. f. n. . . . . . περιποίησις *(4047)*
περιποίησιν, acc. sg. f. n. . . . . id.
(4047) **περιποίησις**, εως, ἡ [§5.E.c] *a laying up, keeping; an acquiring or obtaining, acquisition,*
1 Thess. 5:9; 2 Thess. 2:14; *a saving, preservation,* Heb. 10:39; *a peculiar possession,
specialty,* Eph. 1:14; 1 Pet. 2:9
περιποιοῦνται, 3 pers. pl. pres. mid.
indic. περιποιέω *(†4046)*

περιρήξαντες, nom. pl. m. aor. act. part. (Acts
16:22, GNT, WH & NA | περιρρήξαντες,
MT & TR) . . . . περι(ρ)ρήγνυμι *(4048)*
περιρρήξαντες, nom. pl. m. aor. act. part.
(Acts 16:22, MT & TR | περιρήξαντες,
GNT, WH & NA) . . . . id.
(4048) **περι(ρ)ρήγνυμι**, fut. περι(ρ)ρήξω [§36.5]
(περί + ῥήγνυμι) *to break or tear all
around; to strip off,* Acts 16:22
(4049) **περισπάω**, ῶ, fut. περισπάσω [§22.2] (περί
+ σπάω) *to draw off from around; to
wheel about; to distract;* pass. *to be dis-
tracted, over-busied,* Luke 10:40
(4050) **περισσεία**, ας, ἡ, nom. sg. f. n. [§2.B.b; 2.2]
superabundance, Rom. 5:17; 2 Cor. 8:2;
10:15; James 1:21
περισσείαν, acc. sg. f. n. . . . . περισσεία *(4050)*
περισσεύει, 3 pers. sg. pres. act.
indic. περισσεύω *(4052)*
περισσεύειν, pres. act. infin. . . . . id.
περισσεύετε, 2 pers. pl. pres. act. indic. . . id.
περισσεύῃ, 3 pers. sg. pres. act. subj. . . . . id.
περισσεύητε, 2 pers. pl. pres. act. subj. . . id.
περισσευθήσεται, 3 pers. sg. fut. pass. indic.
[§14.N] . . . . id.
(4051) **περίσσευμα**, ατος, τό, nom. sg. neut. n.
[§4.D.c] *more than enough, residue over
and above,* Mark 8:8; *abundance, exuber-
ance,* Matt. 12:34; Luke 6:45; *superabundance, affluence,* 2 Cor. 8:13, 14
περισσεύματα, acc. pl. neut. n. . . περίσσευμα *(4051)*
περισσεύματος, gen. sg. neut. n. . . . . id.
περισσεύομεν, 1 pers. pl. pres. act.
indic. περισσεύω *(4052)*
περισσεῦον, acc. sg. neut. pres. act. part. . id.
περισσεύονται, 3 pers. pl. pres. mid. indic.
(Luke 15:17, GNT, WH & NA | περισ-
σεύουσιν, MT & TR) . . . . id.
περισσεύοντες, nom. pl. m. pres. act. part. id.
περισσεύοντος, gen. sg. neut. pres. act. part. id.
περισσεύουσα, nom. sg. f. pres. act. part. id.
περισσεύουσιν, 3 pers. pl. pres. act. indic.
(Luke 15:17, MT & TR | περισσεύονται,
GNT, WH & NA) . . . . id.
περισσεύσαι, 3 pers. sg. aor. act. opt.
{1 Thess. 3:12} . . . . id.
περισσεῦσαι, aor. act. infin. {2 Cor. 9:8} . id.
περισσεῦσαν, nom. sg. neut. aor. act. part. id.
περισσεύσαντα, acc. pl. neut. aor. act. part. id.
περισσεύσῃ, 3 pers. sg. aor. act. subj. . . . . id.
(4052) **περισσεύω**, 1 pers. sg. pres. act. indic., fut.
περισσεύσω [§13.M] *to be over and above,
to be superfluous,* Matt. 14:20; Mark
12:44; Luke 21:4, et al.; *to exist in full
quantity, to abound, be abundant,* Rom.

5:15; 2 Cor. 1:5; *to increase, be augmented,* Acts 16:5; *to be advanced, be rendered more prominent,* Rom. 3:7; of persons, *to be abundantly gifted, richly furnished, abound,* Luke 15:17; Rom. 15:13; 1 Cor. 14:12; 2 Cor. 8:7, et al.; *to be possessed of a full sufficiency,* Phil. 4:12, 18; *to abound* in performance, 1 Cor. 15:58; *to be a gainer,* 1 Cor. 8:8; in N.T. trans., *to cause to be abundant,* 2 Cor. 4:15; 9:8; Eph. 1:8; *to cause to be abundantly furnished, cause to abound,* 1 Thess. 3:12; pass. *to be gifted with abundance,* Matt. 13:12; 25:29

περισσόν, nom. sg. neut. adj.
{Matt. 5:37} . . . . περισσός *(4053)*
περισσόν, acc. sg. neut. adj. {Matt. 5:47}   id.

(4053) **περισσός,** ή, όν [§7.F.a] *over and above,* Matt. 5:37; *superfluous,* 2 Cor. 9:1; *extraordinary,* Matt. 5:47; compar. *more, greater,* Matt. 11:9; 23:14, et al.; *excessive,* 2 Cor. 2:7; adverbially, περισσόν, *in full abundance,* John 10:10; περισσότερον, and ἐκ περισσοῦ, *exceedingly, vehemently,* Mark 6:51; 7:36; 1 Cor. 15:10; Eph. 3:20, et al.; τὸ περισσόν, *pre-eminence, advantage,* Rom. 3:1

περισσοτέρα, dat. sg. f. compar. adj.
[§8.4] . . . . περισσός *(4053)*
περισσοτέραν, acc. sg. f. compar. adj. . . . id.
περισσότερον, acc. sg. m. compar. adj.
{Matt. 11:9} . . . . id.
(4054) περισσότερον, nom. sg. neut. compar. adj.
{Mark 12:33} . . . . id.
περισσότερον, acc. sg. neut. compar. adj.
{Mark 12:40} . . . . id.
(4056) **περισσοτέρως,** adv., *more, more abundantly, more earnestly, more vehemently,* Mark 15:14; 2 Cor. 7:13, et al.; *exceedingly,* Gal. 1:14
περισσοῦ, gen. sg. neut. adj. . . . . . . περισσός *(4053)*
(4057) **περισσῶς,** adv., *much, abundantly, vehemently,* Acts 26:11; *more, more abundantly,* Matt. 27:23; Mark 10:26
(4058) **περιστερά,** ᾶς, ἡ [§2.B.b] *a dove, pigeon,* Matt. 3:16; 10:16, et al.
περιστεραί, nom. pl. f. n. . . . . περιστερά *(4058)*
περιστεράν, acc. sg. f. n. . . . . id.
περιστεράς, acc. pl. f. n. . . . . id.
περιστερῶν, gen. pl. f. n. . . . . id.
περιτεμεῖν, 2 aor. act. infin. . . . . . . περιτέμνω *(4059)*
περιτέμνειν, pres. act. infin. . . . . id.
περιτέμνεσθαι, pres. pass. infin. . . . . id.
περιστεμνέσθω, 3 pers. sg. pres. pass. imper.   id.
περιτέμνετε, 2 pers. pl. pres. act. indic. . .   id.

περιτέμνησθε, 2 pers. pl. pres. pass.
subj. . . . . περιτέμνω *(4059)*
περιτεμνόμενοι, nom. pl. m. pres. pass. part.
(Gal. 6:13, GNT, WH, TR & NA | περιτετμημένοι, MT) . . . . id.
περιτεμνομένῳ, dat. sg. m. pres. pass. part.   id.
(4059) **περιτέμνω,** fut. περιτεμῶ [§27.1.b] perf. pass. περιτέτμημαι, 2 aor. περιέτεμον [§27.4.b] (περί + τέμνω) *to cut around; to circumcise, remove the prepuce,* Luke 1:59; 2:21, et al.; met. Col. 2:11; mid. *to submit to circumcision,* Acts 15:1, et al.
περιτετμημένοι, nom. pl. m. perf. pass. part.
(Gal. 6:13, MT | περιτεμνόμενοι, GNT, WH, TR & NA) . . . . περιτέμνω *(4059)*
περιτετμημένος, nom. sg. m. perf. pass. part.   id.
περιτιθέασιν, 3 pers. sg. pres. act. indic. Att.
for περιτιθεῖσιν [§28.6] . . . . περιτίθημι *(4060)*
περιτίθεμεν, 1 pers. pl. pres. act. indic. . . . *(4060)*
(4060) **περιτίθημι,** fut. περιθήσω, aor. περιέθηκα, 2 aor. pass. περιέθην [§28.V] (περί + τίθημι) *to place around, put about or around,* Matt. 21:33; 27:28, et al.; met. *to attach, bestow,* 1 Cor. 12:23
περιτμηθῆναι, aor. pass. infin. . . . . περιτέμνω *(4059)*
περιτμηθῆτε, 2 pers. pl. aor. pass. subj. (Acts 15:1, GNT, WH & NA | περιτέμνησθε, MT & TR) . . . . id.
(4061) **περιτομή,** ῆς, ἡ, nom. sg. f. n. [§2.B.a] *circumcision, the act or custom of circumcision,* John 7:22, 23; Acts 7:8; *the state of being circumcised, the being circumcised,* Rom. 2:25, 26, 27; 4:10; meton. *the circumcision, those who are circumcised,* Rom. 3:30; 4:9; met. spiritual *circumcision* of the heart and affections, Rom. 2:29; Col. 2:11; meton. *persons* spiritually *circumcised,* Phil. 3:3
περιτομῇ, dat. sg. f. n. . . . . περιτομή *(4061)*
περιτομήν, acc. sg. f. n. . . . . id.
περιτομῆς, gen. sg. f. n. . . . . id.
περιτρέπει, 3 pers. sg. pres. act.
indic. . . . . περιτρέπω *(4062)*
(4062) **περιτρέπω,** fut. περιτρέψω [§23.1.a] (περί + τρέπω) *to turn about; to bring round* into any state, Acts 26:24
(4063) **περιτρέχω,** 2 aor. περιέδραμον [§36.1] (περί + τρέχω) *to run about, run up and down,* Mark 6:55
περιφέρειν, pres. act. infin. . . . . περιφέρω *(4064)*
περιφέρεσθε, 2 pers. pl. pres. pass. imper. (Heb. 13:9, TR | παραφέρεσθε, GNT, WH, MT & NA) . . . . id.
περιφερόμεναι, nom. pl. f. pres. pass. part. (Jude 12, TR | παραφερόμεναι, GNT,

WH, MT & NA) . . . . περιφέρω *(4064)*

περιφερόμενοι, nom. pl. m. pres. pass. part.   id.

περιφέροντες, nom. pl. m. pres. act. part.   id.

(4064) **περιφέρω**, fut. περιοίσω, aor. περιήνεγκα, 2 aor. περιήνεγκον [§36.1] (περί + φέρω) *to bear or carry about*, Mark 6:55; 2 Cor. 4:10; pass. *to be borne about hither and thither, to be whirled about, driven to and fro*, Eph. 4:14; Heb. 13:9; Jude 12

περιφρονείτω, 3 pers. sg. pres. act. imper. . . . . περιφρονέω *(4065)*

(4065) **περιφρονέω**, ῶ, fut. περιφρονήσω [§16.P] (περί + φρήν) *to contemplate, reflect on; to despise, disregard*, Tit. 2:15

περίχωρον, acc. sg. f. adj. . . . . περίχωρος *(4066)*

(4066) **περίχωρος**, ον, nom. sg. m. adj. [§7.2] (περί + χώρα) *circumjacent*; ἡ περίχωρος, sc. γῆ, *an adjacent or circumjacent region, country round about*, Matt. 14:35; Mark 1:28; meton. *inhabitants of the region round about*, Matt. 3:5

περιχώρου, gen. sg. f. adj. . . . . περίχωρος *(4066)*

περιχώρῳ, dat. sg. f. adj. . . . . id.

(†4067) **περίψημα**, ατος, τό, nom. sg. neut. n. [§4.D.c] (περιψάω, *to wipe on every side*) *filth which is wiped off; offscouring*; met. 1 Cor. 4:13

περπερεύεται, 3 pers. sg. pres. mid./pass. dep. indic. . . . . περπερεύομαι *(4068)*

(4068) **περπερεύομαι**, fut. περπερεύσομαι (πέρ-περος, *braggart*) *to vaunt one's self*, 1 Cor. 13:4

Περσίδα, acc. sg. f. n. . . . . Περσίς *(4069)*

(4069) **Περσίς**, ίδος, ἡ [§4.2.c] *Persis*, pr. name, Rom. 16:12

(4070) **πέρυσι**, adv., *last year, a year ago*, 2 Cor. 8:10; 9:2

πεσεῖν, 2 aor. act. infin. [§37.1] . . . . . . πίπτω *(4098)*

πεσεῖται, 3 pers. sg. fut. mid. dep. indic. . . id.

πέσετε, 2 pers. pl. 2 aor. act. imper. (Luke 23:30; Rev. 6:16, GNT, MT, TR & NA | πέσατε, WH) . . . . id.

πέσῃ, 3 pers. sg. 2 aor. act. subj. . . . . . . id.

πέσητε, 2 pers. pl. 2 aor. act. subj. . . . . . . id.

πεσόν, nom. sg. neut. 2 aor. act. part. . . . id.

πεσόντα, acc. sg. m. 2 aor. act. part. . . . . id.

πεσόντας, acc. pl. m. 2 aor. act. part. . . . id.

πεσόντες, nom. pl. m. 2 aor. act. part. . . . id.

πεσοῦνται, 3 pers. pl. fut. mid./pass. dep. indic. . . . . id.

πεσών, nom. sg. m. 2 aor. act. part. . . . . . id.

πέσωσι(ν), 3 pers. pl. 2 aor. act. subj. . . . id.

(‡4072) **πετάομαι**, ῶμαι, a later form for πέτομαι, Rev. 4:7; 14:6; 19:17

πετεινά, nom. pl. neut. n.

{Matt. 8:20} . . . . πετεινόν *(4071)*

πετεινά, acc. pl. neut. n. {Matt. 6:26} . . . id.

(4071) **πετεινόν**, οῦ, τό [§3.C.c] (neut. of πετεινός, ή, όν, *winged, flying*, from πέτομαι) *a bird, fowl*, Matt. 6:26; 8:20, et al.

πετεινῶν, gen. pl. neut. n. . . . . πετεινόν *(4071)*

πέτηται, 3 pers. sg. pres. mid./pass. dep. subj. . . . . πέτομαι *(4072)*

(4072) **πέτομαι**, fut. πετήσομαι and πτήσομαι, *to fly*

πετομένοις, dat. pl. neut. pres. mid./pass. dep. part. (Rev. 19:17, GNT, WH, MT & NA | πετωμένοις, TR) . . . . πέτομαι *(4072)*

πετόμενον, acc. sg. m. pres. mid./pass. dep. part. (Rev. 14:6, GNT, WH, MT & NA | πετώμενον, TR) . . . . id.

πετομένου, gen. sg. m. pres. mid./pass. dep. part. (Rev. 8:13, GNT, WH, MT & NA | πετωμένου, TR) . . . . id.

πετομένῳ, dat. sg. m. pres. mid./pass. dep. part. (Rev. 4:7, GNT, WH, MT & NA | πετωμένῳ, TR) . . . . id.

(4073) **πέτρα**, ας, ἡ, nom. sg. f. n. [§2.B.b] *a rock*, Matt. 7:24, 25, et al.; met. Rom. 9:33; 1 Pet. 2:8; *crags, clefts*, Rev. 6:15, 16; *stony ground*, Luke 8:6, 13

πέτρᾳ, dat. sg. f. n. . . . . πέτρα *(4073)*

πέτραι, nom. pl. f. n. . . . . id.

πέτραις, dat. pl. f. n. . . . . id.

πέτραν, acc. sg. f. n. . . . . id.

πέτρας, gen. sg. f. n. {Mark 15:46} . . . . . id.

πέτρας, acc. pl. f. n. {Rev. 6:15} . . . . id.

Πέτρε, voc. sg. m. n. . . . . Πέτρος *(4074)*

Πέτρον, acc. sg. m. n. . . . . id.

(4074) **Πέτρος**, ου, ὁ, nom. sg. m. n. [§3.C.a] *a stone*; in N.T. the Greek rendering of the surname Cephas, given to the Apostle Simon, and having, therefore, the same sense as πέτρα, *Peter*, Matt. 4:18; 8:14, et al.

Πέτρου, gen. sg. m. n. . . . . id.

Πέτρῳ, dat. sg. m. n. . . . . id.

πετρῶδες, acc. sg. neut. adj. . . . . . . πετρώδης *(4075)*

πετρώδη, acc. pl. neut. adj. . . . . id.

(4075) **πετρώδης**, ες [§7.G.b] *like rock; stony, rocky*, Matt. 13:5, 20; Mark 4:5, 16

πετωμένοις, dat. pl. neut. pres. mid./pass. dep. part. (Rev. 19:17, TR | πετομένοις, GNT, WH, MT & NA) . . . . πετάομαι *(‡4072)*

πετώμενον, acc. sg. m. pres. mid./pass. dep. part. (Rev. 14:6, TR | πετόμενον, GNT, WH, MT & NA) . . . . id.

πετωμένου, gen. sg. m. pres. mid./pass. dep. part. (Rev. 8:13, TR | πετομένου, GNT, WH, MT & NA) . . . . id.

πετωμένῳ, dat. sg. m. pres. mid./pass. dep. part. (Rev. 4:7, TR | πετομένῳ, GNT,

WH, MT & NA) . . . . πετάομαι (‡4072)
πεφανερώμεθα, 1 pers. pl. perf. pass. indic.
[§21.U] . . . . φανερόω (5319)
πεφανερῶσθαι, perf. pass. infin. . . . . id.
πεφανέρωται, 3 pers. sg. perf. pass. indic. id.
πεφιλήκατε, 2 pers. pl. perf. act. indic.
[§16.5] . . . . φιλέω (5368)
πεφίμωσο, 2 pers. sg. perf. pass. imper. φιμόω (5392)
πεφορτισμένοι, nom. pl. m. perf. pass.
part. φορτίζω (5412)
πεφυσιωμένοι, nom. pl. m. perf. pass.
part. φυσιόω (5448)
πεφυσιωμένων, gen. pl. m. perf. pass. part. id.
πεφυτευμένην, acc. sg. f. perf. pass.
part. φυτεύω (5452)
πεφωτισμένους, acc. pl. m. perf. pass. part.
[§26.1] . . . . φωτίζω (5461)
πηγαί, nom. pl. f. n. . . . . πηγή (4077)
(4076) **πήγανον**, ου, τό [§3.C.c] *rue,* a plant, *ruta graveolens* of Linnaeus
πήγανον, acc. sg. neut. n. . . . . πήγανον (4076)
πηγάς, acc. pl. f. n. . . . . πηγή (4077)
(4077) **πηγή**, ῆς, ἡ, nom. sg. f. n. [§2.B.a] *a source, spring, fountain,* James 3:11, 12; *a well,* John 4:6; *an issue, flux, flow,* Mark 5:29; met. John 4:14
πηγῇ, dat. sg. f. n. . . . . πηγή (4077)
πηγῆς, gen. sg. f. n. . . . . id.
(4078) **πήγνυμι**, and πηγνύω, fut. πηγνύξω, aor. ἔπηξα [§36.5] *to fasten; to pitch* a tent, Heb. 8:2
(4079) **πηδάλιον**, ου, τό [§3.C.c] (πηδόν, *the blade of an oar) a rudder,* Acts 27:40; James 3:4
πηδαλίου, gen. sg. neut. n. . . . . πηδάλιον (4079)
πηδαλίων, gen. pl. neut. n. . . . . id.
πηλίκοις, dat. pl. neut. adj. . . . . πηλίκος (4080)
(4080) **πηλίκος**, η, ον, nom. sg. m. adj. [§10.7.c] *how large,* Gal. 6:11; *how great* in dignity, Heb. 7:4
πηλόν, acc. sg. m. n. . . . . πηλός (4081)
(4081) **πηλός**, οῦ, ὁ [§3.C.a] *moist earth, mud, slime,* John 9:6, 11, 14, 15; *clay,* potter's *clay,* Rom. 9:21
πηλοῦ, gen. sg. m. n. . . . . πηλός (4081)
(4082) **πήρα**, ας, ἡ [§2.B.b] *a leather bag or sack* for provisions, *scrip, wallet,* Matt. 10:10; Mark 6:8, et al.
πήραν, acc. sg. f. n. . . . . πήρα (4082)
πήρας, gen. sg. f. n. . . . . id.
πῆχυν, acc. sg. m. n. [§5.5] . . . . πῆχυς (4083)
(4083) **πῆχυς**, εως, ὁ [§5.E.c] pr. *cubitus, the forearm;* hence, *a cubit,* a measure of length, equal to the distance from the elbow to the extremity of the little finger, usually considered as equivalent to a foot and one half,

or 17 inches and one half, John 21:8; Rev. 21:17; met. of time, *a span,* Matt. 6:27; Luke 12:25
πηχῶν, gen. pl. m. n. . . . . πῆχυς (4083)
(4084) **πιάζω** (a later form for πιέζω, derived from the Doric) fut. πιάσω, aor. ἐπίασα [§26.1] *to press;* in N.T. *to take or lay hold of,* Acts 3:7; *to take, catch* fish, etc., John 21:3, 10; Rev. 19:20; *to take, seize, apprehend, arrest,* John 7:30, 32, 44, et al.
πιάσαι, aor. act. infin. . . . . πιάζω (4084)
πιάσας, nom. sg. m. aor. act. part. . . . . . . id.
πιάσωσιν, 3 pers. pl. aor. act. subj. . . . . . . id.
πίε, 2 pers. sg. 2 aor. act. imper. [§37.1] . πίνω (4095)
(4085) **πιέζω**, fut. πιέσω, perf. pass. πεπίεσμαι [§26.1] *to press, to press or squeeze down, make compact by pressure,* Luke 6:38
πιεῖν, 2 aor. act. infin. . . . . πίνω (4095)
πίεσαι, 2 pers. sg. fut. mid. dep. indic. [§37.1] id.
πίεσθε, 2 pers. pl. fut. mid. dep. indic. . . . id.
πίεται, 3 pers. sg. fut. mid. dep. indic. . . . id.
πίετε, 2 pers. pl. 2 aor. act. imper. . . . . . . id.
πίῃ, 3 pers. sg. 2 aor. act. subj. . . . . id.
πίητε, 2 pers. pl. 2 aor. act. subj. . . . . id.
(4086) **πιθανολογία**, ας, ἡ [§2.B.b; 2.2] (πιθανός, *persuasive,* πείθω + λόγος) *persuasive speech, plausible discourse,* Col. 2:4
πιθανολογίᾳ, dat. sg. f. n. . . . . . . πιθανολογία (4086)
πιθοῖς, dat. pl. m. adj. (1 Cor. 2:4, WH | πειθοῖς, GNT, WH, MT & NA) . . . πιθός (‡3981)
(‡3981) **πιθός**, ή, όν, *persuasive, skillful,*
πικραίνεσθε, 2 pers. pl. pres. pass.
imper. πικραίνω (4087)
(4087) **πικραίνω**, fut. πικρανῶ [§27.1.c] *to embitter, render bitter,* Rev. 10:9; pass. *to be embittered, be made bitter,* Rev. 8:11; 10:10; met. pass. *to be embittered, to grow angry, harsh,* Col. 3:19
πικρανεῖ, 3 pers. sg. fut. act. indic. . πικραίνω (4087)
(4088) **πικρία**, ας, ἡ, nom. sg. f. n. [§2.B.b; 2.2] *bitterness,* Acts 8:23; Heb. 12:15; met. *bitterness* of spirit and language, *harshness,* Rom. 3:14; Eph. 4:31
πικρίας, gen. sg. f. n. . . . . πικρία (4088)
πικρόν, acc. sg. m. adj. {James 3:14} . πικρός (4089)
πικρόν, acc. sg. neut. adj. {James 3:11} . . id.
(4089) **πικρός**, ά, όν [§7.1] *bitter,* James 3:11; met. *bitter, harsh,* James 3:14
(4090) **πικρῶς**, adv., *bitterly,* Matt. 26:75; Luke 22:62
Πιλάτον, acc. sg. m. n. (TR | Πιλᾶτον, GNT, MT & NA | Πειλᾶτον, WH) . . . . Πιλᾶτος (4091)
Πιλᾶτον, acc. sg. m. n.Πιλᾶτος (GNT, MT & NA | Πιλάτον, TR | Πειλᾶτον, WH) id.
(4091) **Πιλᾶτος**, ου, ὁ, nom. sg. m. n. [§3.C.a] *Pi-*

late, pr. name (GNT, MT & NA |
Πιλάτος, TR | Πειλᾶτος, WH)

Πιλάτου, gen. sg. m. n. (GNT, MT, TR &
NA | Πειλάτου, WH) . . . . Πιλᾶτος *(4091)*

Πιλάτῳ, dat. sg. m. n. (GNT, MT, TR & NA
| Πειλάτῳ, WH) . . . . id.

(‡4130) **πίμπλημι**, or πλήθω, fut. πλήσω, aor. pass.
ἐπλήσθην [§23.1.c; 23.4] *to fill*, Matt.
27:48, et al.; pass. *to be filled* mentally, *be
under full influence*, Luke 1:15; 4:28, et al.;
to be fulfilled, Luke 21:22; of stated time,
to be brought to a close, arrive at its close,
Luke 1:23, 57; 2:6, 21, 22

πίμπρασθαι, pres. pass. infin. . . . . . . πίμπρημι *(4092)*

(4092) **πίμπρημι**, fut. πιμπρήσω, *to set on fire, burn,
inflame;* in N.T. pass., *to swell from inflam-
mation*, Acts 28:6

πίνακι, dat. sg. f. n. . . . . πίναξ *(4094)*

(4093) **πινακίδιον**, ου, τό [§3.C.c] *a small tablet* for
writing

πινακίδιον, acc. sg. neut. n. . . . . . . πινακίδιον *(4093)*

πίνακος, gen. sg. m. n. . . . . πίναξ *(4094)*

(4094) **πίναξ**, ακος, ὁ [§4.2.b] pr. *a board or plank;*
in N.T. *a plate, platter, dish* on which food
was served, Mark 14:8, 11, et al.

πίνει, 3 pers. sg. pres. act. indic. . . . . πίνω *(4095)*

πίνειν, pres. act. infin. . . . . id.

πίνετε, 2 pers. pl. pres. act. indic. . . . . . . id.

πινέτω, 3 pers. sg. pres. act. imper. . . . . . . id.

πίνῃ, 3 pers. sg. pres. act. subj. . . . . id.

πίνητε, 2 pers. pl. pres. act. subj. . . . . id.

πίνοντες, nom. pl. m. pres. act. part. . . . . id.

πίνουσιν, 3 pers. pl. pres. act. indic. . . . . id.

(4095) **πίνω**, 1 pers. sg. pres. act. indic., fut. πίομαι
and πιοῦμαι, 2 aor. ἔπιον, perf. πέπωκα
[§37.1] *to drink*, Matt. 6:25, 31; 26:27, 29,
et al. freq.; trop. of the earth, *to drink in,
imbibe*, Heb. 6:7 {Mark 10:38–39}

πίνω, 1 pers. sg. pres. act. subj.
{Mark 14:25} . . . . πίνω *(4095)*

πίνων, nom. sg. m. pres. act. part. . . . . . . id.

(4096) **πιότης**, ητος, ἡ [§4.2.c] (πίων, *fat*) *fatness,
richness*, Rom. 11:17

πιότητος, gen. sg. f. n. . . . . πιότης *(4096)*

πιοῦσα, nom. sg. f. 2 aor. act. part. . . . . πίνω *(4095)*

πιπρασκομένων, gen. pl. m. pres. pass.
part. . . . . πιπράσκω *(4097)*

(4097) **πιπράσκω**, perf. πέπρακα, perf. pass. πέπραμαι, aor. pass. ἐπράθην [§36.3]
(redupl. from περάω, *to bring from a distance to sell*) *to sell*, Matt. 13:46; 18:25,
et al.; met. with ὑπό, pass. *to be sold
under, to be a slave to, be devoted to*, Rom.
7:14

πίπτει, 3 pers. sg. pres. act. indic. . . . . . πίπτω *(4098)*

πίπτοντες, nom. pl. m. pres. act. part. (Mark
13:25, GNT, WH & NA | ἐκπίπτοντες,
MT & TR) . . . . πίπτω *(4098)*

πιπτόντων, gen. pl. neut. pres. act. part. . id.

(4098) **πίπτω**, fut. πεσοῦμαι, perf. πέπτωκα, 2 aor.
ἔπεσον, and, in N.T., aor. ἔπεσα [§37.1]
to fall, Matt. 15:27; Luke 10:18; *to fall, fall
prostrate, fall down*, Matt. 17:6; 18:29;
Luke 17:16; *to fall down* dead, Luke 21:24;
to fall, fall in ruins, Matt. 7:25, 27; Luke
11:17; met. *to fall, come by chance*, as a
lot, Acts 1:26; *to fall, to fail, become null
and void, fall to the ground*, Luke 16:17;
to fall into a worse state, Rev. 2:5; *to come
to ruin*, Rom. 11:11; Heb. 4:11; *to fall* into
sin, Rom. 11:22; 1 Cor. 10:12; *to fall* in judgment, by condemnation, Rev. 14:8; *to fall
upon, seize*, Rev. 11:11; *to light* upon, Rev.
7:16; *to fall* under, *incur*, James 5:12

(4099) **Πισιδία**, ας, ἡ [§2.B.b; 2.2] *Pisidia*, a country of Asia Minor

Πισιδίαν, acc. sg. f. n. . . . . Πισιδία *(4099)*

Πισιδίας, gen. sg. f. n. (Acts 13:14, MT & TR
| Πισιδίαν, GNT, WH & NA) . . . . id.

πιστά, acc. pl. neut. adj. . . . . πιστός *(4103)*

πιστάς, acc. pl. f. adj. . . . . id.

πιστέ, voc. sg. m. adj. . . . . id.

πίστει, dat. sg. f. n. . . . . πίστις *(4102)*

πίστευε, 2 pers. sg. pres. act. imper. . . . πιστεύω *(4100)*

πιστεύει, 3 pers. sg. pres. act. indic. . . . . . id.

πιστεύειν, pres. act. infin. . . . . id.

πιστεύεις, 2 pers. sg. pres. act. indic. . . . . . id.

πιστεύεται, 3 pers. sg. pres. pass. indic. . . . id.

πιστεύετε, 2 pers. pl. pres. act. indic.
{John 10:25–26} . . . . id.

πιστεύετε, 2 pers. pl. pres. act. imper.
{John 10:37–38} . . . . id.

πιστεύῃ, 3 pers. sg. pres. act. subj. (Mark
11:23; John 17:21, GNT, WH & NA |
πιστεύσῃ, MT & TR) . . . . id.

πιστεύητε, 2 pers. pl. pres. act. subj. . . . . . id.

πιστευθῆναι, aor. pass. infin. . . . . id.

πιστεύομεν, 1 pers. pl. pres. act. indic. . . . . id.

πιστεύοντα, acc. sg. m. pres. act. part. . . . . id.

πιστεύοντας, acc. pl. m. pres. act. part. . . id.

πιστεύοντες, nom. pl. m. pres. act. part. . . id.

πιστεύοντι, dat. sg. m. pres. act. part. . . . . id.

πιστευόντων, gen. pl. m. pres. act. part. . . id.

πιστεύουσι(ν), 3 pers. pl. pres. act. indic.
{John 6:64} . . . . id.

πιστεύουσι(ν), dat. pl. m. pres. act. part.
{John 1:12} . . . . id.

πιστεῦσαι, aor. act. infin. . . . . id.

πιστεύσαντας, acc. pl. m. aor. act. part. . . id.

πιστεύσαντες, nom. pl. m. aor. act. part. . . id.

πιστευσάντων, gen. pl. m. aor. act.
part. . . . . πιστεύω *(4100)*
πιστεύσας, nom. sg. m. aor. act. part. . . . id.
πιστεύσασα, nom. sg. f. aor. act. part. . . . id.
πιστεύσασι(ν), dat. pl. m. aor. act. part.
[§4.3.c] . . . . id.
πιστεύσατε, 2 pers. pl. aor. act. imper. (John
10:38, MT & TR | πιστεύετε, GNT, WH
& NA) . . . . id.
πιστεύσει, 3 pers. sg. fut. act. indic. . . . . . id.
πιστεύσετε, 2 pers. pl. fut. act. indic. . . . . id.
πιστεύσῃ, 3 pers. sg. aor. act. subj. (Mark
11:23; John 17:21, MT & TR | πιστεύῃ,
GNT, WH & NA | John 12:47, πιστεύσῃ,
MT & TR | φυλάξῃ, GNT, WH & NA) id.
πιστεύσῃς, 2 pers. sg. aor. act. subj. . . . . . id.
πιστεύσητε, 2 pers. pl. aor. act. subj. . . . . id.
πιστεύσομεν, 1 pers. pl. fut. act. indic. . . . id.
πίστευσον, 2 pers. sg. aor. act. imper. . . . . id.
πιστευσόντων, gen. pl. m. fut. act. part. (John
17:20, TR | πιστευόντων, GNT, WH, MT
& NA) . . . . id.
πιστεύσουσιν, 3 pers. pl. fut. act. indic. . . id.
πιστεύσω, 1 pers. sg. fut. act. indic. or aor.
act. subj. {John 20:25} . . . . id.
πιστεύσω, 1 pers. sg. aor. act. subj.
{John 9:36} . . . . id.
πιστεύσωμεν, 1 pers. pl. aor. act. subj. . . . id.
πιστεύσωσι(ν), 3 pers. pl. aor. act. subj. . . id.
(4100) **πιστεύω**, 1 pers. sg. pres. act. indic., fut.
πιστεύσω [§13.M] perf. πεπίστευκα, *to believe, give credit to*, Mark 1:15; 16:13; Luke
24:25; intrans. *to believe, have a mental
persuasion*, Matt. 8:13; 9:28; James 2:19;
to believe, be of opinion, Rom. 14:2; in
N.T. πιστεύειν ἐν, εἰς, ἐπί, *to believe in or
on*, Matt. 18:6; 27:42; John 3:15, 16, 18;
absol. *to believe, be a believer* in the religion of Christ, Acts 2:44; 4:4, 32; 13:48;
trans. *to intrust, commit to the charge or
power of*, Luke 16:11; John 2:24; pass. *to
be intrusted with*, Rom. 3:2; 1 Cor. 9:17
πιστεύων, nom. sg. m. pres. act. part. πιστεύω *(4100)*
πίστεως, gen. sg. f. n. . . . . πίστις *(4102)*
πιστή, nom. sg. f. adj. . . . . πιστός *(4103)*
πιστήν, acc. sg. f. adj. . . . . id.
πιστῆς, gen. sg. f. adj. . . . . id.
πιστικῆς, gen. sg. f. adj. . . . . πιστικός *(4101)*
(4101) **πιστικός**, ή, όν [§7.F.a] (πιστός) *genuine, un-
adulterated,* or (πίνω) *liquid,* Mark 14:3;
John 12:3
πίστιν, acc. sg. f. n. . . . . πίστις *(4102)*
(4102) **πίστις**, εως, ἡ, nom. sg. f. n. [§5.E.c]
(πείθομαι) *faith, belief, firm persuasion,*
2 Cor. 5:7; Heb. 11:1; *assurance, firm con-*

viction, Rom. 14:23; *ground of belief, guarantee, assurance,* Acts 17:31; *good faith,
honesty, integrity,* Matt. 23:23; Gal. 5:22;
Tit. 2:10; *faithfulness, truthfulness,* Rom.
3:3; in N.T. *faith* in God and Christ, Matt.
8:10; Acts 3:16, et al. freq.; ἡ πίστις, *the
matter of Gospel faith,* Acts 6:7; Jude 3,
et al.
πιστοί, nom. pl. f. adj. . . . . πιστός *(4103)*
πιστοῖς, dat. pl. m. adj. . . . . id.
πιστόν, acc. sg. m. adj. {1 Tim. 1:12} . . . . id.
πιστόν, nom. sg. neut. adj. {1 Cor. 4:17} . id.
πιστόν, acc. sg. neut. adj. {3 John 5} . . . . id.
(4103) **πιστός**, ή, όν, nom. sg. m. adj. [§7.F.a]
faithful, true, trusty, Matt. 24:45;
25:21, 23; Luke 12:42; 2 Tim. 2:2; *put in
trust,* 1 Cor. 7:25; *true, veracious,* Rev. 1:5;
2:13; *credible, sure, certain, indubitable,*
Acts 13:34; 1 Tim. 1:15; *believing, yield-
ing belief and confidence,* John 20:27; Gal.
3:9; spc. *a* Christian *believer,* Acts 10:45;
16:1, 15; 2 Cor. 6:15; πιστόν, *in a true-
hearted manner, right-mindedly,* 3 John 5
πιστοῦ, gen. sg. m. adj. . . . . πιστός *(4103)*
πιστούς, acc. pl. m. adj. . . . . id.
(4104) **πιστόω**, ῶ, fut. πιστώσω [§20.T] *to make
trustworthy;* pass. *to be assured, feel sure
belief,* 2 Tim. 3:14
πιστῷ, dat. sg. m. adj. . . . . πιστός *(4103)*
πιστῶν, gen. pl. m. adj. . . . . id.
πίω, 1 pers. sg. 2 aor. act. subj. [§37.1] . . πίνω *(4095)*
πίωμεν, 1 pers. pl. 2 aor. act. subj. . . . . . id.
πιών, nom. sg. m. 2 aor. act. part. . . . . . . id.
πίωσιν, 3 pers. pl. 2 aor. act. subj. . . . . . . id.
πλάκες, nom. pl. f. n. . . . . πλάξ *(4109)*
πλανᾷ, 3 pers. sg. pres. act. indic.
{Rev. 13:14} . . . . πλανάω *(4105)*
πλανᾷ, 3 pers. sg. pres. act. subj. (Rev. 20:3,
MT | πλανήσῃ, GNT, WH, TR & NA) id.
πλανᾶσθαι, pres. pass. infin. [§19.S] (Rev.
2:20, TR | πλανᾷ, GNT, WH, MT & NA
| Matt. 24:24, WH | πλανῆσαι, GNT,
MT, TR & NA) . . . . id.
πλανᾶσθε, 2 pers. pl. pres. pass. indic.
{Matt. 22:29} . . . . id.
πλανᾶσθε, 2 pers. pl. pres. pass. imper.
{1 Cor. 6:9} . . . . id.
πλανάτω, 3 pers. sg. pres. act. imper. . . . . id.
(4105) **πλανάω**, ῶ, fut. πλανήσω, aor. ἐπλάνησα
[§18.R] *to lead astray, cause to wander;*
pass. *to go astray, wander about, stray,*
Matt. 18:12, 13; 1 Pet. 2:25; met. *to mislead, deceive,* Matt. 24:4, 5, 11, 24; pass.
to be deceived, err, mistake, Matt. 22:29;
to seduce, delude, John 7:12; pass. *to be*

seduced *or* wander from the path of virtue, *to sin, transgress,* Tit. 3:3; Heb. 5:2; James 5:19, et al.

(4106) **πλάνη,** ης, ἡ, nom. sg. f. n. [§2.B.a] *a wandering; deceit, deception, delusion, imposture, fraud,* Matt. 27:64; 1 Thess. 2:3; *seduction, deceiving,* Eph. 4:14; 2 Thess. 2:11; 1 John 4:6; *error, false opinion,* 2 Pet. 3:17; *wandering* from the path of truth and virtue, *perverseness, wickedness, sin,* Rom. 1:27; James 5:20; 2 Pet. 2:18; Jude 11

πλάνῃ, dat. sg. f. n. . . . . πλάνη *(4106)*
πλανηθῇ, 3 pers. sg. aor. pass. subj. . . πλανάω *(4105)*
πλανηθῆτε, 2 pers. pl. aor. pass. subj. . . . . id.
πλάνης, gen. sg. f. n. . . . . πλάνη *(4106)*
πλανῆσαι, aor. act. infin. . . . . πλανάω *(4105)*
πλανήσῃ, 3 pers. sg. aor. act. subj. . . . . . . id.
πλανήσουσι(ν), 3 pers. pl. fut. act. indic. . id.
πλανῆται, nom. pl. m. n. . . . . πλανήτης *(4107)*

(4107) **πλανήτης,** ου, ὁ [§2.B.c] *a rover, roving, a wanderer, wandering;* ἀστὴρ πλανήτης, *a wandering star,* Jude 13

πλάνοι, nom. pl. m. adj. . . . . πλάνος *(4108)*
πλάνοις, dat. pl. neut. adj. . . . . id.

(4108) **πλάνος,** η, ον, and ος, ον, nom. sg. m. adj., *a wanderer, vagabond;* also act. *deceiving, seducing; a deceiver, impostor,* Matt. 27:63; 2 Cor. 6:8; 1 Tim. 4:1; 2 John 7

πλανῶμεν, 1 pers. pl. pres. act. indic. πλανάω *(4105)*
πλανώμενα, nom. pl. neut. pres. pass. part. (1 Pet. 2:25, MT & TR | πλανώμενοι, GNT, WH & NA) . . . . id.
πλανώμενοι, nom. pl. m. pres. pass. part. id.
πλανωμένοις, dat. pl. m. pres. pass. part. id.
πλανώμενον, acc. sg. neut. pres. pass. part. id.
πλανῶν, nom. sg. m. pres. act. part. . . . . . id.
πλανῶνται, 3 pers. pl. pres. pass. indic. . . id.
πλανῶντες, nom. pl. m. pres. act. part. . . . id.
πλανώντων, gen. pl. m. pres. act. part. . . . id.

(4109) **πλάξ,** πλακός, ἡ [§4.2.b] *a flat broad surface; a table, tablet,* 2 Cor. 3:3; Heb. 9:4

πλαξί(ν), dat. pl. f. n. [§4.3.a] . . . . πλάξ *(4109)*
πλάσαντι, dat. sg. m. aor. act. part. . . πλάσσω *(4111)*

(4110) **πλάσμα,** ατος, τό, nom. sg. neut. n. [§4.D.c] *a thing formed or fashioned;* spc. *a potter's vessel,* Rom. 9:20

(4111) **πλάσσω,** or πλάττω, fut. πλάσω, aor. ἔπλασα, aor. pass. ἐπλάσθην [§26.3] *to form, fashion, mould,* Rom. 9:20; 1 Tim. 2:13

πλαστοῖς, dat. pl. m. adj. . . . . πλαστός *(4112)*

(4112) **πλαστός,** ή, όν [§7.F.a] *formed, fashioned, moulded;* met. *fabricated, counterfeit, delusive,* 2 Pet. 2:3

πλατεῖα, nom. sg. f. adj. {Rev. 21:21} . πλατύς *(4116)*

(4113) **πλατεῖα,** ας, ἡ, nom. sg. f. n. [§2.B.b; 2.2] (pr. f. of πλατύς) *a street, broad way,* Matt. 6:5; 12:19; Luke 10:10, et al. {Matt. 7:13}

πλατείαις, dat. pl. f. n. . . . . πλατεῖα *(4113)*
πλατείας, gen. sg. f. n. {Rev. 11:8} . . . . . id.
πλατείας, acc. pl. f. n. {Luke 10:10} . . . . id.
πλατειῶν, gen. pl. f. n. . . . . id.

(4114) **πλάτος,** ους, τό, nom. sg. neut. n. [§5.E.b] *breadth,* Eph. 3:18; Rev. 20:9; {Rev. 21:16 (2×)}

πλάτος, acc. sg. neut. n. {Rev. 20:9} . . πλάτος *(4114)*
πλατύνθητε, 2 pers. pl. aor. pass. imper. . . . . πλατύνω *(4115)*
πλατύνουσι(ν), 3 pers. pl. pres. act. indic. . id.

(4115) **πλατύνω,** fut. πλατυνῶ, perf. pass. πεπλάτυμαι, aor. pass. ἐπλατύνθην [§27.2.a] *to make broad, widen, enlarge,* Matt. 23:5; pass. met. of the heart, from the Hebrew, *to be expanded* with kindly and genial feelings, 2 Cor. 6:11, 13

(4116) **πλατύς,** εῖα, ύ [§7.H.g] *broad, wide,* Matt. 7:13

(4117) **πλέγμα,** ατος, τό [§4.D.c] *anything plaited or intertwined; a braid* of hair, 1 Tim. 2:9

πλέγμασιν, dat. pl. neut. n. . . . . πλέγμα *(4117)*
πλεῖν, pres. act. infin. . . . . πλέω *(4126)*
πλεῖον, nom. sg. neut. compar. adj. {Matt. 12:42} . . . . πλείων *(4119)*
πλεῖον, acc. sg. neut. compar. adj. {Matt. 20:10} . . . . id.
πλείονα, acc. sg. m. compar. adj. {John 15:2} id.
πλείονα, acc. sg. f. compar. adj. {John 7:31} id.
πλείονα, acc. pl. neut. compar. adj. {Rev. 2:19} . . . . id.
πλείονας, acc. pl. m. compar. adj. . . . . . . id.
πλείονες, nom. pl. m. compar. adj. . . . . . . id.
πλείονος, gen. sg. f. compar. adj. . . . . id.
πλειόνων, gen. pl. m. compar. adj. {2 Cor. 2:6} . . . . id.
πλειόνων, gen. pl. neut. compar. adj. {Luke 11:53} . . . . id.
πλείοσι(ν), dat. pl. m. compar. adj. . . . . . . id.
πλείους, nom. pl. m. compar. adj. {Acts 19:32} . . . . id.
πλείους, nom. pl. f. compar. adj. {Acts 24:11} id.
πλείους, acc. pl. f. compar. adj. {Acts 21:10} id.
πλεῖσται, nom. pl. f. adj. . . . . πλεῖστος *(4118)*
πλεῖστον, nom. sg. neut. adj. . . . . id.

(4118) **πλεῖστος,** η, ον, nom. sg. m. adj. [§8.2] *most; very great,* Matt. 11:20; 21:8; τὸ πλεῖστον, as an adv., *at most,* 1 Cor. 14:27; superlative of πολύς

πλείω, acc. pl. neut. compar. adj. (Matt. 26:53, GNT, WH & NA | πλείους, MT & TR) . . . . πλείων *(4119)*

(4119) **πλείων**, ονος, ὁ, ἡ [§8.2] (compar. of πολύς) more in number, Matt. 21:36; 26:53; more in quantity, Mark 12:43; Luke 21:3; οἱ πλείονες, or πλείους, the greater part, the majority, Acts 19:32; 27:12; the more, 1 Cor. 9:19; 2 Cor. 4:15; neut. πλεῖον, as an adv., more, Luke 7:42; ἐπὶ πλεῖον, more, of time, longer, further, Acts 24:4; of space, more widely, Acts 4:17; 2 Tim. 2:16; 3:9; for the positive, much, of time, long, Acts 20:9; more, higher, greater, more excellent, of higher value, Matt. 5:20; 6:25

(4120) **πλέκω**, fut. πλέξω [§23.1.b] to interweave, weave, braid, plait, Mark 15:17; John 19:2

πλέξαντες, nom. pl. m. aor. act. part. . πλέκω (4120)

πλέον, acc. sg. neut. compar. adj. {Acts 15:28} . . . . πλείων (4119)

πλέον, acc. sg. neut. pres. act. part. {Acts 27:6} . . . . πλέω (4126)

πλεονάζει, 3 pers. sg. pres. act. indic. πλεονάζω (4121)

πλεονάζοντα, acc. sg. m. pres. act. part. {Phil. 4:17} . . . . id.

πλεονάζοντα, nom. pl. neut. pres. act. part. {2 Pet. 1:8} . . . . id.

(4121) **πλεονάζω**, fut. πλεονάσω, aor. ἐπλεόνασα [§26.1] (πλείων, πλέον) to be more than enough; to have more than enough, to have in abundance, 2 Cor. 8:15; to abound, be abundant, 2 Thess. 1:3; 2 Pet. 1:8; to increase, be augmented, Rom. 5:20; to come into wider action, be more widely spread, Rom. 6:1; 2 Cor. 4:15; in N.T. trans. to cause to abound or increase, to augment, 1 Thess. 3:12

πλεονάσαι, 3 pers. sg. aor. act. opt. πλεονάζω (4121)

πλεονάσασα, nom. sg. f. aor. act. part. . . id.

πλεονάσῃ, 3 pers. sg. aor. act. subj. . . . . . id.

πλεονέκται, nom. pl. m. n. . . . . . . πλεονέκτης (4123)

πλεονέκταις, dat. pl. m. n. . . . . id.

πλεονεκτεῖν, pres. act. infin. . . . . πλεονεκτέω (4122)

(4122) **πλεονεκτέω**, ῶ, fut. πλεονεκτήσω [§16.P] (πλείων, πλέον, + ἔχω) to have more than another; to take advantage of; to overreach, make gain of, 2 Cor. 7:2; 12:17, 18; to wrong, 1 Thess. 4:6; to get the better, or an advantage of, 2 Cor. 2:11

πλεονεκτηθῶμεν, 1 pers. pl. aor. pass. subj. [§17.Q] . . . . πλεονεκτέω (4122)

(4123) **πλεονέκτης**, ου, ὁ, nom. sg. m. n. [§2.B.c] one who has or claims to have more than his share; a covetous, avaricious person, one who defrauds for the sake of gain, 1 Cor. 5:10, 11; 6:10; Eph. 5:5

(4124) **πλεονεξία**, ας, ἡ, nom. sg. f. n. [§2.B.b; 2.2]

some advantage which one possesses over another; an inordinate desire of riches, covetousness, Luke 12:15, et al.; grasping, overreaching, extortion, Rom. 1:29; 1 Thess. 2:5, et al.; a gift exacted by importunity and conferred with grudging, a hard-wrung gift, 2 Cor. 9:5; a scheme of extortion, Mark 7:22

πλεονεξίᾳ, dat. sg. f. n. . . . . πλεονεξία (4124)

πλεονεξίαι, nom. pl. f. n. . . . . id.

πλεονεξίαις, dat. pl. f. n. (2 Pet. 2:14, TR | πλεονεξίας, GNT, WH, MT & NA) . . id.

πλεονεξίαν, acc. sg. f. n. . . . . id.

πλεονιξίας, gen. sg. f. n. . . . . id.

πλέοντας, acc. pl. m. pres. act. part. . . . πλέω (4126)

πλεόντων, gen. pl. m. pres. act. part. . . . . id.

(4125) **πλευρά**, ᾶς, ἡ [§2.B.b] pr. a rib; the side of the body, John 19:34; 20:20, 25, 27; Acts 12:7

πλευράν, acc. sg. f. n. . . . . πλευρά (4125)

(4126) **πλέω**, fut. πλεύσομαι and πλευσοῦμαι [§35.1; 35.3] aor. ἔπλευσα, perf. πέπλευκα, to sail, Luke 8:23; Acts 21:3; 27:2, 6, 24

πλέων, nom. sg. m. pres. act. part. (Rev. 18:17, GNT, WH, MT & NA | πλοίων, TR) . . . . πλέω (4126)

πληγαί, nom. pl. f. n. . . . . . . πληγή (4127)

πληγαῖς, dat. pl. f. n. . . . . id.

πληγάς, acc. pl. f. n. . . . . id.

(4127) **πληγή**, ῆς, ἡ, nom. sg. f. n. [§2.B.a] a blow, stroke, stripe, Luke 10:30; 12:48; meton. a wound, Acts 16:33; Rev. 13:3, 12, 14; from the Hebrew, a plague, affliction, calamity, Rev. 9:20; 11:6

πληγῇ, dat. sg. f. n. . . . . πληγή (4127)

πληγήν, acc. sg. f. n. . . . . id.

πληγῆς, gen. sg. f. n. . . . . id.

πληγῶν, gen. pl. f. n. . . . . id.

πλήθει, dat. sg. neut. n. . . . . πλῆθος (4128)

πλήθη, nom. pl. neut. n. . . . . id.

(4128) **πλῆθος**, ους, τό, nom. sg. neut. n. [§5.E.b] fulness, amplitude, magnitude; a multitude, a great number, Luke 1:10; 2:13; 5:6; a multitude, a crowd, throng, Mark 3:7, 8; Luke 6:17, et al. {Luke 23:27}

πλῆθος, acc. sg. neut. n. {Luke 5:6} . . πλῆθος (4128)

πλήθους, gen. sg. neut. n. . . . . id.

πληθύναι, 3 pers. sg. aor. act. opt. (2 Cor. 9:10, MT & TR | πληθυνεῖ, GNT, WH & NA) . . . . πληθύνω (4129)

πληθυνεῖ, 3 pers. sg. fut. act. indic. (2 Cor. 9:10, GNT, WH & NA | πληθύναι, MT & TR) . . . . id.

πληθυνθείη, 3 pers. sg. aor. pass. opt. . . . . id.

πληθυνθῆναι, aor. pass. infin. . . . . id.

πληθυνόντων, gen. pl. m. pres. act.
part. . . . . πληθύνω *(4129)*

(4129) **πληθύνω,** fut. πληθυνῶ, aor. ἐπλήθυνα, aor.
pass. ἐπληθύνθην [§27.1.a,f; 27.3] trans.
to multiply, cause to increase, augment,
2 Cor. 9:10; Heb. 6:14; pass. *to be multiplied, increase, be accumulated,* Matt.
24:12; Acts 6:7; 7:17, et al.; intrans. *to
multiply, increase, be augmented,* Acts 6:1

πληθυνῶ, 1 pers. sg. fut. act. indic. . . πληθύνω *(4129)*
πληθύνων, nom. sg. m. pres. act. part. . . . id.

(4130) **πλήθω,** or **πίμπλημι,** *to fill;* pass. *to be filled*
mentally, *be under full influence; to be ful-
filled*

πλήκτην, acc. sg. m. n. . . . . πλήκτης *(4131)*

(4131) **πλήκτης, ου, ὁ** [§2.B.c] *a striker, one apt to
strike; a quarrelsome, violent person,*
1 Tim. 3:3; Tit. 1:7

(4132) **πλήμμυρα, ας** and **ης, ἡ** [§2.B.b] (πλήμμη, *the
flow of the sea,* πλήθω) *the flood-tide; a
flood, inundation,* Luke 6:48

πλημμύρας, gen. sg. f. n. (Luke 6:48, MT &
TR | πλημμύρης, GNT, WH &
NA) . . . . πλήμμυρα *(4132)*
πλημμύρης, gen. sg. f. n. (Luke 6:48, GNT,
WH & NA | πλημμύρρας, MT & TR) id.

(4133) **πλήν,** adv. (πλέον) *besides, except,* Mark
12:32; Acts 8:1; 20:23; as a conj. *but, however, nevertheless,* Matt. 18:7; Luke 19:27;
Eph. 5:33, et al.; equivalent to ἀλλά, Luke
6:35; 12:31; Acts 27:22

πλήρεις, nom. pl. m. adj. {Acts 19:28} πλήρης *(4134)*
πλήρεις, acc. pl. m. adj. {Acts 6:3} . . . . . . id.
πλήρεις, acc. pl. f. adj. {Matt. 15:37} . . . . id.
πλήρη, acc. sg. m. adj. . . . . id.

(4134) **πλήρης, ές** nom. sg. m. adj. [§7.4.a] (πλέος,
full) full, filled, Matt. 14:20; 15:37; *full* of
disease, Luke 5:12; met. *full of, abounding in, wholly occupied with, completely
under the influence of, or affected by,* Luke
4:1; John 1:14; Acts 9:36, et al.; *full, complete, perfect,* Mark 4:28 {Acts 7:55}

πλήρης, nom. sg. f. adj. {Acts 9:36} . . πλήρης *(4134)*
πληροῖς, 2 pers. sg. pres. act. subj. . . . πληρόω *(4137)*
πληρούμενον, nom. sg. neut. pres. pass. part. id.
πληρουμένου, gen. sg. m. pres. mid. part.
(transitive) . . . . id.
πληροῦν, pres. act. infin. . . . . id.
πληροῦσθε, 2 pers. pl. pres. pass. imper.
[§21.U] . . . . id.
πληροῦται, 3 pers. sg. pres. pass. indic. (Gal.
5:14, MT & TR | πεπλήρωται, GNT,
WH & NA) . . . . id.
πληροφορείσθω, 3 pers. sg. pres. pass.
imper. . . . . πληροφορέω *(4135)*

(4135) **πληροφορέω, ῶ,** fut. πληροφορήσω, aor.
ἐπληροφόρησα [§16.P] (πλήρης + φορέω)
*to bring full measure, to give in full; to
carry out fully, to discharge completely,*
2 Tim. 4:5, 17; pass. of things, *to be fully
established* as a matter of certainty, Luke
1:1; of persons, *to be fully convinced, assured,* Rom. 4:21

πληροφορηθείς, nom. sg. m. aor. pass. part.
[§17.Q] . . . . πληροφορέω *(4135)*
πληροφορηθῇ, 3 pers. sg. aor. pass. subj. . id.
πληροφόρησον, 2 pers. sg. aor. act. imper. id.

(4136) **πληροφορία, ας, ἡ** [§2.B.b; 2.2] *full conviction, firm persuasion, assurance,* 1 Thess.
1:5; Col. 2:2, et al.

πληροφορίᾳ, dat. sg. f. n. . . . . . . πληροφορία *(4136)*
πληροφορίαν, acc. sg. f. n. . . . . id.
πληροφορίας, gen. sg. f. n. . . . . id.

(4137) **πληρόω, ῶ,** fut. πληρώσω, perf. πεπλήρωκα,
aor. ἐπλήρωσα [§20.T] *to fill, make full,
fill up,* Matt. 13:48; 23:32; Luke 3:5; *to
fill up* a deficiency, Phil. 4:18, 19; *to pervade,* John 12:3; Acts 2:2; *to pervade* with
an influence, *to influence fully, possess
fully,* John 16:6; Acts 2:28; 5:3; Rom. 1:29;
Eph. 5:18, et al.; *to complete, perfect,* John
3:29; Eph. 3:19, et al.; *to bring to an end,*
Luke 7:1; *to perform fully, discharge,* Matt.
3:15; Acts 12:25; 13:25; 14:26; Rom. 13:8;
Col. 4:17; *to consummate,* Matt. 5:17; *to
realize, accomplish, fulfil,* Luke 1:20; 9:31;
Acts 3:18; 13:27; from the Hebrew, *to set
forth fully,* Rom. 15:19; Col. 1:25; pass. of
time, *to be fulfilled, come to an end, be
fully arrived,* Mark 1:15; Luke 21:24; John
7:8, et al.; of prophecy, *to receive fulfillment,* Matt. 1:22, et al. freq.

πληρωθείσης, gen. sg. f. aor. pass.
part. . . . . πληρόω *(4137)*
πληρωθέντων, gen. pl. neut. aor. pass. part. id.
πληρωθῇ, 3 pers. sg. aor. pass. subj. . . . . . id.
πληρωθῆναι, aor. pass. infin. . . . . id.
πληρωθήσεται, 3 pers. sg. fut. pass. indic. id.
πληρωθήσονται, 3 pers. pl. fut. pass. indic. id.
πληρωθῆτε, 2 pers. pl. aor. pass. subj. . . . id.
πληρωθῶ, 1 pers. sg. aor. pass. subj. . . . . id.
πληρωθῶσι(ν), 3 pers. pl. aor. pass. subj. . id.

(4138) **πλήρωμα, ατος, τό,** nom. sg. neut. n. [§4.D.c]
*that which fills up; full measure, entire con-
tents,* Mark 8:20; 1 Cor. 10:26, 28; *com-
plement, full extent, full number,* Gal. 4:4:
Eph. 1:10; *that which fills up a deficiency,
a supplement, a patch,* Matt. 9:16; *fulness,
abundance,* John 1:16; *full measure,* Rom.
15:29; *a fulfilling, perfect performance,*

Rom. 13:10; *complete attainment* of entire belief, *full acceptance,* Rom. 11:12; *full development, plenitude,* Eph. 4:13; Col. 1:19; 2:9 {Eph. 1:23}

πλήρωμα, acc. sg. neut. n.
{Eph. 3:19} . . . . πλήρωμα *(4138)*

πληρώματα, acc. pl. neut. n. . . . . id.

πληρώματι, dat. sg. neut. n. . . . . id.

πληρώματος, gen. sg. neut. n. . . . . id.

πληρῶσαι, 3 pers. sg. aor. act. opt.
{Rom. 15:13} . . . . πληρόω *(4137)*

πληρῶσαι, aor. act. infin. {Col. 1:25} . . . . id.

πληρώσαντες, nom. pl. m. aor. act. part. . id.

πληρώσατε, 2 pers. pl. aor. act. imper. . . . id.

πληρώσει, 3 pers. sg. fut. act. indic. . . . . . id.

πληρώσεις, 2 pers. sg. fut. act. indic. . . . . id.

πληρώσῃ, 3 pers. sg. aor. act. subj. . . . . . . id.

πληρώσονται, 3 pers. pl. fut. mid. dep. indic.
(Rev. 6:11, TR | πληρώσωσι, MT | πληρωθῶσι(ν), GNT, WH & NA) . . . . id.

πληρώσωσι, 3 pers. pl. aor. act. subj. (Rev. 6:11, MT | πληρωθῶσι(ν), GNT, WH & NA | πληρώσονται, TR) . . . . id.

πλήσαντες, nom. pl. m. aor. act. part. (John 19:29, MT & TR | GNT, WH & NA omit) . . . . πίμπλημι (‡4130)

πλήσας, nom. sg. m. aor. act. part. . . . . . id.

πλησθείς, nom. sg. m. aor. pass. part. . . . id.

πλησθῆναι, aor. pass. infin. (Luke 21:22, GNT, WH, MT & NA | πληρωθῆναι, TR) . . . . id.

πλησθῇς, 2 pers. sg. aor. pass. subj. . . . . . id.

πλησθήσεται, 3 pers. sg. fut. pass. indic. . id.

(4139) **πλησίον,** adv. (πέλας, idem) *near, near by,* John 4:5; ὁ πλησίον, *a neighbor,* Matt. 19:19; Rom. 15:2, et al.; a friendly *neighbor,* Matt. 5:43

(4140) **πλησμονή,** ῆς, ἡ [§2.B.a] *a filling up;* met. *gratification, satisfaction,* Col. 2:23

πλησμονήν, acc. sg. f. n. . . . . πλησμονή *(4140)*

(4141) **πλήσσω,** fut. πλήξω, 2 aor. pass. ἐπλήγην [§24.9] *to strike, smite;* from the Hebrew, *to smite, to plague, blast,* Rev. 8:12

πλοῖα, nom. pl. neut. n. (Mark 4:36, GNT, WH & NA | πλοιάρια, MT & TR) πλοῖον *(4143)*

πλοῖα, acc. pl. neut. n. {Luke 5:2} . . . . . . id.

πλοιάρια, nom. pl. neut. n.
{John 6:23} . . . . πλοιάριον *(4142)*

πλοιάρια, acc. pl. neut. n. {John 6:24} . . . id.

(4142) **πλοιάριον,** ου, τό, nom. sg. neut. n. [§3.C.c] (dimin. of πλοῖον) *a small vessel, boat,* Mark 3:9, et al.

πλοιαρίῳ, dat. sg. neut. n. . . . . πλοιάριον *(4142)*

(4143) **πλοῖον,** ου, τό, nom. sg. neut. n. [§3.C.c] *a vessel, ship, bark,* whether large or small,

Matt. 4:21, 22; Acts 21:2, 3, et al. {Matt. 14:24}

πλοῖον, acc. sg. neut. n. {Matt. 14:22} . πλοῖον *(4143)*

πλοίου, gen. sg. neut. n. . . . . id.

πλοίῳ, dat. sg. neut. n. . . . . id.

πλοίων, gen. pl. neut. n. . . . . id.

(4144) **πλόος,** οῦς, οῦ, ὁ, and later, πλοῦς, πλοός, ὁ [§3.3] *sailing, navigation, voyage,* Acts 21:7; 27:9, 10

πλοός, gen. sg. m. n. . . . . πλόος *(4144)*

πλοῦν, acc. sg. m. n. . . . . id.

πλούσιοι, nom. pl. m. adj. . . . . πλούσιος *(4145)*

πλουσίοις, dat. pl. m. adj. . . . . id.

πλούσιον, acc. sg. m. adj. . . . . id.

(4145) **πλούσιος,** α, ον, nom. sg. m. adj. [§7.1] *rich, opulent, wealthy;* and pl. οἱ πλούσιοι, *the rich,* Matt. 19:23, 24; 27:57, et al.; met. *rich, abounding in, distinguished for,* Eph. 2:4; James 2:5; Rev. 2:9; 3:17; *rich* in glory, dignity, bliss, etc., 2 Cor. 8:9

πλουσίου, gen. sg. m. adj. . . . . πλούσιος *(4145)*

πλουσίους, acc. pl. m. adj. . . . . id.

(4146) **πλουσίως,** adv., *richly, largely, abundantly,* Col. 3:16, et al.

πλουτεῖν, pres. act. infin. . . . . πλουτέω *(4147)*

(4147) **πλουτέω,** ῶ, fut. πλουτήσω, perf. πεπλούτηκα, aor. ἐπλούτησα [§16.P] *to be or become rich,* Luke 1:25; 1 Tim. 6:9; trop. Luke 12:21; met. *to abound in, be abundantly furnished with,* 1 Tim. 6:18; *to be* spiritually *enriched,* 2 Cor. 8:9, et al.

πλουτήσαντες, nom. pl. m. aor. act. part. . . . . πλουτέω *(4147)*

πλουτήσῃς, 2 pers. sg. aor. act. subj. . . . . id.

πλουτήσητε, 2 pers. pl. aor. act. subj. . . . . id.

πλουτιζόμενοι, nom. pl. m. pres. pass. part. . . . . πλουτίζω *(4148)*

πλουτίζοντες, nom. pl. m. pres. act. part. . id.

(4148) **πλουτίζω,** fut. πλουτίσω, aor. ἐπλούτισα [§26.1] *to make rich, enrich;* met. *to enrich* spiritually, 1 Cor. 1:5; 2 Cor. 6:10; 9:11

πλοῦτον, acc. sg. m. n. . . . . πλοῦτος *(4149)*

(4149) **πλοῦτος,** ου, ὁ, nom. sg. m. n. [§3.C.a] (neut. in the nom. and acc. τὸ πλοῦτος) *riches, wealth, opulence,* Matt. 13:22; Luke 8:14; in N.T., πλοῦτος τοῦ θεοῦ, or Χριστοῦ, *those rich benefits, those abundant blessings which flow from God or Christ,* Eph. 3:8; Phil. 4:19; meton. *richness, abundance, copiousness,* Rom. 2:4; 11:33; 2 Cor. 8:2; meton. *a* spiritual *enriching,* Rom. 11:12 {Eph. 1:18}

πλοῦτος, nom. sg. neut. n.
{Col. 1:27} . . . . πλοῦτος *(4149)*

πλοῦτος, acc. sg. neut. n. {Eph. 1:7} . . . . id.

πλούτου, gen. sg. m. n. . . . . πλοῦτος *(4149)*

πλουτοῦντας, acc. pl. m. pres. act.
part. . . . . πλουτέω *(4147)*

πλουτῶν, nom. sg. m. pres. act. part. . . . . id.

πλύνοντες, nom. pl. m. pres. act. part. (Rev. 22:14, with τὰς στολὰς αὐτῶν, GNT, WH & NA | ποιοῦντες τὰς ἐντολὰς αὐτοῦ, MT & TR) . . . . πλύνω *(4150)*

(4150) **πλύνω,** fut. πλυνῶ, aor. ἔπλυνα [§27.1.a,f] *to wash garments,* Rev. 7:14

πνέῃ, 3 pers. sg. pres. act. subj. . . . . πνέω *(4154)*

πνεῖ, 3 pers. sg. pres. act. indic. [§35.1] . . . id.

πνέοντα, acc. sg. m. pres. act. part. . . . . . id.

πνέοντος, gen. sg. m. pres. act. part. . . . . id.

πνεούσῃ, dat. sg. f. pres. act. part. . . . . . . id.

(4151) **πνεῦμα,** ατος, τό, nom. sg. neut. n. [§4.D.c] *wind, air in motion,* John 3:8; *breath,* 2 Thess. 2:8; the substance *spirit,* John 3:6; *a spirit, spiritual being,* John 4:24; Acts 23:8, 9; Heb. 1:14; *a bodiless spirit, specter,* Luke 24:37; *a foul spirit,* δαιμόνιον, Matt. 8:16; Luke 10:20; *spirit,* as a vital principle, John 6:63; 1 Cor. 15:45; the human *spirit, the soul,* Matt. 26:41; 27:50; Acts 7:59; 1 Cor. 7:34; James 2:26; *the spirit* as the seat of thought and feeling, *the mind,* Mark 8:12; Acts 19:21, et al.; *spirit, mental frame,* 1 Cor. 4:21; 1 Pet. 3:4; *a characteristic spirit, an influential principle,* Luke 9:55; 1 Cor. 2:12; 2 Tim. 1:7; *a pervading influence,* Rom. 11:8; *spirit, frame of mind,* as distinguished from outward circumstances and actions, Matt. 5:3; *spirit* as distinguished from outward show and form, John 4:23; *spirit, a divinely bestowed spiritual frame,* characteristic of true believers, Rom. 8:4; Jude 19; *spirit, latent spiritual import, spiritual significance,* as distinguished from the mere letter, Rom. 2:29: 7:6; 2 Cor. 3:6, 17; *spirit,* as a term for a process superior to a merely natural or carnal course of things, by the operation of the Divine Spirit, Rom. 8:4; Gal. 4:29; *a spiritual dispensation,* or *a sealing energy of the Holy Spirit,* Heb. 9:14; THE HOLY SPIRIT, Matt. 3:16; 12:31; John 1:32, 33, et al.; *a gift of the Holy Spirit,* John 7:39; Acts 19:2; 1 Cor. 14:12, et al.; *an operation or influence of the Holy Spirit,* 1 Cor. 12:3; et al.; *a spiritual influence, an inspiration,* Matt. 22:43; Luke 2:27; Eph. 1:17; *a professedly divine communication,* or, *a professed possessor of a spiritual communication,* 1 Cor. 12:10; 2 Thess. 2:2; 1 John 4:1, 2, 3 {Mark 1:12}

πνεῦμα, acc. sg. neut. n. {Mark 1:10} . πνεῦμα *(4151)*

πνεύμασι(ν), dat. pl. neut. n. . . . . id.

πνεύματα, nom. pl. neut. n. {Rev. 16:14} . id.

πνεύματα, acc. pl. neut. n. {Rev. 16:13} . . id.

πνεύματι, dat. sg. neut. n. . . . . id.

πνευματικά, acc. pl. neut. adj. . . πνευματικός *(4152)*

πνευματικαῖς, dat. pl. f. adj. . . . . id.

πνευματικάς, acc. pl. f. adj. . . . . id.

πνευματικῇ, dat. sg. f. adj. . . . . id.

πνευματικῆς, gen. sg. f. adj. . . . . id.

πνευματικοί, nom. pl. m. adj. . . . . id.

πνευματικοῖς, dat. pl. m. adj. {1 Cor. 3:1} id.

πνευματικοῖς, dat. pl. neut. adj. {1 Cor. 2:13} id.

πνευματικόν, nom. sg. neut. adj. {1 Cor. 15:44, 46} . . . . id.

πνευματικόν, acc. sg. neut. adj. {1 Cor. 10:3-4} . . . . id.

(4152) **πνευματικός,** ή, όν, nom. sg. m. adj. [§7.F.a] *spiritual, pertaining to the soul,* as distinguished from what concerns the body, Rom. 15:27; 1 Cor. 9:11; *spiritual, pertaining to the nature of spirits,* 1 Cor. 15:44; τὰ πνευματικὰ τῆς πονηρίας, i.q. τὰ πνεύματα τὰ πονηρά, *evil spirits,* Eph. 6:12; *spiritual, pertaining or relating to the influences of the Holy Spirit,* of things, Rom. 1:11; 7:14, et al.; τὰ πνευματικά, *spiritual gifts,* 1 Cor. 12:1; 14:1; *superior in process to the natural course of things, miraculous,* 1 Cor. 10:3; of persons, *gifted with a spiritual frame of mind, spiritually affected,* 1 Cor. 2:13, 15; *endowed with spiritual gifts, inspired,* 1 Cor. 14:37

πνευματικῶν, gen. pl. neut. adj. . πνευματικός *(4152)*

(4153) **πνευματικῶς,** adv., *spiritually, through spiritual views and affections,* 1 Cor. 2:14; *spiritually, in a spiritual sense, allegorically,* Rev. 11:8

πνεύματος, gen. sg. neut. n. . . . . πνεῦμα *(4151)*

πνευμάτων, gen. pl. neut. n. . . . . id.

(4154) **πνέω,** fut. πνεύσω [§35.3] later, πνεύσομαι and πνευσοῦμαι, aor. ἔπνευσα, *to breathe; to blow,* as the wind, Matt. 7:25, 27, et al.

(4155) **πνίγω,** fut. πνίξω, πνίξομαι, and πνιξοῦμαι, aor. ἔπνιξα [§23.1.b; 23.2] *to stifle, suffocate, choke,* Mark 5:13; *to seize by the throat,* Mark 18:28

πνικτόν, acc. sg. neut. adj. . . . . πνικτός *(4156)*

(4156) **πνικτός,** ή, όν [§7.F.a] *strangled, suffocated;* in N.T. τὸ πνικτόν, *the flesh of animals killed by strangulation or suffocation,* Acts 15:20, 29; 21:25

πνικτοῦ, gen. sg. neut. adj. . . . . πνικτός *(4156)*

πνικτῶν, gen. pl. neut. adj. (Acts 15:29, GNT, WH & NA | πνικτοῦ, MT & TR) . . . id.

(4157) **πνοή, ῆς, ἡ** [§2.B.a] *breath, respiration,* Acts 17:25; *a wind, a blast of wind, breeze,* Acts 2:2

πνοήν, acc. sg. f. n. . . . . πνοή *(4157)*

πνοῆς, gen. sg. f. n. . . . . id.

πόδα, acc. sg. m. n. [§4.2.c] . . . . πούς *(4228)*

πόδας, acc. pl. m. n. . . . . id.

πόδες, nom. pl. m. n. . . . . id.

ποδήρη, acc. sg. m. adj. . . . . ποδήρης *(4158)*

(4158) **ποδήρης, ες** [§7.G.b] (ποῦς + ἄρω, *to fit*) *reaching to the feet;* as subst. sc. ἐσθής, *a long, flowing robe reaching down to the feet,* Rev. 1:13

ποδός, gen. sg. m. n. . . . . πούς *(4228)*

ποδῶν, gen. pl. m. n. . . . . id.

(4159) **πόθεν,** adv., *whence? whence,* used of place, etc. Matt. 15:33; met. of a state of dignity, Rev. 2:5; used of origin, Matt. 21:25; of cause, source, author, etc., Matt. 13:27, 54, 56; Luke 1:43; *how? in what way?* Mark 8:4; 12:37

ποία, nom. sg. f. interrogative pronoun {Luke 6:34} . . . . ποῖος *(4169)*

ποῖα, acc. pl. neut. interrogative pronoun {Luke 24:19} . . . . id.

ποίᾳ, dat. sg. f. interrogative pronoun . . . . id.

ποίαν, acc. sg. f. interrogative pronoun . . . id.

ποίας, gen. sg. f. interrogative pronoun {Luke 5:19} . . . . id.

ποίας, acc. pl. f. interrogative pronoun {Matt. 19:18} . . . . id.

ποιεῖ, 3 pers. sg. pres. act. indic. {John 11:47} . . . . ποιέω *(4160)*

ποίει, 2 pers. sg. pres. act. imper. {Luke 10:28} . . . . id.

ποιεῖν, pres. act. infin. . . . . id.

ποιεῖς, 2 pers. sg. pres. act. indic. . . . . id.

ποιεῖσθαι, pres. mid. infin. {1 Pet. 1:10, 15} id.

ποιεῖσθαι, pres. pass. infin. {1 Tim. 2:1} . . id.

ποιεῖσθε, 2 pers. pl. pres. mid. imper. . . . . id.

ποιεῖται, 3 pers. sg. pres. mid. indic. . . . . . id.

ποιεῖτε, 2 pers. pl. pres. act. indic. {1 Cor. 10:31a} . . . . id.

ποιεῖτε, 2 pers. pl. pres. act. imper. {1 Cor. 10:31b} . . . . id.

ποιείτω, 3 pers. sg. pres. act. imper. . . . . . id.

(4160) **ποιέω, ῶ,** fut. ποιήσω, perf. πεποίηκα, aor. ἐποίησα [§16.P] *to make, form, construct,* Matt. 17:4; Mark 9:5; John 2:15; of God, *to create,* Matt. 19:4; Acts 4:24; *to make, prepare* a feast, etc., Matt. 22:2; Mark 6:21; met. *to make, establish, ratify,* a covenant, Heb. 8:9; *to make, assume, consider, regard,* Matt. 12:33; *to make, effect, bring to pass, cause to take place, do, accomplish,*

Matt. 7:22; 21:21; Mark 3:8; 6:5; 7:37; met. *to perfect, accomplish, fulfil, put in execution* a purpose, promise, etc., Luke 16:4; 19:48; *to cause, make,* Matt. 5:32; John 11:37; Acts 24:12; *to make gain, gain, acquire,* Matt. 25:16; Luke 19:18; *to get, procure,* Luke 12:33; *to make, to cause to be or become* a thing, Matt. 21:13; 23:15; *to use, treat,* Luke 15:19; *to make, constitute, appoint* to some office, Matt. 4:19; Mark 3:14; *to make, declare to be,* 1 John 1:10; 5:10; *to do, to perform, execute, practise, act,* Matt. 5:46, 47; 6:2, 3; *to commit* evil, Matt. 13:41; 27:23; *to be devoted to, follow, practise,* John 3:21; 5:29; Rom. 3:12; *to do, execute, fulfil, keep, observe, obey,* precepts, etc., Matt. 1:24; 5:19; 7:21, 24, 26; *to bring evil upon, inflict,* Acts 9:13; *to keep, celebrate* a festival, Matt. 26:18; *to institute the celebration of* a festival, Heb. 11:28; ποιεῖν τινα ἔξω, *to cause to leave* a place, i.q. ἔξω ἄγειν, *to lead or conduct out,* Acts 5:34; *to pass, spend* time, *continue for* a time, Matt. 20:12; Acts 15:33; 18:23; James 4:13; *to bear,* as trees, *yield, produce,* Matt. 3:8, 10; 7:17, 18, 19; with a substantive or adjective it forms a periphrasis for the verb corresponding to the noun or adjective, e.g. δῆλον ποιεῖν, i.q. δηλοῦν, *to make manifest, betray,* Matt. 26:73; ἐκδίκησιν ποιεῖν, i.q. ἐκδικεῖν, *to vindicate, avenge,* Luke 18:7, 8; ἔκθετον ποιεῖν, i.q. ἐκτιθέναι, *to expose* infants, Acts 7:19; ἐνέδραν ποιεῖν, i.q. ἐνεδρεύειν, *to lie in wait,* Acts 25:3; ἐξουσίαν ποιεῖν, i.q. ἐξουσιάζειν, *to exercise power or authority,* Rev. 13:12; κρίσιν ποιεῖν, i.q. κρίνειν, *to judge, act as judge,* John 5:27; λύτρωσιν ποιεῖν, i.q. λυτροῦν, *to deliver, set free,* Luke 1:68; μονὴν ποιεῖν, i.q. μένειν, *to remain, dwell,* John 14:23; πόλεμον ποιεῖν, i.q. πολεμεῖν, *to make or wage war, fight,* Rev. 11:7; συμβούλιον ποιεῖν, i.q. συμβουλεύεσθαι, *to consult together, deliberate,* Mark 3:6; συνωμοσίαν ποιεῖν, i.q. συνομνύναι, and συστροφὴν ποιεῖν, i.q. συστρέφεσθαι, *to conspire together, form a conspiracy,* Acts 23:12, 13; φανερὸν ποιεῖν, i.q. φανεροῦν, *to make known, betray,* Matt. 12:16; ἀναβολὴν ποιεῖσθαι, i.q. ἀναβάλλεσθαι, *to delay, procrastinate,* Acts 25:17; βέβαιον ποιεῖσθαι, i.q. βεβαιοῦν, *to confirm, render firm and sure,* 2 Pet. 1:10; δεήσεις ποιεῖσθαι, i.q. δεῖσθαι, *to pray, offer prayer*, Luke 5:33; ἐκβολὴν ποιεῖσθαι, i.q. ἐκβάλλειν, *to cast out, throw overboard*, Acts 27:18; καθαρισμὸν ποιεῖσθαι, i.q. καθαρίζειν, *to cleanse* from sin, Heb. 1:3; κοινωνίαν ποιεῖσθαι, i.q. κοινωνεῖν, *to communicate in liberality, bestow alms*, Rom. 15:26; κοπετὸν ποιεῖν, i.q. κόπτεσθαι, *to lament, bewail*, Acts 8:2; λόγον ποιεῖσθαι, *to regard, make account of*, Acts 20:24; μνείαν ποιεῖσθαι, i.q. μνησθῆναι, *to call to mind*, Rom. 1:9; μνήμην ποιεῖσθαι, *to remember, retain in memory*, 2 Pet. 1:15; πορείαν ποιεῖσθαι, i.q. πορεύεσθαι, *to go, journey, travel*, Luke 13:22; πρόνοιαν ποιεῖσθαι, i.q. προνοεῖσθαι, *to take care of, provide for*, Rom. 13:14; σπουδὴν ποιεῖσθαι, i.q. σπουδάζειν, *to act with diligence and earnestness*, Jude 3

ποιῇ, 3 pers. sg. pres. act. subj. . . . . . . , ποιέω *(4160)*

(4161) **ποίημα**, ατος, τό, nom. sg. neut. n. [§4.D.c] *that which is made or done; a work, workmanship, creation*, Rom. 1:20; met. Eph. 2:10

ποιήμασι(ν), dat. pl. neut. n. . . . . ποίημα *(4161)*
ποιῇς, 2 pers. sg. pres. act. subj. . . . . . ποιέω *(4160)*
ποιῆσαι, aor. act. infin. . . . . id.
ποιήσαιεν, 3 pers. pl. aor. act. opt. (Luke 6:11, GNT, WH & NA | ποιήσειαν, MT & TR) . . . . id.
ποιησάμενοι, nom. pl. m. aor. mid. part. (Acts 23:13, GNT, WH & NA | πεποιηκότες, MT & TR) . . . . id.
ποιησάμενος, nom. sg. m. aor. mid. part. id.
ποιήσαντες, nom. pl. m. aor. act. part. . . . id.
ποιήσαντι, dat. sg. m. aor. act. part. . . . . . id.
ποιήσας, nom. sg. m. aor. act. part. . . . . . id.
ποιήσασαν, acc. sg. f. aor. act. part. . . . . . id.
ποιήσασθαι, aor. mid. infin. . . . . id.
ποιήσατε, 2 pers. pl. aor. act. imper. . . . . id.
ποιησάτω, 3 pers. sg. aor. act. imper. . . . . id.
ποιήσει, 3 pers. sg. fut. act. indic. {Heb. 13:6} . . . . id.
ποιήσει, dat. sg. f. n. {James 1:25} . . . ποίησις *(4162)*
ποιήσειαν, 3 pers. pl. aor. act. opt. (Aeolic) [§13.11.b note] (Luke 6:11, MT & TR | ποιήσαιεν, GNT, WH & NA) . . . . . ποιέω *(4160)*
ποιήσεις, 2 pers. sg. fut. act. indic. . . . . . id.
ποιήσετε, 2 pers. pl. fut. act. indic. . . . . . id.
ποιήσῃ, 3 pers. sg. aor. act. subj. . . . . id.
ποιήσῃς, 2 pers. sg. aor. act. subj. . . . . . . id.
ποιήσητε, 2 pers. pl. aor. act. subj. . . . . . . id.

(4162) **ποίησις**, εως, ἡ [§5.E.c] *a making; an acting, doing, performance; observance* of a law, James 1:25

ποιησόμεθα, 1 pers. pl. fut. mid. dep. indic.

(John 14:23, GNT, WH & NA | ποιήσομεν, MT & TR) . . . . ποιέω *(4160)*
ποιήσομεν, 1 pers. pl. fut. act. indic. . . . . id.
ποίησον, 2 pers. sg. aor. act. imper. . . . . . id.
ποιήσουσιν, 3 pers. pl. fut. act. indic. . . . . id.
ποιήσω, 1 pers. sg. fut. act. indic. {Luke 12:18} . . . . id.
ποιήσω, 1 pers. sg. aor. act. subj. {Luke 12:17} . . . . id.
ποιήσωμεν, 1 pers. pl. aor. act. subj. . . . . id.
ποιήσων, nom. sg. m. fut. act. part. . . . . . id.
ποιήσωσι(ν), 3 pers. pl. aor. act. subj. . . . id.
ποιηταί, nom. pl. m. n. . . . . ποιητής *(4163)*
ποιῆτε, 2 pers. pl. pres. act. subj. . . . . . . ποιέω *(4160)*

(4163) **ποιητής**, οῦ, ὁ, nom. sg. m. n. [§2.B.c] *a maker; the maker or author* of a song or poem, *a poet*, Acts 17:28; *a doer; a performer* of the enactments of a law, Rom. 2:13, et al.

ποιητῶν, gen. pl. m. n. . . . . ποιητής *(4163)*
ποικίλαις, dat. pl. f. adj. . . . . ποικίλος *(4164)*
ποικίλης, gen. sg. f. adj. . . . . id.
ποικίλοις, dat. pl. m. adj. . . . . id.

(4164) **ποικίλος**, η, ον [§7.F.a] *of various colors, variegated, checkered; various, diverse, manifold*, Matt. 4:24, et al.

ποίμαινε, 2 pers. sg. pres. act. imper. ποιμαίνω *(4165)*
ποιμαίνει, 3 pers. sg. pres. act. indic. . . . . id.
ποιμαίνειν, pres. act. infin. . . . . id.
ποιμαίνοντα, acc. sg. m. pres. act. part. . . id.
ποιμαίνοντες, nom. pl. m. pres. act. part. id.

(4165) **ποιμαίνω**, fut. ποιμανῶ, aor. ἐποίμανα [§27.1.c,e] *to feed, pasture, tend a flock*, Luke 17:7; 1 Cor. 9:7; trop. *to feed* with selfish indulgence, *to pamper*, Jude 12; met. *to tend, direct, superintend*, Matt. 2:6; John 21:16, et al.; *to rule*, Rev. 2:27

ποιμάνατε, 2 pers. pl. aor. act. imper. . . . . ποιμαίνω *(4165)*
ποιμανεῖ, 3 pers. sg. fut. act. indic. . . . . . id.
ποιμένα, acc. sg. m. n. . . . . ποιμήν *(4166)*
ποιμένας, acc. pl. m. n. . . . . id.
ποιμένες, nom. pl. m. n. . . . . id.
ποιμένων, gen. pl. m. n. . . . . id.

(4166) **ποιμήν**, ένος, ὁ, nom. sg. m. n. [§4.2.e] *one who tends flocks or herds, a shepherd, herdsman*, Matt. 9:36; 25:32; met. *a pastor, superintendent, guardian*, John 10:11, 14, 16, et al.

(4167) **ποίμνη**, ης, ἡ, nom. sg. f. n. [§2.B.a] *a flock* of sheep, Luke 2:8; 1 Cor. 9:7; meton. *a flock* of disciples, Matt. 26:31; John 10:16

ποίμνην, acc. sg. f. n. . . . . ποίμνη *(4167)*
ποίμνης, gen. sg. f. n. . . . . id.

(4168) **ποίμνιον**, ου, τό, nom. sg. neut. n. [§3.C.c] (contr. for ποιμένιον, *a flock*) *a flock*; met.

a flock of Christian disciples, Acts
20:28, 29; 1 Pet. 5:2, 3 {Luke 12:32}

ποίμνιον, acc. sg. neut. n. {1 Pet. 5:2} ποίμνιον *(4168)*

ποιμνίου, gen. sg. neut. n. . . . . id.

ποιμνίῳ, dat. sg. neut. n. . . . . id.

ποῖον, acc. sg. m. interrogative pronoun
{1 Pet. 1:11} . . . . ποῖος *(4169)*

ποῖον, nom. sg. neut. interrogative pronoun
1 Pet. 2:20) . . . . id.

ποῖον, acc. sg. neut. interrogative pronoun
{John 10:32} . . . . id.

(4169) **ποῖος**, οἵα, οἷον, interrogative pronoun
[§10.7.a] *of what kind, sort, or species,*
John 12:33; 21:19; *what? which?* Matt.
19:18; 21:23, 24, 27, et al.

ποίου, gen. sg. m. interrogative pronoun ποῖος *(4169)*

ποιοῦμαι, 1 pers. sg. pres. mid. indic.
[§17.Q] . . . . ποιέω *(4160)*

ποιοῦμεν, 1 pers. pl. pres. act. indic. . . . . . id.

ποιούμενοι, nom. pl. m. pres. mid. part. . . id.

ποιούμενος, nom. sg. m. pres. mid. part. . id.

ποιοῦν, nom. sg. neut. pres. act. part. . . . . id.

ποιοῦντα, acc. sg. m. pres. act. part.
{John 5:19} . . . . id.

ποιοῦντα, nom. pl. neut. pres. act. part.
{Rev. 16:14} . . . . id.

ποιοῦνται, 3 pers. pl. pres. mid. indic. . . . id.

ποιοῦντας, acc. pl. m. pres. act. part. . . . . id.

ποιοῦντες, nom. pl. m. pres. act. part. . . . id.

ποιοῦντι, dat. sg. m. pres. act. part.
{James 4:17} . . . . id.

ποιοῦντι, dat. sg. neut. pres. act. part.
{Matt. 21:43} . . . . id.

ποιοῦντος, gen. sg. m. pres. act. part. . . . . id.

ποιοῦσι(ν), 3 pers. pl. pres. act. indic.
{Matt. 23:3, 5} . . . . id.

ποιοῦσιν, dat. pl. m. pres. act. part.
{James 3:18} . . . . id.

ποιῶ, 1 pers. sg. pres. act. indic. {John 5:36} id.

ποιῶ, 1 pers. sg. pres. act. subj. {John 6:38} id.

ποίῳ, dat. sg. m. interrogative pronoun
{John 12:33} . . . . ποῖος *(4169)*

ποίῳ, dat. sg. neut. interrogative pronoun
{Acts 4:7} . . . . id.

ποιῶμεν, 1 pers. pl. pres. act. subj. . . . . . ποιέω *(4160)*

ποιῶν, nom. sg. m. pres. act. part. . . . . . . id.

ποιῶσι(ν), 3 pers. pl. pres. act. subj. . . . . . id.

πόλει, dat. sg. f. n. . . . . πόλις *(4172)*

πόλεις, nom. pl. f. n. {Rev. 16:19} . . . . . . id.

πόλεις, acc. pl. f. n. {Matt. 9:35} . . . . id.

πολεμεῖ, 3 pers. sg. pres. act. indic. . . πολεμέω *(4170)*

πολεμεῖτε, 2 pers. pl. pres. act. indic. . . . . id.

(4170) **πολεμέω**, ῶ, fut. πολεμήσω, aor. ἐπολέμησα
[§16.P] *to make or wage war, fight,* Rev. 2:16;
12:7, et al.; *to battle, quarrel,* James 4:2

πολεμῆσαι, aor. act. infin. . . . . πολεμέω *(4170)*

πολεμήσουσι(ν), 3 pers. pl. fut. act. indic. id.

πολεμήσω, 1 pers. sg. fut. act. indic. . . . . id.

πόλεμοι, nom. pl. m. n. . . . . πόλεμος *(4171)*

πόλεμον, acc. sg. m. n. . . . . id.

(4171) **πόλεμος**, ου, ὁ, nom. sg. m. n. [§3.C.a] *war,*
Matt. 24:6; Mark 13:7; *battle, engagement,*
combat, 1 Cor. 14:8; Heb. 11:34; *battling,*
strife, James 4:1, et al.

πολέμους, acc. pl. m. n. . . . . πόλεμος *(4171)*

πολέμῳ, dat. sg. m. n. . . . . id.

πολέμων, gen. pl. m. n. . . . . id.

πόλεσιν, dat. pl. f. n. . . . . πόλις *(4172)*

πόλεων, gen. pl. f. n. . . . . id.

πόλεως, gen. sg. f. n. . . . . id.

πόλιν, acc. sg. f. n. . . . . id.

(4172) **πόλις**, εως, ἡ, nom. sg. f. n. [§5.E.c] *a city,*
an enclosed and walled town, Matt.
10:5, 11; 11:1; meton. *the inhabitants of a*
city, Matt. 8:34; 10:15; with a gen. of person, or a personal pronoun, *the city* of any
one, *the city* of one's birth or residence,
Matt. 9:1; Luke 2:4, 11; ἡ πόλις, *the city,*
κατ' ἐξοχήν, *Jerusalem,* Matt. 21:18;
28:11; met. *a place of permanent residence,*
abode, home, Heb. 11:10, 16; 13:14

πολῖται, nom. pl. m. n. . . . . πολίτης *(4177)*

πολιτάρχας, acc. pl. m. n. . . . . . . πολιτάρχης *(4173)*

(4173) **πολιτάρχης**, ου, ὁ [§2.B.c] (πόλις + ἄρχω)
a ruler or prefect of a city, city magistrate,
Acts 17:6, 8

(4174) **πολιτεία**, ας, ἡ [§2.B.b; 2.2] *the state of be-*
ing a citizen; citizenship, the right or priv-
ilege of being a citizen, freedom of a city
or state, Acts 22:28; *a commonwealth,*
community, Eph. 2:12

πολιτείαν, acc. sg. f. n. . . . . πολιτεία *(4174)*

πολιτείας, gen. sg. f. n. . . . . id.

πολιτεύεσθε, 2 pers. pl. pres. mid./pass. dep.
imper. . . . . πολιτεύω *(†4176)*

(4175) **πολίτευμα**, ατος, τό, nom. sg. neut. n.
[§4.D.c] *the administration of a common-*
wealth; in N.T. equivalent to πολιτεία, *a*
community, commonwealth, Phil. 3:20

(†4176) **πολιτεύω**, fut. πολιτεύσω [§13.M] intrans. *to*
be a citizen; trans. *to govern a city or state,*
administer the affairs of a state; pass. *to*
be governed; in N.T. *to order one's life and*
conduct, converse, live, in a certain manner as to habits and principles, Acts 23:1;
Phil. 1:27

πολίτην, acc. sg. m. n. (Heb. 8:11, GNT, WH
& NA | πλησίον, MT & TR) . . . . πολίτης *(4177)*

(4177) **πολίτης**, ου, ὁ, nom. sg. m. n. [§2.B.c] *a cit-*
izen, Luke 15:15; 19:14; Acts 21:39

πολιτῶν, gen. pl. m. n. . . . . πολίτης *(4177)*

πολλά, nom. pl. neut. adj.

    {1 Cor. 12:14} . . . . πολύς *(4183)*

πολλά, acc. pl. neut. adj. {1 Cor. 12:12} . . id.

πολλαί, nom. pl. f. adj. . . . . id.

πολλαῖς, dat. pl. f. adj. . . . . id.

(4178) **πολλάκις**, adv., *many times, often, frequently,*
    Matt. 17:15; Mark 5:4; 9:22, et al.

πολλαπλασίονα, acc. pl. neut.

    adj. . . . . πολλαπλασίων *(4179)*

(4179) **πολλαπλασίων**, ον [§7.G.a] (a later equivalent
    to πολλαπλάσιος, from πολύς) *manifold,*
    many times more, Luke 18:30

πολλάς, acc. pl. f. adj. . . . . πολύς *(4183)*

πολλή, nom. sg. f. adj. . . . . id.

πολλῇ, dat. sg. f. adj. . . . . id.

πολλήν, acc. sg. f. adj. . . . . id.

πολλῆς, gen. sg. f. adj. . . . . id.

πολλοί, nom. pl. f. adj. . . . . id.

πολλοῖς, dat. pl. m. adj. {Luke 7:21} . . . . id.

πολλοῖς, dat. pl. neut. adj. {Acts 1:3} . . . . id.

πολλοῦ, gen. sg. m. adj. {Acts 15:32} . . . . id.

πολλοῦ, gen. sg. neut. adj. {Acts 22:28} . . id.

πολλούς, acc. pl. m. adj. . . . . id.

πολλῷ, dat. sg. m. adj. {1 Cor. 2:3} . . . . . id.

πολλῷ, dat. sg. neut. adj. {1 Cor. 12:22} . . id.

πολλῶν, gen. pl. m. adj. {Luke 2:34} . . . . id.

πολλῶν, gen. pl. f. adj. {Luke 2:35} . . . . . id.

πολλῶν, gen. pl. neut. adj. {Luke 12:7} . . id.

πολύ, nom. sg. neut. adj. {Luke 6:17} . . . . id.

πολύ, acc. sg. neut. adj. {Luke 5:6} . . . . . id.

(4180) **πολυλογία**, ας, ἡ [§2.B.b; 2.2] (πολύς +
    λόγος) *wordiness, loquacity,* Matt. 6:7

πολυλογίᾳ, dat. sg. f. n. . . . . πολυλογία *(4180)*

(4181) **πολυμερῶς**, adv. (πολυμερής, *consisting of*
    many parts, πολύς + μέρος) *in many parts*
    or parcels, Heb. 1:1

πολύν, acc. sg. m. adj. . . . . πολύς *(4183)*

(4182) **πολυποίκιλος**, ον, nom. sg. m. adj. [§7.2]
    (πολύς + ποικίλος) *exceedingly various,*
    multifarious, multiform, manifold; by impl.
    immense, infinite, Eph. 3:10

(4183) **πολύς**, πολλή, πολύ, nom. sg. m. adj., gen.
    πολλοῦ, πολλῆς, πολλοῦ [§7.7.a] *great* in
    magnitude or quantity, *much, large,* Matt.
    13:5; John 3:23; 15:8; pl. *many,* Matt. 3:7;
    in time, *long,* Matt. 25:19; Mark 6:35;
    John 5:6; οἱ πολλοί, *the many, the mass,*
    Rom. 5:15; 12:5; 1 Cor. 10:33; τὸ πολύ,
    much, 2 Cor. 8:15; πολύ, as an adv., *much,*
    greatly, Mark 12:27; Luke 7:47; of time,
    ἐπὶ πολύ, *a long time,* Acts 28:6; μετ᾽ οὐ
    πολὺ, *not long after,* Acts 27:14; followed
    by a compar., *much,* 2 Cor. 8:22; πολλῷ,
    much, by much, Matt. 6:30; Mark 10:48;

τὰ πολλά, as an adv., *most frequently, gen-*
    erally, Rom. 15:22; πολλά, as an adv.,
    much, greatly, vehemently, Mark 1:45;
    3:12; of time, *many times, frequently,*
    often, Matt. 9:14

(4184) **πολύσπλαγχνος**, ον, nom. sg. m. adj. [§7.2]
    (πολύς + σπλάγχνον) *very merciful, very*
    compassionate, James 5:11

πολυτελεῖ, dat. sg. m. adj. . . . . πολυτελής *(4185)*

πολυτελές, nom. sg. neut. adj. . . . . id.

(4185) **πολυτελής**, ές [§7.G.b] (πολύς + τέλος) *ex-*
    pensive, costly, Mark 14:3; 1 Tim. 2:9; *of*
    great value, very precious, 1 Pet. 3:4

πολυτελοῦς, gen. sg. f. adj. . . . . . . πολυτελής *(4185)*

πολύτιμον, acc. sg. m. adj. . . . . πολύτιμος *(4186)*

(4186) **πολύτιμος**, ον [§7.2] (πολύς + τιμή) *of great*
    price, costly, precious, Matt. 13:46; John
    12:3

πολυτιμότερον, nom. sg. neut. compar. adj.
    (1 Pet. 1:7, GNT, WH & NA | πολὺ
    τιμιώτερον, MT & TR) . . . . πολύτιμος *(4186)*

πολυτίμου, gen. sg. f. adj. . . . . id.

(4187) **πολυτρόπως**, adv. (πολύτροπος, *manifold,*
    various, πολύς + τρόπος) *in many ways,*
    in various modes, Heb. 1:1

(4188) **πόμα**, ατος, τό [§4.D.c] (πέτομαι, perf. pass.
    of πίνω) *drink,* 1 Cor. 10:4; Heb. 9:10

πόμα, acc. sg. neut. n. . . . . πόμα *(4188)*

πόμασι(ν), dat. pl. neut. n. . . . . id.

πονηρά, nom. sg. f. adj.
    {Matt. 12:39} . . . . πονηρός *(4190)*

πονηρά, nom. pl. neut. adj. {John 3:19} . . id.

πονηρά, acc. pl. neut. adj. {Matt. 9:4} . . . id.

πονηρᾷ, dat. sg. f. adj. . . . . id.

πονηραί, nom. pl. f. adj. . . . . id.

πονηρᾶς, gen. sg. f. adj. . . . . id.

πονηρέ, voc. sg. m. adj. . . . . id.

(4189) **πονηρία**, ας, ἡ [§2.B.b; 2.2] pr. *badness, bad*
    condition; in N.T. *evil disposition* of mind,
    wickedness, mischief, malignity, Matt.
    22:18, et al.; pl. πονηρίαι, *wicked deeds,*
    villanies, Mark 7:22; Acts 3:26

πονηρίᾳ, dat. sg. f. n. . . . . πονηρία *(4189)*

πονηρίαι, nom. pl. f. n. . . . . id.

πονηρίαν, acc. sg. f. n. . . . . id.

πονηρίας, gen. sg. f. n. . . . . id.

πονηριῶν, gen. pl. f. n. . . . . id.

πονηροί, nom. pl. m. adj. . . . . πονηρός *(4190)*

πονηροῖς, dat. pl. m. adj. {3 John 10} . . . id.

πονηροῖς, dat. pl. neut. adj. {2 John 11} . . id.

πονηρόν, acc. sg. m. adj. {1 John 2:13-14} id.

πονηρόν, nom. sg. neut. adj. {Acts 19:15} . id.

πονηρόν, acc. sg. neut. adj. {Acts 28:21} . id.

(4190) **πονηρός**, ά, όν, nom. sg. m. adj. [§7.1] *bad,*
    unsound, Matt. 6:23; 7:17, 18; *evil, afflic-*

tive, Eph. 5:16; 6:13; Rev. 16:2; *evil, wrongful, malignant, malevolent,* Matt. 5:11, 39; Acts 28:21; *evil, wicked, impious,* and τὸ πονηρόν, *evil, wrong, wickedness,* Matt. 5:37, 45; 9:4; *slothful, inactive,* Matt. 25:26; Luke 19:22; ὁ πονηρός, *the evil one, the devil,* Matt. 13:19, 38; John 17:15; *evil eye, i.q.* φθονερός, *envious,* Matt. 20:15; Mark 7:22; impl. *covetous, niggardly,* Matt. 7:11

πονηρότερα, acc. pl. neut. compar. adj. . . . . πονηρός *(4190)*

πονηροῦ, gen. sg. m. adj. {2 Thess. 3:3} .   id.

πονηροῦ, gen. sg. neut. adj. {1 Thess. 5:22}   id.

πονηρούς, acc. pl. m. adj. . . . .   id.

πονηρῷ, dat. sg. m. adj. {1 John 5:19} . . .   id.

πονηρῷ, dat. sg. neut. or m. adj. {Matt. 5:39} . . . .   id.

πονηρῶν, gen. pl. m. adj. {2 Thess. 3:2} .   id.

πονηρῶν, gen. pl. neut. adj. {Luke 3:19} .   id.

πόνον, acc. sg. m. n. (Col. 4:13, GNT, WH & NA | ζῆλον, MT & TR) . . . . πόνος *(4192)*

(4192) **πόνος**, ου, ὁ, nom. sg. m. n. [§3.C.a] (πένομαι) *labor, travail; pain, misery, anguish,* Rev. 16:10, 11; 21:4

πόνου, gen. sg. m. n. . . . . πόνος *(4192)*

Ποντικόν, acc. sg. m. adj. . . . . Ποντικός *(4193)*

(4193) **Ποντικός**, ή, όν, *belonging to, or an inhabitant of,* Πόντος, Acts 18:2

(4194) **Πόντιος**, ου, ὁ, nom. sg. m. n. [§3.C.a] *Pontius,* pr. name, Acts 4:27

Ποντίου, gen. sg. m. n. . . . . Πόντιος *(4194)*

Ποντίῳ, dat. sg. m. n. (Matt. 27:2, MT & TR | GNT, WH & NA omit) . . . . Πόντος *(4195)*

Πόντον, acc. sg. m. n. . . . .   id.

(4195) **Πόντος**, ου, ὁ, *Pontus,* country of Asia Minor

Πόντου, gen. sg. m. n. . . . . Πόντος *(4195)*

πόνων, gen. pl. m. n. . . . . πόνος *(4192)*

(4196) **Πόπλιος**, ου, ὁ [§3.C.a] *Publius,* pr. name, Acts 28:7, 8

Ποπλίου, gen. sg. m. n. . . . . Πόπλιος *(4196)*

Ποπλίῳ, dat. sg. m. n. . . . .   id.

(4197) **πορεία**, ας, ἡ [§2.B.b; 2.2] *a going, progress; a journey, travel,* Luke 13:22; *from the Hebrew, way* of life, *business, occupation,* James 1:11

πορείαις, dat. pl. f. n. . . . . πορεία *(4197)*

πορείαν, acc. sg. f. n. . . . .   id.

πορεύεσθαι, pres. mid./pass. dep. infin. . . . . πορεύομαι *(4198)*

πορεύεσθε, 2 pers. pl. pres. mid./pass. dep. imper. . . . .   id.

πορεύεται, 3 pers. sg. pres. mid./pass. dep. indic. . . . .   id.

πορευθείς, nom. sg. m. aor. pass. dep. part.   id.

πορευθεῖσα, nom. sg. f. aor. pass. dep. part. . . . . πορεύομαι *(4198)*

πορευθεῖσαι, nom. pl. f. aor. pass. dep. part.   id.

πορευθέντα, acc. sg. m. aor. pass. dep. part. (Acts 27:3, MT & TR | πορευθέντι, GNT, WH & NA) . . . .   id.

πορευθέντες, nom. pl. m. aor. pass. dep. part.   id.

πορευθέντι, dat. sg. m. aor. pass. dep. part. (Acts 27:3, GNT, WH & NA | πορευθέντα, MT & TR) . . . .   id.

πορευθῇ, 3 pers. sg. aor. pass. dep. subj. .   id.

πορευθῆναι, aor. pass. dep. infin. . . . .   id.

πορευθῆτε, 2 pers. pl. aor. pass. dep. subj.   id.

πορεύθητι, 2 pers. sg. aor. pass. dep. imper.   id.

πορευθῶ, 1 pers. sg. aor. pass. dep. subj. .   id.

πορευθῶσιν, 3 pers. pl. aor. pass. dep. subj.   id.

(4198) **πορεύομαι**, 1 pers. sg. pres. mid./pass. dep. indic., fut. πορεύσομαι, aor. (pass. form) ἐπορεύθην [§14.N] (mid. of πορεύω, *to convey, transport,* from πόρος) *to go, pass from one place to another,* Matt. 17:27; 18:12; *to go away, depart,* Matt. 24:1; 25:41; John 14:2, 3; trop. *to go away, depart,* from life, *to die,* Luke 22:22; *to go, pass on one's way, journey, travel,* Matt. 2:8, 9; Luke 1:39; 2:41; πορεύομαι ὀπίσω, *to go after, to become a follower or partisan,* Luke 21:8; or, *to pursue after, be devoted to,* 2 Pet. 2:10; *from the Hebrew, to go or proceed* in any way or course of life, *live* in any manner, Luke 1:6; 8:14; Acts 9:31

πορευόμεναι, nom. pl. f. pres. mid./pass. dep. part. (Acts 9:31, MT & TR | πορευομένη, GNT, WH & NA) . . . . πορεύομαι *(4198)*

πορευομένη, nom. sg. f. pres. mid./pass. dep. part. (Acts 9:31, GNT, WH & NA | πορευόμεναι, MT & TR) . . . .   id.

πορευόμενοι, nom. pl. m. pres. mid./pass. dep. part. . . . .   id.

πορευομένοις, dat. pl. m. pres. mid./pass. dep. part. . . . .   id.

πορευόμενον, acc. sg. m. pres. mid./pass. dep. part. {Acts 1:11} . . . .   id.

πορευόμενον, nom. sg. neut. pres. mid./pass. dep. part. {Luke 9:53} . . . .   id.

πορευόμενος, nom. sg. m. pres. mid./pass. dep. part. . . . .   id.

πορευομένου, gen. sg. m. pres. mid./pass. dep. part. . . . .   id.

πορευομένους, acc. pl. m. pres. mid./pass. dep. part. . . . .   id.

πορευομένῳ, dat. sg. m. pres. mid./pass. dep. part. . . . .   id.

πορευομένων, gen. pl. m. pres. mid./pass.

dep. part. . . . . πορεύομαι *(4198)*

πορεύου, 2 pers. sg. pres. mid./pass. dep.

    imper. . . . . id.

πορεύσεται, 3 pers. sg. fut. mid. dep. indic. id.

πορεύσῃ, 2 pers. sg. fut. mid. dep. indic. . id.

πορεύσομαι, 1 pers. sg. fut. mid. dep. indic. id.

πορευσόμεθα, 1 pers. pl. fut. mid. dep. indic.

    (James 4:13, GNT, WH & NA | πορευ-

    σώμεθα, MT & TR) . . . . id.

πορεύσονται, 3 pers. pl. fut. mid. dep. indic. id.

πορευσώμεθα, 1 pers. pl. aor. mid. dep. subj.

    (James 4:13, MT & TR | πορευσόμεθα,

    GNT, WH & NA) . . . . id.

πορεύωμαι, 1 pers. sg. pres. mid./pass. dep.

    subj. . . . . id.

(4199) **πορθέω,** ῶ, fut. πορθήσω [§16.P] (a collateral

    form of πέρθω) *to lay waste, destroy;* impl.

    to harass, ravage, Acts 9:21; Gal. 1:13, 23

πορθήσας, nom. sg. m. aor. act. part. . πορθέω *(4199)*

πορισμόν, acc. sg. m. n. . . . . πορισμός *(4200)*

(4200) **πορισμός,** οῦ, ὁ, nom. sg. m. n. [§3.C.a]

    (πορίζομαι, *to furnish to one's self, acquire,*

    gain, mid. of πορίζω, *to furnish, supply*)

    a providing, procuring; meton. *source of*

    gain, 1 Tim. 6:5, 6

Πόρκιον, acc. sg. m. n. . . . . Πόρκιος *(4201)*

(4201) **Πόρκιος,** ου, ὁ, *Porcius,* pr. name

πόρναι, nom. pl. f. n. . . . . πόρνη *(4204)*

(4202) **πορνεία,** ας, ἡ, nom. sg. f. n. [§2.B.b; 2.2] *for-*

    nication, whoredom, Matt. 15:19; Mark

    7:21; Acts 15:20, 29; *concubinage,* John

    8:41; *adultery,* Matt. 5:32; 19:9; *incest,*

    1 Cor. 5:1; *lewdness, uncleanness,* genr.,

    Rom. 1:29; from the Hebrew, put symbol-

    ically for *idolatry,* Rev. 2:21; 14:8

πορνείᾳ, dat. sg. f. n. . . . . πορνεία *(4202)*

πορνεῖαι, nom. pl. f. n. . . . . id.

πορνείαν, acc. sg. f. n. . . . . id.

πορνείας, gen. sg. f. n. {John 8:41} . . . . . id.

πορνείας, acc. pl. f. n. {1 Cor. 7:2} . . . . . . id.

πορνεῦσαι, aor. act. infin. . . . . πορνεύω *(4203)*

πορνεύσαντες, nom. pl. m. aor. act. part. id.

(4203) **πορνεύω,** fut. πορνεύσω, aor. ἐπόρνευσα

    [§13.M] *to commit fornication or whore-*

    dom, 1 Cor. 6:18; 10:8; Rev. 2:14, 20; from

    the Hebrew, *to commit* spiritual *fornica-*

    tion, practise idolatry, Rev. 17:2; 18:3, 9

πορνεύωμεν, 1 pers. pl. pres. act.

    subj. . . . . πορνεύω *(4203)*

πορνεύων, nom. sg. m. pres. act. part. . . . id.

(4204) **πόρνη,** ης, ἡ, nom. sg. f. n. [§2.B.a] (περνάω,

    or πέρνημι, *to sell*) *a prostitute, a whore,*

    harlot, an unchaste female, Matt.

    21:31, 32; from the Hebrew, *an idolatress,*

    Rev. 17:1, 5, 15

πόρνῃ, dat. sg. f. n. . . . . πόρνη *(4204)*

πόρνην, acc. sg. f. n. . . . . id.

πόρνης, gen. sg. f. n. . . . . id.

πόρνοι, nom. pl. m. n. . . . . πόρνος *(4205)*

πόρνοις, dat. pl. m. n. . . . . id.

(4205) **πόρνος,** ου, ὁ, nom. sg. m. n. [§3.C.a] *a cat-*

    amite; in N.T. *a fornicator, impure person,*

    1 Cor. 5:9, 10, 11; 6:9, et al.

πόρνους, acc. pl. m. n. . . . . πόρνος *(4205)*

πορνῶν, gen. pl. f. n. . . . . πόρνη *(4204)*

(4206) **πόρρω,** adv. (a later form of πρόσω, from

    πρό) *forward, in advance, far advanced;*

    far, far off, at a distance, Matt. 15:8; Mark

    7:6

(4207) **πόρρωθεν,** adv., *from a distance, from afar,*

    Heb. 11:13; *at a distance, far, far off,* Luke

    17:12

(†4208) **πορρώτερον,** adv., *farther* (Luke 24:28, GNT,

    WH & NA | πορρωτέρω, MT & TR)

(4208) **πορρωτέρω,** adv. (compar. of πόρρω) *farther,*

    beyond (Luke 24:28, MT & TR | πορ-

    ρώτερον, GNT, WH & NA)

(4209) **πορφύρα,** ας, ἡ [§2.B.b] *purpura, murex,* a

    species of shell-fish that yielded the pur-

    ple dye, highly esteemed by the ancients,

    its tint being a bright crimson; in N.T. *a*

    purple garment, robe of purple, Luke 16:19;

    Rev. 17:4; 18:12, et al.

πορφύρᾳ, dat. sg. f. n. (Rev. 17:4, TR |

    πορφυροῦν, GNT, WH, MT &

    NA) . . . . πορφύρα *(4209)*

πορφύραν, acc. sg. f. n. . . . . id.

πορφύρας, gen. sg. f. n. (Rev. 18:12, GNT,

    WH, TR & NA | πορφυροῦ, MT) . . . id.

(†4210) **πορφύρεος,** α, ον [§7.4.c] *purple, crimson,*

    John 19:2, 5; Matt. 27:28, 31, et al.

(4211) **πορφυρόπωλις,** ιδος, ἡ, nom. sg. f. n. [§5.E.c]

    (f. of πορφυροπώλης, πυρφύρα + πωλέω)

    a female seller of purple cloths

πορφυροῦ, gen. sg. neut. adj. (Rev. 18:12, MT

    | πορφύρας, GNT, WH, TR &

    NA) . . . . πορφύρεος *(†4210)*

πορφυροῦν, acc. sg. neut. adj. . . . . id.

πόσα, acc. pl. neut. correlative or interroga-

    tive pronoun . . . . πόσος *(4214)*

πόσαι, nom. pl. f. correlative or interrogative

    pronoun . . . . id.

(4212) **ποσάκις,** adv., *How many times? How often?*

    Matt. 18:21; 23:37; Luke 13:34

πόσας, acc. pl. f. correlative or interrogative

    pronoun . . . . πόσος *(4214)*

πόσει, dat. sg. f. n. . . . . πόσις *(4213)*

πόσην, acc. sg. f. correlative or interrogative

    pronoun . . . . πόσος *(4214)*

ποσί(ν), dat. pl. m. n. [§4.3.b] . . . . πούς *(4228)*

(4213) **πόσις**, εως, ἡ, nom. sg. f. n. [§5.E.c] *drinking; drink, beverage,* John 6:55; Rom. 14:17; Col. 2:16

πόσοι, nom. pl. m. correlative or interrogative pronoun . . . . πόσος *(4214)*

πόσον, nom. sg. neut. correlative or interrogative pronoun {Matt. 6:23} . . . . id.

πόσον, acc. sg. neut. correlative or interrogative pronoun {Luke 16:5, 7} . . . . id.

(4214) **πόσος**, η, ον, nom. sg. m. correlative or interrogative pronoun to ὅσος + τόσος [§10.7.b] *How great? How much?* Matt. 6:23; Luke 16:5, 7; 2 Cor. 7:11; πόσῳ, adverbially before a comparative, *How much? By how much?* Matt. 7:11; 10:25; Heb. 10:29; of time, *How long?* Mark 9:21; of number, pl. *How many?* Matt. 15:34; 16:9, 10, et al.

πόσους, acc. pl. m. correlative or interrogative pronoun . . . . πόσος *(4214)*

πόσῳ, dat. sg. neut. correlative or interrogative pronoun . . . . id.

πόσων, gen. pl. neut. correlative or interrogative pronoun . . . . id.

ποταμοί, nom. pl. m. n. . . . . ποταμός *(4215)*

ποταμόν, acc. sg. m. n. . . . . id.

(4215) **ποταμός**, οῦ, ὁ, nom. sg. m. n. [§3.C.a] *a river, stream,* Mark 1:5; Acts 16:13; met. and allegorically John 7:38; Rev. 22:1, 2; *a flood, winter torrent,* for χείμαρρος ποταμός, Matt. 7:25, 27

ποταμοῦ, gen. sg. m. n. . . . . ποταμός *(4215)*

ποταμούς, acc. pl. m. n. . . . . id.

ποταμοφόρητον, acc. sg. f. adj. . . . . ποταμοφόρητος *(4216)*

(4216) **ποταμοφόρητος**, ον [§7.2] (ποταμός + φορητός, from φορέω) *borne along or carried away by a flood or torrent,* Rev. 12:15

ποταμῷ, dat. sg. m. n. . . . . ποταμός *(4215)*

ποταμῶν, gen. pl. m. n. . . . . id.

ποταπαί, nom. pl. f. adj. . . . . ποταπός *(4217)*

ποταπή, nom. sg. f. adj. . . . . id.

ποταπήν, acc. sg. f. adj. . . . . id.

ποταποί, nom. pl. m. adj. . . . . id.

(4217) **ποταπός**, ή, όν, nom. sg. m. adj. [§7.F.a] a later form of ποδαπός, *Of what country?* in N.T. equivalent to ποῖος, *What? Of what manner? Of what kind or sort?* Luke 1:29; 7:39; denoting admiration, *What? What kind of? How great?* Matt. 8:27; Mark 13:1, et al.

ποταπούς, acc. pl. m. adj. . . . . ποταπός *(4217)*

(4218) **ποτέ**, an enclitic particle of time, *once, some time or other,* either past or future; *formerly,* John 9:13; *at length,* Luke 22:32;

at any time, ever, Eph. 5:29; Heb. 2:1; intensive after interrogatives, *ever,* 1 Cor. 9:7; Heb. 1:5, et al. {John 9:13}

(4219) **πότε**, interrogative particle, *When? At what time?* Matt. 24:3; 25:37, 38, 39, 44; ἕως πότε, *Till when? How long?* Matt. 17:17, et al. {John 10:24}

(4220) **πότερον**, acc. sg. neut. adj. as an interrogative adv., *Whether?*

(†4220) **πότερος**, α, ον, *Which of the two? Whether?* John 7:17

(4221) **ποτήριον**, ου, τό, nom. sg. neut. n. [§3.C.c] (ποτήρ, πότος, πίνω) *a vessel for drinking, cup,* Matt. 10:42; 23:25, 26; meton. *the contents of a cup, liquor contained in a cup,* Luke 22:20; 1 Cor. 10:16; from the Hebrew, *the cup or potion* of what God's administration deals out, Matt. 20:22, 23; Rev. 14:10, et al. {Luke 22:20b}

ποτήριον, acc. sg. neut. n. {Luke 22:20a} . . . . ποτήριον *(4221)*

ποτηρίου, gen. sg. neut. n. . . . . id.

ποτηρίῳ, dat. sg. neut. n. . . . . id.

ποτηρίων, gen. pl. neut. n. . . . . id.

πότιζε, 2 pers. sg. pres. act. imper. . . . . ποτίζω *(4222)*

ποτίζει, 3 pers. sg. pres. act. indic. . . . . . id.

(4222) **ποτίζω**, fut. ποτίσω, Att. ποτιῶ, perf. πεπότικα, aor. ἐπότισα [§26.1] *to cause to drink, give drink to,* Matt. 10:42, et al.; met. 1 Cor. 3:2; Rev. 14:8; *to water, irrigate,* met. 1 Cor. 3:6, 7, 8

ποτίζων, nom. sg. m. pres. act. part. . . . ποτίζω *(4222)*

(4223) **Ποτίολοι**, ων, οἱ, *Puteoli,* a town of Italy, Acts 28:13

Ποτιόλους, acc. pl. m. n. . . . . Ποτίολοι *(4223)*

ποτίσῃ, 3 pers. sg. aor. act. subj. . . . . . ποτίζω *(4222)*

πότοις, dat. pl. m. n. . . . . πότος *(4224)*

(4224) **πότος**, ου, ὁ [§3.C.a] *a drinking; a drinking together; drinking-bout, compotation,* 1 Pet. 4:3

(4225) **πού**, an enclitic indefinite particle, *somewhere, in a certain place,* Heb. 2:6; 4:4; with numerals, *thereabout* {Rom. 4:19}

(4226) **ποῦ**, an interrogative particle of place, *Where? In what place?* direct, Matt. 2:2; Luke 8:25; John 1:39; indirect, Matt. 2:4; John 1:40; *whither,* John 3:8; 7:35; 13:36 {Rom. 3:27}

(4227) **Πούδης**, εντος, ὁ, nom. sg. m. n. [§4.2.d] *Pudens,* pr. name, Latin, 2 Tim. 4:21

(4228) **πούς**, ποδός, ὁ, nom. sg. m. n. [§4.2.c] *the foot,* Matt. 4:6; 5:35; 7:6; 22:44; 28:9; Luke 1:79; Acts 5:9; Rom. 3:15, et al.

(4229) **πρᾶγμα**, ατος, τό, nom. sg. neut. n. [§4.D.c] *a thing done, fact, deed, work, transaction,*

Luke 1:1; James 3:16; *a matter, affair,* Matt. 18:19; Rom. 16:2; *a matter* of dispute, 1 Cor. 6:1; *a thing,* genr., Heb. 10:1; 11:1; τὸ πρᾶγμα, an euphemism for *profligacy,* perhaps, 1 Thess. 4:6 {James 3:16}

πρᾶγμα, acc. sg. neut. n. {Acts 5:4} .. πρᾶγμα *(4229)*

(4230) **πραγματεία, ας, ἡ** [§2.B.b; 2.2] *an application to a matter of business;* in N.T. *business, affair, transaction,* 2 Tim. 2:4

πραγματείαις, dat. pl. f. n. (2 Tim. 2:4, GNT, MT, TR & NA | πραγματίαις, WH) . . . . πραγματεία *(4230)*

(4231) **πραγματεύομαι,** fut. πραγματεύσομαι [§15.O] *to be occupied with or employed in any business, do business; to trade, traffic,* Luke 19:13

πραγματεύσασθαι, aor. mid. dep. infin. (Luke 19:13, WH | πραγματεύσασθε, GNT, MT, TR & NA) . . . . πραγματεύομαι *(4231)*

πραγματεύσασθε, 2 pers. pl. aor. mid. dep. imper. . . . . id.

πράγματι, dat. sg. neut. n. . . . . πρᾶγμα *(4229)*

πράγματος, gen. sg. neut. n. . . . . id.

πραγμάτων, gen. pl. neut. n. . . . . id.

πραεῖς, nom. pl. m. adj. [§7.8] . . . . . . πραῢς *(4239)*

πράεος, gen. sg. neut. adj. (1 Pet. 3:4, MT | πραέως, GNT, WH & NA | πρᾳέος, TR) . . . . id.

πράεος, gen. sg. neut. adj. (1 Pet. 3:4, TR | πραέος, MT | πραέως, GNT, WH & NA) . . . . id.

πραέως, gen. sg. neut. adj. (1 Pet. 3:4, GNT, WH & NA | πράεος, MT | πρᾳέος, TR) id.

πραθέν, nom. sg. neut. aor. pass. part. . . . . πιπράσκω *(4097)*

πραθῆναι, aor. pass. infin. . . . . id.

(4232) **πραιτώριον, ου, τό,** nom. sg. neut. n. [§3.C.c] (Latin, *praetorium,* from *praetor*) when used in reference to a camp, *the tent of the general or commander-in-chief;* hence, in reference to a province, *the palace in which the governor of the province resided,* Matt. 27:27; Mark 15:16; Acts 23:35, et al.; *the camp occupied by the praetorian cohorts at Rome, the praetorian camp,* or, *the Roman emperor's palace,* Phil. 1:13 {Mark 15:16}

πραιτώριον, acc. sg. neut. n. {Matt. 27:27} . . . . πραιτώριον *(4232)*

πραιτωρίῳ, dat. sg. neut. n. . . . . id.

πράκτορι, dat. sg. m. n. . . . . πράκτωρ *(4233)*

(4233) **πράκτωρ, ορος, ὁ,** nom. sg. m. n. [§4.2.f] *an exactor of dues or penalties; an officer* who enforced payment of debts by imprisonment, Luke 12:58

πρᾶξαι, aor. act. infin. . . . . πράσσω *(4238)*

πράξαντες, nom. pl. m. aor. act. part. . . . id.

πραξάντων, gen. pl. m. aor. act. part. . . . id.

πράξας, nom. sg. m. aor. act. part. (1 Cor. 5:2, GNT, WH & NA | ποιήσας, MT & TR) id.

πράξει, dat. sg. f. n. . . . . πρᾶξις *(4234)*

πράξεις, acc. pl. f. n. . . . . id.

πράξεσιν, dat. pl. f. n. . . . . id.

πράξετε, 2 pers. pl. fut. act. indic. . . . πράσσω *(4238)*

πράξῃς, 2 pers. sg. aor. act. subj. . . . . . . id.

πρᾶξιν, acc. sg. f. n. . . . . πρᾶξις *(4234)*

(4234) **πρᾶξις, εως, ἡ** [§5.E.c] *operation, business, office,* Rom. 12:4; πρᾶξις, and πράξεις, *actions, mode of acting, ways, deeds, practice, behavior,* Matt. 16:27; Luke 23:51, et al.

(4235) **πραός, εῖα, ον,** nom. sg. m. n. [§7.8] *mild; gentle, kind* (Matt. 11:29, TR | πραός, MT | πραῢς, GNT, WH & NA)

(†4235) **πραός, εῖα, ον,** nom. sg. m. n., *mild; gentle, king* (Matt. 11:29, MT | πραός, TR | πραῢς, GNT, WH & NA)

(4236) **πραότης,** or πραΰτης, ητος, ἡ [§4.2.c] *meekness, forbearance,* 1 Cor. 4:21; Gal. 5:23; *gentleness, kindness, benevolence,* 2 Cor. 10:1, et al.

πραότητα, acc. sg. f. n. (Col. 3:12; 1 Tim. 6:11; Tit. 3:2, MT | πραότητα, TR | πραϋπαθίαν, GNT, WH & NA) . πραότης *(4236)*

πραότητα, acc. sg. f. n. (Col. 3:12; 1 Tim. 6:11; Tit. 3:2, TR | πραότητα, MT | πραϋπαθίαν, GNT, WH & NA) . . . . . id.

πραότητι, dat. sg. f. n. (2 Tim. 2:25, MT | πραότητι, TR | πραΰτητι, GNT, WH & NA) . . . . id.

πραότητι, dat. sg. f. n. (2 Tim. 2:25, TR | πραότητι, MT | πραΰτητι, GNT, WH & NA) . . . . id.

πραότητος, gen. sg. f. n. (1 Cor. 4:21; 2 Cor. 10:1; Gal. 6:1; Eph. 4:2, MT | πραότητος, TR | πραΰτητος, GNT, WH & NA) . . id.

πραότητος, gen. sg. f. n. (1 Cor. 4:21; 2 Cor. 10:1; Gal. 6:1; Eph. 4:2, TR | πραότητος, MT | πραΰτητος, GNT, WH & NA) . id.

(4237) **πρασιά, ᾶς, ἡ** [§2.B.b; 2.2] *a small area or bed in a garden;* trop. *a company of persons disposed in squares;* from the Hebrew, πρασιαὶ πρασιαί, *by areas, by squares,* like beds in a garden, Mark 6:40

πρασιαί, nom. pl. f. n. . . . . πρασιά *(4237)*

πράσσει, 3 pers. sg. pres. act. indic. . . πράσσω *(4238)*

πράσσειν, pres. act. infin. . . . . id.

πράσσεις, 2 pers. sg. pres. act. indic. . . . id.

πράσσετε, 2 pers. pl. pres. act. imper. . . . id.

πράσσης, 2 pers. sg. pres. act. subj. . . . . . id.

πράσσοντας, acc. pl. m. pres. act.
part. πράσσω *(4238)*
πράσσοντες, nom. pl. m. pres. act. part. . id.
πράσσοντι, dat. sg. m. pres. act. part. . . . id.
πράσσουσι(ν), 3 pers. pl. pres. act. indic.
(Acts 17:7, GNT, WH, MT & NA |
πράττουσιν, TR) . . . . id.
πράσσουσι(ν), dat. pl. m. pres. act. part.
{Rom. 1:32} . . . . id.
(4238) **πράσσω**, 1 pers. sg. pres. act. indic., or
πράττω, Acts 17:7, fut. πράξω, perf.
πέπραχα, aor. ἔπραξα [§26.3] *to do, execute, perform, practise, act, transact,* and
of evil, *to commit,* Luke 22:23; 23:15; John
3:20; Acts 26:9, 20, 26, 31, et al.; *to fulfil, obey, observe* a law, Rom. 2:25; *to do
to* any one, Acts 16:28; 5:35; *to occupy
one's self with, be engaged in, busy one's
self about,* Acts 19:19; 1 Thess. 4:11; absol. *to fare,* Acts 15:29; Eph. 6:21; *to exact, require, collect* tribute, money lent,
etc., Luke 3:13; 19:23
πράσσων, nom. sg. m. pres. act.
part. πράσσω *(4238)*
πράττειν, pres. act. infin. (Acts 19:36, TR |
πράσσειν, GNT, WH, MT & NA) . . . id.
πράττουσιν, 3 pers. pl. pres. act. indic. (Acts
17:7, TR | πράσσουσι(ν), GNT, WH,
MT & NA) . . . . id.
(‡4236) **πραϋπάθια**, ας, ἡ [§2.B.b; 2.2] (πραΰς +
πάθος, from πάσχω) *meekness, gentleness
of mind, kindness,* 1 Tim. 6:11
πραϋπαθίαν, acc. sg. f. n. (1 Tim. 6:11, GNT,
WH & NA | πραότητα, MT | πραότητα,
TR) . . . . πραϋπάθια *(‡4236)*
(4239) **πραΰς**, εῖα, ύ, nom. sg. m. adj. [§7.8] i.q.
πρᾶος, *meek, gentle, kind, forgiving,* Matt.
5:5; *mild, benevolent, humane,* Matt. 21:5;
1 Pet. 3:4
(4240) **πραΰτης**, ητος, ἡ, nom. sg. f. n. [§4.2.c] i.q.
πραότης, *meekness, mildness, forbearance,*
1 Pet. 3:15; *gentleness, kindness,* James
1:21; 3:13 (Gal. 5:23, GNT, WH & NA
| πραότης, MT | πραότης, TR)
πραΰτητα, acc. sg. f. n. (Col. 3:12; Tit. 3:2,
GNT, WH & NA | πραότητα, MT |
πραότητα, TR) . . . . πραΰτης *(4240)*
πραΰτητι, dat. sg. f. n. (2 Tim. 2:25; James
1:21; 3:13, GNT, WH & NA | πραότητι,
MT | πραότητι, TR) . . . . id.
πραΰτητος, gen. sg. f. n. (1 Cor. 4:21; 2 Cor.
10:1; Gal. 6:1; Eph. 4:2; 1 Pet. 3:15; GNT,
WH & NA | πραότητος, MT | πραό-
τητος, TR) . . . . id.
(†4241) **πρέπει**, 3 pers. sg. pres. act. indic. impersonal

verb, *it becomes, it is fitting, it is proper,
it is right,* etc., and part. πρέπον, *becoming, suitable, decorous,* etc., Matt. 3:15;
1 Cor. 11:13; Eph. 5:3; 1 Tim. 2:10, et al.
πρέπον, nom. sg. neut. pres. act. part. πρέπει *(†4241)*
(4242) **πρεσβεία**, ας, ἡ [§2.B.b; 2.2] *eldership, sen-
iority; an embassy, legation; a body of am-
bassadors, legates,* Luke 14:32; 19:14
πρεσβείαν, acc. sg. f. n. . . . . πρεσβεία *(4242)*
πρεσβεύομεν, 1 pers. pl. pres. act.
indic. πρεσβεύω *(4243)*
(4243) **πρεσβεύω**, 1 pers. sg. pres. act. indic., fut.
πρεσβεύσω [§13.M] (πρέσβυς, *an old
man, an ambassador*) *to be elder; to be an
ambassador, perform the duties of an ambassador,* 2 Cor. 5:20; Eph. 6:20
πρεσβύτας, acc. pl. m. n. . . . . πρεσβύτης *(4246)*
πρεσβυτέρας, acc. pl. f. adj. . . . . πρεσβύτερος *(4245)*
(4244) **πρεσβυτέριον**, ου, τό, nom. sg. neut. n.
[§3.C.c] *a body of old men, an assembly
of elders; the Jewish Sanhedrin,* Luke
22:66; Acts 22:5; *a body of elders* in the
Christian church, *a presbytery,* 1 Tim. 4:14
πρεσβυτερίου, gen. sg. neut. n. . πρεσβυτέριον *(4244)*
πρεσβύτεροι, nom. pl. m. adj.
{Acts 4:23} . . . . πρεσβύτερος *(4245)*
πρεσβύτεροι, voc. pl. m. adj. {Acts 4:8} . . id.
πρεσβυτέροις, dat. pl. m. adj. . . . . id.
(4245) **πρεσβύτερος**, τέρα, τερον, nom. sg. m. adj.
[§7.1] (compar. of πρέσβυς) *elder, senior;
older, more advanced in years,* Luke 15:25;
John 8:9; Acts 2:17; *an elder* in respect of
age, *person advanced in years,* 1 Tim.
5:1, 2; pl. spc. *ancients, ancestors, fathers,*
Matt. 15:2; Heb. 11:2; as an appellation
of dignity, *an elder,* local *dignitary,* Luke
7:3; *an elder, member of the Jewish Sanhedrin,* Matt. 16:21; 21:23; 26:3, 47,
57, 59; *an elder or presbyter* of the Christian church, Acts 11:30; 14:23, et al. freq.
πρεσβυτέρου, gen. sg. m. adj. . . πρεσβύτερος *(4245)*
πρεσβυτέρους, acc. pl. m. adj. . . . . id.
πρεσβυτέρῳ, dat. sg. m. adj. . . . . id.
πρεσβυτέρων, gen. pl. m. adj. . . . . id.
(4246) **πρεσβύτης**, ου, ὁ, nom. sg. m. n. [§2.C.c] *an
old man, aged person,* Luke 1:18; Tit. 2:2;
Philemon 9
πρεσβύτιδας, acc. pl. f. n. . . . . πρεσβῦτις *(4247)*
(4247) **πρεσβῦτις**, ιδος, ἡ [§4.2.c] *an aged woman,*
Tit. 2:3
(4248) **πρηνής**, ές, nom. sg. m. adj. [§7.G.b] *prone,
head-foremost;* πρηνὴς γενόμενος, *falling
head-long,* Acts 1:18
(4249) **πρίζω**, or πρίω, aor. pass. ἐπρίσθην [§26.1]
to saw, saw asunder, Heb. 11:37

(4250) **πρίν**, adv., *before,* of time, Matt. 26:34, 75; Mark 14:72; πρὶν ἤ, *sooner than, before,* Matt. 1:18; Luke 2:26, et al.

(4251) **Πρίσκα**, ης, ἡ, nom. sg. f. n., *Prisca,* pr. name (1 Cor. 16:19, GNT, WH & NA | Πρίσκιλλα, MT & TR)

Πρίσκαν, acc. sg. f. n. . . . . Πρίσκα *(4251)*

(4252) **Πρίσκιλλα**, ης, ἡ, nom. sg. f. n. [§2.3] *Priscilla,* pr. name

Πρίσκιλλαν, acc. sg. f. n. . . . . Πρίσκιλλα *(4252)*

(4253) **πρό**, prep. with a gen., *before,* of place, *in front of, in advance of,* Matt. 11:10; Luke 1:76; Acts 5:23; *before,* of time, Matt. 5:12; Luke 11:38; before an infin. with the gen. of the article, *before, before that,* Matt. 6:8; Luke 2:21; *before, above, in preference,* James 5:12; 1 Pet. 4:8

προαγαγεῖν, 2 aor. act. infin. . . . . προάγω *(4254)*

προαγαγών, nom. sg. m. 2 aor. act. part. [§13.7.d] . . . . id.

προάγει, 3 pers. sg. pres. act. indic. . . . . . id.

προάγειν, pres. act. infin. . . . . id.

προάγοντες, nom. pl. m. pres. act. part. . . id.

προάγουσαι, nom. pl. f. pres. act. part. . . id.

προαγούσας, acc. pl. f. pres. act. part. . . . id.

προαγούσης, gen. sg. f. pres. act. part. . . . id.

προάγουσιν, 3 pers. pl. pres. act. indic. . . id.

(4254) **προάγω**, fut. προάξω [§23.1.b] 2 aor. προήγαγον (πρό + ἄγω) *to lead, bring, or conduct forth, produce,* Acts 12:6; 16:30; 25:26; intrans. *to go before, to go first,* Matt. 2:9; 21:9; Mark 6:45; 1 Tim. 5:24; part. προάγων, ουσα, ον, *preceding, previous, antecedent,* 1 Tim. 1:18; Heb. 7:18; hence, in N.T., trans. *to precede,* Matt. 14:22, et al.; *to be in advance of,* Matt. 21:31

προάγων, nom. sg. m. pres. act. part. προάγω *(4254)*

προαιρεῖται, 3 pers. sg. pres. mid./pass. dep. indic. (2 Cor. 9:7, MT & TR | προήρηται, GNT, WH & NA) . . . προαιρέομαι *(4255)*

(4255) **προαιρέομαι**, οῦμαι, fut. προαιρήσομαι [§17.Q] (πρό + αἱρέω) *to prefer, choose;* met. *to purpose, intend considerately,* 2 Cor. 9:7

(4256) **προαιτιάομαι**, ῶμαι, fut. προαιτιάσομαι (πρό + αἰτιάομαι, from αἰτία) pr. *to charge beforehand; to convict beforehand,* Rom. 3:9, since the charges in the case in question were drawn from Scripture

(4257) **προακούω** (πρό + ἀκούω) *to hear beforehand;* aor. προήκουσα, *to have heard of previously, or already,* Col. 1:5

(4258) **προαμαρτάνω** (πρό + ἁμαρτάνω) *to sin before;* perf. προημάρτηκα, *to have*

already sinned, have sinned heretofore, 2 Cor. 12:21; 13:2

προάξω, 1 pers. sg. fut. act. indic. . . . προάγω *(4254)*

(4259) **προαύλιον**, ου, τό [§3.C.c] (πρό + αὐλή) *the exterior court* before an edifice, Mark 14:68; Matt. 26:71

προαύλιον, acc. sg. neut. n. . . . . . . προαύλιον *(4259)*

(4260) **προβαίνω**, fut. προβήσομαι, 2 aor. προὔβην, part. προβάς [§37.1] (πρό + βαίνω) *to go forward, advance,* Matt. 4:21; Mark 1:19; *to advance* in life, Luke 1:7, 18; 2:36

προβαλλόντων, gen. pl. m. pres. act. part. (Acts 19:33, TR | προβαλόντων, GNT, WH, MT & NA) . . . . προβάλλω *(4261)*

(4261) **προβάλλω**, fut. προβαλῶ, 2 aor. προὔβαλον [§34.1.b] (πρό + βάλλω) *to cast before, project; to put or urge forward,* Acts 19:33; *to put forth,* as a tree its blossoms, etc., Luke 21:30

προβαλόντων, gen. pl. m. aor. act. part. . . . . προβάλλω *(4261)*

προβάλωσιν, 3 pers. pl. 2 aor. act. subj. . . id.

προβάς, nom. sg. m. 2 aor. act. part. . . . . προβαίνω *(4260)*

πρόβατα, nom. pl. neut. n. {John 10:3a} . . . . πρόβατον *(4263)*

πρόβατα, acc. pl. neut. n. {John 10:3b} . . id.

προβάτια, acc. pl. neut. n. (John 21:16, 17, WH | πρόβατα, GNT, MT, TR & NA) . . . . προβάτια *(†4263)*

προβατικῇ, dat. sg. f. adj. . . . . . . προβατικός *(4262)*

(4262) **προβατικός**, ή, όν [§7.F.a] *belonging or pertaining to sheep;* ἡ προβατική, (πύλη) *the sheep-gate,* John 5:2

(†4263) **προβάτια**, ου, τό, dimin. of πρόβατον, *a little sheep,* John 21:16, 17.

(4263) **πρόβατον**, ου, τό, nom. sg. neut. n. [§3.C.c] *a sheep,* Matt. 7:15; 9:36; 10:16; met. Matt. 10:6; 15:24, et al. {Acts 8:32}

πρόβατον, acc. sg. neut. n. {Luke 15:6} . . . . πρόβατον *(4263)*

προβάτου, gen. sg. neut. n. . . . . id.

προβάτων, gen. pl. neut. n. . . . . id.

προβεβηκότες, nom. pl. m. perf. act. part. . . . . προβαίνω *(4260)*

προβεβηκυῖα, nom. sg. f. perf. act. part. . . id.

(4264) **προβιβάζω**, fut. προβιβάσω [§26.1] (πρό + βιβάζω) *to cause any one to advance, to lead forward; to advance, push forward,* Acts 19:33; met. *to incite, instigate,* Matt. 14:8

προβιβασθεῖσα, nom. sg. f. aor. pass. part. . . . . προβιβάζω *(4264)*

(4265) **προβλέπω**, fut. προβλέψω [§23.1.a] (πρό + βλέπω) *to foresee;* mid. *to provide before-*

hand, Heb. 11:40

προβλεψαμένου, gen. sg. m. aor. mid.
part. . . . . προβλέπω *(4265)*

προγεγονότων, gen. pl. neut. perf. act.
part. προγίνομαι *(4266)*

προγεγραμμένοι, nom. pl. m. perf. pass. part.
[§23.7] . . . . προγράφω *(4270)*

(4266) **προγίνομαι,** perf. προγέγονα [§37.1] (πρό +
γίνομαι) *to be or happen before, be previously done or committed;* προγεγονώς,
bygone, previous, Rom. 3:25

προγινώσκοντες, nom. pl. m. pres. act.
part. . . . . προγινώσκω *(4267)*

(4267) **προγινώσκω,** fut. προγνώσομαι, 2 aor.
προέγνων, perf. pass. προέγνωσμαι
[§36.3] (πρό + γινώσκω) *to know beforehand, to be previously acquainted with,*
Acts 26:5; 2 Pet. 3:17; *to determine on
beforehand, to fore-ordain,* 1 Pet. 1:20; *in
N.T., from the Hebrew, to foreknow, to appoint as the subjects of future privileges,*
Rom. 8:29; 11:2

προγνώσει, dat. sg. f. n. . . . . πρόγνωσις *(4268)*

πρόγνωσιν, acc. sg. f. n. . . . . id.

(4268) **πρόγνωσις,** εως, ἡ [§5.E.c] *foreknowledge,
prescience; in N.T. previous determination,
purpose,* Acts 2:23; 1 Pet. 1:2

προγόνοις, dat. pl. m. n. . . . . πρόγονος *(4269)*

(4269) **πρόγονος,** ου, ὁ [§3.C.a] *born earlier, elder;
a progenitor,* pl. *progenitors; parents,*
1 Tim. 5:4; *forefathers, ancestors,* 2 Tim.
1:3

προγόνων, gen. pl. m. n. . . . . πρόγονος *(4269)*

(4270) **προγράφω,** fut. προγράψω, perf. pass.
προγέγραμμαι [§23.6; 23.7] 2 aor. pass.
προεγράφην (πρό + γράφω) *to write
before or aforetime,* Rom. 15:4; Eph. 3:3;
*to make a subject of public notice; to set
forth unreservedly and distinctly,* Gal. 3:1;
to designate clearly, Jude 4

πρόδηλα, nom. pl. neut. adj. . . . . . . πρόδηλος *(4271)*

πρόδηλοι, nom. pl. f. adj. . . . . id.

πρόδηλον, nom. sg. neut. adj. . . . . id.

(4271) **πρόδηλος,** ον [§7.2] (πρό + δῆλος) *previously manifest, before known; plainly manifest, very clear, prominently conspicuous,*
1 Tim. 5:24, 25; Heb. 7:14

(4272) **προδίδωμι,** fut. προδώσω [§30.Z] (πρό +
δίδωμι) *to give before, precede in giving;*
Rom. 11:35; *to give up, abandon, betray*

προδόται, nom. pl. m. n. . . . . προδότης *(4273)*

(4273) **προδότης,** ου, ὁ, nom. sg. m. n. [§2.B.c] *a be-
trayer, traitor,* Luke 6:16; Acts 7:52; 2 Tim.
3:4

προδραμών, nom. sg. m. 2 aor. act.

part. . . . . προτρέχω *(4390)*

(4274) **πρόδρομος,** ον, ὁ, ἡ, nom. sg. m. adj.
(δραμεῖν) *a precursor, forerunner, one who
advances to explore and prepare the way,*
Heb. 6:20

προεβίβασαν, 3 pers. pl. aor. act. indic. (Acts
19:33, MT & TR | συνεβίβασαν, GNT,
WH & NA) . . . . προβιβάζω *(4264)*

προέγνω, 3 pers. sg. aor. act. indic.
[§36.3] . . . . προγινώσκω *(4267)*

προεγνωσμένου, gen. sg. m. perf. pass. part.   id.

προεγράγη, 3 pers. sg. 2 aor. pass. indic.
[§24.6] . . . . προγράφω *(4270)*

προέγραψα, 1 pers. sg. aor. act. indic. . . .   id.

προέδραμε(ν), 3 pers. sg. 2 aor. act. indic.
[§36.1] . . . . προτρέχω *(4390)*

προέδωκεν, 3 pers. sg. aor. act.
indic. προδίδωμι *(4272)*

προεθέμην, 1 pers. sg. 2 aor. mid. indic.
[§28.W] . . . . προτίθημι *(†4388)*

προέθετο, 3 pers. sg. 2 aor. mid. indic. . . .   id.

προεῖδον, part. προιδών, 2 aor. of
προοράω . . . . προοράω *(4308)*

προείπαμεν, 1 pers. pl. aor. act.
indic. . . . . προεῖπον *(‡4277)*

προεῖπε(ν), 3 pers. sg. 2 aor. act. indic.
[§35.7] . . . . id.

(‡4277) **προεῖπον,** 1 pers. sg. 2 aor. act. indic., *to say,
speak*

προείρηκα, 1 pers. sg. perf. act. indic.
[§36.1] . . . . προοράω *(4308)*

προειρήκαμεν, 1 pers. pl. perf. act. indic.   id.

προείρηκεν, 3 pers. sg. perf. act. indic. . . .   id.

προειρηκέναι, perf. act. infin. (Heb. 10:15,
MT & TR | εἰρηκέναι, GNT, WH &
NA) . . . . id.

προειρημένων, gen. pl. m. perf. pass. part.   id.

προείρηται, 3 pers. sg. perf. pass. indic. (Heb.
4:7, GNT, WH & NA | εἴρηται, MT &
TR) . . . . id.

προέκοπτε(ν), 3 pers. sg. imperf. act.
indic. . . . . προκόπτω *(4298)*

προέκοπτον, 1 pers. sg. imperf. act. indic.   id.

προέκοψεν, 3 pers. sg. aor. act. indic. . . .   id.

προέλαβε(ν), 3 pers. sg. 2 aor. act. indic.
[§36.2] . . . . προλαμβάνω *(4301)*

προελέγομεν, 1 pers. pl. imperf. act.
indic. . . . . προλέγω *(4302)*

προελεύσεται, 3 pers. sg. fut. mid. dep. indic.
[§36.1] . . . . προέρχομαι *(4281)*

προελθόντες, nom. pl. m. 2 aor. act. part.   id.

προελθών, nom. sg. m. 2 aor. act. part. . .   id.

προέλθωσιν, 3 pers. pl. 2 aor. act. subj. . .   id.

(4276) **προελπίζω,** fut. προελπίσω [§26.1] (πρό +
ἐλπίζω) *to repose hope and confidence in*

a person or thing *beforehand,* Eph. 1:12

(4278) **προενάρχομαι,** fut. προενάρξομαι [§23.1.b] (πρό + ἐνάρχομαι) *to begin before* a particular time, 2 Cor. 8:6, 10

προενήρξασθε, 2 pers. pl. aor. mid. dep. indic. . . . . προενάρχομαι *(4278)*

προενήρξατο, 3 pers. sg. aor. mid. dep. indic.   id.

(4279) **προεπαγγέλλομαι,** aor. προεπηγγειλάμην [§27.1.d] (πρό + ἐπαγγέλλομαι) *to promise beforehand, or aforetime,* Rom. 1:2

προέπεμπον, 3 pers. pl. imperf. act. indic. . . . . προπέμπω *(4311)*

προεπηγγείλατο, 3 pers. sg. aor. mid. dep. indic. . . . . προεπαγγέλλομαι *(4279)*

προεπηγγελμένην, acc. sg. f. perf. mid./pass. dep. part. (2 Cor. 9:5, GNT, WH & NA | προκατηγγελμένην, MT & TR) . . . . id.

(4281) **προέρχομαι,** fut. προελεύσομαι, 2 aor. προῆλθον [§36.1] (πρό + ἔρχομαι) *to go forwards, advance, proceed,* Matt. 26:39; Mark 14:35; Acts 12:10; *to precede, go before* any one, Luke 22:47; *to precede* in time, *be a forerunner or precursor,* Luke 1:17; *to outgo, outstrip in going,* Mark 6:33; *to travel in advance of* any one, *precede,* Acts 20:5, 13; 2 Cor. 9:5

προεστῶτες, nom. pl. m. perf. act. part. [§35.8] . . . . προΐστημι *(4291)*

προέτειναν, 3 pers. pl. aor. act. indic. [§27.1.d] (Acts 22:25, GNT, WH & NA | προέτεινεν, MT & TR) . . . . προτείνω *(4385)*

προέτεινεν, 3 pers. sg. aor. act. indic. (Acts 22:25, MT & TR | προέτειναν, GNT, WH & NA) . . . . id.

(4282) **προετοιμάζω,** fut. προετοιμάξω [§26.1] (πρό + ἑτοιμάζω) *to prepare beforehand;* in N.T. *to appoint beforehand,* Rom. 9:23; Eph. 2:10

(4283) **προευαγγελίζομαι,** fut. προευαγγελίσομαι, *to announce joyful tidings beforehand,* Gal. 3:8

προευηγγελίσατο, 3 pers. sg. aor. mid. dep. indic. [§23.5] . . . . προευαγγελίζομαι *(4283)*

προεφήτευον, 3 pers. pl. imperf. act. indic. [§34.2] (Acts 19:6, MT & TR | ἐπροφήτευον, GNT, WH & NA) . . προφητεύω *(4395)*

προεφητεύσαμεν, 1 pers. pl. aor. act. indic. (Matt. 7:22, MT & TR | ἐπροφητεύσαμεν, GNT, WH & NA) . . . . id.

προεφήτευσαν, 3 pers. pl. aor. act. indic. (Matt. 11:13, MT & TR | ἐπροφήτευσαν, GNT, WH & NA) . . . . id.

προεφήτευσε(ν), 3 pers. sg. aor. act. indic.   id.

προέφθασεν, 3 pers. sg. aor. act. indic. [§37.1] . . . . προφθάνω *(4399)*

προεχειρίσατο, 3 pers. sg. aor. mid. dep. indic. . . . . προχειρίζομαι *(4400)*

προεχόμεθα, 1 pers. pl. pres. mid./pass. dep. indic. . . . . προέχω *(†4284)*

(†4284) **προέχω,** fut. προέξω (πρό + ἔχω) *to have or hold before;* intrans. and mid. *to excel, surpass, have advantage or pre-eminence,* Rom. 3:9

προεωρακότες, nom. pl. m. perf. act. part. [§36.1] . . . . προοράω *(4308)*

προήγαγον, 1 pers. sg. 2 aor. act. indic. [§13.7.d] . . . . προάγω *(4254)*

προῆγεν, 3 pers. sg. imperf. act. indic. . . . id.

(4285) **προηγέομαι,** οῦμαι, fut. προηγήσομαι [§17.Q] (πρό + ἡγέομαι) *to go before, precede, lead onward;* met. *to endeavor to take the lead of, vie with,* or, *to give precedence to, to prefer,* Rom. 12:10

προηγούμενοι, nom. pl. m. pres. mid./pass. dep. part. . . . . προηγέομαι *(4285)*

προηκούσατε, 2 pers. pl. aor. act. indic. προακούω *(4257)*

προῆλθον, 3 pers. pl. 2 aor. act. indic. προέρχομαι *(4281)*

προηλπικότας, acc. pl. m. perf. act. part. . . . . προελπίζω *(4276)*

προημαρτηκόσι(ν), dat. pl. m. perf. act. part. . . . . προαμαρτάνω *(4258)*

προημαρτηκότων, gen. pl. m. perf. act. part.   id.

προῄρηται, 3 pers. sg. perf. mid. indic. (2 Cor. 9:7, GNT, WH & NA | προαιρεῖται, MT & TR) . . . . προαιρέομαι *(4255)*

προήρχετο, 3 pers. sg. imperf. mid./pass. dep. indic. . . . . προέρχομαι *(4281)*

προητιασάμεθα, 1 pers. pl. aor. mid. dep. indic. [§13.2] . . . . προαιτιάομαι *(4256)*

προητοίμασεν, 3 pers. sg. aor. act. indic. . . . . προετοιμάζω *(4282)*

προθέσει, dat. sg. f. n. . . . . πρόθεσις *(4286)*

προθέσεως, gen. sg. f. n. . . . . id.

πρόθεσιν, acc. sg. f. n. . . . . id.

(4286) **πρόθεσις,** εως, ἡ, nom. sg. f. n. [§5.E.c] *a setting forth or before;* οἱ ἄρτοι τῆς προθέσεως, and ἡ πρόθεσις τῶν ἄρτων, *the shewbread,* the twelve loaves of bread, corresponding to the twelve tribes, which were *set out* in two rows upon the golden table in the sanctuary, Matt. 12:4; Mark 2:26; Luke 6:4; Heb. 9:2; *predetermination, purpose,* Acts 11:23; 27:13; Rom. 8:28; 2 Tim. 3:10, et al.

(4287) **προθεσμία,** ας, ἡ [§2.B.b; 2.2] (pr. f. of προθέσμιος, *before appointed,* πρό + θεσμός) sc. ἡμέρα, *a time before appointed, set or appointed time,* Gal. 4:2

προθεσμίας, gen. sg. f. n. . . . . προθεσμία *(4287)*

(4288) **προθυμία, ας, ἡ,** nom. sg. f. n. [§2.B.b; 2.2] *promptness, readiness, alacrity of mind, willingness,* Acts 17:11; 2 Cor. 8:11, 12, 19; 9:2

προθυμίαν, acc. sg. f. n. . . . . προθυμία *(4288)*

προθυμίας, gen. sg. f. n. . . . . id.

πρόθυμον, nom. sg. neut. adj. . . . . . πρόθυμος *(4289)*

(4289) **πρόθυμος, ον** [§7.2] (πρό + θυμός) *ready in mind, prepared, prompt, willing,* Matt. 26:41; Mark 14:38; τὸ πρόθυμον, i.q. ἡ προθυμία, *readiness, alacrity of mind,* Rom. 1:15

(4290) **προθύμως,** adv., *promptly, with alacrity, readily, willingly, heartily, cheerfully,* 1 Pet. 5:2

προϊδοῦσα, nom. sg. f. 2 aor. act. part. [§36.1] . . . . προοράω *(4308)*

προϊδών, nom. sg. m. 2 aor. act. part. . . . id.

πρόϊμον, acc. sg. m. adj. (James 5:7, GNT, WH & NA | πρώϊμον, MT & TR) . . . . πρόϊμος *(‡4406)*

(‡4406) **πρόϊμος, ον,** *early*

προϊστάμενοι, nom. pl. m. pres. mid. part. . . . . προΐστημι *(4291)*

προϊστάμενον, acc. sg. m. pres. mid. part. id.

προϊστάμενος, nom. sg. m. pres. mid. part. id.

προϊσταμένους, acc. pl. m. pres. mid. part. id.

προΐστασθαι, pres. mid. infin. [§29.Y] . . . id.

(4291) **προΐστημι,** fut. προστήσω [§29.X] (πρό + ἵστημι) *to set before;* met. *to set over, appoint with authority;* intrans. 2 aor. προῦστην, perf. προέστηκα, part. προεστώς, and mid. προΐσταμαι, *to preside, govern, superintend,* Rom. 12:8; 1 Thess. 5:12; 1 Tim. 3:4, 5, 12; 5:17; mid. *to undertake resolutely, to practise diligently, to maintain the practice of,* Tit. 3:8, 14

προκαλούμενοι, nom. pl. m. pres. mid. part. . . . . προκαλέω *(†4292)*

(†4292) **προκαλέω, ῶ,** fut. προκαλέσομαι [§17.Q; 22.1] (προκαλέω, *to call forth, invite to stand forth,* from πρό + καλέω) *to call out, challenge to fight; to provoke, irritate with feelings of ungenerous rivalry,* Gal. 5:26

προκαταγγείλαντας, acc. pl. m. aor. act. part. [§27.1.d] . . . . προκαταγγέλλω *(4293)*

(4293) **προκαταγγέλλω,** fut. προκαταγελῶ [§27.1.b] (πρό + καταγγέλλω) *to declare or announce beforehand, foretell, predict,* Acts 3:18, 24; 7:52; 2 Cor. 9:5

(4294) **προκαταρτίζω,** fut. προκαταρτίσω [§26.1] (πρό + καταρτίζω) *to make ready, prepare, or complete beforehand*

προκαταρτίσωσι(ν), 3 pers. pl. aor. act. subj. . . . . προκαταρτίζω *(4294)*

προκατήγγειλαν, 3 pers. pl. aor. act. indic. (Acts 3:24, TR | κατήγγειλαν, GNT, WH, MT & NA) . . . . προκαταγγέλλω *(4293)*

προκατήγγειλε(ν), 3 pers. sg. aor. act. indic. id.

προκατηγγελμένην, acc. sg. f. perf. pass. part. (2 Cor. 9:5, MT & TR | προεπηγγελμένην, GNT, WH & NA) . . . . id.

(4295) **πρόκειμαι,** fut. προκείσομαι [§33.DD] (πρό + κεῖμαι) *to lie or be placed before;* met. *to be proposed or set before,* as a duty, example, reward, etc., Heb. 6:18; 12:1, 2; Jude 7; *to be at hand, be present,* 2 Cor. 8:12

προκειμένης, gen. sg. f. pres. mid./pass. dep. part. . . . . πρόκειμαι *(4295)*

προκείμενον, acc. sg. m. pres. mid./pass. dep. part. . . . . id.

πρόκεινται, 3 pers. pl. pres. mid./pass. dep. indic. . . . . id.

πρόκειται, 3 pers. sg. pres. mid./pass. dep. indic. . . . . id.

προκεκηρυγμένον, acc. sg. m. perf. pass. part. (Acts 3:20, TR | προκεκυρωμένην, GNT, WH, MT & NA) . . . . προκηρύσσω *(4296)*

προκεκυρωμένην, acc. sg. f. perf. pass. part. . . . . προκυρόω *(4300)*

προκεχειρισμένον, acc. sg. m. perf. pass. part. (Acts 3:20, GNT, WH, MT & NA | προκεκηρυγμένον, TR) . . . . προχειρίζομαι *(4400)*

προκεχειροτονημένοις, dat. pl. m. perf. pass. part. . . . . προχειροτονέω *(4401)*

προκηρύξαντος, gen. sg. m. aor. act. part. . . . . προκηρύσσω *(4296)*

(4296) **προκηρύσσω,** fut. προκηρύξω [§26.3] (πρό + κηρύσσω) *to announce publicly;* in N.T. *to announce before,* Acts 3:20; 13:24

(4297) **προκοπή, ῆς, ἡ,** nom. sg. f. n. [§2.B.a] *advance upon a way;* met. *progress, advancement, furtherance,* Phil. 1:12; 1 Tim. 4:15

προκοπήν, acc. sg. f. n. . . . . προκοπή *(4297)*

(4298) **προκόπτω,** fut. προκόψω [§23.1.a] (πρό + κόπτω) pr. *to cut* a passage *forward; to advance, make progress; to advance,* as time, *to be far spent,* Rom. 13:12; met. *to advance* in wisdom, age, or stature, Luke 2:52; seq. ἐν, *to make progress or proficiency in,* Gal. 1:14;, προκόπτω ἐπὶ πλεῖον, *to proceed or advance* further, 2 Tim. 2:16; 3:9; προκόπτω ἐπὶ τὸ χεῖρον, *to grow* worse and worse, 2 Tim. 3:13

προκόψουσιν, 3 pers. pl. fut. act.

indic. . . . . προκόπτω   (4298)

(4299) πρόκριμα, ατος, τό [§4.D.c] (προκρίνω, *to prejudge, prefer*) *previous judgment, prejudice, prepossession,* or, *preference, partiality,* 1 Tim. 5:21

προκρίματος, gen. sg. neut. n. . . . . πρόκριμα (4299)

(4300) προκυρόω, ῶ, fut. προκυρώσω [§20.T] (πρό + κυρόω) *to sanction and establish previously, ratify and confirm before,* Gal. 3:17

προλαμβάνει, 3 pers. sg. pres. act.
indic. . . . . προλαμβάνω (4301)

(4301) προλαμβάνω, fut. προλή(μ)ψομαι, 2 aor. προέλαβον [§36.2] (πρό + λαμβάνω) *to take before* another, 1 Cor. 11:21; trop. *to anticipate, do beforehand,* Mark 14:8; *to take by surprise;* pass. *be taken unexpectedly, be overtaken, be taken by surprise,* Gal. 6:1

(4302) προλέγω, 1 pers. sg. pres. act. indic., fut. προλέξω, aor. προεῖπα, 2 aor. προεῖπον, perf. προείρηκα [§36.1] (πρό + λέγω) *to tell beforehand, to foretell,* Matt. 24:25; Acts 1:16; Rom. 9:29; 2 Cor. 13:2; Gal. 5:21; 1 Thess. 3:4, et al.

προλημφθῇ, 3 pers. sg. aor. pass. subj. (Gal. 6:1, GNT, WH & NA | προληφθῇ, MT & TR) . . . . προλαμβάνω (4301)

προληφθῇ, 3 pers. sg. aor. pass. subj. (Gal. 6:1, MT & TR | προλημφθῇ, GNT, WH & NA) . . . . id.

(4303) προμαρτύρομαι (πρό + μαρτύρομαι) pr. *to witness or testify beforehand; to declare beforehand, predict,* 1 Pet. 1:11

προμαρτυρόμενον, nom. sg. neut. pres. mid./pass. dep. part. . . . . προμαρτύρομαι (4303)

προμελετᾶν, pres. act. infin. (Luke 21:14, GNT, MT & NA | προμελετᾷν, WH & TR) . . . . προμελετάω (4304)

(4304) προμελετάω, ῶ, fut. προμελετήσω [§18.R] (πρό + μελετάω) *to practise beforehand; to premeditate,* Luke 21:14

προμεριμνᾶτε, 2 pers. pl. pres. act. imper. . . . . προμεριμνάω (4305)

(4305) προμεριμνάω, ῶ, fut. προμεριμνήσω [§18.R] (πρό + μεριμνάω) *to be anxious or solicitous beforehand, to ponder before hand,* Mark 13:11

προνοεῖ, 3 pers. sg. pres. act. indic. . προνοέω (4306)

(4306) προνοέω, ῶ, fut. προνοήσω [§16.P] (πρό + νοέω) *to perceive beforehand, foresee; to provide for,* 1 Tim. 5:8; mid. *to provide for one's self;* by impl. *to apply one's self to a thing, practise, strive to exhibit,* Rom. 12:17; 2 Cor. 8:21

(4307) πρόνοια, ας, ἡ [§2.B.b; 2.2] *forethought; providence, provident care,* Acts 24:2; *provision,* Rom. 13:14

πρόνοιαν, acc. sg. f. n. . . . . πρόνοια (4307)

προνοίας, gen. sg. f. n. . . . . id.

προνοοῦμεν, 1 pers. pl. pres. act. indic. (2 Cor. 8:21, GNT, WH & NA | προνοούμενοι, MT & TR) . . . . προνοέω (4306)

προνοούμενοι, nom. pl. m. pres. mid. part.   id.

(4308) προοράω, ῶ, fut. προόψομαι, perf. προεώρακα, 2 aor. προεῖδον [§36.1] (πρό + ὁράω) *to foresee,* Acts 2:31; Gal. 3:8; *to see before,* Acts 21:29; in N.T. *to have vividly present to the mind, to be mindful of,* Acts 2:25

(4309) προορίζω, fut. προορίσω [§26.1] (πρό + ὁρίζω) *to limit or mark out beforehand; to design definitely beforehand, ordain beforehand, predestine,* Acts 4:28; Rom. 8:29, 30, et al.

προορίσας, nom. sg. m. aor. act. part. . . . . προορίζω (4309)

προορισθέντες, nom. pl. m. aor. pass. part.   id.

προορώμην, 1 pers. sg. imperf. mid. indic. (Acts 2:25, GNT, WH & NA | προωρώμην, MT & TR) . . . . id.

προπαθόντες, nom. pl. m. 2 aor. act. part. . . . . προπάσχω (4310)

(4310) προπάσχω (πρό + πάσχω) 2 aor. προέπαθον [§36.4] *to experience previously,* of ill treatment, 1 Thess. 2:2

προπάτορα, acc. sg. m. n. (Rom. 4:1, GNT, WH & NA | πατέρα, MT & TR) . . . . προπάτωρ (‡3962)

(‡3962) προπάτωρ, ορος, ὁ [§4.2.f] (πρό + πατήρ) *a grandfather; a progenitor, or ancestor*

προπεμπόντων, gen. pl. m. pres. act. part. . . . . προπέμπω (4311)

(4311) προπέμπω, fut. προπέμψω [§23.1.a] (πρό + πέμπω) *to send on before; to accompany or attend out of respect, escort, accompany for a certain distance on setting out on a journey,* Acts 15:3; 20:38; 21:5, et al.; *to furnish with things necessary for a journey,* Tit. 3:13; 3 John 6

προπεμφθέντες, nom. pl. m. aor. pass. part. . . . . προπέμπω (4311)

προπεμφθῆναι, aor. pass. infin. . . . . id.

προπέμψας, nom. sg. m. aor. act. part. . . . id.

προπέμψατε, 2 pers. pl. aor. act. imper. . . id.

προπέμψητε, 2 pers. pl. aor. act. subj. . . . id.

πρόπεμψον, 2 pers. sg. aor. act. imper. . . . id.

προπετεῖς, nom. pl. m. adj. . . . . . . προπετής (4312)

προπετές, acc. sg. neut. adj. . . . . . . id.

(4312) προπετής, ές [§7.G.b] (πρό + πίπτω) *falling*

forwards; meton. *precipitate, rash,* Acts 19:36; 2 Tim. 3:4

(4313) **προπορεύομαι,** fut. προπορεύσομαι [§14.N] (πρό + πορεύομαι) *to precede, go before,* Acts 7:40; Luke 1:76

προπορεύσῃ, 2 pers. sg. fut. mid. dep. indic. . . . . προπορεύομαι *(4313)*

προπορεύσονται, 3 pers. pl. fut. mid. dep. indic. . . . . id.

(4314) **πρός,** prep., with a genitive, *from;* met. *for the benefit of,* Acts 27:34; with a dative, *near, by, at, by the side of, in the vicinity of,* Mark 5:11; Luke 19:37; with an accusative, used of the place to which anything tends, *to, unto, towards,* Matt. 2:12; 3:5, 13; *at, close upon,* Matt. 3:10; Mark 5:22; *near to, in the vicinity of,* Mark 6:45; after verbs of speaking, praying, answering to a charge, etc., *to,* Matt. 3:15; 27:14; of place where, *with, in, among, by, at,* etc., Matt. 26:55; Mark 11:4; Luke 1:80; of time, *for, during,* Luke 8:13; 1 Cor. 7:5; *near, towards,* Luke 24:29; of the end, object, purpose for which an action is exerted, or to which any quality, etc., has reference, *to,* John 4:35; Acts 3:10; 27:12; before an infin. with τό, *in order to, that, in order that,* Matt. 6:1; 13:30; 26:12; *so as to, so that,* Matt. 5:28; of the relation which any action, state, quality, etc., bears to any person or thing, *in relation to, of, concerning, in respect to, with reference to,* Matt. 19:8; Luke 12:41; 18:1; 20:19; *as it respects, as it concerns, with relation to,* Matt. 27:4; John 21:22, 23; *according to, in conformity with,* Luke 12:47; 2 Cor. 5:10; *in comparison with,* Rom. 8:18; *in attention to,* Eph. 3:4; of the actions, dispositions, etc., exhibited with respect to any one, whether friendly, *towards,* Gal. 6:10; Eph. 6:9; or unfriendly, *with, against,* Luke 23:12; Acts 23:30; after verbs signifying to converse, dispute, make a covenant, etc., *with,* Luke 24:14; Acts 2:7; 3:25

(4315) **προσάββατον,** ου, τό, nom. sg. neut. n. [§3.C.c] (πρό + σάββατον) *the day before the sabbath, sabbath-eve,* Mark 15:42

προσάγαγε, 2 pers. sg. 2 aor. act. imper. [§13.7.d] . . . . προσάγω *(4317)*

προσαγαγεῖν, 2 aor. act. infin. (Acts 12:6, WH | προαγαγεῖν, GNT, MT, TR & NA) . id.

προσαγάγῃ, 3 pers. sg. 2 aor. act. subj. . . id.

προσαγαγόντες, nom. pl. m. 2 aor. act. part. id.

προσάγειν, pres. act. infin. . . . . id.

προσαγορευθείς, nom. sg. m. aor. pass.

part. . . . . προσαγορεύω *(4316)*

(4316) **προσαγορεύω,** fut. προσαγορεύσω [§13.M] (πρός + ἀγορεύω, *to speak*) *to speak to, accost, to name, denominate; to nominate, declare,* Heb. 5:10

(4317) **προσάγω,** fut. προσάξω, 2 aor. προσήγαγον [§13.7.d] *to lead or conduct to, bring,* Luke 9:41; Acts 16:20; *to conduct to the presence of, to procure access for,* 1 Pet. 3:18; *to bring near; to near,* in a nautical sense, Acts 27:27

(4318) **προσαγωγή,** ῆς, ἡ [§2.B.a] *approach; access, admission,* to the presence of any one, Rom. 5:2; Eph. 2:18

προσαγωγήν, acc. sg. f. n. . . . . . . προσαγωγή *(4318)*

(4319) **προσαιτέω, ῶ,** fut. προσαιτήσω [§16.P] (πρός + αἰτέω) *to ask for in addition; to ask earnestly, beg; to beg alms,* Mark 10:46; Luke 18:35; John 9:8

(‡5185) **προσαίτης,** ου, ὁ, nom. sg. m. n. [§2.B.c] *a beggar, mendicant* (Mark 10:46; John 9:8, GNT, WH & NA | τυφλός, MT & TR)

προσαιτῶν, nom. sg. m. pres. act. part. . . . . προσαιτέω *(4319)*

(4320) **προσαναβαίνω,** fut. προσαναβήσομαι, 2 aor. προσανέβην [§37.1] (πρός + ἀναβαίνω) *to go up further,* Luke 14:10

προσανάβηθι, 2 pers. sg. 2 aor. act. imper. . . . . προσαναβαίνω *(4320)*

(4321) **προσαναλίσκω,** fut. προσαναλώσω [§36.4] (πρός + ἀναλίσκω) *to consume besides; to expend* on a definite object, Luke 8:43

προσαναλώσασα, nom. sg. f. aor. act. part. (Luke 8:43, GNT, MT, TR & NA | WH omits) . . . . προσαναλίσκω *(4321)*

προσαναπληροῦσα, nom. sg. f. pres. act. part. . . . . προσαναπληρόω *(4322)*

(4322) **προσαναπληρόω, ῶ,** fut. προσαναπληρώσω [§20.T] (πρός + ἀναπληρόω) *to fill up by addition; to supply* deficiencies, 2 Cor. 9:12; 11:9

(4323) **προσανατίθημι** [§28.V] (πρός + ἀνατίθημι) *to lay upon over and above;* mid. *to put one's self in free communication with, to confer with,* Gal. 1:16; *to confer upon, to propound as a matter of consideration,* Gal. 2:6

προσανεθέμην, 1 pers. sg. 2 aor. mid. indic. [§28.W] . . . . προσανατίθημι *(4323)*

προσανέθεντο, 3 pers. pl. 2 aor. mid. indic. id.

προσανεπλήρωσαν, 3 pers. pl. aor. act. indic. . . . . προσαναπληρόω *(4322)*

(4324) **προσαπειλέω, ῶ,** fut. προσαπειλήσω [§16.P] (πρός + ἀπειλέω) *to threaten in addition, utter additional threats,* Acts 4:21

προσαπειλησάμενοι, nom. pl. m. aor. mid.
     part. [§17.Q] .... προσαπειλέω *(4324)*
(4325) **προσδαπανάω**, ῶ, fut. προσδαπανήσω
     [§18.R] (πρός + δαπανάω) *to spend be-*
     sides, expend over and above, Luke 10:35
προσδαπανήσῃς, 2 pers. sg. aor. act.
     subj. .... προσδαπανάω *(4325)*
προσδεξάμενοι, nom. pl. m. aor. mid. dep.
     part. .... προσδέχομαι *(4327)*
προσδέξησθε, 2 pers. pl. aor. mid. dep. subj.   id.
(4326) **προσδέομαι**, fut. προσδεήσομαι [§37.1] (πρός
     + δέομαι) *to want besides or in addition,*
     Acts 17:25
προσδεόμενος, nom. sg. m. pres. mid./pass.
     dep. part. .... προσδέομαι *(4326)*
προσδέχεσθε, 2 pers. pl. pres. mid./pass. dep.
     imper. .... προσδέχομαι *(4327)*
προσδέχεται, 3 pers. sg. pres. mid./pass. dep.
     indic. ....   id.
(4327) **προσδέχομαι**, fut. προσδέξομαι [§23.1.b]
     (πρός + δέχομαι) *to receive, accept; to*
     receive, admit, grant access to, Luke 15:2;
     to receive, admit, accept, and with οὐ,
     to reject, Heb. 11:35; *to submit to,* Heb.
     10:34; *to receive kindly,* as a guest, *en-*
     tertain, Rom. 16:2; *to receive, admit,*
     as a hope, Acts 24:15; *to look or wait*
     for, expect, await, Mark 15:43; Luke 2:25,
     et al.
προσδεχόμενοι, nom. pl. m. pres. mid./pass.
     dep. part. .... προσδέχομαι *(4327)*
προσδεχομένοις, dat. pl. m. pres. mid./pass.
     dep. part. ....   id.
προσδεχόμενος, nom. sg. m. pres. mid./pass.
     dep. part. ....   id.
προσδέχονται, 3 pers. pl. pres. mid./pass.
     dep. indic. ....   id.
προσδοκᾷ, 3 pers. sg. pres. act.
     indic. .... προσδοκάω *(4328)*
(4328) **προσδοκάω**, ῶ, fut. προσδοκήσω [§18.R] *to*
     look for, be expectant of, Matt. 11:3; Luke
     7:19, 20; Acts 3:5; 2 Pet. 3:12, 13, 14; *to*
     expect, Acts 28:6; *to wait for,* Luke 1:21;
     8:40; Acts 10:24; 27:33; absol. *to think,*
     anticipate, Matt. 24:50; Luke 12:46
(4329) **προσδοκία**, ας, ἡ [§2.B.b; 2.2] *a looking for,*
     expectation, anticipation, Luke 21:26; me-
     ton. *expectation, what is expected or an-*
     ticipated, Acts 12:11
προσδοκίας, gen. sg. f. n. .... προσδοκία *(4329)*
προσδοκῶμεν, 1 pers. pl. pres. act. indic.
     {2 Pet. 3:13} .... προσδοκάω *(4328)*
προσδοκῶμεν, 1 pers. pl. pres. act. subj.
     {Luke 7:19–20} ....   id.
προσδοκῶν, nom. sg. m. pres. act. part. .   id.

προσδοκῶντας, acc. pl. m. pres. act.
     part. .... προσδοκάω *(4328)*
προσδοκῶντες, nom. pl. m. pres. act. part.   id.
προσδοκῶντος, gen. sg. m. pres. act. part.   id.
προσδοκώντων, gen. pl. m. pres. act. part.   id.
προσδραμών, nom. sg. m. 2 aor. act. part.
     [§36.1] .... προστρέχω *(4370)*
(4330) **προσεάω**, ῶ, fut. προσεάσω [§22.2] (πρός +
     ἐάω) *to permit an approach,* Acts 27:7
(4331) **προσεγγίζω**, fut. προσεγγίσω [§26.1] (πρός
     + ἐγγίζω) *to approach, come near,* Mark
     2:4
προσεγγίσαι, aor. act. infin. (Mark 2:4, MT
     & TR | προσενέγκαι, GNT, WH &
     NA) .... προσεγγίζω *(4331)*
προσεδέξασθε, 2 pers. pl. aor. mid. dep.
     indic. .... προσδέχομαι *(4327)*
προσεδέχετο, 3 pers. sg. imperf. mid./pass.
     dep. indic. ....   id.
προσεδόκων, 3 pers. pl. imperf. act.
     indic. .... προσδοκάω *(4328)*
προσεδρεύοντες, nom. pl. m. pres. act. part.
     (1 Cor. 9:13, MT & TR | παρεδρεύοντες,
     GNT, WH & NA) .... προσεδρεύω *(4332)*
(4332) **προσεδρεύω**, fut. προσεδρεύσω [§13.M]
     (πρός + ἕδρα) *to sit near;* met. *to wait or*
     attend upon, have charge of, 1 Cor. 9:13
προσέθετο, 3 pers. sg. 2 aor. mid.
     indic. .... προστίθημι *(4369)*
προσέθηκε(ν), 3 pers. sg. aor. act. indic. .   id.
προσειργάσατο, 3 pers. sg. aor. mid. dep.
     indic. [§13.4] (Luke 19:16, MT & TR |
     προσηργάσατο, GNT, WH &
     NA) .... προσεργάζομαι *(4333)*
προσεῖχον, 3 pers. pl. imperf. act.
     indic. .... προσέχω *(4337)*
προσεκαλέσατο, 3 pers. sg. aor. mid. dep.
     indic. (Luke 18:16, GNT, WH & NA |
     προσκαλεσάμενος, MT &
     TR) .... προσκαλέω *(†4341)*
προσεκλήθη, 3 pers. sg. aor. pass. indic. (Acts
     5:36, MT | προσεκλίθη, GNT, WH &
     NA | προσεκολλήθη, TR) ... προσκλίνω *(‡4347)*
προσεκληρώθησαν, 3 pers. pl. aor. pass.
     indic. [§21.U] .... προσκληρόω *(4345)*
προσεκλίθη, 3 pers. sg. aor. pass. indic. (Acts
     5:36, GNT, WH & NA | προσεκλήθη,
     MT | προσεκολλήθη, TR) ... προσκλίνω *(‡4347)*
προσεκολλήθη, 3 pers. sg. aor. pass. indic.
     [§19.S] (Acts 5:36, TR | προσεκλίθη,
     GNT, WH & NA | προσεκλήθη,
     MT) .... προσκολλάω *(4347)*
προσέκοψαν, 3 pers. pl. aor. act.
     indic. .... προσκόπτω *(4350)*
προσεκύλισε(ν), 3 pers. sg. aor. act.

indic. . . . . προσκυλίω *(4351)*
προσεκύνει, 3 pers. sg. imperf. act.
indic. . . . . προσκυνέω *(4352)*
προσεκύνησαν, 3 pers. pl. aor. act. indic. .   id.
προσεκύνησεν, 3 pers. sg. aor. act. indic. .   id.
προσεκύνουν, 3 pers. pl. imperf. act. indic.   id.
προσελάβετο, 3 pers. sg. 2 aor. mid. indic.
[§36.2] . . . . προσλαμβάνω *(4355)*
προσελάβοντο, 3 pers. pl. 2 aor. mid. indic.   id.
προσεληλύθατε, 2 pers. pl. 2 perf. act. indic.
[§36.1] . . . . προσέρχομαι *(4334)*
πρόσελθε, 2 pers. sg. 2 aor. act. imper. . . .   id.
προσελθόντες, nom. pl. m. 2 aor. act. part.   id.
προσελθόντων, gen. pl. m. 2 aor. act. part.   id.
προσελθοῦσα, nom. sg. f. 2 aor. act. part.   id.
προσελθοῦσαι, nom. pl. f. 2 aor. act. part.   id.
προσελθών, nom. sg. m. 2 aor. act. part. .   id.
προσενέγκαι, 2 aor. act. infin. id. (Mark 2:4,
    GNT, WH & NA | προσεγγίσαι, MT &
    TR) . . . . προσφέρω *(4374)*
προσενέγκας, nom. sg. m. aor. act. part.
    [§36.1] . . . .   id.
προσένεγκε, 2 pers. sg. 2 aor. act. imper. .   id.
προσενέγκῃ, 3 pers. sg. aor. act. subj. . . .   id.
προσένεγκον, 2 pers. sg. 2 aor. act. imper.
    (Matt. 8:4, GNT, WH & NA | προσ-
    ένεγκε, MT & TR) . . . .   id.
προσενεχθείς, nom. sg. m. aor. pass. part.   id.
προσενήνοχεν, 3 pers. sg. 2 perf. act. indic.
    Att. for προσήνοχε [§36.1] . . . .   id.
προσέπεσαν, 3 pers. pl. aor. act. indic. (Matt.
    7:25, GNT, WH & NA | προσέπεσον,
    MT & TR) . . . . προσπίπτω *(4363)*
προσέπεσε(ν), 3 pers. sg. 2 aor. act. indic.
    [§37.1] . . . .   id.
προσέπεσον, 3 pers. pl. 2 aor. act. indic.
    (Matt. 7:25, MT & TR | προσέπεσαν,
    GNT, WH & NA) . . . .   id.
προσέπιπτεν, 3 pers. sg. imperf. act. indic.
    (Mark 3:11, MT & TR | προσέπιπτον,
    GNT, WH & NA) . . . .   id.
προσέπιπτον, 3 pers. pl. imperf. act. indic.
    (Mark 3:11, GNT, WH & NA | προσ-
    έπιπτεν, MT & TR) . . . .   id.
προσεποιεῖτο, 3 pers. sg. imperf. mid. indic.
    (Luke 24:28, MT & TR | προσεποιή-
    σατο, GNT, WH & NA) . . . . προσποιέω *(†4364)*
προσεποιήσατο, 3 pers. sg. aor. mid. indic.
    (Luke 24:28, GNT, WH & NA | προσ-
    εποιεῖτο, MT & TR) . . . .   id.
(4333) **προσεργάζομαι,** fut. προσεργάσομαι (πρός
    + ἐργάζομαι) pr. *to work in addition; to*
    gain in addition in trade, Luke 19:16
προσέρρηξεν, 3 pers. sg. aor. act. indic. [§36.5]
    (Luke 6:48, 49, GNT, WH & NA |

προσέρρηξεν, MT & TR) . . προσρήγνυμι *(4366)*
προσέρρηξεν, 3 pers. sg. aor. act. indic. (Luke
    6:48, 49, MT & TR | προσέρηξεν, GNT,
    WH & NA) . . . .   id.
προσέρχεσθαι, pres. mid./pass. dep.
    infin. . . . . προσέρχομαι *(4334)*
προσέρχεται, 3 pers. sg. pres. mid./pass. dep.
    indic. . . . .   id.
(4334) **προσέρχομαι,** fut. προσελεύσομαι, 2 aor.
    προσῆλθον, perf. προσελήλυθα [§36.1]
    (πρός + ἔρχομαι) *to come or go to* any
    one, *approach,* Matt. 4:3, 11; 5:1; 8:19, 25,
    et al. freq.; trop. *to come or go to, ap-*
    proach, draw near, spiritually, Heb. 7:25;
    11:6; 4:16; 1 Pet. 2:4; met. *to assent to, ac-*
    cede to, concur in, 1 Tim. 6:3
προσερχόμενοι, nom. pl. m. pres. mid./pass.
    dep. part. . . . . προσέρχομαι *(4334)*
προσερχόμενον, acc. sg. m. pres. mid./pass.
    dep. part.   id.
προσερχομένου, gen. sg. m. pres. mid./pass.
    dep. part.   id.
προσερχομένους, acc. pl. m. pres. mid./pass.
    dep. part.   id.
προσέρχονται, 3 pers. pl. pres. mid./pass.
    dep. indic. . . . .   id.
προσερχώμεθα, 1 pers. pl. pres. mid./pass.
    dep. subj.   id.
προσέσχηκε(ν), 3 pers. sg. perf. act.
    indic. . . . . προσέχω *(4337)*
προσέταξε(ν), 3 pers. sg. aor. act.
    indic. . . . . προστάσσω *(4367)*
προσετέθη, 3 pers. sg. aor. pass. indic.
    [§28.10] . . . . προστίθημι *(4369)*
προσετέθησαν, 3 pers. pl. aor. pass. indic.   id.
προσετίθει, 3 pers. sg. imperf. act. indic.
    [§31.2] . . . .   id.
προσετίθεντο, 3 pers. pl. imperf. pass. indic.
    [§28.W] . . . .   id.
πρόσευξαι, 2 pers. sg. aor. mid. dep.
    imper. . . . . προσεύχομαι *(4336)*
προσευξάμενοι, nom. pl. m. aor. mid. dep.
    part. . . . .   id.
προσευξάμενος, nom. sg. m. aor. mid. dep.
    part. . . . .   id.
προσεύξασθαι, aor. mid. dep. infin. . . . . .   id.
προσευξάσθωσαν, 3 pers. pl. aor. mid. dep.
    imper. . . . .   id.
προσεύξηται, 3 pers. sg. aor. mid. dep. subj.   id.
προσεύξομαι, 1 pers. sg. fut. mid. dep. indic.   id.
προσευξόμεθα, 1 pers. pl. fut. mid. dep. indic.
    (Rom. 8:26, MT | προσευξώμεθα, GNT,
    WH, TR & NA) . . . .   id.
προσεύξωμαι, 1 pers. sg. aor. mid. dep. subj.   id.
προσευξώμεθα, 1 pers. pl. aor. mid. dep. subj.

(Rom. 8:26, GNT, WH, TR & NA |
προσευξόμεθα, ΜΤ) ...... προσεύχομαι *(4336)*
προσευχαί, nom. pl. f. n. .... προσευχή *(4335)*
προσευχαῖς, dat. pl. f. n. .... id.
προσευχάς, acc. pl. f. n. .... id.
προσεύχεσθαι, pres. mid./pass. dep.
    infin. .... προσεύχομαι *(4336)*
προσεύχεσθε, 2 pers. pl. pres. mid./pass. dep.
    imper. .... id.
προσευχέσθω, 3 pers. sg. pres. mid./pass. dep.
    imper. .... id.
προσεύχεται, 3 pers. sg. pres. mid./pass. dep.
    indic. .... id.
(4335) **προσευχή**, ῆς, ἡ, nom. sg. f. n. [§2.B.a] *prayer,*
    Matt. 17:21; 21:13, 22; Luke 6:12; Acts
    1:14, et al.; meton. *a place where prayer*
    is offered, an oratory, perhaps, Acts
    16:13, 16
προσευχῇ, dat. sg. f. n.
    {Matt. 21:22} .... προσευχή *(4335)*
προσεύχῃ, 2 pers. sg. pres. mid./pass. dep.
    subj. {Matt. 6:6} .... προσεύχομαι *(4336)*
προσευχήν, acc. sg. f. n. .... προσευχή *(4335)*
προσευχῆς, gen. sg. f. n. .... id.
προσεύχησθε, 2 pers. pl. pres. mid./pass. dep.
    subj. .... προσεύχομαι *(4336)*
(4336) **προσεύχομαι**, 1 pers. sg. pres. mid./pass. dep.
    indic., fut. προσεύξομαι, imperf.
    προσηυχόμην, aor. προσηυξάμην [§13.3]
    to pray, offer prayer, Matt. 5:44; 6:5, 6,
    et al.
προσευχόμεθα, 1 pers. pl. pres. mid./pass.
    dep. indic. .... προσεύχομαι *(4336)*
προσευχομένη, nom. sg. f. pres. mid./pass.
    dep. part. .... id.
προσευχόμενοι, nom. pl. m. pres. mid./pass.
    dep. part. .... id.
προσευχόμενον, acc. sg. m. pres. mid./pass.
    dep. part. {Luke 9:18} .... id.
προσευχόμενον, nom. sg. neut. pres.
    mid./pass. dep. part. {Luke 1:10} ..... id.
προσευχόμενος, nom. sg. m. pres. mid./pass.
    dep. part. .... id.
προσευχομένου, gen. sg. m. pres. mid./pass.
    dep. part. .... id.
προσεύχονται, 3 pers. pl. pres. mid./pass. dep.
    indic. .... id.
προσεύχωμαι, 1 pers. sg. pres. mid./pass. dep.
    subj. .... id.
προσευχῶν, gen. pl. f. n. .... προσευχή *(4335)*
προσέφερεν, 3 pers. sg. imperf. act.
    indic. .... προσφέρω *(4374)*
προσέφερον, 3 pers. pl. imperf. act. indic. id.
προσεφώνει, 3 pers. sg. imperf. act.
    indic. .... προσφωνέω *(4377)*

προσεφώνησε(ν), 3 pers. sg. aor. act.
    indic. .... προσφωνέω *(4377)*
πρόσεχε, 2 pers. sg. pres. act. imper. προσέχω *(4337)*
προσέχειν, pres. act. infin. .... id.
προσέχετε, 2 pers. pl. pres. act. imper. ... id.
προσέχοντας, acc. pl. m. pres. act. part. . id.
προσέχοντες, nom. pl. m. pres. act. part. . id.
(4337) **προσέχω**, fut. προσέξω [§36.4] (πρός + ἔχω)
    to have in addition; to hold to, bring near;
    absol. *to apply* the mind to a thing, *to give*
    heed to, attend to, observe, consider, Acts
    5:35; Heb. 2:1; 2 Pet. 1:19; *to take care of,*
    provide for, Acts 20:28; when followed by
    ἀπό, μή, or μήποτε, *to beware of, take*
    heed of, guard against, Matt. 6:1; 7:15; *to*
    assent to, yield credence to, follow, adhere
    or be attached to, Acts 8:6, 10, 11; 16:14;
    to give one's self up to, be addicted to, en-
    gage in, be occupied with, 1 Tim. 1:4; 3:8,
    et al.
προσεῶντος, gen. sg. m. pres. act.
    part. .... προσεάω *(4330)*
προσῆλθαν, 3 pers. pl. 2 aor. act.
    indic. .... προσέρχομαι *(4334)*
προσῆλθε(ν), 3 pers. sg. 2 aor. act. indic. . id.
προσῆλθον, 3 pers. pl. aor. act. indic. [§35.12] id.
(4338) **προσηλόω**, ῶ, fut. προσηλώσω [§20.Τ] (πρός
    + ἧλος) *to nail to, affix with nails,* Col.
    2:14
προσήλυτοι, nom. pl. m. n. ..... προσήλυτος *(4339)*
προσήλυτον, acc. sg. m. n. .... id.
(4339) **προσήλυτος**, ου, ὁ [§3.C.a,b] pr. *a newcomer,*
    a stranger; in N.T. *a proselyte, convert from*
    paganism to Judaism, Matt. 23:15; Acts
    2:10; 6:5; 13:43
προσηλύτων, gen. pl. m. n. ..... προσήλυτος *(4339)*
προσηλώσας, nom. sg. m. aor. act.
    part. .... προσηλόω *(4338)*
προσήνεγκα, 1 pers. sg. aor. act. indic.
    [§36.1] .... προσφέρω *(4374)*
προσήνεγκαν, 3 pers. pl. aor. act. indic. .. id.
προσηνέγκατε, 2 pers. pl. aor. act. indic. . id.
προσήνεγκε(ν), 3 pers. sg. aor. act. indic. . id.
προσηνέχθη, 3 pers. sg. aor. pass. indic. .. id.
προσηνέχθησαν, 3 pers. pl. aor. pass. indic.
    (Matt. 19:13, GNT, WH & NA | προσ-
    ηνέχθη, ΜΤ & TR) .... id.
προσηργάσατο, 3 pers. sg. aor. mid. indic.
    (Luke 19:16, GNT, WH & NA | προσ-
    ειργάσατο, ΜΤ & TR) ... προσεργάζομαι *(4333)*
προσήρχοντο, 3 pers. pl. imperf. mid./pass.
    dep. indic. .... προσέρχομαι *(4334)*
προσηυξάμεθα, 1 pers. pl. aor. mid. dep.
    indic. (Acts 21:5, ΜΤ & TR | προσευ-
    ξάμενοι, GNT, WH & NA) . προσεύχομαι *(4336)*

προσηύξαντο, 3 pers. pl. aor. mid. dep. indic.
[§13.3] .... προσεύχομαι (4336)
προσηύξατο, 3 pers. sg. aor. mid. dep. indic. id.
προσηύχετο, 3 pers. sg. imperf. mid./pass.
dep. indic. .... id.
προσήχθη, 3 pers. sg. aor. pass. indic. (Matt.
18:24, WH | προσηνέχθη, GNT, MT, TR
& NA) .... προσάγω (4317)
προσθεῖναι, 2 aor. act. infin.
[§28.V] .... προστίθημι (4369)
προσθείς, nom. sg. m. 2 aor. act. part. ... id.
προσθές, 2 pers. sg. 2 aor. act. imper. [§38.7] id.
πρόσκαιρα, nom. pl. neut. adj. .. πρόσκαιρος (4340)
πρόσκαιροι, nom. pl. m. adj. .... id.
πρόσκαιρον, acc. sg. f. adj. .... id.
(4340) **πρόσκαιρος**, ον, nom. sg. m. adj. [§7.2] (πρός
+ καιρός) opportune; in N.T. continuing
for a limited time, temporary, transient,
Matt. 13:21; Mark 4:17; 2 Cor. 4:18; Heb.
11:25
προσκαλεῖται, 3 pers. sg. pres. mid./pass. dep.
indic. .... προσκαλέω (†4341)
(†4341) **προσκαλέω**, ῶ, fut. προσκαλέσομαι [§22.1]
perf. (pass form) προσκέκλημαι (mid. of
προσκαλέω, to call to, summon, invite,
from πρός + καλέω) to call to one's self,
summon, Matt. 10:1; 15:10, 32; 18:2, et
al.; to invite, Acts 2:39; to call to the performance of a thing, appoint, Acts 13:2;
16:10
προσκαλεσάμενοι, nom. pl. m. aor. mid. dep.
part. .... προσκαλέω (†4341)
προσκαλεσάμενος, nom. sg. m. aor. mid.
dep. part. .... id.
προσκαλεσάσθω, 3 pers. sg. aor. mid. dep.
imper. .... id.
προσκαλέσηται, 3 pers. sg. aor. mid. dep.
subj. .... id.
προσκαρτερεῖτε, 2 pers. pl. pres. act.
imper. .... προσκαρτερέω (4342)
(4342) **προσκαρτερέω**, ῶ, fut. προσκαρτερήσω
[§16.P] (πρός + καρτερέω) to persist in
adherence to a thing; to be intently engaged
in, attend constantly to, Acts 1:14; 2:42;
Rom. 13:6, et al.; to remain constantly in
a place, Acts 2:46; to constantly attend
upon, continue near to, be at hand, Mark
3:9; Acts 8:13; 10:7
προσκαρτερῇ, 3 pers. sg. pres. act.
subj. .... προσκαρτερέω (4342)
προσκαρτερήσει, dat. sg. f. n. προσκαρτέρησις (4343)
(4343) **προσκαρτέρησις**, εως, ἡ [§5.E.c] perseverance, unremitting continuance in a thing,
Eph. 6:18
προσκαρτερήσομεν, 1 pers. pl. fut. act.

indic. .... προσκαρτερέω (4342)
προσκαρτεροῦντες, nom. pl. m. pres. act.
part. .... id.
προσκαρτερούντων, gen. pl. m. pres. act.
part. .... id.
προσκαρτερῶν, nom. sg. m. pres. act. part. id.
προσκέκλημαι, 1 pers. sg. perf. mid./pass.
dep. indic. [§22.4] .... προσκαλέω (†4341)
προσκέκληται, 3 pers. sg. perf. mid./pass.
dep. indic. .... id.
(4344) **προσκεφάλαιον**, ου, τό [§3.C.c] (πρός +
κεφαλή) pr. a cushion for the head, pillow;
also, a boat-cushion, Mark 4:38
προσκεφάλαιον, acc. sg.
neut. n. .... προσκεφάλαιον (4344)
(4345) **προσκληρόω**, ῶ, fut. προσκληρώσω [§20.T]
(πρός + κληρόω) pr. to assign by lot;
in N.T., aor. mid. (pass. form) προσ-
εκλη ρώθην, to adjoin one's self to, associate with, follow as a disciple, Acts
17:4
πρόσκλησιν, acc. sg. f. n. (1 Tim. 5:21, MT
& TR | πρόσκλισιν, GNT, WH &
NA) .... πρόσκλησις (†4346)
(†4346) **πρόσκλησις**, εως, ἡ [§5.E.c] (πρός + καλέω)
advocacy, or, perhaps, partiality 1 Tim.
5:21
(‡4347) **προσκλίνω**, fut. προσκλινῶ (πρός + κλίνω)
pr. to make to lean upon or against a thing;
met., aor. mid. (pass. form) προσεκλίθην,
to join one's self to, follow as an adherent,
Acts 5:36
πρόσκλισιν, acc. sg. f. n. (1 Tim. 5:21, GNT,
WH & NA | πρόσκλησιν, MT &
TR) .... πρόσκλισις (4346)
(4346) **πρόσκλισις**, εως, ἡ [§5.E.c] pr. a leaning upon
or towards a thing; met. a leaning towards
any one, inclination of mind towards, partiality, 1 Tim. 5:21
(4347) **προσκολλάω**, ῶ, fut. προσκολλήσω [§18.R]
(πρός + κολλάω) pr. to glue to; in N.T.,
aor. mid. (pass. form) προσεκολλήθη, fut.
προσκολληθήσομαι, to join one's self to
any one, follow as an adherent, Acts 5:36;
to cleave closely to, Matt. 19:5; Mark 10:7;
Eph. 5:31
προσκολληθήσεται, 3 pers. sg. fut. pass.
indic. .... προσκολλάω (4347)
(4348) **πρόσκομμα**, ατος, τό, nom. sg. neut. n. [§4.D.c]
a stumbling, Rom. 9:32, 33; 1 Pet. 2:8;
met. a stumbling-block, an occasion of sin-
ning, means of inducing to sin, Rom. 14:13;
1 Cor. 8:9; met. a moral stumbling, a shock
to the moral or religious sense, a moral em-
barrassment, Rom. 14:20 {1 Cor. 8:9}

πρόσκομμα, acc. sg. neut. n.
{Rom. 14:13} . . . . πρόσκομμα (4348)
προσκόμματος, gen. sg. neut. n. . . . . id.

(4349) **προσκοπή**, ῆς, ἡ [§2.B.a] pr. *a stumbling; offence;* in N.T. *an offence, shock, ground of exception,* 2 Cor. 6:3
προσκοπήν, acc. sg. f. n. . . . . προσκοπή (4349)
προσκόπτει, 3 pers. sg. pres. act.
indic. . . . . προσκόπτω (4350)
προσκόπτουσι(ν), 3 pers. pl. pres. act. indic. id.

(4350) **προσκόπτω**, fut. προσκόψω [§23.1.a] (πρός + κόπτω) *to dash against, to beat upon,* Matt. 7:27; *to strike* the foot *against,* Matt. 4:6; Luke 4:11; *to stumble,* John 11:9, 10; met. *to stumble at, to take offence at,* Rom. 9:32; 14:21; 1 Pet. 2:8
προσκόψῃς, 2 pers. sg. aor. act.
subj. . . . . προσκόπτω (4350)
προσκυλίσας, nom. sg. m. aor. act.
part. . . . . προσκυλίω (4351)

(4351) **προσκυλίω**, or προσκυλίνδω, fut. προσ-κυλίσω [§13.M] (πρός + κυλίω) *to roll to or against,* Matt. 27:60; Mark 15:46
προσκυνεῖ, 3 pers. sg. pres. act.
indic. . . . . προσκυνέω (4352)
προσκυνεῖν, pres. act. infin. . . . . id.
προσκυνεῖτε, 2 pers. pl. pres. act. indic. . . id.

(4352) **προσκυνέω**, ῶ, fut. προσκυνήσομαι and προσκυνήσω, aor. προσεκύνησα [§16.P] (πρός + κυνέω, *to kiss*) *to do reverence or homage by kissing the hand;* in N.T. *to do reverence or homage by prostration,* Matt. 2:2, 8, 11; 20:20; Luke 4:7; 24:52; *to pay* divine *homage, worship, adore,* Matt. 4:10; John 4:20, 21; Heb. 1:6, et al.; *to bow one's self in adoration,* Heb. 11:21
προσκυνῆσαι, aor. act. infin. . . . . προσκυνέω (4352)
προσκυνήσαντες, nom. pl. m. aor. act. part. id.
προσκυνήσατε, 2 pers. pl. aor. act. imper. id.
προσκυνησάτωσαν, 3 pers. pl. aor. act.
imper. . . . . id.
προσκυνήσει, 3 pers. sg. fut. act. indic. . . id.
προσκυνήσεις, 2 pers. sg. fut. act. indic. . id.
προσκυνήσετε, 2 pers. pl. fut. act. indic. . id.
προσκυνήσῃς, 2 pers. sg. aor. act. subj. . . id.
προσκύνησον, 2 pers. sg. aor. act. imper. . id.
προσκυνήσουσι(ν), 3 pers. pl. fut. act. indic. id.
προσκυνήσω, 1 pers. sg. aor. act. subj. . . . id.
προσκυνήσων, nom. sg. m. fut. act. part. id.
προσκυνήσωσι(ν), 3 pers. pl. aor. act. subj. id.
προσκυνηταί, nom. pl. m. n. . . προσκυνητής (4353)

(4353) **προσκυνητής**, οῦ, ὁ [§2.B.c] *a worshipper,* John 4:23
προσκυνοῦμεν, 1 pers. pl. pres. act.
indic. . . . . προσκυνέω (4352)

προσκυνοῦντας, acc. pl. m. pres. act.
part. . . . . προσκυνέω (4352)
προσκυνοῦντες, nom. pl. m. pres. act. part. id.
προσκυνοῦσα, nom. sg. f. pres. act. part. . id.
προσκυνοῦσι(ν), 3 pers. pl. pres. act. indic.
(Rev. 4:10, MT & TR | προσκυνήσουσιν, GNT, WH & NA) . . . . id.
προσλαβεῖν, 2 aor. act. infin. [§36.2] (Acts 27:34, MT & TR | μεταλαβεῖν, GNT, WH & NA) . . . . προσλαμβάνω (4355)
προσλαβόμενοι, nom. pl. m. 2 aor. mid.
part. . . . . id.
προσλαβόμενος, nom. sg. m. 2 aor. mid.
part. . . . . id.
προσλαβοῦ, 2 pers. sg. 2 aor. mid. imper. id.

(4354) **προσλαλέω**, ῶ, fut. προσλαλήσω [§16.P] (πρός + λαλέω) *to speak to, converse with,* Acts 13:43; 28:20
προσλαλῆσαι, aor. act. infin. . . . . προσλαλέω (4354)
προσλαλοῦντες, nom. pl. m. pres. act. part. id.
προσλαμβάνεσθε, 2 pers. pl. pres. mid.
imper. . . . . προσλαμβάνω (4355)

(4355) **προσλαμβάνω** [§36.2] *to take besides;* mid. προσλαμβάνομαι, fut. προσλή(μ)ψομαι, 2 aor. προσελαβόμην, *to take to one's self, assume, take as a companion or associate,* Acts 17:5; 18:26; *to take,* as food, Acts 27:33, 34, 36; *to receive kindly or hospitably, admit to one's society and friendship, treat with kindness,* Acts 28:2; Rom. 14:1, 3; 15:7; Philemon 12, 17; *to take or draw to one's self* as a preliminary to an address of admonition, Matt. 16:22; Mark 8:32

(†4356) **πρόσλημψις**, εως, ἡ, nom. sg. f. n., *acceptance* (Rom. 11:15, GNT, WH & NA | πρόσληψις, MT & TR)

(4356) **πρόσληψις**, εως, ἡ, nom. sg. f. n. [§5.E.c] *an assuming; a receiving, reception* (Rom. 11:15, MT & TR | πρόσλημψις, GNT, WH & NA)
προσμεῖναι, aor. act. infin. [§27.1.d] προσμένω (4357)
προσμείνας, nom. sg. m. aor. act. part. . . id.
προσμένει, 3 pers. sg. pres. act. indic. . . . id.
προσμένειν, pres. act. infin. . . . . id.
προσμένουσι(ν), 3 pers. pl. pres. act. indic. id.

(4357) **προσμένω**, fut. προσμενῶ [§27.1.a] (πρός + μένω) *to continue, remain, stay* in a place, 1 Tim. 1:3; *to remain or continue with* any one, Matt. 15:32; Mark 8:2; Acts 18:18; *to adhere to,* Acts 11:23; met. *to remain constant in, persevere in,* Acts 13:43; 1 Tim. 5:5

(4358) **προσορμίζω**, fut. προσορμίσω [§26.1] (πρός + ὁρμίζω, from ὅρμος, *a station for ships*) *to bring a ship to its station or to land;* mid. *to come to the land,* Mark 6:53

προσοφείλεις, 2 pers. sg. pres. act. indic. . . . . προσοφείλω *(4359)*

(4359) **προσοφείλω,** fut. προσοφειλήσω [§35.5] (πρός + ὀφείλω) *to owe besides or in addition,* Philemon 19

(4360) **προσοχθίζω,** fut. προσοχθίσω [§26.1] (πρός + ὀχθίζω, *to be vexed, offended) to be vexed or angry at,* Heb. 3:10

(4361) **πρόσπεινος,** ον, nom. sg. m. adj. [§7.2] (πρός + πεῖνα) *very hungry,* Acts 10:10

προσπεσοῦσα, nom. sg. f. 2 aor. act. part. προσπίπτω *(4363)*

προσπήξαντες, nom. pl. m. aor. act. part. προσπήγνυμι *(4362)*

(4362) **προσπήγνυμι,** fut. προσπήξω [§36.5] (πρός + πήγνυμι) *to fix to, affix to,* Acts 2:23

(4363) **προσπίπτω,** fut. προσπεσοῦμαι, 2 aor. προσέπεσον [§37.1] (πρός + πίπτω) *to fall or impinge upon or against* a thing; *to fall down to* any one, Mark 3:11; 7:25, et al.; *to rush violently upon, beat against,* Matt. 7:25

(†4364) **προσποιέω,** ῶ, fut. προσποιήσω [§16.P] (πρός + ποιέω) *to add or attach;* mid. *to attach to one's self; to claim or arrogate to one's self; to assume the appearance of, make a show of, pretend,* Luke 24:28

προσποιούμενος, nom. sg. m. pres. mid./pass. dep. part. (John 8:6, TR | GNT, WH, MT & NA omit) . . . . προσποιέω *(†4364)*

(4365) **προσπορεύομαι,** fut. προσπορεύσομαι [§14.N] (πρός + πορεύομαι) *to go or come to* any one, Mark 10:35

προσπορεύονται, 3 pers. pl. pres. mid./pass. dep. indic. . . . . προσπορεύομαι *(4365)*

(4366) **προσρήγνυμι,** fut. προσρήξω [§36.5] (πρός + ῥήγνυμι) *to break or burst upon, dash against,* Luke 6:48, 49

(4367) **προστάσσω,** or προστάττω, fut. προστάξω [§26.3] (πρός + τάσσω) pr. *to place or station at or against; to enjoin, command, direct,* Matt. 1:24; 8:4; 21:6; Mark 1:44, et al.; *to assign, constitute, appoint,* Acts 17:26

(4368) **προστάτις,** ιδος, ἡ, nom. sg. f. n. [§4.2.c] (f. of προστάτης, *one who stands in front or before; a leader; a protector, champion, patron,* from προΐστημι) *a patroness, protectress,* Rom. 16:2

προστεθῆναι, aor. pass. infin. [§28.10] . . . . προστίθημι *(4369)*

προστεθήσεται, 3 pers. sg. fut. pass. indic.   id.

προστεταγμένα, acc. pl. neut. perf. pass.

part. προστάσσω *(4367)*

προστεταγμένους, acc. pl. m. perf. pass. part. (Acts 17:26, GNT, WH, MT & NA | προτεταγμένους, TR) . . . . id.

προστῆναι, 2 aor. act. infin. [§29.X] . . . . προστίθημι *(4369)*

(4369) **προστίθημι,** fut. προσθήσω, aor. pass. προσετέθην [§28.V; 28.10] (πρός + τίθημι) *to put to or near; to lay with or by the side of,* Acts 13:36; *to add, superadd, adjoin,* Matt. 6:27, 33; Luke 3:20; Acts 2:41, et al.; from the Hebrew, προστίθεμαι, before an infinitive, and the participle προσθείς, before a finite verb, denote *continuation,* or *repetition,* Luke 19:11; 20:11, 12; Acts 12:3

προστρέχοντες, nom. pl. m. pres. act. part. προστρέχω *(4370)*

(4370) **προστρέχω,** 2 aor. προσέδραμον [§36.2] (πρός + τρέχω) *to run to,* or *up,* Mark 9:15; 10:17; Acts 8:30

(4371) **προσφάγιον,** ου, τό [§3.C.c] (πρός + φαγεῖν) *what is eaten besides;* hence, genr. *victuals, food,* John 21:5

προσφάγιον, acc. sg. neut. n. . . . . προσφάγιον *(4371)*

πρόσφατον, acc. sg. f. adj. . . . . . . πρόσφατος *(4372)*

(4372) **πρόσφατος,** ον [§7.2] (πρός + πέφαμαι, from φάω, *to slay*) pr. *recently killed;* hence, genr. *recent, new, newly or lately made,* Heb. 10:20

(4373) **προσφάτως,** adv., *newly, recently, lately,* Acts 18:2

πρόσφερε, 2 pers. sg. pres. act. imper. . . . . προσφέρω *(4374)*

προσφέρει, 3 pers. sg. pres. act. indic. . . .   id.

προσφέρειν, pres. act. infin. . . . .   id.

προσφέρεται, 3 pers. sg. pres. pass. indic.   id.

προσφέρῃ, 3 pers. sg. pres. act. subj. . . . .   id.

προσφέρῃς, 2 pers. sg. pres. act. subj. . . .   id.

προσφερόμεναι, nom. pl. f. pres. pass. part.   id.

προσφέρονται, 3 pers. pl. pres. pass. indic.   id.

προσφέροντες, nom. pl. m. pres. act. part.   id.

προσφερόντων, gen. pl. m. pres. act. part.   id.

προσφέρουσιν, 3 pers. pl. pres. act. indic. {Heb. 10:1} . . . .   id.

προσφέρουσιν, dat. pl. m. pres. act. part. (Mark 10:13, MT & TR | αὐτοῖς, GNT, WH & NA) . . . .   id.

(4374) **προσφέρω,** fut. προσοίσω, aor. προσήνεγκα, 2 aor. προσήνεγκον [§36.1] (πρός + φέρω) *to bear or bring to,* Matt. 4:24; 25:20; *to bring to or before* magistrates, Luke 12:11; 23:14; *to bring near to, apply to,* John 19:29; *to offer, tender, proffer,* as money, Acts 8:18; *to offer, present,* as gifts,

oblations, etc. Matt. 2:11; 5:23; Heb. 5:7; *to offer* in sacrifice, Mark 1:44; Luke 5:14; *to offer up* any one as a sacrifice to God, Heb. 9:25, 28; 11:17, et al.; mid. *to bear one's self towards, behave or conduct one's self towards, to deal with, treat* any one, Heb. 12:7

προσφέρων, nom. sg. m. pres. act. part. . . . . προσφέρω *(4374)*

προσφέρωσιν, 3 pers. pl. pres. act. subj. (Luke 12:11, MT & TR | εἰσφέρωσιν, GNT, WH & NA) . . . . id.

προσφιλῆ, nom. pl. neut. adj. . . . . προσφιλής *(4375)*

(4375) **προσφιλής**, ές [§7.G.b] (πρός + φίλος) *friendly, amicable, grateful, acceptable,* Phil. 4:8

(4376) **προσφορά**, ᾶς, ἡ, nom. sg. f. n. [§2.B.b] pr. *a bringing to;* in N.T. *an offering, an act of offering up* or *sacrificing,* Heb. 10:10; trop. Rom. 15:16; *an offering, oblation, a thing offered,* Eph. 5:2; Heb. 10:5, 8; *a sacrifice, victim offered,* Acts 21:26; 24:17

προσφορᾷ, dat. sg. f. n. . . . . προσφορά *(4376)*

προσφοράν, acc. sg. f. n. . . . . id.

προσφορᾶς, gen. sg. f. n. {Heb. 10:10} . . . id.

προσφοράς, acc. pl. f. n. {Heb. 10:8} . . . . id.

(4377) **προσφωνέω**, ῶ, fut. προσφωνήσω [§16.P] (πρός + φωνέω) *to speak to, address,* Matt. 11:16; Luke 7:32; 13:12, et al.; *to address, harangue,* Acts 22:2; *to call* to one's self, Luke 6:13

προσφωνοῦντα, nom. pl. neut. pres. act. part. (Matt. 11:16, GNT, WH & NA | προσφωνοῦσι(ν), MT & TR) . . . . . προσφωνέω *(4377)*

προσφωνοῦσι(ν), dat. pl. m. pres. act. part. id.

πρόσχυσιν, acc. sg. f. n. . . . . πρόσχυσις *(4378)*

(4378) **πρόσχυσις**, εως, ἡ [§5.E.c] (προσχέω, *to pour out upon, besprinkle,* from πρός + χέω) *an effusion, sprinkling,* Heb. 11:28

προσψαύετε, 2 pers. pl. pres. act. indic. . . . . προσψαύω *(4379)*

(4379) **προσψαύω**, fut. προσψαύσω [§13.M] (πρός + ψαύω, *to touch*) *to touch upon, touch lightly,* Luke 11:46

πρόσωπα, nom. pl. neut. n. {Rev. 9:7} . . . . πρόσωπον *(4383)*

πρόσωπα, acc. pl. neut. n. {Rev. 7:11} . . . id.

προσωπολημπτεῖτε, 2 pers. pl. pres. act. indic. (James 2:9, GNT, WH & NA | προσωπολημπτεῖτε, MT & TR) . . . . προσωπολημπτέω *(†4380)*

(†4380) **προσωπολημπτέω**, ῶ, *to show partiality,* James 2:9

(‡4381) **προσωπολήμπτης**, ου, ὁ, nom. sg. m. n. *one who shows partiality* (Acts 10:34, GNT,

WH & NA | προσωπολήπτης, MT & TR)

(‡4382) **προσωπολημψία**, ας, ἡ, nom. sg. f. n., *respect of persons, partiality* (Rom. 2:11; Eph. 6:9; Col. 3:25, GNT, WH & NA | προσωπολημψία, MT & TR)

προσωπολημψίαις, dat. pl. f. n. (James 2:1, GNT, WH & NA | προσωπολημψίαις, MT & TR) . . . . προσωπολημψία *(‡4382)*

προσωποληπτεῖτε, 2 pers. pl. pres. act. indic. (James 2:9, MT & TR | προσωπολημπτεῖτε, GNT, WH & NA) προσωποληπτέω *(4380)*

(4380) **προσωποληπτέω**, ῶ, fut. προσωποληπτήσω [§16.P] *to accept or respect the person* of any one, *to pay regard to external appearance, condition, circumstances,* etc., *to show partiality to,* James 2:9

(4381) **προσωπολήπτης**, ου, ὁ, nom. sg. m. n. [§2.B.c] (πρόσωπον + λαμβάνω) *a respecter of persons* (Acts 10:34, MT & TR | προσωπολήμπτης, GNT, WH & NA)

(4382) **προσωποληψία**, ας, ἡ, nom. sg. f. n. [§2.B.b; 2.2] *respect of persons, partiality* (Rom. 2:11; Eph. 6:9; Col. 3:25, MT & TR | προσωπολημψία, GNT, WH & NA)

προσωποληψίαις, dat. pl. f. n. (James 2:1, MT & TR | προσωπολημψίαις, GNT, WH & NA) . . . . προσωποληψία *(4382)*

(4383) **πρόσωπον**, ου, τό, nom. sg. neut. n. [§3.C.c] (πρός + ὤψ) *the face, countenance, visage,* Matt. 6:16, 17; 17:2, 6; according to late usage, *a person, individual,* 2 Cor. 1:11; hence, *personal presence,* 1 Thess. 2:17; from the Hebrew, πρόσωπον πρὸς πρόσωπον, *face to face, clearly, perfectly,* 1 Cor. 13:12; *face, surface, external form, figure, appearance,* Matt. 16:3; Luke 12:56; *external circumstances, or condition* of any one, Matt. 22:16; Mark 12:14; πρόσωπον λαμβάνειν, *to have respect to the external circumstances* of any one, Luke 20:21; Gal. 2:6; ἐν προσώπῳ, *in presence of,* 2 Cor. 2:10; ἀπὸ προσώπου, *from the presence of, from,* Acts 3:19; also, *from before,* Acts 7:45; εἰς πρόσωπον, and κατὰ πρόσωπον, *in the presence of, before,* Acts 3:13; 2 Cor. 8:24; also, *openly,* Gal. 2:11; κατὰ πρόσωπον ἔχειν, *to have before one's face, to have* any one *present,* Acts 25:16; ἀπὸ προσώπου, *from,* Rev. 12:14; πρὸ προσώπου, *before,* Acts 13:24 {Matt. 17:2}

πρόσωπον, acc. sg. neut. n. {Matt. 17:6} . . . . πρόσωπον *(4383)*

προσώπου, gen. sg. neut. n. ...... πρόσωπον *(4383)*
προσώπῳ, dat. sg. neut. n. .... id.
προσώπων, gen. pl. neut. n. .... id.
προσωρμίσθησαν, 3 pers. pl. aor. pass. indic.
   [§26.1] .... προσορμίζω *(4358)*
προσώχθισα, 1 pers. sg. aor. act.
   indic. .... προσοχθίζω *(4360)*
προσώχθισε(ν), 3 pers. sg. aor. act. indic. . id.

(4384) **προτάσσω**, or προτάττω, fut. προτάξω
   [§26.3] (πρό + τάσσω) *to place or arrange*
   in front; to assign beforehand, foreordain,
   Acts 17:26

(4385) **προτείνω**, fut. προτενῶ [§27.1.c] (πρό +
   τείνω) *to extend before; to stretch out,* Acts
   22:25

προτέραν, acc. sg. f. adj. .... πρότερος *(4387)*

(4386) **πρότερον**, acc. sg. neut. adj.

(4387) **πρότερος**, α, ον [§7.1; 8.6] (compar. of πρό)
   former, prior, Eph. 4:22; τὸ πρότερον, as
   an adv., *before, formerly,* John 6:62, et al.

προτεταγμένους, acc. pl. m. perf. pass. part.
   (Acts 17:26, TR | προστεταγμένους,
   GNT, WH, MT & NA) ...... προτάσσω *(4384)*

(†4388) **προτίθημι**, fut. προθήσω [§28.V] (πρό +
   τίθημι) *to place before; to set forth, propose
   publicly,* Rom. 3:25; mid. προτίθεμαι, *to
   purpose, determine, design beforehand,*
   Rom. 1:13; Eph. 1:9

(†4389) **προτρέπω**, fut. προτρέψω [§23.1.a] (πρό +
   τρέπω) *to turn forwards; to impel; to excite, urge, exhort,* Acts 18:27

προτρεψάμενοι, nom. pl. m. aor. mid.
   part. .... προτρέπω *(†4389)*

(4390) **προτρέχω**, 2 aor. προέδραμον [§36.1] (πρό
   + τρέχω) *to run before, or in advance,*
   Luke 19:4; John 20:4

(4391) **προϋπάρχω**, fut. προϋπάρξω [§23.1.b] (πρό
   + ὑπάρχω) imperf. προϋπῆρχον, *to be
   before, or formerly,* Luke 23:12; Acts 8:9

προϋπῆρχεν, 3 pers. sg. imperf. act. indic.
   (Acts 8:9, GNT, MT, TR & NA | προ-
   υπῆρχεν, WH) .... προϋπάρχω *(4391)*
προϋπῆρχον, 3 pers. pl. imperf. act. indic. id.
προφάσει, dat. sg. f. n. .... πρόφασις *(4392)*
πρόφασιν, acc. sg. f. n. .... id.

(4392) **πρόφασις**, εως, ἡ [§5.E.c] (πρό + φαίνω) pr.
   *that which appears in front, that which is
   put forward to hide the true state of things;
   a fair show or pretext,* Acts 27:30; *a specious cloak,* Matt. 23:13; 1 Thess. 2:5; *an
   excuse,* John 15:22

προφέρει, 3 pers. sg. pres. act. indic. προφέρω *(4393)*

(4393) **προφέρω**, fut. προοίσω [§36.1] (πρό + φέρω)
   *to bring before, present; to bring forth or
   out, produce,* Luke 6:45 (2×)

προφῆται, nom. pl. m. n. .... προφήτης *(4396)*
προφήταις, dat. pl. m. n. .... id.
προφήτας, acc. pl. m. n. .... id.

(4394) **προφητεία**, ας, ἡ, nom. sg. f. n. [§2.B.b; 2.2]
   prophecy, a prediction of future events,
   Matt. 13:14; 2 Pet. 1:20, 21; *prophecy, a
   gifted faculty of setting forth and enforcing
   revealed truth,* 1 Cor. 12:10; 13:2, et al.;
   *prophecy, matter of divine teaching set
   forth by special gift,* 1 Tim. 1:18

προφητείᾳ, dat. sg. f. n. .... προφητεία *(4394)*
προφητεῖαι, nom. pl. f. n. .... id.
προφητείαν, acc. sg. f. n. .... id.
προφητείας, gen. sg. f. n. {1 Tim. 4:14} .. id.
προφητείας, acc. pl. g. n. {1 Tim. 1:18} .. id.
προφητεύειν, pres. act. infin. ..... προφητεύω *(4395)*
προφητεύητε, 2 pers. pl. pres. act. subj. . id.
προφητεύομεν, 1 pers. pl. pres. act. indic. id.
προφητεύουσα, nom. sg. f. pres. act. part. id.
προφητεύουσαι, nom. pl. f. pres. act. part. id.
προφητεῦσαι, aor. act. infin. .... id.
προφητεύσαντες, nom. pl. m. aor. act. part. id.
προφήτευσον, 2 pers. sg. aor. act. imper. . id.
προφητεύσουσι(ν), 3 pers. pl. fut. act. indic. id.

(4395) **προφητεύω**, fut. προφητεύσω, aor.
   προεφήτευσα [§13.M] *to exercise the function of a* προφήτης; *to prophesy, to foretell the future,* Matt. 11:13; *to divine,* Matt.
   26:68; Mark 14:65; Luke 22:64; *to prophesy, to set forth matter of divine teaching
   by special faculty,* 1 Cor. 13:9; 14:1, et al.

προφητεύων, nom. sg. m. pres. act.
   part. .... προφητεύω *(4395)*
προφητεύωσιν, 3 pers. pl. pres. act. subj. . id.
προφήτῃ, dat. sg. m. n. (Mark 1:2, GNT, WH
   & NA | προφήταις, MT & TR) προφήτης *(4396)*
προφήτην, acc. sg. m. n. .... id.

(4396) **προφήτης**, ου, ὁ, nom. sg. m. n. [§2.B.c] (πρό
   + φημί) pr. *a spokesman for* another; spc.
   a spokesman or interpreter for a deity; *a
   prophet, seer,* Tit. 1:12; in N.T. *a prophet,
   a divinely commissioned and inspired person,* Matt. 14:5; Luke 7:16, 39; John 9:17,
   et al.; *a prophet* in the Christian church,
   *a person gifted for the exposition of divine
   truth,* 1 Cor. 12:28, 29, et al.; *a prophet,
   a foreteller of the future,* Matt. 1:22, et al.
   freq.; οἱ προφῆται, *the prophetic scriptures
   of the Old Testament,* Luke 16:29, et al.

προφητικόν, acc. sg. m. adj. .... προφητικός *(4397)*

(4397) **προφητικός**, ή, όν [§7.F.a] *prophetic, uttered
   by prophets,* Rom. 16:26; 2 Pet. 1:19

προφητικῶν, gen. pl. m. adj. .... προφητικός *(4397)*
προφῆτιν, acc. sg. f. n. .... προφῆτις *(4398)*

(4398) **προφῆτις**, ιδος, ἡ, nom. sg. f. n. [§4.2.c] *a*

prophetess, a divinely gifted female teacher,
Luke 2:36; Rev. 2:20

προφήτου, gen. sg. m. n. . . . . προφήτης *(4396)*

προφητῶν, gen. pl. m. n. . . . . id.

(4399) **προφθάνω,** fut. προφθάσω, and προφθή-
σομαι, aor. προέφθασα [§37.1] (πρό +
φθάνω) *to outstrip, anticipate; to anticipate* any one in doing or saying a thing,
be beforehand with, Matt. 17:25

(4400) **προχειρίζομαι,** fut. προχειρίσομαι [§26.1]
(πρό + χείρ) *to take into the hand, to
make ready for use or action; to constitute,
destine,* Acts 22:14; 26:16

προχειρίσασθαι, aor. mid. dep.
infin. . . . . προχειρίζομαι *(4400)*

(4401) **προχειροτονέω,** ῶ, fut. προχειροτονήσω
[§16.P] (πρό + χειροτονέω) pr. *to elect
before; to foreappoint,* Acts 10:41

Πρόχορον, acc. sg. m. n. . . . . Πρόχορος *(4402)*

(4402) **Πρόχορος,** ου, ὁ [§3.C.a] *Prochorus,* pr.
name, Acts 6:5

προώρισε(ν), 3 pers. sg. aor. act.
indic. προορίζω *(4309)*

προοωρώμην, 1 pers. sg. imperf. mid. indic.
(Acts 2:25, MT & TR | προορώμην,
GNT, WH & NA) . . . . προοράω *(4308)*

(4403) **πρύμνα,** ης, ἡ, nom. sg. f. n. [§2.3] (πρυμνός,
*last, hindmost) the hinder part of a vessel,
stern,* Mark 4:38, et al.

πρύμνῃ, dat. sg. f. n. . . . . πρύμνα *(4403)*

πρύμνης, gen. sg. f. n. . . . . id.

(4404) **πρωΐ,** adv., *in the morning, early,* Matt. 16:3;
20:1; Mark 15:1; Acts 28:23, et al.; *the
morning watch,* which ushers in the dawn,
Mark 13:35

(4405) **πρωΐα,** ας, ἡ, nom. sg. f. n. (pr. f. of πρώϊος,
α, ον, *in the morning, early)* sc. ὥρα,
morning, the morning hour, Matt. 21:18;
27:1; John 21:4 (John 18:28, TR | πρωΐ,
GNT, WH, MT & NA)

πρωΐας, gen. sg. f. n. . . . . πρωΐα *(4405)*

πρώϊμον, acc. sg. m. adj. (James 5:7, MT &
TR | πρόϊμον, GNT, WH & NA) πρώϊμος *(4406)*

(4406) **πρώϊμος,** η, ον [§7.F.a] *early,* James 5:7

πρωϊνόν, acc. sg. m. adj. . . . . πρωϊνός *(4407)*

(4407) **πρωϊνός,** ή, όν, nom. sg. f. n. adj. (a later
form of πρώϊος) *belonging to the morn-
ing, morning,* Rev. 2:28 (Rev. 22:16, GNT,
MT, TR & NA | πρωινός, WH)

(†4408) **πρῷρα,** ας, ἡ, nom. sg. f. n. [§2.B.b] *the fore-
part of a vessel, prow,* Acts 27:30, 41

πρώρας, gen. sg. f. n. (Acts 27:30, MT & TR
| πρῴρης, GNT, WH & NA) . . . . πρῷρα *(†4408)*

πρῴρης, gen. sg. f. n. (Acts 27:30, GNT, WH
& NA | πρώρας, MT & TR) . . . . id.

πρῶτα, nom. pl. neut. adj. {Rev. 21:4} πρῶτος *(4413)*

πρῶτα, acc. pl. neut. adj. {Rev. 2:5} . . . . id.

(4409) **πρωτεύω,** fut. πρωτεύσω [§13.M] *to be first,
to hold the first rank or highest dignity,
have the pre-eminence, be chief,* Col. 1:18

πρωτεύω, nom. sg. m. pres. act.
part. . . . . πρωτεύω *(4409)*

πρώτη, nom. sg. f. adj. . . . . πρῶτος *(4413)*

πρώτῃ, dat. sg. f. adj. . . . . id.

πρώτην, acc. sg. f. adj. . . . . id.

πρώτης, gen. sg. f. adj. . . . . id.

πρῶτοι, nom. pl. m. adj. . . . . id.

πρώτοις, dat. pl. m. adj. {Mark 6:21} . . . id.

πρώτοις, dat. pl. neut. adj. {1 Cor. 15:3} . id.

(4410) **πρωτοκαθεδρία,** ας, ἡ [§2.B.b; 2.2] (πρῶτος
+ καθέδρα) *the first or uppermost seat,
the most honorable seat,* Matt. 23:6; Mark
12:39; Luke 11:43; 20:46

πρωτοκαθεδρίαν, acc. sg. f. n. πρωτοκαθεδρία *(4410)*

πρωτοκαθεδρίας, acc. pl. f. n. . . . . id.

(4411) **πρωτοκλισία,** ας, ἡ [§2.B.b; 2.2] (πρῶτος +
κλισία) *the first place of reclining* at table, *the most honorable place at table,*
Matt. 23:6; Mark 12:39; Luke 14:7, 8;
20:46

πρωτοκλισίαν, acc. sg. f. n. . . . . πρωτοκλισία *(4411)*

πρωτοκλισίας, acc. pl. f. n. . . . . id.

πρῶτον, acc. sg. m. adj. {Matt. 17:27} πρῶτος *(4413)*

πρῶτον, nom. sg. neut. adj. {Rev. 4:7} . . . id.

πρῶτον, acc. sg. neut. adj. {Rev. 13:12} . . id.

(4412) **πρῶτον,** adv., *first in time, in the first place,*
Mark 4:28; 16:9; τὸ πρῶτον, *at the first,
formerly,* John 12:16; 19:39; *first in dignity, importance,* etc., *before all things,*
Matt. 6:33 {Luke 12:1}

(4413) **πρῶτος,** η, ον, nom. sg. m. adj. [§8.6] (superl.
of πρό, as if contr. from πρότατος) *first
in time, order,* etc., Matt. 10:2; 26:17; *first
in dignity, importance,* etc., *chief, principal, most important,* Mark 6:21; Luke
19:47; Acts 13:50; 16:12; *as an equivalent
to the compar.* πρότερος, *prior,* John
1:15, 30; 15:18; Matt. 27:64; *adverbially,
first,* John 1:42; 5:4; 8:7

πρωτοστάτην, acc. sg. m. n. . . . πρωτοστάτης *(4414)*

(4414) **πρωτοστάτης,** ου, ὁ [§2.B.c] (πρῶτος +
ἵστημι) pr. *one stationed in the first rank
of an army; a leader; a chief, ringleader,*
Acts 24:5

πρωτότοκα, acc. pl. neut. adj. . . . πρωτότοκος *(4416)*

(4415) **πρωτοτόκια,** ων, τά [§3.C.c] *the rights of
primogeniture, birthright,* Heb. 12:16

πρωτοτόκια, acc. pl. neut. n. . . . . πρωτοτόκια *(4415)*

πρωτότοκον, acc. sg. m. adj. . . . πρωτότοκος *(4416)*

(4416) **πρωτότοκος,** ον, nom. sg. m. adj. [§7.2]

(πρῶτος + τίκτω) *first-born*, Matt. 1:25;
Luke 2:7; Heb. 11:28; in N.T. *prior in generation*, Col. 1:15; *a first-born* head of a spiritual family, Rom. 8:29; Heb. 1:6; *first-born*, as possessed of the peculiar privilege of spiritual generation, Heb. 12:23

πρωτοτόκων, gen. pl. m. adj. ... πρωτότοκος *(4416)*
πρώτου, gen. sg. m. adj. {John 19:32} πρῶτος *(4413)*
πρώτου, gen. sg. neut. adj. {Rev. 13:12} .. id.
πρώτους, acc. pl. m. adj. .... id.
πρώτῳ, dat. sg. m. adj. {Luke 16:5} .... id.
πρώτῳ, dat. sg. neut. adj. {Matt. 21:28} . id.
πρώτων, gen. pl. m. adj. {Matt. 20:8} ... id.
πρώτων, gen. pl. f. adj. {Acts 17:4} .... id.
πρώτων, gen. pl. neut. adj. {Matt. 12:45} . id.
(‡4413) **πρώτως**, adv., *for the first time* (Acts 11:26, GNT, WH & NA | πρῶτον, MT & TR)
πταίει, 3 pers. sg. pres. act. indic. ..... πταίω *(4417)*
πταίομεν, 1 pers. pl. pres. act. indic. ..... id.
πταίσει, 3 pers. sg. fut. act. indic. (James 2:10, MT & TR | πταίσῃ, GNT, WH & NA) id.
πταίσῃ, 3 pers. sg. aor. act. subj. (James 2:10, GNT, WH & NA | πταίσει, MT & TR) id.
πταίσητε, 2 pers. pl. aor. act. subj. ...... id.
(4417) **πταίω**, fut. πταίσω, aor. ἔπταισα [§13.M] *to cause to stumble*; intrans. *to stumble, stagger, fall; to make a false step*; met. *to err, offend, transgress*, Rom. 11:11; James 2:10; 3:2(2×); met. *to fail* of an object, 2 Pet. 1:10
(4418) **πτέρνα**, ης, ἡ [§2.3] *the heel*, John 13:18
πτέρναν, acc. sg. f. n. .... πτέρνα *(4418)*
πτέρυγας, acc. pl. f. n. .... πτέρυξ *(4420)*
πτέρυγες, nom. pl. f. n. .... id.
(4419) **πτερύγιον**, ου, τό [§3.C.c] *a little wing; the extremity, the extreme point* of a thing; *a pinnacle, or apex* of a building, Matt. 4:5; Luke 4:9
πτερύγιον, acc. sg. neut. n. .... πτερύγιον *(4419)*
πτερύγων, gen. pl. f. n. .... πτέρυξ *(4420)*
(4420) **πτέρυξ**, υγος, ἡ [§4.2.b] (πτέρον, idem.) *a wing, pinion*, Matt. 23:37; Luke 13:34, et al.
(4421) **πτηνόν**, ου, τό (pr. neut. of πτηνός, ή, όν, *winged*, from πέτομαι) *a bird, fowl*, 1 Cor. 15:39
πτηνῶν, gen. pl. neut. adj. .... πτηνόν *(4421)*
(4422) **πτοέω**, ῶ, fut. πτοήσω [§16.P] aor. pass. ἐπτοήθην, *to terrify, affright*; pass. *to be terrified, be in consternation*, Luke 21:9; 24:37
πτοηθέντες, nom. pl. m. aor. pass. part. [§17.Q] .... πτοέω *(4422)*
πτοηθῆτε, 2 pers. pl. aor. pass. subj. ..... id.
πτόησιν, acc. sg. f. n. .... πτόησις *(4423)*

(4423) **πτόησις**, εως, ἡ [§5.E.c] *consternation, dismay*, 1 Pet. 3:6
Πτολεμαΐδα, acc. sg. f. n. .... Πτολεμαΐς *(4424)*
(4424) **Πτολεμαΐς**, ΐδος, ἡ [§4.2.c] *Ptolemais*, a city on the sea-coast of Galilee: the modern *Acre*, Acts 21:7
πτύξας, nom. sg. m. aor. act. part. .. πτύσσω *(4428)*
(4425) **πτύον**, ου, τό, nom. sg. neut. n. [§3.C.c] *a fan, winnowing-shovel*, Matt. 3:12; Luke 3:17
πτυρόμενοι, nom. pl. m. pres. pass. part. .... πτύρω *(4426)*
(4426) **πτύρω**, *to scare, terrify*; pass. *to be terrified, be in consternation*, Phil. 1:28
πτύσας, nom. sg. m. aor. act. part. .... πτύω *(4429)*
(4427) **πτύσμα**, ατος, τό [§4.D.c] *spittle, saliva*, John 9:6
πτύσματος, gen. sg. neut. n. .... πτύσμα *(4427)*
(4428) **πτύσσω**, fut. πτύξω, aor. ἔτυξα [§26.3] *to fold; to roll up* a scroll, Luke 4:20
(4429) **πτύω**, fut. πτύσω, aor. ἔπτυσα [§13.M] *to spit, spit out*, Mark 7:33; 8:23; John 9:6
(4430) **πτῶμα**, ατος, τό, nom. sg. neut. n. [§4.D.c] *a fall; a dead body, carcass, corpse*, Matt. 24:28; Mark 6:29 {Rev. 11:8}
πτῶμα, acc. sg. neut. n. {Rev. 11:9} ... πτῶμα *(4430)*
πτώματα, nom. pl. neut. n. (Rev. 11:8, TR | πτῶμα, GNT, WH, MT & NA) ..... id.
πτώματα, acc. pl. neut. n. {Rev. 11:9} ... id.
πτῶσιν, acc. sg. f. n. .... πτῶσις *(4431)*
(4431) **πτῶσις**, εως, ἡ, nom. sg. f. n. [§5.E.c] *a fall, crash, ruin*, Matt. 7:27; met. *downfall, ruin*, Luke 2:34
πτωχά, acc. pl. neut. adj. .... πτωχός *(4434)*
(4432) **πτωχεία**, ας, ἡ, nom. sg. f. n. [§2.B.b; 2.2] *begging; beggary; poverty*, 2 Cor. 8:2, 9; Rev. 2:9
πτωχείᾳ, dat. sg. f. n. .... πτωχεία *(4432)*
πτωχείαν, acc. sg. f. n. .... id.
(4433) **πτωχεύω**, fut. πτωχεύσω [§13.M] *to be a beggar; to be or become poor, be in poverty*, 2 Cor. 8:9
πτωχή, nom. sg. f. adj. .... πτωχός *(4434)*
πτωχοί, nom. pl. m. adj. .... id.
πτωχοῖς, dat. pl. m. adj. .... id.
πτωχόν, acc. sg. m. adj. .... id.
(4434) **πτωχός**, ή, όν, nom. sg. m. adj. *reduced to beggary, mendicant; poor, indigent*, Matt. 19:21; 26:9, 11, et al.; met. spiritually *poor*, Rev. 3:17; by impl. *a person of low condition*, Matt. 11:5; Luke 4:18; 7:22; met. *beggarly, sorry*, Gal. 4:9; met. *lowly*, Matt. 5:3; Luke 6:20
πτωχούς, acc. pl. m. adj. .... πτωχός *(4434)*
πτωχῷ, dat. sg. m. adj. .... id.
πτωχῶν, gen. pl. m. adj. .... id.

(4435) **πυγμή,** ῆς, ἡ [§2.B.a] (πύξ) *the fist;* πυγμῇ, *together with the fore-arm,* or, *with care, carefully,* Mark 7:3

πυγμῇ, dat. sg. f. n. . . . . πυγμή *(4435)*

πυθέσθαι, 2 aor. mid. dep. infin. [§36.2] (John 13:24, GNT, MT, TR & NA | εἰπέ, WH) . . . . πυνθάνομαι *(4441)*

πυθόμενος, nom. sg. m. 2 aor. mid. dep. part. id.

(4436) **Πύθων,** ωνος, ὁ [§4.2.e] *Python,* the name of the mythological serpent slain by Apollo, thence named the Pythian; later, equivalent to ἐγγαστρίμαντις, *a soothsaying ventriloquist;* πνεῦμα πύθωνος, i.q. δαιμόνιον μαντικόν, *a soothsaying demon,* Acts 16:16

πύθωνα, acc. sg. m. n. (Acts 16:16, GNT, WH & NA | πύθωνος, MT & TR) . . . . πύθων *(4436)*

πύθωνος, gen. sg. m. n. (Acts 16:16, MT & TR | πύθωνα, GNT, WH & NA) . . . . id.

πυκνά, acc. pl. neut. adj. . . . . πυκνός *(4437)*

πυκνάς, acc. pl. f. adj. . . . . id.

(4437) **πυκνός,** ή, όν [§7.F.a] *dense, thick; frequent,* 1 Tim. 5:23; πυκνά, as an adverb, *frequently, often,* Luke 5:33; so the compar. πυκνότερον, *very frequently,* Acts 24:26

πυκνότερον, acc. sg. neut. compar. adj. . . . . πυκνός *(4437)*

(†4438) **πυκτεύω,** 1 pers. sg. pres. act. indic., fut. πυκτεύσω [§13.M] (πύκτης, *a boxer,* from πύξ) *to box, fight as a pugilist,* 1 Cor. 9:26

πύλαι, nom. pl. f. n. . . . . πύλη *(4439)*

πύλας, acc. pl. f. n. . . . . id.

(4439) **πύλη,** ης, ἡ, nom. sg. f. n. [§2.B.a] *a gate,* Matt. 7:13, 14; Luke 7:12; Acts 12:10, et al.; πύλαι ᾅδου, *the gates of hades, the nether world and its powers, the powers of destruction, dissolution,* Matt. 16:18

πύλῃ, dat. sg. f. n. . . . . πύλη *(4439)*

πύλην, acc. sg. f. n. . . . . id.

πύλης, gen. sg. f. n. . . . . id.

(4440) **πυλών,** ῶνος, ὁ [§4.2.e] *a gateway, vestibule,* Matt. 26:71; Luke 16:20; *a gate,* Acts 14:13; Rev. 21:12, 13, 15, 21, 25, et al.

πυλῶνα, acc. sg. m. n. . . . . πυλών *(4440)*

πυλῶνας, acc. pl. m. n. . . . . id.

πυλῶνες, nom. pl. m. n. . . . . id.

πυλῶνος, gen. sg. m. n. . . . . id.

πυλώνων, gen. pl. m. n. . . . . id.

πυλῶσιν, dat. pl. m. n. . . . . id.

πυνθάνεσθαι, pres. mid./pass. dep. infin. . . . . πυνθάνομαι *(4441)*

(4441) **πυνθάνομαι,** 1 pers. sg. pres. mid./pass. dep. indic., fut. πεύσομαι, 2 aor. ἐπυθόμην [§36.2] *to ask, inquire,* Matt. 2:4; Luke 15:26, et al.; *to investigate, examine* judi-

cially, Acts 23:20; *to ascertain by inquiry, understand,* Acts 23:34

(4442) **πῦρ,** πυρός, τό, nom. sg. neut. n. [§4.2.f] *fire,* Matt. 3:10; 7:19; 13:40, et al. freq.; πυρός, used by Hebraism with the force of an adjective, *fiery, fierce,* Heb. 10:27; *fire* used figuratively to express various circumstances of severe trial, Luke 12:49; 1 Cor. 3:13; Jude 23 {Mark 9:48}

πῦρ, acc. sg. neut. n. {Mark 9:43} . . . . . . πῦρ *(4442)*

(4443) **πυρά,** ᾶς, ἡ [§2.B.b] *a fire, heap of combustibles,* Acts 28:2, 3

πυράν, acc. sg. f. n. . . . . πυρά *(4443)*

πύργον, acc. sg. m. n. . . . . πύργος *(4444)*

(4444) **πύργος,** ου, ὁ, nom. sg. m. n. [§3.C.a] *a tower,* Matt. 21:33; Mark 12:1; Luke 13:4; genr. *a castle, palace,* Luke 14:28

πυρέσσουσα, nom. sg. f. pres. act. part. . . . . πυρέσσω *(4445)*

πυρέσσουσαν, acc. sg. f. pres. act. part. . . . id.

(4445) **πυρέσσω,** or πυρέττω, fut. πυρέξω [§26.3] *to be feverish, be sick of a fever,* Matt. 8:14; Mark 1:30

πυρετοῖς, dat. pl. m. n. . . . . πυρετός *(4446)*

(4446) **πυρετός,** οῦ, ὁ, nom. sg. m. n. [§3.C.a] *scorching and noxious heat; a fever,* Matt. 8:15; Mark 1:31, et al.

πυρετῷ, dat. sg. m. n. . . . . id.

πυρί, dat. sg. neut. n. . . . . πῦρ *(4442)*

(4447) **πύρινος,** η, ον [§7.F.a] pr. *of fire, fiery, burning; shining, glittering,* Rev. 9:17

πυρίνους, acc. pl. m. adj. . . . . πύρινος *(4447)*

πυρός, gen. sg. neut. n. [§4.2.f] . . . . πῦρ *(4442)*

πυροῦμαι, 1 pers. sg. pres. pass. indic. [§21.U] . . . . πυρόω *(4448)*

πυρούμενοι, nom. pl. m. pres. pass. part. . . id.

πυροῦσθαι, pres. pass. infin. . . . . id.

(4448) **πυρόω,** ῶ, fut. πυρώσω [§20.T] *to set on fire, burn;* pass. *to be kindled, be on fire, burn, flame,* Eph. 6:16; 2 Pet. 3:12; Rev. 1:15; met. *to fire* with distressful feelings, 2 Cor. 11:29; of lust, *to be inflamed, burn,* 1 Cor. 7:9; *to be tried with fire,* as metals, Rev. 3:18

πυρράζει, 3 pers. sg. pres. act. indic. πυρράζω *(4449)*

(4449) **πυρράζω,** fut. πυρράσω [§26.1] *to be fiery-red,* Matt. 16:2, 3

(4450) **πυρρός,** ά, όν, nom. sg. m. adj. [§7.1] *of the color of fire, fiery-red* (Rev. 6:4; 12:3, GNT, TR, WH & NA | πυρός, MT)

(†4450) **Πύρρος,** ου, ὁ [§3.C.a] *Pyrrhus,* pr. name Πύρρου, gen. sg. m. n. (Acts 20:4, GNT, WH & NA | MT & TR omit) . . . . . . Πύρρος *(†4450)*

πυρώσει, dat. sg. f. n. . . . . πύρωσις *(4451)*

πυρώσεως, gen. sg. f. n. . . . . id.

(4451) πύρωσις, εως, ἡ [§5.E.c] *a burning, confla-gration*, Rev. 18:9, 18; met. *a fiery test* of trying circumstances, 1 Pet. 4:12

(4452) -πω, an enclitic particle, *yet*, see μήπω *(3380)*; μηδέπω *(3369)*; οὔπω *(3768)*; οὐδέπω *(3764)*; and πώποτε *(4455)*

πωλεῖ, 3 pers. sg. pres. act. indic. . . . . . πωλέω *(4453)*

πωλεῖται, 3 pers. sg. pres. pass. indic. [§17.Q]   id.

(4453) πωλέω, ῶ, fut. πωλήσω [§16.P] *to sell*, Matt. 10:29; 13:44, et al.

πωλῆσαι, aor. act. infin. . . . . id.

πωλήσας, nom. sg. m. aor. act. part. . . . . id.

πωλήσατε, 2 pers. pl. aor. act. imper. . . . . id.

πωλησάτω, 3 pers. sg. aor. act. imper. (Luke 22:36, GNT, WH, TR & NA | πωλήσει, MT) . . . . id.

πωλήσει, 3 pers. sg. fut. act. indic. (Luke 22:36, MT | πωλησάτω, GNT, WH, TR & NA) . . . . id.

πώλησον, 2 pers. sg. aor. act. imper. . . . . . id.

πῶλον, acc. sg. m. n. . . . . πῶλος *(4454)*

(4454) πῶλος, ου, ὁ [§3.C.a] *a youngling; a foal or colt*, Matt. 21:2, 5, 7; Mark 11:2, et al.

πωλούμενον, acc. sg. neut. pres. pass. part. . . . . πωλέω *(4453)*

πωλοῦνται, 3 pers. pl. pres. pass. indic. (Luke 12:6, GNT, WH & NA | πωλεῖται, MT & TR) . . . . id.

πωλοῦντας, acc. pl. m. pres. act. part. . . . id.

πωλοῦντες, nom. pl. m. pres. act. part. . . id.

πωλούντων, gen. pl. m. pres. act. part. . . . id.

πωλοῦσιν, dat. pl. m. pres. act. part. . . . . id.

(4455) πώποτε, adv. (πω + πότε) *ever yet, ever, at any time,* Luke 19:30; John 1:18, et al.

(4456) πωρόω, ῶ, fut. πωρώσω [§20.T] (πῶρος, *a stony concretion*) *to petrify; to harden;* in N.T. *to harden* the feelings, John 12:40; pass. *to become callous, unimpressible,* Mark 6:52; 8:17; Rom. 11:7; 2 Cor. 3:14

πωρώσει, dat. sg. f. n. . . . . πώρωσις *(4457)*

πώρωσιν, acc. sg. f. n. . . . . id.

(4457) πώρωσις, εως, ἡ, nom. sg. f. n. [§5.E.c] *a hardening;* met. *hardness* of heart, *callous-ness, insensibility,* Mark 3:5; Rom. 11:25; Eph. 4:18

(4458) -πως, an enclitic particle, *in any way, by any means,* see εἴπως, *(1513)* and μήπως *(3381)* {Rom. 11:14}

(4459) πῶς, adv., *How? In what manner? By what means?* Matt. 7:4; 22:12; John 6:52; used in interrogations which imply a negative, Matt. 12:26, 29, 34; 22:45; 23:33; Acts 8:31; put concisely for *How is it that? How does it come to pass that?* Matt. 16:11; 22:43; Mark 4:30; John 7:15; with an in-direct interrogation, *how, in what manner,* Matt. 6:28; 10:19; Mark 11:18; put for τί, *What?* Luke 10:26; put for ὡς, as a par-ticle of exclamation, *how, how much, how greatly,* Mark 10:23, 24 {Rom. 10:14–15}

Ρ

(4460) Ῥαάβ, ἡ, *Rahab,* pr. name, indecl.

(4461) Ῥαββί, ὁ, indecl. (later Hebrew רַבִּי, from רַב, which was deemed less honorable) *Rabbi, my master, teacher, doctor* (Matt. 23:7, 8; 26:25, 49, et al., GNT, MT, TR & NA | Ῥαββεί, WH)

(4462) Ῥαββονί, or Ῥαββουνί, indecl. (later Hebrew רִבּוֹן, Aramaic with suffix רִבּוֹנִי) *Rabboni, my master,* the highest title of honor in the Jewish schools (Mark 10:51; John 20:16, GNT, MT, TR & NA | Ῥαββονεί, WH)

(4462) Ῥαββουνί, same signif. as Ῥαββονί

ῥαβδίζειν, pres. act. infin. . . . . ῥαβδίζω *(4463)*

(4463) ῥαβδίζω, fut. ῥαβδίσω [§26.1] aor. ἐρράβδισα, aor. pass. ἐρραβδίσθην, *to beat with rods,* Acts 16:22; 2 Cor. 11:25

ῥάβδον, acc. sg. f. n. . . . . ῥάβδος *(4464)*

(4464) ῥάβδος, ου, ἡ, nom. sg. f. n. [§3.C.b] *a rod, wand,* Heb. 9:4; Rev. 11:1; *a rod* of cor-rection, 1 Cor. 4:21; *a staff,* Matt. 10:10; Heb. 11:21; *a scepter,* Heb. 1:8; Rev. 2:27

ῥάβδου, gen. sg. f. n. . . . . ῥάβδος *(4464)*

ῥάβδους, acc. pl. f. n. (Matt. 10:10, MT & TR | ῥάβδον, GNT, WH & NA) . . . . id.

ῥαβδοῦχοι, nom. pl. m. n. . . . . ῥαβδοῦχος *(4465)*

(4465) ῥαβδοῦχος, ου, ὁ [§3.C.a] (ῥάβδος + ἔχω) *the bearer of a wand* of office; *a lictor, sergeant,* a public servant who bore a bun-dle or rods before the magistrates as insig-nia of their office, and carried into execution the sentences they pronounced, Acts 16:35, 38

ῥαβδούχους, acc. pl. m. n. . . . . . . ῥαβδοῦχος *(4465)*

ῥάβδῳ, dat. sg. f. n. . . . . ῥάβδος *(4464)*

(†4466) Ῥαγαύ, ὁ, *Ragau,* pr. name, indecl. (Luke 3:35, GNT, WH & NA | Ῥαγαῦ, MT & TR)

(4467) ῥαδιούργημα, ατος, τό, nom. sg. neut. n. [§4.D.c] (ῥᾳδιουργέω, *to do easily, to act recklessly;* ῥᾴδιος, *easy,* and ἔργον) pr. *anything done lightly, levity; reckless con-duct, crime,* Acts 18:14

(4468) ῥᾳδιουργία, ας, ἡ [§2.B.b; 2.2] *facility of do-ing* anything; *levity in doing; recklessness, profligacy, wickedness,* Acts 13:10

ῥαδιουργίας, gen. sg. f. n. . . . . . . ῥαδιουργία *(4468)*

(‡4481) Ῥαιφάν, ὁ, pr. name, indecl. *Rephan* (Acts 7:43, GNT & NA | Ῥεμφάν, MT & TR | Ῥομφά, WH)

(4469) ῥακά, *Raca,* an Aramaic term of bitter contempt, *worthless fellow,* Matt. 5:22

(4470) ῥάκος, ους, τό [§5.E.b] *a piece torn off; a bit of cloth, cloth*

ῥάκους, gen. sg. neut. n. . . . . ῥάκος *(4470)*

(4471) Ῥαμᾶ, ἡ, indecl. *Rama,* a city of Judea

ῥαντίζουσα, nom. sg. f. pres. act. part. . . . . ῥαντίζω *(4472)*

(4472) ῥαντίζω, fut. ῥαντίσω [§26.1] aor. ἐρράντισα, perf. pass. ἐρράντισμαι (ῥαίνω, idem) *to sprinkle, besprinkle,* Heb. 9:13, 19, 21; met. and by impl. *to cleanse by sprinkling, purify, free from pollution,* Heb. 10:22

ῥαντισμόν, acc. sg. m. n. . . . . ῥαντισμός *(4473)*

(4473) ῥαντισμός, οῦ, ὁ [§3.C.a] pr. *a sprinkling;* met. *a cleansing, purification, lustration,* Heb. 12: 24; 1 Pet. 1:2

ῥαντισμοῦ, gen. sg. m. n. . . . . . . ῥαντισμός *(4473)*

ῥαπίζει, 3 pers. sg. pres. act. indic. (Matt. 5:39, GNT, WH & NA | ῥαπίσει, MT & TR) . . . . ῥαπίζω *(4474)*

(4474) ῥαπίζω, fut. ῥαπίσω, aor. ἐρράπισα [§26.1] (ῥαπίς, *a rod*) *to beat with rods; to strike with the palm of the hand, cuff, clap,* Matt. 5:39; 26:67

ῥαπίσει, 3 pers. sg. fut. act. indic. (Matt. 5:39, MT & TR | ῥαπίζει, GNT, WH & NA) . . . . ῥαπίζω *(4474)*

(4475) ῥάπισμα, ατος, τό [§4.D.c] *a blow with the palm of the hand, cuff, slap,* Mark 14:65; John 18:22; 19:3

ῥάπισμα, acc. sg. neut. n. . . . . ῥάπισμα *(4475)*

ῥαπίσμασιν, dat. pl. neut. n. . . . . id.

ῥαπίσματα, acc. pl. neut. n. . . . . id.

ῥαφίδος, gen. sg. f. n. . . . . ῥαφίς *(4476)*

(4476) ῥαφίς, ίδος, ἡ [§4.2.c] (ῥάπτω, *to sew, sew together*) *a needle,* Matt. 19:24; Mark 10:25; Luke 18:25

(4477) Ῥαχάβ, ἡ, *Rachab,* pr. name, indecl., Matt. 1:5

(4478) Ῥαχήλ, ἡ, *Rachel,* pr. name, indecl., Matt. 2:18

(4479) Ῥεβέκκα, ας, ἡ, nom. sg. f. n., *Rebecca,* pr. name, Rom. 9:10

(†4480) ῥέδη, ης, ἡ [§2.B.a] (Latin, *rheda*) *a carriage with four wheels* for travelling, *a chariot,* Rev. 18:13

ῥεδῶν, gen. pl. f. n. . . . . ῥέδη *(†4480)*

(4481) Ῥεμφάν, or Ῥεφάν, ὁ, indecl. (the original passage, Amos 5:26, has כִּיּוּן; the LXX has Ῥαιφάν, the Egyptian name for the

planet Saturn) *Remphan,* the name of an idol, Acts 7:43 (MT & TR | Ῥαιφάν, GNT & NA | Ῥομφά, WH)

ῥεραντισμένοι, nom. pl. m. perf. pass. part. (Heb. 10:22, GNT, WH & NA | ἐρραντισμένοι, MT & TR) . . . . ῥαντίζω *(4472)*

ῥεύσουσιν, 3 pers. pl. fut. act. indic. . . . . ῥέω *(4482)*

(4482) ῥέω, fut. ῥεύσω, ῥεύσομαι [§35.3] aor. ἔρρευσα, *to flow*

(4483) ῥέω, an obsolete form, from which perf. εἴρηκα, perf. pass. εἴρημαι, aor. pass. ἐρρήθην, and ἐρρέθην, part. ῥηθείς [§36.1] *to say, speak,* Matt. 1:22; 2 Cor. 12:9; Rev. 7:14, et al.; *to speak of,* Matt. 3:3; *to direct, command, prescribe,* Matt. 5:21, et al.; *to address* one *as* anything, *to call, name,* John 15:15, et al.

(4484) Ῥήγιον, ου, τό [§3.C.c] *Rhegium,* a city at the southwestern extremity of Italy, Acts 28:13

Ῥήγιον, acc. sg. neut. n. . . . . Ῥήγιον *(4484)*

(4485) ῥῆγμα, ατος, τό, nom. sg. neut. n. [§4.D.c] *a rent; a crash, ruin,* Luke 6:49

(4486) ῥήγνυμι, or ῥήσσω, fut. ῥήξω, aor. ἔρρηξα [§36.5] *to rend, shatter; to break or burst in pieces,* Matt. 9:17; Mark 2:22; Luke 5:37, et al.; *to rend, lacerate,* Matt. 7:6; *to cast or dash* upon the ground, *convulse,* Mark 9:18; Luke 9:42; absol. *to break forth* into exclamation, Gal. 4:27

ῥήγνυνται, 3 pers. pl. pres. pass. indic. . . . . ῥήγνυμι *(4486)*

ῥηθείς, nom. sg. m. aor. pass. part. (of aor. pass. ἐρρήθην) used in connection with λέγω, φημί, and εἰπεῖν . . . . ῥέω *(4483)*

ῥηθέν, nom. sg. neut. aor. pass. part. {Matt. 21:4} . . . . id.

ῥηθέν, acc. sg. neut. aor. pass. part. {Matt. 22:31} . . . . id.

(4487) ῥῆμα, ατος, τό, nom. sg. neut. n. [§4.D.c] *that which is spoken; declaration, saying, speech, word,* Matt. 12:36; 26:75; Mark 9:32; 14:72; *a command, mandate, direction,* Luke 3:2; 5:5; *a promise,* Luke 1:38; 2:29; *a prediction, prophecy,* 2 Pet. 3:2; *a doctrine* of God or Christ, John 3:34; 5:47; 6:63, 68; Acts 5:20; *an accusation, charge, crimination,* Matt. 5:11; 27:14; from the Hebrew, *a thing,* Matt. 4:4; Luke 4:4; *a matter, affair, transaction, business,* Matt. 18:16; Luke 1:65; 2 Cor. 13:1, et al. {Luke 1:37}

ῥῆμα, acc. sg. neut. n. {Luke 1:38} . . . . . ῥῆμα *(4487)*

ῥήμασι(ν), dat. pl. neut. n. . . . . id.

ῥήματα, nom. pl. neut. n. {John 15:7} . . . id.

ῥήματα, acc. pl. neut. n. {John 14:10} . . . id.

ῥήματι, dat. sg. neut. n. . . . . ῥῆμα *(4487)*

ῥήματος, gen. sg. neut. n. . . . . id.

ῥημάτων, gen. pl. neut. n. . . . . id.

ῥήξει, 3 pers. sg. fut. act. indic. . . . . . ῥήγνυμι *(4486)*

ῥῆξον, 2 pers. sg. aor. act. imper. . . . . id.

ῥήξωσιν, 3 pers. pl. aor. act. subj. . . . . . . id.

(4488) **Ῥησά,** ὁ, *Rhesa,* pr. name, indecl.

ῥήσσει, 3 pers. sg. pres. act. indic. . . . ῥήγνυμι *(4486)*

ῥήτορος, gen. sg. m. n. . . . . ῥήτωρ *(4489)*

(4489) **ῥήτωρ,** ορος, ὁ [§4.2.f] *an orator, advocate,*
Acts 24:1

(4490) **ῥητῶς,** adv. (ῥητός, ῥέω) *in express words,*
expressly, 1 Tim. 4:1

(4491) **ῥίζα,** ης, ἡ, nom. sg. f. n. [§2.3] *a root* of a
tree, Matt. 3:10; 13:6; met. ἔχειν ῥίζαν, or
ἔχειν ῥίζαν ἐν ἑαυτῷ, *to be rooted* in faith,
Matt. 13:21; Mark 4:17; Luke 8:13; met.
cause, source, origin, 1 Tim. 6:10; Heb.
12:15; by synec. *the trunk, stock* of a tree,
met. Rom. 11:16, 17, 18; met. *offspring,*
progeny, a descendant, Rom. 15:12; Rev.
5:5; 22:16

ῥίζαν, acc. sg. f. n. . . . . ῥίζα *(4491)*

ῥίζης, gen. sg. f. n. . . . . id.

(4492) **ῥιζόω,** ῶ, fut. ῥιζώσω [§20.T] *to root, cause*
to take root; perf. pass. part. ἐρριζωμένος,
firmly rooted, strengthened with roots;
met. *firm, constant, firmly fixed,* Eph.
3:18; Col. 2:7

ῥιζῶν, gen. pl. f. n. . . . . ῥίζα *(4491)*

(4493) **ῥιπή,** ῆς, ἡ [§2.B.a] pr. *a rapid sweep, jerk;*
a wink, twinkling of the eye, 1 Cor. 15:52

ῥιπῇ, dat. sg. f. n. . . . . ῥιπή *(4493)*

ῥιπιζομένῳ, dat. sg. m. pres. pass. part. ῥιπίζω *(4494)*

(4494) **ῥιπίζω,** fut. ῥιπίσω [§26.1] (ῥιπίς, *a fan or bel-*
lows, from ῥίπτω) *to fan, blow, ventilate;*
to toss, agitate, e.g. the ocean by the wind,
James 1:6

(4495) **ῥιπτέω,** ῶ, frequent and repeated action, *to*
toss repeatedly, toss up with violent gesture, Acts 22:23

ῥιπτούντων, gen. pl. m. pres. act. part. ῥιπτέω *(4495)*

(4496) **ῥίπτω,** fut. ῥίψω, aor. ἔρριψα [§23.1.a; 23.2]
perf. pass. ἔρριμμαι [§23.7] *to hurl, throw,*
cast; to throw or cast down, Matt. 27:5;
Luke 4:35; 17:2; *to throw or cast* out, Acts
27:19, 29; *to lay down, set down,* Matt.
15:30; pass. *to be dispersed, scattered,*
Matt. 9:36

ῥῖψαν, nom. sg. neut. aor. act. part. . . . ῥίπτω *(4496)*

ῥίψαντες, nom. pl. m. aor. act. part. . . . . id.

ῥίψας, nom. sg. m. aor. act. part. . . . . . . id.

ρμδ΄, abbreviated numeral, *one hundred forty*
four (Rev. 7:4, TR; Rev. 14:1, 3, MT & TR
| ἑκατον καὶ τεσσαράκοντα τέσσαρες,

GNT, WH & NA)

(4497) **Ῥοβοάμ,** ὁ, *Roboam,* pr. name, indecl.

(4498) **Ῥόδη,** ης, ἡ, nom. sg. f. n., *Rhoda,* pr. name,
Acts 12:13

Ῥόδον, acc. sg. f. n. . . . . Ῥόδη *(4498)*

(4499) **Ῥόδος,** ου, ἡ [§3.C.a] *Rhodes,* an island in
the Mediterranean, south of Caria, Acts
21:1

(4500) **ῥοιζηδόν,** adv. (ῥοῖζος, *a whizzing, a rushing*
noise) with a noise, with a crash, etc., 2 Pet.
3:10

(‡4481) **Ῥομφά,** pr. name, *Rompha* (Acts 7:43, WH
| Ῥαιφάν, GNT & NA | Ῥεμφάν, MT
& TR)

(4501) **ῥομφαία,** ας, ἡ, nom. sg. f. n. [§2.B.b; 2.2]
pr. *a* Thracian *broad-sword; a sword,* Rev.
1:16; 2:12; by meton. *war,* Rev. 6:8; met.
a thrill of anguish, Luke 2:35

ῥομφαίᾳ, dat. sg. f. n. . . . . ῥομφαία *(4501)*

ῥομφαίαν, acc. sg. f. n. . . . . id.

(4502) **Ῥουβήν,** ὁ, *Reuben,* pr. name, indecl., Rev.
7:5

(4503) **Ῥούθ,** ὁ, *Ruth,* pr. name, indecl., Matt. 1:5

Ῥοῦφον, acc. sg. m. n. . . . . Ῥοῦφος *(4504)*

(4504) **Ῥοῦφος,** ου, ὁ [§3.C.a] *Rufus,* pr. name

Ῥούφου, gen. sg. m. n. . . . . Ῥοῦφος *(4504)*

ῥύεσθαι, pres. mid./pass. dep. infin. . . ῥύομαι *(4506)*

ῥύεται, 3 pers. sg. pres. mid./pass. dep. indic.
(2 Cor. 1:10, MT & TR | ῥύσεται, GNT,
WH & NA) . . . . id.

ῥύμαις, dat. pl. f. n. . . . . ῥύμη *(4505)*

ῥύμας, acc. pl. f. n. . . . . id.

(4505) **ῥύμη,** ης, ἡ [§2.B.a] (ῥύω, *to draw) pr. a rush*
or sweep of a body in motion; *a street,* Acts
9:11; 12:10; *a narrow street, lane, alley,* as
distinguished from πλατεῖα, Matt. 6:2;
Luke 14:21

ῥύμην, acc. sg. f. n. . . . . ῥύμη *(4505)*

(4506) **ῥύομαι,** fut. ῥύσομαι, aor. ἐρρυσάμην [§14.N]
to drag out of danger, *to rescue, save,* Matt.
6:13; 27:43; later also aor. pass. ἐρρύσθην,
to be rescued, delivered, Luke 1:74; Rom.
15:31; 2 Thess. 3:2; 2 Tim. 4:17

ῥυόμενον, acc. sg. m. pres. mid./pass. dep.
part. . . . . ῥύομαι *(4506)*

ῥυόμενος, nom. sg. m. pres. mid./pass. dep.
part. . . . . id.

(‡4510) **ῥυπαίνω,** *to make filthy, defile*

ῥυπανθήτω, 3 pers. sg. aor. pass. imper. (Rev.
22:11, GNT, WH & NA | ῥυπαρευθήτω,
MT | ῥυπωσάτω, TR) . . . . ῥυπαίνω *(‡4510)*

ῥυπαρᾷ, dat. sg. f. adj. . . . . ῥυπαρός *(4508)*

ῥυπαρευθήτω, 3 pers. sg. aor. pass. imper.
(Rev. 22:11, MT | ῥυπανθήτω, GNT, WH
& NA | ῥυπωσάτω, TR) . . . ῥυπαρεύομαι *(‡4510)*

(‡4510) **ῥυπαρεύομαι**, fut. ῥυπαρεύσομαι (ῥυπαρός) *to be filthy, squalid*; met. *to be polluted*

(4507) **ῥυπαρία**, ας, ἡ [§2.B.b; 2.2] *filth*; met. moral *filthiness, uncleanness, pollution*, James 1:21
    ῥυπαρίαν, acc. sg. f. n. . . . . ῥυπαρία (4507)

(4508) **ῥυπαρός**, ά, όν, nom. sg. m. adj. [§7.1] *filthy, squalid, sordid, dirty*, James 2:2; met. *defiled, polluted* (Rev. 22:11, GNT, MT, WH & NA | ῥυπῶν, TR)

(4509) **ῥύπος**, ου, ὁ [§3.C.a] *filth, squalor*, 1 Pet. 3:21
    ῥύπου, gen. sg. m. n. . . . . ῥύπος (4509)

(4510) **ῥυπόω**, ῶ, fut. ῥυπώσω [§20.T] *to be filthy*; met. *to be* morally *polluted*, Rev. 22:11 (2×)
    ῥυπῶν, nom. sg. m. pres. act. part. (Rev. 22:11, TR | ῥυπαρός, GNT, WH, MT & NA) . . . . ῥυπόω (4510)
    ῥυπωσάτω, 3 pers. sg. aor. act. imper. (Rev. 22:11, TR | ῥυπαρευθήτω, MT | ῥυπανθήτω, GNT, WH & NA) . . . . ῥυπόω (4510)
    ῥῦσαι, 2 pers. sg. aor. mid. dep. imper. ῥύομαι (4506)
    ῥυσάσθω, 3 pers. sg. aor. mid. dep. imper. id.
    ῥύσει, dat. sg. f. n. . . . . ῥύσις (4511)
    ῥύσεται, 3 pers. sg. fut. mid. dep. indic. . . . . ῥύομαι (4506)
    ῥυσθέντας, acc. pl. m. aor. pass. part. . . . id.
    ῥυσθῶ, 1 pers. sg. aor. pass. subj. . . . . . . id.
    ῥυσθῶμεν, 1 pers. pl. aor. pass. subj. . . . . id.

(4511) **ῥύσις**, εως, ἡ, nom. sg. f. n. [§5.E.c] *a flowing*; a morbid *flux*, Mark 5:25; Luke 8:43, 44
    ῥυτίδα, acc. sg. f. n. . . . . ῥυτίς (4512)

(4512) **ῥυτίς**, ίδος, ἡ [§4.2.c] (ῥύω, *to draw*) *a wrinkle*; met. *a* disfiguring *wrinkle, flaw, blemish*, Eph. 5:27
    Ῥωμαϊκοῖς, dat. pl. neut. adj. (Luke 23:38, MT & TR | GNT, WH & NA omit) . . . . Ῥωμαϊκός (4513)

(4513) **Ῥωμαϊκός**, ή, όν [§7.F.a] *Roman, Latin*, Luke 23:38
    Ῥωμαῖοι, nom. pl. m. adj. . . . . Ῥωμαῖος (4514)
    Ῥωμαίοις, dat. pl. m. adj. . . . . id.
    Ῥωμαῖον, acc. sg. m. adj. . . . . id.

(4514) **Ῥωμαῖος**, ή, όν, nom. sg. m. adj. [§7.F] *Roman; a Roman citizen*, John 11:48; Acts 2:10; 16:21, et al.
    Ῥωμαίους, acc. pl. m. adj. . . . . Ῥωμαῖος (4514)

(4515) **Ῥωμαϊστί**, adv., *in the Roman language, in Latin*, John 19:20
    Ῥωμαίων, gen. pl. m. adj. . . . . Ῥωμαῖος (4514)

(4516) **Ῥώμη**, ης, ἡ [§2.B.a] *Rome*
    Ῥώμῃ, dat. sg. f. n. . . . . Ῥώμη (4516)
    Ῥώμην, acc. sg. f. n. . . . . id.
    Ῥώμης, gen. sg. f. n. . . . . id.

(4517) **ῥώννυμι**, or ῥωννύω, fut. ῥώσω [§36.5] *to strengthen, render firm*; pass. perf. ἔρρωμαι, *to be well, enjoy firm health*; imperative ἔρρωσο, ἔρρωσθε, at the end of letters, like the Latin *vale, farewell*, Acts 15:29; 23:30

Σ

σά, nom. pl. neut. 2 pers. possessive pronoun {Luke 15:31} . . . . σός (4674)
σά, acc. pl. neut. 2 pers. possessive pronoun {Luke 6:30} . . . . id.

(4518) **σαβαχθανί**, indecl. (Aramaic שְׁבַקְתַּנִי, from שְׁבַק, *to leave, forsake*) *sabacthani, thou hast forsaken me* (σαβαχθάνι, MT | σαβαχθανεί, WH) interrogatively, *Hast thou forsaken me?* preceded with λαμᾶ, *Why?* Matt. 27:46; Mark 15:34

(4519) **σαβαώθ** (Hebrew צְבָאוֹת, pl. of צָבָא) *hosts, armies*, Rom. 9:29; James 5:4
    σάββασι(ν), dat. pl. neut. n. [§6.8] . σάββατον (4521)
    σάββατα, acc. pl. neut. n. . . . . id.

(4520) **σαββατισμός**, οῦ, ὁ, nom. sg. m. n. [§3.C.a] (σαββατίζω, i.q. Hebrew שָׁבַת, from which it is formed, *to cease or rest from labor*, and thus *keep sabbath*) pr. *a keeping of a sabbath; a state of rest, a sabbath-state*, Heb. 4:9

(4521) **σάββατον**, ου, τό, nom. sg. neut. n. [§3.C.c] (Hebrew שַׁבָּת) pr. *cessation from labor, rest; the* Jewish *sabbath*, both in the sg. and pl., Matt. 12:2, 5, 8; 28:1; Luke 4:16; *a week*, sg. and pl., Matt. 28:1; Mark 16:9, et al.; pl. *sabbaths, or times of sacred rest*, Col. 2:16 {Mark 2:27a}
    σάββατον, acc. sg. neut. n. {Mark 2:27b} . . . . σάββατον (4521)
    σαββάτου, gen. sg. neut. n. . . . . id.
    σαββάτῳ, dat. sg. neut. n. . . . . id.
    σαββάτων, gen. pl. neut. n. . . . . id.

(4522) **σαγήνη**, ης, ἡ [§2.B.a] (σαγή, from σάττω, *to load*) *a large net, drag*, Matt. 13:47
    σαγήνῃ, dat. sg. f. n. . . . . σαγήνη (4522)
    Σαδδουκαῖοι, nom. pl. m. n. . . . Σαδδουκαῖος (4523)

(4523) **Σαδδουκαῖος**, ου, ὁ [§3.C.a] *a Sadducee, one belonging to the sect of the Sadducees*, which, according to the Talmudists, was founded by one צָדוֹק, *Sadoc*, about three centuries before the Christian era: they were directly opposed in sentiments to the Pharisees, Matt. 3:7; 16:1, 6, 11, 12; 22:23, 34, et al.

Σαδδουκαίους, acc. pl. m. n. . . Σαδδουκαῖος *(4523)*
Σαδδουκαίων, gen. pl. m. n. . . . . id.

(4524) **Σαδώκ**, ὁ, *Sadoc*, pr. name, indecl.
σαίνεσθαι, pres. pass. infin. . . . . σαίνω *(4525)*

(4525) **σαίνω**, fut. σανῶ, aor. ἔσηνα and ἔσανα
[§27.1.c,e] pr. *to wag* the tail; *to fawn, flat-
ter, cajole;* pass. *to be cajoled; to be
wrought upon, to be perturbed,* 1 Thess.
3:3

(4526) **σάκκος**, ου, ὁ, nom. sg. m. n. [§3.C.a]
(Hebrew שַׂק) *sackcloth,* a species of very
coarse black cloth made of hair, Rev. 6:12;
a mourning garment of *sackcloth,* Matt.
11:21; Luke 10:13; Rev. 11:3
σάκκους, acc. pl. m. n. . . . . σάκκος *(4526)*
σάκκῳ, dat. sg. m. n. . . . . id.

(4527) **Σαλά**, ὁ, *Sala,* pr. name, indecl., Luke 3:35

(4528) **Σαλαθιήλ**, ὁ, *Salathiel,* pr. name, indecl.
Σαλαμῖνι, dat. sg. f. n. . . . . Σαλαμίς *(4529)*

(4529) **Σαλαμίς**, ῖνος, ἡ [§4.2.e] *Salamis,* a city in the
island of Cyprus, Acts 13:5

(4530) **Σαλείμ**, indecl. *Salim,* pr. name of a place
(John 3:23, GNT, WH, TR & NA |
Σαλήμ, MT)
σαλευθῆναι, aor. pass. infin. [§14.N] . . σαλεύω *(4531)*
σαλευθήσονται, 3 pers. pl. fut. pass. indic. id.
σαλευθῶ, 1 pers. sg. aor. pass. subj. . . . . . id.
σαλευόμενα, nom. pl. neut. pres. pass. part. id.
σαλευόμενον, acc. sg. m. pres. pass. part. id.
σαλευομένων, gen. pl. neut. pres. pass. part. id.
σαλεύοντες, nom. pl. m. pres. act. part. . . id.
σαλεῦσαι, aor. act. infin. . . . . id.

(4531) **σαλεύω**, fut. σαλεύσω, aor. ἐσάλευσα
[§13.M] *to make to rock, to shake,* Matt.
11:7; 24:29; Luke 6:48; Acts 4:31, et al.;
met. *to stir up, excite* the people, Acts
17:13; *to agitate, disturb* mentally, Acts
2:25; 2 Thess 2:2; pass. impl. *to totter, be
ready to fall, be near to ruin,* met. Heb.
12:27

(4532) **Σαλήμ**, ἡ, *Salem,* pr. name, indecl.

(4533) **Σαλμών**, ὁ, *Salmon,* pr. name, indecl.

(4534) **Σαλμώνη**, ης, ἡ [§2.B.a] *Salmone,* a promontory, the eastern extremity of Crete, Acts
27:7
Σαλμώνην, acc. sg. f. n. . . . . Σαλμώνη *(4534)*

(4535) **σάλος**, ου, ὁ [§3.C.a] *agitation, tossing, rolling,* spc. of the sea, Luke 21:25
σάλου, gen. sg. m. n. . . . . σάλος *(4535)*
σάλπιγγα, acc. sg. f. n. . . . . σάλπιγξ *(4536)*
σάλπιγγας, acc. pl. f. n. . . . . id.
σάλπιγγες, nom. pl. f. n. . . . . id.
σάλπιγγι, dat. sg. f. n. . . . . id.
σάλπιγγος, gen. sg. f. n. . . . . id.

(4536) **σάλπιγξ**, ιγγος, ἡ, nom. sg. f. n. [§4.2.b] *a*
trumpet, Matt. 24:31; 1 Thess. 4:16, et al.
σαλπίζειν, pres. act. infin. . . . . σαλπίζω *(4537)*

(4537) **σαλπίζω**, fut. σαλπίγξω and σαλπίσω [§26.2]
aor. ἐσάλπιγξα and ἐσάλπισα, *to sound
a trumpet,* Rev. 8:6, 7, 8, 10, 12, 13, et al.
σαλπίσει, 3 pers. sg. fut. act. indic. . . σαλπίζω *(4537)*
σαλπίσῃς, 2 pers. sg. aor. act. subj. . . . . . id.

(4538) **σαλπιστής**, οῦ, ὁ [§2.B.c] *a trumpeter,* Rev.
18:22
σαλπιστῶν, gen. pl. m. n. . . . . . . σαλπιστής *(4538)*
σαλπίσωσι(ν), 3 pers. pl. aor. act.
subj. . . . . σαλπίζω *(4537)*

(4539) **Σαλώμη**, ης, ἡ, nom. sg. f. n., *Salome,* pr.
name

(4540) **Σαμάρεια**, ας, ἡ, nom. sg. f. n. [§2.B.b; 2.2]
Samaria, the city and region so called (Acts
8:14, GNT, MT, TR & NA | Σαμαρία,
WH)
Σαμαρείᾳ, dat. sg. f. n. (Acts 1:8, GNT, MT,
TR & NA | Σαμαρίᾳ, WH) . . . . Σαμάρεια *(4540)*
Σαμάρειαν, acc. sg. f. n. (Acts 15:3, GNT,
MT, TR & NA | Σαμαρίαν, WH) . . . . id.
Σαμαρείας, gen. sg. f. n. (Luke 17:11; John
4:4, 5, 7; Acts 8:1, 9; 9:31, GNT, MT, TR
& NA | Σαμαρίας, WH) . . . . id.
Σαμαρεῖται, nom. pl. m. n. (John 4:40, MT
& TR | Σαμαρῖται, GNT, WH &
NA) . . . . Σαμαρείτης *(4541)*
Σαμαρείταις, dat. pl. m. n. (John 4:9, MT &
TR | Σαμαρίταις, GNT, WH & NA) . id.

(4541) **Σαμαρείτης**, ου, ὁ, nom. sg. m. n. [§2.B.c] *a
Samaritan,* an inhabitant of the city or re-
gion of Σαμάρεια, *Samaria,* applied by the
Jews as a term of reproach and contempt,
Matt. 10:5; John 4:9; 8:48, et al. (Luke
10:33; 17:16; John 8:48, MT & TR |
Σαμαρίτης, GNT, WH & NA)
Σαμαρείτιδος, gen. sg. f. n. (John 4:9, MT
& TR | Σαμαρίτιδος, GNT, WH &
NA) . . . . Σαμαρεῖτις *(4542)*

(4542) **Σαμαρεῖτις**, ιδος, ἡ, nom. sg. f. n. [§4.2.c] *a
Samaritan woman* (John 4:9, MT & TR
| Σαμαρίτις, GNT, WH & NA)
Σαμαρειτῶν, gen. pl. m. n. (Matt. 10:5; Luke
9:52; John 4:39; Acts 8:25, MT & TR |
Σαμαριτῶν, GNT, WH & NA) Σαμαρείτης *(4541)*
Σαμαρῖται, nom. pl. m. n. (John 4:40, GNT,
WH & NA | Σαμαρεῖται, MT &
TR) . . . . Σαμαρίτης *(‡4541)*
Σαμαρίταις, dat. pl. m. n. (John 4:9, GNT,
WH & NA | Σαμαρείταις, MT & TR) id.

(‡4541) **Σαμαρίτης**, ου, ὁ, nom. sg. m. n. *a Samaritan* (Luke 10:33; 17:16; John 8:45, GNT,
WH & NA | Σαμαρείτης, MT & TR)
Σαμαρίτιδος, gen. sg. f. n. (John 4:9, GNT,

WH & NA | Σαμαρείτιδος, MT &
TR) . . . . Σαμαρῖτις (†4542)

(†4542) **Σαμαρῖτις,** ιδος, ἡ, nom. sg. f. n. *a Samaritan woman* (John 4:9, GNT, WH & NA | Σαμαρεῖτις, MT & TR)

Σαμαριτῶν, gen. pl. m. n. (Matt. 10:5; Luke 9:52; John 4:39; Acts 8:25, GNT, WH & NA | Σαμαρειτῶν, MT & TR) . . . . Σαμαρίτης (‡4541)

(4543) **Σαμοθράκη,** ης, ἡ [§2.B.a] *Samothrace,* an island in the northern part of the Aegean sea, Acts 16:11

Σαμοθρᾴκην, acc. sg. f. n. . . . . . . Σαμοθρᾴκη (4543)
Σάμον, acc. sg. f. n. . . . . Σάμος (4544)

(4544) **Σάμος,** ου, ἡ [§3.C.b] *Samos,* a celebrated island in the Aegean sea, Acts 20:15

(4545) **Σαμουήλ,** ὁ, *Samuel,* pr. name, indecl.

(4546) **Σαμψών,** ὁ, *Samson,* pr. name, indecl., Heb. 11:32

σανδάλια, acc. pl. neut. n. . . . . . . σανδάλιον (4547)

(4547) **σανδάλιον,** ου, τό [§3.C.c] (pr. dimin. of σάνδαλον) *a sandal,* a sole of wood or hide, covering the bottom of the foot, and bound on with leathern thongs, Mark 6:9; Acts 12:8

(4548) **σανίς,** ίδος, ἡ [§4.2.c] *a board, plank,* Acts 27:44

σανίσιν, dat. pl. f. n. . . . . σανίς (4548)

(4549) **Σαούλ,** ὁ, *Saul,* pr. name, indecl. I. *Saul, king of Israel,* Acts 13:21 II. *The Apostle Paul,* Acts 9:4, et al.

σαπρά, acc. pl. neut. adj. . . . . σαπρός (4550)
σαπρόν, acc. sg. m. adj. {Matt. 12:33b} . . id.
σαπρόν, nom. sg. neut. adj. {Matt. 7:17, 18} id.
σαπρόν, acc. sg. neut. adj. {Matt. 12:33a} id.

(4550) **σαπρός,** ά, όν, nom. sg. m. adj. [§7.1] pr. *rotten, putrid;* hence, *bad, of a bad quality,* Matt. 7:17, 18; 12:33; Luke 6:43; *refuse,* Matt. 13:48; met. *corrupt, depraved, vicious, foul, impure,* Eph. 4:29

(4551) **Σαπφείρη,** ης, ἡ, *Sapphira,* pr. name, Acts 5:1

Σαπφείρῃ, dat. sg. f. n. (Acts 5:1, MT & TR | Σαπφίρῃ, GNT & NA) . Σαπφείρη (4551)

(4552) **Σάπφειρος,** ου, ἡ, nom. sg. f. n. [§3.C.b] (Hebrew ספּיר) *a sapphire,* a precious stone of a blue color in various shades, next in hardness and value to the diamond (Rev. 21:19, MT & TR | Σάπφιρος, GNT, WH & NA)

(‡4551) **Σαπφίρη,** ης, ἡ, *Sapphira,* pr. name
Σαπφίρῃ, dat. sg. f. n. (Acts 5:1, GNT, WH & NA | Σαπφείρῃ, MT & TR) . Σαπφίρη (‡4551)

(†4552) **σάπφιρος,** ου, ἡ, nom. sg. f. n., *a sapphire* (Rev. 21:19, GNT, WH & NA | Σάπφειρος, MT & TR)

(4553) **σαργάνη,** ης, ἡ [§2.B.a] *twisted or plaited work; a network of cords like a basket, basket of ropes,* etc. 2 Cor. 11:33

σαργάνῃ, dat. sg. f. n. . . . . id.

(4554) **Σάρδεις,** εων, αἱ [§5.E.c] *Sardis,* the chief city of Lydia

Σάρδεις, acc. pl. f. n. . . . . Σάρδεις (4554)
Σάρδεσιν, dat. pl. f. n. . . . . id.

(4555) **σάρδινος,** ου, ὁ [§3.C.a] *a sardine,* a precious stone of a blood-red color, Rev. 4:3

σαρδίνῳ, dat. sg. m. n. (Rev. 4:3, TR | σαρδίῳ, GNT, WH, MT & NA) σάρδινος (4555)

(†4556) **σάρδιον,** ου, τό, nom. sg. neut. n. *carnelian,* a reddish precious stone (Rev. 21:20, GNT, WH, MT & NA | σάρδιος, TR)

(4556) **σάρδιος,** ου, ὁ, nom. sg. m. n., *a carnelian* (Rev. 21:20, TR | σάρδιον, GNT, WH, MT & NA)

σαρδίῳ, dat. sg. neut. n. (Rev. 4:3, GNT, WH, MT & NA | σαρδίνῳ, TR) . . . . . σάρδιος (4556)

(4557) **σαρδόνυξ,** υχος, ἡ, nom. sg. f. n. [§4.2.b] (σάρδιον + ὄνυξ) *sardonyx,* a gem exhibiting the color of the carnelian and the white of the calcedony, intermingled in alternate layers

(4558) **Σάρεπτα,** ων, τά, nom. pl. neut. n., *Sarepta,* a city of Phoenicia, between Tyre and Sidon, Luke 4:26

σάρκα, acc. sg. f. n. . . . . σάρξ (4561)
σάρκας, acc. pl. f. n. . . . . id.
σαρκί, dat. sg. f. n. . . . . id.
σαρκικά, nom. pl. neut. adj.
{2 Cor. 10:4} . . . . σαρκικός (4559)
σαρκικά, acc. pl. neut. adj. {1 Cor. 9:11} . id.
σαρκικῇ, dat. sg. f. adj. . . . . id.
σαρκικῆς, gen. sg. f. adj. (Heb. 7:16, MT & TR | σαρκίνης, GNT, WH & NA) . . . id.
σαρκικοί, nom. pl. m. adj. . . . . id.
σαρκικοῖς, dat. pl. m. adj. (1 Cor. 3:1, MT & TR | σάρκινοις, GNT, WH & NA) id.
σαρκικοῖς, dat. pl. neut. adj. {Rom. 15:27} id.

(4559) **σαρκικός,** ή, όν, nom. sg. m. adj. [§7.F.a] *fleshly; pertaining to the body, corporeal, physical,* Rom. 15:27; 1 Cor. 9:11; *carnal, pertaining to the flesh,* 1 Pet. 2:11; *carnal, subject to the propensity of the flesh,* Rom. 7:14; *carnal, low in spiritual knowledge and frame,* 1 Cor. 3:1, 3; *carnal, human* as opposed to divine, 2 Cor. 1:12; 10:4; *carnal, earthly,* Heb. 7:16 (Rom. 7:14, MT & TR | σάρκινος, GNT, WH & NA)

σαρκικῶν, gen. pl. f. adj. . . . . σαρκικός (4559)
σαρκίναις, dat. pl. f. adj. . . . . σάρκινος (4560)
σαρκίνης, gen. sg. f. adj. (Heb. 7:16, GNT, WH & NA | σαρκικῆς, MT & TR) . . id.

σαρκίνοις, dat. pl. m. adj. (1 Cor. 3:1, GNT, WH & NA | σαρκικοῖς, MT & TR) . . . . σάρκινος *(4560)*

(4560) **σάρκινος,** η, ον, nom. sg. m. adj. [§7.F.a] *of flesh, fleshly,* 2 Cor. 3:3 (Rom. 7:14, GNT, WH & NA | σαρκικός, MT & TR)

σαρκός, gen. sg. f. n. . . . . σάρξ *(4561)*

σαρκῶν, gen. pl. f. n. . . . . id.

(4561) **σάρξ,** σαρκός, ἡ, nom. sg. f. n. [§4.2.b] *flesh,* Luke 24:39; John 3:6, et al.; *the human body,* 2 Cor. 7:5; *flesh, human nature, human frame,* John 1:13, 14; 1 Pet. 4:1; 1 John 4:2, et al.; *kindred,* Rom. 11:14; *consanguinnity, lineage,* Rom. 1:3; 9:3, et al.; *flesh, humanity, human beings,* Matt. 24:22; Luke 3:6; John 17:2, et al.; *the circumstances of the body, material condition,* 1 Cor. 5:5; 7:28; Philemon 16, et al.; *flesh, mere humanity, human fashion,* 1 Cor. 1:26; 2 Cor. 1:17; *flesh* as the seat of passion and frailty, Rom. 8:1, 3, 5, et al.; *carnality,* Gal. 5:24; *materiality, material circumstance,* as opposed to the spiritual, Phil. 3:3, 4; Col. 2:18; *a material system or mode,* Gal. 3:3; Heb. 9:10

σαροῖ, 3 pers. sg. pres. act. indic. . . . . . σαρόω *(4563)*

(4562) **Σαρούχ,** ὁ, *Saruch,* pr. name, indecl. (Luke 3:35, TR | Σερούχ, GNT, WH, MT & NA)

(4563) **σαρόω,** ῶ, fut. σαρώσω [§20.T] perf. pass. σεσάρωμαι (i.q. σαίρω) *to sweep, to cleanse with a broom,* Matt. 12:44; Luke 11:25; 15:8

(4564) **Σάρρα,** ας, ἡ, nom. sg. f. n., *Sara, Sarah,* pr. name

Σάρρᾳ, dat. sg. f. n. . . . . Σάρρα *(4564)*

Σάρρας, gen. sg. f. n. . . . . id.

(4565) **Σαρών,** ῶνος, ὁ [§4.2.e] *Saron,* a level tract of Palestine, between Caesarea and Joppa

Σαρῶνα, acc. sg. m. n. (Acts 9:35, GNT, WH & NA | Ἀσσάρωνα, MT | Σαρωνᾶν, TRs | Σάρωνα, TRb) . . . . Σαρών *(4565)*

Σαρωνᾶν, acc. sg. m. n. (Acts 9:35, TRs | Σαρῶνα, GNT, WH & NA | Ἀσσάρωνα, MT | Σάρωνα, TRb) . . . . id.

σάτα, acc. pl. neut. n. . . . . σάτον *(4568)*

(4566) **Σατᾶν,** ὁ, *Satan,* indecl. (2 Cor. 12:7, MT & TR | Σατανᾶ, GNT, WH & NA)

Σατανᾶ, gen. sg. m. n. {Mark 1:13} . Σατανᾶς *(4567)*

Σατανᾶ, voc. sg. m. n. {Mark 8:33} . . . . . id.

Σατανᾷ, dat. sg. m. n. . . . . id.

Σατανᾶν, acc. sg. m. n. . . . . id.

(4567) **Σατανᾶς,** ᾶ, ὁ, nom. sg. m. n. [§2.4] and once 2 Cor. 12:7, Σατᾶν, ὁ, indecl. (Hebrew שָׂטָן) *an adversary, opponent, enemy,* per-

haps, Matt. 16:23; Mark 8:33; Luke 4:8; elsewhere, *Satan, the devil,* Matt. 4:10; Mark 1:13, et al.

(4568) **σάτον,** ου, τό [§3.C.c] (Hebrew סְאָה, Aramaic סָאתָא) *a satum or seah,* a Hebrew measure for things dry, containing, as Josephus testifies, (*Ant.* 9.85) an Italian modius and one half, or 24 sextarii, and therefore equivalent to somewhat less than three gallons English, Matt. 13:33; Luke 13:21

Σαῦλον, acc. sg. m. n. . . . . Σαῦλος *(4569)*

(4569) **Σαῦλος,** ου, ὁ, nom. sg. m. n., *Saul,* the Hebrew name of the Apostle Paul, Σαούλ with a Greek termination

Σαύλου, gen. sg. m. n. . . . . Σαῦλος *(4569)*

Σαύλῳ, dat. sg. m. n. . . . . id.

(4570) **σβέννυμι,** fut. σβέσω, aor. ἔσβεσα [§36.5] *to extinguish, quench,* Matt. 12:20; 25:8; Mark 9:44, 46, 48, et al.; met. *to quench, damp, hinder, thwart,* 1 Thess. 5:19

σβέννυνται, 3 pers. pl. pres. pass. indic. . . . . σβέννυμι *(4570)*

σβέννυται, 3 pers. sg. pres. pass. indic. . . . id.

σβέννυτε, 2 pers. pl. pres. act. imper. . . . . id.

σβέσαι, aor. act. infin. . . . . id.

σβέσει, 3 pers. sg. fut. act. indic. . . . . id.

(4571) **σέ** (and σε, enclitic) acc. sg. 2 pers. personal pronoun . . . . σύ *(4771)*

σεαυτόν, acc. sg. m. 3 pers. reflexive pronoun . . . . σεαυτοῦ *(4572)*

(4572) **σεαυτοῦ,** ῆς, οῦ, gen. sg. m. 3 pers. reflexive pronoun [§11.K.d] *of thyself,* and dat. σεαυτῷ, ῇ, ῷ, *to thyself,* etc. Matt. 4:6; 8:4; 19:19, et al.

σεαυτῷ, dat. sg. m. 3 pers. reflexive pronoun . . . . σεαυτοῦ *(4572)*

(4573) **σεβάζομαι,** fut. σεβάσομαι, aor. pass. ἐσεβάσθην [§26.1] (σέβας, *adoration,* from σέβομαι) *to feel dread of* a thing; *to venerate, adore, worship,* Rom. 1:25

(4574) **σέβασμα,** ατος, τό [§4.D.c] *an object of religious veneration and worship,* Acts 17:23; 2 Thess. 2:4

σέβασμα, acc. sg. neut. n. . . . . σέβασμα *(4574)*

σεβάσματα, acc. pl. neut. n. . . . . id.

σεβαστῆς, gen. sg. f. adj. . . . . σεβαστός *(4575)*

σεβαστόν, acc. sg. m. adj. . . . . id.

(4575) **σεβαστός,** ή, όν [§7.F.a] pr. *venerable, august;* ὁ Σεβαστός, i.q. Latin *Augustus,* Acts 25:21, 25; *Augustan,* or, *Sebastan,* named from the city Sebaste, Acts 27:1

σεβαστοῦ, gen. sg. m. adj. . . . . σεβαστός *(4575)*

σέβεσθαι, pres. mid./pass. dep. infin. . σέβομαι *(4576)*

σέβεται, 3 pers. sg. pres. mid./pass. dep.

indic. . . . . σέβομαι *(4576)*

(4576) **σέβομαι,** *to stand in awe; to venerate, reverence, worship, adore,* Matt. 15:9; Acts 19:27, et al.; part. σεβόμενος, η, ον, *worshiping, devout, pious,* a term applied to proselytes to Judaism, Acts 13:43, et al.

σεβομένας, acc. pl. f. pres. mid./pass. dep. part. . . . . σέβομαι *(4576)*

σεβομένη, nom. sg. f. pres. mid./pass. dep. part. . . . . id.

σεβομένοις, dat. pl. m. pres. mid./pass. dep. part. . . . . id.

σεβομένου, gen. sg. m. pres. mid./pass. dep. part. . . . . id.

σεβομένων, gen. pl. m. pres. mid./pass. dep. part. . . . . id.

σέβονται, 3 pers. pl. pres. mid./pass. dep. indic. . . . . id.

σειομένη, nom. sg. f. pres. pass. part. . . . σείω *(4579)*

(4577) **σειρά,** ᾶς, ἡ [§2.B.b] *a cord, rope, band;* in N.T. *a chain,* 2 Pet. 2:4

σειραῖς, dat. pl. f. n. (2 Pet. 2:4, GNT, MT, TR & NA | σειροῖς, WH) . . . . σειρά *(4577)*

σειροῖς, dat. pl. m. n. (2 Pet. 2:4, WH | σειραῖς, GNT, MT, TR & NA) . . . σειρος *(†4577)*

(†4577) **σειρος,** οῦ, ὁ, *a pitfall, a den or cave*

σεισμοί, nom. pl. m. n. . . . . σεισμός *(4578)*

σεισμόν, acc. sg. m. n. . . . . id.

(4578) **σεισμός,** οῦ, ὁ, nom. sg. m. n. [§3.C.a] pr. *a shaking, agitation, concussion; an earthquake,* Matt. 24:7; 27:54, et al.; *a tempest,* Matt. 8:24

σεισμῷ, dat. sg. m. n. . . . . σεισμός *(4578)*

σείσω, 1 pers. sg. fut. act. indic. (Heb. 12:26, GNT, WH & NA | σείω, MT & TR) σείω *(4579)*

(4579) **σείω,** 1 pers. sg. pres. act. indic., fut. σείσω, aor. ἔσεισα [§13.M] *to shake, agitate,* Heb. 12:26; Rev. 6:13; pass. *to quake,* Matt. 27:51; 28:4; met. *to put in commotion, agitate,* Matt. 21:10 (Heb. 12:26, MT & TR | σείσω, GNT, WH & NA)

(4580) **Σεκοῦνδος,** ου, ὁ, nom. sg. m. n., *Secundus,* pr. name (Acts 20:4, GNT, MT, TR & NA | Σέκουνδος, WH)

(4581) **Σελεύκεια,** ας, ἡ [§2.B.b; 2.2] *Seleucia,* a city of Syria, west of Antioch, on the Orontes, Acts 13:4

Σελεύκειαν, acc. sg. f. n. (Acts 13:4, GNT, MT, TR & NA | Σελευκίαν, WH) . . . . Σελεύκεια *(4581)*

(4582) **σελήνη,** ης, ἡ, nom. sg. f. n. [§2.B.a] *the moon,* Matt. 24:29; Mark 13:24, et al.

σελήνῃ, dat. sg. f. n. . . . . σελήνη *(4582)*

σελήνης, gen. sg. f. n. . . . . id.

σεληνιάζεται, 3 pers. sg. pres. mid./pass. dep.

indic. . . . . σεληνιάζομαι *(4583)*

(4583) **σεληνιάζομαι,** fut. σεληνιάσομαι [§26.1] *to be lunatic,* Matt. 4:24; 17:15

σεληνιαζομένους, acc. pl. m. pres. mid./pass. dep. part. . . . . σεληνιάζομαι *(4583)*

(†4584) **Σεμεΐν,** ὁ, *Semei,* pr. name, indecl. (Luke 3:26, GNT & NA | Σεμεείν, WH | Σεμεεί, MT & TR)

σεμίδαλιν, acc. sg. f. n. . . . . σεμίδαλις *(4585)*

(4585) **σεμίδαλις,** εως, ἡ [§5.E.c] *the finest flour,* Rev. 18:13

σεμνά, nom. pl. neut. adj. . . . . σεμνός *(4586)*

σεμνάς, acc. pl. f. adj. . . . . id.

(4586) **σεμνός,** ή, όν [§7.F.a] *august, venerable; honorable, reputable,* Phil. 4:8; *grave, serious, dignified,* 1 Tim. 3:8, 11; Tit. 2:2

(4587) **σεμνότης,** ητος, ἡ [§4.2.c] pr. *majesty; gravity, dignity, dignified seriousness,* 1 Tim. 2:2; 3:4

σεμνότητα, acc. sg. f. n. . . . . σεμνότης *(4587)*

σεμνότητι, dat. sg. f. n. . . . . id.

σεμνότητος, gen. sg. f. n. . . . . id.

σεμνούς, acc. pl. m. adj. . . . . σεμνός *(4586)*

(4588) **Σέργιος,** ου, ὁ [§3.C.a] *Sergius,* pr. name, Acts 13:7

Σεργίῳ, dat. sg. m. n. . . . . Σέργιος *(4588)*

(‡4562) **Σερούχ,** ὁ, *Serug,* proper name (Luke 3:35, GNT, WH, MT & NA | Σαρούχ, TR)

σεσαλευμένον, acc. sg. neut. perf. pass. part. . . . . σαλεύω *(4531)*

σεσαρωμένον, acc. sg. m. perf. pass. part. [§21.U] . . . . σαρόω *(4563)*

σέσηπε(ν), 3 pers. sg. 2 perf. act. indic. . σήπω *(4595)*

σεσιγημένου, gen. sg. neut. perf. pass. part. . . . . σιγάω *(4601)*

σεσοφισμένοις, dat. pl. m. perf. pass. part. . . . . σοφίζω *(4679)*

σέσωκε(ν), 3 pers. sg. perf. act. indic. . σῴζω *(†4982)*

σεσωρευμένα, acc. pl. neut. perf. pass. part. . . . . σωρεύω *(4987)*

σεσωσμένοι, nom. pl. m. perf. pass. part. (Eph. 2:5, 8, GNT, WH, MT & NA | σεσωσμένοι, TR) . . . . σῴζω *(†4982)*

σέσωσται, 3 pers. sg. perf. pass. indic. [§37.2] (Acts 4:9, MT & TR | σέσωται, GNT, WH & NA) . . . . id.

σέσωται, 3 pers. sg. perf. pass. indic. (Acts 4:9, GNT, WH & NA | σέσωσται, MT & TR) . . . . id.

σῇ, dat. sg. f. 2 pers. possessive pronoun . σός *(4674)*

(4589) **Σήθ,** ὁ, *Seth,* pr. name, indecl., Luke 3:38

(4590) **Σήμ,** ὁ, *Sem, Shem,* pr. name, indecl., Luke 3:36

(4591) **σημαίνω,** fut. φαμανῶ, aor. ἐσήμηνα and ἐσήμανα [§27.1.c,e] (σῆμα, *a sign, mark*)

to indicate by a sign, to signal; to indicate, intimate, John 12:33; *to make known, communicate,* Acts 11:28; Rev. 1:1; *to specify,* Acts 25:27

σημαίνων, nom. sg. m. pres. act.
part. .... σημαίνω (4591)

σημᾶναι, aor. act. infin. .... id.

σημεῖα, nom. pl. neut. n.
{Mark 16:17} .... σημεῖον (4592)

σημεῖα, acc. pl. neut. n. {Mark 13:22} ... id.

σημείοις, dat. pl. neut. n. .... id.

(4592) **σημεῖον,** ου, τό, nom. sg. neut. n. [§3.C.c] (σῆμα) *a sign, a mark, token,* by which anything is known or distinguished, Matt. 16:3; 24:3; 2 Thess. 3:17; *a token, pledge, assurance,* Luke 2:12; *a proof, evidence, convincing token,* Matt. 12:38; 16:1; John 2:18; in N.T. *a sign, wonder, remarkable event, wonderful appearance, extraordinary phenomenon,* 1 Cor. 14:22; Rev. 12:1, 3; 15:1; *a portent, prodigy,* Matt. 24:30; Acts 2:19; *a wonderful work, miraculous operation, miracle,* Matt. 24:24; Mark 16:17, 20; meton. *a sign, a signal character,* Luke 2:34 {Matt. 12:39b,c}

σημεῖον, acc. sg. neut. n.
{Matt. 12:38–39a} .... σημεῖον (4592)

σημειοῦσθε, 2 pers. pl. pres. mid.
imper. .... σημειόω (4593)

(4593) **σημειόω,** ῶ, fut. σημειώσω [§20.T] *to mark, inscribe marks upon;* mid. *to mark for one's self, note,* 2 Thess. 3:14

σημείων, gen. pl. neut. n. .... σημεῖον (4592)

(4594) **σήμερον,** adv., *to-day, this day,* Matt. 6:11, 30; 16:3; 21:28; *now, at present,* Heb. 13:8; 2 Cor. 3:15; ἡ σήμερον, sc. ἡμέρα, sometimes expressed, *this day, the present day,* Acts 20:26; ἕως or ἄχρι τῆς σήμερον, *until this day, until our times,* Matt. 11:23; 27:8, et al. freq.

σήν, acc. sg. f. 2 pers. possessive pronoun σός (4674)

(4595) **σήπω,** *to cause to putrify, make rotten;* mid. σήπομαι, 2 perf. σέσηπα [§25.1] *to putrify, rot, be corrupted or rotten,* James 5:2

(4596) **σηρικός,** ή, όν [§7.F.a] (σήρ, *a silkworm*) *silk, of silk, silken;* τὸ σηρικόν, *silken stuff, silk,* Rev. 18:12

σηρικοῦ, gen. sg. neut. adj. (Rev. 18:12, MT & TR | σιρικοῦ, GNT, WH & NA) . σηρικός (4596)

(4597) **σής,** σητός, ὁ, nom. sg. m. n. [§4.2.c] *a moth,* Luke 12:33 {Matt. 6:19, 20}

σῆς, gen. sg. f. 2 pers. possessive pronoun
{Matt. 24:3} .... σός (4674)

σητόβρωτα, nom. pl. neut. adj. . σητόβρωτος (4598)

(4598) **σητόβρωτος,** ον [§7.2] (σής + βιβρώσκω)

moth-eaten, James 5:2

(4599) **σθενόω,** ῶ, fut. σθενώσω, aor. ἐσθένωσα [§20.T] (σθένος, *strength*) *to strengthen, impart strength,* 1 Pet. 5:10

σθενώσαι, 3 pers. sg. aor. act. opt. (1 Pet. 5:10, TR | σθενώσει, GNT, WH, MT & NA) .... σθενόω (4599)

σθενώσει, 3 pers. sg. fut. act. indic. (1 Pet. 5:10, GNT, WH, MT & NA | σθενώσαι, TR) .... id.

σιαγόνα, acc. sg. f. n. .... σιαγών (4600)

(4600) **σιαγών,** όνος, ἡ [§4.2.e] *the jaw-bone;* in N.T. *the cheek,* Matt. 5:39; Luke 6:29

σιγᾶν, pres. act. infin. (Acts 12:17, GNT, MT & N | σιγᾷν, WH & TR) .... σιγάω (4601)

σιγάτω, 3 pers. sg. pres. act. imper. ..... id.

σιγάτωσαν, 3 pers. pl. pres. act. imper. ... id.

(4601) **σιγάω,** ῶ, fut. σιγήσω [§18.R] perf. pass. σεσίγημαι, *to be silent, keep silence,* Luke 9:36; 20:26, et al.; trans. *to keep in silence, not to reveal, to conceal;* pass. *to be concealed, not to be revealed,* Rom. 16:25

(4602) **σιγή,** ῆς, ἡ, nom. sg. f. n. [§2.B.a] *silence,* Acts 21:40; Rev. 8:1

σιγῆς, gen. sg. f. n. .... σιγή (4602)

σιγῆσαι, aor. act. infin. .... σιγάω (4601)

σιγήσῃ, 3 pers. sg. aor. act. subj. (Luke 18:39, GNT, WH & NA | σιωπήσῃ, MT & TR) id.

σιδηρᾷ, dat. sg. f. adj. .... σιδήρεος (4603)

σιδηρᾶν, acc. sg. f. adj. .... id.

(4603) **σιδήρεος,** οῦς, σιδήρεα, ᾶ, οῦν, contr. οῦς, ᾶ, οῦν [§7.4.c] *made of iron,* Acts 12:10; Rev. 2:27; 9:9; 12:5; 19:15

(4604) **σίδηρος,** ου, ὁ [§3.C.a] *iron,* Rev. 18:12

σιδήρου, gen. sg. m. n. .... σίδηρος (4604)

σιδηροῦς, acc. pl. m. adj. .... σιδήρεος (4603)

(4605) **Σιδών,** ῶνος, ἡ [§4.2.e] *Sidon,* a celebrated city of Phoenicia

Σιδῶνα, acc. sg. f. n. .... Σιδών (4605)

Σιδῶνι, dat. sg. f. n. .... id.

(†4606) **Σιδωνία,** ας, ἡ (sc. χώρα) *the country or district of Sidon*

Σιδωνίας, gen. sg. f. n. (Luke 4:26, GNT, WH & NA | Σιδῶνος, MT & TR) .. Σιδωνία (†4606)

Σιδωνίοις, dat. pl. f. adj. .... Σιδώνιος (4606)

(4606) **Σιδώνιος,** ία, ιον, *Sidonian; an inhabitant of* Σιδών, *Sidon,* Acts 12:20

Σιδῶνος, gen. sg. f. n. .... Σιδών (4605)

(4607) **σικάριος,** ου, ὁ [§3.C.a] (Latin *sicarius,* from sica, *a dagger, poniard*) *an assassin, bandit, robber,* Acts 21:38

σικαρίων, gen. pl. m. n. .... σικάριος (4607)

(4608) **σίκερα,** τό, indecl. (Hebrew שֵׁכָר) *strong or inebriating drink,* Luke 1:15

Σιλᾷ, dat. sg. m. n. (GNT, WH & NA | Σίλα,

MT & TR) . . . . Σιλᾶς (†4609)

Σιλᾶν, acc. sg. m. n. (GNT, WH & NA |
Σίλαν, MT & TR) . . . . id.

(†4609) **Σιλᾶς**, ᾶ, ὁ, nom. sg. m. n. [§2.4] *Silas*, pr.
name, in Luke, Acts 15:22, et al.;
Σιλουανός, in Paul, 2 Cor. 1:19, et al.; and
Peter, 1 Pet. 5:12 (GNT, WH & NA |
Σίλας, MT & TR)

(4610) **Σιλουανός**, οῦ, ὁ, nom. sg. m. n. [§3.C.a]
Silvanus, pr. name
Σιλουανοῦ, gen. sg. m. n. . . . . Σιλουανός (4610)

(4611) **Σιλωάμ**, ὁ, indecl. *Siloam, a pool or fountain
near Jerusalem*
σιμικίνθια, acc. pl. neut. n. . . . . . σιμικίνθιον (4612)

(4612) **σιμικίνθιον**, ου, τό [§3.C.c] (Latin
semicinctium, from *semi, half*, and *cingo,
to gird) an apron*, Acts 19:12

(‡4826) **Σιμεών**, ὁ, indecl. pr. name *Simeon* (Luke
2:25, 34; 3:30, TR | Συμεών, GNT, WH,
MT, TRs & NA)

(4613) **Σίμων**, ωνος, ὁ, nom. sg. m. n. [§4.2.e]
Simon, pr. name   I. *Simon Peter*, Matt.
4:18, et al. freq.   II. *Simon (the Canaan-
ite) Zelotes*, Matt. 10:4; Acts 1:13, et al.
III. *Simon, brother of Jesus*, Matt. 13:55;
Mark 6:3   IV. *Simon, the leper*, Matt.
26:6; Mark 14:3   V. *Simon, the Pharisee*, Luke 7:40, et al.   VI. *Simon of Cyrene*, Matt. 27:32, et al.   VII. *Simon,
father of Judas Iscariot*, John 6:71, et al.
VIII. *Simon, the sorcerer*, Acts 8:9, et al.
IX. *Simon, the tanner, of Joppa*, Acts 9:43;
10:6, et al. {Luke 7:43}

Σίμων, voc. sg. m. n. {Luke 7:40} . . . . . Σίμων (4613)

Σίμωνα, acc. sg. m. n. . . . . id.

Σίμωνι, dat. sg. m. n. . . . . id.

Σίμωνος, gen. sg. m. n. . . . . id.

(4614) **Σινᾶ**, τό, indecl. *Mount Sina, Sinai*, in Arabia
(Acts 7:30, 38; Gal. 4:24, 25, GNT, MT,
TR & NA | Σινά, WH)
σινάπεως, gen. sg. neut. n. . . . . σίναπι (4615)

(4615) **σίναπι**, εως, τό [§5.4] *mustard;* in N.T. probably the shrub, not the herb, *Khardal, Sal-
vadora Persica L.*, the fruit of which
possesses the pungency of mustard, Matt.
13:31; 17:20, et al.
σινδόνα, acc. sg. f. n. . . . . σινδών (4616)

σινδόνι, dat. sg. f. n. . . . . id.

(4616) **σινδών**, όνος, ἡ [§4.2.e] *sindon;* pr. *fine In-
dian cloth; fine linen;* in N.T. *a linen garment, an upper garment or wrapper of fine
linen*, worn in summer by night, and used
to envelope dead bodies, Matt. 27:59;
Mark 14:51, 52; 15:46; Luke 23:53

(4617) **σινιάζω**, fut. σινιάσω [§26.1] (σινίον, *a sieve*)

to sift; met. *to sift* by trials and tempta-
tions, Luke 22:31

σινιάσαι, aor. act. infin. . . . . σινιάζω (4617)

(‡4596) **σιρικός**, ή, όν (σήρ, *a silkworm) silk, of silk,
silken;* τὸ σηρικόν, *silken stuff, silk*, Rev.
18:12

σιρικοῦ, gen. sg. neut. adj. (Rev. 18:12, GNT,
WH & NA | σηρικοῦ, MT &
TR) . . . . σιρικός (‡4596)

σῖτα, acc. pl. m. n. [§6.7] (Acts 7:12, MT &
TR | σιτία, GNT, WH & NA) . . . . . σῖτος (4621)

σιτευτόν, acc. sg. m. adj. . . . . σιτευτός (4618)

(4618) **σιτευτός**, ή, όν [§7.F.a] (σιτεύω, *to feed or fatten*, σῖτος) *fed, fatted*, Luke 15:23, 27, 30

σιτία, acc. pl. neut. n. (Acts 7:12, GNT, WH
& NA | σῖτα, MT & TR) . . . . σιτίον (‡4621)

(‡4621) **σιτίον**, ου, τό [§3.C.c] *provision of corn, food*

σιτιστά, nom. pl. neut. adj. . . . . σιτιστός (4619)

(4619) **σιτιστός**, ή, όν (σιτίζω, *to fatten*, from σῖτος)
fatted, a fatling, Matt. 22:4

(†4620) **σιτομέτριον**, ου, τό [§3.C.c] (σῖτος + μετρέω)
a certain measure of grain distributed for
food at set times to the slaves of a family,
a ration, Luke 12:42

σιτομέτριον, acc. sg. neut. n. . . . σιτομέτριον (†4620)

σῖτον, acc. sg. m. n. . . . . σῖτος (4621)

(4621) **σῖτος**, ου, ὁ, *corn, grain, wheat*, Matt. 3:12;
13:25, 29, 30; Mark 4:28, et al.; pl. σῖτα,
bread, food, Acts 7:12

σίτου, gen. sg. m. n. . . . . σῖτος (4621)

(‡4966) **Σιχέμ**, *Sychem*, a city of Samaria (Acts 7:16,
TRb | Συχέμ, GNT, WH, MT, TRs &
NA)

(4622) **Σιών**, ὁ, or τό, indecl. *Mount Sion*

σιώπα, 2 pers. sg. pres. act. imper. . . . σιωπάω (4623)

(4623) **σιωπάω**, ῶ, fut. σιωπήσω, aor. ἐσιώπησα
[§18.R] *to be silent, keep silence, hold one's
peace*, Matt. 20:31; 26:63, et al.; σιωπῶν,
silent, dumb, Luke 1:20; met. *to be silent,
still, hushed, calm*, as the sea, Mark 4:39

σιωπήσῃ, 3 pers. sg. aor. act. subj. . . σιωπάω (4623)

σιωπήσῃς, 2 pers. sg. aor. act. subj. . . . . . id.

σιωπήσουσιν, 3 pers. pl. fut. act. indic. (Luke
19:40, GNT, WH & NA | σιωπήσωσιν,
MT & TR) . . . . id.

σιωπήσωσιν, 3 pers. pl. aor. act. subj. . . . id.

σιωπῶν, nom. sg. m. pres. act. part. . . . . . id.

σκάνδαλα, acc. pl. neut. n. . . . . . σκάνδαλον (4625)

σκανδαλίζει, 3 pers. sg. pres. act.
indic. σκανδαλίζω (4624)

σκανδαλίζεται, 3 pers. sg. pres. pass. indic.   id.

σκανδαλίζῃ, 3 pers. sg. pres. act. subj. . . . id.

σκανδαλίζονται, 3 pers. pl. pres. pass. indic.   id.

(4624) **σκανδαλίζω**, fut. σκανδαλίσω, aor. ἐσκαν-
δάλισα [§26.1] pr. *to cause to stumble;*

met. *to offend, vex,* Matt. 17:27; *to offend, shock, excite feelings of repugnance,* John 6:61; 1 Cor. 8:13; pass. *to be offended, shocked, pained,* Matt. 15:12; Rom. 14:21; 2 Cor. 11:29; σκανδαλίζεσθαι ἔν τινι, *to be affected with scruples or repugnance towards any one* as respects his claims or pretensions, Matt. 11:6; 13:57, et al.; met. *to cause to stumble* morally, *to cause to falter or err,* Matt. 5:29; 18:6, et al.; pass. *to falter, fall away,* Matt. 13:21, et al.

σκανδαλίση, 3 pers. sg. aor. act.
     subj. σκανδαλίζω *(4624)*
σκανδαλισθῇ, 3 pers. sg. aor. pass. subj. .   id.
σκανδαλισθήσεσθε, 2 pers. pl. fut. pass.
     indic. . . . . id.
σκανδαλισθήσομαι, 1 pers. sg. fut. pass.
     indic. . . . . id.
σκανδαλισθήσονται, 3 pers. pl. fut. pass.
     indic. . . . . id.
σκανδαλισθῆτε, 2 pers. pl. aor. pass. subj.   id.
σκανδαλίσω, 1 pers. sg. aor. act. subj. . . .   id.
σκανδαλίσωμεν, 1 pers. pl. aor. act. subj.   id.
(4625) **σκάνδαλον,** ου, τό, nom. sg. neut. n. [§3.C.c]
     (a later equivalent to σκανδάληθρον) pr.
     a trap-spring; also genr. *a stumbling-block, anything against which one stumbles, an impediment;* met. *a cause of ruin, destruction, misery,* etc., Rom. 9:33; 11:9; *a cause or occasion of sinning,* Matt. 18:7(3×); Luke 17:1; *scandal, offence, cause of indignation,* 1 Cor. 1:23; Gal. 5:11 {1 John 2:10}
σκάνδαλον, acc. sg. neut. n.
     {Rev. 2:14} . . . . σκάνδαλον *(4625)*
σκανδάλου, gen. sg. neut. n. . . . . id.
σκανδάλων, gen. pl. neut. n. . . . . id.
σκάπτειν, pres. act. infin. . . . . σκάπτω *(4626)*
(4626) **σκάπτω,** fut. σκάψω, aor. ἔσκαψα [§23.1.a; 23.2] *to dig, excavate,* Luke 6:48; 13:8; 16:3
(4627) **σκάφη,** ης, ἡ [§2.B.a] pr. *anything excavated or hollowed; a boat, skiff,* Acts 27:16, 30, 32
σκάφην, acc. sg. f. n. . . . . σκάφη *(4627)*
σκάφης, gen. sg. f. n. . . . . id.
σκάψω, 1 pers. sg. aor. act. subj. . . . σκάπτω *(4626)*
σκέλη, acc. pl. neut. n. . . . . σκέλος *(4628)*
(4628) **σκέλος,** ους, τό, pl. τὰ σκέλη [§5.E.b] *the leg,* John 19:31, 32, 33
(4629) **σκέπασμα,** ατος, τό [§4.D.c] (σκεπάζω, *to cover*) *covering; clothing, raiment,* 1 Tim. 6:8
σκεπάσματα, acc. pl. neut. n. . . . . σκέπασμα *(4629)*
Σκευᾶ, gen. sg. m. n. . . . . Σκευᾶς *(4630)*

(4630) **Σκευᾶς,** ᾶ, ὁ [§2.4] *Sceva,* pr. name
σκεύει, dat. sg. neut. n. . . . . σκεῦος *(4632)*
σκεύεσιν, dat. pl. neut. n. . . . . id.
σκεύη, nom. pl. neut. n. {Rev. 2:27} . . . . id.
σκεύη, acc. pl. neut. n. {Matt. 12:29} . . . . id.
(4631) **σκευή,** ῆς, ἡ [§2.B.a] *apparatus; tackle,* Acts 27:19
σκευήν, acc. sg. f. n. . . . . σκευή *(4631)*
(4632) **σκεῦος,** ους, τό, nom. sg. neut. n. [§5.E.b]
     a vessel, utensil for containing anything, Mark 11:16; Luke 8:16; Rom. 9:21; *any utensil, instrument;* σκεύη, *household stuff, furniture, goods,* etc., Matt. 12:29; Mark 3:27, et al.; *the mast of a ship,* or, *the sail,* Acts 27:17; met. *an instrument, means, organ, minister,* Acts 9:15; σκεύη ὀργῆς and σκεύη ἐλέους, *vessels of wrath,* or, *of mercy, persons visited by punishment,* or, *the divine favor,* Rom. 9:22, 23; *the vessel or frame* of the human individual, 1 Thess. 4:4; 1 Pet. 3:7 {Acts 9:15}
σκεῦος, acc. sg. neut. n. {Acts 10:11} . σκεῦος *(4632)*
σκηναῖς, dat. pl. f. n. . . . . σκηνή *(4633)*
σκηνάς, acc. pl. f. n. . . . . id.
σκήνει, dat. sg. neut. n. . . . . σκῆνος *(4636)*
(4633) **σκηνή,** ῆς, ἡ, nom. sg. f. n. [§2.B.a] *a tent, tabernacle;* genr. *any temporary dwelling; a tent, booth,* Matt. 17:4; Heb. 11:9; *the tabernacle* of the covenant, Heb. 8:5; 9:1, 21; 13:10; allegor. *the* celestial or true *tabernacle,* Heb. 8:2; 9:11; *a division or compartment of the tabernacle,* Heb. 9:2, 3, 6; *a small portable tent or shrine,* Acts 7:43; *an abode or seat* of a lineage, Acts 15:16; *a mansion, habitation, abode, dwelling,* Luke 16:9; Rev. 13:6
σκηνῇ, dat. sg. f. n. . . . . σκηνή *(4633)*
σκηνήν, acc. sg. f. n. . . . . id.
σκηνῆς, gen. sg. f. n. . . . . id.
(4634) **σκηνοπηγία,** ας, ἡ, nom. sg. f. n. [§2.B.b; 2.2] (σκῆνος + πήγνυμι) pr. *a pitching of tents or booths;* hence, *the feast of tabernacles or booths,* instituted in memory of the forty years' wandering of the Israelites in the desert, and as a season of gratitude for the ingathering of harvest, celebrated during eight days, commencing on the 15th of Tisri
σκηνοποιοί, nom. pl. m. n. . . . . . σκηνοποιός *(4635)*
(4635) **σκηνοποιός,** οῦ, ὁ (σκηνή + ποιέω) *a tent-maker*
(4636) **σκῆνος,** ους, τό [§5.E.b] (equivalent to σκηνή) *a tent, tabernacle;* met. *the* corporeal *tabernacle,* 2 Cor. 5:1, 4
σκηνοῦντας, acc. pl. m. pres. act.

part. σκηνόω *(4637)*

σκηνοῦντες, nom. pl. m. pres. act. part. . . . id.

σκήνους, gen. sg. neut. n. . . . . σκῆνος *(4636)*

(4637) **σκηνόω**, ῶ, fut. σκηνώσω, aor. ἐσκήνωσα [§20.T] *to pitch tent, encamp; to taberna-cle, dwell in a tent; to dwell, have one's abode*, John 1:14; Rev. 7:15; 12:12; 13:6; 21:3

(4638) **σκήνωμα**, ατος, τό [§4.D.c] *a habitation, abode, dwelling*, Acts 7:46; *the* corporeal *tabernacle* of the soul, 2 Pet. 1:13, 14

σκήνωμα, acc. sg. neut. n. . . . . σκήνωμα *(4638)*

σκηνώματι, dat. sg. neut. n. . . . . id.

σκηνώματος, gen. sg. neut. n. . . . . id.

σκηνώσει, 3 pers. sg. fut. act. indic. . σκηνόω *(4637)*

(4639) **σκιά**, ᾶς, ἡ, nom. sg. f. n. [§2.B.b; 2.2] *a shade, shadow*, Mark 4:32; Acts 5:15; met. *a shadow, a shadowing forth, adumbra-tion*, in distinction from ἡ εἰκών, the per-fect image or delineation, and τὸ σῶμα, the reality, Col. 2:17; Heb. 8:5; 10:1; *gloom*; σκιὰ θανάτου, *death-shade, the thickest darkness*, Matt. 4:16; Luke 1:79

σκιᾷ, dat. sg. f. n. . . . . σκιά *(4639)*

σκιάν, acc. sg. f. n. . . . . id.

(4640) **σκιρτάω**, ῶ, fut. σκιρτήσω, aor. ἐσκίρτησα [§18.R] *to leap*, Luke 1:41, 44; *to leap, skip, bound* for joy, Luke 6:23

σκιρτήσατε, 2 pers. pl. aor. act.

imper. . . . . σκιρτάω *(4640)*

(4641) **σκληροκαρδία**, ας, ἡ [§2.B.b; 2.2] (σκληρός + καρδία) *hardness of heart, obduracy, obstinacy, perverseness*, Matt. 19:8; Mark 10:5; 16:14

σκληροκαρδίαν, acc. sg. f. n. . . σκληροκαρδία *(4641)*

σκληρόν, nom. sg. neut. adj. . . . . . . σκληρός *(4642)*

(4642) **σκληρός**, ά, όν, nom. sg. m. adj. [§7.1] *dry, hard*; met. *harsh, severe, stern*, Matt. 25:24; *vehement, violent, fierce*, James 3:4; *grievous, painful*, Acts 9:5; 26:14; *grating* to the mind, *repulsive, offensive*, John 6:60; *stubborn, contumacious*, Jude 15

(4643) **σκληρότης**, ητος, ἡ [§4.2.c] *hardness*; met. σκληρότης τῆς καρδίας, *hardness of heart, obduracy, obstinacy, perverseness*, Rom. 2:5

σκληρότητα, acc. sg. f. n. . . . . σκληρότης *(4643)*

σκληροτράχηλοι, voc. pl. m.

adj. . . . . σκληροτράχηλος *(4644)*

(4644) **σκληροτράχηλος**, ον [§7.2] (σκληρός + τράχηλος) *stiff-necked, obstinate, refrac-tory*

σκληρύνει, 3 pers. sg. pres. act.

indic. σκληρύνω *(4645)*

σκληρύνητε, 2 pers. pl. pres. act. subj. . . . id.

σκληρυνθῇ, 3 pers. sg. aor. pass.

subj. σκληρύνω *(4645)*

(4645) **σκληρύνω**, fut. σκληρυνῶ, aor. ἐσκλήρυνα [§27.1.a,f] *to harden*; met. *to harden mor-ally, to make stubborn*, Heb. 3:8, 15; 4:7; as a negation of ἐλεεῖν, *to leave to stub-bornness and contumacy*, Rom. 9:18; mid. and pass. *to put on a stubborn frame, be-come obdurate*, Acts 19:9; Heb. 3:13

σκληρῶν, gen. pl. m. adj.

{James 3:4} . . . . σκληρός *(4642)*

σκληρῶν, gen. pl. neut. adj. {Jude 15} . . . id.

σκολιά, nom. pl. neut. adj. . . . . σκολιός *(4646)*

σκολιᾶς, gen. sg. f. adj. . . . . id.

σκολιοῖς, dat. pl. m. adj. . . . . id.

(4646) **σκολιός**, ά, όν [§7.1] *crooked, tortuous*, Luke 3:5; met. *perverse, wicked*, Acts 2:40; Phil. 2:15; *crooked, peevish, morose*, 1 Pet. 2:18

(4647) **σκόλοψ**, οπος, ὁ, nom. sg. m. n. [§4.2.a] *anything pointed*; met. *a thorn, a plague*, 2 Cor. 12:7

σκόπει, 2 pers. sg. pres. act. imper. . . σκοπέω *(4648)*

σκοπεῖν, pres. act. infin. . . . . id.

σκοπεῖτε, 2 pers. pl. pres. act. imper. . . . . id.

(4648) **σκοπέω**, ῶ, fut. σκοπήσω [§16.P] *to view at-tentively, watch, reconnoiter; to see, ob-serve, take care, beware*, Luke 11:35; Gal. 6:1; *to regard, have respect to*, 2 Cor. 4:18; Phil. 2:4; *to mark, note*, Rom. 16:17; Phil. 3:17

σκοπόν, acc. sg. m. n. . . . . σκοπός *(4649)*

(4649) **σκοπός**, οῦ, ὁ [§3.C.a] (σκέπτομαι, *to look around, survey*) *a watcher*; also, *a distant object on which the eye is kept fixed; a mark, goal*, Phil. 3:14

σκοποῦντες, nom. pl. m. pres. act. part. (Phil. 2:4, GNT, WH & NA | σκοπεῖτε, MT & TR) . . . . σκοπέω *(4648)*

σκοπούντων, gen. pl. m. pres. act. part. . . id.

σκοπῶν, nom. sg. m. pres. act. part. . . . . id.

σκορπίζει, 3 pers. sg. pres. act.

indic. . . . . σκορπίζω *(4650)*

(4650) **σκορπίζω**, fut. σκορπίσω, aor. ἐσκόρπισα [§26.1] *to disperse, scatter*, John 10:12; 16:32; *to dissipate, waste*, Matt. 12:30; Luke 11:23; *to scatter abroad* one's gifts, *give liberally*, 2 Cor. 9:9

σκορπίοι, nom. pl. m. n. . . . . σκορπίος *(4651)*

σκορπίοις, dat. pl. m. n. . . . . id.

σκορπίον, acc. sg. m. n. . . . . id.

(4651) **σκορπίος**, ου, ὁ [§3.C.a] *a scorpion, scorpio Afer* of Linn., a large insect, sometimes sev-eral inches in length, shaped somewhat like a crab and furnished with a tail terminat-ing in a stinger from which it emits a dan-

gerous poison, Luke 10:19; 11:12, et al.

σκορπίου, gen. sg. m. n. .... σκορπίος *(4651)*

σκορπισθῆτε, 2 pers. pl. aor. pass.
subj. .... σκορπίζω *(4650)*

σκορπίων, gen. pl. m. n. .... σκορπίος *(4651)*

σκότει, dat. sg. neut. n. .... σκότος *(4655)*

σκοτεινόν, nom. sg. neut. adj. (Luke 11:34,
GNT, MT, TR & NA | σκοτινόν,
WH) .... σκοτεινός *(4652)*

σκοτεινόν, acc. sg. neut. adj. (Luke 11:36,
GNT, MT, TR & NA | σκοτινόν, WH)   id.

(4652) **σκοτεινός**, ή, όν [§7.F.a] *dark, darkling,* Matt.
6:23; Luke 11:34, 36

(4653) **σκοτία**, ας, ἡ, nom. sg. f. n. [§2.B.b; 2.2]
darkness, John 6:17; 20:1; *privacy,* Matt.
10:27; Luke 12:3; met. *moral or spiritual
darkness,* John 1:5(2×); 8:12; 12:35, 46,
et al.

σκοτίᾳ, dat. sg. f. n. .... σκοτία *(4653)*

σκοτίας, gen. sg. f. n. .... id.

(4654) **σκοτίζω**, fut. σκοτίσω [§26.1] *to darken,
shroud in darkness;* pass. *to be darkened,
obscured,* Matt. 24:29; Luke 23:45; met.
to be shrouded in moral *darkness, to be be-
nighted,* Rom. 1:21, et al.

σκοτισθῇ, 3 pers. sg. aor. pass. subj. . σκοτίζω *(4654)*

σκοτισθήσεται, 3 pers. sg. fut. pass. indic.   id.

σκοτισθήτωσαν, 3 pers. pl. aor. pass. imper.   id.

(4655) **σκότος**, ους, τό, nom. sg. neut. n. [§5.E.b]
but, according to ordinary Greek usage, ου,
ὁ, Heb. 12:18, *darkness,* Matt. 27:45; Acts
2:20; *gloom* of punishment and misery,
Matt. 8:12; 2 Pet. 2:17; met. moral or spiritual *darkness,* Matt. 4:16; John 3:19; Eph.
5:11; *a realm of* moral *darkness,* Eph. 5:8;
6:12 {Matt. 27:45}

σκότος, acc. sg. neut. n.
{Matt. 25:30} .... σκότος *(4655)*

σκότους, gen. sg. neut. n. .... id.

(4656) **σκοτόω**, ῶ, fut. σκοτώσω [§20.T] *to darken,
shroud in darkness,* Rev. 16:10

σκότῳ, dat. sg. m. n. (Heb. 12:18, MT & TR
| ζόφῳ, GNT, WH & NA) ...... σκότος *(4655)*

σκύβαλα, acc. pl. neut. n. .... σκύβαλον *(4657)*

(4657) **σκύβαλον**, ου, τό [§3.C.c] *offal, dung, sweep-
ings, refuse*

(4658) **Σκύθης**, ου, ὁ, nom. sg. m. n. [§2.B.c] *A
Scythian, a native of Scythia,* the modern
Mongolia and Tartary

σκυθρωποί, nom. pl. m. adj. .... σκυθρωπός *(4659)*

(4659) **σκυθρωπός**, όν and ή, όν (σκυθρός, *stern,
gloomy,* and ὤψ) *of a stern, morose, sour,
gloomy, or dejected countenance,* Matt.
6:16; Luke 24:17

σκῦλα, acc. pl. neut. n. .... σκῦλον *(4661)*

σκύλλε, 2 pers. sg. pres. act. imper. .. σκύλλω *(4660)*

σκύλλεις, 2 pers. sg. pres. act. indic. .... id.

σκύλλου, 2 pers. sg. pres. pass. imper. ... id.

(4660) **σκύλλω**, fut. σκυλῶ, perf. pass. ἔσκυλμαι
[§27.1.b; 27.3] *to flay, lacerate;* met. *to vex,
trouble, annoy,* Mark 5:35; Luke 7:6; 8:49;
pass. met. ἐσκυλμένοι, *jaded, in sorry
plight,* Matt. 9:36

(4661) **σκῦλον**, ου, τό [§3.C.c] *spoils stripped off an
enemy;* σκῦλα, *spoil, plunder, booty,* Luke
11:22

(4662) **σκωληκόβρωτος**, ον, nom. sg. m. adj.
(σκώληξ + βιβρώσκω) *eaten of worms,
consumed by worms*

(4663) **σκώληξ**, ηκος, ὁ, nom. sg. m. n. [§4.2.b] *a
worm;* met. *gnawing anguish,* Mark 9:44,
46, 48

(4664) **σμαράγδινος**, η, ον [§7.F.a] *of smaragdus or
emerald,* Rev. 4:3

σμαραγδίνῳ, dat. sg. m. adj. (Rev. 4:3, GNT,
WH, TR & NA | σμαραγδίνων,
MT) .... σμαράγδινος *(4664)*

σμαραγδίνων, gen. pl. neut. adj. (Rev. 4:3,
MT | σμαραγδίνῳ, GNT, WH, TR &
NA) .... id.

(4665) **σμάραγδος**, ου, ὁ, nom. sg. m. n. [§3.C.a]
smaragdus, the emerald, a gem of a pure
green color; but under this name the ancients probably comprised all stones of a
fine green color

(4666) **σμύρνα**, ης, ἡ (Hebrew מוֹר) *myrrh,* an aromatic bitter resin, or gum, issuing by incision, and sometimes spontaneously, from
the trunk and larger branches of a small
thorny tree growing in Egypt, Arabia, and
Abyssinia, much used by the ancients in un-
guents, Matt. 2:11; John 19:39

(4667) **Σμύρνα**, ης, ἡ [§2.3] *Smyrna,* a maritime city
of Ionia, in Asia Minor

(4668) **Σμυρναῖος**, α, ον, *Smyrnean; an inhabitant of
Smyrna,* Rev. 1:11; 2:8

Σμυρναίων, gen. pl. m. n. (Rev. 2:8, TR |
Σμύρνῃ, GNT, WH, MT &
NA) .... Σμυρναῖος *(4668)*

Σμύρναν, acc. sg. f. n. {Rev. 1:11} ... Σμύρνα *(4667)*

σμύρναν, acc. sg. f. n. {Matt. 2:11} .. σμύρνα *(4666)*

Σμύρνῃ, dat. sg. f. n. (Rev. 2:8, GNT, WH,
MT & NA | Σμυρναίων, TR) .... Σμύρνα *(4667)*

σμύρνης, gen. sg. f. n. .... σμύρνα *(4666)*

(4669) **σμυρνίζω**, fut. σμυρνίσω [§26.1] *to mingle or
impregnate with myrrh,* Mark 15:23

(4670) **Σόδομα**, ων, τά, nom. pl. neut. n. [§3.C.c] *So-
dom,* one of the four cities of the vale of
Siddim, now covered by the Dead sea

Σοδόμοις, dat. pl. neut. n. .... Σόδομα *(4670)*

Σοδόμων, gen. pl. neut. n. . . . . Σόδομα *(4670)*

(4671) σοί, dat. sg. 2 pers. personal pron. (enclitic
   σοι) [§11.K.b] {Luke 5:23} . . . .   σύ *(4771)*

σοί, nom. pl. m. 2 pers. possessive pron.
   {Luke 5:33} . . . .   σός *(4674)*

(4672) **Σολομών**, ῶντος or ῶνος, ὁ, nom. sg. m. n.
   [§4.2.d] *Solomon*, pr. name
Σολομῶνα, acc. sg. m. n. (Matt. 1:6, GNT,
   WH, MT & NA | Σολομῶντα,
   TR) . . . . Σολομών *(4672)*
Σολομῶνος, gen. sg. m. n. . . . .   id.
Σολομῶντα, acc. sg. m. n. (Matt. 1:6, TR |
   Σολομῶνα, GNT, WH, MT & NA) . .   id.
Σολομῶντος, gen. sg. m. n. . . . .   id.
σόν, nom. sg. neut. 2 pers. possessive pron.,
   John 18:35 . . . .   σός *(4674)*
σόν, acc. sg. neut. 2 pers. possessive pron.
   {Matt. 20:14} . . . .   id.

(4673) **σορός**, οῦ, ἡ [§3.C.b] *a coffer; an urn for receiving the ashes of the dead; a coffin; in
   N.T. a bier,* Luke 7:14
σοροῦ, gen. sg. f. n. . . . . σορός *(4673)*

(4674) **σός**, σή, σόν, nom. sg. m. 2 pers. possessive
   pron. [§11.3] *thine, yours,* Matt. 7:3, 22,
   et al.; οἱ σοί, *thy kindred, friends,* etc.,
   Mark 5:19; τὸ σόν and τὰ σά, *what is
   thine, thy property, goods,* etc., Matt.
   20:14; 25:25; Luke 6:30

(4675) σοῦ, or enclitic σου, gen. sg. 2 pers. personal
   pron. . . . .   σύ *(4771)*
σουδάρια, acc. pl. neut. n. . . . . σουδάριον *(4676)*

(4676) **σουδάριον**, ου, τό [§3.C.c] (Latin *sudarium*)
   a handkerchief, napkin, etc., Luke 19:20;
   John 11:44, et al.
σουδάριον, acc. sg. neut. n. . . . . . . σουδάριον *(4676)*
σουδαρίῳ, dat. sg. neut. n. . . . .   id.
σούς, acc. pl. m. 2 pers. possessive pron. . σός *(4674)*

(4677) **Σουσάννα**, ης, ἡ, nom. sg. f. n. [§2.3] *Su-
   sanna,* pr. name (Luke 8:3, GNT, TR, WH
   & NA | σωσάννα, MT)

(4678) **σοφία**, ας, ἡ, nom. sg. f. n. [§2.B.b; 2.2] *wisdom* in general, *knowledge,* Matt. 12:42;
   Luke 2:40, 52; 11:31; Acts 7:10; *ability,*
   Luke 21:15; Acts 6:3, 10; practical *wisdom,
   prudence,* Col. 4:5; *learning, science,* Matt.
   13:54; Mark 6:2; Acts 7:22; scientific *skill,*
   1 Cor. 1:17; 2:1; professed *wisdom,* human *philosophy,* 1 Cor. 1:19, 20, 22; 2:4,
   5, 6, et al.; superior *knowledge and enlightenment,* Col. 2:23; in N.T. divine *wisdom,* Rom. 11:33; Eph. 3:10; Col. 2:3;
   revealed *wisdom,* Matt. 11:19; Luke 11:49;
   1 Cor. 1:24, 30; 2:7; Christian *enlightenment,* 1 Cor. 12:8; Eph. 1:8, 17; Col.
   1:9, 28; 3:16; James 1:5; 3:13

σοφίᾳ, dat. sg. f. n. . . . .   σοφία *(4678)*
σοφίαν, acc. sg. f. n. . . . .   id.
σοφίας, gen. sg. f. n. . . . .   id.

(4679) **σοφίζω**, fut. σοφίσω, aor. ἐσόφισα [§26.1] *to
   make wise, enlighten,* 2 Tim. 3:15; mid. *to
   invent skilfully, devise artfully,* pass. 2 Pet.
   1:16
σοφίσαι, aor. act. infin. . . . . σοφίζω *(4679)*
σοφοί, nom. pl. m. adj. . . . . σοφός *(4680)*
σοφοῖς, dat. pl. m. adj. . . . .   id.

(4680) **σοφός**, ή, όν, nom. sg. m. adj. [§7.F.a] *wise*
   generally, 1 Cor. 1:25; *shrewd, sagacious,
   clever,* Rom. 16:19; 1 Cor. 3:10; 6:5;
   learned, intelligent, Matt. 11:25; Rom.
   1:14, 22; 1 Cor. 1:19, 20, 26, 27; 3:18; in
   N.T. divinely *instructed,* Matt. 23:34; *furnished with* Christian *wisdom,* spiritually
   enlightened James 3:13; *all-wise,* Rom.
   16:27; 1 Tim. 1:17; Jude 25
σοφούς, acc. pl. m. adj. . . . . σοφός *(4680)*
σοφῷ, dat. sg. m. adj. . . . .   id.
σοφῶν, gen. pl. m. adj. . . . .   id.
σοφώτερον, nom. sg. neut. compar. adj.
   [§8.1.4] . . . .   id.

(4681) **Σπανία**, ας, ἡ [§2.B.b; 2.2] *Spain*
Σπανίαν, acc. sg. f. n. . . . . Σπανία *(4681)*
σπαράξαν, nom. sg. neut. aor. act.
   part. . . . . σπαράσσω *(4682)*
σπαράξας, nom. sg. m. aor. act. part. (Mark
   9:26, GNT, WH & NA | σπαράξαν, MT
   & TR) . . . .   id.
σπαράσσει, 3 pers. sg. pres. act. indic. . . .   id.

(4682) **σπαράσσω**, or σπαράττω, fut. σπαράξω, aor.
   ἐσπάραξα [§26.3] pr. *to tear, lacerate;* by
   impl. *to agitate greatly, convulse, distort by
   convulsions,* Mark 1:26; 9:20, 26; Luke
   9:39

(4683) **σπαργανόω**, ῶ, fut. σπαργανώσω [§20.T]
   (σπάργανον, *a bandage; swaddling-cloth*)
   to swathe, wrap in swaddling-cloths, Luke
   2:7, 12
σπαρείς, nom. sg. m. 2 aor. pass. part.
   [§27.4.a,b] . . . . σπείρω *(4687)*
σπαρέντες, nom. pl. m. 2 aor. pass. part. .   id.
σπαρῇ, 3 pers. sg. 2 aor. pass. subj. . . . . .   id.
σπασάμενος, nom. sg. m. aor. mid.
   part. . . . . σπάω *(4685)*

(4684) **σπαταλάω**, ῶ, fut. σπαταλήσω [§18.R] (σπα-
   τάλη, *riot, luxury*) *to live luxuriously, vo-
   luptuously, wantonly,* 1 Tim. 5:6; James
   5:5
σπαταλῶσα, nom. sg. f. pres. act.
   part. . . . . σπαταλάω *(4684)*

(4685) **σπάω**, ῶ, fut. σπάσω [§22.2] perf. ἔσπακα,
   aor. mid. ἐσπασάμην, *to draw, pull; to*

draw a sword, Mark 14:47; Acts 16:27

(4686) **σπεῖρα**, ας, or ης, ἡ, nom. sg. f. n. [§2.2] *anything twisted or wreathed, a cord, coil, band, etc.; a band of soldiers, company, troop;* used for a Roman *maniple,* or, *cohort,* Matt. 27:27; Acts 10:1; *the* temple guard, John 18:3, 12

σπεῖραι, aor. act. infin. . . . . σπείρω (4687)
σπεῖραν, acc. sg. f. n. . . . . σπεῖρα (4686)
σπείραντι, dat. sg. m. aor. act. part. (Matt. 13:24, GNT, WH & TRb, NA | σπεί-
ροντι, MT & TRs) . . . . σπείρω (4687)
σπείραντος, gen. sg. m. aor. act. part. (Matt. 13:18, GNT, WH & NA | σπείροντος, MT & TR) . . . . id.
σπείρας, nom. sg. m. aor. act. part. . . . . id.
σπείρει, 3 pers. sg. pres. act. indic. . . . . . id.
σπείρειν, pres. act. infin. . . . . id.
σπείρεις, 2 pers. sg. pres. act. indic. . . . . id.
σπείρεται, 3 pers. sg. pres. pass. indic. . . . id.
σπείρῃ, 3 pers. sg. pres. act. subj. . . . . . . id.
σπείρης, gen. sg. f. n. [§2.2] . . . . σπεῖρα (4686)
σπειρόμενοι, nom. pl. m. pres. pass. part. σπείρω (4687)
σπείροντι, dat. sg. m. pres. act. part. . . . . id.
σπείροντος, gen. sg. m. pres. act. part. (Matt. 13:18, MT & TR | σπείραντος, GNT, WH & NA) . . . . id.
σπείρουσιν, 3 pers. pl. pres. act. indic. . . . id.

(4687) **σπείρω**, fut. σπερῶ, aor. ἔσπειρα [§27.1.c,d] 2 perf. ἔσπορα, 2 aor. pass. ἐσπάρην [§27.5; 27.4.a] *to sow* seed, Matt. 6:26; 13:3, 4, 18, 24, 25, 27, 37, 39; in N.T. used with variety of metaphors, Matt. 13:19; 25:24; 1 Cor. 9:11; 2 Cor. 9:6; Gal. 6:7, et al.

σπείρων, nom. sg. m. pres. act. part. . σπείρω (4687)
σπεκουλάτορα, acc. sg. m. n. (Mark 6:27, GNT, WH, MT & NA | σπεκουλάτωρα, TR) . . . . σπεκουλάτωρ (4688)

(4688) **σπεκουλάτωρ**, ορος, ὁ [§4.2.f] (Latin *speculator*) *a sentinel, life-guardsman,* a kind of soldiers who formed the body-guard of princes, etc., one of whose duties was to put criminals to death, Mark 6:27

σπεκουλάτωρα, acc. sg. m. n. (Mark 6:27, TR | σπεκουλάτορα, GNT, WH, MT & NA) . . . . σπεκουλάτωρ (4688)
σπένδομαι, 1 pers. sg. pres. pass. indic. . . . . σπένδω (4689)

(4689) **σπένδω**, fut. σπείσω [§27.1] *to pour out a libation or drink-offering;* in N.T. mid. *to make a libation of one's self* by expending energy and life in the service of the Gospel, Phil. 2:17; pass. *to be in the act of*

being sacrificed in the cause of the Gospel, 2 Tim. 4:6

(4690) **σπέρμα**, ατος, τό, nom. sg. neut. n. [§4.D.c] *seed,* Matt. 13:24, 27, 37, 38; *semen virile,* Heb. 11:11; *offspring, progeny, posterity,* Matt. 22:24, 25; John 7:42; *a seed* of future generations, Rom. 9:29; in N.T. met. *a seed or principle* of spiritual life, 1 John 3:9 {Matt. 13:38}

σπέρμα, acc. sg. neut. n. {Matt. 13:37} . . . . σπέρμα (4690)
σπέρμασιν, dat. pl. neut. n. . . . . id.
σπέρματι, dat. sg. neut. n. . . . . id.
σπέρματος, gen. sg. neut. n. . . . . id.
σπερμάτων, gen. pl. neut. n. . . . . id.

(4691) **σπερμολόγος**, ον, nom. sg. m. adj. [§7.2] (σπέρμα + λέγω, *to pick*) pr. *seed-picking; one who picks up and retails scraps of information; a babbler,* Acts 17:18

σπεύδοντας, acc. pl. m. pres. act. part. σπεύδω (4692)

(4692) **σπεύδω**, fut. σπεύσω, aor. ἔσπευσα [§23.1.c; 23.2] trans. *to urge on, impel, quicken; to quicken* in idea, *to be eager for the arrival of,* 2 Pet. 3:12; intrans. *to hasten, make haste,* Acts 20:16; 22:18; the part. has the force of an adverb, *quickly, hastily,* Luke 2:16; 19:5, 6

σπεύσαντες, nom. pl. m. aor. act. part. σπεύδω (4692)
σπεύσας, nom. sg. m. aor. act. part. . . . . . id.
σπεῦσον, 2 pers. sg. aor. act. imper. . . . . . id.
σπήλαια, acc. pl. neut. n. . . . . σπήλαιον (4693)
σπηλαίοις, dat. pl. neut. n. . . . . id.

(4693) **σπήλαιον**, ου, τό, nom. sg. neut. n. [§3.C.c] (σπέος, *a cavern*) *a cave, cavern, den* {John 11:38}

σπήλαιον, acc. sg. neut. n. {Matt. 21:13} . . . . σπήλαιον (4693)
σπιλάδες, nom. pl. f. n. . . . . σπιλάς (4694)

(4694) **σπιλάς**, άδος, ἡ [§4.2.c] *a sharply-cleft portion of rock;* in N.T. *a flaw, stigma,* Jude 12

σπίλοι, nom. pl. m. n. (2 Pet. 2:13, GNT, WH & NA | σπῖλοι, MT & TR) . . . . . σπίλος (‡4696)
σπῖλοι, nom. pl. m. n. (2 Pet. 2:13, MT & TR | σπίλοι, GNT, WH & NA) . . . . . id.
σπίλον, acc. sg. m. n. (Eph. 5:27, GNT, WH & NA | σπῖλον, MT & TR) . . . . id.
σπῖλον, acc. sg. m. n. (Eph. 5:27, MT & TR | σπίλος, GNT, WH & NA) . . . . id.

(‡4696) **σπίλος**, and σπῖλος, ου, ὁ [§3.C.a] *a spot, stain, blot;* a moral *blot,* Eph. 5:27; 2 Pet. 2:13

σπιλοῦσα, nom. sg. f. pres. act. part. . σπιλόω (4695)

(4695) **σπιλόω**, ῶ, fut. σπιλώσω [§20.T] *to spot, soil;*

to contaminate, defile, James 3:6; Jude 23

σπλάγχνα, nom. pl. neut. n.
{Philemon 12} . . . . σπλάγχνον *(4698)*

σπλάγχνα, acc. pl. neut. n. {Philemon 20}   id.

(4697) **σπλαγχνίζομαι,** 1 pers. sg. pres. mid./pass.
dep. indic., fut. σπλαγχνίσομαι, aor. pass.
ἐσπλαγχνίσθην [§26.1] *to be moved with
pity or compassion,* Matt. 9:36; 14:14;
20:34; Luke 7:13, et al.; *to compassionate,* Matt. 18:27

σπλαγχνισθείς, nom. sg. m. aor. pass. dep.
part. . . . . σπλαγχνίζομαι *(4697)*

σπλάγχνοις, dat. pl. neut. n. . . . . . σπλάγχνον *(4698)*

(4698) **σπλάγχνον,** ου, τό [§3.C.c] but usually, and
in N.T. only in pl. τὰ σπλάγχνα, ων, *the
chief intestines, viscera; the entrails, bowels,* Acts 1:18; met. *the heart, the affections
of the heart, the tender affections,* Luke
1:78; 2 Cor. 6:12; Phil. 1:8, et al.; meton.
a cherished one, dear as one's self, Philemon 12

σπόγγον, acc. sg. m. n. . . . . σπόγγος *(4699)*

(4699) **σπόγγος,** ου, ὁ [§3.C.a] *a sponge,* Matt.
27:48; Mark 15:36; John 19:29

(4700) **σποδός,** οῦ, ἡ, nom. sg. f. n. [§3.C.b] *ashes,*
Matt. 11:21, et al.

σποδῷ, dat. sg. m. n. . . . . σποδός *(4700)*

(4701) **σπορά,** ᾶς, ἡ [§2.B.b] *a sowing; seed sown;*
met. generative *seed, generation,* 1 Pet. 1:23

σπορᾶς, gen. sg. f. n. . . . . σπορά *(4701)*

(4702) **σπόριμος,** ον [§7.2] *sown, fit to be sown;* in
N.T. τὰ σπόριμα, *fields which are sown,
fields of grain, cornfields,* Matt. 12:1; Mark
2:23; Luke 6:1

σπορίμων, gen. pl. m. adj. . . . . σπόριμος *(4702)*

σπόρον, acc. sg. m. n. . . . . σπόρος *(4703)*

(4703) **σπόρος,** ου, ὁ, nom. sg. m. n. [§3.C.a] *a sowing;* in N.T. *seed, that which is sown,* Mark
4:26, 27; Luke 8:5, 11; met. *the seed sown
in almsgiving,* 2 Cor. 9:10

σπουδάζοντες, nom. pl. m. pres. act.
part. σπουδάζω *(4704)*

(4704) **σπουδάζω,** fut. σπουδάσω and σπουδάσομαι
[§26.1] perf. ἐσπούδακα, aor. ἐσπούδασα,
*to hasten; to be in earnest about, be bent
upon,* Gal. 2:10; *to endeavor earnestly,
strive,* Eph. 4:3, et al.

σπουδαῖον, acc. sg. m. adj. . . . . . . σπουδαῖος *(4705)*

(4705) **σπουδαῖος,** α, ον [§7.1] *earnest, eager, forward,* 2 Cor. 8:17, 22; compar. neut.
σπουδαιότερον, as an adv., *earnestly, sed-
ulously,* 2 Tim. 1:17

σπουδαιότερον, acc. sg. m. compar. adj.
[§8.4] {2 Cor. 8:22} . . . . σπουδαῖος *(4705)*

(4706) **σπουδαιότερον,** acc. sg. neut. compar. adj.

used adverbially (2 Tim. 1:17, MT & TR
| σπουδαίως, GNT, WH & NA)

(4707) **σπουδαιότερος,** nom. sg. m. compar. adj.

(4708) **σπουδαιοτέρως,** compar. adv., *more earnestly*

(4709) **σπουδαίως,** adv., *earnestly, eagerly, diligently,*
Luke 7:4; Tit. 3:13; compar. σπουδαι-
οτέρως, *more earnestly,* Phil. 2:28

σπουδάσατε, 2 pers. pl. aor. act.
imper. . . . . σπεύδω *(4692)*

σπούδασον, 2 pers. sg. aor. act. imper. . . . id.

σπουδάσω, 1 pers. sg. fut. act. indic. . . . . id.

σπουδάσωμεν, 1 pers. pl. aor. act. subj. . . id.

σπουδῇ, dat. sg. f. n. . . . . σπουδή *(4710)*

(4710) **σπουδή,** ῆς, ἡ [§2.B.a] *haste;* μετὰ σπουδῆς,
with haste, hastily, quickly, Mark 6:25;
Luke 1:39; *earnestness, earnest application,
diligence,* Rom. 12:8, 11; 2 Cor. 7:11, 12,
et al.

σπουδήν, acc. sg. f. n. . . . . σπουδή *(4710)*

σπουδῆς, gen. sg. f. n. . . . . id.

σπυρίδας, acc. pl. f. n. (Matt. 15:37; 16:10;
Mark 8:8, GNT, MT, TR & NA |
σφυρίδας, WH) . . . . σπυρίς *(4711)*

σπυρίδι, dat. sg. f. n. (Acts 9:25, GNT, MT,
TR & NA | σφυρίδι, WH) . . . . id.

σπυρίδων, gen. pl. f. n. (Mark 8:20, GNT,
MT, TR & NA | σφυρίδων, WH) . . . . id.

(4711) **σπυρίς,** ίδος, ἡ [§4.2.c] *a basket, hand-basket
for provisions,* Matt. 15:37; 16:10; Mark
8:8, 20; Acts 9:25

(4712) **στάδιον,** ου, τό, pl. στάδια and στάδιοι, pr.
a fixed standard of measure; a stadium, the
eighth part of a Roman mile, and nearly
equal to a furlong, containing 201.45
yards, Luke 24:13, et al.; *a race-course, a
race,* 1 Cor. 9:24

σταδίους, acc. pl. neut. n. . . . . στάδιον *(4712)*

σταδίῳ, dat. sg. neut. n. . . . . id.

σταδίων, gen. pl. neut. n. . . . . id.

σταθείς, nom. sg. m. aor. pass. part.
[§29.6] . . . . ἵστημι *(2476)*

σταθέντα, acc. sg. m. aor. pass. part. . . . . id.

σταθέντες, nom. pl. m. aor. pass. part. . . . id.

σταθῇ, 3 pers. sg. aor. pass. subj. . . . . . . id.

σταθῆναι, aor. pass. infin. . . . . id.

σταθήσεσθε, 2 pers. pl. fut. pass. indic. (Mark
13:9, GNT, WH, TRs & NA | ἀχθή-
σεσθε, TRb) . . . . id.

σταθήσεται, 3 pers. sg. fut. pass. indic. . . id.

σταθῆτε, 2 pers. pl. aor. pass. subj. (Col. 4:12,
GNT, WH & NA | στῆτε, MT & TR) id.

(4713) **στάμνος,** ον, nom. sg. m. adj., *a wine-jar; a
pot, jar, urn, vase*

στάντος, gen. sg. m. 2 aor. act. part. . . ἵστημι *(2476)*

στάς, nom. sg. m. 2 aor. act. part. [§29.X] id.

στᾶσα, nom. sg. f. 2 aor. act. part. .... ἵστημι *(2476)*

στάσει, dat. sg. f. n. .... στάσις *(4714)*

στάσεις, acc. pl. f. n. (Acts 24:5, GNT, WH & NA | στάσιν, MT & TR) .... id.

στάσεως, gen. sg. f. n. .... id.

(‡4955) **στασιαστής**, οῦ, ὁ [§2.B.c] *a partisan*

στασιαστῶν, gen. pl. m. n. (Mark 15:7, GNT, WH & NA | συστασιαστῶν, MT & TR) .... στασιαστής *(‡4955)*

στάσιν, acc. sg. f. n. .... στάσις *(4714)*

(4714) **στάσις**, εως, ἡ, nom. sg. f. n. [§5.E.c] *a setting; a standing; an* effective *position, an* unimpaired *standing or dignity,* Heb. 9:8; *a gathered party, a group;* hence, *a tumultuous assemblage, popular outbreak,* Mark 15:7; Acts 19:40, et al.; *seditious movement,* Acts 24:5; *discord, dispute, dissension,* Acts 15:2; 23:7, 10

(4715) **στατήρ**, ῆρος, ὁ [§4.2.f] (ἵστημι, *to weigh*) pr. *a weight; a stater,* an Attic silver coin, equal in value to the Jewish shekel, or to four Attic or two Alexandrian drachmas, and equivalent to about eighty cents of American money, Matt. 17:27

στατῆρα, acc. sg. m. n. .... στατήρ *(4715)*

σταυρόν, acc. sg. m. n. .... σταυρός *(4716)*

(4716) **σταυρός**, οῦ, ὁ, nom. sg. m. n. [§3.C.a] *a stake; a cross,* Matt. 27:32, 40, 42; Phil. 2:8; by impl. *the punishment of the cross, crucifixion,* Eph. 2:16; Heb. 12:2; meton. *the crucifixion* of Christ in respect of its import, *the doctrine of the cross,* 1 Cor. 1:17, 18; Gal. 5:11; 6:12, 14; met. in the phrases αἴρειν, or βαστάζειν, or λαμβάνειν τὸν σταυρὸν αὑτοῦ, *to take up, or bear one's cross, to be ready to encounter any extremity,* Matt. 10:38; 16:24, et al.

σταυροῦ, gen. sg. m. n. {Matt. 27:40} .... σταυρός *(4716)*

σταύρου, 2 pers. sg. pres. act. imper. (Luke 23:21(2×), GNT, WH & NA | Σταύρωσον, MT & TR) .... σταυρόω *(4717)*

σταυροῦνται, 3 pers. pl. pres. pass. indic. . id.

σταυροῦσι(ν), 3 pers. pl. pres. act. indic. . id.

(4717) **σταυρόω**, ῶ, fut. σταυρώσω [§20.T] aor. ἐσταύρωσα, perf. pass. ἐσταύρωμαι, *to fix stakes;* later, *to crucify, affix to the cross,* Matt. 20:19; 23:34; met. *to crucify, to mortify, to deaden, to make a sacrifice of,* Gal. 5:24; pass. *to be cut off* from a thing, as by a violent death, *to be come dead to,* Gal. 6:14

σταυρῷ, dat. sg. m. n. .... σταυρός *(4716)*

σταυρωθῇ, 3 pers. sg. aor. pass. subj. σταυρόω *(4717)*

σταυρωθῆναι, aor. pass. infin. .... id.

σταυρωθήτω, 3 pers. sg. aor. pass. imper. .... σταυρόω *(4717)*

σταυρῶσαι, aor. act. infin. .... id.

σταυρώσαντες, nom. pl. m. aor. act. part. id.

σταυρώσατε, 2 pers. pl. aor. act. imper. .. id.

σταυρώσετε, 2 pers. pl. fut. act. indic. ... id.

σταύρωσον, 2 pers. sg. aor. act. imper. ... id.

σταυρώσω, 1 pers. sg. fut. act. indic. .... id.

σταυρώσωσιν, 3 pers. pl. aor. act. subj. .. id.

σταφυλαί, nom. pl. f. n. (Rev. 14:18, GNT, WH, TR & NA | σταφυλή, MT) σταφυλή *(4718)*

σταφυλάς, acc. pl. f. n. (Matt. 7:16, GNT, WH & NA | σταφυλήν, MT & TR) .. id.

(4718) **σταφυλή**, ῆς, ἡ, nom. sg. f. n. [§2.B.a] (σταφίς, *a raisin*) *a cluster or bunch of grapes,* Matt. 7:16; Luke 6:44 (Rev. 14:18, MT | σταφυλαί, GNT, WH, TR & NA)

σταφυλήν, acc. sg. f. n. .... σταφυλή *(4718)*

στάχυας, acc. pl. m. n. .... στάχυς *(4719)*

στάχυϊ, dat. sg. m. n. .... id.

στάχυν, acc. sg. m. n. {Mark 4:28} ..... id.

Στάχυν, acc. sg. m. n. {Rom. 16:9} ... Στάχυς *(4720)*

(4719) **στάχυς**, υος, ὁ [§5.E.g] *an ear of corn,* Matt. 12:1; Mark 2:23; 4:28; Luke 6:1

(4720) **Στάχυς**, υος, ὁ, *Stachys,* pr. name

στέγει, 3 pers. sg. pres. act. indic. ..... στέγω *(4722)*

(4721) **στέγη**, ης, ἡ [§2.B.a] *a roof, flat roof* of a house, Matt. 8:8; Mark 2:4; Luke 7:6

στέγην, acc. sg. f. n. .... στέγη *(4721)*

στέγομεν, 1 pers. pl. pres. act. indic. ... στέγω *(4722)*

στέγοντες, nom. pl. m. pres. act. part. ... id.

(4722) **στέγω**, fut. στέξω [§23.1.b] *to cover; to hold off, to hold in;* hence, *to hold out against, to endure patiently,* 1 Cor. 9:12; 13:7; absol. *to contain one's self,* 1 Thess. 3:1, 5

στέγων, nom. sg. m. pres. act. part. ... στέγω *(4722)*

(†4723) **στεῖρα**, ας, ἡ, nom. sg. f. n., *barren, incapable of bearing children* {Luke 1:7}

στεῖρα, voc. sg. f. n. {Gal. 4:27} .... στεῖρα *(†4723)*

στείρᾳ, dat. sg. f. n. .... id.

στεῖραι, nom. pl. f. n. .... id.

(4723) **στεῖρος**, α, ον [§7.1] *sterile; barren, not bearing children,* Luke 1:7, 36; 23:29; Gal. 4:27

στέλλεσθαι, pres. mid. infin. .... στέλλω *(4724)*

στελλόμενοι, nom. pl. m. pres. mid. part. id.

(4724) **στέλλω**, fut. στελῶ, perf. ἔσταλκα [§27.1.b; 27.2.b] aor. ἔστειλα [§27.1.d] pr. *to place in set order, to arrange; to equip; to despatch; to stow; to contract;* mid. *to contract one's self, to shrink; to withdraw from, avoid, shun,* 2 Cor. 8:20; 2 Thess. 3:6

(4725) **στέμμα**, ατος, τό [§4.D.c] (στέφω, *to encircle*) *a crown; a fillet, wreath,* Acts 14:13

στέμματα, acc. pl. neut. n. . . . . στέμμα *(4725)*
στεναγμοῖς, dat. pl. m. n. . . . . στεναγμός *(4726)*
(4726) **στεναγμός,** οῦ, ὁ [§3.C.a] *a sighing, groaning,*
    groan, Acts 7:34; an inward *sighing, as-*
    piration, Rom. 8:26
στεναγμοῦ, gen. sg. m. n. . . . . . . στεναγμός *(4726)*
στενάζετε, 2 pers. pl. pres. act.
    imper. . . . . στενάζω *(4727)*
στενάζομεν, 1 pers. pl. pres. act. indic. . . . id.
στενάζοντες, nom. pl. m. pres. act. part. . id.
(4727) **στενάζω,** fut. στενάξω, aor. ἐστέναξα [§26.2]
    to groan, sigh, Rom. 8:23; 2 Cor. 5:2, 4;
    Heb. 13:17; *to sigh* inwardly, Mark 7:34;
    to give vent to querulous or censorious feel-
    ings, James 5:9
στενή, nom. sg. f. adj. . . . . στενός *(4728)*
στενῆς, gen. sg. f. adj. . . . . id.
(4728) **στενός,** ή, όν [§7.F.a] *narrow, strait,* Matt.
    7:13, 14; Luke 13:24
στενοχωρεῖσθε, 2 pers. pl. pres. pass.
    indic. . . . . στενοχωρέω *(4729)*
(4729) **στενοχωρέω,** ῶ, fut. στενοχωρήσω [§16.P]
    (στενός + χώρα) *to crowd together into*
    a narrow place, straiten; pass. met. *to be*
    in straits, to be cooped up, to be cramped
    from action, 2 Cor. 4:8; *to be cramped* in
    feeling, 2 Cor. 6:12
(4730) **στενοχωρία,** ας, ἡ, nom. sg. f. n. [§2.B.b; 2.2]
    pr. *narrowness of place, a narrow place;*
    met. *straits, distress, anguish,* Rom. 2:9;
    8:35; 2 Cor. 6:4; 12:10
στενοχωρίαις, dat. pl. f. n. . . . . . . στενοχωρία *(4730)*
στενοχωρούμενοι, nom. pl. m. pres. pass.
    part. . . . . στενοχωρέω *(4729)*
στερεά, nom. sg. f. adj. . . . . στερεός *(4731)*
στερεᾶς, gen. sg. f. adj. . . . . id.
στερεοί, nom. pl. f. adj. . . . . id.
(4731) **στερεός,** ά, όν, nom. sg. m. adj. [§7.1]
    (perhaps kindred with ἵστημι) *stiff, hard;*
    of food, *solid,* as opposed to what is liq-
    uid and light, Heb. 5:12; *firm, steadfast,*
    2 Tim. 2:19; 1 Pet. 5:9
(4732) **στερεόω,** ῶ, fut. στερεώσω, aor. ἐστερέωσα
    [§20.T] *to render firm; to strengthen,* Acts
    3:7, 16; *to settle,* Acts 16:5
(4733) **στερέωμα,** ατος, τό [§4.D.c] pr. *what is solid*
    and firm; met. *firmness, steadfastness, con-*
    stancy, Col. 2:5
στερέωμα, acc. sg. neut. n. . . . . στερέωμα *(4733)*
Στεφανᾶ, gen. sg. m. n. . . . . Στεφανᾶς *(4734)*
(4734) **Στεφανᾶς,** ᾶ, ὁ [§2.4] *Stephanas,* pr. name
στέφανοι, nom. pl. m. n. . . . . στέφανος *(4735)*
στέφανον, acc. sg. m. n. {Matt. 27:29} . . id.
Στέφανον, acc. sg. m. n. {Acts 6:5} Στέφανος *(4736)*
(4735) **στέφανος,** ου, ὁ, nom. sg. m. n. [§3.C.a]

(στέφω, *to encircle*) *that which forms an*
    encirclement; a crown, Matt. 27:29; Rev.
    4:4, 10; *a chaplet, wreath,* conferred on a
    victor in the public games, 1 Cor. 9:25;
    met. *a crown, reward, prize,* 2 Tim. 4:8;
    James 1:12; *a crown, ornament, honor,*
    glory {Phil. 4:1}
(4736) **Στέφανος,** ου, ὁ, nom. sg. m. n. *Stephanus,*
    Stephen, pr. name {Acts 6:8}
Στεφάνου, gen. sg. m. n. . . . . Στέφανος *(4736)*
στεφάνους, acc. pl. m. n. . . . . στέφανος *(4735)*
στεφανοῦται, 3 pers. sg. pres. pass. indic.
    [§21.U] . . . . στεφανόω *(4737)*
(4737) **στεφανόω,** ῶ, fut. στεφανώσω, aor.
    ἐστεφάνωσα [§20.T] *to encompass; to*
    crown; to crown as victor in the games,
    2 Tim. 2:5; met. *to crown, adorn, deco-*
    rate, Heb. 2:7, 9
Στεφάνῳ, dat. sg. m. n. . . . . Στέφανος *(4736)*
στήθη, acc. pl. neut. n. . . . . στῆθος *(4738)*
στῆθι, 2 pers. sg. 2 aor. act. imper.
    [§29.2] . . . . ἵστημι *(2476)*
(4738) **στῆθος,** ους, τό, and pl. τὰ στήθη [§5.E.b]
    the breast, Luke 18:13; 23:48; John 13:25,
    et al.
στῆθος, acc. s. neut. n. . . . . στῆθος *(4738)*
στήκει, 3 pers. sg. pres. act. indic. . . . . στήκω *(4739)*
στήκετε, 2 pers. pl. pres. act. indic.
    {Phil. 1:27} . . . . id.
στήκετε, 2 pers. pl. pres. act. imper.
    {Phil. 4:1} . . . . id.
στήκητε, 2 pers. pl. pres. act. subj. (1 Thess.
    3:8, TR | στήκετε, GNT, MT, WH &
    NA) . . . . id.
στήκοντες, nom. pl. m. pres. act. part. (Mark
    3:31, GNT, WH & NA | ἑστῶτες, MT
    & TR) . . . . id.
(4739) **στήκω,** a late equivalent to ἕστηκα, *to stand,*
    Mark 11:25; met. *to stand* when under
    judgment, *to be approved,* Rom. 14:4; *to*
    stand firm, be constant, persevere, 1 Cor.
    16:13, et al.
στῆναι, 2 aor. act. infin. [§29.X] . . . . . ἵστημι *(2476)*
(4740) **στηριγμός,** οῦ, ὁ [§3.C.a] pr. *a fixing, settling;*
    a state of firmness, fixedness; met. *firm-*
    ness of belief, *settle frame* of mind, 2 Pet.
    3:17
στηριγμοῦ, gen. sg. m. n. . . . . στηριγμός *(4740)*
(4741) **στηρίζω,** fut. στηρίξω, aor. ἐστήριξα [§26.2]
    to set fast; to set in a certain position or
    direction, Luke 9:51; met. *to render* mentally
    steadfast, *to settle, confirm,* Luke 22:32;
    Rom. 1:11, et al.; perf. pass. ἐστήριγμαι,
    to stand immovable, Luke 16:26; met. *to*
    be mentally *settled,* 2 Pet. 1:12

στηρίζων, nom. sg. m. pres. act. part. (Acts
 18:23, WH | ἐπιστηρίζων, GNT, MT, TR
 & NA) . . . . στηρίζω *(4741)*
στηρίξαι, aor. act. infin. {1 Thess. 3:2} στηρίζω *(4741)*
στηρίξαι, 3 pers. sg. aor. act. opt.
 {2 Thess. 2:17} . . . . id.
στηρίξατε, 2 pers. pl. aor. act. imper. . . . . id.
στηρίξει, 3 pers. sg. fut. act. indic. . . . . . . id.
στήριξον, 2 pers. sg. aor. act. imper. (Rev. 3:2,
 TR | στήρισον, GNT, WH & NA |
 τήρησον, MT | Luke 22:32, MT & TR
 | στήρισον, GNT, WH & NA) . . . . . . id.
στήρισον, 2 pers. sg. aor. act. imper. (Luke
 22:32, GNT, WH & NA | στήριξον, MT
 & TR | Rev. 3:2, GNT, WH & NA |
 στήριξον, MT & TR) . . . . id.
στηριχθῆναι, aor. pass. infin. . . . . id.
στῆσαι, aor. act. infin. . . . . ἵστημι *(2476)*
στήσαντες, nom. pl. m. aor. act. part. . . . id.
στήσει, 3 pers. sg. fut. act. indic. . . . . id.
στήσῃ, 3 pers. sg. aor. act. subj. . . . . id.
στήσῃς, 2 pers. sg. aor. act. subj. . . . . id.
στήσητε, 2 pers. pl. aor. act. subj. (Mark 7:9,
 GNT & NA | τηρήσητε, MT, TR &
 WH) . . . . id.
στήσονται, 3 pers. pl. fut. mid. dep. indic. id.
στῆτε, 2 pers. pl. 2 aor. act. subj. [§29.3] (Col.
 4:12, MT & TR | σταθῆτε, GNT, WH &
 NA) . . . . id.
στῆτε, 2 pers. pl. 2 aor. act. imper.
 {Eph. 6:14} . . . . id.
στιβάδας, acc. pl. f. n. (Mark 11:8, GNT, WH
 & NA | στοιβάδας, MT & TR) . . στιβάς *(‡4746)*
(‡4746) **στιβάς**, άδος, ἡ, *a stuffing of leaves, boughs,*
 etc.; meton. *a bough, branch*
(4742) **στίγμα**, ατος, τό [§4.D.c] (στίζω, *to prick; to*
 burn in marks, brand) a brand-mark
στίγματα, acc. pl. neut. n. . . . . στίγμα *(4742)*
(4743) **στιγμή**, ῆς, ἡ [§2.B.a] (στίζω) pr. *a point;* met.
 a point of time, *moment, instant*
στιγμῇ, dat. sg. f. n. . . . . στιγμή *(4743)*
στίλβοντα, nom. pl. neut. pres. act.
 part. . . . . στίλβω *(4744)*
(4744) **στίλβω**, fut. στίλψω [§23.1.a] *to shine, glisten*
(4745) **στοά**, ᾶς, ἡ [§2.B.b; 2.2] *a colonnade, piazza,*
 cloister, covered walk supported by col-
 umns, John 5:2; 10:23; Acts 3:11; 5:12
στοᾷ, dat. sg. f. n. . . . . στοά *(4745)*
στοάς, acc. pl. f. n. . . . . id.
στοιβάδας, acc. pl. f. n. (Mark 11:8, MT &
 TR | στιβάδας, GNT, WH &
 NA) . . . . στοιβάς *(4746)*
(4746) **στοιβάς**, άδος, ἡ [§4.2.c] (στείβω, *to tread*)
 a stuffing of leaves, boughs, etc.; meton.
 a bough, branch

(‡4770) **Στοϊκός**, η, όν, *Stoic*
Στοϊκῶν, gen. pl. m. adj. (Acts 17:18, GNT,
 MT & NA | Στωϊκῶν, TR | Στωικῶν,
 WH) . . . . Στοϊκός *(‡4770)*
στοιχεῖα, nom. pl. neut. n.
 {2 Pet. 3:10, 12} . . . . στοιχεῖον *(4747)*
στοιχεῖα, acc. pl. neut. n. {Gal. 4:3} . . . . id.
στοιχεῖν, pres. act. infin. . . . . στοιχέω *(4748)*
(4747) **στοιχεῖον**, ου, τό [§3.C.c] (dimin. of στοῖχος,
 a row, a straight rod or rule, from στείχω,
 to go in a straight line) *an element; an el-*
 ement of the natural universe, 2 Pet.
 3:10, 12; *an element or rudiment* of any intellectual or religious system, Gal. 4:3, 9;
 Col. 2:8, 20; Heb. 5:12
στοιχεῖς, 2 pers. sg. pres. act. indic. . . στοιχέω *(4748)*
στοιχείων, gen. pl. neut. n. . . . . στοιχεῖον *(4747)*
(4748) **στοιχέω**, ῶ, fut. στοιχήσω [§16.P] (στοῖχος,
 a row) pr. *to advance in a line;* met. *to*
 frame one's conduct by a certain rule, Acts
 21:24; Rom. 4:12; Gal. 5:25; 6:16; Phil.
 3:16
στοιχήσουσιν, 3 pers. pl. fut. act.
 indic. . . . . στοιχέω *(4748)*
στοιχοῦσι(ν), dat. pl. m. pres. act. part. . . id.
στοιχῶμεν, 1 pers. pl. pres. act. subj. . . . id.
στολαί, nom. pl. f. n. (Rev. 6:11, MT & TR
 | στολή, GNT, WH & NA) . . . . στολή *(4749)*
στολαῖς, dat. pl. f. n. . . . . id.
στολάς, acc. pl. f. n. . . . . id.
(4749) **στολή**, ῆς, ἡ, nom. sg. f. n. [§2.B.a]
 equipment; dress; a long garment, flowing
 robe, worn by priests, kings, and persons
 of distinction, Matt. 12:38; 16:5, et al.
 (Rev. 6:11, GNT, WH & NA | στολαί,
 MT & TR)
στολήν, acc. sg. f. n. . . . . στολή *(4749)*
(4750) **στόμα**, ατος, τό, nom. sg. neut. n. [§4.D.c]
 the mouth, Matt. 12:34; 15:11, 17, 18;
 21:16, et al.; *speech, words,* Matt. 18:16;
 2 Cor. 13:1; *command of speech, facility*
 of language, Luke 21:15; from the Hebrew,
 ἀνοίγειν τὸ στόμα, *to make utterance, to*
 speak, Matt. 5:2; 13:35, et al.; also, used
 of the earth, *to rend, yawn,* Rev. 12:16;
 στόμα πρὸς στόμα λαλεῖν, *to speak*
 mouth to mouth, face to face, 2 John 12;
 3 John 14; *the edge or point* of a weapon,
 Luke 21:24; Heb. 11:34 {Rev. 13:2}
στόμα, acc. sg. neut. n. {Rev. 12:16} . . . στόμα *(4750)*
στόματα, acc. pl. neut. n. . . . . id.
στόματι, dat. sg. neut. n. . . . . id.
στόματος, gen. sg. neut. n. . . . . id.
στομάτων, gen. pl. neut. n. . . . . id.
στόμαχον, acc. sg. m. n. . . . . στόμαχος *(4751)*

(4751) **στόμαχος**, ου, ὁ [§3.C.a] pr. *the gullet* leading to the stomach; hence, *later, the stomach* itself, 1 Tim. 5:23

(4752) **στρατεία**, ας, ἡ [§2.B.b; 2.2] *a military expedition, campaign;* and genr. *military service, warfare;* met. *the Christian warfare,* 2 Cor. 10:4; 1 Tim. 1:18

στρατείαν, acc. sg. f. n. . . . . στρατεία (4752)
στρατείας, gen. sg. f. n. . . . . id.
στρατεύεται, 3 pers. sg. pres. mid. indic. [§15.O] . . . . στρατεύω (†4754)
στρατεύῃ, 2 pers. sg. pres. mid. subj. . . . . id.

(4753) **στράτευμα**, ατος, τό [§4.D.c] *an army,* Matt. 22:7, et al.; *an armed force, corps,* Acts 23:10, 27; *troops, guards,* Luke 23:11

στράτευμα, acc. sg. neut. n. . . . . . στράτευμα (4753)
στρατεύμασιν, dat. pl. neut. n. . . . . id.
στρατεύματα, nom. pl. neut. n. {Rev. 19:14} id.
στρατεύματα, acc. pl. neut. n. {Rev. 19:19} id.
στρατεύματι, dat. sg. neut. n. . . . . id.
στρατεύματος, gen. sg. neut. n. . . . . id.
στρατευμάτων, gen. pl. neut. n. . . . . id.
στρατευόμεθα, 1 pers. pl. pres. mid. indic. . . . . στρατεύω (†4754)
στρατευόμενοι, nom. pl. m. pres. mid. part. id.
στρατευόμενος, nom. sg. m. pres. mid. part. id.
στρατευομένων, gen. pl. f. pres. mid. part. id.
στρατεύονται, 3 pers. pl. pres. mid. indic. id.

(†4754) **στρατεύω**, fut. στρατεύσω [§13.M] and mid. στρατεύομαι (στρατός, *an army*) *to perform military duty, serve as a soldier,* Luke 3:14; 1 Cor. 9:7; 2 Tim. 2:4; *to battle,* James 4:1; 1 Pet. 2:11; *to be* spiritually *militant,* 2 Cor. 10:3; 1 Tim. 1:18

στρατηγοί, nom. pl. m. n. . . . . . . στρατηγός (4755)
στρατηγοῖς, dat. pl. m. n. . . . . id.

(4755) **στρατηγός**, οῦ, ὁ, nom. sg. m. n. [§3.C.c] (στρατός + ἄγω) *a leader or commander of an army, general; a* Roman *praetor, provincial magistrate,* Acts 16:20, 22, 35, 36, 38; στρατηγὸς τοῦ ἱεροῦ, *the captain or prefect of the temple,* the chief of the Levites who kept guard in and around the temple, Luke 22:4, 52; Acts 4:1; 5:24, 26

στρατηγούς, acc. pl. m. n. . . . . . . στρατηγός (4755)

(4756) **στρατιά**, ᾶς, ἡ [§2.B.b; 2.2] (στρατός) *an army, host;* from the Hebrew, στρατιὰ οὐράνιος, or τοῦ οὐρανοῦ, *the heavenly host,* the host of heaven, the hosts of angels, Luke 2:13; *the stars,* Acts 7:42

στρατιᾷ, dat. sg. f. n. . . . . στρατιά (4756)
στρατιᾶς, gen. sg. f. n. . . . . id.
στρατιῶται, nom. pl. m. n. . . . . . στρατιώτης (4757)
στρατιώταις, dat. pl. m. n. . . . . id.
στρατιώτας, acc. pl. m. n. . . . . id.

στρατιώτῃ, dat. sg. m. n. . . . . . . στρατιώτης (4757)
στρατιώτην, acc. sg. m. n. . . . . id.

(4757) **στρατιώτης**, ου, ὁ, nom. sg. m. n. [§2.B.c] *a soldier,* Matt. 8:9; 27:27, et al.; met. *a soldier* of Christ, 2 Tim. 2:3

στρατιωτῶν, gen. pl. m. n. . . . . . στρατιώτης (4757)

(4758) **στρατολογέω**, ῶ, fut. στρατολογήσω [§16.P] (στρατός + λέγω) *to collect or levy an army, enlist troops*

στρατολογήσαντι, dat. sg. m. aor. act. part. . . . . στρατολογέω (4758)
στρατοπεδάρχῃ, dat. sg. m. n. (Acts 28:16, TR | στρατοπεδάρχῳ, MT | GNT, WH & NA omit) . . . . στρατοπεδάρχης (4759)

(4759) **στρατοπεδάρχης**, ου, ὁ [§2.B.c] (στρατόπεδον + ἄρχω) *a commandant of a camp; legionary tribune;* perhaps, *the prefect of the praetorian camp;,* Acts 28:16

(†4759) **στρατοπέδαρχος**, ου, ὁ, *a military commander*

στρατοπεδάρχῳ, dat. sg. m. n. (Acts 28:16, MT | στρατοπεδάρχῃ, TR | GNT, WH & NA omit) . . . . στρατοπέδαρχος (†4759)

(4760) **στρατόπεδον**, ου, τό [§3.C.c] (στρατός + πέδον, *ground, plain*) pr. *the site of an encampment; an encampment;* meton. *an army,* Luke 21:20

στρατοπέδων, gen. pl. neut. n. . . στρατόπεδον (4760)
στραφείς, nom. sg. m. 2 aor. pass. part. [§24.10] . . . . στρέφω (4762)
στραφεῖσα, nom. sg. f. 2 aor. pass. part. . id.
στραφέντες, nom. pl. m. 2 aor. pass. part. id.
στραφῆτε, 2 pers. pl. 2 aor. pass. subj. . . . id.
στραφῶσιν, 3 pers. pl. 2 aor. pass. subj. (John 12:40, GNT, WH & NA | ἐπιστραφῶσι(ν), MT & TR) . . . . id.
στρεβλοῦσιν, 3 pers. pl. pres. act. indic. . . . . στρεβλόω (4761)

(4761) **στρεβλόω**, ῶ, fut. στρεβλώσω [§20.T] (στρεβλή, *a windlass, a wrench, instrument of torture, rack*) pr. *to distort* the limbs *on a rack;* met. *to wrench, distort, pervert*

στρέφειν, pres. act. infin. . . . . στρέφω (4762)
στρεφόμεθα, 1 pers. pl. pres. pass. indic. . id.

(4762) **στρέφω**, fut. στρέψω, aor. ἔστρεψα [§23.1.a; 23.2] 2 aor. pass. ἐστράφην [§24.10] *to twist; to turn,* Matt. 5:39; *to make a change* of substance, *to change,* Rev. 11:6; absol. *to change or turn* one's course of dealing, Acts 7:42; mid. *to turn one's self about,* Matt. 16:23; Luke 7:9, et al.; *to turn back,* Acts 7:39; *to change one's direction, to turn* elsewhere, Acts 13:46; *to change one's course of principle and conduct, to* *be converted,* Matt. 18:3

στρέψον, 2 pers. sg. aor. act. imper. . . στρέφω *(4762)*

στρηνιάσαντες, nom. pl. m. aor. act.
part. . . . . στρηνιάω *(4763)*

(4763) **στρηνιάω, ῶ,** fut. στρηνιάσω [§22.2] *to be wanton, to revel, riot,* Rev. 18:7, 9

(4764) **στρῆνος,** ους, τό [§5.E.b] (στρηνής, *strong, hard) headstrong pride; wantonness, luxury, voluptuousness,* Rev. 18:3

στρήνους, gen. sg. neut. n. . . . . στρῆνος *(4764)*

στρουθία, nom. pl. neut. n. . . . . . . στρουθίον *(4765)*

(4765) **στρουθίον,** ου, τό [§3.C.c] (dimin. of στρουθός) *any small bird,* spc. *a sparrow,* Matt. 10:29, 31; Luke 12:6, 7

στρουθίων, gen. pl. neut. n. . . . . . . στρουθίον *(4765)*

(4766) **στρώννυμι,** or στρωννύω, fut. στρώσω, aor. ἔστρωσα, perf. pass. ἔστρωμαι [§36.5] (by metath. for στορέννυμι) *to spread, to strew,* Matt. 21:8; Mark 11:8; *to spread* a couch, Acts 9:34; used of a supper-chamber, pass. *to have the couches spread, to be prepared, furnished,* Mark 14:15; Luke 22:12

στρῶσον, 2 pers. sg. aor. act.
imper. . . . . στρώννυμι *(4766)*

στυγητοί, nom. pl. m. adj. . . . . . . στυγητός *(†4767)*

(†4767) **στυγητός,** ή, όν, and ός, όν (στυγέω, *to hate) hateful, odious, detested*

(4768) **στυγνάζω,** fut. στυγνάσω, aor. ἐστύγνασα [§26.1] (στυγνός, *gloomy) to put on a gloomy and downcast look,* Mark 10:22; of the sky, *to lower,* Matt. 16:3

στυγνάζων, nom. sg. m. pres. act.
part. . . . . στυγνάζω *(4768)*

στυγνάσας, nom. sg. m. aor. act. part. . . . id.

στῦλοι, nom. pl. m. n. . . . . στῦλος *(†4769)*

στῦλον, acc. sg. m. n. . . . . id.

(†4769) **στῦλος,** ου, ὁ, nom. sg. m. n. [§3.C.a] *a pillar, column,* Rev. 10:1; used of persons of authority, influence, etc., *a support or pillar* of the Church, Gal. 2:9; Rev. 3:12; *a support* of true doctrine, 1 Tim. 3:15

(4770) **Στωϊκός,** ή, όν [§7.F.a] *stoic, belonging to the sect of the Stoics,* founded by Zeno, and deriving their name from the *portico,* στοά, where he taught

Στωϊκῶν, gen. pl. m. adj. (Acts 17:18, TR | Στωικῶν, WH | Στοϊκῶν, GNT, MT, NA) . . . . Στωϊκός *(4770)*

(4771) **σύ,** nom. sg. 2 pers. personal pronoun, gen. σοῦ, dat. σοί, acc. σέ, and enclitic σου, σοι, σε, pl. ὑμεῖς [§11.K.b] *thou,* Matt. 1:20; 2:6 et al. freq.

(4772) **συγγένεια,** ας, ἡ [§2.B.b; 2.2] *kindred; kinsfolk, kinsmen, relatives,* Luke 1:61; Acts 7:3, 14

συγγενείᾳ, dat. sg. f. n. (Luke 1:61, MT & TR | συγγενείας, GNT, WH & NA) . . . . συγγένεια *(4772)*

συγγένειαν, acc. sg. f. n. . . . . id.

συγγενείας, gen. sg. f. n. . . . . id.

συγγενεῖς, nom. pl. m. adj.
{Luke 1:58} . . . . συγγενής *(4773)*

συγγενεῖς, acc. pl. m. adj. {Luke 14:12} . . id.

συγγενέσι(ν), dat. pl. m. adj. (Mark 6:4; Luke 2:44, MT & TR | συγγενεῦσιν, GNT, WH & NA) . . . . id.

συγγενεῦσιν, dat. pl. m. adj. (Mark 6:4; Luke 2:44, GNT, WH & NA | συγγενέσι(ν), MT & TR) . . . . id.

συγγενῆ, acc. sg. m. adj. . . . . id.

(4773) **συγγενής,** ές, nom. sg. m. adj. [§7.G.b] (σύν + γένος) *kindred, akin;* as a subst. *a kinsman or kinswoman, relative;* Mark 6:4; Luke 1:36, 58, et al.; *one nationally akin, a fellow-countryman,* Rom. 9:3 {John 18:26}

συγγενής, nom. sg. f. adj. (Luke 1:36, MT & TR | συγγενίς, GNT, WH & NA) . . . . συγγενής *(4773)*

(†4773) **συγγενίς,** ίδος, ἡ, nom. sg. f. n., *a kinswoman* (Luke 1:36, GNT, WH & NA | συγγενής, MT & TR)

συγγενῶν, gen. pl. m. adj. . . . . συγγενής *(4773)*

(4774) **συγγνώμη,** ης, ἡ [§2.B.a] (συγγινώσκω, *to agree in judgment with) pardon; concession, leave, permission,* 1 Cor. 7:6

συγγνώμην, acc. sg. f. n. . . . . συγγνώμη *(4774)*

(4775) **συγκάθημαι** (σύν + κάθημαι) *to sit in company with,* Mark 14:54; Acts 26:30

συγκαθήμενοι, nom. pl. m. pres. mid./pass. dep. part. (Acts 26:30, GNT, MT, TR & NA | συνκαθήμενοι, WH) . . . συγκάθημαι *(4775)*

συγκαθήμενος, nom. sg. m. pres. mid./pass. dep. part. (Mark 14:54, GNT, MT, TR & NA | συνκαθήμενος, WH) . . . . id.

(4776) **συγκαθίζω,** fut. συγκαθίσω [§26.1] (σύν + καθίζω) trans. *to cause to sit with, seat in company with,* Eph. 2:6; intrans. *to sit in company with; to sit down together,* Luke 22:55

συγκαθισάντων, gen. pl. m. aor. act. part. (Luke 22:55, GNT, MT, TR & NA | συνκαθισάντων, WH) . . . . συγκαθίζω *(4776)*

(4777) **συγκακοπαθέω, ῶ,** fut. συγκακοπαθήσω [§16.P] (σύν + κακοπαθέω) *to suffer evils along with* any one; *to be enduringly adherent,* 2 Tim. 1:8

συγκακοπάθησον, 2 pers. sg. aor. act. imper. (2 Tim. 1:8, GNT, MT, TR & NA | συνκακοπάθησον, WH) . . συγκακοπαθέω *(4777)*

συγκακουχεῖσθαι, pres. mid./pass. dep. infin.

(Heb. 11:25, GNT, MT, TR & NA |
συνκακουχεῖσθαι, WH) . συγκακουχέομαι (†4778)

(†4778) **συγκακουχέομαι, οῦμαι** (σύν + κακουχέω)
to encounter adversity along with any one
συγκαλεῖ, 3 pers. sg. pres. act. indic. (Luke
15:6, 9, GNT & NA | συνκαλεῖ, WH |
Luke 15:6, συνκαλεῖται, MT & TR | Luke
15:9, συνκαλεῖ, MT & TR) . . . συγκαλέω (4779)
συγκαλεῖται, 3 pers. sg. pres. mid. indic. (Luke
15:9, MT & TR | συγκαλεῖ, GNT & NA
| συνκαλεῖ, WH) . . . . id.
συγκαλεσάμενος, nom. sg. m. aor. mid. part.
(Luke 9:1; 23:13; Acts 10:24, GNT, MT,
TR & NA | συνκαλεσάμενος, WH) . . id.
συγκαλέσασθαι, aor. mid. infin. (Acts 28:17,
GNT, MT, TR & NA | συνκαλέσασθαι,
WH) . . . . id.

(4779) **συγκαλέω, ῶ,** fut. συγκαλέσω [§22.1] (σύν
+ καλέω) *to call together, convoke,* Mark
15:16; mid. *to call around one's self,* Luke
9:1, et al.
συγκαλοῦσιν, 3 pers. pl. pres. act. indic.
(Mark 15:16, GNT, MT, TR & NA |
συνκαλοῦσιν, WH) . . . . συγκαλέω (4779)

(4780) **συγκαλύπτω,** fut. συγκαλύψω, perf. pass.
συγκεκάλυμμαι [§23.1.a; 23.7] (σύν +
καλύπτω) *to cover altogether, to cover up;*
met. *to conceal,* Luke 12:2

(4781) **συγκάμπτω,** fut. συγκάμψω [§23.1.a] (σύν +
κάμπτω) *to bend or bow together; to bow
down* the back of any one afflictively, Rom.
11:10
σύγκαμψον, 2 pers. sg. aor. act. imper. (Rom.
11:10, GNT, MT, TR & NA | σύνκαμ-
ψον, WH) . . . . συγκάμπτω (4781)

(4782) **συγκαταβαίνω,** fut. συγκαταβήσομαι [§37.1]
(σύν + καταβαίνω) *to go down with* anyone
συγκαταβάντες, nom. pl. m. 2 aor. act. part.
(Acts 25:5, GNT, MT, TR & NA | συν-
καταβάντες, WH) . . . . συγκαταβαίνω (4782)

(4783) **συγκατάθεσις, εως, ἡ,** nom. sg. f. n. [§5.E.c]
assent; in N.T. *accord, alliance* (2 Cor.
6:16, GNT, MT, TR & NA | συνκατά-
θεσις, WH)
συγκατατεθειμένος, nom. sg. m. perf.
mid./pass. dep. part. (Luke 23:51, GNT,
MT, TR & NA | συνκατατεθειμένος,
WH) . . . . συγκατατίθημι (†4784)

(†4784) **συγκατατίθημι** (σύν + κατατίθημι) *to set
down together with;* mid. *to assent, accord*

(4785) **συγκαταψηφίζω,** fut. συγκαταψηφίσω [§26.1]
(σύν, καταψηφίζω, ψῆφος) *to count, number with*
συγκατεψηφίσθη, 3 pers. sg. aor. pass. indic.
(Acts 1:26, GNT, MT, TR & NA |

συνκαταψηφίζω, WH) . . . συγκαταψηφίζω (4785)
συγκεκαλυμμένον, nom. sg. neut. perf. pass.
part. . . . . συγκαλύπτω (4780)
συγκεκερασμένους, acc. pl. m. perf. pass.
part. (Heb. 4:2, GNT & NA | συγκε-
κραμένος, TR | συνκεκραμένους, MT |
συνκεκερασμένους, WH) . . συγκεράννυμι (4786)
συγκεκλεισμένοι, nom. pl. m. perf. pass. part.
(Gal. 3:23, MT & TR | συγκλειόμενοι,
GNT, WH & NA) . . . . συγκλείω (4788)
συγκεκραμένος, nom. sg. m. perf. pass. part.
(Heb. 4:2, TR | συγκεκερασμένους, GNT
& NA | συνκεκραμένους, MT | συν-
κεκερασμένους, WH) . . . . . συγκεράννυμι (4786)

(4786) **συγκεράννυμι,** or συγκερανύω, fut.
συγκεράσω, aor. συνεκέρασα, perf. συγ-
κέκραμαι [§36.5] (σύν + κεράννυμι) *to mix
with, mingle together, commingle; to blend,*
1 Cor. 12:24; pass. *to be combined,* Heb. 4:2
συγκεχυμένη, nom. sg. f. perf. pass. part.
(Acts 19:32, GNT, MT, TR & NA |
συνκεχυμένη, WH) . . . . συγχέω (4797)
συγκέχυται, 3 pers. sg. perf. pass. indic. (Acts
21:31, MT & TR | συγχύννεται, GNT &
NA | συνχύννεται, WH) . . . . id.

(4787) **συγκινέω, ῶ,** fut. συγκινήσω [§16.P] (σύν +
κινέω) *to move together, agitate, put in tur-
moil; to excite,* Acts 6:12
συγκλειόμενοι, nom. pl. m. pres. pass. part.
(Gal. 3:23, GNT & NA | συγκεκλεισ-
μένοι, MT & TR | συνκλειόμενοι,
WH) . . . . συγκλείω (4788)

(4788) **συγκλείω,** fut. συγκλείσω [§22.4] (σύν +
κλείω) *to shut up together, to hem in; to
enclose,* Luke 5:6; met. *to band* under a
sweeping sentence, Rom. 11:32; Gal. 3:22;
pass. *to be banded* under a bar of disability,
Gal. 3:23
συγκληρονόμα, acc. pl. neut. adj. (Eph. 3:6,
GNT, MT, TR & NA | συνκληρονόμα,
WH) . . . . συγκληρονόμος (4789)
συγκληρονόμοι, nom. pl. m. adj. (Rom. 8:17,
GNT, MT, TR & NA | συνκληρονόμοι,
WH) . . . . id.
συγκληρονόμοις, dat. pl. m. adj. (1 Pet. 3:7,
GNT & NA | συγκληρονόμοι, MT &
TR | συνκληρονόμοι, WH) . . . . id.

(4789) **συγκληρονόμος, ον** [§7.2] (σύν + κληρονόμος)
pr. *a coheir,* Rom. 8:17; *a fellow-participant,*
Eph. 3:6; Heb. 11:9; 1 Pet. 3:7
συγκληρονόμων, gen. pl. m. adj. (Heb. 11:9,
GNT, MT, TR & NA | συνκληρονόμων,
WH) . . . . συγκληρονόμος (4789)
συγκοινωνεῖτε, 2 pers. pl. pres. act. imper.
(Eph. 5:11, GNT, MT, TR & NA |

συνκοινωνεῖτε, WH) . . . . . . συγκοινωνέω *(4790)*

(4790) **συγκοινωνέω**, ῶ, fut. συγκοινωνήσω [§16.P]
to be a joint partaker, participate with a
person; in N.T. *to mix one's self up* in a
thing, *to involve one's self, be an accomplice in,* Eph. 5:11; Rev. 18:4; *to sympathize actively in, to relieve,* Phil. 4:14
συγκοινωνήσαντες, nom. pl. m. aor. act. part.
(Phil. 4:14, GNT, MT, TR & NA |
συνκοινωνήσαντες, WH) . . . συγκοινωνέω *(4790)*
συγκοινωνήσητε, 2 pers. pl. aor. act. subj.
(Rev. 18:4, GNT, MT, TR & NA |
συνκοινωνήσητε, WH) . . . . id.

(4791) **συγκοινωνός**, όν, nom. sg. m. adj. (σύν +
κοινωνός) *one who partakes jointly; a co-
participant,* Rom. 11:17; *a copartner* in service, *fellow,* 1 Cor. 9:23; Phil. 1:7; *a sharer,*
Rev. 1:9 (Rom. 11:17; 1 Cor. 9:23; Rev. 1:9,
GNT, MT, TR & NA | συνκοινωνός, WH)
συγκοινωνούς, acc. pl. m. adj. (Phil. 1:7,
GNT, MT, TR & NA | συνκοινωνούς,
WH) . . . . συγκοινωνός *(4791)*

(4792) **συγκομίζω**, fut. συγκομίσω [§26.1] (σύν +
κομίζω) *to bring together, collect; to prepare for burial, take charge of the funeral*
of any one, *bury,* Acts 8:2
συγκρῖναι, aor. act. infin. (2 Cor. 10:12, GNT,
MT, TR & NA | συνκρῖναι,
WH) . . . . συγκρίνω *(4793)*
συγκρίνοντες, nom. pl. m. pres. act. part.
(1 Cor. 2:13; 2 Cor. 10:12, GNT, MT, TR
& NA | συνκρίνοντες, WH) . . . . id.

(4793) **συγκρίνω**, fut. συγκρινῶ [§27.1.a] (σύν +
κρίνω) *to combine, compound; to compare,
to estimate by comparing with* something
else, or, *to match,* 2 Cor. 10:12(2×); *to explain, to illustrate,* or, *to suit,* 1 Cor. 2:13
συγκύπτουσα, nom. sg. f. pres. act. part.
(Luke 13:11, GNT, MT, TR & NA |
συνκύπτουσα, WH) . . . . συγκύπτω *(4794)*

(4794) **συγκύπτω**, fut. συγκύψω [§23.1.a] (σύν +
κύπτω) *to bend or bow together; to be
bowed together, bent double*

(4795) **συγκυρία**, ας, ἡ [§2.B.b; 2.2] (συγκυρέω, *to
happen together,* σύν + κυρέω, *to hap-
pen) concurrence, coincidence, chance, ac-
cident;* κατὰ συγκυρίαν, *by chance,
accidentally,* Luke 10:31
συγκυρίαν, acc. sg. f. n. . . . . συγκυρία *(4795)*
συγχαίρει, 2 pers. sg. pres. act. indic. (1 Cor.
12:26; 13:6, GNT, MT, TR & NA |
συνχαίρει, WH) . . . . συγχαίρω *(4796)*
συγχαίρετε, 2 pers. pl. pres. act. imper. (Phil.
2:18, GNT, MT, TR & NA | συνχαίρετε,
WH) . . . . id.

(4796) **συγχαίρω**, 1 pers. sg. pres. act. indic., 2 aor.
συνεχάρην [§27.4.b] (σύν + χαίρω) *to re-
joice with* any one, *sympathize in joy,* Luke
15:6, 9; Phil. 2:17, 18; met. 1 Cor. 12:26;
to sympathize in the advancement of,
1 Cor. 13:6 (Phil. 2:17, GNT, MT, TR &
NA | συνχαίρω, WH)
συγχάρητε, 2 pers. pl. 2 aor. pass. dep. imper.
(Luke 15:6, 9, GNT, MT, TR & NA |
συνχάρητε, WH) . . . . συγχαίρω *(4796)*

(4797) **συγχέω**, and later, συγχύνω, imperf. συνέχεον
and συνέχυννον, perf. pass. συγκέχυμαι,
aor. pass. συνεχύθην [§35.1; 36.1] (σύν +
χέω) *to pour together, mingle by pouring
together;* hence, *to confound, perplex,
amaze,* Acts 2:6; *to confound* in dispute,
Acts 9:22; *to throw into confusion, fill with
uproar,* Acts 19:32; 21:27, 31

(4798) **συγχράομαι**, ῶμαι, fut. συγχρήσομαι [§18.R]
(σύν + χράομαι) *to use at the same time
with another, use in common; to have social intercourse with, associate with*
συγχρῶνται, 3 pers. pl. pres. mid./pass. dep.
indic. (John 4:9, GNT, MT, TR & NA |
συνχρῶνται, WH) . . . . συγχράομαι *(4798)*
συγχύννεται, 3 pers. sg. pres. pass. indic. (Acts
21:31, GNT & NA | συγκέχυται, MT &
TR | συνχύννεται, WH) . . . . . συγχύν(ν)ω *(‡4797)*

(‡4797) **συγχύν(ν)ω**, *to throw into confusion, fill with
uproar,*
συγχύσεως, gen. sg. f. n. . . . . σύγχυσις *(4799)*

(4799) **σύγχυσις**, εως, ἡ [§5.E.c] pr. *a pouring together;* hence, *confusion, commotion, tu-
mult, uproar,* Acts 19:29

(4800) **συζάω**, ῶ, fut. συζήσω [§25.2] (σύν + ζάω)
to live with; to continue in life with any
one, 2 Cor. 7:3; *to co-exist in life with* another, Rom. 6:8; 2 Tim. 2:11

(4801) **συζεύγνυμι**, fut. συζεύξω, aor. συνέζευξα
[§31.BB] (σύν + ζεύγνυμι, *to yoke) to yoke
together;* trop. *to conjoin, join together,
unite,* Matt. 19:6; Mark 10:9
συζῆν, pres. act. infin. (2 Cor. 7:3, GNT, MT
& NA | συζῆν, TR | συνζῆν, WH) . συζάω *(4800)*
συζήσομεν, 1 pers. pl. fut. act. indic. (Rom.
6:8; 2 Tim. 2:11, GNT, MT, TR & NA
| συνζήσομεν, WH) . . . . id.
συζητεῖν, pres. act. infin. (Mark 1:27; 8:11;
Luke 22:23; 24:15, GNT, MT, TR & NA
| συνζητεῖν, WH) . . . . συζητέω *(4802)*
συζητεῖτε, 2 pers. pl. pres. act. indic. (Mark 9:16,
GNT, MT, TR & NA | συνζητεῖτε, WH)   id.

(4802) **συζητέω**, ῶ, fut. συζητήσω [§16.P] (σύν +
ζητέω) *to seek, ask,* or *inquire with* another;
to deliberate, debate, Mark 1:27; 9:10; *to*

hold discourse with, argue, reason, Mark 8:11; 12:28; Acts 6:9; *to question, dispute, cavil*, Mark 9:14, 16, et al.

συζητήσεως, gen. sg. f. n. (Acts 15:2, 7 TR | ζητήσεως, GNT, WH & NA | συζητήσεως, Acts 15:7, MT | ζητήσεως, Acts 15:2, MT) . . . . συζήτησις *(4803)*

συζήτησιν, acc. sg. f. n. (Acts 28:29, MT & TR | GNT, WH & NA omit) . . . . . . id.

(4803) **συζήτησις**, εως, ἡ [§5.E.c] *mutual discussion, debate, disputation*, Acts 15:2, 7; 28:29

(4804) **συζητητής**, nom. sg. m. n. [§2.B.c] *a disputant, controversial reasoner, sophist* (1 Cor. 1:20, GNT, MT, TR & NA | συνζητητής, WH)

συζητοῦντας, acc. pl. m. pres. act. part. (Mark 9:14, GNT, MT, TR & NA | συνζητοῦντας, WH) . . . . συζητέω *(4802)*

συζητοῦντες, nom. pl. m. pres. act. part. (Mark 9:10; Acts 6:9, GNT, MT, TR & NA | συνζητοῦντες, WH) . . . . id.

συζητούντων, gen. pl. m. pres. act. part. (Mark 12:28, GNT, MT, TR & NA | συνζητούντως, WH) . . . . id.

σύζυγε, voc. sg. m. adj. (Phil. 4:3, GNT, MT, TR & NA | σύνζυγε, WH) . . . . . σύζυγος *(4805)*

(4805) **σύζυγος**, ον [§7.2] *a yoke-fellow; an associate, fellow-laborer, coadjutor*, Phil. 4:3

(4806) **συζωοποιέω**, ῶ, fut. συζωοποιήσω [§16.P] (σύν + ζωοποιέω) *to quicken together with another; to make a sharer in the quickening of another*, Eph. 2:5; Col. 2:13

σῦκα, acc. pl. neut. n. . . . . σῦκον *(4810)*

(4807) **συκάμινος**, ου, ἡ, and ὁ, *a sycamore-tree*, i.q. συκομοραία, q.v.

συκαμίνῳ, dat. sg. m. adj. . . . . συκάμινος *(4807)*

(4808) **συκῆ**, ῆς, ἡ, nom. sg. f. n. [§2.B.a] contr. for συκέα, *a fig-tree, ficus carica* of Linn., Matt. 21:19, et al.

συκῆ, dat. sg. f. n. . . . . συκῆ *(4808)*

συκῆν, acc. sg. f. n. . . . . id.

συκῆς, gen. sg. f. n. . . . . id.

(†4809) **συκομοραία**, or συκομορέα, ας, ἡ [§2.B.b; 2.2] (σῦκον + μόρον, *a mulberry*) equivalent to συκόμορος, *the fig-mulberry, ficus sycamorus* of Linn., a tree whose leaves resemble those of the mulberry, and its fruit that of the fig-tree

συκομορέαν, acc. sg. f. n. (Luke 19:4, GNT, WH & NA | συκομωραίαν, MT & TR) . . . . συκομοραία *(†4809)*

συκομωραίαν, acc. sg. f. n. (Luke 19:4, MT & TR | συκομορέαν, GNT, WH & NA) id.

(4810) **σῦκον**, ου, τό [§3.C.c] *a fig*, Matt. 7:16, et al.

(4811) **συκοφαντέω**, ῶ, fut. συκοφαντήσω [§16.P] (συκοφάντης, pr. among the Athenians, *an informer against those who exported figs contrary to law*, σῦκον, φαίνω) *to inform against; to accuse falsely;* by impl. *to wrong by false accusations or insidious arts; to extort* money *by false informations*, Luke 3:14; 19:8

συκοφαντήσητε, 2 pers. pl. aor. act. subj. . . . . συκοφαντέω *(4811)*

σύκων, gen. pl. neut. n. . . . . σῦκον *(4810)*

(4812) **συλαγωγέω**, ῶ, fut. συλαγωγήσω [§16.P] (σύλη, or σῦλον, and ἄγω) *to carry off as a prey or booty;* met. *to make victims of imposture*, Col. 2:8

συλαγωγῶν, nom. sg. m. pres. act. part. συλαγωγέω *(4812)*

(4813) **συλάω**, ῶ, fut. συλήσω, aor. ἐσύλησα [§18.R] (σύλη, or σῦλον, *the right of seizing the goods of a merchant in payment*) *to strip, rob; to rob, encroach upon*, 2 Cor. 11:8

συλλαβεῖν, 2 aor. act. infin. . . . . συλλαμβάνω *(4815)*

συλλαβέσθαι, 2 aor. mid. infin. . . . . id.

συλλαβόμενοι, nom. pl. m. 2 aor. mid. part. id.

συλλαβόντες, nom. pl. m. 2 aor. act. part. id.

συλλαβοῦσα, nom. sg. f. 2 aor. act. part. . id.

συλλαβοῦσι(ν), dat. pl. m. 2 aor. act. part. id.

συλλαλήσας, nom. sg. m. aor. act. part. συλλαλέω *(4814)*

συλλαλοῦντες, nom. pl. m. pres. act. part. id.

(4814) **συλλαλέω**, ῶ, fut. συλλαλήσω [§16.P] (σύν + λαλέω) *to talk, converse, or confer with*, Matt. 17:3; Mark 9:4, et al.

συλλαμβάνου, 2 pers. sg. pres. mid. imper. . . . . συλλαμβάνω *(4815)*

(4815) **συλλαμβάνω**, fut. συλλή(μ)ψομαι, 2 aor. συνέλαβον, perf. συνείληφα, aor. pass. συνελήφθην [§36.2] (σύν + λαμβάνω) *to catch up; to seize, apprehend*, Matt. 26:55; Acts 1:16, et al.; *to catch*, as prey, Luke 5:9; *to conceive, become pregnant*, Luke 1:24, 31, 36; 2:21; met. James 1:15; mid. *to help, aid, assist*, Luke 5:7; Phil. 4:3

συλλέγεται, 3 pers. sg. pres. pass. indic. . . . . συλλέγω *(4816)*

συλλέγοντες, nom. pl. m. pres. act. part. . id.

συλλέγουσι(ν), 3 pers. pl. pres. act. indic. . id.

(4816) **συλλέγω**, fut. συλλέξω [§23.1.b] (σύν + λέγω) *to collect, gather*, Matt. 7:16; 13:28, et al.

συλλέξατε, 2 pers. pl. aor. act. imper. συλλέγω *(4816)*

συλλέξουσιν, 3 pers. pl. fut. act. indic. . . . id.

συλλέξωμεν, 1 pers. pl. aor. act. subj. . . . id.

συλλημφθέντα, acc. sg. m. aor. pass. part. (Acts 23:27, GNT, WH & NA | συλληφθέντα, MT & TR) . . . . συλλαμβάνω *(4815)*

συλλημφθῆναι, aor. pass. infin. (Luke 2:21, GNT, WH & NA | συλληφθῆναι, MT &

TR) . . . . συλλαμβάνω *(4815)*

συλλήμψη, 2 pers. sg. fut. mid. dep. indic. (Luke 1:31, GNT, WH & NA | συλλήψη, MT & TR) . . . . id.

συλληφθέντα, acc. sg. m. aor. pass. part. (Acts 23:27, MT & TR | συλλημφθέντα, GNT, WH & NA) . . . . id.

συλληφθῆναι, aor. pass. infin. (Luke 2:21, MT & TR | συλλημφθῆναι, GNT, WH & NA) id.

συλλήψη, 2 pers. sg. fut. mid. dep. indic. (Luke 1:31, MT & TR | συλλήμψη, GNT, WH & NA) . . . . id.

(4817) **συλλογίζομαι**, fut. συλλογίσομαι [§26.1] (σύν + λογίζομαι) *to reckon up together; to consider, deliberate, reason,* Luke 20:5

(†4818) **συλλυπέομαι**, οῦμαι [§17.Q] (σύν + λυπέομαι) *to be grieved together with; to be grieved,* Mark 3:5

συλλυπούμενος, nom. sg. m. pres. mid./pass. dep. part. . . . . συλλυπέομαι *(†4818)*

συμβαίνειν, pres. act. infin. . . . . συμβαίνω *(4819)*

συμβαίνοντος, gen. sg. neut. pres. act. part.   id.

(4819) **συμβαίνω**, fut. συμβήσομαι, 2 aor. συνέβην [§37.1] (σύν + βαίνω) *to stand with the feet near together; to step or come together; to happen, befall, fall out,* Mark 10:32, et al.

συμβαλεῖν, 2 aor. act. infin. (Luke 14:31, GNT, MT, TR & NA | συνβαλεῖν, WH) . . . . συμβάλλω *(4820)*

συμβάλλουσα, nom. sg. f. pres. act. part. (Luke 2:19, GNT, MT, TR & NA | συν-βάλλουσα, WH) . . . . id.

(4820) **συμβάλλω**, fut. συμβαλῶ [§27.2.d] (σύν + βάλλω) pr. *to throw together;* absol. *to meet and join,* Acts 20:14; *to meet* in war, *to encounter, engage with,* Luke 14:31; *to encounter* in discourse or dispute, Acts 17:18; *to consult together,* Acts 4:15; mid. *to contribute, be of service to, to aid,* Acts 18:27; συμβάλλειν ἐν τῇ καρδίᾳ, *to revolve in mind, ponder upon,* Luke 2:19

συμβάντων, gen. pl. m. 2 aor. act. part. . . . . συμβαίνω *(4819)*

συμβασιλεύσομεν, 1 pers. pl. fut. act. indic. (2 Tim. 2:12, GNT, MT, TR & NA | συνβασιλεύσομεν, WH) . . . . συμβασιλεύω *(4821)*

συμβασιλεύσωμεν, 1 pers. pl. aor. act. subj. (1 Cor. 4:8, GNT, MT, TR & NA | συνβασιλεύσωμεν, WH) . . . . id.

(4821) **συμβασιλεύω**, fut. συμβασιλεύσω [§13.M] (σύν + βασιλεύω) *to reign with;* met. *to enjoy honor and felicity with,* 1 Cor. 4:8; 2 Tim. 2:12

συμβέβηκε(ν), 3 pers. sg. perf. act. indic. [§37.1] . . . . συμβαίνω *(4819)*

συμβεβηκότι, dat. sg. neut. perf. act. part.   id.

συμβεβηκότων, gen. pl. neut. perf. act. part. . . . . συμβαίνω *(4819)*

συμβιβαζόμενον, nom. sg. neut. pres. pass. part. (Eph. 4:16; Col. 2:19, GNT, MT, TR & NA | συνβιβαζόμενον, WH) συμβιβάζω *(4822)*

συμβιβάζοντες, nom. pl. m. pres. act. part. (Acts 16:10, GNT, MT, TR & NA | συνβιβάζοντες, WH) . . . . id.

(4822) **συμβιβάζω**, fut. συμβιβάσω [§26.1] (σύν + βιβάζω) pr. *to cause to come together; to unite, knit together,* Eph. 4:16; Col. 2:2, 19; *to infer, conclude,* Acts 16:10; by impl. *to prove, demonstrate,* Acts 9:22; in N.T. *to teach, instruct,* 1 Cor. 2:16

συμβιβάζων, nom. sg. m. pres. act. part. (Acts 9:22, GNT, MT, TR & NA | συνβιβάζων, WH) . . . . συμβιβάζω *(4822)*

συμβιβάσει, 3 pers. sg. fut. act. indic. (1 Cor. 2:16, GNT, MT, TR & NA | συνβιβάσει, WH) . . . . id.

συμβιβασθέντες, nom. pl. m. aor. pass. part. (Col. 2:2, GNT & NA | συμβιβασθέντων, MT & TR | συνβιβασθέντες, WH) . . . id.

συμβιβασθέντων, gen. pl. m. aor. pass. part. (Col. 2:2, MT & TR | συμβιβασθέντες, GNT & NA | συνβιβασθέντες, WH) . id.

συμβουλεύσας, nom. sg. m. aor. act. part. συμβουλεύω *(4823)*

(4823) **συμβουλεύω**, 1 pers. sg. pres. act. indic., fut. συμβουλεύσω [§13.M] (σύν + βουλεύω) *to counsel, advise, exhort,* John 18:14; Rev. 3:18; mid. *to consult together, plot,* Matt. 26:4, et al.

(4824) **συμβούλιον**, ου, τό [§3.C.c] *counsel, consultation, mutual consultation,* Matt. 12:14; 22:15, et al.; *a council of counsellors,* Acts 25:12

συμβούλιον, acc. sg. neut. n. . . . . συμβούλιον *(4824)*

συμβουλίου, gen. sg. neut. n. . . . . id.

(4825) **σύμβουλος**, ου, ὁ, nom. sg. m. n. [§3.C.a] (σύν + βουλή) *a counsellor; one who shares one's counsel,* Rom. 11:34

(4826) **Συμεών**, ὁ, *Symeon, Simeon,* pr. name, indecl. I. *Simeon, son of Juda,* Luke 3:30   II. *Simeon, son of Jacob,* Rev. 7:7   III. *Simeon, a prophet of Jerusalem,* Luke 2:25, 34   IV. *Simeon, or Simon Peter,* Acts 15:14; 2 Pet. 1:1   V. *Simeon, called Niger,* Acts 13:1

συμμαθηταῖς, dat. pl. m. n. . . . . . συμμαθητής *(4827)*

(4827) **συμμαθητής**, οῦ, ὁ [§2.B.c] (σύν + μαθητής) *a fellow-disciple*

συμμαρτυρεῖ, 3 pers. sg. pres. act. indic. (Rom. 8:6, GNT, MT, TR & NA | συνμαρτυρεῖ, WH) . . . . συμμαρτυρέω *(4828)*

(4828) **συμμαρτυρέω**, ῶ, fut. συμμαρτυρήσω [§16.P]

(σύν + μαρτυρέω) *to testify or bear witness together with* another, *add testimony,* Rom. 2:15; 8:16; 9:1

συμμαρτυροῦμαι, 1 pers. sg. pres. mid./pass. dep. indic. (Rev. 22:18, TR | μαρτυρῶ, GNT, MT, WH & NA) .... συμμαρτυρέω *(4828)*

συμμαρτυρούσης, gen. sg. f. pres. act. part. (Rom. 2:15; 9:1, GNT, MT, TR & NA | συνμαρτυρούσης, WH) .... id.

(4829) **συμμερίζομαι,** fut. συμμερίσομαι [§26.1] (σύν + μερίζω) *to divide with* another so as to receive a part to one's self, *share with, partake with*

συμμερίζονται, 3 pers. pl. pres. mid./pass. dep. indic. (1 Cor. 9:13, GNT, MT, TR & NA | συμμερίζονται, WH) .. συμμερίζομαι *(4829)*

συμμέτοχα, acc. pl. neut. adj. (Eph. 3:6, GNT, MT, TR & NA | συνμέτοχα, WH) .... συμμέτοχος *(4830)*

συμμέτοχοι, nom. pl. m. adj. (Eph. 5:7, GNT, MT, TR & NA | συνμέτοχοι, WH) .. id.

(4830) **συμμέτοχος,** ον [§7.2] (σύν + μέτοχος) *a partaker with* any one, *a joint partaker,* Eph. 3:6; 5:7

συμμιμηταί, nom. pl. m. n. (Phil. 3:17, GNT, MT, TR & NA | συνμιμηταί, WH) .... συμμιμητής *(4831)*

(4831) **συμμιμητής,** οῦ, ὁ [§2.B.c] (σύν + μιμέομαι) *an imitator together with* any one, *a joint-imitator*

συμμορφιζόμενος, nom. sg. m. pres. pass. part. (Phil. 3:10, GNT, WH & NA | συμμορφούμενος, MT & TR) .... συμμορφίζω *(‡4833)*

(‡4833) **συμμορφίζω,** fut. συμμορφίσω [§26.1] (σύν + μορφίζω) *to conform to*

σύμμορφον, acc. sg. neut. adj. ... σύμμορφος *(4832)*

(4832) **σύμμορφος,** ον [§7.2] (σύν + μορφή) *of life form, assimilated, conformed,* Rom. 8:29; Phil. 3:21

συμμορφούμενος, nom. sg. m. pres. pass. part. (Phil. 3:10, MT & TR | συμμορφιζόμενος, GNT, WH & NA) συμμορφόω *(4833)*

συμμόρφους, acc. pl. m. adj. .... σύμμορφος *(4832)*

(4833) **συμμορφόω,** ῶ, fut. συμμορφώσω [§20.T] (σύν + μορφόω) *to conform to*

συμπαθεῖς, nom. pl. m. adj. ...... συμπαθής *(4835)*

(4834) **συμπαθέω,** ῶ, fut. συμπαθήσω [§16.P] *to sympathize with,* Heb. 4:15; *to compassionate,* Heb. 10:34

(4835) **συμπαθής,** ές [§7.G.b] (σύν + πάθος, πάσχω) *sympathizing, compassionate,* 1 Pet. 3:8

συμπαθῆσαι, aor. act. infin. (Heb. 4:15, GNT, MT, TR & NA | συνπαθῆσαι, WH) .... συμπαθέω *(4834)*

συμπαραγενόμενοι, nom. pl. m. 2 aor. mid.

dep. part. (Luke 23:48, GNT, MT, TR & NA | συνπαραγενόμενοι, WH) .... συμπαραγίνομαι *(4836)*

(4836) **συμπαραγίνομαι,** 2 aor. συμπαρεγενόμην [§37.1] (σύν + παραγίνομαι) *to be present together with; to come together, convene,* Luke 23:48; *to stand by or support* one judicially, 2 Tim. 4:16

(4837) **συμπαρακαλέω,** ῶ, fut. συμπαρακαλέσω [§22.1] (σύν + παρακαλέω) *to invite, exhort* along with others; *to animate* in company with others; pass. *to share in mutual encouragement*

συμπαρακληθῆναι, aor. pass. infin. (Rom. 1:12, GNT, MT, TR & NA | συνπαρακληθῆναι, WH) .... συμπαρακαλέω *(4837)*

συμπαραλαβεῖν, 2 aor. act. infin. (Acts 15:37, GNT, MT, TR & NA | συνπαραλαβεῖς, WH) .... συμπαραλαμβάνω *(4838)*

συμπαραλαβόντες, nom. pl. m. 2 aor. act. part. (Acts 12:25, GNT, MT, TR & NA | συνπαραλαβόντες, WH) .... id.

συμπαραλαβών, nom. sg. m. 2 aor. act. part. (Gal. 2:1, GNT, MT, TR & NA | συνπαραλαβών, WH) .... id.

συμπαραλαμβάνειν, pres. act. infin. (Acts 15:38, GNT & NA | συμπαραλαβεῖν, MT & TR | συνπαραλαμβάνειν, WH) id.

(4838) **συμπαραλαμβάνω,** 2 aor. συμπαρέλαβον [§36.2] (σύν + παραλαμβάνω) *to take along with, take as a companion,* Acts 12:25; 15:37, 38; Gal. 2:1

(4839) **συμπαραμένω,** fut. συμπαραμενῶ [§27.1.a] (σύν + παραμένω) *to remain or continue with or among*

συμπαραμενῶ, 1 pers. sg. fut. act. indic. (Phil. 1:25, MT & TR | παραμενῶ, GNT, WH & NA) .... συμπαραμένω *(4839)*

συμπαρεγένετο, 3 pers. sg. 2 aor. mid. dep. indic. (2 Tim. 4:16, MT & TR | παρεγένετο, GNT, WH & NA) .. συμπαραγίνομαι *(4836)*

(4840) **συμπάρειμι** (σύν + πάρειμι) *to be present with* any one

συμπαρόντες, nom. pl. m. pres. part. (Acts 25:24, GNT, MT, TR & NA | συνπαρόντες, WH) .... συμπάρειμι *(4840)*

συμπάσχει, 3 pers. sg. pres. act. indic. (1 Cor. 12:26, GNT, MT, TR & NA | συνπάσχει, WH) .... συμπάσχω *(4841)*

συμπάσχομεν, 1 pers. pl. pres. act. indic. (Rom. 8:17, GNT, MT, TR & NA | συνπάσχομεν, WH) .... id.

(4841) **συμπάσχω,** fut. συμπείσομαι [§36.4] (σύν + πάσχω) *to suffer with, sympathize,* 1 Cor. 12:26; *to suffer as* another, *endure corres-*

ponding sufferings, Rom. 8:17

(4842) συμπέμπω, fut. συμπέμψω [§23.1.a] (σύν + πέμπω) *to send with* any one, 2 Cor. 8:18, 22

συμπεριλαβών, nom. sg. m. 2 aor. act. part. (Acts 20:10, GNT, MT, TR & NA | συνπεριλαβών, WH) . . . συμπεριλαμβάνω *(4843)*

(4843) συμπεριλαμβάνω, fut. συμπεριλή(μ)ψομαι [§36.2] (σύν + περιλαμβάνω) *to embrace together; to embrace*, Acts 20:10

(4844) συμπίνω, fut. συμπίομαι and συμπιοῦμαι, 2 aor. συνέπιον [§37.1] (σύν + πίνω) *to drink with* any one, Acts 10:41

(‡4098) συμπίπτω, *to fall together, collapse, fall in*, Luke 6:49

συμπληροῦσθαι, pres. pass. infin. (Luke 9:51, GNT, MT, WH, TR & NA | Acts 2:1, GNT, MT, TR & NA | Acts 2:1, συνπληροῦσθαι, WH) . . . . . . συμπληρόω *(4845)*

(4845) συμπληρόω, ῶ, fut. συμπληρώσω [§20.T] (σύν + πληρόω,) *to fill, fill up, fill full*, Luke 8:23; pass., of time, *to be completed, have fully come*, Luke 9:51; Acts 2:1

συμπνίγει, 3 pers. sg. pres. act. indic. (Matt. 13:22, GNT, MT, TR & NA | συνπνίγει, WH) . . . . συμπνίγω *(4846)*

συμπνίγονται, 3 pers. pl. pres. pass. indic. (Luke 8:14, GNT, MT, TR & NA | συνπνίγονται, WH) . . . . id.

συμπνίγουσι(ν), 3 pers. pl. pres. act. indic. (Mark 4:19, GNT, MT, TR & NA | συνπνίγουσιν, WH) . . . . id.

(4846) συμπνίγω, fut. συμπνιξοῦμαι [§23.1.b] (σύν + πνίγω) *to throttle, choke; trop. to choke the growth or increase of seed or plants*, Matt. 13:22; Mark 4:7, 19; Luke 8:14; *to press upon, crowd, throng*, Luke 8:42

συμπολῖται, nom. pl. m. n. (Eph. 2:19, GNT, MT, TR & NA | συνπολῖται, WH) . . . . συμπολίτης *(4847)*

(4847) συμπολίτης, ου, ὁ [§2.B.c] (σύν + πολίτης) *a fellow-citizen*, met. Eph. 2:19

(4848) συμπορεύομαι, fut. συμπορεύσομαι [§14.N] (σύν + πορεύομαι) *to go with, accompany*, Luke 7:11; 14:25; 24:15; *to come together, assemble*, Mark 10:1

συμπορεύονται, 3 pers. pl. pres. mid./pass. dep. indic. (Mark 10:1, GNT, MT, TR & NA | συνπορεύονται, WH) . συμπορεύομαι *(4848)*

συμπόσια, acc. pl. neut. n. . . . . συμπόσιον *(4849)*

(4849) συμπόσιον, ου, τό [§3.C.c] *a drinking together; a feast, banquet; a festive company*; in N.T. pl. συμπόσια, *mess-parties*, Mark 6:39

(4850) συμπρεσβύτερος, ου, ὁ, nom. sg. m. n. [§3.C.a] (σύν + πρεσβύτερος) *a fellow-*

elder, fellow-presbyter

συμφέρει, 3 pers. sg. pres. act. indic. συμφέρω *(4851)*

συμφέρον, acc. sg. neut. pres. act. part. . . . id.

συμφερόντων, gen. pl. neut. pres. act. part. id.

(4851) συμφέρω, fut. συνοίσω, aor. συνήνεγκα, 2 aor. συνήνεγκον [§36.1] (σύν + φέρω) *to bring together, collect*, Acts 19:19; absol. *to con- duce to, be for the benefit* of any one, *be pro- fitable, advantageous, expedient*, 1 Cor. 6:12; *to suit best, be appropriate*, 2 Cor. 8:10; neut. part. τὸ συμφέρον, *good, benefit, profit, ad- vantage*, Acts 20:20; 1 Cor. 7:35; impers. συμφέρει, *it is profitable, advantageous, expedient*, Matt. 5:29, 30; 19:10, et al.

(4852) σύμφημι, 1 pers. sg. pres. indic., [§33.DD; 33.1] (σύν + φημί) pr. *to affirm with; to assent* (Rom. 7:16, GNT, MT, TR & NA | σύνφημι, WH)

σύμφορον, acc. sg. neut. adj. (1 Cor. 7:35; 10:33, GNT, WH & NA | συμφέρον, MT & TR) . . . . σύμφορος *(‡4851)*

(‡4851) σύμφορος, ον [§7.2] *profitable, expedient*, 1 Cor. 7:35; 10:33

συμφυεῖσαι, nom. pl. f. 2 aor. pass. part., Luke 8:7 . . . . συμφύω *(4855)*

(4853) συμφυλέτης, ου, ὁ [§2.B.c] (σύν + φυλή) pr. *one of the same tribe; a fellow-citizen, fellow-countryman*

συμφυλετῶν, gen. pl. m. n. . . . . . συμφυλέτης *(4853)*

σύμφυτοι, nom. pl. m. adj. . . . . σύμφυτος *(4854)*

(4854) σύμφυτος, ον [§7.2] (σύν + φύω) pr. *planted together, grown together*; in N.T. met. *grown together, closely entwined or united with*, Rom. 6:5

(4855) συμφύω, fut. συμφύσω, 2 aor. pass. συνεφύην [§24.11] (σύν + φύω) *to make to grow to- gether*; pass. *to grow or spring up with*, Luke 8:7

συμφωνεῖ, 3 pers. sg. pres. act. indic. (Luke 5:36, MT & TR | συμφωνήσει, GNT, WH & NA) . . . . συμφωνέω *(4856)*

(4856) συμφωνέω, ῶ, fut. συμφωνήσω [§16.P] *to sound together, to be in unison, be in ac- cord*; trop. *to agree with, accord with* in purport, Acts 15:15; *to harmonize with, be congruous, suit with*, Luke 5:36; *to agree with, make an agreement*, Matt. 18:19; 20:2, 13; Acts 5:9

συμφωνήσας, nom. sg. m. aor. act. part. . . . . συμφωνέω *(4856)*

συμφωνήσει, 3 pers. sg. fut. act. indic. (Luke 5:36, GNT, WH & NA | συμφωνεῖ, MT & TR) . . . . id.

(4857) συμφώνησις, εως, ἡ, nom. sg. f. n. [§5.E.c] *uni- son, accord; agreement, concord*, 2 Cor. 6:15

συμφωνήσωσιν, 3 pers. pl. aor. act.
subj. . . . . συμφωνέω *(4856)*

(4858) **συμφωνία**, ας, ἡ [§2.B.b; 2.2] *symphony, harmony of sounds, concert of instruments, music,* Luke 15:25
συμφωνίας, gen. sg. f. n. . . . . συμφωνία *(4858)*

(4859) **σύμφωνος**, ον [§7.2] (σύν + φωνή) *agreeing in sound;* met. *accordant, harmonious, agreeing,* and neut. τὸ σύμφωνον, *accord, agreement,* 1 Cor. 7:5
συμφώνου, gen. sg. neut. adj. . . . . . σύμφωνος *(4859)*
συμφωνοῦσιν, 3 pers. pl. pres. act.
indic. . . . . συμφωνέω *(4856)*

(4860) **συμψηφίζω**, fut. συμψηφίσω [§26.1] (σύν + ψηφίζω, ψῆφος) *to calculate together, compute, reckon up,* Acts 19:19
σύμψυχοι, nom. pl. m. adj. (Phil. 2:2, GNT, MT, TR & NA | σύνψυχοι, WH) . . . σύμψυχος *(4861)*

(4861) **σύμψυχος**, ον [§7.2] (σύν + ψυχή) *united in mind, at unity*

(4862) **σύν**, prep. governing a dat., *with, together with,* Matt. 25:27; 26:35; 27:38; *attendant on,* 1 Cor. 15:10; *besides,* Luke 24:21; *with, with the assistance of,* 1 Cor. 5:4; *with, in the same manner as,* Gal. 3:9; εἶναι σύν τινι, *to be with any one, to be in company with, accompany,* Luke 2:13; 8:38; *to be on the side of, be a partisan of any one,* Acts 4:13; 14:4; οἱ σύν τινι, *those with any one, the companions of any one,* Mark 2:26; Acts 22:9; *the colleagues, associates of any one,* Acts 5:17, 21
συναγαγεῖν, 2 aor. act. infin. [§13.7.d] συνάγω *(4863)*
συναγάγετε, 2 pers. pl. 2 aor. act. imper. . id.
συναγάγῃ, 3 pers. sg. 2 aor. act. subj. . . . . id.
συναγαγόντες, nom. pl. m. 2 aor. act. part. id.
συναγαγούσῃ, dat. sg. f. 2 aor. act. part. . id.
συναγαγών, nom. sg. m. 2 aor. act. part. . id.
συνάγει, 3 pers. sg. pres. act. indic. . . . . . . id.
συνάγεσθε, 2 pers. pl. pres. pass. imper. (Rev. 19:17, TR | συνάχθητε, GNT, MT, WH & NA) . . . . id.
συνάγεται, 3 pers. sg. pres. pass. indic. (Mark 4:1, GNT, WH & NA | συνήχθη, MT & TR) id.
συνάγετε, 2 pers. pl. pres. act. indic. (Matt. 13:30, WH | συναγάγετε, GNT, MT, TR & NA) . . . . id.
συνάγονται, 3 pers. pl. pres. pass. indic. . . id.
συνάγουσιν, 3 pers. pl. pres. act. indic. . . . id.

(4863) **συνάγω**, 1 pers. sg. pres. act. indic., fut. συνάξω, 2 aor. συνήγαγον [§13.7.d] perf. pass. συνῆγμαι, aor. pass. συνήχθην [§23.7; 23.4] fut. pass. συναχθήσομαι [§23.3.b] (σύν + ἄγω) *to bring together, collect, gather,* as grain, fruits, etc., Matt. 3:12;

6:26; 13:30, 47; *to collect* an assembly, *convoke;* pass. *to convene, come together, meet,* Matt. 2:4; 13:2; 18:20; 22:10; in N.T. *to receive with kindness and hospitality, to entertain,* Matt. 25:35, 38, 43, et al.
συναγωγαῖς, dat. pl. f. n. . . . . συναγωγή *(4864)*
συναγωγάς, acc. pl. f. n. . . . . id.

(4864) **συναγωγή**, ῆς, ἡ, nom. sg. f. n. [§2.B.a] *a collecting, gathering; a* Christian *assembly or congregation,* James 2:2; *the congregation* of a synagogue, Acts 9:2, et al.; hence, the place itself, *a synagogue,* Luke 7:5, et al.
συναγωγῇ, dat. sg. f. n. . . . . συναγωγή *(4864)*
συναγωγήν, acc. sg. f. n. . . . . id.
συναγωγῆς, gen. sg. f. n. . . . . id.
συναγωγῶν, gen. pl. f. n. . . . . id.
συναγών, nom. sg. m. pres. act. part. . συνάγω *(4863)*

(4865) **συναγωνίζομαι**, fut. συναγωνίσομαι [§26.1] (σύν + ἀγωνίζομαι) *to combat in company with* any one; *to exert one's strength with, to be earnest in aiding,* Rom. 15:30
συναγωνίσασθαι, aor. mid. dep.
infin. . . . . συναγωνίζομαι *(4865)*

(4866) **συναθλέω**, ῶ, fut. συναθλήσω [§16.P] (σύν + ἀθλέω) pr. *to contend on the side of* any one; in N.T. *to co-operate vigorously with* a person, Phil. 4:3; *to make effort in the cause of, in support of* a thing, Phil. 1:27
συναθλοῦντες, nom. pl. m. pres. act.
part. . . . . συναθλέω *(4866)*

(4867) **συναθροίζω**, fut. συναθροίσω [§26.1] (σύν + ἀθροίζω, *to gather,* ἀθρόος) *to gather; to bring together, convoke,* Acts 19:25; pass. *to come together, convene,* Luke 24:23; Acts 12:12
συναθροίσας, nom. sg. m. aor. act.
part. . . . . συναθροίζω *(4867)*
συναίρει, 3 pers. sg. pres. act. indic. . συναίρω *(4868)*
συναίρειν, pres. act. infin. . . . . id.

(4868) **συναίρω**, fut. συναρῶ [§27.1.c] (σύν + αἴρω) *to take up* a thing *with* any one; in N.T. συναίρειν λόγον, *to adjust accounts, reckon* in order to payment, Matt. 18:23, 24; 25:19

(4869) **συναιχμάλωτος**, ον, nom. sg. m. adj. (σύν + αἰχμάλωτος) *a fellow-captive,* Rom. 16:7; Col. 4:10; Philemon 23
συναιχμαλώτους, acc. pl. m.
adj. . . . . συναιχμάλωτος *(4869)*

(4870) **συνακολουθέω**, ῶ, fut. συνακολουθήσω [§16.P] (σύν + ἀκολουθέω) *to follow in company with, accompany,* Mark 5:37; Luke 23:49
συνακολουθῆσαι, aor. act.
infin. . . . . συνακολουθέω *(4870)*
συνακολουθῆσασαι, nom. pl. f. aor. act. part. (Luke 23:49, MT & TR | συνακολουθοῦσαι, GNT, WH & NA) . συνακολουθέω *(4870)*

συνακολουθοῦσαι, nom. pl. f. aor. act. part.
(Luke 23:49, GNT, WH & NA | συν
ακολουθήσασαι, MT & TR) . . . .   id.

συναλιζόμενος, nom. sg. m. pres. mid./pass.
dep. part. . . . . συναλίζω *(4871)*

(4871) **συναλίζω**, fut. συναλίσω [§26.1] (σύν +
ἁλίζω, *to collect*) *to cause to come together, collect, assemble, congregate;* mid.
to convene to one's self

(‡4900) **συναλλάσσω** (σύν + ἀλλάσσω) *to negotiate or
bargain with* any one; *to reconcile,* Acts 7:26

(4872) **συναναβαίνω**, fut. συναναβήσομαι, 2 aor.
συνανέβην [§37.1] (σύν + ἀναβαίνω) *to
go up, ascend with* any one, Mark 15:41;
Acts 13:31

συναναβᾶσαι, nom. pl. f. 2 aor. act.
part. . . . . συναναβαίνω *(4872)*
συναναβᾶσιν, dat. pl. m. 2 aor. act. part. .   id.

(4873) **συνανάκειμαι**, fut. συνανακείσομαι [§33.DD]
(σύν + ἀνάκειμαι) *to recline with* any one
at table, Matt. 9:10; 14:9, et al.

συνανακείμενοι, nom. pl. m. pres. mid./pass.
dep. part. . . . . συνανάκειμαι *(4873)*
συνανακειμένοις, dat. pl. m. pres. mid./pass.
dep. part. . . . .   id.
συνανακειμένους, acc. pl. m. pres. mid./pass.
dep. part. . . . .   id.
συνανακειμένων, gen. pl. m. pres. mid./pass.
dep. part. . . . .   id.

(4874) **συναναμίγνυμι** (σύν + ἀναμίγνυμι, *to mix,
mingle*) *to mix together with, commingle;*
mid. met. *to mingle one's self with, to associate with, have familiar intercourse with,*
1 Cor. 5:9, 11; 2 Thess. 3:14

συναναμίγνυσθαι, pres. mid.
infin. . . . . συναναμίγνυμι *(4874)*
συναναμίγνυσθε, 2 pers. pl. pres. mid. imper.
(2 Thess. 3:14; MT & TR | συναναμίγ
νυσθαι, GNT, WH & NA) . . . .   id.

(4875) **συναναπαύομαι**, fut. συναναπαύσομαι
[§14.N] (σύν + ἀναπαύομαι) *to experience
refreshment in company with* any one
συναναπαύσωμαι, 1 pers. sg. aor. mid. dep.
subj. . . . . συναναπαύομαι *(4875)*
συνανέκειντο, 3 pers. pl. imperf. mid./pass.
dep. indic. . . . . συνανάκειμαι *(4873)*

(4876) **συναντάω**, ῶ, fut. συναντήσω [§18.R] (σύν
+ ἀντάω, ἀντί) *to meet with, fall in with,
encounter, to meet,* Luke 9:37; 22:10; Acts
10:25; Heb. 7:1, 10; *to occur, happen to,
befall,* Acts 20:22

συναντήσας, nom. sg. m. aor. act.
part. συναντάω *(4876)*
συναντήσει, 3 pers. sg. fut. act. indic. . . . .   id.
συνάντησιν, acc. sg. f. n. (Matt. 8:34, MT &

TR | ὑπάντησιν, GNT, WH &
NA) . . . . συνάντησις *(4877)*

(4877) **συνάντησις**, εως, ἡ [§5.E.c] *a meeting,* Matt.
8:34

συναντήσοντα, acc. pl. neut. fut. act.
part. συναντάω *(4876)*
συναντιλάβηται, 3 pers. sg. 2 aor. mid. dep.
subj. . . . . συναντιλαμβάνομαι *(4878)*
συναντιλαμβάνεται, 3 pers. sg. pres.
mid./pass. dep. indic. . . . .   id.

(4878) **συναντιλαμβάνομαι**, fut. συναντιλή(μ)ψομαι
[§36.2] (σύν + ἀντιλαμβάνομαι) pr. *to
take hold of with* any one; *to support, help,
aid,* Luke 10:40; Rom. 8:26

συνάξει, 3 pers. sg. fut. act. indic. . . . συνάγω *(4863)*
συνάξω, 1 pers. sg. fut. act. indic. . . . . . .   id.

(4879) **συναπάγω**, fut. συναπάξω [§23.1.b] (σύν +
ἀπάγω) *to lead or conduct away with; to
seduce;* pass. *to be led away, carried astray,*
Gal. 2:13; 2 Pet. 3:17; mid. *to conform
one's self willingly to* certain circumstances, Rom. 12:16

συναπαγόμενοι, nom. pl. m. pres. mid.
part. συναπάγω *(4879)*
συναπαχθέντες, nom. pl. m. aor. pass. part.   id.
συναπεθάνομεν, 1 pers. pl. 2 aor. act.
indic. . . . . συναποθνήσκω *(†4880)*
συναπέστειλα, 1 pers. sg. aor. act.
indic. . . . . συναποστέλλω *(4882)*
συναπήχθη, 3 pers. sg. aor. pass.
indic. . . . . συναπάγω *(4879)*
συναποθανεῖν, 2 aor. act.
infin. . . . . συναποθνήσκω *(†4880)*

(†4880) **συναποθνήσκω**, 2 aor. συναπέθανον [§36.4]
(σύν + ἀποθνήσκω) *to die together with*
any one, Mark 14:31; 2 Cor. 7:3; met. *to
die with,* in respect of a spiritual likeness,
2 Tim. 2:11

(4881) **συναπόλλυμι**, 2 aor. mid. συναπωλόμην
[§36.5] (σύν + ἀπόλλυμι) *to destroy together with* others; mid. *to perish or be destroyed with* others, Heb. 11:31

(4882) **συναποστέλλω**, fut. συναποστελῶ, aor.
συναπέστειλα [§27.1.b,d] (σύν +
ἀποστέλλω) *to send forth together with*
any one, 2 Cor. 12:18

συναπώλετο, 3 pers. sg. 2 aor. mid.
indic. . . . . συναπόλλυμι *(4881)*
συνᾶραι, aor. act. infin. [§27.1.f] . . . . συναίρω *(4868)*

(4883) **συναρμολογέω**, ῶ, fut. συναρμολογήσω
[§16.P] (σύν + ἁρμολογέω, from ἁρμός,
a joint, + λόγος) *to join together fitly, fit
or frame together, compact,* Eph. 2:21; 4:16

συναρμολογουμένη, nom. sg. f. pres. pass.
part. [§17.Q] . . . . συναρμολογέω *(4883)*

συναρμολογούμενον, nom. sg. neut. pres. pass. part. . . . . συναρμολογέω *(4883)*

(4884) **συναρπάζω**, fut. συναρπάσω [§26.1] (σύν + ἀρπάζω) *to snatch up, clutch; to seize and carry off suddenly,* Acts 6:12; *to seize with force and violence,* Luke 8:29; pass. of a ship, *to be caught and swept on* by the wind, Acts 27:15

συναρπάσαντες, nom. pl. m. aor. act. part. . . . . συναρπάζω *(4884)*

συναρπασθέντος, gen. sg. neut. aor. pass. part. id.

συναυξάνεσθαι, pres. pass. infin. . . . . συναυξάνομαι *(†4885)*

(†4885) **συναυξάνομαι**, fut. συναυξήσομαι [§35.5] (σύν + αὐξάνω) *to grow together* in company

συναχθέντες, nom. pl. m. aor. pass. part. . . . . συνάγω *(4863)*

συναχθέντων, gen. pl. m. aor. pass. part. . id.

συναχθῆναι, aor. pass. infin. [§23.4] . . . . . id.

συναχθήσεται, 3 pers. sg. fut. pass. indic. (Matt. 25:32, MT & TR | συναχθή-σονται, GNT, WH & NA) . . . . id.

συναχθήσονται, 3 pers. pl. fut. pass. indic. id.

συνάχθητε, 2 pers. pl. aor. pass. imper. (Rev. 19:17, GNT, MT, WH & NA | συνά-γεσθε, TR) . . . . id.

συνδεδεμένοι, nom. pl. m. perf. pass. part. . . . . συνδέω *(4887)*

σύνδεσμον, acc. sg. m. n. . . . . . . σύνδεσμος *(4886)*

(4886) **σύνδεσμος**, ου, ὁ, nom. sg. m. n. [§3.C.a] *that which binds together; a ligature,* Col. 2:19; *a band* of union, Eph. 4:3; Col. 3:14; *a bundle,* or, *bond,* Acts 8:23

συνδέσμῳ, dat. sg. m. n. . . . . σύνδεσμος *(4886)*

συνδέσμων, gen. pl. m. n. . . . . id.

(4887) **συνδέω**, fut. συνδήσω [§37.1] (σύν + δέω) *to bind together;* in N.T. pass. *to be in bonds together,* Heb. 13:3

(4888) **συνδοξάζω**, fut. συνδοξάσω [§26.1] (σύν + δοξάζω) in N.T. *to glorify together with, to exalt to a state of dignity and happiness in company with, to make to partake in the glorification* of another

συνδοξασθῶμεν, 1 pers. pl. aor. pass. subj. συνδοξάζω *(4888)*

σύνδουλοι, nom. pl. m. n. . . . . σύνδουλος *(4889)*

σύνδουλον, acc. sg. m. n. . . . . id.

(4889) **σύνδουλος**, ου, ὁ, nom. sg. m. n. [§3.C.a] (σύν + δοῦλος) *a fellow-slave, fellow-servant,* Matt. 24:49, et al.; *a fellow-minister* of Christ, Col. 1:7, et al.

συνδούλου, gen. sg. m. n. . . . . σύνδουλος *(4889)*

συνδούλους, acc. pl. m. n. . . . . id.

συνδούλων, gen. pl. m. n. . . . . id.

(4890) **συνδρομή**, ῆς, ἡ, nom. sg. f. n. [§2.B.a]

(συνέδραμον) *a running together, concourse,* Acts 21:30

συνέβαινεν, 3 pers. sg. imperf. act. indic. (1 Cor. 10:11, GNT, WH & NA | συν-έβαινον, MT & TR) . . . . συμβαίνω *(4819)*

συνέβαινον, 3 pers. pl. imperf. act. indic. (1 Cor. 10:11, MT & TR | συνέβαινεν, GNT, WH & NA) . . . . id.

συνέβαλεν, 3 pers. sg. 2 aor. act. indic. [§27.2.d] (Acts 20:14, MT & TR | συνέβαλλεν, GNT, WH & NA) συμβάλλω *(4820)*

συνεβάλετο, 3 pers. sg. 2 aor. mid. indic. . id.

συνέβαλλεν, 3 pers. sg. imperf. act. indic. (Acts 20:14, GNT, WH & NA | συν-έβαλεν, MT & TR) . . . . id.

συνέβαλλον, 3 pers. pl. imperf. act. indic. id.

συνέβαλον, 3 pers. pl. 2 aor. act. indic. (Acts 4:15, TR | συνέβαλλον, GNT, MT, WH & NA) id.

συνέβη, 3 pers. sg. 2 aor. act. indic. [§37.1] . . . . συμβαίνω *(4819)*

συνεβίβασαν, 3 pers. pl. aor. act. indic. (Acts 19:33, GNT, WH & NA | προεβίβασαν, MT & TR) . . . . συμβιβάζω *(4822)*

συνεβουλεύσαντο, 3 pers. pl. aor. mid. indic. συμβουλεύω *(4823)*

(4891) **συνεγείρω**, fut. συνεγερῶ [§37.1] (σύν + ἐγείρω) *to raise up with* any one; *to raise up with* Christ by spiritual resemblance of His resurrection, Eph. 2:6; Col. 2:12; 3:1

συνέδραμε(ν), 3 pers. sg. 2 aor. act. indic. . . . . συντρέχω *(4936)*

συνέδραμον, 3 pers. pl. 2 aor. act. indic. . id.

συνέδρια, acc. pl. neut. n. . . . . συνέδριον *(4892)*

(4892) **συνέδριον**, ου, τό, nom. sg. neut. n. [§3.C.c] (σύν + ἕδρα) pr. *a sitting together, assembly,* etc.,; in N.T. *the Sanhedrin,* the supreme council of the Jewish nation, Matt. 5:22; 26:59; meton. *the Sanhedrin,* as including the members and place of meeting, Luke 22:66; Acts 4:15, et al.; genr. *a judicial council, tribunal,* Matt. 10:17; Mark 13:9 {Matt. 26:59}

συνέδριον, acc. sg. neut. n. {Luke 22:66} . . . . συνέδριον *(4892)*

συνεδρίου, gen. sg. neut. n. . . . . id.

συνεδρίῳ, dat. sg. neut. n. . . . . id.

συνέζευξεν, 3 pers. sg. aor. act. indic. . . . . συζεύγνυμι *(4801)*

συνεζήτει, 3 pers. sg. imperf. act. indic. [§34.1.c] . . . . συζητέω *(4802)*

συνεζωοποίησε(ν), 3 pers. sg. aor. act. indic. (Col. 2:13, GNT, MT, TRb, WH & NA | συνεζωποίησεν, TRs) . . . . συζωοποιέω *(4806)*

συνέθεντο, 3 pers. pl. 2 aor. mid. indic. . . . . συντίθημι *(†4934)*

συνέθλιβον, 3 pers. pl. imperf. act.

indic. . . . . συνθλίβω *(4918)*

συνειδήσει, dat. sg. f. n. . . . . συνείδησις *(4893)*

συνειδήσεσιν, dat. pl. f. n. . . . . id.

συνειδήσεως, gen. sg. f. n. . . . . id.

συνείδησιν, acc. sg. f. n. . . . . id.

(4893) **συνείδησις,** εως, ή, nom. sg. f. n. [§5.E.c] (συνειδέναι) *consciousness,* Heb. 10:2; *a present idea, persisting notion, impression of reality,* 1 Cor. 8:7; 1 Pet. 2:19; *conscience,* as an inward moral impression of one's actions and principles, John 8:9; Acts 23:1; 24:16; Rom. 9:1; 2 Cor. 1:12, et al.; *conscience,* as the inward faculty of moral judgment, Rom. 2:15; 13:5; 1 Cor. 8:7, 10, 12; 10:25, 27, 28, 29; 2 Cor. 4:2; 5:11, et al.; *conscience,* as the inward moral and spiritual frame, Tit. 1:15; Heb. 9:14

(†4894) **συνεῖδον,** 2 aor. of συνοράω, part. συνιδών [§36.1] *to see under one range of view; to take a deliberate glance* of a state of matters, Acts 12:12; 14:6

συνειδυίας, gen. sg. f. perf. act. part. (Acts 5:2, MT & TR | συνειδυίης, GNT, WH & NA) . . . . σύνοιδα *(‡4894)*

συνειδυίης, gen. sg. f. perf. act. part. (Acts 5:2, GNT, WH & NA | συνειδυίας, MT & TR) . . . . id.

συνείληφεν, 3 pers. sg. perf. act. indic. (Luke 1:36, GNT, WH & NA | συνειληφυῖα, MT & TR) . . . . συλλαμβάνω *(4815)*

συνειληφυῖα, nom. sg. f. perf. act. part. [§36.2] (Luke 1:36, MT & TR | συνείληφεν, GNT, WH & NA) . . . . id.

(4895) **σύνειμι,** fut. συνέσομαι [§12.L] (σύν + εἰμί) *to be with, be in company with,* Luke 9:18; Acts 22:11

(4896) **σύνειμι,** part. συνιών [§33.4] (σύν + εἶμι) *to come together, assemble,* Luke 8:4

συνείπετο, 3 pers. sg. imperf. mid./pass. dep. indic. συνέπομαι *(4902)*

(4897) **συνεισέρχομαι,** 2 aor. συνεισῆλθον [§36.1] (σύν + εἰσέρχομαι) *to enter with* any one, John 18:15; *to embark with,* John 6:22

συνεισῆλθε(ν), 3 pers. sg. 2 aor. act. indic. . . . . συνεισέρχομαι *(4897)*

συνείχετο, 3 pers. sg. imperf. pass. indic. . . . . συνέχω *(4912)*

συνείχοντο, 3 pers. pl. imperf. pass. indic. . . . id.

συνεκάθισεν, 3 pers. sg. aor. act. indic. [§34.1.c] . . . . συγκαθίζω *(4776)*

συνεκάλεσαν, 3 pers. pl. aor. act. indic. . . . . συγκαλέω *(4779)*

(4898) **συνέκδημος,** ου, ὁ, nom. sg. m. n. [§3.C.a] (σύν + ἔκδημος, *a traveller to foreign countries*) *one who accompanies* another *to for-*

eign countries, fellow-traveller, Acts 19:29; 2 Cor. 8:19

συνεκδήμους, acc. pl. m. n. . . . . . . συνέκδημος *(4898)*

συνεκέρασε(ν), 3 pers. sg. aor. act. indic. συγκεράννυμι *(4786)*

συνεκίνησαν, 3 pers. pl. aor. act. indic. . . . . συγκινέω *(4787)*

συνέκλεισαν, 3 pers. pl. aor. act. indic. . . . . συγκλείω *(4788)*

συνέκλεισε(ν), 3 pers. sg. aor. act. indic. . . . id.

συνεκλεκτή, nom. sg. f. adj. . . . . . συνεκλεκτός *(4899)*

(4899) **συνεκλεκτός,** ή, όν [§7.F.a] (σύν + ἐκλεκτός) *chosen along with* others; *elected* to Gospel privileges *along with,* 1 Pet. 5:13

συνεκόμισαν, 3 pers. pl. aor. act. indic. . . . . συγκομίζω *(4792)*

συνέλαβεν, 3 pers. sg. 2 aor. act. indic. . . . . συλλαμβάνω *(4815)*

συνέλαβον, 3 pers. pl. 2 aor. act. indic. . . . . id.

συνελάλησε(ν), 3 pers. sg. aor. act. indic. . . . . συλλαλέω *(4814)*

συνελάλουν, 3 pers. pl. imperf. act. indic. . . id.

(4900) **συνελαύνω,** fut. συνελάσω, aor. συνήλασα [§36.2] (σύν + ἐλαύνω) pr. *to drive together; to urge to meet;* in N.T. *to urge* to union, Acts 7:26

συνέλεξαν, 3 pers. pl. aor. act. indic. . . . συλλέγω *(4816)*

συνεληλύθεισαν, 3 pers. pl. pluperf. act. indic. . . . . id.

συνεληλυθότας, acc. pl. m. perf. act. part. . id.

συνεληλυθυῖαι, nom. pl. f. perf. act. part. . . . . συνέρχομαι *(4905)*

συνελθεῖν, 2 aor. act. infin. . . . . id.

συνέλθη, 3 pers. sg. 2 aor. act. subj. . . . . . . id.

συνελθόντα, acc. sg. m. 2 aor. act. part. . . . id.

συνελθόντας, acc. pl. m. 2 aor. act. part. . . id.

συνελθόντες, nom. pl. m. 2 aor. act. part. . id.

συνελθόντων, gen. pl. m. 2 aor. act. part. . . id.

συνελθούσαις, dat. pl. f. 2 aor. act. part. . . id.

συνελογίσαντο, 3 pers. pl. aor. mid. dep. indic. συλλογίζομαι *(4817)*

συνενέγκαντες, nom. pl. m. 2 aor. act. part. . . . . συμφέρω *(4851)*

συνέξουσι(ν), 3 pers. pl. fut. act. indic. . . . . συνέχω *(4912)*

συνεπαθήσατε, 2 pers. pl. aor. act. indic. . . . . συμπαθέω *(4834)*

συνεπέθεντο, 3 pers. pl. 2 aor. mid. indic. (Acts 24:9, GNT, WH & NA | συνέθεντο, MT & TR) . . . . συνεπιτίθεμαι *(‡4934)*

συνεπέμψαμεν, 1 pers. pl. aor. act. indic. . . . . συμπέμπω *(4842)*

συνέπεσεν, 3 pers. sg. 2 aor. act. indic. (Luke 6:49, GNT, WH & NA | ἔπεσε(ν), MT & TR) . . . . συμπίπτω *(‡4098)* συνεπέστη, 3 pers. sg. 2 aor. act.

indic. . . . . συνεφίστημι *(4911)*

(4901) **συνεπιμαρτυρέω**, ῶ, fut. συνεπιμαρτυρήσω [§16.P] (σύν + ἐπιμαρτυρέω) *to join in according attestation; to support by attestation, to confirm, sanction*

συνεπιμαρτυροῦντος, gen. sg. m. pres. act.

part. . . . . συνεπιμαρτυρέω *(4901)*

συνεπίομεν, 1 pers. pl. 2 aor. act.

indic. συμπίνω *(4844)*

(‡4934) **συνεπιτίθεμαι** (σύν + ἐπιτίθημι) *to set upon along with, assail at the same time; to unite in impeaching,* Acts 24:9

συνεπληροῦντο, 3 pers. pl. imperf. pass.

indic. . . . . συμπληρόω *(4845)*

συνέπνιγον, 3 pers. pl. imperf. act.

indic. . . . . συμπνίγω *(4846)*

συνέπνιξαν, 3 pers. pl. aor. act. indic. . . . id.

(4902) **συνέπομαι**, imperf. συνειπόμην [§13.4] (σύν + ἔπομαι, *to follow*) *to follow with, attend, accompany,* Acts 20:4

συνεπορεύετο, 3 pers. sg. imperf. mid./pass.

dep. indic. . . . . συμπορεύομαι *(4848)*

συνεπορεύοντο, 3 pers. pl. imperf. mid./pass.

dep. indic. id.

συνεργεῖ, 3 pers. sg. pres. act. indic. συνεργέω *(4903)*

(4903) **συνεργέω**, ῶ, fut. συνεργήσω [§16.P] *to work together with, to co-operate,* etc., 1 Cor. 16:16; 2 Cor. 6:1; *to assist, afford aid to,* Mark 16:20; *to be a motive principle,* James 2:22; absol. *to conspire actively* to a result, Rom. 8:28

συνεργοί, nom. pl. m. adj. . . . . συνεργός *(4904)*

συνεργόν, acc. sg. m. adj. . . . . id.

(4904) **συνεργός**, όν, nom. sg. m. adj. (σύν + ἔργον) *a fellow-laborer, associate, coadjutor,* Rom. 16:3, 9, 21; 2 Cor. 1:24, et al.

συνεργοῦντες, nom. pl. m. pres. act.

part. . . . . συνεργέω *(4903)*

συνεργοῦντι, dat. sg. m. pres. act. part. . . id.

συνεργοῦντος, gen. sg. m. pres. act. part. . id.

συνεργούς, acc. pl. m. adj. . . . . συνεργός *(4904)*

συνεργῷ, dat. sg. m. adj. . . . . id.

συνεργῶν, gen. pl. m. adj. . . . . id.

συνέρχεσθε, 2 pers. pl. pres. mid./pass. dep.

indic. . . . . συνέρχομαι *(4905)*

συνέρχεται, 3 pers. sg. pres. mid./pass. dep.

indic. . . . . id.

συνέρχησθε, 2 pers. pl. pres. mid./pass. dep.

subj. . . . . id.

(4905) **συνέρχομαι**, 2 aor. συνῆλθον [§36.1] (σύν + ἔρχομαι) *to come together; to assemble,* Mark 3:20; 6:33; 14:53; *to cohabit* matrimonially, Matt. 1:18; 1 Cor. 7:5; *to go or come with* any one, *to accompany,* Luke

23:55; Acts 9:39; *to company with, associate with,* Acts 1:21, et al.

συνερχόμενοι, nom. pl. m. pres. mid./pass.

dep. part. . . . . συνέρχομαι *(4905)*

συνερχομένων, gen. pl. m. pres. mid./pass.

dep. part. id.

συνέρχονται, 3 pers. pl. pres. mid./pass. dep.

indic. . . . . id.

συνέσει, dat. sg. f. n. . . . . σύνεσις *(4907)*

συνέσεως, gen. sg. f. n. . . . . id.

συνεσθίει, 3 pers. sg. pres. act. indic. συνεσθίω *(4906)*

συνεσθίειν, pres. act. infin. . . . . id.

(4906) **συνεσθίω**, 2 aor. συνέφαγον [§36.1] (σύν + ἐσθίω) *to eat with,* 1 Cor. 5:11; *by impl. to associate with, live on familiar terms with,* Luke 15:2; Gal. 2:12

σύνεσιν, acc. sg. f. n. . . . . σύνεσις *(4907)*

(4907) **σύνεσις**, εως, ἡ [§5.E.c] pr. *a sending together, a junction,* as of streams; met. *understanding, intelligence, discernment, sagaciousness,* Luke 2:47; 1 Cor. 1:19, et al.; meton. *the understanding, intellect, mind,* Mark 12:33

συνεσπάραξεν, 3 pers. sg. aor. act.

indic. . . . . συσπαράσσω *(4952)*

συνεσταλμένος, nom. sg. m. perf. pass.

part. . . . . συστέλλω *(4958)*

συνεσταυρώθη, 3 pers. sg. aor. pass. indic.

[§21.U] . . . . συσταυρόω *(4957)*

συνεσταύρωμαι, 1 pers. sg. perf. pass. indic. id.

συνεσταυρωμένοι, nom. pl. m. perf. pass.

part. . . . . id.

συνέστειλαν, 3 pers. pl. aor. act. indic.

[§27.1.d] . . . . συστέλλω *(4958)*

συνέστηκε(ν), 3 pers. sg. perf. act. indic.

[§29.X] . . . . συνίστημι *(4921)*

συνεστήσατε, 2 pers. pl. aor. act. indic. . . id.

συνεστῶσα, nom. sg. f. perf. act. part.

[§35.8] . . . . id.

συνεστῶτας, acc. pl. m. perf. act. part. . . id.

συνέσχον, 3 pers. pl. 2 aor. act. indic.

[§36.4] . . . . συνέχω *(4912)*

συνέταξε(ν), 3 pers. sg. aor. act.

indic. . . . . συντάσσω *(4929)*

συνετάφημεν, 1 pers. pl. 2 aor. pass. indic.

[§24.8.b] . . . . συνθάπτω *(4916)*

σύνετε, 2 pers. pl. 2 aor. imper. (Mark 7:14, GNT, WH & NA | συνίετε, MT & TR) . . . . συνίημι *(4920)*

συνετέθειντο, 3 pers. pl. pluperf. mid. indic.

[§28.10] . . . . συντίθημι *(†4934)*

συνετέλεσεν, 3 pers. sg. aor. act. indic. (Matt. 7:28, MT & TR | ἐτέλεσεν, GNT, WH & NA) . . . . συντελέω *(4931)*

συνετήρει, 3 pers. sg. imperf. act.

indic. συντηρέω *(4933)*

(4908) **συνετός, ή, όν** [§7.F.a] *intelligent, discerning, sagacious, wise, prudent,* Matt. 11:25; Luke 20:21, et al.

συνετῷ, dat. sg. m. adj. . . . . συνετός *(4908)*
συνετῶν, gen. pl. m. adj. . . . . id.
συνευδοκεῖ, 3 pers. sg. pres. act.
indic. . . . . συνευδοκέω *(4909)*
συνευδοκεῖτε, 2 pers. pl. pres. act. indic. . id.

(4909) **συνευδοκέω, ῶ,** fut. συνευδοκήσω [§16.P] (σύν + εὐδοκέω) *to approve with* another; *to accord with in principle,* Rom. 1:32; *to stamp approval,* Luke 11:48; Acts 8:1; 22:20; *to be willing, agreeable,* 1 Cor. 7:12, 13

συνευδοκοῦσι(ν), 3 pers. pl. pres. act.
indic. . . . . συνευδοκέω *(4909)*
συνευδοκῶν, nom. sg. m. pres. act. part. . id.

(†4910) **συνευωχέομαι, οῦμαι,** fut. συνευωχήσομαι [§17.Q] (σύν + εὐωχέομαι, *to feast, banquet*) *to feast together with,* 2 Pet. 2:13; Jude 12

συνευωχούμενοι, nom. pl. m. pres. mid./pass.
dep. part. . . . . συνευωχέομαι *(†4910)*
συνέφαγεν, 3 pers. sg. 2 aor. act. indic. (Acts 11:3, WH | συνέφαγες, GNT, MT, TR & NA) . . . . συνεσθίω *(4906)*
συνέφαγες, 2 pers. sg. 2 aor. act. indic. (Acts 11:3, GNT, MT, TR & NA | συνέφαγεν, WH) . . . . id.
συνεφάγομεν, 1 pers. pl. 2 aor. act. indic.   id.

(4911) **συνεφίστημι** [§29.X] (σύν + ἐφίστημι) *to set together upon;* intrans. 2 aor. συνεπέστην, *to assail together,* Acts 16:22

συνεφωνήθη, 3 pers. sg. aor. pass.
indic. . . . . συμφωνέω *(4856)*
συνεφώνησας, 2 pers. sg. aor. act. indic. . id.
συνέχαιρον, 3 pers. pl. imperf. act.
indic. . . . . συγχαίρω *(4796)*
συνέχει, 3 pers. sg. pres. act. indic. . . . συνέχω *(4912)*
συνέχεον, 3 pers. pl. imperf. act. indic.
[§35.1] . . . . συγχέω *(4797)*
συνέχομαι, 1 pers. sg. pres. pass.
indic. . . . . συνέχω *(4912)*
συνεχομένη, nom. sg. f. pres. pass. part. . id.
συνεχόμενον, acc. sg. m. pres. pass. part. . id.
συνεχομένους, acc. pl. m. pres. pass. part. . id.
συνέχοντες, nom. pl. m. pres. act. part. . . id.
συνέχουσι(ν), 3 pers. pl. pres. act. indic. . . id.
συνεχύθη, 3 pers. sg. aor. pass. indic. . συγχέω *(4797)*
συνέχυνε(ν), 3 pers. sg. imperf. act. indic.
(Acts 9:22, MT & TR | συνέχυννεν, GNT, WH & NA) . . . . id.
συνέχυννεν, 3 pers. sg. imperf. act. indic. (Acts 9:22, GNT, WH & NA | συνέχυνε(ν),

MT & TR) . . . . συγχέω *(4797)*

(4912) **συνέχω,** fut. συνέξω [§36.4] (σύν + ἔχω) pr. *to hold together; to confine, shut up close;* τὰ ὦτα, *to stop the ears,* Acts 7:57; *to confine, straiten,* as a besieged city, Luke 19:43; *to hold, hold fast, have the custody of* any one, Luke 22:63; *to hem in, urge, press upon,* Luke 8:45; *to exercise a constraining influence on,* 2 Cor. 5:14; pass. *to be seized with, be affected with,* as fear, disease, etc., Matt. 4:24; Luke 4:38, et al.; *to be in a state of* mental *constriction, to be hard pressed* by urgency of circumstances, Luke 12:50; Acts 18:5; Phil. 1:23

συνεψήφισαν, 3 pers. pl. aor. act.
indic. . . . . συμψηφίζω *(4860)*
συνήγαγεν, 3 pers. sg. 2 aor. act. indic.
[§13.7.d] . . . . συνάγω *(4863)*
συνηγάγετε, 2 pers. pl. 2 aor. act. indic. . . id.
συνηγάγομεν, 1 pers. pl. 2 aor. act. indic.   id.
συνήγαγον, 3 pers. pl. 2 aor. act. indic. . . id.
συνήγειρε(ν), 3 pers. sg. aor. act.
indic. . . . . συνεγείρω *(4891)*
συνηγέρθητε, 2 pers. pl. aor. pass. indic. . id.
συνηγμένα, acc. pl. neut. perf. pass.
part. συνάγω *(4863)*
συνηγμένοι, nom. pl. m. perf. pass. part. . id.
συνηγμένων, gen. pl. m. perf. pass. part. . id.

(4913) **συνήδομαι,** 1 pers. sg. pres. mid./pass. dep. indic., fut. συνησθήσομαι (σύν + ἥδομαι, *to be pleased, delighted*) *to be pleased along with* others; *to congratulate; to delight in, approve cordially,* Rom. 7:22

(4914) **συνήθεια, ας, ἡ,** nom. sg. f. n. [§2.B.b; 2.2] (συνήθης, *accustomed, familiar, customary,* from σύν + ἦθος) *intercourse; use, custom; an established custom, practice,* John 18:39; 1 Cor. 11:16

συνηθείᾳ, dat. sg. f. n. (1 Cor. 8:7, GNT, WH & NA | συνειδήσει, MT & TR) . συνήθεια *(4914)*
συνήθειαν, acc. sg. f. n. . . . . id.
συνήθλησαν, 3 pers. pl. aor. act.
indic. . . . . συναθλέω *(4866)*
συνηθροισμένοι, nom. pl. m. perf. pass.
part. . . . . συναθροίζω *(4867)*
συνηθροισμένους, acc. pl. m. perf. pass. part.
(Luke 24:33, MT & TR | ἠθροισμένους, GNT, WH & NA) . . . . id.
συνῆκαν, 3 pers. pl. aor. act. indic.
[§32.CC] . . . . συνίημι *(4920)*
συνήκατε, 2 pers. pl. aor. act. indic. . . . . . id.
συνηκολούθει, 3 pers. sg. imperf. act. indic.
(Mark 14:52, GNT, WH & NA | ἠκολούθει, TR | ἠκολούθησεν, MT) . . . . συνακολουθέω *(4870)*

συνήλασεν, 3 pers. sg. aor. act. indic. (Acts 7:26, MT & TR | συνήλλασσεν, GNT, WH & NA) . . . . συνελαύνω *(4900)*

συνῆλθαν, 3 pers. pl. 2 aor. act. indic. (Acts 10:45, GNT, WH & NA | συνῆλθον, MT & TR) . . . . συνέρχομαι *(4905)*

συνῆλθε(ν), 3 pers. sg. 2 aor. act. indic. . . id.

συνῆλθον, 3 pers. pl. 2 aor. act. indic. [§36.1] id.

συνηλικιώτας, acc. pl. m. n. . . . συνηλικιώτης *(4915)*

(4915) **συνηλικιώτης**, ου, ὁ [§2.B.c] (σύν + ἡλικιώτης, idem, from. ἡλικία) *one of the same age, an equal in age*

συνήλλασσεν, 3 pers. sg. imperf. act. indic. (Acts 7:26, GNT, WH & NA | συνή-λασεν, MT & TR) . . . . . . συναλλάσσω *(‡4900)*

συνήντησεν, 3 pers. sg. aor. act. indic. . . . . συναντάω *(4876)*

συνήργει, 3 pers. sg. imperf. act. indic. . . . . συνεργέω *(4903)*

συνηρπάκει, 3 pers. sg. pluperf. act. indic. . . . . συναρπάζω *(4884)*

συνήρπασαν, 3 pers. pl. aor. act. indic. . . . id.

συνήρχετο, 3 pers. sg. imperf. mid./pass. dep. indic. . . . . συνέρχομαι *(4905)*

συνήρχοντο, 3 pers. pl. imperf. mid./pass. dep. indic. id.

συνῆσαν, 3 pers. pl. imperf. indic. [§12.L] . . . . σύνειμι *(4895)*

συνήσθιεν, 3 pers. sg. imperf. act. indic. . . . . συνεσθίω *(4906)*

συνήσουσι(ν), 3 pers. pl. fut. act. indic. . συνίημι *(4920)*

συνῆτε, 2 pers. pl. 2 aor. act. subj. [§32.CC] id.

συνήχθη, 3 pers. sg. aor. pass. indic. . συνάγω *(4863)*

συνήχθησαν, 3 pers. pl. aor. pass. indic. . . . id.

(4916) **συνθάπτω**, fut. συνθάψω, 2 aor. pass. συνετάφην [§24.8.b] (σύν + θάπτω) *to bury with;* pass. in N.T. *to be buried with* Christ symbolically, Rom. 6:4; Col. 2:12

συνθλασθήσεται, 3 pers. sg. fut. pass. indic. . . . . συνθλάω *(4917)*

(4917) **συνθλάω**, ῶ, fut. συνθλάσω, fut. pass. συν-θλασθήσομαι [§22.2.4] (σύν + θλάω, *to break*) *to crush together; to break in pieces, shatter,* Matt. 21:44; Luke 20:18

συνθλίβοντα, acc. sg. m. pres. act. part. . . . . συνθλίβω *(4918)*

(4918) **συνθλίβω**, fut. συνφλίψω [§23.1.a] (σύν + θλίβω) *to press together; to press upon, crowd, throng,* Mark 5:24, 31

συνθρύπτοντες, nom. pl. m. pres. act. part. . . . . συνθρύπτω *(4919)*

(4919) **συνθρύπτω**, fut. συνθρύψω [§23.1.a] (σύν + θρύπτω) *to crush to pieces;* met. *to break the heart of any one, to make to quail*

συνιᾶσιν, 3 pers. pl. pres. act. indic. [§28.6]

(2 Cor. 10:12, GNT, WH & NA | συν-ιοῦσιν, MT & TR) . . . . συνίημι *(4920)*

συνιδόντες, nom. pl. m. 2 aor. act. part. [§36.1] . . . . συνεῖδον *(†4894)*

συνιδών, nom. sg. m. 2 aor. act. part. . . . id.

συνιείς, nom. sg. m. pres. act. part. (Matt. 13:23, GNT, WH & NA | συνιῶν, MT & TR) . . . . συνίημι *(4920)*

συνιέναι, pres. act. infin. . . . . id.

συνιέντες, nom. pl. m. pres. act. part. (Eph. 5:17, MT & TR | συνίετε, GNT, WH & NA) . . . . id.

συνιέντος, gen. sg. m. pres. act. part. . . . . id.

συνίετε, 2 pers. pl. pres. act. indic. {Mark 8:17} . . . . id.

συνίετε, 2 pers. pl. pres. act. imper. {Matt. 15:10} . . . . id.

(4920) **συνίημι**, fut. συνήσω, and συνήσομαι, aor. συνῆκα, 2 aor. subj. συνῶ, and in N.T. 3 pers. pl. pres. συνιοῦσιν (as if from συνιέω) part. συνιῶν and συνιών [§32.CC] (σύν + ἵημι, *to send*) pr. *to send together;* met. *to understand, comprehend thoroughly,* Matt. 13:51; Luke 2:50; 18:34; 24:45; *to perceive clearly,* Matt. 16:12; 17:13; Acts 7:25; Rom. 15:21; Eph. 5:17; absol. *to be well-judging, sensible,* 2 Cor. 10:12; *to be* spiritually *intelligent,* Matt. 13:13, 14, 15; Acts 28:26, 27, et al.; *to be* religiously *wise,* Rom. 3:11

συνιόντος, gen. sg. m. pres. part. [§33.4] . . . . σύνειμι *(4896)*

συνιοῦσι(ν), 3 pers. pl. pres. act. indic. (of συνιέω) . . . . συνίημι *(4920)*

συνιστάνειν, pres. act. infin. (of συνιστάνω) . . . . συνίστημι *(4921)*

συνιστάνομεν, 1 pers. pl. pres. act. indic. (of συνιστάνω) . . . . id.

συνιστάνοντες, nom. pl. m. pres. act. part. (2 Cor. 4:2, GNT, WH & NA | συνι-στῶντες, MT & TR) . . . . id.

συνιστανόντων, gen. pl. m. pres. act. part. (of συνιστάνω) . . . . id.

συνιστάντες, nom. pl. m. pres. act. part. (2 Cor. 6:4, GNT & NA | συνιστῶντες, MT & TR | συνιστάνοντες, WH) . . . . id.

(4921) **συνιστάνω**, 1 pers. sg. pres. act. indic., *to place in a striking point of view, to evince* (Gal. 2:18, GNT, WH & NA | συνίστημι, MT & TR)

συνιστάνων, nom. sg. m. pres. act. part. (2 Cor. 10:18, GNT, WH & NA | συν-ιστῶν, MT & TR) . . . . συνιστάνω *(4921)*

συνίστασθαι, pres. pass. infin. [§29.Y] . . . . συνίστημι *(4921)*

(4921) **συνίστημι**, 1 pers. sg. pres. act. indic., and

later, συνιστάω, and συνιστάνω, fut.
συστήσω [§29.X] (σύν + ἵστημι) to place
together; to recommend to favorable attention, Rom. 16:1; 2 Cor. 3:1; 10:18, et al.;
to place in a striking point of view, to
evince, Rom. 3:5; 5:8; Gal. 2:18; intrans.
perf. συνέστηκα, part. συνεστώς, to stand
beside, Luke 9:32; to have been perman-
ently framed, Col. 1:17; to possess consistence, 2 Pet. 3:5

συνίστησι(ν), 3 pers. sg. pres. act.
indic. . . . . συνίστημι (4921)

συνιστῶν, nom. sg. m. pres. act. part. (of
συνιστάω | 2 Cor. 10:18, MT & TR |
συνιστάνων, GNT, WH & NA) . . . . . id.

συνιστῶντες, nom. pl. m. pres. act. part. (of
συνιστάω | 2 Cor. 4:2; 6:4, MT & TR |
2 Cor. 4:2, συνιστάνοντες, GNT, WH &
NA | 2 Cor. 6:4, συνιστάντες, GNT &
NA. WH has συνιστάνοντες) . . . . id.

συνιῶν, nom. sg. m. pres. act. part. (of
συνιέω) . . . . συνίημι (4920)

συνιῶσι(ν), 3 pers. pl. pres. act. subj. . . . . id.

συνοδεύοντες, nom. pl. m. pres. act.
part. . . . . συνοδεύω (4922)

(4922) **συνοδεύω**, fut. συνοδεύσω [§13.M] (σύν +
ὁδεύω) to journey or travel with, accompany on a journey

(4923) **συνοδία**, ας, ἡ [§2.B.b; 2.2] (σύν + ὁδός) pr.
a journeying together; meton. a company
of fellow-travellers, caravan, Luke 2:44

συνοδίᾳ, dat. sg. f. n. . . . . συνοδία (4923)

(‡4894) **σύνοιδα**, 1 pers. sg. perf. act. indic., a perf.
with the sense of a present, part. συνειδώς
[§37.1] to share in the knowledge of a
thing; to be privy to, Acts 5:2; to be con-
scious; οὐδὲν σύνοιδα, to have a clear conscience, 1 Cor. 4:4

(4924) **συνοικέω**, ῶ, fut. συνοικήσω [§16.P] (σύν +
οἰκέω) to dwell with; to live or cohabit
with, 1 Pet. 3:7

συνοικοδομεῖσθε, 2 pers. pl. pres. pass. indic.
[§17.Q] . . . . συνοικοδομέω (4925)

(4925) **συνοικοδομέω**, ῶ [§16.P] (σύν + οἰκοδομέω)
to build in company with any one; pass.
to be built in along with, form a constituent part of a structure

συνοικοῦντες, nom. pl. m. pres. act.
part. . . . . συνοικέω (4924)

(4926) **συνομιλέω**, ῶ, fut. συνομιλήσω [§16.P] (σύν
+ ὁμιλέω) pr. to be in company with; to
talk or converse with, Acts 10:27

συνομιλῶν, nom. sg. m. pres. act.
part. . . . . συνομιλέω (4926)

(4927) **συνομορέω**, ῶ, fut. συνομορήσω [§16.P] (σύν

+ ὁμορέω, to border upon, from ὁμός +
ὅρος) to be contiguous, adjoin

συνομοροῦσα, nom. sg. f. pres. act.
part. . . . . συνομορέω (4927)

συνόντων, gen. pl. m. pres. part. . . . . . σύνειμι (4895)

(4928) **συνοχή**, ῆς, ἡ, nom. sg. f. n. [§2.B.a] pr. a being held together; compression; in N.T.
met. distress of mind, anxiety, Luke 21:25;
2 Cor. 2:4

συνοχῆς, gen. sg. f. n. . . . . συνοχή (4928)

(4929) **συντάσσω**, or συντάττω, fut. συντάξω
[§26.3] (σύν + τάσσω) pr. to arrange or
place in order together; in N.T. to order,
charge, direct, Matt. 26:19; 27:10

συνταφέντες, nom. pl. m. 2 aor. pass. part.
[§24.8.b] . . . . συνθάπτω (4916)

(4930) **συντέλεια**, ας, ἡ, nom. sg. f. n. [§2.B.b; 2.2]
a complete combination, a completion,
consummation, end, Matt. 13:39, 40, 49;
24:3; 28:20; Heb. 9:26

συντελείᾳ, dat. sg. f. n. . . . . συντέλεια (4930)

συντελείας, gen. sg. f. n. . . . . id.

συντελεῖσθαι, pres. pass. infin.
[§17.Q] . . . . συντελέω (4931)

συντελέσας, nom. sg. m. aor. act. part. . . id.

συντελεσθεισῶν, gen. pl. f. aor. pass. part. id.

συντελέσω, 1 pers. sg. fut. act. indic. . . . . id.

(4931) **συντελέω**, ῶ, fut. συντελέσω [§22.1] (σύν +
τελέω) pr. to bring to an end altogether;
to finish, end, Matt. 7:28; to consummate,
Rom. 9:28; to ratify a covenant, Heb. 8:8;
pass. to be terminated, Luke 4:2; Acts
21:27; to be fully realized, Mark 13:4

συντελῶν, nom. sg. m. pres. act.
part. . . . . συντελέω (4931)

(4932) **συντέμνω**, fut. συντεμῶ, perf. τέτμηκα
[§27.2.d] perf. pass. τέτμημαι (σύν +
τέμνω) pr. to cut short, contract by cutting
off; met. to execute speedily, or from the
Hebrew, to determine, decide, decree, Rom.
9:28(2×)

συντέμνων, nom. sg. m. pres. act.
part. . . . . συντέμνω (4932)

συντετμημένον, acc. sg. m. perf. pass. part.
[§27.3] (Rom. 9:28, MT & TR | GNT,
WH & NA omit) . . . . id.

συντετριμμένον, acc. sg. m. perf. pass. part.
[§23.7.8] . . . . συντρίβω (4937)

συντετριμμένους, acc. pl. m. perf. pass. part.
(Luke 4:18, MT & TR | GNT, WH & NA
omit) . . . . id.

συντετρίφθαι, perf. pass. infin. . . . . id.

(4933) **συντηρέω**, ῶ, fut. συντηρήσω [§16.P] (σύν +
τηρέω) to keep safe and sound, Matt. 9:17;
Luke 5:38; to observe strictly, or, to secure

from harm, protect, Mark 6:20; *to preserve in memory, keep carefully in mind,* Luke 2:19

συντηροῦνται, 3 pers. pl. pres. pass. indic.
[§17.Q] . . . . συντηρέω *(4933)*

(†4934) **συντίθημι** [§28.V] (σύν + τίθημι) *to place together;* 2 aor. mid. συνεθέμην, perf. συντέθειμαι [§28.W; 28.10] *to agree together, come to a mutual understanding,* John 9:22; Acts 23:20; *to bargain, to pledge one's self,* Luke 22:5; *to second* a statement, Acts 24:9

(4935) **συντόμως,** adv., *concisely, briefly,* Acts 24:4

συντρεχόντων, gen. pl. m. pres. act. part. συντρέχω *(4936)*

(4936) **συντρέχω,** 2 aor. συνέδραμον [§36.1] (σύν + τρέχω) *to run together, flock together,* Mark 6:33; Acts 3:11; *to run in company with* others, met. 1 Pet. 4:4

συντρίβεται, 3 pers. sg. pres. pass. indic. συντρίβω *(4937)*

συντριβήσεται, 3 pers. sg. 2 fut. pass. indic. [§24.3] . . . . id.

συντρῖβον, nom. sg. neut. pres. act. part. (Luke 9:39, GNT, WH, MT & NA | συντρίβον, TR) . . . . id.

(4937) **συντρίβω,** fut. συντρίψω, perf. pass. συντέτριμμαι [§23.1.a; 23.7] fut. pass. συντριβήσομαι (σύν + τρίβω) *to rub together; to shiver,* Mark 14:3; Rev. 2:27; *to break, break in pieces,* Mark 5:4; John 19:36; *to break down, crush, bruise,* Matt. 12:20; met. *to break the power of* any one, *deprive of strength, debilitate,* Luke 9:39; Rom. 16:20; pass. *to be broken* in heart, *be contrite,* Luke 4:18

(4938) **σύντριμμα,** ατος, τό, nom. sg. neut. n. [§4.D.c] *a breaking, bruising;* in N.T. *destruction, ruin,* Rom. 3:16

συντρίψασα, nom. sg. f. aor. act. part. . . . . συντρίβω *(4937)*

συντρίψει, 3 pers. sg. fut. act. indic. . . . . . id.

(4939) **σύντροφος,** ον, nom. sg. m. adj. [§7.2] (συντρέφω, *to nurse, bring up together,* σύν + τρέφω) *nursed with* another; *one brought up or educated with* another, Acts 13:1

(4940) **συντυγχάνω,** 2 aor. συνέτυχον [§36.2] (σύν + τυγχάνω) *to meet or fall in with;* in N.T. *to get to, approach,* Luke 8:19

συντυχεῖν, 2 aor. act. infin. . . . . . συντυγχάνω *(4940)*

(4941) **Συντύχη,** ης, ἡ [§2.B.a] *Syntyche,* pr. name

Συντύχην, acc. sg. f. n. . . . . Συντύχη *(4941)*

συνυπεκρίθησαν, 3 pers. pl. aor. pass. indic. [§27.3] . . . . συνυποκρίνομαι *(4942)*

(4942) **συνυποκρίνομαι** (σύν + ὑποκρίνομαι) aor. (pass. form) συνυπεκρίθην, *to dissemble, feign with,* or *in the same manner as* another

(4943) **συνυπουργέω,** ῶ, fut. συνυπουργήσω [§16.P] (σύν + ὑπουργέω, *to render service,* from ὑπό + ἔργον) *to aid along with* another, *help together*

συνυπουργούντων, gen. pl. m. pres. act. part. . . . . συνυπουργέω *(4943)*

συνωδίνει, 3 pers. sg. pres. act. indic. . . . . συνωδίνω *(4944)*

(4944) **συνωδίνω,** fut. συνωδινῶ [§27.1.a] (σύν + ὠδίνω, *to be in birth-pangs*) pr. *to travail at the same time with;* trop. *to be altogether in throes,* Rom. 8:22

(4945) **συνωμοσία,** ας, ἡ [§2.B.b; 2.2] (συνόμνυμι, *to swear together,* from σύν + ὄμνυμι) *a banding by oath; a combination, conspiracy*

συνωμοσίαν, acc. sg. f. n. . . . . συνωμοσία *(4945)*

συνῶσι(ν), 3 pers. pl. 2 aor. act. subj. συνίημι *(4920)*

(4946) **Συρακοῦσαι,** ῶν, αἱ, *Syracuse,* a celebrated city of Sicily, Acts 28:12

Συρακούσας, acc. pl. f. n. . . . . . . Συρακοῦσαι *(4946)*

σύρει, 3 pers. sg. pres. act. indic. . . . . . σύρω *(4951)*

(4947) **Συρία,** ας, ἡ [§2.B.b; 2.2] *Syria,* an extensive country of Asia

Συρίαν, acc. sg. f. n. . . . . Συρία *(4947)*

Συρίας, gen. sg. f. n. . . . . id.

σύροντες, nom. sg. m. pres. act. part. . . σύρω *(4951)*

(4948) **Σύρος,** ου, ὁ, nom. sg. m. n., *a Syrian*

(†4949) **Συροφοίνικισσα,** or Συροφοίνισσα, ης, ἡ, nom. sg. f. n. [§2.3] *a Syrophenician woman,* Phenicia being included in Syria, Mark 7:26

Σύρτην, acc. sg. f. n. (Acts 27:17, MT | σύρτιν, GNT, WH, NA & TR) . . . Σύρτις *(4950)*

σύρτιν, acc. sg. f. n. (Acts 27:17, GNT, WH, TR & NA | Σύρτην, MT) . . . . id.

(4950) **Σύρτις,** εως, ἡ [§5.E.c] *a shoal, sand-bank, a place dangerous on account of shoals,* two of which were particularly famous on the northern coast of Africa, one lying near Carthage, and the other, *the syrtis major,* lying between Cyrene and Leptis, which is probably referred to in Acts 27:17

(4951) **σύρω,** *to draw, drag,* John 21:8; Rev. 12:4; *to force away, hale* before magistrates, etc., Acts 8:3; 14:19; 17:6

σύρων, nom. sg. m. pres. act. part. . . . . . σύρω *(4951)*

(4952) **συσπαράσσω,** or συσπαράττω}, fut. συσπαράξω [§26.3] (σύν + σπαράσσω) *to tear to pieces; to convulse altogether,* Luke 9:42

(4953) **σύσσημον,** ου, τό [§3.C.c] (σύν + σῆμα) *a concerted signal*
σύσσημον, acc. sg. neut. n. .... σύσσημον *(4953)*
σύσσωμα, acc. pl. neut. adj. (Eph. 3:6, GNT, MT, TR & NA | σύνσωμα, WH) .... σύσσωμος *(4954)*

(4954) **σύσσωμος,** ον [§7.2] (σύν + σῶμα) *united in the same body;* met. pl. *joint members* in a spiritual body, Eph. 3:6

(4955) **συστασιαστής,** οῦ, ὁ [§2.B.c] (συστασιάζω, *to join in a sedition with,* from σύν + στάσις) *an accomplice in sedition, associate in insurrection*
συστασιαστῶν, gen. pl. m. n. (Mark 15:7, MT & TR | στασιαστῶν, GNT, WH & NA) .... συστασιαστής *(4955)*

(4956) **συστατικός,** ή, όν [§7.F.a] *commendatory, recommendatory,* 2 Cor. 3:1 (2×)
συστατικῶν, gen. pl. m. adj. .... συστατικός *(4956)*

(4957) **συσταυρόω,** ῶ, fut. συσταυρώσω, perf. pass. συνεσταύρωμαι, aor. pass. συνεσταυρώθην [§21.U] (σύν + σταυρόω) *to crucify with* another, Matt. 27:44; Mark 15:32; John 19:32; pass. met. *to be crucified with* another in a spiritual resemblance, Rom. 6:6; Gal. 2:20
συσταυρωθέντες, nom. pl. m. aor. pass. part. (Matt. 27:44, GNT, MT, TR & NA | συνσταυρωθέντες, WH) .... συσταυρόω *(4957)*
συσταυρωθέντος, gen. sg. m. aor. pass. part. (John 19:32, GNT, MT, TR & NA | συνσταυρωθέντος, WH) .... id.

(4958) **συστέλλω,** fut. συστελῶ, aor. συνέστειλα [§27.1.b,d] perf. pass. συνέσταλμαι [§27.3] (σύν + στέλλω) *to draw together, contract, straiten; to enwrap;* hence, i.q. περιστέλλω, *to lay out, prepare for burial,* Acts 5:6; pass. *to be shortened,* or, *to be environed with trials,* 1 Cor. 7:29
συστενάζει, 3 pers. sg. pres. act. indic. (Rom. 8:22, GNT, MT, TR & NA | συστενάζει, WH) .... συστενάζω *(4959)*

(4959) **συστενάζω,** fut. συστενάξω [§26.2] (σύν + στενάζω) *to groan altogether*
συστοιχεῖ, 3 pers. sg. pres. act. indic. (Gal. 4:25, GNT, MT, TR & NA | συνστοιχεῖ, WH) .... συστοιχέω *(4960)*

(4960) **συστοιχέω,** ῶ, fut. συστοιχήσω [§16.P] (σύν + στοιχέω) pr. *to be in the same row with;* met. *to correspond to,* Gal. 4:25
συστρατιώτῃ, dat. sg. m. n. (Philemon 2, GNT, MT, TR & NA | συνστρατιώτῃ, WH) .... συστρατιώτης *(4961)*
συστρατιώτην, acc. sg. m. n. (Phil. 2:25, GNT, MT, TR & NA | συνστρατιώτην,

WH) .... συστρατιώτης *(4961)*

(4961) **συστρατιώτης,** ου, ὁ [§2.B.c] (σύν + στρατιώτης) *a fellow-soldier;* met. *a fellow-soldier, co-militant,* in the service of Christ, Phil. 2:25; Philemon 2
συστρεφομένων, gen. pl. m. pres. pass. part. (Matt. 17:22, GNT, WH & NA | ἀναστρεφομένων, MT & TR) .... συστρέφω *(4962)*

(4962) **συστρέφω,** fut. συστρέψω [§23.1.a] (σύν + στρέφω) *to turn or roll together; to collect, gather*
συστρέψαντος, gen. sg. m. aor. act. part. .... συστρέφω *(4962)*

(4963) **συστροφή,** ῆς, ἡ [§2.B.a] *a gathering, concourse, tumultuous assembly,* Acts 19:40; *a combination, conspiracy,* Acts 23:12
συστροφήν, acc. sg. f. n. .... συστροφή *(4963)*
συστροφῆς, gen. sg. f. n. .... id.
συσχηματίζεσθε, 2 pers. pl. pres. mid./pass. imper. (Rom. 12:2, GNT, MT, TR & NA | συνσχηματίζεσθε, WH) ... συσχηματίζω *(4964)*
συσχηματιζόμενοι, nom. pl. m. pres. mid./pass. part. (1 Pet. 1:14, GNT, MT, TR & NA | συνσχηματιζόμενοι, WH) ... id.

(4964) **συσχηματίζω** (σύν + σχηματίζω, *to form,* from σχῆμα) *to fashion in accordance with;* mid./pass. *to conform or assimilate one's self to,* met. Rom. 12:2; 1 Pet. 1:14

(4965) **Συχάρ,** ἡ, indecl. *Sychar,* a city of Samaria, John 4:5

(4966) **Συχέμ,** ἡ, indecl. *Sychem,* a city of Samaria, or ὁ, *Shechem,* proper name (Acts 7:16, GNT, MT, TRs, WH & NA | Σιχέμ, TRb)

(4967) **σφαγή,** ῆς, ἡ [§2.B.a] *slaughter,* Acts 8:32; Rom. 8:36; James 5:5
σφαγήν, acc. sg. f. n. .... ·σφαγή *(4967)*
σφαγῆς, gen. sg. f. n. .... id.
σφάγια, acc. pl. neut. n. .... σφάγιον *(4968)*

(4968) **σφάγιον,** ου, τό [§3.C.c] *a victim* slaughtered in sacrifice, Acts 7:42

(4969) **σφάζω,** or Att. σφάττω, fut. σφάξω, aor. ἔσφαξα, 2 aor. pass. ἐσφάγην [§26.3] perf. pass. ἔσφαγμαι, *to slaughter, kill, slay;* pr. used of animals killed in sacrifice, etc., Rev. 5:6, 9, 12; 13:8; of persons, etc., 1 John 3:12; Rev. 6:4, 9; 18:24; *to wound mortally,* Rev. 13:3
σφάξουσιν, 3 pers. pl. fut. act. indic. (Rev. 6:4, GNT, WH & NA | σφάξωσι(ν), MT & TR) .... σφάζω *(4969)*
σφάξωσι(ν), 3 pers. pl. aor. act. subj. (Rev. 6:4, MT & TR | σφάξουσιν, GNT, WH & NA) .... id.

(4970) **σφόδρα,** adv. (pr. neut. pl. of σφοδρός, *vehe-*

ment, violent, strong) much, greatly, exceedingly, Matt. 2:10; 17:6, et al.

(4971) σφοδρῶς, adv. (from σφοδρός) *exceedingly, vehemently*

σφραγῖδα, acc. sg. f. n. . . . . σφραγίς *(4973)*

σφραγῖδας, acc. pl. f. n. . . . . id.

σφραγῖδων, gen. pl. f. n. . . . . id.

(4972) σφραγίζω, fut. σφραγίσω, aor. ἐσφράγισα, perf. pass. ἐσφράγισμαι, aor. pass. ἐσφραγίσθην [§26.1] *to seal, stamp with a seal,* Matt. 27:66; *to seal up, to close up, conceal,* Rev. 10:4; 22:10; *to set a mark upon, distinguish by a mark,* Rev. 7:3, 8; *to seal, to mark distinctively* as invested with a certain character, John 6:27; mid. *to set one's own mark upon, seal as one's own, to impress with a mark of acceptance,* 2 Cor. 1:22; *to obtain a quittance of, to deliver over safely* to any one, Rom. 15:28; absol. *to set to one's seal, to make a solemn declaration,* John 3:33

σφραγίζωμεν, 1 pers. pl. pres. act. subj. (Rev. 7:3, TRs | σφραγίσωμεν, GNT, MT, TRb, WH & NA) . . . . σφραγίζω *(4972)*

(4973) σφραγίς, nom. sg. f. n. σφραγίς, ίδος, ἡ [§4.2.c] *a seal, a signet ring,* Rev. 7:2; *an inscription on a seal, motto,* 2 Tim. 2:19; *a seal, the impression of a seal,* Rev. 5:1, et al.; *a seal, a distinctive mark,* Rev. 9:4; *a seal, a token, proof,* 1 Cor. 9:2; *a token* of guarantee, Rom. 4:11

σφραγισάμενος, nom. sg. m. aor. mid. part. . . . . σφραγίζω *(4972)*

σφραγίσαντες, nom. pl. m. aor. act. part. id.

σφραγίσεται, 3 pers. sg. fut. mid. dep. indic. (2 Cor. 11:10, TRs | φραγήσεται, GNT, WH, MT, TRb & NA) . . . . id.

σφραγίσῃς, 2 pers. sg. aor. act. subj. . . . . id.

σφραγῖσιν, dat. pl. f. n. . . . . σφραγίς *(4973)*

σφράγισον, 2 pers. sg. aor. act. imper. σφραγίζω *(4972)*

σφραγίσωμεν, 1 pers. pl. aor. act. subj. (Rev. 7:3, GNT, MT, TRb, WH & NA | σφραγίζωμεν, TRs) . . . . id.

σφυδρά, nom. pl. neut. (Acts 3:7, GNT, WH & NA | σφυρά, MT & TR) . . . . σφυδρόν *(†4974)*

(†4974) σφυδρόν, οῦ, τό, *ankle*

σφυρίδας, acc. pl. f. n. (Matt. 15:37; 16:10; Mark 8:8, WH | σπυρίδας, GNT, MT, TR & NA) . . . . σφυρίς *(‡4711)*

σφυρίδι, dat. sg. f. n. (Acts 9:25, WH | σπυρίδι, GNT, MT, TR & NA) . . . . . . id.

σφυρίδων, gen. pl. f. n. (Mark 8:20, WH | σπυρίδων, GNT, MT, TR & NA) . . . . id.

(‡4711) σφυρίς, ίδος, ἡ, a flexible mat-*basket* for carrying provisions

σφυρά, nom. pl. neut. n. (Acts 3:7, MT & TR | σφυδρά, GNT, WH & NA) . . . . . σφυρόν *(4974)*

(4974) σφυρόν, οῦ, τό [§3.C.c] *the ankle;* pl. τὰ σφυρά, *the ankle bones, malleoli,* Acts 3:7

(4975) σχεδόν, adv. (ἔχω, σχεῖν) pr. *near,* of place; hence, *nearly, almost,* Acts 13:44; 19:26; Heb. 9:22

(4976) σχῆμα, ατος, τό, nom. sg. neut. n. [§4.D.c] (σχεῖν) *fashion, form; fashion, external show,* 1 Cor. 7:31

σχήματι, dat. sg. neut. n. . . . . σχῆμα *(4976)*

σχῆτε, 2 pers. pl. 2 aor. act. subj. (2 Cor. 1:15, GNT, WH & NA | ἔχητε, MT & TR) ἔχω *(2192)*

σχίζει, 3 pers. sg. pres. act. indic. (Luke 5:36, MT & TR | σχίσει, GNT, WH & NA) . . . . σχίζω *(4977)*

σχιζομένους, acc. pl. m. pres. pass. part. . id.

(4977) σχίζω, fut. σχίσω, aor. ἔσχισα, aor. pass. ἐσχίσθην [§26.1] *to split,* Matt. 27:51; *to rend, tear asunder,* Matt. 27:51; Luke 5:36, et al.; mid. *to open or unfold* with a chasm, Mark 1:10; pass. met. *to be divided* into parties or factions, Acts 14:4; 23:7

σχίσας, nom. sg. m. aor. act. part. (Luke 5:36, GNT, WH & NA | MT & TR omit) . . . . σχίζω *(4977)*

σχίσει, 3 pers. sg. fut. act. indic. (Luke 5:36, GNT, WH & NA | σχίζει, MT & TR) id.

(4978) σχίσμα, ατος, τό, nom. sg. neut. n. [§4.D.c] *a rent,* Matt. 9:16; Mark 2:21; met. *a division* into parties, *schism,* John 7:43; 9:16, et al.

σχίσματα, nom. pl. neut. n. {1 Cor. 1:10} . . . . σχίσμα *(4978)*

σχίσματα, acc. pl. neut. n. {1 Cor. 11:18} . id.

σχίσωμεν, 1 pers. pl. aor. act. subj. . . . . σχίζω *(4977)*

σχοινία, acc. pl. neut. n. . . . . σχοινίον *(4979)*

(4979) σχοινίον, ου, τό [§3.C.c] (σχοῖνος, *a rush*) pr. *a cord made of rushes;* genr. *a rope, cord,* John 2:15; Acts 27:32

σχοινίων, gen. pl. neut. n. . . . . σχοινίον *(4979)*

σχολάζητε, 2 pers. pl. pres. act. subj. (1 Cor. 7:5, MT & TR | σχολάσητε, GNT, WH & NA) . . . . σχολάζω *(4980)*

σχολάζοντα, acc. sg. m. pres. act. part. . . id.

(4980) σχολάζω, fut. σχολάσω [§26.1] *to be unemployed, to be at leisure; to be at leisure* for a thing, *to devote one's self entirely* to a thing, 1 Cor. 7:5; *to be unoccupied, empty,* Matt. 12:44

σχολάσητε, 2 pers. pl. aor. act. subj. (1 Cor. 7:5, GNT, WH & NA | σχολάζητε, MT & TR) . . . . σχολάζω *(4980)*

(4981) **σχολή, ῆς, ἡ** [§2.B.a] *freedom from occupa-*
tion; later, ease, leisure; a school, Acts 19:9
σχολῇ, dat. sg. f. n. . . . . σχολή *(4981)*
σχῶ, 1 pers. sg. 2 aor. act. subj. [§36.4] .. ἔχω *(2192)*
σχῶμεν, 1 pers. pl. 2 aor. act. subj. (Matt.
    21:38, GNT, WH & NA | κατάσχωμεν,
    MT & TR | σχῶμεν, 1 John 2:28, GNT,
    WH & NA | ἔχωμεν, MT & TR) . . . . id.
σῷ, dat. sg. m. 2 pers. possessive pron.
    {Matt. 7:3} . . . . σός *(4674)*
σῷ, dat. sg. neut. 2 pers. possessive pron.
    (Matt. 7:22) . . . . id.
σώζει, 3 pers. sg. pres. act. indic. (1 Pet. 3:21,
    WH & TR | σῴζει, GNT, MT &
    NA) . . . . σῴζω *(†4982)*
σῴζει, 3 pers. sg. pres. act. indic. (1 Pet. 3:21,
    GNT, MT & NA | σώζει, WH & TR) id.
σώζειν, pres. act. infin. (Heb. 5:7; 7:25, WH
    & TR | σῴζειν, GNT, MT & NA) . . . id.
σῴζειν, pres. act. infin. (Heb. 5:7; 7:25, GNT,
    MT & NA | σώζειν, WH & TR) . . . . id.
σώζεσθαι, pres. pass. infin. (Acts 27:20, WH
    & TR | σῴζεσθαι, GNT, MT & NA) . id.
σῴζεσθαι, pres. pass. infin. (Acts 27:20, GNT,
    MT & NA | σώζεσθαι, WH & TR) .. id.
σώζεσθε, 2 pers. pl. pres. pass. indic. (1 Cor.
    15:2, WH & TR | σῴζεσθε, GNT, MT
    & NA) . . . . id.
σῴζεσθε, 2 pers. pl. pres. pass. indic. (1 Cor.
    15:2, GNT, MT & NA | σώζεσθε, WH
    & TR) . . . . id.
σώζεται, 3 pers. sg. pres. pass. indic. (1 Pet.
    4:18, Wh & TR | σῴζεται, GNT, MT &
    NA) . . . . id.
σῴζεται, 3 pers. sg. pres. pass. indic. (1 Pet.
    4:18, GNT, MT & NA | σώζεται, WH &
    TR) . . . . id.
σώζετε, 2 pers. pl. pres. act. imper. (Jude 23,
    WH & TR | σῴζετε, GNT, MT & NA) id.
σῴζετε, 2 pers. pl. pres. act. imper. (Jude 23,
    GNT, MT & NA | σώζετε, WH & TR) id.
σωζόμενοι, nom. pl. m. pres. pass. part. (Luke
    13:23, WH & TR | σῳζόμενοι, GNT, MT
    & NA) . . . . id.
σῳζόμενοι, nom. pl. m. pres. pass. part. (Luke
    13:23, GNT, MT & NA | σωζόμενοι,
    WH & TR) . . . . id.
σωζομένοις, dat. pl. m. pres. pass. part.
    (1 Cor. 1:18; 2 Cor. 2:15, WH & TR |
    σῳζομένοις, GNT, MT & NA) . . . . . . id.
σῳζομένοις, dat. pl. m. pres. pass. part.
    (1 Cor. 1:18; 2 Cor. 2:15, GNT, MT & NA
    | σωζομένοις, WH & TR) . . . . id.
σωζομένους, acc. pl. m. pres. pass. part. (Acts
    2:47, WH & TR | σῳζομένους, GNT,

MT & NA) . . . . σῴζω *(†4982)*
σῳζομένους, acc. pl. m. pres. pass. part. (Acts
    2:47, GNT, MT & NA | σωζομένους,
    WH & TR) . . . . id.
σωζομένων, gen. pl. m. pres. pass. part. (Rev.
    21:24, TR | GNT, WH, MT & NA omit) id.
(†4982) **σῴζω,** fut. σώσω, perf. σέσωκα, aor. ἔσωσα,
    aor. pass. ἐσώθην, perf. pass. σέσωσμαι
    [§37.1] *to save, rescue; to preserve safe and*
    unharmed, Matt. 8:25; 10:22; 24:22;
    27:40, 42, 49; 1 Tim. 2:15; σῴζειν εἰς, *to*
    bring safely to, 2 Tim. 4:18; *to cure, heal,*
    restore to health, Matt. 9:21, 22; Mark
    5:23, 28, 34; 6:56, et al.; *to save, preserve*
    from being lost, Matt. 16:25; Mark 3:4;
    8:35; σῴζειν ἀπό, *to deliver from, set free*
    from, Matt. 1:21; John 12:27; Acts 2:40;
    in N.T. *to rescue* from unbelief, *convert,*
    Rom. 11:14; 1 Cor. 1:21; 7:16; *to bring*
    within the pale of saving privilege, Tit. 3:5;
    1 Pet. 3:21 (or, as others, *to save,* in the full-
    est force of the term: see the context of
    these two passages); *to save* from final ruin,
    1 Tim. 1:15; pass. *to be brought within the*
    pale of saving privilege, Acts 2:47; Eph.
    2:5, 8 (or, according to others, *to be ac-*
    tually saved); *to be in the way of salvation,*
    1 Cor. 15:2; 2 Cor. 2:15 (compare, how-
    ever, with this last passage, Luke 13:23;
    Acts 2:47)
σωθῇ, 3 pers. sg. aor. pass. subj. . . . . . σῴζω *(†4982)*
σωθῆναι, aor. pass. infin. . . . . id.
σωθήσεται, 3 pers. sg. fut. pass. indic. . . . id.
σωθήσῃ, 2 pers. sg. fut. pass. indic. . . . . id.
σωθήσομαι, 1 pers. sg. fut. pass. indic. . . . id.
σωθησόμεθα, 1 pers. pl. fut. pass. indic. . id.
σώθητε, 2 pers. pl. aor. pass. imper.
    {Acts 2:40} . . . . id.
σωθῆτε, 2 pers. pl. aor. pass. subj.
    {John 5:34} . . . . id.
σωθῶ, 1 pers. sg. aor. pass. subj. . . . . id.
σωθῶσι(ν), 3 pers. pl. aor. pass. subj. . . . . id.
(4983) **σῶμα,** ατος, τό, nom. sg. neut. n. [§4.D.c] *the*
    body of an animal; *a living body,* Matt.
    5:29, 30; 6:22, 23, 25; James 3:3; *a per-*
    son, individual, 1 Cor. 6:16; *a dead body,*
    corpse, carcass, Matt. 14:12; 27:52, 58;
    Heb. 13:11; *the human body* considered as
    the seat and occasion of moral imperfec-
    tion, as inducing to sin through its appe-
    tites and passions, Rom. 7:24; 8:13; genr.
    a body, a material substance, 1 Cor. 15:37,
    38, 40; *the substance, reality,* as opposed
    to ἡ σκιά, Col. 2:17; in N.T. met., *the ag-*
    gregate body of believers, *the body* of the

Church, Rom. 12:5; Col. 1:18, et al. {1 Cor. 6:19}

σῶμα, acc. sg. neut. n. {1 Cor. 6:18} . . . σῶμα *(4983)*

σώματα, nom. pl. neut. n. {1 Cor. 6:15} . . id.

σώματα, acc. pl. neut. n. {Rom. 12:1} . . . id.

σώματι, dat. sg. neut. n. . . . . id.

σωματική, nom. sg. f. adj. . . . . . σωματικός *(4984)*

(4984) **σωματικός, ή, όν** [§7.F.a] *bodily, of or belonging to the body,* 1 Tim. 4:8; *corporeal, material,* Luke 3:22

σωματικῷ, dat. sg. neut. adj. . . . σωματικός *(4984)*

(4985) **σωματικῶς,** adv., *bodily, in a bodily frame,* Col. 2:9

σώματος, gen. sg. neut. n. . . . . σῶμα *(4983)*

σωμάτων, gen. pl. neut. n. . . . . id.

(4986) **Σώπατρος, ου, ό,** nom. sg. m. n. [§3.C.a] *Sopater,* pr. name

σωρεύσεις, 2 pers. sg. fut. act. indic. . σωρεύω *(4987)*

(4987) **σωρεύω,** fut. σωρεύσω [§13.M] (σωρός, *a heap*) *to heap or pile up,* Rom. 12:20; met. pass. *to be laden* with sins, 2 Tim. 3:6

σῶσαι, aor. act. infin. . . . . σῴζω *(†4982)*

(‡4677) **Σωσάννα, ης, ή,** nom. sg. f. n., pr. name, *Susanna* (Luke 8:3, MT | Σουσάννα, GNT, TR, WH & NA)

σώσαντος, gen. sg. m. aor. act. part. . . σῴζω *(†4982)*

σώσας, nom. sg. m. aor. act. part. . . . . . . id.

σωσάτω, 3 pers. sg. aor. act. imper. . . . . . id.

σώσει, 3 pers. sg. fut. act. indic. . . . . id.

σώσεις, 2 pers. sg. fut. act. indic. . . . . id.

Σωσθένην, acc. sg. m. n. . . . . Σωσθένης *(4988)*

(4988) **Σωσθένης, ου, ό,** nom. sg. m. n. [§2.B.c] *Sosthenes,* pr. name

(4989) **Σωσίπατρος, ου, ό,** nom. sg. m. n., *Sosipater,* pr. name

σῶσον, 2 pers. sg. aor. act. imper. . . . . σῴζω *(†4982)*

σώσω, 1 pers. sg. fut. act. indic. {Rom. 11:14} id.

σώσω, 1 pers. sg. aor. act. subj. {John 12:47} id.

σώσων, nom. sg. m. fut. act. part. . . . . . . id.

(4990) **σωτήρ, ῆρος, ό,** nom. sg. m. n. [§4.2.f] *a savior, preserver, deliverer,* Luke 1:47; 2:11; Acts 5:31, et al.

σωτῆρα, acc. sg. m. n. . . . . σωτήρ *(4990)*

σωτῆρι, dat. sg. m. n. . . . . id.

(4991) **σωτηρία, ας, ή,** nom. sg. f. n. [§2.B.b; 2.2] *a saving, preservation,* Acts 27:34; Heb. 11:7; *deliverance,* Luke 1:69, 71; Acts 7:25; *salvation,* spiritual and eternal, Luke 1:77; 19:9; Acts 4:12; Rev. 7:10; *a being placed in a condition of salvation* by an embracing of the Gospel, Rom. 10:1, 10; 2 Tim. 3:15; *means or opportunity of salvation,* Acts 13:26; Rom. 11:11; Heb. 2:3, et al.; ἡ σωτηρία, *the* promised *deliverance* by the Messiah, John 4:22

σωτηρίαν, acc. sg. f. n. . . . . σωτηρία *(4991)*

σωτηρίας, gen. sg. f. n. . . . . id.

σωτήριον, nom. sg. neut. adj. {Acts 28:28} . . . . σωτήριος *(†4992)*

(4992) σωτήριον, acc. sg. neut. adj. {Luke 2:30} . id.

(†4992) **σωτήριος, ον,** nom. sg. m. adj. [§7.2] *imparting salvation, saving,* Tit. 2:11; neut. τὸ σωτήριον, equivalent to σωτηρία, Luke 2:30; 3:6; Acts 28:28; Eph. 6:17

σωτηρίου, gen. sg. neut. adj. . . . . . σωτήριος *(†4992)*

σωτῆρος, gen. sg. m. n. . . . . σωτήρ *(4990)*

σώφρονα, acc. sg. m. adj. . . . . σώφρων *(4998)*

σώφρονας, acc. pl. m. adj. {Tit. 2:2} . . . . id.

σώφρονας, acc. pl. f. adj. {Tit. 2:5} . . . . id.

σωφρονεῖν, pres. act. infin. . . . . . . σωφρονέω *(4993)*

(4993) **σωφρονέω, ῶ,** fut. σωφρονήσω, aor. ἐσωφρόνησα [§16.P] *to be of a sound mind, be in one's right mind, be sane,* Mark 5:15; *to be calm,* 2 Cor. 5:13; *to be sober-minded, sedate, staid,* Tit. 2:6; 1 Pet. 4:7; *to be of a modest, humble mind,* Rom. 12:3

σωφρονήσατε, 2 pers. pl. aor. act. imper. . . . . σωφρονέω *(4993)*

(4994) **σωφρονίζω,** fut. σωφρονίσω [§26.1] pr. *to render* any one σώφρων, *to restore to a right mind; to make sober-minded, to steady* by exhortation and guidance, Tit. 2:4

σωφρονίζωσι(ν), 3 pers. pl. pres. act. subj. . . . . σωφρονίζω *(4994)*

(4995) **σωφρονισμός, οῦ, ό** [§3.C.a] *a rendering sound-minded; calm vigor of mind,* 2 Tim. 1:7

σωφρονισμοῦ, gen. sg. m. n. . . . σωφρονισμός *(4995)*

σωφρονοῦμεν, 1 pers. pl. pres. act. indic. . . . . σωφρονέω *(4993)*

σωφρονοῦντα, acc. sg. m. pres. act. part. . id.

(4996) **σωφρόνως,** adv., *in the manner of a person in his right mind; soberly, staidly, temperately,* Tit. 2:12

(4997) **σωφροσύνη, ης, ή** [§2.B.a] *sanity, soundness of mind, a sane mind,* Acts 26:25; female *modesty,* 1 Tim. 2:9, 15

σωφροσύνης, gen. sg. f. n. . . . . . . σωφροσύνη *(4997)*

(4998) **σώφρων, ον** [§7.G.a; 7.3] (σῶς, sound, and φρήν) *of a sound mind, sane; staid, temperate, discreet,* 1 Tim. 3:2; Tit. 1:8; 2:2; *modest, chaste,* Tit. 2:5

T

τά, nom. pl. neut. article, {1 John 3:10} . . ό *(3588)*

τά, acc. pl. neut. article {1 John 2:15} . . . . id.

(†4999) **ταβέρνη, ης, ἡ** (Latin *taberna*) *a tavern, inn*

ταβερνῶν, gen. pl. f. n. . . . . ταβέρνη (†4999)

(5000) **Ταβιθά, ἡ** (Aramaic טְבִיתָא) i.q. Δορκάς, *an antelope, Tabitha*, pr. name (Acts 9:36, 40, GNT, MT, TR & NA | Ταβειθά, WH)

(5001) **τάγμα, ατος, τό** [§4.D.c] pr. *anything placed in order*; in N.T. *order of* succession, 1 Cor. 15:23

τάγματι, dat. sg. neut. n. . . . . id.

τάδε, acc. pl. neut. demonstrative pron. . . ὅδε (3592)

ταῖς, dat. pl. f. article . . . . ὁ (3588)

τακτῇ, dat. sg. f. adj. . . . . τακτός (5002)

(5002) **τακτός, ή, όν** [§7.F.a] pr. *arranged; fixed, appointed, set*, Acts 12:21

(5003) **ταλαιπωρέω, ῶ**, fut. ταλαιπωρήσω, perf. τεταλαιπώρηκα [§16.P] *to endure severe labor and hardship; to be harassed; to suffer compunction*, James 4:9

ταλαιπωρήσατε, 2 pers. pl. aor. act. imper. . . . . ταλαιπωρέω (5003)

(5004) **ταλαιπωρία, ας, ἡ**, nom. sg. f. n. [§2.B.b; 2.2] *toil, difficulty, hardship; calamity, misery, distress*, Rom. 3:16; James 5:1

ταλαιπωρίαις, dat. pl. f. n. . . . . . ταλαιπωρία (5004)

(5005) **ταλαίπωρος, ον**, nom. sg. m. adj. [§7.2] pr. *enduring severe effort and hardship*; hence, *wretched, miserable, afflicted*, Rom. 7:24; Rev. 3:17

τάλαντα, acc. pl. neut. n. . . . . τάλαντον (5007)

ταλαντιαία, nom. sg. f. adj. . . . . . ταλαντιαῖος (5006)

(5006) **ταλαντιαῖος, αία, αῖον** [§7.1] *of a talent weight, weighing a talent*, Rev. 16:21

(5007) **τάλαντον, ου, τό** [§3.C.c] (ταλάω, *to sustain*) *the scale of a balance; a talent*, which as a weight was among the Jews equivalent to 3000 shekels, i.e., as usually estimated, 114 lbs. 15 dwts. Troy; while the Attic talent, on the usual estimate, was only equal to 56 lbs. 11 oz. Troy, Matt. 18:24; 25:15, 16, 20, 24, 25, 28

τάλαντον, acc. sg. neut. n. . . . . τάλαντον (5007)

ταλάντων, gen. pl. neut. n. . . . . id.

(5008) **ταλιθά** (Aramaic טְלִיתָא) *talitha*, i.q. κοράσιον, *a damsel, maiden* (Mark 5:41, GNT, MT, TR & NA | ταλειθά, WH)

ταμείοις, dat. pl. neut. n. . . . . ταμεῖον (5009)

(5009) **ταμεῖον, ου, τό**, nom. sg. neut. n., equivalent to ταμιεῖον (ταμιεύω, to be ταμίας, *manager, storekeeper*) *a storehouse, granary, barn*, Luke 12:24; *a chamber, closet, place of retirement and privacy*, Matt. 6:6; 24:26; Luke 12:3 {Luke 12:24}

ταμεῖον, acc. sg. neut. n. {Matt. 6:6} . ταμεῖον (5009)

(‡3568) **τανῦν**, adv. *at present, now* (Acts 20:32; 27:22, TRs | τὰ νῦν, GNT, MT, TRb, WH & NA)

ταξάμενοι, nom. pl. m. aor. mid. part. τάσσω (5021)

τάξει, dat. sg. f. n. . . . . τάξις (5010)

τάξιν, acc. sg. f. n. . . . . id.

(5010) **τάξις, εως, ἡ** [§5.E.c] *order, regular disposition, arrangement; order, series, succession*, Luke 1:8; *an order, distinctive class*, as of priests, Heb. 5:6; 7:11; *order, good order*, 1 Cor. 14:40; *orderliness, well-regulated conduct*, Col. 2:5

ταπεινοῖς, dat. pl. m. adj. . . . . ταπεινός (5011)

(5011) **ταπεινός, ή, όν**, nom. sg. m. adj. [§7.F.a] *low* in situation; of condition, *humble, poor, mean, depressed*, Luke 1:52; 2 Cor. 7:6; James 1:9; met. of the mind, *humble, lowly, modest*, Matt. 11:29; Rom. 12:16, et al.

ταπεινούς, acc. pl. m. adj. . . . . ταπεινός (5011)

ταπεινοῦσθαι, pres. pass. infin. . . . . ταπεινόω (5013)

ταπεινόφρονες, nom. pl. m. adj. (1 Pet. 3:8, GNT, WH & NA | φιλόφρονες, MT & TR) . . . . ταπεινόφρων (‡5391)

(5012) **ταπεινοφροσύνη, ης, ἡ** [§2.B.a] *lowliness or humility of mind and deportment, modesty*, Acts 20:19; Eph. 4:2; Phil. 2:3, et al.

ταπεινοφροσύνη, dat. sg. f. n. ταπεινοφροσύνη (5012)

ταπεινοφροσύνην, acc. sg. f. n. . . . . id.

ταπεινοφροσύνης, gen. sg. f. n. . . . . id.

(‡5391) **ταπεινόφρων, ον** [§7.G.a] (ταπεινός + φρήν) *humble-minded*

(5013) **ταπεινόω, ῶ**, fut. ταπεινώσω, aor. ἐταπείνωσα [§20.T] *to bring low, depress, level*, Luke 3:5; met. *to humble, abase*, Phil. 2:8; mid. *to descend to, or live in, a humble condition*, 2 Cor. 11:7; Phil. 4:12; *to humble, depress the pride of*, any one, Matt. 18:4; mid. *to humble one's self, exhibit humility and contrition*, James 4:10; *to humble* with respect to hopes and expectations, *to depress* with disappointment, 2 Cor. 12:21

ταπεινωθήσεται, 3 pers. sg. fut. pass. indic. [§21.U] . . . . ταπεινόω (5013)

ταπεινώθητε, 2 pers. pl. aor. pass. imper. . id.

ταπεινῶν, nom. sg. m. pres. act. part. . . . . id.

ταπεινώσει, 3 pers. sg. fut. act. indic. {Matt. 18:4} . . . . id.

ταπεινώσει, dat. sg. f. n. {Acts 8:33} . . . . ταπείνωσις (5014)

ταπεινώσεως, gen. sg. f. n. . . . . id.

ταπεινώσῃ, 3 pers. sg. aor. act. subj. ταπεινόω (5013)

ταπείνωσιν, acc. sg. f. n. . . . . ταπείνωσις (5014)

(5014) **ταπείνωσις, εως, ἡ** [§5.E.c] *depression; meanness, low estate, abject condition*, Luke 1:48; Acts 8:33; Phil. 3:21; James 1:10

ταρασσέσθω, 3 pers. sg. pres. pass. imper. . . . . τἀράσσω (5015)

ταράσσοντες, nom. pl. m. pres. act.
part. . . . . ταράσσω *(5015)*

(5015) **ταράσσω**, or ταράττω, fut. ταράξω, aor.
ἐτάραξα, perf. pass. τετάραγμαι, aor.
pass. ἐταράχθην [§26.3] *to agitate, trou-*
ble, as water, John 5:4, 7; met. *to agitate,*
trouble the mind; with fear, *to terrify, put*
in consternation, Matt. 2:3; 14:26; with
grief, etc., *to disquiet, affect with grief, anx-*
iety, etc., John 12:27; 13:21; with doubt,
etc., *to unsettle, perplex,* Acts 15:24; Gal.
1:7, et al.

ταράσσων, nom. sg. m. pres. act.
part. . . . . ταράσσω *(5015)*
ταραχαί, nom. pl. f. n. (Mark 13:8, MT &
TR | GNT, WH & NA omit) . . . . . ταραχή *(5016)*

(5016) **ταραχή**, ῆς, ἡ [§2.B.a] *agitation, troubling,* of
water, John 5:4; met. *commotion, tumult,*
Matt. 13:8
ταραχήν, acc. sg. f. n. (John 5:4, MT & TR
| GNT, WH & NA omit) . . . . ταραχή *(5016)*
ταραχθῇ, 3 pers. sg. aor. pass. subj. . ταράσσω *(5015)*
ταραχθῆτε, 2 pers. pl. aor. pass. subj. . . . . id.

(5017) **τάραχος**, ου, ὁ, nom. sg. m. n. [§3.C.a]
agitation, commotion; perturbation, con-
sternation, terror, Acts 12:18; *excitement,*
tumult, public contention, Acts 19:23
Ταρσέα, acc. sg. m. n. . . . . Ταρσεύς *(5018)*

(5018) **Ταρσεύς**, έως, ὁ, nom. sg. m. n. [§5.E.d] *of,*
or a native of Ταρσός, *Tarsus,* the metropolis of Cilicia, Acts 9:11; 21:39
Ταρσόν, acc. sg. f. n. . . . . Ταρσός *(5019)*

(5019) **Ταρσός**, οῦ, ἡ, *Tarsus,* the chief city of Cilicia, and birth-place of the Apostle Paul
Ταρσῷ, dat. sg. f. n. . . . . Ταρσός *(5019)*

(5020) **ταρταρόω**, ῶ, fut. ταρταρώσω [§20.T]
(Τάρταρος, *Tartarus,* which in the mythol-
ogy of the ancients was that part of Hades,
where the wicked were confined and tormented) *to cast or thrust down to Tartarus*
or Gehenna
ταρταρώσας, nom. sg. m. aor. act.
part. . . . . ταρταρόω *(5020)*
τάς, acc. pl. f. article . . . . ὁ *(3588)*
τασσόμενος, nom. sg. m. pres. pass.
part. . . . . τάσσω *(5021)*

(5021) **τάσσω**, or τάττω, fut. τάξω, aor. ἔταξα, perf.
pass. τέταγμαι [§26.3] *to arrange; to set,*
appoint, in a certain station, Luke 7:8;
Rom. 13:1; *to set, devote,* to a pursuit,
1 Cor. 16:15; *to dispose, frame,* for an object, Acts 13:48; *to arrange, appoint,* place
or time, Matt. 28:16; Acts 28:23; *to allot,*
assign, Acts 22:10; *to settle, decide,* Acts
15:2

ταῦροι, nom. pl. m. n. . . . . ταῦρος *(5022)*

(5022) **ταῦρος**, ου, ὁ [§3.C.a] *a bull, beeve,* Matt.
22:4, et al.
ταύρους, acc. pl. m. n. . . . . ταῦρος *(5022)*
ταύρων, gen. pl. m. n. . . . . id.

(5024) **ταὐτά**, by crasis for τὰ αὐτά, *the same things,*
1 Thess. 2:14; κατὰ ταὐτά, *after, the same*
manner, thus, so, Luke 6:23, 26; 17:30
(1 Thess. 2:14, TR | τὰ αὐτά, GNT, WH,
MT & NA)
ταῦτα, nom. pl. neut. demonstrative pron.
{Matt. 6:33} . . . . οὗτος *(3778)*
ταῦτα, acc. pl. neut. demonstrative pron.
{Matt. 6:32} . . . . id.

(5025) **ταύταις**, dat. pl. f. demonstrative pron. . . . id.
(5025) **ταύτας**, acc. pl. f. demonstrative pron. . . . id.
(5026) **ταύτῃ**, dat. sg. f. demonstrative pron. . . . . id.
(5026) **ταύτην**, acc. sg. f. demonstrative pron. . . . id.
(5026) **ταύτης**, gen. sg. f. demonstrative pron. . . . id.

(5027) **ταφή**, ῆς, ἡ [§2.B.a] *burial, the act of bury-*
ing, sepulture, Matt. 27:7
ταφήν, acc. sg. f. n. . . . . ταφή *(5027)*
τάφοις, dat. pl. m. n. . . . . τάφος *(5028)*
τάφον, acc. sg. m. n. . . . . id.

(5028) **τάφος**, ὁ, nom. sg. m. n. [§3.C.a] *a sepulchre,*
Matt. 23:27, 29; 27:61, 64, 66; 28:1; met.
Rom. 3:13
τάφου, gen. sg. m. n. . . . . τάφος *(5028)*
τάφους, acc. pl. m. n. . . . . id.

(5029) **τάχα**, adv., pr., *quickly, soon; perhaps, pos-*
sibly, Rom. 5:7; Philemon 15
τάχει, dat. sg. neut. n. . . . . τάχος *(5034)*

(5030) **ταχέως**, adv., *quickly, speedily; soon, shortly,*
1 Cor. 4:19; Gal. 1:6; *hastily,* Luke 14:21;
16:6, et al.; *with inconsiderate haste,*
1 Tim. 5:22
ταχινή, nom. sg. f. adj. . . . . ταχινός *(5031)*
ταχινήν, acc. sg. f. adj. . . . . id.

(5031) **ταχινός**, ή, όν [§7.F.a] *swift, speedy,* 2 Pet. 2:1;
near at hand, impending, 2 Pet. 1:14

(5032) **τάχιον**, compar. adv. (pr. neut. of ταχίων,
compar. of ταχύς) *more swiftly, more*
quickly, more speedily, John 20:4; Heb.
13:19; *quickly, speedily,* John 13:27, et al.

(5033) **τάχιστα**, superl. adv. (pr. neut. of the superl.
of ταχύς) [§8.5] *most quickly, most speed-*
ily, very quickly; ὡς τάχιστα, *as soon as*
possible, Acts 17:15

(5034) **τάχος**, ους, τό [§5.E.b] *swiftness, speed,*
quickness, celerity; ἐν τάχει, *with speed,*
quickly, speedily; soon, shortly, Luke 18:8;
Acts 25:4; *hastily, immediately,* Acts 12:7,
et al.

(5035) **ταχύ**, adv., *quickly, speedily, hastily,* Matt.
28:7, 8; *soon, shortly, immediately,* Matt.

5:25; *suddenly,* Rev. 2:5, 16; 3:11, et al.; *easily, readily,* Mark 9:39; pr. neut. of ταχύς

(5036) **ταχύς**, εῖα, ύ, nom. sg. m. adj. [§7.H.g] *swift, fleet, quick;* met. *ready, prompt,* James 1:19

(5037) **τε**, or **τέ**, a combinatory enclitic particle; serving either as a lightly-appending link, Acts 1:15; *and,* Acts 2:3; or as an inclusive prefix, Luke 12:45; *both,* Luke 24:20; Acts 26:16, et al.

τεθέαμαι, 1 pers. sg. perf. mid./pass. dep. indic. [§22.2] . . . . θεάομαι (2300)

τεθεάμεθα, 1 pers. pl. perf. mid./pass. dep. indic. . . . . id.

τεθέαται, 3 pers. sg. perf. mid./pass. dep. indic. . . . . id.

τέθεικα, 1 pers. sg. perf. act. indic. [§28.9.d] . . . . τίθημι (5087)

τεθείκατε, 2 pers. pl. perf. act. indic. . . . . id.

τεθεικώς, nom. sg. m. perf. act. part. . . . . id.

τεθειμένος, nom. sg. m. perf. pass. part. (John 19:41, GNT, WH & NA | ἐτέθη, MT & TR) . . . . id.

τέθειται, 3 pers. sg. perf. pass. indic. (Mark 15:47, GNT, WH & NA | τίθεται, MT & TR) . . . . id.

τεθεμελιωμένοι, nom. pl. m. perf. pass. part. . . . . θεμελιόω (2311)

τεθεμελίωτο, 3 pers. sg. pluperf. pass. indic. (for ἐτεθεμελίωτο) [§13.8.f] . . . . id.

τεθεραπευμέναι, nom. pl. f. perf. pass. part. . . . . θεραπεύω (2323)

τεθεραπευμένον, acc. sg. m. perf. pass. part. id.

τεθεραπευμένῳ, dat. sg. m. perf. pass. part. id.

τεθῇ, 3 pers. sg. aor. pass. subj. [§28.10] τίθημι (5087)

τεθῆναι, aor. pass. infin. . . . . id.

τεθησαυρισμένοι, nom. pl. m. perf. pass. part. . . . . θησαυρίζω (2343)

τεθλιμμένη, nom. sg. f. perf. pass. part. θλίβω (2346)

τεθνάναι, 2 perf. act. infin. [§35.8] (Acts 14:19, MT & TR | τεθνηκέναι, GNT, WH & NA) . . . . θνήσκω (2348)

τεθνήκασι(ν), 3 pers. pl. perf. act. indic. . . id.

τέθνηκε(ν), 3 pers. sg. perf. act. indic. [§38.2] . . . . id.

τεθνηκέναι, perf. act. infin. (Acts 14:19, GNT, WH & NA | τεθνάναι, MT & TR) . . id.

τεθνηκότα, acc. sg. m. perf. act. part. . . . id.

τεθνηκότος, gen. sg. m. perf. act. part. . . id.

τεθνηκώς, nom. sg. m. perf. act. part. [§36.4] id.

τεθραμμένος, nom. sg. m. perf. pass. part. [§35.9] . . . . τρέφω (5142)

τεθραυσμένους, acc. pl. m. perf. pass. part. . . . . θραύω (2352)

τεθυμένα, nom. pl. neut. perf. pass. part. . θύω (2380)

τεθῶσιν, 3 pers. pl. aor. pass. subj. [§28.10] . . . . τίθημι (5087)

τείχη, nom. pl. neut. n. . . . . τεῖχος (5038)

(5038) **τεῖχος**, ους, τό, nom. sg. neut. n. [§5.E.b] *a wall* of a city, Acts 9:25, et al. {Rev. 21:14}

τεῖχος, acc. sg. neut. n. {Rev. 21:12} . . . τεῖχος (5038)

τείχους, gen. sg. neut. n. . . . . id.

τεκεῖν, 2 aor. act. infin. [§37.1] . . . . . . τίκτω (5088)

τέκῃ, 3 pers. sg. 2 aor. act. subj. . . . . id.

τεκμηρίοις, dat. pl. neut. n. . . . . τεκμήριον (5039)

(5039) **τεκμήριον**, ου, τό [§3.C.c] (τέκμαρ, *a fixed mark*) *a sign, indubitable token, clear proof*

τέκνα, nom. pl. neut. n. {1 John 3:1–2} . . . . τέκνον (5043)

τέκνα, acc. pl. neut. n. {1 John 5:2} . . . . . id.

τέκνα, voc. pl. neut. n. {Mark 10:24} . . . . id.

τεκνία, voc. pl. neut. n. . . . . τεκνίον (5040)

(5040) **τεκνίον**, ου, τό (dimin. of τέκνον) *a little child;* τεκνία, an endearing appellation, *my dear children,* John 13:33; Gal. 4:19; 1 John 2:1, et al.

τεκνογονεῖν, pres. act. infin. . . . . . τεκνογονέω (5041)

(5041) **τεκνογονέω**, ῶ, fut. τεκνογονήσω [§16.P] (τέκνον + γίγνομαι) *to bear children; to rear a family,* 1 Tim. 5:14

(5042) **τεκνογονία**, ας, ἡ [§2.B.b; 2.2] *the bearing of children, the rearing of a family,* 1 Tim. 2:15

τεκνογονίας, gen. sg. f. n. . . . . . . τεκνογονία (5042)

τέκνοις, dat. pl. neut. n. . . . . τέκνον (5043)

(5043) **τέκνον**, ου, τό, nom. sg. neut. n. [§3.C.c] *a child, a son or daughter,* Matt. 2:18; Luke 1:7, et al.; pl. *descendants, posterity,* Matt. 3:9; Acts 2:39; *child, son,* as a term of endearment, Matt. 9:2; Mark 2:5; 10:24; pl. *children, inhabitants, people,* of a city, Matt. 23:37; Luke 19:44; from the Hebrew, met. *a child* or *son* in virtue of discipleship, 1 Cor. 4:17; 1 Tim. 1:2; 2 Tim. 1:2; Tit. 1:4; Philemon 10; 3 John 4; *a child* in virtue of gracious acceptance, John 1:12; 11:52; Rom. 8:16, 21; 1 John 3:1; *a child* in virtue of spiritual conformity, John 8:39; Phil. 2:15; 1 John 3:10; *a child of,* one characterized by some condition or quality, Matt. 11:19; Eph. 2:3; 5:8; 1 Pet. 1:14; 2 Pet. 2:14 {Rev. 12:5}

τέκνον, acc. sg. neut. n. {Rev. 12:4} . . τέκνον (5043)

τέκνον, voc. sg. neut. n. {Matt. 9:2} . . . . id.

(5044) **τεκνοτροφέω**, ῶ, fut. τεκνοτροφήσω [§16.P] (τέκνον + τρέφω) *to rear a family,* 1 Tim. 5:10

τέκνου, gen. sg. neut. n. . . . . τέκνον (5043)

τέκνῳ, dat. sg. neut. n. . . . . id.

τέκνων, gen. pl. neut. n. . . . . id.

τέκτονος, gen. sg. m. n. . . . . τέκτων *(5045)*

(5045) **τέκτων**, ονος, ὁ, nom. sg. m. n. [§4.2.e] *an artisan;* and spc. *one who works in wood, a carpenter,* Matt. 13:55; Mark 6:3

τελεῖ, 3 pers. sg. pres. act. indic. . . . . . . τελέω *(5055)*

τελεία, nom. sg. f. adj. . . . . τέλειος *(5046)*

τέλειοι, nom. pl. m. adj. . . . . id.

τελείοις, dat. pl. m. adj. . . . . id.

τέλειον, acc. sg. m. adj. {James 1:25} . . . . id.

τέλειον, nom. sg. neut. adj. {Rom. 12:2} . id.

τέλειον, acc. sg. neut. adj. {James 1:4} . . . id.

(5046) **τέλειος**, εία, ειον, nom. sg. m. adj. [§7.1] *brought to completion; fully accomplished, fully developed,* James 1:4; *fully realized, thorough,* 1 John 4:18; *complete, entire,* as opposed to what is partial and limited, 1 Cor. 13:10; *full grown, of ripe age,* 1 Cor. 14:20; Eph. 4:13; Heb. 5:14; *fully accomplished* in Christian enlightenment, 1 Cor. 2:6; Phil. 3:15; Col. 1:28; *perfect* in some point of character, *without shortcoming* in respect of a certain standard, Matt. 5:48; 19:21; Col. 4:12; James 1:4; 3:2; *perfect, consummate,* Rom. 12:2; James 1:17, 25; compar. *of higher excellence and efficiency,* Heb. 9:11

τελειοτέρας, gen. sg. f. compar. adj. [§8.4] . . . . τέλειος *(5046)*

(5047) **τελειότης**, ητος, ἡ [§4.2.c] *completeness, perfectness,* Col. 3:14; *ripeness* of knowledge or practice, Heb. 6:1

τελειότητα, acc. sg. f. n. . . . . τελειότης *(5047)*

τελειότητος, gen. sg. f. n. . . . . id.

τελειοῦμαι, 1 pers. sg. pres. pass. indic. [§21.U] . . . . τελειόω *(5048)*

τελειοῦται, 3 pers. sg. pres. pass. indic. (2 Cor. 12:9, MT & TR | τελεῖται, GNT, WH & NA) . . . . id.

(5048) **τελειόω**, ῶ, fut. τελειώσω, perf. τετελείωκα, aor. ἐτελείωσα [§20.T] *to execute fully, discharge,* John 4:34; 5:36; 17:4; *to reach the end of, run through, finish,* Luke 2:43; Acts 20:24; *to consummate, place in a condition of finality,* Heb. 7:19; *to perfect* a person, *advance a person to final completeness* of character, Heb. 2:10; 5:9; 7:28; *to perfect* a person, *advance a person to a completeness* of its kind, which needs no further provision, Heb. 9:9; 10:1, 14; pass. *to receive fulfillment,* John 19:28; *to be brought to the goal, to reach the end of one's course,* Luke 13:32; Phil. 3:12; Heb. 11:40; 12:23; *to be fully developed,* 2 Cor. 12:9; James 2:22; 1 John 2:5; 4:12, 17; *to be completely organized, to be closely*

embodied, John 17:23

τελεῖται, 3 pers. sg. pres. pass. indic. (2 Cor. 12:9, GNT, WH & NA | τελειοῦται, MT & TR) . . . . τελέω *(5055)*

τελεῖτε, 2 pers. pl. pres. act. indic. . . . . . . id.

τελειωθείς, nom. sg. m. aor. pass. part. . . . . τελειόω *(5048)*

τελειωθῇ, 3 pers. sg. aor. pass. subj. . . . . . id.

τελειωθῶσι(ν), 3 pers. pl. aor. pass. subj. . id.

τελείων, gen. pl. m. adj. . . . . τέλειος *(5046)*

(5049) **τελείως**, adv., *perfectly,* 1 Pet. 1:13

τελειῶσαι, aor. act. infin. . . . . τελειόω *(5048)*

τελειωσάντων, gen. pl. m. aor. act. part. . id.

τελειώσας, nom. sg. m. aor. act. part. (John 17:4, GNT, WH & NA | ἐτελείωσα, MT & TR) . . . . id.

(5050) **τελείωσις**, εως, ἡ, nom. sg. f. n. [§5.E.c] *a completing; a fulfillment, an accomplishment* of predictions, promised, etc.; Luke 1:45; *finality* of function, *completeness* of operation and effect, Heb. 7:11

τελειώσω, 1 pers. sg. aor. act. subj. . . τελειόω *(5048)*

τελειωτήν, acc. sg. m. n. . . . . τελειωτής *(5051)*

(5051) **τελειωτής**, οῦ, ὁ [§2.B.c] *a finisher, one who completes and perfects* a thing; *one who brings through to final attainment,* Heb. 12:2; cf. ch. 2:10

τελέσητε, 2 pers. pl. aor. act. subj. . . . . τελέω *(5055)*

τελεσθῇ, 3 pers. sg. aor. pass. subj. . . . . . id.

τελεσθῆναι, aor. pass. infin. . . . . id.

τελεσθήσεται, 3 pers. sg. fut. pass. indic. . id.

τελεσθήσονται, 3 pers. pl. fut. pass. indic. (Rev. 17:17, GNT, WH & NA | τελεσθῇ, TR | τελεσθῶσιν, MT) . . . . id.

τελεσθῶσιν, 3 pers. pl. aor. pass. subj. . . . id.

(5052) **τελεσφορέω**, ῶ, fut. τελεσφορήσω [§16.P] (τελεσφόρος, from τέλος + φέρω) *to bring to maturity,* as fruits, etc.; met. Luke 8:14

τελεσφοροῦσι(ν), 3 pers. pl. pres. act. indic. . . . . τελεσφορέω *(5052)*

τελέσωσι(ν), 3 pers. pl. aor. act. subj. . . τελέω *(5055)*

τελευτᾷ, 3 pers. sg. pres. act. indic. . τελευτάω *(5053)*

τελευτᾶν, pres. act. infin. (Luke 7:2, GNT, MT & NA | τελευτᾷν, WH & TR) . . id.

τελευτάτω, 3 pers. sg. pres. act. imper. . . . id.

(5053) **τελευτάω**, ῶ, fut. τελευτήσω, perf. τετελεύτηκα, aor. ἐτελεύτησα [§18.R] *to end, finish, complete;* absol. *to end* one's life, *to die,* Matt. 2:19; 15:4; 22:25, et al.

(5054) **τελευτή**, ῆς, ἡ [§2.B.a] *a finishing, end;* hence, *end* of life, *death, decease,* Matt. 2:15

τελευτῆς, gen. sg. f. n. . . . . τελευτή *(5054)*

τελευτήσαντος, gen. sg. m. aor. act. part. . . . . τελευτάω *(5053)*

τελευτῶν, nom. sg. m. pres. act. part. . . . . id.

(5055) **τελέω, ῶ,** fut. τελέσω [§22.1] perf. τετέλεκα, aor. ἐτέλεσα, *to finish, complete, conclude,* an operation, Matt. 11:1; 13:53; 19:1, et al.; *to finish* a circuit, Matt. 10:23; *to fulfil, to carry out into full operation,* Rom. 2:27; Gal. 5:16; James 2:8; *to pay* dues, Matt. 17:24, et al.; pass. *to be fulfilled, realized,* Luke 12:50; 18:31, et al.; of time, *to be ended, elapse,* Rev. 15:8; 20:3, 5, 7
τέλη, nom. pl. neut. n. {1 Cor. 10:11} .. τέλος *(5056)*
τέλη, acc. pl. neut. n. {Matt. 17:25} ..... id.

(5056) **τέλος, ους, τό,** nom. sg. neut. n. [§5.E.b] *an end attained, consummation; an end, closing act,* Matt. 24:6, 14; 1 Cor. 15:24, et al.; *full performance, perfect discharge,* Rom. 10:4; *fulfillment, realization,* Luke 22:37; *final dealing,* developed *issue,* James 5:11; *issue, final stage,* 1 Cor. 10:11; *issue, result,* Matt. 26:58; Rom. 6:21, 22; 1 Pet. 1:9; antitypical *issue,* 2 Cor. 3:13; *practical issue,* 1 Tim. 1:5; *ultimate destiny,* Phil. 3:19; Heb. 6:8; 1 Pet. 4:17; *an impost, due,* Matt. 17:25; Rom. 13:7; εἰς τέλος, *to the full,* 1 Thess. 2:16; εἰς τέλος, *continually,* Luke 18:5; εἰς τέλος, μέχρι, ἄχρι τέλους, *throughout,* Matt. 10:22; Mark 13:13; John 13:1; Heb. 3:6, 14; 6:11; Rev. 2:26 {Matt. 24:14}
τέλος, acc. sg. neut. n. {Matt. 24:13} .. τέλος *(5056)*
τέλους, gen. sg. neut. n. .... id.
τελοῦσα, nom. sg. f. pres. act. part. ... τελέω *(5055)*
τελῶναι, nom. pl. m. n. .... τελώνης *(5057)*
τελώνην, acc. sg. m. n. .... id.

(5057) **τελώνης, ου, ὁ,** nom. sg. m. n. [§2.B.c] (τέλος + ὠνέομαι) *one who farms the public revenues;* in N.T. *a publican, collector of imposts, tax gatherer,* Matt. 5:46; 9:10, 11; 10:3, et al.

(5058) **τελώνιον, ου, τό** [§3.C.c] *a custom-house, toll-house; collector's office,* Matt. 9:9; Mark 2:14; Luke 5:27
τελώνιον, acc. sg. neut. n. .... τελώνιον *(5058)*
τελωνῶν, gen. pl. m. n. .... τελώνης *(5057)*
τέξεται, 3 pers. sg. fut. mid. dep. indic. [§37.1] .... τίκτω *(5088)*
τέξῃ, 2 pers. sg. fut. mid. dep. indic. .... id.

(5059) **τέρας, ατος, τό** [§4.2.c] *a prodigy, portent,* Acts 2:19; *a signal act, wonder, miracle,* John 4:48; Acts 2:43, et al.
τέρασι(ν), dat. pl. neut. n. .... τέρας *(5059)*
τέρατα, nom. pl. neut. n. {Acts 2:43} .... id.
τέρατα, acc. pl. neut. n. {Acts 2:19} ..... id.
τεράτων, gen. pl. neut. n. .... id.

(5060) **Τέρτιος, ου, ὁ,** nom. sg. m. n., *Tertius,* pr. name

(5061) **Τέρτυλλος, ου, ὁ,** nom. sg. m. n., *Tertullus,* pr. name
Τερτύλλου, gen. sg. m. n. .... Τέρτυλλος *(5061)*
τέσσαρα, nom. pl. neut. numeral {Rev. 4:6} .... τέσσαρες *(5064)*
τέσσαρα, acc. pl. neut. numeral {John 19:23} id.

(5062) **τεσσαράκοντα, οἱ, αἱ, τά,** numeral, *forty,* Matt. 4:2, et al. (MT & TR | τεσσεάκοντα, GNT, WH & NA)
τεσσαρακονταετῆ, acc. sg. m. adj. (Acts 13:18, MT & TR | τεσσερακονταετῆ, GNT, WH & NA) .... τεσσαρακονταετής *(5063)*

(5063) **τεσσαρακονταετής, ές,** nom. sg. m. adj. [§7.G.b] (τεσσαράκοντα + ἔτος) *of forty years* (Acts 7:23, MT & TR | τεσσερακονταετής, GNT, WH & NA)
τέσσαρας, acc. pl. m. numeral {Rev. 4:4} .... τέσσαρες *(5064)*
τέσσαρας, acc. pl. f. numeral {John 11:17} id.

(5064) **τέσσαρες, ** nom. pl. m. numeral, Att. τέτταρες, ων, οἱ, αἱ, neut. τέσσαρα, Att. τέτταρα [§9.I.d] *four,* Matt. 24:31; Mark 2:3, et al. {Rev. 11:16}
τέσσαρες, nom. pl. f. numeral {Rev. 14:1} .... τέσσαρες *(5064)*
τεσσαρεσκαιδεκάτη, nom. sg. f. adj. .... τεσσαρεσκαιδέκατος *(5065)*
τεσσαρεσκαιδεκάτην, acc. sg. f. adj. .... id.

(5065) **τεσσαρεσκαιδέκατος, η, ον** (τέσσαρες, καί, + δέκατος) *the fourteenth,* Acts 27:27, 33
τέσσαρσιν, dat. pl. m. numeral {Rev. 7:2} .... τέσσαρες *(5064)*
τέσσαρσιν, dat. pl. f. numeral {Rev. 20:8} id.
τέσσαρσιν, dat. pl. neut. numeral {Acts 12:4} id.
τεσσάρων, gen. pl. m. numeral {Rev. 21:17} id.
τεσσάρων, gen. pl. neut. numeral {Rev. 15:7} id.

(‡5062) **τεσσεράκοντα, οἱ, αἱ, τά,** numeral, *forty* (GNT, WH & NA | τεσσαράκοντα, MT & TR)
τεσσερακονταετῆ, acc. sg. m. adj. (Acts 13:18, GNT, WH & NA | τεσσαρακονταετῆ, MT & TR) ... τεσσερακονταετής *(‡5063)*

(‡5063) **τεσσερακονταετής, ές,** nom. sg. m. adj. *forty years* (Acts 7:23, GNT, WH & NA | τεσσαρακονταετής, MT & TR)
τεταγμέναι, nom. pl. f. perf. pass. part. τάσσω *(5021)*
τεταγμένοι, nom. pl. m. perf. pass. part. . id.
τέτακται, 3 pers. sg. perf. pass. indic. [§26.3] id.
τεταραγμένοι, nom. pl. m. perf. pass. part. .... ταράσσω *(5015)*
τετάρακται, 3 pers. sg. perf. pass. indic. . id.

(5066) **τεταρταῖος, αία, αῖον,** nom. sg. m. adj. [§7.1] *on the fourth day,* John 11:39
τετάρτη, dat. sg. f. adj. .... τέταρτος *(5067)*

τετάρτην, acc. sg. f. adj. . . . . τέταρτος *(5067)*
τετάρτης, gen. sg. f. adj. . . . . id.
τέταρτον, nom. sg. neut. adj. {Rev. 4:7} . . id.
τέταρτον, acc. sg. neut. adj. {Rev. 6:8} . . . id.
(5067) **τέταρτος**, η, ον, nom. sg. m. adj. [§7.F.a]
    fourth, Matt. 14:25, et al.
τετάρτου, gen. sg. neut. adj. . . . . τέταρτος *(5067)*
τεταχέναι, pres. act. infin. (Acts 18:2, MT |
    διατεταχέναι, GNT, WH, TR &
    NA) . . . . τάσσω *(5021)*
τετελείωκεν, 3 pers. sg. perf. act.
    indic. . . . . τελειόω *(5048)*
τετελείωμαι, 1 pers. sg. perf. pass. indic.
    [§21.U] . . . . id.
τετελειωμένη, nom. sg. f. perf. pass. part. id.
τετελειωμένοι, nom. pl. m. perf. pass. part. id.
τετελειωμένον, acc. sg. m. perf. pass. part. id.
τετελειωμένων, gen. pl. m. perf. pass. part. id.
τετελείωται, 3 pers. sg. perf. pass. indic. . id.
τετέλεκα, 1 pers. sg. perf. act. indic. . . . τελέω *(5055)*
τετέλεσται, 3 pers. sg. perf. pass. indic.
    [§22.5.6] . . . . id.
τετελευτηκότος, gen. sg. m. perf. act. part.
    (John 11:39, GNT, WH & NA | τεθνη-
    κότος, MT & TR) . . . . τελευτάω *(5053)*
τέτευχε(ν), 3 pers. sg. perf. act. indic. [§36.2]
    (Heb. 8:6, TR | τέτυκε(ν), GNT, WH,
    MT & NA) . . . . τυγχάνω *(5177)*
τετήρηκα, 1 pers. sg. perf. act. indic. . . . τηρέω *(5083)*
τετήρηκαν, 3 pers. pl. perf. act. indic. [§35.13]
    (John 17:6, GNT, WH & NA | τετηρή-
    κασι(ν), MT & TR) . . . . id.
τετήρηκας, 2 pers. sg. perf. act. indic. . . . id.
τετηρήκασι(ν), 3 pers. pl. perf. act. indic.
    (John 17:6, MT & TR | τετήρηκαν, GNT,
    WH & NA) . . . . id.
τετήρηκεν, 3 pers. sg. perf. act. indic. . . . id.
τετηρημένην, acc. sg. f. perf. pass. part.
    [§17.Q] . . . . id.
τετηρημένοις, dat. pl. m. perf. pass. part. id.
τετηρημένους, acc. pl. m. perf. pass. part.
    (2 Pet. 2:4, TR | τηρουμένους, GNT,
    WH, MT & NA) . . . . id.
τετήρηται, 3 pers. sg. perf. pass. indic. . . id.
τετιμημένου, gen. sg. m. perf. pass. part.
    [§19.S] . . . . τιμάω *(5091)*
(‡5075) **τετρα(α)ρχέω**, ῶ, fut. τετρα(α)ρχήσω
    [§16.P] *to be tetrarch, rule as tetrarch,* Luke
    3:1 (3×)
(‡5076) **τετρ(α)άρχης**, ου, ὁ, nom. sg. m. n. [§2.B.c]
    (τετράς + ἄρχω) *a tetrarch;* pr. one of a
    sovereign body of four; in N.T., according
    to later usage, a provincial sovereign un-
    der the Roman emperor, Matt. 14:1; Luke
    3:19; 9:7; Acts 13:1

τετρ(α)άρχου, gen. sg. m. n. . . τετρ(α)άρχης *(‡5076)*
τετρα(α)ρχοῦντος, gen. sg. m. pres. act.
    part. . . . . τετρα(α)ρχέω *(‡5075)*
(5068) **τετράγωνος**, ον [§7.2] (τέσσαρες + γωνία)
    four-angled, quadrangular, square, Rev.
    21:16
τετράγωνος, nom. sg. f. adj. . . . . τετράγωνος *(5068)*
τετραδίοις, dat. pl. neut. n. . . . . τετράδιον *(5069)*
(5069) **τετράδιον**, ου, τό [§3.C.c] (dimin. of τετράς)
    a set of four, quaternion; a detachment of
    four men, Acts 12:4
(5070) **τετρακισχίλιοι**, αι, α, nom. pl. m. numeral
    (τετράκις, *four times,* and χίλιοι) *four*
    thousand, Matt. 15:38, et al.
τετρακισχιλίους, acc. pl. m.
    numeral . . . . τετρακισχίλιοι *(5070)*
τετρακισχιλίων, gen. pl. m. numeral . . . . id.
τετρακόσια, acc. pl. neut.
    numeral . . . . τετρακόσιοι *(5071)*
(5071) **τετρακόσιοι**, αι, α, numeral, *four hundred,*
    Acts 5:36, et al.
τετρακοσίοις, dat. pl. neut.
    numeral . . . . τετρακόσιοι *(5071)*
τετρακοσίων, gen. pl. neut. numeral . . . . . id.
(5072) τετράμηνον, nom. sg. neut. adj. (John 4:35,
    TR | τετράμηνος, GNT, WH, MT &
    NA) . . . . τετράμηνος *(†5072)*
(†5072) **τετράμηνος**, ον, nom. sg. m. adj. [§7.2]
    (τέσσαρες + μήν) *of four months, four*
    months in duration (John 4:35, GNT, WH,
    MT & NA | τετράμηνον, TR)
(5073) **τετραπλόος**, οῦς, ῆ, οῦν [§7.4.b] (τετράς)
    quadruple, fourfold, Luke 19:8
τετραπλοῦν, acc. sg. neut. adj. . . . τετραπλόος *(5073)*
τετράποδα, nom. pl. neut. adj.
    {Acts 10:12} . . . . τετράπους *(5074)*
τετράποδα, acc. pl. neut. adj. {Acts 11:6} . id.
τετραπόδων, gen. pl. neut. adj. . . . . id.
(5074) **τετράπους**, ουν [§4.2.c] (τέσσαρες + πούς)
    four-footed; pl. τὰ τετράποδα, sc. ζῶα,
    quadrupeds, Acts 10:12; 11:6; Rom. 1:23
τετραυματισμένους, acc. pl. m. perf. pass.
    part. . . . . τραυματίζω *(5135)*
τετραχηλισμένα, nom. pl. neut. perf. pass.
    part. . . . . τραχηλίζω *(5136)*
τετύφλωκεν, 3 pers. sg. perf. act.
    indic. τυφλόω *(5186)*
τετυφωμένοι, nom. pl. m. perf. pass.
    part. . . . . τυφόω *(5187)*
τετύφωται, 3 pers. sg. perf. pass. indic.
    [§21.U] . . . . id.
τέτυχε(ν), 3 pers. sg. 2 perf. act. indic. (Heb.
    8:6, GNT, WH, MT & NA | τέτευχε(ν),
    TR) . . . . τυγχάνω *(5177)*
(5077) **τεφρόω**, ῶ, fut. τεφρώσω [§20.T] (τέφρα,

ashes) to reduce to ashes, to consume, destroy

τεφρώσας, nom. sg. m. aor. act. part.   τεφρόω *(5077)*

τεχθείς, nom. sg. m. aor. pass. part.
   [§37.1] . . . . τίκτω *(5088)*

(5078) **τέχνη, ης, ἡ** [§2.B.a] *art, skill,* Acts 17:29; *an art, trade, craft,* Acts 18:3; Rev. 18:22

τέχνῃ, dat. sg. f. n. (Acts 18:3, GNT, WH & NA | τέχνην, MT & TR) . . . . τέχνη *(5078)*

τέχνην, acc. sg. f. n. (Acts 18:3, MT & TR | τέχνῃ, GNT, WH & NA) . . . . id.

τέχνης, gen. sg. f. n. . . . . id.

τεχνῖται, nom. pl. m. n. . . . . τεχνίτης *(5079)*

τεχνίταις, dat. pl. m. n. . . . . id.

(5079) **τεχνίτης, ου, ὁ,** nom. sg. m. n. [§2.B.c] *an artisan, artificer; workman, mechanic,* Acts 19:24, 38; Rev. 18:22; *an architect, builder,* Heb. 11:10

τῇ, dat. sg. f. article . . . . ὁ *(3588)*

τῇδε, dat. sg. f. demonstrative pron.
   [§10.J.a] . . . . ὅδε *(3592)*

τήκεται, 3 pers. sg. pres. pass. indic. . . . τήκω *(5080)*

(5080) **τήκω,** fut. τήξω [§23.1.b] *to dissolve, render liquid;* pass. *to be liquefied, melt*

(5081) **τηλαυγῶς,** adv. (τηλαυγής, *widely resplendent,* from τῆλε, *afar,* + αὐγή) *clearly, plainly, distinctly*

τηλικαῦτα, nom. pl. neut. demonstrative pron. τηλικοῦτος *(5082)*

τηλικαύτης, gen. sg. f. demonstrative pron.   id.

(5082) **τηλικοῦτος,** αὕτη, οῦτο, nom. sg. m. demonstrative pron. [§10.7.8] (τηλίκος, *so great*) *so great,* 2 Cor. 1:10; Heb. 2:3; James 3:4; Rev. 16:18

τηλικούτου, gen. sg. m. demonstrative pron. τηλικοῦτος *(5082)*

τήν, acc. sg. f. article . . . . ὁ *(3588)*

τήνδε, acc. sg. f. demonstrative pron. . . . . ὅδε *(3592)*

τηρεῖ, 3 pers. sg. pres. act. indic.
   {John 14:24} . . . . τηρέω *(5083)*

τήρει, 2 pers. sg. pres. act. imper. {Rev. 3:3}   id.

τηρεῖν, pres. act. infin. . . . . id.

τηρεῖσθαι, pres. pass. infin. [§17.Q] . . . . . id.

τηρεῖτε, 2 pers. pl. pres. act. imper. . . . . . id.

(5083) **τηρέω, ῶ,** fut. τηρήσω, perf. τετήρηκα, aor. ἐτήρησα [§16.P] (τηρός, *watching, watchful*) *to keep watch upon, guard,* Matt. 27:36, 54; 28:4; Acts 12:6; *to watch over protectively, guard,* 1 John 5:18; Rev. 16:15; *to mark attentively, to heed,* Rev. 1:3; *to observe practically, keep strictly,* Matt. 19:17; 23:3; 28:20; Mark 7:9; John 8:51, et al.; *to preserve, shield,* John 17:15; *to store up, reserve,* John 2:10; 12:7; 1 Pet. 1:4; 2 Pet. 2:4, 9, 17, et al.; *to keep in custody,*

Acts 12:5; 16:23, et al.; *to maintain,* Eph. 4:3; 2 Tim. 4:7; *to keep* in a condition, John 17:11, 12; 1 Cor. 7:37; 2 Cor. 11:9; 1 Tim. 5:22; James 1:27

τηρῇ, 3 pers. sg. pres. act. subj. . . . . . . τηρέω *(5083)*

τηρηθείη, 3 pers. sg. aor. pass. opt. . . . . . . id.

τηρηθῆναι, aor. pass. infin. . . . . id.

τηρῆσαι, aor. act. infin. . . . . id.

τηρήσαντας, acc. pl. m. aor. act. part. . . . id.

τηρήσατε, 2 pers. pl. aor. act. imper. . . . . id.

τηρήσει, 3 pers. sg. fut. act. indic.
   {John 14:23} . . . . id.

τηρήσει, dat. sg. f. n. {Acts 5:18} . . . . τήρησις *(5084)*

τηρήσετε, 2 pers. pl. fut. act. indic. (John 14:15, GNT, WH & NA | τηρήσατε, MT & TR) . . . . τηρέω *(5083)*

τηρήσῃ, 3 pers. sg. aor. act. subj. . . . . . . id.

τηρήσῃς, 2 pers. sg. aor. act. subj. . . . . . . id.

τηρήσητε, 2 pers. pl. aor. act. subj. . . . . . id.

τήρησιν, acc. sg. f. n. . . . . τήρησις *(5084)*

(5084) **τήρησις, εως, ἡ,** nom. sg. f. n. [§5.E.c] *a keeping, custody;* meton. *a place of custody, prison, ward,* Acts 4:3; met. *practical observance, strict performance,* 1 Cor. 7:19

τήρησον, 2 pers. sg. aor. act. imper. . . . τηρέω *(5083)*

τηρήσουσιν, 3 pers. pl. fut. act. indic. . . . id.

τηρήσω, 1 pers. sg. fut. act. indic. . . . . . . id.

τηροῦμεν, 1 pers. pl. pres. act. indic. . . . . id.

τηρούμενοι, nom. pl. m. pres. pass. part. . id.

τηρουμένους, acc. pl. m. pres. pass. part. (2 Pet. 2:4, GNT, WH, MT & NA | τετηρημένους, TR) . . . . id.

τηροῦντες, nom. pl. m. pres. act. part. . . . id.

τηρούντων, gen. pl. m. pres. act. part. . . . id.

τηρῶ, 1 pers. sg. pres. act. indic. . . . . id.

τηρῶμεν, 1 pers. pl. pres. act. subj. . . . . . id.

τηρῶν, nom. sg. m. pres. act. part. . . . . . id.

τῆς, gen. sg. f. article . . . . ὁ *(3588)*

τι, nom. sg. neut. indefinite pron. [§10.4]
   {John 5:14} . . . . τις *(5100)*

τι, acc. sg. neut. indefinite pron. {John 5:19}   id.

τί, nom. sg. neut. interrogative pron. [§10.J.f]
   {Luke 23:31} . . . . τίς *(5101)*

τί, acc. sg. neut. interrogative pron.
   {Luke 23:34} . . . . id.

Τιβεριάδος, gen. sg. f. n. . . . . Τιβεριάς *(5085)*

(5085) **Τιβεριάς, άδος, ἡ** [§4.2.c] *Tiberias,* a city of Galilee, built by Herod Antipas, and named in honor of Tiberius

(5086) **Τιβέριος, ου, ὁ** [§3.C.a] *Tiberius,* the third Roman emperor

Τιβερίου, gen. sg. m. n. . . . . Τιβέριος *(5086)*

τιθέασιν, 3 pers. pl. pres. act. indic. (for τιθεῖσι) [§28.6] . . . . τίθημι *(5087)*

τιθείς, nom. sg. m. pres. act. part. . . . . . . id.

τιθέναι, pres. act. infin. . . . . τίθημι *(5087)*

τιθέντες, nom. pl. m. pres. act. part. . . . . . id.

τίθεται, 3 pers. sg. pres. pass. indic. [§28.8.a]
    (Mark 15:47, MT TR | τέθειται, GNT,
    WH & NA) . . . . id.

τιθέτω, 3 pers. sg. pres. act. imper. . . . . . . id.

(5087) **τίθημι**, 1 pers. sg. pres. act. indic., fut. θήσω,
aor. ἔθηκα, perf. τέθεικα, 2 aor. ἔθην, 2
aor. mid. ἐθέμην [§28.V.W] aor. pass.
ἐτέθην, perf. pass. τέθειμαι, pluperf.
ἐτεθείμην [§28.10] *to place, set, lay,* Matt.
5:15; Mark 6:56; Luke 6:48, et al.; *to produce* at table, John 2:10; *to deposit, lay,*
Matt. 27:60; Luke 23:53; Acts 3:2; *to lay
down,* Luke 19:21, 22; John 10:11, 15,
17, 18; 1 John 3:16, et al.; *to lay aside, put
off,* John 13:4; *to allocate, assign,* Matt.
24:51; Luke 12:46; *to set, constitute, appoint,* John 15:16; Acts 13:47; Heb. 1:2; *to
render, make,* Matt. 22:44; Rom. 4:17;
1 Cor. 9:18; mid. *to put* in custody, Matt.
14:3; Acts 4:3; *to reserve,* Acts 1:7; *to commit* as a matter of charge, 2 Cor. 5:19; *to
set,* with design, in a certain arrangement
or position, Acts 20:28; 1 Cor. 12:18, 28;
1 Thess. 5:9; 1 Tim. 1:12; pass. 1 Tim. 2:7;
2 Tim. 1:11; 1 Pet. 2:8; τιθέναι τὰ γόνατα,
to kneel down, Mark 15:19; Luke 22:41;
Acts 7:60; 9:40; 20:36; 21:5; τίθεσθαι ἐν
τῇ καρδίᾳ, *to lay to heart, ponder,* Luke
1:66; also, εἰς τὰς καρδίας, Luke 21:14;
τίθεσθαι ἐν τῇ καρδίᾳ, *to design, resolve,*
Acts 5:4; also, ἐν πνεύματι, Acts 19:21;
also, βουλήν, Acts 27:12; τίθεσθαι εἰς τὰ
ὦτα, *to give attentive audience to, to listen to retentively,* Luke 9:44

τίθησι(ν), 3 pers. sg. pres. act. indic. . . . τίθημι *(5087)*

τίκτει, 3 pers. sg. pres. act. indic. . . . . . τίκτω *(5088)*

τίκτῃ, 3 pers. sg. pres. act. subj. . . . . id.

τίκτουσα, nom. sg. f. pres. act. part. . . . . id.

(5088) **τίκτω**, fut. τέξω and τέξομαι, 2 aor. ἔτεκον,
perf. τέτοκα, aor. pass. ἐτέχθην [§37.1] *to
bear, bring forth* children, Matt. 1:21, 23,
et al.; trop. *to bear, produce,* as the earth,
yield, Heb. 6:7; met. *to give birth to,* James
1:15

τίλλειν, pres. act. infin. . . . . τίλλω *(5089)*

τίλλοντες, nom. pl. m. pres. act. part. . . . id.

(5089) **τίλλω**, fut. τιλῶ [§27.1.b] *to pull, pluck off,*
Matt. 12:1; Mark 2:33; Luke 6:1

τίμα, 2 pers. sg. pres. act. imper. . . . . . . τιμάω *(5091)*

τιμᾷ, 3 pers. sg. pres. act. indic. . . . . id.

(5090) **Τίμαιος**, ου, ὁ, *Timaeus,* pr. name, Mark
10:46

Τιμαίου, gen. sg. m. n. . . . . Τίμαιος *(5090)*

τιμαῖς, dat. pl. f. n. . . . . τιμή *(5092)*

τιμᾶς, acc. pl. f. n. . . . . id.

τιμᾶτε, 2 pers. pl. pres. act. imper. . . . . τιμάω *(5091)*

(5091) **τιμάω**, ῶ, fut. τιμήσω, aor. ἐτίμησα [§18.R]
*to estimate in respect of worth; to hold in
estimation, respect, honor, reverence,* Matt.
15:4, 5, 8; 19:19; Mark 7:10, et al.; *to
honor* with reverent service, John
5:23(4×); 8:49; *to treat with honor, manifest consideration towards,* Acts 28:10; *to
treat graciously, visit with marks of favor,*
John 12:26; mid. *to price,* Matt. 27:9

(5092) **τιμή**, ῆς, ἡ, nom. sg. f. n. [§2.B.a] (τίω, *to
price*) *a pricing, estimate of worth; price,
value,* Matt. 27:9; *price paid,* Matt. 27:6;
meton. *a thing of price,* and collectively,
precious things, Rev. 21:24, 26; *preciousness,* 1 Pet. 2:7; substantial *value,* real
worth, Col. 2:23; *careful regard, honor,
state of honor, dignity,* Rom. 9:21; Heb.
5:4; *honor* conferred, *observance, veneration,* Rom. 2:7, 10; 12:10; *mark of favor
and consideration,* Acts 28:10

τιμῇ, dat. sg. f. n. . . . . τιμή *(5092)*

τιμήν, acc. sg. f. n. . . . . id.

τιμῆς, gen. sg. f. n. . . . . id.

τιμήσατε, 2 pers. pl. aor. act. imper. . . . τιμάω *(5091)*

τιμήσει, 3 pers. sg. fut. act. indic. . . . . id.

τιμήσῃ, 3 pers. sg. aor. act. subj. (Matt. 15:5,
TR & MT | τιμήσει, Matt. 15:6, GNT,
WH & NA) . . . . id.

τίμια, nom. pl. neut. adj. . . . . τίμιος *(5093)*

τιμίαν, acc. sg. f. adj. . . . . id.

τίμιον, acc. sg. m. adj. . . . . id.

(5093) **τίμιος**, α, ον, nom. sg. m. adj. [§7.1] *precious,
costly, of great price,* 1 Cor. 3:12; Rev.
18:12; *precious, dear, valuable,* Acts 20:24;
1 Pet. 1:7, 19; *honored, esteemed, re-
spected,* Acts 5:34; Heb. 13:4

(5094) **τιμιότης**, ητος, ἡ [§4.2.c] *preciousness, costli-
ness;* meton. *precious things, valuable merchandise,* Rev. 18:19

τιμιότητος, gen. sg. f. n. . . . . τιμιότης *(5094)*

τιμίου, gen. sg. f. adj. . . . . τίμιος *(5093)*

τιμίους, acc. pl. m. adj. . . . . id.

τιμίῳ, dat. sg. m. adj. {Rev. 17:4} . . . . id.

τιμίῳ, dat. sg. neut. adj. {1 Pet. 1:19} . . . . . id.

τιμιωτάτου, gen. sg. neut. superlative adj.
    [§8.4] . . . . id.

τιμιωτάτῳ, dat. sg. m. superlative adj. . . . id.

τιμιώτερον, nom. sg. neut. compar. adj. (1 Pet.
1:7, with πολύ, MT & TR | πολυτιμό-
τερον, GNT, WH & NA) . . . . id.

Τιμόθεε, voc. sg. m. n. . . . . Τιμόθεος *(5095)*

Τιμόθεον, acc. sg. m. n. . . . . id.

(5095) **Τιμόθεος,** ου, ὁ, nom. sg. m. n. [§3.C.a] *Timotheus, Timothy,* pr. name

Τιμοθέου, gen. sg. m. n. . . . . Τιμόθεος *(5095)*

Τιμοθέῳ, dat. sg. m. n. . . . . id.

τιμῶ, 1 pers. sg. pres. act. indic. . . . . . . τιμάω *(5091)*

τιμῶν, nom. sg. m. pres. act. part. . . . . . . id.

(5096) **Τίμων,** ωνος, ὁ [§4.2.e] *Timon,* pr. name, Acts 6:5

Τίμωνα, acc. sg. m. n. . . . . Τίμων *(5096)*

(5097) **τιμωρέω,** ῶ, fut. τιμωρήσω [§16.P] aor. pass. ἐτιμωρήθην (τιμωρός, *an aider, an avenger,* from τιμή + αἴρω) *to succor, to avenge,* any one; in N.T. *to punish,* Acts 22:5; 26:11

τιμωρηθῶσιν, 3 pers. pl. aor. pass. subj. [§17.Q] . . . . τιμωρέω *(5097)*

(5098) **τιμωρία,** ας, ἡ [§2.B.b; 2.2] *punishment,* Heb. 10:29

τιμωρίας, gen. sg. f. n. . . . . τιμωρία *(5098)*

τιμωρῶν, nom. sg. m. pres. act. part. τιμωρέω *(5097)*

τιμῶσι, 3 pers. pl. pres. act. indic. {John 5:23b} . . . . τιμάω *(5091)*

τιμῶσι, 3 pers. pl. pres. act. subj. {John 5:23a} . . . . id.

τινά or τινα, acc. sg. m. indefinite pron. {Acts 18:2} . . . . τις *(5100)*

τινά or τινα, acc. sg. f. indefinite pron. {Acts 16:16} . . . . id.

τινά or τινα, nom. pl. neut. indefinite pron. {2 Pet. 3:16} . . . . id.

τινά or τινα, acc. pl. neut. indefinite pron. {Acts 25:19} . . . . id.

τίνα, acc. sg. m. interrogative pron. {John 18:7} . . . . τίς *(5101)*

τίνα, acc. sg. f. interrogative pron. {John 18:29} . . . . id.

τίνα, nom. pl. neut. interrogative pron. {John 10:6} . . . . id.

τινάς or τινας, acc. pl. m. indefinite pron. {Acts 9:2} . . . . τις *(5100)*

τινάς or τινας, acc. pl. f. indefinite pron. {Acts 9:19} . . . . id.

τίνας, acc. pl. m. interrogative pron. {John 13:18} . . . . τίς *(5101)*

τίνας, acc. pl. f. interrogative pron. {1 Thess. 4:2} . . . . id.

τινές or τινες, nom. pl. m. indefinite pron. {Luke 6:2} . . . . τις *(5100)*

τινές or τινες, nom. pl. f. indefinite pron. {Luke 8:2} . . . . id.

τίνες, nom. pl. m. interrogative pron. . . . . τίς *(5101)*

τινί or τινι, dat. sg. m. indefinite pron. {Luke 12:15} . . . . τις *(5100)*

τινί or τινι, dat. sg. f. indefinite pron. {Luke 18:2} . . . . id.

τινί or τινι, dat. sg. neut. indefinite pron. {Gal. 6:1} . . . . τις *(5100)*

τίνι, dat. sg. m. interrogative pron. {John 12:38} . . . . τίς *(5101)*

τίνι, dat. sg. neut. interrogative pron. {Matt. 5:13} . . . . id.

τινός or τινος, gen. sg. m. indefinite pron. {Luke 20:28} . . . . τις *(5100)*

τινός or τινος, gen. sg. neut. indefinite pron. {Luke 22:35} . . . . id.

τίνος, gen. sg. m. interrogative pron. {John 13:22} . . . . τίς *(5101)*

τίνος, gen. sg. neut. interrogative pron. {1 John 3:12} . . . . id.

(5099) **τίνω,** fut. τίσω [§27.1.a and note] *to pay; to pay* a penalty, *incur* punishment, 2 Thess. 1:9

τινῶν or τινων, gen. pl. m. indefinite pron. {Acts 24:1} . . . . τις *(5100)*

τινῶν or τινων, gen. pl. f. indefinite pron. {Acts 25:13} . . . . id.

τινῶν or τινων, gen. pl. neut. indefinite pron. {Acts 27:44} . . . . id.

τίνων, gen. pl. m. interrogative pron. {2 Tim. 3:14} . . . . τίς *(5101)*

τίνων, gen. pl. neut. interrogative pron. {1 Tim. 1:7} . . . . id.

(5100) **τις,** τις, τι nom. sg. m. indefinite pron. [§10.J.e] *a certain one, some one,* Matt. 12:47, et al.; pl. *some, certain, several,* Luke 8:2; Acts 9:19; 2 Pet. 3:16, et al.; *one, a person,* Matt. 12:29; Luke 14:8; John 6:50, et al.; combined with the name of an individual, *one,* Mark 15:21, et al.; *as it were, in a manner, a kind of,* Heb. 10:27; James 1:18; *any* whatever, Matt. 8:28; Luke 11:36; Rom. 8:39, et al.; τις, *somebody* of consequence, Acts 5:36; τι, *something* of consequence, Gal. 2:6; 6:3; τι, *anything* at all, *anything* worth account, 1 Cor. 3:7; 10:19; τι, *at all,* Phil. 3:15; Philemon 18 {Luke 11:1}

τις, nom. sg. f. indefinite pron. {Luke 11:27} . . . . τις *(5100)*

(5101) **τίς,** τίς, τί, nom. sg. m. interrogative pron. [§10.J.1] strictly of direct inquiry, *Who? What?* Matt. 3:7; 5:13; 19:27; equivalent to πότερος, *Whether? which* of two things? Matt. 9:5; Mark 2:9; Phil. 1:22; neut. τι, *Why? Wherefore?* Matt. 8:26; 9:11, 14; τί ὅτι, *Why is it that?* Mark 2:16; John 14:22; neut. τί, *What?* as an empathic interrogative, Acts 26:8; τί, *How very!* Matt. 7:14; in indirect question, Matt. 10:11; 12:3, et al. {Matt. 12:11}

τίς, nom. sg. f. interrogative pron.
{Matt. 12:48} .... τίς *(5101)*

τισί(ν), dat. pl. m. indefinite pron.
{Heb. 10:25} .... τις *(5100)*

τίσι(ν), dat. pl. m. interrogative pron.
{Heb. 3:17, 18} .... τίς *(5101)*

τίσουσιν, 3 pers. pl. fut. act. indic. ..... τίνω *(5099)*

Τιτίου, gen. sg. m. n. (Acts 18:7, GNT, WH
& NA | MT & TR omit) .... Τίτιος *(‡5103)*

(‡5103) **Τίτιος,** ου, ὁ, *Titius,* pr. name

τίτλον, acc. sg. m. n. .... τίτλος *(5102)*

(5102) **τίτλος,** ου, ὁ [§3.C.a] (Latin *titulus*) *an in-
scribed roll, superscription,* John 19:19, 20

Τίτον, acc. sg. m. n. .... Τίτος *(5103)*

(5103) **Τίτος,** ου, ὁ, nom. sg. m. n., *Titus,* pr. name

Τίτου, gen. sg. m. n. .... Τίτος *(5103)*

Τίτῳ, dat. sg. m. n. .... id.

τό, nom. sg. neut. article {1 John 1:7} .... ὁ *(3588)*

τό, acc. sg. neut. article {1 John 2:17} .... id.

τοιᾶσδε, gen. sg. f. demonstrative
pron. .... τοιόσδε *(5107)*

τοιαῦτα, acc. pl. neut. demonstrative
pron. .... τοιοῦτος *(5108)*

τοιαῦται, nom. pl. f. demonstrative pron. .. id.

τοιαύταις, dat. pl. f. demonstrative pron. .. id.

τοιαύτας, acc. pl. f. demonstrative pron. ... id.

τοιαύτη, nom. sg. f. demonstrative pron. ... id.

τοιαύτην, acc. sg. f. demonstrative pron. ... id.

(5105) **τοιγαροῦν** (τοι, γάρ, + οὖν) a doubly strengthened form of the particle τοι, *well then, so
then, wherefore,* 1 Thess. 4:8; Heb. 12:1

(5106) **τοίνυν,** a strengthening of the particle τοι, by
the enclitic νυν, *well then, therefore now,
therefore,* Luke 20:25; 1 Cor. 9:26, et al.

(5107) **τοιόσδε,** τοιάδε, τοιόνδε [§10.8] a more point-
edly demonstrative form of τοῖος, *such as
this; such as follows,* 2 Pet. 1:17

τοιοῦτο, acc. sg. neut. demonstrative pron.
(Matt. 18:5, GNT, WH & NA | τοιοῦτον,
MT & TR) .... τοιοῦτος *(5108)*

τοιοῦτοι, nom. pl. m. demonstrative pron. id.

τοιούτοις, dat. pl. m. demonstrative pron.
{1 Cor. 16:16} .... id.

τοιούτοις, dat. pl. neut. demonstrative pron.
{1 Cor. 7:15} .... id.

τοιοῦτον, acc. sg. m. demonstrative pron.
{Acts 22:22} .... id.

τοιοῦτον, acc. sg. neut. demonstrative pron.
(Matt. 18:5, MT & TR | τοιοῦτο, GNT,
WH & NA | Acts 21:25, MT & TR;
GNT, WH & NA omit) .... id.

(5108) **τοιοῦτος,** τοιαύτη, τοιοῦτο, and τοιοῦτον,
nom. sg. m. demonstrative pron. [§10.7.a]
a lengthened and more demonstrative form
of τοῖος, *such, such like, of this kind or*

sort, Matt. 18:5; 19:14; *such, so great,*
Matt. 9:8; Mark 6:2; ὁ τοιοῦτος, *such a
fellow,* Acts 22:22; also, *the one alluded to,*
1 Cor. 5:1; 2 Cor. 2:6, 7; 12:2, 3, 5

τοιούτου, gen. sg. m. demonstrative
pron. .... τοιοῦτος *(5108)*

τοιούτους, acc. pl. m. demonstrative pron. id.

τοιούτῳ, dat. sg. m. demonstrative pron. . id.

τοιούτων, gen. pl. m. demonstrative pron. (1 Tim.
6:5, MT & TR | GNT, WH & NA omit) id.

τοιούτων, gen. pl. f. demonstrative pron.
{Gal. 5:23} .... id.

τοιούτων, gen. pl. neut. demonstrative pron.
{Eph. 5:27} .... id.

τοῖς, dat. pl. m. article {1 John 1:1} ..... ὁ *(3588)*

τοῖς, dat. pl. neut. article {2 John 1} ..... id.

τοίχε, voc. sg. m. n. .... τοῖχος *(5109)*

(5109) **τοῖχος,** ου, ὁ [§3.C.a] *a wall* of a building, as
distinct from a city wall or fortification
(τεῖχος) Acts 23:3

(5110) **τόκος,** ου, ὁ [§3.C.a] *a bringing forth; offspring;* met. *produce* of money lent, *interest, usury,* Matt. 25:27; Luke 19:23

τόκῳ, dat. sg. m. n. .... τόκος *(5110)*

τολμᾷ, 3 pers. sg. pres. act. indic.
{2 Cor. 6:1} .... τολμάω *(5111)*

τολμᾷ, 3 pers. sg. pres. act. subj.
{2 Cor. 11:21} .... id.

τολμᾶν, pres. act. infin. (Phil. 1:14, GNT, MT
& NA | τολμᾶν, WH & TR) .... id.

(5111) **τολμάω,** ῶ, fut. τολμήσω, aor. ἐτόλμησα
[§18.R] *to assume resolution* to do a thing,
Mark 15:43; Rom. 5:7; Phil. 1:14; *to make
up the mind,* 2 Cor. 10:12; *to dare,* Acts 5:13;
7:32; *to presume,* Matt. 22:46; Mark 12:34;
Luke 20:40; John 21:12; Rom. 15:18; Jude
9; *to have the face,* 1 Cor. 6:1; absol. *to assume a bold bearing,* 2 Cor. 10:2; 11:21

(5112) **τολμηρότερον,** adv. (from τολμηρότερος, α,
ον,) [§7.1] (compar. of τολμηρός, *bold,*
from τολμάω) *bolder;* neut. τολμηρότερον, as an adv., *more boldly, with more
confidence, more freely* (Rom. 15:15, GNT,
MT, TR & NA | τολμηροτέρως, WH)

(†5112) **τολμηροτέρως,** adv., *more boldly* (Rom.
15:15, WH | τολμηρότερον, GNT, MT,
TR & NA)

τολμῆσαι, aor. act. infin. .... τολμάω *(5111)*

τολμήσας, nom. sg. m. aor. act. part. .... id.

τολμήσω, 1 pers. sg. fut. act. indic. ..... id.

τολμηταί, nom. pl. m. n. .... τολμητής *(5113)*

(5113) **τολμητής,** οῦ, ὁ [§2.B.c] *one who is bold;* in
a bad sense, *a presumptuous, audacious
person,* 2 Pet. 2:10

τολμῶ, 1 pers. sg. pres. act. indic. .... τολμάω *(5111)*

τολμῶμεν, 1 pers. pl. pres. act. indic. . τολμάω *(5111)*

(5114) **τομώτερος**, α, ον, nom. sg. m. adj. [§7.1]
(compar. of τόμος, *cutting, sharp, keen,*
from τέμνω, *to cut*) *keener, sharper*

τόν, acc. sg. m. article . . . . ὁ *(3588)*

(5115) **τόξον**, ου, τό [§3.C.c] *a bow,* Rev. 6:2

τόξον, acc. sg. neut. n. . . . . τόξον *(5115)*

(5116) **τοπάζιον**, ου, τό, nom. sg. neut. n., *a topaz,*
a gem of a yellowish color, different from
the modern topaz

τόποις, dat. pl. m. n. . . . . τόπος *(5117)*

τόπον, acc. sg. m. n. . . . . id.

(5117) **τόπος**, ου, ὁ, nom. sg. m. n. [§3.C.a] *a place,
locality,* Matt. 12:43; Luke 6:17, et al.; *a
limited spot or ground,* Matt. 24:15; 27:33;
John 4:20; Acts 6:13, et al.; *a precise spot
or situation,* Matt. 28:6; Mark 16:6; Luke
14:9, et al.; *a dwelling place, abode, mansion, dwelling, seat,* John 14:2, 3; Acts
4:31; *a place* of ordinary deposit, Matt.
26:52; *a place, passage* in a book, Luke
4:17; *place* occupied, *room, space,* Luke
2:7; 14:9, 22; *place, opportunity,* Acts
25:16; Heb. 12:17; *place, condition, position,* 1 Cor. 14:16

τόπου, gen. sg. m. n. . . . . τόπος *(5117)*

τόπους, acc. pl. m. n. . . . . id.

τόπῳ, dat. sg. m. n. . . . . id.

τόπων, gen. pl. m. n. . . . . id.

τοσαῦτα, nom. pl. neut. demonstrative pron.
{1 Cor. 14:10} . . . . τοσοῦτος *(5118)*

τοσαῦτα, acc. pl. neut. demonstrative pron.
{Gal. 3:4} . . . . id.

τοσαύτην, acc. sg. f. demonstrative pron. . id.

τοσοῦτο, acc. sg. neut. demonstrative pron.
(Heb. 7:22, GNT, WH & NA | τοσοῦτον,
MT & TR) . . . . id.

τοσοῦτοι, nom. pl. m. demonstrative pron. id.

τοσοῦτον, acc. sg. m. demonstrative pron.
[§10.8] {Heb. 4:7} . . . . id.

τοσοῦτον, nom. sg. neut. demonstrative pron.
(Rev. 21:16, TR | GNT, MT, WH & NA
omit) . . . . id.

τοσοῦτον, acc. sg. neut. demonstrative pron.
{Heb. 12:1} . . . . id.

(5118) **τοσοῦτος**, τοσαύτη, τοσοῦτο and τοσοῦτον
[§10.7.b] a lengthened and more demonstrative form of τόσος, *so great, so much,*
Matt. 8:10; 15:33; *so long,* of time, John
14:9; pl. *so many,* Matt. 15:33, et al.

τοσούτου, gen. sg. neut. demonstrative
pron. . . . . τοσοῦτος *(5118)*

τοσούτους, acc. pl. m. demonstrative pron. id.

τοσούτῳ, dat. sg. m. demonstrative pron.
(John 14:9, GNT, MT, TR & NA | το-

σοῦτον, WH) . . . . τοσοῦτος *(5118)*

τοσούτῳ, dat. sg. neut. demonstrative pron.
{Heb. 10:25} . . . . id.

τοσούτων, gen. pl. m. demonstrative pron. id.

(5119) **τότε**, adv., of time, *then, at that time,* Matt.
2:17; 3:5; 11:20; *then, thereupon,* Matt.
12:29; 13:26; 25:31; ἀπὸ τότε, *from that
time,* Matt. 4:17; 16:21; ὁ τότε, *which then
was,* 2 Pet. 3:6

(5120) τοῦ, gen. sg. m. article {1 John 1:3} . . . . . . ὁ *(3588)*

(5120) τοῦ, gen. sg. neut. article {1 John 3:24} . . id.

(5121) **τοὐναντίον** (by crasis for τὸ ἐναντίον) *that
which is opposite;* as an adv., *on the contrary, on the other hand,* 2 Cor. 2:7; Gal.
2:7; 1 Pet. 3:9

(5122) **τοὔνομα** (by crasis for τὸ ὄνομα) *the name;*
in the acc. *by name,* Matt. 27:57

τούς, acc. pl. m. article . . . . ὁ *(3588)*

(5123) **τουτέστι(ν)** (by crasis for τοῦτ' ἔστι(ν)) *that
is, which signifies, which implies,* Acts
19:4, et al. (Acts 1:19, TRs | τοῦτ' ἔστι(ν),
GNT, WH, MT, TRb & NA)

(5124) τοῦτο, nom. sg. neut. demonstrative pron.
[§10.J.c] {John 6:61} . . . . οὗτος *(3778)*

(5124) τοῦτο, acc. sg. neut. demonstrative pron.
{John 6:65} . . . . id.

(5125) τούτοις, dat. pl. m. demonstrative pron.
{Jude 14} . . . . id.

(5125) τούτοις, dat. pl. neut. demonstrative pron.
{Jude 10} . . . . id.

(5126) τοῦτον, acc. sg. m. demonstrative pron. . . id.

(5127) τούτου, gen. sg. m. demonstrative pron.
{John 6:51} . . . . id.

(5127) τούτου, gen. sg. neut. demonstrative pron.
{John 6:61} . . . . id.

(5128) τούτους, acc. pl. m. demonstrative pron. . . id.

(5129) τούτῳ, dat. sg. m. demonstrative pron.
{John 13:24} . . . . id.

(5129) τούτῳ, dat. sg. neut. demonstrative pron.
{John 13:35} . . . . id.

(5130) τούτων, gen. pl. m. demonstrative pron.
{Acts 5:38} . . . . id.

(5130) τούτων, gen. pl. f. demonstrative pron.
{Acts 5:36} . . . . id.

(5130) τούτων, gen. pl. neut. demonstrative pron.
{Acts 5:32} . . . . id.

(5131) **τράγος**, ου, ὁ [§3.C.a] *a he-goat,* Heb. 9:12,
13, 19; 10:4

τράγων, gen. pl. m. n. . . . . τράγος *(5131)*

(5132) **τράπεζα**, ης, ἡ, nom. sg. f. n. [§2.3] (τετράς,
four, and πέζα, *a foot*) *a table, an eating-
table,* Matt. 15:27; Mark 7:28; Heb. 9:2;
by impl. *a meal, feast,* Rom. 11:9; 1 Cor.
10:21; *a table or counter* of a money-
changer, Matt. 21:12; *a bank,* Luke 19:23;

by impl. pl. *money matters,* Acts 6:2

τραπέζαις, dat. pl. f. n. . . . . τράπεζα *(5132)*

τράπεζαν, acc. sg. f. n. . . . . id.

τραπέζας, acc. pl. f. n. . . . . id.

τραπέζης, gen. sg. f. n. . . . . id.

τραπεζίταις, dat. pl. m. n. (Matt. 25:27, GNT, MT, TR & NA | τραπεζείταις, WH) . . . . τραπεζίτης *(5133)*

(5133) **τραπεζίτης,** ου, ὁ [§2.B.c] *a money-changer, broker, banker,* who exchanges or loans money for a premium, Matt. 25:27

(5134) **τραῦμα,** ατος, τό [§4.D.c] (τιτρώσκω, *to wound) a wound,* Luke 10:34

τραύματα, acc. pl. neut. n. . . . . τραῦμα *(5134)*

(5135) **τραυματίζω,** fut. τραυματίσω, aor. ἐτραυμάτισα [§26.1] *to wound,* Luke 20:12; Acts 19:16

τραυματίσαντες, nom. pl. m. aor. act. part. . . . . τραυματίζω *(5135)*

τραχεῖαι, nom. pl. f. adj. . . . . τραχύς *(5138)*

τραχεῖς, acc. pl. m. adj. . . . . id.

(5136) **τραχηλίζω,** fut. τραχηλίσω, perf. pass. τετραχήλισμαι [§26.1] pr. *to gripe the neck; to bend the neck back,* so as to make bare or expose the throat, as in slaughtering animals, etc.; met. *to lay bare in view,* Heb. 4:13

τράχηλον, acc. sg. m. n. . . . . τράχηλος *(5137)*

(5137) **τράχηλος,** ου, ὁ [§3.C.a] *the neck,* Matt. 18:6, et al.; ἐπιθεῖναι ζυγὸν ἐπὶ τὸν τράχηλον, *to put a yoke upon the neck* of any one, met. *to bind to a burdensome observance,* Acts 15:10; ὑποτιθέναι τὸν τράχηλον, *to lay down one's neck* under the axe of the executioner, *to imperil one's life,* Rom. 16:4

(5138) **τραχύς,** εῖα, ύ [§7.H.g] *rough, rugged, uneven,* Luke 3:5; εἰς τραχεῖς τόπους, *on a rocky shore,* Acts 27:29

Τραχωνίτιδος, gen. sg. f. n. . . . . . Τραχωνῖτις *(5139)*

(5139) **Τραχωνῖτις,** ιδος, ἡ [§4.2.c] *Trachonitis,* part of the tetrarchy of Herod Antipas, the north-easternmost habitable district east of the Jordan

(‡4999) **Τρεῖς Ταβέρναι,** *the Three Taverns,* the name of a small place on the Appian road, according to Antonius, 33 Roman miles from Rome, Acts 28:15

(5140) **τρεῖς,** οἱ, αἱ, τά, nom. pl. m. numeral, [§9.1.c] *three,* Matt. 12:40, et al. {Acts 10:19}

τρεῖς, nom. pl. f. numeral {Rev. 6:6} . . . τρεῖς *(5140)*

τρεῖς, acc. pl. m. numeral {Acts 7:20} . . . id.

τρεῖς, acc. pl. f. numeral {Acts 9:9} . . . . . id.

τρέμουσα, nom. sg. f. pres. act. part. . . τρέμω *(5141)*

τρέμουσι(ν), 3 pers. pl. pres. act. indic. . . id.

(5141) **τρέμω** (τρέω, idem) *to tremble, be agitated*

from fear, Mark 5:33; Luke 8:47; Acts 9:6; by impl. *to fear, be afraid,* 2 Pet. 2:10

τρέμων, nom. sg. m. pres. act. part. (Acts 9:6, TR | GNT, WH, MT & NA omit) . τρέμω *(5141)*

τρέφει, 3 pers. sg. pres. act. indic. . . . . . τρέφω *(5142)*

τρέφεσθαι, pres. pass. infin. . . . . id.

τρέφεται, 3 pers. sg. pres. pass. indic. (Rev. 12:14, GNT, WH, TR & NA | τρέφηται, MT) . . . . id.

τρέφηται, 3 pers. sg. pres. pass. subj. (Rev. 12:14, MT | τρέφεται, GNT, WH, TR & NA) . . . . id.

(5142) **τρέφω,** fut. θρέψω [§35.4] aor. ἔθρεψα, perf. pass. τέθραμμαι [§35.9] *to thicken; to nourish; to feed, support, cherish, provide for,* Matt. 6:26; 25:37, et al.; *to bring up, rear, educate,* Luke 4:16; *to gorge, pamper,* James 5:5

τρέφωσιν, 3 pers. pl. pres. act. subj. (Rev. 12:6, GNT, WH, TR & NA | ἐκτρέφωσιν, MT) . . . . τρέφω *(5142)*

τρέχει, 3 pers. sg. pres. act. indic. . . . . . τρέχω *(5143)*

τρέχετε, 2 pers. pl. pres. act. imper. . . . . . id.

τρέχῃ, 3 pers. sg. pres. act. subj. . . . . id.

τρέχοντες, nom. pl. m. pres. act. part. . . . id.

τρέχοντος, gen. sg. m. pres. act. part. . . . id.

τρεχόντων, gen. pl. m. pres. act. part. . . . id.

τρέχουσι(ν), 3 pers. pl. pres. act. indic. . . . id.

(5143) **τρέχω,** 1 pers. sg. pres. act. indic., fut. θρέξομαι, and δραμοῦμαι, 2 aor. ἔδραμον [§36.1] *to run,* Matt. 27:48; 28:8, et al.; *to run a race,* 1 Cor. 9:24; met. 1 Cor. 9:24, 26; Heb. 12:1; in N.T. *to run* a certain course of conduct, Gal. 5:7; *to run* a course of exertion, Rom. 9:16; Gal. 2:2; Phil. 2:16; *to run, to progress freely, to advance rapidly,* 2 Thess. 3:1 {1 Cor. 9:26}

τρέχω, 1 pers. sg. pres. act. subj. {Gal. 2:2} . . . . τρέχω *(5143)*

τρέχωμεν, 1 pers. pl. pres. act. subj. . . . . . id.

(‡5168) **τρῆμα,** ατος, τό (τιτράω, or τίτρημι, *to bore,* perf. pass. τέτρημαι) *an aperture*

τρήματος (βελόνης) gen. sg. neut. n. (Luke 18:25, GNT, WH & NA | τρυμαλιᾶς ῥαφίδος, MT & TR) . . . . τρῆμα *(‡5168)*

τρία, nom. pl. neut. numeral {1 Cor. 13:13} . . . . τρεῖς *(5140)*

τρία, acc. pl. neut. numeral {Luke 13:21} . id.

(5144) **τριάκοντα,** οἱ, αἱ, τά, indecl. numeral, *thirty,* Matt. 13:8, 23, et al.

τριακονταοκτώ, indecl. numeral, *thirty-eight* (John 5:5, TRs | τριάκοντα καὶ ὀκτώ, GNT, WH, MT, TRb & NA)

(5145) **τριακόσιοι,** αι, α, numeral, *three hundred,* Mark 14:5; John 12:5

τριακοσίων, gen. pl. m. numeral .. τριακόσιοι *(5145)*

(5146) **τρίβολος**, ου, ὁ [§3.C.a] (τρεῖς + βέλος) pr. *three-pronged;* as a subst. *a caltrop;* a plant, *land caltrop, a thorn,* Matt. 7:16; Heb. 6:8

τριβόλους, acc. pl. m. n. . . . . τρίβολος *(5146)*

τριβόλων, gen. pl. m. n. . . . . id.

(5147) **τρίβος**, ου, ἡ [§3.C.b] (τρίβω, *to rub, wear*) *a beaten track; a road, highway,* Matt. 3:3; Mark 1:3; Luke 3:4

τρίβους, acc. pl. f. n. . . . . τρίβος *(5147)*

(5148) **τριετία**, ας, ἡ [§2.B.b; 2.2] (τρεῖς + ἔτος) *the space of three years,* Acts 20:31

τριετίαν, acc. sg. f. n. . . . . τριετία *(5148)*

τρίζει, 3 pers. sg. pres. act. indic. . . . . . . τρίζω *(5149)*

(5149) **τρίζω**, fut. τρίσω [§26.1] *to creak, to utter a creaking, stridulous, grating sound; to gnash, grind* the teeth, Mark 9:18

(5150) τρίμηνον, acc. sg. neut. adj. . . . . . . τρίμηνος (†5150)

(†5150) **τρίμηνος**, ὃν (τρεῖς + μήν) *the space of three months,* Heb. 11:23

(5151) **τρίς**, adv., *three times, thrice,* Matt. 26:34, 75, et al.; ἐπὶ τρίς, *to the extent of thrice, as many as three times,* Acts 10:16; 11:10

τρισί(ν), dat. pl. m. numeral {Luke 12:52} . . . . τρεῖς *(5140)*

τρισί(ν), dat. pl. f. numeral {Mark 15:29}   id.

(5152) **τρίστεγον**, ου, τό [§3.C.c] (neut. of τρίστεγος, *having three stories,* from τρεῖς + στέγη) *the third floor, third story,* Acts 20:9

τριστέγου, gen. sg. neut. n. . . . . τρίστεγον *(5152)*

τρισχίλιαι, nom. pl. f. numeral . . . . τρισχίλιοι *(5153)*

(5153) **τρισχίλιοι**, αι, α (τρεῖς + χίλιοι) numeral, *three thousand,* Acts 2:41

τρίτη, nom. sg. f. adj. . . . . τρίτος *(5154)*

τρίτῃ, dat. sg. f. adj. . . . . id.

τρίτην, acc. sg. f. adj. . . . . id.

τρίτης, gen. sg. f. adj. . . . . id.

τρίτον, acc. sg. m. adj. {Luke 20:12} . . . . id.

τρίτον, nom. sg. neut. adj. {Rev. 4:7} . . . . id.

τρίτον, acc. sg. neut. adj. {Rev. 12:4} . . . . id.

(5154) **τρίτος**, η, ον, nom. sg. m. adj. [§7.F.a] *third,* Matt. 20:3; 27:64; ἐκ τρίτου, *the third time, for the third time,* Matt. 26:44; τὸ τρίτον, sc. μέρος, *the third part,* Rev. 8:7, 12; τρίτον and τὸ τρίτον, as an adv., *the third time, for the third time,* Mark 14:41; Luke 23:22

τρίτου, gen. sg. m. adj. {2 Cor. 12:2} .. τρίτος *(5154)*

τρίτου, gen. sg. neut. adj. {Matt. 26:44} . id.

τρίχα, acc. sg. f. n. [§4.2 note] . . . . θρίξ *(2359)*

τρίχας, acc. pl. f. n. . . . . id.

τρίχες, nom. pl. f. n. . . . . id.

(5155) **τρίχινος**, η, ον, nom. sg. m. adj. [§7.F.a] *of hair, made of hair,* Rev. 6:12

τριχῶν, gen. pl. f. n. . . . . θρίξ *(2359)*

τριῶν, gen. pl. m. numeral {Rev. 8:13} .. τρεῖς *(5140)*

τριῶν, gen. pl. f. numeral {Rev. 9:18} . . . . id.

Τριῶν Ταβερνῶν, gen. pl. m. n. . . . . Τρεῖς Ταβέρναι (‡4999)

(5156) **τρόμος**, ου, ὁ, nom. sg. m. n. [§3.C.a] pr. *a trembling, quaking; trembling* from fear, *fear, terror, agitation of mind,* Mark 16:8; *anxious diffidence,* under solemn responsibility, 1 Cor. 2:3; *reverence, veneration, awe,* 2 Cor. 7:15; Eph. 6:5; Phil. 2:12

τρόμου, gen. sg. m. n. . . . . τρόμος *(5156)*

τρόμῳ, dat. sg. m. n. . . . . id.

(5157) **τροπή**, ῆς, ἡ [§2.B.a] (τρέπω, *to turn*) *a turning round; a turning back, change, mutation,* James 1:17

τροπῆς, gen. sg. f. n. . . . . τροπή *(5157)*

τρόπον, acc. sg. m. n. . . . . τρόπος *(5158)*

(5158) **τρόπος**, ου, ὁ, nom. sg. m. n. [§3.C.a] (τρέπω, *to turn*) *a turn; mode, manner, way,* Jude 7; ὃν τρόπον, + καθ' ὃν τρόπον, *in which manner, as, even as,* Matt. 23:37; Acts 15:11, et al.; κατὰ μηδένα τρόπον, *in no way, by no means,* 2 Thess. 2:3; ἐν παντὶ τρόπῳ, and παντὶ τρόπῳ, *in every way, by every means,* Phil. 1:18; 2 Thess. 3:16; *turn* of mind or action, *habit, disposition,* Heb. 13:5

(5159) **τροποφορέω**, ῶ, fut. τροποφορήσω, aor. ἐτροποφόρησα [§16.P] (τρόπος + φορέω) *to bear with the disposition, manners, and conduct* of any one, Acts 13:18

τρόπῳ, dat. sg. m. n. . . . . τρόπος *(5158)*

τροφάς, acc. pl. f. n. . . . . τροφή *(5160)*

(5160) **τροφή**, ῆς, ἡ, nom. sg. f. n. [§2.B.a] *nutriment, nourishment, food,* Matt. 3:4, et al.; *provision, victual,* Matt. 24:45; *sustenance, maintenance,* Matt. 10:10; met. *nutriment* of the mind, Heb. 5:12, 14

τροφήν, acc. sg. f. n. . . . . τροφή *(5160)*

τροφῆς, gen. sg. f. n. . . . . id.

Τρόφιμον, acc. sg. m. n. . . . . Τρόφιμος *(5161)*

(5161) **Τρόφιμος**, ου, ὁ, nom. sg. m. n. [§3.C.a] *Trophimus,* pr. name

(5162) **τροφός**, οῦ, ἡ, nom. sg. f. n. [§3.C.b] *a nurse,* 1 Thess. 2:7

(5163) **τροχιά**, ᾶς, ἡ [§2.B.b; 2.2] *a wheel-track; a track, way, path,* met. Heb. 12:13

τροχιάς, acc. pl. f. n. . . . . τροχιά *(5163)*

τροχόν, acc. sg. m. n. . . . . τροχός *(5164)*

(5164) **τροχός**, οῦ, ὁ [§3.C.a] pr. *a runner; anything orbicular, a wheel; drift, course,* with which signification the word is usually written τρόχος, James 3:6

(†5165) **τρυβλίον**, ου, τό [§3.C.c] *a bowl, dish,* Matt.

26:23; Mark 14:20

τρυβλίον, acc. sg. neut. n. . . . . τρυβλίον (†5165)

τρυβλίῳ, dat. sg. neut. n. . . . . id.

(5166) **τρυγάω**, ῶ, fut. τρυγήσω, aor. ἐτρύγησα [§18.R] (τρύγη, *ripe fruits*) *to harvest, gather,* fruits, and spc. grapes, Luke 6:44; Rev. 14:18, 19

τρύγησον, 2 pers. sg. aor. act. imper. . τρυγάω (5166)

τρυγόνων, gen. pl. f. n. . . . . τρυγών (5167)

(5167) **τρυγών**, όνος, ἡ [§4.2.e] (τρύζω, *to murmur*) *a turtle-dove*

τρυγῶσι(ν), 3 pers. pl. pres. act. indic. τρυγάω (5166)

(5168) **τρυμαλιά**, ᾶς, ἡ [§2.B.b; 2.2] (τρύμη, from τρύω, *to rub, wear*) *a hole, perforation; eye* of a needle, Mark 10:25; Luke 18:25

τρυμαλιᾶς, gen. sg. f. n. . . . . τρυμαλιά (5168)

(5169) **τρύπημα**, ατος, τό [§4.D.c] (τρυπάω, τρύπη, *a hole*, from τρύω) *a hole; eye* of a needle, Matt. 19:24

τρυπήματος, gen. sg. neut. n. (Matt. 19:24, GNT, MT, TR & NA | τρήματος, WH) . . . . τρύπημα (5169)

(5170) **Τρύφαινα**, ης, ἡ [§2.3] *Tryphaena,* pr. name

Τρύφαιναν, acc. sg. f. n. . . . . Τρύφαινα (5170)

(5171) **τρυφάω**, ῶ, fut. τρυφήσω, aor. ἐτρύφησα [§18.R] *to live delicately and luxuriously,* James 5:5

(5172) **τρυφή**, ῆς, ἡ [§2.B.a] (θρύπτω, *to break small, to enfeeble, enervate*) *delicate living, luxury,* Luke 7:25; 2 Pet. 2:13

τρυφῇ, dat. sg. f. n. . . . . τρυφή (5172)

τρυφήν, acc. sg. f. n. . . . . id.

(5173) **Τρυφῶσα**, ης, ἡ [§2.3] *Tryphosa,* pr. name, Rom. 16:12

Τρυφῶσαν, acc. sg. f. n. . . . . Τρυφῶσα (5173)

Τρῳάδα, acc. sg. f. n. (Acts 16:8; 20:6; 2 Cor. 2:12, GNT, MT, WH, NA | Τρωάδα, TR) . . . . Τρωάς (†5174)

Τρῳάδι, dat. sg. f. n. (Acts 20:5; 2 Tim. 4:13, GNT, MT, WH, NA | Τρωάδι, TR) . . id.

Τρῳάδος, gen. sg. f. n. (Acts 16:11, GNT, MT, WH, NA | Τρωάδος, TR) . . . . id.

(†5174) **Τρῳάς**, άδος, ἡ [§4.2.c] *Troas,* a city on the coast of Phrygia, near the site of ancient Troy

τρώγοντες, nom. pl. m. pres. act. part. τρώγω (5176)

(5175) **Τρωγύλλιον**, ου, τό [§3.C.c] *Trogyllium,* a town and promontory on the western coast of Ionia, opposite Samos

Τρωγυλλίῳ, dat. sg. neut. n. (Acts 20:15, MT & TR | GNT, WH & NA omit) . . . . Τρωγύλλιον (5175)

(5176) **τρώγω**, fut. τρώξομαι, 2 aor. ἔτραγον [§36.1] pr. *to crunch; to eat,* Matt. 24:38; from the Hebrew, ἄρτον τρώγειν, *to take food, par-*

take of a meal, John 13:18

τρώγων, nom. sg. m. pres. act. part. . . . τρώγω (5176)

τυγχάνοντα, acc. sg. m. pres. act. part. (Luke 10:30, MT & TR | GNT, WH & NA omit) . . . . τυγχάνω (5177)

τυγχάνοντες, nom. pl. m. pres. act. part. . id.

(5177) **τυγχάνω**, fut. τεύξομαι, perf. τετύχηκα and τέτευχα, 2 aor. ἔτυχον [§36.2] *to hit* an object; *to attain to, to obtain, acquire, enjoy,* Luke 20:35; Acts 24:3, et al.; intrans. *to happen, fall out, chance;* part. τυχών, οὖσα, όν, *common, ordinary,* Acts 19:11; 28:2; neut. τυχόν, as an adv., *it may be, perchance, perhaps,* 1 Cor. 16:6; εἰ τύχοι, *as it so happens, as the case may be,* 1 Cor. 14:10; 15:37; *to be* in a certain condition, Luke 10:30

(5178) **τυμπανίζω**, fut. τυμπανίσω, aor. pass. ἐτυμπανίσθην [§26.1] (τύμπανον, *a drum*) pr. *to beat a drum; to drum upon;* in N.T. *to bastinade, beat to death with rods and clubs,* Heb. 11:35

(†5179) **τυπικῶς**, adv., *figuratively, typically* (1 Cor. 10:11, GNT, WH & NA | τύποι, MT & TR)

τύποι, nom. pl. m. n. . . . . τύπος (5179)

τύπον, acc. sg. m. n. . . . . id.

(5179) **τύπος**, ου, ὁ, nom. sg. m. n. [§3.C.a] pr. *a blow; an impress; a print, mark,* of a wound inflicted, John 20:25; *a delineation; an image, statue,* Acts 7:43; *a formula, scheme,* Rom. 6:17; *form, purport,* Acts 23:25; *a figure, counterpart,* 1 Cor. 10:6; *an* anticipative *figure, type,* Rom. 5:14; 1 Cor. 10:11; *a model pattern,* Acts 7:44; Heb. 8:5; *a moral pattern,* Phil. 3:17; 1 Thess. 1:7; 2 Thess. 3:9; 1 Tim. 4:12; 1 Pet. 5:3

τύπους, acc. pl. m. n. . . . . τύπος (5179)

τύπτειν, pres. act. infin. . . . . τύπτω (5180)

τύπτεσθαι, pres. pass. infin. . . . . id.

τύπτοντες, nom. pl. m. pres. act. part. . . . id.

τύπτοντι, dat. sg. m. pres. act. part. . . . . . id.

(5180) **τύπτω**, fut. τύψω [§23.2] aor. ἔτυφα, *to beat, strike, smite,* Matt. 24:49; 27:30, et al.; *to beat* the breast, as expressive of grief or strong emotion, Luke 18:13; 23:48; in N.T. met. *to wound or shock* the conscience of any one, 1 Cor. 8:12; from the Hebrew, *to smite* with evil, *punish,* Acts 23:3

(5181) **Τύραννος**, ου, ὁ [§3.C.a] *Tyrannus,* pr. name, Acts 19:9

Τυράννου, gen. sg. m. n. . . . . Τύραννος (5181)

τυρβάζῃ, 2 pers. sg. pres. pass. indic. (Luke 10:41, MT & TR | θορυβάζῃ, GNT, WH

& NA) . . . . τυρβάζω *(5182)*

(5182) **τυρβάζω**, fut. τυρβάσω [§26.1] (τύρβη, *tumult*) *to stir up, render turbid; to throw into a state of perturbation, disquiet;* mid. *to trouble one's self, be troubled, be disquieted,* Luke 10:41

Τυρίοις, dat. pl. m. n. . . . . Τύριος *(5183)*

(5183) **Τύριος**, ου, ὁ, *a Tyrian, an inhabitant* of Τύρος, *Tyre,* Acts 12:20

Τύρον, acc. sg. f. n. . . . . Τύρος *(5184)*

(5184) **Τύρος**, ου, ἡ [§3.C.b] *Tyrus, Tyre,* a celebrated and wealth commercial city of Phoenicia

Τύρου, gen. sg. f. n. . . . . Τύρος *(5184)*

Τύρῳ, dat. sg. f. n. . . . . id.

τυφλέ, voc. sg. m. adj. . . . . τυφλός *(5185)*

τυφλοί, nom. pl. m. adj. {Matt. 21:14} . . . id.

τυφλοί, voc. pl. m. adj. {Matt. 23:16, 17} . id.

τυφλοῖς, dat. pl. m. adj. . . . . id.

τυφλόν, acc. sg. m. adj. . . . . id.

(5185) **τυφλός**, ή, όν, nom. sg. m. adj. [§7.F.a] *blind,* Matt. 9:27, 28; 11:5; 12:22; met. mentally *blind,* Matt. 15:14; 23:16, et al.

τυφλοῦ, gen. sg. m. adj. . . . . τυφλός *(5185)*

τυφλούς, acc. pl. m. adj. . . . . id.

(5186) **τυφλόω**, ῶ, fut. τυφλώσω, perf. τετύφλωκα [§20.T] *to blind, render blind;* met. John 12:40; 1 John 2:11; 2 Cor. 4:4

τυφλῷ, dat. sg. m. adj. . . . . τυφλός *(5185)*

τυφλῶν, gen. pl. m. adj. . . . . id.

τυφόμενον, acc. sg. neut. pres. pass. part. . . . . τύφω *(†5188)*

(5187) **τυφόω**, ῶ, fut. τυφώσω, perf. pass. τετύφωμαι [§21.U] (τῦφος, *smoke,* from τύφω) *to besmoke;* met. *to possess with the fumes* of conceit; pass. *to be demented with conceit, puffed up,* 1 Tim. 3:6; 6:4; 2 Tim. 3:4

(†5188) **τύφω**, fut. θύψω [§35.4] *to raise a smoke;* pass. *to emit smoke, smoke, smoulder,* Matt. 12:20

τυφωθείς, nom. sg. m. aor. pass. part. . τυφόω *(5187)*

(5189) **τυφωνικός**, ή, όν, nom. sg. m. adj. [§7.F.a] (τυφῶν, *typhoon, a hurricane*) *stormy, tempestuous*

τυχεῖν, 2 aor. act. infin. [§36.2] . . . . . τυγχάνω *(5177)*

Τυχικόν, acc. sg. m. n. (2 Tim. 4:12; Tit. 3:12, GNT, MT, TR & NA | Τύχικον, WH) . . . . Τυχικός *(5190)*

(5190) **Τυχικός**, ου, ὁ, nom. sg. m. n., *Tychicus,* pr. name (Acts 20:4; Eph. 6:21; Col. 4:7, GNT, MT, TR & NA | Τύχικος, WH)

Τυχικοῦ, gen. sg. m. n. (Eph. 6:24, TRs | GNT, WH, MT, TRb & NA omit) Τυχικός *(5190)*

τύχοι, 3 pers. sg. 2 aor. act. opt. . . . . τυγχάνω *(5177)*

τυχόν, acc. sg. neut. 2 aor. act. part. . . . . . id.

τυχοῦσαν, acc. sg. f. 2 aor. act. part. . . . . id.

τυχούσας, acc. pl. f. 2 aor. act. part. . τυγχάνω *(5177)*

τυχών, nom. sg. m. 2 aor. act. part. . . . . . id.

τύχωσι(ν), 3 pers. pl. 2 aor. act. subj. . . . . id.

τῷ, dat. sg. m. article {1 John 2:24} . . . . ὁ *(3588)*

τῷ, dat. sg. neut. article {1 John 1:6} . . . . . id.

τῶν, gen. pl. m. article {1 John 3:16} . . . . id.

τῶν, gen. pl. f. article {1 John 2:2} . . . . . . id.

τῶν, gen. pl. neut. article {1 John 5:21} . . id.

Υ

(5191) **ὑακίνθινος**, η, ον [§7.F.a] *hyacinthine, resembling the hyacinth in color,* Rev. 9:17

ὑακινθίνους, acc. pl. m. adj. . . . . . . ὑακίνθινος *(5191)*

(5192) **ὑάκινθος**, ου, ὁ, nom. sg. m. n. [§3.C.a] *a hyacinth,* a gem resembling the color of the *hyacinth flower*

ὑαλίνη, nom. sg. f. adj. . . . . ὑάλινος *(5193)*

ὑαλίνην, acc. sg. f. adj. . . . . id.

(5193) **ὑάλινος**, η, ον [§7.F.a] *made of glass; glassy, translucent,* Rev. 4:6; 15:2

(5194) **ὕαλος**, ου, ὁ, nom. sg. m. n. [§3.C.a] *a transparent stone, crystal;* also, *glass* (Rev. 21:21, GNT, TR, WH & NA | ὕελος, MT)

ὑάλῳ, dat. sg. m. n. (Rev. 21:18, GNT, TR, WH & NA | ὑέλῳ, MT) . . . . ὕαλος *(5194)*

ὕβρεσιν, dat. pl. f. n. . . . . ὕβρις *(5196)*

ὕβρεως, gen. sg. f. n. . . . . id.

ὑβρίζεις, 2 pers. sg. pres. act. indic. . . . ὑβρίζω *(5195)*

(5195) **ὑβρίζω**, fut. ὑβρίσω, aor. ὕβρισα [§13.3] *to run riot;* trans. *to outrage,* Matt. 22:6; Luke 11:45, et al.

ὕβριν, acc. sg. f. n. . . . . ὕβρις *(5196)*

(5196) **ὕβρις**, εως, ἡ [§5.E.c] *violent wantonness, insolence; contumelious treatment, outrage,* 2 Cor. 12:10; *damage* by sea, Acts 17:10

ὑβρίσαι, aor. act. infin. . . . . ὑβρίζω *(5195)*

ὕβρισαν, 3 pers. pl. aor. act. indic. . . . . . . id.

ὑβρισθέντες, nom. pl. m. aor. pass. part. . id.

ὑβρισθήσεται, 3 pers. sg. fut. pass. indic. . id.

ὑβριστάς, acc. pl. m. n. . . . . ὑβριστής *(5197)*

ὑβριστήν, acc. sg. m. n. . . . . id.

(5197) **ὑβριστής**, οῦ, ὁ [§2.B.c] *an overbearing, wantonly violent person,* Rom. 1:30; 1 Tim. 1:13

ὑγιαίνειν, pres. act. infin. . . . . ὑγιαίνω *(5198)*

ὑγιαίνοντα, acc. sg. m. pres. act. part. . . . id.

ὑγιαίνοντας, acc. pl. m. pres. act. part. . . . id.

ὑγιαίνοντες, nom. pl. m. pres. act. part. . . id.

ὑγιαινόντων, gen. pl. m. pres. act. part. . . id.

ὑγιαινούσῃ, dat. sg. f. pres. act. part. . . . id.

ὑγιαινούσης, gen. sg. f. pres. act. part. . . . id.

ὑγιαίνουσι(ν), dat. pl. m. pres. act. part. . . id.

(5198) ὑγιαίνω, fut. ὑγιανῶ [§27.1.c] *to be hale, sound, in health,* Luke 5:31; 7:10; *to be safe and sound,* Luke 15:27; met. *to be healthful or sound* in faith, doctrine, etc., Tit. 1:13; 2:2; part. ὑγιαίνων, ουσα, ον, *sound, pure, uncorrupted,* 1 Tim. 1:10, et al.

ὑγιαίνωσιν, 3 pers. pl. pres. act. subj. . ὑγιαίνω (5198)
ὑγιεῖς, acc. pl. m. adj. . . . . ὑγιής (5199)
ὑγιῆ, acc. sg. m. adj. . . . . id.

(5199) ὑγιής, ές, nom. sg. m. adj. [§7.G.b] *hale, sound, in health,* Matt. 12:13; 15:31, et al.; met. of doctrine, *sound, pure, wholesome,* Tit. 2:8 {John 5:9}

ὑγιής, nom. sg. f. adj. {Matt. 12:13} . . . . ὑγιής (5199)

(5200) ὑγρός, ά, όν [§7.1] (ὕω, *to wet) pr. wet, moist, humid;* used of a tree, *full of sap, fresh, green,* Luke 23:31

ὑγρῷ, dat. sg. neut. adj. . . . . ὑγρός (5200)
ὕδασιν, dat. pl. neut. n. [§4.3.b] . . . . ὕδωρ (5204)
ὕδατα, nom. pl. neut. n. {John 3:23} . . . . id.
ὕδατα, acc. pl. neut. n. {Matt. 14:28} . . . . id.
ὕδατι, dat. sg. neut. n. . . . . id.
ὕδατος, gen. sg. neut. n. . . . . id.
ὑδάτων, gen. pl. neut. n. . . . . id.

(5201) ὑδρία, ας, ἡ [§2.B.b; 2.2] *a water-pot, pitcher,* John 2:6, 7; *a bucket, pail,* John 4:28

ὑδρίαι, nom. pl. f. n. . . . . ὑδρία (5201)
ὑδρίαν, acc. sg. f. n. . . . . id.
ὑδρίας, acc. pl. f. n. . . . . id.
ὑδροπότει, 2 pers. sg. pres. act.
    imper. . . . . ὑδροποτέω (5202)

(5202) ὑδροποτέω, ῶ, fut. ὑδροποτήσω [§16.P] (ὑδροπότης, ὕδωρ + πίνω) *to be a water-drinker*

(5203) ὑδρωπικός, ή, όν, nom. sg. m. adj. [§7.F.a] (ὕδρωψ, the *dropsy,* from ὕδωρ) *dropsical*

(5204) ὕδωρ, ὕδατος, τό, nom. sg. neut. n. [§4.2.c] *water,* Matt. 3:11, 16; 14:28, 29; 17:15; John 5:3, 4, 7; *watery fluid,* John 19:34; ὕδωρ ζῶν, *living water, fresh flowing water,* John 4:11; met. of spiritual refreshment, John 4:10; 7:38 {John 4:14}

ὕδωρ, acc. sg. neut. n. {John 4:15} . . . . . ὕδωρ (5204)
ὑετόν, acc. sg. m. n. . . . . ὑετός (5205)

(5205) ὑετός, οῦ, ὁ, nom. sg. m. n. [§3.C.a] (ὕω, *to rain) rain,* Acts 14:17, et al.

ὑετούς, acc. pl. m. n. . . . . ὑετός (5205)
υἱέ, voc. sg. m. n. . . . . id.

(5206) υἱοθεσία, ας, ἡ, nom. sg. f. n. [§2.B.b; 2.2] (υἱός + τίθημι) *adoption, a placing in the condition of a son,* Rom. 8:15, 23; 9:4; Gal. 4:5; Eph. 1:5

υἱοθεσίαν, acc. sg. f. n. . . . . υἱοθεσία (5206)
υἱοθεσίας, gen. sg. f. n. . . . . id.
υἱοί, nom. pl. m. n. {Mark 2:19} . . . . . . υἱός (5207)

υἱοί, voc. pl. m. n. {Acts 13:26} . . . . υἱός (5207)
υἱοῖς, dat. pl. m. n. . . . . id.
υἱόν, acc. sg. m. n. . . . . id.

(5207) υἱός, οῦ, ὁ, nom. sg. m. n. [§3.C.a] *a son,* Matt. 1:21, 25; 7:9; 13:55, et al. freq.; *a legitimate son,* Heb. 12:8; *a son* artificially constituted, Acts 7:21; Heb. 11:24; *a descendant,* Matt. 1:1, 20; Mark 12:35, et al.; in N.T. *the young* of an animal, Matt. 21:5; *a spiritual son* in respect of conversion or discipleship, 1 Pet. 5:13; from the Hebrew, *a disciple,* perhaps, Matt. 12:27; *a son* as implying connection in respect of membership, service, resemblance, manifestation, destiny, etc., Matt. 8:12; 9:15; 13:38; 23:15; Mark 2:19; 3:17; Luke 5:34; 10:6; 16:8; 20:34, 36; John 17:12; Acts 2:25; 4:36; 13:10; Eph. 2:2; 5:6; Col. 3:6; 1 Thess. 5:5; 2 Thess. 2:3; υἱὸς θεοῦ, κ.τ.λ., *son of God* in respect of divinity, Matt. 4:3, 6; 14:33; Rom. 1:4, et al.; also, in respect of privilege and character, Matt. 5:9, 45; Luke 6:35; Rom. 8:14, 19; 9:26; Gal. 3:26; ὁ υἱὸς τοῦ θεοῦ, κ.τ.λ., a title of the Messiah, Matt. 26:63; Mark 3:11; 14:61; John 1:34, 50; 20:31, et al.; υἱὸς ἀνθρώπου, *a son of man, a man,* Mark 3:28; Eph. 3:5; Heb. 2:6; ὁ υἱὸς τοῦ ἀνθρώπου, a title of the Messiah, Matt. 8:20, et al. freq.; as also, ὁ υἱὸς Δαβίδ, (Δαυίδ) Matt. 12:23, et al.

υἱοῦ, gen. sg. m. n. . . . . υἱός (5207)
υἱούς, acc. pl. m. n. . . . . id.
υἱῷ, dat. sg. m. n. . . . . id.
υἱῶν, gen. pl. m. n. . . . . id.

(5208) ὕλη, ης, ἡ [§2.B.a] *wood, a forest;* in N.T. *firewood, a mass of fuel,* James 3:5

ὕλην, acc. sg. f. n. . . . . ὕλη (5208)

(5209) ὑμᾶς, acc. pl. 2 pers. personal pron. [§11.K.b] . . . . σύ (4771)

(5210) ὑμεῖς, nom. pl. 2 pers. personal pron. . . . . id.

(†5211) Ὑμέναιος, ου, ὁ, nom. sg. m. n. [§3.C.a] *Hymenaeus,* pr. name

ὑμετέρα, nom. sg. f. 2 pers. possessive
    pron. . . . . ὑμέτερος (5212)
ὑμετέρᾳ, dat. sg. f. 2 pers. possessive pron. id.
ὑμετέραν, acc. sg. f. 2 pers. possessive pron. id.
ὑμετέρας, gen. sg. f. 2 pers. possessive pron. id.
ὑμέτερον, acc. sg. m. 2 pers. possessive pron. {John 15:20} . . . . id.
ὑμέτερον, acc. sg. neut. 2 pers. possessive pron. {Luke 16:12} . . . . id.

(5212) ὑμέτερος, α, ον, nom. sg. m. 2 pers. possessive pron. [§11.3] (ὑμεῖς) *your, yours,* Luke 6:20; John 7:6; 15:20, et al.

ὑμετέρῳ, dat. sg. m. 2 pers. possessive pron.
{John 8:17} . . . . ὑμέτερος *(5212)*
ὑμετέρῳ, dat. sg. neut. 2 pers. possessive pron.
{Rom. 11:31} . . . . id.
(5213) ὑμῖν, dat. pl. 2 pers. personal pron. . . . . . . σύ *(4771)*
(5214) **ὑμνέω**, ῶ, fut. ὑμνήσω, aor. ὕμνησα [§16.P]
to hymn, praise, celebrate or worship with
hymns, Acts 16:25; absol. *to sing a hymn,*
Matt. 26:30; Mark 14:26
ὑμνήσαντες, nom. pl. m. aor. act. part. ὑμνέω *(5214)*
ὑμνήσω, 1 pers. sg. fut. act. indic. . . . . . . id.
ὕμνοις, dat. pl. m. n. . . . . ὕμνος *(5215)*
(5215) **ὕμνος**, ου, ὁ [§3.C.a] *a song; a hymn, son of*
praise to God, Eph. 5:19; Col. 3:16
ὕμνουν, 3 pers. pl. imperf. act. indic. . . ὑμνέω *(5214)*
(5216) ὑμῶν, gen. pl. 2 pers. personal pron. . . . . σύ *(4771)*
ὑπ᾽, by apostrophe for ὑπό . . . . ὑπό *(5259)*
ὕπαγε, 2 pers. sg. pres. act. imper. . . . . ὑπάγω *(5217)*
ὑπάγει, 3 pers. sg. pres. act. indic. . . . . . . id.
ὑπάγειν, pres. act. infin. . . . . id.
ὑπάγεις, 2 pers. sg. pres. act. indic. . . . . . . id.
ὑπάγετε, 2 pers. pl. pres. act. imper. . . . . . id.
ὑπάγῃ, 3 pers. sg. pres. act. subj. (Rev. 14:4,
GNT, MT, TR & NA | ὑπάγει, WH) . id.
ὑπάγητε, 2 pers. pl. pres. act. subj. . . . . . . id.
ὑπάγοντας, acc. pl. m. pres. act. part. . . . id.
ὑπάγοντες, nom. pl. m. pres. act. part. . . . id.
(5217) **ὑπάγω**, 1 pers. sg. pres. act. indic., fut. ὑπάξω
[§23.1.b] (ὑπό + ἄγω) *to lead or bring un-*
der; to lead or bring from under; to draw
on or away; in N.T. intrans. *to go away,*
depart, Matt. 8:4, 13; 9:6; ὕπαγε ὀπίσω
μου, *Get behind me! Away! Begone!* Matt.
4:10; 16:23; *to go,* Matt. 5:41; Luke 12:58,
et al.; *to depart* life, Matt. 26:24
(5218) **ὑπακοή**, ῆς, ἡ, nom. sg. f. n. [§2.B.a] *a heark-*
ening to; obedience, Rom. 5:19; 6:16; 1 Pet.
1:14; *submissiveness,* Rom. 16:19; 2 Cor.
7:15; *submission,* Rom. 1:5; 15:18; 16:26;
2 Cor. 10:5; Heb. 5:8; 1 Pet. 1:2, 22; *com-*
pliance, Philemon 21
ὑπακοῇ, dat. sg. f. n. . . . . ὑπακοή *(5218)*
ὑπακοήν, acc. sg. f. n. . . . . id.
ὑπακοῆς, gen. sg. f. n. . . . . id.
ὑπακούει, 3 pers. sg. pres. act. indic. ὑπακούω *(5219)*
ὑπακούειν, pres. act. infin. . . . . id.
ὑπακούετε, 2 per. pl. pres. act. indic.
{Rom. 6:16} . . . . id.
ὑπακούετε, 2 pers. pl. pres. act. imper.
{Eph.6:1} . . . . id.
ὑπακούουσι(ν), 3 pers. pl. pres. act. indic.
{Luke 8:25} . . . . id.
ὑπακούουσι(ν), dat. pl. m. pres. act. part.
{2 Thess. 1:8} . . . . id.
ὑπακοῦσαι, aor. act. infin. . . . . id.

(5219) **ὑπακούω**, fut. ὑπακούσομαι (ὑπό + ἀκούω)
to give ear, hearken; to listen, Acts 12:13;
to obey, Matt. 8:27; Mark 1:27, et al.; in
N.T. *to render submissive acceptance,* Acts
6:7; Rom. 6:17; 2 Thess. 1:8; Heb. 5:9; absol. *to be submissive,* Phil. 2:12
(5220) **ὕπανδρος**, ον, nom. sg. f. adj. (ὑπό + ἀνήρ)
bound to a man, married
(5221) **ὑπαντάω**, ῶ, fut. ὑπαντήσω [§18.R] (ὑπό +
ἀντάω) *to meet,* Matt. 8:28; Luke 8:27;
John 11:20, 30; 12:18
ὑπαντῆσαι, aor. act. infin. (Luke 14:31, GNT,
WH & NA | ἀπαντῆσαι, MT &
TR) . . . . ὑπαντάω *(5221)*
ὑπάντησιν, acc. sg. f. n. . . . . ὑπάντησις *(5222)*
(5222) **ὑπάντησις**, εως, ἡ [§5.E.c] *a meeting, act of*
meeting, John 12:13
ὑπάρξεις, acc. pl. f. n. . . . . ὕπαρξις *(5223)*
ὕπαρξιν, acc. sg. f. n. . . . . id.
(5223) **ὕπαρξις**, εως, ἡ [§5.E.c] *goods possessed, sub-*
stance, property, Acts 2:45; Heb. 10:34
ὑπάρχει, 3 pers. sg. pres. act. indic. . . ὑπάρχω *(5225)*
ὑπάρχειν, pres. act. infin. . . . . id.
(5224) ὑπάρχοντα, acc. sg. m. pres. ·act. part.
{Acts 17:27} . . . . id.
(5224) ὑπάρχοντα, nom. pl. neut. pres. act. part.
{Luke 11:21} . . . . id.
(5224) ὑπάρχοντα, acc. pl. neut. pres. act. part.
{Luke 12:33} . . . . id.
ὑπάρχοντας, acc. pl. m. pres. act. part. . . id.
ὑπάρχοντες, nom. pl. m. pres. act. part. . . id.
ὑπάρχοντος, gen. sg. m. pres. act. part.
{Acts 4:37} . . . . id.
ὑπάρχοντος, gen. sg. neut. pres. act. part.
{Acts 19:40} . . . . id.
ὑπαρχόντων, gen. pl. neut. pres. act. part. . id.
ὑπαρχούσης, gen. sg. f. pres. act. part. . . . id.
ὑπάρχουσι(ν), 3 pers. pl. pres. act. indic.
{Acts 21:20} . . . . id.
ὑπάρχουσιν, dat. pl. neut. pres. act. part.
{Matt. 24:47} . . . . id.
(5225) **ὑπάρχω**, fut. ὑπάρξω [§23.1.b] (ὑπό + ἄρχω)
to begin; to come into existence; to exist;
to be, subsist, Acts 19:40; 28:18; *to be in*
possession, to belong, Acts 3:6; 4:37; neut.
pl. part. τὰ ὑπάρχοντα, *goods, posses-*
sions, property, Matt. 19:21; Luke 8:3; *to*
be, Luke 7:25; 8:41, et al.
ὑπάρχων, nom. sg. m. pres. act. part. ὑπάρχω *(5225)*
ὑπάρχωσι(ν), 3 pers. pl. pres. act. subj. . . id.
ὑπέβαλον, 3 pers. pl. 2 aor. act. indic.
[§27.2.d] . . . . ὑποβάλλω *(5260)*
ὑπέδειξα, 1 pers. sg. aor. act.
indic. . . . . ὑποδείκνυμι *(5263)*
ὑπέδειξεν, 3 pers. sg. aor. act. indic. . . . . . id.

ὑπεδέξατο, 3 pers. sg. aor. mid. dep.

indic. . . . . ὑποδέχομαι *(5264)*

ὑπέθηκαν, 3 pers. pl. aor. act. indic.

[§28.V] . . . . ὑποτίθημι *(5294)*

ὑπείκετε, 2 pers. pl. pres. act. imper. . . ὑπείκω *(5226)*

(5226) **ὑπείκω,** fut. ὑπείξω [§23.1.b] (ὑπό + εἴκω)
to yield, give way; absol. *to be submissive,*
Heb. 13:17

ὑπέλαβεν, 3 per. sg. 2 aor. act. indic.

[§24.9] . . . . ὑπολαμβάνω *(5274)*

ὑπελείφθην, 1 pers. sg. aor. pass. indic.

[§23.4] . . . . ὑπολείπω *(5275)*

ὑπέμειναν, 3 pers. pl. aor. act. indic. (Acts
17:14, GNT, WH & NA | ὑπέμενον, MT
& TR) . . . . ὑπομένω *(5278)*

ὑπεμείνατε, 2 pers. pl. aor. act. indic. . . . . id.

ὑπέμεινε(ν), 3 pers. sg. aor. act. indic.

[§27.1.d] . . . . id.

ὑπέμενον, 3 pers. pl. imperf. act. indic. (Acts
17:14, MT & TR | ὑπέμειναν, GNT, WH
& NA) . . . . id.

ὑπεμνήσθη, 3 pers. sg. aor. act. indic.

[§22.5] . . . . ὑπομιμνήσκω *(†5279)*

ὑπεναντίον, nom. sg. neut. adj. . . . ὑπεναντίος *(5227)*

(5227) **ὑπεναντίος,** α, ον [§7.1] (ὑπό + ἐναντίος)
over against; contrary, adverse; ὁ
ὑπεναντίος, *an opponent, adversary,* Heb.
10:27; *untoward, inimical,* Col. 2:14

ὑπεναντίους, acc. pl. m. adj. . . . . . ὑπεναντίος *(5227)*

ὑπενεγκεῖν, 2 aor. act. infin. [§36.1] . ὑποφέρω *(5297)*

ὑπενόουν, 1 pers. sg. imperf. act. indic.

{Acts 25:18} . . . . ὑπονοέω *(5282)*

ὑπενόουν, 3 pers. pl. imperf. act. indic.

{Acts 27:27} . . . . id.

ὑπεπλεύσαμεν, 1 pers. pl. aor. act. indic.

[§35.3] . . . . ὑποπλέω *(5284)*

(5228) **ὑπέρ,** prep. with a genitive, *above, over;* met.
in behalf of, Matt. 5:44; Mark 9:40; John
17:19, et al.; *instead of* beneficially, Philemon 13; *in maintenance of,* Rom. 15:8;
for the furtherance of, John 11:4; 2 Cor.
1:6, 8, et al.; *for the realization of,* Phil.
2:13; equivalent to περί, *about, concerning,* with the further signification of interest or concern in the subject, Acts 5:41;
Rom. 9:27; 2 Cor. 5:12; 8:23; 2 Thess. 2:1,
et al.; with an acc., *over, beyond;* met. *beyond, more than,* Matt. 10:37; 2 Cor. 1:8,
et al.; used after comparative terms, Luke
16:8; 2 Cor. 12:13; Heb. 4:12; in N.T. as
an adv., *in a higher degree, in fuller measure,* 2 Cor. 11:23

ὑπεραιρόμενος, nom. sg. m. pres. pass.

part. ὑπεραίρω *(†5229)*

(†5229) **ὑπεραίρω** (ὑπέρ + αἴρω) *to raise or lift up*

above or over; mid. *to lift up one's self;*
met. *to be over-elated,* 2 Cor. 12:7; *to bear
ones' self arrogantly, to rear a haughty
front,* 2 Thess. 2:4

ὑπεραίρωμαι, 1 pers. sg. pres. pass.

subj. ὑπεραίρω *(†5229)*

(5230) **ὑπέρακμος,** ον, adj. [§7.2] (ὑπερ + ἀκμή,
a point, prime) past the bloom of life,
1 Cor. 7:36

(5231) **ὑπεράνω,** adv. (ὑπέρ + ἄνω) *above, over, far
above;* of place, Eph. 4:10; Heb. 9:5; of
rank, dignity, etc., Eph. 1:21

ὑπεραυξάνει, 3 pers. sg. pres. act.

indic. . . . . ὑπεραυξάνω *(5232)*

(5232) **ὑπεραυξάνω,** fut. ὑπεραυξήσω [§35.5] (ὑπέρ
+ αὐξάνω) *to increase exceedingly,*
2 Thess. 1:3

ὑπερβαίνειν, pres. act. infin. . . . . . ὑπερβαίνω *(5233)*

(5233) **ὑπερβαίνω,** fut. ὑπερβήσομαι [§37.1] (ὑπέρ
+ βαίνω) *to overstep; to wrong, aggrieve,*
1 Thess. 4:6

ὑπερβάλλον, nom. sg. neut. pres. act. part.
{Eph. 1:19} . . . . ὑπερβάλλω *(5235)*

ὑπερβάλλον, acc. sg. neut. pres. act. part.
(Eph. 2:7, GNT, WH & NA | ὑπερβάλ-
λοντα, MT & TR) . . . . id.

ὑπερβάλλοντα, acc. sg. m. pres. act. part.
(Eph. 2:7, MT & TR | ὑπερβάλλον,
GNT, WH & NA) . . . . id.

(5234) **ὑπερβαλλόντως,** adv., *exceedingly, above
measure,* 2 Cor. 11:23

ὑπερβάλλουσαν, acc. sg. f. pres. act.

part. ὑπερβάλλω *(5235)*

ὑπερβαλλούσης, gen. sg. f. pres. act. part.   id.

(5235) **ὑπερβάλλω,** fut. ὑπερβαλῶ [§27.1.b] (ὑπέρ +
βάλλω) pr. *to cast* or *throw over or beyond, to overshoot;* met. *to surpass, excel;*
part. ὑπερβάλλων, ουσα, ον, *surpassing,*
2 Cor. 3:10; 9:14, et al.

(5236) **ὑπερβολή,** ῆς, ἡ, nom. sg. f. n. [§2.B.a] pr.
*a throwing beyond, an overshooting; ex-
traordinary amount or character, tran-
scendency,* 2 Cor. 12:7; 4:7; καθ'
ὑπερβολήν, adverbially, *exceedingly, extremely,* Rom. 7:13; 2 Cor. 1:8, et al.

ὑπερβολῇ, dat. sg. f. n. . . . . ὑπερβολή *(5236)*

ὑπερβολήν, acc. sg. f. n. . . . . id.

(†5237) **ὑπερεῖδον,** 2 aor. of ὑπεροράω [§36.1] *to look
over or above* a thing; met. *to overlook,
disregard; to bear with,* Acts 17:30

(5238) **ὑπερέκεινα,** adv. (ὑπέρ, ἐκεῖνα) *beyond,*
2 Cor. 10:16

(‡4057) **ὑπερεκπερισσοῦ,** adv. (ὑπέρ, εκ, + περισσοῦ)
*in over abundance; beyond all measure, super-
abundantly,* Eph. 3:20; 1 Thess. 3:10; 5:13

ὑπερεκτείνομεν, 1 pers. pl. pres. act.
indic. . . . . ὑπερεκτείνω *(5239)*

(5239) **ὑπερεκτείνω**, fut. ὑπερεκτενῶ [§27.1.c] (ὑπέρ
+ ἐκτείνω) *to over-extend, over-stretch,*
2 Cor. 10:14

ὑπερεκχυν(ν)όμενον, acc. sg. neut. pres. pass.
part. . . . . ὑπερεκχύν(ν)ω *(5240)*

(5240) **ὑπερεκχύν(ν)ω** (ὑπέρ + ἐκχύν(ν)ω) *to pour
out above measure or in excess;* pass. *to
run over, overflow,* Luke 6:38

ὑπερεντυγχάνει, 3 pers. sg. pres. act.
indic. . . . . ὑπερεντυγχάνω *(5241)*

(5241) **ὑπερεντυγχάνω** (ὑπέρ + ἐντυγχάνω) *to intercede for,* Rom. 8:26

ὑπερεπερίσσευσεν, 3 pers. sg. aor. act.
indic. . . . . ὑπερπερισσεύω *(5248)*

ὑπερεπλεόνασε(ν), 3 pers. sg. aor. act.
indic. . . . . ὑπερπλεονάζω *(5250)*

ὑπερέχον, acc. sg. neut. pres. act.
part. . . . . ὑπερέχω *(5242)*

ὑπερέχοντας, acc. pl. m. pres. act. part. . . . id.
ὑπερέχοντι, dat. sg. m. pres. act. part. . . . . id.
ὑπερέχουσα, nom. sg. f. pres. act. part. . . . id.
ὑπερεχούσαις, dat. pl. f. pres. act. part. . . . id.

(5242) **ὑπερέχω**, fut. ὑπερέξω (ὑπέρ + ἔχω) *to hold
above;* intrans. *to stand out above, to over-
top;* met. *to surpass, excel,* Phil. 2:3; 4:7;
τὸ ὑπερέχον, *excellence, pre-eminence,*
Phil. 3:8; *to be higher, superior,* Rom. 13:1;
1 Pet. 2:13

(5243) **ὑπερηφανία**, ας, ἡ, nom. sg. f. n. [§2.B.b; 2.2]
haughtiness, arrogance, Mark 7:22

ὑπερήφανοι, nom. pl. m. adj. . . . ὑπερήφανος *(5244)*
ὑπερηφάνοις, dat. pl. m. adj. . . . . id.

(5244) **ὑπερήφανος**, ον [§7.2] (ὑπέρ + φαίνω) pr.
conspicuous above, supereminent; met. *as-
suming, haughty, arrogant,* Luke 1:51;
Rom. 1:30; 2 Tim. 3:2; James 4:6; 1 Pet.
5:5

ὑπερηφάνους, acc. pl. m. adj. . . . ὑπερήφανος *(5244)*
ὑπεριδών, nom. sg. m. aor. act.
part. ὑπερεῖδον *(†5237)*

(‡5228) **ὑπερλίαν**, adv. (ὑπέρ + λίαν) *in the highest
degree, pre-eminently, especially, superla-
tively* (2 Cor. 11:5; 12:11, GNT, MT, WH
& NA | ὑπὲρ λίαν, TR)

(5245) **ὑπερνικάω**, ῶ, fut. ὑπερνικήσω [§18.R] (ὑπέρ
+ νικάω) *to overpower in victory; to be
abundantly victorious, prevail mightily,*
Rom. 8:37

ὑπερνικῶμεν, 1 pers. pl. pres. act.
indic. ὑπερνικάω *(5245)*

ὑπέρογκα, acc. pl. neut. adj. . . . . . ὑπέρογκος *(5246)*

(5246) **ὑπέρογκος**, ον [§7.2] (ὑπέρ + ὄγκος) pr.
over-swollen, overgrown; of language,

swelling, pompous, boastful, 2 Pet. 2:18;
Jude 16

(5247) **ὑπεροχή**, ῆς, ἡ [§2.B.a] *prominence;* met. *excellence, rare quality,* 1 Cor. 2:1; *eminent
station, authority,* 1 Tim. 2:2

ὑπεροχῇ, dat. sg. f. n. . . . . ὑπεροχή *(5247)*
ὑπεροχήν, acc. sg. f. n. . . . . id.

ὑπερπερισσεύομαι, 1 pers. sg. pres. pass.
part. . . . . ὑπερπερισσεύω *(5248)*

(5248) **ὑπερπερισσεύω**, fut. ὑπερπερισσεύσω
[§13.M] (ὑπέρ + περισσεύω) *to superabound; to abound still more,* Rom. 5:20;
mid. *to be abundantly filled, overflow,*
2 Cor. 7:4

(5249) **ὑπερπερισσῶς**, adv. (ὑπέρ + περισσῶς) *su-
perabundantly, most vehemently, above all
measure,* Mark 7:37

(5250) **ὑπερπλεονάζω**, fut. ὑπερπλεονάσω [§26.1]
(ὑπέρ + πλεονάζω) *to superabound, be in
exceeding abundance, over-exceed,* 1 Tim.
1:14

(5251) **ὑπερυψόω**, ῶ, fut. ὑπερυψώσω [§20.Τ] (ὑπέρ
+ ὑψόω) *to exalt supremely,* Phil. 2:9

ὑπερύψωσε(ν), 3 pers. sg. aor. act.
indic. ὑπερυψόω *(5251)*

ὑπερφρονεῖν, pres. act. infin. . . . . ὑπερφρονέω *(5252)*

(5252) **ὑπερφρονέω**, ῶ, fut. ὑπερφρονήσω [§16.P]
(ὑπέρ + φρονέω) *to overween, have lofty
thoughts, be elated,* Rom. 12:3

(5253) **ὑπερῷον**, ου, τό [§3.C.c] (pr. neut. of
ὑπερῷος, *upper,* from ὑπέρ) *the upper part
of a house, upper room, or chamber,* Acts
1:13; 9:37, 39; 20:8

ὑπερῷον, acc. sg. neut. n. . . . . ὑπερῷον *(5253)*
ὑπερῴῳ, dat. sg. neut. n. . . . . id.

ὑπεστειλάμην, 1 pers. sg. aor. mid. indic.
[§27.1.d] . . . . ὑποστέλλω *(5288)*

ὑπέστελλε(ν), 3 pers. sg. imperf. act. indic. id.
ὑπέστρεφον, 3 pers. pl. imperf. act.
indic. ὑποστρέφω *(5290)*

ὑπέστρεψα, 1 pers. sg. aor. act. indic. . . . . id.
ὑπέστρεψαν, 3 pers. pl. aor. act. indic. . . . id.
ὑπέστρεψε(ν), 3 pers. sg. aor. act. indic. . . id.
ὑπεστρώννυον, 3 pers. pl. imperf. act.
indic. . . . . ὑποστρώννυμι *(5291)*

ὑπετάγη, 3 pers. sg. 2 aor. pass. indic.
[§26.3] . . . . ὑποτάσσω *(5293)*

ὑπετάγησαν, 3 pers. pl. 2 aor. pass. indic. id.
ὑπέταξας, 2 pers. sg. aor. act. indic. . . . . . id.
ὑπέταξε(ν), 3 pers. sg. aor. act. indic. . . . . id.
ὑπέχουσαι, nom. pl. f. pres. act. part. . ὑπέχω *(5254)*

(5254) **ὑπέχω**, fut. ὑπέξω [§36.4] (ὑπό + ἔχω) pr.
to hold under; to render, undergo, suffer,
Jude 7

ὑπεχώρησε(ν), 3 pers. sg. aor. act.

indic. . . . . ὑποχωρέω *(5298)*

ὑπῆγον, 3 pers. pl. imperf. act. indic. . . ὑπάγω *(5217)*

ὑπήκοοι, nom. pl. m. adj. . . . . ὑπήκοος *(5255)*

(5255) **ὑπήκοος**, ον, nom. sg. m. adj. [§7.2] *giving ear; obedient, submissive,* Acts 7:39; 2 Cor. 2:9; Phil. 2:8

ὑπήκουον, 3 pers. pl. imperf. act.
indic. . . . . ὑπακούω *(5219)*

ὑπήκουσαν, 3 pers. pl. aor. act. indic. . . . id.

ὑπηκούσατε, 2 pers. pl. aor. act. indic. . . . id.

ὑπήκουσε(ν), 3 pers. sg. aor. act. indic. . . id.

ὑπήνεγκα, 1 pers. sg. aor. act. indic.
[§36.1] . . . . ὑποφέρω *(5297)*

ὑπήντησαν, 3 pers. pl. aor. act. indic. ὑπαντάω *(5221)*

ὑπήντησεν, 3 pers. sg. aor. act. indic. . . . . id.

ὑπηρέται, nom. pl. m. n. . . . . ὑπηρέτης *(5257)*

ὑπηρέταις, dat. pl. m. n. . . . . id.

ὑπηρέτας, acc. pl. m. n. . . . . id.

ὑπηρετεῖν, pres. act. infin. . . . . ὑπηρετέω *(5256)*

(5256) **ὑπηρετέω**, ῶ, fut. ὑπηρετήσω, aor. ὑπηρέτησα, *to subserve,* Acts 13:36; *to relieve, supply,* Acts 20:34; *to render kind offices,* Acts 24:23

ὑπηρέτῃ, dat. sg. m. n. . . . . ὑπηρέτης *(5257)*

ὑπηρέτην, acc. sg. m. n. . . . . id.

(5257) **ὑπηρέτης**, ου, ὁ [§2.B.c] (ὑπό + ἐρέτης, *a rower*) pr. *an under-rower, a rower, one of a ship's crew; a minister, attendant, servant; an attendant* on a magistrate, *a lictor, apparitor, officer,* Matt. 5:25; *an attendant or officer* of the Sanhedrin, Matt. 26:58; *an attendant, or servant* of a synagogue, Luke 4:20; *a minister, attendant, assistant* in any work, Luke 1:2; John 18:36, et al.

ὑπηρέτησαν, 3 pers. pl. aor. act.
indic. . . . . ὑπηρετέω *(5256)*

ὑπηρέτησας, nom. sg. m. aor. act. part. . . id.

ὑπηρετῶν, gen. pl. m. n. . . . . ὑπηρέτης *(5257)*

ὑπῆρχε(ν), 3 pers. sg. imperf. act.
indic. . . . . ὑπάρχω *(5225)*

ὑπῆρχον, 3 pers. pl. imperf. act. indic. . . . id.

(5258) **ὕπνος**, ου, ὁ [§3.C.a] *sleep,* Matt. 1:24, et al.; met. spiritual *sleep,* religious *slumber,* Rom. 13:11

ὕπνου, gen. sg. m. n. . . . . ὕπνος *(5258)*

ὕπνῳ, dat. sg. m. n. . . . . id.

(5259) **ὑπό**, prep., with a genitive, pr. *under;* hence used to express influence, causation, agency; *by,* Matt. 1:22, et al. freq.; *by the agency of, at the hands of,* 2 Cor. 11:24; Heb. 12:3; with acc., *under,* with the idea of motion associated, Matt. 5:15, et al.; *under,* John 1:49; 1 Cor. 10:1; *under subjection to,* Rom. 6:14; 1 Tim. 6:1, et al.; of time, *at, about,* Acts 5:21

(5260) **ὑποβάλλω**, fut. ὑποβαλῶ, aor. ὑπέβαλον [§27.2.d] (ὑπό + βάλλω) *to cast under;* met. *to suggest, instigate; to suborn,* Acts 6:11

ὑπογραμμόν, acc. sg. m. n. . . . . . ὑπογραμμός *(5261)*

(5261) **ὑπογραμμός**, οῦ, ὁ [§3.C.a] (ὑπογράφω). pr. *a copy to write after;* met. *an example for imitation, pattern,* 1 Pet. 2:21

ὑποδέδεκται, 3 pers. sg. perf. mid./pass. dep.
indic. [§23.7] . . . . ὑποδέχομαι *(5264)*

ὑποδεδεμένους, acc. pl. m. perf. pass.
part. . . . . ὑποδέω *(5265)*

(5262) **ὑπόδειγμα**, ατος, τό [§4.D.c] *a token, intimation; an example,* proposed for imitation or admonition, John 13:15; Heb. 4:11; James 5:10; 2 Pet. 2:6; *a copy,* Heb. 8:5; 9:23

ὑπόδειγμα, acc. sg. neut. n. . . . . . . ὑπόδειγμα *(5262)*

ὑποδείγματα, acc. pl. neut. n. . . . . id.

ὑποδείγματι, dat. sg. neut. n. . . . . id.

(5263) **ὑποδείκνυμι**, fut. ὑποδείξω [§31.BB] (ὑπό + δείκνυμι) *to indicate,* Acts 20:35; *to intimate, suggest,* Matt. 3:7; Luke 3:7; 6:47; 12:5; Acts 9:16

ὑποδείξω, 1 pers. sg. fut. act.
indic. ὑποδείκνυμι *(5263)*

ὑποδεξαμένη, nom. sg. f. aor. mid. dep.
part. . . . . ὑποδέχομαι *(5264)*

(5264) **ὑποδέχομαι**, fut. ὑποδέξομαι, perf. ὑποδέδεγμαι [§23.7] (ὑπό + δέχομαι) *to give reception to; to receive as a guest, entertain,* Luke 10:38; 19:6; Acts 17:7; James 2:25

(5265) **ὑποδέω**, fut. ὑποδήσω, perf. pass. ὑποδέδεμαι [§37.1] (ὑπό + δέω) *to bind under,* mid. *to bind under one's self, put on one's own feet,* Acts 12:8; *to shoe,* Eph. 6:15; pass. *to be shod,* Mark 6:9

(5266) **ὑπόδημα**, ατος, τό [§4.D.c] *anything bound under; a sandal,* Matt. 3:11; 10:10, et al.

ὑπόδημα, acc. sg. neut. n. . . . . ὑπόδημα *(5266)*

ὑποδήματα, acc. pl. neut. n. . . . . id.

ὑποδήματος, gen. sg. neut. n. . . . . id.

ὑποδημάτων, gen. pl. neut. n. . . . . id.

ὑπόδησαι, 2 pers. sg. aor. mid. imper. ὑποδέω *(5265)*

ὑποδησάμενοι, nom. pl. m. aor. mid. part. id.

(5267) **ὑπόδικος**, ον, nom. sg. m. adj. [§7.2] (ὑπό + δίκη) *under a legal process;* also, *under a judicial sentence; under verdict* to an opposed party in a suit, *liable to penalty, convict,* Rom. 3:19

ὑποδραμόντες, nom. pl. m. 2 aor. act. part.
[§36.1] . . . . ὑποτρέχω *(5295)*

(5268) **ὑποζύγιον**, ου, τό, nom. sg. neut. n. [§3.C.c] (pr. neut. of ὑποζύγιος, *under a yoke,* from

ὑπό + ζυγόν) *an animal subject to the yoke, a beast of draught or burden;* in N.T. spc. *an ass,* Matt. 21:5; 2 Pet. 2:16

ὑποζυγίου, gen. sg. neut. n. . . . . ὑποζύγιον *(5268)*

(5269) **ὑποζώννυμι,** fut. ὑποζώσω (ὑπό + ζώννυμι) *to gird under,* of persons; *to undergird a ship with cables, chains,* etc., Acts 27:17

ὑποζώννυντες, nom. pl. m. pres. act. part. ὑποζώννυμι *(5269)*

(5270) **ὑποκάτω,** adv. (ὑπό + κάτω) *under, beneath, underneath,* Mark 6:11; 7:28, et al.; met. Heb. 2:8

(5271) **ὑποκρίνομαι,** fut. ὑποκρινοῦμαι (ὑπό + κρίνω) *to answer, respond; to act a part upon the stage;* hence, *to assume a counterfeit character; to pretend, feign,* Luke 20:20

ὑποκρινομένους, acc. pl. m. pres. mid./pass. dep. part. . . . . ὑποκρίνομαι *(5271)*

ὑποκρίσει, dat. sg. f. n. . . . . ὑπόκρισις *(5272)*

ὑποκρίσεις, acc. pl. f. n. (1 Pet. 2:1, GNT, MT, TR & NA | ὑπόκρισιν, WH) . . . . id.

ὑποκρίσεως, gen. sg. f. n. . . . . id.

ὑπόκρισιν, acc. sg. f. n. . . . . id.

(5272) **ὑπόκρισις,** εως, ἡ, nom. sg. f. n. [§5.E.c] *a response, answer; histrionic personification, acting; hypocrisy, simulation,* Matt. 23:28; Mark 12:15, et al.

ὑποκριτά, voc. sg. m. n. . . . . ὑποκριτής *(5273)*

ὑποκριταί, nom. pl. m. n. {Matt. 6:5} . . . . id.

ὑποκριταί, voc. pl. m. n. {Matt. 15:7} . . . . id.

(5273) **ὑποκριτής,** οῦ, ὁ [§2.B.c] *the giver of an answer or response; a stageplayer, actor;* in N.T. *a moral or religious counterfeit, a hypocrite,* Matt. 6:2, 5, 16; 7:5, et al.

ὑποκριτῶν, gen. pl. m. n. . . . . ὑποκριτής *(5273)*

ὑπολαβών, nom. sg. m. 2 aor. act. part. . . . . ὑπολαμβάνω *(5274)*

ὑπολαμβάνειν, pres. act. infin. (3 John 8, GNT, WH & NA | ἀπολαμβάνειν, MT & TR) . . . . id.

ὑπολαμβάνετε, 2 pers. pl. pres. act. indic. . . id.

(5274) **ὑπολαμβάνω,** 1 pers. sg. pres. act. indic., fut. ἀπολή(μ)ψομαι, 2 aor. ὑπέλαβον [§36.2] (ὑπό + λαμβάνω) *to take up,* by placing one's self underneath what is taken up; *to receive as a guest, support,* 3 John 8; *to catch away, withdraw,* Acts 1:9; *to take up* discourse by continuation; hence, *to answer,* Luke 10:30; *to take up* a notion, *to think, suppose,* Luke 7:43; Acts 2:15

(‡2640) **ὑπόλειμμα,** ατος, τό, nom. sg. neut. n. [§4.D.c] *a remnant* (Rom. 9:27, GNT, WH & NA | κατάλειμμα, MT & TR)

(5275) **ὑπολείπω,** fut. ὑπολείψω [§23.1.a] (ὑπό + λείπω) *to leave remaining, leave behind;*

pass. *to be left surviving,* Rom. 11:3

(5276) **ὑπολήνιον,** ου, τό [§3.C.c] (ὑπό + ληνός) *a vat,* placed under the press, ληνός, to receive the juice, Mark 12:1

ὑπολήνιον, acc. sg. neut. n. . . . . ὑπολήνιον *(5276)*

(5277) **ὑπολιμπάνω** (ὑπό + λιμπάνω, *to leave*) equivalent to ὑπολείπω, *to leave behind,* 1 Pet. 2:21

ὑπολιμπάνων, nom. sg. m. pres. act. part. . . . . ὑπολιμπάνω *(5277)*

ὑπομείναντας, acc. pl. m. aor. act. part. (James 5:11, GNT, WH & NA | ὑπομένοντας, MT & TR) . . . . ὑπομένω *(5278)*

ὑπομείνας, nom. sg. m. aor. act. part. . . . . . id.

ὑπομεμενηκότα, acc. sg. m. perf. act. part. [§27.2.d] . . . . id.

ὑπομένει, 3 pers. sg. pres. act. indic. . . . . . . id.

ὑπομενεῖτε, 2 pers. pl. fut. act. indic. . . . . . id.

ὑπομένετε, 2 pers. pl. pres. act. indic. . . . . . id.

ὑπομένομεν, 1 pers. pl. pres. act. indic. . . . . id.

ὑπομένοντας, acc. pl. m. pres. act. part. (James 5:11, MT & TR | ὑπομείναντας, GNT, WH & NA) . . . . id.

ὑπομένοντες, nom. pl. m. pres. act. part. . . id.

(5278) **ὑπομένω,** 1 pers. sg. pres. act. indic., fut. ὑπομενῶ [§27.1.a] aor. ὑπέμεινα (ὑπό + μένω) intrans. *to remain or stay behind,* when others have departed, Luke 2:43; trans. *to bear up under, endure, suffer patiently,* 1 Cor. 13:7; Heb. 10:32; absol. *to continue firm, hold out, remain constant, persevere,* Matt. 10:22; 24:13, et al.

ὑπομίμνησκε, 2 pers. sg. pres. act. imper. (2 Tim. 2:14; Tit. 3:1, GNT & NA | ὑπομίμνησκε, WH, MT & TR) . . . . ὑπομιμνήσκω *(†5279)*

ὑπομιμνήσκειν, pres. act. infin. (2 Pet. 1:12, GNT & NA | ὑπομιμνήσκειν, WH, MT & TR) . . . . id.

(†5279) **ὑπομιμνήσκω,** fut. ὑπομνήσω [§36.4] (ὑπό + μιμνήσκω) *to put in mind, remind,* John 14:26; Tit. 3:1; 2 Pet. 1:12; Jude 5; *to suggest recollection of, remind* others *of,* 2 Tim. 2:14; 3 John 10; mid. ὑπομιμνήσκομαι, aor. (pass. form) ὑπεμνήσθην, *to call to mind, recollect, remember,* Luke 22:61

ὑπομνῆσαι, aor. act. infin. . . . . . . ὑπομιμνήσκω *(†5279)*

ὑπομνήσει, 3 pers. sg. fut. act. indic. {John 14:26} . . . . id.

ὑπομνήσει, dat. sg. f. n. {2 Pet. 1:13} . . . . ὑπόμνησις *(5280)*

ὑπόμνησιν, acc. sg. f. n. . . . . id.

(5280) **ὑπόμνησις,** εως, ἡ [§5.E.c] *a putting in mind, act of reminding,* 2 Pet. 1:13; 3:1; *remem-*

brance, recollection, 2 Tim. 1:5
ὑπομνήσω, 1 pers. sg. fut. act.
indic. . . . . ὑπομιμνήσκω (†5279)
(5281) ὑπομονή, ῆς, ἡ, nom. sg. f. n. [§2.B.a] *patient
endurance,* 2 Cor. 12:12; Col. 1:11, et al.;
patient awaiting, Luke 21:19; *a patient
frame of mind, patience,* Rom. 5:3, 4;
15:4, 5; James 1:3, et al.; *perseverance,*
Rom. 2:7; *endurance* in adherence to an
object, 1 Thess. 1:3; 2 Thess. 3:5; Rev. 1:9;
ἐν ὑπομονῇ and δι' ὑπομονῆς, *constantly,
perseveringly,* Luke 8:15; Rom. 8:25; Heb.
12:1; *an enduring* of affliction, etc., *the act
of suffering, undergoing,* etc., 2 Cor. 1:6;
6:4
ὑπομονῇ, dat. sg. f. n. . . . . ὑπομονή (5281)
ὑπομονήν, acc. sg. f. n. . . . . id.
ὑπομονῆς, gen. sg. f. n. . . . . id.
ὑπονοεῖτε, 2 pers. pl. pres. act. indic. ὑπονοέω (5282)
(5282) ὑπονοέω, ῶ, fut. ὑπονοήσω [§16.P] (ὑπό +
νοέω) *to suspect; to suppose, deem,* Acts
13:25; 25:18; 27:27
(5283) ὑπόνοια, ας, ἡ [§2.B.b; 2.2] *suspicion, sur-
mise,* 1 Tim. 6:4
ὑπόνοιαι, nom. pl. f. n. . . . . ὑπόνοια (5283)
(5284) ὑποπλέω, fut. ὑποπλεύσομαι [§35.3] (ὑπό +
πλέω) *to sail under; to sail under* the lee,
or, *to the south of,* an island, etc., Acts
27:4, 7
ὑποπνεύσαντος, gen. sg. m. aor. act.
part. . . . . ὑποπνέω (5285)
(5285) ὑποπνέω, fut. ὑποπνεύσω [§35.1.3] (ὑπό +
πνέω) *to blow gently,* as the wind, Acts
27:13
(5286) ὑποπόδιον, ου, τό, nom. sg. neut. n. [§3.C.c]
(ὑπό + πούς) *a footstool,* James 2:3, et al.
{Matt. 5:35}
ὑποπόδιον, acc. sg. neut. n.
{Luke 20:43} . . . . ὑποπόδιον (5286)
ὑποστάσει, dat. sg. f. n. . . . . ὑπόστασις (5287)
ὑποστάσεως, gen. sg. f. n. . . . . id.
(5287) ὑπόστασις, εως, ἡ, nom. sg. f. n. [§5.E.c]
(ὑφίσταμαι, *to stand under,* ὑπὸ ἵστημι)
pr. *a standing under; a taking* of a thing
*upon one's self; an assumed position, an
assumption* of a specific character, 2 Cor.
11:17; *an engagement undertaken* with regard to the conduct either of others, *a
vouching,* 2 Cor. 9:4; or of one's self, *a
pledged profession,* Heb. 3:14; *an assured
impression, a mental realizing,* Heb. 11:1;
a substructure, basis; subsistence, essence,
Heb. 1:3
ὑποστείληται, 3 pers. sg. aor. mid.
subj. ὑποστέλλω (5288)

(5288) ὑποστέλλω, fut. ὑποστελῶ, aor. ὑπέστειλα
[§27.1.b,d] (ὑπό + στέλλω) pr. *to let down,
to stow away; to draw back, withdraw,*
Gal. 2:12; mid. *to shrink back, quail, re-
coil,* Heb. 10:38; *to keep back, suppress,
conceal,* Acts 20:20, 27
(5289) ὑποστολή, ῆς, ἡ [§2.B.a] *a shrinking back,*
Heb. 10:39
ὑποστολῆς, gen. sg. f. n. . . . . ὑποστολή (5289)
ὑπόστρεφε, 2 pers. sg. pres. act.
imper. . . . . ὑποστρέφω (5290)
ὑποστρέφειν, pres. act. infin. . . . . id.
ὑποστρέφοντι, dat. sg. m. pres. act. part. . id.
(5290) ὑποστρέφω, fut. ὑποστρέψω [§23.1.a] (ὑπό +
στρέφω) *to turn back, return,* Mark 14:40;
Luke 1:56; 2:39, 43, 45, et al.
ὑποστρέφων, nom. sg. m. pres. act.
part. . . . . ὑποστρέφω (5290)
ὑποστρέψαι, aor. act. infin. . . . . id.
ὑποστρέψαντες, nom. pl. m. aor. act. part. id.
ὑποστρέψαντι, dat. sg. m. aor. act. part. . id.
ὑποστρέψας, nom. sg. m. aor. act. part.
(Mark 14:40, MT & TR | GNT, WH &
NA omit) . . . . id.
ὑποστρέψασαι, nom. pl. f. aor. act. part. . id.
ὑποστρέψω, 1 pers. sg. fut. act. indic. . . . id.
(5291) ὑποστρώννυμι, or ὑποστρωννύω, fut.
ὑποστρώσω [§36.5] (ὑπό + στρώννυμι)
to stow under, spread underneath, Luke
19:36
ὑποταγέντων, gen. pl. m. 2 aor. pass.
part. . . . . ὑποτάσσω (5293)
(5292) ὑποταγή, ῆς, ἡ [§2.B.a] *subordination,* 1 Tim.
3:4; *submissiveness,* 2 Cor. 9:13; Gal. 2:5;
1 Tim. 2:11
ὑποταγῇ, dat. sg. f. n. {2 Cor. 9:13} . ὑποταγή (5292)
ὑποταγῇ, 3 pers. sg. 2 aor. pass. subj. [§26.3]
{1 Cor. 15:28} . . . . ὑποτάσσω (5293)
ὑποταγήσεται, 3 pers. sg. 2 fut. pass. indic. id.
ὑποταγησόμεθα, 1 pers. pl. 2 fut. pass. indic. id.
ὑποτάγητε, 2 pers. pl. 2 aor. pass. imper. . id.
ὑποτάξαι, aor. act. infin. . . . . id.
ὑποτάξαντα, acc. sg. m. aor. act. part. . . . id.
ὑποτάξαντι, dat. sg. m. aor. act. part. . . . id.
ὑποτάξαντος, gen. sg. m. aor. act. part. . . id.
ὑποτάσσεσθαι, pres. mid. infin. . . . . id.
ὑποτάσσεσθε, 2 pers. pl. pres. mid. imper. id.
ὑποτασσέσθω, 3 pers. sg. pres. mid. imper. id.
ὑποτασσέσθωσαν, 3 pers. pl. pres. pass.
imper. (1 Cor. 14:34, GNT, WH & NA |
ὑποτάσσεσθαι, MT & TR) . . . . id.
ὑποτάσσεται, 3 pers. sg. pres. pass. indic. id.
ὑποτάσσησθε, 2 pers. pl. pres. pass. subj. id.
ὑποτασσόμεναι, nom. pl. f. pres. pass. part. id.
ὑποτασσομένας, acc. pl. f. pres. pass. part. id.

ὑποτασσόμενοι, nom. pl. m. pres. pass. part. . . . . ὑποτάσσω *(5293)*

ὑποτασσόμενος, nom. sg. m. pres. pass. part.   id.

(5293) **ὑποτάσσω**, or ὑποτάττω, fut. ὑποτάξω [§26.3] (ὑπό + τάσσω) *to place or arrange under; to subordinate,* 1 Cor. 15:27; *to bring under influence,* Rom. 8:20; pass. *to be subordinated,* 1 Cor. 14:32, et al.; *to be brought under a state or influence,* Rom. 8:20; mid. *to submit one's self, render obedience, be submissive,* Luke 2:51; 10:17, et al.

ὑποτεταγμένα, acc. pl. neut. perf. pass. part.   id.

ὑποτέτακται, 3 pers. sg. perf. pass. indic. .   id.

ὑποτιθέμενος, nom. sg. m. pres. mid. part. . . . . ὑποτίθημι *(5294)*

(5294) **ὑποτίθημι**, fut. ὑποθήσω [§28.V] (ὑπό + τίθημι) *to place under; to lay down* the neck beneath the sword of the executioner, *to set on imminent risk,* Rom. 16:4; mid. *to suggest, recommend to attention,* 1 Tim. 4:6

(5295) **ὑποτρέχω**, 2 aor. ὑπέδραμον [§36.1] (ὑπό + τρέχω) *to run under;* as a nautical term, *to sail under* the lee of, Acts 27:16

ὑποτύπωσιν, acc. sg. f. n. . . . . . . ὑποτύπωσις *(5296)*

(5296) **ὑποτύπωσις**, εως, ἡ [§5.E.c] (ὑποτυπόω, *to sketch,* from ὑπό + τυπόω) *a sketch, delineation; a form, formula, presentment, sample,* 2 Tim. 1:13; *a pattern, a model representation,* 1 Tim. 1:16

ὑποφέρει, 3 pers. sg. pres. act. indic. ὑποφέρω *(5297)*

(5297) **ὑποφέρω**, aor. ὑπήνεγκα, 2 aor. ὑπήνεγκον [§36.1] (ὑπό + φέρω) *to bear under; to bear up under, support, sustain,* 1 Cor. 10:13; *to endure patiently,* 1 Pet. 2:19; *to undergo,* 2 Tim. 3:11

(5298) **ὑποχωρέω**, ῶ, fut. ὑποχωρήσω [§16.P] (ὑπό + χωρέω) *to withdraw, retire,* Luke 5:16; 9:10

ὑποχωρῶν, nom. sg. m. pres. act. part. . . . . ὑποχωρέω *(5298)*

ὑπωπιάζῃ, 3 pers. sg. pres. act. subj. (Luke 18:5, GNT, TR, WH & NA | ὑποπιάζῃ, MT) . . . . ὑπωπιάζω *(5299)*

(5299) **ὑπωπιάζω**, 1 pers. sg. pres. act. indic., fut. ὑπωπιάσω [§26.1] (ὑπώπιον, *the part of the face below the eyes,* from ὑπό + ὤψ) pr. *to strike one upon the parts beneath the eye; to beat black and blue;* hence, *to discipline by hardship, coerce,* 1 Cor. 9:27; met. *to weary* by continual importunities, *pester,* Luke 18:5

(5300) **ὗς**, ὑός, ὁ, nom. sg. f. n. [§5.E.g] *a hog, swine, boar or sow,* 2 Pet. 2:22

(5301) **ὕσσωπος**, ου, ὁ, ἡ, τό (Hebrew אֵזוֹב) *hyssop,* in N.T., however, not the plant usually so named, but probably the caper plant; *a bunch of hyssop,* Heb. 9:19; *a hyssop stalk,* John 19:29

ὑσσώπου, gen. sg. m. (f. or neut.) . . ὕσσωπος *(5301)*

ὑσσώπῳ, dat. sg. m. (f. or neut.) . . . .   id.

ὑστερεῖ, 3 pers. sg. pres. act. indic. . . ὑστερέω *(5302)*

ὑστερεῖσθαι, pres. pass. infin. . . . .   id.

(5302) **ὑστερέω**, ῶ, fut. ὑστερήσω, aor. ὑστέρησα, perf. ὑστέρηκα [§16.P] *to be behind* in place or time, *to be in the rear; to fall short of, be inferior to,* 2 Cor. 11:5; 12:11; *to fail of, fail to attain,* Heb. 4:1; *to be in want of, lack,* Luke 22:35; *to be wanting,* Mark 10:21; absol. *to be defective, in default,* Matt. 19:20; 1 Cor. 12:24; *to run short,* John 2:3; mid. *to come short of* a privilege or standard, *to miss,* Rom. 3:23; absol. *to come short, be below standard,* 1 Cor. 1:7; *to come short* of sufficiency, *to be in need, want,* Luke 15:14; 2 Cor. 11:8; Phil. 4:12; Heb. 11:37; *to be a loser, suffer detriment,* 1 Cor. 8:8; in N.T. ὑστερεῖν ἀπό, *to be backwards with respect to, to slight,* Heb. 12:15

ὑστερηθείς, nom. sg. m. aor. pass. part. . . . . ὑστερέω *(5302)*

ὑστερηκέναι, perf. act. infin. . . . .   id.

(5303) **ὑστέρημα**, ατος, τό [§4.D.c] *a shortcoming, defect;* personal *shortcoming,* 1 Cor. 16:17; Phil. 2:30; Col. 1:24; 1 Thess. 3:10; *want, need, poverty, penury,* Luke 21:4; 2 Cor. 8:13, 14, et al.

ὑστέρημα, acc. sg. neut. n. . . . . ὑστέρημα *(5303)*

ὑστερήματα, acc. pl. neut. n. . . . .   id.

ὑστερήματος, gen. sg. neut. n. . . . .   id.

ὑστέρησα, 1 pers. sg. aor. act. indic. . ὑστερέω *(5302)*

ὑστερήσαντος, gen. sg. m. aor. act. part. .   id.

ὑστερήσατε, 2 pers. pl. aor. act. indic. . . .   id.

ὑστερήσεως, gen. sg. f. n. . . . . ὑστέρησις *(5304)*

ὑστέρησιν, acc. sg. f. n. . . . .   id.

(5304) **ὑστέρησις**, εως, ἡ [§5.E.c] *want, need,* Mark 12:44; Phil. 4:11

ὑστέροις, dat. pl. m. adj. . . . . ὕστερος *(5306)*

(5305) **ὕστερον**, adv., *after, afterwards,* Matt. 4:2; 22:27, et al. pr. neut. of ὕστερος

(5306) **ὕστερος**, α, ον, nom. sg. m. adj. [§7.1] *posterior* in place or time; *subsequent,* 1 Tim. 4:1 (Matt. 21:31, WH | πρῶτος, GNT, MT, TR & NA)

ὑστερούμεθα, 1 pers. pl. pres. pass. indic. . . . . ὑστερέω *(5302)*

ὑστερούμενοι, nom. pl. m. pres. pass. part.   id.

ὑστερουμένῳ, dat. sg. m. pres. pass. part.

(1 Cor. 12:24, GNT, WH & NA | ὑστε-
ροῦντι, MT & TR) . . . . ὑστερέω *(5302)*

ὑστεροῦνται, 3 pers. pl. pres. pass. indic. . . id.

ὑστεροῦντι, dat. sg. m. pres. pass. part. (1 Cor.
12:24, MT & TR | ὑστερουμένῳ, GNT,
WH & NA) . . . . id.

ὑστερῶ, 1 pers. sg. pres. act. indic. contr. . . id.

ὑστερῶν, nom. sg. m. pres. act. part. . . . . . id.

ὑφ’, by apostrophe for ὑπό before an
aspirate . . . . ὑπό *(5259)*

(5307) **ὑφαντός**, η, ον, nom. sg. m. adj. [§7.F.a]
(ὑφαίνω, *to weave*) *woven,* John 19:23

ὕψει, dat. sg. neut. n. . . . . ὕψος *(5311)*

ὑψηλά, acc. pl. neut. adj. . . . . ὑψηλός *(5308)*

ὑψηλοῖς, dat. pl. neut. adj. . . . . id.

ὑψηλόν, nom. sg. neut. adj. {Luke 16:15} . . id.

ὑψηλόν, acc. sg. neut. adj. {Matt. 4:8} . . . . id.

(5308) **ὑψηλός**, ή, όν [§7.F.a] *high, lofty, elevated,*
Matt. 4:8; 17:1, et al.; τὰ ὑψηλά, *the high-
est* heaven, Heb. 1:3; *upraised,* Acts 13:17;
met. *highly esteemed,* Luke 16:15; φρονεῖν
τὰ ὑψηλά, *to have lofty thoughts, be
proud, overween,* Rom. 12:16

ὑψηλότερος, nom. sg. m. compar. adj. . . ὑψηλός *(5308)*

ὑψηλοῦ, gen. sg. m. adj. . . . . id.

ὑψηλοφρόνει, 2 pers. sg. pres. act. imper.
(Rom. 11:20, MT & TR | ὑψηλά, GNT,
WH & NA) . . . . ὑψηλοφρονέω *(5309)*

ὑψηλοφρονεῖν, pres. act. infin. . . . . id.

(5309) **ὑψηλοφρονέω**, ῶ, fut. ὑψηλοφρονήσω [§16.P]
(ὑψηλός + φρονέω) *to have lofty
thoughts, be proud, overweening, haughty,*
Rom. 11:20; 1 Tim. 6:17

ὑψίστοις, dat. pl. neut. adj. . . . . ὕψιστος *(5310)*

(5310) **ὕψιστος**, η, ον, nom. sg. m. adj. [§7.F.a] *highest, loftiest, most elevated;* τὰ ὕψιστα,
from the Hebrew, *the highest* heaven, Matt.
21:9; Mark 11:10; met. ὁ ὕψιστος, *the
Most High,* Mark 5:7, et al.; superlative
of ὕψος

ὑψίστου, gen. sg. m. adj. . . . . ὕψιστος *(5310)*

(5311) **ὕψος**, ους, τό, nom. sg. neut. n. [§5.E.b]
height, Eph. 3:18; Rev. 21:16; met. *exal-
tation, dignity, eminence,* James 1:9; from
the Hebrew, *the height* of heaven, Luke
1:78; 24:49 {Eph. 3:18}

ὕψος, acc. sg. neut. n. {Eph. 4:8} . . . . ὕψος *(5311)*

ὕψους, gen. sg. neut. n. . . . . id.

(5312) **ὑψόω**, ῶ, fut. ὑψώσω, aor. ὕψωσα [§20.T]
to raise aloft, lift up, John 3:14; 8:28; met.
to elevate in condition, *uplift, exalt,* Matt.
11:23; 23:12; Luke 1:52

ὑψωθείς, nom. sg. m. aor. pass. part.
[§21.U] . . . . ὑψόω *(5312)*

ὑψωθεῖσα, nom. sg. f. aor. pass. part. (Matt.

11:23; Luke 10:15, MT & TR | ὑψωθήσῃ,
GNT, WH & NA) . . . . id.

ὑψωθῆναι, aor. pass. infin. . . . . ὑψόω *(5312)*

ὑψωθήσεται, 3 pers. sg. fut. pass. indic. . . . id.

ὑψωθήσῃ, 2 pers. sg. fut. pass. indic. (Matt.
11:23; Luke 10:15, GNT, WH & NA |
ὑψωθεῖσα, MT & TR) . . . . id.

ὑψωθῆτε, 2 pers. pl. aor. pass. subj. . . . . . . id.

ὑψωθῶ, 1 pers. sg. aor. pass. subj. . . . . id.

(5313) **ὕψωμα**, ατος, τό, nom. sg. neut. n. [§4.D.c]
height, Rom. 8:39; *a towering* of self-
conceit, *presumption,* 2 Cor. 10:5 {Rom.
8:39}

ὕψωμα, acc. sg. neut. n. {2 Cor. 10:5} . . . ὕψωμα *(5313)*

ὑψῶν, nom. sg. m. pres. act. part. . . . . ὑψόω *(5312)*

ὑψώσει, 3 pers. sg. fut. act. indic. . . . . id.

ὕψωσε(ν), 3 pers. sg. aor. act. indic. . . . . . . id.

ὑψώσῃ, 3 pers. sg. aor. act. subj. . . . . id.

ὑψώσητε, 2 pers. pl. aor. act. subj. . . . . id.

Φ

φάγε, 2 pers. sg. 2 aor. act. imper. . . . . . . ἐσθίω *(2068)*

φαγεῖν, 2 aor. act. infin. . . . . id.

φάγεσαι, 2 pers. sg. fut. mid. dep. indic.
[§35.6; 36.1] . . . . id.

φάγεται, 3 pers. sg. fut. mid. dep. indic. . . . id.

φάγετε, 2 pers. pl. 2 aor. act. imper. . . . . . . id.

φάγῃ, 3 pers. sg. 2 aor. act. subj. . . . . id.

φάγῃς, 2 pers. sg. 2 aor. act. subj. . . . . id.

φάγητε, 2 pers. pl. 2 aor. act. subj. . . . . id.

φάγοι, 3 pers. sg. 2 aor. act. opt. . . . . id.

φάγονται, 3 pers. pl. 2 fut. mid. dep. indic. . id.

φαγόντες, nom. pl. m. 2 aor. act. part. . . . . id.

(5314) **φάγος**, ου, ὁ, nom. sg. m. n. [§3.C.a] *a glut-
ton,* Matt. 11:19; Luke 7:34

(5315) **φάγω**, 1 pers. sg. 2 aor. act. subj. . . . . ἐσθίω *(2068)*

φάγωμεν, 1 pers. pl. 2 aor. act. subj. . . . . . . id.

φάγωσι(ν), 3 pers. pl. 2 aor. act. subj. . . . . . id.

φαιλόνην, acc. sg. m. n. (2 Tim. 4:13, GNT,
MT, TRs & NA | φελόνην, WH &
TRb) . . . . φαιλόνης *(‡5341)*

(‡5341) **φαιλόνης**, or φελόνης, ου, ὁ (by metath.
for φαινόλης, Latin *paenula*) *a thick
cloak* for travelling, with a hood, 2 Tim.
4:13

φαίνει, 3 pers. sg. pres. act. indic. . . . . . . φαίνω *(5316)*

φαίνεσθε, 2 pers. pl. pres. pass. indic.
{Matt. 23:28} . . . . id.

φαίνεσθε, 2 pers. pl. pres. pass. indic. or
imper. {Phil. 2:15} . . . . id.

φαίνεται, 3 pers. sg. pres. mid./pass. indic. . id.

φαίνῃ, 3 pers. sg. pres. act. subj. (Rev. 8:12,

TR | φάνη, GNT, WH, MT & NA) . φαίνω *(5316)*

φαινομένη, nom. sg. f. pres. mid./pass. part. id.

φαινομένου, gen. sg. m. pres. mid./pass. part. id.

φαινομένων, gen. pl. neut. pres. mid./pass. part. . . . . id.

φαίνονται, 3 pers. pl. pres. mid./pass. indic. id.

φαίνοντι, dat. sg. m. pres. mid. or. pass. part. id.

(5316) **φαίνω,** fut. φανῶ, perf. πέφαγκα [§27.1.c; 27.2.a]· 2 aor. pass. ἐφάνην [§27.4.b] *to cause to appear, bring to light; absol. to shine,* John 1:5; 5:35; 2 Pet. 1:19; 1 John 2:8; Rev. 1:16; 8:12; 21:23; mid./pass. *to be seen, appear, be visible,* Matt. 1:20; 2:7, 13, 19, et al.; τὰ φαινόμενα, *things visible, things obvious to the senses,* Heb. 11:3; φαίνομαι, *to appear, seen, be in appearance,* Matt. 23:27; Luke 24:11; *to appear in thought, seen in idea, be a notion,* Mark 14:64, et al.

φαίνων, nom. sg. m. pres. act. part. . . . . . φαίνω *(5316)*

φαίνωσιν, 3 pers. pl. pres. act. subj. . . . . . . id.

(†5317) **Φάλεγ,** ὁ, *Phalec,* pr. name, indecl. (Luke 3:35, MT | Φαλέκ, GNT, WH, TR & NA)

(5317) **Φαλέκ,** ὁ, *Phalec,* pr. name, indecl. (Luke 3:35, GNT, WH, TR & NA | φάλεγ, MT)

φανεῖται, 3 pers. sg. fut. mid. dep. indic. . φαίνω *(5316)*

φανερά, nom. sg. f. adj. {1 Tim. 4:15} . . . . φανερός *(5318)*

φανερά, nom. pl. neut. adj. {1 John 3:10} . . id.

φανεροί, nom. pl. m. adj. . . . . id.

φανερόν, acc. sg. m. adj. {Mark 3:12} . . . . id.

φανερόν, nom. sg. neut. adj. {Luke 8:17a} . id.

φανερόν, acc. sg. neut. adj. {Luke 8:17b} . . id.

(5318) **φανερός,** ά, όν [§7.1] *apparent, conspicuous, manifest, clear, known, well-known,* Mark 4:22; 6:14; Gal. 5:19, et al.; ἐν φανερῷ, *openly,* Matt. 6:4, 6; also, *in outward guise, externally,* Rom. 2:28

φανερούμενοι, nom. pl. m. pres. pass. part. . . . . φανερόω *(5319)*

φανερούμενον, nom. sg. neut. pres. pass. part. . . . . id.

φανεροῦντι, dat. sg. m. pres. act. part. . . . . id.

φανερούς, acc. pl. m. adj. . . . . φανερός *(5318)*

φανεροῦται, 3 pers. sg. pres. pass. indic. . . . . φανερόω *(5319)*

(†5319) **φανερόω,** ῶ, fut. φανερώσω, aor. ἐφανέρωσα [§20.T] perf. pass. πεφανέρωμαι [§21.U] *to bring to light, to set in a clear light; to manifest, display,* John 2:11; 7:4; 9:3, et al.; *to evince,* Rom. 1:19; 2 Cor. 7:12; *to declare, make known,* John 17:6; *to disclose,* Mark 4:22; 1 Cor. 4:5; Col. 4:4; *to reveal,* Rom. 3:21; 16:26; Col. 1:26, et al.; *to present to view,* John 21:1, 14; pass. *to*

make an appearance, Mark 16:12, 14; spc. of Christ, *to be personally manifested,* John 1:31; Col. 3:4; 1 Pet. 1:20; 5:4; 1 John 3:5, et al.; *to be laid bare, appear in true character,* 2 Cor. 5:10, 11

φανερῷ, dat. sg. neut. adj. . . . . φανερός *(5318)*

φανερωθεῖσαν, acc. sg. f. aor. pass. part. . . . . φανερόω *(5319)*

φανερωθέντες, nom. pl. m. aor. pass. part. (2 Cor. 11:6, MT & TR | φανερώσαντες, GNT, WH & NA) . . . . id.

φανερωθέντος, gen. sg. m. aor. pass. part. . id.

φανερωθῇ, 3 pers. sg. aor. pass. subj. . . . . . id.

φανερωθῆναι, aor. pass. infin. . . . . id.

φανερωθήσεσθε, 2 pers. pl. fut. pass. indic. . id.

φανερωθῶσιν, 3 pers. pl. aor. pass. subj. . . . id.

(5320) **φανερῶς,** adv., *manifestly; clearly, plainly, distinctly,* Acts 10:3; *openly, publicly,* Mark 1:45; John 7:10

φανερώσαντες, nom. pl. m. aor. act. part. (2 Cor. 11:6, GNT, WH & NA | φανερωθέντες, MT & TR) . . . . φανερόω *(5319)*

φανερώσει, 3 pers. sg. fut. act. indic. {1 Cor. 4:5} . . . . id.

φανερώσει, dat. sg. f. n. {2 Cor. 4:2} . . . . φανέρωσις *(5321)*

(5321) **φανέρωσις,** εως, ἡ, nom. sg. f. n. [§5.E.c] *an evidencing, clear display,* 2 Cor. 4:2; *an outward evidencing* of a latent principle, *active exhibition,* 1 Cor. 12:7

φανέρωσον, 2 pers. sg. aor. act. imper. . . . . φανερόω *(5319)*

φανερώσω, 1 pers. sg. aor. act. subj. . . . . . . id.

φανῇ, 3 pers. sg. 2 aor. pass. subj. . . . . . . φαίνω *(5316)*

φανῇς, 2 pers. sg. 2 aor. pass. subj. . . . . . . id.

φανήσεται, 3 pers. sg. 2 fut. pass. indic. [§27.4.c] . . . . id.

(5322) **φανός,** οῦ, ὁ [§3.C.a] *a torch, lantern, light,* John 18:3

(5323) **Φανουήλ,** ὁ, *Phanuel,* pr. name, indecl., Luke 2:36

φανταζόμενον, nom. sg. neut. pres. pass. part. . . . . φαντάζω *(5324)*

(5324) **φαντάζω,** fut. φαντάσω [§26.1] *to render visible, cause to appear;* pass. *to appear, be seen;* τὸ φανταζόμενον, *the sight, spectacle,* Heb. 12:21

(5325) **φαντασία,** ας, ἡ [§2.B.b; 2.2] pr. *a rendering visible; a display; pomp, parade,* Acts 25:23

φαντασίας, gen. sg. f. n. . . . . φαντασία *(5325)*

(5326) **φάντασμα,** ατος, τό, nom. sg. neut. n. [§4.D.c] *a phantom, specter,* Matt. 14:26; Mark 6:49

φανῶμεν, 1 pers. pl. 2 aor. pass. subj. . . . φαίνω *(5316)*

φανῶν, gen. pl. m. n. . . . . φανός *(5322)* φανῶσι(ν), 3 pers. pl. 2 aor. pass. subj. . . φαίνω *(5316)*

(5327) **φάραγξ**, αγγος, ἡ, nom. sg. f. n. [§4.2.b] *a cleft, ravine, dell*, Luke 3:5

(5328) **Φαραώ**, ὁ, *Pharaoh*, pr. name, indecl.

(5329) **Φαρές**, ὁ, *Phares*, pr. name, indecl. (Matt. 1:3; Luke 3:33, GNT, WH & NA | φάρες, MT & TR)

φαρισαῖε, voc. sg. m. n. . . . . φαρισαῖος *(†5330)*

φαρισαῖοι, nom. pl. m. n. {Matt. 23:2} . . . . id.

φαρισαῖοι, voc. pl. m. n. {Matt. 23:13} . . . . id.

φαρισαίοις, dat. pl. m. n. . . . . id.

(†5330) **φαρισαῖος**, ου, ὁ, nom. sg. m. n. [§3.C.a] *a Pharisee, a follower of the sect of the Pharisees,* a numerous and powerful sect of the Jews, distinguished for their ceremonial observances, and apparent sanctity of life, and for being rigid interpreters of the Mosaic law; but who not unfrequently violated its spirit by their traditional interpretations and precepts, to which they ascribed nearly an equal authority with the Old Testament Scriptures, Matt. 5:20; 12:2; 23:14, et al.

φαρισαίου, gen. sg. m. n. . . . . φαρισαῖος *(†5330)*

φαρισαίους, acc. pl. m. n. . . . . id.

φαρισαίων, gen. pl. m. n. . . . . id.

(5331) **φαρμακεία**, ας, ἡ, nom. sg. f. n. [§2.B.b; 2.2] (φάρμακον, *a drug) employment of drugs* for any purpose; *sorcery, magic, enchantment,* Rev. 9:21; 18:23 (Gal. 5:20, GNT, MT, TR & NA | φαρμακία, WH)

φαρμακεία, dat. sg. f. n. (Rev. 18:23, GNT, MT, TR & NA | φαρμακία, WH) . . . . φαρμακεία *(5331)*

φαρμακειῶν, gen. pl. f. n. (Rev. 9:21, TR | φαρμάκων, GNT, WH, MT & NA) . . . id.

(5332) **φαρμακεύς**, έως, ὁ [§5.E.d] pr. *one who deals in drugs; an enchanter, magician, sorcerer,* Acts 21:8

φαρμακεῦσι(ν), dat. pl. m. n. (Rev. 21:8, TR | φαρμακοῖς, GNT, WH, MT & NA) . . . . φαρμακεύς *(5332)*

φαρμακοί, nom. pl. m. n. . . . . φαρμακός *(5333)*

φαρμακοῖς, dat. pl. m. n. (Rev. 21:8, GNT, WH, MT & NA | φαρμακεῦσ(ν), TR) . id.

(‡5331) **φάρμακον**, ου, τό, *a drug; an enchantment; magic potion, charm*

(5333) **φαρμακός**, οῦ, ὁ [§3.C.a] *a sorcerer,* Rev. 21:8; 22:15

φαρμάκων, gen. pl. neut. n. (Rev. 9:21, GNT, WH, MT & NA | φαρμακειῶν, TR) . . . . φάρμακον *(‡5331)*

φασί(ν), 3 pers. pl. pres. indic. [§33.1] . . . . . φημί *(5346)*

(5334) **φάσις**, εως, ἡ, nom. sg. f. n. [§5.E.c] *report, information,* Acts 21:31

φάσκοντας, acc. pl. m. pres. act. part. (Rev.

2:2, TR | GNT, WH, MT & NA omit) . . . . φάσκω *(5335)*

φάσκοντες, nom. pl. m. pres. act. part. . . . . id.

(5335) **φάσκω**, equivalent to φημί, imperf. ἔφασκον, *to assert, affirm,* Acts 24:9; 25:19; Rom. 1:22; Rev. 2:2

(5336) **φάτνη**, ης, ἡ [§2.B.a] *a manger, crib,* Luke 2:7, 12, 16; 13:15

φάτνη, dat. sg. f. n. . . . . φάτνη *(5336)*

φάτνης, gen. sg. f. n. . . . . id.

φαῦλα, acc. pl. neut. adj. . . . . φαῦλος *(5337)*

φαῦλον, nom. sg. neut. adj. {James 3:16} . . id.

φαῦλον, acc. sg. neut. adj. {Rom. 9:11} . . . . id.

(5337) **φαῦλος**, η, ον [§7.F.a] *sorry, vile, refuse; evil, wicked;* John 3:20; 5:29; Tit. 2:8; James 3:16

(5338) **φέγγος**, ους, τό [§5.E.b] *light, splendor,* Matt. 24:29; Mark 13:24; Luke 11:33

φέγγος, acc. sg. neut. n. . . . . φέγγος *(5338)*

(5339) **φείδομαι**, 1 pers. sg. pres. mid./pass. dep. indic., fut. φείσομαι [§23.1.c] *to spare, be thrifty of; to spare, be tender of,* Rom. 8:32; *to spare,* in respect of hard dealing, Acts 20:29; Rom. 11:21; 1 Cor. 7:28; 2 Cor. 1:23; 13:2; 2 Pet. 2:4, 5; absol. *to forbear, abstain,* 2 Cor. 12:6

φειδόμενοι, nom. pl. m. pres. mid./pass. dep. part. . . . . φείδομαι *(5339)*

φειδόμενος, nom. sg. m. pres. mid./pass. dep. part. . . . . id.

(5340) **φειδομένως**, adv., *sparingly, parsimoniously,* 2 Cor. 9:6 (2×)

φείσεται, 3 pers. sg. fut. mid. dep. indic. (Rom. 11:21, GNT, WH, MT & NA | φείσηται, TR) . . . . φαίνω *(5316)*

φείσηται, 3 pers. sg. aor. mid. dep. subj. (Rom. 11:21, TR | φείσεται, GNT, WH, MT & NA) . . . . id.

φείσομαι, 1 pers. sg. fut. mid. dep. indic. . . id.

φελόνην, acc. sg. f. n. (2 Tim. 4:13, WH & TRb | φαιλόνην, GNT, MT, TRs & NA) . . . . φελόνης *(5341)*

(5341) **φελόνης**, *a thick cloak* for travelling, with a hood, 2 Tim. 4:13

φέρε, 2 pers. sg. pres. act. imper. . . . . . . φέρω *(5342)*

φέρει, 3 pers. sg. pres. act. indic. . . . . id.

φέρειν, pres. act. infin. . . . . id.

φέρεσθαι, pres. pass. infin. . . . . id.

φέρετε, 2 pers. pl. pres. act. indic. {John 18:29} . . . . id.

φέρετε, 2 pers. pl. pres. act. imper. {John 2:8} id.

φέρῃ, 3 pers. sg. pres. act. subj. . . . . id.

φέρητε, 2 pers. pl. pres. act. subj. . . . . id.

φερομένην, acc. sg. f. pres. pass. part. . . . . . id.

φερομένης, gen. sg. f. pres. mid./pass. part. . . id.

φερόμενοι, nom. pl. m. pres. pass. part. .. φέρω (5342)

φέρον, nom. sg. neut. pres. act. part. . . . . . . id.

φέροντες, nom. pl. m. pres. act. part. . . . . . id.

φέρουσαι, nom. pl. f. pres. act. part. . . . . . . id.

φέρουσαν, acc. sg. f. pres. act. part. . . . . . . id.

φέρουσι(ν), 3 pers. pl. pres. act. indic. . . . . . id.

(5342) **φέρω**, fut. οἴσω, aor. ἤνεγκα, 2 aor. ἤνεγκον, aor. pass. ἠνέχθην [§36.1] *to bear, carry,* Mark 2:3, et al.; *to bring,* Matt. 14:11, 18, et al.; *to conduct,* Matt. 17:17; John 21:18, et al.; *to bear, endure,* Rom. 9:22; Heb. 12:20; 13:13; *to uphold, maintain, conserve,* Heb. 1:3; *to bear, bring forth, produce,* Mark 4:8; John 12:24; 15:2, et al.; *to bring forward, advance, allege,* John 18:29; Acts 25:7; 2 Pet. 2:11; *to offer, ascribe,* Rev. 21:24, 26; absol. used of a gate, *to lead,* Acts 12:10; pass. *to be brought* within reach, *offered,* 1 Pet. 1:13; *to be brought in, to enter,* Heb. 9:16; *to be under a moving influence, to be moved, be instinct,* 2 Pet. 1:21; mid. *to rush, sweep,* Acts 2:2; *to proceed, come forth, have utterance,* 2 Pet. 1:17, 18, 21; *to proceed, make progress,* Heb. 6:1; used of a ship, *to drive* before the wind, Acts 27:15, 17

φερώμεθα, 1 pers. pl. pres. pass. subj. . . . . φέρω (5342)

φέρων, nom. sg. m. pres. act. part. . . . . id.

φεῦγε, 2 pers. sg. pres. act. imper. . . . . . . φεύγω (5343)

φεύγει, 3 pers. sg. pres. act. indic. . . . . id.

φεύγετε, 2 pers. pl. pres. act. imper. . . . . . id.

φευγέτωσαν, 3 pers. pl. pres. act. imper. . . . id.

(5343) **φεύγω**, fut. φεύξομαι, 2 aor. ἔφυγον [§24.9] absol. *to flee, take to flight,* Matt. 2:13; 8:33, et al.; *to shrink, stand fearfully aloof,* 1 Cor. 10:14; *to make escape,* Matt. 23:33; trans. *to shun,* 1 Cor. 6:18; 1 Tim. 6:11; 2 Tim. 2:22; *to escape,* Heb. 11:34

φεύξεται, 3 pers. sg. fut. mid. dep. indic. . . . . φεύγω (5343)

φεύξονται, 3 pers. pl. fut. mid. dep. indic. . . id.

Φήλικα, acc. sg. m. n. . . . . Φῆλιξ (5344)

Φήλικι, dat. sg. m. n. . . . . id.

Φήλικος, gen. sg. m. n. . . . . id.

(5344) **Φῆλιξ**, ικος, ὁ, nom. sg. m. n. [§4.2.b] *Felix,* pr. name {Acts 24:22}

Φήλιξ, voc. sg. m. n. {Acts 24:3} . . . . . . Φῆλιξ (5344)

(5345) **φήμη**, ης, ἡ, nom. sg. f. n. [§2.B.a] pr. *a celestial or oracular utterance; an utterance; fame, rumor, report,* Matt. 9:26; Luke 4:14

(5346) **φημί**, 1 pers. sg. pres. indic., fut. φήσω, imperf. ἔφην [§33.DD] (φάω) *to utter, tell forth; to say, speak,* Matt. 8:8; 14:8; 26:34, 61; *to say, allege, affirm,* Rom. 3:8, et al.

φησί(ν), 3 pers. sg. pres. indic. [§33.1] . . . . . φημί (5346)

Φῆστε, voc. sg. m. n. . . . . Φῆστος (5347)

Φῆστον, acc. sg. m. n. . . . . id.

(5347) **Φῆστος**, ου, ὁ, nom. sg. m. n. [§3.C.a] *Festus,* pr. name

Φήστου, gen. sg. m. n. . . . . Φῆστος (5347)

Φήστῳ, dat. sg. m. n. . . . . id.

(5348) **φθάνω**, fut. φθήσομαι and φθάσω, aor. ἔφθασα, 2 aor. ἔφθην [§37.1] *to be beforehand with; to outstrip, precede,* 1 Thess. 4:15; absol. *to advance, make progress,* 2 Cor. 10:14; Phil. 3:16; *to come up* with, *come upon, be close at hand,* Matt. 12:28; 1 Thess. 2:16; *to attain* an object of pursuit, Rom. 9:31

φθαρῇ, 3 pers. sg. 2 aor. pass. subj. . . . . φθείρω (5351)

φθαρήσονται, 3 pers. sg. 2 fut. pass. indic. (2 Pet. 2:12, GNT, WH & NA | καταφθαρήσονται, MT & TR) . . . . id.

φθαρτῆς, gen. sg. f. adj. . . . . φθαρτός (5349)

φθαρτοῖς, dat. pl. neut. adj. . . . . id.

φθαρτόν, acc. sg. m. adj. {1 Cor. 9:25} . . . . id.

φθαρτόν, nom. sg. neut. adj. (1 Cor. 15:54, GNT, MT, TR & NA | WH omits) . . . id.

φθαρτόν, acc. sg. neut. adj. {1 Cor. 15:53} . . id.

(5349) **φθαρτός**, ή, όν [§7.F.a] *corruptible, perishable,* Rom. 1:23; 1 Cor. 9:25, et al.

φθαρτοῦ, gen. sg. m. adj. . . . . φθαρτός (5349)

φθάσωμεν, 1 pers. pl. aor. act. subj. . . . . φθάνω (5348)

φθέγγεσθαι, pres. mid./pass. dep. infin. . . . . φθέγγομαι (5350)

(5350) **φθέγγομαι**, fut. φθέγξομαι, aor. ἐφθεγξάμην [§23.5] *to emit a sound; to speak,* Acts 4:18; 2 Pet. 2:16, 18

φθεγγόμενοι, nom. pl. m. pres. mid. dep. part. . . . . φθέγγομαι (5350)

φθεγξάμενον, nom. sg. neut. aor. mid./pass. dep. part. . . . . id.

φθείρει, 3 pers. sg. pres. act. indic. . . . . . . φθείρω (5351)

φθειρόμενον, acc. sg. m. pres. pass. part. . . id.

φθείρονται, 3 pers. pl. pres. pass. indic. . . . id.

φθείρουσιν, 3 pers. pl. pres. act. indic. . . . . . id.

(5351) **φθείρω**, fut. φθερῶ, perf. ἔφθαρκα [§27.1.c; 27.2.b] aor. ἔφθειρα, aor. pass. ἐφθάρην [§27.1.d; 27.4.a] (φθέω, idem) *to spoil, ruin,* 1 Cor. 3:17; 2 Cor. 7:2; *to corrupt,* morally *deprave,* 1 Cor. 15:33; 2 Cor. 11:3, et al.

φθερεῖ, 3 pers. sg. fut. act. indic. . . . . φθείρω (5351)

φθινοπωρινά, nom. pl. neut. adj. . . . . φθινοπωρινός (5352)

(5352) **φθινοπωρινός**, ή, όν [§7.F.a] (φθινόπωρον, *the latter part of autumn,* from φθίνω, *to wane,* and ὀπώρα) *autumnal, sere, bare*

φθόγγοις, dat. pl. m. n. . . . . φθόγγος (5353)

(5353) **φθόγγος**, ου, ὁ, nom. sg. m. n. [§3.C.a] *a vocal sound*, Rom. 10:18; 1 Cor. 14:7

(5354) **φθονέω**, ῶ, fut. φθονήσω, aor. ἐφόνησα [§16.P] *to envy*, Gal. 5:26

φθόνοι, nom. pl. m. n. . . . . φθόνος (5355)

φθόνον, acc. sg. m. n. . . . . id.

(5355) **φθόνος**, ου, ὁ, nom. sg. m. n. [§3.C.a] *envy, jealously, spite*, Matt. 27:18; Mark 15:10, et al.

φθόνου, gen. sg. m. n. . . . . φθόνος (5355)

φθονοῦντες, nom. pl. m. pres. act. part. φθονέω (5354)

φθόνους, acc. pl. m. n. . . . . φθόνος (5355)

φθόνῳ, dat. sg. m. n. . . . . id.

(5356) **φθορά**, ᾶς, ἡ, nom. sg. f. n. [§2.B.b] *corruption, decay, ruin, corruptibility, mortality*, Rom. 8:21; 1 Cor. 15:42; meton. *corruptible, perishable substance*, 1 Cor. 15:50; *killing, slaughter*, 2 Pet. 2:12; spiritual *ruin*, Gal. 6:8; Col. 2:22; met. moral *corruption, depravity*, 2 Pet. 1:4; 2:12, 19

φθορᾷ, dat. sg. f. n. . . . . φθορά (5356)

φθοράν, acc. sg. f. n. . . . . id.

φθορᾶς, gen. sg. f. n. . . . . id.

φιάλας, acc. pl. f. n. . . . . φιάλη (5357)

(5357) **φιάλη**, ης, ἡ [§2.B.a] *a bowl, shallow cup, patera*, Rev. 5:8; 15:7; 16:1, 2, 3, 4, et al.

φιάλην, acc. sg. f. n. . . . . φιάλη (5357)

φιλάγαθον, acc. sg. m. adj. . . . . . . φιλάγαθος (5358)

(5358) **φιλάγαθος**, ον [§7.2] (φίλος + ἀγαθός) *a lover of goodness*, or, *of the good, a fosterer of virtue*, Tit. 1:8

(5359) **Φιλαδέλφεια**, ας, ἡ [§2.B.b; 2.2] *Philadelphia, a city of Lydia, near Mount Tmolus*

Φιλαδελφείᾳ, dat. sg. f. n. (Rev. 3:7, GNT, MT, TR & NA | Φιλαδελφίᾳ, WH) . . . . Φιλαδέλφεια (5359)

φιλαδέλφειαν, acc. sg. f. n. (Rev. 1:11, GNT, MT, TR & NA | Φιλαδελφίαν, WH) . id.

(5360) **φιλαδελφία**, ας, ἡ, nom. sg. f. n. [§2.B.b; 2.2] *brotherly love*; in N.T. *love of the* Christian *brotherhood*, Rom. 12:10; 1 Thess. 4:9, et al.

φιλαδελφίᾳ, dat. sg. f. n. . . . . . . φιλαδελφία (5360)

φιλαδελφίαν, acc. sg. f. n. . . . . id.

φιλαδελφίας, gen. sg. f. n. . . . . id.

φιλάδελφοι, nom. pl. m. adj. . . . . φιλάδελφος (5361)

(5361) **φιλάδελφος**, ον [§7.2] (φίλος + ἀδελφός) *brother-loving*; in N.T. *loving the members of the* Christian *brotherhood*, 1 Pet. 3:8

(5362) **φίλανδρος**, ον (φίλος + ἀνήρ) *husband-loving; conjugal*

φιλάνδρους, acc. pl. f. n. . . . . φίλανδρος (5362)

(5363) **φιλανθρωπία**, ας, ἡ, nom. sg. f. n. [§2.B.b; 2.2] (φιλάνθρωπος, *loving mankind, hu-*

mane, from φίλος + ἄνθρωπος) *philanthropy, love of mankind*, Tit. 3:4; *benevolence, humanity*, Acts 28:2

φιλανθρωπίαν, acc. sg. f. n. . . . . φιλανθρωπία (5363)

(5364) **φιλανθρώπως**, adv., *humanely, benevolently, kindly*, Acts 27:3

(5365) **φιλαργυρία**, ας, ἡ, nom. sg. f. n. [§2.B.b; 2.2] *love of money, covetousness*, 1 Tim. 6:10

φιλάργυροι, nom. pl. m. adj. . . . . φιλάργυρος (5366)

(5366) **φιλάργυρος**, ον [§7.2] (φίλος + ἄργυρος) *money-loving, covetous*, Luke 16:14; 2 Tim. 3:2

φίλας, acc. pl. f. n. (pr. f. of φίλος) . . . . φίλη (‡5384)

φίλαυτοι, nom. pl. m. adj. . . . . φίλαυτος (5367)

(5367) **φίλαυτος**, ον [§7.2] (φίλος + αὐτός) *self-loving; selfish*, 2 Tim. 3:2

φίλε, voc. sg. m. n. . . . . φίλος (5384)

φιλεῖ, 3 pers. sg. pres. act. indic. . . . . . . φιλέω (5368)

φιλεῖς, 2 pers. sg. pres. act. indic. . . . . id.

(5368) **φιλέω**, ῶ, fut. φιλήσω, aor. ἐφίλησα [§16.P] pr. *to manifest some act or token of kindness of affection; to kiss*, Matt. 26:48; Mark 14:44; Luke 22:47; *to love, regard with affection, have affection for*, Matt. 10:37; John 5:20; *to like, be fond of, delight in* a thing, Matt. 23:6; Rev. 22:15; *to cherish inordinately, set store by*, John 12:25; followed by an infin. *to be wont*, Matt. 6:5

(‡5384) **φίλη**, ης, ἡ [§2.B.a] *a female friend*, Luke 15:9

φιλήδονοι, nom. pl. m. adj. . . . . . . φιλήδονος (5369)

(5369) **φιλήδονος**, ον [§7.2] (φίλος + ἡδονή) *pleasure-loving; a lover of pleasure*, 2 Tim. 3:4

(5370) **φίλημα**, ατος, τό [§4.D.c] *a kiss*, Luke 7:45; 22:48; Rom. 16:16, et al.

φίλημα, acc. sg. neut. n. . . . . φίλημα (5370)

φιλήματι, dat. sg. neut. n. . . . . id.

Φιλήμονα, acc. sg. m. n. (Philemon 25, TRs | GNT, WH, MT, TRb & NA omit) . . . . φιλήμων (5371)

Φιλήμονι, dat. sg. m. n. . . . . id.

(5371) **Φιλήμων**, ονος, ὁ [§4.2.e] *Philemon*, pr. name, Philemon 1

φιλῆσαι, aor. act. infin. . . . . φιλέω (5368)

φιλήσω, 1 pers. sg. aor. act. subj. . . . . id.

(5372) **Φίλητος**, ου, ὁ, nom. sg. m. n., *Philetus*, pr. name (2 Tim. 2:17, GNT, MT, TRb, WH & NA | Φιλητός, TRs)

(5373) **φιλία**, ας, ἡ, nom. sg. f. n. [§2.B.b; 2.2] *affection, fondness, love*, James 4:4

Φίλιππε, voc. sg. m. n. . . . . Φίλιππος (5376)

Φιλιππήσιοι, voc. pl. m. n. . . . . . . Φιλιππήσιος (5374)

(5374) **Φιλιππήσιος**, ου, ὁ, *a Philippian, a citizen of* Φίλιπποι, *Philippi*, Phil. 4:15

Φιλιππησίους, acc. pl. m. n. (Phil. 4:23, TRs | GNT, WH, MT, TRb & NA omit) . . . . Φιλιππήσιος *(5374)*

(5375) **Φίλιπποι**, ων, οἱ, *Philippi, a considerable city of Macedonia, east of Amphipolis,* Phil. 1:1

Φιλίπποις, dat. pl. m. n. . . . . Φίλιπποι *(5375)*

Φίλιππον, acc. sg. m. n. . . . . Φίλιππος *(5376)*

(5376) **Φίλιππος**, ου, ὁ, nom. sg. m. n. [§3.C.a] *Philip,* pr. name   I. *Philip, the Apostle,* Matt. 10:3, et al.   II. *Philip, the Evangelist,* Acts 6:5, et al.   III. *Philip, son of Herod the Great and Mariamne,* Matt. 14:3, et al.   IV. *Philip, son of Herod the Great and Cleopatra,* Matt. 16:13; Luke 3:1

Φιλίππου, gen. sg. m. n. . . . . Φίλιππος *(5376)*

Φιλίππους, acc. sg. m. n. . . . . Φίλιπποι *(5375)*

Φιλίππῳ, dat. sg. m. n. . . . . Φίλιππος *(5376)*

Φιλίππων, gen. sg. m. n. . . . . Φίλιπποι *(5375)*

φιλόθεοι, nom. pl. m. adj. . . . . φιλόθεος *(5377)*

(5377) **φιλόθεος**, ον [§7.2] (φίλος + θεός) *God-loving, pious; a lover of God,* 2 Tim. 3:4

φίλοι, nom. pl. m. adj. . . . . φίλος *(5384)*

φίλοις, dat. pl. m. adj. . . . . id.

Φιλόλογον, acc. sg. m. n. . . . . Φιλόλογος *(5378)*

(5378) **Φιλόλογος**, ου, ὁ, *Philologus,* pr. name, Rom. 16:15

φίλον, acc. sg. m. adj. . . . . φίλος *(5384)*

(5379) **φιλονεικία**, ας, ἡ, nom. sg. f. n. [§2.B.b; 2.2] *a love of contention; rivalry, contention,* Luke 22:24

(5380) **φιλόνεικος**, ον, nom. sg. m. adj. [§7.2] (φίλος + νεῖκος, *contention*) *fond of contention; contentious, disputations,* 1 Cor. 11:16

(†5381) **φιλοξενία**, ας, ἡ [§2.B.b; 2.2] *kindness to strangers, hospitality,* Rom. 12:13; Heb. 13:2

φιλοξενίαν, acc. sg. f. n. . . . . φιλοξενία *(†5381)*

φιλοξενίας, gen. sg. f. n. . . . . id.

φιλόξενοι, nom. pl. m. adj. . . . . φιλόξενος *(5382)*

φιλόξενον, acc. sg. m. adj. . . . . id.

(5382) **φιλόξενος**, ον [§7.2] (φίλος + ξένος) *kind to strangers, hospitable,* 1 Tim. 3:2; Tit. 1:8; 1 Pet. 4:9

(5383) **φιλοπρωτεύω** (φίλος + πρωτεύω) *to love or desire to be first or chief, affect preeminence,* 3 John 9

φιλοπρωτεύων, nom. sg. m. pres. act. part. . . . . φιλοπρωτεύω *(5383)*

(5384) **φίλος**, η, ον, nom. sg. m. adj., *loved, dear;* as a subst., *a friend,* Luke 7:6; 11:5, 6, 8, et al.; *a congenial associate,* Matt. 11:19; Luke 7:34; James 4:4; used as a word of courteous appellation, Luke 14:10

(5385) **φιλοσοφία**, ας, ἡ [§2.B.b; 2.2] *a love of*

science; systematic philosophy; in N.T. *the philosophy* of the Jewish gnosis, Col. 2:8

φιλοσοφίας, gen. sg. f. n. . . . . φιλοσοφία *(5385)*

(5386) **φιλόσοφος**, ου, ὁ [§3.C.a] (φίλος + σοφία) pr. *a lover of science, a systematic philosopher,* Acts 17:18

φιλοσόφων, gen. pl. m. n. . . . . φιλόσοφος *(5386)*

φιλόστοργοι, nom. pl. m. adj. . . . . φιλόστοργος *(5387)*

(5387) **φιλόστοργος**, ον [§7.2] (φίλος + στοργή, *natural affection*) *tenderly affectionate,* Rom. 12:10

(5388) **φιλότεκνος**, ον (φίλος + τέκνον) *loving one's children, duly parental,* Tit. 2:4

φιλοτέκνους, acc. pl. f. adj. . . . . φιλότεκνος *(5388)*

φιλοτιμεῖσθαι, pres. mid./pass. dep. infin. . . . . φιλοτιμέομαι *(5389)*

(5389) **φιλοτιμέομαι**, οῦμαι, fut. φιλοτιμήσομαι [§17.Q] (φιλότιμος, *studious of honor or distinction,* φίλος + τιμή) pr. *to be ambitious of honor;* by impl. *to exert one's self to accomplish a thing, use one's utmost efforts, endeavor earnestly,* Rom. 15:20; 2 Cor. 5:9; 1 Thess. 4:11

φιλοτιμούμεθα, 1 pers. pl. pres. mid./pass. dep. indic. . . . . φιλοτιμέομαι *(5389)*

φιλοτιμούμενον, acc. sg. m. pres. mid./pass. dep. part. . . . . id.

φιλοῦντας, acc. pl. m. pres. act. part. . . . . φιλέω *(5368)*

φιλούντων, gen. pl. m. pres. act. part. . . . . . id.

φίλους, acc. pl. m. adj. . . . . φίλος *(5384)*

φιλοῦσι(ν), 3 pers. pl. pres. act. indic. . . . φιλέω *(5368)*

φιλόφρονες, nom. pl. m. adj. (1 Pet. 3:8, MT & TR | ταπεινόφρονες, GNT, WH & NA) . . . . φιλόφρων *(5391)*

(5390) **φιλοφρόνως**, adv., *with kindly feeling or manner, courteously,* Acts 28:7

(5391) **φιλόφρων**, ον [§7.G.a] (φίλος + φρήν) *kindly minded, benign, courteous,* 1 Pet. 3:8

φιλῶ, 1 pers. sg. pres. act. indic. {John 2:15, 16, 17} . . . . φιλέω *(5368)*

φιλῶ, 1 pers. sg. pres. act. subj. {Rev. 3:19}   id.

φιλῶν, nom. sg. m. pres. act. part. {John 12:25} . . . . id.

φίλων, gen. pl. m. adj. {John 15:13} . . . . . φίλος *(5384)*

φιμοῦν, pres. act. infin. . . . . φιμόω *(5392)*

(5392) **φιμόω**, ῶ, fut. φιμώσω, aor. ἐφίμωσα, perf. pass. πεφίμωμαι, aor. pass. ἐφιμώθην [§20.T; 21.U] (φιμός, *a muzzle*) *to muzzle,* 1 Cor. 9:9; 1 Tim. 5:18; met. and by impl. *to silence, put to silence;* pass. *to be silent, speechless,* Matt. 22:12, 34; Mark 1:25, et al.; trop. pass. *to be hushed,* as winds and waves, Mark 4:39

φιμώθητι, 2 pers. sg. aor. pass. imper. . . . φιμόω *(5392)*

φιμώσεις, 2 pers. sg. fut. act. indic. . . . . id.

Φλέγοντα, acc. sg. m. n. . . . . Φλέγων (5393)

(5393) **Φλέγων**, οντος, ὁ [§4.2.d] *Phlegon*, pr. name, Rom. 16:14

φλογά, acc. sg. f. n. . . . . φλόξ (5395)

φλογί, dat. sg. f. n. . . . . id.

φλογιζομένη, nom. sg. f. pres. pass. part. . . . . φλογίζω (5394)

φλογίζουσα, nom. sg. f. pres. act. part. . . . . id.

(5394) **φλογίζω**, fut. φλογίσω [§26.1] *to set in a flame, kindle, inflame*, James 3:6(2×)

φλογός, gen. sg. f. n. . . . . φλόξ (5395)

(5395) **φλόξ**, φλογός, ἡ, nom. sg. f. n. [§4.2.b] (φλέγω, *to burn, blaze*) *a flame*, Luke 16:24; Acts 7:30, et al.

(5396) **φλυαρέω**, ῶ, fut. φλυαρήσω [§16.P] *to talk folly*; in N.T. trans. *to prate about or against* any one, 3 John 10

φλύαροι, nom. pl. f. adj. . . . . φλύαρος (5397)

(5397) **φλύαρος**, ον (φλύω, *to boil over, bubble*; met. *to babble*) *a prater, tattler*, 1 Tim. 5:13

φλυαρῶν, nom. sg. m. pres. act. part. . . . . φλυαρέω (5396)

φοβεῖσθαι, pres. mid./pass. dep. infin. [§17.Q] . . . . φοβέω (5399)

φοβεῖσθε, 2 pers. pl. pres. mid./pass. dep. imper. . . . . id.

φοβερά, nom. sg. f. adj. . . . . φοβερός (5398)

φοβερόν, nom. sg. neut. adj. . . . . id.

(5398) **φοβερός**, ά, όν [§7.1] *fearful; terrible*, Heb. 10:27, 31; 12:21

(5399) **φοβέω**, ῶ, fut. φοβήσω [§16.P] *to terrify, frighten*; aor. mid. (pass. form) ἐφοβήθην, fut. φοβηθήσομαι, *to fear, dread*, Matt. 10:26; 14:5, et al.; *to fear reverentially, to reverence*, Mark 6:20; Luke 1:50; Acts 10:2; Eph. 5:33; Rev. 11:18, et al.; *to be afraid to do a thing*, Matt. 2:22; Mark 9:32, et al.; *to be reluctant, to scruple*, Matt. 1:20; *to fear, be apprehensive*, Acts 27:17; 2 Cor. 11:3; 12:20; *to be fearfully anxious*, Heb. 4:1; absol. *to be fearful, afraid, alarmed*, Matt. 14:27; 17:6, 7; Mark 16:8, et al.; *to be fearfully impressed*, Rom. 11:20

φοβῇ, 2 pers. sg. pres. mid./pass. dep. indic. . . . . φοβέω (5399)

φοβηθείς, nom. sg. m. aor. pass. dep. part. . id.

φοβηθεῖσα, nom. sg. f. aor. pass. dep. part. . id.

φοβηθέντες, nom. pl. m. aor. pass. dep. part. id.

φοβηθῇ, 3 pers. sg. aor. pass. dep. subj. . . . id.

φοβηθῇς, 2 pers. sg. aor. pass. dep. subj. . . . id.

φοβηθήσομαι, 1 pers. sg. fut. pass. dep. indic. id.

φοβηθῆτε, 2 pers. pl. aor. pass. dep. subj. {Luke 12:4, 5a} . . . . id.

φοβήθητε, 2 pers. pl. aor. pass. dep. imper. {Luke 12:5b,c} . . . . id.

φοβηθῶμεν, 1 pers. pl. aor. pass. dep. subj. . . . . φοβέω (5399)

φοβῆται, 3 pers. sg. pres. mid./pass. dep. subj. . . . . id.

φόβητρα, nom. pl. neut. n. . . . . φόβητρον (5400)

(5400) **φόβητρον**, ου, τό [§3.C.c] *something which inspires terror; terrific prodigy or portent*, Luke 21:11

φόβοι, nom. pl. m. n. . . . . φόβος (5401)

φόβον, acc. sg. m. n. . . . . id.

(5401) **φόβος**, ου, ὁ, nom. sg. m. n. [§3.C.a] (φέβομαι, *to be affrighted, to flee*) *fear, terror, affright*, Matt. 14:26; Luke 1:12; *astonishment, amazement*, Matt. 28:8; Mark 4:41; *trembling solicitude*, 1 Cor. 2:3; 2 Cor. 7:15; meton. *a terror, an object or cause of terror*, Rom. 13:3; *revererential fear, awe*, Acts 9:31; Rom. 3:18; *respect, deference*, Rom. 13:7; 1 Pet. 2:18

φόβου, gen. sg. m. n. {Luke 5:26} . . . . id.

φοβοῦ, 2 pers. sg. pres. mid./pass. dep. imper. {Luke 5:10} . . . . φοβέω (5399)

φοβοῦμαι, 1 pers. sg. pres. mid./pass. dep. indic. . . . . id.

φοβούμεθα, 1 pers. pl. pres. mid./pass. dep. indic. . . . . id.

φοβούμεναι, nom. pl. f. pres. mid./pass. dep. part. . . . . id.

φοβούμενοι, nom. pl. m. pres. mid./pass. dep. part. . . . . id.

φοβουμένοις, dat. pl. m. pres. mid./pass. dep. part. . . . . id.

φοβούμενος, nom. sg. m. pres. mid./pass. dep. part. . . . . id.

φόβῳ, dat. sg. m. n. . . . . φόβος (5401)

(5402) **Φοίβη**, ης, ἡ [§2.B.a] *Phoebe*, pr. name, Rom. 16:1

Φοίβην, acc. sg. f. n. . . . . Φοίβη (5402)

Φοίβης, gen. sg. f. n. (Rom. 16:27, TRs | GNT, WH, MT, TRb & NA omit) . . . . id.

Φοίνικα, acc. sg. m. n. . . . . Φοῖνιξ (5405)

φοίνικας, acc. pl. m. n. (Rev. 7:9, MT | φοίνικες, GNT, WH, TR & NA) . . . φοῖνιξ (†5404)

φοίνικες, nom. pl. m. n. (Rev. 7:9, GNT, WH, TR & NA | φοίνικας, MT) . . . . id.

(5403) **Φοινίκη**, ης, ἡ, *Phoenice, Phoenicia*, a country on the east of the Mediterranean, between Palestine and Syria, anciently celebrated for commerce, Acts 11:19; 15:3; 21:2

Φοινίκην, acc. sg. f. n. . . . . Φοινίκη (5403)

Φοινίκης, gen. sg. f. n. . . . . id.

φοινίκων, gen. pl. m. n. . . . . φοῖνιξ (†5404)

(†5404) **φοῖνιξ**, ικος, ὁ [§4.2.b] *the palm-tree, the date-palm, phoenix dactylifera* of Linn., John

12:13; Rev. 7:9

(5405) **Φοῖνιξ**, ικος, ὁ, *Phoenix, Phoenice*, a city, with a harbor, on the southeast coast of Crete

φονέα, acc. sg. m. n. . . . . φονεύς *(5406)*

φονεῖς, nom. pl. m. n. {Acts 7:52} . . . . . . id.

φονεῖς, acc. pl. m. n. {Matt. 22:7} . . . . . . id.

φονεύεις, 2 pers. sg. pres. act. indic. (James 2:11, GNT, WH & NA | φονεύσεις, MT & TR) . . . . φονεύω *(5407)*

φονεύετε, 2 pers. pl. pres. act. indic. . . . . . id.

(5406) **φονεύς**, έως, ὁ, nom. sg. m. n. [§5.E.d] *a homicide, murderer*, Matt. 22:7; Acts 3:14, et al.

φονευσάντων, gen. pl. m. aor. act. part. . . . . φονεύω *(5407)*

φονεύσεις, 2 pers. sg. fut. act. indic. . . . . . . id.

φονεύσῃ, 3 pers. sg. aor. act. subj. . . . . id.

φονεύσῃς, 2 pers. sg. aor. act. subj. . . . . id.

φονεῦσι(ν), dat. pl. m. n. . . . . φονεύς *(5406)*

(5407) **φονεύω**, fut. φονεύσω, aor. ἐφόνευσα [§13.M] *to put to death, kill, stay*, Matt. 23:31, 35, et al.; absol. *to commit murder*, Matt. 5:21, et al.

φόνοι, nom. pl. m. n. . . . . φόνος *(5408)*

φόνον, acc. sg. m. n. . . . . id.

(5408) **φόνος**, ου, ὁ [§3.C.a] *a killing, slaughter, murder*, Matt. 15:19; Mark 7:21; 15:7, et al.

φόνου, gen. sg. m. n. . . . . φόνος *(5408)*

φόνῳ, dat. sg. m. n. . . . . id.

φόνων, gen. pl. m. n. . . . . id.

φορεῖ, 3 pers. sg. pres. act. indic. . . . . . . φορέω *(5409)*

φορέσομεν, 1 pers. pl. fut. act. indic. (1 Cor. 15:49, GNT, TR & NA | φορέσωμεν, WH & MT) . . . . id.

φορέσωμεν, 1 pers. pl. aor. act. subj. (1 Cor. 15:49, WH & MT | φορέσομεν, GNT, TR & NA) . . . . id.

(5409) **φορέω**, ῶ, fut. φορήσω and φορέσω [§22.1] aor. ἐφόρεσα, *to bear; to wear*, Matt. 11:8; 1 Cor. 15:49, et al.

(5410) **Φόρον**, ου, τό (Latin, *forum*) *a forum, marketplace*; Φόρον Ἀππίου, *Forum Appii*, the name of a small town on the Appian way, according to Antoninus, forty-three Roman miles from Rome, or about forty English miles, Acts 28:15

φόρον, acc. sg. m. n. . . . . φόρος *(5411)*

(5411) **φόρος**, ου, ὁ [§3.C.a] *tribute, tax*, strictly such as is laid on dependent and subject people, Luke 20:22; 23:2; Rom. 13:6, 7

Φόρου, gen. sg. neut. n. . . . . Φόρον *(5410)*

φοροῦντα, acc. sg. m. pres. act. part. . . . . φορέω *(5409)*

φοροῦντες, nom. pl. m. pres. act. part. . . . . id.

φόρους, acc. pl. m. n. . . . . φόρος *(5411)*

φορτία, acc. pl. neut. n. . . . . φορτίον *(5413)*

φορτίζετε, 2 pers. pl. pres. act. indic. . . . φορτίζω *(5412)*

(5412) **φορτίζω**, fut. φορτίσω, perf. pass. πεφόρτισμαι [§26.1] (φόρτος, *a load*) *to load, lade, burden*; met. Matt. 11:28; Luke 11:46

φορτίοις, dat. pl. neut. n. . . . . φορτίον *(5413)*

(5413) **φορτίον**, ου, τό, nom. sg. neut. n. [§3.C.c] *a load, burden*; of a ship, *freight, cargo*, Acts 27:10; met. *a burden* of imposed precepts, etc., Matt. 23:4; Luke 11:46(2×); of faults, sins, etc., Gal. 6:5 {Matt. 11:30}

φορτίον, acc. sg. neut. n. {Gal. 6:5} . . . φορτίον *(5413)*

φορτίου, gen. sg. neut. n. (Acts 27:10, GNT, WH, MT & NA | φόρτου, TR) . . . . . . id.

(5414) **φόρτος**, ου, ὁ [§3.C.a] *a load, burden; freight, cargo*, Acts 27:10

φόρτου, gen. sg. m. n. (Acts 27:10, TR | φορτίου, GNT, WH, MT & NA) . . . φόρτος *(5414)*

φορῶν, nom. sg. m. pres. act. part. . . . . . φορέω *(5409)*

(5415) **Φορτουνάτος**, or Φουρτουνάτος, ου, ὁ, *Fortunatus*, pr. name

Φορτουνάτου, gen. sg. m. n. (1 Cor. 16:17, GNT, WH & NA | φουρτουνάτου, MT & TR) . . . . Φορτουνάτος *(5415)*

(5416) **φραγέλλιον**, ου, τό [§3.C.c] (Latin *flagellum*) *a whip, scourge*, John 2:15

φραγέλλιον, acc. sg. neut. n. . . . . . . φραγέλλιον *(5416)*

(5417) **φραγελλόω**, ῶ, fut. φραγελλώσω [§20.T] *to scourge*, Matt. 27:26; Mark 15:15

φραγελλώσας, nom. sg. m. aor. act. part. . . . . φραγελλόω *(5417)*

φραγῇ, 3 pers. sg. 2 aor. pass. subj. . . . φράσσω *(5420)*

φραγήσεται, 3 pers. sg. 2 fut. pass. indic. (2 Cor. 11:10, GNT, MT, TRb, WH & NA | σφραγίσεται, TRs) . . . . id.

φραγμόν, acc. sg. m. n. . . . . φραγμός *(5418)*

(5418) **φραγμός**, οῦ, ὁ [§3.C.a] *a fence, hedge; a hedgeside path*, Matt. 21:33; Mark 12:1; Luke 14:23; met. *a parting fence*, Eph. 2:14

φραγμοῦ, gen. sg. m. n. . . . . φραγμός *(5418)*

φραγμούς, acc. pl. m. n. . . . . id.

(5419) **φράζω**, fut. φράσω, aor. ἔφρασα [§26.1] pr. *to propound in distinct terms, to tell*; in N.T. *to explain, interpret, expound*, Matt. 13:36; 15:15

φράσον, 2 pers. sg. aor. act. imper. . . . . . φράζω *(5419)*

(5420) **φράσσω**, or φράττω, fut. φράξω, aor. ἔφραξα [§26.3] *to fence in*; by impl. *to obstruct, stop, close up*, Heb. 11:33; met. *to silence, put to silence*, Rom. 3:19; 2 Cor. 11:10

(5421) **φρέαρ**, φρέατος, τό, nom. sg. neut. n. [§4.2.c] *a well, cistern*, Luke 14:5; *a pit*, Rev. 9:1, 2 {John 4:11}

φρέαρ, acc. sg. neut. n. {John 4:12} . . . φρέαρ (5421)

φρέατος, gen. sg. neut. n. . . . . id.

φρεναπατᾷ, 3 pers. sg. pres. act.
  indic. . . . . φρεναπατάω (5422)

φρεναπάται, nom. pl. m. n. . . . . . φρεναπάτης (5423)·

(5422) **φρεναπατάω**, ῶ, fut. φρεναπατήσω [§18.R]
  (φρήν + ἀπατάω) *to deceive the mind; to
  deceive, impose on,* Gal. 6:3

(5423) **φρεναπάτης**, ου, ὁ [§2.B.c] *a deceiver, seducer,*
  Tit. 1:10

φρεσί(ν), dat. pl. f. n. . . . . φρήν (5424)

(5424) **φρήν**, ενός, ἡ [§4.2.e] pr. *the diaphragm, mid-
  riff; the mind, intellect,* 1 Cor. 14:20(2×)

φρίσσουσι(ν), 3 pers. pl. pres. act.
  indic. . . . . φρίσσω (5425)

(5425) **φρίσσω**, or φρίττω, fut. φρίξω, perf.
  πέφρικα, aor. ἔφριξα [§26.3] *to be ruffled,
  to bristle; to shiver, shudder* from fear,
  James 2:19

φρονεῖ, 3 pers. sg. pres. act. indic.
  {Rom. 14:6} . . . . φρονέω (5426)

φρόνει, 2 pers. sg. pres. act. imper. (Rom.
  11:20, GNT, WH & NA | ὑψηλοφρόνει,
  MT & TR) . . . . id.

φρονεῖν, pres. act. infin. . . . . id.

φρονεῖς, 2 pers. sg. pres. act. indic. . . . . . . id.

φρονείσθω, 3 pers. sg. pres. pass. imper. (Phil.
  2:5, MT & TR | φρονεῖτε, GNT, WH &
  NA) . . . . id.

φρονεῖτε, 2 pers. pl. pres. act. indic.
  {Phil. 3:15} . . . . id.

φρονεῖτε, 2 pers. pl. pres. act. imper.
  {Phil. 2:5} . . . . id.

(5426) **φρονέω**, ῶ, fut. φρονήσω, aor. ἐφρόνησα
  [§16.P] *to think, to mind; to be of opinion,* Acts 28:22; Phil. 1:7; *to take thought,
  be considerate,* Phil. 4:10; *to entertain sentiments or inclinations* of a specific kind,
  to be minded, Rom. 12:16; 15:5; 1 Cor.
  13:11; 2 Cor. 13:11; Gal. 5:10; Phil. 2:2;
  3:16; 4:2; *to be in a* certain *frame of mind,*
  Rom. 12:3; Phil. 2:5; *to imagine, entertain
  conceit,* 1 Cor. 4:6; *to heed, pay regard to,*
  Rom. 14:6; *to incline to, be set upon, mind,*
  Matt. 16:23; Mark 8:33; Rom. 8:5; Phil.
  3:15, 19; Col. 3:2

(5427) **φρόνημα**, ατος, τό, nom. sg. neut. n. [§4.D.c]
  frame of thought, will, mind, Rom. 8:6,
  7, 27

φρονήσει, dat. sg. f. n. . . . . φρόνησις (5428)

φρονήσετε, 2 pers. pl. fut. act. indic. . φρονέω (5426)

(5428) **φρόνησις**, εως, ἡ [§5.E.c] *a thoughtful frame,
  sense, rightmindedness,* Luke 1:17; *intelligence,* Eph. 1:8

φρονῆτε, 2 pers. pl. pres. act. subj. . . . φρονέω (5426)

φρόνιμοι, nom. pl. m. adj.
  {Matt. 10:16} . . . . φρόνιμος (5429)

φρόνιμοι, nom. pl. f. adj. {Matt. 25:2, 4, 9}   id.

φρονίμοις, dat. pl. m. adj. {1 Cor. 10:15} .   id.

φρονίμοις, dat. pl. f. adj. {Matt. 25:8} . . .   id.

(5429) **φρόνιμος**, η, ον, nom. sg. m. adj. [§7.F.a] *considerate, thoughtful, prudent, discreet,*
  Matt. 7:24; 10:16; 24:45, et al.; *sagacious,
  wise,* Rom. 11:25; 12:16; 1 Cor. 4:10;
  10:15; 2 Cor. 11:19

φρονίμῳ, dat. sg. m. adj. . . . . φρόνιμος (5429)

(5430) **φρονίμως**, adv., *considerately, providently,*
  Luke 16:8

φρονιμώτεροι, nom. pl. m. compar. adj.
  [§8.4] . . . . φρόνιμος (5429)

φρονοῦντες, nom. pl. m. pres. act.
  part. . . . . φρονέω (5426)

φρονοῦσιν, 3 pers. pl. pres. act. indic. . . . id.

(5431) **φροντίζω**, fut. φροντίσω, perf. πεφρόντικα,
  aor. ἐφρόντισα [§26.1] (φροντίς, *thought,
  care,* from φρονέω) *to be considerate, be
  careful,* Tit. 3:8

φροντίζωσι(ν), 3 pers. pl. pres. act.
  subj. . . . . φροντίζω (5431)

φρονῶμεν, 1 pers. pl. pres. act. subj. . φρονέω (5426)

φρονῶν, nom. sg. m. pres. act. part. . . . . . id.

(5432) **φρουρέω**, ῶ, fut. φρουρήσω [§16.P]
  (φρουρός, *a watcher, guard*) *to keep
  watch;* trans. *to guard, watch,* with a military guard, 2 Cor. 11:32; *to keep* in a condition of restraint, Gal. 3:23; *to keep* in a
  state of settlement or security, Phil. 4:7;
  1 Pet. 1:5

φρουρήσει, 3 pers. sg. fut. act. indic. φρουρέω (5432)

φρουρουμένους, acc. pl. m. pres. pass. part.
  [§17.Q] . . . . id.

(5433) **φρυάσσω**, fut. φρυάξω, aor. ἐφρύαξα [§26.3]
  in classical usage φρυάσσομαι, pr. *to snort,
  neigh, stamp,* etc.; as a high-spirited horse;
  hence, *to be noisy, fierce, insolent, and tumultuous, to rage, tumultuate,* Acts 4:25

(5434) **φρύγανον**, ου, τό [§3.C.c] (φρύγω, or
  φρύσσω, *to parch*) *a dry twig, branch,* etc.,
  faggot, Acts 28:3

φρυγάνων, gen. pl. neut. n. . . . . φρύγανον (5434)

(5435) **Φρυγία**, ας, ἡ [§2.B.b; 2.2] *Phrygia,* an inland
  province of Asia Minor

Φρυγίαν, acc. sg. f. n. . . . . Φρυγία (5435)

Φρυγίας, gen. sg. f. n. (1 Tim. 6:21, TRs |
  GNT, WH, MT, TRb & NA omit) . . .   id.

φυγεῖν, 2 aor. act. infin. [§24.9] . . . . . . φεύγω (5343)

(†5436) **Φύγελος**, ου, ὁ, nom. sg. m. n., *Phygellus,* pr.
  name (2 Tim. 1:15, GNT, WH, MT & NA
  | Φύγελλος, TR)

(5437) **φυγή**, ῆς, ἡ, nom. sg. f. n. [§2.B.a] *a fleeing,* *flight,* Matt. 24:20; Mark 13:18

φύγητε, 2 pers. pl. 2 aor. act. subj. .... φεύγω *(5343)*

φυέν, nom. sg. neut. 2 aor. pass. part.

    [§24.11] .... φύω *(5453)*

φυλαί, nom. pl. f. n. .... φυλή *(5443)*

φυλαῖς, dat. pl. f. n. .... id.

φυλακαῖς, dat. pl. f. n. .... φυλακή *(5438)*

φύλακας, acc. pl. m. n. {Acts 12:19} ... φύλαξ *(5441)*

φυλακάς, acc. pl. f. n. {Acts 22:4} ... φυλακή *(5438)*

φύλακες, nom. pl. m. n. .... φύλαξ *(5441)*

(5438) **φυλακή,** ῆς, ἡ, nom. sg. f. n. [§2.B.a] *a keeping watch, ward, guard,* Luke 2:8; *a place of watch, haunt,* Rev. 18:2; *a watch, guard, body of guards,* Acts 12:10; *ward, custody, imprisonment,* 2 Cor. 6:5; 11:23; Heb. 11:36; *durance,* 1 Pet. 3:19; *a place of custody, prison,* Matt. 14:10; 25:39, 44; *a watch or division,* of the night, which in the time of our Savior was divided into four watches of three hours each, called ὀψέ, μεσονύκτιον, ἀλεκτοροφωνία and πρωΐα, or πρωΐ, Matt. 14:25; 24:43; Mark 6:48; Luke 12:38(2×)

φυλακῇ, dat. sg. f. n. .... φυλακή *(5438)*

φυλακήν, acc. sg. f. n. .... id.

φυλακῆς, gen. sg. f. n. .... id.

(5439) **φυλακίζω,** fut. φυλακίσω [§26.1] *to deliver into custody, put in prison, imprison,* Acts 22:19

φυλακίζων, nom. sg. m. pres. act. part. .... φυλακίζω *(5439)*

φυλακτήρια, acc. pl. neut. n. ... φυλακτήριον *(5440)*

(5440) **φυλακτήριον,** ου, τό [§3.C.c] *the station of a guard or watch; a preservative, safeguard;* hence, *a phylactery or amulet,* worn about the person; from which circumstance the word is used in the N.T. as a term for the Jewish *Tephillin* or *prayer-fillets,* which took their rise from the injunction in Deut. 6:8; 11:18; Matt. 23:5

(5441) **φύλαξ,** ακος, ὁ [§4.2.b] *a watchman, guard, sentinel,* Acts 5:23; 12:6, 19

φυλάξαι, aor. act. infin. .... φυλάσσω *(5442)*

φυλάξατε, 2 pers. pl. aor. act. imper. .... id.

φυλάξει, 3 pers. sg. fut. act. indic. ...... id.

φυλάξῃ, 3 pers. sg. aor. act. subj. (John 12:47, GNT, WH & NA | πιστεύσῃ, MT & TR) .... id.

φυλάξῃς, 2 pers. sg. aor. act. subj. ...... id.

φύλαξον, 2 pers. sg. aor. act. imper. ..... id.

φυλάς, acc. pl. f. n. .... φυλή *(5443)*

φυλάσσειν, pres. act. infin. ... φυλάσσω *(5442)*

φυλάσσεσθαι, pres. mid. infin. .... id.

φυλάσσεσθε, 2 pers. pl. pres. mid. imper. . id.

φυλάσσῃ, 3 pers. sg. pres. act. subj. ..... id.

φυλασσόμενος, nom. sg. m. pres. pass. part. .... φυλάσσω *(5442)*

φυλάσσοντες, nom. pl. m. pres. act. part. id.

φυλάσσοντι, dat. sg. m. pres. act. part. ... id.

φυλάσσου, 2 pers. sg. pres. mid. imper. ... id.

φυλάσσουσιν, 3 pers. pl. pres. act. indic. . id.

(5442) **φυλάσσω,** or φυλάττω, fut. φυλάξω, aor. ἐφύλαξα [§26.3] *to be on watch, keep watch,* Luke 2:8; *to have in keeping,* Acts 22:20; *to have in custody,* Acts 28:16; *to keep* under restraint, *confine,* Luke 8:29; Acts 12:4; 23:35; *to guard, defend,* Luke 11:21; *to keep safe, preserve,* John 12:25; 17:12; 2 Thess. 3:3; 2 Pet. 2:5; Jude 24; *to keep* in abstinence, *debar,* Acts 21:25; 1 John 5:21; *to observe* a matter of injunction or duty, Matt. 19:20; Mark 10:20; Luke 11:28; 18:21; Acts 7:53; 16:4; 21:24, et al.; mid. *to be on one's guard, beware,* Luke 12:15; 2 Tim. 4:15; 2 Pet. 3:17

φυλάσσων, nom. sg. m. pres. act. part. .... φυλάσσω *(5442)*

(5443) **φυλή,** ῆς, ἡ [§2.B.a] *a tribe,* Matt. 19:28; 24:30; Luke 2:36; *a people, nation,* Rev. 1:7; 5:9, et al.

φυλήν, acc. sg. f. n. .... φυλή *(5443)*

φυλῆς, gen. sg. f. n. .... id.

φύλλα, nom. pl. neut. n. {Rev. 22:2} . φύλλον *(5444)*

φύλλα, acc. pl. neut. n. {Matt. 21:19} .... id.

(5444) **φύλλον,** ου, τό [§3.C.c] *a leaf,* Matt. 21:19, et al.

φυλῶν, gen. pl. f. n. .... φυλή *(5443)*

φύουσα, nom. sg. f. pres. act. part. ... φύω *(5453)*

(5445) **φύραμα,** ατος, τό, nom. sg. neut. n. [§4.D.c] (φυράω, *to mix, mingle by kneading,* etc.) *that which is mingled and reduced to a uniform consistence by kneading, beating, treading,* etc.; *a mass* of potter's clay, Rom. 9:21; of dough, 1 Cor. 5:6; Gal. 5:9; met. Rom. 11:16 {1 Cor. 5:7}

φύραμα, acc. sg. neut. n. {1 Cor. 5:6} φύραμα *(5445)*

φυράματος, gen. sg. neut. n. .... id.

φύσει, dat. sg. f. n. .... φύσις *(5449)*

φύσεως, gen. sg. f. n. .... id.

φυσικά, nom. pl. neut. adj. .... φυσικός *(5446)*

φυσικήν, acc. sg. f. adj. .... id.

(5446) **φυσικός,** ή, όν [§7.F.a] *natural, agreeable to nature,* Rom. 1:26, 27; *following the instinct of nature,* as animals, 2 Pet. 2:12

(5447) **φυσικῶς,** adv., *naturally, by natural instinct,* Jude 10

φύσιν, acc. sg. f. n. .... φύσις *(5449)*

φυσιοῖ, 3 pers. sg. pres. act. indic. .... φυσιόω *(5448)*

φυσιούμενος, nom. sg. m. pres. pass. part. id.

φυσιοῦσθε, an irreg. form for φυσιῶσθε, 2

pers. pl. pres. pass. subj. [§21.U] .. φυσιόω *(5448)*
φυσιοῦται, 3 pers. sg. pres. pass. indic. . . .   id.

(5448) **φυσιόω**, ῶ, fut. φυσιώσω [§20.T] perf. pass.
πεφυσίωμαι, used in N.T. as an equivalent
to φυσάω, *to inflate, puff up;* met. *to in-*
flate with pride and vanity, 1 Cor. 8:1; pass.
to be inflated with pride, *to be proud, vain,*
arrogant, 1 Cor. 4:6, 19; 5:2; 8:1; 13:4, et
al.

(5449) **φύσις**, εως, ἡ, nom. sg. f. n. [§5.E.c] *essence,*
Gal. 4:8; *native condition, birth,* Rom.
2:27; 11:21, 24; Gal. 2:15; Eph. 2:3; *na-*
tive species, kind, James 3:7; *nature, nat-*
ural frame, 2 Pet. 1:4; *nature, native*
instinct, Rom. 2:14; 1 Cor. 11:14; *nature,*
prescribed course of nature, Rom.1:26
φυσιώσεις, nom. pl. f. n. . . . . φυσίωσις *(5450)*

(5450) **φυσίωσις**, εως, ἡ [§5.E.c] pr. *inflation;* met.
inflation of mind, *pride,* 2 Cor. 12:20

(5451) **φυτεία**, ας, ἡ, nom. sg. f. n. [§2.B.b; 2.2] *plan-*
tation, the act of planting; a plant, met.
Matt. 15:13
φυτεύει, 3 pers. sg. pres. act. indic. . . . φυτεύω *(5452)*
φυτεύθητι, 2 pers. sg. aor. pass. imper. . . .   id.

(5452) **φυτεύω**, fut. φυτεύσω, aor. ἐφύτευσα [§13.M]
(φυτόν, *a plant,* from φύω) *to plant, set,*
Matt. 21:33; Luke 13:6, et al.; met. Matt.
15:13; *to plant* the Gospel, 1 Cor. 3:6, 7, 8
φυτεύων, nom. sg. m. pres. act. part. . φυτεύω *(5452)*

(5453) **φύω**, fut. φύσω, perf. πέφυκα [§13.M] 2 aor.
pass. ἐφύην [§24.11] *to generate, produce;*
pass. *to be generated, produced;* of plants,
to germinate, sprout, Luke 8:6; intrans. *to*
germinate, spring or grow up, Heb. 12: 15

(5454) **φωλεός**, οῦ, ὁ [§3.C.a] *a den, lair, burrow,*
Matt. 8:20; Luke 9:58
φωλεούς, acc. pl. m. n. . . . . φωλεός *(5454)*
φωναί, nom. pl. f. n. . . . . φωνή *(5456)*
φωναῖς, dat. pl. f. n. . . . .   id.
φωνάς, acc. pl. f. n. . . . .   id.
φωνεῖ, 3 pers. sg. pres. act. indic.
{Matt. 27:47} . . . . φωνέω *(5455)*
φώνει, 2 pers. sg. pres. act. imper.
{Luke 14:12} . . . .   id.
φωνεῖτε, 2 pers. pl. pres. act. indic. . . . . . .   id.

(5455) **φωνέω**, ῶ, fut. φωνήσω, aor. ἐφώνησα
[§16.P] *to sound, utter a sound;* of the
cock, *to crow,* Matt. 26:34, 74, 75; *to call,*
or cry out, exclaim, Luke 8:8, 54; 16:24;
23:46; *to call to,* Matt. 27:47; Mark 3:31,
et al.; *to call, entitle,* John 13:13; *to call,*
summon, Matt. 20:32, et al.; *to invite* to
a feast, Luke 14:12

(5456) **φωνή**, ῆς, ἡ, nom. sg. f. n. [§2.B.a] *a sound,*
Matt. 24:31; John 3:8; Rev. 4:5; 8:5; *a cry,*

Matt. 2:18; *an* articulate *sound, voice,*
Matt. 3:3, 17; 17:5; 27:46, 50; *voice,*
speech, discourse, John 10:16, 27; Acts
7:31; 12:22; 13:27; Heb. 3:7, 15; *tone of*
address, Gal. 4:20; *language, tongue, di-*
alect, 1 Cor. 14:10
φωνῇ, dat. sg. f. n. . . . . φωνή *(5456)*
φωνηθῆναι, aor. pass. infin. . . . . φωνέω *(5455)*
φωνήν, acc. sg. f. n. . . . . φωνή *(5456)*
φωνῆς, gen. sg. f. n. . . . .   id.
φωνῆσαι, aor. act. infin. . . . . φωνέω *(5455)*
φωνῆσαν, nom. sg. neut. aor. act. part. (Mark
1:26, GNT, WH & NA | κράξαν, MT &
TR) . . . .   id.
φωνήσαντες, nom. pl. m. aor. act. part. . . .   id.
φωνήσας, nom. sg. m. aor. act. part. . . . .   id.
φωνήσατε, 2 pers. pl. aor. act. imper. (Mark
10:49, GNT, WH & NA | φωνηθῆναι,
MT & TR) . . . .   id.
φωνήσει, 3 pers. sg. fut. act. indic. . . . . .   id.
φωνήσῃ, 3 pers. sg. aor. act. subj. (John 13:38,
GNT, WH, MT & NA | φωνήσει, TR)   id.
φώνησον, 2 pers. sg. aor. act. imper. . . . .   id.
φωνοῦντες, nom. pl. m. pres. act. part. (Mark
3:31, MT & TR | καλοῦντες, GNT, WH
& NA) . . . .   id.
φωνοῦσι(ν), 3 pers. pl. pres. act. indic. . . .   id.
φωνῶν, gen. pl. m. n. . . . . φωνή *(5456)*

(5457) **φῶς**, φωτός, τό, nom. sg. neut. n. [§4.2.c]
(contr. for φάος) *light,* Matt. 17:2; 2 Cor.
4:6; *daylight, broad day,* Matt. 10:27; Luke
12:3; *radiance, blaze of light,* Matt. 4:16;
Acts 9:3; 12:7, et al.; *an instrument or*
means of light, a light, Matt. 6:23; Acts
16:29; *a fire,* Mark 14:54; Luke 22:56;
from the Hebrew, *the light* of God's
presence, 2 Cor. 11:14; 1 Tim. 6:16; met.
the light of Divine truth, spiritual *illumi-*
nation, Luke 16:8; John 3:19; Rom. 13:12;
Eph. 5:8; 1 Pet. 2:9; 1 John 1:7; 2:8, 9, 10,
et al.; *a source or dispenser of* spiritual
light, Matt. 5:14; John 1:4, 5, 7, 8, 9; 8:12;
9:5, et al.; pure *radiance,* perfect *bright-*
ness, 1 John 1:5 {John 3:19a}
φῶς, acc. sg. neut. n. {John 3:19b, 20} . . . φῶς *(5457)*

(5458) **φωστήρ**, ῆρος, ὁ, nom. sg. m. n. [§4.2.f] *a*
cause of light, illuminator; a light, lumi-
nary, Phil. 2:15; *radiance,* or, *luminary,*
Rev. 21:11
φωστῆρες, nom. pl. m. n. . . . . φωστήρ *(5458)*

(5459) **φωσφόρος**, ον, nom. sg. m. adj. (φῶς +
φέρω) *light-bringing;* sc. ἀστήρ, *Lucifer,*
the morning star, met. 2 Pet. 1:19
φῶτα, acc. pl. neut. n. . . . . φῶς *(5457)*
φωτεινή, nom. sg. f. adj. (Matt. 17:5, GNT,

MT, TR & NA | φωτινή, WH) . φωτεινός *(5460)*
φωτεινόν, nom. sg. neut. adj. (Matt. 6:22;
    Luke 11:34, 36a,b, GNT, MT, TR & NA
    | φωτινόν, WH) . . . . id.
(5460) **φωτεινός**, ή, όν [§7.F.a] *radiant, lustrous,*
    Matt. 17:5; *enlightened, illuminated,* Matt.
    6:22; Luke 11:34, 36(2×)
φωτί, dat. sg. neut. n. . . . . φῶς *(5457)*
φωτιεῖ, 3 pers. sg. fut. act. indic. Attic [§35.11]
    (Rev. 22:5, MT | φωτίζει, TR | φωτίσει,
    GNT, WH & NA) . . . . φωτίζω *(5461)*
φωτίζει, 3 pers. sg. pres. act. indic. . . . . . . id.
φωτίζῃ, 3 pers. sg. pres. act. subj. . . . . id.
(5461) **φωτίζω**, fut. φωτίσω, aor. ἐφώτισα [§26.1] *to*
    light, give light to, illuminate, shine upon,
    Luke 11:36; Rev. 18:1; met. *to enlighten*
    spiritually, John 1:9; Eph. 1:18; 3:9; Heb.
    6:4; 10:32; *to reveal, to bring to light, make*
    known, 1 Cor. 4:5; 2 Tim. 1:10
φωτίσαι, aor. act. infin. . . . . φωτίζω *(5461)*
φωτίσαντος, gen. sg. m. aor. act. part. . . . id.
φωτίσει, 3 pers. sg. fut. act. indic. . . . . id.
φωτισθέντας, acc. pl. m. aor. pass. part. . id.
φωτισθέντες, nom. pl. m. aor. pass. part. . id.
φωτισμόν, acc. sg. m. n. . . . . φωτισμός *(5462)*
(5462) **φωτισμός**, οῦ, ὁ [§3.C.a] *illumination; a shin-*
    ing forth, effulgence, 2 Cor. 4:4, 6
φωτός, gen. sg. neut. n. . . . . φῶς *(5457)*
φώτων, gen. pl. neut. n. . . . . id.

Χ

χαῖρε, 2 pers. sg. pres. act. imper. . . . . . χαίρω *(5463)*
χαίρει, 3 pers. sg. pres. act. indic. . . . . id.
χαίρειν, pres. act. infin. . . . . id.
χαίρετε, 2 pers. pl. pres. act. imper. . . . . . id.
χαίρῃ, 3 pers. sg. pres. act. subj. . . . . id.
χαίρομεν, 1 pers. pl. pres. act. indic. . . . . id.
χαίροντες, nom. pl. m. pres. act. part. . . . id.
χαιρόντων, gen. pl. m. pres. act. part. . . . id.
χαίρουσιν, 3 pers. pl. pres. act. indic. (Rev.
    11:10, GNT, WH, MT & NA | χαροῦσιν,
    TR) . . . . id.
(5463) **χαίρω**, 1 pers. sg. pres. act. indic., fut.
    χαιρήσω, and, later, χαρήσομαι, 2 aor.
    ἐχάρην [§27.4.b] *to rejoice, be glad, be joy-*
    ful, be full of joy, Matt. 2:10; 5:12; 18:13;
    Mark 14:11; Rom. 12:12; 2 Cor. 2:3;
    imper. χαῖρε, χαίρετε, a term of salutation,
    Hail! Matt. 26:49; λέγω χαίρειν, *to greet,*
    2 John 10, 11; infin. χαίρειν, an epistolary
    forth, *Health!* Acts 15:23
χαίρωμεν, 1 pers. pl. pres. act. subj. . . . χαίρω *(5463)*

χαίρων, nom. sg. m. pres. act. part. . . . χαίρω *(5463)*
(5464) **χάλαζα**, ης, ἡ, nom. sg. f. n. [§2.3] *hail,* Rev.
    8:7; 11:19; 16:21(2×)
χαλάζης, gen. sg. f. n. . . . . χάλαζα *(5464)*
χαλάσαντες, nom. pl. m. aor. act.
    part. . . . . χαλάω *(5465)*
χαλασάντων, gen. pl. m. aor. act. part. . . id.
χαλάσατε, 2 pers. pl. aor. act. imper. . . . . id.
χαλάσω, 1 pers. sg. fut. act. indic. . . . . . . id.
(5465) **χαλάω**, ῶ, fut. χαλάσω [§22.2] aor. ἐχάλασα,
    to slacken; to let down, lower, Mark 2:4;
    Luke 5:4, et al.
(5466) **Χαλδαῖος**, ου, ὁ, *a Chaldean, a native of Chal-*
    dea, a country of central Asia, which seems
    to have included Mesopotamia, Acts 7:4
Χαλδαίων, gen. pl. m. n. . . . . Χαλδαῖος *(5466)*
χαλεποί, nom. pl. m. adj. . . . . χαλεπός *(5467)*
(5467) **χαλεπός**, ή, όν [§7.F.a] *hard, rugged; furious,*
    ferocious, Matt. 8:28; *trying,* 2 Tim. 3:1
(5468) **χαλιναγωγέω**, ῶ. fut. χαλιναγωγήσω [§16.P]
    (χαλινός + ἄγω) pr. *to guide with a bri-*
    dle; met. *to bridle, control, sway,* James
    1:26; 3:2
χαλιναγωγῆσαι, aor. act. infin. . χαλιναγωγέω *(5468)*
χαλιναγωγῶν, nom. sg. m. pres. act. part. id.
(5469) **χαλινός**, οῦ, ὁ [§3.C.a] *a bridle, bit, curb,*
    James 3:3; Rev. 14:20
χαλινούς, acc. pl. m. n. . . . . χαλινός *(5469)*
χαλινῶν, gen. pl. m. n. . . . . id.
χαλκᾶ, acc. pl. neut. adj. . . . . χάλκεος *(5470)*
(5470) **χάλκεος**, or χαλκοῦς, έα, εον, or ῆ, οῦν
    [§7.4.B] *brazen,* Rev. 9:20
(5471) **χαλκεύς**, έως, ὁ, nom. sg. m. n. [§5.E.d] pr.
    a coppersmith; hence, genr. *a worker in*
    metals, smith, 2 Tim. 4:14
(5472) **χαλκηδών**, όνος, ὁ, nom. sg. m. n. [§4.2.e]
    chalcedony, the name of a gem, generally
    of a whitish, bluish, or gray color, suscep-
    tible of a high and beautiful polish, and of
    which there are several varieties, as the
    onyx, modern carnelian, etc.
(5473) **χαλκίον**, ου, τό [§3.C.c] *a vessel, copper,*
    brazen utensil, Mark 7:4
χαλκίων, gen. pl. neut. n. . . . . χαλκίον *(5473)*
(5474) **χαλκολίβανον**, ου, τό [§3.C.c] *orichalcum,*
    fine bronze, a factitious metal of which
    there were several varieties, the white being
    of the highest repute, or, *deep-tinted frank-*
    incense, Rev. 1:15; 2:18
χαλκολιβάνῳ, dat. sg. neut. n. . χαλκολίβανον *(5474)*
χαλκόν, acc. sg. m. n. . . . . χαλκός *(5475)*
(5475) **χαλκός**, οῦ, ὁ, nom. sg. m. n. [§3.C.a] *copper,*
    also, *bronze,* Rev. 18:12; *a brazen musical in-*
    strument, 1 Cor. 13:1; *copper money,* Matt.
    10:9; *money* in general, Mark 6:8; 12:41

χαλκοῦ, gen. sg. m. n. . . . . χαλκός *(5475)*

χαλῶσι(ν), 3 pers. pl. pres. act. indic. . χαλάω *(5465)*

(5476) **χαμαί,** adv., *on the ground, to the earth,* John 9:6; 18:6

(5477) **Χαναάν,** ὁ, *Canaan,* the ancient name of Palestine (WH, MT & TR | Χανάαν, GNT & NA)

Χαναναία, nom. sg. f. adj. . . . . . . Χαναναῖος *(†5478)*

(†5478) **Χαναναῖος,** αία, αῖον [§7.1] *Canaanitish, of Canaan,* Matt. 15:22

(5479) **χαρά,** ῆς, ἡ, nom. sg. f. n. . [§2.B.b] *joy, gladness, rejoicing,* Matt. 2:10; 13:20, 44; 28:8, et al.; meton. *joy, cause of joy, occasion of rejoicing,* Luke 2:10; Phil. 4:1; 1 Thess. 2:19, 20; *bliss,* Matt. 25:21, 23

χαρᾷ, dat. sg. f. n. . . . . χαρά *(5479)*

(5480) **χάραγμα,** ατος, τό [§4.D.c] (χαράσσω, *to notch, engrave*) *an imprinted mark,* Rev. 13:16, et al.; *sculpture,* Acts 17:29

χάραγμα, acc. sg. neut. n. . . . . χάραγμα *(5480)*

χαράγματα, acc. pl. neut. n. (Rev. 13:16, MT | χάραγμα, GNT, WH, TR & NA) . . . id.

χαράγματι, dat. sg. neut. n. . . . . id.

χαράγματος, gen. sg. neut. n. (Rev. 15:2, TR | GNT, WH, MT & NA omit) . . . . . . id.

χάρακα, acc. sg. m. n. . . . . χάραξ *(5482)*

(5481) **χαρακτήρ,** ῆρος, ὁ, nom. sg. m. n. [§4.2.f] *a graver, graving-tool; an engraven or impressed device; an impress, exact expression,* Heb. 1:3

(5482) **χάραξ,** ακος, ὁ [§4.2.b] *a stake; a pale; a* military *palisade, rampart,* formed from the earth thrown out of the ditch, and stuck with sharp stakes or palisades, Luke 19:43

χαράν, acc. sg. f. n. . . . . χαρά *(5479)*

χαρᾶς, gen. sg. f. n. . . . . id.

χαρῆναι, 2 aor. pass. dep. infin. . . . . . . χαίρω *(5463)*

χαρήσεται, 3 pers. sg. 2 fut. pass. dep. indic. id.

χαρήσομαι, 1 pers. sg. 2 fut. pass. dep. indic. id.

χαρήσονται, 3 pers. pl. 2 fut. pass. dep. indic. id.

χάρητε, 2 pers. pl. 2 aor. pass. dep. imper. (Luke 6:23, GNT, WH, MT & NA | χαίρετε, TR) . . . . id.

χαρῆτε, 2 pers. pl. 2 aor. pass. dep. subj. {Phil. 2:28} . . . . id.

χαρίζεσθαι, pres. mid./pass. dep. infin. . . . . χαρίζομαι *(5483)*

χαρίζεσθε, 2 pers. pl. pres. mid./pass. dep. indic. . . . . id.

(5483) **χαρίζομαι,** fut. χαρίσομαι, aor. ἐχαρισάμην, fut. pass. χαρισθήσομαι, aor. pass. ἐχαρίσθην [§26.1] *to gratify; to bestow* in kindness, *grant* as a free favor, Luke 7:21; Rom. 8:32; *to grant the deliverance* of a person in favor to the desire of others, Acts

3:14; 27:24; Philemon 22; *to sacrifice* a person to the demands of enemies, Acts 25:11; *to remit, forgive,* Luke 7:42; 2 Cor. 2:7, 10

χαριζόμενοι, nom. pl. m. pres. mid./pass. dep. or pass. part. . . . . χαρίζομαι *(5483)*

χάριν, acc. sg. f. n. [§4.4] {Luke 1:30} . . χάρις *(5485)*

(5484) **χάριν,** adv., used as a particle or preposition governing the genitive case, *on account of,* Luke 7:47; Eph. 3:1, 14; 1 John 3:12; *for the sake of, in order to,* Gal. 3:19; Tit. 1:5, 11; Jude 16; *on the score of,* 1 Tim. 5:14; from the accusative of χάρις {Luke 7:47}

(5485) **χάρις,** ιτος, ἡ, nom. sg. f. n. [§4.2.c] *pleasing show, charm; beauty, gracefulness; a pleasing circumstance, matter of approval,* 1 Pet. 2:19, 20; *kindly bearing, graciousness,* Luke 4:22; *a beneficial opportunity, benefit,* 2 Cor. 1:15; Eph. 4:29; *a charitable act, generous gift,* 1 Cor. 16:3; 2 Cor. 8:4, 6, et al.; *an act of favor,* Acts 25:3; *favor, acceptance,* Luke 1:30, 52; Acts 2:47; 7:10, 46; *free favor, free gift, grace,* John 1:14, 16, 17; Rom. 4:4, 16; 11:5, 6; Eph. 2:5, 8; 1 Pet. 3:7; *free favor* specially manifested by God towards man in the Gospel scheme, *grace,* Acts 15:11; Rom. 3:24; 5:15, 17, 20, 21; 6:1; 2 Cor. 4:15, et al.; *a gracious provision, gracious scheme, grace,* Rom. 6:14, 15; Heb. 2:9; 12:28; 13:9; *gracious dealing* from God, *grace,* Acts 14:26; 15:40; Rom. 1:7; 1 Cor. 1:4; 15:10; Gal. 1:15, et al.; *a commission graciously devolved* by God upon a human agent, Rom. 1:5; 12:3; 15:15; 1 Cor. 3:10; 2 Cor. 1:12; Gal. 2:9; Eph. 3:8; *grace, graciously bestowed* divine *endowment or influence,* Luke 2:40; Acts 4:33; 11:23; Rom. 12:6; 2 Cor. 12:9, et al.; *grace, a graciously vouchsafed* spiritual *position,* Acts 11:23; Rom. 5:2; Gal. 5:4; 2 Pet. 3:18; *an emotion correspondent to what is pleasing or kindly; sense of obligation,* Luke 17:9; *a grateful frame of mind,* 1 Cor. 10:30; *thanks,* Luke 6:32, 33, 34; Rom. 6:17; 1 Cor. 15:57, et al.; χάριν or χάριτας καταθέσθαι, *to oblige, gratify,* Acts 24:27; 25:9

χαρισάμενος, nom. sg. m. aor. mid. dep. part. . . . . χαρίζομαι *(5483)*

χαρίσασθαι, aor. mid. dep. infin. . . . . id.

χαρίσασθε, 2 pers. pl. aor. mid. dep. imper. id.

χαρίσεται, 3 pers. sg. fut. mid. dep. indic. id.

χαρισθέντα, acc. pl. neut. aor. pass. part. . id.

χαρισθῆναι, aor. pass. infin. ...... χαρίζομαι *(5483)*
χαρισθήσομαι, 1 pers. sg. fut. pass. indic. ..... id.

(5486) **χάρισμα,** ατος, τό, nom. sg. neut. n. [§4.D.c]
    a free favor, free gift, Rom. 5:15, 16; 6:23;
    2 Cor. 1:11, et al.; *benefit,* Rom. 1:11; a di-
    vinely conferred *endowment,* 1 Cor. 12:4,
    9, 28, 30, 31, et al. {Rom. 5:15}
χάρισμα, acc. sg. neut. n.
    {Rom. 1:11} .... χάρισμα *(5486)*
χαρίσματα, nom. pl. neut. n. {Rom. 11:29} ..... id.
χαρίσματα, acc. pl. neut. n. {Rom. 12:6} . ..... id.
χαρίσματι, dat. sg. neut. n. .... id.
χαρίσματος, gen. sg. neut. n. .... id.
χαρισμάτων, gen. pl. neut. n. .... id.
χάριτα, acc. sg. f. n. .... χάρις *(5485)*
χάριτας, acc. pl. f. n. (Acts 24:27, MT & TR
    | χάριτα, GNT, WH & NA) .... id.
χάριτι, dat. sg. f. n. .... id.
χάριτος, gen. sg. f. n. .... id.

(5487) **χαριτόω,** ῶ, fut. χαριτώσω, perf. pass.
    κεχαρίτωμαι [§21.U] *to favor, visit with fa-*
    vor, to make an object of favor, to gift;
    pass. *to be visited with free favor, be an*
    object of gracious visitation, Luke 1:28
χαροῦσιν, 3 pers. pl. fut. act. indic. (Rev.
    11:10, TR | χαίρουσιν, GNT, WH, MT
    & NA) .... χαίρω *(5463)*

(5488) **Χαρράν,** ἡ, indecl. *Charran,* a city in the
    northern part of Mesopotamia, Acts 7:2, 4

(5489) **χάρτης,** ου, ὁ [§2.4] *paper,* 2 John 12
χάρτου, gen. sg. m. n. .... χάρτης *(5489)*

(5490) **χάσμα,** ατος, τό [§4.D.c] (χαίνω, to gape,
    yawn) a *chasm, gulf,* Luke 16:26
χάσμα, acc. sg. neut. n. .... χάσμα *(5490)*
χείλεσι(ν), dat. pl. neut. n. .... χεῖλος *(5491)*
χειλέων, gen. pl. neut. n. .... id.
χείλη, acc. pl. neut. n. .... id.

(5491) **χεῖλος,** ους, τό [§5.E.b] a *lip,* and pl. τὰ
    χείλη, *the lips,* Matt. 15:8; Rom. 3:13, et
    al.; trop. χεῖλος τῆς θαλάσσης, *the sea-*
    shore, Heb. 11:12; meton. *language, dia-*
    lect, 1 Cor. 14:21
χεῖλος, acc. sg. neut. n. .... χεῖλος *(5491)*
χειμαζομένων, gen. pl. m. pres. pass.
    part. .... χειμάζω *(5492)*

(5492) **χειμάζω,** fut. χειμάσω [§26.1] (χεῖμα, *a storm*)
    to excite a tempest, toss with a tempest;
    pass. *to be storm-tossed,* Acts 27:18

(5493) **χείμαρρος,** ου, ὁ [§3.C.a] (χεῖμα + ῥέω)
    winter-flowing; as a subst. *a stream which*
    flows in winter, but is dry in summer, *a*
    brook, John 18:1
χειμάρρου, gen. sg. m. n. .... χείμαρρος *(5493)*

(5494) **χειμών,** ῶνος, ὁ, nom. sg. m. n. [§4.2.e]
    (χεῖμα) *stormy weather,* Matt. 16:3; a

storm, tempest, Acts 27:20; *winter,* Matt.
    24:20, et al.
χειμῶνος, gen. sg. m. n. .... χειμών *(5494)*

(5495) **χείρ,** χειρός, ἡ, nom. sg. f. n. [§6.4.f] *a hand,*
    Matt. 3:12; 4:6; 8:15, et al. freq.; from the
    Hebrew, χεὶρ Κυρίου, a special *operation*
    of God, Acts 11:21; 13:3; ἐν χειρί, *by*
    agency, Acts 7:35; Gal. 3:19
χεῖρα, acc. sg. f. n. .... χείρ *(5495)*

(5496) **χειραγωγέω,** ῶ, fut. χειραγωγήσω [§16.P] *to*
    lead by the hand, Acts 9:8; 22:11

(5497) **χειραγωγός,** οῦ, ὁ [§3.C.a] (χείρ + ἀγωγός,
    a leader) *one who leads another by the*
    hand, Acts 13:11
χειραγωγούμενος, nom. sg. m. pres. pass.
    part. [§17.Q] .... χειραγωγέω *(5496)*
χειραγωγοῦντες, nom. pl. m. pres. act.
    part. .... id.
χειραγωγούς, acc. pl. m. n. ...... χειραγωγός *(5497)*
χεῖρας, acc. pl. f. n. .... χείρ *(5495)*
χεῖρες, nom. pl. f. n. .... id.
χειρί, dat. sg. f. n. .... id.

(5498) **χειρόγραφον,** ου, τό [§3.C.c] (χείρ + γράφω)
    handwriting; a written form, literal instru-
    ment, as distinguished from a spiritual dis-
    pensation, Col. 2:14
χειρόγραφον, acc. sg. neut. n. ... χειρόγραφον *(5498)*
χεῖρον, nom. sg. neut. adj.
    {Mark 2:21} .... χείρων *(5501)*
χεῖρον, acc. sg. neut. adj. {Mark 5:26} ... . id.
χείρονα, nom. pl. neut. adj. .... id.
χείρονος, gen. sg. f. adj. .... id.
χειροποίητα, acc. pl. neut. adj. . χειροποίητος *(5499)*
χειροποιήτοις, dat. pl. m. adj. .... id.
χειροποίητον, acc. sg. m. adj. .... id.

(5499) **χειροποίητος,** ον [§7.2] (χείρ + ποιητός,
    made, from ποιέω) *made by hand, artifi-*
    cial, material, Mark 14:58; Acts 7:48, et al.
χειροποιήτου, gen. sg. f. adj. ... χειροποίητος *(5499)*
χειρός, gen. sg. f. n. .... χείρ *(5495)*

(5500) **χειροτονέω,** ῶ, fut. χειροτονήσω [§16.P] (χείρ
    + τείνω) *to stretch out the hand; to con-*
    stitute by voting; to appoint, constitute,
    Acts 14:23; 2 Cor. 8:19
χειροτονηθείς, nom. sg. m. aor. pass. part.
    [§17.Q] .... χειροτονέω *(5500)*
χειροτονηθέντα, acc. sg. m. aor. pass. part.
    (2 Tim. 4:22, TRs | GNT, WH, MT, TRb
    & NA omit) .... id.
χειροτονήσαντες, nom. pl. m. aor. act. part. ..... id.
χειρῶν, gen. pl. f. n. {Matt. 4:6;
    1 Tim. 4:14} .... χείρ *(5495)*

(5501) **χείρων,** ον, nom. sg. m. adj. [§8.5] (irregular
    compar. of κακός) *worse,* Matt. 9:16;
    more severe, John 5:14; Heb. 10:29

{1 Tim. 5:8}

χείρων, nom. sg. f. adj. {Matt. 27:64} . χείρων (5501)

(†5502) **Χερουβείν, τά,** indecl. *cherubim* (Heb. 9:5, WH | Χερουβίμ, GNT, MT, TR & NA)

(†5502) **Χερουβίμ, τά** (Hebrew כְּרוּבִים) *cherubim,* the emblematic figures, representing cherubim, on the ark (Heb. 9:5, GNT, MT, TR & NA | Χερουβείν, WH)

χερσί(ν), dat. pl. f. n. [§6.4.f] . . . . χείρ (5495)

(5503) **χήρα, ας, ἡ,** nom. sg. f. n. [§2.B.b] (pr. f. of χῆρος, *bereft) a widow,* Matt. 23:14; Luke 4:26, et al.

χῆραι, nom. pl. f. n. . . . . χήρα (5503)

χήραις, dat. pl. f. n. . . . . id.

χήραν, acc. sg. f. n. . . . . id.

χήρας, acc. pl. f. n. . . . . id.

χηρῶν, gen. pl. f. n. . . . . id.

(5504) **χθές,** adv., *yesterday* (John 4:52; Acts 7:28; Heb. 13:8, MT & TR | ἐχθές, GNT, WH & NA)

χίλια, nom. pl. neut. numeral {Rev. 20:2, 4, 6} . . . . χίλιοι (5507)

χίλια, acc. pl. neut. numeral {Rev. 20:3, 5, 7} id.

χιλιάδες, nom. pl. f. n. . . . . χιλιάς (5505)

χιλιάδων, nom. pl. f. n. . . . . id.

χιλίαρχοι, nom. pl. m. n. . . . . . . χιλίαρχος (‡5506)

χιλιάρχοις, dat. pl. m. n. . . . . id.

χιλίαρχον, acc. sg. m. n. . . . . id.

(‡5506) **χιλίαρχος, ου, ὁ,** nom. sg. m. n. [§3.C.a] (χίλιοι + ἄρχω) *a chiliarch, commander of a thousand men;* hence, genr. *a commander, military chief,* Mark 6:21; Rev. 6:15; 19:18; spc. *a legionary tribune,* Acts 21:31, 32, 33, 37, et al.; *the prefect* of the temple, John 18:12

χιλιάρχῳ, dat. sg. m. n. . . . . χιλίαρχος (‡5506)

χιλιάρχων, gen. pl. m. n. . . . . id.

(5505) **χιλιάς, άδος, ἡ** [§4.2.c] the number *one thousand, a thousand,* Luke 14:31; Acts 4:4, et al.

χιλίας, acc. pl. f. numeral . . . . χίλιοι (5507)

χιλιάσιν, dat. pl. f. n. . . . . χιλιάς (5505)

(5507) **χίλιοι, αι, α,** numeral, *a thousand,* 2 Pet. 3:8; Rev. 11:3, et al.

χιλίων, gen. pl. m. numeral . . . . χίλιοι (5507)

(5508) **Χίος, ου, ἡ** [§3.C.b] *Chios,* an island near the coast of Asia Minor, in the Aegean sea, between Samos and Lesbos, Acts 20:15

Χίου, gen. sg. f. n. . . . . Χίος (5508)

(5509) **χιτών, ῶνος, ὁ,** nom. sg. m. n. [§4.2.e] *a tunic, vest,* the inner garment which fitted close to the body, having armholes, and sometimes sleeves, and reaching below the knees, Matt. 5:40; 10:10; pl. χιτῶνες, *clothes, garments* in general, Mark 14:63

χιτῶνα, acc. sg. m. n. . . . . χιτών (5509)

χιτῶνας, acc. pl. m. n. . . . . id.

(5510) **χιών, όνος, ἡ,** nom. sg. f. n. [§4.2.e] *snow,* Matt. 28:3; Mark 9:3; Rev. 1:14

χλαμύδα, acc. sg. f. n. . . . . χλαμύς (5511)

(5511) **χλαμύς, ύδος, ἡ** [§4.2.e] *chlamys,* a species of *cloak;* a Roman military commander's *cloak, paludamentum,* Matt. 27:28, 31

χλευάζοντες, nom. pl. m. pres. act. part. (Acts 2:13, MT & TR | διαχλευάζοντες, GNT, WH & NA) . . . . χλευάζω (5512)

(5512) **χλευάζω,** fut. χλευάσω, aor. ἐχλεύασα [§26.1] (χλεύη, *jest) to jeer, scoff,* Acts 2:13

(5513) **χλιαρός, ά, όν,** nom. sg. m. adj. [§7.1] (χλίω, *to become warm) warm, tepid; lukewarm,* Rev. 3:16

(5514) **Χλόη, ης, ἡ** [§2.B.a] *Chloe,* pr. name, 1 Cor. 1:11

Χλόης, gen. sg. f. n. . . . . Χλόη (5514)

χλωρόν, acc. sg. neut. adj. . . . . χλωρός (5515)

(5515) **χλωρός, ά, όν,** nom. sg. m. adj. [§7.1] (χλόη, *the first tender shoot of vegetation) pale green; green, verdant,* Mark 6:39; Rev. 8:7; 9:4; *pale, sallow,* Rev. 6:8

χλωρῷ, dat. sg. m. adj. . . . . χλωρός (5515)

(5516) **χξϛ′,** *six hundred and sixty-six,* the number denoted by these letters; viz., χ′ = 600, ξ′ = 60, ϛ′ = 6 (Rev. 13:18, MT & TR | ἑξακόσιοι ἑξήκοντα ἕξ, GNT, WH & NA)

χοϊκοί, nom. pl. m. adj. . . . . χοϊκός (5517)

(5517) **χοϊκός, ή, όν,** nom. sg. m. adj. [§7.F.a] *of earth, earthy,* 1 Cor. 15:47, 48, 49

χοϊκοῦ, gen. sg. m. adj. . . . . χοϊκός (5517)

χοίνικες, nom. pl. m. n. . . . . χοῖνιξ (5518)

(5518) **χοῖνιξ, ικος, ἡ,** nom. sg. m. n. [§4.2.b] *a choenix,* an Attic measure for things dry, being the 48th part of a medimnus, consequently equal to the 8th part of the Roman modius, and nearly equivalent to about one quart, being considered a sufficient daily allowance for the sustenance of one man, Rev. 6:6 (2×)

χοῖροι, nom. pl. m. n. . . . . χοῖρος (5519)

(5519) **χοῖρος, ου, ὁ, ἡ,** pr. *a young swine; a swine, hog, or sow,* Matt. 8:30, 31, 32, et al.

χοίρους, acc. pl. m. n. . . . . χοῖρος (5519)

χοίρων, gen. pl. m. n. . . . . id.

χολᾶτε, 2 pers. pl. pres. act. indic. . . . . χολάω (5520)

(5520) **χολάω, ῶ,** fut. χολάσω (χολή, considered as the seat or cause of anger and of melancholy) pr. *to be melancholy;* used later as an equivalent to χολοῦμαι, *to be angry, incensed,* John 7:23

(5521) **χολή, ῆς, ἡ** [§2.B.a] *the bile, gall;* in N.T. a

bitter ingredient, as *wormwood,* Matt. 27:34; χολὴ πικρίας, *intense bitterness,* met. *thorough disaffection* to divine truth, *utter estrangement,* Acts 8:23

χολήν, acc. sg. f. n. . . . . χολή *(5521)*
χολῆς, gen. sg. f. n. . . . . id.

(5522) **χόος**, or χοῦς, gen. χοός, dat. χοΐ, acc. χοῦν [§3.3] (χέω, *to pour) earth dug out and heaped up; loose earth, dirt, dust,* Mark 6:11; Rev. 18:19

(†5523) **Χοραζείν, ἡ,** indecl. *Chorazin* (Matt. 11:21; Luke 10:13, WH | Χοραζίν, Matt. 11:21, Luke 10:13, GNT, MT, TR & NA | Luke 10:13, Χωραζίν, TR)

(5523) **Χοραζίν, ἡ,** indecl. *Chorazin,* a town of Galilee, probably near Bethsaida and Capernaum

χορηγεῖ, 3 pers. sg. pres. act. indic. . . χορηγέω *(5524)*

(5524) **χορηγέω, ῶ,** fut. χορηγήσω [§16.P] (χορός + ἡγέομαι) *to lead a chorus;* at Athens, *to defray the cost of a chorus;* hence, *to supply funds; to supply, furnish,* 2 Cor. 9:10; 1 Pet. 4:11

χορηγῆσαι, 3 pers. sg. aor. act. opt. (2 Cor. 9:10, MT & TR | χορηγήσει, GNT, WH & NA) . . . . χορηγέω *(5524)*
χορηγήσει, 3 pers. sg. fut. act. indic. (2 Cor. 9:10, GNT, WH & NA | χορηγῆσαι, MT & TR) . . . . id.

(5525) **χορός, οῦ, ὁ** [§3.C.a] *dancing* with music, Luke 15:25

χορτάζεσθαι, pres. pass. infin. . . . . . χορτάζω *(5526)*
χορτάζεσθε, 2 pers. pl. pres. pass. imper. . id.

(5526) **χορτάζω,** fut. χορτάσω, aor. ἐχόρτασα [§26.1] pr. *to feed or fill with grass, herbage,* etc., *to fatten;* used of animals of prey, *to satiate, gorge,* Rev. 19:21; of persons, *to satisfy with food,* Matt. 14:20; 15:33, 37; met. *to satisfy* the desire of any one, Matt. 5:6, et al.

χορτάσαι, aor. act. infin. . . . . χορτάζω *(5526)*
χορτασθῆναι, aor. pass. infin. . . . . id.
χορτασθήσεσθε, 2 pers. pl. fut. pass. indic. id.
χορτασθήσονται, 3 pers. pl. fut. pass. indic. id.

(5527) **χόρτασμα, ατος, τό** [§4.D.c] *pasture, provender* for cattle; *food, provision, sustenance,* for men, Acts 7:11

χορτάσματα, acc. pl. neut. n. . . . . . χόρτασμα *(5527)*
χόρτον, acc. sg. m. n. . . . . χόρτος *(5528)*

(5528) **χόρτος, ου, ὁ,** nom. sg. m. n. [§3.C.a] *an enclosure; pasture-ground; fodder* for beasts; in N.T. *herbage, verdure,* Matt. 6:30; 14:19, et al.; *a plant* of corn, Matt. 13:26; Mark 4:28

χόρτου, gen. sg. m. n. . . . . χόρτος *(5528)*

χόρτους, acc. pl. m. n. (Matt. 14:19, MT & TR | χόρτου, GNT, WH & NA) . . χόρτος *(5528)*
χόρτῳ, dat. sg. m. n. . . . . id.
χορῶν, gen. pl. m. n. . . . . χορός *(5525)*
Χουζᾶ, gen. sg. m. n. . . . . Χουζᾶς *(5529)*

(5529) **Χουζᾶς, ᾶ, ὁ** [§2.4] *Chuzas, Chuza,* pr. name, Luke 8:3

χοῦν, acc. sg. m. n. . . . . χόος *(5522)*

(5530) **χράομαι, ῶμαι,** fut. χρήσομαι [§35.2] *to use, make use of, employ,* Acts 27:17; 1 Cor. 7:31, et al.; *to avail one's self of,* 1 Cor. 7:21; 9:12, 15; *to use, to treat, behave towards,* Acts 27:3; 2 Cor. 13:10

(5532) **χρεία, ας, ἡ,** nom. sg. f. n. [§2.B.b; 2.2] *use; need, necessity, requisiteness,* Eph. 4:29; Heb. 7:11; personal *need, an* individual *want,* Acts 20:34; Rom. 12:13; Phil. 2:25; 4:16, 19; χρείαν ἔχω, *to need, require, want,* Matt. 6:8; 14:16; Mark 2:25; John 2:25; ἐστὶ χρεία, *there is need,* Luke 10:42; τὰ πρὸς τὴν χρείαν, *necessary things,* Acts 28:10, et al.; *a necessary business, affair,* Acts 6:3

χρείαις, dat. pl. f. n. . . . . χρεία *(5532)*
χρείαν, acc. sg. f. n. . . . . id.
χρείας, gen. sg. f. n. {Acts 6:3} . . . . id.
χρείας, acc. pl. f. n. {Acts 28:10} . . . . id.
χρεοφειλέται, nom. pl. m. n. (Luke 7:41, GNT, WH & NA | χρεωφειλέται, MT & TR) . . . . χρεοφειλέτης *(†5533)*

(†5533) **χρεοφειλέτης, ου, ὁ,** *debtor*

χρεοφειλετῶν, gen. pl. m. n. (Luke 16:5, GNT, WH & NA | χρεωφειλετῶν, MT & TR) . . . . χρεοφειλέτης *(†5533)*
χρεωφειλέται, nom. pl. m. n. (Luke 7:41, MT & TR | χρεοφειλέται, GNT, WH & NA) . . . . χρεωφειλέτης *(5533)*

(5533) **χρεωφειλέτης, ου, ὁ** [§2.B.c] (χρέος, *a debt,* + ὀφειλέτης) *one who owes a debt, a debtor,* Luke 7:41; 16:5

χρεωφειλετῶν, gen. pl. m. n. (Luke 16:5, MT & TR | χρεοφειλετῶν, GNT, WH & NA) . . . . χρεωφειλέτης *(5533)*

(5534) **χρή,** impersonal verb, *there is need or occasion, it is necessary, it is requisite; it behoves, it becomes, it is proper,* James 3:10

χρῇζει, 3 pers. sg. pres. act. indic. . . . . . χρῄζω *(5535)*
χρῄζετε, 2 pers. pl. pres. act. indic. . . . . . id.
χρῄζῃ, 3 pers. sg. pres. act. subj. . . . . id.
χρῄζομεν, 1 pers. pl. pres. act. indic. . . . . id.

(5535) **χρῄζω** (χρεία) *to need, want, desire,* Matt. 6:32; Luke 11:8; 12:30; Rom. 16:2; 2 Cor. 3:1

(5536) **χρῆμα, ατος, τό** [§4.D.c] *anything useful, or needful;* pl. *wealth, riches,* Mark 10:23, 24;

Luke 18:24; *money*, Acts 8:18, 20; 24:26;
sg. *price*, Acts 4:37

χρῆμα, acc. sg. neut. n. . . . . χρῆμα *(5536)*

χρήμασιν, dat. pl. neut. n. (Mark 10:24, MT
& TR | GNT, WH & NA omit) . . . . id.

χρήματα, nom. pl. neut. n. {Acts 24:26} . id.

χρήματα, acc. pl. neut. n. {Acts 8:18} . . . id.

χρηματίζοντα, acc. sg. m. pres. act.
part. χρηματίζω *(5537)*

(5537) **χρηματίζω**, fut. χρηματίσω, aor. ἐχρημάτισα
[§26.1] *to have dealings, transact business;
to negotiate; to give answer on delibera-
tion;* in N.T. *to utter a divine communication,* Heb. 12:25; pass. *to be divinely
instructed, receive a revelation or warning
from God,* Matt. 2:12, 22; Luke 2:26; Acts
10:22; Heb. 8:5; 11:7; intrans. *to receive
an appellation, be styled,* Acts 11:26; Rom.
7:3

χρηματίσαι, aor. act. infin. . . . . . . χρηματίζω *(5537)*

χρηματίσει, 3 pers. sg. fut. act. indic. . . . . id.

χρηματισθείς, nom. sg. m. aor. pass. part. id.

χρηματισθέντες, nom. pl. m. aor. pass. part. id.

(5538) **χρηματισμός**, οῦ, ὁ, nom. sg. m. n. [§3.C.a]
in N.T. *a response from God, a divine communication, oracle,* Rom. 11:4

χρημάτων, gen. pl. neut. n. . . . . χρῆμα *(5536)*

χρῆσαι, 2 pers. sg. aor. mid. dep.
imper. χράομαι *(5530)*

χρησάμενος, nom. sg. m. aor. mid. dep. part. id.

χρῆσθ' (for χρηστά) acc. pl. neut. adj. (1 Cor.
15:33, TR | χρηστά, GNT, WH, MT &
NA) . . . . χρηστός *(5543)*

χρήσιμον, acc. sg. neut. adj. . . . . . . χρήσιμος *(5539)*

(5539) **χρήσιμος**, η, ον, or ον, *useful, profitable,*
2 Tim. 2:14

χρῆσιν, acc. sg. f. n. . . . . χρῆσις *(5540)*

(5540) **χρῆσις**, εως, ἡ [§5.E.c] *use, employment; manner of using,* Rom. 1:26, 27

χρῆσον, 2 pers. sg. aor. act. imper. . . κίχρημι *(‡5531)*

χρηστά, acc. pl. neut. adj. (1 Cor. 15:33, GNT,
WH, MT & NA | χρῆσθ', TR) . . χρηστός *(5543)*

χρηστεύεται, 3 pers. sg. pres. mid./pass. dep.
indic. χρηστεύομαι *(5541)*

(5541) **χρηστεύομαι**, fut. χρηστεύσομαι [§14.N] *to be
gentle, benign, kind,* 1 Cor. 13:4

χρηστοί, nom. pl. m. adj. . . . . χρηστός *(5543)*

(5542) **χρηστολογία**, ας, ἡ [§2.B.b; 2.2] (χρηστός +
λόγος) *bland address, fair speaking,* Rom.
16:18

χρηστολογίας, gen. sg. f. n. . . . . χρηστολογία *(5542)*

χρηστόν, nom. sg. neut. adj. . . . . . . χρηστός *(5543)*

(5543) **χρηστός**, ή, όν, nom. sg. m. adj. [§7.F.a]
useful, profitable; good, agreeable, Luke
5:39; *easy,* as a yoke, Matt. 11:30; *gentle, be-*

nign, kind, obliging, gracious, Luke 6:35;
Eph. 4:32; Rom. 2:4; 1 Pet. 2:3; *good* in
character, disposition, etc., *virtuous,* 1 Cor.
15:33

χρηστότερος, nom. sg. m. compar. adj. [§8.4]
(Luke 5:39, MT & TR | χρηστός, GNT,
WH & NA) . . . . χρηστός *(5543)*

(5544) **χρηστότης**, ητος, ἡ, nom. sg. f. n. [§4.2.c] pr.
utility; goodness, kindness, gentleness,
Rom. 2:4; 11:22, et al.; *kindness* shown,
beneficence, Eph. 2:7; *goodness, virtue,*
Rom. 3:12

χρηστότητα, acc. sg. f. n. . . . . . . χρηστότης *(5544)*

χρηστότητι, dat. sg. f. n. . . . . id.

χρηστότητος, gen. sg. f. n. . . . . id.

χρήσωμαι, 1 pers. sg. aor. mid. dep.
subj. . . . . χράομαι *(5530)*

χρῆται, 3 pers. sg. pres. mid./pass. dep. subj.
[§35.2] . . . . id.

χρίσας, nom. sg. m. aor. act. part. . . . . . χρίω *(5548)*

(5545) **χρῖσμα**, ατος, τό, nom. sg. neut. n. [§4.D.c]
pr. *anything which is applied by smearing;
ointment, unguent;* in N.T. *an anointing,
unction,* in the reception of spiritual privileges {1 John 2:27}

χρῖσμα, acc. sg. neut. n. {1 John 2:20} χρῖσμα *(5545)*

Χριστέ, voc. sg. m. n. . . . . Χριστός *(5547)*

Χιστιανόν, acc. sg. m. n. . . . . Χριστιανός *(5546)*

(5546) **Χριστιανός**, οῦ, ὁ, nom. sg. m. n. *a Christian,
follower of Christ,* Acts 11:26; 26:28; 1 Pet.
4:16

Χριστιανούς, acc. pl. m. n. . . . . . . Χριστιανός *(5546)*

Χριστόν, acc. sg. m. n. . . . . Χριστός *(5547)*

(5547) **Χριστός**, οῦ, ὁ, nom. sg. m. n. [§3.C.a] pr.
anointed; ὁ Χριστός, *the Christ, the
Anointed One,* i.q. Μεσσίας, *the Messiah,*
Matt. 1:16, 17; John 1:20, 25, 42, et al.
freq.; meton. *Christ, the word or doctrine
of Christ,* 2 Cor. 1:19, 21; Eph. 4:20;
Christ, a truly Christian frame of doctrine
and affection, Rom. 8:10; Gal. 4:19; *Christ,
the Church of Christ,* 1 Cor. 12:12; *Christ,
the* distinctive *privileges of the Gospel of
Christ,* Gal. 3:27; Phil. 3:8; Heb. 3:14

Χριστοῦ, gen. sg. m. n. . . . . Χριστός *(5547)*

Χριστῷ, dat. sg. m. n. . . . . id.

(5548) **χρίω**, fut. χρίσω, aor. ἔχρισα [§22.4] *to
anoint;* in N.T. *to anoint,* by way of insti-
tuting to a dignity, function, or privilege,
Luke 4:18; Acts 4:27; 10:38; 2 Cor. 1:21;
Heb. 1:9

χρονιεῖ, 3 pers. sg. fut. act. indic. Att. [§35.11]
(Heb. 10:37, MT & TR | χρονίσει, GNT,
WH & NA) . . . . χρονίζω *(5549)*

χρονίζει, 3 pers. sg. pres. act. indic. . . . . . id.

χρονίζειν, pres. act. infin. . . . . χρονίζω (5549)

χρονίζοντος, gen. sg. m. pres. act. part. . .   id.

(5549) **χρονίζω**, fut. χρονίσω, Att. χρονιῶ, aor. ἐχρόνισα [§26.1] *to while, spend time; to linger, delay, be long*, Matt. 24:48; 25:5; Luke 1:21; 12:45; Heb. 10:37

χρονίσει, 3 pers. sg. fut. act. indic. (Heb. 10:37, GNT, WH & NA | χρονιεῖ, MT & TR) . . . . χρονίζω (5549)

χρόνοις, dat. pl. m. n. . . . . χρόνος (5550)

χρόνον, acc. sg. m. n. . . . .   id.

(5550) **χρόνος**, ου, ὁ, nom. sg. m. n. [§3.C.a] *time, whether in respect of duration or a definite point of its lapse*, Matt. 2:7; 25:19, et al. freq.; *an epoch, era*, marked *duration*, Acts 1:7; 1 Thess. 5:1

(5551) **χρονοτριβέω**, ῶ, fut. χρονοτριβήσω [§16.P] (χρόνος + τρίβω) *to spend time, while away time, linger, delay*, Acts 20:16

χρονοτριβῆσαι, aor. act. infin. . . . χρονοτριβέω (5551)

χρόνου, gen. sg. m. n. . . . . χρόνος (5550)

χρόνους, acc. pl. m. n. . . . .   id.

χρόνῳ, dat. sg. m. n. . . . .   id.

χρόνων, gen. pl. m. n. . . . .   id.

χρυσᾶ, nom. pl. neut. adj. {2 Tim. 2:20} . . . . χρύσεος (5552)

χρυσᾶ, acc. pl. neut. adj. {Rev. 9:20} . . . .   id.

χρυσᾶν, acc. sg. f. adj. (Rev. 1:13, GNT, WH & NA | χρυσῆν, MT & TR) . . . .   id.

χρυσᾶς, acc. pl. f. adj. . . . .   id.

(5552) **χρύσεος**, η, ον, and contr. οῦς, ῆ, οῦν [§7.4.b] *golden, of gold*, 2 Tim. 2:20; Heb. 9:4, et al.

χρυσῆ, nom. sg. f. adj. . . . . χρύσεος (5552)

χρυσῆν, acc. sg. f. adj. (Rev. 1:13, MT & TR | χρυσᾶν, GNT, WH & NA) . . . .   id.

(5553) **χρυσίον**, ίου, τό nom. sg. neut. n. [§3.C.c] (dimin. from χρυσός) *gold*, Heb. 9:4; 1 Pet. 1:7; Rev. 21:18, 21; spc. *gold when coined or manufactured; golden ornaments*, 1 Pet. 3:3; *gold coin, money*, Acts 3:6; 20:33; 1 Pet. 1:18

χρυσίον, acc. sg. neut. n. {Rev. 3:18} . χρυσίον (5553)

χρυσίου, gen. sg. neut. n. . . . .   id.

χρυσίῳ, dat. sg. neut. n. . . . .   id.

χρυσίων, gen. pl. neut. n. . . . .   id.

(5554) **χρυσοδακτύλιος**, ον, nom. sg. m. adj. [§7.2] (χρυσός + δακτύλιος) *having rings of gold on the fingers*

χρυσοῖ, nom. pl. m. adj. (Rev. 9:7, MT | ὅμοιοι χρυσῷ, GNT, WH, TR & NA) . . . . χρύσεος (5552)

(5555) **χρυσόλιθος**, ου, ὁ, nom. sg. m. n. (χρυσός + λίθος) *chrysolite*, a name applied by the ancients to all gems of a gold color; spc.

the modern *topaz*, Rev. 21:20

χρυσόν, acc. sg. m. n. . . . . χρυσός (5557)

(5556) **χρυσόπρασος**, ου, ὁ, nom. sg. m. n. [§3.C.a] (χρυσός + πράσσω, *a leek*) *a chrsoprase, a species of gem of a golden green color like that of a leek*

(5557) **χρυσός**, οῦ, ὁ, nom. sg. m. n. [§3.C.a] *gold*, Matt. 2:11; 23:16, 17; meton. *gold ornaments*, 1 Tim. 2:9; *gold coin, money*, Matt. 10:9, et al.

χρυσοῦ, gen. sg. m. n. {Rev. 18:12} . . . χρυσός (5557)

χρυσοῦ, gen. sg. neut. adj. {Rev. 9:13} . . . . χρύσεος (5552)

χρυσοῦν, acc. sg. m. adj. {Rev. 8:3} . . . . .   id.

χρυσοῦν, acc. sg. neut. adj. {Rev. 17:4} . . .   id.

χρυσοῦς, acc. pl. m. adj. . . . .   id.

(5558) **χρυσόω**, ῶ, fut. χρυσώσω, perf. pass. κεχρύσωμαι [§21.U] *to gild, overlay with gold, adorn or deck with gold*, Rev. 17:4; 18:16

χρυσῷ, dat. sg. m. n. . . . . χρυσός (5557)

χρυσῶν, gen. pl. f. adj. . . . . χρύσεος (5552)

χρῶ, 2 pers. sg. pres. mid./pass. dep. imper. . . . . χράομαι (5530)

χρώμεθα, 1 pers. pl. pres. mid./pass. dep. indic. . . . .   id.

χρώμενοι, nom. pl. m. pres. mid./pass. dep. part. . . . .   id.

(5559) **χρώς**, χρωτός, ὁ [§4.2.c] *the skin; the body*; Acts 19:12

χρωτός, gen. sg. m. n. . . . . χρώς (5559)

χωλοί, nom. pl. m. adj. . . . . χωλός (5560)

χωλόν, acc. sg. m. adj. {Matt. 18:8} . . . . .   id.

χωλόν, nom. sg. neut. adj. {Heb. 12:13} . .   id.

(5560) **χωλός**, ή, όν, nom. sg. m. adj. [§7.F.a] *crippled in the feet, limping, halting, lame*, Matt. 11:5; 15:30, 31, et al.; met. *limping, weak*, spiritually, Heb. 12:13; *maimed, deprived of a foot*, for ἀναπηρός, Mark 9:45

χωλοῦ, gen. pl. m. adj. (Acts 3:11, TR | GNT, WH, MT & NA omit) . . . . χωλός (5560)

χωλούς, acc. pl. m. adj. . . . .   id.

χωλῶν, gen. pl. m. adj. . . . .   id.

(5561) **χώρα**, ας, ἡ, nom. sg. f. n. [§2.B.b] (χῶρος, idem.) *space, room; a country, region, tract, province*, Mark 5:10; Luke 2:8; *a district, territory, environs*, Matt. 8:28; meton. *the inhabitants of a country, region, etc.*, Mark 1:5; Acts 12:20; *the country*, as opposed to the city or town, Luke 21:21; *a field, farm*, Luke 12:16; John 4:35

χώρᾳ, dat. sg. f. n. . . . . χώρα (5561)

(‡5523) **Χωραζίν**, ἡ, indecl. name, *Chorazin* (Luke 10:13, TR | Χοραζίν, GNT, WH, MT & NA)

χώραις, dat. pl. f. n. . . . . χώρα *(5561)*
χώραν, acc. sg. f. n. . . . . id.
χώρας, gen. sg. f. n. {John 11:55} . . . . . . id.
χώρας, acc. pl. f. n. {John 4:35} . . . . id.
χωρεῖ, 3 pers. sg. pres. act. indic. . . . . . χωρέω *(5562)*
χωρεῖν, pres. act. infin. . . . . id.
χωρείτω, 3 pers. sg. pres. act. imper. . . . . id.
(5562) **χωρέω, ῶ,** fut. χωρήσω, aor. ἐχώρησα [§16.P]
to make room, either by motion or capac-
ity; *to move, pass,* Matt. 15:17; *to proceed,*
go on, 2 Pet. 3:9; *to progress, make way,*
John 8:37; trans. *to hold* as contents, *con-*
tain, afford room for, Mark 2:2; John 2:6;
21:25; met. *to give* mental *admittance to,*
to yield accordance, Matt. 19:11, 12; *to ad-*
mit to approbation and esteem, *to regard*
cordially, 2 Cor. 7:2
χωρῆσαι, aor. act. infin. . . . . χωρέω *(5562)*
χωρήσατε, 2 pers. pl. aor. act. imper. . . . . id.
χωρήσειν, fut. act. infin. (John 21:25, WH |
χωρῆσαι, GNT, MT, TR & NA) . . . . . id.
χωρία, nom. pl. neut. n. . . . . χωρίον *(5564)*
χωρίζεσθαι, pres. pass. infin. . . . . χωρίζω *(5563)*
χωρίζέσθω, 3 pers. sg. pres. pass. imper. . id.
χωρίζεται, 3 pers. sg. pres. mid. indic. . . id.
χωρίζέτω, 3 pers. sg. pres. act. imper. . . . id.
(5563) **χωρίζω,** fut. χωρίσω, aor. ἐχώρισα [§26.1] *to*
sunder, sever, disunite, Matt. 19:6; Rom.
8:35, 39; aor. mid. (pass. form) ἐχωρί-
σθην, perf. κεχώρισμαι, *to dissociate one's*
self, to part, 1 Cor. 7:10, 11, 15; *to with-*
draw, depart, Acts 1:4; 18:1, 2; Philemon
15; *to be aloof,* Heb. 7:26
(5564) **χωρίον, ου, τό** [§3.C.c] (pr. dimin. of χῶρος)
a place, spot; Matt. 26:36; Mark 14:32; *a*
field, farm, estate, domain, John 4:5; Acts
1:18, et al.
χωρίον, acc. sg. neut. n. . . . . χωρίον *(5564)*
χωρίου, gen. sg. neut. n. . . . . id.
(5565) **χωρίς,** adv., *apart,* John 20:7; *apart from,*
parted from, John 15:5; James 2:18,
20, 26; *alien from,* Eph. 2:12; *apart from,*
on a distinct footing from, 1 Cor. 11:11;
apart from, distinct from, without the
intervention of, Rom. 3:21, 28; 4:6; *apart*
from the company of, *independently of,*
1 Cor. 4:8; Heb. 11:40; *without* the
presence of, Heb. 9:28; *without* the agency
of, John 1:3; Rom. 10:14; *without* the employment of, Matt. 13:34; Mark 4:34;
Heb. 7:20, 21; 9:7, 18, 22; *without,* Luke
6:49; Phil. 2:14; 1 Tim. 2:8; 5:21; Philemon 14; Heb. 10:28; 11:6; 12:8, 14; *clear*
from, Heb. 7:7; *irrespectively of,* Rom.
7:8, 9; *without reckoning, besides,* Matt.

14:21; 15:38; 2 Cor. 11:28; *with the excep-*
tion of, Heb. 4:15
χωρίσαι, aor. act. infin. . . . . χωρίζω *(5563)*
χωρίσει, 3 pers. sg. fut. act. indic. . . . . . . id.
χωρισθείς, nom. sg. m. aor. pass. part. (mid.
signif.) . . . . id.
χωρισθῇ, 3 pers. sg. aor. pass. indic. (mid. signif.) id.
χωρισθῆναι, aor. pass. infin. (mid. signif.) id.
χωρίων, gen. pl. neut. n. . . . . χωρίον *(5564)*
χῶρον, acc. sg. m. n. . . . . χῶρος *(5566)*
(5566) **χῶρος, ου, ὁ** [§3.C.a] *Corus,* or *Caurus, the*
northwest wind; meton. *the northwest*
quarter of the heavens, Acts 27:12
χωροῦσαι, nom. pl. f. pres. act. part. . . χωρέω *(5562)*
χωροῦσι(ν), 3 pers. pl. pres. act. indic. . . . id.

Ψ

ψαλλέτω, 3 pers. sg. pres. act. imper. . ψάλλω *(5567)*
ψάλλοντες, nom. pl. m. pres. act. part. . . id.
(5567) **ψάλλω,** fut. ψαλῶ, aor. ἔψηλα [§27.1.b,ε]
(ψάω, *to touch*) *to move by a touch, to*
twitch; to touch, strike the strings or chords
of an instrument; absol. *to play on a*
stringed instrument; to sing to music; in
N.T. *to sing praises,* Rom. 15:9; 1 Cor.
14:15; Eph. 5:19; James 5:13
ψαλμοῖς, dat. pl. m. n. . . . . ψαλμός *(5568)*
ψαλμόν, acc. sg. m. n. . . . . id.
(5568) **ψαλμός, οῦ, ὁ** [§3.C.a] *impulse, touch,* of the
chords of a stringed instrument; in N.T. *a*
sacred song, psalm, 1 Cor. 14:26; Eph.
5:19, et al.
ψαλμῷ, dat. sg. m. n. . . . . ψαλμός *(5568)*
ψαλμῶν, gen. pl. m. n. . . . . id.
ψαλῶ, 1 pers. sg. fut. act. indic. . . . . . ψάλλω *(5567)*
ψευδαδέλφοις, dat. pl. m. n. . . . ψευδάδελφος *(5569)*
(5569) **ψευδάδελφος, ου, ὁ** [§3.C.a] (ψευδής +
ἀδελφός) *a false brother, a pretended*
Christian, 2 Cor. 11:26; Gal. 2:4
ψευδαδέλφους, acc. pl. m. n. . . . ψευδάδελφος *(5569)*
ψευδαπόστολοι, nom. pl.
m. n. . . . . ψευδαπόστολος *(5570)*
(5570) **ψευδαπόστολος, ου, ὁ** (ψευδής + ἀπόστολος) *a false apostle, pretended minister of*
Christ, 2 Cor. 11:13
ψεύδει, dat. sg. neut. n. . . . . ψεῦδος *(5579)*
ψευδεῖς, acc. pl. m. adj. . . . . ψευδής *(5571)*
ψεύδεσθε, 2 pers. pl. pres. mid./pass. dep.
imper. ψεύδω (‡5574)
ψευδέσι(ν), dat. pl. m. adj. . . . . ψευδής *(5571)*
(5571) **ψευδής, ές** [§7.G.b] *false, lying,* Acts 6:13; Rev.
2:2; in N.T. pl. *maintainers of* religious

falsehood, corrupters of the truth of God, Rev. 21:8

ψευδοδιδάσκαλοι, nom. pl.
m. n. .... ψευδοδιδάσκαλος (5572)

(5572) ψευδοδιδάσκαλος, ου, ὁ (ψευδής + διδάσκαλος) a false teacher, one who inculcates false doctrines, 2 Pet. 2:1

(5573) ψευδολόγος, ον [§7.2] (ψευδής + λέγω) false-speaking, 1 Tim. 4:2

ψευδολόγων, gen. pl. m. adj. .... ψευδολόγος (5573)

(5574) ψεύδομαι, 1 pers. sg. pres. mid./pass. dep.
indic. .... ψεύδω (‡5574)

(5576) ψευδομαρτυρέω, ῶ, fut. ψευδομαρτυρήσω [§16.P] to bear false witness, give false testimony, Matt. 19:18; Mark 14:56, 57, et al.

ψευδομαρτυρήσεις, 2 pers. sg. fut. act.
indic. .... ψευδομαρτυρέω (5576)
ψευδομαρτυρήσῃς, 2 pers. sg. aor. act. subj.   id.

(5577) ψευδομαρτυρία, ας, ἡ [§2.B.b; 2.2] false witness, false testimony, Matt. 15:19; 26:59

ψευδομαρτυρίαι, nom. pl. f. n. ψευδομαρτυρία (5577)
ψευδομαρτυρίαν, acc. sg. f. n. .... id.
ψευδομαρτύρων, gen. pl. m. n. ψευδόμαρτυς (†5575)

(†5575) ψευδόμαρτυς, υρος, ὁ [§4.2.f] (ψευδής + μάρτυς) a false witness, Matt. 26:60(2×); 1 Cor. 15:15

ψευδομάρτυρες, nom. pl. m. n. ψευδόμαρτυς (†5575)
ψευδόμεθα, 1 pers. pl. pres. mid./pass.
indic. .... ψεύδω (‡5574)
ψευδόμενοι, nom. pl. m. pres. mid./pass.
part. .... id.
ψεύδονται, 3 pers. pl. pres. mid./pass. indic.   id.
ψευδοπροφῆται, nom. pl. m. n. ψευδοπροφήτης (5578)
ψευδοπροφήταις, dat. pl. m. n. .... id.
ψευδοπροφήτην, acc. sg. m. n. .... id.

(5578) ψευδοπροφήτης, ου, ὁ, nom. sg. m. n. [§2.B.c] (ψευδής + προφήτης) a false prophet, one who falsely claims to speak by divine inspiration, whether as a foreteller of future events, or as a teacher of doctrines, Matt. 7:15; 24:24, et al.

ψευδοπροφήτου, gen. sg. m. n. ψευδοπροφήτης (5578)
ψευδοπροφητῶν, gen. pl. m. n. .... id.

(5579) ψεῦδος, ους, τό, nom. sg. neut. n. [§5.E.b] falsehood, John 8:44; Eph. 4:25; 2 Thess. 2:9, 11; 1 John 2:27; in N.T. religious falsehood, perversion of religious truth, false religion, Rom. 1:25; the practices of false religion, Rev. 21:27; 22:15 {Rev. 14:5}

ψεῦδος, acc. sg. neut. n. {Rev. 22:15} . ψεῦδος (5579)
ψεύδους, gen. sg. neut. n. .... id.
ψευδόχριστοι, nom. pl. m. n. .. ψευδόχριστος (5580)

(5580) ψευδόχριστος, ου, ὁ [§3.C.a] (ψευδής +

χριστός) a false Christ, pretended Messiah, Matt. 24:24; Mark 13:22

(‡5574) ψεύδω, fut. ψεύσω [§23.1.c] to deceive; mid. to speak falsely or deceitfully, utter falsehood, lie, Matt. 5:11; Rom. 9:1, et al.; trans. to deceive, or attempt to deceive, by a lie, Acts 5:3

(5581) ψευδώνυμος, ον [§7.2] (ψευδής + ὄνομα) falsely named, falsely called, 1 Tim. 6:20

ψευδωνύμου, gen. sg. f. adj. .... ψευδώνυμος (5581)
ψεύσασθαι, aor. mid. dep. infin. ..... ψεύδω (‡5574)

(5582) ψεῦσμα, ατος, τό [§4.D.c] a falsehood, lie; in N.T. delinquency, Rom. 3:7

ψεύσματι, dat. sg. neut. n. .... ψεῦσμα (5582)
ψεῦσται, nom. pl. m. n. .... ψεύστης (5583)
ψεύσταις, dat. pl. m. n. .... id.
ψεύστην, acc. sg. m. n. .... id.

(5583) ψεύστης, ου, ὁ, nom. sg. m. n. [§2.B.c] one who utters a falsehood, a liar, John 8:44, 55, et al.; in N.T. a delinquent, Rom. 3:4

(5584) ψηλαφάω, ῶ, fut. ψηλαφήσω, aor. ἐψηλάφησα [§18.R] to feel, handle Luke 24:39; to feel or grope for or after, as persons in the dark, Acts 17:27

ψηλαφήσατε, 2 pers. pl. aor. act.
imper. .... ψηλαφάω (5584)
ψηλαφήσειαν, 3 pers. pl. aor. act. opt. Oeol.
[§13.11 note] .... id.
ψηλαφωμένῳ, dat. sg. neut. pres. pass. part.   id.
ψηφίζει, 3 pers. sg. pres. act. indic. ... ψηφίζω (5585)

(5585) ψηφίζω, fut. ψηφίσω [§26.1] to reckon by means of pebbles, compute by counters; hence genr. to compute, reckon, calculate, Luke 14:28; Rev. 13:18

ψηφισάτω, 3 pers. sg. aor. act. imper. . ψηφίζω (5585)
ψῆφον, acc. sg. f. n. .... ψῆφος (5586)

(5586) ψῆφος, ου, ἡ [§3.C.b] a small stone, pebble; a pebble variously employed, especially in a ballot; hence, a vote, suffrage, Acts 26:10; a pebble or stone; probably given as a token, Rev. 2:17(2×)

ψιθυρισμοί, nom. pl. m. n. ...... ψιθυρισμός (5587)

(5587) ψιθυρισμός, οῦ, ὁ (ψιθυρίζω, to whisper) a whispering; a calumnious whispering, detraction, 2 Cor. 12:20

ψιθυριστάς, acc. pl. m. n. .... ψιθυριστής (5588)

(5588) ψιθυριστής, οῦ, ὁ [§2.B.c] (ψιθυρίζω) a whisperer; a calumnious whisperer, detractor, Rom. 1:29

(5589) ψιχίον, ου, τό [§3.C.c] (dimin. of ψίξ, a fragment, morsel) a morsel, crumb, bit, Matt. 15:27; Mark 7:28; Luke 16:21

ψιχίων, gen. pl. neut. n. .... ψιχίον (5589)
ψυγήσεται, 3 pers. sg. 2 fut. pass. indic.

[§24.8.c] . . . . ψύχω *(5594)*

ψυχαί, nom. pl. f. n. . . . . ψυχή *(5590)*

ψυχαῖς, dat. pl. f. n. . . . . id.

ψυχάς, acc. pl. f. n. . . . . id.

ψύχει, dat. sg. neut. n. . . . . ψῦχος *(5592)*

(5590) **ψυχή**, ῆς, ἡ, nom. sg. f. n. [§2.B.a] *breath; the principle of animal life; the life,* Matt. 2:20; 6:25; Mark 3:4; Luke 21:19; John 10:11, et al.; *an inanimate being,* 1 Cor. 15:45; *a* human *individual, soul,* Acts 2:41; 3:23; 7:14; 27:37; Rom. 13:1; 1 Pet. 3:20; *the* immaterial *soul,* Matt. 10:28; 1 Pet. 1:9; 2:11, 25; 4:19, et al.; *the soul* as the seat of religious and moral sentiment, Matt. 11:29; Acts 14:2, 22; 15:24; Eph. 6:6, et al.; *the soul,* as a seat of feeling, Matt. 12:18; 26:38, et al.; *the soul, the inner self,* Luke 12:19 {Luke 12:23}

ψυχή, voc. sg. f. n. {Luke 12:19} . . . . ψυχή *(5590)*

ψυχῇ, dat. sg. f. n. . . . . id.

ψυχήν, acc. sg. f. n. . . . . id.

ψυχῆς, gen. sg. f. n. . . . . id.

ψυχική, nom. sg. f. adj. . . . . ψυχικός *(5591)*

ψυχικοί, nom. pl. m. adj. . . . . id.

ψυχικόν, nom. sg. neut. adj. . . . . id.

(5591) **ψυχικός**, ή, όν, nom. sg. m. adj. [§7.F.a] *pertaining to the life or the soul;* in N.T. *animal,* as distinguished from spiritual subsistence, 1 Cor. 15:44, 46; *occupied with mere animal things, animal, sensual,* 1 Cor. 2:14; James 3:15; Jude 19

(5592) **ψῦχος**, ους, τό, nom. sg. neut. n. [§5.E.b] *cold,* 2 Cor. 11:27 {John 18:18}

ψῦχος, acc. sg. neut. n. {Acts 28:2} . . . ψῦχος *(5592)*

(5593) **ψυχρός**, ά, όν, nom. sg. m. adj. [§7.1] *cool, cold,* Matt. 10:42; met. Rev. 3:15, 16

ψυχροῦ, gen. sg. neut. adj. . . . . ψυχρός *(5593)*

(5594) **ψύχω**, fut. ψύξω, 2 aor. pass. ἐψύγην, 2 fut. ψυγήσομαι [§24.8.c] *to breathe; to cool;* pass. *to be cooled;* met. of affection, Matt. 24:12

ψυχῶν, gen. pl. f. n. . . . . ψυχή *(5590)*

ψώμιζε, 2 pers. sg. pres. act. imper. . . ψωμίζω *(5595)*

(5595) **ψωμίζω**, fut. ψωμίσω [§26.1] (ψωμός, *a bit, morsel*) pr. *to feed by morsels;* hence, genr. *to feed, supply with food,* Rom. 12:20; *to bestow in supplying food,* 1 Cor. 13:3

(5596) **ψωμίον**, ου, τό [§3.C.c] (dimin. of ψωμός, from. ψάω, *to break into bits*) *a bit, morsel, mouthful,* John 13:26, 27, 30

ψωμίον, acc. sg. neut. n. . . . . ψωμίον *(5596)*

ψωμίσω, 1 pers. sg. aor. act. subj. . . . ψωμίζω *(5595)*

ψώχοντες, nom. pl. m. pres. act. part. . ψώχω *(5597)*

(5597) **ψώχω**, fut. ψώξω [§23.1.b] (ψάω) *to rub in pieces,* as the ears of grain

Ω

(5598) **Ω, ω**, *Omega,* the last letter of the Greek alphabet, hence, met. τὸ Ω, *the last,* Rev. 1:8, 11; 21:6; {Rev. 22:13}

(5599) **ὦ**, interjection *O!* {Matt. 15:28}

(5600) **ὦ**, 1 pers. sg. pres. subj. {John 9:5} . . . . . . εἰμί *(1510)*

ᾧ, dat. sg. m. relative pron. {Acts 10:6} . . . . ὅς *(3739)*

ᾧ, dat. sg. neut. relative pron. {Acts 10:12} id.

(5601) **Ὠβήδ**, ὁ, *Obed,* pr. name indecl. (Matt. 1:5; Luke 3:32, MT & TR | Ἰωβήδ, GNT & NA | Luke 3:32, Ὠβήλ, WH)

ᾠδαῖς, dat. pl. f. n. . . . . ᾠδή *(5603)*

(5602) **ὧδε**, adv., *thus; here, in this place,* Matt. 12:6, 41; ὧδε ἤ ὧδε, *here or there,* Matt. 24:23; τὰ ὧδε, *the state of things here,* Col. 4:9; met. *herein, in this thing,* Rev. 13:10, 18; *hither, to this place,* Matt. 8:29; 14:18, et al.

(5603) **ᾠδή**, ῆς, ἡ [§2.B.a] (contr. for ἀοιδή, from ἀείδω) *an ode, song, hymn,* Eph. 5:19; Col. 3:16; Rev. 5:9; 14:3; 15:3

ᾠδήν, acc. sg. f. n. . . . . ᾠδή *(5603)*

(5604) **ὠδίν**, ῖνος, ἡ, nom. sg. f. n. (pr. ὠδίς, ῖνος, ἡ,) *the throe,* of a woman in travail, *a birth-pang,* 1 Thess. 5:3; pl. met. *birth-throes, preliminary troubles* to the development of a catastrophe, Matt. 24:8; Mark 13:9; from the Hebrew, *a stringent band, a snare, noose,* Acts 2:24

ὠδῖνας, acc. pl. f. n. . . . . ὠδίν *(5604)*

ὠδίνουσα, nom. sg. f. pres. act. part. . . ὠδίνω *(5605)*

(5605) **ὠδίνω**, 1 pers. sg. pres. act. indic., fut. ὠδινῶ [§27.1.a] *to be in travail,* Gal. 4:27; Rev. 12:2; met. *to travail with, to make effort to bring to* spiritual *birth,* Gal. 4:19

ὠδίνων, gen. pl. f. n. . . . . ὠδίν *(5604)*

ᾠκοδομήθη, 3 pers. sg. aor. pass. indic. [§13.2] (John 2:20, MT & TR | οἰκοδομήθη, GNT, WH & NA) . . . οἰκοδομέω *(3618)*

ᾠκοδόμησε(ν), 3 pers. sg. aor. act. indic. . id.

ᾠκοδόμητο, 3 pers. sg. pluperf. pass. indic. id.

ᾠκοδόμουν, 3 pers. pl. imperf. act. indic. . id.

ὦμεν, 1 pers. pl. pres. subj. . . . . εἰμί *(1510)*

ὡμίλει, 3 pers. sg. imperf. act. indic. [§13.2] . . . . ὁμιλέω *(3656)*

ὡμίλουν, 3 pers. pl. imperf. act. indic. . . . id.

ὡμοιώθη, 3 pers. sg. aor. pass. indic. . ὁμοιόω *(3666)*

ὡμοιώθημεν, 1 pers. pl. aor. pass. indic. . . id.

ὡμολόγησας, 2 pers. sg. aor. act. indic. . . . . ὁμολογέω *(3670)*

ὡμολόγησε(ν), 3 pers. sg. aor. act. indic. . id.

ὡμολόγουν, 3 pers. pl. imperf. act. indic. . id.

(5606) **ὦμος**, ου, ὁ [§3.C.a] *the shoulder,* Matt.

23:4; Luke 15:5

ὤμοσα, 1 pers. sg. aor. act. indic. ..... ὀμνύω (3660)

ὤμοσε(ν), 3 pers. sg. aor. act. indic. ..... id.

ὤμους, acc. pl. m. n. .... ὦμος (5606)

(5607) ὤν, nom. sg. m. pres. part. {Heb. 5:8a} .. εἰμί (1510)

ὤν, gen. pl. m. relative pronoun
{Heb. 5:8b} .... ὅς (3739)

ὤν, gen. pl. f. relative pronoun {Acts 9:36} id.

ὤν, gen. pl. neut. relative pronoun
{Acts 22:10} .... id.

ὠνείδιζον, 3 pers. pl. imperf. act.
indic. .... ὀνειδίζω (3679)

ὠνείδισε(ν), 3 pers. sg. aor. act. indic. ... id.

(5608) ὠνέομαι, οῦμαι, fut. ὠνήσομαι, aor.
ὠνησάμην [§17.Q] to buy, purchase, Acts
7:16

ὠνήσατο, 3 pers. sg. aor. mid. dep.
indic. .... ὠνέομαι (5608)

ὠνόμασε(ν), 3 pers. sg. aor. act.
indic. .... ὀνομάζω (3687)

ὠνομάσθη, 3 pers. sg. aor. pass. indic. ... id.

(5609) ὠόν, οῦ, τό [§3.C.c] an egg, Luke 11:12

ὠόν, acc. sg. neut. n. .... ὠόν (5609)

(5610) ὥρα, ας, ἡ, nom. sg. f. n. [§2.B.b] a limited
portion of time, marked out by part of a
settled routine or train of circumstances;
a season of the year; time of day, Matt.
14:15; Mark 6:35; 11:11; an hour, Matt.
20:3; John 11:9, et al.; in N.T. an eventful
season, 1 John 2:18 (2×); Rev. 3:10; 14:7;
due time, John 16:21; Rom. 13:11; a destined period, hour, Matt. 26:45; Mark
14:35; John 2:4; 7:30, et al.; a short period, Matt. 26:40; John 5:35; 2 Cor. 7:8;
Gal. 2:5; 1 Thess. 2:17; Philemon 15; a
point of time, time, Matt. 8:13; 24:42;
Luke 2:38, et al.

ὥρᾳ, dat. sg. f. n. .... ὥρα (5610)

ὧραι, nom. pl. f. n. .... id.

ὡραίᾳ, dat. sg. f. adj. .... ὡραῖος (5611)

ὡραίαν, acc. sg. f. adj. .... id.

ὡραῖοι, nom. pl. m. adj. .... id.

(5611) ὡραῖος, α, ον [§7.1] timely, seasonable; in
prime, blooming; in N.T. beautiful, Matt.
23:27; Acts 3:2, 10; Rom. 10:15

ὥραν, acc. sg. f. n. .... ὥρα (5610)

ὥρας, gen. sg. f. n. {Acts 23:23} .... id.

ὥρας, acc. pl. f. n. {Acts 19:34} .... id.

ὠργίσθη, 3 pers. sg. aor. pass. indic. ... ὀργίζω (3710)

ὠργίσθησαν, 3 pers. pl. aor. pass. indic. .. id.

ὤρθριζε(ν), 3 pers. sg. imperf. act.
indic. .... ὀρθρίζω (3719)

ὥρισαν, 3 pers. pl. aor. act. indic. ..... ὁρίζω (3724)

ὥρισε(ν), 3 pers. sg. aor. act. indic. ...... id.

ὡρισμένῃ, dat. sg. f. perf. pass. part. .... id.

ὡρισμένον, acc. sg. neut. perf. pass. part. ὁρίζω (3724)

ὡρισμένος, nom. sg. m. perf. pass. part. . id.

ὥρμησαν, 3 pers. pl. aor. act. indic. ... ὁρμάω (3729)

ὥρμησε(ν), 3 pers. sg. aor. act. indic. .... id.

ὤρυξεν, 3 pers. sg. aor. act. indic. ... ὀρύσσω (3736)

(5612) ὠρύομαι, fut. ὠρύσομαι [§14.N] to howl; to
roar, as a lion, 1 Pet. 5:8

ὠρυόμενος, nom. sg. m. pres. mid./pass. dep.
part. .... ὠρύομαι (5612)

ὠρχήσασθε, 2 pers. pl. aor. mid. dep.
indic. .... ὀρχέομαι (3738)

ὠρχήσατο, 3 pers. sg. aor. mid. dep. indic. id.

ὠρῶν, gen. pl. f. n. .... ὥρα (5610)

(5613) ὡς, adv., as, correlatively, Mark 4:26; John
7:46; Rom. 5:15, et al.; as, like as, Matt.
10:16; Eph. 5:8, et al.; according as, Gal.
6:10, et al.; as, as it were, Rev. 8:8, et al.;
as, Luke 16:1; Acts 3:12, et al.; before numerals, about, Mark 5:13, et al.; conj. that,
Acts 10:28, et al.; how, Rom. 11:2, et al.;
when, Matt. 28:9; Phil. 2:23; as an exclam-
atory particle, how, Rom. 10:15; equivalent
to ὥστε, accordingly, Heb. 3:11; also, on
condition that, provided that, Acts 20:24;
ὡς εἰπεῖν, so to speak, Heb. 7:9

(5614) ὡσαννά (Hebrew הוֹשִׁיעָה־נָּא) Hosanna! save
now, succor now, Matt. 21:9, 15, et al.

(5615) ὡσαύτως, adv. (ὡς + αὕτως, αὐτός) just so,
in just the same way or manner, likewise,
Matt. 20:5; 21:30, et al.

(5616) ὡσεί, adv. (ὡς + εἰ) as if; as it were, as, like,
Matt. 3:16; 9:36, et al.; with terms of number or quantity, about, Matt. 14:21; Luke
1:56; 22:41, 59

(5617) Ὡσηέ, ὁ, Osee, Hosea, pr. name, indecl.
(Rom. 9:25, GNT, MT, TRb, WH & NA
| Ὡσηέ, TRs)

ὦσι(ν), 3 pers. pl. pres. subj. {Mark 3:14} εἰμί (1510)

ὠσί(ν), dat. pl. neut. n. [§4.3.b] {Matt.
13:15} .... οὖς (3775)

(5618) ὥσπερ, adv. (ὡς + περ) just as, as, like as,
Matt. 6:2; 24:38; 1 Thess. 5:3, et al.

(5619) ὡσπερεί, adv. (ὥσφερ + εἰ) just as if; as it
were, 1 Cor. 15:8

(5620) ὥστε, conj. (ὡς + τε) so that, so as that, so
as to, Matt. 8:24; Mark 2:12; Acts 14:1;
Gal. 2:13; as an illative particle, therefore,
consequently, Matt. 12:12; 23:31, et al.; in
N.T. as a particle of design, in order that,
in order to, Luke 9:52

ὦτα, nom. pl. neut. n. {Matt. 13:16} ..... οὖς (3775)

ὦτα, acc. pl. neut. n. {Matt. 13:43} ..... id.

(†5621) ὠτάριον, ου, τό (dimin. of ὠτίον) an ear,
Matt. 14:47

ὠτάριον, acc. sg. neut. n. .... ὠτάριον (†5621)

(5621) ὠτίον, ου, τό, in N.T. simply equivalent to οὖς, *an ear,* Matt. 26:51; Mark 14:47; Luke 22:51; John 18:10, 26

ὠτίον, acc. sg. neut. n. . . . . ὠτίον *(5621)*

ὠτίου, gen. sg. neut. n. . . . . id.

ὤφειλε(ν), 3 pers. sg. imperf. act.
indic. . . . . ὀφείλω *(3784)*

ὠφείλετε, 2 pers. pl. imperf. act. indic. (1 Cor. 5:10, GNT, WH & NA | ὀφείλετε, MT & TR) . . . . id.

ὠφείλομεν, 1 pers. pl. imperf. act. indic. . id.

ὤφειλον, 1 pers. sg. imperf. act. indic. . . . id.

ὠφελεῖ, 3 pers. sg. pres. act. indic. . . . ὠφελέω *(5623)*

(5622) ὠφέλεια, ας, ἡ, nom. sg. f. n. [§2.B.b; 2.2] *help; profit, gain, advantage, benefit,* Rom. 3:1; Jude 16

ὠφελείας, gen. sg. f. n. . . . . ὠφέλεια *(5622)*

ὠφελεῖται, 3 pers. sg. pres. pass.
indic. . . . . ὠφελέω *(5623)*

ὠφελεῖτε, 2 pers. pl. pres. act. indic. . . . . . id.

(5623) ὠφελέω, ῶ, ὠφελήσω, aor. ὠφέλησα [§16.P]

to help, profit, benefit, Matt. 27:24; Mark 7:11; Rom. 2:25, et al.

ὠφεληθεῖσα, nom. sg. f. aor. pass.
part. . . . . ὠφελέω *(5623)*

ὠφεληθῇς, 2 pers. sg. aor. pass. subj. . . . . id.

ὠφελήθησαν, 3 pers. pl. aor. pass. indic. . id.

ὠφεληθήσεται, 3 pers. sg. fut. pass. indic. (Matt. 16:26, GNT, WH & NA | ὠφελεῖται, MT & TR) . . . . id.

ὠφελήσει, 3 pers. sg. fut. act. indic. . . . . . id.

ὠφέλησεν, 3 pers. sg. aor. act. indic. . . . . . id.

ὠφελήσω, 1 pers. sg. fut. act. indic. . . . . . id.

ὠφέλιμα, nom. pl. neut. adj. . . . . . . ὠφέλιμος *(5624)*

(5624) ὠφέλιμος, ον, nom. sg. m. adj. [§7.2] *profitable, useful, beneficial; serviceable,* 1 Tim. 4:8(2×); 2 Tim. 3:16; Tit. 3:8

ὠφελοῦμαι, 1 pers. sg. pres. pass.
indic. . . . . ὠφελέω *(5623)*

ὤφθη, 3 pers. sg. aor. pass. indic. . . . . . . ὁράω *(3708)*

ὤφθην, 1 pers. sg. aor. pass. indic. [§36.1] . . id.

ὤφθησαν, 3 pers. pl. aor. pass. indic. . . . . id.

APPENDIX: CROSS-REFERENCE LIST
OF STRONG'S VARIANTS

The following is a cross-reference listing of lexical entries which can be found in their proper alphabetical order in the lexicon but are out of numerical sequence because they are variant spellings or variant forms of the Strong's number cited. This list makes it possible to locate these forms by number within the main body of the work.

(‡1) Ἄλφα, between (255) and (256)
(‡3) Ἀββαδών, between (5) and (6)
(‡30) ἄγγος, between (32) and (33)
(‡86) Ἅιδης, between (125) and (126)
(‡90) ἀφθορία, between (862) and (863)
(‡127) δέος, between (1189) and (1190)
(‡138) αἱρέω, between (141) and (142)
(‡157) αἰτίωμα, between (159) and (160)
(‡196) ἀκριβής, between (197) and (198)
(‡217) ἄλα, between (210) and (211)
(‡294) ἀμφιάζω, between (292) and 293
(‡303) ἀναμέσον, between (362) and (363)
(‡376) ἀνάπειρος, between (374) and (375)
(‡448) ἀνέλεος, between (415) and (416)
(‡450) ἀναπηδάω, between (375) and (376)
(‡473) ἀνθ', between (435) and (436)
(‡508) ἀνάγαιον, between (311) and (312)
(‡617) ἀνακυλίω, between (351) and (352)
(‡621) ἐπιλείχω, between (1952) and (1953)
(‡643) ἐπισκευάζομαι, between (1980) and (1981)
(‡650) ἀφυστερέω, between (879) and (880)
(‡681) περιάπτω, between (4014) and (4015)
(‡689) Ἀδμίν, between (95) and (96)
(‡693) ἀργυροῦς, between (696) and (697)
(‡697) πάγος, between (3803) and (3804)
(‡717) Μαγεδών, between (3094) and (3095)
(‡729) ἄραφος, between (689) and (690)
(‡730) ἄρσην, between (733) and (734)
(‡760) Ἀσάφ, between (761) and (762)
(‡782) ἀπασπάζομαι, between (537) and (538)
(‡821) ἀτιμάω, between (818) and (819)
(‡881) Ἄχας, between (884) and (885)
(‡885) Ἀχίμ, between (886) and (887)
(‡906) ἀμφιβάλλω, between (292) and (293)
(‡916) καταβαρύνω, between (2599) and (2600)
(‡920) βάρ, between (911) and (912)

(‡987) δυσφημέω, between (1425) and (1426)
(‡1003) Βοές, between (994) and (995)
(‡1007) Βεώρ, between (961) and (962)
(‡1011) βουλεύομαι, between (1009) and (1010)
(‡1046) Γερασηνός, between (1085) and (1086)
(‡1081) γένημα, between (1079) and (1080)
(‡1125) ἐνγράφω, between (1728) and (1729)
(‡1125) καταγράφω, between (2608) and (2609)
(‡1138) Δαυίδ, between (1160) and (1161)
(‡1155) δανίζω, between (1157) and (1158)
(‡1157) δανιστής, between (1158) and (1159)
(‡1163) δέον, between (1189) and (1190)
(‡1174) δεισιδαίμων, between (1175) and (1176)
(‡1349) καταδίκη, between (2613) and (2614)
(‡1486) εἴωθα, between (1536) and (1537)
(‡1492) οἶδα, between (3608) and (3609)
(‡1494) ἱερόθυτος, between (2410) and (2411)
(‡1495) εἰδωλολατρία, between (1496) and (1497)
(‡1503) ἔοικα, between (1857) and (1858)
(‡1530) ἐκπηδάω, between (1600) and (1601)
(‡1534) εἶτεν, between (1535) and (1536)
(‡1536) εἴ, between (1487) and (1488)
(‡1545) ἐκβαίνω, between (1543) and (1544)
(‡1573) ἐγκακέω, between (1457) and (1458)
(‡1573) ἐνκακέω, between (1765) and (1766)
(‡1650) ἐλεγμός, between (1648) and (1649)
(‡1653) ἐλεάω, between (1648) and (1649)
(‡1714) ἐμπί(μ)πρημι, between (1705) and (1706)
(‡1739) ἐνδώμησις, between (1746) and (1747)
(‡1752) εἴκενεν, between (1511) and (1512)
(‡1760) διενθυμέομαι, between (1326) and (1327)
(‡1766) ἔνατος, between (1728) and (1729)
(‡1768) ἐνενήκοντα, between (1752) and (1753)
(‡1769) ἐνεός, between (1752) and (1753)
(‡1831) διεξέρχομαι, between (1326) and (1327)
(‡1856) ἐκσῴζω, between (1612) and (1613)

(‡1888)	αὐτόφωρος, between (848) and (849)
(‡1902)	ἐπενδύω, between (1903) and (1904)
(‡1904)	ἐπεισέρχομαι, between (1898) and (1899)
(‡1944)	ἐπάρατος, between (1883) and (1884)
(‡1966)	ἔπειμι, between (1896) and (1897)
(‡1976)	ἐπιρράπτω, between (1977) and (1978)
(‡1999)	ἐπίστασις, between (1987) and (1988)
(‡2027)	ἐπικέλλω, between (1945) and (1946)
(‡2045)	ἐραυνάω, between (2037) and (2038)
(‡2095)	εὖγε, between (2103) and (2104)
(‡2127)	κατευλογέω, between (2720) and (2721)
(‡2136)	Εὐωδία, between (2175) and (2176)
(‡2145)	εὐπάρεδρος, between (2137) and (2138)
(‡2148)	εὐρακύλων, between (2146) and (2147)
(‡2206)	ζηλεύω, between (2204) and (2205)
(‡2214)	ἐκζήτησις, between (1567) and (1568)
(‡2274)	ἐσσόομαι, between (2074) and (2075)
(‡2276)	ἥσσων, between (2269) and (2270)
(‡2296)	ἐκθαυμάζω, between (1569) and (1570)
(‡2309)	ἐθέλω, between (1479) and (1480)
(‡2397)	εἰδέα, between (1489) and (1490)
(‡2442)	ὁμείρομαι, between (3655) and (3656)
(‡2448)	Ἰωδά, between (2492) and (2493)
(‡2466)	Ἰσσαχάρ, between (2475) and (2476)
(‡2490)	Ἰωανάν, between (2488) and (2489)
(‡2496)	Ἀρνί, between (720) and (721)
(‡2509)	καθώσπερ, between (2531) and (2532)
(‡2584)	Καφαρναούμ, between (2746) and (2747)
(‡2620)	ἐνκαυχάομαι, between (1765) and (1766)
(‡2640)	ὑπόλειμμα, between (5274) and (5275)
(‡2652)	κατάθεμα, between (2616) and (2617)
(‡2653)	καταθεματίζω, between (2616) and (2617)
(‡2730)	κατοικίζω, between (2733) and (2734)
(‡2735)	διόρθωμα, between (1356) and (1357)
(‡2736)	κατωτέρω, between (2737) and (2738)
(‡2743)	καυστηριάζω, between (2741) and (2742)
(‡2744)	ἐγκαυχάομαι, between (1460) and (1461)
(‡2792)	κιννάμωμον, between (2796) and (2797)
(‡2802)	Καῦδα, between (2737) and (2738)
(‡2854)	κολλύριον, between (2855) and (2856)
(‡2857)	Κολασσαί, between (2851) and (2852)
(‡2858)	Κολασσαεύς, between (2851) and (2852)
(‡2927)	κρυφαῖος, between (2930) and (2931)
(‡2944)	κυκλεύω, between (2942) and (2943)
(‡2945)	κύκλος, between (2943) and (2944)
(‡2955)	κατακύπτω, between (2633) and (2634)
(‡2982)	λαμμᾶ, between (2984) and (2985)
(‡2982)	λεμα, between (3011) and (3012)
(‡2982)	λιμά, between (3039) and (3040)
(‡2992)	λαός, between (2994) and (2995)
(‡3004)	εἶπον, between (1512) and (1513)
(‡3028)	λήμψις, between (3024) and (3025)
(‡3062)	λοιπός, between (3063) and (3064)
(‡3104)	Μεννά, between (3303) and (3304)
(‡3156)	Μαθθαῖος, between (3102) and (3103)
(‡3157)	Μαθθάν, between (3102) and (3103)
(‡3158)	Μαθθάτ, between (3102) and (3103)
(‡3159)	Μαθθίας, between (3102) and (3103)
(‡3166)	αὐχέω, between (849) and (850)
(‡3199)	μέλει, between (3190) and (3191)
(‡3344)	μετατρέπω, between (3346) and (3347)
(‡3363)	ἵνα μή, between (2443) and (2444)
(‡3395)	ἔλιγμα, between (1662) and (1663)
(‡3449)	μόχθος, between (3451) and (3452)
(‡3461)	δισμυριάς, between (1364) and (1365)
(‡3497)	Ναιμάν, between (3483) and (3484)
(‡3501)	νεώτερος, between (3512) and (3513)
(‡3502)	νοσσός, between (3556) and (3557)
(‡3507)	ὁμίχλη, between (3658) and (3659)
(‡3568)	τανῦν, between (5009) and (5010)
(‡3615)	οἰκειακός, between (3608) and (3609)
(‡3627)	οἰκτίρω, between (3629) and (3630)
(‡3641)	ὀλίγως, between (3643) and (3644)
(‡3708)	εἶδον, between (1490) and (1491)
(‡3726)	ἐνορκίζω, between (1774) and (1775)
(‡3762)	οὐθείς, between (3764) and (3765)
(‡3837)	πανταχῇ, between (3835) and (3836)
(‡3851)	παραβολεύομαι, between (3849) and (3850)
(‡3859)	διαπαρατριβή, between (1275) and (1276)
(‡3962)	προπάτωρ, between (4310) and (4311)
(‡3964)	πατρολῴας, between (3969) and (3970)
(‡3981)	πιθός, between (4086) and (4087)
(‡3987)	πειράομαι, between (3985) and (3986)
(‡4016)	παρεμβάλλω, between (3924) and (3925)
(‡4057)	ἐκπερισσοῦ, between (1599) and (1600)
(‡4057)	ἐκπερισσῶς, between (1599) and (1600)
(‡4057)	ὑπερεκπερισσοῦ, between (5238) and (5239)
(‡4072)	πετάομαι, between (4070) and (4071)
(‡4098)	συμπίπτω, between (4844) and (4845)
(‡4130)	πίμπλημι, between (4091) and (4092)
(‡4225)	μήπου or μή που, between (3379) and (3380)
(‡4236)	πραϋπάθια, between (4238) and (4239)
(‡4277)	προεῖπον, between (4275) and (4276)
(‡4332)	παρεδρεύω, between (3917) and (3918)
(‡4347)	προσκλίνω, between (4345) and (4346)
(‡4381)	προσωπολήμπτης, between (4379) and (4380)
(‡4382)	προσωπολημψία, between (4379) and (4380)
(‡4406)	πρόϊμος, between (4290) and (4291)
(‡4413)	πρώτως, between (4416) and (4417)
(‡4476)	βελόνη, between (955) and (956)
(‡4481)	Ῥαιφάν, between (4468) and (4469)
(‡4481)	Ῥομφά, between (4500) and (4501)
(‡4510)	ῥυπαίνω, between (4506) and (4507)
(‡4510)	ῥυπαρεύομαι, between (4506) and (4507)
(‡4541)	Σαμαρίτης, between (4542) and (4543)
(‡4551)	Σαπφίρη, between (4552) and (4553)
(‡4562)	Σερούχ, between (4588) and (4589)
(‡4565)	Ἀσσάρων, between (787) and (788)
(‡4596)	σιρικός, between (4617) and (4618)
(‡4621)	σιτίον, between (4618) and (4619)
(‡4677)	Σωσάννα, between (4987) and (4988)
(‡4687)	ἐπισπείρω, between (1986) and (1987)
(‡4696)	σπίλος, between (4694) and (4695)
(‡4711)	σφυρίς, between (4974) and (4975)
(‡4746)	στιβάς, between (4741) and (4742)
(‡4770)	Στοϊκός, between (4746) and (4747)
(‡4797)	συγχύν(ν)ω, between (4798) and (4799)
(‡4826)	Σιμεών, between (4612) and (4613)
(‡4833)	συμμορφίζω, between (4831) and (4832)
(‡4851)	σύμφορος, between (4852) and (4853)
(‡4867)	ἀθροίζω, between (119) and (120)
(‡4894)	σύνοιδα, between (4923) and (4924)

(‡4900) συναλλάσσω, between *(4871)* and *(4872)*
(‡4934) συνεπιτίθεμαι, between *(4901)* and *(4902)*
(‡4955) στασιαστής, between *(4713)* and *(4714)*
(‡4966) Συχέμ, between *(4621)* and *(4622)*
(‡4999) **Τρεῖς Ταβέρναι**, between *(5139)* and *(5140)*
(‡5062) τεσσεράκοντα, between *(5065)* and *(5066)*
(‡5063) τεσσερακονταετής, between *(5065)* and *(5066)*
(‡5075) τετρα(α)ρχέω, between *(5067)* and *(5068)*
(‡5076) τετρ(α)άρχης, between *(5067)* and *(5068)*
(‡5103) **Τίτιος**, between *(5101)* and *(5102)*
(‡5168) τρῆμα, between *(5148)* and *(5149)*
(‡5182) θορυβάζομαι, between *(2349)* and *(2350)*
(‡5185) προσαίτης, between *(4319)* and *(4320)*

(‡5228) ὑπερλίαν, between *(5244)* and *(5245)*
(‡5331) φάρμακον, between *(5332)* and *(5333)*
(‡5341) φαιλόνης, between *(5315)* and *(5316)*
(‡5384) φίλη, between *(5368)* and *(5369)*
(‡5391) ταπεινόφρων, between *(5012)* and *(5013)*
(‡5392) κημόω, between *(2777)* and *(2778)*
(‡5504) ἐχθές, between *(2188)* and *(2189)*
(‡5506) χιλίαρχος, between *(5504)* and *(5505)*
(‡5512) διαχλευάζω, between *(1315)* and *(1316)*
(‡5523) **Χωραζίν**, between *(5561)* and *(5562)*
(‡5531) κίχρημι, between *(2797)* and *(2798)*
(‡5574) ψεύδω, between *(5580)* and *(5581)*
(‡5601) 'Ιωβήδ, between *(2492)* and *(2493)*